Francess G Halpenny

DICTIONARY OF CANADIAN BIOGRAPHY

DICTIONARY OF CANADIAN BIOGRAPHY

DICTIONNAIRE BIOGRAPHIQUE DU CANADA

GENERAL EDITOR

DAVID M. HAYNE

DIRECTEUR ADJOINT

ANDRÉ VACHON

UNIVERSITY OF TORONTO PRESS

LES PRESSES DE L'UNIVERSITÉ LAVAL

DICTIONARY
OF CANADIAN
BIOGRAPHY

VOLUME II

1701 TO 1740

UNIVERSITY OF TORONTO PRESS

ENGLISH TRANSLATION OF FRENCH BIOGRAPHIES

J. F. Flinn, *Chairman* / J. S. Wood

FRENCH TRANSLATION OF ENGLISH BIOGRAPHIES

Claire Dagneau Wells, *Chairman*

© University of Toronto Press and
Les Presses de l'université Laval, 1969
Printed in Canada

Regular Edition: SBN 8020 3240 0
Laurentian Edition: SBN 8020 3249 4

CONTENTS

INTRODUCTION TO VOLUME II

THE *Dictionary of Canadian Biography/Dictionnaire biographique du Canada* was founded in 1959, having been made possible by a generous bequest left to the University of Toronto by a public-spirited Toronto business man, the late James Nicholson (1861–1952); the story of this bequest will be found in the General Introduction in Volume I of the *Dictionary*. Two years later, in 1961, the *Dictionary* became a bilingual enterprise when the authorities of l'Université Laval in Quebec undertook responsibility for a French edition. Since that time volumes of the *Dictionary* have been prepared jointly in the Toronto and Quebec offices of the DCB/DBC, under the immediate auspices of University of Toronto Press and Les Presses de l'université Laval.

Volume I of the *Dictionary of Canadian Biography/Dictionnaire biographique du Canada*, devoted to persons of Canadian interest who died between the years 1000 and 1700 A.D., appeared in 1966. The present volume, the second of the series, continues the chronological sequence begun in Volume I: it contains biographies of persons who died between 1701 and 1740. Future volumes will appear approximately every two years to a total of twenty or more, thus providing a complete record of the activities of all noteworthy inhabitants of Canada from earliest times to the ultimate date of publication.

Volume II continues Volume I not only in its chronological arrangement but also in its principles of selection and in the demands made on its contributors. Preliminary studies undertaken in the Toronto and Quebec offices of the *Dictionary* first produced a rough working list of some 1,200 names of persons who died in the forty years embraced by the volume. Subsequently, in consultation with numerous specialists in Canada and abroad, this total was reduced to about 600; the resulting *Preliminary Name List*, published in January 1967, was distributed widely for comment and further suggestions. In the volume as it is now issued there are 578 biographies, distributed as follows:

New France	377
Acadia	44
Newfoundland	39
English and New Englanders	36
Indians	36
Hudson's Bay Company	27
Île Royale	19

Geographically, the range of Volume II is greater than that of Volume I, reflecting the gradual expansion of Canadian activity in the early years of the 18th century: figures in this volume are found from Newfoundland to Lake Winnipeg, from Hudson Bay to New Orleans.

As in Volume I, biographies have been assigned in one of seven categories of length. The shortest are notes of 200 words, the longest extended studies of 10,000 words or more. Two of the biographies in Volume II are of the maximum length; 209 are notes of 200 words or less; the remainder range between these two limits.

The 152 contributors who have written articles for Volume II have been carefully selected for their specialized knowledge of the period and the persons treated in the volume. Their names will be found in the list of "Contributors" on page 705. Their articles, written in either English or French, have been prepared according to the general recommendations contained in the DCB/DBC's *Directives to Contributors*, the key paragraph of which reads as follows:

> Each biography should be an informative and stimulating treatment of its subject, presented in readable form. All factual information should be precise and accurate, and be based upon reliable (preferably primary) sources. Biographies should not, however, be mere catalogues of dates and events, or compilations of previous studies of the same subject. The biographer should try to give the reader an orderly account of the personality and achievements of the subject, *against the background of the period in which the person lived and the events in which he or she participated.* It is evident that such biographies cannot be written to any one specification, but it is expected that the biographer will attempt, within the space available, to appraise the circumstances shaping his subject's character and career, enumerating the parts played by ancestry, parentage, education, physical and social environment, and other formative influences; that he will make discreet use of relevant anecdote; and that he will conclude his biography by an equitable and discriminating evaluation of the subject's strengths and weaknesses, successes and failures, and probable place in Canadian history.

After submission, all articles were carefully checked by the *Dictionary*'s editors for factual accuracy, historical interpretation, and readability. Correspondence with the contributor at every stage ensured that the final text of each biography was acceptable to both contributor and editors. The biographies were then carefully translated into the other Canadian language and the final manuscript of the two parallel volumes, English and French, was prepared. Each volume includes, in addition to the biographies, a preliminary essay on the administration of New France, designed to assist the reader to relate the 377 New France biographies, a glossary of Indian tribal names, a general bibliography, and a detailed nominal index with cross-references to Volume I biographies and others yet to be published.

The preparation of Volume II has required, apart from the indispensable contribution of the writers of articles, the constant efforts and watchfulness of editorial, research, and translation staffs of approximately thirty persons. Their names, together with those of consultants and friends of the *Dictionary*, will be found on the following pages.

DAVID M. HAYNE
ANDRÉ VACHON

STAFF OF THE DICTIONARY

THE PUBLICATION of Volume II is the culmination of four years of painstaking work by staff members in the Toronto and Quebec offices of the *Dictionary*.

In Toronto, under the direction of Mrs Mary McD. Maude, Volume II biographies have been edited by Miss Jean Norman, Mr John St. James, Mr John Bryden, and Mr Douglas Hay, after preliminary work had been done by Mrs Constance P. McFarland; administrative and secretarial services have been provided by Mrs D. A. Sutherland (formerly Miss J. Elizabeth Cragg), Miss Paula M. M. Brine, and Miss Barbara Goldstein; and research assistance has been furnished by Miss Maud M. Hutcheson, Mrs Phyllis Creighton, Messrs S. A. Barker, K. Cassidy, and A. J. Cowan.

In Quebec, under the leadership of M. Gaston Tisdel, Volume II biographies have been edited by Mme Germaine Van Coillie, Mlle Huguette Filteau, and MM. Michel Paquin and André Côté, after preliminary work had been done by Mlles Céline Dupré and Olga Jurgens; administrative and secretarial services have been provided by Mme Marika Cancelier, assisted at different times by Mmes Nicole Baspeyre and Céline Massicotte and Mlle Danielle Decottignies; research and editorial assistance has been furnished by Mme Gilberte Massey, Mlle Louise-Hélène Boileau, Professor Elzéar Lavoie, and MM. Léon Thériault and Marc-André Poulin. Mlle Françoise Hudon and M. Roch-André Rompré have given help during all stages of the printing of the volume.

ACKNOWLEDGEMENTS

THIS SECTION of Volume I of the *Dictionary of Canadian Biography/Dictionnaire biographique du Canada* began with a grateful reference to the generous co-operation and sustained enthusiasm of Mrs James Nicholson. It would have been natural, and equally appropriate, to speak here of her continuing interest and devotion during the preparation of Volume II. Unfortunately, it is instead an unhappy duty to record that Mrs Nicholson died, in her ninety-fourth year, on 8 March 1969, just as Volume II was being prepared for the press. In her death the *Dictionary* has lost a precious link with its benefactor, and an irreplaceable friend and supporter.

Those of us who are responsible for the day-to-day preparation of the DCB/DBC cannot help but be constantly grateful for the assistance and encouragement provided by institutions and individuals. Two organizations have been particularly generous in their support: the Canada Council, which by a direct grant of $17,000 underwrote part of the costs of Volume II, and the Centennial Commission, which by liberally subventioning the *Dictionary*'s Ottawa research office established for nineteenth-century biographical investigations indirectly assisted the preparation of Volume II in a number of ways.

The largest group of individuals to whom we are indebted is made up of our distinguished contributors, whose names will be found on page 705. Without them, the *Dictionary* in its present form could not exist. Some of them, and in particular Professor Yves F. Zoltvany, have provided special assistance by acting as consultants for the volume: Professors W. J. Eccles, Harold Hickerson, Fathers René Baudry, c.s.c., and Jacques Valois, o.f.m., Dr C. Bruce Fergusson and Dr Gordon M. Day, Miss Alice M. Johnson, Messrs Donald Chaput, Antonio Dansereau, p.s.s., Donald J. Horton, Peter N. Moogk, Bernard Pothier, C. J. Russ, F. J. Thorpe, and Lt-Cdr. Michael Godfrey. Mme Louise Dechêne, Mlle M.-A. Menier, M. Étienne Taillemite, and M. Jacques Mathieu assisted in the preparation of the General Bibliography and elsewhere.

Throughout the preparation of Volume II we have again enjoyed the most willing cooperation from the libraries and archives of Canada and other countries. We are particularly grateful to the administrators and staffs of those institutions to which we have appealed most frequently: in Toronto, the University of Toronto Library, the Metropolitan Toronto Libraries, the Ontario Legislative Library and the Public Archives of Ontario; in Quebec, la Bibliothèque générale de l'Université Laval, les Archives du Séminaire de Québec, les Archives du Québec, and la Bibliothèque de la Législature; in Ottawa, the Public Archives of Canada.

In less specific ways, but no less constantly, the authorities of the University of

Toronto and of l'Université Laval have shown themselves sensible of the needs of the *Dictionary* and have smoothed its path. Particularly has this been true of the officers of the two university presses: Mr Marsh Jeanneret, Miss Eleanor Harman and Mr Harald Bohne at University of Toronto Press, and M. Georges Laberge and M. Lucien Zérounian at Les Presses de l'université Laval, have guided and encouraged the DCB/DBC staff at every turn, enabling them to avoid the many pitfalls that might have beset such a large publishing venture.

A special word of thanks, which by its brevity is utterly inadequate to express the debt it records, goes to Miss Francess G. Halpenny for replacing the General Editor during his absence and for giving him the benefit of her valuable advice at every stage of the preparation of Volume II.

DICTIONNAIRE BIOGRAPHIQUE DU CANADA   DICTIONARY OF CANADIAN BIOGRAPHY

Editorial Notes

PROPER NAMES

Persons have been entered under family name rather than title, pseudonym, popular name, nickname, or name in religion, an arrangement which has the advantage of bringing together prominent members of the same family [*see* LE MOYNE, GRIMINGTON, LENEUF, etc.]. Where possible, the form of the surname is based on the actual signature (although contemporary spelling of names was often erratic) and is given in the language of origin and in the spelling of the period: DENYS, which later became "Denis," and so on.

FRENCH NAMES

In the case of French family names, "La," "Le," "Du," and "Des" (but not "de") are considered as part of the name and are capitalized. Compound French names and titles abound in this period: PIERRE LE MOYNE d'Iberville et d'Ardillières; Jean-Baptiste de LA CROIX de Chevrières de Saint-Vallier; etc. In such cases, cross-references are made in the text from the compounds to the main name-entry: from "Iberville" and "Ardillières" to "Le Moyne"; and from "Chevrières" and "Saint-Vallier" to "La Croix." First names appear in the modern form: "Jean" rather than "Jehan"; "Noël" rather than "Noel."

NAMES OF MARRIED WOMEN AND NUNS

Married women and *religieuses* have been entered under their maiden names, with cross-references from their husbands' names or their names in religion: JOYBERT de Soulanges et de Marson, Louise-Élisabeth de (Rigaud de Vaudreuil); JUCHEREAU de La Ferté, JEANNE-FRANÇOISE, *dite* de Saint-Ignace.

INDIAN NAMES

Indian names have presented a particular problem, since an Indian might be known by his own name (spelled in a variety of ways by the French, English, or Dutch, unfamiliar with Indian languages), by a French or English nickname, and often by a French baptismal name. Since there can now be no certainty as to the original spelling, the entry has been given in the form of the Indian name found in sources such as *JR* (Thwaites); *NYCD* (O'Callaghan and Fernow); La Potherie, *Histoire*; and so on. An effort has been made to include the major variants of the original name, as well as the nicknames, with appropriate cross-references in the text. When the Indian name is not known, as is often the case with women, Indians are classified under their baptismal name.

CROSS-REFERENCES

For each first mention, in an individual biography, of a person who also has a biography in Volume II, the family name is printed in capitals and small capitals: Lawrence ARMSTRONG; Saint-Vallier [LA CROIX]. If there are two or more persons of the same family name, the first names also appear in capitals and small capitals: ALPHONSE TONTY; HENRI TONTY.

ASTERISKS

An asterisk following a name indicates either that the person has a biography in Volume I: Louis de Buade* de Frontenac, or that he will receive a biography in a subsequent volume: Jean-Baptiste Le Moyne* de Bienville; Gilles Hocquart*.

PLACE-NAMES

The spelling most often encountered in the documents and maps of the period has been employed, in the original language. Complete consistency, however, has not been possible, nor has it been thought desirable. The English edition cites very well-known place-names in their present-day English form: St Lawrence River, Quebec, Montreal, but uses Trois-Rivières rather than Three Rivers. The modern form has also been used when no agreement exists among 18th-century writers.

Alternative and more familiar forms of place-names are included in parentheses after the original. The alternative is usually the modern name, based whenever possible on the *Gazetteers of Canada* issued by the Canadian Board on Geographical Names, Ottawa. Where biographies include both French and English protagonists, the alternative place-names in the English edition may be the French form: for example, Moose Fort (Fort Saint-Louis or Monsipi), or Nashwaak (Naxouat).

In the present state of Canadian toponymy, no one work has been found entirely satisfactory. The following works have been useful as guides: for French names, Marcel Trudel, *Atlas historique* (1961, rev. ed. 1968); *JR* (Thwaites); and P.-G. Roy, *Inv. concessions*; for Acadian names, Ganong, "Historic sites in New Brunswick"; for HBC names, HBRS, XXI, XXII (Rich), XXV (Davies and Johnson); for Indian names, *NYCD* (O'Callaghan and Fernow), and *Handbook of American Indians* (Hodge); for Newfoundland names, E. R. Seary, *Toponymy of the Island of Newfoundland, check-list no.1, Sources, maps* (1959); *Check-list no.2, Names, I, The Northern peninsula* (1960) (mimeographed; to be published).

QUOTATIONS

Quotations have been translated when the language of the original passage is different from that of the text. All passages quoted from relatively standard works, such as the *Jesuit Relations*, are given in the generally accepted English translation of those works, a fact which will account for some variant spellings between text and quotation and some irregularities. Direct quotations correspond to the originals, except in one particular. The "expanded method" has been used in the transcriptions of quotations from early documents and printed works; "i" is changed to "j" and "v" to "u" ("ivin" becomes "juin"); and some "u's" are changed to "v's" ("liue" becomes "live"). The original accents have been retained and contractions have been expanded.

DATES

The discrepancy between Old Style (Julian calendar, used in England until 1752) and New Style (Gregorian calendar, used in Italy, Spain, Portugal, and France from 1582) affects every biography in Volume II. Most biographies, of course, present no problem: dates in those based entirely on English documents can be assumed to be Old Style; and in those based exclusively on French sources, New Style. But where an article draws on both English and continental or Quebec sources, authors have been asked to make the dates in the article uniformly Old or New Style and to indicate after the first date given (o.s.) or (N.s.). It should be noted that: (*a*) Old Style dates were 10 days behind New Style dates throughout the year in the 17th century and 11 days behind in the 18th century; (*b*) the Old Style new year began 25 March and the New Style new year on 1 January (for Old Style dates between January and 25 March, the year is indicated as 1685/86).

BIBLIOGRAPHIES

In order to avoid lengthy repetition, sources cited in five or more individual bibliographies are listed there in shortened form and are cited in full in the General Bibliography (pp. 677–703). The individual bibliographies are generally arranged alphabetically according to the five sections of the General Bibliography—manuscript sources, primary printed sources, reference works, studies, and journals. Wherever possible, references to manuscript material give the location of the original documents, rather than copies. Many abbreviations are used in these bibliographies, especially for archival sources; a list of these can be found on p. 2.

In general the items in individual bibliographies are the sources as listed by the contributors, but these items have been supplemented by a considerable amount of bibliographical investigation in the DCB/

DBC offices. Some special bibliographical comments by contributors appear within square brackets.

A description of the bibliographical style will be found in Constance McFarland, "The development of French and English styles for the DCB/DBC's bibliographies," *Papers of the Bibliographical Society of Canada*, III (1964), 27–37.

TRANSLATION INTO ENGLISH (a note by the Committee for the English Translation of French biographies)

In translating into English the biographies submitted originally in French to the DCB/DBC, the translators have tried to render the sense of the French text as faithfully as possible, while producing a clear and readable English version. At times the concision and brevity of the French necessitated a rather longer development in the English, but they have tried to avoid stylistic embellishments that would have misrepresented the French text.

Wherever possible, the translators have avoided using two distinct English words to translate the same French one in different passages or biographies, and also the use of a single English term to represent two or more French ones found in different contexts. Nevertheless the vagaries of the two languages have sometimes thwarted this desire for consistency; the French word "procureur" means both a legal representative and the financial officer of an ecclesiastical community, and it has been translated in some places as "attorney," and elsewhere as "bursar." On the other hand, English usage does not distinguish between "procureur" in the latter meaning and its synonym "économe"; thus the single English word "bursar" will be found doing duty for both. The greatest difficulty has of course been in trying to find suitable English equivalents for terms drawn from the political, religious, social, or economic background of 17th- and 18th-century life. The presence in the English version of occasional French words (e.g., *haute, moyenne, et basse justice*; *maître des comptes*; *donné*), which have no exact equivalent in English usage, will identify our least successful efforts in this direction. Occasional obscurity or ambiguity may have resulted from the difficulty of determining the precise meaning of certain words or expressions taken more or less directly from documents of the period, which are themselves not always free of obscurity or ambiguity. In accordance with editorial policy, full names of companies and institutions, such as "Compagnie de la Nouvelle-France" or "Conseil Souverain," have not been translated.

The Administration of New France

ANDRÉ VACHON

IT WAS ONLY gradually, with the emergence of new needs occasioned by its territorial and demographic expansion, that New France received its administrative structures. These were not to attain their complete and final form until about 1720. For nearly a century the internal administrative apparatus was in continual evolution, particularly under the influence of the different régimes that were imposed on the colony: those of the Compagnie de la Nouvelle-France or Compagnie des Cent-Associés (1627–63), the Compagnie des Indes Occidentales (1664–74), and the royal government (1663–64; 1674–1760). These administrative institutions, therefore, should not only be described in their state of perfection, but a brief outline of their origin and development should also be given; in this way the reader of this dictionary, perhaps less familiar with the French period of our history, will not be totally baffled by the complexity of operation, more apparent than real, of the various bodies—military, civil, and judicial—which controlled the life of the colony at any given moment.

Compagnie des Cent-Associés (1627–63). New France had always been under the authority of the king, but this authority had so far been exercised only in remote fashion, through the intermediary of monopoly companies little concerned with their commitments and of inactive viceroys, both of whom were under the somewhat vague jurisdiction of the admiral of France. But in October 1626, wishing to bring colonial affairs under control, Richelieu had himself appointed "grand master, head, and superintendent general of French navigation and trade." The cardinal abolished the offices of admiral of France and viceroy of New France, annulled the existing monopolies, and on 29 April 1627 established the "Compagnie des Cent-Associés for trade in Canada," and made over New France to it, "with full seigneurial rights of ownership and justice." As seigneurs of New France, the Cent-Associés were made responsible for administering it under Richelieu's supervision, acting in the name and under the authority of Louis XIII, and according to the terms of their charter.

The first form of government adopted for Canada was extremely simple. On presentation of three candidates by the company, Richelieu chose and presented in his turn to the king the one who, "in the absence of his lordship the cardinal," would command in New France "for the king's service." Samuel de Champlain* was the first appointee, but was named by the company, and only provisionally. It was his successor, Charles Huault* de Montmagny, who received the first royal commission. In theory, the governor was to be appointed "for a three-year period," but it was apparently only after 1645 that his term of office was thus limited, being made renewable once only from 1648 on. The governor held all powers: the military command, civil direction of the colony, and enforcement of the decrees of the council of state; in addition he was empowered to pass judgement finally and without appeal, both in civil and criminal proceedings, but with the collaboration, in difficult cases, of some officers or notables [Noël Juchereau* Des Chatelets; Achille Bréhaut* Delisle]. Besides the governor himself and his occasional advisers, the machinery of the law consisted of merely one law-officer, a humble clerk of court—often the governor's secretary—who also played the part of a notary but did not bear the title officially [Laurent Bermen*]. Only the financial management of the colony, entrusted to the agent (or general clerk) of the company in Canada [Derré* de Gand], was outside the governor's purview. The latter had a deputy who was in command at Trois-Rivières [Bréhaut Delisle; François de Champflour*]. After Richelieu's death in 1642 New France came under the jurisdiction of a secretary of state responsible for foreign affairs, but this changed nothing in the internal administration of the colony; in that year 1642, however, Montreal was founded, and Paul de Chomedey* de Maisonneuve filled the role of governor there.

The first important change occurred in 1647, two years after the formation of the Communauté des Habitants. Indeed, the king established, in association with the community, a managing and supervisory council formed of the governor general (Montmagny), the superior of the Jesuits, and the governor of Montreal (27 March 1647). This council, often called the first council of New France—and sometimes council of the fur trade—to distinguish it from the Conseil Souverain, was enlarged the following year (5 March 1648): on it were to sit, as well as the governor general [Louis d'Ailleboust* de Coulonge] and the superior of the Jesuits [Jérôme Lalemant*; Paul Ragueneau*], any former governor general living in Canada and two councillors (three in the absence of a former governor) elected by the other members of the council after consultation with the syndics of the inhabitants of Quebec, Montreal, and Trois-Rivières [Jean-Paul Godefroy*; Robert Giffard*]. The local governors of Montreal and Trois-Rivières had a seat on the council and the right to speak and vote there when they were visiting Quebec. This council had important functions: the administration of public funds—carried out until 1645 by the agent of the Cent-Associés—the surveillance of trade, the enforcement of public order, and the appointment of various officials, such as the admiral of the fleet [Jean-Paul Godefroy], the clerk of the warehouses [Jean Gloria*], and in particular a secretary of the council authorized to practise as a notary [Guillaume Audouart*, the first notary in Canada]. The appearance of this administrative machinery, however, in no way diminished the role of the governors general, whose commissions continued to grant the same powers as in the past. It appears moreover that the governor enjoyed a right of veto in the council; that was normal, since he had ultimate responsibility for the entire administration of the colony. It was on him, for example, and not on the council, that on 29 March 1649 the Cent-Associés, who had hitherto reserved this privilege to themselves, conferred the power to make land grants and assign sites.

Another improvement in the administrative organization of New France was made in 1651, when Governor Jean de Lauson* established at Quebec a regular tribunal, the seneschal's court, charged with rendering justice in the name of the Compagnie des Cent-Associés, which possessed seigneurial rights of *haute justice* in New France. Under the honorary responsibility of a grand seneschal [Jean de Lauson* (junior)], this *seigneurial* (as opposed to *royal*) court was made up of a lieutenant general for civil and criminal affairs (a judge) [Le Vieux*], a special lieutenant (a deputy judge) [Sevestre*], and a seigneurial attorney [Louis-Théandre Chartier*]. (The duties of the attorney were to institute proceedings in the name of the holder of the power of justice, and to watch over the interests of the latter and in general of those subject to law by obtaining judgements

proportionate to the offences. In the seigneurial tribunals he was called "seigneurial attorney," in royal jurisdictions "king's attorney," and in the Conseil Souverain "attorney general".) The seneschal's court of Quebec had its clerk of court [Rolland Godet*], who generally practised as a notary also, and at least one court officer or process-server (often called "sergeant," or even "process-server and sergeant," the two terms being in actual fact synonymous) [Michel Fillion*; Jean Levasseur*]. At about the same period Trois-Rivières also received a seneschal's court, a tribunal composed of a lieutenant general for civil and criminal affairs [Michel Leneuf* Du Hérisson; Pierre BOUCHER] and a seigneurial attorney [Maurice Poulin* de La Fontaine]; Séverin AMEAU held the offices of clerk of court, notary, and process-server at the same time. Montreal Island, the property of the Société de Notre-Dame de Montréal, had had its own seigneurial court since 1648. It was made up of a judge, Maisonneuve himself, a seigneurial attorney, and a clerk of court [Jean de Saint-Père*] who customarily practised as a notary, and sometimes even as a notary, process-server, and surveyor [Bénigne Basset*]. The appeals from these courts were heard by the governor general, who was always empowered to pass final judgement without appeal, whereas the seneschal's courts of Quebec and Trois-Rivières received appeals from the seigneurial courts of justice that were being set up in their district, like those of Lauson [Charles Sevestre] and Beaupré [Louis Rouer* de Villeray] in the region of Quebec.

Despite the existence of a council and various tribunals, the governor general's authority remained intact, and was still exercised in all spheres of civil and military activity, including that of justice. But on 7 March 1657 the king reorganized the council of 1647 and 1648: composed of the governor general, a director appointed by the Compagnie des Cent-Associés, and four councillors elected for two years (two by the inhabitants of Quebec, the other two by those of Montreal and Trois-Rivières respectively), the new council received numerous legislative, executive, and judiciary powers, but above all it was made responsible for the commerce, fur trade, and financial management of the colony. Despite the increased importance of this council, the governor still retained the liberty to act at his discretion; in reality this was becoming more difficult. A second statute, obtained like the first by the Cent-Associés, is dated 13 May 1659. It decreed that cases of all kinds should be referred in the first instance to the judges set up by the company, that appeals should be taken to the *parlement* of Paris except for matters of very little consequence or requiring immediate judgement, and that the governor no longer had authority to suspend or revoke law-officers, the king reserving this right to himself after due investigation. One might as well say that the governor immediately lost almost all his prerogatives (which were considerable) in the field of justice, and even the possibility of exercising effective control over the legal system. The real power, in the field of justice, passed into the hands of the seigneurial attorney of the company in Quebec. Consequently, from then on the governor found himself ill-placed for intervening directly in matters of law and order, and still more so for imposing on his colleagues in the council an authority about which he himself could have no illusions.

First Royal Government (1663–64). This reduction of the powers of the governor general was only the prelude to radical changes which were to be brought about abruptly in 1663. In March of that year the Cent-Associés handed their resignation to the king and returned New France to him. The whole administrative structure of the colony, founded on the seigneurial rights of the company, collapsed. The king replaced it by an administrative system similar to that of the French provinces, which comprised a governor general, a Conseil Souverain, and an intendant. But the Sieur Robert, who was nominated to be intendant of New France, did not come to Canada; the legislative, executive, and judicial powers were divided temporarily between the governor and the Conseil Souverain, who were to administer the colony under the direct authority of Louis XIV.

The Conseil Souverain was created in April 1663. It was composed of the governor general [Augustin de Saffray* de Mézy], the vicar apostolic [François de LAVAL], who from 1661 on had sat on the preceding council, or in his absence the senior ecclesiastic in the colony, five councillors [Louis Rouer; Mathieu Damours* de Chauffours], a king's attorney [Jean Bourdon*], and a clerk of court (or secretary; he was also called "clerk of court and secretary") [Jean-Baptiste Peuvret* Demesnu]. "Conjointly and in concert," the governor and the vicar apostolic were to appoint annually the other members of the council and receive their oath of allegiance. From the opening session of the council, however, a member extraordinary sat there by right: the royal commissary, Louis Gaudais-Dupont*, who was in the colony only temporarily, but whom the king had made a member of this body.

Just like the provincial *parlements* which had inspired it, the Conseil Souverain was essentially a supreme court of justice, responsible, in addition to its purely legal functions, for the recording (or transcription in the registers of insinuations) of royal ordinances—which it thus implemented in the colony; like the *parlements* also, it possessed (after 1667) the right of remonstrance, and had the power to make regulatory rulings (that is, to settle provisionally and on a suppletory basis questions which the customary law and the ordinances did not cover). But in 1663 this council, as the result of an intendant's absence, found itself entrusted with an important administrative and political role which the French *parlements* did not have: it was to control the colony's finances, supervise the fur-trade, maintain law and order, regulate commerce, appoint judges, law-officers, and notaries, and finally it could designate councillors to see that its decisions were carried out. On the legal plane, the council played the double role of an appeal court and a court of first instance, for both civil and criminal affairs; an appeal against its sentences could be made only to the king's council. Furthermore, the Conseil Souverain was responsible for exercising surveillance over the entire legal machinery of New France.

Without delay, the council gave its attention to organizing the colony's judicial system, which had been wiped out by the resignation of the Cent-Associés. Using its right to act as a court of first instance, it did not deem it necessary to give Quebec another royal tribunal; but Montreal and Trois-Rivières still had to be provided for. On 18 Oct. 1663 the council ratified the establishment of a royal seneschal's court at Montreal, and the appointment by the governor general and the vicar apostolic of a royal judge for civil and criminal affairs, a king's attorney [Charles Le Moyne* de Longueuil et de Châteauguay], and a clerk of court practising also as a notary [Bénigne Basset*]; this tribunal also had a process-server. A month later, on 17 Nov. 1663, the council organized a royal court of justice at Trois-Rivières, appointing to it a royal judge [Pierre Boucher], a king's attorney [Poulin de La Fontaine], a clerk of court and a notary [Ameau]; a process-server was also assigned to this jurisdiction. Appeals against sentences passed by these two royal courts were heard by the Conseil Souverain, as were those of the seigneurial courts of the region of Quebec.

In this administrative system of 1663, which was to last only a year, the governor general had again lost some of his powers: all civil administration had passed into the hands of the council; in the legal sphere he was now simply the president of the Conseil Souverain; in the vast field of public order he could intervene only conjointly with the council; he had to share with the vicar apostolic the appointing of councillors and the granting of seigneuries. In his own right, there now remained to this once all-powerful personage military affairs, a rather general supervisory duty, and of course a great moral authority as personal representative of the king in New France.

Compagnie des Indes Occidentales (1664–74). Scarcely a year had passed since the resignation of the Cent-Associés when Louis XIV, influenced by Colbert, created in May 1664 the Compagnie des Indes Occidentales, and granted New France to it, "with full ownership and rights of seigneurial justice." Once more the colony was to experience seigneurial administration, albeit in a somewhat mitigated form. By the company's charter the king reserved to himself the prerogative of granting their commissions to the governors and officers of the Conseil Souverain, who were to be chosen and appointed by the company; to the latter belonged the right of commissioning all the other officials and law-officers. Nevertheless, it was Louis XIV who appointed the governors, and later on the intendants; in turn the governors and intendants appointed the councillors. This infringement of the company's charter was a constant source of trouble in the administration of the colony: the king's men, in their attempts to impose royal policy everywhere and control the law-officers, fought with the company's men. The whole mechanism of administrative institutions was disrupted for some 10 years.

From 1664 to 1674 New France was therefore subject to a double metropolitan authority: that of the king, which was normally exercised through the intermediary of the "minister" Colbert (he was to become secretary of state for the Marine in 1669), and that of the Compagnie des Indes Occidentales, which was represented at Quebec by its agent general. In the numerous conflicts over jurisdiction that resulted from this division of authority, it was the company that gave way most often, so much so that the seigneurial structures provided for in the charter of 1664 soon began to show stronger and stronger traces of royal influence.

The entry of the Compagnie des Indes Occidentales upon the Canadian scene had profound repercussions on the institutions set up in 1663. The Conseil Souverain, at the same time as it allowed the company's agent general to take a seat on the council, had to make over to the company the supervision of the fur trade, the regulating of commerce, and the appointment of judges, law-officers, and notaries, as well as sharing with it the control of colonial finances; only its

powers with respect to finance and to the maintenance of law and order, which it shared with the company and the governor respectively, still distinguished the Conseil Souverain from the *parlements* of France. For his part the governor, in the sphere of military affairs, became theoretically an agent of the company, whose entire jurisdiction in this field was affirmed by the charter of 1664. On this point, however, as on many others, the king changed his mind; through the governors, whom he appointed himself, he kept military and diplomatic control of New France. Finally, judges, law-officers, and notaries could no longer cite their royal titles as legal authority; once again the administration of justice depended on a seigneurial régime.

Had it not been for the arrival at Quebec, in the autumn of 1665, of the first intendant of New France [Jean Talon*], who had been appointed by the king on the preceding 23 March, some kind of balance might have been established in the administration of the colony. But the "intendant responsible for justice, public order, and finance" had such varied and extensive powers that his integration into the administrative structure more or less shattered it. No sphere of civil administration escaped him entirely. Being responsible for justice, and being a common law judge who could not be appealed against, he would in actual fact control the Conseil Souverain, of which he was a part, in addition to appointing its members by agreement with the governor, and even the company, with its seigneurial right of *haute justice*. In the very large sphere of law and order, his function as civil administrator and the multiplicity of his powers were going to confer unusual authority on him, even if here he had to act in conjunction with the governor and the council. Finance, until recently controlled by the company in consultation with the council, from now on came exclusively under him. In short, in everything which did not exceed the limits of his functions, that is to say in everything which was not exclusively military or religious, he could do or decree whatever was necessary or useful for the king's service. A latecomer to the colony, the intendant could play a commanding role only if he were dressed in the spoils taken from others: those of the company, deprived of the control of finance, and at the very least threatened in its rights of justice, and even in its monopoly of trade to the extent that it no longer controlled legislation concerned with public order; those of the Conseil Souverain, returned to the status of a provincial *parlement* if we except its share in the maintenance of law and order; finally those of the governor, who was reduced more than ever to looking after military and diplomatic affairs and to a more and more general supervisory role—and whose expenditure, even in those spheres exclusively in his jurisdiction, would henceforth be authorized by the intendant.

The same year that Intendant Talon arrived (1665), another personage landed at Quebec, entrusted with an extraordinary task and armed with extraordinary powers: the lieutenant general Alexandre de Prouville* de Tracy, who has often been wrongly styled a viceroy. A personal envoy of Louis XIV, the lieutenant general had to play the part of pacifier in the colony, both from the military and the civil point of view. Indeed, while the Iroquois war was at its height, a serious conflict had been festering at Quebec between Governor Saffray de Mézy and Bishop Laval, which was partially paralyzing the administration. Tracy's orders were to put an end to the wars and the quarrels. For the duration of his stay (1665–67) he had authority and precedence over the governor general [Daniel de Rémy* de Courcelle], who thereby, temporarily and for the first time, lost the first rank. Everything considered, however, Tracy had roughly the powers of a governor general. Moreover his commission served subsequently as a model for those of the governors general, with this exception, that from the strictly military point of view it conferred on him far greater liberty of action than the governors general received, for they were obliged to have their policy approved by the court.

At the end of 1665, as a result of the conflict between Saffray de Mézy and Laval and of the changes that had occurred since 1664, justice in the colony was in need of a complete overhaul. The Conseil Souverain had not met since the preceding 6 July, thus depriving the town of Quebec of any court of first instance and leaving the other jurisdictions without a court of appeal. At Trois-Rivières and Montreal the "royal" courts had been more or less maintained, but the judges and law-officers, who had been appointed under the royal régime, had not yet been confirmed in office by the company, and they sat irregularly. At Quebec, to prevent the inconveniences resulting from the paralysis of the council, the intendant heard cases and gave judgement himself. On 6 Dec. 1666 the Conseil Souverain was finally reorganized, on the same footing as in 1663, but including the intendant, who seems to have replaced the agent of the company; there is no further mention of the latter as a member of the council.

At the beginning of 1667, using its rights of justice, the Compagnie des Indes Occidentales established at Quebec a court of seigneurial justice—the provost court of Quebec—responsible for hearing in first instance all cases relating "to affairs of justice, public order, trade or navigation, whether they be civil or criminal," and for receiving appeals from the seigneurial jurisdictions. This court consisted of a lieutenant general for civil and criminal affairs [Louis-Théandre Chartier de Lotbinière], a seigneurial attorney [Peuvret Demesnu], and a clerk of court [Gilles Rageot*]. That same year the company set up a similar tribunal at Trois-Rivières. Appeals from these two courts came before the Conseil Souverain, in the same way as those from the seigneurial court of Montreal, which had succeeded the royal seneschal's court of 1663; the latter had been abolished in September 1666 because it was violating the rights of the Sulpicians, who as seigneurs of the island had the right of *haute justice*.

As long as the lieutenant general, Prouville de Tracy, stayed in the colony, the institutions, once set up, functioned more or less normally, without the representatives of the Compagnie des Indes Occidentales being too sharply beset by the royal power. But Tracy's departure (1667) really set hostilities in motion. The Intendants Talon and Claude de Boutroue* d'Aubigny tried to impose royal authority everywhere, even when this authority, by the wish of the king himself, was supposed to be expressed only through the intermediary of the company. For example, they wanted to attach to the royal power the notaries, who, in principle and in law, came under the seigneurial jurisdictions of Quebec, Montreal, and Trois-Rivières, and who, under the company's régime, could in no way lay claim to the title of royal notaries. The intendant, nonetheless, forced them to practise as royal notaries [Gilles Rageot], and seized the power of appointing notaries [Jean Cusson]. The intendant likewise took into his own hands the granting of seigneuries, a realm in which the company, as the owner of New France, had an unmistakable right to act alone. Consequently, by the end of Talon's second stay in 1672, the company had long since given up claiming its rights. For his part Governor Louis de Buade* de Frontenac, who had no intendant with him before 1675, ignored it completely. In 1674 Louis XIV put an end to the inglorious career of this company, which had already passed into the background, and resumed possession of the vast territory of New France.

Second Royal Government (1674–1760). At the time when the royal government began, the great administrative institutions of the colony were already created. For another half-century, it is true, they were to evolve somewhat, and gradually to be completed and take precise shape, but the general framework erected from 1663 on was to remain unchanged. The whole administration, both civil and military, would depend on the governor general and the intendant, and justice, of which the pyramidal organization had been sketched out from 1663 to 1667, would have at its summit the Conseil Souverain, a sort of supreme court which would pass judgements without appeal in Canada.

In theory the jurisdiction of the governor general, the intendant, and the Conseil Souverain extended to the whole of New France, that is to the totality of French possessions in North America; in practice, because of distances and the difficulty of communications, Acadia and Louisiana had their own governments, which were authorized to correspond directly with the mother country. The inhabited area of the colony—Canada properly so called—was divided into three governments, or administrative territories, centring around the towns of Quebec, the capital and also the episcopal see, Trois-Rivières, and Montreal. The government of Quebec extended, on the north shore, from Les Éboulements to Grondines, and on the south shore from Rimouski to Deschaillons; that of Trois-Rivières, from Sainte-Anne-de-La-Pérade to Maskinongé on the north shore and from Saint-Pierre-les-Becquets to Yamaska on the south; to the west of Maskinongé and Yamaska, the government of Montreal had as its limits the last farms in the region of Châteauguay and Vaudreuil. The west and the *pays d'en haut*, which were fur-trading and mission territories where a whole network of forts sprang up, were direct dependencies of the authorities of New France, at Quebec.

From 1674 to 1760 New France was under the authority of the king, whose representative and spokesman for colonial affairs was the minister of Marine (or more exactly the secretary of state for the Marine). During the regency, however, as a result of the temporary abolition of the offices of secretary of state, royal authority was exercised over New France through the intermediary of the council of Marine (1715–23). But the accession of Louis XV brought a return to the old formula. In France the ministry of Marine took the place of a ministry of colonies, the colonies, however, being clearly subordinated to the former, as a study of the correspondence of the minister and of the budgets of New France makes quite plain.

The principal function of the governor general, the first person in the hierarchy of the colony, who was appointed by the king and removable at his pleasure, was to represent the person of the sovereign in New France. Consequently he held authority over all orders in Canada, and had to maintain them in their obedience to the king and their respect for the monarchy. In all matters, even in those which did not belong to his immediate jurisdiction, he was required to support with his prestige—which was great, as were the honours that were rendered to him—and with his authority the intendant, the Conseil Souverain, and in general all officers responsible for the colony's welfare and the king's service. In exceptionally grave circumstances, and if he deemed them prejudicial to the country's welfare and the interests of the state, he had the power to oppose the decisions of the intendant himself, on condition, however, that he justified his conduct fully before the minister and the king. This great moral authority, which was conferred on him by his dignity as the monarch's personal representative, explains why he was acknowledged to have a kind of joint jurisdiction, with the intendant, in the fields of population and colonization, trade and industry, maintenance of order, and religion (supervision of clergy, of religious communities, and of hospitals), although in all sections of economic and social life the intendant was the initiator, promoter, and indispensable king-pin. Again in his capacity as the representative of the sovereign, the original owner of the "domain" from which they were taken, he shared with the intendant the granting of seigneuries, and, with him, delivered judgement in the legal disputes and contestations that might result.

Beyond these general powers derived from his pre-eminent status as the king's representative, the governor general had special attributions in two spheres where his jurisdiction was exclusive: military affairs and diplomatic relations. He acted in the colony as commander or general in chief of the armies, with authority over any commander or general who might land there on behalf of the king. He commanded the troops, presided over the council of war, was responsible for fortifications and could decide alone on peace or war with the Indians. He directed the colony's diplomacy with the Indian tribes (as with the English colonies of America) and thereby exerted his authority over the *pays d'en haut* and the territories of the west, which were studded with forts and trading-posts and traversed by Indians. It was he who appointed the commandants of the posts and forts, making of them agents of his Indian policy; it was he also who issued fur-trading licences (*congés*), but in conjunction with the intendant, because of commercial implications; finally he had a certain jurisdiction over the mission territories, the missionaries too being in some sort agents of French policy [JACQUES and JEAN DE LAMBERVILLE].

The only limitations imposed on the governor general, in the military and diplomatic spheres, might come to him from Versailles (which authorized him to decide alone on the building of stockaded forts, for example, but not on the building of stone forts), but also from the intendant, to the extent that the latter held absolute control over the colony's finances, since all expenditures, for military, diplomatic, or other purposes, had to be determined and authorized by him. It is true that the governor shared in the preparation of the colony's budget, which he submitted to the minister jointly with the intendant; but once this budget was accepted he was, for any expenditure not explicitly provided for, at the mercy of his powerful colleague . . . give or take 10,000 *livres*. To the governor, indeed, was turned over the revenue from the sale of fur-trading licences and from the leasing of posts; from this he was allowed to deduct, before paying it into the treasury, up to 10,000 *livres* for gratuities and charity.

In his specifically military duties the governor general was assisted by a general staff authorized to sit as a council of war, and constituted by the combined general staffs of each of the Canadian governments. Indeed the governor general had a military deputy, the local governor in each of the governments of Montreal [Louis-Hector de CALLIÈRE] and Trois-Rivières [Claude de RAMEZAY]; he himself filled the role of local governor for the government of Quebec. The governor general and each of the two local governors were flanked by a king's lieutenant [Louis de LA PORTE de Louvigny; Claude-Michel Bégon*], a town major (*major*) [François LE VERRIER de Rousson], and an assistant town major (*aide-major*). Under the presidency of the governor general, therefore, these officers taken together, along with the intendant, who sat by right on all councils of war, and the chief engineer, who was responsible for the fortifications [Gaspard Chaussegros* de Léry], formed the colony's general staff.

The governor general commanded both the colonial regular troops (*troupes de la Marine*) garrisoned in New France and the colonial militia, which was organized in its final form in 1669. In the 18th century the regular troops in Canada numbered 28 companies, each having at least 4 officers: a captain, a lieutenant, an ensign on the active list, and a second ensign. The main body of the troops was billeted in the government of Montreal, near the colony's strategic points and the waterways leading to them. For its part the militia grouped all able-bodied male settlers from 16 to 60, except for military officers, law-officers, and officials. Under the command of the local

staffs, the militia had its own cadres: each government had at its head a colonel, a major, and an adjutant (*aide-major*), and each parish provided at least one company, comprising a very variable number of militiamen, whose officers were a captain, a lieutenant, an ensign, and a sergeant; in the towns the companies were distributed by districts [René-Louis CHARTIER de Lotbinière]. Although he was general in chief of New France, the governor general did not have the power to appoint the officers of the general staff, or even, in the case of the regular troops, to grant promotions; he could only recommend to the minister and the king candidates for higher rank or for decorations (in particular for the prestigious cross of the order of Saint-Louis). As far as the militia was concerned, however, the right of appointment and promotion belonged to him exclusively.

As a result of his virtually exclusive jurisdiction over the posts of the *pays d'en haut*, the governor had some share with the intendant in the administration of justice (in addition to that which he already had in the granting of seigneuries). Indeed the commandants of these posts, who were appointed by the governor, rendered justice in the area of their jurisdiction. It was a rather rough and ready sort of military justice; appeals against it had to come before both the intendant, who was responsible for justice in the colony, and the governor, who authorized its exercise in the commissions which he issued to the commandants of distant posts. In the same way, because of the possible repercussions on relations with the Indians, the governor and the intendant heard together the Indians' complaints and claims, resulting from thefts of which they might have been victims at the hands of Frenchmen.

If he had to share certain of his duties, particularly with the governor, the intendant, the third person in the colonial hierarchy—after the governor general and the bishop—was none the less the strongest man in New France by the number, extent, and importance of his powers. Appointed by the king and removable at his pleasure, he had the title of "intendant responsible for justice, public order, and finance," to which was going to be added, for Bigot*, that of intendant for the Marine. He was the highest civil dignitary of the colony, and in that capacity could expect honours scarcely less than those to which the governor, the king's personal representative, was entitled. In addition, as the public funds were at his disposal, the intendant, by allocating contracts and other privileges, was able to muster a sizable following in the colony.

Everything that was not within the exclusive jurisdiction of the governor general and the bishop came under the intendant alone, required his participation, or was carried out under his authority. To go back to the very terms of his commission, the duties of the intendant concerned the vast spheres of justice, public order, and finance. He had first of all to see that "good and prompt" justice was rendered to all without distinction; he therefore had to exercise constant supervision over tribunals, judges, and law-officers, and see to the execution of decrees, edicts, ordinances, and regulations. By virtue of this general duty and his special responsibilities, the intendant could either call before himself any case, civil or criminal, that was pending before the courts, or send back to a regular tribunal an affair referred to him, or again, revoke a sentence passed by the Conseil Souverain if he deemed it contrary to the interests of justice, or even on occasion depart from the habitual procedures. He did not, however, have the right to appoint judges and law-officers, whom he could remove only in quite exceptional circumstances and with the obligatory participation of the governor general. Nevertheless, he did appoint and could suspend the clerk of the marshalcy, process-servers, and notaries, as well as surveyors. He was himself the only competent judge in cases of crimes against the security of the state, in actions relating to public order, the levying of dues, smuggling, the fur trade or the king's domain, and in all questions concerning the seigneurial regime, in respect to which he was the interpreter of the customary law. Appeal could be made against the intendant's judgements only to the king's council, the Conseil Souverain of Quebec being inferior to the intendant (who was moreover the real president of this tribunal; the governor was its honorary president). In summary cases, which he had the right to hear, the intendant's judgement was without appeal.

Also under the intendant's control was the very large sector concerned with the maintenance of public order, that is to say everything that concerned not only law and order but also in a general way the whole colonial administration. In New France administrative regulations were aimed principally at increasing the population, developing land holdings, and establishing trade and industry, all of these being sectors which were under the intendant's jurisdiction, although the governor general normally countersigned ordinances on these subjects and the Conseil Souverain occasionally played a role in these matters with the intendant, accompanied or not by the governor. Breaches of regulations and ordinances concerned with public order came exclusively under the intendant, who was authorized to pronounce sentence in all cases.

In the sphere of finance the intendant's authority was in practice absolute in the colony; only the governor general could, theoretically, oppose him in this area, and then only for extremely serious reasons. The intendant held the funds and could alone authorize even the smallest expenditures. Moreover, he had exclusive jurisdiction over the levying and collection of the dues in force in the colony, particularly those of the Domaine d'Occident in Canada (or king's domain), over imposts (taxes), of which he controlled the receipt and disbursement (the king alone being able to order the tax itself), over the circulation of currency in the colony and over "card money" (playing cards used as currency to relieve the shortage of coin [see Jacques de MEULLES]), which was countersigned by the governor general and by the comptroller of the Marine at Quebec. Likewise the intendant, as manager of the possessions of the crown, had jurisdiction over those of the distant posts which were carrying on trade on the king's behalf. Since he was the only one holding the funds and authorizing their outlay, the intendant was alone entitled to give orders for public works (except in the case of fortifications, where the governor had to act with him) and to make purchases in the name of the state. In short the whole civil life of the colony, including its seigneurial life, was animated, directed, and controlled by the intendant.

To assist him in his duties the intendant appointed subdelegates, who were occasional rather than permanent officials, sometimes commissioned for very short periods (during a brief absence of the intendant for example), and having a mandate which could be very general [René-Louis Chartier] or restricted to one particular matter. Thus a councillor or notary could be appointed the intendant's subdelegate with the sole purpose of settling a dispute, conducting an inquiry, or carrying out a precise task [François GENAPLE]. The number of these delegates could vary a great deal, according to contingencies. At Montreal, however, which was "the place in Canada where there were always the most troops," the intendant was represented permanently by the commissary of the Marine [CLAIRAMBAULT d'Aigremont], who was his subdelegate by right. From 1733 on, the latter was a member of the Conseil Souverain in his own right, and could even preside over it in the intendant's absence.

Under the intendant three groups of officials evolved: those of the "offices" of the Marine, those of the Domaine d'Occident, and finally the chief road officer and his subordinates. To the offices of the Marine were entrusted the king's storehouses and the care of the provisions, ammunition, and other merchandise which were the property of the state. These offices were under the direction of the comptroller of the Marine [Clairambault d'Aigremont], who was responsible for the management and accounts of the king's store-houses and who resided at Quebec. Under his orders were two staffs, one at Quebec the other at Montreal, both made up of a keeper of stores, a treasurer, and writers (book-keepers), that is, some 30 officials. For his part the director of the Domaine d'Occident was entrusted with the administration of certain territories being exploited for the benefit of the king (the king's domain, or the Tadoussac trading concession), and with the collection of certain dues, such as the levy of 25 per cent on beaver furs and of 10 per cent on moose hides, and the other levy of 10 per cent on wines, spirits, and tobacco. His staff included a comptroller, visitors (inspectors), a captain of the guards, and writers, that is, altogether (apart from the guards) fewer than 10 men. As for the chief road officer, he was in charge of the building and repair of roads and bridges, the alignment of houses in the towns, the upkeep of paved thorough-fares, in a word the system of roads, as his title indicates [PIERRE ROBINAU de Bécancour]. He had clerks who assisted him or replaced him in case of absence [Genaple].

This two-headed administration, founded on a division of powers between the governor general and the intendant, was however embodied and as it were unified in the person of the militia captain, who at the level of the parish and the seigneury represented both the governor and the intendant, the military and the civil authorities. In reality only the governor had jurisdiction over him, but the intendant often entrusted him with the application, in the territory for which he was responsible, of certain regulations and ordinances, with the supervision and even the direction of road-building operations, etc. In this respect the militia captain, although a copyholder, was above the seigneur.

The militia captain's civil role was nevertheless reduced in seigneuries provided with a court of justice: the intendant then instructed the officers of the tribunal to see to the execution of his ordinances. These minor courts were not without importance: if indeed the seigneury was the culmination, the focal point of the administration of the colony, it was at the same time the starting point for the administration of justice, which from jurisdiction to jurisdiction went right up to the king.

Until the end of the 17th century the right of *haute, moyenne, et basse justice* was granted fairly liberally to the seigneurs of the colony; subse-quently this right was restricted to *basse justice* only, it being left to the royal jurisdictions to hear cases of any real importance. The seigneur possess-ing rights of justice was required to appoint law-officers on his lands to whom the intendant granted commissions. These seigneurial courts of justice bore different names, which do not however reflect any dissimilarity between them: there were seneschal's courts, provost courts, bailiff's courts, but in general one spoke rather of seigneurial (or subordinate) justice, or else of seigneurial jurisdictions. These courts of first instance were composed of a judge (called a "seneschal" [Jacques BARBEL], a "provost," a "bailiff" or a "seigneurial" judge, as the case might be), a seigneurial attorney [Hilaire BERNARD], a clerk of court (who most often practised also as a notary [Paul VACHON]), and a process-server [Antoine-Olivier QUINIARD]. These officials were paid by the seigneur, in whose name they dispensed justice. Appeals from the seigneurial courts came before the royal jurisdiction of the government to which they were answerable.

Indeed, in each of the three governments, Quebec, Trois-Rivières, and Montreal, a royal court sat; it was called provost court at Quebec (between about 1680 and 1717 we also come across the expression "provost and admiralty court of Quebec"), and royal jurisdiction at Trois-Rivières and Montreal. The provost court of Quebec, a court of first instance in civil and criminal matters, was also responsible for hearing cases concerning maritime trade (until 1719), and served as an appeal court for the seigneurial jurisdictions of the government. This court, created in 1667 by the Compagnie des Indes Occidentales, was in theory abolished in 1674 by the resignation of the company; nevertheless, it continued to sit [Louis-Théandre Chartier de Lotbinière] and was officially "re-established" in 1677. The royal jurisdiction of Trois-Rivières, itself born of a court (or jurisdiction) set up in 1667 by the Compagnie des Indes Occidentales, had a history similar to that of the provost court of Quebec and played the same role in its own locality, but did not concern itself with maritime trade. At Montreal things developed differently. The Sulpicians, seigneurs of Montreal since 1663, did indeed possess their own seigneurial tribunal; they dispensed justice until 1693, when a royal jurisdiction similar to that of Trois-Rivières was set up at Montreal by order of the king. The Sulpicians then gave up appointing law-officers, except for the clerk of court or keeper of the registry, of which they remained the owners. In addition to their specifically judicial powers, these jurisdictions registered or "insinuated" in the registers provided for that purpose the commis-sions of their officers, and in certain cases various documents, for example marriage contracts, wills, and donations. Appeals from these tribunals came before the Conseil Souverain.

These royal jurisdictions were made up of the following law-officers, appointed by the king (with the exception of the process-servers): a lieutenant general for civil and criminal affairs (royal judge) [René-Louis Chartier], assisted (except at Trois-Rivières where this office did not exist) by a local lieutenant (deputy royal judge) from 1695 on at Quebec and from 1712 at Montreal [Paul DUPUY], a king's attorney [Louis BOULDUC], and a clerk of court [Pierre RIVET Cavelier] assisted by registry clerks and process-servers [Jean-Baptiste POT-TIER]. The royal notaries [Jacques Barbel], who were ancillary law-officers, were attached to these royal jurisdictions. In the absence of lawyers in the colony—where they were never permitted to practise their profession—notaries, clerks of court, process-servers, even ordinary private persons, were authorized to appear as practitioners before all the courts in New France and to represent parties and set out facts, but not to plead. These practitioners were not by virtue of this law-officers, and their remuneration was a matter of arrangement between them and the litigants whose interests they were espousing.

In 1677 the judicial machinery of the colony was equipped for criminal matters with a marshalcy having at its head a grand provost [Philippe Gaultier* de Comporté] assisted by a clerk of court [René Hubert]—both appointed by the king—and by six archers. The marshalcy was never truly a tribunal: it was responsible rather for seeking out criminals, conducting preliminary investigations (interrogations), and making up the dossier to be handed over to the king's attorney so that the holding of a trial might be ordered. The criminal was shut up in the "royal prisons," under guard of the prison keeper (also called "jailer" and "guardian of the prisons") [François Genaple; Antoine ADHÉMAR; Michel LEPAILLEUR de Laferté]. Judicial torture and punishments were carried out by the executioner (or hangman) [Jean RATTIER], appointed by the Conseil Souverain.

In addition to these royal jurisdictions, there still existed at Quebec a diocesan officiality, an ecclesiastical tribunal created by Bishop Laval in 1660 but not recognized officially by the state until 1684. This tribunal, of which the official (judge), promoter (attorney), and clerk of court [Jacques Barbel] were appointed by the bishop, was a court of first instance for civil and criminal cases in which an ecclesiastic or a religious was involved. Appeals from this ecclesiastical juris-diction came before the Conseil Souverain.

The judicial organization of the colony was completed in 1719, when the admiralty court of Quebec sat for the first time; this court had been created two years earlier to lighten the load of the provost court of Quebec, which for many years had served as an admiralty court. This tribunal had judicial and administrative powers. It had to deal in the first instance, in civil and criminal affairs, with all cases concerned with maritime trade and with the Marine in general, and in time of war to decide on the validity of captures; furthermore, its officers had to ensure the maintenance of law and order in ports, docks, and harbours, regulate fishing, see to the salvaging and care of wreckage and derelict objects, and enforce observance of the laws and regulations concerning smuggling by sea. The officers of the admiralty court of Quebec, who were appointed by the grand admiral of France, in whose name they administered justice, and who were approved by the king, were three in number: a lieutenant general (judge) [Jean-Baptiste COUIL-LARD de Lespinay], an attorney [Nicolas-Gaspard Boucault*], and a clerk of court [Jean-Claude LOUET]. To this tribunal was answerable the harbour-master captain (or port captain) [Louis PRAT], who was formerly under the intendant's direct authority and whose principal duties were to ensure, with the help of a lieutenant and a harbour-master having the rank of sub-lieutenant, the maintenance of law and order in the port, and to prevent ships' captains and private individuals from throwing into the roadstead stones or any other object which might damage ships. Under the orders of these officers worked dock-masters, inter-preters, brokers, gaugers, loaders and unloaders of ballast, etc. The receiver, attached to the same tribunal, delivered to the ships their licences, or permits to leave port. Appeals from this court came before the Conseil Souverain.

Crowning the whole judicial organization of the country was the Conseil Souverain. In the 18th century it pronounced judgement only in cases of appeal, and of its administrative rights it retained only those of registration and remonstrance; it still took part in the maintenance of law and order, but only in the intendant's presence and so to speak on his express instructions. The number of councillors, which was five in 1663 in addition to the governor general, the vicar apostolic, and, after 1665, the intendant, was increased to seven in 1675 (these councillors being from then on appointed for life by the king). In 1703 the name of the council was changed to that of Conseil Supérieur, and the number of councillors in-creased to 12, one of them being an ecclesiastical councillor. With the governor, the bishops, and the intendants, the 12 councillors, the attorney general [Mathieu-Benoît COLLET], and the clerk of court or secretary, the Conseil Supérieur therefore comprised 17 persons, to whom was added in 1733 the commissary of the Marine at Montreal. In 1742 the king gave seats on the council to four assessors, in theory law students who were appointed for three years, and who, except on very rare occasions, were present only in an advisory capacity. Thus composed, the Conseil Supérieur judged appeals from the royal jurisdictions, the admiralty court, and the officiality. Appeal could be made against its judgements only to the king's council in France.

Such, in their elegant simplicity, were the administrative structures of New France. To complete the too brief description that we have given of them, it would have been necessary to analyse much more searchingly the way they operated, to evaluate their advantages and disadvantages, and especially to describe the spirit that inspired them. But the aim here was, on a modest scale, to reconstitute the framework within which moved so many persons whose careers are outlined in the early volumes of this dictionary. Indeed, in reading the biographies devoted to these persons the reader will see these administrative structures come to life, will discover their intentions and their purposes, and will appraise their results.

Glossary of Indian Tribal Names

THIS GLOSSARY INCLUDES the tribal names that appear most frequently in the biographies of Volume II. It is designed to assist the reader in identifying and locating geographically those tribes involved in the development of New France and encountered during western explorations. Full names of authors of the articles will be found in the list of "Contributors," page 705. Unsigned articles have been compiled by the staff of the *Dictionary*.

The following sources have been used in the preparation of the Glossary; shortened titles are listed in full in the General Bibliography. Gabriel Archer, "The relation of Captain Gosnold's voyage," *Mass. Hist. Soc. Coll.*, 3d ser., VIII (1843), 72–81. W. M. Beauchamp, *A history of the New York Iroquois now commonly called the Six Nations* (Albany, 1905). Louis Binford, "An ethnohistory of the Nottoway, Meherrin and Weanock Indians of Southeastern Virginia," *Ethnohistory*, XIV (1967), no.4, 103–218. T.-M. Charland, *Histoire des Abénakis d'Odanak* (Montréal, 1964). William Coats, *The geography of Hudson's Bay ... between the years 1727 and 1751 ...*, ed. John Barrow (Hakluyt Soc. pub., London, 1852). G. M. Day, "The identity of the Sokokis," *Ethnohistory*, XII (1965), 237–49. *Découvertes et établissements des Français* (Margry). Arthur Dobbs, *An account of the countries adjoining to Hudson's Bay ...* (London, 1744). *Journals and letters of La Vérendrye* (Burpee). Charles Gill, *Notes sur de vieux manuscrits Abénakis* (Montréal, 1886). Daniel Gookin, "An historical account of the doings and sufferings of the Christian Indians in New England," American Antiquarian Soc. *Trans. and Coll.*, II (Cambridge, 1836), [423]–534; "Historical collections of the Indians in New England," *Mass. Hist. Soc. Coll.*, 1st ser., I (1792), 141–232. L. K. Gahan, "The Nipmucks and their territory," *Mass. Archaeological Soc. Bull.*, II (1940), no.2, 2–6. *Handbook of American Indians* (Hodge). Samuel Hearne, *A journey from Prince of Wales's fort in Hudson's Bay to the northern ocean, 1769, 1770, 1771, and 1772*, ed. Richard Glover (Toronto, 1958). Alexander Henry, *Travels and adventures in Canada and the Indian territories, between the years 1760 and 1766*, ed. James Bain (Toronto, 1901). William Hubbard, *The history of the Indian wars in New England* (Boston and London, 1677; new ed., Roxbury, 1865). HBRS, XXV (Davies and Johnson). *Indian tribes* (Blair). [James Isham], *James Isham's observations on Hudson's Bay, 1743 ...*, ed. with an Intro. by E. E. Rich (HBRS pub., XII, London and Toronto, 1949). Francis Jennings, "Glory, death and transfiguration; the Susquehannock Indians in the seventeenth century," American Philosophical Soc. *Proc.* (Philadelphia), CXII, no.1 (1968). Jenness, *Indians of Canada*. *JR* (Thwaites). *Jug. et délib.* Lahontan, *New voyages* (Thwaites). La Potherie,

Histoire (1722). *Livingston Indian records* (Leder). Alexander MacKenzie, *Voyages from Montreal ... through the continent of North America, to the Frozen and Pacific Oceans, in the years 1789 and 1793 ...* (London, 1801). J.-A. Maurault, *Histoire des Abénakis depuis 1605 jusqu'à nos jours* (Sorel, 1866). *Michigan Pioneer Coll.*, XXXIII, XXXIV. Christopher Middleton, *A vindication of the conduct of Captain C. Middleton ... for discovering a North-West Passage to the Western American Ocean ...* (London, 1743). *NYCD* (O'Callaghan and Fernow). A. C. Parker, *An analytical history of the Seneca Indians* (Rochester, N.Y., 1926); *The constitution of the Five Nations* (Albany, 1916). Joseph Robson, *An account of six years residence in Hudson's Bay from 1733 to 1736 and 1744 to 1747 ...* (London, 1752). F. G. Speck, *The Iroquois, a study in cultural evolution* (Cranbrook Institute of Science Bull. no.23, Bloomfield Hills, Mich., 1945); "Native tribes and dialects of Connecticut, a Mohegan-Pequot diary," Bureau of American Ethnology *Annual Report*, XLIII (1928), 199–287; "Territorial subdivisions and boundaries of the Wampanoag, Massachusett, and Nauset Indians," *Indian Notes and Monographs* (New York), [miscellaneous ser.], XLIV (1928), 7–152. P. A. W. Wallace, *The white roots of peace* (Philadelphia, 1946). Wis. State Hist. Soc. *Coll.*, XVI, XVII.

Abenakis; in French Abénaquis. A loose alliance of tribes in the area of what is now Maine and New Brunswick, which included, among others, the Malecites, Micmacs, Passamaquoddys, Penobscots, Norridgewocks, Pigwackets, and possibly the Sokokis. All these tribes spoke similar dialects. Hunting and fishing were important activities, but maize was grown for winter food, and by the 18th century the fur trade played a very important part in tribal economies. In the 17th and 18th centuries the Abenakis were dependable allies of the French, and made many raids on New England during wars between the colonies. The French considered them an important barrier to attack from the south. In the wake of losses suffered in war many of them moved to the French mission villages of Saint-François and Bécancour. *See* NORRIDGEWOCKS, PENOBSCOTS, PIGWACKETS, SAINT-FRANÇOIS ABENAKIS. D.H.

Agniers. *See* MOHAWKS
Aiouez. *See* IOWAS

Algonkian (Algonquian); in French Algique, Algonkienne. Refers to the family of languages spoken by numerous peoples in north central and northeastern parts of the United States and almost the entire eastern sub-Arctic of Canada. This family of languages was part of a larger family of dialects, languages, and language families, including Muskogean, an important language family in the southeastern United States, whose member groups were distributed over about half of the occupied land of precontact North America. This term is not to be confused with ALGONKIN.   H.H.

Algonkins (Algonquins). A congeries of closely related but politically separate tribes of the Chippewa-Ottawa-Algonkin branch of the Algonkian language family occupying chiefly the Ottawa River valley and also a region north of Lake Huron where they merged with Chippewas and Ottawas. Other neighbours with a similar culture were the Montagnais, the Naskapis and the Crees to the north and east. The Algonkins were game hunters, fishermen, and wild food gatherers. They made extensive use of birch bark. They participated energetically as trappers in the French fur trade. During the second half of the 17th century many of their settlements suffered from attacks by the Five Nations Iroquois, resulting in wide-scale dispersal north and northwest of their original locations in the Ottawa valley.   H.H.

Amikwas; in French Amikoués. An Algonkian people living on and adjacent to the north shore of Lake Huron, and also sporadically at Lake Nipissing, mentioned by French traders and missionaries from the mid-17th to mid-18th centuries, by which time they were no longer referred to as a separate people. The Amikwas were an autonomous branch of the association of related groups who after French contact came together to form the Chippewa (Saulteux) tribe. Their early history is closely linked to that of the Chippewas, and there is a strong probability that they comprised merely the beaver clan of that tribe. They were primarily hunters and fishermen and played a prominent role as trappers, perhaps at times as middlemen, in the French fur trade. *See* CHIPPEWAS.   H.H.

Andastes. *See* SUSQUEHANNOCKS
Androscoggins. *See* AROSAGUNTACOOKS
Aoyatanouns. *See* WEAS

Arosaguntacooks. A tribe engaged on the French side in the colonial wars of the early 18th century, commonly identified with the Abenakis of the Androscoggin River in Maine. *See also* SAINT-FRANÇOIS ABENAKIS.   G.M.D.

Assiniboins; in French Assinipoil, etc.; also known as Stones or Stoneys. This was a large Dakota Siouan-speaking congeries of woodland-prairie bands detached from one of the western Dakota divisions in the mid-17th century. The Assiniboins in the late 17th and early 18th centuries occupied the international boundary region around Lake of the Woods and Red River of the North extending northward to an undetermined distance. Their settlements interpenetrated with those of closely allied Algonkian-speaking Crees. With the Crees they were continuously at enmity with their Dakota congeners. It is probable that the fur trade was responsible for their fragmenting from their kinsmen. Because of their northerly position, they had access to the trade at Hudson Bay and elsewhere. During the last half of the 18th century, Assiniboins with western Crees gradually moved to the high plains where they hunted bison on horseback. *See* STONES.   H.H.

Assistaeronons (Assistagueronons). *See* MASCOUTENS

Athapaskans; northern division known as the Déné. The tribes that are within the larger Athapaskan linguistic family but who are culturally related and inhabit the Arctic drainage and parts of the western drainage of Hudson Bay are frequently referred to as the Déné. This group includes the present-day tribes known as the Beavers, Chipewyans, Dogribs, Hares, Yellowknives, and Slaveys. They formed the last major bloc of Canadian Indians to be brought directly into the European fur trade. After 1717 when Fort Prince of Wales was established at Churchill River the only tribe which was in continuous contact there for years was the Chipewyans, then known to the Hudson's Bay Company men only as the Northern Indians. In 1715 William STUART, accompanied by THANADELTHUR, a Chipewyan woman, and a number of Crees, had travelled north from York to try to make peace between the Crees and the Chipewyans and thus to establish trade relations with the latter. The Chipewyans were the largest tribe of the Déné and were distributed widely to the west and northwest of Hudson Bay. Their exact aboriginal territorial boundaries, as well as those of all the Déné tribes, remain vague, because the Crees had already dislocated peoples to the north and west. Cree territory had vastly expanded by the time the first references to any Déné are made. At a later date the Chipewyans ranged from Churchill River west to the Peace River, north on the Slave River to Great Slave Lake and, from there, northeast into the Barrens adjoining Eskimo territory. The early descriptions of the Northern Indians' difficulties in travelling to Fort Prince of Wales suggest that only those northwest of Hudson Bay were attempting direct trade relations and were coming from long distances (probably 200 miles or more). This implies that the term Northern Indians in the 1700s usually referred to a Chipewyan sub-group, the Caribou Eaters (Mangeurs de Caribou). The Caribou Eaters are the most northerly of the Chipewyans and, unlike their southern woodland tribesmen, exploited the Barrens seasonally. The Copper Indians (Couteaux Jaunes) were the only other Déné tribe specifically identified in the first half of the 18th century. Now known as the Yellowknives, they are linguistically and culturally closely related to the Chipewyans. Their designation as "Copper Indians" dates from 1714 when they were reported as Indians who made copper implements and who roamed in a distant area of rich copper deposits that the Hudson's Bay Company attempted numerous times in the 18th century to locate. The only possible contact with these Indians, with the exception of one or two who came to Fort Prince of Wales with Northern Indians, would have been by Stuart in 1715. The Copper Indians lived to the west of their Northern Indian neighbours and were located (by Samuel Hearne*) in 1771 on the Coppermine River and to the eastward. The Dogribs (Platscotés de Chiens) were also mentioned a few times in early accounts. These references must be considered a general designation based on hearsay reports for some one or more tribes of the Déné group. Henry KELSEY's Dogside (1691), LE ROY de La Potherie's Attimospiquaies (1753), and Arthur Dobbs* Plascotez de Chiens (1744) cannot be considered specific references to the Dogribs who inhabited the area between Great Slave Lake and Great Bear Lake in historic times. The Slaveys (Esclaves), are not specifically mentioned in the 18th-century accounts. Slave is a generic term used by the Hudson's Bay Company to refer to slaves of the Algonkians. The most frequent slaves in this specific period were Chipewyans captured by the Crees. The Slavey tribe of more recent designation is located at the southwest end of Great Slave Lake and on the headwaters of the Mackenzie River. The Beaver Indians (Castors) were not identified as a tribe until visited by Alexander Mackenzie* in 1793. They were probably inhabiting the area between Lake Athabasca and the Rocky Mountains before the Crees pushed them further west and up the Peace River. The Hares (Peaux-de-Lièvres) were identified by Mackenzie in 1793; they inhabit the area north and west of Great Bear Lake to the Mackenzie River.

B.C.G. and J.HM

Attiwandaronk. *See* NEUTRALS
Beaver Indians. *See* ATHAPASKANS
Beaver People. *See* AMIKWAS

Beothuk ("Red Indians"); in French Béothuk (Peaux-Rouges). The first aborigines encountered by early European visitors to Newfoundland; they probably belonged to a distinct linguistic family confined to Newfoundland and were exterminated by European fishermen and the Micmacs. The last known survivor died in captivity in 1829.

Cahokias. One of the most important of the tribal divisions of the central Algonkian Illinois; they may have been living separately in their own village when first encountered by Cavelier* de La Salle in 1682. By the 1690s they were living with kindred Tamaroas in a large agricultural village on the east bank of the Mississippi nearly opposite the present St Louis. Like other Illinois they suffered heavy losses from warfare and disease. *See* ILLINOIS, TAMAROAS. H.H.

Canibas. *See* NORRIDGEWOCKS

Caribou Eaters. *See* ATHAPASKANS
Cat Nation. *See* ERIES
Caughnawaga Indians. *See* IROQUOIS, MISSION INDIANS, MOHAWKS

Cayugas; in French Goyogouins; their own term for themselves being variously interpreted as People of the Swamp, Great Pipe People, and People Where the Locusts Were Taken Out. One of the member tribes of the Iroquois Confederacy, the Cayugas lived between the Onondagas and Senecas in territory on either side of the present Cayuga Lake in west central New York State. Like all other league members, the Cayugas were agriculturalists, growing maize, beans, and squash. They also hunted deer and other woodland game. Together with the Oneidas they constituted the minor governing group in Confederacy politics known as the Younger Brothers. Following the American Revolution the majority of Cayugas moved to a reservation on the Grand River in Ontario, southwest of Hamilton, where they reside today. Of all the member tribes of the Confederacy, they tended to be the most conservative in the 19th century and even down to the present. *See* IROQUOIS, FIVE NATIONS CONFEDERACY, MOHAWKS, ONONDAGAS, SENECAS. H.H. and A.E.

Chickasaws; in French Chicachas. A leading Muskogean tribe, in the 18th century the Chickasaws lived in the area which is now Pontotoc and Union counties in northern Mississippi. They also claimed a much larger area, including the present state of Tennessee and northern Alabama. Warlike and independent, they dominated the area, and Chickasaw was the *lingua franca* of all the tribes on the lower Mississippi. The Chickasaws, always enemies of the French, especially resented French trade relations with their enemies the Choctaws. In the early 18th century the English, friendly with the Chickasaws, were attempting to enter the Mississippi valley, and this fact, and Chickasaw raids on Mississippi convoys, made the French determined to defeat the Chickasaws. In 1736 a force under d'Artaguiette attacked them in their home territory, but the result was a massacre of the French [*see* FRANÇOIS-MARIE BISSOT de Vinsenne]. The Chickasaws resisted successfully again in the war of 1739–40.

Chipewyans. *See* ATHAPASKANS

Chippewas (Ojibwas); in French Saulteurs, Sauteux. Originally located in the region adjacent to northern Lake Huron and eastern Lake Superior, the Chippewas had come by the late 18th century to occupy a region extending from lower Ontario to eastern Saskatchewan, including extensive areas in the Great Lakes, Mississippi, and Hudson Bay drainages. Basically a hunting and fishing people, the Chippewas also made use of wild rice and other wild plants including the sugar maple. They were renowned for their skill in the use of birch bark, especially in the manufacture of canoes. Chippewas played a prominent role in the fur trade as trappers and middlemen. Their warfare with the Dakota Sioux, with whom they had once been trading allies, was a prominent feature of the frontier. When the first contact with them was made, the Chippewas were divided into several local bands which probably were patrilineal clans. From 1670 to 1736 the bands consolidated, permitting the establishment of villages, the largest of which, amounting to about 1,000 persons, was located at Chequamegon peninsula in western Lake Superior. The Chippewas were never organized politically above the village level, but comprised a congeries of related bands and villages. *See* COUNCIL OF THE THREE FIRES. H.H.

Comanches; in French Padoucas. A nomadic plains tribe who hunted buffalo, they were known to be living in the western part of the present state of Kansas in 1719. That year DUTISNÉ encountered them, and reported that they were mortal enemies of the Pawnees and had prevented the Spaniards from visiting that tribe. The Comanches' enmity towards other western tribes threatened the French system of alliances until VÉNIARD de Bourgmond re-established good relations.

Copper Indians. *See* ATHAPASKANS

Council of the Three Fires; in French, Confédération des Trois-Feux. A designation for the central Algonkian Chippewas, Ottawas, and Potawatomis indicating the close alliance, if not confederation, among them. The Chippewas and Ottawas spoke dialects of one language; Potawatomi is considered a related but separate language. The "Council" was a political fiction probably invented in the first half of the 18th century by members of the three tribes who had established joint villages in the St Joseph River region west of Detroit. In later times, after moving westward to the Illinois country, they became known to British and American traders and government agents as the "United Nations of Chippewa, Ottawa, and Potawatomi Indians." The origin of the villages, whose main membership was Potawatomi, is obscure, and they represent but a minute fragment of the membership of those tribes. The fiction of confederation was based on actual linguistic and cultural similarities, which indicate that their separation had taken place in late prehistoric times. *See* CHIPPEWAS, OTTAWAS, POTAWATOMIS. H.H.

Cranes. *See* MIAMIS

Crees; in French Cris, a shortened form of Kristinaux. An Algonkian-speaking people closely related to the Montagnais-Naskapis, the Crees comprised a great number of related, but autonomous, villages and bands. At the height of their expansion in the late 18th century they occupied a region including most of the southern half of the Hudson Bay coast,

extending westward to include large portions of what is now northern Ontario, Manitoba, Saskatchewan, and eastern Alberta. This expansion resulted in diversification into four main divisions: Swampy, Rocky, Woods, and Plains. The ancestral Crees were probably confined to the region contiguous to James Bay, including the inland lakes and waterways in the Shield. There they hunted wild fowl, moose, and woodland caribou, which with fish and wild plant products provided their subsistence. From the mid-17th century Crees were active in the French and British fur trade as trappers and as middlemen to far inland tribes, including the Blackfeet and northern Athapaskans. They traded at the HBC posts on James Bay, where they were known as Home Indians, and they figured prominently in the explorations of Pierre Gaultier* de La Vérendrye. Close allies of the Siouan Assiniboins, they were at various periods bitter foes of the Dakota Sioux, Blackfeet, and Chipewyans. *See* MASKEGONS, MONSONIS. H.H.

Culs-Coupez. *See* OTTAWAS
Dakotas. *See* SIOUX
Dogribs. *See* ATHAPASKANS
Dogsides. *See* ATHAPASKANS

Eries; in French Ériés (Nation du Chat). The Eries, or Cat Nation (People of the Long-Tailed—Eastern—Puma), were linguistic cousins of the Iroquois. Their territory and agricultural settlements were, according to the *Jesuit Relations*, situated east of the present Lake Erie. Much confusion surrounds their identity as a separate group; at times they were confused with the Awenrehronons (Wenros) and a more cryptic tribal entity known as the Black Minquas. Because they had sheltered Huron fugitives after the destruction of Huronia in 1649, the Eries were subjected to the vengeance of the Iroquois Confederacy, and were themselves defeated and absorbed by the Iroquois in 1654–57. *See* IROQUOIAN, IROQUOIS, WENROS. H.H. and A.E.

Etchemins. *See* MALECITES
Fire People. *See* MASCOUTENS

Five Nations Confederacy; in French Cinq-Nations. A designation for the political alliance, or league, of the Mohawks, Oneidas, Onondagas, Cayugas, and Senecas, established *c.* 1570 by two half-legendary heroes, Dekanahwideh and Hiawatha. Also called the Iroquois League, or Confederacy of the Five Nations. Sometime between 1712 and 1722 the Tuscaroras, a linguistically related tribe from Carolina, moved north in small groups into Confederacy territory and were accepted as the sixth nation. Thereafter the Confederacy was called the Six Nations. During the latter half of the 17th century and much of the 18th, many dispossessed remnants of small coastal tribes were given asylum in territory controlled by the league; such asylum did not constitute equal status with the older member tribes of the league. The Confederacy had its political capital in the territory of the Onondaga tribe, located near the present Syracuse, New York, and Onondaga chiefs, like TEGANISSORENS, had much influence on league decisions. As with all other Iroquoians, the tribes of the Confederacy depended for their subsistence on agriculture, raising maize, beans, and squash in river bottoms. Hunting and fishing provided substantial food. Also, as everywhere, the matrilineal clan system was in effect, fields being owned jointly by female members of matrilineages. *See* IROQUOIAN, IROQUOIS.

H.H. and A.E.

Folles Avoines. *See* MENOMINEES

Foxes (Mesquakies, or Red Earth People); in French Renards, Outagamis. Originally located in the lower peninsula of Michigan, they migrated, probably under pressure from Iroquois, to the Green Bay (Baie des Puants) area where they were first contacted by French traders and missionaries in the 1660s. The Foxes spoke a central Algonkian language closely related to Sauk, Kickapoo, and Mascouten, the languages of the peoples with whom they were often allied and who had migrated with them. All these tribes lived in villages where they raised maize, beans, and squash; they held annual communal hunts for deer and bison. Drawn into the fur trade at an early date, they had a shortage of beaver in their own country, but, occupying strategic positions on the important Fox-Wisconsin River trade route to the Mississippi, they demanded a share in the trade as middlemen or in the form of tolls. At the beginning of the 18th century the Foxes were on friendly terms with New France and her Indian allies [*see* NORO], but after the Chippewa massacre of a Fox village near Detroit in 1712 [*see* PEMOUSSA] the Foxes became a major source of disruption. Their raids were aggravated, in French eyes, by attempts to ally themselves with the English. Temporarily subdued in 1716 [*see* OUACHALA], the Foxes finally suffered defeat in 1730 and 1731–32, when the French took prisoner their greatest war-chief, KIALA. In 1733 many joined the Sauks and with them began a movement westward, first to the Mississippi, then across it into Iowa where some of the associated Sauk and Fox peoples continue to live today. *See* SAUKS.   H.H.

Gaspesians. *See* MICMACS
Gens du Lac. *See* MDEWAKANTONS
Goyogouins. *See* CAYUGAS
Hares. *See* ATHAPASKANS
Home Indians. *See* CREES

Hurons (from the Old French *hure*, a "bristly head"). They were divided into four separate tribes: The Bear (Attignawantan); the Cord (Attignueenongnahac); the Rock (Ahrendarrhonon); and the Deer (Tahontaenrat). When Iroquois attacks led to the dispersal of the Huron confederacy early in 1649, many Hurons took refuge among the neighbouring Tionontatis (Petuns), who were closely allied to them in language and culture. Most of these refugees belonged to the Attignawantan tribe and came from the village of Ossossane, which by that time was largely Christian. In December 1649, however, the Tionontatis and their Huron guests were driven out of southern Ontario by the Iroquois, who did not wish to see the Huron trade fall into the hands of yet another tribe. About 800 Tionontatis and Hurons made an orderly retreat northward towards Lake Michigan. Although mostly Tionontatis, these people came to be known as the Wyandots, a corruption of *Wendat*, the old name the Hurons had applied to themselves. Between 1653 and 1670, the Wyandots wandered in the region of the upper Great Lakes, participating in the fur trade and living with and being influenced by the Ottawas and Potawotamis. In 1670 the Hurons founded a settlement at Mackinac. In 1701 the chief KONDIARONK attended the peace conference convened at Montreal by CALLIÈRE, and the Hurons were persuaded to move to the vicinity of Fort Pontchartrain, which the French had just constructed at Detroit. About 1738 there was a division among the Wyandots. Some remained in the Detroit area and their descendants now reside near Sandwich, Ontario; the others, under war-chief Orontony, or Nicholas, moved to Sandusky, Ohio. After many wanderings the latter group finally settled on the Wyandotte Reservation in Oklahoma. The Wyandot language died out in the first half of this century. *See* HURONS OF LORETTE, IROQUOIAN.

B.G.T.

Hurons of Lorette. After the overthrow of the Huron confederacy in 1649, a portion of the Huron people fled to Quebec and finally settled at Lorette, where they still reside. In the spring of 1650, about 300 Christian Huron refugees, who had spent the winter living under French protection on Christian Island in Georgian Bay, asked to be taken to Quebec. In March 1651 they settled on Île d'Orléans. There they were joined by the Hurons who had settled at Sillery as early as 1640 and by other Christian Hurons who arrived from what is now Ontario. The following year most of the Hurons at Quebec who belonged to the Ahrendarrhonon and Attignawantan tribes were forced to settle among the Onondaga and Mohawk tribes respectively. Most of the Hurons who remained at Quebec were of the Attingueenongnahac tribe. The Hurons continued to reside close to the fort at Quebec until 1668, when they settled at Beauport, where they began to cultivate land in the traditional Huron manner. In 1669 they moved to Sainte-Foy, where they were joined by some Christian Iroquois. In 1673 the expanding population moved to Ancienne Lorette and in 1697 to Jeune Lorette. For the past hundred years most of their income has been derived from the manufacture of snowshoes, moccasins, and baskets. The Hurons of Lorette are noted for their devotion to Christianity. Although they have retained their sense of ethnic identity, they have intermarried extensively with French Canadians and ceased to speak Huron in the early part of the 19th century. *See* HURONS.   B.G.T.

Illinois. Adapted by the French from *Iliniwek*, the People, for a number of closely related tribes, chief among whom were the Kaskaskias, Cahokias, Peorias, Tamaroas, and Michigameas. The Illinois were distinct from Miami tribes who spoke different dialects of the same central Algonkian language. The Illinois were first met by Marquette* and Jolliet* in 1673 on the Illinois and Mississippi rivers, and throughout the French régime they lived in numerous agricultural villages on both banks of the Mississippi and its eastern tributaries in southern Iowa, northern Missouri, and Illinois. Maize, beans, and squash were staple foods, and communal bison hunts were conducted on foot west of the Mississippi during the summer. They traded furs to the French who from the 1680s established forts and, later, settlements in their country. Internecine warfare, first with the Iroquois, later with the Sioux, Foxes, and Chickasaws, combined with smallpox and other diseases, caused a severe reduction in their numbers; by the 19th century they were virtually extinct. Aboriginally the Illinois were probably organized in extended matrilocal families.   H.H.

Iowas; in French Aiouez. A Chiwere Siouan tribe closely related in language and social organization to the Winnebagos of the Green Bay (Baie des Puants) region, the Iowas occupied a large portion of the state which bears their name. Like neighbouring central Algonkians and Siouans, the Iowas were village farmers who made intensive use of river beds to raise maize, beans, and squash. Their reliance on wooden digging implements did not permit them to cultivate the rich but toughly sodded prairie lands. There, however, they conducted communal bison hunts on foot during the summer. They trapped fur game in winter, carrying pelts to French posts at Green Bay and on the upper Mississippi River. The Iowas did not figure prominently in the warfare that characterized intertribal relations in the late 17th and 18th centuries but seem for the most part to have maintained a position of neutrality. *See* WINNEBAGOS.   H.H.

Iroquoian; in French, Huronne-iroquoise; generally refers to the linguistic family composed of the Hurons, Iroquois (League of Five Nations), Neutrals, Susquehannocks, Eries, Tuscaroras, Nottaways, Meherrins, Cherokees, Wenros, and the Laurentian "Iroquois" encountered by Cartier* in 1534. The member groups of this language family were largely concentrated in the eastern Great Lakes region of Canada and the United States; but small groups, as well as the numerous Cherokees, were distributed in the southeastern piedmont and tidewater regions of the middle Atlantic and southern United States. This family of languages was part of a larger family of distantly related language families, including Siouan and Caddoan, whose member groups were distributed over the western Great Lakes and Mississippi valley of early North America. In specific usage the term might be used in reference to the league, or Five Nations Confederacy; it is also occasionally used as an adjective (i.e., Iroquoian costume, village). *See* IROQUOIS, FIVE NATIONS CONFEDERACY.   H.H. and A.E.

Iroquois; derived from the Algonkian word, Irinakhoiw, literally, Real Adders, figuratively, Rattlesnakes, with the French suffix *-ois*. Also referred to by some Algonkian tribes as Mingwes, Mingos, Nadowas, Maquas, and Massawomekes A generic term applied to a congeries of five closely related and politically unified tribes inhabiting villages in central New York State in a line running westward from present Amsterdam, N.Y., up the Mohawk River and through the Finger Lakes to the Genesee River. The member tribes were organized into a league variously referred to by themselves as Kayanerenh-Kowa, The Great Peace, or Kanonsionni, The Long-House. The former term implied their unity of purpose, the latter called to mind the unity of their member tribes by allusion to the closeness of family apartments in their bark long-houses. From east to west the member tribes were the Mohawks, Oneidas, Onondagas, Cayugas, and Senecas. During the 17th century the Iroquois overcame the other tribes drawn into the fur trade by their desire for European manufactured trade goods and firearms. The Hurons, close linguistic relatives, were subdued in this period and most were absorbed into the Iroquois population. In the late 17th century expeditions were led by BRISAY de Denonville and Louis de Buade* de Frontenac, governors of New France, against the Iroquois, but attempts to establish a peace were also made during these years. The peace conference of 1701 convened at Montreal by Louis-Hector de CALLIÈRE marks a watershed in Iroquois-French relations. In the 18th century the Iroquois largely played the role of a "buffer state" between New France and the English colonies on the Atlantic coast. The life of the Onondaga chief TEGANISSORENS reflects the shifts in the Iroquois position through these years. *See* IROQUOIAN, FIVE NATIONS CONFEDERACY.
                                               H.H. and A.E.

Kansas. A Siouan-speaking tribe of some 1,600 people, closely affiliated in language and in migration legend with the Osages, Quapaws, Omahas, and Poncas. The name is derived from one of the 16 patrisibs into which the Kansas were divided. According to Marquette*'s map, the Kansas must have been located in 1674 on the lower Kansas River. In 1724 Étienne de VÉNIARD de Bourgmond visited them at a village along the Missouri River at the present site of Doniphan, Kansas. By 1740 the Kansas had retired to a point near Salt Creek, north of the present Leavenworth, Kansas. Near this village the French established Fort Cavagnolle, probably before 1740. Some time after 1757 the Kansas moved to the Kansas River, establishing a village at the mouth of the Blue River. The movement of the Kansas to the Missouri River locations probably followed their involvement in the fur trade, and they early became one of the better armed tribes in the area. Their relocation on the Kansas River seems related to tribal dislocations accompanying westward thrusts and migrations by the Cheyennes, Dakotas, Sauks and Foxes, and Iowas in pursuit of hunting and trade advantages. After 1750 the Kansas apparently directed their summer and fall buffalo hunts southwesterly to the great bend of the Arkansas, and developed a sporadic alliance with the Osages. There is some doubt whether the Guas identified by the Coronado expedition were Kansas, or the Escansaques met by Juan de Oñate in 1601 somewhere in southern Kansas.   F.W.V.

Kaskaskias. One of the largest and perhaps the most important of the tribal divisions of the central Algonkian Illinois, others being the Cahokias, Peorias, Tamaroas, and Michigameas. When first encountered by the French in the 1670s the Kaskaskias lived in a large agricultural village on the upper Illinois River, but dispersed in hundreds of hunting parties during the winter. Bison were taken during the summer on the prairies west of the Mississippi by large communal parties hunting on foot. Under the pressure of Iroquois attacks during the 1680s, the Kaskaskias gradually moved down the Illinois, finally settling during the first decade of the 18th century on the Mississippi near the mouth of the river that bears their name. Attacks by the Foxes from 1713 to 1738 led to an almost complete withdrawal from the Illinois region. The Kaskaskia village on the Illinois was singular in that it included members of all the other Illinois tribes. The establishment of the first important French post, Fort Saint-Louis, opposite their village at Le Rocher (Starved Rock) on Lake Peoria by Cavelier* de La Salle and HENRI TONTY in 1682–83, may have been a cause. *See* ILLINOIS.   H.H.

Kickapoos; in French Kicapous. Like their close central Algonkian kinsmen, the Foxes, Sauks, and Mascoutens, the Kickapoos settled southwest of Green Bay (Baie des Puants) in the region between the Fox River (Wisconsin) and the Illinois River, during the last decade of the 17th century. During most of the French régime the Kickapoos were closely identified with the Foxes and Mascoutens in intertribal warfare, and at times aided the Foxes in their wars with the French. The Kickapoos were village farmers and raised maize, beans, and squash. Like other central Algonkians, they carried on annual communal hunts for deer and bison, and also trapped for the fur trade. They are remarkable in their later history for their extensive migrations, being the first of the central Algonkians to adopt a Plains culture; during the 19th century large numbers of Kickapoos migrated to Mexico where a group of them is found today. *See* FOXES. H.H.

Kiskakons. *See* OTTAWAS
Kristinaux. *See* CREES
League of the Iroquois. *See* FIVE NATIONS CONFEDERACY.

Mahicans (Mohicans); in French also Loups. A powerful tribe to the east of the Five Nations Confederacy, which inhabited the Hudson valley and extended into Massachusetts. They are related to but distinct from the Mohegans, an Algonkian tribe who lived in what is now Connecticut. They settled first at Schodac, on an island in the vicinity of Albany, N.Y., in 40 villages. After attacks by the Mohawks, they moved in 1664 to what is now Stockbridge, Mass. Another migration formed the largest part of the Schaghticokes. The French used the term "Loups" for the latter, and for the Munsees and Delawares, as well as for the related Mahicans. In 1730 a large group of the Stockbridge Mahicans moved to the area of Wyoming, Pa., and later to Ohio. *See* SCHAGHTICOKES.

Malecites (Etchemins); in French Malécites (Etchemins). A tribe closely resembling the Micmacs (early writers confused the two), which lived along the Saint John River in New Brunswick. Their territory stretched north beyond the drainage basin of the Saint John River and, to the south, also included a part of what is now the state of Maine. *See* ABENAKIS.

Mascoutens (central Algonkian for Prairie People, but also known as Fire People); in French also called Nation du Feu, and often referred to as Assistagueronons, Assistaeronons. A central Algonkian people closely related generically and by alliance to the Kickapoos, Sauks, and Foxes; like the others, by the 18th century they lived southwest of Green Bay (Baie des Puants) in the region between the upper Fox and Illinois Rivers, and also in the Milwaukee River region. Tracing the history of the Mascoutens is difficult because none of them are living today. They probably merged during the last part of the 18th century with Sauk, Fox, and Kickapoo congeners. The Mascoutens were woodland village farmers and also carried on communal hunts on the prairies during the summer. They fought as allies of the Foxes at various times against the Illinois, Ottawas, Chippewas, and other Indian enemies, and occasionally against the French. *See* FOXES, KICKAPOOS.   H.H.

Maskegons (Algonkian for People of the Swamp); in French, Moskégon. Probably a term for the Swampy Crees or a branch of them, living on and inland from the southwest shore of James Bay. They may also have been the same, or part of the same group as the Monsonis who, as auxiliaries of the Crees, figured in the explorations of Pierre Gaultier* de La Vérendrye, 1730–49. The term may also, or alternatively, have been applied to Chippewa-speaking groups living in the marshy country between Lake of the Woods and Lake Winnipeg at the end of the 18th and during the first half of the 19th centuries. *See* CHIPPEWAS, CREES, MONSONIS.

H.H.

Mdewakantons; also called by the French Gens du Lac after the Mille Lacs lake region in Minnesota and other lake sites in the Mississippi headwaters region, where they lived. This was the Dakota Siouan tribal division most frequently mentioned by the French, beginning with Father Louis HENNEPIN and DANIEL GREYSOLON Dulhut in 1680. The Mdewakantons traded furs at posts on the upper Mississippi at Lake Pepin (near Lake City, Minn.) at various times between 1685 and 1751, and also to Chippewa middlemen living on Chequamegon Peninsula of Lake Superior between 1680 and 1736. The Mdewakantons played a prominent role in the intertribal wars of that period, fighting the Foxes, Illinois, Crees, and Assiniboins. They were often courted by Algonkian and French traders, their country being rich in fur game. The Chippewa alliance with the Mdewakantons was broken in 1736 when the French established direct trade with the latter and with their foes, the Crees. Towards the end of the 18th century the Mdewakantons abandoned their woodland villages because of Chippewa pressure and founded new villages in the prairie region of southeastern Minnesota. *See* SIOUX.

H.H.

Menominees (central Algonkian signifying Wild Rice People); invariably referred to by the French as Folles Avoines. The Menominees, who spoke a distinctive central Algonkian language, occupied most of the region between the northwest shore of Lake Michigan including Green Bay (Baie des Puants) and the south shore of eastern Lake Superior, perhaps in conjunction with certain Chippewa groups. Unlike other central Algonkians, the Menominees apparently had occupied since aboriginal times the region in which they were first encountered by the French in the mid-17th century. A woodland village people, they relied chiefly on wild rice (*zizania aquatica*), fish, and large game, especially Virginia deer, for subsistence, and were energetic trappers for the fur trade. This tribe maintained a position of neutrality in intertribal warfare throughout the French régime and after. Their social organization was similar to that of the neighbouring Chippewas: patrilineal clans divided into several sets, or phratries, within which marriage could not occur.

H.H.

Metchigamias. *See* MICHIGAMEAS

Miamis; in French also Oumamis. The generic term for six related but autonomous tribes, perhaps aboriginally totemic clans, including as the three most important: Piankeshaws, Weas, and Atchatchakangouens (Cranes); also, Kilatekas, Mengakonkias, and Pepicokeas. After 1700 the term Miami, although persisting as the generic name, was applied specifically to the Crane division. In the 19th century divisional distinctions were lost. The Miamis spoke dialects of one central Algonkian language closely related to the dialects of Illinois. When first encountered in the 1670s the Miamis had moved from the southwestern Lake Michigan area to the Fox-Wisconsin River area. After establishing villages at various locations in Wisconsin and Illinois, including the mouth of the Wisconsin River, during the first decade of the 18th century, the various divisions moved east to establish permanent villages on the St Joseph, Maumee, and Wabash rivers in Michigan, Ohio, and Indiana. The Cranes, or Miamis proper, had their villages on the Maumee. Some Miamis also settled at Detroit, where they were involved in the LE PESANT affair of 1706. The Miamis cultivated maize, beans, and squash, hunted large prairie and woodland game, and trapped for the fur trade. Led by chiefs like CHICHIKATELO, they were important allies of the French, who maintained posts and garrisons in their country. The Miamis warred against the Foxes and Chickasaws. In 1733 they suffered badly from smallpox. *See* PIANKESHAWS, WEAS.

H.H.

Michigameas; in French, Metchigamias. At the time of first contact with the Europeans they were the southernmost of the tribal divisions of the Illinois, some other divisions being the Cahokias, Kaskaskias, Peorias, and Tamaroas. The Michigameas apparently detached themselves from the others in early historical times. In 1700–1 they joined the Tamaroas in their village on the Mississippi, a few miles south of the Missouri junction, perhaps as a result of pressure from Caddoan enemies to the south. Later, in the 1720s, the Michigameas were associated with the Kaskaskias who were said to have adopted them but continued to live with the Tamaroas in an agricultural village on the east bank of the Mississippi, in the present Randolph County, Ill. *See* ILLINOIS, TAMAROAS. H.H.

Micmacs (etymologically "the allies," Souriquois, Gaspesians [in French Gaspésiens], Miscouiens). A member tribe of the Abenaki Confederacy, which, at the time of its discovery, occupied Nova Scotia, Cape Breton Island, the northern portion of New Brunswick, and Prince Edward Island. They are the Souriquois of the *Jesuit Relations* and the Gaspesians of Le Clercq*. The tribe adopted agriculture, accepted the Christian teachings of the missionaries, intermarried freely with the French colonists, and, like their neighbours the Malecites, remained allies of the French throughout the wars of the 17th and 18th centuries.

Miscouiens. *See* MICMACS

Mission or **Praying Indians.** The Christianized Indians who lived in the missions of New France. The principal groups were the Iroquois of Sault-Saint-Louis (Caughnawaga); the Iroquois of the Mountain (at Lac des Deux-Montagnes, or Oka, after

xxxiii

1720); the Abenakis of Saint-François and Bécancour; and the Hurons of Lorette. *See* HURONS OF LORETTE, SAINT-FRANÇOIS ABENAKIS.

Missisaugas; in French Mississagues. A Chippewa-speaking tribe, possibly the eagle clan, or totem, of the autonomous but associated clans which were the ancestors of the modern Chippewas. In Chippewa their name signifies "large outlet" and refers to their village at the mouth of the Mississaga River of northern Lake Huron where they maintained a sturgeon fishery in summer. Like their close kinsmen they were fishermen, hunters, and energetic trappers. They were not then cultivators, but like other Algonkians in the upper Great Lakes region, traded hides to farming neighbours to the south for maize. The Missisaugas appear to have detached themselves from westward-moving Chippewas in the late 17th century. Some moved south to the Detroit area about 1700 and later gravitated east to the lower peninsula of Ontario as allies or trading partners of the New York Iroquois; others remained in the Lake Huron area. *See* CHIPPEWAS.

H.H.

Missouris. A Siouan-speaking people estimated to number around 1,000 at the time of French contact. Missouri, meaning Great Muddy, is an Algonkian term. The Missouri name, Niutachi (Those Who Arrived at the Mouth), is a sobriquet commemorating their decision to settle at the mouth of the Grand River. In legend the Missouris, along with the Otos and Iowas, were said to have split off from the Winnebagos at the time the latter elected to migrate no further than the Green Bay (Baie des Puants) area. VÉNIARD de Bourgmond located a Missouri village on the north side of the Missouri River in 1714, and Fort Orléans was built nearby in 1723. When Fort Orléans was abandoned for an establishment farther up the Missouri among the Kansas (Fort Cavagnolle), the Missouri Indians arranged to settle south of the Missouri several miles from the Little Osages. In 1785 the Missouris were reported to number about 120 men, or an estimated population of little more than 500. In their early association with the Little Osages, the Missouris profited by slave and horse raids among Caddoan-speaking groups to the west, and their successes led to the use of the word "Panis" (a general term for these Caddoan speakers at the time) for slave. Toward the end of the 18th century the Missouris suffered such a drastic population decline because of epidemics and war that the majority migrated to the Otos and several families joined the Osages and Kansas. F.W.V.

Mistassinis, in French Mistassins. The Mistassini Indians speak a dialect of Cree, the latter being a part of the Algonkian language family. The term "Mistassini" in their dialect means Huge Rock and refers to an immense boulder resting on a sandy beach near the outlet of Lake Mistassini. They revered it as the residence of the god of good

and bad weather. Numbering several hundred in the late 17th century, by 1730 the Mistassinis had been reduced by European diseases to a small group. They have inhabited the area of Lakes Mistassini and Albanel for over 300 years. The Mistassinis were an inland group, who in the early 1700s were primarily hunters of big game, especially caribou, exploiting an immense territory. Although they continued to be big game hunters for another 200 years, they were, even at this period, augmenting their hunting by trapping fur-bearing animals to exchange for European commodities. No doubt the French knew of the Mistassinis by the early 1600s but the first reference to them by name was not made until 1642–43. Father Charles Albanel* met them in 1672, and during the following years the Mistassinis were encountered by fur traders who established temporary posts in the territory of the Indians. During the summer the Mistassinis also travelled either to Lac Saint-Jean or to Rupert House on James Bay. At the close of the 17th century, interest in the area of the Mistassinis decreased; then, in 1720, Father Pierre LAURE began his work in the area and was the first to provide a general, albeit limited, description of the Mistassini Indians. *See* CREES. E.S.R.

Mohawks; in French Agniers. Over two dozen names have been applied to this group, their own reference for themselves being Kaniengehaga, People of the Place of the Flint. The Mohawks were the easternmost member of the Five Nations Confederacy; as the ritual Keepers of the Eastern Door of the Longhouse, they "defended" the eastern borders of Iroquois territory. In the federal councils of the league, the Mohawks were ranked among the Elder Brothers (Mohawks, Onondagas, Senecas). In 1609 the Mohawks first came in contact with Europeans. Their rough treatment at the hands of Champlain* has been thought to be the basis for their enmity towards the French over the following 150 years. During the 17th century the Mohawks, led by chiefs like TEKARIHOKEN, continually harassed French settlements along the St Lawrence, although Jesuit missionaries such as Simon Le Moyne* and JACQUES DE LAMBERVILLE visited them during intermittent periods of peace. The establishment of a Dutch trading post at Fort Orange (the present Albany, N.Y.) afforded the Mohawks and cognate Iroquois tribes a source of firearms to carry out their wars. About 1668, owing to the influence of several missionaries, a small number of Mohawks were converted to Christianity and left their homeland in central New York to settle near Montreal at Sault-Saint-Louis (Caughnawaga). *See* IROQUOIS, FIVE NATIONS CONFEDERACY, MISSION INDIANS.

H.H. and A.E.

Mohicans. *See* MAHICANS

Monsonis (Algonkian for Moose). The name may refer to a clan, or totemic affiliation, but it is more probably a reference to their moose hunting. The

Monsonis were a division of the Woods or Swampy Crees with whom they eventually merged. During the French régime they inhabited the country adjacent to southwestern James Bay and also the international boundary region between Lake Superior and Lake Winnipeg. They were prominent partners of other Crees and Assiniboins in the accounts of Pierre Gaultier* de La Vérendrye. They were hunters, trappers, and fishermen, and participated to some extent in wars against the Sioux. Like the rest of the Crees, their early social organization is not known, but they were probably less sedentary than the central Algonkians to the south. *See* CREES, MASKEGONS. H.H.

Montagnais; a French name referring to the upland regions to the north of the lower St Lawrence, where these northern Algonkians lived. They and the Naskapis occupied the greater part of the Labrador peninsula, except the northern coastal region and much of the east shore of Hudson Bay, occupied by Eskimos. Montagnais-Naskapi dialects are similar to dialects of Cree, and their culture merges into that of the Woods and Swampy Crees. The Montagnais were in the fur trade even before Champlain*'s coming and were trappers and middlemen throughout the French régime. They resided mostly in wooded areas where moose, fish, and fur game provided their main subsistence, while the Naskapis occupied barren grounds where they hunted the caribou. Although their social organization in early times is not known, the Montagnais maintained large settlements at fisheries on the St Lawrence River and inland lakes, scattering in small bands for the winter hunts. Some groups also engaged in communal hunts for sea mammals, especially seals. *See* CREES, NASKAPIS. H.H.

Moskégon. *See* MASKEGONS
Nadouessioux. *See* SIOUX

Narragansetts, Nipmucs, Wampanoags. These eastern Algonkians lived in northeastern Connecticut, Rhode Island, and eastern Massachusetts. (The Nipmucs may have been merely the inhabitants of the "Nipmuc country," rather than an ethnic entity.) All three groups subsisted by agriculture, fishing, and hunting, and spoke closely related languages. Chief Massasoit of the Wampanoags made a treaty with the Pilgrims which lasted for 55 years, but his son, Philip, roused his tribe against the English colonists in 1675-76 [see CHURCH]. The Narragansetts joined Philip, as did the Nipmucs, many of whom had been considered Christians by the English. King Philip's War caused great damage to the colonists and brought disaster upon the defeated Indians. A few of the survivors remained in their homeland, but the majority fled west and north. *See* SCHAGHTICOKES. G.M.D.

Naskapis. The congeries of northern Algonkian bands occupying in general the northern and northwestern portions of the region of the great Montag-nais-Naskapi family; their dialects merge into those of both Montagnais and Crees whose cultures theirs greatly resembles. The main distinction between Montagnais and Naskapis was the greater proclivity of the latter for communal caribou hunting in barren grounds, the former being more associated with woodland hunting, trapping, and fishing. Naskapis, with little access to coastal and riverine trading posts, were not in early times as integrated into the fur trade as Montagnais, but probably received in some areas trade goods through Montagnais and Cree middlemen, the former coming inland from the St Lawrence, the latter from the East Main of Hudson Bay. Little is known of early Naskapi social organization, but reliance on the communal caribou hunt would imply the existence of large social groups for at least part of the year. *See* CREES, MONTAGNAIS. H.H.

Nassawaketons. *See* OTTAWAS
Nation du Chat. *See* ERIES
Nation du Feu. *See* MASCOUTENS

Neutrals (called Attiwandaronk by the Hurons); in French Neutres. This Iroquoian-speaking tribe occupied the territory in southwestern Ontario between the Niagara River on the east, Lake Erie on the south, Lake St Clair on the west and an indeterminate northern boundary roughly 75 miles from Huronia. They were a small confederacy of agricultural people who raised a surplus of tobacco for trading purposes. Situated between the Iroquois Confederacy on the east and the Huron Confederacy to the northwest, the Neutrals remained uncommitted during conflicts between the two groups. They gave asylum to refugees from other war-torn tribal groups, particularly to the Eries with whom they were closely identified. In 1650-51 the Neutral Confederacy was itself subjugated and its remnants were absorbed by the Iroquois League. *See* IROQUOIAN. H.H. and A.E.

Nez-Percés. *See* AMIKWAS

Nipissings; in French Népissingues, Nipissiriniens. In Algonkian, People of the Little Water, so named from the location of their villages on Lake Nipissing. A central Algonkian-speaking people of the Chippewa-Ottawa-Algonkian language group, they, like the others, were middlemen in the French fur trade, trading mainly with Crees to the north. They were also fishermen, hunters, and trappers. Although they grew little maize, they obtained ample supplies through trade with neighbouring and allied Hurons and others in exchange for hides. The Nipissings, like Chippewas, had exogamous patrilineal clans, or totems, and like other central Algonkians lived, when conditions permitted, in permanent villages, leaving them only seasonally to hunt, trap, and trade. *See* CHIPPEWAS, OTTAWAS. H.H.

Nipmucs. *See* NARRAGANSETTS

Norridgewocks; in French, Canibas. An important division of the Abenakis, the Norridgewocks usually lived at the village of that name (now Old Point, south Madison) on the Kennebec River in Maine. Led by chiefs like MOG and supported by Father Sébastien RALE, their Jesuit missionary, they fought for the French during the War of the Spanish Succession, carrying scalps and prisoners to Quebec. The Penobscots, Pigwackets, and other Abenaki tribes also remained allied to the French. After the treaty of Utrecht in 1713, however, the Norridgewocks were the tribe principally affected by the spread of English settlement east of the Kennebec and up the river valley. WOWURNA and other chiefs protested and then harassed the English settlers, until Massachusetts declared war on the Abenakis in 1722. Rale was killed by the English in 1724, and most of the Norridgewocks moved to Saint-François in Canada. They joined the Penobscots in making peace in 1727, and many of the Norridgewocks returned to their native village at that time. Greatly reduced in numbers from the beginning of the century, they did not actively resist the quickening pace of English settlement. Their village was attacked again by the English in 1749, and most of them moved to Saint-François in 1754. *See* ABENAKIS, SAINT-FRANÇOIS ABENAKIS, PENOBSCOTS, PIGWACKETS.　　D.H.

Northern Indians. *See* ATHAPASKANS

Nottoways; in French, Ontationoués. A small Iroquoian-speaking group residing along the Nottoway River in Virginia, their own name being Cheroenhaka, meaning possibly Fork of a River. The term Nottoway appears to be a generic Algonkian term, meaning Serpent or Beast, which is used in reference to all alien speakers. (There is also a Nottaway River flowing into Hudson Bay, which may well be an indication of Iroquois attacks in that area, although there is no historic connection between the Canadian Nottaway and the Virginia Nottoway Rivers.) In 1757 a small group of Nottoway Indians from Virginia participated in the English campaign against the French Fort Duquesne. *See* IROQUOIAN.　　H.H. and A.E.

Ojibwas. *See* CHIPPEWAS

Oneidas; in French Onneiouts. The name stems from the Iroquois term Tiioneniote, figuratively, People of the Upright Stone. Like their close kinsmen, the Mohawks, and all other members of the league, the Oneidas were village farmers and raised maize, beans, and squash. They also carried on extensive seasonal hunting, fishing, and collecting of wild plant foods. In the league's political organization the Oneidas, along with the Cayugas, were designated Younger Brothers. Oneida territory extended approximately from the present Utica, N.Y., west to Oneida Lake. Father Pierre MILLET visited the Oneidas; GOUENTAGRANDI, an Oneida woman, was baptized by him and later moved to the mission at

Sault-Saint-Louis (Caughnawaga). *See* IROQUOIS, FIVE NATIONS CONFEDERACY.　　H.H. and A.E.

Onneiouts. *See* ONEIDAS

Onondagas; in French Onontagués; their own term for themselves being, Ononta ge, figuratively, People of the Hills. The Onondagas were the most centrally located of the five Iroquois tribes forming the confederacy, their geographic location being the reason they were designated the federal capital of the league. As members of the Elder Brothers in the political functions of the league, they acted as mediators between the Elder Brothers (Mohawks and Senecas) and Younger Brothers (Oneidas and Cayugas). All major questions and decisions affecting the member tribes were deliberated at Onondaga, and their chiefs, like TEGANISSORENS, OHONSIOWANNE, and ARADGI, were very influential. Onondaga territory extended from the western shore of Oneida Lake westward to Skaneateles Lake, in New York State. During most of the years of conflict between New France and the English colonies the Onondagas, like the rest of the league's members, allied themselves with the English. From time to time Jesuit missionaries established themselves at Onondaga—JEAN and JACQUES DE LAMBERVILLE are two examples—but were seldom successful in achieving conversions. CHARLES LE MOYNE de Longueuil and PAUL LE MOYNE de Maricourt were both adopted by the tribe and attempted to influence the Iroquois in favour of New France. The Onondagas survive to the present day on a modest reservation in their old homeland south of the city of Syracuse. *See* IROQUOIS, FIVE NATIONS CONFEDERACY.　　H.H. and A.E.

Onontagués. *See* ONONDAGAS
Ontationoués. *See* NOTTOWAYS

Osages. French derivation from Washazhe, Children of the Waters, a subdivision or phratry of the Hunkah moiety. A Siouan-speaking people of approximately 6,000, the Osages were divided by the end of the 18th century into three major village-bands: Great Osages, Little Osages, and Osages of the Oaks or Arkansas Osages. Marquette* in 1673 located the Osages south of the Missouri and probably intended to situate them in their traditional settlements on the Upper Osage River, Vernon County, Missouri. Attracted by opportunities offered by the fur trade a group later known as the Little Osages took up residence on the south bank of the Missouri near Wakenda Creek early in the 18th century and remained associated with the Missouri Indians in that vicinity until 1790 or 1800. The Arkansas Osages developed a permanent village a few miles north of Claremore, Oklahoma. The Osages dominated trade between the Missouri and Arkansas and Red Rivers during the 18th century and apparently drove the Caddoan-speaking predecessors (Paniouassa) of the Wichita Indians from settlements in eastern Oklahoma by

1750. The seasonal cycle followed by the Osages included fall and winter use of the Ozark Plateau in Missouri and northern Arkansas and a summer and fall buffalo hunt into Oklahoma and Kansas as far west as the Great Saline.   F.W.V.

Otos. A Siouan-speaking people affiliated linguistically and in migratory legend with the Missouris, Iowas, and Winnebagos. Their early population is estimated at around 1,000. According to legend, a chief's son seduced the daughter of another chief and led to the separation of the Otos and the Missouris; hence, the sobriquet, Wa'to'tana or "lechers." Marquette* (1673) locates the Otos vaguely in what may be western Iowa. Around 1680 they are reported on the upper Iowa and Blue Earth (Minn.) rivers. Shortly after 1700 the Otos crossed the Missouri River and established themselves in southeastern Nebraska, while continuing to hunt in southwestern Iowa around the headwaters of the Grand River. In 1785 the Oto village was described as in the middle of a prairie, on a low hill, some 15 leagues up the Platte River. In 1720 the Otos joined the Pawnees and some French traders in repulsing the Spanish expedition to the Platte River headed by Villazur. *See* IOWAS, MISSOURIS, WINNEBAGOS.   F.W.V.

Ottawas (Algonkian for Traders); in French Outaouais. This term was applied throughout the 17th century to upper Great Lakes Algonkians including Nipissings, Saulteux (Chippewas), and others engaging as middlemen. In the more classic sense the term was applied to four tribes sharing a common language and culture: Sinagos, Kiskakons (Culs-Coupez), du Sable, and Nassawaketons. These may aboriginally have been based in separate patrilineal clan sets, or phratries. The divisions no longer exist. The Ottawas replaced the Hurons, decimated by New York Iroquois attacks in 1649–50, as middlemen, but were themselves forced by Iroquois attacks to abandon their original villages on the shores and islands of northern Lake Huron, migrating, with Nipissings, as far north as Lake Nipigon, and as far south as Chequamegon on western Lake Superior. Returning to Manitoulin Island and Michilimackinac in the 1670s, many joined Cadillac [LAUMET] at Detroit in 1700, some remaining thereafter in lower Michigan, others returning a few years later to old residences to the north. The Ottawas grew maize, fished, hunted, and trapped. They were allies of the French, as CHINGOUESSI, MISCOUAKY, and KOUTAOILIBOE pointed out at the Montreal peace conference of 1700–1, and fought actively against other tribes and the British. In 1706, however, the Detroit Ottawas, led by LE PESANT and OUTOUTAGAN, attacked the Miamis and Hurons who also lived there. The whole French system of tribal alliances in the west was endangered, but the initiatives of KINONGÉ and Koutaoiliboe restored peace. *See* CHIPPEWAS, COUNCIL OF THE THREE FIRES, POTAWATOMIS.   H.H.

Ottawas du Sable. *See* OTTAWAS
Ouenros. *See* WENROS
Ouiatanons. *See* WEAS
Ouinipegons. *See* WINNEBAGOS
Ousakis. *See* SAUKS
Outagamis. *See* FOXES
Outaouais. *See* OTTAWAS
Ouyatanons. *See* WEAS
Padoucas. *See* COMANCHES
Panis. *See* PAWNEES

Papinachois. The early missionaries locate these Indians in the highlands between the Mistassini region and Labrador; they are ancestors of present-day Montagnais-Naskapis.

Passamaquoddys; in French Pesmocodys. A small tribe which belonged to the Abenaki Confederacy but which spoke a dialect similar to that of the Malecites. The Passamaquoddys occupied all the regions around Passamaquoddy Bay, the Sainte-Croix River and Schoodic Lake, on the boundary between Maine and New Brunswick.

Pawnees (Horn People); in French Panis. The Pawnees belonged to the Caddoan linguistic family and lived in the valley of the Platte River in what is now Nebraska. How their name also came to be given to any Indian slave is not known; when DUTISNÉ visited them in 1719, however, they received him coldly because they had been told by the Osages that the Frenchman was looking for slaves.

Pégouakis. *See* PIGWACKETS

Penobscots; in French Pentagouets. An important division of the Abenakis, they inhabited the land about Penobscot Bay and the Penobscot River in Maine. Their principal village was at Pentagouet (now Castine), and in language and customs they closely resembled the Norridgewocks. Like them, too, they fought the colonists during King Philip's war [*see* CHURCH] and raided the New England frontier during King William's and Queen Anne's wars. Their allegiance to the French was maintained by common interest and by the influence of such men as JEAN-VINCENT and BERNARD-ANSELME D'ABBADIE de Saint-Castin, and Father Pierre de La Chasse*. After the treaty of Utrecht the Penobscots joined the Norridgewocks and other Abenakis in resisting encroaching English settlement on their lands, a resistance that culminated in war with Massachusetts [*see* MOG]. Their chief WENEMOUET was the first to make peace in 1725, causing a rift between them and the other Abenakis, particularly those in Canada. After 1749 they did not fight against the English, and unlike the Norridgewocks did not join the Saint-François Abenakis near Quebec. They are now one of the most numerous remaining New England tribes, and still live on part of their ancestral lands at Oldtown, on the Penobscot River. *See* ABENAKIS, NORRIDGEWOCKS, SAINT-FRANÇOIS ABENAKIS.   D.H.

Pentagouets. *See* PENOBSCOTS

Peorias. One of the more important and populous tribal divisions of the Illinois, some others being the Cahokias, Kaskaskias, Tamaroas, and Michigameas. When first encountered by Marquette* and Jolliet* in 1673 they were living in one or more villages on the west bank of the Mississippi near its junction with the Missouri. Later they were found near the lake on the Illinois River which bears their name. Eventually, owing to war and disease, they, like other Illinois, suffered such losses as to become virtually extinct. *See* ILLINOIS. H.H.

Pesmocodys. *See* PASSAMAQUODDYS
Petun Hurons. *See* HURONS

Piankeshaws; in French Peanquishas. One of the three most important of the Miami tribes, the others being the Weas and Atchatchakangouens (Miamis proper). A central Algonkian farming-hunting village people first encountered by the French in the 1670s, the Piankeshaws, during the last decades of the 17th century, separated from other Miamis, who were moving east. The Piankeshaws established villages, first on the Illinois River, later at the Fox-Wisconsin portage, on the west bank of the Mississippi nearly opposite the mouth of the Wisconsin, and in the Chicago region. In the early 18th century they too moved eastward, finally founding a village on the Wabash River, a few miles south of Lafayette, Ind. Except for a brief excursion in the 1730s to the area of what is now Vincennes, Ind., they remained near Lafayette until the 19th century. Like the other Miami tribes they trapped for the fur trade, and, as allies of the French, participated in the warfare which characterized intertribal relations in the Great Lakes region. *See* MIAMIS, WEAS. H.H.

Pigwackets; in French, Pégouakis. A division of the Abenakis who lived at the head of the Saco River, Maine; their principal village was located at the present Fryeburg. NESCAMBIOUIT, ATECOUANDO, and other chiefs of the tribe fought on the French side in King William's and Queen Anne's wars, but the tribe was greatly weakened by losses inflicted on them in 1725 during Massachusetts' war with the Abenakis [*see* MOG]. The survivors were absorbed by other tribes; many of them moved to Saint-François in Canada. *See* ABENAKIS, SAINT-FRANÇOIS ABENAKIS. D.H.

Plains Crees. *See* CREES
Platcotés de Chiens (Platscotés de Chiens). *See* ATHAPASKANS

Potawatomis (central Algonkian for People of the Place of the Fire); in French, Potéouatamis. They must be distinguished from the Mascoutens, another central Algonkian tribe, called People of the Fire. Potawatomi language and culture were closely related to those of the Chippewas and Ottawas, but they were the most distinct of the three peoples, having a different language. The Potawatomis were highly mobile during the French period, moving from aboriginal locations in the lower peninsula of Michigan first to Sault Ste Marie, then to the Green Bay (Baie des Puants) area where they were encountered by the French in the late 1660s. During the early 17th century they were variously located near Detroit, along the St Joseph River in Michigan and Indiana, and in the Milwaukee area. In the latter two places some of their villages included small numbers of Chippewa and Ottawa migrants from the north, with whom they became known jointly as the Council of the Three Fires, or United Nations. The Potawatomis were important in the network of French Indian allies in the west, and chiefs like OUENEMEK and OUNANGUISSÉ had real influence on the policy of New France. The Potawatomis were village maize farmers and during the summer hunted prairie game. They were energetic trappers in the fur trade. Like the Chippewas and Menominees, they were divided into patrilineal clans organized in exogamous phratry sets. *See* CHIPPEWAS, COUNCIL OF THE THREE FIRES, MASCOUTENS. H.H.

Prairie People. *See* MASCOUTENS
Puants. *See* WINNEBAGOS
"Red Indians." *See* BEOTHUKS
Renards. *See* FOXES
Rocky Crees. *See* CREES, STONES
Sacs. *See* SAUKS

Saint-François Abenakis. The inhabitants of a mission village on the Saint-François River near its confluence with the St Lawrence, probably settled between 1660 and 1670. The first occupants were apparently Sokokis. There appear to have been Abenakis and "Loups" in the village before 1700. In 1705 or 1706, the mission of Saint-François de Sales moved from the lower falls of the Chaudière River to the Saint-François, bringing many Abenakis from Maine and some additional Sokokis and "Loups," so that in 1711 the village was estimated to contain 260 warriors, perhaps 1,300 persons. This population was reduced by epidemics and the colonial wars in which they were always allies of the French. Then between the outbreak of the American Revolution and 1800, Saint-François received numerous new inhabitants from the upper Connecticut River and from Missisquoi, at the mouth of the Missisquoi River on Lake Champlain. Until at least 1816, the band was known officially as the Abenakis and Sokokis of Saint-François. The present name conceals the Sokoki element but may nevertheless be accurate, since the Sokokis probably spoke an Abenaki dialect. The assertion, often repeated in the last 60 years, that the Abenakis of the Androscoggin River were the dominant group at Saint-François, remains to be proved and is probably incorrect. The idea seems to have originated in a fancied resemblance between place names on the Androscoggin River and the early Abenaki name for Saint-François, namely *Arsi-kantekȣ*, literally Empty Cabin River. Saint-François probably absorbed most of the fugitives from western New England—the Sokokis, Penacooks, Pigwackets, Piscataquas, Saco Indians, Nipmucs, and Schaghticokes. The Androscoggin Indians retired to the nearby mission of Bécancour. *See* ABENAKIS, PIGWACKETS, SCHAGHTICOKES, SOKOKIS.   G.M.D.

Sakis. *See* SAUKS
Santees. *See* SIOUX

Sauks (Sacs); in French also Ousakis, Sakis. A central Algonkian tribe closely related in language and culture to the Foxes, Kickapoos, and Mascoutens; they had a village at the mouth of the Fox River on Green Bay (Baie des Puants). The Sauks generally maintained an alliance with the Foxes, but did not participate as much as their allies in intertribal wars and wars against the French, perhaps because of their close proximity to French trading posts and missions at Green Bay. In 1733 the Sauks welcomed Fox refugees from their wars with the French, and from that date the history of the two tribes is indistinguishable. After that, gradual movement westward took them first to the Mississippi, thence across it into Iowa. Like their kinsmen, the Sauks were village people who cultivated maize, beans, and squash, hunted large game during the summer, and trapped for the fur trade during the winter. *See* FOXES.   H.H.

Sauteurs, Sauteux. *See* CHIPPEWAS

Schaghticokes. Inhabitants of a village on the Hoosac River near its confluence with the Hudson River. In 1676 and 1677, Governor Andros of New York settled the site with refugees from the southern New England tribes who had been defeated in King Philip's War. It probably had a population of 1,000 by 1678. A band of "North Indians" (Sokokis), moved down from Canada in 1685 to join them. Discontent developed, and groups began to leave as early as 1698. The French made a persistent effort to attract the Schaghticokes away from the English, and they succeeded to the extent that there were only 12 families left by 1754. These also fled and joined the Canadian Abenakis. The various components of the village and the groups which subsequently withdrew have never been identified, and their origins may never be ascertained. Their identity has been further confused by the fact that they came to share with the Mahicans the names Loups (French) and River Indians (English). *See* MAHICANS, SOKOKIS.   G.M.D.

Senecas; in French Tsonnontouans, Djiionondowanen-a-ka being their own designation for themselves, literally, People of the Big Hill. The Senecas were the westernmost member of the Five Nations Confederacy; as the ritual Keepers of the Western Door of the Longhouse, they "defended" the western borders of Iroquois territory. In population the Senecas were, and still are, the most numerous of the member nations in the league. In the federal councils of the league the Senecas ranked with the Mohawks and Onondagas as members of the Elder Brothers, a legislative segment of the federal council. The Seneca chiefs AOUENANO, CAGENQUARICHTEN, TEKANOET, and TONATAKOUT, were involved in negotiations with the French during the late 17th and early 18th centuries. Louis-Thomas CHABERT de Joncaire was adopted by the Senecas and was one of a few Canadians who were able to influence the Iroquois during this period. Along with other members of the league, the Senecas were village farmers who raised maize, beans, and squash. They also depended on seasonal hunting, fishing, and gathering. Following the upheaval of the American Revolution, the majority of the Senecas managed to remain in their traditional homeland in western New York State where they reside on reservations today. *See* IROQUOIS, FIVE NATIONS CONFEDERACY.   H.H. and A.E.

Sinago Ottawas. *See* OTTAWAS

Sioux; from Nadouessioux (French spelling for a central Algonkian term for Little Snakes, or Enemies; also called Dakotas, which in Siouan means the People). Numerous bands and villages of this Dakota Siouan tribe were located in the Mississippi headwaters region, along the Minnesota River, and west to the eastern watershed of the Missouri below the Great Bend. The French referred to two divisions, Sioux of the Woods and Sioux of the Prairies. The former comprised those tribes known today as Santees, the latter, tribes from whom are descended the modern Yanktons, Yanktonais, and Tetons. The Santees, especially the Mdewakanton division, had most contact with the French, beginning about 1680 and, with interruptions due to intertribal warfare and distance, lasting throughout the French régime. The Santee Sioux were woodland village people cultivating a little maize, but relying chiefly on wild rice and other natural products including bison, which they hunted on foot in large communal parties on the prairies to the south and west. At first trading allies of the Chippewas of Chequamegon peninsula, the Sioux began in 1736 to include them among their many Algonkian foes in warfare which lasted well into the 19th century. *See* MDEWAKANTON.   H.H.

Slaveys. *See* ATHAPASKANS
Socoquis. *See* SOKOKIS

Sokokis. The Socoquiois and Socoquis of the French, the Soquachjck of the Dutch, the Onejagese of the Iroquois, the North Indians and Squakheags of the English. An Algonkian-speaking tribe occupying the upper Connecticut River valley from Northfield, Mass., possibly to the headwaters. When Europeans first met the Sokokis in 1642 this tribe had treaty relations with the Iroquois. Prior to this they had been friendly with the Algonkins, and by 1650 they were at war with the Iroquois. An attack by the Iroquois in 1663 was disastrous to both sides. It made the Iroquois sue for peace and brought about the temporary withdrawal of the Sokokis from the southern part of their territory. Some Sokokis were living at Montreal by 1662, and after this they became well known at Saint-François, Trois-Rivières, Schaghticoke, and Chambly. They appear to have been the first settlers of Saint-François and they retained their separate identity in this mixed village until the late 19th century. Since 1832 the Sokokis have merged with the Indians of the Saco River in Maine. *See* SAINT-FRANÇOIS ABENAKIS, SCHAGHTICOKES. G.M.D.

Souriquois. *See* MICMACS

Stones, Stoneys. Although some doubt exists at present whether this might be an appellation for Rocky Crees, it is most likely that the term refers in most, if not all, instances to the Assiniboins, whose name in central Algonkian roughly means People of the Stone. *See* ASSINIBOINS. H.H.

Susquehannocks (known to the Hurons as Andasto-guehronnons, which the French shortened to Andastes or Andastogues, to the Dutch as Minquas or White Minquas, and to the English as Conestogas and Susquehannahs). They inhabited the country around upper Chesapeake Bay and the Susque-hannah River valley. They were intermittently at war with the Iroquois League; Étienne Brûlé* once induced them to aid Champlain and the Hurons in a raid on the Iroquois in central New York. The Susquehannocks maintained a close alliance with the Hurons, although they did not provide military aid against the Iroquois League at the time of the Huron dispersal. Between 1638 and 1655 Swedish settlers provided a trading outlet for the Susque-hannocks. After 1655 it was chiefly the Dutch, and later the English, who traded with them. By the year 1676 the Susquehannocks were for the most part subjugated and absorbed by the Iroquois League. After 1700 their former territory became a sanctuary residence for remnant Indian groups who were refugees from white conflict and was under the administration and protection of the Iroquois Con-federacy. *See* FIVE NATIONS CONFEDERACY, IROQUOIS. H.H. and A.E.

Swampy Crees. *See* CREES, MASKEGONS, MONSONIS

Tamaroas; in French, Tamarois. One of the tribal divisions of the historic Illinois, the Tamaroas shared a village with the Cahokias, another Illinois tribe, on the east bank of the Mississippi nearly opposite the present St Louis. In 1701 they broke off from the Cahokias and probably joined still another Illinois tribe, the Kaskaskias, who at the time were moving down to the Mississippi from Lake Peoria (Illinois River). Like other Illinois, they suffered heavy losses from warfare and disease

throughout the French, British, and American periods. *See* CAHOKIAS, ILLINOIS, KASKASKIAS. H.H.

Tionontatis. *See* HURONS
Tsonnontouans. *See* SENECAS

Tuscaroras; in French Tuscarorens, Skaruren or Esaurora being their own designation, literally, Hemp Gatherers. Originally located in North Carolina when first encountered by Europeans, the Tuscaroras, as a result of continual warfare between themselves and English colonists during the late 17th and early 18th century, moved north between 1712 and 1722. They had applied for and received asylum from the federal council of the Iroquois League. During the balance of the 18th century they lived under the tutelage of the member Oneidas, and became an unofficial non-voting member of the Younger Brothers in the federal council. Like their linguistic kinsmen, the other Iroquoian tribes, the Tuscaroras were primarily an agricultural people. *See* IROQUOIAN, IROQUOIS, FIVE NATIONS CON-FEDERACY, ONEIDAS. H.H. and A.E.

Wampanoags. *See* NARRAGANSETTS

Weas; in French Aoyatanouns, Ouiatanons, Ouyata-nons, etc. One of the three most important of the Miami tribes, the others being the Piankeshaws and Atchatchakangouens (Miamis proper), a central Algonkian village farming people first met by the French in the 1670s in the region southwest of Green Bay (Baie des Puants). After locating their villages at various places in Wisconsin and Illinois, including Fort Saint-Louis on Lake Peoria of the Illinois River, in the 1680s and Chicago in 1696, they finally in 1708 moved east to the upper Wabash River at Lafayette, Ind. Like other Miami tribes, the Weas were allied with the French and partici-pated in warfare on their behalf, chiefly against the Foxes in Wisconsin and the Chickasaws to the south. Like other tribes in their region they suffered heavy losses during the smallpox epidemic of 1733. *See* MIAMIS, PIANKESHAWS. H.H.

Wendats. V. HURONS

Wenros; in French Ouenros, Awenrohronons, being a Huron Iroquois designation meaning literally The People of the Place of the Floating Scum. This term probably refers to their residence around or near the present Cuba, N.Y., where a natural pond of petroleum, or oil spring, is located. As a result of both disease and constant warfare with the Iroquois, by 1640 the remnants of this group had taken refuge among both the Neutrals and the Hurons and were absorbed. The Wenros appear to have been a member of the Iroquoian linguistic family, and an agricultural people. *See* HURONS, IROQUOIAN. H.H. and A.E.

Winnebagos; in French Puants, Ouinipegons (in

central Algonkian, People of the Stinking Water). The Winnebagos spoke a language related to the Chiwere division of Siouan, which was spoken by the neighbouring Iowas. When first encountered by the explorer Jean Nicollet* de Belleborne in 1634, they were living at Green Bay (Baie des Puants). At that time and later they occupied the Door peninsula east of Green Bay and at various times such rivers as the Fox, Wisconsin, Rock, and Milwaukee in Wisconsin and Illinois. After their numbers had been severely reduced by disease and warfare with Algonkians in the mid-17th century, the Winnebagos increased in population until by mid-18th century they had become important in the fur trade, in warfare, and in forest diplomacy. They were woodland village maize farmers who also relied on wild rice, fish, and large woodland and prairie game. They were grouped in patrilineal clans organized in two sets, or moieties, which had ceremonial and social functions including exogamy (the rule requiring that marriage take place outside the moiety). H.H.

Woods Crees. *See* CREES, MONSONIS
Wyandots. *See* HURONS
Yellowknives. *See* ATHAPASKANS

BIOGRAPHIES

List of Abbreviations

AAQ Archives de l'archevêché de Québec
ACND Archives de la congrégation de Notre-Dame, Montréal
AE Archives du Ministère des Affaires étrangères, Paris
AHDM Archives des religieuses hospitalières de Saint-Joseph de l'Hôtel-Dieu de Montréal
AHDQ Archives de l'Hôtel-Dieu de Québec
AJJ Archives judiciaires de Joliette
AJM Archives judiciaires de Montréal
AJQ Archives judiciaires de Québec
AJTR Archives judiciaires de Trois-Rivières
AMUQ Archives du monastère des Ursulines de Québec
AN Archives nationales, Paris
ANDM Archives paroissiales de Notre-Dame de Montréal
ANDQ Archives paroissiales de Notre-Dame de Québec
APQ Archives de la province de Québec. Now AQ
AQ Archives du Québec
ARSI Archivum Romanum Societatis Iesu, Rome
ASGM Archives des Sœurs Grises de Montréal
ASJ Archives de la Société de Jésus
ASJCF Archives de la Société de Jésus, province du Canada français
ASQ Archives du Séminaire de Québec
ASSM Archives du Séminaire de Saint-Sulpice de Montréal
BM British Museum
BN Bibliothèque nationale, Paris
BRH *Bulletin des recherches historiques*

CCHA Canadian Catholic Historical Association
CF *Canada français*
CHA Canadian Historical Association
CHR *Canadian Historical Review*
CTG Archives du Comité technique du génie, Paris
DAB *Dictionary of American Biography*
DBF *Dictionnaire de biographie française*
DCB *Dictionary of Canadian Biography*
DNB *Dictionary of National Biography*
HBC Hudson's Bay Company
HBRS Hudson's Bay Record Society
IOA Inventaire des œuvres d'art du Québec
JJ *Journal des Jésuites*
JR *Jesuit Relations and allied documents*
MPA *Mississippi Provincial Archives*
NF *Nova Francia*
NYCD *Documents relative to the colonial history of the State of New York*
PAC Public Archives of Canada
PANS Public Archives of Nova Scotia
PRO Public Record Office, London
RC *Revue canadienne*
RHAF *Revue d'histoire de l'Amérique française*
RSCT *Royal Society of Canada Transactions*
RUL *Revue de l'université Laval*
SCHEC Société canadienne de l'histoire de l'Église catholique
SGCF Société généalogique canadienne-française
SHA Archives du Service historique de l'armée, Paris
SHQ Société historique de Québec
USPG United Society for the Propagation of the Gospel

BIOGRAPHIES

A

ABBADIE DE SAINT-CASTIN, BERNARD-ANSELME D', fourth baron of the name, French officer, commander in Acadia; b. 1689 at Pentagouet, son of JEAN-VINCENT D'ABBADIE de Saint-Castin and Pidianske (Marie-Mathilde), an Indian woman; d. 1720 in Béarn.

After Jean-Vincent de Saint-Castin's departure for France in 1701, western Acadia was in a precarious state. It was above all important to regain control over the Abenakis. As the situation was daily getting worse, Governor Brouillan [MOMBETON], seeing that the baron was not returning, decided in 1704 to appeal to his son Bernard-Anselme. This young man, a pupil at the Petit Séminaire of Quebec, was still only 15. But Brouillan thought that, being born and brought up in his mother's tribe, and rigorously trained by his father, he would have the necessary standing and competence. He was not wrong. Bernard-Anselme rallied his tribe, and immediately proved himself equal to the task. The war of harassment against the settlers in New England flared up again more violently than ever. Young Saint-Castin showed the extent of his bravery in the defence of Port-Royal (Annapolis Royal, N.S.) first from 8 to 16 June (N.S.), then from 20 to 31 Aug. 1707 [*see* MARCH]. In the course of several bitter fights, he played a leading role at the head of his Abenakis and of the settlers, so much so that the new governor, Daniel d'AUGER de Subercase, in a letter dated 22 September addressed to the minister, had no hesitation in recommending him for the rank of ensign.

Meanwhile the news of Jean-Vincent's death had arrived. Reduced to inactivity as a result of several wounds received in the battle of 31 August, the fourth Baron de Saint-Castin took advantage of the occasion to get married. On 31 Oct. 1707, in the Port-Royal that he had so stoutly defended, he married Marie-Charlotte Damours de Chauffours, daughter of LOUIS DAMOURS, seigneur of Jemseg, one of Jean-Vincent's comrades in arms at the capture of Pemaquid (1696). In December the baron's sisters married Philippe Mius d'Entremont and Alexandre Le Borgne* de Belle-Isle respectively; thus the Saint-Castins, Franco-Abenaki half-breeds, became linked by marriage with the best Acadian families. On 20 December, in a further letter to the minister, Subercase recommended Bernard-Anselme for the rank of lieutenant, with command of the Indians in Acadia. The court granted him this latest responsibility on 6 June 1708.

Bernard-Anselme began by dividing his time between Port-Royal, where he had his family residence, and Pentagouet, his native village, which remained an advanced bastion of the Acadian defences. But he was not really an Abenaki chief in the absolute sense, as his father had been, and he devoted little of his effort to trading; he continued to be a French officer, entrusted with command of the Indians, as he had been appointed by the king. For living expenses, he was content with his pay. But the following year he adopted a quite different type of activity. He fitted out a ship and became a privateer. He joined forces with other famous privateers, Pierre Morpain*, Pierre MAISONNAT, *dit* Baptiste, and DANIEL ROBINAU, who gave a lot of trouble to the English; in the year 1709 alone they sank 35 of their ships and took 470 of them prisoner.

However, Port-Royal was doomed, for New England had vowed to avenge the humiliating defeat of 1707. While the unfortunate Subercase was vainly asking Versailles for help, Queen Anne was giving substantial assistance to the colonies of Massachusetts, Connecticut, New Hampshire, and Rhode Island, to enable them to organize a formidable expedition. On 5 Oct. 1710 the governor of Virginia, Sir Francis NICHOLSON, at the head of 2,000 soldiers borne on 36 ships, laid siege to Port-Royal. Subercase had only 158 regular soldiers and 127 militiamen to put up against him; he resisted the invader for a week, and finally capitulated on 13 October. A week later Saint-Castin, who knew nothing of what had happened, appeared before Port-Royal, which had already been rebaptized Annapolis Royal. His ship was captured, but he managed to escape and take to the woods.

The English hastened to make him enticing offers if he would agree to come over to them; nothing could better show the extent to which the son had inherited the prestige and power of the

Abbadie de Saint-Castin

father. Naturally, he declined these offers; he only consented to set out for Quebec with the act of capitulation, letters from Subercase, and an English major, LIVINGSTON, who wanted to see the Marquis RIGAUD de Vaudreuil.

Appointed by Vaudreuil to the command of the whole of Acadia, the baron stayed only a month at Quebec. He left it on 18 Jan. 1711, armed with precise instructions: to keep the Indians hostile towards New England, and to maintain the Acadians in their loyalty to the French crown. Saint-Castin settled at Pentagouet, and for two years carried on his double mission as best he could. In 1711 Saint-Castin's Abenakis harassed the English garrison at Annapolis Royal. The following year Saint-Castin was appointed lieutenant.

On 16 April 1713, however, the treaty of Utrecht, which handed Acadia over to England, was signed. As France kept Cape Breton Island (or Île Royale), efforts were made to encourage the Acadians and Abenakis to go there. Saint-Castin spent the winter of 1713–14 with his tribe, at the falls on the Penobscot River. The Indians did not want to give up their country, and in the spring the baron withdrew alone to the Saint John River. He reflected then that the time had finally come to go to France to straighten out his affairs. He had already been giving thought to this matter, and from 1707 on he had toyed with the idea of setting out. Subercase, who needed him too much, had been opposed to his going, and had asked the minister to intervene to terminate the disputes which were depriving the baron of his family estate. Saint-Castin had thereupon been content with sending a power of attorney to Subercase's brother-in-law, Jacques de Sarraute-Marjolet.

Saint-Castin and his wife left Acadia on one of the last boats to sail in 1714, and arrived in Béarn at the end of the year. Alas! Bernard-Anselme, in the negotiations concerning his estate, was not to be much luckier than his father. If, as it appears, Sarraute won his case against Jean de Labaig, Jean-Vincent's opponent, he refused in his turn to furnish a full accounting to Bernard-Anselme! Threatened with a lawsuit by Saint-Castin, he invoked the question of domicile, and returned to the charges of illegitimate birth. The court, which was very anxious to send the young baron back to Canada, took up the affair again with the intendant in Pau. It none the less dragged on, and was complicated by a lawsuit with the Chevalier de Florence over another part of the estate. In 1717 Bernard-Anselme was admitted into the States of Béarn, in the order of the nobility. In the spring of 1720 he drafted a memoir intended for the minister on the "Services rendus par les sieurs de Saint-Castin, père et fils, dans le pays de Canada en la Nouvelle-France." He died the same year, at the beginning of autumn.

By his marriage with Marie-Charlotte Damours de Chauffours he had only three children, all daughters: Marie-Anselme, born in 1711 at Quebec; Brigitte, who was a pupil of the Ursulines of Quebec; and Louise, born in 1716 at Pau. Bernard-Anselme's widow lived at Pau until 1734 and died there, after sustaining a lawsuit before the *parlement* of Navarre.

GEORGES CERBELAUD SALAGNAC

AN, Col., B, 29–30, 32, 34–37; C^{11D}, 6–8. Charlevoix, *History* (Shea), V. *Coll. de manuscrits relatifs à la N.-F.*, II, III. "Correspondance de Vaudreuil," APQ *Rapport, 1938–39, 1946–47, 1947–48.* "Lettres et mémoires de F.-M.-F. Ruette d'Auteuil," 46. *NYCD* (O'Callaghan and Fernow), IX.

ABBADIE DE SAINT-CASTIN, JEAN-VINCENT D', baron, French officer and Abenaki chief; b. 1652 at Saint-Castin (in Béarn, now the department of Basses-Pyrénées); d. 1707 at Pau.

The man who was to become one of the principal chiefs of the Abenakis came from a well-established noble family of Béarn. An Abbadie de Maslacq appears in the general enumeration of the households in the viscountship of Béarn which was drawn up in 1385 by order of Gaston Phébus. In 1581 the noble estate of Saint-Castin entered the Abbadie family by marriage. In 1654 Jean-Jacques I obtained authorization from Louis XIV for the erection of this fief into a barony. In 1649 this first Baron de Saint-Castin had married Isabeau de Béarn-Bonasse, a lady of high estate, since she was descended from a branch of the house of Foix.

The couple had three children: Jean-Jacques II, born in 1650, Marie, born in 1651, and Jean-Vincent, born in 1652, the same year that his mother was to be carried off by the plague. So our younger son from Béarn was motherless when he was still only a few months old. We have no knowledge whatever of the childhood and early adolescence of the younger Saint-Castin. He must have received the education peculiar to the young nobles of that period, based on a knightly conception of the military art, and with a rudimentary minimum of general knowledge. We are scarcely surprised to see his name mentioned as an ensign on the muster-rolls of the Carignan-Salières regiment, in Chambly*'s company, bound for Canada in 1665. At that time, Jean-Vincent was only thirteen! Exceptional though it was, this was not unique; we know that on several occasions very young men served in the king's armies. And a younger son from Béarn (or from Gascony) must often have been obliged to venture out very early to seek his fortune. Had not this young man already lost his father? The question may well be asked, since in a deed of sale dated 24 Feb. 1666 Jean-Jacques II, his elder brother, signed as the second Baron de Saint-Castin. The father's death would provide a suitable explanation of the younger son's joining the army, where his birth and education secured him the rank of ensign.

It is probable that in 1666 Jean-Vincent took part with his regiment in the campaign of the Marquis de Tracy [Prouville*] against the Iroquois. But it is not until 1670 that we see his name mentioned again. In July of that year, the treaty of Breda having restored Acadia to France, he went, still an ensign, with Captain Andigné* de Grandfontaine, the new governor of Acadia, and Lieutenant Pierre de Joybert* de Soulanges et de Marson to Penobscot Bay, to retake possession of the fort captured by the English 16 years before. It was the first contact the young 18-year-old officer had made with this almost virgin country that was to become his home.

Grandfontaine established himself at Pentagouet (on the Penobscot River), and Saint-Castin did likewise. The place was what one might call a "hot spot," right in the middle of contested territory. Indeed, the French maintained that the boundary of Acadia was at the Kennebec River, the English put it as far back as the Penobscot River, and the most enthusiastic of the Bostonians even wanted to make it the Sainte-Croix River! While these disputes were going on between white men, in the coastal region the country remained also and above all the domain of the Penobscots, and in the forests of the interior that of the other Abenaki tribes. Saint-Castin was entrusted with several missions which enabled him to study the men and the country.

In 1673 Grandfontaine was replaced by Jacques de Chambly as governor of Acadia. The following year, when everything was peaceful, Saint-Castin was to become acquainted, somewhat brutally, with Dutch pirates who were allied with the Bostonians. Chambly, with 30 men, was able to hold out for only an hour against 110 assailants; he was taken prisoner. Saint-Castin, after being tortured with a brimstone match, managed to escape. He hid for a few days among the Indians, who were already his friends, then set off through the woods towards Quebec. During the four years that the ensign, in the eagerness of his youth, had roamed everywhere through the colony on the Penobscot, an advanced bastion of Catholic France in immediate contact with Puritan New England, he had already admirably understood all the problems of this veritable Indian "march."

And while Saint-Castin was making his report at the Château Saint-Louis, Buade* de Frontenac, good judge that he was, was sizing him up. The governor general of Canada saw how this young, intelligent, and enthusiastic officer could be utilized; on the spot he proposed a line of conduct for him that was to set the pattern for his whole life. The mission that he entrusted to him did not take the form of a written order; it was discreetly mentioned in the "Mémoire des services rendus par les sieurs de Saint-Castin, père et fils, dans le pays de Canada en la Nouvelle-France," drawn up in 1720 by Jean-Vincent's son, BERNARD-ANSELME; in it we read: "[Saint-Castin] had the good fortune to escape and to make his way to Quebec to receive the governor's orders, which were to urge the Abenakis and other nations throughout the whole colony of Acadia to adopt the interests of the king of France." Furthermore, the rest of Jean-Vincent's life shows clearly enough what was at stake in this mission.

In the same year, 1674, the young man became the third Baron de Saint-Castin on the death of his elder brother, who left no posterity. But the time had not come to go and collect inheritances, and the ensign threw himself unreservedly into the adventure awaiting him. From that time on Saint-Castin, who seems to have been no longer subject to any official authority, appears to have divested himself almost entirely of his position as a French officer. He divided his time between a Penobscot tribe, which finally adopted him, and his dwelling at Pentagouet, a mere pied-à-terre which must have comprised a factory and a storehouse for merchandise, for he also began to engage in trade.

Saint-Castin chose a wife in his tribe. According to tradition the Indian baroness was very pretty. Moreover she was not a mere nobody, since she was the daughter of the great Penobscot chief Madokawando. Saint-Castin knew how to conciliate love and political acumen. The Algonkin name of this bronze-skinned spouse must have been Pidianske or Pidiwamiska, and her Christian name Marie-Mathilde, unless two distinct women are involved. Saint-Castin has been accused, without too much proof, of having had several wives, legitimately or as concubines, and of having lived a dissolute existence deep in the Acadian forests. These are insinuations spread abroad by his enemies, which were to be utilized later in the attempt to contest his right to the family inheritance. It is true that the baron's marriage took place at first according to Indian custom, perhaps before 1678, but it is certain that in the last quarter of 1684, at Pentagouet, Father JACQUES BIGOT, the Jesuit missionary to the Abenakis, acting on the express order of Bishop LAVAL of

Abbadie de Saint-Castin

Quebec, received the consent of the couple according to Catholic rite.

Saint-Castin was entirely an Abenaki, to the extent of making the interests of his new compatriots his own. If he engaged in the fur trade, if he maintained close business relations with Boston, in defiance of the rules of the French administration, it was precisely because being more Abenaki than French he no longer considered himself affected by them. But as the French needed an alliance with the Abenakis, the court, the governors general of Canada, and the governors of Acadia always dealt tactfully with the baron and treated him with the consideration due his rank. Officially, moreover, this rank remained a modest one, for Saint-Castin avoided ostentation in everything. Until his death in 1698, Madokawando was the sole great chief of the Penobscots; he had his lieutenants who were in command of the warriors, led expeditions, and parleyed with the enemy when truces were made. But it was known everywhere that nothing was done without his son-in-law's advice, and that the latter had only to express a wish for it to be instantly complied with.

After Saint-Castin had settled among the Abenakis, King Philip (Pometacom) and his warriors ravaged New England in 1675 [*see* CHURCH]. The Penobscots and the Abenakis did not enter the struggle until 1676, after an attack had been made on one of their chiefs. One may reasonably suppose that Saint-Castin began to exercise his talents as a military counsellor on the occasion of this war. Indeed, the people of his nation displayed consummate skill at it, holding in check at every point, from the Penobscot River to Salmon Falls, N.H., and even beyond, 700 regular troops, and even inflicting humiliating defeats upon them. With the return of peace the governor of New York, Sir Edmund Andros, hastened to have a fort constructed at Pemaquid, between the Penobscot and Kennebec Rivers.

But the strategy and superior equipment of the Abenakis had not failed to intrigue and worry the people of Boston and New York. They endeavoured to find out what might be behind this, and they finally learned of the existence of "a reduced French officer, who had married a daughter of Madokawando, and kept a trading house at Penobscot, where he considered himself as independent, being out of the limits of any established government . . . ." (Belknap) They then lost no time in making him advances to win him over. But Saint-Castin rejected the English offers. The Bostonians then thought they could intimidate him. As the joint frontier commission had not yet taken any decision about this part of Acadia, in 1686 Judge John Palmer of New York ordered

wine stored on Abenaki territory to be seized and called upon the baron to apply to His Britannic Majesty for the land grant of Pentagouet, on condition, of course, that he take the oath of allegiance to the British monarch! This meant that Saint-Castin had to commit himself, which he promptly did by addressing his request for a land grant to the court at Versailles.

In that same year BRISAY de Denonville recommended him for the governorship of Acadia, if Perrot* were to leave his post. Saint-Castin set out for Canada with a detachment of Abenakis in order to take part in Denonville's expedition against the Iroquois (1687). Andros took advantage of this absence to pillage the baron's dwelling at Pentagouet. He tried also to suborn Madokawando, but to no avail. When the War of the League of Augsburg broke out (1689), the Penobscots and the other Abenakis resumed their forays against the English settlers with greater vigour than ever, not hesitating to put even towns to fire and sword by extraordinarily daring surprise attacks. In 1690 Madokawando and Saint-Castin personally commanded the Penobscots who joined RENÉ ROBINAU de Portneuf's column, which was sent from Canada to attack the town of Casco (near present Portland, Me.) on the Atlantic. The same year, alerted by the spies whom he maintained in New England, Saint-Castin was able to give Frontenac timely warning of Phips*'s preparations against Quebec. Saint-Castin had become a thorn in the English side. In 1692 Phips did not scruple to hire two deserters to murder Saint-Castin, but the plot was thwarted by two Acadians, Jean SERREAU de Saint-Aubin and Jacques Petitpas.

For a long time Frontenac had been toying with a plan to strike at the heart of New England by attacking Boston or New York, and he kept on badgering the court to carry it out. Meanwhile PIERRE LE MOYNE d'Iberville had been instructed to destroy the fort at Pemaquid, which constituted a permanent threat to Acadia. Saint-Castin gave the bold sailor valuable assistance with his warriors, who had been joined by the Passamaquoddys and the Malecites. Pemaquid fell on 15 Aug. 1696 under the combined action launched by Iberville's fleet and the land forces.

Madokawando died in 1698, probably leaving the position of principal chief of the Penobscots to his son-in-law. But when peace returned at the end of 1699, Saint-Castin, always concerned for his independence, quickly resumed his commercial operations with New England, without worrying about the French regulations. Once more accusations were levelled against him, and despite a favourable report by Governor Brouillan [MOM-

6

BETON], the baron decided to return to France, to clear himself and (finally!) to straighten up his personal affairs. He left Pentagouet at the end of 1701. Once at Versailles, he had no difficulty in dispelling Pontchartrain's prejudices. In 1702 he arrived in his native Béarn. His brother-in-law, the judge Jean de Labaig, his sister Marie's husband, was waiting for him armed to the teeth, ready to sink the estate, of which he had to render an account, into a morass of legal procedure. With a skill worthy of a better cause, Labaig managed things so well that he piled one obstacle upon another, after having already done all he could to prove that Jean-Vincent's birth was illegitimate. The court, which wanted to send Saint-Castin back as quickly as possible to Acadia, where he was needed more than ever, intervened energetically in the *parlement* of Pau to hasten the passing of judgement. It was all in vain. In 1707, exhausted by quibbling and chicanery, Jean-Vincent d'Abbadie, third Baron de Saint-Castin, died at Pau without seeing Acadia again.

He left several children, of whom only some are known to us: his eldest son, Bernard-Anselme, born in 1689; then Joseph*; another son whose first name we do not know; and two daughters, Thérèse and Anastasie, who on the same day, 4 Dec. 1707, married Philippe Mius d'Entremont and Alexandre Le Borgne* de Belle-Isle respectively. Another boy, Jean-Pierre, who studied at the Petit Séminaire of Quebec, died at the age of eight. Another daughter, Ursule, is thought to have married Louis Damours de Freneuse in 1715.

GEORGES CERBELAUD SALAGNAC

AN, Col., B, 16, 19, 22, 25; C¹¹D, 2–6. BN, MS, Clairambault 874, ff.167, 171, 381; 880, f.302; NAF 7485, f.178. "Mass. Archives," XXXVI, 78, 96, 206; XXXVII, 40, 101, 102.

Charlevoix, *History* (Shea), III, IV, V. Church, *King Philip's war* (Dexter), I, II. *Coll. de manuscrits relatifs à la N.-F.*, I, II. "Correspondance de Vaudreuil," APQ *Rapport, 1939–40*. Dièreville, *Relation of voyage to Port Royal* (Webster). William Hubbard, *The history of the Indian wars in New England* (Boston and London, 1677; new ed., Roxbury, 1865). Hutchinson, *Hist. of Mass.-bay* (1765). Lahontan, *Nouveaux voyages*, II. La Potherie, *Histoire* (1722). Increase Mather, *A brief history of the war with the Indians in New England* (Boston and London, 1676). *Mémoires des commissaires*, I, xxiv–xxv, 51; *Memorials of the English and French commissaries*, I, 29, 122. Daniel Neal, *The history of New-England . . . to the year 1700 . . .* (2v., London, 1720), I, II. *NYCD* (O'Callaghan and Fernow), IX. P.-G. Roy, *Inv. concessions*, IV, 44.

J. P. Baxter, *The pioneers of New France in New England, with contemporary letters and documents* (Albany, 1894). Jeremy Belknap, *The history of New Hampshire* (2d ed., 3v., Boston, 1813), I, 130–31. Bernard, *Le drame acadien*. Coleman, *New England captives*. Pierre Daviault, *Le baron de Saint-Castin, chef abénaquis* (Montréal, 1939). Dufau de Maluquer, "Notice généalogique sur la maison d'Abbadie de Maslacq," *RSCT*, 2d ser., I (1895), sect.I, 73. Lauvrière, *La tragédie d'un peuple*. Robert Le Blant, *Une figure légendaire de l'histoire acadienne: le baron de Saint-Castin* (Dax, [1934]). J.-A. Maurault, *Histoire des Abénakis depuis 1605 jusqu'à nos jours* (Sorel, 1866). Rameau de Saint-Père, *Une colonie féodale*. Robert Rumilly, *Histoire des Acadiens* (2v., Montréal, [1955]). Sylvester, *Indian wars*. W. D. Williamson, *The history of the state of Maine, from its first discovery*, A.D. *1602, to the separation*, A.D. *1820, inclusive* (2v., Hallowell, Me., 1832).

"Les barons de Saint-Castin," *BRH*, IX (1903), 222–23; *see also* "A propos du sieur de Saint-Castin," *BRH*, XLI (1935), 611. Ganong, "Historic sites in New Brunswick," 313. Gorham Munson, "St. Castin: a legend revisited," *Dalhousie Review* (Halifax), XLV (1965–66), 338–60.

ACOUTSINA (also written **Acountsina**), Eskimo girl, about 20 years old in 1717, captive of AUGUSTIN LE GARDEUR de Courtemanche at the latter's trading post on Baie de Phélypeaux (previously Baie des Espagnols and today Brador Bay), on the north shore of the St Lawrence, at the entrance to the Strait of Belle Isle. She lived there from 1717 to 1719.

With a young companion, whose name we do not know, Acoutsina played the part of family helper, and was considered as a member of the Courtemanche family. She learned enough French to serve as an interpreter when need arose, and to teach the rudiments of the Eskimo language to Courtemanche's successor, his step-son, François Martel* de Brouague. Brouague's and ANTOINE-DENIS RAUDOT's writings refer to her habitually as "the young slavegirl," "the young Indian girl," the "esquimaude" (which takes this grammatical form back at least 250 years), the "esquimaute," or the "esquimote."

The young captive was the daughter of the chief Ouibignaro, who came to the fort on the Baie de Phélypeaux in 1719 and took his daughter back. He was accompanied on that occasion by numerous Eskimos and by another chief, Camerlique, who seems to have been of European origin if we interpret the girl's statements correctly. We possess very little information about these three persons. Acoutsina's accounts, noted down at the time and known only in manuscript form, likewise contained brief descriptions of Eskimo customs and legends. In particular, Acoutsina informed her "French family" that there existed in the north beings "without a fundament" and pygmies; she thus led Raudot to believe that certain of Jacques

7

Acoutsina

Cartier*'s tales, reported to be mythical, might not be entirely void of truth.

The problem that first arises is to ascertain whether Acoutsina and her people were really Eskimos. Indeed J. A. Burgesse has shown that the "Eskimos" in the first register of births, marriages, and deaths of the Tadoussac domain were Papinachois or Naskapis (of the Algonkian family). The word *esquimau*, a French term dating from the beginning of the colony, is derived from an Algonkian word *eisimeow* (or its equivalent), meaning "eater of raw flesh." Originally, therefore, this word applied not only to the real Eskimos, but equally to nordic Amerindians leading a rather wretched life, such as the Naskapis. One might more readily believe that Acoutsina and her people were Beothuks, the true "Red Indians" who lived in Newfoundland; these disappeared entirely with Sarah Shanawdithit* who died in captivity in 1829, when a belated effort was being made to save this ethnic group; unfortunately no other Beothuk was ever discovered.

These two hypotheses must be eliminated. Acoutsina and her people are indeed Eskimos. The following facts allow us to affirm this. Courtemanche, like his contemporary Pierre Constantin and their predecessor Louis Jolliet*, had set up fur-trading posts on the borders of the Eskimo country, between the Strait of Belle Isle and Mingan. Their object was even to establish friendly relations with these people and bring them into the orbit of French commerce. They frequently met Eskimos and attempted to organize trade with them. They could hardly be mistaken as to their identity. They had in their service Montagnais Indians who spoke a dialect closely allied to that of the Naskapis, and who could not have been mistaken as to the ethnic relationship of the Eskimos in question. Moreover, these Montagnais hunters were well acquainted with the Beothuks, the "red men" who were at that time confined to central Newfoundland. The names of the Indians and Eskimos, transcribed after being heard by ears trained to French sounds, underwent inevitable distortion; however, the three names quoted above can easily be interpreted as Eskimo terms. According to Roderick MacGregor, Acoutsina seems to be a transformation of *akutsiarq*, which could be translated as "the beautiful apron" (*aku* referring to the wide back part of the mother's parka). The nearest word to Ouibignaro is *uiviquartok*, meaning "inclined to be difficult." Camerlique can be explained by *kamilik*, meaning "he has boots." For anyone acquainted with the Eskimo language, in which the phoneme *r* is often reduced to a single very attenuated roll, the two forms seem almost homonyms. Furthermore,

these names are quite consistent with Eskimo thinking. Brouague, who learned from Acoutsina to speak a little Eskimo, quotes from his vocabulary the word *annanâ*, which in that language means "mother." Finally, several ethnological traits described by Acoutsina are characteristics of Eskimo culture.

Acoutsina and Ouibignaro—for we must leave aside Camerlique, who was probably of foreign origin—do not seem to have been the only Eskimos in contact with the French in this period. Indeed, a letter from a Father François dated 20 Oct. 1732 contains this passage: "I counted on having the privilege of giving you a detailed account of matters relating to the Eskimo natives, but it will be extremely brief, for this is all I could get out of the young Eskimo woman who lives at Beauport; not being very familiar as yet with the French language, she could not express herself adequately, or even understand clearly what she was being asked." According to the few pieces of information that one can glean from this letter, it is clear that reference is being made to Eskimos and not to Naskapis or to Beothuks. In this period it was only the Eskimos who were able to come and steal from the French fishermen on the north bank of the St Lawrence.

Acoutsina's story and the statements she made permit us to assess Euro-Eskimo relations a century after the establishment of the French colony. Of the three linguistic families in eastern Canada (the Algonkian, the Iroquoian, and the Eskimo), only the small Eskimo-speaking tribes remained long hostile 'o the European element. Their coastal territory, of arctic type, ran southwest from the Strait of Belle Isle to near the Mingan Islands. Beyond, to the west, lived their traditional enemies the Montagnais, whom they always designated in their language by terms of contempt—*erpalik*, for example, which meant "who has nits"—or "the enemy." Seasonal cod-fishermen and Eskimos encroached on each other. The Eskimos wanted to take advantage of the opportunity to get nails, and like the Beothuks of Newfoundland they could think of nothing more practical than burning the boats.

The French posts on the Strait of Belle Isle attempted, however, to establish friendly contacts with them, in order to organize fur-trading with these refractory Amerindians. It was at this point that the Sieur de Courtemanche appeared on the scene. On 16 Oct. 1716 M. Lair, Courtemanche's chaplain, wrote from Baie de Phélypeaux to Madame de Courtemanche, who was then at Bayonne: "All conceivable means must be employed to win over the Eskimos. Those means are: 1) forbid the French to fire on them; 2) try to entice or catch a few of them, treat them well in all sorts of ways, and send them back with gifts for themselves and their compatriots; 3) urge a few bold and clever Frenchmen to go among them in order to try to bring them round, or at least to appeal to the Frenchmen who are believed to be among them [for deserters sometimes banded together with the natives] to persuade them to trade with the French. To this end promise to give good rewards to these Frenchmen. . . ."

Madame de Courtemanche was apparently a masterful woman who had her say in the affairs of the post. We may wonder whether the chaplain was not trying to obtain the agreement of the mistress of the house first, in order to win over the husband subsequently. Or he may have assumed responsibility for a plan conceived by Courtemanche, in order to get it more readily accepted by the wife. Both hypotheses can be put forward.

In the autumn of 1716 Courtemanche met some Eskimos, and urged them to return the following year for fur-trading. They came on 25 May 1717, faithful to the rendezvous, and camped within gunshot of the fort. With 18 men (French and Montagnais), Courtemanche went to the Eskimo camp, where they threatened to ill-treat him. While he was exhorting the chief, the natives took to their shallops; the women, first in, were quickly joined by the men, who began to shoot arrows at the French. Courtemanche therefore intercepted a shallop occupied by 12 persons, and managed to seize a woman, two girls, and a small boy. The latter died shortly after being duly baptized.

After Courtemanche's death in June 1717, his step-son Brouague directed the fur-trading post on Baie de Phélypeaux. During the next two years nothing more was seen of the Eskimos. Brouague's letters no longer mention the woman, but only the two girls, and particularly the elder of the two, Acoutsina, who was 18 or 20 years old. Both girls were still living at the post in 1719.

Meanwhile Brouague (letter dated 9 Sept. 1718) was applying himself to the task of learning the Eskimo language from Acoutsina, who was living with Madame de Courtemanche as a member of the family. Despite her easy life among understanding whites who assumed the role of parents in relation to their captives, Acoutsina "still has a strong desire to return to her nation," wrote Brouague in September 1718. "I consoled her by giving her the hope," he added, "that she would be returned to her parents."

What French she had learned enabled Acoutsina to convey information to her masters concerning Eskimo customs, and also mythical ideas or legends based on false interpretations. She likewise told them how certain Europeans had settled among them, one being a shipwrecked sailor whom they apparently called "good old Nicolas," and with whom the administration at Quebec tried to get into contact. Raudot's correspondence contains a letter, written after 1717, to "good old Nicolas," seeking his collaboration in the task of bringing the two peoples together. We have no idea whether the letter reached its destination, the more so because we do not know whether this person really existed.

In September 1719, having become commandant "of all the shore of Bras d'Or with power to settle disputes there," Brouague reported the following: his scouts, who were constantly on the watch, informed him of the presence of Eskimos on Île aux Bois, an opportunity he had long been waiting for. Leaving his men at a distance, he advanced unarmed towards the Eskimos, accompanied only by Acoutsina, who made herself known. Her father, chief Ouibignaro, was with the group. At sunset he went with Brouague to the fort, entreating him to leave his daughter with him, and saying that he would bring her back the next day. Some 30 Eskimos then came to join them and feasted at the fort. Ouibignaro recognized Acoutsina's young companion as a relation of his, and begged to have both girls, to which Brouague readily agreed. To the eager expressions of gratitude addressed to Madame de Courtemanche, who had treated the girls so well, a pessimistic note was added. Camerlique, one of their principal chiefs despite his foreign origin (if Acoutsina's information was correct), declared that they must all be killed, including Madame de Courtemanche. Acoutsina began to weep, but she was reassured instantly, and the Eskimos even promised no longer to burn the shallops of the French fishermen. During the reunion the chaplain, Lair—no doubt Acoutsina's French teacher—handed her a book so that she could give her kindred a demonstration of her knowledge. After the exchange of gifts the two parties separated, and thus ends the story of Acoutsina, who was not heard of again.

This fine beginning had no sequel. The Eskimos did not return; they continued their depredations against the French fishermen, then against the English, and carried on like this until the Moravian Brethren, Protestant missionaries from central Europe and the spiritual descendants of John Huss, came 50 years later to settle on the coast of Labrador.

JACQUES ROUSSEAU

The Sieur de Brouague's letters, the main source of information about Acoutsina, Camerlique and Ouibignaro are found in AN, Col., C^{11A}, 109. C^{11A}, 122 contains various documents of which Raudot's

9

letters correspond, except for minute differences, to letters 44–89 in *Relation par lettres de l'Amérique septentrionale, années 1709 et 1710*, éd. Camille de Rochemonteix (Paris, 1904). Raudot's letters in C^{11A} end with these words: "Here is the end by M. Raudot, the younger. I have already sent you the first lot and half of the second." At this point Pierre Margry adds: "This statement was made by Raudot the younger about the Sieur de Louvigny's memoir about the savages. See his letter of 24 Sept. 1709." For some of Brouague's other letters see AN, Col., C^{11A}, 37, f.405; 41, ff.57–63; 43, ff.149–61. [J.R.]

"Mémoire de M. de Brouague, commandant pour le roi à la cote de Labrador . . . ," APQ *Rapport, 1922–23*, 368–74. La Morandière, *Hist. de la pêche française de la morue*. J. A. Burgesse, "Esquimaux in the Saguenay," *Primitive Man* (Washington), XXII (1949), 23–32. Charles de La Morandière, "Les Français au Labrador au XVIIIe siècle," Académie de marine, *Communications et mémoires*, II (Paris, 1956–57), 24–59. Jacques Rousseau, "Le dernier des Peaux-Rouges," *Cahiers des Dix*, XXVII (1962), 47–76; "L'origine et l'évolution du mot esquimau," *Cahiers des Dix*, XX (1955), 179–98.

ADAMS (Adems; after 1727 he used the spelling **Adames), JOSEPH,** Hudson's Bay Company employee; b. *c.* 1700; d. 1737.

One of several children born to William, a labourer, and Katherine Adams, Joseph was baptized 4 May 1700 in Woodford parish, Essex. On 1 June 1705, he was fitted out by the parish and bound to serve the HBC until he was 24. Assuming that he was baptized shortly after birth, it would appear that Adams was sent to Albany at the tender age of five years. There he was educated by the chief factors and learned the Cree language; he was fitted out with new clothes each year according to the terms of his indenture. Adams soon proved to be a good apprentice and a trustworthy servant. There was considerable correspondence between London and Albany concerning his age and the expiry date of his indenture. In 1714 Anthony BEALE, HBC governor, estimated that Adams was 18 years old; either Adams was big for his age or Beale hoped that by deliberately overestimating Adams' age the time of his indenture would be lessened. Finally in 1722, upon the recommendation of Thomas McCliesh*, who succeeded Henry KELSEY as governor for the HBC overseas, Adams was entertained at £16 per annum retroactive to 11 Sept. 1721 because for the 1721–22 season he had wintered as trader on the East Main. For reasons of health he spent the 1723–24 season in England.

Adams acted as deputy to Joseph MYATT from 1727–28 until Myatt's death on 9 June 1730, whereupon Adams took over command. With William BEVAN he did a survey of Moose River in July 1728 and located the site of the original Moose Factory. The London committee had intended that Adams supervise the establishment of a factory at Moose in 1730–31, but Myatt's death necessitated Adams' staying at Albany. He sent Thomas RENDER and John Jewer to build the post, although he had reservations about their capabilities. In October 1731 his reservations proved accurate and he had to visit Moose because the men refused to work under Render.

Adams was supposed to be recalled in 1735 and again in 1736, and was to be replaced by Thomas McCliesh, but on both occasions McCliesh upon arrival in the bay was "sore afflicted with ailments" and had to return to England. The winter of 1735–36 was a particularly busy one for Adams; in January 1736 he heard that Moose factory had been destroyed by fire on 26 Dec. 1735, and later he wrote to the committee: "we have strained ourselves to the utmost to assist them."

During his long tenure as governor, Adams carried out considerable rebuilding of Albany Factory to make it more defensible. He failed to decrease the consumption of brandy by company servants, a trend that had started in the 1720s and continued throughout the 1730s. The London committee felt that the loss of five Albany servants by drowning and the destruction of Moose resulted from excessive drinking. A sharp reduction in the Albany fur returns was caused by the establishment of Moose Factory, by the competition of Pierre Gaultier* de La Vérendrye's posts, and also by the anonymous coureurs de bois who seemed to have established temporary posts on both the Moose and Albany rivers.

Adams died on 29 Sept. 1737, shortly after his return to England with his three-year-old halfbreed daughter, Mary. His will, which was proved on 12 Jan. 1738, listed bequests to his sister Mary and to his executors, Captains George Spurrell and Christopher Middleton*; the greater part of his estate was left in trust for the benefit of his infant daughter.

G. E. THORMAN

HBC Arch. A.6/3 (letters outward, 1705, 1713); A.6/4 (letters outward, 1718–19, 1720, 1722, 1724, 1726); A.6/5 (letters outward, 1727, 1729–37); B.3/a/5–6, 9–11, 14–25 (Albany journals between 1713 and 1737). HBRS, XXV (Davies and Johnson).

ADDEAWANDO (Adeawanadon, Adeawando). *See* ATECOUANDO

ADEMS. *See* ADAMS

ADHÉMAR DE SAINT-MARTIN, ANTOINE, royal notary, clerk of court, process-server,

Adhémar de Saint-Martin

surveyor, and prison keeper; b. *c.* 1639, son of Michel Adhémar, a bourgeois of Saint-Salvy in the town of Albi (in the province of Languedoc), and of Cécile Gasche; d. 15 April 1714 at Montreal.

Among the troops who landed at Quebec with M. de Chastelard de Salières on 17 Aug. 1665 was a soldier named Saint-Martin, in the company of M. de Saurel*; in Saint-Martin one is tempted to recognize Antoine Adhémar, all the more because it was at Sorel that the latter began his civil career, as royal notary in 1668. (In all probability, therefore, Adhémar took part in the expedition into the Mohawk country.) On 3 Nov. 1673, when Frontenac [Buade*] appointed him "royal process-server and serjeant-at-law for the whole of Canada," Adhémar was still living at Sorel, but received acts regularly in the seigneuries of Cap-de-la-Madeleine, Sainte-Anne de la Pérade, Batiscan, Champlain, and even Chambly. He was about to go and set himself up at Champlain. According to documents dated 1681, 1682, and 1684, he added to his offices of royal notary and process-server those of prison keeper at Trois-Rivières, clerk of court, and sworn surveyor: enough to keep him busy!

It was at Champlain that on 28 Aug. 1683 Geneviève Sageot, whom he had married on 10 Oct. 1667 at Quebec, died at the age of 33, leaving him four children. Adhémar remarried twice at Cap-de-la-Madeleine, where he seems to have lived from 1684: on 8 Feb. 1684 he took as his wife Marie Sédilot, the widow of René Blanchet by her second marriage, who died soon after the birth of a daughter; and on 20 Jan. 1687 he married Michelle, the daughter of the notary Jean CUSSON, who bore him a sixth child.

At the time of his third marriage Adhémar was about to move to Montreal, where he had been summoned by DOLLIER de Casson, to replace Hilaire Bourgine* as clerk of the court for seigneurial justice. On 2 May 1687 Casson gave him his commission. Pursuing his career, but confining himself now to his responsibilities as notary and clerk of court, Adhémar also devoted much attention to the interests of the widow and under-age children of his brother-in-law Jean Aubuchon, who had been murdered in 1685. A large number of deeds, in which he appears in his capacity as guardian, concern this estate. After acting as court clerk for the seigneurs of Montreal from 1687 on, he was transferred by a commission dated 17 Nov. 1693 to the new royal jurisdiction of Montreal, to which he was to remain attached until his death. For a short time in 1703, he held the office of acting lieutenant-general there.

On leaving the Trois-Rivières region in 1687, Adhémar had sold his land at Champlain to his brother-in-law, Jean Cusson; Jacques Babie had bought from him his "two oxen and the cow which are at M. Cusson's" for 140 *livres*. Thus, although he had made no declaration to this effect at the time of the 1681 census, Adhémar did have some cattle, and probably a few acres under cultivation. But he does not seem to have had a particular liking for the country, or rather he seems to have preferred the atmosphere of the town. In Montreal he rapidly became recognized as the notary of the merchants dealing in furs and the coureurs de bois.

His correspondence, which has been partially preserved, shows that once he was at Montreal he continued to maintain relationships with the settlers at Champlain, particularly with the merchant Jacques Babie, and afterwards with the latter's widow. From it we learn, among other things, that in the autumn of 1687 Adhémar, who had just settled at Montreal, was very ill, "and even in danger of dying." Adhémar was the confidential agent of Babie and of many others: he was entrusted with the most varied tasks, which he undertook moreover with good grace.

Adhémar owned some houses at Montreal and lived there in fairly comfortable circumstances. But he went after his debtors ruthlessly: the Registre du bailliage et des audiences enumerates no fewer than 155 suits that he instituted. Despite all this, the sums owing to him in February 1711 amounted to 2,066 *livres*, 8 *sols*, 3 *deniers*. The difficulty he experienced in recovering his money did not prevent him from being charitable: he was one of the first three directors of the office of the needy (Bureau des pauvres) at Montreal, and in 1695, after the fire in the Hôtel-Dieu of Montreal, he subscribed 20 *livres* for its reconstruction. This man, obliging, hard-headed in business but responsive to those in distress, was also a careful official who earned praise in 1690 for his way of keeping the records. Unfortunately the last years of his life were saddened by his differences with his son-in-law, Deniau-Destaillis. After Adhémar's death, Deniau and Tessier, his other son-in-law, started a dispute concerning his estate which was taken before the Conseil Souverain.

On 15 April 1714 Intendant Bégon* gave Jean-Baptiste Adhémar*, Antoine's eldest son, a commission as a royal notary, in succession to his father.

ANDRÉ VACHON

AJM, Greffe d'Antoine Adhémar, 1668–1714; Greffe d'Hilaire Bourgine, 17 mai 1686, 27 juin 1689; Greffe de Pierre Cabazié, 27 déc. 1685, 27 déc. 1688, 21 août 1689, 18 oct. 1689, 29 avril 1690, 15 mai 1690, 13 avril 1691; Greffe de Claude Maugue, 5 nov. 1688, 2 juin 1695, 29 févr. 1696; Greffe de Pierre Raimbault, 16 févr. 1711; Registre du bailliage et des audiences.

Adiawonda

AJQ, Greffe de Gilles Rageot, 9 oct. 1667. AJTR, Greffe de Séverin Ameau, 24 déc. 1680, 20 juin 1683, 4 janv. 1687; Greffe de Jean Cusson, 8 févr. 1684. AQ, Antoine Adhémar; NF, Doc. de la jur. des T.-R., I, 28, 55; NF, Ins. de la Prév. de Québec, I, 387; NF, Ord. des int., VI, 66; VII, 5f. *Jug. et délib.*, I, II, III, IV, VI. Recensement du Canada, 1681 (Sulte). A. Roy, *Inv. greffes not.*, V, VI. Godbout, "Nos ancêtres," 464f. Massicotte, "Les tribunaux et les officiers de justice," *BRH*, XXXVII (1931), 127, 183, 188, 190. Mondoux, *L'Hôtel-Dieu de Montréal*, 247. "Les notaires au Canada." J.-E. Roy, *Histoire du notariat*, I, 147, 151f, 202, 221, 363, 382. Régis Roy et Malchelosse, *Le régiment de Carignan*, 103. Sulte, *Mélanges historiques* (Malchelosse), I, 104–17. Vachon, *Histoire du notariat*, 41, 43.

ADIAWONDA. *See* ATECOUANDO

AGRAIN, JEAN-ANTOINE D', Comte, assistant town major and infantry captain, knight of the order of Saint-Louis, b. probably at Le Puy-en-Velay (Le Puy), murdered on the Labadeck River, Île Royale (Baddeck River, Cape Breton Island), 23 Jan. 1722.

On the recommendation of his uncle, the Marquis d'Urfé, Agrain was appointed assistant town major at Île Royale on 29 June 1715, and was to take his post at Port-Toulouse (St Peters); however, he did not reach the colony until August 1716, and by 1719 had obtained leave to return to France after threatening to resign his commission. Early in 1720 he was in France, raising workers for the fortifications at Île Royale and the Windward Islands. On 27 March he concluded an agreement with his uncle Jugues d'Agrain Du Mazel for a joint investment in goods to be purchased at Lyons and Le Puy-en-Velay and sold by Agrain at Île Royale.

Before returning briefly to Louisbourg that summer, Agrain had been promoted captain and had obtained official approval for a project to ship timber from Île Royale to the Rochefort shipyards. By December 1720 Agrain was back in France with wood samples, and the following March a specific contract concerning the type and quantity of wood to be supplied was drawn up. Returning to Île Royale later in 1721, Agrain immediately encountered problems—wood cut by his men during the previous winter was unacceptable and shortage of funds was pressing. He wintered at the lumbering site on the Labadeck River, and on 23 December was awarded the order of Saint-Louis. One month later two of his workmen murdered him in revenge for maltreatment and alleged starvation. His estate, encumbered with debts, was involved in legal wrangles until 1732. Although Saint-Ovide de Brouillan [Mombeton*] described Agrain in 1718 as "a very good officer," he emerges as a rather reckless man whose ambitious schemes lacked the forethought necessary to bring them to a successful conclusion.

JOHN HUMPHREYS

AN, Col., B, 37, f.124; 40–41; 42, f.466; 44, 45, 47–50, 54, 55; C¹¹ᴮ, 1–4, 5, ff.136–47; 6, ff.261–82; 7–9; C¹¹ᶜ, 15, pièces 160, 194, 196, 232, 234; D²ᶜ, 222 (Alphabet Laffilard); E, 1, ff.2–28 (printed in *NF* (1930), 404–10 [50–56], 110–17); Marine, B¹, 8, 51, 52, 55, ff.105–13. *NF*, V (1930), 118–20. McLennan, *Louisbourg*, 66. [McLennan erroneously states that Agrain was murdered by "two Indians in his employment"; the record of the murder trial, in AN, Col., C¹¹ᴮ, 6, proves the accused were Frenchmen engaged by Agrain to work on his project for the exploitation of Île Royale timber. J.H.]

AIGREMONT, FRANÇOIS CLAIRAMBAULT D'. *See* CLAIRAMBAULT

AILLEBOUST D'ARGENTEUIL, PIERRE D', soldier; b. at Quebec, 19 June 1659, son of Charles-Joseph d'Ailleboust* Des Muceaux and Catherine Legardeur de Repentigny; d. at Montreal, 15 March 1711.

Argenteuil belonged to two of the most prominent families of New France. In November 1687 he married Marie-Louise, daughter of PIERRE DENYS de La Ronde, at Quebec and in the 1690s he obtained the seigneuries of the Îles Bourdon and of Argenteuil from his father. Argenteuil became a half-pay lieutenant in 1690, and in 1710 he reached his highest rank, captain of a company.

Throughout the 1690s Argenteuil made many trips to the Michilimackinac region. He led several fur trade convoys back to Montreal, and Buade* de Frontenac often praised his work. In the early 1700s Argenteuil was at the Detroit post, working closely with Cadillac [LAUMET]. He also figured prominently in the LE PESANT affair of 1706–7 and its aftermath—the Miami troubles of 1708. Argenteuil went with JEAN-PAUL LEGARDEUR de Saint-Pierre, his cousin, from Detroit to Michilimackinac where Le Pesant was apprehended and returned to Detroit for trial. In 1708, Argenteuil convinced the Sagina Ottawas to go to Cadillac's aid at Detroit. The reports of this event disparage Cadillac's role, but Argenteuil performed well and had the confidence of all the warring factions.

In 1709 Argenteuil was in the east, and played a prominent role in the assaults on the forts at St John's, Newfoundland [see LLOYD]. In the summer of 1710, Argenteuil was back in the Ottawa country, where he succeeded in making peace among the various Algonkian tribes. RIGAUD de

Vaudreuil was so impressed that in October of the same year he sent Argenteuil to the Iroquois country on a peace mission.

Argenteuil's most important assignment came in March 1711 when Vaudreuil appointed him leader of a major expedition to the western country. His orders were to make contact with all the warriors of the western tribes, gather them at Detroit, then lead them east to fight against the English and the Iroquois. Argenteuil never went on this mission, as he died of apoplexy in Montreal on 15 March 1711, only days after he had received his orders.

Frontenac and Vaudreuil both entrusted Argenteuil with important missions. Even CLAIRAMBAULT d'Aigremont, who wrote damaging reports about Cadillac and his officers, several times wrote that Argenteuil "has as much influence over savages as anyone can have . . . but, in other ways, he has little discretion."

Of Argenteuil's 11 children, several were prominent in military and fur-trading affairs. Argenteuil's widow died on 5 Nov. 1747.

DONALD CHAPUT

AN, Col., C^11A, 24, f.208v; 28, ff.165–73v. Charlevoix, *History* (Shea). "Correspondance de Frontenac (1689–99)," APQ *Rapport*, *1927–28*, 159; *1928–29*, 381. "Correspondance de Vaudreuil," APQ *Rapport*, *1939–40*, 389, 401; *1946–47*, 390–91, 413, 444. *Michigan Pioneer Coll.*, XXXIII, 342–46, 350–61, 374, 382, 385–86, 424–52, 487–91, 497–502, 534. *NYCD* (O'Callaghan and Fernow), IX, 676, 847–48, 855. Recensement du Canada, 1666 (APQ *Rapport*), 108. A. Roy, *Inv. greffes not.*, VII, 46. P.-G. Roy, "Ce que Callières pensait de nos officiers," 321–33; *Inv. concessions*. Wisconsin State Hist. Soc. *Coll.*, XVI. Godbout, "Nos ancêtres," APQ *Rapport*, *1951–53*, 470–71. Tanguay, *Dictionnaire*, I, 152; III, 223.

AILLEBOUST DE MANTHET, NICOLAS D', soldier, fur-trader; baptized 12 April 1663 at Montreal, son of Charles-Joseph d'Ailleboust* Des Muceaux and Catherine Legardeur; d. 1709 at Hudson Bay.

He rose by successive stages in his military career, and on 1 April 1702 reached the rank of captain. From 1684 on he had been a companion of DANIEL GREYSOLON Dulhut in the *pays d'en haut*, and on 16 Oct. 1689 took part with him in a raid on a group of Senecas at Lac des Deux-Montagnes. The same year, having barely landed to take up his second mandate as governor, Buade* de Frontenac sent him with all speed to Cataracoui (Fort Frontenac), in order to stop the fort from being abandoned and destroyed, as ordered by BRISAY de Denonville. But it was already too late: CLÉMENT Du Vuault de Valrennes

had blown up the fortifications. In January 1690, with Le Moyne* de Sainte-Hélène, he directed the raid planned by Frontenac against Schenectady. On 18 February, at nightfall, the party, made up of 210 men of whom 114 were Canadians, attacked the English post. When they withdrew some hours later, they left behind them some 60 dead, smoking ruins, and a helpless population that sought refuge at Albany. The next day they headed back to Montreal with 25 captives.

In 1693, during the War of the League of Augsburg, Nicolas de Manthet, together with ROBUTEL de La Noue and AUGUSTIN LE GARDEUR de Courtemanche, led a party of 625 men who were sent on an expedition against the Mohawks in the region of Albany. The expedition left Montreal on 25 January and three weeks later reached the territory where war was to be waged. After setting fire to villages and capturing 300 persons, two-thirds of whom were women and children, the party, burdened with its prisoners, turned back and made for Montreal. On the way home it was twice attacked by Anglo-Mohawk bands who inflicted only light casualties, but who delayed its progress and thus exposed its members to starvation; this danger became a disaster when the thaw had ruined the provisions in the caches. The captives were set free. A few soldiers starved to death. More than a hundred had to remain on the spot to await help. The others managed with difficulty to get to Montreal, after ridding themselves of their muskets and blankets in order to travel more lightly.

It was on a similar expedition, this time against Albany Fort on Hudson Bay, that the Sieur de Manthet perished in July 1709. RIGAUD de Vaudreuil had ordered him to seize this fort, but the undertaking resulted in a failure attributable, in the governor's opinion, to the excessive recklessness of the soldiers and an inadequate knowledge of the area.

Like all soldiers of his stamp, Nicolas de Manthet served on several occasions as a diplomatic agent among the Indian allies; it was above all important, particularly during the first two intercolonial conflicts, to keep them within the sphere of French influence. In 1703 Vaudreuil said of him that no one at that time had so much ascendancy over the Indians and even over the French in the *pays d'en haut*.

Official missions to the west apparently served as a cover for trafficking in pelts on a fairly large scale. In 1706 Vaudreuil and JACQUES RAUDOT were obliged to apologize to the minister on Nicolas de Manthet's behalf, stating that on his journeys towards the posts on the Great Lakes he had to take the goods required to meet his own

Ailleboust Des Muceaux

needs. Manthet was a shareholder of the Compagnie de la Colonie and maintained business relations with CHARLES AUBERT de La Chesnaye. Official correspondence and notarial acts show that he was involved in the fur trade from 1699 up to the year of his death, 1709, when he was sentenced to pay 3,039 *livres* to the Sieur REGNARD Duplessis, the agent general of the Compagnie de la Colonie.

On 9 June 1696 Nicolas d'Ailleboust de Manthet had married Françoise Denys de La Ronde, Guillaume Bouthier's widow; by her he had six daughters whom we know of and perhaps a seventh about whom we have no information.

JEAN BLAIN

AN, Col., B, 23, f.26. *Coll. de manuscrits relatifs à la N.-F.*, I, 482–531. Charlevoix, *Histoire* (1744), III, 184–88; IV, 57f. "Correspondance de Vaudreuil," APQ *Rapport, 1938–39, 1939–40, 1942–43.* P.-G. Roy, "Ce que Callières pensait de nos officiers," *BRH*, XXVI (1920), 327; *Inv. ord. int.*, I, 21, 71. [François Vachon] de Belmont, *Histoire du Canada*, 30. Godbout, "Nos ancêtres," APQ *Rapport, 1951–53*, 471f. Eccles, *Frontenac*, 224f., 252–54. Aegidius Fauteux, *La famille d'Ailleboust* (Montréal, 1917), 122–26. P.-G. Roy, "Philippe Clément Du Vuault De Valrennes," *BRH*, XI (1905), 195.

AILLEBOUST DES MUCEAUX (Musseaux), JEAN-BAPTISTE D', half-pay lieutenant, business man; b. 27 March 1666 at Montreal, son of Charles-Joseph d'Ailleboust* Des Muceaux and Catherine Legardeur; d. and buried 2 Sept. 1730 at Montreal.

He first chose a military career, and was promoted in 1690 to the rank of half-pay lieutenant. The following year he quit the service, left Quebec to go to Montreal, and devoted his energies to the wine trade, which led him to travel in the *pays d'en haut.*

Jean-Baptiste d'Ailleboust is chiefly known through a curious ruling handed down with respect to him by Bishop Saint-Vallier [LA CROIX] on 26 May 1719, which by refusing absolution censured his relations with his servant, the daughter of Paul Haguenier. The penalty was imposed not only on the guilty couple but also on d'Ailleboust's wife and the concubine's father, who were expected to use their influence to bring to their senses the husband and the daughter respectively.

On 19 April 1689, at Quebec, Jean-Baptiste d'Ailleboust had married Anne Le Picard, Vital Oriol's widow, who was buried on 20 July 1736 at Montreal. He had 16 children.

JEAN BLAIN

Caron, "Inventaire de documents," APQ *Rapport, 1941–42*, 192. "Estat des employs vaquans ausquels Monsieur le comte de Frontenac ... a pourvu en l'année 1691 en attendant les commissions de sa majesté," *BRH*, XIII (1907), 309. P.-G. Roy, *Inv. ord. int.*, I, 92, 205. Godbout, "Nos ancêtres," APQ *Rapport, 1951–53*, 472. Aegidius Fauteux, *La famille d'Ailleboust* (Montréal, 1917), 140–42. Gosselin, *L'Église du Canada*, I, 394f.

ALDEN, JOHN, New England sea-captain and trader; b. 1625 or 1626 in Plymouth, Mass., son of John Alden, the *Mayflower* Pilgrim, and Priscilla Mullens; d. in Boston, 14 March 1701/2.

For many years Alden was the commander of a sloop in the colonial service, supplying eastern forts with provisions and stores. In 1688 and 1689 he made trading voyages to Port-Royal (Annapolis Royal, N.S.) and Les Mines (Grand Pré, N.S.). He made a truce with the Indians at Sagadahoc in November 1690. Earlier that year he had taken part in the capture of Port-Royal under Phips*, and had gone with Captain Cyprian Southack* to reduce La Hève and Chedabouctou (Guysborough, N.S.).

The following year Alden was master of the vessel carrying Colonel Edward Tyng*, newly appointed governor of Acadia, to Port-Royal and the Saint John River. Also on board were Alden's son, William, and the Boston merchant John NELSON. At the Saint John River, their vessel was captured by the French frigate, *Soleil d'Afrique*, commanded by SIMON-PIERRE DENYS de Bonaventure and carrying the new French governor of Acadia, Robinau* de Villebon. Alden was sent to Boston on parole with a letter to the governor requesting an exchange of prisoners. Villebon sought the return of about 60 soldiers captured by Phips in 1690. Alden's son and Colonel Tyng were held as hostages, and Nelson was sent to Quebec. Alden returned to the Saint John in May 1692, bringing with him only six French soldiers. Villebon sent two men to take them ashore, but Alden landed the soldiers on an island and carried these two men off with him when he set sail for Boston. Villebon protested Alden's conduct, accusing him of bad faith in the matter of the prisoners. Alden's son and Colonel Tyng were subsequently sent to France.

Earlier in 1692, Alden had been accused of witchcraft and sent to Salem, where he was in jail for 15 weeks. He escaped and was eventually cleared of the charge in 1693. In 1696 he took part in an unsuccessful attempt to drive Villebon from his fort on the Saint John River. Two years later he was one of the commissioners sent to Pentagouet (on Penobscot Bay) to settle the preliminary terms for peace with the Abenakis.

Alden was married twice. He had one child, a

daughter, by his first wife, Elizabeth. His second wife, whom he married 1 April 1660, was a widow, Elizabeth Everill, daughter of William Phillips of Boston and Saco. She and Alden had 12 children, seven of whom died young.

CHARLES BRUCE FERGUSSON

AN, Col., C¹¹ᴬ, 12, f.4 (calendared in PAC *Report, 1885*, lvii). Charlevoix, *History* (Shea), V. *Coll. de manuscrits relatifs à la N.-F.*, II, III. Hutchinson, *Hist. of Mass.-bay* (Mayo), II, 36–37. "Journal of expedition against Port Royal, 1690." *NYCD* (O'Callaghan and Fernow), IX, 527, 532. PRO, *CSP, Col., 1689–92.* Webster, *Acadia*, 32–34, 37–39. "Alden genealogy," *New Eng. Hist. and Geneal. Register*, LII (1898), 162–67. Brebner, *New England's outpost*, 51–52. Pierre Daviault, *Le baron de Saint-Castin, chef abénaquis* (Montréal, 1939).

ALLARD DE SAINTE-MARIE, JEAN-JOSEPH D', infantry captain, knight of the order of Saint-Louis; b. *c.* 1670 in Provence; d. 25 March 1730 at Louisbourg, Île Royale (Cape Breton Island).

Sainte-Marie began his military career in 1686, served in Flanders during the War of the League of Augsburg, and was wounded at Valcour in 1689. In 1698 he became a member of the king's bodyguard, but in 1701 he sought a post in the colonies and was sent to Placentia (Plaisance) as a lieutenant in the Compagnie de Villemarceau. By 1706 he had married the sister-in-law of the governor, PASTOUR de Costebelle, whose praise he earned by his work on the Crèvecœur battery. He was promoted captain in 1712 and moved to Louisbourg with his company two years later.

His most important mission during his years at Louisbourg came in 1718, when he was sent to Canso (Canceau) and thence to Boston to protest an English attack led by Captain SMART on Canso in September of that year. During the 1720s he consistently offered to raise an artillery company for the Louisbourg garrison, but was unable to gain approval for this project. He received the order of Saint-Louis in February 1724, but his hopes of becoming commander of the Royal Battery foundered when this post was garrisoned by detachments rather than a full company. Sainte-Marie seems to have been a steady, conscientious officer with a talent for engineering, but Costebelle also noted that he lacked supporters because of his "excessive thrift."

JOHN HUMPHREYS

AN, Col., B, 22, f.149; 29, 30, 36, 37, 38, 45, 47, 49, 50, 54; C¹¹ᴮ, 1, 2, ff.290–93; 3, f.113; 4–5, 7, 9, 10; C¹¹ᶜ, 3–6, 15; D²ᶜ, 222 (Alphabet Laffilard); E, 3, f.1; Marine, B¹, 8, 19, ff.486v–89v; 20–21, 50; C⁷, 4,

ff.1–25; Section Outre-Mer, G¹, 406, 467; Dépôt des fortifications des colonies, carton 2, no.116. *Coll. de manuscrits relatifs à la N.-F.*, III, 34–35, 46. Fauteux, *Les chevaliers de Saint-Louis.* McLennan, *Louisbourg*, 35, 37, 38, 63, 77.

ALLONNE, MADELEINE DE ROYBON D'. *See* ROYBON

ALOIGNY DE LA GROYE, CHARLES-HENRI D', lieutenant, garrison adjutant, military commandant, knight of the order of Saint-Louis, naval captain; b. *c.* 1662 in the province of Poitou, son of Louis d'Aloigny and Charlotte de Chasteigner; he took the title of Marquis de La Groye after the death of his father and his older brother; d. in the autumn of 1714, in the shipwreck of the *Saint-Jérôme* on Sable Island.

Charles-Henri d'Aloigny, who was a midshipman at Rochefort, sailed for Canada in 1683 with the rank of lieutenant in the land forces. His 30 years in New France were distinguished by an active military career. He was promoted captain in 1688 by BRISAY de Denonville, and this appointment was confirmed by a royal order dated 1 March 1691. He received a commission in 1692 as sub-lieutenant in the navy.

In 1695 Aloigny accompanied CRISAFY on an expedition to re-establish Fort Frontenac. In September of that year, on learning that small groups of Indian prowlers were setting traps and ambushes for the French, Frontenac [Buade*] and CALLIÈRE dispatched supporting troops to various points, and Aloigny was assigned the task of leading a detachment in the direction of Boucherville to surprise the Indians who were pillaging crops.

In 1700 Aloigny was appointed commandant of Fort Frontenac for some months, replacing Louvigny [LA PORTE], who had been arrested "for having acted contrary to the king's orders." In 1702 Aloigny was appointed garrison adjutant, succeeding Daniel d'AUGER de Subercase who had been appointed governor of Placentia (Plaisance). From this time on Aloigny received one military promotion after another. He was commandant of the troops in 1704, a position that he held until his death, at which time the king deemed it advisable not to make any further appointments to the position. He was created a knight of the order of Saint-Louis in 1705, and two years later he received a commission as lieutenant-commander.

For reasons of health he had to return to France in 1708; in 1709 he was back in the colony, pursuing his military activity. That same year he was promoted commander in the navy, and the following year naval captain. In the autumn of

Ameau

1714, after being ill for eight months, during which "he was several times at death's door," he sailed on the *Saint-Jérôme* to return to France. The ship was wrecked on Sable Island.

Apparently La Groye was a good soldier; Frontenac, in 1691, considered him a "brave officer, very devoted to the service, and a gentleman." Callière, for his part, described him in 1701 as a "good officer."

On 5 Nov. 1703 Charles-Henri d'Aloigny had married Geneviève Macard, daughter of Nicolas Macard and Marguerite Couillard. Married first to Charles Bazire*, then to François PROVOST, she had been widowed twice. No children were born of her marriage with Aloigny.

NOËL BÉLANGER

N.-G. Boucault, "État présent du Canada," APQ *Rapport, 1920–21*, 35. "Correspondance de Frontenac (1689–98)," APQ *Rapport, 1927–28*, 66. "Correspondance de Vaudreuil," APQ *Rapport, 1938–39*, 96. *Jug. et délib.* A. Roy, *Inv. greffes not.*, XIX. *Royal Fort Frontenac* (Preston and Lamontagne), 387, 391, 399, 467. Taillemite, *Inventaire analytique, série B*, I. P.-G. Roy, *La ville de Québec*, II, 56, 430.

AMEAU, *dit* Saint-Séverin, SÉVERIN, soldier, royal notary, clerk of court, court officer, and school teacher; b. 1620, son of Jean Ameau and Françoise Remogis of the parish of Saint-Sauveur in Paris; buried 9 May 1715 at Trois-Rivières.

Ameau, a garrison soldier, signed a contract at Trois-Rivières on 19 June 1649, and therefore must have been in Canada since at least the preceding summer. Because of his education it was not long before he began to act as notary and clerk of court at Trois-Rivières (1651 or 1652); he also drew up acts as court officer there. Justice at Trois-Rivières was still only seigneurial, but it was soon to boast of the epithet "royal," by virtue of a decision by the new Conseil Souverain. On 17 Nov. 1663 Pierre BOUCHER was appointed royal judge, Maurice Poulin* de La Fontaine king's attorney, and Ameau clerk of court; Quentin Moral was appointed royal notary but does not seem to have taken up the office, which was entrusted on 28 June 1664 to Séverin Ameau. For the humble tabellion of the small town this was a dazzling promotion; henceforth he was authorized to receive acts in the whole government of Trois-Rivières, and for a time in 1668 his services were even required at Quebec. Ameau was a conscientious civil servant, being reprimanded only once in 50 years. He had reached the age of 81 when in 1701 the intendant, Champigny [BOCHART], appointed the notary Jean-Baptiste POTTIER to succeed him.

Séverin Ameau lived an active and peaceful life.

He was already 42 when, on 7 Feb. 1662 at Trois-Rivières, he married Madeleine Baudoin, who was 23. They had two sons and one daughter. Like all his colleagues in the rural areas, the notary Ameau also farmed. In 1667 he owned 4 head of cattle and 6 acres of land under cultivation; in 1681 he had 6 head of cattle, 12 acres under cultivation, and a musket. More than one colonist who had less to do than he could not show as much. It is true, however, that in 1666 and 1681 Ameau had in his employ a "domestic," who was probably assigned to working the farm. Ameau lived at Trois-Rivières, in a house "consisting of a living-room, a cellar, and an attic," which was situated on a lot with a frontage of 30 feet on Rue Saint-Jean, running back to a depth of 24 feet along Rue Saint-Pierre. He had bought this lot on 7 May 1662 from Guillaume Cotentin, *dit* Lavallée, for the sum of 425 *livres*.

On 1 May 1665 Jacques Leneuf* de La Poterie granted Ameau a lot measuring three-quarters of an acre in area on Île Ronde, where Ameau had already acquired from Jean Garnier, *dit* Nadeau, on 10 July 1662, a piece of land measuring one and a half *arpents* by five. On 3 Aug. 1665 Nicolas Marsolet* granted him a piece of land measuring 3 *arpents* by 60 at Arbre-à-la-Croix, on the shore of the St Lawrence. On 25 June 1668 Ameau also owned in the *censive* (seigneurial area) of Trois-Rivières two pieces of land, each measuring 5 *arpents* by 20; one, on the Saint-Maurice, had been granted by Pierre Boucher on 27 July 1656, the other, on the St Lawrence, by the Compagnie de la Nouvelle-France on 5 May 1659.

Ameau's long career was only slightly troubled by two or three minor judicial disputes and by a theft of which he was the victim in 1673. Four thieves, equipped with a skeleton key, broke into Ameau's house one night and stole wine, spirits, and a quantity of eels. They received various sentences, including the repayment of 12 *livres* 5 *sols* on condition that Ameau agreed to pay half the court costs. A strange sentence indeed, which Ameau appealed to the Conseil Souverain! It was a good thing he did: the guilty persons were punished, and he received 50 *livres* in compensation. In 1686, as a result of having acted in a moment of spite, it was he who paid 50 *livres* to a woman whom he had brought from Trois-Rivières to Quebec on legal matters just at the period when the council was on vacation. She was the wife of Pierre Boulanger, a merchant from Cap-de-la-Madeleine with whom he was quarrelling at the time.

Séverin Ameau endeavoured to be of help to the community. In a request to the intendant dated 28 May 1687 he wrote: ". . . for 35 years now [he] has continuously held the office of court clerk in the jurisdiction of Trois-Rivières. And in addition [he] has always exerted himself to render service to the population of the aforementioned place, either in teaching the children or in participating in the singing at divine service held in the church of the aforementioned place . . . ."

Such was the existence of this model citizen, who died in 1715 at the venerable age of 95 or 96, nine years after his wife, who had been buried 13 Nov. 1706.

ANDRÉ VACHON

AJQ, Greffe de Romain Becquet, 16 oct. 1680; Greffe de Laurent Bermen, 19 juin 1649; Greffe de Pierre Duquet, 6 nov. 1684. AJTR, Greffe de Séverin Ameau. ASQ, Polygraphie, III, 133. *Jug. et délib.*, I, 58f., 654f., 725–27, 752f.; II, 811f.; III, 91. *Papier terrier de la Cie des I.O.* (P.-G. Roy), 305–8. Recensement du Canada, 1666 (APQ *Rapport*). Recensements du Canada, 1667, 1681 (Sulte). A. Roy, *Inv. greffes not.*, XI, 49–137. P.-G. Roy, *Inv. coll. pièces jud. et not.*, II, 403. Godbout, "Nos ancêtres," APQ *Rapport, 1951–53*, 486f.; *1953–55*, 502f. "Les notaires au Canada," 16f. J.-E. Roy, *Histoire du notariat*, I, 60–62, 191, 202, 313.

AMIOT (Amyot) DE VINCELOTTE, CHARLES-JOSEPH, navigator, naval lieutenant, militia commander, seigneur; b. 23 March 1665 at Quebec, son of Charles Amiot* and Geneviève de Chavigny; buried 9 May 1735 in the same town.

Charles-Joseph received his elementary education at the Jesuit college in Quebec; then he studied the principles of navigation, doubtless under the direction of Martin Boutet*. In 1680 he received from his mother the fief of Vincelotte (Cap Saint-Ignace) that she herself had received in 1672 from Talon*. At 19, in 1684, he enlisted in the militia. He drew up a will the same year, before leaving "to travel and go to war in the king's service against the Iroquois." We find him again in 1693 when he presented a petition—successfully—to Louis de Buade* de Frontenac and BOCHART de Champigny asking that his fief be enlarged; he wished, he wrote, to "contribute to the utmost of his ability to the development of this colony and work hard to establish himself there."

When Governor Frontenac died in 1698, two of the colony's officers, RIGAUD de Vaudreuil and CALLIÈRE, aspired to succeed him. Each wished to be the first to notify the court of the governor's death and to seek the nomination. During the winter of 1698–99 Amiot was charged with this mission by Rigaud de Vaudreuil and Champigny, while AUGUSTIN LE GARDEUR de Courtemanche was chosen for the same purpose by Callière. A race took place between the two emissaries, each wishing to be the first at court. Amiot de Vincelotte was the last to arrive, although only a few hours after Courtemanche, and Callière was granted the governor generalship.

In 1703 the seigneur Amiot was recommended for the post of attorney of the provost's court of Quebec. He was described in a document as "the person in this country whom we know to be most capable of filling this position. He is active, is intelligent, and has applied himself to the study of the ordinances and of the customary law of Paris, which he knows well." He did not obtain the post, which was entrusted to his step-father, Jean-Baptiste COUILLARD de Lespinay, who had married Geneviève de Chavigny in 1680. Perhaps this can be seen as one of the causes of the subsequent rivalry between Amiot and Couillard.

Amiot next carried out several expeditions in 1703–4 to the shores of Newfoundland, under the command of the privateer Jean LÉGER de La Grange and of Claude Pauperet. In 1706 he was chosen to go privateering off the shores of New England, serving as a lieutenant under Louis Denys* de La Ronde. In particular, they both fought a hard battle against John MARCH, who laid siege to Port-Royal on 26 May 1707 (6 June N.S.). After their victory over the English they carried the good news to the king, and took advantage of the opportunity to ask for help for an expedition against Boston. The French government approved the project, but was unable to give them any other ship except the *Vénus*, a rather poorly equipped frigate; they nevertheless sailed it for two years, and made numerous captures. Did Amiot subsequently take part in other military enterprises? We do not know. The last mention of his activity in this field is in 1727 when he was appointed commander of the militia forces on the south shore of the St Lawrence. We know, however, that in 1718 he sought, apparently in vain, a commission as ensign and the position of lieutenant of the port of Quebec.

Did Amiot de Vincelotte have a particular liking for wrangling and rivalry? It may be thought so. In any case he spent much of the money that came from his privateering and his seigneury on long and useless legal actions. In 1724, after his mother's death, Amiot brought several lawsuits against his step-father; "he boasted that he had some 15 lawsuits to bring [against him]." He even claimed from him "six spoons, six forks and one silver cup."

On 19 Feb. 1691, at Montreal, Charles Amiot de Vincelotte had married Marie-Gabrielle, daughter of Jean-Vincent Philippe de Hautmesnyl. Thirteen children were born of this marriage. Nevertheless in 1727 he sought a separation.

17

Amours

After a full life, he died at the age of 70 at Quebec.

NOËL BÉLANGER

AJQ, Greffe de Gilles Rageot, 10 juillet 1684. AQ, NF, Coll. de pièces jud. et not., 580, 607; NF, Ord. des int., XII, 128f.; NF, Registres d'intendance, I, 9. "Mémoire de Gédéon de Catalogne sur les plans des seigneuries et habitations des gouvernements de Québec, les Trois-Rivières et Montréal," *BRH*, XXI (1915), 330. Ivanhoë Caron, "Le fief Cap Saint-Ignace," *BRH*, XX (1914), 365–69. P.-G. Roy, "Charles-Joseph Amyot Vincelotte," *BRH*, XXV (1919), 306–15.

AMOURS. *See* DAMOURS

AMYOT. *See* AMIOT

ANDRÉ, LOUIS, Jesuit priest, missionary; b. 28 May 1631 at Saint-Rémy-de-Provence, Bouches-du-Rhône, France; d. 19 Sept. 1715 at Quebec.

Louis André entered the Society of Jesus at Lyons on 12 Sept. 1650. After the customary Jesuit training in teaching and ecclesiastical studies, he came to New France, arriving at Quebec on 7 June 1669. The following summer he was sent to the Ottawa mission of Sault Ste Marie with Father Gabriel Druillettes*, a missionary of broad experience who guided André in his early dealings with the Indians. André spent the season of 1670–71 with a band of Ottawas, refugees from Chagouamigon (Chequamegon Bay on Lake Superior), wintering on Manitoulin Island. Returning to Sault Ste Marie in 1671, Father André began twelve years of missionary labour in the Baie des Puants (Green Bay) area, devoting much of his effort to the Menominees, the Wild Rice People, who dwelt along the Menominee River. In 1683, André was recalled to Saint-Ignace (Saint Ignace, Michigan) and worked there until 1684 when he was recalled to Quebec. At the age of 54, after so many years of missionary life, André was assigned to teach philosophy and later Latin, a task which occupied him until 1690. Possibly it was this period of comparative repose that enabled him to compile his valuable Algonkin and Ottawa dictionary as well as his "Préceptes, phrases et mots," a little conversational manual which is still preserved.

In 1690, at the advanced age of 60, Father André again became a missionary to the Indians, this time on the Saguenay, physically one of the most difficult mission areas in New France. After two years at Chicoutimi (1690–92), André spent the next six years (1692–98) at Montreal and Quebec, devoting himself to the Indians in those areas. Some of his time during those years was spent with the Indians on the Sept-Îles below Tadoussac. Records regarding André during his last years of active life are somewhat confusing. It is believed that from 1698 to 1700 he was at the mission of Saint-François-de-Sales on the Chaudière River. Father André apparently ended his active work about 1705. He died at Quebec on 19 Sept. 1715, having spent 46 years in New France.

JOSEPH P. DONNELLY, S.J.

ASJCF, Louis André, Extraits des préceptes, phrases et mots de la langue algonquine, outaouaise pour un missionnaire nouveau. *JR* (Thwaites). Ivanhoë Caron, "Prêtres séculiers et religieux," 201. J.-A. Maurault, *Histoire des Abénakis depuis 1605 jusqu'à nos jours* (Sorel, 1866), 276f. Rochemonteix, *Les Jésuites et la N.-F. au XVIIe siècle*, III, 369. A. E. Jones, "A sketch of Father Louis André S.J., an early Wisconsin missionary," *U.S. Catholic Hist. Mag.*, III (1890), 26–40.

ANGILLIERS. *See* LARGILLIER

ANGO DES MAIZERETS, LOUIS, priest, vicar general and canon of Quebec, superior of the seminary; b. January 1636 in Normandy; d. 23 April 1721 at Quebec.

His parents' names are not known; we do know, however, that he was the eldest of a noble Norman family which owned a *château* at Argentan and was well-to-do, since it put aside for him an annual income of 1,200 *livres* when he renounced his patrimony. This income was paid to him until his death by his nephews, one of whom was Ango de La Mothe, a lawyer in the *parlement* of Rouen and seigneur of Montgomery.

Louis Ango Des Maizerets studied at the Jesuit colleges in La Flèche and Paris. In Paris he met François de LAVAL, the future bishop of Quebec, and became his colleague in the community founded by Father Bagot, as well as in the secret society called *Les Bons Amis*. In 1653 he also became associated with the Hermitage at Caen, a school for spiritual instruction under the direction of the lay apostle Jean de Bernières de Louvigny. Bishop Laval's departure for New France in 1659 decided the direction that Ango's life would take. He entered holy orders and was ordained a priest on 29 Sept. 1662 in Paris. That same autumn Bishop Laval returned to France, and there, with the aim of strengthening the church in Canada, founded by an ordinance published 26 March 1663 the seminary of Quebec, which was destined to recruit and give cohesion to the clergy of the colony.

Ango Des Maizerets

Abbé Louis Ango Des Maizerets belonged to the first contingent destined for the seminary of Quebec. In May 1663 Abbé Hugues Pommier*, Father Pierre RAFFEIX, a Jesuit, and he sailed for Canada with their bishop. The crossing took nearly four months, during which Ango Des Maizerets almost died of scurvy. They landed at Quebec on 15 September and moved into a new building which served both as presbytery and as bishop's palace and which became at the same time the birthplace of the seminary. The other founding priests were Henri de Bernières*, the first superior, Jean Dudouyt*, and Thomas Morel*. Five seminarists, 3 from France and 2 from Canada, and some domestics, including Denis Roberge, Bishop Laval's servant, constituted a rather imposing personnel for this seminary. The priests concerned themselves as much with the ministry of the parish as with the training of clerics. To make clear this double vocation, Bishop Laval, when he established the first parish of Quebec in 1664, created one chapter for both it and the seminary.

According to his contemporaries, Abbé Louis Ango Des Maizerets does not seem to have had a very prepossessing appearance; his voice was weak and his health was poor. Outstanding qualities made up for these weaknesses. Indeed he fulfilled several functions, sometimes concurrently. He was the second superior of the seminary and then held this office, alternately with M. de Bernières, for 31 years, for the periods 1672–73, 1683–85, 1688–93, and 1698–1721. When he was not the superior, he held the office of first assistant and, at irregular intervals, that of procurator; he also occasionally ministered as parish priest at Ange-Gardien and at the cathedral.

From its beginning, in 1668, Bishop Laval entrusted to him the direction of the Petit Séminaire. Candidates for the priesthood were boarded there, and attended classes at the Jesuit college, on the site of the present city hall. But their moral upbringing was the responsibility of the seminary, which in addition was given the task of associating with them a group of young Hurons in an effort to Frenchify them. It was Abbé Ango Des Maizerets who, inspired by Bishop Laval, had drawn up the first set of regulations for the institution and who directed it for a good part of his life.

When the chapter of Quebec was instituted in 1684, he was one of the first canons, with the dignity of archdeacon and later of precentor. On several occasions he was responsible for the spiritual guidance of the Sisters of the Hôtel-Dieu or those of the Hôpital Général, and Bishop Laval even made him his vicar general. He retained this

title under the succeeding bishop, although, through the arbitrary action of Bishop Saint-Vallier [LA CROIX], this worthy priest was one day victim of an interdict which debarred him from all functions in the diocese. He and his colleagues in the seminary and the chapter, Henri de Bernières and Charles de GLANDELET, had been imprudent enough to appeal to the Conseil Souverain against a decision by the bishop in a disciplinary matter, as the ecclesiastical law of the time allowed them to do. Their common punishment lasted several months, to the great vexation of the whole population. Bishop Saint-Vallier had a change of heart, and two of his former victims, Ango Des Maizerets and Glandelet, were the first to request his return in 1711 when the court wanted to keep him in France.

As superior of the seminary Ango Des Maizerets also had to overcome severe material losses caused by Phips*' siege in 1690 and the two great fires of 1701 and 1705. Each time, with Bishop Laval's encouragement, he raised the seminary again from its ruins.

Ango Des Maizerets celebrated his golden jubilee in the priesthood on 29 Sept. 1712. His health was beginning to arouse serious concern. In 1721 he was struck down by an attack of paralysis, and it was from his bed that he dictated his will on 10 April, although he was unable to sign it. All that remained for him to do was to sign over to the seminary the instalments of his life annuity, which, it must be added, he had always deposited faithfully in the general treasury. His final illness lasted only two weeks. After his death the procurator of the seminary, JEAN-BAPTISTE GAULTIER de Varennes, eulogized him in the ledger: "On 23 April 1721, Louis Ango Des Maizerets . . . the Superior and one of the founders of the seminary of Quebec, which he directed in this capacity for nearly 40 years in an edifying manner and to everyone's great satisfaction, died after receiving the last rites of the Church. . . . All Canada is indebted to him for educating our youth, to which task he applied himself for nearly 50 years. . . ."

Some of Abbé Louis Ango Des Maizerets' writings have been preserved: the account of the consecration of the new classical college in 1677, the earliest regulations and decisions of the council of the community, and the "reasons for and against the union of the Seminary of Saint-Sulpice with the Séminaire des Missions étrangères," a union which Bishop Laval had envisaged for a time before his resignation to give the church in Canada greater accord and solidity.

HONORIUS PROVOST

19

Anne de Sainte-Agnès

For further background see also the biographies of Henri de Bernières* (*DCB*, I, 91–92) and François de LAVAL. ASQ, Chapitre, 6, 10, 19, 21, 31; Lettres, M, 7, 8; N, 87; MSS, 239; Séminaire, I, 15; II, 40; V, 15; VI, 52c; LXXXV, 5; XCV, 4, 13, 24, 39, 42. Louis Bertrand de Latour, *Mémoires sur la vie de M. de Laval, premier évêque de Québec* (Cologne, 1761), 3, 6, 32, 34, 107, 153. Auguste Gosselin, *Vie de Mgr de Laval*, I, 379, 557; II, 233f. Rochemonteix, *Les Jésuites et la N.-F. au XVIIIᵉ siècle*, I, 95f. *L'Abeille* (Québec), I, 15 (4 janv. 1849); II, 16 (7 mars 1850). P.-E. Gosselin, "Mémoire sur l'abbé Louis Ango de Maizerets," SCHEC *Rapport, 1942–43*, 39–45.

ANNE DE SAINTE-AGNÈS. *See* BOURDON

AOUENANO (Awenano, Awanano), Seneca civil chief and Iroquois negotiator; fl. 1699–1701.

Aouenano played a leading role in the negotiations with the French which led to the peace treaty of 1701. He was one of eight Seneca civil chiefs, who were appointed by virtue of their war experiences, their mother's lineage, their gravity, and their persuasive eloquence. These mature, and often elderly, men served as peacekeepers among their people and as envoys in external relations. Aouenano dealt primarily with the French while other Seneca chiefs treated with the agents of New York province.

Aouenano's entire family was killed in the summer of 1699 when Indian allies of the French invaded the Seneca lands. He evidently contained his desire for revenge and attempted to bring hostilities to an end. In that same year, he and a Seneca chief called Assichqua sent a messenger to the governor of New France with two belts of wampum to discuss peace. The Onondaga chiefs told the English that this was a private mission without Seneca or other Iroquois authorization. Governor CALLIÈRE answered the message of the two chiefs by sending back two wampum belts as a sign of favour.

On 18 July 1700, Aouenano arrived in Montreal with TONATAKOUT and two other Seneca chiefs and the Onondaga sachems ARADGI and OHONSIO-WANNE. Their embassy sought an end to attacks by the French allies and requested a general exchange of prisoners. Although the ambassadors claimed to speak for the entire Iroquois league, the Mohawks excepted, Callière would not accept them as such and he demanded that the Cayugas and Oneidas send their own deputies.

Two weeks before the arrival of the six ambassadors in Montreal, another Iroquois delegation at Albany had asked the English to press the French and their Indian allies into extending the peace established by the Treaty of Ryswyck to the Iroquois. The English refused to give them military aid and left the Iroquois no option but to obtain what terms they could from the French.

Four of the ambassadors to Montreal were left with the French while the others with Father BRUYAS, CHABERT de Joncaire and PAUL LE MOYNE de Maricourt returned to gather the prisoners held by the Iroquois and to collect deputies from the Cayugas and Oneidas.

Aouenano was present at the final peace conference held through July and August 1701 at Montreal. His major contribution was a conciliatory funeral oration pronounced over the body of KONDIARONK, chief of the Michilimackinac Hurons. On behalf of the four Iroquois nations present, he called upon their enemies to partake of Kondiaronk's desire for reconciliation.

The peace treaty signed on 4 Aug. 1701, and later accepted by the Mohawks, was a turning point in French-Iroquois relations. By the terms of the treaty, the Iroquois were to remain neutral in any French-English conflict. Moreover, should they be wronged by one of the French allies, they had to accept mediation by the French before retaliating. The Iroquois accepted these restraints on their freedom of action only because of their weakened state, the absence of English military support, and the combined threat of the French and their Indian partners.

PETER N. MOOGK

AN, Col., C¹¹ᴬ, 18, pp.46–51; 19, pp.78–86 (copies in PAC). [The PAC transcript of AN, Col., C¹¹ᴬ, 18 (p. 46) gives the date of the Indians' arrival in Montreal as 17 July; the microfilmed original (f.81) gives 18 July.] La Potherie, *Histoire* (1722), IV, 135–46, 230–31. *NYCD* (O'Callaghan and Fernow), IV, 658, 694; IX, 708, 711. Y. F. Zoltvany, "Philippe de Rigaud de Vaudreuil, governor of New France (1703–1725)," unpublished Ph.D. thesis, University of Alberta, 1963, 54–55.

APTHORP, ALEXANDER, warehouse-keeper for the HBC at York Fort, 1714–18; member of James KNIGHT's expedition; d. *c.* 1720.

Alexander Apthorp was with James Knight in 1714 when, on behalf of the HBC, he accepted from the French the restoration of York Fort (Fort Bourbon) according to the provision made in the treaty of Utrecht. Little is known about Apthorp, whose surviving York Fort account books for 1714–17 are excellent examples of the type of book-keeping practised in Hudson Bay in the 18th century. Apthorp's only surviving letter, which is not as lucid as his accounts, describes the effect of the flood at York Fort in the spring of 1715.

In 1718 Apthorp returned to London with Knight who was planning an expedition to the north of Churchill in search of the Strait of Anian and the copper and gold deposits he had learned about from the Northern Indians. Knight sailed from London in 1719 accompanied by Apthorp, one of the seven members of the expedition who have been identified. The expedition's two ships met with disaster near the southeast corner of Marble Island in 1720; the exact fate of Apthorp and his companions remains unknown.

ALICE M. JOHNSON

HBC Arch. B.239/d/7–9 (York account books, 1714–17). HBRS, XXV (Davies and Johnson), 51–53 (Apthorp's letter to the company).

ARADGI, Onondaga sachem, described by the Senecas as "a great favourite of the French"; we know him only from a few events in 1700 and 1702.

In 1698 the Iroquois had begun to discuss a peace treaty with the French, but they were unwilling to include in this peace the tribes to the west who were allies of the French, since these tribes were competing with them for furs. In 1699, however, an Iroquois attack on the Miami Indians led to reprisals by the Ottawas, Illinois, and other tribes, and serious Iroquois losses. The following winter, Aradgi visited the Oneidas to tell them that the two Iroquois tribes who were in the greatest danger, the Senecas and the Cayugas, were planning to discuss with the French a general treaty that would involve the tribes to the west. Aradgi asked the Oneidas to inform the English of this, no doubt because he hoped that with English support the Iroquois could avoid making concessions to the French. A snowstorm prevented the immediate forwarding of his message.

In April 1700, Aradgi was at Onondaga, where he acted as spokesman at a meeting of the Iroquois sachems with Colonel Peter SCHUYLER. In July, the Senecas reported to the English that Aradgi and AOUENANO, a sachem from their tribe, had set out for Canada to negotiate with the French. The Senecas stressed that this journey had been undertaken without tribal authorization. Since the Iroquois concluded a treaty with the French in 1701 [see TEGANISSORENS], we are justified in suspecting that the Senecas' denial of responsibility for Aradgi's action was made only to maintain good relations with the English. Although he was not at the 1701 peace conference, Aradgi appears to have accompanied a group of Onondaga and Cayuga sachems on a mission to Canada in 1702.

BRUCE G. TRIGGER

Charlevoix, *History* (Shea). La Potherie, *Histoire.* *NYCD* (O'Callaghan and Fernow), IV, 658–61, 694, 998.

ARCE, LOUIS-ARMAND DE LOM D'. *See* LOM

ARDILLIÈRES, PIERRE LE MOYNE D'IBERVILLE ET D'. *See* LE MOYNE

ARGENSON, PIERRE DE VOYER D'. *See* VOYER

ARGENTEUIL, PIERRE D'AILLEBOUST D'. *See* AILLEBOUST

ARMSTRONG, LAWRENCE, lieutenant-governor of Nova Scotia, 1724/25–1739; lieutenant-colonel of Philipps' Regiment (later the 40th Foot), 1720–39; b. 1664 in Ireland; committed suicide at Annapolis Royal, N.S., 6 Dec. 1739. It is not known which of the three branches of the Irish Armstrongs he was born into, but all three contributed distinguished officers and engineers to the British service in the 18th century.

In the early 1690s Armstrong joined a regiment raised in Ireland, and saw service in Marlborough's campaigns on the Continent until 1711, when the regiment was detached from the Duke's forces to join Sir Hovenden WALKER's expedition against Quebec. When several of Walker's ships were wrecked on the night of 22–23 August (o.s.) off Île-aux-Oeufs, Armstrong suffered the first of the reverses that were to mark his career in Canada. He was cast up on the littered shore with only his clothes, having lost his money, his personal effects, and the equipment of his entire company.

Armstrong's men formed part of the force that was detached from the battered Walker expedition in September to reinforce the garrison at Annapolis Royal. The former Port-Royal had been captured from the French only a year before; but already its new masters were floundering in the problems of exercising British control over Nova Scotia from an isolated fort. The garrison was poorly clothed and demoralized because of Governor Samuel VETCH's inability to pay his New England agent for supplies; the arrival of the destitute reinforcements aggravated the situation so much that Armstrong and his fellow captains had little choice but to use their own pay to support their companies.

By 1712 the officers of the garrison had settled into a pattern of semi-poverty, continuing debt and petty quarrels that was to prevail for 30 years. Armstrong, possessing an erratic temperament and strong convictions, soon succumbed to the closeted atmosphere. The officers, ". . . a multitude . . . whose jarrs about Command and Rank create one Endless trouble, . . ." became involved in heated polemics about the virtues of the

Armstrong

Protestant succession. As a member of an Irish family who had been "great sufferers for the Protestant Interest," Armstrong was hardly the type to have doubts about the question; and reacting to the pro-Jacobite remarks of George VANE, a fellow officer, at the mess table he smashed a wine decanter over his head. In 1714 he fell out with the gentle CAULFEILD, Vetch's successor as governor, and quarrelled with the local New Englanders, one of whom, William Winniett*, accused Armstrong of uttering "virulous Conceptions" against him.

Armstrong's debts accumulated as the problems of supporting his company increased, and with his Boston creditors pressing him he went to England in 1715 to seek redress. In February 1715/16 he presented his case to the Lords of Trade, who arranged to reimburse him for his losses. He spent four years in England, living on his pay and compensation.

When he returned to Nova Scotia in 1720, the province's situation held greater promise. Colonel Richard Philipps* was governor, with orders to form a civil government, secure the Acadians' allegiance, and consolidate British control. The orphaned "independent companies" had been formed into a regiment of foot under Philipps. The latter established a provincial council consisting of the regimental officers and New England civilians, and Armstrong, as the new major of the regiment, was given a council seat.

He took little part in council meetings, being dispatched to Louisbourg in the fall of 1720 to negotiate with the French governor, Saint-Ovide de Brouillan [Mombeton*], for the return of property seized by Indians from the New England fishermen at Canso (Canseau). The Canso area had posed a delicate problem for French, British, and New England authorities since 1718, when Captain Thomas SMART, commanding the *Squirrel*, plundered the French fishermen there on the grounds that the fishery was in British-held territory. Responsibility for encouraging the Indians to raid the New Englanders in 1720 was disavowed by Saint-Ovide at Louisbourg; but Philipps sent Armstrong to deliver a stiff protest to the governor and press for compensation. Saint-Ovide received Armstrong politely, and by giving him every assistance in collecting evidence from French fishermen in the Canso area skilfully underlined the fact that the British had never given satisfaction for the 1718 incident.

Throughout his career Armstrong shared Philipps' view that the Canso fishery was a significant asset to the province. In fact, by this time Armstrong's ideas about Nova Scotia were firmly set, and were to undergo little evolution.

Like Philipps, he favoured Protestant immigration as a logical confirmation of conquest; yearned for a strong military force that would overawe the Acadians and Indians; recognized the importance of securing the Acadians' allegiance, or at least their neutrality; and chafed under the inability of the government at Annapolis Royal to control the province.

Aside from this basic attitude, Armstrong shared little with Philipps. The two men took an instant dislike to each other. Philipps distrusted his major, fearing the latter's influence with the authorities in England, while Armstrong made no effort to hide his contempt for the governor. He was in financial straits again, his company's provisions having been lost in shipwrecks on two occasions in 1720. Philipps refused to bear the cost of one of these setbacks, and blocked Armstrong's attempts to get leave.

Armstrong, now a lieutenant-colonel, returned to Annapolis from Canso in 1721 and took advantage of Philipps' absence to hurry to England. His movements during the next four years are obscure. He bombarded the Lords of Trade with requests for compensation for his Canso losses, obtaining substantial repayment with the help of friends and relatives in the government. He took a house in Westminster, lived comfortably, and seems to have kept in close touch with the political machine of the Duke of Newcastle. On his own request he was appointed lieutenant-governor of Nova Scotia, effective 8 Feb. 1724/25. Philipps was at this time living in England, although still holding the governorship; John DOUCETT was lieutenant-governor of the town and fort of Annapolis Royal.

Armstrong's first period of residence as lieutenant-governor (May 1725 until the fall of 1729) was marked by a determined attempt to solve local problems, by quarrels with the council and with members of the Roman Catholic clergy, such as Father GAULIN, and by complete failure to achieve the progress he so earnestly desired for the province. After a year at Canso, where he vainly hoped to establish a large permanent settlement of fishermen, he came to Annapolis Royal resolved to settle the Acadian issue. On 25 Sept. 1726 he met the Annapolis Acadians at the fort, where he presented an oath requiring them to be "true subjects," to swear "submission and obedience," and to affirm (an Armstrong touch) that "no hopes of Absolution from any in Holy Orders" would move them from their allegiance.

Predictably, the Acadians requested exemption from bearing arms. Armstrong replied that British law prevented Roman Catholics from serving in the army in any event, "His Majesty having so many faithful Protestant subjects first to provide for." J. B. Brebner suggests that this was an ingenious dodge on Armstrong's part, but it is equally plausible that Armstrong's reaction was a spontaneous one, entirely in character. After some discussion he agreed to have the exemption written on the margin of the document "in order to get them over by Degrees." Another attempt was made to impose an unqualified oath in September 1727. This time the Annapolis Acadians asked for several conditions, including the exemption from bearing arms and the provision of more priests. Armstrong and his council reacted sternly, arresting four Acadian deputies, including Abraham BOURG; three of them were briefly imprisoned.

Armstrong's last attempt to deal with the issue was made a month later, when he sent Ensign Robert WROTH to the Acadian settlements to achieve by diplomacy what had been lost in September by imperiousness. Wroth gave the Acadians a written confirmation of the exemption from military service, a concession that Armstrong and the council refused to ratify. It does not appear that the Acadians were officially informed that the modified oath was annulled; and the net result of Armstrong's efforts was simply to strengthen the Acadians' belief that they were entitled to neutral status in war time.

His attempts to impose the oath tell much about Armstrong. It was characteristic of him to meet a problem head-on, without much subtlety, and with an insistence on complete success that made disappointment inevitable. His prejudices, although standard for the times, ensured defeat in the Nova Scotian situation. He distrusted the priests, with some justification during his first residence, and did not yet recognize the pragmatic value of consistently cultivating their support. His chances of ever obtaining an unqualified oath from the Annapolis Acadians were effectively wrecked in 1728 by his violent treatment of their priest, Father René-Charles de BRESLAY. For reasons which remain obscure because of contradictory evidence, Armstrong believed that the priest was interfering in secular matters, and Breslay was forced to hide in the woods after his house was pillaged on the angry lieutenant-governor's orders.

Other difficulties beset Armstrong during this period. The merchants at Annapolis engaged in clandestine trade with the Acadians and French at will. Perhaps because of his experiences with the garrison's New England contractors, and certainly because of their "antimonarchical" tendencies, he quarrelled with the local New Englanders, who reciprocated by petitioning against him to the Board of Trade. His problems were compounded

by a corrosive and perennial feud with Major Alexander Cosby*, a council member and Philipps' brother-in-law.

The complaints which accumulated against Armstrong were probably responsible to some degree for Philipps' reappearance in Nova Scotia in 1729. Yet it is not clear that the authorities were greatly dissatisfied with Armstrong. He left Nova Scotia as soon as Philipps arrived, but was back in 1731 bearing a new commission, the orders for Philipps' recall, and an entitlement to Philipps' pay.

For the next eight years Armstrong wrestled mostly with routine problems. His inconsistency, as usual, made his work more difficult than necessary. He had always believed in using Acadians as rent-gatherers and notaries, and as far back as 1727 had appointed Prudent Robichaud* as notary for the Annapolis area. Yet in 1737 he dismissed Alexandre Bourg*, who had been appointed for the Minas district by Philipps, and replaced him with Louis-François Mangeant*, dit Saint-Germain, a French-Canadian of doubtful character who had fled Quebec after killing a man in an alleged affair of honour, and who was detested by the Acadians for his peremptoriness and his earlier part in the Breslay affair. At the same time Armstrong was urging the home authorities to allow Acadians to become justices of the peace in an official, regular sense—an obvious impossibility under the British laws governing Roman Catholics. Nevertheless, in spite of these aberrations he seems to have made a genuine attempt to rule the Acadians wisely, arbitrating their numerous disputes with unaccustomed patience—or resignation—and applying himself assiduously to the most mundane details of administration. Despite his suspicions about the priests, and a few quarrels with them, he avoided outright clashes, and even gained an admission from Saint-Ovide that he was tolerant towards their religion.

His relations with the garrison and council, however, worsened in this period. The continuous personality clashes, the failure of his hopes to attract settlers to the province and establish new townships, the lack of encouragement from home, and a tendency to "Melancholy fitts" wore him down until he became an aged caricature of himself. On 6 Dec. 1739 he "put a Period to his life with his own Hands" and was found with "five Wounds in his Breast and his sword Lying carelessly by him in his bed." The officers held an inquest and discreetly attributed his death to "Lunacy."

Armstrong was a difficult man to his contemporaries, and is a difficult man to judge now, for his character and career were full of contradictions. He considered the Acadians "a Rebellious crew," an "ungovernable people," but tried frequently if clumsily to cultivate their loyalty and support. His deep-rooted distrust of the priests was not universal, being reserved for regular priests, and he was generally on amicable terms with their secular brethren. No one was more aware than he that British control of the province lacked substance, and yet he seemed genuinely mystified whenever the prestige of his position failed to command respect and obedience from the Acadians. His reports to the home authorities reveal a mixture of shrewd assessment and administrative myopia, of objectivity and gross exaggeration.

Until J. B. Brebner produced a deft analysis of the man in 1927 (*New England's outpost*), Armstrong suffered at the hands of historians of the Acadian period, notably Édouard Richard and H.-R. Casgrain. This is understandable, since Armstrong clearly displayed bad temper, arrogance, impatience, and lack of perception in dealing with people. Yet, with the possible exception of his harsh treatment of Breslay, he cannot be accused of questionable motives, and was fiercely dedicated to British retention of Nova Scotia. Nor can he be charged with oppressing the Acadians, for he had neither the force at his disposal nor the mandate to do so; and his characteristically exaggerated language provides no safe clue that he really had the inclination. It is worth noting that Armstrong's unpleasant traits have obscured the fact that he had a minor effect on the Acadians and the future of the province.

Indeed, it could be said that personality is largely irrelevant to an assessment of any resident authority's influence on events in Nova Scotia during this confused period. Philipps brought blandishments and poise to his attempts to get an unqualified oath from the Acadians, and concluded the business by retreating drastically from his demands. Paul Mascarene*, who followed Armstrong and understood the Acadians better than his predecessors, enjoyed some success in dealing with them; but he could not solve the basic problem of the oath, and recognized the futility of the attempt. Armstrong, with a more simplistic outlook, based his hopes on imperiousness and the imaginary prestige of the lieutenant-governor's position. He failed too, and not only because of his unsuitability for the post. A good part of the fault lay with a British government which was occupied with greater things than Nova Scotia, and which could bring little interest, less understanding, and no coherent policy to bear on the problems of the far-away province.

As a man Armstrong may justly be considered a complex, quarrelsome, and unlikeable individual whose traits were aggravated by the frustrating circumstances under which he lived. As an administrator he shared with Philipps the responsibility for the Acadians' conviction that their status was an officially neutral one, for their first understanding that they were exempt from bearing arms came during his regime. In summary, he has a place as one of the men who laboured with little guidance and support to keep Nova Scotia at least nominally British in a period when Walpole's policies precluded any consolidation of overseas empire.

MAXWELL SUTHERLAND

AN, Col., B, 53, 59, 65; C^{11B}, 8 (*see also* calendars for these series in PAC *Report*, *1905*, *1887*). Mass. Hist. Soc., Gay papers, V. N.B. Museum, Webster Coll., pkt.200. PAC, Nova Scotia A, 3–7; 8, pp. 19, 133; 9; 12–14; 15, pp.33–210; 16; 17, p.283; 19–24 (*see also* PAC *Report*, *1894*). PRO, C.O. 217/3. *Coll. doc. inédits Canada et Amérique* (*CF*), I (1888). *N.S. Archives*, I, II, III. PAC *Report*, *1905*, II, App. A, 70–72. PRO, *B.T.Journal*, *1734/35 to 1741*; *CSP, Col.*, *1720–21*, *1722–23*, *1724–25*, *1726–27*, *1728–29*, *1730*, *1732*, *1733*, *1734–35*, *1735–36*, *1737*. *Walker expedition* (Graham). *Army list of 1740* (Army Hist. Research Soc. Reprint, Sheffield, 1931), 43. John Burke, *A genealogical and heraldic history of the commoners of Great Britain and Ireland* (4v., London, 1838), IV, 338–49. Le Jeune, *Dictionnaire*, I. W. P. Bell, *The "foreign protestants" and the settlement of Nova Scotia* (Toronto, 1961). Brebner, *New England's outpost*. Casgrain, *Les Sulpiciens en Acadie*. McLennan, *Louisbourg*. Édouard Richard, *Acadia; missing links of a lost chapter in American history, by an Acadian* (Montreal and New York, 1895). Robert Rumilly, *Histoire des Acadiens* (2v., Montréal, [1955]), II. Waller, *Samuel Vetch*. H.-R. Casgrain, "Éclaircissements sur la question acadienne," *RSCT*, 1st ser., VI (1888), 38–44.

ARNOLD (Arnall, Arnol, Arnald), WILLIAM, master of a sloop trading from New England to Newfoundland; fl. 1713–16.

William Arnold was one of several New England men held suspect by the English government for the illegal practice of "Seducing away great Numbers of Fishermen, and Seamen, and transporting 'em to New England." The laws of the period encouraged the use of the Newfoundland fisheries as a training ground for seamen for the English navy. A certain proportion of "green" men were sent out each year to the fishing grounds to learn the art of seamanship. Many of these men preferred a period of indenture in the colonies, and eventual freedom there, to the risk of being seized by the press gangs of Bristol and Portsmouth. Thus it was not difficult for men of

Arnold's trade to "seduce" these seamen away to New England at the end of the fishing season.

A major source of information about Arnold and the irregularities of the Newfoundland fisheries is the "Schedule of Trade and Fishery of Newfoundland" for 1715, which was prepared by Captain Falkingham of the *Gibraltar*, and included in the report submitted to the Admiralty by the commodore of the Newfoundland convoy, Thomas KEMPTHORNE. This "Schedule" informs us that William Arnold, master of a Boston vessel, sailed into Trepassey with a cargo of provisions, rum, and sheep, and that he exported a cargo of "passengers." Arnold sailed a 70-ton, plantation-built vessel which had a crew of seven men, and carried no guns. Other contemporary documents record that Arnold brought 80 sheep, provisions, and stores to Newfoundland from Boston in 1714–15. He returned there from New England the following year (1716) in the ship *Friendship* with a similar cargo. Captain Kempthorne complained of Arnold to the Board of Trade for illegally transporting seamen to New England. A postscript to Kempthorne's report stated that Arnold was "one whose impudent practice this way deserves correction above any others."

Little is known about Arnold's personal life other than that he was married to the former Mary Holyoke in Boston. The ceremony was performed by a Presbyterian minister, the Rev. Benjamin Wadsworth, on 17 Sept. 1713.

ANN MARIE NIELSEN

PRO, C.O. 194/4, f.389; 194/6, ff.20, 194. Boston, Registry Dept., *Records relating to the early history of Boston*, ed. W. H. Whitmore, W. S. Appleton, *et al.* (39v., Boston, 1876–1909), XXVIII: *Boston marriages, 1700–1751* (1898). PRO, *CSP, 1714–15, 1716–17.* C. B. Judah, *The North American fisheries and British policy to 1713* (University of Illinois studies in the social sciences, XVIII, nos.3–4, 1932, distributed 1933). Lounsbury, *British fishery at Nfld.* Prowse, *History of Nfld.* John Reeves, *History of the government of the island of Newfoundland, with an Appendix; containing the acts of parliament made respecting the trade and fishery* (London, 1793), 37–38, 56–57, 66; App., xxx. R. H. Tait, *Newfoundland: a summary of the history and development of Britain's oldest colony from 1497 to 1939* (Harrington Park, N. J., 1939), 19–21. R. G. Lounsbury, "Yankee trade at Newfoundland," *New Eng. Q.*, III (1930), 607–26.

ASCUMBUIT (Assacambuit). *See* NESCAMBIOUIT

ASSUROWLAWAY. *See* WAXAWAY

ATCHAMISSEY. *See* SCATCHAMISSE

ATECOUANDO (Athiconando, Decwando, Descouando, Adeawando, Addeawando, Adiawonda, Adeawanadon, Athurnando, Beawando, Dewando, Deowando, Edewancho, Ontaniendo), a prominent chief of the Pigwacket tribe of the Abenakis; fl. 1701–26.

Those spellings of his name which are not obvious disfigurements by copyists fall into two groups yielding different Abenaki names, *attek8ehaṅnedo*, "the Deer Spirit-power," and *atiéhaṅnedo*, "the Dog Spirit-power." The fact that two Abenaki names emerge seems to be coincidence, since the sequence of events makes it likely that there was only one person behind the many spellings. In fact, Edward Tyng* employed both Decwando and Deowando for the same person in one letter. The Decwando series has been preferred here; RAMEZAY and Bégon*, quoting Father Joseph Aubéry* who knew both the chief and the Abenaki language, wrote Athiconando (the latter form is meaningless but was probably miscopied from Athicouando). Aubéry himself wrote Atecouando.

In the earliest documents there are suggestions that Atecouando was a Penacook, and he appears to have been working for war in the uneasy summer of 1688 which preceded the outbreak of King William's War. On 29 Nov. 1690 he witnessed the truce and exchange of prisoners made between the Abenakis and the English "upon the water in canoes" at Sagadahoc, at the mouth of the Kennebec River, Maine. In 1701 he began to appear as an important chief representing the Pigwackets in their negotiations with the English. On 3 June of that year six Abenaki chiefs signed a peace with New England and promised to try to bring those Indians then in Canada into the agreement. They refused to stop travelling to Canada, however, since they would then be wholly dependent on the English for trade supplies, and they also objected to receiving English missionaries. Atecouando signed as one of the two chief sachems of "Narrackamagog." In December of the same year he was one of the two "Sagamores of Arrocomecoog" who sent Sampson Hegan, Bomoseen, and other messengers to Boston. (The Indian fort of "Narracomecock" was at the head of the Saco River and was probably equivalent to Pigwacket (Pequawket, now Fryeburg, Me.); it should not be confused with a place of a similar name on the Androscoggin River.) Atecouando was one of the Pigwacket chiefs at the 1702 treaty at Sagadahoc and one of three chiefs from Pigwacket and Penacook (now Concord, N.H.) who signed the treaty at Casco Bay on 20 June 1703. NESCAMBIOUIT was also a prominent Pigwacket chief, but Atecouando seems to have become the

Aubert de La Chesnaye

principal chief of the tribe by about 1706, since at this time he led his entire village to Canada to settle at the mission on the Saint-François (St Francis) river.

During Queen Anne's War some of the Pigwackets scattered to other missions, and many died. At the end of the war in 1713 the Penobscots and Norridgewocks made peace with the English [see Mog], and in July of the following year Atecouando and other Pigwacket chiefs ratified the treaty at Portsmouth, N.H. The Indians were anxious to have trading posts established to the east. They reasserted their claim to the land but invited the English to live at Cocheco (Dover, N.H.) and Saco, Me. At the last minute the English declared that the Indians were the queen's subjects and that therefore the queen owned all the land eastward. It is doubtful whether the Indians understood the claim and its implications.

In the winter of 1714–15 Atecouando's family returned to Pigwacket to hunt and to plant their fields the following spring. In August 1715, he returned to Saint-François to ask RIGAUD de Vaudreuil for permission to remove all the Indians there and at Bécancour, together with their missionary, Father Aubéry, to Pigwacket. He had the further hope of attracting some "Loup" Indians, probably Schaghticokes, from the vicinity of Fort Orange (Albany, N.Y.). Since Saint-François was important for the defence of New France, the French tried to dissuade him from returning to the ancient home of his tribe. He persisted, however, perhaps because of the superiority of English trade goods, and formed a village of about 25 warriors. He promised to return to Canada in case of another war. On 12 Aug. 1717, he was one of the chiefs who signed the ratification of the 1713 and 1714 treaties at Georgetown, Me. [see WOWURNA]. Some of his tribe attended a meeting at Georgetown in July 1721 and one at Norridgewock (now Old Point in south Madison, Me.) in October of that year, but it is not known whether Atecouando was among them.

In 1722, the hostilities known to New England historians as Lovewell's War broke out between the English and the Abenakis. It appears likely that Atecouando kept his promise and returned to Saint-François at this time, since he apparently did not take part in the raids by a band of Pigwackets led by Paugus. He probably returned to Pigwacket late in 1726. Although Jacob Wendell's census had listed only seven men in the Pigwacket tribe that year, John Gyles's* census in November listed "Edewancho" as chief of 24 warriors there.

This is the last certain appearance of Atecouando in history. At the treaty signed at Falmouth (Portland, Me.) in July 1727 [see WENEMOUET],

the Pigwacket chiefs were not listed separately, but among the Arosaguntacook chiefs from Saint-François we find "Suzack, son of Beawando," suggesting Sozap, son of Atecouando. This may be an indication that the latter was already dead or too infirm to travel to Falmouth. Some Indians remained at Pigwacket until King George's War began in 1744, when a few joined the English and the majority probably returned to Saint-François. More than 20 years after the treaty of Falmouth, a Jérôme Atecouando* began to appear as a grand chief of the Saint-François nation, but his connection with the earlier Atecouando is uncertain. Jérôme may have been the son of Atecouando of Pigwacket and the "Saarom" of the Falmouth treaty, or was possibly younger than Sozap and therefore not distinguished in the document.

GORDON M. DAY

Archives du Séminaire de Nicolet, Que., Joseph Aubéry, "Dictionnaire Abnaquis-François," 157, 161, 183, 242, 258, 435; "Dictionnaire François-Abnaquis," 128. AN, Col., B, 38, f.452; C¹¹ᴬ, 35, ff.62–65. *Coll. de manuscrits relatifs à la N.-F.*, III, 23, 58. "Correspondance de Vaudreuil," APQ *Rapport, 1947–48*, 296–305, 332. *Documentary hist. of Maine*, V, 164–66; VI, 436; IX, 145; X, 50–51, 87–95; XXIII, 31–32, 67–69, 291. *JR* (Thwaites), LXVII, 28–37; LXIX, 72–73. Maine Hist. Soc. *Coll.*, 1st ser., III (1853), 355–58, 361–75, 377–412. Mather, *Magnalia Christi Americana*, 609–10. New Eng. Hist. and Geneal. *Register*, XX, 9. *NYCD* (O'Callaghan and Fernow), IX, 904. Penhallow, *Hist. of wars with Eastern Indians* (1859), 16.

Frederick Kidder, *The Abenaki Indians; their treaties of 1713 and 1717* . . . (Portland, 1859), 20–23; *The expeditions of Capt. John Lovewell* . . . (Boston, 1865), 108.

AUBERT DE LA CHESNAYE, CHARLES, merchant, fur-trader, seigneur, financier, member of the Conseil Souverain of New France, ennobled by Louis XIV on 24 March 1693, New France's leading businessman of the 17th century; b. in Amiens, 12 Feb. 1632; died in Quebec, 20 Sept. 1702.

He was the son of Jacques Aubert and Marie Goupy (or Goupil). In La Chesnaye's marriage contracts and his letters of nobility, the occupation of his father is given either as "comptroller" or "intendant of the fortifications of the town and citadel of Amiens"; but in the birth certificate of his sister Anne in 1629, the father is referred to simply as Jacques Aubert "painter holding shop in Paris." Possibly the latter became intendant at a subsequent date, for the family does appear to have been well-connected socially. Acting as Anne's godparents were a son and daughter of the

Aubert de La Chesnaye

Duc de Chaulnes, the military governor of Picardy. Charles' godfather was Charles Parmentier, the Duc's *maître d'hôtel*. Mention is also made, in a notarial deed of 1695, of a second son, Louis, who was residing in Antwerp and acting as the business agent of the princes of Uzel and Brussels.

How and when La Chesnaye acquired his fortune is not known, but the possibility of a family inheritance would appear to be ruled out. In his last will written in August 1702, he described his parents simply as "worthy people" and himself as "quite poor" when he arrived in Canada in 1655 as the agent of a group of Rouen merchants. This position must have been an important factor in his early career. In 1660, these Rouen merchants and Toussaint Guénet, a French financier, concluded an important treaty with René Robinau* de Bécancour, who represented the colony. It gave the Guénet syndicate exclusive control of the Canadian import trade for an annual fee of 10,000 *livres* and the right to collect the 25 per cent and 10 per cent taxes on beaver pelts and moosehides for an additional amount of 50,000 *livres*. The habitants considered these terms excessively generous and they managed to have the treaty rescinded by the royal council in March 1662. For two years, however, La Chesnaye had helped to manage an important enterprise and it may well have been during this period that he launched his own business career.

Shortly after the cancellation of the treaty, La Chesnaye negotiated his first major business transaction. In October 1663 the Conseil Souverain held a public auction to find a leaseholder for the Tadoussac fur trade monopoly and the taxes on beaver pelts and moosehides. Several bidders appeared on the first day, but the field was soon narrowed down to two men: La Chesnaye and Claude Charron*. Competition now became keen. Each man outbid the other in turn and the price offered for the lease rose gradually from 38,000 to 46,000 *livres* which Charron offered on the morning of the fourth day. That afternoon the customary three candles were lit to signify that the auction was about to close; but before the third flame had flickered out La Chesnaye had managed to snatch victory from his rival with a final bid of 46,500 *livres*. The lease was to run for three years and 15,000 *livres* were payable in advance at the start of each year.

La Chesnaye had other important business interests besides the beaver trade. He owned a large store in Quebec in which he kept a stock of merchandise valued at approximately 50,000 *livres*. In November 1664, he and several other merchants were accused by the syndics representing the habitants of having sold their merchandise at prices higher than those set by the council the preceding June. In reply to this charge, La Chesnaye admitted that the price he had demanded for shoes had exceeded the prescribed rates, but he claimed that he had thought that the tariff applied only to itinerant merchants and not to those who had their residence in the colony. He also pointed out that the habitants paid for their purchases in beaver pelts, whose value had remained constant in Canada but had declined sharply in France. To have followed the tariff under those circumstances would have resulted in heavy financial losses. The council was not impressed by these arguments and imposed fines on the guilty merchants. Only in 1670 did it set a new price scale for the pelts, following renewed complaints by La Chesnaye and his colleagues about the harmful effect the high value of beaver was having on their affairs.

Soon after his arrival in the colony La Chesnaye began to acquire land. In 1659 he purchased for 1,000 *livres* 70 acres on Coteau Sainte-Geneviève, one of the colony's most favoured sites for agriculture by virtue of its proximity to Quebec, and a lot on Rue du Sault-au-Matelot in Lower Town where he built a spacious home in the 1660s. He became co-seigneur of Beaupré in 1662 when he bought the share of Olivier Letardif* in the company founded in 1638 to develop the large domain extending from the Montmorency River to Cap Tourmente. Bishop LAVAL, who had arrived in Canada in 1659, was also interested in obtaining this attractive seigneury, which was almost fully settled, and La Chesnaye was instrumental in helping him achieve his goal. Between 1662 and 1664, acting as the procurator of the seigneury, La Chesnaye sold his own share and those of several other members of the company to the bishop. He did not, however, sever all his connections with Beaupré. In 1668 he obtained from the new seigneur a subfief with a frontage of approximately 10 *arpents* on the St Lawrence River in the parish of Ange-Gardien and purchased another, somewhat larger, from JEAN-BAPTISTE LEGARDEUR de Repentigny in Château-Richer.

The fur trade, the sale of merchandise, and agriculture were thus the three basic ventures on which La Chesnaye built his career. Except for the fur trade, however, economic conditions in the colony limited rather than favoured business opportunities. Agricultural expansion was severely hindered by the small population, the Iroquois wars, the absence of external markets, and the fur trade's superior economic appeal. Until the 1690s, when card money became well established, the colony lacked a currency. This factor, joined to the impoverished condition of the habitants,

27

Aubert de La Chesnaye

obliged the colonial merchants to sell on credit and they frequently experienced great difficulty in the recovery of debts. La Chesnaye, in brief, enjoyed none of the opportunities of the business class after 1713, which was favoured by a long period of peace, a population that was relatively large, a market at Louisbourg for agricultural products, and the creation by means of state assistance of fairly important industries such as the shipyards and the Saint-Maurice ironworks.

In May 1664, as part of the crown's vast programme of colonial reorganization, Canada became the property of the newly established Compagnie des Indes Occidentales. The company was granted a 40-year monopoly of the commerce of Canada including the Tadoussac fur trade and the taxes on beaver pelts and moosehides. Shortly afterwards, Jean Talon* began his famous campaign to restrict these company rights. He claimed that the monopoly discouraged the spirit of enterprise among the settlers, hindered the growth of trade, and, generally speaking, was an obstacle to the progress of the colony. His solution was to make the trade free or place it in the hands of a new company composed of himself and the principal Canadian settlers.

La Chesnaye had been named agent of the Compagnie des Indes Occidentales in 1666 and he sharply criticized Talon's proposition. In a memoir submitted to the court in 1667 he argued that no company could replace the Compagnie des Indes Occidentales unless it had at its disposal an initial capital fund of 1,300,000 *livres*. He calculated that this amount, which could not possibly be raised in the colony, would be required to buy up the company's unsold pelts and its stock of merchandise, and to attend to the colony's immediate needs. As for freedom of trade, La Chesnaye did not consider it a practical solution for he did not believe that a sufficient number of merchants would be interested in trading with Canada to satisfy its needs. La Chesnaye may have communicated his views orally to Colbert during a trip to France in 1665, for the minister used arguments very similar to his to turn down Talon's recommendations in 1666. The will of the intendant, however, finally prevailed. During a visit to France in 1669 he obtained the abolition of the Compagnie des Indes Occidentales's monopoly.

In taking his stand La Chesnaye had no doubt been thinking of the interests of his employer, but other considerations also appear to have been involved. As a strongly established and well connected businessman, he obviously did not believe that the colony could flourish without the protection of powerful financial interests. Having witnessed the sorry performance of the Compagnie des Habitants in the 1650s, it is not surprising that he should have found Talon's recommendations distasteful for they would once again deliver the colony into the hands of petty, dishonest businessmen. In this affair, furthermore, La Chesnaye believed that the intendant had been trying to serve his own interests rather than those of the colony. In a memoir written many years later, he stated that Talon had campaigned against the Compagnie des Indes Occidentales's monopoly because he expected that its cancellation would enable him to increase his private trade in articles he imported into the colony free of freight and insurance charges.

This friction between La Chesnaye and Talon fortunately did not prevent them from cooperating on some important projects. In 1670, La Chesnaye went into lumbering, a sector of the Canadian economy which the intendant was hoping to develop. Two years later, Talon granted to him, Charles Bazire*, and PIERRE DENYS de La Ronde the seigneury of Percé, to be used as a base for a fishing industry. La Chesnaye and La Ronde formed a company in which the former invested 13,874 *livres* and the latter 8,324 *livres*. Thus around La Chesnaye's main interests, which consisted of the fur trade, the Quebec store, and agriculture, there emerged a network of secondary activities such as lumbering, fishing, a brickyard after 1679, and for a short time mining.

In 1672, La Chesnaye sizably enlarged the scope of his operations when he leased from the Compagnie des Indes Occidentales, for 47,000 *livres* annually, the financial rights which it still exercised in Canada. These consisted basically of the proceeds from the taxes on beaver pelts and moosehides which had yielded a profit of 70,000 *livres* in 1670. The acquisition of these important revenues probably explains his decision to take up residence in La Rochelle, whose seaport was the nerve centre of commerce between Canada and France. There, he would be able to look after the marketing of his pelts and would also be close to the high circles of French finance. To collect the taxes in Canada and to manage his other affairs, he appointed his associate Charles Bazire.

From 1672 until his return to Canada in 1678, La Chesnaye figured prominently in La Rochelle's bustling commercial life. He soon won the confidence of the city's other merchants who twice elected him to the *cour consulaire*, which rendered judgments in mercantile cases. Alone or with his partners Jean Grignon, Jean Gitton, and Étienne Joulin, he owned several vessels ranging in size from 60 to 300 tons which plied the sea between La Rochelle, Quebec, Percé, the West Indies, Amsterdam, and Hamburg with cargoes of fur, fish, and assorted merchandise. Thus La Chesnaye used his years in France to expand his business and to make commercial contacts in several countries of Europe.

In 1674, Louis XIV abolished the Compagnie des Indes Occidentales. The next year he ceded to a syndicate of French financiers, acting under the name of Jean Oudiette and known as the Compagnie de la Ferme, several important commercial privileges in Canada and some of the other French colonies for 350,000 *livres* annually. The Compagnie de la Ferme's Canadian rights consisted of the Tadoussac fur trade, the proceeds of the tax on beaver pelts and moosehides, and on the wines and spirits entering the colony, and the exclusive right to market Canadian beaver in France. It was obliged, however, to purchase all the beaver pelts brought to its stores at four *livres* ten *sols* per pound weight. Three days after the conclusion of this treaty, Oudiette leased his Canadian rights to La Chesnaye for 119,000 *livres* annually, with 20,000 *livres* payable in advance. By means of this transaction, La Chesnaye gained complete control of the Canadian beaver trade, but he soon found that he lacked the resources to support such an enormous enterprise. As a result of the expansionist policy pursued by Governor Louis de Buade* de Frontenac, far more pelts were being produced in Canada than the French market could absorb; but La Chesnaye could make no adjustment to meet these conditions for he was obliged by the terms of the Oudiette treaty to purchase all the beaver brought to him. By 1677 he was practically crushed by an enormous debt of 1,000,000 *livres*. Fortunately he was rescued by a group of powerful financiers, including Louis Carrel and Hugues Mathé, receivers general of finance for the generalities of Paris and Champagne, who brought fresh capital to the venture. The transactions that followed are far from clear, but it would appear that the new group gained control of over 80 per cent of the Canadian farm. La Chesnaye retained the balance but sold most of it for 43,000 *livres* in 1680.

The death of Charles Bazire on 15 Dec. 1677 obliged La Chesnaye to return to Canada to settle the claims made by the heirs of the deceased on some of the assets of the partnership. The matter was complicated, for the association between the two men had not been formalized by any deed, and several transactions of concern to the partnership had been entered into by Bazire in his own name. Finally, in settlement of their claims, La Chesnaye offered the heirs either one-third of all the assets he had held in common with Bazire—in the form of seigneuries, merchandise, *rentes*, and loans—or 130,000 *livres*, payable in cash, merchandise, and

title deeds to some of the accounts receivable. The heirs preferred the second, perhaps as the less complicated of the two alternatives, and relinquished all claims on the remaining assets of the partnership.

This was not the end of the affair, however. Following the death of Bazire the French shareholders in the Compagnie de la Ferme had also sent an agent, Josias Boisseau*, to Canada to examine the state of their affairs. Shortly after his arrival in the colony, he and La Chesnaye became involved in a violent quarrel. According to the agent, discord had broken out because he had tried to prevent La Chesnaye from defrauding his associates of large sums of money. The intendant, Jacques Duchesneau*, and the author of an anonymous memoir of 1681, however, presented a vastly different picture of the affair. They claimed that Boisseau, who had allied himself with Frontenac, had defied with impunity both the intendant's and La Chesnaye's efforts to regulate his conduct and had built a fortune of 50,000 *livres* at the expense of the company. This version gains considerable support from a dispatch addressed to Bishop Laval by the Abbé Jean Dudouyt*, the bishop's representative in Paris, in which the latter wrote that Boisseau would be hard put to account for his actions, which had caused the company heavy losses, if Frontenac were not there to protect him. Boisseau was dismissed from office in 1681 by order of the court.

These problems were not the only ones to occupy La Chesnaye's attention in the late 1670s. When he returned to the colony he found it split into two rival groups by Frontenac and Cavelier* de La Salle's attempt to monopolize the western fur trade. La Chesnaye allied himself with the merchants who were opposed to this design, which would ruin them beyond repair if it should succeed, and became one of their leaders. It was he who was primarily responsible for grouping them in 1682 into a company—the Compagnie du Nord—which turned their attention towards Hudson Bay. Because of the prominent position he occupied in their ranks, La Chesnaye was soon bitterly attacked by members of the rival camp. In an anonymous memoir of 1680, he and his principal allies, JACQUES LE BER, Charles Le Moyne*, and Philippe Gaultier* de Comporté, were accused of trading openly with the Indians within the colonial boundaries, of smuggling furs to the English, and of sending numerous canoes into the west in defiance of the royal ordinances. These accusations probably contained considerable truth but the court appears never to have paid much attention to them. This may have been the work of Duchesneau who energetically defended

Aubert de La Chesnaye

La Chesnaye in his dispatches; but perhaps the government simply realized that it would be both unwise and unjust to antagonize a man who was playing a role of vital importance in the colony's economic life.

In 1680, the syndicate of financiers which had relieved La Chesnaye of the Canadian farm judged that the operation had become unprofitable and surrendered the lease to Jean Oudiette. It next had to decide how to dispose of its remaining assets in Canada, consisting of merchandise, furs, and sums of money owed to it by a large number of French and Indians. The syndicate could have pressed for the recovery of these debts, but this would have taken time and probably necessitated numerous lawsuits. Rather than follow such a course of action, it preferred to transfer the title to all its debts and assets to La Chesnaye for the sum of 410,000 *livres*, payable in four equal annual instalments. This transaction—worth nearly $1,000,000 in present-day currency—is a turning-point in his career. Although the value of the debts is not given, it must have been considerably higher than the purchase price because of the risks involved in their recovery. La Chesnaye thus appears to have staked the better part of his fortune on a speculative venture which could result either in a sizable profit or a ruinous loss.

As security for payment, he mortgaged all his own assets and properties. The notarial inventory in which these are listed is an important document, for it provides a comprehensive picture of the state of his fortune in 1681. Its total value was then 476,000 *livres* made up of five principal categories: accounts receivable, 175,000 *livres*; *contrats de rente*, 100,000 *livres*; merchandise, 50,000 *livres*; his house on Rue du Sault-au-Matelot, 60,000 *livres*; farms and seigneuries, 66,000 *livres*. Several hundred notarial deeds in which a broad range of business transactions are recorded shed a great deal of light on the manner and spirit in which La Chesnaye administered this fortune. The image that emerges from these documents is not that of a selfish merchant uniquely interested in increasing his wealth, but that of a man who was intensely concerned with the development of the colony. Unlike the itinerant merchant, who took the profits from his Canadian trade back to France with him, La Chesnaye invested his gains in the colony and loaned them to the settlers. Unfortunately, these practices were largely responsible for his eventual ruin, which probably explains why so few people followed his example.

La Chesnaye dealt with people from all classes of society. He sold merchandise on credit for amounts ranging from a few *livres* to several thousand. Because of the disappearance of his account books, the profits he realized on these transactions are not known, but the price he charged for shoes in the 1660s suggests that he drove a hard bargain. He also made many cash loans to seigneurs and habitants, usually to enable them to improve their properties. On 1 Oct. 1666, he loaned 10,600 *livres* to Bishop Laval to permit him to meet a payment on the seigneury of Beaupré. On 25 Feb. 1679, he loaned 3,000 *livres* to Charles Cadieu de Courville, a habitant of Beauport, and 4,135 *livres* to Joseph Giffard, the seigneur, to enable them to repair existing buildings and put up new ones. These loans were made in return for *contrats de rente*, which were much like modern savings bonds. They yielded an annual interest rate of 5 to 5½ per cent, but bore no maturity date. As long as interest payments were made there was apparently no way to compel the debtor to repay the principal. At first sight this type of investment would appear ill suited to the needs of a businessman since it froze large amounts of capital. But in the context of the depressed long-term economic cycle that prevailed in the French world from 1630 to 1730 approximately, an investment that yielded 5 per cent interest was probably considered good.

La Chesnaye also had a large amount of money invested in land. He acquired his first acres in 1659 and continued to increase his holdings thereafter until he became the most important landowner of his day. His purpose in acquiring farms and seigneuries was not speculation nor merely the social prestige connected with the ownership of land. He was essentially an agricultural entrepreneur who wanted to base part of his business on the sale of wheat, peas, and other staple crops. By 1685, he had apparently achieved a measure of success, for he then settled part of a debt with a shipment of wheat worth 23,000 *livres*. That same year he and two other merchants undertook to supply the colony with an emergency stock of flour to be used in case of famine.

His seigneuries can be divided into two categories. There were those like Repentigny, Rivière-du-Loup, and Kamouraska that he acquired when they were little more than wilderness tracts, and whose development proved to be costly indeed. He spent 35,000 and 33,000 *livres* on Rivière-du-Loup and Repentigny respectively, but their commercial value was only 18,000 and 16,000 *livres* in 1680. Uncleared seigneuries were apparently worthless, for Kamouraska, which remained undeveloped until the 1690s, is not listed in the inventory of 1681. Then, there were the holdings in the vicinity of Quebec that were highly productive and very valuable. The arriere-fief of Charlesville in the seigneury of Beaupré, granted to La Chesnaye and Charles Bazire by Bishop Laval in 1677, had 16 tenants and was worth 6,000 *livres*. A fully equipped 70-acre farm in the Coteau Sainte-Geneviève was valued at 20,000 *livres* in 1680, and another in the same area was sold for 9,000 *livres* in 1679. Most of these estates, it should be pointed out, were not under La Chesnaye's direct management but, like Repentigny, were leased for cash, or, like Charlesville, were farmed out on a sharecropping agreement.

While he was negotiating his great transaction with the Compagnie de la Ferme, La Chesnaye was also laying the foundations of the Canadian-based Hudson Bay company that became known as the Compagnie du Nord. The French government approved of the formation of this trading organization which might succeed in diverting large quantities of prime beaver pelts from the British Hudson's Bay Company. In 1679 the French director of trade, Francesco Bellinzani, arranged a meeting between La Chesnaye and Pierre-Esprit RADISSON, who were both in Paris at the time. The two men consulted together on the means of forming the company and it was finally agreed that Radisson would lead the first commercial expedition to the bay in return for 25 per cent of the profits. In Canada the new governor, Le Febvre* de La Barre, who had replaced Frontenac in 1682, encouraged other merchants to join the enterprise and some 193,000 *livres* were eventually invested in it. La Chesnaye was by far the most important shareholder with an investment of 90,000 *livres*.

The arrival of La Barre as governor had enabled La Chesnaye to expand his operations in yet another direction. As long as Frontenac had been in office the Great Lakes and Mississippi Valley regions had been controlled by La Salle and closed to the other merchants of the colony. La Barre, however, who was hostile to La Salle, deprived him of his posts and placed La Chesnaye and his group in possession of Fort Frontenac. A party of malcontents, led by the intendant, Jacques de MEULLES, construed this gesture as proof of the existence of a partnership between the governor and La Chesnaye, and painted a dark picture of its effects on the colony. They claimed that the governor and his partner had over 30 canoes in the west under the command of DANIEL GREYSOLON Dulhut and that a large portion of their fur was being diverted to the English. De Meulles even stated that it was to defend these commercial interests that La Barre, acting on the advice of La Chesnaye, had decided to wage war on the Iroquois. This contention was taken up 30 years later by GÉDÉON DE CATALOGNE. In his *Recueil* he claimed that La Barre, in order to eliminate all competition from the west, had authorized the Iroquois to plunder the traders who could not produce his personal permit. The governor had opted for war after the Indians had overstepped these limits and attacked canoes belonging to La Chesnaye.

How true were these accusations? Independent evidence shows that those relating to La Chesnaye's western trading operations were well founded. In 1685, the furs and merchandise which he had in the west were valued at 100,000 *livres*. His implication in the contraband trade with the English seems established beyond question by the trading permit issued to him by the New York government in 1684. Some of his letters of the mid-1680s establish his connection with the Greysolon brothers, Dulhut and La Tourette. The statements of de Meulles and Catalogne about the origins of the war, however, are not acceptable. For it appears incredible that La Chesnaye would have wantonly exposed to destruction at the hands of the Iroquois a colony which he had worked so hard to develop and in which he had enormous sums invested. If he did advise La Barre to make war on the Five Nations it must have been because he was convinced that a display of force was necessary to overawe these Indians who had recently invaded the territory of the Illinois and seemed on the verge of waging a general war on Canada.

The year 1682 seems to be the watershed in La Chesnaye's career. The years preceding that date had been marked by several major business transactions and the expansion of his affairs. Afterwards, although the downward trend cannot be graphed with precision, decline gradually set in. Two factors—the Iroquois war and the fire which ravaged the Lower Town of Quebec in August 1682—appear to have been principally responsible for this turn in his fortunes. The heavy material losses suffered by the colony during its war with the Five Nations no doubt made it difficult for La Chesnaye to recover from the habitants the debts which he had purchased from the Compagnie de la Ferme. As for the fire, it destroyed 55 buildings including several warehouses. La Chesnaye's properties were spared, but he loaned large sums of money to his stricken fellow-citizens to enable them to rebuild their homes. He thus depleted his cash reserves at a time when he still owed 213,000 *livres* to the Compagnie de la Ferme, which was pressing him relentlessly for a settlement. He finally discharged his debt in 1685 by transferring to his creditors the 100,000 *livres* of fur and merchandise which he had in the west, a shipment of wheat worth 23,000 *livres*, and his share of 90,000 *livres* in the Compagnie du Nord.

31

Aubert de La Chesnaye

Up to that time La Chesnaye's connection with the Hudson Bay trade had not been a profitable one. The Compagnie du Nord, plagued by misfortune and Radisson's treachery, had suffered losses of 273,426 *livres*.

For the balance of the 1680s, however, there was no noticeable change in the tempo of La Chesnaye's activities. He rejoined the Compagnie du Nord in which he had a share of 22,268 *livres* in 1691. He continued to sell large quantities of merchandise on credit or the instalment plan and to make cash loans to finance serious projects. On 8 Oct. 1683, he sold 12,000 *livres* of merchandise to René Gaultier* de Varennes, payable in furs, field crops, and cash over a 12-year period. Some three months later, in return for a *rente* of 650 *livres*, he loaned 13,000 *livres* to Étienne Landron and Jean Joly to enable them to build a bakery. He also continued to increase his seigneurial holdings. Some of his important acquisitions between 1683 and 1688 were Madawaska, on the Saint John River, granted by La Barre and de Meulles; Yamaska, on the south shore of the St Lawrence near Trois-Rivières, donated by MICHEL LENEUF de La Vallière (the elder); Saint-Jean-Port-Joli, below Quebec, acquired from Noël Langlois in settlement of a debt of 1,160 *livres*; Le Bic, also below Quebec, from CHARLES DENYS de Vitré in settlement of another debt of 2,050 *livres*. In 1689, La Chesnaye and a few other merchants were granted the concession of Blanc-Sablon including a part of the coast of Labrador and of Newfoundland by BRISAY de Denonville and BOCHART de Champigny for the cod and whale fisheries.

Denis RIVERIN, who had sublet the Tadoussac trade from 1682 to 1685, complained that his affairs were gravely prejudiced by La Chesnaye's extensive lower St Lawrence holdings. He stated that Indians who usually dealt at Tadoussac were now trading across the St Lawrence at Rivière-du-Loup and Le Bic where La Chesnaye had posted his agents. These furs were then sent down the Saint John River, which passed through Madawaska, to Port-Royal (Annapolis Royal, N.S.), where La Chesnaye owned a trading counter. From there they could be shipped to France duty-free since the taxes of 25 per cent and 10 per cent levied on Canadian furs did not extend to Acadia. In 1684 the court issued an ordinance forbidding the settlers of the lower St Lawrence to trade with the Indians, but it modified its decision the following year. The settlers were then authorized to engage in the Indian trade but ordered not to trespass on the Tadoussac domain.

The documentation available on La Chesnaye for the 1690s suggests rather than tells of increasing financial difficulties. His relationship with his partner, Jean GOBIN, is most revealing in this respect. In 1690, La Chesnaye, his son FRANÇOIS, and Gobin formed a private company. Nothing is known of the nature of this operation but it obviously did not flourish. In 1699, the two Auberts withdrew, leaving two vessels and merchandise worth 102,000 *livres* in the possession of Gobin, on condition that he pay off the firm's debts within two years. Notarial documents also record the existence of large personal debts. La Chesnaye owed Gobin 83,264 *livres* as a result of three transactions made in 1692 and 1694. He also owed 51,681 *livres* to European correspondents and Canadian creditors, for which he signed eight separate obligations before the notary Louis CHAMBALON on 18 April 1695. It may have been to settle some of these debts that he began to dispose of his seigneuries. Île Dupas and Chicot were sold for 1,500 *livres*, in 1690; Charlesville and Yamaska for 6,250 and 3,333 *livres* respectively, in 1694; Repentigny for 15,000 *livres*, in 1700.

In spite of these financial difficulties, La Chesnaye remained active throughout the 1690s. In 1691, he became a member of a fishing company formed by Champigny and ten years later undertook to supply the government with 60 masts annually for a period of ten years. He also devoted much attention to the development of his seigneuries below Quebec. Twenty-seven settlers and their families took up residence in Kamouraska between 1694 and 1700 and the value of the seigneury rose to 12,000 *livres* by the latter date. It was also during those final years of his life that his prestige in the colony reached its peak. In 1693, Louis XIV granted him letters of nobility as a reward for the many years he had devoted to the development of the Canadian economy. Two years later, he succeeded the deceased Charles Legardeur* de Tilly as councillor in the Sovereign Council of New France. The office should in fact have reverted to one of Tilly's sons, PIERRE-NOËL LEGARDEUR de Tilly, but the latter ceded it to La Chesnaye in settlement of a debt of 6,500 *livres* which he was incapable of paying. With this office in the colonial magistrature and his letters of nobility, La Chesnaye's social metamorphosis was complete. The *bourgeois* had become a *gentilhomme*.

Ennoblement, however, was not followed by a loss of interest in mercantile pursuits. Until the end of his life, La Chesnaye remained the undisputed leader of the Canadian business community. In 1700, he became the leading shareholder of the Compagnie de la Colonie, which leased the beaver trade from the Compagnie de la Ferme. His investment in this corporation amounted to 25,000 *livres* divided into 500 shares, of which 120 had been transferred from the books of the Compagnie du Nord, which the Compagnie de la Colonie had absorbed, and 380 purchased on credit. In 1700, he went to France with MATHIEU-FRANÇOIS MARTIN de Lino to negotiate better terms with the Paris bankers, Pasquier, Bourlet, and Goy, who acted as the company's correspondents. Their mission was successful, for the bankers increased the amount of their loan and reduced the interest rate from 10% to 8%. La Chesnaye was back in Canada in 1701 and he died the following year on 20 September.

On 26 August he had prepared his last will. This document is illuminating, for it shows what thoughts preoccupied him as death drew near. In it he stated that he had never felt much attachment for worldly goods but had simply worked for the progress of the colony "courageously and earnestly." He asked forgiveness for the many wrongs and injustices, both great and small, which he had probably committed during a long career devoted to business, but added that he could recall no specific offensive action "against any of his fellow men." He requested the celebration of a daily mass in perpetuity for the repose of his soul and those of his Canadian friends with whom he had possibly entered into business intrigues, a simple funeral service, and burial in the paupers' cemetery of the Hôtel-Dieu of Quebec. It is almost as if, by means of this final gesture, La Chesnaye hoped to appear before the Almighty in the same destitute condition as the poor of the colony next to whom he would be buried.

La Chesnaye had been married three times to daughters of prominent Canadian families. On 6 Feb. 1664, he married Catherine-Gertrude, 15-year-old daughter of Guillaume Couillard* and Guillemette Hébert*, a daughter of Louis Hébert*. She died that same year, shortly after giving birth to a son. His second wife, Marie-Louise Juchereau de La Ferté, was the daughter of Jean Juchereau* de La Ferté and Marie Giffard. Their marriage was celebrated on 10 Jan. 1668, and she died in La Rochelle on 7 March 1678, at the age of 26. On 11 Aug. 1680, La Chesnaye took his third wife, Marie-Angélique, 19-year-old daughter of Pierre Denys de La Ronde and Catherine Leneuf. She died in Quebec on 8 Nov. 1713. Eleven of the 18 children born of these marriages lived to adulthood. Two of the six daughters became nuns at the Quebec Hôtel-Dieu and the four others married officers of the sword and the robe in Canada and Île Royale. Of the five sons only one, François, known as the Sieur de Maur et de Mille-Vaches, appears to have shown any inclination for business. Two of his brothers, Charles and Louis*, entered the army: the former in France, where he was killed between 1690 and 1693; the latter in Canada, where he joined the colonial regular troops. Pierre, known as the Sieur de Gaspé, appears to have spent his life on his seigneuries and to have devoted himself to agriculture. He was the great-grandfather of Philippe Aubert* de Gaspé, the author of *Les Anciens Canadiens*. Details of the career of Louis, known as the Sieur Duforillon, who died in France in 1721, are not known.

Settling the estate proved to be a matter of extreme complexity and the question finally had to be referred to the Conseil Supérieur in 1708. La Chesnaye's fortune, according to Claude de RAMEZAY, his brother-in-law, had once amounted to 800,000 *livres*. His assets at his death consisted of his Quebec house, his seigneuries, 43,000 *livres* of merchandise, and approximately 282,000 *livres* of *rentes* and accounts receivable, of which 200,000 *livres* had to be written off as bad debt. Liabilities totalled 420,000 *livres*. In 1700, to simplify the settlement of the estate, La Chesnaye had donated 24,500 *livres* in *rentes* and landed property to each of his three sons from his second marriage. This amount was increased to 30,000 *livres* in 1708 and it then became the turn of the creditors to salvage what they could from the balance of the estate. The sale of La Chesnaye's last seigneuries in 1709 helped to settle some of the debts, but most of the claims made against the estate appear never to have been paid.

In its essentials, the career of Charles Aubert de La Chesnaye closely resembles that of the pious and austere bourgeois of 17th-century France. Some historians have pointed out that the deeply Catholic society of the *ancien régime* never fully approved of the bourgeois way of life that was based on profit and illegitimate gain. The bourgeois, in an effort to dissipate these misgivings and win acceptance, used part of their money to make bequests and donations to churches and religious communities. The case of La Chesnaye seems to corroborate this thesis. He was a member of the Congregation of the Virgin Mary and a generous benefactor of religious communities and charitable institutions. He was opposed to the sale of brandy to the Indians. Following the great fire which ravaged Quebec in 1682 he made generous loans to help fellow-Canadians rebuild their homes.

In his private life La Chesnaye seems to have practised the austerity that was encouraged by the church in New France. The most useful document on this aspect of his personality is the inventory of his belongings that was made following his death. It shows that his house, despite its impressive proportions, was functionally furnished—in one

Aubert de La Chesnaye

room hung curtains made from old tablecloths— and that his wardrobe was simple. He usually seems to have dressed in a pair of red or grey flannel trousers, a jacket and jerkin made of serge, and an old beaver hat. His only concessions to luxury were a wig and five shirts trimmed with lace. The inventory also tells us something of his taste in reading. All but three of the 35 books he owned dealt with religious themes. Among the latter were the works of Saint François de Sales, an important figure of the French religious revival of the early 17th century.

La Chesnaye, however, was not satisfied with his bourgeois status. From an early date, like many wealthy and ambitious members of the French third estate, he was strongly attracted to the nobility. Born plain Charles Aubert, he soon added de La Chesnaye to his name. This quest for noble status might also help to explain his eagerness to acquire seigneuries. It is doubtful that he was thinking only of economic return when he spent large sums to develop land, for the same amount invested in the fur trade and the fisheries would have enabled him to net a higher profit. He may also have been thinking of the social prestige which the ownership of fine estates alone could confer.

The religious side of La Chesnaye's personality and his efforts to enter the ranks of the nobility should not be allowed to obscure the fact that the driving force in his career had been the spirit of gain. Systematically, he reinvested his capital in productive ventures in order to realize still greater profits. His house on Rue du Sault-au-Matelot became the seat of an economic empire that extended in all directions and controlled the material resources of New France as well as the lives of a great number of habitants who had mortgaged their properties in return for cash loans. With money, in other words, came power, the quest for which cannot be discounted as a factor in La Chesnaye's career.

YVES F. ZOLTVANY

[The information on the Aubert family is based on Série E of the Archives de la Somme (Amiens). This series contains La Chesnaye's birth certificate. The passage dealing with La Chesnaye's years in La Rochelle is based on material in the Archives de la Charente-Maritime (La Rochelle). La Chesnaye's relationship with the Compagnie des Indes Occidentales and the Compagnie de la Ferme from 1672 to 1681 is based essentially on AN, G⁷, 1312; Archives de la Charente-Maritime, greffe Teuleron; AN, Paris, greffe Beaudry. La Chesnaye's great transaction of 1681 was passed in Beaudry's greffe.

The Archives des Colonies series, particularly C¹¹ᴬ, record many of the important events of La Chesnaye's career, such as his relationship with Talon, Frontenac, La Barre, and his connection with the Compagnie du Nord. The Archives judiciaires de Québec, which contain several hundred notarial deeds covering a broad range of business transactions, are indispensable for understanding the manner and spirit in which La Chesnaye administered his affairs. The *registres de la prévôté* in the Quebec provincial archives record a great number of lawsuits in which La Chesnaye was usually suing for the recovery of debts. Y.F.Z.]

AAQ, Registres d'insinuation A. Archives de la Charente-Maritime (La Rochelle), B 4192, 5672–5680; E, Minutes Teuleron, Drouyneau, Pénigaud. Archives de La Somme (Amiens), E, Registre des baptêmes, mariages et sépultures de la paroisse St Michel. AJM, Greffe d'Antoine Adhémar. AJQ, Greffes de Guillaume Audouart, Romain Becquet, Louis Chambalon, Pierre Duquet, Michel Fillion, François Genaple, Florent de La Cetière, Gilles Rageot. AN, G⁷, pièce 1312; Col., B, 16; C¹¹ᴬ, 2–22, 125; F²ᴬ, 13; F³, 2. ASQ, C4; C17; Lettres, N; MSS, 20. AQ, NF, Registres de la Prévôté de Québec; Registres divers et pièces détachées du Conseil Supérieur.

Coll. de manuscrits relatifs à la N.-F. Juchereau, *Annales* (Jamet). *Jug. et délib.* Le Blant, *Histoire de la N.-F. Lettres de noblesse* (P.-G. Roy). *Papier terrier de la Cie des I.O.* (P.-G. Roy), 131–36. P.-G. Roy, *Inv. concessions.* Eccles, *Canada under Louis XIV.* Bernard Groethuysen, *L'Église et la bourgeoisie* (Origines de l'esprit bourgeois en France, I, 5ᵉ éd., Paris, 1956). Lanctot, *History of Canada*, I, II. Robert Mandrou, *La France aux XVIIᵉ et XVIIIᵉ siècles* (Paris, 1967). P.-G. Roy, *La famille Aubert de Gaspé* (Lévis, 1907). Guy Frégault, "La Compagnie de la colonie," *Revue de l'université d'Ottawa*, XXX (1960), 5–29, 127–49.

AUBERT DE LA CHESNAYE, FRANÇOIS, seigneur of **Maur** and of **Mille-Vaches,** member of the Conseil Supérieur, director general of the Compagnie de l'Île Saint-Jean; baptized 9 Jan. 1669 at Quebec. He perished at sea off Île Royale (Cape Breton Island) during the night of 27–28 Aug. 1725.

François Aubert was the first child of CHARLES AUBERT de La Chesnaye and his second wife Marie-Louise Juchereau de La Ferté. On 12 April 1695, at Quebec, he married Anne-Ursule Denys de La Ronde, daughter of PIERRE DENYS de La Ronde. He had six children by this marriage. His wife having died on 30 Jan. 1709, he married on 12 Oct. 1711, at Beauport, Marie-Thérèse de La Lande Gayon, widow of PAUL LE MOYNE de Maricourt, who bore him another eight children. She died on 1 May 1738 at Quebec.

As early as 1670 he had become seigneur of Mille-Vaches by a deed of gift. Like his father, he devoted himself to trade. In 1697 he had difficulties with Louis Buade* de Frontenac over an English ship which he had captured on his way back from France. On 29 Oct. 1703 he was installed as a member of the transformed and enlarged Conseil Supérieur. He inherited the seigneury of Maur from his uncle, PAUL-AUGUSTIN JUCHEREAU, in the autumn of 1714.

In 1722 he was director general of the Compagnie de l'Île Saint-Jean (Prince Edward Island), formed by the Comte de Saint-Pierre to develop this island. The aim of this undertaking was not purely commercial, for also in question was the creation of a French colony to replace Acadia, which had fallen into the hands of the English. It was hoped that the Acadians would emigrate to it more readily than to Île Royale, for which they showed little liking. A subdelegate of the intendant, Robert Potier* Dubuisson, had been appointed to the settlement in 1722, with the object of giving it greater autonomy in relation to Île Royale, which was causing loss to the settlement by its competition in fishing. The Comte de Saint-Pierre, a courtier greedy for profit rather than a colonizer, let the company decline, and it found itself contending with both the fishermen from Cape Breton and those from Saint-Malo. François Aubert, the financial director, was soon beset by the creditors. Bankruptcy had to be declared in the autumn of 1724, and Aubert went to France on the *Héros* to be present at the liquidation.

It was while returning to New France the following year on the *Chameau* that he lost his life. The ship went down with all hands off Île Royale. Aubert left his family an inheritance burdened with debt. The Maur seigneury was confiscated and finally adjudged in 1734 to the Hôtel-Dieu of Quebec for 19,000 *livres*; 10,000 were in payment of a debt to the nuns, and the rest went to the heirs of the first seigneur, Jean Juchereau* de Maur. The Hospitallers gave it the name of seigneury of the Poor, since the revenue from it was used to sustain the needy.

LUCIEN CAMPEAU

AJQ, Greffe de Romain Becquet, 2 juillet 1670. AN, Col., C¹¹ᴮ, 7. *Jug. et délib.* A. Roy, *Inv. greffes not.*, XVIII, XIX. Eccles, *Frontenac*, 303–13. Harvey, *French régime in P.E.I.*, 40–55. Lorin, *Le comte de Frontenac*, 471. P.-G. Roy, *La famille Juchereau Duchesnay*.

AUCHAGAH (the name is written thus in La Vérendrye's journal, but is sometimes spelled **Ochagach** or **Ochakah, Ochagac**), a Cree who frequented Fort Kaministiquia, fur trading establishment of Pierre Gaultier* de La Vérendrye; *fl.* 1729.

Questioned by La Vérendrye about means of reaching the fabled "Western Sea," Auchagah sketched for him a map showing, among others, the Grand Portage–Nantoüagan (Pigeon River) route. He evidently held this to be superior to the Kaministiquia River route hitherto followed by the few European travellers who had ventured beyond Lake Superior.

Writing to Beauharnois* de La Boische, governor of New France, in 1729, La Vérendrye calls Auchagah "the man most capable of guiding a party and with whom there would be no fear of our being abandoned on the way." Auchagah agreed to act as guide, though it is not known whether he did accompany La Vérendrye when he journeyed over the suggested route in 1732. The new route pleased the explorer and the Kaministiquia one was thereafter abandoned.

The route suggested by Auchagah thus became the great highway to the northwest. At its eastern end, long the fur traders' rendezvous, there came into being Grand Portage, the imposing western headquarters of the North West Company. In 1783 the Pigeon River became a part of the international boundary, and the commerce of the Northwest reverted to the "all-Canadian" Kaministiquia route.

K. R. MACPHERSON

Copies of Auchagah's map are in the PAC, Map Div., H2-902-1737; the Ayer Collection of the Newberry Library, Chicago; and the Kohl Collection of the Library of Congress. [La Vérendrye], *Journals and letters of La Vérendrye* (Burpee), 52–53. Wis. State Hist. Soc. *Coll.*, XVII, 102–3. J. P. Bertrand, *Highway of destiny; an epic story of Canadian development* (New York, 1959), 79. [Bertrand states that Auchagah guided La Vérendrye across the Lake of the Woods in 1732. This, however, seems doubtful. K.R.M.] L. J. Burpee, *Pathfinders of the great plains; a chronicle of La Vérendrye and his sons* (Toronto, 1914), 15–17. N. M. Crouse, *La Vérendrye, fur trader and explorer* (Toronto and Ithaca, N.Y., 1956), 44–47.

AUGER DE SUBERCASE, DANIEL D', company captain and garrison adjutant in Canada, governor of Placentia (Plaisance), then of Acadia; b. 12 Feb. 1661 at Orthez (department of Basses-Pyrénées), son of Jourdain and Marie or Madeleine de Boyrie, baptized in the Protestant church at Orthez; d. 20 Nov. 1732 at Cannes (now Cannes-L'Écluse, department of Yonne).

The family's original name was Dauger, later changed to d'Auger. Jean Dauger, a rich merchant and *bourgeois* of Nay, in Béarn, purchased several noble estates, including the lay abbey of Subercase, near Asson. By virtue of these holdings he was ennobled on 6 July 1616, and sat in the States of Béarn. His two sons, Jean and Jourdain, inherited his domains.

Daniel first served for some ten years in the land forces, and in 1684 was a captain in the

Auger de Subercase

Régiment de Bretagne. He entered the Marine shortly afterwards, recruited a company of 50 men for Canada, and obtained command of it. No sooner had he landed at Quebec in 1687 than he set off with his contingent on a campaign against the Senecas [see BRISAY de Denonville]. In the summer of 1689, at Verdun, he was in command of a flying column of 200 men. After the Lachine massacre in August, Subercase wanted to pursue the Iroquois, but RIGAUD de Vaudreuil forbad it. The following year he was at Île d'Orléans, to prevent a landing by Phips*. Three years later he was appointed lieutenant-commander, then promoted garrison adjutant in place of Joseph de MONIC, with a gratuity of 500 *livres*. He showed himself very energetic in this post, but his difficult character gave rise to protracted differences with Louis TANTOUIN de La Touche, the commissary of the Marine. In 1696, he took part as adjutant general in the expedition led by Buade* de Frontenac against the Onondagas. The governor and the intendant recommended him to the minister, asking an increase in salary for him and sending him to France to carry their dispatches and report on the state of the troops. He was back in Canada the same year. On 15 Oct. 1700 his name appeared with those of the principal officers of the colony on the list of shareholders of the Compagnie de La Ferme du Roi. On 1 April 1702 he succeeded Monic as governor of Placentia, with 1,700 *livres* by way of salary and gratuity. He immediately went to France in order to settle some personal affairs, and did not take up his post until the following year. Philippe PASTOUR de Costebelle carried on in his absence.

When he arrived at Placentia Subercase found the settlement in a sorry state. Monic, who had been acting governor for five years, had done nothing but quarrel with his officers. The stockade and platforms of the fort were rotten, and the earthworks were collapsing as a result of the action of the sea. The garrison of 150 men had been recruited in haphazard fashion and was poorly armed and poorly housed, and many soldiers were deserting to the enemy. The civil population was continually short of supplies and merchandise, and was exploited by the merchants. Subercase's first concern was to put the colony's defences in order. In August 1703, a few weeks after his arrival, Placentia just managed to escape a siege. First two English ships came to cruise off the coast. Subercase was able to call in the French fishermen in time, and only a few vessels were captured, along with the post of Saint-Pierre. By a raid on Ferryland (Forillon) he then took some prisoners, and learned from them that a fleet of 33 sail, assembled at St John's under the command of

Admiral John GRAYDON, was assigned to attack the French post. On 24 August three ships did in fact come and anchor off Petit Plaisance. But the crew of a Saint-Malo boat captured by the English warned them that the post was prepared to resist. These ships did not venture to attack, and were content to lie in wait for the fishing boats. Finally the arrival of two French warships, the *Juste* and the *Hasardeux*, persuaded them to sail off. With relief, Subercase immediately busied himself with consolidating his positions.

By energetic measures he improved the existence and the morale of the soldiers. During the winter, with the help of the settlers, and by utilizing local materials, he had the fortifications rebuilt, and protected them with a dike. He also concerned himself with providing more food supplies by growing cereals, in order to be able to raise and feed poultry, ewes, and livestock. He had a marsh drained and on it set up kitchen-gardens from which he gathered vegetables to feed the settlers. These resources, added to the hauls of fish, partly made up for the inadequate supplies coming from France.

As soon as he had arrived, Subercase had proposed to the court to attack St John's. The expedition was authorized and prepared in 1704. A party of 100 men, Canadians and Indians, came from Canada, under the command of M. de Beaucourt. With the soldiers of the garrison, the settlers, fishermen, and Indians, the expedition comprised 450 men. Among the officers were Jacques TESTARD de Montigny and Jacques L'HERMITTE, who had been members of the expedition of MOMBETON de Brouillan and PIERRE LE MOYNE d'Iberville in 1696. Delayed by continual rains and supply difficulties, the expedition did not set out until 8 January 1705. A brigantine carrying a mortar and bombs went at the same time to Bay Bulls (Baie des Taureaux). Their progress, in bitterly cold weather, through snow-covered forests traversed by rivers that had to be forded, was extremely laborious. The troops captured Bay Bulls and Petty Harbour (Petit Havre), and on 31 January were a league from St John's. It had been decided to attempt a surprise attack at dawn on 1 February. But the guides were not familiar with the region, the approaches had not been sufficiently reconnoitred, the distance was greater than had been anticipated, and the difficulty of marching in the snow disorganized the troops. The advance guard arrived alone in sight of the fort, and was received with heavy fire. Subercase fell back upon the port and the houses of the little town, which he occupied, together with two batteries, but he did not dare to attack the fort. He waited 33 days in vain for the arrival of the brigantine. At last he decided to try an escalade, but had to give it up in face of the opposition of the Indians and militiamen commanded by John MOODY and Robert LATHAM. As the fishing season was approaching, he had to abandon the siege. However, the governor sent Montigny, with a party of 70 men, to the north of the island, in order to destroy the settlements on Conception and Trinity Bays. All the posts were destroyed as far as Bonavista, except Carbonear. In all the expedition took 1,200 prisoners, who had to be released for want of provisions with which to feed them; only 80 were brought back to Placentia. It had spiked or cast overboard 40 cannon, burned one ship, taken or destroyed 2,000 shallops and 200 wagons. Pillaging yielded only 2,600 *livres* in cash, but Subercase estimated the losses inflicted on the enemy at 4 millions. This havoc could not, however, obliterate the fact that St John's, the centre of resistance, remained intact, and that the campaign had missed its principal objective. The relative want of success nonetheless earned for Subercase the minister's congratulations, tempered with a note of regret.

Subercase's expedition brought a little relief to the colony. The English prisoners were welcome reinforcements for the fishermen, and the morale of the troops was restored in consequence. Subercase, with the help of masons from France, had part of the fort rebuilt in stone. He also encouraged the organizing of privateering crews, made up of Canadians, young adventurers from Placentia, and Micmacs from Cape Breton Island. These parties harassed the English settlements, both by sea and by land. A census of 1705 mentions 450 settlers, distributed throughout the various French posts in Newfoundland. Several settlers, including the governor himself, maintained large fisheries; a few merchants were trading with Canada, and the first steps were being taken to organize agriculture. The governor planned to establish a hospital, in order to look after the sick from the town and from the fishing vessels; he proposed to put the Religious Hospitallers of Quebec in charge of it, and to provide for its maintenance by imposing a levy of a hundredweight of cod per vessel. Thus, despite the war, the colony gradually grew stronger, although its existence was still precarious. The material and moral conditions of life had improved. Finally, a new phenomenon, relations between the governor and the officers were harmonious. Order and peace prevailed in this strangely mixed population composed of soldiers, fishermen, privateers, and Indians. These results were due in large measure to the governor's energy, courage, and devotion to the king's service. It was no doubt this meritorious

conduct that the court wished to reward in making him a knight of the order of Saint-Louis in 1705, and in granting him, on 10 April 1706, the governorship of Acadia, which had been vacant since Brouillan's death.

The new governor landed at Port-Royal (Annapolis Royal, N.S.) on 28 October. By his conciliatory attitude he made an excellent impression on SIMON-PIERRE DENYS de Bonaventure, the colony's administrator, and on Mathieu de GOUTIN, but he found the colony in a woeful state. Everything was in short supply, and he had to have stockings and shoes for the officers bought secretly in Boston. In order to meet his needs and those of the administration, he borrowed 1,000 *livres* and made 6,000 *livres* worth of card money. The fort, eroded by the rains, caved in in three places. A wrangling spirit pervaded the population and the garrison, while the English were constantly threatening the colony with their privateers and warships, which cruised unchallenged near the coasts. Reviving the ideas of Brouillan and Bonaventure, Subercase proposed to populate the east coast, build a strong fort there, and even transport the capital there. He requested gifts for the Indians and the appointment of a French officer, BERNARD-ANSELME D'ABBADIE de Saint-Castin, to command them. During the autumn he had the fortifications repaired and the frigate *Biche* completed, and asked Quebec for a crew and more troops. The following spring Vaudreuil did indeed send him 60 Canadians, both sailors and soldiers. These reinforcements came at the right moment, for on 6 June (26 May, o.s.), the day after their arrival, Colonel John MARCH, coming from Boston with some 20 ships and 1,600 men, appeared at the entry to the Port-Royal basin.

Their numerical superiority gave the assailants cause to hope for an easy victory. But the governor organized the defence energetically: he summoned all the settlers to the fort, sent several parties to harry the enemy, and led several sallies himself. During one of them he had his horse killed under him. These skirmishes caused fairly severe losses to the enemy. However, they had prepared entrenchments, and on 16 June they attempted an assault which was checked by the artillery of the fort. At the same time Saint-Castin, at the head of a band of 35 settlers and Abenakis, succeeded in trapping in an ambush a party that was busy setting fire to some houses, and he himself killed 10 or 12 men. This foray, added to the rumour of a big gathering of 300 to 400 settlers and some 100 Indians, robbed the besiegers of any courage they had left. They returned to their ships and weighed anchor. The beleaguered fort's only casualties were one man killed and a few wounded. The

Auger de Subercase

assailants had lost 40 to 50 men, but they had wrought considerable havoc by burning down many houses, killing livestock, and uprooting grain and crops.

The respite that followed was of short duration. The governor of Boston, Dudley, was not prepared to accept the humiliation of this set-back. He persuaded his council to send reinforcements of 600 men to March, and ordered him to resume the attack. The fleet, with some additional units, therefore re-appeared before Port-Royal on 20 August, and effected a landing on the opposite shore. Colonel Wainwright, a commander under March's orders, then had encampments set up opposite and above the fort, with the intention of forcing a way through. Subercase immediately sent a party of Indians and settlers which surprised the advance guard, killed six of its men, and took two prisoners. For its part the garrison cannonaded the positions of the enemy so vigorously that it forced them to withdraw into the woods. They then went down again towards their ships, and a large detachment crossed the river. Saint-Castin, posted in that spot with some 60 Abenakis, greeted them with several volleys of musket shots, and before the superiority of numbers withdrew slowly, sniping as he went. In order to prevent an assault on the fort, Subercase went out with 250 men and had solid retrenchments built at the Ruisseau du Moulin (Allain River). Before this obstacle the enemy hesitated, and began to fall back. Le Poupet de La Boularderie and Saint-Castin rushed forward with 60 men to cut off their retreat, and accidentally ended up in the midst of a much larger band which was resting in a field of grain. A sharp hand-to-hand tussle followed, with axes and musket butts, during which La Boularderie and Saint-Castin were wounded, together with some 15 of their companions. The ensign Antoine de Saillans, seriously wounded, died a few days later. In that day alone the enemy had lost 120 men. They remained a few more days without attempting anything, and, as the French were constantly receiving fresh reinforcements of Indians and settlers, they feared they might be taken in the rear and re-embarked on 1 September. Subercase, in appreciation of his conduct during these two sieges, received from the court a gratuity of 2,000 *livres*, which was later changed into a pension of 600 *livres*.

The following autumn was rather difficult at Port-Royal. The two sieges had ruined a good number of settlers, for whom the governor vainly sought an indemnity. The supply ship *Loire* brought no goods. The governor was forced to give his sheets and shirts to the sick, and to sell his silver table-service to pay for repairs to the fort.

In 1708 and 1709 France, sorely tried by reverses in Europe, could not send any substantial reinforcements: the new recruits were mere children, two-thirds of the muskets exploded in one's hands, and the soldiers and officers no longer received their pay. Subercase was fortunately able to obtain the help of the Saint-Domingue privateers, particularly that of Pierre Morpain*, who brought provisions, cloth, and ammunition to Port-Royal. Saint-Castin and the governor himself fitted out ships for privateering and took prizes. But this privateering brought reprisals, and a heavy raid from the direction of Canada, headed by Jean-Baptiste Hertel de Rouville, further alarmed the English colonies. Samuel Vetch and Francis Nicholson went to England to ask for help, and were well received. Subercase, foreseeing fresh attacks, also asked France for assistance. The minister replied to him that the treasury was empty, and that "the king would abandon the colony if it continues to be such a burden." Settlers and soldiers had the impression of being forsaken by their king, who no longer even paid his debts. Discontent and discord once again spread like a disease. Clergy and officers denounced the governor to the court, accusing him of imposing his arbitration in the settlement of lawsuits, misusing his authority, and tolerating libertinage and over-indulgence in intoxicating liquors. On his side Subercase complained of his officers: one of the captains was weak in the head, another was clearly out of his mind; others were dishonest or negligent, the engineer was an eccentric, and the governor declared that he would have "as much need of a madhouse as of barracks." An epidemic of purpura decimated Port-Royal and was the final blow to the morale of the population.

It was in these circumstances that on 5 Oct. 1710 General Francis Nicholson's fleet appeared before Port-Royal. It comprised a landing force of 2,000 men (3,400 according to Subercase), made up of one regiment of English regulars and four regiments of militiamen raised by Massachusetts, Connecticut, Rhode Island, and New Hampshire, and carried in 36 vessels, 7 of which were warships. Subercase had fewer than 300 men to set against them: about 150 soldiers of the garrison, some 100 militiamen, a few Canadians, and some privateers. The Indians, ill rewarded for their help in the earlier sieges and dissatisfied with the low price offered by the French for their beaver furs, kept their distance. The English disembarked on both sides of the river, and Subercase, unsure of his soldiers, did not dare attempt a sortie; no one would have come back! The English immediately marched on the fort; but brisk artillery fire checked their advance. They had to take cover, dig trenches, mount batteries, in short undertake a regular siege. After a few days they succeeded in setting up a battery, sheltered from the French fire, on ground of a different level; from there they cannonaded the fort, and a galliot hurled bombs into it for several nights. This bombardment had a disastrous effect on the morale of the besieged. CHARLES DE SAINT-ÉTIENNE de La Tour was seriously wounded, and a bomb blew off a corner of the powder magazine. The panic-stricken settlers asked the governor to surrender, and that very evening five soldiers and 50 militiamen deserted. The next day Subercase convened a council of officers, and all were of the opinion that they should ask for a capitulation. On his side, Nicholson sent a summons to surrender. Subercase, while refusing to acknowledge the alleged rights contained in this summons, accepted the principle of a surrender. There was an exchange of hostages and envoys, and the capitulation was discussed and signed on 13 October. This capitulation, a fairly liberal one, granted the honours of war; the governor could retain, at his choice, six cannon and two mortars; the settlers within a radius of three miles, by taking an oath of allegiance, could keep their possessions and remain; otherwise they had two years in which to withdraw. The garrison, made up of 156 soldiers, came out with drums beating and flags flying, and dragging a small mortar. Honour was saved, but the sight of these starving soldiers in rags and tatters, many of whom were no more than adolescents, saddened even the victors. As he handed over the keys of the fort to Nicholson, Subercase expressed the hope of returning to pay him a visit the following spring! Colonel Vetch assumed command of the fort, with a garrison of 450 men. The French garrison, the civil officials, and a few families, amounting to a little over 250 persons, sailed for France on three ships; they reached Nantes on 1 December. Subercase, accused of negligence by some officers, and reprimanded by Vaudreuil and the minister, was summoned before a court martial at Rochefort, but rapidly acquitted.

In the first months of 1711, Pontchartrain, belatedly convinced of Acadia's importance, outlined vague plans for retaking Port-Royal. To this end he wanted to send Subercase to serve at Quebec under Vaudreuil's orders, while continuing to pay his salary as governor. But Subercase refused in disgust. Two years later the treaty of Utrecht ceded Acadia to England for good. We know little about the years which followed Subercase's return to France. He retired from the service and lived on his estates in Béarn.

In 1716 the minister wrote to François de Beauharnois* de La Boische, asking him to consult Subercase in order to prepare new plans for the recapture of Acadia. In 1719 Subercase was living at Jurançon, near Pau. He continued to draw a captain's pension of 600 *livres* a year. He died on 20 Nov. 1732 at Cannes, in the department of Yonne. A ledger-stone marks his grave in the church of this village. He had married Marie-Anne Du Bourget and had had one son, for whom, in a letter of 1707, he requested an ensign's commission. He also had several nephews, one of whom, called the "Chevalier de Subercase," served for some time under his orders at Placentia before returning to Béarn. Subercase was the last and probably the most remarkable governor of French Acadia.

RENÉ BAUDRY

AN, Col., B, 11–32; C¹¹ᶜ, 4–5; C¹¹ᴰ, 5–7; Marine, B², 167, f.122; 223, f.595; Section Outre-Mer, Dépôt des fortifications des colonies, carton 2, nos.67–68; G³, 2053, pièce 14. BN, MS, Clairambault 1307, f.48; Fr. 10207, f.205.

Charlevoix, *History* (Shea), IV, V. *Coll. de manuscrits relatifs à la N.-F.*, I, II. "Correspondance de Frontenac (1689–99)," APQ *Rapport, 1927–28, 1928–29*. "Journal of Colonel Nicholson at the capture of Annapolis, 1710," N.S. Hist. Soc. *Coll.*, I (1878), 59ff. *Mémoires des commissaires*, II, 340; IV, 444–45; *Memorials of the English and French commissaries*, I, 627. *NYCD* (O'Callaghan and Fernow), IX, 853, 927. Penhallow, *Hist. of wars with Eastern Indians* (1824), 55, 62ff. PAC *Report, 1899*, Supp., 26. PRO, *B.T.Journal, 1704–1708/9, 1708/9–1714/15*. See also the account of the August 1707 attack from the *Gazette de France* (Paris), 25 Feb. 1708, reproduced at the end of Dièreville's *Relation of voyage to Port Royal* (Webster), 318–20.

Brebner, *New England's outpost*. La Morandière, *Hist. de la pêche française de la morue*, I, 491–501, 502–3. Lanctot, *Histoire du Canada*, II, 144. Lauvrière, *La tragédie d'un peuple*. Parkman, *A half-century of conflict*, ch.6. Rameau de Saint-Père, *Une colonie féodale*, I, 329–55. Robert Rumilly, *Histoire des Acadiens* (2v., Montréal, [1955]), I, 174–91. Waller, *Samuel Vetch*. "Daniel Auger, sieur de Subercase," *BRH*, XVI (1910), 176–81. Robert Le Blant, "Daniel d'Auger de Subercase, Gouverneur de Plaisance, 1703–5," *NF*, VII (1932), 1–80; "Dauger de Subercaze," in *DBF*; "Nobilière du Béarn," *Revue hist. et archéol. du Béarn*, 1940. É.-Z. Massicotte, "Les familles de Sabrevois, Sabrevois de Sermonville et Sabrevois de Bleury," *BRH*, XXX (1924), 107. P.-G. Roy, "Daniel Auger de Subercase," *BRH*, XXIII (1917), 55.

AULNEAU (de La Touche), JEAN-PIERRE, priest, Jesuit; b. 21 April 1705 at Moûtiers-sur-le-Lay (department of Vendée); d. 8 June 1736.

Father Aulneau was the eldest of a family of five

children. One of his brothers was a Jesuit; another, Michel, was a Sulpician, and his only sister was a nun at Fontenay. He studied at the seminary of Luçon, then on 12 Dec. 1720 he entered the noviciate at Bordeaux. He studied philosophy at Pau (1722–25), where he taught for a year, then he was a teacher at La Rochelle (1726–28) and Poitiers (1728–30). He studied theology in Poitiers (1730–34). On 12 Aug. 1734, already a priest, he landed at Quebec, after a difficult crossing on the *Ruby*. On 15 August he was laid low by the illness that had wrought havoc on the ship, and on two occasions he was near death's door. When he had recovered his health, he prepared for his theological examinations at the Jesuit college in Quebec and passed them during Lent the following year.

Father Aulneau was assigned to accompany those who were searching for the western sea, towards which La Vérendrye [Gaultier*] had begun to make his way. He was instructed to search out "new natives never seen before." He was averse to leaving without the help of another priest, but he set out at the beginning of June 1735 to join La Vérendrye at Montreal. After spending two weeks at Sault-Saint-Louis with his friend, Father François Nau, he left Montreal on 21 June with the explorer. On 27 July he left Michilimackinac after an eight-day halt. Three hundred leagues of the journey were to a great extent covered in the midst of smoke and flames from a forest fire that had been lit by the Indians. On 23 October they finally landed at Fort Saint-Charles, which had been built in 1732. The post stood on the west shore of Lake of the Woods, in Cree country. The Assiniboins occupied another part of the same lake.

Father Aulneau was supposed to go on with the Assiniboins until they reached a tribe that was still unknown to the French, the Kaotiouaks or Ouantchipouanes, who were later called the Mandans. These Indians were said to be sedentary. They lived 250 leagues farther west, grew corn, owned horses, and hunted the buffalo. Their skin was white, and they were known for their gentleness. The Jesuit was supposed to learn their language and supply information concerning them.

In the spring of 1736 La Vérendrye sent his eldest son, JEAN-BAPTISTE [GAULTIER], to Michilimackinac with 19 men to get supplies. Father Aulneau went with them, to visit Father Saint-Pé. On the first evening of their trip, 8 June 1736, the party stopped for the night on an island in Lake of the Woods. A band of Sioux took them by surprise. They were all massacred and decapitated. The bodies were found on 20 June by some Frenchmen. On 17 September La Vérendrye had the bodies of his son and the missionary, together with the heads of the others, brought for burial in the chapel of Fort Saint-Charles. This disaster put an end to the project of a mission to the Mandans.

LUCIEN CAMPEAU

"Lettres du père Aulneau," APQ *Rapport, 1926–27*, 259–330. Le Jeune, *Dictionnaire*, I, 98f.; II, 112–16. Rochemonteix, *Les Jésuites et la N.-F. au XVIIIe siècle*, I, 212–25. Paul Desjardins, "Le projet de mission du Père Aulneau chez les Mandanes," SCHEC *Rapport, 1948–49*, 55–69.

AUTEUIL DE MONCEAUX, FRANÇOIS-MADELEINE-FORTUNÉ RUETTE D'. *See* RUETTE

AVAUGOUR, LOUIS D', Jesuit priest, missionary; b. 1669 in France; d. 4 Feb. 1732 at Paris.

Louis d'Avaugour entered the Society of Jesus at Paris in 1696 when he was 27, an unusually advanced age for entrance, which generally took place about age 17. Avaugour completed his noviciate (1696–98), and then came to Quebec before receiving holy orders. He was tonsured and given minor orders by Bishop Saint-Vallier [LA CROIX] in the chapel of the Quebec seminary on 19 Sept. 1699. It is not known when he was raised to the priesthood.

Father Avaugour's first active missionary work appears to have been done at Lorette where he was stationed some time before 1710. He soon acquired a penetrating insight into the character of the Huron Indians and in 1710 submitted a lengthy report on the state of that mission to Father Joseph GERMAIN, superior of the Jesuits in Canada. This document describes in intimate detail the daily life of the Huron Christians at Lorette and inveighs with stinging asperity against those who debauched the Indians with spirits. Avaugour warned that drunkenness among the Indians would not only cause them to reject Christianity, but also in the long run cause the loss of the colony to France.

About 1720 Father Avaugour was sent to the Illinois mission where he laboured until shortly before 1726 when he was recalled to France to assume the office of procurator in Paris for the Jesuits in Canada and Louisiana. The post was a particularly difficult one during the years he held it. Towards the end of the 18th century the French Jesuits had been given charge of missions in China, Constantinople, Martinique, and Santo Domingo. These newly assigned fields drained off much of the Jesuit manpower which might otherwise have been sent to New France. The lack of adequate recruits was felt chiefly in the mission area of the present state of Maine, where the activity of the English tended to disrupt the Jesuits' efforts among the Abenakis and other tribes which had been traditionally loyal to France.

In Louisiana the Jesuits became involved in a none too edifying controversy with the Capuchins. Father Nicolas-Ignace de Beaubois*, Jesuit superior in the colony of Louisiana, quite imprudently offended Father Raphael, superior of the Capuchins, by officiating at religious functions at New Orleans without permission of Father Raphael, who was the vicar-general of the bishop of Quebec for that area. When the colonists took sides in the controversy, the matter was referred to France and Father Avaugour, as procurator in Paris for the French Jesuits in North America, was obliged to intervene. After continuing for several years, the rather undignified dispute was solved by the recall of Beaubois in 1728.

Father Avaugour died at Paris on 4 Feb. 1732.

JOSEPH P. DONNELLY, S.J.

Caron, "Inventaire de documents," APQ *Rapport, 1939–40*, 348; *1940–41*, 425, 428; *1941–42*, 219, 226, 236, 245, 251, 259. *JR* (Thwaites), LXVI, 146–73. Delanglez, *French Jesuits in Louisiana*. O'Neill, *Church and state in Louisiana*. Rochemonteix, *Les Jésuites et la N.-F. au XVIIe siècle*, III, 678–87; *Les Jésuites et la N.-F. au XVIIIe siècle*, I, 133–39, 273–314.

AVENEAU, CLAUDE, Jesuit, missionary; b. 25 Dec. 1650 at Laval (department of Mayenne); d. 14 Sept. 1711 at Quebec.

Claude Aveneau entered the noviciate in Paris in 1669. Two years later he was appointed to the Jesuit college in Arras, where he taught for seven years. He then studied philosophy for a year at the Collège Louis-le-Grand in Paris and did four years of theology at Bourges, where he was ordained a priest in 1683. After the third year of his noviciate at Rouen, he left for Canada in 1685.

He was first sent to the mission at Sillery. The following year he was assigned to the mission to the Ottawas of the Great Lakes. The Jesuits had also just opened a mission for the Miamis, who had taken refuge at the mission of Saint-Joseph (in Michigan). It was there that from 1689 on Father Aveneau spent the better part of his life. In 1702 he incurred the displeasure of Cadillac [LAUMET], the commandant at Detroit. Cadillac had had the higher authorities approve a project of his to found at Detroit a post which would be larger than the one at Montreal, and where the whites and the various Indian tribes of the region would live in perfect harmony. It was first necessary to attract the Indians to the post. And it was at this point that Cadillac's noble plan proved unrealistic. For the most part, the Indians did not feel drawn towards Detroit. Moreover, taught by experience, the missionaries considered the Frenchifying of the Indians, their living together with the whites, and the brandy trade to be disastrous for their apostolate. Cadillac accused them of having prevented his plan from being realized. The only documents that we have concerning the matter are by Cadillac, and it is known that he was not always trustworthy. We know that Cadillac, feeling the Miamis from the St Joseph river were too slow in coming, blamed Aveneau, removed him from his post, and replaced him by a Recollet who did not speak the language and did not have the confidence of the faithful. The result was disturbances and opposition by the Miamis to the French. In 1708 Governor Vaudreuil [RIGAUD] and Intendant RAUDOT reported Cadillac's misuse of authority to the minister. Father Aveneau returned to the Miamis, and order was restored.

In 1711, as Father Aveneau was very ill, it was decided to send him to Quebec to recover his health. It was a deplorable necessity, to force a 300-mile trip by canoe upon a man who was already exhausted. He died at Quebec on 14 Sept. 1711. Father Joseph GERMAIN, who wrote the account of his life, praised his patience, his fortitude, and his charity towards all, friend and foe alike.

LÉON POULIOT, S.J.

ASJCF, 492. "Correspondance de Vaudreuil," APQ *Rapport, 1939–40*, 451. *Découvertes et établissements des Français* (Margry), V, 239. *JR* (Thwaites), LXIII, 302. George Paré, *The Catholic Church in Detroit, 1701–1888* (Detroit, 1951), 78–140. Rochemonteix, *Les Jésuites et la N.-F. au XVIIe siècle*, III, 477, 512ff.; *Les Jésuites et la N.-F. au XVIIIe siècle*, I, 65ff.

AWANANO (Awenano). *See* AOUENANO

AWENEMWET. *See* WENEMOUET

B

BACQUEVILLE DE LA POTHERIE, CLAUDE-CHARLES LE ROY DE LA POTERIE, *dit. See* LE ROY

BALEY (Bayly, Bayley), HENRY, HBC captain and governor; d. 20 Dec. 1701.

After serving as chief mate to Captain Leonard

Baptiste

Edgcombe*, Baley was given command of the company's fireship, *Prosperous*, in 1692. In the summer of the same year he sailed to Hudson Bay as part of the expedition under James KNIGHT to recover the James Bay posts, which had been in the hands of the French since 1686. Baley, who was wounded in action when Albany was retaken in the summer of 1693, was recommended by Knight for "behaving himself well." He returned to England that year in the *Royal Hudson's Bay* (Capt. Michael GRIMINGTON). In 1694 Baley commanded the *Dering* [III] to and from the bay, calling both at York, where Thomas Walsh was governor, and at Albany. Later that year York surrendered to the French.

Baley did not return to the bay until 1696 when he was again in command of the *Dering* in the expedition, comprising ships of both HBC and the Royal Navy, organized to recapture York Fort. The fort was taken in August of the same year, and in accordance with his instructions Baley assumed the governorship. The triumph was short-lived. York was to fall into French hands again the following summer. After PIERRE LE MOYNE d'Iberville had beaten the English ships in the bay, he opened fire on York Fort; Baley did not capitulate immediately, but sought to arouse the fighting spirit of his men by promising £40 to their widows—an offer that did not meet with enthusiasm. He then sent two men—one of them Henry KELSEY—to negotiate surrender terms with Iberville. The English request to keep the company's beaver was not granted, but otherwise the conditions of surrender were mild, and the governor was accorded all the honours of war. Baley arrived back in London in December 1697.

The following year he was assigned to the *Pery* and sailed to Albany. He served in James Bay under Knight, spending part of the time on the East Main. In 1700 Baley commanded the *Pery* on the return trip to England. He remained in the company's employ in London until his death on 20 Dec. 1701. He left his widow, Judith, sole executrix of his will.

MAUD M. HUTCHESON

HBC Arch. A.1/19–25; A.6/5; A.14/6; A.15/5. HBRS, XX (Rich and Johnson); XXV (Davies and Johnson). *Kelsey papers* (Doughty and Martin).

BAPTISTE, PIERRE MAISONNAT, *dit.* See MAISONNAT

BARAT. *See* BARRAT

BARBAUCANNES (Barbocant), PHILIPPE ÉNAULT (Esnault, Hénaut) DE. *See* ÉNAULT

BARBEL, JACQUES, soldier, merchant, seigneur, clerk of court, secretary to the intendant Michel Bégon*, seigneurial judge, and royal notary; b. *c.* 1670 at Le Havre-de-Grâce, in the diocese of Rouen, son of Charles Barbel and Catherine Provost; d. at Quebec, where he was buried 30 July 1740 in the church of the Recollets.

To give an exact account of Barbel's astonishing activity and his omnipresence in the region of Quebec from 1703 on, a whole book would have to be devoted to him, although it was some time before he began to be noticed. It is evident that he was very young when he arrived in the colony, since he had already turned up at Quebec on 17 Nov. 1687, at the signing of the marriage contract between François Dumas and Marie de Montmainier. He was at that time a sergeant of the garrison. Then we lose sight of him until he reappears in 1698, when he married Louise-Renée Toupin on 5 November at Beauport. Suddenly, in 1700, he became almost famous: on 20 April Louis XIV himself had granted him a commission as royal notary at Montreal. But what is more surprising still is that Barbel remained at Quebec, without availing himself of his appointment. In 1703, according to François-Madeleine-Fortuné de RUETTE d'Auteuil, he was a "domestic" in the king's warehouses, although this expression should not be taken literally.

The year 1703, however, rich in various events, was to mark a turning-point in Barbel's career that might have been disastrous. On 27 January his wife was buried, leaving him with three children. The youngest, a few days old, passed away soon afterwards, probably struck down, like his mother, by the smallpox epidemic. Among the many victims was Alexandre PEUVRET de Gaudarville, whose widow, Marie-Anne Gaultier de Comporté, Barbel "seduced" and "made pregnant." Everyone cried scandal: Barbel had taken advantage of the "dismay" and "solitude" of a widow who was still a minor. IGNACE JUCHEREAU Duchesnay, Peuvret's brother-in-law, dragged Barbel before the courts, but the affair petered out in the registry of the Conseil Souverain. According to Ruette d'Auteuil, the new governor Philippe de RIGAUD de Vaudreuil protected Barbel. *Lettres de cachet* were issued from France against the guilty pair; this time it is believed to have been JACQUES RAUDOT who suppressed the proceedings. Shortly before this liaison was known, it is probable (although Ruette d'Auteuil affirmed the contrary), Barbel had been appointed seneschal judge of Lauson, 12 May 1703, and on 4 June royal notary at Quebec. Finally, quickly forgetting his fleeting love affair, Barbel married again on 26 November; his second wife was Marie-Anne Le Picart. Truth to tell, the scandal was not the first that the colony had known, and was of short duration.

From the time of his second appointment as royal notary, Barbel, who had made only two brief appearances, in 1700, before the Conseil Souverain, began an active career as a legal practitioner; as an attorney, he regularly represented parties in their absence, or if need be assisted them. It even happened that, at the same session of the council, he conducted two or three cases simultaneously. Barbel was often opposed to the notary Florent de LA CETIÈRE, representing the other side, and on 5 Dec. 1707 he accused La Cetière of having acted on certain occasions for both defendant and plaintiff at once, and furthermore of being sometimes involved in the same actions as clerk of court and process-server, which proved to be correct. Several times Barbel acted as a guardian, and still more often as an elected syndic or trustee for estates in abeyance, among others those of CHARLES AUBERT de La Chesnaye, Nicolas Volant, and Olivier MOREL de La Durantaye. In these various capacities, he often appeared before the courts and concluded numerous settlements.

Already seneschal judge of Lauson, a royal notary, and a prominent legal practitioner at Quebec, Barbel was on the way to other offices: on 22 Aug. 1712 he was appointed judge of bailiff's court of the Beaupré seigneury, and the following 27 August court clerk of the officiality, a post which he still held in 1725; on 15 Sept. 1714 and again in 1716, he was said to be secretary to Michel Bégon; in addition he was chief court clerk of the Conseil Supérieur from 8 Feb. 1721 to October 1722, and acting clerk of the provost court of Quebec from 31 Aug. 1725 to 23 April 1726; furthermore, Bégon having empowered Pierre HAIMARD to be in charge as king's attorney in the provost court of Quebec in the event of the occupant's absence, Barbel was himself appointed, on 22 June 1716, as Haimard's deputy. All things considered, a fine judicial career for a man who in 1703 had almost experienced to his own detriment the rigours of the law!

Barbel was moreover a merchant, concerning himself with maritime trade, and a seigneur as well. In 1710 he was the owner of a brigantine, the *Saint-Antoine*, and in 1719 of another ship, the *Aimable*. Perhaps he travelled to France in 1711–12, when he was said to be "absent," on business. Be that as it may, like all his *confrères*, he had difficulty recovering moneys owing to him, but he knew how to avenge himself by not paying his own debts. Perhaps to acquire prestige, he bought the arriere-fief of Argentenay, on the Île d'Orléans, in two lots: one from Joseph Perrot on 10 March 1716, and the other from Bertrand Perrot on 27 March 1722. His title of seigneur brought him little but trouble. On 19 Oct. 1716 his fief was seized in accordance with feudal law by Guillaume GAILLARD, the seigneur of Île d'Orléans, and Barbel had to plead his case over a long period in order to obtain replevin. Then in 1726 some of his furniture was seized from his home; the same thing was done in 1728 by the merchant Louis Bazil*, who also had put up for auction three pieces of land in the fief that belonged to Barbel; they brought in 995 *livres*. In 1732, in their turn, the Hospitallers of the Hôtel-Dieu actually seized the arriere-fief, but Barbel extricated himself from this difficulty somehow or other. After his death, Argentenay was finally adjudged by law, on 13 Oct. 1744, to Pierre Trottier* Desauniers.

In 1739 Barbel had resigned from his office as judge of the Beaupré seigneury, but had retained that of royal notary. At that time he was living in Rue Saint-Louis, in the house where Montcalm* later died. This house had to be given up by Barbel's family after his death, because they were unable to pay the arrears of rent with which it was burdened. Barbel's estate was moreover so encumbered that his heirs accepted it only without liability to debts beyond the assets descended. Barbel was survived by his third wife, Marie-Madeleine Amiot, whom he had married 22 Oct. 1719, and seven children, out of the 15 that he had had by his first two marriages. His registry contained 1,361 minutes, and the mere list of the documents found at his house, relative to lawsuits with which he had been concerned, fills 18 notebooks of 24 pages each.

Jacques Barbel had undoubtedly a good deal of ambition and energy, and an incredible capacity for work, but, as the proverb says, grasp all lose all.

ANDRÉ VACHON

AAQ, Registres d'insinuation B, 187. AJM, Greffe d'Antoine Adhémar; Registres des audiences (1709), 385f., 397, 400, 403, 406, 440. AJQ, Greffe de Jacques Barbel, 1703–40; Greffe de Claude Barolet, 29 déc. 1740, 3 févr. 1741; Greffe de Louis Chambalon, 21 mars 1703, 25 oct. 1710; Greffe d'Étienne Dubreuil, 20 avril 1716; Greffe de François Genaple, 24 oct. 1698, 22, 24 nov. 1703; Greffe de J.-C. Louet, 22 oct. 1719, 22 mars, 25 juillet 1722, 19 avril, 11 juillet 1723, 25 nov. 1728, 6 nov. 1732; Greffe de J.-C. Panet, 16 mai 1749; Greffe de Gilles Rageot, 17 nov. 1687; Greffe de Pierre Rivet, 10 mars 1716. AQ, NF, Coll. de pièces jud. et not., 2020, 2040½; NF, Ins. Cons. sup., V, 53, 135v. et seq.; NF, Ins. de la Prév. de Québec, II, 107–9, 176; III, 342; NF, Ord. des int., VI, 249f.; VII½, 34; IX, 1. ASQ, Paroisse de Québec, 4; Polygraphie,

Barbier

XXI, 64; XXII, 40; Séminaire, XX, O, 10, 29; XXI; XXV, 18.

Édits ord., II, 526f. *Jug. et délib.*, IV, V, VI. "Lettres et mémoires de F.-M.-F. Ruette d'Auteuil," 18–20, 55. *Ord. comm.* (P.-G. Roy), II, 314f. Recensement de Québec, 1716 (Beaudet). P.-G. Roy, *Inv. concessions*, I, 97–100; *Inv. jug. et délib., 1716–1760.* Gareau, "La prévôté de Québec," 120ff. Godbout, "Nos ancêtres," APQ *Rapport, 1953–55*, 473ff. P.-G. Roy, "Les secrétaires des gouverneurs et intendants de la Nouvelle-France," *BRH*, XLI (1935), 100. Jean Langevin, *Notes sur les archives de N.-D. de Beauport* (2v., Québec, 1860–63), I, 62f. J.-E. Roy, *Histoire du notariat.* P.-G. Roy, *L'Île d'Orléans* (Québec, 1928), 101f. P.-B. Casgrain, "La maison d'Arnoux où Montcalm est mort," *BRH*, IX (1903), 8–11.

BARBIER, MARIE, *dite* **de l'Assomption,** sister of the Congrégation de Notre-Dame; baptized 1 May 1663, daughter of Gilbert Barbier, *dit* Le Minime, master carpenter, surveyor, seigneurial attorney and churchwarden of the parish of Ville-Marie, and of Catherine de La Vau; d. 19 May 1739.

We are partially familiar with Marie Barbier's youth through the letters which she wrote to her director, Charles de GLANDELET. She relates to him, among other things, her youthful vanities, the intervention of the Virgin who saved her from an attempted rape, and various mystical experiences she underwent. From the age of 14 she was a boarder and perhaps an "aspirant" with the Sisters of the Congrégation de Notre-Dame, since in 1679 she was admitted as a novice and in 1684 her religious profession was confirmed by a "donation *inter vivos*." She was the first Montreal woman to enter the congregation of Marguerite Bourgeoys*.

During her probationary period she offered up special devotion to the Infant Jesus, on the recommendation of a preacher. This somewhat naïve theologian claimed that such devotion was very effective in obtaining forgiveness of sins, for children, he said, never harbour resentment. Marie's sense of guilt over her peccadillos of the past, and her simple faith, therefore led her to maintain a constant dialogue with the Holy Child. He became her recourse and help in daily tasks, so much so that she put him "in charge" of the bread when her duties summoned her elsewhere. According to Abbé Glandelet, this trust enabled Marie to accomplish the most extraordinary feats: sick people who ate rolls "shaped like a round flat biscuit" and made in honour of the Infant Jesus were cured; flour and other provisions were multiplied in times of scarcity; a storm which flooded the granary containing this flour left it intact; a fire on Île d'Orléans was stopped. The Congrégation de Notre-Dame has had restored a primitive picture of the Infant Jesus that tradition still associates with Sister Barbier's name.

In 1685 Marie Barbier, accompanied by Sister Mayrand, went to the parish of Sainte-Famille on Île d'Orléans and founded a school. In 1686 she was recalled to Quebec, and took part in the founding of the almshouse of La Providence. Bishop Saint-Vallier [LA CROIX] had conceived this project after being delighted with the similar institution established by Marguerite Bourgeoys at Ville-Marie.

Marie Barbier returned to Île d'Orléans in 1689 and remained there until she left for Ville-Marie in 1691. In the following year, 1692, she was appointed assistant, and in 1693 became superior, succeeding Mother Bourgeoys; she remained in office until 1698. Shortly after her election she came into conflict with Bishop Saint-Vallier over the rule of the congregation. Saint-Vallier, incapable of conceiving that a nun might have a life which extended beyond the cloister, rewrote Sister Bourgeoys' original rule. Several articles, inapplicable to a teaching congregation working in a developing colony, could be followed only in a cloister. The prelate came expressly to Ville-Marie to impose on the nuns solemn vows, the payment of a dowry, and also a special vow of obedience to the bishop. He even threatened to require from them a written acceptance of his proposals. They succeeded, however, in persuading Bishop Saint-Vallier to postpone the enforcement of the ruling until after his return from France, where he was to consult M. Louis Tronson, the superior of the Sulpicians in Paris. The council of the congregation, under Marie Barbier's guidance, sent a very detailed petition to Tronson. The latter prevailed upon the bishop to accept some changes, but the revision took four years. The rule of 1698 did, however, preserve some articles decreed by the prelate.

In 1700 Marie Barbier had to enter the Hôtel-Dieu of Quebec, "to be cured ... of a cancer in her breast." She had developed the tumour following an excessively harsh penance, when she was wearing under her dress, near the breast, an instrument with iron points. Michel SARRAZIN, "as skilful a surgeon as he was a clever doctor," performed the surgical operation on 29 May—perhaps the first operation for cancer in Canada. Mother JUCHEREAU de Saint-Ignace tells us in the *Annales* that Marie Barbier "returned to Montreal, completely cured."

After that Sister Barbier occupied several administrative posts while continuing to teach and work until her death, on 19 May 1739; she was 76.

Marie Barbier knew how to inflict great

suffering on herself; so excessive were some of her penances that she was to regret them. It is to be noted that in the petition against the 1694 rule she asked that no mortification of the flesh be imposed, urging that this should be an individual choice made by each sister on the advice of her director. Marie Barbier's mystic life will continue to be somewhat obscure so long as we do not know the precise extent of Abbé Glandelet's influence on her spiritual training.

M. Eileen Scott, c.n.d.

AJM, Greffe de Bénigne Basset, 20 déc. 1684; Greffe de Claude Maugue, 11 août 1679; Greffe de Jean de Saint-Père, 5 nov. 1650. ANDM, Registres des baptêmes, mariages et sépultures. ASQ, Congrégation Notre-Dame, 198 : [Charles de Glandelet], Recueil touchant la S[œur Marie Barbier], fille séculière de la Congrégation de Notre-Dame.... Juchereau, *Annales* (Jamet). *Histoire de la congrégation de Notre-Dame de Montréal* (9v., Montréal, 1910, 1941), II, IV. [É.-M. Faillon], *Vie de la Sœur Bourgeoys, fondatrice de la Congrégation de Notre-Dame de Villemarie en Canada, suivie de l'histoire de cet institut jusqu'à ce jour* (2v., Ville-Marie [Montréal], 1853), II.

BARLEY (Barlow). *See* Berley

BARRAT, CLAUDE, clerk of court and notary at Placentia (Plaisance), Newfoundland; b. *c.* 1658 at Troyes; d. after 1711.

Claude Barrat married Jeanne Quisence at Saint-Malo in 1681. A census made in Newfoundland records his presence at Saint-Pierre in 1691; two years later he was employing ten lads who were learning the fishing trade. On 15 March 1696, on the recommendation of Governor Brouillan [Mombeton], he was appointed notary and clerk of court at Placentia. He continued to concern himself with fishing, but things went badly. He embezzled a sum of money, and as a result he was dismissed from office by Joseph de Monic, administrator in Brouillan's absence. His wife then went to Acadia, where she set up a business and kept a tavern at Port-Royal (Annapolis Royal, N.S.). Brouillan, now in Acadia, endeavoured to obtain for Barrat the position of clerk of court at Port-Royal. In the meantime Barrat had secured his reinstatement, but Monic did not want to let him leave before he had paid his debts.

Madame Barrat continued to live at Port-Royal, under the governor's protection: he sent soldiers to work for her, and entered the name of her son, who was still a small boy, on the muster-roll of the garrison. Mathieu de Goutin and Abel Maudoux*, the parish priest of Port-Royal, in agreement for once, cried shame: Madame Barrat diluted by half the wine she sold to the soldiers, and she lived at the governor's house. The bishop of Quebec intervened, and the king ordered her to be sent back to her husband. She preferred to go to France in 1704. Brouillan went there also on leave, but died on his return to Acadia the following year. Madame Barrat returned to Port-Royal, thinking she would rejoin him there, but Justinien Durand*, the new parish priest, asked that she be sent away a second time.

At Placentia Claude Barrat, who was still in debt, sold his house in 1706. His possessions were seized in 1708, and he gave his son a power of attorney to settle his affairs. Barrat went to France and requested that his son succeed to his office, but the latter was deemed unfit for it. According to the censuses taken at Placentia, Barrat, his wife, and two sons were still living there in 1711.

Claude Barrat's minutes as a notary and some of his official acts as clerk of court have been preserved. But his wife's romantic adventures have brought him more notoriety than his notary's pen.

René Baudry

AN, Col., B, 19, f.29; 23, f.164v; 25, f.63v; 29, f.380v; C¹¹c, 1–2; C¹¹ᴰ, 4, ff.109, 316; 5, f.197; F³, 54, ff.425–26; Section Outre-Mer, G¹, 467/1; G³, 2053, pièces 69, 139, 144. *Coll. de manuscrits relatifs à la N.-F.*, II, 417. "Recensements de Terreneuve et Plaisance," SGCF *Mémoires*, XI (1960), 79, 84; XIII (1962), 244, 247.

BARTHÉLEMY, MICHEL, priest, Sulpician, missionary; b. 1638 in the diocese of Paris; d. 11 April 1706 at Montreal.

Barthélemy arrived in Montreal in 1665. In the autumn of 1668 M. Thubières* de Queylus sent him, along with Dollier de Casson, to spend the winter among the Algonkins in order to learn their language and become familiar with their way of life, but the experiment was cut short. Not long after, perhaps in 1672, he went off to serve as a missionary to the Iroquois who had recently settled on the north shore of Lake Ontario, on the Bay of Kenté (Quinte); he joined Claude Trouvé and François de Salignac* de La Mothe-Fénelon, who had been there since 1668. He remained not quite seven years, endeavouring with his fellow religious to learn the Indians' language, and to give instruction particularly to the young Indians, occasionally baptizing the dying, children or adults. But by 1675, because of the inconstant character of the Iroquois, serious thought was being given to abandoning the mission, and in 1680 this step reluctantly had to be taken.

Barthélemy returned to Montreal in 1679 and first became the school-master at the Iroquois

Basset

mission of La Montagne which M. Bailly* had been directing for three years. Then the following year we find him at Ville-Marie, where he was in charge of singing at the parish church and looked after the French primary schools in cooperation with M. Souart*. But ministering to the Indians still attracted him. He learned the Algonkins' language, not to go as a missionary to their country but to take care of those among them who, old or sick, came in rather great numbers to seek aid from the French at Ville-Marie.

In 1686 he was sent to found the parish of Rivière-des-Prairies, north of Montreal Island. He is supposed to have built the first chapel there around 1690, but in 1692 he was obliged to return to the seminary at Montreal because of the depopulation of his parish resulting from the incessant incursions by the Iroquois; in 1689 he himself had been besieged in the mill at Rivière-des-Prairies by a band of Indians.

On his return to Montreal he took up again his office of curate and his ministry to the Algonkins. His concern for them was truly admirable. He was not content with taking care of them himself, but every year for nearly 30 years he requested that aid be furnished them, either by settling them on the Rivière de l'Assomption, or by joining them with the Iroquois at the fort at La Montagne, or by building lodges for them near Ville-Marie. But, although people admired his zeal and did not wish to discourage him, the reply was always that his projects appeared too costly or impracticable. He also urged that other missionaries study the Algonkin language, which he alone knew, and he offered his services to teach it to them in six months. In the end his insistence had favourable results. Thanks to it, the famous Algonkin mission of Île aux Tourtres, at the west end of Montreal Island, was founded in 1703 by M. de BRESLAY, parish priest of Sault-Saint-Louis.

Michel Barthélemy died at Montreal 11 April 1706.

ANTONIO DANSEREAU, P.S.S.

Further information on the Quinté mission will be found in the biographies of François de Salignac* de La Mothe-Fénelon [*DCB*, I, 599–601] and Claude TROUVÉ. ASSM, Correspondance des supérieurs généraux. Dollier de Casson, *Histoire du Montréal*. [Louis Tronson], *Correspondance de M. de Tronson, troisième Supérieur de la Compagnie de Saint-Sulpice: Lettres choisies*, [*16 juillet 1676–15 janv. 1700*], éd. A.-L. Bertrand (3v., Paris, 1904), II. Allaire, *Dictionnaire*. C.-P. Beaubien, *Le Sault-au-Récollet: ses rapports avec les premiers temps de la colonie* (Montréal, 1898). Faillon, *Histoire de la colonie française*. Henri Gauthier, *Sulpitiana* (Montréal, 1926). Pierre Rousseau, *Saint-Sulpice et les missions catholiques* (Montréal, 1930); "Une mission éphémère, Kenté,"

Bulletin de l'Association des Anciens Élèves du Collège de Montréal, XX (1930), 1–50.

BASSET, DAVID, Huguenot merchant active in Newfoundland and New England; fl. 1687–1701; d. 17 Aug. 1724 in the West Indies.

Basset seems to have been an inhabitant of Acadia originally; some time before 1682 he married a Mary Laverdure, by whom he was to have six children. This woman may possibly have been the daughter of the Acadian settler Pierre Melanson *dit* La Verdure [*see* Charles Melanson*]. Basset established himself in Boston and became actively engaged in trade between New England and Newfoundland, shipping tobacco, sugar, and other provisions in return for fish. In the autumn of 1687, he came into conflict with the governor of Placentia (Plaisance), Antoine Parat*, who accused Basset of carrying to Boston two Huguenots the governor had wanted to send to France. As a punishment for his alleged offence, Basset's ship and goods were confiscated, and he himself was sent to France to be imprisoned at Bayonne. However, Parat was later reprimanded for his actions—evidently the governor owed Basset money. The latter, through the help of influential friends, was pardoned on condition that he return and settle at Port-Royal (Annapolis Royal, N.S.). He was allowed to go to Boston to fetch his family, but did not return.

In 1690 he served as master of the *Porcupine* under Captain Cyprian Southack* at the capture of Port-Royal by Phips*, and later took part in a coastal raid at La Hève and in the destruction of Fort Saint-Louis, the trading post of the Compagnie des Pêches sédentaires de l'Acadie [*see* Bergier*] at Chedabouctou (Guysborough, N.S.). The following year he captured a French vessel in the St Lawrence and raided the Baie des Chaleurs. He continued to be active in privateering and trading for some time, both on the east coast of North America and in the West Indies. He owned shares in various ships, including the *Trial* and the *William and John*.

In 1697, Basset was captured by Pierre MAISONNAT, *dit* Baptiste, at Cap Sable and taken to Fort Nashwaak (Naxouat) on the Saint John River. Governor Villebon [Robinau*] hoped that with good treatment he could secure Basset's much-needed services as a pilot. Basset agreed to serve and was once again allowed to go and fetch his family from Boston. He returned without them in December 1698 and was arrested by Villebon and sent to France as a dangerous person. When Governor Bellomont of Massachusetts protested this action, Basset was released and allowed to return to Acadia. Villebon was reprimanded for his inconsistent conduct towards Basset and was ordered to restore the latter's confiscated property.

In October 1700, Villebon's temporary successor, CLAUDE-SÉBASTIEN DE VILLIEU gave Basset permission to go to Boston for his wife. Basset returned early the next year, and departed again for Boston two months later. When he arrived in Acadia in June of 1701, still without his family, he was arrested by Villieu. Little is known of Basset's activities from this time until his death in the West Indies in 1724. His throat was slit as he lay sleeping on the quarter-deck of his ship.

M. C. ROSENFIELD

AN, Col., B, 15, f.8; C^{11C}, 1, f.85; F^3, 6, ff.303, 307. Mass. Hist. Soc., Parkman papers, XXX. "Mass. Archives," VII, 64, 101; XXXVII, 93–95; LXI, 446, 447, 558, 558a, 559. *Coll. de manuscrits relatifs à la N.-F.*, II, 335, 336. "Journal of expedition against Port Royal, 1690," 63. *Mémoires des commissaires*, II, 333; and *Memorials of the English and French commissaries*, I, 620–21. Taillemite, *Inventaire analytique, série B*, I. Webster, *Acadia*, 23, 72–73, 102, 116, 162. *New Eng. Hist. and Geneal. Register*, XV (1861), XXIX (1875). Murdoch, *History of Nova-Scotia*, I, 240–42, 247. T. B. Wyman, *The genealogies and estates of Charlestown in the county of Middlesex and Commonwealth of Massachusetts, 1629–1818* (Boston, 1879).

BASSET, JEAN, priest; b. *c.* 1645 in France; d. 20 Nov. 1715 at Pointe-aux-Trembles (Neuville).

Although we have no detailed knowledge of Basset's origins, we do know that when he arrived at Quebec in 1675, together with a contingent for the seminary composed of at least three other ecclesiastics, he came from the parish of Sainte-Croix, in the diocese of Lyons. He was ordained priest at the seminary on 21 December of the same year. Although his name appears on the list of members of the community of the seminary in 1692, he always devoted himself to ministering to a parish: at the cathedral (1675–78), on Île d'Orléans (1678–80), at Pointe-aux-Trembles (1680–81), at Repentigny and neighbouring places (1682–84), and again at Pointe-aux-Trembles (1684–1715), where he died on 20 Nov. 1715; he was buried in the church there the next day.

He had made a donation on 1 Aug. 1715 to the Congrégation de Notre-Dame of a piece of land and a farm. It was only after much negotiation that in 1685 he had succeeded in endowing his parish with a convent of these sisters. He had gone on a pilgrimage to Ancienne Lorette with Mother Bourgeoys* for this purpose. Philéas Gagnon has noted that for want of a notary in his region, Abbé Basset drafted a large number of acts for the settlers; these acts are deposited today in the registries of various notaries.

HONORIUS PROVOST

AAQ, Notre-Dame de Québec. AJQ, Greffe de Jacques Barbel, 1er août 1715. ANDQ, Registres des baptêmes, mariages et sépultures. ASQ, Évêques, 171; Paroisses diverses, 90; Polygraphie, XXII, 20, 22. [É.-M. Faillon], *Vie de la Sœur Bourgeoys, fondatrice de la Congrégation de Notre-Dame de Villemarie en Canada, suivie de l'histoire de cet institut jusqu'à ce jour* (2v., Villemarie [Montréal], 1853). Auguste Gosselin, *Vie de Mgr de Laval*, II, 691. David Gosselin, "Saint-Laurent de l'île d'Orléans," *BRH*, V (1899), 259. P.-G. Roy, "Saint-François de Sales de la Pointe-aux-Trembles," *BRH*, III (1897), 129.

BATILLY, FRANÇOIS-MARIE MARGANE DE. *See* MARGANE

BAUDEAU (Boudeau), PIERRE, surgeon-major; b. 1643; arrived in New France in 1692 (according to a note by Frontenac [Buade*], whose correspondence with the court recounts the circumstances of Baudeau's appointment); buried in Montreal in 1708.

In 1692 Michel SARRAZIN, one of the most famous Canadian doctors and naturalists, decided to enter the Jesuit order. Frontenac relates that he was obliged to replace the practitioner by a person "who arrived here before the said Sieur Sarrazin left to go to France, and who [Baudeau] is a very skilful man, expert in his profession, loved and esteemed by everybody here, and who has served for a long time in the land and naval forces." Subsequently Sarrazin changed his mind and studied medicine in Paris. Frontenac requested the minister to continue to give Sarrazin his support, "but I ask you above all," he went on, "to withdraw nothing of what is due to the Sieur Baudeau, surgeon-major, a man who must at all costs be retained."

From 4 Oct. to 7 Nov. 1693 and from 22 Feb. to 31 March 1695, Baudeau served at the Hôtel-Dieu of Quebec, as he did from 22 Aug. to 30 Oct. 1708; he was assigned to the women's ward there.

In 1705, Baudeau was performing his duties at Montreal; he had occasion to examine a soldier of M. de RAMEZAY, Jean Du Tartre (de Tard), *dit* La Verdure, who had received a sword wound during a brawl that involved the brothers Rocbert* de La Morandière and some soldiers of the garrison. Baudeau was buried 4 Nov. 1708 at Notre-Dame de Montréal.

HERVÉ BIRON

AHDQ, Registres de l'Hôtel-Dieu de Québec. AJM, Registres d'état civil de Notre-Dame de Montréal. AN, Col., C^{11A}, 10–16. AQ, Manuscrits relatifs à

Baudry

l'histoire de la N.-F., 2e série, VIII, 196. *Jug. et délib.*, V, 465–71, 914. "Correspondance de Frontenac (1689–99)," APQ *Rapport, 1928–29*, 343. [The printed document gives Baudoin instead of Baudeau, but the manuscript clearly mentions Baudeau.] Ahern, *Notes pour l'histoire de la médecine*, 37, 38, 478. Arthur Vallée, *Un biologiste canadien: Michel Sarrazin, 1659–1735, sa vie, ses travaux et son temps* (Québec, 1927), 24, 157.

BAUDRY (Beaudry), *dit* **Des Butes (Desbutes), GUILLAUME,** gunsmith, gold- and silversmith; b. 2 Oct. 1657 at Quebec; d. 1732 at Trois-Rivières.

On 13 July 1682 Guillaume Baudry married Jeanne Soullard, who was "fifteen to sixteen years old," an armourer's daughter, at Quebec. He subsequently settled at Trois-Rivières. On 4 March 1689·and 14 Jan. 1693 he received two grants of fiefs from René Robinau* de Bécancour. The Baudrys had 15 children, one of whom, Jean-Baptiste, who exercised the craft of gunsmith, was among the original inhabitants of Detroit.

Only one piece of craftsmanship by Guillaume Baudry has been recorded. It was he who engraved the lead plaque for the cornerstone of the Recollet church at Trois-Rivières; on 11 July 1710 ANTOINE-DENIS RAUDOT came to lay it officially. In 1713 this church was the object of a royal gratuity of 500 *livres*.

On 18 Feb. 1726 Baudry was summoned to court by the surgeon Alavoine*, who claimed 174 *livres* from him, but Baudry was successful in having the account appraised by the Quebec doctor, SARRAZIN.

Guillaume Baudry, *dit* Des Butes, was buried on 26 Feb. 1732 at Trois-Rivières.

MAURICE CARRIER

AJTR, Greffe de Séverin Ameau, 17 sept. 1680, 4 mars 1689, 14 janv., 24 août 1693; Registres d'état civil de Notre-Dame-de-la-Conception, 26 fév. 1732. Tanguay, *Dictionnaire*, I, 310. Jouve, *Les Franciscains et le Canada: aux Trois-Rivières*, 95–96, 146. Télesphore Saint-Pierre, *Histoire des Canadiens du Michigan et du comté d'Essex, Ontario* (Montréal, 1895), 157.

BAUDRY DE LAMARCHE, JACQUES, purchaser of Lamothe Cadillac's [LAUMET] rights at Detroit, attorney in France of the Charon brothers; baptized 13 Sept. 1676, at Trois-Rivières, son of Urbain Baudry, *dit* Lamarche, and Madeleine Boucher; d. after 1738, probably in France.

Very little is known about Jacques Baudry de Lamarche. The son of a Trois-Rivières edge-tool maker, he moved to France at an unknown date

and made his home in Paris. Around 1723 he purchased Cadillac's rights to certain properties at Detroit, consisting of several buildings which had deteriorated, a mill, some cattle, and an undetermined area of both cleared and uncleared land. An attorney, Véron* de Grandmesnil, was appointed by Baudry to take possession of these but he soon became involved in difficulties with Philippe de RIGAUD de Vaudreuil and ALPHONSE TONTY over the extent and general state of the properties in question. Disputes over these matters continued for at least five years. During this time, Baudry plagued the ministry of Marine with claims and counter-claims and Grandmesnil laid his case before the governor and intendant in New France.

A decade passed before the name of Jacques Baudry reappeared in the history of New France. In 1738 he was asked to serve as general and special attorney for the Frères Hospitaliers de la Croix, a charitable order founded by François CHARON in Montreal. A merger with the Frères de la Salle, or Frères des Écoles Chrétiennes, was being contemplated, and Baudry was to collect outstanding debts and oversee the union. This is the last known reference to him in French documents.

C. J. RUSS

AN, Col., B, 46–50; C11A, 45–50. P.-G. Roy, *Inv. ord. int.*, I, 254, 265. É.-Z. Massicotte, "Inventaire des documents et des imprimés concernant la communauté des frères Charon et l'Hôpital Général de Montréal sous le régime français," APQ *Rapport, 1923–24*, 187. Tanguay, *Dictionnaire*, I, 31f.; II, 152 [Tanguay's confusion about Jacques Baudry's parents is evident; it is certain that Jacques Baudry, son of Urbain Baudry, was never married in New France. C.J.R.]. Aegidius Fauteux, "Jacques Baudry de Lamarche," *BRH*, XXXVII (1931), 203f.

BAUGY, LOUIS-HENRI DE, *dit* Chevalier de Baugy; b. at a date unknown; d. 1720 in Paris. He came from a noble family of the province of Berry; his father, Guillaume de Baugy, was a king's counsellor and captain of light horse in the regiments of Cardinal Mazarin.

Baugy sailed for Canada from La Rochelle on the night of 12–13 July 1682 on the *Saint-François-Xavier*. He arrived at Quebec in October together with Le Febvre* de La Barre, who was succeeding Buade* de Frontenac. The new governor, under pressure from the group of merchants who envied the advantages enjoyed by Cavelier* de La Salle in the Great Lakes region, undertook to deprive the latter of his possessions. He entrusted this mission to MOREL de La Durantaye, a former captain in the Régiment de Chambellay, to whom he assigned the Chevalier de Baugy as lieutenant. By their commission dated 1 and 15 March 1683 and the instructions which followed on 20 April, they were both under orders to seize the canoes of the coureurs de bois who did not have a fur-trading licence; to urge the Illinois, Tionontatis, and Miamis to take their pelts to Montreal; to keep watch over La Salle, and to seize his possessions if the accusations levelled against him proved to be correct.

On 23 April 1683 the two agents left Quebec for Michilimackinac, where they arrived on 2 July. While La Durantaye was setting himself up at Michilimackinac, Baugy proceeded towards Fort Saint-Louis des Illinois. On the way, when he was 15 leagues from the fort, he met La Salle, who was returning to Montreal from the Mississippi. Baugy informed him of his mission, and La Salle deferred to him. La Salle wrote a letter to his partner HENRI TONTY, the commandant of Fort Saint-Louis, asking him to receive Baugy courteously. Tonty obeyed; he handed over command of the fort to La Barre's envoy, but he remained on the spot in order to attend to La Salle's interests.

Between Tonty and Baugy, who was looking after the interests of La Barre, there was frequent friction. Baugy tried in vain to entice away Tonty's men who, in return for an increase in wages and promises of grants of land, remained loyal to La Salle. On 21 March 1684 the two rivals had to forget their quarrels to organize the defence of the fort, which was threatened by 200 Iroquois. The siege lasted six days. Baugy dispatched a courier to Michilimackinac. Thanks to the support of a party of Illinois, however, they succeeded in repelling the Iroquois well before the arrival of La Durantaye and his men. When La Durantaye reached the fort on 21 May he brought with him precise orders from La Barre: Tonty was to leave the fort and Baugy to take over sole command there.

While Baugy was enjoying a monopoly of the fur trade among the Illinois, La Salle was successfully pleading his case at Versailles. Reinstated in his privileges by the king, La Salle dispatched Tonty to Fort Saint-Louis as governor of the fort. Tonty presented himself at Fort Saint-Louis on 26 June 1685. The tables were turned: Baugy was obliged in his turn to leave the fort and go back to Quebec.

We find no trace of Baugy in any records until the spring of 1687, when he took part as BRISAY de Denonville's aide-de-camp in the campaign against the Senecas. The valuable account which he left of this action demonstrates a great concern for exactness and precision. Denonville highly appreciated his aide-de-camp's services during this campaign, and thought fit to recognize his merit by granting him the honour of a company in Canada.

Baugy did not die in 1689, as Margry states, but went to France in November of that year. He never returned to Canada. As seigneur of Villecien, Villevallier, Fay, and other places, he lived in his *château* at Villecien. On 19 Feb. 1696 he was appointed captain-major at Saint-Julien-du-Sault. He died in Paris on 19 Feb. 1720 and was buried in the chapel of his *château* at Fay.

JEAN HAMELIN

Baugy, *Journal* (Serrigny). *Découvertes et établissements des Français* (Margry), V, 4–7. *Ord. comm.* (P.-G. Roy), II, 3–33, 43. Eccles, *Frontenac*. E. R. Murphy, *Henry de Tonty, fur trader of the Mississippi* (Baltimore, 1941). Benjamin Sulte, "Les Tonty," *RSCT*, 1st ser., XI (1893), sect.I, 3–31.

BAYLEY (Bayly). *See* BALEY

BEALE, ANTHONY, succeeded John FULLARTINE as governor and chief commander for the HBC in James Bay; b. *c.* 1664; d. 13 April 1731 (o.s.) at Prince of Wales Fort.

Anthony Beale joined the HBC as an apprentice in 1678. It is not known exactly where he obtained his initial experience of life in James Bay, or whether he ever came under the direct eye of Governor Charles Bayly*, but the latter's successor, John Nixon*, referred to him as "Anthoney Beale alias Small Cole" in the list of men who were to spend the winter of 1682–83 at Albany Fort. As Beale did not return to England in 1685, when his apprenticeship ended, his father requested that the governor and committee allow his son to come back by the supply-ship of 1686. This application was granted, but circumstances intervened to delay young Beale's return until 1687. The ship that sailed for James Bay in the spring of 1686 was wrecked in Hudson Strait on the outward voyage, and even before that disaster occurred Pierre de Troyes* had led a party overland from Montreal to capture the company's posts (in spite of peace existing between the English and French crowns). Beale was among the men made prisoner when Governor Henry Sergeant* surrendered Albany Fort on 16 July. Fortunately for Beale, on his release, he was not one of the 22 miserable wretches who were left to drag out an existence in James Bay during the winter of 1686–87. Instead he was among the 50 or so people from Moose Fort, Rupert River, and Albany Fort who reached York Fort in the

Beale

"Weake Leaky" *Colleton* yacht. Governor George Geyer* accommodated these unexpected arrivals either at York Fort or at New Severn during the ensuing winter.

Beale reached London in the autumn of 1687. With two associates he delivered a statement to the committee on 18 November criticizing the way in which Sergeant had surrendered Albany Fort and hinting at other complaints which could be made about his conduct.

Beale was re-engaged by the HBC but the duties he was expected to carry out for £12 per annum were not specified. He was, however, experienced in bayside conditions and must have been considered a useful member of the expedition led by Captain John Marsh*, which sailed from the Thames in the spring of 1688 with the object of re-establishing the company's right to trade in Albany River without annoying the French, or "Disturbing them" unless they began hostilities. Orders for the recapture of Albany Fort (now called Sainte-Anne) were not given because the truce between the English and French crowns was not due to expire until 1 Jan. 1688/89. The expedition was a complete failure and by the spring of 1689 all the surviving members of the English party were prisoners of PIERRE LE MOYNE d'Iberville. Later in the season most of the Englishmen were released, but several of the most experienced were sent overland to New France with the obvious aim of depriving the HBC of their future services. Anthony Beale was among this number. Because war had broken out between England and France earlier that year, Beale and his companions endured "miserable Servitude" in New France until the summer of 1691 when they were sent to France and imprisoned at La Rochelle. Beale's wife Mary (whom he must have married after returning to England in 1687) was among those who petitioned Queen Mary on 1 Oct. 1691 for help in getting their husbands released.

The war continued, but Beale was freed in time to enter into a more financially rewarding contract with the HBC and to sail from the Thames in the *Royal Hudson's Bay* (Capt. Michael GRIMINGTON) in the spring of 1692 as a member of the expedition, led by Captain James KNIGHT, to recapture Albany Fort. After wintering on Gilpin Island off the East Main, Knight mounted the attack on 22 June 1693; as the French were only about six in number the English party was able to overcome their resistance without difficulty.

Beale's third term of employment in James Bay (which began with the committee's order to Knight to have "some Regard" for him as an old servant) was a lengthy one, lasting until 1708. During this time he rose from the position of an experienced and useful assistant to that of governor. The period was a particularly critical one in the company's history, but Beale himself was not again involved in any clash with the French because, from 1690 to 1697, their efforts against the HBC were directed to the Port Nelson area and they did not attack Albany Fort again until 1709. But Beale's career might have suffered a third interruption or indeed have been ended if the treaty of Ryswick (1697) had operated in Hudson Bay. As events turned out, York Fort remained in French possession after Iberville's naval victory off Hayes River in 1697, and Albany Fort, which should have been exchanged for it, was retained by the HBC and remained its only possession in Hudson Bay until 1714. With England's entry into the War of the Spanish Succession in 1702 the threat of an attack on Albany was renewed.

The stages by which Beale rose to the highest position at Albany Fort were gradual. He served there under Governor Knight from 1693 to 1697, and was one of John Fullartine's "few hands" in 1697–98. In the winters of 1698–99 and 1699–1700 Beale was responsible to Knight for the East Main trade which was carried on from an island base off the coast, and when the governor again left for England in the autumn of 1700 he made Beale deputy to the new governor, Fullartine. Beale's appointment was confirmed by a commission from the committee in 1701. He spent one more winter (1700–1) as chief trader off the East Main, but after that he fulfilled his duties at Albany, and Henry KELSEY managed the East Main trade. It was partly Beale's reputation as "a very careful, honest man" who understood the company's business "as well as most men that ever were in it," that earned him his appointment as governor in 1705. The commission sent to Beale that year constituted him governor and chief commander of Albany, Moose, and Rupert Rivers, and of all the territories within Hudson Bay and Strait, as well as upon the East and West Mains. But in reality Beale's powers did not extend beyond James Bay because the French were still in possession of York Fort (renamed Fort Bourbon).

With all due ceremony Beale's commission was read to the assembled inmates of Albany Fort on 13 Sept. 1705 and Fullartine embarked on the *Hudson's Bay* [II] for England. But he returned to the fort on 25 September to report that Captain Michael Grimington was sick, and that after the ship had run aground it had not been possible to get her out of Albany River until it was too late in the season to risk the voyage to England. The council met to discuss the awkward situation that had now arisen and, according to the minutes (which Fullartine signed as one of the members), agreed unanimously that the *Hudson's Bay* should winter at Gilpin Island off the East Main where Fullartine would trade on behalf of the company. But Fullartine (according to Beale, whose account of the affair is the only one to survive) had second thoughts and argued that he was still governor. Beale, however, firmly refused to yield even though Fullartine probably claimed that his commission from the crown (which had not been revoked) entitled him to resume command. It was by crediting Beale's account with only £100 (his salary as deputy governor) for the season 1705–6 that the company expressed its disapproval, and although Beale pressed his claim he did not receive the additional £100 until June 1710.

Beale's letter of 23 July 1706 to the governor and committee is the second written from Albany Fort to survive in the company's archives. It is the letter of a blunt man who did not hesitate to scold the committee for its shortcomings, especially in omitting to send a ship annually to Albany River to relieve the needs, not only of employees, but of Indians who had grown dependent on the company's goods. Beale's Albany Fort journal for the season 1705–6 is of particular interest; it is the first from any trading post to survive in the company's archives, and the short matter-of-fact entries reveal a great deal about life and duties at the bayside under the threat of attack from the French. Although he had had little or no formal education, Beale was commanding in the summer of 1706 the sole British possession in Hudson Bay with but 27 men and the prospect of only irregular communication with London. Beale's term as governor ended in 1708 when he returned to England at his own request.

An accusation of illicit trading in furs was brought against Beale in 1710, and though a lengthy investigation took place, no record remains to show the result. Whatever the verdict, the governor and committee were glad to secure Beale's services at short notice in 1711. This was because James Knight was prevented by illness from going to Albany Fort to relieve John Fullartine and because the deputy governor on the spot, Henry Kelsey, having formerly expressed a wish to return home, could not be relied on to remain. It was undoubtedly with the experience of 1705 in mind that Beale requested, and obtained, from the queen a commission in order "Better to maintain his Government." By it he was constituted governor and commander-in-chief in place of John Fullartine of all the company's posts in the Bottom of the Bay, particularly of those on Albany, Moose, and Rupert Rivers, and of all others which had been newly settled or recovered from the enemy; in fact Albany Fort was still the only HBC possession in operation. Beale was also commanded to act both defensively and offensively against the French.

The arrival of not only Beale but also his former deputy, Nathaniel BISHOP, on 26 Sept. 1711 after a bad passage in the *Pery* (Capt. Richard WARD) was a blow to Kelsey, who had been left as governor on Fullartine's departure the previous month and who now had to drop into a subordinate position. Both Kelsey and Beale were deserving but circumstances had favoured Beale at a time when the HBC had only one settlement and a number of employees worthy of recognition and promotion. Like Beale they too had loyally endured privations while prisoners of the French and had acquired experience and ability in the fur trade.

By the time Beale's contract expired in 1714 the situation in Hudson Bay had changed. The Treaty of Utrecht (1713), which ended the war in Europe, provided for the restoration of York Fort to the HBC. James Knight was sent by the company to York Fort as commander-in-chief, and because Richard Staunton* who was already at Albany was willing to serve there as chief factor responsible to Knight, Beale was recalled to England.

Beale applied for re-employment in 1718 but there was no station for him to fill. Although the situation was unchanged in 1720 he was engaged at £50 per annum to serve under Kelsey at York Fort. Orders were sent to Kelsey stating that Beale, who was to be employed where he would be most useful, was to have a seat on the council and be treated "very Civilly." Beale, who was in command at York Fort during Kelsey's voyage northwards to trade with Eskimos in the summer of 1721, received his official appointment as "second" later that year. From 1722 to 1726 he served for £60 per annum in a similar capacity under Kelsey's successor, Thomas McCliesh*. Beale spent his last season at York Fort (1726–27) in command when McCliesh was absent in England and then went to Churchill River (Fort Prince of Wales) as "chief commander." He had been sent there to revive the trade and also to clear up the disorders which had grown while his predecessor, the young and inexperienced Richard Norton*, had been in charge. These tasks were performed by Beale to the satisfaction of the committee, but he was now approaching 70 years of age and in 1730, on account of failing health, he requested leave to return to England the following year. He died, however, on 13 April 1731. Thomas BIRD who assumed command recorded that Beale was buried with full honours at Fort Prince of Wales on the following day. Beale was survived by his wife (apparently his second one), Joanna, and their daughter, Frances, who were domiciled in

England, as were all families of company employees at this period.

Beale's rise from humble beginnings is evidence enough of character and purpose. His abilities were limited, perhaps because of lack of much experience in the world beyond Hudson Bay, but his courage, loyalty and knowledge of the fur trade and Indians were important to the HBC, particularly during the time when it had only a precarious foothold in Hudson Bay.

ALICE M. JOHNSON

[Besides the journal mentioned above, Beale was responsible for four others kept at Albany, one at York Fort, and two at Fort Prince of Wales. Details of the references to Beale in the HBC archives can be found in HBRS, XXV (Davies and Johnson), which also includes his letters to the company. The background to the period is covered in detail in HBRS, XXI (Rich). A.M.J.]

BEAR, The. *See* LE PESANT

BEAUBASSIN. *See* LENEUF

BEAUCHÊNE, ROBERT CHEVALIER, *dit.* *See* CHEVALIER

BEAUDRY. *See* BAUDRY

BEAUHARNOIS DE BEAUMONT ET DE VILLECHAUVE, CLAUDE DE, French naval officer, midshipman (1 Jan. 1691), sub-lieutenant in the navy (1 Jan. 1696), lieutenant-commander (1 July 1703), commander (25 Nov. 1712), captain (17 March 1727), seigneur; b. 22 Sept. 1674 at Saint-Laurent near Orléans, son of François de Beauharnois de La Boische (Boeche) and Marguerite-Françoise Pyvart (Pinard) de Chastullé; d. 17 Jan. 1738 at La Boische or La Chaussée, buried at Saint-Laurent. He married Renée Hardouineau at La Rochelle 11 May 1713. They had two sons: François, b. 8 Feb. 1714, and Claude* (called the *chevalier*), b. in Rochefort 16 Jan. 1717.

Brother of Charles de Beauharnois* de La Boische, governor general of New France, and of François*, intendant, Claude was sixth son in a family of seven sons and seven daughters. He never resided in Canada, but on several occasions (1703, 1711, 1712, 1723) he commanded the vessels which annually brought munitions, troops, and the king's orders to the colony. His first trip to Quebec appears to have been in 1703 as commander of the *Seine*, carrying munitions and some private cargo and returning to La Rochelle with masts and beaver pelts. In July 1711 he was placed in command of the *Héros* with orders to take troops and supplies to Quebec in preparation for the imminent invasion of an English expedition led by Sir Hovenden WALKER. His instructions, characteristic of French naval policy throughout most of the 18th century, required him to proceed with extreme caution and restraint. The destruction of part of Walker's fleet forestalled the invasion, permitting Claude to arrive at Quebec on 7 November without incident. It may have been he who brought to Quebec a small English ship captured that fall. When he set sail for France the same month he took with him JACQUES RAUDOT who had been recalled as intendant of New France. Claude again commanded the *Héros* on its voyage to Quebec in 1712, bringing his sister Jeanne-Élisabeth and her husband Michel Bégon*, the new intendant. He made similar trips to Saint-Domingue in 1726 and 1732. In May and June of 1734, during the War of the Polish Succession, he commanded three ships in the Baltic campaign.

He was mentioned for distinctive service, along with his brothers, in the king's proclamation of 1707 erecting François's Acadian seigneury into the barony of Beauville. On 12 April 1729 he and his brother Charles received jointly the seigneury of Villechauve on the St Lawrence River. Neither Charles nor Claude appears to have made much effort to attract settlers to their seigneury. Presumably because Charles had no children the seigneury reverted to the king on his death in 1749.

In 1750 Claude's eldest son, François, requested that the seigneury be regranted to him, which it was on 14 June of that year. On 7 June 1763 François sold his seigneury to Michel Chartier de Lotbinière for 24,000 *livres*. It is quite possible that payment was made in some form of paper currency circulating in New France at the time, worth only a fraction of its face value. In this case it is uncertain how much—if any—of the 24,000 *livres* François was able to redeem in French *livres*. He may have been trying to take advantage of Louis XV's declaration of February 1763 in which the king voiced his intention to redeem Canadian bills of exchange.

According to Alexandre Mazas (*Histoire de l'ordre militaire de Saint-Louis*), both Claude de Beauharnois and his brother Charles were decorated with the cross of the order of Saint-Louis on the same day, 28 June 1718. Another brother, Guillaume*, and Claude's son, Claude, received the cross of Saint-Louis on other occasions. This, along with the fact that all the Beauharnois were career officers in the navy, probably explains why they have frequently been confused. In February 1738 the delegates in France of the chapter of Quebec wrote to their superiors in Quebec that Claude de Beauharnois had died, and that he had been "highly regarded in the navy, especially by M. de Maurepas, as a good officer."

S. DALE STANDEN

AJQ, Contrat de mariage de Claude de Beauharnois, Chevalier de Beaumont, capitaine de frégate, avec Mademoiselle Renée Hardouineau (before Masson and Soullard, notaries at La Rochelle, 11 May 1713). AN, Col., B, 23, ff.191v–93, 204v, 205–6; 33, ff.171–75, 176v; Marine, C¹, 154, ff.171, 189; 157, f.273; 161; Marine, C⁷, 20, f.12. PAC, FM 6, B, 9, ff.23v, 114v–16v. Charlevoix, *Histoire* (1744), II, 356. "Correspondance de Vaudreuil," APQ *Rapport, 1946–47*, 460; *1947–48*, 155f., 160f., 171. *Documents relating to Canadian currency during the French period* (Shortt), II, 963, 973. Juchereau, *Annales* (Jamet), 364, 369, 379 [The last reference is to Guillaume, rather than, as Jamet thought, Claude. S.D.S.]. P.-G. Roy, *Inv. concessions*, IV, 191, 227f.; *Inv. jug. et délib., 1717–1760*, II, 73. Fauteux, *Les chevaliers de Saint-Louis*, 109, 119f., 149f. Georges Lacour-Gayet, *La Marine militaire de la France sous le règne de Louis XV* (Paris, 1902), 118–20, 530, 534. Alexandre Mazas, *Histoire de l'ordre militaire de Saint-Louis depuis son institution en 1693 jusqu'en 1830* (2ᵉ éd., 3v., Paris, 1860–61), II, 117f. Auguste Gosselin, "Charles de Beauharnais," *BRH*, VII (1901), 293–301. Olivier, "Le gouverneur de Beauharnois," *BRH*, II (1896), 189. J.-E. Roy, "Notes sur l'intendant Bégon," *BRH*, IV (1898), 269. P.-G. Roy, "Le mariage manqué du chevalier de Beauharnois," *BRH*, LI (1945), 139–42; "Les marquisats, comtés, baronnies et châtellenies dans la Nouvelle-France," *BRH*, XXI (1915), 47f. Régis Roy, "Michel Bégon," *BRH*, VIII (1902), 167; "François de Beauharnois," *BRH*, VII (1901), 302–9. "La seigneurie de Villechauve ou Beauharnois," *BRH*, XXXIV (1928), 276f. Benjamin Sulte, "Les Beauharnois au Canada," *BRH*, VIII (1902), 115f. [The author confuses Claude with his son of the same name, and his brother Guillaume. S.D.S.]. Henri Têtu, "Le chapitre de la cathédrale de Québec et ses délégués en France (1723–1773)," *BRH*, XVI (1910) 232, 238.

BEAULIEU ET DE LA GROSSARDIÈRE, JACQUES GOURDEAU (Gourdau) DE. *See* GOURDEAU

BEAUMARCHAIS, Sieur de. *See* JUCHEREAU DE SAINT-DENYS

BEAUMONT ET DE VILLECHAUVE, CLAUDE DE BEAUHARNOIS DE. *See* BEAUHARNOIS

BEAWANDO, *See* ATECOUANDO

BÉCANCOUR, PIERRE ROBINAU DE. *See* ROBINAU

BÉCART DE GRANVILLE ET DE FONVILLE, CHARLES (he signed **Fonville,** but was readily called Sieur de **Granville**), king's attorney, draughtsman, and cartographer; baptized 31 May 1675 at Quebec, son of Pierre Bécart de Granville and Marie-Anne Macard; d. 2 Jan. 1703 at Quebec, and buried the same day in the church there.

The son of an officer in the Carignan-Salières regiment, Charles first intended to follow a military career. In 1694 he was an ensign in the Marine, then, at least in 1695 and 1696, he served on the frigate *Bouffonne*. It therefore seemed that he was to follow the example of his brother Louis, who was two years older than he and who had begun his career in the navy in France in 1687. But it was Jean-Baptiste, born in 1670, king's attorney in the provost court of Quebec since 1695, that he was to succeed. When Jean-Baptiste died on 23 April 1699, CALLIÈRE and BOCHART de Champigny asked the minister to consent to nominate to this post young Charles Bécart, who would reach his majority the following year. On 20 April 1700 the king signed the desired commission, and on 11 October the Conseil Souverain admitted Bécart to his office as king's attorney. But two years later Bécart, still a bachelor, was attacked by the smallpox epidemic which was ravaging the colony at that time, and on 2 Jan. 1703 he died.

Charles Bécart had a great talent for drawing; according to Callière and Champigny he was even a genius. He had prepared some maps, and an admirable *Vue de Québec* (1699?). In 1700 he declared himself ready to teach cartography, which the intendant and the governor thought he alone was capable of doing. Their enthusiasm for Bécart's gifts was long shared by historians, who credited him with sketches published in 1930 in Paris and entitled *Les Raretés des Indes*. These drawings are now attributed to Louis Nicolas, a defrocked Jesuit who had been a missionary in New France from 1667 to 1675. But the fact remains that Bécart, as is proved by his maps and more especially by his *Vue de Québec*, had a good deal of talent, spontaneity, and freshness, and that his premature death deprived New France of a remarkable artist.

ANDRÉ VACHON

Jug. et délib., IV, 487. P.-G. Roy, *Inv. ins. Cons. souv.*, 100. Gareau, "La prévôté de Québec," 106f. Godbout, "Nos ancêtres," APQ *Rapport, 1953–55*, 531f. Le Jeune, *Dictionnaire*, I, 716. Tanguay, *Dictionnaire*, I, 42, 401. Harper, *Painting in Canada*. Morisset, *La peinture traditionnelle au C. f.*, 18f. P.-G. Roy, *La famille Bécard de Grandville* (Lévis, 1914); *Fils de Québec*, I, 92f., 97f.

Beevin

BERGER, JEAN, painter; b. *c.* 1681 at Saint-Dizier-au-Mont-d'Or, near Lyons, son of Jean-Claude Berger and Éléonore Montalan; d. after 1709.

Berger arrived in Quebec between 1700 and 1704 as a soldier. Quebec and Montreal had at that time a considerable number of prisoners captured in New England, and in particular a curious person, Pendleton Fletcher, with whom Berger became acquainted. Fletcher, along with a certain James Adams, a prisoner at Montreal, was convicted of making counterfeit card money. Berger was suspected of being an accomplice and was thrown into prison, but was freed pending an inquiry. The case was apparently not carried any further, and Berger seems to have profited from a fortunate combination of circumstances.

On 17 April 1706 he married in the church of Notre-Dame de Québec Rachel Storer (who had been rebaptized Marie-Françoise the day before), daughter of Jeremiah Storer and Ruth Masters. She had been born about 1687 at Wells (Maine), and with her older sister Priscilla and her cousin Mary had been carried off by Abenaki Indians at the same time as Adams and Fletcher.

In 1707 Berger was in business at Montreal as a painter. He was no doubt making a living after a fashion from his painting when the bad company he kept brought about his downfall. One evening in February 1709, two unknown persons gave the apothecary Claude de Saint-Olive a severe beating. Berger was accused of this misdeed and was imprisoned, but succeeded in proving his innocence. He would have been freed if the demon of music—for he was also a song-writer and singer—had not led him to compose a spiteful song in ten verses ridiculing Saint-Olive. In the heat of inspiration he allowed himself, to his misfortune, to attribute his incarceration to the venality of the "Gentlemen of the law." At first he was sentenced by the jurisdiction of Montreal to pay small fines to the king and Saint-Olive, to be put in the *carcan*, and to be banished. He appealed this sentence to the Conseil Supérieur, which not only

confirmed it but also banished him from the whole of Canada. Such severity towards an amiable scamp, who had just spent some months in prison undeservedly, leads us to believe that the authorities had simply been waiting for a pretext to rid the colony of him.

What happened then to Berger and his wife? They are never mentioned in the correspondence which Mary Storer carried on with her family. In 1729, however, Jeremiah Storer left part of his estate to Rachel "Bargee." It is therefore very probable that Berger settled in one of the English colonies.

We know nothing certain about Berger's work except that in 1706 he painted an altar frontal for the church of La Sainte-Famille on Île d'Orléans. Among the anonymous portraits of the time we may probably attribute to him those of Zacharie-François and JEAN-BAPTISTE HERTEL, which are now in the McCord Museum at McGill University.

JULES BAZIN

AJM, Greffe de Michel Lepailleur de Laferté, 21 déc. 1707. AJQ, Greffe de Jacques Barbel, 17 avril 1706; Greffe de Louis Chambalon, 26 août 1704. ANDM, Registres des baptêmes, mariages et sépultures. ANDQ, Registres des baptêmes, mariages et sépultures. AQ, NF, Ord. des int., I, 13f. ASQ, C 12. *Jug. et délib.*, V, 305, 1025. P.-G. Roy, *Inv. coll. de pièces jud. et not.*, I, 47, 301; *Inv. ins. Cons. souv.*, I, 119f.; *Inv. ord. int.*, I, 5f. Raymond Boyer, *Les crimes et les châtiments au Canada français du XVIIᵉ au XXᵉ siècle* (Montréal, 1966), 429–31. Coleman, *New England captives.* J. R. Harper, *Painting in Canada: a history* (Toronto, 1966). É.-Z. Massicotte, *Faits curieux de l'histoire de Montréal* (Montréal, 1922), 36–42. Gérard Morisset, *Coup d'œil sur les arts en Nouvelle-France* (Québec, 1941); *La peinture traditionnelle au C.f.*, 34f. J. R. Harper, "La galerie de portraits de la famille Hertel de Rouville," *Vie des Arts* (Montréal), XLVII (1967), 17f. É.-Z. Massicotte, "Le châtiment d'un chansonnier à Montréal au XVIIIᵉ siècle," *BRH*, XXII (1916), 46–49. Gérard Morisset, "Le peintre chansonnier Jean Berger," *La Patrie* (Montréal), 25 févr. 1951, 26. P.-G. Roy, "Les lettres de naturalité sous le régime français," *BRH*, XXX (1924), 225–32.

BERGIER, MARC, priest, missionary, vicar general of the bishop of Quebec for the missions in the Mississippi valley and superior of the missionaries of the seminary of Quebec in that region; b. *c.* 1667 at Tain, in the diocese of Vienne in the province of Dauphiné (probably Tain-l'Hermitage, department of Drôme); d. 9 Nov. 1707 at the Tamaroa mission (Cahokia, Ill.).

Marc Bergier arrived in Quebec in 1698. On 30 July 1699 he was received as a member of the Séminaire des Missions Étrangères of Quebec, and the next day he was appointed vicar general of

Bishop Saint-Vallier [LA CROIX] for the Mississippi region.

At this time he introduced himself as a "doctor of laws," the son of Jean-Jacques Bergier, a priest in retirement at the Hôpital Général of Vienne. He explained that his father had entered the priesthood shortly after becoming a widower, when Marc was still only a child four years of age. Unfortunately the missionary did not say where he had been educated, nor what were the circumstances that brought him to New France.

On 7 Feb. 1700, after an arduous six-month trip, Bergier arrived among the Tamaroas in company with the young ecclesiastic, Michel Buisson de Saint-Cosme, who was his helper until 1703. The vicar general was to succeed the founder of the Sainte-Famille mission, JEAN-FRANÇOIS BUISSON de Saint-Cosme (1667–1706), his companion's older brother.

Being entrusted with the care of what was a "disputed vineyard," Bergier in his turn soon came into conflict with the Jesuits, who continued to claim the Tamaroas' village as their exclusive spiritual fief. Indeed, a month later, Fathers Pierre-François Pinet and Joseph de Limoges came to take up the task of Saint-Cosme's rival, Father Julien Bineteau, who had died. The change in protagonists merely extended the quarrel over the Tamaroas. At the beginning, however, Bergier compromised with the Jesuits to avoid a scandal, while waiting for Bishop Saint-Vallier to settle the dispute. He contented himself with ministering to the handful of Frenchmen in the locality. Besides, it was difficult for him to compete with Pinet, since he possessed neither Pinet's gift for languages nor his missionary experience in the Illinois country.

After living for two years among the Tamaroas, Bergier complained of being still "a missionary without a mission, a superior without a command, and a vicar general without authority." The fact was that the Jesuits were unwilling to recognize the jurisdiction of the bishop of Quebec and his delegate. They even went further, according to Bergier, and resorted to the shabbiest means to prevent him from learning the Indian language with the aim of keeping a monopoly on the conversion of the Indians. "They would like to possess the right and the left in the kingdom of Jesus Christ," declared the missionary, frustrated in his field of action.

In the spring of 1702, however, Bergier was out of patience, and in order to obey Bishop LAVAL and Bishop Saint-Vallier he decided to carry out his duties among the Indians. He had been supplying his adversaries for eight months but henceforth was willing to let them have mass wine only in

exchange for Illinois Indians whom he could evangelize. He even went so far as to lay Pinet under an interdict. On the orders of his superior, Father GABRIEL MAREST, Pinet ignored the interdict. The vicar general consequently regretted having come to such an extremity. "So now we have confusion, scandal, and division in the village," exclaimed Bergier, "with altar against altar, missionary against missionary, Indians against Indians!" He even had doubts about the validity of his interdict, which the Jesuits disputed. More and more the Jesuits cried persecution, and pretended that they were the victims of the priests of the Missions Étrangères everywhere in the world, linking the quarrel over the Tamaroas with that of the Chinese rites.

But when Father Pinet finally learned that the arbitrators appointed by the king had a year before settled the dispute in favour of the seminary of Quebec, he gave way and on 14 June went to establish himself two leagues away among the Kaskaskias. Clear-sighted as he was, Bergier did not consider that because of this settlement he was out of his difficulties. He was too well aware of his limitations. "In this I recognize that the secrets of providence are truly impenetrable, and that God does not judge after the fashion of men," he said, "for the fact that He has taken this mission away from that Father to entrust it to me seems contrary to all reason, and I fear that it is a result of His justice upon me and upon the Indians for having responded so badly, all of us, to His favours. There they are, reduced to dry breasts. May God make them abundant, through His infinite mercy!"

As Bergier had foreseen, the mission to the Tamaroas was to make only slow progress under his direction, although at the time he was recognized to be the best missionary of the Missions Étrangères in the Mississippi country. The main obstacle to his apostolate was the impossibility, after Michel Buisson de Saint-Cosme's departure, of his accompanying the Indians on their summer and winter hunts. Having lost his assistant, he could hardly absent himself. At the beginning of 1707, however, he had to do so, to go to seek supplies at Mobile. He took advantage of his stay there to appease the violent quarrels between the civil and religious authorities of the locality.

Bergier applied himself to his ministry with fervour and great rigour. He raised several questions touching upon the celebration of baptism and marriage, as well as the observance of the Sabbath among the Indians: the solutions proposed by the Jesuits did not satisfy him. He moreover displayed a detachment and a trust in providence that were uncommon. In his opinion the missionaries should have looked to the generosity of the Indians for their subsistence rather than engaging in the fur trade, which associated the priests in the Indians' eyes with rich merchants. Despite the notorious poverty of the missions in the Mississippi country, he even reproached the bishop of Quebec for sending him too much money.

Bergier was indeed an ascetic whose extreme austerity caused fears for his health. His colleagues' misgivings were justified since he died 9 Nov. 1707 "with his stomach full of abscesses internally and externally, without any doctor or surgeon other than God alone." His death resulted from an epidemic during which he had lavished his attentions without stint upon the Indians. His death was esteemed to be even more heroic than that of St Francis Xavier, since the missionary to the Tamaroas had not been able to find support during his solitary agony in thinking of the fruits of his ministry.

The Indians mourned him, after having ill treated him. They bestowed upon him their highest praise, saying that Bergier was truly a man.

CÉLINE DUPRÉ

ASQ, Lettres, M, 38, p.29; N, 133; O, 41; P, 8, p.10; R, 29, 30, 41–73, 86; S, 101; Polygraphie, IX, 11, 26, 27. JR (Thwaites). Old Cahokia, a narrative and documents illustrating the first century of its history, ed. J. F. McDermott et al. (St Louis, 1949). Provost, Le Séminaire de Québec: documents et biographies, 435f. Alvord, Illinois country, I, 117, 139. Delanglez, French Jesuits in Louisiana, 20–23, 37–39, 62f., 379–86. Giraud, Histoire de la Louisiane française, I. Gosselin, Vie de Mgr de Laval, II, 463–94. Rochemonteix, Les Jésuites et la N.-F. au XVIIᵉ siècle, III, 550–73; Les Jésuites et la N.-F. au XVIIIᵉ siècle, I, 254–63. J. H. Schlarman, From Quebec to New-Orleans: the story of the French in America . . . Fort Chartres (Belleville, Ill., 1929).

BERLEY (Barley, Barlow), GEORGE, HBC captain; d. 1720?

Berley's date and place of birth are unknown but he was certainly an Englishman, and presumably he was a young man when he joined the HBC in 1708 as a gunner at £50 a year for three years. He served his term in the bay and then returned from Fort Albany to England in the ship Hudson's Bay [II] (Capt. Joseph DAVIS) in 1711.

It is not known what he did for the next 5 years. Probably he went to sea as a mate, for in 1716 he was given command of the HBC's new frigate Albany. She was a small vessel of about 80 tons designed especially "to go into Albany River," built by James Taylor, and launched early in 1716. Berley was obviously a competent seaman who

enjoyed the confidence of his superiors and peers. He took the Albany on her first voyage to Fort Albany in 1716 and Thomas McCliesh*, chief at the fort, wrote on 12 September that 5 to 9 September was spent getting the Albany frigate into Fort Albany; "Had not Captain Berley been a brisk hardy man the ship had been lost before he arrived in this road, off the Bay of Vapuska." McCliesh at the same time referred his superiors to Berley for a character reference for himself.

Berley made two more voyages in the Albany, to Fort Albany in 1717 and to Churchill in 1718. In 1719 as a successful and experienced HBC captain he and his ship were selected to join James KNIGHT's expedition. She sailed with the Discovery (Capt. David VAUGHAN) from the Thames to seek minerals and the northwest passage and was wrecked on Marble Island in 1719 or 1720, where everyone on the expedition perished.

A later George Berley, who distinguished himself as a gunner defending Fort Albany in 1739, may have been his son.

ERNEST S. DODGE

Founding of Churchill (Kenney). HBRS, XXI (Rich); XXV (Davies and Johnson).

BERMEN DE LA MARTINIÈRE, CLAUDE DE, esquire, seigneurial judge, seigneur, councillor in the Conseil Souverain and first councillor of the Conseil Supérieur, lieutenant general of the provost court of Quebec, acting attorney general of the Conseil Souverain from December 1681 to September 1682, and subdelegate of the intendant, Michel Bégon*, in 1714; b. 30 May 1636 at La Ferté-Vidame (department of Eure-et-Loir); d. 14 April 1719 at Quebec.

The son of Louis Bermen de La Martinière, a lawyer in the parlement of Paris, and Françoise Juchereau, La Martinière came to Canada in 1662 at the invitation of his relative, Nicolas Juchereau* de Saint-Denis. On 7 July 1664 he married Anne Després, the widow of Jean de Lauson* (the younger), the former grand seneschal of New France. La Martinière thus became the owner of the vast seigneury of Lauson, which was cleared and settled over the next 20 years, largely as a result of his efforts.

Like his father, La Martinière chose a legal career. Between 1662 and 1678 he served as the seigneurial judge of Beauport, Beaupré, Notre-Dame-des-Anges, and Île d'Orléans. In 1678 he resigned these positions to accept an appointment on the Conseil Souverain. There he soon displayed his aggressive temperament. In 1680 he investigated François-Marie Perrot*'s illegal fur-trading activities and issued such a scathing indictment of

Bermen de La Martinière

them that Governor Frontenac [Buade*] sought to have the inquiry discontinued. La Martinière, however, did not back down. With the support of the Conseil Souverain he completed his inquiry the following year.

La Martinière's career on the Conseil Souverain was interrupted in 1684 when he led a supply convoy to Port Nelson (Fort Bourbon) on Hudson Bay, where the Compagnie du Nord had established a post in 1682. When he arrived there he discovered that the post was in English hands and he was obliged to retreat. On the way back to Canada in 1685 the expedition captured the English vessel *Perpetuana Merchant*—the only achievement of the venture.

Upon his return to Quebec La Martinière was unjustly criticized by Governor BRISAY de Denonville for lack of aggressive action against the English. He was also sharply reprimanded by Seignelay [Colbert] for having been absent from the Conseil Souverain and in the employ of a commercial company; he was told to choose between the two positions. Although his salary of 1,200 *livres* as commander for the Compagnie du Nord far outweighed his earnings as councillor, La Martinière, who had suffered through an agonizing winter on Hudson Bay, chose to remain on the Conseil Souverain.

La Martinière's career as councillor was interrupted a second time in 1689. The death of his wife in March of that year had placed his title to the seigneury of Lauson in jeopardy, and he sailed to France, where he remained until the summer of 1691 defending his possessions. Litigation dragged on until 1699 when La Martinière was finally obliged to surrender his title to Thomas Bertrand, a Paris merchant, who had acquired the seigneury in payment of debts owed by a son of Anne Després, Charles-Joseph de Lauson. This reduced La Martinière's properties to the small seigneury of La Martinière or Beauchamp, adjoining Lauson, which had been granted to him in 1692.

On his return to the colony, La Martinière resumed his seat on the Conseil Souverain. In 1694 this body clashed once more with Frontenac, and La Martinière's report of the episode to Louis Phélypeaux, the minister of Marine, caused the authorities to censure the governor for his conduct. On 5 May 1700 La Martinière was appointed keeper of the seal of the Conseil Souverain, and on 1 June 1703 lieutenant general of the provost court of Quebec. He was promoted to the position of first councillor of the Conseil Supérieur on 5 May 1710, despite some differences with the intendant, JACQUES RAUDOT, and kept this position until his death.

On 9 April 1697 La Martinière's second marriage, to Marie-Anne Cailleteau, took place at Quebec. This union, which produced five children (two died in childhood), increased La Martinière's financial burden just when the loss of Lauson had deprived him of his major source of income. Some relief came in 1712 in the form of an annual pension of 200 *livres*, but this was far from sufficient. Consequently, La Martinière applied for a fur-trading licence (*congé*), which he sold to finance his daughter's education as a nun, and wrote his relative, the Duc de Saint-Simon, the famous author of memoirs, asking him to provide for his two sons.

In 1714 La Martinière, who on 27 April was appointed subdelegate of the intendant, became involved in the most controversial episode of his career. In the summer of that year, while Bégon was away in Montreal, La Martinière charged that the intendant had formed a grain monopoly that was causing a near famine in the colony and he sought to break it by means of police regulations. The Conseil Supérieur, acting immediately on this report, instructed the attorney general to draw up relief measures. When Bégon returned to Quebec he furiously claimed that this action constituted a direct challenge to his authority. Although the council was forced to accept the intendant's rebuke, bread riots subsequently occurred outside Quebec, giving some support to La Martinière's allegations. The intendant then accused La Martinière of having instigated these riots, but the latter successfully answered the charges.

La Martinière died on 14 April 1719 and the following day he was buried in the church of Notre-Dame at Quebec. He was survived by his third wife, Marie Molin, whom he had married on 4 Aug. 1710; Anne Cailleteau had died on 30 Nov. 1708. One daughter, Jeanne-Françoise, a nun, and two sons, Claude-Antoine, who went on to a distinguished military career in Canada, and Jean-Baptiste, who later left Quebec to reside in the Antilles, also survived him.

EDWARD H. BORINS

AN, Col., B, 9, ff.45, 110; C^{11A}, 6, ff.406–7; 7, ff.73, 211. "Les congés de traite accordés en 1717," *BRH*, XXIX (1923), 271. "Correspondance de Vaudreuil," APQ *Rapport, 1938–39, 1939–40, 1942–43, 1946–47, 1948–49. Documents relating to Canadian currency during the French period* (Shortt), I, 231, 265–67. *Documents relating to Hudson Bay* (Tyrrell). *Jug. et délib.*, I, II, III, IV, VI. "Lettres de Claude Bermen de La Martinière," *BRH*, XXXVIII (1932), 18–39. A. Roy, *Inv. greffes not.*, III, IV, VII, XVIII, XIX. P.-G. Roy, *Inv. concessions*, IV, 59.

Charland, "Notre-Dame de Québec: le nécrologe de la crypte," 176. Cahall, *Sovereign Council of New*

Bernard de La Rivière

France, 102, 107–11, 133–38. J. Delalande, *Le Conseil souverain de la Nouvelle-France* (Québec, 1927). Eccles, *Frontenac*, 146f., 302–4. Fauteux, *Essai sur l'industrie sous le régime français*. J.-E. Roy, *Claude de Bermen, Sieur de La Martinière, 1639–1719* (Lévis, 1891) [a good portion of this work, which is a brief biography, contains important documents]. E. H. Borins, "La Compagnie du Nord, 1682–1700," unpublished M.A. thesis, McGill University, 1968, 60–62, 80–87. P.-G. Roy, "Une supplique de M. de Bermen de La Martinière," *BRH*, XXXV (1929), 382–84 [contains an excerpt from a letter written by La Martinière to the Duc de Saint-Simon].

BERNARD DE LA RIVIÈRE (Darivière), HILAIRE, mason, building contractor, "architect," royal surveyor, court officer, legal practitioner, seigneurial attorney, and notary; b. *c.* 1640 in France; buried 1 Dec. 1729 at Quebec.

Hilaire Bernard de La Rivière was a building contractor. It was in this capacity that in 1688 Bishop Saint-Vallier [LA CROIX], who was at the time in France, engaged him to direct the work of enlarging the cathedral of Quebec and of building a church in Lower Town, the future Notre-Dame des Victoires. Once in Canada, La Rivière asked Intendant Champigny [BOCHART] to commission him as "royal measurer and surveyor"; this was done on 20 July 1689, even more easily perhaps since—as the intendant mentions—he had already exercised the same functions in France. He came to Canada with his wife, Marguerite Gillet. As far as we know, the couple had no children. Madame La Rivière was drowned at Sept-Îles, in 1693, when the *Carossol* was shipwrecked on the way back to France.

Having decided to stay in Canada, Bernard de La Rivière, displaying an enthusiasm and ambition worthy of a much younger man, made a remarkable career for himself. As an architect and contractor—two terms which were at that time more or less synonymous—he did a great deal of building, particularly in stone. On 28 Sept. 1692, with his *confrère* François de LAJOÜE, he undertook to do the stonework for the new fort of Quebec, as well as for the governor's residence, and on 3 June 1693, with the same partner, to build the Saint-Jean gate, according to the plans by Boisberthelot* de Beaucours. He also worked a great deal for private individuals, and trained several apprentices. His competence was acknowledged: the judges of the Conseil Souverain regularly commissioned him to "inspect" works or buildings and make reports on his findings. Nor did Bernard de La Rivière remain idle as a surveyor; theodolite in hand, he ranged tirelessly through all the seigneuries in the government of Quebec.

In 1707, without giving up any of his former occupations, he launched straight into another career. On 14 January Intendant JACQUES RAUDOT appointed him court officer to the Conseil Supérieur, and on the following 7 May notary and process-server in the *côtes* (land divisions) of the government of Quebec, "so long as there are no other notaries or serjeants at law [process-servers] established in the aforesaid places." Then, on 15 July 1711, he was appointed seigneurial attorney of the Lauson seigneury. On 6 November of the same year, Raudot allowed him to receive ratification at Quebec of any deeds which he might have drawn up on the *côtes*. (This did not give him the right to exercise the profession of notary at Quebec, as has been claimed, but only to have ratified there deeds made in the absence of one of the parties.)

Hilaire de La Rivière embarked upon his career as a legal officer and notary when he was nearly 70 years old. But the most remarkable thing is that all of his functions necessitated constant journeys, in winter as in summer, to all corners of the government of Quebec, and this in the extremely arduous conditions of the time, when the canoe and the snow-shoe were virtually the only means of getting around. His commission of 1707 made him the first of those itinerant notaries who covered one seigneury after another, with their pack on their back, in search of clients. Philippe Aubert de Gaspé, in his *Anciens Canadiens*, has given a picturesque description of these roving members of the body of notaries. As a process-server, Bernard de La Rivière had to serve notices, writs, decrees, and ordinances in the most remote places: on 10 Feb. 1710, for example, Jacques BARBEL was sentenced to pay him 36 *livres* for the six days taken up "in the journey that he [Bernard] made to serve on Julien Laigne living at Tilly a decree of this Council." As a surveyor, Bernard was in demand in seigneuries as far from Quebec as Sainte-Anne de la Pocatière to the east and Sainte-Anne de la Pérade to the west. His numerous and repeated absences prevented him from officiating as a legal practitioner; only rarely did he act in this capacity before the council.

This tireless walker did not cease his surveying trips until 1723, at the age of 83. His vigour was declining. The following year, on 26 Aug. 1724, in a commission that resembled a medical bulletin, Intendant Michel Bégon* appointed François Rageot* court officer to the Conseil Supérieur, "in view of the infirmity of the Sieur Hilaire Bernard de La Rivière which does not make it possible for him, because of his great age, to continue working." La Rivière received his last notarial act on 7 Oct. 1725. We know that on 30

June 1726 he was paralysed, but he lived another three and a half years.

Bernard de La Rivière had remarried 3 Nov. 1694 at Quebec; his second wife, Marie-Madeleine Voyer, bore him nine children, of whom three girls and one boy, born between 1703 and 1708, were still dependent on him in 1720. His family responsibilities must perhaps be considered as the reason for his protracted career. He had become a widower a second time at the beginning of October 1711, and on 22 Sept. 1712, at Beauport, he had married Gabrielle d'Anneville, Mathieu Lagrange's widow, who was buried 13 Oct. 1728 at Quebec.

When one contemplates the admirable activity of this old man, one inevitably thinks of La Fontaine's fable beginning: "An octogenarian was planting. . . ." But, in life as in the fable, it was the old man who was right.

André Vachon

AJQ, Greffe d'Hilaire Bernard de La Rivière, 1707–25; Greffe de Louis Chambalon, 22 oct. 1693, 2 nov. 1694, 31 janv., 21 mars 1695, 31 mai 1702, 8 mars 1715; Greffe d'Étienne Dubreuil, 20 sept. 1712, 30 juin 1726, 10 juillet 1729; Greffe de François Genaple, 3 oct., 25, 29 nov. 1688, 4 mai, 28 sept., 9 nov. 1692, 29 mai 1695, 22 oct. 1696, 2 oct. 1698; Greffe de Gilles Rageot, 2 mars, 28 mai 1691, 22 nov. 1692. AQ, NF, Coll. de pièces jud. et not., 254, 2036; NF, Ins. Cons. sup., III, 9f., 44f.; VI, 31v *et seq.*; NF, Ins. de la Prév. de Québec, I, 629, 707, 731; II, 353; III, 295, 306; NF, Ord. des int., I, 83v *et seq.*, 101v; IV, 17v. *Jug. et délib.*, III, IV, V, VI. *Ord. comm.* (P.-G. Roy), II, 183. Recensement de Québec, 1716 (Beaudet). A. Roy, *Inv. greffes not.*, VIII, 238–74. P.-G. Roy, *Inv. jug. et délib.*, *1716–1760*, VII, 44f., 62f. Godbout, "Nos ancêtres," APQ *Rapport*, *1955–57*, 420–22. Philippe Aubert de Gaspé, *Les anciens Canadiens* (Québec, 1863), 351f., 410. Auguste Gosselin, *Henri de Bernières, premier curé de Québec* (Les Normands au Canada, Québec, 1902), 160f., 374f. Jean Langevin, *Notes sur les archives de N.-D. de Beauport* (2v., Québec, 1860–63), I, 102. J.-E. Roy, *Histoire du notariat*, I, 109, 134, 158–60. P.-G. Roy, *La ville de Québec*, I, 520 (plate facing); II, 424f. J.-E. Roy, "La cartographie et l'arpentage sous le régime français," *BRH*, I (1895), 38–40, 53f.

BERTHIER, ISAAC, called Alexandre after 1665, captain in the Régiment de l'Allier and often called captain in the Carignan regiment, seigneur; son of Pierre Berthier and Marguerite Bariac; b. 1638 at Bergerac in the bishopric of Périgueux; d. 1708 on his seigneury of Bellechasse.

We have little information about Isaac Berthier before his arrival in New France. His promotion in the army was rapid, for he landed at Quebec on 30 June 1665 at the head of his own company; at that time he was with the troops brought from the West Indies by Prouville* de Tracy.

A few months after his arrival Isaac Berthier, who was a Huguenot, embraced the Roman Catholic religion. On that occasion he probably changed his first name and adopted that of Alexandre, which has led some historians to believe that there were two Captain Berthiers in Canada. One may well doubt this. The only two references to Isaac Berthier are in 1665; they are contained in a marriage contract drawn up on 12 Aug. 1665 at Quebec, which he witnessed, and in the register of abjurations of the archbishopric of Quebec, under the date of 8 Oct. 1665. After that we lose all trace of the name. As for Alexandre Berthier, the name appears for the first time on 1 May 1666, in the "Registre des confirmations" of the archbishopric of Quebec. In his correspondence with Colbert, Talon* speaks only of the "Sieur Berthier"; if there had been two Captain Berthiers, the intendant would not have omitted to specify whether Isaac or Alexandre was meant. However, the certificate of Alexandre junior's marriage at Notre-Dame de Québec on 4 Oct. 1702 provides us with the best proof: in it we read that Alexandre senior is a "former captain in the régiment de l'aliers," the regiment to which Isaac Berthier belonged. Hence we are presumably concerned with one and the same person.

After being billeted with his men at Quebec during the winter of 1665–66, Captain Berthier was appointed commandant of Fort de l'Assomption (Saint-Jean, Quebec), then named with Pierre de Saurel* to command the rear-guard of the troops during Prouville de Tracy's 1666 expedition against the Mohawks. He returned to France with the soldiers of the Carignan regiment, and came back in 1670 to Canada, where on 11 Oct. 1672, in the parish church of Notre-Dame de Québec, he married Marie Legardeur de Tilly, sister of Catherine who had married Pierre de Saurel in 1668. Eighteen days later he received from Talon the Bellechasse seigneury (Berthier-en-bas), and the following year he bought the seigneury of the Sieur Hugues Randin* (Berthier-en-haut or Villemur), which was considerably enlarged by a subsequent land grant. Meanwhile he had taken part in two expeditions against the Iroquois.

After 1674 Alexandre Berthier devoted himself particularly to agriculture and to the settling of his seigneuries. The data of the 1681 census show that he was the largest farmer on the Villemur fief. In the same year, Buade* de Frontenac pointed out in a report that Berthier and several associates had "five canoes and ten men engaged in fur-trading in the woods." Some while later, he went to live on his seigneury of Berthier-en-bas, and as

Bertier

captain of the militia of that seigneury he led his own company at the time of BRISAY de Denonville's expedition against the Senecas in 1687.

Although he was not a personage of the first rank, Alexandre Berthier enjoyed a certain esteem, since the authorities invited him to the assemblies of notables. At the meeting organized by Frontenac in 1678 to discuss the brandy trade, Berthier and his brother-in-law Pierre de Saurel declared themselves jointly in favour of such trading. As a seigneur, Berthier also took part in the council of war in Quebec in 1682. It is therefore not surprising that Le Febvre* de La Barre considered proposing him for the post of governor of Montreal in 1683.

Alexandre Berthier died at the end of 1708 at Berthier-en-bas. Five years before his death he had bequeathed all his possessions to his daughter-in-law, Marie-Françoise Viennay-Pachot, Alexandre junior's widow; at his death he also left her with the burden of a 24-year-old lawsuit that he had brought against the seigneuress of Rivière-du-Sud (Montmagny, Quebec), Geneviève Després, over the boundaries of their seigneuries.

ULRIC LÉVESQUE

AJQ, Greffe de Louis Chambalon, 3 juin 1699, 18 juin 1704. AQ, NF, Cahiers d'intendance, I, 6, ff.238–43; 7, ff.310–19. Caron, "Inventaire de documents," APQ Rapport, 1939–40, 207. "Correspondance de Frontenac (1672–82)," APQ Rapport, 1926–27, 123. "Correspondance échangée entre la cour de France et l'Intendant Talon pendant ses deux administrations dans la Nouvelle-France," APQ Rapport, 1930–31, 39, 45, 61. Découvertes et établissements des Français (Margry), I, 407f. Jug. et délib. JR (Thwaites), L, 140; LXII, 156. Recensement du Canada, 1681 (Sulte). A. Roy, Inv. greffes not., XVIII, 347f.; XIX, 121. P.-G. Roy, Inv. concessions, II, 179–83, 187–89; Inv. ord. int., I, 38, 68f.

Bonnault, "Le Canada militaire," 275, 333. Régis Roy et Malchelosse, Le régiment de Carignan. Sulte, Mélanges historiques (Malchelosse), VIII. M. Berneval, "Régiment de l'Allier," NF, V (1930), 316. "La famille Berthier," BRH, XX (1914), 379f. Amédée Gosselin, "Les deux capitaines Berthier," BRH, IX (1903), 310f. S.-A. Moreau, "Le capitaine Berthier," BRH, IX (1903), 273f. P.-G. Roy, "Les deux capitaines Berthier," BRH, IX (1903), 56–58; "La mort de M. de Berthier," BRH, XXII (1916), 209–10; "La seigneurie de Bellechasse ou Berthier," BRH, XXVII (1921), 65–74. Régis Roy, "Isaac et Alexandre Berthier, capitaines au régiment de Carignan," RSCT, 3d ser., VII (1913), sect.i, 125–37. H. Têtu, "Les abjurations à Québec en 1665," BRH, XI (1905), 26.

BERTIER (Berthier), MICHEL, king's surgeon at the Hôtel-Dieu of Quebec; b. 1695 in France, son of Antoine Bertier and Antoinette Cochon, both of Saumur (Anjou); d.5 Sept. 1740 at Quebec.

Michel Bertier collaborated on many occasions with Michel SARRAZIN, particularly in 1727 at the bedside of the second bishop of Quebec, Jean-Baptiste de LA CROIX de Chevrières de Saint-Vallier. Thirteen years later Bertier was to assist another bishop on his death bed, François POURROY de Lauberivière, stricken with typhus contracted while tending the typhus cases on the *Rubis* during an Atlantic crossing. Bishop Lauberivière's death brought down upon Bertier the wrath of Canon Pierre Hazeur* de L'Orme. In a subsequent letter, the fiery and quarrelsome canon accused Bertier of having "in no small way contributed to hastening the death of our poor bishop by the brusque nature of his treatments: it was the all too frequent blood-lettings that brought about a stroke and then occasioned the death of our dear prelate. . . ." However, Bertier's heroic death during this same epidemic disproves flatly the canon's diagnosis. In fact it was while tending the typhus cases from the *Rubis* at the Hôtel-Dieu that Bertier, weakened by working night and day, contracted the terrible disease and succumbed on 5 Sept. 1740. He was buried in the church of Notre-Dame de Québec.

On 17 Sept. 1724 he had married Marie-Anne Denys, daughter of the provost marshal Paul DENYS de Saint-Simon and Marie-Madeleine de Peiras. Only one of the seven children of this union survived their father.

In those far-off times, infectious diseases were rife in New France, and a close watch had to be kept on the ships coming up the St Lawrence. For this reason, about 1720 Michel Bégon* established what may be called a period of quarantine, and the first member of the profession responsible for the supervision and inspection of ships was Michel Bertier. Ten years later an epidemic of smallpox ravaged the colony and, according to the intendant, Gilles Hocquart*, affected more than 2,000 people, of whom a large proportion perished; Bertier again displayed an unsurpassed devotion to duty, as did also his *confrères*, Sarrazin and Joseph Benoist*. Consequently Hocquart asked the king, on their behalf, for a small recognition "in consideration of the extraordinary service which they have given, with as much unselfishness as courage."

CHARLES-MARIE BOISSONNAULT

AN, Col., C¹¹ᴬ, 60. Charland, "Notre-Dame de Québec: le nécrologe de la crypte," 209. Abbott, History of medicine, 27f., 30. Ahern, Notes pour l'histoire de la médecine, 49f. P.-G. Roy, "La quarantaine sous le régime français," in Les petites choses de notre histoire (Lévis, 1919), I, 129–33. Henri Têtu, "Le chapitre de la cathédrale de Québec et ses délégués en France (1723–1773)," BRH, XIV (1908), 131.

BESCHEFER, THIERRY, priest, Jesuit, missionary, superior of the Canadian mission; b. 25 March 1630 at Châlons-sur-Marne (province of Champagne); d. 4 Feb. 1711 at the Jesuit college in Reims.

Thierry Beschefer entered the noviciate at Nancy, in the ecclesiastical province of Champagne, on 24 May 1647. If we are to believe what we read in the registers of the society, we gather that he had superior intellectual gifts which won him his colleagues' esteem. By the time he was in his second noviciate year he was teaching at Pont-à-Mousson, where from 1650 to 1653 he devoted himself to the study of philosophy. He then taught in several Jesuit colleges. On finishing his studies and being ordained a priest in 1661 he taught rhetoric, again at Pont-à-Mousson, then classics at the college in Metz. He must have done his Third Year at Nancy, since he made his profession at the noviciate there on 15 Aug. 1664.

On 19 June 1665 Beschefer arrived at Quebec on Captain Le Gagneur's ship, which likewise carried four companies of the Carignan-Salières regiment. His superiors immediately urged him to study the Huron language at Quebec. The energy with which Prouville* de Tracy undertook at that time to subdue the Iroquois gave the most turbulent members of the Five Nations, the Mohawks and the Oneidas, cause for reflection, and in the summer of 1666 an embassy from the two tribes appeared at Quebec and asked for peace talks. The lieutenant general then decided to send Father Beschefer, with some of the envoys, as ambassadors to the English, the new masters of New Amsterdam (New York). The Jesuit departed 20 July 1666, accompanied by an interpreter, Jacques de Cailhault de La Tesserie, and a *donné*, Charles Boquet*. By 28 July, however, he was back at Quebec with his whole escort: the embassy had been stopped at Trois-Rivières by the news that the Mohawks had massacred three Frenchmen and captured M. de Lerole Canchy, M. de Tracy's cousin.

Beschefer went back to studying the Huron language. According to the register for 1667 he was sent in the last months of that year to spend the winter on the Îles Percées (across from Boucherville); it is more probable that he spent it at Pierre BOUCHER's newly cleared farm at Boucherville. In 1668 Beschefer was appointed superior of the mission to the Algonkins at Cap-de-la-Madeleine; this mission post was in decline then because of the disorders arising from the trade in spirits and does not seem to have been kept up after 1670, when Beschefer left it. Father Jean Pierron*, another native of Champagne, was at the time in charge of the Martyrs' mission in the Mohawk country, one

of the most unrewarding of the period because of the influence which the inhabitants of Albany had on these Indians. In 1670 Pierron came to Quebec to seek help, and Beschefer was sent to aid him, along with Father François Boniface. During the years 1670–71, 84 persons were baptized at the mission, but 74 of these neophytes died after receiving the sacrament, most of them being children under seven years of age.

On 12 July 1671 Father Claude Dablon* took over the office of rector of the Jesuit college in Quebec and superior general of the mission. In 1672 he called Beschefer to Quebec and entrusted to him the duties of minister of the college, prefect of studies, prefect of the church and confessor, and catechist at the church. During the whole of Father Dablon's superiorship Beschefer fulfilled these functions, to which he added that of chaplain of the prison of Quebec. On 6 Aug. 1680 he became superior in his turn. His administration coincided with the renewal of the Iroquois peril, for the fear which had kept the cantons quiet since Tracy's campaigns had been dispelled. The governor of New York, Thomas Dongan, was planning to dominate all trade to the north and west by using the Iroquois, to whom he offered prices for their furs that the French could not compete with. The Iroquois began systematically to destroy the most distant allies of the French, with the intention of falling upon the colony along the St Lawrence when they had isolated it. Meanwhile Buade* de Frontenac left Canada and was succeeded by Le Febvre* de La Barre. On 10 Oct. 1682 the new governor convened an assembly of the notables of the country at the Jesuit college. Beschefer, as the superior, attended it with Fathers Dablon and Frémin*. The peril was lucidly analysed and energetic measures were decided upon. But we know that the governor's indecision and blunders served only to make the Iroquois more daring.

In a letter to the provincial in Paris dated 21 Oct. 1683 Father Beschefer, as superior, reported on the state of the missions. The most distant were assigned to three large districts, each with a superior responsible to Quebec. The Tadoussac mission covered all the basin of the Saguenay up to its source, both shores of the St Lawrence as far as its mouth, and part of the Maritimes. It was directed by Father François de CRESPIEUL, who was aided by two missionaries and who followed the nomads over this territory on their hunting and trading expeditions. The mission to the Ottawas was run by Father Jean ENJALRAN, whose assistants ranged over the three lakes, Huron, Michigan, and Superior, and even at this time were going among the Sioux. The mission to the Iroquois was divided among the Five Cantons and was under the direction of Father JEAN DE LAMBERVILLE. Finally, closer to Quebec and directly dependent upon it were: the mission to the Hurons at Lorette, the mission at Sillery, where several Abenakis had just arrived seeking refuge, the mission at Sault-Saint-Louis (Caughnawaga), to which came Christians abandoning the Iroquois tribes. The main difficulty encountered by the missionaries was the Indians' fondness for spirits, a fondness which the European traders, English, Dutch, or French, exploited shamelessly.

On 18 Aug. 1686 Beschefer was replaced as superior by Father Claude Dablon and again became prefect of studies at the college, adviser to the mission, and confessor at the church. He was to carry out these duties until 1690. Two letters, all that remains of a close correspondence with M. Cabart de Villermont, are the only documents by him that we have for this period. The first, dated 19 Sept. 1687, recounts in detail BRISAY de Denonville's expedition against the Senecas (1687) and a military exploit by PIERRE LE MOYNE d'Iberville in the Hudson Bay region (1686). The second letter, written on the 22 October following, gives information concerning Canada's riches in natural resources, several samples of which the Jesuit sent to France.

In 1690 the provincial of France recalled Beschefer to Paris to be procurator of the Canadian mission, with his residence at the Collège Louis-le-Grand. However Beschefer gave up this charge and sailed again for Canada in the summer of 1691, but he was obliged to take advantage of a meeting with another ship to return to France because of illness. He went back to his native province of Champagne and lived at the Jesuit college in Reims, where he served as minister and prefect of the church. In 1707, as his health was declining, he no longer had any role but that of confessor. From 1709 on he is referred to as an old man but nevertheless retained the office of adviser. He died two years later, having almost reached the age of 81.

LUCIEN CAMPEAU

ARSI, Francia 23 and 24; Gallia 10, ff.153–54. JR (Thwaites). *Catalogi sociorum et officiorum provinciae Campaniae Societatis Iesu ab anno 1616 ad annum 1773*, éd. L. Carrez (10v., Châlons, Paris, Lille, 1897–1914).

BEVAN (Beevin, Beven), WILLIAM, HBC sloopmaster; chief at Moose Fort; fl. 1723–37.

William Bevan, who was described as a "diligent, careful" man, sailed from London to Albany Fort in 1723 as mate of the *Beaver* sloop. Four years later he succeeded George Gunn as master. Bevan, like Gunn, was "deficient in the language," but because no better man was available, he also took over as trader at the vessel's winter base on the Eastmain River.

In anticipation of the building of a new post near the mouth of Moose River, Bevan and Joseph ADAMS were sent there from Albany Fort in 1728 to take soundings. They began their journey of about 100 miles along the flat coast of James Bay, but their boat soon became leaky, and they were obliged to continue by canoe. The exchange of craft undoubtedly gave Bevan some experience of the dangers faced by Indians who could travel from Moose River to Albany Fort only during the short summer season [*see* SCATCHAMISSE]. Then, as now, the few suitable landing places were unapproachable except at high tide; furthermore, there were no migrating geese to satisfy the hungry, wind-bound traveller. While in Moose River Bevan and Adams discovered the site of the post which Pierre de Troyes* had captured from the HBC in 1686.

In 1732, two years after Moose Fort was established, Bevan was made "Chief Factor and Commander" there. Like his predecessors, John Jewer and Thomas RENDER, Bevan found the men at Moose Fort given to "Mutiny and Sottishness," and he apparently had little control over them. This state of affairs, together with Bevan's own laxity—he accepted without close investigation a bad-tempered cook's explanation that the "prodigious Smoak" in the kitchen was caused by "the steem of the dishwater on the hot Bricks"—led to the destruction by fire of Moose Fort in the space of two hours on the night of 26 Dec. 1735. An Indian girl lost her life and three HBC men died afterwards from exposure and hunger. After collecting the scattered remains of property and food, and making temporary shelter, Bevan set the men to work rebuilding Moose Fort.

Bevan, whose contract had been renewed by the HBC in 1736 before news of the fire reached London, was recalled to England in 1737 and was succeeded at Moose by Richard Staunton*.

ALICE M. JOHNSON

HBC Arch. B.135/a/3–5 (Moose Fort journals, 1732–35). HBRS, XXV (Davies and Johnson) includes several letters from Bevan and the Moose Fort council.

BIGOT, FRANÇOIS, seigneurial attorney, royal notary, court officer, son of François Bigot, *dit* Lamothe, and Marguerite Drapeau; b. sometime between 1643 and 1645 in France; buried 28 Oct. 1708 at Champlain.

François Bigot arrived in Canada with his parents and his sister Marie in 1662 or shortly before, and lived at first with his father, who was one of Pierre BOUCHER's farmers at Cap-de-la-

Madeleine. He seems to have had a deep love for the land, and was a farmer a long time, if not all his life. On 30 June 1666 he received from Quentin Moral two grants of land, each measuring two *arpents* by 40, in the fief of Arbre-à-la-Croix. This must have been some sort of confirmation of a grant already made, for as early as 1667 Bigot declared that he had six acres under cultivation there. But he soon went and settled in the Prairies Marsolet, having acquired there a piece of land measuring three *arpents* by 40 from Pierre Durand on 12 Sept. 1669, for the sum of 80 *livres*; he increased this holding by buying a like amount from Mathieu Brunet on 14 April 1679, and by 1704, thanks to a grant of 13 *arpents* by 40 made to him by GÉDÉON DE CATALOGNE, Bigot had rounded off his property nicely. Meanwhile he had rented the domain of the Marsolet fief, but he relinquished his lease on 4 March 1678. In 1681 he possessed in his own right 6 head of cattle, 13 acres of cleared land, and 3 muskets.

We do not exactly know how it happened, but at the beginning of the 18th century Bigot was holding certain legal offices: in 1702 and 1704 he was styled seigneurial attorney of the Champlain seigneury, and certainly from 1704 on he was drawing up documents as a court officer in the royal jurisdiction of Trois-Rivières. In addition, on 8 Oct. 1702 he was acting as a notary, an office that he kept until his death. His registry is now lost, but we know two of the acts that he received.

It was in the Prairies Marsolet that Bigot brought up his 11 children. He had first married, in 1666, Catherine Baillargeon, who died childless sometime between 1670 and 1672. He remarried 24 Oct. 1672 at Château-Richer, his second wife being Marie Bouchard d'Orval, who was buried 19 June 1717 at Champlain. When Bigot died in 1708 he left three children under age; the act of guardianship was drawn up on 9 Aug. 1710, and the inventory of the estate on the 26 August following. In this estate were a few books that throw light upon the naïve faith of the time: *Le Nouveau Testament, Le martyre d'André, catéchiste, Petite délimitation de la dévotion à l'Ange Gardien, La vie de Ste-Catherine de Sienne*; and a single secular work, *Le parfait notaire*.

ANDRÉ VACHON

AJM, Greffe d'Antoine Adhémar, 14, 16 avril 1679, 15 mars 1704, 11 oct. 1712. AJQ, Greffe de Claude Auber, 25 juin 1663; Greffe de Louis Chambalon, 7 oct. 1697; Greffe de Pierre Duquet, 4 mars 1678. AJTR, Greffe de Séverin Ameau, 12 sept. 1669, 28 juin 1670, 17 nov. 1673, 5 févr. 1674; Greffe de Jacques de La Touche, 8 déc. 1665, 30 juin 1666; Greffe de Daniel Normandin, 3 mars 1704, 12 juillet 1719; Greffe de J.-B. Pottier, 9, 26 août, 28 nov. 1710.

Jug. et délib., IV, 677; V, 37, 250, 727f., 873. Recensement du Canada, 1666 (APQ *Rapport*). Recensements du Canada, 1667, 1681 (Sulte). Godbout, "Nos ancêtres," APQ *Rapport*, 1955–57, 458f. "Les notaires au Canada," 9f. Tanguay, *Dictionnaire*, I, 51. Cloutier, *Histoire de la paroisse de Champlain*, I, 57–62, 127; II, 68. Raymond Douville, "Quel François Bigot fut notaire royal," *BRH*, LXII (1956), 89–91. André Vachon, "François Bigot dit Lamothe fut-il notaire royal?" *BRH*, LXI (1955), 129–32.

BIGOT, JACQUES, priest, Jesuit, missionary to the Abenakis, brother of VINCENT BIGOT; b. 26 July 1651 at Bourges, France; d. April 1711 at Quebec.

Jacques Bigot had entered the Jesuit noviciate in Paris on 9 Sept. 1667. When he arrived in Canada in 1679 he was assigned to the mission to the Algonkins at Sillery, near Quebec, where the Abenakis, fleeing from the war being waged against them by the English, were taking refuge. Sillery was soon no longer adequate to receive these immigrants. The soil, which had been badly farmed by its former settlers, was exhausted, and firewood was no longer to be found in the proximity of the dwellings. Father Bigot settled the Abenakis near the falls on the Chaudière River, on ground for which he obtained a grant on 1 July 1683 from Le Febvre* de La Barre and de MEULLES.

This new mission, which was named Saint-François de Sales, became the most zealous in North America. In his 1684 report the missionary wrote: "Everyone in this country agrees that no one has ever seen a tribe here receive so readily the teachings of our mysteries." Every year Father Bigot went on a preaching trip to the Abenakis who had remained in Acadia. In 1687 he was instructed by BRISAY de Denonville to go to the region of Boston in order to urge the Abenakis to settle at his mission, so as to increase the number of inhabitants and so that they might join the French in case of attack. Two years later the village on the Chaudière numbered not fewer than 600 souls. In 1690, in a report to Seignelay [Colbert], Denonville rejoiced that "the good relations that he had with these Indians, thanks to the Jesuits and in particular to two priests, the Bigot brothers, has ensured the success of all the attacks they have made upon the English."

In the autumn of 1691 Father Bigot went to France, taking with him the Abenakis' vow to Our Lady of Chartres and a large wampum belt for the canons of the cathedral. In return the canons gave him, to take back to the Abenakis, a large chemise in a reliquary, which he took back with him to Quebec in the spring of 1694.

In September 1698 Father Bigot went for a few months to replace his brother Vincent, who was

Bigot

ill, at Naurakamig, an Abenaki village in Acadia. The following month he accompanied the Abenakis to the seaside to treat for peace with the captain of an English ship. These negotiations came to nothing, as the captain of the ship proposed that the Indians expel the French missionaries and replace them by Protestant clergymen. Father Bigot was back at Quebec in the spring of 1699.

As the land at the falls on the Chaudière had become unproductive for growing corn, Father Bigot decided in 1700 to transfer the mission to the shores of the Saint-François River, where a certain number of Sokokis and Abenakis had been settled since 1676 at least. There he obtained as a grant for his Indians a good part of the seigneuries of Saint-François and Pierreville. According to the testimony of Bacqueville de La Potherie [LE ROY], who visited him in his bark cabin in 1701, Father Bigot's life in the midst of his Indians was given over completely to spreading the gospel. Drunkenness was the great evil that he had to combat. And as this vice was caused by vagabondism, he strove to induce those Indians who practised it to settle down at the mission. The sight of the orderly life which was led and of the veritable fervour which reigned there, together with the exhortations of the good Christians, contributed even more than the missionary's urgings to bringing the profligates back into the strait and narrow path.

Bigot had to leave the Saint-François mission in the autumn of 1707 or at the beginning of 1708. He was stricken by a lingering disease and retired to live at Quebec, where he died in April 1711.

THOMAS CHARLAND, O.P.

AN, Col., C¹¹A, 8, ff.108, 129, 132, 132v, 176, 177, 183, 193v, 235, 238, 239v; 9, ff.121, 130v, 159, 159v; 11, 185v. [*Jacques Bigot*], *Copie d'une lettre escrite par le père Jacques Bigot de la Compagnie de Jésus l'an 1684, pour accompagner un collier de pourcelaine envoié par les Abnaquis de la mission de Sainct François de Sales dans la Nouvelle-France au tombeau de leur sainct patron à Annecy* (Manate [New York], 1858); *Relation de ce qui s'est passé de plus remarquable dans la mission Abnaquise de Sainct Joseph de Sillery, et dans l'establissement de la Nouvelle Mission de Sainct François de Sales, l'année 1684. Par le R. P. Jacques Bigot de la Compagnie de Jésus* (Manate [New York], 1857); *Relation de ce qui s'est passé de plus remarquable dans la mission Abnaquise de sainct Joseph de Sillery, et de sainct François de Sales, l'année 1685. Par le R. P. Jacques Bigot, de la Compagnie de Jésus* (Manate [New York], 1858); *Relation de la mission Abnaquise de St. François de Sales l'année 1702, par le Père Jacques Bigot, de la Compagnie de Jésus* (New York, 1865). *Documents inédits concernant la Compagnie de Jésus*, éd. Auguste Carayon (28v., Poitiers et Paris, 1863–74), XI, 277. *JR* (Thwaites), LXII, LXIII, LXIV. Father Bigot's letter which Carayon and Thwaites date as 26 Oct. 1699 should be 26 Oct. 1698 according to A.-L. Leymarie, *Exposition rétrospective des colonies françaises de l'Amérique du Nord. Catalogue illustré* (Paris, 1929), 278. *NYCD* (O'Callaghan and Fernow), IX, 354, 440. J.-A. Maurault, *Histoire des Abénakis depuis 1605 jusqu'à nos jours* (Sorel, 1866). Rochemonteix, *Les Jésuites et la N.-F. au XVIIᵉ siècle*, III, 226–29, 289–90, 377, 395–96, 407, 437–39.

BIGOT, VINCENT, priest, Jesuit, missionary to the Abenakis, brother of JACQUES BIGOT; b. 15 May 1649 at Bourges, France; d. 7 Sept. 1720 in Paris.

Vincent Bigot had entered the Jesuit noviciate in Paris on 2 Sept. 1664. He arrived in Canada in 1680 and was first attached, in 1681–82, to the Algonkin mission at Sillery, then in 1682–83 to the mission to the Iroquois at La Prairie-de-la-Magdeleine. He returned to Sillery in 1683 and was superior of the mission until 1690. Then, when his brother Jacques returned to France, he took his place at the Saint-François de Sales mission at the falls on the Chaudière River. In 1694 he went to found the mission to the Abenakis at Pentagouet in Acadia. He directed this mission for more than seven years, transferring it in 1698 to Naurakamig on the Androscoggin River. This locality was better suited to farming. He baptized the majority of the Indians of this village. During the summer of 1698 he fell ill and was replaced for some months by his brother Jacques, whose place he took at the Chaudière mission. It was from there that on 25 Sept. 1699 he wrote to renew the union of prayers between the Abenakis and the canons of the cathedral of Chartres, to whom he sent a belt, six feet long, composed of 11 strings of wampum. In return the canons sent the Abenakis a small silver statue of the Virgin, a copy of an ancient wooden statue which is kept in the underground church of the cathedral of Chartres.

According to tradition it was Vincent Bigot who founded the Abenaki mission at Bécancour in 1700; in reality this mission was founded by Father Sébastien RALE, but not until after 1705. Bigot returned to his Acadian mission in 1700, but was withdrawn from it by his superior the following year. It was claimed that he was not sufficiently zealous in keeping his Abenakis attached to the interests of France. On 6 Oct. 1701 Brouillan [MOMBETON] the governor of Port-Royal (Annapolis Royal, N.S.), wrote to the minister, Pontchartrain: "It is certain . . . that he has not been able to prevent the Indians from entering into negotiations with the English and that these negotiations have progressed to the point where they have received the presents and have promised to make peace with them."

After attending the meeting of the Indian tribes which opened on 25 July 1701 at Montreal to ratify the peace of 1700, Vincent Bigot went to aid his brother at the Saint-François mission, concerning himself particularly with training the Abenakis in church singing. From 1704 to 1710 he was at Quebec, where he held the office of superior general of the Jesuit missions in Canada. During these years he had rescued from the hands of the Abenakis two English prisoners: Marie-Anne Davis, who became a nun at the Hôtel-Dieu of Quebec in 1710, and Esther Wheelwright*, who entered the Ursuline convent in Quebec and was elected superior in 1760. In 1713 Father Bigot returned to France, where he held the office of procurator of the missions in Canada until his death on 7 Sept. 1720.

THOMAS CHARLAND, O.P.

[Vincent Bigot], *Relation de ce qui s'est passé de plus remarquable dans la mission des Abnaquis à l'Acadie, l'année 1701* (Manate [New York], 1858). Caron, "Inventaire de documents," APQ *Rapport, 1940–41*, 437. *Coll. de manuscrits relatifs à la N.-F.*, II, 386. *JR* (Thwaites), LXXI. T.-M. Charland, *Histoire des Abénakis d'Odanak* (Montréal, 1964), 56. A.-L. Leymarie, *Exposition rétrospective des colonies françaises de l'Amérique du Nord. Catalogue illustré* (Paris, 1929), 278–79. J.-A. Maurault, *Histoire des Abénakis depuis 1605 jusqu'à nos jours* (Sorel, 1866). Rochemonteix, *Les Jésuites et la N.-F. au XVIIe siècle*, III, 226, 229, 282, 290, 298, 302, 377, 406, 437–39, 443.

BIRD, THOMAS, HBC chief at Albany Fort, 1737–39; d. 1739.

Nothing is known about Thomas Bird's origin or the circumstances of his entry into the HBC. He sailed from London in 1719 in the *Hudson's Bay* [III] (Capt. Richard WARD), which was wrecked off Cape Tatnum on 24 August. After working as book-keeper at York Fort, Bird was transferred to Fort Prince of Wales, Churchill River, in 1720. Except for two short periods, when he held temporary command, he served successively under Nathaniel BISHOP, Richard Norton*, Anthony BEALE, and again Richard Norton. Bird was recalled to England in 1733. His failure to reach even the rank of second before 1731 was apparently due to the lack of respect shown him by the men at Churchill River.

In 1734 Bird was re-engaged as second at Albany Fort; he held that position until 1737 when he became chief on the retirement of Joseph ADAMS. Bird's death, probably "hastened by an immoderate use of liquors," occurred at Albany on 21 June 1739. He was succeeded by Rowland WAGGONER and survived by a child living in England.

It is unlikely that this Thomas Bird was related to his contemporary of the same name who was secretary to the HBC and died in London in 1735.

ALICE M. JOHNSON

[Letters to the Governor and Committee written by Bird and his colleagues at Fort Prince of Wales and Albany Fort are printed in HBRS, XXV (Davies and Johnson). The volume also includes references to manuscript journals kept by Bird and housed in the HBC archives. A.M.J.]

BISHOP, NATHANIEL, joined the HBC in 1686 and died as master of the company's Churchill River post on 30 June 1723.

Bishop was employed at York Fort from 1686 to 1693 when he sailed for England. He returned to York the following year, and became a prisoner of the French when they captured the post on 4 Oct. 1694. He was back in London early in 1696, rejoined the company, and helped recapture York later that year, only to become PIERRE LE MOYNE d'Iberville's prisoner when the French again took the fort in 1697. He arrived back in London in time to sail to Albany on the company's supply-ship in 1698.

After a short stay in England, from 1703 to 1705, Bishop returned to James Bay as deputy to Governor Anthony BEALE. The two sailed for England in 1708, and returned to their old positions in James Bay for another three-year spell in 1711. In 1715 Bishop was again at Albany as second to Thomas McCliesh*, who spoke highly of him in letters to the company. During the next five years, Bishop frequently wintered on the East Main; he returned to England in 1720. In 1721 he was appointed master at Churchill River (Fort Prince of Wales), but he could not take over the post until the following year as the supply-ship *Hannah* was unable to reach Churchill. Meanwhile Richard Staunton* remained in charge of the post. On 5 April 1723 Bishop fell sick of what he believed to be gout and died on 30 June. Richard Norton* and Thomas BIRD temporarily assumed "charge" at Churchill, and notified the company's committee in London of Bishop's death.

RICHARD GLOVER

HBRS, XXI (Rich); XXV (Davies and Johnson). *Kelsey papers* (Doughty and Martin). Morton, *History of the Canadian west*.

BISSOT, FRANÇOIS-JOSEPH, merchant and navigator, bourgeois of Quebec, co-seigneur of Mingan; b. 19 May 1673, son of François Byssot* de La Rivière and Marie Couillard; d. 11 Dec. 1737 at Quebec.

Bissot de Vinsenne

François-Joseph Bissot is known to us particularly through his efforts to develop the land grant of Mingan, which his father had received from the Compagnie des Cent-Associés in 1661 and which extended from "Île aux Œufs . . . as far as Sept-Îles and into Grande Anse, towards the Esquimaux country where the Spaniards usually fish." On 9 Nov. 1695 he formed a company with Louis Jolliet* and his wife Claire-Françoise Bissot, Charles Jolliet, and Charles-François Bissot, to trade at Mingan for five years, but by the following year Jolliet was working alone there.

Bissot nonetheless spent several years at Mingan: at least two of his children were born there, in 1716 and 1718. He hunted seal and traded with the Indians, endeavouring, as he was later to emphasize to the minister, to make contact with them 100 miles inland and prevent them from having dealings with the Hudson's Bay Company. Between these more or less lengthy stays he lived at Quebec, where he finally retired in 1733.

That year François-Joseph Bissot leased Mingan to his son-in-law, Jean de Lafontaine* de Belcour, but the contract, which was signed on 29 April, was cancelled on 13 September of the same year. On 14 Sept. 1734 he rented this land grant to the Sieurs Fleury* de La Gorgendière and Trottier* Desaulniers for two years. Finally, by a contract signed on 15 March 1736, he let it out for nine years to Jean-Louis Volant* d'Haudebourg, who was to pay him 1,200 *livres* each year.

From 1733 on he redoubled his efforts to have his ownership titles ratified. Having lost the documents in a fire, and fearing that his estates would revert to the king's domain, he wrote to Maurepas, to explain the work that he had carried out at Mingan and the disbursements that he had made. As he received no answer, he wrote to him again in 1737. This time the minister asked Beauharnois* de La Boische and Hocquart* to make the necessary inquiries and recommendations, but it was too late, for Bissot had already died when the letter reached New France.

François-Joseph Bissot's other activities are not well known. In 1731, by agreement with the councillor Martin Chéron, he sought authorization to drag for anchors lost in the roadstead of Quebec; anticipating rather heavy expenses, he asked to be exempted from the dues to be paid. His request was supported by Beauharnois and Hocquart in their letter of 24 Oct. 1731 to the minister. We know of two lawsuits brought by Bissot: one in 1729, against the parish council of Quebec, concerning a pew in the cathedral, the other against the Sieur Vaucour, a navigator.

François-Joseph Bissot was married on 4 Feb. 1698 to Marie Lambert Dumont; he had 9 children, 6 daughters and 3 sons. He died on 11 Dec. 1737 at Quebec and was buried the next day.

NIVE VOISINE

AJQ, Greffe de Claude Barolet, 29 avril 1733, 14 sept. 1734, 15 mars 1736; Greffe de Guillaume Roger, 9 nov. 1695. A. Roy, *Inv. greffes not.*, XVIII, 201. P.-G. Roy, *Inv. concessions*, III, 190. Godbout, "Nos ancêtres," APQ *Rapport, 1957–58*, 385f. P.-G. Roy, *Le sieur de Vincennes, fondateur de l'Indiana et sa famille* (Québec, 1919).

BISSOT DE VINSENNE (Vincennes), FRANÇOIS-MARIE, eldest son of JEAN-BAPTISTE BISSOT de Vinsenne and of Marguerite Forestier, second ensign in the troops of Canada and half-pay lieutenant in those of Louisiana, commandant of the posts of the Ouyatanons (Weas), near modern Lafayette, Indiana, and of the Peanguichias (Piankeshaws), subsequently called Vincennes, on the Ouabache (Wabash) River; b. 17 June 1700 in Montreal; burned by the Chickasaws near the present site of Fulton, Mississippi, 25 March 1736.

Vinsenne spent almost his entire life among the Miami Indians. A letter he wrote in 1733 shows that he was only 13 years old when he first accompanied his father on a visit to this tribe. In 1718 he was posted among the Ouyatanon Miamis, who lived on the upper Ouabache, and within the next four years was appointed commandant of the Ouyatanon post. Although he was still only a cadet in the colonial troops, this young officer was already noted for his skill in handling the Indians.

In the mid 1720s the area in which Vinsenne was posted was assuming great strategical importance. By using the river system of the Ouabache and the Belle Rivière (Ohio) the English, who had been intensifying their pressure on the west since the treaty of Utrecht, would be able to enter the Mississippi valley and disrupt communications between Canada and Louisiana. The Compagnie des Indes, to which the ownership of the southern colony had been granted in 1717, feared that this incursion would entail the loss of the Illinois country and might eventually cause the ruin of the French North American empire. To cope with the British threat, it revived the plans which had first been formulated in 1713 to build a post in the region where the Ouabache, the Rivière des Cheraquis (Tennessee), and the Cumberland River made their junction with the Belle Rivière. The commanding officer who would be posted at this crucial point would be expected to cooperate with Vinsenne in blocking English penetration of the west and protecting communications between the two French colonies.

Because of its inability or unwillingness to make the expenditures necessary to build this post and to stock it with merchandise for the Indians, the company did not carry out its plan. To maintain control of the region it relied on Vinsenne, whose influence over the Miamis gave him considerable power. Thus, while he was still under Canadian jurisdiction, this officer gradually became an agent of Louisiana. He held the rank of half-pay lieutenant in the troops of the southern colony and also received an annual subsidy from its government consisting of a gratuity of 300 *livres*, which was added to his regular salary, and a sum of 800 *livres* for the purchase of gifts for the Indians.

In 1730 Vinsenne severed his connections with Canada by moving down the Ouabache with his Indians. On 1 July of the following year the Compagnie des Indes ceded Louisiana to the crown and immediately afterwards steps were taken to have a post erected near the junction of the Ouabache and the Belle Rivière. Vinsenne appears to have begun the construction of this establishment late in 1731 and to have completed it early the following year. In 1733 he described it in one of his dispatches to Jean-Baptiste Le Moyne* de Bienville, the governor of Louisiana. It was located some 80 miles up the Ouabache, near the present site of Vincennes, Indiana, and consisted of two buildings surrounded by a palisade. Five Indian tribes that could field between 600 and 700 warriors lived nearby in four villages. The commandant complained that a lack of troops and merchandise was making it difficult for him to control these natives. On occasion, in order to present them with gifts, he had to borrow from travellers or draw upon his personal belongings. The situation was further complicated in 1735 when the English appeared on the Belle Rivière and made efforts to win the Indians to their side.

Early in 1736, Vinsenne and several Miami warriors set off for Fort de Chartres in the Illinois country to join forces with Pierre d'Artaguiette who was preparing an expedition against the Chickasaws. This warlike nation, which inhabited an area made up roughly of the present state of Tennessee and of the northern parts of Mississippi and Alabama, had an alliance with the English of the Carolinas and for several years had been harassing the settlements of the French and attacking their convoys on the Mississippi River. Finally, Bienville had decided to make war on them. The campaign plans which he drew up called for his force and that of d'Artaguiette to meet in Chickasaw country and to march together against the enemy.

D'Artaguiette's army, made up of approximately 140 Frenchmen and 266 Indians, was the first to arrive at the rendezvous. With supplies running low and the Indians showing signs of restlessness, the commander decided to capture three small Chickasaw villages in order to seize their provisions. The attack began early on the morning of 25 March. The first two villages were easily taken and the assault on the third was under way when several hundred Chickasaw warriors appeared on the scene to lend their support to their beleaguered tribesmen. D'Artaguiette's scouts had failed to notice that the three villages formed part of a much larger complex which lay half concealed in the surrounding hills. Abandoned by the Miamis and the Illinois who had panicked and fled, d'Artaguiette ordered the rest of his army to retreat, but with the Chickasaws in furious pursuit he was obliged to stop and give battle. Despite a valiant stand by the French and their Iroquois and Arkansas auxiliaries they were soon overwhelmed by superior numbers. The Chickasaws killed several of them during the engagement and also took some 20 prisoners, including d'Artaguiette, Vinsenne, Louis d'Ailleboust de Coulange (the younger), Saint-Ange [Pierre Groston], Louis-Marie-Charles Dutisné and the Jesuit Antoine Sénat, who had accompanied the expedition as chaplain.

For the events that follow the principal sources are the account of a Chickasaw slave woman and that of Drouet de Richerville, who was taken prisoner but who managed to escape after spending two years in captivity. The captives, except for a few who were set aside to be tortured later or to be used in prisoner exchanges, were led into the centre of one of the villages where they mounted two pyres which had been prepared by the Chickasaw women. These were then set ablaze. The victims suffered this torment without flinching. Led by Father Sénat they sang hymns and canticles in firm voices, even as the flames were engulfing them.

Vinsenne was survived by his half-breed wife, Marie Longpré, the daughter of a wealthy settler of Kaskaskia, whom he had married in 1733, and by two daughters. His memory, like that of his father, was long revered by the Miamis.

YVES F. ZOLTVANY

AN, Col., B, 35, 43; C^{11A}, 44, 52, 56, 63; C^{13A}, 9, 11, 16, 17, 19, 20; D^{2C}, 222; F^{3}, 24. *Découvertes et établissements des Français* (Margry), VI.

Alvord, *Illinois country*. N. M. Belting, *Kaskaskia under the French régime* (University of Illinois studies in the social sciences, XXIX, no.3, Urbana, 1948), 77. J. P. Dunn, *The mission to the Ouabache* (Ind. Hist. Soc. pub., III, no.4, Indianapolis, 1902). Pierre Heinrich, *La Louisiane sous la Compagnie des Indes, 1717–1731* (Paris, [1908]). Rochemonteix, *Les Jésuites*

Bissot de Vinsenne

et la N.-F. au XVIIIᵉ siècle, I. P.-G. Roy, Sieur de Vincennes identified (Ind. Hist. Soc. pub., VII, no.1, Indianapolis, [1917]).

BISSOT DE VINSENNE (Vincennes), JEAN-BAPTISTE, second ensign in the colonial regular troops, agent of New France among the Miami Indians; b. 19 Jan. 1668 in Quebec; d. 1719 among the Miamis near the present site of Fort Wayne, Indiana.

Bissot de Vinsenne was one of 12 children of François Byssot* de La Rivière and Marie Couillard. Claire-Françoise, a daughter of this marriage, married Louis Jolliet*, the discoverer of the Mississippi. Jean-Baptiste entered the seminary of Quebec in 1676 but, being unfit for the ecclesiastical state, left this institution in 1680. On 20 Oct. 1687, as he was preparing to leave for France to seek employment, he asked the Conseil Souverain to grant him his letters of majority so that he might have the right to administer his property.

We next hear of Vinsenne in 1694. At that time he had returned to Canada and had apparently decided to make his career in the west. In 1694 and 1695 he sold the properties which he owned in the colony, consisting of half the seigneury of Vincennes, lands in the seigneury of Lauson, and certain rights in the seigneury of Mingan on the north shore of the St Lawrence. Towards 1695 he was named second ensign in the colonial regular troops and the following year was sent by Frontenac [Buade*] to command among the Miami Indians, who inhabited the territory southeast of Lake Michigan. In 1704, the governor, Philippe de Rigaud de Vaudreuil, informed the court that Vinsenne enjoyed much influence over this important tribe and that New France stood in great need of his services.

Vinsenne was not above trading with the Indians when he went on his diplomatic missions to the interior. He did so in 1704 when Vaudreuil sent him among the Miamis for the purpose of urging them to offer compensation to the Senecas whom they had recently attacked. This misuse of his commission greatly angered Pontchartrain, the minister of Marine, and may explain why Vinsenne never won promotion in the colonial troops. Vaudreuil, however, did not lose confidence in his agent. He continued to regard him as the colony's leading expert on Miami affairs and to make frequent use of his services.

From 1712 until 1719 Vinsenne appears to have resided permanently with the Miamis, arbitrating their quarrels with the Illinois and urging them to make war on the Foxes. After 1715, one of his principal responsibilities was to prevent his Indians from falling under English control. To achieve this end he was instructed by Vaudreuil to exhort them to move away from the Maumee River, where they had recently settled, and to return to their old village near Fort Saint-Joseph at the southeastern tip of Lake Michigan. Only a few of the Miamis had complied when Vinsenne died in 1719. For this reason, the governor decided to consolidate French control of the Maumee River area by sending the experienced Jacques-Charles Renaud Dubuisson to establish a garrisoned post there in 1721.

On 19 Sept. 1696, in Montreal, Vinsenne had married Marguerite Forestier, daughter of Antoine Forestier, surgeon, and of Marie-Madeleine Le Cavelier. They had four daughters and three sons, one of whom was François-Marie.

YVES F. ZOLTVANY

AJM, Greffe d'Antoine Adhémar, 6 sept. 1696. AJQ, Greffe de Louis Chambalon, 25 oct. 1694, 22 févr., 9 mars 1695, 21 mai 1703. AN, Col., B, 27, 39; C¹¹ᴬ, 22, 24, 33, 34, 35, 40, 42, 124; D²ᶜ, 47. "Correspondance de Vaudreuil," APQ Rapport, 1938–39, 1947–48. Jug. et délib., II, 799, 834–35; III, 189–90. P.-G. Roy, Inv. concessions, III, 19; Sieur de Vincennes identified (Ind. Hist. Soc. pub., VII, no.1, Indianapolis, [1917]).

BLAINVILLE, JEAN-BAPTISTE CÉLORON DE. See CÉLORON

BLAISE DES BERGÈRES DE RIGAUVILLE, NICOLAS, officer, commandant of Fort Niagara, seigneur; b. 1679 at Estampes (France), son of RAYMOND BLAISE Des Bergères de Rigauville, captain, and of Anne Richard de Goigni; buried 11 July 1739 in the church of Berthier-en-bas (Bellechasse).

On 29 July 1685, when he was about six, Nicolas Blaise Des Bergères, accompanying his father to New France, arrived at Quebec. As a cadet, he showed an aptitude for a military career, so much so that in 1696 His Majesty granted him a commission as an ensign "subject to his being 18." As Des Bergères had not reached the required age, Louis de Buade* de Frontenac was unable to have him appointed an ensign until 1698. In 1703 he was with his father, who was then commandant of Fort Frontenac. He may have succeeded the latter as commandant of Fort Chambly in 1709.

He was promoted lieutenant in 1726, and was in command at Fort Niagara from 1730 to 1736. In July 1730 the garrison of the fort revolted against Des Bergères' discipline and threatened him with death. The instigators of the revolt were taken to Montreal to be tried. Three of them were sentenced to death, but succeeded in escaping the day before they were to be executed. On 20 March 1736 the state, in recognition of the excellent services of this active and intelligent officer, conferred on him the rank of company commander.

On 4 April 1712, at Quebec, Nicolas Blaise Des Bergères had married Marie-Françoise Viennay-Pachot, widow of Alexandre Berthier, junior, and daughter of François Viennay-Pachot* and of CHARLOTTE-FRANÇOISE JUCHEREAU de Saint-Denis. As a dowry, the young widow brought him two seigneuries: Berthier-en-bas (Bellechasse), where the couple lived, and Berthier-en-haut (Villemur), which they sold to Pierre de Lestage, a Montreal merchant, on 26 April 1718. From their marriage nine children were born: one was Jean-Baptiste-Marie Blaise* Des Bergères de Rigauville, an officer, who was among the first Canadians to be named to the Legislative Council by Carleton* in 1775; another was Charles-Régis, priest and canon of the chapter of Quebec.

Nicolas Blaise Des Bergères died on his seigneury, probably on 10 July 1739. He was buried the following day in the church of Berthier-en-bas.

MARCEL BELLAVANCE

AJQ, Greffe de Florent de La Cetière, 10 mars 1712. AQ, NF, Registres d'intendance, III. "Correspondance de Frontenac (1689–99)," APQ *Rapport, 1928–29*, 301, 317, 344, 363, 368. P.-G. Roy, *Inv. coll. pièces jud. et not.*, I, 79; *Inv. concessions*, II. *Royal Fort Frontenac* (Preston and Lamontagne). P.-G. Roy, *Les officiers d'état-major*. Salone, *La colonisation de la Nouvelle-France*. Sulte, *Mélanges historiques* (Malchelosse), IX. Aegidius Fauteux, "Raymond Blaise," *BRH*, XXXIII (1927), 283. P.-G. Roy, "La famille Viennay-Pachot," *BRH*, XXI (1915), 339; "La seigneurie Bellechasse ou Berthier," *BRH*, XXVII (1921), 65–74. Benjamin Sulte, "Nicolas des Bergères de Rigauville," *BRH*, VIII (1902), 249–51.

BLAISE DES BERGÈRES DE RIGAUVILLE, RAYMOND (he sometimes signed **des Bergères**), captain, commandant of Forts Niagara, Frontenac, and Chambly, town major of Trois-Rivières; b. 1655 in the diocese of Saint-Pierre at Orléans (department of Loiret), son of Jean Blaise Des Bergères and Marie Boucher; d. 21 July 1711 at Montreal.

Des Bergères is believed to have served for seven years in the second company of the king's musketeers. On 5 March 1685, some months before his departure for America, he was promoted captain in the colonial regular troops. He then joined the officers and soldiers accompanying the new governor, BRISAY de Denonville, whose mission in Canada was to check the Indian menace and to oppose English designs on the territory belonging to France. About three years before, the

Iroquois, encouraged this time by Governor Dongan of New York and the merchants of Albany, had started waging guerilla warfare again.

Des Bergères' wife, Anne Richard de Goigni, was probably already dead when he arrived in Quebec, on 29 July 1685, with his son NICOLAS, who was six years of age.

Upon Denonville's arrival New France immediately took the offensive. In 1686, while the Chevalier de Troyes* and the LE MOYNE brothers were seizing the English forts on Hudson Bay, the governor was preparing a great punitive expedition against the Senecas south of Lake Ontario. The expedition, in which Des Bergères took part, reached the lake in July 1687. As the Indians had fled before the army's advance, the French formally took possession of the territory after burning the villages and destroying the crops. Denonville then built a stockade fort at Niagara to close the route by which beaver might be taken to the English and to assure future communications with the west. Command of the fort was entrusted to the Chevalier de Troyes and that of the garrison to Raymond Blaise Des Bergères.

The winter of 1687–88 was a tragic one at Niagara. Scurvy broke out among the garrison and nearly all the men succumbed to it, including the Chevalier de Troyes, who died on 8 May 1688. Only 12 soldiers and their officer, Des Bergères, survived.

The captain was not to remain long in command of the fort. Its destruction was, in fact, one of the conditions for peace imposed upon Denonville by Dongan, who was arming the Iroquois against the French. Faced in the summer of 1688 with the bloody guerilla warfare waged by the Mohawks along the Richelieu River, the French governor ordered the evacuation of Niagara, as he was to order that of Fort Frontenac the following year under the same circumstances. Des Bergères thus left the fort in mid-September 1688 and immediately returned to Montreal with his garrison.

Some months after his return from Niagara Des Bergères succeeded Captain François Lefebvre, Sieur Duplessis, as commandant of Fort Saint-Louis at Chambly. The Sieur Duplessis' reluctance to give up command of this important post was perhaps the cause of hostility between the two men. In any case on 15 July 1689, after an altercation, the two captains fought a duel in which Des Bergères was slightly wounded. The duelists were immediately arrested and imprisoned, and their case was examined the next day at Montreal. After a long inquiry the matter finally came before the Conseil Souverain on the following 16 November. Both were "acquitted of the accusation brought against them because of the duel." The Sieur

Blaise Des Bergères

Duplessis was, however, sentenced to pay 600 *livres* to Des Bergères as well as court costs.

Despite this incident Des Bergères kept his post at Chambly. He was to remain there until 1696. Because of its geographical situation Chambly was of the utmost strategic importance, especially in those difficult years when the colony had to bear up against the combined attacks of the Indians and English and to launch its own offensives.

On 12 Oct. 1691 the intendant, BOCHART de Champigny, complained to the minister about Des Bergères who, according to him, was using up "a considerable quantity of provisions, munitions, and warehouse equipment." When the minister told him of this accusation, Buade* de Frontenac replied on 15 Sept. 1692 that these expenditures "were real" and were well employed. At the same time he expressed his satisfaction with Des Bergères in the following terms: "But what I can tell you without being untruthful is that there is no one here in command of a fort who keeps things in as good state as he does, who is more vigilant, and in whom one must put greater trust . . . his post is the most sought after and the most exposed of all. It is one of the keys to the country, and our enemies are before its stockades almost every day, so that it is necessary to be as alert as I know he is to alleviate the anxiety that I would have for it, if someone less attentive were in his place." Des Bergères may even have contributed out of his own pocket to the rebuilding of the fort in 1693. In recognition of his excellent services the governor granted him that year a gratuity of 500 *livres*.

On 8 Nov. 1694, at Montreal, Des Bergères married Jeanne-Cécile Closse, widow of Jacques Bizard*, town major of Montreal and seigneur of Île Bizard, and daughter of Lambert Closse*. Eminent personages, such as M. de CALLIÈRE, were present at the marriage.

Two years after his marriage Des Bergères gave up command of Fort Chambly. This took place at the moment when Frontenac was preparing to lead a strong expedition against the Onondagas. Naturally the governor retained the services of the man whose qualities he had praised so highly some years before. The expedition left Montreal at the beginning of July 1696 and some days later reached Fort Frontenac; it had been restored the preceding summer by the Chevalier Thomas Crisafy* who had died in Montreal in February 1696. The governor pursued his campaign in August, having entrusted the defence of the fort to the Marquis Antoine de CRISAFY, brother of the Chevalier, and to Raymond Blaise Des Bergères. The expedition was completely successful and was back at Montreal in September.

Des Bergères too probably returned to Montreal, where he must have lived with his family until 1700. During these few years his wife bore him three children, of whom only one, Marie-Joseph, born 3 May 1698, lived. Madame Des Bergères died on 4 Feb. 1700 at Montreal.

Left alone with a two-year-old baby and Nicolas, who was 21 by then, Des Bergères took up his career again. The command of Fort Frontenac was vacant as a result of the removal and arrest of LA PORTE de Louvigny, who had been engaged in the fur trade illegally. Des Bergères was in command at this post until 1704; his son Nicolas was a member of the garrison. In this position Des Bergères again showed himself deserving of the confidence of the authorities of the colony, as is attested by the reaction on the part of RIGAUD de Vaudreuil and François de Beauharnois* de La Boische to the possibility of Des Bergères' nomination to the newly created post of king's lieutenant at Trois-Rivières. "The latter is required for the king's service at Fort Frontenac, where he is in command," they wrote to the minister on 15 Nov. 1703.

In 1707 Des Bergères was called to command Fort Chambly for the second time. The gravity of the military situation made necessary the presence of an experienced officer in this post, for the rumour persisted of an invasion by the English via the Richelieu River.

From that time forth it appears that Des Bergères aspired to the quiet life which a permanent and well-paid appointment would procure for him. The post of town major of Trois-Rivières had been vacant since the death of MICHEL GODEFROY de Linctôt on 18 May 1709. Des Bergères asked for the office and was granted it in May 1710. Previously he may have left his son Nicolas in command of Fort Chambly; on 13 Nov. 1709, at Île Dupas, he had married Marguerite Vauvril de Blason, the widow of Lambert Boucher*, Sieur de Grandpré. He died on 21 July 1711 at the Hôtel-Dieu of Montreal.

Raymond Blaise Des Bergères lived in Canada at the period of the first open struggles between New France and New England. In his capacity as commandant of forts which were situated at strategic places, Des Bergères was one of the artisans of French supremacy in America, a supremacy which was seriously compromised by the treaty of Utrecht.

MARCEL BELLAVANCE

AJM, Greffe d'Antoine Adhémar, 8 nov. 1694; Registres d'état civil de Notre-Dame de Montréal, novembre 1694, janvier 1697, octobre 1699, février 1700, juillet 1711. "Correspondance de Frontenac (1689–99)," APQ *Rapport, 1927–28*, 114–22, 123–28. *Jug. et délib.*, III, 364–67. Lahontan, *Nouveaux voyages*, I, 123f., 168f., 276f. *NYCD* (O'Callaghan and Fernow), IX, 651f., 664f., 714. *Royal Fort Frontenac* (Preston and Lamontagne), 391f., 397–401, 402. P.-G. Roy, *Les officiers d'état-major.* Lanctot, *Histoire du Canada*, II. G. F. G. Stanley, *Canada's soldiers; the military history of an unmilitary people* (Toronto, 1960). Sulte, *Mélanges historiques* (Malchelosse), IX. Raymond Douville, "Deux officiers 'indésirables' des troupes de la Marine," *Cahiers des Dix*, XIX (1954). Aegidius Fauteux, "Raymond Blaise," *BRH*, XXXIII (1927), 283–84. É.-Z. Massicotte, "Duel et coups d'épée à Montréal sous le régime français," *BRH*, XXI (1915), 356. P.-G. Roy, "Les commandants du fort Niagara," *BRH*, LIV (1948), 133; "Le duel sous le régime français," *BRH*, XIII (1907), 132; "Raymond-Blaise des Bergères," *BRH*, XXII (1916), 227–35. Benjamin Sulte, "Nicolas des Bergères," *BRH*, VIII (1902), 249–51; "Raymond des Bergères de Rigauville," *BRH*, VIII, 212–15.

BLANCHARD, GUILLAUME, early settler on the Petitcodiac River; b. at Port-Royal (Annapolis Royal, N.S.), 1650; son of Jean Blanchard and Radegonde Lambert; d. 1716.

In 1672 Guillaume married Huguette Gougeon, daughter of Antoine Gougeon and Jeanne Chabrat. They had 12 children between 1674 and 1698. In July 1698, Blanchard and two of his sons joined Pierre TIBAUDEAU on the latter's second expedition to the Chipoudy (Shepody) River. The Blanchards, sailing in their own boat, explored the Petitcodiac before returning to Port-Royal in the autumn. In the summer of 1699 they returned to the Petitcodiac and established a small settlement, known for a time as "Village des Blanchard," probably near the present site of Hillsborough, N.B. Blanchard returned again the next year, and in 1701 he left two sons, a daughter, and her husband to spend the winter on the Petitcodiac.

Legal suits had been threatened by CLAUDE-SÉBASTIEN DE VILLIEU on behalf of his father-in-law, MICHEL LENEUF de La Vallière (the elder), resident at Beaubassin, who claimed the Chipoudy and Petitcodiac settlements as part of his seigneury. A declaration of 1703 by the Conseil d'État, repeated in 1705, confirmed the settlers in the possession of their land, but also stated that La Vallière was to have seigneurial rights over the land. La Vallière's successful claim destroyed the settlers' hope of obtaining seigneurial rights for themselves and their descendants. The Blanchard family continued to grow, and numerous Blanchards, probably descendants of Guillaume, were enumerated among the more than 300 Petitcodiac settlers in 1752.

MAUD HODY

AN, Col., B, 27, f.153; C¹¹D, 3, ff.225–26; 4, ff.178–83; 5, ff.81–83 (copies in PAC); Section Outre-Mer, G¹, 466 (Recensements de l'Acadie, 1671, 1686, 1693, 1698, 1700, 1701; copies in Archives de l'université de Moncton). PANS, MS docs., XX. Rameau de Saint-Père, *Une colonie féodale*, I, 239, 243–47, 254, 267–69; II, 333–37. Ganong, "Historic sites in New Brunswick," 316.

BLAWBEK (Blewbeck). *See* CAGENQUARICHTEN

BLEURY, JACQUES-CHARLES DE SABREVOIS DE. *See* SABREVOIS

BOCHART DE CHAMPIGNY, JEAN, Sieur de **Noroy** et de **Verneuil,** chevalier, intendant of New France, 1686–1702; b. after 1645, son of Jean Bochart de Champigny, intendant of Rouen, and Marie Boivin; d. December 1720 at Hâvre-de-Grâce, France.

On 22 July 1686 Jean Bochart de Champigny, accompanied by his pregnant wife and two of his sons, set sail from La Rochelle to take up his appointment as intendant of New France. Fortunately the voyage was not as prolonged as Atlantic crossings could be at that time of year. In mid-September, they arrived at Quebec in good health and a few days after disembarking Madame de Champigny, née Marie-Madeleine de Chaspoux, Dame de Verneuil et Du Plessis-Savari, gave birth to a daughter. It was likely during these first days in the colony that Champigny had the copy of the bronze head of Louis XIV by Bernini placed on a pedestal in the market place in Lower Town. This extraordinarily fine work he had brought with him so that the Canadians could know what their monarch looked like. It still stands in the same place today. On the 23d of the month Champigny's commission as intendant of justice, civil administration, and finance, dated April 1686, was registered by the Conseil Souverain. For the ensuing 16 years, longer than any intendant except Hocquart*, he was to be accountable to Louis XIV and the minister of Marine for the social well-being, internal security, economic prosperity, and the maintenance of law and order in New France. For discharging these onerous responsibilities he received a salary of 12,000 *livres* a year; not enough to meet the living expenses of a man in his station. As compensation, however, he had the prestige and authority that went with the office, made manifest by his personal body-guard of five archers and large staff of junior officials. Although his official status in the colony ranked beneath that of the governor, and in a tangential way below that of the bishop, yet the exercising of his powers affected the people, for good or ill, in far more ways than did that of either of his superiors.

Champigny's appointment was unique in one respect; unlike all the other senior officials in the colony, before and after him, he had not held

Bochart de Champigny

office under the crown before. Unfortunately very little is known of his pre-Canadian career. The documents that might have supplied this information were likely lost when the château at Champigny, near Paris, was destroyed during the Franco-Prussian war. That he had not served an apprenticeship in more junior posts is surprising, particularly since he must have been in his mid-thirties when he left for Canada—his eldest son was made a sub-lieutenant in the navy in 1688.

It is even more surprising in the light of the fact that some eight generations of the Bochart family had served the crown in one administrative capacity or another. The first Bochart of whom mention is found, Guillaume, was a native of Vézelay in Burgundy. He appears to have done nothing more noteworthy than acquire the fief of Noroy; but with his son Jean, who in 1440 became a counsellor in the *parlement*, the family began its steady rise in the world. During the ensuing two centuries Bocharts were prominent in the legal profession, acquired considerable wealth, and contracted marriage alliances with leading families of both the robe and the sword; families such as the Montmorencys, the Tronsons, and the La Portes. Bishop LAVAL was a Montmorency, the superior of the Sulpicians in Paris was a Tronson, and both acknowledged their kinship to Champigny. Cardinal Richelieu on the distaff side was the most notable member of the La Porte family. By 1596 a Bochart was a councillor of state and had acquired the fief of Champigny. Then, in 1624, Jean Bochart, Seigneur de Champigny, de Noroy et de Bouconvilliers was appointed superintendent of finance and controller general. Four years later he became first president of the *parlement* of Paris. It was one of his numerous grandsons, Jean Bochart VIII, who came to serve the crown in New France. Thus, the Baron de Lahontan [LOM D'ARCE], officer of the colonial regular troops, wrote the truth when he remarked: "This new intendant is a member of one of the most illustrious families of the Robe in France."

The governor general of the colony, Jacques-René de BRISAY, Marquis de Denonville, informed the minister that he could not thank him enough for his happy choice of intendant and he expressed the wish that the king might be so fortunate as to be served by men as faithful and disinterested throughout his realm. These good relations among the senior officials had been sought by the minister and the expectation may explain why Champigny, despite his lack of experience in the royal service, was selected for such an onerous position. The two preceding intendants, de MEULLES and Duchesneau*, had proven incapable of working in harmony with the incumbent governors, devoting too much of their time to squabbling and even open conflict. The colony's administration had suffered greatly in consequence, and the minister was determined to have no more of it. To the surprise of many in the colony, and the disappointment of certain fractious elements with a penchant for fishing in troubled waters, he was not disappointed.

It was indeed fortunate that these cordial relations existed during the first three years of Champigny's intendancy, for the colony was on the eve of a cruel war that was to endure for 13 years. Champigny was to see large sections of the colony laid waste by the Five Nations of the Iroquois Confederacy, see a New England fleet and army assault Quebec, and was to play no small part in its slow struggle to a decisive victory in a war waged from the Atlantic to Hudson Bay and west beyond the Mississippi. During these same troubled years French sovereignty, and his responsibilities, were pushed far into the interior of the continent, beyond the Great Lakes, and down the Mississippi Valley. Within the confines of the central colony on the banks of the St Lawrence he was instrumental in diversifying and strengthening the colonial economy. The strains of war, and a growing population, also brought serious social problems requiring the establishment of new institutions and the rapid expansion of existing rudimentary ones.

Educated at a Jesuit college, then the best schools in Europe, and subsequently in the law, Champigny was clearly a man of exceptional intelligence. He showed himself to be an efficient administrator, introducing reforms where needed and never sparing himself in times of stress. Perhaps the personal attribute that was most conspicuous was his strength of character. When he believed himself to be in the right he could not be swayed, either by the governor or even by the minister. Indeed, on more than one important issue he obliged the minister to give way even though he thereby placed his career in jeopardy. What is more important, on these occasions events proved his judgment to have been sound. Unlike Frontenac [Buade*], with whom he served for nine years, Champigny does not appear to have possessed great personal charm. His official correspondence shows little evidence of wit or humour, albeit dispatches to the minister are not good vehicles for those qualities. In these dispatches, however, he sometimes employed biting irony, verging on sarcasm, even with the minister. As a courtier he would have been a distinct failure, but as a royal official he eventually succeeded in earning the respect of both the minister and Louis XIV.

Bochart de Champigny

In an age when deep religious feeling was giving way to a more secular, worldly outlook, where the influence of the counter-Reformation was waning and scepticism and libertinism becoming prevalent, Champigny was patently a sincerely religious man. This allowed his enemies—with his character and his position he had many—to accuse him of being too much influenced by the clergy, when there was a conflict between secular and clerical authority. Yet the evidence indicates the contrary. Whenever he felt that the clergy in the colony were encroaching on the royal authority he opposed them, earning the sincere displeasure of the bishop on occasion. Although he would not suffer fools or scoundrels, he was a humane man. This is evidenced by some of the social legislation that he introduced. It must be remembered, however, that this attitude towards the individual and society was a distinctive feature of the age of Louis XIV, particularly during Pontchartrain's administration.

In time of war compassion is frequently forgotten, particularly when the war is waged against a relentless and cruel foe. Champigny's most important task upon assuming his duties was to assist Denonville in his plans for a campaign against the western Iroquois, who threatened the French hold on the west and who had become extremely aggressive in recent years. This campaign, launched in 1687, was planned with very great care by Denonville, as, indeed, it needed to be. To move an army, composed largely of French regular troops of doubtful quality, several hundred miles into the Canadian wilderness to attack a foe as wily, numerous, and ferocious as was this powerful tribe was no small undertaking. That Champigny deserves much of the credit for the careful logistic planning there is no gainsaying.

Surprise was one of the chief elements upon which Denonville counted for success. To ensure it, and also to have available hostages for exchange should any of the French be captured, Denonville took prisoner all the Iroquois encountered on the way up the St Lawrence to Fort Frontenac. This was clearly a legitimate act of war. Before the main body of the army reached Lake Ontario Champigny went ahead to Fort Frontenac (Cataracoui) with a small advance party to make preparations for the army's arrival and subsequent advance into the enemy's territory. Encamped near the fort were two parties of Iroquois; one of them was taken prisoner by a force sent by Denonville, but the other, some 30 men and 90 women and children, were invited by Champigny to the fort for a feast. Once within the stockade they were seized and the men bound and tethered. When Denonville and the army reached the fort a detach-ment was sent to capture another group of nearby Iroquois. Subsequently all the prisoners were sent back to Montreal and, in blind obedience to a directive from the minister that any able-bodied Iroquois captured during the campaign be sent to France to serve in the galleys, 36 of the 58 male Iroquois were sent to France. Two years later, at Denonville's behest, they were sent back to Quebec. Some, however, had died either in the galleys or during the voyage.

Most of the contemporaries who commented on these events regarded Denonville's and Champigny's actions as justified, but some condemned one or the other, or both. Unfortunately, in doing so they gave exaggerated and quite erroneous accounts of the circumstances, confusing Iroquois captured by force with those taken by guile, imputing wrong motives to the wrong people and exaggerating the consequences. Latter-day historians have, for the most part, merely compounded the confusion. When a close analysis of the motives, circumstances, and consequences of the events is made, the fact remains that the capture of the one small party of Iroquois by Champigny at Fort Frontenac was effected in a distinctly dubious manner. At the same time it must be said that there is no evidence whatsoever that it changed the course of events. To claim, as some historians have done, that this act of treachery brought about the so-called Lachine massacre two years later is contradicted by too much evidence to warrant any degree of credence.

With New France again in a state of war the defences of the colony had to be strengthened—they were, indeed, almost non-existent—and in this task Denonville was very ably assisted by Champigny. As a result of his exertions during and after the campaign Denonville's health was ruined and he asked to be recalled. Champigny was upset when he learned that Denonville's request had been granted and that the Comte de Frontenac was to replace him.

From the moment that Frontenac arrived in the colony, his relations with Champigny were strained, but they never quite reached the breaking point. To some degree their difficulties were caused by their differing temperaments. Frontenac's flamboyance and his insatiable appetite for flattery, which allowed sycophants ample scope to exercise their talents, grated on Champigny but he responded to these character traits only with disdain. On the other hand, Champigny's bureaucratic rigidity, at times, must have irritated Frontenac whose attitude towards government directives was frequently cavalier. Their more serious disputes centred about questions of policy and, for the first six years of their association,

Bochart de Champigny

Frontenac had sufficient support in the ministry of Marine to force Champigny to give way. During these years a friend of Frontenac's, Jean-Baptiste de Lagny, the intendant of commerce, was in charge of Canadian affairs. The minister, Louis Phélypeaux de Pontchartrain, a kinsman of Frontenac's, paid little attention to what was going on in the colony. Champigny was very critical of Frontenac's military policy, as were Hector de CALLIÈRE, the governor of Montreal, who was responsible for the tactical direction of the war, and Philippe de RIGAUD de Vaudreuil, commanding officer of the colonial regular troops. Champigny considered that Frontenac's raids of 1690 on the border settlements of New York and New England would hinder the enemy's war effort but little, and that a single concerted attack to destroy the Iroquois' main base, Albany, would be far more effective. The governor of New York shared Champigny's view and was relieved that Frontenac neglected to make the attempt. Later in the war, however, Champigny, Callière, and Vaudreuil were able to bring enough pressure to bear on Frontenac to force him to alter his Fabian strategy. The success of this change forced the Iroquois to come to terms and prevented a wholesale defection of the western nations allied with the French.

Champigny's proper role in military affairs was only indirectly concerned with strategy but the success of these operations depended in no small measure on how efficiently he discharged his duties. He was responsible for paying and supplying the troops, providing them with arms, munitions, canoes and boats, and arranging for their billets in the forts or with civilians in the towns, since there were no barracks in the colony. He also had to arrange for their hospitalization, serve as executor of their wills on occasion, and when hostilities ceased he had to dispose of surplus military supplies. The building and maintenance of the colony's fortifications was also his responsibility, as was the safekeeping of prisoners of war and their eventual exchange.

After familiarizing himself with colonial conditions Champigny introduced several notable reforms in the military system. It was the custom in the colonial regular troops for the captain of each company to pay his men, and issue them with uniforms and rations. As the captains expected to make a profit on these transactions, too often their men were clad in rags and inadequately fed. In Europe this had not been too serious an abuse since the French during this period fought their wars on other countries' territory, hence the men could forage for themselves at the expense of the enemy's civilian population. In Canada, however,

they could not do so and, given the severity of the climate, the regular soldiers suffered considerable hardship. Champigny put a stop to this practice in 1687 by importing supplies of clothing and issuing it to the men on repayment. Two years later he extended this system to their rations. His successor, François de Beauharnois* de La Boische later complained that he had charged only 3 *livres* 6 *sols* per man for rations worth 3 *livres* 9 *sols*. Then, in 1692, Champigny introduced a form of battle dress for the Canadian army on active service. Previously the troops had been clothed in a pale grey coat with red or blue facings—blue for the men, red for sergeants—grey knee breeches and stockings, shirt, cravat, and a wide brimmed hat. This uniform was adequate for European parade-ground soldiering, but quite unsuitable for the Canadian climate and terrain. Champigny therefore designed and had the men issued with the type of clothing worn by coureurs de bois.

Frequently the colony's budget proved inadequate and Champigny had to face the wrath of the minister when he exceeded it. The excessive rate of wear and tear on equipment during campaigns in the wilderness was something that the minister consistently failed to comprehend. In 1693, when he was taken severely to task on this subject, Champigny sent the minister a stinging reply, informing him in great detail what the frequent campaigns required. "If all this," he wrote, "and an infinity of other things could be done without expense in a new country half ruined by war, it would be a most admirable secret which, with all my heart, I wish I had been able to discover in order to satisfy His Majesty and please you."

To send a rebuke such as this to the minister required either considerable strength of character or the recklessness of desperation, and Champigny was not notably reckless. It is hardly to be wondered at that rumours now began to circulate that certain officials in the ministry of Marine were gloating over the likelihood of his imminent dismissal from office.

Champigny also made himself unpopular with some of the regular officers by his attempts to have the colonial regular troops play a greater role in military operations. Although he was forced to agree with Frontenac that the regular troops were of little use in campaigns against the Iroquois until they had had several years' experience in this guerila-type warfare, he still felt that they could be employed more effectively. As it was, the Canadian habitants in the ranks of the militia were doing most of the fighting and the regular troops were used as a labour force. This arrangement had been inaugurated as an emergency measure by Champigny's predecessor, de Meulles, but Champigny believed that it was being grossly abused. He discovered that the soldiers were eager to work in a civilian capacity since they earned good wages and were free of military duties and discipline. Their captains, however, would only release them if they made no claim for their military pay and, what was worse, the captains forced the men to hand over part of their wages. The men, for the most part, were willing to do this and the method of paying the troops made it difficult to check the abuse. Periodically a muster parade was called by the intendant or his deputy, heads were counted, and the captains received money to pay those present. The captains made very sure that all their men were on hand for these parades, but when they were needed for a war party they were not available and the militia were called out instead. Champigny, in frustration, eventually suggested that the best way to eliminate these abuses, and make the regular soldiers a more effective fighting force, would be to discharge them all and make them get married. Then they would settle on the land and in a few years become habitants, fit for active service in the militia. Needless to say, the recommendation was not adopted.

The main reason why Champigny was so concerned about the continual use of militia rather than regular troops for military operations was the dire effects it had on the social and economic fabric of the colony, for whose well-being he was directly responsible. Soldiers were expendable but the habitants were the backbone of colonial society. In 1691, after touring the upper colony, where the Iroquois raids had caused great devastation, he wrote: "I found the people living above Trois-Rivières in a state of great misery and the whole countryside ruined by the enemy, with the exception of the area around Boucherville and the forts, to which all the families have been forced to retire, which prevents them working on their distant fields or raising cattle except in very small numbers because of the limited space available in the forts. They dare not venture out because of the enemy who appears from time to time. What is even more grievous is the number of habitants crippled in the war and the poor widows who, having lost their husbands in the fighting, have trouble in obtaining bread for their children."

In an attempt to alleviate hardship for the poor, and to eliminate a grave social abuse, Champigny in 1688 had the Conseil Souverain establish a new institution to provide a comprehensive system of poor relief. The legislation brought into being Bureaux des Pauvres in the three towns, Quebec, Trois-Rivières, and Montreal. These offices were staffed by the local parish priest and three directors, and cared for the poor in their areas. They were required to collect alms for this purpose from the more well-to-do and see to their distribution. Those of the poor who could work were found employment, those who could not were given aid enough to suffice for their needs. Once the offices had begun to function begging was forbidden, except in the most desperate cases, and fines were imposed on anyone who encouraged it by granting alms at his door to unlicensed beggars. Champigny and the Conseil Souverain had three main aims in view when they drafted this legislation: to ensure that no one starved, to find useful work for all those capable of working, and to put an end to the public annoyance created by hordes of mendicants, some of whom preferred to beg rather than to work for a living. Their purpose was, clearly, not merely to protect the more well-to-do but also to ensure the well-being of the less fortunate members of society. This *règlement* is worthy of note not merely because it is one of the earliest examples of comprehensive welfare legislation in Canada, but also because its spirit was basically humane; every effort was made to safeguard the basic dignity of those it sought to aid, as well as to serve the interests of society as a whole.

In the founding of this institution, as in many other matters, Champigny had to work closely with the clergy. Although he, like his wife, was a very religious man, he never forgot for a moment that he was a senior royal official. During his tenure of office there was no real conflict between church and state, but there were differences of opinion on matters that affected both. It must be remembered that the officials who represented the authority of the crown were also members of the church served by the clergy; there was never any basic disagreement on ends, only occasionally on means. Thus Champigny refused to grant the bishop exclusive control of the royal subvention to the clergy, and he was upheld by the minister. The king and the minister of Marine were anxious to have resident priests established in as many of the more populated parishes as possible; the bishop preferred to have his secular priests based at the Quebec seminary and travelling about the colony, spending a few weeks at each in turn. Champigny opposed the bishop firmly on this point. Similarly, he was not in entire agreement with the Jesuits who, for the best of reasons, wished a total ban on the trading of liquor to the Indians and, indeed, wanted all but missionaries excluded from the distant Indian villages. Champigny sympathized with their motives but considered these measures impractical and sought only to eradicate abuses as far as possible. When Frontenac and Bishop

Bochart de Champigny

Saint-Vallier [LA CROIX] became embroiled in a violent dispute over the playing of Molière's *Tartuffe* by the governor's company of amateur players in 1694, Champigny sought to mediate but upon seeing that it was impossible, withdrew to the sidelines. The minister later was mildly critical of him for not having supported the governor, but, all things considered, Champigny showed sound judgement in declining to become involved.

Similarly, in his relations with the Conseil Souverain, over whose deliberations he presided, Champigny preserved a necessary aloofness which did much to suppress the latent tendency for intrigue and faction amongst the members of that body. On one occasion, when there was a serious meat shortage in the Quebec district, Frontenac and some members of the council favoured fixing the prices of this commodity to prevent profiteering and ensure fair shares for all. Champigny opposed the measure on principle, claiming that fixed prices would not increase the supply; if anything, they would have the contrary effect. His was the novel—for that age—argument of the free market concept. Frontenac, however, pointed out that while waiting for high prices to stimulate production many people would have been deprived of meat entirely. Champigny then agreed to call a public assembly and submit the issue to it. When this was done the majority showed itself in favour of regulating the prices and Champigny immediately issued an ordinance in accordance with the popular verdict. There was, of course, nothing novel about this procedure; such public assemblies were held quite regularly to discover the views of the people before legislation was enacted. When all food was in short supply Champigny did not hesitate to distribute rations from the military stores to the civilian population.

Unfortunately certain other differences of opinion between Champigny and Frontenac on policy questions were not so easily reconciled—royal policy governing the fur trade, for example. The king and the minister of Marine still subscribed to the policy laid down by Colbert that, as far as possible, the trade with the Indians in furs should be carried on at Montreal and Trois-Rivières and the Canadians forbidden to voyage to the west to trade in the Indian villages. The purpose of this policy was to keep the Canadians in the colony, employed in agriculture, fishing, lumbering, and ancillary industries, not roaming about the interior of the continent part of the year and living in idleness the rest of the time. The Canadians, however, had consistently defied the restrictive edicts and Colbert, in 1681, had moderated them by allowing the governor and intendant to issue 25 fur-trading licences (*congés*) a year. Each licence allowed one canoe bearing three men to voyage to the west to trade. Champigny made a determined effort to prevent this privilege being abused but his efforts were continually thwarted by Frontenac who allowed more than double the number to leave the colony to trade every year. Similarly the king's injunction of 1679 forbidding the transport of brandy to the Indian villages was rejected by Frontenac. When, in 1693, Champigny issued ordinances forbidding anyone to take more than a modest amount of brandy for his own use on voyages up country, Frontenac issued an ordinance of his own overruling that of the intendant. Champigny was also defeated in his attempt to revoke Frontenac's granting of a monopoly on the fur trade in the entire Illinois country, a vast area south of the Great Lakes, to HENRI TONTY and François DAUPHIN de La Forest, the heirs of his late associate, Cavelier* de La Salle. Frontenac had no legal sanction whatsoever for this, but, with the support of his friend de Lagny in the ministry of Marine, he was able to ride roughshod over Champigny's protests.

Eventually, however, a radical change occurred in the attitude of the minister towards Frontenac and Champigny. Previously, whenever there was a difference of opinion between them, Frontenac's views carried the day. When anything went wrong in the colony, Champigny, not Frontenac, was held to blame; and in their several disputes it was the same. But in 1695 the minister was obliged to take a closer look at colonial affairs, and what he discovered forced him to conclude that Champigny had not always been wrong or misguided. The cause of this change in attitude was the discovery that the company holding the monopoly on the marketing of beaver fur in France, which was the mainstay of the fur trade—hence of the French empire in North America—had an unsalable surplus of 1,500,000 *livres* worth of the commodity. This company paid the crown 550,000 *livres* a year for the monopoly and the lease expired in 1697. Clearly, it might well prove difficult to find anyone willing to take a new lease. The consequent large financial loss to the crown, just at a time of heavy war expenditures, would prove intolerable. The minister immediately began to investigate how this situation had arisen and he concluded that Frontenac was mainly responsible because he had refused to abide by the edicts governing the fur trade.

The minister and Louis XIV now enunciated a much more restrictive policy, ordering that all but one post in the Illinois country be abandoned, the garrisons withdrawn, and no more permits issued for trading voyages to the west. Although Champigny had strongly opposed Frontenac's circumvention of the earlier edicts, he supported the governor's decision not to implement the decree. Champigny then advised the minister that to withdraw from the west in this fashion, with the war still on, would be folly. He suggested a compromise that would have allowed the French to maintain their control of the west and, at the same time, would have curbed the abuses that had resulted in the surplus of beaver. Unfortunately, the minister eased his restrictions, allowing more posts to be retained, but he ignored Champigny's suggested reforms; thus the abuses continued unabated. Yet from this time on the minister's marginal notations in the Canadian dispatches indicate approval of Champigny's recommendations and disapproval of, frequently anger with, those of Frontenac. Consequently, when in 1696 the governor, in a high-handed manner interfered in a judicial case to do with a ship prize, nullified the decree of the court, overruled an ordinance of the intendant and rendered judgement himself, the minister not only refused to sanction his actions but issued an edict confirming Champigny's ordinance and his general handling of the case. Frontenac was ordered, in the strongest terms, never to do anything of the sort again.

The governor was, however, incapable of self-restraint and a few weeks later he came into violent conflict with Champigny when he again intervened in a judicial matter. This time he acted to protect his protégé, Lamothe Cadillac [LAUMET], commandant at Michilimackinac, who was being prosecuted by the intendant for having grossly abused his authority and made a mockery of both justice and the edicts governing the fur trade. Fortunately, this dispute between Champigny and Frontenac, which looked as if it might get completely out of hand, was reconciled by the intervention of Vaudreuil and an influential visitor to the colony, the Marquis de Coutré. The moral victory was clearly Champigny's but he was still rather bitter. Moreover, the legal issues involved were vital ones. He therefore asked the minister to decide once and for all whether or not the governor could force the officers of justice to defer to his opinions, or to veto the judgements of the intendant. In actual fact the governor had this authority, but he could use it only in the most drastic circumstances, when, for instance, the security of the colony was at stake. He certainly was not justified in using his authority merely to allow one of his following to evade justice.

Before the minister and Louis XIV were required to rule in this issue Frontenac died. Before his death he made his peace with Champigny, who subsequently wrote to the minister: "You may perhaps find it hard to believe, my lord, that I was deeply moved by his death in spite of the strained relations that had existed between us. The truth of the matter is that our misunderstandings sprang solely from a divergence of opinion as to what was best for the king's service. As private persons we never quarrelled. Also I must state that during his last illness he used me most civilly; it would be ungrateful of me not to acknowledge the fact." It is quite likely that Champigny's feelings were not momentarily overcome by the sombre event, and that he spoke the truth. He gave no evidence of being an emotional man and his frequent disputes with Frontenac on policy matters really occupied but little time. The dispatches to the court are naturally replete with them, and might lead one to believe that this state of affairs was constant; but these dispatches were sent only once a year, giving an account of all that transpired during the preceding twelve months. It could easily be that a dispatch would make much of a dispute lasting only a few days, while the fact that the governor and intendant had carried on their work in a reasonably amiable fashion during the rest of the year would be passed over in silence. In military matters he must have been able to work with Frontenac most of the time; had he not, the conduct of the war would have been impossible.

With Frontenac's successor, Louis-Hector de Callière, who had been governor of Montreal, Champigny's relations were better. Champigny and Callière were in basic agreement on the major policy questions and cooperated admirably in their execution, particularly in their attempts to control the western fur trade, hold the Iroquois in check, and maintain the alliances with the western nations. Together they negotiated the treaty of 1701 with the Iroquois and some 30 other Indian nations, which restored peace to the west. Michel Bégon* wrote of it: "Messieurs de Callières and Champigny have acquired immortal glory by reconciling all the differing interests of these peoples who have arranged among themselves a peace which, in its results, will be very advantageous to our country." What did make their relationship difficult was Callière's testy personality. He took umbrage over trivialities and was continually at odds with the senior officers of the regular troops over petty questions of precedence and protocol. At least part of the trouble likely stemmed from the fact that Callière suffered severely from gout. Moreover, in his relations with Champigny he was perhaps too acutely aware that the intendant was on very good terms with Vaudreuil, who had been his unsuccessful rival for the governor general's post and with

Bochart de Champigny

whom his own relations were strained. Although Champigny's patience was severely tried on occasion there were no serious disputes. It has been asserted that Champigny himself had been a contender for the post of governor general, but there is no evidence whatsoever to support this contention and a good deal that convincingly refutes it.

Certainly Champigny could not have devoted too much of his time to disputing with the governors; he had far too many responsibilities to have been able to afford this luxury. He had to anticipate the needs of the colony in foodstuffs and other vital supplies a year ahead of time, calculate how much the colony could provide for itself, then arrange for the balance to be imported the following summer. He was also required to do everything possible to stimulate the economy and, considering the handicaps under which he laboured, he accomplished a great deal. In 1687 the minister had instructed him, "this colony will never be stable as long as it cannot subsist on its own, and the people cannot obtain from it all the absolute necessities of life."

In agriculture several factors combined to hinder production—the destruction of crops, livestock, and farm buildings by the Iroquois and the absence of so many men either on trading ventures to the west or on military campaigns with the militia. A more enduring factor was that Canada was bypassed by the European agricultural revolution of the late 17th and 18th centuries. Farming methods persisted in the old, inefficient way, made worse by the profligacy of frontier conditions. Too many of the habitants were content to grow only enough for their own needs. Moreover, the staple food was wheat bread, average consumption being a pound and a half per person per day, and both the climate and the soil were unsuitable for this grain. Consequently crop failures were frequent, though no more so than in France. Only occasionally was there a surplus of wheat or flour for export. Champigny did all he could to stimulate production, but it was difficult to make the conservative habitants change their ways. He did get them to raise hemp, flax, and more sheep for the production of rope and clothing, but again they were reluctant to produce more than sufficed for themselves.

In his attempts to stimulate the fishing industry to produce for the export market he also had scant success. Lack of capital for ships and tackle, lack of salt supplies in the colony, and the depredations of English privateers in the Gulf, were the main hindrances. Champigny persuaded the minister to provide subsidies for fishing tackle, and with this aid CHARLES DENYS de Vitré did enjoy some suc-

cess in the whale and porpoise fishery, his boats bringing in 70 whales in 1701 and 97 porpoises the following year. In an attempt to encourage by example, Champigny and Frontenac, in partnership with two Quebec merchants, refurbished a ship prize and sent it to the Grand Banks. Within a year it was recaptured by the English and Champigny bemoaned the fact that he had thereby lost 4,000 *livres*. To provide the much needed salt for the sedentary fishing industry Champigny had a supply sent out on the king's ships and sold it at a modest profit for the crown to the fishermen, but the minister, with his habitual shortsightedness, subsequently took him severely to task for not charging all that the traffic would bear. Despite these problems, fishing for the local market did thrive and after the war expanded down the Gulf to Labrador.

The industry to which Champigny devoted most of his attention was the production of timber, more particularly ship masts. In the age of sail the tall, perfectly proportioned pine trees required for main masts were as vital to a maritime nation as oil was later to be. Without an adequate supply of masts and spars, ships were useless hulks. The main source of supply of the essential main masts was Russia and the Baltic states. Both England and France were eager to rid themselves of this dependence on a foreign source of supply and to obtain masts, along with other naval supplies, from their American colonies. Neither state enjoyed much success. In Canada Champigny had the forests surveyed, obtained royal subsidies, had master craftsmen sent from France, and managed to have a considerable number of masts, and also oak planks, produced. The main problem was to get them across the Atlantic to the French ship yards. The bottleneck here was a shortage of flutes, the long, stern-loading ships needed to transport masts. Year after year some 90 great masts would be ready for shipment and no more than 12 could be exported. Champigny suspected that the timber merchants of the Pyrenees were not eager to face Canadian competition and were making difficulties. Another factor was the high cost of Canadian masts and timber, but this was inevitable in an infant industry and the same problem was encountered by the English. Yet a beginning was made and the industry managed to keep its head above water, awaiting better times. The number of sawmills in the colony did increase but most of the timber they produced was consumed locally during these years.

Champigny also tried to stimulate trade with the West Indies, but in war time this was too risky a business to have much success. As soon as the war ended, a promising trade sprang up

Bochart de Champigny

between merchants in Quebec and New England, but the minister, Pontchartrain, would have none of it. He forbade all trade with the English colonies, fearing that they might provide the colony with goods that France could have supplied. The trade continued, clandestinely, chiefly by the Lake Champlain–Richelieu River route between Albany and Montreal. French wines, brandy, silks, and beaver pelts moved south in exchange for English woollens needed to compete with the Hudson's Bay Company in the fur trade. The intendant and the governor, Callière, claimed that they were doing all they could to stop this trade, but the benefits to the colony were obvious, and there is reason to believe that they did not over-exert themselves.

During his last years in the colony Champigny was deeply concerned with the various attempts to organize a company to take over the beaver monopoly, one which would function without reducing the prices paid in Canada in spite of the depressed state of the market. Several proposals were put forward and there was a great deal of intrigue between rival groups. Champigny's sympathies were clearly with the Canadians and he was rebuked by the minister for this manifest partiality. Eventually the Canadian fur-traders proposed forming a company to market the furs themselves. Champigny, however, was very sceptical and advised that it was extremely doubtful that the Canadians could succeed in this venture, but the minister rejected his views and accepted the merchants' proposal. This Canadian company, the Compagnie du Canada, organized in 1700, quickly encountered difficulties with which it could not cope and in 1706 it collapsed.

In another sphere of activity Champigny was able to accomplish something—town planning. From 1688 on the population of Montreal began to increase rapidly and some persons owning vacant land within the town walls began to take advantage of the increased demand by charging exorbitant prices to rent or sell. Champigny quickly put a stop to this by decreeing that no one could own more than one acre of land within the town; all owners of vacant land had to build a stone house within a year of the decree. Persons with surplus land who did not wish to build had to dispose of it within six months. At the same time Champigny ordered the streets widened to 30 feet.

One particular innovation introduced by Champigny should earn him the respect of historians. In 1698 he proposed the establishment of Canadian archives to preserve all edicts, ordinances, and royal declarations for future reference. The following year the archives came

into existence with the clerk of the Conseil Souverain serving as Canada's first archivist. Another of Champigny's proposals was the creation of a Canadian Estates General. In a rather mysterious dispatch dated 15 Oct. 1700, he suggested that if the minister decided to make the colony a *pays d'état*—several provinces in France had this form of local assembly—the governing body should consist of the governor, who would preside, the bishop, the intendant, who would have a deliberative voice and chair the meetings, two deputies from the clergy, two from the Conseil Souverain, a judge from each of the three towns, two seigneurs from each of the three governments, Quebec, Montreal, and Trois-Rivières, three merchants from Quebec, two from Montreal, and one from Trois-Rivières. "In this assembly," he wrote, "the affairs of the colony would be settled by the plurality of votes and whatever tax the colony was required to impose would be provided for." Nothing, however, came of this proposal and the Canadians escaped the threat of having to impose taxes on themselves.

The following year, 1701, Champigny was gratified to learn that he had been appointed by the king to the post of intendant at Le Havre. In the autumn of 1702, when his replacement arrived, he and his wife left Quebec, but this by no means marked the end of his concern with Canada. While at Le Havre he served for several years as the minister's adviser on Canadian affairs. The Canadian dispatches were sent to him for his comments and recommendations. He also prepared memoirs on the more important issues for the minister's guidance and his views carried considerable weight.

One question that must be asked of any government official, then as now, is whether or not he took advantage of his position for private profit. In Champigny's case one can say only that he was either honest or extremely clever. In any bureaucracy, suspicion, malicious gossip, whispered accusations, and backbiting are endemic. It would be difficult to find any official in New France who was not accused of wrong-doing of one sort or another. Champigny was no exception. Yet what is striking is that only two such accusations against him have come to light. One is an anonymous letter by a disgruntled soldier accusing his superior officers of all manner of crimes, and linking Champigny and Vaudreuil, the commanding officer of the colonial regular troops, with them. Not much credence need be given this testimony. The other, however, may carry more weight. It is a letter of Father N. Tremblay of the Missions Étrangères to the retired bishop, Monsignor Laval, dated Paris, 19 June 1705, three

Boisbriand

years after Champigny had left Canada. It briefly states that the Missions Étrangères had been informed that Champigny had made a personal profit of over 25,000 *livres* a year on the food and clothing provided for the regular troops in the colony. "Men who are very certain of it have so informed me," wrote Father Tremblay. It would have been easy for Champigny to have lined his pockets in this manner but, as so many men would be affected, it is difficult to see how he could have done so without arousing comment long before 1705. Certainly had Frontenac even suspected that Champigny was guilty of malversation he would have been quick to report it to the minister. That he did not do so requires that the charge repeated by Father Tremblay be, at most, treated as "not proven" in the Scottish legal sense.

All things considered, Champigny's career as intendant of New France can perhaps best be summed up as that of a competent, conscientious, senior civil servant. He was not an initiator of great projects; the times were not propitious for such things. His fundamental concern with social values made him a staunch opponent of unbridled western expansion which, in his view, sapped the strength of the colony. Like Colbert, he was far-sighted enough to see that greedy attempts to seize the whole of North America before the economy and the social fabric of the central colony had been firmly consolidated would court disaster. In military affairs he showed a good grasp of strategy and the tactics needed to achieve its aims. His efforts to sustain the fighting forces of New France during the darkest days of the war contributed in no small degree to their success. It may well be that the presence of at least one of his sons in the colonial troops made him more acutely aware of their needs and difficulties. His relations with the three governors under whom he served left much to be desired as far as Frontenac and Callière were concerned, but the administration of the colony never suffered as a result. Perhaps the best testimonial to this intendant was that of Mother JEANNE-FRANÇOISE JUCHEREAU of the Hôtel-Dieu at Quebec who remarked of Champigny, after he had called to pay his final respects before sailing for France: "He was a good man, humane, and well liked."

W. J. ECCLES

[Unfortunately, no private papers or correspondence by or to Champigny are known to have survived. His dispatches to the minister are contained in AN, Col., C[11A]; the minister's dispatches to him are in AN, Col., B. A good deal of pertinent material is contained in AN, Col., F[3]; the PAC has microfilm copies. The ASQ has several pertinent documents, particularly in Lettres, N. The *Jugements et délibérations du Conseil souverain de la Nouvelle-France* contains a great deal of relevant material. Regrettably, few of Champigny's *édits* and ordinances have survived.

On the origins of the office of intendant, the articles by Edmond Esmonin in *Études sur la France des XVIIe et XVIIIe siècles* should be consulted. Gustave Lanctot's early work, *L'administration de la Nouvelle-France* (Paris, 1929), is useful, and Cahall, *The Sovereign Council of New France*, is essential to the understanding of the role of the intendant in the administration of justice. F. M. Hammang, in *The Marquis de Vaudreuil, New France at the beginning of the eighteenth century* (Bruges, 1938), discusses the part played by Champigny in Canadian affairs after his return to France. Rochemonteix, *Les Jésuites et la Nouvelle-France au XVIIIe siècle*, contains much information on Champigny's relations with the members of that order. Eccles, *Canada under Louis XIV*, and *Frontenac*, deal with Champigny's Canadian career in some detail. Thérèse Prince-Falmagne, *Un marquis du grand siècle, Jacques-René de Brisay de Denonville, gouverneur de la Nouvelle-France, 1637–1710* (Montréal, 1965), discusses Denonville's relations with Champigny. Régis Roy's brief notes, "Jean Bochart," *BRH*, VII (1901), 325–27, and "Champigny," *BRH*, XX (1914), 80–81, provide some genealogical information, but they also contain errors of fact. W.J.E.]

BOISBRIAND, PIERRE DUGUÉ DE. *See* DUGUÉ

BOISHÉBERT, HENRI-LOUIS DESCHAMPS DE. *See* DESCHAMPS

BONAVENTURE, SIMON-PIERRE DENYS DE. *See* DENYS

BONNER, JOHN, Massachusetts mapmaker and mariner; b. *c.* 1643, possibly in London; d. 30 Jan. 1725/26 at Boston.

After his arrival in Boston about 1670 he was owner or master of many vessels, including the sloop *Mary* in Phips*'s Canadian expedition of 1690 and the brigantine *Hope*, which he piloted to Quebec under a flag of truce in 1706 to bring home the Rev. JOHN WILLIAMS (author of *The redeemed captive*). This experience gave him a reputation as being the New Englander with the best knowledge of the passage up the Canada River (St Lawrence) to Quebec and resulted in his impressment into the service of Admiral Sir Hovenden WALKER's expedition against that city in 1711. He served as pilot of the flagship *Edgar*, and after part of the fleet was wrecked west of Anticosti Island his counsel against proceeding to Quebec was heeded and the fleet returned to England without accomplishing its objective.

Bonner returned to Boston and spent his

Bouat

remaining years pursuing his maritime interests. His map of Boston, published in 1722, was the first engraved map of that town. He also made a plan of the Boston waterfront in 1714 and a draft of the entrance to Boston harbour in 1716. Bonner was married four times. He was survived by two children, Jane and John, born of his second marriage (to Mary Clark).

The *Boston News-Letter* of 3 Feb. 1725/26 made the following assessment of his contribution to Massachusetts: "One of the best acquainted with the Coasts of North America, of any of his time; of great Knowledge and Judgment in Marine Affairs; [he] was very much consulted, improved and relied upon by the Government as a Principal Pilate, in our Marine Expeditions, and with diligent Care and Faithfulness discharged his Trust."

ROBERT L. WAGNER

Boston News-Letter, 26 Aug., 18 Nov. 1706, 3 Feb. 1725/26. "Journal of expedition against Port Royal, 1690," 54–66. PRO, *CSP, Col., 1711–12. 1690, Sir William Phips devant Québec* (Myrand), 197. *Suffolk County Court records, 1671–1680* (2v., Col. Soc. Mass. pub., XXIX–XXX, Boston, 1933), II, 31–35. *Walker expedition* (Graham). *DAB. New Eng. Hist. and Geneal. Register*, V (1851), 174; XIV (1860), 240. *The memorial history of Boston including Suffolk county, Massachusetts, 1630–1880*, ed. Justin Winsor (4v., Boston, 1880–81), II, liii.

BOUAT, FRANÇOIS-MARIE, lieutenant general at the court of royal jurisdiction at Montreal, seigneur of Terrebonne and merchant; baptized 25 March 1676 at Montreal, son of Abraham Bouat and Marguerite de Névellet; buried 18 May 1726 in the same town.

Bouat is an example of the type of junior official who did not hesitate to combine the functions of a judge with those of a dealer in furs. The son of a tavern-keeper, he engaged in trade at a very early age, and was convicted in 1695 for trafficking in spirits. Until 1709 he seems to have frequented the main fur-trading routes, particularly those in the *pays d'en haut* and upper Louisiana. On 20 April 1709 his appointment to the post of lieutenant to the provost marshal of Montreal put an end to his trips into the hinterland, but not to his business affairs. In general, his duties consisted of ensuring public order at Montreal with the aid of archers that were placed at his disposal. In 1711, while retaining his post in the marshalcy, he received a commission as special lieutenant at the court of royal jurisdiction at Montreal, and in that capacity he was required to assist the lieutenant general, Jacques-Alexis FLEURY Deschambault, in his function as royal judge for civil and criminal affairs. Following Deschambault's death Bouat

went to France in 1715, and there succeeded in acquiring for himself the post of lieutenant general, for which he received a commission on 27 April 1716. He was to perform his duties as a royal judge until his death.

This did not mean that Bouat neglected his interest in trade; his pronounced liking for trafficking resulted in his being suspended from office and sentenced by a court martial to a month in prison in 1718, when in contravention of RIGAUD de Vaudreuil's orders he had fitted out three canoes, instead of two, which he intended for ALPHONSE TONTY, the commandant at Detroit. Claude de RAMEZAY, the governor of Montreal, informed of the judge's disobedience before the hired crews set out, had demanded that Bouat conform rigorously to Vaudreuil's authorization. Bouat carried on without turning a hair. When convicted his only recourse was to the king. He did not fail to avail himself of this by making use of the support of his sister Marguerite, Antoine PASCAUD's wife, who was a creditor of Ramezay and who asserted that the governor of Montreal was making this matter a pretext for wreaking vengeance. In June 1720 the king ratified the sentence passed by the court martial, but nevertheless reinstated Judge Bouat in office. The king took the opportunity to reprimand the prevaricator and to affirm that the position he occupied forbad him to trade in any way, either directly or as a middleman. The warning remained a dead letter. There is a document showing that the judge was still engaged in trading in 1724.

Bouat was involved in another incident which pitted Governor Vaudreuil against Intendant Bégon*. Following the fire which had devastated the oldest part of Montreal in 1721, Vaudreuil had ordered then and there that the market should henceforth be held elsewhere, on a site farther to the north; Bouat, who refused to listen to this view, allowed the market to be reopened in the same place. Ramezay attempted to have Vaudreuil's order carried out, but Bouat went to Quebec and informed Intendant Bégon; the latter, jealous of his prerogatives, decided to renew the ordinance of 1706 that established the site of the market at the original spot. The affair was brought before the council of Marine, which settled the dispute in favour of the intendant and thereby allowed Bouat to crow in triumph.

On 1 Oct. 1718 Judge Bouat undertook to purchase the seigneury of Terrebonne, by virtue of a contract signed with Marie-Catherine de Saint-Georges, Louis LE CONTE Dupré's widow. But he kept it only two years: on 12 Sept. 1720 he sold it again to Louis Lepage* de Sainte-Claire, the parish priest of Île Jésus, whose name has

81

Boucher

remained linked with the first efforts at establishing Canadian industry.

On 18 May 1726 François-Marie Bouat was buried at Montreal. On 7 June 1700, at Quebec, he had first married Madeleine Lambert Dumont, daughter of Eustache Lambert Dumont and Sophie Vanneck. By this marriage he had 13 children, 7 of whom survived their mother, who died in December 1722. Eight months later, on 8 Aug. 1723, he married Agathe Legardeur de Repentigny, who bore him two children.

JEAN BLAIN

AJM, Greffe de Pierre Raimbault, 1 oct. 1718, 12 sept. 1720. P.-G. Roy, *Inv. concessions*, III, 116–22. Godbout, "Nos ancêtres," APQ *Rapport, 1959–60*, 284f. É.-Z. Massicotte, "La famille Bouat," *BRH*, XXX (1924), 39–45, 198, 409; "Les juges de Montréal sous le régime français, 1648–1760," *BRH*, XXVII (1921), 181; "La maréchaussée à Montréal," *BRH*, XXII (1916), 16–18.

BOUCHER, PIERRE, Sieur de **Grosbois**, interpreter, soldier, governor of Trois-Rivières, royal judge, founder and seigneur of Boucherville; son of Gaspard Boucher and Nicole Lemer (Lemaire); baptized 1 Aug. 1622 at Mortagne, in Perche (France); d. 19 April 1717 at Boucherville.

In answer to the appeal of his fellow-countryman Robert Giffard* to settle in Canada, Gaspard Boucher sold his farm at Mortagne on 1 Feb. 1634. We have no written undertaking on Gaspard Boucher's part towards Robert Giffard, but it is possible that Gaspard was one of a group which sailed for New France that same year. Some historians have expressed the opinion that on this first voyage he brought his wife, Nicole Lemer, and his children: Pierre the eldest, Nicolas, Marie, and Marguerite, who had all four been baptized at Mortagne; we do not know where his youngest daughter Madeleine was born, perhaps on the way over. Alfred Cambray, who supports the idea that the family arrived in 1634, thinks that they were on a ship commanded by Captain de Ville, which may also have carried Abbé Jean Le Sueur* and Jean Bourdon*. On the other hand, Madame Pierre Montagne states that these last two passengers accompanied Robert Giffard and his family on a ship commanded by Captain de Nesle. Madame Montagne also hints vaguely that the Boucher family was part of this group in 1634.

In a report drafted in 1695 Pierre Boucher stated that he had been brought to Canada in 1635 at the age of 13. If Gaspard Boucher came over in 1634, he may have returned the following year to fetch his family and his belongings; it was during a voyage in this year that he is thought to have had an altercation with his compatriot Thomas Giroux. The act by Guillaume Tronquet, dated 12 Sept. 1638, that records this incident, specifies that Boucher and his family made the crossing on a ship commanded by Captain de Ville. Now the four ships that sailed in 1634 were commanded by Du Plessis-Bochart*, Nesle, Bontemps, and Lormel. Captain de Ville, however, may have commanded one of the "eight large ships" mentioned in the 1635 *Relation* under the date of 4 July, six of which anchored at Tadoussac before proceeding to Quebec.

Gaspard Boucher, a carpenter by profession, was hired by the Jesuits to work on their farm at Notre-Dame-des-Anges. It has been affirmed that the religious took over the children's education, and in particular that of Pierre. However, in the acts which concern them, the latter's sisters stated that they could neither write nor sign their name. Pierre was the Jesuits' pupil particularly during his stay in Huronia, where he went in 1637 and where he remained until 1641 as an assistant to the missionaries. During these four years he shared the Indians' life, observed their customs, and learned their dialects. On 11 April 1640, at Téanaostaiaé (St Joseph II), he was seriously wounded in one arm during a revolt by the Hurons, when Fathers Brébeuf* and Chaumonot* were severely beaten and threatened with burning at the stake.

As soon as the young man returned to Quebec, Governor Huault* de Montmagny took him into his service as a soldier, but especially as an interpreter and agent to the Indian tribes. In this capacity he took part in all the parleys of the authorities with the Indians and acquired valuable experience which was to stand him in good stead all his life. He went everywhere with the governor, who obtained rapid promotion for him. From private he became corporal, and shortly afterwards sergeant. He is known to have been at Ville-Marie on 18 May 1642, when this post was established. On 20 August following, at the mouth of the Richelieu, he took part in the battle that the small French force had to fight with the Iroquois. Boucher admired greatly "the courage and gallant bearing" of the governor, as well as the latter's skilful diplomacy during the peace negotiations. In 1644 Boucher was appointed official interpreter and clerk at the fort of Trois-Rivières, and quickly made himself indispensable. He played an active role, particularly on the occasion of the important discussions in 1645 in which the Mohawk chief Kiotseaeton* was the dominant figure. It was Pierre Boucher, accompanied by his brother-in-law Toussaint Toupin and a Mohawk, who on 23 Jan. 1646 brought to Quebec [*see* Kiotseaeton] the letters which refuted the false allegations made by the Huron Tandihetsi concerning the treaty just concluded. On 14 February Boucher brought back to Trois-Rivières the Hurons who had carried to Quebec the account of the death of Father Anne de Noüe*. He was already the key figure in the little town of Trois-Rivières.

Pierre Boucher's parents came to settle at Trois-Rivières soon after his appointment. The first mention of Gaspard's presence there is on 21 March 1646, when the governor made him a land grant of 24 acres situated between the lands owned by Jean-Paul Godefroy* and by Étienne de La Fond. On 30 Jan. 1645, at Quebec, the latter had married Pierre Boucher's sister Marie. Incidentally it is surprising that no trace is to be found anywhere of the last years and death of Gaspard Boucher and his wife. Pierre Boucher himself never alludes to these details. On 19 June 1652 Nicole Lemer is referred to as being a godmother at Trois-Rivières; subsequently there is no further mention of her. As for Gaspard, it has been asserted that he died in a fire that destroyed his house; this is based on a somewhat ambiguous statement made by his daughter Madeleine, who on 27 June 1668 affirmed that the title to the land grant of 1646 "has been burned with the said Gaspard Boucher's house, in which it [he?] was . . ." Whether she is talking about the title or the owner himself we do not know, although if it had been the latter the *Relations* or the parish register would have mentioned it. The last reference to Gaspard Boucher is on 20 May 1662, when he brought an action against Jacques Besnard. At that time Pierre Boucher was in France.

From 1645 on, Pierre Boucher lived permanently in the little town of Trois-Rivières. He took part in the defence of the fort, which was exposed to Iroquois attacks. In 1646 he went with his fellow-citizens, mostly improvised soldiers, to the Rivière Puante (Bécancour), where the presence of hostile Indians had been detected. "We lost some men," he wrote later, "the enemy having withdrawn without loss because of the poor leadership of our commanders." From then on his character as a leader, sharpened by the uninterrupted state of war, began to take shape. In 1648 and 1649 the little French colony on the banks of the St Lawrence was more than ever threatened with annihilation. Ville-Marie was no longer a sure outpost; one could count only on the town of Trois-Rivières "to stop the enemy from throwing himself upon a defenceless Quebec, the capture of which would spell the ruin of the country." The governor of Trois-Rivières in those unhappy years was Jacques Leneuf* de La Poterie, who was more of a businessman than a soldier and who was, moreover, often

absent. Louis d'Ailleboust* had just replaced Montmagny as governor, and a rapid visit to Trois-Rivières convinced him that Pierre Boucher was the real leader of the community. He appointed him "captain of the town" and had important discussions with him, as an outcome of which he asked him to prepare a plan of defence; the implementation of this plan was later to be the object of an official ordinance.

Pierre Boucher's idea was to bring about as soon as possible a radical transformation of the settlers' buildings, until then scattered at random, "some here, some there, according to the desire and convenience of each person," to quote the author of the *Relation*. Indeed a reconstituted plan of the land grants of the period shows that they covered approximately the area of the present lower town. This scattered population was too easy a target for Iroquois attacks. The suggestion made by Boucher, which the ordinance authorized him to carry out, was that the farms should be concentrated and the families enclosed within an *enceinte* of solid stockades; over these, guard-houses, which the governor had recommended should be set up, would keep a continuous watch. Each settler was to help in building the *enceinte*, practise handling weapons, and take his turn on the watch. Some of them, on various pretexts, tried to evade the orders. But the captain was relentless. Each man had to contribute his hours of corvée and all families had to resign themselves to living within the stockade. This initiative represents the first serious effort to organize the defence of the little town by its own settlers.

On 6 June 1651 Pierre Boucher was confirmed in his post of captain of the town. Du Plessis-Kerbodot [Guillemot*] was its acting governor and at the same time commander of the flying column. The recent attacks, the corpses of settlers found each day in their fields, and especially the deaths of four inhabitants of Cap-de-la-Madeleine, among them the notary Florent Boujonnier, revolted the governor, and he decided to launch a massive sortie to exterminate the Iroquois bands. Fearing a reverse, Captain Boucher was opposed to it, and he himself remained inside the fort with a few able-bodied men. This conflict of authority was to be resolved by the slaughter of 19 Aug. 1652, when 22 settlers and soldiers, including the governor, were massacred in the woods around the town.

As a result of this defeat, the settlers thought the situation was hopeless. The majority of family heads had perished. Of the first 40 settlers of Trois-Rivières not 10 remained. The whole colony, especially the population of Quebec, was at bay. The authorities wondered whether they would not be forced to leave the country. Panic spread even

Boucher

to those who had put their trust in providence. Mother Catherine de Saint-Augustin [Simon*], speaking in the name of her community, wrote: "We are not hastening to complete the rest of our buildings because of our uncertainty as to whether we shall stay here long." Marie de l'Incarnation [Guyart*] was still more explicit: "Plans are being made to leave everything," she wrote, "and to bring ships from France to save those who escape falling into the hands of our enemies." Pierre Boucher himself echoed this possibility. An ordinance that he issued on 10 Aug. 1653 contains these lines: "Despite the uncertainty of the times caused by the enemy, being in doubt as to whether we must vacate the country or not. . . ." However, he himself refused to despair, and he was soon to have the opportunity to try out his system of defence, all the more because he received a commission as acting governor in the absence of Jacques Leneuf.

On 23 Aug. 1653, one year after the massacre of Du Plessis-Kerbodot and his men, a force of 600 Iroquois, divided into three bands, encircled the post of Trois-Rivières. The Indians employed their usual tactics. They carried off the animals and burned the crops and the buildings outside the fort. Then they attacked the fort itself, where Pierre Boucher was mounting guard with the 40 or so able-bodied men, most of them adolescents and old persons, at his disposal. The defenders exercised unremitting vigilance, and each assault by the enemy was energetically repulsed. Consequently after nine days of siege the Iroquois, despairing of gaining possession of the fort, asked for peace negotiations. Fearing a trap, the governor went outside the fort alone, both to avoid exposing his improvised soldiers to a surprise attack and to keep concealed the weakness of his forces. We do not know the arguments that the shrewd commander may have used to induce the enemy chiefs to accept his own conditions. He wrote later: "The peace was concluded on the conditions that they would hand over to me all the prisoners they had in their army, whether they were French or Indian, that they would go and get those whom they were holding in their villages and bring them back within 40 days, and that the most important among the Iroquois nations would come with presents to Quebec to seek peace from our governor M. de Lauzon, and to conclude it. This was carried out in every particular. And when they went away, they left me six of their children as hostages." When he learned of this unhoped-for victory, Governor Jean de Lauson* said to Pierre Boucher: "It was fortunate that you held your post so well. For if the enemy had taken Trois-Rivières, the whole country would have been lost."

The writer of the *Relation* of that year hastened to note: "This event was so sudden, this change in barbarian minds so surprising, that one must admit that a spirit superior to that of human beings guided this task."

It was not until after this exploit, however, that Boucher officially received the title of commander of the fort which he had just saved. Lauson's ordinance bears the date of 23 August, the first day of the Iroquois' attack, but the report sent by Boucher to the governor expressly mentions that his appointment was subsequent to the event, and that it was granted to him as a reward for his success on that occasion. Likewise his appointment as governor, which was dated 1 Oct. 1654 and bore the mention "titular governor," was accorded to him after he had actually assumed the office. Meanwhile he had been entrusted with other responsibilities. From 1651 on he had been "churchwarden in charge of charitable activities in the parish." On various occasions he performed the duties of civil and criminal judge, which obliged him to give rulings on disputes between neighbours, cheating at cards, and petty thefts. His unruffled outlook on life enabled him to realize that successive trials had not made his fellow-citizens any wiser. Trading in spirits became once more the major activity of the settlers, who abandoned their families and went off on business again. In short, the little town of Trois-Rivières was far from being the place where Boucher's dream of establishing a seigneury in keeping with his ideas could be made a reality.

In 1657, even though his fellow-townsmen had just elected him by vote "king's councillor in the council established at Quebec," he requested permission from the governor to give up his official functions and to retire to what he called "his property." He did in fact own some land grants in the region. He chose that of Sainte-Marie, at Cap-de-la-Madeleine, a domain of 200 acres in area. We realize, when we read the minutes of the notaries of the period, and particularly those of Claude Herlin, how much importance Pierre Boucher attached to the protection of the settlers who agreed to become his copyholders. Reference is continually made in these minutes to redoubts, bastions, and stockades. Boucher continued to protect his fellow-countrymen, even despite themselves, for the danger of Iroquois attacks still existed, especially in 1658 and 1659. The settlers of Cap-de-la-Madeleine were spared, and on 27 April 1660 the superior of the missions, Father Jérôme Lalemant*, pointed out "the heavy expenditures made by the Sieur Boucher to support all Cap-de-la-Madeleine against the Iroquois, and the expenditures that he made to set himself up there."

On his arrival at Quebec on 31 Aug. 1661, Governor Dubois* Davaugour was not slow to realize the deplorable state of the colony. He swiftly took two important decisions: he placed a Jesuit, Father Ragueneau*, "at the head of a general council for the service of the king and the welfare of the country"; then he proposed to send a delegate familiar with the country to the new king, Louis XIV, to plead the colony's cause. The governor could not choose this special envoy himself, for he had just arrived. Although the historian Sulte has advanced a contrary hypothesis, it was by common agreement with the Jesuits and the colony's notables that the governor named Pierre Boucher, to whom he had just brought letters of nobility obtained by Lauson on his return to Paris. Indeed, Boucher knew the colony better than anyone. He had brilliant feats of arms to his credit. He had lived in close association with the governors, which had permitted him to acquire a certain distinction of manner and bearing. Furthermore, Davaugour gave him, as Boucher has noted himself, a "Memorandum of instructions concerning the manner in which I was to behave and to whom I was to address myself, which I followed exactly."

Pierre Boucher sailed for Paris on 22 October, bearing dispatches from the governor, one of which was an important letter addressed to the Prince de Condé. He also brought letters from the Jesuits in Canada to their house in Paris, the procurator of which was his old friend Father Paul Le Jeune*, who undoubtedly made his mission easier for him. We can accept, with Father Léon Pouliot, that Father Le Jeune's Épître au Roi, which introduces the Relation of 1661, and which received the imprimatur on 20 Jan. 1662, was inspired by Pierre Boucher's presence in Paris, and was intended to support the arguments of the young delegate. The lines that Boucher devotes to the royal audience in his "Mémoire" of 1695 are restrained: "I had the honour of speaking to the king, who questioned me about the state of the country, of which I gave him an accurate account, and His Majesty promised me that he would help the country and take it under his protection; which he has done." Boucher also had interviews with various persons of the court, including the Prince de Condé and Colbert; the latter asked him for a written report on the resources of this country and the reasons for keeping it for France.

When he sailed again from La Rochelle on 15 July 1662, Boucher could count on the two ships, the 100 soldiers, the provisions, and the munitions promised by the king. He had himself recruited "a hundred working men," having borrowed money to pay for their crossing. The return journey was long and arduous; the Aigle d'or and the Saint-Jean-Baptiste ran into fierce storms. Some 60 men, "both soldiers and workmen," died at sea. The rumour spread that these people had died of the plague, which was false, but for a long time Boucher had to house his recruits himself. He made his report to Davaugour, who handed over to him his commission as governor of Trois-Rivières.

The success of Pierre Boucher's mission marks a turning point in the history of New France. His presence among the most influential persons of the kingdom resulted in much curiosity and sympathy being aroused for his country. His report, to the writing of which he applied himself on his return, increased interest in New France. It was intelligent, sincere, rational propaganda, which reinforced on the human and economic level what was already known of this country through the Relations des Jésuites. The happiest outcome of this little work was the sending of the troops of the Carignan regiment and the coming of the Marquis de Tracy [Prouville*] and Intendant Talon*. At last France was taking the fate of its distant colony seriously.

The new governor, Saffray* de Mézy, confirmed Boucher in his post of governor. Almost at the same time, on 17 Nov. 1663, the Conseil Souverain conferred on him the office of royal judge, a position that he gave up the following year in favour of Michel Leneuf*. He had become the dominant figure in the colony, and successive governors and military leaders, as soon as they arrived, sought his opinions and his advice. The Marquis de Tracy in particular, whom he accompanied at the time of the famous 1666 expedition against the Mohawks, showed high esteem for him. But this man, who enjoyed all the honours and was favoured with the confidence of everyone, lofty or lowly, was not satisfied. This country, which was continually in a state of war, should be a country at peace. He wanted to set the example himself, and had, moreover, been thinking of it for a long time. In 1667, while he was still governor of Trois-Rivières and seigneur of Sainte-Marie, he took a far-reaching decision which he persuaded the governor, Rémy* de Courcelle, and the viceroy, the Marquis de Tracy, to accept. He proposed to go and settle in the heart of the Indian country, on his seigneury of Îles Percées, later called Boucherville. He had just married his eldest daughter Marie to the brave officer René Gaultier* de Varennes, to whom, with the agreement of the authorities, he entrusted his post as governor. Boucher enumerated the reasons for this decision in a document which has come down to us and which shows his greatness of mind and his strongly developed social sense. In it is discernible the

Boucher

disappointment that he felt when he saw his fellow-countrymen, for whom he had many times risked his life and of whom some were related to him, leading a life which did not conform to the ideal that he had set for himself. Indeed, Boucher's mother-in-law, Jeanne Énard, widow of Christophe Crevier, and his two brothers-in-law, were deeply incriminated in the inquiries of the Conseil Souverain into the trade in spirits, and the man who replaced him as judge, Michel Leneuf, was not equal to his task. These incidents were doubtless the reason for his decision to have "a place in this country where honest people may live in peace."

He was 45 years old, and thus began the last, and also the longest and most peaceful stage in his career. Henceforth he would devote himself to the realization of his most cherished dream: to develop a seigneury according to his own conception, with settlers judiciously chosen and ready to accept a flexible discipline. On 4 April 1673 he assembled at the seigneurial manor-house the 37 copyholders who had proved their worth, and handed them the titles to their land grants. The seigneurial dues were trifling; just what was required to meet communal needs, for he farmed his lands himself. Peace and mutual help attended the growth of the seigneury. Children were born, and the Bouchers set the example. In the parish register, Jeanne Boucher heads the list of baptisms.

In less than 15 years Boucherville became the ideal seigneury. It conformed in all particulars to the plan which Boucher had himself elaborated in his report to Colbert. The 1681 census lists the settlers, their families, their trades, the number of acres being farmed. The seigneur himself had 100 acres under cultivation: he was not listed as having any servants, for his sons were old enough to work. This perfect organization commanded the attention of the authorities and of travellers. This seigneury "is one of the finest and richest properties in the colony," remarked the intendant, BOCHART de Champigny; and according to GÉDÉON DE CATALOGNE its settlers "are the most prosperous in the government of Montreal."

Like Champlain* and Talon, Pierre Boucher believed in the possibility of creating a new people by the union of French men and Indian women. He gave the example himself by marrying, in 1649, a Huron girl, a pupil of the Ursulines of Quebec, Marie Ouebadinskoue, otherwise called Marie-Madeleine Chrestienne. The young woman died in December of the same year while giving birth to a child, who did not live. Boucher next married, in 1652, a fellow-countrywoman, Jeanne Crevier, who was the daughter of Christophe Crevier, the pioneer from Rouen, and who had come from

France with her parents. Fifteen children were born of this marriage. The sons adopted various names, chosen for the most part by Pierre Boucher himself and inspired by his native Perche. They formed the Montarville, Montbrun, Grosbois, Grandpré, Montizambert, La Bruère, La Perrière, and Boucherville families. The daughters married into the Gaultier de Varennes, Legardeur, Daneau de Muy, and Sabrevois de Bleury families. By the interplay of marriages, the Montizambert branch became English and Protestant after the cession of 1763. Another line, the Montbruns, went to the Illinois country and gained renown in the fields of politics, the army, and medicine. Others settled in Mauritius, the West Indies, Louisiana, and France.

Pierre Boucher's descendants are certainly among the most numerous left by the emigrants who came to settle in New France in the 17th century. This makes still more accurate the appreciation which BRISAY de Denonville sent in 1686 to Seignelay, the minister of Marine and Colbert's son: "It is the family that has worked the hardest for the good of the colony, having neglected nothing of what is required to further it. The father was one of the first founders of the colony under M. d'Avaugour. Held in esteem by His Excellency your late father, he was for a long time governor of Trois-Rivières. His seigneury is one of the finest in this country."

During his old age, Pierre Boucher wrote his "Mémoires," a chronological succession of the events in which he had been involved. It is a kind of record book, a series of notes which, although somewhat sketchy and unpretentious, are filled with an abundance of small details that are not unimportant for a better knowledge of his period. The deep meaning that this man endeavoured to give to his life is revealed especially in his spiritual testament which he entitled "My last wishes," and which has an original and touching simplicity. Tradition has it that for several years after his death the parish priests of Boucherville read the text of his testament from the pulpit on New Year's day. The parishioners recognized themselves in it. "I do not leave you great wealth," he acknowledged, "but the little that I do leave you has been very properly acquired. I have done what I could to leave you more, I have neglected nothing to that end, having indulged in no foolish expense, as you all know; but it did not please God, who is the master, to give me more. I leave you for friends many persons of rank and distinction and many honest people. I leave you no enemies for my part, as far as I know. I have done what I could to live without reproach; try to do the same." After this preamble, he had for his wife and children, whom he named in order of birth, an appropriate sentence, which was in accordance with the temperament of each one and which shows how united the family was. His principal piece of writing remains from certain points of view the propaganda work of 1663, of which we pointed out earlier the influence and the significance, but the serene philosophy revealed in the text expressing his last wishes and the text giving the reasons that prompted him to settle at Boucherville make us understand better the moral worth of this man and the secret of his influence on his contemporaries. Father Léon Pouliot summed up in one sentence Pierre Boucher's exceptional life when he wrote that he was "the most estimable and the greatest Canadian of his time; a distinction that none can take from him."

He died in his manor-house at Boucherville on 19 April 1717 at the age of 95 years, 82 of which were spent in New France. He lived for 20 years under Louis XIII, 73 under Louis XIV, and 2 under Louis XV. He could have known the first 13 governors and the first 7 intendants of his country of adoption.

RAYMOND DOUVILLE

AJTR, Registres des audiences de la cour de juridiction civile et criminelle. AN, Col., E, dossier Pierre Boucher. Archives du séminaire de Trois-Rivières, Collection Montarville Boucher de La Bruère. BN, MS, NAF 23607. [Pierre Boucher], *Histoire véritable et naturelle des mœurs et productions du pays de la Nouvelle-France, vulgairement dite le Canada* (Paris, 1664; Société historique de Boucherville Pub., I, 1964). *JR* (Thwaites). *JJ* (Laverdière et Casgrain). "Ordonnances inédites de Pierre Boucher, gouverneur des Trois-Rivières," *BRH*, XXXII (1926), 187–92.

Bonnault, "Le Canada militaire," 517–18. A.-A. Cambray, *Robert Giffard, premier seigneur de Beauport et les origines de la Nouvelle-France* (Cap-de-la-Madeleine, 1932). Archange Godbout, *Les pionniers de la région trifluvienne* (Trois-Rivières, 1934). [Louis Lalande], *Une vieille seigneurie, Boucherville* (Montréal, 1890). Séraphin Marion, *Un pionnier canadien, Pierre Boucher* (Québec, 1927). Mme Pierre Montagne, *Tourouvre et les Juchereau* (Société canadienne de généalogie pub., XIII, Québec, 1965). Kathryn de Monbreun Whitefort, *A genealogy and history of Jacques Timothé Boucher, sieur de Monbreun* (Ann Arbor, 1939). Montarville Boucher de La Bruère, "Pierre Boucher," *Cahiers des Dix*, II (1937), 237–60; "Pierre Boucher, colonisateur," *Cahiers des Dix*, III (1938), 165–90.

BOUDEAU. *See* BAUDEAU

BOUILLET DE LA CHASSAIGNE (Chassagne), JEAN, esquire, career soldier, knight of the order of Saint-Louis; b. June 1654 at Paray (Paray-le-Monial, department of Saône-et-Loire), son of Gaudefroy Bouillet and Anne Bartaud; d. 31 Jan. 1733 at Montreal.

Jean Bouillet was of noble descent; his father was a lawyer in the *parlement* of Paray and seigneur of the fief of La Chassagne. Being of a noble family, he could allow himself to envisage a brilliant military career. He was posted to the Régiment de Navarre in 1672, and quickly became an ensign, then a lieutenant (1675). In 1677 he was promoted to the rank of captain in the Régiment de Condé, and ten years later obtained command of a company of the colonial regular troops serving in Canada.

In 1690 he was commandant at Fort Lachine, where during the following winter he took part in a sortie against the Iroquois. Midshipman in 1693, captain again in 1694 and a naval sub-lieutenant the following year, La Chassaigne then vegetated for some 15 years, probably in a post in the Montreal region. But like every nobleman he had ambition, and he secured the support of people capable of obtaining advancement for him. LE ROY de La Potherie, in 1701, described him as one of the rare persons who won the esteem of CALLIÈRE "and who applauds his every action with affected admiration." This judgement is probably exaggerated, but it is partly confirmed by the numerous requests which he made after 1703, with the support of the governor and the intendant, to have at one time a king's lieutenancy at Trois-Rivières or in Acadia, at another a cross of the order of Saint-Louis, an honour which he finally obtained on 7 July 1711.

At the time of RAMEZAY's unsuccessful expedition against the Iroquois in 1709, La Chassaigne was in command of the 100 soldiers of the king's troops who were taking part in it. The following year he became town major of Montreal, then held in turn the posts of town major of Quebec (1716), king's lieutenant at Montreal (1720), governor of Trois-Rivières (1726), and governor of Montreal (1730), a post that he was still holding at the time of his death. During his term as governor of Trois-Rivières he had been on a mission to Burnet, the governor of New York, to urge him to have Fort Oswego, which had been erected in violation of the treaty of Utrecht, pulled down; this mission earned him from Burnet's pen the compliment of being called a person of "great merit."

On 28 Oct. 1699, at Montreal, he had married Marie-Anne Le Moyne, daughter of CHARLES LE MOYNE de Longueuil. Even if La Chassaigne was considered a good officer by Callière and RIGAUD de Vaudreuil, it is apparent to us that this fortunate alliance with one of the most celebrated families of Canada helped him in his career. Was it not the Baron de Longueuil whom he replaced as town major of Montreal in 1710, and from one of his brothers-in-law that 20 years later he took over the post of governor of Montreal?

At that time a military career did not enrich those who followed it, and La Chassaigne was no exception to the rule. In 1711 he was sentenced by the Conseil Supérieur to repay the sum of 797 *livres* which he had borrowed from Jean-Baptiste CÉLORON de Blainville. In a will that he made in 1727 he bequeathed the majority of his possessions in France to the Hôtel-Dieu Saint-Joseph of the town of Paray, but significantly enough there was no reference in this will to possessions that he might have had in Canada. In 1733 a generous pension of 3,000 *livres* was granted to him by the king, but he was not able to enjoy it, since he died before knowing of its existence.

Jean Bouillet left no descendants, and his wife ended her days in the Ursuline convent at Trois-Rivières. Another Bouillet, Claude, of whom he was the great-uncle, went to Canada around 1730; three daughters and one son survived him there.

ULRIC LÉVESQUE

AJQ, Greffe de Florent de La Cetière, 4 oct. 1727. Charlevoix, *Histoire* (1744), II, 59, 336. "Correspondance de Vaudreuil," APQ *Rapport, 1938–39*, 17, 156; *1939–40*, 398, 441, 459; *1942–43*, 433, 437; *1946–47*, 393, 401, 426, 459. *Jug. et délib.*, VI, 248–50. "Liste des officiers de guerre qui servent en Canada (octobre 1722) dressée par le gouverneur de Vaudreuil," *BRH*, XXXVI (1930), 207. "Un mémoire de Le Roy de La Potherie sur la Nouvelle-France adressé à M. de Pontchartrain, 1701–1702," *BRH*, XXII (1916), 214. P.-G. Roy, "Ce que Callières pensait de nos officiers," 321. Fauteux, *Les chevaliers de Saint-Louis*. "Rolle des officiers qui servent en Canada . . . (5 octobre 1692)," *BRH*, XXXIV (1928), 559.

J.-B.-A. Ferland, *La France dans l'Amérique du Nord* (3ᵉ éd., 2v., Montréal, 1929), II, 160, 278, 329. Alex. Jodoin et J.-L. Vincent, *Histoire de Longueuil et de la famille de Longueuil* (Montréal, 1889), 156. E. Demaizière, "Un bourguignon, gouverneur de Montréal. Jean Bouillet de La Chassagne," *NF*, I (1926), 132–34. J.-E. Roy, "Le patronage dans l'armée," *BRH*, II (1896), 114. P.-G. Roy, "Jean Bouillet de La Chassaigne," *BRH*, XI (1905), 144; "Les officiers d'état-major," *RC*, 3ᵉ sér., XXII (1918), 290. Benjamin Sulte, "Les gouverneurs des Trois-Rivières," *BRH*, II (1896), 72.

BOULDUC, LOUIS, soldier, settler, bourgeois, king's attorney; b. *c.* 1648 or 1649, son of Pierre Boulduc, master apothecary-herbalist of the Rue Saint-Jacques, in the parish of Saint-Benoît in Paris, and of Gilette Pijart; d. sometime between 1699 and 1701 in France.

Boulduc landed 17 Aug. 1665 at Quebec with Andigné* de Grandfontaine's company in the Carignan regiment. On 20 Aug. 1668 he married there Élisabeth Hubert, daughter of an attorney in the *parlement* of Paris. The couple settled at Charlesbourg, on a piece of land of 40 acres acquired from Jacques Bédard on 7 Oct. 1669 at a cost of 800 *livres*. But Boulduc, city dweller that he was, had only a short-lived interest in agricultural work. On 18 Nov. 1672 he rented a house at Quebec, and on 29 Oct. 1674 he was mentioned as a bourgeois of that town; meanwhile, on 26 Aug. 1674, he had sold his land for the sum of 850 *livres*. Apparently on the recommendation of Frontenac [Buade*], he was given the appointment, by royal letters dated 15 April 1676, of king's attorney for the provost court of Quebec, at a salary of 300 *livres*. On 31 August following, after taking the customary oath, he was installed in office.

During the period of Frontenac's first governorship, which was marked by incessant quarrels among rival factions, one could not with impunity side with the irascible governor. If he did not already know it, Boulduc was going to learn it to his cost, particularly because Frontenac proposed to use him and the provost court to check the Conseil Souverain. But the choice of Boulduc was hardly a fortunate one, if we are to believe Duchesneau*, who was personally involved in the intrigues, and Denonville [BRISAY], who in 1685 had time to conduct his own inquiry. Boulduc, wrote Duchesneau, "is accused of extortion, theft in all the houses where he is tolerated, continual debauchery and profligacy"; for his part, Denonville considered him "an out-and-out scoundrel who should never be tolerated in such an office."

The councillors never ceased harrying this over vulnerable official, in an attempt to discredit him and thereby to compromise the provost court. The struggle began in earnest after Louis XIV, in May 1677, had restored the provost court of Quebec to its original authority, and confirmed the attorney Boulduc in his post. Frontenac's protégé could expect some serious opposition. On 13 Nov. 1680 Duchesneau struck the first blow in a letter to the minister, and in January 1681 Boulduc, accused of embezzlement, was brought before the Conseil Souverain. Following a complaint lodged against him by a Bayonne merchant who perhaps wanted to take revenge, Boulduc was soon to see the councillors extend their indiscreet inquiries to his whole life, public and private. By virtue of a decree of 28 April he was suspended, and replaced temporarily by Pierre Duquet*. This was the signal for a rare outburst of fury: the factions tore at each other unremittingly in a fight to the finish, for which Boulduc was in reality scarcely anything more than the occasion and the pretext. Finally, after 14 months of outright brawling, the council found

Boulduc guilty of embezzlement—this was on 20 March 1682—and declared that he had forfeited his office.

It may be surmised that Frontenac, when back in France, did not forsake his protégé, for by a decree dated 10 March 1685 Louis XIV granted Boulduc's family one third of his salary, and asked the intendant to restore Boulduc to his post if he were deemed to have been sufficiently punished. Denonville vigorously opposed the former attorney's return, with the result that on 4 June 1686 the king dismissed the wretched Boulduc for good.

Madame Boulduc had gone back to France in 1685, provided with a pass by Denonville, who declared himself happy to "rid the country of a rather poor piece of goods." Boulduc followed her, perhaps the year after. They left behind "children who are dependent upon the charity of honest folk." The Boulducs had indeed three sons and two (or three) daughters whose ages ranged from 9 to 17 years. The youngest girl, who may or may not have been still alive, was Frontenac's god-daughter. They all remained in the colony and took the name of Bolduc. As for the parents, they died in France, apparently without seeing their children again.

Who would venture to pass final judgement on Boulduc? Whatever may have been his faults, he was perhaps above all the victim of a troubled age. Intendant de MEULLES seems to have thought so: "Much passion having been stirred up in this affair, the King would be wise to reinstate this magistrate," he wrote on 12 Nov. 1686.

ANDRÉ VACHON

[On 8 Feb. 1700, in his son René's marriage contract, Louis Boulduc—then in France—is described as living (Greffe Jacob); on 7 Nov. 1701, in the contract of his son Jacques he is described as deceased (Greffe Jacob). We can then conclude that he died in France between the summer of 1699 and that of 1701. A.V.]

AJQ, Greffe de Romain Becquet, 18 nov. 1672, 26 août 1674; Greffe de Pierre Duquet, 7 oct. 1669; Greffe de Leconte, 8 août 1668; Greffe de Gilles Rageot, 26 août 1674, 8 nov. 1675. AQ, NF, Ins. de la Prév. de Québec, I, 299, 543. "Correspondance de Frontenac (1672–82)," APQ *Rapport, 1926–27*, 140. *Jug. et délib.*, I, II. "Lettres et mémoires de F.-M.-F. Ruette d'Auteuil," 5f., 23. Recensement du Canada, 1681 (Sulte). P.-G. Roy, *Inv. Ins. Cons. souv.*, 67f. Gareau, "La prévôté de Québec," 104f. Godbout, "Nos ancêtres," APQ *Rapport, 1957–59*, 429f. Le Jeune, *Dictionnaire*, I, 200f. P.-G. Roy, "Louis Boulduc ou Bolduc," *BRH*, XXII (1916), 65–70. Régis Roy, "Boulduc," *BRH*, XXVI (1920), 13.

BOULER (Bowler), ROBERT, captain in the Royal Navy; commodore of the Newfoundland convoy and temporary governor, 1724–27; b. *c.* 1676; d. 1734.

Robert Bouler was appointed 5th lieutenant in the *Royal William* in 1696 and was promoted captain of the *Experiment* in 1707. After several years of uneventful service at sea, he was appointed commodore of the Newfoundland convoy and governor for the summer of 1724. He held this appointment again in 1725 and 1726. In 1727, in command of the *Argyle*, he was appointed commodore and governor for St John's and the northern parts of the island; Captain John St. Lo in the *Ludlow Castle*—under Bouler's orders until reaching Newfoundland waters—became commodore and governor of Placentia and the south coast. Bouler's answers to the customary Heads of Enquiry were perfunctory and stereotyped, and in 1726 the Board of Trade and Plantations noted that they expected the commodore to be more "punctual" in his answers.

The state of Newfoundland in the 1720s was critical. The fishery was at a low ebb, and many of the fishing admirals were turning to trade: "The Admirals of the fishing ships seem more diligent in their shops and storehouses ashore than in taking and curing of fish, however the cheife reasons of the fish being not so good as it used to be, is that the fish do not come in so early as heretofore so that the great part of the summer season being over the latter part is most attended with wet, and that prevents their being thoroughly cur'd." Drunkenness, corruption, and crime were rife in the settlement; Bouler reported that the "number of families who keep private houses" was 257, and the number "who keep taverns, 74." Despite sporadic attempts by the inhabitants to set up local governing bodies [*see* JAGO], no permanent or efficient authority was established. Many of the impoverished and debt-ridden inhabitants fled to New England as "indentured servants"; Bouler noted that the taking of bonds from masters of New England ships to prevent this traffic was virtually useless, as the offending ships merely waited until the commodore left. In 1725 Bouler reported a complaint by George SKEFFINGTON that certain individuals had interfered with his salmon fisheries; the commodore investigated the matter and ordered two of the offenders to be flogged, "with a catt of nine tails on the bare back."

After his last return from Newfoundland Bouler was placed on half-pay and did not serve at sea again. He died 27 July 1734.

MICHAEL GODFREY

PRO, Adm. 2/51, pp.439f. (orders and instructions), 6 (commission and warrant books), 51/63 (captain's log of H.M.S. *Argyle*), 51/558 (captain's log of H.M.S.

Boullard

Ludlow Castle); C.O. 194/7, 194/8; *CSP, Col., 1724–25, 1726–27.* Charnock, *Biographia navalis*, III. Lounsbury, *British fishery at Nfld.*

BOULLARD, ÉTIENNE, priest, canon, capitular vicar, parish priest of Beauport and Quebec, superior of the seminary of Quebec; b. 1658 at Château-du-Loir (province of Maine); d. 1733 at Quebec.

Étienne Boullard was ordained a priest in 1682 and arrived in New France in 1684. He was immediately appointed parish priest for the new parish of Beauport, which he directed until 1719. From 1692 on he belonged to the seminary of Quebec, since his name appears on the list of members of the community. In 1700 he became a canon in the chapter, and for a long time he held the offices of theologal and official. In 1724, upon Abbé THIBOULT's death, he became superior of the seminary for two years, and as he was "agreeable to everyone" he was appointed priest of the parish of Notre-Dame de Québec in 1725 and remained in that charge until his death.

In 1705, along with Dufournel*, the parish priest of Ange-Gardien, he entered into the quarrel of the tithes. The preceding year Louis XIV had abolished the allocation which allowed for a supplement to be paid to certain parish priests. Convinced that the ecclesiastical tax as it was being levied was insufficient to support certain of their colleagues decently and wishing to stir up public opinion, Abbés Boullard and Dufournel announced to their parishioners that they were going to exact the tithe not only on grain, but also "on everything that the soil produces, whether cultivated or not, and on animals, such as hay from the low-lying meadows, fruits, flax and hemp, sheep, and other items." Boullard even mentioned a seventh precept of the church which supposedly rendered the payment of tithes obligatory. He may not have been innovating completely, since the catechism published by Bishop Saint-Vallier [LA CROIX] in 1702 recalled the precept: "He shall not marry out of season; he shall pay his tithes correctly," but the settlers were much surprised at the abbé's interpretation and grumbled loudly about it when the masses were over. RUETTE d'Auteuil immediately intervened, called a meeting of the Conseil Supérieur, and made a long indictment of the two priests. Boullard and his colleague were summoned to explain their conduct; this they did on 22 Dec. 1705, but their claim was dismissed and, despite a request by all the clergy of the colony in 1707, the civil authorities decided to authorize only the tithe on grain.

In 1701 Abbé Boullard had to deal with a marriage "à la gaumine." Louis de Montéléon, an officer in the colonial regular troops, wanted to marry Marie-Anne-Josette L'Estringant de Saint-Martin. He sought the permission of the vicar general, GLANDELET, who refused it until he had furnished proof that he was not already married. On 7 Jan. 1711, being unwilling to wait any longer, Montéléon and his fiancée, accompanied by witnesses, went to the church of Beauport and took advantage of the wedding service of Simon Touchet and Geneviève Gagnier to exchange their vows of consent clearly and publicly. Abbé Boullard, who was officiating, immediately turned away from the altar and protested energetically, even asking those present to leave the church. At the moment of the final benediction he declared that a marriage contracted thus was "an outrage upon the authority of the church," and said "other things as well of a sort to fill with horror those who were witnesses to such a crime." Upon his return to the presbytery he again took the guilty pair to task, then drew up a declaration that he sent to the vicar general, Glandelet. Before legal action was begun, however, Boullard proposed meeting the two young people "to try by gentleness and suavity" to bring them around to a better way of thinking. He half succeeded, since the Sieur de Montéléon publicly asked forgiveness during mass for the parish and promised to quit Mlle de L'Estringant. But on the girl's side there was no giving way. Boullard left it to the Conseil Supérieur to hear the case, annul the marriage, and order that the girl be confined in the convent of the Hôtel-Dieu until the marriage was regularized, which took place the 16 February following.

Abbé Boullard is above all famous for the part that he played in the quarrel surrounding Bishop Saint-Vallier's death, which occurred during the night of 25–26 December 1727. When it occurred the canons of the chapter elected M. Boullard capitular vicar to administer the diocese and authorized him to preside over the obsequies in the cathedral. But M. de Lotbinière [Chartier*], the pro-dean and archdeacon of the chapter and Saint-Vallier's vicar general, who was unpopular, insisted on presiding; he was supported by the bishop's executor, Intendant DUPUY, who was intent on fulfilling Saint-Vallier's wish to be buried in the Hôpital Général. Dupuy called upon the two parties to appear before him on 2 Jan. 1728. The canons refused to admit the intendant's competence in this matter, or even that of the Conseil Supérieur, and the meeting did not take place. That same evening, it was learned that, upon Dupuy's order, the funeral service had been held in the Hôpital Général before the appointed time. Boullard was one of the first to arrive on the scene. "Because of the outrage that had been committed," and in view of the refusal of the mother superior, Geneviève Duchesnay de Saint-Augustin, to appear before him, he placed the Hôpital Général under interdict and removed her from office.

This resulted in a dispute between the Conseil Supérieur, the intendant, and M. de Lotbinière on one hand, and the chapter of Quebec and M. Boullard on the other. The latter was sentenced to a fine of 1,000 *livres* and forbidden "to make any jurisdictional act as vicar general." He nevertheless increased his authoritative acts and his threats of excommunication, with the result that the Ursulines and the Nuns Hospitallers complained that he was "perturbing" them. He was summoned by the Conseil Supérieur and appeared before it on 8 March to deliver a written statement of nine pages which was supposed to prove that he had been rightfully elected capitular vicar and that the judgements pronounced against him were null in law. It was during this meeting that Beauharnois* de La Boische intervened to calm people's minds. When he was informed of the matter, the king re-established order: Dupuy was recalled, the distraints and fines were annulled, and some blame was cast upon the chapter.

Abbé Boullard was not the sole person responsible for all these incidents, but his lack of tact and goodwill contributed to inflaming the dispute. It was he who defended the right of the chapter fiercely, who readily made use of ecclesiastical penalties against the religious communities, and who had directed the canon's last acts of resistance to M. de Lotbinière. The least that can be said is that his interventions were rarely conducive to re-establishing peace.

Abbé Boullard died 28 Sept. 1733 and was buried the next day in the crypt of Notre-Dame de Québec.

NIVE VOISINE

Caron, "Inventaire de documents," APQ *Rapport, 1940–41, 1941–42. Jug. et délib.*, V, 184, 211, 230; VI. *Mandements des évêques de Québec* (Têtu et Gagnon), I, 522f. Étienne Marchand, "Les troubles de l'Église du Canada en 1728," *BRH*, III (1897), 117–21. "Les mariages à la gaumine," APQ *Rapport, 1920–21*, 366–407. "Mémoire de M. Dupuy, Intendant de la Nouvelle-France, sur les troubles arrivés à Québec en 1727 et 1728, après la mort de Mgr de Saint-Vallier," APQ *Rapport, 1920–21*, 78–105. Provost, *Le Séminaire de Québec: documents et biographies*, 24. PAC *Report, 1904*, 116. P.-G. Roy, *Inv. jug. et délib., 1717–1760*, I, 340–45.

Allaire, *Dictionnaire*. Gosselin, *L'Église du Canada*, IV, V. Lanctot, *Histoire du Canada*, III, 40–41. *Monseigneur de Saint-Vallier et l'Hôpital Général de Québec*. Auguste Gosselin, "Charles de Beauharnais," *BRH*, VII (1901), 293–301; "Un épisode de l'histoire de la dîme au Canada (1705–1707)," *RSCT*, 2nd ser., IX (1903), sect.I, 45–63. Alfred Rambaud, "La vie orageuse et douloureuse de Mgr de Saint-Vallier," *RUL*, IX (1954), 90–108. P.-G. Roy, "Un poème héroï-comique," *BRH*, III (1897), 114–16.

BOURDON, ANNE, *dite* **de Sainte-Agnès,** first Canadian superior of the Ursulines in New France; b. 29 Aug. 1644 at Quebec, daughter of Jean Bourdon*, attorney general of New France, and Jacqueline Potel; d. 4 Nov. 1711.

As early as 23 Aug. 1648 the "Registre des entrées des pensionnaires" mentions the girl's presence at the Ursuline seminary: "Her mother brought her there through fear of the Iroquois." Anne, a precocious child, applied to enter the order of the Ursulines of Quebec at the age of 14. She was admitted to the noviciate on 8 Sept. 1658, and made her profession on 30 Sept. 1660. Bishop LAVAL received the young Ursuline's vows, "a thing which had never occurred before in Canada." The wording of the vows required her "to concern herself to the best of her ability with the teaching of little French and Indian girls." Hence the necessity of learning the Algonkian, Huron, and even Iroquois languages. Anne Bourdon had as her teacher of Indian languages Marie de l'Incarnation [Guyart*], who wrote in 1668: "My task during the winter mornings is to teach Indian languages to my young sisters."

Although a seigneur, M. Bourdon did not possess the 3,000 *livres* required for his daughter Anne's dowry. Marie de l'Incarnation gave him eight years to complete his payments. According to the terms of the contract drawn up by the notary Guillaume Audouart*, the entire sum was to be paid in cash, in beaver furs, and in funds to be received from his estate. On 12 Oct. 1660 M. Bourdon donated his arriere-fief of Sainte-Anne to the Ursulines. On 14 July 1664 Marie de l'Incarnation announced that she had received from M. Bourdon the sum of 1,000 *livres* "all in good beaver." Finally in 1666 the dues of Sister Anne Bourdon were discharged by the payment of 1,000 *livres tournois*.

During her religious career Anne Bourdon assumed the most important offices in the convent. She was in turn depositary, secretary of the chapter, zelatrice, assistant superior, and mistress of novices. In addition, she distinguished herself as the annalist or author of the *Vieux Récit*. After the fire of 1686 she reconstructed from memory the 50 years of archives that had been destroyed. For this task she was well fitted by her qualities of birth, mind, and heart. On 7 June 1700, although Bishop Laval wanted another French superior, the members of the chapter gave their votes to Mother Anne Bourdon de Sainte-Agnès.

Bourdon

Having been with the Ursulines since her childhood, she had known the foundresses and had been reared in their way of thinking. Moreover, in her family, she had heard the problems of the colony and the kingdom discussed. Furthermore, she possessed a superior intelligence, and an orderly and inquisitive mind. The last words she wrote reveal her faith and her patriotism: "They [the English] put their trust in their number; as for us, Lord, our trust is in your protection."

A "violent and incurable pleurisy" carried her off on 4 Nov. 1711; "her saintly life," the *Registres* say, "having spared her all dread of death."

MARIE-EMMANUEL CHABOT

AMUQ, Constitution manuscrite des Ursulines de Québec (1647); Registre des entrées des pensionnaires. *JJ* (Laverdière et Casgrain), 250. Marie Guyart de l'Incarnation, *Lettres* (Richaudeau), II. *DCB*, I, 111–13. Le Jeune, *Dictionnaire*, I, 225–27. P.-G. Roy, *A travers l'histoire des Ursulines de Québec* (Lévis, 1939), 40. *Les Ursulines de Québec* (1866–78), I, 224–27, 299, 449, 472–73; II, 42, 74–78.

BOURDON, JACQUES, process-server, clerk of court, and notary; baptized 5 June 1645 in the church of Saint-Godard at Rouen, son of Jean Bourdon and Marguerite Legris; buried 7 Aug. 1724 at Boucherville.

In our opinion, J.-Edmond Roy has wrongly identified Jacques Bourdon with the "J. Bourdon" who was a clerk in the court registry of the Conseil Souverain in 1664. It was rather at Montreal, in the autumn of 1666, that Bourdon began his career, as a process-server. But by 9 Oct. 1667 he had been dismissed from his office by Judge Charles-Joseph d'Ailleboust* Des Muceaux. Although he owned a few acres of land at Longueuil, he settled at Boucherville, where on 8 Feb. 1672 he married Marie Ménard and on 19 March 1673 bought from his father-in-law a piece of land measuring 2 *arpents* by 25. In 1681 he had only two acres under cultivation, and his live-stock consisted of one cow. It is true that since 1677 he had been acting as process-server, clerk of court, and notary of the Boucherville seigneury, but Pierre BOUCHER was soon to remove him from office on 15 June 1683. Bourdon none the less continued to call himself a notary, by what authority is not very clear: mention has been made of a commission granted by Intendant Bégon*, which is probable. He exercised his profession until 1720, contending with the seigneurial notary for a clientele that was small in any event, with the result that in 1739 Louis-Claude Danré* de Blanzy found only 158 minutes in his registry. This was very little on which to bring up a family of 14 chil-

dren. Fortunately, on 26 Aug. 1702, he had received another commission as process-server. His wife survived him by two years and was buried 2 July 1726 at Boucherville.

ANDRÉ VACHON

AJM, Greffe de Bénigne Basset, 27 nov. 1666, 15 août 1671, 18 oct. 1676; Greffe de Jacques Bourdon; Greffe de Thomas Frérot, 3 janv. 1672, 19 mars 1673; Greffe de Marien Tailhandier, 14, 26 mars 1713, 14 avril 1718, 28 nov. 1725. Recensement du Canada, 1681 (Sulte). P.-G. Roy, *Inv. coll. pièces jud. et not.*, II, 404. Godbout, "Nos ancêtres," APQ *Rapport, 1959–60*, 340f. É.-Z. Massicotte, "Les tribunaux et les officiers de justice," BRH, XXXVII (1931), 128. "Les notaires au Canada," 27. [Louis Lalande], *Une vieille seigneurie, Boucherville* (Montréal, 1890), 401f. J.-E. Roy, *Histoire du notariat*, I, 209f., 337.

BOURDON, MARGUERITE, *dite* **de Saint-Jean-Baptiste,** Augustinian Hospitaller of the Hôtel-Dieu of Quebec, one of the foundresses of the Hôpital Général; b. 12 Oct. 1642 at Quebec, daughter of Jean Bourdon*, attorney general of New France, and of Jacqueline Potel; d. 11 Oct. 1706.

Marguerite, one of Jean Bourdon's four daughters by his first marriage, was raised by nuns, as were her sisters, Marie, Geneviève, and ANNE. She remained with the Ursulines until she was 14. Although the Ursulines would have "very much liked to have her with them," Marguerite returned to live with her parents, who considered that she was too young to make up her mind. Although she was liked and sought after in the society in which she moved—Jean de Lauson*, the governor's son, even asked for her hand—she nevertheless chose to join the Religious Hospitallers of the Hôtel-Dieu. She was received into the order on 23 Jan. 1657 and made her profession on 15 Oct. 1658 under the name of Saint-Jean-Baptiste.

At the Hôtel-Dieu Marguerite played an increasingly important role. Her zeal in the service of the poor caused her to be named several times to the post of second and then of first hospitaller. Because of her piety she was appointed vestry-nun. Finally, her sense of order and exactitude contributed to her being elected assistant superior twice.

The founding of the Hôpital Général somewhat upset this peaceful existence. On his arrival in New France in 1688, Bishop Saint-Vallier [LA CROIX], who wanted to found a hospital for the infirm, bought a house in the Upper Town of Quebec and entrusted its management to the Congrégation de Notre-Dame. In 1692 the hospice was moved to the convent of Notre-Dame-des-Anges [*see* FILIASTRE] on the banks of the St Charles River, and the Hospitallers of the Hôtel-Dieu were asked to take over the running of the new hospital. At first they attempted to refuse, and proposed instead building an annex to their convent where the infirm would be cared for; Bishop Saint-Vallier did not accept this proposal and persisted in his request. Finally the nuns had to accede to the bishop's desires. In 1693, then, they signed the founding deed and appointed four nuns. Marguerite Bourdon was one of those chosen, along with two other choir nuns, Mothers LOUISE SOUMANDE de Saint-Augustin and Geneviève Gosselin de Sainte-Madeleine, and a lay sister, Sister Madeleine Bâcon de la Résurrection. They moved into their new convent on 1 April 1693; Mother Saint-Jean-Baptiste, although she was not appointed superior, was entrusted by virtue of being the eldest with the task of directing her companions under the authority of the superior of the Hôtel-Dieu, Mother Juchereau de Saint-Ignace [JUCHEREAU de La Ferté]. It was, however, Louise Soumande de Saint-Augustin who was chosen as superior in the first elections, held in 1694.

In this hospice, where there was no lack of work, Mother Saint-Jean-Baptiste exerted herself without stint. In 1699 she had an attack of spitting blood and fell ill with a dangerous lung ailment. As her illness persisted, she was taken to the Hôtel-Dieu where she could receive better care. She came back only after six weeks, a little better but not perfectly recovered, and she had to remain some time without working, which did not prevent her from being elected assistant superior in April 1699.

These elections had increased in importance, since an ordinance by Bishop Saint-Vallier had just separated the two communities of the Hôtel-Dieu and the Hôpital Général, a measure which almost brought about the disappearance of the latter. Indeed, when the religious of the Hôtel-Dieu presented a memoir to the Comte de Pontchartrain to have certain points defined more accurately, the minister ordered the dissolution of the community of the Hôpital Général and the transfer of all the religious to the Hôtel-Dieu. But the authorities of the colony sought a means of lessening the effect of the minister's order and decided to send back to the mother house only the superior, Mother Gabrielle Denis de l'Annonciation, and the novices. Bishop Saint-Vallier himself went to France and succeeded in saving his work and the young community; the religious returned to the Hôpital Général.

Marguerite Bourdon died 11 Oct. 1706. Mother Saint-Augustin paid her this final tribute: "As I have always been responsible for temporal affairs,

it was a great comfort for me to have in her example support in maintaining discipline within the house. She set the young sisters great examples of fervour, discipline, and mortification. In the midst of our sorrow we have the consolation of seeing her die as she had lived, bearing the precious mark of predestination."

NIVE VOISINE

Juchereau, *Annales* (Jamet). Casgrain, *Histoire de l'Hôtel-Dieu de Québec. Monseigneur de Saint-Vallier et l'Hôpital Général de Québec.*

BOURG, ABRAHAM, deputy representing Upper Cobequid, Nova Scotia, 1720–26; b. at Port-Royal (Annapolis Royal, N.S.) 1662, son of Antoine Bourg and Antoinette Landry; married in 1683 Marie Brun, daughter of Vincent and Marie Breaux; date of death unknown.

Abraham Bourg was one of the deputies chosen by the Nova Scotia Council to represent the Acadian districts in 1720, under the governorship of Richard Philipps*. He was apparently released from his duties in 1726 at his own request, because of lameness and infirmity. On 16 Sept. 1727 he, Francis Richards, and the deputies Charles Landry and Guillaume Bourgeois refused to take the oath of allegiance to George II. Lieutenant-Governor Lawrence ARMSTRONG maintained, moreover, that they had assembled the inhabitants a day earlier than they had been ordered. Armstrong charged that "instead of persuading them to their duty by solid arguments of which they were not incapable they [the deputies] frightened them . . . by representing the oath so strong and binding that neither they nor their children should ever shake off the yoke."

For their alleged opposition they were committed to prison. It was ordered that Bourg, however, "in consideration of his great age," should be allowed to leave the province as soon as possible, but without his goods. As the others were released after a short time, it appears unlikely that Abraham Bourg actually left. An oath of 1730 bears a signature which may be his. It is not known when Bourg died, but it may have been after 13 April 1736, when Marie Brun's burial record identifies her as the wife (not widow) of Abraham Bourg.

MAUD HODY

Archives of the Bishop's House, Yarmouth, N.S., Registre de baptêmes, mariages, et sépultures pour la paroisse Saint-Jean-Baptiste à Annapolis Royal, 1727–1755 (copy in Archives de l'université de Moncton). AN, Section Outre-Mer, G¹, 466 (Recensements de l'Acadie, 1671, 1686, 1693, 1698, 1701, 1703 [Port-Royal], 1714 [Cobequid]; copies in Archives de

93

Bourgeois

l'université de Moncton). PANS, MS docs., XVII, Letter of Lawrence Armstrong, 17 Nov. 1727 (printed in PRO, CSP, Col., 1726–27); XXII, 150, 153, 160, 216ff. (printed in N.S. Archives, III). PANS, Oath of loyalty to George II, 1730 (no. 7 in box of original oaths).

BOURGEOIS, JACQUES (Jacob), surgeon, colonizer, founder of Beaubassin; b. sometime between 1618 and 1621 in France, probably at Couperans-en-Brie (department of Seine-et-Marne); d. 1701 at Port-Royal (Annapolis Royal, N.S.); founder of the Bourgeois family in Acadia.

Before leaving France, Bourgeois had entered the medical profession. He came to Port-Royal in 1642 with 18 families that Governor Menou* d'Aulnay brought with him on one of his voyages. Bourgeois' father, also named Jacques, was an army officer at Port-Royal and was the brother-in-law of Germain Doucet, Sieur de La Verdure, Aulnay's assistant. In 1654 Sedgwick* seized Port-Royal, and as by the terms of the capitulation soldiers were to be repatriated, Jacques Bourgeois senior returned to France; his son remained in Acadia, where he became the ancestor of a large number of descendants. In 1643 Bourgeois had married Jeanne, Guillaume Trahan's daughter, who was born in France in 1631; they had ten children, seven girls and three boys.

At Port-Royal, Jacques Bourgeois became a farmer and shipbuilder. He traded with the Bostonians, particularly with John NELSON and William Phips*; he learned their language, and was the interpreter for the French in their dealings with the English. In 1672 he sold a part of his holdings at Port-Royal in order to settle, with his sons Charles and Germain and two of his sons-in-law, in the Chignecto Basin, thus becoming the first promoter of settlement in this region; he built a flour-mill and a saw-mill there. A few years later, in 1676, the region was made into a seigneury, the holder of which was MICHEL LENEUF de La Vallière (the elder), a nobleman born at Trois-Rivières; the new fief, 100 square leagues in extent, was named Beaubassin. As La Vallière brought in settlers and indentured employees from Canada, two distinct establishments adjoined each other at Beaubassin; but a clause in the title to the land grant protected the interests of Jacques Bourgeois and the other Acadian settlers established on the domain; it was not long before the two elements of the population merged into one.

The Chignecto region provided Jacques Bourgeois and the whole settlement with fertile marshes, and high ground suitable for farming. The Shediac portage was an important relay station in the sea communications between Acadia and Canada and a strategic position commanding the isthmus and Baie Française (Bay of Fundy). By the time of the expulsion of the Acadians, Beaubassin had become one of the most prosperous places in Acadia.

The distinguished colonist had settled at Port-Royal again before 1699; he died there, an octogenarian, in 1701. The family name was perpetuated by two of his three sons: Charles, born in 1646, who married Anne Dugas in 1668; and Germain, born about 1650, who married his first wife, Marguerite Belliveau, in 1673 and his second wife, Madeleine Dugas, in 1682; the third son, Guillaume, left only a daughter.

CLÉMENT CORMIER

AN, Col., C^{11D}, 3, f.191. Coll. de manuscrits relatifs à la N.-F., I, 149. Recensement de l'Acadie, 1686 (BRH), 681. Placide Gaudet, "Acadian genealogy and notes," PAC Report, 1905, II, pt.III, 1; App. A, 1; see also his Notes généalogiques (preserved in PAC and the Archives de l'université de Moncton), and his studies in the Évangéline (Moncton), 5 Feb. and 10 Dec. 1942. Arsenault, Hist. et généal. des Acadiens, 61–63, 361. Rameau de Saint-Père, Une colonie féodale, I, 167–69, 171–72, 175; II, 335.

BOURGMOND, ÉTIENNE DE VÉNIARD DE. See VÉNIARD

BOUVART, MARTIN (baptized **Samuel**), priest, Jesuit, superior of the mission in New France; b. 15 Aug. 1637 at Chartres; d. 10 Aug. 1705 at Quebec.

Martin Bouvart did his literary studies at Blois and studied philosophy for two years at the University of Paris. With the help of an uncle who was a Jesuit, he was admitted into the noviciate in Paris on 10 Aug. 1658. In 1660 he was a teacher at Amiens, and six years later he again studied philosophy at La Flèche. He taught at Eu, and in 1668 returned to La Flèche for his theology. During his third year of probation at Rouen, in 1672, he received assurance that he would be sent to Canada, but his mother was so grieved by this that she fell seriously ill. In the spring of 1673 he was sent to Nantes, with no very precise destination. There he found Father Antoine SILVY, and the two were immediately scheduled to sail together from La Rochelle for Quebec.

The two Jesuits arrived in New France on 30 Sept. 1673, and Bouvart was given the task of assisting Father Joseph-Marie Chaumonot*, the priest to the Hurons at Notre-Dame-de-Foy. Thus he took part in the creation of the Notre-Dame-de-Lorette mission; the plan for this had been decided upon, and it was carried out between December 1673 and November 1674. In the autumn of 1676 he succeeded Father Guillaume Matthieu as professor of theology at the Jesuit college in Quebec and also became procurator of the mission. Until 1698 he devoted himself to teaching rhetoric, philosophy, and theology. It was he who had the greatest share in the training of the young clerics of the colony.

On 25 Aug. 1698 he was appointed rector of the college and superior general of the mission. His term as superior was marked by several quarrels between the Jesuits and Bishop Saint-Vallier [LA CROIX]. The latter, who had returned to Canada in 1697 with an admonishment from Louis XIV to keep the peace, had a few differences with the Society of Jesus. The bishop of Quebec wanted to make himself agreeable towards the priests of the seminary, with whom he had previously quarrelled; the Jesuits, however, had to put up with some vexations. Saint-Vallier took away from them the primary school which they were holding in their college, and the direction of the Congrégation des Messieurs de Québec; he forbade the college to give debates and theatrical performances. Furthermore, he accused the Fathers of teaching probabilism, which would contribute to laxity of morals. In addition, he asked the Jesuits to leave the church and house at Notre-Dame-de-Lorette, which they had built at great cost, because he wanted to make a parish out of the mission [see COUVERT]. Finally, Bouvart had to compromise with Saint-Vallier over the mission to the Tamaroas [see BERGIER]. In these quarrels Bouvart deemed it advisable to make concessions, to the great annoyance of his advisers, who reproached him in their letters to the general of the society with a lack of courage. He himself asked to be relieved of his office at the end of his first three-year term, but he was maintained in it for an entire second term, during which he had a second quarrel with the bishop of Quebec. The latter published a *Catéchisme* and *Rituel* that are usually described as "moral Jansenism." Bouvart made a criticism of them which the Sorbonne, at Saint-Vallier's request, condemned as "rash, conducive to schism and to the revolt of the flock against the minister, and very insulting to His Excellency the bishop of Quebec."

In August 1704 Father VINCENT BIGOT replaced Bouvart. The latter, whose health was already frail, died on 10 Aug. 1705 at the Jesuit college in Quebec.

LUCIEN CAMPEAU

ARSI, Gallia, 110/I, 110/II. *JR* (Thwaites), LXXV, LXXVI. Rochemonteix, *Les Jésuites et la N.-F. au XVIIᵉ siècle*, III, 373, 550–89. Alfred Rambaud, "La vie orageuse et douloureuse de Mgr de Saint-Vallier," *RUL*, IX (1954), 100–1.

BOWLER. *See* BOULER

BRANDEAU, ESTHER, young Jewish girl, b. *c.* 1718, probably at Saint-Esprit near Bayonne, in the diocese of Dax; lived at Quebec 1738–39; d. at a date unknown.

The arrival of Esther Brandeau, a young girl about 20 years old who was disguised as a boy and gave her name as Jacques La Fargue, created a veritable stir at Quebec in September 1738. Chance having disclosed her true identity, Intendant Hocquart* had her arrested and taken to the Hôpital Général. On 15 September the commissary of Marine, Varin*, subjected her to an interrogation which is our only source of information about her past. On 21 April 1739 the minister wrote in this connection: "I do not know whether one can trust implicitly the declaration made by the so-called Esther Brandeau." Be that as it may, according to this declaration Esther was the daughter of David Brandeau, a merchant at Saint-Esprit near Bayonne. Around 1733 her parents put her on a Dutch ship to send her to her brother and one of her aunts at Amsterdam. The ship was wrecked, she was saved by one of the crew, and was given shelter by a certain Catherine Churiau, a resident of Biarritz. It was from this time that she decided to wear male clothes. The commissary reporting her words explained her decision thus: "she [Catherine Churiau] made her eat pork and other kinds of meat that were forbidden to the Jews, and she resolved in due course never to return to the house of her father and mother, in order to enjoy the same liberty as the Christians."

Subsequently Esther Brandeau led a somewhat unsettled existence. She was in turn a ship's boy at Bordeaux, an errand boy for a tailor at Rennes, a domestic in the service of the Recollets at Clissay, in the employ of a baker at Saint-Malo, in the service of a Sieur La Chapelle, an infantry captain at Vitré, arrested for theft at Noisel near Nantes, and finally hired at La Rochelle as a ship's boy on the *Saint-Michel*, which was bound for Canada. All this, of course, under different borrowed names.

At a period when a monolithic religious structure was so firmly established, her arrival in New France was a source of intense embarrassment to Intendant Hocquart. Seeking instructions from the minister, he wrote: "Since her arrival at Quebec her conduct has been fairly restrained. She appears desirous of being converted to Catholicism." The minister replied: "I shall be very gratified to learn of her conversion. You must furthermore treat her in accordance with the way she behaves in the colony." It seems, however,

Breslay

that the "restrained" conduct of the beginning and the favourable disposition towards conversion did not last long. On 27 Sept. 1739 Hocquart wrote to the minister: "She is so flighty that she has been unable to adapt herself, either in the Hôpital Général or in several other houses ... Her conduct has not been precisely bad, but she is so fickle, that at different times she has been as much receptive as hostile to the instructions that zealous ecclesiastics have attempted to give her; I have no alternative but to send her away."

At the time the authorities of the colony considered it important, at least officially, that the inhabitants abide by Catholic orthodoxy. A non-Catholic immigrant in New France could look forward only to conversion or deportation. It was the same with non-orthodox Catholics [see POULET]. The deportation of Esther Brandeau very quickly became an "official matter"; even the king took a hand in it, and decided that the state would pay the young delinquent's return passage. On 25 Jan. 1740 he wrote to the admiral of France: "My cousin the Sieur Hocquart ... has embarked at Quebec on the ship *Comte de Matignon* of La Rochelle the so-called Esther Brandeau, a Jewess whom he had to send back to France in execution of my orders." After this letter from the king we hear no more of Esther Brandeau. She had most probably re-embarked in the autumn of 1739.

Esther Brandeau had remained in the colony only a year, long enough however to attract the attention of the highest authorities in New France. She was certainly the first Jewish person—and at the time perhaps the only one—to set foot in the colony.

GASTON TISDEL

PAC *Report, 1886,* xxxiii–xxxv. P.-G. Roy, *La ville de Québec,* I, 147–48. B. G. Sack, *History of the Jews in Canada,* trans. Ralph Novek (Montreal, [1965]), 6–9. Denis Vaugeois, *Les Juifs et la Nouvelle-France* (Trois-Rivières, 1968).

BRESLAY, RENÉ-CHARLES (Charles-René) DE, priest, Sulpician, missionary, vicar general of the bishopric of Quebec; b. June 1658 in Le Mans (Maine, France); d. in Paris 4 Dec. 1735.

After ten years as "gentleman in waiting in the privy chamber of the king," Breslay entered the order of Saint-Sulpice, and was professed in 1689. He requested, and on 1 Feb. 1694 was granted, the opportunity of serving the church in New France. He arrived on 3 Aug. 1694 and was stationed in Montreal, first as curate (1694–96), then as parish priest of the church of Notre-Dame (1696–1703). Named parish priest of Sault-Saint-Louis at the extremity of Montreal Island in March 1703, he

was instrumental in establishing on Îles de Vaudreuil a mission which centred on Île-aux-Tourtres. The mission was for the benefit of the Algonkins whose language Father Breslay had previously mastered and whom he had induced to move to this location.

His 16-year sojourn at Île-aux-Tourtres was marked by the establishment of a parish at Sainte-Anne-du-Bout-de-l'île; his disagreement with Governor RIGAUD de Vaudreuil concerning the brandy trade, which Breslay opposed; his parochial duties at Pointe-Claire (1716–19); and his assistance towards the construction of a canal to bypass Sault-Saint-Louis (Lachine rapids), which had been initiated by DOLLIER de Casson.

Sparked by a desire to plead the cause of his missions and the church's stand on the brandy question before the home authorities, Father Breslay returned to France (1719–20) where he encountered the Comte de Saint-Pierre who had been granted Île Saint Jean (P.E.I.) and neighbouring islands. At the invitation of the latter and with the eager concurrence of M. Lechassier, superior general of the Sulpician order, Father Breslay became the first parish priest on Île Saint Jean in April 1720. At this time, he was also made vicar general of the bishopric of Quebec. Aided by M. Métivier, he established a parish at Port-La-Joie (near present-day Charlottetown), where in 1722 was dedicated a church to St John the Evangelist. He also executed the manifold duties falling to him as missionary priest at Beaubassin (Chignecto) and other centres, especially Malpèque (Malpeque Bay, P.E.I.), which was frequented in the summer by the Micmacs. Lechassier had dreamed of establishing a seminary on Île Saint-Jean, but Father Breslay thought this premature and advised against it. To alleviate the financial burden of supporting parish priests, the Comte de Saint-Pierre suggested procuring representatives of a mendicant order for missionary work. To this end, Father Breslay returned to France on 29 April 1723.

Then followed a short stint as parish priest at Louisbourg (Île Royale), until in November 1724, at the request of the inhabitants, he was appointed to Annapolis Royal (formerly Port-Royal) where he was received officially by the council. Breslay was assigned a building at the extremity of the fort (known as Fort Mohawk), to be utilized as a parish house and a church. Of his welcome he wrote, "I had the honour to be received very graciously by Mr. Doucet [DOUCETT], the lieutenant-governor." Later, however, Breslay received harsh treatment at the hands of Lieutenant-Governor ARMSTRONG. In a letter to Governor Philipps*, Breslay claimed the lieutenant-governor had turned against him when he found himself unable to fulfil Armstrong's request for a loan. By 1728, faced with the threat of imprisonment at the hands of Armstrong, Father Breslay was obliged to flee to a Micmac encampment where he remained for 14 months. He was reinstated in his parish after Philipps arrived at Annapolis Royal late in 1729. The next year Breslay went to Paris where he retired to a Sulpician seminary. He died there on 4 Dec. 1735.

Throughout his lifetime, Father Breslay adhered tenaciously to his religious ideals. Unfortunately, these brought him constantly into conflict with the civil authorities.

E. A. CHARD

AN, Col., B, 27, 29, 33, 34, 35, 36, 37, 46, 47, 48, 53, 54, 55; C¹¹ᴬ, 36, 37. "Correspondance de Vaudreuil," APQ *Rapport, 1938–39, 1939–40*. PAC *Report, 1905*, II, App. A, 70–72, gives a transcript of Breslay's letter to Governor Philipps. Allaire, *Dictionnaire*, III. Le Jeune, *Dictionnaire*. Tanguay, *Répertoire du clergé*.

Brebner, *New England's outpost*. Casgrain, *Les Sulpiciens en Acadie*. Henri Gauthier, *La Compagnie de Saint-Sulpice au Canada* (Montréal, 1912); *Sulpitiana* (Montréal, 1926). Harvey, *French régime in P.E.I.* J. C. MacMillan, *The early history of the Catholic Church in Prince Edward Island* (Quebec, 1905). Édouard Richard, *Acadie, reconstruction d'un chapitre perdu de l'histoire d'Amérique*, éd. M.-J.-H. Beaudé [Henri d'Arles] (3v., Québec and Boston, 1916–21), I. Pierre Rousseau, *Saint-Sulpice et les missions catholiques* (Montréal, 1930), 112, 123, 132–34. A. B. Warburton, *A history of Prince Edward Island from its discovery in 1534 until the departure of Lieutenant-Governor Ready in A.D. 1831* (Saint John, N.B., 1923). Olivier Maurault, "L'île aux Tourtes," in *Marges d'histoire* (3v., Montréal, 1929–30), III, 155–64.

BRICAULT DE VALMUR, LOUIS-FRÉDÉRIC, secretary to Intendant Gilles Hocquart* from 1729 to 1737; b. 1690 or 1691; d. at Quebec, 27 June 1738.

It is probable that Valmur came to New France in September 1729 with Hocquart, the newly appointed financial commissary, as the latter's personal choice for the post of secretary. This was an office of great trust and Hocquart was thoroughly acquainted with Valmur's background and character. In 1731 he described him to the minister as well-born, of a respected Parisian family, and having a brother who was a notary in Paris. In addition, he was ". . . intelligent, hardworking and . . . has studied law." Valmur resided at the intendant's palace in Quebec and, during the early 1730s, gradually expanded his activities to include the normal work of the intendancy as well as special administrative tasks like the pre-

paration of the seigneurial terrier. He appears also to have developed some private interests, for in 1733 he joined a group of entrepreneurs seeking to establish an ironworks at Saint-Maurice (*see* FRANÇOIS POULIN). Actually, such involvement by a royal official in a colonial enterprise was in line with Hocquart's own philosophy, and the intendant continued to favour Valmur in his reports to France, asking, for example, that he be promoted king's writer. The minister, however, refused to allow this while Valmur continued in the role of secretary. Hocquart therefore dismissed Valmur from that post in 1737 and again petitioned for a commission as writer for him. This time the request was granted, but Valmur died before the news arrived by the first vessels in 1738. He was buried in the crypt of Notre-Dame.

DONALD J. HORTON

AN, Col., B, 57, p.66; C¹¹ᴬ, 55, 59, 68, 70. Charland, "Notre-Dame de Québec: le nécrologe de la crypte," 208. P.-G. Roy, "Les secrétaires des gouverneurs et intendants de la Nouvelle-France," *BRH*, XLI (1935).

BRIDGES, TIMOTHY, captain in the Royal Navy; commodore of the Newfoundland convoy, 1704 and 1705; b. *c.* 1670; d. some time after 1708.

In 1702 Timothy Bridges was appointed to the command of the *Looe*, and served in this ship as commodore of the Newfoundland convoy for 1704 and 1705. He arrived at St John's in the summer of 1704 to find the settlement split into two factions. Serious charges were being made against Captain Thomas LLOYD, the military commander of the garrison, and Bridges advised him to return to England to clear himself of the allegations. After appointing Lieutenant MOODY to replace Lloyd, Bridges sailed for England in the autumn of 1704.

During the winter Moody successfully repulsed a French attack on St John's, but when Bridges returned the following spring he found considerable friction between Moody and many of the inhabitants. In October 1705, Lloyd returned to Newfoundland with the rank of major, having been reinstated as military commander. The following month, Bridges sailed for England with Moody as a passenger. The *Looe* was wrecked on the Isle of Wight, but both officers survived. After acquittal by court martial for the loss of his ship, Bridges was appointed to the command of the *Kingston* in the West Indies. Some time later he was dismissed from the service for misconduct, and was not employed again at sea after 1708.

Bridges' place in Canadian history is a very secondary one. His answers to the Board of Trade and Plantations' customary Heads of Enquiry are

Brisay de Denonville

brief and uninspired; and his interest lies rather in the role he played in the struggle between Lloyd and Moody.

MICHAEL GODFREY

PRO, Adm. 6 (commission and warrant books); C.O. 194/3; *CSP, Col., 1704–5, 1706–8.* Charnock, *Biographia navalis,* III.

BRISAY DE DENONVILLE, JACQUES-RENÉ DE, marquis, colonel and brigadier of the Queen's Dragoons, inspector-general of Dragoons, governor general of New France, 1685–1689, major-general, deputy-governor for the dukes of Bourgogne, Anjou, and Berry; b. 10 Dec. 1637, d. 22 Sept. 1710.

The Brisay family of Poitou by the 17th century could trace its ancestry for 500 years, claiming descent from Torquatus Byrsarius who, in 852, was charged by Charles the Bald with the defence of the lands between the Loire and Vilaine rivers against Viking and Breton assaults. Consanguinity was also claimed with the counts of Anjou and the Plantagenet kings of England. By the 11th century the seigneury of Brisay had been established on the left bank of the Vienne.

Pierre de Brisay, born 1523, son of François de Brisay and Marie de Hémard, inherited the seigneury of Denonville, located in Beauce near Chartres, from his mother and became the first Brisay de Denonville. Pierre, a nephew of the Cardinal Charles de Hémard de Denonville, entered the church and was appointed archdeacon of Mâcon, and subsequently abbé of Saint-Père-en-Vallée near Chartres from which he derived considerable revenue. Between 1563 and 1568, however, he turned Huguenot and at the age of 52 married Jacqueline, 25-year-old daughter of Claude d'Orléans. Their son Jacques gained the succession to the seigneury of Denonville and by 1606 he was the senior member of the clan. A staunch Huguenot, he entered the army, served as a captain of cavalry, and died at the siege of Breda in 1625.

His son, Pierre de Brisay, born in 1607, inherited the titles seigneur de Denonville, vicomte de Montbazillac, seigneur de Bellavilliers, seigneur châtelain de Thiville, seigneur marquis d'Avesnes, seigneur de Chesnay. Emulating his father, he took up the career of arms and served first in the Netherlands as a cornet in the light horse under the Maréchal de Châtillon. In 1628 he married Louise d'Alès de Corbet, daughter of a Huguenot aide-de-camp and gentleman in waiting of Louis XIII. Both families ranked as members of the lower nobility; that is, they were not among the great families of France hence they had to struggle

to advance their fortunes, and they enjoyed fair success. In 1636 Pierre de Brisay and his wife abjured the Protestant faith and returned to the church of Rome. In 1642 Pierre de Brisay was named a gentleman in waiting by Louis XIII and in 1653 he was appointed king's counsellor in the councils of state and finance. By 1668 he was a major-general in the armies of Louis XIV.

Fourteen children were born of this marriage: six died in infancy. The seventh child, Jacques-René, future governor general of New France, was born a year after his parents' conversion, but the stern Calvinist background in which his parents had been raised left its mark. All his life, Jacques-René was very devout and a staunch supporter of the clergy.

At that time the only careers open to members of the nobility were the army and the church, or rustication on their estates. Of the six sons of Pierre de Brisay who attained maturity, three entered the army, three the church, and one, Charles de Brisay d'Huillé, combined both careers as a tonsured knight of the order of St John of Jerusalem. He was killed fighting the Turks in Crete. As the eldest son Jacques-René took the title Marquis de Denonville and entered the army at an early age. His later correspondence indicates that his schooling had not been prolonged. By 1663 he was a captain in the Régiment Royal and the following year took part in the North African campaign of the Duc de Beaufort against the Algerian pirates. Three years later he was serving in the Netherlands and in January 1668 he was commissioned captain in the Dragoons. That same year, in November, he married Catherine Courtin, daughter of Germain Courtin de Tangeux. He served throughout the Dutch war, which began in 1672, and made a name for himself as not merely a brave soldier but also a very capable officer. In consequence he was commissioned lieutenant-colonel in 1673 of the Queen's Dragoons, and colonel-lieutenant in 1675. In 1681 he was appointed inspector-general of Dragoons for the provinces of Flanders, Picardy, Artois, and Hainaut, and on 30 March 1683 was promoted brigadier. The following year Louis XIV appointed him to succeed Le Febvre* de La Barre as governor general of New France. His commission was dated 1 Jan. 1685. The appointment carried with it 24,000 *livres* a year; not over generous, all things considered. The king, however, purchased Denonville's regiment from him for 60,000 *livres* and then gave it to the Marquis de Murcé, a nephew of Madame de Maintenon.

Exactly why Denonville was chosen is not known, but La Barre had to be replaced. Ten years earlier the Iroquois, after a decade of peace, had adopted an aggressive policy aimed at driving the French out of the west and diverting the fur trade from Montreal to Albany with themselves as middlemen. The then governor, Louis de Buade*, Comte de Frontenac, had attempted to curb this policy by appeasing the Five Nations, which had merely encouraged them to become more aggressive. La Barre attempted to restore the French position by military means and failed dismally. He did succeed in one thing, however; he forced Louis XIV and Colbert, the minister of Marine, to take more effective measures for the preservation of French power in North America.

In August 1684 Spain and the Empire had made peace with France, and thus Louis XIV was able to choose a governor general for the colony from among his senior officers of proven ability. There is no evidence to indicate that Denonville owed his appointment to influence at the court, or to anything but his demonstrated military competence and probity. In a dispatch to the intendant of New France, Jacques de MEULLES, the Marquis de Seignelay, minister of Marine, wrote: "He is one of the most esteemed officers in the kingdom. His Majesty chose him as a man who by his virtue will work for the good of religion, by his valour and his experience will restore the affairs that M. de La Barre has virtually abandoned in the shameful peace that he made with the Iroquois, and by his wisdom will avoid all manner of difficulties and troubles with you."

In the five months that elapsed between receiving his commission and sailing for Quebec, Denonville was not idle. He garnered all the information he could concerning New France, then outlined for the minister's approval the action that he thought would have to be taken. When the minister ordered 500 reinforcements for the regular troops serving in the colony, Denonville personally supervised their recruitment and made sure their equipment was of the best. In these matters his attention to detail was meticulous. Eight or nine half-pay lieutenants volunteered to serve under him as sergeants with his assurance that they would be restored to commissioned rank as vacancies occurred. This was an excellent testimonial to the confidence he inspired.

Upon arrival at La Rochelle with his pregnant wife and his daughters aged 14 and 3, Denonville was appalled by the cramped, foul conditions on the troop ships and immediately petitioned the minister to have other arrangements made, but to no avail. He then asked for 40 supernumerary troops to replace those he anticipated would not survive the crossing. This too was denied. Because of his wife's condition he took passage on a mer-

chant vessel. Sharing the captain's table with them was the newly appointed bishop of Quebec, Jean-Baptiste de LA CROIX de Saint-Vallier, a very austere but energetic prelate.

On 1 August Denonville and his family arrived safely at Quebec where, a few weeks later, the Marquise de Denonville was safely delivered of a daughter. Towards the end of the month the troop ships arrived and the governor's worst fears were realized. On one ship 60 of the troops died of typhus or scurvy, and on the other 80 were more dead than alive. The facilities of the Hôtel-Dieu at Quebec were taxed to the limit with over 300 victims of fever. To make matters worse, the troops sent earlier were in a bad way; many had died of influenza that had swept through the colony the previous year; of the remainder over a quarter were unfit for service, and 44 of them Denonville shipped back to France.

Within a few weeks of his arrival Denonville had travelled from Quebec to Fort Frontenac (Cataracoui, now Kingston, Ont.) and back, observing everything, and he was shocked by much that he saw. He was, in fact, the first governor to have any care for the state of Canadian society and to attempt reforms. The seigneuries, he noted, and the habitations on them, were too spread out, rendering their defence almost impossible. Canadian youth, living in close proximity to the Indians, had adopted many of their ways, some good, most bad. To his stern, puritanical gaze they appeared debauched, undisciplined, lacking in respect for all authority. Worst of all were the seigneurs' sons. He noted that these young Canadians were fine physical specimens, robust and vivacious. What was needed was a means to channel and control their energies. He recommended that some of them should be sent to France and commissioned in the Guards and other permanent regiments. At his request the king granted six commissions for the regular troops serving in the colony, to be issued by Denonville and the intendant to Canadian gentlemen. This experiment proved so successful that Denonville recommended that no more officers be sent from France. From this time on Canadian society was to be dominated by the military with their aristocratic values.

As a long-term measure Denonville, with a 400-*livre* subvention from the crown, established a navigation school at Quebec to train Canadians as pilots, a career for which they showed great aptitude. He also took steps to have better charts made of the St Lawrence than the Dutch ones currently in use. At the same time he asked the minister to see to it that no more indigent nobles were sent out and he succeeded in obtaining modest

Brisay de Denonville

pensions for certain noble families who had served the colony well in earlier years but had since been reduced to penury.

Drunkenness, he declared, was a major vice. Every rogue and idler had but one ambition: to open a tavern and avoid labour on the land. Half the houses in the colony were, he claimed, grog shops. To curb the attendant abuses he enacted strict regulations governing taverns. Drunkards and those leading debauched lives were, on conviction by the courts, to be placed in the stocks to suffer public humiliation. As for the sale of liquor to the Indians, he fully concurred with the clergy on its deplorable consequences and he did all he could to check the trade.

He also took steps to curb long standing abuses in the fur trade. In conjunction with the intendant the governor was empowered to grant 25 fur-trading licences (*congés*) a year, each of which entitled the holder to send a canoe load of goods to trade in the west. His predecessors had granted excessive numbers of these trading licences to those who had known how to gain their favour and Denonville was reliably informed that there were some 600 coureurs de bois continually out of the colony. This had resulted in the abandonment of farms, in families becoming a charge on the public, and in merchants being owed vast sums for trade goods issued on credit. Although the worst abuses were caused by a handful of these men, Denonville was determined to impose order. He restricted the number of licences to 25 and issued them only to poorer families who had been excluded from such favours in the past, thereby making enemies of some of the more influential families in the colony. Licence holders now had to declare the names of the three voyageurs allowed per canoe, and the goods being shipped. The voyageurs had to register at Montreal or Trois-Rivières on their departure and return, and obtain a certificate of good conduct from the missionaries at the western posts.

He also gave it as his opinion that the establishment of posts in the west had been a serious mistake, resulting in the weakening of the colony, huge expense, and involvement in all manner of inter-tribal disputes. Far from curbing tribes hostile to the French these posts were, he claimed, a serious liability owing to the difficulty and cost of supplying them, particularly in war-time. Like Colbert he believed it would have been far better to concentrate French resources in the central colony, have the Indians come to Montreal to trade and keep the Canadians employed in fishing in the Gulf rather than having them push ever farther west into the wilderness, becoming more Indian than French in their values and attitudes.

But to decry the situation was one thing; to curb it, let alone stop it, proved to be impossible.

Closer to home Denonville found much to occupy his attention. The three towns he regarded as fire traps, and measures had to be taken to guard against conflagrations. He would have liked to see an iron foundry established to utilize the rich iron ore deposits near Trois-Rivières for the manufacture of stoves which would have reduced the fire hazard. This, however, he had to admit was out of the question for the time being owing to a lack of capital and technical skills in the colony. At Montreal, which was without defences of any sort, he set the troops to work building a palisade, and at Quebec he had a new magazine for arms and powder built since the existing one was a menace to the entire area. As he pointed out, were a flying spark to ignite the roof, not only would the resulting explosion do great damage but the colony would be virtually defenceless until fresh ammunition supplies could be brought from France.

He quickly discovered that the intendant was trafficking in the king's stores for his private profit. He reported this to the minister who immediately recalled Jacques de Meulles and sent in his place Jean BOCHART de Champigny, an old friend of Denonville. This removed the possibility of a renewal of the earlier conflicts between governor and intendant in the Conseil Souverain. In fact, Denonville informed the minister that he wished to absent himself from its meetings. He had, he declared, more than enough to attend to and not being a lawyer he felt he could contribute little to the council's deliberations. The minister, however, feared that this would establish a dangerous precedent but he did agree that Denonville need attend only when the council requested him to give his opinion.

These domestic problems, however, faded almost to insignificance when contrasted with the external dangers that menaced the colony. Just as he was the first governor to attempt serious social reforms, so was Denonville the first to see clearly the magnitude of the threat to Canada's security. His instructions had been explicit on the need to remove the Iroquois threat, preferably without resort to war. He explained to the minister that the menace was more than just the Iroquois' attempts to drive the French out of the western fur trade. The colony was threatened from the south by the English of New York, and from the north by English control of Hudson Bay. He recommended that the best solution to the threat from the south would be for Louis XIV to purchase the province of New York from James II. That done, the Iroquois would be obliged to keep the peace. There was, however, little chance of this taking place, and Denonville, within a few weeks of his arrival, became convinced that the Iroquois would not abide by the terms of La Barre's treaty; sooner or later, at a time of their choosing, they would attack the French settlements. All that restrained them was their desire to seduce the western nations out of the French alliance first; one enemy at a time was always their policy. Under these circumstances Denonville decided it would be far better to attack them first, but very careful preparations were needed before launching an invasion of the Iroquois country.

While these preparations were being made Denonville dealt with the Hudson Bay menace. Although English and French diplomats in London were arranging a treaty of neutrality prior to a final settlement of their territorial claims in North America, Denonville sent an expedition of 105 men, led by Pierre de Troyes*, an officer in the colonial regular troops, overland from Montreal to James Bay. They exceeded their rather vague written orders, captured the three English posts at the Bottom of the Bay along with 50,000 prime beaver pelts, and left Canadian garrisons at the forts, thereby removing this threat on the northern flank of the Canadian fur trade empire.

In the south, meanwhile, the Irish Catholic governor of New York, Thomas Dongan, had sent an expedition of Albany fur-traders, guided by renegade Canadian coureurs de bois, to trade with the Ottawas at Michilimackinac, offering them goods at much lower prices than did the French. It was from this tribe that the Canadians obtained the bulk of their furs, and if they defected Canada would have been ruined. At the same time Dongan had entered into a cool but courteous correspondence with Denonville, offering to co-operate in keeping the peace in the west and soliciting Denonville's aid in obtaining 25,000 *livres* back pay he claimed was owed him by the French crown for his services with James, Duke of York, in the armies of Louis XIV prior to the restoration of the Stuarts in England.

This Albany trading venture convinced Denonville that the French hold on the west could be maintained only by the same means he had employed in James Bay. He learned that Dongan planned to send another expedition to Michilimackinac the following year; the Ottawas were wavering in their loyalty, succumbing to English and Iroquois blandishments to forget their traditional enmity with the Five Nations and trade with Albany. Whenever the Iroquois encountered Canadian canoes in the west they pillaged them, demonstrating their contempt for the French.

Denonville knew that he lacked sufficient troops to destroy the Iroquois in one campaign. He had barely enough to attack one flank of the Five Nations, and simultaneous attacks were needed on both flanks, on both the Mohawks and the Senecas at once, driving them in on the centre so that they would be forced to stand and fight. He appealed to the minister for additional forces but he had no assurance that they would be forthcoming. Time was not on his side. He needed time to fortify the defenceless settlements, and as a long range policy he recommended that the Canadian settlements be relocated, the homes be clustered in villages rather than stretched out along the river; but for the moment he did not dare even to build block houses in the exposed seigneuries lest the Iroquois should take alarm and begin spoiling attacks. All he could do was disguise his intentions from the Iroquois for as long as possible, then launch his full strength against the Senecas, the strongest, most aggressive, and most distant of the Five Nations.

Despite the tight security precautions, it was impossible to hide the fact that something was afoot and the Onondagas got wind of it. When, early in 1687, they proposed a conference at Fort Frontenac to reconcile differences Denonville agreed, and when Father JEAN DE LAMBERVILLE, the Jesuit missionary at Onondaga went to Quebec to make arrangements, Denonville did not inform him of his intentions lest Lamberville, wittingly or unwittingly, should betray to the Iroquois the plans for the campaign. He feared that, were they to learn of it, they would mass sizable forces to ambush his army at the rapids along the St Lawrence, and at the same time attack the settlements. The safety of the army and the settlers, and the success of the campaign, depended on keeping the enemy guessing and immobilized until the French forces were in position to strike a telling blow.

Supplies were sent well in advance to Fort Frontenac and the western posts. The officers in the west were given detailed instructions where and when they were to join the army with as many Indian allies and coureurs de bois as they could muster. Detachments were ordered to block the main routes to Michilimackinac and seize the Albany traders should they venture across the lakes.

On 13 June 1687 the expedition left Montreal: 832 colonial regulars, over 900 Canadian militia, and some 400 Indian allies. A few days earlier a convoy had reached Quebec bringing 800 additional regulars, but it was impossible to incorporate them in the expedition at that late hour.

As the army made its way up the turbulent St Lawrence the advance party captured several

Brisay de Denonville

Iroquois lurking along the river. At Fort Frontenac Intendant Champigny, who had gone on ahead of the main force, seized some Cayugas and Oneidas by dubious means to prevent them carrying word of the army's approach to the Iroquois villages south of the lake. Another party of so-called Neutral Iroquois, from a village near the fort, was subsequently seized for the same reason. All told, some 50 to 60 men and 150 women and children were made captive. They were sent back to Montreal to serve as hostages in case any of the French were captured by the Iroquois.

The day after Denonville's arrival at Fort Frontenac came word that two parties of Albany traders had been captured en route to Michilimackinac. They too were sent to Montreal and held in jail for a while. The Canadian renegades who had guided them were given a summary trial and shot. The Albany merchants were to make no further attempts to trade north of the Great Lakes. That dangerous threat had been eliminated.

The assault on the Senecas, however, was not as successful. After one brief skirmish the enemy fled into the depths of the forest and the Indian allies of the French refused to pursue them. Casualties on both sides were light, but the Seneca villages and their food supplies were systematically destroyed. Denonville then proceeded with his main force to Niagara where a blockhouse was built at the mouth of the river and the men given an opportunity to visit the falls. Leaving a garrison of 100 men under the Sieur de Troyes at the new fort, Denonville took the army back to Montreal, arriving there on 13 August without incident. The campaign had achieved as much as he had expected, but not as much as he had desired.

Before embarking on the campaign Denonville had received orders from the minister to take as many Iroquois prisoners as he could and ship them to France to serve as rowers in the royal galleys. He complied by sending 36 of the 58 male prisoners to France, but he made it plain that he would rather not have done so. He requested that they be well treated and sent back to Canada when the time came to arrange a peace settlement with the Five Nations; this was, in fact, done but only 13 actually returned, the others having succumbed to disease in France or on the voyage. Under the circumstances it would have been wiser to keep these Iroquois prisoners in the colony, ready to be exchanged when needed.

Much ink has been spilled over this incident, and all manner of consequences attributed to it that have no basis whatsoever in fact. Most of these Iroquois were legitimate prisoners of war, and compared to the manner in which the Five Nations treated their prisoners this group was relatively well treated. Service in the French galleys was by no means as horrible as romantic literature has made it appear. Yet when all this has been said, the fact remains that Denonville's reluctant compliance with orders was an error in judgement. Moreover, his enemies, and later generations of hostile historians, were able to distort the facts and damage his reputation.

One thing the campaign had done was to confirm Denonville's estimate that much larger forces than he had available were needed to conquer the Five Nations in a single campaign. In his dispatches to the minister he now made it plain that unless he had a total force of 4,000 men and food supplies sufficient for two years, it would be far better to arrange a peace settlement. The alternative would be a long-drawn-out war of attrition with heavy casualties and the destruction of the more exposed settlements. To impress upon the minister the urgency of the situation Denonville sent Louis-Hector de CALLIÈRE, governor of Montreal and second in command, to Versailles with a plan for the conquest of New York. This plan called for a force of 800 men to go from Canada to raze Albany while a naval force of 6 frigates with 1,200 men sailed directly from France to capture Manhattan and use it as a base to ravage the New England coast as far as Boston. These expeditions, Denonville and Callière claimed, had a far better chance of success than had campaigns on the Iroquois villages in the remote depths of the forest. With New York devastated, the Iroquois flank would be turned and they would be forced to accept French terms for peace.

Meanwhile, disease had taken a heavy toll in the colony; of a total population of 11,000, over 1,400 had died, and Iroquois war parties were inflicting casualties in the Montreal area. At Fort Niagara the garrison was kept prisoner by marauding Iroquois and 89 died of scurvy. At Fort Frontenac it was the same: 100 died there, and the Iroquois burned the out-buildings and the cattle. Denonville therefore, to gain a respite, entered into peace negotiations with the chiefs of three of the Five Nations. He was most insistent that all the Indian nations allied with the French be included. Despite the fact that while the negotiations were taking place the Iroquois ambushed and pillaged three canoes of western Indians en route to trade at Montreal, killing some and taking the survivors prisoner to the Iroquois villages, a peace settlement was finally arranged, to be ratified at Montreal by all the Five Nations the following year. In the meantime hostilities were suspended. Two months later, however, the settlement was threatened. A party of Hurons led by KONDIARONK, fearing that the peace would merely result in the Iroquois concentrating their entire strength against his people, ambushed a party of Iroquois ambassadors on their way to Montreal to confer with Denonville. Kondiaronk tried to make it appear that he had acted on orders of the French, but the garrison at Fort Frontenac was able to disabuse the Iroquois of this notion and the incident failed to have the consequences hoped for by Kondiaronk and later attributed to it by some historians.

During the ensuing months Denonville did his best to strengthen the colony's defences but the Canadians, reassured by the peace negotiations and the absence of Iroquois war parties, took little interest. As Denonville foresaw, some of them would later pay for this neglect with their lives.

The spring of 1689 became summer and there was no word from the Iroquois, nor did the ships arrive from France with supplies and instructions from the minister. In the English colonies Sir Edmund Andros, governor of New England and New York, was doing his best to prevent direct negotiations between the Iroquois and the French, claiming that the Five Nations were subjects of the British crown, and that the French had therefore to negotiate with him, not with the Iroquois. This claim the French and the Iroquois rejected, yet it served to delay ratification of the treaty until word was received in New England of the outbreak of hostilities between England and France following on the Glorious Revolution that put William and Mary on the English throne. Denonville, however, was unaware that England and France were at war.

When the Iroquois were informed by the English at Albany that a state of war existed they abandoned all thought of peace with Canada. Previously, the governor of New York, obeying orders from Whitehall, had tried to prevent them from attacking the Canadian settlements but had encouraged their aggressive policy in the west. Now they were free to launch assaults on Canada and they believed they could count on English support. While Denonville, still ignorant of these developments, was impatiently awaiting the Iroquois ambassadors to ratify the peace treaty, the Five Nations were massing their forces. At dawn on 5 August, an estimated 1,500 of their warriors struck at the unsuspecting settlements at Lachine, a few miles from Montreal. Although the loss of life was not nearly as great as was later claimed—in fact, 24 were killed, some 70 to 90 were taken prisoner of whom 42 never returned, and 56 of 77 homes were destroyed—the sudden ferocity of the attack was a devastating blow.

Denonville has been accused of failing to respond adequately. With the benefit of hindsight it is possible to argue that he could have counter-attacked more effectively, but given the circumstances, the fragmentary, incoherent, and exaggerated reports on the enemy's movements that reached him, the orders he gave were the only sound ones he could have given. He could give only general orders and expect the local commander of the troops, Philippe de RIGAUD de Vaudreuil, to use his own judgement. The failure to take advantage of the situation as it developed, and to launch a telling counter-attack, must be blamed on Vaudreuil rather than on Denonville. With the advantage of surprise and stealth the Iroquois had scored the first of several such victories in a war that was to endure for ten years. Yet they did not have things all their own way. Shortly after the attack at Lachine, a small party of Canadians sent out by Denonville encountered an Iroquois war party on the Lac des Deux-Montagnes. Without loss to themselves they killed 18 of the enemy and took three prisoners who were subsequently burned alive in the Place Royale at Montreal in retaliation for the treatment meted out by the Iroquois to the Canadians they captured. To the east, Denonville loosed the Abenakis against the New England settlements where they created havoc comparable to that wrought by the Iroquois at Lachine.

With Iroquois war parties roaming about the settlements Denonville was forced to abandon all thought of maintaining a garrison at Fort Frontenac. Niagara had had to be abandoned earlier because of the supply problem. Fort Frontenac could serve no military purpose: its garrison was kept prisoner by a handful of Iroquois lurking about, and it required convoys of several hundred men to keep it supplied. On 24 September Denonville sent orders to the commandant CLÉMENT Du Vuault de Valrennes to blow up the fort and return to Montreal with the surviving members of the garrison.

Three weeks later the long-delayed ships arrived from France, bringing with them Callière and Louis de Buade, Comte de Frontenac, appointed to succeed Denonville as governor general. It has frequently been asserted that Frontenac was reappointed to save the colony from the consequences of Denonville's inept stewardship, as evidenced by the Lachine massacre and the abandonment of Fort Frontenac. Such assertions are refuted by the chronology of events. Frontenac had been appointed to succeed Denonville in April 1689, four months before the Iroquois attack on Lachine. In fact, Louis XIV and the minister, in a dispatch dated 1 May 1689, expressed their complete satisfaction with the

Brisay de Denonville

measures taken by Denonville. They also sanctioned the abandonment of Fort Frontenac, should he deem it necessary. Then, on 31 May, Louis XIV signed the order for Denonville to return to France. In it he stated that because of the war in Europe he had decided to recall Denonville "to employ you in my armies where I am persuaded that you will serve me with the same zeal and the same success as you have done in the past." Subsequently, however, Paul de Beauvillier, Duc de Saint-Aignan, persuaded the king to appoint Denonville his deputy as governor to the king's grandson, Louis de France, Duc de Bourgogne, in recognition of Denonville's 33 years of service in the royal armies. Denonville had intimated in 1688 that he would like to be recalled if the minister rejected his proposals on the policy to be pursued for the protection of the colony, and with war raging in Europe there was no possibility of the colony receiving the support requested. In addition, Denonville's health was not good; he had worn himself out with his exertions, and for this reason alone he deserved to be relieved of his duties. There is, however, no evidence to indicate that Denonville was recalled for any reason other than that stated by Louis XIV.

Denonville had arrived in New France just after the Iroquois had imposed a humiliating peace on the French and an epidemic had decimated its population. The morale of the Canadians had been low, the colony defenceless. He was eminently successful in blocking attempts by the governor of New York to displace the French in the west and divert the fur trade from Montreal to Albany. He also weakened the hold of the English on Hudson Bay by seizing and retaining their forts in James Bay. With the meagre forces available he restored the military balance, demonstrating to the Iroquois that their most distant villages could be destroyed. With unpalatable directness he made very plain to the minister of Marine what was needed to make the colony secure from attack. When the stipulated forces were denied him he followed his instructions and secured a peace treaty with honourable terms. That this peace endured only a few months was not his fault; he had no control over the events in Europe which sparked the Iroquois assault on the settlements at Lachine. It is not without significance that his successor was eventually given the forces that Denonville had declared to be necessary to crush the Iroquois, yet it took nine years of savage fighting to bring the latter to terms.

In the field of civil administration also Denonville made a notable contribution, introducing reforms that were to have a profound effect on Canadian society. In this, however, as in military affairs, he was to a degree his own worst enemy. The post of governor general was basically a political position, and Denonville's character made him unsuited for the role. He was no courtier. He was transparently honest, and he was a perfectionist. He demanded much, perhaps too much, of others, and he demanded more of himself. When anything went wrong he always took the blame; when things went right he gave the credit to his subordinates or to God. He left the colony immediately after the Iroquois had scored an initial victory, and his successor, in his dispatches to the court, not only made the situation appear far worse than it actually was, but maintained that Denonville was entirely to blame. Others in the colony, however, expressed sincere regret at his departure. All things considered, the colony had good cause to be grateful to him.

Denonville and his family sailed from Quebec in mid-November and arrived at La Rochelle on 26 December after a stormy crossing. The following month he made his report to the minister. That both Seignelay and Louis XIV were satisfied with his conduct of affairs in Canada is evidenced by his being raised to the rank of major-general. On 25 Aug. 1690 he was appointed deputy-governor to the Duc d'Anjou, and on 24 Aug. 1693 he was given the same responsibility for Charles de France, Duc de Berry. His declining years were, however, embittered by the disgrace of his son, a colonel of infantry, who was cashiered on orders of the king for surrendering his regiment without a fight to George Hamilton, Earl of Orkney, at the battle of Blenheim in 1704. Six years later, on 22 Sept. 1710, the old marquis died at his *château*. He was buried on the 24th in the crypt of the *château* chapel.

W. J. ECCLES

[The primary source material dealing with Denonville's tenure as governor general, most of it contained in Archives des Colonies, C[11A], F[3], and B series, is to be found in the Archives Nationales, Paris. The PAC has microfilm copies and transcripts, as does the AQ. Other documents are to be found at the ASQ and at the New York State Archives in Albany. Transcripts of the latter are contained in *NYCD* (O'Callaghan and Fernow). The Baron de Lahontan's self-extolling account of events, *New Voyages* (Thwaites), was written after a lapse of several years and has to be treated sceptically.

There is one published biography of Denonville, by Thérèse Prince-Falmagne, *Un marquis du grand siècle, Jacques René de Brisay de Denonville, gouverneur de la Nouvelle-France, 1637–1710* (Montréal, [1965]), valuable for the information it provides on Denonville's antecedents. Among the more useful articles in learned journals are Jean Leclerc, "Denonville et ses captifs iroquois," *RHAF*, XIV (1960–61), 545–58;

Brossard

XV (1961–62), 41–58; "Le rappel de Denonville," *RHAF*, XX (1966–67), 380–408; and W. J. Eccles, "Denonville et les galériens iroquois," *RHAF*, XIV (1960–61), 408–29.

The period of Denonville's tenure of office in Canada is discussed in all the histories of the period but the earlier ones are marred by prejudice and slipshod scholarship. The "established" version is well presented in Parkman, *Count Frontenac and New France* (1877). A "revisionist" interpretation is provided in Eccles, *Canada under Louis XIV*. W.J.E.]

BROSSARD, JEAN-FRANÇOIS, ploughman and settler; b. 1654 in France, d. December 1716 at Port-Royal (Annapolis Royal, N.S.).

He came to Acadia in 1671, and settled at Port-Royal, where around 1681 he married Catherine Richard, daughter of Michel Richard and Madeleine Blanchard. With Pierre TIBAUDEAU he took part in founding a settlement at Chipoudy. In the spring of 1700 one of Jean-François Brossard's sons went with Tibaudeau and some other young men to Chipoudy. The young scout chose a lot for his father and made a start on the settlement. Jean-François and his wife visited the new settlement and were delighted with it. However, the pioneer did not go to live there himself.

The Brossards had 10 children, 6 boys and 4 girls. One of the sons, Pierre, settled at Pisiquit. Two others, Joseph and Alexandre, lived at Chipoudy on properties which had been granted to their wives, Agnès and Marguerite, granddaughters of Pierre Tibaudeau. The two young Brossards bore the surname of Beausoleil, after their native village near Port-Royal. Later, Alexandre settled at Petitcodiac, a village founded by Guillaume BLANCHARD; Joseph, who distinguished himself in skirmishes against the English in 1755, took up his abode at a place called Le Cran, now Stoney Creek. The Brossards of Louisiana and those of Cape Breton are descended from Alexandre and Joseph.

CLÉMENT CORMIER

AN, Section Outre-Mer, G¹, 466 (Recensements de l'Acadie, 1686, 1693, 1698, 1700, 1701, 1703). Archives de l'université de Moncton, Placide Gaudet and A. E. Daigle, Personal papers on Acadian genealogies. PANS, MS docs., XXVI (parish register of Port-Royal, 31 Dec. 1716). Arsenault, *Hist. et généal. des Acadiens*, I, 368. Rameau de Saint-Père, *Une colonie féodale*, I, 246, 254, 255, 256, 258–59, 261, 266–67. [On the "marriages" of Brossard's daughters, described by Rameau, *see* the bibliography for Pierre TIBAUDEAU.]

BROSSARD, URBAIN, master mason, son of Mathurin Brossard and Michelle Bidaut; b. 1633 or 1634 at La Flèche, province of Anjou; buried 10 April 1710 at Montreal.

Brossard came to Ville-Marie with the contingent of 1653. He had been engaged as a mason and settler and applied himself all his life to building and farming.

His first undertaking dates from 30 Nov. 1658, when he agreed to start the following May to build a house for Raphaël-Lambert Closse*. In 1660 François Bailly* took him into partnership for three years. Six years later, in association with Michel Bouvier he built a house for Pierre Chauvin. In 1672, with Gilles Devennes and Bouvier, he erected a vast house at Lachine for Jean Milot, a maker of edge-tools and merchant from Montreal. At the top of the contract a sketch signed by Brossard (his partners could not write) shows the lay-out of this building. It measured 50 feet by 25, had a pavilion roof, and comprised a ground floor and two upper storeys, two chimneys, a forge, a well, and an outside oven. In 1676 Brossard, with the same two partners, built a house for DANIEL GREYSOLON Dulhut, and in 1680, with Bouvier alone, a house for Philippe Dufresnoy Carion.

The next ten years are marked only by works of secondary importance: foundations, half-timbered field-stone gables and attics, chimneys and fireplaces. Then came a series of important works: in 1690, in partnership with Michel Dubuc, a house for the merchant Claude Pothier; in 1692 houses for Pierre Legardeur* de Repentigny and Claude Dudevoir, the first in association with Étienne Campot, the other with Jean Mars; in 1695 an extensive enlargement to Jean-Vincent Philippe de Hautmesnyl's house; finally, in 1704, in collaboration with Jean Deslandes, a mill on the seigneury of Pierre de SAINT-OURS.

Brossard was a good mason and knew how to cut stone; on occasion he even acted as the supplier of stone and quarryman. His contracts inform us of the methods of work and the building practices of his time. From them we see that works were generally carried out by masons in partnership, with joint responsibility, and not by a single contractor. These masons generally engaged only "their labour and their tools," and as there were a score of them in and around Montreal, they felt no need to train apprentices. The use of cut stone was rare; most often people were content with "boulders or field-stones." Finally, the frequency of half-timbered field-stone construction must be noted, an ancient building method which was to continue in use into the following century.

In 1660 Brossard had married Urbaine, the only daughter of Sébastien Hodiau, who also came originally from La Flèche. Urbaine died in 1681, after bearing him eight children, among them Catherine, who married the mason Jean Sareau, and Madeleine, who married the maker of

Brouillan

edge-tools François Campot, the son of the mason Étienne Campot.

JULES BAZIN

AJM, Greffe d'Antoine Adhémar; Greffe de Bénigne Basset; Greffe d'Hilaire Bourgine; Greffe de Claude Maugue; Greffe de Pierre Raimbault. *Jug. et délib.*, II, 734. Recensement du Canada, 1666 (APQ *Rapport*). Recensements du Canada, 1667, 1681 (Sulte). R.-J. Auger, *La grande recrue de 1653* (SGCF pub., I, Montréal, 1955). *DCB*, I, 78. [Faillon], *Histoire de la colonie française*, II, 536. Morisset, *L'architecture en Nouvelle-France*, 129. É.-Z. Massicotte, "Maçons, entrepreneurs, architectes," *BRH*, XXXV (1929), 133–34.

BROUILLAN, JACQUES-FRANÇOIS DE MOMBETON DE. *See* MOMBETON

BRUSLÉ (Brulé), MICHEL, priest, Recollet, missionary to the Micmacs; b. 1673; d. 7 Sept. 1724 at Montreal.

Michel Bruslé entered the noviciate of the Recollets of the province of Saint-Denis when he was 16 and made his profession in 1690. He was ordained a deacon at Trèves 22 Dec. 1696, and he received the priesthood the following year. In 1698 Father Michel sailed for Canada together with Father Olivier GOYER, the provincial commissioner for the Recollet mission in New France.

During the first six years he served three centres of colonization; on 10 June 1699, when registering an act at Saint-François-du-Lac, he signed as "missionary at Verchères, Contrecœur, Saint-Ours, and other surrounding places." In 1705 he was called back to Quebec and became "missionary to the Micmacs" of the Gulf of St Lawrence. He held this office for 17 years without interruption. Occasionally during this period, when he was in the region, he said mass and served as parish priest at Rimouski, Baie Saint-Paul, Ristigouche, and Port-La-Joie (near Charlottetown, P.E.I.).

The main centres of his mission were Ristigouche, Miramichi, and Nipisiguit (Bathurst, N.B.), which all belonged to the seigneury of Richard Denys* de Fronsac, whose widow, Françoise Cailleteau, married Pierre Rey Gaillard, an artilleryman, at Quebec in 1694. The latter was much more interested in the trade in pelts than in his official duties and his properties. It was in connection with this commerce that he and his wife were to attack Father Michel, accusing him of doing them great harm by engaging in it himself, "so that he is a merchant and a trader with the Indians rather than a missionary and mendicant according to the statutes of the order of St Francis." To put an end to this quarrel, the financial commissary for Île Royale (Cape Breton

Island), Pierre-Auguste de SOUBRAS, asked Father Michel and Abbé Antoine GAULIN, missionary to the Indians at Antigonish, to draw up a report on the matter for him. On 4 Dec. 1716 the missionaries denounced the scandalous practices of Rey Gaillard who, to obtain game and pelts, attracted the Indians daily with liquor.

No formal condemnation was pronounced against Father Michel. On the contrary, Soubras entrusted him with an important mission: to unite his Micmacs with those at Antigonish, and move them to the Acadian shore of Canso Strait, as close to Île Royale as possible.

In 1722 Father Michel was relieved of his mission and ministered temporarily to Baie Saint-Paul and Petite-Rivière. Two years later he became superior of the Recollets of the convent at Montreal, where he died.

JACQUES VALOIS

AJJ, Registres d'état civil de Joliette. AJTR, Registres d'état civil de Saint-François-du-Lac. AN, Col., C^{11B}, 1, ff.337, 431; 2, ff.44, 189; 3, f.270; Marine, B^1, 8, f.540; Section Outre-Mer, G^1, 411. AQ, NF, Coll. de pièces jud. et not., 490½.

BRUYAS, JACQUES, Jesuit missionary to the Iroquois tribes, author, interpreter, and deputy of the governor general in negotiations with the Iroquois and English; b. 13 July 1635 at Lyons; d. 15 June 1712.

Bruyas became a Jesuit novice at the age of 16, on 11 Nov. 1651, and in 1666 joined the Canadian mission. He arrived at Quebec on 3 August on the *Saint-Joseph*. Within a year he was assigned to the Iroquois missions which were being reopened after the expedition against the Mohawks and Oneidas led by Prouville* de Tracy and Rémy* de Courcelle. The terms of the peace which resulted from this expedition included an agreement that the Iroquois furnish hostages as security for the missionaries who would be sent to their cantons. After receiving the blessing of Bishop LAVAL, Bruyas left Quebec on 14 July 1667, accompanied by "some Frenchmen and some Iroquois that were instructed during their captivity and are now very good Christians." He was delayed for more than a month at Fort Sainte-Anne, at the mouth of Lake Champlain, by a party of hostile Mohicans.

Bruyas arrived in the village of the Oneidas in September. He soon had his chapel dedicated to St François-Xavier, and said mass there for the first time on St Michael's day. Although he found a few Christianized Indians to form the nucleus of a congregation, most of the Oneidas were insolent and hostile. The opposition of the medicine-men and the Indians' adherence to their old religion further complicated Bruyas' task. His first report to his superior reached Quebec on 15 Dec. 1667, by Huron runner. Another communication of 21 Jan. 1668 indicated that Bruyas was hindered in his apostolic labours by the prevalent drunkenness and licentiousness of the Indians, and by threats to his life following certain dreams to which the tribesmen were much attached. He did not as yet understand the Iroquois language, and could not, therefore, supply accurate information about the attitudes of the Indians towards the French and towards Catholicism. He believed the military campaign of Tracy had rendered the Oneidas more amenable to the gospel; nevertheless, he had succeeded in baptizing only 60 sickly infants and 4 adults. In general, however, the Oneidas were beginning to treat him with respect, had permitted him to instruct the catechumens and had regaled him with their "squash and beans and Indian corn flavoured with smoked fish."

During his first sojourn at Oneida Father Bruyas had found a Christian Huron, François Tonsahoten*, who, though he did not openly practise his religion, had told his Erie wife, Catherine Gandeacteua*, to attend to the instructions of the missionary. It was she who taught him the Oneida dialect.

The English and Dutch continued to provide the Iroquois with prodigious quantities of brandy and wine which resulted in their being "incessantly drunk," and beatings and murders ensued. New Netherlands had passed into English hands and the governor of New York, Francis Lovelace, gave Bruyas and his co-religionists to understand that he was not opposed to their evangelical labours but that French trade in the Iroquois country must cease. In April 1668, Bruyas received as his assistant Father Julien GARNIER, the first Jesuit ordained in Canada. Bruyas' position became almost untenable in August of the following year when news was received that some Oneidas had been robbed of their furs and killed by French traders near Montreal, that one hostage at Montreal had been flogged, and another was in irons.

Bruyas had been weakened by a tertian fever and by a famine during which he survived on dried frogs. The arrival of 60 kegs of brandy from "New Holland" on 16 Aug. 1669 decided him to leave for Lake Oneida in order to avoid the inevitable brawls and disorders in the village. He seems to have regained some strength and courage as a result of a six-day meeting of the six Jesuit missionaries in the Iroquois cantons, which was convened on 26 August at Onondaga to discuss strategy. Upon his return to the mission on 6 September he found the brandy frenzy at its height. A few weeks later an epidemic struck the community; many infants were baptized before they died. By 20 November he could write that "the lack of drink makes me enjoy a great rest." His trials were not so soon ended, however. On 3 April 1670 traders returned with 40 kegs of brandy, which he foresaw were destined "to disturb our devotions during the coming Easter Holy days." The following day he left to spend a fortnight with Father MILLET at Onondaga.

Father Bruyas was now transferred to the Mohawks and became in 1670 the superior of the Iroquois missions. Opposition and disappointments continued to mark his evangelical labours. In 1673 when the chieftain Togouiroui*, known to the French as the "Great Mohawk," was converted and settled with numerous fellow tribesmen on the banks of the St Lawrence, the Mohawks of Tionnotoguen reproached Bruyas with having plotted to depopulate the cantons. Bruyas gave a wampum belt to attest that neither he nor Father Garnier had instigated Togouiroui's decision to move to a reserve. The following year was more encouraging and saw the conversion of the aged but influential Mohawk medicine-man, Pierre Assendasé. By 1676, Bruyas' position was secure enough for him to be able to set up a statue of the Virgin Mary and to introduce special litanies to the Immaculate Conception on Saturdays and Sundays. A letter dated 31 July informs us that he had recently baptized more than 40 persons there; most of them had, however, "already taken possession of heaven." The next summer three Indian converts arrived to assist him as catechizers.

In 1679 his 12 years of ministry in the Iroquois cantons ended and he took charge of the mission at Sault-Saint-Louis (Caughnawaga), the reserve near Montreal. Father CHAUCHETIÈRE spent 1681 with him at this mission and reported that Bruyas was responsible for the spiritual needs of the savages "and is a father to them for both their bodies and their souls." His fight for temperance never ceased and he reported that over 100 Indians came to the reserve to escape the drunken debaucheries in their villages. Nevertheless, when disorders fomented by brandy erupted at the reserve many returned to their cantons. A letter addressed to Governor Buade* de Frontenac, in April 1691, reveals Bruyas' understanding of the Mohawks. From August 1693 to August 1698, he was superior of the Canadian mission and made his headquarters in Quebec. He then returned to Caughnawaga.

His consummate skill as a negotiator was demonstrated in Boston in 1699 [see MICHEL LENEUF de La Vallière de Beaubassin, the elder]. In 1700 he accompanied PAUL LE MOYNE de

Buisson de Saint-Cosme

Maricourt to the Onondagas to negotiate peace terms. Bruyas was well received as an official envoy of Governor CALLIÈRE; he delivered the appropriate wampum and recalled the ties that the missionaries had sought to establish between the Iroquois and the French. Bruyas told the delegates of the five cantons assembled at Onondaga on 10 Aug. 1700 that, although the Dutch had promised to send them a gunsmith if they would reject the Catholic missionaries and take a Protestant pastor (the Reverend Debelius of Fort Orange), the governor of New York, Bellomont, wished to enslave them. The Dutch envoy who was present left in anger and defeat. Nineteen deputies from the Oneidas, Onondagas, Senecas, and Cayugas started for Montreal with 13 French prisoners. The governor received them on 8 September but would make only a temporary peace as he insisted on the return of all prisoners and a union of all the tribes in subscribing to the peace terms.

In June of 1701, Bruyas was again sent to the Onondagas to continue the negotiations, particularly to persuade the Mohawks and Oneidas to take part in the peace conference. On this occasion he decided not to oppose openly plans for Anglican missionary work among the Hurons, but warned the Iroquois that if they agreed to the requests of the agents of Governor Bellomont and did not attend the Montreal peace talks they could expect nothing in future from the French governor. The Iroquois delegates proceeded to Montreal. There at the conference in August 1701 Bruyas conveyed the governor's message to the Huron chief, KONDIARONK. By the terms of the treaty concluded there, Bruyas' objective of having the Iroquois cantons reopened to the Jesuit missionaries was achieved.

Noted for his linguistic abilities, Bruyas left a grammar of the Mohawk language, *Radices verborum iroquaeorum*, as well as a catechism and a prayer-book in Mohawk.

Bruyas remained active at the Caughnawaga mission until his death there on 15 June 1712.

C. J. JAENEN

ARSI, Gallia 110/I, ff.108–20. ASJ, France (Chantilly), Fonds Brotier, 162. ASJCF, Collection générale, Série A, f.XI(b). Jacques Bruyas, "Radical words of the Mohawk language, with their derivatives," New York University Regents, *Annual Report on condition of state cabinet*, XVI (1863), 3–123; *Radices verborum iroquaeorum* (Shea's Library of American linguistics, X, 1862). Charlevoix, *Histoire* (1744), III, 363f. Claude Dablon, *Relation de ce qui s'est passé de plus remarquable aux missions des peres de la Compagnie de Jésus de la Nouvelle-France les années 1671 et 1672* (Paris, 1673); *Relation de ce qui s'est passé de plus remarquable aux missions des peres de la Compagnie de Jésus en Nouvelle-France les annés 1672 et 1673* (New York, 1861). François Élesban de Guilhermy, *Ménologe de la Compagnie de Jésus . . . , assistance de France, comprenant les missions de l'Archipel, de la Syrie, . . . du Canada, de la Louisiane . . . ,* éd. [Jacques Terrien] (2 part., Paris, 1892), première partie, 742–44. Marie Guyart de l'Incarnation, *Letters* (Marshall) [English trans.], 329, 338–43, 417–20. *JR* (Thwaites). *JJ* (Laverdière et Casgrain). *Jug. et délib.*, I, 742. La Potherie, *Histoire* (1722), IV, 152f., 186, 241. [F.-J. Le Mercier], *Relation de ce qui s'est passé . . . aux années mil six cens soixante-sept et mil six cens soixante-huit* (Paris, 1669). *Mission du Canada. Relations inédites de la Nouvelle-France (1672–1679) pour faire suite aux anciennes relations (1615–1673)*, éd. F. Martin (2v., Paris, 1861), II, 10–11. *Relation des affaires du Canada en 1696. Avec des Lettres des pères de la Compagnie de Jésus depuis 1696 jusqu'en 1702* (New York, 1895), 29–30. [Jeremias Van Rensselaer], *Correspondence of Jeremias Van Rensselaer, 1651–1674*, ed. A. J. F. Van Laer (Albany, 1932), 450f. *Liste des missionnaires-jésuites, Nouvelle France et Louisiane, 1611–1800* (Montréal, 1929). F.-X. Noiseux, *Liste chronologique des évêques et des prêtres tant séculiers que réguliers, employés au service de l'église . . .* (Québec, 1834). J. G. Shea, *History of the Catholic Church in the United States* (4v., New York, 1886–92), I, 284–304.

BUISSON DE SAINT-COSME, JEAN-FRANÇOIS, priest, canon, bursar of the seminary of Quebec; baptized 26 Nov. 1660 at Quebec; d. 15 March 1712 at Quebec.

Father Buisson was the son of Gervais Buisson, "Bisson" according to his signature, and of Marie Lereau. The family came from Saint-Cosme-de-Vair, in the bishopric of Le Mans, which explains the surname given him. But as there was another family of Buissons who came from the same place, and particularly since there was another Jean-François BUISSON de Saint-Cosme (1667–1706) in that family, who in turn became a priest of the seminary, an unofficial distinction had to be decided upon. In point of fact the older man, the one in whom we are interested, was never called and never signed himself anything else than "Buisson, priest," whereas the second one, the missionary, was ordinarily called "St-Cosme." The latter also had a younger brother, Michel, who was in turn a missionary and a parish priest and who signed himself, to be different: "Buisson de St-Cosme."

Abbé Buisson entered the Petit Séminaire of Quebec on 4 Sept. 1674. He must have finished his classical studies before 27 Sept. 1682, since Bishop LAVAL gave him the tonsure on that date. He received all the orders in the course of 1683, including the priesthood on 30 November. When the chapter of Quebec was set up the following year, he was appointed a canon. In addition he fulfilled temporarily the functions of chaplain of the Hôtel-Dieu of Quebec (1684–85), and later (1707–12) he was spiritual director of the Ursulines. In 1687 consideration was given to sending him as a missionary to Acadia. But the bishop could no longer assign him to a distant ministry, as he was needed too much at the seminary.

In 1684, when he was 24, he became bursar of the house and was to retain that office until 1710, although from 1707 on he had a deputy, JEAN-BAPTISTE GAULTIER de Varennes. This long period of administration was perhaps not the most critical, but it was the most active and eventful one in the history of the seminary under the French régime. The large-scale building programme, which had been started in 1675, was continued. The seminary went through the alarm and the damages caused by Phips*'s attack in 1690, and even destruction by fire on two occasions, in 1701 and 1705. Despite the warnings of the superiors of the seminary in Paris, the religious in Quebec wanted to rebuild on a larger and sounder basis; one can appreciate the bursar's situation in this unfavourable conjuncture. After the second fire, the worry about the reconstruction which had to be supervised and the debts which had to be contracted may have contributed to sapping his health, thus requiring the appointment of an assistant bursar. Nevertheless, someone wrote of him: "M. Buisson is very anxious that our refectory be pleasant and also that the boys be well fed."

Despite these vicissitudes, the work of the seminary did not suffer too serious an interruption. The result was that the procurator of the seminary in Paris, Abbé Henri-Jean Tremblay*, worn with toil and confident in the abilities of his colleague in Quebec, proposed on 5 June 1712 that Buisson come to take his place. Even if it had proved acceptable, this proposition arrived too late. Buisson was in fact dead, having succumbed to measles on 15 March. He had been buried on the same day in the cathedral.

HONORIUS PROVOST

AJQ, Greffe de Pierre Duquet, 24 mai 1671. ASQ, Annales du Petit Séminaire; Chapitre, 40; Lettres, N, 86, 125; O, 53; Paroisse de Québec, 23. Charland, "Notre-Dame de Québec: le nécrologe de la crypte," 173. Tanguay, *Dictionnaire*. Casgrain, *Histoire de l'Hôtel-Dieu de Québec*, 574. Gosselin, *Vie de Mgr de Laval*, II, 692. *Les Ursulines de Québec (1866–78)*, II, 37. Amédée Gosselin, "Les Buisson de Saint-Cosme, prêtres," *BRH*, XXX (1924), 195–98.

BUISSON DE SAINT-COSME, JEAN-FRAN-ÇOIS, priest of the seminary of Quebec, founder of the Sainte-Famille mission to the Tamaroas;

b. 30 Jan. 1667 at Lauson, son of Michel Buisson (Bisson), *dit* Saint-Cosme and Suzanne Delicérasse (de Lizeiras); murdered in 1706 in the Mississippi country.

The family of the Abbé Buisson came originally from Saint-Cosme-de-Vair (department of Sarthe) in France [see JEAN-FRANÇOIS BUISSON de Saint-Cosme (1660–1712)]. This place-name, which was often used, without commas, with the Buissons' name to indicate their place of origin, finally became part of their surname. In his explanation of this onomastic peculiarity Monsignor Amédée Gosselin wrote concerning Jean-François the missionary: "He was the son of Michel Buisson, de Saint-Cosme, naturally, and of Suzanne...." It was probably this sentence which, misunderstood, caused the English-language historian Webster to say, basing himself upon Gosselin, that Michel's son was an illegitimate child, whereas he was born three years after his parents' marriage.

When he was eight, Buisson de Saint-Cosme entered the Petit Séminaire of Quebec. In 1690 he was received into the priesthood. In choosing to serve the church he had followed a vocation that was, so to speak, a family one. Indeed, his younger brother Michel also became a priest, his sister Marie-Françoise joined the nuns of the Hôtel-Dieu, and another sister, who has not been identified, received the habit of the Congrégation de Notre-Dame from Bishop Saint-Vallier [LA CROIX]. As for the parents, they gave up their station as well-to-do settlers to "give" themselves to the seminary of Quebec and administered its farm on Île Jésus.

Buisson de Saint-Cosme was parish priest for the parish of Les Mines (Grand Pré) in Acadia from 1692 (or earlier) till 1698, during the stormy period of Governor Joseph Robinau* de Villebon's administration. Like other priests in the colony he was accused of meddling in temporal affairs. His recall was even discussed. At the same time certain of his superiors said that they were "distressed" by his "attitudes" and by his "supply of conceit" which modest talents did not redeem.

He was chosen nonetheless to become one of the pioneers in the missionary work carried on by the seminary of Quebec in the Mississippi Valley [see DAVION]. In April 1699, with the aim of acting as a link between the mission to the Taensas and Quebec, which were 1,000 leagues (about 2,760 miles) apart, Buisson de Saint-Cosme settled among the Tamaroas on the east bank of the Mississippi, six leagues downstream from its junction with the Missouri.

His church was barely finished when Father Julien Bineteau arrived unexpectedly in May. He had been sent from Pimitoui (Peoria) by the

Bulteau

Jesuits; the latter did not look kindly upon these gentlemen of the Missions Étrangères who were coming to work in their territories. According to the assertions of the priests of the seminary and of the explorer HENRI TONTY, the Society of Jesus considered as part of its mission to the Illinois a village some 220 miles (80 leagues) away which had never been evangelized. Saint-Cosme's adversaries claimed a prior right to carry on the apostleship to the Tamaroas, particularly because of the "flying missions" which they had conducted among these Indians when they came to Pimitoui or during their summer migrations. Consequently the Jesuits challenged the validity of the letters patent issued 14 July 1698. Bishop Saint-Vallier, by these letters patent, officially authorized the directors of the seminary of Quebec to create a mission in the Tamaroa country in case, the bishop specified, "other missionaries who did not belong to their body endeavoured, perhaps by virtue of letters patent granted them by us previously, to exclude them from the right to settle among the Indians called Tamaroas and to carry on missions."

Father Bineteau accordingly entered into open competition with Saint-Cosme. According to the latter the Jesuit did everything in his power to prevent him from learning the prayers and the catechism in the Illinois language. Father Jacques GRAVIER even forbade him expressly to exercise any ministry, among either the French or the Indians.

When Marc BERGIER replaced him at the Sainte-Famille mission, Saint-Cosme went off to the lower Mississippi in July 1700. He took the place of the vicar general, François de Montigny*, among the Natchez. His apostolate there did not bear fruit because of his limited gift for languages, the fact that the Indians lived widely dispersed, and their customs, which made them ill disposed to receiving the message of the gospel. We might add that he was not fond of the Indians and even called for servants who were "capable of standing up to the most wicked Indian," for, he said, "it is awkward for a missionary to have to punch an Indian."

Saint-Cosme's misgivings were well founded, for at the end of 1706, while going down to Mobile, he was killed by the arrows of the Chitimachas. According to a document in the Bibliothèque Nationale in Paris, the origin and author of which seem to be unknown, it was supposedly discovered after his death that Saint-Cosme had been the lover of the Natchez' Great Sun, that is to say the Indian woman who ruled over them. He was even supposed to have had a son by her, the Natchez chief named Saint-Cosme

who in 1729 directed the massacre of the French by his tribe. These assertions may seem rather ironical if one bears in mind the intransigence which the missionary demonstrated to those about him as regards morals and the vigour with which he stigmatized throughout his correspondence the debauchery of the French and the depravity of the Indians.

CÉLINE DUPRÉ

ASQ, Lettres, M, 30, 37; N, 114, 117, 121, 122; O, 7, 12, 49; R, 26–40 (correspondance de Buisson de Saint-Cosme, 30 août 1698–8 janv. 1706), 53, 82; MSS, 29; Missions, 49; Polygraphie, IX, 17, 24, 25. BN, MS, NAF 2550, f.115. Noël Baillargeon, "Les missions du séminaire de Québec dans la vallée du Mississipi 1698–1699," AQ *Rapport, 1965*, 13–56. Caron, "Inventaire de documents," APQ *Rapport, 1939–40, 1940–41. Découvertes et établissements des Français* (Margry), IV, 250; V, 408, 433–35. *Fleur de Lys and Calumet: being the Pénicaut narrative of a French adventure in Louisiana*, ed. and tr. R. G. McWilliams (Baton Rouge, La., 1953), 70f. *JR* (Thwaites). Webster, *Acadia*, 194.

Godbout, "Nos ancêtres," APQ *Rapport, 1955–57*, 438ff. Delanglez, *French Jesuits in Louisiana*, 63. Giraud, *Histoire de la Louisiane française*, I. O'Neill, *Church and state in Louisiana*. Rochemonteix, *Les Jésuites et la N.-F. au XVIIᵉ siècle*, III, 538f., 567; *Les Jésuites et la N.-F. au XVIIIᵉ siècle*, I, 258–60. Amédée Gosselin, "Les Buisson de Saint-Cosme, prêtres," *BRH*, XXX (1924), 195–98.

BULTEAU, GUILLAUME, priest, Recollet; b. 1666, made his profession in the ecclesiastical province of Saint-André (province of Flanders) in 1689; d. 9 Nov. 1716 at Quebec.

From 1694 on Father Bulteau was at the convent in Montreal. During the night of 23–24 Feb. 1695, together with his superior, Father JOSEPH DENYS, and another Recollet, he went to the aid of the nuns of the Hôtel-Dieu, whose establishment was destroyed by fire. That same year he supplied for the parish priest of Trois-Rivières, Luc FILIASTRE, during his absence, and registered acts on 17 and 25 September and again on 6 October. Two years later he was listed in the census as a missionary at Contrecœur, and in 1699 he was at Varennes.

In 1700 Father Bulteau succeeded Father Filiastre as superior of the Recollets of Montreal. It was in his capacity as superior that he attended the general assembly of the Indians that was held in Montreal from 3 to 8 September. Along with the superiors of the Sulpicians and Jesuits, Father Bulteau signed the official report of this assembly, after the Chevalier de CALLIÈRE, BOCHART de Champigny, RIGAUD de Vaudreuil, and some other prominent personages.

On 16 Oct. 1701, at Varennes, he baptized Marie-Marguerite Dufrost* de Lajemmerais, the

Cagenquarichten

future Madame d'Youville, foundress of the Grey Nuns. In 1705, impelled by a completely understandable zeal, Father Bulteau, who was at the time "in residence" in Quebec, entrusted to Maurice Déry, a settler at Charlesbourg, an illegitimate child whose father, known only to Bulteau, was to pay 50 *livres* a year to the adoptive father. Yet Déry received only 25 *livres* the first year. On several occasions he reminded the Recollet that he already had several mouths to feed. After being patient for four years, on 15 Dec. 1709 Déry was authorized by an ordinance from JACQUES RAUDOT to have the religious summoned before PIERRE RAIMBAULT, the intendant's subdelegate in Montreal, and to demand the name of the child's father, so that he could claim what was due him.

In 1712 Father Bulteau was again the superior in Montreal, at the time when the syndic for the Recollets, Jean Soumande, ratified in their name a contract with Pierre Janson*, *dit* Lapalme, master mason, by which Janson undertook to build the portal of the Recollets' church for 1,800 *livres*.

On 6 Nov. 1716, some days before his death, Father Bulteau, who had returned to Quebec, signed, in his capacity as former guardian of the convent in Montreal, a petition dealing with responsibilities. This petition was addressed by five Recollets of the Canadian mission to the provincial and the definitors of the province of Saint-Denis. The next day the same Recollets signed another petition addressed to M. de Vaudreuil, asking him to support their suggestions to the provincial. Two days later Father Bulteau died, after 22 years of apostolate in Canada.

JACQUES VALOIS

AN, Col., C11A, 19, f.41. ASSM, Documents Faillon, X, 635. PAC *Report, 1899*, Supp., 100–1. "Les Iroquois à Montréal en 1700 (3 septembre 1700)," *BRH*, XXXVII (1931), 375–83. [É.-M. Faillon], *Vie de Mademoiselle Mance et histoire de l'Hôtel-Dieu de Villemarie dans l'île de Montréal en Canada* (2v., Ville-Marie [Montréal], 1854), II, 103. Albertine Ferland-Anger, *Mère d'Youville* (Montréal, 1945), 267–72. Hugolin [Stanislas Lemay], *Le père Joseph Denis, premier récollet canadien (1657–1736)* (2v., Québec, 1926), II, 123–31. Jouve, *Les Franciscains et le Canada: aux Trois-Rivières*, 59–60.

C

CABANAC, FRANÇOIS DESJORDY MO-REAU DE. *See* DESJORDY

CABANAC (Cabanas), JOSEPH DESJORDY DE. *See* DESJORDY

CABAZIÉ, PIERRE, court officer, jail-keeper, acting king's attorney and judge, clerk in the court registry, and notary; b. *c.* 1641 in the region of Toulouse, son of Pierre Cabazié, royal notary, and Delphine Desbordes; buried 14 July 1715 at Montreal.

Cabazié's long judicial career began on 23 Jan. 1673, when by virtue of a commission from DOLLIER de Casson he became serjeant-at-law (court officer) of the bailiff's court of Montreal for the *côte* Saint-Martin. The following year, on 25 September, when Bénigne Basset* had been suspended for four months, the Conseil Souverain appointed Cabazié acting notary. But while continuing to draw up documents as a court officer, he practised the profession of notary without interruption from 1674 to 1693, receiving 172 acts. He was moreover a clerk in the registry of the bailiff's court from 1674 to 1678 and from 1680 to 1691, and also acted as jail-keeper around 1683. In 1693, when royal justice was set up in Montreal, Cabazié left the seigneurs' court; from 17 Nov. 1693 till his death he was a royal court officer; he also served as acting king's attorney from 1696 to 1701, and as acting lieutenant-general in 1698, 1700, 1702, 1703, and 1705. On 23 July 1669, at Quebec, he had married Jeanne Guiberge, who was about 13 years of age.

ANDRÉ VACHON

AJM, Greffe de Pierre Cabazié. *Jug. et délib.* A. Roy, *Inv. greffes not.*, X, 5–27. Massicotte, "Les tribunaux et les officiers de justice," *BRH*, XXXVII (1931), 127, 179, 180, 182, 187, 189, 252f. "Les notaires au Canada," 26. J.-E. Roy, *Histoire du notariat*, I, 145f.

CADILLAC, ANTOINE LAUMET, *dit* **DE LAMOTHE.** *See* LAUMET

CAGENQUARICHTEN (Kajnquiratiton, also probably **Kanaharighton, Kanakarighton),** also called **Blawbek (Blewbeck),** leading sachem, or hereditary chief, of the Senecas; fl. 1699–1726.

In September 1699, Cagenquarichten, called the chief sachem of the Senecas, visited the Onondagas to inform them that a number of Senecas had been killed and scalped by warriors of the Ojibwa (Dowaganhae) tribe, while hunting near their village. Although the Iroquois were at peace with

111

Callière

the French at this time, they were still at odds with tribes to the north and west, who were allies of the French and competitors with the Iroquois in the fur trade. Until they suffered heavy losses in 1699, the Iroquois were unwilling to include these tribes in any peace treaty. Cagenquarichten proposed to the Onondagas that they should go to Canada to ask the French to put a stop to the raids of their western allies, but the pro-English party at Onondaga persuaded him to refer the Senecas' complaint to the English officials in Albany, rather than to the French. This was done soon afterwards.

In 1714, Cagenquarichten visited Albany to ask the governor, Robert Hunter, to send a smith to settle midway between the Senecas and the Cayugas to repair their guns and hatchets.

In the 1720s Cagenquarichten was regarded as a good friend of the English. Prior to 1720 some unknown event had resulted in his being deposed as sachem; the English were anxious to have him reinstated in office. In May 1720, Peter SCHUYLER and Robert Livingston visited the Senecas and presented a belt of wampum to their council with the request that Cagenquarichten be reappointed sachem. This was done. In 1722, Cagenquarichten travelled to Albany with some Indians who had just returned from Canada. Cagenquarichten may have visited Canada with this delegation, although this is not certain.

A Seneca sachem by the name of Kanakarighton was among the Seneca, Cayuga, and Onondaga sachems who signed the treaty of 1726, by which the Iroquois placed their lands under the protection of the British crown. At this time Kanakarighton criticized the Onondagas for telling CHARLES LE MOYNE de Longueuil that the French could construct a stone fort on Seneca land near Niagara, and stated that the Senecas had been to Niagara to protest the French action. There appears to be no reason to doubt that this man and Cagenquarichten were one and the same.

BRUCE G. TRIGGER

NYCD (O'Callaghan and Fernow), IV, V.

CALLIÈRE, LOUIS-HECTOR DE (usually spelled **Callières** but he signed without the "s"), *chevalier*, captain in France, governor of Montreal, governor general of New France, knight of the order of Saint-Louis; b. at Thorigny-sur-Vire, province of Normandy, on 12 Nov. 1648; d. at Quebec on 26 May 1703.

The family came originally from the province of Angoumois where, in 1490, the king's commissioners recognized the nobility of Jehan de Callières. Two years later, by his marriage to Perrette Du Fort, this Jehan de Callières came into possession of the seigneury of Clérac in Saintonge which subsequently became the family's principal place of residence.

Jacques de Callières, the father of Louis-Hector, was born in Touraine at an unknown date. He became a follower of the powerful families of Matignon and Orléans-Longueville whose protection enabled him to become brigadier-general in the royal army and governor of the town of Cherbourg in Normandy in 1644. While holding this position he found time to indulge his taste for literature. He wrote several books, including a *Lettre héroïque à la duchesse de Longueville sur le retour de M. le prince*, and was also a founding member of the academy of Caen in 1652. He died at Cherbourg in 1662. In 1643 he had married Madeleine Potier de Courcy, daughter of the seigneur of Courcy, near Coutances. Two daughters and two sons were born of their marriage.

François, the eldest, was elected to the French Academy in 1689 and also served with distinction in Louis XIV's diplomatic corps. He was sent to Poland in 1670 to promote the candidacy of the Duc de Longueville to the throne of that country and was one of the three French plenipotentiaries who negotiated the treaty of Ryswick in 1697. Afterwards he became one of the king's four private secretaries and in 1701, thanks to his ability to imitate the royal handwriting and to his mastery of the French language, succeeded Toussaint Rose as the secretary "who held the pen." His duties, designed to save the monarch time and fatigue, consisted of writing in a hand and style similar to those of the king letters and memoirs to dignitaries and foreign heads of state and of signing them with the royal name. Such a position of trust gave Callières great power which he frequently used to further the career of Louis-Hector in Canada.

The latter had entered the French army towards 1664 and had participated in several of the military campaigns of Louis XIV. The name of his regiment is not known for certain. The minister of Marine referred to him as a former infantry captain in the Régiment de Navarre when he appointed him to succeed François-Marie Perrot* as governor of Montreal in 1684, but Callière himself stated that he had served in the Régiment de Piémont. Like his brother, Louis-Hector had an able mind and his dealings with the Indians showed that he was a skilful negotiator. He soon impressed Governor Le Febvre* de La Barre as a man of much experience, prudence, and wisdom. As for his personality, it can best be described as the opposite of mellow. He had the sense of discipline and the habit of command of the career soldier, an inflated feeling of self-importance, and a can-tankerous disposition that was not improved by recurring attacks of gout.

The recent outbreak of the Iroquois war had enhanced the importance of the government of Montreal. Because of its geographical location, Montreal was not only the area most exposed to Iroquois attacks but also the base where all offensive operations against these Indians were organized. Thus, the governor of this district had to act as a military leader and also take measures to assure the safety of the civilian population. Callière showed that he had the will and the ability to assume such responsibilities; BRISAY de Denonville informed the minister that "in this place [he is] governor, commissary, keeper of stores and munitions, and does any job connected with the service." Soon, the governor came to regard him as the colony's ablest military officer and he did not hesitate to increase his powers. He annexed both shores of the St Lawrence as far as Lac Saint-Pierre to the government of Montreal after detaching them from that of Trois-Rivières. To prevent discord from breaking out in the colony should the position of governor general become vacant through death or disease, he asked the minister of Marine to name Callière second in command in all of Canada. The ministry at first balked at this request but finally granted it in 1687.

Meantime, New France was being faced with a mounting Iroquois threat which it found nearly impossible to contain. In 1687, seconded by Callière and RIGAUD de Vaudreuil, the newly arrived commander of the troops, Denonville had invaded the territory of the western Iroquois at the head of a large army. The expedition, however, totally failed to intimidate the Five Nations and also underscored the difficulties and hardships of wilderness campaigning against such an elusive foe. The experience was not lost on Denonville and Callière. To crush the Iroquois, the two men worked out a scheme that was not lacking in originality and boldness: the conquest and occupation of New York. The memoirs which Callière personally presented at Versailles early in 1689 enumerated the principal advantages France would derive from the possession of this colony: the subjugation of the Iroquois who, finding themselves deprived of their supply of English arms and ammunition, would be obliged to come to terms with the French; the security of the cod-fisheries; and the possession of a fertile province with one of the finest harbours in America. To execute this design, the governor of Montreal asked for two frigates and an army of 2,000 men. With this army he would capture Albany and then proceed to attack New York on the land side while the two frigates blockaded the harbour and bombarded the town. Louis XIV approved the project after making a few modifications in it and decreed that Callière would become the governor of the conquered province. However, a series of delays seriously retarded the arrival of the ships off the North American coast and the whole enterprise had to be abandoned.

There was to be little rest for Callière after his return to Canada late in 1689. France and England were now at war and the conflict with the Five Nations was entering a new and more violent phase. Iroquois war parties prowled in the district of Montreal and constantly threatened the lives and properties of the population. Callière, how-ever, had put the area in a state of defence. Montreal had been enclosed with a strong palisade, and redoubts made of staves fourteen feet high had been built on each seigneury to provide the inhabitants with protection against Iroquois forays. Callière was also kept busy organizing military expeditions and sending them in pursuit of the Iroquois whenever their presence was reported in his district. On occasion, he commanded these expeditions personally, but most of the time they were led by Vaudreuil or veteran officers of the colonial regular troops. Knowing that Montreal was in good hands, Buade* de Frontenac intervened but little in the affairs of the upper colony and spent most of his time in Quebec where he devoted his attention to the war's strategical aspect. In 1694, partly no doubt as a result of the governor's good reports, Callière was awarded the coveted cross of Saint-Louis, an honour for which Frontenac had to wait until 1697.

Callière did not fully reciprocate Frontenac's esteem for he had serious doubts about the soundness of the governor's war policy. On several occasions, Frontenac had ordered a virtual cessa-tion of hostilities to allow Iroquois deputies to come to Quebec with peace proposals. Callière for his part greatly doubted that the Iroquois sincerely desired peace. In his opinion, their real aim was to keep the French inactive so that they might rest their forces, garner a good stock of furs, and negotiate a peace settlement with the western allies of New France. Then they might resume the war more vigorously than before. This assessment, as events showed, was a fairly accurate one and by 1696 Frontenac decided that the military expedi-tion favoured by Callière could no longer be deferred. On 4 July an army of over 2,000 men, made up of colonial regular troops, militiamen, and Indian auxiliaries left Montreal. Later that month it disembarked on the south shore of Lake

Callière

Ontario and advanced on the Onondaga settlements. Callière, suffering from gout, came in front on a horse which had been specially transported for him from Montreal on a flatboat; Frontenac, feeling the weight of his 74 years, was carried along behind the army in an armchair. Although this force failed to make contact with the enemy, it ravaged the territory of the Onondagas and Oneidas and struck a terrible blow at the fighting spirit of the Iroquois.

When Frontenac died on 28 Nov. 1698, Callière automatically became acting governor general, but Vaudreuil was a contender for the permanent commission. Callière, however, was able to out-manœuvre his rival. Using speed and secrecy he gave his application to an envoy, AUGUSTIN LE GARDEUR de Courtemanche, and sent him to France by way of the English colonies. The time thus gained proved decisive. Courtemanche reached Versailles a few hours before Vaudreuil's emissary, Charles-Joseph AMIOT de Vincelotte, and handed Callière's dispatches to his brother François who then took them to Louis XIV. When Pontchartrain, Vaudreuil's protector, approached the monarch with the news of Frontenac's demise, he was informed that His Majesty was already aware of the development and had granted the position of governor to François de Callières for his brother.

Meantime winter had closed in and sealed off the colony from the outside world. What had happened in France would not be known before spring, but until then Callière was the acting governor and he lost no opportunity to impress his dignity upon his political rivals. He behaved insufferably towards the intendant BOCHART de Champigny who was a Vaudreuil supporter; he obliged the Conseil Souverain to register his provisions as acting governor, although there was absolutely no need for such a formality; finally, on one occasion when he reviewed the troops, he insisted upon the salute that was reserved for field marshals. For Vaudreuil, the naval commissary TANTOUIN de La Touche, and the comptroller LE ROY de La Potherie, all this was simply too much and they sent their indignant protests to the minister. La Potherie was especially scathing in his remarks. Unlike Vaudreuil, who was "very much a gentleman," the comptroller claimed that Callière was "hard and insensitive" and had not earned the esteem of four people in the whole colony. As for the Iroquois, he added tartly, it was fortunate that they were at present holding their peace for Callière was in no condition to lead an army against them, being "in bed all year, stricken with gout and another infirmity which prevents him from sitting." It must have come as no surprise to anyone when both Champigny and La Potherie left the colony shortly after Callière's appointment was made official.

Callière became governor two years after the treaty of Ryswick had ended hostilities between England and France. The main problem now facing him was the negotiation of a firm treaty between the Iroquois, New France, and all her Indian allies. This task was enormously complicated. Bellomont, the governor of New York, maintained that the Iroquois were British subjects who were included in the terms of the treaty of Ryswick and he made every effort to thwart their negotiations with the French. Furthermore, Callière had to deal with some thirty different tribes, many of whom had been warring on one another or on the Iroquois since time immemorial. To bring about a reconciliation under such circumstances required consummate diplomatic skill.

Resolving these problems took almost three years. The Iroquois, out of consideration for the English, were at first reluctant to negotiate with the French. In 1699, three of their deputies called on Callière and attempted to move the site of the talks to Albany, but the governor replied that these could be held only in Montreal. In subsequent meetings, to induce the Iroquois to send an official delegation to Canada, Callière taunted them with Bellomont's claim that they were British subjects without the right to speak for themselves and threatened them with an invasion of their cantons if they refused to enter into negotiations. The western Indians, however, who had not discontinued their raids on the Iroquois, finally settled the matter. The Iroquois initially asked the English to grant them protection against these attacks, but when it became evident that no help was forthcoming from that quarter they had no choice but to turn to the French.

In July 1700, two Onondaga and four Seneca chiefs arrived in the colony, announced their desire for peace, and asked Callière to allow Father BRUYAS, CHABERT de Joncaire, and PAUL LE MOYNE de Maricourt—three men who enjoyed great prestige among the Iroquois—to accompany them to their cantons to speak in favour of a treaty. Callière agreed to this and their mission was crowned with success. The three Frenchmen were back in the colony in September with a 19-man delegation representing all the nations except the Mohawks, and 13 French prisoners liberated by the Iroquois as proof of the sincerity of their intentions. These delegates met with those of the mission Indians, Abenakis, Hurons, and Ottawas and peace terms were agreed upon. Callière then announced that a great assembly would take place the following summer when all prisoners would be exchanged and the treaty solemnly ratified.

Early the following summer the deputies began to arrive in Montreal. As their canoes came in sight of the town the occupants raised their paddles in salute and the French cannon returned the greeting. By July, 1,300 Indians of over 30 different tribes from areas as far apart as the Atlantic coast and the headwaters of the Mississippi had assembled and the sessions began. For several days delegation after delegation appeared before Callière with its charges and counter-charges, claims and counterclaims. As expected, the return of the prisoners proved to be the most troublesome point. Many of them had died or been killed in captivity; others had been adopted and would not be given up. It is no small tribute to Callière's ability that he was able to prevail upon the deputies to leave this problem to him to settle as best he could. With this matter disposed of, the treaty could be drawn up. All the tribes agreed to live at peace with each other and not to strike back when attacked as in the past, but to take their grievance to the governor of New France who would obtain redress. Equally important, Callière extracted a promise from the Iroquois to remain neutral in any future conflict between the French and the English. Thus, New York was stripped of its first line of offence and defence and the governor of New France became the arbiter of peace over a vast portion of North America.

Meantime, Callière was reaping the results of the reckless overtrading in beaver which had marked the Frontenac era. The market in France was saturated with this product, prices in Canada were falling as a result, and Louis XIV decided to take drastic measures to reduce the flow of beaver pelts into the colony. In May 1696 he issued an edict that suppressed the 25 fur-trading licences (*congés*), abolished the principal western posts, and ordered the coureurs de bois to return to civilization. Callière immediately realized that this legislation threatened to undermine New France's network of alliances with the Indian tribes. Low prices in Montreal might well drive the natives to Albany into the arms of the English; moreover the abolition of the posts and licences made it more difficult to control the allies and facilitated English infiltration of the west. The governor did something to offset the effects of tumbling prices when, in typically strong-handed fashion, he compelled the newly established Compagnie de la Colonie to sell merchandise to the Indians at special rates; but he was unable to convince the minister of the need to re-establish the posts and licences.

Callière, however, did not elude the royal instructions, but made a resolute attempt to enforce the ban on trade in the west. In 1699, he confiscated the trade goods that two Montreal merchants were endeavouring to send to their agents at Michilimackinac. The following year he arrested La Porte de Louvigny, the commandant of Fort Frontenac, for having illegally engaged in the fur trade. Such sternness probably shocked a population which had grown accustomed to Frontenac's laxity, but it also yielded appreciable results. In 1699 and 1700, Champigny and Callière reported that coureurs de bois were returning to the colony as they exhausted their supplies of trade goods. But a radical reorientation of France's western policy would soon ruin this attempt to revive Colbert's old compact colony system.

In 1700 and 1701, Louis XIV decided to consolidate his control of North America from the Great Lakes to the Gulf of Mexico by founding new settlements at Detroit and on the lower Mississippi in Louisiana. The reasons for the foundation of Louisiana lay in European dynastic politics. Charles II, the last of the Spanish Hapsburgs, had died on 1 Nov. 1700, and bequeathed to Louis XIV's grandson, Philippe d'Anjou, the entire Spanish inheritance. By founding a colony on the lower Mississippi that would protect Mexico from the aggressive designs of the English plantations on the Atlantic coast, Louis XIV hoped to demonstrate to Spain that now that it was under a Bourbon king it could rely on French support. As for Detroit, memoirs submitted by Cadillac [Laumet] seemed to prove among other things that a post there would block English expansionism in the region of the Great Lakes. Thus, by means of these two new settlements, France hoped to control all of North America west of the Appalachians and close it to the English.

Callière had serious misgivings about this general policy but he was unable to have it modified. Although he thought that the Detroit project was good on the whole, he did detect two "major obstacles." First, the Iroquois might take offence at a settlement built on their hunting grounds and renew their war on Canada. Second, and here Callière uncovered the basic flaw, Detroit would draw the western allies close to the Iroquois cantons. Such proximity would facilitate the growth of trade relations between them and commercial intercourse might eventually give rise to a political connection. Much more important for the preservation of the west, he thought, was the re-establishment of the old trading posts and of the licences. All Pontchartrain would state in reply was that the Detroit project should be put through unless "insurmountable difficulties"

Callière

were discovered. Thus, Callière deferred to ministerial wishes and cooperated with Cadillac to assure the success of his venture.

If Callière had reservations about Detroit and Cadillac, he felt nothing but hostility towards Louisiana and its founder, PIERRE LE MOYNE d'Iberville. Detroit, although it had some objectionable features, was at least under Canadian jurisdiction, but Louisiana was a separate colony carved out of territory hitherto governed from Quebec. This in itself would probably have sufficed to annoy Callière; but to make matters worse the new colony soon became a refuge for renegade coureurs de bois and a competitor of Canada for the fur trade of the interior. The angry governor urged the court to adopt measures to correct this situation which, he claimed, was ruining his colony. He suggested that Louisiana be placed under his command, that coureurs de bois who retired there after violating the laws of Canada be arrested, and that Louisiana be forbidden to receive beaver pelts and be permitted only the trade in buffalo hides and other products of the southern part of the continent. The minister, however, refused to grant Callière jurisdiction over Louisiana because it was much easier to send orders there directly from France than by way of Quebec. He also refused to arrest the coureurs de bois who had deserted from Canada since he wished to make use of them to begin the settlement of the new colony. Orders were issued to compel these people to pay their Canadian debts and to prevent Louisiana from receiving beaver, but they do not appear to have been enforced.

Callière, therefore, had little influence over decisions affecting western policy, but he played an important role in shaping the strategy followed by New France during the War of the Spanish Succession. When this conflict broke out in 1702, Pontchartrain urged the governor to conclude an offensive alliance with the Iroquois and authorized him to strike a major blow at the English colonies. Callière, however, did not share this aggressive mood. The colonial budget, in his opinion, would have to be increased by 50,000 to 60,000 *livres* to finance a large-scale military operation. As for the Iroquois, the most that could be expected from them for the time being was the neutrality they had promised to observe in 1701; incursions against the upper New York settlements, he thought, would almost certainly induce these Indians to break their agreement with the French in order to come to the aid of their old allies. Against New England, on the other hand, the governor authorized the Abenakis to resume the border warfare interrupted by the treaty of Ryswick. The speech he made to a group of these Indians

who appeared at Quebec in December 1702 suggests that his strategy here was dictated by the need to make the French alliance profitable in the eyes of this fierce tribe. In this speech, he informed the deputies that the plunder they would gather on their raids, joined to the gifts they would receive from the French, would enable them to live more comfortably in time of war than in time of peace. Callière's views on the conduct of the war were approved by Pontchartrain and became the basis of French strategy in America for the duration of the War of the Spanish Succession. A truce with New York was to be combined with a little war on New England.

On Ascension day in May 1703, Callière was attending high mass in the Quebec cathedral. Suddenly he suffered a haemorrhage and began to vomit blood. He was immediately taken back to his residence at the Château Saint-Louis, but it was already apparent that the end was near. On 25 May the notary Louis CHAMBALON was summoned to the dying man's bedside to draw up his last will and testament. Being the apostolic syndic of the Recollets, Callière asked to be buried in their church and left them the sum of 1,200 *livres* for the completion of their convent. He directed that his wardrobe and silverware be divided between his secretary, Hauteville, his *maître d'hôtel*, Beaufort, and his valet, Gillet. Since he had not married he left all his other possessions to his brother François. Feebly, in an almost illegible scrawl, the governor signed the document which Chambalon held out to him. The following day he was dead.

Callière had been the type of governor whom people fear and obey but do not love. Many had resented him for his severity, his imperious ways, the inflexible manner in which he enforced royal orders; but they had also respected him for his integrity and his high concept of public duty. There were no doubt some who breathed a sigh of relief at his passing, but those who appreciated sound government paid him high tribute. Father Charlevoix* stated that Callière was "justly regretted as the most accomplished General the colony had yet had, and the man who had rendered it the most important services." In her annals of the Quebec Hôtel-Dieu, Mother JUCHEREAU de La Ferté wrote: "all those who knew his ability feel that we did not deserve such a governor." These testimonies were not undeserved. Callière had been one of the principal artisans of the French victory during the second Iroquois war, the diplomat who negotiated the great peace of 1701, and the strategist who shaped New France's policy for the War of the Spanish Succession. In the history of the colony, there probably never was an abler and more devoted servant of the French monarchy.

Yves F. Zoltvany

AJQ, Greffe de Louis Chambalon, 25 mai 1703. AN, Col., B, 12, 13, 15, 16, 17; 19, 20, 22, 23; C^{11A}, 6–21; C^{11E}, 14; D^{2C}, 49; F^3, 2, 6, 8. BN, MS, Cabinet des titres, dossiers bleus, 148. Charlevoix, *Histoire.* "Correspondance de Frontenac (1689–1699)," APQ *Rapport, 1927–28,* 1–211; *1928–29,* 247–384. "Un éloge funèbre du gouverneur de Callières," APQ *Rapport, 1921–22,* 226–32. Juchereau, *Annales* (Jamet). La Potherie, *Histoire* (1753). Le Blant, *Histoire de la N.-F.,* 270n. *NYCD* (O'Callaghan and Fernow), IX, X. "Testament de Louis-Hector de Callières, gouverneur de la Nouvelle-France," APQ *Rapport, 1920–21,* 320ff.

Eccles, *Canada under Louis XIV; Frontenac.* Giraud, *Histoire de la Louisiane française,* I. Lanctot, *Histoire du Canada,* II. C. Vigen, *Notice sur les de Callières de Normandie et leurs rapports avec ceux de Saintonge* (Ligugé, s.d.). "Le frère de notre gouverneur de Callières," *BRH,* XXXIII (1927), 48–51. M. Godefroy, "Le chevalier de Callières, gouverneur de Canada (1648–1703)," *Revue catholique de Normandie,* VIII (1898–99), 5–19, 158–70, 228–41, 310–24, 456–69; IX (1899–1900), 5–17. H. Jouan, "A propos de Jacques-François et Louis-Hector de Callières," *Mémoires de la société académique de Cherbourg* (1890), 1–18; "Les de Callières (Jacques et Louis-Hector): Un nouveau point douteux d'histoire locale éclairci," *Mémoires de la société académique de Cherbourg* (1891), 52f. (This very short note contains an extract from the birth certificate of Louis-Hector de Callière, proving that he was born at Thorigny-sur-Vire, in the province of Normandy, on 12 Nov. 1648.) H. Moulin, "Les deux Callières, Jacques et François," *Mémoire de l'Académie des belles-lettres de Caen* (1883), 136–56. Benjamin Sulte, "La famille de Callières," *RSCT,* 1st ser., VIII (1890), sect.I, 91–112; "La signature royale," *BRH,* XXI (1915), 75–77.

CALVARIN, GOULVEN, originally from Vannes, in Brittany, priest of the Séminaire des Missions Étrangères in Paris and of the seminary of Quebec, parish priest and missionary; d. 26 Nov. 1719 in the Mississippi region.

Before coming to Canada Abbé Goulven Calvarin had been a missionary to Île Bourbon (Réunion). Wishing to devote himself to Indian missions, he joined the seminary of Quebec in 1703. The directors were on the point of sending him to the Mississippi region when a letter from Abbé Henri-Jean Tremblay* dissuaded them from doing so. Abbé Calvarin, stated the procurator of the seminary, was too old to learn the Indian languages and would never be of any use in a mission. Goulven Calvarin did not go to a mission, but was made parish priest of Pointe-à-la-Caille (Montmagny). He lived there from 1704 till 1708, then went on to direct the parish and the

École des Arts et Métiers at Saint-Joachim until 1712.

Abbé Calvarin doubtless possessed remarkable qualities, for the directors of the seminary of Quebec chose him to join their ranks in 1710. Bishop Saint-Vallier [La Croix] appointed him canon on 26 Nov. 1712 and promoter of the officiality on 30 Nov. 1716. He had nevertheless not given up thinking of the missions, and when he was asked to go to take charge of the mission to the Tamaroas, he accepted. On 10 May 1718 the missionary left, in company with two *confrères* from the seminary of Quebec, Abbés Jean-Paul Mercier and René Thaumur de La Source. But Abbé Calvarin had over-estimated his strength; he arrived among the Tamaroas in a state of complete exhaustion and died some months later, on 26 Nov. 1719.

Noël Baillargeon

AAQ, Registres d'insinuation B, 189, 244. ASQ, C13, 51, 297; Chapitre, 40; Lettres, N, 123; O, 41; Missions, 43, 73c; Paroisse de Québec, 2; Paroisses diverses, 57, 59b; Polygraphie, VII, 80. *Édits ord.,* II, 163.

CAMPBEL (Campbell). *See* Saint-Étienne de La Tour, Agathe (Marie-Agathe) de

CAMPBELL, COLIN, H.M. sub-commissioner for prizes and one of his brother James Campbell's agents in Newfoundland; fl. 1699–1710.

Colin Campbell first visited Newfoundland in 1699 on behalf of his brother to investigate the trading potentialities of the colony. In 1700 he settled at "Pontegarve," in Conception Bay, as agent and factor. When the War of the Spanish Succession began and the French attacked Carbonear in 1702, Campbell, Thomas Edwards, and others moved to an island in Conception Bay; Campbell then returned to England to petition the government for military protection. By 1704 he was back in St John's as a sub-commissioner for prizes, presumably captured French ships or colonial vessels contravening the navigation acts. Some traders complained of his irregularities—selling three prizes "clandestinely" and transferring timber reserved for the navy from the fort to his house.

On 28 April 1705 Colin Campbell was ordered by John Moody to return to England on the commandeered New England sloop *Friendship* to carry a report to the Board of Trade on Auger de Subercase's attack on St John's on 21 Jan. 1704/5, and a complaint against the engineer John Roope. Campbell was captured by a French privateer and arrived in England in June 1705.

Cannehoot

He reported to the board that Subercase, with 600 men, including 150 Indians and Canadians under TESTARD de Montigny, marched to Bay Bulls, Petty Harbour, and then to St John's. There they destroyed 120 houses and all stages and flakes. They laid siege unsuccessfully to the fort, commanded by John Moody and Robert LATHAM. On 23 February the French marched south to Fair Ellens, ravaging the coast, and carrying to Placentia (Plaisance) 200 male inhabitants of St John's, including Campbell. Colin Campbell apparently obtained his release at Fair Ellens. According to this report, the French lost 200 men but the English only three.

Richard Sampson, one of Campbell's servants who had accompanied him to England, reported to the board in June 1705 that the French had spared four houses in St John's, one of them being Campbell's. With this unfavourable report, the matter rested for a number of years. On 20 March 1710 John Moody contradicted Sampson's report in front of the board. He stated that Campbell obtained a truce of four or five days from Subercase during which time Campbell undertook the hazardous trip to the "South Castle" to give encouragement to Latham. Because the fort then refused to surrender, Subercase forced Campbell to travel five days on foot carrying part of his plunder. He then left Campbell alone to make his way back to St John's. Moody's statement was supported by Archibald CUMINGS and James Campbell.

The next month Campbell presented to the Board of Trade and Plantations a petition from Poole merchants asking that the commodores and fishing admirals have power to appoint J.P.s, constables, and militia during winter, but only to bind over cases for settlement by the commodores in the summer: a slight modification of the old West Country appeal against civil government. In February 1705/6 Colin sailed from Plymouth and was again captured. After being prisoner at Saint-Malo until 1709, he returned to England. He joined his brother in reporting to the board—which had been investigating for several years the cases of Moody and LLOYD—Moody's heroic defence of St John's in 1705, and Lloyd's negligence and his oppression of the inhabitants. It appears that Colin Campbell did not return to Newfoundland.

James Campbell's operations in Newfoundland were large: he claimed his losses in 1705 and 1708 were £10,737. From 1702 he was active in petitioning for men-of-war to capture Placentia, adequate convoys for the fishing fleets, and the fortification of Trinity Harbour and Ferryland. He was considered by the board an important informant on colonial matters. From 1713 on, he acted as agent for Moody and Taverner*, and it would appear that the preventive officer in Newfoundland, Cumings, reported to him.

C. P. MCFARLAND

PRO, C.O. 194/4; *Acts of P.C., col. ser., 1680–1720, Unbound papers*; *B.T.Journal, 1704–1708/9, 1708/9–1714/15, 1714/15–1718*; *CSP, Col., 1702–3, 1704–5, 1706–8, 1708–9, 1709–10, 1711–12, 1714–15*. Lounsbury, *British fishery at Nfld.*

CANNEHOOT (Cannehouet). *See* TEKANOET

CAPTAIN JOSEPH. *See* WOWURNA

CAPTAIN SWAN. *See* SWAN

CARHEIL, ÉTIENNE DE, Jesuit priest, missionary; b. 20 Nov. 1633 at Carentoir, France; d. 27 July 1726 at Quebec.

Étienne de Carheil entered the Jesuit noviciate at Paris on 30 Aug. 1653. Ordained in 1666, he set out for Quebec where he arrived on 6 August. After two years of preparation, Carheil was assigned in 1668 to work among the Cayugas at the mission of Saint-Joseph. He remained labouring in that area for the next 15 years, but without gaining many converts. Carheil found that the Indians generally rejected Christianity because they feared that baptism brought sickness and death to those tribes who had accepted it, and also because neophytes were required to abjure former superstitions and hitherto accepted codes of morality. Father Charlevoix*, who knew Carheil personally, reported that despite the missionary's lack of success in attracting converts, he was highly esteemed by the Indians who knew him.

In 1683, Carheil, together with other Jesuit missionaries working among the Iroquois, was recalled to Quebec because of the threat of war between the French and the Iroquois. On his return to Quebec, Carheil was assigned to teach grammar in the college which the Jesuits conducted there. In 1686, he was sent as a missionary to the Ottawa and Huron Indians and stationed at the mission of Saint-Ignace near the Straits of Mackinac.

After four years at Saint-Ignace, Carheil's influence over the Indians was sufficiently effective for him to be able to dissuade them from forming an anti-French alliance with the Iroquois. In a lengthy letter, dated 17 Sept. 1690, Carheil outlined to Governor Frontenac [Buade*] why the Ottawas wavered in their loyalty, pointing out that the Iroquois, by a series of raids, had seemed to demonstrate that the French could hardly defend themselves much less aid their Indian allies.

However, Carheil succeeded in inducing the Ottawas to meet with Frontenac during the summer of 1690, and at the parley they disavowed any intention of forming an alliance with the Iroquois. Eleven years later, in 1701, Governor CALLIÈRE sought to effect a general peace among all the Indian tribes; the eloquence of the Huron chief KONDIARONK, called the Rat, won the day for the plan. Kondiaronk, who had embraced Christianity through Carheil's instruction, declared, according to Charlevoix, that he respected only two Europeans, Frontenac and Carheil.

With the exploration of the Mississippi Valley, Saint-Ignace became a rendezvous for French traders whose presence exercised an unfavourable influence on the Indians frequenting the mission. Before 1690, Carheil and other missionaries held the traders in check by excluding from the area any who debauched the Indians. This situation changed radically in 1690 when Fort Buade was built quite near the mission. The fort's garrison soon consorted with the natives to the moral detriment of the latter. Consequently the missionaries complained that instead of protecting the mission the soldiers were trading with the Indians and debauching them with liquor. The situation grew worse when Cadillac [LAUMET], who cordially disliked the Jesuits, became commandant in 1694. Matters came to a head in 1696 when the crown ordered the closing of the western posts. Cadillac, however, had no intention of compliantly abandoning his opportunity to reap the rich profits which his position offered. Returning to France, he procured permission to establish a post at Detroit, using his own funds. When the new centre opened in 1701, Cadillac induced many Indians from Saint-Ignace to migrate to his post. Carheil opposed the move, as did most of the Jesuit missionaries at Saint-Ignace, because he believed that Cadillac would give the Indians too little encouragement to lead Christian lives. On 30 Aug. 1702 Carheil wrote a lengthy letter to Callière, outlining why the Jesuits objected to the situation. Despite the efforts of the Jesuits at Saint-Ignace, the Indians migrated to Cadillac's new post in such numbers that the mission near the Straits of Mackinac had to be abandoned and the mission buildings burned to the ground. A few years later when Fort Michilimackinac was erected by the French on the southern shore of the straits, the Jesuits again established a mission, but by this time Carheil's career was over. During the remainder of his life, he devoted himself to the care of the French at Quebec and Montreal.

Charlevoix notes that Carheil's contemporaries considered him a man of great talents and solid virtues. He is said to have spoken the Iroquois and Huron languages with as much ease as his native French. Carheil left a two-volume treatise on Huron called *Racines Hurones*.

JOSEPH P. DONNELLY, S.J.

Charlevoix, *History* (Shea), III, 116–17; IV, 55–57. *Découvertes et établissements des Français* (Margry), V, 204, 223–24, 235–37. *JR* (Thwaites). *NYCD* (O'Callaghan and Fernow), IX, 360, 587. P. Orhand, *Un admirable inconnu: le révérend père Étienne de Carheil* (Paris, [1897]). Rochemonteix, *Les Jésuites et la N.-F. au XVIIe siècle*, III, 497–527. J. G. Shea, *History of the Catholic Church in the United States* (4v., New York, 1886–92), I, 286–94, 297, 303, 328, 332.

CARREROT, PIERRE, settler and fisherman, keeper of stores at Placentia (Plaisance) and on Île Royale (Cape Breton Island), receiver of dues at the admiralty court of Louisbourg; b. *c.* 1667 at Bayonne; d. 1732 at Louisbourg.

Carrerot, who had been established at Placentia at least since 1690, married that same year Marie, widow of a certain Charpentier and daughter of Thomas Picq (also written Piet and Pitt), who came originally from England. In 1702 Carrerot received a commission as keeper of stores, a function that he had been fulfilling since 1692. He was the holder of five tracts of land with houses and fishing rooms, and regularly employed between 10 and 20 men who served as sailors and fishermen; this made him one of the most important settlers in the colony. When he went to Île Royale, he worked his fishing concession at La Baleine (Baleine Cove), where in 1717 he employed as many as 27 men, but he seems gradually to have abandoned fishing in order to support his sons in their commercial ventures. In 1724 we find him established at Louisbourg, having temporarily resumed his former office of keeper of stores, which had been left vacant by his son Philippe*. It was perhaps not until about 1730 that he was made receiver of dues at the admiralty court, since the collection of these had long been carried out by its attorney.

Carrerot died on 2 May 1732. His sons Philippe and André*, his daughter Marie-Anne, widow of Quentin de La Salle, former assistant town major of Placentia, as well as a grandson, Louis Delort, born of the first marriage of Guillaume Delort and Françoise-Ovide Carrerot, deceased, divided between them the slender proceeds of his estate, from which Delort was to claim—in vain—payment of a dowry of 1,500 *livres*.

LOUISE DECHÊNE

Casson

AN, Col., B, 17, 23; C¹¹ᴮ, 1–13; C¹¹ᶜ, 1–7; E, 64 (dossier de Pierre Carrerot); Section Outre-Mer, G¹, 406–7, 462, 466, 467 (copies in PAC); G², 181; G³, 2055, 2056–58.

CASSON, FRANÇOIS DOLLIER DE. *See* DOLLIER

CATALOGNE, GÉDÉON (DE) (he signed "Catalougne," the Béarnais way, but most official documents refer to him as "Catalogne"; he used the particle "de" sometimes, whereas some of his relatives used it and some did not), surveyor, cartographer, and sub-engineer; b. 1662 at Arthez, Béarn, son of Gédéon Catalougne and Marie de Capdeviolle, grandson of Gédéon Catalougne; married 11 Aug. 1690 at Montreal, Marie-Anne Lemire, daughter of Jean Lemire* and Louise Marsolet; father of nine children including JOSEPH; d. 5 July 1729 at Louisbourg.

In his youth, Catalogne must have been instructed in mathematics, particularly geometry; but, being a Protestant, he could not have been trained for a commission in the corps of engineers. Evidently he came to Canada in 1683 under the *nom de guerre* of "La Liberté," serving as a soldier and surveyor in the colonial regular troops and taking part in both Le Febvre* de La Barre's campaign against the Iroquois (1684) and the attacks against English posts on Hudson Bay led by the Chevalier de Troyes* (1686). In 1687, after his conversion to Roman Catholicism, he was commissioned. As an ensign, he participated in several campaigns against the Iroquois and the English, including the siege of Quebec led by Phips*, and supervised the construction of various earthworks and stockade fortifications. After being promoted in 1691, at Buade* de Frontenac's request, to the rank of half-pay lieutenant, he continued his surveying, building, and general military duties; and BOCHART de Champigny described him as a "good officer and *honnête homme*." In 1700, as a licensed surveyor, he undertook for 9,000 *livres* to construct a canal at Lachine for the Sulpicians [*see* DOLLIER de Casson]; but his survey must have been inadequate for, among other things, he did not foresee the large amount of solid rock which would have to be excavated and removed. The canal was not finished.

He became a lieutenant in 1704, took part in the raid led by AUGER de Subercase in 1705 against St John's, Newfoundland, and helped to strengthen the colony's defences on the Richelieu River invasion route. Most important during the war of 1703–13, however, was his detailed mapping of the three administrative districts of Canada, beginning about 1708 and culminating in the well-known survey reports of 1712 and 1715. During the same period he sought recognition from the Académie des Sciences for two scientific papers: one in 1706 on longitude and the drift of ships and the other in 1710 on a method of taking soundings; the academy was unable to adopt them. The intendants, JACQUES and ANTOINE-DENIS RAUDOT, who were most impressed with his work, recommended a captaincy for him; but the court would do no more than name him sub-engineer, with a supplementary salary of some 200 *livres* per annum. He held this post at Montreal from 1712 until 1720, preparing plans and maps, and directing work on the *enceinte*; and occasionally assisting with the works at Quebec. Slowly he moved up the seniority list until, by 1720, he was second in line for a captaincy.

That year the Comte de Saint-Pierre, proprietor of Île Saint-Jean (Prince Edward Island), asked for Catalogne, "an excellent person, who understands the work that has to be done and is more suitable than any other for such a settlement." He assisted Saint-Pierre until 1723, when he finally received the promotion he had been seeking: a captaincy and command of one of the companies at Louisbourg; but he lost the status—and pay—of sub-engineer. While in Canada settling various property transactions in 1722–23, he joined master-builder Jean Maillou*, of Quebec, with the object of underbidding Michel-Philippe ISABEAU for some of the works at Louisbourg. He was sure, he told the minister in November 1724, that far from conflicting with his military responsibilities such a partnership would be in the interests of the service—in addition to providing the supplementary income which Catalogne required to support the large family he had left behind in Canada.

Naturally the climate of Île Saint-Jean appealed to Catalogne more than that of Louisbourg; he could not think of a better arrangement than to command a company on the island. Therefore, after nothing had come of Maillou's bid, Catalogne informed the minister that the people of the island, which had been returned to the royal domain, wanted him to take command. He could do that economically, he suggested, if he were paid a flat sum for feeding and clothing his company, by purchasing supplies for the lowest possible Louisbourg price and keeping them for two years in storehouses built large enough for the purpose. The minister, however, had no plans for raising the tiny garrison of Île Saint-Jean to company strength, nor was he impressed with Catalogne's plan.

Catalogne was too enterprising to be satisfied with garrison life at Louisbourg. He had acquired, on the Miré (Mira) River, property which he was developing both for its limestone quarries and for its fertile soil: on it he was growing barley, oats, several kinds of vegetables, melons, and tobacco. At his own expense he had found that agriculture in certain districts of Île Royale (Cape Breton Island) was possible but costly if scarce hired labour were used; but the Miré, he said, could support 500 resident families, and livestock could be imported and bred there with profit.

At his death in 1729, Catalogne held property in Louisbourg, on the Miré, in Quebec, and in Montreal; the Quebec property was the fief of Les Prairies-Marsolet, first conceded to his wife's grandfather, Nicolas Marsolet*. The Montreal property on the Saint-Pierre River was acquired from the Sulpicians in 1690. It was natural for the author of the 1712 and 1715 reports, a surveyor, to place a high value on land; but the total economic worth of his own holdings remains unknown.

His most important legacies are his maps and plans, his reports of 1712 and 1715 on the seigneuries and his *Recueil de ce qui s'est passé au Canada, au sujet de la guerre tant des Anglais que des Iroquois, depuis l'année 1682*. Although not all of Catalogne's maps and plans have survived, and although some for which he was responsible may not have been attributed to him, there are extant a map of the district ("gouvernement") of Quebec in three parts and one of the district of Trois-Rivières in two. All dated 1709 and drawn by JEAN-BAPTISTE DE COUAGNE, they illustrate the corresponding portions of the 1712 survey report by Catalogne on the seigneuries by showing the boundaries of the grants and the names of the seigneurial families. Those of the district of Montreal are missing. Other maps extant are a plan of Montreal and a map of the St Lawrence River in two parts, drawn by Catalogne and published in 1723 at Paris by king's geographer Moullart Sanson. There is also evidence that Catalogne drew a plan of Chambly in 1711 and one of the *enceinte* of Montreal in 1715.

Catalogne's survey of the seigneuries, the first version of which was dated 1712 and which was revised in 1715, arose from a study finished in 1708 which was limited to the district of Montreal. Catalogne, who had undertaken the work himself with support from the elder Raudot, asked the minister whether the king would like him to survey the seigneuries of the whole of Canada. Pontchartrain thought that the task might be shared with LEVASSEUR de Neré and Boisberthelot* de Beaucours; but the Raudots, to whose discretion the matter was left, preferred to have Catalogne do the whole job himself. Some of the shortcomings of the report may stem directly from this decision, as Catalogne was required to attend to his other duties at the same time; in fact he pleaded lack of time for failing to show the total area of land under cultivation and for omitting certain seigneuries.

The report set out to survey Canada district by district and seigneur by seigneur, indicating ". . . both the natural and the adventitious products, and the quality and ownership of the lands." It was observed that many seigneuries had not been developed, thus confirming that which had influenced Versailles in issuing the edicts of 1711 ordering the return of undeveloped seigneuries to the king and of undeveloped *rôtures* to the seigneur. Catalogne made no attempt to describe the undeveloped lands, however, or to ascribe reasons for their primitive state. The revision of 1715 (which, unlike its predecessor, has not been published) corrected some errors and specified "the seigneuries on which justice is administered"; but its main object was to make the paper more practical: to emphasize improvements which could really be carried out. These reports were, however, no panacea: they provided topographical and resource information, at least some of which was new to the administrators and policy-makers of the time.

The *Recueil* is partly a chronicle based on hearsay and partly a memoir, with all the defects and the usefulness of these types of source: subjectivity and errors in recollection, but details which complement contemporary documents. Written no earlier than the autumn of 1716, it is a version of events from 1682 until that year. It is of value for the details it provides of those events, particularly military, in which Catalogne took part, such as the raids on the James Bay forts in 1686 and on St John's in 1705, and it is interesting for the character assessments which Catalogne makes of some of his contemporaries. In other respects, it must be read with caution.

F. J. THORPE

[The maps and plans attributed to Catalogne are to be found in the British Museum and the Bibliothèque Nationale, with copies in the Public Archives of Canada, Ottawa. Another map, of Montreal, in the Archives du Comité Technique du Génie (Paris) may or may not be attributable to Catalogne and there is speculation as to whether the Montreal plan of 1723 (see below) is a copy, reduced, of the mission one of 1707 (article of Mme M. Azard cited below).

The "Recueil" is to be found in AN, Col., F³, 2, ff.100–29. It was published in Le Blant (see below) pp.170–272 and previously in less accurate and incomplete versions dated 1871 (Société Historique et

Catalogne

Littéraire de Québec) and 1883 (in *Coll. de manuscrits relatifs à la N.-F.*, I). The nature of the two earlier publications is described in Le Blant, pp.154–56.

AJM, Greffe de Jacques David, 28 juillet 1721, 22 sept. 1721; Greffe de Claude Maugue, 24 oct. 1692; Greffe de J.-B. Pottier, 2 févr. 1690, 9 août 1690, 31 oct. 1700; Greffe de J.-C. Raimbault, 19 juin 1726, 25 août 1728, 31 août 1728, 15 févr. 1730, 26 juin 1730, 9 août 1731, 13 mars 1732. AJQ, Greffe de François Genaple, 3 juin 1696. AN, Col., B, 29, ff.124v, 334v, 335f., 400–1; 33, f.162; 34, ff.344, 461v–63v; 35, f.306v; 40, ff.490f.; 41, ff.533v, 534f.; 45, f.293v; 48, f.973; 49, f.722v; 52, f.593v; 58, f.483; C¹¹ᴬ, 20, f.74; 24, f.163; 28, ff.250f.; 33, ff.15f., 209f.; 34, ff.113–14v, 328v; 120, f.180; C¹¹ᴮ, 5, f.13; 7, f.12; C¹¹ᶜ, 16, ff.13–15; C¹¹ᴱ, 13, ff.156–57; C¹¹ᴳ, 3, ff.159f., 183; 4, ff.97f.; D²ᶜ, 47; 57, ff.29, 54; 60, f.3v; E, 65, pièces 2, 3, 5, 11; F³, 2, ff.358f.; 6, ff.392f.; Section Outre-Mer, G¹, 406. PAC, Map div., H2/312 [1708] (BM, King's Maps, CXIX, 22); H3/340; H12/1112 (1723); V2/300 (1709), sheets I–V (BN, Cartes et plans, Portefeuille 127, div. 2, pièces I–V).

Documents relating to seigniorial tenure (Munro), 94–151. Le Blant, *Histoire de la N.-F.*, 87–272. "M. de Catalogne et le canal de la rivière Saint-Pierre," *BRH*, XIII (1907), 88–90. P.-G. Roy, *Inv. coll. pièces jud. et not.*, I, 66; II, 310. Trudel, *Atlas historique* (1961).

Harris, *The seigneurial system*. M.-M. Azard-Malauie, "Commentaires et réflexions sur quelques documents de l'exposition 'L'Amitié franco-canadienne' organisée à Montréal et à Québec en 1967," *RHAF*, XXI (1968), 770–72. Aegidius Fauteux, "Gédéon de Catalogne," *La Patrie* (Montréal), 9 juin 1934, 40–42. Ernest Marceau, "Les origines des canaux du Canada," *RC*, 3ᵉ sér., II (1908), 432–33. F.J.T.]

CATALOGNE, JOSEPH DE, soldier and officer in the colonial regular troops; b. 5 May 1694 at Montreal, son of GÉDÉON and Marie-Anne Lemire; married Marie-Charlotte Renaud Dubuisson (d. June 1734), daughter of JACQUES-CHARLES; they had one child, Louis-François-Gédéon* (b. 14 Feb. 1734); d. 10 Oct. 1735 on Île Royale (Cape Breton Island).

Catalogne enlisted in the colonial regular troops about 1714 and was commissioned in 1722 as a second ensign. After he had served three years in Canada in this capacity, his father sought a promotion for him, but was told that Joseph was 14th in line. The minister did agree, however, to a transfer to his father's company at Louisbourg. In 1730, the year following his father's death, he became an ensign and then, within two months, a lieutenant. In August 1732, while en route to Canada, where he was conducting 60 seamen, he was shipwrecked at Port d'Orléans (Ingonish Harbour, N.S.) and lost all his personal effects, valued at 512 *livres*. In 1734, he commanded a party sent by Saint-Ovide [Mombeton*] to two Cape

Breton outports to investigate violations of fishing ordinances.

F. J. THORPE

AN, Col., B, 49, f.722v *et seq.*; 50, f.514v; 54, f.506; 55, f.574; 64, ff.466, 479v, 484v; C¹¹ᴮ, 15, f.65; C¹¹ᶜ, 16, f.14; C¹¹ᴳ, 7, f.190; D²ᶜ, 47, ff.359–60; 60, ff.6, 9v; 222/1, p. 121 (copy in PAC); E, 65; Section Outre-Mer, G¹, 406/3, pp.379, 397 (transcript in PAC). Le Blant, *Histoire de la N.-F.* McLennan, *Louisbourg*, 49. [There does not seem to be any evidence, other than McLennan's claim, that Joseph wrote a treatise on the magnet and thereby gained a seat in the Académie des Sciences. F.J.T.]

CATCHAMISSE. *See* SCATCHAMISSE

CAULFEILD, THOMAS, soldier, lieutenant-governor at Annapolis Royal 1711–17; baptized on 26 March 1685 in England; d. 2 March 1716/17 (o.s.).

A member of an Oxfordshire family which settled in Ireland at the beginning of the 17th century, Thomas Caulfeild was a son of William, 2d Viscount Charlemont, and Anne, daughter of Dr James Margetson, archbishop of Armagh.

Caulfeild saw military service in Spain in 1702 and 1705, and in 1710 took part in the successful expedition against Port-Royal (Annapolis Royal, N.S.) led by Francis NICHOLSON. The following year he participated in the disastrous expedition against Quebec under Sir Hovenden WALKER. While returning from Quebec, Brigadier-General JOHN HILL appointed Caulfeild, "a gentleman that has served very well, to be deputy governour [at Annapolis Royal], which was absolutely necessary for keeping good order and discipline in the garrison." Caulfeild was confirmed in this post on 16 Oct. 1712, when he was commissioned lieutenant-governor of the garrison, replacing Sir Charles HOBBY. He was also made captain of an independent company of foot.

Caulfeild was in command in Nova Scotia from October 1711 to June 1712, during the absence of Governor Samuel VETCH. Although the inhabitants of the district of Annapolis had taken the oath of allegiance early in 1711, many of the Acadians outside that area were hostile, and the Indians had not come to terms. Caulfeild did his best to make his fort more defensible and to keep discipline in a garrison whose mutinous tendencies were aggravated by a shortage of clothing and bedding and by an impending lack of provisions. Governor Vetch returned to Annapolis Royal in June 1712, and remained there until the end of the summer of 1713. In October of that year Francis Nicholson who, unknown to Vetch, had been commissioned governor of Nova Scotia in October

1712, directed Caulfeild to take over the government from Vetch. Nicholson did not come to Nova Scotia until the summer of 1714, and then remained only a few months.

Meantime, on 5 Nov. 1713, Caulfeild summoned all the inhabitants of Annapolis and made known to them Queen Anne's declaration concerning the continued occupancy of Acadia and Newfoundland by French subjects [*see* NICHOLSON]. He reported that the chief inhabitants seemed to be satisfied and willing to continue on their lands, which he thought would be of great service to the garrison. At first the French authorities endeavoured to induce the Acadians to migrate to Île Royale, where Louisbourg had been founded. With the permission of the local British officials, the French sent Captains Louis Denys* de La Ronde and JACQUES D'ESPIET de Pensens to Nova Scotia in August 1714 to visit the Acadian settlements and tell the Acadians what inducements they were prepared to offer them to move. A few Acadians did go to Île Royale and nearly all of them in the emotion of the moment signified their willingness to go to French territory. It was soon seen, however, that the Acadians were in general reluctant to leave their homes. Nicholson wrote from Boston on 20 Nov. 1714 to advise Caulfeild to do what he could to prevent French agents from coming into Nova Scotia and to keep a close watch on all proceedings, especially those in which the French missionaries were involved.

Learning of the accession of George I, Caulfeild proclaimed the new monarch at Annapolis Royal late in 1714. The oaths of allegiance were taken by the garrison and the English inhabitants. The French refused, but did sign a paper recognizing George I as the legitimate sovereign and certifying that they would never do anything contrary to his service while they remained there. As soon as the season permitted, Caulfeild sent French-speaking officers to the other Acadian settlements to proclaim George I. This was done early in 1715 by Thomas Button and Peter Capon, who found the Acadians unwilling to take the oath. The Indians on the Saint John River also refused, and declared that they no longer sold their furs at Annapolis Royal because of the exorbitant prices of merchandise there.

Caulfeild was rather critical of Nicholson. He thought that the governor had tried to stop the soldiers' pay in England and ruin their credit in Boston, and that he was too rash in telling the soldiers and English inhabitants to have no contact with the French and in shutting the gates of the garrison against them, whereas their produce was required for subsistence. Nicholson was removed from his post in January 1714/15. Vetch

succeeded to the governorship but never returned to Nova Scotia.

Caulfeild realized the importance of retaining the French inhabitants in Nova Scotia. He stated in a letter to the Board of Trade dated 1 Nov. 1715, that if the French remained they would be of great benefit to the colony, but that if they left they would strengthen the enemy. He also stressed the advantage to be derived from having some English inhabitants sent to Nova Scotia, especially industrious labourers, pitch and tar makers, carpenters, and smiths. To promote trade with the Indians and to encourage them to come to Annapolis Royal to sell furs and feathers, he recommended that a king's magazine be established there.

During his term in office, Caulfeild faced the problem of settling disputes among the inhabitants. He did not think that he had authority to establish courts of judicature, so he sought instructions in the matter. He felt that he would be blameworthy if he took no notice of injustice, and was desirous of cultivating as good an understanding among the people as possible. Thus, pending instructions from London, he continued or revived the practice begun in the winter of 1710–11 of referring disputes among the Acadians to a court composed of officers and Acadians. Like Vetch, however, Caulfeild found himself hampered by a lack of direction from the British government. In addition, he went deeply into debt to procure needed provisions for the garrison, and bore this burden until his death.

CHARLES BRUCE FERGUSSON

PRO, C.O. 217/1, ff.60–63, 83–84, 86–87, 135–36, 206, 291, 301, 315–19, 345, 359–60, 362, 368, 370, 384–85, 388, 390; 217/3, ff.31, 49–54, 60–61, 69, 84–85, 103. *Coll. doc. inédits, Canada et Amérique* (*CF*), I (1888), 110–13, 155–71. *N.S. Archives, II.* N.S. Hist. Soc., *Coll.,* I (1878), IV (1884). PRO, *CSP, Col., 1711–12, 1712–14, 1714–15, 1716–17.* J. B. and A. P. Burke, *A genealogical and heraldic history of the peerage and baronetage, the Privy Council, knightage and companionage,* ed. A. W. Thorpe (80th ed., London, 1921). Dalton, *English army lists,* IV, 261–62; V, 288–90; VI, 184, 190. Brebner, *New England's outpost.* Dalton, *George the First's army* I, 222–40, 248, 313. Waller, *Samuel Vetch.* F.-J. Audet, "Governors, lieutenant-governors, and administrators of Nova Scotia, 1604–1932" (bound typescript in PANS, n.d.).

CAVELIER, JEAN, priest, Sulpician, explorer, elder brother of Robert Cavelier* de La Salle; b. 27 Oct. 1636 at Rouen, son of Jean Cavelier, a wholesale haberdasher, and of Catherine Geest; d. 24 Nov. 1722 at Rouen.

Jean Cavelier was a member of a rich family belonging to the upper bourgeoisie of the provinces.

Cavelier

We have no details on his life before 1658, the date at which he entered the Sulpician seminary in Paris. Four years later he was ordained priest.

On 7 Sept. 1666, at the same time as DOLLIER de Casson, he arrived at Montreal, where he was a parish priest until 1676. That year he was involved in a dispute with a certain Pierre Cavelier; he attempted to have the latter's house and land in Montreal seized. Then in October 1679, while preparing to leave for France, he tried to recover the money which he had advanced to his brother, Robert Cavelier de La Salle, who had been in New France since 1667. On 23 November the Conseil Souverain rendered a judgement which allowed him to obtain a fairly large sum. This so ruined La Salle's credit in the colony that he wrote in a letter: "[Jean] has done . . . all that the bitterest enemy could do."

Finally, in November, Jean Cavelier left for France, where he remained until 1684, when his brother chose him as a member of his expedition to the Mississippi country [see DOUAY; GRAVIER; HENNEPIN]. Although he played only a secondary role in this expedition, Jean Cavelier has left us a journal written some years later. According to Barthélemy*, one of his travelling companions, he was the butt of his brother's capricious temperament. Indeed, Barthélemy claimed that La Salle "almost starved him . . . allotting him only a handful of flour a day." Several historians have labelled this story as ridiculous.

After La Salle's tragic death, which occurred on 19 March 1687 near La Trinité, Abbé Cavelier and the remainder of the explorer's companions reached Fort Saint-Louis-des-Illinois on 14 September. The Sulpician, concealing his brother's death, presented to HENRI TONTY a note signed by La Salle before his murder, and asked Tonty to supply him with the wherewithal to meet the costs of a journey to France which his brother wanted him to make. To comply with Cavelier's request, Tonty gave him some beaver furs, and on 13 July 1688 Jean Cavelier reached Montreal. Instead of revealing La Salle's death, he preferred to let people believe that he was still alive. He tells us himself in his journal that he had "concealed his [brother's] death from M. the Governor General of Canada," and that he was taking good care "not to let anyone know it." This behaviour seems strange, for if the governor had been aware of the expedition's failure early enough he could have done something to save the survivors abandoned near the Mississippi delta. This was at least the opinion expressed by BRISAY de Denonville in a letter addressed to Seignelay [Colbert] in January 1690. Cavelier seems to have acted in this way with the object of obtaining for himself the assets owed to the creditors of his brother, who was acknowledged to be insolvent.

After spending a month at Montreal, where according to Henri Joutel (author of an account of La Salle's last expedition), he concerned himself chiefly with business, the Abbé went to Quebec, then to Île Percée, and sailed on 4 Sept. 1688; he reached La Rochelle on 9 October. But instead of going directly to Paris he preferred to make a pilgrimage to Saumur, then to Mont-Saint-Michel, and after that to go to Rouen. It was only at the beginning of December that he met Seignelay, after M. Tronson, his superior, had urged him to make his report to the minister.

Subsequently Cavelier was to lose all interest in the Mississippi expedition, as is evidenced by a letter that Tronson wrote on 1 June 1690 to Bishop Saint-Vallier [LA CROIX]: "Monsieur Cavelier's plan to charter a vessel has fallen through, he is entirely taken up at Rouen with straightening out what is left of his business affairs, which long absences have reduced to a sorry state; it is sad to see such a good worker spending a part of his life in difficulties of this kind."

It was at this period that Cavelier wrote the journal of the expedition. The text was to be presented to Seignelay, no doubt with a view to obtaining some pecuniary advantages and defending his brother's memory. This explains why scant credibility can be attached to the document.

Jean Cavelier spent his last days at Rouen, probably at his niece's house, where he died a rich man on 24 Nov. 1722.

JEAN-GUY PELLETIER

[Jean Cavelier], *The journal of Jean Cavelier, the account of a survivor of La Salle's Texas expedition, 1684–1688*, trans. and annotated by Jean Delanglez (Chicago, 1938). Charlevoix, *Histoire* (1744), II. *Découvertes et établissements des Français* (Margry), II, III. [Henri Joutel], *Journal historique du dernier voyage que feu M. de La Sale fit dans le golfe de Mexique . . . où l'on voit l'histoire tragique de sa mort & plusieurs choses curieuses du nouveau monde . . .*, rédigé et mis en ordre par Monsieur De Michel (Paris, 1713). *Jug. et délib.*, II. Le Jeune, *Dictionnaire*. Rochemonteix, *Les Jésuites et la N.-F. au XVIIe siècle*, III. Jean Delanglez, "The authorship of the journal of Jean Cavelier," *Mid-America*, XXV (1943; new ser. XIV), 220–23. George Paré, "The St-Joseph mission," *Mississippi Valley Hist. Review*, XVII (1930–31), 24–54.

CAVELIER, PIERRE RIVET. *See* RIVET

CÉLORON DE BLAINVILLE, JEAN-BAPTISTE, midshipman, lieutenant, captain, knight of the order of Saint-Louis; baptized 19 Feb. 1660 in the church of Saint-Sauveur in Paris, son of Antoine Céloron, king's counsellor, and of Marie Rémy; nephew of Pierre RÉMY, parish priest of Lachine; d. 4 June 1735 at Montreal.

Jean-Baptiste Céloron probably came to Canada in 1684. He was in Montreal in 1688, when he was found guilty of playing billiards on Easter Monday, during vespers, which was forbidden at that time. In 1691 he was a half-pay captain. The following year he was granted the former fief of Blainville. Ten years later he received a commission as captain of a company of colonial regular troops, replacing the Sieur de Merville. In 1704 he asked for leave and returned to France to put his affairs in order. He was to return to Canada in the autumn of the following year.

During his stay in Paris Céloron de Blainville roused in his family an interest in Canada. As a result of his efforts he received in 1707 two sums of money, which he made over to the Ursulines of Trois-Rivières, and in 1708 he settled an annuity on them in the name of his sister in Paris, Catherine Céloron.

In June 1705 he accused Pierre de Saint-Ours*, the younger, of violating his sixteen-year-old daughter, Hélène, but by September Saint-Ours had been freed of this charge. Saint-Ours married the girl in 1710. On 7 July 1711 the minister wrote to the intendant, Bégon*: "As the big lawsuit between the Saint-Ours and Blainville families has been settled with a marriage, it is advisable for the peace of the two families that the proceedings of this affair be forgotten. . . ."

Later Céloron de Blainville engaged in the fur trade in the *pays d'en haut*, without much success, however. This is proven by three transfers of letters of credit in favour of Pierre YOU de La Découverte, Mademoiselle Picoté de Belestre, and Jean BOUILLET de La Chassaigne, two recognizances, one to Jean Loubinois de Tourneuve for the sum of 1,593 *livres*, the other to Pierre Trottier* Désauniers for 1,691 *livres*, and a lawsuit before the bench of the royal jurisdiction of Montreal in 1721.

Jean-Baptiste Céloron de Blainville was married four times and had eight children. By his first marriage, which took place in Paris, he had a son who became a Recollet. Then in 1686, in Montreal, he married Hélène Picoté de Belestre, mother of François de LA FRENAYE. They had seven children, one of whom, Pierre-Joseph Céloron* de Blainville, won fame as a soldier. On the death of his second wife Céloron de Blainville married Geneviève Damours de Chauffours, daughter of Mathieu Damours*, in 1703. And in 1704 he married Geneviève-Gertrude, daughter of Charles Legardeur* de Tilly. He was created a knight of the order of Saint-Louis on 4 April 1730, though he had solicited this honour since 1712. His superiors noted that he was only a fairly good officer. This no doubt explains why the archives contain nothing special about his military career. He died on 4 June 1735 at Montreal.

ROLAND-J. AUGER

AAQ, Registres d'insinuation C. AJM, Greffe d'Antoine Adhémar, 2 oct. 1693, 29 nov. 1701, 7 janv., 28 sept. 1705, 8 juillet, 11 oct., 18 nov. 1707, 23 janv. 1708, 16 avril 1710, 17 févr. 1712; Greffe de Bénigne Basset, 16 juin 1692; Greffe de Jacques David, 26, 30 août 1721. AN, Col., C¹¹ᴬ, 24, ff.214, 237; 31, ff.5–28. Caron, "Inventaire de documents," APQ *Rapport*, *1940–41*, 352. "Correspondance de Vaudreuil," APQ *Rapport*, *1938–39*, 22, 36. PAC *Report*, *1899*, Supp., 352, 376, 446, 457, 480; *1904*, App.K, 131. P.-G. Roy, *Inv. coll. pièces jud. et not.*, I; *Inv. concessions*, V, 153. Fauteux, *Les chevaliers de Saint-Louis*. [Faillon], *Histoire de la colonie française*, 341. Désiré Girouard, *Lake St. Louis, old and new, and Cavelier de La Salle* (Montréal, 1893), 211. É.-Z. Massicotte, "Évocations du vieux Montréal," *Cahiers des Dix*, III (1938), 145. P.-G. Roy, "La famille Céloron de Blainville," *BRH*, XV (1909), 302–14, 329–50, 360–76.

CHABERT DE JONCAIRE, LOUIS-THOMAS, esquire, called **Sononchiez** by the Iroquois, member of the governor's guards and lieutenant in the colonial regular troops, agent and interpreter for New France among the Iroquois; born in Saint-Rémi de Provence, near Arles, *c.* 1670; died at Fort Niagara, 29 June 1739.

The son of Antoine-Marie de Joncaire, esquire, and Gabrielle Hardi, Joncaire probably came to Canada in the late 1680s as cavalry sergeant in the governor's guards. Soon after his arrival he was captured by the Senecas, who decided to put him to death. What happened immediately afterwards is uncertain. In 1709 Joncaire told the intendant, ANTOINE-DENIS RAUDOT, that when one of the chiefs tried to burn his fingers as a preliminary torment, he struck him in the face with his fist and broke his nose. This display of spirit had so impressed the Senecas that they not only spared his life but also adopted him into their tribe. Joncaire's son, Daniel*, makes no mention of such an incident in a memoir written shortly after 1760. He simply states that his father had been captured by the Senecas and was about to be burnt when he was adopted by one of the women of the tribe. Whatever may be the correct version, there can be no doubt that an intimate relationship between the Iroquois and Joncaire began during his captivity and lasted until his death many years later. The Indians, on the one hand, gave him their friendship and their trust. Joncaire, on the

Chabert de Joncaire

other, mastered their language and acquired a complete understanding of their mentality. He was thus in a position to render precious services to New France whenever there were negotiations to be conducted with this important tribe.

With Father BRUYAS and PAUL LE MOYNE de Maricourt, Joncaire played a significant role in the discussions that led to the peace treaty of 1701, ending the second Iroquois war. In the summer of 1700 these three men accompanied two Onondaga and four Seneca chiefs to the Iroquois cantons and managed to prevail upon all the nations except the Mohawks to send an official delegation to Canada to negotiate a treaty with the French and their native allies. During the War of the Spanish Succession which broke out in 1702, he and CHARLES LE MOYNE de Longueuil, who wielded great influence over the Onondagas, were chosen by Governor Philippe de RIGAUD de Vaudreuil to carry out the most important part of his wartime policy—preserving Iroquois neutrality. To achieve this end, Joncaire alternately appealed to the interests of the Senecas by presenting them with gifts and played upon their fears by threatening them with an attack by the western Indians if they should break their treaty with New France. For such a threat to carry weight it was important that the Iroquois pursue their traditional policy of excluding the western Indians from the Albany trade; if they granted them a right of way to that city, as the halfbreed agent Montour, who was employed by the New York merchants, was urging them to do, the western Indians would no longer have compelling reasons to make war on the Five Nations should the French ask them to do so.

On Vaudreuil's orders Joncaire set out to eliminate Montour. In the summer of 1709 the two men and their followers met by accident in Iroquois country. Feigning friendliness, Joncaire invited Montour to smoke with him and produced some tobacco. The Albany agent accepted and took out his knife to cut it. Joncaire then remarked on the smallness of the knife and asked for it so that he might give him a better one. Not suspecting anything, Montour handed his knife to the Frenchman. The latter immediately flung it away and one of his followers then crushed Montour's skull with a hatchet which had been concealed under his coat.

As this incident shows, Joncaire did not hesitate to use deceit when it served his purpose, although his success with the Indians appears to have been due primarily to his ability to establish a psychological link with them. This was strikingly demonstrated in August 1711. New France was being threatened with an English attack and

Vaudreuil had summoned 800 Indians from a dozen different tribes to Montreal to renew the alliance with them. The crucial moment came during a banquet on 7 August when these allies were asked to declare themselves against the English. It was then that Joncaire and Michel Maray* de La Chauvignerie, who served Longueuil as interpreter among the Onondagas, stood up before the assembly, brandished hatchets, and broke into the war song. Soon all the Indians joined in, thus asserting their solidarity with the French.

It was again thanks to Joncaire that New France was able to build a fort at Niagara, on Seneca territory, in 1720. This was a location of great strategic importance, for it commanded the portage around the falls which was used by a great number of western Indians when they travelled towards the English and French settlements for purposes of trade. When Vaudreuil learned that the English were planning to occupy it he sent Joncaire to the Senecas with instructions to gain their assent to a French post. Early in 1720, Joncaire presented himself at their settlements and convened an assembly of the chiefs. When they had gathered he informed them that he had always derived much pleasure from his visits among them. In fact, he went on, he would come even more frequently if he had a house of his own to which he could withdraw. The chiefs replied that as one of their sons he was free to build a house for himself wherever he chose. This is what Joncaire had been hoping to hear. He hurried to Fort Frontenac, chose eight soldiers, and proceeded directly to Niagara. On the east side of the river, some eight miles below the falls, the group built a trading house and displayed the French colours. By this somewhat unscrupulous exploitation of the Seneca trust in him, Joncaire had once more gained his ends.

Joncaire commanded at Niagara until 1726. In 1723 he again demonstrated his great influence over the Iroquois by obtaining their permission to replace the original trading house by a wooden stockade large enough to hold 300 defenders. In 1731, he was chosen by Governor Charles de Beauharnois* de La Boische to command a group of Shawnees who had migrated from the Susquehanna to the Allegheny River. His mission was to prevent them from trading with the English and if possible to induce them to move their village farther west, preferably to Detroit, where French influence was greater. Joncaire was apparently working at this task when he died at Fort Niagara on 29 June 1739.

On 1 March 1706, in Montreal, he had married Marie-Madeleine Le Gay, the 17-year-old daughter of Jean-Jérôme Le Gay, Sieur de Beaulieu, merchant and bourgeois of Montreal, and Madeleine Just. Of the ten children born of this marriage between 1707 and 1723, two played a part in the colony's history. The eldest son, Philippe-Thomas*, was presented by his father to the Senecas at the age of ten, became a captain in the colonial regular troops, and died in Canada shortly after the conquest. His brother Daniel, known as the Sieur de Chabert et de Clausonne, was a prominent figure in the Niagara region during the Seven Years War. Implicated in "the Canada affair," he spent some time in the Bastille following the conquest and after his release returned to America to die at Detroit in 1771. According to Bacqueville de La Potherie [LE ROY], Joncaire also had had a wife among the Iroquois whom he had married in the 1690s.

Courageous and arrogant, ruthless and unscrupulous, hated and feared by the English whose intrigues and designs he so frequently uncovered and disrupted, admired by the Iroquois who considered him one of their own, Joncaire was a mighty agent of French influence among the Indians for over 40 years. It was with men like him that France built her wilderness empire in America.

YVES F. ZOLTVANY

AN, Col., C^{11A}, 18–70 contains a great number of references to Joncaire. AJM, Greffe d'Antoine Adhémar, 1 March 1706. Charlevoix, *Histoire*. Colden, *History of the Five Nations* (1747). *Livingston Indian Records* (Leder). *NYCD* (O'Callaghan and Fernow), IV, V, IX. Wraxall, *An abridgement of Indian affairs* (McIlwain). F. H. Severance, *An old frontier of France: the Niagara region and adjacent lakes under French control* (2v., New York, 1917).

CHABOULIÉ (Chaboillez), CHARLES, sculptor and carpenter, son of Jean Chaboulié, sculptor and carpenter, and of Marie Le Hour, of the parish of Saint-Rémi in Troyes (province of Champagne). He was born *c*. 1638, if we are to believe his death certificate, dated 20 Aug. 1708, in which he was said to be about 70; on the other hand, in the certificate of his marriage on 13 Oct. 1704 to Angélique Dandonneau Du Sablé, who was 21, he admitted to being *about* 50.

The date of his arrival in Canada is not known. Massicotte has speculated that the founder of the Brothers Hospitallers, François CHARON de La Barre, brought him back with him in 1700 after a voyage to France. It is now known that before coming to Montreal Chaboulié spent some years at Quebec and even was almost married there. He probably took part in the construction on the Place d'Armes of the Recollet monastery which

began in July 1693, and he certainly had a strong influence on the school of sculpture in that town.

On 6 May 1701 he was at Montreal and put himself at the disposal of the Brothers Hospitallers. At that time Charon perhaps intended to open an arts and crafts school with the help of Chaboulié and PIERRE LE BER. If that was so, his project was not realized, for on 7 May 1702 Chaboulié, whose enthusiasm for his tardily discovered calling had disappeared, entered into partnership with a cousin, Laurent Rousseau, *dit* Larose, a former sergeant in the colonial regular troops. Rousseau was to farm their land on the *côte* Saint-Laurent, while Chaboulié would finish the tabernacle in the Recollet chapel. Afterwards they were to live together on the fruits of their respective trades. In 1704 Chaboulié took on Charles Achard as an apprentice and undertook to teach him his sculptor's art and the carpenter's trade. Various facts lead us to believe that he was very kind; the inventory of his belongings after his death shows us that he made a comfortable living not only from his work as a sculptor, but also from carpentry.

Chaboulié had friendly connections with the sculptor Noël LEVASSEUR. In 1702, still a bachelor, he undertook to leave all his property to Levasseur's first-born.

Only remnants of Chaboulié's work are left. His important works for the chapels of the Hôtel-Dieu and the Congrégation de Notre Dame were destroyed when these buildings were burned, and the Recollets' tabernacle has disappeared. Some madonnas, one of which is in the Hôtel-Dieu, are attributed to him, as are some turned and carved candlesticks in the Hôpital Général.

His wife remarried in 1710 and about ten years later went to settle in the west; she died in 1764 at Detroit. By her marriage with Chaboulié she had three children, two daughters and a son, Charles, born in 1706, who was to be the forebear of numerous traffickers and later dealers in furs. At least two of them were intimately associated with the great bourgeois of the Compagnie du Nord-Ouest. Among the other prominent members of the family should be mentioned the notary Louis Chaboillez and the Abbé Augustin Chaboillez.

JULES BAZIN

AHDM, Livre de comptes, I (1705–1708). AJM, Greffe d'Antoine Adhémar, 6 mai 1701, 7 mai 1702, 31 mars, 8 oct. 1704; Greffe de Michel Lepailleur de Laferté, 13 mai 1703, 16 janv. 1707. AJQ, Greffe de Louis Chambalon, 6 juillet 1694, 29 juin 1695; Greffe de Guillaume Roger, 9 oct. 1695. ANDM, Registres des baptêmes, mariages et sépultures. É.-Z. Massicotte, "Inventaire des documents et des imprimés concernant la communauté des frères Charon de

Chachagouesse

l'Hôpital Général de Montréal sous le régime français," APQ *Rapport, 1923–24*, 173, 193. Gosselin, *L'Église du Canada*, I, 120. Gérard Morisset, *Coup d'œil sur les arts en Nouvelle-France* (Québec, 1941), 32, 155. É.-Z. Massicotte, "L'apprentissage au bon vieux temps," *BRH*, XLIV (1938), 365; "Les Chaboillez: une famille de traitants au XVIIIᵉ et au XIXᵉ siècles," *BRH*, XXVIII (1922), 184–88; "Quelques sculpteurs montréalais sous la domination française," *BRH*, XXXIV (1928), 538.

CHACHAGOUESSE (Chachagwessiou, Chachagouache, Chachagonache, Chachagonesse, Nicanapé), Illinois chief of Le Rocher (Starved Rock); fl. 1674–1712.

For more than 40 years Chachagouesse was a powerful chief and astute negotiator for the Illinois Indians. Father Jacques Marquette*, with whom he travelled for some 15 days in November of 1674 on Marquette's expedition to establish a mission among the Illinois, described him as "greatly esteemed among his people, partly because he engages in the fur trade." Marquette added that Chachagouesse and his companions were hard bargainers who seldom gave more for a robe than a Frenchman would, even when dealing with their own tribesmen.

In 1712, Renaud Dubuisson, commandant at Detroit, selected Chachagouesse, whom he described as a man of great authority, to travel to Montreal with Makisabi, a Potawatomi chief, to negotiate a peace settlement between the Illinois and the Miamis. Dubuisson, stressing the importance of such a peace, claimed that the Miamis had threatened to remove themselves to the Oyau River at the end of Lake Erie—the very place where the English were planning to build a fort. Throughout the deliberations, Chachagouesse, who was accompanied by his daughter, assumed a modest, beseeching pose, but despite the elaborate metaphors of his Indian oratory, he was firmly resolved to conclude peace only on condition that Frenchmen, preferably a ten-man garrison, be sent to enforce its terms and to resume trade with the Illinois. Governor Rigaud de Vaudreuil yielded to this demand and agreed to send Pierre de Liette with Chachagouesse to the Illinois and Jean-Baptiste Bissot de Vinsenne to the Miamis.

Donald J. Horton

AN, Col., C¹¹ᴬ, 33, ff.91–94, 101–2. *Early narratives of the northwest, 1634–1699*, ed. L. P. Kellogg (Original narratives of early American history, [XVII], New York, 1917), 263–66. *JR* (Thwaites), LIX, 167–75. *Michigan Pioneer Coll.*, XXXIII, 550, 559–61. *NYCD* (O'Callaghan and Fernow), IX, 865. Wis. State Hist. Soc. *Coll.*, XVI, 285. Eccles, *Frontenac*, 328–33.

CHACORNACLE (Chacornac, Chacornade), JOANNÈS DE. *See* Joannès

CHAIGNEAU (Du Chaigneau), LÉONARD, priest, Sulpician, bursar, director of schools, missionary; b. 1663 in the diocese of Limoges (France); d. 1711 at Montreal.

He entered the Society of Saint-Sulpice in 1687 and arrived in Canada on 15 August of the following year. From 1690 to 1693 he was entrusted with the bursarship of the seminary of Montreal. At that period this office was an extensive one. It comprised practically all the temporal administration of the seigneuries: the collection of the tithes and seigneurial dues, the management of the seigneurs' domain, the construction of mills, roads, parish buildings, the maintenance of the priests of Saint-Sulpice in Canada. Each year the bursar had to give a report on his administration to the ecclesiastics of the seminary in Paris, who were the seigneurs of Montreal Island. In Canada, he was answerable to some degree to the procurator [*see* Chèze]. In all matters, particularly those involving expenditure of money, the procurator superior and the bursar were supposed to take action only if they were in agreement. In case of disagreement, the question had to be referred to the council, which decided by a majority vote. Such were the principal terms of the administration of the seminary of Montreal at the time when M. Chaigneau became bursar.

According to M. Louis Tronson, the superior general, Chaigneau always executed his work carefully, and never received anything but favourable comments in Canada. It was because of his administrative abilities that on two occasions after 1693, for a few months in 1696–97 and in 1704–5, he was called in to help rectify a financial situation that was getting out of hand.

In 1696, by an act dated 15 December, Dollier de Casson placed him officially in charge of the parish schools of Montreal. He had already been taking care of them for three years: in May 1694 he had addressed a report to Bishop Saint-Vallier [La Croix] on the equipment of the schools at Ville-Marie, and the following year he had fitted out a fairly large house for the children, at a cost of 2,500 *livres*.

In 1699 his career as a parish priest began. He inaugurated his ministry on Montreal Island by serving two already established parishes: Pointe-aux-Trembles from 1699 to 1702, and Rivière-des-Prairies from 1702 to 1703. In 1704 he became the priest and missionary for the centres of settlement that were beginning to develop along the banks of the St Lawrence between Repentigny and Trois-Rivières. He applied himself to his new functions conscientiously and devotedly. He was not afraid to lay aside the ecclesiastical habit occasionally to work as a labourer, build and daub walls, quarry rocks, cut and burn wood. He had, besides, a talent for discovering resources, for accomplishing many things with little help, for making do in situations where there was nothing. People were constantly surprised at the good order which he knew how to maintain in handling the revenues of the parishes where he served, and which he left free of debts. On 14 July 1707 he was appointed priest of the parish of Notre-Dame-de-l'Assomption-de-Repentigny, one of the oldest parishes in the region. After one year he was recalled to the seminary of Ville-Marie, where he died on 23 Dec. 1711. Several acts signed by him in 1710 and 1711 allow us to suppose that after his return to Montreal he may have occupied the position of bursar and assistant procurator, which became vacant on M. Cailhe's death in July 1708.

ANTONIO DANSEREAU, P.S.S.

ASSM, Correspondance des supérieurs généraux; Section des requêtes et ordonnances. Caron, "Inventaire de documents," APQ *Rapport, 1939–40*, 317; *1940–41*, 402. [Louis Tronson], *Correspondance de M. de Tronson, troisième supérieur de la Compagnie de Saint-Sulpice: Lettres choisies*, [*16 juillet 1676–15 janv. 1700*], éd. A.-L. Bertrand (3v., Paris, 1904), II. Allaire, *Dictionnaire*. Hormidas Magnan, *Dictionnaire historique et géographique des paroisses, missions et municipalités de la province de Québec* (Arthabaska, Qué., 1925). Azarie Couillard Després, *Histoire de Sorel, de ses origines à nos jours* (Montréal, 1926). Gauthier, *Sulpitiana* (Montréal, 1926). *Histoire des paroisses du diocèse de Montréal* (Annuaire de Montréal, II, Montréal, 1867–82). É.-Z. Massicotte, "Fondation d'une communauté de frères instituteurs à Montréal en 1686," *BRH*, XXVIII (1922), 40.

CHAMBALON, LOUIS, merchant and royal notary; b. *c.* 1663; originally from Notre-Dame de Mirebeau in the bishopric of Poitiers, son of Louis Chambalon, a doctor, and of Marie Prieur; buried 15 June 1716 in the parish church of Quebec.

Chambalon arrived in Canada in 1688 or shortly before. He was first a clerk with Messrs Hazeur, merchants at Quebec. On 2 Oct. 1689, in return for a salary of 1,000 *livres* a year and the right to do a little fur-trading on his own account, he promised Nicolas PERROT that he would accompany him into the Ottawa country as his assistant business agent. He left for the *pays d'en haut* in March 1690, and probably came back in the spring of 1691. On 12 June of that year, at Quebec, he married Marie-Anne Pinguet, the widow of his former employer, Léonard Hazeur Des Ormeaux. From that time on Chambalon's

public role was that of a merchant, importing all sorts of products from France and supplying the voyageurs engaged in the fur trade. It was perhaps with an eye to his business that he sought the grant of an arriere-fief measuring three leagues by six in the seigneury of Ristigouche (on Baie des Chaleurs), which Pierre Rey Gaillard granted him on 17 June 1698.

After Gilles Rageot*'s death at the beginning of 1692, Chambalon the merchant had received from Champigny [BOCHART] a commission as royal notary, which was confirmed by Louis XIV on 10 April 1694. Chambalon practised until his death and was the busiest notary of his time. His registry contains nearly 4,000 minutes. Being related through his first wife to the bourgeoisie of the colony, he had as his clients the élite of Quebec society, and his services were often sought by the governors and intendants. He did not try to hold several offices at the same time, and he never appeared before the Conseil Souverain as a legal practitioner.

To all appearances Chambalon was less impecunious than his colleagues, but it is not certain that this was true in reality. He was, for example, one of the shareholders in the Compagnie de la Colonie, having subscribed 4,000 *livres*; but a memorandum of the period affirms that he had no money and many debts. In truth, that was the sad fate of nearly all business men in New France; they retained from the fur trade a very small portion of the profits, almost all of which were pocketed by the suppliers and ship-owners of the mother country. Chambalon's situation was to become still worse. Suffering terribly from gout and violent chest pains, so much so that he was helpless two months out of three, he had to give up his business activities, probably around 1706. In 1707, because of Chambalon's decreased activity, the intendant appointed Jean-Étienne DUBREUIL notary at Quebec. Two years later Chambalon sought from the king a pension, which he does not appear to have received. In 1710, in an effort to keep his practice, which was still impressive, he took on a clerk, René-Claude Barolet*, who was appointed notary in 1728.

Having lost his first wife in April 1694, Chambalon had taken as his second wife Geneviève Roussel, on 9 August of the same year. By his first marriage he had two children, who did not live, and none by the second. He did however look after his first wife's son, Charles Hazeur, who was ordained a priest in 1706, and also Catherine-Madeleine Renaud de Desmeloizes, who lived in his home and later became an Ursuline. In 1699 he also sheltered a cousin, François Aubert, who caused him some unpleasantness. Indeed, Aubert

Champigny

"led astray" one of Chambalon's servants in Chambalon's own house. The servant became pregnant, the matter was brought before the courts, and as for Chambalon, he was sentenced to advance Aubert 50 *livres* to meet the child's most pressing needs. This was certainly a humiliating experience for the worthy notary, whose piety, it was said, "was edifying to the whole town of Quebec," and who was furthermore, around this period, one of the directors of the Hôpital Général. In reality, however, Chambalon had no part in this scandal, any more than he had in the Mareuil* affair or in that of the *prie-dieu*, in which he had been involved despite himself, in his role as notary, in 1694.

Geneviève Roussel survived her husband and lived until October 1738.

ANDRÉ VACHON

AJQ, Greffe de Gilles Rageot, 11 juin 1691; Greffe de Guillaume Roger, 8 août 1694. AQ, NF, Ins. de la Prév. de Québec, I, 760; III, 121; IV, 333. "Correspondance de Vaudreuil," APQ *Rapport, 1942–43*, 424; *1946–47*, 445. *Jug. et délib.* "Lettre de M. de Lamothe Cadillac, 28 sept. 1694," APQ *Rapport, 1923–24*, 81, 84. *Ord. comm.* (P.-G. Roy), II, 235f. P.-G. Roy, *Inv. concessions*, IV, 54. "Liste générale des intéressés en la compagnie de la colonie du Canada, et des actions qu'ils y ont prises," *BRH*, XL (1934), 498. Tanguay, *Dictionnaire*, I, 112. J.-E. Roy, *Histoire du notariat*, I. P.-G. Roy, *La ville de Québec*, II, 498. *Les Ursulines de Québec* (1863–66), II, 216.

CHAMPIGNY, JEAN BOCHART DE. *See* BOCHART

CHAMPION DE CICÉ, LOUIS-ARMAND, priest, Sulpician, missionary in Canada, vicar apostolic to Siam; b. 24 Sept. 1648 at Bruz, in the diocese of Rennes, son of Charles Champion de Cicé and Judith Thévin; d. 1727 in Siam.

While still young he showed an inclination for missionary work. He entered the seminary of Saint-Sulpice in Paris and asked to be sent to Canada, where he arrived in 1674. He replaced his *confrère*, Salignac* de La Mothe-Fénelon, at the mission to the Iroquois at Kenté (Quinte). In collaboration with Claude TROUVÉ, the mission superior, Joseph Mariet, Ranuyer, and some others, he worked at evangelizing the Cayugas who hunted and fished in this region.

In 1681 he was recalled to France by family matters. He left the Society of Saint-Sulpice to enrol in the Société des Missions Étrangères, which entrusted him with an important mission in China. In 1699 he was back again in France, when the famous quarrel of the "Missions d'Orient" broke out. He took sides with his congregation against the Jesuits, who tolerated the survival of pagan rites among their converts. On being informed of his abilities and his zeal, the pope appointed him vicar apostolic to Siam. He was consecrated in 1701 at Saint-Brieuc, with the title of bishop of Sabula, and left immediately for the Orient. He founded numerous charitable works and always maintained good relations with the ruling dynasty. He died in April 1727, leaving behind him the memory of an active priest who was esteemed by all.

ARMAND YON

PAC, FM 17, A 3, 21, f.12. Henri Gauthier, *Sulpitiana* (Montréal, 1926). Olivier Maurault, *Nos Messieurs* (Montréal, 1936). Comte E.-L.-M.-A. de Palys, *Un Breton en Indo-Chine au XVIII⁰ siècle: notice sur Monseigneur de Cicé* (Vannes, 1892).

CHAMPY, GÉLASE, priest, Recollet, provincial commissioner; b. 1657 at Sézanne; d. 1 Dec. 1738 at Saint-Germain en Laye.

Gélase Champy entered the Recollet order in 1678. He must have been appointed guardian of the convent in Quebec at the provincial chapter held in Paris on 5 June 1701, for on 1 Oct. 1702 he was in office. Indeed he took part in a meeting of the council of the Franciscan mission in Canada, presided over by Father JOSEPH DENYS, the provincial commissioner. This assembly, held at Quebec and attended also by Fathers Luc FILIASTRE and Élisée Crey, the superiors of Trois-Rivières and Montreal, had to approve the settlement of certain debts. The council decided to part with a house belonging to the mission; CALLIÈRE, the apostolic syndic of the Recollets, was also present, and signed the minutes.

Father Champy did not know at the time that on 26 June 1703, less than a year later, he would have the painful duty of delivering Callière's funeral oration. Mother JEANNE-FRANÇOISE JUCHEREAU de Saint-Ignace, who reported the event, added: "without doubt he gave him well merited praise, for one could not say enough good of this great man." She wrongly attributed to Champy the title of provincial commissioner, an office that he was to hold from 1707 to 1710. In November 1703 Father Champy went to France to attend the provincial chapter which was to be held in Paris on 18 April 1704. During his four-year stay in France he made use of his talents as an orator; they were much sought after particularly by the Recollets of the Rue du Bac. In addition, he kept the cause of the missions in Canada well to the fore, so much so that in 1707 the provincial chapter of Paris appointed him provincial commissioner of the Canadian mission and president (guardian) of the convent in Quebec. He succeeded Father Apollinaire Luteau.

His term of office was marked by no outstanding achievement. We may note that on 6 June 1708, in the chapel of his convent, he officiated at the burial of PIERRE DENYS de La Ronde, the father of the first Canadian Recollet, Father Joseph. Champy's last official act in Canada was the signing of a petition dated 21 Oct. 1709; this document, addressed to the intendant, JACQUES RAUDOT, and cosigned by all the superiors of the communities of men and women, requested that the annual allowance, which was slow in coming, be finally paid.

We do not know the date of his return to France. We do know, however, that from 1716 on he devoted himself to preaching in the Franciscan convents of Saint-Jean de Belleville, Saint-Sauveur, and Paris. He died on 1 Dec. 1738 at the age of 81 and after 60 years of religious life.

JACQUES VALOIS

BN, MS, NAF 1827, f.81. "Un éloge funèbre du gouverneur de Callières," APQ *Rapport, 1921–22*, 228–32. *Gazette de France* (Paris), 29 juillet 1703. Juchereau, *Annales* (Jamet), 312. Jouve, *Les Franciscains et le Canada: aux Trois-Rivières*, 74, 78, 87, 90.

CHANGOUESSI (Changouessy, Changouossy).
See CHINGOUESSI

CHAPTES, JEAN-LOUIS DE LA CORNE DE.
See LA CORNE

CHARLY SAINT-ANGE, JEAN-BAPTISTE (he signed Charly), Montreal merchant, colonel of militia, churchwarden; b. 17 Aug. 1668 in Montreal; d. 9 Nov. 1728 in Quebec.

He was the eldest surviving son of André Charly, *dit* Saint-Ange, and Marie Dumesnil, both of whom were brought as immigrants to Montreal by Chomedey* de Maisonneuve in the 1650s. Jean-Baptiste appears to have been held in high esteem by his contemporaries as was his father before him. In 1707 and 1724 he was elected churchwarden of Notre-Dame de Montréal and at some time was appointed colonel of militia. He improved upon his father's economic position by engaging in the fur trade. In 1691 he was hired by a Montreal merchant to make a trip to the Ottawa country to trade. By 1700 he had become a merchant and creditor himself, and was an original shareholder in the ill-fated Compagnie de la Colonie. Improvements to his house in Montreal in 1691, the acquisition of a house in Quebec and another in Montreal prior to 1715, and the probable purchase of a tract of land on Île Jésus in 1712, attest to his increasing affluence. The depressed state of the fur trade during the War of the Spanish Succession seems not to have harmed him seriously. With the revival of the trade Charly emerged a respectable merchant, financing numerous expeditions to the western posts after 1720.

On 3 July 1701 he married the eldest daughter of Louis LE CONTE Dupré, Marie-Charlotte, who died in 1705. On 18 Sept. 1722 he married Louise-Catherine d'Ailleboust de Manthet, daughter of NICOLAS; after his death, Louise-Catherine married Pierre-Jacques*, only son of Pierre PAYEN de Noyan (17 Nov. 1731). Jean-Baptiste left a prosperous business to his sons by his first marriage, Jacques Charly and Louis Charly Saint-Ange, in spite of a successful law suit by his widow over the inheritance. Louis in particular became a very prominent merchant in Montreal, investing heavily in the western trade and in several speculative mining ventures. Jacques, though less successful in trade, married Thérèse Charest, only daughter of the wealthy Étienne Charest, seigneur of Lauson.

Jean-Baptiste's only surviving son by his second marriage, Jean-Baptiste-François (b. 1728), chose a military career. In 1750 he obtained a commission as ensign in the troops of Île Royale (Cape Breton Island), and in 1758 was transferred to Canada where he served with distinction in the campaign of 1759. For this he was appointed major of Île Gorée in Senegal in 1766. Thus, by acquiring social status and fortune through the fur trade, Jean-Baptiste opened for his sons the major avenues of advancement: a substantial business in the fur trade; marriage into a prominent family; and a commission in the colonial regular troops.

Jean-Baptiste Charly died while on a trip to Quebec in 1728. His respectable position in the colony is reflected by the fact that he was buried in the cathedral of Notre-Dame de Québec on 9 November, under the name Jean-Baptiste Saint-Ange, Sieur de Charly.

S. DALE STANDEN

Jug. et délib., VI, 900, 926f., 1015f., 1022–26, 1071f. PAC *Report*, 1899, Supp., 101, 110. P.-G. Roy, *Inv. jug. et délib., 1717–1760*, I, 222, 225; II, 213f.; III, 3, 24. P.-G. et A. Roy, *Inv. greffes not.*, I, 154, 196; VI, 64; IX, 184; X, 78; XII; XIX, 514; XXI. Charland, "Notre-Dame de Québec: le nécrologe de la crypte," 180f. Massicotte, "Répertoire des engagements pour l'Ouest." Tanguay, *Dictionnaire*, I, 117, 153; III, 19, 266; VI, 265.

Aegidius Fauteux, *La famille d'Ailleboust* (Montréal, 1917), 126–28. P.-G. Roy, *La famille Charly Saint-Ange* (Lévis, 1945), 1–15 [This book is in error about the age of Jean-Baptiste Charly's sons when he died in 1728. s.d.s.]. R.-L. Séguin, *La civilisation traditionnelle de l' "Habitant" aux XVIIᵉ et XVIIIᵉ*

Charly Saint-Ange

siècles (Montréal, [1967]), 319–21, 328. "Les familles Roy au Canada," *BRH*, XXXI (1925), 527. O. Lapalice, "Louis Charly Saint-Ange, marguillier de Notre-Dame de Montréal," *BRH*, XXXIV (1928), 426–29.

CHARLY SAINT-ANGE, MARIE-CATHE-RINE, *dite* **du Saint-Sacrement,** known in religion, in the Congrégation de Notre-Dame, as Sister Saint-Ange and from 1700 on as Sister du Saint-Sacrement; b. 1666 at Ville-Marie; superior general of the Congrégation, 1708–11, 1717–19; d. at Ville-Marie 1719.

Her father, André Charly, *dit* Saint-Ange, originally from the parish of Saint-Gervais in Paris, arrived in 1651 in Montreal, where he acquired and farmed a piece of land near the river. In 1654 he married Marie Dumesnil. Four of their daughters belonged to the community founded by Sister Bourgeoys*.

Catherine joined the young community when she was 13 and became one of its most active and influential members. She was only 27 when she was elected counsellor to the new superior, Sister Marie BARBIER. Five years later she was entrusted with the office of novice-mistress. In 1698, when each sister of the Congrégation de Notre-Dame gave up her family name to assume a name in religion, Sister Charly chose that of Sister Saint-Ange.

Catherine Charly's memory is forever linked with that of Sister Bourgeoys' death in January 1700. An account based upon the letters of the sisters of the Congrégation de Notre-Dame, which are reproduced by GLANDELET in his monograph, tells us that, upon learning that Sister Saint-Ange was going to die, Sister Bourgeoys prayed God to take her in place of this young sister; some days later, when Sister Saint-Ange had recovered her health, Sister Bourgeoys died. As a mark of gratitude Sister Saint-Ange called herself Sister du Saint-Sacrement, the name in religion which Sister Bourgeoys had taken in 1698.

Elected superior-general in 1708, Sister Charly, *dite* du Saint-Sacrement, proved to be a woman of remarkable wisdom in the face of great difficulties which threatened the community at that time. Vaudreuil [RIGAUD] and JACQUES RAUDOT, who were aware of Bishop Saint-Vallier's [LA CROIX] desire to make the Congrégation de Notre-Dame a cloistered community and who disapproved of it, wrote to Pontchartrain to obtain a formal written interdiction of this project. But the king's reply went beyond the expectations of the governor and the intendant, who thus unintentionally jeopardized the stability of the Congrégation. The minister replied in fact that His Majesty would never allow his sisters to be cloistered or to take

vows, and that if they were doing so, he insisted that the minister forbid it. But the privilege of taking vows, which had been granted the Congrégation de Notre-Dame in 1698, ensured the community of a prestige and stability which facilitated the recruiting of members. The annals of the Congrégation de Notre-Dame have preserved the letters which were written by Sister Catherine Charly to Pontchartrain, Bishop Saint-Vallier, and the Marquise de Maintenon, whom she asked "to use her influence with the King." In these letters she shows herself to be admirably adroit: while using very respectful formulae, she succeeds in expressing clearly her desire to see His Majesty continue to forbid the sisters to be cloistered but not forbid them to take vows. The king did not grant her request, but the superior-general was sufficiently skilful to get around the difficulty; in agreement with the civil and ecclesiastical authorities of the country she continued to have simple vows pronounced, but in secret. After the king's death and Pontchartrain's departure, Raudot was instructed by the ministry of Marine to settle virtually by himself all these matters concerning Canada, which put an end to the intervention by the government of France in the question of the nuns' vows.

Sister Catherine Charly was re-elected superior in 1717 and had to cope with pecuniary difficulties during this period. She died in the exercise of this office in January 1719.

HÉLÈNE BERNIER

ACND, Charles Glandelet, Le vray esprit de Marguerite Bourgeoys et de l'Institut des sœurs séculières de la Congrégation de Notre-Dame établie à Ville-Marie en l'Isle de Montréal en Canada, 1701. ANDM, Registres des baptêmes, mariages et sépultures. [É.-M. Faillon], *Vie de la Sœur Bourgeoys, fondatrice de la Congrégation de Notre-Dame de Villemarie en Canada, suivie de l'histoire de cet institut jusqu'à ce jour* (2v., Ville-Marie [Montréal], 1853). Albert Jamet, *Marguerite Bourgeoys, 1620–1700* (2v., Montréal, 1942). "La famille Charly Saint-Ange," *BRH*, LI (1945), 91–105.

CHARON DE LA BARRE, FRANÇOIS (he signed fs Charon), merchant, founder of the Brothers Hospitallers of the Cross and of St Joseph, as well as of the Hôpital Général of Montreal; b. 7 Sept. 1654 at Quebec, son of Claude Charron* and Claude Camus (Le Camus); d. shortly after 9 July 1719 at sea on board the king's flute *Chameau*.

Mother JEANNE-FRANÇOISE JUCHEREAU de Saint-Ignace tells us that his parents sent him to France to study, which would explain his fine handwriting. The son of a rich notable of Quebec, François Charon chose to live at Montreal, the cross-roads for the trade in pelts, where he became a money-lender to the fur-traders. His father must have helped him, for on 25 Oct. 1684, when the joint estate of his parents was being divided up shortly after his mother's death, François acknowledged that he owed his father the sum of 10,000 *livres* in French money, by a promissory note dated 30 Oct. 1683. In August 1683 Charon was one of the four Montreal merchants who had Cavelier* de La Salle's furs at Fort Frontenac seized. In partnership with Charles Catignon, the king's storekeeper at Quebec, François prospered. During the summer of 1688 alone the partners advanced more than 40,000 *livres* in money and goods to those holding fur-trading permits. At the bottom of the notarial recognizances are to be found the names of the most important fur-traders of the time.

On 4 Aug. 1687 François had been chosen to be the guardian of the under-age children of his father and his father's second wife Élisabeth Damours. On the preceding 27 April he had signed an act before the notary Gilles Rageot* by virtue of a power of attorney from his father. Claude Charron seems therefore to have died sometime between these two dates.

According to various leases, François Charon lived at Montreal in houses rented on Rue Saint-Paul; in the one belonging to Jean-Vincent Philippe de Hautmesnyl he fell so seriously ill in the autumn of 1687 that he had to dictate his will on 26 November. The will was revoked on 12 March 1688; this time Charon was living in the house of the widow Le Moyne [Thierry], situated on the Place du Marché. In his will François Charon left the major part of his possessions to the poor of the town, and he revoked it, not to deprive them but in order to assist them more effectively. It seems that in the face of death life had appeared to him in a new light, and having recovered his health he resolved to follow henceforth the precepts of the gospels by practising charity. In this frame of mind he decided to found an almshouse at Montreal for old men in need.

The religious spirit which had presided over the founding of Ville-Marie was still very much alive there. The brothers PIERRE LE BER and Jean Le Ber Du Chesne, along with Jean Fredin, joined with Charon to make his charitable project into a reality. This project, solidly based on the associates' fortunes and their honesty, inspired confidence in the people of Montreal, who showed their generosity through gifts, legacies, annuities, and loans on favourable terms. The benefits conferred by this almshouse were so evident that as early as 28 Oct. 1688 DOLLIER de Casson, representing the seigneurs of Montreal Island, granted

the associates nine acres of land at Pointe-à-Callières. The associates' aim was clearly stated in the deed of grant: "to join together to found a hospital for men in this place, and . . . create for it a community of Brothers of Charity." On 3 Oct. 1689 Charon dissolved the company that he had formed with Charles Catignon, and gave up the guardianship of his half-brother, on 25 May 1691, in order to devote himself more freely to the building of his hospice. He obtained from the Conseil Souverain on 31 Aug. 1692 the authorization to begin construction. By 17 October of that year, before the notary Antoine ADHÉMAR, Charon signed the first contract with Jean Tessier, *dit* Lavigne, by the terms of which the latter would furnish the lime, at 60 *sous* a barrel, the fieldstone, and the quoins necessary for constructing the building.

Soon a handsome three-storey stone building with a slate roof—the future Hôpital Général—could be seen rising outside the town's walls. It had a frontage of 90 feet and a depth of 30, and was flanked by two 30-foot wings; it contained 24 rooms in addition to the offices. Sister Marie MORIN, the annalist of the Hôtel-Dieu, wrote that it "already surpasses all the others in accommodation." On 1 June 1694 the first needy person was admitted, Pierre Chevalier, an idiot of about 40 years of age.

The recruiting of the Brothers Hospitallers continued as well as could be expected, despite the death of Jean Le Ber Du Chesne, killed by an Iroquois arrow on 31 Aug. 1691. He had bequeathed his land grant at Pointe Saint-Charles to the associates. When Jean Fredin went to France in 1700, never to return, the founders were reduced to two. But already some recruits had joined this nucleus and as early as 2 Oct. 1694 Bishop Saint-Vallier [LA CROIX] granted them permission to live as a community, to perform the duties of Hospitallers, to construct a small belfry to ring for services, to have mass said, and to keep the Holy Sacrament. Once he had obtained the local authorizations, Charon applied for royal assent, without which no establishment had any chance of surviving in New France. The letters patent signed by Louis XIV on 15 April 1694 stipulated that "this almshouse is authorized to receive poor orphan children, [the] crippled, the old men, the infirm, and other needy members of their sex . . . to teach crafts to the aforesaid children and to give them the best possible education, all this under the jurisdiction of the heads of the colony." In their joint letter of 20 Oct. 1699, CALLIÈRE and BOCHART de Champigny wrote: "A House which will be useful to the colony is that of the Brothers Hospitallers which has been established in

Charon de La Barre

Montreal. It has so far cost the country nothing, yet it does a great deal of good. There is a ward full of poor people . . . they are well cared for there."

Bishop LAVAL, writing that same year to Abbé Tremblay, superior of the Missions Étrangères in Paris, said: "Render all possible service to M. Charon as to the missionaries themselves. He is a true servant of God." Charon had indeed lent two of his brothers to the missionaries of the seminary of Quebec for their missions to the Tamaroas. One of them, Brother Alexandre Turpin, remained there for two years, and François de Montigny* praises him as follows: "Brother Alexandre, a Hospitaller from Montreal, who had accompanied us on this journey and who had edified us the whole way by his worthy behaviour and principally by his charity towards our sick people, having gone to the sick child, baptized him without any difficulty, the mother having no fear of him." The Indian women used to flee at the approach of the Black Robes, with the result that the priests were not able to administer baptism to dying children. Brother Alexandre took the missionary's place on this occasion, and perhaps on others too.

The work of Charon also received encouragement from Louis XIV. Indeed, on 5 May 1700, the king granted an annual gratuity of 1,000 *livres* for the work of the Hôpital Général of Montreal. Bishop Saint-Vallier then delegated his vicar-general, Joseph de LA COLOMBIÈRE, to form the associates into a religious community according to canonical rules. The community of the Brothers Hospitallers of the Cross and of St Joseph was thus regularly established. It should be noted that the official documents from the court refer to them only as the Hospitallers of Montreal or the associates of M. Charon. The people called them the Charon Brothers.

On 25 April 1701 the brothers adopted a uniform habit which their constitutions described as follows: "The habits of the brothers are simple and modest, rather like the frock-coat of the ecclesiastics. The jacket, breeches, and stockings will be black, as will be the habit. The professed will be distinguished from the novices by a woollen cross which they will wear on the breast over their habit and which will come down over the top of the jacket. The bands and cuffs may be of cambric provided they are not too costly." On 17 May 1702 six brothers, headed by François Charon, pronounced the simple provisional vows of religion according to the Rule of St Augustine in the presence of M. de La Colombière who was assisted by M. VACHON de Belmont. Pierre Le Ber, however, declined to take vows and to wear the uniform habit, although he continued to live in the almshouse until his death on 11 March 1707.

François Charon had cleared fairly easily all the stages involved in setting up his foundation, but as soon as he tried to make a religious community of it he ran up against a host of difficulties, particularly the king's opposition. In a letter dated 30 June 1707, Pontchartrain [Jérôme Phélypeaux] clearly indicated the king's prohibitions, which had been outlined in several letters since 1700. Louis XIV forbad the brothers to take religious vows, to wear a uniform habit, and to call themselves brothers. This refusal to permit the taking of religious vows undermined enthusiasm; some brothers left the community and nobody came forward to fill the ranks. No spiritual master was ready to take on the responsibility of moulding these men of goodwill into a cohesive whole. Charon, who had been elected superior in 1704, was well aware of this, since he attempted, in vain, to unite his community with that of Saint-Sulpice or with the seminary of Quebec. On 6 June 1708, the king repeated his orders, but Charon de La Barre had already gone to France in the autumn of 1707 to plead his cause before the court. RUETTE d'Auteuil claimed in his report of 1712 that Charon was still dancing attendance upon the minister: "Charon, an intelligent man, keenly observant in all things and capable of making good reports, has been languishing in Paris for five years, vainly seeking permission to return to Canada to give support to his establishment, which is in the last stages of collapse."

In accordance with the letters patent authorizing the foundation, which prescribed the teaching of crafts to orphans, and after securing specific letters patent to this end dated 30 Aug. 1699, Charon made several attempts to create some small industries. He had set up three crafts at the Hôpital Général, and, in 1719, on the occasion of his last trip to France, he hired "the Sieurs Darles and Souste, workers and manufacturers of silk and woollen stockings," in order to establish a factory. He had made one other attempt, to establish a brewery. This lucrative operation soon became a source of vexations, even occasionally of disorders. Having lost grain and beer for lack of proper milling, Charon decided to build himself a mill on the grounds of the hospital. As milling was the exclusive privilege of the seigneurs, there resulted stubborn and protracted differences between the Sulpicians, who were seigneurs of Montreal Island, and the Hospitallers. Charon de La Barre was thus carrying on many enterprises at once. In 1700 he had requested permission to open a hospital for the sick at the post at Detroit which Cadillac [LAUMET] proposed to establish.

134

The court had rejected his plan on receiving a report by the Sieur CLAIRAMBAULT d'Aigremont, who had been instructed to inquire into it.

Finally, Charon wished to accomplish more than the letters patent of 15 April 1694 required. There was already a primary school at the Hôpital Général, and Charon tried in vain, from about 1708 on, to extend teaching to the country districts. It was not until 1717 that Bégon* endorsed this initiative, and that Charon went to France to obtain royal approval. In the spring of 1718, provided with his letters patent, Charon returned to Canada with six schoolmasters. The king granted an annual allowance of 3,000 *livres*, on the express condition that there be maintained at least six masters for the free teaching of boys in the country districts. Once the schoolmasters who had been so painfully recruited here and there in France got to Canada, they did not persevere for long in their teaching. The tenacious Charon undertook another round of recruiting on French soil in 1719. He was returning with six other schoolmasters on board the king's flute the *Chameau*, when death overtook him on the 17th day of the crossing. To execute his will, which had been dictated 9 July 1719 at 1 PM to the Sieur de Saint-Eugène, king's clerk, he had appointed Louis Turc* de Castelveyre, one of the six schoolmasters.

Previously on 2 Feb. 1710, in a solemn deed, François Charon had given over to the poor of the Hôpital Général all the sums of money which he had personally paid for the building of the hospital; the chapel alone had cost 49,414 *livres*. He had endowed Montreal with its first hospice for old men, at a total cost of 23,016 *livres*. Charon was the founder of the only male community ever created in Canada. His charity and piety were beyond dispute. Deploring his death, Bishop Saint-Vallier wrote: "what consoles us all is that his death was as saintly as his life." At Montreal this bereavement was marked by public prayers.

Bishop Saint-Vallier, acting, as he believed, in accordance with the founder's views, appointed Louis Turc, who adopted the name in religion of Brother Chrétien, superior of the community. It was at that time composed of five of the original Hospitallers although 22 had been admitted since the beginning. Before entering upon his office, Brother Chrétien had an inventory of the community's possessions drawn up by the notary Adhémar on 25 Oct. 1719.

However, Brother Chrétien did not have the business sense possessed by François Charon, and during his administration from 1720 to 1735 the community suffered a number of disappointments. In 1731, for lack of schoolmasters, the king withdrew from the Brothers Hospitallers the annual allowance of 3,000 *livres*, and Bishop Pierre-Herman Dosquet* forbad the brothers to receive other persons. In addition, following a legal action that lasted five years, they were obliged to pay their creditors 24,419 *livres*, 19 *sols*, 10 *deniers*. This debt, added to the already considerable ones owed by the hospital, hastened its ruin. The judgement pronounced in April 1735 recognized Brother Chrétien's integrity but also his deplorable incompetence. In 1747 there remained at the hospice only three octogenarian brothers, who begged the authorities to relieve them of the administration both of this vast, broken-down building and of the four old men who were vegetating in it. The hospital activity launched by François Charon had lasted for 53 years by the time it passed into the skilful hands of Mme d'Youville [Dufrost*].

IN COLLABORATION WITH
ALBERTINE FERLAND-ANGERS

AJM, Greffe d'Antoine Adhémar; Greffe de Bénigne Basset, 26 nov. 1687, 3 oct. 1689; Greffe de Pierre Raimbault. AN, Col., B, 29, ff.194, 374; 40; C¹¹ᴬ, 39, ff.391, 393; 40, f.23; 41, f.170; 82; F³, 7, f.1. ANDQ, Registres des baptêmes, mariages et sépultures, 9 sept. 1654. ASGM, Concession par M. Dollier de Casson à M. Charon, 28 oct. 1688; Constitution pour les Frères Hospitaliers de la Croix et de Saint Joseph, observations de la règle de Saint Augustin; Lettres patentes de confirmation de l'Hôpital-général de Montréal et Maîtres d'école, 1ᵉʳ févr. 1718; Lettres patentes pour l'établissement d'un Hôpital à Ville-Marie dans l'Île de Montréal, 15 avril 1694; Lettres patentes pour l'établissement des manufactures d'arts et métiers à l'Hôpital-général de Montréal, 30 mai 1699; Registre de l'admission des pauvres et des sépultures; Registre des vêtures, professions, sépultures et visites canoniques des Frères Hospitaliers, 1701–1748; Testament de Frère Charon de La Barre, 9 juillet 1719. ASQ, Fonds Verreau, M. Saberdache; Lettres, R, 41–73. Juchereau, *Annales* (Jamet). "Lettres et mémoires de F.-M.-F. Ruette d'Auteuil," APQ *Rapport, 1922–23*, 1–114.

É.-Z. Massicotte, "Inventaire des documents et des imprimés concernant la communauté des frères Charon et l'Hôpital Général de Montréal sous le régime français," APQ *Rapport, 1923–24*, 163–201. Camille Bertrand, *Histoire de Montréal* (2v., Paris et Montréal, 1935, 1942. [É.-M. Faillon], *Vie de Mme d'Youville, fondatrice des Sœurs de la Charité de Villemarie dans l'Île de Montréal en Canada* (Ville-Marie [Montréal], 1852). Gosselin, *L'Église du Canada.*

CHARTIER DE LOTBINIÈRE, RENÉ-LOUIS, esquire, seigneur, deputy attorney general, councillor, lieutenant general on the bench of the provost and admiralty courts of Quebec, sub-delegate of the intendant, militia officer, and agent

Chartier de Lotbinière

general of the Compagnie de la Colonie; baptized 14 Nov. 1641 in the church of Saint-Nicolas-des-Champs in Paris, son of Louis-Théandre Chartier* de Lotbinière and Élisabeth Damours; d. 3 June 1709 at Quebec.

Born of a family that had been ennobled at the beginning of the 15th century, René-Louis Chartier was the grandson of the famous René-Pierre Chartier, doctor in ordinary to Louis XIII and professor of surgery at the Collège Royal. The Chartiers were connected by marriage with some of the better families of France; thus, through his mother, René-Louis was related to Jean de Lauson* (senior), formerly intendant of the provinces of Provence, Guyenne, and Dauphiné, director of the Compagnie des Cent-Associés, and future governor of New France. The Lotbinière family probably came to Canada with Lauson, who landed at Quebec on 13 Oct. 1651.

Not yet ten years old when he arrived, René-Louis was at an age to receive vivid and lasting impressions. A gigantic river, immense mountains and forests, decked out in their autumn colours, endless expanses, and the half-naked Indians who hastened to meet the ship in their swift bark canoes—could a little boy ever forget all these things? René-Louis was also at the age at which one adapts best to a new life. He attended the Jesuit college in Quebec. There he met every day with dauntless missionaries, discoverers and geographers as well as apostles, who sailed fabulous rivers and lakes and preached the gospel to distant tribes with strange customs. How little he must have missed the confined, noisy, muddy Paris of his time! When the boy was nearing the end of his classical studies, Governor VOYER d'Argenson arrived at Quebec. In a play improvised for the occasion and presented at the college on 28 July 1658, René-Louis played the role of the "spirit of the forests, the interpreter for the strangers." Spirit of the forests! Could the erstwhile little Parisian have dreamt of a finer title?

Upon his return into the wings of the improvised stage at the Jesuit college, René-Louis Chartier disappears from our sight for several years. (Is it not within the power of spirits to disappear thus, without leaving any trace?) He is mentioned once, on 29 Jan. 1662, when Dubois* Davagour granted him some pieces of land on the St Charles River which had belonged to the Recollets (and which Chartier gave back to them 23 Oct. 1670, when they returned to Canada). Then all is silence until 1666. We encounter him briefly at Quebec in 1667 and 1668, then meet him again in 1670. It is impossible to say how he spent all this time. If we had the eyes of Lynkeus, we should perhaps catch frequent glimpses of him as, wearing snowshoes

and carrying a musket, he tirelessly scoured the woods around Quebec, which abounded in game. He was undoubtedly used to long excursions in the forest, as he was to demonstrate on two occasions in 1666.

Rémy* de Courcelle was preparing his ill-starred adventure into the Iroquois country. A few Canadian settlers joined the soldiers, who had recently arrived from France. René-Louis Chartier was one of them. Hastily prepared and carried out in winter by troops who had no experience of the country, the expedition was fraught with extraordinary difficulties because of the excessive cold and the lack of food. Like the good Canadian that he had become, René-Louis would have come out of it very well, had it not been for a slight wound that he had received in action and the fact that on the way back he was dazzled by the snow and ice and lost his sight for three days. The little army encountered nothing but disappointments and returned without achieving any of its designs of conquest. A new and more ambitious attempt was made in September 1666. This time the Mohawk villages were ravaged, and on 17 October they were officially taken over. In his capacity as "lieutenant of a company of Quebeck citizens" Chartier de Lotbinière signed the report, which was drawn up in Iroquois territory by the royal notary Pierre Duquet*.

After his return from the first expedition Chartier, who in 1666 and 1667 was still living in his father's home, had composed a burlesque poem (a *genre* much in fashion in France), which recounted "Monsieur de Courcelles' trip" into the Iroquois country in 510 lines (500 octosyllabics and 10 alexandrines). It is certainly the first poem written by a Canadian, or by a Frenchman educated in New France, to receive historical mention. This is, moreover, the principal merit of this curious poem: it is long, boring, and hardly poetic, to tell the truth, but not without documentary value. Among the least objectionable lines may be mentioned the following:

> Après ces beaux exploits et ces travaux
> guerriers
> Grand Courcelle admirant l'objet de vos
> lauriers
> En sérieux je diray que les peines dherculle
> Que celles dAllexandre & dAuguste et de
> Julle
> Ont eu beaucoup desclat mais leur ont moins
> cousté ...

> After these noble exploits and these toils of
> war,
> Great Courcelle, admiring the deeds which
> earned you your laurels

136

In all seriousness I shall say that the labours
    of Hercules,
Of Alexander, Augustus, and Caesar,
Received great renown but cost them less
    effort . . .

In toying with the muse in this way René-Louis
perhaps had in mind that Alain Chartier, who died
in 1455, whose direct descendant he was and to
whom he owed his noble rank, had been in his
time a prose-writer of merit, if not a great poet—
which we have not forgotten in our own day.

At the beginning of 1670, except for his military
role of 1666, René-Louis Chartier had not yet
performed any public function. Had this young
nobleman been content with an idle existence
devoted entirely to hunting and rambles, or was he
studying law with his father, the principal law
officer in the seneschal's and then the provost
court of Quebec? The latter hypothesis is almost
certainly correct, unless he had gone to study in
Paris. On 13 Jan. 1670, in any event, he was
installed in the office of deputy attorney general to
the Conseil Souverain. But from the death of Jean
Bourdon* on 12 Jan. 1668 to the appointment of
Denis-Joseph Ruette* d'Auteuil on 29 May 1674,
there was no regularly appointed attorney general
to the council, and it was the deputy who carried
out the duties of the office. This was, consequently, a heavy responsibility which Chartier,
who was only 28, could not have assumed if he
had not been thoroughly versed in law and
procedure. Chartier's appointment, which was an
annual one, was renewed 12 Jan. 1671, 28 Mar.
1672, 16 Jan. 1673 (when he took the oath of
loyalty to the king demanded by Buade* de
Frontenac), and 15 Jan. 1674. An additional proof
of the authorities' satisfaction may be seen in his
appointment as a councillor on 29 May 1674,
when his name was put forward by the Compagnie
des Indes occidentales. Chartier was 32, and the
future looked bright. On 26 April 1675 Louis XIV
appointed him a councillor for life. Among the
councillors, whose number was raised from 5 to 7,
he held the fifth place. In 1674, at the time of his
installation, he had been assigned the last place,
since he was the most recently appointed. He had
protested and had claimed a right to be treated
with greater respect, as being the only councillor
to hold his appointment from the king: a matter
of precedence, of which his century has given us
many examples.

René-Louis' father, however, who had been
lieutenant general for civil and criminal affairs of
the provost court of Quebec since 1666, was
preparing to resign his post. It may be supposed
that, in accord with the spirit of the age, he

requested insistently that his son succeed him. The
office of judge of the provost court of Quebec was,
in fact, one of great prestige and much more
remunerative than that of councillor, which at that
time carried with it a salary of only 300 *livres* a
year. René-Louis was, in fact, appointed on
1 May 1677, replacing his father; on 25 October
he was installed by councillors Louis Rouer* de
Villeray and CHARLES DENYS de Vitré. His salary
was 500 *livres*. For 26 years Chartier was to
discharge his duties as a judge to everyone's
satisfaction; his reputation grew from year to year,
as did the esteem in which he was held. Duchesneau*, BRISAY de Denonville, BOCHART de
Champigny, Frontenac, the king himself, one after
another praised his honesty and his competence,
drawing attention to the services he rendered the
colony; on 28 Dec. 1698 he was appointed judge
of the admiralty court, although the setting up of
this tribunal was delayed until 1717; Bishop
Saint-Vallier [LA CROIX] for his part made
Chartier one of the directors of the Hôpital
Général of Quebec. On many occasions he was
called upon to sit on the Conseil Souverain when
a councillor was absent. In addition he was subdelegate to the intendant in 1677, 1687, 1689, 1690,
and 1706. In the last-mentioned year, for example,
his judicial powers were very wide, proof of the
confidence in his judgement and knowledge.

Throughout his honourable career Chartier de
Lotbinière continued, as a militia officer, to take
part in the defence of the colony. In the autumn of
1666 he was a lieutenant in a company, and on
2 June 1673 he was promoted to lieutenant-
colonel of the militia of Quebec. On 6 July 1684
he received from Le Febvre* de La Barre a commission as officer commanding the regiment of
Quebec (204 men), and in this capacity he accompanied the governor in his expedition against the
Iroquois; in the absence of Denonville, who in
1687 carried the war into the *pays d'en haut*, it was
Chartier de Lotbinière who was in command at
Quebec; on 6 June 1690 he was appointed colonel
of a company of Quebec militiamen and took part
in the defence of the town during the siege by
Phips*. In New France the nobility of the robe
knew how to take up the sword with courage
when the need arose.

René-Louis Chartier's competence and devotion were soon to be rewarded and his worth
recognized. On 1 June 1703 Louis XIV appointed
him chief councillor of the Conseil Supérieur.
From that time on he ranked fourth in the
hierarchy of the colony, being preceded only by
the governor, the intendant, and the bishop. Even
before his installation on 26 Nov. 1703 Chartier
had had a petition addressed to the court asking

Chartier de Lotbinière

that he be paid an annual gratuity of 250 *livres* "which [would permit] him to do honour to his office"; the position of chief councillor, which was worth 450 *livres*, did not, he explained, bring in as much as did that of lieutenant general, to which were attached fees as well as a salary of 500 *livres*, yet it entailed greater expense. When he was chief councillor, Rouer de Villeray had received such a gratuity; the king likewise granted one to Chartier. It was important that this high officer maintain his rank fittingly.

Life was on the grand scale in the colony, and particularly at Quebec, where one's prestige was proportionate to the magnificence of one's table, clothes, and retinue. The gentry dreamt of living like princes, the bourgeoisie gave in to the lure of luxury and lived on the scale of the nobility, and the peasants indulged in the habits and comforts of the bourgeoisie:

> Tout petit prince a des ambassadeurs.
> Tout marquis veut avoir des pages.
>
> (La Fontaine)
>
> Every princeling has ambassadors.
> Every marquis wants to have pages.

Everything went on in New France as if people had adopted the improvidence of the nomadic Indian, living from day to day and not minding the cost. Too often, to maintain a social rank he had usurped, a person had to go every day a little more deeply into debt. The outward display ill concealed the extreme poverty of these needy colonials in their homes. The greatest fortunes were based upon neglected bonds and unpaid debts. CHARLES AUBERT de La Chesnaye, for example, the most powerful businessman of his time, died insolvent. This was not, however, the end of Chartier de Lotbinière.

In June 1701 the notaries Louis CHAMBALON and CHARLES RAGEOT took an inventory of the joint estate of René-Louis Chartier and Marie-Madeleine Lambert, married 24 Jan. 1678 at Quebec. This document permits us to appraise Chartier's fortune at that time: 2,692 *livres*, 4 *sols*, 4 *deniers* in personal property, implements, and farm animals; 318 *livres*, 9 *sols*, 4 *deniers* in cash; and debts receivable amounting to 4,924 *livres*, 1 *sol*, 8 *deniers*. That is to say, 7,934 *livres*, 15 *sols*, 4 *deniers* on the credit side, from which must be deducted liabilities totalling 1,929 *livres*, 6 *sols*, 6 *deniers*, which leaves 6,005 *livres*, 8 *sols*, 10 *deniers*. To this sum must be added the value of the house which he had under construction at that time and for which he had already paid out 6,000 *livres*, his seigneury of Lotbinière measuring three and a half leagues by six (acquired by grants dated 3 Nov. 1672, 1 April 1685, and 25 March 1695, and by a purchase on 22 Feb. 1686), the farm land belonging to the seigneury with its mill, its two houses, and its barns, his properties at Quebec, and some assets, including his library, which he possessed in his own right. In other words, a respectable fortune of at least some 20,000 *livres*.

The house in which Chartier lived, on Rue Saint-Louis, was small and had only one storey. It consisted of a kitchen with a pantry, a parlour in which there was a bed, a bedroom, the lieutenant general's study which also served as his bedroom, a cellar, and an attic. In it lived Chartier, his second wife, Françoise Jachée, whom he had married on 16 May 1701, and the six surviving children of the ten that Marie-Madeleine Lambert had borne him. The family had no servant. Except in the parlour which, when required, was turned into a dining-room, the furniture and utensils were broken, worn out, of little value. The parlour displayed a sumptuousness devoid of any extravagance: 12 wild-cherry chairs, an armchair, a settee, a panelled buffet which served as a table, a spinet (a rare instrument in New France), an old pedestal table, two mirrors, one of which measured 20 inches by 16, three pieces of tapestry-work in *point de Hongrie*, a pair of iron firedogs with copper knobs, of a total value of 400 *livres*. Listed for use at receptions and preserved carefully in Chartier's study were 12 silver spoons and forks, a dish, and two salt-cellars, likewise in silver, all valued at 416 *livres*, 5 *sols*, on the basis of 45 *livres* the mark. While at Versailles the great king continued to eat with his fingers, the lieutenant general of Quebec, on the days when he received, was not unaware of the refinements of the new code of etiquette.

At the time of his second marriage Chartier yielded to the temptation of trying his luck in commercial ventures. In 1701 he was one of the directors of the Compagnie de la Nouvelle-France, to which he had subscribed 1,000 *livres*. In addition, on 13 Nov. 1704 he paid out 7,711 *livres* in card money and entered into partnership with Jean LÉGER de La Grange to operate a ship that had been taken from the English, but which was soon recaptured by them. The affairs of the Compagnie de la Nouvelle-France went badly; in the period from 1700 to 1704 it lost 300,000 *livres*. At the king's request the board of directors, composed of five members, was abolished, and the running of its affairs was entrusted to an agent general, assisted by a private agent. Chartier de Lotbinière and Georges REGNARD Duplessis were chosen. Chartier was appointed 11 Sept. 1705 with a salary of 1,000 *livres*. In 1706 Regnard received preference over Chartier, who withdrew. The chief councillor added little to his modest wealth in these operations; in 1708 JACQUES RAUDOT stated that he did not have "a large fortune."

At his death the wonder-struck little boy of 1651 was chief councillor to the Conseil Supérieur, and one of his nephews, RIGAUD de Vaudreuil, was governor of New France. He left behind him the memory of an upright and competent man whose services to the colony were countless. Governors and intendants had been unanimous in praising him unreservedly. Arriving in Quebec at the age of ten, René-Louis Chartier de Lotbinière had received his schooling in Canada and had returned to France only twice, in 1674 and 1691; he had become a true Canadian.

ANDRÉ VACHON

AJQ, Greffe de Romain Becquet, 1, 12 avril 1674, 3 sept., 28 déc. 1677; Greffe de Louis Chambalon, 18 oct. 1697, 9 oct. 1698, 1 févr. 1699, 14 mai, 13 juin 1701, 3, 10 nov. 1702, 29 janv. 1703. AQ, Coll. P.-G. Roy, Chartier de Lotbinière; NF, Cahiers d'intendance, II, 496–98, 502, 512; NF, Foi et hommage, I, 169; NF, Ins. Cons. sup., II, 139f et seq.; NF, Ins. de la Prév. de Québec, I, 327; NF, Ord. des int., I, 1, 46; NF, Registres d'intendance, I, 44f.; IV, 12; Seigneuries, Lotbinière. ASQ, Lettres, N, 14, 121; Polygraphie, III, 113; XLVI, 16; Séminaire, XXXV, 23.

"Acte d'association entre Jean Léger de La Grange et René-Louis Chartier de Lotbinière," BRH, XXIV (1918), 99–101. "La compagnie de 1666: procès-verbal de prise de possession des forts d'Agnié, 17 octobre 1666," BRH, XIII (1907), 350f. "Correspondance de Frontenac," APQ Rapport, 1926–27, 62, 80, 129; 1928–29, 345. "Correspondance de Vaudreuil," APQ Rapport, 1942–43. Documents relating to Canadian currency during the French period (Shortt), I, 87, 117–22. "L'expédition de M. de La Barre contre les Iroquois en 1684," BRH, XXXI (1925), 55. Jug. et délib. Pièces et documents relatifs à la tenure seigneuriale, [II], 302, 315f., 364, 408. Recensement du Canada, 1666 (APQ Rapport). Recensements du Canada, 1667, 1681 (Sulte). P.-G. Roy, Inv. concessions; Inv. ins. Cons. souv.; Inv. ord. int., I. André Vachon, "Inventaire des biens de René-Louis Chartier de Lotbinière (Québec, 13–17 juin 1701)," RHAF, XXI (1968), 308–24. "Vers burlesques," BRH, XXXIII (1927), 264–82.

DCB, I, 201–3. Gareau, "La prévôté de Québec," 61, 129, 134f. Tanguay, Dictionnaire, I, 120. Luc Lacourcière, Anthologie poétique de la Nouvelle-France (XVIIᵉ siècle) (Textes d'auteurs canadiens, V, Québec, 1966 [polycopié]), 89–101. Raymond Douville, "Trois seigneuries sans seigneurs," Cahiers des Dix, XVI (1951), 135–50. A. de Léry McDonald, "René-Louis de Lotbinière, premier conseiller au Conseil supérieur," BRH, XXXIII (1927), 585–87. P.-G. Roy, "René-Louis Chartier de Lotbinière," BRH, XXXIII (1927), 257–64. André Vachon, "De quelques erreurs au sujet de René-Louis Chartier de Lotbinière," BRH, LXIX (1967), 139–42; "Seize documents concernant René-Louis Chartier de Lotbinière," BRH, LXIX (1967), 99–107.

CHÂTELLERAULT, MICHEL ROY, dit. See ROY

CHAUCHETIÈRE, CLAUDE, Jesuit missionary, mathematician, artist, and mystic; b. at Saint-Porchaire-de-Poitiers in Aquitaine, on 7 Sept. 1645; d. 17 April 1709.

When 17 years old Chauchetière was present at the death of a priest who was on the point of departing for the Canadian mission field and said, "that made me feel that it was good to give oneself to God." He entered the Jesuit novitiate at Bordeaux in 1663 on his 18th birthday. He felt much attracted to Canada because the possibilities for suffering and sacrifice seemed especially great there. He applied himself to his spiritual preparation for such evangelical labours. In spite of his fervour "and his constant desire always to do the will of God" it seemed to him that his spiritual progress was slow and that each day undid the work previously accomplished. From 1665 to 1667 he studied philosophy at Poitiers and then instructed at Tulle, La Rochelle, and Saintes successively. At the end of December 1672, he saw Father Louis Mercier who gave him some lessons in Huron. Chauchetière at this time learned the rosary in Huron and found consolation in praying in that language.

He came to Canada in 1677 (some say 1674) and spent one year at the Huron mission at Quebec prior to his assignment to the Iroquois mission, Saint-François-Xavier, at Sault-Saint-Louis (Caughnawaga). His name is found in the registers of La Prairie and Lorette in 1677. In that year Kateri Tekakwitha*, one of the converts at the Mohawk village of Gandawagué, came to Saint-François-Xavier and gave the leadership the new community required. Chauchetière was much impressed by her mystical experiences and her deep spirituality; he had scarcely expected to find such spiritual depth among the native converts. Kateri Tekakwitha lived at the mission of Saint-François-Xavier until her death on 17 April 1680. The following year Father Chauchetière painted a portrait in oils of the Indian maiden and wrote a brief biography of the "lily of the Mohawks." He attributed to her intercession his seemingly miraculous escape from the mission chapel, which collapsed during a gale.

In 1682 Father Chauchetière put his artistic talents to further use. Employing a technique used

Chaudillon

by Pierron* among the Mohawks a decade earlier, he introduced at the Caughnawaga reserve paintings of biblical scenes and illustrations of the sacraments and of the seven deadly sins. These were bound into small books which the Indians could readily take with them to the fields and forests.

His numerous writings are always picturesque and entertaining, as well as instructive. The narrative of 19 years of labour at the Caughnawaga mission is rapid in its pace and permeated with the mysticism of its author. His letters indicate a deep concern for the spiritual and temporal welfare of the Iroquois converts and the 100 or so French families for whom he was pastor from 1678 to 1685. His pamphlet on drunkenness discussed the chief social problem confronting his colleagues who sought to convert and Frenchify the tribesmen. He described such effects of the liquor trade as loss of life and property, sexual deviation, and aggressiveness caused by drunkenness, but he offered no new or effective means of social control.

Chauchetière did not enjoy good health. In 1692 he suffered from severe headaches and erysipelas and soon afterwards was weakened by a "bloody flux." He wrote that during a visit to Fort Frontenac (Cataracoui) he was attacked by scurvy. His eyesight began to fail him during the later years of his ministry but he refused to wear spectacles.

In 1694 his 16 years of service as a missionary to the Iroquois of La Prairie ended. On 20 September he wrote to a friend in Bordeaux that he was to have gone with PIERRE LE MOYNE d'Iberville to Hudson Bay "to teach a class in mathematics on the ship." He was replaced by Father SILVY, then at the last moment MAREST was substituted. Chauchetière then expected to be sent to the Huron mission at Michilimackinac, but instead he was sent to Montreal to teach the boys "navigation, fortification, and other mathematical subjects." He described his occupation as that of "proto-regent of Villemarie" and teacher of mathematics to 12 or 15 pupils, including some young officers. He reported in 1694 having two or three pupils who were on ships and one who was the assistant pilot of one of the king's vessels.

In addition to teaching mathematics each afternoon from four to five o'clock he was expected to hear confessions on Sundays, and on the first Sunday of the month he was required to preach in the parish church. The latter duty he does not seem to have relished and he commented, "I must preach but I have no sermons." He had always been much interested in scientific concepts, as his correspondence and relations reveal, and he took care to observe carefully and to record

eclipses, parhelions, earthquakes, and other natural phenomena. His descriptions of the fauna and flora are vivid.

Chauchetière's ministry at Montreal was hardly a peaceful one. He shared the Jesuits' suspicion of the Sulpicians who were influential on the island. He had many confrontations with Bishop Saint-Vallier [LA CROIX], who on more than one occasion threatened him with interdiction. Chauchetière found his position made more difficult by the fact that he was confessor to Governor CALLIÈRE of Montreal, a bitter enemy of the bishop. When Chauchetière was so bold as to object to the numerous restrictions and reserved cases imposed by Saint-Vallier, the bishop questioned both the missionary's motives and his moral integrity.

Little is known concerning the later life of Chauchetière except that he remained faithful to his calling until his death at Quebec on 17 April 1709.

C. J. JAENEN

ASJ, France (Chantilly), Fonds Brotier, 162, ff.78–88, 108–20. ASJCF, Collection générale, Série A, ff.VIII(b), XI(a), 1, 5; XI(b); XII(a) (PAC, FM 17, 6–3); 343. Charlevoix, *History* (Shea), IV, 283. Claude Chauchetière, *Narration annuelle de la Mission du Sault depuis la fondation jusqu'à l'an 1686*; *La vie de la b. Catherine Thegakouita dite à présent la Sainte Sauvagesse* (Manate [New York], 1887). *JR* (Thwaites), LX, LXII, LXIV, LXXI. *Jug. et délib.*, I, 511. *Lettres édifiantes et curieuses escrites des missions étrangères par quelques missionnaires de la Compagnie de Jésus* (30v., Paris, 1707–73; nouv. éd., 26v., Paris, 1870–83), XII, 119–211. François Élesban de Guilhermy, *Ménologe de la Compagnie de Jésus . . . , assistance de France, comprenant les missions de l'Archipel de la Syrie, . . . du Canada, de la Louisiane . . .*, éd. [Jacques Terrien] (2 part., Paris, 1892), première partie, 511–13. F.-N. Noiseux, *Liste chronologique des évêques et des prêtres tant séculiers que réguliers, employés au service de l'église . . .* (Québec, 1834). Rochemonteix, *Les Jésuites et la N.-F. au XVIIe siècle*, III, 641–78.

CHAUDILLON, ANTOINE, surgeon, settler; b. 1643 at Saint-Martin-d'Ygrande in the former province of Bourbonnais, son of Claude Chaudillon and Antoinette Tin; d. 1707 at Pointe-aux-Trembles (Montreal).

On 26 May 1672 Chaudillon married Marie Boucher, 18 years of age, the daughter of François Boucher, one of the first settlers at Sillery, and of Florence Gareman. The couple lived at Sorel from 1674 to 1684, then at Pointe-aux-Trembles, near Montreal, where Chaudillon died and was buried on 6 Oct. 1707. His wife lived until 16 Dec. 1713. Five children were born of this marriage.

In the 1681 census Chaudillon is listed as a

surgeon and settler at Sorel. His livestock consisted of six head of cattle, and his farm included 16 acres under cultivation.

Chaudillon was wounded in the battle of 2 July 1690 against the Iroquois, fought at Rivière-des-Prairies, on the small stream called the Grou. In *À travers les registres* Tanguay writes that Chaudillon died in the battle; in reality he was carried off as a prisoner and was later released along with Pierre Payet, *dit* Saint-Amour. He was called upon several times to take part in inquiries into various sensational affairs which engrossed the settlement at Montreal. Thus in 1703 he examined a new-born infant whose throat had been cut, and also Marie-Anne Esmond, a young girl who was suspected of being the mother and murderess of the child.

HERVÉ BIRON

J.-A. Lebœuf, *Complément au Dictionnaire généalogique Tanguay* (1ʳᵉ série, Montréal, 1957), 39. É.-Z. Massicotte, "Les chirurgiens, médecins, etc., de Montréal sous le régime français," APQ *Rapport, 1922–23*, 137. Tanguay, *Dictionnaire*, I, 122. Abbott, *History of medicine*, 19, 20. Ahern, *Notes pour l'histoire de la médecine*, 100, 314. Azarie Couillard Després, *Histoire de Sorel, de ses origines à nos jours* (Montréal, 1926), 59. H.-A. Scott, *Une paroisse historique de la Nouvelle-France: Notre-Dame de Sainte-Foy: histoire civile et religieuse d'après les sources* (Québec, 1902), 296. Sulte, *Hist. des Can. fr.*, V, 74.

CHAUFFOURS, LOUIS DAMOURS DE. *See* DAMOURS

CHAUMONT, ALEXANDRE DE, chevalier, marshal of the camps and armies of the king, seigneur (France), officer in the Carignan regiment, aide-de-camp and captain of the guards of Alexandre de Prouville* de Tracy, ambassador to Siam in 1685; b. *c.* 1640, son of Alexandre de Chaumont, seigneur of Athieules, member of a branch of the Quitry family, and of Isabelle Du Bois Des Cours, daughter of Adrien, seigneur of Fafières; d. 28 Jan. 1710.

The Chevalier de Chaumont came to New France in early 1665, carrying the minister's instructions to Tracy for the latter's Canadian campaign. He had been given a commission to serve as Tracy's aide-de-camp and was soon awarded the additional title of captain of the guards. He was described by Intendant Talon* as an assiduous and useful officer. Talon, in fact, selected him to join a group of distinguished persons who were to build houses in one of the new model villages to be established near Quebec. But by mid-summer 1666, Chaumont was more seriously engaged in assisting Tracy and Rémy* de Courcelle in organizing an army to attack the Mohawk canton. Although his duty obliged him to remain close to Tracy throughout the ensuing expedition, the account given in the *Jesuit Relations* singled him out as an officer whose conduct was most exemplary. He was present when the main Mohawk village, Andaraque, was taken and he witnessed the formal ceremonies held to claim the neighbouring lands for Louis XIV. Chaumont sailed to France in the fall of 1666 to report personally to the minister on the Iroquois war, but does not appear to have returned to the colony. In 1675 he was in the navy and brought news of the war in Sicily to Versailles. In later years he became a royal musketeer and, in 1685, served as a special French ambassador to Siam, where he signed a trading agreement.

DONALD J. HORTON

AN, Col., C¹¹ᴬ, 22, ff.112, 221, 315, 325, 410. Bibliothèque de la Chambre des députés (Paris), MS, 292, ff.3–31. BN, MS, Fr. 22673, ff.114, 173, 268; Mélanges de Colbert, 273, f.259. Charlevoix, *History* (Shea), III, 90. "La compagnie de 1666: procès-verbal de prise de possession des forts d'Agnié, 17 octobre 1666," *BRH*, XIII (1907), 351. "Correspondance échangée entre la cour de France et l'Intendant Talon pendant ses deux administrations dans la Nouvelle-France," APQ *Rapport, 1930–31*, 38, 45, 52, 56, 61. *JR* (Thwaites), L, 147, 199. *JJ* (Laverdière et Casgrain), 348f.

Eccles, *Canada under Louis XIV*, 41–44. Lucien Lanier, *Étude historique sur les relations de la France et du royaume de Siam, de 1662 à 1703* . . . (Versailles, 1883). Ernest Lavisse et Alfred Rambaud, *Histoire générale, du IVᵉ siècle à nos jours* (12v., Paris, 1892–1901), VI, 916. Benjamin Sulte, *Mélanges historiques* (Malchelosse), VII, 58, 62–64; VIII, 32, 54, 57, 85, 131; "Officiers de Carignan," *BRH*, XVII (1911), 194.

CHAVIGNY LACHEVROTIÈRE, FRANÇOIS DE, esquire, seigneur; b. 6 July 1650 on the Île d'Orléans, son of François de Chavigny and Éléonore de Grandmaison*; buried 14 Feb. 1725 at Deschambault.

In 1670 he was one of the partners of the explorer Daumont* de Saint-Lusson, who was sent by Talon* to look for a copper mine in the Ottawa country. The following year, at Sault Ste Marie, a report was drawn up of the proceedings by which Saint-Lusson took possession of the western country, and on it appears Chavigny's signature.

Although Jolliet* and Chavigny signed in a notary's presence a contract dated 1 Oct. 1672 and a declaration dated 3 October in connection with a new expedition to the west, Chavigny does not seem to have taken part in this expedition; it was put off till the middle of May 1673, and it is

Chevalier

known that he was at Fort Frontenac in July 1673, at the time of the inspection by Frontenac [Buade*].

During his missions Chavigny rendered valuable services which, however, received scant recompense. In 1674 his mother bequeathed to him the fief of Chavigny, which was subsequently known by the name of La Chevrotière. Without neglecting the development of his seigneury, Chavigny took on a job in 1712 as an employee of the Tadoussac trading sub-concession.

His first wife, whom he had married at Quebec in June 1675, was Antoinette de Poussans. They had a daughter, Louise, whose godfather was Frontenac. In April 1699, Geneviève Guion Desprez became his second wife. Of this marriage were born five daughters and a son, who was baptized François. In the autumn of 1724 Chavigny fell ill and died at the beginning of the following year, at 75 years of age. His wife lived for 30 years after his death.

JEAN-JACQUES LEFEBVRE

AJQ, Greffe de Romain Becquet, 19 juin 1675; Greffe de Louis Chambalon, 18 avril 1699. ANDQ, Registres des baptêmes, mariages et sépultures. *Jug. et délib.* A. Roy, *Inv. greffes not.*, III, 135, 269; XVIII, 232–33. P.-G. Roy, *Inv. concessions*, I, 157f.; III, 68ff. Tanguay, *Dictionnaire*, I, 163; III, 267. P.-G. Roy, *La famille de Chavigny de la Chevrotière* (Lévis, 1916).

CHEVALIER, *dit* **Beauchêne**, **ROBERT**, soldier, adventurer and privateer, writer of memoirs; b. 23 April 1686 at Pointe-aux-Trembles (Montreal), son of Jacques Chevalier and Jeanne Vilain; d. December 1731 at Tours (France).

In Beauchêne's biography reality and legend overlap. It is now certain that this person did exist and left memoirs, but the story that he told was considerably amplified and modified by Alain-René Lesage.

Let us first summarize the incidents of his life which are vouched for by documents, or which appear probable. The circumstances of his birth are certain. At the age of 20, he and his two elder brothers Paul and Jean entered into an agreement with Lamothe Cadillac [LAUMET] to take a canoe full of merchandise to Detroit and to bring back pelts. It also appears likely that he took part in an expedition against Orange (Albany, N.Y.) and Corlar (Schenectady). In 1707 he was one of the group of Canadians recruited by CHARLES-JOSEPH AMIOT de Vincelotte to go to Port-Royal (Annapolis Royal, N.S.) and make up the crew of the frigate, the *Biche*; he then served under the privateer captain Pierre Morpain*.

After a lucrative career in privateering, he is supposed, according to Lesage, to have gone to France. He is thought to have lived for a while at Brest, Saint-Malo, and Nantes, and to have died at Tours during a brawl. In fact, his death certificate, dated 11 Dec. 1731, has been found in the parish registers of that city. He is supposed to have left an autobiography which his wife is said to have entrusted to Lesage, who published it under the following title: *Les avantures de monsieur Robert Chevalier, dit de Beauchêne, capitaine de flibustiers dans la Nouvelle-France.*

The authenticity of these memoirs has been hotly disputed. Charles Bourel de La Roncière and A.-L. Leymarie believed them to be authentic. Gilbert Chinard, Aegidius Fauteux, and Gustave Lanctot have subjected them to close scrutiny and have rejected a good portion of them. It seems certain that Chevalier did indeed draft the biographical notes which served as an outline for Lesage. The general framework of the story, the names of obscure personages such as Abbé Périac (Priat*), episodes such as the unsuccessful expedition against Corlar, the journey to Acadia, the enlistment with Morpain, and numerous details correspond to historical reality and could not have been invented.

On the other hand, the *Avantures* mention several fictitious personages, such as Legendre, frequently confuse names and dates, and contain anachronisms and manifest exaggerations. These inaccuracies may be explained by the unreliability of the memory of the author, who drafted his recollections long after the events, but also by the intervention of Lesage. The latter not only touched up the style but also introduced lengthy expansions, for example the one about "marriages in Canada," inspired by Lahontan [LOM D'ARCE]; in addition he invented the long, fantastic story of the Comte de Monneville, which occupies half the book.

In short, Chevalier was a boastful and unscrupulous adventurer who had the good fortune to encounter a writer of talent who could bring him out of obscurity and transform him into the hero of a novel.

RENÉ BAUDRY

[Alain-René] Lesage, *Les avantures de monsieur Robert Chevalier, dit de Beauchêne, capitaine de flibustiers dans la Nouvelle-France* (2v., Paris, 1732). Several of the subsequent editions are incorrectly entitled: *Les aventures du Chevalier de Beauchêne.* Massicotte, "Répertoire des engagements pour l'Ouest," 240–41. Tanguay, *Dictionnaire.*
Charles Bourel de La Roncière, *Histoire de la marine française* (6v., Paris, 1899–1932), VI, 508–16. Gilbert Chinard, *L'Amérique et le rêve exotique dans la littérature française au XVIIe et au XVIIIe siècle* (Paris, 1913), 271–79. Gustave Lanctot, *Faussaires et*

faussetés en histoire canadienne (Montréal, 1948), 130–47. Gilbert Chinard, "Les aventures de Chevalier de Beauchêne, de Lesage," *Revue du XVIIIᵉ siècle* (Paris), I (1913), 279–93. Aegidius Fauteux, "Les aventures du chevalier de Beauchêne," *Cahiers des Dix*, II (1937), 7–33. Robert Le Blant, "Les études historiques sur la colonie française d'Acadie, 1603–1713," *Revue d'histoire des colonies* (Paris), XXXV (1948), 105. A.-L. Leymarie, "Robert Chevalier *dit* de Beauchêne, capitaine de flibustiers dans la Nouvelle-France (1686–1731)," *NF*, V (1930), 358–62 [4–8].

CHEVRIÈRES DE SAINT-VALLIER, JEAN-BAPTISTE DE LA CROIX DE. *See* LA CROIX

CHÈZE, FRANÇOIS, priest, Sulpician, procurator of the Sulpician seminary at Montreal; b. 7 May 1683 at Vallore in the diocese of Clermont (France); d. 24 May 1740 at Montreal.

François Chèze entered the Sulpician order in 1711, three years after his ordination, and arrived in Canada the following year. He was first attached to the parish of Ville-Marie, and in 1724 he was appointed parish priest of Longue-Pointe but only for a few months. He soon returned to the parish of Notre-Dame, probably to assist M. François Citoys de Chaumeaux, who since 1712 had held simultaneously the offices of "secretary, bursar, and procurator of the seigneurs of Montreal Island." It is believed that M. Chèze had been entrusted with the office of procurator.

It is not easy to determine the duties of this office under the French régime. Until 1670, the procurator also served as the superior of the Sulpician order in Canada. It was to him that the superior general in Paris, in the name of the seigneurs of Montreal Island, gave his procuration, which conferred upon him the authority to make land grants, appoint and dismiss legal officers, levy seigneurial dues, and generally sign all documents necessary for the administration of the colony. In all the documents on which his name appeared, he had to indicate that he was the procurator of the seigneurs. This designation does not seem to have been used for other members of the seminary apart from the superiors of Montreal before 1707, at which time M. Cailhe, the bursar since 1697, had begun to style himself in certain documents "secretary, bursar, and procurator of the seigneurs." In this latter case, the office of procurator does not seem to have been anything but that of a secretary whose responsibility it was to draft petitions, ordinances, deeds concerning land grants, sales, and rentals, and on occasion to act in the name of the seigneurs in matters of a secondary nature, in which he alone signed certain leases or petitions of little importance. M. Chèze is thought to have exercised this function for three

or four years at the most, since in a deed dated 4 Sept. 1728 it was M. Louis Normant de Faradon who was named as procurator.

In 1728 Chèze became a curate once more, and was also entrusted with the direction of the Confrérie des Dames de la Sainte-Famille, which he reorganized; he wrote a short historical account of it, which is recorded at the beginning of the first registry of the association. He had the reputation of being a great preacher and a great confessor. He died on 24 May 1740 at the seminary.

ANTONIO DANSEREAU, P.S.S.

ASSM, Section des biographies; Section des requêtes et ordonnances. Caron, "Inventaire de documents," APQ *Rapport*, *1940–41*, 430. Étienne Marchand, "Les troubles de l'Église du Canada en 1728," *BRH*, III (1897), 133. Allaire, *Dictionnaire*. Gauthier, *Sulpitiana*. Odoric-M. [Jouve], "Étude historique et critique sur les actes du Frère Didace Pelletier, Récollet," *BRH*, XVII (1911), 92, 172.

CHICHIKATELO (Chichicatato) chief of the Miamis at St Joseph River, devoted to the French and to Catholicism; d. 1701.

Chichikatelo was the emissary of the Miami Indians to Governor CALLIÈRE's peace conference of 1701 between the French, their allies, and the Iroquois. An accomplished orator, highly regarded by both his own people and the French, he was described by LE ROY de La Poterie as "a personage of singular merit, with a bearing reminiscent of that of the Roman Emperors." In his address to the tribes assembled at Montreal, he expressed an intense desire for peace, despite the fact that the Iroquois had burned his son to death a few years earlier. To demonstrate his good faith, he presented eight Iroquois prisoners, some of whom had been ransomed from other tribes, and he intimated that he would have brought more had his people not been obliged to travel with their Huron neighbours, being unaccustomed themselves to the use of canoes. Alluding to the failure of the Iroquois to bring their prisoners, he expressed misgivings about their sincerity but resolved to turn over his captives nevertheless, trusting in God to punish those who violated the treaty's terms.

During the discussions which followed the formal ratification of the peace, Chichikatelo scorned those allied chieftains who were demanding guarantees from Callière for their safe return west. He contended that such matters were decided by God alone and, when he himself fell fatally ill a few days later, he asked only that his people not blame the French. So greatly did he symbolize fidelity to the French, that future Miami delegations to Governor RIGAUD de Vaudreuil used his name in expressions of allegiance and in begging forgiveness for the periodic crimes of their tribesmen.

In 1702, Father Claude AVENEAU, a missionary at St Joseph River, opposed LAUMET, *dit* de Lamothe Cadillac's efforts to gather all the Miami Indians at Detroit on the grounds that Governor Callière's last instructions to Chichikatelo in 1701 had been to bring the Miami nation together at St Joseph River. The missionary took this stand even though Chichikatelo's family was evidently prepared to migrate to Detroit.

DONALD J. HORTON

AN, Col., C¹¹ᴬ, 19, f.42; 20, f.220v; 21, ff.68–68v, 85–86. Charlevoix, *History* (Shea), V, 143–44. *Indian tribes* (Blair), II, 136. La Potherie, *Histoire* (1722), IV, 207–8, 233, 244–45, 254–55, 260–62. *Michigan Pioneer Coll.*, XXXIII, . 123–24. *NYCD* (O'Callaghan and Fernow), IX, 723.

CHINGOUESSI (Changouessi, Changouessy, Changouossy, Jangouessy, Sangouessy) Ottawa Sinango chief from Michilimackinac; fl. 1695–1701.

Chingouessi came to Quebec in July of 1698 to report to Governor Buade* de Frontenac that his neighbours, the Kiskakons and Ottawas du Sable, were on the point of abandoning Michilimackinac. Claiming to have stood resolutely against such a move, he now expressed fear that his loyalty to the French had endangered his life and, with high dramatic sense, asked Frontenac to provide him with an antidote for poison. At the governor's behest, he agreed to attend an assembly of Indians at Montreal with the aim of convincing the most dissident chiefs that they could escape Iroquois slaughter only by remaining together at Michilimackinac. The mission was apparently successful and henceforth Chingouessi stood high in French esteem.

In 1701, he was the Ottawa Sinango delegate to the peace conference convened by CALLIÈRE in Montreal between the French, their allies, and the Iroquois. In discussions concerning the fur trade, he joined several other chiefs in submitting that since beaver were becoming increasingly scarce, the French should accept more miscellaneous pelts from the Michilimackinac tribes. During the actual peace negotiations, he apologized for having brought so few of his Iroquois prisoners but, with disarming candour, explained that he had eaten most of them. Even so, to demonstrate his desire for peace, he presented an Iroquois woman and child whom he had ransomed.

DONALD J. HORTON

AN, Col., C¹¹ᴬ, 13, ff.28–30v; 19, f.42. Charlevoix, *History* (Shea), V, 143–44. La Potherie, *Histoire* (1722),

IV, 23, 94–97, 204, 233, 244. *NYCD* (O'Callaghan and Fernow), IX, 606, 683, 723.

CHOLENEC, PIERRE, priest, Jesuit, missionary; b. 10 June 1641 at Saint-Pol-de-Léon in Lower Brittany; d. 30 Oct. 1723 at Quebec.

Father Cholenec entered the Jesuit order in Paris on 8 Sept. 1659. Having an easy-going mind and amiable disposition, he did not make one think of his native land, "where the laws of salvage encouraged wreckers." While he was still doing his philosophical studies he was appointed prefect to Prince Rinaldo d'Este.

After completing his theology at the Collège Louis-le-Grand in Paris, he set out for Canada in 1674. The following year he was at Kentaké (La Prairie de la Magdeleine), where he distinguished himself as a preacher and spiritual director. There he met Jacques LARGILLIER, *dit* Le Castor, and Pierre Porteret, two *donnés* who had assisted Father Jacques Marquette* in his last hours. The detailed account which he immediately prepared was the first of several relations of this death. In the autumn of 1677, at the Saint-François-Xavier mission to the Iroquois, he welcomed Kateri Tekakwitha*, who had just come from the Mohawk canton. As did his *confrères* in the mission, and as he did also with all those under his direction, he sought to christianize her rather than frenchify her. More than once this missionary point of view aroused Governor Buade* de Frontenac's anger.

From 1683 to 1688 Father Cholenec worked at Lorette, but he then returned to the Iroquois mission, of which he was the superior from 1695 to 1699. At that time he wrote a biography of Kateri Tekakwitha, in a natural, correct style. In 1700 he was the superior of the Jesuits in Montreal but he afterwards returned to Saint-François-Xavier, where he held the office of superior from 1712 to 1722. He composed another life of Kateri Tekakwitha, intended for the *Lettres édifiantes*, and, in Latin, a letter and a biography of the Iroquois virgin destined for the general of the Jesuits in Rome. This last letter was followed by an account of the martyrdom of several Indians of his mission which was insufficiently known.

Shortly before his death, Cholenec enjoyed the happiness of living in the new Jesuit residence, which had been built by his efforts at the very centre of the new mission site, and which is still inhabited by this order today. He died on 30 Oct. 1723 at the Jesuit college in Quebec.

HENRI BÉCHARD, S.J.

ASJCF, 748; Varia, V, 6. ASQ, MSS, 374. *Beatificationis et canonizationis servae Dei Catharinae Tekawitha virginis indianae positio super virtutibus*

(Rome, 1940). Claude Dablon, *Relation de ce qui s'est passé de plus remarquable aux missions des peres de la Compagnie de Jésus en la Nouvelle-France, les années 1673 à 1679* (New York, 1860). *JR* (Thwaites). *Lettres édifiantes et curieuses escrites des missions étrangères par quelques missionnaires de la Compagnie de Jésus* (30v., Paris, 1707–73), XII, XIII. E. J. Devine, *Historic Caughnawaga* (Montreal, 1922). A. E. Jones, «*Ѕendake Ehen*» *or old Huronia* (Toronto, 1909). Rochemonteix, *Les Jésuites et la N.-F. au XVIIᵉ siècle*, III, 597–612.

CHURCH, BENJAMIN, soldier and Indian fighter; b. 1639 at Plymouth, Mass., son of Richard Church, who had migrated from England about 1630, and Elizabeth (Warren) Church; d. 17 Jan. 1717/18 (o.s.) at Little Compton, R.I.

The Church family lived in various Massachusetts towns while Richard Church worked as a carpenter. One of nine children, Benjamin was brought up in his father's trade. Aside from this, however, nothing is known of his youth. He was married 26 Dec. 1667 to Alice Southworth, daughter of Constant and Elizabeth (Collier) Southworth of Duxbury, Mass. Six years later Church took up land at Saconet (Sogkonate, modern Little Compton, R.I.), which was then part of Plymouth colony.

In June 1675 he learned from some Indian friends that the chief of the Wampanoag tribe, Metacomet (Metacom, Pometacom), known as King Philip, whose village was on Mount Hope peninsula at the north end of Narragansett Bay, intended to make war on the English. Church reported this intelligence on 16 June to the governor of Plymouth colony. Philip's hot-blooded warriors began looting and burning on 20 June. Church was given command of a mixed scouting force of English and friendly Indians. The Wampanoags escaped to the eastward, fought a pitched battle on 19 July, and fled to the north into Massachusetts Bay. The Nipmucks and Narragansetts joined with them in warfare, and the latter were defeated in the battle of the Great Swamp in December 1675. Church was wounded and earned a reputation for aggressiveness and personal bravery. In August 1676 his company ambushed and killed Philip. Church cut off his head to exhibit.

With the return of peace, Church was appointed a magistrate in Saconet. He acquired other lands and in 1680 helped establish the town of Bristol (R.I.), which he represented in the General Court in 1682. At the outbreak of King William's War (War of the League of Augsburg) in 1689, he was commissioned a major and commander of the Plymouth forces to be sent eastward to Maine. On 18 Sept. 1689 he landed at Fort Loyal (at Falmouth, now Portland), where Silvanus DAVIS was in command. A few days later he engaged besieging Indians in a six-hour battle. He then marched up and down the coast and drove off the Indians who were menacing Fort Loyal; they returned the following spring, however, supported by French forces, and took the fort.

In September 1690, Church was commissioned again to lead an expedition "against the Common Enemy, Indian & French their Aiders and Abettors," in an attempt to secure the eastern borders. With 300 English and Indians from Plymouth and Massachusetts Bay, he sailed to Casco Bay and marched to the Androscoggin River, only to find the Indian fort at Pejepscot (Brunswick, Me.) deserted. He recovered some English captives at another fort at modern Lewiston and burned the place. Church fought two more skirmishes on his way back and left some men to guard the Wells settlement. As with the previous expedition, Church felt that the compensation he later received was inadequate.

The third campaign into Maine took place in the summer of 1692. At this time Church assisted in the building of Fort William Henry at Pemaquid. The fourth expedition, in 1696, landed at Penobscot Bay in September in a vain search for JEAN-VINCENT D'ABBADIE de Saint-Castin and his forces. Saint-Castin had participated in raids on Maine settlements, the latest being the capture of Fort William Henry with PIERRE LE MOYNE d'Iberville early in August. After a skirmish with Indians, Church returned to his ships and decided to sail northeast to Beaubassin (Chignecto). As the inhabitants fled, his forces seized the town and destroyed most of the houses. The expedition moved back to the mouth of the Saint John River and carried off 12 cannon and shot hidden for a new fort. Fearing that the river might be too low for safe passage, Church decided against attacking the fort at Nashwaak (Naxouat, opposite modern Fredericton, N.B.) commanded by Governor Robinau* de Villebon. Upon embarking, however, he met another squadron under Colonel John Hathorne, who had orders to proceed upriver to attack the fort. The French were well prepared for the attack, thanks to the scouting of DANIEL ROBINAU de Neuvillette, Villebon's brother, and the attempted siege failed.

In March 1703/4, in the first year of Queen Anne's War (War of the Spanish Succession), Church proposed himself to Governor Dudley of Massachusetts as the leader of another expedition eastward to revenge the Franco-Indian attack on Deerfield, Mass., on 29 February [*see* Rev. John WILLIAMS]. Dudley commissioned him a colonel for the undertaking and authorized him to conduct coastal raids as far as Port-Royal (Annapolis Royal, N.S.). On the way Church captured, on Green Island near Penobscot Bay, three Frenchmen and an Indian who guided him to Penobscot (Pentagouet, modern Castine, Me.), where some French and Indians were attacked. Among those taken was Saint-Castin's half-breed daughter. Church was informed that two French officers, M. Gourdon and Michel Chartier*, were building a fort at Passamaquoddy, and he went there next. Gourdon was taken prisoner, but Chartier escaped.

On 20 June (1 July, N.S.) the expedition reached Les Mines (Grand Pré). Church summoned the inhabitants to surrender, which they did. He then burned the town, broke open the dikes, and cut the crops. On the night of the 22d he captured Pigiguit and the next day took Cobequid (Truro, N.S.). The avenging force sailed to Port-Royal, but after a council of war on 4 July decided to try to seize the town. Instead, Church went up to the head of Chignecto Bay and despoiled Beaubassin again before returning home via Passamaquoddy and Penobscot Bays. Once more Church felt himself poorly rewarded and he retired from military service.

In 1705 he was living in Little Compton again, and in 1715 he dictated to his son Thomas his *Entertaining passages relating to Philip's War . . . as also of expeditions more lately made against the common enemy, and Indian rebels, in the eastern parts of New-England.* On 17 January 1717/18 he was thrown from his horse, broke a blood vessel, and bled to death. His wife, Alice, survived him only seven weeks, leaving seven children.

Church was a devout man who considered that in his military campaigns he was acting as the avenging arm of God. His efforts in the defence of New England and in retaliatory raids on Acadia did much to boost New England morale, and there can be little doubt that Church's leadership and initiative paved the way for the capture of Port-Royal in 1710.

HOWARD H. PECKHAM

[Church's autobiographical book, *Entertaining passages . . .*, which offers the most complete account of his military activities, was first published in 1716 and today is a book of extreme rarity. It has been edited in two volumes, with copious footnotes and additional biographical introductions, by H. M. Dexter: *History of King Philip's war* (Boston, 1865–67). The second volume is subtitled *The history of the eastern expeditions. . . .* The Maine Historical Society has published occasional letters of Church, remarkable for their orthography, in its *Collections*, as has the Massachusetts Historical Society in its *Proceedings*. He is mentioned in various documents published in New Plymouth colony, *Records of the colony of New Plymouth in New England (1620–1692)*, ed. N. B. Shurtleff and David Pulsifer (12v., Boston, 1855–61), V, VI, VII.

French accounts of the 1704 expedition can be found in AN, Col., C¹¹ᴰ; *Coll. de manuscrits relatifs à la N.-F.*, II, 416–21; and Rameau de Saint-Père, *Une colonie féodale*, I, 326–28, who mentions some skirmishes around Port-Royal after the council of war of 4 July 1704 which are not described in English accounts of the incident.

Other sources on Church's life include: *Documentary hist. of Maine*, IX. PRO, *CSP, Col., 1689–92, 1704–5*. DAB. Hutchinson, *Hist. of Mass.-bay* (Mayo), II, 109–10. Murdoch, *History of Nova-Scotia*, I, 272–74. Parkman, *A half-century of conflict* (1893), I, 116–20. H. H. Peckham, *The colonial wars, 1689–1762* (Chicago, 1964). Webster, *Acadia*. H.H.P.]

CICÉ, LOUIS-ARMAND CHAMPION DE. *See* CHAMPION

CLAIRAMBAULT D'AIGREMONT, FRANÇOIS, naval commissary in Canada; baptized 26 March 1659 at Nuits-sur-Armançon (department of Yonne); d. a bachelor 1 Dec. 1728 at Quebec.

Claude Clairambault, François' father, was first a merchant, and then became a judge and royal notary at Nuits. François was a first cousin of Nicolas Clairambault (1643–1730), chief clerk of the Marine, of Charles Clairambault (1645–1720), commissary-general of the Marine, and of Pierre Clairambault (1651–1740), the famous genealogist of the king's orders. The Clairambaults, who had been established at Séboncourt (department of Aisne), may have emigrated to the region of Nuits-sur-Armançon around 1630. The name Aigremont came from a small farm situated in the parish of Étivey in the canton of Noyers (Yonne), which by 1666 had fallen into ruin. The Clairambaults were not therefore originally from Franche-Comté, as P.-G. Roy thought.

We do not know very much about the early part of François' career. He seems to have been involved for some time in the tax-farms of the Domaine d'Occident, and on 15 May 1685 Louis XIV bestowed on him the estates without claimants which were available at Saint-Domingue and on the Îles d'Amérique. Thanks no doubt to family influence, he entered the service of the Marine at Dunkirk as an "inspector," at a date which cannot be exactly ascertained. On 26 Nov. 1683 the intendant of the Marine at Dunkirk, Patoulet, wrote to the minister in praise of Aigremont, "who has worked here for some years with extraordinary diligence and wisdom, coupled with well-tried loyalty." On 1 July 1684 he became Patoulet's secretary. In a petition of 1716 he was to claim that he had worked "for three years in the offices of the Marine during M. de Seignelay's time"; he did not specify at what period, probably around 1685. On 1 July 1690 we find him serving as secretary to Seignelay's relative Louvigny d'Orgemont, who was intendant of the Marine at Le Havre. He held this position until 1 June 1701, when he received a commission as naval commissary in Canada, where he was to replace TANTOUIN de La Touche; he landed at Quebec from the *Seine* on 4 Sept. 1701. He was reported at that time to be a "very upright and capable man and a steady worker." But the following year the king made the office of commissary a venal one, and Clairambault found himself called upon to purchase an appointment in order to be continued in office. He who never ceased to complain that he had been born without possessions could not raise the 30,000 *livres* required, and he gave vent to some bitterness when he declared "that he found it hard, after 20 years of uninterrupted and unselfish service, to have been sent so far to obtain a position only to be allowed to enjoy it for so short a time."

Intendant François de Beauharnois* de La Boische, who appreciated him, arranged matters by taking him on as a secretary with a supplementary salary of 400 *livres*, and in 1703 appointed him his subdelegate at Montreal, so that there was scarcely any change in his duties.

Quite clearly Clairambault was highly esteemed. In 1705 Pontchartrain recommended him to Intendant JACQUES RAUDOT, and in 1707 an important mark of confidence was conferred on him when he was given the mission of inspecting the trading posts in the interior, "to examine," the minister wrote to him, "what trade is done there, and to ascertain exactly the state in which these posts are, and whether those who are in command there are not engaging in illicit trading . . . you must investigate on the spot the usefulness or otherwise of each post . . . because according to what you write His Majesty will decide to maintain the useful ones and abandon the others."

Clairambault left Montreal on 5 June 1708, and carried out his mission with care. He summed up his conclusions in a long report dated 14 Nov. 1708, which received the approval of the minister. "His Majesty has found so much good faith in it that he has decided to follow the opinions expressed." When Raudot went back to France he entrusted the intendancy to Clairambault in the interim, and the latter held the office for nearly a year (November 1711–October 1712). Bégon*, Raudot's successor, wrote that "the knowledge

and views of the Sieur d'Aigremont will be very helpful"; consequently, at the end of 1712, he appointed him comptroller of the Marine, instructed him to salvage the wreckage of the English fleet lost in the St Lawrence, and requested a gratuity for him. But the coffers of the kingdom were empty, and all the unfortunate comptroller received was a letter from the minister assuring him that he was "very happy with the way in which you are serving in Canada."

As the acquiring of commissaryships by purchase was abolished in 1716, Clairambault asked to be reinstated in his rank, and this request was enthusiastically supported by RIGAUD de Vaudreuil and Bégon, who once again praised his rectitude and his ability. He therefore received another commission on 17 Feb. 1717. In 1724, again on the recommendation of Vaudreuil and Bégon, he was granted an increase in pay of 600 *livres*. But the end of his career was saddened by the fire which burned down the intendant's palace at Quebec on 28 Dec. 1725, and in which he lost all he owned—little enough in any case— about 4,000 *livres* in furniture, silver, and clothes. The administrators asked for an indemnity on his behalf, but apparently did not obtain it. In 1728 Intendant CLAUDE-THOMAS DUPUY was recalled, and Clairambault was again put in charge in the interim. On 12 October he gave judgement against the intendant, sentencing him to pay various sums owing to the king's treasury. On 20 October he put his name to an ordinance concerning the beaver trade. He died the same year, and was buried on 4 December in the cathedral of Quebec.

Clairambault, wrote the governor general, Charles de Beauharnois* de La Boische, was "universally regretted . . . his unselfishness was so great during his lifetime that when he died there was not enough money to bury him." Rarely has an official been the object of such a chorus of praise, given without the slightest reservation.

ÉTIENNE TAILLEMITE

Archives de la Côte d'Or (Dijon), C 2885, 307. Archives d'Yonne (Auxerre), B, suppl. 225. AN, Col., B, 22, f.275v; 23, ff.103v., 235; 27, f.30; 29, ff.89, 126; 30, ff.131, 169; 33, f.367v; 34, f.322; 35, f.306; 36, f.405; 37, f.141v; C^{11A}, 18, f.42; 19, ff.98, 223, 225; 20, ff.75v, 121, 217, 218; 21, f.104v; 22, f.206v; 29, f.26; 31, f.172; 32, ff.10, 222v; 33, ff.15v, 113, 131v, 260; 34, ff.104, 322; 35, f.232; 36, ff.27, 170; 45, f.70; 46, ff.6, 20, 189, 425; 49, ff.147, 532; 50; E, 82; Marine, C², 55; Minutier, XCV, 41. BN, MS, Cabinet des titres, dossiers bleus, 189, 4919f.

Charland, "Notre-Dame de Québec: le nécrologe de la crypte," 181. Le Jeune, *Dictionnaire*. P.-G. Roy, "Les commissaires ordinaires de la marine en la

Clément Du Vuault

Nouvelle-France," *BRH*, XXIV (1918), 53; "François Clairambault d'Aigremont," *BRH*, XII (1906), 114–18; "Jean-Baptiste de Silly," *BRH*, XXII (1916), 313.

CLÉMENT DU VUAULT (Vault) DE VAL-RENNES, PHILIPPE, captain in the colonial regular troops, served with distinction in Canada 1685–93; b. 1647; d. prior to 1708.

At the age of 14 Valrennes killed a man but escaped punishment; a few months later, in 1662, he was commissioned an ensign in the Régiment de l'Épinay. In 1665 he was promoted lieutenant and in 1672 captain. He subsequently served for 13 years in the Normandy militia (*bataillons de campagne*) and in the Régiment de Normandie, Louis de Buade*, Comte de Frontenac's old regiment. He was commissioned a captain in the colonial regular troops in 1685 and came to Canada with the reinforcements sent with the Marquis de Denonville [BRISAY]. He appears to have become acclimatized to the Canadian environment without difficulty, for on 7 April 1687 he married a Canadian girl, Jeanne Bissot, a grand-daughter of Louis Hébert* and sister-in-law of Louis Jolliet*.

In 1687 Valrennes commanded one of the four columns of colonial regulars in the expedition against the Senecas. The following year, in July, he took over the command of Fort Frontenac (Cataracoui). This was a dangerous assignment since the fort was besieged by the Iroquois. The garrison was, in fact, kept prisoner, threatened with scurvy, and unable to hamper the movements of the enemy in any way. To keep the fort's 50-man garrison supplied required convoys of several hundred men. For these reasons Denonville, after the massive Iroquois assault on the settlements at Lachine in August 1689, sent word to Valrennes to blow up the fort and retire to Montreal with the garrison. Denonville instructed him to mine the walls, set slow fuses, and then retire with his men as swiftly as possible, for all the Iroquois in the vicinity would be sure to come swarming when they heard the explosion. The fleeing garrison was some distance away when the mines exploded and they assumed that the fort had been destroyed. Later it was discovered that some of the charges had not gone off; only five small breaches had been made in the walls. Valrennes did, however, succeed in getting the garrison safely to Montreal and the intendant, Jean BOCHART de Champigny, exonerated him from all blame for the mishap. Champigny informed the minister that Valrennes was one of the bravest and most prudent officers they had. He requested the minister to grant Valrennes a gratuity and a word or two of en-couragement, expressing the satisfaction in which his conduct was held; this to encourage the other officers to emulate him.

Two years later, in August 1691, a force composed of 146 Mohawks and Mahicans, and 120 Albany militiamen, led by Major Peter SCHUYLER, invaded the settlements south of Montreal. When the governor of the district, Hector de CALLIÈRE, received word of their approach he massed 700–800 colonial regular troops and militiamen around the fort at La Prairie de la Magdelaine. Shortly before dawn on 11 August during a rain storm, the invading force took the French by surprise, inflicted heavy casualties, and then retreated swiftly towards the Richelieu River. Fearing that the enemy might attack the fort at Chambly, Callière had earlier sent 160 men, colonial regulars, militia, and Indian allies, commanded by Valrennes, to block the road. Hearing the heavy firing at La Prairie, Valrennes obeyed the cardinal rule of 17th century warfare and marched his force to the sound of the guns. Halfway between the two forts he met the retiring enemy, flushed with their earlier success. Swiftly and coolly he marshalled his men in three ranks behind two fallen tree trunks. Five or six of his men were wounded during this manoeuvre but Valrennes made the ranks hold their fire until the enemy were within pistol range. The Albany forces charged and were met by measured volleys at close quarters. Their losses were heavy but the rest came on through the pall of powder smoke. For over an hour there was bloody hand-to-hand fighting; muskets were wielded as clubs, tomahawks, knives, and bare hands were used, and the air was filled with shrill war cries and the screams of mortally wounded men. It was the most savage engagement of the war. The Albany forces, with their great superiority of numbers, over two to one, finally fought their way through and fled. Valrennes' men were too exhausted to pursue them.

Afterwards, both sides greatly exaggerated the losses they had inflicted. Major Peter Schuyler stated that the Albany losses had been 37 dead and 31 wounded. The French admitted to losing 45 killed and 60 wounded, most of them in the first attack at La Prairie. All the French accounts agreed on one thing, that Valrennes had saved the day. The Albany militia made no further attempts to invade Canadian territory. From that day on the Iroquois had to bear the brunt of the fighting alone. In his dispatches to the court Frontenac was unstinting in his praise of Valrennes, declaring that "Nothing can equal the fearlessness with which the Sieur de Valrenne conducted himself. His calm expression and the coolness with which he gave his orders put heart into everyone."

Frontenac also pleaded with the minister to intervene in a law suit that Valrennes' brother-in-law had instituted at Beauvais to deny Valrennes his share of his mother's estate. Frontenac declared that Valrennes was too valuable an officer to be allowed to return to France to fight the case, but he should not have to suffer in consequence. When the minister granted this request Valrennes, with the strong support of both Frontenac and Champigny, submitted a plea to the king for letters of rehabilitation to pardon him for having killed a man 31 years earlier. His persistent brother-in-law had dredged up this old crime to nullify the *lettres d'état* granted Valrennes the year before to halt the legal proceedings at Beauvais.

This request the king was also pleased to grant but in 1693 Valrennes was stricken with paralysis, the result of old wounds. Frontenac and Champigny gave him leave to return to France, accompanied by his two valets, to seek a cure. While in France he requested that he be given the first vacant governorship in Canada, and be made a knight of the order of Saint-Louis. To substantiate his claim for membership in this order he stated that he was the senior of the captains in the colonial regular troops serving in Canada, had served 33 years in the king's armies, was a descendant of the first four marshals of France, and bore the scars of several wounds.

Despite his enviable military record—every year in his appraisal of the officers serving in Canada Champigny had given him the highest rating, "Very good officer, a brave man, suited to the country,"—these requests were denied. Instead, his commission as captain in the Canadian regulars was renewed and in 1695 he was accorded a brevet as *enseigne de vaisseau*. In 1696, his health apparently not having responded to treatment, he was retired on a pension of 600 *livres* a year. After that date his name ceases to appear on the roll of officers on the Canadian establishment. Of him could fairly be said that he epitomized the values of his class and of his age. Without men of his quality it is doubtful if New France could have survived as long as it did.

W. J. ECCLES

AN, Col., C¹¹ᴬ, 10, pp.194–98; 11, pp.236, 286, 300–2; 12, pp.31, 60, 279; D²ᶜ, 47, pp.51, 68, 90, 106, 114, 128, 142, 152, 180, 215; 222/2, p.288; F³, 6, pp.383–404 (PAC transcripts). *NYCD* (O'Callaghan and Fernow), III, 800–5 [this contains Major Peter Schuyler's journal of his expedition to Canada in 1691]. [François Vachon] de Belmont, *Histoire du Canada.* Tanguay, *Dictionnaire.* Eccles, *Frontenac.* Lanctot, *Histoire du Canada.* P.-G. Roy, "Philippe Clément Du Vuault De Valrennes," *BRH*, XI (1905), 193–203.

CLÉRIN, DENIS D'ESTIENNE DU BOURGUÉ DE. *See* ESTIENNE

CLIGNANCOUR, RENÉ DAMOURS DE. *See* DAMOURS

COLLET, MATHIEU-BENOÎT, lawyer in the *parlement* of Paris, king's counsellor, attorney general to the Conseil Supérieur of Quebec from 1712 to 1727; b. *c.* 1671 in France, son of Benoît Collet, lawyer in the *parlement* of Paris, and of Antoinette Thomé, of Lyons; d. 5 March 1727 at Quebec.

When Collet was appointed attorney general to the Conseil Supérieur on 14 June 1712, this post had been vacant for nearly six years: François RUETTE d'Auteuil, who had been dismissed in June 1707, had been in France since the previous autumn; Jessé Leduc Des Fontaines was chosen to replace him but died in September 1710, a few days after arriving at Quebec and before he could be installed; Goussé, Collet's immediate predecessor, never came to Canada. Collet reached Quebec in the autumn of 1712 aboard the ship *Héros*, presented his letters of appointment to the council on 14 October, and was installed in office three days later. Charles MACARD, whom the council had designated in 1707 to carry on in the interval, had petitioned for the post without success.

During the 15 years that Collet held the office of attorney general, he devoted himself conscientiously and with meticulous care to assisting the council in its task of dispensing justice. His extreme concern to ensure that the rules of law be strictly respected in all matters, civil or criminal, occasionally provoked retaliations. Thus he was reproached for providing his services free, but the king supported him, "His Majesty's intention being that justice in the Counseil Supérieur shall be administered free of charge." At times Collet's enthusiasm was judged excessive and incurred disapproval, although his sole preoccupation in acting thus was to guide the members of the council more effectively in their decisions. He had for example made it his practice, when a case presented some difficult question, to state the grounds on which he based his conclusions as well as the conclusions themselves. He even went so far as to refuse to withdraw during the deliberations, as he was supposed to do. Collet was given to understand, however, that councillors had rightly complained of such behaviour, which, though well intentioned, could only "hinder the judges in their decisions."

As attorney general it was his duty to see that

Collet

the king's orders were carried out in the colony, and he always gave this matter the most careful attention. In 1714, for example, he denounced the pretensions of officers in command of the king's ships and rebuked their contempt for the court to which they were answerable. He protested too against MARTIN de Lino's remarks that certain articles of an ordinance could not be complied with, and demonstrated the contrary, concluding in slightly peremptory fashion: "This proves that the councillor has spoken about something which he does not understand."

Collet did not however propose to limit his role to that of a mere watchdog of the law. From his first months in office, he undertook to point out to the authorities in France the difficulties, given the local conditions, of applying rigorously certain provisions of royal legislation. Consequently he was invited to send "reasoned reports on the basis of which His Majesty can reach a decision." Collet preferred to present these reports in person and he, therefore, requested and obtained permission to go to France; this he did in the autumn of 1716.

The series of nine reports that he submitted to the council of Marine during 1717 bears abundant testimony to his professional competence, as well as to the interest he had taken in his official tasks. These reports contain several projects for reorganization or reform, and remain the most durable and significant accomplishment of his career, though they did not all meet with a favourable reception.

After Collet had pointed out that it would be an advantage if the businessmen of Quebec and Montreal could meet to discuss business matters, as was the custom in all the commercial towns of France, a decree to this effect was drafted and immediately adopted by the council of state on 11 May 1717; each group of businessmen was authorized to choose a spokesman to be its syndic. Collet defended commercial interests in two reports, which were not however followed up: one concerned the payment of bills of exchange; in the other, he acted on the settlers' behalf, requesting permission for them to form a new company for trading in beaver pelts and proposing an agreement to this end. The forming of the Compagnie d'Occident, however, brought these last suggestions to nought.

To Collet also goes the credit for having been the first to propose that a law school be set up in Quebec. From the time of his arrival in Canada he had been in a position to see how detrimental to the administration of justice was the inadequate training of the judges; rare indeed were those, even among the members of the Conseil Supérieur, who could boast that they possessed some knowledge of the law. At first Collet had taken active steps to improve this undesirable situation by seeking to inform the councillors about the rules that should guide their decisions, but he had only drawn censure upon himself. From then on it seemed to him that the only sure way of correcting this deplorable state of affairs was legal training. In order that "those who aspire to offices in the judicature may be properly informed," he offered to give lessons in French law. He asked only that he should be provided with "some books." The council of Marine, which examined the proposal on 17 March 1717, declared in favour of it, but on condition that Collet would be willing to agree to run his school "free of charge," adding that "if subsequently the utility of this school is recognized, some recompense may be given him for this work." At a cost of 500 *livres*, the attorney general had the legal works necessary for his project purchased in Paris. For their part RIGAUD de Vaudreuil and Bégon* declared themselves ready to support to the utmost Collet's "good intentions." Despite all these encouragments, the law school did not come into existence until 1733, when the project was taken up again, this time successfully, by Louis-Guillaume Verrier*, Collet's successor.

Again it was Collet who initiated one of the most important legislative measures of the French régime concerning the organization of the notarial profession. A royal declaration of 2 Aug. 1717, applicable to all the colonies, requiring the preservation of notaries' minutes, resulted from the long report in which Collet pointed out the necessity of obliging notaries to classify their acts in chronological order, and of setting up a system of inventory and safe-keeping for the registries of deceased notaries. Despite its urgent nature, however, this reform was not put into effect until ten years later.

Among all the questions with which Collet had to deal, it was to the administration of justice that he devoted the most attention. All his efforts in this field were aimed at providing readier access to the courts, while at the same time discouraging the inevitable plaintiffs who were too fond of litigation. The three reports on the subject that he submitted to the council of Marine in 1717 are the best proof of this intention. In them he suggested various measures designed to reduce delays as much as possible, and to suppress the costly and useless procedures which by unduly prolonging lawsuits discredited justice in the minds of the settlers. Furthermore he volunteered to draft an ordinance which would replace in the colonies the great ordinance of 1667 on civil procedure (commonly called the *Code civil*); certain provisions of the code, though valid in the mother country, had to be changed to be more in keeping with the needs of Canada, and several others had already been modified or abrogated by special regulations and edicts. Collet proposed to assemble into one code, which he suggested calling the *Code civil pour la Nouvelle-France et autres colonies françaises*, a large number of legislative texts, the majority of which were poorly understood because they had not been put into print; he considered that this would be a useful service to the many honest litigants, victims of their own ignorance, who had been left to the mercy of legal practitioners adept in the art of instigating "a proliferation of legal actions" that were vexatious and ruinous.

These proposals, however, did not meet with approval, and this is to be regretted. The desire to ensure legislative uniformity throughout the kingdom—the obvious reflection of a policy of centralization—inevitably interfered with all local particularisms; Collet's projects on the contrary tended to accentuate them. On the other hand his suggestion for drawing up a code of procedure for the colonies seemed to have a stronger hold on the attention of the council of Marine. The council then inquired where Collet planned to do this work, how much time he would need for it, and what it would cost. Collet replied that it would be more convenient for him to work in France, that he would need 1,000 *livres* in addition to his salary, and that he confidently anticipated that his text would be ready before the ships sailed the following year. Whereupon the council rejected the attorney general's proposal, intimating to him that "it [would] be better for him to return to Canada, where his presence [would] be more useful to the colony."

The last of Collet's reports dealt with the new parishes. In it he argued against the bishop's claim that the decision to build new churches and to break up old parishes should rest solely with him, whereas the custom of the kingdom required that such action be taken only after an inquiry had been made as to its expediency or inexpediency, and after all the parties concerned had been heard. The bishop's intention to act independently, again asserted by Saint-Vallier [LA CROIX] in a petition addressed to the king's council on 3 Nov. 1717, had given rise to several differences which Collet hoped to be able to bring to an end. In 1720, as growing needs made a new division of parishes necessary, the king decided to have an inquiry *supra commodo et incommodo* instituted, in order to effect a redistribution of parish districts. Collet was chosen to conduct this inquiry. From 4 Feb. to 3 June 1721 he covered both shores of the St Lawrence, accompanied by a clerk of court, Nicolas-Gaspard Boucault*. The attorney general's reports resulted in a joint ruling by the governor, the intendant, and the bishop on 20 Sept. 1721, dividing the colony into 82 parish districts. This ruling was confirmed by the king on the following 3 March.

During his stay in France Collet seems to have been in financial straits. Because of his position as lawyer in the *parlement*, the king had granted to him, as to his two predecessors Leduc and Goussé, an annual gratuity of 1,000 *livres* in addition to his salary. Fearing that he would be affected by the recent decision to reduce all pensions, Collet appealed to the council of Marine. The latter was of the opinion that, as his services had given satisfaction, he should be permitted to retain his gratuity intact. Although the order for this payment was consequently given, Collet received nothing, and in the autumn of 1717 he gave up the idea of returning to Canada. In 1718 he reminded the council that his gratuity for two and a half years was still owing to him, and that he was "not in a position to leave Paris and proceed to his destination unless he was paid." He repeated his request the following year, and finally sailed for Quebec, where he arrived in September 1719. He resumed his functions in the Conseil Supérieur on 2 October after three years spent in France. He immediately ordered the registration of some 15 edicts, declarations, letters patent, and decrees of the council of state issued during his absence.

On 7 Jan. 1713, at Quebec, Collet had married Élisabeth, daughter of Paul DENIS de Saint-Simon. They had one son, Mathieu, who was born and baptized 3 Nov. 1713, but who died the following 8 October. Collet's wife had died two weeks before, on 24 Sept. 1714. Collet did not remarry.

At the time of his death on 5 March 1727, he was living in the house of his sister-in-law Marie-Anne Denis de Saint-Simon, wife of the surgeon Michel BERTIER, in a separate annex with its entrance on Rue des Pauvres facing the ramparts, in the Saint-Nicolas quarter of Quebec. He was buried with his wife and son in the crypt of the church of Notre-Dame in Quebec, 7 March 1727.

On the eve of his death, he had made his will, before the notary LOUET senior, constituting his sister-in-law his residuary legatee. On learning of his death, Intendant DUPUY immediately had the seals affixed to the house, because of the presence there of the numerous public documents that Collet kept stored in his home and also the books which the state had bought to enable him to run a law school. Altogether these books, which he had

Collins

kept on hand, constituted a meagre library of no more than 25 legal works, which are listed in detail in the inventory of the estate.

On 15 Sept. 1724, Collet had acquired at an agreed rent a piece of land on which he had had built the house where he lived. Shortly before his death, he had also purchased from Louis Rouer* d'Artigny some land on Chemin Saint-Jean. He sometimes assumed the title of Seigneur de La Fortière.

Nicolas Lanouiller*, one of those who aspired to succeed him in the post of attorney general, carried on the duties of this office until the installation of Louis-Guillaume Verrier on 17 Sept. 1728.

ANDRÉ MOREL

AJQ, Greffe de Jacques Barbel, 31 déc. 1712; Greffe de Jean-Claude Louet, 15 sept. 1724, 29 juillet 1725, 4 mai 1726; Registres d'état civil de Notre-Dame de Québec, 1713, 1714, 1727. AN., Col., B, 34, ff. 17v–18, 41v, 59–60; 35, f.86v; 36, f.408v; 37, f.190v; 38, ff.205v–206; 39, ff.120v–121, 134, 255v; 40, ff.113v–114; 41, f.84v; C¹¹ᴬ, 34, ff.441–46, 496–98, 505; 37, ff.128–29, 161–67, 260–64, 270–76, 278–83, 291–308; 38, f.38; 42, ff.181–85; 47, f.130; 49, f.169; F³, 10, ff.257–60v; 11, ff.24–26v. AQ, NF, Ins. Cons. sup., III, 52; NF, Registres du Cons. sup., 1717–1719. Édits ord., I, III. Gérard Filteau, La naissance d'une nation, tableau du Canada en 1755 (2v., Montréal, 1937), I. Jug. et délib., VI, 523–24, 1206–7. "Procès-verbaux du procureur général Collet" (Caron), 262–380. PAC Report, 1899, Supp. A. Roy, Inv. greffes not., X. P.-G. Roy, Inv. contrats de mariage, II, 67; Inv. ins. Cons. souv., 124, 185; Inv. jug. et délib., 1717–1760, I, VI, VII; Inv. testaments, I, 130. Charland, "Notre-Dame de Québec: le nécrologe de la crypte," 180, 346. "Liste des officiers de justice de la Nouvelle-France (1722)," BRH, XXXVI (1930), 152. "Liste des personnes auxquelles le Conseil a accordé le passage pour le Canada sur la flûte l'Éléphant (1718)," BRH, XXXIV (1928), 759. Cahall, Sovereign Council of New France, 106, 159. Guy Frégault, La civilisation de la Nouvelle-France (1713–1744) (Montréal, 1944). Gosselin, L'Église du Canada, I. J.-E. Roy, Histoire du notariat, I, 281–97. P.-G. Roy, La ville de Québec, II, 237–38, 293–94. Vachon, Histoire du notariat, 26. Ignotus [Thomas Chapais], "Notes et souvenirs," La Presse (Montréal), 6 déc. 1902. Édouard Fabre-Surveyer, "Louis-Guillaume Verrier (1690–1758)," RHAF, VI (1952), 159–74.

COLLINS, JOHN, governor and commander-in-chief of the fort and harbour of St John's, Newfoundland; fl. 1706–20.

The merchant John Collins first appears in September 1706 when he was appointed a captain and his son an ensign of militia in St John's by Commodore Underdown. After Captain LLOYD and the garrison of St John's were captured by the

French in the winter of 1708–9, Collins as commander of the militia tried unsuccessfully to retake the fort, but he was captured and taken as a prisoner to Placentia (Plaisance), where he was held for several months. According to Collins, St John's was "lost by [Lloyd's] neglect." Collins was released after signing a declaration in May 1709 before Costebelle [PASTOUR] that the French had done nothing contrary to the articles of war and that he and other St John's merchants such as William Keen* would fulfil the financial conditions of the surrender imposed by the French commander Saint-Ovide [Mombeton*].

Collins and Allen Southmayd were able to send the Board of Trade and Plantations a description of the fortification at Placentia: there was a force of 50 men in the castle, which could hold at most 150 men, and the harbour contained 43 sail, including 1 man-of-war and 6 to 8 armed ships. Probably as an acknowledgement of his leadership in 1708, the commodore of the naval escort in 1709, Captain Joseph TAYLOUR, appointed Collins governor and commander-in-chief of the fort and harbour of St John's and of the coast between Ferryland and Carbonear Island. Collins' authority empowered him to appoint captains and other officers as necessary. Almost immediately Collins petitioned Colonel NICHOLSON, commander of the expedition against Port-Royal (Annapolis Royal, N.S.), to furnish supplies to support the 470 persons in the garrison through the winter. He also wrote his brother, the Rev. Edward Collins, minister at Wimbledon, Surrey, recounting the "miserable, hard winter" they had had, and asking his brother to present his case to the board. He submitted the usual petitions for repayment of his expenses in regaining the fort, which Commodore CROWE commended in 1711. He also petitioned to be kept on as governor, and his case was supported by the Duke of Leeds. In 1712 the next commodore, Sir Nicholas TREVANION, confirmed him as governor of Fort William, and he continued to be referred to as governor at least until 1720.

It is difficult to determine the duties of the "governor" after the war with France ended in 1713 with the treaty of Utrecht. Nicholson and then Philipps* were nominally governors of Placentia and Nova Scotia, and as there was no civil government until 1729, the commodores continued to adjudicate disputes when they visited the island in the summer and to complain about the lawlessness of the long rowdy winters. In 1716 the Board of Trade recommended that two judges be elected by the inhabitants before the departure of the fleet. As for Collins' suitability for the post of governor or magistrate, Commodore Passenger thought that "no man liveing in . . . Newfoundland is fit to govern," whereas Commodore Scott thought Keen and Collins "fitly qualify'd for the preserving of order."

It would appear that Collins' prosperity increased as did that of the fishery, after the serious decline of 1711 to 1714. In 1720 Commodore Percy noted that despite previous orders Collins and seven other merchants had refused to relinquish the stages of fishing admirals that they had "engrossed." John Collins was probably dead before 1723, when the principal inhabitants of St John's drew up a Lockian petition for civil government [see JAGO].

C. P. MCFARLAND

PRO, C.O. 194/4; *Acts of P.C., col. ser., 1680–1720*; *B.T.Journal, 1704–1708/9, 1708/9–1714/15*; *CSP, Col., 1706–8, 1708–9, 1710–11, 1711–12, 1712–14, 1717–18, 1719–20, 1720–21*; *C.T.Papers, 1714–19*. Rogers, *Newfoundland*.

CONSTANTIN, NICOLAS-BERNARDIN, Recollet priest; b. 1664; d. September 1730.

Father Constantin must have been one of the four Recollets who came to Canada in 1696. His name appears in the records for the first time on 8 Nov. 1697 at Trois-Rivières; on 20 Feb. 1698 he recorded another act there. In 1701 he was apparently a missionary at Sorel and Berthier, since he figures as such on the list of parish priests to whom the king gave allowances in "the present year of 1701," a list that was closed on 15 October of that year. In 1702 on 22 July, 4 and 12 August, he held services at Batiscan, which was at that time without a parish priest. During February and March 1703 he served at Saint-François de Sales, on Île Jésus.

Father Constantin was at Montreal in 1706. He served at Longueuil and was always ready to assist parish priests in the region and to help out in parishes where there was no one to officiate. The following year he was to be found at La Prairie de la Magdeleine and Saint-François de Sales and in 1710 at Lachenaye.

It was doubtless in the parish of Saint-François de Sales that Father Constantin served on a more regular basis. Abbé Louis Lepage de Sainte-Claire, who had been appointed priest of this parish and officiant at Lachenaye, appealed to the Recollets of Montreal for help in securing replacements during his numerous absences. It was Father Constantin who became, as it were, his curate, but he did not take the title until 2 March 1721; he retained the office until 18 September of that year.

In 1724 Father Constantin again served at Lachenaye and Varennes, and in 1726 at La Prairie de la Magdeleine. We encounter him for the last time on 23 March 1729, when he baptized a pair of twins at the request of the parish priest of Longueuil, the Sulpician Joseph Isambart. He died "in Canada ... September 1730, at the age of 66."

JACQUES VALOIS

Archives des Franciscains de Québec, Fonds Jouve-Godbout, Table générale des Frères Mineurs, f.41. AJJ, Registres d'état civil de Lachenaie. AJTR, Registres d'état civil de Batiscan. AN, Col., B, 19; F⁵ᴬ, 3, f.25.

COSTEBELLE, PHILIPPE DE PASTOUR DE. *See* PASTOUR

COUAGNE, CHARLES DE, *maître d'hôtel*, fur trader, land owner, merchant, and entrepreneur; b. in 1651 in the parish of Clion, archdiocese of Bourges, son of Charles de Couagne and Renée Greffière; d. in Montreal in 1706.

Couagne first appears in the documents of New France as an employee of Buade* de Frontenac. Benjamin Sulte wrongly calls him a valet. His position as the governor's *maître d'hôtel* indicates that he held a high status within Frontenac's entourage. Shortly after his marriage Couagne established himself in the Montreal area. His commercial activities, like those of other prominent merchants, were varied: he speculated in real estate in Sorel, Boucherville, and Montreal; he took an active part in the trade of the *pays d'en haut* as a direct employer of coureurs de bois, and also extended significant sums in credit to others engaged in the fur trade—in some years he lent as much as 20,000 *livres*. He engaged in wholesale and retail merchandising in Montreal from 1683 until his death. He also bought and leased cattle and wood lots, and was concerned with supplying the food staple, bread.

Couagne was married twice: to Anne Mars in 1680, and in 1685 to Marie Godé. The latter, after the death of Couagne, married Derivon de Budemon. Couagne had 11 children; one of his daughters married FRANÇOIS POULIN de Francheville. His sons, particularly René*, played an active role in the commercial life in the colony till the conquest; JEAN-BAPTISTE was a military engineer who served in Canada and Île Royale (Cape Breton Island). After 1760 his descendants tried to claim that they were of the nobility.

Couagne's health began deteriorating in 1704 and, after an illness of two years, he died between 22 and 28 Aug. 1706. He left a surprisingly large estate: the net assets—which included, however, many due bills and obligations—totalled 226,547 *livres* 17 *sols*. His succession involved litigation over a long period of time. The sons accused the mother of concerning herself, especially after her remarriage, with only the assets of the estate and not the liabilities.

CAMERON NISH

AJM, Greffe d'Antoine Adhémar, 23 juillet 1701, 22, 28 août 1706. AJQ, Greffe de Pierre Duquet, 19 nov. 1680; Greffe de Florent de La Cetière, 3 mai 1704. AQ, NF, Coll. de pièces jud. et. not., 284, 323, 352. PAC, FM 24, Collection Baby, L 3, pp.25,128–25,136.

COUAGNE, JEAN-BAPTISTE DE, surveyor and military engineer in Canada and Île Royale (Cape Breton Island); b. 1687 probably at Montreal, the son of CHARLES DE COUAGNE (d. 1706) and Marie Godé (d. 1729); m. 28 Sept. 1720, at Louisbourg, Marguerite-Madeleine de Gannes de Falaise (d. 1733); father of Michel and Jean-François (the former an engineer at Louisbourg and in Canada); d. 22 Jan. 1740 at Louisbourg.

In 1708 GÉDÉON DE CATALOGNE, a business associate of Charles de Couagne, engaged Jean-Baptiste as his surveyor-assistant in mapping the jurisdictions (*gouvernements*) of Quebec, Trois-Rivières, and Montreal. The young Couagne was the draftsman of the maps for at least the first two. He continued to serve as a surveyor and mapmaker in Canada until, in 1713, he was commissioned ensign and posted to Île Royale to take part in the reconnaissance of the new colony there.

From 1713 to 1716 he assisted Jacques L'HERMITTE in surveying the island and earned commendation for his talent in design and for his stamina and diligence. In 1714 with Louis Denys* de La Ronde and JEAN-BAPTISTE HERTEL de Rouville he conducted a small party of Acadians (who were considering an invitation to settle on Île Royale instead of becoming British subjects) into the region of the La Brador (Bras d'Or) lakes. Although his report of January 1715 mentions some arable land and timber resources north of the Grand Lac de La Brador (Great Bras d'Or), it emphasizes that south of it neither the timber nor the soil was of good quality, the only profitable resource being the cod fishery, which could be exploited through the use of the good natural harbours. Most of the Acadians had returned home, there to remain. In August 1715 Couagne helped to build a fort for those who had settled at Port Toulouse (St Peters).

In 1717 he began a long career as a resident assistant-engineer on Île Royale, serving first under Jean-François de VERVILLE, director of fortifications, and subsequently under Étienne Verrier*, engineer-in-chief; he held this post until his death. Although not a member of the corps of engineers, Couagne was accepted as a competent engineer: Verville, for example, was prepared to put him in charge of work at Port-Dauphin (Englishtown, N.S.) in 1717; he usually shared supervision of the work at Louisbourg between 1718 and 1724 when Verville wintered in France; and on those occasions when Verrier returned to France on leave, the same arrangement obtained. Not brilliant—he was never more than a good second to Verville or Verrier—he combined diligence with integrity, retaining a sense of objectivity in the midst of those personal and procedural wrangles which marked the tenure of Verville. The usefulness and devotion to service of Couagne were matters on which even bitter enemies could agree, so that while his colleague Pierre-Jérôme Boucher*, for example, could be called "a creature of Verville" after the latter's departure from Louisbourg, Couagne was nobody's "creature." Once established at Louisbourg, Couagne rarely left, and then only to go to Canada on family business. After his wife's death in 1733, his health began to decline.

He moved slowly up the promotion scale of the colonial regular troops, becoming a lieutenant in 1719 and a half-pay captain in 1732, the rank he held at his death. With Fontenay during the first three years, and Boucher thereafter, Couagne drafted many of the plans for fortifications and buildings on Île Royale which are credited to Verville and Verrier, as well as many of the estimates and construction accounts. Some specific tasks which were assigned to him were the surveying in 1716 of shore-lines for fishermen at Louisbourg; the designing of accommodation for new troops in 1719 and the repairing of a bakery and a house for officers; the drafting of plans for a house for the financial commissary (1721); and the preparation in 1723, during the absence of Verville, of emergency defences against possible raids by pirates.

F. J. THORPE

AN, Col., B, 35, ff.57, 249; 36, ff.423, 433v; 38, f.253; 39, f.266; 41, f.592; 42, f.481; 44, ff.560, 574v; 48, f.953; 49, f.701; 50, ff.595–97; 52, ff.588–93; 53, ff.602v–6; 57, ff.743, 757; C^{11A}, 48, f.202; C^{11B}, 1, ff.11, 87–89, 247, 291–315v; 2, ff.131, 259; 3, ff.153–53v; 4, ff.107, 145, 147, 216, 237–41; 5, ff.25–34, 58, 218–19, 238–40v, 349, 403, 405, 414–16; 6, ff.69–70, 114, 145, 152, 182, 313; 7, ff.132, 261, 331; 9, f.60; 11, ff.14–15, 74–79v; 12, f.22; 13, ff.200–4v; 14, ff.298–302; 22, ff.139, 143; D^{2C}, 60, f.18; 222, p.168 (copy in PAC); E, 94, f.1; F^3, 51, ff.39–40, 128, 132. PAC, Map div., A/300 (1709); R/300 (1709); VI/900, sect.I and II ([1711]).

A. Roy, *Inv. greffes not.*, V, 126, 181, 201. Le Blant, *Histoire de la N.-F.*, 135. McLennan, *Louisbourg*.

COUILLARD DE LESPINAY, JEAN-BAP-TISTE (Lépinay, L'Épine, L'Espinay), ensign,

Couillard de Lespinay

captain of the guards of the tax-farm, attorney of the provost court, lieutenant-general of the admiralty court, seigneur; son of Louis Couillard* de Lespinay and Geneviève Després; baptized at Quebec 2 May 1657; buried 8 March 1735 at Quebec.

Jean-Baptiste Couillard de Lespinay, the eldest son of the first seigneur of Rivière-du-Sud, had a double career as administrator and seigneur. On 24 Oct. 1680 he married Geneviève de Chavigny, widow of Charles Amiot*. From her first marriage she had had one son, Charles-Joseph AMIOT de Vincelotte, who was to have numerous conflicts with his step-father.

On 15 May 1691, after serving as ensign and captain of the guards of the tax-farm, Couillard de Lespinay received from Buade* de Frontenac a commission as captain of the port of Quebec. Curiously enough, neither the king, Louis XIV, nor the admiral of France confirmed this appointment, so that in 1702 a report stressed that "a port captain would be very necessary," and that one could hardly find "a man of greater uprightness and with more experience of such matters than he [Lespinay]." However, CALLIÈRE and Beauharnois* de La Boische were opposed, for according to them "the Sieur de Lépinay is not qualified either by his birth or by his services for such a position." On the other hand, in 1703 these same governmental authorities recommended him for the post of king's attorney of the provost and admiralty courts of Quebec, but they changed their minds and later put forward the name of his step-son Charles-Joseph Amiot. Nevertheless, on 10 Oct. 1705 Couillard received from JACQUES RAUDOT the order to take over the functions of attorney during the absence of the Sieur Thierry, who was detained in France by illness. He deputized in this office until 9 June 1708, when the king appointed him officially to the post. He exercised this function until 1716. On 27 April of that year, the king granted him the office of special lieutenant of the provost court, but Couillard was to act as lieutenant-general until the installation of Pierre André* de Leigne, on 10 Oct. 1719. In January 1718 Couillard was granted the commission of lieutenant-general in the admiralty court of Quebec. From October 1719 until his death, he performed the two functions of special lieutenant of the provost court and lieutenant-general of the admiralty court.

These duties obliged Couillard de Lespinay to live in Quebec, where he resided in Rue Sous-le-Fort. He nonetheless remained co-seigneur of Rivière-du-Sud. On 4 Aug. 1671 at the same time as did his brothers LOUIS and Jacques, he had received a land grant of 100 acres, situated between

Rivière-du-Sud and Rivière des Vases. On his father's death in 1678, he had inherited, as the eldest son, half of the Rivière-du-Sud seigneury. In 1701 he was granted the fief of Lespinay and purchased the fief of Saint-Luc. As the owner of a fairly extensive domain, he, like his brother Louis, proved himself to be a wise seigneur who made numerous land grants. He was, moreover, obliged to defend part of his property, first in 1693 against Nicolas Gamache, seigneur of L'Islet, and a second time, after the death of his wife in 1724, against Amiot de Vincelotte, his step-son, who boasted that he had some 15 lawsuits to bring against him and who obtained only half of an unidentified fief.

Jean-Baptiste Couillard de Lespinay was always acknowledged to be a "very worthy man"; the authorities praised his "loyalty, integrity, experience and attachment to the service of His Majesty." A fervent Christian, he was a member of the Marian congregation for men and one of the benefactors of the religious communities of Quebec. He was buried in the paupers' cemetery at Quebec.

NIVE VOISINE

AQ, Azarie Couillard Després. "Un mémoire de Le Roy de La Potherie sur la Nouvelle-France adressé à M. de Pontchartrain, 1701–1702," BRH, XXII (1916), 214–16. Azarie Couillard Després, Histoire des seigneurs de la Rivière-du-Sud et leurs alliés canadiens et acadiens (Saint-Hyacinthe, Qué., 1912); La première famille française au Canada, ses alliés et ses descendants (Montréal, 1906). P.-G. Roy, "Jean-Baptiste Couillard de Lespinay," BRH, XXVI (1920), 3–10.

COUILLARD DE LESPINAY, LOUIS, co-seigneur of Rivière-du-Sud; baptized 29 Nov. 1658 at Quebec, son of Louis Couillard*, Sieur de Lespinay, and of Geneviève Després; buried 15 May 1728 at Saint-Pierre du Sud.

Louis Couillard de Lespinay gradually built up a large fief. On 4 Aug. 1671 he received from his father, as a settlement of portion by anticipation, an arriere-fief of "four arpents in the said seigneury of Rivière-du-Sud, fronting on the St Lawrence River and extending to a depth of 40 arpents." On 29 Nov. 1685, conjointly with his brother Jacques, he inherited half of the Rivière-du-Sud seigneury of which his mother had had possession since her husband's death in 1678; this part became his completely when he bought out his brother Jacques in 1690.

During all these years, Louis Couillard proved to be a good administrator. In 1700 he won a sensational lawsuit against Isaac (Alexandre) BERTHIER, seigneur of Bellechasse, over the boundaries of his seigneury. Under his stimulus,

Coulanges de Levilliers

settling progressed rapidly and the number of settlers increased steadily, so much so that around 1720 the seigneury of Rivière-du-Sud was the second in size from the point of view of population.

This growth made necessary the opening of roads to the interior. Louis Couillard thus became one of the creators of the "king's road." In 1713 he obtained an ordinance from the king requiring the settlers of Saint-Thomas and Saint-Pierre to work on roads and bridges, under penalty of fines. As there was a good deal of stalling and opposition, Michel Bégon* issued a new decree on 22 April 1720. A start was thus made on the organization of road-building in New France.

Louis Couillard de Lespinay was buried on 15 May 1728. He had been married four times. On 23 Oct. 1680 he married Marie Vandry, by whom he had two children who died young. On 4 May 1688 he married Marie Fortin, who bore him 11 children. He married Marguerite Bélanger in 1712, became a widower in 1717, and two years later took as his fourth wife Louise Nolin, by whom he had three children.

NIVE VOISINE

Jug. et délib. A. Roy, *Inv. greffes not.*, III, 64. Azarie Couillard Després, *Histoire des seigneurs de la Rivière-du-Sud et leurs alliés canadiens et acadiens* (Saint-Hyacinthe, Qué., 1912). F.-J. Audet, "La seigneurie de la Rivière du Sud," *BRH*, VI (1901), 117–19. Azarie Couillard Després, "En marge de l'histoire de la Rivière-du-Sud, *BRH*, XXI (1915), 116–22.

COULANGES DE LEVILLIERS. *See* PETIT

COULON DE VILLIERS, NICOLAS-ANTOINE, captain; b. 20 March 1683 at Mantes, son of Raoul-Guillaume, Sieur de Villiers-en-Arthies, and of Louise, daughter of Antoine de La Fosse, seigneur of Valpendant; d. 1733.

His family formed part of the rich provincial nobility. We know nothing about his youth, but he seems to have arrived at Quebec in the summer of 1700. On 26 April of that year, he had received from the king the expectancy of an ensignship in Canada.

CALLIÈRE named him an ensign in October. In 1703 Coulon de Villiers was garrisoned at Montreal, where his name appears in several notarial acts. He seems to have married in 1705, for on 7 December of that year, before the notary Abel Michon, he signed a marriage contract with Angélique Jarret de Verchères, Madeleine*'s sister. On 1 July 1715 he was promoted lieutenant on the active list.

He was appointed in 1725 commandant at the post on the St Joseph River (Michigan). There

we find his name in the register of baptisms under the date 26 Aug. 1725. On 25 Nov. 1730, in the same register, he is called "seigneur of Verchères." Although there is no mention of his name in the list of land grants, it may be that he inherited a part of the Verchères seigneury through his wife.

It was from 1730 on that Coulon de Villiers' life became somewhat more eventful. He had to contend with some Fox who had taken refuge in a small fort on the bank of the St Joseph River. He recorded in his account of the expedition that "the siege of their fort lasted 23 days; they were reduced to eating leather, and we were little better off." Taking advantage of a stormy night, the Indians tried to flee, but the French slaughtered several of them. Coulon de Villiers then sent one of his sons to Quebec to notify the governor of this success. On 18 June 1731 he personally took to Montreal the chief of the Foxes, who begged for mercy for the lives of those of his subjects who had escaped the slaughter.

It was probably on this occasion that Governor Beauharnois* de La Boische appointed him commandant of the post at Baie des Puants (Green Bay). He was also promoted captain on 1 April 1733. Coulon de Villiers did not enjoy his new position for long. On 16 September he once more had to fight against the Foxes, who had taken refuge among the Sauks at the other end of Baie des Puants. He tried to force his way into their small fort, but the Indians began to fire; one of his sons, whose name we do not know, was killed. Coulon de Villiers himself met the same fate, as did his son-in-law François Regnard Duplessis (who had married Marie-Madeleine), Jean-Baptiste-René Legardeur de Repentigny, and some other Frenchmen.

Coulon de Villiers had been a brave officer, but the minister of Marine, in a letter addressed to Beauharnois on 12 April 1735, said that his "rash and foolhardy conduct" might have been the cause of his death.

He had seven boys and six girls; two of his sons, Joseph*, Sieur de Jumonville, and Louis*, became famous. On 13 April 1734 Madame de Villiers was granted a pension of 300 *livres*. She died the same year and was buried on 30 December.

JEAN-GUY PELLETIER

ASQ, MSS, 132, 133. "The St-Joseph baptismal register," ed. George Paré and M. M. Quaife, *Mississippi Valley Hist. Review*, XIII (1926), 201–39. P.-G. Roy, *La famille Jarret de Verchères* (Lévis, 1908). Amédée Gosselin, "Notes sur la famille Coulon de Villiers," *BRH*, XII (1906), 161–79, 193–218, 225–46, 296. George Paré, "The St-Joseph mission," *Mississippi Valley Hist. Review*, XVII (1930–31), 24–54.

COURTEMANCHE, AUGUSTIN LE GAR-DEUR DE. *See* Le Gardeur

COURVAL, JEAN-BAPTISTE POULIN DE. *See* Poulin

COUTURE, GUILLAUME (he sometimes signed himself **Cousture**), carpenter, a *donné* of the Society of Jesus, discoverer, interpreter, diplomat, judge of the seneschal's court, first settler at Lévis; b. *c.* 1616 at Saint-Godard-de-Rouen (province of Normandy), son of Guillaume Couture and Madeleine Mallet; d. 1701.

It is impossible, by reference to existing documents, to determine the year of his arrival in New France. The Jesuits, who in their *Relations* never tire of praising his devotion and his courage, furnish no information on this point. The years 1639 and 1640 seem the most likely. He may have made the crossing in the spring of 1640 at the same time as René Goupil* and Father René Ménard*, and have undertaken to be an assistant to the Jesuits before he left France. His vocation as a *donné* may have been inspired by Goupil, who was already one. In an act dated 26 June 1641 at Quebec, in which he bequeathed to his mother and sister the modest amount of landed property left to him in France by his father, he styled himself "servant of the reverend Fathers of the Society of Jesus in the Huron mission in New France." He set off shortly afterwards for Huronia, taking with him various items for the missionaries. It was the first of his long trips. He returned to Quebec the following spring, with Fathers Isaac Jogues* and Charles Raymbaut*, who was gravely ill; they were accompanied by a few Indian chiefs, among whom was the famous Ahatsistari*. Altogether there were 25 travellers in 4 canoes.

Scarcely 15 days after their arrival, Jogues and Couture, accompanied this time by René Goupil, set out once more for the Huron country. The expedition was an important one, for the Indian chiefs, who had come to Quebec on an official mission, were returning to their country at the same time, having been assured of the protection of the French authorities against their Iroquois enemies. On 1 Aug. 1642, 12 canoes, carrying some 40 persons, left Trois-Rivières. The departure did not escape the vigilant eyes of the enemy sentries. On the first evening of the journey, when the convoy had barely reached the entry to Îles-du-Sud in Lac Saint-Pierre, they halted for the night [*see* Ahatsistari*]. The next day, at dawn, they were on the point of setting out when scouts discovered tracks of Indians on the shore. They started all the same, but less than half an hour later the little band heard firing and returned

hastily to land. Goupil, a novice in forest lore, was quickly captured. Jogues, who had hidden for a moment in the undergrowth, surrendered himself to the Iroquois in order not to abandon his companions. Couture thought the missionary was in a safe place and managed to flee; but not finding him anywhere and not wanting to leave him, he returned towards the site of the ambush. On the way he encountered five Iroquois; one of them took aim at him, but missed his target; Couture fired in his turn and killed his adversary. The four others captured him, and as the dead man was their chief Couture experienced Indian vengeance for the first time. His nails were torn out, his joints were broken, and then the palms of his hands were slowly pierced. One finger was sawn off with a shell. Couture bore all this without a cry, for not far away his companions were suffering in silence. The prisoners who had not been killed outright were borne off to the Mohawk villages, where further tortures awaited them. All were stripped naked, and were forced to pass between two rows of men armed with whips and clubs who struck them in turn. Couture headed this ghastly procession, which was repeated in each village.

In accordance with Indian custom, Couture was turned over to the family of the chief whom he had killed, so that they could dispose of him as they thought fit. He was made to witness the horrible death meted out to the chief Ahatsistari, details of which he later gave to Father Jogues. He was then adopted by a widow of the tribe, who dressed his wounds and treated him well. He was to acknowledge later to Jogues that, despite the proposals that were made to him, he remained faithful to his vows as a *donné*.

Goupil was murdered on 29 September 1642. Jogues succeeded in escaping in November 1643, with the complicity of the Dutch near by, and eventually got to France. Couture could have joined him, but he did not want to compromise the missionary's flight, and decided to wait for another opportunity. He continued to improve his knowledge of the Iroquois language, observe customs, and note particularly the intentions of the chiefs. He adapted himself readily to his new kind of life, and his peaceful attitude won him the confidence of the members of the council. One *Relation* mentions that "the Iroquois held him in esteem and high repute, as one of the first men in their nation. Consequently he assumed the position of a captain among them, having acquired this prestige by his prudence and wisdom." Léo-Paul Desrosiers was correct in writing that "Couture is therefore the first Frenchman to win a great influence in the Iroquois country, after

Couture

being adopted there, and, right in this enemy territory, to play a role favourable to France. Like several of his successors, he was to rise within this strange nation from the state of prisoner to that of chief."

Thus in July 1645 he accompanied the chief Kiotseaeton*, the recognized diplomat and great warrior of the Mohawk tribe, to a council held at Trois-Rivières by the governor general, Huault* de Montmagny, and François de Champflour*, the commandant and local governor. Couture was dressed in Iroquois style, like his companions. He identified himself, but everyone, including Father Jogues, who had returned from France some time before, hesitated to recognize him, for all hope of seeing him again had been lost. "As soon as Couture was recognized," notes the *Relation* of 1645, "each person threw himself on his neck. They looked on him as a man come back to life who gives joy to all who thought him dead, or at least in danger of spending the rest of his existence in a most bitter and barbarous captivity."

It was indeed with a genuine desire for peace that the Mohawks brought back their precious prisoner, for Couture had convinced them of the friendly intentions of the French. But Couture's idea went still further: he would have liked to be the instigator of a permanent peace between all the Indian nations and the French colony. To this end he agreed to return with the Iroquois ambassadors, to try to encourage them to open serious peace negotiations with the Hurons.

When he returned in the spring of 1646 from this embassy to the Mohawks, Couture sought from the Jesuits authorization to break his vows as a *donné*, because he intended to get married: perhaps he wanted to marry an Iroquois girl with a view to strengthening the alliance between Indians and whites. The superior, Jérôme Lalemant*, gave his consent on 26 April. Couture continued his peace parleys at Trois-Rivières and Quebec with the chiefs of the various nations. He was on the point of succeeding when on 18 Oct. 1646 Father Jogues, who since his escape had returned twice to the Mohawks as an emissary, and his companion Jean de La Lande* were murdered. Negotiations were broken off. The Algonkins and Hurons were secretly delighted, for they alone would retain the friendship of the French. Couture, in no way discouraged, went to the Huron country in 1647 to try to renew the treaties of alliance. His efforts were fruitless, but on his return the population of Trois-Rivières and the loyal Indians welcomed him warmly at the instigation of Father Jacques Buteux*, who had a high regard for him and who in a report dated 1652 called him "the worthy Couture." A similar welcome was given him at Sillery, "with joy on the part of all the Huron, Algonkin and Annieh-ronnon [Mohawk] Indians," as the *Journal des Jésuites* noted.

In this same year, 1647, Couture entered into partnership with François Byssot* de La Rivière, and went to settle at Pointe-Lévy, on the Lauson seigneury. He agreed to clear a tract of land and erect a main building for his partner, the latter providing the money and materials. The building was finished in the autumn; Byssot gave Couture 200 *livres* for his work, and allowed him to remain in the house until he had completed his own dwelling on a neighbouring piece of land. On 15 Oct. 1648 both obtained official title to their land grants from the seigneur, Jean de Lauson*. On 18 Nov. 1649 Couture married Anne, one of the three Esmard sisters, who had come together from Niort, in the province of Poitou. [The others were Barbe, wife of Olivier Letardif*, and Madeleine, wife of the son of Zacarie Cloutier*.] The marriage ceremony, presided over by Abbé Le Sueur*, took place "in the house of the said Sieur Couture at Pointe-Lévy," according to the register of the Roman Catholic church in Quebec.

Although Couture wanted to stay quietly on his property and make it bear fruit, his knowledge of Indian languages and his experience of life in the woods were often made use of by the authorities. There can be no doubt that in the relation of Father Buteux the detailed part that concerned Father Jogues' captivity was to a large extent inspired by Couture. Apart from a few Hurons, he was the sole witness of it. He was called upon in 1657 to be an interpreter for the founding of a mission among the Onondagas, a mission earnestly requested by the tribe itself. In 1661 he agreed to take part, along with Fathers Gabriel Druillettes* and also Claude Dablon*, Denis Guyon, and François Pelletier, in an expedition sent by Governor VOYER d'Argenson to discover the northern sea. The Indian guides, dreading the presence of Iroquois in the region, abandoned the French at the watershed. Two years later Couture accepted Governor Dubois* Davaugour's invitation to assume command of an expedition to accompany "the Indians northwards as far and as long as he shall deem it expedient for the service of the king and the good of the country: and he may go himself or send others to winter with them, if he thinks that his own safety may thereby be ensured and that some public advantage may ensue." The expedition was an important one: to find an inland route to the northern sea. Two Frenchmen, Pierre Duquet*, later a notary, and Jean Langlois, a shipwright, accompanied Couture; the others were Indians. In all there were 44 canoes. In an affidavit which he swore in 1688, Couture went over the itinerary they had followed: the group left Quebec in mid-May, started up the Saguenay River, and reached Lake Mistassini on 26 June. A sudden storm left a foot of snow. The group pushed on, and reached a river [Rupert] "that empties into the Northern Sea." The French were unable to continue on their route, for the Indian guides refused to go any farther. Couture thus affirmed in 1688 that in 1663 he was unable to make his way to the northern sea. Nevertheless, this daring expedition permitted him to become acquainted with the vast region to the north of the St Lawrence, a region peopled with Indian tribes whose customs were very different from and more peaceful than those of the Iroquois and Hurons. In 1665 he arranged with Charles Amiot*, Noël Jérémie*, and Sébastien Prouvereau that they would accompany Father Henri NOUVEL, who was going to preach the gospel to the Papinachois. The following year he was delegated by the governor to go to New Holland to protest against the murder of two French officers by the Mohawks. He went to the Iroquois and ordered them to hand over the murderers, under threat of a punitive expedition. He returned to Quebec on 6 September with two Mohawks, one of whom was the leader of the group that had killed Lieutenant Chazy.

This episode marks the end of Guillaume Couture's adventurous career. From that time on he seldom left his domain at Pointe-Lévy. The 1667 census places him there, with his wife and nine children. He had 20 acres under cultivation and 6 head of cattle. In turn or simultaneously he held the most important offices in the seigneury: captain of the militia, clerk of court, "judge of the seneschal's court for the Lauzon shore." According to an act of 16 Nov. 1684, drawn up by Nicolas Métru, he may also have acted as a notary. In 1675 he requested a resident parish priest for the seigneury, where the copyholders were beginning to be numerous. Owing to the scarcity of priests, he did not obtain one until 1690. Through these different sources, one can feel that he was the moving spirit of the newly formed seigneury. Yet in the 1681 census he reported only the humble title of carpenter.

One can give only an approximate idea of the last years of his life, which were those of an ordinary settler of the earliest period. The attack on Quebec by Phips* in 1690 put the inhabitants of the south shore of the St Lawrence in a state of alert. It is probable that the former hero did not dissociate himself from the defence plans, but we have no precise indication as to his participation in them. The archives of the Conseil Souverain

have preserved the details of misunderstandings that arose sometimes between Couture and Byssot, at other times between the two pioneers and the other copyholders of the seigneury. An analysis of these documents clearly indicates that Couture did not seem to be easy to get along with, and that he intended to see that his rights were respected. According to the same documents, he appears sometimes to have exceeded his prerogatives as judge and captain of the seigneury. Nonetheless, on several occasions he was invited to sit on the Conseil Souverain, in the absence of regular members. Meanwhile the majority of his ten children had formed connections by marriage with people of good family. Thus, in 1678 Marie married François Vézier, and five years later Claude Bourget; in 1680 Marguerite married Jean Marsolet, son of Nicolas Marsolet* de Saint-Aignan; in 1688 Louise married Charles-Thomas Couillard de Beaumont.

His wife Anne Esmard was buried at Pointe-Lévy on 15 Jan. 1700. On 28 June following, Guillaume Couture acknowledged that he owed to "his younger son" Joseph-Oger Couture, Sieur de La Cressonnière, the sum of 600 *livres* for having assisted his father and mother during the last six years, and "even long before." On 14 Nov. 1701 an inventory was made of the possessions of "the late Guill. Couture, during his lifetime judge of the seneschal's court for the Lauzon shore, and Anne Hemard." He therefore died before this date, and we do not know the place where this hero of the early days of the colony is buried.

RAYMOND DOUVILLE

JR (Thwaites). *JJ* (Laverdière et Casgrain). *Jug. et délib.*, I, 417, 438; II, 674. *Ici ont passé* (Société hist. du Saguenay pub., II, Chicoutimi, 1934). Jean Delanglez, *Louis Jolliet, vie et voyages* (Montréal, 1950). L.-P. Desrosiers, *Iroquoisie* (Montréal, 1947). Archange Godbout, *Les pionniers de la région triffuvienne* (Trois-Rivières, 1934). J.-E. Roy, *Le premier colon de Lévis: Guillaume Couture* (Lévis, 1884). F.-X. Talbot, *La vie d'Isaac Jogues: un saint parmi les sauvages* (Paris, 1937). Lucien Campeau, "Un site historique retrouvé," *RHAF*, VI (1952), 31. Jean Côté, "L'institution des donnés," *RHAF*, XV (1961), 344–78. Archange Godbout, "Les trois sœurs Esmard," SGCF *Mémoires*, I (1944–45), 197–200.

COUTURIER, *dit* **Le Bourguignon, PIERRE,** architect; b. *c.* 1665 at Arc-en-Barrois, diocese of Langres, son of Michel Couturier and Marie Guillier (?); buried 8 Jan. 1715 at Montreal.

Couturier probably came to Canada in 1697. On his arrival he entered into partnership with the masons Gilbert Maillet and Jean Deslandes, to build houses for JEAN-BAPTISTE D'AILLEBOUST Des

Couvert

Muceaux and Jean Boudor. In 1700, alone this time, he built a house for Étienne Rocbert* de La Morandière and put up for PAUL LE MOYNE de Maricourt, according to his design, "the masonry foundations for a house, outbuildings, and outhouse . . . at *Pres de Ville*." The absence of any mention in the archives leads us to think that Couturier's activity was then probably limited for three or four years to works of minor importance (foundations and chimneys).

The year 1705 was marked by two important undertakings: the building of the Château de Ramezay and of the first Recollet convent in stone. In connection with the latter, Couturier was sued for bad workmanship and failure to complete it. Apparently, absorbed by the building of the Ramezay house, he neglected the work on the convent and thus, in view of his slowness, the Recollets had it continued by other masons. The difference was settled out of court.

In 1707 Couturier won the contract over two competitors for the ground floor of the new prison in Montreal. This building, the plans for which had been prepared by Boisberthelot* de Beaucours, was to be completed later; the first part of the undertaking comprised only the foundations, a lodge for the keeper, two cells, and latrines. The work, which was carefully done, extended over two years. At the end of 1708 Couturier entered into an agreement with the parish council of Notre-Dame to cut all the stone necessary for joining the frontispiece of the bell-tower to the façade of the parish church. He had also received that year a commission as surveyor, but he does not seem to have exercised that profession.

In 1709 and 1710 Couturier took on large-scale repair work on the half-timbered field-stone houses of Jean-Marie Bouat and Pierre Biron. The following year he built for Pierre YOU de La Découverte, on the Place d'Armes, a house with two storeys, a cellar, and an attic. In 1712 he built the church at Boucherville. His last work, a bridge, is known to us only through the mention made of it in the repertory of the notary Antoine ADHÉMAR on 8 June 1712.

Although he was a master mason and stone-cutter, Couturier is most often called an architect, which means that he was a master mason who was capable of preparing a plan and, merely by a simple estimate, of giving correct proportions to buildings and their outline. The various contracts that he entered into contain interesting details concerning building methods in use at the beginning of the 18th century; in another connection, his contracts of partnership with other masons and for the hiring of masons, hodmen, apprentices, and labourers (in 1713 for example he agreed to teach stone-cutting to two masons), furnish us with valuable information about the organization of labour at that time.

On 11 Jan. 1700 Couturier married Marguerite Payet of Pointe-aux-Trembles (near Montreal). They had 13 children. Two daughters married into the Janson dynasty: Charlotte, who married Louis, a stone-cutter, and Marie-Joseph, wife of Louis' brother Dominique*, who was a king's architect when he died.

JULES BAZIN

AJM, Greffe d'Antoine Adhémar; Greffe de Michel Lepailleur de Laferté; Greffe de Pierre Raimbault; Registres des audiences (1702–1706), V, 755ff. ANDM, Registres des baptêmes, mariages et sépultures. *Jug. et délib.*, IV, 308, 338. É.-Z. Massicotte, "Les arpenteurs de Montréal," *BRH*, XXV (1919), 223; "Maçons, entrepreneurs, architectes," *BRH*, XXXV (1929), 137f. Tanguay, *Dictionnaire*, I, 148; III, 190f.

COUVERT, MICHEL-GERMAIN DE, priest, Jesuit, missionary; b. 5 Jan. 1653 in the diocese of Bayeux; d. 1715 at Quebec.

On 5 Nov. 1672 he entered the Jesuit noviciate in Paris. He seemed destined for the highest offices in his order when, having completed his preparation, he asked for and obtained permission to go to Canada as a missionary. He arrived in 1690, the year of the expedition led by Phips* against Quebec. Couvert has left us a "Relation de la defaite des Anglois à Québec." In this eye-witness account the facts are dated exactly and presented in a sober style.

In 1691 he was appointed to the Huron mission at Notre-Dame-de-Lorette, located three leagues from Quebec on the seigneury of Saint-Gabriel, which belonged to the Jesuits. He had the privilege of living there with Father Chaumonot*, whose long career was reaching its end. In 1694 Father Couvert became the superior of this mission.

In 1697, at the request of Bishop Saint-Vallier [LA CROIX], the Jesuits gave up their residence and four acres of land around the church to facilitate the setting up in this locality of a parish for the French. Nouvelle Lorette than became Ancienne Lorette, and the Huron mission, henceforth located near the falls on the St Charles River at three leagues' distance from Quebec, was called Jeune Lorette (Loretteville). It was while Father Couvert was superior that this change of location took place, as did the building of a church at the mission which preserves several treasures from Ancienne Lorette. Father Couvert submitted with humility to this administrative measure, which was desired by the bishop and which he turned to the best possible account.

The Hurons, whose earlier fervour had fallen

off somewhat, again became an exemplary Christian community under Father Couvert's guidance. Crippled with infirmities, he withdrew to the college in Quebec, where the lofty quality of his inner life was a source of edification to all. Certain historians say that he died in 1713, others in 1714, and others still in 1715. The last date, it seems, is the correct one, for his obituary letter, written by Father Joseph-Louis GERMAIN and dated at Quebec on 1 Nov. 1715, begins as follows: "This is to inform Your Reverence of the loss which our Mission suffered these past days in the person of Father Michel de Couvert...." He had lived for 25 years in Canada and was, according to Father Rochemonteix*, one of the most consummate apostles in New France.

LÉON POULIOT, S.J.

ASJCF, 410; Fonds Rochemonteix, 4010, 285, printed in *JR* (Thwaites), LXIV, 40–52, and in *1690, Sir William Phips devant Québec* (Myrand), 115–20. L. St-G. Lindsay, *Notre-Dame de la Jeune-Lorette en la Nouvelle-France, étude historique* (Montréal, 1900) Rochemonteix, *Les Jésuites et la N.-F. au XVIIe siècle*, III, 247n., 393n.

CRESPIEUL, FRANÇOIS DE, priest, Jesuit, missionary to the Montagnais Indians; b. 16 March 1639 at Arras, son of Jean de Crespieul, a lawyer, and of Marguerite Théry, baptized by his uncle, canon Antoine Théry; d. December 1702.

François de Crespieul entered the noviciate in Tournai on 27 Sept. 1658, then studied philosophy at the Jesuit college in Douai; he did his classical studies at the college in Lille, where from 1662 to 1666 he taught, chiefly in the senior class. During his years of teaching, Crespieul wrote five letters to the general of the Jesuits in Rome, Father Jean-Paul Oliva, to obtain the favour of joining the missions in India, or Martinique, or New France.

In the spring of 1670, as soon as he was ordained a priest, Crespieul sailed on the Sieur Denis Guyon's ship with another young missionary, Father Jacques Robaud, for the missions in Canada. The crossing of the Atlantic was a long and arduous one. A contagious disease broke out among the soldiers and claimed several victims, among them Robaud, who died on 15 July 1670 when he landed at Tadoussac.

The superior of the Jesuit college in Quebec entrusted Father Crespieul with the task of teaching Latin and Greek in the senior class, while requiring him to complete his theological studies. In addition, he was to take lessons in the Montagnais language. As his teacher he had Father Charles Albanel*, who had an excellent knowledge of this language and its dialects.

On 29 Oct. 1671 Crespieul arrived at Tadoussac to begin his arduous missionary work. His parish, comprising all the Montagnais territory, stretched from Île-aux-Coudres to Sept-Îles and from Tadoussac to Lake Mistassini, and took in Chicoutimi, Métabetchouan, and Nekoubau. The missionary ranged in every direction through this immense country of forests, leading the same life as his nomadic Montagnais. He wrote: "The life of a missionary to the Montagnais is a long, slow martyrdom ... during the winter the missionary sits or kneels nearly the whole day long, exposed to almost continual smoke.... He eats when there is something to eat, and when he is offered something ... suffering and affliction are the lot of these holy and painful missions." Despite these highly unsatisfactory living conditions, Crespieul remained 30 years in this mission country. He was assisted by Father Bonaventure Fabvre, who in 1688 replaced Father Antoine Dalmas* among the Montagnais. For nearly 11 years Fabvre travelled through the huge Montagnais mission, at a time when Father Crespieul, sick and exhausted by his missionary work and by hardships of all kinds, found himself obliged to live at Chicoutimi. Father Fabvre died on 6 Dec. 1700 at Quebec.

In 1696, Father Crespieul was honoured with the title of "apostolic vicar" (?) to the Montagnais tribe. At the end of July 1702 he returned to Quebec, where the superior appointed him an adviser. He died at the end of December of the same year, a victim of the smallpox epidemic raging at Quebec. "He died from the fatigue that he incurred while visiting the sick, and from compassion for the public distress for which he saw no remedy, as the whole town had become nothing more than a general hospital."

Father Crespieul had shown special devotion to Marie-Catherine de Saint-Augustin [Simon*]. As he noted in his journal, it was in consideration of this devotion that "The Reverend Mother Saint-Ignace, superior of the Nuns Hospitallers, presented [to him] in 1693 an important relic of the blessed Mother Catherine de Saint-Augustin, contained in a small mother of pearl shrine sent by Bishop Du Linot."

LORENZO ANGERS

AAQ, Manuscrit montagnais. AHDQ, Annales, 1636–1716. AMUQ, Annales manuscrites du monastère des Ursulines de Québec, I, 116. ASQ, MSS, 360. Archives de la Société historique du Saguenay, Documents relatifs à la jeunesse de François de Crespieul, compilés par Pierre de Lattre, s.j. *JR* (Thwaites), LIX, LX, LXXI. "Reglemens concernant

Crisafy

le bon estat de la mission de Tadoussac par François de Crespieul," *BRH*, VI (1900), 269–73. Rochemonteix, *Les Jésuites et la N.-F. au XVIIe siècle*, III, 415–29.

CRISAFY, ANTOINE DE, marquis, military man, captain, commandant, king's lieutenant, governor of Trois-Rivières, knight of the order of Saint-Louis; b. at Messina (Sicily), son of Mathieu de Crisafy and Françoise de Grimaldi; buried 6 May 1709 at Trois-Rivières.

Antoine de Crisafy had acquired the rank of lieutenant-colonel and commanded an infantry regiment in the army of the Duc de Vivonne, marshal of France, when Sicily revolted against the Spaniards. He was "disabled in one arm" at the capture of Descalette. He had prevailed upon his younger brother, Thomas*, a knight of Malta, to join the revolt, and they both had to flee their native island; this cost them the confiscation of all their assets, which were considerable. They went to the principality of Monaco, which belonged to the Grimaldi family and where they had estates.

According to certain authors the Crisafy brothers were cast into the Bastille in 1683 (no doubt as the result of a brawl), and were soon released on condition that they agreed to serve in the colonies. We know that they were appointed to lead two of the seven companies that Louis XIV sent to New France in 1684 at Governor Le Febvre* de La Barre's request. The captaincies granted to the two brothers bear the date of 3 April of that year. Four companies, theirs among them, landed at Quebec on 24 September, at about the same time as the governor was returning from his pathetic expedition against the Iroquois.

It was under Brisay de Denonville's governorship that the Crisafys first gave evidence of their technical training and bravery. These officers, who came originally from a country where cold is unknown, adapted themselves to the harsh Canadian climate, even though their health deteriorated as a result. In 1686 they accompanied the governor on an expedition against the Senecas. Denonville held them in high esteem, and informed the minister that "of the officers of the colonial regular troops there are none capable of commanding a post of 100 men, unless it be the Crisafys, who are more sensible than anybody else; that he cannot praise too highly the two brothers, who are diligent and well-deserving; that talent is necessary to command at Niagara, where the best [officer] is not very good." The Marquis de Rompré, a company captain, was offended at this preference on the governor's part, claiming that he was the most senior sub-lieutenant. However, the companies of the Crisafy brothers had been formed before his, and this chronological priority, reinforced by their real competence, prevailed. The Marquis de Rompré went back to France, and the Crisafys continued to give proof of their valour and experience. Until the death of Thomas on 29 Feb. 1696, the complimentary remarks made by authorities of the court and of the colony referred to both of them.

Antoine distinguished himself particularly in 1692, when Governor Callière entrusted him with the command of the troops at Sault-Saint-Louis. By using guile he succeeded in thwarting the attempts of 800 Iroquois who had made plans to destroy the French colony. After this exploit Callière's friendship for Crisafy never faltered. In 1696, at the time of Buade* de Frontenac's expedition against the Iroquois, Crisafy, with Captain Raymond Blaise Des Bergères, was made responsible for guarding the recently constructed fort of Onondaga, where the boats, supplies, and ammunition required for the expedition were located.

Following his 13 years of devoted service to the French colony in America, and on the recommendation of Frontenac and Callière, the court created for him the post of king's lieutenant at Montreal. His appointment was dated 15 March 1697 and signed by Frontenac on 26 October. In May 1698 he was made a knight of the order of Saint-Louis, at the same time as Frontenac and Callière. The king, in a letter of 19 June addressed to Rigaud de Vaudreuil, authorized the latter to invest all three. On 30 October of the same year the Sulpicians, as seigneurs of Montreal, made Crisafy a land grant, in the form of a noble fief, without rights of justice, at Côte-des-Neiges.

As a result of the powers which he possessed as king's lieutenant, Crisafy became acting governor of Montreal when Callière replaced Frontenac as governor general in 1699. According to Le Roy de La Potherie, it was even thought that he might obtain the post, and his appointment was expected. However, Vaudreuil was chosen and Callière had Crisafy appointed king's lieutenant at Quebec, replacing François Provost, who was appointed governor of Trois-Rivières. He thus became one of the principal figures in New France, and was drawn into the bickerings over precedence and abuses of authority—the contagious disease endemic in high administrative circles. Traces of his ridiculous disagreements with Intendant Bochart de Champigny, Claude de Ramezay, his successor at Montreal, and François Provost, his predecessor, are recorded in official correspondence. He even created his own "prie-Dieu incident," by stationing on one side of his chair in the church of the Recollets three lackeys, and on the other three soldiers from the Château Saint-Louis. These various incidents unfortunately tarnished his not inconsiderable reputation as a military strategist.

François Provost having died on 1 June 1702, Crisafy obtained the post of governor of Trois-Rivières, exactly a year later. His immediate neighbourhood consisted of 32 houses in the upper town, that is to say within the walls, and 17 houses outside the walls. It was the smallest of the three governments, but Crisafy seems to have made the best of it, for he took part in almost all the social and religious activities, and he seems to have won the esteem of those under his jurisdiction. He died while in office, and was buried on 6 May 1709 in the parish church.

On 17 Feb. 1700, while he was king's lieutenant at Quebec, Crisafy had married Marie-Claire Ruette d'Auteuil, who was 15 years old and was the daughter of the attorney general. The young wife accompanied her husband to Trois-Rivières, but, having a sickly constitution, she had to return to Quebec on her mother's advice, and died there on 9 Oct. 1705. After Marie-Claire's death difficulties about the estate arose between RUETTE d'Auteuil and his son-in-law. Both accepted the arbitration of the Marquis de Vaudreuil and of Cadillac [LAUMET] to settle the dispute. Crisafy ended his life in most respectable fashion, in the manor-house he occupied as governor of Trois-Rivières, and in the company of his faithful servant Émery Jarry.

The notary POTTIER drew up a detailed inventory of the possessions of this picturesque career soldier, who left no relative in this country.

RAYMOND DOUVILLE

AJQ, Greffe de Florent de La Cetière, 29 mars 1706. AJTR, Greffe de J.-B. Pottier, 26 nov. 1706. AN, Col., B, 20. Charlevoix, *Histoire* (1744), II, 95–97, 125, 170. P.-G. Roy, *Inv. coll. pièces jud. et not.*, I, 204. Fauteux, *Les chevaliers de Saint-Louis*. P.-G. Roy, *Les officiers d'état-major*. J.-B.-A. Ferland, *Cours d'histoire du Canada (1534–1759)* (1re éd., 2v., Québec, 1861–65), II, 274–82. Jouve, *Les Franciscains et le Canada: aux Trois-Rivières*. Lionel Groulx, "Le Gallicanisme au Canada sous Louis XIV," *RHAF*, I (1947), 68. Jean Leclerc, "Denonville et ses captifs iroquois," *RHAF*, XIV (1960), 548. É.-Z. Massicotte, "Le Marquis de Crisafy, seigneur de la Côte-des-Neiges," *BRH*, XL (1934), 431–32. Benjamin Sulte, "M. de Galiffet," *BRH*, V (1899), 348.

CROWE, JOSIAS, commodore of the Newfoundland convoy, 1711; d. 21 Sept. 1714.

The first mention we have of Crowe is as captain of the *St Paul* in 1691. He held many subsequent commands during the French wars.

In 1695 he convoyed the American merchant fleet, and in 1701 served the New England station, thus gaining some experience of the working of English colonial administration.

In 1711 Crowe was appointed commodore of the annual convoy to Newfoundland. He was instructed to report on French activities, on the fishery, the inhabitants, and the fishing vessels, and was required to enforce the provisions of the Newfoundland Act of 1699. When he inquired precisely what penalties he was authorized to inflict, he caused a flurry in the administrative dovecots and was finally told only to use "the most effectual method . . . for remedying several irregularities that stil continue to be practis'd in those parts."

Crowe was on station at St John's from August to October, and took his duties seriously. He attempted in his proclamation of 28 August to check drunkenness by prohibiting the sale of drink to any but strangers on "the Sabbath day," and by providing fines for drunken behaviour, though it was far from clear who would enforce these penalties. The proclamation must have been printed or produced in multiple form, since a copy was to be put up in every tavern.

Commodores, in carrying out their somewhat loosely defined duties, normally consulted fishing captains and leading inhabitants. Crowe did so rather more publicly and elaborately than usual. He assembled an informal body composed of "the commanders of merchant ships, merchants, and chief inhabitants," and attempted to work out "rules and orders" for the improvement of local conditions. His decisions were then promulgated under 16 heads. These are known as "Crowe's Laws" but they are less than a code and are of a dubious legislative character. A number were judicial or quasi-judicial decisions in disputes between inhabitants, or between inhabitants and visiting fishermen. Drunken excess was again denounced; servants were to be punished if they attempted to serve two masters. The 1699 act was to be enforced by dispossessing inhabitants who had occupied fishing-rooms held by fishing vessels at any time since 1685, and by punishing those who, during winter, interfered with stages, flakes, and cook-rooms belonging to the annual fishing ships. A voluntary levy of fish was to be raised for the pastor, Reverend Jacob RICE. John COLLINS, a leading inhabitant of St John's, was confirmed as "deputy governor" in military affairs; rules were laid down for the use of tenements within the fort as places of refuge, there being still no regular garrison. Seamen were to patrol at night to guard against French spies. All inhabitants were to be in winter quarters by 1 October and were not to

Cuillerier

leave without the permission of the local governors, nine of whom, including Collins, were given charge of the principal settlements and placed at the head of the local militia. Many of these provisions had been instituted between 1708 and 1710 to deal with wartime emergencies. Though Crowe was more thorough than some commodores and conducted his activities with more publicity and formality than most, historians like Prowse who regarded "Crowe's Laws" as foreshadowing some kind of representative government were mistaken.

Crowe's suggestions for reform were sensible if not original. A governor resident all the year round, one "impowered to put the laws in execution," was essential for the health of the colony. Crowe took a sensible line too on the many infractions of the trade restrictions. He thought few of these infractions were serious, and some it was undesirable to remedy. New England shipping, for example, was responsible for many breaches, but it brought essential provisions to the island. His report, dated 31 October, was fuller and more critical than usual, but otherwise it followed traditional lines.

Sir Nicholas Trevanion, his successor as commodore, in 1712, followed his procedure almost to the letter but subsequent convoy captains did not find so much publicity and ceremony necessary.

D. B. Quinn

The Fulham papers in the Lambeth palace library, ed. W. W. Manross (Oxford, 1965), 3. PRO, *B.T. Journal, 1708/9–1714/15*; CSP, *Col., 1701, 1710–11, 1711–12, 1712–14*. Charnock, *Biographia navalis*, II. M. A. Field, "The development of government in Newfoundland, 1638–1713," unpublished M.A. thesis, University of London, 1924. Prowse, *History of Nfld.* Rogers, *Newfoundland*.

CUILLERIER, RENÉ, indentured employee of the Hôtel-Dieu of Montreal, settler; b. *c.* 1639, probably at Véron, in the diocese of Angers, son of Julien Cuillerier and Julienne Faifeu; d. *c.* 1712 at Montreal.

René Cuillerier arrived in New France on 7 Sept. 1659. On 8 June 1659, at La Rochelle, he had signed before the notary A. Demontreau an undertaking with Sister Judith Moreau* de Brésoles, the superior of the Hôtel-Dieu of Montreal. By this contract he became a servant at the hospital in Ville-Marie for an annual salary of 75 *livres*. By the autumn he was at Montreal, and on 25 Oct. 1661, with some settlers assisted by members of the garrison and led by Abbé Guillaume Vignal*, Cuillerier went to Île de la Pierre, in the St Lawrence, to quarry materials

with which to complete the building of the first seminary at Montreal. He had cause to rue it, for the Iroquois were roaming the neighbourhood. The latter attacked the workers, killed some of them, wounded others, and captured Vignal, Claude de Brigeac*, Cuillerier, and Jacques Dufresne.

Cuillerier and Brigeac were carried off into captivity among the Oneidas. They were subjected to a beating and Cuillerier had his nails torn out. The Indians then decided to burn the two Frenchmen. Death was first meted out to Brigeac, but Cuillerier was saved by an Indian woman who asked to adopt him "in order that he might take the place of her brother."

During his captivity, which lasted 19 months, Cuillerier met other fellow-sufferers: Michel Messier, *dit* Saint-Michel, and Urbain Tessier-Lavigne. In the spring of 1663 Cuillerier took advantage of a hunting trip with the Oneidas, who had been joined by some Mohawks and captive Frenchmen, to flee in the direction of New Holland. He went to Fort Orange, whence he made his way to Boston, and finally reached Quebec.

Cuillerier was back in Montreal at the end of the summer, and resumed his service with the Religious Hospitallers of the Hôtel-Dieu. On 20 May 1665 he settled on Montreal Island, having obtained from the Sulpicians a land grant of 45 acres. This land was to form part of the Verdun fief, which was granted to him in 1671. He took part in the founding of the parish of Lachine and in 1675 became its first churchwarden. The following year his fortified house received the name Fort Cuillerier. At the time of the 1681 census he had 32 acres under cultivation and owned 6 muskets, one pistol, and 6 head of cattle.

On 22 March 1712 Cuillerier, who had been ill for some time, made his will in the presence of Michel de Villermaula, parish priest of Lachine. His last will and testament was deposited in Jean-Baptiste Adhémar*'s registry on 26 Jan. 1716. Even if the date of his death is unknown to us, a notarial act of 27 Jan. 1718, signed before the notary Adhémar and deposited in Michel Lepailleur's registry, indicates that Madame Lucault had "been the widow of her said husband for more than five years."

On 13 April 1665, in the chapel of the Hôtel-Dieu of Montreal, René Cuillerier had married Marie Lucault, daughter of Léonard Barbeau, *dit* Lucault, and of Barbe Poisson. Sixteen children were born of this marriage; seven of them were baptized at Montreal and the others at Lachine.

Claude Perrault

AJM, Greffe de J.-B. Adhémar; Greffe de Michel Lepailleur de Laferté; Registre d'état civil de Lachine; Registres d'état civil de Notre-Dame de Montréal. Archives de Saint-Sulpice, Paris, François Citoys de Chaumaux, Estat des concessions faites par les seigneurs de Montréal. *JJ* (Laverdière et Casgrain). Recensements du Canada, 1667, 1681 (Sulte). Camille Bertrand, *Monsieur de La Dauversière, fondateur de Montréal et des Religieuses hospitalières de Saint-Joseph 1597–1659* (Montréal, 1947), 230. [Faillon], *Histoire de la colonie française.* Archange Godbout, *Les passagers du Saint-André; la recrue de 1659* (Société généalogique canadienne-française, V, Montréal, 1964). Mondoux, *L'Hôtel-Dieu de Montréal*, 239, 246, 247.

CUMINGS, ARCHIBALD, Newfoundland merchant and customs official; b. *c.* 1667; d. sometime after 1726.

Archibald Cumings was evidently of Scottish origin, but no details about his early life have been found. He began trading at St John's, Newfoundland, in 1698 and acquired property there and at Ferryland; his losses in the French winter attack of 1704–5 were heavy. In March 1706 he was appointed government agent for prizes in Newfoundland, probably in association with the CAMPBELL brothers. In October 1708, as part of the policy of building up a small body of royal officials in Newfoundland, Cumings was given the additional post of customs officer by the commissioners of the customs. This office was created in an attempt to curb illegal trade in Newfoundland; however, as the vice-admiralty court, created at the same time, failed to materialize [*see* SMITH], Cumings was powerless to do anything more effective than report. In connection with his new appointment Cumings left for England on 25 Oct. 1708, and so was not present when the French captured and destroyed St John's the following winter.

During the next few seasons, Cumings spent much of his time in England. He made several reports on Newfoundland to the Board of Trade; like John MOODY, who later became deputy-governor of Placentia, he recommended the fortification of Ferryland (Forillon) instead of St John's. In 1710 he claimed to have remitted, as tenths and perquisites of the Admiralty, £2,000 from Newfoundland for prizes; for this he eventually received £100 plus expenses. With Francis NICHOLSON, Moody, and the Campbell brothers, he was consulted in 1712 about the possible treaty settlement with the French, and he expressed the view that they should not be given any fishing rights in Newfoundland or be allowed to fortify Cape Breton. Cumings' report from St John's in October 1712 was the first to stress the bad fishing

which was to plague the fishermen in eastern Newfoundland for some years; his news in October 1713 was little better. In February 1715 he had a four-page pamphlet, *Considerations on the trade to Newfoundland* printed and laid before the Board of Trade. Cumings believed that Newfoundland should have a governor and a proper legal system, so that the colonists there "may be governed a[s] Brittains and not live like a banditie or forsaken people." Cumings also proposed that there be some system of entry and clearance for shipping in Newfoundland to help curb the illegal trade.

By 1715 Cumings felt that he had served long enough in Newfoundland; and in 1716 he was appointed customs officer at Boston and prize officer for New England. He served there actively for a decade, and submitted several useful reports on the fishing off New England and in the Bay of Fundy (Baie Française). A false report of his death was circulating in 1723, but he is last heard of at Boston on 23 Aug. 1726.

Archibald Cumings showed considerable tenacity in his Newfoundland duties. As customs officer the most he could do was report on the fishery and on trade with the colony, but he did this fully and well. As prize officer he was able to act by getting condemnations when the commodore of the convoy was present. Once the war was over, prizes and the emoluments from their disposal disappeared, and this almost certainly helped him decide to move to New England. On the Newfoundland situation, Cumings was shrewd and forthright; he always spoke up for the colonists and was a strong protagonist of the institution of a civil government and judicature. His opinion was respected by the Board of Trade, though he did not succeed in eradicating its prejudices against the Newfoundland settlements.

D. B. QUINN

Archibald Cumings, *Considerations on the trade to Newfoundland* (London, [1715]). PRO, *B.T.Journal, 1704–1708/9, 1708/9–1714/15, 1722/23–1728; CSP, Col., 1704–5, 1706–8, 1708–9, 1710–11, 1711–12, 1712–14, 1714–15, 1716–17, 1717–18, 1719–20, 1721–22, 1722–23, 1724–25, 1726–27; C.T.Books, 1710; C.T.Papers, 1702–7.* M. A. Field, "The development of government in Newfoundland, 1638–1713," unpublished M.A. thesis, University of London, 1924. Lounsbury, *British fishery at Nfld.* Rogers, *Newfoundland.*

CUSSON, JEAN, farmer, seigneurial attorney, clerk of court, royal notary, and acting king's attorney; b. 1632 or around 1635–36 at Clair, near Rouen (province of Normandy), son of Jean

Damours de Chauffours

Cusson and Jacqueline Pépin; d. 8 April 1718 at Saint-Sulpice.

It has been said with a good deal of justice that the settlers of New France, craftsmen or soldiers rather than farmers, attracted moreover by the fur trade, had only a slight interest in farming. For many of them, cultivating their land remained a marginal activity and simply constituted, in the final analysis, a necessary means of supplementing their income but one which they endured impatiently and got rid of at the first opportunity. Yet there were true habitants; Jean Cusson belonged to that group. After his marriage on 16 Sept. 1656, at Trois-Rivières, to Marie Foubert, a girl 15 years of age who originally came from Rouen, Cusson settled down at Cap-de-la-Madeleine. By 1667 the couple owned 7 head of cattle and 28 acres of land under cultivation, a quite extraordinary achievement. Certainly Cusson had sufficient means to take on hired men, such as François Vannasse (who was already there in 1666) and Jean Pilon, the first being 25 years of age, the other 40, both of them being listed in the 1667 census as living in his home. And despite the offices which he was to occupy in the realm of justice, Cusson did not neglect his farming; in 1681 he declared 6 head of cattle and 40 acres!

In 1669, just at the time when the Jesuits, who were the seigneurs of Cap-de-la-Madeleine, gave Cusson a commission as notary, seigneurial attorney, and clerk of court, the intendant, Boutroue* d'Aubigny, was engaged at Quebec in a struggle to take away from the Compagnie des Indes Occidentales the right of appointing notaries and to restrict the powers of the seigneurs in the realm of justice. Although he gladly admitted Cusson to his offices as seigneurial attorney and court clerk, the intendant authorized him to act as notary only provisionally, and on the express condition that he take the title of royal notary. Soon the seigneurs were to have only the right of presenting notaries, the appointment itself falling within the intendant's competence. Cusson acted as notary at Cap-de-la-Madeleine until 1687, and then in the seigneury of Champlain from 1687 to 1700. In 1700 he moved to Montreal, where he carried on his functions for four years. He lived at Pointe-aux-Trembles. In 1704, at about 70 years of age, Cusson retired, but he came out of retirement for a short time in 1707–8, when he was acting king's attorney for Montreal.

Cusson and his wife had 12 children. They all reached adult age, which was rather rare for the period.

André Vachon

AJJ, Registres d'état civil de Saint-Sulpice. AJTR, Greffe de Séverin Ameau, 31 août 1656. AQ, NF, Ord. des int., I, 49. F.-L. Desaulniers, "Le greffe de Jean Cusson," BRH, X (1904), 51–57. Jug. et délib., I, II, III. Ord. comm. (P.-G. Roy), I, 88f. Recensement du Canada, 1666 (APQ Rapport). Recensements du Canada, 1667, 1681 (Sulte). Massicotte, "Les tribunaux et les officiers de justice," BRH, XXXVII (1931), 189, 304. "Les notaires au Canada," 25. J.-E. Roy, Histoire du notariat I, 162, 201f., 211f. Vachon, Histoire du notariat 19f.

D

DAMOURS (d'Amours) DE CHAUFFOURS, LOUIS, Acadian seigneur, fur-trader and soldier; baptized 16 May 1655 at Quebec, eldest surviving son of Mathieu Damours* de Chauffours and Marie Marsolet; buried 9 May 1708 at Port-Royal (Annapolis Royal, N.S.).

On 20 Sept. 1684 Louis Damours received a seigneurial grant in Acadia on the Rechibucto river where he had built a fortified trading post and residence two years earlier. On 1 Oct. 1686 he married at Quebec Marguerite Guyon, daughter of Simon Guyon; her sister Louise* married his brother Mathieu Damours* de Freneuse in the same year. He and Marguerite had three children. On 7 October 1686, he obtained grants near Forts Jemseg and Nashwaak (Naxouat) on the Saint John River, previously issued to Pierre de Joybert* de Soulanges. He moved there with his family, presumably to be near two of his brothers, René Damours de Clignancour and Mathieu Damours de Freneuse, who had already settled on the Saint John.

Later he had established a store, was pursuing the fur trade with the Indians, and farming his land. He and his brothers were severely criticized by Governor Robinau* de Villebon who claimed that they were disreputable and overfond of liquor, and that they had failed to improve their grants of land. Much the same charges were levelled by Villebon at other settlers and officials and it seems clear that there was an unfortunate atmosphere of intrigue, bickering, and trouble making which may have been sparked in part by Villebon's own illegal involvement in the fur trade. In any case his treatment of the Damours brothers earned him the censure of the minister of Marine, Pontchartrain.

In 1695 Louis Damours purchased John Gyles*, a captive of the Malecite Indians, whose published account of his experiences contains considerable information about the Saint John area of that period. In August 1696, Damours participated in the attack by a mixed Indian and French force led by PIERRE LE MOYNE d'Iberville and JEAN-VINCENT D'ABBADIE de Saint-Castin on Fort William Henry at Pemaquid in New England. Damours commanded his own vessel in this expedition, and after the capture of Pemaquid he took the garrison to Boston. In October of that same year a New England force led by Hathorne made a raid along the Saint John. Although Damours was absent in France at the time, his buildings, crops, and livestock—constituting probably the largest farm of that time in the area— were spared thanks to a note from Gyles to the commander requesting that he do so. Gyles was later freed by Damours for this act of loyalty.

Owing to damage caused to his property by a high freshet in 1701 and the decision of Governor de Brouillan [MOMBETON] to abandon defences on the Saint John, Damours determined to move to Port-Royal. Brouillan appealed to the court for aid for Damours, as the latter was in serious financial straits. It was also about this time that his wife died. With France and England at war in Acadia once more, Damours joined the French forces and was taken prisoner in 1703. He spent slightly more than two years as a captive in Boston, returning to Port-Royal in 1706, where he died two years later. He was aptly termed by Brouillan "the mainstay of the inhabitants and the savages" during his years as a seigneur on the Saint John River.

GEORGE MACBEATH

AN, Col., B, 16, ff.41–42; 19, f.37; C¹¹D, 2, ff.244, 244v, 246, 277, 278; 3, ff.18, 157v; 4, ff.62, 144v, 214v, 323v; 5, ff.112, 282v; Section Outre-Mer, Dépôt des fortifications des colonies, carton 2, no.56. *Coll. de manuscrits relatifs à la N.-F.*, I, 386; II, 96, 183, 190, 215, 302, 389, 390, 408, 455, 463. [John Gyles], *Memoirs of odd adventures* ... (Boston, 1736; repr., Cincinnati, 1869). *Jug. et délib.*, III, 399, 547, 555, 562, 783. A. Roy, *Inv. greffes not.*, VII, 37. P.-G. Roy, *Inv. concessions*, IV, 2–3, 57; *Inv. contrats de mariage*, II, 120. Webster, *Acadia*. Tanguay, *Dictionnaire*, I, III.
Azarie Couillard Després, *Histoire des seigneurs de la Rivière-du-Sud et leurs alliés canadiens et acadiens* (Saint-Hyacinthe, Qué., 1912), 108–11. W. O. Raymond, *The River St John, its physical features, legends and history from 1604 to 1784*, ed. J. C. Webster (Sackville, N.B., 1943). Ganong, "Historic sites in New Brunswick." P.-G. Roy, "Mathieu Damours de Chauffours," *BRH* XXXII (1926), 385–92.

DAMOURS (d'Amours) DE CLIGNANCOUR, RENÉ, seigneur, and fur-trader; baptized 9 Aug. 1660 at Quebec, the son of Mathieu Damours* de Chauffours and Marie Marsolet; fl. 1684–1710.

On 20 Sept. 1684, René Damours received a grant of land in Acadia extending along both banks of the Saint John River from Medoctec (Meductic) to Grand-Sault (Grand Falls), a distance of over ninety miles. He devoted less attention than his brothers to farming, clearing only 15 acres in a dozen years. He seems to have preferred trade with the Indians, and it is believed that he kept retainers for this purpose at Medoctec, the largest Indian village on the Saint John. Some of the charges of licentiousness and failure to clear land, levelled by Governor Robinau* de Villebon against the Damours brothers, may have been true in René's case during his first years on the Saint John, but positive proof is lacking.

On 13 Oct. 1689 at Quebec, Damours married Françoise-Charlotte, daughter of Charles Legardeur* de Tilly. They journeyed to Acadia where they took up residence, not on René's own property but at Aucpac on Cléoncoré Island (now Eccles Island), which belonged to his brother, LOUIS. Indications are that, while remaining an active fur-trader, he gradually devoted more attention to farming. A census of 1698 shows that he, his wife, and four children were still living on Cléoncoré Island, where he was raising cattle, hogs, and poultry, and growing some grain.

When Hathorne attacked Fort Saint-Joseph (Nashwaak) on 18 Oct. 1696, Damours was given joint command, along with the privateer Pierre MAISONNAT, *dit* Baptiste, of the force of Indians participating in its defence. The next day, when ordered to harry the New England force then withdrawing, he and Baptiste found it impossible to persuade the Indians to follow.

It seems that he moved his family to Port-Royal shortly after the evacuation of Fort Saint-Joseph by Villebon in 1698. However, he continued to participate in Indian raids on New England settlements. He was present when Port-Royal was captured by English and colonial forces under NICHOLSON in the fall of 1710. Later, he was sent to Governor Vaudreuil [RIGAUD] by the Acadian settlers living in the Port-Royal area with a letter (dated 13 Nov. 1710) in which they complained of harsh treatment by VETCH, then commander at Port-Royal. This is the last record we have of René Damours.

GEORGE MACBEATH

Dandonneau

AN, Col., C¹¹ᴰ, 2, ff.244, 244v, 246, 278; 3, f.18; 7, f.98. Charlevoix, *History* (Shea), V, 235. *Coll. de manuscrits relatifs à la N.-F.*, I, 386; II, 244. *Jug. et délib.*, III, 399. P.-G. Roy, *Inv. concessions*, IV, 1; VI, 65; *Inv. contrats de mariage*, II, 119. Webster, *Acadia*, 94, 106, 110, 170. Tanguay, *Dictionnaire*, I, 154. Arsenault, *Hist. et généal. des Acadiens*, I, 59, 66, 381. Murdoch, *History of Nova-Scotia*, I, 321. W. O. Raymond, *Glimpses of the past; history of the river St John, A.D. 1604–1784* (Saint John, N.B., 1905). Ganong, "Historic sites in New Brunswick," 312.

DANDONNEAU, PIERRE, *dit* **Lajeunesse,** settler; baptized 25 Oct. 1624 at La Rochelle (France), son of Jacques Dandonneau and Isabelle Fain; d. 1702 at Champlain.

Pierre Dandonneau was one of the most earnest and tenacious settlers in the early years of the colony. He does not even seem to have engaged in fur-trading. He arrived in Canada around 1647, was sent to the little town of Trois-Rivières, and worked first for Jean Godefroy* de Lintot as an indentured employee. A land grant was made to him on 21 April 1652, and he quickly became one of the chief settlers of the locality. When, on 16 Jan. 1653, he signed his marriage contract with Françoise Jobin, a "king's daughter" (*fille du roi*) living at the Sieur de Lintot's house, personages as influential as the governor of the town, Jacques Leneuf* de La Poterie, and Pierre BOUCHER, the commandant of the fort, were present. Dandonneau acquired land grants on the islands situated at the mouth of the St Maurice River.

In 1664 he left Trois-Rivières and moved with his family to Champlain, where he was one of the first to receive land grants. He bought from the Sieur Besnard, *dit* Saint-André, a piece of land, two acres of which were already cleared, then on 17 March 1665 the local seigneur, Pézard* de La Tousche, made him a land grant in his own right. Dandonneau remained permanently on the Champlain seigneury, contributed a great deal to its development, and died there in 1702. By his marriage with Françoise Jobin he had ten daughters and three sons; one of the latter, Louis, Sieur Du Sablé, was seigneur of Île Dupas, and married his daughter Marie-Anne to the discoverer Pierre Gaultier* de La Vérendrye.

RAYMOND DOUVILLE

Archives du séminaire de Trois-Rivières, Collection Henri Désilets et Montarville Boucher de La Bruère. P.-G. Roy, *Inv. concessions*, V, 190. Cloutier, *Histoire de la paroisse de Champlain*. Archange Godbout, *Les pionniers de la région trifluvienne* (Trois-Rivières, 1934). Sulte, *Mélanges historiques* (Malchelosse), XVIII, XX.

DANEAU DE MUY, NICOLAS, knight of the order of Saint-Louis, town major of Quebec and governor-designate of Louisiana; b. 1651, in Beauvais, France, son of Jacques Daneau and Catherine Driot; d. 28 Jan. 1708, at Havana, Cuba.

Nicolas embarked on a military career, was commissioned lieutenant in 1674 and appointed captain in the Régiment de Normandie in 1678. He entered the service of the colonial regular troops as a captain in 1685 and the same year came to Canada with the reinforcements brought by the Marquis de Denonville [BRISAY].

Between 1685 and 1687 Nicolas was stationed at Montreal, where the garrison troops were employed by CALLIÈRE strengthening the fortifications of Montreal with a palisade. The young captain found time nevertheless to pay court to Geneviève Bissot, widow of the surgeon Louis Maheut*. Changing his mind, he jilted the widow and, in the spring of 1687, married Marguerite Boucher (1663–1698), the third daughter of Pierre BOUCHER, former governor of Trois-Rivières and seigneur of Boucherville. The widow was mollified by the payment of 350 *livres*. Following his wife's death in 1698, Nicolas married Catherine d'Ailleboust Des Muceaux (1669–1755), sister of PIERRE D'AILLEBOUST d'Argenteuil, in 1702. A son by the first marriage, Jacques-Pierre* (1695–1755), followed in his father's footsteps as a soldier and received the cross of the order of Saint-Louis in 1754.

In 1687 Nicolas took part in Denonville's expedition against the Iroquois, an affair which brought no credit to the commander and little to the troops. He was present at Quebec during the siege of that city by Phips* and in the following year, 1691, he was one of the men assembled by Callière at La Prairie de la Magdelaine to guard the country against hostile incursions from New York. One hundred and sixty men were placed under the command of Philippe CLÉMENT Du Vuault, sieur de Valrennes, and sent to Chambly to watch the line of the Richelieu. On 11 August they were attacked by Mohawks and Albany militia led by Major Peter SCHUYLER. Although Valrennes' men were for the most part inexperienced, they successfully routed the enemy. Among those specially mentioned for their coolness and bravery on this occasion was "the Sieur de Muyet." His good work then and subsequently led the Comte de Frontenac [Buade*] to write that Nicolas Daneau de Muy was one of his "bravest officers," and that he had "distinguished himself during the ten years he has been in the country." Charlevoix* said of him that he was "an officer of merit and one of the ablest then in the colony."

168

There was scarcely an action during the years which followed in which Nicolas was not a participant. He was captain of a company of regulars which formed part of RIGAUD de Vaudreuil's command during Frontenac's expedition against the Onondagas in the summer of 1696. And no sooner was this expedition brought to a conclusion than he was placed in charge of a contingent of Canadians and sent to Placentia (Plaisance) to take part in the operations against the English settlements in Newfoundland. Not only did Nicolas acquit himself creditably in the military operations which followed, but he also displayed his political talents by helping to reconcile the rival commanders, PIERRE LE MOYNE d'Iberville and Jacques-François de MOMBETON de Brouillan, governor of Placentia. When the conquest of the island was completed Nicolas did not follow Iberville to Hudson Bay but returned with his contingent to Quebec in the summer of 1697.

Sometime after his return from Newfoundland, Nicolas was made commandant of Fort Chambly, an appointment which he held for several years. In 1703 it was proposed to elevate Chambly from a simple fort to an administrative sub-division of the government of Montreal and to place M. Daneau de Muy in charge. He was, however, appointed garrison adjutant at Quebec on 14 June 1704. Believing that he was entitled to a more senior appointment, de Muy returned to France in 1705. As a result of his solicitations he was offered the post of king's lieutenant of the island of Cayenne. He hesitated to accept an appointment which would take his wife and family from Canada to a small island off the shores of South America. About this time—the date is uncertain, probably 1706 or 1707—he was awarded the cross of the order of Saint-Louis. In 1707 he was nominated governor of Louisiana. He never took up this appointment; he died in Havana, Cuba, in January 1708, while en route to New Orleans.

GEORGE F. G. STANLEY

AN, Col., C¹¹A, 14, f.282; C¹¹D, 3, ff.27–40. Charlevoix, *History* (Shea), IV, V. "Correspondance de Frontenac (1689–99)," *APQ Rapport, 1928–29*, 297. "Correspondance de Vaudreuil," *APQ Rapport, 1938–39*, 17, 121; *1947–48*, 309. *NYCD* (O'Callaghan and Fernow), IX. P.-G. Roy, "Ce que Callières pensait de nos officiers," 323. Taillemite, *Inventaire analytique, série B*, I.

Fauteux, *Les chevaliers de Saint-Louis*. Le Jeune, *Dictionnaire*. É.-Z. Massicotte, "Les commandants du Fort Chambly," *BRH*, XXXI (1925), 455. Tanguay, *Dictionnaire*. [François Daniel], *Histoire des grandes familles françaises du Canada* (Montréal, 1867). J.-B.-A. Ferland, *Cours d'histoire du Canada (1534–1759)* (2ᵉ éd., 2v., Québec, 1882), II. Frégault,

Iberville, 219. O'Neill, *Church and state in Louisiana*. J.-E. Roy, *Histoire de la seigneurie de Lauzon* (5v., Lévis, 1897–1904), I. Sulte, *Hist. des Can. fr.*, V, 119; VI, 26–27; *Mélanges historiques* (Malchelosse), IX, 17. J.-E. Roy, "François Bissot, sieur de la Rivière," *RSCT*, 1st ser., X (1892), sect.I, 39. P.-G. Roy, "Nicolas Daneau de Muy," *BRH*, X (1904), 345–50; "Nicolas Daneau de Muy et ses enfants," *Cahiers des Dix*, XVIII (1953), 160–61.

DARCE. *See* LOM

DARIVIÈRE. *See* BERNARD

DAUPHIN DE LA FOREST, FRANÇOIS, employee of Cavelier* de La Salle at Fort Frontenac (Cataracoui, now Kingston, Ont.), holder of the trading concession of Saint-Louis-des-Illinois, captain, manager, and commandant at Detroit; b. *c*. 1649 in Paris, son of Gabriel de La Forest, lieutenant of the provost of Île-de-France, and of Jeanne Noreau; d. 15 Oct. 1714 at Quebec.

According to the Cavelier family, La Forest had not been born a nobleman, and it was simply as a clerk that La Salle is believed to have brought him to Canada in 1675 to manage Fort Frontenac or Cataracoui (now Kingston), which had just been granted to La Salle. While on his travels, he left La Forest to act as his attorney and to assume command with the title of garrison adjutant. La Forest went regularly to Montreal, about five days' journey from Cataracoui, to buy merchandise and hire men. In September 1682 he brought to Montreal the Onondaga chief TEGANISSORENS, the representative sent by the Five Nations to the governor. The profits from the fur-trading at Cataracoui were security for the loans contracted by La Salle; consequently La Forest's management was closely watched and even criticized by the Sieur François Plet (Pellet), a cousin and principal creditor of La Salle, as well as by the merchants of the colony who had advanced funds. The merchants gained the day, and in 1683 La Barre [Le Febvre*] seized La Salle's two trading concessions, namely Cataracoui and Fort Saint-Louis-des-Illinois, in order to hand them over to the merchants. The following year, however, the king ordered the governor to return these properties and to give his full protection to M. de La Forest, who after accompanying La Salle to France returned to take command at Cataracoui.

But now that the Iroquois were taking their furs to the English, the post was ruined. Therefore when, in 1685, Denonville [BRISAY] set up a garrison there, La Forest, having no news of his employer, went up the lakes to join HENRI TONTY at Saint-Louis-des-Illinois, where the fur trade

169

was more profitable and there was less competition. As La Salle had disappeared and Tonty had set off in search of him, La Forest took over command at Fort Saint-Louis and managed everything himself, making the fur-trading contracts and purchasing goods. To comply with the governor's orders, he had in addition to raise parties of Illinois to harry the English fur-traders and the Iroquois.

In 1689, setting forth these services rendered to the colony, La Forest asked for the trading concession at Saint-Louis-des-Illinois for himself and for Tonty. This was granted to them the following year, but the undertaking was to prove onerous in the long run. Indeed, in exchange for the exclusive right to the fur trade throughout the territory, the court demanded an ever increasing participation in the war against the Iroquois. The repeated levying of men, the cost of which devolved upon the trading concessionaires, was a charge against the revenues which they could get from trade. In 1684, as governor of the Illinois country, La Salle had granted La Forest a captain's commission, but it was not until 1691 that the latter was entered on the list of officers maintained in the colony. Obviously, the emoluments from this appointment alone were not enough to enable La Forest to exploit his trading concession. Consequently, when in 1696 the king decided to close all the posts in the west except for Saint-Louis, but on condition that no fur-trading be carried on there, Frontenac [Buade*] was able to reply that the measure meant abandoning the grant. Despite the governor's reiterated protests, the court maintained its prohibition. The decision no longer affected Tonty, who had made his share over to his brother before going down to Mobile. As for La Forest, he managed to stay on at Saint-Louis-des-Illinois until 1702, when the governor ordered him to come back east if he wanted to enjoy the commission as a captain on the active list at Placentia (Plaisance), which had just been granted to him.

In the autumn of that same year La Forest was installed in command of his company, but he refused to go to Placentia, and seems to have spent at most 18 months in garrison at Trois-Rivières before receiving in 1705 an order to serve at Fort Pontchartrain (Detroit); this was due to the recommendation of LAUMET, *dit* de Lamothe Cadillac. In 1710 the latter was appointed governor of Louisiana, and the minister gave "the command of Detroit to the Sieur de La Forest, a second-rate individual, with the undeclared intention of letting this establishment, which is a bad one, drop, without abandoning it publicly after having supported it for so long." At the same

time, while giving compensation to Lamothe, La Forest had agreed to run the post with the profits from the seigneury and a fur-trading licence limited to 20,000 *livres* for beaver. But this new undertaking was to be still more difficult than the one at Saint-Louis-des-Illinois, in view of the high costs required to maintain the garrison. Involved in a lawsuit with Lamothe after being similarly involved with the Tonty brothers, vainly endeavouring to get the heirs of La Salle to recognize a promissory note which the latter was said to have signed for him, caught up in the stormy affairs of CHARLOTTE-FRANÇOISE JUCHEREAU de Saint-Denis, whom he had married in 1702, La Forest died at Quebec in 1714. He left a complicated inheritance, which his family in France finally rejected.

LOUISE DECHÊNE

AE, Mém. et doc., Amérique, 3. AN, Col., B, 15, 16, 22, 27, 29, 32–37; C^{11A}, 5, 7, 8, 20, 21, 29, 32–34; C^{11E}, 15; C^{13C}, 3, f.151; D^{2D}, carton 1; E, 246 (dossier de La Forest); F^3, 2, 4–6. BN, MS, NAF 9279, f.105; 9290, 9293, 9304 (Margry). "Correspondance de Frontenac (1689–99)," APQ *Rapport, 1927–28, 1928–29.* "Estat des employs vaquans ausquels Monsieur le comte de Frontenac ... a pourvue en l'année 1691 en attendant les commissions de sa majesté," *BRH,* XIII (1907), 339. *Jug. et délib.,* I. Le Blant, *Histoire de la N.-F.,* 270n. A. Roy, *Inv. greffes not.,* V, 92, 122, 142, 184–85; XVIII, XIX, XX.

Charland, "Notre-Dame de Québec: le nécrologe de la crypte," 174. Le Jeune, *Dictionnaire.* Gabriel Gravier, *Cavelier de La Salle de Rouen* (Paris, 1871); *Découvertes et établissements de Cavelier de La Salle, de Rouen, dans l'Amérique du Nord ...* (Paris, 1870). "Notes sur les seigneuries du district de Rimouski," *BRH,* XVII (1911), 313.

DAVID, JACQUES, merchant, court clerk, and royal notary; b. *c.* 1684 at Notre-Dame-de-la-Platée, in the diocese of Castres (province of Languedoc); son of Paul David and Marie Montet; buried 17 Oct. 1726 at Montreal.

The truth of the matter is that we know very little about Jacques David. The earliest evidence of his presence in Canada is his marriage contract, which was received 12 Sept. 1715 by Florent de LA CETIÈRE. Five days later, at Quebec, he married Marie-Louise Normandin, who was about 19. She was the daughter of the inn-keeper, Laurent Normandin, *dit* Le Sauvage, and a niece of the notary, Daniel NORMANDIN. At the time of the Quebec census in 1716 the couple was living on Rue Sous-le-Fort, probably with Marie-Louise's parents. David declared himself to be a merchant and gave his age as 28, his wife's as 20.

We know nothing of the circumstances in which David moved to Montreal, where the first of his five children was baptized 9 Oct. 1717. In the summer of 1718 he was acting court clerk there. But on 20 September he took over the Montreal registry on a three-year lease, effective from the following 1 January. On 10 March 1719 Intendant Bégon* ratified the agreement that had been reached between the Sulpician seminary, who owned the registry, and Jacques David; it authorized David to practise as court clerk—which he had already started doing. Two months later, on 8 May, Bégon appointed David royal notary. This was to be expected: the offices of court clerk and notary often went together in New France. At his death David left a minute-book that was quite extensive, considering the fact that he had practised for only seven years, while continuing till the end to have charge of the Montreal registry.

Nothing is known of David's private life except that he lived in a house on the Place d'Armes that he had rented on 4 Oct. 1720 for 240 *livres* a year, paying 60 *livres* in cash.

ANDRÉ VACHON

AJM, Greffe de Jacques David, 1719–1726; 4 oct. 1720. AJQ, Greffe de Florent de La Cetière, 12 sept. 1715. AQ, NF, Ord. des int., VI, 324v *et seq.*, 326v *et seq. Édits ord.*, II, 290f. Recensement de Québec, 1716 (Beaudet). P.-G. Roy, *Inv. jug. et délib., 1717–1760*, I, 251, 297. Massicotte, "Les tribunaux et les officiers de justice," *BRH*, XXXVII (1931), 190f., 305. Tanguay, *Dictionnaire*, III, 255.

DAVION, ALBERT, member of the community of the seminary of Quebec, parish priest on Île d'Orléans, and missionary in Louisiana; b. at Saint-Omer in the province of Artois; d. 1726 in the parish of his birth.

Abbé Albert Davion arrived in Quebec 24 May 1690. He was first the parish priest at Saint-Jean and Saint-François on the Île d'Orléans, then in 1698 he was chosen by Bishop Saint-Vallier [LA CROIX] and the directors of the seminary of Quebec to go with Abbé Jean-François BUISSON de Saint-Cosme (1667–1706) to found missions in Louisiana under the direction of Abbé François de Montigny. According to Abbé Henri-Jean Tremblay*, procurator of the seminary of Quebec in Paris, he was "a very good priest," but in such poor health that life in the wilds did not suit him at all. Abbé Davion and his fellow religious set out from Lachine 2 July 1698, accompanied by 12 paddlers. The travellers followed the Ottawa route and reached Fort Michilimackinac 8 September. There they found the explorer HENRI TONTY, who guided them as far as the Arkansas Indian country, which they reached 27 December. On 4 Jan. 1699 the expedition continued on its way and stopped 200 miles farther south, among the Tunicas, where

Davion agreed to found a mission. But Abbé Montigny and he decided first to go on as far as Fort Maurepas on Biloxi Bay (Biloxi, Mississippi). On his return from this voyage Davion settled among the Tunicas, on the banks of the Yazoo River (Miss.). He devoted himself to this tribe, occasionally staying for long periods in the French settlements on Mobile Bay (Alabama).

In 1722 he retired to New Orleans. But the Capuchins, to whom the missions in Lower Louisiana now belonged, asked for his recall. Abbé Davion sailed for France in 1725 and withdrew to live with his family, where he died 8 April 1726 after a short illness.

NOËL BAILLARGEON

AAQ, Copies de documents, Série A: Église du Canada, III, 9f. ASQ, Évêques, 172; Lettres, N, 48, 123; R, 64, 77; Missions, 73, 73c, 102; Paroisses diverses, 47–48. Noël Baillargeon, "Les missions du séminaire de Québec dans la vallée du Mississipi 1698–1699," AQ *Rapport, 1965*, 13–70. *Découvertes et établissements des Français* (Margry), VI, 247. *MPA* (Rowland and Sanders), II, 346n. Arthur Maheux, "La bibliothèque du missionnaire Davion au XVIIIe siècle," *CF*, 2e série, XXVII (1939–40), 650f.

DAVIS, JOSEPH, seaman employed by the HBC off and on between 1692 and 1715.

Davis served under Captain James KNIGHT in the expedition of 1692–93, which recaptured Fort Albany from the French, and stayed in James Bay until 1697. He rejoined the company in 1702, sailing to James Bay in that year and returning to England in 1703. He did the same as commander of the *Pery* frigate in 1706–7, and in 1708 took the *Eastmain* sloop to Albany, returning in the *Hudson's Bay* [II] (Capt. Michael GRIMINGTON). After the death of Grimington, Davis commanded this ship on voyages to Albany in 1710–11, 1712, and 1713–14.

In 1715 he was sent to York Fort as captain of the newly built supply ship, *Hudson's Bay* [III], but failed to reach that post although he was reported as coming within 15 miles of it. The consequences of his failure were serious: the company in London received no furs from York for its annual sale; James Knight, governor at York, missed the year's supply of trade goods. For want of those goods he could not fulfil his promise, given by the HBC explorer William STUART to the Chipewyan Indians, to start trading at Churchill in 1715–16. Accordingly Davis was dismissed from the company's service. So he disappears from Canadian history, a man more important for what he failed to do than for anything he did.

RICHARD GLOVER

Davis

HBRS, XXI (Rich); XXV (Davies and Johnson). Morton, *History of the Canadian west*.

DAVIS, SILVANUS (Sylvanus), land-agent and speculator, coastal trader, militia captain, and commander of Fort Loyal at Falmouth (Portland, Me.); b. *c.* 1635; d. 19 April 1703 (o.s.) in Hull (Nantasket, Mass.).

Davis' origins and early history are obscure. From 1659 on he acquired lands in Maine on the Damariscotta, the Kennebec and nearby rivers, and on Casco Bay; his trading activities with the Indians, the settlers, and also the French date from this period. In the early 1680s he moved from the Kennebec to Falmouth, where he was a leading landowner and businessman, operator of a saw-mill, a grist-mill, and a store, while carrying on his coastal trade. In 1686 he was made a justice of the peace, and in 1691 he became one of the representatives of Maine in the Massachusetts Council.

A militia captain in King Philip's War, Davis continued his military activities after his move to Falmouth, commanding Fort Loyal, the principal English strong point on Casco Bay; he held this post in 1689 and again in May 1690, when the fort's new commander withdrew to Boston for aid as a large force of French and Indians under the command of RENÉ ROBINAU de Portneuf and AUGUSTIN LE GARDEUR de Courtemanche approached. The attack, one of Buade* de Frontenac's planned strikes against the English colonies, began on 16 May (26 May, N.S.). On 20 May, after a siege of five days, Fort Loyal surrendered; Davis was one of the few to survive the massacre which followed. He was fairly well treated on the long journey to the St Lawrence, and had considerable freedom during his four months in Quebec. He was there throughout the unsuccessful siege by the Phips* expedition, and was one of the prisoners exchanged for Phips's French captives when the fleet withdrew in October 1690. On his return Captain Davis wrote an account of the fall of Fort Loyal, of his conversation with Frontenac, and of his experiences and impressions during the siege.

Later in the 1690s he moved to Massachusetts, retaining some of his interests in Maine, and settled finally in Hull, where he remained until his death in 1703. A man of energy and enterprise, ambitious, a shrewd businessman, Davis was also an experienced Indian fighter, a good disciplinarian, and a courageous commander.

ALICE R. STEWART

["Mass. Archives," XXXVI, 72, 73. Suffolk County Court House (Boston, Mass.), Registry of Probate, 2806. *Documentary hist. of Maine*, IV, 390, 459–63; V, 7, 8, 10, 11, 95–96; VI; VII, 358. "Provincial charter of 1691, October 7, 1691," in *Trans., 1913–14* (Col. Soc. Mass. pub., XVII, Boston, 1915), 35, 38, 39n. *Vital records of Hull, Mass. to the year 1850*, comp. T. W. Baldwin (Boston, 1911), 65.

Valuable evidence of Davis' contacts with French traders can be found in [Henri Brunet], "Letters of an Acadian trader, 1674–1676" ed. L.-A. Vigneras, *New Eng. Q.*, XIII (March 1940), 98–110. There are a number of contemporary or nearly contemporary accounts of the siege and fall of Fort Loyal, both from French and from English sources. There is some disagreement on details such as the dates, the use by Portneuf of conventional methods of siege warfare, what French and Indian leaders were present, whether or in what manner a pledge of protection was given to the inhabitants when the fort surrendered, and their subsequent treatment. Later historians reflect to some extent these differences in the early sources. A detailed, emotional account from the English side was written by Davis himself after his return from captivity, "Declaration of Sylvanus Davis inhabitant of the town of Falmouth in the province of Maine, in New England, concerning the cruel, treacherous and barbarous management of a war against the English in the eastern parts of New England by the cruel Indians . . . ," *Mass. Hist. Soc. Coll.*, 3d ser., I (1825), 101–12; *see also*: Cotton Mather, *Magnalia Christi Americana*, II, 523–25. For the French version of the attack see MONSEIGNAT's account in AN, Col., C¹¹A, 11 (printed in *Coll. de manuscrits relatifs à la N.-F.*, I, 498–99 and in *NYCD* (O'Callaghan and Fernow), IX, 472–73); Monseignat refers to Davis as "Denis." *See also*: La Potherie, *Histoire* (1722), III, 76–81; Le Clercq, *First establishment of the faith* (Shea), II, 293ff.; Charlevoix, *History* (Shea), II, 132–37. Later accounts include J. T. Hull, *The siege and capture of Fort Loyall . . . 1690* (o.s.) (Portland, Me., 1885), 24–67, 69ff.; Parkman, *Count Frontenac and New France* (1891), 228–31; Eccles, *Frontenac*, 225–27. For the fullest treatment of Davis' experiences as a prisoner in Quebec and the details of his exchange, including his own story, *see*: *1690, Sir William Phips devant Québec* (Myrand).

The following sources were also found useful for the life of Davis: C. J. Binney, "New England genealogies," I, 39, 39a–e (this work is a manuscript collection of genealogical material in the library of the New Eng. Hist. and Geneal. Soc.). Hutchinson, *Hist. of Mass.-bay* (Mayo), I, 293–94. *Genealogical dictionary of Maine and New Hampshire*, ed. Sybil Noyes *et al.* (Portland, Me., 1928–39). W. D. Spencer, *Maine immortals* (Augusta, Me., 1932), 89–98. A.R.S.]

DECANESORA. *See* TEGANISSORENS

DECWANDO. *See* ATECOUANDO

DEGOUTIN (Degoutins). *See* GOUTIN

DEHORNÉ. *See* HORNÉ

DELAUNAY, CHARLES, coureur de bois, tanner; b. in Quebec, 30 May 1648; d. in Montreal, 26 Feb. 1737.

Pierre Delaunay, the father of Charles, was born in Fresnay-le-Boesme in Maine in 1616. He came to Canada in 1635 as a clerk of the Compagnie des Cent-Associés and married Françoise Pinguet in Quebec on 7 Nov. 1645. He was killed by the Iroquois on 28 Nov. 1654.

Like many other Canadians, Charles was initially attracted to the life of the coureur de bois. He was a member of the party which HENRI TONTY led to the Gulf of Mexico in 1686 in an unsuccessful attempt to rescue the ill-fated expedition of Cavelier* de La Salle. Following his marriage in 1695 to Marie-Anne Legras (by whom he was to have 13 children) he settled in Montreal. There he opened a tannery with Gérard Barsalou in 1700. When the two men dissolved their partnership six years later JACQUES RAUDOT decreed by an ordinance that they would be the only two tanners authorized to ply their trade in Montreal and he laid down in some detail their rights and obligations. Shortly afterwards Delaunay took on an indentured employee, Gabriel Lenoir, *dit* Rolland, who became his partner in 1713 and married his daughter, Marie-Joseph, in 1714.

Charles Delaunay is admittedly a minor figure, but he is not without historical significance. His career as a tanner, which can be studied in some detail in numerous notarial documents, provides valuable information on one of the important crafts of the French régime and on the general nature of business practices in the colony.

Yves F. Zoltvany

AJM, Greffe d'Antoine Adhémar, 12 déc. 1695; Greffe de Pierre Raimbault, 9 sept. 1731. *Découvertes et établissements des Français* (Margry), III, 436–50. *Jug. et délib.*, III, IV, VI. A. Roy, *Inv. greffes not.*, IV, V, VI, XI, XII, XVII, XXI. P.-G. Roy, *Inv. ord. int.*, I, 48. Massicotte, "Répertoire des engagements pour l'Ouest," 195. Tanguay, *Dictionnaire*, I, 171; III, 297–98. Fauteux, *Essai sur l'industrie sous le régime français*, II, 413–29. Francis Parkman, *La Salle and the discovery of the great west* (Boston, 1887), 428–30. Ivanhoë Caron, "Les censitaires du côteau Sainte-Geneviève (banlieue de Québec) de 1636 à 1800," *BRH*, XXVII (1921), 97–108.

DELHALLE (De la Halle), CONSTANTIN, priest, Recollet, founder and parish priest of Sainte-Anne du Détroit; killed 1 June 1706 at Detroit.

Tanguay has confused Delhalle with Father Nicolas-Bernardin CONSTANTIN. For his part Charlevoix*, although distinguishing him from Constantin, calls him Nicolas-Bernardin-Constan-tin De Lhalle. Furthermore, the spelling of his name varies a great deal over the years: Dehalle (Simple Bocquet), De L'halle and Delahalle (Bonaventure Liénard), de L'Halle (Gosselin), Challe (Massicotte), de LHalle (Jouve).

According to Shea, Delhalle arrived in Canada on 1 June 1696. He accompanied Lamothe Cadillac [LAUMET] at the time of the creation of Detroit, and himself founded the first church in Michigan, which he dedicated to St Anne on 26 July 1701. During a council of the Hurons held in the fort at Detroit on 4 Dec. 1701, in the absence of Delhalle, Cadillac asserted "that the Black Robes [the Jesuits] do not speak effectively today because they are vexed at my bringing with me a Grey Robe [a Recollet], and because priests are to come who have white collars [priests from the Missions Étrangères]. This annoys them because they would like to be the only ones."

Meanwhile Father Constantin had returned from the *pays d'en haut*, for we find in the parish registers of Champlain a certificate of baptism dated 25 Sept. 1701 and signed by him, which is evidence of his passing through that parish. In June 1702 he was at Trois-Rivières, where he officiated as the parish priest. He apparently returned then to Detroit, since Cadillac stressed that he was there in a letter dated 25 September of the same year.

On 5 Oct. 1703 a fire destroyed the chapel at Detroit and Father Constantin's house, as well as the residences of Cadillac and HENRI TONTY. The registers of this parish were also destroyed. The first act in the new register was the certificate of baptism of Marie-Thérèse, Cadillac's daughter, which was dated 2 Feb. 1704. "This register, containing only three pages, has been preserved, and is the oldest register of the first French parish in the West. . . ."

Father Constantin was present at several councils held by the Indians at Detroit, in particular that of 8 June 1704, when the Indians accused the governor, RIGAUD de Vaudreuil, of having deceived them and considered abandoning the post. On 8 March 1706 LE PESANT, the chief of the Ottawas du Sable, complained of the murders committed by the Shawnees, the Sioux, and the Miamis and wanted to go to war against them.

Father Constantin was killed on 1 June of the same year. Charlevoix recounts the event in these words: "The Recollet Father Constantin, chaplain of the fort, was walking in his garden, ignorant of all that was going on. Some Ottawas seized and bound him; but John le Blanc [OUTOUTAGAN], one of their chiefs, who had taken part in the assembly at Montreal, where the general peace was signed, unbound him, and begged him to go and tell the Commandant that they had no designs on the French, and that he besought him to stop firing on them. As that religious was about entering the fort, some flying Miamis overtook him, and a volley of musketry was fired upon them by Ottawas who perceived them. Father Constantin was struck and fell dead on the spot."

His body was buried in the cemetery of his parish. A certain veneration became attached to his name (miracles have even been attributed to his intercession), and the Recollets who succeeded one another at this post, particularly Fathers Simple Bocquet and Bonaventure Liénard, took special care of his mortal remains.

JACQUES VALOIS

AJTR, Registres d'état civil de Champlain. AN, Col., C¹¹ᴬ, 26, f.106; C¹¹ᴱ, 14, f.125. Charlevoix, *History* (Shea), V, 185–86. *Découvertes et établissements des Français* (Margry), V, 190–91, 259–61. PAC *Report*, *1899*, Supp., 45. "Le récollet Constantin Delhalle," *BRH*, XX (1914), 92. Tanguay, *Répertoire du clergé*, 78. Gosselin, *L'Église du Canada*, III, 334–36. J. G. Shea, *History of the Catholic Church in the United States* (4v., New York, 1886–92), I, 620–24; *History of the Catholic missions among the Indian tribes of the United States* (New York, 1855), 376. *The American Cath. Hist. Researches* (Philadelphia), XIII (1896). É.-Z. Massicotte, "Les deux Pères de l'Halle," *BRH*, VIII (1902), 149–50. N. Saint-Pierre, "Lamothe-Cadillac et la fondation de Détroit," *BRH*, XIX (1913), 129–51.

DELIETTE. *See* LIETTE

DEMESNU DE GAUDARVILLE, ALEXANDRE PEUVRET. *See* PEUVRET

DENONVILLE, JACQUES-RENÉ BRISAY DE. *See* BRISAY

DENYS, JOSEPH (baptized **Jacques**), priest, first Canadian Recollet, provincial commissioner; b. 7 Nov. 1657 at Trois-Rivières, son of PIERRE DENYS de La Ronde and Catherine Leneuf de La Poterie; d. 25 Jan. 1736 at Quebec.

Joseph Denys was descended from illustrious Canadian families. His maternal grandfather, Jacques Leneuf* de La Poterie, had arrived in Canada in 1636 and had made his permanent home at Trois-Rivières in 1640. His paternal grandfather, Simon Denys* de La Trinité, spent some years in Acadia (1632–50), then settled at Quebec. His father, after his marriage in 1665, lived for some years at Trois-Rivières, and around 1661 he also went to live at Quebec.

Jacques, the second child of a family that was to number 12, was born on 7 Nov. 1657 at Trois-

Rivières. He was baptized the next day by the Jesuit Pierre Bailloquet*, and received the Christian name of his maternal grandfather. At the age of 11, that is on 21 Aug. 1669, he entered the Petit Séminaire of Quebec, which had opened its doors the preceding year. Was he already contemplating the priesthood? The arrival of the Recollets in 1670 no doubt made him think about the religious life, for at 20 he entered the Franciscan noviciate, thus becoming the first priest to serve his noviciate in Canada.

The habit was conferred upon him by Father Potentien OZON, the superior of the convent of Notre-Dame-des-Anges. He received the name of Joseph, no doubt in memory of the patron whom the Recollets of 1615 had given to Canada. The following year, 1678, Father Valentin LEROUX heard the religious profession made by Brother Joseph, who immediately went to France for his theological studies and was ordained priest there in 1682. His superiors sent him back to Canada, where he devoted himself to preaching, hearing confessions, and conducting religious services for the settlers.

In 1683, after a brief period of apprenticeship, the young priest found himself plunged into the great adventure of successively establishing parishes and holding superiorships, which were to lead him to the top of his province. For some ten years his father, Pierre Denys, had been a partner with CHARLES AUBERT de La Chesnaye in a fishing undertaking at Percé. The two had been joint owners of the seigneury of Île Percée since 1677 when a third owner, Charles Bazire*, had died. Probably the father suggested to the Recollet authorities that his son should come to Percé, and offered to assist in the building of a church there. However that may be, the Recollet reached Percé in 1683, accompanied by Brother Didace Pelletier*, a carpenter by trade. As soon as they arrived, they started to build a church and complete the missionaries' residence, where for ten years the Recollet Father Exupère Dethunes* had been living. Le Clercq* states that this was the first church in the locality. It was dedicated to the apostle St Peter. Opposite Percé, on Bonaventure Island, the Recollets had another mission, with a church dedicated to St Claire. Its architect was perhaps Father Joseph.

During the six years of his missionary service at Percé, Joseph Denys served in a dual capacity: as a minister to the residents, who were few in number and relatively fervent, and to the fluctuating and mixed population found there in the fishing season. At those periods he had to fight the abuses pointed out by Bishop Saint-Vallier [LA CROIX] on his visit in 1686: failure to attend divine service and lack of respect towards it, working on Sundays, theft, drunkenness, profligacy, and quarrelling.

In September 1689 the Recollets opened a mission at Placentia (Plaisance), Newfoundland. Father Xiste Le Tac was its superior and Joseph Denys was appointed parish priest with the title and function of vicar general. His task was no easier than at Percé. In February 1690, 45 English privateers surprised Placentia. The Recollet echoed the general anxiety in his representations to the minister; he begged His Excellency to have compassion on nearly 30 families who were exposed not only to the usual cruelty of the English, but also to the inhumanity of wretches who respected neither religion nor law. He himself risked his life to disarm a murderer who threatened to kill whosoever dared to approach him.

In March 1692 Louis XIV officially recognized all present and future establishments of the Recollets of Canada, Acadia, and Newfoundland, including those on the islands of Saint-Pierre and at Plaisance. That same year Father Joseph received new instructions from his superiors: to found at Montreal an establishment for the Recollets. M. Tronson, the superior general of the Sulpicians, states the reasons to Buade* de Frontenac: "to remove all cause for complaint where we are concerned and to leave all consciences free." Father Denys therefore became the founder of the first Recollet convent at Ville-Marie. In cooperation with the syndic of the Recollets, Bertrand Arnaud, a Montreal merchant, he acquired about four and a half acres of land, and within two months the residence and chapel were built. It was only a temporary construction, for 12 years later the convent was rebuilt in stone.

The following year, 1693, the community was completely installed, and on 15 October Bishop Saint-Vallier was able to write: "The land acquired by the Recollets is so attractive that there is a place for one of the finest and largest convents; the garden is in perfect condition, and I do not believe that there is a more splendid one in Canada."

In March 1694 Father Joseph took part, with his fellow religious, in the first synod held at Montreal by Bishop Saint-Vallier. In May of the same year the incident known as the "*prie-dieu* affair" burst upon his convent. On 10 May, in the church of the Recollets at Montreal, two novices took the habit [see La Frenaye]; Bishop Saint-Vallier and M. de Callière took part in this ceremony. The bishop was of the opinion that the *prie-dieu* intended for the governor was in a more honourable place than his was, and asked Father Denys, the superior of the convent, to have it removed; the latter obeyed the bishop. Knowing nothing about the incident, the officers who entered the church put the gover-

nor's *prie-dieu* back in its accustomed place. The bishop got angry and tried to force the governor to sit elsewhere, and on the latter's refusal he left the church.

The next day the bishop ordered the Recollets to remove all the *prie-dieu*, including his own. The governor having had them put back by his soldiers, the bishop placed the church under interdict, and it was closed to the faithful. Knowing that they were in no way responsible for this dispute between the civil and religious authorities, the Recollets nevertheless obeyed, believing that their submission would represent sufficient satisfaction for the alleged insult that had been received on their premises, and that the bishop would lift the interdict after a few days. Two months went by during which all attempts at reconciliation came up against the demands of the bishop. Convinced that matters were going to drag on, the Recollets took their stand on their privileges and canonical exemptions, drew up a report of the affair, made a protest to the bishop, and reopened their church. The bishop issued three monitions to induce the religious to submit to authority. They obstinately refused. Then Bishop Saint-Vallier resorted to the supreme measure: a personal interdiction on each religious of Montreal, on pain of excommunication. The Recollets paid no heed to this, and continued to keep their church open and to carry on their ministry. The Conseil Souverain of Quebec, before which the affair was brought, referred it to the council of state in France. The latter declared that as the bishop had exceeded his powers and acted without sufficient information, there were grounds for deciding in favour of those who complained of misuse of authority. These contentions lasted from May 1694 to the end of October 1695.

It does not seem that Father Joseph Denys received any rebuke from his superiors over this affair, for in 1696 he was nominated to assume the direction of the community of Quebec, the most important Recollet mission in Canada.

During these years at Quebec he experienced a double sorrow: the death of his mother, aged about 60, on 24 Oct. 1697, and the following year, on 28 November, the death of the Comte de Frontenac, the Recollets' syndic. Father Joseph complied with the last will and testament of the governor, who had expressed the desire to be buried in the church of the Recollets. He also intended to transport the governor's heart to France, but it is not known whether he was able to do this.

As superior he was present on 27 Feb. 1698 at the third synod summoned by Bishop Saint-Vallier, in the course of which 23 statutes were adopted. He also took part on 3 Oct. 1699 in the meeting of the representatives of the three estates, called with a

175

Denys de Bonaventure

view to better regulating the farming-out of the trade in furs.

In 1699 Father Joseph ceased to be guardian of the convent in Quebec, and went to France for the affairs of the mission. He returned with the title of provincial commissioner of the mission, succeeding Father GOYER. He discharged these important duties for five years, and then became once more an ordinary religious. He devoted himself to his ministry as parish priest at Cap-Saint-Ignace and at Saint-Michel until the autumn of 1707, when he undertook another journey to France and returned holding the office of novice-master of the convent at Quebec. Two years later, in 1709, he was appointed guardian and priest of the parish of Trois-Rivières, where he was to remain until 1717. He had a stone church built there which remained standing until the fire of 24 June 1908. During his stay at Trois-Rivières he accepted responsibility for a certain time for the spiritual direction of the Ursulines.

Father Joseph, being a former provincial commissioner and of Canadian origin, was interested in the future of the Recollets in Canada. Hence on 6 Nov. 1716 he signed a petition addressed to the provincial and council of definitors of the ecclesiastical province of New France. He suggested among other things that the provincial commissioner should not be attached to any community, so that he could always be fair and equitable in the allotment of religious and in the distribution of the alms which the king gave to the mission; he further suggested that the provincial commissioner should have a council composed of the local superiors and of the three most senior members of the convent where this council would sit, and that the said council should have authority to decide on the spot, without having recourse to the council of definitors in France, upon matters concerning the mission.

Freed of his responsibilities as superior and as parish priest of Trois-Rivières, Joseph Denys then devoted his attention to the cause of Brother Didace Pelletier, who had died in great sanctity on 21 Feb. 1699 and whose body was buried in the chapel of the Recollets at Trois-Rivières. Father Joseph had been his confessor for 14 years, and his travelling companion for still longer. In 1718 he went to France with a whole dossier containing a summary of Brother Didace's life, as well as reports of allegedly miraculous acts attributed to the religious. He took steps to present his case for beatification to Rome, and even planned to write a detailed biography of his confidant, but we do not know whether he carried out his project.

While he was returning from one of his numerous journeys to France, Father Joseph stopped at Île Royale and stayed there from the month of October 1722 until the spring of the following year. In 1727 he returned there, this time as vicar general of Bishop Saint-Vallier with residence at Louisbourg. In an act dated 8 April 1728 he called himself "provincial commissioner of the Recollets of Paris and vicar-general in all the new colony of Île Royale."

It was at Louisbourg that he learned of the death of his bishop, Saint-Vallier, which occurred on 26 Dec. 1727. Both advanced in age, and among the oldest priests in Canada, they had contributed greatly to the building of the young Canadian church. Father Joseph returned to Quebec in 1729; he was 71. There he was to finish his days, in the peace of mind brought by prayer. After an illness of three days, he died on 25 Jan. 1736. People wrote at that time that he had died in great sanctity. He left tangible marks of his work at Montreal, Trois-Rivières, Quebec, Percé, Île Royale, and Placentia.

JACQUES VALOIS

AN, Col., B, 38, ff.166, 195; C[11A], 120, f.150. AQ, NF, Doc. de la jur. de T.-R., 18. ASQ. BN, MS, Fr. 9097, f.20. "L'affaire du prie-dieu à Montréal, en 1694," APQ *Rapport, 1923–24,* 71–110. Hugolin [Stanislas Lemay], *L'établissement des Récollets à l'île Percée (1673–1690)* (Québec, 1912); *L'établissement des Récollets à Montréal, 1692* (Montréal, 1911); *L'établissement des Récollets de la province de Saint-Denis à Plaisance en l'île de Terre-Neuve, 1689* (Québec, 1911); *Le père Joseph Denis, premier récollet canadien (1657–1736)* (2v., Québec, 1926). Jouve, *Les Franciscains et le Canada: aux Trois-Rivières,* 90–111.

DENYS DE BONAVENTURE, SIMON-PIERRE, naval officer and administrator, b. at Trois-Rivières, 22 June 1659, son of PIERRE DENYS de La Ronde and Catherine Leneuf; m. in 1693 Jeanne Jannière, widow of Jean-François Bourdon*, Sieur de Dombourg; d. at Rochefort, 7 Feb. 1711, and was buried there in the church of Saint-Louis.

Bonaventure's date of birth is frequently given as 15 Feb. 1654 but family papers show this to be the birth date of his uncle, Simon-Pierre Denys de Saint-Pierre, with whom he is sometimes confused. Saint-Pierre was the son of Simon Denys* de La Trinité and Françoise Du Tartre. He became a lieutenant in the colonial regular troops, and while still young was wounded in an encounter with the Iroquois, taken prisoner, and burned. Le Jeune states that Bonaventure was married first in 1686 to Geneviève Couillard, but according to the family records she was the wife of another of his uncles, Pierre Denys Du Tartre.

Denys de Bonaventure

Bonaventure entered the colonial regular troops and was employed by the Compagnie du Nord, a trading company formed in 1682 by Canadian and French merchants [see Charles Aubert de La Chesnaye]. He also directed at this time a fishery, established at Île Percée by his father, who had obtained a concession of land in 1672 for this purpose. Bonaventure was not, however, free from interruption in this activity. During a period of eight months, from the autumn of 1685 to the summer of 1686, he had to accompany Intendant de Meulles on a voyage to Acadia, commanding a small vessel and crew. Subsequently he made a trip to France to seek payment for this service and to petition for the maintenance of his fisheries.

Bonaventure's fortunes were soon affected by the wars with the English. In 1690 the English raided and destroyed the fishing establishments at Île Percée. In the same year Bonaventure, in command of the *Saint-Francois-Xavier*, accompanied Pierre Le Moyne d'Iberville in the *Sainte-Anne* to attack York Fort in Hudson Bay. The expedition failed to take this fort but threatened the New Severn post, which was burned down by its commander, Thomas Walsh. Iberville wintered at the bay but Bonaventure sailed for Quebec with a cargo of furs, changing his destination to France when he learned that Sir William Phips* was besieging the town. In 1691, in command of the *Soleil d'Afrique*, Bonaventure carried Robinau* de Villebon, new governor of Acadia, to the Saint John River. At the Saint John, they captured a New England vessel carrying John Alden, John Nelson, and Colonel Edward Tyng*. In 1692, Bonaventure, captain of the 34-gun frigate, the *Envieux*, and Iberville, in the 38-gun *Poli*, convoyed six merchantmen to Quebec, taking three prizes en route. Iberville was to have headed another attack on York Fort but the season was too advanced, so he helped Bonaventure to carry supplies to Acadia. The *Poli* and the *Envieux* cruised the coast, were driven apart in a storm, and returned to France separately. In 1693, Bonaventure and Iberville, in the *Indiscret* and the *Poli* respectively, sailed for Quebec whence they were to leave for another attack on York, but again the season was too far advanced. Bonaventure spent 1694 and 1695 carrying supplies to Acadia and cruising the coast in the *Envieux*.

In 1696 Bonaventure and Iberville, together with Jean-Vincent d'Abbadie de Saint-Castin and his band of Abenakis, captured and destroyed Fort William Henry at Pemaquid. The ships then sailed for Placentia (Plaisance). Bonaventure carried the governor of Placentia, Brouillan [Mombeton], and his forces to a rendezvous near St John's, while Iberville led a detachment overland across

the Avalon Peninsula. Brouillan and Iberville went on to capture St John's but Bonaventure returned to France with dispatches in the *Profond*.

During the next four years Bonaventure was again transporting provisions to Acadia. In 1701, when Brouillan succeeded Villebon as governor of Acadia, Bonaventure was appointed second in command. Brouillan rebuilt the fort at Port-Royal (Annapolis Royal, N.S.), destroyed by the English in 1690, and Bonaventure was named king's lieutenant there on 2 Feb. 1702. In July 1704, when an English force led by Colonel Church ravaged some Acadian settlements and laid siege to the fort, Bonaventure was absent at Les Mines (Minas). Brouillan sailed for France in December 1704 leaving Bonaventure in command, but died shortly after returning to Acadia, in September 1705. Bonaventure petitioned for the post of governor, but in spite of his record of service and his popularity with the inhabitants the appointment was denied him, owing to reports which had reached France of his liaison with the widowed Madame Louise Damours de Freneuse [Guyon*]. On 22 May 1706 Auger de Subercase, formerly governor at Placentia, was named governor of Acadia.

In June 1707 the English under Colonel March again laid siege to Port-Royal, but withdrew when Bernard-Anselme d'Abbadie de Saint-Castin arrived with a band of Abenakis. During this siege Bonaventure was ill in bed in the fort. The enemy destroyed farms and burned houses in the vicinity, including Bonaventure's house and all his effects. The English returned in August and again laid siege to the fort, but withdrew with the arrival of Saint-Castin and after some sharp skirmishes with the French and the Indians.

Efforts were made to strengthen the fort at Port-Royal while French and Indian raids on New England settlements continued and privateers preyed on English shipping, the cargoes helping to provision Port-Royal. In 1710 the English determined to attack Port-Royal in force. On 29 September (N.S.; 18 September, O.S.) a large expedition under Colonel Nicholson sailed from Boston, and on 13 October Port-Royal capitulated. The garrison, including Bonaventure, was transported to La Rochelle. Bonaventure then submitted a plan to the minister for the recapture of Port-Royal. He was not to know that Port-Royal was irretrievably lost. He died at Rochefort in 1711.

Talebearing seems to have been a common pastime in Port-Royal. Bonaventure was accused not only of an affair with Madame de Freneuse but also of trading on his own account with the colonists in the Acadian settlements and, worse, with the English. It was also alleged that he was

Denys de La Ronde

malingering during the siege in June 1707. There is evidence that his association with Madame de Freneuse cost him promotion, but it is not apparent that the authorities in France took the other accusations very seriously, for he had the confidence of the governors under whom he served. He may have been named a knight of the order of Saint-Louis, for he is referred to as such in the marriage record of his son, Claude-Élisabeth, on 25 Nov. 1748.

Bonaventure's career was shaped by the troubled times in which he lived. He was a soldier and spent the greater part of his life engaged in his country's struggle against the English in America. He seems to have been an active and a likeable man, possibly not overburdened with moral scruples, and a commander who carried out his duties capably and vigorously.

A. J. E. LUNN

AN, Col., B, 16, 17, 19, 20, 22, 23, 25, 27, 29, 32; C¹¹ᴬ, 8; C¹¹ᴰ, 2, 4, 5, 6. "Mass. Archives," II, 611–11b. PAC, FM 18, H 13 (Denys family papers). *Coll. de manuscrits relatifs à la N.-F.*, II, III. "Correspondance de Frontenac (1689–99)," APQ *Rapport*, 1927–28, 1928–29. "Correspondance de Vaudreuil," APQ *Rapport*, 1938–39. *Jug. et délib.*, III, IV, V. Webster, *Acadia*.

Fauteux, *Les chevaliers de Saint-Louis*. Le Jeune, *Dictionnaire*. Tanguay, *Dictionnaire*. N. M. Crouse, *Lemoyne d'Iberville: soldier of New France* (Toronto, [1954]). Frégault, *Iberville*. La Morandière, *Hist. de la pêche française de la morue*, I, 370ff. Murdoch, *History of Nova-Scotia*. Robert Rumilly, *Histoire des Acadiens* (2v., Montréal, [1955]). Pierre Daviault, "Mme de Freneuse et M. de Bonaventure," *RSCT*, 3d ser., XXXV (1941), sect.I, 37–56. "Simon-Pierre de Bonaventure," *BRH*, XXXVIII (1932), 437.

DENYS DE LA RONDE, PIERRE, landowner and businessman, b. 8 Oct. 1631 at Saint-Vincent de Tours, son of Simon Denys* de La Trinité and his first wife, Jeanne Dubreuil. On 23 Aug. 1655 he married Catherine Leneuf (1640–1697), daughter of Jacques Leneuf* de La Poterie, governor of Trois-Rivières. He died in Quebec and was buried 8 June 1708 in the church of the Recollets.

Denys de La Ronde engaged in numerous business enterprises. He owned lots in Lower Town, Quebec, and on 14 Aug. 1655 he bought the brewery in Quebec and was still operating it in 1664. When he married in 1655 he settled at Trois-Rivières and was associated with his father-in-law's shipping company. In 1657 he bought a farm at *côte* Sainte-Geneviève near Quebec and leased it. He moved from Trois-Rivières to Quebec in 1661, or soon after, and on 2 March 1662 obtained from the Jesuits a grant of land, 2 arpents by 40, on the St Charles River. Five years

later he had half of it under cultivation. Subsequently his grant was increased and he also obtained land nearby at Bourg-Royal which he rented. On 4 March 1663 he was one of the 17 merchants to whom Governor Pierre Dubois* Davaugour leased the Tadoussac trading concession.

Talon* on 20 July 1672 granted Denys de La Ronde, CHARLES AUBERT de La Chesnaye, and Charles Bazire* a tract of land extending from Percé to Mal Baie; there they established a sedentary fishery for seals, porpoises, cod, and all other fish in the seas and rivers, which Denys de La Ronde managed. A few years later there were buildings at Percé to store fish and to lodge crews, a house for the commandant, a chapel and lodging for two Recollets, a few houses for settlers, and 100 acres of cleared land. At Petite Rivière (Saint-Pierre de la Mal Baie) there were lodgings for 15 men, a storehouse, farm buildings, a garden, and 30 acres of cleared land. The enterprise did not prosper however. By 1676 the partners wished to withdraw and Denys de La Ronde petitioned the government for compensation for his ruinous expenditures. On 18 Oct. 1677 most of the grant was ceded to JACQUES LE BER of Montreal and by 1685 the seigneury eventually reverted to a cousin of Denys de La Ronde, Richard Denys* de Fronsac, acting for his father, Nicolas Denys*. The grant had originally been taken from the holdings of Nicolas Denys. The settlements were destroyed by raiders from New England in 1690.

Meanwhile by 1676 Denys de La Ronde's sight was failing, and he evidently was blind three years later when Buade* de Frontenac petitioned the king for help for him. Denys de La Ronde turned over his seigneury on the St Charles to a farmer, then on 1 Sept. 1680 bought a house in Upper Town, Quebec, on Rue Saint-Louis, adjoining the property of the Recollets, and lived there on rents from his properties. In 1691 he and his wife gave up their house to the Recollets as a hospice in return for an annual income and the use of a house on the Recollets' land at the corner of Rues Sainte-Anne and Desjardins. Denys de La Ronde had always had a close and friendly relationship with the Recollets. One of his sons, Jacques, became Father JOSEPH DENYS, the first Canadian Recollet. Both Denys de La Ronde and his wife were buried in the Recollets' church in Quebec.

A. J. E. LUNN

PAC, FM 18, H 13 (Denys family papers). Denys, *Description and natural history* (Ganong). P.-G. Roy, *Inv. concessions*, II, 127. P.-G. et A. Roy, *Inv. greffes not.*, I, 60, 71; II, 10; III, 152, 185. Hugolin [Stanislas Lemay], *Le père Joseph Denis, premier récollet* canadien (1657–1736) (2v., Québec, 1926). Sulte, Hist. des Can. fr., V. Hugolin [Stanislas Lemay], "L'établissement des Récollets à l'isle Percée 1673–1690," BRH, XVII (1911), 339–52, 369–80.

DENYS DE SAINT-SIMON, PAUL, provost of the marshalcy, member of the Conseil Souverain; b. 13 June 1649, baptized in the church of Saint-Sauveur in Paris, son of Simon Denys* de La Trinité and Françoise Du Tartre; married Marie-Madeleine de Peiras, sister of Jean-Baptiste de PEIRAS, on 18 Jan. 1678; d. in Quebec, 14 Oct. 1731.

From August 1671 to August 1672 Denys de Saint-Simon accompanied the Jesuit Charles Albanel*, on an arduous journey from Tadoussac to James Bay for the purpose of claiming the territory for France and of christianizing the Indians. In accordance with his instructions from Talon*, he planted the arms of France at Lake Nemiskau on 9 July 1672.

In 1678 Denys de Saint-Simon was appointed lieutenant of the marshalcy or "Prévôté des Maréchaux." The marshalcy had been established in Canada by royal edict of 9 May 1677. It was a body of law enforcement officers, called "archers," headed by a provost. The office of lieutenant, second in command to the provost, is said to have been created especially for Denys de Saint-Simon. Denys was named provost of the marshalcy on 24 May 1689, after the death of the first incumbent. The office carried an annual stipend of 500 livres. Denys continued to hold it until 12 May 1714 when he relinquished it to his son, Charles Denys* de Saint-Simon. In 1710 Denys was appointed temporarily to the Conseil Souverain and in 1714 was given permission to attend sessions; he received a permanent appointment to it on 1 April 1717. Towards the end of 1717 he was acting as attorney general.

Denys de Saint-Simon also had farming and commercial interests. The census of 1681 shows that he had land under cultivation. In 1700 he took shares in the Compagnie de la Colonie, formed to exploit the beaver trade. It is probable that, like other prominent members of the colony, Denys de Saint-Simon continued to invest in land and in commercial ventures, but his principal contribution appears to have been his public service as lieutenant and provost of the marshalcy and as a member of the Conseil Souverain.

A. J. E. LUNN

Documents relating to Canadian currency during the French period (Shortt), I, 404, 436, 446. Édits ord., I, 97. JR (Thwaites), XXXIV, 246f.; LVI, 149–217, 303. PAC Report, 1899, Supp.; 1923, App.D. P.-G. Roy, "Les conseillers au Conseil souverain de la Nouvelle-France," RSCT, 3d ser., IX (1915), sect.I, 179. Sulte, Hist. des Can. fr., III, 57; V, 15, 54; VII, 41. Jacques Rousseau, "Les voyages du père Albanel au lac Mistassini et à la baie James," RHAF, III (1950), 556–86. P.-G. Roy, "Prévôt de la maréchaussée en la Nouvelle-France," BRH, VII (1901), 368f.

DENYS DE VITRÉ, CHARLES, landowner, fisherman, member of the Conseil Souverain; b. 8 March 1645 at Tours, son of Simon Denys* de La Trinité and Françoise Du Tartre; married first on 18 Oct. 1668 at Quebec, Catherine de Loustelneau (1648–1698), daughter of Charles de Loustelneau and Charlotte de Buday Fleury of Paris, and secondly on 18 March 1700, Marie-Charlotte, daughter of Jean Chrétien; d. in Quebec and was buried there 9 Jan. 1703.

Vitré belonged to a prominent family and distinguished himself by his efforts to develop commercial fisheries in the St Lawrence. As a result of his position and his contribution to the economic life of the colony, he was recognized, encouraged, and, as far as possible, supported by the governor and intendant. He was appointed a member of the Conseil Souverain in 1673, at the age of 28, and continued as a member for the rest of his life. He was granted a succession of seigneuries, some primarily for the purpose of establishing fisheries, and he acquired land in and near Quebec.

Vitré's properties were: Bellevue, between Contrecœur and Verchères, granted in 1672 and sold in 1678; Le Bic, granted in 1675 and sold in 1688; a lot acquired in 1683 in Lower Town (Quebec) near the present church of Notre-Dame-des-Victoires; Vitré or Montapeine, between Beaumont and Lauson, granted in 1683 and ultimately inherited by his eldest daughter, Marie-Gabrielle; Trois-Pistoles, granted in 1687 and exchanged for Jean Rioux's seigneury on Île d'Orléans in 1696; a lot on the Champlain quay in Quebec, acquired in 1692; a seigneury at Antigonish, in Acadia, granted in 1697; an arriere-fief in the Jesuits' seigneury of Notre-Dame-des-Anges near Quebec, granted in 1699.

Vitré formed partnerships and let contracts for the exploitation of his properties and of the fisheries. For example, Le Bic, which was granted originally in part for the establishment of fisheries, was let to a resident contractor on half shares. Trois-Pistoles was leased to Denis RIVERIN, a director of the Compagnie du Nord. Each year Vitré sent fishing expeditions to the lower St Lawrence. He rented or purchased fishing vessels and engaged active partners who conducted the actual operation, sharing costs and profits. Vitré was particularly interested in developing porpoise fisheries, which might give valuable returns in oil and skins, but was limited by lack of capital. Finally, in 1701, he entered into partnership with two wealthy merchants of Quebec, FRANÇOIS HAZEUR and Pierre Peire, and with some help from the government in France, which provided rope for nets, he established a porpoise fishery at Kamouraska. The crown awarded Vitré a gratuity of 550 *livres* for the establishment of the porpoise fisheries and in November 1702, after a successful season, the governor and intendant requested that the subsidy be continued in view of Vitré's proposal to expand the enterprise. Vitré died, however, in January 1703, victim of an influenza epidemic.

A. J. E. LUNN

PAC, FM 18, H 13 (Denys family papers). *Coll. de manuscrits relatifs à la N.-F.* "Procès-verbaux du procureur général Collet" (Caron), 372, 375, 378. PAC *Report, 1899*, Supp. A. Roy, *Inv. greffes not.*, VIII, XVIII, XIX. P.-G. Roy, *Inv. concessions*, I, III, IV; *Inv. contrats de mariage*, II, 159; "Les conseillers au Conseil souverain de la Nouvelle-France," *RSCT*, 3d ser., IX (1915), sect.I, 176. Sulte, *Hist. des Can. fr.* "La famille Des Champs de Boishébert," *BRH*, XII (1906), 78. A. J. E. Lunn, "Economic development in New France, 1713–1760," unpublished Ph.D. thesis, McGill University, 1943. "Notes sur les seigneuries du district de Rimouski," *BRH*, XVII (1911), 240, 244. P.-G. Roy, "Charles Denys de Vitré, conseiller au Conseil souverain," *BRH*, XXIV (1918), 225–42.

DEOWANDO. *See* ATECOUANDO

DEREZY. *See* PERROT

DES BERGÈRES. *See* BLAISE

DES BUTES, GUILLAUME BAUDRY, *dit.* *See* BAUDRY

DESCHAMBAULT, JACQUES-ALEXIS FLEURY. *See* FLEURY

DESCHAMPS DE BOISHÉBERT, HENRI-LOUIS, esquire, assistant town major of Quebec, captain in the colonial regular troops, commandant of Detroit; b. at Rivière-Ouelle, 7 Feb. 1679; d. at Quebec, 6 June 1736.

The Deschamps family came from Normandy where they had been known as esquires and *chevaliers* since the 15th century. Henri-Louis, the fourth son of JEAN-BAPTISTE-FRANÇOIS and Catherine-Gertrude Macard, joined the colonial regular troops in the late 1690s. The various capacities in which he served until his promotion to the rank of lieutenant in 1715 and the praise that he won from his superiors show that he was a versatile and able soldier. In 1702, Governor CALLIÈRE sent him to Michilimackinac to report on the activities of CHARLES JUCHEREAU de Saint-Denys and Pierre-Charles LE SUEUR, who were suspected of illegal fur-trading. Boishébert discovered that these two men, and several others as well, were openly trafficking with the Indians in defiance of the royal ordinances, but his efforts to intervene were met with scorn and derision. "It is very fine and honourable for me, Monsieur, to be charged with your orders," he wrote to Callière, "but it is also very vexatious to have only ink and paper as my sole force to carry them out."

For the greater part of the War of the Spanish Succession Boishébert served outside Canada. In 1705 he helped to guard the harbours of Newfoundland and participated in the capture of three English vessels near Boston. Two years later he sailed aboard a privateer commanded by ALEXANDRE LENEUF de La Vallière de Beaubassin which campaigned fruitlessly on the Atlantic. In 1710 he was chosen to lead the convoy of reinforcements which RIGAUD de Vaudreuil was sending to Acadia to help Governor AUGER de Subercase ward off English attacks. In spite of this assistance, Port Royal (Annapolis Royal, N.S.) capitulated to a British force on 2 October and Boishébert returned to Canada. For the remainder of the war he worked on the fortifications of Quebec as the assistant of the chief engineer, Boisberthelot* de Beaucours. In 1713 he inspected the Labrador coast and drew maps that were sent to the ministry of Marine.

After a voyage to France in 1716, Boishébert took up residence in Quebec where he had been appointed assistant town major. He also concerned himself with the development of his seigneury of La Bouteillerie on which his father had spent some 50,000 *livres*, but which yielded only an annual revenue of 900 *livres*. In 1721, the government granted to Boishébert and Philippe Peire jointly the exclusive right to exploit the porpoise fisheries off La Bouteillerie and Kamouraska and an annual subsidy of 400 *livres*. Unfortunately, the enterprise did not prosper and the government discontinued its support in 1732.

Boishébert was promoted to the rank of captain in 1728 and two years later was appointed commandant of Detroit. At approximately the same time the colonial authorities inaugurated a new policy for that post to eliminate the abuses which had long prevailed there. Henceforth, the commanding officer was strictly forbidden to engage in the fur trade. To cover the cost of salaries, administration, and gifts to the Indians, he was allowed to sell permits to persons wishing to trade at his post. In his report on the state of the colony written in 1730, Payen* de Noyan stated that this system assured the commandant of a revenue of 8,000 to 10,000 *livres* annually.

By following this new policy, Boishébert, unlike Lamothe Cadillac [LAUMET] and ALPHONSE TONTY, his two most famous predecessors, was able to maintain good relations with the Detroit settlers. He also took a special interest in the development of agriculture and the wheat crop increased to approximately 1,470 bushels in 1735. Finally, he was quite successful in his dealings with the Indians. In 1732 and 1733 several war parties set out from Detroit against the Foxes and the Chickasaws.

Boishébert appears to have left Detroit in 1734. He died suddenly of apoplexy in Quebec on 6 June 1736.

On 10 Dec. 1721, he had married Louise-Geneviève de Ramezay, the daughter of the governor of Montreal, Claude de RAMEZAY. Judging from the many signatures of Canadian notables that appear on the marriage contract, this must have been an event of considerable social importance. Madame de Boishébert died at the Quebec Hôpital Général on 13 Oct. 1769. Three daughters and two sons had been born of their marriage. One daughter became a nun and the other two married into the leading Canadian families of Saint-Ours Deschaillons and Tarieu de Lanaudière. The elder son, Claude-Louis, died in infancy. The second, Charles Deschamps* de Boishébert et de Raffetot, entered the colonial troops in 1742, at the age of 15, and played a prominent part in the campaigns of the War of the Austrian Succession and the Seven Years War.

YVES F. ZOLTVANY

AJM, Greffe de Michel Lepailleur de Laferté, 10 juin 1721. AN, Col., B, 27, 29, 33, 35, 38, 39, 41, 42, 59; C¹¹ᴬ, 20, 29, 30, 31, 40, 52, 54, 56, 57, 59, 65; C¹¹ᴳ, 3, 5; D²ᶜ, 47, 49; F³, 10, 12. "Correspondance de Vaudreuil," APQ *Rapport*, 1946–47, 426, 459; *1947–48*, 155, 169, 238, 282, 305, 338. *Lettres de noblesse* (P.-G. Roy), II, 32–58. *Michigan Pioneer Coll.*, XXXIII, XXXIV. P.-G. Roy, *Inv. ord. int.*, I, 194–96, 199. Eccles, *Canada under Louis XIV*, 245. Fauteux, *Essai sur l'industrie sous le régime français*. Guy Frégault, *François Bigot, administrateur français* (2 v., Ottawa, 1948). P.-G. Roy, *La famille Des Champs de Boishébert* (Lévis, 1906). Benjamin Sulte, "Jean-Baptiste-François Des Champs de La Bouteillerie," *BRH*, XII (1906), 112–13.

DESCHAMPS DE LA BOUTEILLERIE, JEAN-BAPTISTE-FRANÇOIS, seigneur of Rivière-Ouelle; baptized 1646 at Cliponville, son of Jean Deschamps, seigneur of Costecoste, Montaubert, and Landres (France), and of Élisabeth Debin; buried 16 Dec. 1703 at Rivière-Ouelle. His title La Bouteillerie came from his paternal grandmother, Suzanne La Bouteiller, Dame de La Bouteillerie.

It was long believed that Jean-Baptiste-François Deschamps de La Bouteillerie had come to America in 1665 with the Carignan regiment, but this is not the case. He sailed in June 1671 on the *Saint-Jean-Baptiste* "with two carpenters, two masons, and four labourers to clear land not exceeding 1,000 acres which the king had given him." Michel-Claude Guibert, who reports this fact, adds that the ship also carried "100 men, 120 king's daughters [*filles du roi*], 50 sheep and ewes, 10 asses and she-asses, cloth, blankets, and many other things for man's everyday life and use." The arrival of this nobleman greatly pleased Talon*, who stressed that "if persons of this quality readily take this route, Canada will soon be filled with people capable of maintaining it well."

On 29 Oct 1672 Deschamps de La Bouteillerie was granted the seigneury of Rivière-Ouelle by Talon. He went there shortly afterwards with some settlers, who in 1681 constituted 11 families with a total of 62 persons, and who had already brought under cultivation 132 acres of land. Apart from a few journeys to Quebec, Deschamps de La Bouteillerie spent his life at Rivière-Ouelle among his copyholders, who slowly increased in number and reached a total of 105 persons in 1698 and 302 in 1739. He was one of the few men of his rank to devote himself solely to his seigneury and to developing it rapidly. He was buried on 16 Dec. 1703 under his seigneurial pew.

On 24 Oct. 1672 Deschamps de La Bouteillerie married Catherine-Gertrude Macard, daughter of Nicolas and Marguerite Couillard. Six children were born of this marriage; one of them, Charles-Joseph (1674–1726), became a priest and canon of the cathedral of Quebec, and another, HENRI-LOUIS, Sieur de Boishébert, inherited the fief. After his first wife's death in 1681, Deschamps de La Bouteillerie married again in April 1701; his second wife was Jeanne-Marguerite Le Chevalier, widow of Robert Lévesque, one of his first copyholders.

NIVE VOISINE

P.-G. Roy, *Inv. concessions*, II, 249; *Inv. contrats de mariage*, II, 165. Adolphe Michaud, *Généalogie des familles de la Rivière Ouelle depuis l'origine de la paroisse jusqu'à nos jours* (Québec, 1908). Sulte, *Hist. des Can. fr.*, IV, 47. "Jean-Baptiste-François Des Champs de La Bouteillerie," *BRH*, XII (1906), 75–77. "Le sieur Des Champs de La Bouteillerie," *BRH*, XXXVII (1931), 54.

DESCOUANDO. *See* ATECOUANDO

Des Friches de Meneval

DES FRICHES DE MENEVAL, LOUIS-ALEXANDRE, governor of Acadia, fl. 1687–1703.

We possess little precise information on Meneval's past history before he came to Canada. Charlevoix* and several others after him believed that he was a member of the Robinau family. But Meneval himself lists his titles in several documents, thus establishing his true identity. Some biographers thought he was the son of Artus Des Friches, Seigneur of Brasseuse and related to the celebrated Genoese family of the Dorias, but this relationship has not been confirmed. It seems more probable that he descended from another branch of the Des Friches family which lived in the Orléanais. He certainly belonged to the army, for BRISAY de Denonville informs us that he had won Turenne's esteem, and Gargas says that he had served at Indret, near Nantes. On 1 March 1687, when he was appointed governor of Acadia in place of Perrot*, on the Marquis de Chevry's recommendation, he was still only a company lieutenant. The following 5 April he received detailed instructions, of which a draft annotated in the minister's hand has come down to us. According to this he was to encourage colonization and agriculture and prevent the English from trading and fishing in Acadia. He was to receive a salary of 3,000 *livres*, and before he left he was, given a gratuity of 1,000 *livres*.

The new governor sailed on a ship belonging to the Compagnie de la pêche sédentaire de l'Acadie, bound for Chedabouctou (Guysborough, N.S.); from there the king's frigate the *Friponne*, on her return trip from Quebec, took him to Port-Royal (Annapolis Royal, N.S.), which he did not reach until the beginning of October. He had been preceded by two new officers, Gargas, a writer in the Marine, and Miramont, officer in command of the troops, who brought with them a contingent of 30 soldiers, munitions, and a sum of 4,000 *livres* for the reconstruction of the fort. Meneval's first concern was to examine Perrot's accounts and oblige him to pay the arrears owed the soldiers. He also made inquiries about Perrot's illicit trading activities, but did not push his investigation very far. The season was too far advanced to undertake the restoration of the fort; moreover the governor was undecided as to whether it would not be better to build a new fort at Pentagouet (on the Penobscot River) or on the Saint George River, in order to protect the frontier. At the beginning of December he sent reports of his observations to the minister, to M. de Lagny, director general of trade, and to the Marquis de Chevry, the director of the Compagnie de la pêche sédentaire, and complained about his officers.

The following year, 1688, the *Friponne* returned to Acadia, bringing 30 more soldiers, which raised the strength of the garrison to 90, of whom some 20 remained at Chedabouctou. The same ship also brought an engineer, Pasquine*, whose task was to inspect the posts and prepare plans for a fort. This engineer worked out an extensive project for Port-Royal, but the minister, who was anxious to save money, refused to approve it. The *Friponne* brought in addition two new officers, Soulègre, captain of the troops, and Mathieu de GOUTIN. The latter acted in the dual capacity of judge and clerk of court, and Meneval completed the organization of justice by entrusting the office of attorney to Pierre Chenet Dubreuil.

In the autumn of 1688, Meneval addressed to the minister a long report, in which he painted a pessimistic picture of his government: the cost of living was high; there was a shortage of flour and of workers; some of the soldiers were old and disabled and had ceased to be of any use; the contingent of the preceding year had received bad muskets and that of 1688 had only 19 muskets between 30 soldiers, so that half of them were without arms; the surgeon was a drunkard, and the court had neglected to supply funds with which to pay him; a hospital and medical supplies were needed; his own gratuity had not been renewed, and he sought permission to go to France to report to the minister and settle some personal affairs. This indictment contained a few positive elements: Meneval, like Denonville, suggested that soldiers be allowed to marry and to become settlers; he also recommended that fishing, the country's best resource, be developed by advancing loans to the settlers and protecting the coasts with armed barks; the settlement at Les Mines (Grand Pré, N.S.) was developing, and he had issued a few ordinances. He ended his letter by saying that the English "very much wanted Acadia."

While the minister was asking for information about the frontiers of Acadia and the king was sending ambassadors to negotiate in England, the Bostonians set about deciding the question in a more effective manner. A few months previously the governor of New England, Andros, had come to Pentagouet to summon JEAN-VINCENT D'ABBADIE de Saint-Castin to acknowledge allegiance to the English, and had pillaged the fort. In the fall of 1688, almost at the time when Meneval was writing and the *Friponne* was on her way to Port-Royal, pirates from Massachusetts pillaged the fort at Chedabouctou and captured the company's ship. This act of piracy, under the very nose of the king's frigate, humiliated the governor, who blamed the commander of the *Friponne*, Beauregard, for arriving too late; but the latter defended himself by casting the blame on the governor, whose orders he had been merely following. These seizures caused the loss of 12,000 *livres* in merchandise that was intended for the settlers of Port-Royal, and the governor also lost his supplies. The situation, already bad, was to become disastrous a few months later, when in May 1689 William of Orange, the new king of England, declared war on France. It could be anticipated that despite the 1686 treaty of neutrality this war between the mother countries would unleash open hostilities in the colonies, particularly in Acadia, which was the most exposed and most poorly defended frontier region.

In this perilous situation, when the whole population ought to have rallied to the defence of the country, internal quarrels rent the colony. Conflicts of prestige and personality clashes set the governor and his chief collaborator, de Goutin, at variance. Each had his party and pestered the court with reports; Meneval accused de Goutin and his friends, among them Lamothe Cadillac [LAUMET], of insubordination and intrigue, while de Goutin accused the governor of protecting the priests, encouraging trading by the English, and interfering in the administration of justice. Meanwhile English frigates were cruising in Baie Française (Bay of Fundy); soldiers and settlers were short of everything, the more so because the supply ships had not yet arrived. Irritated at being opposed, suffering from gout, fearing that his authority would be compromised, foreseeing English attacks, and afraid of being held responsible for events, Meneval asked to be recalled. In a letter to Chevry in September 1689 he said that he was determined to go to France even without authorization, "preferring a hundred times to remain three years in the Bastille rather than one single week here."

The ships did arrive eventually, however, on 5 October 1689. One of them brought to Acadia a new engineer, Saccardy*. The court had instructed him to build a fort at Port-Royal forthwith and sent a further sum of 5,000 *livres*. Saccardy had the old fort rased completely and drew up a plan for a vast *enceinte* with four bastions, enclosing the governor's house, the church, a mill, and the guard-houses; it would also be able to hold barracks and receive the settlers in case of attack. Saccardy set to work briskly, and in 16 days, with the help of the soldiers, settlers, and 40 sailors, succeeded in building half of his *enceinte*. But the ship had to leave again; Saccardy received from Buade* de Frontenac an order to re-embark, leaving the fort unfinished. Robinau* de Villebon, Meneval's lieutenant, was also ordered to go to France, thus leaving the governor without an officer.

The raids carried out by the Abenakis following the sacking of Pentagouet, the confiscation of fishing vessels off the Acadian coasts, and the attacks launched by Frontenac during the winter of 1689–90 had alarmed and incensed the English colonies. The merchants of Salem and Boston got up a subscription, and in the spring of 1690 the government of Massachusetts organized a campaign against the Acadian settlements, command of which was entrusted to William Phips*. The expedition was composed of 7 ships, armed with 78 cannon and carrying 736 men, 446 of them being militiamen. The squadron set sail on 23 April (O.S.; 3 May N.S.), and after calling at Pentagouet and other posts it entered the basin of Port-Royal on 9 May (19 May). Meneval, alerted the same evening by the sentries, had a gun fired to warn the settlers, but only three hastened to the fort. The next day Phips came up the river and sent for the governor. Meneval had only 70 soldiers; the unfinished *enceinte* remained open and its 18 cannon had not been brought into firing positions; 42 young men of Port-Royal were absent. Any resistance therefore appeared useless. Meneval sent Abbé LOUIS PETIT to discuss the terms of surrender.

Phips accepted a capitulation under the following conditions: the fort, the cannon, and the merchandise belonging to the king and the company would be handed over to him; the officers and soldiers would retain their liberty and be transported to Quebec; the settlers would keep their possessions and enjoy the free exercise of their religion. But Phips refused to sign a written capitulation, declaring that his word as a general was sufficient. The next day, Sunday 11 May (21 May), Meneval himself went on board the flagship, and Phips repeated his promises in the presence of de Goutin. Meanwhile some soldiers of the garrison pillaged the company's warehouse and the English troops went on shore. When Phips saw how weak the fort and the garrison were, he was sorry that he had granted such generous terms and made the pillaging a pretext for breaking his word. He had the soldiers imprisoned in the church and confined the governor to his house, under the guard of a sentry. And then organized pillaging began: for 12 days the militiamen ransacked houses and gardens, seized the wheat and the clothes of the settlers, and killed their cattle; they sacked the church, demolished and burned the stockade. Before leaving, they forced the settlers to take an oath of allegiance and elect a council of six notables, presided over by Charles La Tourasse*, to administer justice and see that good order was preserved until the government of Massachusetts had appointed an administration. Then Phips sailed away again, taking the governor as a prisoner, together with Abbés Petit and Trouvé and some 50 soldiers; the remainder had fled to Les Mines.

In Boston, Meneval first spent three months closely guarded in a house; then he complained to the council of Massachusetts, which censured Phips and ordered him to return Meneval's clothes and money to him, but Phips handed back to him only 1,000 *livres* and a few bits of old clothing. Meneval next obtained a passport for London, but Phips, fearing disclosures, had him put in prison again. Meneval succeeded however in getting his freedom, and sailed for France on a small 25-tonner chartered by Dongan. He reached Paris on 6 April 1691, and asked for an audience with Pontchartrain. He had left his papers and a power of attorney with John Nelson, in order to proceed with claims against Phips. But Nelson's imprisonment and the appointment of Phips as governor, followed by his death, prevented these claims from being followed up. During the succeeding years, Meneval gave his views on a plan of attack against Boston and on the boundary question. In 1700 he tried a final approach to the minister, with the object of getting the commissaries to obtain reimbursement for him from Phips' widow and heirs, but it seems clear that these requests had no success. He died around 1703 or 1709.

Meneval's career as governor was not very brilliant. Doubtless he had qualities; he appeared to be honest and anxious to serve well. If, of necessity, he tolerated trading with the English, nothing proves that he took part in it himself. His reports reveal intelligence and a good understanding of the situation. But he showed himself to be of a difficult and captious disposition; barely had he arrived when he proceeded to complain of his first aides, Gargas and Miramont. In the exercise of his authority he was often arbitrary and immoderate, condemning people to prison for trifles and taking excessive steps, such as the exile of the Morin family. As a soldier, he was scarcely effective in the defence of Port-Royal; despite the court's decision to rebuild the fort in 1687, he hesitated, decided nothing, then left all the responsibility to the engineers; he was blamed severely for this by Seignelay. At the time of the siege, he appeared in somewhat of a hurry to capitulate; Perrot and Frontenac looked with disapproval on a surrender made without even a show of resistance. But Meneval was perhaps more to be pitied than blamed. He was ill, poorly aided, and probably little prepared to hold a command which carried such heavy responsibilities. He became discouraged and took a dislike to the country, and his letters present a long string of lamentations. In a word, in the difficult circumstances in which he exercised his mandate, he made the mistake of displaying only rather ordinary qualities, whereas what would have been required was exceptional courage and talents.

RENÉ BAUDRY

AN, Col., B, 13, ff.144, 184f.; 15, ff.34f.; C¹¹ᴬ, 9, f.214; 10, 11; C¹¹ᴰ, 2, ff.78–83v, 94, 96–104, 104–6v, 112v, 115, 126–30, 134–43, 153–58; C¹¹ᴱ, 1, f.43; E, 309 (dossier Meneval); F¹ᴬ, 3, f.52; Section Outre-Mer, Dépôt des fortifications des colonies, carton 2, nos.56–57. BN, MS, Clairambault 884, ff.189–97. "Mass. Archives," XXXVI, 233, 262, 263a; XXXVII, 176, 178. *Acadiensia Nova* (Morse), I, 135f., 171, 196, 203f. Charlevoix, *Histoire*, II, 52; III, 75. *Coll. de manuscrits relatifs à la N.-F.*, I, 396–99, 406, 410–13, 433–36, 502–3; II, 6–8, 10–12, 40–44, 239–40, 253–54. "Correspondance de Frontenac (1689–99)," APQ *Rapport, 1927–28*, 42. *Édits ord.*, III, 89. "Journal of expedition against Port Royal, 1690." *Jug. et délib.*, III, 189, 274. "Lettre du ministre à M. de Menneval, gouverneur de l'Acadie," *BRH*, XXVII (1921), 147–48. Webster, *Acadia*, 182f.

Parkman, *Count Frontenac and New France* (1891), 235–40. Rameau de Saint-Père, *Une colonie féodale*, I, 165; II, 324. Archange Godbout, "Les Morin d'Acadie," SGCF *Mémoires*, I (1944), 101–10. P.-G. Roy, "Qui était M. de Meneval . . .?" APQ *Rapport, 1920–21*, 297–307. Régis Roy, "M. de Meneval," *BRH*, XXVIII (1922), 271.

DESGOUTINS. *See* Goutin

DESHAYES, JEAN (he sometimes signed **Deshaies**), marine surveyor and royal hydrographer of New France; d. 18 Dec. 1706 at Quebec.

Nothing is known of his family background; however, in 1668 Jean Deshayes was already a man of recognized ability. In that year Colbert wished to buy the secret of a new method of calculating longitude from a foreign scholar, and it was Deshayes who was ordered to test its validity. Two years later he departed for Acadia to test a similar theory at sea. At that time he was a poor mathematics teacher. The engineer Saint-Columbe described him as "a man of strong good sense." Deshayes occupied himself with teaching and navigational problems in France until 1681 when, along with two other scientists, he was ordered to undertake an expedition to Gorée off Cape Verde and to the islands of Martinique and Guadaloupe in the West Indies. It was probably as a result of this venture that he was sent to New France to make a hydrographic survey of the St Lawrence River.

He arrived in Quebec in August 1685 and, although in frail health, accompanied Governor Brisay de Denonville on a journey to Fort Frontenac (Cataracoui, now Kingston, Ont.), landing at frequent intervals to observe and calculate latitudes and to draw a map. During the next year, he was fully occupied in carrying out a detailed hydrographic survey of the St Lawrence below Quebec. In November, for some unknown reason, he left the colony without completing the survey. Nevertheless, this work became the basis for a chart of the river that was published around 1700 on the recommendation of the Académie Royale des Sciences; a second edition appeared in 1715. These charts were the first engraved maps devoted solely to the St Lawrence River. They became a basic navigational tool of the pilots and masters of New France and served as such until the final years of the French régime.

It was probably because of the appearance of this chart rather than by any influence exerted on his behalf, that Deshayes was appointed royal hydrographer of New France in 1702. He arrived back in the colony that same year, and for the next four years taught navigation and pilotage to the youth of the colony. In 1703, he was appointed deputy engineer. During the following year, he drew a chart of the north shore of the St Lawrence to show Augustin Le Gardeur de Courtemanche's voyage of exploration to Labrador.

Deshayes seems never to have married. At his death he left few possessions beyond a library which deserves mention only because it was exceptional among private libraries in New France—it contained no religious books. Besides being the author of a very significant chart, Deshayes published a revised edition of *L'Usage du compas de proportion de D. Henrion* (Paris 1681; second edition, 1685). He also wrote *La théorie et pratique du nivellement*, which appeared in 1685, with a second edition in 1695.

JAMES S. PRITCHARD

AN, Col., B, 23, f.218; C^{11A}, 7. ASQ, Polygraphie, II, 34. BN, MS, Coll. d'Anville, Ge DD 2987 (8658). PAC, Map div., copies of maps and charts by Deshayes. *Histoire de l'Académie royale des sciences, 1699* (Paris, 1702). "Lettre du gouverneur de Beauharnois au ministre," *BRH*, LI (1945), 302. *Recueil de cartes, plans et vues relatifs aux États-Unis et au Canada, New York, Boston, Montréal, Québec, Louisbourg (1651–1731)*, éd. A. L. Pinart (Paris, 1893). *Catalogue général des livres imprimés de la bibliothèque nationale* (197v., Paris, 1897–1967), XXIX, 386–87.

L. A. Brown, *The story of maps* (Boston, 1949), 220–24. Henry Harrisse, *Notes pour servir à l'histoire, à la bibliographie et à la cartographie de la Nouvelle-France et des pays adjacents, 1545–1700* (Paris, 1872). Jean Delanglez, "Franquelin, mapmaker," *Mid-America* (Chicago), XXV (1943; new ser., XIV), 29–74. Didier Neuville, "Les établissements scientifiques de l'ancienne marine," *Revue maritime et coloniale*, LIX (1878), 60–94. J. S. Pritchard, "French developments in hydrography with particular reference to the St Lawrence River during the reign of Louis XIV (1665–1709)," unpublished M.A. thesis, University of Western Ontario, 1965. Antoine Roy, "Ce qu'ils lisaient," *Cahiers des Dix*, XX (1955), 199–215. P.-G. Roy, "Jean Deshayes, hydrographe du roi," *BRH*, XXII (1916), 129–33.

DESJORDY DE CABANAC, JOSEPH (sometimes written **Cabanas**), captain in the colonial regular troops, town major of Trois-Rivières; b. 1657 at Carcassonne, France; d. 1713 at Champlain. Joseph was the youngest son of Pierre de Jordy and Louise de Rathery; his brothers were Melchior and Pierre-François, the latter the father of François Desjordy Moreau.

Joseph entered the military service of the king in 1676 as a subaltern in the king's regiment. In 1680 he transferred to the Régiment de Picardie and five years later became a lieutenant in the colonial regular troops at Rochefort. The same year, 1685, he accompanied his nephew, François, to Canada on the *Diligente* as part of Brisay de Denonville's command. In 1687 he went with Denonville's troops to Cataracoui (Fort Frontenac), but the expedition against the Iroquois ended in a humiliating compromise and Joseph returned to Montreal with his company. Though he gained no honours in this expedition, he served with some distinction against Phips* in 1690. He, along with Claude-Sébastien de Villieu and Duclos de Beaumanoir, were given special mention in dispatches for their attacks upon the enemy's camp east of the St Charles River.

Owing to the weakness of the colony, the practice was adopted of billeting soldiers and their officers throughout the rural areas to provide protection against the Indian raiders. The officers were usually billeted with the seigneurs; and it is hardly surprising that many officers formed marital alliances with the Canadian seigneurial families. This was true of Joseph, who in November 1691 married Madeleine, daughter of Étienne Pézard* de La Tousche, seigneur of Champlain. Joseph's nephew, François, was present and signed the marriage contract and marriage certificate. To her husband, Madeleine brought the fief and house called "Le Moteux."

In 1695 Joseph received from Governor Frontenac [Buade*] and the intendant, Bochart de Champigny, the fief of Cabanac on the Richelieu River. Some confusion exists with respect to this

Desjordy Moreau de Cabanac

seigneury. The act of ratification gives the name of François Desjordy as the grantee of the seigneury on the Richelieu; but, since there is no record of François ever having made any grants from a seigneury on the Richelieu and proof exists that Joseph did make such grants, clearly there was an error on the part of the copyist. In 1695 or 1696, on the death of his father-in-law, Joseph Desjordy became co-seigneur of Champlain with his brother-in-law, Étienne de La Tousche.

In 1696 Joseph was promoted to the rank of captain and was given a company of colonial troops. CALLIÈRE considered him a good officer. In 1709 he was given the temporary post of commander of Trois-Rivières on the death of the Marquis de CRISAFY. Finally, three years later, after the intervention of the governor, RIGAUD de Vaudreuil, the king appointed Joseph Desjordy de Cabanac major of Trois-Rivières in succession to RAYMOND BLAISE Des Bergères, in June 1712. Less than a year later, on 25 April 1713, Joseph Desjordy died at Champlain. His claim and that of his brother Melchior to nobility had been confirmed by Louis XIV on 23 Jan. 1703.

GEORGE F. G. STANLEY

AN, Col., C¹¹A, 12. *NYCD* (O'Callaghan and Fernow), IX, 488. "Procès-verbaux du procureur général Collet" (Caron), 315–18, 372. E.-J. Auclair, *Les de Jordy de Cabanac, histoire d'une ancienne famille noble du Canada* (Montréal, 1930). Sulte, *Hist. des Can. fr.*, V, 119. P.-G. Roy, "Les officiers d'état-major," *RC*, 3ᵉ sér., XXII (1918), 299–300.

DESJORDY MOREAU DE CABANAC, FRANÇOIS (Sourdy), knight of the order of Saint-Louis, commandant of Fort Frontenac, 1696, commandant of Fort Chambly, 1711–12, town major of Trois-Rivières, 1720–26; b. 1666 at Carcassonne, France, only son of Pierre-François de Jordy and Élisabeth de Pradines; d. 1726 at Trois-Rivières.

In 1682, at the age of 16, François became a cadet in the Régiment de Besançon. Three years later, he was commissioned lieutenant and came to Canada on board the *Diligente* with his uncle, JOSEPH DESJORDY de Cabanac, as an officer of the colonial regular troops en route to New France as reinforcements for BRISAY de Denonville. Stationed in Montreal from 1685 to 1687 under CALLIÈRE, François Desjordy Moreau may well have taken part in the ill-fated Denonville expedition against the Iroquois in 1687. He was certainly present at the defence of Quebec against Phips* in 1690, when his name appears as de Sourdy. The same name is mentioned as belonging to one of the officers participating in the Indian warfare follow-

ing the repulse of Phips. Typical of the actions at this time was the expedition led by the Sieurs CLAUDE GUILLOUET d'Orvilliers and Boisberthelot* de Beaucours to the island of Toniata (Grenadier Island, near Brockville) in 1692 in which François was one of the participants. In the same year he was mentioned in the "Rolle des Officiers qui servent en Canada" as a half-pay captain and assessed as a good officer and a brave man.

In 1694 François found himself at odds with Bishop Saint-Vallier [LA CROIX]. For his scandalous conduct in maintaining MARGUERITE DIZY, wife of Jean Desbrieux, at Batiscan as his mistress, François was placed under an interdict by the bishop (not an excommunication as stated by Gosselin). After an altercation between the parish priest of Batiscan, Nicolas FOUCAULT, and François and his uncle Joseph the matter went before the Conseil Supérieur. The Cabanac-Desbrieux affair was one of several issues which marked the strained relations between Saint-Vallier and Buade* de Frontenac. Although the interdict was maintained no action was taken against the two Desjordys. Both were friends of Frontenac, and much too well connected in France. Subsequently, however, the hot-blooded young officer was sent to cool his heels at Fort Frontenac in 1696. The same year he served as a captain under RIGAUD de Vaudreuil's command during Frontenac's expedition against the Iroquois.

In October 1696, François received the seigneury of Des Aulnets on the Chaudière river and a month later married Anne Nolan (1674–1703), the daughter of Pierre Nolan, a merchant of Ville-Marie. Three daughters were born of this marriage. After Anne's death in 1703, François took as his second wife, in 1705, Louise-Catherine Robinau (1677–1757), daughter of René Robinau* de Bécancour, Baron de Portneuf. Louise-Catherine brought her husband the seigneury of Îles Bouchard, and it was there that the Desjordy family raised their seven children, four of whom were sons.

Meanwhile François continued his military career. In 1709 he accompanied RAMEZAY's expedition against NICHOLSON and in 1711–12, commanded at Fort Chambly in succession to RAYMOND BLAISE Des Bergères. On 28 June 1718 he was awarded the cross of Saint-Louis and in 1720 he followed FRANÇOIS MARIAUCHAU d'Esgly as town major of Trois-Rivières. His uncle, Joseph Desjordy, had held the same appointment, 1712–1713. In 1725 an order was issued appointing François Desjordy de Saint-Georges commandant, an appointment equivalent to governor, of Trois-Rivières. Apparently the name "Saint-Georges"

186

Dessailliant

was added in error. It is the only instance in which this name appears as part of Desjordy's title.

Early in 1726 François Desjordy Moreau died at Trois-Rivières, where he was buried on 16 February of that year. His widow survived him by 31 years. She died in her manor at Îles Bouchard in September 1757.

GEORGE F. G. STANLEY

AN, Col., C¹¹ᴬ, 13, ff.64–66, 95–98; F³, 7, ff.198–270. Charlevoix, *History* (Shea), V, 12, 218–19. *NYCD* (O'Callaghan and Fernow), IX, 649, 655. *Royal Fort Frontenac* (Preston and Lamontagne), 467. Fauteux, *Les chevaliers de Saint-Louis*, 111–12. É.-Z. Massicotte, "Les commandants du Fort Chambly," *BRH*, XXXI (1925), 455. E.-J. Auclair, *Les de Jordy de Cabanac, histoire d'une ancienne famille noble du Canada* (Montréal, 1930). Eccles, *Frontenac*, 299–300. Sulte, *Mélanges historiques* (Malchelosse), XIV, 69.

DESLIETTES. See LIETTE

DES MAIZERETS, LOUIS ANGO. See ANGO

DESMAREST, CLAUDE-JOSEPH LE ROY. See LE ROY

DES MUCEAUX (MUSSEAUX), JEAN-BAPTISTE D'AILLEBOUST. See AILLEBOUST

DESSAILLIANT, MICHEL, *dit* **Richeterre,** artist and painter, lived successively at Montreal, Detroit, and Quebec; fl. 1701–23.

In 1701 he was at Montreal, as is proved by a note acknowledging receipt of 40 *livres* for the portrait of Madame de Repentigny. Five years later he was staying at Detroit, where he may have painted a retable for Cadillac [LAUMET]. In 1708 he returned to Montreal and then went to Quebec, where he became one of the most sought-after painters.

He painted principally to order, concentrating on religious themes. Three of his ex-votos have been preserved at Sainte-Anne de Beaupré. The first, entitled *Madame de Riverin et ses enfants*, was painted at Quebec in 1703. Madame, *née* Angélique Gaultier, is kneeling with her three daughters and her son before St Anne, who is seated on a cushion of clouds. This picture constitutes an interesting document on the way women and children dressed in that period. An ex-voto, painted in 1710 or 1711, recalls the shipwreck of the *Saincte-Anne*; this picture was given by Captain Charles Édouin to his crew in 1711, after their ship the *Saincte-Anne*, which had been dispatched from Newfoundland by Subercase [AUGER], had been miraculously saved from a storm (1709). This ship can be seen breaking up

under the fury of the waves, curling magnificently and depicted in faded greens and reddish ochres; on the deck Father Antoine GAULIN (entrusted with a message from Subercase for the governor) implores the protection of St Anne.

The *Livre de Comptes* of Sainte-Anne de Beaupré shows that "on 6 Feb. 1716 there was received from M. Roger for a solemn mass with a picture, 14 *livres*." The ex-voto, entitled *M. Roger*, commemorates the miraculous rescue, through the intercession of St Anne, of this Quebec merchant, whose ship was caught in the ice. The design is more carefully worked out than in the case of the two preceding paintings: St Anne and the Virgin dominate the upper part of the picture, while from the ship, with its sails full spread, the human cargo drops off one by one and takes to frail boats.

It is the Hôtel-Dieu of Quebec, however, that possesses the most lifelike of Dessailliant's ex-votos, that of *L'Ange-Gardien*. The rather crude colouring, the artlessness of the little girl whose rosy face is enlivened by small, intelligent black eyes, the generous treatment given to the angel with his bluish wings and ample white tunic: these are all characteristics of a work that monastic tradition has enveloped in legend.

Dessailliant has also left some portraits, most of which are in a very bad state of preservation. The Hôtel-Dieu of Quebec possesses those of *Mère Louise de Soumande de Saint-Augustin* (1708), *Madame Régnard Duplessis* depicted in the person of St Helen (1707), *Jeanne-Françoise Juchereau, dite de Saint-Ignace* (1723), and *L'Abbé Joseph Séré de la Colombière* (1723). We should also mention the portraits of *Jean-Baptiste Hertel, chevalier de Rouville* (c. 1710), *Zacharie François Hertel, sieur de la Fresnière* (c. 1710), and the *Cheavlier La Corne de Saint-Luc* (undated).

The ex-votos are, however, the most interesting part of Dessailliant's works. The art of the ex-voto enjoyed considerable popularity in French Canada for nearly two centuries. Threatened by the perils of the untamed forces of sea and forest, exposed to the hazards of wars and calamities of all kinds, the settlers offered thanks to heaven by asking often unknown artists, craftsmen, and painters to express on canvas the favours which the settlers had received. These pictures were presented to sanctuaries and monasteries, where all could see them and be moved to piety by them. St Anne, whose cult seems to have crossed the seas with the Bretons, as the many ex-votos in the sanctuary of Beaupré testify, was thus the object of numerous testimonies. These works, inspired by intense faith and gratitude, and having a mediaeval air about them, often escape the rules of art and sometimes attain to the sublime. The ex-votos are to our

Devarenne

painting what tales are to our literature: a precious jewel.

MAURICE CARRIER

AJQ, Greffe de Pierre Rivet, 25 oct. 1710. IOA, Hôtel-Dieu de Québec, J-4, 1–10; Notre-Dame-des-Victoires, D-7; Rivière Ouelle, E-5; Sainte-Anne de Beaupré, A-4, A-5, A-7, A-10, A-11, A-12, B-1, B-2, B-3, B-5, C-4. Harper, *Painting in Canada*. Gérard Morisset, *Peintres et tableaux* (2v., Les arts au Canada français, Québec, 1936–37), I, 33–59; *La peinture traditionnelle au C.f.*, 35. Claude Picher, "Les ex-voto," *Canadian Art* (Ottawa), XVIII (1961), no.4.

DEVARENNE (De Varenne). *See* GAULTIER

DEWANDO. *See* ATECOUANDO

DIÈREVILLE (Dierville, Dière de Dièreville), French surgeon and writer, author of an account of a voyage to Acadia; b. in France, perhaps at Pont-l'Évêque (department of Calvados); fl. 1699–1711.

The name Dièreville is not unknown in Normandy. An act dated 26 Nov. 1625, concerning one Jehan Dièreville, of Saint-Thomas de Touques, has been found in the registry of the tabellions of Honfleur. Moreover, several Dières were at Honfleur at the beginning of the 17th century, among them Guyon and Jacques Dières, who were sea captains. Now Honfleur and Touques are not far from Pont-l'Évêque, where Dièreville is supposed to have been born.

The two forms, Dièreville and Dière de Dièreville, are found in documents existing at Pont-l'Évêque. Dierville, without initials or a first name, occurs in a report by a contemporary, Joseph Pitton de Tournefort, and on the labels of the Acadian plants (about 25 specimens) preserved in the herbarium of the Muséum d'Histoire Naturelle in Paris. These labels were written partly by Sébastien Vaillant, a botanist of the time. We do not know the first name of the person in question, and the initial N., first used in Father Le Jeune's *Dictionnaire*, is not borne out by any known document. Nor do we know anything about the dates of his birth and death. The year 1670, sometimes mentioned as his birth-date, is only an approximation.

In 1698 Michel Bégon, intendant of La Rochelle, had a secretary named Pierre Dières. As this happens to be the Michel Bégon who had instructed Dièreville to write the account of his voyage to Acadia, and as the author dedicated it to him, it is legitimate to suppose that this Pierre Dières and Dière de Dièreville might be of the same family. According to a somewhat obscure note made by Delavaud and Dangibeaud, editors of *Lettres de Michel Bégon*, one of Pierre's brothers, Jacques-Christophe, may have been commissary-general of the Marine for provisions at Saint-Jean-d'Angély. Now, as Michel Bégon was known for his rather pronounced nepotism, it is understandable that his solicitude should have extended equally to his secretary's brothers. Moreover, we know from Dièreville's account that he had three brothers, and, through the archives of Calvados, that he owned property near the village of Reux in the neighbourhood of Pont-l'Évêque. One may even wonder whether he was not born in that village rather than at Pont-l'Évêque. This is sometimes asserted, although without precise supporting documents.

Before 1699 Dièreville seems to have studied surgery at the Hôtel-Dieu in Paris, if we are to believe a passage in his account, and before 1701 he published some poems in the *Mercure galant*. But the principal event in his life was his journey to Acadia. On 20 Aug. 1699 he left La Rochelle on board the *Royalle Paix*, in the capacity of supercargo, that is, of an agent appointed by the ship-owner and responsible for watching over the cargo. He reached Port-Royal (Annapolis Royal, N.S.) in Acadia on 13 October, after a voyage of 54 days. He spent a year in the country in search of information about the region and the French and Amerindian populations; he also gathered plants. On 6 Oct. 1700 he sailed for Europe, and reached La Rochelle on 9 November. On 21 December of the following year he became a surgeon at the hospice of Pont-l'Évêque, a post which he was still occupying on 10 April 1711.

Apart from that, nothing is known of him. Only his account and the plants he gathered in Acadia contribute to his fame. He brought back specimens of *Chelone acadiensis* (today *Chelone glabra*), which were types used by Tournefort when he described the species in 1706, and also the *Diervilla acadiensis* (today *Diervilla Lonicera*), a species of a genus which Tournefort dedicated to him. In his description Tournefort pays tribute to Dièreville as follows: "I know only one species of this genus, which M. Dierville, a surgeon of Pont-l'Évêque and very knowledgeable on the subject of plants, has brought from Acadia."

Michel Bégon—to whom Plumier dedicated the genus *Begonia*, and whose son of the same name, Michel*, was to become intendant of New France —suggested to Dièreville that he write his account in verse, but the author's friends did not approve of this. To please everybody, Dièreville sacrificed 5,000 lines of verse and kept only 2,529, the rimed stanzas alternating with prose. The result clearly demonstrates that Dièreville, in abandoning the

188

lines, did not deprive the nation of any appreciable part of its poetic heritage!

The account bears the title of *Relation du voyage du Port Royal de l'Acadie, ou de la Nouvelle France*, and was published at Rouen in 1708. The author describes in detail the life aboard ship, not forgetting the cabin boy who was whipped to calm the wind and the loss overboard of part of the cargo. He shows a particular interest in fauna, and recounts his hunting and fishing trips, the fine drifting snow (which he calls *foudrille*) of the Canadian winter, the methods of making spruce beer and maple sugar; he describes the country of the aboiteaux (dikes), the customs of the Indians (and particularly their way of reviving drowned people by enemas of tobacco smoke), and the cooking of the Amerindians, the Acadians, and the seafarers. Culinary memories stimulate this gourmet, and the space that he allots to them makes of his account the first important work in the gastronomical literature of Canada.

The account, which was well received at the time, formed the subject of a long bibliographical study in the *Journal des Scavans* in 1708. It sold well, owing to the infatuation of a public that thirsted for exoticism. Boisard, wrongly, judged the publication severely. Others exaggerated its significance. The truth lies between the two extremes. The author has neither the accuracy, the acuteness of observation, nor the knowledge of the facts possessed by someone like Pierre BOUCHER. The work is doubtless rather superficial, but at a period when so much remained to be discovered in Canada, Dièreville does furnish some new information. Certain ethnological details are not to be found elsewhere. Moreover, reaching as he did the great mass of amateurs, he helped to create in the mother country a climate favourable to Acadia and to New France.

JACQUES ROUSSEAU

[There were three printings of Dièreville's *Relation* in 1708. In the third, the editor added an account of an attack on Port-Royal by New England, taken from the *Gazette* of 25 Feb. 1708. In 1710, another edition—apparently unauthorized—appeared in Amsterdam, then an English translation in 1714, and an abridged German version in 1751. In 1885, L. U. Fontaine re-edited the work in Quebec, leaving out the spicy sections and the account of the return voyage. Finally in 1933, the Champlain Society of Toronto published a critical edition (with an English translation), prepared by Mr. and Mrs. Clarence Webster, and entitled: *Relation of the voyage to Port Royal in Acadia or New France*. J.R.]

Archives du Calvados (Caen), Tabellionnage de Honfleur, 26 nov. 1625. *Documents relatifs à la marine normande et à ses armements aux XVIe et XVIIe siècles . . .* , éd. Charles et Paul Bréard (Rouen, 1889).

Journal des scavans (Paris), 1er série, 1708, 513–21. *Lettres de Michel Bégon*, éd. L. Delavaud et Charles Dangibeaud (3v., Archives historiques de la Saintonge et de l'Aunis, XLVII–XLIX, Paris, 1925–35), I, 35. [Joseph] Pitton de Tournefort, "Suite de l'établissement de quelques nouveaux genres de plantes," *Histoire de l'Académie royale des Sciences*, 1706 (Paris, 1707), 83–87. Ferdinand Hoefer, *Nouvelle biographie universelle[-générale]* . . . (46v., Paris, 1852–66), XIV (1855). Frédéric Lachèvre, *Bibliographie des recueils collectifs de poésies publiés de 1597 à 1700* (4v., Paris, 1901–5), III, 314. Le Jeune, *Dictionnaire*. L.-G. Michaud, *Biographie universelle ancienne et moderne* . . . (nouv. éd., 45v., Paris, 1854–65), XI. François Boisard, *Notices biographiques, littéraires et critiques sur les hommes du Calvados qui se sont fait remarquer par leurs actions ou par leurs ouvrages* (Caen, 1848). Marie-Victorin, *Flore laurentienne* (Montréal, 1935). Robert Le Blant, "Les études historiques sur la colonie française d'Acadie, 1603–1713," *Revue d'histoire des colonies* (Paris), XXXV (1948), 104. Gérard Malchelosse, "La bibliothèque acadienne," *Cahiers des Dix*, XIX (1954), 281.

DI LIETTO. *See* LIETTE

DIZY, MARGUERITE, surgeon, wife of Jean Desbrieux (Debrieux, De Broyeux, and Des Broyeux); baptized 11 Feb. 1663 at Trois-Rivières, daughter of Pierre Dizy, *dit* Montplaisir, and Marie Drouillet (or Drouillard), sister of MICHEL-IGNACE; d. after 11 April 1730.

Had it not been for all the commotion which accompanied her amorous intrigue with the soldier FRANÇOIS DESJORDY de Cabanac, Marguerite Dizy would have received scant attention from historians. At 14 years of age, on 4 Feb. 1677, she signed a marriage contract with Jean Desbrieux, whom she married soon afterwards. She had a son by him, François, who was two years old in 1681. In that year's census the couple was reported to be living at Batiscan; the items enumerated were one rifle, five head of cattle, and six *arpents* under cultivation. Judging by a contract of 3 June 1673, Desbrieux' land was worked by farmers or indentured employees, while the owner devoted most of the year to his fur-trading expeditions in the direction of the Ottawa and Nipissing Indian countries.

The lonely Marguerite was not unresponsive to the advances of François Desjordy, a half-pay captain of the colonial regular troops stationed near Batiscan. In Desbrieux' absence, it was not long before they were living together. On 9 Feb. 1694, as the scandal had been going on "for several years," the parish priests of Batiscan and Champlain, the Sieurs FOUCAULT and Bouquin*, read from the pulpit a pastoral letter from Bishop Saint-Vallier [LA CROIX] which forbade the lovers

189

Dizy

Desjordy and Desbrieux to enter these two churches. (There was, however, no question of an excommunication, as has sometimes been asserted.) The affair rapidly became complicated as regards Desjordy and his friend Jacques-François Hamelin* de Bourgchemin, Marguerite Dizy's brother-in-law, but this is not the place to recount the ins and outs of it. In March, Marguerite Dizy addressed a first petition to the Conseil Souverain, requesting annulment of the pastoral letter and reparation for the offence of which she claimed she was the victim. Alert to the possible encroachment of the church upon matters concerning the state, Frontenac [Buade*] intervened in the dispute, and the suit was referred to the king's privy council and was quickly forgotten.

Marguerite Dizy, who had become a widow on 27 Aug. 1699, settled the affairs of her husband, who had died at Montreal apparently while in full activity, and from that time on we often lose sight of her. She continued, however, to live at Batiscan, on scarcely better terms with her parish priest than at the time of the Sieur Foucault. In fact on 20 June 1704 Intendant François de Beauharnois* passed judgement against the widow Desbrieux, who was accused of having slandered Boy, the parish priest of Batiscan, and of having broadcast these calumnies. (In 1721, perhaps by an ironic trick of fate, Marguerite Dizy was to bring an action against Charles Duteau, *dit* Tourville, who was guilty of slandering her and her family.)

It seems that Marguerite Dizy practised the profession of surgeon; at least it was in this capacity that on 11 April 1730 she signed a certificate in a case involving wounding. The date of her death is not known.

ANDRÉ VACHON

AJM, Greffe d'Antoine Adhémar, 4 févr. 1677; Greffe de Claude Maugue, 29 mai 1682, 11 sept. 1693, 30 août 1696; Greffe de J.-B. Pottier, 22, 23 sept. 1697. AJQ, Greffe de Louis Chambalon, 15 oct. 1700, 30 oct. 1714. AJTR, Greffe de J.-B. Pottier, 12 oct. 1700, 14 nov. 1701; Greffe de Michel Roy, 3, 10 juin 1673, 4 août 1673. "L'affaire du prie-dieu à Montréal, en 1694," APQ *Rapport, 1923–24*. "Un compte de 'chirurgienne'," *BRH*, XXXII (1926), 167. *Jug. et délib.*, III, IV, V. Recensement du Canada, 1681 (Sulte). *Catalogue du Château de Ramezay* (Montréal, 1962), 151, no.1914. Ahern, *Notes pour l'histoire de la médecine*, 171f. Eccles, *Frontenac*, 299f., 303. Gosselin, *L'Église du Canada*, I, 114f. Raymond Douville, "Deux officiers 'indésirables' des troupes de la Marine," *Cahiers des Dix*, XIX (1954), 67–98.

DIZY, *dit* **Montplaisir, MICHEL-IGNACE,** soldier, traveller, farmer, seigneurial judge; baptized 16 Aug. 1661 at Trois-Rivières, son of Pierre Dizy and Marie Drouillet (or Drouillard), brother

of MARGUERITE; buried 13 Feb. 1723 at Champlain.

Michel-Ignace Dizy did not succeed in resisting the lure of adventure which won over the youth of the Trois-Rivières region in the 17th century. With his brother, Charles, and his future father-in-law, René Baudouin, he is thought to have accompanied Cavelier* de La Salle, for he obtained a grant of land at Fort Saint-Louis in the Miami country on 1 Dec. 1682. We find Michel-Ignace at Cataracoui the following summer, with a group of militiamen from his native region. He held the rank of lieutenant in Jean-Amador Godefroy's company. He was back at Champlain before 2 Dec. 1683, the date on which he deposited the title to his land grant at Fort Saint-Louis in the registry of the notary Antoine ADHÉMAR.

His brother Charles and René Baudouin continued to travel in the west, but Michel-Ignace settled at Champlain on a land grant received from his father in return for a loan of 1,000 *livres*, amassed on his earlier fur-trading trips. On 6 Feb. 1690 he married Marie-Jeanne Baudouin, and, having bought some land from CHARLES AUBERT de La Chesnaye on 5 July 1690, he divided his time from then on between the cultivation of his farm and his office as seigneurial judge. In the latter capacity he was rebuked by the Conseil Souverain in 1713 for having failed in a proceeding to follow "the ordinances and customary law of Paris." This did not prevent him from enjoying until his death the confidence of his fellow-countrymen.

RAYMOND DOUVILLE

AJM, Greffe d'Antoine Adhémar, 1, 2 déc. 1683. AJQ, Greffe de Gilles Rageot, 5 juillet 1690. AJTR, Greffe de Séverin Ameau, 8 oct. 1685, 6 févr. 1690. *Jug. et délib.*, V, 346f.; VI, 625, 917. Godbout, "Nos ancêtres," APQ *Rapport, 1951–53*, 503. Cloutier, *Histoire de la paroisse de Champlain*, I, II. Eddie Hamelin, *La paroisse de Champlain* (Trois-Rivières, 1933). Jean Delanglez, "A calendar of La Salle's travels 1643–1683," *Mid-America*, XXII (1940; new ser., XI), 304f.

DOLLIER DE CASSON, FRANÇOIS, cavalry captain, priest, Sulpician, military chaplain, explorer, superior of the Sulpicians in New France (1671–74 and 1678–1701) and as such seigneur of Montreal Island, parish priest of Trois-Rivières, then of Ville-Marie (Montreal), vicar general of the diocese of Quebec, architect, and historian; b. 1636 in the *château* of Casson-sur-l'Erdre in Lower Brittany, in the diocese of Nantes; d. 27 Sept. 1701 in Montreal.

François Dollier's parents, Charles de Casson and Françoise de Cailleux, belonged to the bourgeois and military gentry and had a certain fortune. The arms of the family, "of gules with three fesses argent, bend azure brochant," also bore spur rowels as a sign of their knightly and martial ancestry.

Dollier had at least two sisters. One of them, born in 1643 at Bellé near Nantes, became superior of the Benedictine nuns of the convent of Le Calvaire in Angers. She took the name Julienne-Angélique de Jésus Pâtissant and died on 16 Sept. 1686, loved and praised by her sisters in religion because of her humility and charity. The other married Gabriel Peschart, Sieur and Baron de Bossac, and guaranteed her brother François a life annuity of 1,200 *livres*. During his convalescence in France, 1676–78, Dollier withdrew to their *château* and acted as preceptor to their son.

Like many other young men of that period Dollier learned life by experience in the army. He was, besides, made for the job physically, possessing such extraordinary strength that he could carry two men sitting in his hands. A photograph of a painting, which may be of him, shows him to be fairly old and of what seems to be an imposing stature; the unwrinkled face, the features, strong but devoid of harshness, the lofty brow, the determined mouth and chin, and the frank look give him a virile appearance. He served as a cavalry captain under the orders of Marshal de Turenne, and his bravery won him the general's esteem.

After three years of military life Dollier joined the Sulpicians to continue his studies and become a priest. Most of the early documents of the Sulpician seminary in Paris have unfortunately been destroyed and no trace can be found of his stay there. The reconstruction of his activities in Canada is just as difficult because of the enormous gaps in the archives of the seminary in Montreal. The correspondence of Tronson, his superior in Paris, and the *Histoire du Montréal* by Dollier himself constitute practically the only important sources of information that we have about him.

It is, therefore, Dollier himself who tells us that he was one of three "victims" designated by the superior of Saint-Sulpice to go to Canada. He arrived in Quebec on 7 Sept. 1666 and left a week later as military chaplain accompanying Prouville* de Tracy's expedition against the Mohawks. He did not greatly appreciate this first contact with New France; besides the difficulties of the trip, he had to spend part of his nights hearing confessions and put up with severe rationing of victuals. He described this regime as a "noviciate in abstinence," and his captain as "the grand master of fasting [worthy of] serving as the master in this matter among the Fathers of the Desert." He was weakened so much by these restrictions

that he was unable to go to the aid of a man who was drowning.

He had not yet recovered from this expedition and from a faulty blood-letting done by a surgeon when his superior chose him, in the autumn of 1666, to take the succour of religion to 60 soldiers garrisoned at Fort Sainte-Anne on Île Lamothe in Lake Champlain. He decided to leave despite his weakness and was successful in persuading some ten soldiers to escort him a part of the way. On his arrival he found that two-thirds of the garrison were suffering from scurvy; thanks to his zealous care he was able to save most of them.

When he arrived back at Montreal at the beginning of the summer of 1667, Dollier was sent to serve as parish priest at Trois-Rivières. For a year he carried out the duties of his charge in this small parish of a few hundred inhabitants. In the autumn of 1668 he went off as a missionary to the Nipissing Indians to learn the Algonkian language. Perhaps he also learned to smoke there, for it was later said that he was extremely fond of tobacco. He spent the winter with a chief who owned a young slave, a native of the regions to the south. His enthusiasm aroused by what this Indian told him, Dollier informed his superior of the possibilities of evangelization among the "Ottawa tribes" in the Mississippi region. Being anxious to open up new fields where the Sulpicians could carry the gospel, Queylus [Thubières*] approved Dollier's missionary projects. Dollier then went down to Quebec to obtain the necessary permission from the civil and religious authorities and to prepare his trip and his stay among the Indians. He "had made up his mind never to return [to Montreal] if he could find a tribe that would be willing to receive him." At the governor's request, however, he agreed to join an expedition of the adventurous Robert Cavelier* de La Salle. But the superior of the Sulpicians, who distrusted La Salle, replaced the person designated to accompany Dollier, Michel BARTHÉLEMY, by René Bréhant* de Galinée, who had some knowledge of geography.

The team of explorers, composed of 22 Europeans and some Algonkian interpreters, left Montreal on 6 July 1669. The travellers reached Lake Ontario at the beginning of the month of August. The lack of a good interpreter—La Salle finally admitted his ignorance of the Iroquois language—and the unwillingness of the Senecas to supply them with a guide held them up for nearly a month. A meeting with an Iroquois who was going home and who offered to guide them got them out of their difficulty. They followed the south shore of Lake Ontario, crossed the Niagara River, and went north as far as Tinaouataoua

Dollier de Casson

(near the present city of Hamilton). There they met Adrien Jolliet, Louis*' brother, who was returning from a mission to the Great Lakes. He described to them the route to follow to reach the "Ottawa tribes" and the possibilities for evangelization among the Potawatomis, and indicated to them the place where he had left a canoe. This encounter revived the missionaries' enthusiasm. It had, however, the opposite effect on La Salle. The unscrupulous adventurer made a pretext of a slight ailment caused by fever to abandon the Sulpicians.

Accompanied by seven men and equipped with three canoes, the Sulpicians proceeded on their way as far as the north shore of Lake Erie, where they decided to spend the winter. The wealth of flora and fauna enabled them to collect rapidly a large supply of food and to spend a quiet period. Dollier often maintained that this stay in the solitude of the great open spaces was of more value for their eternal existence than the best ten years elsewhere; he even went so far as to express the wish that he might die in the middle of the woods rather than surrounded by his *confrères* at the seminary. This almost mystical joy did not prevent Dollier from thinking of the political aims of the trip; on 23 March 1670 he raised a cross and took official possession of the territory in the name of the king of France. He signed the act drawn up at this time, "François Dollier, priest from the diocese of Nantes in Brittany."

The next day the missionaries set off again in order to arrive as quickly as possible among the Indians of the Mississippi country. Shortly after their departure, however, Bréhant de Galinée lost his canoe with its contents. Being left with only two canoes and no provisions, they were about to give up, when they accidentally discovered the canoe that had been left by Jolliet, at the same time as a herd of deer arrived within reach of their muskets. This was only a respite. Some days later a gale arose during the night and the raging waves carried off Dollier's canoe. The missionary lost his most precious possession, the portable altar with all its accessories. After deliberating, the Sulpicians decided to return to Montreal.

Out of a spirit of adventure and to become widely acquainted with the region, they made their return via the "northern route," which was well known to the Jesuits and the coureurs de bois. After going up the Detroit River and Lake Huron, they arrived at the mission at Michilimackinac, then crossed Georgian Bay and reached Montreal on 18 June 1670 via Lake Nipissing and the Ottawa River. The trip had lasted 347 days and had ended partly in failure. But if the missionary undertaking had failed, the political administrators

were for their part satisfied with the results. The Sulpicians had not discovered Lakes Ontario, Erie, and Huron, but they had proved conclusively that these lakes were all connected. In addition, as the first Europeans to enter the Niagara River from Lake Ontario, they had taken official possession of this country, made an exact geographical survey, and left an account of their expedition. This journal, Bréhant de Galinée's work, was published successively by the Société Historique de Montréal in 1875, by Margry in 1879, and by Coyne in *Papers and Records* of the Ontario Historical Society in 1903. Dollier, who had also written an account of the expedition, deemed his companion's superior to his own and destroyed his manuscript.

Dollier firmly hoped to go back among the Indians shortly after his return to Montreal in June 1670, but war between the Algonkins and Iroquois forced him to put off his project. He accompanied, however, the 56 volunteers who had been gathered together by Rémy* de Courcelle to go to quiet the Iroquois on Lake Ontario in the summer of 1670. He was back from this brief expedition by mid-August, and at that time he replaced Queylus as superior at Montreal.

The new superior's task did not promise to be an easy one, for the population of Montreal had tripled since his arrival in Canada and was composed in large measure of soldiers, who were more interested in the fur trade than in farming. Moreover, this outpost received every year a large contingent of Indians who had come to bring their furs. As superior, Dollier had to carry out the duties of a seigneur with powers of *haute justice*; these made firmness and diplomacy necessary, and he acquitted himself honourably.

Following his appointment as superior, Dollier devoted his time to various tasks that he had his heart set on: the organization of the town, the construction of a church, and the writing of his *Histoire du Montréal*. As the population of Ville-Marie was approaching 1,500, the construction of a parish church was imperative. Dollier drew up the plan for it, chose and blessed the site, and laid one of the first stones on 30 June 1672. The church of Notre-Dame was opened for services in 1678 and was completed on 16 June 1683 with the consecration of its bell. It served the parish until 1829.

Wishing to organize the development of the town, Dollier laid out the first streets in 1672 with the help of the notary and surveyor Bénigne Basset*. He marked out the Rues Saint-Joseph, Saint-Pierre, Saint-Paul, Saint-Charles, Saint-François, du Calvaire, Saint-Lambert, Saint-Gabriel, and Notre-Dame and forced acceptance of his work by refusing to let the inhabitants sow crops where he had laid out these streets. In addition, he gave a stern reminder to the holders of land grants of their obligation to take up residence.

Meanwhile Dollier wrote his *Histoire du Montréal*. Pierre Margry discovered this manuscript in Paris in 1844 and Louis-Joseph Papineau* had it copied on the government's behalf. The Société Historique de Montréal published it in 1868. It was reprinted the following year in the *Revue Canadienne* and in 1871 by the Quebec Literary and Historical Society. The most recent and best edition of this text is, however, that published by Ralph Flenley in 1928.

Being the first historian of Montreal, Dollier gives us information unavailable elsewhere about the founding of the town, its pioneers, and the first quarter-century of its existence. Following the model of the famous *Relations*, he summarizes the main events of the colony year by year and goes well outside the limits of his society's activities. If, in imitation of the Jesuits—and of most of his contemporaries—he gives way to the desire to edify the reader and makes providence the prime cause of events, he nevertheless gives more importance and space to the political, economic, and military factors which had an influence upon the development of the colony.

Dollier endeavoured in addition to bring forward only indisputable facts, facts that were based upon authentic witness and were often recounted by the very people who had played a role in Montreal's beginnings. Despite his good faith and his desire to stick to the truth—he warned his readers that his account might contain errors and omissions—he could not, however, discern the element of distortion or exaggeration that sentimentality and an interval of 20 years had been able to add to the oral tradition concerning certain facts, such as "Dollard*'s exploit."

"Without any doubt Dollier was not a professional writer," as Roger Duhamel notes; however, he did manifest some concern for the way he wrote: "If the manner of writing history allowed me . . . , but since historical discourse no longer allows me this liberty. . . ." This Sulpician, neither a mystic nor a poet, knew how to observe, listen, and relate, and was not afraid to sprinkle his account with anecdotes, such as that of the woman who remarried even before her first husband had been buried, and that about Martine Messier*, who saved herself from death thanks to a firm grip on a particularly sensitive region of an Iroquois, but who boxed the ear of a Montrealer who had embraced her to show his joy. Dollier also made use of irony, attributing the origin of the place-name Lachine to the derision that greeted La Salle's failure to find a passage to China. He also

left behind him unforgettable phrases that historians and patriots delighted in citing later. Among them is Chomedey* de Maisonneuve's proud reply to the governor: "My honour is at stake, and you will consider it right that I go there [to Montreal] to begin a colony, even if all the trees on this island were to be transformed into Iroquois." For these reasons and because it is an indispensable source for the history of Montreal and the colony, Dollier's work has had considerable influence on French-Canadian historiography. In general Dollier established for a long time the character, the achievement, or the reputation of the inhabitants of Montreal.

Dollier also concerned himself with enforcing respect for the seigneurial rights of the seminary of Saint-Sulpice. In 1672 he protested vigorously to the governor of Montreal, François-Marie Perrot*, who had imprisoned the attorney of the bailiff's court, Jean-Baptiste Migeon* de Branssat, without good reason. Two years later he sent a formal remonstrance to Buade* de Frontenac, who had empowered Gilles de Boyvinet, the lieutenant-general of the jurisdiction of Trois-Rivières, to hear cases concerning coureurs de bois of Montreal. Dollier wrote that he would have brought the matter into the open by applying to the Conseil Souverain if his respect and deference for the governor, together with his distrust of him since Perrot's imprisonment, had not held him back, especially since Frontenac might have thought that the seigneurs of Montreal Island were trying to prevent his orders from being carried out. Three days later Abbé Salignac* de La Mothe-Fénelon preached his famous sermon which appeared to all to be an attack against the use of authority as practised by Frontenac. The latter's vigorous reaction is comprehensible; informed of Fénelon's sermon at the same time as he received Dollier's notice, it was easy for him to believe that this was all part of a concerted attack by the Sulpicians and to take Dollier's allusions for threats. Exasperated by the superior's refusal later to come to Quebec to give evidence about the Fénelon affair because of illness—Dollier had fallen through the ice on the preceding 14 February, had remained partially immersed for several hours, and had not yet recovered from this accident —Frontenac obliged him to comply with the subpoena on pain of seizure of his community's temporalities. The Sulpician stayed at the seminary at Quebec, where two legal officers had to go to obtain his version of the matter. His testimony added nothing since, being ill, he had not heard the sermon. He requested, however, and obtained an indemnity of 100 *livres* for his trip.

In the autumn of 1674 Dollier went to France to

Dollier de Casson

complete his convalescence. There is no evidence that he wanted to get away to calm people's minds or to lend support to the version of the facts that Fénelon and Perrot, who accompanied him on this voyage, were going to give. He did not reach the home of his sister, Madame de.Bossac, until the spring of 1676. He then acted as preceptor to her son. Having recovered his health he obtained his superior's agreement and left his family surreptitiously to return to Montreal in 1678.

At the time of his arrival in the colony tension was running high among the administrators: "I found there," he wrote to his sister, "a general estrangement and a state of disunion which extended over the whole of Canada. . . . The governor [Buade de Frontenac] and the intendant [Duchesneau*] were on very bad terms. I ventured to intervene in this matter, and God gave it his blessing. These two great Canadian trees are already uniting their branches." Dollier's superior in Paris recognized the importance of his intervention, saying that Dollier had been received as an angel of peace. A conciliatory spirit was, moreover, one of the outstanding characteristics of Dollier's personality and won him the praise of all his contemporaries. He was a great diplomat and was successful in winning Bishop LAVAL over to his side after Queylus' departure in 1671. Although he was a friend of the former, he was nevertheless the confidential agent of Bishop Saint-Vallier [LA CROIX], who appointed him vicar general and wrote as a compliment to him: "Their superior [of the Sulpicians] is a person of merit and grace, who has received from God a marvellous gift of discernment for putting those under his direction in posts according to their various talents. He possesses the art of humouring persons of all sorts, and his prudence, together with his gentleness and his other virtues, has won him the esteem and affection of all manner of people." Dollier maintained excellent relations with the religious in New France: Jesuits, Recollets, and the priests of the Séminaire des Missions Étrangères; with the latter, moreover, he entered into a spiritual union in 1688.

Dollier was involved in only one serious conflict, the crisis of 1694–97, which grew out of the "affair of the *prie-dieu*." In 1694 the Recollets had invited the governor of Montreal and the bishop to the inauguration of their church, but Saint-Vallier was relegated to the background. A quarrel resulted the following year which was strewn with accusations, ordinances, and even interdicts; the situation had become so bitter by the fall of 1694, the bishop had to go to France to justify his conduct. Dollier, who was vicar general at the time, was drawn into the quarrel. He supported the bishop and put pressure on the minister for Saint-

Vallier's return to Canada. He did this on Saint-Vallier's express order, said Laval, and perhaps also through fear of seeing a Jesuit appointed bishop. Dollier, however, remained objective and honest. He considered for a moment taking advantage of this crisis and of his powers to take over the missions which were being disputed by the Jesuits and Recollets, at least according to Laval, but he thought better of it, allowed the Recollets to settle with the Ottawas, calmed people's minds, and brought about a general reconciliation.

This gift for bringing people together again and making himself liked by all was not, however, exercised in a way that would be detrimental to the Sulpicians, for Dollier could be firm when need arose. If he supported Saint-Vallier at the time of this crisis, he nonetheless made clear to him how he thought when he wrote to him that the bishop of Quebec would be acting in a cowardly manner if he resigned his functions because of the opposition of a community, which, however, Dollier does not identify. He had used the same firmness and frankness with the Indians when the great chief Garakontié* asked him for land on Montreal Island, on the plea that his lands were not as good; Dollier replied to him in public that he was lying.

His frankness, his understanding of problems, and his office, along with his experience of life in Canada, brought him great authority. Thus, when the governor, Le Febvre* de La Barre, convened in 1682 an assembly of the notables of the country to discuss the Iroquois peril, Dollier was requested to set forth Montreal's situation. On the religious plane his competence was similarly recognized by Bishop Saint-Vallier, who made him his vicar general for the Montreal region and who, at the time he returned to France in 1694, ordered the vicar general for the region of Quebec to get in touch with Dollier if need arose.

As superior Dollier had to organize the internal life of his religious institution. According to Tronson, the superior in Paris, and Souart*, a former superior at Ville-Marie, the seminary of Montreal functioned well under him. But Dollier was above all a man of action. He built a new seminary, into which the Sulpicians moved in 1686. He gave his support to the other religious communities in the Montreal region. He organized a collection which brought in 8,000 *livres* for the rebuilding of the Hôtel-Dieu, obtained spiritual and material aid for the Congrégation de Notre-Dame, and accepted the office of administrator of the Hôtel-Dieu on Jeanne Mance*'s death. Finally the superior in Paris asked him to limit his activities and ordered him to give up his office as administrator of the hospital. Nevertheless

Dollier helped François CHARON de La Barre to prepare the founding of his institute of the Brothers Hospitallers of St Joseph, even to the extent of sheltering them for a while. He also founded parishes around Ville-Marie and administered the Sulpician missions at Montreal and in Acadia. He was appointed parish priest of Ville-Marie in 1694 but does not seem to have exercised this ministry; in the act of creation of the Bureaux des Pauvres in 1698 M. de BRESLAY's name was inserted as assuring the functions of parish priest at Ville-Marie.

Dollier also gave his attention to encouraging education in Montreal. Ever since they had been invited to do so by the king in 1668, the Sulpicians had been teaching the Indians. If it is doubtful that Dollier himself taught them, he nevertheless gave a great deal of attention to this activity, which gave an opportunity for evangelization. A few days before his departure for the west in 1669 he had offered to the young Indians showing the most talent and goodwill two prizes of 1,000 *livres* to assist them in pursuing their studies. Governor Courcelle, moreover, entrusted him with 1,000 *livres* for the education of a young Iroquois girl. For another young Indian girl who had been educated at Montreal Dollier obtained a dowry of 150 *livres* to allow her to marry a Frenchman. He welcomed the Charon Brothers' primary school into the seminary itself, lodging both masters and pupils there. But Tronson censured this initiative: "It had been decided to accommodate the children in the house and to take charge of feeding them without having obtained permission from here . . . That a spiritual union be established with the Charon Brothers or Hermits, that responsibility be assumed for their conduct and their rule of life, that they be aided with advice: all very well; but that is enough!"

The superior in Paris was going to have other difficulties with his *confrère* in Montreal, for Dollier's prodigality did not extend only to religious institutions. Being a man full of life and fond of company, Dollier extended liberal hospitality to the governor, the intendant, and the ecclesiastical dignitaries when they were staying in Montreal. It even appears that certain people carried off valuable articles, for money was the least of the worries of the superior of Montreal. Tronson finally warned Dollier: "If the seminary of Montreal is ruined through lack of funds, I wash my hands of it."

This man who enjoyed life was nonetheless respectful of religious principles and strict in their application. For example he opposed the church-warden, Jean Arnaud, who wanted to increase the receipts of the church by allowing the ladies to distribute in turn bread which had been blessed and to take up the collection, as in France of yore. But Dollier saw in this custom a cause of sin rather than a source of revenue: the persons chosen were selected more for their beauty and their charms than for their upright life, and he always refused to grant the ladies this favour.

Dollier realized, however, that there is some distance between principles and practice, and when he was face to face with actual reality he sometimes became less unbending in his position. Thus, in his *Histoire du Montréal* he violently denounced the use of spirits, without which, he wrote, "we would have thousands of conversions among the Indians." He recognized, nevertheless, that he could do nothing to prevent this trade. He even went further: at the same time as he was severely criticizing the traders' behaviour, "he felt that he had to give in to the settlers by granting them, in a document signed by himself, the right . . . to sell wine, spirits, and other beverages generally at retail." In commenting upon this authorization Faillon wrote that, according to Dollier, "Canada had greater need of fat purses than of empty ones."

The former cavalry captain did not disown his previous military history. He did not accompany La Barre, but he probably took part in BRISAY de Denonville's expedition.

During his last 20 years Dollier devoted much time and money to a project that was dear to him, the digging of the Lachine canal. The idea of constructing this canal was not Dollier's; nor did Abbé Fénelon, who had spoken of it in 1670, attribute to himself the credit for this idea. In 1680 Dollier popularized the subject again, worked out schemes and plans, and immediately embarked upon the digging. In the realization of this project he saw two important advantages: it would allow canoes coming from the Great Lakes to avoid the rapids at Sault-Saint-Louis in travelling to Montreal, and it would permit the building of flour mills on the banks of the canal. Dollier also hoped that the receipts from these mills would make up for the expenses incurred in the construction work. The superior in Paris, however, refused to give his approval, for fear of entering into too great expense. Dollier, who was already busy finishing the parish church and assuring the security of Montreal against the Iroquois, put off the realization of his project.

The idea was taken up again in 1689. The intendant, BOCHART de Champigny, Abbé Pierre RÉMY, and the engineer GÉDÉON DE CATALOGNE supported it, and the intendant facilitated the task by issuing an ordinance instructing the settlers of the Sulpicians' seigneury to pay their dues. The same day Dollier ordered his copyholders to go to

195

Dollier de Casson

work digging the canal. The massacre of the inhabitants of the village of Lachine by the Iroquois in 1689 put a brutal end to the work.

Dollier was not discouraged. His superior's opposition did, however, dampen his ardour. In 1692 Tronson wrote to him: "I cannot hide from you that you have the reputation of undertaking too much, and among the examples given of this people do not fail to mention the canal which you have undertaken and which you want to continue." The project seemed to have come to nothing.

The enterprising and strong-willed Sulpician could not, however, accept defeat. In 1697 he undertook a more modest project, the Saint-Gabriel canal, which would connect the waters of Lac Saint-Pierre with those of the Petite Rivière to supply more water for the town mill. Once again Tronson expressed his disapproval, wanted assurances about the chances of success of the project, and expressed concern about the cost of completing this canal. The lack of money and the hardness of the rock brought about another failure.

The stubborn superior of Montreal made another attempt the following year, venturing upon the "great undertaking." Gédéon de Catalogne had given him a detailed report—although it was frequently inaccurate—about the possibilities of digging the Lachine canal. Subsequently Catalogne was accused of having tried to take advantage of Dollier's senility to enrich himself at the Sulpicians' expense, but this accusation was false, since the superior, attended by the bursar, Michel Caille, signed on 30 Oct. 1700 a detailed contract before the notary Antoine ADHÉMAR and laid down deadlines for the progress of the work before payment would be made. Catalogne contracted to dig a channel 12 feet wide and 9 feet deep and to finish the work in June 1701. For their part the Sulpicians supplied all the tools, provisions, and money to the amount of 13,000 *livres* in deferred payments. In Paris a reprimand followed the initial astonishment. Tronson complained that "in Montreal the practice is always to go ahead and do what one wants to do first, and then to let us know about it here." If he had believed for a moment that "necessity would teach him [Dollier] to be economical," he was quite wrong. The work did not proceed as had been foreseen; the difficulties piled up. When it ran into rock, the work was delayed and the cost grew. Dollier did not live to see the end of the work, for he died on 27 Sept. 1701, when it was two-thirds completed. Shortly after the project was abandoned.

Dollier was buried in the parish church and Grandet, who had known him well, eulogized him in the following terms: "He had acquired universal esteem and repute in the whole of Canada through the tactfulness of his address, his open and polite manners, and his conversation, which was easy and full of kindness and accompanied by an air of nobility, a bearing and a dignity that, devoid of pretence or affectation, won him all hearts and conferred upon him a commanding authority which was irresistible." But all this literature—these repetitious praises, the admiration which he roused through his many qualities combined—all this was expressed much more simply by the Indians, who said: "There is a man!"

JACQUES MATHIEU

AJM, Greffe d'Antoine Adhémar, 30 oct. 1700. AN, Col., C¹¹ᴬ, 3, f.56. AQ, Dollier de Casson, Histoire de Montréal, 1640–1672 [In addition, this deposit contains a photograph of a portrait said to be that of Dollier de Casson.]. ASQ, Chapitre, I, 13; Congrégation Notre-Dame, 11; Lettres, M, 21, 22, 23; O, 36; Polygraphie, IV, 20; XXIV, 12a, 24; Séminaire, I, 20. PAC, FM 17, 7–2, 1, pp.11–16.

"Acte de remontrance des seigneurs de Montréal au sujet des usurpations du Sieur de Boyvinet," *BRH*, XXXI (1925), 291–93. [Dollier de Casson], *Histoire du Montréal 1640–1672* (Société historique de Montréal *Mémoires*, IV, 1868); *Histoire du Montréal 1640–1672*, *RC*, 1ᵉʳ sér., VI (1869); *Histoire du Montréal 1640–1672* (Lit. and Hist. Soc. of Quebec, 1871); *A history of Montreal 1640–1672 . . .*, ed. and trans. by Ralph Flenley (Toronto, 1928). René de Bréhant de Galinée, "Exploration of the Great Lakes 1669–1670 . . .," ed. J. H. Coyne, Ont. Hist. Soc., *Papers and Records*, IV (1903). "Procès-verbal d'une assemblée tenue à Québec le 10 octobre 1682," *BRH*, XXX (1924), 249–52. Saint-Vallier, *Estat présent de l'Église* (1856). É.-Z. Massicotte, "Maçons, entrepreneurs, architectes," *BRH*, XXXV (1929), 132–42.

[Faillon], *Histoire de la colonie française*. Raphael Bellemare, " 'Le bureau des pauvres' de Montréal," *BRH*, V (1899), 279–80. R. Bonin, "Le canal Lachine sous le régime français," *BRH*, XLII (1936), 265–99. "Un Breton supérieur du Séminaire de Montréal," *NF*, III (1927–28), 183–86. Roger Duhamel, "Dollier de Casson," *Cahiers de l'Académie canadienne-française*, VIII (1964), 131–36. Ovide Lapalice, "Le pain bénit à Notre-Dame de Montréal," *BRH*, XXVII (1921), 153–60. É.-Z. Massicotte, "Ville Marie-Montréal," *BRH*, XX (1914), 125. Olivier Maurault, "Les aumôniers de troupes . . . sous le régime français," *Cahiers des Dix*, XXX (1965), 9–17; "Études sur Dollier de Casson," *Revue trimestrielle canadienne (L'Ingénieur)*, IV (1919), 361–70; "Les origines de l'enseignement secondaire à Montréal," *Cahiers des Dix*, I (1936), 95–104; "Les Sulpiciens seigneurs de Montréal," *Revue trimestrielle canadienne*, XXVIII (1942), 237–53. J.-M. Paradis, "Le lieu d'hivernement de l'expédition Dollier-Galinée," *Mémoires de Diplômes d'études supérieures*, Université Laval, 1967. Robert Roquebrune, "Deux historiens de Montréal au XVIIᵉ siècle," *CF*, 2ᵉ sér., XXI (1933), 19–30. F. Uzureau, "L'abbé Dollier de

Casson, supérieur du Séminaire de Montréal," *CF*, 2ᵉ sér., XII (1924), 134–39.

DOUAY, ANASTASE, priest, Recollet, naval chaplain; b. at La Quesnoy, in Hainaut, Belgium (now department of Nord, France); d. in Mexico.

We are familiar with only a part of the life of Anastase Douay, a Recollet of the ecclesiastical province of Saint-Antoine in Artois. His name is attached almost exclusively to the two expeditions which he made in Louisiana in search of the mouth of the Mississippi, the first with Cavelier* de La Salle (1684–1687), the second with PIERRE LE MOYNE d'Iberville (1698–99).

Douay had the happy thought of making manuscript notes. He lost those of the first expedition in various shipwrecks, and those of the second were stolen from him, together with his breviary. Thanks to the historian Chrestien Le Clercq*, to whom he entrusted "a précis of what he was able to recover of them, for which the reader," he said, "will perhaps be more grateful to me than if I composed it in my own style," we have some precious information concerning La Salle's expedition. Although the party, which originally comprised more than 320 persons, left La Rochelle on 24 July 1684, the chaplain's account does not begin until 22 April 1686, when La Salle set out with some 20 companions to try to discover, by an overland route, the mouth of the Mississippi. Douay describes the little band's eventful stay among the Cenis Indians, and on its return the triple murder, by Pierre Duhaut and his accomplices, of Crevel de Moranget, La Salle's nephew, Nika, a Shawnee hunter, and the explorer's servant; he was present at the death of his leader, shot down by Duhaut, gave him absolution, and closed his eyes, burying him "as well as possible with a cross [which he placed] on his grave."

Despite reservations that have been expressed as to the plausibility of Le Clercq's account, we have no reason to maintain, as the envious Joutel has suggested, that he falsified Douay's narration. As Douay was the sole eye-witness of the drama, his account remains more acceptable than those of Joutel, GRAVIER, or HENNEPIN, who copied it at the same time as they made bold to challenge it.

After La Salle's death, Douay returned to Quebec on 27 July 1688, and on 20 August sailed for France to give an account of the facts to the Marquis de Seignelay [Colbert]. He remained in France, and we know from Hennepin that he was vicar of the Recollet convent at Cambrai in 1698.

Far from casting any light on the Mississippi question, La Salle's last expedition had given rise to new riddles. On 16 July 1698 Pontchartrain, minister of Marine, wrote to Bégon*, the intendant at La Rochelle, that he was sending Father Anastase to him from Paris, to be chaplain of the *Badine*, a frigate which was accompanying the *Marin*: his previous experience might be of some help to Le Moyne d'Iberville, the leader of the new expedition which set out from La Rochelle on 5 September in search of the mouth of the Mississippi. Three months later, on 3 March 1699 to be exact, Douay "[had] the joy" of saying mass and singing the *Te Deum* "on sighting the Mississippi River."

For the second time the chronicler Douay suffered a profound disappointment. On 24 or 31 March he was robbed of his scrip, which contained his breviary and a short handwritten account of all that had happened on the voyage. The religious thought that it had been stolen by an Indian who had embarked with him at Ommans. The next day he went to the Indians' village to try to recover it. The chief, although indignant at the accusation made against one of his tribe, agreed to assemble all his people. In vain Father Anastase sought to move them by his tears; the breviary and the manuscript remained undiscovered, "which left him inconsolable."

On 4 May 1699, in a petition addressed to the Sacred Congregation of the Propaganda, it was requested that Father Anastase Douay be given the powers of prefect apostolic for Louisiana. However, in April of the same year, Douay had refused Le Moyne d'Iberville's invitation to remain at the new mission. Iberville wrote in the log-book of the *Badine* that Douay preferred to return to France and live for the rest of his life in his convent. Did Douay modify his decision after the official petition, and assume the high office of prefect apostolic? We have no document which can throw light on this question. Furthermore, we know nothing about the end of Father Anastase's life. The necrology of the Recollets mentions only the place of his death: Mexico.

JACQUES VALOIS

Découvertes et établissements des Français (Margry) IV, 70, 124, 125, 157, 169, 190, 235, 237f., 247, 273. Le Clercq, *Premier établissement de la foy*, II. J. G. Shea, *Discovery and exploration of the Mississippi Valley* ... (New York, 1852), 197–229. Delanglez, *French Jesuits in Louisiana.* Frégault, *Iberville*, 264ff. Henry Harrisse, *Notes pour servir à l'histoire, à la bibliographie et à la cartographie de la Nouvelle-France et des pays adjacents, 1545–1700* (Paris, 1872), 159, 163–65. O'Neill, *Church and state in Louisiana.* J. G. Shea, *History of the Catholic Church in the United States* (4v., New York, 1886–92), I, 340–51. "L'assassinat de Cavelier de La Salle," *BRH*, XLIII (1937), 146–48. Viator, "La mort de Cavelier de La Salle," *BRH*, III (1897), 175.

Doucett

DOUCETT, JOHN, captain, lieutenant-governor of the fort of Annapolis Royal, N.S., 1717–26, and administrator of the government of Nova Scotia, 1717–20 and 1722–26; born probably in England; d. 19 Nov. 1726 at Annapolis Royal.

Although presumed to be of French descent, Doucett was, as he himself put it, "a Stranger to the French Tongue." He received several military commissions from 1702 on, and was appointed lieutenant-governor of the garrison of Annapolis Royal on 25 May 1717, succeeding Thomas CAULFEILD. Richard Philipps*, the new governor of Nova Scotia, remained in England to gather information and arrange for instructions about his responsibilities; meanwhile Doucett went out to Nova Scotia, arriving at Annapolis Royal on 28 Oct. 1717.

He was concerned to find the fort in ruins and the garrison unruly because of lack of pay and shortage of clothing, and he took steps to remedy this situation. Scandalized by the non-allegiance of the Acadians, who formed the bulk of the population, Doucett drafted an oath for their signature. Within a few days of his arrival, he summoned the neighbouring Acadians to sign it, and early in December he sent a copy of it to Peter Mellanson (Pierre Melanson?) of Minas to be translated into French and made public there. He also urged Father Félix Pain*, the French priest at Minas, not to influence the inhabitants against swearing allegiance to George I.

Doucett's efforts with respect to the oath were of little avail. The Acadians of Annapolis replied that unless the garrison could protect them from the Indians they dared not take the oath. Otherwise, they could only take an oath not to take up arms against England, France, or any of their subjects or allies. Doucett regarded this dread of the Indians as mere pretence, and believed that the Acadians feared their priests more than the Indians.

The reply from Minas was received on 10 Feb. 1717/18. The inhabitants refused to sign the oath for three alleged reasons: it did not assure them freedom of religion; upon taking the oath they would be threatened by the Indians; and their ancestors had never taken such an oath. The Acadians later sent messengers to Louisbourg to ask the governor, Joseph de Saint-Ovide de Brouillan [Mombeton*], for his advice.

Doucett proposed to Vaudreuil [RIGAUD] at Quebec and to Brouillan that mutual efforts be made to cement the peace between Britain and France. In his letter to Vaudreuil, dated 15 April 1718, he expressed his desire that those Acadians who were inclined to become British subjects should be free to do so, and asked that Vaudreuil order all those who would not to withdraw to French territory. In his letter of 15 May 1718 he complained to Brouillan about French encroachments on the fisheries of Nova Scotia, as well as about the French failure to comply with the agreement signed by the Acadians with Louis Denys* de La Ronde in 1714, in which they signified their willingness to leave Nova Scotia. Doucett considered the agreement annulled, but was willing to allow any Acadians who still wished to leave to do so.

Brouillan replied, in July, that he had no knowledge of French encroachment on the British fishery, that in his opinion the Canso (Canseau) Islands belonged to France, and that the failure of the Acadians to emigrate was attributable to obstacles raised by the former governor, Francis NICHOLSON, and others who did not wish them to carry off their goods. Vaudreuil's reply was similar in substance. He also requested Doucett not to allow English vessels to sail the Saint John River which, Vaudreuil claimed, was under French control. Doucett was convinced that Vaudreuil's claim to the Saint John was without foundation for that river was "much about the center of Nova Scotia." The gravity of the matter, however, was emphasized by letters from Vaudreuil to Louis Allain of Annapolis, which fell into Doucett's hands. Vaudreuil told Allain that the Saint John was not under English control and that the Acadians could obtain land along it by applying to Father LOYARD who had authority to make such grants. The boundary dispute was clearly more than academic, for the French claimed that only the peninsula of Nova Scotia fell within the ancient limits of Acadia as ceded to Great Britain by the treaty of Utrecht.

The subject of trade also bristled with difficulties. Smuggling was prevalent, and there was considerable trade between Île Royale (Cape Breton Island) and the Acadian settlements at Minas and Cobequid. Doucett hoped that measures would be taken to prevent clandestine trade and encroachments on the fishery, and in letters dated 6 Feb. 1717/18 to the Lords of Trade and to the secretary of state he pointed out the advantages of having three or four sloops, of four or six guns each, cruising between the Strait of Canso (Grand Passage de Fronsac) and Mount Desert Island (Île des Monts Déserts), and in the Bay of Fundy. Doucett continued to press for this support, but although his advice was sound, effective action was not taken immediately. In the meantime, in September 1718, French fishermen at Canso were plundered by a New England vessel commanded by Thomas SMART. When, in turn, English fishermen at Canso were raided in 1720 by French and Indians, a company of troops was stationed there for the ensuing winter, and Captain Thomas Durell, in the *Seahorse*, provided protection for the fishery in 1721.

Governor Philipps arrived at Annapolis Royal about the middle of April 1720, and on 25 April established His Majesty's Council of Nova Scotia, with Doucett as president. Philipps took up residence at Canso in the summer of 1721, remaining there until his return to England late in 1722, when he left Doucett in command at Annapolis Royal.

The need for winning over the Indians of Nova Scotia had become obvious to Doucett, and on 13 Dec. 1718 he urged Philipps to apply to the Lords of Trade for presents for the Indians. In the summer of 1721 these arrived and early in 1722 Philipps gave a feast at Canso for the Indian chiefs. The Indians solemnly promised their friendship. Relations between the Abenakis and the government of Massachusetts had been steadily worsening, however [*see* MOG]. In mid-June Abenaki raids began at the Kennebec River, and simultaneously the Indians made a sudden and unprovoked attack upon shipping in the Bay of Fundy and along the eastern coast of Nova Scotia. Reports were received that the Indians had captured 18 trading vessels in the bay and 18 fishing boats off the eastern coast. Doucett heard that the Indians' design was to capture Annapolis Royal. Seizing as hostages 22 Indians who happened to be encamped nearby, he sent a sloop to Canso for Philipps' instructions and to warn the fishermen and traders along the coast to be on their guard. Doucett's initiative at Annapolis Royal and Philipps' actions at Canso thwarted the Indians' plans. Doucett later expressed the belief that Father GAULIN's mission Indians had taken part in the plundering.

A definite peace with the Indians was not established in New England until 1727 [*see* WENEMOUET], but the war in Nova Scotia officially ended with the ratification of the peace at Annapolis Royal on 4 June 1726. Among the Indians present were Joseph Nepomoit (Nipimoit) of Saint John, and representatives of the Cape Sable, Shubenacadie, La Have, Minas, and Annapolis River Indians. It cost Doucett nearly £300 in presents and feasts to achieve this peace, but the ratification gave him a measure of satisfaction.

Lawrence ARMSTRONG was commissioned lieutenant-governor of Nova Scotia on 8 Feb. 1724/25; Doucett continued as president of the council, as well as lieutenant-governor of Annapolis Royal. By August 1726 Doucett had received permission for a leave of absence of some months, but he remained in Annapolis Royal until his death in November.

Doucett's wife was with him in Nova Scotia but her name is unknown. In 1721 they had a family of six children. In 1723, Isabella and Honoria Doucett, aunts and guardians of four of John Doucett's children, petitioned the War Office on their behalf.

CHARLES BRUCE FERGUSSON

Mass. Hist. Soc., Gay papers, II, III, IV. PAC, Nova Scotia A, 9, 15, 16, 17 (calendared in PAC *Report, 1894,* 30–34, 51–61). PANS, MS docs., XVII, 8. PRO, C.O. 217/2, ff.129–30, 135, 175–77, 182, 186–89, 192–97, 200, 202, 207–9, 211, 213, 215–17, 220–21, 230–31, 237–38, 254–56, 260–61; 217/3, ff.26–27, 31, 47, 103–4, 151; 217/4, ff.43, 113–19, 128–30, 132, 134, 155–56, 182–85, 208; 217/5, ff.1–2, 66–68; 217/30, ff.1f.; 217/31, ff.65–68, 71; 218/1, ff.173–76, 187–88, 190–92, 241–46, 254; 218/2, ff.12–13, 17, 25–36; W.O. 71/6, 345.
Coll. doc. inédits Canada et Amérique (CF), I (1888), 116–20, 170–73. *Coll. de manuscrits relatifs à la N.-F.,* II, 213–15. *NYCD* (O'Callaghan and Fernow), IX, 892, 936, 945, 948–49. *N.S. Archives,* II, III. PRO, *CSP, Col., 1717–18, 1722–23, 1726–27.* Dalton, *English army lists,* V, 148, Brebner, *New England's outpost.* Dalton, *George the First's army,* I, 222, 248, 313. F.-J. Audet, "Governors, lieutenant-governors, and administrators of Nova Scotia, 1604–1932" (bound typescript in PANS, n.d.).

DRISY. *See* PERROT

DRUÉ, JUCONDE, Recollet, architectural designer and painter, born in Paris 1664; entered the Recollet order 1683; died after 1726, possibly in Paris *c.* 1739.

Drué's chief importance in the history of New France is as the designer who popularized the type of church plan and interior decoration known, after the religious order in whose chapels it first appeared, as *à la récollette.* This style was first introduced to New France by the painter-architect Claude François*, Frère Luc, the church he designed for the Recollets during his stay in Quebec from August 1670 to November 1671 being modelled on the Recollet church in Paris, still extant as the Villemin Military Hospital opposite the Gare de l'Est. In 1692 the Quebec church was sold to Bishop Saint-Vallier [LA CROIX] for use as the Hôpital Général, and the Recollets acquired another property near the Château Saint-Louis. Here they were to build a new church and monastery in 1693 to the designs of Juconde Drué.

Before coming to Canada—probably in 1692— Drué had been trained in painting and architectural design at the Recollet monastery in Paris where Frère Luc lived. Drué not only followed his teacher's precepts in designing the 1693 Recollet

Drué

church of Quebec but also incorporated in it most of the interior woodcarving from the earlier Recollet church which Frère Luc had built; under the terms of sale to Saint-Vallier the Recollets were allowed to take these fittings with them. Though this first building by Drué in Quebec was damaged during the siége of 1759 and destroyed by fire in 1796, its appearance is well known from the exterior and interior drawings which Richard Short* made of it, and published in 1761.

In basic form the building was a long barrel-vaulted rectangle, without transepts; on either side of the end wall were altars, framed by free-standing columns on pedestals carrying straight entablatures. Between these columns was a deep recess, whose walls supported a tall tower and spire, and against the flat end wall was a main altar framed like the side ones, but with double instead of single columns and an elliptical pediment giving the effect of a triumphal arch. This arrangement was instantly popular and widely imitated in the colony. Drué himself helped spread this vogue by repeating it in several works. He is thought to have designed the third church of Sainte-Anne de Beaupré (rebuilding begun 1689, interior from 1694 on). To him also has been attributed the Petit Hermitage, or Chapelle Saint-Roch, erected in 1694 by the Recollets on the east side of the St Charles River. He also apparently designed the 1706 Recollet church of Montreal (which Pierre Janson*, dit Lapalme, contracted to finish in 1712), and the churches of Saint-Joseph (1721) and Saint-Nicolas (begun 1721, completed 1728) on the Lauson shore. Not one of the five buildings now survives. Gérard Morisset has also attributed to Drué the design for the third parish church of Trois-Rivières, built 1710–13; this church was in an area traditionally under strong Recollet influence, and the interior decoration, begun in 1730, was under the direction of Augustin Quintal*, Drué's pupil and his successor as chief designer for the Recollets. The lavishly carved interior of this Trois-Rivières church, executed by Gilles Bolvin*, was, until its destruction by fire in 1908, one of the greatest achievements of Quebec art, and the first of a brilliant series of interiors created jointly by Quintal and Bolvin which directly carried on and developed the precedent set by Drué.

Other examples of Drué's influence on church design during the French régime include the first church of Ange-Gardien (built 1675–76, interior decoration begun after 1694 under curé Gaspard Dufournel*, destroyed 1931), the redecoration of the chapel of the Hôpital Général (begun 1697, still extant with many later alterations), the second church of Pointe-aux-Trembles, Montreal (built 1705–9, decorated from 1726 on by Pierre-Noël Levasseur*, destroyed 1937), the first church of Yamachiche (probably designed by Drué's follower Augustin Quintal in the early 1730s), and the chapel of the Ursulines in Quebec (built 1720–22, decorated 1734–39 by the Levasseurs, remodelled in 1902 and still extant). After 1763, churches à la récollette were severely criticized by Bishop Briand*, but despite his strictures Drué's precedent and influence lived on into the 19th century to be brilliantly revived and given classic expression in the great church designs of Thomas Baillairgé*.

That Drué's artistic talents were recognized by his contemporaries is evident from the fact that in 1700 the Conseil Souverain chose him as "arbitre-estimateur" in a litigious affair between the sculptor Denis MALLET and the Jesuits. However, for Drué himself his artistic career was only a small part of his life's work, and most of his time was devoted to missionary and ecclesiastical activities. In 1692 he is referred to as "prêtre missionnaire" at Notre-Dame-des-Anges (Quebec), and in 1693 we find him at Saint-Augustin de Portneuf. From 1693 to 1698, he interrupted his ministry there to become the first chaplain of the Hôpital Général of Quebec. In 1700, Drué went back to missionary work which led him successively to Charlesbourg (1700), Ancienne Lorette (1701), Sainte-Anne de la Pérade (1718), Saint-Antoine de Tilly (1719–20), Saint-Joseph de Chambly (1721, 1723–24), and to Pointe à la Chevelure (1721–23). In July 1726, we find him in Montreal—the last mention of him in Canada.

ALAN GOWANS

AAQ, Registres d'insinuation A, 419. Archives des Franciscains de Québec, Dossier Juconde Drué. AJQ Greffe de François Genaple, 17 sept. 1692, 10 janv. 1693. Charlevoix, Histoire (1722), III, 74f. Jug. et délib., IV, 487, 495; V, 211. Richard Short, Twelve views of the principal buildings in Québec (London, 1761). Caron, "Prêtres séculiers et religieux," 290. R.-É. Casgrain, Histoire de la paroisse de l'Ange-Gardien (Québec, 1902). J.-C. Gamache, Histoire de Saint-Roch de Québec et de ses institutions 1829–1929 (Québec, 1929), 24f. Gosselin, L'Église du Canada, I. Alan Gowans, Church architecture in New France (Toronto, 1955). Jouve, Les Franciscains et le Canada: aux Trois-Rivières; Les frères mineurs à Québec, 1615–1905, simple coup d'œil historique (Québec, 1906), 80f. Monseigneur de Saint-Vallier et l'Hôpital Général de Québec. Gérard Morisset, Coup d'œil sur les arts en Nouvelle-France (Québec, 1941). J.-E. Roy, Histoire de la seigneurie de Lauzon (5v., Lévis, 1897–1904), II, 96f. P.-G. Roy, A travers l'histoire de l'Hôtel-Dieu de Québec (Lévis, 1939); Les vieilles églises de la province de Québec, 1647–1800 (Québec, 1925). Ramsay Traquair, The old architecture of Québec (Toronto, 1947). Gérard Morisset, "Thomas Baillargé," Technique (Québec), XXIV (1949), 471.

DU BOURGUÉ DE CLÉRIN, DENIS D'ESTIENNE. *See* ESTIENNE

DUBREUIL, JEAN-ÉTIENNE, shoemaker, court officer, seigneurial attorney, and royal notary; b. *c.* 1666, son of Jean Dubreuil and Catherine Lemarinier of the parish of Saint-Médéric in Paris; d. 4 June 1734 and buried the following day at Quebec.

In March 1681 there was a Dubreuil among the governor general's guards. Was he Jean-Étienne, who was barely 15 years old, or a relative whom he presumably had accompanied or followed to Canada? We cannot say. Jean-Étienne Dubreuil was in any event at Quebec in the autumn of 1691, carrying on the shoemaker's craft. On 29 Sept. 1693 he took on Charles Saulcier as an apprentice for four years. He was also verger of the parish of Notre-Dame in Quebec around 1697. These humble beginnings did not prevent him from acceding to some relatively important offices which certainly were more prestigious, if not more profitable. On 8 Nov. 1704 he was appointed by Intendant François de Beauharnois* court officer to the Conseil Supérieur, and was admitted to the office on 15 December following. Then on 26 Nov. 1707, in view of the infirmities with which the lawyer CHAMBALON was afflicted and which often prevented him from working, JACQUES RAUDOT appointed Dubreuil notary. When a report on his "character" was received on 7 December, Dubreuil was authorized to practise as a notary. Like many of his *confrères,* he was soon going to hold three offices simultaneously: on 2 June 1710 he received a commission as attorney for the seigneury of Notre-Dame-des-Anges. The "character" report was received 14 June. We do not know how long he retained this office. Finally, on 31 Aug. 1725, the very day of René Hubert's death, he was appointed, at the king's discretion, to succeed him as first court officer to the Conseil Supérieur; he was admitted on 1 October. The king approved this promotion on 14 May 1726, with the result that on 7 October following another ceremony was held to install the new incumbent.

Dubreuil was married three times: the first time, on 26 Nov. 1691, to Marguerite Le Gardeur, who was buried 29 Dec. 1702 during the smallpox epidemic, at Quebec; the second time, on 14 May 1703, to Marie-Anne Chevalier, who was buried 5 April 1711; and finally, on 12 Feb. 1713, to Marie-Jeanne Routier, Jacques Voyer's widow, who survived him by three years. His first two wives each bore him five children. The Dubreuil family lived in Upper Town, near the bakery belonging to the seminary on Rue Sainte-Famille. Dubreuil owned various pieces of land and at the beginning of his career engaged in some dealings in real estate. Being burdened with a large family, however, he did not become rich. When he was still a shoemaker he had invested 1,000 *livres* in the Compagnie de la Colonie; in 1708—when he was court officer and notary—Raudot wrote laconically that "he has nothing." Alas! the poverty of legal officers under the French régime.

ANDRÉ VACHON

AJQ, Greffe de Louis Chambalon, 29 sept. 1693, 14 oct. 1705; Greffe de François Genaple, 25 nov. 1691, 13 mai 1703; Greffe de Jacques Pinguet, 18 août 1734; Greffe de François Rageot, 31 janv., 9 févr. 1713. AQ, NF, Coll. de pièces jud. et not., 907, 2034½, 2037¾, 2055; NF, Ins. Cons. sup., II, 154v; III, 44f.; VI, 47v *et seq.*, 88; NF, Ins. de la Prév. de Québec, I, 684; II, 126, 346; III, 138; NF, Ord. des int., IV, 17v. *Jug. et délib. Ord. comm.* (P.-G. Roy), II, 324. Recensement de Québec, 1716 (Beaudet). "Liste générale des intéressés en la compagnie de la colonie du Canada, et des actions qu'ils y ont prises," *BRH,* XL (1934), 499. Tanguay, *Dictionnaire,* I, 206.

DUBUISSON, JACQUES-CHARLES RENAUD. *See* RENAUD

DU CHAIGNEAU. *See* CHAIGNEAU

DUCHESNAY, IGNACE JUCHEREAU. *See* JUCHEREAU

DUFROST DE LA JEMERAIS, CHRISTOPHE, nephew of Pierre Gaultier* de La Vérendrye and his "second in command" in the venture to discover the "Western Sea"; b. 6 Dec. 1708 at Varennes, last child of François-Christophe Dufrost de La Gemerais and Marie-Renée Gaultier de Varennes; d. 10 May 1736 at Fort Maurepas, a bachelor.

The name was most often written, in France, Dufro or Dufrost de la Gesmeraye or de la Gesmerais, and in Canada, Dufrost de La Gemerais, de La Jemerais, or de La Jemmeraye. Young Christophe signed himself "La Jemerais."

Christophe, the youngest of the family, entered the army very young. He served at Fort Saint-Philippe des Miamis from 1723 to 1725; he was appointed a cadet in 1726 and continued to serve at Saint-Philippe until 1727 when he went to Fort Beauharnois des Sioux, built by René Boucher de La Perrière in that year. In 1728 Boucher de La Perrière had to leave the fort, and La Jemerais remained temporarily in charge of the post during the winter. Towards the end of the season, young Dufrost, accompanied by a few soldiers and a group of Indians, including several Fox chiefs, went to the St Joseph River to see the commandant

Dugay

of the fort, and continued on to Montreal, leaving Fort Beauharnois without a garrison. He carried out this mission at the request of the Indians, who had several misdeeds to be pardoned for. On the way these Indians, afraid of the presence of their enemies, particularly of the Ottawas, abandoned the party; La Jemerais had to go on with his soldiers, and reached Montreal on 31 Aug. 1729.

In 1731 he went with his uncle La Vérendrye on his first expedition towards the western sea, and they began the construction of Fort Saint-Pierre, at the western extremity of Lac La Pluie (Rainy Lake); the following year he accompanied the explorer to Lac des Bois (Lake of the Woods) and helped him to build Fort Saint-Charles there. In the spring of 1733 he went to within a few leagues of Lac Ouinipigon (Lake Winnipeg), together with his cousin JEAN-BAPTISTE GAULTIER de La Vérendrye, in search of a suitable site for the building of a fort. Then he made his way eastwards, in order to inform the governor of the new discoveries.

Returning to the west in 1734, he replaced his uncle at Fort Saint-Charles; on 9 March 1734, as a result of a request of Madame de Vaudreuil [JOYBERT], he was appointed second ensign. La Jemerais wrote to the governor on 23 July 1735 to inform him of the commercial activities of the posts. He was instructed to visit the Mandans in the Missouri region, and the following year was sent to Fort Maurepas on the Rivière Rouge, where, during the winter, he fell seriously ill. He died on 10 May 1736, while his two La Vérendrye cousins, who had been sent to his aid, were trying to bring him back to Fort Saint-Charles, using a route that no other Frenchman was to follow before the conquest of Canada. He was buried "at the Fourche des Roseaux," near the present village of Letellier in Manitoba.

La Jemerais had a fairly good education, was familiar with cartography, and knew how to "measure an elevation." He has left us the first French map of the west, which is also the best. It is dated 1 Oct. 1733, and the final drawing is by the engineer Gaspard-Joseph Chaussegros* de Léry.

The father of Christophe, François-Christophe was a descendant of the old noble family of the Dufrosts, which according to authentic documents goes back to 1409. François-Christophe was the son of Christophe Dufrost, Sieur de Boissemances, and of Marguerite de La Forest, Dame de La Gemerais; the latter belonged like her husband to the nobility of Brittany, and she transmitted her last title to her new family.

François-Christophe obtained a post as midshipman in 1683, and two years later he came to Canada with BRISAY de Denonville. On 17 March 1687 he was appointed an ensign and served at Fort Niagara (1687–88). In his report of 1689 Louis de Buade* de Frontenac had nothing but praise for François-Christophe, and in 1692 gave him a commission as lieutenant, which was confirmed by the court on 1 March 1693. On 5 May 1695 he became a sub-lieutenant, and on 15 June 1705 was appointed captain. In the meantime he served a few years (1696–99) at Fort Frontenac (Cataracoui; now Kingston, Ontario). He died on 1 June 1708 at Montreal.

On 18 Jan. 1701, at Varennes, François-Christophe Dufrost had married Marie-Renée Gaultier de Varennes, daughter of René Gaultier* de Varennes and Marie Boucher and granddaughter of Pierre BOUCHER. They had three sons and three daughters, all born at Varennes; one, Marie-Marguerite*, was to become the foundress of the Sisters of Charity of the Hôpital Général in Montreal.

ANTOINE CHAMPAGNE

AE, Mém. et doc., Amérique, 8, ff.46, 69. AJM, Greffe d'Antoine Adhémar, 10 janv. 1701; Greffe de J.-B. Adhémar, 6 mai 1731; Greffe de Jacques David, 27 mai, 1726; Greffe de C.-J. Porlier, 22 mai 1734; Greffe de J.-C. Raimbault, 2 juillet, 21 août 1732; Registres des congés, 1721–1726. AJQ, Greffe de J.-B. Peuvret Demesnu, 12 déc. 1712. AN, Col., C¹¹ᴬ, 11, ff.28f.; 51, ff.131, 135f.; C¹¹ᴱ, 16, f.134; D²ᶜ, 47, ff.49–62; E, 263; F³, 2, ff.489–91; 12, ff.85–87. Service hydrographique de la Marine (Paris), Dépôt des cartes et plans de la Marine, 4044B, 39, 85.

Découvertes et établissements des Français (Margry), VI. [La Vérendrye], *Journals and letters of La Vérendrye* (Burpee). "Lettres du père Aulneau," APQ *Rapport, 1926–27*, 290. Wis. State Hist. Soc. *Coll.*, XVII. L. J. Burpee, *The search for the western sea* (London, 1908; rev. ed., Toronto, 1935). Parkman, *A half-century of conflict.* L.-A. Prud'homme, "Documents sur la découverte du Nord-Ouest," Société hist. de Saint-Boniface *Bull.*, I (1911).

DUGAY (Duguay), JACQUES, surgeon; b. *c.*1647 at Semur-en-Auxois (department of Côte-d'Or), France, son of Michel Dugay, sworn master surgeon, and of Catherine Laubret; buried 13 March 1727 at Trois-Rivières.

On 21 Nov. 1672, shortly after his arrival in New France, Dugay married Jeanne Baudry, daughter of one of the original settlers of Trois-Rivières, Urbain Baudry, *dit* La Marche. In addition to giving the sum of 300 *livres* Baudry undertook, by way of a dowry to his daughter, to lodge the young couple in his own home and keep them for a year. Jeanne Baudry died 22 Nov. 1700. She had had 11 children.

For more than half a century Jacques Dugay practised the art of medicine at Trois-Rivières. As he was for many years the only surgeon practising there, he must have treated nearly all the local families. It was probably he who attended the Recollet brother Didace Pelletier* during the illness preceding his death. He contributed in good measure to the possible beatification of Brother Pelletier by testifying several times in support of persons who claimed to have been cured through his intercession. Dugay also attended in his last moments the Marquis de CRISAFY, governor of Trois-Rivières, who died 6 May 1709. Most of the notarial inventories of the period have entries under his name for fees for medical care, operations, deliveries, and medicine.

On 29 April 1709 Dugay remarried; his second wife was Anne Baillargeon. He died at 80 years of age and was buried in the cemetery of the Ursulines' hospital. He left behind him a reputation as a modest and conscientious practitioner.

RAYMOND DOUVILLE

AJTR, Greffe de Séverin Ameau. A. Roy, *Inv. greffes not.*, XI, 95, 229. Ahern, *Notes pour l'histoire de la médecine*, 191. Raymond Douville, *Visages du vieux Trois-Rivières* (Trois-Rivières, 1955). L.-E. Duguay, *Généalogie de la famille de Pierre Duguay* (2v., Trois-Rivières, 1923), II. Jouve, *Les Franciscains et le Canada: aux Trois-Rivières. Les Ursulines des Trois-Rivières depuis leur établissement jusqu'à nos jours* (4v., Trois-Rivières, 1888–1911). Odoric-M. [Jouve], "Étude historique et critique sur les actes du Frère Didace Pelletier, Récollet," *BRH*, XVII (1911).

DUGUÉ DE BOISBRIAND, PIERRE, protégé and officer of Buade* de Frontenac, commandant in the Illinois country; b. 21 Feb. 1675 at Ville-Marie (Montreal); second son of Michel-Sidrac Dugué* de Boisbriand, seigneur of Mille-Îles, and of Marie Moyen Des Granges; d. 7 June 1736.

Dugué began his military career under the aegis of Count Frontenac as a half-pay ensign in the colonial regular troops, but in 1694 was promoted to the rank of ensign. His first military assignment was as second in command, under Captain SAINT-OURS in 1695. The following year he served with PIERRE LE MOYNE d'Iberville, his cousin, in an attack on Newfoundland. Dugué's last encounter with the English took place in 1697 when he accompanied Iberville's expedition to recapture York Fort (Fort Bourbon) in Hudson Bay. After a very difficult voyage from Placentia (Plaisance), Iberville defeated a squadron of three English war-ships and forced Henry BALEY, the commander of the fort, to surrender. Iberville then returned to France leaving his brother, JOSEPH LE MOYNE de Serigny, in command, probably with Dugué as his lieutenant.

After the treaty of Ryswick (September 1697), Dugué was brought to France. Meanwhile Iber-

ville had made an exploratory trip to the mouth of the Mississippi to continue the work of Cavelier* de La Salle. In 1699 he made a second voyage and Dugué went with him as an officer of the marine, serving on the frigate *Renommée.* Iberville established Fort de Mississipi on Biloxi Bay which de Maltot and Louis Denys* de La Ronde commanded first, followed by Iberville's brother, Le Moyne* de Bienville. Dugué's position as town major of Biloxi had been confirmed by royal order in August 1699.

In 1702 the two Le Moyne brothers founded the city of Mobile in which a number of officers, including Dugué de Boisbriand, received grants of land. Two years later, Dugué, on the instructions of Bienville, escorted 70 Chickasaws to a peace conference with the Choctaws, but the latter massacred the envoys in front of Dugué and his force of 25 French soldiers. Dugué was wounded in the fight, and the Choctaws endeavoured to show their regret by sending him back to Mobile with an escort of 300 warriors. Although there is no information concerning Dugué for the next ten years, it appears that he lived in Mobile during that period. In 1714 when Bienville became governor, he took over Natchez and Fort Saint-Jérôme; he intended to place the latter under Dugué's command, but it was committed instead to Captain Chavagne de Richebourg.

In 1716 Dugué became garrison adjutant. The following year he was named commandant of Mobile and the surrounding country. At this point he was granted leave to return to France. In Paris, Dugué was considered a man of importance, for the Compagnie d'Occident had just taken over Antoine Crozat's monopoly of trade from the lands of the Illinois to the coast, and the company was seeking advice as to what it should do. As a result, in the spring of 1718 Dugué returned to Louisiana on board the *Duchesse de Noailles* with a commission as first king's lieutenant and member of the council of Louisiana; a few months later he was commissioned commandant of the Illinois. In December of that year with a strong force of soldiers and some miners who wished to hunt for minerals, Dugué left for the Jesuit mission at Kaskaskia, arriving there on 13 May 1719. The following year, he built Fort de Chartres 16 miles to the northwest. He remained there for a number of years, and, although a hunchback, became very popular with the Indians owing to his knowledge of their language and his interest in their welfare. He sought to push farther into the interior but inter-tribal wars, rising costs of provisions, and difficulties with RIGAUD de Vaudreuil, governor of New France, prevented him.

By 1720 the Compagnie des Indes had fallen into

Du Lescöat

serious difficulties, largely through internal squabbles. In 1724 Bienville, accused of misgovernment, returned to France, and the governorship was assumed by Dugué. The latter, however, did not remain in power long, for complaints were made against him as well; when he refused to cooperate with Jacques de La Chaise, who had been sent out to investigate, he also was recalled. In France he was censured, deprived of his rank, and dismissed from the royal service. In 1730, however, he was granted a pension of 800 *livres* by the king. On 7 June 1736 he died in France. Contrary to Msgr Tanguay's statement Dugué never married.

W. STANFORD REID

AE, Mém. et doc., Amérique, 1, ff.5–8. AN, Col., B, 29, 35; C¹³ᴬ; Marine, B²; B³. *Découvertes et établissements des Français* (Margry), V, 587–672. *MPA* (Rowland and Sanders). Tanguay, *Dictionnaire*, I, 210. Alvord, *Illinois country*. N. M. Belting, *Kaskaskia under the French régime* (University of Illinois studies in the social sciences, XXIX, no.3, Urbana, 1948). Giraud, *Histoire de la Louisiane française*. HBRS, XXI (Rich). O'Neill, *Church and state in Louisiana*. "La famille Du Gué de Boisbriand," *BRH*, XXIV (1918), 193–200. Benjamin Sulte, "Michel-Sidrac Dugué, sieur de Boisbriand," *BRH*, X (1904), 221–23.

DU LESCÖAT, JEAN-GABRIEL-MARIE LE PAPE. *See* LE PAPE

DULHUT, DANIEL GREYSOLON. *See* GREYSOLON

DU LUTH. *See* GREYSOLON

DU MESNIL DE NORREY (DUMESNIL-PÂTÉ), JACQUES LE PICARD. *See* LE PICARD

DUPLESSIS, ANTOINE-OLIVIER QUINIARD, *dit. See* QUINIARD

DUPLESSIS, GEORGES RÉGNARD. *See* RÉGNARD

DUPONT, M. *See* POULET

DUPONT, SIMÉON, priest, Recollet, b. 1671 in Paris; d. 17 Sept. 1732 at Trois-Rivières.

We do not know the exact date of Father Siméon Dupont's arrival in Canada. His first act entered in the parish register of Trois-Rivières is dated 21 Nov. 1701, when he was assisting Father Luc FILIASTRE. While ministering tirelessly to the neighbouring parishes, he also carried out the duties of curate in the parish of Trois-Rivières until 1716. He was then appointed superior of the

community of Recollets in that town; he also took on the office of priest of the parish, deputizing in the absence of Father Antoine MARTIN de Lino, who did not arrive until October 1717.

Can we maintain, as does the historian Jouve, that from 1702 to 1724 "he prepared and supervised the building of the churches of five future parishes," namely those of Maskinongé, Rivière-du-Loup (Louiseville), and Yamachiche, on the north shore, and Baie-du-Febvre and Nicolet on the south shore? We do know that on 1 Jan. 1716 Judge René GODEFROY de Tonnancour initialled the register of Nicolet at the request of Father Dupont, "a priest serving the parish of the Nativité de la Sainte Vierge et de Saint-Pierre in the seigneuries of Bécancour and Dutort." In addition, the Recollet made the first entry in the registry of Bécancour on 12 January of the same year. On 22 July 1722 Father Siméon signed as a witness the deed of gift donating the land on which the church had been built to the parish council of Nicolet; this gift was made so that a presbytery could be erected and a garden prepared there for the missionary. It is therefore certain that he organized these missions, served them for more than 12 years, and endowed some parishes with their first registers, although this does not mean that he actually built the churches.

Father Dupont made his last entry in the register of Trois-Rivières on 10 Oct. 1731. Exhausted by long and arduous missionary trips, he died the following year at the age of 61, after 44 years in the church.

JACQUES VALOIS

Archives de l'évêché de Nicolet, carton Bécancour. Archives de la Seine-Inférieur, H (clergé régulier), récollets, 5. AJTR, Greffe de Pierre Petit; Registres d'état civil de Trois-Rivières, 21 nov. 1701, 10 oct. 1731. AQ, NF, Doc. de la jur. des T.-R. "Procès-verbaux du procureur général Collet" (Caron), 281–83. J.-É. Bellemare, *Histoire de la Baie-Saint-Antoine, dit Baie-du-Febvre, 1683–1911* (Montréal, 1911). Jouve, *Les Franciscains et le Canada: aux Trois-Rivières*, 124, 294, 305, 310.

DUPONT DE NEUVILLE, NICOLAS, member of the Conseil Souverain, keeper of the seals; b. *c.* 1632, son of Jean Dupont, receiver general for the salt granary of Vervins in the province of Picardy, and of Marie Gauchet; buried 26 April 1716 in the parish church of Notre-Dame de Québec.

By 1652 Nicolas was probably in New France, where he was engaged in trade. In 1665 he was churchwarden of Notre-Dame de Québec. He returned to France before 1668, and on 18 March 1669, in Paris, he signed his marriage contract with

Jeanne Gaudais; their first child was baptized on 19 Dec. 1669 at Quebec. Two sons and three daughters were born of this marriage; no male descendants survived, since the elder son died soon after birth and the younger was drowned at the age of 11. Nicolas Dupont has often been confused with Louis Gaudais-Dupont, but has finally been distinguished from him.

Louis XIV ennobled Dupont by letters patent on 30 April 1669. On the following 13 January he was admitted to the Conseil Souverain and received his life appointment from the king on 26 April 1675. He was appointed councillor and keeper of the seals on 1 June 1703.

On 20 Dec. 1670 Nicolas Dupont had bought from Zacharie Cloutier* the arriere-fief of La Clouterie (or La Cloutièrerie) in the Beauport seigneury. He made it over as a dowry to his daughter Françoise-Thérèse on 10 May 1687, on the occasion of her marriage to François-Marie Renaud* d'Avène de Desmeloizes. He also acquired the seigneury which has borne the names of Dombourg, Pointe-aux-Trembles, and Neuville, and which adjoins the Maur seigneury on the west. It was bought from Jean-François Bourdon* de Dombourg on 12 Nov. 1680 and enlarged on 27 April 1683 by a land grant from Le Febvre* de La Barre and de MEULLES. This domain also passed to the family of Renaud d'Avène de Desmeloizes after the grandfather's death.

Nicolas Dupont was a prominent person in his day. On 7 Nov. 1678 he was given the task of bearing to the king the opinions of an assembly of notables regarding the sale of spirits to the Indians. He enjoyed the confidence of Frontenac [Buade*] without being his tool. In August 1685 Intendant de Meulles, who was obliged to go and spend the winter in Acadia, delegated his powers to him during his absence. It was then that Dupont came into conflict with another delegate of the intendant, Jean-Baptiste Migeon*, a Montreal merchant, appointed to examine the suits against those who were trading with the English. He meant to prevent Migeon from carrying on his activity at Quebec, where he lived himself. On 8 Nov. 1685 the Conseil Souverain confirmed the freedom of the Montreal judge to "continue wherever it is his concern—even in Quebec—to institute proceedings as he has been delegated to do by the Intendant." In June 1704 Dupont contributed money to a maritime venture led by Jean LÉGER de La Grange against the English in Newfoundland. On 5 Oct. 1713, he gave an acre and a half of land at Pointe-aux-Trembles to the Sisters of the Congrégation de Notre-Dame "to found a mission there for teaching the young girls of his seigneury."

Dupont was the senior member of the Conseil Supérieur, when he passed away at the age of 84. His wife had died before him, on 16 Sept. 1707. One of their daughters, Marie-Madeleine, married PAUL LE MOYNE de Maricourt on 29 Oct. 1691 at Quebec.

LUCIEN CAMPEAU

Jug. et délib. P.-G. Roy, Inv. concessions, I, 40ff.; II, 22ff. DCB, I, 114, 232, 325, 572.

DU PONT DE RENON, MICHEL (sometimes called **Du Pont de Saint-Pierre**), officer of the garrison in Acadia and on Île Royale (Cape Breton Island); b. at Serignac, Saintonge; drowned 4 Sept. 1719 at Port-Dauphin, Île Royale (Englishtown, N.S.).

Renon was the son of Hugues Du Pont and Marie Du Hérauld de Gourville, and the brother of FRANCOIS DU PONT Duvivier and Louis Du Pont* Duchambon. On 26 Feb. 1710 he married at Port-Royal (Annapolis Royal, N.S.) Anne Desgoutins, the daughter of the highest-ranking officer of the civil establishment of Acadia, Mathieu de GOUTIN, and Jeanne Tibaudeau. Renon and his wife had five children.

Renon came to Acadia from France in 1702 as a lieutenant in the company of his brother Duvivier. In 1705 he was acting assistant town major. On the surrender of Port-Royal to the English under NICHOLSON in 1710, he returned to France where he remained until his appointment as assistant town major in the new colony of Île Royale in 1713. In June 1715 he succeeded to the captaincy of his late brother, François. Governor PASTOUR de Costebelle had occasion to write favourably in 1715 of Renon's devotion in the king's service.

Following her husband's death in 1719, Renon's widow married in 1724 the subdelegate of the intendant for Port-Dauphin, Michel Hertel* de Cournoyer.

BERNARD POTHIER

AN, Col., B, 23, 27, 36, 37; C^{11B}, 1; C^{11D}, 5, 7; D^{2C}, 47; Section Outre-Mer, G^1, 406; G^3, 2056. PANS, MS docs., XXVI (parish register of Port-Royal), 34. Le Jeune, Dictionnaire, I, 443. McLennan, Louisbourg.

DU PONT DUVIVIER, FRANÇOIS, sublieutenant in the navy, captain in Acadia and Île Royale (Cape Breton Island); b. 5 Sept. 1676 at Serignac, Saintonge, d. 31 Oct. or 1 Nov. 1714 in Louisbourg.

Duvivier was the second of nine sons and one daughter of Hugues Du Pont and Marie Du Hérauld de Gourville. Two brothers, MICHEL DU PONT de Renon and Louis Du Pont* Duchambon, also served in Acadia and Île Royale. Duvivier married on 12 Jan. 1705 Marie Mius d'Entremont, the daughter of Jacques Mius, Baron de

Duprac

Pobomcoup, and Anne de Saint-Étienne de La Tour, a daughter of Charles de Saint-Étienne* de La Tour. From this union there came seven children: François* (b. April 1705), Joseph-Michel, Joseph, Louis, and Michel* were all born in Port-Royal (Annapolis Royal, N.S.); Anne-Marie in Serignac; and Marie-Joseph (b. in 1715 after her father's death) in Louisbourg.

Duvivier was a midshipman at Rochefort from 1692 until 1702. That year he was awarded the rank of sub-lieutenant in the navy and the captaincy of a new company of colonial regular troops in Acadia. Though the governor of Acadia, Daniel d'Auger de Subercase, expressed satisfaction with Duvivier's conduct when the English under John March attacked Port-Royal in 1707, he described him in 1708 as "negligent beyond imagination . . . totally lacking in experience and emulation . . . [but] nevertheless a good fellow."

Duvivier's chief claim to notoriety in the colony was the irregular circumstances of his marriage in January 1705 before the Recollet Félix Pain*. He had failed to secure the permission of either his family or the commanding officer at Port-Royal. The commander, Simon-Pierre Denys de Bonaventure, lamented that such alliances between officers and young women of obscure birth and humble circumstances could not but seriously affect their careers and their diligence in the king's service. Though in Port-Royal the incident aroused the passions of those involved, as well as the curiosity of the settlers, the ministry was content to write letters reprimanding Duvivier and the superior of the Recollets in France for the insubordination of the priests of the order in Acadia.

Following the surrender of Port-Royal to the British under Nicholson in 1710, Duvivier returned to France. In June 1712 he was awarded the command of a company in Canada but failed to leave Paris in time to embark, for which negligence he was severely reprimanded by the minister of Marine. He sailed finally in 1713 from La Rochelle as a captain in the expedition which officially founded the colony of Île Royale. Undoubtedly because of his previous Acadian connections, he was sent that summer to Nova Scotia to encourage and organize the removal of the Acadians to the new French colony.

At his death in the autumn of 1714, his widow was awarded a small pension. She remained for several years in Île Royale before moving to Paris where she was reported as residing in 1734. At least three of Duvivier's sons entered the service in Île Royale where they soon acquired the reputation of being more zealous for trade than for the military.

Bernard Pothier

AN, Col., B, 23–37; C¹¹ᴮ, 1, 20; C¹¹ᶜ, 7, ff.215v, 224v; C¹¹ᴰ, 5–7; Section Outre-Mer, G³, 2039, 2056. PANS, MS docs., XXVI (parish register of Port-Royal), 11.

DUPRAC, JEAN-ROBERT, mason, court clerk, and seigneurial notary; b. c. 1646, son of Jacques Duprac, master sculptor, and of Françoise Lamoureux; originally from the parish of Saint-Porchère in Poitiers (province of Poitou); buried 30 Aug. 1726 at Beauport.

Duprac arrived in Canada in 1674 at the latest, since, on 6 Jan. 1675, he signed a marriage contract with Marguerite Vachon, daughter of the notary Paul Vachon. On 14 June 1676 Duprac was "a settler at Beauport." He was a mason by trade, and in 1681 he had only two acres under cultivation and five head of cattle. Like many colonists in New France, artisans by trade and often town-dwellers by birth, he probably had no taste for farm work. He must therefore have welcomed his appointment, on 1 Dec. 1693, as notary in the seigneury of Beauport, replacing Paul Vachon. Although we do not know precisely when, Duprac likewise succeeded his father-in-law as notary and clerk of court for the neighbouring seigneury of Notre-Dame-des-Anges. He continued in practice until 1723.

Duprac had nine children by Marguerite Vachon, who died 24 June 1703 of smallpox; his son Noël, who was baptized 21 Sept. 1681, was eventually to succeed him. As the son-in-law and the father of notaries, and a notary himself, Duprac was no exception in New France, where official charges were often handed down as if they were part of a heritage and somehow belonged to a family's patrimony.

André Vachon

AJQ, Greffe de J.-R. Duprac, 1693–1723; Greffe de Michel Fillion, 6 janv. 1675; Greffe de Paul Vachon, 14 juin 1716. AQ, NF, Registres de la Prévôté de Québec, 25 janv. 1694. *Jug. et délib.* Recensement du Canada, 1681 (Sulte). Tanguay, *Dictionnaire,* I, 217. Jean Langevin, *Notes sur les archives de N.-D. de Beauport* (2v., Québec, 1860–63). J.-E. Roy, *Histoire du notariat,* I, 166f., 342, 345.

DUPRAT. *See* Prat

DUPRÉ (Dupré, *dit* **Le Conte).** *See* Le Conte

DUPRÉ, FRANÇOIS, member of the community of priests of the seminary of Quebec, first parish priest of Champlain, second parish priest of Quebec; b. c. 1648 in France; d. 29 June 1720 at Ancienne-Lorette.

In September 1675, on returning from his second

trip to France, Bishop LAVAL brought back with him a young priest from the diocese of Chartres, François Dupré. Nothing seems to be known today about his origins. All we know of his family is that at the beginning of 1704 he had a brother who was a tradesman in Orléans, another who had been a surgeon and assistant medical officer with the army in Italy and who had died the previous summer, a sister who lived somewhere in France, and a nephew in Canada, probably the Philippe Dupré who was ordained 1 Jan. 1704 by Bishop Laval.

François Dupré first served as a missionary of the seminary of Quebec; then in the autumn of 1678 he became the first parish priest of Champlain. At this period he also served Batiscan, whose parishioners he was obliged to pursue before the Conseil Souverain in 1682 to obtain payment of the tithes. In 1683 he was responsible for about 320 souls. His church was a modest wooden chapel with a thatched roof, 55 ft. long and 25 ft. wide. The following year the parish of Champlain was set up for the second time, and *Maître* Dupré took solemn possession of it on 10 June 1685.

He resigned his office 17 March 1687 to succeed Henri de Bernières* at the head of the parish of Notre-Dame in Quebec. Four days later his installation took place in the cathedral, where the next day "to the ringing of the bell and at the end of the minor canonical hours" he was received as an honorary canon of the chapter of Quebec.

He had been chosen "as the person most apt for maintaining concord between the religious and the clergy" but was to become, probably very much despite himself, one of the numerous subjects of dispute between Bishop Saint-Vallier [LA CROIX] and the priests of the seminary of Quebec. The bishop, it seems, was a long time in pardoning them for appointing a parish priest for Quebec when he himself was absent. In 1693 he even attacked M. Dupré violently, demanding his resignation and threatening to suspend him from the execution of the duties with which he had just been entrusted as first assistant to the superior of the seminary. The members of the seminary regularly retorted that they had acted by virtue of the powers granted them by the union of the parish and the seminary of Quebec at a time when the successor to Bishop Laval was still only his vicar general.

For several years, however, they envisaged replacing at the head of the parish of Quebec someone who admitted to "having difficulty in remaining there because of his limited aptitude for expressing himself in his sermons." Did M. Dupré's indiscretion turn the scale? "M. le

Curé is charged with being unable to keep anything secret," wrote the procurator in Paris to the officers of the seminary in June 1707. "It is for this reason," he continued, "that it is claimed that no one would dare confide any matter either to M. Dupré or to M. Desmaizerais [ANGO Des Maizerets]. On the following 6 July Abbé Henri-Jean Tremblay* added however: "I believe that he must be truly humble if he agrees to resign, and if he reverts to a position such as that at Trois-Rivières."

François Dupré was capable of such humility; he resigned his office on 10 October and ended his days as parish priest at Ancienne-Lorette, where he was buried in the sanctuary of the church. "I have committed myself completely to being directed by my superiors. I have always found my peace in that," said his letter of resignation.

From 1701 to 1707 he had been spiritual director of the Ursulines, who appreciated his devotion, his wisdom, and his knowledge.

CÉLINE DUPRÉ

AAQ, Copies de documents, Série A; Église du Canada, I, 20; Registres d'insinuation A, 560, 690. ASQ, Chapitre, 21, 31, 198i, p.14; Lettres, M, 19, pp.34f.; 23, 24, 29, pp.3f.; 30, pp.37–40; 31, 38, pp.21f.; O, 37, p.20; 39, pp.33f.; 41, 45, p.1; 48; R, 6; Paroisse de Québec, 3a, 14–18; Paroisses diverses, 32, 33, 34; Polygraphie, XVIII, 54; XXII, 22, 22a; Séminaire, I, 11. Caron, "Inventaire de documents," APQ *Rapport, 1939–40, 1940–41. Jug. et délib. Mandements des évêques de Québec* (Têtu et Gagnon), I, 122. Provost, *Le Séminaire de Québec: documents et biographies*, 184, 421. Cyprien Tanguay, *A travers les registres* (Montréal, 1886), 113. Cloutier, *Histoire de la paroisse de Champlain*. Auguste Gosselin, *Henri de Bernières, premier curé de Québec* (Les Normands au Canada, Québec, 1902). *Les Ursulines de Québec* (1866–78), II, 36.

DUPUY, CLAUDE-THOMAS (the name was sometimes written **Du Puy** or **Dupuis,** but he signed Dupuy), lawyer, *maître des requêtes,* intendant of New France from 1725 to 1728; b. 10 Dec. 1678 in Paris, only son of Claude Dupuy and Élisabeth Aubry; married, on 6 June 1724, Marie-Madeleine Lefouyn, by whom he had no children; d. 15 Sept. 1738 at the Château de Carcé, near Rennes.

The intendant's family came originally from Ambert, in the province of Auvergne. Jacques Dupuy, the great-grandfather of Claude-Thomas, lived there at the beginning of the 17th century. A document of 1611 calls him a merchant. His son Étienne was styled a merchant and bourgeois of Ambert, and was a clerk in the bailiff's court of that town. From 1648 on, Étienne enjoyed the

Dupuy

designation of "honourable man," a sign of social progress. Of his numerous sons, Thomas and Claude are the best known. The former made a fortune in the manufacture of paper, an industry very wide-spread in Auvergne at that time, and in various tax farms. He acquired several seigneuries, in particular that of Grandrif, which he added to his name. His son bought the office of king's secretary-counsellor, "maison et couronne de France," in the *parlement* of Pau, which conferred nobility upon him at the same time. His line has continued down to our day under the name of La Grandrive.

Étienne's second son, Claude, the father of Claude-Thomas, left Ambert to try his luck in Paris, where fortune smiled on him. He usually called himself a bourgeois of Paris and a paper-maker with his own shop; but the sale of paper, facilitated by his brother's activity in Auvergne, did not absorb all his energies; he lent money, speculated on houses, and was soon to be found ·buying offices for his son, which was an investment for the bourgeois of the time as well as a means of social advancement.

On 20 June 1676 he had married Élisabeth Aubry, who also belonged to the well-to-do Paris bourgeoisie, since she brought him a dowry of 10,000 *livres*, 8,000 of which were in ready money. But although Claude's father-in-law was only a comptroller of La Bûche in Paris his brother-in-law, Charles Aubry, was a lawyer in the *parlement*. The· family was moving finally towards the bar. Jacques-Charles Aubry, Charles' son, became between 1715 and 1735 one of the most famous lawyers in Paris.

Claude-Thomas Dupuy also chose this career. From 1688 to 1696 he studied at the Collège de Beauvais, two doors away from his father's house, which in that period had an excellent reputation. When he left it he enrolled in the Faculty of Law, where in 1698 he took his baccalaureate and in 1699 his licentiate. Shortly afterwards he entered the *parlement* as a lawyer, and in 1701 his parents bought for him the office of "king's counsellor, His Majesty's lawyer on the presidial bench of the Châtelet in Paris." In 1708 he became advocate general in the *grand conseil*; in his letters of appointment he is styled "chevalier." In 1720 he bought the office of *maître des requêtes*, which was worth something like 200,000 *livres*. *Maîtres des requêtes* had important duties, but it must be particularly noted that the office was normally a stepping-stone to higher posts, especially to an intendancy or to the council of state.

Towards the end of 1722 the new *maître des requêtes* decided, apparently for financial reasons (either substantial losses incurred through the failure of the system or ill-inspired land deals), to resign his office; and in the spring of 1723 he received his letters as honorary *maître des requêtes*, which allowed him to attend the meetings and express opinions there, but without receiving the emoluments of the post. He thus remained almost three years without an office, that is to say until his appointment in October 1725 to the intendancy in Canada; this is a somewhat surprising fact, for which a valid explanation has not yet been found.

Let us begin by noting all the unusual elements of the Dupuy case. It hardly ever happened that one became *maître des requêtes* if one's parents had not themselves held such offices for at least one or two generations. To a certain extent Claude-Thomas Dupuy appears like an upstart in this world of highly placed Parisian magistrates. It was partly Claude Dupuy's money that enabled his son to make headway. Louis Moreri, in *Le grand dictionnaire historique ou le mélange curieux de l'histoire sacrée et profane* .... (1759), was himself struck by the personal worth of Claude-Thomas; he worked his way up, he tells us, "by his own merit." This remark is the more significant because we are not aware that Dupuy had any "patron," that is to say a highly placed and influential person who would have been capable of furthering his candidacy for the various posts that he occupied.

But at the beginning of June 1726 he left Paris for a quite new adventure. He set out for Quebec, to take on there very different duties from those which had hitherto occupied him. He came to replace Michel Bégon*, who had held the intendancy since 1712.

In 1723 the latter had indeed asked the king to replace him in the post of intendant of Canada. Edme-Nicolas Robert, who was appointed at the beginning of 1724, did not come to Canada, since he died suddenly in July on the boat that was bringing him to New France. The following year the Sieur de Chazel also disappeared, in the shipwreck of the *Chameau* within sight of the shores of Cape Breton Island. On the news of his death Dupuy presented his candidacy for the still vacant post. The colonial office accepted at once, for it considered "that there are few persons in the Marine who are fitted for this position."

The new intendant took possession of his office on 2 Sept. 1726. He was to remain only two years in Canada. In the normal discharge of his duties, Dupuy displayed competence and perspicacity, but in a critical moment he showed so little restraint and self-possession that the minister decided to recall him.

The first duty of an intendant of New France was to administer justice; "good and prompt justice," said the instructions. Having spent his life in the highest courts of the mother country, Dupuy cannot have met many problems in the cases that came before him at Quebec. In what remains to us of his enactments nothing appears abnormal, except that one might perhaps reproach him with showing a certain partiality towards seigneurs, to the detriment of copyholders. With him justice was expeditious; a sentence was sometimes pronounced on the very day of the offence.

People, who were perhaps merely repeating the comments which he had made himself on his own action, have accused him of being excessively severe in his judgements. However, a close examination of the relevant documents reveals nothing of this kind. Among other things, he has been taken to task over the fine of 200 *livres* imposed on a young man who had sold spirits illegally, but this severity, which is in no way excessive, was justified by the fact that he wanted to make an example of him.

The maintenance of order also came under the intendant, and in the 18th century this included all the internal administration of the colony. By going through Dupuy's correspondence it is possible to establish that he reflected a great deal about the problems posed by the colonization of North America. He saw first its vertical dimension, that is the relationship of colony to mother country. On this point the court's instructions were clear: the "colony of Canada is good only to the extent that it can be useful to the kingdom." After studying the Canadian setting, he concluded as follows: first, Canada offered France "inexhaustible wealth," of which unfortunately full advantage could not be taken, either through ignorance or through lack of manpower. Secondly, Canadians were in the process of becoming a new people, who were different from the French, and whom the mother country, unless she were careful, would soon find it hard to control. "The colony is on the verge of ruin," he wrote in 1727, "unless we are assisted with men and money." He asked the French government to invest in Canada in shipbuilding, and in the establishment of glassworks and potteries, which were all industries requiring large quantities of wood. He particularly asked that new blood be injected to help the Canadians, whose spirit of independence had impressed him, to develop. A strong colony would be of service to the mother country in many ways. His appeal fell on deaf ears.

Then came the horizontal dimension, the integration of New France in the North American setting. Two salient facts engaged his attention: the presence of the English, and Franco-Indian relations. Dupuy recognized with considerable

perspicacity the sharpness of the sword which the Anglo-Saxons held poised over the colony. He had not been there for a year before the English were installed, and firmly, at Oswego on Lake Ontario. "Now we are reduced to being on the defensive in our own country!" he exclaimed. He asked for an energetic effort by the mother country: "Moderate efforts will do more at present than great projects that would be implemented too late," a prediction that was to be realized 30 years later, during the Seven Years' War.

Being a good jurist, he did not hesitate to state his theory concerning the rights of the French over the territories of the Iroquois after the treaty of Utrecht. Burnet had used the fact that the French had asked the consent of the Iroquois before reconstructing Fort Niagara as an argument to show that the territories in question were in truth Indian property. But, Dupuy hastened to retort, this "consent . . . does not prove anything in a country which is a colony and newly discovered, as we have at all times shared everything with the natives by common consent." Hence the consent of the natives was the basis of joint ownership of the territories. Dupuy saw proof of this consent in the fact that the Indians called the king of France their father and the French their brothers. A fragile confirmation indeed, but the notion of joint ownership is interesting.

Dupuy also concerned himself with the exploitation of the colony, that is to say the development of its economy. Being of the opinion that the fur trade was destined to die out rapidly, he decided to concentrate his efforts on the products of the soil. For example, he encouraged the growing of hemp; but his success was short-lived. He tried, but in vain, to persuade the mother country to build vessels in Canada. Everywhere he came up against insurmountable obstacles: the lack of outlets for the produce, the dearth of specialized workmen; when all was said or done the mother country could not make up its mind to invest heavily in Canada, and this would have been the only way to get out of the impasse.

With regard to law and order in the towns Dupuy had very decided views; he wanted to set the taverns to rights, and to this end he issued ordinances that many considered excessive and untimely. But it was town-planning that particularly interested him. He wanted to make the town of Quebec into a beautiful capital. He repaired the streets, laid out squares, and planned to put fountains and basins in them. Governor Charles de Beauharnois* de La Boische was shocked by an expenditure that he deemed useless, and the king's engineer, Chaussegros* de Léry, was annoyed at not having been consulted. Dupuy had indeed

209

Dupuy

decided everything on his own initiative, and had even thought of directing the construction work himself.

As to the financial situation, which he subsequently prided himself on having clarified, it must be admitted that during the first months of his intendancy he conducted a fairly extensive investigation in this direction. The reports of his successors confirmed his conclusions: the court never sent enough money, and as a rule it arbitrarily reduced the requests of its administrators, with the result that there was a lack of currency, sometimes a tragic lack, in the colony. Moreover, the court did not stop pedlars from draining off this currency. Above all, the minister was unwilling to admit that the costs of administration went on increasing with the general growth of the colony. Brutal reminders of these truths were unpalatable to him, and in the autumn of 1728 he was shocked to discover that in the last months of his administration Dupuy, whose thoughts were elsewhere, had pretty well neglected financial details; several accounts were not in order, and workmen whom he had taken on had not been paid. When Maurepas wrote to Hocquart* in the spring of 1729, to advise him to pay particular attention to His Majesty's finances, he told him bluntly: "His Majesty is informed that financial matters in the colony are not in order, that accounts of expenditures are four years behind and have not been closed, and that those of the warehouses have not been closed since 1 Oct. 1726 either." We may wonder, moreover, whether Dupuy, whose own finances were never in perfect shape, was well qualified to manage those of the king.

The minister's dissatisfaction and disapproval also extended to another sphere: the intendant's relations with certain persons, particularly the governor, Beauharnois. Each year in his instructions the king brought up insistently a point considered essential: perfect understanding between the governor and the intendant. The first contact had raised hopes of a harmonious and durable relationship, but nothing came of it. By the end of 1726 Beauharnois, who was touchy, had the impression that Dupuy, insatiable of honours, wanted to equal him in prestige and power. At that moment a climate of tension between the two was created. Not a month passed without a heated squabble breaking out, whether it was over a marriage to be authorized or a drum to be supplied to the troops. Each time the incident, often trivial in itself, assumed the proportions of an event. The general was not as learned as the magistrate, but he had a caustic style; from his pen have come lapidary sentences on the subject of the intendant,

which historians have taken pleasure in repeating. Following the quarrel over the drum, he said to the minister: "If we had crossed the tropic on our way here, I might have thought that he had been touched with madness, since there is no common sense in any of his requests." Then, when he pointed out that Dupuy would not listen to reason, his comment was: "He hearkens to no one, he fancies that he has become a god." They came to the point where they detested each other thoroughly; "I have only to say white for him to say black," remarked Beauharnois; "I have only to be of one opinion for him to be of another." In fact the governor always had the impression that his rights were being encroached upon, and for his part Dupuy saw the dark designs of Beauharnois everywhere, and accused him of being involved in the fur trade.

There was probably an incompatibility of temperament between the two men; but it must certainly be admitted also that they were diametrically opposed both by their origin and by their professional training. Dupuy spent his life in the magistracy and came from a bourgeois family, for whom the king's service was something new; that is why the intendant, at every turn, made it known that he had served His Majesty such and such a number of years; he even went so far as to identify his ideas and wishes with those of the sovereign. "The latter even had to remind him, in 1727, that he was only the second person in the colony." For Beauharnois, on the other hand, whose whole family history had been bound up for more than two centuries with the magistracy and the royal services, this had become a natural thing, about which there was never any question in his correspondence. And as for his own career, he had spent it almost entirely in the Marine; he knew nothing about the legal mind and easily got lost in the subtle turns of a parliamentarian's arguments. Hence we can more readily understand why they were at variance from the beginning of their joint administration to the end.

To be sure, all these difficulties annoyed the minister: however, he saw nothing irreparable in the situation. But such was not his reaction when at the end of May 1728 he received the report, dispatched to him by the chapter of Quebec, concerning the events which had marked the beginning of that year.

Bishop Saint-Vallier [LA CROIX], who had died during the night of 26 Dec. 1727, had chosen Intendant Dupuy as his executor. The latter took his role very seriously. Early on the morning of 26 December, he affixed seals to the bishop's possessions, transmitted the seals of the diocese, the emblems of authority, to the canons, and proclaimed the beginning of the regale. For their part the canons, having met immediately, elected Étienne BOULLARD as capitular vicar. On 31 December a dispute broke out in the chapter as to who should preside at the funeral, which had been set for 4 January. Chartier* de Lotbinière maintained that this honour belonged to him, in his capacity as archdeacon. Boullard, as capitular vicar, claimed it for himself. Lotbinière conceived the unfortunate notion of taking the dispute to the intendant, who summoned the canons for 2 January. The latter, questioning his authority in matters of ecclesiastical discipline, refused to appear. Dupuy was extremely annoyed at this. He then made a strange decision: as it had been reported to him that the canons wanted to remove the bishop's body to transport it to the cathedral and bury it there, contrary to the bishop's last will and testament, he decided to advance the date of the funeral. Without warning anybody, either among the clergy or the congregation of Quebec, he ordered Lotbinière to proceed forthwith—it was early afternoon on 2 January—with the interment of the bishop, which the archdeacon did, before the astonished eyes of the nuns and paupers of the Hôpital Général. Boullard reacted immediately: he placed the chapel of the Hôpital Général under interdict and deposed the mother superior. Dupuy replied at once that these acts were invalid; first because Boullard had not shown his letters of appointment, and secondly because in any case his election was worthless, since he had just discovered that there was a coadjutor in France who had automatically taken office. The canons were summoned to the Conseil Supérieur for the following Monday, 5 January.

Thus began the battle between the chapter, led by Boullard, and the Conseil Supérieur, directed by Dupuy. The latter's weapons were ordinances and fines, the former's interdicts and threats of excommunication. The January and February meetings of the council were almost entirely given over to violent, impassioned speeches by the intendant against the canons and particularly against Boullard. The affair came to such a pass that the governor considered it his duty to intervene. He came in person to the Conseil Supérieur and forbad the intendant to arraign Canon Boullard, despite the writ that had been issued shortly before. This intervention did not convince Dupuy, who challenged the governor's authority in legal matters and countermanded his orders. The wrangling continued in this way until the end of May.

These dissensions had created a great stir in the colony. The clergy had become divided. Several officers had to make a difficult choice between two authorities whose orders were contradictory. This all caused great wonderment among the people. The king was quickly informed of events. At the end of January the canons, with the governor's connivance and despite the intendant's veto, sent one of their members as a representative to Paris via New England. The latter reached Versailles before the end of May, and a few days later it was decided to recall the intendant. The minister was astonished at the numerous irregularities of procedure perpetrated by Dupuy, and was shocked by his intemperate language as well as by his ill-timed decisions. It was not understood at Versailles how such an experienced magistrate could act in such an ill-advised fashion. The truth is that at bottom Dupuy lacked the prudence that a good administrator needs; he never doubted his own ideas or rather he would not give them up, for in his opinion the authority with which the king had invested him gave them an inviolable character and put them above discussion.

He gave free rein to his passionate feelings; his speeches are full of violent diatribes against all who dared to oppose him, be they members of the chapter, religious, or officers. He seems to have delighted in this dispute, which allowed him to give public expression to his ideas on the superiority of the civil power over the church. But we must recognize, as moreover the court did, that his legal knowledge had limitations. The nonvacancy of the episcopal see was far from being established, and in all these questions of ecclesiastical law, with which he was less familiar, he ought to have shown more discretion and prudence. Furthermore, the minister approved Beauharnois' intervention in the Conseil Supérieur, even if this was extraordinary. Indeed the governor, the sovereign's personal representative in the colony, possessed supreme authority there. It was his duty, by virtue of his letters of appointment, to "maintain and keep the peoples in peace, quiet, and tranquillity." It seemed to him—the minister shared his opinion—that the "tranquillity" of the colony was threatened by Dupuy's behaviour.

One may legitimately ask oneself whether the latter was not induced to act as he did because of the prejudice, shared by many magistrates, that their profession was superior to that of the military. "If force were not controlled by law," Charles Loyseau had written at the beginning of the 17th century, "robbery and brigandage would prevail." Dupuy's attitude might well derive from such an outlook.

The king's decision vexed him sorely; and the grief that this brutal recall caused him was further aggravated by some very unpleasant occurrences.

211

Dupuy

As he had incurred heavy debts (65,000 *livres*) during his two-year stay in Quebec, an order of restraint was obtained against him. Of the 50-odd bales that he had brought with him to Quebec he took back to France only a few clothes and some papers. The sale of his possessions was subsequently carried out; he had to send back to France his library, for which there were no purchasers at Quebec, and his astronomical instruments, which would have had to go for a ridiculous price. The intendant emerged from his Canadian adventures profoundly humiliated and completely ruined. No one, on his return to the mother country, would offer him a position. But the king took pity on his misfortune, and granted him an annual pension of 1,500 *livres*.

Dupuy did not, however, lose heart. One might even say that his return to France heralded the beginning of a new career, a scientific one. Dupuy was a cultured man, he passed for a scholar; the doctor at the Hôtel-Dieu of Quebec, Michel SARRAZIN, had a high esteem for his learning. It has been possible to verify that this reputation was not overrated. Indeed we know the composition of his library, which contained more than 1,000 volumes. Its main features should be noted: a prominence given to the Bible, of which he possessed the text in several languages; a well-stocked and well-balanced legal section; an important place devoted to the arts and sciences, music, and mechanics, among other subjects. We know by cross-checking that Dupuy's interest in these fields, the last in particular, was not merely theoretical. Had he not transported with him to Quebec a well-equipped physics laboratory containing many models made by himself?

This long-standing interest in experiments in mechanics occupied the last years of his life. He constructed hydraulic machines, some of which were fairly widely talked of and were mentioned in the scientific reviews of the period. On three occasions inquirers from the Académie des Sciences came to see his inventions. Their report on the visit was favourable; they stated: "Monsieur Dupuy's pump is very good, and its capacity is at least as great as that of any pump so far shown before the academy." The king's *privilège* was then granted to his widow, for at that date (1741), the inventor had been dead for three years. He had died on 15 Sept. 1738 at the Château de Carcé, near Rennes, where he had been asked to come to "pump out the waters" which were filling the mines at Pontpéan. But as his death had interrupted the experiment it was his pupil, M. de Gensanne, who had completed it, and apparently with success. The experiment had no sequel, however, and it is easy to understand why: it was based on the principles of Cartesian physics, which was already at that time disappearing under the attacks of the Newtonians. There too Dupuy's success was ephemeral.

Finally, to what can we attribute Dupuy's original failure as an intendant in Canada? We can draw on several details for an answer. First his psychology: we have noted his inflexibility, his inadaptability. This natural rigidity had no doubt been strengthened by Jansenist influence, which appears evident in Dupuy. His inclination towards violence probably did not help in the execution of duties in which contacts with the public were so frequent. As for prudence, he seems to have been devoid of it; he did not know how to wait, to play his hand skilfully, to dissimulate. A long family tradition in the king's service would have given him more tact, would have taught him the art of compromise. It is also evident that his previous training had ill prepared him for his post as intendant in New France. His whole career had been spent in Paris courts where he was never alone in making decisions, where he was only one cog among many others, several of whom were his superiors. He found himself in Quebec with extensive power in his hands, and with no equal except the governor, whom moreover he could not bear to acknowledge as his superior.

After his administration, the court deemed it wise to return to the traditional practice of appointing to the Canadian intendancy an officer from the Marine cadres, experienced in office work and administrative routine.

JEAN-CLAUDE DUBÉ

Archives de l'Hôpital-Général de Québec, Annales, I. Archives municipales d'Ambert. AN, MM, Registres, Faculté de droit, 1049–1193; V, Grande Chancellerie; V⁴, Requêtes de l'Hôtel; V⁵, Grand Conseil; Col., B, 47–53; C¹¹ᴬ, 48–52; E; F¹ᴬ. AQ, NF, Ord. des int.; NF, Registres du Cons. sup. Bibliothèque de l'Académie des Sciences (Paris), MS, Registres de l'Académie. Bibliothèque Mazarine (Paris), MS, 3455. BN, MS, Cabinet des titres, P.O. 2959. Minutier Central (Paris), Études, XVII, LII.

Documents relating to Canadian currency during the French period (Shortt). *Édits ord.*, II. Louis de Héricourt, *Les loix ecclésiastiques de France* . . . (Paris, 1719). *Histoire de l'Académie royale des sciences, 1735* (Paris, 1738). *Machines et inventions approuvées par l'Académie royale des sciences, depuis son établissement jusqu'à présent . . . avec leur description: dessinées et publiées par M. Gallon* (7v., Paris, 1735–77). "Mémoire de M. Dupuy, Intendant de la Nouvelle-France, sur les troubles arrivés à Québec en 1727 et 1728, après la mort de Mgr de Saint-Vallier, évêque de Québec," APQ *Rapport, 1920–21*, 78–105.

Louis Moreri, *Le grand dictionnaire historique, ou le mélange curieux de l'histoire sacrée et profane* . . .

(10v., Paris, 1759). Louis Apcher, *Les Dupuy de la Grandrive: leurs papeteries de la Grandrive et Barot, leur parent, l'intendant du Canada, Claude-Thomas Dupuy* (Paris, 1937). Maurice Daumas, *Les cabinets de physique au XVIIe et XVIIIe siècles* (Paris, 1953). J.-C. Dubé, *Claude-Thomas Dupuy, Intendant de la Nouvelle-France, 1678–1738* (Montréal, 1968). Auguste Gosselin, *Mgr de Saint-Vallier et son temps* (Evreux, 1898). Maurice Daumas, "Les constructeurs français d'appareils scientifiques au XVIIe siècle," *Thalès* (Paris), 1948. Guy Frégault, "Essai sur les finances canadiennes (1700–1750)," *RHAF*, XII (1958–59), 307–23, 459–85; XIII (1959–60), 30–45, 157–83. Ignotus [Thomas Chapais], "Notes et souvenirs," *La Presse* (Montréal), 19 oct., 9 nov. 1901. Roland Mousnier, "Note sur les rapports entre les gouverneurs de provinces et les intendants dans la première moitié du XVIIe siècle," *Revue historique* (Paris), CCXXVIII (1962), 339–50. R. Petit, "Les bibliothèques des hommes du Parlement de Paris au XVIIe siècle," Mémoire de Diplômes des Études Supérieures, Sorbonne, 1954. H. M. Thomas, "A Canadian Pooh-Bah," *Dalhousie Review* (Halifax), XII (1927–28), 69–79.

DUPUY DE LISLOYE, PAUL, esquire, soldier, seigneur, king's attorney, and special lieutenant of the provost court of Quebec; b. *c.* 1637 at Beaucaire (province of Languedoc), son of Simon Dupuy and Suzanne Boschette (or Brusquet), "people of great integrity and of good character"; d. 20 Dec. 1713 and buried the next day in the cathedral of Quebec.

Paul Dupuy landed at Quebec in the autumn of 1665 as an ensign in Maximy's company of the Carignan-Salières regiment. When military operations had ended, he decided to stay in Canada. On 22 Oct. 1668, at Quebec, he married one of Louis Hébert*'s descendants, Jeanne Couillard, granddaughter of Guillaume Couillard* de Lespinay, who was born in June 1654. By the terms of the marriage contract the young couple received from Jeanne's father and mother, Louis Couillard* de Lespinay and Geneviève Després, half of Île-aux-Oies (which actually included two islands: a larger and a smaller one) and half of Île-aux-Grues, the other half going to their cousins, Pierre BÉCARD de Grandville and Anne Macard, another granddaughter of Guillaume Couillard. At first Dupuy and his wife seem to have lived mainly at Quebec, where they had two children baptized, in 1669 and 1671. In 1669 Dupuy returned to Beaucaire, perhaps to put his affairs there in order. He came back in 1670, bearing a passport from the governor of Beaucaire—a document which establishes beyond doubt Dupuy's place of birth, about which several historians have been in error. On 17 Oct. 1671, with a view to settling permanently on Île-aux-Oies, Dupuy made an arrangement with Bécard de Grandville by which the Sieur de Lisloye was to be the owner of the larger Île-aux-Oies and Bécard of the smaller one and of Île-aux-Grues. Dupuy and his family probably took up residence on their domain in 1671 or 1672, since their third child was baptized there by a missionary in the winter of 1672–73.

They lived the peaceful life of farming seigneurs. In 1681 the population of the island was 39, including Dupuy's family, which counted six children and employed two servants. Five settlers, one of them still a bachelor, had taken up land. Dupuy had 24 head of cattle and 20 acres under cultivation, and his copyholders had 64 cattle and 21 acres. Dupuy rarely went to Quebec but lived on his island "like a saint," according to the annalist of the Hôtel-Dieu of Quebec, "devoting several hours to prayer every day, reading edifying works, delivering on all Sundays and feast days an exhortation to his servants and the country people from all the surrounding area who gathered in his home to listen to him speak of God. . . . Several of them have assured us," continued the annalist, "that no preacher had ever impressed them as much."

When he was in his fifties Dupuy was to be drawn out of his retreat and his island by BRISAY de Denonville and BOCHART de Champigny. When Louis XIV dismissed Louis BOULDUC, king's attorney for the provost court of Quebec, and ordered the governor and the intendant to find a successor to him, they chose Dupuy. He was appointed on 17 Oct. 1686 and on 24 October he was called to his office and took the oath. Dupuy displayed extraordinary integrity and impartiality. Consequently, when René-Louis CHARTIER de Lotbinière, the lieutenant-general of the provost court, was absent on a trip to France in 1691, Dupuy was appointed by the council to replace him until his return. In 1692 he collected and catalogued all the records of proceedings of the provost court, arranged them in order, and initialled them. The preservation of these precious registers is perhaps due to him. Nevertheless, and despite the zeal of its officers, the provost court could not cope with its task, as the matters with which it had to deal became more numerous every year. When Louis XIV finally consented to appoint a second judge to help the lieutenant-general, it was Paul Dupuy whom he named on 1 June 1695 to hold the office of special lieutenant to the provost court. Dupuy was admitted to the Conseil Souverain in September 1696. His salary was set by the king at 500 *livres*. He was to remain titular special lieutenant to the provost court until his death, although from 10 Nov. 1710 on he acted as lieutenant-general in the absence of the

Durand de La Garenne

occupant, Denis RIVERIN, who was living in France.

Paul Dupuy's outside activities were, however, not negligible. Mindful of his first profession, he took part, with the rank of major, in the expeditions led in 1684 by Le Febvre* de La Barre and in 1687 by Denonville against the Senecas. Again, he demonstrated freely his virtue of charity, which was extolled by the Nuns Hospitallers of Quebec, by concerning himself from the time of its creation with the Bureaux des Pauvres, of which he was for several years the treasurer and one of the directors. When the Hôpital Général of Quebec was founded, he became *ex officio* one of its administrators. Having the responsibility of a large family and not being rich, he could hardly give of his own money; nevertheless he sought out benefactors, the Sieur REGNARD Duplessis for example, the treasurer of the Marine, for the charitable works which he had at heart. Even though he was an officer of the provost court, acting judge of the Conseil Souverain, a legal practitioner on occasion, Dupuy could not afford a dowry for his daughter, who had joined the Nuns Hospitallers, nor pay his debts to the Sieur Peire, a Quebec businessman, who sued him in 1711. Being obviously in difficult financial straits, Dupuy sold his seigneury of Île-aux-Oies to the Nuns Hospitallers of the Hôtel-Dieu of Quebec. It was given over to them in 1711, but the contract was not signed until 14 Feb. 1713. Dupuy was paid 12,000 *livres* for it, but 3,000 *livres* were kept by the Nuns Hospitallers for the unpaid dowry of one of his daughters, the second to take the veil as a member of this community.

This law officer, who had been chosen in 1698 to become the first judge of the admiralty court, a tribunal whose creation was finally delayed until 1717, whose name was put forward in 1706 for a post as councillor on the Conseil Supérieur, and upon whom was bestowed in 1697 a seigneury in Acadia measuring three leagues by three, nevertheless died in poverty, without having been able to obtain for his son the reversion of his office that he had solicited since 1703. He would probably have been spared this destitution if he had remained deaf to the appeal from Denonville and Champigny in 1686 and had stayed on his domain on Île-aux-Oies, of which the fertility and the yield astonished the Nuns Hospitallers of Quebec. In addition to poverty he had to suffer many bereavements. His wife died in 1702, and when he in turn passed away, only 4 of his 15 children (some sources say 13) survived him.

Paul Dupuy paid dearly for his decision to serve his fellow-countrymen, but he earned their esteem and gratitude, and hence posterity's. He remains forever the honest, upright man, the fair, painstaking judge, whom governors and intendants praised: "one of the wisest and most disinterested officers" of his period.

ANDRÉ VACHON

AJQ, Greffe de Florent de La Cetière, 14 févr. 1713; Greffe de Gilles Rageot, 10 juillet 1677. AQ, Paul Dupuis; NF, Ins. de la Prév. de Québec, I, 543, 663; II, 1; III, 192, 456; NF, Registres d'intendance, IV 11f. "Correspondance de Frontenac (1689–1698)," APQ *Rapport, 1928–29*, 293, 306. "Correspondance de Vaudreuil," APQ *Rapport, 1938–39*, 53, 85, 116, 130; *1939–40*, 409, 460. *Jug. et délib.*, III, IV. Juchereau, *Annales* (Jamet). P.-G. Roy, *Inv. concessions*, I, 215f., 224f.; *Inv. ins. Cons. souv.*, 68. Bonnault, "Le Canada militaire," 277, 295. Gareau, "La prévôté de Québec," 51–146. Sulte, *Hist. des Can. fr.*, V, 78. N.-E. Dionne, "L'île aux Oies," *BRH*, VII (1901), 47–51; "Paul Dupuis, sieur de Lislois," *BRH*, VII (1901), 218–21.

DURAND DE LA GARENNE (first name unknown), writer then commissary of the Marine, judge of the admiralty court at Placentia (Plaisance); fl. 1691–1715.

At first an employee at the port of Rochefort, Durand came to Placentia in 1699, as a writer in the Marine. The following year the king entrusted him with the office of commissary, and he was promoted subdelegate of the intendant of Quebec in 1701. His many duties included that of looking after troops, supplies, and fortifications, which resulted in conflicts with Joseph de MONIC, whose ill-will he had to endure. He got on better with AUGER de Subercase, and went through the St John's campaign with him (1705). He went to France the following year and returned in 1707, having been appointed judge of the admiralty court. In 1710 he took a census of the settlers at Plaisance and in the neighbouring district. The next year he proposed that the settlers of Newfoundland and of the island of Saint-Pierre be transported to Île Royale (Cape Breton Island).

Like all the officers at Placentia, he went in for fishing on his own account, and in 1711 he contributed to the fitting out of a privateer. This ship was captured as it left the port, and Durand had to share in paying the captain's ransom. This mishap seems to have upset his business, for in succeeding years we find him being prosecuted for debts, and he owed money to the treasurer of the Marine. After the treaty of Utrecht he was given the task, with PASTOUR de Costebelle, of preparing the evacuation of Placentia. But his accounts were in utter confusion. He was also accused of misappropriating and selling articles coming from the capture of St John's in 1709. Instead of going to Île Royale, however, La Garenne slipped away to Saint-Domingue, where his brother, Durand de Beauval, was a receiving agent. He died there, opportunely, on 12 Oct. 1715, leaving the clerks of the Marine with the responsibility for liquidating the accounts of the lost colony. The French national archives contain a good number of his letters and reports on the business affairs of Placentia during the 15 years that he was employed there.

RENÉ BAUDRY

AN, Col., B, 22–23, 25, 27, 29–30, 32–35, 37–38; C^{11B}, 1, f.120; C^{11C}, 2–7, 16; E, 93 (dossier Costebelle); F^3, 54, ff.421–30; Section Outre-Mer, G^1, 467 (recensements de Plaisance, 1706, 1710; printed in SGCF *Mémoires*, XI (1960), 80–81); G^3, 2053–55. *Coll. de manuscrits relatifs à la N.-F.*, II, 565. Le Blant, *Histoire de la N.-F.*, 256; *Philippe de Pastour de Costebelle*, 94, 115, 168.

DUTISNÉ, CLAUDE-CHARLES (Tissenay, Tisnet, Visseri), captain in the colonial regular troops in Louisiana, commandant at Forts Natchitoches, de Chartres, and Natchez, seigneur; b. in the parish of Saint-Germain-l'Auxerrois, Paris, son of Claude-Charles Dutisné and Catherine Du Cloux; d. 1730, in the Illinois country.

In his *Histoire de la Louisiane française* Émile Lauvrière wrote that Dutisné joined the colonial regular troops because he was not tall enough for the French army. On 15 June 1705 he was commissioned ensign in the troops of New France. Later that year he sailed for Quebec where he married Marie-Anne Gaultier de Comporté on 6 Feb. 1708. By this marriage he became seigneur of Champigny and Gaudarville, for Marie-Anne was the widow of Alexandre PEUVRET de Gaudarville. She died in 1711, and Dutisné married Marguerite Margane de Lavalterie in Quebec on 28 Oct. 1713.

In March 1714 Dutisné led 12 Canadians to the Ouabache (Wabash) River where he was to meet Jean-Baptiste Quenet with 20 to 24 Canadians from Quebec and Pierre DUGUÉ de Boisbriand from the Illinois. Their mission was to build a fort and trading post to impede English contact with the Miamis and the Natchez. As neither of the other two parties arrived, Dutisné and his men left the Ouabache and made their way to Île Dauphine (Dauphine Island, Ala.). This journey took them through the Kaskaskia region of the Illinois country, where Dutisné discovered some silver mines. Upon arriving in Louisiana he submitted a report to the governor, Lamothe Cadillac [LAUMET] who, characteristically enough, promptly took credit for the find.

In the fall of 1714, Dutisné was promoted lieutenant, and in this capacity assisted in the construction of Fort Rosalie among the Natchez. He served at Fort Rosalie (later Fort Natchez) as second in command until he received orders to build a post on the island of the Natchitoches (72 leagues up the Red River), where he remained as commandant for two years. During this time he submitted a memoir to the Compagnie des Indes recommending the construction of a post in the Yazoo country (Yazoo River area, Miss.) to put an end to the trade which the English from Carolina were carrying on in that area. The company considered his suggestion, but took no immediate action. In 1718, with a compass as his only guide, Dutisné passed through Alibamu country on foot on his way northward to Quebec, wintered there, and returned with his family to the Illinois country.

In 1719 he was commissioned captain, and was sent by Jean-Baptiste Le Moyne* de Bienville to establish contact with the Missouri Indians. He travelled from the Illinois country along the Missouri River to the site of present-day Kansas City, where the Missouris greeted him in friendly fashion but refused to let him advance farther. This action forced Dutisné to return down the Missouri to the mouth of the Osage River, which he followed to the land of the Osage Indians. Again he was well received, but every effort was made to discourage him from penetrating any farther. Nevertheless, he crossed the Arkansas River and travelled 40 leagues in four days to the villages of the Pawnees (Panis). His reception there was hostile, for the Osages had sent word that Dutisné had come to take slaves. The Pawnees twice tested his bravery by holding a hatchet over his head and on both occasions he dared them to strike. Although favourably impressed by Dutisné's display of courage, the Pawnees refused to let him proceed farther west where their mortal enemies, the Padoucas (Comanches), lived. Dutisné was therefore obliged to return to the Illinois country.

The significance of Dutisné's travels cannot be denied. He established relations with three tribes in territory previously unexplored, discovered silver deposits in the Osage country, and ascertained that the Spaniards had visited the Pawnees on more than one occasion but had since found the route to their settlements barred by the Padoucas. Moreover, his experiences at each village had shown that there existed a demand for French trade goods.

In 1720 the infantry companies of Dutisné and Pierre d'Artaguiette were stationed at the newly founded Fort de Chartres six leagues north of Kaskaskia (Ill.). Their first two years at this post were tranquil ones, but in 1722 the Illinois at Pimitoui and Le Rocher (Starved Rock) were attacked by the Foxes, and Boisbriand, commandant of the region, appealed to Dutisné and d'Artaguiette for assistance. These three men led a party of 100 to the defence of their allies, but the Foxes retreated before their arrival. Subsequently stability returned to the area, and Dutisné was able to depart for New Orleans.

On 21 Oct. 1723 Dutisné was appointed to replace Boisbriand as commandant among the Illinois, and he took up residence at Fort de Chartres. Confusion and fear reigned throughout the Illinois country during his command, for the Foxes had resumed their harassment of the French allies. Although a temporary peace had been negotiated by Constant Le Marchand de Lignery, Dutisné was far from satisfied, for it protected only the lake tribes and did not improve the situation to the south, where the French were under constant threat of attack. In 1725 he asked to be removed from Fort de Chartres because of illness, and was appointed commandant of Fort Rosalie. After resuming command of Fort de Chartres in 1729, he was shot in the cheek by a Fox Indian, and died the following year from the effects of this wound.

Dutisné's first wife bore him three sons, Louis-Marie-Charles, Charles, and Louis-Marie-Joseph. The eldest son, Louis-Marie-Charles, served in the Illinois country for several years. He led a convoy from the Missouris to Fort de Chartres in 1725 and, although there is no record of his activities during the next few years, one may assume that he continued to work among the Indians of the region, for he was chosen to accompany Pierre Groston de Saint-Ange to the country of the Missouris in 1734. In March of 1736 he participated in Pierre d'Artaguiette's campaign against the Chickasaws, which cost the lives of several young officers. Louis-Marie-Charles Dutisné and François-Marie Bissot de Vinsenne were among the casualties.

Some of his contemporaries questioned his morals, but it cannot be gainsaid that Claude-Charles Dutisné devoted the last 16 years of his life to active service in the interests of Louisiana. He was a true pioneer, travelling through at least 15, and perhaps as many as 25, of the present United States. He was a man whose life was determined by his desire for adventure.

C. J. Russ

AN, Col., C¹¹A, 22, p.253; 31, p.232 (copies in PAC); C¹³A, 3, f.853; 4, ff.82, 318, 605, 1019; 7, f.136; 12, ff.178, 293; 21, f.22; D²C, 222/1, p.273 (copy in PAC). AJQ, Greffe de Louis Chambalon, 24 avril 1708; Greffe de François Genaple, 4 févr. 1708. Charlevoix, *History* (Shea), VI, 28–32, 71, 120–22. "Correspondance de Vaudreuil," APQ *Rapport*, 1947–48, 271, 283. *Découvertes et établissements des Français* (Margry), V, 512–44, 564, 615; VI, 309–15. P.-G. Roy, *Inv. concessions*, I, 272–73; *Inv. ord. int.*, I, 90–91. Wis. State Hist. Soc. *Coll.*, III, 155; XVI. Le Jeune, *Dictionnaire*, II, 720. Tanguay, *Dictionnaire*, III, 582.

Alvord, *Illinois country*, I, 157n, 175, 178. Giraud, *Histoire de la Louisiane française*, III, 373–74, 380–81. Pierre Heinrich, *La Louisiane sous la Compagnie des Indes, 1717–1731* (Paris, [1908]), 112–15, 182–83. Émile Lauvrière, *Histoire de la Louisiane française, 1673–1939* (Louisiana, 1940), 156, 172, 184–87, 292–95, 302, 305, 381. C. L. Vogel, *The Capuchins in French Louisiana (1722–1766)* (Washington, 1928), 106–8.

DUVIVIER, FRANÇOIS DU PONT. *See* Du Pont

DU VUAULT DE VALRENNES, PHILIPPE CLÉMENT. *See* Clément

E

EDEWANCHO. *See* Atecouando

ÉLIE, JACQUES, fifth official executioner in Canada; b. *c.* 1682 in the village of Parcoul, in the province of Saintonge; d. 23 May 1710 on the shores of the Duchesne River, in the seigneury of Deschaillons.

Élie arrived in New France when quite young and lived first in Acadia, where he was condemned to death at Port-Royal. As there was no executioner in Acadia, he was sent to Quebec to be hanged. In November 1705 he was in the prison of the Conciergerie when, Canada having been without an executioner for two years, the Conseil Souverain asked him to fill the office of hangman. He accepted, on condition that his life be spared.

Jacques Élie was a rogue of the worst sort, and as soon as he was released he started stealing again and continued to do so despite frequent stays in prison.

On 7 Oct. 1707 he married Marie-Joseph Maréchal at Quebec. She bore him two sons. Provoked beyond measure by the insults which the inhabitants of Quebec heaped upon them, the Élies decided to flee to New England. They entrusted their fate to the Pawnee Indian Nicolas, who undertook to serve as their guide. But after one day's travelling, during the night of 23 May 1710 while Jacques Élie, his wife, and two children were sleeping, the Pawnee murdered them, robbed them, and fled. The hangman Élie and his family were buried on the site of the crime.

ANDRÉ LACHANCE

AHDQ, Registres des malades, 1709–12. AJQ, Registre d'état civil de Notre-Dame de Québec. AQ, NF, Coll. de pièces jud. et not., 377, 447; NF, Dossiers du Cons. sup., Mat. crim., III, 193ff. *Jug. et délib.*, V, 192. André Lachance, *Le bourreau au Canada sous le régime français* (SHQ Cahiers d'histoire, XVIII, 1966), 67–72. Marcel Trudel, *L'esclavage au Canada français; histoire et conditions de l'esclavage* (Québec, 1960), 225.

ÉNAULT (Esnault, Hénaut) DE BARBAU-CANNES (Barbocant), PHILIPPE, physician and prominent early settler in Acadia; b. at Saumur, France, in 1651; d. after 1708.

About 1676 Énault was hired as an employee of Nicolas Denys* at Nipisiguit (Bathurst, N.B.) where Richard Denys* de Fronsac was in charge. Here he practised medicine and appears to have been used by Denys as a supervisor in both fishing and farming activities. Soon after his arrival he built a house on the southern shore of the Nipisiguit river at its mouth.

Recruiting employees of his own, Énault engaged in fishing on a large scale and also developed a trade in furs with the Micmac Indians living in the area. He did not neglect his land, however; we know that he had some cattle, and Father Chrestien Le Clercq* tells us that he farmed "with success and [harvested] wheat beyond what [was] necessary for the support of his family." To grind his wheat he built a grist mill operated by water power. Le Clercq, an early missionary in the region, speaks well of Énault, of his successful colonizing, and of the support Énault gave him in his missionary endeavours.

In 1689, Énault received a grant from the crown covering a league on either side of the mouth of the Nipisiguit river and measuring some two leagues in depth. With this he was given the freedom to trade with the Indians, to hunt, and to fish. Difficulties soon arose, however, for on 26 May 1690 Jean GOBIN, a Quebec merchant, was given a large seigneurial grant on the Nipisiguit which included Énault's grant. Gobin ceded the land to Richard Denys two days later. The latter evidently pressed for the removal of Énault from his land. On 29 Aug. 1691, after they had taken their case before the Conseil Souverain, Denys and Énault reached an agreement whereby the latter would retain his land and pay Denys 100 *sols* rent every

two years. Two years later, in August 1693, Énault received a seigneurial grant on the Pocmouche river, north of the Miramichi. The two grants on the Nipisiguit and the Pocmouche were confirmed by the Conseil Souverain in 1703 and 1705 respectively.

After Énault's death—he was still alive in 1708—his several children, by a Micmac woman whom he had married about 1679, abandoned the lands and went to live with the Indians. With time, Énault's property rights lapsed.

GEORGE MACBEATH

Le Clercq, *New relation of Gaspesia* (Ganong). *Jug. et délib.*, III, 553–55; IV, 835–37; V, 143–44. *Ord. comm.* (P.-G. Roy), II, 196–97. "Richard Denys, sieur de Fronsac, and his settlements in northern New Brunswick," Historical-geographical documents relating to New Brunswick, ed. W. F. Ganong, 4, N.B. Hist. Soc. *Coll.*, [III], no.7 (1907), 7–54. P.-G. Roy, *Inv. concessions*, IV, 40–46; *Inv. ins. Cons. souv.*, 80, 105. Ganong, "Historic sites in New Brunswick," 300–1, 304, 309.

ENJALRAN, JEAN, Jesuit priest, missionary; b. 10 Oct. 1639 at Rodez, France; d. 18 Feb. 1718 in the same city.

Jean Enjalran entered the Society of Jesus at Toulouse on 18 Sept. 1656. After completing the novitiate he taught at Cahors, Pamiers, and Aurillac. He did his ecclesiastical studies at Toulouse and Tournon. After his ordination he taught philosophy at Toulouse (1673–75) and was prefect of studies there during the academic year 1675–76.

Enjalran reached Quebec on 22 July 1676. Shortly after his arrival, on 13 October, he wrote a lengthy letter describing conditions in New France. After a year at Sillery studying the Algonkian tongue, the new recruit was assigned to the Ottawa mission with his headquarters at Saint-Ignace. Enjalran is said to have become an expert in the Ottawa language, thereby gaining great influence over those tribesmen, as well as the Hurons dwelling at the mission. With only four years of mission experience, Enjalran was appointed, in 1681, superior of the Ottawa mission, a position which he held until 1688.

In 1683 the French erected Fort Buade at Saint-Ignace and gave the command of the garrison to the very able Olivier MOREL de La Durantaye who continued in the office until 1690. Enjalran was most helpful to the commandant during Governor Le Febvre* de La Barre's unsuccessful campaign against the Iroquois, encouraging the Hurons and Ottawas to join the conflict under the command of La Durantaye. Three years later, in 1687, Enjalran played a major role in convincing the Ottawas and Hurons to join the French again, when Governor BRISAY de Denonville launched another attack against the Iroquois. In that campaign Enjalran was chaplain of the forces from the west and was himself wounded in battle, though not seriously.

The following year, 1688, Enjalran went to France. After 1688 Enjalran's name does not appear in the annual list of Jesuits attached to the mission of New France. He clearly did return, however, and was active in the controversy between Cadillac [LAUMET] and the Jesuits regarding the removal of the Ottawas and Hurons from Saint-Ignace to Fort Pontchartrain at Detroit.

After La Durantaye was replaced by LA PORTE de Louvigny as commandant of Fort Buade in 1690, the Jesuit missionaries constantly complained of the bad influence which the soldiers at the fort exercised on the Indians. Most of the missionaries contended that the Indians should not be put in contact with Europeans until they had had sufficient experience with Europeans to enter their sophisticated world. Further, the Jesuits contended that since they alone had been commissioned by the bishop of Quebec to effect the conversion of the Indians no other group of priests should be allowed to begin a mission field, or at least not start one near an already existing mission. When Cadillac obtained authority to open his post at Detroit, he proposed inviting the Recollets to act as post chaplains and to serve the French population which he hoped would grow up around the fort [see DELHALLE]. As for the Indians, Cadillac planned to invite the Jesuit missionaries from Saint-Ignace to transfer their mission effort, along with their neophytes, to the new post.

Father Enjalran did not share the opinion of his fellow Jesuits regarding mission policy. He believed that isolating the Indians was not feasible. In his view, the Indians should be taught to speak French, adopt French customs, and enter into the society of their French neighbours as quickly as possible. Further, Enjalran felt that Cadillac's establishment at Detroit was strategically important and should be encouraged by the presence of Jesuit missionaries. Since the difference of opinion between Enjalran and his fellow Jesuits was on a question of policy, the matter was referred to Father Claude Dablon*, superior of all the Jesuits in New France, who ruled in favour of Father Enjalran's opponents. Dablon withdrew Enjalran from missionary work.

Before his departure from Canada, Father Enjalran performed one final important service. In 1700 Governor CALLIÈRE despatched him with LE GARDEUR de Courtemanche to induce the Ottawas to attend the great peace parley held at Montreal during the summer of 1701. Enjalran was not only helpful in persuading the Indians to attend the meeting, but he was also able to convince the Ottawas to surrender two Iroquois prisoners, whom he brought back to Montreal. When the western tribes met with Callière Enjalran acted as the official interpreter for them.

Enjalran left Canada shortly after 27 Aug. 1702. He died 16 years later in his native town of Rodez.

JOSEPH P. DONNELLY, S.J.

Charlevoix, *History* (Shea), V, 150, 153. *Découvertes et établissements des Français* (Margry), V, 207, 211–12. *JR* (Thwaites), LX, 104–47; LXI, 103–47; LXIII, 175. *NYCD* (O'Callaghan and Fernow), IX. Rochemonteix, *Les Jésuites et la N.-F. au XVIIᵉ siècle*, III, 511–12.

ERIZY. *See* PERROT

ESCHAILLONS, PIERRE DE SAINT-OURS D'. *See* SAINT-OURS

ESCHAMBAULT. *See* FLEURY

ESGLY. *See* MARIAUCHAU

ESNAULT. *See* ÉNAULT

ESPIET DE PENSENS, JACQUES D', esquire, officer of the colonial regular troops in Acadia, Placentia (Plaisance), and Île Royale (Cape Breton Island), councillor of the Conseil Supérieur of Île Royale, king's lieutenant and commandant of Île Saint-Jean (Prince Edward Island), knight of the order of Saint-Louis; native of Aignan, diocese of Auch; d. 1737 in France.

Jacques de Pensens began his long career in North America at Placentia where he was named ensign on 1 May 1698. In 1705 he was promoted assistant town major and moved to Port-Royal (Annapolis Royal, N.S.). De Pensens remained in Acadia only a few years, but his later career shows that he was in the colony sufficiently long to win the Acadians' respect and affection. He returned to Placentia in the summer of 1708 and took part during the winter of 1708–9 in the expedition led by Saint-Ovide de Brouillan [Mombeton*] against the English fort at St John's (commanded by Thomas LLOYD). Charlevoix* records that de Pensens played a conspicuous role in the attack and was the first to enter the fort.

In 1713 the treaty of Utrecht ended the struggle between France and England but confirmed the English in possession of all Newfoundland and Acadia. The garrison and settlers of Placentia prepared to move to Cape Breton Island where a new colony was to be founded. De Pensens, who had been promoted lieutenant in 1712, was among those officers who signed the act whereby the French took possession of the island. It was hoped that the Acadians would also move to Île Royale. In the summer of 1714 de Pensens and Louis Denys* de La Ronde were sent to Acadia to try and persuade the Acadians to relocate. De Pensens promised that all who did so would be granted a year's rations. However, this help was not forthcoming; also the English put obstacles in the Acadians' way, and there was no mass emigration.

In 1715 de Pensens (who had been named a captain the preceding year) was made commandant at Port Toulouse (St Peters, N.S.), one of the three fortified areas on Île Royale. The financial commissary, Pierre-Auguste de SOUBRAS, emphasized to him the importance of trying to attract the Acadians to that area—one of the few regions suitable for agriculture. De Pensens spent the next ten years in garrison duty at either Louisbourg or Port Toulouse. He returned to France for a year's leave in 1718 and successfully forwarded his own career. While there he was granted the cross of the order of Saint-Louis, and the following year he and François-Marie Desgoutins* were named titular councillors on the Conseil Supérieur of Louisbourg with a salary of 300 *livres* per year. De Pensens held the post until 1733 when he was appointed king's lieutenant of Île Saint-Jean. He undertook two missions to Canso (Canseau) in these years: one in 1720 to investigate the difficulties between the English and French fishermen there [*see* SMART and HIRIBERRY], and the other in 1726 to meet with Lieutenant-Governor Lawrence ARMSTRONG.

The final stage in de Pensens' career began in 1725 when he was told to prepare to take possession of Île Saint-Jean the following spring in the name of the king. The islands of Saint-Jean, Miscou, and Magdelaine, and adjacent isles had been granted in 1719 to the Comte de Saint-Pierre; some attempt had been made by the company he formed to settle Île Saint-Jean at that time [*see* GOTTEVILLE]. By 1724, however, the company was bankrupt, and in 1725 the island was virtually deserted. Though the post constituted an independent command of an administrative unit it must have seemed to de Pensens a demotion; he was not to take his full company, but only a detachment of 25 or 30 men—a totally inadequate force for such a remote yet exposed area. Saint-Ovide, governor of Île Royale, urged that de Pensens be given the position of king's lieutenant and that at least one or two companies be assigned to him, but to no avail. De Pensens left for Île

Saint-Jean on 27 June 1726 with the ensign Alphonse Tonty and 26 men. It was not until 1733 that de Pensens finally received a commission as king's lieutenant for Île Saint-Jean, for a term of five years.

The administrative problems which the command entailed were many; settling the island was the most pressing. The Acadians did not immediately move to the island as had been hoped. De Pensens reported in 1726 that they feared falling under the control of a company. The exclusive fishing rights which had been granted to the Comte de Saint-Pierre had been revoked by the council of Marine in 1726, but not until 1730 were the islands reunited to the royal domain. There was no priest until 1727 when Father Félix Pain* was sent to be missionary there, and even then he was not resident all the year round. In 1728 the census listed only 336 persons on the island; in 1730 the figure was 325. In that year de Pensens reported that he had hired an Acadian who had a boat to transport goods and livestock from Baie Verte. There was some improvement in the next few years: the 1734 census listed 572 persons. In fact, the Acadians, always the chief source of population, did not move in numbers to the island until after the War of the Austrian Succession when thousands arrived. But before the war only a few areas of the island were settled: Port La Joie (near present-day Charlottetown), the administrative centre, Rivière du Nord-Est (Hillsborough River), Havre de la Pointe de l'Est (Tranchemontagne, now South Lake), Havre Saint-Pierre (St Peters Harbour), the most populous area, Capodiche (Savage Harbour), Tracadie, Malpeque, and Trois-Rivières, where Jean-Baptiste Roma*'s company was established (on Brudenell Point). Some fishing was done at Port La Joie and Pointe de l'Est, but the main fishing establishment was Havre Saint-Pierre. In 1726 there were 18 shallops and 1 schooner engaged in the cod-fishery on the island; in 1734, 39 shallops and 1 schooner. During these years there were always a few boats engaged in the coasting trade between Île Royale and Île Saint-Jean as well.

On his arrival de Pensens reported that there were so few improved lands as to be hardly worth mentioning. He wrote that in 1727 only seven colonists sowed any grain, but that the yield was promising. Port La Joie and the Rivière du Nord-Est were the places where most land was cultivated though some farming was done at Malpeque, Tracadie, and even Havre Saint-Pierre. The Micmacs had a permanent headquarters at Malpeque where they grew corn.

Discipline of the troops stationed on the island was a continual problem for de Pensens. Saint-

Estienne Du Bourgué

Ovide reported in 1735 that the soldiers there thought of themselves as "galley-slaves" and were convinced that they would spend the rest of their lives on the island. Desertions to Acadia were frequent—as were desertions to the French colonies from the English garrison in Acadia. De Pensens himself does not seem to have been too fond of living on the island; he was reprimanded several times for spending the winter at Louisbourg.

De Pensens' career was cut short by sickness. He first complained of poor health in 1719 and by the 1730s he was unable to continue working. He was ill in the fall of 1735, and in 1736 Robert Du Haget commanded in his absence. In 1736 de Pensens returned to France on leave—without much expectation of ever returning. Saint-Ovide wrote in November, "it seems to me that this officer is in no condition at all to be able to continue his service, since he cannot withstand the harsh climate of this country. . . ." De Pensens retired on 1 April 1737 with a pension of 800 *livres* and died a few months later. Louis Du Pont* Duchambon succeeded to his command.

De Pensens was involved in numerous commercial enterprises. At various times he owned several pieces of property in Île Royale. In 1720 he sold a small lot and house in Louisbourg for 600 *livres*, and in 1736 he sold another lot, house, and stone storehouse for 11,000 *livres*. He also developed a fishing establishment on Îles Michaux but was forced to sell it in 1718, when officers were forbidden to engage in fishing. He was part owner of the schooner *Vénus*, which was leased to a Saint-Jean-de-Luz merchant in 1726 for 4,000 *livres* to be paid in wine, liquor, and other goods.

Suspicion of illicit dealing also fell on de Pensens. He was mentioned in accusations brought against Saint-Ovide in 1728. The latter was charged with trading illegally, and de Pensens was said to have looked after the business which was all done in the names of two Louisbourg merchants, Joseph Lartigue* and Michel Daccarette. Nothing came of these charges, however. De Pensens was implicated in a dubious transaction for the contract for the Louisbourg fortifications along with François Ganet* and Gratien d'Arrigrand. Evidently this association became known when de Pensens' will was read. Saint-Ovide was thought to have been involved as well, which he denied. Nevertheless the affair contributed to his loss of the governorship.

De Pensens had three nephews in the colonial regular troops in Île Royale whose careers he fostered: Jean-Georges d'Espiet, Pierre-Paul d'Espiet de La Plagne, seigneur of Margouet, and Jean d'Espiet, chevalier de Pensens. All three became captains in the troops and were granted crosses of the order of Saint-Louis.

De Pensens seems to have been a fairly good though unambitious officer. He was not particularly interested in the details of administering a small and widespread population; he seems to have spent as little time as possible on the island. He was, however, always well informed of the conditions there and was instrumental in establishing the settlements on a firm basis. He supported the Acadians in their quest for land concessions and for aid from the crown in their first year on the island. He and Robert Potier* Dubuisson, the subdelegate of the intendant for the island, worked in harmony. De Pensens was, in short, a man of his times—a good and brave soldier, interested in furthering his family and in improving his financial condition, casually conscientious in discharging his responsibilities, and paternal in his attitude towards those he commanded.

MARY McD. MAUDE

Archives de la Charente-Maritime (La Rochelle), Amirauté de Louisbourg, B 266, ff.77–78v. AN, Col., B, 20–67; C¹¹ᴮ, 1–29; C¹¹ᶜ, 8, 9; C¹¹ᴰ, 5–7; Section Outre-Mer, G¹, 406, ff.7v, 25v; 466/3; 467/2; G², 192/1, pp.7–7v, 20v–21; G³, 2039, 12 sept. 1736; 2041, 27 sept. 1750; 2056, 13 nov. 1717; 2057, 1720, pièce 1, 24 févr. 1720; 2058, 3 déc. 1726. Charlevoix, *History* (Shea). Taillemite, *Inventaire analytique, série B.* Fauteux, *Les chevaliers de Saint-Louis.* Harvey, *French régime in P.E.I.* Le Blant, *Philippe de Pastour de Costebelle.* McLennan, *Louisbourg.*

ESTIENNE DU BOURGUÉ DE CLÉRIN, DENIS D', cavalry sergeant, lieutenant, assistant town major; b. *c.* 1660 at Aix-en-Provence, son of Denis d'Estienne Du Bourgué, king's counsellor in the *parlement* of Provence, and of Françoise Desvoges de Clérin; buried 24 Feb. 1719 at Montreal.

A second lieutenant in the Régiment de Vendôme in 1672, the Sieur de Clérin had served in 1680 as a sergeant in the Queen's Dragoons and a cornet in the same regiment in 1682. According to CALLIÈRE he is supposed to have arrived in Canada in 1685 as a half-pay ensign. In 1687 he was appointed an ensign on the active list. In 1688 Clérin was at Fort Niagara, and the following year at Montreal, where he was promoted second lieutenant with the position of assistant town major. He kept this office until his death, and was appointed a half-pay lieutenant in 1691 and in 1695 was placed on the active list. In 1700, learning that illicit trafficking in furs was being conducted by the Sieur de Louvigny [LA PORTE], the commandant of Fort Frontenac, Callière sent Clérin and JOANNÈS de Chacornacle to straighten out the situation on the spot. After this mission, which was carried out successfully, the governor in his report dated 15 Oct. 1701 noted concerning Clérin: "A good officer who discharges his duty well." In 1706 Clérin became the Recollets' syndic in Montreal.

On 24 April 1691 he had married Jeanne Le Selle, daughter of Barbe Poisson and Gabriel Celles Duclos, in Montreal. Six children were born of this marriage. Clérin died leaving his wife in poor circumstances: on 26 June 1720 Vaudreuil granted her a fur-trading licence.

JEAN-JACQUES LEFEBVRE

ANDM, Registres des baptêmes, mariages et sépultures. *Jug. et délib.*, V, 715f. A. Roy, *Inv. greffes not.*, IV, 499f.; V, 130, 139. *Royal Fort Frontenac* (Preston and Lamontagne). É.-Z. Massicotte, "Congés et permis déposés ou enregistrés à Montréal sous le régime français," APQ *Rapport, 1921–22*, 193. Tanguay, *Dictionnaire*, I, 193. Aegidius Fauteux, "Le sieur de Clérin," *BRH*, XXXIII (1927), 255f. Placide Gaudet, "Réponses," *BRH*, XXIII (1917), 64. É.-Z. Massicotte, "M. D'Estienne du Bourgué de Clérin, aide-major de Montréal," *BRH*, XXII (1916), 319f.; "Où et quand mourut M. de Clérin," *BRH*, XXXVI (1930), 729f. Régis Roy, "D'Estienne du Bourget," *BRH*, XXXII (1926), 689f.

F

FALAISE (Falaize), LOUIS DE GANNES DE. *See* GANNES

FÉZERET, RENÉ, gunsmith; b. *c.* 1642, son of Claude Fézeret, master locksmith, and of Suzanne Guillebaut, of the parish of Saint-Sauveur in La Rochelle; d. 31 July 1720 at Montreal.

On the strength of some entries in account-books of the parish council, Fézeret is considered to have been the first goldsmith in Montreal, but his activity in this field was limited to minor repairs. On the other hand, he often called himself the first gunsmith in New France, meaning no doubt the first in time. This assertion is perhaps true, for his father, who had come to Quebec sometime between 1643 and 1647, returned to France before 1652, and came back to Montreal with the contingent of 1659. It was probably during this stay in France that Fézeret learned his gunsmith's trade.

Fézeret affords an intriguing example of someone who rose in society. To be a tradesman, then a member of the bourgeoisie, and finally a seigneur whose daughter married into the nobility of the long robe (she married François-Gabriel de Thiersant), required adroitness, tact, and perseverance; Fézeret lacked none of these qualities. He was, moreover, greatly helped by his wife, Marie Carlié, whom he married in Montreal on 11 Nov. 1670; a stubbornly litigious person she kept the jurisdiction of Montreal and the Conseil Souverain busy.

In his early years Fézeret was content to practise his trade. Then he began to acquire pieces of land in all sorts of places, even as far away as Louisiana. Finally he obtained the fiefs of Saint-Charles and Bonsecours on the Yamaska River. He eagerly took to fur-trading, and in 1703 he also formed a

company "to continue the search for . . . a silver mine . . . on the Rivière du Lièvre." He was at first successful in business, but then suffered such reverses that in 1705 the list of his creditors was posted in the three governments of the country.

His wife died in 1717, and seven months later Fézeret married Marie Philippe, the 45-year-old widow of Jean Legras, a former Montreal merchant. Of the eight children of his first marriage only the youngest, Marie-Joseph, who had been baptized 17 Feb. 1692 under the name of Marie-Rose, survived him. His three sons were "killed and maimed in the king's service," in Louisiana. The eldest of his grandsons, François-Henri de Thiersant, married the daughter of a member of the Académie française; the youngest, Pierre-François, became a priest.

JULES BAZIN

AJM, Greffe d'Antoine Adhémar; Greffe de Bénigne Basset; Greffe d'Hilaire Bourgine; Greffe de Jacques David; Greffe de Michel Lepailleur de Laferté; Greffe de Claude Maugue; Greffe de Pierre Raimbault. AJQ, Greffe de Louis Chambalon, 25 oct. 1703. ANDM, Registres des baptêmes, mariages et sépultures. *Jug. et délib.*, I, III, IV.

Fauteux, *Essai sur l'industrie sous le régime français*, I, 26. Ovide Lapalice, *Histoire de la seigneurie Massue et de la paroisse de Saint-Aimé* (s.l., 1930). Télesphore Saint-Pierre, *Histoire des Canadiens du Michigan et du comté d'Essex, Ontario* (Montréal, 1895), 68. Ramsay Traquair, *The old silver of Quebec* (Toronto, 1940), 27. É.-Z. Massicotte, "Les actes de foi et hommage conservés à Montréal," *BRH*, XXVI (1920), 94; "La Saint-Eloi et la corporation des armuriers à Montréal, au XVIIᵉ siècle," *BRH*, XXIII (1917), 343–46.

FILIASTRE, LUC, priest, Recollet, provincial commissioner; b. 1646 at Rouen; d. 15 Sept. 1721 at Quebec.

Filiastre

He joined the Recollets of the ecclesiastical province of Saint-Denis in 1668, received the tonsure and the minor orders in his native town on 19 Sept. 1670, the subdiaconate on 2 Feb. 1671, and was admitted into the priesthood the following year.

Father Luc Filiastre arrived in Canada in September 1677, together with the provincial commissioner, Father Valentin LEROUX, and two other Recollets. Immediately upon arrival he devoted himself to parish work. We find him at Charlesbourg in July 1678, at Saint-François-du-Lac on 25 July 1680, and on the Saint-Michel river on 28 Jan. 1681. At the time the minutes of the taking-over of the land of the seneschalsy by the Recollets were signed in Quebec on 12 Nov. 1681, he styled himself "director of the Third Order." During the summer of 1682, having assumed the office of chaplain to the governor-general, he went to Montreal to meet the Indians who had come down to trade their pelts. With François DOLLIER de Casson, the superior of the Sulpicians, he was present at the audience given by Frontenac [Buade*] to the representative from the five Iroquois tribes, and countersigned the report on it.

By a capitular act dated 13 June 1683, the Recollets of Notre-Dame-des-Anges named Fathers Luc Filiastre and Joseph DENYS as their delegates to the new governor, M. de La Barre [Le Febvre*], who was at the time absent from Quebec; they were "to inform him of our peaceable and obedient conduct, until such time as it shall please His Majesty to permit us to enjoy without let or hindrance the gift which in his goodness he has conferred upon us," in other words the grant of the land of the seneschalsy. This step was decided upon following the bishop's injunction ordering the Recollets to pull down the bell-turret of their hospice at Quebec [see HENRI LE ROY].

After this delicate mission, Father Filiastre went to France in the autumn of 1683. In Paris, he preached the Advent sermons of 1687 and the Lenten sermons of 1688 in the parish of La Villette. In 1689 he sailed for Canada with Frontenac, who was returning to New France; the *Ambuscade* and the *Fourgon* reached Chedabouctou (Guysborough, N.S.) on 12 September, and Father Filiastre was at Quebec a month later. Filiastre combined the posts of provincial commissioner and guardian of the convent of Notre-Dame-des-Anges at Quebec: since 1670 the same person had held these two offices simultaneously.

There were various noteworthy events in the administration of the new commissioner, who had to concern himself with all the Recollet missions in New France. In Newfoundland the French settlement at Placentia (Plaisance), which had been served by his community for only nine months, was pillaged in February 1690 by English privateers. In August of that year, at Percé, another post entrusted to the Recollets, pirates from New England burned down the church, the missionaries' residence, and the surrounding houses. Less than two months later, an English squadron commanded by Phips* laid siege to Quebec.

To these anxieties was added the unwilling cession of Filiastre's convent to Bishop Saint-Vallier [LA CROIX]. The latter had just founded the Hôpital Général at Quebec, provisionally set up in a house belonging to the nuns of Marguerite Bourgeoys*, and was looking for a larger building and piece of land; he resolved to take over the convent of the Recollets at Quebec. He proposed that they sell him Notre-Dame-des-Anges, in return for permission to replace their hospice by a regular convent and for payment to them of a "sum of 8,000 *livres* in currency of this country." The council of definitors of the royal convent at Versailles gave its agreement to this transaction. Father Filiastre and his fellow religious accepted this offer, albeit with regret, for fear of alienating the prelate's goodwill. On 13 Sept. 1692 Father Hyacinthe Perrault*, the new provincial commissioner, signed the contract for the sale. In a letter of 10 Oct. 1692 addressed to the provincial and the definitors of the province of Saint-Denis, Frontenac was to emphasize this fear clearly: "I was perhaps more reluctant than any of the Fathers of your order to see you lose a convent to the building and embellishment of which I had made a modest contribution, but on the other hand, seeing that it was impossible to ensure that the bishop's heart would remain well disposed towards you if the exchange that he proposed were refused, and considering that this was the sole means of obtaining lasting peace for you, I was of the opinion that I must pay no further heed to the pride that I might have in my handiwork, and that you should likewise on your side close your eyes to your temporal concerns in order to think solely of everyone's edification and convenience . . . we have tried to get from the bishop not the full amount that your convent was worth, but at least all that the scanty resources that he has for completing a work as great as the one he is beginning allowed him to give you."

Delighted with the successful result of his approach to the king and the provincial of Saint-Denis, Bishop Saint-Vallier, then in France, had authorized the establishment of the Recollets at Montreal and Trois-Rivières; he had himself requested the letters patent for these foundations, which were delivered in March 1692. It was Father

Fleury Deschambault

Joseph Denys who founded the convent at Montreal, and the founding of the convent at Trois-Rivières was entrusted to Father Luc Filiastre. To Father Filiastre's position as superior of the new convent was soon added that of priest of the parish, in the place of Abel Maudoux*, whom the bishop sent to Port-Royal (Annapolis Royal, N.S.). The new parish priest entered his first act on 10 Nov. 1693, and the last of his triennium on 21 Sept. 1696. After this he became "director of the Ursuline Ladies," who had been established at Trois-Rivières since 1697. Starting in November 1700, in place of Father Samuel Entheaume, Father Filiastre was appointed parish priest a second time in Trois-Rivières.

A few years later, Filiastre settled a delicate matter during the absence of the superior of the convent at Quebec, Father Apollinaire Luteau. In the course of the year 1706, RIGAUD de Vaudreuil and JACQUES RAUDOT imposed a public corvée; Louis LA PORTE de Louvigny wanted to make the Recollets of Quebec take part in the digging for the fortifications of the town. Father Filiastre considered it his duty to protest on the grounds that his convent was exceedingly poor. In point of fact, in a memorandum of 14 June 1704 addressed to the governor and the intendant, the king deemed it proper that "those of the secular clergy who have dwellings outside the presbytery, and the communities which have large estates, should contribute to public corvées." The Recollets had no such possessions, and were therefore exempt from the corvées. Louvigny persisted and called Father Filiastre a rebel against the king's orders. Filiastre, a peace-loving person, agreed to have his community take some part in the public corvée. Louvigny himself stated this in a letter to the minister dated 21 Oct. 1706.

After 28 years of toil, prematurely aged by the heavy responsibilities he had taken on, Father Filiastre retired to the calm of the cloister, occasionally exercising his ministry in the pulpit and the confessional of the convent church in Quebec. In 1719, he celebrated at Quebec his fiftieth anniversary in holy orders. He died two years later.

JACQUES VALOIS

AAQ, Registres d'insinuation A, 282. AJQ, Greffe de François Genaple, 19 juin 1683, 11 oct. 1705. AJTR, Greffe de J.-B. Pottier. AN, Col., C¹¹ᴬ, 6, ff.33, 36. Archives de Saint-Sulpice, Paris, Correspondance, XIV, f.157. Archives de la Seine-Maritime (Rouen), G.9747, ff.12, 13, 30 (clergé séculier). Caron, "Inventaire de documents," APQ Rapport, 1940–41, 391f. "Correspondance de Vaudreuil," APQ Rapport, 1938–39, 55, 151. Le Tac, Histoire chronologique de la N.-F. (Réveillaud), 199. Sulte, Hist. des Can. fr., V, 53.

FLEURY DESCHAMBAULT (d'Eschambault), JACQUES-ALEXIS, bailiff, king's attorney then royal judge at Montreal, founder of the seigneury and village of Deschambault; b. c. 1642, son of Jacques Fleury and Perrine Gabar; buried 31 March 1715 at Montreal. He descended from a noble family, and came originally from the parish of Saint-Jean de Montaigu in the lower part of the province of Poitou.

He came to Quebec at the beginning of 1671; he was then a "doctor of laws and lawyer in the parlement." On 19 Nov. 1671, barely six months after his arrival, he married Marguerite de Chavigny, the widow of Thomas Douaire de Bondy and the mother of four children. His mother-in-law, Éléonore de Grandmaison*, widow of François de Chavigny, owned a fief on the banks of the St Lawrence, near Portneuf; it was one league wide by three leagues deep, and little cultivation had so far been done on it. She first granted her son-in-law, on 22 April 1674, a piece of land with a frontage of 10 arpents. Jacques-Alexis went to settle on it with his family, and the 1681 census lists him as having already 20 acres of land under cultivation and 16 head of cattle. Two years later, in 1683, Éléonore de Grandmaison made over the whole seigneury to him, in exchange for a piece of land on the Île d'Orléans. Deschambault was still the only settler on this seigneury. He undertook to develop it, with the help of his children. The following year the new seigneur took part in the expedition of La Barre [Le Febvre*] against the Senecas. He served on that occasion as assistant adjutant in the Quebec battalion. A census taken in 1688 shows that he was energetically developing his land: he had 3 domestics, 39 acres under cultivation, 37 in pasture, and 34 head of cattle. Four families of settlers were established there and three others were in the process of becoming so. Deschambault was living on the yield from the land and from fishing, and he had had a manor-house and a mill built. In addition, the seigneury bore his name.

A considerable change took place in his life in 1690, allowing him to abandon his existence as a country seigneur and to return to the town and resume his legal studies. The Sulpicians, the seigneurs of Montreal, held the right to administer justice on the island; their bailiff, Migeon* de Branssat, had just resigned because of his advanced age and his manifold activities. The Sulpicians thought of the former lawyer Deschambault as his replacement. But Deschambault had difficulty in getting accepted. Migeon was against him, and the Conseil Souverain, which was anxious to abolish seigneurial justice, caused delays, so that the new judge, who was appointed by Abbé DOLLIER de

Fonblanche

Casson in August 1690, was not able to take up his office until the 21 November following. On that occasion he delivered a formal address, the text of which has been preserved. In one of his first cases, he incurred the displeasure of the council, which reprimanded him and annulled his decision.

As the population on and around Montreal Island was growing, the king, in agreement with the Sulpicians, established royal justice in the region by an edict dated 15 March 1693. The Conseil Souverain named CHARLES JUCHEREAU de Saint-Denys the first lieutenant general for civil and criminal affairs; at the same time Deschambault became king's attorney, which meant a reduction in his responsibilities. He accepted this tolerably well, however, and was on close terms with his colleague. In 1696 he had to cease exercising his office temporarily, in order to accompany Frontenac [Buade*] on his expedition against the Iroquois; he was then commanding the Montreal militia forces. In 1698, for several months, he served as judge in place of Juchereau, who made a journey to France. He replaced him again in 1701, for a longer period, when Juchereau, who was possessed by a desire for adventure, obtained a three-year leave and set off for the Mississippi country. When news of this adventurous magistrate's death reached Montreal, two candidates sought his post: Deschambault and Migeon de La Gauchetière, the former judge's son. In 1706, on the advice of Intendant RAUDOT, Deschambault was officially appointed lieutenant general for civil and criminal affairs for Montreal,

He was called upon to judge several difficult cases, and in one of them, having too readily given credence to the tittle-tattle of some female gossips, he suffered the bitter humiliation of being suspended for a month by the Conseil Souverain in order to "study the ordinances," and of being sentenced to pay the costs of the lawsuit. He also came into conflict several times with Governor Philippe de RIGAUD de Vaudreuil, who wished to protect his old friends in Montreal. Deschambault complained to the court at Versailles, and the governor inflicted harsh reprisals upon him, even going so far as to have the judges' pew in the church at Montreal suppressed. These vexations did not however harm his career, and he continued to serve as judge until an advanced age. He died in March 1715 at Montreal, having contributed to the administration of justice in various capacities for 25 years. One of his last legal acts was a curious police regulation by which he ordered the inhabitants of Montreal to keep up "the footways" (wooden sidewalks) before their houses, and forbad them to allow their pigs to run about the streets.

He had had seven children by his first marriage, to Marguerite de Chavigny. The eldest, Jacques* (1672–98), was a missionary in Acadia; the second, Charles (1674–1742), went to France and became a businessman and ship-owner at La Rochelle; Joseph* (1676–1755), Sieur de La Gorgendière, married Claire Jolliet, the explorer's daughter, and continued the Canadian line of the family; Charlotte (1683–1755) married François LE VERRIER, then Pierre de Rigaud* de Cavagnial, Marquis de Vaudreuil; Simon-Thomas, Sieur de La Janière, went to settle in Martinique.

After Marguerite de Chavigny's death in 1705, Deschambault married, on 9 July 1708, Marguerite-Renée Denys, widow of Thomas de Lanouguère* and daughter of PIERRE DENYS de La Ronde and Catherine Leneuf. He thus became, by the interplay of marriages, the father-in-law of Madeleine de Verchères [Jarret*]. He had no children by this second marriage, and his widow survived him.

RENÉ BAUDRY

AN, Col., B, 32. f.14v; 33, f.381; 34, ff.344, 358; 35, f.307; C¹¹ᴬ, 31, f.176; 33, ff.199, 201; C¹¹ᴳ, 2, f.118v; 3, ff.29ff.; 4, ff.203ff.; 5, ff.37ff. "L'expédition de M. de La Barre contre les Iroquois en 1684," *BRH*, XXXI (1925), 55. *Jug. et délib.*, II, VI. É.-Z. Massicotte, "Ordonnance inédite de M. de Fleury Deschambault, concernant les rues de Montréal, en 1715," *BRH*, XXII (1916), 81. "Recensement de la seigneurie d'Eschambault (1688)," *RHAF*, IX (1954–55), 439. Massicotte, "Les tribunaux et les officiers de justice," *RSCT*, 3d ser., X (1916), sect.I, 275, 284, 286.

[François Daniel], *Histoire des grandes familles françaises du Canada* (Montréal, 1867), 371–96. Aegidius Fauteux, "Réponse," *BRH*, XXXVIII (1932), 59. J.-J. Lefebvre, "La famille Fleury d'Eschambault de La Gorgendière," SGCF *Mémoires*, III (1948–49), 152–74. P.-G. Roy, "Jacques-Alexis de Fleury Deschambault," *BRH*, XXXVII (1931), 705–13.

FONBLANCHE, JEAN MARTINET DE. *See* MARTINET

FONDS (FOND), JEAN DE. *See* RODRIGUE

FONVILLE (GRANVILLE), CHARLES BÉCART DE. *See* BÉCART

FORANT, ISAAC-LOUIS DE, naval officer, knight of the order of Saint-Louis, third governor of Île Royale (Cape Breton Island); b. probably in the mid-1680s, at La Tremblade (department of Charente-Maritime), 25 miles southwest of Rochefort; d. unmarried on 10 May 1740, at Louisbourg. He was the grandson of Job de Forant (1612–92) who, following his conversion from Calvinism, rose to the rank of rear-admiral in the French navy in 1686.

Isaac-Louis de Forant entered the naval service as a midshipman at Rochefort on 19 Nov. 1703. On 1 Nov. 1705 he became sublieutenant in the navy, and on 12 Nov. 1712, lieutenant-commander. He was for several years the commander of the king's vessel *Héros*, which he sailed frequently to Louisbourg and Quebec in the 1720s and 1730s.

On 1 April 1739, Forant, a naval captain since October 1731, was named governor of Île Royale; François Bigot* was appointed financial commissary at the same time. Though Forant voiced his displeasure at so menial an appointment, when his colleagues were serving in the colonies as governors general, Maurepas, the minister of Marine, persuaded him to accept the appointment with good grace.

The authorities, in appointing Forant and Bigot to Île Royale, obviously counted on them to solve the serious problems and to end the disorders of scandalous proportions which were retarding the progress of the entire colony. In his instructions of 26 May 1739, Maurepas singled out the lax discipline of both the officers and troops. He urged that stringent measures be taken to curb absenteeism and excessive drinking. He also urged action be taken to end irregularities respecting guard duties, the distribution of food rations and merchandise from the stores, and the payment of wages and supplementary earnings to the troops, all of which served to perpetuate the problems of indiscipline and low morale.

After consultations with his predecessor, Joseph de Mombeton* de Saint-Ovide de Brouillan, Forant, with a domestic staff of four men and two women, sailed with Bigot from Île d'Aix aboard the *Jason* on 30 July 1739. He disembarked at Louisbourg on 10 September. His first official action was to inspect the assembled troops; in his first dispatch to the minister he candidly stated that they were the worst he had ever seen. Following the inspection, Forant gathered all the captains in his quarters at the Château Saint-Louis and read to them pertinent passages from the minister's observations of the previous May. In Forant's words, the officers "seemed extremely moved by the unfavourable opinions communicated to you about their behaviour," and seemed determined to show the minister that they were not so wholly to blame as his informants would have had him believe.

During the following two weeks, Forant rid the garrison of its most glaringly unsatisfactory elements. By discharging only the incapacitated and the obviously inept, retaining temporarily those who did not conform to official stipulations as to size, and with the recruits of 1739, he was able to keep the companies at 56 men each. Though he begged for 100 more recruits "[so that he could] continue the reforms and make the troops acceptable," only 60 men were sent in 1740. He obtained sheets and mattresses for the barracks, which were so infested with vermin that on summer nights soldiers preferred to take their blankets to the top of the ramparts and sleep in the open air. Forant also founded an artillery school to serve the needs of Louisbourg, which depended on the efficiency of its artillery.

The problem of liquor was equally pressing, but Forant and Bigot observed in a joint dispatch in November 1739 that the officers' canteens were considerably less obnoxious than the many cabarets of Louisbourg. Maurepas, in a letter of 7 May 1740, expressed his strong disapproval of any laxity in coming to grips with so obvious a cause of disorder. "It would seem," he wrote, "that you are determined to let them continue to exist. . . . I could not give my approval to the position you have taken on this question."

In the meantime, however, Forant became seriously ill in late April, and on 10 May 1740 he died of an inflammation of the lungs. Bigot, who wrote glowingly of his superior's qualities, had Forant interred beneath the Château Saint-Louis chapel. His remains, though not positively distinguished from those of a fellow officer, were discovered by archaeologists in 1964.

When he made his will Forant was obviously in the final agony, judging from his six laboured attempts to affix an adequate signature. After bequeathing to his colleague Bigot his eleven-volume set of Moreri's *Grand dictionnaire historique* and to the governor's residence his tapestries and paintings, which were numerous and of fine quality, he asked that something be given to his domestics and those who had assisted him in his illness. In a gesture which was unparalleled in Louisbourg's short history, he stipulated that the residue of his estate be used to provide eight bursaries for the education at the Louisbourg convent of the Congrégation de Notre-Dame of daughters of Île Royale officers. After some disagreement on the part of Forant's sister and only heir, Marguerite de Forant, to whom Bigot had sent her brother's furnishings, a compromise was reached in October 1741, whereby the sisters would dispose of 32,000 *livres* from the estate, while the residue was awarded to Mademoiselle de Forant. The following year, in June 1742, the fund was invested in France at 5 per cent per annum.

It would seem from the handful of contemporary

references that Isaac-Louis de Forant was held in the highest esteem by all. Though Maurepas' admiration of his devotion to duty and his talent might be conventional, François de Beauharnois*, who as intendant of Rochefort from 1710–11 to 1739 knew Forant well, wrote in 1739 of his and Bigot's "agreeableness and good attitude." Forant was eulogized both by his king's lieutenant, François Le Coutre* de Bourville, and by his friend Bigot. The anonymous *Habitant de Louisbourg* wrote in the 1740s: "By his humaneness and gentleness he deserved to be a leader of men. He was feared because he was loved."

Since Forant served as governor of Île Royale for only eight months, it is pure speculation to draw conclusions about what permanent value his reforms would have had, if he had lived. Conversely, notwithstanding both his failure to act vigorously on the problem of liquor at Louisbourg and the mutiny and siege which his immediate successors had to deal with, Forant's achievements were sufficiently positive that his brief administration should not be written off as of no lasting importance.

IN COLLABORATION

Archives Maritimes, Port de Rochefort, E, 364, 366, 368. AN, Col., B, 68, 69, 72; C^{11B}, 21, 22; D^{2C}, 222; Marine, C^1, 161; 4JJ, 7, 8; Section Outre-Mer, G^2, 185; G^3, 2046. *Louisbourg in 1745; the anonymous Lettre d'un habitant de Louisbourg (Cape Breton) containing a narrative by an eye-witness of the siege in 1745*, ed. George Wrong (Toronto, 1897). Le Jeune, *Dictionnaire*. Guy Frégault, *Bigot* (2v., Montréal, 1948), I. Lauvrière, *La tragédie d'un peuple*. McLennan, *Louisbourg*.

FORESTIER, ANTOINE, surgeon at the Hôtel-Dieu of Ville-Marie, medico-legal expert; b. 1646, son of Jean Forestier and Françoise Ricard, both from Sévérac-le-Château, in Rouergue; buried 7 Nov. 1717 at Montreal.

Antoine Forestier was considered, according to Ahern, "one of the most prominent doctors of Montreal." By a contract signed before the notary Claude Maugue*, he entered the service of the Hôtel-Dieu of Ville-Marie on 20 Aug. 1681, at the same time as the surgeon Jean MARTINET de Fonblanche. The agreement stipulated, among other things, that for three-month periods and at an annual salary of 75 *livres* each surgeon in turn was to tend the patients in the hospital. Throughout his long career—he died in his seventy-second year—Antoine Forestier, often in conjunction with Jean Martinet, acted as a medico-legal expert. Hence his signature is to be found at the end of several documents and certificates of various kinds.

In those far-off days, despite or perhaps because

of the fact that New France was sparsely populated, quarrels were numerous, and often were only settled finally before the Conseil Souverain. Consequently the medico-legal expert was frequently called in to conduct a physical and medical examination of the persons who complained of having been struck and beaten. The *Jugements et délibérations du Conseil souverain* report in particular a series of lawsuits resulting from charges laid by women against other women. One of the worst insults that could be levelled against a woman was to accuse her of bearing the marks of the lash and the fleur-de-lis. On many occasions, at the request of the court, Forestier had to carry out examinations to verify whether libel had occurred. His signature also appeared on a medico-legal appraisal—believed to be the first of its kind—following an accident involving a vehicle.

At that period surgeons were required to give free treatment to military officers; on 24 April1711 Forestier brought about the abolition of this practice by having the courts decree that except during their stay in hospital officers should pay fees as the other patients did.

On 25 Nov. 1670, at Montreal, Antoine Forestier had married Marie-Madeleine Le Cavelier, aged 14, the daughter of Robert Le Cavelier, *dit* Deslauriers, armourer, and Adrienne Duvivier, both of Montreal. They had 18 children, one of whom was Antoine-Bertrand Forestier*, who became in his turn "the leading surgeon of his time at Montreal."

CHARLES-MARIE BOISSONNAULT

AJM, Greffe de Bénigne Basset, 3 nov. 1670; Greffe de Claude Maugue, 20 août 1681. *Jug. et délib.*, III, 567f.; IV, 830, 893, 900. A. Roy, *Inv. greffes not.*, IX, 15, 30. É.-Z. Massicotte, "Les chirurgiens de Montréal au XVIIe siècle," *BRH*, XX (1914), 255; XXVII (1921), 42; "Les chirurgiens, médecins, etc., de Montréal sous le régime français," APQ *Rapport, 1922–23*, 135, 148, 149f. Abbott, *History of medicine*, 19f. Ahern, *Notes pour l'histoire de la médecine*, 226–30.

FOTHERBY, CHARLES, captain in the Royal Navy, commodore of the Newfoundland convoy, 1714; b. c. 1670–75; d. 1 Aug. 1720.

As captain of the 40-gun *Lark*, Fotherby sailed with Sir George Rooke on his expedition to the Mediterranean in 1704. There he served with notable success, particularly in the defence of Gibraltar, when both Rooke and Sir John LEAKE were absent with the main part of the fleet.

Fotherby was commodore of the Newfoundland convoy in 1714 and his report, like that of KEMPTHORNE for the following year, shows how far the regulations for the fishery were ignored at this time. He notes that few of the fishing ships in Newfoundland had a certificate of clearance from an English port, "wether by neglect or otherwaise I could not tell." The stipulation that a certain number of "green men" be included in the crew of each ship coming from England was probably being flouted, and, despite Fotherby's orders to the contrary, there was a steady migration of "land men" from Newfoundland to New England. French brandy was being smuggled through Placentia (Plaisance), and although Fotherby did not go there himself he was informed that most of the inhabitants of the French settlement had left. His report illustrates the general decline and uncertainty which characterized the colony and the fishery just after the treaty of Utrecht.

C. M. ROWE

PRO, *CSP, Col., 1714–15.* Charnock, *Biographia navalis,* III. Lounsbury, *British fishery at Nfld.*

FOUCAULT, NICOLAS, originally from Paris, member of the seminary of Quebec, parish priest, missionary; killed in 1702 by Indians of the Coroas tribe.

Nicolas Foucault was still only a seminarist when he landed at Quebec in June, 1688. Bishop Saint-Vallier [LA CROIX] conferred minor orders and the subdiaconate upon him on 22 August and 30 November of that year, and ordained him priest on 3 Dec. 1689.

After his ordination Abbé Foucault was sent to the parish of Batiscan, where he ministered to everyone's satisfaction, since Bishop Saint-Vallier appointed him titular parish priest on 23 Sept. 1693. In 1700 the seminary of Quebec chose him to go to work with Abbé Marc BERGIER among the Tamaroas. The choice of candidates must have been limited, because Abbé Henri-Jean Tremblay* wrote to the superior of the seminary to say that he did not understand how Foucault could have been sent to the Mississippi region: "His health is very bad," he wrote, "and I am afraid that he will not long survive in that country." The procurator acknowledged however that Nicolas Foucault had all the other qualities necessary for "working there successfully."

Abbé Foucault arrived at the mission to the Tamaroas on 28 April 1701. His stay was brief. At the request of Bergier or of Iberville [PIERRE LE MOYNE], he went to work among the Arkansas Indians. At the beginning of 1702 he left these barbarous Indians, who were indifferent to his teaching, and went with three companions to join Abbé DAVION. On the way the travellers, who were ill, stopped among the Coroas in order to hire the services of four Indians to paddle their canoe. Coveting Abbé Foucault's well-filled coffer, the four Coroas seized the opportunity to murder the travellers in their sleep. Davion, who had come to meet Foucault, found the bodies of the victims shortly afterwards.

NOËL BAILLARGEON

AAQ, Registres d'insinuation A, 235, 281. ASQ, Lettres, N, 121, 122; O, 28, 29; R, 50, 53, 60, 62; Paroisses diverses, 31; Polygraphie, IX, 24, 27. Giraud, *Histoire de la Louisiane française,* I.

FRANCHEVILLE, FRANÇOIS POULIN DE. *See* POULIN

FRANCHEVILLE, PIERRE, priest, secretary to Bishop LAVAL, parish priest; son of Marin Terrier de Repentigny et de Francheville, originally from the province of Normandy, and of Jeanne Jallot, from the province of Poitou; baptized 14 July 1649 at Trois-Rivières; d. at Longueuil and buried 7 Aug. 1713 at Montreal.

Bishop Laval was later to write of Francheville: "He was brought up at the seminary from the time he was quite small." A school in the presbytery, headed by Martin Boutet*, had indeed existed before the creation (in 1668) of the Petit Séminaire of Quebec. As early as 1666 Francheville, a student at the Jesuit college, publicly defended a thesis in philosophy, together with Louis Jolliet*, and the following year he took part, with Amador MARTIN, in a disputation "on the whole of philosophy with honours." Francheville received the tonsure 8 Oct. 1667. From 1670 he acted as secretary to Bishop Laval until the latter left for France in 1671. The bishop made his appointment as secretary official on his return in 1675. Francheville was ordained on 18 Sept. 1676. He was a member of the community of the seminary, and parts of the regulations ratified in 1683 are in his handwriting.

At the time of the proceedings brought against François Salignac* de La Mothe-Fénelon, Francheville was fined for having failed to obey two summonses by the Conseil Souverain in October 1674, arguing that holy canons forbade him to appear before a secular court on a criminal matter.

Francheville served as parish priest at Beauport (1678–81), Saint-Pierre, on Île d'Orléans (1681–1689), Rivière-Ouelle (1689–92), Cap-Saint-Ignace and Saint-Thomas (1692–98), and finally at Longueuil (1701–13). It was during his stay at Rivière-Ouelle that, armed with a musket, he led his parishioners in repelling an attempted landing by the troops led by Phips* in 1690.

HONORIUS PROVOST

AAQ, Registres d'insinuation A, 79, 102. ASQ,

Franquelin

Lettres, N, 97; Paroisses diverses, 51; Polygraphie, VII, 10; Séminaire, I, 25a; XCV, 23f. *JJ* (Laverdière et Casgrain), 345, 355. "Le procès de l'abbé de Fénelon devant le Conseil souverain de la Nouvelle-France en 1674," APQ *Rapport, 1921–22*, 129, 175, 182f. Jean Langevin, *Notes sur les archives de N.-D. de Beauport* (2v., Québec, 1860–63), I, 22, 24, 30, 118.

FRANQUELIN, JEAN-BAPTISTE-LOUIS, cartographer, king's hydrographer at Quebec; b. *c.* 1651 at Saint-Michel de Villebernin (Indre), came to Canada in 1671; d. in France after 1712.

Franquelin came to Canada to trade, and says that he was quite successful in his first three years. In fact, he seems to have made sufficient profits to keep himself for the following nine years—unless his host, Jean Juchereau* de La Ferté, was supporting him. In 1674, the governor, Buade* de Frontenac, persuaded him to give up trading in order to devote his time to mapmaking. Louis Jolliet* had returned to Quebec after his exploration of the Mississippi River, and had drawn a map of his route from memory. The governor wished to have a larger, more polished and complete map to send to Paris. So from 1674 to 1693, Franquelin drew maps to accompany the dispatches to France of the governors and intendants. Among these were the largest and most artistic maps made in Canada in the 17th century. It is likely that he learned this art as a boy, for cartography was being taught in the colleges of France at the time. Franquelin's career at Quebec suggests that when coming to Canada he brought with him his drafting instruments, paints, and brushes. Thus he was the only person in Quebec equipped to do a professional job. He won notice by colouring his maps and decorating the unexplored regions with trees, beaver and caribou.

By 1675, he had completed his "Map of the discovery of Sr. Jolliet." It showed the canoe route, with portages, from Montreal to the western end of Lake Superior, to the Mississippi, and on to the Gulf of Mexico. It was a large map, measuring 100 by 67 centimetres. Franquelin's earlier maps were signed *Joannes Ludovicus Franquelin pinxit*, which suggests that he had a classical education, and liked the old-world tradition. He was ten years at Quebec before adopting the colonial custom of signing his work in the vernacular.

In 1681, he showed courage and independence in producing a map of North America in four parts, each measuring 100 by 68 centimetres. Richelieu had decreed in 1634 that longitude was to be measured from Hierro (in the Canary Islands), but on this map Franquelin stated that he measured longitude eastward from the Azores. However, neither the governor nor the intendant of New France, nor the authorities in Paris considered that Franquelin was flouting French law in so doing. As he marked Cape Race (Newfoundland) at longitude 338° (measured eastward), it seems that by the "Azores" he meant Corvo, the most westerly of the northern chain of the Azores. Cape Race was reckoned 22° west of it. From mariners he had learned that the safe route from France to Canada was by way of the Azores. On passing Corvo, they would change course to 22° north of west, and after moving 22° of longitude west of Corvo, were generally in sight of Cape Race. Corvo was considered to be the most westerly land of the continent of Europe, and Cape Race the nearest point of North America to it.

In November 1683, governor Le Febvre* de La Barre sent his dispatches to Paris with the 22-year-old PIERRE LE MOYNE d'Iberville, and the maps illustrating them with their author, Franquelin, who travelled at his own expense. Cavelier* de La Salle, who went to France at the same time, got Franquelin's ear, and in Paris the following year, Franquelin signed his "Map of Louisiana or of the voyages of Sr. de la Salle and of the countries which he discovered between New France and the Gulf of Mexico in the years 1679, 80, 81 and 82." This map has been most extensively copied. The original measured 180 by 140 centimetres, but most copies are on a reduced scale. From La Rochelle, La Salle sailed in 1684 on his expedition to the Gulf of Mexico, while Franquelin made for Quebec.

In 1685, Le Febvre's recently arrived successor, BRISAY de Denonville, wrote to the minister of Marine of the need for a teacher of navigation at Quebec, since the subject had not been taught since the death of Boutet* de Saint-Martin in 1683. Denonville recommended either Franquelin or Louis Jolliet. Franquelin was chosen. The news of his appointment was brought to Quebec in 1686 by BOCHART de Champigny, who had come to replace de MEULLES as intendant. Franquelin did not want to accept the appointment, since teaching would make inroads on his time for mapmaking, and the salary of 400 *livres* a year was altogether too low. To rent a house large enough to accommodate all those seeking instruction in navigation would cost, he said, 300 *livres* a year. He did not mention a further embarrassment. He was no longer a bachelor, for on 4 Feb. 1683 he had married Élisabeth Chesné (or Chesnay), daughter of the notary Claude Auber*, recently widowed and the mother of eight children. Franquelin had discovered that ten people could not live as cheaply as one, especially when that one was not used to living cheaply. In spite of all these obstacles, he accepted the appointment on the orders of the governor, who held out hope of an increase in salary.

In 1686 he signed his name to a map adding the title "king's geographer," and the following year received his commission as "the king's hydrographer at Quebec," thereafter adding this title to his signature. But he was not content with his position. Denonville and Champigny thought up a possible solution to his difficulties, which would suit them as well. They were not at all satisfied with the engineer Villeneuve*, who was slow in drawing plans, so they wrote to the minister of Marine suggesting that Franquelin be given Villeneuve's salary (as well as his own) and turn over the teaching of navigation to the Jesuits. When, in 1688, no reply to their suggestion had been received from the minister, Franquelin made another voyage to France at his own expense to plead his cause. He brought with him a most beautiful map of all then-known North America, in answer to a request by the court for a map showing the boundary lines between New France and New England. With the map, he presented a petition in which he repeated his arguments for an increase in salary. He asked that he be given, in addition to his present salary, that of an engineer in Canada, for should he continue to teach and to turn out maps annually, he would have to employ a draughtsman. Louis XIV was sympathetic, and wrote to the governor and the intendant that he would be willing to approve the appointment of Franquelin as engineer, if Denonville so wished. Meanwhile, Villeneuve was to be sent to France, and in his absence his salary was to be given to Franquelin. The king sidestepped the question of Franquelin's permanently holding two jobs.

Franquelin returned to Quebec, and Villeneuve was given leave of absence. But in Quebec, in that summer of 1689, the news about Franquelin and Villeneuve was overshadowed by other news. The ships brought word that France was at war with England, the Netherlands, and Spain and that Denonville was to be replaced as governor of New France by Frontenac, who was coming with instructions to attack Albany by land and Manhattan by sea. When Frontenac arrived at Quebec in October, he found the colony in a state of fear, after the terrible massacre by the Iroquois at Lachine in August. Only the Iroquois were ready for war. Denonville and Villeneuve were counted as fortunate when they sailed from Quebec in November. In France, Denonville again urged that Franquelin be relieved of his task of teaching, since he was not interested in it and the Jesuits would do it better.

Franquelin was acting engineer from November 1689 until at least June 1691, when he drew the plans of the battery at Quebec. It was an exciting time. In October 1690, Sir William Phips* appeared before Quebec with his fleet, and blockaded and besieged the city for eight days. The erecting of emergency defences became Franquelin's duty, and Frontenac commended him for his efficiency.

In 1691, Frontenac had Franquelin draw maps of the coast of New England for an invasion from the sea, but the ship carrying the maps was lost on its way to France. In 1692 (after Villeneuve had returned to Quebec), Frontenac sent Franquelin on the *Envieux* to scout the coast of New England, and then to proceed to Paris to draw whatever maps were needed. With him he sent the adventurer Lamothe Cadillac [LAUMET], who knew the New England coast. The two arrived in France in November 1692, and the following year Franquelin completed a well-drawn map of the coast of New England, which showed "the way by land and by sea from Boston to Manhattan." The same year, he drew a map of the town, bay, and surroundings of Boston, "verified by the Sr. de la Motte [*alias* Cadillac]."

Franquelin and Cadillac had been in Paris only a month when Villeneuve appeared there unexpectedly, after quitting his job in Quebec. Events started to move rapidly for Franquelin. He lost little time in applying for Villeneuve's position, but on 1 March 1693 the king decreed that Franquelin was to stay in Paris that year to draw maps of New England, and he appointed LEVASSEUR de Neré, a friend of Frontenac, to be engineer at Quebec. Franquelin appealed to the king, stating that he could not support his family on the salary assigned to the royal hydrographer, and that he had been heavily in debt when he left Quebec. He suggested that if, in recognition of his years of unrewarded service, his family could be brought to France, he would settle it on some property which he owned in Touraine, and return to Canada alone. The king gave orders that Franquelin's wife, eight children, and two maids were to be given free transportation on the first of his majesty's ships leaving Quebec for France. On 4 November, Champigny reported that he had given orders for Franquelin's wife and family to be provided with all necessities for their return on the *Carossol*. By the end of the year, the last ship of the season from Quebec reached France and brought the news that the *Carossol*, when about 350 miles downstream from Quebec, had hit a reef and foundered. Only a few of the crew were saved. In a memoir to the minister of Marine, written while he was distraught, Franquelin pleaded for pity. He now found himself bereft of his wife and ten of 13 children and of the financial assistance which she was bringing to reimburse

Franquelin

those friends who were kind enough to advance him money during his stay in Paris. Mutual agreement was reached. Franquelin was offered free transportation to Quebec, and in April his name was on the passenger list of the *Charente*. In May the king informed Frontenac and Champigny that Franquelin, his hydrographer, was returning to Quebec. But in November, the governor and intendant seemed somewhat annoyed as they wrote from Quebec to the minister that Franquelin had not arrived, contrary to the king's dispatch. Why Franquelin did not return to Canada in 1694 is a matter for speculation. It is possible that he was retained in Paris at the request of the then near-almighty Le Prestre de Vauban. France was still at war, and dreamed of driving the English from North America. Franquelin could draw maps of strategic points in North America.

The fact is that Franquelin did not return to Canada in 1694, or the following two years. He remained in good standing with the king. In January 1697, he was working for Vauban, who was keeping him very busy. Louis Jolliet had been to Paris between December 1695 and March 1696 and had returned to Quebec with word that he was to succeed Franquelin as professor of hydrography at Quebec. His commission as king's hydrographer at Quebec was dated 30 April 1697. For this year we have a map of the Mississippi River signed and dated (at Paris): *J. B. Louis Franquelin, Hydr. & Geogr. du Roy, 1697.* The map professes to show the results of LE SUEUR's explorations of the Mississippi from the mouth of the Wisconsin River northwards. In 1695, Le Sueur had been as far north as Red Wing, Minn. In the winter of 1696-97, he was in Paris. Franquelin's next known map is signed and dated: *Jean Baptiste Louis Franquelin, Geographe du Roy, 1699.* It depicts, in four parts, New France, including the Mississippi Valley, and takes account of the discoveries of La Salle's last expedition, as recorded by Le Clercq*.

Louis Jolliet died in the year 1700, before the last ships of the year had left Quebec for France. On 18 May 1701, the king formally appointed Franquelin, as he himself had requested, professor of hydrography at Quebec. Yet Franquelin did not come to Canada in 1701, nor the following year. We do not know why. In 1703, Jean DES-HAYES was appointed to the post. After Deshayes died in December 1706, the governor and intendant asked that the Jesuits be invited to fill his place. In 1708, their request was granted, and the Jesuits remained responsible to the crown for the teaching of hydrography at Quebec until the end of the French régime.

In 1701, Franquelin had asked to be appointed hydrographer at Quebec but we have no evidence that he either asked for or was offered the position left vacant by the death of Deshayes. In 1708, he drew a little map of New France, admirably executed, and dedicated to Jérôme Phélypeaux, minister of the Marine and secretary of state, "by his most humble, most obedient and most faithful servant Franquelin." This dedication reminds us that Vauban (with whom Franquelin had been associated) fell from the king's favour in 1707 and died in disgrace that same year. Franquelin's small map, more beautiful than useful, could have been a token of loyalty offered to the king's minister. It may have been a parting gift.

When and where Franquelin died we do not know. We know that he was certified as living when his daughter Élisabeth signed a marriage contract with Joseph Lemieux in 1712, and that his daughter Marie-Anne reported him as deceased when she signed her marriage contract with Jacques Quesnel in 1730. In the year 1708 he was in Paris. Before he died he may have retired to Touraine. Never prominent among the constellations through which he passed, he fades from our sight. As a bachelor, he showed himself a retiring young man, an artistic dreamer wedded to map-making. His sudden awakening to the need for adequate recompense for his work followed his marriage. After the death of his wife he started, in Paris, to dream dreams. He would return to Canada, survey all the settled lands in New France, plot roads from Quebec to Albany, Boston, and Acadia, and search for a shorter overland route to Hudson Bay. He never evinced a desire to see his children at Quebec. His passage for Canada was booked, but he did not sail. It would seem that when he had to choose between travel and his studio, the lure of his paint-box and colours decided the issue.

M. W. BURKE-GAFFNEY

BN, MS, Clairambault 879, f.294, "Mémoire touchant les voyages que Franquelin hydrographe du roy en Canada a fait a Quebec et a Paris." Charlevoix, *History* (Shea), II. *Coll. de manuscrits relatifs à la N.-F.*, I, 346, 451, 471; II, 94, 117, 124, 155, 253. "Correspondance de Frontenac (1689–99)," APQ *Rapport, 1927–28*, 97, 144, 174, 208, *JR* (Thwaites). *Jug. et délib.*, III. Le Clercq, *Premier établissement de la foy*, II. Gabriel Marcel, *Reproductions de cartes et de globes relatifs à la découverte de l'Amerique du XVIe au XVIIIe siècle* (Paris, 1893), plates 6, 22, 40. PAC *Report, 1899*, Supp. *Recueil des cartes, plans et vues relatifs aux États-Unis et au Canada, New York, Boston, Montréal, Québec, Louisbourg (1651–1731)*, éd. A. L. Pinart (Paris, 1893), plates 3, 4, 10. A. Roy, *Inv. greffes not.*, IV, 190. P.-G. Roy, *Inventaire de pièces sur la côte de Labrador conservées aux Archives de la Province de Québec* (2v., Québec, 1940–42), I, 254–56. Tanguay, *Dictionnaire*, I.

Jean Delanglez, *Life and voyages of Louis Jolliet, 1645–1700* (Institute of Jesuit Hist. pub., Chicago, 1948), 54, 57, 78–81, 85, 90–91, 141, 147, 188–89, 194–95, 197, 205, 236, 239–40. Amédée Gosselin, *L'instruction au Canada sous le régime français (1635–1760)* (Québec, 1911), 326–41. Henry Harrisse, *Notes pour servir à l'histoire, à la bibliographie et à la cartographie de la Nouvelle-France et des pays adjacents, 1545–1700* (Paris, 1872), 194, 197–202, 205–7 209, 211–14. Gabriel Marcel, *Cartographie de la Nouvelle-France; supplément à l'ouvrage de M. Harrisse* (Paris, 1885), 10–14.

Jean Delanglez, "Franquelin, mapmaker," *Mid-America*, XXV (1943; new ser., XIV), 29–74; "The discovery of the Mississippi," *Mid-America*, XXVII (1945; new ser., XVI), 219–31; this article includes a letter from Jolliet to Frontenac. Auguste Gosselin, "Encore le P. de Bonnécamps (1707–1790)," *RSCT*, 2d ser., III (1897), sect.I, 93–117. P.-G. Roy, "Un hydrographe du roi à Québec: Jean-Baptiste-Louis Franquelin," *RSCT*, 3d ser., XIII (1919), sect.I, 47–59.

FULLARTINE, JOHN (the name is sometimes written **Fullertine** or **Fullerton**, but he signed **Fullartine**), succeeded James KNIGHT as governor and chief commander for the HBC in James Bay; b. *c.* 1652; d. October 1738 in London.

When John Fullartine of Edinburgh joined the HBC in 1683 he was described as a "tradesman," but no mention of the craft in which he served his apprenticeship has so far been found. He can claim to be among the first Scotsmen employed by the company and his engagement was probably one result of Governor John Nixon*'s recommendation that men from over the border should be recruited because they came from "a hard country to live in," and would not only accept lower wages, but be "better content with their dyet then Englishmen."

Fullartine sailed to James Bay in the *Diligence* (Capt. Nehemiah Walker*) and gained his initial experience in the fur trade at the post on Rupert River. When the company issued instructions to Henry Sergeant*, governor of the James Bay posts, to obtain isinglass from Eastmain River Fullartine was named as one of the men to be sent there. The project was not carried out, however, so presumably Fullartine remained at Rupert River where he was in September 1685, when Hugh Verner*, chief factor, received warning from Zacharie Jolliet of a threatened French attack on the company's posts. As soon as winter travel became possible Fullartine was sent to Albany Fort to warn Sergeant and to get advice. Fullartine was there on 16 July 1686 (o.s.) when the threat became a reality and Governor Sergeant surrendered to Pierre de Troyes*. Fullartine was one of the prisoners who, on release, sailed northwards in the overcrowded *Colleton* to spend the winter of 1686–87 either at York Fort or New Severn; he returned to England the following autumn.

The capture of Albany and the other James Bay posts took place while England and France were at peace. In 1688 the truce existing between the two crowns caused the HBC to limit the first objective of the expedition, which it sent to Albany River under Captain John Marsh*, to re-establishing trade. Marsh was instructed to avoid conflict with the French who, under PIERRE LE MOYNE d'Iberville, were at Albany Fort (renamed Sainte-Anne). Fullartine was a member of this abortive expedition and by the second week of March 1689 he and his surviving companions were prisoners of the French. Later in the season he was one of the selected number sent overland to New France. As England and France were then at war, he was kept for two years in "miserable Servitude" before being sent to France and imprisoned at La Rochelle. His wife was among those who petitioned Queen Mary for help in getting their husbands freed. Release came about the spring of 1692, and he returned to London.

Fullartine entered into a new contract with the HBC and sailed from the Thames in the *Royal Hudson's Bay* (Capt. Michael GRIMINGTON) in June 1692. The expedition, supported by the *Pery* (Capt. Charles Cotesworth) and the *Prosperous* (Capt. Henry BALEY), proposed to recapture Albany Fort from the French. James Knight was in command and before sailing he was requested by the committee "to have some Regard" for its old servant John Fullartine. After calling at York Fort the ships sailed to Gilpin Island off the East Main and Fullartine was one of the 127 men who wintered there, 1692–93, "under the government of Captain James Knight." Albany Fort was taken on 22 June 1693 without difficulty, though resistance was put up by the few Frenchmen left there. Fullartine was commended by the committee for having been "soe forward in the Performance" of his duty. It appears that in the season 1693–94 Fullartine traded for the company (and himself) on Gilpin Island, earning thereby the committee's thanks and a reminder that private trade was against standing orders.

When Knight sent his deputy, Stephen Sinclair, back to England in 1694, he appointed Fullartine to the vacancy and the choice met with approval in London. In 1697, when Knight determined to delay no longer in returning to England, he left Fullartine in command. Undoubtedly Fullartine looked forward with reasonable confidence to the company's confirming his position and appointing him governor, but events were even then occurring

Fullartine

in Hudson Bay to cause him future disappointment. The French, having diverted their aggressive efforts from James Bay to the more coveted Port Nelson area, had for the second time in four years captured York Fort (renamed Fort Bourbon). Fullartine should have received supplies and news from England in 1697 by the *Dering* [III] (Capt. Michael Grimington), but this vessel "hardly Escaping" on 26 August during the battle off Hayes River which preceded the surrender of York Fort to Iberville, returned directly to England. Fullartine, with his "few hands," was thus left without replenishments of supplies and trading goods, and also without news. How soon he learned about the company's losses is not known, but he possibly heard reports of the surrender of York Fort from Indians during the following winter. He certainly learned about the company's changed fortunes when the supply-ships arrived from England in the summer of 1698; his own expectation of being appointed governor was disappointed. It was expected that Albany Fort would be exchanged with the French for York Fort under articles 7 and 8 of the treaty of Ryswick; with this transaction in mind, the company had prevailed upon Knight to return to Albany as its chief representative. The commissioners did not agree about the disposal of York Fort, however, with the result that the treaty of Ryswick never operated in Hudson Bay, and Albany Fort remained in the company's possession. It was to be the only English fort in the bay until 1714 when the company's rights in Hudson Bay were restored to it under the treaty of Utrecht (1713).

Fullartine served as deputy governor until Knight returned to London in 1700, and then acted as governor during the 1700–1 season. On the arrival of the supply-ship in 1701 he received the company's commission constituting him governor and chief commander of Albany, Moose, and Rupert Rivers, and of all the territories within Hudson Strait and Bay as well as upon the East and West Main. Anthony BEALE was appointed his deputy. Fullartine's commission, unlike Knight's, was unsupported by one from the crown because the company had been advised by counsel that its own commission was sufficient by virtue of the charter of 2 May 1670. But in 1702, when England had entered the War of the Spanish Succession, the company thought it necessary "in order to the better Defence" of Albany to obtain and send to Fullartine a commission from Queen Anne. This constituted him governor and chief commander of the places named in the company's commission, and of any "since new Erected, Settled, discovered or Recovered & which formerly have been or of Right

doe belong to us & are or were Granted by the Charter" to the HBC.

Fullartine's letter of 2 Aug. 1703 acknowledging the commission is the first of any written from Albany Fort to survive in the HBC archives. It reviews in an outspoken manner the problems and difficulties at Albany when war in Europe was increasing the costs of supplies and limiting the sales of furs. Fullartine remarks that if the trade was not profitable enough to defray the cost of sending a ship annually from London, "it will soon not be worth the keeping" because repeated disappointments make "all men sick" of the country. His complement, after the ship sailed for England in 1703, was 35 men and boys.

Fullartine had asked to return to England "the next year" as he was intermittently "sadly tortured with the gravel and stone," but he was obliged to wait until 1705 for the appearance of the next ship. Acting on Fullartine's recommendation the committee had appointed Anthony Beale his successor. On 13 September, when the business for 1704–5 was finished, Fullartine called the men together and read the new governor's commission. He then went aboard the *Hudson's Bay* [II] expecting to return to England, but Captain Michael Grimington was ill and his ship could not be got out of Albany River. It is not known whether Fullartine reported in writing to the committee on the argument that developed between himself and Beale; only Beale's version of events has survived. According to this the Albany council members, including Fullartine, met and agreed that the vessel should winter at Gilpin Island off the East Main where he, Fullartine, would trade on behalf of the company. But a little later Fullartine suddenly "Grew very Angrey and Assumed the Government," and threatened "to tie Neck and Heels" any who hindered him. Beale, knowing him "to be given to passion," refused to yield, and Fullartine gave way. There were no more disagreements, but talebearing by "some knaves" caused Fullartine to resolve not to re-enter Albany Fort; on his return from Gilpin Island in the summer of 1706 he "made his Lodging in a Tent" until he boarded the ship for England.

On 21 Oct. 1706 Fullartine was welcomed to London by the committee and when outstanding salaries were settled early in the next year he, not Beale, was allowed the governor's remuneration for the season 1705–6. The committee's support of Fullartine presumably rested on the royal commission of 1702 which had not been cancelled.

Fullartine was engaged by the company early in March 1708 to go again to Albany Fort as Beale had asked to return home. In its instructions issued to Fullartine just before he sailed the following

May, the committee remarked that he was appointed governor and chief commander "bejond the Seas" according to the company's commission, which was "dignifyed and Confirmed" by the queen's commission. He was ordered to try to settle a post at Moose River if he found that the French had taken Albany; but all was well and he settled down to what was to be his last period of service overseas. Because the company did not send a ship to Albany in 1709 and because the *Hudson's Bay* [II] (Capt. Joseph Davis) which it sent in 1710 could not return to England until 1711, the committee received no news direct from Fullartine between the autumns of 1708 and 1711 when he himself returned. But news had been received from an unexpected source late in April or early in May 1710. Four Mohawk chiefs from New England, who had come to London to petition Queen Anne for aid against the French, accepted an invitation to "take A Colation" with the governor and committee at Hudson's Bay House. It was at this party that one of the guests informed his hosts that there had been an unsuccessful French attack on Albany Fort. He had knowledge of it because he had been in Canada when the French party had returned. The information given by this Mohawk chief, together with that contained in Fullartine's no longer extant report (from which the committee apparently quoted to inspire Joseph Isbister* at Albany Fort during the War of the Austrian Succession), and that conveyed in the scattered references to the affair found in correspondence and accounts, reveals that the attack took place on or about 26 June 1709. Fullartine, it appears, was warned of the approach of the French by a friendly Indian, Jack Tuckey. The attackers numbered about 100 (including 30 Indians) and in the fight lost their 2 leaders and 16 men. The company's only casualties were James Fidler and Oliver Stricklar; these two men, who were absent from the fort at the time of the attack, were ambushed and killed on their way back.

Fullartine was welcomed home by the committee on 2 Oct. 1711. By the time the general court was held on 27 November following, he had acquired enough HBC stock to allow for his election to the committee. His first-hand knowledge and experience of the fur trade and of life in Rupert's Land were undoubtedly invaluable to his fellow members who never had ventured through Hudson Strait. Fullartine was a conscientious HBC committee member for many years until his death, in October 1738, at Newington Green, Middlesex.

John Fullartine was one of the first employees of the HBC who not only rose from one of the lower ranks in the company's service to that of governor overseas, but also served on the London committee. He was employed in the bay at a time when the company's affairs were threatened by French aggression, and his loyalty and courage were recognized. He had the ability to gain the respect of Indians as well as of the men under his command; and he successfully managed the company's trade. His progress from the status of tradesman to that of governor overseas was slow but steady, and the pattern of his promotion at the bayside set a precedent which was followed on many occasions in the 18th century. Fullartine's attendance at the weekly meetings of the London committee was regular, but as only decisions were recorded in the minutes it is not known how much influence, if any, he had on company policy. During his lifetime Fullartine became a legend. The story of his defence of Albany became garbled with the passing years (Samuel Hearne*'s version is evidence of this) and then forgotten. All surviving information about this incident in the HBC's records has now been examined and once again Fullartine's part in maintaining the company's rights in Hudson Bay is recognized.

ALICE M. JOHNSON

[Fullartine's only surviving letter is printed in HBRS, XXV (Davies and Johnson), which also lists the pertinent sources in the HBC archives. For background information on the company's trade and financial position during Fullartine's career, *see* HBRS, XXI (Rich.) His death is mentioned in *The Historical Register* (London), XXIII (1738), 40, and his will, dated 17 March 1736 (proved 20 Oct. 1738) is in Somerset House, P.C.C., Brodrepp, f.232. A.M.J.]

G

GADOIS, PIERRE, Montreal Island farmer, armourer, gunsmith, witchcraft victim; b. 1632 in Saint-Germain-des-Prés parish near Bellême in Perche; d. 8 May 1714 in Montreal.

Pierre Gadois was the eldest son of Pierre Gadoys* (1594–1667) and came to Canada with his parents. The family arrived at Ville-Marie (Montreal) about 1647 after a sojourn in the Quebec region. Pierre the younger was, according to Marguerite Bourgeoys*, the first altar-boy in

Gaillard

the frontier settlement of Ville-Marie. He was probably trained in gunsmithery by Jean La Forest [Tavernier] and possibly transmitted his skill to his brother, Jean-Baptiste (1641–1728), who also became a gunsmith.

On 12 Aug. 1657, Pierre Gadois was married to Marie Pontonnier by Father Claude Pijart* who pronounced the customary "nulloque Legitimo impedimento detecto." Yet there was indeed an impediment. Mlle Pontonnier had wed Gadois in preference to another suitor. The rejected lover was René Besnard, *dit* Bourjoly, a corporal in the Ville-Marie garrison, who openly declared that the marriage would be forever sterile. When the bride failed to conceive in the first year of marriage, Besnard was accused of having made the groom impotent by an incantation over a thrice-knotted string.

Upon the complaint of the injured couple and others, a seigneurial tribunal was convened in November 1658 to investigate the charges of sorcery against René Besnard. The defendant denied any association with witchcraft even though, he claimed, Gadois' wife had offered him the fullest intimacies if he would acknowledge the deed and break the spell. When faced with testimony that he had boasted suggestively in public of "knowing how to tie the knot," Besnard replied that he had been speaking about the lacing of his hose. Sieur Chomedey* de Maisonneuve, as acting magistrate, sent the corporal to prison and later into exile.

Bishop LAVAL repeated the marriage blessing after an ecclesiastical investigation and on 30 Aug. 1660, the required three years after the first marriage having elapsed, he declared the marriage null "because of permanent impotence caused by witchcraft." Marie Pontonnier remarried two months later, but Gadois delayed his second essay at matrimony until 20 April 1665, when he took Jeanne Besnard (no relation to René) as his spouse. His second wife bore 14 children, with twins as a final *tour de force*.

Pierre Gadois had an honourable public life. In the 1660s he served in the defence of Ville-Marie as a militiaman and as a member of the Saint-Pierre river cooperative farming community, which guarded the southern approach to Ville-Marie. In the next decade, Gadois moved into a new house on Rue Notre-Dame, opposite the first seminary. He now devoted more of his time to his craft as armourer-gunsmith and participated in the religious and social activities of the St Éloi society of armourers. As a churchwarden he supervised in 1672 the construction of a public well in the Place d'Armes. The 1681 census listed Gadois as the relatively prosperous owner of 30 cultivated acres.

Two years later, he arranged an advantageous marriage for his eldest daughter, Jeanne-Françoise, to the merchant Antoine Hattanville. In later years, Gadois supplemented his income by selling town lots and by leasing out his farmlands. Pierre Gadois, the respected Montreal burgher, would soon be eclipsed by his more famous son, Jacques Gadois*, *dit* Mauger (1686–1750), the silversmith and merchant.

PETER N. MOOGK

AJM, Greffe de Bénigne Basset, 29 nov. 1672, 11 sept. 1673, 21 avril 1675; Greffe d'Hilaire Bourgine, 30 nov. 1689; Greffe de Pierre Cabazié, 30 mars 1685; Greffe de Claude Maugue, 28 mars 1678; Greffe de Jean de Saint-Père, 6 mai 1657; Registres d'état civil de Notre-Dame de Montréal, mariages (1643–70), 235, 267–68, 297; baptêmes, mariages, sépultures (1714), 62. AJTR, Greffe de J.-B. Pottier, 6 juin 1690, 5 oct. 1696. ASSM, armoire 7, tiroir 4 (28 oct. 1694); tiroir 25 (3 juillet 1670, 19 juin 1678); tiroir 40 (15 oct. 1683, 25 févr. 1690, 14 sept. 1694, 6 août 1710); tiroir 46 (1 déc. 1695, 1695 s.d., 4 févr. 1700); tiroir 51 (7 oct. 1683). *Ord. comm.* (P.-G. Roy), I, 266–77. Recensement du Canada, 1666 (APQ *Rapport*).

É.-Z. Massicotte, "La milice de 1663," *BRH*, XXXII (1926), 408. Raymond Boyer, *Les crimes et les châtiments au Canada français du XVIIᵉ au XXᵉ siècle* (Montréal, 1966), 293–95. R.-L. Séguin, *La sorcellerie au Canada français du XVIIᵉ au XIXᵉ siècle* (Montréal, 1961), 9–21. *Canadian Antiquarian and Numismatic J.* (Montréal), 3d ser., XIII (1916), 13. É.-Z. Massicotte, "La Saint-Eloi et la corporation des armuriers à Montréal, au XVIIᵉ siècle," *BRH*, XXIII (1917), 343–46.

GAILLARD, GUILLAUME, businessman, seigneur of the Île d'Orléans and member of the Conseil Supérieur; b. *c.* 1669 at Villeneuve-la-Comtesse, bishopric of Saintes, son of Hilaire Gaillard and Catherine Leduc; d. 1729.

At the age of 16, Gaillard had come to New France to be a servant of Jean-François Hazeur, Sieur de Petit-Marais, a Montreal merchant, but as the latter had died before Gaillard arrived, in 1685, the young man went to Quebec. On 22 April 1703, in his capacity as churchwarden, he signed an agreement between the seminary and the parish council of Notre-Dame de Québec. Intendant JACQUES RAUDOT said of him, on 28 Oct. 1709: "[He] is a capable man who has a fine understanding of judicial affairs, and who even worked for a long time under the late Sieur de Villeray, first councillor...." His inventory, drawn up by the notary Henry Hiché* on 11 Jan. 1730, mentions more than 25 volumes of law, which proves that he had acquired a sound juridical training.

On 27 May 1690 he married Marie-Catherine Neveu (Nepveu), who bore him 13 children. His first wife died in 1715, and he married again in 1719; his second wife was Louise-Catherine Denys, Dominique Bergeron's widow.

In an act signed on 6 May 1707 before the notary CHAMBALON, Gaillard went into partnership with ALEXANDRE LENEUF de Beaubassin, a lieutenant in the colonial regular troops, and Joseph Riverin, another merchant, with the intention of fitting out the ship *Nostre-Dame de Victoire* "to go privateering ... on and in the neighbourhood of Cape Breton, the island of Newfoundland, the Grand Banks, and surrounding areas." Beaubassin provided the ship, of 80 to 90 tons draught, which was under construction at Quebec, and which would be armed with 6 iron cannon and manned by 100 officers and men. Gaillard was to obtain the provisions and "all utensils that will be required both for the service of the cabin and for the crew." As for Riverin, he was to rig out the vessel with sails, grappling-irons, and so on. The profits were to be divided between the three partners and the crew. Thomas MOORE, an Irishman from the Île d'Orléans, was taken on as ship's master and pilot; but the vessel put to sea too late and returned in the autumn having captured nothing.

On 20 March 1712, Gaillard acquired for 24,000 *livres* in French currency the seigneury of the island and countship of Saint-Laurent (Île d'Orléans), which he bought from François Berthelot, a counsellor in the *parlement* of Paris [*see* CHARLOTTE-FRANÇOISE JUCHEREAU]. Six years later, he acquired for Intendant Michel Bégon* the Grandpré fief, in the Notre-Dame-des-Anges seigneury, the property of Françoise Duquet, widow of Olivier MOREL de La Durantaye.

On 20 Jan. 1710 Gaillard was called upon to sit temporarily in the Conseil Supérieur. Louis XIV signed the letters of permanent appointment on the following 5 May.

The death of Bishop Saint-Vallier [LA CROIX], during the night of the 26 Dec. 1727, gave rise to an extremely violent conflict between the upper clergy on the one hand, and Intendant DUPUY and the two members of the Conseil Supérieur, the Sieurs Gaillard and Rouer* d'Artigny, on the other [*see* BOULLARD and Louis-Eustache Chartier* de Lotbinière]. Gaillard, "given special powers on behalf of the Hôpital Général," took part in preparing the obsequies of the bishop in the chapel of the institution, against the wish of the chapter. On 16 Feb. 1728, Gaillard was deputed by the council to lay information against all those who had contravened the council's decrees with respect to the canons of the chapter. After a long series of vicissitudes, the governor exiled Gaillard to Beauport and Artigny to Beaumont, but both took refuge at the intendant's house. The king dis-

approved of the governor's action, while at the same time dismissing Dupuy and replacing him by Gilles Hocquart*. The latter received orders to reprimand the councillor severely, as if he had been found guilty.

This long imbroglio impaired Gaillard's health. He was reinstated in his functions on 4 Oct. 1729 but died on 12 November and was buried the next day in the crypt of the church of Notre-Dame de Québec.

HERVÉ BIRON

AJQ, Greffe de Louis Chambalon; Greffe de François Genaple. AQ, NF, Ins. Cons. sup., VI, 6; NF, Ord. des int., XIV; NF, Registres du Cons. sup., 20 janv. 1727–28 juin 1728. Caron, "Inventaire de documents," APQ *Rapport*, 1941–42, 285–90. "La flibuste du sieur Leneuf de Beaubassin en 1707," APQ *Rapport*, 1922–23, 348–55. *Mandements des évêques de Québec* (Têtu et Gagnon), I, 522. PAC *Report*, 1904, App.K, 116. P.-G. Roy, *Inv. concessions*, I, 76. J. Delalande, *Le Conseil souverain de la Nouvelle-France* (Québec, 1927), 213–27. "La famille Gaillard de Saint-Laurent," *BRH*, XLI (1935), 193–212.

GALAN (GALAND, GALLANT). *See* HACHÉ-GALLANT

GALLARD (Gallar, Galard), CHARLOTTE, nun, Religious Hospitaller, mistress of novices, depositary, and superior of the Religious Hospitallers of St Joseph in Montreal; b. 1648 at Angers, daughter of René Gallard, king's counsellor to the bench of the provost court of Angers, and of Claude de Faye; d. 10 March 1725 at Montreal.

While still a young novice at the Hôtel-Dieu in Beaufort-en-Vallée, Sister Gallard fell gravely ill. She recovered after promising to devote her life to the service of the sick in the community of the Religious Hospitallers of St Joseph at the Hôtel-Dieu of Montreal, and left her convent 27 May 1681. She sailed for Ville-Marie in the company of Sister Françoise MAUMOUSSEAU. Despite delicate health, Sister Gallard held important offices. The first time the Hôtel-Dieu was burned, 24 Feb. 1695, she provided for the wants of the sick in her capacity as depositary of the poor, and her zeal assured in great measure the success of the work of reconstruction. Subsequently she became mistress of novices, then superior for the first time, from 1702 to 1708, and for a second time in 1711.

In a long letter dated 22 Oct. 1713, which she wrote to the superior of the Hôtel-Dieu of La Flèche, she gave interesting details about life at the hospital, the Indians' customs, and her own situation. She said that her great age—she was 64—would require that she be relieved of all tasks. Her consolation, she wrote, was that she was leaving a

Gamelin

flourishing community, composed entirely of Canadian nuns, since she was now the only French one. Her desire for rest was not granted, however, since she remained superior until 1717 and was to hold the office again from 1720 till her death.

In 1721 the hospital and convent were ravaged by fire once more. Mother Gallard, who was superior at the time, directed the community with a skilful hand and took the necessary steps to assure the continuation of the missionary work. She died at the age of 77 without having the joy of seeing the convent finished.

HÉLÈNE BERNIER

AHDM, Annales, 328f.; Mère Chauvelier, Livre ou second recueil de lettres circulaires, 147–56. Mondoux, L'Hôtel-Dieu de Montréal.

GAMELIN, IGNACE, Montreal merchant (usually confused with his second son of the same name); b. in 1663, probably in the Trois-Rivières area, the eldest son of Michel Gamelain* and Marguerite Crevier; d. at the age of 76 in Montreal and buried on 9 Jan. 1739.

Ignace Gamelin married Marguerite Le Moyne, the daughter of Jean Le Moyne and Madeleine de Chavigny, on 10 Nov. 1693, in the parish of Batiscan. They appear to have had nine children, most of whom died before their father. The eldest son, Jacques-Alexis (bap. 14 June 1697 and buried in 1730), and the second child, Ignace* (bap. 10 Dec. 1698), were born when the Gamelin family was still in the environment of Batiscan. They were domiciled in Montreal by 1702, but probably lived in rented quarters. Gamelin is not listed as a house-owner in the census of 1731. It was not until 1732 that his son Ignace began building his own house.

Evidence is lacking to distinguish Gamelin clearly from his son of the same name, who played an important rôle in the commercial life of the colony. It would be natural to presume that since his son did not reach his majority until 1723, documents signed "Ignace Gamelin" before that date should concern the father. However, a verification of the signatures indicates that the son entered contractual obligations before his majority. Moreover, it seems certain that it was the younger Gamelin who formed a partnership with POULIN de Francheville in 1732 for the development of the St Maurice Forges. Indeed, in a memorandum dated 1742, three years after his father's death, he mentions his participation in the ironworks with Francheville.

Gamelin's brother, Pierre, was the founder of the Gamelin, dit Châteauvieux, or Gamelin-Maugras line.

CAMERON NISH

AJM, Greffe de J.-B. Pottier; Greffe de Joseph-Charles Raimbault. AN, Col., C¹¹ᴬ, 109–10. Collection Lafontaine (Sir George Williams Univ., Montreal), Registre de la paroisse de Batiscan; Registre de la cure de Montréal. Recensement du Canada, 1667 (Sulte). Bonnault, "Le Canada militaire," 261–527. É.-Z. Massicotte, "Congés et permis déposés ou enregistrés à Montréal sous le régime français," APQ Rapport, 1921–22, 189–225; "Répertoire des engagements pour l'Ouest," 191–466.

GANNES DE FALAISE (Falaize), LOUIS DE, officer in the colonial regular troops in Canada and Acadia, knight of the order of Saint-Louis; b. October 1658 at Buxeuil, province of Poitou; d. 25 Feb. 1714 at La Rochelle; eldest son of Louis de Gannes, seigneur de Falaise, "gendarme d'une compagnie du Roi," and Françoise Le Bloy, brother of François de Gannes* de Falaise, and a relative of the Argensons.

De Gannes became a midshipman at Rochefort in 1683, a lieutenant in Canada in 1687, and a captain in Acadia in 1696. In 1704 he was appointed major in Acadia. Though he was severely reprimanded in 1705 for his lack of diligence, his superiors had frequent occasion in the years following to write favourably of his contribution to the service. After the surrender of Port-Royal (Annapolis Royal, N.S.) in 1710, he went back to France, then returned to Quebec where he received the cross of the order of Saint-Louis in 1713. That same year he was appointed major of the new colony of Île Royale (Cape Breton Island) but died at La Rochelle in February 1714 before leaving for his new post.

He was married three times: in 1691, in Quebec, to Barbe, a daughter of Simon Denys* de La Trinité and Françoise Du Tartre; in 1695, in Montreal, to Louise, daughter of Charles Legardeur* de Tilly and Geneviève Juchereau de Maur; and in 1700, in Acadia, to Marguerite, daughter of MICHEL LENEUF de La Vallière, the elder, and Marie Denys. He had one child from his first marriage and 12 from his third. His widow lived first at Île Royale, then at Trois-Rivières, where she died in April 1760.

BERNARD POTHIER

AN, Col., B, 13–36; C¹¹ᴰ, 4, f.99; 5, f.122v; E, 197 (dossier de Gannes), pièce 1. Lettres de noblesse (P.-G. Roy), II, 71–90. Webster, Acadia. Aegidius Fauteux, Les chevaliers de Saint-Louis; "La famille de Gannes," BRH, XXXI (1925), 271–85. É.-Z. Massicotte et Régis Roy, Armorial du Canada français (2ᵉ série, Montréal, 1918), 108. J.-B.-A. Allaire, "Biographie canadienne," BRH, XIX (1913), 343–44.

GARGOT, FRANÇOIS LORIT, dit. See LORIT

236

GARNIER, JULIEN, priest, Jesuit, missionary, superior of the mission in New France; b. 6 Jan. 1643 in the diocese of Saint-Brieuc in the province of Brittany; d. 30 Jan. 1730 at Quebec.

Julien Garnier entered the Society of Jesus in Paris on 25 Sept. 1660. Two years later, on 27 Oct. 1662, he arrived at Quebec, where for three years he taught at the Jesuit college while preparing for the missions by studying the Indian languages. On 10 April 1666 he received the priesthood from Bishop LAVAL. He was the first Jesuit to be ordained a priest in Canada. Of his first mass, which was celebrated on 12 April, one may read in the *Journal des Jésuites*: ". . . we gave a dinner in our reception-room, as on the feast of St. Ignatius, to all the authorities, and to the six [Indian] captains who were at Quebec." Under Father Jérôme Lalemant*'s guidance Garnier continued his theological studies, which were approved in an examination "on the whole of theology, in keeping with the custom of the Society" on 12 April 1668.

At the end of that month he went to join Father Jacques BRUYAS among the Oneidas, and a few months later he went to live with the Onondagas. In his mind the latter was a temporary mission, but when he wanted to rejoin his post the Indians objected. As he argued that he could not remain at Onontagué without a chapel and without a companion, the great chieftain Garakontié*, who was still a heathen, did not hesitate to take up the challenge. Some days later the chapel was up, and Garakontié was on his way to Quebec to obtain some companions for Father Garnier; it was in this way that the Iroquois missions acquired Fathers Pierre MILLET and Étienne de CARHEIL.

Father Garnier toiled in the Iroquois country until 1685, not without some merit, for he encountered a great deal of hostility. He wrote of the problems of converting the Iroquois: "One of the great obstacles encountered is found in dreams, which seem to constitute this country's sole Divinity, to which [the Iroquois] defer in all things." In his relation for 1672 Garnier recounts that the Iroquois believe that "the black-gowned men are here only as spies, and convey all information to Onnontio—that is, to Monsieur the governor." Also, more than one attempt was made upon his life; Garnier affirms that "humanly speaking, my life depends on that little girl's health . . . [or] on the march of a French army to this country." In a letter addressed to Le Febvre* de La Barre and dated 23 April 1684 Garnier opposed military action against the Iroquois, which would have compromised the missions. After BRISAY de Denonville's expedition in 1687 missionary work in the Iroquois country did become impossible, and Garnier then exercised his ministry at Sault-Saint-Louis until he was appointed superior of the mission at Lorette, near Quebec, in 1691. In 1694, however, he returned to Sault-Saint-Louis.

At the discussions preceding the great peace treaty concluded in 1701 at Montreal, Garnier translated CALLIÈRE's speech into Huron. This peace treaty permitted the reopening of the Iroquois missions, and in 1702 Garnier, accompanied by VAILLANT de Gueslis, went back to his missionary field, devoting himself this time particularly to the Senecas. In 1709, at the instigation of Peter SCHUYLER, four of the Five Cantons denounced the treaty of 1701, and Garnier again returned to Sault-Saint-Louis. In 1716 he became superior of all the missions in New France; he held this office for three years. In a short, unpublished account devoted to him, Father Félix Martin wrote: "During his administration the accusation of engaging in trade was revived against the missionaries and complaints were carried as far as Rome. The archives of the Gesù contain a letter by Father Garnier, dated 21 Oct. 1718 and addressed to his general, in which he explains what had given rise to this calumny. Pelts were, so to speak, the country's currency. Farmers used them to pay their rent. They were given in particular to the church to pay for masses. This was money which after a certain period had to be converted into coin."

Father Garnier had known Father Joseph Lafitau* intimately from 1712 till 1716. The latter, in a famous work, bore this witness to Garnier: "Above all I have profited from the knowledge of a former Jesuit missionary named Father Julien Garnier, who had devoted himself to the missions from the time of his noviciate and who spent more than 60 years in them. . . . He knew the Algonkian language fairly well, but he was master particularly of the Huron language and the five Iroquois dialects . . . ; it was, I say, in my dealings with this virtuous missionary, with whom I was intimately acquainted, that I derived all that I have to say here about the Indians."

When his three years as superior were at an end, Father Garnier returned to Sault-Saint-Louis, where he worked until 1728. He died on 31 Jan. 1730 at the college in Quebec, after 67 years and 3 months of missionary work. Of all the Jesuits who came from France in the 17th century, he was the one who worked and lived longest in Canada.

LÉON POULIOT, S.J.

ASJCF, 269. *JR* (Thwaites). Joseph Lafitau, *Mœurs des sauvages amériquains comparées aux mœurs des premiers temps* (2v., Paris, 1724). Campbell, *Pioneer priests*, I, 312–33. Eccles, *Canada under Louis XIV*,

Gaudarville

133. Rochemonteix, *Les Jésuites et la N.-F. au XVIIe siècle*, III, 383ff.

GAUDARVILLE, ALEXANDRE PEUVRET DEMESNU DE. *See* Peuvret

GAULIN, ANTOINE, priest of the Séminaire des Missions Étrangères in Quebec, missionary to the Abenakis and Micmacs of Acadia and Nova Scotia; born at Sainte-Famille, Île d'Orléans 17 April 1674, son of François Gaulin, farmer, and Marie Rocheron; ordained priest at Quebec, 21 Dec. 1697; died at Quebec 7 March 1740.

Gaulin came to Acadia in 1698, and the following year replaced Father Thury* as missionary to the Abenakis at Pentagouet (near Castine, Maine); Father Philippe Rageot served as his assistant. In this early period Gaulin committed himself to fighting the brandy trade operated by CLAUDE-SÉBASTIEN DE VILLIEU. On 5 Oct. 1702, he was named vicar-general in Acadia by ANGO Des Maizerets.

It was at this time that Gaulin revived Thury's plans to gather the Indians of the Penobscot area into a large mission near Canso, far from New England. The plan was thwarted in 1707, however, when the English captured the supplies intended for the new mission. War with the English intervened, and that same year Gaulin, with BERNARD-ANSELME D'ABBADIE de Saint-Castin, led his Indians to meet the invading English commanded by Colonel John MARCH. After the capture of Port-Royal (renamed Annapolis Royal) in 1710, Gaulin, acting on instructions from Pontchartrain, had his Indians raid and harass the English to prevent them from becoming solidly established in Nova Scotia. The English garrison was commanded at this time by Samuel VETCH and by his lieutenant Sir Charles HOBBY. Gaulin was unable to lead an all out attack on Annapolis Royal, however, because the ship bringing clothing, arms, and munitions to his Indians was captured by the English.

Between 1717 and 1720, after France had founded a new colony on Île Royale (Cape Breton Island), Gaulin succeeded in bringing together a great number of Micmacs from the peninsula in a large mission at Antigonish—within English territory but close to Île Royale. Later he established missions at Cape Sable, La Hève (La Have), Shubenacadie and Mirligueche (near Lunenburg).

Gaulin and fellow missionaries Justinien Durand* and Félix Pain* were less successful in encouraging many Acadians to move to Île Royale. In 1718 Gaulin went to France to solicit assistance "for the benefit of religion and the advantage of the colony." With increased funds he was able, in 1727, to carry out a census of Acadians in Nova Scotia, and with his assistant, Michel Courtin, to translate prayers and a catechism into the Micmac language. His new resources also enabled Gaulin to perform better his duties of proselytizing, maintaining among the Acadians some loyalty for France, and preventing the Indians from signing a peace treaty with the English. These activities led Lawrence ARMSTRONG, the English lieutenant-governor at Annapolis Royal, to call him before the executive council in 1726; the council restricted him to the post of curate at Minas (Les Mines). At the same time the French were accusing him of encouraging peace between the English and the Indians; however, the accusations were subsequently proven false. His health was now broken by years of service; he lived quietly at Minas until 1731 and then at Annapolis until 1732 when he retired to Quebec.

Gaulin was feared by the English because of his powerful influence among the Indians and Acadians, trusted by the French as their chief contact with the Indians, and beloved by the Indians for whose welfare he went deeply into debt.

Gaulin is depicted in an *ex-voto* at Sainte-Anne de Beaupré, in which he is a passenger on a storm-tossed ship being saved by Saint Anne.

DAVID LEE

AN, Col., B, 27, f.28; 29, ff.7, 29; 33, f.42; 34, ff.85, 111v; 35, f.32; 36, ff.445, 447, 448; 37, f.226; 42, f.472; 48, f.410; 49, f.705; 50, f.581; 52, f.586; 53, f.24; 55, f.563; 57, f.744; 58, f.516; C^{11A}, 18, ff.139–41; C^{11B}, 1, f.249; 2, f.237; 3, f.42; 4, f.251; 5, f.358; 6, f.77; C^{11D}, 4, f.45; 6, f.250; 7, f.177; 8, f.3. ASQ, Fonds Amédée-Gosselin, 49; Polygraphie, IX, 23c. PAC, Nova Scotia A, 15, pp.150ff.; Nova Scotia B, 1, pp.96–97, 99–101, 104ff.

Coll. doc. inédits Canada et Amérique (*CF*), I (1888), 190–93. *Coll. de manuscrits relatifs à la N.-F.*, II, 336–37, 385, 466, 504, 566; III, 126–27. "Correspondance de Vaudreuil," APQ *Rapport, 1939–40*, 337. *N.S. Archives*, I, 68–69; II, 77; III, 204. Allaire, *Dictionnaire.* Caron, "Prêtres séculiers et religieux," 295.

Bernard, *Le drame acadien.* Casgrain, *Les Sulpiciens en Acadie.* Gosselin, *L'Église du Canada*, I, 368; II, 229. Harvey, *French régime in P.E.I.* A. A. Johnston, *A history of the Catholic Church in eastern Nova Scotia [1611–1827]* (1v. to date, Antigonish, 1960), I. McLennan, *Louisbourg.* Gérard Morisset, *Peintres et tableaux* (2v., Les arts au Canada français, Québec, 1936–37), I, 54. P.-G. Roy, *L'île d'Orléans* (Québec, 1928), 363–65. R. V. Bannon, "Antoine Gaulin (1674–1740): an apostle of early Acadie," CCHA *Report, 1952*, 49–59.

GAULTIER DE LA VÉRENDRYE, JEAN-BAPTISTE (he also signed **La Verendrye**),

Gaultier de La Vérendrye

eldest son of Pierre Gaultier* de La Vérendrye and Marie-Anne Dandonneau; b. 3 Sept. 1713 on Île Dupas, baptized two days later in the church of the Visitation on Île Dupas, the baptism being recorded in the register of Saint-Pierre at Sorel, the only parish in the region to have a resident priest at that time; d. 6 June 1736, a bachelor.

Jean-Baptiste's name is to be found in a "list of 28 cadets commissioned by the court in 1731, and whose pay is to begin on 1 Jan. 1732." This listing indicates that, as was customary, he must have received military training at Montreal before that date, and doubtless he received part of his education there.

In 1731 he was a member of the first team to head towards the west under his father's command. On 19 April he hired men for the west, and on 28 April, with Nicolas Sarrazin, an ironsmith and armourer, and Eustache Gamelin-Châteauvieux, a merchant, he formed one of the four secondary companies set up for the purpose of trading. This association was to last three years, and Jean-Baptiste had the right to one quarter of the revenues. Having completed the building of Fort Saint-Pierre at Lac à la Pluie (Rainy Lake) in the autumn of the same year, he spent a hard winter there with his cousin CHRISTOPHE DUFROST de La Jemerais; the following spring he took a load of furs to Michilimackinac. In the autumn of 1732 he arrived at Fort Saint-Charles, which was then being built, after being caught in the ice on Lac des Bois (Lake of the Woods) and forced to leave his cargo temporarily ten leagues from the fort. In the spring of 1733 he went with La Jemerais as far as the Barrière aux Esturgeons on the Ouinipigon (Winnipeg) River and apparently built a small fort there. He had to return to Fort Saint-Charles without completing his journey, however, because of the demands of the merchants, who refused to finance the building of new settlements. In September 1733 La Vérendrye (senior) sent him to Fort Saint-Pierre to meet the canoes from Montreal. He was back the following month.

In January 1734 he went with his father to Fort Saint-Pierre, among the Crees and Monsonis, who talked of nothing but war against the southern Sioux. The explorer succeeded in calming them, but he had to agree to leave them Jean-Baptiste as a witness and counsellor for another expedition that they were planning against the Mascoutens, Winnebagos or Prairie Sioux. This took place in the spring of 1734, and Jean-Baptiste set out from Fort Saint-Charles with the Crees, who had "adopted" him as one of theirs, and the Monsonis; but as the Indians did not conform to the conditions laid down by La Vérendrye to his son, the latter left the expedition. He went to the Rivière

Rouge (Red River) to build the first Fort Maurepas. This fort, at first intended for the Crees, was about six miles to the north of the present small town of Selkirk. Jean-Baptiste remained in charge of the fort until he was replaced by La Jemerais in the autumn of 1735. In a letter written from Fort Maurepas to the governor, Charles de Beauharnois* de La Boische on 7 June 1735, Jean-Baptiste said: "I have established a fort at Lac Ouinipigon (Lake Winnipeg), five leagues up the Rivière Rouge." According to La Jemerais, he came across 300 "lodges" there belonging to the Assiniboins, and obtained from them interesting information about the Mandans.

In the meantime La Vérendrye (senior) was on his way to Montreal, and on 18 May 1735, with his son Jean-Baptiste, Christophe Dufrost, and other persons, he formed a new commercial company to replace the earlier ones. Jean-Baptiste spent the winter of 1735–36 at Fort Saint-Charles. The situation was becoming very trying, for the merchants had not sent in time the merchandise agreed upon, and it had remained at Grand Portage. On 5 June Jean-Baptiste and 20 other Frenchmen, among them Father AULNEAU, left Fort Saint-Charles to go and fetch provisions and the merchandise. Surprised by Sioux marauders, they were all massacred the next morning on a small island in Lac des Bois; their bodies were later transported to Fort Saint-Charles and buried in the chapel.

Jean-Baptiste de La Vérendrye, who had come to the west at the age of 18, seemed particularly well qualified to help his father, who from the outset entrusted several important missions to him. His father wrote to the minister, Maurepas, on 11 May 1733: "I contented myself [after the mutiny at Grand Portage in 1731] with sending my nephew who is my 'second in command', and my son who is my 'third in command' . . . to build a fort at Thekamamihouen or Lac de la Pluie. . . ." Jean-Baptiste became "second in command" on La Jemerais' death on 10 May 1736. He had learned the Monsoni language and served as an interpreter.

Jean-Baptiste de La Vérendrye's share in the construction of Fort Maurepas makes him the equal of his father and one of the founders of the present province of Manitoba.

ANTOINE CHAMPAGNE

AE, Mém. et doc., Amérique, 8, ff.46–69. AJM, Greffe de J.-B. Adhémar, 28 avril 1731. AN, Col., C^{11A}, 67, ff.168–71; C^{11E}, 16, ff.156–59, 182–86, 189–90, 282–90, 303; D^{2C}, 43, f.30; E, 263; F^3, 2 ff.489–91; 12, f.248. PAC, FM 18, B 12. Service hydrographique de la Marine (Paris), Dépôt des cartes et plans de la Marine, 4044B, 85. *Découvertes et établissements des Français* (Margry), VI. [La

Gaultier de Varennes

Vérendrye], *Journals and letters of La Vérendrye* (Burpee). "Lettres du père Aulneau," APQ *Rapport, 1926–27*, 290. Wis. State Hist. Soc. *Coll.*, XVII.

L. J. Burpee, *The search for the western sea* (London, 1908; rev. ed., Toronto, 1935). Parkman, *A half-century of conflict*. L.-A. Prud'homme, "Documents sur la découverte du Nord-Ouest," Société hist. de Saint-Boniface *Bull.*, I (1911).

GAULTIER (Gauthier, Gautier) DE VARENNES (Devarenne, De Varenne), JEAN-BAPTISTE, priest, procurator of the seminary of Quebec, canon, penitentiary and archdeacon of the chapter, vicar-general, member of the Conseil Supérieur; b. probably 2 Oct. 1677 at Trois-Rivières, son of René Gaultier* de Varennes, governor of Trois-Rivières, and of Marie Boucher, daughter of Pierre BOUCHER; died 30 March 1726 at Quebec.

Jean-Baptiste, older brother of the discoverer Pierre Gaultier* de La Vérendrye, entered the Petit Séminaire of Quebec in September 1688, when he was about 11 years of age. He was brought there by Bishop Saint-Vallier [LA CROIX], who had just returned from France after his consecration as bishop, and by Abbé Des Maizerets [ANGO]. There he completed all his studies, including theology, between September 1697 and 3 Dec. 1700, the date of his ordination as a priest by Bishop LAVAL in the seminary chapel.

Until 1706 he was a curate at the cathedral. Priests serving in the parish were members of the seminary, consequently Varennes was received into it in 1701 and was given the task of directing the young theological students. On 2 Oct. 1702 he became a canon in the chapter; in 1716 he was the penitentiary, and finally, in the last years of his life, archdeacon and vicar-general of the diocese. In addition, on 4 Jan. 1724, the king appointed him councillor and clerk of the Conseil Supérieur, to fill the vacancy caused by the death of Abbé Joseph de LA COLOMBIÈRE.

Quite apart from all these dignities, which were primarily honorary, from 1707 till his death Abbé Varennes devoted himself above all to his office as procurator of the seminary, in which task he aided and ultimately succeeded Abbé JEAN-FRANÇOIS BUISSON de Saint-Cosme (1660–1712). The seminary was carrying at this time a debt of 60,000 *livres*. Varennes concerned himself particularly with administering the seigneuries and managing the farms and mills which were run by the seminary. It became apparent that Varennes' administration was more and more disastrous. He was rebuked for not following the directors' orders, for borrowing too much, and for refusing to produce accounts of his management. The

superiors of the seminary in Paris, upon which the seminary in Quebec was dependent, became so alarmed at the situation that they advised the procurator to hand in his resignation. Instead of doing so, Varennes drew up a long report, dated 1 Sept. 1723, justifying his administration from 1707 on. He attributed the disastrous situation to several factors: "the two fires that, as is known, the seminary suffered at four years' interval . . . the fire that ravaged Île Jésus . . . the loss at sea of a ship laden with effects belonging to us, and the capture of another by the enemy . . . the extremely high price of everything . . . the receiving of missionaries at all times without requiring any recompense from them . . . the necessity of paying as much for a piece of land as for a whole Canadian seigneury . . . the detaching and sending [forth] of missionaries, with considerable expense incurred, both for them and for the servants who accompany them . . . after all, I cannot cease believing that God gives His blessing to this undertaking and that He gives us back in other ways what we spend thus. What is true, is that all this does not appear to have increased our revenues."

During this period another subject of concern arose: the friction between priests born in Canada and those from France, who always kept for themselves the positions of authority in the seminary. It is probable that Abbé Varennes was at the head of the Canadian faction. In 1723, on being warned of this dispute, the superiors in Paris gave their colleagues at Quebec some wise admonitions on the direction of the church in Canada.

Bishop Saint-Vallier recognized Varennes' talents and qualities by appointing him archdeacon and vicar-general. He even chose him to be his executor, thus indicating his confidence in him. Varennes died 30 March 1726 a year before the bishop himself died.

Abbé Varennes may have been a touchy administrator, but he was recognized as a exemplary priest: given to self mortification and filled with liturgical zeal, he was discreet and capable in directing young people, and was faithful in observing regulations.

HONORIUS PROVOST

ASQ, C 14, 235–36; Lettres, M, 28, 47, 59; N, 109, 116, 134; R, 35; Séminaire, IV, 119; V, 64; VIII, 1; XV, 58. Charland, "Notre-Dame de Québec: le nécrologe de la crypte," 180. Tanguay, *Dictionnaire*, I, 258. Gosselin, *L'Église du Canada*, I, 389f., 439. J.-E. Roy, "Les conseillers au Conseil souverain de la Nouvelle-France," *BRH*, I (1895), 179. P.-G. Roy, "Les conseillers clercs au Conseil souverain de la

Nouvelle-France," *BRH*, XXII (1916), 352. Benjamin Sulte, "La Vérenderie avant ses voyages au Nord-Ouest," *BRH*, XXI (1915), 103. Henri Têtu, "Le chapitre de la cathédrale de Québec et ses délégués en France (1723–1773)," *BRH*, XVI (1910), 138.

GAY (Guay), ROBERT-MICHEL, priest, Sulpician, missionary, first superior of the mission at Lac des Deux Montagnes (Oka); b. 1663 at Autun; d. 29 July 1725 at Montreal.

After being ordained a priest, M. Gay joined the Sulpicians on 10 May 1687 and left for Canada in April 1688. Upon his arrival on 15 August his superiors entrusted to him the mission at La Montagne. While there he undertook an extensive study of the Indian languages, "receiving lessons in Algonkian from his *confrère* BARTHÉLEMY, in Huron from M. Mariet; from M. Belmont [VACHON] himself lessons in Iroquois." It seems clear that M. Gay had a certain success in his study of the Indian languages, since "there remained some scraps of an Algonkian grammar, which disappeared in the lamentable fire of 15 June 1877."

When the La Montagne mission moved to Sault-au-Récollet in September 1696, M. Gay followed his flock. During his whole life as a missionary, but especially when at La Montagne and Sault-au-Récollet, the valiant Sulpician made it his duty to accompany the members of his mission when they went to war, thus following the advice of his superior general. But he was not content just to act as chaplain; having extraordinary influence over his neophytes and being of a powerful build and dauntless courage, he was always in the front rank of his Indians during combats. Soon his exploits brought him from M. Tronson a recommendation to be prudent. "We have learned from the accounts of the war just how great has been your bravery. It is a worthy form of zeal to risk oneself for the safety of one's brothers and for the colony and our religion: but in order that God may bless your zeal and that it may not take you too far, always accompany it with obedience." It seems that M. Gay did not immediately moderate his warlike ardour, for M. Tronson had to make new appeals for prudence the following year.

Some years later, in 1698, the missionary expressed a desire to return to France, but DOLLIER de Casson succeeded in dissuading him, to the greater good of the Indians. As the years went by, M. Gay, realizing the importance of the presence of missionaries among the Indians, bequeathed on 29 October 1707, together with Messrs Maurice Quéré de Tréguron and Vachon de Belmont, a sum, the income from which was to serve in perpetuity for the maintenance of a priest in the service of the Indian missions.

As the proximity of the town constituted a danger for his flock, who were inclined towards drunkenness, M. Gay and his superior remonstrated to the council of Marine, which soon consented to moving the mission to Lac des Deux Montagnes. This move took place in 1721, and M. Gay became the first superior of this mission. He kept this post until his death, which occurred on 29 July 1725 at the seminary in Montreal.

This missionary had spent 37 years in the service of the missions in the Montreal region, and he was one of the great figures among the Sulpicians of his period. He fully deserved the recognition accorded by "his Indians" and the whole colony at the time of his burial in the church of Notre-Dame, for "according to the reports of the time, he exhibited in this function the virtues of an apostle and the qualities of an army general."

JEAN-MARC PARADIS

PAC, FM 17, A 7–2, 1, v.2. [François Vachon] de Belmont, *Histoire du Canada*. [Louis Tronson], *Correspondance de M. de Tronson, troisième Supérieur de la Compagnie de Saint-Sulpice: Lettres choisies,* [*16 juillet 1676–15 janv. 1700*], éd. A.-L. Bertrand (3v., Paris, 1904), II.
A.-L. Bertrand, *Bibliothèque sulpicienne ou histoire littéraire de la compagnie de Saint-Sulpice* (3v., Paris, 1900), I. René Desrochers, *Le Sault-au-Récollet* (Montréal, 1936). Henri Gauthier, *La Compagnie de Saint-Sulpice au Canada* (Montréal, 1912); *Sulpitiana* (Montréal, 1926). Olivier Maurault, *Nos Messieurs* (Montréal, 1936); *Quand Saint-Sulpice allait en guerre* (Montréal, 1940). Pierre Rousseau, *Saint-Sulpice et les missions catholiques* (Montréal, 1930). L.-P. Desrosiers, "Correspondance de M. Magnien," *Cahiers des Dix*, IX (1944), 199–227. Olivier Maurault, "Les vicissitudes d'une mission sauvage," *Revue trimestrielle canadienne* (*L'Ingénieur*), XVI (1930).

GENAPLE DE BELLEFONDS, FRANÇOIS, carpenter, legal practitioner, jailer, process-server, acting clerk of court, royal notary, clerk of the chief road officer, subdelegate of the intendant, churchwarden, and seigneur; b. *c.* 1643, son of Claude Genaple and Catherine Coursier, of the parish of Saint-Merri in Paris; d. 6 Oct. 1709 at Quebec and buried the next day.

Genaple probably arrived in the colony in 1664 or a little before. He was then a carpenter. He settled at Sillery, on a piece of land 2 *arpents* by 60, which he had purchased from Jacques Le Meilleur on 24 Nov. 1665. A few months earlier, on 7 Aug. 1665, he had signed a marriage contract with Marie-Anne de La Porte, a Parisian like himself, and he had married her at Quebec on 12 October.

Genaple de Bellefonds

Two of Genaple's first three children were baptized at Sillery, and the last six at Quebec, where the family seems to have established itself towards the end of 1671 or in 1672, while keeping, at least until 1678, the property at Sillery. This land, situated on the Saint-Michel road, consisted of ten acres under cultivation in 1667 and was probably worked by tenant-farmers from 1672 on.

Genaple was fairly well educated. By giving up farming to go and live in the town, he probably hoped to work his way into colonial officialdom. He began modestly: on 11 Oct. 1673 Buade* de Frontenac, who apparently was protecting him, appointed him "process-server and royal serjeant-at-law serving the whole of Canada." A year later, on 5 Nov. 1674, Genaple appeared before the Conseil Souverain for the first time as a legal practitioner. At about the same period he became jailer of the Quebec prisons; in any event he was occupying that post on 25 June 1675, and on occasion this position caused him difficulties to which we shall return later.

If his activities as process-server, jailer, and practitioner, combined perhaps with the occasional exercise of his craft as a carpenter, provided some kind of subsistence for his small family, Genaple nevertheless continued to seek some high office which might increase his income. In the autumn of 1673 fortune had seemed to smile on him. The notary Romain Becquet*, who had decided to resign, had agreed to make over his minutes to Genaple; consequently, on 18 Oct. 1673, Frontenac had granted the latter a commission as "royal notary and tabellion in the jurisdiction of the town of Quebec"; but on 21 November he had revoked this commission, probably as a result of opposition from the Compagnie des Indes Occidentales, either because it wanted to reserve the right to appoint notaries, or because it questioned the status of royal notary which notaries in the seigneurial jurisdiction of Quebec had enjoyed since Talon*'s time. In 1677 Genaple again encountered some opposition. It came this time from the court officers of the Conseil Souverain, who were then at loggerheads with those of the provost court of Quebec, and who criticized Genaple for discharging two incompatible functions, those of process-server and jailer. Indeed, the law forbad this pluralism. But the Conseil Souverain failed to give an opinion on this particular aspect of the question, and Genaple escaped with no more than a fright. It was only five years later—ten years after he established himself at Quebec—that he was finally able to realize his ambition of becoming a notary: on 9 April 1682 Becquet sold him his minutes for 500 *livres*, on condition that he was received as a notary before All Saints' day; Intendant de MEULLES appointed him royal notary on 22 October to replace Becquet, who had died at the end of April.

Shortly before 1685 certain intrigues had formed around Gilles Rageot*, with the object of taking away from him his office as clerk of the provost court of Quebec and giving it to the ambitious Genaple. Intendant de Meulles appears to have been the instigator of the affair. Having obtained from the king a blank clerk of court's commission, he, on 10 March 1685, certainly entered Genaple's name on it, to replace Rageot, "[whose] infirmities," he asserted, "have rendered [him] incapable of serving." Rageot, it is true, "was subject to epileptic fits," but that had not prevented him from discharging his duties since 1666, when he was already suffering from this disease. The evicted clerk of court took his case to the Conseil Souverain, which after having admitted Genaple to his office changed its mind, and decided to write to the king on Rageot's behalf. While awaiting the court's orders, the council insisted that the records and archives of the provost court be deposited in a cupboard with two locks, of which Rageot had one key and Genaple the other, and that the first continue to make out the writs in his own hand whereas Genaple would sign them, Rageot receiving three quarters of the emoluments and Genaple only one quarter, as a fee for signing. This ruling after the manner of Solomon prevailed until 24 Sept. 1686; on that day Rageot was reinstated in his office following a new commission which had been signed by the king on 24 (or 29) May and which at the same time cancelled that given to Genaple.

From 1690 on at least, and until his death, Genaple was clerk of the chief road officer of New France. The administrative importance of this office was all the greater because the official in charge of the roads system, the Sieur PIERRE ROBINAU de Bécancour, was often conspicuous by his protracted absences. In 1695 Genaple was churchwarden of the parish council of Quebec, and in 1701 churchwarden in charge. Finally, on 16 May 1706, he was appointed subdelegate of the intendant, ANTOINE-DENIS RAUDOT, "to settle," in the latter's absence, "matters which may arise in the Compagnie de la Colonie in this country." Churchwarden in charge, the intendant's subdelegate, here at last was something to give some prestige to a man who arrived in the colony as a carpenter, was all his life jailer of the Quebec prisons, and had scarcely performed anything but tasks that were relatively obscure or that—like the notariat—conferred no right to the honours to which at that time people were so partial. True, on

25 Feb. 1690, after requesting it from Frontenac, our jailer had acquired the enviable title of seigneur of Longues-Vues, a piece of land situated on the Saint John River in Acadia. This land, granted with rights of justice, apparently remained uncultivated, Genaple contenting himself with his new-found and slightly gratuitous designation of seigneur.

In 1692 Genaple had drawn attention upon himself by raising before the Conseil Souverain the question of inventories. This matter, long since settled in France, had not been regulated in any way in the colony. Consequently the lieutenants general and the king's attorneys of the three royal jurisdictions assumed the right of drawing up inventories. Genaple knew his authorities—he possessed in fact a certain number of law books—and basing himself on French jurisprudence he addressed a petition to the council. "As early as the year 1317," he said, "it was enacted and ordained by edict of the king that only notaries were empowered to make inventories and divisions of property, all officers of justice being forbidden to undertake the same." After a long historical account Genaple concluded that it was only inventories and divisions that had been "ordered by a verdict after full argument on both sides and after being contested before the court and without misrepresentation [that fall] to the judge . . . , and when it [is] a question of right of aubaine, default of heirs, and vacant property." Genaple therefore asked that only notaries be authorized to make inventories and divisions of property, save in the exceptional cases covered by French law. This well documented petition remained unanswered. It was not until 1708 that the council decided that inventories should be made "concurrently" by lieutenants general and notaries "according as they shall be required from them."

In spite of the fact that in the second half of his career Genaple held positions of some importance, one cannot avoid the impression that he always remained first and foremost a jailer. He lived with his family in the prisons of the intendant's palace, and that in the long run was enough to affect his character and mark him profoundly. His task was moreover a thankless one: several times he was reprimanded by the Conseil Souverain for having let prisoners escape; furthermore, he had differences with the officers of justice, particularly with Louis-Théandre Chartier de Lotbinière in the La Corruble affair. The atmosphere in which he lived daily, the difficulties that he experienced in making his way in Quebec officialdom, the numerous setbacks that he suffered, among which the escapes were not the least important, all this embittered the ex-carpenter, the more so because he found himself powerless to keep in the path of virtue his own son Jean-François, who became involved in some shady affairs and even served a term in prison. Genaple's bitterness caused him on occasion to use immoderate language, particularly in 1685 and 1701, when he showed disrespect towards the governor general. In both cases he was forced to make a formal apology before the council and to offer his excuses to the governor.

On Genaple's death, which occurred on 6 Oct. 1709, his widow inherited his minutes. According to custom she was entitled to deliver copies of them for payment. Neither this occasional activity nor her occupation of midwife could assure her a livelihood, however, for Genaple had left her only "little wealth." Therefore she obtained from the intendant, on 26 Jan. 1710, permission to succeed her husband as keeper of the prisoners in the intendant's palace, her son Joseph, "who lives with her in the said prisons," agreeing to answer for her. She married René Hubert on 22 Nov. 1711 at Quebec, where she was buried on 28 June 1718.

ANDRÉ VACHON

AJQ, Greffe de Pierre Duquet, 7 août 1665; Greffe de Michel Fillion, 24 nov. 1665; Greffe de François Genaple, 1682–1709; Greffe de Gilles Rageot, 9 avril 1682. AQ, NF, Coll. de pièces jud. et not., 174, 2606; NF, Ins. Cons. sup., II, 44v *et seq.*, 52, 92v *et seq.*, 108; NF, Ins. de la Prév. de Québec, I, 260, 261, 264, 445; NF, Ord. des int., I, 46; IV, 7v *et seq.* "Correspondance de Vaudreuil," APQ *Rapport, 1942–43*, 402. Claude Dablon, "Aveu et dénombrement de la seigneurie de Sillery pour les Révérends Pères Jésuites (1678)," APQ *Rapport, 1943–44*, 15. *Jug. et délib.*, I–IV. *Ord. comm.* (P.-G. Roy), I, 151f., 153f., 155f.; II, 9–11, 92. *Pièces et documents relatifs à la tenure seigneuriale*, [II], 396f. Recensements du Canada, 1666 (APQ *Rapport*); 1667, 1681 (Sulte). A. Roy, *Inv. greffes not.*, VII, 1–192. P.-G. Roy, *Inv. concessions*, IV, 44. Gareau, "La prévôté de Québec," 112. "Les notaires au Canada," 25f. Tanguay, *Dictionnaire*, I, 262. Vachon, "Inv. critique des notaires royaux," *RHAF*, IX (1955–56), 432f. J.-E. Roy, *Histoire du notariat*, I. P.-G. Roy, *Toutes petites choses du régime français* (2v., Québec, 1944), I, 122f., 210f. Vachon, *Histoire du notariat*, 22f., 39. "La bibliothèque de François Genaple," *BRH*, XLIV (1938), 143. "La discipline d'autrefois," *BRH*, XXXVII (1931), 352f.

GEOFFROY, LOUIS, priest, Sulpician, missionary, vicar and parish priest at Port-Royal (Annapolis Royal, N.S.), grand vicar of the bishop of Quebec, founder of schools, churches, and a convent; b. 1660 or 1661 in Paris; d. 1 May 1707 in Quebec at the Hôtel-Dieu.

Geoffroy began his studies for the priesthood at the Séminaire des Trente-Trois. In 1683 he proceeded to the Paris seminary to study theology, and left two years later with minor orders. He then spent three months at the Séminaire des Missions Étrangères in preparation for missionary work in the Orient. While at this seminary he met Bishop Laval, Bishop Saint-Vallier [La Croix], and Abbé Dudouyt*, all of whom urged him to work in New France. Early in 1685 he was ordained by Laval and made preparations to leave for the colony, first pledging himself to the service of the Sulpician order.

Geoffroy was one of six Sulpicians to sail from La Rochelle with Saint-Vallier in June 1685. He took up residence in Acadia the following year, serving at Port-Royal as vicar until 1690, and as parish priest from 1690 to 1692. He not only laid the foundations of primary education in the seaboard colony but also built several schools at his own expense. Unfortunately, much of his work was destroyed in 1690 when attacks by William Phips* and English pirates in turn devastated the Port-Royal district. Frustrated at every turn by illegal trading, petty rivalries among the officers, and the destruction suffered at the hands of the enemy, Geoffroy asked to be moved to the stable centre of the colony. On 1 Jan. 1692, he was appointed parish priest of La Prairie de la Magdeleine and was officially installed the following September.

Geoffroy was in France from 1695 to 1697, settling family matters, regaining his health, and studying moral theology. He returned to La Prairie de la Magdeleine in 1697, with the additional responsibility of serving the Champlain and Batiscan missions. In 1703 he became parish priest of Contrecœur, and served at Sorel in 1703–4. He had also been appointed vicar general of the rural parishes in the diocese and in this position supervised the construction of presbyteries and churches. He became known as the grand architect of the diocese, for he built stone churches in Champlain, Sorel, and Contrecœur, and spent his own money on the construction of a convent in Champlain for the sisters of the Congrégation de Notre-Dame. For a while he considered returning to France, but the shortage of clergy in the colony encouraged him to remain. He died in Quebec in 1707.

Geoffroy's life in North America began with hardship and frustration in Acadia but was followed by a period of accomplishment in Canada. Because his projects were often greater than Saint-Vallier's financial resources, Geoffroy contributed more than 8,000 *livres* of his own funds to carry out the work of developing the diocese.

C. J. Russ

ASSM, Correspondance générale, 2ᵉ partie, lettres de M. Leschassier, 13, 216, 273; lettres de M. Tronson, IV, 461; VI, 183, 226. Caron, "Inventaire de documents," APQ *Rapport, 1939–40*, 264, 275, 305, 321; *1940–41*, 401, 407. Allaire, *Dictionnaire*, I, 236f. Caron, "Prêtres séculiers et religieux," 262f. Henri Gauthier, *Sulpitiana* (Montréal, 1926), 210f. Le Jeune, *Dictionnaire*, I, 695. F.-J. Audet, *Contrecœur: famille, seigneurie, paroisse, village* (Montréal, 1940), 83, 86, 87. Casgrain, *Les Sulpiciens en Acadie*. Morisset, *L'architecture en Nouvelle-France*, 132. Pierre Rousseau, *Saint-Sulpice et les missions catholiques* (Montréal, 1930), 126–31.

GEORGEMÉ, SÉRAPHIN, priest, Recollet, missionary, provincial commissioner for Canada; b. *c.* 1659, d. 1705 in Paris.

He joined the Recollets in Paris in 1679. He was ordained a priest in 1684, and was a lecturer in theology until 1686. The following year, the provincial chapter of Paris appointed him guardian of the convent of Notre-Dame-des-Anges at Quebec and provincial commissioner for Canada. He arrived in Canada in 1688. In his capacity as guardian and commissioner he had to pit himself against the bishop of Quebec concerning the burial of one of his religious. The trouble began on 11 Dec. 1688, when Bishop Saint-Vallier [La Croix] forbad him to have Father Nicolas Cadart, who had just died, buried in the cemetery of the hospice of Notre-Dame-des-Anges. According to the bishop, burials were the exclusive right of the priest of the parish. The next day Father Georgemé replied, asserting the age-old rights of his order, which were based on apostolic concessions and had been approved by Bishop Laval. In a letter addressed to him on 13 December, Bishop Saint-Vallier repeated his prohibition, at the same time suggesting that the priest sing the service in the cathedral or conduct it behind closed doors in his convent. The Recollet replied on 14 December, and under the cover of apparently sincere apologies he none the less stood his ground. Moreover, on 17 December, in the name of the Recollets, he addressed a kind of remonstrance to the bishop on the subject of his refusal to allow Father Cadart solemn burial; among the signatories are to be found the names of Fathers Xiste Le Tac and Ambroise Pélerin. It seems that the solemn service was indeed held, followed by burial in the community cemetery, since on 18 December Bishop Saint-Vallier wrote to Father Georgemé to convey to the Recollets his displeasure at their disobedience.

This long and hasty correspondence between the two ecclesiastics brings out clearly the personality of the superior of the Recollets: an enlightened man, on the whole level-headed, but courageous and firm when necessary. It was this firmness that Bishop Saint-Vallier had occasion to praise in speaking of him in a letter written 3 March 1693 to Father Joseph DENYS: "I hope that God will reward the firmness of Father Séraphin [Georgemé], your *confrère.*" Bishop Saint-Vallier was then maintaining the same position as Father Georgemé, opposing officers who were keeping for themselves part of their soldiers' pay. He asked the parish priests to refuse them absolution. This recommendation created problems for the confessors. A few years later, however, the theologians of the Sorbonne decided in favour of the bishop and Father Georgemé.

In 1691 Father Georgemé exercised his ministry on the Durantaye seigneury, and during his stay it was he who entered almost all the acts in the registry. On 13 Sept. 1692 he signed the deed by which the convent of Notre-Dame-des-Anges was sold to Bishop Saint-Vallier [*see* Luc FILIASTRE]. At that time he was still a lecturer in theology at Quebec.

He went back to France in 1694, and the following year he was in Paris, according to Abbé Tronson's letter to DOLLIER de Casson: "Father Séraphin, who came to see me twice at Ivry, talked to me about everything with moderation. . . ." Perhaps Tronson was alluding to the relations of Father Georgemé with Bishop Saint-Vallier, which have been mentioned earlier! On 27 Feb. 1698 Father Georgemé was back in Canada, since he took part in the third synod at Quebec. He did not play a leading role in this assembly, nor did the 33 secular and regular priests who participated. Bishop Saint-Vallier, the only legislator, reserved that role for himself.

Father Georgemé returned to France in the autumn of 1700. He was elected provincial councillor at the chapter meeting held in Paris in 1701. He died 27 Aug. 1705 in Paris, at the age of 46 and after 26 years in holy orders.

GABRIEL-M.-RÉAL DUMAS

AAQ, Registres d'insinuation A, ff.236, 237, 240, 244, 248, 250, 419, 481; Registres d'insinuation B, f.47. Archives des Franciscains de Québec, Dossier Séraphin Georgemé. Caron, "Inventaire de documents," APQ *Rapport, 1939–40*, 289. *Mandements des évêques de Québec* (Têtu et Gagnon), I, 195, 367. Gosselin, *L'Église du Canada*, IV, 206. Hugolin [Stanislas Lemay], *L'établissement des Récollets à Montréal, 1692* (Montréal, 1911), 49. Jouve, *Les Franciscains et le Canada: aux Trois-Rivières*, 73. J.-E. Roy, *Histoire de la seigneurie de Lauzon* (5v., Lévis, 1897–1904), I, lxxx. Marie-Antoine [Roy], *Saint-Michel de la Durantaye [notes et souvenirs]: 1678–1929* (Québec, 1929), 32, 79. Henri Têtu, *Histoire du palais épiscopal du Québec* (Québec, 1896), 36.

GERMAIN, JOSEPH-LOUIS (but he signed Joseph), Jesuit missionary and professor of theology at the college in Quebec; born in Auvergne on 3 Jan. 1633; died at Quebec early in 1722.

Germain entered the Jesuit novitiate at Toulouse on 21 Sept. 1656 and was ordained in 1676. He began a long and distinguished teaching career in 1662–63 at Saint-Flour, where he taught humanities. He was then placed in charge of philosophy at the college in Béziers (1663–65), at Cahors (1665–67) and at Toulouse (1667–71). In 1671 he went to Clermont-Ferrand to teach theology, remaining there five years. In 1676 he was back at the novitiate at Toulouse as minister for one year, and then as rector from 1677 to 1685. During the next two years he was at the college of Pamiers.

In 1687 Germain was accepted for the Canadian mission and arrived at Quebec on 4 June of that year. He taught both philosophy and theology at the Jesuit college at Quebec until 1710. From 10 Sept. 1710 to 1 Oct. 1716 he was the superior of the Canadian missions of his order, having had some previous experience in that responsible position during the absence of Father BOUVART in 1699. The college at Quebec remained his ordinary place of residence during this period. In October 1718 he left for a visit to France. The records indicate that he died at Quebec in January or February 1722.

During his teaching career at the college in Quebec between 40 and 50 students came twice daily from the seminary to be instructed by the Jesuits. It was Father Germain who organized two congregations dedicated to the Blessed Virgin Mary at the college, one for the clergy and the other for the students. He never pretended to scholarly or to administrative abilities. On the contrary, he protested that he was quite unable to draft communications suitable for the information of Roman officials. Nevertheless, he seemed completely engrossed in his teaching duties and expressed satisfaction with the academic achievements of the pupils he instructed at the college at Quebec over a 23-year period.

Numerous extant letters written by Father Germain between 1693 and 1718 indicate a very precise understanding of the political implications and importance of the Iroquois missions of his order. The threat posed by the English located to the south of New France was a recurrent theme in his correspondence. His letters are also a valuable source of information concerning the intercolonial wars, particularly the events of 1711–13. It was he who ordered the Jesuits, who had left the Iroquois cantons in 1709 because of fear of a general attack on the French colony, to return to their mission stations in 1711. He also played a dominant role in organizing popular preparations and allaying general fears during the WALKER expedition of 1711.

C. J. JAENEN

AN, Col., C¹¹ᴬ, 32. ARSI, Gallia 110/I, ff.85, 96a, 102, 114, 147; 110/II, 66, 67, 110, 124, 131. ASJCF. *JR* (Thwaites), LXVI, LXXI. *Jug. et délib.*, V, 660.

GIBSONE, SIR JOHN, colonel, commander of land forces sent to Newfoundland in 1697; b. Ratho, near Edinburgh, 1637; d. 24 Oct. 1717.

Gibsone entered the Dutch army and gained a captain's commission in 1675. He came to England in 1688 with the invasion forces of William of Orange and obtained an English commission as lieutenant-colonel in February 1689. He got his first regimental command in 1694 and was lieutenant-governor of Portsmouth from May 1689 until his death.

In 1697 Gibsone was appointed commander of the 2,000 men sent to Newfoundland with a naval force under Sir John Norris*. The combined expedition was to recover the English settlements captured for the French in 1696 by PIERRE LE MOYNE d'Iberville and Brouillan [MOMBETON], to remove the French from Placentia (Plaisance), and to secure a permanent military establishment at St John's. Early in 1697 the Board of Trade had received accounts of the "devastation of the English settlements in Newfoundland," in which the inhabitants and fishermen of St John's described the hardships and deprivation they had endured before finally capitulating, gave details of the number of colonists who had been killed or forced to leave, and reported the French threat to seize the whole of the Newfoundland fishing trade and even "to take all New England next year." In spite of the urgency of the situation, the punitive expedition under Gibsone and Norris was late in arriving in Newfoundland and inactive when it did arrive.

St John's was found to be deserted and was reoccupied. Handicapped by lack of materials and provisions, Gibsone nevertheless set about the construction of shore batteries and a fort. These were not completed, however, nor was anything done about driving the French from Placentia. When a French naval squadron under the Marquis de Nesmond appeared off St John's in August 1697, neither side attacked. Gibsone returned to England in October 1697, leaving behind a garrison of 300 under Major Thomas HANDASYDE, and the situation in Newfoundland was temporarily resolved by the Peace of Ryswick.

Gibsone had no further direct contact with Newfoundland but was frequently in attendance on the Lords of Trade and Plantations to advise on the situation at St John's; he regularly pressed for better support to be given to the colony. He thus became involved in the long-standing dispute between the colonists and the Western Adventurers. Unlike Norris, who favoured the West Country men, Gibsone urged stronger and more extensive fortifications and the establishing of a settled government: "I do not mean a military government but the civil and Church government also." Gibsone's recommendations were to go unheeded for another 30 years, however, and a cryptic marginal note was added to one of his letters: "he will accomplish nothing."

Although after 1700 Gibsone was mainly concerned with affairs at Portsmouth, as late as 1710 he was still advocating a new fort at Ferryland (Forillon). He died in 1717, aged eighty.

C. M. ROWE

PRO, *Acts of P.C., col. ser., 1680–1720*; *CSP, Col., 1696–97*, no.586 (account of the capture of St John's by the French); *1697–98, 1704–5, 1706–8, 1710–11*. *DNB*. Lounsbury, *British fishery at Nfld.* Prowse, *History of Nfld.*

GILL, MICHAEL, mariner of Charlestown, Mass.; b. *c.* 1673 at Dover, England; m. Relief Dowse on 26 May 1696 (o.s.); d. 14 June 1720 at Charlestown, father of at least ten children.

In 1698 Gill was trading with Canada in a 40-ton vessel, handling mixed cargoes. He traded also with the outposts at Bonavista and other parts of Newfoundland. On 18 Aug. 1704 (29 August, N.S.), when Bonavista was attacked by a French fleet under Jean LÉGER de La Grange, Gill was the only English captain to escape after a six-hour battle. An account of this incident in the *Flying Post* of London stated that "had they [the French] taken Captain Gill they would not have left house stage or goods in the harbour; all which is owing... to the courage and conduct of Captain Gill."

Little is known of the extent of Gill's trade with Canada, but he was active in trading with the southern parts of America, the West Indies, and Europe and owned shares in many vessels. He engaged in land transactions at Charlestown and at the time of his death he held, from Harvard College, a lease on one of the ferry boats going to Boston.

Gill's eldest son, Michael (1699–1773), settled in Newfoundland in 1748 and rose to be the first colonel of the militia; Nicholas, possibly a son or grandson, was chief magistrate at St John's. A grandson, Moses, became lieutenant-governor of Massachusetts (1794–1800).

M. C. ROSENFIELD

"Mass. Archives," VII, IX. Mass. Hist. Soc., J.

Davis Coll., 161.G.50 (Gill's will). Charlevoix, *History* (Shea), V, 169. *Harvard College records* (3v., Col. Soc. Mass. pub., XV–XVI, XXXI, Boston, 1925, 1935), II, 444, 468. *New Eng. Hist. and Geneal. Register*, VII (1853), 149; XVI (1862), 38; XXIX (1875); XXX (1876); XXXI (1877). Prowse, *History of Nfld.*, 239–41 (contains account from *Flying Post*, 10 March 1704/5). T. B. Wyman, *The genealogies and estates of Charlestown in the county of Middlesex and Commonwealth of Massachusetts, 1629–1818* (Boston, 1879), 408–9.

GILLAM, BENJAMIN, sea captain and adventurer; b. 23 March 1662/63, son of Zachariah Gillam* and Phoebe Phillips; d. 14 May 1706.

Benjamin Gillam's chief claim to fame is his role in the triangular drama that took place in the Port Nelson area of Hudson Bay in 1682. With a group of 14 New England colleagues, all "very resolute fellows," he sailed the *Bachelor's Delight* from New England on 21 June 1682 to Nelson River, intending to trespass on the monopoly of the HBC. Even as the group set about establishing themselves, Benjamin's father Zachariah, captain of the *Prince Rupert* and an employee of the HBC, was approaching the bay with a new governor, John Bridgar*. About the same time, RADISSON was bringing a French party from Canada into Hayes River.

By a combination of guile, luck, and superior knowledge of the area, Radisson outwitted his opponents. Zachariah Gillam perished when his ship was crushed in the ice in October 1682, and the following year Radisson captured the posts held by the HBC and by the interlopers from New England, taking Bridgar and the young Gillam prisoner. After his release by the governor of New France, Le Febvre* de La Barre, Benjamin returned to Boston to find himself under arrest. The collector of customs for New England, Edward Randolph, had been empowered to take this drastic action against him, but circumstances soon changed in Gillam's favour. His interloping activities against the HBC were disregarded, and his status as a British subject was upheld. Indeed, the HBC was to argue its claim to vast possessions in Hudson Bay on the fact that Gillam had reached Port Nelson in advance of Radisson's party.

The association of the Gillams with Hudson Bay seems to terminate about 1684, but the name reappears in British records in the 1690s, when the family was engaged in building ships for English merchants.

Benjamin Gillam died on 14 May 1706. His will, dated 28 April 1701, mentions his wife, Abigail, and two daughters, Abigail (born 1684) and Ann (born 1688).

MAUD M. HUTCHESON

HBRS, IX (Rich); XI, XX (Rich and Johnson). PRO, *Acts of P.C., col. ser., 1680–1720. New Eng. Hist. and Geneal. Register*, XIX (1865). Nute, *Caesars of the wilderness.*

GLANDELET, CHARLES DE, priest, writer, teacher, preacher, secretary to Bishop Saint-Vallier [LA CROIX], superior of various communities of nuns, ninth superior of the seminary of Quebec, vicar general; b. 1645 at Vannes in the province of Brittany; d. 1 July 1725 at the Ursuline convent in Trois-Rivières.

Abbé Charles de Glandelet was a man who spent an active life and whose many talents did not always meet with unanimous appreciation. On his arrival in Canada in August 1675 he took up residence in the seminary of Quebec while working in the secretariat of the bishopric. Several documents in the "Livre du Secrétariat" were recopied by him, in particular "the acts against [Thubières*] de Queylus." In 1678 he was appointed second assistant to the superior of the seminary and retained this office until 1684. From that time on Abbé Glandelet became the champion of the rights of the seminary of Quebec, an attitude which was to be the source of a great deal of friction with Bishop Saint-Vallier, who was considered to be "suspicious and susceptible in the extreme, even in France." The bishop's personal manner was certainly displeasing to the members of the seminary. According to Glandelet, during meetings the bishop "begins by using sweet words and acting in a flattering and gentle manner; but as soon as he is opposed he displays the indignation and out-bursts of anger which turn one's mind and heart against him."

The bishop's demands were numerous; he wanted to extend his authority to fields as diverse as the temporal administration of the seminary, its internal regulations, the upkeep of ecclesiastics who were not attached to it, the acceptance of the children for the Petit Séminaire, whom the bishop would have liked to place there gratuitously, and the appointment of priests to charges which depended on the seminary, in particular that of Quebec. Despite these difficulties, Abbé Glandelet displayed real abilities as an administrator. In his correspondence with the authorities of the Séminaire des Missions Étrangères in Paris, on which the seminary of Quebec was dependent, he made discerning remarks concerning the general regulations which should be in force in all the seminaries, but at the same time he advocated adjustments which were necessitated by the particular circumstances of life in Canada. The very terms of the union between the seminary of Quebec and that in Paris made some compromises

Glandelet

necessary because of the distance separating the two establishments. Glandelet showed particular reticence about the right of appointment of a superior by persons who did not know the possible incumbent or who might send an inexperienced man to Canada. One point, however, was clear in the assistant superior's mind: it concerned the "sharing in common" which should be practised "at least by the officers who will be in charge of each seminary." An expression that returns constantly in his writings is "detachment from worldly possessions." He put this principle into application himself when on 7 Nov. 1679 he gave all his property to the seminary, on condition that the authorities provide for the needs of his mother, who had crossed with him to Canada and did sewing at the seminary.

In 1684 Abbé Glandelet was appointed canon of the cathedral and first theologal of the chapter in addition to assuming the role of procurator to the bishop and the chapter. He owed his appointment to Bishop LAVAL, who considered him worthy to figure among the first 13 titular canons appointed in Canada. After Bishop Laval's retirement relations became strained between Bishop Saint-Vallier and the canons. The points of contention concerned the chapter's jurisdiction, its own statutes, the appointment and rank of the canons and their responsibilities with regard to the parish of Quebec, the choice of precentors, etcetera. The bishop would have liked to arrange everything according to his point of view. Besides, according to Glandelet, "His Excellency's prejudices are so great, the unfavourable impressions that he has acquired of us so strong, that most of what we say and do he turns to our disadvantage."

Despite these difficulties Canon Glandelet was proposed by the authorities of the Séminaire des Missions Étrangères in Paris for the office of superior of the seminary, as early as 1687, "for the good and the edification of the church in Canada." In their letter to the priests in Quebec they added that Glandelet might also assist the parish priest of Quebec in his ministry, in particular in the field of preaching, "for it is of capital importance that this function be performed as much as possible by some ecclesiastic who will do so gracefully." It is difficult to form an accurate idea of Glandelet as a preacher. We know that he pronounced the first funeral oration for Bishop Laval. He undoubtedly had a more resounding success when in January 1694 he delivered a sermon in the cathedral in which he fulminated against plays and openly condemned the persons who took part in these productions. Some days later Bishop Saint-Vallier issued a pastoral letter which was distinctly unfavourable to the plays

staged by Buade* de Frontenac in the Château Saint-Louis during the winter of 1693. On the other hand, it seems that after being a popular preacher Glandelet saw his audience desert him little by little, supposedly because he adhered too blindly in his sermons to what the bishop wanted him to say, "while being careless in the teachings that he gave."

The years 1692–93 were painful ones. At this time, indeed, relations between the bishop and Abbé Glandelet became so bad that, according to a nun of the Congrégation de Notre-Dame, the bishop forbad Glandelet to exercise his office as assistant superior and withdrew from him permission to hear confessions. It is, moreover, certain that the bishop of Quebec had asked the superiors of the seminary in Paris to recall to France Abbé Glandelet and his friend, ANGO Des Maizerets, the superior of the seminary. M. Brisacier, the superior of the Séminaire des Missions Étrangères in Paris, replied to this request, saying: "the king's intention is that in the event that His Excellency the Bishop of Quebec is not satisfied with their conduct at the end of a year after notification of the regulations which have been laid down today, His Excellency the Bishop may send back to France the aforementioned gentlemen, whom we enjoin with all our strength to obey with the respect they owe His Majesty and their bishop."

This letter, dated 20 Jan. 1692 at Paris, had no sequel, since the seminary in Paris could find no one to replace the two ecclesiastics. They were, moreover, "canons and dignitaries." The direction of the seminary could very well be taken away from them, but they could not be deprived of their benefices. Be that as it may, relations certainly improved, since we find Glandelet in a new function in 1697, that of vicar general to the bishop of Quebec. He was delighted, but took care in announcing the news to point out that "the good Lord takes pleasure in establishing His works by ways that seemed certain to destroy them." We find the vicar general, in the exercise of his functions, conducting a succession of inquiries among the Ursulines of Quebec to gather evidence relative to claims of extraordinary cures for a nun and one of the boarders in the convent obtained through the instrumentality of Brother Didace Pelletier*.

In addition to his position as an official of the diocese, Glandelet held several superiorships concurrently: that of the Ursulines of Trois-Rivières, which he held from the founding of the convent in 1697 till his death; that of the Ursulines of Quebec from 1700 till 1715, and that of the nuns of the Hôtel-Dieu of Quebec from 1710 on. He also found time to write. We are indebted to him for the text of an office of the Holy Family done in collaboration with a religious from France, as well as the biographical accounts of the first two superiors of the Congrégation de Notre-Dame, Marguerite Bourgeoys* and Marie BARBIER. Was he the author of the commentaries which accompany the manuscript copy of the Comte de Frontenac's funeral oration, pronounced on 19 Dec. 1698 by Father Olivier GOYER? The Recollet exaggerates indeed the praises addressed to Frontenac, and the annotator attacks with a biting pen:

> "To judge fairly
> The oration made to the glory
> Of a hero of sad memory
> Nothing is lacking but the truth."

In the notes which accompany his study on Frontenac and his times, George Stewart says that Abbé Casgrain told him that these remarks were due to Abbé Charles de Glandelet.

Finally in 1721 Abbé Glandelet became the ninth superior of the seminary of Quebec. He remained in this office until 1723. This appointment was undoubtedly no surprise, as his name had been suggested for the post on various occasions.

Was Glandelet a Jansenist? Several accusations on this point have been made against him. The Ursulines of Quebec were somewhat "prejudiced" against him. What may seem strange is that he himself suspected certain people of practising Jansenism, in particular one Merlac*, who had in his possession M. Arnauld's *Lettres*. In 1714 Glandelet left Quebec temporarily for the Ursuline convent in Trois-Rivières. It seems that there was a connection between this departure and the Jansenist doctrine. At the very least Abbé Glandelet was rigid in his morals and austere in his principles. One has only to read the regulations of the seminary of Quebec to ascertain the painful requirements laid down by the Abbé. He himself lived a life of labour, mortification, and detachment from worldly possessions. His will, drawn up in his hand on 27 Nov. 1716, shows that he possessed nothing "which does not belong on several scores to the Séminaire des Missions Étrangères in Quebec, of which I have the honour of being a member ...."; it also indicates that "in addition I have made to it [the seminary] a donation of the little wealth I had when I came to Canada by a private act written and signed by my hand the seventh day of November one thousand six hundred and seventy nine. ..." Why then did Glandelet make his second will in 1716? He explained that he had taken certain personal

belongings to the convent of the Ursulines in Trois-Rivières, and he asked the members of the seminary "to be so kind as to leave them with them as a favour to, and for the benefit of, their community." He took advantage of the occasion to ask pardon of all the members of the seminary for anything that was blameworthy in his conduct and "for all the bad examples that I have set."

In 1723 Abbé Glandelet, crippled with infirmities, left Quebec for the Ursuline convent in Trois-Rivières, where he ended his days. His death occurred on 1 July 1725; at this point, therefore, a correction must be made to Tanguay, who said that he died in June. His body was probably taken to Quebec, since there is nothing to be found in the bishop's palace at Trois-Rivières on the subject of his burial.

"He was generally mourned and died as he had lived, that is to say in sentiments that make us believe without difficulty that he has gone to harvest the fruit of his labours and to share the glory that God reserves for those who have served Him with as much ardour and loyalty as he did throughout his life." This was the eulogy, no doubt merited, that Canons Pierre Hazeur* and Jean-Marie de La Corne* bestowed upon Abbé Glandelet after his death. Thus disappeared, in the words of Abbé Honorius Provost, "one of the most distinguished and most representative priests of the seminary."

NOËL BÉLANGER

ACND, Charles Glandelet, Le vray esprit de Marguerite Bourgeoys et de l'Institut des sœurs séculières de la Congrégation Notre-Dame établie à Ville-Marie en l'Isle de Montréal en Canada, 1701. ASQ, Chapitre, 16, 17, 30, 31, 32, 41, 306; Congrégation Notre-Dame, 65; Lettres, M, 6, 7, 38; P, 11; MSS, 198; Polygraphie, II, 28; Séminaire, I, 31a; VI, 73u; XVII, 35; LI, XCII, 17; XCV, 4a, 7, 24. Juchereau, *Annales* (Jamet). Provost, *Le Séminaire de Québec: documents et biographies*, 421–22. Caron, "Prêtres séculiers et religieux," 230. Gosselin, *L'Église du Canada*, IV; *Vie de Mgr de Laval*. George Stewart, "Frontenac and his times," in *Narrative and critical history of America*, ed. Justin Winsor (8v., Boston and New York, 1884–89), IV, 397. "Le récollet Olivier Goyer," *BRH*, I (1895), 65f. Odoric-M. [Jouve], "Étude historique et critique sur les actes du Frère Didace Pelletier, Récollet," *BRH*, XVII (1911), 87.

GLEDHILL, SAMUEL, lieutenant-governor of Placentia (Plaisance); b. 7 April 1677, at Horbury, near Wakefield, Yorkshire, younger son of Robert Gledhill, cloth-dresser, and Isabella (Atkinson); d. 1735 or 1736.

Educated at Wakefield Grammar School and privately, Samuel Gledhill ran away from home before the age of twelve to join the army but was

Gledhill

brought back again. Later, with his parents' consent, he entered the navy and served Captain (later Admiral Sir) Hovenden WALKER as his secretary. Gledhill went to Spain, where he was kidnapped, and was sold as a slave in the West Indies. After his release he returned to Spain and Italy. Commissioned lieutenant in 1702 and lieutenant-colonel in 1707, he served in England and in the Low Countries; at the siege of Douai he was wounded and taken prisoner by the French.

In 1702 Gledhill had married Isabella Richmond of Carlisle, by whom he was to have at least nine children. In 1710 he contested a parliamentary seat in Carlisle, but without success. In 1712, however, he was made lieutenant-governor of Carlisle with the substantive rank of captain in General Stanhope's regiment of foot. When peace came, Gledhill found that life as a half-pay captain did not suit him; he fell out with his wife's family and spent some time at The Hague before receiving an appointment, through the patronage of the Duke of Argyll, as lieutenant-governor of Placentia, Newfoundland, in succession to Martin Purcell, who, in 1717, had replaced John MOODY.

On the voyage out to take up his new post, Gledhill and his family were shipwrecked off Ferryland Head on 3 Sept. 1719, but were rescued and eventually reached Placentia. Gledhill was armed with sufficient capital to buy the rights to many houses and fishing-rooms which Moody had acquired when the French left Placentia. As lieutenant-governor of Placentia, Gledhill was nominally responsible to Richard Philipps*, the governor of Nova Scotia and Placentia; on his arrival in Newfoundland, Gledhill took over command of two companies of Philipps' regiment, and received an allocation of £2,500 for additional fortifications. In 1720, however, Philipps issued orders that the garrison at Placentia be reduced to a single company of 40 men and that the inhabitants of Newfoundland be induced to transfer to Nova Scotia. Gledhill had to acquiesce in the establishment cut, and the fortification works were left unfinished, but he refused to display proclamations that the inhabitants were to leave unless he was ordered to do so by the secretary of state "in whose province lies this land."

The value of Gledhill's official salary and allowances he later estimated at £688 15s., but he was determined to exploit his position to the full. By 1727 he had 24 properties and a capital of over £11,000. Many of his "plantations" were in the names of his eight children—including three daughters born in Newfoundland, named Placentia, America, and Carolina. He invested heavily too in ships, and in 1727 he wrote to a relative, "I've so disposed my Affairs, that from what ever

Corner of the Compass the Wind Blows, it shall serve some one of my Children's Vessels, each of which is to be an owner."

In 1726 his wife and children went home, and his wife died soon after reaching England. In his rambling letters and notes, Gledhill frequently comments on his solitary state; eventually, however, one of his sons, Joseph, rejoined him and was edged into the captaincy of Gledhill's company. Joseph also assisted his father in many business ventures. In 1731 Gledhill claimed a community of 30 households with a winter population of 179 (plus the garrison), almost all of whom depended on him in some way. His new warehouse monopolized domestic commerce as well as the trade with the summer fishing population of some 2,000 men. He divided up Great Beach and leased it and other shore properties annually for fishing stages and cook-rooms. Some of his boats were manned as fishing vessels by members of the garrison, others were hired out to visiting fishing captains. His ships traded across the Atlantic and he had a man of business in London. He even began shipbuilding at Placentia.

When he first arrived in Newfoundland Gledhill was assiduous in suggesting improvements, such as the construction of a road between Placentia and St John's, and several times he met costs for his men when supplies went astray. As he became increasingly absorbed in business, however, he gave less attention to Fort Frederick at Placentia and its garrison, and often failed to answer official letters, claiming never to have received them.

Although Gledhill paid little attention to the orders of his superior, Philipps, he made use of his position as lieutenant-governor when dealing with the commodores of the annual convoys to Newfoundland. Gledhill refused to acknowledge the superior authority of the convoy commodores, whose supervisory visits he resented, maintaining that he was responsible only to Philipps. Gledhill collaborated closely, however, with the fishing admirals who normally dealt with disputes arising during the fishing season.

Gledhill's activities were bound to bring him into collision with the Board of Trade and Plantations and with the English merchants concerned in the Newfoundland fishery. The latter were determined to check the activities of the Newfoundland settlers, to maintain prior rights to shore facilities, and to control commerce in the colony. At various times between 1722 and 1727 complaints against Gledhill were made by merchants of London, Bristol, Poole, Dartmouth, Bideford, Barnstable, and Whitehaven. He was accused of monopolizing the trade in wines, spirits, and woollen goods, of maintaining the beaches as his private property and charging high rates for their use; his shipbuilding project was also condemned as it would exhaust the supply of raw materials used for building stages and cookrooms. It was claimed that he removed from their houses persons he did not like, and filled Placentia with Jacobites, Irish papists, and transported felons. A former member of the garrison, Thomas Salmon, brought serious charges against him: Gledhill, he claimed, had driven him out of his fishing business, seized his house, and cruelly treated his wife and daughter. Gledhill managed, however, to find witnesses to discredit Salmon.

By 1727 the complaints against the lieutenant-governor began to be taken seriously, and in 1728 the Board of Trade reported to the Duke of Newcastle that "so disorderly a person could not be allowed to continue." Gledhill's pay was stopped and in May 1729, when Captain Henry Osborn was designated governor of Newfoundland and commander-in-chief, Gledhill was put under his orders and instructed to come home. He duly appeared with witnesses and evidence at the end of 1729, and, after hearings before the privy council committee, he was restored to his command on 11 June 1730. After his return to Newfoundland with reinforcements for his depleted company, in August 1731, there was less friction with the authorities at home, perhaps because Newfoundland—at last—had a permanent governor to whom the lieutenant-governor of Placentia was directly responsible. Gledhill could no longer play off his absent superior, the governor of Nova Scotia, against the annual convoy commodores. Moreover, after his return in 1731 Gledhill had to share his local influence with the newly appointed justices of the peace. In the fall of 1731 George Clinton*, the first of many royal officials to hold the double position of governor and commodore, reported that Placentia was difficult to manage: "these are a set of people that no one person living can please." But by and large Gledhill, now old and prosperous, gave no more trouble. In 1733 the governor, Lord Muskerry [MacCarthy], made no complaints about him.

Samuel Gledhill seems to have been absent from Placentia in September 1735 and had died before 26 May 1736, when his son, Captain Joseph Gledhill, took over his depleted and decrepit company, and the poorly maintained Fort Frederick. How much of Gledhill's fortune survived him does not appear to be known.

Samuel Gledhill represents a stage in the development of settled authority in Newfoundland. As a military officer with a limited income from the government, he took some responsibility for local government, but was soon attracted to set up

as landowner, merchant, and monopolist. Undoubtedly he exploited his position at the government's expense and was guilty of many technical offences against trade regulations. How far he was guilty of oppression and cruelty as well is hard to say, though he was certainly arbitrary in his treatment of competitors. His naive letters and autobiographical sketch show him to have been pleased with his success. His example demonstrates clearly that it was possible for an individual settler, established in a newly acquired part of Newfoundland, to build up a substantial locally based commerce and a large private fortune.

D. B. QUINN

W. H. Chippindall, *Memoirs of Lt.-Col. Samuel Gledhill, lieutenant governor of Placentia and commander-in-chief of Newfoundland from 1719 to 1727, to which is prefixed a connected narrative of his life by his descendant, Colonel W. H. Chippindall* (Kendal, 1910). PRO, *Acts of P.C., col. ser., 1720–45*; *B.T.Journal, 1718–22, 1722/23–1728, 1728/29–1734, 1734/35–1741*; *CSP, Col., 1719–20, 1720–21, 1722–23, 1724–25, 1728–29, 1730, 1731, 1735–36, 1737*; *C.T.Papers, 1720–28*; *C.T.Books and Papers, 1731–34, 1735–38*. Lounsbury, *British fishery at Nfld.* Prowse, *History of Nfld.* Rogers, *Newfoundland.*

GOBIN, JEAN, merchant; b. 1646 at Tours; d. 11 July 1703 at Quebec.

Shortly after his arrival in Canada in the early 1680s, Gobin established himself as a merchant and shipper. In 1685 his name appeared on the list of directors of the Compagnie du Nord. After Philippe Gaultier* de Comporté's death in 1687, Gobin acted as his children's guardian, but this led to a lengthy legal dispute in which Gobin was accused of profiting at the expense of Comporté's heirs and was ordered to return a substantial sum of money. In 1688 Gobin was granted property in Quebec's Lower Town. On 14 April 1689 he and several partners obtained fishing rights in the Gulf of St Lawrence, and in 1690 he was granted a seigneury in Acadia, which he sold within a year. Gobin's partner in several interests, including a tannery and brickyard, as well as an investment in the Compagnie de la Colonie, was the colony's leading merchant, CHARLES AUBERT de La Chesnaye.

Gobin died insolvent in 1703. Both he and his wife Gabrielle Bécasseau were buried in the crypt of the church of Notre-Dame de Québec. They left no children.

EDWARD H. BORINS

AN, Col., C¹¹ᴬ, 6, f.431; 15, f.86; 125, ff.88, 89, 368–70. *Jug. et délib.*, II, III, IV. A. Roy, *Inv. greffes not.*, III, IV, VII, XVIII, XIX. P.-G. Roy, *Inv. concessions*, IV, 39, 45; *Inv. ins. Cons. souv.* Charland,

Godefroy de Lintot

"Notre-Dame de Québec: le nécrologe de la crypte," 170. Fauteux, *Essai sur l'industrie sous le régime français*, I, 156.

GODEFROY DE LINTOT, MICHEL, esquire, captain in the colonial regular troops, town major of Trois-Rivières, seigneur; baptized 21 Oct. 1637, eldest son of Jean Godefroy* de Lintot and Marie Leneuf; d. 18 May 1709, at Trois-Rivières.

Lintot was the first white child to be born and baptized at Trois-Rivières. On 2 Sept. 1664, he married Perrinne Picoté de Belestre, and four years later became seigneur of Dutort, which had been donated to him by his uncle, Michel Leneuf* Du Hérisson. In the ensuing decade, Godefroy settled a dozen inhabitants on this seigneury.

Lintot was appointed an ensign in 1667 on the recommendation of Alexandre de Prouville* de Tracy and was successively promoted to the ranks of half-pay captain in 1687 and of full captain in 1700. He became town major of Trois-Rivières in 1702, a position which he held until his death. There is no evidence that he served in any of the military engagements of the period. Some writers have credited him with participation in Jacques TESTARD de Montigny's 1705 Newfoundland campaign, but the Lintot referred to in the narrative of this expedition was Michel's son, René.

Like his father before him, Michel was burdened with a large family. Of his 12 children, René and six daughters married, three of the latter choosing officers of the colonial regular troops. Michel apparently left little money at his death in 1709, for his widow was compelled to appeal to the state for financial assistance.

C. J. RUSS

AJTR, Greffe de Séverin Ameau, 22 févr. 1672, 6 août 1673, 2 sept., 21 nov. 1674, 22 févr., 13 sept. 1676; Greffe de J.-B. Pottier, 14 juin 1704; Registres d'état civil de Trois-Rivières. AN, Col., C¹¹ᴬ, 2, f.232. "Correspondance de Vaudreuil," APQ *Rapport, 1939–40*, 403; *1942–43*, 402, 423. "L'expédition de M. de Montigny à Terreneuve en 1705," APQ *Rapport, 1922–23*, 293–98. P.-G. Roy, *Inv. concessions*, I, 150f.; *La famille Godefroy de Tonnancour* (Lévis, 1904). Benjamin Sulte, *Histoire de la ville des Trois-Rivières et de ses environs, depuis la découverte jusqu'à l'année 1637* (Montréal, 1870).

GODEFROY DE SAINT-PAUL, JEAN-AMADOR, esquire, interpreter, captain of the Trois-Rivières militia, fur-trader, seigneur; baptized at Trois-Rivières on 18 July 1649, son of Jean Godefroy* de Lintot and Marie Leneuf; d. 10 Sept. 1730, at Trois-Rivières.

In August 1682, Saint-Paul acted as interpreter for the Miamis and Kiskakons during a conference held in Montreal, which would seem to indicate that he had previously spent some time in the west. In 1684 and 1687 he accompanied, as captain of the Trois-Rivières militia, the expeditions of Governors Le Febvre* de La Barre and BRISAY de Denonville against the Iroquois. In the late 1680s and early 1690s he and Antoine Lepellé, his partner and future son-in-law, traded with the Ottawas.

By 1706, Saint-Paul's interests had grown to include the eastern cod fisheries. In that year, RIGAUD de Vaudreuil and JACQUES RAUDOT granted him a seigneury in Labrador consisting of five leagues frontage by ten leagues depth on both sides of the Grande Rivière (Quitzezaqui). He continued to make his home in Trois-Rivières, however, and to trade with the tribes nearby. He had no doubt mastered the language of the Algonkins; he was accorded the privilege of selling them beer and cider on their visits to Trois-Rivières.

Saint-Paul was married twice, and outlived both his wives. Marguerite Jutrat, whom he married in Trois-Rivières on 12 Nov. 1675, bore him two daughters. After her death, he married Françoise Lepellé in Trois-Rivières on 22 July 1682. She gave birth to six children, and predeceased him by three years.

C. J. RUSS

AJM, Greffe d'Antoine Adhémar, 22 juillet 1682, 13, 16, 17 sept. 1694; Greffe de Bénigne Basset, 2, 3 août 1688. AJTR, Greffe de Severin Ameau, 17 nov. 1675, 7 juillet 1698. AN, Col., C¹¹ᴬ, 6, ff.4–25, 476–79. *NYCD* (O'Callaghan and Fernow), IX, 334. P.-G. Roy, *Inv. concessions*, IV, 188–89; *Inv. ord. int.*, I, 127; *La famille Godefroy de Tonnancour* (Lévis, 1904).

GODEFROY DE TONNANCOUR, RENÉ, king's attorney, lieutenant-general of Trois-Rivières, seigneur of La Pointe-du-Lac; baptized 12 May 1669 at Trois-Rivières; son of Louis Godefroy de Normanville, king's attorney, and of Marguerite Seigneuret; grandson of Jean Godefroy* de Lintot; buried 21 Sept. 1738 at Trois-Rivières.

Tonnancour was only ten when his father died and could not immediately succeed to his father's position. Indeed, the intendant, Duchesneau*, wrote on 10 Nov. 1679 that "the office of king's attorney at Trois-Rivières is vacant because of the death of the Sieur de Normanville, who has left a son who shows much promise." He suggested that the office be kept for him, to which the king willingly assented. Thus the office remained vacant until 1695, the year in which he took the position.

On 12 May 1714 Tonnancour succeeded Jean LECHASSEUR as lieutenant-general for civil and criminal affairs for the jurisdiction of Trois-

Godefroy de Vieuxpont

Rivières. He also acted as syndic for the Recollets in the same town; in this capacity he watched over their temporal interests and supervised the construction of a monastery and church for the religious community. The Ursulines, who established a convent and a hospital in the town, also found in him a protector. Finally, he made the Charon Brothers a gift of a piece of land for the setting-up of a boys' school.

In 1718 Tonnancour obtained confirmation for his family of the ennoblement which had been granted in 1668 but which had never been registered. He gave some attention, without much success, to his seigneury of La Pointe-du-Lac which he had inherited from his father; the latter, through his marriage with Marguerite Seigneuret when she was only nine, had added to his domain the adjacent land belonging to his father-in-law. On it Tonnancour tried to settle some Indians, who eked out a miserable existence in wretched lodges until about the end of the French régime.

On 8 Oct. 1731 Beauharnois* de La Boische and Hocquart* had rendered a glowing tribute to the jurist: "The Sieur de Tonnancour, in his capacity of subdelegate of the intendant and as an intelligent and good judge, settles summarily almost all the disputes in the government of Trois-Rivières."

In a spirit of humility Tonnancour had asked to be buried in the cemetery rather than in the parish church. The Ursulines wrote that the deceased had always been "the counsellor, stay, and support of all those who had recourse to his protection." The burial certificate, drawn up by the parish priest of Trois-Rivières, notes the moral qualities of the deceased during his life as well as during his illness.

By his marriage in 1693 to Marguerite Ameau, the daughter of the notary Séverin AMEAU, he had five sons and five daughters. Two of the daughters became Ursulines. The eldest son, Antoine-Charles*, became a priest and then a canon of the chapter of Quebec. The continuator of the line was Louis-Joseph, born 27 March 1712.

HERVÉ BIRON

AJTR, Registres d'état civil de Trois-Rivières. AN, Col., C¹¹ᴬ, 4–6. *Jug. et délib.*, II, IV, V, VI. *Lettres de noblesse* (P.-G. Roy), I, 197f. P.-G. Roy, *Inv. concessions*, I, III; *Inv. jug. et délib., 1717–1760*, I, 210, 266. Alexandre Dugré, *La Pointe-du-Lac* (Trois-Rivières, 1943), 14–21. Jouve, *Les Franciscains et le Canada: aux Trois-Rivières*, 58, 91, 152ff., 276. P.-G. Roy, *La famille Godefroy de Tonnancour* (Lévis, 1904), 33–43. Sulte, *Mélanges historiques* (Malchelosse), XIX, 12f., 16–18, 30–34.

GODEFROY DE VIEUXPONT (Vieux-Pont),

JOSEPH, interpreter, fur-trader, militia captain; b. 20 July 1645 at Trois-Rivières, sixth child of Jean Godefroy* de Lintot and Marie Leneuf; d. *c.* 1716. Governor Huault* de Montmagny had been his godfather.

In 1649 his uncle, the Sieur Michel Leneuf* Du Hérisson, had been granted the fief of Vieuxpont: "one league of land along the St Lawrence River, in the locality of Trois-Rivières and going up the said river, by five leagues in depth, extending into the said lands and places not already granted." Leneuf made a donation of his land to his nephew by a private agreement dated 15 Nov. 1667. The new seigneur rendered fealty and homage at Quebec on 7 July 1668.

Louis de Buade* de Frontenac allowed Vieuxpont to enlarge his seigneury by granting him a new concession on 23 Aug. 1674. It consisted of 15 acres, comprising the territory stretching "from the third to the fourth river." He rendered fealty and homage for this on 26 Aug. 1677.

On 14 Nov. 1674 Frontenac suggested to the minister of the Marine that interpreters for the Huron and Algonkian languages be appointed: "The 200 *écus* that I am told the directors of the company have allotted to the post of grand master of the waters and forests, which appears to me an office of little utility in Canada at present, would be better used for this purpose and would not increase their expenses. If you were to approve of my suggestion, the Sieurs LeMoyne and Vieux-Pont will be very suitable for such a position."

Apparently Vieuxpont, backed up by Frontenac's friendship, was participating in the fur trade illegally; at least this was the accusation made by Intendant Duchesneau* before M. de Seignelay. On the occasion of the governor's conference with the Ottawas at Montreal, in September 1682, Vieuxpont served as his interpreter. The purpose of the meeting was to establish peace with the Indians and to urge them to trade with the French. But Frontenac had already been recalled. Le Febvre* de La Barre replaced him, and on 10 October, at Quebec, he held an assembly of the notables at which Vieuxpont was present. They decided to show an energetic attitude towards the Iroquois, and this was the origin of the disastrous wars that marked La Barre's régime.

On 12 Nov. 1682 the new governor took up again his predecessor's idea: "One of the persons who is the most necessary for the king's service in this country is an interpreter of the various Indian languages, and we can hardly do without such a person in the present state of affairs. We have here a nobleman called M. de Vieux-Pont, who understands them all and speaks them well. It would be proper for the king to grant him the maintenance that is given to company captains on half-pay, in order that the intendant and I may use his services more freely and divert him without misgivings from his own affairs."

In 1687, at the time of BRISAY de Denonville's expedition against the Senecas, Vieuxpont was captain of the militia at Trois-Rivières. He commanded a company formed of settlers from that region. During the siege of Quebec in 1690, he was wounded by fire from the English ships. A contemporary account says: "The Sieur de Vieuxpont's musket was carried away and his arm dislocated by one of the shots."

On 21 Oct. 1675, at Trois-Rivières, Vieuxpont had married Catherine, daughter of Maurice Poulin* de La Fontaine and Jeanne Jallot. Ten children were born of this marriage. Vieuxpont is thought to have died around 1716.

HERVÉ BIRON

Coll. de manuscrits relatifs à la N.-F., I, 524. "Correspondance de Frontenac (1672–82)," APQ *Rapport, 1926–27,* 76. É.-Z. Massicotte, "Inventaire des actes de foi et hommage conservés aux archives judiciaires de Montréal," APQ *Rapport, 1921–22,* 102. P.-G. Roy, *Inv. concessions,* I, 286f. Bonnault, "Le Canada militaire," 519. P.-G. Roy, *La famille Godefroy de Tonnancour* (Lévis, 1904). Sulte, *Mélanges historiques* (Malchelosse), XI.

GOFFE, EDMUND, soldier and politician; b. *c.* 1670 at Cambridge, Mass., son of Samuel and Hannah (Bernard) Goffe; married Hannah Lynde, daughter of Samuel Lynde, in May 1696; was married, a second time, 24 June 1728, to Mrs. Mary Norden, widow of Colonel Nathaniel Norden of Marblehead, Mass.; d. 16 Oct. 1740, at Cambridge, without issue.

From the size of his fines while a student at Harvard, Goffe seems to have been "the most obstreperous undergraduate of his day" (C. K. Shipton). Upon graduation in 1692 Goffe entered public life, as befitted a member of a prominent Massachusetts family. His early career consisted of odd jobs such as constable and surveyor. In 1710 he served as a lieutenant-colonel in the expedition against Port-Royal (Annapolis Royal, N.S.) under Francis NICHOLSON, but scarcely distinguished himself. On his return he was taken to court charged with using his position to defraud the colony. A conviction was obtained, but later reversed. In 1711 Goffe participated in the preparations for Sir Hovenden WALKER's expedition to Canada. Four years later he was one of two commissioners appointed to negotiate with the Cape Sable Indians when they seized some 27 New England fishing vessels.

Representing Cambridge in the Massachusetts General Court in 1716, 1720, and 1721, Goffe served on a committee dealing with Indian affairs. He relinquished his seat in the General Court in 1721 to become commander of the forces to be sent against the eastern Indians. He occupied this post for about three years, until he was once again accused of fraud. Goffe's remaining years brought him considerable financial difficulties. In 1733 Governor Jonathan Belcher referred to him as "a poor bankrupt lost wretch." C. K. Shipton has said of his military career that "Col. Goffe's services . . . were not so notable for fighting as for a system of graft which he and some of his fellow officers developed."

DONALD F. CHARD

"Journal of Colonel Nicholson at the capture of Annapolis, 1710," N.S. Hist. Soc. *Coll.,* I (1878), 69. *Journals of the House of Representatives of Massachusetts* (25v., Mass. Hist. Soc. pub., Boston, 1919–50), I, 48, 56, 58; III, 17. *N.S. Archives, II.* Sylvester, *Indian wars,* III, 186–87. Shipton, *Sibley's Harvard graduates,* IV, 57, 58. L. R. Paige, *History of Cambridge, Massachusetts, 1630–1877* (Boston, 1877) 403.

GOTTEVILLE DE BELILE, ROBERT-DAVID, lieutenant-commander, captain of a company of colonial regular troops, commandant of the Compagnie de l'Île Saint-Jean, knight of the order of Saint-Louis; fl. 1696–1724.

Gotteville de Belile joined the navy in 1696, and was commissioned sub-lieutenant in 1705. In June 1709 he was with the forces that arrived in Placentia (Plaisance) to help Governor PASTOUR de Costebelle defend it and the recently captured St John's against any English attack. Costebelle described him as a "capable officer . . . devoted to the service."

Gotteville was made captain of a fire-ship in 1712; he was promoted lieutenant-commander in 1719. Shortly after he was named captain of a company of colonial regular troops and commandant of the Compagnie de l'Île Saint-Jean. Saint-Jean (Prince Edward Island), Miscou, and adjacent isles had been granted to the Comte de Saint-Pierre in August 1719, on condition that he colonize them. Gotteville arrived in Louisbourg on 23 Aug. 1720 on his way to Île Saint-Jean and was joined by Louis Denys* de La Ronde. La Ronde and the engineer GÉDÉON DE CATALOGNE had been assigned to help in establishing the settlement. Two of the company's ships, carrying 300 colonists, had already gone to Île Saint-Jean. The company's headquarters were established at Port La Joie (near present-day Charlottetowr) and the colonists settled there and at Havre

Saint-Pierre (St Peters Harbour) and Tranche-montagne (South Lake) on the north coast.

Gotteville de Belile was soon faced with the problem of defending the company's fisheries. In July 1721, according to Saint-Ovide [Mombeton*], the governor of Île Royale (Cape Breton Island), Gotteville had armed a small boat and a shallop. Gotteville maintained that fishermen from Île Royale were fishing for cod in waters granted to the Comte de Saint-Pierre and were depriving the inhabitants of Havre Saint-Pierre and Tranche-montagne of their livelihood. Fishing boats belonging to two Île Royale fishermen were seized—an action which had important legal repercussions. The fishermen took their case to the admiralty officers at Louisbourg, who decided in their favour and ordered Gotteville to pay damages and costs. When the latter appealed to the Conseil Supérieur of Louisbourg the judgement was upheld. The case then came to the attention of the king's council which, by a decree of 22 March 1722, reversed the decision, and granted the Comte de Saint-Pierre exclusive fishing rights in the waters enclosed by the islands and within a league of their shores. The decree also removed all litigation arising from these fishing rights from the jurisdiction of the admiralty at Louisbourg and ruled that all such cases would be heard by the financial commissary of Louisbourg, Jacques-Ange Le Normant* de Mézy.

Gotteville de Belile left the island in 1722 because of poor health, and Boisberthelot* de Beaucours, an officer of the Louisbourg garrison, succeeded him as commandant for a two-year term. Gotteville retired with a pension of 500 *livres* and was granted a gratuity of 300 *livres* on 3 April 1724.

MARY McD. MAUDE

Archives de la Charente-Maritime (La Rochelle), Amirauté de Louisbourg, B, 265, ff.16–18. AN, Col., B, 44, 45; C¹¹ᴮ, 5–7; C¹¹ᶜ, 6; C¹¹ᴳ, 12, ff.26–27v; Marine, C¹, 161; Section Outre-Mer, G¹, 411, ff.1v, 2, 9, 12. Fauteux, *Les chevaliers de Saint-Louis.* Harvey, *French régime in P.E.I.* McLennan, *Louisbourg.*

GOUENTAGRANDI, baptized **Suzanne**; Oneida woman who saved the life of Father Pierre MILLET after his capture by the Iroquois in 1689; died in Caughnawaga after 1738.

Gouentagrandi is described as being of the "first nobility" of her tribe. She was related to Gannassatiron who helped her to protect Millet. Throughout her lifetime Gouentagrandi was one of the staunchest adherents of the French faction among her people.

Little is known about her life prior to 1691. In that year Father Millet wrote that he had baptized her, together with her daughter and husband (chief Manchot) on a previous visit to the Oneidas. This was probably between 1671 and 1684. He added that since that time she had saved not only his own life but the lives of several French who had been taken prisoner by the Iroquois.

Father Millet was captured in 1689 by the Onondagas, during the siege of Fort Frontenac. He was handed over to the Oneidas and taken to their chief town. Gouentagrandi went out to greet him as he neared the town, unbound his hands, and provided him with fresh clothing. Her husband, who was given charge of the prisoner, informed the Oneidas that Millet came as a missionary, not as a captive, and that it was the business of the hereditary chiefs, not the ordinary people, to decide his fate. Millet lived in Gouentagrandi's house for three weeks, awaiting the meeting that was to consider what should be done with him. Gouentagrandi looked after him during this period and brought him children to baptize and Christian Indians for confession. After the warriors returned from their attack on Lachine, she had to move Millet from one cabin to another to conceal him.

There is little doubt that Gouentagrandi played an important role in the Iroquois council's decision to turn Millet over to her kinsman Gannassatiron. She probably also encouraged Gannassatiron to adopt Millet and to have him made a sachem. Thereafter, Millet was able to live among the Oneidas as an honoured and influential "guest," but although he was adopted by Gannassatiron, Millet continued to live in Gouentagrandi's cabin. She was outspoken in her opposition to English demands that the Oneidas should expel him from their country. She is also credited with foiling a Mohawk plot to kidnap Millet on the pretext of having him come to confess some Christians living among them.

In September 1693, Gouentagrandi accompanied the Oneida sachem, Tareha*, on his unenviable mission to inform Buade* de Frontenac that the French would have to negotiate the peace with the Oneidas through the English officials at Albany. Gouentagrandi is reported to have accompanied Tareha because of her desire to meet Frontenac. Charlevoix* reports that in spite of his anger at Tareha's mission Frontenac was extremely flattered by Gouentagrandi's visit and "seemed to regard this woman as something more than an Iroquois squaw." Charlevoix drew an affectionate and naïve parallel between her visit to Frontenac and that paid by the Queen of Sheba to King Solomon.

Gourdeau de Beaulieu

In 1696, when French soldiers under the command of Philippe de RIGAUD de Vaudreuil attacked the Oneida village, Gouentagrandi (described in the *Jesuit Relations* as "the famous Christian woman of Onneiout who saved father millet's life") came out to meet them and offered to go with 80 of her tribe to live among the Iroquois who had already settled in Canada. While she was back in the village advising her people to surrender, the French attacked the settlement and burned it. After the attack, 30 Oneida surrendered to the French and were taken back to Canada. These must have included Gouentagrandi, who from this time appears to have lived at Sault Saint-Louis (Caughnawaga). The Senecas under TEKANOET stayed at her house en route to the 1701 peace conference at Montreal. Charlevoix saw her there in 1708 and in 1738 she visited Quebec where she was received by the governor at the Château Saint-Louis. She also visited the convents of the city, including that of the Ursulines. She was reported at that time to be over 100 years old. In his *History of New France*, published in 1744, Charlevoix reports that she died "in a happy old age, after long edifying that town [Caughnawaga] by the constant practice of all Christian virtues."

BRUCE G. TRIGGER

Charlevoix, *History* (Shea), IV, 244–45. *JR* (Thwaites), LXIV, 67–107; LXV, 27. E. J. Devine, *Historic Caughnawaga* (Montreal, 1922), 113–14. [The evidence in *JR* (Thwaites), LXV, 27, makes it unlikely that Gouentagrandi moved to Caughnawaga in 1694, as Devine claims; the suggestion that Gouentagrandi was married to Tareha also seems erroneous. B.G.T.]

GOURDEAU (Gourdau) DE BEAULIEU ET DE LA GROSSARDIÈRE, JACQUES, merchant and bourgeois; baptized 8 July 1660 at Quebec, son of Jacques Gourdeau, notary and clerk of the seneschal's court of Quebec, and of Éléonore de Grandmaison*; d. 2 July 1720.

On 26 Feb. 1691, at Quebec, he married Marie Bissot, daughter of François Byssot* de La Rivière, widow of Claude Porlier, by whom he had seven children; she was buried on 24 July 1719 in the cathedral at Quebec.

In Quebec Jacques Gourdeau owned a house on Rue Sous-le-Fort, and on Île d'Orléans he owned the arriere-fiefs of La Grossardière, with a frontage of 40 *arpents* and running the whole depth of the island, and Beaulieu, with a frontage of 15 *arpents* and extending for half the depth of the island. He did not work these domains himself; instead he farmed them out and sold certain parts of them. In 1703 he rendered fealty and homage to the Comtesse de Saint-Laurent [CHARLOTTE-FRANÇOISE JUCHEREAU] for these two arriere-fiefs which were situated in her countship. In 1698 he had bought from Pierre Rey Gaillard, a commissary of artillery and the guardian of Richard Denys* de Fronsac's children, a fief measuring three leagues by six in the seigneury of Miramichi; he sold this land again in February 1699. The same year his brother-in-law Charles-François Bissot made over to him the entitlement to profits and revenues which he held over fur-trading rights in the seigneury of Mingan.

Here and there one finds an indication of the activities of Gourdeau in the 1690s with a number of family connections. In 1691 Gourdeau gave up his rights to the estate of his brother Antoine, who had died at sea on board the *Saint-François Xavier*. With Louis Jolliet*, his brother-in-law, he was appointed in 1694 trustee of the interests of the Montagnais girl Marie-Madeleine Tetesigaguoy, who was involved in litigation over the annulment of her marriage with NICOLAS, son of Noël Jérémie*. In 1696 he was named a guardian of the children of Claude Porlier, his wife's previous husband. During the same year he bought from LOUIS COUILLARD, for 17 *sols* each, all the salmon which the latter had caught. In 1697 he acted as attorney for his brother-in-law FRANÇOIS-JOSEPH BISSOT, and was commissioned to go to Sept-Îles to get belongings that had not been lost in the wreck of the *Corossol*.

From 1702 on, he was away from Quebec, and engaged indentured employees to carry on fur-trading in Acadia (Peremoneoudy). During that time he left the care of his property to his wife. She seems subsequently to have followed her husband, since in 1704 the two of them, "in their projected absence," gave power of attorney to the notary Jacques BARBEL, and in 1715 they gave it to the notary Louis CHAMBALON. Gourdeau was mentioned as "formerly a merchant in Quebec" in 1707, during proceedings in which he was represented by an attorney. It seems that Gourdeau and his wife were again present in Quebec in 1716, however, when they vainly brought an action to prevent the seizure of their house, which had been sold by court order eight years before. In 1732 Gourdeau's son Pierre-Jacques, who had long been absent from Quebec, claimed under *beneficium inventorii* the assets which had belonged to his father.

ANTONIO DROLET

AQ, NF, Coll. pièces jud. et not., 3725; Seigneuries, Île d'Orléans. *Jug. et délib.*, I, III, IV. A. Roy, *Inv. greffes not.*, XVIII, XIX. P.-G. Roy, *Inv. concessions*, I, IV, 51; V, 1, 33; *Inv. contrats de mariage*, III, 132. Régis Roy, "Armoirie de la famille Gourdeau,"

Goutin

Annales de l'institut canadien-français d'Ottawa, III (1924), 2.

GOUTIN (sometimes written **Degoutin, Degoutins, Desgoutins,** but he signed **De Goutin**), **MATHIEU DE,** king's counsellor, lieutenant general for justice in Acadia, king's writer in Acadia and Île Royale (Cape Breton Island); b. in France, probably in the 1660s; d. in Île Royale 25 Dec. 1714.

Our knowledge of de Goutin previous to his coming to Acadia is meagre. He himself refers to having participated in five campaigns, probably as a commissariat clerk, with the Régiment de la Couronne. He secured his appointment to Acadia through the influence of the Marquis de Chevry, a director of the Compagnie de la Pêche Sédentaire de l'Acadie, whose father he had previously served as secretary.

De Goutin came to Acadia in 1688, and soon married, in the words of Governor DES FRICHES de Meneval, "foolishly, a peasant's daughter," Jeanne Tibaudeau, the daughter of Pierre TIBAUDEAU and Jeanne Terriot. By her he had the following children: François-Marie*, Abraham (or Alexandre), Anne, Mathieu, Marguerite, Jacques, Marie-Joseph, Antoine, Joseph, Jeanne, Magdelaine, and Louise.

Upon his arrival at Port-Royal, de Goutin found himself the busiest official of the colony. As lieutenant general he heard all civil and criminal suits, and those pertaining as well to public order, navigation and trade. As king's writer he was the subdelegate of the intendant of New France. He administered the king's accounts, munitions, and supplies, and was inspector of crown works. With such extensive duties it was perhaps inevitable that his performance should give rise to many of the quarrels in which he became embroiled. As early as 1689 Meneval wrote the minister that de Goutin was "an undeserving, worthless character, . . . [who is] quite stubbornly convinced of his ability, . . . [and] sure that the two offices he holds will give him a rank and authority here which are, if not above, at least equal to that of the governor." Specifically, Meneval accused him of seeking to incite the garrison, the inhabitants, and the Indians to disobedience and to contempt not only of the governor's authority, but of that of the clergy as well. On this latter point, Meneval reported that de Goutin and his friends "degrade [the] lives and characters [of the clergy] to the great contempt of religion." De Goutin countered that Meneval meddled with his functions "[doing] everything without informing me in any way," and instructing the inhabitants "not to acknowledge me as their judge." He went on to accuse the clergy of illegal trade, and of "intimidating the consciences" of the inhabitants.

As a result of these quarrels the minister ordered de Goutin back to France. In the meantime, however, Sir William Phips* had captured Port-Royal in May 1690. After being taken prisoner and later released, de Goutin went first to the Saint John River, and then to Canada. He returned to Port-Royal the following year before sailing to France, probably in 1692. There, in 1692 and 1693, he presumably regained the favour of the authorities, and in February 1693, amid references to his "ability, courage and devotion to duty," he was instructed to return to Acadia. De Goutin's relations with Meneval's successor, Joseph Robinau* de Villebon, appear to have been without incident for several years. During this time he had been confirmed in the possession of two wilderness tracts, one on the Mouscoudabouet (Musquodoboit) River in 1692, the other at La Pointe-aux-Chesnes, on the Saint John River, in 1696. There is no evidence that he undertook any improvements on either property. On 27 March 1696 he obtained leave to return to France to attend to family affairs. Before departing, he accompanied PIERRE LE MOYNE d'Iberville in his attack on the English fort at Pemaquid in August; he sent an account of this expedition to the minister. While in France he spent five weeks at the ministry of Marine.

He returned to Acadia in 1697, arriving at Fort Nashwaak (Naxouat) on 10 August. For some reason it was only upon his return to Acadia that de Goutin's relations with Villebon became uneasy, judging from the dispatches in which he reported at length on the alleged misconduct of his superior. He also clashed with CLAUDE-SÉBASTIEN DE VILLIEU, accusing him of selling for his own profit the foodstuffs he received for the soldiers of his company, and with SIMON-PIERRE DENYS de Bonaventure, on the latter's alleged affair with Mme de Freneuse [Louise Guyon*].

The question as to whether de Goutin was suited to his duties in Acadia recurred during the governorship of Jacques-François de Brouillan [MOMBETON]. Though the new governor's first impression of de Goutin was favourable, he soon reported that de Goutin was "hardly in a position to make good judgments . . . because a third of the settlers are relatives of his wife." De Goutin agreed to refer cases involving his wife's relatives to the king's attorney. Brouillan then contended that because of the extent and variety of his duties, de Goutin "has trouble doing any one of his jobs well." Indeed, de Goutin himself complained that he had "no set time for drinking and eating, [for]

257

Goyer

I am more busy on feast days and Sundays than on workings days, [because] the settlers use these days to conduct their business when they come to Mass." Brouillan's most serious contention was that de Goutin was leading a cabal of officers aimed at undermining the governor's authority. To this de Goutin somewhat facetiously replied that what the governor called a cabal was nothing more than "three or four friends, honourable people, who are close because they like each other's company ... [and who are] called cabalists ... because they have not bowed before the beast."

By contrast, de Goutin's relations with Governor AUGER de Subercase were strikingly cordial. The minister had issued the terse warning to de Goutin: "Should you give him cause for complaint ... you would not be able to stay in. this country." De Goutin appears to have been very careful, and in 1707 Subercase advised the minister that he "fulfils properly the duties of his office." The minister in turn appeared to show increased confidence in de Goutin, for in 1708 and again in 1710 he instructed him in no uncertain terms to report everything that might appear contrary to the king's interest, including Subercase's conduct.

Following the surrender of Port-Royal to Francis NICHOLSON in 1710, de Goutin returned to France with his family in 1711. In 1714 he was appointed king's writer at Île Royale. After his death on Christmas day 1714, his widow and children remained at Île Royale, where for a time they received rations from the crown. Their eldest son, François-Marie, followed his father into the civil administration of Île Royale, and at least five daughters married officers, four in Île Royale.

Traditionally, Mathieu de Goutin has been described, somewhat unfairly, as an "unscrupulous mischief maker." Though his arrogance and vanity are quite apparent, it would appear nevertheless that he was a capable official. Indeed, his superiors persisted in recognizing this for 22 years. Because one of the functions of effective civil officials was to serve as a restraint upon the otherwise near-absolute power of the governor, it is perhaps as much for this reason, as for his alliances among the inhabitants, that Mathieu de Goutin also enjoyed the confidence of the Acadian peasantry, who had acquired long before a natural distaste for the inflexibility of colonial administration.

BERNARD POTHIER

AN, Col., B, 15–17, 19, 20, 22, 23, 25, 27, 29, 32, 35, 39; C¹¹ᴮ, 1, 2, 13; C¹¹ᶜ, 2, 7, 16; C¹¹ᴰ, 2–7; E, 209; Section Outre-Mer, G¹, 406; G³, 2037, 2040, 2047, 2056, 2058.

Charlevoix, *Histoire* (1744), II, 111. *Coll. de manuscrits relatifs à la N.-F.*, II, 224, 466, 480, 492. "Extrait de la relation faitte par Mʳ de Gouttin de la prisse du fort de Pimiquid," *PAC Report, 1912*, App. F, 73–74. Le Jeune, *Dictionnaire*, I, 503–4.

Bernard, *Le drame acadien*, 179–83, 189n, 196. Casgrain, *Les Sulpiciens en Acadie*, 120–23. Parkman, *A half-century of conflict* (1892), I. Webster, *Acadia*, 6, 9, 174–77. Pierre Daviault, "Mme de Freneuse et M. de Bonaventure," *RSCT*, 3d ser., XXXV (1941), sect.ı, 37–56. É.-Z. Massicotte, "Mathieu De Goutin, lieutenant civil et criminel de l'Acadie," *BRH*, LI (1945), 221–22.

GOYER, OLIVIER, priest, Recollet, provincial commissioner of the Recollets of Canada; b. 1663 in France; d. 8 Oct. 1721 in Paris.

Olivier Goyer made his profession in 1680 with the Recollets of Paris. Six years later he became a lecturer in theology. Between 1695 and 1698 he preached Lenten sermons to the Recollets, while continuing his teachings.

In 1698 Goyer went to Canada as provincial commissioner and lived in Quebec. He was Governor Buade* de Frontenac's confessor and was at his bedside until he breathed his last on 28 Nov. 1698. The funeral took place on 1 December, but the official service, presided over by Bishop Saint-Vallier [LA CROIX], was not held until 19 December, at the Recollet convent. Father Goyer pronounced the funeral oration for the illustrious deceased before the highest ecclesiastical and civil dignitaries in Canada. On 13 Jan. 1699 Goyer signed an act accepting a legacy of 1,500 *livres* which Frontenac had left to the Recollets for celebrating masses for the peace of his soul.

On 26 Oct. 1699 he certified the accuracy of a copy of the first written report of the holy acts of the late Recollet brother Didace Pelletier*. On 8 Sept. 1700 he arrived at Placentia (Plaisance), whence he withdrew two of the three Recollets who had been there, since the mission had been handed over to the Recollets of Brittany. Then he went to France, arriving at La Rochelle on 29 Nov. 1700. In France he continued to teach theology and preach Advent and Lenten sermons in various convents of his order. He died at the convent of Saint-Denis in Paris on 8 Oct. 1721, after 41 years in holy orders.

Father Goyer seems to have been an impressive preacher. His funeral oration for Frontenac was much admired by his contemporaries but has been much criticized by the historians. That is easily explained. At 35 years of age he had just arrived in the country as superior of the Recollets of

Canada, and had to compose hastily, in a few days, a portrait of the famous governor of New France. The funeral oration, an oratorical *genre* which had been rendered famous by Bossuet, was in great favour in the 17th century. The preachers in the colony used it and sometimes abused it. What did Father Goyer do? He followed the fashion of the period, in keeping with which long speeches furnished above all the pretext for a glorious panegyric of the deceased. Rochemonteix said that Father Goyer's oration was "from beginning to end the panegyric of M. de Frontenac, who possesses only virtues and qualities, and the finest at that. . . ." This Jesuit, however, also exaggerates, for in his oration Goyer criticized Frontenac's conduct on the matter of liquor; he did it in terms that were adroitly chosen but nonetheless disapproving. In short, while praising the noble aspects of the governor's life, Father Goyer did not sacrifice the truth in any way. Moreover, the Recollet was well informed, as all the details of his biography of the deceased show. Among other facts he pointed out the death of Frontenac's son, François-Louis killed, according to him, at the head of a regiment which he commanded in the service of the bishop of Münster, an ally of France. Most authors have accepted Goyer's version of this incident.

Pierre-Georges Roy, who was the first person to publish this funeral oration in French, inserted after the text the "Remarques" which appear to be by Abbé GLANDELET and not, as Jacques Viger maintained, by Abbé Bertrand* de Latour. The commentary provides the opposite view to certain of Father Goyer's assertions. From this standpoint they are interesting, but they would require being verified in their turn. Wherever the truth lies, it must be admitted that Father Goyer's funeral oration is well constructed and betokens a sense of classical style in the author as well as indisputable gifts as an orator.

GABRIEL-M.-RÉAL DUMAS

The text of the funeral oration is found in BN, MS, Fr. 13516, ff.163–95; P.-G. Roy published it in *BRH*, I (1895), 66–76, 82–89, followed by "Remarques sur l'oraison funèbre de feu M. de Frontenac prononcée en l'église des Récollets de Québec, le 19 décembre 1698, par le P. Olivier Goyer, commissaire des Recollets," in *BRH*, I (1895), 95–108. Archives des Franciscains de Québec, Dossier Olivier Goyer. AN, L, 941. Gosselin, *L'Église du Canada*, I, 30ff. Rochemonteix, *Les Jésuites et la N.-F. au XVIIᵉ siècle*, III, 96. P.-G. Roy, *La ville de Québec*, II, 428, 544; "Le fils de Frontenac," *BRH*, III (1897), 140.

GRANDE TERRE, LA. *See* OHONSIOWANNE

GRANDMESNIL, ÉTIENNE VERON DE. *See* VERON

GRANVILLE ET DE FONVILLE, CHARLES BÉCART DE. *See* BÉCART

GRAVIER, JACQUES, priest, Jesuit, missionary to the Ottawas, founder of the Illinois mission; b. 17 May 1651 at Moulins; d. 17 (or 23, or 26) April 1708 at Mobile (Alabama).

Gravier entered the Society of Jesus in the fall of 1670 and made his novitiate at Paris. From 1672 until 1680 he taught and tutored in the Jesuit schools of Hesdin, Eu, and Arras. These assignments he interrupted for a year of philosophy at the Collège Louis-le-Grand in Paris (1678–79); he returned to the same institution for his theological studies (1680–84). His intelligence and education would later appear in his letters where he wrote perspicaciously on theological and canonical questions. After his third year of theology he was ordained a priest, and after the fourth set out promptly for Canada. He sojourned briefly at the college in Quebec, and then spent a year at Sillery studying Algonquin (1685–86).

Called westward to the Ottawa mission, he went to Saint-Ignace and there wrote out in his own serious, space-sparing hand the solemn profession of four vows on 2 Feb. 1687. For 21 more years he would live the dedication of this day.

In 1689 he went to take up residence among the Illinois tribes—first at Starved Rock on the Illinois River. He prepared a grammar of their language, and by founding this mission carried out the promise made almost two decades before by Jacques Marquette*. In 1696 he was named "Superior of the Missions among the Ottawa, the Illinois, the Miami, and others"; in this capacity he had to return to Michilimackinac. Quebec's Bishop Saint-Vallier [LA CROIX] named him his vicar general for these missions. With typical tenacity Gravier strove to retain the Tamaroa mission as part of the bishop of Quebec's original 1690 commission to the Jesuits, but had to yield to the adamant Saint-Vallier, who entrusted the village to the Quebec seminary priests.

Gravier canoed downriver to the primitive Louisiana settlements in November 1700; during a year of ministry to French and Indians, he won the lasting friendship and esteem of Jean-Baptiste Le Moyne* de Bienville. In turn, Gravier, as a good linguist, was impressed by Bienville's knowledge of Indian languages. He left the Gulf Coast colony in February 1702 for the return to the Illinois country. During 1702–4 he was again among "his Illinois," and in 1705 was named

Graydon

superior of that mission, now separately administered.

In the autumn of 1705 an aroused Peoria attacked Gravier, as he later reported, "in hatred of the faith," letting fly five arrows without warning or provocation; the deep wound in his arm was crudely or perhaps maliciously treated with the result that infection set in and the pain grew worse. Despairing of healing in the wilds, he made the arduous trip to Mobile in midwinter (1705–6), and, still without relief, sailed for France in late 1706. (Both in Mobile and in Paris he took the side of Bienville against Henri Roulleaux de La Vente, a priest of the Séminaire des Missions Étrangères, and Nicolas de LA SALLE, the commissary.) Whatever alleviation he obtained, it was clear that he would suffer from the wound for the rest of his life; with this knowledge he sailed back to Mobile, arriving in February 1708, and made preparations to return to his post among the Peorias. The infection of the wound and the fatigue of his travels thwarted his plans. Death came to his fever-racked frame while he was in or quite near old Mobile.

CHARLES E. O'NEILL

AN, Col., B, 29, ff.260v, 261, 263v, 265; C¹³ᴬ, 1, ff.504–7, 570–81, 582; Marine, 3JJ, 389, f.19. ARSI, Gallia 110/II, ff.269–70v, 271–72v, 273v. ASJ, France (Chantilly), Fonds Brotier, 105. ASQ, Lettres, R, 82, 83; Lettres, M, 38, 39; Lettres, S, 102. BN, MS, Fr. 6453, ff.18ff. Library of Congress (Washington), Jesuit Relations MSS. *Découvertes et établissements des Français* (Margry), IV, 5. [Jacques Gravier], *Lettre du P. Jacques Gravier, le 23 février 1708, sur les affaires de la Louisiane* (New York, 1865); *Relation ou journal du voyage de r.p. Jacques Gravier de la Compagnie de Jésus, en 1700 depuis le pays des Illinois jusqu'à l'embouchure du Mississipi* (New York, 1859). *JR* (Thwaites), LXV, 100–79; LXVI, 32–34, 120–43. *Lettres édifiantes et curieuses escrites des missions étrangères* (nouv. éd., 14v., Lyon, 1819), IV, 209.

Delanglez, *French Jesuits in Louisiana*. O'Neill, *Church and state in Louisiana*. Rochemonteix, *Les Jésuites et la N.-F. au XVIIᵉ siècle*, III, 538, 547, 688–90.

GRAYDON, JOHN, vice-admiral; commodore of the Newfoundland convoy and temporary governor, 1701; b. *c.* 1666; d. 1726.

Graydon was appointed second lieutenant in 1686 and lieutenant two years later. Promoted captain in 1689 he was present at the battle off Beachy Head, 1690, and at Barfleur, 1692.

In 1701 Graydon, commanding the *Assistance*, was appointed commodore of the Newfoundland convoy and governor. The Newfoundland Act of 1699 had been drafted with a view to improving the lax and lawless state of affairs which had

hitherto prevailed in that island. The act, which replaced the earlier Western Charters, gave judicial powers to the commodore and administrative powers to the fishing admirals of each harbour. The Board of Trade and Plantations wished to learn if the act had improved conditions. Graydon was instructed to investigate and report on the Heads of Enquiries with which he was supplied. His replies cover a wide field and are informative. He reported that the act was still largely disregarded by the fishing admirals, although the Lord's day was duly observed. He described conditions in the fishing industry and the manner of livelihood of the inhabitants. Graydon reported that the French had better and more extensive fishing facilities than the English, that the garrison at Placentia (Plaisance) consisted of 3 companies of 30 men each, and that 60 guns had recently been landed. With Graydon went George LARKIN, who was commissioned to report on an act for the suppression of piracy in the plantations.

After returning to England, Graydon was promoted to rear-admiral in 1702 and served under Admiral Sir George Rooke in the squadron supporting the landing of British troops and the assault on Vigo. Promoted vice-admiral in March 1702/3 Graydon was appointed to the command of a squadron with orders to sail to Jamaica without delay and there raise a force sufficient to attack and capture the French settlement at Placentia. On 18 March, off Ushant, a French squadron under Jean-Baptiste Ducasse was sighted, returning after an engagement with Vice-Admiral Benbow. In view of his orders Graydon did not attack and even recalled the *Montague* which had opened fire. This decision was to weigh heavily against him in the future.

At Jamaica the ships of his squadron were found to be in poor shape and he incurred the wrath of the merchants for impressing seamen from their service (as in fact he had the legal power to do). Many merchants wrote to the Board of Trade and Plantations to complain against what they considered illegal impressment and Graydon's high-handed attitude [*see* HANDASYDE]. One writer described him as "moros and ill-tempered." Despite obstruction Graydon managed to raise a force numerically superior to that of the French at Placentia. On arrival off Newfoundland, on 2 Aug. 1703, Graydon summoned a council of war on board the *Boyne* at St Mary's Bay. Amongst the officers present were Rear-Admiral Sir William WHETSTONE and the military commander of the garrison at St John's, Captain Michael RICHARDS. In view of the crank and ill-found condition of the ships, much sickness amongst the seamen and troops, and rumours—

possibly spread by French deserters—of a very strong force at Placentia it was decided that an attack might well meet with disaster. The squadron sailed for England without making any attempt at the reduction of Placentia. Richards, who had asked for permission to return on the grounds of ill health, embarked for the passage home, leaving Lieutenant Thomas LLOYD in command at St John's.

On his return Graydon was faced with the extreme displeasure of the government and, from some quarters, with accusations of actual cowardice. His failure to attack Ducasse's squadron, the angry protests of the merchants of Jamaica (who may have had "interest" at home), and his decision not to attack Placentia may have influenced the government against him. He was not brought to trial by court martial, but the House of Lords deprived him of his pension. He died in retirement, 12 March 1725/26.

A portrait of Graydon by Kneller hangs in the Painted Hall of the Royal Naval College, Greenwich.

MICHAEL GODFREY

PRO, Adm. 6/107; C.O. 194/2, 195/3. Campbell, *Lives of the admirals*, III. PRO, *B.T. Journal, 1704–1708/9*; *CSP, Col., 1701, 1702, 1702–3, 1704–5*. Charnock, *Biographia navalis*, II. *DNB*. Lounsbury, *British fishery at Nfld*.

"GREAT WORLD." *See* OHONSIOWANNE

GREYSOLON DE LA TOURETTE, CLAUDE, esquire, fur-trader, brother of DANIEL GREYSOLON Dulhut; b. *c.* 1660, probably at Saint-Germain-Laval; d. after 1716, in France, probably at Lyons.

The date of La Tourette's arrival in New France is uncertain. He may have come with Dulhut in 1675 or perhaps only in 1682, when the latter returned to the colony after having unsuccessfully sought from Seignelay the grant of a seigneury in the lands he might discover west of Lake Superior. In 1683, holding Governor Le Febvre* de La Barre's commission, the two brothers set out together for the western Great Lakes with a convoy of 15 canoes.

La Tourette's duties in the west consisted in administering the posts which his brother founded on Lake Nipigon and at Kaministiquia. This involved establishing commercial relations with the Indians living on the lands between Lake Superior and Hudson Bay and making voyages to Montreal to purchase trade goods and to hire indentured employees. There are indications that La Tourette was highly successful in this work. In 1687, during one of his visits to the colony, he informed Governor Denonville [BRISAY] that over 1,500 Indians had come to his posts to trade. When he returned to the west in 1688 he took with him a party of 200 men, 30 of them being his own employees. By that date, Dulhut's western career had come to an end, but La Tourette continued to operate the two posts until approximately 1693.

He probably returned to France in the mid 1690s; little is known of his life after that. The fur trade had apparently made him wealthy, however, for in 1700 he loaned to the procurators of the city of Lyons, where he had taken up residence, the sum of 10,800 *livres*. In New France, meantime, the shareholders of the former Compagnie de La Ferme du Roi were taking action against him before the Conseil Supérieur for the recovery of a sum of 3,186 *livres* loaned to him by CHARLES AUBERT de La Chesnaye in 1685. This lawsuit, in which La Tourette was represented by a deputy, continued until 1716 when a judgment was rendered ordering him to pay the amount in question. This is the last reference to him in Canadian documents. There is no evidence to support the theory that he returned to America to command a post in the Illinois country in 1728.

YVES F. ZOLTVANY

[Isolated references to La Tourette can be found in several books and articles, but these are unreliable. The most common errors consist in calling him Charles instead of Claude and in maintaining that he arrived in Canada in 1675, accompanied Dulhut on his expedition to the west in 1678, and returned to command a post in the Illinois country in 1728. No evidence has been found to support any of these three contentions. Y.F.Z.]

AN, Col., C^{11A}, 6, 9; F^3, 7. *Découvertes et établissements des Français* (Margry), VI. *Jug. et délib.*, III, V, VI. P.-G. et A. Roy, *Inv. greffes not.*, I, IV, V, XI, XVIII. É.-Z. Massicotte, "Daniel de Greysolon, sieur du Lhut, Claude de Greysolon, sieur de La Tourette, et Jean Jacques Patron," *BRH*, XXXIII (1927), 139–47.

GREYSOLON DULHUT (sometimes written **Du Lhut** or **Du Luth**), **DANIEL,** esquire, ensign, *gendarme* of the king's household, coureur de bois, explorer, founder of western posts, captain in the colonial regular troops; b. *c.* 1639 at Saint-Germain-Laval; d. in Montreal, 25 Feb. 1710.

The Greysolons came from the region of Saint-Germain-Laval, near Lyons. Genealogical evidence indicates that they were of the middle class but Dulhut enjoyed the title of esquire. At some point in its history, then, the family must have entered the ranks of the lesser nobility.

Little is known of Dulhut's early years. From his correspondence, which contains a few classical

Greysolon Dulhut

allusions and passages of some literary value, it can be inferred that he was a man of education. His career in France was a military one. In 1657 he is mentioned as an ensign in the Régiment de Lyon and around 1665 he joined the Gendarmes, an élite regiment of the royal household to which only noblemen were admitted. As a member of this regiment he served in the army commanded by Condé in 1674. On 11 August at Seneffe, this force of 100,000 men defeated the Dutch under William of Orange. Dulhut participated in the bloody encounter as the squire of the Marquis de Lassay, one of Condé's aides-de-camp.

In a letter written to the Marquis de Seignelay in 1682, Dulhut stated that he had made two voyages to New France before 1674. Although nothing is known of their nature and purpose it was during those early visits to the colony that he began to think of travelling to the land of the Sioux, the powerful tribe settled near the headwaters of the Mississippi. This is the project to which he devoted himself in earnest after his return to Canada in 1675. He acquired a house in Montreal, mingled with the Indians, and was even given three slaves by a group of Sioux as a sign of their friendship. Two of his relatives already settled in the colony may have been of some assistance to him at this stage of his career. His uncle Jacques Patron, a Montreal merchant, may have been interested in the commercial aspect of the proposed venture and possibly provided funds to finance it. His brother-in-law, Lussigny, an officer in Buade* de Frontenac's guards, perhaps introduced him to the governor. Frontenac already knew that the Lake Superior area was a virtually untapped source of prime beaver pelts. In 1676, he had sent Hugues Randin* to Sault Ste Marie to arbitrate a settlement between the Sioux and their neighbours in order to open the area to French commerce. Since then Colbert had, on two occasions, forbidden trading outside the limits of the colony. Perhaps because of these prohibitions Frontenac did not authorize Dulhut to carry out his project.

Dulhut decided therefore to leave Montreal secretly on 1 Sept. 1678 with seven French followers and his three Indian slaves. His purpose was to negotiate a permanent peace between the Sioux, Chippewas, and other tribes dwelling west and north of Lake Superior and link up this pacified area firmly with New France. He also hoped to prevent the Crees and Monsonis from taking their pelts to the English on Hudson Bay. In 1678, these Indians had been plundered by the Ottawas who acted as middlemen between them and New France [see KINONGÉ]; as a result of this unhappy experience they had decided to take their trade to the bay unless they could have dealings with the French. To prevent these two northern nations from defecting to the English, Dulhut thought that direct trade should be carried out with them, even if it meant bypassing the Ottawa middlemen.

The expedition wintered at Sault Ste Marie and, on 2 July 1679, raised the arms of France in the great village of the Nadouesioux. Similar ceremonies took place in surrounding settlements to serve notice on the English that these lands were now claimed by Louis XIV. All the tribes who were visited were also invited to send representatives to a general assembly to discuss the terms of a peace treaty. This meeting took place on Lake Superior in September and Dulhut had the satisfaction of seeing the many tribes represented agree to a general reconciliation. To cement these frail new bonds of friendship, he arranged for several intertribal marriages and encouraged the Indians to carry out their winter hunt together.

Dulhut had also sent three of his men westward with a Sioux war party. How far they went is not known but they returned in the summer of 1680 with salt and the assurances of their Indian guides that it came from a great lake, 20 days' journey to the west, whose waters were not fit for drinking. Dulhut concluded that the western sea was within reach and he set out from Lake Superior toward the Mississippi. When he reached the river he learned that three of Cavelier* de La Salle's men, including the Recollet Louis HENNEPIN, had been captured by the Sioux and carried off as slaves. Dulhut pursued the Indians and finally caught up with them somewhere on the upper Mississippi. Although they apologized and readily freed their captives, Dulhut prudently decided to turn back. By committing this act of hostility against the French, with whom they had just concluded a treaty, the Sioux had shown how untrustworthy they were and he was obviously unwilling to proceed with his discovery under such uncertain auspices. After berating the Indians for their conduct he took La Salle's men aboard his canoes and returned to Michilimackinac.

Meantime, in Quebec, Intendant Jacques Duchesneau* was complaining loudly about Dulhut whom he described as the chief of the renegade coureurs de bois and as Frontenac's partner in the fur trade. In a dispatch to the minister the intendant claimed that shipments of fur were being sent not only to Jacques Patron and to the governor but also to the English and that the entire western fur trade might eventually be diverted to the latter. Learning of the intendant's accusations Dulhut hurried back to the colony to defend himself in March 1681. He arrived three months before the proclamation of Colbert's amnesty for all the coureurs de bois, and Duchesneau demanded that he be jailed as a renegade. Frontenac, however, who had now become a protector of the explorer, refused to allow this and sent him to France instead to convince the minister of his innocence.

In France Dulhut presented Seignelay with an account of his voyage to the Mississippi and defended himself against the accusation of having violated the edict of 1676, which forbad going into the woods to trade. Dulhut maintained that his purpose had been to arbitrate a peace treaty between several Indian tribes. He also asked for permission to continue his explorations and for the grant of a seigneury in the lands he might discover. Had this request been granted he would perhaps have established a commercial empire for himself similar to La Salle's south of the Great Lakes. The court, however, had just instituted the system of the 25 fur-trading licences (*congés*) in yet another effort to restrict the number of persons deserting the colony and was hardly in the mood to encourage voyages of discovery, which, more often than not, were simply trading expeditions in disguise. Furthermore La Salle, who had powerful supporters at the court, was hostile to Dulhut, whom he probably regarded as a potential competitor. These obstacles were too great to overcome. Dulhut succeeded in clearing himself of the accusations made against him, but his requests were turned down.

When he returned to Canada in the autumn of 1682 Frontenac had been recalled and Le Febvre* de La Barre was assuming office in his place. Dulhut soon won favour with the new governor and became one of his principal lieutenants. Early in 1683, holding a three-year commission from La Barre, he returned to the regions of the western Great Lakes and the upper Mississippi with a convoy of 15 canoes. His mission had a double purpose: to reduce to discipline the tribes of the northwest, an urgent necessity in view of the imminence of war with the Iroquois; and to prevent the northern nations from taking their pelts to the English on Hudson Bay. During the next three years Dulhut exerted himself continuously to achieve these ends. He commandeered the services of licensed traders to help fortify Michilimackinac, reprimanded the Potawatomis for their lukewarm attitude toward the French, and renewed his peace-making efforts among the Foxes, Sioux, and Chippewas. The last of these nations was especially difficult to manage as was demonstrated in 1684 when four of its warriors murdered two French traders. When one of the culprits appeared at the Jesuit mission of Sault Ste Marie the staff of 12 on duty there did not dare to arrest him, fearing the reprisals of his tribe. Dulhut, as soon as he learned of the incident, hurried to the mission, rounded up the suspects, including the chief Achinaga and his two sons, and put them on trial. Achinaga was acquitted and his younger son pardoned, but the two others who had been found guilty were executed before 400 Indians. By coldly meting out this punishment, Dulhut taught the natives that the French were a people to be respected and feared.

In 1684 and 1685, French positions in the west were strengthened by the building of two trading posts. They were located on Lake Nipigon and at Kaministiquia, at the western extremity of Lake Superior, and were placed under the command of Dulhut's younger brother CLAUDE GREYSOLON de La Tourette. The intendant Jacques de MEULLES promptly denounced these activities. He informed the court that the real purpose of the posts, which were too far from Hudson Bay to prevent the Indians from going there to trade, was to promote Dulhut's private interests and that La Barre's commission was an exclusive charter to the Lake Superior trade. The accusation contains some truth, for Dulhut and La Tourette engaged in commerce on an extensive scale. This is shown by a letter written by Dulhut to his creditor CHARLES AUBERT de La Chesnaye, in 1684, in which he asked for an advance of money and stated that he had more than 800 beaver robes at Michilimackinac with which to make the repayment the following year. But the intendant was wrong in suggesting that these activities were not harming the English for Hudson's Bay Company officials claimed in 1686 that Dulhut had cost them £20,000 in lost trade.

Important military services were added to these economic ones. In 1684, when La Barre undertook his abortive campaign against the Iroquois, Dulhut, MOREL de La Durantaye, and Nicolas PERROT raised 500 warriors among the western nations and marched them to Niagara to lend support to the main contingent. La Barre's successor, BRISAY de Denonville, also recognized Dulhut's ability and his influence over the Indians and frequently called upon his services. In 1685 and 1686, English and Dutch merchants from Albany had appeared at Michilimackinac and carried out a sizable trade with the Indians almost in the shadow of the French post. To prevent further intrusions into New France's trading empire, Denonville decided to build posts at the Toronto portage and at Detroit, two important entry points into the west. Dulhut was given the task of erecting the one at Detroit, which was called Fort Saint-Joseph and garrisoned with 50 men. In 1687, when the governor organized his great campaign against the Senecas, Dulhut and other French commanders in the west mustered 400 warriors and operated a perfectly timed junction with the main army on Lake Ontario.

Instead of returning to Lake Superior after this last campaign Dulhut came back to Canada. No reason has been given, but it may have been the onset of gout, a disease from which he suffered constantly during his last 20 years and which finally incapacitated him in 1702. At first, however, he was still able to take part in the Iroquois war. In 1689 he defeated a party of 22 of these Indians on the Lac des Deux-Montagnes and, as a reward, was made half-pay captain. Nothing more is heard of him until 1696 when he accompanied the army Frontenac was leading against the Onondagas and Oneidas as far as Fort Frontenac, where he remained in command. The following year he was promoted to the rank of captain.

After the Fort Frontenac command, Dulhut retired into private life. Unmarried and apparently only attended by a servant, La Roche, who ministered to him during his long illness, he lived his last 15 years uneventfully in Montreal. In June 1701 he rented the house he owned jointly with La Tourette to Philippe de RIGAUD de Vaudreuil for 400 *livres* annually and may then have moved to the home of the tanner Charles DELAUNAY, where he was living in 1709. In March of that year he drew up his last will and testament to which he added a codicil the following February. He left 800 *livres* to the Recollets, 100 *livres* to the Congrégation de Notre-Dame, and 300 to his servant. The biggest part of the estate, however, was a sum of some 11,766 *livres* owed to him by Delaunay. Dulhut asked only for the repayment of 4,000 *livres* and deeded the balance to the tanner's wife and children.

He died in Montreal on 25 Feb. 1710, and was buried in the Recollet chapel. He left the reputation of having been an *honnête homme* and a brave and loyal officer.

Dulhut has often been compared to La Salle and in so far as both men opened new territories to French commerce and influence they do have something in common. Unlike that of La Salle, however, Dulhut's career as an explorer was short-lived, and since he wrote little, the geographical knowledge he obtained of the upper Mississippi and its affluents was not widely diffused. The two men also differed in character. La Salle was imaginative and impulsive but without organizational ability; Dulhut, although somewhat lacking in *élan*, was steady-going and reliable, two attributes that no doubt explain why the three governors under whom he served made him one of their chief agents in the west. By virtue of his numerous activities in that region he appears as one of the principal architects of the alliance between New France and the Lake Superior tribes. But by showing how one could trade directly with those remote nations he irritated the Ottawa middlemen and must be regarded as one of those responsible for their coolness towards the French during some stages of the Iroquois war.

YVES F. ZOLTVANY

AJM, Greffe d'Antoine Adhémar; Greffe de Michel Lepailleur. AN, Col., B, 11, 16, 19, 20; C¹¹ᴬ, 5, 6, 7, 8, 9, 10, 14, 20; C¹¹ᴱ, 16; D²ᶜ, 47; F³, 2, 6, 7. "Correspondance de Frontenac," APQ *Rapport, 1926–27, 1927–28, 1928–29. Découvertes et établissements des Français* (Margry), II, V, VI. HBRS, XXI (Rich). *Jug. et délib.*, V.

C. W. Colby, *Canadian types of the old régime, 1608–1698* (New York, 1908). Eccles, *Canada under Louis XIV.* Lionel Groulx, *Notre grande aventure; l'empire français en Amérique du Nord (1535–1760)* (Montréal, [1958]). Kellogg, *French régime.* Lorin, *Le comte de Frontenac.* Antoine d'Eschambault, "La vie aventureuse de Daniel Greysolon, sieur Dulhut," *RHAF*, V (1951–52), 320–39. Gérard Malchelosse, "Un gentilhomme coureur de bois: Daniel Greysolon, sieur Du Lhut," *Cahiers des Dix*, XVI (1951), 195–232.

GRIMINGTON, MICHAEL, sometimes written **Gryminton** or **Grymington,** HBC captain; d. 15 June 1710 at Harwich, Essex, England.

Nothing is known about Michael Grimington's origin or his life before he became a seaman in the HBC's new 40-ton frigate *Albemarle* (Capt. Thomas Draper*) in 1680, but the possibility of his having made earlier voyages to Hudson Bay should not be ruled out. The *Albemarle*'s destination was Charlton Island in James Bay, but Draper was ordered to call en route at Severn River and, if he found it suitable for settlement, to remain there and establish a trading post. How far these orders were followed is doubtful, but no settlement was made, so Grimington spent the winter of 1680–81 in James Bay and, the following autumn, returned to London in the *Albemarle*.

Grimington was employed in James Bay during the season 1682–83, going out in the *Lucy* (Capt. Nicholas Reymer) and returning in the *Diligence* (Capt. Nehemiah Walker*). The committee must have heard exceptionally good reports of Grimington's ability, because it took the unusual course, not long after his arrival in London, of securing his agreement to go back to the bay in 1684 and to serve there for three years. Confirmation of the committee members' good opinion is evident not only in a much more remunerative contract made longer in advance than customary, but also in remarks to Governor

Henry Sergeant* in their letter of 1684 when they referred to Grimington's particular knowledge of the navigation at the mouths of Albany and Moose Rivers.

After taking an "Oath of fidelity to the Company" Grimington sailed as second mate in the chartered ship *John and Thomas* (Capt. Leonard Edgcombe*) for James Bay where he was to command "the Yatch," one of the three small vessels stationed there and used for lightering as well as local exploration. The reference to the yacht suggests the *Colleton*, but it is not certain that Grimington was given command of that particular vessel on arrival in James Bay.

In the spring of 1685 the committee members decided that Thomas Phipps*, chief warehouse-keeper in James Bay, should be governor in the Port Nelson area instead of John Abraham*. They accordingly sent instructions to Sergeant to provide a passage for Phipps in the first available coastal vessel, which was to be commanded by that "skillfull Coaster," Michael Grimington. The *Hayes* sloop made the passage northwards before the end of navigation in 1685 and Grimington wintered at York Fort where he was to be stationed for the future. His ability as a coaster was put to the test in the following summer when he sailed the *Hayes* through driving ice from Port Nelson to the mouth of Churchill River. There, during the explorations made by Grimington and his companions (John Abraham, Francis Hildsley, Martin Johnson, John Warner and Benjamin Wallis) relics of Jens Munk*'s 1619–20 expedition were found.

When the supply-ship from London reached York Fort later that summer (1686) it was learned that the vessel bound for the James Bay posts, the *Happy Return* (Capt. William Bond*), had been lost in Hudson Strait, so Governor George Geyer* sent Grimington in the *Hayes* with a cargo of supplies for the relief of their southern colleagues. It was then not known at York Fort that, although the English and French were not at war, the HBC posts on Moose, Rupert, and Albany Rivers had been captured by Pierre de Troyes* and all the inmates taken prisoner. Somewhere on the passage southwards Grimington must have unknowingly passed the *Colleton* in which the majority of those who had been released were going to York Fort. How soon he learned that the James Bay posts were occupied by the French under PIERRE LE MOYNE d'Iberville can only be guessed. The fact that the *Hayes* was not captured until 14 June 1687 (the date on which Grimington's wages ceased according to HBC records) indicates that in the passage southwards the *Hayes* was delayed by the early onset of winter, that

Grimington was obliged to find safe quarters off the East Main, perhaps at Gilpin Island, and that he did not get in touch with Albany Fort as soon as winter travel became possible because he had learned from Indians that the French were in occupation. His aim would therefore be to try to slip back unnoticed to Port Nelson as soon as ice conditions allowed in 1687. It is highly probable that he was trying to do just this on 14 June when the *Hayes* encountered the *Craven*, an HBC ship which had been captured and armed by the French. Besides Frenchmen, the latter vessel was carrying some of the Englishmen, who had barely survived the winter, to Rupert River en route to Nemiskau and New France. At the time the *Hayes* was captured (and two of her crew killed), Grimington was on an island cutting timber with which to mend her rudder. And there the French left him for 15 days. He was almost dead when they took him away to join the party bound for New France. The account of the capture of the *Hayes* and of the events which followed was given to the HBC in London on 17 Jan. 1688 by Edward Coles and eight other men. It appears that the party arrived at Quebec on 12 September and that with the exception of Michael Grimington and John Egremon, who were detained against their wills, all were found passage in ships bound for France.

Through its governor, Lord Churchill, the HBC brought the circumstances of Grimington's detention to the notice of the king. This "excellent Seaman in those parts," it claimed, was being held "to teach them the Navigation of the Bay" to the detriment of the company and contrary to his duty and allegiance as a British subject. Royal aid was sought in getting the irregularity brought to the notice of the French king so that instructions ordering release might be sent to the governor of Canada in 1688. Grimington reached London via La Rochelle in the early part of 1689.

In the following June Grimington sailed from the Thames as chief mate in the company's new ship, the 150-ton *Royal Hudson's Bay* (Capt. Leonard Edgcombe). The 70-ton *Northwest Fox* (Capt. John Ford) sailed in company. Edgcombe's ship was carrying supplies to the expedition led by John Marsh* which had sailed in 1688 to re-establish trade in Albany River and, as war had recently been declared between England and France, Edgcombe was ordered to take offensive action against the French should they still be in occupation of the forts in James Bay. When the vessels were about 30 leagues off the Scilly Islands they were attacked by three French privateers. Ford surrendered, but Edgcombe and Grimington fought for about eight hours and

Grimington

escaped. However, their disabled ship had to be taken back to Plymouth to be refitted. Desertion of seamen, lack of a convoy, and above all the danger of beginning a voyage to Hudson Bay so late in the season, made it necessary to abandon the venture for that year, so Grimington spent the winter of 1689–90 in England. The committee expressed its appreciation of his conduct by presenting him with a piece of plate (valued at £10) in the form of a tankard bearing the company's coat of arms.

In 1690 Grimington was given command of what had been the HBC's 120-ton pink *Dering*. This had been renamed *Prosperous* and with royal consent converted into a fireship for the protection of the *Royal Hudson's Bay* (Capt. Edgcombe) and the *Dering* [II] (Capt. James Young*). Their captains and Grimington carried letters of marque. After escorting the two vessels to York Fort, Grimington was to winter there if needed by Governor Geyer and, at the opening of navigation in 1691, to explore "Dering River" to the north of Churchill River and "to fix a Factorie there." Although Grimington wintered in the bay it is not known whether he sailed to this unidentified river before returning to England in the autumn of 1691.

Grimington next sailed from London in 1692 as a member of the expedition sent to recapture Albany (renamed Sainte Anne) Fort. The committee recommended him to the leader, James KNIGHT, as one "very fitt both to advise & Execute," and made him commander of the *Royal Hudson's Bay*. From York Fort on, Grimington was "chiefe or Admirall"; he, Charles Cotesworth of the *Pery*, and Henry BALEY of the *Prosperous* carried letters of marque. The expedition wintered on Gilpin Island and in June 1693, after the few remaining Frenchmen were overcome, Albany Fort came back into the HBC's possession. Grimington, his part in that venture being finished, returned to London. "Severall omisions" on his part earned him a severe reprimand and on being re-engaged he was warned against entertaining his warrant officers without the approval of the committee. It is thus obvious that his offence during 1692–93 had been over-familiarity with lower ranks to the detriment of discipline.

Grimington successfully commanded the *Royal Hudson's Bay* to and from York and Albany Forts in 1694, but as no supply-ships were sent to the bay in 1695 he remained in England. In 1696 he again commanded the *Royal Hudson's Bay* and carried a letter of marque, but on this voyage he sailed not only with the HBC's ship *Dering* (the third of that name and under the command of Henry Baley) and *Knight* (Capt. Nicholas Smithsend*), but also with H.M. ships *Bonaventure* (Capt. William

Allen) and *Seaford* (Capt. Grange). The aim of this expedition was to recapture York Fort, which had been taken by Iberville in the autumn of 1694. This purpose was accomplished (though the French again took the fort the following year) and according to orders Grimington brought the *Dering* back to England in the same year. When the *Bonaventure* was off the Scillies, it was attacked by a French man-of-war. Grimington was accused of running away, but the committee members were apparently satisfied with whatever explanation he gave them.

In 1697 the HBC's ships *Royal Hudson's Bay* (Capt. Nicholas Smithsend) and *Dering*, commanded by Grimington, were convoyed by H.M. ships *Hampshire* (Capt. John Fletcher*) and (until she was lost in Hudson Strait) *Owner's Love* (Capt. Loyd). Grimington was ordered to sail to James Bay after calling at York Fort and to return to England in the same season, but he could not follow these instructions because the ships encountered Iberville's *Pélican* off Hayes River on 26 August. In the battle which resulted Grimington, "hardly Escapeing," returned to England with nine wounded men aboard. The *Hampshire* was sunk and the *Royal Hudson's Bay* captured. Although Grimington's voyage "was not so successfull as could have been wished," the committee were well satisfied that "he had done his utmost in all Respects."

York Fort (Fort Bourbon) was not returned to the HBC until 1714; thus, from 1698, the company's ships sailed to its only possession, Albany Fort, in James Bay. As commander of the *Dering* [III] Grimington made successful return voyages there in 1698 and 1699. He remained in England in 1700 because Albany Fort was thought not to be in need of supplies, but he made a successful voyage there and back in 1701 as captain of the 100-ton *Pery*. The peace which had lasted between England and France since 1697 ended in May 1702. Grimington, in command of the newly built 160-ton *Hudson's Bay* [II], experienced inevitable difficulties in getting seamen and in joining convoys and, as a result, his arrival in James Bay occurred so late in the season that he was obliged to winter on Gilpin Island before even delivering the cargo at Albany. He returned to England in 1703.

Grimington remained in the HBC's employ even though vessels were no longer sent annually to the bay. He took the *Hudson's Bay* to Albany in 1705 but she ran aground in Albany River while he was sick, and the homeward voyage had to be postponed until the next year. This postponement caused the differences which arose between John FULLARTINE and Anthony BEALE. Grimington's next voyage to Albany, out and home, was successfully made in the *Hudson's Bay* in 1708, and he was again in command of her in 1710 when he sailed from the Thames on what proved to be his last voyage. He died at Harwich, Essex, on 15 June and was buried there two days later. The *Hudson's Bay* continued to Albany under the command of Joseph DAVIS.

Grimington was survived by his wife Anne and by a son, MICHAEL.

Throughout his long service Grimington was entirely concerned with marine affairs in Hudson Bay and the Thames. His lax behaviour in 1692–93 may have prejudiced his appointment as governor of York Fort in 1696 to the advantage of Henry Baley, though there is no proof that Grimington aspired to the position. His skill as a navigator was unquestioned as was also his loyalty during one of the most decisive periods in the history of the HBC.

ALICE M. JOHNSON

[References to Michael Grimington and his sailing instructions (1690–96) are found in HBRS, XI, XX (Rich and Johnson). HBRS, XXV (Davies and Johnson) contains biographical information. A.M.J.]

GRIMINGTON, MICHAEL, the younger, HBC seaman; son of Michael GRIMINGTON; fl. 1698–1719.

Grimington's marine experience was gained in James Bay. His first recorded voyage was made there from London in 1698 and was followed by two years' service as a seaman in the *Pery* (Capt. Henry BALEY) based in the bay. As a seaman he also wintered in James Bay in 1702–3 and 1705–6. His next HBC voyage, in the *Pery* (Capt. Richard WARD), ended in shipwreck on arrival in Albany River; so Grimington once more wintered in James Bay (1711–12) before returning to London.

Grimington was employed during 1713–18 in the bayside marine service. Although he commanded the *Prosperous* hoy from 1714, it was DAVID VAUGHAN who sailed her northwards from Albany to York in 1716 preparatory to her taking part, under Grimington's command, in the establishing of Churchill in 1717. Any reputation Grimington may have earned as a seaman was ruined by drunkenness. His consequent unreliability led to complaints against him by James KNIGHT and Henry KELSEY and resulted in his recall to England in 1718. Grimington sailed to and from Albany in 1719 as chief mate of the *Mary* (Capt. James Belcher); after this date his name disappeared from HBC records.

ALICE M. JOHNSON

Founding of Churchill (Kenney). HBRS, XXV (Davies and Johnson).

GROSBOIS. *See* BOUCHER

GROSTON (Grotton) DE SAINT-ANGE, ROBERT, officer in the colonial regular troops in the Illinois country; b. at Châtillon-sur-Seine, diocese of Langres, province of Champagne, son of Jean Groston and Marie Rebourceau; d. before June 1740.

The date of Robert Groston's arrival in Canada is unknown, but in 1736 Le Moyne* de Bienville said that he had been in the king's service for over 50 years. In 1692 he married Marguerite Crevier, by whom he had six sons and two daughters. Marguerite was buried at Montreal, 7 June 1707. On 24 March 1718 he married Élisabeth, daughter of François Chorel (Sorel) and Marie-Anne Aubuchon. According to Charlevoix*, Saint-Ange was his escort on the voyage down the Mississippi in 1721. Soon after that, Saint-Ange was serving in the Illinois country, where he brought his second wife, their only child, Élisabeth, and two sons by his first marriage: Pierre (bap. 17 Nov. 1693) and Louis, Sieur de Bellerive (bap. 16 Oct. 1698).

On 30 May 1722 Saint-Ange was commissioned ensign on half pay and in 1723 was sent up the Missouri with VÉNIARD de Bourgmond to build Fort d'Orléans. He was in the first party dispatched towards the Padouca (Comanche) country (western Kansas) in 1724, but when Bourgmond led a second expedition there later that year, Saint-Ange (half-pay lieutenant since December 1722) remained in command at Fort d'Orléans. In 1725 he was again in command while Bourgmond was escorting his party of Missouri Indians to France.

Some time later Saint-Ange returned to serve again in the eastern Illinois country. He bought a house near Fort de Chartres in 1729 and in 1730 succeeded to the command of that post, from which he led a successful campaign against the Fox Indians. About 1734 he was superseded by Pierre d'Artaguiette and on 16 Dec. 1738, in recognition of services, was commissioned half-pay captain, though news of his promotion apparently had not reached him by the time of his death, reported to Versailles by Bienville in June 1740.

His son Pierre, commissioned half-pay ensign 19 Dec. 1722, died a lieutenant in the Chickasaw disaster in 1736 [*see* FRANÇOIS-MARIE BISSOT DE VINSENNE]. In 1738 Robert Groston de Saint-Ange was mentioned in the "Registre des donations" at Fort de Chartres as guardian of Pierre's daughter Marie-Rose and son Pierre, both minors. Robert Groston's daughter Élisabeth married François Coulon de Villiers in 1740 and died at Fort de Chartres 6 March 1755. Saint-Ange's widow was

Grymington

buried at Fort de Chartres 23 Feb. 1762, said to be 79 years old, although Tanguay gives the date of her baptism as 1 April 1691.

JOHN FRANCIS MCDERMOTT

The name is sometimes written Groston de Saint-Ange, sometimes Grotton, *dit* Saint-Ange; the *de* has no noble significance. Archives of Illinois State Hist. Library (Springfield), Registre des donations, Fort de Chartres. Archives of the Missouri Hist. Soc. (St Louis), Fort de Chartres, records of the church of Sainte-Anne. AN, Col., B, 43, f.124; 66, f.365; C¹³ᴬ, 21, f.181; 25, f.94. *Découvertes et établissements des Français* (Margry), VI. Wis. State Hist. Soc. *Coll.*, XVIII.

Tanguay, *Dictionnaire*, I, 285; III, 69, 199; IV, 382. N. M. Belting, *Kaskaskia under the French régime* (University of Illinois studies in the social sciences, XXIX, no.3, Urbana, 1948). Marc de Villiers Du Terrage, *La découverte du Missouri et l'histoire du fort d'Orléans (1673–1728)* (Paris, 1925). W. B. Douglas, "The Sieurs de St. Ange," Ill. State Hist. Soc. *Trans., 1909* (Ill. State Hist. Lib. pub., XIV, Springfield, 1910), 135–46.

GRYMINGTON (Gryminton). *See* GRIMINGTON

GUAY. *See* GAY

GUESDRON, JULIEN, priest, Recollet, guardian, acting provincial commissioner, provincial; b. 1667, apparently at Cambrai; d. 1735 at Versailles.

Father Guesdron first entered the secular clergy, and it was after he had received the subdiaconate that he asked to be admitted to the Recollets in 1687; he received the diaconate at Rouen 17 Dec. 1689 and the priesthood probably the following year.

He sailed from Rochefort for Canada on 20 May 1699. In his capacity as guardian of the convent of Quebec, on 26 October of that same year he signed the "Actes du Frère Didace Pelletier," attesting to two cures attributed to this Recollet brother [*see* Pelletier*].

At the end of the summer of 1700 he replaced Father Olivier GOYER as acting provincial commissioner of the Recollets in Canada. During his stay in Canada he served at Lauson and Trois-Rivières; he then served as chaplain at Port-Dauphin (Englishtown, N.S.), and as a missionary and officiating priest at Louisbourg.

In the autumn of 1701 he returned to France, where he was guardian of the convent of Metz (1704–10) and novice master. In August 1722 he was elected provincial of the Recollets of the province of Saint-Denis (1722–25), and on 9 July 1731 he was re-elected for three years. He was appointed on 30 July of that year by a papal brief

apostolic commissioner to settle a difference which had arisen between the Recollets of the province of Dauphiné and those of Lyons. On 30 April 1735 he died at the convent of Versailles, at 68 years of age, after 48 years in holy orders.

GABRIEL-M.-RÉAL DUMAS

AAQ, Registres d'insinuation A, f.536. Archives des Franciscains de Québec, Dossier Julien Guesdron. AN, Col., B, 20, f.176v. Archives de la Seine-Maritime (Rouen), G.9755, f.25 (clergé séculier). Rom. Bibli. Corsiniana, codex 912, Lettere. *Recueil des instructions données aux ambassadeurs et ministres de France . . . [1648–1791]*, éd. Gabriel et Jean Hanotaux (3v., Paris, 1888–1913), III, 157 n.2.

GUESLIS, FRANÇOIS VAILLANT DE. *See* VAILLANT

GUILLIMIN, CHARLES (also **Guillimen**, although this form was not used in New France), wealthy merchant, fitter-out of ships, commission agent, shipbuilder, militia commander, councillor in the Conseil Supérieur; b. 1676; d. at Quebec, 27 Feb. 1739.

The Guillimin family, which formed part of the younger branch of one of the most venerable noble houses of Brittany, dwelt in the seaport and fishing centre of Concarneau (Finistère). Guillaume Guillimin, Charles' father, was a lawyer in the *parlement* of Brittany. The details of Charles' early life are not known, but he apparently came to New France in the late 1600s with at least enough capital to enter ambitiously into a number of colonial enterprises. Through investments in the St Lawrence fisheries, in shipbuilding and in trade with metropolitan merchants, he soon became "one of the richest merchants of Quebec." He also appears to have acquired a measure of military distinction during this early phase of his colonial career. He claimed, for example, that in the heat of Sir William Phips*'s naval assault on Quebec in 1690, he had successfully mounted two batteries on the heights of the Cul de Sac in order to harass the disabled English vessels taking refuge below. In 1704, furthermore, he commanded the Quebec militia on an expedition organized by the Marquis de Vaudreuil [RIGAUD] against the New England settlements.

But Guillimin was first and foremost a merchant; through the first quarter of the 18th century he devoted the bulk of his energy to augmenting both his wealth and his commercial influence. In 1710, for instance, he entrenched himself more solidly within the Canadian business community by marrying Françoise Lemaître, the widowed daughter of a Montreal merchant. He also developed fishing establishments in the Baie

Guillouet d'Orvilliers

des Chaleurs and on the Îles de la Madeleine; constructed seven or eight seagoing vessels at Quebec; erected several large houses and at least one store in Quebec and Montreal; and acted as commission agent for Madame Pascaud, widow of ANTOINE, of La Rochelle—one of the French merchants who carried on a heavy trade with New France. As Governor Charles de Beauharnois* de La Boische and Intendant Gilles Hocquart* later testified: "it is true that this individual has carried out substantial business undertakings in this country...." They pointed out too that Guillimin had always been a good citizen, devoted to the public interest. He had proven as much in 1712, when he loaned 40,000 *livres* to the king's treasurer at Quebec during a financial crisis. Indeed, his services were acknowledged publicly on 20 Sept. 1721 by his installation as a councillor in the Conseil Supérieur of New France.

Yet, as was so often the case in New France, circumstances eventually conspired to wipe out Guillimin's fortune. To begin with, the decision by French authorities to devalue Canadian card money forced him to shoulder a severe loss when his 40,000 *livres* loan was, at last, repaid. He incurred still more devastating losses when several of his trading vessels were sunk during the 1720s. Before long, his creditors began to hound him with lawsuits. He attempted to recoup at least a portion of his disappearing affluence by means of a suit against Madame Pascaud over alleged injustices in her dealings with him as her commission agent, but his action was finally thwarted by the minister, Maurepas. So low had Guillimin's fortunes sunk by the early 1730s, he was obliged to petition the minister for a pension. But despite the strong support of the governor and intendant, Guillimin was refused; Maurepas also declined, in 1736, to absolve him of a 1,300 *livres* debt to the king's store. Although he continued his efforts to re-establish his maritime commerce, he was evidently a poor man when he died in 1739— leaving to his children, particularly Charles and Guillaume, the task of mending the family's fortunes. Guillimin's career had followed a pattern that was not untypical of many of New France's merchants: apparent prosperity and increasing social prestige dissipated almost at an instant by administrative decisions taken in France and by the normal vicissitudes of the Canadian economy.

DONALD J. HORTON

AN, Col., B, 44, 57–61, 64; C¹¹A, 36, 66, 71–72; E, 215; Section Outre-Mer, G³, 2038 (Greffe de J.-C. Desmaret, 20 oct. 1732). *Documents relating to Canadian currency during the French period* (Shortt), II, 744. Le Jeune, *Dictionnaire*, I, 726f. Tanguay, *Dictionnaire*, IV, 420. Cahall, *Sovereign Council of New France*. Cameron Nish, "La bourgeoisie et les mariages, 1729–1748," *RHAF*, XIX (1965–66), 595. P.-G. Roy, "La famille Guillimin," *BRH*, XXIII (1917), 97–116.

GUILLOUET D'ORVILLIERS, CLAUDE, officer who served in Canada and Guiana; b. 11 June 1668 on the island of St Kitts (West Indies), the son of RÉMY GUILLOUET and Anne-Marie Le Febvre de La Barre; married Marie-Claude de Vicq de Pontgibaud on 1 Feb. 1706; d. 12 Dec. 1728, on board the *Paon* while on his way back to France.

In 1685 Orvilliers was a lieutenant serving in Canada. On 1 March 1687 he obtained a captain's commission and received command of a company, with which he campaigned against the Senecas, distinguishing himself particularly during an ambush laid by the Indians for the Marquis de Denonville [BRISAY]. He then served at Fort Frontenac under the orders of his father, whom he ultimately replaced. In 1690 he took part in operations around Quebec with a party of Hurons from the mission at Lorette. On 11 Aug. 1691 he again drew attention to himself by the brilliant manner in which he backed up CLÉMENT Du Vuault de Valrennes in the battle of La Prairie against the Iroquois, when a numerically inferior French force defeated the enemy in hand-to-hand fighting, killing nearly 200 of them. "Since the colony has been established there has never been such a strong or vigorous action," wrote Frontenac [Buade*]. Frontenac, on 20 Nov. 1690, had requested a sub-lieutenant's commission for Orvilliers, "who is serving in this country with great ardour and who seeks out eagerly any opportunity to distinguish himself."

Orvilliers was finally promoted sub-lieutenant on 1 Jan. 1692, and in February of that year was put in command of a party of 120 Frenchmen and 205 Indians who were to proceed inland in the direction of Fort Frontenac (Cataracoui); he was, however, seriously burned when a bucket of boiling water was upset over him and had to hand over command to Boisberthelot* de Beaucours. In 1693 he returned to France and then served in the Marine. He became lieutenant of a free company at Rochefort on 23 Dec. 1696, and on 1 Nov. 1705 he was promoted lieutenant-commander, taking over command of the free company at Rochefort that same year. In 1706 he was in command of the *Gaillard*, on which he took his father to Guiana. He then carried out various transport missions to Guiana, Martinique, and Santo Domingo (Haiti) while in command of various ships: in 1707, the *Saemslack*; in 1711, the *Profond*; in 1712, the *Renommée*; and in 1713, the

269

Guillouet d'Orvilliers

Héros. On 25 Nov. 1712 he was promoted commander and also became a knight of the order of Saint-Louis; the following year he was appointed king's lieutenant at Moulins, and on 22 May 1715 he became governor of Guiana, the office having become vacant following his father's death and the retirement of Commander Béthune.

He arrived at Cayenne in September 1716 and applied himself to the development of the colony, at the same time continuing to maintain good relations with the Indians through the Jesuit mission at Kourou. In 1724 he proposed to the minister an ambitious plan for settlement in the regions of the Oyapock and Marouini Rivers which foreshadowed the one that Choiseul tried to bring into being at Kourou in 1764; Orvilliers directed in person the development of a vast land grant that he had obtained in association with ANTOINE-DENIS RAUDOT and the Sieur Pierre de Forcade. He developed the district of Approuague, founded the post of Oyapock, took an interest in the search for minerals, in botany, and in the introduction of new kinds of crops, such as tobacco and coffee.

Claude d'Orvilliers had four sons: Claude, who served as an officer in Guiana and Santo Domingo; Gilbert, who was governor of Guiana from 1749 to 1763; Louis, who had a brilliant naval career and was lieutenant general of the naval forces when he died in 1792; and Paul, who was a captain in the Régiment de Navarre.

ÉTIENNE TAILLEMITE

AN, Col., B, 13, f.146; 28, ff.59, 161, 169, 393, 503, 511; 31, f.26; 33, f.103; 35, ff.4, 6v, 44v, 83v 205; 36, f.202; 37, f.124; 39; 41; 44; 47; 50; 52; C^{11A}, 11, ff.63, 108, 169, 235, 236; 12, ff.93, 97v, 359; C^{14}, 8–14; D^{2C}, 222, f.397; E, 188 (dossier de Forcade); Marine, C^1, 161; C^7, 231. Archives personnelles du général d'Esclaibes, château de Saternault, par l'Arbret (Pas-de-Calais). Le Jeune, *Dictionnaire*.

GUILLOUET D'ORVILLIERS, RÉMY, officer who served in Canada and French Guiana; b. *c.* 1633, son of Jean Guillouet, a lawyer in the *parlement*, and of Marguerite Gascoing. In 1666, at La Rochelle, he married Anne-Marie Le Febvre, the legitimized daughter of Antoine Le Febvre* de La Barre, the future governor general of Canada. He died 18 Aug. 1713 at Cayenne (French Guiana).

In 1651 Orvilliers was an ensign in the Régiment de Conti; he was promoted captain in 1657, then he was transferred to the Régiment de Poitou. In 1667 he was in command of the five companies of this unit that were detached to the West Indies, with his headquarters on St Kitts Island. In 1669 he returned to France to serve in the Régiment d'Harcourt. He went to Canada in 1682 as captain of the guards of his father-in-law, Governor General Le Febvre de La Barre, and took part in the campaign against the Iroquois, commanding the rearguard. In 1685 Denonville [BRISAY] appointed him commander of Fort Frontenac (Cataracoui), replacing DAUPHIN de La Forest, who was to "go to the Illinois on business for M. de La Salle [Cavelier*]." Guillouet took part in 1687 in the expedition against the Senecas, then returned to Fort Frontenac, where he was rejoined by his son CLAUDE and in 1688 he went back to France.

His conduct was always judged favourably by his chiefs, and Father Charlevoix* could write: "M. d'Orvilliers, commandant of the post at Cataracoui, was one of the officers in the colony on whose prudence, ability, and steadfastness the governor generals of New France relied the most."

Orvilliers continued his career in Guiana, where he was appointed a captain on 13 Jan. 1689 and king's lieutenant on 18 Aug. 1690. In 1694 he spent some time in France, and on several occasions in 1697 and in the period 1700–1 he took over command during the absence of Governor Férolles. The latter reproached him for his lack of order but recognized his ability. On 9 March 1706 Orvilliers was appointed governor of Guiana, and in this office he was very active. No doubt relying upon his experience in Canada, he endeavoured to improve relations with the Indians by safeguarding their freedom, sending them Jesuit missionaries, giving them grants of land, and settling them in villages near Cayenne. He also assigned several officers to the task of exploring the interior of the country, which was virtually unknown at that time, and he fought against the claims of the Portuguese in the region of the Oyapock River. The Jesuit Father Gouyé, procurator of the missions in South America, praised him; the commissary, Albon, likewise declared that Orvilliers possessed many good qualities, despite his impetuous nature. Probably annoyed by Orvilliers' stormy differences with the king's lieutenant Grandval [Morthon], Pontchartrain [Phélypeaux] rebuked him on several occasions for governing too harshly. Orvilliers, who was made a knight of the order of Saint-Louis on 28 July 1705, left one son, Claude, who succeeded him as governor of Guiana.

ÉTIENNE TAILLEMITE

AN, Col., B, 11, f.81v; 14, ff.75, 302, 544v; 18, ff.199, 586v; 21, ff.188, 349v, 437v, 690; 24, f.135v; 26, f.147; 28, ff.44, 49, 87, 157, 176, 212, 225, 448; 31, ff.50, 194, 287, 376, 456, 482, 623; 33, ff.30v, 62v, 96v; 34, ff.103, 104v, 116, 133, 135v; 35, ff.610v–616v; C^{11A}, 2; C^{14}, 3–7; Marine, C^1, 161; C^7, 231. Archives personnelles du général d'Esclaibes, château de

Saternault, par l'Arbret (Pas-de-Calais). Charlevoix, *Histoire* (1722), II, 313. Le Jeune, *Dictionnaire*.

GUION (Guyon), FRANÇOIS, privateer operating on the coasts of Acadia and New England; b. 3 March 1666, son of Denis Guion and Élisabeth Boucher of Île d'Orléans; married Marie-Anne Roberge, 4 April 1688; d. before 12 July 1701.

Guion is mentioned several times in Robinau* de Villebon's journals, sometimes in association with another privateer, Baptiste (Pierre MAISONNAT), but the name François is used there only once. References to Guion the elder and Guion the younger have increased the difficulty of identification, as have the numerous repetitions of similar names in the Guion family. Webster stated that Guion was born in 1635, but this seems to be the birth date of an uncle of the same name. C. Alice Baker completely confused Guion with Baptiste. Two notarial documents have been found, however—one of them Guion's marriage contract and the other referring to the sale of prizes—which bear identical signatures of François Guion, and enable us to identify him as the man born in 1666.

Guion was a brother-in-law of Antoine LAUMET, *dit* de Lamothe Cadillac, who married the former's sister Marie-Thérèse, but not of LOUIS DAMOURS de Chauffours and Mathieu Damours* de Freneuse, as Antoine Bernard has stated. They married two of his cousins. Guion's younger brother Joseph sometimes accompanied him as his lieutenant and sometimes operated separately. They were among those referred to by Bernard as "sea-wolves," who were based at Port-Royal (Annapolis Royal, N.S.), Beaubassin (Chignecto) and Les Mines (Grand Pré, N.S.) at this time and who preyed on English shipping, especially fishing boats.

On 4 June 1695 François Guion took three prizes from an English frigate which went on a rock south of Grand Manan, and by September of that year he had captured nine more fishing vessels, five of which he ransomed for 1,500 *livres*. As Guion's home was in Quebec he took many of his prizes there for disposal, and there is a record of his brother Joseph's recruiting in 1695 for the crew of François' sloop *Philibusquier*.

In April or May 1696 Guion's vessel was captured by an English frigate and he was taken prisoner to Boston. He was soon released in an exchange for English prisoners taken by PIERRE LE MOYNE d'Iberville at Pemaquid. He was back at Port-Royal in late summer bringing word that an English force was being assembled at Boston for an attack on the French settlements, especially Villebon's Fort Saint-Joseph (Nashwaak) on the Saint John River.

Nothing more seems to be recorded about Guion's activities after this date, but his career was a brief one for, according to Tanguay, he was already dead when his fifth child was born in July 1701. As his wife requested an inventory of his estate in August, it is probable that Guion had died shortly before the birth of his last child.

W. AUSTIN SQUIRES

AJM, Greffe de Michel Lepailleur de Laferté, 19 janv. 1702. *Coll. de manuscrits relatifs à la N.-F.*, II, 222, 250, 282. *Jug. et délib.*, III, 513–16. *NYCD* (O'Callaghan and Fernow), IX, 617, 643, 667. A. Roy, *Inv. greffes not.*, VII, 51; XVIII, 191, 322. P.-G. Roy, *Inv. testaments*, I, 274. Webster, *Acadia*, 77–78, 81, 82, 148, 149, 150–51, 178. Tanguay, *Dictionnaire*, I, 296. Bernard, *Le drame acadien*, 189, 220. C. A. Baker, "The adventures of Baptiste," Pocumtuck Valley Memorial Assoc. *Hist. and proc., 1899–1904*, IV (Deerfield, Mass., 1905), 342–477. Régis Roy, "Le flibustier Baptiste," *BRH*, V (1898), 11–12. *See also* É.-Z. Massicotte, "Flibustiers montréalais," *BRH*, XLII (1936), 583–84.

GUYOTTE, ÉTIENNE, priest, Sulpician, missionary at Lachine and at Sorel, parish priest of Notre-Dame de Montréal, ecclesiastical superior of the sisters of the Congrégation de Notre-Dame; b. between 1639 and 1644 in Gray, a small town about 30 miles from Besançon; d. 1701 in either Paris or Bourges.

Guyotte entered the order of Saint-Sulpice on 10 March 1674. He departed for New France the following year, and served as a missionary at both Lachine and nearby Fort de La Présentation for three years. Although Lachine was not considered large enough to support a resident priest, Guyotte was able to build a church there in 1676. The following year he became involved in a dispute with an important Lachine merchant, François LENOIR, *dit* Rolland, who was trading alcohol with the Indians and encouraging drunkenness. When Bishop François de LAVAL placed Rolland under interdict for his trading activities, Guyotte excluded the merchant from public prayers. Then, when Rolland appeared for mass, Guyotte ordered the verger to eject him from the church.

In 1678 Guyotte was recalled to France to work in the diocese of Besançon. He left New France in October with François LE FEVRE but his mind was set on returning; in May 1682 he was at La Rochelle awaiting passage to the colony. In October of that year he was appointed parish priest of Notre-Dame de Montréal, an office which included supervision of the parish school. By 1685, however, the number of priests in the parish was

271

insufficient to operate the school satisfactorily and it was turned over to the parish council of Notre-Dame.

From December 1686 to July 1687, Guyotte served at Sorel as a missionary, and from 1687 to 1692 was ecclesiastical superior of the sisters of the Congrégation de Notre-Dame. By 1690 he was causing his superiors much concern; he was not only offensive, imperious, and moody, but also insisted on issuing rebukes to individual parishioners from the pulpit. He publicly refused to grant communion to a woman who was wearing powder and jewellery, instead of admonishing her privately during confession. He then refused absolution to certain women whom he denounced as witches. Louis Tronson, superior of the seminary of Saint-Sulpice in Paris, had no alternative but to recall him in 1693.

Guyotte spent 1694 in Gray and approached Tronson early in 1695 to ask that he be returned to New France, but the superior refused this request. Tronson took this position in spite of petitions asking for Guyotte's return sent to François DOLLIER de Casson, to Bishop Saint-Vallier [LA CROIX], and to the Paris seminary. The petition sent to the seminary was signed by 40 persons including the Montreal merchant, JACQUES LE BER. Subsequently, Guyotte was considered for work in several seminaries, and was finally sent to Bourges to assist in the administration of the parish attached to the seminary there.

In spite of being refused permission to return to New France as a Sulpician priest, he remained loyal to his vocation and to his order, and even declined offers from the Frères Hospitaliers de la Croix to supervise their Montreal hospital. Death overtook him suddenly in 1701 while he was delivering a sermon.

C. J. RUSS

ASSM, Biographies: Étienne Guyotte; Pierre Rémy; Correspondance générale, 2e partie, lettres de M. Tronson, I, 42; II, 156; III, 196, 256; V, 101. Henri Gauthier, *Sulpitiana* (Montréal, 1926), 214f.

H

HACHÉ-GALLANT, MICHEL (the name was originally Larché; the forms **Haché**, *dit* **Gallant, Galan,** and **Galand** also appear), settler in Acadia and Île Saint-Jean (Prince Edward Island), founder of the Haché and the Gallant families of the Maritimes; b. *c.* 1663, d. 1737.

Michel Haché-Gallant's origins are obscure. He is probably the son of Pierre Larché, originally of the parish of Saint-Pierre in Montdidier, bishopric of Beauvais, and of Adrienne Langlois. Pierre Larché had died by 1668, and Michel was raised in Trois-Rivières at the home of Jacques Leneuf* de La Poterie, father of MICHEL LENEUF de La Vallière, senior. The latter seems to have taken Michel Larché with him to Acadia to his seigneury of Beaubassin. Rameau de Saint-Père writes of La Vallière and his seigneury, "among the indentured employees, we find . . . an active and intelligent young man named Haché Galand, who was [La Vallière's] business representative, serjeant-at-arms, and confidential agent." In 1690 Michel Haché married Anne Cormier; they had 12 children, 7 boys and 5 girls. At the time of his marriage he was described as militia captain of the Beaubassin shore.

After the loss of Port-Royal (Annapolis Royal, N.S.) to the English under Francis NICHOLSON in 1710 and the subsequent cession of Acadia to England by the treaty of Utrecht in 1713, a number of Acadians moved to the nearby French possessions of Île Royale (Cape Breton Island) and Île Saint-Jean. Michel Haché was among these; in 1720 he moved with his family to Île Saint-Jean and settled at Port La Joie (near Charlottetown), a settlement which had just been founded. He was named port captain of Port La Joie about that time, and he and his wife were among the most respected settlers there.

Michel Haché-Gallant went through the ice at the mouth of the Rivière du Nord (North River) and was drowned on 10 April 1737. His body was recovered on 17 July and he was buried in the cemetery of Port La Joie the same day.

PATRICE GALLANT

AN, Col., C11B, 1, ff.104–5; Section Outre-Mer, G1, 411, f.31; 466 (Recensements de l'Acadie). Placide Gaudet, Notes généalogiques (preserved in PAC and Archives de l'université de Moncton). Tanguay, *Dictionnaire*, I, 589. Arsenault, *Hist. et généal. des Acadiens*, II, 590–91. Patrice Gallant, *Michel Haché-Gallant et ses descendants* (1v. paru, Rimouski, 1958), I, 3–10. Rameau de Saint-Père, *Une colonie féodale*, I, 171.

HAIMARD, PIERRE, merchant, procurator-syndic, judge of the provost court, deputy attorney general; b. 1674 at Du Mesny in the

Hamare de La Borde

bishopric of Reims, son of Étienne Haimard and Martine Hurault; d. 12 Sept. 1724 at Quebec.

Pierre Haimard came to New France around 1690 and at first took service as a domestic, but he had much greater ambitions. He was already running a business in Quebec on Rue du Cul-de-Sac in Lower Town in 1695.

On 10 Nov. 1707 the governor and the intendant granted him the Paspébiac seigneury on Baie des Chaleurs, with the right of *haute, moyenne et basse justice*. In 1719 Haimard bought the Mont-Louis seigneury, situated in the lower reaches of the St Lawrence; it had been part of the estate of Nicolas Bourlet,.of Paris, although Haimard had been in possession of it for several years. In 1721, as a seigneur, Haimard required "all those who held documents giving title to land grants to present them to him within a month, to settle and be in residence on their land, otherwise it would be rejoined to the seigneurial domain."

In addition to his business in Quebec, Pierre Haimard engaged in the fishing trade, particularly on his Mont-Louis seigneury. He set up a drying-ground for cod there and employed Jean Flibot, Étienne Rondeau, André Demay, and Pierre Pruneau to look after his trade in cod. He had ordinances issued forbidding "the inhabitants of Quebec and the surrounding districts who go to fish at Mont-Louis to sell any spirits or other intoxicating liquor to his employees, on pain of losing their own catch." He also owned establishments on the Îles de la Madeleine "for the killing of seals and walrus." On one occasion he even had seized "the oil and barbels of a whale" which had been stolen from him.

Being a very active man with a well developed business sense, Pierre Haimard took part in the fitting out of a king's frigate in Acadia, in collaboration with some other people from Quebec. He added to his income by collecting accounts, in his capacity as attorney, for a number of merchants in France.

He was a man of sound judgement, and his personal services were often called upon: as guardian (for Louis Jolliet*'s children, in 1700), surrogate guardian, procurator, executor, and so on. It was especially as syndic for the creditors of the two large estates of CHARLES AUBERT de La Chesnaye and Jean GOBIN, the director of the Compagnie du Nord, that Pierre Haimard had to call all his powers into play. His role was not an easy one, for all Aubert's assets were in the form of landed property and there was very little ready money. For that reason this estate was not finally settled until 12 years after Pierre Haimard's death.

Pierre Haimard died at Quebec and was buried in the cathedral on 12 Sept. 1724, where on 1 Sept. 1698 he had married Louise Guillot, Gabriel Gosselin's widow. She had two children whom her husband adopted; he even made Louis Gosselin a donee *inter vivos*; this donation was the cause of a lawsuit of which all the ins and outs are to be found in the records of the Conseil Supérieur. It was not until 10 April 1753, nearly 30 years after his death, that Pierre Haimard's estate was finally wound up.

From the documents at our disposal it is clear that Pierre Haimard was a man of character and a firm will. A mere domestic in 1690, he became a merchant in 1695, judge of the provost court for the Notre-Dame-des-Anges seigneury in 1704, deputy attorney general at the Conseil Supérieur from November 1706 to July 1710, and finally seigneur of Paspébiac in 1707 and of Mont-Louis in 1719.

ROLAND-J. AUGER

AJM, Greffe de Louis-Claude Danré de Blanzy, 24 févr. 1749. AQ, NF, Cahiers d'intendance, II, 647–49; NF, Foi et hommage, II, 130; NF, Ins. Cons. sup., III, 38f.; NF, Ord. des int., I, III. *Jug. et. délib.*, III, IV, V, VI. A. Roy, *Inv. greffes not.*, XIX. P.-G. Roy, *Inv. coll. pièces jud. et not.*, II, 238; "Biographies canadiennes," *BRH*, XXII (1916), 22–25.

HAMARE (Hamard) DE LA BORDE, JEAN-BAPTISTE-JULIEN, lawyer, merchant, attorney of the provost and admiralty courts of Quebec; b. 29 June 1693 in Paris, son of Julien Hamare and Gratiane Moreau; d. probably after 1729.

Julien Hamare de La Borde, who was a lawyer in the *parlement* of Paris, arrived in New France before 19 Nov. 1720, since on that date, before the notary LA CETIÈRE, he signed his contract of marriage with Geneviève Lambert. They had a son, who died in 1721, and a daughter, Geneviève-Louise, who was baptized at Quebec in 1723. As soon as he arrived in the colony, Hamare seems to have engaged in fur-trading, for according to a lawsuit started in 1723 and settled in 1724 he had sold furs in the amount of 1,200 *livres* to Louis Lambert in 1721.

On 10 Feb. 1722 the king appointed Hamare attorney of the provost court of Quebec, and on 12 March of the same year, on the presentation of the Comte de Toulouse [Louis-Alexandre de Bourbon], he also obtained the post of attorney of the admiralty court of Quebec. On 5 October the inquiry into his character was ordered; this was done on 10 October, and two days later Hamare was admitted to the office of attorney.

Having obtained permission from the king to go to France for his personal affairs, Hamare sailed on board the *Éléphant* with Intendant Bégon*

Handasyde

in September 1726. Before leaving he sold his house to Joseph Féré Du Buron, a regular officer. This sale gave rise to a lawsuit in which his mother-in-law, Marie-Renée Roussel, Gabriel Lambert's widow, was his proxy. Hamare won his case on 27 March 1730, when Du Buron was obliged to pay the 2,000 *livres* that he owed him.

Jean-Baptiste-Julien Hamare does not seem to have returned to New France. We do not know the date of his death, but he was still living in 1729, for in that year he sent a letter to Canada.

BERNARD WEILBRENNER

AQ, Julien Hamard de La Borde. ASQ, Paroisse de Québec, 35. P.-G. Roy, *Inv. coll. pièces jud. et not.*, I, 182, 184; *Inv. ins. Cons. souv.*, 164f., 185; *Inv. jug. et délib., 1717–1760*, I, 22, 100; II, 164, 165, 198; *Inv. ord. int.*, II, 20. Gareau, "La prévôté de Québec," 108f.

HANDASYDE, THOMAS, commander of the English forces at St John's, 1697–98; governor of Jamaica, 1702–11; d. 1712.

As a junior officer Handasyde fought in campaigns in Ireland and Flanders. He was promoted major in Colonel John GIBSONE's regiment, 16 March 1694, and sailed in the expedition for the re-capture of St John's, Newfoundland, in 1697. On arrival, St John's was found abandoned and destroyed, and the soldiers were put to work re-constructing the fort and other defences under the supervision of the engineer, Michael RICHARDS. As provisions were very scarce, Colonel Gibsone decided to take the regiment home, leaving some 300 men under the command of Major Handasyde. Gibsone recommended Handasyde as a candidate for the governorship of Newfoundland, describing him as a "good, worthy man, of courage and conduct, who has served the King 24 years." On his return to England in 1698, Handasyde reported that, although 214 men had died from hardship and malnutrition, the fortifications had been rebuilt. As ordered, he had formed a Newfoundland Independent Company of 53 men to constitute a permanent garrison for St John's. (Military engineers at that time held no army rank, and it was in this company that Richards received his commission as captain, as did Robert LATHAM some years later.)

On 20 June 1702, Handasyde received commissions as colonel of the 22d regiment and as lieutenant-governor of Jamaica. He became governor of the island soon after his arrival, and in 1703 the Earl of Peterborough described Handasyde as "one of the best infantry officers we have." That same year, on the arrival of Vice-Admiral GRAYDON's squadron, destined for the

ill-fated expedition to Placentia (Plaisance), Handasyde did all he could to provide the fleet with provisions, and assist in the embarkation of the soldiers, but he resented Graydon's wholesale impressment of men. He forwarded the protests of 18 ship-masters and merchants to the Board of Trade and Plantations, and he despatched a letter to Graydon himself, with a request to return at least the landsmen he had taken.

Handasyde was promoted to major-general on 1 Jan. 1710, and returned to England in 1711. In 1712 he resigned his commission as colonel of the 22d regiment in favour of his son Roger, and died soon afterwards.

MICHAEL GODFREY

PRO, *CSP, Col., 1697–98, 1702, 1702–3, 1710–11, 1711–12; CSP, Dom., 1702–3*, 537 (Earl of Peterborough's letter). Dalton, *English army lists*, II–V. Prowse, *History of Nfld.*

HAOUILAMEK, *See* OUENEMEK

HARRISON, JOHN, minister, chaplain in the expedition against Port-Royal (Annapolis Royal, N.S.), 1710, chaplain to the garrison at Annapolis Royal, 1710–20, member of the first council of Nova Scotia, 1720, fl. 1710–21.

In May 1710 Harrison crossed from England to Boston in the *Dragon* as chaplain to Commodore GEORGE MARTIN, who had been appointed commander of Her Majesty's ships in the expedition against Port-Royal. On 18 Sept. 1710 (o.s.), Harrison sailed with the fleet to Port-Royal. After its capture he conducted a service of thanksgiving in the chapel on 10 October. The following day Colonel Francis NICHOLSON, at a council of war, and upon the recommendation of Commodore Martin, appointed Harrison chaplain to the garrison at Annapolis Royal. For the next three years, Harrison diligently ministered to the garrison and to the residents who were members of the Church of England.

On 7 Nov. 1713, he obtained leave of absence to go to Boston on private business. While there he was concerned with the interests of the church at Annapolis Royal as his letter of 23 November to Francis Nicholson attests. Early in March 1715/16 Harrison was reported to have gone to England from Annapolis Royal. He returned there on 15 Nov. 1716, bringing with him clothing for the garrison.

When the first civil council in Nova Scotia was instituted on 25 April 1720, Governor Richard Philipps* appointed Harrison as one of its members. Four days later Harrison was designated a member of a committee of council appointed to draft an order to the French inhabitants living along the Annapolis River to choose their representatives. He attended meetings of the council until 16 Aug. 1720.

Shortly afterwards he went back to England. On 5 Sept. 1725, Lieutenant-Governor Lawrence ARMSTRONG declared that Harrison was still in England, and that he had been away from Nova Scotia for about four years. It seems unlikely that he later returned to Nova Scotia. He was probably still alive in 1732, for on 23 November of that year, after the garrison chaplain, Reverend Richard WATTS, had petitioned for a patent for the church land, Armstrong confirmed a grant in Annapolis Royal to John Harrison, also chaplain, and his successors in office.

CHARLES BRUCE FERGUSSON

Nova Scotia, Dept. of Lands and Forests, Crown land records, I, 26–27 (copies in PANS). PANS, MS docs., VIII, 4. PRO, C.O. 217/2, ff.78–79; 217/4, f. 274. USPG, Letters and reports of missionaries of SPG, A, VIII, 568–75; IX, 391 (copies in PANS). "Letters and other papers relating to the early history of the Church of England in Nova Scotia," in N.S. Hist. Soc. *Coll.*, VII (1891), 89–91; *see also* N.S. Hist. Soc. *Coll.*, I (1878), 86. *N.S. Archives*, II, III. PRO, *CSP, Col.*, *1710–11, 1714–15, 1720–21, 1724–25, 1734–35*. Dalton, *English army lists*. C. W. Vernon, *Bicentenary sketches and early days of the church in Nova Scotia* (Halifax, 1910), 1, 3, 27–32.

HAUTMESNIL, FRANÇOIS PHILIPPE(S) DE. *See* PHILIPPE(S)

HAZEUR, FRANÇOIS, prominent Quebec merchant and entrepreneur, seigneur, member of the Compagnie du Nord and the Compagnie de la Colonie, councillor in the Conseil Supérieur; b. in France, *c.* 1638; d. in Quebec, 28 June 1708.

The son of François Hazeur, a bourgeois of Brouage, and Marie Proust, he immigrated to Canada in the late 1660s with two brothers, Jean-François, Sieur de Petit-Marais, and Léonard, Sieur Des Ormeaux, and two sisters, Madeleine and Marie-Anne. They were joined by their mother and younger sister, Jeanne-Louise, following the death of their father about 1672. Jean-François and Léonard went into commerce. Of the three sisters, Jeanne-Louise and Madeleine became nuns at the Hôtel-Dieu of Quebec, and Marie-Anne married Jean Sébille, a Quebec merchant.

François took up residence in Quebec where, on 21 Nov. 1672, he married Anne Soumande, daughter of the merchant Pierre Soumande and Simonne Côté. His business relations included the La Rochelle merchants Jean Gitton and Jean Grignon, Philippe Gaultier* de Comporté, and his father-in-law. It may have been with their support that he opened a store in Quebec, which soon became a flourishing enterprise, and that he began to engage in the fur trade. By the early 1680s, Hazeur had become a prominent member of the Canadian business community. He was particularly active in the fur trade, equipping numerous canoes for the west and purchasing fur-trading licences (*congés*) from the original grantees. When the Compagnie du Nord was formed in 1682 for the purpose of exploiting the Hudson Bay trade, Hazeur lost no time in joining its ranks. His investment of 17,521 *livres* in 1691 was the fourth in importance, after those of the Compagnie de la Ferme, CHARLES AUBERT de La Chesnaye, and JACQUES LE BER.

In 1688 and 1689, Hazeur began to diversify his economic activities. He formed a partnership with Soumande and Grignon which acquired control of the seigneury of Malbaie, a thickly wooded area containing many types of timber suitable for naval construction. Under the management of the three partners, the seigneury soon became the chief Canadian centre of the lumber industry. Two sawmills were built on the site, sheds and buildings put up, roads opened, and 25 to 30 workers employed in the enterprise. In 1689 Hazeur reported that the seigneury could produce annually 30,000 feet of plank, 2,000 feet of sheathing, and up to 100 masts.

Unfortunately the enterprise did not prosper, although two carpenters sent from France in 1687 had pronounced the wood to be of good quality. In 1692, Hazeur stated that he and his partners had spent 85,000 *livres* to date and recovered only a small part of their investment. Many factors had caused this state of affairs. In the spring of 1690 flooding had severely damaged the installations, and further destruction had been wrought in the fall of that year by the English expedition which was on its way to attack Quebec. The greatest handicap of all, however, appears to have been a lack of adequate transportation facilities, which prevented the partners from making sizable shipments to France. As a result, wood which had been cut for three years was still in storage and wasting away for want of a market. To correct the situation, Hazeur asked the king to place one or two of his large flutes at the partners' disposal every year; failure to do this, he warned, would probably compel them to abandon the venture.

By the late 1690s, Hazeur's interests had shifted from lumbering to other areas of the economy. On 20 Sept. 1697, he and Denis RIVERIN were granted the seigneury of Anse-de-l'Étang, in the lower St Lawrence, where they planned to exploit

Hazeur

a slate quarry. Neither man, however, took an active interest in the development of this seigneury; they had become too involved in other projects. On 16 Feb. 1701, Hazeur had formed a partnership with CHARLES DENYS de Vitré and Pierre Peire to engage in the porpoise fisheries in the section of the St Lawrence facing Rivière Ouelle and Kamouraska. The crown granted them a five-year monopoly as well as an annual gratuity of 550 *livres*. Following the death of Vitré on 9 Jan. 1703, the two surviving partners received additional support in the form of fishing equipment and in 1705 their monopoly was renewed for 15 years. This enterprise, however, met with the same ill fortune as Hazeur's venture into lumbering. By 1704, he and Peire had incurred expenses of 50,000 *livres*, and two years later their debts had risen to 60,000 *livres*. In 1707, they were in serious difficulty. Production was down to 40 barrels of oil and the minister informed Hazeur that the product was defective and overpriced.

From 1705, Hazeur also had fishing interests in Newfoundland. In that year he was granted the seigneury of Portachoix on the northwestern shore of the island and he entered into a partnership with a habitant named Pierre Constantin who agreed to settle there to hunt and fish. How this enterprise fared financially is not known but it appears never to have been more than a minor operation.

Hazeur had also retained important interests in the fur trade. On 22 Oct. 1693, he formed an association with La Chesnaye, Charles MACARD, Jean Le Picard, François Viennay-Pachot* and Jean GOBIN, which acquired the lease of the Tadoussac trade from a Paris bourgeois named Jean-François Chalmet. In 1700, the ownership of the Tadoussac domain passed to the newly formed Compagnie de la Colonie of which Hazeur had become a shareholder. Soon afterwards, the company leased it to Hazeur and Riverin for a period of eight years at 12,700 *livres* per year. Hazeur made a substantial effort to restore the trade of this region which had been stagnating for many years before. Unfortunately, economic conditions in the early 18th century did not lend themselves to such an operation. The beaver trade was severely depressed, and the hazards facing navigation as a result of the outbreak of the War of the Spanish Succession were causing a sizable increase in the price of trade goods. By 1708, Hazeur had lost between 40,000 and 50,000 *livres* in the Tadoussac trade and his sons claimed that this was the principal cause of his financial ruin.

The only enterprise which apparently showed a steady profit during all these years and which probably was the source of capital for most of Hazeur's other undertakings was his Quebec store. His customers, like those of La Chesnaye, came from every walk of life and were scattered over the whole colony. In May and June 1695, 13 recognizances, representing a total sum of 20,202 *livres*, to cover important credit transactions were passed before the Montreal notary Bénigne Basset* alone. In February 1708, it had become necessary for Hazeur to appoint a manager, Pierre Normandin, to look after his affairs in Montreal, Trois-Rivières, Batiscan, and Champlain.

Meantime, Hazeur had become a respected and prominent member of Canadian society. His house on the Place Royale in Lower Town was reportedly the finest in Quebec. He was much esteemed by the religious orders for his frequent acts of generosity and also by Governor Frontenac [Buade*] who, on his deathbed, named him and Charles de MONSEIGNAT co-executors of his last will and testament. In 1703, Hazeur was appointed to the Conseil Supérieur in place of the deceased La Chesnaye and he acquitted himself very well of his new duties. According to JACQUES RAUDOT, Hazeur had worked hard to familiarize himself with the functions of his office and he soon became the equal of the more experienced councillors.

Hazeur died insolvent on 28 June 1708, "missed by everyone because of his merit, his virtue, and his uprightness," according to Philippe de RIGAUD de Vaudreuil and Raudot. He was survived by his second wife, Élisabeth Barbe, the daughter of Sylvain Barbe, a bailiff of the Châtelet de Paris, and Jeanne Girardin, whom he had married in Quebec on 16 Jan. 1696, four years after the death of his first wife, and by five of 13 children, all of them born of his first marriage. These included JEAN-FRANÇOIS, lawyer in the *parlement* of Paris, Joseph-Thierry*, priest of the parish of Saint-François on Île d'Orléans and subsequently a member of the chapter of Quebec, and Pierre, who became known as Canon Hazeur* de L'Orme. He was appointed parish priest of Champlain in 1707 and, like his brother before him, became a member of the chapter of Quebec in 1722. Marie-Anne-Ursule, the sole surviving daughter, married the king's surgeon Michel SARRAZIN.

For over 30 years François Hazeur had been one of New France's most important and enterprising businessmen and he might have amassed considerable wealth had it not been for his disastrous ventures into lumbering, fishing and the Tadoussac trade. His failure in these areas should not be imputed primarily to any personal shortcomings but to the unfavourable economic conditions of the period.

YVES F. ZOLTVANY

AJM, Greffe d'Antoine Adhémar; Greffe d'Hilaire Bourgine; Greffe de Claude Maugue. AJQ, Greffe de Romain Becquet; Greffe de Louis Chambalon; Greffe de Pierre Duquet; Greffe de François Genaple; Greffe de Gilles Rageot. AJTR, Greffe de J.-B. Pottier. AN, Col., B, 16, 23, 27, 29, 42; C¹¹ᴬ, 6, 7, 9, 10, 11, 12, 15, 22, 24, 27, 28, 29, 125; C¹¹ᴳ, 3; F³, 6, 7, 8, 9. "Correspondance de Frontenac (1689–99)," APQ *Rapport*, 1927–28. "Correspondance de Vaudreuil," APQ *Rapport, 1938–39; 1939–40; 1946–47; 1947–48.* Juchereau, *Annales* (Jamet). *Jug. et délib.* P.-G. Roy, *Inv. concessions*, III, IV; *Inv. ord. int.*, I. Fauteux, *Essai sur l'industrie sous le régime français.* P.-G. Roy, *La ville de Québec.* E. H. Borins, "La Compagnie du Nord, 1682–1700," unpublished M.A. thesis, McGill University, 1968. N.-E. Dionne, "Les caveaux de la basilique Notre-Dame de Québec," *BRH*, IV (1898), 130–34. "La famille Hazeur," *BRH*, XLI (1935), 321–49. P.-G. Roy, "Charles Denys de Vitré, conseiller au Conseil souverain," *BRH*, XXIV (1918), 225–42; "Notes sur François Hazeur," *BRH*, XXXII (1926), 705–11. Victor Tremblay, "Le moulin de Hazeur," *BRH*, LV (1949), 123–25.

HAZEUR, JEAN-FRANÇOIS, lawyer in the *parlement* of Paris, special lieutenant of the provost court of Quebec, councillor in the Conseil Supérieur; baptized 16 July 1678 in Quebec, son of FRANÇOIS HAZEUR and Anne Soumande; buried 14 May 1733 in Quebec.

At the age of nine, Jean-François entered the seminary of Quebec, where he studied for four years. In 1694, he enrolled at the Jesuit college of Clermont in Paris to study theology, and in 1700 proceeded to the Jesuit noviciate at Quimper in Brittany. He never joined the Society of Jesus, however, preferring instead to go into law. He became a lawyer in the *parlement* of Paris and was back in New France by 1708. During most of these years in France he had been supported by his father who had paid him an annual pension of 150 *livres* from 1694 until 1700 and one of 350 *livres* after that date. His brothers had also loaned him considerable sums of money.

On 4 March 1708, the cream of Quebec society gathered to witness the drawing up of the marriage contract between Jean-François and Catherine Martin de Lino, whose wedding had been arranged to take place on the 20th of that month. Over 100 persons signed the document, including the governor, the two intendants, the senior councillors, Quebec provost court officials, treasurers and senior officers of the colonial regular troops, and friends and relatives. This impressive assembly provides some indication of the prestige which the Hazeur and Martin de Lino families enjoyed in the colony.

Following the death of François Hazeur on 28 June 1708, Jean-François and his two brothers, Joseph-Thierry* and Pierre*, attempted to carry on, apparently without success, his fishing operations in the St Lawrence River. They were also granted the lease of the Tadoussac trade for a four-year period without charge in consideration of the losses suffered by their father. Jean-François, for his part, applied for the position which his father had held in the Conseil Supérieur, claiming that it had been promised to him *en survivance* in 1703. His application was turned down, however, although it was supported by Intendant JACQUES RAUDOT, and he had to settle for the position of special lieutenant of the Quebec provost court, a position which he held from 1710 until 1712.

Finally, in 1712, the death of Augustin ROUER de Villeray created a vacancy on the Conseil Supérieur, which was filled by Jean-François. He continued to serve as councillor for another 21 years. The only incident that marked this long tenure occurred in 1728, when he was obliged to apologize to the ministry of Marine for having wrongly supported Intendant CLAUDE-THOMAS DUPUY in his dispute with the clergy.

Jean-François died in Quebec in May 1733. He was survived by his wife, Catherine, who was buried in Quebec on 13 Dec. 1740, and by two of seven children. The eldest, François-Marie-Joseph, served in the Louisiana colonial regular troops as an ensign and lieutenant, and then held the position of commandant among the Alibamus during the 1730s and 1740s. His younger brother, Louis-Ignace, settled in Saint Domingue where he worked as an inspector in a sugar refinery, and later married a mulatress.

C. J. RUSS

AJQ, Greffe de Louis Chambalon, 3, 4 mars 1708; Greffe de François Genaple, 17 mai 1700. AN, Col., C¹¹ᴬ, 28, f.45; 29, ff.144–45; 32, f.15; 50, ff.135–38. "Correspondance de Vaudreuil," APQ *Rapport, 1947–48,* 146, 185. P.-G. Roy, *La ville de Québec,* I, 417–18. "La famille Hazeur," *BRH*, XLI (1935), 321–49. P.-G. Roy, "Une série de belles signatures," *BRH*, XLIV (1938), 181–83. Henri Têtu, "Le chapitre de la cathédrale de Québec et ses délégués en France (1723–1773)," *BRH*, XIII (1907), 224–43; XVI (1910), 161–75.

THE HEAVY. *See* LE PESANT

HÉNAUT. *See* ÉNAULT

HENNEPIN, LOUIS (baptized **Antoine**), priest, Recollet, missionary, explorer, historiographer; b. 12 May 1626 at Ath, in Belgium, son of Gaspard Hennepin, a butcher, and of Norbertine Leleu; d. *c.* 1705.

Louis Hennepin attended the École latine in the

Hennepin

town of Ath (province of Hainaut), and did his classical studies there. Around the age of 17 he donned the rough homespun of the Franciscans at the convent of Béthune (department of Pas-de-Calais), and began his noviciate under the direction of Father Gabriel de La Ribourde*. He continued his studies at the convent of Montargis (department of Loiret), with Father Paul Huet* as his master, then entered the priesthood.

Imbued with sincere missionary fervour, and adventurous into the bargain, he immediately sought to give free expression to his zeal and his natural inclination. After a period of time spent with his sister Jeanne at Ghent, where he acquired some knowledge of Flemish, he set out for Rome with the object of interesting the higher authorities of the order in his missionary ideal. He received permission to visit a number of sanctuaries and monasteries in Italy and Germany on the way back, "Whereby," he wrote, "I began to satisfy my natural curiosity." When he reached the low countries Hennepin settled at Hal (province of Brabant), on the order of the provincial superior, Father Guillaume Herincx. For a year he carried on a preaching ministry, then he went to Artois, staying in the convents situated along the coast: Biez, Calais, Dunkirk. His romantic mind caught fire when he heard the sailors' stories, some of them strange ones. Indeed Hennepin, hiding behind tavern doors, drank in the adventurous seamen's words. "I would have spent whole days and nights in this occupation, which I found so pleasant," he wrote in the *Nouvelle découverte*, "because I always learned something new about the beauty, fertility, and wealth of the countries where these people had been."

During the war started by Louis XIV in 1672 he devoted himself in Holland to the care of the wounded and sick; in 1673 he spent eight months in this fashion at Maastricht (Netherlands). A contagious illness obliged him to rest for a time; once he was cured, he took up his task again and was present at the battle of Seneffe (Hainaut) on 11 Aug. 1674.

The following year, on 22 April 1675, Louis XIV asked the Recollets to send five missionaries to New France in the near future. The superiors chose Fathers Chrestien Le Clercq*, Luc Buisset, Zénobe Membré*, Louis Hennepin, and Denis Moquet (the latter, who was sick, stayed in Europe). At the end of May 1675, with Cavelier* de La Salle, the missionaries left Europe.

The eager missionary lost no time in getting to work. He gave the Advent and Lent sermons at the Hôtel-Dieu of Quebec on Bishop LAVAL's invitation, and went through countryside and village, preaching the gospel at Cap-Tourmente,

Trois-Rivières, Sainte-Anne de Beaupré, and Bourg-Royal. In the spring of 1676 he went to Lake Ontario to replace Father Léonard Duchesne at Cataracoui (Fort Frontenac, now Kingston, Ont.). Hennepin's activity never flagged; with his *confrère* Luc Buisset, he built a "mission house" which was soon frequented by many Iroquois.

In 1678 Hennepin went back to Quebec to take up priestly duties there. La Salle, who had returned from Europe (15 September) with royal authorization to explore the western part of New France, handed the missionary a letter from Father Hyacinthe Lefebvre, his provincial superior; the latter requested Hennepin to accompany the explorer on his travels. Armed with the articles indispensable for his task of disseminating the gospel, the missionary arrived at Fort Frontenac.

A few days later (18 November) the odyssey began: 16 passengers boarded a brigantine of 10 tons, commanded by the Sieur La Motte* de Lucière; with about a month's advance on La Salle, Lucière's mission was to build a fort and a bark at Niagara. Braving the inclemency of an already late season, the sailing-ship succeeded in reaching the Niagara River on 6 December; on 8 December it was at Niagara Falls, "the most beautiful and altogether the most terrifying waterfall in the universe."

It was not long before the travellers encountered the first difficulties of the daring undertaking: the disquieting presence of Indians ever on the watch, the lack of provisions, and the discontent and grumblings of the members of the crew. They nonetheless laid a bark down as early as January (1679), and built Fort Conti during the winter. On 11 May, on La Salle's orders, Hennepin went down to Fort Frontenac to bring back to Niagara his two *confrères*: Gabriel de La Ribourde and Zénobe Membré.

From 7 Aug. 1679 to 29 Feb. 1680 Hennepin accompanied Cavelier de La Salle on his explorations [for the description of this voyage *see* Cavelier* de La Salle]; from Fort Crèvecœur La Salle then sent him with an advance guard towards the upper Mississippi. Together with Michel Accault and Antoine Auguel, *dit* Le Picard Du Guay, Hennepin left in a canoe carrying a cargo worth about 1,100 *livres*. Hennepin claimed that he made his way to the mouth of the Mississippi between 29 February and 25 March; he had returned from there by 10 April. "After paddling all night, heading in a northerly direction," wrote Hennepin, "we found ourselves quite far from [the] mouth [of the Illinois river]." On 11 April, at two o'clock in the afternoon, there suddenly appeared 33 canoes carrying Sioux Indians on a warlike expedition against neighbouring tribes. The French were seized immediately, but their lives were spared thanks to the pipe of peace and the gifts that they proffered; but the Sioux forced the three travellers to follow them to their village. In the midst of the war fleet the French canoe, handled by vigorous Indians, went about 250 leagues along the River Colbert (Mississippi). On "the nineteenth day of navigation, five leagues" from a waterfall that Hennepin was to name "Saint-Antoine de Pade," the Indians went ashore, hid their canoes, and broke that of the French to pieces. Then followed a forced march of five days over marshes, lakes, and rivers to the Sioux village, situated in the Thousand Lakes region. When the escort finally reached the village, around 21 April 1680, Hennepin was exhausted; a steam bath after the Indian fashion revived him. Having been adopted by the chief, Aquipaguetin, and his six wives, Father Louis was able to take advantage of his painful captivity to study the habits, customs, and language of the tribe.

In July the village scattered for the hunting season. After "making a hole in the ground in which to put [his] silver chalice and [his] papers until he returned from hunting," Hennepin went south with the "Great Chief Ouasicoudé." During this expedition on the Wisconsin River there occurred the chance meeting with DANIEL GREYSOLON Dulhut and five Frenchmen, who were visiting the Sioux (25 July); on 14 Aug. 1680 all were back in the village.

At the end of September the great chief of the Sioux gave the French permission to leave, and even drew on a piece of paper the route they could follow. "With this map," wrote Hennepin, "we set out, eight Frenchmen in two canoes." After wintering at Michilimackinac, the travellers started out for Quebec in Easter week (between 6 and 13 April 1681). The same year Louis Hennepin landed at Le Havre and retired to the convent of Saint-Germain-en-Laye to write up an account of his odyssey.

The *Description de la Louisiane*, published on 5 Jan. 1683 in Paris, had the most unqualified success: the work went through several editions, and was translated into Italian, Dutch, and German. The monk became a celebrity overnight for readers hungering for exotic stories and delighted by the description of the Mississippi and its rich valley. For a time the Recollet's name was honoured: he was vicar of the convent of Le Cateau-Cambrésis in 1683, and superior of the convent of Renty from 1684 to 1687. But for reasons that are still not known, Hennepin suddenly fell into disgrace; he was relegated to the convent of Saint-Omer, and subsequently expelled from the ecclesiastical province of Artois. In Hainaut, where he took refuge, the Recollet resided for five years (1687–92) at Gosselies, as chaplain of the Recollet Sisters. Once more harried by the civil and ecclesiastical authorities, Hennepin had to leave this last residence. It was then that he tried to interest the king of England in the rich countries recently discovered. Thanks to the protection of William Blathwayt, William III's secretary of war, and to the intervention of the Baron de Malqueneck, the Elector of Bavaria's favourite, Hennepin obtained permission to go to Holland at the king's expense, in order to publish his books and prepare for his crossing to America.

In 1696 Louis Hennepin, dressed in lay attire (the wearing of the ecclesiastical or religious habit being forbidden in Holland), left Belgium and made for Amsterdam, where he counted on publishing his works. His plan was thwarted by "serious obstacles." By agreement with the Count of Athlone, a Dutch general in William III's service, Hennepin set out for Utrecht. At first he lodged at the house of Martin Van Blacklandt; but the latter's wife, a shrew tainted with jansenism, made life impossible for him. He then withdrew to the house of a pious widow, Dame Renswore.

For three or four months Hennepin assisted the Dominican Louis van der Dostyne, the priest of Notre-Dame-du-Rosaire; his ministry embraced for the most part French-speaking refugees. On 1 March, in the name of their co-religionists, 58 citizens signed a petition asking authorization to establish a missionary station for French-speaking Catholics at Utrecht. Their request remained unanswered, and on 5 May Hennepin, exasperated by the slanderous rumours that continued to circulate with regard to him, began to preach, despite a formal interdict imposed by Pierre Codde, the vicar apostolic and an uncompromising Jansenist. The latter ordered Father Dostyne to close his chapel to the Recollet, then, from the pulpits of the churches of Utrecht, forbad the churchgoers to attend Father Hennepin's sermons or masses said by him, on pain of sin (2 June).

This fresh conflict with the religious authorities of Holland still did not succeed in bringing this extraordinary man to heel. He found the time and the means to publish the *Nouvelle découverte* in 1697, then the *Nouveau voyage* in 1698, two works which recount his alleged trip down the Mississippi and add numerous details concerning his short stay in America and his troubled life in Europe. In his third book he directly attacked the vicar apostolic. Indeed *La morale pratique du Jansénisme* (1698) exposed the vexatious conduct of Pierre Codde and his acolyte Jacques Cats towards him,

Hennepin

denounced Dutch jansenism, and revealed some of Hennepin's personal grievances. Shortly afterwards the authorities of the city of Utrecht gave him notice to leave.

Before quitting this city for Rome (around 18 July), Hennepin took a step as surprising as it was unaccountable; he called on the French ambassador at The Hague, M. de Bonrepaus, requesting him to obtain permission for him to return to France and go back to America. "One might thus prevent this restless spirit from prompting the English and the Dutch to set up other establishments in America," the ambassador wrote on 26 June. In reply to this letter, Pontchartrain [Phélypeaux] informed the ambassador on 9 July that the king of France would grant the request. The following year (May 1699), however, Louis XIV changed his mind; he plainly forbad Hennepin to set foot on American soil on pain of arrest.

From 1699 on Father Hennepin's life still remains rather obscure to us; a few salient facts, however, permit us to reconstruct its last moments. In December 1699, while at Rome, he sought and obtained authorization to retire to the convent of Saint-Bonaventure-sur-le-Palatin, "for the purpose of attending to the salvation of his own soul there, after working for so many years for the salvation of his fellow-men." Two years later (March 1701) we find him at the convent of *Ara cœli*, on the Capitoline Hill; apparently, we are informed in a document, he had "wheedled his way around Cardinal Spada, who was supplying funds for a new mission to the Mississippi countries." Finally, from Belgium (July 1701), Hennepin dispatched to the sovereign pontiff a petition "to be granted the right and authority to devote himself to the conversion of apostate religious in Holland"; this permission was not granted.

Louis Hennepin's story is still incomplete. In the present state of our knowledge we can at best put forward hypotheses on the most controversial problems raised by the life of this turbulent personage. Belgian by birth but French by education, he had lived in an environment of intrigues and cabals. The *Description de la Louisiane* earned him a glory and celebrity that were rapidly effaced by a sensational fall from favour; he was expelled from France, then pursued, hunted down to the point where he no longer felt safe, "whatever service I had rendered in all the places I had lived in until then." It was at that time that he took refuge with William III, an ally of his country. In taking this step, should Hennepin be seen in the guise of an adventurer with few qualms as to what methods he adopted to realize his plans? As the

reasons for his expulsion are still ill-defined, it is rather difficult to answer this question satisfactorily.

A man of well-tempered, enterprising, and combative character, Hennepin had to collaborate with one whose personality was as strong as his: Cavelier de La Salle. Clashes occurred, inevitably. Did La Salle subsequently become the intriguer who worked through the civil and religious authorities to bring about the Recollet's downfall? Hennepin affirms this, but it remains to be proved.

When he came to America there was an underlying rivalry between Jesuits and Recollets. The first enjoyed the support of the bishop, the second, brought to Canada to counterbalance the influence of the sons of St Ignatius, were given a more receptive hearing by the civil authorities, who were even to criticize the bishop of Quebec for his distrust of the Recollets. In such a context, the stir made by this restless monk during his stay in New France can easily be guessed at. Moreover, mischievous rumours and libellous accusations were rife concerning the Recollet, who laid himself so readily open to reproaches. Too many writers, working from these malicious reports, have painted an unfavourable picture of him.

Louis Hennepin had a rather strange personality, made up of a mixture of qualities and defects that were equally marked. Undoubtedly, in Europe and America, he was a zealous propagator of the faith, sincerely attached to the Church; his *Morale pratique du jansénisme* is ample proof of this. In his autobiography—nothing for the moment justifies our calling in question the sincerity of this testimony, despite undeniable exaggerations—he appears again to be a generous man, giving of himself unstintingly. In Europe he lavished care upon the injured and the sick at the risk of his own life; when he was superior at Renty he rebuilt the convent, at Gosselies he directed the work for the reconstruction of the chapel. During his expeditionary voyage, in America, he intervened to put down revolts, prevent defections, and calm the Indians; in 1679, when they had to disembark in Lake Dauphin, he did not hesitate to jump into the water and pull the canoe to the shore, carrying "our worthy, elderly Recollet [Gabriel de La Ribourde]" on his shoulders.

A fearless disseminator of the faith, but also an independent person, disagreeable into the bargain, he more than once antagonized his associates, provoked dissension, and made enemies for himself. At the time of the crossing in 1675, imbued with a compulsive zeal, he took to task a group of girls, on the pretext that they "were making a lot of noise with their dancing, and thus preventing the sailors from getting their rest during the night"; this intervention started up a rather serious verbal battle between the monk and Cavelier de La Salle. In Canada he administered the sacraments without the bishop's authorization; during his captivity among the Sioux, he made enemies of his two companions, Michel Accault and Antoine Auguel. In France, he firmly opposed his superiors who wanted to send him back to America; finally, in Holland, he preached and celebrated mass despite the opposition of the ecclesiastical authorities. All the wrongs were perhaps not on Father Hennepin's side, but this conduct offered material for the most regrettable rumours.

Should one encumber the picture by including in it such unflattering epithets as plagiarist, lying, shameless, impudent, which have been lavishly applied to him by many authors? Did Hennepin really go down the mighty Mississippi in 30 days as he claimed he did? "I assure you before God that my account is faithful and honest, and that you can believe everything that is reported there." In his *Description de la Louisiane* Hennepin warned the reader that he proposed to write another book. Did he then make no mention of certain facts "in order not to cause distress to the Sieur de La Salle"? The studies so far undertaken, with the aim of answering these questions, are distinctly unfavourable to Louis Hennepin. In any case, these points remain to be cleared up before a decisive answer can be given.

In his day, Louis Hennepin was the most fashionable of popular authors; his work had no fewer than 46 editions. No doubt as a writer he does not possess the flavour of a Gabriel Sagard*, for example; he was not always careful about details, and his style often lacks elegance. Nevertheless, he writes spontaneously, sometimes gives iridescent colours to his pictures, paints enthusiastically the flora and fauna of the country, and describes perceptively the Indian tribes, their way of life, their customs, and their beliefs.

Let us at least leave to this enigmatic personage the glory which is his due: that of having shared in the discoveries made in New France and of having succeeded in making them known to Europe.

JEAN-ROCH RIOUX

Louis Hennepin, *Description de la Louisiane, nouvellement découverte au sud-ouest de la Nouvelle-France par ordre du Roy. Avec la carte du pays; les mœurs et la manière de vivre des sauvages* (Paris, 1683); *Nouvelle découverte d'un très grand pays situé dans l'Amérique entre Le Nouveau-Mexique et la mer glaciale. Avec les cartes et les figures nécessaires et de plus l'histoire naturelle et moralle et les avantages qu'on en peust tirer par l'établissement des colonies. Le tout dédié à sa majesté Britannique Guillaume III* (Utrecht, 1697);

Nouveau voyage d'un païs plus grand que l'Europe. Avec les réflections des entreprises du Sieur de la Salle sur les mines de Ste Barbe etc. Enrichi de la carte, de figures expressives, des mœurs et manière de vivre des sauvages du nord et du sud, de la prise de Québec, ville capitale de la Nouvelle-France, par les Anglois, et avantages qu'on peut retirer du chemin racourci de la Chine et du Japon, par le moien de tant de vastes contrées et de nouvelles colonies. Avec approbation et dédié à sa majesté Guillaume III Roy de la Grande Bretagne (Utrecht, 1698); *La morale pratique du jansénisme . . .* (Utrecht, 1698).

Father Hennepin's works have been published in several editions in various languages: see Jérôme Goyens, "Coup d'œil sur les œuvres littéraires du père Hennepin," *Archivum Franciscanum Historicum* (Florence, Italy), XVIII (1925), 341–45; and Hugolin [Stanislas Lemay], *Bibliographie des bibliographies du P. Louis Hennepin* (Notes bibliographiques pour servir à l'histoire des Récollets au Canada, IV, Montréal, 1933).

The following are some of the most important and most recent studies on Father Louis Hennepin: Jean Delanglez, *Hennepin's Description of Louisiana, a critical essay* (Institute of Jesuit history pub., Chicago, 1941); Jérôme Goyens, "Le P. Louis Hennepin, o.f.m., missionnaire au Canada au XVIIe siècle. Quelques jalons pour sa biographie," *Archivum Franciscanum Historicum*, XVIII (1925), 318–41, 473–510. [Goyens' work should be used with caution; his arguments are not always firmly documented, and some of his conclusions have been shown to be wrong. J.-R.R.]

Father Hugolin [Stanislas Lemay] has published a series of articles on Hennepin in the journal *Nos Cahiers*: "Son allégeance politique et religieuse," I (1936), 316–46; "Les *Observationes* de Pierre Codde, vicaire apostolique de Hollande," II (1937), 5–37; "Une obédience pour l'Amérique en 1696, et départ pour la Hollande," II (1937), 149–79; "Aux prises avec les jansénistes," II (1937), 245–80; "A Utrecht, ses efforts pour y obtenir une station missionnaire en 1697," II (1937), 375–419; "Devant Rome," III (1938), 17–68; "A Paris, 1682," III (1938), 105–40; "Devant l'histoire," III (1938), 245–76, 341–74. As well, Lemay has published "Une étude bibliographique et historique sur *La Morale pratique du jansénisme du père Louis Hennepin*," *RSCT*, 3d ser., XXXI (1937), sect.I, 127–49. Finally, he has gathered together and published some documents under the title *Bibliographie du Père Louis Hennepin, récollet. Les pièces documentaires* (Montréal, 1937).

Armand Louant, "Le P. Louis Hennepin. Nouveaux jalons pour sa biographie," *Revue d'histoire ecclésiastique* (Louvain, Belgium), XLV (1950), 186–211; LII (1957), 871–76; "Précisions nouvelles sur le Père Hennepin, missionnaire et explorateur," *Bulletin de la classe des lettres et des sciences morales de l'Académie royale de Belgique* (Brussels), XLII (1956), 5e sér., 215–76. [The author examines Hennepin's case in the light of the latest scientific studies and new documents discovered in governmental archives at Mons; two autograph letters in particular identify Louis as one of Gaspard Hennepin's four sons. J.-R.R.]

Heracouansit

C.-M. Morin, "Du nouveau sur le récollet Louis Hennepin," *RHAF*, I (1947–48), 112–17. H.-A. Scott, "Un coup d'épée dans l'eau, ou, Une nouvelle apologie du P. Louis Hennepin," *RSCT*, 3d ser., XXI (1927), sect.i, 113–60. J. Stengers, "Hennepin et la découverte du Mississipi," *Bulletin de la société royale belge de géographie d'Anvers*, 1945, 61–82.

HERACOUANSIT. *See* Mog

HERTEL DE LA FRESNIÈRE, JOSEPH-FRANÇOIS, officer, interpreter, commandant, seigneur; baptized 3 July 1642 at Trois-Rivières, son of Jacques Hertel* and Marie Marguerie; buried 22 May 1722 at Boucherville.

The man whom his contemporaries nicknamed "the Hero" grew up in an atmosphere of continual wars, his native town of Trois-Rivières being the principal advanced post against Iroquois attacks. He was therefore schooled from his youth to believe that danger was always present, and must be conquered by toughness. He was brought up by a wonderful and courageous mother, who had had her share of trials: her only brother, François Marguerie*, was drowned in 1648 and her husband died by accident three years later, leaving three infant children: François, the eldest, and two girls.

François Hertel wrote in his report of 1712 that his first experience of soldiering went back to 1657, when he was 15. An act of 26 August of that year does indeed describe him as a soldier. Hence he took part many times in the defence of the town of Trois-Rivières, which after the massacre of its principal settlers on 19 Aug. 1652 had to rely on every one capable of handling a weapon. Between times he worked at clearing the land. An act of 21 Jan. 1654 drawn up by the notary Ameau informs us that he felled the trees of an island, inherited from his father, which he wanted to seed in order to support his mother and his young sisters. At the same time he prevented the Iroquois from hiding on it.

In the last week of July 1661, having rashly left the fortified *enceinte*, he was captured by four marauding Iroquois who took him to their village, where he was subjected to torture. The incidents of this captivity are known through the three letters that he succeeded in smuggling out to Father Simon Le Moyne* at Onondaga, and which were reproduced in the *Relation* of 1660–61, as was the anonymous story of a French captive of which he is suspected of being the author. An old Indian woman adopted him; from her he learned the Iroquois language, and at the same time he observed the tribe's customs. Taking advantage of a time when his protectress was absent, he managed to escape, and got to Montreal and then to Trois-Rivières, whereas all his relatives and friends thought he was dead.

François Hertel appears to have been a captive about two years. He was back before 3 Oct. 1663, for on that day he was present at Guillaume de Larue's marriage. For a few years after that he led the life of an ordinary settler. On 22 Sept. 1664 he was married at Montreal, then returned to Trois-Rivières, where he served as an Iroquois interpreter as well as being a member of the local garrison. As he himself was to write later, "he was in all the parties of men made up both by the governors and by other officers, and was active in a number of small engagements to repel the forays that they [the Iroquois] were making against our homes." He was a member of Governor Rémy* de Courcelle's useless expedition in the spring of 1666, and of the more realistic one led by the lieutenant general, Prouville* de Tracy, in the autumn of the same year. In 1673 he went with Buade* de Frontenac on an expedition to Lake Ontario, and took part in the building of Fort Frontenac (Cataracoui, now Kingston, Ont.). In 1678 he was sent by the authorities on a mission to Hudson Bay. He yielded to the temptation of fur-trading and returned from this expedition with a large cargo which was seized on his arrival at Quebec. By order of the Conseil Souverain he was put in prison and sentenced to pay a fine of 2,000 *livres* and to have his furs confiscated. For lack of proof that he had been trading unlawfully, he was soon released and returned to his home town. He wanted to ensure the education of his children, and in 1681 he entrusted this task to the teacher Pierre Bertrand, who had already studied at the University of Paris.

It was then that his sequence of military exploits really began. Governor Le Febvre* de La Barre, on the advice of his counsellors, entrusted him with the command of all the tribes who were allies of the French, a responsibility which he continued to exercise under Brisay de Denonville. In the face of the continual ambushes to which his family and all the settlers were exposed, Hertel devised war tactics, derived from Indian methods, in which he initiated his sons: the surprise attack. Other Canadian-born commanders were to use such tactics as well, but apparently never with such fire, speed, and success. What history calls "Hertel's raids" count among the most ingenious and fruitful military feats of that period.

Frontenac had confidence in these tactics, and decided to put them to the test in chastising the New England leaders for inspiring and encouraging the Lachine massacre. We know that at the beginning of 1690 the bold governor raised three parties of soldiers who were to start out from the capital of each of the three governments, and by a similar surprise attack lay waste different villages.

Hertel's objective was Salmon Falls, or more exactly the neighbouring fort of Rollinsford. He had recruited some 25 volunteers from his native town, among them his three eldest sons, his nephew Louis Crevier who was also his mother's godson, and other relatives by marriage, including Nicolas Gastineau, junior, and Jacques Maugras, senior. An equal number of Indians, namely 20 Sokokis and 5 Algonkins, who were recruited at Saint-François-du-Lac, joined the group. After a hard winter march of two months, the little band reached the outskirts of Salmon Falls during the night of 27 March. Hertel divided his detachment into three groups, which took advantage of the darkness to swoop down upon the fort and the village simultaneously. Within two hours every-thing was completely wiped out. Historians and chroniclers do not agree as to the precise number of victims. According to Abbé Maurault, who based himself on Monseignat, there were 43 Englishmen killed, 54 taken prisoner, 27 houses burned down, and 2,000 head of cattle lost. The English chroniclers do not put the number of dead as higher than 30, the majority men; furthermore, they consider the figure of 2,000 head of cattle a gross exaggeration. Of the French group two were killed, one being Jacques Maugras, and one was taken prisoner.

Hertel, with his survivors and prisoners, was already on the way back when an Indian scout informed him that a troop of soldiers and settlers was heading towards them. According to Mon-seignat there were 250 of them. Scales sets the number at 100, and Charles H. Lincoln at 140. Hertel placed his men among the bushes, and when the enemy stepped on to the narrow bridge over the little Wooster River the troop burst upon them. Some 20 Englishmen were killed, and the others, thrown into confusion by this sudden attack and the Indians' war whoops, took to their heels. The French victory was clouded by Louis Crevier's death and by the wound that Zacharie Hertel* received in the knee, a wound which for want of immediate attention was to leave him a cripple for life. Committing to some of his men the care of the captives, most of them women and children, Hertel went immediately to help RENÉ ROBINAU de Portneuf's Quebec detachment, which was on its way towards the English post of Casco (Falmouth). Meanwhile Gastineau was returning post-haste to Quebec to convey to Frontenac the news of the victory.

The tactics had proved their worth, and were not to be abandoned. The Hertels, father and sons, rapidly became the terror of the English and the enemy Indians. Their feats were beyond number. They turned up everywhere. They had scarcely got back from the raid on Salmon Falls when they were at Quebec, which was being besieged by Phips*. Then, despite his wound, Zacharie took part the following year in a combat in the course of which he was taken prisoner; he was to remain in the hands of the Iroquois for three years.

From 1709 to 1712 François Hertel was com-mandant of Fort Frontenac, where he rendered valuable services, for according to RIGAUD de Vaudreuil "he understands almost all the Indian languages." During this time, in the words of Charlevoix* who was quoting a letter from Frontenac, he "distinguished himself on every occasion at the head of the militiamen of Trois-Rivières." Each year the exploits grew in number. Hertel was right when he stated in his report of 1712 that "During all the wars no party of men or expedition has been made ready that has not included the father and some of his sons." At one time he and seven of his sons were serving with the troops at the same time. After he retired, it was his pride to say that all his sons had borne arms in the defence of Canada.

In view of Hertel's bravery and record of service, Frontenac tried from 1689 on to obtain letters of nobility for him. For a long time the court turned a deaf ear. He was promised them in 1691, but the document did not arrive. As com-pensation he was granted a military promotion. The humble name Hertel meant nothing in France. In a royal dispatch dated 30 June 1707 Vaudreuil and JACQUES RAUDOT were informed: "With regard to those [the letters of nobility] which have been promised to the Sieur Hertel, it is necessary, in order to draw them up, to have a report giving the reasons for which they are to be granted. The reasons must be strong for obtaining such a favour, his services are not great enough for that." The objection was further made that being poor he would be unable to maintain his rank among the colonial nobility. Finally in 1716, more than a quarter of a century after Frontenac's first inquiry, Governor Rigaud de Vaudreuil was able to put into his hands the parchment so much desired and so highly deserved.

François Hertel died in 1722 and was buried on 22 May at Boucherville. Saladin, the parish priest, wrote laconically on the death certificate that "Brother Louis, the schoolmaster, and several others" were present. Such was the funeral oration of one of the colony's greatest heroes. A few months before Charlevoix had visited him and had remarked that he was "in full strength and health; the whole colony paid tribute to his virtue and merit."

Hertel de Moncours

By his marriage with Marguerite de THAVENET, the sister of Jacques de Chambly*'s fiancée, François Hertel had inherited the seigneury of Chambly, for which he rendered fealty and homage on 11 Oct. 1694. Subsequently he divided it up for the benefit of some of his sons. On 19 May 1701 he again rendered fealty and homage for a piece of land with a frontage of two leagues adjoining the Rouville seigneury. It was around this time that he went to reside there permanently; settlers, the majority former soldiers, had already been established there for several years. The surname La Fresnière passed to his eldest son Zacharie. The others adopted various names, several of which are still extant: Hertel de Rouville, JEAN-BAPTISTE; Hertel de Cournoyer, Jacques* and Lambert; Hertel de Chambly, René and Michel; Hertel de Beaulac, Claude; Hertel de Saint-Louis, Louis; Hertel de Moncours, PIERRE, born in 1687, godson of the Chevalier de Troyes*; and Hertel de Saint-Francois, Joseph*.

It may be added that a complete study of the martial exploits of François Hertel and his sons has not yet been made. Rarely, in the defence of a nation, have the limits of courage been pushed so far.

RAYMOND DOUVILLE

AJM, Greffe d'Antoine Adhémar, 19 mai 1701. AJTR, Greffe de Séverin Ameau, 21 janv. 1654, 4 nov. 1681; Registres d'état civil de Trois-Rivières. Charlevoix, *Histoire* (1744), I, 354; II, 50f. 83. "Correspondance de Frontenac (1689–99)," APQ *Rapport, 1927–28*, 36, 37, 53, 109. "Correspondance de Vaudreuil," APQ *Rapport, 1938–39*, 62; *1939–40*, 364, 412, 454; *1942–43*, 436; *1947–48*, 161, 164. *JR* (Thwaites). P.-G. Roy, *Inv. concessions*, II, 196f. T.-M. Charland, *Histoire des Abénakis d'Odanak* (Montréal, 1964); *Histoire de Saint-François-du-Lac* (Ottawa, 1942). Coleman, *New England captives*. Albert Gravel, *Pages d'histoire régionale* (Sherbrooke, 1966). C. H. Lincoln, *Narratives of the Indian Wars, 1675–1699* (New York, 1959). Lorin, *Le comte de Frontenac*. J.-A. Maurault, *Histoire des Abénakis depuis 1605 jusqu'à nos jours* (Sorel, 1866). John Scales, *History of Dover, New Hampshire . . .* (Manchester, N.H., 1923). Sulte, *Mélanges historiques* (Malchelosse), IX. Robert La Roque de Roquebrune, "Les Demoiselles de Thavenet," *NF*, V (1930), 86–91.

HERTEL DE MONCOURS (MONTCOURT), PIERRE, b. at Trois-Rivières on 19 March 1687, the 10th child of JOSEPH-FRANÇOIS HERTEL de La Fresnière and Marguerite de THAVENET; d. 28 Feb. 1739.

Pierre de Moncours and his brothers entered the colonial military service. Their education consisted in participating in raiding parties rather than in formal training, and they became particularly adept in relations with the indigenous peoples. In 1731, Moncours' brother, Zacharie Hertel* de La Fresnière, was sent to build a palisaded fort, later named Fort Saint-Frédéric, at Pointe à la Chevelure on Lake Champlain; Moncours went there in command of the garrison. After suffering some losses in the great Montreal fire of 1734 he was sent to command at Baie des Puants (Green Bay, Wis.). In this region the previous year Nicolas-Antoine COULON de Villiers had unsuccessfully attempted to exterminate the Fox tribe. Moncours undertook to cooperate with the traders who were at that post, but in 1736 Charles de Beauharnois* de La Boische wrote to the minister, Maurepas, complaining that his appointee at Baie des Puants had disobeyed orders and locked up some traders. The governor recalled Moncours the following year.

On 17 Nov. 1721 at Montreal, Pierre de Moncours married Thérèse, daughter of Paul d'Ailleboust* de Périgny and niece of the famous brothers, NICOLAS, PIERRE, and JEAN-BAPTISTE D'AILLEBOUST. From this marriage two children were born, of whom one, Pierre, became an officer in the colonial troops. Hertel de Moncours died on 28 Feb. 1739. His son was killed at Niagara in 1759.

C. C. J. BOND

AN, Col., C¹¹ᴬ, 54, f.134; 65, f.152; D²ᶜ, 222. Provost, "Inventaire de documents," 595. Gagnon, "Noms propres au Canada français," 94. Le Jeune, *Dictionnaire*, II, 297. Tanguay, *Dictionnaire*, I, 152; IV, 497. P.-G. Roy, *Hommes et choses du fort Saint-Frédéric* (Montréal, 1946), 158ff. "La famille Margane de Lavaltrie," *BRH*, XXIII (1917), 42.

HERTEL DE ROUVILLE, JEAN-BAPTISTE, ensign, lieutenant, captain on Île Royale (Cape Breton Island), commandant of Port-Dauphin (Englishtown, N.S.), knight of the order of Saint-Louis; b. 26 Oct. 1668 at Trois-Rivières, third son of FRANÇOIS HERTEL and Marguerite de THAVENET; buried 30 June 1722 on Île Royale.

Like all the members of his family, Hertel de Rouville took up soldiering at an early age. He had already gained some experience in a number of skirmishes before he accompanied his father and two of his brothers in Governor BRISAY de Denonville's campaign against the Senecas in 1687. He was also on the expedition led by his father which razed the village of Salmon Falls in the winter 1690–91, and a few months later he helped in the resistance that Quebec put up against Phips*. When he had barely reached his majority he was already fit to command the surprise attacks of which his father had perfected the tactics.

The first important raid directed by Hertel de Rouville occurred in 1704, and took the same form as the one against Salmon Falls in which he had participated 13 years before, except that the party was larger: 250 men, of whom 50 were Canadians and 200 were Abenaki and Iroquois Indians from Sault-Saint-Louis (Caughnawaga). This time it was a question of avenging the Abenakis, who had just been the victims of a bloody raid and who had asked RIGAUD de Vaudreuil for help. Among the French volunteers were four of the commander's brothers. The expedition had no precise objective; the intention was to make reprisals. Fate willed that the target should be the little town of Deerfield, on the outskirts of which the assailants arrived in the night of 28–29 February (10–11 March, N.S.). Thanks to the snow piled up along the stockades they slipped silently inside and the massacre began: 54 settlers were killed (Bancroft puts it at 47) and about 120 were taken prisoner. The latter included the minister JOHN WILLIAMS, whose wife had been killed in the raid, and three of his children. On the French side there were three dead and some 20 wounded, among them Rouville himself. In the autumn of the same year Hertel de Rouville was in command of a group of Abenakis at Placentia (Plaisance), where he went to give assistance to AUGER de Subercase. At that time he took possession of an English fort.

Four years later, in 1708, the governor put Rouville and Jean-Baptiste de Saint-Ours* Deschaillons in command of an expedition of the same type. The objective this time was to be the seaport of Portsmouth (N.H.). When an epidemic broke out among the allied Indians, they took this as a bad omen and at the last minute refused to join the expedition. With barely 200 fighting men, the commanders deemed it unwise to attack the fortified post, and chose the harmless little village of Haverhill on the Merrimack River. The church and surrounding houses were burned down and some 15 people killed, including the minister Benjamin Rolfe and his wife. On their way back the small party, delayed by its prisoners (the majority women, old men, and children), was attacked by a detachment led by Captain Ayer. A fight took place, and the French forced the enemy to flee. Among the dead were Pierre JARRET de Verchères and René Hertel* de Chambly, Hertel de Rouville's brother. Another Verchères, Louis, was taken prisoner.

In the summer of 1709, at the request of Vaudreuil and of the allied Indians who had specifically asked for him as their leader, Hertel directed another raid on the outskirts of Deerfield, to forestall a possible attack against Montreal. The English losses amounted to several dead and two men who were made prisoner, John Arms and his brother-in-law Joseph Closson, who were taken to Sault-Saint-Louis and condemned to run the gauntlet, a great attraction for the Indians. The French authorities vainly tried to exchange Arms, an officer, for Verchères, an ensign; the English reserved the right to exchange the latter for a daughter of the minister Williams.

Joseph Dudley, the governor of Boston, sought to make a compromise with Vaudreuil. There were several exchanges of prisoners, but the threat of reprisals was in the air. For some time every village in New England was on the alert. This was what the French authorities, who it must be said treated the English prisoners humanely, were after. Hertel de Rouville and his men had become the terror of the soldiers and settlers. Prodigious bravery and speed of execution had done much to create the reputation of a great warrior that was attached to the name Hertel de Rouville. It must be admitted, however, that his most impressive exploits had been accomplished against defenceless people, and that to preserve the goodwill of his Indian allies he had been constrained to permit the carrying out of acts of barbarity that were unworthy of civilized beings. On the other hand, the psychological effect of these unexpected attacks was considerable. It is understandable that this commander, trained in Indian methods of combat, was never favourably reported on by the English chroniclers and historians who have recounted these events. Ansel Phelps describes him thus: "An officer of great courage, but pre-eminently cruel and vindictive." Relating the massacre at Haverhill, George Wingate Chase speaks of "the infamous Hertel de Rouville, the sacker of Deerfield."

Subsequently the authorities tried to entrust Hertel with quieter missions, for his health no longer allowed him to make spectacular excursions. In 1710 he was sent as a representative to Boston with one of his most loyal lieutenants, Simon Dupuy, to try to settle the details of certain agreements with the English leaders. On 24 Feb. 1713 the minister of Marine instructed M. de Vaudreuil to select "40 or 50 of the best workers" in New France and to send them to Cape Breton Island to work on the fortifications there; in this activity they were to be under the command of the Sieur Hertel de Rouville. The latter went there with his family, which he housed at Port-Toulouse (St Peters). He signed with the other officers the act authorizing the taking over of the island. The following year Governor PASTOUR de Costebelle sent him, with Captain Louis Denys* de La Ronde and the engineer JEAN-BAPTISTE DE COUAGNE, to explore the island's north shore. In 1715, on the strength of the report he had submitted, Rouville received orders to take his men to Port-Dauphin to build a fortress there, containing a warehouse, a forge, a bakery, barracks, and a hospital. The work was pushed ahead briskly and completed before winter; this won Rouville the esteem of the island's governor, who called him a "phoenix of toil."

The establishments on Cape Breton Island were designed primarily for defence, and Hertel de Rouville was a man who preferred taking the offensive. The authorities realized this, and on 14 Oct. 1716 Vaudreuil asked the council of Marine to send him back to New France, "Because he does not know anybody better fitted to be sent among these Indian nations . . . both because of the ascendancy that he has over these nations and furthermore because he is capable of opposing all the ventures that the English might undertake in this part of the continent." The council yielded to the governor's request, and Rouville was informed of it on 7 July 1717. But the order was countermanded, for an English attack from the direction of Acadia was anticipated, and Rouville's presence was thought to be likely to give the enemy pause. In 1719 he went to France to raise a contingent to reinforce the Port-Dauphin garrison. He was still commandant of this fort when he died prematurely, at the age of 54. He was buried on 30 June 1722, about a month after his father.

Hertel de Rouville had been made a knight of the order of Saint-Louis on 23 Dec. 1721, a few months before his death. He had been married twice. On 23 Nov. 1698, at Trois-Rivières, he had married Jeanne Dubois, who died less than two years later. On 6 Feb. 1708 he married Marie-Anne Baudouin, the eldest daughter of the Quebec doctor Gervais Baudouin*. The marriage contract, drawn up two days earlier by the notary GENAPLE, had been the occasion for an impressive ceremony in the residence of the intendants, JACQUES and ANTOINE-DENIS RAUDOT, in the presence of Governor Vaudreuil, his wife, and the principal civil and military figures of the town. Several children were born of this union, among them Jean-Baptiste-François, who like his father took up a military career, and was made a knight of the order of Saint-Louis in 1762, and René-Ovide, born 6 Sept. 1720 at Port-Toulouse, who became a judge, and to the great despair of his mother married the flighty Louise André de Leigne.

On 8 Jan. 1694 Hertel de Rouville had obtained from Governor Buade* de Frontenac a seigneury adjoining his father's, to which he gave his name. One can understand why he was never able to develop it. Before he left for Acadia he had decided to reside at Montreal, in a house in Rue Saint-Paul which Madame Baudouin had given her daughter

as a marriage settlement. In 1724 his widow rendered fealty and homage to the governor for the Rouville seigneury, and at the same time obtained a gratuity of 300 *livres* paid out of the royal treasury, "in consideration of her husband's services."

RAYMOND DOUVILLE

For more complete bibliographical information, *see* JOSEPH-FRANÇOIS HERTEL de La Fresnière.

AJQ, Greffe de François Genaple, 4 févr. 1708. *Coll. de manuscrits relatifs à la N.-F.*, I, 455–61, 497f. "Correspondance de Vaudreuil," APQ *Rapport*, *1938–39*, 28, 43, 44, 54, 56, 62; *1939–40*, 428, 431f.; *1942–43*, 428, 429; *1947–48*, 151, 167, 196, 197, 228, 327, 334. Fauteux, *Les chevaliers de Saint-Louis*. Albert Gravel, *Pages d'histoire régionale* (Sherbrooke, 1966).

HILL, JOHN, military commander of the British expedition against Quebec in 1711; b. before 1685; d. 19 June 1735.

John, better known as Jack, Hill was the brother of Queen Anne's favourite, Abigail Hill (Mrs. Masham), and a "poor relation" of the Duchess of Marlborough. Neither a transcription of the epitaph on his tombstone, nor the records of Somerset House disclose the date and place of his birth. We know only that he was born before 1685, the birth year of his younger sister Alice. Sarah Churchill paid for his schooling at St Alban's, and then had him appointed successively as page of honour to Anne's consort, the Prince of Denmark, as groom of the bedchamber to the Duke of Gloucester, and finally as aide de camp to her husband. In 1702 he became captain and lieutenant-colonel in the Coldstream Guards, and three years after assuming this customary double rank he succeeded his uncle, Brigadier Stanhope, as colonel of the regiment known as the 11th Foot. In 1707 this regiment was nearly wiped out at Almansa in northern Spain, but Hill was able to reorganize it in time for the Flanders campaign of 1709.

Despite Marlborough's strong opposition he was appointed brigadier-general in 1710, and given command of some 5,300 troops participating in the WALKER expedition against Quebec. In suggesting Hill to the Queen, Henry St John, later Viscount Bolingbroke, can have had little thought of the man's capacity (although it was by no means undistinguished), but he did see the wisdom of supporting the brother of Mrs. Masham, whose friendship as the queen's favourite he anxiously cultivated. Moreover, the appointment was a further blow to Marlborough, whose powers and prestige, along with those of the Whigs, were already undermined.

Following the disaster by shipwreck at the entrance of the St Lawrence River during the night of 22–23 Aug. 1711, Hill had little difficulty in persuading the distracted admiral to abandon further efforts to take Quebec, or even Placentia, and he returned with him to England in early October of the same year. Like Admiral Walker's, Hill's career did not immediately suffer as a result of the disaster. The Tories were now in command; scarcely a month after the survivors returned, the Duke of Marlborough was dismissed from all his offices. Consequently, instead of suffering disgrace, Hill was promoted major-general in July 1712, and in the same year commanded the force sent to hold Dunkirk as security during the negotiations preceding the treaty of Utrecht. Not until the return of the Whigs with the accession of George I in 1714 was he deprived of his regiment.

Hill died in London on 19 June 1735, leaving his estate to his nephew, Samuel, second Baron Masham.

GERALD S. GRAHAM

Letters and correspondence, public and private, by the Right Honourable Henry St. John, Lord visc. Bolingbroke during the time he was secretary of state, ed. Gilbert Parke (4v., London, 1798), I. *Walker expedition* (Graham); the editor's Introduction to this volume contains further bibliographical material. Dalton, *English army lists*, V. *DNB*. W. S. Churchill, *Marlborough, his life and times* (4v., London, 1933–38), I.

HILL, SAMUEL, ship's captain and sometime captive of the French; b. 14 Dec. 1668 (o.s.) at Saco, Me., one of triplets among eight children of Roger Hill (who had arrived with his father Peter from Plymouth, Eng., 22 March 1632/33), and Sarah Mary Cross Hill; d. *c.* 1732.

Hill, considered "a most valuable and useful citizen" of Wells, Me., was captain of a packet employed in bringing provisions to Maine ports. He married Elizabeth Austin, daughter of Samuel Austin and Elizabeth Gooch, and lived on the Austin farm at Wells. They had four children. His elder brother John had commanded the small fort at Saco during King William's War (the War of the League of Augsburg).

At the outbreak of Queen Anne's War (War of the Spanish Succession), Hill's youngest son was killed and he and the rest of his family were carried captive to Quebec after the French and Indian attack on Wells, 10 Aug. 1703 (21 August, N.S.), led by ALEXANDRE LENEUF de Beaubassin. Governor RIGAUD de Vaudreuil sent Hill to Boston in 1705 to arrange an exchange of prisoners. Hill estimated there were 117 captives at Quebec and 70 with the Indians. He was returned to

Quebec in a vessel commanded by Samuel VETCH, and was accompanied by AUGUSTIN LE GARDEUR de Courtemanche. The latter had brought a peace proposal, now rejected by New England, from the French governor. Hill was finally released with his family, and they arrived in Boston on 21 Nov. 1706 aboard the *Hope* (piloted by John BONNER).

It seems probable that Hill was enlisted among the pilots to guide Admiral Sir Hovenden WALKER's fleet in the unsuccessful attempt of 1711 to conquer New France.

G. M. WALLER

Coll. de manuscrits relatifs à la N.-F., II, 435. *Documentary hist. of Maine*, IV, 80ff., 141; V, 410, 423, 431, 441–43, 466. *Walker expedition* (Graham). *Colonial and revolutionary families of Pennsylvania*, ed. Wilfred Jordan (15v. in progress, New York, 1911–), new ser., V (1934), 643. *Genealogical dictionary of Maine and New Hampshire*, ed. Sybil Noyes *et al.* (Portland, Me., 1928–39), 329. E. E. Bourne, *The history of Wells and Kennebunk from the earliest settlements to the year 1820* (Portland, Me., 1875), 245–55, 261–63, 286–88, 303, 331. Coleman, *New England captives*, I.

HILTON, WINTHROP, colonel, military leader of New Hampshire; b. *c.* 1671, probably at Dover, N.H., son of Edward Hilton and Ann Dudley, the grand-daughter of Governors John Winthrop and Thomas Dudley; married Ann, daughter of Humphrey Wilson; d. 23 June 1710 (o.s.) at Epping, near Exeter, N.H.

Little is known of Hilton's early years, which were probably spent in the family's fishing and lumbering operation. He seems to have been active in the mast-making business to the time of his death. By the winter of 1703 he had risen to the rank of major in the provincial forces and was leading parties against the Indians (principally the Abenakis). Although his efforts at this time were not successful, he was to earn the bitter hatred of the Indians for his later successes. In 1704 he was appointed a lieutenant-colonel and served under Colonel Benjamin CHURCH on his expedition along the eastern coast to Port-Royal (Annapolis Royal, N.S.). During the winter of 1704/5, Hilton led a force of 250 English and 20 Indians against the Abenaki settlement at Norridgewock (Narantsouak) on the Kennebec where the Jesuit Father RALE had built a church and mission. The heavy snow delayed Hilton's force, and Father Rale and the Indians evacuated the village before they arrived. The New Englanders burned the abandoned wigwams and chapel.

In the spring of 1706 Hilton led a small force of 24 men to the Penobscot, and went as far as Chignecto, but had only limited success. In the

Hiou

summer, with 64 men, he marched against a large body of French and Indians who were on their way to the Piscataqua, but he had to return owing to lack of provisions. In December Hilton was appointed a judge of the Court of Common Pleas. After an unsuccessful attempt to reach Norridgewock in February 1706/7, Hilton was put in command of a regiment of 220 men, which was to form part of a larger force under Colonel John MARCH, heading east against Port-Royal. This force, which sailed in May 1707, consisted of over 1,000 soldiers and almost 500 sailors. Though they greatly outnumbered the Port-Royal forces, the New Englanders failed in two attempts to take the town. As did most of the officers, Hilton had to struggle to clear his name from the disgrace associated with this expedition in the minds of fellow New Englanders.

The next few years saw Hilton leading various other military expeditions, with little success; for example, in 1708/9 he went with 170 men against Pigwacket (Pequawket, modern Fryeburg, Me.) and Norridgewock, but failed to encounter the enemy. In the autumn of 1709 or early spring of 1710, he was appointed a member of the provincial council, but died before he could take up his appointment. Hilton was killed in an Indian raid as he and some of his associates in the mast business were barking trees at Epping, N.H. He was buried near by, on his own land on the west bank of the river, and was survived by his wife and four daughters. A son, Winthrop, was born posthumously. Hilton had considerable land holdings and many areas in New Hampshire bear his name. Dover, settled by the family, was originally known as Hilton's Point.

M. C. ROSENFIELD

"Mass. Archives," II, 156c. Mass. Hist. Soc., Belknap papers, 61.A.18–38; Greenough Coll. *Coll. de manuscrits relatifs à la N.-F.*, II. *Documentary hist. of Maine*, IX. Hutchinson, *Hist. of Mass.-bay* (1768), II. Mass. Hist. Soc. *Coll.*, 6th ser., III (1889). PRO, *CSP, Col., 1704–5, 1706–8, 1708–9, 1711–12*.

New Eng. Hist. and Geneal. Register, I (1847), 71; VII (1853), 51–52; XXVI (1872), 435. James Savage, *A genealogical dictionary of the first settlers of New England . . .* (4v., Boston, 1860–62; 2d ed., Baltimore, 1965), II. C. H. Bell, *History of the town of Exeter, New Hampshire* (Exeter, 1888). Coleman, *New England captives*, I. Murdoch, *History of Nova-Scotia*, I. J. G. Palfrey, *History of New England* (4v., Boston, 1858–75), IV. Parkman, *A half-century of conflict* (1893), I. Rameau de Saint-Père, *Une colonie féodale*, I. Sylvester, *Indian wars*, III.

HIOU. *See* YOU

288

HIRIBERRY, JOANNIS DE (less frequently spelled **Hiribery, Hirriberry,** with numerous other variants), "bourgeois merchant, and former magistrate of the town of St. Jean de Luz," fisherman; fl. 1718–22.

Hiriberry was the most persistent claimant against the seizures made at Canso (Canceau) in September 1718 by Captain Thomas SMART. The apparent failure of the Massachusetts authorities to make the restitution ordered by the Lords Justices in June 1719 induced Hiriberry to appeal to London. By the end of 1720, no doubt mainly because of the support given him by Cardinal Dubois and the French council, he had obtained a letter of credit from Cragg, the British Secretary of State for the Southern Department, to the value of £200 (one-hundredth of the sum he claimed, but one-tenth of the value estimated by the British authorities). Despite the growing disinterest of his French supporters, evident by the spring of 1721, and their desertion during the following year, he continued to press his claims, and in April 1722 was offered a grant of £800. However, no record has been found to indicate whether this offer was accepted, or whether the subsequent requests he persisted in making were any more successful.

Joannis de Hiriberry was at once a victim and an abettor in the Anglo-French contest for the North American fisheries. Whether French diplomacy was inspired or embarrassed by his case might be open to question; but the Canso incident of September 1718 would probably not have reached the dimensions it attained had it not been for his pertinacity.

G. P. BROWNE

AN, Col., C¹¹ᴮ, 3, 5, 6. PRO, C.O. 5/867; *CSP, Col., 1719*. McLennan, *Louisbourg*. For a more complete bibliography on the Canso dispute, *see* the bibliography for Thomas Smart.

HOBBY, SIR CHARLES, Massachusetts merchant, knighted July 1705; lieutenant-governor of Annapolis Royal, N.S., June–October 1711; b. in Boston *c.* 1665; d. in London, 1715.

Charles Hobby was the son of William and Ann Hobby of Boston. His father was a merchant of considerable wealth, and Hobby followed his father's mercantile career. As a young man he went to Jamaica where he lived from at least June 1692 (he was later knighted, ostensibly for bravery during an earthquake in that month) until he returned to Boston early in 1700. There he went into partnership with his brother-in-law John Coleman and was for a time one of the leading merchants in the town. Wealth and connections brought local prestige and Hobby became a selectman for Boston, justice of the peace for Suffolk County, captain of the Ancient and Honourable Artillery Company, colonel of the Boston regiment of the Massachusetts militia, and eventually warden of King's Chapel.

Hobby's influence was in part the result of his early acquaintance with Governor Joseph Dudley, but beginning in 1703, he and the governor quarrelled frequently over the latter's awards and penalties to Hobby's privateering ships. Early in 1705 Hobby took his complaints to London, where he quickly found himself the representative of a number of diverse groups—the Boston merchants, the Puritan divines of Massachusetts, the proprietary supporters in New Hampshire—all wishing to see Dudley removed. For the next two years Hobby worked with these groups and with friends at court to get the governor displaced, using as his main charge the governor's "conspiracy" with Samuel VETCH, another Boston merchant, to trade with the French in the current war. The charges against Dudley were scheduled to be heard at the Board of Trade in February 1706/7 (o.s.); then, at the last minute, Hobby decided not to appear.

Why? Probably he was impressed with the strength of Dudley's connections at Whitehall; he had also come under the influence of some of Dudley's close friends, including Francis NICHOLSON; most important, Vetch himself may already have suggested the possibility of collaborating in an attack on Canada. In any event Hobby returned to Boston the following year and made his peace with Dudley; within a few months of the reconciliation Hobby volunteered to join Vetch's expedition against Port-Royal and was chosen to go with his Boston regiment.

After many delays the expedition sailed in September 1710, under Nicholson's command. In October Port-Royal fell to the British and Vetch was made governor of the fort (soon to be renamed Annapolis Royal) and of a three-mile surrounding area. Hobby was second in command. The following June Vetch left for Boston to plan a full-scale attack on Quebec and Hobby was left in charge of Annapolis. The garrison he commanded was by now reduced by disease and desertion, while the fort was beginning to fall into disrepair. Furthermore, they were surrounded by hostile French and Indians organized under BERNARD-ANSELME D'ABBADIE de Saint-Castin, who were daily awaiting supplies in order to attack the fort. Hobby soon received news that Sir Hovenden WALKER, commander of the Quebec expedition, was sending 200 New Englanders to reinforce the Annapolis garrison and in

return demanded that Hobby return 100 British Marines and all the mortars and ordnance stores he could spare. Hobby called a council of war. Fearful of a French attack the officers at first decided the fort could spare neither men nor supplies and sent Walker word to this effect. Vetch, however, encouraged Walker to repeat his order at the end of July and this time Hobby complied.

Meanwhile, the French and Indians had become more aggressive. Early in June, a detachment of about 70 men, sent from Annapolis to harass a nearby Indian settlement and restore the transportation of wood to the fort, was ambushed by Indians about 12 miles north of Annapolis Royal (near modern Bridgetown); some 30 soldiers were killed. Shortly afterwards a force of about 200 French and Indians laid siege unsuccessfully to the fort. Otherwise Hobby's term of office was uneventful. He repaired the fort and, despite a great shortage of supplies, managed to hold the garrison together for the brief period of his command.

After the failure of the Quebec expedition, Vetch returned to Annapolis Royal in October, bringing Thomas CAULFEILD to replace Hobby. The latter went back to Boston and resumed his mercantile activity for the next two and a half years. His Boston business was unsuccessful but he retained his interest in Nova Scotia and invested heavily in real estate and building there. When Vetch quarrelled with Nicholson, Hobby went to England in the spring of 1714 with Nicholson's encouragement to seek the governorship of Nova Scotia for himself. He and Nicholson drew up charges of maladministration against Vetch, which they submitted to the Board of Trade.

Soon after Hobby's arrival in England, however, Queen Anne died and Hobby, ever the opportunist and observing Nicholson's prospects temporarily dimmed under the new king, once again cultivated the friendship of Vetch. It was hardly coincidence that Hobby's testimony against Vetch at the Board of Trade (18 Jan. to 4 Feb. 1714/15) was strikingly ineffectual and that Vetch recommended him for the lieutenant-governorship immediately afterward. Hobby was thus in line to be lieutenant-governor again, when he died in London in 1715, leaving a widow and a son.

Hobby's estate was insolvent. In 1706 he had purchased rights to half the proprietary lands in New Hampshire; his Boston creditors and his son John tried unsuccessfully for more than ten years in New Hampshire courts to have his land rights converted to payment of his debts. His insolvency has been attributed to "high living"; more likely it was the result of simple business incompetence

Holdsworth

combined with the failure of his privateering, his New Hampshire lands, and his command at Annapolis to pay off as he expected. As a politician and military commander he was equally unlucky; in all his activities he was above all a rank opportunist, even by the standards of an age of opportunism.

ALISON OLSON

Boston, Registry Dept., *Records relating to the early history of Boston*, ed. W. H. Whitmore, W. S. Appleton, *et al.* (39v., Boston, 1876–1909), I: [*Boston tax lists, etc., 1674–95*] (1876); VII: *Boston records, 1660–1701* (1881); IX: *Boston births, baptisms, marriages, and deaths, 1630–1699* (1883); XI: *Records of Boston selectmen, 1701–1715* (1884). "Correspondance de Vaudreuil," APQ *Rapport, 1946–47*, 430–31. Hutchinson, *Hist. of Mass.-bay* (Mayo). Mass. Hist. Soc. *Coll.*, 5th ser., VI (1879); 6th ser., V (1892). [Cotton Mather], *Diary of Cotton Mather* (2v., New York, [1957?]), I, II. New Hampshire provincial papers, *Documents and records relating to the province of New Hampshire* (40v. in progress, Concord, 1867–   ), III, IV. *N.S. Archives, II.* N.S. Hist. Soc. *Coll.*, IV (1884). *Probate records of the province of New Hampshire*, ed. A. S. Batchellor *et al.* (24v. in progress, Concord, 1907–   ), I. PRO, *B.T.Journal, 1704–1708/9, 1708/9–1714/15; CSP, Col., 1701, 1702, 1702–3, 1704–5, 1706–8, 1708–9, 1710–11, 1711–12, 1712–14, 1714–15. Walker expedition* (Graham).

The book of dignities, ed. Joseph Haydn and rev. Horace Ockerby (3d ed., London, 1894). *New Eng. Hist. and Geneal. Register*, XXIV (1870), XXIX (1875). James Savage, *A genealogical dictionary of the first settlers of New England . . .* (4v., Boston, 1860–62; 2d ed., Baltimore, 1965), II. Shipton, *Sibley's Harvard graduates*, VI, 246. Society of Colonial Wars, *Annual register of officers and members* (New York, 1896); *Register of officers and members, 1897–98* (New York, 1898); *General register, 1899–1902* (New York, 1902). W. H. Whitmore, *The Massachusetts civil list . . . 1630–1774* (Albany, 1870).

Nathaniel Adams, *Annals of Portsmouth* (Portsmouth, N.H., 1825). Bernard and Lotte Bailyn, *Massachusetts shipping 1697–1714* (Cambridge, Mass., 1959). Jeremy Belknap, *The history of New Hampshire* (Philadelphia, 1784); ed. John Farmer (Dover, N.H., 1831). Brebner, *New England's outpost*. Calnek, *History of Annapolis. Commonwealth history of Massachusetts*, ed. A. B. Hart (5v., New York, 1927–30), II. J. A. Doyle, *English colonies in America* (5v., New York, 1882–1907), III. Everett Kimball, *The public life of Joseph Dudley; a study of the colonial policy of the Stuarts in New England, 1660–1715* (New York, 1911). *The memorial history of Boston including Suffolk county, Massachusetts, 1630–1880*, ed. Justin Winsor (4v., Boston, 1880–81), II. Murdoch, *History of Nova-Scotia*, I. Kenneth Murdock, *Increase Mather, foremost American Puritan* (Cambridge, Mass., 1925). O. A. Roberts, *History of the military company of the Massachusetts, now called the Ancient and Honorable artillery company of Massachusetts 1637–1888* (4v., Boston, 1895–1901), I. Waller, *Samuel Vetch.* D. C. Harvey, "History in stone and bronze," *Dalhousie Review* (Halifax), XII (1932–33), 69–76.

HOLDSWORTH, ARTHUR, fishing captain and merchant in Newfoundland; b. 1668, son of Arthur Holdsworth (1624–90), fishing captain, ship-owner, and merchant of Dartmouth, Devonshire; d. 1726.

Arthur, with his brother Robert, helped develop the family business with Newfoundland and Portugal. It was the custom in Newfoundland that the first fishing captain to arrive at each harbour was the fishing admiral for the season. In 1700 Robert Holdsworth in the *Nicholas* (with Arthur accompanying him) was admiral at St John's. At a party given in Fort William by Capt. Michael RICHARDS, Arthur Holdsworth resented the supercilious remarks of the garrison commander, Capt. William Lilburne, and challenged him to a duel. Lilburne retired hurt after a single touch, though he claimed to have inflicted three wounds on Holdsworth. Lilburne was accused by Richards of cowardice, and was dismissed and brought home by the commodore, Capt. Stafford Fairborne. Arthur Holdsworth thus became a centre of controversy as recriminations continued in England. That the Holdsworths were unpopular may be seen from the support of some 40 fishing captains, many of them from Plymouth, for Lilburne against Holdsworth.

Rivalry between the western fishing ports may partly account for this animosity, but it was also caused by an innovation by the Holdsworths in their way of doing business. They had developed, though they did not in fact initiate, the practice of bringing out each season a large number of passengers or by-boatmen. These men would fish on their own account for the season, but hand over a share of their catch to the Holdsworths; most of the other fishing captains restricted fishing to the regular crew. In 1701 George LARKIN noted that Holdsworth made it his business "in the beginning of the year . . . to ride from one Market Town to another in the West of England on purpose to get passengers," and promised that if one of the Holdsworths should be admiral in any harbour he would see to it that the by-boatmen got a fishing-room normally reserved for a ship's crew. This was a discouragement to the Western Adventurers since the by-boatmen could afford to sell their fish more cheaply than the regular fishermen. In 1701, Arthur Holdsworth, again in the *Nicholas*, was fishing admiral at St John's and distributed no fewer than 236 passengers among the fishing-rooms, much to the disgust of the other captains. This killing seems to have been enough for him, however; in the following seasons he was on good terms with his fellow captains and cooperated with them.

Holdsworth was a merchant as well as a fishing captain. He occupied a house in St John's during the fishing season, and in 1702 undertook to bring out Portland stone, in ballast, for the fort. His brother, Robert, incited Major Thomas LLOYD to hire out soldiers to the fishing captains in 1704. The following year, Arthur Holdsworth was one of those who wrote from Newfoundland to thank the Bishop of London for sending out the new clergyman, Jacob RICE. In 1706 he registered a complaint that some of his fellow captains were throwing ballast into the harbour. Holdsworth seems to have worked closely with Lloyd, and was one of those who defended him against the accusations made in 1708.

Vice-admiral in 1708, Holdsworth was admiral again in 1709 when he arrived to find St John's destroyed by the French. He advocated the rapid restoration of Fort William, supplying some materials for emergency repairs, and urged that a strong garrison be maintained. Similar recommendations were made by the commodore, Capt. Joseph TAYLOUR. Holdsworth had a good head for business; for many years from 1702 onwards, he worked in close association with Henry Hayman, the influential Plymouth fishing captain. In 1711 Holdsworth's possession of the house in St John's was confirmed. After 1711, however, Holdsworth seems slowly to have relinquished his personal contacts with Newfoundland, though it is likely that he visited Placentia (Plaisance) on at least one occasion. His ships continued to take part in the Newfoundland fishery, his son, a third Arthur, taking his place as captain.

Arthur Holdsworth married Elizabeth, daughter of Henry Lane of Dartmouth. Her first husband, Capt. Roger Vavasor, had been killed at sea in 1696, and Holdsworth brought up her son, Henry, in his own household. Elizabeth and Arthur Holdsworth had four surviving children, a son and three daughters. Apart from his house in Newfoundland, Holdsworth owned extensive property in and around Dartmouth. His Dartmouth home was Mount Gilpin, and he also built a country house at Widdicombe, near Torcross. He died on 9 Nov. 1726 and was buried in St Petrok's church, Dartmouth.

Holdsworth's was one of a number of west-country seafaring and merchant families which had large stakes in the Newfoundland fishery over three or more generations. Arthur Holdsworth was a good example of the type; at first he attempted to enlarge his profits by unorthodox methods, but he was pulled back by his fellow captains and thereafter devoted himself to developing their strong collective interests.

D. B. QUINN

Dartmouth Municipal Records (in Exeter Public Library), leases of a house in Modbury, Devon, 1719 (Z7/Box 12), and of Perrings Pallace and Town Pallace, Dartmouth, 1725 (DD63900–63902, 63908). Somerset House, Principal Probate Registry, Holdsworth's will (dated 1 Nov. 1726, proved 5 June 1727). PRO, *CSP, Col., 1701, 1704–5, 1706–8, 1708–9, 1711–12, 1724–25*; *B.T.Journal, 1708/9–1714/15*. M. A. Field, "The development of government in Newfoundland, 1638–1713," unpublished M.A. thesis, University of London, 1924, 218–22. Innis, *Cod fisheries*, 109. Prowse, *History of Nfld*. Percy Russell, *Dartmouth, a history of the port and town* (London and New York, 1950), 122–24, 141–42. *Devon and Cornwall Notes and Queries* (Exeter), XIV (1927), 261. Devonshire Assoc., Exeter, *Trans.*, XXXII (1900), 513–14; XLV (1913), 239–41.

HOPKINS, SAMUEL, HBC employee; fl. 1715–31.

In 1715 Hopkins was taken from Christ's Hospital, London, as an apprentice for seven years, and sent to Albany Factory to keep accounts; James KNIGHT was instructed to "be very kind to him, and give him all the encouragemt." possible. Despite the London committee's complaints about his ornate handwriting, his wages were increased to £20 per annum in 1722. On 3 Oct. 1722 he deserted his post and went up the river with two Home Indians (Indians employed by the company), who had come down to Albany for winter credit. He spent the winter inland, but it is impossible to determine how far he penetrated. He returned to Albany on 1 May 1723 and was placed under house arrest by Governor Joseph MYATT. He broke arrest by scaling the wall on 17 May and tried to persuade some Indians to let him accompany them up the river. The Indians refused, and two men sent by Governor Myatt easily recaptured him. Hopkins was sent to England and appeared before the London committee whose members were no more impressed with his reasons for "eloping his employment" than Myatt had been. His wages were docked for the time he was absent.

The company re-employed him "out of charity" in 1724 and sent him to York Fort where he worked under Thomas McCliesh* who described him as "naturally honest" and "very obliging." Hopkins served first as steward and then, at a much increased salary, as book-keeper from 1727 to 1731, when he returned to England. He must have married while in England in 1723–24, for payments to his wife are recorded in December

Horné

1726. That neither Myatt nor the London committee seemed interested in Hopkins' experiences may demonstrate the company's lack of interest in inland exploration from Albany, or it may be evidence that Hopkins wintered not far from the port.

G. E. THORMAN

HBRS, XXV (Davies and Johnson).

HORNÉ (Dehorné), *dit* **Laneuville, JACQUES DE,** soldier, royal notary, and process-server; b. in 1664 (according to Tanguay); he came from Dieppe (province of Normandy), and was the son of Jacques de Horné and Catherine Duval; buried 7 March 1730 at Sainte-Croix.

Horné came to Canada as a soldier in the colonial regular troops. On 24 Jan. 1702, at Saint-Laurent on the Île d'Orléans, he married Marie Sivadier. From 1704 until his death, Horné practised as royal notary and process-server. His commission has not been found, but we know that his jurisdiction extended along the north and south shores of the St Lawrence from the Chaudière falls to the government of Trois-Rivières. He was one of those itinerant notaries of the French régime, who had to be continually on the move in search of a scanty clientele. His territory covered 25 leagues, on the two shores of the St Lawrence, which he had to cross in summer by canoe, in winter by making his way over the ice. His job was certainly no sinecure.

As he lived at Notre-Dame-de-Bonsecours, Horné was in 1723 a member of the parish of Saint-Antoine de Tilly. But, in agreement with the settlers of Bonsecours and Maranda, he recognized as parish priest only the missionary to Sainte-Croix. On 30 Dec. 1723 Bégon* called these refractory parishioners to order. Shortly afterwards Horné lost a child, whom he had buried at Sainte-Croix. The parish priest of Saint-Antoine immediately lodged a complaint, as a result of which the intendant, on 10 March 1724, suspended Horné from his offices as notary and process-server for setting a bad example, and sentenced him to a fine of 20 *livres*. The intendant reinstated him on 27 April following, when he had paid the tithe, the fine, and the burial dues for his child.

Horné died in 1730 and was buried at ... Sainte-Croix!

ANDRÉ VACHON

AJQ, Greffe de Louis Chambalon, 3 avril 1702. AQ, NF, Ord. des int., VI, 275; X, 12. Caron "Inventaire de documents," APQ *Rapport, 1941–42,* 251. *Édits ord.,* II, 207, 289. "Les notaires au Canada," 33. Tanguay, *Dictionnaire,* III, 281. J.-E. Roy, *Histoire du notariat,* I, 161f., 225.

HYOU. *See* You

I

IBERVILLE ET D'ARDILLIÈRES, PIERRE LE MOYNE D'. *See* LE MOYNE

ISABEAU, MICHEL-PHILIPPE, contractor for the construction of the citadel at Louisbourg, 1719–24; son of Arnoud Isabeau; Parisian, possibly of Norman origin; d. after 20 Nov. 1724 aboard the *Victoire* en route from Louisbourg to France.

Having visited Louisbourg in 1717, Isabeau contracted on 7 March 1719 to build the King's Bastion and Château Saint-Louis according to VERVILLE's plans. He worked from the spring of 1720 until the autumn of 1724. Reports that his prices were higher than the average for the colony, that he claimed additional profits by exploiting loopholes in his contract, and that he trafficked in goods, especially drink, with the soldier-labourers he employed, were offset by Verville's support, by the speed of his work during the fine summer of 1722, and by official displeasure with Jacques-Ange Le Normant* de Mézy, his chief critic.

After his death he was succeeded by François Ganet*. Investigation revealed neglect in the work, without establishing how much of it was Isabeau's. Extensive repair to the fortifications was necessary; quantities of fill had to be removed; and, in part because of the vagueness of his contract, Isabeau owed the crown for supplies and labour. In 1731 the net balance payable to his sister, Madame Planton, and his other heirs was reckoned at some 9,400 *livres*.

F. J. THORPE

AN, Col., B, 39, f.277v; 42, f.487; 44, f.566v; 48, f.925; 49, ff.697v, 703, 707–8v; 50, ff.586v, 597v–99; 54, f.520v; C¹¹ᴮ, 4, ff.278–82; 5, ff.58–67v, 220–21v, 386–88, 420–22; 6, ff.127, 170–73v, 235–42v, 293–94v; 7, ff.12, 361–62, 370–72; 8, ff.8–20v, 215; 9, ff.231–50v; 10, ff.242–45; 12, ff.60–61v, 122–43; 13, f.106 *et seq.* McLennan, *Louisbourg,* 45, 55.

J

JACKSON, JOHN, first chaplain to the garrison at St John's, Newfoundland; d. 1717.

The details of Jackson's birth, education, and early life are obscure. He may have served as chaplain for the expedition to Newfoundland under Sir John Norris* and GIBSONE in 1697. In 1700 he was appointed first chaplain to the garrison at St John's, and the following year sailed with his wife and eight children to Newfoundland. Unfortunately the arrival of Jackson at St John's on 12 July 1701 was not to improve the already strained atmosphere there. He consistently supported the soldiers and the inhabitants against what he considered to be the tyrannical oppression of the officers of the garrison. However, many felt that his attitude and his behaviour only worsened the situation: "[he] sowed discord among the inhabitants and goaded the soldiers to mutiny."

Soon after his arrival Jackson wrote to the Bishop of London, complaining of ill-treatment and insults from Captain Powell and Lieutenant Francis of the Independent Company. His complaint was passed on to the queen, and the Board of Trade and Plantations sent instructions that the minister was not to be abused by the military. This probably did not make for happier relations with the officers of the local forces. A little later there are reports that "Dr. Jackson . . . drank to the confusion and damnation of Captain Michael RICHARDS, and became intoxicated." When Thomas LLOYD became the commander of the garrison on Richards' return to England in 1703, the battle reached its climax. Jackson complained of Lloyd's notorious brutality and extortion to Captain Timothy BRIDGES, commodore of the convoy for 1704, supporting these accusations with petitions and memorials from those who had suffered at Lloyd's hands.

Apart from his specific quarrels with the garrison commanders, Jackson did not find life in Newfoundland easy. The accommodation provided for him in Fort William was unsatisfactory, and he moved into a house rented from a local merchant, Colin CAMPBELL. Later, difficulties arose over the rent, and eventually Jackson managed to secure a more suitable house inside the fort. He had made the point that his military commission as chaplain entitled him to the second best residence after that of the garrison commander: "Is Mr. LATHAM, who has no commission, and as Chief Mason ought to be preferred to a barrick, to be preferred in that place before me?"

In 1702 Jackson received a benefaction of £30 and a salary of £50 *per annum* from the Society for the Propagation of the Gospel, which must materially have assisted him, as he had difficulty in obtaining his official salary, and some of the inhabitants cheated him of his tithe, which was due to him according to the value of a catch of fish.

While Bridges, Richards, and Lloyd were in London in the winter of 1704–5, they reported to the Board of Trade on Jackson's behaviour, and suggested that he was a disruptive element at St John's. On 1 March 1705, the board wrote to the bishop of London asking that Jackson be replaced: "We are convinced that the irregular proceedings [in Newfoundland] have been in great measure occasioned by the violent temper and scandalous life of Mr. Jackson the minister." Early in November 1705 Jackson and his family—now 11 children—left Newfoundland in the *Falkland*, in the same convoy as the *Looe* carrying Bridges and John MOODY. On the night of 19 December, the *Falkland* was driven ashore on the long, flat sands of Sandwich Bay off Deal. There was no loss of life, but the turn of the tide flooded the ship and the Jackson family lost most of their possessions. On reaching London the family took up quarters at "Star Inn near ye Monument," and Jackson wrote to the Board of Trade begging to be excused from immediate attendance as he was suffering from the effects of shipwreck. He received a kindly reply and indeed from this time the board seems to have revised its opinion of Jackson. In 1706 the board issued a certificate "in favour of Mr. Jackson," and wrote to the bishop of London: "we commend this unfortunate man to your charity."

Jackson went to Dursley in Gloucestershire in 1709 and became curate there. In 1710 he was inducted as rector of Uley, and the same year married a Mary Bissett; it is quite probable that his first wife died in Newfoundland. Jackson's last letter to the board, in support of his old friend, Moody, is dated 2 April 1710 from Uley.

One of the most controversial characters in early Newfoundland history, Jackson has been denounced as "coarse and cruel," and as "one whose way of living . . . did instead of hindering vice . . . rather increase it." Yet it must be remembered that many of those who signed memorials for and against officials in Newfoundland had no idea what they were signing, and blatant forgery of documents and signatures was common. That

Jacob

Jackson's task as chaplain at St John's was a difficult one cannot be denied, and there is some indication that he tried to carry out his work conscientiously; he set to work to build a church in St John's and attempted to curb some of the outrageous brutality that was rife in the settlement. Certificates from the soldiers and inhabitants at St John's testify to Jackson's "sober and peaceable life." It seems fairly certain, however, that Jackson was cantankerous, bad-tempered and factious; his morality and personal integrity were repeatedly questioned.

MICHAEL GODFREY

Alumni Oxonienses, ed. Joseph Foster (4v., Oxford, [1891–92?]) seems to have confused the Newfoundland John Jackson with another John Jackson, who was inducted as rector of Weston Birt in 1702 and died in 1738.
Gloucester, England, Records of the Diocesan Registry. PRO, Adm. 1/1777 (captains' letters); 51/354. *Classified digest of the records of the Society for the Propagation of the Gospel in foreign parts 1701–1892* (London, 1893). PRO, *CSP, Col., 1700, 1701, 1702, 1702–3, 1704–5, 1706–8*; *CSP, Dom., 1700–2*. Dalton, *English army lists*, IV. Prowse, *History of Nfld.*

JACOB, ÉTIENNE, court officer, serjeant of the Conseil Souverain, seigneurial notary, judge of the bailiff's court of Beaupré and Île d'Orléans, son of Étienne Jacob and Jeanne Bellejambe, of Saint-Germain in Paris; b. *c.* 1648; d. after 10 April 1726.

He arrived in New France before 4 July 1665, for on that date he was a domestic of Antoine Berson, *dit* Chatillon, on the Beaupré shore. He was to spend his life in that locality. It was at Quebec, however, that on 14 Oct. 1670 he married a king's girl (*fille du roi*), Jeanne Fressel, who was 17 years old and had a dowry of 850 *livres*.

After being an ordinary settler, he was nominated on 4 Jan. 1676 by Bishop LAVAL as court officer of the seigneurial jurisdiction of Beaupré. On 10 April 1683 he was further promoted to the office of clerk of court and notary for the same jurisdiction. Finally, on 12 March 1689, Jacob was promoted judge of the bailiff's court of Beaupré; the investigation into his character and his swearing-in took place on the 28th of the same month. Jacob became, moreover, judge of the bailiff's court for the countship of Saint-Laurent (Île d'Orléans) on 25 May 1703, and took the oath on 5 June. Because of "the infirmities of his age," Jacob's appointment as judge of Beaupré was revoked on 22 Aug. 1712, but he carried on his practice as seigneurial notary.

The date of Jacob's death remains unknown, although we do know that his last act is dated 10 Aug. 1726.

HONORIUS PROVOST

AJQ, Greffe de Claude Auber, 4 juillet 1665; Greffe de Romain Bequet, 31 août 1670; Greffe d'Étienne Jacob, 10 août 1726. AQ, NF, Coll. pièces jud. et not., 2016. ASQ, Séminaire, VI, 53, 82; XX–XXV. *Jug. et délib.*, II, III, IV, VI. A. Roy, *Inv. greffes not.*, III, 48; VII, 193. P.-G. Roy, *Inv. contrats de mariage*, III, 239. Tanguay, *Dictionnaire*, I, 315. J.-E. Roy, *Histoire du notariat*, I, 137, 170.

JACQUIÉS, *dit* **Leblond, JEAN,** sculptor and painter, b. 1688 in the parish of Sainte-Catherine in Brussels; son of Luc Jacquiés and Barbe Segris (Seygris); d. after 1724.

He arrived in Canada about 1712, and on 24 Nov. 1715 married Catherine Guillemote at Montreal; they had at least three children.

Jacquiés, *dit* Leblond, worked especially in the region of Trois-Rivières. On 28 June 1716 he undertook to make the altar of the Ursuline church there; the contract bears the signature of Father Joseph DENYS, the parish priest of Trois-Rivières at that time. On 23 Feb. 1721 the parish priest of Saint-François-du-Lac, Jean-Baptiste Dugast, ordered from him a tabernacle similar "to the one which he, Leblond, previously made for the Recollet fathers in that town [Trois-Rivières] and which is now on the high altar of their church." In addition to the necessary wood, Jacquiés received 350 *livres* in money and 20 pounds of tobacco.

Of his work as a sculptor there remain only two bas-reliefs intended for the first church of Yamachiche, a madonna, and fragments of the tabernacle of Saint-François-du-Lac. Only two pictures permit us to form an idea of his talents as a painter: *Marie Madeleine repentante* and *Madone tenant son enfant*.

The two extant bas-reliefs represent St Joseph and St Simon. In these one notices a certain stiffness and an absence of artifice, which recall in a way the ingenuousness of the old masters of the Middle Ages. The statue of the Virgin is more elaborate without being fussy. The artist's Flemish ancestry is more evident in the two paintings. These also display a certain rigidity in composition, but it is pleasantly softened by the complicated drapery and the well-arranged colours.

We lose all trace of Jacquiés after 1724, the year in which one of his children was baptized. We know however that his wife returned to Montreal and died there in 1734.

MAURICE CARRIER

AJM, Registres d'état civil de Notre-Dame de Montréal (1715), 141, 142, 154. IOA, Cap-de-la-Madeleine, A-5, A-6; Trois-Rivières, A-9, B-11, B-12. É.-Z. Massicotte, "Quelques sculpteurs montréalais sous la domination française," *BRH*, XXXIV (1928), 538–40. Tanguay, *Dictionnaire*, IV, 575. Jouve, *Les Franciscains et le Canada: aux Trois-Rivières*, 76. Morisset, *La peinture traditionnelle au C.f.*, 38.

JAGO, JOHN, minister at St John's, Newfoundland; b. 1684; d. sometime after 1724. Son of George Jago of Egloskerry, Cornwall, John Jago was educated at Exeter College, Oxford. Little is known of his early ministry, except that in 1717 he was vicar of St Keverne, Cornwall.

By 1723 Jago was acting as minister in St John's, Newfoundland. Disorder and crime were rampant in the town; debts were collected by force and the local inhabitants were ruthlessly exploited. As the British government ignored repeated recommendations and appeals for some form of civil government to be established in the settlement, the leading property owners of St John's decided in 1723 to form an association "for the mutual preservation of H.M. peace, and the protection of us and ours, during the winter, that is, until the arrival of a British fishing ship in this harbour." The subscribers, who were to forfeit £50 bail if they broke any of the articles of association, elected three men (including the minister, Jago) as justices. Commodore Robert BOULER, reporting to the Board of Trade and Plantations in 1724, mentioned that the three justices had held regular courts during the winter months and had settled a number of local disputes.

After this period of service in Newfoundland, nothing more is heard of Jago. He may have returned to England, but he seems to have held no further ecclesiastical positions.

CARSON I. A. RITCHIE

PRO, C.O. 194/7. *Index to the Act Books of the Archbishops of Canterbury, 1663–1859*, compiled E. H. W. Dunkin, extended and edited Claude Jenkins and E. A. Fry (2v., British Record Soc., LV, LXIII, 1929, 1938), I. PRO, *CSP, Col., 1724–25. Alumni Oxonienses*, ed. Joseph Foster (4v., Oxford, [1891–92?]).

JANGOUESSY. See CHINGOUESSI

JARRET DE VERCHÈRES, PIERRE, officer; b. 1679 or 1680 at Verchères (Canada); son of François Jarret de Verchères and Marie Perrot; killed 1708.

His family came from the province of Dauphiné.

An attempt has been made, wrongly, to link him with the Verchères de La Réole, from the region of Bordeaux. Pierre Jarret de Verchères' father, who was born in 1641, was the son of Jean Jarret and Claudine Pécaudy, of Saint-Chef, near the hamlet of Verchères in the archbishopric of Vienne. François arrived in New France at the age of 24 with the Carignan-Salières regiment, as an ensign in the company of his uncle, Antoine Pécaudy de Contrecœur. When the regiment was recalled to France in 1667, the young soldier decided to make his home in Canada, in accordance with the wish of the king, Louis XIV, who encouraged the settling of soldiers in the colony to increase the safety of its population. Two years later, on 16 Sept. 1669, at Sainte-Famille (Île d'Orléans), he married a young girl of 14.

Writing to the minister on 2 Nov. 1672, Buade* de Frontenac requested for François Jarret de Verchères letters of nobility, which apparently he never obtained. The next day Talon* granted him as a fief, with rights of seigneury and justice, "a piece of land half a league wide by one league in depth, fronting on the St Lawrence River, and extending down from the Sieur de Grandmaison's land grant towards the unassigned lands as far as those of the Sieur Vitrez. . . ." This seigneury was subsequently to be enlarged by the addition of Île aux Prunes and Île Longue and another league of depth. In November 1674 the governor again asked Colbert for a reward for the good services of Verchères, who, acting on his order, had harried coureurs de bois as far as 200 leagues above Montreal, alienating many persons' good will in doing so.

The founder of Verchères, while he worked at bringing his domain under cultivation, did not abandon soldiering. At the time of BRISAY de Denonville's expedition against the Senecas in 1687, he was captain of a militia company in Alexandre BERTHIER's battalion. In 1691 he received from Frontenac a commission as ensign in the troops in Canada, which the king ratified on 1 March 1693. He was promoted lieutenant on 15 April 1694, then made a lieutenant on half pay.

François died on 26 Feb. 1700, leaving his family in poverty. He had had 12 children, of whom Pierre was the fifth. Pierre was to follow in his father's footsteps, and even in those of his mother, who in 1690 had held out almost single-handed against the Iroquois in a 48-hour siege. Young Pierre early received his baptism of fire. When he was about 12 years old, he defended the fort of Verchères for a week, side by side with his famous sister Madeleine* and his younger brother Alexandre. It was doubtless of Pierre that the heroine spoke in 1699, when she requested of the

Jeanne-Françoise

Comtesse de Maurepas: ". . . that the good you would like to do me at least redound to the advantage of one of my brothers who is a cadet in our troops. If it is your pleasure, have him made an ensign. He has experience in the service, he has been on several expeditions against the Iroquois. . . ." Her wish was granted and the young man received the desired rank.

On 29 Aug. 1708 he took part in the attack on Haverhill, a village in Massachusetts, with a detachment of 100 Frenchmen and a smaller number of Indians led by Jean-Baptiste de Saint-Ours Deschaillons and JEAN-BAPTISTE HERTEL de Rouville. After putting the village to fire and sword, the assailants were withdrawing at dawn when they fell into an ambush laid by some 60 English. In these two engagements there were 18 wounded and 10 killed on the Canadian side; among the dead was Pierre Jarret de Verchères.

CÉLINE DUPRÉ

AN, Col., C^{11A}, 18, f.69; F^3, 5, f.427. Baugy, *Journal* (Serrigny), 84. "Correspondance de Frontenac (1672–82)," APQ *Rapport, 1926–27*, 18, 68. "Correspondance de Vaudreuil," APQ *Rapport, 1939–40*, 430–32, 438, 457f. *Lettres de noblesse* (P.-G. Roy), II. PAC *Report, 1899*, 6–7. P.-G. Roy, Inv. concessions, III, 27–34. Taillemite, *Inventaire analytique, série B*, I, 54, 56. Bonnault, "Le Canada militaire," 287, 486. Coleman, *New England captives*. P.-G. Roy, *La famille Jarret de Verchères* (Lévis, 1908); *BRH*, XIV (1908), 209–17, 240–54, 271–85, 299–303. Pierre Saint-Olive, *Les Dauphinois au Canada. Essai de catalogue des Dauphinois qui ont pris part à l'établissement du régime français au Canada, suivi d'une étude sur un Dauphinois canadien: Antoine Pécody de Contrecœur* (Paris, 1936), 27f., 94. Aegidius Fauteux, "La famille Jarret," *BRH*, XXX (1924), 253–56, 278.

JEANNE-FRANÇOISE DE SAINT-IGNACE. *See* JUCHEREAU

JÉRÉMIE, *dit* LAMONTAGNE, NICOLAS, interpreter and clerk for the trading-posts in the king's domain and on Hudson Bay; bap. at Sillery, 16 Feb. 1669, fourth of the 12 children of Noël Jérémie* and Jeanne Pelletier; d. 19 Oct. 1732 at Quebec.

In 1676 Noël Jérémie was clerk at Métabetchouan, a trading-post which Pierre Bécart de Granville had just set up. In 1690 he was at Chicoutimi with his son Nicolas, who was then 21, and later, in 1693, at Tadoussac, still acting as clerk for the fur trade in the king's domain and with his son Nicolas still under his orders. At that time he was an assiduous visitor to the post on the Îlets Jérémie, situated 87 miles to the east of Tadoussac, where the Papinachois Indians from

the headwaters of the Bersimis and the rivers of the region came to barter their furs. Noël and Nicolas Jérémie had therefore almost completely covered the king's domain, which besides Tadoussac, Chicoutimi, and the Îlets Jérémie, had only one other firmly established post, that on the Moisie River.

It was in honour of Noël Jérémie (and perhaps also of his son Nicolas) that the Îlets Jérémie were named. Frequent references to this place-name were already to be found in the "Miscellaneorum liber" (1691–1780), which is a continuation of the "Second registre de Tadoussac" and which was drawn up in particular by the Jesuit missionaries Pierre LAURE, Claude Coquart*, and Jean-Baptiste de La Brosse. According to one opinion, which however lacks confirmation, the Côte de la Montagne at Quebec also owes its name to Noël Jérémie, who is supposed to have owned a *pied-à-terre* near there.

Nicolas Jérémie was baptized in 1669 at Sillery and was brought up at Batiscan. In 1693 he married the Montagnais Indian Marie-Madeleine Tetesigaguoy at Lac Saint-John. Father CRESPIEUL solemnized the marriage. Since Nicolas was under 25, the legal age of majority at that time, and as the ordinances concerning marriages between French and Indians had not been respected, the Conseil Souverain annulled the marriage in 1694, at the request of Nicolas' father; the petitioner was however sentenced to provide for the Indian girl, for whom Jacques GOURDEAU and Louis Jolliet* were appointed guardians.

After this episode Nicolas lived for some years in the Hudson Bay region, in the service of the state and various trading companies. Nicolas died in 1732 and was buried in the basilica of Quebec. In 1735 Françoise Bourrot, whom he had married at Quebec in 1707, married a businessman and navigator, Charles Boucher de Boucherville. She died 3 Aug. 1758. By this marriage Nicolas had only one daughter, Françoise, who was 22 in 1745. Nicolas' daughter does not seem to have married; his brothers on the other hand had numerous descendants, who retained only the surnames Douville, Dauville, Beaurivage, and Lamontagne. All the families that bear these names, however, do not necessarily go back to Noël Jérémie.

A sister of Nicolas Jérémie, Catherine (1664–1744), was one of the earliest herbalists in Canada. She treated her children and neighbours with medicinal herbs, and she is even supposed to have sent botanical specimens to France. In 1681, at Champlain where her parents were dwelling at the time after living at Batiscan, she married Jacques Aubuchon, by whom she had a daughter. She married again, in 1688, at Batiscan, her second husband being Michel LEPAILLEUR, a Quebec notary, who settled in Montreal in 1703. By her marriage with him she had 10 or 11 children.

Nicolas Jérémie entered history with his "Relation du détroit et de la baie d'Hudson," first published in 1720 at Amsterdam but perhaps written as early as 1714. For Jean-Frédéric Bernard, the compiler of the *Recueil de voyages au nord* in 1732, the author becomes simply 'Monsieur Jérémie," but there is no doubt that it, was Nicolas, and not his father Noël, as has been believed previously. The contents of the book deal with history, ethnology, animal and vegetable life, and it is in the last three areas that it makes an important albeit succinct contribution. It was at this time that several notions entered scientific literature. If it has not been too much touched up by copyists or editors, the account, which is written in a lively manner, reveals excellent training. In 1744 Charlevoix* gave this appreciation of the work: "I knew the author [no doubt during his stay in Canada in 1708 or during his second trip in 1720], who was a worthy man and an experienced traveller. His account is very instructive and written with discernment."

Jérémie's work, written after his return for good from Hudson Bay, is concise but nonetheless accurate. Except for the historical portion, it is the work of an eye-witness. "I note down nothing," he wrote, "until I have seen and examined it myself: and in order not to advance anything on the word of others, I have visited nearly all the places which I speak of." It is essentially a narration and a report. The author first groups his material by subjects: early history, description of the country and its fauna, the conquest by the French of parts of Hudson Bay, a phase with which he had been intimately associated; then he comes back to the fauna. At this point his narration turns into a report on the future prospects of the Hudson Bay territory and the regions to the west. It is evident that this report was destined for someone close to the king's counsellors, perhaps even for the minister. As access to the work is not easy, it is advisable to give a short analysis of its contents.

Nicolas first recounts briefly the history of the discovery of Hudson Bay and of the trips that had been made there before his own in 1694. He then dwells at greater length on what he observed himself. He describes among other things the topography of the territory; the ice conditions, which turn the bay into a sea closed to navigation for more than nine months of the year; and the pronounced magnetic variation from the North, giving indications which permit conjectures about a magnetic pole that was not yet known. His special interest is in the fauna: after brief des-

criptions of the walrus, caribou, and beaver (whose dam and lodge he studies) and a mention of all the animals that had some economic importance, he introduces his readers to an animal that frequented the Rivière Danoise (the Churchill River, which had been discovered by Jens Munk*, the leader of a Danish expedition in 1619–20). These animals are "a sort of ox which we call *Bœufs musquez* (musk-oxen), because they smell so strongly of musk that in certain seasons of the year it is impossible to eat their meat." His description of the musk-ox is probably the first of this mammal. Even the name of the beast seems to be mentioned in French for the first time. The long, fine, silky wool of the musk-ox particularly interested Jérémie, and in 1708 he took some of it to France to "have made for himself stockings that were finer than silk ones." One of the next appearances of the musk-ox would be in the *Histoire* by La Potherie (LE ROY), which likewise recounts the capture of Fort Nelson and which, though written about the same time as Jérémie's "Relation", was not published until 1753.

Jérémie's description of the musk-ox remains a classic document in the history of zoology, but it should be pointed out that the drawing of what is identified as the "wild ox of the Mississippi and Hudson Bay" in the 1720 edition is that of the buffalo rather than the musk-ox, the two animals obviously having been confused by the illustrator, as the caption proves. The animal's horns and the hunters' dress show without the slightest doubt that the drawing is the work of an artist who had never seen the animal, rather than of Jérémie himself.

Quite naturally, Jérémie's attention was drawn particularly to hunting and fishing. He was the representative of a fur-trading company, and he also had to see that the garrison was fed. The products of hunting and fishing, piled up at the beginning of the winter and kept frozen in the snow, would keep almost till the spring. Hares and partridge were so abundant that according to his calculations the 80 men of the garrison would have consumed in one winter 90,000 partridges and 25,000 hares, which amounts to 4 partridges and 1 hare a day per man.

At Fort Bourbon even a vegetable garden was planted, in which grew "good lettuce, green cabbages, and other vegetables of the same sort which we salted down to make soup during the winter." This was surely one of the earliest attempts, if not the first, to carry on agriculture in Canada at this latitude.

The "Relation" refers to the existence, far to the west of Hudson Bay, in the Dogrib Indian country, of "a mine of red copper, so abundant

Jérémie

and so pure that, without treating it in the forge but just as they gather it in the mine, they simply hit it between two stones and make out of it anything they wish. I have very often seen some of it, because our Indians used to bring some back every time they went to war in those parts." This is one of the earliest mentions, supported by specimens, of the existence of copper in the northwest territories.

The author was interested in the Amerindian peoples, particularly the Eskimos, whom he described at length, and the *Platscotés de Chiens* (a name which designates in particular an Athapaskan band known today in English as the Dogribs), who lived farther west and who "are at war with our Savanais." The latter were the Swampy Crees, or Maskegons (from the Algonkian *moskeg*, meaning peat-bog or swamp, called in popular French-Canadian speech *savane*). He likewise mentions the Assiniboins (of the Sioux family), the *Kristinaux* (today the Crees), and the *Sauteux* (comprising part of the Chippewas and, like the preceding groups, belonging to the Algonkian family), who lived in the region of Lake Winnipeg and had dealings with the natives who carried on trade with Fort Bourbon. During his stay in the Hudson Bay region Jérémie was to try to have exploration carried out to the west and southwest, beyond the hydrographic basin in which he was living.

Although we do not always know whether he was referring to the Eskimos, the Athapaskans, or the Algonkians, the author reports several specific characteristics concerning the natives. These include notes on their dwellings (tents of moose or caribou skins), the use of snow-shoes, the sharing of belongings with the less fortunate (as the author's precise text implies, the natives did not have our notion of property rights, and for them nature's goods were to be at everyone's disposal), their primitive religion, the almost ritual suicide of the old people, aided by their children, and finally the cannibalism which was imposed by necessity: "I have seen one man," he wrote, "who, after eating his wife and their six children, said that he had not been touched until the last one that he had eaten, because he loved him more than the others, and that, on opening the head to eat the brain, he had been moved by the feeling that a father must have for his children, and that he had not had the strength to break his bones in order to suck the marrow from them."

The part played by Jérémie himself in the Hudson Bay region began in 1694. Previously (1682–83), Chouart* Des Groseilliers and RADISSON had gained control of the mouths of the Nelson and Hayes Rivers and the trading-post became Fort Bourbon. Subsequently the site returned to the English, who were still established there in 1694, when PIERRE LE MOYNE d'Iberville came to seize it with the *Poli* and another ship commanded by his brother JOSEPH LE MOYNE de Serigny (the *Charante*, according to Jérémie, but according to Prud'homme, Rich, and Tyrrell the *Salamandre*). Nicolas Jérémie came with Iberville on the *Poli* and set himself up at Fort Bourbon as "ensign and interpreter of the languages of the Indians, and commercial director." He was indeed the representative of a fur-trading company, the Compagnie du Nord or Compagnie de la baie d'Hudson, which was to be succeeded in January 1701 by the Compagnie du Canada, known popularly as the Compagnie des Castors and Compagnie du Pays. When Iberville set off again for France in September, he left Gabriel Testard* de La Forest in command of the fort, with a company of 67 men.

In September 1696 the English came back. On the day following their arrival, 6 September, when they were preparing to land, Jérémie was given the task of opposing them with 14 men. "As we were lying in ambush in dense thickets, and as I took care to have my men fire at the right moment, one after another, each time I saw an armed longboat appear, the English promptly returned aboard ship." For lack of supplies, the fort had to capitulate. But contrary to "the terms of capitulation, which were most advantageous," wrote Jérémie, "they broke their promises; for instead of putting us on French territory, with all our belongings, as they had promised, they took us to England and threw us into prison, while our pelts and other belongings were plundered." The conditions of capitulation were, however, ambiguous and could be interpreted differently by the two sides, as KELSEY's diary shows.

Four months later Jérémie crossed to France, and at the beginning of 1697 he went directly to Placentia (Plaisance) to rejoin Iberville, who was in command of four ships, *Pélican, Palmier, Profond*, and *Vespe* (*Wesp*), and who returned to Hudson Bay. On 8 Sept. 1697 Jérémie took part in the capture of the former Fort Bourbon, of which Serigny became governor on Iberville's departure for Europe. In 1698 Serigny likewise departed, leaving his relative, JEAN-BAPTISTE LE MOYNE de Martigny, in command, while Jérémie fulfilled the duties of lieutenant and interpreter.

Jérémie also continued to direct the fur trade until 1707, and after asking for leave several times he returned to France by way of Quebec, where he married Françoise Bourot, the widow of Jean Chaviteau, a ship's captain. As soon as he arrived in Europe, he was proposed to the court as commander of Fort Bourbon. He therefore left in 1708 from La Rochelle, with a new garrison. As it was too late in the year to enter Hudson Strait, which was usually blocked early by the ice, they had to spend the winter at Placentia. Jérémie consequently wrote to the person to whom he was later to address his "Relation" (whom the editor in Amsterdam simply calls *Monsieur*) and who seems to have been the minister or at least someone in high authority: "We were obliged to put into Plaisance, from where I had the honour of writing you to ask your permission to obtain supplies from Canada, and you were so kind as to give your assent." The permission no doubt allowed him to go to Quebec, where his wife perhaps was—we do not know whether he had taken her with him to France right after his marriage, or whether she accompanied him later to Fort Bourbon.

During the summer of 1709 Jérémie went, then, to Fort Bourbon, where he was to be governor for six years. The situation at the fort was not always perfectly secure. The forest and water furnished much of their food, but the articles needed for barter were lacking. The company, which made a profit from the fur trade, neglected its shipments. From 1709 to 1713 we are told not a single French ship reached Hudson Bay. In 1713 "The Gentlemen of the Company sent a ship which brought us all kinds of provisions and merchandise for trading, of which the Indians had great need. For they had been waiting for four years, because I had no more merchandise to trade with them; this resulted in many of them dying of starvation, as they have forgotten how to use bows and arrows since the Europeans have been bringing them fire-arms."

The scarcity of their reserves forced Jérémie to keep the powder, which was in danger of running out, for the garrison. In 1712 this situation brought about the massacre of eight of his best men, whom he had sent out to hunt. Since he was unable after that to keep up both Fort Bourbon and Fort Phélipeaux, a subordinate post on the Hayes River, he ordered the garrison of the latter to withdraw; but as he had not had time to have the 100 pounds of powder remaining in the abandoned fort carried away, the Indians seized it, which brought the garrison to the brink of famine by the spring. Fortunately the ship which arrived in 1713 delivered them from these difficulties.

In 1714 Jérémie received from the court an order, along with letters from the Comte de Pontchartrain, to hand the post over to the English (*see* James KNIGHT), in accord with the terms of the treaty of Utrecht. We have hardly any information about his subsequent career. We know that he returned to Quebec and that, shortly before he wrote his "Relation", Intendant Bégon*

asked to see him in order to obtain information concerning western exploration.

It appears that Jérémie wrote his account while in France, at a date unknown to us, and that he did so at the request of one of the king's counsellors, perhaps the minister in 1708, who does not seem to have given up all designs on Hudson Bay. As the form of his narrative suggests, Jérémie had probably been given the task of writing down all that he knew about Hudson Bay, James Bay, and the surrounding regions. "If you wish," he wrote, "when I am in Canada I shall consult with some people who have been to that country several times." This country was James Bay, with which he was not familiar. The "Relation" ends with a memoir concerning future prospects. Fort Bourbon, he wrote, could produce "more than 100,000 *livres* profit every year. In 1713 I had not been sent 8,000 *livres* of cargo in all, and in 1714 I did business for goods worth more than 120,000 *livres*, which I brought with me when I was relieved by the English. In my opinion, this post would be one of the best in America, if only a little money were spent on it."

At a time when Hudson Bay had become English territory, except for short periods, Jérémie's account is one of the rare documents by a Frenchman who had lived for some years in those regions. The descriptions that the author gives of the life of the natives furnish Canadian ethnology with precious data: Jérémie spent a rather long time in the country; his testimony is not that of a passing traveller. Finally, his account of the campaigns by the French in Hudson Bay under Iberville's command, which he had witnessed and taken part in, provides precise details about this phase of history.

JACQUES ROUSSEAU

Nicolas Jérémie's "Relation du Détroit et de la Baie d'Hudson" was first published in the *Recueil d'arrests et autres pièces pour l'établissement de la Compagnie d'Occident* (Amsterdam, 1720); the second edition of the "Relation" appeared in *Recueil de voyages au Nord* (Amsterdam, 1732), III. A third edition, based on the edition of 1732 but compared with that of 1720, was entitled: "Relation du Détroit et de la Baie d'Hudson par Monsieur Jérémie," with Intro. by J.-H. Prud'homme, published in the Société hist. de Saint-Boniface *Bull.*, II (1912); some spelling changes have been made in this edition and three short passages, which added little to the text, have been deleted. The fourth edition was published in English: *Twenty years of York Factory, 1694–1714: Jérémie's account of Hudson Strait and Bay*, tr. from the French ed. of 1720 with notes and Intro. by Robert Douglas and J. N. Wallace (Ottawa, 1926). According to *JR* (Thwaites), LXXI, 252, Jérémie's work first appeared

Joannès de Chacornacle

in Amsterdam in 1710; this is an error and should read 1720.

AAQ, Registres des missions des Postes du Roy, Miscellaneorum liber. ASQ, MSS, 360. Charlevoix, *Histoire. Documents relating to Hudson Bay* (Tyrrell). HBRS, XXI (Rich); XXV (Davies and Johnson). *Kelsey papers* (Doughty and Martin). Le Jeune, *Dictionnaire*. Tanguay, *Dictionnaire*; the sections dealing with the Jérémie family need considerable revision. Damase Potvin, *Les Îlets-Jérémie: histoire d'une ancienne mission du Domaine du roi* (Québec, 1928). L.-A. Prud'homme, "La baie d'Hudson," *RSCT*, 3d ser., III (1909), sect.i, 3–36. A. Rhéaume, "Nicolas Jérémie," *BRH*, IX (1903), 246. Benjamin Sulte, "Noël et Nicolas Jérémie," *BRH*, XIII (1907), 90–92. [J.R.]

JOANNÈS DE CHACORNACLE (Chacornac, Chacornade), officer; b. 1672 in the province of Picardy; d. 1707 at Placentia (Plaisance).

Little is known of his origins. No one, it seems, has discovered his certificates of baptism and marriage, which would supply his whole name, the names of his father and mother, and his exact place of birth. Our information about this officer comes almost solely from the correspondence exchanged between the court of France and the colonial authorities, and it always omits his given name. That of François-Augustin has been attributed to him, probably by confusion with Baron François-Augustin Joannès* de Chacornacle (1683–1754), captain of the garrison at Trois-Rivières and knight of the order of Saint-Louis. They were likely brothers, although the second was born in Paris. The latter's parents are known: Balthazar de Joannès, knight, baron, and captain in the dragoons, and Catherine Mortier.

Strangely enough, on 5 May 1734 the Baron de Joannès had entered in the registry of Trois-Rivières a document concerning a certain Joannès de Chacornacle which, since it was dated 1692, could only have belonged to his older brother. This certificate of good and faithful services coincides, moreover, with certain details furnished by CALLIÈRE in 1701 concerning the Sieur de Chacornacle's career before he came to Canada. He had first been a cadet for two years; as his commanding officer had recommended him to Versailles for his "good conduct" and his "assiduity in the service," in 1692 he was promoted second lieutenant in Montauban's company in the Régiment d'Agenais. The following year he was commissioned a lieutenant in the Régiment Royal-Vaisseaux.

In 1694 he became a lieutenant on half pay and went to New France. An order from the king dated 23 May 1695 retained him in his rank in the forces in Canada. In the spring of 1700 the governor of the colony sent him, at the head of a detachment of soldiers, to seize the pelts which Louis de LA PORTE de Louvigny, the commandant of Fort Frontenac, had obtained through illegal transactions in the fur trade. He executed his mission efficiently.

In the summer of 1701 he was one of the lieutenants of ALPHONSE TONTY, the captain of the force which was with Lamothe Cadillac [LAUMET] at the founding of Detroit. Then, on 1 Feb. 1702, he became captain of a company of infantry in Acadia. Three years later we find him at Placentia, where he died in 1707.

He was highly regarded by his superiors and was, in Callière's opinion, "a good officer."

CÉLINE DUPRÉ

Jug. et délib., IV, 499–502. *NYCD* (O'Callaghan and Fernow), IX, 714. P.-G. Roy, "Ce que Callières pensait de nos officiers," 331. *Royal Fort Frontenac* (Preston and Lamontagne), 202, 400, 471. Taillemite, *Inventaire analytique, série B*, I. [François Daniel] *Le vicomte C. de Léry, lieutenant-général de l'empire français, ingénieur en chef de la grande armée, et sa famille ...* (Montréal, 1867), 208. Sulte, *Hist. des Can. fr.*, V, 148, 151. Raymond Douville, "Deux officiers 'indésirables' des troupes de la Marine," *Cahiers des Dix*, XIX (1954), 83–98. É.-Z. Massicotte, "Le sieur de Chacornacle," *BRH*, XXXIV (1928), 183. Benjamin Sulte, "Les Tonty," *RSCT*, 1st ser., XI (1893), sect.i, 26.

JOLLIET DE MINGAN, JEAN-BAPTISTE, merchant and trader, involved in fisheries; baptized 11 May 1683, son of Louis Jolliet* and Claire-Françoise Bissot; d. between 1732 and 1735, probably at Mingan.

When Louis Jolliet died in 1700 he left his family and associates a sizable territory in the Gulf of St Lawrence, consisting primarily of Anticosti and the islands and islets of Mingan. The poor quality of the moss-covered soil of the islands and nearby north shore made cultivation of the land unpractical, but the area was valuable nonetheless for it was strategically located for the fur trade and the cod, seal, and salmon fisheries.

In 1703 Jean-Baptiste, his older brother François Jolliet d'Abancourt, and the Bissot brothers, Charles-François and FRANÇOIS-JOSEPH, formed a partnership for the exploitation of the trade and fisheries of the Mingan-Anticosti concessions. Backing the group was FRANÇOIS HAZEUR, the prominent Quebec merchant, who advanced the required merchandise, victuals, and fishing tackle. In 1705, however, both Charles-François Bissot and François Jolliet lost interest in the enterprise, and the latter ceded his share to his brother,

Charles Jolliet d'Anticosti. The following year the association was completely dissolved. Jean-Baptiste remained in possession of the trade and fisheries of Mingan, while his brother Charles exploited Anticosti Island. Between them, the two Jolliets operated four or five trading posts.

On 11 Sept. 1708, at Quebec, Jean-Baptiste had married Marie Mars, daughter of the merchant Simon Mars and Anne de Faye. Since there is no record of their presence in Quebec after that date, one can assume that they moved to Mingan, where Jean-Baptiste lived out the remaining years of his life. Marie gave birth to six daughters and one son, Jean-Joseph, who later became a member of the group that was granted a monopoly of the trade of the Sioux country by Governor Charles de Beauharnois* de La Boische in 1731. After the death of her husband, Marie married Jean-Louis Volant* d'Haudebourg on 18 April 1735; she was buried 28 Feb. 1776.

C. J. Russ

AJQ, Greffe de Louis Chambalon, 5, 7 avril, 19 sept. 1703; 3 juin, 27 sept. 1704; 9 mai, 30 sept. 1705; 24 juillet 1715; Greffe de Jean-Claude Louet, 25 mai 1732. AN, Col., C¹¹ᴬ, 36, ff.501–4. P.-G. Roy, *Inventaire de pièces sur la côte de Labrador conservées aux Archives de la Province de Québec* (2v., Québec, 1940–42), I, 271–73. Wis. State Hist. Soc. *Coll.*, XVII. Bonnault, "Le Canada militaire," 414. Jean Delanglez, *Louis Jolliet, vie et voyages (1645–1700)* (Montréal, 1950). Fauteux, *Essai sur l'industrie sous le régime français*, II, 529–30. Ernest Gagnon, *Louis Jolliet, découvreur du Mississipi et du pays des Illinois, premier seigneur de l'île d'Anticosti* (Montréal, 1946). Pierre Margry, "Louis Jolliet," *RC*, 1ᵉʳᵉ sér., VIII (1871), 931–42; IX (1872), 61–73, 121–38, 205–19.

JONCAIRE, LOUIS-THOMAS CHABERT DE. *See* CHABERT

JOYBERT DE SOULANGES ET DE MARSON, LOUISE-ÉLISABETH DE, Marquise de Vaudreuil (she signed Louise Élisabeth de Joybert before her marriage and Joybert de Vaudreuil afterwards), wife of Philippe de RIGAUD, Marquis de Vaudreuil, governor of New France from 1703 to 1725; mother of 11 children including Pierre*, last governor of New France and the first native-born Canadian to hold that office, and François-Pierre*, governor of Montreal from 1757 to 1760; under-governess of the children of the Duc de Berry; born at Jemseg in Acadia, 18 Aug. 1673; d. in Paris in January 1740.

She was the daughter of Pierre de Joybert* de Soulanges et de Marson, officer in the Carignan-Salières regiment and afterwards a seigneur and administrator in Acadia. Her mother was Marie-Françoise Chartier, daughter of Louis-Théandre Chartier* de Lotbinière, lieutenant general of the provost's court at Quebec. When Joybert died in 1678 his widow moved to Quebec with her son and daughter. Her husband had left her practically penniless but she was fortunately rescued by the government which granted her a pension of 300 *livres*.

Louise-Élisabeth was educated at the Ursuline convent in Quebec. On 21 Nov. 1690, in that city, she married Philippe de Rigaud de Vaudreuil, the commander of the Canadian troops. According to the marriage contract, a dowry of 12,000 *livres* was guaranteed to the bride and a sum of 5,000 *livres* was presented to the groom by his mother-in-law. Because of this marriage, there was some hesitation about naming Vaudreuil governor of New France in 1703. It was feared that his colonial ties and his wife's numerous Canadian relatives would make it impossible for him to rule impartially.

In 1709 Madame de Vaudreuil sailed for France aboard the *Bellone*, despite the hazards of war-time navigation and the scant safety a merchantman of 120 tons provided. The many difficulties her husband was then experiencing in his public and his private life apparently explain her precipitate departure. The War of the Spanish Succession was entering a crucial stage, and more soldiers and equipment were needed in the colony to resist a possible English attack. The governor's relations with the intendants, JACQUES and ANTOINE-DENIS RAUDOT had deteriorated, and their criticism of his administration could dispose the minister unfavourably towards him. Then there were lawsuits over the Vaudreuil estates in Languedoc, and sons whose careers required looking after. For all these reasons Vaudreuil needed someone at Versailles to take charge of his interests and to explain and defend his policy to the minister. In view of the active social role played by women in New France, the choice of his wife to fill this position is not surprising.

Madame de Vaudreuil was most successful at Versailles. She soon won the friendship of Jérôme de Pontchartrain, the minister of Marine, and this powerful figure thereafter took a personal interest in the fortunes of her family. The Marquise was appointed under-governess of the children of the Duc de Berry, the third son of the Grand Dauphin, in 1712. In that same year her husband was made commander of the order of Saint-Louis. Her sons won promotions in the army and the navy. She also made clever political use of her influence by recommending various Canadians for appointments and advancement. In this manner she surrounded herself and her husband with a network of clients. Finally, she was allowed to examine the complaints Pontchartrain received against Vaudreuil and was thus able to identify the latter's enemies and to uncover plots and intrigues against him.

Old foes watched with helpless anger while she consolidated the governor's position. "She controls all the positions in Canada," wrote RUETTE d'Auteuil, Vaudreuil's old *bête noire*. "She writes magnificent letters from all sorts of places to the seaports about the power she can exert over him [Pontchartrain] for their benefit or detriment; she offers her protection, she threatens to use her influence; what is even more certain . . . is that she causes great fear and imposes silence on most of those who could speak against her husband." Denis RIVERIN, another malcontent, moaned: "At present everything is in a wretched state; a mere woman is in control, to the same extent when she is absent as when she is here."

The Marquise came back to the colony in 1721. Her circumstances had greatly changed since that day in 1709 when she had set out for France as an obscure colonial. She returned as a great lady voyaging aboard the king's vessel in the comfort of the captain's quarters, with two of her daughters, their governess, and a chambermaid. Her character also had changed during those years. Those who had known her earlier had praised her modesty. According to the bishop of Quebec, she now wore the air of a person of importance and power.

She returned to France briefly in 1723 when a new minister, Jean-Frédéric de Maurepas, replaced the council of Marine which had administered the colonies since the death of Louis XIV. Apparently she wanted to make certain that the fortunes of her family would not suffer from this change of régime. She was back in the colony the following year but returned to France permanently in the fall of 1725, shortly after the death of her husband.

Madame de Vaudreuil took up residence in Paris where she was reunited with her mother and three of her sons. Her husband had left little money but the government granted her a pension of 3,000 *livres* and also paid her a rent of 1,500 *livres* for the use of her house in Montreal. With this income and additional revenues derived from the Vaudreuil estates in Languedoc, she appears to have lived in modest comfort with her two unmarried daughters. She remained in touch with her Canadian friends and continued to take an active interest in the careers of her sons. She died in January 1740 after a brief illness.

She was an intelligent and extremely ambitious person who devoted her best energies to furthering the fortunes of her family. To her belongs a good part of the credit for the successful careers of Vaudreuil and his sons.

YVES F. ZOLTVANY

Archives de la Haute-Garonne (Toulouse), Commune de Revel, BB.13 (administration communale). AJQ, Greffe de François Genaple, 19 nov. 1690. AN, Col., B, 27, 32, 34, 44, 55; C^{11A}, 21–49; D^{2D}, carton 1; Marine, B^1, B^2, C^7. "Correspondance de Vaudreuil," APQ *Rapport, 1942–43; 1946–47*. Juchereau, *Annales* (Jamet), 346, 399f. "Lettres et mémoires de F.-M.-F. Ruette d'Auteuil," APQ *Rapport, 1922–23*, 50. [Louis de Rouvroy de Saint-Simon], *Mémoires complets et authentiques du duc de Saint-Simon sur le siècle de Louis XIV et la Régence* (21v., Paris, 1929), X, 399.

Guy Frégault, *Le grand marquis, Pierre de Rigaud de Vaudreuil et la Louisiane* (Montréal, 1952). F. M. Hammang, *The Marquis de Vaudreuil, New France at the beginning of the eighteenth century* (Bruges, 1938). P.-G. Roy, *La famille de Rigaud de Vaudreuil* (Lévis, 1938); *La ville de Québec*, II, 24f. *Les Ursulines de Québec* (1863–1866), I, 484. Guy Frégault, "Un cadet de Gascogne: Philippe de Rigaud de Vaudreuil," *RHAF*, V (1951–52), 15–44; "Politique et politiciens au début du XVIIIe siècle," *Ecrits du Canada français* (Montréal), XI (1961), 91–208. Henri Têtu, "Le chapitre de la cathédrale de Québec et ses délégués en France (1723–1773)," *BRH*, XVI (1910), 194, 232, 269f.

JUCHEREAU DE LA FERTÉ, DENIS-JOSEPH, half-pay lieutenant; baptized 20 June 1661 at Quebec, son of Jean Juchereau* de La Ferté and Marie Giffard; died a bachelor; buried 9 Aug. 1709 at Quebec.

La Ferté's presence among the fur-traders of Lake Superior in the autumn of 1683 is referred to in a letter of 12 April 1684 from DANIEL GREYSOLON Dulhut to Governor Le Febvre* de La Barre. La Ferté went down again to Quebec the following spring, no doubt, since he took part in the governor's expedition against the Senecas. He is mentioned as captain of the Cap-Rouge militiamen at the review which was held on 14 Aug. 1684 at Fort Frontenac. On 7 Aug. 1685 he took on Laurent Glory for a journey to the Ottawa country; in 1686 he was to be found at Michilimackinac, whence he was preparing to return to Quebec. He was apparently a member of BRISAY de Denonville's expedition against the Senecas in 1687, which included "La Ferté's company." It was apparently to this Juchereau that Buade* de Frontenac, on 15 Oct. 1691, gave a commission as a half-pay lieutenant.

At the beginning of 1694, La Ferté, together with JEAN-BAPTISTE LE MOYNE de Martigny, a cousin of PIERRE LE MOYNE d'Iberville, and some other officers, was accused of disturbing the peace in Lower Town at Quebec. In the same year he went with Louis Jolliet* on a voyage of exploration to Labrador. He turns up as a midshipman on the *Wesp* in 1697; this was one of the five ships that Iberville was taking that year to regain Fort Nelson, in Hudson Bay. In the spring of the following year La Ferté was sent from France as a messenger to warn Frontenac of the preparations being made by New England against Canada.

There is no further mention of him until 1703, at which time he had a quarrel with an ensign named Noël Chartrain, to whom he administered a severe thrashing. An affair of this kind, between officers, was fairly serious. RIGAUD de Vaudreuil, who was leaving for Montreal at that time, ordered the king's lieutenant, Antoine de CRISAFY, to put Juchereau in prison. The next day Crisafy, on the request of his wife, who was the prisoner's cousin, set him free. Vaudreuil had to imprison him again on his return, thus rousing the ire of the attorney general, François de RUETTE d'Auteuil, and of the latter's son-in-law Crisafy. PAUL DUPUY de Lisloye, the lieutenant of the provost court of Quebec, presided at the trial. Chartrain thought Juchereau's sentence too lenient, and the king allowed an appeal to be made to the Conseil Supérieur, provided that the judges were not related to the defendant. But in 1705 Vaudreuil was able to write that the incident was considered closed. Meanwhile, La Ferté had served as lieutenant to MOREL de La Durantaye, who was in command of the *Joybert*, a brigantine which had been fitted out at Quebec in 1704 for privateering against the English in Newfoundland.

Denis-Joseph Juchereau was never more than a subaltern officer, and apart from his escapades he scarcely attracted any attention. At his death he was buried at the Hôtel-Dieu of Quebec, as were several members of his family.

LUCIEN CAMPEAU

"Correspondance de Vaudreuil," APQ *Rapport, 1938–39*, 22–23, 86. *Découvertes et établissements des Français* (Margry), VI, 44. "Estat des employs vaquans ausquels Monsieur le comte de Frontenac . . . a pourvu en l'année 1691 en attendant les commissions de sa majesté," *BRH*, XIII (1907), 341. "Journal de Louis Jolliet allant à la descouverte de Labrador, 1694," APQ *Rapport, 1943–44*, 195f. P.-G. Roy, *Inv. coll. pièces jud. et not.*, I, 281. Bonnault, "Le Canada militaire," 376. J.-B.-A. Ferland, *Cours d'histoire du Canada (1534–1759)* (2ᵉ éd., 2v., Québec, 1882), II, 190. P.-G. Roy, *La famille Juchereau Duchesnay*, 54–56; *Fils de Québec*, I, 63–65; "Un corsaire canadien: Jean Léger de La Grange," *BRH*, XXIV (1918), 65f.

JUCHEREAU DE LA FERTÉ, JEANNE-FRANÇOISE, *dite* **de Saint-Ignace**, superior of the Religious Hospitallers of the Hôtel-Dieu at Quebec and author of *Les Annales de l'Hôtel-Dieu de Québec, 1636–1716*; b. at Quebec on 1 May 1650, the daughter of Jean Juchereau* de La Ferté, and of Marie Giffard; d. 14 Jan. 1723.

Her religious name was given her by her aunt, Mother Marie-Françoise Giffard*, *dite* Marie de Saint-Ignace, who had called the six-and-a-half year-old girl to her deathbed to bless her and to impress upon her that one day she would take her place at the Hôtel-Dieu. Jeanne-Françoise set aside her mother's dissuasion and prevailed on her to take her to Bishop LAVAL to receive his blessing before entering the monastery on 22 April 1662. She was too young to be accepted as a novice but was permitted to remain as a boarder. Two years later she assumed the novice's white veil and her religious name of Saint-Ignace.

On 8 March 1670 she was named by Bishop Laval to her first position of responsibility within the community; she became trustee of the alms for the poor. She was named trustee for the entire community on 14 Oct. 1673. Her responsibilities increased rapidly: on 1 Dec. 1676 she was appointed assistant to the ailing superior, Mother Marie-Renée de la Nativité; on 19 Dec. 1680 she was elected mistress of the novices for a three-year term; then on 13 Dec. 1683 she was elected superior of her monastery although she was only 33 years old. She was superior for a total of 24 years and assistant for another 12 years.

While superior of the Hôtel-Dieu Mother Juchereau encouraged piety and self-sacrifice, steadfastly promoted policies she believed to be in the best interests of the sisters, and defended orthodoxy. Under her direction, devotions to the Sacred Heart of Mary were introduced in the monastery in 1690, a cult sponsored in France by Jean Eudes and approved in the colony by her counsellors, Bishop Laval and the Abbé Henri de Bernières*. On her re-election as superior in March 1702 she instituted the custom of kissing the feet and hands of the Virgin's statue in recognition of her honorary role as first superior of the community. When the Ursulines were without lodgings Mother Juchereau invited them to share the facilities of the Hôtel-Dieu and personally accompanied them to their new convent when it was completed. Her labours during the epidemics of influenza, measles, and fevers which ravaged New France in 1688 drew high commendation from Governor BRISAY de Denonville. These labours were to be repeated during the epidemics of 1703 and 1711. Her kindness and charity were demonstrated in the hospitality extended to Sarah Garrish, an English girl ransomed from the Abenakis who had killed her family and enslaved her, and to a renegade Benedictine. She was scandalized, however, when

Juchereau de Maur

she discovered the latter held Jansenist views and she quickly rose to the defence of orthodoxy. In 1694 she asked the bishop to remove the Abbé André de Merlac* as counsellor because of his Jansenism and misconduct, and again in 1718 she warned her sisters against the "venom of heresy."

One incident may serve to illustrate her willingness to defend her monastery against whatever she considered detrimental to its development. In 1692 Bishop Saint-Vallier [LA CROIX] suggested that the Hospitallers assume charge of the Hôpital Général founded at the former Recollet monastery of Notre-Dame-des-Anges one league from Quebec [see MARGUERITE BOURDON]. Mother Juchereau refused, saying her sisters were called to minister to the sick in Quebec, not elsewhere. When ordered by Versailles to comply she nevertheless did so with good grace and accompanied four sisters (April 1693) to the Hôpital Général, where she remained for a week assisting in its organization. In 1699 Saint-Vallier called for the services of 12 Hospitallers at the Hôpital Général and requested an annual annuity of 1,200 *livres* for this purpose. When Mother Juchereau again refused to cooperate he manipulated the elections of 20 March to prevent her obtaining any office. Resentment built up between the sisters in the Hôtel-Dieu and those in the Hôpital Général, institutions which were separated on 7 April 1699. Mother Juchereau appealed to the minister of Marine through the good offices of the retired Bishop Laval. In the more peaceful elections of 1700 she was chosen assistant and shortly thereafter communications from France indicated Pontchartrain supported her in her quarrel with Bishop Saint-Vallier. She then played a key role in bringing about a reconciliation between the sisters at the Hôtel-Dieu and those at the Hôpital Général.

Shortly after her election as superior for an eighth term in 1713 Mother Juchereau was struck down by a high fever and paralysis which kept her bed-ridden for years. She was increasingly troubled by catarrh until her death in January 1723. Though reduced to physical inactivity she employed some of the time between 1716 and 1722 in dictating to Mother Régnard* Duplessis de Sainte-Hélène a general history of the monastery and of the colony to 1716. Her *Histoire de l'Hôtel-Dieu de Québec* was published at Montauban in 1751 and republished as *Les Annales de l'Hôtel-Dieu de Québec, 1636–1716* in Quebec in 1939. This important primary source for 17th century history provides details about certain personalities and events not found elsewhere, yet is strangely silent on other points.

Mother Juchereau was devout, intelligent, methodical in her work, and as Denonville observed, "very reasonable, of admirable wisdom and conduct." She was the first Canadian-born superior of her order and the most outstanding member of the second generation of these sisters. Her portrait is at the Hôtel-Dieu in Quebec.

C. J. JAENEN

AHDQ, Lettres, I; Mélanges, IX. AN, Col., C¹¹ᴬ, 7. Juchereau et Duplessis, *Histoire de l'Hôtel-Dieu de Québec*; *Annales* (Jamet). Le Jeune, *Dictionnaire. The Macmillan Dictionary of Canadian Biography*, ed. W. S. Wallace (Toronto, 1963). Casgrain, *Histoire de l'Hôtel-Dieu de Québec*.

JUCHEREAU DE MAUR, PAUL-AUGUSTIN, receiving-agent of the Compagnie de la Colonie de la Nouvelle-France; b. 13 June 1658 at Quebec; d. 1714 at sea.

Paul-Augustin Juchereau was the second son of Jean Juchereau* de La Ferté, seigneur of Maur, member of the Conseil Souverain, and of Marie Giffard, daughter of the seigneur of Beauport. He was the brother of DENIS-JOSEPH JUCHEREAU de La Ferté and JEANNE-FRANÇOISE JUCHEREAU de La Ferté, *dite* de Saint-Ignace, the superior and annalist of the Hôtel-Dieu of Quebec.

He received a remarkable education for the time, and went in for business. His elder brother, Noël, having entered the Jesuit order, in 1685 Paul-Augustin received the seigneury of Maur from his father. This seigneury, of 50 acres, also called Saint-Augustin, was situated near Quebec.

Paul-Augustin went to France in 1700 along with Sieur PASCAUD, to try and obtain freedom of trade for Canadians. He was involved in the creation of the Compagnie de la Colonie, for on 13 July 1701 the company delivered to Juchereau a commission as an "agent appointed to receive the beaver pelts and the tenth part of the moose hides"; he held this position until his death.

When WALKER's fleet broke up on Île-aux-Oeufs in 1711, the poets, Mother Saint-Ignace tells us, exhausted their imagination in putting this shipwreck into verse of every kind and shape. Some of the poems and songs have been preserved in the archives of the Hôtel-Dieu of Quebec including one by Paul-Augustin.

In the autumn of 1714 Juchereau sailed for France on board the *Saint-Jérôme*, which sank near Sable Island. There were only two survivors of this shipwreck; Paul-Augustin perished in it, together with the captain, Lechtier (Lechter) de Chalus, the Marquis d'ALOIGNY, commander of the troops, and François Dumontier, secretary to the Marquis Philippe de RIGAUD de Vaudreuil.

Paul-Augustin, who had remained a bachelor, had bequeathed his possessions to his nephew,

FRANÇOIS AUBERT de La Chesnaye, Sieur de Mille-Vaches, who inherited the seigneury and title of Maur.

ANTONIO DROLET

AN, Col., C¹¹A, 35. *Jug. et délib.* P.-G. Roy, *Inv. coll. pièces jud. et not.*, I, 281; II, 309. Azarie Couillard Després, *La première famille française au Canada, ses alliés et ses descendants* (Montréal, 1906). Hugolin [Stanislaus Lemay], *Vieux papiers, vieilles chansons* (Montréal, 1936). P.-G. Roy, *La famille Juchereau Duchesnay.* E. C. Bailly, "Additional notes on the French-Canadian background of a Minnesota pioneer: Alexis Bailly," *BRH*, LX (1954), 166. Mme Pierre Montagne, "Robert Giffard, futur seigneur de Beauport," SGCF *Mémoires*, XVII (1936), 34. P.-G. Roy, "Paul-Augustin Juchereau de Maure," *BRH*, XXIX (1923), 81; "La seigneurie de Maur ou Saint-Augustin," *BRH*, IX (1903), 83.

JUCHEREAU DE SAINT-DENIS, CHARLOTTE-FRANÇOISE DE, *dite* Comtesse de Saint-Laurent, daughter of Nicolas Juchereau* de Saint-Denis and Marie-Thérèse Giffard; baptized 4 Feb. 1660 at Quebec; d. 28 Dec. 1732 at Quebec and buried on 30 December.

On 27 Feb. 1702 Charlotte-Françoise, acting with the king's approval, purchased for the sum of 41,333 *livres* in French currency the Île d'Orléans, which had been sold by Bishop LAVAL in 1675 to François Berthelot, king's secretary. When he had been ennobled, Berthelot had managed to have the island raised to the countship of Saint-Laurent. When she had acquired possession of the island, Charlotte-Françoise Juchereau took the title of countess, which she retained after her marriage with La Forest [DAUPHIN]. She arranged for her eldest son, born a Pachot by her first marriage, to bear the title also. Having been unable to meet her obligations to Berthelot, however, she had to engage in long legal proceedings, both in Canada and in France, to which she made several trips, and she proved to be a stubborn litigant. Her long struggle in the courts lasted from 1704 to 1713. Having exhausted legal means without success, she abandoned her proceedings only when the king ordered her explicitly to do so, and to return to Canada. The case, which was finally decided in Berthelot's favour, seems to have contributed to the dismissal of RUETTE d'Auteuil, the countess's brother-in-law, who had taken up her defence against RAUDOT.

A large number of notarial acts drawn up between 1698 and 1704 show that Charlotte-Françoise Juchereau was an energetic and enterprising businesswoman. Having obtained separate maintenance from La Forest in 1702, with his authorization in due form to act on his behalf, she continued to carry out transactions of all kinds (sales, purchases, loans, borrowings, ship charters, building contracts) in her own name and through straw men; the sums involved were at times considerable. Meanwhile she kept a careful watch over her children's interests. Nevertheless, she was sometimes in financial straits: in 1704, to honour a debt she owed PIERRE LE MOYNE d'Iberville, she had to sell all her personal goods located on her properties on Île d'Orléans; in 1705 she sold to René Lepage, the seigneur of Rimouski, her fief on the Métis River, which she had inherited from her first husband.

On 17 Dec. 1680, she had married at Beauport François Viennay-Pachot*, a seigneur and businessman left a widower by the death of Jeanne Avamy; Charlotte-Françoise bore him 16 children. On 11 Nov. 1702 she was married again, this time to Captain Dauphin de La Forest.

Charlotte-Françoise earned for herself an unflattering reputation: Portchartrain considered her a "dangerous woman," whereas Raudot called her a "haughty and capricious" merchant who thought that as a countess she could do anything she wished. "People might perhaps have forgiven her vanity and her usurping of the title of countess," he added, "if she had at least paid her bills."

ANTONIO DROLET

Charlevoix, *Histoire* (1744), I, 465. *Jug. et délib.* PAC *Report, 1899*, 213. Tanguay, *Dictionnaire*, I, 328, 457. P.-G. Roy, *La famille Juchereau Duchesnay.* P.-B. Casgrain, "Une autre maison Montcalm à Québec (1759)," *BRH*, VIII (1902), 329–40. Ignotus [Thomas Chapais], "Notes et souvenirs," *La Presse* (Montréal), 5, 19 avril 1902. "Les Juchereau Duchesnay," *BRH*, XXXVIII (1932), 409. P.-G. Roy, "La famille Viennay-Pachot," *BRH*, XXI (1915), 336–42.

JUCHEREAU DE SAINT-DENYS, CHARLES, (known between 1689 and 1698 as the Sieur de **Beaumarchais),** lieutenant and captain in the colonial regular troops, first lieutenant general of the royal jurisdiction of Montreal, receiver of beaver for the Compagnie de la Colonie [*see* CHARLES AUBERT de La Chesnaye], trader, entrepreneur, founder of a tannery on the Ohio River; b. 6 Dec. 1655, baptized 25 December at Quebec, second of 12 children of Nicolas Juchereau* de Saint-Denis and Marie-Thérèse Giffard; d. 27 Aug. 1703 in the Illinois country.

On 21 April 1692 Charles Juchereau married Thérèse-Denise Migeon (1678–1748), daughter of Jean-Baptiste Migeon* de Branssat. They had five children. The Branssat family connections soon worked to good effect; on the death in 1693 of Jean-Baptiste, who had been nominated first royal judge of Montreal, Saint-Denys, an officer in the

Juchereau de Saint-Denys

same company as ALPHONSE TONTY and PIERRE LEGARDEUR de Repentigny, was recommended as "one of the most capable persons who might be chosen" for the newly created office.

One advantage of this position was that it afforded a knowledge of the fur trade, in which Saint-Denys was becoming a leading figure. Though complaining of his limited revenue, Saint-Denys, with his wife and his sister, CHARLOTTE-FRANÇOISE JUCHEREAU, made frequent loans to western traders; in 1693 they loaned 6,996 *livres* to HENRI TONTY and DAUPHIN de La Forest. Stricter regulation of this trade in 1696 made it necessary for Saint-Denys to obtain leave from his duties as judge to represent the merchants in Paris in 1699. He returned the following year to help found the Compagnie du Canada for the export of furs, and became receiver of beaver at a salary of 6,000 *livres*—a vast increase over his stipend as judge. [*See* Antoine PASCAUD.] Further regulations again brought Saint-Denys to Paris in 1700 to protest the royal policies. Instead of relief for his associates, however, he secured a concession, largely through the influence of the Comtesse de Saint-Pierre, to establish a tannery on the lower Ohio.

Saint-Denys did not fail to capitalize on a growing awareness of this area's enormous strategic significance. The Tennessee (Rivière des Cheraquis), Cumberland, Ohio (Belle Rivière), and Mississippi Rivers all flowed together there, with the Wabash (Ouabache) and Missouri not far away. French trappers were already trading illicitly with the English, exposing the fragile settlements of the Mississippi Valley to the imperial designs of the British. The minister of Marine was being urged by many to fortify the area, settle it, or at least police it. Juchereau's establishment would discourage Anglo-French contacts, promote Indian alliances, and possibly become a real asset to the colony. In his search for profit he nonetheless would be serving the royal interests, since he promised that he had not fruitlessly devoted 25 years "to learning the means of establishing a colony and making it a success."

The concession granted to Juchereau carried several conditions. He was permitted to secure any skins for tanning or bleaching except beaver; violation of this clause would mean forfeiture of the concession. He might be absent from his judgeship for three years, selecting two agents to remain behind and supply the expedition or to go in his place. He could take 24 men in 8 canoes, with all necessary supplies, including brandy for his men but not for sale to the Indians. Tan-yards and buildings could be erected wherever necessary. He could mine any deposits of lead or copper. A chaplain approved by the bishop of Quebec or by his vicar general was to go with the expedition.

The scheme drew prolonged objections from Juchereau's colleagues in the Compagnie du Canada, who, perhaps from personal experience, predicted the many abuses he could practise. They complained that the new agreement would "complete their ruin," and urged that the Illinois country not be included as part of Louisiana. PIERRE LE MOYNE d'Iberville, however, who was married to Juchereau's niece, welcomed this increase in his sphere of influence, and even sent soldiers to assist the venture.

In debt by some 40,000 *livres*, Saint-Denys left Montreal with his party on 18 May 1702, and reached Illinois by way of Michilimackinac and the country of the Fox and Mascouten Indians late in the year. At Kaskaskia he secured the services of Jean MERMET as chaplain, and was criticized by a missionary to the Kaskaskias, Father PIERRE-GABRIEL MAREST: "Monsieur Jucherau is prodigal of his promises, but he thinks, in reality, of his own interests."

The party quickly established communications with Louisiana and engaged Mascoutens, and possibly some local coureurs de bois, as hunters. They built a fort about two leagues from the mouth of the Ohio, the exact site of which is not known, although several suggestions have been put forward. They probably established posts throughout the vicinity; one may have been on the site of Fort Massac (1757–1814), and the legend of a massacre at this place may have had its origins in some misfortune dating from Juchereau's time.

With Saint-Denys' death in 1703, perhaps from the epidemic that swept the Mascouten tribe as well as Louisiana, the venture disintegrated. François PHILIPPE de Mandeville, one of the survivors, attempted to salvage an accumulation of several thousand skins—including buffalo, deer, bear, roebuck, panther, and wolf—but many were stolen by the Indians, damaged by moths, or lost in a sudden flooding of the river.

Some 30 survivors of the epidemic finally descended to Mobile; but others joined the unlicensed bands roaming the colony, and some even requested passage to France for their furs. In 1704 Le Moyne* de Bienville complained that the Indians were killing those who remained, and stated that they were "very good men, suitable for this country" if they would only settle somewhere. Apparently they never did, but the idea of a tannery intrigued French officials for many years, and various sites of the "ancien fort ruiné" appeared on maps for decades.

Juchereau's brother Louis* was in charge of the tannery after the departure of Mandeville; Louis had come to Louisiana with Iberville and was prominent in its affairs until his death. Juchereau's son, Joseph-Charles (1696–1765), may have accompanied Louis on an expedition to Mexico.

Saint-Denys was probably sincere in wishing to establish a permanent French settlement, as well as a tannery for quick profits. Had he been successful he would have served the colony as well as himself; a firm nucleus of French power in the Illinois country at that time might have drastically altered the course of empire west of the Alleghenies.

JOHN FORTIER

AN, Col., B, 22, ff.264v–65v; C[11A], 36, ff.402–3, 411–12; C[13A], 1, ff.241–42, 449–64v; C[13B], 1. Charlevoix, *History* (Shea). "Correspondance de Frontenac (1689–99)," APQ *Rapport, 1927–28*, 178; *1928–29*, 380. *Découvertes et établissements des Français* (Margry), IV, 478–79, 487, 586–92, 625–31; V, 349–68, 425–26, 438–39. *Documents relating to Canadian currency during the French period* (Shortt). Ill. State Hist. Lib. Coll., XXIII. *JR* (Thwaites), LXV, LXVI. "Un mémoire de Le Roy de La Potherie sur la Nouvelle-France adressé à M. de Pontchartrain, 1701–1702," *BRH*, XXII (1916), 214–16. *MPA* (Rowland and Sanders). *NYCD* (O'Callaghan and Fernow), IX. Recensement du Canada, 1666 (APQ *Rapport*), 61. *DCB*, I. É.-Z. Massicotte, "La famille Juchereau de Beaumarchais et de Saint-Denis," *BRH*, XXXVI (1930), 528–29; "Répertoire des engagements pour l'Ouest," 206–7. Tanguay, *Dictionnaire*.

Alvord, *Illinois country*. Giraud, *Histoire de la Louisiane française*, I, II, III. P.-G. Roy, *La famille Juchereau Duchesnay*. N. W. Caldwell, "Charles Juchereau de St. Denys: a French pioneer in the Mississippi valley," *Mississippi Valley Hist. Review*, XXVIII (1942), 563–80; "Fort Massac during the French and Indian war," Ill. State Hist. Soc. *J.*, XLIII (1950), 100–19. [Both articles by Caldwell may be considered definitive; the one on Fort Massac is the first of a series of three.] J.-J. Lefebvre, "La succession de Charles Juchereau de Saint-Denis (1655–1703), premier juge royal de Montréal (1693)," APQ *Rapport, 1959–60*, 233–73. P.-G. Roy, "Charles Juchereau de Saint-Denys," *BRH*, XXXII (1926), 441–42.

JUCHEREAU DUCHESNAY, IGNACE (originally from Du Chesné-Vidame, department of Eure-et-Loir), seigneur of Beauport; b. 3 Aug.

1658; d. 7 April 1715, and was buried at Beauport the next day.

Juchereau Duchesnay was the third child of Nicolas Juchereau* and Marie-Thérèse Giffard. On 24 Feb. 1683, at Beauport, he married Marie-Catherine Peuvret, daughter of Jean-Baptiste Peuvret* Demesnu, chief clerk and secretary of the Conseil Souverain, and seigneur. By this marriage he had 17 children. Through him the name of the Juchereaus has been perpetuated in Canada.

On 17 Feb. 1683, the very day that his marriage contract was signed, Juchereau Duchesnay inherited the Beauport seigneury from his uncle Joseph Giffard; he did not, however, exercise his rights to it until 1689. He caused his domain to prosper, and it remained in his family until the end of the seigneurial régime. On 6 Oct. 1704, before the Canadian courts, he lost a lengthy action which he had brought against the Jesuits, with the aim of having corrections made to the boundary between the seigneuries of Notre-Dame-des-Anges and Beauport, as it had been set in the time of Huault* de Montmagny.

In February 1684, in command of the Beauport militia, he took part in the ill-starred expedition of Le Febvre* de La Barre against the Iroquois and showed himself to be a man of courage.

Juchereau Duchesnay is thought by P.-G. Roy to have been PIERRE LE MOYNE d'Iberville's companion on the 1686 expedition to Hudson Bay, under the orders of the Chevalier de Troyes*.

Louis XIV appointed him to the Conseil Supérieur in 1705, but for reasons still unknown he refused to sit on it, and his appointment was given to Michel SARRAZIN two years later.

His wife survived him, living until 15 Feb. 1739, and several of his descendants had distinguished careers in Canada and abroad.

LUCIEN CAMPEAU

Chevalier de Troyes, *Journal* (Caron). P.-G. Roy, *Inv concessions*, I, 33; *Inv. contrats de mariage*, III, 269. Bonnault, "Le Canada militaire," 392–94. P.-G. Roy, *La famille Juchereau Duchesnay*, 175–78. J.-E. Roy, "Les conseillers au Conseil souverain de la Nouvelle-France," *BRH*, I (1895), 178.

K

KAJNQUIRATITON, KANAHARIGHTON (Kanakarighton). *See* CAGENQUARICHTEN

KATALOUIBOIS. *See* KOUTAOILIBOE

KELSEY, HENRY, explorer, mariner, and overseas governor of the HBC; b. *c.* 1667; d. 1724.

Kelsey's reputation rests securely on his journey to the Canadian plains in 1690–92, but this achievement should not be allowed to eclipse his versatility or the solid contributions he made to establishing the HBC. In nearly 40 years of service Kelsey played a part in most of the major events in Hudson Bay. Between 1684 and 1722, there were only three complete years (1704, 1705, and 1713) in which he was absent from the bay. He went out from England for the HBC six times (in 1684, 1694, 1696, 1698, 1706, and 1714); he was twice a prisoner of the French when York Fort was taken, and twice present when it was recovered. He served at Albany when that was the only post in the HBC's possession, and he helped to develop the East Main trade. He was in the first party which tried to settle at Churchill River (1689) and he contributed to the later and sucessful establishment of a post there. He had a rare understanding of Indian languages.

Nothing is known for certain of Kelsey's parentage. A Thomas Kelsey served as an officer in the Parliamentary army and was a major-general of militia in 1655 (*DNB*); another Thomas Kelsey, goldsmith of London, briefly held stock in the HBC in 1679. The likeliest person to have been Henry's father is John Kelsey of East Greenwich, mariner, who died in 1674 and who may have been "one Kelsy, a commander of a fire-ship," mentioned by Pepys (*Diary*, ed. H. B. Wheatley (10v., London, 1898–99), VII, 180). John Kelsey left three sons of whom the first-named was Henry. Our identification rests chiefly on the East Greenwich connexion, for this is where Henry Kelsey's wife came from, where his children were baptized, where he owned two houses, and where he himself died and was buried. A difficulty that has not been resolved, however, is that if Henry Kelsey was the eldest son named in John Kelsey's will he must have been born not later than the summer of 1667, John, the second-named, being baptized on 24 May 1668 (o.s.). This means that when the HBC committee wrote in 1688 of "the Boy Henry Kelsey" (a soubriquet picked up and used by modern writers) he had already reached the age of 21.

Kelsey was apprenticed to the HBC for a term of four years on 15 March 1684. The suggestion has been made that this was his second period of service with the company, the first having run from 1677 to 1684. Kelsey certainly was apprenticed to someone in 1677 for his indenture of that year was in the HBC's possession in 1683. It does not however follow that he must have joined the company at the age of 10: he and his indenture may have been taken over (in or before 1683) from a former master. Even if he joined at an earlier date it is unlikely that he had served in the Bayside ports before he sailed with Captain John Outlaw* in the *Lucy* on 6 May 1684.

Kelsey was posted to the fort at Nelson River which was later resited and styled York Fort. A few weeks after his arrival the place was unsuccessfully attacked by the French, but nothing is recorded of Kelsey's part in the action. The first event which he thought worth entering in his own "Memorandum of my abode in hudsons bay" took place in the winter of 1688–89 when he carried letters (which Indians had failed to get through) from York to New Severn. On the round trip, which took a month, Kelsey was accompanied by an Indian boy. But even before this exploit Kelsey was known to the HBC committee in London as "a very active Lad Delighting much in Indians Compa., being never better pleased than when hee is Travelling amongst them."

In this same dispatch Kelsey was detailed to go with a party to Churchill River, and in the early summer of 1689 the expedition set out from York. Having landed men to build a factory at Churchill, Captain James Young* with Kelsey aboard tried to sail the *Hopewell* north along the coast, and it is at this point that the earliest journal in *The Kelsey papers* begins, "A Journal of a voyage & Journey undertaken by Henry Kelsey to discover & Endeavour to bring to a Commerce ye nothern Indians Inhabiting to ye Northward of Churchill River & also ye dogside Nation." From 17 to 26 June 1689 the *Hopewell*, hampered by ice, made only 20 leagues. Kelsey now suggested to Young that he and an Indian boy (the companion of the previous winter) should try their luck ashore. By his own computation Kelsey and the boy marched 138 miles in a northerly direction, inland but not far from the coast. From almost every point of view the trip was a failure. The going was hilly and stony; musk-ox were seen and described in the journal but game proved scarce; Indian litter was found but no Indians. Worst of all, the boy proved more hindrance than help, and was so apprehensive of danger that Kelsey turned back in disgust on 12 July. He travelled 142 miles back to the point where Young had put him ashore and a further 93 miles to Churchill River. The contrast between the disappointments of this march and the success of Kelsey's journey to the Plains in 1690 is striking. North of Churchill, Kelsey was hampered by his own inexperience but even more by a companion who seems not to have known where he was going. As he tells the story, Kelsey underwent no such traumatic experiences as befell Richard Norton* in these parts nearly 30 years later. But the record for 25 July 1689 suggests that this journey was something more than a country walk: "To day put from ye shore it being dreadfull to behold ye falls we had to pass Considering we had nothing to tye our Raft but small Logline & were forct to shoot 3 Desperate falls ye Raft struck upon two of ym but gott safely over."

Kelsey intended to return to England in 1686 but did not do so. The following summer, on 12 June 1690, he started from York on the journey for which he is chiefly remembered. Until the publication in 1929 of *The Kelsey papers*, the only contemporary account of this expedition was in the parliamentary report of 1749 when two (slightly different) versions of Kelsey's journal were presented to a committee of the House of Commons as evidence of the HBC's active interest in exploration. This journal covers only the period July to September 1691 when Kelsey was inland, and leaves it unclear where he went and with what object. The ambiguity enabled Joseph Robson*, a former employee of the HBC but in 1749 an opponent, to deny the authenticity of the journal and to propagate a version of Kelsey's travels which is far from the truth. Robson, claiming to rest his case on oral traditions in the bay, did not seek to impugn Kelsey personally: he admitted that there had been a journey and that Kelsey had acquitted himself well. But he denied that the expedition had been authorized, let alone ordered, by Governor George Geyer* at York. In Robson's tale Kelsey had run away from Geyer's ill treatment, travelled inland on his own initiative, communicated with Geyer by means of a letter written in charcoal on birchbark (having no proper writing materials), and finally turned up at York with an Indian wife. Thus Kelsey's exploit was construed to the company's discredit. *The Kelsey papers*, containing the author's own version of the 1691 journal and a rhymed prologue dealing with his departure from York in the summer of 1690, together with documentation from the HBC archives, put it altogether beyond doubt that Kelsey's mission was authorized and ordered by Geyer and was a reflection of the London committee's eagerness that such inland journeys should be made. Whether Robson's version was of his own invention or whether he took it in good faith from later traditions in the bay, it is impossible to say.

The main purpose of Kelsey's mission in Geyer's words was "to call, encourage, and invite, the remoter Indians to a Trade with us." Kelsey carried samples of the goods normally available at the bayside, including two long English guns, powder, shot, 20 pounds of Brazil tobacco, a brass kettle, beads, hatchets, a blanket, and a lace-coat. Next year Geyer sent up fresh supplies of the same sort. The HBC at this time was interested in ways of diversifying its trade so as to avoid an undue dependence on furs, and the orders sent to Kelsey in 1691 were to look for mines, minerals, and drugs. Probably his instructions included the pacification of Indian tribes, for war in the interior had long been recognized as a hindrance to trade. In any event Kelsey assumed the role of peacemaker. There is indeed no reason to question Geyer's summary at Kelsey's homecoming: "[he] travelled and endeavoured to keep the Peace among them according to my Order."

The direction taken by Kelsey was southwest from York, and he set out cheerfully (according to Geyer), but "with heavy heart" by his own account. The route from York was probably up Hayes River and Fox River to Moose Lake, the same followed by Anthony Henday* in 1754, but this suggestion has been criticized by Doughty and Martin, editors of *The Kelsey papers*. Less than a month after leaving the bayside Kelsey was "on ye borders of ye stone Indian Country," his estimated distance from York being 600 miles,

> Through Rivers wch run strong with falls
> thirty three Carriages five lakes in all.

(The above is a fair sample of Kelsey's crude verse in the prologue to his journal in *The Kelsey papers*. No explanation has been offered why he wrote in this way.) Here, on 10 July 1690, Kelsey took possession of the land for his masters, naming the spot "deerings point" after Sir Edward Dering, then deputy governor of the HBC. It is on the location of this place that much of the controversy concerning Kelsey's travels has turned. Three suggestions have been canvassed. The first, and least plausible, is Split Lake on Nelson River, which would effectively diminish Kelsey's achievement: this came from L. J. Burpee in 1908 and was virtually withdrawn by him in a later edition of *The search for the western sea* (1935). The second is Cedar Lake, north of Lake Winnipegosis (C. N. Bell). The third, and now most widely accepted, is a bend in the Saskatchewan River about twelve miles below The Pas, Manitoba (A. S. Morton and others). Kelsey appears not to have travelled far from Derings Point in the winter of 1690–91 and was back there by the spring:

> At deerings point after the frost
> I set up their a Certain Cross
> In token of my being there
> Cut out on it ye date of year
> And Likewise for to veryfie the same
> added to it my master sir Edward deerings name.

Kelsey reported to Geyer by letter and received from York fresh supplies and orders. Then on

Kelsey

15 July 1691 he set out from Derings Point "to discover & bring to a Commerce the Naywatame poets." Where he went can never be known with perfect certainty, despite the survival of his journal; but C. N. Bell's summary is the most circumstantial yet made and deserves quotation: "[Kelsey] ascended the Saskatchewan to the Carrot River at a point on which he abandoned his canoes and proceeded on foot, taking three days under starving conditions to pass through the muskeg country, extending for many miles south of the Saskatchewan River, then entered upon the first firm land, with its wild pigeons and moose, and farther south a more open prairie country which afforded an abundance of red deer, where he met the Eagle Creek Assiniboines, and proceeding on reached the Red Deer River, with its 'slate mines,' and, ascending that stream south south-west farther on came to the edge of the timber country, where before him stretched the Great Salt Plain, forty-six miles wide, extending east and west, and on which he met more of the Assiniboine Indians (these from the adjacent Thunder Hill district) he had journeyed so far to treat with, for he was indeed in 'the country of the Assiniboines.' That plain abounded with buffalo, and, crossing it, he again entered a wooded area and high champlain land, replete with ponds and lakes all inhabited by beaver, which was evidently the Touchwood Hills country." In the course of this journey, on 20 Aug. 1691, Kelsey recorded descriptions of the buffalo and grizzly bear, the first white man to do so in the Canadian west.

Kelsey met a large band of Stone or Mountain Indians (Assiniboines) on 25 August, and soon after he made contact with the "Naywatame" with a view to establishing peace between these two tribes according to Geyer's instructions. It is not certain who the "Naywatame" were: Burpee suggests "the Nodwayes or Sioux," and A. S. Morton the Gros Ventres (Atsinas). Kelsey reports his speeches and endeavours briefly and soberly. They were not on the whole successful; nor should it be expected that one young white man 1,000 miles from his friends would be able to heal tribal feuds. The "Naywatame" promised to meet Kelsey at Derings Point next spring and go with him to the Bayside, but fear of attack kept them away. Rich, who called the journey "both in its extent and in its consequences unique in the history of North America," admits Kelsey's failure as peacemaker. Kelsey may have spent the winter of 1691–92 south of the Saskatchewan or he may have gone back to Derings Point: the daily entries in his journal cease on 12 Sept. 1691. He returned to York in the summer of 1692 after an absence of two years. Geyer, who was evidently well pleased, reported Kelsey's arrival "with a good Fleet of Indians" in his letter to London of 9 Sept. 1692.

Such was Kelsey's exploration into the west. At times it was hard, and there may well have been dangers even if we discard with the rest of the fiction Robson's tale of Kelsey's killing two grizzly bears with two shots. Considered purely as a piece of pathfinding, the journey was a major achievement though Kelsey's journal is suggestive of his having travelled always in the company of Indians who knew what they were doing. To say this is not to diminish Kelsey's personal credit but rather to emphasize his outstanding talent for winning the confidence of the Indians whom he accompanied: this talent and a courageous spirit were the best assets for exploring North America. Harder to evaluate are the practical results of the journey. One must question its success as a diplomatic mission. Commercially, however, more may have been achieved; very likely trade at York was advanced, but by how much and for how long is impossible to say. In any case French occupation of York from 1694 to 1696 and from 1697 to 1714 must have reduced the benefits to the HBC. What is beyond dispute is that Kelsey's travels were a triumph of nerve, especially if set against the failure of others to follow his example. In more than half a century after Kelsey made his way to the plains, only two employees of the HBC—William STUART and Richard Norton—performed major inland journeys.

The version of Kelsey's journal in *The Kelsey papers* has an interesting appendix, "an Accot. of those Indians belief & Superstitions." Kelsey was no more anthropologist than he was poet; but perhaps his notes deserve to be regarded as the first "observations" of Indian life and religion by a HBC man, crudely prefiguring the "Observations" of James Isham* and Andrew Graham*.

After wintering at York, Kelsey returned to England; when his wages ceased on 12 Sept. 1693 he had completed nine years service in the bay. He re-enlisted on 25 April 1694, sailed with the summer shipping, and was back at York early in August. A letter written by him on 8 August contains the interesting declaration that "for my own part I shall neither do nor act on any discovery untill I receive further orders from my masters in England." These orders never came and Kelsey made no more inland journeys. This year, 1694, saw a successful French challenge in Hudson Bay: for all but one of the following 20 years York, an obvious starting-point for inland travel, was in French hands, and when the HBC got it back Kelsey was too senior to be spared.

When the ships left for home on 13 Aug. 1694

Kelsey began "A Journal of our wintering by gods assistance at hayes River in ye year of our Lord 1694." Only routine matters were recorded until 14 September when Indians brought news of two ships in the vicinity which proved to be French under PIERRE LE MOYNE d'Iberville. This journal is our principal source of information concerning the leisurely investment of York which followed. Though shots were exchanged on 16 September it was not until 3 October that the French got their mortar into position and were ready, if the English refused to give up the fort, to "reduce it to ashes & give us no quarter." Governor Thomas Walsh thereupon sent Kelsey and another to negotiate with Iberville, and the fort was surrendered on 4 October. There is reason to think that the English garrison—Kelsey included—was turned loose to winter "in the woods & deserts" before shipment to France the following year.

Kelsey and other survivors were back in England at the end of 1695 or early in 1696. His wages had ceased on the day York was given up (the HBC's usual practice) and he was probably short of money and glad to sign on once more on 18 May 1696 for a term of three years. The HBC was planning to recover York with the help of the Royal Navy, and Kelsey's prompt re-engagement and his appointment as third in succession to the governorship are signs that the London committee attached no blame to him for what they regarded as the base surrender of 1694. Kelsey sailed from Gravesend on 2 June 1696 in the *Royal Hudson's Bay* frigate (Capt. Michael GRIMINGTON), part of the mixed HBC and RN fleet. His journal (2 June to 19 July) describes the assembly and departure of this fleet and records speaking with a Swedish ship at sea, from whom the English squadron had news of Iberville. York was duly retaken but Kelsey's journal of this event—if he kept one—has not survived and nothing is known of his part in the action.

Now follows the longest journal in *The Kelsey papers*, though by no means the most interesting, 18 Sept. 1696 to 3 Sept. 1697. Little personal information is to be found in this record of a year's routine, similar to the many post-journals of later date in the HBC archives. It is indeed possible that this *is* a post-journal or draft or copy of one rather than a private document: Kelsey is sometimes mentioned as "Mr. Kelsey" instead of "I," and the record of events at York continues in the journal when Kelsey himself is absent from the fort. The journal closes with a near-repetition of the events of three years earlier. On 19 Aug. 1697 the French were sighted by Indians; on 31 August they landed close to the fort. Bombardment began and the call for surrender came on 2 September.

Governor Henry BALEY was for resistance and "drew up a paper & brought on ye platform to satisfie ye men they should have every one a years pay gratis if they would sign ye same & we kept ye fort." Some signed, others refused. Kelsey's journal reports the incident but without comment and with no indication of his own preference. Surrender was decided on; with two others, Kelsey again negotiated terms with Iberville. Baley's decision was the right one. Iberville in the *Pélican* had already beaten the English ships in the bay and the French force at York (if Kelsey's estimate of 900 is believed) was in overwhelming strength. So ended "a Tedious winter & tragical Journal by me Henry Kelsey." The prisoners appear this time to have been sent to France before winter, and Kelsey was probably back in England by the end of the year. War between France and England had been ended by the treaty of Ryswick, signed in September 1697.

The French held York till 1714 and, though war began again in 1702, the HBC made no attempt to recover it by force. With Iberville's career in the bay ended, and the HBC short of money, stalemate ensued, broken only by an unsuccessful French assault on Albany, the HBC's one remaining fort, in 1709. It was to Albany that Kelsey was sent after entering into a new contract for three years on 25 May 1698. For his fourth passage out he shipped in the *Dering* [III] (Capt. Michael Grimington); a journal of part of this voyage forms the last such record (in point of time) in *The Kelsey papers*. Henceforth Kelsey's life must be reconstructed chiefly from the HBC's archives and from his own brief "Memorandum of my abode."

James KNIGHT was governor at Albany till 1700 when he was succeeded by John FULLARTINE. Kelsey in 1701 was made master of the *Knight* frigate, a vessel of just under 50 tons, which had been sent to the bay in 1696 and was now used for the East Main trade. This trade was controlled from Albany, no permanent factory being built at East Main at this time though it is likely that temporary winter quarters were occupied on Gilpin Island, Baley Island or elsewhere. The *Knight* loaded at Albany with goods and provisions in the late summer, wintered on or off the East Main, and returned in spring. Anthony BEALE ran the business for three winters and Kelsey for four (1701–3 and 1707–9), doubling the duties of master of the vessel and trader. The HBC had some hopes of the East Main trade, both for marten skins and for minerals. Nothing much came of the search for minerals, but furs were taken. Two of Kelsey's seasons (1702–3 and 1708–9) were successful: 3,242 and 3,328 made beaver were the products,

Kelsey

figures not exceeded in the East Main trade till 1729–30, though only a small fraction of what was being taken at Albany.

Kelsey came back to England in 1703, possibly because he was dissatisfied with his wage of £50 a year, possibly for the reason given by Governor Fullartine, "the recovery of his health." Little is known of Kelsey's life between 6 Oct. 1703 when he landed in England and his next contract with the HBC on 28 Nov. 1705; this was his longest time out of the company's service. The terms of the new agreement suggest that he was badly wanted, 10s. a week till he sailed in the following summer, £4 a month as mate on the voyage out, and £100 a year in the bay. Kelsey was now clearly recognized as a competent seaman as well as an efficient officer.

Kelsey's posting was as chief trader at Albany, but "I was kept out of my Imploy a year by Govr Beal." In the winters of 1707–8 and 1708–9 he was back in the East Main trade and it was this that caused him to miss the French attack on Albany in 1709. For the next three years, so far as we know, he remained at Albany where it appears by a letter of 29 May 1710 that amongst other duties he had some responsibility for training: the London committee wrote, "you doe well to Educate the men in Literature but Especially in the Language that in time wee may send them to Travell If wee see it Convenient." The reference to literature is mysterious—possibly it means no more than teaching them to read—but the same letter throws some light on one of the minor puzzles regarding Kelsey. Robson in his attack on the HBC alleged that Kelsey had compiled a "vocabulary of the Indian language, and that the Company had ordered it to be suppressed." There was indeed such a work: "wee have sent you your dixonary Printed," the committee continued, "that you may the Better Instruct the young Ladds with you, in ye Indian Language."

Kelsey left Albany for England in August 1712 in his old ship, the *Knight*, though as passenger not master. His intention was to return to the bay in the following year, and he was appointed to go as deputy to Knight at York, which was about to be handed back to the HBC under the treaty of Utrecht. Delay in preparing documents for the handover caused a year's postponement, and Kelsey was given £100 as compensation for the deferment of his appointment. This concession, and the waiving on this occasion of the normal requirement of one year's notice of resignation, are further indications of the regard in which he was held. Kelsey left England—for the sixth and last time—in June 1714 and was present at the handing over of York on 11 September. For the

next three years he played second fiddle to Knight. The main task was to rebuild the fort which was found in 1714 "all rotten and ready to fall, not scarce defensible against the natives if they have a mind to assault us." Behind Kelsey's laconic note "Exerted my utmost to gett a new fort" must lie a good deal of work and some hardship, notably that caused by the break-up of the ice in the river at 10:00 A.M. on Saturday, 7 May 1715, when the factory had to be evacuated and "if St Paul's had stood there before the deluge there had been none now." Kelsey took over command at York in 1717 when Knight went to establish a new post at Churchill, and when Knight returned to England the following year Kelsey, after 34 years of almost unbroken service to the HBC, was made governor over all the bay settlements, Churchill included.

Knight, back in England, made certain complaints against Kelsey, full particulars of which have not survived. Kenney, Rich, and others have suggested that the accusations centred upon private trade, but the few facts on record are not conclusive. Kelsey was sent a copy of the charges in 1719 with a request for detailed answers, the London committee "being very Unwilling to think that a Person wee had so Good an Opinion of as yourself should forfeit their Estimes." Kelsey's reply is lost but in a letter to Richard Staunton* of 1 Feb. 1720 he referred to "fals asspersions concerning ye Indians and had it not bin for ym it would been very hard with us this winter for they have killed near 100 Deer," which sounds like a defence against a charge of being too soft with Indians. One of the charges, we know, referred to theft by Indians as long before as 1696–97. These are the only complaints against Kelsey recorded in the whole of his service, and it is clear that he strongly resented them. "It is a great Dolor," he wrote to Staunton in 1720, "to be represented so Odiously to Our Masters and tuched in ye most Sensable part yt is a mans reputation wch is more Valuable yn Life itselfe." What caused this friction between two old servants of the HBC is unknown. Knight was now an old man but he can hardly be reckoned senile for he was given command of the HBC's voyage of discovery in 1719. He was an ex-shareholder and member of the London committee, so one would expect the charges he laid against Kelsey to have been taken seriously; but there is no evidence that they were pressed very far, and it is unlikely that the HBC would have left Kelsey in command till 1722 if they had lost confidence in him.

Kelsey's term as governor lasted for four years. Post-journals survive for this period, but there is only one letter to London, a brief note dated

19 June 1719 announcing his departure "on discovery to the northward" and setting out the arrangements made for running affairs in his absence. This "discovery" was a matter of much concern in the closing years of Kelsey's career. Knight set out on his last voyage in this same year to search for gold and the northwest passage and to find death, tragic but not unapt for the fierce old man whose first employment in the bay had been in 1676. Kelsey's own voyage northward in July and August 1719 was quite independent of Knight's; at the time he knew nothing of Knight's plans and the HBC wisely tried to keep them apart. Knight was told not to sail south of latitude 64°N; if he did so, he would come under Kelsey's orders. Kelsey's expedition was in the *Prosperous* hoy, with the *Success* in company, and is briefly described in his "Memorandum": two of the HBC's Indian slaves were exchanged for two Eskimos to be trained as interpreters, and there was some trade in whalebone, oil and "Sea Horse teeth." By his own estimate he sailed as far as 62° 40′N. By the next season (1720) Kelsey knew about Knight's voyage, and this may be why he sent John Hancock to Churchill and thence north instead of going himself to renew the attempt to develop an Eskimo trade. Hancock was back in September with the news that Knight's men had "Spoiled our Trade." As yet there was no inkling of disaster.

In 1721 Kelsey again went north in person, having "Richd. Norton & an Nothern indian on board to show me ye copper," tales of which had been reaching HBC posts. This is the nearest the evidence takes us to a coincidence of purpose between Knight's dreams and Kelsey's realistic aims. Knight's was an expedition with several objectives, gold and other valuable minerals, the northwest passage, whale fishery, all to be searched for north of 64°. Kelsey's voyages in 1719 and 1721 and the two which he dispatched but did not accompany in 1720 and 1722 were limited in intention, stimulated, as the most recent historian of the search for the northwest passage argues, by a concern at the failure of Churchill to pay its way. (Williams, *The British search for the northwest passage*.)

Kelsey's last expedition is succinctly described in the "Memorandum." He called first at Churchill, left there on 13 July 1721, saw parties of Eskimos on 21, 23 July, and 1 August, and began his return on 9 August. From these Eskimos he learned of the loss of Knight's *Albany*, "we seeing things belonging to those vessels," but he was unable to search to the northward, "ye winds did not favour my Intentions of going farther to ye Noward."

Kelsey sent Captain John SCROGGS in the *Whalebone* to the north in 1722, the last of this series of voyages of "discovery." It is surprising in view of Kelsey's finds the previous year that no orders have come to light for searching out the fate of Knight's ships; but there may have been verbal instructions to this effect. Scroggs certainly brought back information sufficient to convince the HBC that Knight and his ships had been lost. Kelsey's interest in the north now ended for with the arrival of the *Mary* from London in 1722 came his recall and his successor, Thomas McCliesh*. No reason was given by the HBC beyond Kelsey's having completed four years as deputy and four as governor; "Wee think it Convenient to Call you home." Kelsey was now in his middle fifties, not a great age for service in a company which had employed such a venerable figure as Knight.

Kelsey reached England on 31 Oct. 1722 and was paid off. In January 1724 he petitioned for appointment as captain of the HBC ship *Hannah*, which suggests that while he may have had enough of continuous residence in the bay he was still game for a summer voyage. In fact the *Hannah* did not sail in 1724 so Kelsey did not get the job. On professional grounds his appointment would have been entirely credible for he was an experienced mariner. When and how he gained this competence is not clear: we know that he commanded the *Knight* in 1701 and was mate in the *Pery* on her Atlantic crossing in 1706. In the "Memorandum" he records, and claims credit for, two major salvage operations in Hudson Bay which testify to skilled seamanship. The first was in 1711 when the *Pery*, out from England, grounded on sand off Albany and was wrecked by a gale. Kelsey reports "Govr Beale Desired me to take charge of ye knight to go down to ye Perry to save what could be of ye Cargo accordingly I did," though Beale's account of the event gives credit neither to Kelsey nor to anyone else. Again, in 1719 when the *Hudson's Bay* [III] frigate was wrecked off Cape Tatnum, Kelsey saved most of the cargo. "I had," he writes, "a narrow escape for my life & If I had not staid till ye 2d of Septr. to get ye cargo on shore their would have been little of it sav'd."

Henry Kelsey died in his own house in Church Street, East Greenwich, and was buried on 2 Nov. 1724. He had married Elizabeth Dix of East Greenwich on 7 April 1698 soon after returning from his second spell as a prisoner of the French; she survived him and was the executrix of his will. Three children are known to have been born to the marriage: Elizabeth (b. 11 July 1704) and Mary (b. 17 March 1706), both born in the only long break in Kelsey's service with the HBC, and

313

Kelsey

John (b. 16 Nov. 1713) born while his father was waiting to return to York. In the registrations of baptism of his children Kelsey is described as "mariner" but in his will made on 2 Jan. 1723 as "gentleman."

Kelsey's earnings in his service to the HBC have been carefully investigated: they were not great. As an apprentice he was promised £8 and two suits at the end of his time: in fact he received £15 in gratuities and wages totalling £36. From 1688 to 1691 he was paid £15 a year, rising to £30 between 1691 and 1693; he received no reward for his exploration north of Churchill in 1689 but a gratuity of £30 for his journey to the plains, which if not the greatest ever made must surely have been one of the cheapest. By 1696 he was earning £35 a year, dropping to £30 when he went to Albany in 1698 and rising to £50 when he took over the East Main trade in 1701. From 1706 he got £100 a year and this (apart from a brief period in 1711 when he was in charge at Albany) remained his wage till he became governor in 1718 at £200 a year. Adding such supplementary payments as "lying-by money" it appears that Kelsey's lifetime of service to the HBC brought him a little less than £2,500. Not surprisingly the provision left for his widow was slight. True he owned the house in which he lived and the one next to it, but in 1730 Elizabeth Kelsey had to petition the HBC for help with the cost of apprenticing her son: she received ten guineas, and another six guineas in 1734 to buy clothes for the son, "She being wholly incapable to do it herself."

The Kelsey papers, which were not known to historians before 1926 and which are now the chief source of information concerning the life of Henry Kelsey, leave a number of questions unanswered. How and where did these papers come into the hands of the Dobbs family, descendants of Arthur Dobbs*, the leader of the critics of the HBC in 1749? The "papers" are entries in a single paper-covered volume, the title-page of which reads "Henry Kelsey his Book being ye Gift of James Hubbud in the year of our Lord 1693." Doughty and Martin, the editors, concluded that Dobbs did not know of the existence of this book when he attacked the HBC in 1749; for Dobbs, three years before Robson's book was published, likewise interpreted Kelsey's journey to the plains as impromptu and unauthorized. A contrary view is pressed by E. E. Rich who thought it probable that Kelsey's journal was copied or abstracted from the HBC's records by Christopher Middleton* and passed by him to Dobbs. "That Dobbs, with a copy of Kelsey's Journal in his possession . . . should have suppressed it . . . is merely an instance of the rancour

with which he challenged the Company's position." There is no evidence to support either view. There is nothing to show that the volume now called *The Kelsey papers* was ever part of the HBC's archives for Middleton to copy or steal. The title page suggests that it was Kelsey's own property, though his action of recording official business in a private book would not have had the company's approval. He may have brought it back to England in 1722 in case Knight's charges against him were revived: the "Memorandum of my abode" (the last document in the book) ends with the arrival of Kelsey's relief and reads like an apologia. Dobbs could have got the volume from Kelsey's family, could even have bought it, before 1749 or after 1749; one's guess at the date must depend on whether one thinks Dobbs a rogue or not.

There is also disagreement about the handwriting of *The Kelsey papers*. Doughty and Martin were of the opinion that the whole of the volume was in Kelsey's hand; Kenney that none of it was except a few lines in an Indian language which appear on pages 60–61 of the printed edition.

Some of these mysteries may in time be cleared up, but it is not rash to say that the HBC archives are unlikely to yield much more information of substance concerning the life of Henry Kelsey. Scraps of biographical information concerning his parentage, early life, and descendants may be found elsewhere, but we must not expect to know a great deal more of the man himself than we do now. It is little enough. What he did is in outline clear, but his character remains, as A. S. Morton said, "illusive." A good deal of what has been written about him consists of generalized inference from his recorded actions. We seldom know what choice was open to him. His letters and journals contain few personal reflections; what can be found (such as the observation already quoted on the value of reputation, or the remark in 1722 "Its but in vain for any man to kick against the fates") are commonplace. He had, one thinks, little formal education; his composition does not rise above the rather low level of HBC officers of the time. Yet he wrote verse which, however crude, was harder to write than prose, and he taught "literature" to the rough-necks in the bay. That he was a man with whom it was possible to quarrel is suggested by the dispute with Beale in 1706 and the break with Governor Knight, but we know the rights and wrongs of neither case. With men under his command Kelsey could certainly be severe, as he showed by flogging two men on Boxing-day 1719 and two more on 10 May following: the journal entries are consistent with his having administered these punishments in person.

314

Undoubtedly his forte was relations with Indians, though Morton may be going a little far in calling him "our first example of that comparatively rare species, the Indianized Englishman."

Perhaps Kelsey preferred Indian to white society, perhaps he pitied the savages and wanted to protect them. We know that he dismissed John Hancock from the council at York for cruelty to Eskimos and "for beating and Useing all Indians Morosly." But for this, and for most of what Kelsey did, sound commercial reasons can be adduced.

K. G. DAVIES

The principal source of information on Kelsey's life is *The Kelsey papers* (Doughty and Martin), which contains the journals cited above and the "Memorandum of my abode in hudsons bay from 1683 to 1722." The date, 1683, is Kelsey's error; he went out in 1684. There are two versions of the journal of 1691 in G.B., Parliament, H.C., *Report from the committee appointed to inquire into the state and condition of the countries adjoining to Hudson's Bay, and of the trade carried on there* ([London], 1749), which also prints brief but important extracts from the HBC records, some of which are no longer extant. References to Kelsey will be found in HBRS, IX (Rich); XI, XX (Rich and Johnson); XXV (Davies and Johnson); and in *The founding of Churchill* (Kenney). Unpublished materials include a number of the HBC's letters to Kelsey, entries of letters from Kelsey while governor to commanders of other posts in the bay, and the relevant post-journals, but these have been searched by Doughty and Martin for their Intro. to *The Kelsey papers*; by J. F. Kenney for "The career of Henry Kelsey," *RSCT*, 3d ser., XXIII (1929), sect.II; and by A. M. Johnson for her biography of Kelsey in HBRS, XXV, wherein will also be found authoritative statements concerning Kelsey's terms of service and earnings, together with the results of careful search for his family history. C. N. Bell, "The journal of Henry Kelsey (1691–1692)," Hist. and Sci. Soc. of Man. *Trans.*, new ser., IV (May, 1928), is a detailed reconstruction of Kelsey's route in 1690–92, though not every conclusion has found general acceptance. HBRS, XXI (Rich), Morton, *History of the Canadian west*, and L. J. Burpee, *The search for the western sea* (London, 1908; rev. ed., Toronto, 1935), all discuss what the latter calls "the Henry Kelsey puzzle." Joseph Robson's case is put forward in his *An account of six years residence in Hudson's-Bay, from 1733 to 1736, and 1744 to 1747* (London, 1752). [K. G. D.]

KEMPTHORNE, THOMAS, captain in the Royal Navy; commodore of the Newfoundland convoy and temporary governor, 1715; b. *c.* 1677; d. 1736.

Thomas Kempthorne is believed to have been a member of the family of Vice-Admiral Sir John Kempthorne of Widecombe, Devonshire. In 1704, in command of the *Roebuck*, he served in the Mediterranean under Vice-Admiral Sir John LEAKE. In 1705 he was tried by court martial for an unsuccessful engagement with a much superior French squadron, and was honourably acquitted.

In 1715, in command of the *Worcester*, he was appointed commodore of the Newfoundland convoy. The Board of Trade and Plantations was concerned about the state of the fishery (after the war and several bad fishing seasons) and recognized the need for regulations, supplementing the Newfoundland Act of 1699, to control the lawlessness in Newfoundland. Kempthorne was, therefore, instructed to take with him a copy of the act and to report on its operation. The *Worcester* sailed from Plymouth 25 May and anchored in Bay Bulls on 8 July. Four days later the conscientious Kempthorne summoned the first of his "Courts for regulating the Fisheries." His subsequent report to the Board presents a vivid picture of contemporary affairs. He described in some detail the methods of fishing, curing, and salting the catch. He found the inhabitants relied for their livelihood almost entirely on fishing, making little use of the country-side for sustenance. Provisions were obtained mostly from New England and Ireland. Kempthorne severely criticized the fishing admirals, who were theoretically responsible for settling disputes. Besides quarrelling amongst themselves, the fishing admirals used their authority to further their own interests. Some became so powerful that they were called "kings" by the Newfoundlanders. They dealt unjustly with their servants, and flouted the Newfoundland Act with impunity, only making a pretence of compliance when a "man of warr" was present. As Kempthorne remarked, "the winter season is a sort of respite from all observance of law or government." He made strong recommendations that some permanent authority be appointed to administer justice during the winter months, for, he claimed, if a consistent policy were established at St John's, "the metropolis of this Island," this would influence the standard of conduct throughout the country.

One of the worst evils of the time was that traders allowed the inhabitants credit for provisions and drink during the winter months; debts were collected, often forcibly, at the end of the fishing season, and further credit then granted, so that men were constantly in debt. This led many to seek asylum in New England. The traffic in indentured servants was on the increase, and there was a constant drain of English seamen and "green men" enticed away by New England shipmasters [see ARNOLD]. To stop this practice Kempthorne suggested the taking of bonds from masters of New England ships. He also suggested that the

Kenougé

New England custom of granting the hired hands a share of the catch should be instituted, as an incentive. Kempthorne, in the *Worcester*, sailed from St John's 15 Oct. 1715, having previously ordered the *Gibraltar*, Capt. Edward Falkingham, to chase away two Spanish ships illegally fishing on the Banks.

In March 1715/16 after considering reports from Kempthorne and from persons concerned about the trade, such as Archibald CUMINGS and James Campbell [*see* Colin CAMPBELL], the Board of Trade and Plantations recommended further legislation to enforce the decisions of the commodores, to provide magistrates during the winter, and to regulate trade. However nothing was done until 1728.

In 1717 Kempthorne was appointed to the command of the *Royal Oak*, taking part, under Admiral Sir George Byng, in the victory over the Spanish fleet off Cape Passero, August 1718. In 1722 he was appointed commissioner of the dockyard, Chatham. He died at Chatham 23 July 1736.

MICHAEL GODFREY

PRO, Adm. 51/1057, pt.10 (captain's log of H.M.S. *Worcester*); C.O. 194/6, 195/6; *CSP, Col., 1714–15, 1716–17*. Charnock, *Biographia navalis*, III. Lounsbury, *British fishery at Nfld*.

KENOUGÉ. *See* KINONGÉ

KIALA (Quiala), Fox chief hostile to the French; fl. 1733–34.

Little is known about Kiala. The French colonial manuscripts make only a few references to him in the years 1733 and 1734. On the basis of this fragmentary evidence, however, Louise P. Kellogg, author of *The French régime in Wisconsin and the Northwest*, concluded that he was a chieftain of great courage and influence, and the principal architect of the policy his tribe followed towards the French from the early 1720s until 1734. She first presented this view in a paper read to the Wisconsin Historical Society in 1907 and it was subsequently accepted by other historians who dealt with the Fox Indians during the French régime.

Following LA PORTE de Louvigny's expedition against the Foxes in 1716, these Indians had become divided into two factions. A pro-French party under OUACHALA sought to maintain good relations with New France; but it was opposed by a war party which gradually gained the upper hand. Kellogg conjectured that the latter was led by Kiala and that his goal, like that of Pontiac* and Tecumseh* at a later date, was to build up a great confederacy of tribes that would rise against the white man's domination of Indian territory. It would have included tribes as far apart as the Abenakis in Acadia, the Sioux at the headwaters of the Mississippi, and the Chickasaws on the frontiers of Louisiana. Had this design been successful, Kellogg states, the French might have been driven from the St Lawrence, the Great Lakes, and the Mississippi.

This theory is difficult to accept. It is true that during the 1720s the Foxes carried on negotiations with the Iroquois, the Chickasaws, and the Abenakis [*see* NESCAMBIOUIT] in order to confirm old alliances and form new ones, but this does not prove the existence of an anti-French conspiracy. The Foxes may simply have been attempting to recruit reinforcements to help them in their war against some of the western tribes. Kellogg's theory is weakened most of all by the silence of the governments of Canada and Louisiana on the subject of an anti-French plot. The officials of these two colonies, who were usually well informed of Indian activities, had a different understanding of the situation. They claimed that the Foxes were waging war in order to foil French attempts to penetrate the lands west of Lake Superior, which were inhabited by the Sioux. The Foxes feared that the sizable trade they carried on with these Indians would be greatly reduced by the competition of European traders.

Governor RIGAUD de Vaudreuil, whose 35 years of service in Canada had taught him to fear the consequences of Indian wars, had followed a conciliatory policy towards the Foxes; but his successor, Charles de Beauharnois* de La Boische, decided to reduce them by military means. His decision was motivated by reports of English intrigue in the west, by renewed acts of violence committed by the Foxes and, perhaps, by the hope of beginning his tenure of office with a spectacular victory over the Indian enemies of New France.

In 1728, the Foxes managed to elude the first army sent against them under the command of LE MARCHAND de Lignery, but they gained only a temporary respite. French diplomacy was at work across the west and the Foxes soon found themselves isolated, ringed by hostile tribes. In 1730, somewhere south of Lake Michigan, they suffered a crushing defeat at the hands of a contingent of 1,400 western Indians, commanded by Nicolas-Antoine COULON de Villiers. In the winter of 1731–32, they were again defeated with heavy losses by an army of Iroquois and Hurons from the Canadian missions. All that was left of them after this battle was a miserable group of approximately 40 warriors and 10 boys who came to the French post at Baie des Puants (Green Bay), begging for peace and their lives. Unable to grant this request on his own authority, the commander, Coulon de Villiers, set out for Montreal with four of the principal Foxes. Two were former chiefs and one of these was Kiala.

They found Beauharnois in a merciless mood. The governor had been exasperated by these Indians, who had blocked the colony's westward expansion and obliged it to wage a costly war, and he laid down terms that amounted to total extermination. The remnants of the tribe were to be transported to Canada and scattered among the missions, and all were to be killed if they made any resistance [see COULON de Villiers]. Kiala, whom the French regarded as the instigator of all the Fox misdeeds, was to be deported to Martinique. His wife, who had followed him to Montreal, was given to the Hurons of Lorette, who adopted her into their tribe.

In September 1734, Kiala was placed aboard the *Saint-François* bound for Martinique. "We must warn you that this man has had a reputation for dauntlessness among his people, who are our enemies, and that he should be closely watched," Beauharnois and Hocquart* wrote to the authorities of that colony. As far as is known, the Fox chieftain died on this tropical island, perhaps as a slave on one of the plantations. His wife, more fortunate, managed to escape from the Hurons and presumably found her way back to her native land.

YVES F. ZOLTVANY

AN, Col., B, 61; C¹¹ᴬ, 47, 50, 57, 61; C¹³ᴬ, 8. Wis. State Hist. Soc. *Coll.*, XVI, XVII. "Calendar of manuscripts in the archives of the Chicago Historical Society," PAC *Report, 1905*, I, lxix. Alvord, *Illinois country.* F.-É. Audet, *Les premiers établissements français au pays des Illinois; la guerre des Renards* (Paris, 1938). L. P. Kellogg, *French régime*; "The Fox Indians during the French régime," Wis. State Hist. Soc. *Proc., 1907* (1908), 142–88.

KINONGÉ (Kenougé, "The Pike," in French "Le Brochet"), a chief of the Ottawas du Sable who spent most of his life at Michilimackinac, an ally of the French; fl. 1660–1713.

The first mention of Kinongé is in 1660, when Father René Ménard* stayed with his family at Kiaonan (now Keweenaw) Bay for the winter. The missionary reproached him with keeping four or five wives, a practice which was often a mark of ability and distinction among the tribes of the Great Lakes. Probably as a result of this dispute, Kinongé "treated the poor Father very badly, and finally forced him to leave and make himself a hut out of fir-branches."

In 1679 DANIEL GREYSOLON Dulhut reported that the Ottawas, led by Kinongé, had plundered Cree fur convoys on Lake Superior the year before, and he feared that the Crees would be driven to trade with the English at Hudson Bay. The Crees threatened revenge, however, and Kinongé decided to trade near the Illinois country.

By the early 1680s he was one of the most influential French allies in the region of the upper lakes. When two French traders were killed by Indians at Kiaonan Bay in 1683, Dulhut used Kinongé's cabin at Michilimackinac for their trial. The executions which followed surprised and shocked the Indians, but Dulhut gave a feast in the cabin the next day to ease Kinongé's "sickness of heart" that sentence had been passed there. A decade later, in 1695, the chief appeared at Montreal at a conference called for the upper lakes Indians. Buade* de Frontenac hoped to make peace between the Ottawas and the Sioux, as warfare between them interfered with the fur trade. He asked that they direct their energies against the Iroquois, promising them troops, arms, and provisions. This offer pleased Kinongé, who replied: "all our young men are gone on the war path, and they will be very glad to find on their return wherewithal to continue."

Kinongé figured in the LE PESANT affair of 1706. The Michilimackinac Ottawas did not join in the attack at Detroit, and in August 1706 Kinongé and others carried this message to Governor RIGAUD de Vaudreuil. Vaudreuil acknowledged that the Michilimackinac Ottawas were innocent and praised the loyalty of Kinongé, but insisted on revenge against Le Pesant. In August 1706 Vaudreuil refused the Iroquois permission to attack Michilimackinac, stating that those Ottawas were innocent of any intrigue. He again mentioned the loyalty of Kinongé.

In June 1707 the governor ordered the Ottawa chiefs to Montreal to explain the affair further. He praised Kinongé, who was present, but was cool towards OUTOUTAGAN and the others. The chiefs, fearing Le Pesant's power, claimed they would have difficulty in apprehending him. Vaudreuil replied that he would instruct Cadillac [LAUMET] to pardon all the Ottawas except Le Pesant, and he insisted on Le Pesant's death. The loyal Kinongé was to deliver this message to Cadillac in Detroit.

At Detroit, in August, Cadillac told the Ottawa chiefs including Kinongé and KOUTAOILIBOE that he would have nothing to do with them until the culprit was delivered. The other chiefs put pressure on Kinongé, because he and Le Pesant were of the same clan. It was decided to send JEAN-PAUL LEGARDEUR de Saint-Pierre and the Ottawa chiefs to Michilimackinac to apprehend Le Pesant and return him to Detroit. This was done, but Cadillac

Knight

apparently allowed him to escape later. Throughout this affair the role of Kinongé was crucial. He was a key messenger between Michilimackinac, Montreal, and Detroit; it is doubtful that Le Pesant would have been so easily apprehended without his help.

Kinongé was mentioned in June 1708, when Father JOSEPH-JACQUES MAREST wrote to Vaudreuil from Michilimackinac, condemning Cadillac for trying to entice the remaining Ottawas to Detroit. Marest pointed out that Kinongé opposed this move. In 1713, Kinongé (called a Kiskakon chief by Vaudreuil) was one of the Michilimackinac Indians who came to Vaudreuil and asked him to send LA PORTE de Louvigny to assist them in a venture against the Foxes.

DONALD CHAPUT

AN, Col., C¹¹A, 6, ff.222–53, 372ff.; 26, ff.75, 106ff., 138; 28, ff.165ff. "Capital punishment in Michigan, 1683: Duluth at Michilimackinac," *Michigan History* (Lansing), L (1966), 349–60. "Correspondance de Vaudreuil," APQ *Rapport, 1939–40*, 380–84, 387–405 *1947–48*, 229. *Découvertes et établissements des Français* (Margry), English MS translation, VI, 49–57, 60ff. *JR* (Thwaites), XLVIII, 117. *Michigan Pioneer Coll.*, XXXIII. *NYCD* (O'Callaghan and Fernow), IX, 594–632, 779–81. Sheldon, *Early history of Michigan*.

KNIGHT, JAMES, HBC governor and explorer; b. 1640?; d. 1719–20?

James Knight was probably born about 1640, since he was said to have been nearly 80 years old when he set out on his last voyage. His birthplace is not known but he was a shipwright or carpenter at Deptford, England, when he first entered the employ of the HBC on 16 May 1676. Most of his life was spent in the company's service. Arriving at James Bay in August 1676, he spent the next five years as a carpenter at £42 per annum, apparently building or repairing the factories at Rupert, Moose, and Albany Rivers. In 1680 he was considered for the post of deputy governor but the appointment went to the surgeon, Walter Farr.

Knight returned to London in August 1681 and on 28 October he reported to the HBC's committee on the factories, the Indians, and the country. The committee members realized that they had a good man, and consulted him frequently while preparations were being made to send an expedition to the bay in 1682. He advised on guns, supplies, and trade goods and, as a shipwright, examined the *Albemarle*. On 8 Feb. 1682 he accepted an appointment as chief factor at Albany Fort with a salary of £70 per annum, but by 11 May the company made him deputy governor

in the bay to John Nixon* and chief factor at Albany, with the wage increased to £100. As he was about to sail, an unexplained quarrel occurred, and on 28 May the captains of the ships *Friendship* and *Lucy* were ordered not to allow Knight on board, but the order was revoked the same day. The following day Knight sailed on the *Friendship*, taking his brother Richard with him as a personal servant.

He spent the next three years at Albany where his trading skill increased the HBC's business along the western shore of the bay. Knight emerges as an able, gruff, rather illiterate man whose practical ability, energy, tenacity, and endurance assured his rapid advancement. He sailed for England in September 1685 aboard the *Owner's Goodwill* (Capt. Richard Lucas*) arriving in the Downs 26 October. In early December he appeared before a sub-committee to answer charges by Governor Henry Sergeant*, Nixon's successor, of private trading, about the worst offence an HBC employee could commit. Knight denied the charges of shipping home beaver skins in 1684 on the *John and Thomas* for his private account and produced documents supporting his contention that they had been addressed and shipped to the company. He was also suspected of being too friendly with the New England traders in the bay, and it was known that he was sympathetic with the New Englanders, a number of whom were employed by the company. The investigating committee was dissatisfied with Knight's evidence but postponed a decision until the return of Governor Sergeant. Since the French under the Chevalier de Troyes* captured the posts at the Bottom of the Bay (James Bay) in 1686, Sergeant's return was delayed and the case against Knight did not come up until November 1687. In the meantime, he submitted suggestions to the company on how the trade could be run more efficiently and expenses reduced. This may have been an effort to help get a favourable decision for his case but, if so, it did not work. Knight's connection with the HBC was severed after the hearing.

It is not known how Knight was employed from late 1687 until 1692 when he again joined the company. In March of that year a secret meeting of the committee was held to consider sending a force to protect York Fort and also to retake the Bottom of the Bay. Probably by arrangement Captain James Knight, now referred to as "of London, Merchant," was waiting in an ante-room. He was offered command of the proposed expedition but showed proper reluctance until, a month later, his own proposals—including a bonus of £500 if he recaptured Fort Albany (Fort Sainte-Anne)—had been considered and accepted.

On 15 June 1692 he was issued royal letters patent making him governor and commander-in-chief of all forts, factories, and territories in Hudson Bay; he was to carry out reprisals and recover by force of arms territory held by the French.

Knight sailed in June 1692 with four ships—the *Royal Hudson's Bay*, *Dering* [II], *Pery*, and *Prosperous*—and 213 men: the most powerful expedition the company had yet sent to the bay. The fleet arrived 29 August at York Factory. The *Dering* returned to England, and Knight, after wintering at Old Factory Island (Gilpin Island) north of Eastmain River, with the other three vessels successfully attacked Albany Fort 22 June 1693. The gratified company voted him a bonus and named a new frigate in his honour. In October 1694 the French under Pierre Le Moyne d'Iberville captured York but the English retook it 31 Aug. 1696. During this time Knight at Albany held the only English fort in the bay. Knight returned to England in 1697 with Captain Thomas Man on the frigate *Pery* and there learned that York Fort had once more been taken by the French. By the Treaty of Ryswick signed 20 Sept. 1697 England and France agreed with certain provisos to restore to each other territories held at the outbreak of the war. In fact the treaty was never put into effect in Hudson Bay; the English remained at Albany and the French at York Fort (renamed Fort Bourbon) on the Hayes River.

To expedite the exchange envisaged in the treaty the company called on Knight, its most experienced man, to resume charge of Albany Fort. This he agreed to do and sailed in early June 1698 on the *Dering* [III] (Capt. Michael Grimington) accompanied by the *Pery* (Capt. Henry Baley). Knight held the *Pery* in the bay and sent the *Dering* back to England. No supply ship was sent out in 1700 and Knight, with provisions at a low ebb, sailed for home in September in the *Pery*. He arrived 3 November, and by mid-November had acquired £400 of HBC stock. This, together with his previous holdings, made him eligible for the committee, to which he was elected. He was re-elected annually until 1713, and during this time apparently lived in London—he is now sometimes referred to as "of London, Gentleman." He attended committee meetings quite regularly and made occasional business trips to Holland. In 1711, Knight agreed to go as governor to Albany, to replace Fullartine, but was prevented by sickness, and Anthony Beale went instead.

The War of the Spanish Succession ended with the Treaty of Utrecht, 31 March 1713. One of its provisions stipulated that France should return all Hudson Bay territories to Great Britain and reimburse the HBC for all damages due it. The company petitioned Queen Anne that the act of cession should be made to its representatives; a royal commission granted this request and authorized Captain James Knight and Henry Kelsey, his deputy, to receive the surrender. The two men embarked on the *Union* frigate, 6 June 1714, and arrived off York Fort, 5 September. On the 11th Knight went ashore and received the formal surrender of Nicolas Jérémie, the French commander.

With the entire bay now in company control there was opportunity to improve and consolidate trade. Knight, who remained on at York as governor, now lent his efforts to stopping the continual warfare between Crees (Home Indians) and Athapascans (Northern Indians) which interfered with the fur trade. His efforts to improve trade received an early set-back, however, when Captain Joseph Davis failed to deliver the cargo from England in 1715. It was also planned that Knight found a post at the Churchill River where an abortive attempt had been made in 1689. Knight was influenced in planning a northern post by several considerations. He wanted to bring in more trade from the Northern Indians, open a new trade with the Eskimos who came south seasonally as far as the Churchill River, and investigate the exciting reports from the Northern Indians of a mine of yellow metal to the northwest. These reports appeared to be substantiated when, on 7 May 1716, William Stuart returned from his long journey inland accompanied by the slave woman, Thanadelthur. After the death of Thanadelthur on 5 Feb. 1717, Knight acquired for "60 skins" another Slave Woman, who was to act as interpreter during the expedition to Churchill.

Knight dispatched an advance party including John Carruthers and William Stuart for the Churchill River in June 1717. He himself followed a month later on the hoy *Success* and spent the winter of 1717–18 at the new settlement at the river's mouth, which was named Fort Prince of Wales, later Churchill. On his departure at the end of the 1717–18 season Richard Staunton* was left in charge. In 1717 Knight wrote the committee requesting that he be recalled the following year. His request was granted. Henry Kelsey was appointed his successor, and in September 1718 Knight left the bay on the *Albany* frigate with hopes of persuading the committee to send an expedition northward to find a way to the gold and copper mines which he was convinced could be reached by sea. He undoubtedly discussed his plans at length with Captain George Berley of the *Albany* and Captain David Vaughan, who was also returning to England as a passenger, for these two were chosen as his captains the following year.

Kondiaronk

Knight explained his proposal to the committee on 18 November and other meetings continued during the winter. On 1 May 1719 the committee finally agreed that Knight go on a voyage of discovery to the north of 64° to seek the Strait of Anian leading into a northwest passage, to enlarge and increase the company's trade, to discover gold and copper mines, and to establish a whaling industry. His ships were to be the *Albany* frigate and the new sloop *Discovery* commanded by his old friends Berley and Vaughan. Knight said farewell to the governor and committee at Gravesend 4 June 1719 and took his departure. The expedition was never again seen by white men. Knight planned to, and apparently did, sail directly to the north of 64° without stopping at any of the Hudson Bay forts. In 1721 Kelsey in a trading voyage to the north found evidence among the Eskimos which left little doubt that the ships had been wrecked. In 1722 Kelsey sent Captain John Scroggs on the sloop *Whalebone* northward. On his return Scroggs stated that both ships had been wrecked and all the men killed by the Eskimos. On 29 September the two ships were written off the company books.

Nearly half a century later the tragic fate of the expedition was discovered by Samuel Hearne* who found remains of two ships, a dwelling, and wreckage in a cove on Marble Island. He returned in 1769 and confirmed from interviews with the Eskimos that this was indeed where the Knight expedition had perished. The Eskimos said that about 50 men were building a house in the late fall of 1719 after their ships had been wrecked. By spring their numbers were greatly reduced and by the end of a second winter only 20 men survived. Five lived until the summer of 1721 when they, too, died.

Sometime during his life James Knight had married. His will, giving his residence as Bisham in Berkshire, probated 23 Sept. 1724, left his estate to his wife Elizabeth. The will also contained a curious reference to Knight's son: "to my son Gilpin Knight one shilling and no more he having been already advanced by me in the world Considerably more than my Circumstances could allow of."

ERNEST S. DODGE

Knight's journal from 14 July to 13 Sept. 1717 has been edited by J. F. Kenny and published with an historical Intro. and Notes under the title *The founding of Churchill*. HBRS, VIII (Rich); XII, XX (Rich and Johnson); XXI (Rich); XXV (Davies and Johnson). *DNB*. Dodge, *Northwest by sea*. Williams, *The British search for the northwest passage*.

KONDIARONK (Gaspar Soiaga, Souoias, Sas-taretsi), known by the French as **"Le Rat"**; a Tionontati or Petun Huron chief at Michilimackinac; b. *c.* 1649; d. 2 Aug. 1701 in Montreal, when participating in peace negotiations between the tribes of the Upper Lakes and the Iroquois.

Following the Iroquois dispersal of the Hurons in 1649, the Tionontati eventually settled at Michilimackinac, the home of several Algonkian tribes. Because they were culturally and linguistically different, the Hurons did not readily integrate with the Algonkian community, being visibly separated from the Kiskakon [Ottawa] village by a thin palisade. Although they were nominally allies of the Algonkians and traded maize to the hunting and fishing bands that gathered at the straits, the Tionontati were ready to make friendly overtures to the Iroquois if they felt their security threatened. Their immediate fear was that the latter, currently warring with the Miamis and the Illinois to the south in an attempt to gain new beaver grounds, would turn their attention to the tribes at the Straits of Mackinac.

A crisis came soon enough. While raiding westward a Seneca leader strayed, was captured by some Winnebagos, and was carried as prize to Michilimackinac. During a meeting with HENRI TONTY in a Kiskakon wigwam the Seneca was murdered by an Illinois. Lest the Iroquois annihilate them, the Mackinac tribes sought the protection of the French governor and it was during negotiations with Louis de Buade* de Frontenac in 1682 that Kondiaronk first was noticed.

While the Ottawa speaker whined that they were like dead men and prayed that their father take pity on them, the Rat acknowledged "that the earth was turned upside down," and reminded Frontenac that the Huron, his erstwhile brother, "is now thy son" and therefore entitled to protection in return for obedience. These blandishments neither convinced Frontenac nor satisfied the Kiskakons, for it was known that the Hurons had sent wampum belts to the Iroquois without confiding in the allies or giving notice to Onontio [the governor]. On being questioned, Kondiaronk claimed that the Huron action had been an attempt to settle the affair of the murdered warrior but the Kiskakons maintained that not only had the Hurons withheld the wampum belts of the Ottawas but they had blamed them for the entire incident. Having trusted the Hurons to placate the Senecas on their behalf, the Ottawas now feared unilateral dealing at their expense.

In spite of Frontenac's efforts to get them to trust one another, both tribes returned to Michilimackinac as uneasy neighbours while Iroquois aggression against the western tribes continued unabated. In 1687 after Jacques-René Brisay de Denonville's invasion of the Seneca country, Kondiaronk and the allies extracted from him, in return for their loyalty, a pledge that the war should not be terminated until the Iroquois were destroyed. Peace might suit the old men of the Iroquois and relieve a harassed French colony, but it posed a threat to the Hurons of Michilimackinac that Kondiaronk perceived. Without the French to divert their attention, the Iroquois would be able to concentrate on their campaigns in the west. In the summer of 1688 Kondiaronk decided to strike a blow for himself. He raised a war party and they set out to take scalps and prisoners.

Arriving at Fort Frontenac (Cataracoui, now Kingston, Ont.) to obtain information, Kondiaronk was amazed to learn from the commander that Denonville was negotiating a peace with the Five Nations, whose ambassadors were momentarily expected there for conduct to Montreal. He was advised to return home at once and to this he assented. Inwardly resenting the French decision, however, Kondiaronk withdrew across the lake to Anse de la Famine (Mexico Bay, near Oswego) where he knew the Onondaga embassy must pass before going on to the fort. Within a week the delegation appeared, composed of four councillors and 40 escorting warriors. The Hurons waited until they began to land and greeted them with a volley as they disembarked. In the confusion, a chief was killed, others were wounded and the rest were taken prisoner.

The captives were no sooner tied securely than Kondiaronk opened a fateful woods-edge council. He represented that he had acted on learning from Denonville that an Iroquois war party would soon pass that way. The chagrined Iroquois, through their chief ambassador, the noted Teganissorens, protested that they were peace envoys voyaging to Montreal. Kondiaronk feigned amazement, then rage and fury, cursing Denonville for betraying him into becoming an instrument of treachery. Then he addressed his prisoners and Teganissorens: "Go, my brothers, I release you and send you back to your people, despite the fact we are at war with you. It is the governor of the French who has made me commit this act, which is so treacherous that I shall never forgive myself for it if your Five Nations do not take their righteous vengeance." When he propped up his words with a present of guns, powder, and balls, the Iroquois were convinced, assuring him on the spot that if the Hurons wanted a separate peace they could have it. As Kondiaronk had lost a man, however, custom entitled him to request a replacement for adoption: the Onondagas gave

him an adopted Shawnee. They then turned back to their villages and the Hurons set out for Michilimackinac. Passing by Fort Frontenac Kondiaronk called on the commandant, and made this chilling boast as he left: "I have just killed the peace; we shall see how Onontio will get out of this business."

The war party reached Michilimackinac in apparent triumph and presented the hapless "Iroquois" to the commandant who, having heard nothing of the intended peace between his government and the Iroquois, promptly condemned the man to be shot. Although the captive protested that this treatment was a violation of diplomatic immunity, Kondiaronk pretended that the man was light-headed and, even worse, afraid to die. Kondiaronk sent for an old Seneca slave to witness the execution, told him his countryman's story, and freed him to carry the word back to the Iroquois. Kondiaronk charged him to relate how badly the French abused the custom of adoption, and how they violated their trust while deceiving the Five Nations with feigned peace negotiations.

Although one member of the Iroquois delegation attacked by Kondiaronk had escaped to Fort Frontenac where the French gave assurances of their innocence in the affair, the damage done to the peace negotiations was irreparable. The message of French perfidy passed rapidly from fire to fire the length of the Iroquois longhouse. The wampum belts were buried and the war kettles hung. Within a year of Kondiaronk's treachery the war parties of the Five Nations descended on the Island of Montreal, sacking Lachine in the summer of 1689. Because of the renewal of French-English hostilities in Europe, the New York colony aided and abetted the Indian attacks but Lom d'Arce, Baron de Lahontan, held the Rat responsible for provoking the Iroquois to the point where it was impossible to appease them.

In the decade of warfare that followed, Kondiaronk's intrigues were numerous. In 1689 he was caught plotting with the Iroquois for the destruction of his Ottawa neighbours and that September, as if to witness his own mischief, he came down to Montreal and returned home unscathed, proving that the French lacked the temerity to hang him. But he was worth more alive than dead. Although it was probably he who was behind the Ottawas' rebuff to Frontenac the following year and their proposed treaty with the Iroquois to trade at Albany, by mid-decade when the Hurons at Michilimackinac were again divided Kondiaronk was leading the pro-French faction with another Huron chief, Le Baron, leading the English-Iroquois opposition, each side having a mixed following of Ottawas. The Baron wanted to ally

Kondiaronk

with the Iroquois to destroy the Miamis, but in 1697 the Rat warned the latter and attacked the former, cutting 55 Iroquois to pieces in a two-hour canoe engagement on Lake Erie. This victory ruined the possibility of a Huron-Iroquois alliance, re-established Kondiaronk's pre-eminence, and helped to restore the tribes at Michilimackinac as children of Frontenac when they came to Montreal to council.

With the Treaty of Ryswick in 1697 ending the conflict in Europe, New York and New France agreed to suspend hostilities. The withdrawal of active English support, combined with the depredations of a long war, prompted the Iroquois to make peace overtures to Frontenac. Negotiations went on for several years and led to the settlement of 1701. Kondiaronk was present whenever the allies conferred. At one of the initial meetings between Frontenac and the Ottawas over a truce with the Iroquois, a Cayuga delegate tried to embarrass the Ottawas by accusing them of having negotiated without the participation of Onontio. Kondiaronk, "the most civilized and considerable person of the Upper Nations," rebuked the Cayuga: "We are in the presence of our father; nothing should be concealed from him, so relate the message carried in the wampum belts that you first addressed to us and to the Ottawas." The discomfited Cayuga declined the challenge.

After Frontenac died, the Rat transferred his respect to Louis-Hector de CALLIÈRE, the new Onontio. In 1700 Callière brought the various tribes together at Montreal to achieve a brittle armistice preparatory to the final settlement. On this occasion the Rat urged the Iroquois to listen to the voice of their father: "Let it not be in a forced or insincere way that you ask him for peace; for my part I return to him the hatchet he had given me, and lay it at his feet. Who will be so bold as to take it up?" For a while the sparks flew thickly on both sides. The Iroquois speaker, having listened calmly to the Rat, replied with spirit: "Onontio had hurled the hatchet into the sky [made war] and what is up there never comes down again; but there was a little string attached to this hatchet by which he pulled it back, and struck us with it. . . ." Here the Rat took charge to remind them that "the Seneca was planning the complete destruction of the French, intending not even to spare his father [Frontenac], whom he intended to put first into the kettle, for an Iroquois threatened to drink his blood from his skull. . . ." Kondiaronk said further of the Iroquois "that their hands were covered with the blood of our allies, that the allies' flesh was even still between their teeth, that their lips were all gory with it,

[and] it was well known that they were lying to hide what was in their hearts." In the Rat's style, one must dissipate the clouds shrouding the Tree of Peace.

The final Indian congress was held the following year. It began 21 July 1701, when Bacqueville de La Potherie [LE ROY], the prime source on the proceedings, went to meet the delegates at the village of the Mission Indians at Sault-Saint-Louis (Caughnawaga). The first flotilla to appear consisted of 200 Iroquois, headed by the ambassadors of the Onondagas, Oneidas, and Cayugas, the Senecas having dropped by the way, and the Mohawks following later. They approached firing their guns and the salute was returned by their brethren, the mission Indians, ranged along the shore. They were properly greeted at the water's edge by a small fire and then led by the arm to the main council lodge where they smoked for a quarter of an hour with great composure. Next they were greeted with the "three rare words" of the ritual of requickening—wiping of tears, clearing of the ears, and opening the throat—to prepare them to speak of peace the next day with Onontio.

The protocol of forest diplomacy demanded the use of metaphor, timing, manipulation of space, and reciprocal action by both parties. The kettle, the hatchet, the road, the fire, the mat, the sun, and the Tree of Peace were each subject to qualifiers appropriate to the mood or intent. Leading or receiving a procession at the woods-edge, taking guests by the arm to the main fire, arranging the council grounds, seating delegates, allowing them to withdraw to consider, and to return to reply, were part of the spatial arrangements. Wiping away tears, exchanging speeches and songs, passing the pipe, throwing wampum belts, returning prisoners, distributing presents, and apportioning the feast were expected of both hosts and guests. All of this belonged to a ritual widely shared in the lower lakes by Iroquoians and Algonkians alike, and surviving as a fragment in the Iroquois Condolence Council.

The following day the Iroquois shot the rapids to the main fire at Montreal, where they were greeted by the crash of artillery. The smoke of their feasting had scarcely disappeared when in their wake came 200 canoes of the French allies—Chippewas, Ottawas, Potawatomis, Hurons, Miamis, Winnebagos, Menominees, Sauks, Foxes, and Mascoutens—over 700 Indians to be received ceremoniously at the landing. The Far Indians performed their specialty, the Calumet Dance, to the accompaniment of gourd rattles, making friends of their hosts.

By 25 July negotiations between the tribes were

fully under way and the Rat spoke of the difficulties encountered in recovering Iroquois prisoners from the allies. He wondered whether the Iroquois would comply in an exchange with sincerity or cheat them of their nephews taken in the past 13 years of war. He suspected that the allies were to be deceived, although they were still willing to leave their prisoners as a gesture of good faith. The next day, however, the Iroquois admitted that they did not have the promised prisoners, saying that as small children they had been given to families for adoption and professing not to be masters of their young people. This excuse annoyed the Hurons and Miamis who had forcibly taken the Iroquois captives away from foster families. Days of wrangling followed.

The Rat, having persuaded his own and allied tribes to bring their Iroquois prisoners to Montreal, was deeply humiliated at being duped, and shortly afterwards succumbed to a violent fever. He came so ill to a council held 1 August to discuss the matter that he could not stand. Yet everyone was glad when he spoke: "He sat down first on a folding stool; [then] a large and comfortable armchair was brought for him so that he could speak with greater ease; he was given some wine to strengthen him but he asked for a herbal drink and it was realized that he wanted syrup of maiden-hair fern," a sovereign Iroquois remedy. Having recovered somewhat, he spoke in a languid tone while the assembly listened intently for nearly two hours, occasionally voicing its approval of his points. Though he was obviously chagrined at the conduct of the Iroquois, his political skill made him take a new tack, and he reviewed at length his own diplomatic role in averting attacks on the Iroquois, in persuading reluctant tribal delegations to come to Montreal, and in recovering prisoners. "We could not help but be touched," wrote La Potherie, "by the eloquence with which he expressed himself, and [could not fail] to recognize at the same time that he was a man of worth." After speaking the Rat felt too weak to return to his hut, and was carried in the armchair to the hospital, where his illness steadily worsened. He died at two A.M.

The Iroquois, who love funerals, came to cover the dead. Sixty strong, they marched in solemn procession with great dignity, led by CHABERT de Joncaire, with TONATAKOUT, the leading Seneca chief, walking at the rear and weeping. When close to the body, they sat in a circle around it, while the appointed chanter continued pacing for a quarter of an hour. He was followed by a second speaker, AOUENANO, who wiped away the tears, opened the throat, and poured in a sweet medicine to re-quicken the mourners. Then producing a belt, he

restored the Sun, urging the warriors to emerge from darkness to the light of peace. He then temporarily covered the body pending the main rites. There were similar gestures by other tribal delegations.

The Rat's funeral was held the following day (3 Aug. 1701). The French wished the Hurons and their allies to know how touched they were by the loss of so considerable a person. Pierre de SAINT-OURS headed a military escort of 60 men, followed by 16 Huron warriors in ranks of 4 wearing beaver robes, faces blackened as a mark of their mourning, and guns reversed; then came clergy and 6 war chiefs bearing the flower-covered coffin on which lay a plumed hat, a sword, and a gorget. Behind the train were the brother and sons of the dead chief, and files of Huron and Ottawa warriors. Madame de Champigny, attended by Philippe de RIGAUD de Vaudreuil, governor of Montreal, and staff officers closed the procession. After the Christian burial service—for the Rat was a convert of the Jesuits—the soldiers and warriors fired two volleys of musketry, one for each of the two cultures represented in the rites. Then each man in passing fired his musket a third time. Kondiaronk was interred in the church of Montreal and his tomb was inscribed: "Here lies the Rat, Huron Chief."

Today no trace of Kondiaronk's grave remains. He lies somewhere near or beneath Montreal's Place d'Armes.

WILLIAM N. FENTON

Charlevoix, *History* (Shea). *Indian tribes* (Blair). *The Iroquois book of rites*, ed. Horatio Hale (Toronto, 1963). Lahontan, *New voyages* (Thwaites). La Poterie, *Histoire* (1722). *NYCD* (O'Callaghan and Fernow), X. W. N. Fenton, *The roll call of the Iroquois chiefs; a study of a mnemonic cane from the Six Nations reserve* (Washington, 1950). Kathleen Jenkins, *Montreal, island city of the St. Lawrence* (Garden City, N.Y., 1966). W. V. Kinietz, *The Indians of the western Great Lakes, 1615–1760* (Ann Arbor, 1940). Parkman, *Count Frontenac and New France* (1891). W. N. Fenton, "An Iroquois condolence council for installing Cayuga chiefs in 1945," Washington Academy of Sciences J., XXXVI (1946), 112–27. A. F. C. Wallace, "Origins of Iroquois neutrality: The grand settlement of 1701," *Pennsylvania History*, XXIV (1957), 223–35.

KOUTAOILIBOE (Katalouibois, Koutaouileone, Outaouliboy), a leading Ottawa chief of the Kiskakon clan, from Michilimackinac; fl. 1700–1712.

In September 1700 Koutaoiliboe represented the four Ottawa clans at CALLIÈRE's peace conference with the Iroquois. The chief promised loyalty to the French and urged that hostilities cease between the Iroquois and western Indians.

La Barre

A year later, Father JOSEPH-JACQUES MAREST, writing from Michilimackinac, mentioned that Koutaoiliboe was one of his most trusted couriers. He carried messages for the French between Michilimackinac, Detroit, and Montreal from then until 1712.

After the LE PESANT affair at Detroit, much bitterness remained between the Ottawas and Miamis. In late summer of 1706, some Detroit Ottawas passed through Michilimackinac on their way to destroy the Miami post on the St Joseph River. They urged their Michilimackinac cousins, led by Onaské and Koutaoiliboe, to join the attack. Father Marest convinced Koutaoiliboe, however, that it would be unwise to attack the Saint-Joseph post, as there were missionaries there. The Ottawas did not relish the idea of another dispute over the death of a priest, such as had recently caused differences at Detroit [see Constantin DELHALLE]. They retired with gifts from Father Marest, who explained to RIGAUD de Vaudreuil: "[Koutaoiliboe] has sufficient intelligence, and influence, and is well affected enough towards us, to deserve to be conciliated."

Koutaoiliboe went to Detroit in August 1707 to attend the councils concerning Le Pesant. After being mistakenly accused by Cadillac [LAUMET] and JEAN-PAUL LEGARDEUR de Saint-Pierre of intrigue in the affair, he and other chiefs were sent with Saint-Pierre and PIERRE D'AILLEBOUST d'Argenteuil to Michilimackinac to get custody of Le Pesant. According to Koutaoiliboe—confirmed by d'Argenteuil and Saint-Pierre—he had much to do with convincing Le Pesant to surrender and go to Detroit. At a council in Montreal in October 1707, Vaudreuil said to Koutaoiliboe: "I know that Kataouliboûé's mind has always been well disposed, and his heart French; I have therefore a real esteem for him." At that time Vaudreuil gave Koutaoiliboe and the other Michilimackinac Ottawas permission to travel freely between Michilimackinac, Detroit, and Montreal, a policy he reaffirmed in July 1708. In July 1710 Koutaoiliboe visited Vaudreuil, reminded him of the Kiskakons' loyalty, and asked that the fort at Michilimackinac, abandoned since 1698, be re-established.

Father Marest wrote to Vaudreuil in June 1712 that the current Fox-French conflict in Detroit [see PEMOUSSA] was further reason for Michilimackinac to be re-established. The letter was sent via Koutaoiliboe, who, according to Marest, agreed with his plans. The missionary said that an Ottawa war chief, Saguina*, would remain in Michilimackinac; Saguina had more influence over the tribe than Koutaoiliboe and was greatly feared by the enemy.

In a subsequent letter Marest explained to Vaudreuil that Koutaoiliboe was upset because Detroit was getting all the supplies and troops, whereas the Michilimackinac Ottawas had more frequently proven their loyalty. Marest claimed that Koutaoiliboe was the only Ottawa who was always loyal to Vaudreuil. Marest was probably correct in his analysis of Koutaoiliboe's views, but it must be remembered that Marest was envious of the shift of French resources from Michilimackinac to Detroit.

Vaudreuil met Koutaoiliboe and OUENEMEK at Montreal in July 1712 to discuss the Fox problem. Koutaoiliboe presented a grandiose plan for destroying the Foxes; Vaudreuil instead agreed with Ouenemek who urged a more cautious approach.

We do not have a report of Koutaoiliboe's death, but in 1706 he was said to be one of the "old men."

DONALD CHAPUT

AN, Col., C¹¹A, 24, f.259; 26, ff.75, 124, 138; 31, ff.114–20; 33, f.77. La Poterie, *Histoire* (1722), IV, 61–62. *Michigan Pioneer Coll.*, XXXIII, 114–15, 346–50, 354–61, 366–67, 553–57. *NYCD* (O'Callaghan and Fernow), IX, 624, 718–19. Sheldon, *Early history of Michigan*, 261–62, 271–75.

L

LA BARRE, FRANÇOIS CHARON DE. *See* CHARON

LA BEAUME (BAUME), MARIEN TAILHANDIER, *dit*. *See* TAILHANDIER

LA BORDE, JEAN - BAPTISTE - JULIEN HAMARE DE. *See* HAMARE

LA BOULARDERIE, LOUIS-SIMON LE POUPET DE. *See* LE POUPET

LA BOUTEILLERIE, JEAN - BAPTISTE - FRANÇOIS DESCHAMPS DE. *See* DESCHAMPS

LA CARDONNIÈRE, AUGUSTIN ROUER DE VILLERAY ET DE. *See* ROUER

LA CETIÈRE, FLORENT DE, upholsterer, tavern-keeper, soldier, royal notary, court officer, clerk of court, judge of seneschal's court, legal practitioner, and seigneur; b. *c.* 1656 (according to the 1716 census), son of Jean de La Cetière and Anne de Bier, of Poitiers; buried 30 Oct. 1728 at Quebec.

The first mention of La Cetière's presence in Canada is on the occasion of his marriage contract, signed before Gilles Rageot* on 10 Nov. 1687. He was then an upholsterer, but speedily took on other jobs: in 1695 he was at one and the same time an upholsterer, a tavern-keeper (and had been since at least the preceding year), a soldier in the Quebec garrison, and a legal practitioner. A man ready to turn his hand to anything, and with never a penny to his name!

He had already been a court officer for a short while when in 1702 he received a commission as royal notary in the provost court of Quebec. The opinions of the persons called to testify to his "character," on 21 June 1702, were completely unfavourable to him: a few years earlier (1695?) he had embarked in secret on a ship leaving for France, in an attempt to desert the garrison and defraud his creditors; he had placed himself in questionable situations, had become bankrupt, was dishonest, had been forbidden to "plead" (as a legal practitioner); in short, he had a bad reputation. Nevertheless, thanks to powerful protection, La Cetière was received into the profession of notary.

In 1704 La Cetière was a clerk in the registry of the provost court of Quebec; in 1707 he unofficially succeeded the principal court clerk, François Rageot*, on the latter's resignation. But heavy, ominous clouds were already gathering over his head. Gradually he had "taken possession of the mind" of Bermen de La Martinière, the lieutenant-general, who became his instrument. Louis XIV demanded his dismissal: on 10 Nov. 1707 Jacques Raudot suspended him. At the same time Barbel denounced him for acting simultaneously on behalf of clients whose interests conflicted. The charge was brought before the Conseil Supérieur, which on 5 December forbade him to offer his services as an attorney for any party in a legal action for three months, and in addition suspended him as a notary and court officer; on 12 December the council ordered a new inquiry into his "character" for the period during which he held his judicial offices; the inquiry took place on the 17th, and two days later the council lifted the suspension from La Cetière, although cautioning him severely against dishonest practices. One may wonder whether the Raudots were not protecting him, as is suggested by the muddle-headed

Ruette d'Auteuil, who mentions La Cetière as one of the intendant's subdelegates around 1706. Any one else would have lost his head and his reputation; but in 1709 La Cetière was again a clerk in the registry of the provost court!

La Cetière continued his career. On 15 Feb. 1710 Jacques Raudot appointed him third court officer of the Conseil Supérieur. He had authorized him on 3 Jan. 1709 to exercise the profession of notary throughout the colony, except within the confines of Montreal and Trois-Rivières. Then in 1713 we find La Cetière a clerk in the court registry of the Conseil Supérieur. The year following, on 21 Feb. 1714, he received another commission, this time as judge of the seneschal's court in the jurisdiction of Beauport, and on the same day he successfully underwent the traditional inquiry concerning his "character."

At the height of his career, this former tavern-keeper who had become a judge permitted himself the luxury of acquiring an arriere-fief, that of Vilmé, in the Lauson seigneury; he paid 1,000 *livres* for it on 22 Jan. 1724.

Beset from all sides by his numerous occupations, La Cetière had little time to be meticulous. After his death in 1728, it was discovered that 214 of the notarial acts received by him were signed neither by himself nor by the witnesses. The council had to ratify them, after an inventory charged to the estate. La Cetière, moreover, left more debts than assets: to his female servant alone he owed 900 *livres* in wages—the price of his arriere-fief and of his seigneurial title!

ANDRÉ VACHON

AJQ, Greffe de Louis Chambalon; Greffe d'Étienne Dubreuil, 22 janv. 1724. AQ, NF, Coll. de pièces jud. et not., 2019, 2034, 2041; NF, Ins. de la Prév. de Québec, III, 566; NF, Ord. des int., I, 26v, 142; IV, 17v *et seq. Jug. et délib.*, III, IV, V, VI. "Lettres et mémoires de F.-M.-F. Ruette d'Auteuil," 55. Recensement de Québec, 1716 (Beaudet). Gareau, "La prévôté de Québec," 116–18. J.-E. Roy, *Histoire du notariat*, I. Vachon, *Histoire du notariat*, 29, 39.

LA CHASSAIGNE, JEAN BOUILLET DE. *See* BOUILLET

LA CHESNAYE. *See* AUBERT

LACHEVROTIÈRE, FRANÇOIS DE CHAVIGNY. *See* CHAVIGNY

LACISERAYE, MICHEL LEFEBVRE, *dit.* *See* LEFEBVRE

LA COLOMBIÈRE, JOSEPH DE, priest, canon, vicar general, archdeacon, ecclesiastical

325

La Colombière

councillor on the Conseil Supérieur, precentor; b. 1651 at Vienne (province of Dauphiné), son of Bertrand de La Colombière, a magistrate, and Marguerite Coindat; d. 18 July 1723 at Quebec.

Joseph, who has been incorrectly called Serré de La Colombière or La Colombière-Serré, was the younger brother of the Jesuit Claude de La Colombière, who was famous for his preaching of the devotion to the Sacred Heart and who was to be beatified in 1929. Joseph had been a lawyer for five or six years when he joined the Sulpicians. Shortly after receiving the priesthood he left for New France and arrived in the colony on 21 July 1682. He was highly recommended by his superior in Paris, M. Tronson, and was considered by him as a possible replacement for DOLLIER de Casson, with whom he went to work at Montreal.

At first he carried out his ministry there to everyone's satisfaction and was confessor for the nuns of the Hôtel-Dieu and the Congrégation de Notre-Dame. In addition, he quickly acquired renown as a sacred orator. In 1690, when he was chaplain to the troops from Montreal who had gone to aid the inhabitants of Quebec during its siege by Phips*, La Colombière preached a sermon as part of the ceremony of thanksgiving for the victory. In the presence of Buade* de Frontenac and the assembled military forces he was not afraid to attribute all the credit for the defeat of the English exclusively to the Virgin. The following year he was recalled to France for having supported the cause of Sister Tardy, a visionary whose influence was a menace to authority in the different religious communities in Montreal.

La Colombière landed in France in the middle of July 1691, along with Bishop Saint-Vallier [LA CROIX]. Despairing of ever obtaining permission to return to New France, he left Saint-Sulpice to go to live in the seminary of the Missions Étrangères. The bishop brought him back to Quebec on 9 Aug. 1692, against Tronson's advice.

It was not long before the former Sulpician fell a victim to the quarrelsome prelate. In December the procedure of his elevation to the canonry was the subject of a serious difference between the bishop and the chapter of Quebec. According to Bishop LAVAL, M. de Merlac*, precentor of the chapter, was trying to destroy Bishop Saint-Vallier's confidence in La Colombière. The latter, for his part, was writing to various religious and civil authorities about the crisis that the church was going through in Canada, a crisis that frightened him, he said, much more than did the Iroquois. He laid the blame for this crisis mainly on Laval's successor and demanded Bishop Saint-Vallier's resignation, as much for the bishop's own spiritual welfare as for the sake of the colony.

Bishop Laval said that providence wanted to use La Colombière "to defend the truth"; he added that "he has an upright and sincere heart and acts in all things with much prudence and truly in the spirit of God; and it seems as if he were sent here this year for the sole purpose of perceiving clearly the evil spirit by which the bishop of Quebec is impelled and animated. . . ."

Saint-Vallier was not long, however, in regaining his esteem for La Colombière, since in 1694 he made him the ecclesiastical superior of the Hôtel-Dieu of Quebec. In addition, on 2 May 1698 he appointed him vicar general, and on the following 14 August archdeacon of the chapter of Quebec, offices which were to be especially heavy during Bishop Saint-Vallier's absence from 1700 till 1713. On 16 June 1703 the bishop added to these offices that of ecclesiastical councillor of the Conseil Supérieur of New France, a position which, unfortunately for the holder's disastrous financial situation, did not entail any remuneration. But in 1709, being dissatisfied with the manner in which La Colombière was carrying out his duties as confessor to the Nuns Hospitallers of the Hôtel-Dieu, Bishop Saint-Vallier relieved him of these duties. La Colombière was definitively restored to favour five years later, and on 11 Jan. 1722 he was promoted to be precentor of the chapter of Quebec. This was the last dignity he achieved.

On 18 July 1723, after being paralyzed for a few days, La Colombière died at the Hôtel-Dieu of Quebec, where he had been living for some years. Although he had been reconciled with the Sulpicians, he had never been able to obtain his readmission among them, which had not prevented the authorities of the order from favouring his appointment to the office of superior of the Charon Brothers [see François CHARON de La Barre], whose work the archdeacon had at heart. He left behind him the memory of an eloquent, cordial man, devoted, modest, charitable, disinterested, and much attached to the worship of the Virgin Mary. He had even been thought of at one time as the coadjutor to Bishop Saint-Vallier. Bishop Laval (whose funeral sermon he later pronounced), the seminary of the Missions Étrangères, and the nuns of the Hôtel-Dieu of Quebec in particular extolled his merits. Pontchartrain for his part said of La Colombière in 1710: "He is a fine person, who is labouring in New France with good results, through the purity of his morals and through his preachings."

What, however, perhaps distinguishes him even more is that, in the troubled period in which he lived, people counted on him "to handle matters gently."

CÉLINE DUPRÉ

La Corne de Chaptes

ASQ, Chapitre, 69, 101, 139a; Lettres, M, 12, 13, 37, 7f.; 38, 36–38; N, 99, 101, 10; 102, 4; 129, 5; O, 12, 7; 45, 48; R, 6; Paroisse de Quebec, 3a, 33; Polygraphie, XVIII, 54. Caron, "Inventaire de documents," APQ Rapport, 1939–40; 1940–41. Juchereau, Annales (Jamet). Jug. et délib., V, VI. Taillemite, Inventaire analytique, série B, I.

Casgrain, Histoire de l'Hôtel-Dieu de Québec. [É.-M. Faillon], Vie de la Sœur Bourgeoys, fondatrice de la Congrégation de Notre-Dame de Villemarie en Canada, suivie de l'histoire de cet institut jusqu'à ce jour (2v., Ville-Marie [Montréal], 1853), I, 378–96. Gosselin, L'Église du Canada, II. Monseigneur de Saint-Vallier et l'Hôpital Général de Québec. Ernest Myrand, M. de la Colombière, orateur: historique d'un sermon célèbre prononcé à Notre-Dame de Québec, le 5 novembre 1690, à l'occasion de la levée du siège de cette ville . . . , suivi des relations officielles de Frontenac, Monseignat et Juchereau de Saint-Ignace . . . (Montréal, 1898). Les Ursulines de Québec (1866–78), II, 27–29. Amédée Gosselin, "Essai de biographie de l'abbé Joseph de La Colombière," RSCT, 3d ser., XXIX (1935), sect.I, 87–108. Alfred Rambaud, "La vie orageuse et douloureuse de Mgr de Saint-Vallier," RUL, IX (1954), 96.

LA CORNE DE CHAPTES, JEAN-LOUIS DE, king's lieutenant at Montreal; b. 23 Oct. 1666 at Chaptes, in the commune of Beauregard-Vendon (department of Puy-de-Dôme), son of Luc de La Corne and Antoinette d'Allemagne; d. 6 May 1732 at Montreal.

In 1685 New France welcomed a young soldier, second lieutenant La Corne, who was descended from a noble family of the province of Auvergne. Only 19 years old, he had already lost an eye in battle. In 1691 Buade* de Frontenac granted him a commission as a lieutenant, which received royal approval on 1 March 1693, the year in which he was wounded in the thigh while on active service. On 4 June 1698 he received a year's leave to go to France; this leave was renewed on 25 May 1699 and 8 June 1701.

Three years later we find him at Fort Frontenac (Cataracoui, now Kingston, Ont.), contending with the Ottawas; the latter were attacking the Iroquois who had pitched their tents not far from Cataracoui. Suspecting La Corne of having been a trouble-maker in this affair, Louis XIV withheld the promotion of a man whom he had always considered up to then "as a good officer." But the authorities of the colony lost no time in establishing his innocence, and on 27 May 1706, at their urgent request, he was promoted captain. The preceding year, according to GÉDÉON DE CATALOGNE, Jean-Louis de La Corne had lost the command of Fort Frontenac because he had had an artillery salute fired in honour of LAUMET, dit de Lamothe Cadillac, who was at that time on

bad terms with Governor RIGAUD de Vaudreuil. On 15 Nov. 1707 Vaudreuil and JACQUES RAUDOT requested the cross of the order of Saint-Louis for La Corne, assuring the minister that the latter was "a very good and brave officer, who is all covered with wounds." However, it was a little more than five years before the king granted La Corne the decoration.

In 1712 La Corne, through the mediation of Vaudreuil, vainly entreated the king to give him the command of Fort Chambly. On the other hand, on 12 May 1714 he became town major of Trois-Rivières, and on 27 April 1716 garrison adjutant in the colonial regular troops at Quebec. In a document dated 1722 appears the following favourable comment by Vaudreuil on La Corne; "He leads a steady life, and performs very well his duties as garrison adjutant. Of the many wounds that he has received, one has cost him an eye and another has maimed him in one arm, but he is capable of marching anywhere where his services may be required." Consequently, on 8 Feb. 1724, the king granted to this disabled officer a pension of 400 livres, and on 23 April 1726 named him king's lieutenant at Montreal. A few months after this last promotion, La Corne informed the new governor, Beauharnois* de La Boische, that the English had incited the Five Nations to destroy the French fort at Niagara. Then, on 13 Feb. 1731, he drafted a report, which was forwarded to the minister, on the need for setting up a trading post at Pointe de la Couronne, on Lake Champlain. That autumn Beauharnois praised La Corne, saying that he was an excellent man, who was active and vigilant, and who loved the service. But his devotion to the king seems to have brought La Corne more wounds and praises than fortune. Indeed, when he died on 6 May 1732, he left his wife in straitened circumstances. Marie Pécaudy de Contrecœur, whom he had married on 11 June 1695, owed the seminary of Quebec, in 1734, 450 livres "for her sons' board."

Jean-Louis de La Corne de Chaptes was the founder of one of the most important families in New France, and four of his sons became knights of the order of Saint-Louis.

CÉLINE DUPRÉ

AN, Col., C¹¹ᴬ, 120, ff.126v., 127ff. ASQ, MSS, 132, 133; Polygraphie, XXII, 28; Séminaire, V, 57. Coll. de manuscrits relatifs à la N.-F., I, 607. "Correspondance de Vaudreuil," APQ Rapport, 1938–39, 66, 80, 95, 127; 1939–40, 402; 1947–48, 183, 226, 260, 270. Lettres de noblesse (P.-G. Roy), I, 217–60. NYCD (O'Callaghan and Fernow), IX. P.-G. Roy, Inv. concessions, II, IV; Inventaire des papiers de Léry conservés aux Archives de la province de Québec

La Croix de Chevrières

(3v., Québec, 1939–40), I, 172f. Taillemite, *Inventaire analytique, série B*, I. Fauteux, *Les chevaliers de Saint-Louis*, 106. P.-G. Roy, *Les officiers d'état-major*, 113–16. Emmanuel de Cathelineau, "Gens d'Auvergne en Canada: l'abbé de La Corne, généalogiste," *NF*, IV (1929), 259–82; "Gens d'Auvergne en Canada: le sieur de Vernerolles et ses amis," *NF*, III (1927–28), 157–61. J.-J. Lefebvre, "Luc Lacorne de Saint-Luc," APQ *Rapport, 1947–48*, 31.

LA CROIX DE CHEVRIÈRES DE SAINT-VALLIER, JEAN-BAPTISTE DE, second bishop of Quebec; b. 14 Nov. 1653 at Grenoble, son of Jean de La Croix de Chevrières de Saint-Vallier and Marie de Sayve; d. 26 Dec. 1727 at Quebec.

Jean-Baptiste de La Croix's family ranked among the best in Dauphiné: country noblemen, officers, magistrates, ambassadors. Jean de La Croix, his great-grandfather, was a talented lawyer and a poet when the fancy struck him; he was first a judge in the *parlement* of Grenoble, then, after he lost his wife, a priest and bishop of Grenoble. Jean-Baptiste's father divided his career between the magistrature at Grenoble and the diplomatic service. He married Marie de Sayve, the daughter of a magistrate at Dijon; they had ten children, three of whom entered religion. The La Croixs were large land owners and in particular owned the *château* of Saint-Vallier on the banks of the Rhone, which had formerly belonged to Diane de Poitiers, King Henry II's famous mistress.

It was in this *château* that Jean-Baptiste's childhood was spent in part. Beyond this we know practically nothing of his youth, other than that he was charitable, that he studied at the Jesuit college in Grenoble, and that he early thought of the priesthood. He entered the seminary of Saint-Sulpice in Paris and at 19 years of age obtained a licentiate in theology, in 1672. Four years later, in 1676, even before he was ordained and thanks to his family's connections, he was appointed almoner in ordinary to Louis XIV. He was not ordained a priest until 1681.

Licence was still the keynote of life at the Sun King's court, and Madame de Montespan continued to reign over the heart and senses of Louis XIV. The young abbé did not, however, let himself be seduced by the apparent brilliance of this "delightful life." No doubt influenced by the whole movement that had been born of the French counter-reformation—although we are badly informed about the stages in his intellectual development—and being a personal friend of the bishop of Grenoble, Le Camus, who was well known for his moral rigour, he immediately exhibited the utmost austerity. Instead of assuming court dress, he kept his cassock, and in his spare time he began to visit regularly hospitals, prisons, and country parishes. In 1683 he founded a hospital with his own money in the little town of Saint-Vallier. Later, in his funeral oration for Bishop Saint-Vallier, Abbé Fornel* was to exclaim dramatically: "What an astonishing sight meets my eyes! Our new Jean-Baptiste purifies himself at the court of kings, in the midst of delights, what a prodigy!"

In 1684 Abbé Saint-Vallier was 31 and already his appointment to a see in France was generally anticipated. At that time his spiritual director, the Jesuit Father Le Valois, rather an influential personage in the ecclesiastical circles of the capital, spoke to him of the see of Quebec. The incumbent of the see, Bishop LAVAL, was thinking of resigning. He proposed to come to France to ask Louis XIV to choose a successor for him. Would Abbé Saint-Vallier agree to be this successor?

An ambitious priest would certainly have refused. Created just ten years before, situated two or three months' sailing time from France, burdened with a harsh climate, the diocese of Quebec in 1684 was perhaps the most wretched and difficult of all the dioceses in mission lands. It was immense, taking in the greater part of the territories that had already been explored in North America: Newfoundland, Acadia, the valley of the St Lawrence, the region of the Great Lakes, and even the whole of the valley of the Mississippi, which Cavelier* de La Salle had just traversed down to its mouth. This diocese on a continental scale was on the other hand scarcely populated. And what diocesans! Nine out of ten were Indians, who were almost completely refractory to Christianity and who were on the brink of resuming the offensive against the French. In the midst of these Indians there was a handful of French settlers, barely more than 10,000. Many of them led a Christian and truly family life, often a pious one; but half of the young men, attracted by the call of adventure and profit, were coureurs de bois, seeking the precious furs. They distributed spirits lavishly, and made the Indians drunk in order to filch their pelts or their women. When they came back from the woods, they led a gay life at Montreal, which had lost much of its original Christian fervour. "Good cheer, women, gambling, liquor, everything goes," observed a contemporary, Baron de Lahontan [LOM d'Arce].

To evangelize the Indians and to keep the French within the bounds of Christianity, however, the clergy in Canada was not lacking in numbers, since there were already about a hundred priests—Jesuits, Sulpicians, Recollets, priests of the Missions Étrangères in Paris—and around a hundred nuns. These priests and nuns, the majority of whom had come from France, were for the most part devoted, of strict orthodoxy and pure morals, but also quarrelsome and fond of litigation. Moreover, financial resources were lacking, and the relations between the church and the colonial authorities were sometimes extremely strained. The root of the quarrel was the question of spirits. Bishop Laval would have liked to limit the importation of spirits and forbid their sale to the Indians. The governors objected. In their view the trade in alcohol was necessary for the development of commerce and for good relations with the Indian tribes. Versailles tended to uphold the governors against Bishop Laval, who was considered too rigorous.

In short, only a truly apostolic priest could accept so onerous a charge as the see of Quebec. Abbé Saint-Vallier had the soul of an apostle. He did not hesitate for one minute in giving his assent. His family protested in vain; he disregarded their objections. In January 1685 Bishop Laval, who had returned to France, offered his resignation to the king and proposed that Abbé Saint-Vallier succeed him. Louis XIV forthwith appointed his young almoner to the see of Quebec. The consecration, however, had to be postponed. Pope Innocent XI, who had been on bad terms with the king since the affair of the Regale and the declaration of the four Articles, was not granting any more bulls of investiture. Abbé Saint-Vallier left for Canada with the title simply of Bishop Laval's vicar general. He hoped that upon his return the quarrel between the pope and the king would have ended and he could receive his bulls.

Abbé Saint-Vallier's first sojourn in Canada lasted 18 months. Despite his lack of training the young priest astonished the clergy by his endurance and his zeal. First he visited Quebec, next all the parishes along the St Lawrence, and finally Montreal. Then, following the inland rivers and lakes, he went with two priests and a small escort to distant Acadia. He left in the spring of 1686 without even waiting for the break-up of the ice. They went from river to river, from lake to lake. Sometimes they had to break the ice to get the canoes through. At one time they thought they would die of starvation. Then came the summer, the unbearable mosquito bites, the humid heat. Everywhere they met Frenchmen or Indians, Abbé Saint-Vallier preached, catechized, rebuked, praised. He ate little, scarcely slept, and worked unceasingly. When he returned to Quebec in the autumn of 1686 he even thought of going inland as far as the Great Lakes.

The clergy in Canada was filled with admiration at such zeal, but it was also frightened. Indeed, it quickly perceived that Saint-Vallier had all the defects of his qualities. Dynamic and enterprising, he was also headstrong, domineering, taking no account of the advice of his associates. He was demanding for his subordinates, as he was for himself. "I do not seek to please people," he had, moreover, stated openly. Finally, he spent his own money lavishly and did the same with that of others. When he left Quebec the seminary found itself 10,000 *livres* deeper in debt.

The superiors of the seminary wrote to give their impressions to Bishop Laval, who had remained in Paris during Saint-Vallier's stay in Canada. They were categorical; despite his zeal and his talents, Abbé Saint-Vallier did not appear to them to be at all the man who was needed to govern the diocese of Quebec. Bishop Laval sided with them and asked Abbé Saint-Vallier to withdraw. Offended, Saint-Vallier refused and was backed up by Louis XIV, who even forbade Bishop Laval to return to Quebec. Bishop Laval was dismayed; his only dream was to die at Quebec, within the church that he had contributed to founding. In his bitterness he accused his successor of having suggested to the court that he be kept in France. Saint-Vallier protested vigorously against this accusation.

In 1688, however, the atmosphere became calmer. As the pope had sent the necessary bulls, Abbé Saint-Vallier could be consecrated bishop at Saint-Sulpice in Paris on 25 Jan. 1688. He immediately begged the king to allow Bishop Laval to return to Canada. Louis XIV let himself be moved. Bishop Laval did not wait an instant to leave. Despite his age and his infirmities, he went on horseback to La Rochelle, whence he sailed immediately for Canada. Some weeks later Saint-Vallier left the capital in his turn and arrived at Quebec on 31 July 1688.

With Bishop Saint-Vallier's return there began for the church in Canada a long period of crisis which lasted no fewer than 16 years, from 1688 to 1704. It started with a violent, and inevitable quarrel between the bishop and his seminary. It was directed by three priests who had deeply wounded Saint-Vallier by asking for his resignation at the beginning of 1687: Bernières*, ANGO Des Maizerets, and GLANDELET. Secondly, Bishop Laval, the founder of the seminary, had granted it privileges which went beyond what was usual. It was not only a house for the preparation of future priests, but also a true religious community which was affiliated with the Séminaire des Missions Étrangères in Paris and included all the parish priests of the colony, in short, all the secular clergy. Three quarters of the clergy in Canada— Recollets, Sulpicians, Jesuits—already escaped the direct authority of the bishop, who found

La Croix de Chevrières

himself, in addition, obliged to share his jurisdiction over his own secular clergy with his seminary.

In the autumn of 1688 Bishop Saint-Vallier demanded an immediate and complete change in the organization of the seminary. The seminary refused, and the bishop spoke of revolt against his lawful authority. His adversaries denounced the prelate's unbearable and tyrannical character and even insinuated that Saint-Vallier had Jansenists in his *entourage*, in particular the vicar general whom he had brought from France, Abbé Merlac*. Bishop Laval, whom his successor's jealousy had forced to leave Quebec to take refuge at Cap Tourmente, sided with the seminary. Quickly all moderation was forgotten on both sides. It must be said that times were hard and nerves were generally on edge. The Iroquois had resumed their massacres of French settlers. The English were coming to besiege Quebec. The mother country sometimes hinted that it would give up Canada.

Finally, to resolve this deadlock, Saint-Vallier went in person in the spring of 1691 to demand arbitration in France. The king named as arbiters the archbishop of Paris and his own confessor, Father La Chaise. Both of them decided in favour of the bishop on the essential points. The seminary of Quebec lost its privileges and came under the usual rule. The bishop returned to Quebec in triumph. Had he not prophesied before his departure: "We shall see whether he was bishop or not"?

Thereupon developed the great quarrels of 1693–94, "terrible years for the church in Canada." It is impossible to go into detail here about these quarrels, which were, besides, often petty but always extremely revealing of Saint-Vallier's temperament, his preferences in doctrinal matters, and the religious atmosphere of the period. Let us say simply that during those two years Saint-Vallier achieved the extraordinary feat of falling out not only with the governor of New France, Frontenac [Buade*], who wanted to have *Tartuffe* played at Quebec but because of the bishop's opposition had to give it up, with the governor of Montreal, CALLIÈRE, and with certain officers of the troops stationed in the colony, but also with the cathedral chapter, the seminary, the Recollets [*see* JOSEPH DENYS], the Jesuits [*see* BOUVART, COUVERT], the nuns of the Hôtel-Dieu of Quebec [*see* JUCHEREAU de Saint-Ignace, MARGUERITE BOURDON], and the nuns of the Congrégation de Notre-Dame [*see* BARBIER]. At the end of the summer of 1694 almost the whole diocese of Quebec was in rebellion against the authority of the bishop.

Reports sent to Louis XIV denounced Saint-Vallier's tyranny. The king ordered the prelate to come to France to justify himself. The bishop obeyed. In December 1694 he was in Paris. After hearing him, Louis XIV urged him to resign. Saint-Vallier refused. He could not be reproached with any serious offence against either morality or doctrine. Perhaps he had only sinned through excessive zeal! But after all, was it not up to subordinates to obey? Moreover, added Saint-Vallier, his adversaries forgot to mention the positive side of the first six years of his episcopate. Had he not founded the Hôpital Général (1692), begun the construction of a palace for the bishop (1688), installed the Jesuits and Recollets at Montreal (1692), contributed to the creation of a new community of brothers hospitallers [*see* François CHARON de La Barre], visited Newfoundland, made a second trip to Acadia (1689), encouraged his diocesans' resistance against the English (1690)? In truth, what bishop in France could say more?

Louis XIV asked the advice of his *entourage*. Madame de Maintenon declined to give an opinion. Fénelon asked to be excused: he was ill informed of the problems of the church in Canada. Bossuet considered that Saint-Vallier was not capable of governing his diocese well, but that if he would not hand in his resignation, he could not be kept in France. That would be contrary to the decisions of the Council of Trent, which made it an obligation for bishops to live in their diocese. Father La Chaise, the king's confessor and a Jesuit with great influence at court, also hesitated to express an opinion. He knew the prelate's irritableness. If the king ever allowed him to return to Canada despite the Jesuits' opposition, would he not seek vengeance by taking all their Indian missions away from them? That would spell the ruin of the Society in North America. Father La Chaise decided to remain neutral.

For two years Saint-Vallier maintained his desire to return to Canada. In 1697 Louis XIV summoned him to Versailles and tried once more to obtain his resignation. Saint-Vallier refused. The king then allowed the bishop to return to Quebec, and Saint-Vallier promised to be "prudent," that is to say, to moderate his zeal.

In the summer of 1697, then, he returned to Quebec. There followed a few months of calm and peace in the diocese. The bishop took advantage of them to authorize a new Ursuline establishment at Trois-Rivières and to become reconciled with his seminary.

But in 1698 a new conflict broke out with the Jesuits over the missions in the Mississippi country. The quarrel originated on the upper Mississippi, where the Jesuits were preaching the gospel to the Illinois Indians in the triangle formed by the Mississippi, the Ohio, and the Great Lakes. They were alone in this immense region. In 1698 the seminary of Quebec, whose purpose was not only the preparation of future priests but also the conversion of the heathen, asked its bishop for the right to go to evangelize the little village of the Tamaroas not far from the junction of the Missouri and the Mississippi. Saint-Vallier, who wanted henceforth only to be on friendly terms with his seminary, gave his consent. Three priests from the seminary of Quebec, BUISSON de Saint-Cosme (1667–1706), DAVION, and Montigny*, went off to live among the Tamaroas. But then the Jesuits raised an outcry. Others were coming to set up missions in their territory! The Tamaroas were Illinois, of the same race and language as all the other Illinois. The evangelization of all the Illinois had been entrusted to the Jesuits by Bishop Saint-Vallier himself in letters patent dated 16 Dec. 1690. It was a flagrant injustice.

The Jesuits displayed all the more anxiety since at that date a great dispute in the Far East was setting them against the priests of the Missions Étrangères, on which depended the seminary of Quebec. The Jesuits in China had allowed their new converts to continue rendering certain obeisance to Confucius and celebrating certain ceremonies in honour of their ancestors. The priests of the Missions Étrangères, who were also evangelizing China, had protested against this attitude on the part of the Jesuits; in their view this was a lapse into idolatry and superstition. The dispute had become more acrimonious, with the Jesuits accusing their adversaries of wanting to take their missions in the Far East from them. From China the controversy had spread to Rome, then to Paris, and finally as far as Canada. The Jesuits' violent reaction in the affair of the Tamaroas is therefore understandable. There were those who wanted to expel them not only from China, but also from America. Firm resistance was called for.

Bishop Saint-Vallier was called upon to settle the conflict. He decided absolutely against the Jesuits. They refused this arbitration. Again an avalanche of contradictory letters descended upon Paris. The king did not know in whose favour to decide, and besides, he could not make anything out of all this uproar over a tiny Indian village lost in the heart of North America. The Missions Étrangères in Paris themselves tended towards a compromise. But Bishop Saint-Vallier was not a man to capitulate, even before the redoubtable Society of Jesus. In 1700 he came to Paris, moved heaven and earth, and finally obtained satisfaction in June 1701. The Tamaroas stayed with the seminary of Quebec. But the Jesuits in Canada were deeply hurt. They denounced the bishop to their general in Rome. One of them even went so far as to describe him as "a terrible scourge which has caused more ravages in the spiritual domain than an enemy army can cause in the temporal. He is a relentless enemy of the Society, who speaks of all Jesuits as scoundrels." For his part the superior wrote: "Under the sheep's skin of the shepherd he hides a wolf who is most enraged against our Society."

Two years after the settlement of the affair of the Tamaroas, while Bishop Saint-Vallier was still in France, a new conflict broke out with the Society of Jesus over this same subject of the missions. This time the theatre was the lower Mississippi. A new colony, Louisiana, had just been founded; who was going to receive the responsibility for evangelizing it? Again the Jesuits and the priests of the Missions Étrangères entered into competition. To avoid all possibility of future discord, the Jesuits demanded a district where their superior would also be the bishop of Quebec's vicar general. Bishop Saint-Vallier flared up: "Never would he make a Jesuit his vicar general." The Society then recalled the three Jesuits who had already been sent to Louisiana. The priests of the Missions Étrangères remained there by themselves.

Having been ill treated by Bishop Saint-Vallier, the Jesuits in Canada took their revenge in rather a cruel way. In 1702 and 1703 the bishop had published a *Catechism* and a *Ritual*: these works were sombre, harsh, austere in inspiration, representative of the tendency most often called "moral Jansenism." To cite only one example, the *Catechism* resolved the formidable problem of the number of the damned and the blessed in the most severe way: "Question: Will the number of the damned be much greater than the number of the blessed? Answer: Yes, the road to perdition is broad, whereas the road which leads to the everlasting life is narrow." Despite this pessimistic note, *Ritual* and *Catechism* were nevertheless perfectly orthodox. Bishop Saint-Vallier, who was still settling his affairs in France, sent some copies of them to Quebec. Father Bouvart, the superior of the Jesuits, read them, leaped to his pen, and wrote a long indictment to prove that the bishop's works lapsed into Arianism, Pelagianism, Jansenism, Lutheranism, and Calvinism. These accusations were based upon certain sentences into which errors had slipped at the time of printing or which had been awkwardly phrased by Bishop Saint-Vallier. For example, the *Ritual* stated: "God usually gives his actual graces to those persons who are prepared to receive a sacrament." In the

La Croix de Chevrières

adverb "usually" Father Bouvart saw a Jansenist affirmation. "Always" was required, or "usually" had to be taken out.

Naturally, the bishop was informed of the Jesuit's criticism and he complained to the Sorbonne, which condemned Bouvart's work as "rash, tending to create schism and revolt in the flock against the shepherd, and most injurious to His Excellency the Bishop of Quebec, who is shamefully treated in it." Despite his indignation, Saint-Vallier was sufficiently shrewd to recognize that if Father Bouvart's criticism often fell into insolence, certain reproaches were perfectly justified. He hastened to publish a second edition of his *Ritual*, which had been much more badly treated than the *Catechism*.

The theological dispute stopped there. It marked the end of this long period of incessant quarrelling which had begun in 1688. Now the bishop was above all to know suffering.

In the month of July 1704 Bishop Saint-Vallier left La Rochelle once more for Canada. He had spent nearly four years in Europe and had even been able to take a trip as far as Rome, where Clement XI had received cordially the first bishop from North America to come to make a visit to the pope. Now the prelate was in a hurry to get back to Quebec and take up again the administration of his diocese.

Alas! At that time the War of the Spanish Succession was raging. France was no longer mistress of the seas. Off the Azores an English fleet attacked the convoy to which Bishop Saint-Vallier's ship belonged. The convoy was scattered and the ship carrying the bishop surrendered. Saint-Vallier was taken prisoner and was even insulted by a sailor who seized him by the throat to take his pectoral cross. Then, with the 16 ecclesiastics in his company, he was taken to England.

Queen Anne was on the throne. She agreed to release the prelate only if Louis XIV on his side set free another ecclesiastic, the dean of the cathedral of Liège, the Baron de Méan, who had been carried off from his cathedral because of his intrigues with France's adversaries. Versailles refused to set the Baron de Méan free, first because he was a dangerous man for France's interests, and then because people were not unhappy to be rid for a time of a bishop who, despite his zeal, had a genius for getting into quarrels. Certain of the prelate's adversaries even hoped that if his captivity were prolonged, he would tender his resignation.

Saint-Vallier did not resign, but for five years he remained a prisoner in little towns on the outskirts of London. Five years of boredom, of inaction, of vexations on the part of the English, of hopes of liberation that were always dashed, of petty quarrels with his ecclesiastical suite, of physical suffering too. Bishop Saint-Vallier was still young; at the beginning of his captivity he was only 51. But the tumultuous existence he had led had worn him out prematurely. In the winter of 1704–5 he even thought that he would die.

In 1709, however, Louis XIV consented to set free the dean of Liège. The English released Bishop Saint-Vallier, who rushed to Paris and immediately asked to leave again for Canada. The news that he had received from his diocese was bad. Bishop Laval had died in 1708: no one could ordain new priests at Quebec. Yet successive epidemics had reduced the numbers of the clergy in Canada. In addition, reports indicated a marked decline in morality, great licentiousness, much greed among the rich, and hostility towards the church on the part of the colonial authorities.

Abbé Glandelet even wrote to his bishop: "Disorders of unchastity are so frequent and so usual, that no one tries to keep them secret any more. Nothing is so common as to see young girls pregnant, and a distinguished person who knows very well everything that is going on in Quebec told me a few days ago that half of Quebec was an outright b. . . . This poor colony greatly needs to have people who would sustain it by their example and their piety. . . . The priests are not backed up . . . and on the contrary the desire seems to be to make them contemptible."

Without doubt Abbé Glandelet's pessimistic descriptions were exaggerated, but they strongly impressed the bishop, who was much inclined himself to believe that almost all his diocesans were living in a state of perdition. Only the bishop's immediate return would make it possible to put a stop to such a flood of vice.

The king did not, however, allow this return, for a renewal of the religious disputes was feared at Versailles. For four years, from 1709 to 1713, Saint-Vallier was forced to remain in France, in what could be called his second exile. He took advantage of it to visit the abbeys which his diocese owned in France, sent some regulations to his clergy, took an interest in the recruiting of new settlers, squabbled with his seminary; above all, he was bored.

In 1711 a long report addressed to the king once more summed up the benefits of Bishop Saint-Vallier's administration. Louis XIV was not moved. In the spring of 1713, after being on the point of death for a short time during the winter of 1711–12, the bishop sent a new letter, formally reminding Louis XIV of his responsibilities as sovereign; in keeping the bishop in

France simply at his own desire, the king was taking upon himself "before God" all the grievous consequences that might result from it. "His Majesty will perhaps be very much surprised one day to see that God will not impute as a fault the fact of having done too much, but that of not having done enough." This time Louis XIV gave in. Without waiting any longer, Saint-Vallier sailed from La Rochelle and landed at Quebec on 17 Aug. 1713. The whole town was there, eager to see its bishop again after an absence of 13 years. They found him aged, tired, changed in appearance. He was no longer the slender, brisk, haughty young bishop of the early years of his episcopate, but a melancholy old man with heavy, drooping shoulders and thick, flabby jowls. During the winter of 1713–14 he again believed that he was going to die. His *entourage* urged him to take some rest. His reply was: "Would I not be only too happy to die in the midst of works undertaken for the glory of God?" As soon as he was well again he resumed his usual tasks, but he had lost his vigour of former years and on several occasions he had to take to his bed.

To these physical sufferings were added moral ones. Doubtless, in the last years of his life, the prelate succeeded in reaching a reconciliation with the Jesuits—one of them, Father La Chasse*, even became his personal confessor and pronounced his funeral oration—and in living on good terms with the Sulpicians, the Recollets, and the various communities of nuns. But grudges subsisted between Bishop Saint-Vallier and his seminary. The parish priests, and particularly those born in Canada, did not like their bishop. The canons likewise found fault with the prelate who, for his part, did not have any particular scruples about reproaching them for their fondness for bourgeois comforts and their laziness. Furthermore, relations between the colonial authorities and the bishop's palace were lacking in cordiality. The governor, RIGAUD de Vaudreuil, was accused of infringing the rights of the church. The bishop called him sharply to order, and when the governor died in 1725 he refused to have the passing-bell tolled at the cathedral.

Such intransigence was undoubtedly maladroit. It helped create a sort of moral isolation about the bishop's old age. In 1713 the king had given him a coadjutor, a Capuchin, Bishop Mornay. He never came to New France, but in October 1727, some months before his death, Bishop Saint-Vallier admitted sadly to Charles de Beauharnois* de La Boische, the new governor-general, that if the coadjutor arrived "everyone would desert him." A poignant admission of New France's disaffection for its old bishop!

In the absence of popularity, Saint-Vallier was respected for his austerity, and he was never so austere as during the last 14 years of his life. In 1713 he had given up his palace to go to live at the Hôpital Général, of which he was the founder. His habits were worn; his apartment was but a single room, with whitewashed walls and furnishings amounting only to a bed, some pieces of furniture, a few shelves of books, and some pious engravings. Gradually he even reached the point of selling the personal belongings he had brought from France, his linen, his shoes, his bed-covers, and his bed itself. Twice a week he observed the most rigorous fast, as he did on the eve of all feast-days of the Blessed Virgin and during all of Lent. During the 40 days of Lent he always invited some poor person to share his only meal. Through humility he had also wanted to be the chaplain of the Hôpital Général. Every day he said mass for the community, then, if the duties of his office left him some leisure time, he visited the sick, administered the last sacraments to the dying, celebrated funeral masses himself, and accompanied the dead to the little cemetery of the Hôpital Général.

This austerity was accompanied by untiring activity to assure the success of orthodoxy and morality in his immense American diocese. He was to be seen creating parishes, building churches, condemning Jansenism on several occasions, pursuing in his pastoral letters libertines, drunkards, traffickers in spirits, and tavern-keepers. Despite his advanced age he was interested even in the most distant regions of his diocese, the islands of the Gulf of St Lawrence, Acadia, the post at Detroit, Louisiana. And, no more than in his youth, was he inclined towards indulgence and optimism. In 1722 he deplored the mediocrity of his flock and added that the spirit of faith was weakening and was dying away "almost entirely" in the hearts of his diocesans. Probably a greatly exaggerated severity, but it is encountered again for example in Mother Régnard* Duplessis de Sainte-Hélène, the superior of the Hôtel-Dieu of Quebec. In 1733 she was to pass this curious judgement on her contemporaries: "We are in an age where I fear everything, for corruption is at its peak; we see pitiful things, similar ones are reported to us, I believe that we are close to the last judgement . . . charity has grown cold, and there remains little faith in the world."

The bishop grew weaker every day. He died on 26 Dec. 1727. He was 74 and had governed the diocese of Quebec for 42 years. One of his last utterances deserves to be quoted, for it epitomizes wonderfully his generosity: "Forget me," he said to the nuns of the Hôpital Général who were

333

Ladan

gathered about him, "but do not forget my poor."

After his death began one of the most famous and picturesque episodes, and one of the least edifying, in the history of the church in Canada [see BOULLARD, Louis-Eustache Chartier* de Lotbinière, CLAUDE-THOMAS DUPUY]. For a year, because of questions of precedence on the day of Bishop Saint-Vallier's funeral and then because of a problem of jurisdiction over the diocese, the clergy of Quebec was to engage in the fiercest of fights, as were most of the colonial authorities, in particular Dupuy and the Conseil Souverain. It seems as if Bishop Saint-Vallier's episcopate, which was born in the midst of disputes, could not end otherwise than in a storm.

Such was Bishop Saint-Vallier's life, a tragic one certainly, stormy and full of suffering. Domineering to the point of despotism, not having received as his share the gift of joy and radiance but, on the contrary, deeply pessimistic and without any indulgence for his contemporaries' weaknesses, more inclined to teach a God of wrath than a God of charity, being in this too faithful a disciple of the French counter-reformation movement, Bishop Saint-Vallier must himself bear the main responsibility for the commotions of his episcopate. But it would be unfair to judge him solely on his real deficiencies of character and doctrine. One must not forget either the difficulty of the times or the complete lack of flexibility on the part of the bishop's adversaries. It must above all be stressed that, despite his faults, through his unremitting activity, his piety and austerity, his untiring charity towards the poor, and the breadth of his legislation Bishop Saint-Vallier undoubtedly contributed to the consolidation of the Catholic church in North America.

ALFRED RAMBAUD

The manuscript sources are, first, essentially in the ASQ, and numerous series have been consulted: Lettres, Polygraphie, Seminaire, Chapitre, Missions, Évêques, Paroisses. It should be noted particularly that the series Lettres contains a copious correspondence exchanged each year between the Séminaire des Missions Étrangères in Paris and the seminary in Quebec. These letters, which sometimes become quite voluminous—50, 100, and even 150 pages—contain an accurate and lively picture, sometimes comic, sometimes dramatic, of most of the episodes which marked Bishop Saint-Vallier's greatly agitated episcopate.

Also valuable are the AAQ, which contain especially copies of documents kept in Paris and Rome, and the AN, particularly Col., C^{11A}, 6 to 52. In addition, the letters to his Canadian correspondents are particularly useful documents; copies of them are in the Municipal Library of Montreal. The Fonds Rochemonteix, kept in the ASJCF, contains copies of the letters in Latin

sent by the Jesuits in Canada to their general in Rome and written with a very free pen. In them are to be found curious details concerning the offensive conducted by Bishop Saint-Vallier against the Society of Jesus from 1698 to 1704.

It is impossible to mention all the printed sources. Above all, Bishop Saint-Vallier's works must be kept in mind: *Catéchisme du diocèse de Québec* (Paris, 1702); *Estat présent de l'Église et de la colonie française dans la Nouvelle-France ...* (Paris, 1688; Québec, 1856 ou 1857); *Rituel du diocèse de Québec* (Paris, 1703), the first edition has 604 pages and the second, of the same year, 671; *Statuts, ordonnances et lettres pastorales* (Paris, 1703). There are also the funeral orations delivered at the time of his death: Joachim Fornel, "Éloge funèbre de Mgr de Saint-Vallier," *BRH*, XIV (1908), 80–87, 110–21; R. P. de La Chasse, *Éloge funèbre de Mgr de Saint-Vallier* (Québec, 1927). Finally, certain reports and correspondence of the period: Duplessis de Sainte-Hélène, "Lettres," *NF*, II (1926–27), 67–78; III (1927–28), 39–56, 171–74; Juchereau, *Annales* (Jamet); Étienne Marchand, "Les troubles de l'Église du Canada en 1728," *BRH*, III (1897), 117–21, 132–38; Georges Poulet, "Récit simple de ce qu'un religieux bénédictin a souffert au Canada au sujet de la bulle Unigenitus," APQ *Rapport, 1922–23*, 276–89; "L'affaire du priedieu à Montréal, en 1694," APQ *Rapport, 1923–24*, 71–110.

The only studies of Bishop Saint-Vallier's episcopate are the two books by Gosselin, which are by now out-of-date: *Mgr de Saint-Vallier et son temps* (Evreux, 1899) and *L'Église du Canada*, I. The author has written an article: "La vie orageuse et douloureuse de Mgr de Saint-Vallier, deuxième évêque de Québec (1653–1727)," *RUL*, IX (1954), 90–108, and at present is completing a thesis on Bishop Saint-Vallier's episcopate. In the absence of a recent synthesis of the life of the bishop of Quebec, there are numerous monographs which permit study of certain episodes in the prelate's life. In particular may be mentioned: Hector Bibeau, "La pensée mariale de Mgr de Saint-Vallier," Diplôme des Études Supérieures Mémoire, Université Laval, 1966. Albert Bois, *Un grand dauphinois: Mgr Jean-Baptiste de la Croix de Chevrières de Saint-Vallier, évêque de Québec* (Domergue, 1942). Amédée Gosselin, "Un épisode de l'histoire du théâtre au Canada," *RSCT*, 1st ser., VI (1888), sect.I, 53–72. *Monseigneur de Saint-Vallier et l'Hôpital-Général de Québec*. Alfred Rambaud, "La querelle du *Tartuffe* à Paris et à Québec," *RUL*, VIII (1954), 421–34. A Canadian priest, Father Plante, is at present completing a study of Bishop Saint-Vallier's theological thought, which seems to him to have been considerably influenced by the whole movement of moral rigorism born of the Counter-Reformation. [A.R.]

LADAN, ADRIEN (Adrian), priest, Recollet, lecturer in theology; b. 1647; d. 3 Nov. 1722 at Montargis, France.

Father Adrien Ladan entered religion in 1666, when he joined the Recollets of the ecclesiastical province of Saint-Denis; he arrived in New France in 1681. His celebrity is due to his quarrels with Bishop LAVAL in what it is customary to call "the affair of the sermon." The bishop entrusted him with preaching the Advent sermons for 1681. On 7 December, the second Sunday of Advent, Father Ladan made reference from the cathedral pulpit to the differences existing between the intendant, Duchesneau*, and the governor, Frontenac [Buade*]. Bishop Laval asked him to refrain rigorously from dealing with this question. On 8 December Father Ladan did the same thing again, and the bishop warned him a second time. The following Sunday the preacher pronounced the words "cabal, division, and partiality."

That was the limit, and Laval summoned him to the archiepiscopal palace to explain himself. Ladan wanted to talk with him in private, but the bishop insisted that his vicars general be present at the interview. In a document dated 19 Dec. 1681 Bishop Laval gave his version of the facts, concluding that "it was up to the King, and not the Church, to put an end to the difference between the Governor and the Intendant." Father Ladan said in reply "that he considered His Excellency either in his role as bishop or as a private individual, that he submitted to him as bishop, but that as a private individual he was not infallible . . . that he had not asked for the pulpit, and that he was ready to quit it rather than act against his conscience." The bishop took him at his word and forbad him to preach. It was a priest from the seminary who finished the Advent addresses on 21 December.

In a request sent at a date that was certainly later than 14 December 1681, Frontenac asked Father Valentin LEROUX, the Recollet superior, to give him in writing an account of the whole matter involving Father Ladan, so that he might inform Louis XIV of it. The superior did indeed write this account, but the document cannot be found. It is to be noted that Frontenac, who had been alluded to directly by Ladan, took less offence at the preacher's words than did Bishop Laval. In his request to the superior he wrote that the Recollet had "spoken [in his sermons] cursorily of the divisions, partiality, and cabals which exist in the country, sermons that we would have listened to with great edification."

Father Ladan remained for three more years in Canada. On 14 June 1683 he signed the protestation by the Recollets of Quebec in the "affair of the bell-tower" [see HENRI LE ROY]. In 1700 we find him at Vitry in France, where he was given permission to receive confessions and to preach. He died 3 Nov. 1722 at Montargis.

JACQUES VALOIS

AAQ, Registres d'insinuation A, 270, 229–31. AN, Col., F³, 6, f.18. Louis Bertrand de Latour, *Mémoires sur la vie de M. de Laval, premier évêque de Québec* (Cologne, 1761), 203–4. Caron, "Inventaire de documents," APQ *Rapport, 1939–40,* 245. PAC *Report, 1899,* 77. Gosselin, *Vie de Mgr de Laval,* II, 99–104.

LA DÉCOUVERTE (Ladescouverte), PIERRE YOU DE. *See* YOU

LA DURANTAYE, OLIVIER MOREL DE. *See* MOREL

LA FAYE, LOUIS-FRANÇOIS DE (when he arrived in Canada he signed **Delafaye**, but from 1704 on he adopted **de la Faye**), priest, Sulpician, founder of the first boys' school at Montreal; b. 1657 in Paris; d. 6 July 1729 at Montreal.

M. de La Faye entered the Sulpician order on 9 Nov. 1684 and was in New France in 1685, when he was only a sub-deacon. He was consecrated a priest in Canada on 26 Sept. 1688. From 1691 to 1728 he was priest of several parishes in the Montreal region. He retired to the seminary of Montreal in 1728 and died the following year at the age of 72. It may be said that in the exercise of his parochial ministry he showed himself to be concerned for the welfare of his parishioners and generous towards the outcasts of fortune.

É.-Z. Massicotte claims that Abbé Gabriel Souart*, a Sulpician, and M. de La Faye, by then an ecclesiastic, "wanted to found at Ville-Marie, towards the end of the seventeenth century, a school of some size, and very probably a community of Teaching Brothers similar to the one which Jean-Baptiste de La Salle . . . a seminarist at Saint-Sulpice, had founded in Paris 6 or 7 years before." For this school, Massicotte continues, on 15 Sept. 1686 they made over a house which they owned in Rue Notre-Dame to a group of laymen, under the leadership of Mathurin Rouillé. "By the agreement entered into by Rouillé in his own name and in that of his companions and successors, it is clear that the intention is to found a community, although the matter is not mentioned specifically on this occasion. . . ." The financial situation of the community deteriorated in 1690, and on 27 Sept. 1693 it was forced to hand over its assets to the parish priest and churchwardens of Ville-Marie. This bankruptcy, which could be foreseen even in 1690, is thought to explain Abbé de La Faye's appointment to Sainte-Anne-de-Bellevue the following year.

In any event, M. de La Faye certainly contributed to the setting up of the first boys' school in Montreal in 1686. That he taught there is likely, since he is not known to have held any other position before 1691. That he may have been both a seminarist and a teacher from 1686 to 1688 was to be expected at this time; moreover M. Tronson already saw a schoolmaster in him: "He does not possess great talents, but he has a very strong sense of duty, and I believe that he is capable of being a schoolmaster at Montreal." We have no knowledge whatsoever of his pedagogical role, however, or of his active participation in the newly created community of teaching brothers. He appears to have been a modest founder, who kept closely guarded the secret of a recently founded community which he considered useful and necessary to perfect the work of his predecessors.

JEAN-MARC PARADIS

AN, Col., C¹¹A, 45. ASQ, Polygraphie, XXII, 20; Séminaire, I, 20. PAC, FM 17, A 7–2, 1, vol.2; FM 18, H 25, 2, pièce 16. Caron, "Inventaire de documents," APQ *Rapport, 1939–40*, 269. [Louis Tronson], *Correspondance de M. de Tronson, troisième Supérieur de la Compagnie de Saint-Sulpice: Lettres choisies, [16 juillet 1676–15 janv. 1700]*, éd. A.-L. Bertrand (3v., Paris, 1904). Henri Gauthier, *La Compagnie de Saint-Sulpice au Canada* (Montréal, 1912); *Sulpitiana* (Montréal, 1926). É.-Z. Massicotte, "Fondation d'une communauté de frères instituteurs à Montréal en 1686," *BRH*, XXVIII (1922), 37–42.

LA FERTÉ. *See* JUCHEREAU

LAFERTÉ, MICHEL LEPAILLEUR DE. *See* LEPAILLEUR

LA FOREST, FRANÇOIS DAUPHIN DE. *See* DAUPHIN

LA FOREST, MARC-ANTOINE DE, writer in the Marine, employed extraordinarily at Rochefort and Placentia (Plaisance), commissary at Port-Toulouse (St Peters, N.S.), then attorney of the Admiralty Court of Louisbourg; b. in France; d. 22 June 1738 at Louisbourg at about the age of 70.

On two occasions, in 1705, and again in 1713 at the time of the French withdrawal from Newfoundland he came to Placentia to perform the functions of commissary during the Sieur DURAND de La Garenne's absence. The financial commissary, Pierre-Auguste de SOUBRAS, retained his services at Île Royale (Cape Breton Island) and entrusted him with the duties of subdelegate, storekeeper, and bailiff at Port-Toulouse. He was appointed king's attorney of the Admiralty Court set up at Louisbourg in 1718. In the same year he refused a commission from the governor to go to Canso (Canseau) with ALLARD de Sainte-Marie

to investigate the recent pillaging. To his new duties at Louisbourg he was to bring the same niggling zeal and quarrelsome disposition that had already made him odious to all the merchants and ships' captains who visited the colony.

He was a widower, who had left behind him in France five children and many debts; in 1718, at Port-Dauphin (Englishtown, N.S.), he married Marie-Anne Courthiau, who bore him ten children. He sought by all possible means to enlarge the scope of his jurisdiction and to increase the number of dues collected and legal proceedings instituted, on which his emoluments depended. He was thwarted by the governor, Saint-Ovide de Brouillan [Mombeton*], who protected commerce, and in 1735 his accounts with the Admiralty Court showed a deficit of 3,300 *livres*, which he had to reimburse directly from his reduced income as a writer on half-pay.

LOUISE DECHÊNE

AN, Col., B, 29, 35; C¹¹B, 1–21; C¹¹C, 1–7; E, 246 (dossier de La Forest); Section Outre-Mer, G¹, 406, 407 (copies in the PAC); 462; G³, 2056. McLennan, *Louisbourg.*

LA FRENAYE, FRANÇOIS DE (baptized **Pierre-Antoine**), deacon, Recollet; b. 8 Oct. 1677 at Montreal, eldest son of Antoine de La Frenaye* de Brucy, a lieutenant in the Régiment d'Auvergne, and of Hélène Picoté de Belestre; d. in May 1705 at Orléans, France.

Pierre-Antoine de La Frenaye was a boarder at the seminary in Quebec and studied at the Jesuit college. In 1683, at the age of 16, he decided in favour of the religious life and entered the noviciate of the Recollets at the convent in Montreal, which had been founded the previous year. He took his vows on 10 May 1694.

Jean-Baptiste CÉLORON de Blainville, the second husband of François' mother, had invited Saint-Vallier [LA CROIX], bishop of Quebec, and Louis-Hector de CALLIÈRE, governor of Montreal, to the ceremony of taking the vows. The presence of these high dignitaries gave a special lustre to this occasion, the first of its kind at Montreal in a male religious community. It resulted in the "affair of the *prie-dieu*" [*see* JOSEPH DENYS].

After completing, according to the usage of the Franciscans of the ecclesiastical province of Saint-Denis, what might be called a second year of training, La Frenaye took courses in philosophy and theology at the convent in Quebec, or perhaps in France, where he is thought to have received the tonsure, the minor orders, and the subdiaconate; these ordinations are not recorded in Quebec. It is certain, however, that he received the diaconate from Bishop LAVAL, in Bishop Saint-Vallier's absence, in the chapel of the seminary on 18 April 1700. Shortly afterwards he returned to France, where he died in 1705, after 12 years in holy orders.

Following the example of his spiritual father St Francis of Assisi, the young religious voluntarily remained a deacon until his death.

JACQUES VALOIS

AAQ, Registres d'insinuation A, 187. AN, K, carton 1238, pièce 48. "L'affaire du prie-dieu à Montréal, en 1694," APQ *Rapport*, *1923–24*, 102. É.-Z. Massicotte, "Le sieur la Fresnaye de Brucy," *BRH*, XXXVI (1930), 644–45.

LA FRESNIÈRE, JOSEPH - FRANÇOIS HERTEL DE. *See* HERTEL

LA GARENNE, DURAND DE. *See* DURAND

LA GRANDE TERRE. *See* OHONSIOWANNE

LA GRANGE, JEAN LÉGER DE. *See* LÉGER

LAGRENÉ, PIERRE DE, priest, Jesuit, missionary, superior of the Jesuit residence in Montreal; b. 12 Oct. 1659 in Paris; d. 24 Nov. 1736 at Quebec.

Pierre de Lagrené entered the noviciate of Paris at the age of 18. He did his philosophical and theological studies at the Jesuit college in La Flèche, taught elementary Latin, classics, and rhetoric for 5 years at the college in Hesdin (department of Pas-de-Calais), and rhetoric for 2 years at the college in Eu (Normandy). He was ordained a priest in 1693, and arrived in Canada the following year.

From 1694 till 1696 he prepared for his apostolate among the Iroquois by studying the Huron language at Notre-Dame de Lorette, under the guidance of Father COUVERT. From 1697 till 1701 and from 1704 till 1707 he was a missionary at Sault-Saint-Louis (Caughnawaga). Then he went to live at the Jesuit residence in Montreal, of which he was superior in 1716. He concerned himself with the construction of the chapel for this residence, consecrated 10 April 1710, and more particularly with the organization of the Congrégation des Hommes de Ville-Marie, which brought together the elite of Montreal society. When the Sulpicians took over this community after the death in 1791 of the last Jesuit in Montreal, Father Bernard Well, they continued to keep it up as Father Lagrené had conceived it.

In 1723 Father Lagrené was appointed to the Jesuit college in Quebec. There, as everywhere else, his life was devoid of any ostentation, but he rendered great services as assistant to the rector, director of the Congrégation de la Sainte-Vierge, and teacher. It was there that he died on 24 Nov. 1736.

LÉON POULIOT, S.J.

ASJCF, 570, 571. Rochemonteix, *Les Jésuites et la N.-F. au XVIIe siècle*, III, 384.

LA GROSSARDIÈRE, JACQUES GOURDEAU (Gourdau) DE BEAULIEU ET DE. *See* GOURDEAU

LA GROYE, CHARLES-HENRI D'ALOIGNY DE. *See* ALOIGNY

LA HALLE, CONSTANTIN DE. *See* DELHALLE

LAHONTAN, LOUIS-ARMAND DE LOM D'ARCE DE. *See* LOM

LA JEMERAIS, CHRISTOPHE DUFROST DE. *See* DUFROST

LA JEUNESSE. *See* DANDONNEAU

LAJOÜE, FRANÇOIS DE, surveyor and geometrician, master mason, architect and contractor, merchant, bourgeois, engineer; b. *c.* 1656 in the Paris region (Saint-Giruault), son of Jacques de La Joue, master surgeon, and Madeleine Guerin; died in Persia in 1719 or shortly before.

François de Lajoüe practised his surveyor's trade in Paris before coming to settle at Quebec in 1689 or shortly before, when he was about 33 years of age. He lived in the home of Pierre MÉNAGE, whose daughter, Marie-Anne, he married on 3 Nov. 1689. Of their marriage were born several daughters; one of them, Marie-Agnès, married Pierre-Noël Levasseur*: another, Marie-Thérèse, married an engineer, La Guer de Morville. The Lajoües lived on Rue Saint-Louis, near the Ménage home, until about 1700; then they had a house built for themselves across from the Fontaine Royale on Rue du Garde-fou. It was in this stone house, with a mansard roof, that Bégon* and his family took refuge when they were driven out of the palace on the tragic evening of 5 or 6 January 1713.

La Joüe's career in Canada lasted barely a quarter of a century, about the same time that Sébastien Le Prestre de Vauban was active in France, and the engineers JACQUES LEVASSEUR de Néré and Boisberthelot* de Beaucours were working in Canada. On 22 Dec. 1689 Lajoüe

Lajoüe

received his commission as royal geometrician and surveyor, at the same time as BERNARD de La Rivière. Subsequently his activities were split between surveys, measuring, and building jobs, interspersed with a short-lived commercial venture. The first big order we know him to have received was the plan for a building 100 feet long which he started constructing for the Nuns Hospitallers in 1691 and of which he made a small model in relief. This building was not finished until 1698. In 1692 he submitted the plans for the construction of the *château* and the new fort. Frontenac [Buade*] declared of the *château* that "it is not without some sort of miracle that I have not been crushed under the ruins of the old building," although he considered it at the same time to be an ornament to the town. This building was not completed until 1700. In 1693, in collaboration with his colleague La Rivière, Lajoüe built the Saint-Jean gate, following Beaucours' plans. Janson*, *dit* Lapalme, and Jean LE ROUGE were the creators of the Saint-Louis gate. The two gates were built on the same model. Lajoüe went to France that same year to inquire into the property titles and inventory of a certain Leboeuf.

In 1700 he directed the construction of the *château* and the new surrounding wall, and he became a shareholder in the Compagnie de la Colonie. He made recommendations in 1702 for the restoration of the church at Sainte-Famille on Île d'Orléans. In 1703 he submitted the plan requested by the seminary for the building of a new presbytery, and the following year he was busy with the Jesuits' church at Sillery. Around that time he ordered from Hulot, the Duc d'Orléans' wood-carver, "a handsome tabernacle," which he wished to offer to the nuns of the Hôtel-Dieu, whose regular architect he was. He paid 400 francs in advance, but was unable to settle the whole amount, as his business affairs had gone badly. The nuns had to have recourse to court action in order to regain the ornament, which had been seized, and it was not until 12 years later, on Assumption Day, that it was placed in the church, at a time when restoration work was being carried out.

In 1708 he presented a project for a system of distributing water to the Hôtel-Dieu. The project mentions specifically "places where it is desired to bring the water furnished by the town of Quebec and which has been granted by M. Talon*." The work was postponed. In 1710 Lajoüe turns up as one of the owners of the *Africain*, a ship of 431 tons stowage; when it went bankrupt, Lajoüe quarrelled with Denis RIVERIN, whom he accused of having drawn him into a bad business deal and of having cheated him. He did work for the Recollets in 1714 and 1715 and perhaps for the Ursulines, for whom he is supposed to have prepared the plans of their church. (In this matter we are dealing with hypotheses which it has been impossible to verify.) There still exists a drawing by him of the seminary which also shows the cathedral and the bishop's palace.

Around 1715 Lajoüe left Canada, placing his belongings in the care of the nuns of the Hôtel-Dieu. In 1717 and 1718 he was mentioned as being absent. A letter from the bishop of Babylon dated 30 July 1719 informs us that he died in Persia, where he was working as an engineer. The inventory of his papers, dated 3 April 1721, is of little interest except for the mention of 16 survey reports "drawn up by La Joue in his capacity as a sworn surveyor." The settlement of Lajoüe's estate, which was without claimants, dragged on until 1743.

Lajoüe's career benefitted from the energetic administration of Governors Frontenac, CALLIÈRE, and Vaudreuil [RIGAUD], and of intendants such as Champigny [BOCHART]. The failure of the attack by Phips* against Quebec and the treaty of Ryswick were favourable to great projects: it was then that Quebec was enclosed for the first time by a regular wall and received its adornment of buildings and steeples. For this construction a group of soldiers, selected for their abilities in this type of work, were backed up by the group from the seminary; this institution had an art school which included Baillif*, Denis MALLET, and Jacques LEBLOND de Latour, and around them moved people such as Lajoüe, Ménage, and La Rivière. After Baillif's tragic and premature death in 1699, Lajoüe played a leading part in construction activity.

The work of the architects was moreover paralleled by that of the carpenters and the artisans who were concerned with decorating the interiors. The limitations imposed on the architects did not apply, however, to the master decorators, whose retables, tabernacles, and baldachins constitute so many imaginary temples drawn from the great models. But the fact is that the kind of building material available and the lack of real opportunities prevented the architect from fully demonstrating his capabilities. Building in Quebec during this period cannot therefore be assessed in terms of personalities and grandiose achievements; it was above all the result of many and various contributions. A multitude of craftsmen persisted, with unequal means, in employing at Quebec old practices imported from France and in adapting them to new conditions. This architecture is characterized by the full use of the site and the utilization of simple elements.

Lajoüe's Parisian origins, his many activities, his orderly form of art, his mysterious death in Persia, all contribute to the legend which grew up around most of our craftsmen.

PIERRE MAYRAND

AJQ, Greffe de Jacques Barbel, 3 mai 1728; Greffe de Louis Chambalon, 3 nov. 1693, 18 sept. 1701, 22 avril 1703; Greffe de François Genaple; Greffe de Jean-Claude Louet, 3 avril 1721; Greffe de Gilles Rageot, 18 févr 1690, 1 déc. 1691; Greffe de Pierre Rivet, 7 avril 1715. Juchereau, *Annales* (Jamet), 281, 421, 442. *Jug. et délib.*, I, II. É.-Z. Massicotte, "Maçons, entrepreneurs, architectes," *BRH*, XXXV (1929), 135. Tanguay, *Dictionnaire*, III, 292. J.-É. Bellemare, *Histoire de la Baie-Saint-Antoine, dit Baie-du-Febvre, 1683–1911* (Montréal, 1911), 18. P.-G. Roy, *Les cimetières de Québec* (Québec, 1941), 110; *La ville de Québec*, I, II. Ramsay Traquair, *The old architecture of Quebec* (Toronto, 1947), 93.

LALIBERTÉ, NICOLAS SENET, *dit. See* SENET

LA MALGUE (La Marche), CHARLES-PAUL DE MARIN DE. *See* MARIN

LA MARCHE, DOMINIQUE DE (baptized François), priest, Recollet, missionary, superior of the Recollets in Acadia, provincial commissioner; b. *c.* 1677 in France; d. 14 Nov. 1738 at Montargis (Loiret).

In 1701 La Marche was ordained a priest at Rouen, and upon being appointed lecturer in philosophy at the convent in Quebec he arrived in Canada in 1702. He returned to France in 1703 or 1704, then finally came back to Canada in 1705. He left Montreal in June 1706 to go to Detroit with Cadillac [LAUMET]; the register of baptisms shows that he was there on 16 Aug. 1706; he remained there until 29 July 1708. In 1709 he was vicar of the convent and professor of philosophy at Quebec. He was then appointed superior of the Recollets on Île Royale (Cape Breton Island), where he arrived 27 Aug. 1713. There he was a member of a committee which had been created to choose a port for a French settlement. The following persons: L'HERMITTE, Saint-Ovide de Brouillan [Mombeton*], JEAN-BAPTISTE DE COUAGNE, Péan* de Livaudière, Eury* de La Perelle, Jacques D'ESPIET de Pensens, Louis Denys* de La Ronde, and Father Dominique de La Marche, chose Havre-à-l'Anglois, which was to be called Louisbourg.

After the treaty of Utrecht in 1713, it was on Île Royale, which remained a French possession, that Father La Marche made his mark because of the numerous reports that he sent to the civil and religious authorities. He visited the principal French posts in Acadia, which had become an English possession, including Port-Toulouse (St Peters, N.S.) and Minas, where he met the leading families of the area. Following these meetings, and in his capacity as superior of the Recollets and vicar general to the bishop of Quebec, on 7 Sept. 1715 he sent to PASTOUR de Costebelle, governor of Île Royale, a report in which he spoke of the Acadians' loyalty to France and their transfer to Île Royale. Afterwards he belonged to a commission of envoys which was responsible for presenting the Acadians' interests to the English and the French authorities. His attempts did not obtain the results that he hoped for. Although the voluntary emigration of the Acadians to Île Royale had been authorized by letter by Queen Anne of England, the authorities on both sides did not lend their cooperation to this project. According to Father La Marche, the Acadians were not to blame for failing to go to Île Royale; it was in good measure the fault of Governor Costebelle, who had decided that the Acadians would remain where they were.

On 2 Jan. 1716 La Marche arrived at Port-Dauphin (Englishtown, N.S.) as chaplain, and he lost no time in building a chapel there. From 1721 to 1726 he was provincial commissioner of the Recollets in Canada. In 1728 he returned to France, where he lived at Montargis, as certain documents mention. It was there that he died on 14 Nov. 1738. The financial commissary, SOUBRAS, had praised him as follows: "A man of genius, active, adroit, and fitted to direct and manage minds."

GABRIEL-M.-RÉAL DUMAS

Archives des Franciscains de Québec, Dossier Dominique de La Marche. AN, Col., B, 39, ff.298v, 302v; C11A, 106, ff.276–84; C11B, 1, ff.259, 415; 2, ff.30, 36–42, 96; C11D, 8, f.40; F3, 50, f.8. L.-M. Le Jeune, *Tableaux synoptiques de l'histoire de l'Acadie...* (Québec, 1918). McLennan, *Louisbourg*.

LA MARGUE (La Marque). *See* MARIN

LAMARRE, *dit* Bélisle, **HENRI** (signed **henry Lamars** *dit* **bellile** and, after 1692, **henrÿ Bélisle**; É.-Z. Massicotte called him Henri Belisle-Levasseur on unknown authority), barber-surgeon at Quebec, Detroit, Champlain, and Pointe-aux-Trembles on Montreal Island; son of Antoine Lamarre and Marguerite Levasseur of Saint-Michel-le-Palus parish in Angers (Maine-et-Loire); d. September 1740 at Pointe-aux-Trembles.

As a general rule, surgeons in New France were men of substance. Bélisle was an unhappy

La Martinière

exception to this rule and he spent much of his life fighting a rear-guard action against his creditors. He was a druggist's son and came to Quebec from Anjou after 1681. On 26 June 1690 he married Catherine Demosny, daughter of the late surgeon Jean Demosny*. The list of friends in their wedding contract, which included two Quebec surgeons, suggests that Bélisle was a recent immigrant to Canada. In the next decade he trained two apprentices and worked throughout the Quebec region. One patient, whose severed leg tendon he failed to rejoin, obtained a miraculous cure at the shrine of Sainte-Anne de Beaupré.

In May 1701 Bélisle was hired by BOCHART de Champigny as a coureur de bois and surgeon to go to Fort Pontchartrain at Detroit in the king's service. Bélisle's wife died during his absence and three of their children were boarded with the Sisters of the Congrégation de Notre Dame at Sainte-Famille, on Île d'Orléans. Two daughters eventually joined this teaching order. On 26 Nov. 1705, Bélisle married Périnne Dandonneau, a Batiscan widow with nine children. The surgeon was at this time establishing a home at Champlain, near Trois-Rivières. His life was far from settled. Notarial records show that he was in Quebec in 1707 and that in 1708, 1709, and 1710 he was at Detroit, where his second wife died in 1711.

Bélisle then moved to a new home, taking up residence in the village of Pointe-aux-Trembles. On 25 Aug. 1712 he married Jeanne Archambault, the eldest daughter of a local farmer. This fruitful match added seven children to the five from the first bed. Whether through sheer vitality or their father's skill, all but one lived to adulthood in an age when infant mortality was high.

Bélisle's population explosion added to his financial difficulties. When his first two wives died, he took legal action to exclude half of each estate from the claims of creditors. He stated that in 1711 he did not even retain enough property to merit an estate inventory. In 1713, his newly wed daughter, Marie-Catherine, and her husband brought Bélisle before a notary to have his promise of a dowry and trousseau recorded. One suspects avarice or financial mismanagement on his part as well as unfortunate circumstances. Perhaps Bélisle had served as a voyageur and investor in the fur trade during the 1706–13 slump.

As a surgeon Bélisle treated patients on Île-Jésus, Montreal Island, and in the south shore hamlets. Frequently he was paid in promissory notes. He purchased the inheritance rights of the children of his first marriage to some Quebec properties, and he accumulated pieces of real estate in the Montreal area, which he leased and later sold. At Pointe-aux-Trembles, he lived in a modest, wooden, *pièces-sur-pièces* house with a stone hearth, a board roof, and paper windows.

Bélisle's financial situation worsened in the 1730s when a nervous disorder deprived him of a steady hand—so essential to his trade. In 1736 he permitted his wife to withdraw her portion from their community of goods and legally to summon Bélisle's other heirs either to renounce their inheritance rights or to contribute to the maintenance of their aged father. Since the children retained their rights, one may assume that they met their legal obligation to support Bélisle.

When Bélisle died in 1740, his assets covered his declared debts. What was left, however, was insufficient to meet his widow's needs. Undeclared debts appeared and more were incurred. A court summons to Bélisle's children to share in the debt-ridden estate went unanswered, and in 1742 the entire legacy was awarded to the poor widow. Somehow, she managed to survive the threat of seizure by creditors of all that she possessed and slowly repaid the claimants. By 1749 she was sufficiently solvent, and attractive, to find another husband.

PETER N. MOOGK

AJM, Greffe d'Antoine Adhémar, 27 mai 1701; Greffe de René Chorel de Saint-Romain, 8 juillet 1732; Greffe de François Comparet, 8 juin 1736, 14 nov. 1740; Greffe de Michel Lepailleur de Laferté, 14 août 1712; Greffe de Simon Sanguinet, 18 août 1742; Greffe de Nicolas Senet, 16 août 1713, 16 mai 1718. AJQ, Greffe de Louis Chambalon, 21 juillet 1692, 1 juillet 1695; Greffe de Jean-Étienne Dubreuil, 27 août 1721, 28 déc. 1722; Greffe de Gilles Rageot, 19 juin 1690; Registres d'état civil de Notre-Dame de Québec, 1690–95, f.36. AJTR, Greffe de J.-B. Pottier, 25 nov. 1705; Greffe d'Étienne Veron de Grandmesnil, 5 juillet 1707. ASQ, Congrégation Notre-Dame, 61; Paroisses diverses, 71. *Jug. et délib.*, V, 308, 571–72; VI, 62. *Michigan Pioneer Coll.*, XXXIV, 237, 256, 257, 263, 266, 294.

Massicotte, "Répertoire des engagements pour l'Ouest," 206. Raymond Douville, *Visages du vieux Trois-Rivières* (Trois-Rivières, 1955); "Chirurgiens, barbiers-chirurgiens et charlatans de la région trifluvienne sous le régime français," *Cahiers des Dix*, XV (1950), 92–94.

LA MARTINIÈRE, CLAUDE BERMEN DE. *See* BERMEN

LAMBERVILLE, JACQUES DE, Jesuit missionary to the Mohawks and Onondagas, younger brother of the missionary JEAN DE LAMBERVILLE; b. 1641, in Rouen; d. 18 April 1710 (some sources say 1711; others give 1718, but this is definitely incorrect), in or near Montreal.

Jacques de Lamberville became a Jesuit at the

age of 20 and taught in various colleges of the society in France before coming to Canada at the age of 34. He was immediately assigned to the Iroquois missions. Lamberville's most illustrious convert was Kateri Tekakwitha*, a retiring young girl partly blinded by smallpox who had escaped the notice of his colleagues and predecessors, Fathers BRUYAS and Frémin*, at Gandaouagué. One day in 1675 as he was making his usual calls from lodge to lodge he came upon her when she had been prevented by an injured foot from joining the other women working in the fields. He was surprised to find that since childhood she had greatly desired to embrace Catholicism. He began her instruction immediately, and his caution and thoroughness in instructing new converts is well illustrated in the case of this young girl for it was not until Easter Sunday 1676 that he baptized her. Her public confession of faith aroused opposition and persecution. Lamberville conspired with some visiting Huron and Iroquois catechizers, during the absence of her uncle and guardian at Albany (Fort Orange) in 1677, to send her secretly to a reserve near Montreal. Although he had been much impressed by the piety and virtue of this young woman he dissuaded her from attempting to found a community of Indian nuns. He knew from his experiences in the Iroquois cantons how little success such a foundation would have. He himself had, nevertheless, reasonably good results; in the two months preceding Easter 1676 he had baptized 13 adults and shortly after Kateri's baptism another seven had been baptized. In his first year he had made about 50 converts, only ten of whom were moribund.

In 1677–78 he joined Father Bruyas and jointly they baptized about 40 persons during the year, most of whom died shortly thereafter. His time among the Mohawks was particularly difficult. On one occasion, for example, a drunken warrior attacked him in the chapel, shot at him, and then attempted to dispatch him with an iron bar. Only the midnight darkness and the Indian's inebriated condition saved the missionary thus surprised at his devotions.

Although his career was not as brilliant as his brother's, it is evident that he was possessed of the same tenacity, courage, and forbearance as Jean. Not until 1684 did Jacques become actively involved in the political role often imposed on the missionaries by royal officials. In that fateful year he was summoned to meet Governor Le Febvre* de La Barre who was launching an expedition against the Senecas. Jacques de Lamberville joined the expedition at La Galette (Ogdensburg) and was ordered to go to his brother Jean at Onondaga to reassure the tribesmen of French goodwill. He

arrived at Onondaga on 17 Aug. 1684 and spent the whole night discussing political and religious affairs with his brother. In the morning the Onondaga chieftains were assembled and messengers were dispatched to the Oneidas, Mohawks, and Cayugas. After La Barre's expedition collapsed, Jacques de Lamberville joined his brother among the Onondagas. It was he who carried the governor's messages to the Iroquois in October.

The year spent at Onondaga with Jean was a relatively successful one, owing in good measure to the improvised practice of medicine and dentistry carried on by the enterprising brothers. When Jean was summoned to Quebec in 1686 by BRISAY de Denonville, Jacques remained among the Onondagas; he was the only missionary left in the Iroquois cantons. He too was soon recalled by Denonville, who was planning a campaign against the Senecas, and was assigned to chaplaincy duties with the garrison at Cataracoui (Fort Frontenac). Shortly after his brother joined him in this duty, Jacques requested an appointment at the Jesuit college in Quebec where he taught fifth and sixth form classes for a year.

In 1689 we find Jacques de Lamberville at Sault-Saint-Louis (Caughnawaga) and two years later, in 1692, he was in residence at Montreal. When the Jesuits were permitted to return to the Iroquois cantons in 1701, Jacques de Lamberville, though now quite old, insisted on returning to the Onondagas where his brother had worked for many years. In obscurity and self-denial he laboured until 1709 when English intrigues had become so effective among the Iroquois that evangelization was virtually impossible. The final trial for Lamberville came when Abraham Schuyler tricked him into returning to Montreal to give an account of alleged English military dispositions and then had some drunken Indians burn his chapel and residence.

Jacques de Lamberville remained in Montreal and was given charge of the business affairs of the Hôtel-Dieu along with the Abbé Henri-Jean Tremblay*. He became momentarily involved in the dissatisfactions expressed with Saint-Vallier's [LA CROIX] episcopacy and he went so far as to state that the bishop should resign because of the divisions he caused among both clergy and laity. Death overtook Jacques de Lamberville on 18 April 1710 at Montreal, according to Father GERMAIN, his superior.

He was eulogized for assiduously mortifying his flesh and preparing for martyrdom. The colonists recounted his rigorous piety and practices of self-abnegation; the Iroquois simply called him "the divine man." It was not surprising that following his decease miracles were alleged to have happened

Lamberville

to persons who merely touched articles which he had used. The official account of his 37 years of apostolic labours in Canada sent to the general of the Society of Jesus in Rome made special mention of his self-mortification and the miracles associated with his possessions.

C. J. Jaenen

AN, Col., C^{11A}, 4–9; C^{11G}, 8, 169. Claude Chauchetière, *La vie de la b. Catherine Thegakouita dite à présent la Sainte Sauvagesse* (Manate [New York], 1887), 179. François Élesban de Guilhermy, *Ménologe de la Compagnie de Jésus . . . , assistance de France, comprenant les missions de l'Archipel, de la Syrie, . . . du Canada, de la Louisiane . . .* , éd. [Jacques Terrien] (2 part., Paris, 1892), première partie, 514. *JR* (Thwaites). Juchereau, *Annales* (Jamet), 199, 297, 346. *Lettres édifiantes et curieuses escrites des missions étrangères par quelques missionnaires de la Compagnie de Jésus* (30 v., Paris, 1707–73; nouv. éd., 26v., Paris, 1780–83), VI, 50. *Mission du Canada: Relations inédites de la Nouvelle-France (1672–1679) pour faire suite aux anciennes relations (1615–1672)* [éd. Felix Martin] (2v., Paris, 1861), II, 104–6. Campbell, *Pioneer priests*, I, 298–311.

LAMBERVILLE, JEAN DE, Jesuit missionary to the Onondagas, diplomat, b. at Rouen, 27 Dec. 1633; d. in Paris, 10 Feb. 1714.

Lamberville completed his literary and philosophical studies at the Jesuit college of Rouen and at the age of 23 entered the noviciate in Paris (3 March 1656), where he taught grammar and humanities and completed his own theological studies. He came to New France in 1669, and was immediately assigned to the Jesuit missions where he remained until 1687, when all missionaries were expelled from the Confederacy and the territory claimed by New York.

Lamberville's first encounter with the Onondagas in their village communities was at the mission of Saint-Jean-Baptiste. His impressions in 1672–73 were that only the superior persons could ever be converted and even so it would be necessary to employ generous presents and force of arms: "two arms, one of gold, the other of steel." Two years later, however, he could report some success, owing partly to the assistance of the converted chieftain Garakontié* who seconded his evangelical efforts. He also began to make good use of the medical supplies sent from France and became especially adept at bleeding and extracting teeth. Of the 72 converts he had won in a year he estimated that no fewer than 40 had died.

In 1676 he baptized some Mahicans who were being cruelly tortured by the Iroquois but was unable to obtain their release. He was himself threatened on several occasions but he remained fearless despite threats of torture, beatings, and death. Much of the opposition, he believed, was aroused by the "jugglers" whose magical practices were now undermined by the new religion and the new medicine. Eventually Lamberville obtained a public confrontation with his bitterest opponents and won from the elders the right to instruct and baptize all captives destined for the stake. Shortly thereafter two women captives were brought to him for baptism before being slowly burned and devoured. His evangelical labours at this period gained few living recruits for the church. Of the seven adults baptized during the course of the year none survived, and of the 45 children baptized almost 40 died soon after receiving the sacrament. His opponents had little difficulty in proving the claim that baptism itself was a cause of death. Nevertheless, his zeal was boundless, for on one occasion he walked 20 leagues to baptize a child whose parents had sent for him. He attributed the lack of success in evangelizing and Frenchifying the Indians to the fact that they were "not capable of reasoning as do the Chinese and other civilized nations," a viewpoint which was in sharp contradiction with the earlier optimistic views of "natural man."

In 1677, as newly appointed superior of the missions among the Five Nations, Lamberville faced increased persecution and hostility, much of it fomented by Dutch and English traders. The latter resented and feared the political implications and economic consequences of Jesuit spiritual ascendancy among the Iroquois tribes. Lamberville always maintained cordial, but strictly correct, relations with the foreigners to the south. On one occasion he returned a stolen gun and powder box to Jeremiah Van Rensselaer, but he explained in an accompanying letter that his humanity would not allow him to return a runaway slave to Albany.

Of 36 children and 23 adults baptized in 1677–78 only 12 survived the epidemics that ravaged the villages. A particularly cruel loss to the missionary was the death of Daniel Garakontié, whom Lamberville attended throughout his last sufferings. He personally made the chieftain's coffin and buried him with all the marks of honour and love he could display in a hostile encampment. The Europeans not only had intensified economic competition and intertribal rivalries, but also had introduced diseases of epidemic proportions.

By 1682 the patient and long-suffering Jean de Lamberville was able to instruct and baptize about 50 children annually, although by and large adults were still beyond his ministration. Resentment against his person, although not against the social and cultural force he represented, seemed to have subsided considerably. The Jesuit superior,

Father BESCHEFER, wrote in 1683 of "the great reputation" Jean de Lamberville and his brother JACQUES enjoyed among the Onondagas and attributed their improving position to their sympathetic understanding of Iroquois culture and to their judicious employment of medicines sent by the Maréchal de Bellefonds.

Lamberville's own correspondence gives a vivid and valuable picture of Onondaga domestic life, detailed accounts of the consequences of the liquor traffic, and insights into the missionaries' use of persuasion and penance to enforce social order. Lamberville alleges that on one expedition against the Illinois the Iroquois devoured 600 captives. Still he did not lose his patience and sympathy towards the tribesmen among whom he lived and laboured.

The royal officials began to see in Lamberville an influential diplomat and skilful negotiator. Cavelier* de La Salle consulted with him among the Onondagas about the building of a fort at Cataracoui. Buade* de Frontenac soon came to visit this new fort, named Fort Frontenac (now Kingston, Ont.) in his honour, and seized the opportunity to preach to the Iroquois himself. Lamberville wrote to his superior that he hoped the powerful exhortations of the governor would result in many conversions "supported as those exhortations were by numerous presents."

Lamberville was soon to emerge as the man of peace, the great diplomat whom the Iroquois could trust but who was betrayed by the French. He had difficulty explaining to the aborigines the complexities of French politics. When the Iroquois pillaged a French fur convoy, because they had been given to understand they should intercept all non-licensed traders, Governor Le Febvre* de La Barre prepared for war while appealing to Lamberville to negotiate the usual reparations required in such circumstances. Lamberville did not suspect the governor's double-dealing, but he did warn him repeatedly of the futility of attempting to divide the Iroquois Confederacy. When La Barre's ill-advised military expedition foundered in 1684 and he found himself out of provisions, encamped in a pestilential swamp at the source of the St Lawrence, with the majority of his men incapacitated by illness, he was forced to accept a humiliating conciliation and to beg Lamberville to make peace for him. Lamberville again warned that a military conquest of the Iroquois cantons would require at least 1,000 soldiers. He was one of the few individuals in the colony who vigorously defended the governor's decision to come to terms with the Iroquois.

When La Barre was recalled, his successor BRISAY de Denonville came to New France with orders to crush the Iroquois. His preparations, unknown to Lamberville, included building a fleet of flat-boats for transport, fortifying Montreal, and gathering arms and ammunition. In 1686 Lamberville, who remained in the Onondaga country with his brother despite insults and ill-treatment, was summoned to Quebec by Denonville and became the unsuspecting instrument of the latter's tactics. Denonville provided him with numerous presents for the tribesmen, commissioned him to invite representatives from the Confederacy to a parley at Fort Frontenac and seemed to accept Lamberville's conciliatory views. Denonville wrote, "This poor father does not suspect our design. He is a clever man; but if I recalled him from his mission our purpose would be suspected and the storm would burst on us." Lamberville assembled 40 chieftains and with difficulty persuaded them to go to Cataracoui to meet the governor in the midsummer of 1687. Denonville, meanwhile, betrayed the missionary's trust and assembled a sizable force at Cataracoui, seizing the Iroquois who were in the immediate vicinity and sending a few score of them to France to serve in the Mediterranean galley fleet. Lamberville learned of this bellicose policy from some English envoys at Onondaga, who had received word through trade contacts in Montreal. These Englishmen urged Lamberville to retire with them to the safety of New York, where Governor Dongan, a Roman Catholic, would afford him safe passage to France. The alternative, they suggested, was almost certain massacre by the Iroquois once they learned of the French betrayal. Lamberville refused their offer of assistance and in the company of eight Iroquois delegates left immediately for Cataracoui to ascertain the facts. On the way they encountered several warriors who had escaped from Denonville's camp. It is a tribute to the esteem the Iroquois had for Lamberville that they did not harm him. Instead, they conducted him safely to the edge of the French encampment. He was unable to change Denonville's plans but he did obtain the release of several notable Iroquois prisoners.

During Denonville's campaign against the Senecas in 1687 Lamberville remained with his brother at Fort Frontenac where he acted as chaplain for a garrison of some 140 men weakened by scurvy. In this capacity he sometimes visited the garrison at Fort Niagara. On one such journey the Iroquois attacked the vessel carrying Lamberville, and during a heated three-quarter-hour battle the latter first prayed and urged the men to fight to the death rather than be captured and tortured, then took part in the fighting himself. In December he was again asked to negotiate with

La Mollerie

the Onondagas, a mission which he willingly accepted although he was already ill with scurvy. He presented two collars to the chieftains, one to urge them to treat the French prisoners well and the other to ease the shame of the Seneca campaign. These tokens were later presented to Governor Dongan who successfully inflamed the Iroquois against the French. Dongan insisted on the release of all Iroquois galley slaves, the abandonment of the Indian reserves, the demolition of the forts at Cataracoui and Niagara, and the restoration of the booty taken from the Senecas.

On his return to Cataracoui Lamberville was so weakened by scurvy that he had to be hauled by sled, more dead than alive, to Montreal in February 1688, where for two and a half years he suffered as much from the attempts to cure him as from the malady. At least he could find some consolation in the fact that because he had contracted the disease while serving the troops, the royal officials defrayed his expenses during all this time and paid those who had cared for him.

Early in 1688 Denonville again asked Lamberville to secure Onondaga neutrality, if nothing more, in the impending Iroquois war, but Lamberville was too ill to go himself to Onondaga. Therefore he sent one of the Iroquois, who had accompanied a mission from Governor Dongan, entrusting him with a message of conciliation. Eventually a deputation headed by La Grande Gueule [Otreouti*] came to Montreal and through the efforts of Lamberville, who dragged himself to the meeting in spite of his desperate illness, reached a truce with Denonville in June 1688. Lamberville on this occasion succeeded in modifying all the conditions set forth by Dongan except the demand for the demolition of Fort Niagara. Denonville had reason to tell Seignelay, the minister of Marine, on 6 Nov. 1688, that Lamberville had "averted the storm that threatened us," commenting also: "how clever he is in controlling the Indian, who is shrewder than you imagine."

When an Iroquois delegation returned seeking definitive peace terms in August 1688, the Huron chieftain KONDIARONK waylaid it, killing some of its members and telling the rest that he had attacked them on orders from the governor. In revenge the Iroquois launched a general attack on the colony, especially on Lachine, on 4 and 5 Aug. 1689. Lamberville's work was ruined.

His superior, noting his precarious health, his bitter disappointment and his advanced age, sent him to France as procurator of the Canadian mission. With the return of Frontenac to New France and the sending of expeditions into English territory, the diplomacy of Lamberville was no longer required. To a friend he confided his desire "that I may end in our dear Canada the few days that remain to me," and the Onondagas sent a request to have him back in their villages. These desires remained unfulfilled at the time of his death in Paris on 10 Feb. 1714 at the age of 81.

C. J. JAENEN

AHDQ, Lettres, I. AN, Col., C^{11A}, 6–9. ARSI, Gallia 110/II, ff.107a, 116. Baugy, *Journal* (Serrigny). Charlevoix, *Histoire* (1744), I, 509–49; II, 282, 333ff. François Élesban de Guilhermy, *Ménologe de la Compagnie de Jésus ..., assistance de France, comprenant les missions de l'Archipel, de la Syrie, ... du Canada, de la Louisiane ...*, éd. [Jacques Terrien] (2 part., Paris, 1892), première partie, 225–77. *JR* (Thwaites). Lahontan, *Nouveaux voyages*, II. La Poterie, *Histoire* (1722), III, 1–58. *Mission du Canada: Relations inédites de la Nouvelle-France (1672–1679) pour faire suite aux anciennes relations (1615–1672)*, [éd. Félix Martin] (2v., Paris, 1861), I, 30–57; II, 39f., 108–14, 196–204, 347. *NYCD* (O'Callaghan and Fernow), III, 488f.; IX, 226–28, 252–62. [Jeremias Van Rensselaer], *Correspondence of Jeremias Van Rensselaer, 1651–1674*, ed. A. J. F. Van Laer (Albany, 1932), 447f. Campbell, *Pioneer priests*, I, 226–45. Rochemonteix, *Les Jésuites et la N.-F. au XVIIe siècle*, III, 154–222.

LA MOLLERIE, JACQUES MALERAY DE NOIRÉ DE. *See* MALERAY

LAMONTAGNE, NICOLAS JÉRÉMIE, *dit. See* JÉRÉMIE

LAMOTHE CADILLAC, ANTOINE LAUMET, *dit* **DE.** *See* LAUMET

LANDON, SIMPLE, priest, Recollet; b. 1641; d. 24 Feb. 1712 at Châlons-sur-Marne.

Landon took his religious vows with the Recollets of the ecclesiastical province of Saint-Denis in 1659 and received all the minor orders in 1663. During the first years of his priesthood he taught philosophy, and around 1669–70 he became a preacher in Paris.

Father Landon was one of the first religious who came to Canada in 1670 to restore the Recollet order which had been prevented, since 1632, from returning to Quebec, where it had been established in 1615. Under the direction of Father Germain Allart*, the minister of the province of Saint-Denis, Fathers Gabriel de La Ribourde*, Hilarion Guénin, Simple Landon, and Brothers Luc François*, a deacon, and Anselme Bardou, a lay brother, sailed from La Rochelle with Intendant Talon* at the end of May 1670. They arrived at

Quebec on 18 August after a voyage fraught with great dangers.

The Recollets were welcomed by the bishop, the governor, the Jesuits, and "the great concourse of inhabitants with all the signs of joy that one might expect from a country where our Fathers were eagerly awaited." The bishop entrusted them with four missions: Île Percée, the Saint John River, Fort Frontenac, and Trois-Rivières.

After superintending the establishment of his religious at Quebec, Father Germain Allart returned to France. Father Hilarion Guénin was assigned to serve Trois-Rivières. At Quebec itself, Father Gabriel de La Ribourde became provincial commissioner and superior of the convent. Father Simple Landon, who lived at the same convent, spent his time ministering to parishes, in particular to Pointe-aux-Trembles (Neuville). On 5 May 1672 he was present at the launching of a building programme to enlarge the Hôtel-Dieu. He returned to France in the autumn of the same year, and there he devoted himself to preaching in the church of the Recollets in Paris.

JACQUES VALOIS

AN, LL, 54, f.113v; 84, f.52v. BN, Imprimés, Recollets, LK⁷, 6743; MS, Fr. 15775, f.198. Juchereau, *Annales* (Jamet), 170. Le Clercq, *Premier établissement de la foy*, II, 91ff.

LANEUVILLE, JACQUES DE HORNÉ, *dit.* *See* HORNÉ

LANGELIER. *See* LARGILIER

LANGLOISERIE, CHARLES - GASPARD PIOT DE. *See* PIOT

LA NOUË, ZACHARIE ROBUTEL DE. *See* ROBUTEL

LA PLACE, LOUIS-HYACINTHE DE, baptized **Jean-Claude,** priest, Recollet, missionary, lecturer in theology, provincial commissioner for Canada; b. 1 Feb. 1673 at Rouen, 14th child of Pierre de La Place and Marie Le Couteux; d. 1737 at Versailles.

In 1691 Louis-Hyacinthe de La Place joined the Recollet order, in which he had been preceded by two of his brothers, Simon* and Eustache. He was ordained a priest in 1696, and in 1704 he was appointed lecturer in theology in the convent of Saint-Denis in Paris. From 1706 to 1709 he was guardian of the convent at Vitry-le-François. Appointed provincial commissioner for Canada in 1709, he sailed 5 May 1710 from Rochefort on the *Africain*, reaching Quebec on 8 September. Thanks to his good qualities and his capable administration he held the office of provincial commissioner for 10 years, although the prescribed period was 3 years. During his visits to the convents in Montreal and Trois-Rivières he exercised his clerical functions, for his name is found in the records of baptisms, marriages, and burials in these localities.

On 28 Oct. 1720 he sailed from Quebec on the *Chameau* and arrived at Rochefort on 8 December. From 1722 to 1725 he was guardian of the convent in Paris. He was elected provincial of the Recollets of the province of Saint-Denis in Paris on 15 July 1725, and was re-elected in 1734. He died at Versailles on 30 Jan. 1737, at 64 years of age and after 45 years in holy orders.

GABRIEL-M.-RÉAL DUMAS

Archives des Franciscains de Québec, Dossier L.-H. de La Place. AN, L, 959; Col., B, 30, f.129; 36, f.388; C¹¹ᴬ, 42, f.1720. Archives de la Seine-Maritime (Rouen), H (clergé régulier), récollets. *Mandements des évêques de Québec* (Têtu et Gagnon), I, 488. Odoric-M. [Jouve], *Les Franciscains et le Canada: aux Trois-Rivières*; "Étude historique et critique sur les actes du Frère Didace Pelletier, Récollet," *BRH*, XVII (1911), 175. Régis Roy, "Les archives de Seine-et-Marne," *BRH*, XXIX (1923), 239.

LA PORTE DE LOUVIGNY, LOUIS DE, lieutenant in France and in Canada, captain in the colonial regular troops, commander of western posts, sub-lieutenant in the navy, town major of Trois-Rivières and of Quebec, knight of the order of Saint-Louis, commander-in-chief of the *pays d'en haut*, governor of Trois-Rivières; b. c. 1662, either in Paris or in Le Mans; lost at sea 27 Aug. 1725.

The son of Jean de La Porte and Françoise Faucrolle or Foucrelle, he is sometimes confused with Lussigny, who was a member of Buade* de Frontenac's guards in the 1670s. Louvigny, however, arrived in New France only in 1683. Prior to that date he had served as a subordinate officer in the Régiment de Navarre for six years.

War between New France and the Iroquois was breaking out when Louvigny arrived in the colony, and in the years that followed he distinguished himself on several expeditions against these Indians. He soon impressed Governor Denonville [BRISAY] who recommended him for a promotion and sent him on a mission to Hudson Bay in 1688. The following year Frontenac returned to Canada and one of his first acts was to send Louvigny to Michilimackinac with 170 men, with orders to reinforce that post and to relieve the commandant,

La Porte de Louvigny

MOREL de La Durantaye. The governor claimed that this change of command was necessary to prevent the Ottawa Indians from coming to terms with the Iroquois, but the intendant, BOCHART de Champigny, thought otherwise. He claimed that La Durantaye was an excellent officer, who had matters well in hand at Michilimackinac, whereas Frontenac's appointee was a fur-trader by instinct. The real reason for the latter's appointment, according to the intendant, had been his willingness to pay Frontenac's secretary 500 *livres* annually in return for the command of the post. Whatever truth there may be in this account, Louvigny turned out to be an able commandant. When he asked to be relieved in 1694, in order to go to France to attend to family matters, Champigny as well as Frontenac warmly commended him for his services.

On 7 Nov. 1699, Louvigny, now a captain and considered one of the colony's best soldiers, was named commanding officer of Fort Frontenac. In the winter that followed, he and his garrison engaged in the fur trade with the Iroquois, thus violating the edict of 1696 that forbad commerce at the western posts. This blunder could have cost him his career. He was immediately placed under arrest by order of Governor CALLIÈRE and it was only at Champigny's insistence that the case be heard by the Conseil Souverain that he avoided trial by court martial. Impressed by his defence and by the Iroquois' plea that he be shown mercy, the Conseil Souverain rendered no verdict but sent Louvigny to France to let the king decide his fate. There he was deprived of the position of town major of Trois-Rivières, which he had recently acquired, but he did not long remain out of favour. On 1 June 1703, he was appointed town major of Quebec.

Louvigny's ability and his influence over the Indians were clearly recognized soon after his return to the colony. In 1705, a group of Ottawas had attacked a Seneca hunting party near Fort Frontenac, killed several of their number, and carried off others as prisoners to Michilimackinac. Unless the Iroquois were promptly offered reparation, the peace treaty they had concluded with New France and her Indian allies in 1701 could well be jeopardized. The new governor, Philippe de RIGAUD de Vaudreuil, chose Louvigny to go to Michilimackinac to free the prisoners and to bring the offending Ottawas back to Montreal for a meeting with the Senecas. The success of this mission helped Louvigny to establish himself as one of the governor's principal lieutenants. On Vaudreuil's recommendation, he was granted the coveted cross of the order cf Saint-Louis in 1708 and was also chosen to command at Michili-

mackinac when this important post, abandoned by royal order since 1696, was re-established in 1712.

Circumstances delayed Louvigny's return to the west until 1716, the year in which he became king's lieutenant. At that time a military campaign had become necessary to subjugate the Fox Indians, whose war on the French and their allies had badly disrupted the fur trade. A first expedition against them having failed in 1715, a second was organized the following year and placed under Louvigny's command. It was made up of some 400 coureurs de bois and a like number of Indian volunteers, the very elements whose unruly behaviour had been largely responsible for the failure of the preceding campaign. With Louvigny commanding, however, the army moved swiftly and in good order from Montreal, by way of Michilimackinac and Detroit, to Baie des Puants (Green Bay), where the Fox stronghold was located. With the aid of saps and mortars they weakened the fortifications and forced the enemy to sue for peace. This feat of arms restored tranquillity in the west and so impressed the court that it granted the commander a gratuity of 3,000 *livres*.

Louvigny had now become a prominent and influential figure in New France. He was no longer simply a subordinate carrying out orders but also participated in policy making. He advised Vaudreuil on the location of the posts that were founded in the west between 1716 and 1721 and also wrote several important memoirs on the policy the French should follow in the interior. In 1720, the position of commander-in-chief of the *pays d'en haut* was specially created for him. The duties consisted in carrying out biennial inspection tours of the western posts to coordinate the activities of the commanding officers and to prevent the brandy trade. The problem of financing such lengthy voyages, however, prevented him from ever exercising these functions.

In 1724, during a visit to France, Louvigny was named governor of Trois-Rivières. Unfortunately, he did not live to take up his post. The *Chameau*, aboard which he was returning to the colony, struck a reef and sank off Cape Breton with no survivors. Louvigny left his wife, Marie Nolan, whom he had married in Quebec on 26 Oct. 1684, three daughters and one son. Six other children had died in infancy. Both Bishop Saint-Vallier [LA CROIX] and Governor Beauharnois* de La Boische implored the court to come to the assistance of this family which had been left in complete penury by the death of the father.

Louvigny had been an outstanding officer. After his misadventure at Fort Frontenac he became a devoted and high-minded servant of New France. As one of Vaudreuil's close counsellors he also helped to shape the course of French western policy during the first quarter of the 18th century.

YVES F. ZOLTVANY

AJQ, Greffe de Pierre Duquet, 26 oct. 1684. AN, Col., B, 13, 16, 22, 23, 25, 29, 32, 33, 34, 37, 38, 39, 42; C¹¹ᴬ, 8–48; C¹¹ᴳ, 2, 3, 4, 5, 6, 8; D²ᶜ, 47; F³, 6, 7, 8, 9, 10. Charlevoix, *Histoire*. "Correspondance de Frontenac (1689–99)," APQ *Rapport, 1927–28, 1928–29*. "Correspondance de Vaudreuil," APQ *Rapport, 1938–39, 1939–40, 1942–43, 1946–47, 1947–48*. *Jug. et délib.*, IV. Wis. State Hist. Soc. *Coll.*, XVI.

F.-É. Audet, *Les premiers établissements français au pays des Illinois; la guerre des Renards* (Paris, 1938). Kellogg, *French régime*. P.-G. Roy, *La famille de La Porte de Louvigny* (Lévis, 1938). "M. de Louvigny était-il protestant?" *BRH*, XX (1914), 380–82.

LA POTHERIE (POTERIE), *dit* **BACQUE-VILLE DE LA POTHERIE, CLAUDE-CHARLES LE ROY DE.** See LE ROY

LARGILLIER (Langelier, Angilliers), JACQUES, called **Le Castor,** trader in furs, settler, a *donné* of the Society of Jesus, companion of Father Jacques Marquette*; b. *c.* 1644 in France, perhaps in the village of Quierzy, in Picardy; d. 4 Nov. 1714 at the post of Kaskaskia, in the Illinois country.

Around 1664 Largillier came to join his uncle Raymond Pajet, *dit* Carcy, who had settled at Quebec, then at Beaupré. Largillier's name is found for the first time in an act of the notary Jacques de La Tousche recorded at Cap-de-la-Madeleine on 20 April 1666, when he made a contract with Adrien Jolliet and Denis Guyon whereby he would undertake a "journey to the Ottawas." The following year he obtained from Jean Bourdon*, seigneur of Dombourg, a land grant which he made over to his cousin Guillaume Pajet on 11 Aug. 1669. He then set out on another journey to the *pays d'en haut*, probably with Adrien Jolliet and Jean Peré*, who had been sent by Talon* "to go and reconnoitre to see whether the copper mine situated to the north of Lake Ontario ... is rich and of easy extraction." On 4 June 1671, at Sault-Sainte-Marie, he was one of the signatories to the act whereby Daumont* de Saint-Lusson took possession of the territories of the West.

Among the records of the period which testify to Largillier's skill as a fur-trader, whence his nickname "Le Castor," must be mentioned the contract entered into on 1 Oct. 1672 before the notary Gilles Rageot* by Louis Jolliet*, several other partners, and himself, to "make together

the journey to the Ottawa Indians [and to] trade in furs with the Indians." Largillier probably took part in Jolliet's expedition to the Mississippi in 1673; the explorer definitely had a high opinion of Largillier's worth as a "canoe man" to include him with his own companions in this way. In 1674 Largillier went with Father Marquette to the Illinois country. In July 1675 he was back in Quebec, with a rich cargo of furs. It is probable that he brought with him at the same time the last writings of Father Marquette, who had died on 18 May, and that he informed Father Claude Dablon* by word of mouth about the illness and death of the missionary, to whom he had given constant and attentive care.

During the following months he disposed of his material possessions to place himself, from 1676 on, at the service of the Jesuits, probably as a *donné*. He does not seem to have taken the usual vows, although he made his solemn promises; he wore lay dress to be freer during his numerous journeys. In 1681 a census records his presence in the Ottawa mission. He accompanied and assisted the missionaries Allouez*, AVENEAU, Albanel*, NOUVEL, and GRAVIER in their trips. From then on his name ceases to appear in notarial acts.

He spent the last years of his life at the Kaskaskia mission in the Illinois country, and the missionaries praised his untiring devotion. Old, infirm, and almost helpless, he was given devoted care by the priests of the mission, who were happy to serve one who had served them so well. Largillier did not survive the epidemic of quartan fever which ravaged this region in 1714, and he died on 4 November, a few weeks after his superior, Father PIERRE-GABRIEL MAREST.

RAYMOND DOUVILLE

AJQ, Greffe de Romain Becquet, 30 juillet 1675; Greffe de Pierre Duquet, 17 mars 1673; Greffe de Gilles Rageot, 1 oct. 1672, 19 oct. 1675. ASJCF, Fonds Rochemonteix, 4025, 10; 4026. *JR* (Thwaites), LXIV, LXVI, LIX, LXXI. *Jug. et délib.*, I, 864. N. M. Belting, *Kaskaskia under the French régime* (University of Illinois studies in the social sciences, XXIX, no.3, Urbana, 1948). Sister Mary Borgias Palm, *Jesuit Missions of the Illinois Country, 1673–1763* (n.p., 1933). Raymond Douville, "Jacques Largillier dit 'le castor,' coureur des bois et 'frère donné'," *Cahiers des Dix*, XXIX (1964), 47–63.

LA RIVIÈRE, GUILLAUME DE LORIMIER DE. See LORIMIER

LA RIVIÈRE, HILAIRE BERNARD DE, See BERNARD

Larkin

LARKIN, GEORGE, barrister in the High Court of Admiralty; d. 1703 or 1704.

"Versed in the forms of Admiralty Courts," Larkin was appointed in April 1701 to make an investigation for the Board of Trade which would take him "first to Newfoundland . . . and from thence ·. . . to New England and so forwards through all the Plantations" where smuggling and piracy were alarmingly on the increase. His mission was made necessary by widespread disregard of two important statutes, the 1699 act for better regulation of the Newfoundland fisheries and the 1700 act for more effectual suppression of piracy. Larkin was furnished with instructions for curbing illicit trade, and empowered to establish courts and procedures for conducting piracy trials.

Instructions of similar nature were issued to Commodore John GRAYDON of the Newfoundland convoy, and the two were to work in concert. By 11 August Larkin had his report ready, written on board the *Assistance* in St John's harbour. "Want of a penalty" accounted for the weakness of the trade regulatory act, and the list of abuses requiring correction was formidable; he condemned the inefficiency of the fishing admirals and their blatant self-interest, naming Arthur HOLDSWORTH as one of the worst offenders. A local merchant, Henry Newman*, was appointed "register" (registrar) of the courts set up for piracy trials, and Larkin "layd downe everything so plaine" that these trials could proceed without error.

From Newfoundland Larkin went on to Boston "where illegal trade and piracy found so general encouragement," and after three days in Philadelphia he found "everyone very shy of me and glad to see me preparing to be gone." In Bermuda he met with grave misfortune, being charged—it seems falsely—with seducing a mulatto servant, and imprisoned. His release from prison was ordered from England in 1703 and he must have died shortly afterwards. A "promise . . . in relation to Mr. Larkin's widow" was brought before the Board of Trade in September 1704.

MAUD M. HUTCHESON

G.B., Parliament, *Proceedings and debates respecting North America* (Stock). *NYCD* (O'Callaghan and Fernow), IV. PRO, *Acts of P.C., col. ser., Unbound papers*; *CSP, Col.,* 1699, 1700, 1701, 1702, 1702–3, 1704–5. Lounsbury, *British fishery at Nfld.* Prowse, *History of Nfld.* Rogers, *Newfoundland.*

LA RONDE, PIERRE DENYS DE. *See* DENYS

LAROSE, JACQUES LE BER, *dit.* *See* LE BER

LARUE, GUILLAUME DE, indentured worker, carpenter, notary, seigneurial judge, originally from the parish of Saint-Maclou (Rouen); b. *c.* 1636, son of Guillaume de Larue and Marie Pouilliot; buried 9 Jan. 1717 at Sainte-Anne de la Pérade.

As he had a good education, Larue became the confidential agent of the Jesuits in their seigneury of Cap-de-la-Madeleine. From 1662 on he was in turn a court officer, seigneurial attorney, clerk of court, and clerk in the court registry. In 1664 he moved to Champlain and was appointed seigneurial notary, then in 1673 judge in the same place. He was also designated in some deeds as judge of the provost court in the seigneury of Batiscan. His duties as a man of law did not cause him to neglect his trade as a carpenter, so that his services were much sought after for the building of mills, barns, and houses. Some of his plans and estimates for the construction of houses have been preserved, and show scrupulous concern for accuracy.

Guillaume de Larue practised the profession of notary from 1664 to 1689. His registry from 9 Jan. 1664 to 18 April 1676, comprising 140 acts, has been preserved at the Palais de Justice of Trois-Rivières. The rest has been destroyed or lost. A few copies appear however in the registers of insinuations or are collated with the registries of other notaries.

Seven children were born of his marriage with Marie Pepin in 1663. Around 1700 he retired and went to live with his son Étienne near Batiscan, and died there 17 years later.

RAYMOND DOUVILLE

AJTR, Greffe de Séverin Ameau; Greffe de Jean Cusson; Greffe de Laurent Du Portail; Greffe de Claude Herlin; Greffe de Jacques de La Touche. *Jug. et délib.,* I, II, V, VI. P.-G. et A. Roy, *Inv. greffes not.,* II, 248; XI, 71. Archange Godbout, *Origine des familles canadiennes-françaises, extrait de l'état civil français* (Lille, 1925). "Les notaires au Canada," 22. Tanguay, *Dictionnaire,* I, 351. Vachon, "Inv. critique des notaires royaux," *RHAF,* X (1956–57), 261. Cloutier, *Histoire de la paroisse de Champlain,* I. J.-E. Roy, *Histoire du notariat,* I, 200, 210, 230. Émile Vaillancourt, *La conquête du Canada par les Normands* (Montréal, 1930).

LA SALLE, NICOLAS DE, colonial administrator, commissary in Louisiana, b. probably at Paris, son of Nicolas de La Salle and Marie Harot; d. 31 Dec. 1710 in (old) Mobile.

La Salle was the brother of Charles de La Salle, commissary general at Marseilles who died in 1695; another brother died in 1690 while serving as financial commissary in Siam.

Nicolas de La Salle accompanied René-Robert Cavelier* de La Salle (no relation) in the possession-taking Mississippi River expedition of 1682. Margry attributes to Nicolas a brief, prosaic narrative of this exploration journey; Nicolas himself claims to have sent to the minister of Marine in 1697 "the memoirs of M. de La Salle." Margry's hesitation and the narrative's impersonal phrasing leave room for doubt in the attribution of authorship of the manuscript. The author notes that he "wrote this relation in 1685; it was given me by the young de La Salle."

In 1700 Nicolas was employed in office work with the navy in Toulon when he asked Pont-chartrain for a more remunerative post in the new Louisiana colony; he recalled his services with Cavelier de La Salle, and reminded the minister of the faithful service of his late brothers. Nicolas needed a higher salary because of his "large family." Given the position of acting commissary, he sailed to Biloxi in the summer of 1701. PIERRE LE MOYNE d'Iberville praised him as being the first to bring to the colony his wife and children; the two oldest, Nicolas and Simon, were eight and seven years of age; the youngest, François, was only two. Nicolas had married Madeleine Chartroux in Toulon on 26 June 1692; presumably she died on the Gulf Coast, for by late 1707 we find him married to Catherine de Berenhard who bore him a son in 1708 and a daughter in 1709. In the two marriages Nicolas was the father of (at least) six children; when he died, his possessions had to be sold at auction for the support of five who survived him.

Serving as "writer performing the functions of commissary" in Louisiana, Nicolas de La Salle administered the royal warehouse with its supplies, and kept the colonial financial accounts of official salaries and expenses. He directed the taking of Louisiana's first census, which he completed and signed on 12 Aug. 1708. Wisely but in vain he urged the sending of farm families needed in the colony; he deplored the libertine life of some 60 coureurs de bois listed as being in the Mississippi valley.

La Salle clashed sharply and continually with Le Moyne* de Bienville, commandant of the colony after Iberville's departure and death. He accused Bienville of profiteering, of domineering behaviour, and of usurpation of the commissary's prerogatives. Indeed, the charges of La Salle led to lengthy investigation of the Le Moyne brothers, and helped keep Bienville from being named governor. However, according to Commissary Martin d'Artaguiette, sent to Louisiana to examine charges and countercharges, La Salle's own accounts were not entirely blameless.

At Mobile, which had succeeded Biloxi as the capital, La Salle found in the pastor, Henri Roulleaux de La Vente, a strong ally in quarrels with the commandant, and the colonists were obliged to choose sides in the bitter division between the leaders' factions.

La Salle's criticism of the site of old Mobile, and his recommendation for moving downriver were factors that contributed to the choice of the city's present site.

He was about to be recalled to France when in old Mobile "he died of the flux on the last day of December" in 1710.

C. E. O'NEILL

Archives of the diocese of Mobile, first register, ff.3v, 6, 6v, 9v, 10v. Archives municipales de Toulon, État civil, GG 85, f.32v; 87, f.224; 92, f.13. AN, Col., C¹³ᴬ, 1, ff.468, 486; 2, ff.1, 17–18, 26–27, 99, 107–11, 133, 226, 324, 593, 633; C¹³ᴮ, pièces 4, 5, 7, 8; Marine, B², 154, ff.524, 642; C², 55, 57. *Découvertes et établissements des Français* (Margry), I, 547–70; IV, 493. [Nicolas de La Salle], *Relation of the discovery of the Mississippi River, written from the narrative of Nicolas de La Salle, otherwise known as the little M. de La Salle*, tr. M. B. Anderson (Chicago, 1898). *MPA* (Rowland and Sanders), III, 17–168; the Index confuses Nicolas de La Salle with another La Salle, probably his son. Giraud, *Histoire de la Louisiane française*, I. O'Neill, *Church and state in Louisiana*.

LASCARIS D'URFÉ, FRANÇOIS-SATURNIN, Sulpician, missionary, member of a noble family from the Forez region; b. 1641 at Baugé, son of Charles-Emmanuel, Marquis d'Urfé et de Baugé, marshal of His Majesty's camps and armies, and of Marguerite d'Allègre; d. 30 June 1701 in his château de Baugé.

Through his great-grandmother, Renée de Savoie-Lascaris, he was related to the illustrious Greek house of Lascaris, which had once occupied the throne of Constantinople.

François-Saturnin Lascaris d'Urfé was admitted on 1 April 1660 to the seminary of Saint-Sulpice in Paris and was ordained a priest in 1665 or 1666. His superior soon sent him, at his request, to Canada, where he arrived in the autumn of 1668. The following year he was assigned to the new mission to the Iroquois at Kenté (Quinte). This was in reality a "flying column," for the missionaries had to move about frequently to accompany the Indians on their hunting expeditions. D'Urfé accompanied his colleague and cousin Salignac* de La Mothe-Fénelon to the mission. Like the latter, he knew the consolations afforded by his ministry as well as its disappointments, for if the Indians received the Black Robes gladly, they nevertheless did not give up their ancestral customs. D'Urfé spent more than four years at Kenté, then in 1674, when his cousin had great difficulties with Governor Buade* de Frontenac, it was he who replaced Fénelon at the mission at Gentilly (Dorval).

For having tried to defend Fénelon, Abbé d'Urfé likewise had to suffer the governor's unpleasantness. In the autumn of 1674 he sailed for France with Fénelon to plead his cause. He prepared a memoir for Colbert. This memoir, clever and at the same time forcible, made mention of the vexations to which he had been subjected: his mail had been opened, he had been deprived of the services of a valet, and Frontenac had expelled him from his office without listening to him. On 13 May 1675 Colbert, whose son had just married d'Urfé's first cousin, wrote to Frontenac: "Monsieur d'Urfé has become a very close relation of mine, since he is a first cousin of my daughter-in-law, which constrains me to ask you to show him some sign of your particular consideration." Although d'Urfé and Frontenac subsequently seem to have made their peace, the accusing manuscript remained in the files. Nevertheless, L. Bertrand, the historiographer of Saint-Sulpice assures us, d'Urfé's memoir "contributed in no small measure to bringing about M. de Frontenac's recall."

The missionary firmly intended to return to Canada, but he was faced with a financial problem; it was decided by his superiors that he should pay the cost of his voyage. Now his family was neither rich nor generous. However, a favourable opportunity presented itself in 1685 when M. de Saint-Vallier [LA CROIX] was named bishop of Quebec; François d'Urfé was recommended to him to act as his guide and counsellor. D'Urfé did not remain long at Quebec but went back to Montreal to rejoin his *confrères*. It was thus that he became in 1686, if not the founder of the parish, at least the first resident priest for the parish of Saint-Louis du Haut de l'Île.

More and more the tendency was to go out to meet the Indians who came to Montreal to trade their furs: Lachine was founded in 1669, Gentilly around 1673. From the registers of landed property it appears that by 1678 there were fiefs all along the shoreline, from Senneville to Gentilly. The name of the fief of Bellevue has remained attached to Sainte-Anne-de-Bellevue, which was first called "du bout de l'île" ("at the end of the island"). If we are to believe tradition, the chapel of Saint-Louis de Haut de l'Île stood on a point which is still called Pointe-à-Caron and which forms part of the present-day Baie d'Urfé.

In the autumn of 1687, after the frequent incursions by the Iroquois against the colony had been resumed, the little parish of Saint-Louis was attacked. D'Urfé narrowly escaped the massacre and could do nothing but bury the dead, among whom was his sole churchwarden, Jean de Lalonde, *dit* l'Espérance. In doing so he acted courageously, although according to his superiors he was not "particularly brave by nature."

He was called back to France on family matters in 1687 and was appointed in turn to various benefices. Then in 1697 he retired to his château of Baugé, where he died in 1701, barely 60 years old. The *Gallia Christiana* informs us that he was buried in the vaults of the Hôtel-Dieu, which is today the hospice, where an inscription recalls the dignity of his life and his unfailing charity.

ARMAND YON

Bibliothèque municipale de Montréal, Fonds Gagnon, Lettres manuscrites des supérieurs de Saint-Sulpice. "Correspondance de Frontenac (1672–1682)," APQ *Rapport*, 1926–27, 82f. *Gallia Christiana in provincias ecclesiasticas ...* (13v., Paris, 1715–85), II, 592. Louis Moreri, *Le grand dictionnaire historique, ou le mélange curieux de l'histoire sacrée et profane ...* (nouv. éd. [par L.-F.-J. de La Barre], 6v., Paris, 1725), V, 329. A.-L. Bertrand, *Bibliothèque sulpicienne ou histoire littéraire de la compagnie de Saint-Sulpice* (3v., Paris, 1900), I, 155. Eccles, *Frontenac*, 69. [Faillon], *Histoire de la colonie française*, III, 493ff. Armand Yon, "Une 'victime' de Frontenac: l'abbé François Lascaris d'Urfé (1641–1701)," SCHEC *Rapport*, 1944–45, 51–67.

LA SOURCE, ANTOINE-DOMINIQUE-RENÉ THAUMUR DE. *See* THAUMUR

LATHAM, ROBERT, mason, engineer, captain; d. 1713.

Of Robert Latham's antecedents nothing is known beyond the fact that he was a master mason. As such he received an appointment as a military engineer and was posted to St John's, Newfoundland, in 1701. There he was engaged in building and strengthening the defences. Latham's first years in Newfoundland were uneventful, except for a dispute with the minister, John JACKSON, about the occupancy of a house inside Fort William. As military chaplain Jackson claimed precedence over Latham, and his claim appears to have been upheld.

When Captain Thomas LLOYD was ordered to return to England in 1704, Lieutenant John MOODY, his successor, fearing a possible attack by the French, appointed Latham acting lieutenant in command of the south battery, sometimes called the South Castle, a strongly built stone defence work. French forces, under AUGER de Subercase, attacked St John's 21 Jan. 1704/5; but both Fort William and the South Castle survived the siege until the French withdrew, with heavy losses, on 23 February. During that time Latham with a dozen or so soldiers and a number of civilian inhabitants repelled repeated French attacks. The English merchant, Colin CAMPBELL, had been taken prisoner and was forced on more than one occasion to approach Latham, under a flag of truce, with the object of inducing him to visit Lieutenant Moody in Fort William and persuade him to surrender. Each time these overtures were repulsed. Allegations were subsequently made that the French had planned an ambush—their Indian allies would have killed Latham on his way to the fort.

Latham was confirmed as a lieutenant in the Newfoundland Independent Company, 2 May 1705. Unfortunately friction arose between Latham and Moody who accused his lieutenant of disobedience and of setting a bad example for the soldiers. In October Moody was superseded by Major Lloyd, who brought with him a brevet captaincy for Latham. Latham remained on very good terms with the new garrison commander. When Moody and Jackson returned to England, the latter continued his feud against Latham—and indirectly against Lloyd—in a report dated 2 Feb. 1706 to the House of Commons: "Mr. Latham as Chief Mason had a large sum sent him yearly to pay labourers, most of which he employed in buying liquors and in trade. . . . He . . . refused to pay me much that is owed, and would not make my lodgings in the fort fit to live in."

Latham was ordered to return to England by the Board of Ordnance in 1707. In a report to the Duke of Marlborough, master-general of the ordnance, dated 13 Dec. 1707, the board stated that Latham had expended considerable sums of money on the fortifications at St John's without rendering any satisfactory accounts. They had, therefore, recalled him "last Summer," appointing George VANE in his place. Major Lloyd wrote to the Board of Trade praising Latham's efficiency and diligence, and stressing his popularity with the inhabitants; Lloyd hoped Latham would be permitted to return the following spring. Despite—or because of—this recommendation Latham was not re-appointed to Newfoundland.

In 1710 the Board of Ordnance appointed Latham as engineer at Fort St Phillip in the island of Menorca. He died there early in 1713.

MICHAEL GODFREY

PRO, W.O. 46/6 (correspondence of the Master-General of the Ordnance); *CSP, Col., 1704–5, 1706–8.* Dalton, *English army lists,* V. Prowse, *History of Nfld.*

Dalton states that Latham was appointed to Menorca in 1712; however, PRO, W.O. 53/448 (Board of Ordnance, bill books for Menorca, 1710)

show that Capt. Robert Latham signed for his first pay in July of 1710 at Fort St Phillip, Menorca.

LA TOUCHE, JEAN-PIERRE AULNEAU DE. *See* AULNEAU

LA TOUCHE, LOUIS TANTOUIN DE. *See* TANTOUIN

LA TOUR. *See* SAINT-ÉTIENNE

LATOUR, JACQUES LEBLOND DE. *See* LEBLOND

LA TOURETTE, CLAUDE GREYSOLON DE. *See* GREYSOLON

LAUBERIVIÈRE, FRANÇOIS-LOUIS DE POURROY DE. *See* POURROY

LAUMET, ANTOINE, *dit* de Lamothe Cadillac, seigneur in Acadia, captain in the colonial regular troops, sub-lieutenant in the navy, commandant of Michilimackinac, founder of Detroit, governor of Louisiana, knight of the order of Saint-Louis, governor of Castelsarrasin in France; a turbulent figure in the history of New France, described by Agnes Laut as among the "great early heroes in North American history" and by W. J. Eccles as "one of the worst scoundrels ever to set foot in New France"; b. at Les Laumets, near Caumont (department of Tarn-et-Garonne), 5 March 1658; d. at Castelsarrasin, 15 Oct. 1730.

Boastful, ingenious, quarrelsome, not too scrupulous about adhering to the truth, Antoine Laumet was a true son of Gascony. He has gone down in history with the impressive noble pedigree he invented for himself, consisting of the title of esquire, a coat of arms, the noble alias of de Lamothe Cadillac, and a father who was counsellor in the prestigious *parlement* of Toulouse. The truth is quite different. Cadillac's baptismal certificate, preserved in the parish of Saint-Nicolas-de-la-Grave, shows that his father, Jean Laumet, was a humble provincial magistrate, and his mother, Jeanne Péchagut, of bourgeois stock. Assuming a noble identity was of course a common practice in 17th-century France, but Cadillac may have hoped to gain more by this than merely social prestige. The thorough manner in which he blurred over his real origins, going so far as to alter the name of his mother to Malenfant on his wedding certificate of 25 June 1687, has led several historians to believe that for some reason or other he wished to make it impossible for anyone to inquire about his real identity.

351

Laumet

Little is known of Cadillac's life before he came to Canada. It is clear from his voluminous American correspondence which, although untrustworthy, is invariably witty and well written, that he received a good education. On occasion he even ventured into the field of scholarship with rather startling results. While commanding at Michilimackinac he wrote a report to prove that the western Indians were closely related to the Jews. As for his claim to have held a commission in the French army, it is almost invalidated by the contradictory statements he made about his rank and regiment. In 1690 he told a clerk of the ministry of Marine that he had been an infantry captain; the following year he informed Frontenac [Buade*] that he had held the rank of lieutenant in the Régiment Clairambault; in a memorial of the mid 1720s to the ministry of Marine he had demoted himself to a cadet in the Régiment de Dampierre-Lorraine.

About 1683 Cadillac landed in Acadia as an obscure immigrant and settled in Port-Royal (Annapolis Royal, N.S.). Shortly afterwards he took service under François GUION, a privateer who had stopped there to equip his vessel. While serving under Guion he gained an extensive knowledge of the New England coast which later made him a valuable man in the eyes of the French government. He also had the opportunity to visit Guion's home at Beauport, near Quebec, where he fell in love with Marie-Thérèse, the daughter of François' elder brother, Denis. They were married in Quebec on 25 June 1687, and returned to Acadia where Cadillac was granted a seigneury of 25 square miles on the Douaguek River (Union River, Me.).

Cadillac never developed this wilderness tract; fighting with the governor, DES FRICHES de Meneval, kept him far too busy for that. Cadillac, it seems, had formed a trading partnership with Soulègre, commandant of the Port-Royal garrison, and Mathieu de GOUTIN, the chief commissary. When Meneval informed Soulègre and de Goutin that as officers they were forbidden to engage in trade, the three partners schemed against him. They sought to alienate the priests from him and, when this failed, tried to turn the people against the priests by urging them not to pay the tithe. Meneval was soon complaining in the strongest terms about the three cronies. "This Cadillac," he stated in one dispatch, "who is the most uncooperative person in the world, is a scatter-brain who has been driven out of France for who knows what crimes." A clerk of the ministry of Marine who had occasion to speak with Cadillac shortly afterwards had much the same impression of him: "He was recognized as being very sharp indeed,

and quite capable of the practices Mr de Menneval noted."

In the summer of 1691 Cadillac arrived at Quebec with his family and not a penny to his name. In May of the previous year his Acadia habitation had been destroyed, along with several other houses in the vicinity of Port Royal, by Sir William Phips*. Never had Cadillac's prospects been bleaker, but they soon began to brighten perceptibly. Although the court had been alerted by Meneval to the type of man he was, it still considered that with his knowledge of the Atlantic seaboard he might render valuable service should an attack be launched against Boston or New York. Frontenac was therefore instructed to grant Cadillac employment in the royal service and to help him in every possible way. The governor, who had taken an instant liking to the glib, boisterous Gascon was only too happy to oblige and made him a lieutenant in the colonial regular troops. In 1692, Cadillac made a reconnaissance trip along the New England coast with Jean-Baptiste FRANQUELIN, the mapmaker, and submitted to the royal government a detailed and accurate report on the geography of the area. In recognition of this service he was promoted to the rank of captain in October 1693. The following year, Frontenac appointed him commandant of Michilimackinac, at the junction of Lake Huron and Lake Michigan.

Michilimackinac was the most important military and trading station held by New France in the western country. To command there at the height of the Iroquois war was a heavy responsibility. Basically the duties of the commandant were threefold: to keep all the western tribes in the French alliance, to make them live in harmony with each other, and to induce them to wage war relentlessly on the Five Nations. It is quite odd that Frontenac and his secretary, Charles de MONSEIGNAT, the author of the annual "Relation of the most Remarkable Canadian Occurrences," should have asserted that Cadillac was acquitting himself very well in this work when the facts they reported proved the exact contrary. Cadillac was unable to prevent the Hurons and Iroquois from exchanging embassies for the purpose of concluding a peace treaty; he was unable to preserve harmony between the various western tribes, much less persuade them to form a large striking force to attack the Iroquois. In 1697, when Cadillac returned to Canada, Monseignat reported that affairs in the Great Lakes region were "extremely confused."

Cadillac may have been a failure as a commandant but he proved to be very adroit as a fur-trader. When he arrived at Michilimackinac late in 1694, his capital assets consisted only of his captain's pay of 1,080 *livres* annually. Three years later he sent to France letters of exchange valued at 27,596 *livres* 4 *sols* which represented only a part of his net profits. These gains were realized in two ways: by selling unlimited quantities of brandy to the Indians, a practice which both angered and distressed the Jesuits, Father CARHEIL and Father JOSEPH MAREST; and by fleecing the coureurs de bois, few of whom dared to complain because they knew that Cadillac was protected by Frontenac. The commissary of the king's troops, Louis TANTOUIN de La Touche, best summed up the nature of Cadillac's tenure as commandant when he stated: "Never has a man amassed so much wealth in so short a time and caused so much talk by the wrongs suffered by the individuals who advance funds to his sort of trading ventures."

On 21 May 1696, the situation in the west was drastically altered. To reduce the flow of beaver pelts into the colony, a flow which had saturated the French market, Louis XIV issued an edict which abolished the fur-trading licences *(congés)* and ordered the withdrawal of the garrisons from the principal western posts. This law obliged Cadillac to return to Canada, where he arrived on 29 Aug. 1697, with a large flotilla of canoes bearing nearly 176,000 pounds of beaver pelts. By that date, in order to keep the western tribes under French influence, Louis XIV had issued a second edict which allowed the retention of the posts of Fort Frontenac, Michilimackinac, and Saint-Joseph des Miamis. The ban on trade in the west, however, was not lifted and the governor claimed that this restriction made the reoccupation of the posts unfeasible since it deprived the men of their chief means of subsistence. As for Cadillac, he was not interested in returning to the hinterland if he could not engage in the fur trade. In 1698 he sailed for France to present to the court a new programme for the west which is the master-stroke of his career—the colonization of Detroit.

What Cadillac proposed to establish at Detroit was not a garrisoned post such as the one he had commanded at Michilimackinac but a small colony where a considerable body of Frenchmen would settle and where all the western tribes would regroup. Such a settlement, Cadillac promised, would serve military, economic, cultural, and moral ends. Militarily, it would prevent English expansion in the Great Lakes region and, being located on the doorstep of the Iroquois, would enable the French to send a large army against them at a moment's notice in case of war. Economically, since the Indians would be far too busy moving to their new home from scattered points in the west to find time for hunting, Detroit would help slow down the beaver trade. Culturally, a large white settlement at the centre of the continent would facilitate the Frenchification of the western tribes. Morally, the exploitation of the Indians by the coureurs de bois which took place in the depths of the wilderness would cease at Detroit where civil and religious personnel would be present to supervise transactions between them.

Pontchartrain, the minister of Marine, was impressed by these arguments, but he prudently decided to refer the whole matter to Louis-Hector de CALLIÈRE and Jean BOCHART de Champigny before making a decision. The reaction of these officials was hardly enthusiastic. The intendant claimed that even if Cadillac did succeed in grouping all the western tribes in one place this would be of no advantage to New France since ancestral rivalries would soon cause them to fly at each other's throats. Callière feared that the Iroquois might be offended by a settlement built on their hunting grounds and renew their war on Canada. Furthermore, by drawing the western allies close to the Five Nations, Detroit would make it easy for all these Indians to trade together and perhaps eventually to conclude an alliance detrimental to the French. The merchants were also alarmed. Detroit, they realized, commanded one of the main commercial cross-roads of the Great Lakes country and whoever controlled it could rapidly become the master of the whole fur trade. Taken aback by the strength of the opposition, Cadillac, who had returned to Canada in the spring of 1699, hurried back to France in the fall to refute these objections. With his powers of persuasion he was able to overcome Pontchartrain's hesitations. In the dispatches of 1700, the governor and intendant were told to put the project into execution, unless "insurmountable obstacles" were discovered.

With ALPHONSE TONTY as his first lieutenant, Cadillac arrived at Detroit with 100 men in the summer of 1701. Two years later Philippe de RIGAUD de Vaudreuil became governor of New France and almost immediately the two men were at loggerheads. Personality differences made some friction between them inevitable. A descendant of an old family of the military nobility, formerly a member of the crack Musketeers, the new governor regarded the slick Gascon *parvenu* with contempt. The root of the quarrel, however, lay in policy, not personalities. By his actions at Detroit soon after his arrival there, Cadillac showed that he wanted to make himself the master of the northwest. In 1704 he was granted the ownership of his post and on a number of occasions afterwards he asked Pontchartrain to make the area under his command into a separate government. Vaudreuil, for much the same reasons as Callière, considered that Cadillac's experiment was essentially unsound. He favoured a return to the traditional pattern of posts and fur-trading licences into which Detroit, shorn of its pretences of becoming the unique post in the west and the place of residence of all the western tribes, would fit as one of several garrisoned posts. Such a system, however, would also have made it impossible for Cadillac to rise to the position of power to which he aspired. He therefore decided that Vaudreuil was an enemy who had to be destroyed.

His anti-Vaudreuil campaign was cleverly conducted. He began by winning the support of two powerful Canadian notables: Claude de RAMEZAY, the governor of Montreal, and RUETTE d'Auteuil, the attorney general of the Conseil Supérieur, battle-hardened by many years of political infighting with Frontenac. The trio—shades of Acadia!—accused Vaudreuil of persecuting Cadillac and plotting to bring about the downfall of Detroit. Why? Because this new settlement was a challenge to his control of the fur trade. "The great project of the Canadian authorities," stated Cadillac, "is to establish Michilimackinac on the basis of fur-trading licences and coureurs de bois. This is the great inducement offered by the governor general, and it allows him to be, so to speak, in command of trade." To hammer the point home, d'Auteuil added that Vaudreuil had experienced "extreme displeasure to see placed in a post that might interfere with his trade a man who was put there by someone other than himself and on whom he could not count for support in his greedy designs."

Vaudreuil was not endowed with Cadillac's mental agility, but he invariably struck with force and deadly accuracy once he had assessed a situation. So it was in this case. Cadillac, Ramezay, and d'Auteuil, he claimed, far from being allied by common feelings of concern for the welfare of the colony, simply shared the common ambition of profiting from the Detroit fur trade. Furthermore, their anticipated gains would not materialize through legal trading channels but through contraband. This was the reason why Cadillac was asking that his zone of command become a separate government, since he could then trade with the English, secure in the knowledge that no one could call him to account for his actions. He had won Ramezay to his side by giving him a stake in his settlement; he had completed arrangements with PIERRE LE MOYNE d'Iberville to ship beaver down the Mississippi; he had gone so far as to offer Vaudreuil himself 500 to 600 *pistoles* annually in return for an agreement not to interfere with

his commerce. If he should succeed in his plans, Canada would be ruined irreparably.

Only Pontchartrain could settle this dispute but he hesitated a long time before taking action. Cadillac's memoirs of 1698 and 1699 had deeply impressed him and for many years afterwards in thinking about Detroit he considered "that one way of retaining possession of North America was to prevent the English and other nations from penetrating inland." That Vaudreuil, to satisfy his personal ambition, should be plotting to overthrow this important settlement was judged intolerable. In June 1706 the governor was sternly warned to mend his ways or suffer the full consequences of royal displeasure. But even as these words were being written doubts were growing in the minister's mind about Cadillac's character and the soundness of his policy. The air of independence assumed by the commandant of Detroit, his extravagant vocabulary, and the wild accusations he hurled at the governor, the intendant, and the Jesuits lent support to the complaints about his insubordination, arrogance, and irresponsibility. Moreover, it was fast becoming evident that his Indian policy was a failure. In 1706 and 1707, in what came to be known as the LE PESANT affair, the Hurons, Ottawas, and Miamis who had settled near Detroit came to blows and almost plunged the west into war. Upon hearing of this development, Pontchartrain finally decided that the time had come to clear the air once and for all. In November 1707 he appointed François CLAIRAMBAULT d'Aigremont to investigate and report on conditions in the west.

D'Aigremont's report, submitted in November 1708, was a crushing indictment of Cadillac as a profiteer and of his policy as a menace to French control of the interior. It began by pointing out that Detroit was not the highly developed settlement which Cadillac was describing in his dispatches in order to induce the minister to separate it from Canada. Besides the military garrison and a few hundred Indians there were but 62 French settlers and 353 acres of land under cultivation. Over this domain Cadillac exercised a tyrannical rule which had earned him the hatred of white and red man alike. Tradesmen were obliged to pay him large sums of money for the right to ply their craft; a jug of brandy, which cost two to four *livres* in Canada, sold for 20 at Detroit.

The report also confirmed the governor's fears about the adverse effect Detroit might have on the French network of Indian alliances. This outpost, for all practical purposes, had become a satellite of New York's commercial sphere; almost all its fur crop ended up in English hands. As for the Iroquois, they lost no opportunity to trade with the French allies, sometimes allowing them to travel as far as Albany to trade directly with the English, and gradually winning them to their side by these tactics. "This shows," concluded d'Aigremont, "that the Iroquois have taken advantage of the period since the founding of Detroit to win over our allies in order to have them on their side in case of war, which would certainly be the case."

It was impossible for Pontchartrain to go on supporting Cadillac after this devastating report, but it was also difficult for the minister to punish him severely. To have done so after upholding him for so long would have been tantamount to admitting his own mistake; rather than share in the discomfiture of his former favourite Pontchartrain preferred to pack him off to Louisiana as governor. François DAUPHIN de La Forest, who had succeeded Tonty as Cadillac's first lieutenant, became the commandant of Detroit. The confidential jottings of a clerk of the ministry of Marine explain the reasons for this appointment. La Forest was considered a mediocre officer without enough ability to command a western post. By putting him in charge of Detroit, Pontchartrain hoped to bring about the collapse of this discredited settlement. He would thus rid himself of a troublesome problem without having to take the embarrassing step of reversing his former policy.

Louisiana, of which Cadillac was appointed governor on 5 May 1710, was without a doubt the most dismal colony in the French empire. Founded by Iberville ten years before, it had a total population of 300 to 400 persons, ridden by vice and disease, who eked out a precarious existence on the shores of the Gulf of Mexico. The French government, its coffers drained dry by the War of the Spanish Succession, could do little for the development of this territory and was hoping to transfer it to Antoine Crozat, one of the richest men in France. To overcome the financier's understandable reluctance about such an undertaking, Pontchartrain turned to Cadillac who had gone back to France after leaving Detroit instead of following instructions and proceeding directly to Louisiana. Cadillac presented Crozat with memoirs which spoke of the gulf colony as a land of immense mineral wealth. Like the minister of Marine 12 years before, the millionaire entrepreneur could not keep himself from falling under the amazing Gascon's spell. In September 1712 a company was formed for the development of Louisiana to which Crozat contributed 600,000 to 700,000 *livres* and Cadillac his administrative talents. This arrangement, it seems, made Cadillac believe that he would be Crozat's principal representative in Louisiana; but other officials appointed by the company and the crown deprived him of much of the authority he hoped to wield and also appreciably reduced the possibilities of personal enrichment.

Cadillac landed in Louisiana in June 1713 and he was not impressed by what he saw. The colony, he informed the minister, was a "wretched place" inhabited by "gallows-birds with no respect for religion and addicted to vice." Prospects of future development, he went on, hinged entirely on the discovery of mines and the establishment of trade relations with Mexico. Cadillac made a serious effort to implement this two-point programme. Soon after his arrival, he sent an overland expedition towards Mexico under the command of Louis Juchereau* de Saint-Denis. Unfortunately, Spain's policy proscribed trade between her colonies and foreign powers and the expedition completely failed in its purpose. As a prospector, Cadillac was more successful. In 1716 he personally inspected the Illinois country where he located a copper mine.

Meantime, true to his old self, Cadillac was quarrelling furiously with his colleagues in government. Even before landing in Louisiana he had managed to antagonize the colony's newly appointed financial commissary—the equivalent of the Canadian intendant—Jean-Baptiste Du Bois Duclos. During the voyage across the Atlantic aboard the *Baron de La Fauche* Cadillac warned Duclos that it would be dangerous to quarrel with him because he had a superior mind. Duclos conceded that Cadillac was a dangerous man, not because of his superior mind, which he judged to be quite mediocre except when his own interests were involved, but because he was "very troubled and very restless" and "the most barefaced liar I had ever seen." Then, soon after landing in Louisiana, Cadillac began to quarrel with the king's lieutenant, Jean-Baptiste Le Moyne* de Bienville. According to Bienville, the trouble began when he offended Cadillac by refusing to marry his daughter, Marie-Madeleine; thereafter, he complained, he was treated like a corporal. On one occasion the assistant town major paid Bienville a visit to inform him in the governor's name that he was a "dolt" and a "fop." Cadillac, unfortunately, did not limit himself to namecalling. Out of spite he obstructed Bienville's work among the Indian tribes and Louisiana's relations with the native populations sharply deteriorated.

By 1716, Crozat had wearied of Cadillac whom he held responsible for the colony's stagnation and even suspected of concealing Louisiana's real wealth in order to profit from it personally. Cadillac, for his part, had wearied of Crozat whom he accused of breach of contract. The decision to

355

Laumet

recall the governor was taken at the financier's insistence on 3 March 1716, but it was only in the summer of the following year that Cadillac with his whole family sailed out of Mobile Bay for France. A career of 34 years in the colonies had come to an inglorious end.

On 27 September 1717, less than one month after arriving in France, Cadillac and his eldest son, Antoine, were clapped in the Bastille where they remained until 8 February. The charge against them was that "of having made improper statements against the government of France and of the colonies." Crozat's monopoly had recently been transferred to the Compagnie de l'Occident which, to encourage immigration to Louisiana, described the colony as another Eldorado. Cadillac, for his part, regarded Louisiana as "a monstrous confusion" and he protested publicly and loudly against the company's fanciful description. Lest he jeopardize its entire publicity campaign it was deemed prudent to remove him from circulation for a few months.

Subsequently, however, the ministry of Marine repented the harshness with which it had treated Cadillac. It granted him the cross of the order of Saint-Louis and paid all his salary arrears as governor of Louisiana, even for the period from 1710 to 1712, when he had not yet taken up his position, and for 1718, after he had lost it. Emboldened by these successes, Cadillac next attempted to recover the possession of Detroit, including the exclusive right to the trade of the post, but after studying his petition the council granted him only the ownership of some of the land, buildings, and cattle. Cadillac did not profit from this ruling since he never returned to Detroit nor did he send a deputy there. In 1723, he purchased the governorship of Castelsarrasin, a small town 12 miles from Montauban, carrying an annual salary of 120 *livres*. He died there on 15 Oct. 1730. His last seven years in France are as obscure as the 25 which preceded his coming to America.

A critical examination of the thousands of pages of archival material relating to Cadillac inevitably leads the historian to the conclusion that he most definitely was not one of the "great early heroes" and probably deserves to be ranked with the "worst scoundrels ever to set foot in New France." How, then, did the Cadillac myth originate? Perhaps in three ways. First, because the settlement he founded in 1701 grew into one of the principal cities of the United States, it was to be expected that civic-minded Detroiters with a taste for history would seek to make him into a great man. Secondly, Cadillac's correspondence taken in isolation creates the illusion that he was a devoted, able, and far-seeing servant of the crown who had to struggle unceasingly against the persecutions and petty schemes of less gifted men. Thirdly, Cadillac was anticlerical. His hostility to the Jesuits, his fulminations against what he once termed "an odious, ecclesiastical domination that is quite intolerable" endeared him to English Protestant historians as one of the few persons in the history of New France who dared assert his independence of priestly control and defend the prerogatives of the state against the church. Thus, with the passing of time, an individual who had never been anything but a cunning adventurer in search of personal enrichment came to be regarded as one of the great figures of the French régime in America.

YVES F. ZOLTVANY

[The bulk of the manuscript material on Cadillac is in the following series: AN, Col., B, 16–42; C^{11A}, 12–43; C^{11D}, 2; C^{11E}, 14, 15; C^{11G}, 1–6; C^{13A}, 2–4; D^{2C}, 47, 49, 51; F^3, 2, 7, 8, 9, 10; Marine, B^1, 1–55. Bibliothèque de l'Arsenal (Paris), Archives de la Bastille, 10631, 12482. BN, MS, Clairambault 849, 882; NAF 9274, 9279, 9299 (Margry).

Some of these documents have been published by Pierre Margry, *Découvertes et établissements des Français*, V, but this compilation must be used with circumspection since documents hostile to Cadillac have been either edited or omitted. More satisfactory is "The Cadillac Papers," edited by C. M. Burton and published in *Michigan Pioneer Coll.*, XXXIII, 36–716; XXXIV, 11–303. A fairly balanced picture of Cadillac will emerge if this compilation is used in conjunction with the correspondence of Philippe de Rigaud de Vaudreuil, published in APQ *Rapport, 1938–39*, 12–179; *1939–40*, 355–463; *1942–43*, 369–443; *1946–47*, 371–460; *1947–48*, 137–339.

Readers interested in the evolution of historical opinion on Cadillac should consult the works given below. C. M. Burton, *Cadillac's village* (Detroit, 1896); *A sketch of the life of Antoine de la Mothe Cadillac, the founder of Detroit* (Detroit, 1895); and Agnes Laut, *Cadillac, knight errant of the wilderness . . .* (Indianapolis, 1931) are highly favourable to Cadillac, particularly the last which, although it claims to be based on the sources, reads like a bad historical novel. Between 1944 and 1951 the Jesuit Jean Delanglez published a series of scholarly articles on Cadillac: "Cadillac's early years in America," *Mid-America*, XXVI (1944), 3–39; "Antoine Laumet, alias Cadillac, commandant at Michilimackinac," XXVII (1945), 108–32, 188–216, 232–56; "The genesis and building of Detroit," XXX (1948), 75–104; "Cadillac at Detroit," XXX (1948), 152–76; "Cadillac, proprietor of Detroit," XXXII (1950), 155–88, 226–58; "Cadillac's last years," XXXIII (1951), 3–42. This series of articles utterly destroys the Cadillac myth. Eccles, *Frontenac*; Giraud, *Histoire de la Louisiane française*; and Y. F. Zoltvany, "New France and the west," deal with Cadillac at Michilimackinac, Detroit, and in Louisiana, and are all equally critical of him.

E. Forestié, *Lamothe-Cadillac, fondateur de la ville de Détroit* (Montauban, 1907), is the only serious inquiry into Cadillac's early years in France. Y.F.Z.]

LAURE, PIERRE-MICHEL, priest, Jesuit, missionary to the Saguenay region; b. 17 Sept. 1688 at Orléans, France; d. 22 Nov. 1738 at Les Éboulements.

Pierre-Michel Laure, who had joined the Jesuits in Paris on 29 Oct. 1707, was assigned to the missions in Canada. On 29 Oct. 1711 he arrived at Quebec, where he spent four years as a teacher at the Jesuit college. In 1716 he was in charge of the library; this is the first mention of this office in the annals of the house. Reference is also made to the fact that he was studying painting. On 27 Aug. 1713 he had received the tonsure and the minor orders in the chapel of the Hôpital Général. It was there, in June 1719, that, upon completion of his theological studies, he was ordained subdeacon, deacon, and priest by Bishop Saint-Vallier [LA CROIX]. The following year he was entrusted with the task of setting up again the missions to the Montagnais in the Saguenay region, which for 18 years, since Father François de CRESPIEUL's death, had been virtually abandoned. He left for Chicoutimi on 1 June 1720.

At Chicoutimi he was received with manifestations of joy, but he soon became greatly distressed at the sad state of the mission and its people: "an old, tumble-down chapel . . ., no Indian had any tincture of our Holy Religion other than a great desire to learn the principles of it. The young people had never heard anyone speak about it, the older ones mumbled only a few jumbled scraps of the Lord's Prayer and the *Ave Maria* which had come down from their forefathers. Licentiousness, which reigned supreme among them, polygamy, drunkenness, even more, in a word all the disorders that the most vulgar libertinism engenders were the idols that these poor, blind creatures adored, to the exclusion of all else. . . ." Faced with this spectacle, in which he could see the measure of the task awaiting him, he suffered cruelly from finding himself alone, without accommodation or help, and above all unable to remedy the evil immediately; the Algonkin language, which he had learned at the college in Quebec, did not permit him to make himself understood sufficiently by the Montagnais.

He had the good luck to find on the spot a remarkably intelligent and cultivated Indian, who spoke French well, Marie Outchiouanish, the wife of Nicolas Pelletier (Peltier). He became her pupil and made rapid progress. "She directed my studies rigorously," he wrote, "and at the first word that she heard me pronounce she said to the others: 'That's it! Our father has spoken our language, I shall no longer speak French to him.' Despite my entreaties she kept her word; and by dint of making her pupil guess she brought him to the point where he could preach the mystery at Christmas without any notes." Later on he added: "A short oration of about three quarters of an hour on the Gospel."

In the meantime a liveable house had been built for him. At Christmas he had the satisfaction of seeing his poor chapel filled with well-disposed faithful, some of whom had made a trip of more than 100 leagues to get there; "almost all" had confessed and had received communion, to the great edification of the Frenchmen who were employed at the trading-post.

This first wintering-over, in a hastily built house devoid of comfort, was a hard one for Father Laure. "Being unwell, at the first sign of spring, he arranged for someone to take him to Quebec, where he planned to spend some time." But he could not stay there long. Even before the Indian hunters had arrived back, he had returned to Chicoutimi. The rumour had spread that because of discouragement he had given up his mission; finding this report false led the Montagnais to demonstrate their good feelings. He won them over completely during an epidemic which raged among them during the spring of that year, 1721. The malady broke out suddenly; it was believed that it came from the plague at Marseilles, and had been brought in in contaminated bales of blankets. Hardly had the tent village been set up than it took on the appearance of a camp of persons stricken by the plague. In three weeks 25 adults and a number of children were carried off. Night and day, unceasingly, Father Laure succoured his poor people. He was strengthened by several conversions and by some edifying deaths; but he became so exhausted that "in the interval of rest" that followed it was as it were "impossible for him to say even four words" in the Montagnais language.

He then hastened off to visit the Montagnais at Tadoussac, who had been awaiting him for a long time. "I found these people so well disposed towards the Christian religion," he wrote, "that I could not get out of spending the winter with them." The wintering-over took place eight leagues from there, at Anse de Bon-Désir, where 120 adults, a number of whom were occupied hunting seals, had come together for religious services. He spent four winters in a row there. In 1723 he built a chapel and a house for the missionary. From there, during the summer, he carried on his ministry to the mission at Chicoutimi and to the Papinachois at the post on the Îlets Jérémie, on the shore of the St Lawrence.

Laval

Hostility on the part of the fur-trading clerks led Father Laure to give up this well-organized and promising mission in 1725 and to go to take up residence at Chicoutimi, an arrangement which corresponded with the desires of the Indians from the interior of the Saguenay region. Repairs were made to the house he was to live in, and in the autumn construction was begun on a new chapel, in which he celebrated the first mass on 15 Aug. 1726. He worked on this chapel himself, gave "the first ax-stroke," and with his own hands made the altar, the fittings, and the interior decorations (sculpture and painting), for he was skilful at this work. The little church, carefully built of cedar, was to last exactly 130 years. Father Laure did the same sort of work on his new house, which was begun in 1728.

It was at Chicoutimi that he regularly spent the winter, except in 1733 and probably in 1736, when he went to Quebec. From Chicoutimi, as previously when he was at Bon-Désir, he used to go, usually twice a year, to visit the groups scattered about his vast domain, which stretched from Sept-Îles to Lake Mistassini. In addition to his regular missions, he used to go wherever he was needed.

Father Laure made the suggestion that some small plots of Indian corn be cultivated near the trading posts and that modest Indian industries be established, such as making bark canoes, to keep the men and women occupied during the summer and to augment their livelihood. Affirming that he had "carried out the experiment successfully," he also proposed the creation of "a small fund sufficient to keep some children on a modest scale and in the Indian manner, so that, when these children had been looked after for a winter by worthy old women . . . and had duly received instruction, they would return to their parents in the spring and impart their doctrine. . . ." In addition, he added, these catechizing guardians "would prepare skins, make robes, beaver hoods, moccasins, snow-shoes, and would render other services in the house which it is difficult to do without in winter."

He would have liked to go to Labrador to found a mission and did some soliciting towards that end, but had no success. In 1737, after 18 years of apostolate in the king's domain, Father Laure was appointed resident missionary at Les Éboulements. He returned to carry on his ministry at Tadoussac in July 1738; this was his last visit to the Saguenay region. He died 22 Nov. 1738 at Les Éboulements.

In a long account, dated at Chicoutimi in March 1730, Father Laure described the country, the tribes that inhabited it, and the first ten years of his missionary activity. This text contains important geographical and ethnological data; it also mentions two places which have never been identified: an "industrious river" ("rivière industrieuse") at Lake St John, and a "marble cave" of a strange sort to the east of Lake Mistassini. The author refers in his account to previous relations, the texts of which we do not possess except that of a letter from Tadoussac in 1724 in which he criticizes the Montagnais severely.

Father Laure also left us an "Apparat français-montagnais," some maps of the king's domain, labelled "Domaine du Roy en Canada," all of them dedicated to the dauphin, and finally a map marked "Le cours de Pitchitaouitchetz ou du Saguenay" ("The course of Pitchitaouitchetz or the Saguenay River"), dedicated to the Marquis de Beauharnois* the governor of Canada, and bearing the date 1731.

VICTOR TREMBLAY, P.D.

Two of Father Laure's manuscripts are preserved at the archbishop's palace in Quebec; one contains a short catechism in the Algonkin language, with the questions to be asked at baptisms and the forms of prayers; the other consists of prayers and songs in the Montagnais language, a catechism, also in Montagnais, recommendations for missionaries, and other small matters, and at the end the text of his letter written at Tadoussac in 1724, which is followed by some brief remarks. The theological college of the Oblate Fathers in Ottawa has in its possession the copy of his "Apparat français-montagnais," his manuscript of "Prières et catéchisme" written in 1728, a copy of his "Alphabet et prières en langue montagnaise" which was published later, in 1767, and a small hand-written lexicon of Montagnais terms, "Les parties dù corps humain." [v. t.]

AAQ, Registres des missions des Postes du Roy, Miscellaneorum Liber. ASJCF, 554; Cahier des vœux, f.33v; Lettres de l'intendant Hocquart relatives aux missions du Saguenay. JR (Thwaites). "Le clergé de la Nouvelle-France," BRH, LIV (1948), 82, 216. Bibliothèque de la Compagnie de Jésus. Première partie: bibliographie par les Pères Augustin et Aloys de Backer. Second partie: histoire par le Père Auguste Carayon, éd. Carlos Sommervogel (9v., Bruxelles et Paris, 1890–1900), IV, 1561. Rochemonteix, Les Jésuites et la N.-F. au XVIIe siècle, III, 432.

LAVAL, FRANÇOIS DE, bishop *in partibus* of Petraea, vicar apostolic in New France (1658–74), first bishop of Quebec (1674–88); b. 30 April 1623 at Montigny-sur-Avre (department of Eure-et-Loir), in the diocese of Chartres (France) and baptized François-Xavier; son of Hugues de Laval, seigneur of Montigny, Montbaudry, Alaincourt, and Revercourt, and of Michelle de Péricard; d. 6 May 1708 at Quebec and buried 9 May in the cathedral there.

François de Laval was descended from the

younger branch of one of the noblest families in France, the Montmorencys, whose origins are believed to go back to pagan Gaul. A Montmorency, in fact, is supposed to have been the first of the nobles of the kingdom of France to receive baptism with Clovis from St Rémi at Reims in 496. The battlecry "Dieu ayde au premier baron chrestien [God aid the first Christian baron]," which was also the motto of this line and is found in Bishop Laval's arms, perpetuated the memory of this glorious event. The title of "First Barons of France," which was likewise borne by the Montmorencys, was no less deserved: this family gave the church and the kingdom several cardinals, 6 constables, 12 marshals, 4 admirals, and a great number of generals and civil, naval, and military officers. In the 13th century Mathieu de Montmorency, called the great Constable of France, took as his second wife Emme de Laval, who was also of noble birth. Their son Guy took his mother's name; François de Laval was descended from him.

Through his mother, Michelle de Péricard, daughter of the seigneur of Saint-Étienne, in Normandy, François de Laval belonged to a family of the legal nobility which had supplied the *parlement* of Rouen with several officers of the crown and the church with numerous prelates. Indeed, the see of Évreux was occupied about that time by a brother of Madame de Laval, François de Péricard, who was to play an important role in young François's life.

Despite their noble birth the seigneur of Montigny and his wife, who were both of proven piety and virtue, were not possessed of a large fortune: the fief of Montigny, the most important of the four which they held, was in reality only a good-sized market-town. The family's financial situation was soon to become rather precarious, and François was one day to have to devote himself to restoring it.

Hugues de Laval and his wife had six sons and two daughters, one of whom, Isabelle, a posthumous child, died at the age of seven months. Henri, the fifth son, entered the Benedictine order and became prior of La Croix-Saint-Lauffroy; Anne-Charlotte took the veil with the Nuns of the Blessed Sacrament and became their superior. Destined by his family for the ecclesiastical state, to which he aspired himself, François received the tonsure and took holy orders at the age of eight and a half, as was the custom of the period, soon after entering the Jesuit college at La Flèche, which was attended by the sons of the best families of France. François was to spend ten years, from 1631 to 1641, in this famous institution, pursuing his literary and philosophical studies

with great success. In 1637, his uncle, François de Péricard, bishop of Évreux, appointed him a canon of the cathedral of his diocese. Even though it was not large—it was increased in 1639—this benefice came just at the right time. Added to his family's meagre resources, it allowed François to continue his studies, which for a time had been endangered by his father's death on 11 Sept. 1636.

The years that he spent at La Flèche were, in a way, decisive for François de Laval. Under the enlightened guidance of the Jesuits he advanced rapidly in the paths of piety and virtue, soon earning admission into the Congrégation de la Sainte Vierge, which was at the time directed by Father Jean Bagot. His resolution to devote himself to God in the priesthood dated from that period, as did his interest in the Canadian missions; these were held much in honour at the college where lived some of the greatest apostles of the French possessions in America. Being constantly in contact with the sons of St Ignatius, François got to know them, was imbued with their spirituality, and became sincerely attached to them. "God alone," he wrote in 1659, "knows how much I am indebted to your Society [the Society of Jesus], which warmed me in its breast when I was a child, nourished me with its salutary doctrine in my youth, and has not ceased since then to encourage and guide me. ... [The Jesuits] taught me to love God and have been my guides in the path of salvation and the Christian virtues...."

In 1641 François went to Paris and lived at the Collège de Clermont, also run by the Jesuits, to study theology. He was proceeding at a good pace towards the priesthood when two tragic events in rapid succession struck him cruel blows: his two older brothers were killed. François, who had enlisted in Condé's army, fell in 1644 at Freiburg, and Gabriel, who was serving in Turenne's army, was killed in 1645 at Nordlingen. François, who inherited the patrimony and the family obligations, took the name of Abbé de Montigny. His mother, with the powerful backing of the bishop of Évreux, begged him to leave the ecclesiastical state, to marry, and to uphold the honour of his house. François was immovable but nevertheless decided to interrupt his studies momentarily. He returned to Montigny, put the family's affairs in order, and soon went back to the Collège de Clermont, this time with the encouragement of the bishop of Évreux. In 1646 he was ordained subdeacon, the following year deacon, and on 1 May 1647 priest.

At 24 years of age, François was well prepared for a ministry that, it appears from the most authoritative testimony, was fruitful. At Paris he

Laval

had again met Father Bagot and several of his associates of the Congrégation at La Flèche. They had come together once more in the society called the Bons Amis and continued as a group their work of seeking their spiritual improvement. François stood out in this group through his piety, zeal, and virtue. In the year following his ordination he devoted himself to caring for the sick, teaching abandoned children, and administering his patrimony. In 1648 he resigned his canonry at Évreux. Shortly afterwards, in December, he was appointed archdeacon of the same diocese, which at that time comprised 155 parishes and 4 chapels. It was a heavy task. But, wrote M. de LA COLOMBIÈRE, "the regularity of his visits, his fervour in carrying them out, the improvements that he effected and the order that he established in the parishes, the relief of the poor, his application to all sorts of good works, all these things indicated clearly that although he was not a bishop, he had the mind and ability of one and that there were no services that the church could not expect from such a great person." In 1649 he had obtained from the University of Paris a licentiate in canon law, which he required for carrying out his duties as archdeacon.

From 1642 on at least François de Laval had secretly dreamed of being a missionary. The Bons Amis, with whom he remained in close touch during his years as archdeacon, shared his aspirations. This society was, besides, the cradle of the Séminaire des Missions Étrangères in Paris. In 1652 the Jesuit, Alexandre de Rhodes, was looking, with the pope's permission, for candidates who would accept appointments as vicars apostolic in Tonkin and Indochina. After consulting with Father Bagot and the Bons Amis, he chose François Pallu, Bernard Picques, and François de Laval, who were approved by Rome and the court. François de Laval was destined for Tonkin. But the appointment soon began to drag on. The Congregation for the Propagation of the Faith, which disapproved of the excessive independence of the Jesuits in the mission countries, feared that the proposed candidates were too closely linked with them, all the more since they had declared their readiness to join the Society of Jesus. Moreover, Portugal was firmly opposed to French bishops being sent to the Far East. The project was given up in 1654. Whatever his future activity was to be, François de Laval decided to prepare for it henceforth in prayer and seclusion. In 1654, without even keeping the pension to which he was entitled, he resigned the archdeaconry of Évreux—which might have led him to the bishopric—in favour of his friend Henri-Marie Boudon and made over to his younger brother

Jean-Louis his patrimony and his birthright. (Hugues, the youngest of his brothers, had died in 1642 at about 12 years of age.) When these last links with the world had been broken, he set off for Caen.

François went to knock at the door of the Hermitage, which was directed by M. Jean de Bernières de Louvigny. One of the great mystics of his time, M. de Bernières, although a layman, had been chosen as teacher and spiritual director by some of the most pious and virtuous persons in France. Since 1649 the Hermitage had sheltered a small community of priests and laymen who devoted themselves to preaching and charitable activities and who led an austere and severely regulated life. François de Laval, who was an "intimate friend" of M. de Bernières, put his admirable maxims into practice: he combined charitable works with prayer and preaching and, as he had done in Paris, engaged in helping the poor and the sick, in the great tradition of St Vincent de Paul. In between, he reformed a monastery whose rule had become lax and brought out into the open, even before the court, the rights of a community of nuns hospitallers which was threatened with spoliation. He was, furthermore, the administrator and confessor of two communities of nuns, and in 1657 he earned from Bishop Servien an unequivocal commendation (which was given upon oath): he was described as a priest "of great piety," "prudent and of unusually great competence in business matters," who had set "fine examples" of virtue in the diocese of Bayeux.

But once again there was a movement on foot to endow New France with a bishopric. This movement had originated in 1645 with the Associates of Montreal, but it had subsequently encountered many obstacles. In January 1657 the Associates put forward a candidate, the Sulpician Gabriel de Thubières* de Levy de Queylus. Although he was accepted by the assembly of the clergy of France, Abbé Queylus was not received favourably by the Jesuits. They, declining an invitation from the queen mother, Anne d'Autriche, to have one of their members appointed to the episcopal see of Quebec, submitted the name of their former pupil, François de Laval. Being anxious that the new bishop should be on good terms with the Jesuits in Canada, the queen mother and the court approved this choice. François de Laval was informed at the Hermitage of the plans which had been made for him. He could not, however, foresee the difficulties with which his path would henceforth be strewn.

The choice of François de Laval and the circumstances surrounding his appointment to the episcopal see of New France were, in fact, going to stir up and bring into the open the latent conflict which was developing in this colony, for the ecclesiastical jurisdiction over it was being disputed by Rome and the archbishop of Rouen quietly but with great determination and tenacity.

Since the 16th century the pope had not had any direct authority over missions. He had to go through the kings, who had the right of advowson, the bishops, who extended their influence beyond the boundaries of their dioceses, and the superiors general of the great missionary orders, which had acquired wide autonomy. The general of the Jesuits, for example, and his provincials in France could found missions without even consulting the Holy See. Thus, on their arrival in Canada in 1625 and when they came back again in 1632 the Jesuits held their powers from Rome, but through the intermediary of their general. In 1622, however, with the object of centralizing the administration of all missions and putting them directly under the control of the Holy See, the pope had created the Congregation for the Propagation of the Faith. The Congregation had thenceforth attempted, with great prudence and diplomacy but rather limited success, to reduce the virtually complete independence of the Jesuits in mission countries.

In Canada, however, the missionaries of the Society of Jesus were to lose gradually the quiet assurance that they had enjoyed at the beginning. The arrival in 1639 of the Ursulines and Nuns Hospitallers—particularly the latter, who had been induced by the archbishop of Rouen to promise that they would recognize his jurisdiction over their community—contributed especially to alarming the Jesuits about the validity of the religious professions which they might be called upon to receive or the marriages among settlers which they solemnized, relying solely upon their powers as missionaries. Did their jurisdiction extend beyond the strictly missionary ministry to the Indians? They were less and less certain about it. To ask the Congregation for the Propagation of the Faith for wider powers would mean that they would be putting themselves under its complete domination and would, moreover, be a departure from the Society's traditional policy, which their general in Rome defended fiercely. Besides, the archbishop of Rouen, who had no doubts about the legality of his jurisdiction over New France, was gradually but irreversibly imposing his episcopal authority upon the young colony.

Two events were to cause the Jesuits in Canada to lean towards Rouen. In 1645 and 1646, on the one hand, the Associates of Montreal were working for the creation of a bishopric in Canada and proposed a candidate of their choosing, Abbé Thomas Le Gauffre. If they were successful, the autonomy of the Jesuits in New France was finished. On the other hand, in 1646 the new general of the Jesuits had given in to the pressure exercised by the Congregation for the Propagation of the Faith and had ceded back to it, in reality, most of his powers as far as missions were concerned. At this juncture the Jesuits in Canada hesitated, deliberated cautiously, and finally in 1648 accepted the jurisdiction of the Congregation for the Propagation of the Faith by asking it for new powers; but at the same time they sought from the archbishop of Rouen letters, which they accepted in 1649, making their superior in Quebec his vicar general. This last step, on which not even their general was consulted, was kept a secret until 1653, one so well kept that despite her close connections with the Jesuits Marie de l'Incarnation [Guyart*] did not suspect anything. The powers of a vicar general were broader than those conferred by the Congregation for the Propagation of the Faith and gave the Jesuits greater reassurance about the validity of the religious professions and marriages. In 1653, therefore, they made public their dependence upon Rouen and ceased to correspond with the Congregation for the Propagation of the Faith after that date. Of the two options presented them, they had chosen the one which imposed fewer restrictions upon them: the Rouen formula left them greater authority and autonomy than that of Rome would have done.

In refusing the candidate of the assembly of the clergy of France in January 1657 the Jesuits were not rejecting Abbé Queylus as a person, but rather the threat that he represented for the independence of the church in Canada, which they intended to restore and to secure for good. Secretly they proposed to the court a candidate of their choosing, François de Laval. They wanted to make him the titular bishop of Quebec. For 18 months they pushed this matter in Paris and Rome, apparently without the archbishop of Rouen, François II de Harlay de Champvallon, having the slightest suspicion of it. The fact was that, once their candidate had been appointed and consecrated, they intended to separate the church in Canada completely from the archbishopric of Rouen. In their minds the bishop of Quebec should be directly responsible to the pope. Of course, Harlay would not have been of that opinion.

In January 1657, then, Louis XIV wrote to the pope, presenting to him his candidate for the bishopric of Quebec, *Father* François de Laval. Rome first wanted to know to what community

361

this *father* belonged. This was the first cause of delay. Then someone forgot to forward the canonical information. Time passed. Backed by the court of France, the Jesuits kept applying pressure. Months went by. Everyone was becoming impatient; the number of memoranda kept increasing, help was sought from the cardinals in Rome, but to no avail. Only François de Laval remained silent and as though indifferent, to the surprise of those who were supporting his candidature most strongly. It was not he who had sought this appointment; perhaps mindful of the Tonkin affair, he waited at the Hermitage, without doing anything to influence Rome's decision, which would be the expression of God's will for him.

Rome's delay in reaching a decision came, to tell the truth, from the Congregation for the Propagation of the Faith. Once more it was feared there that through François de Laval, who had been closely linked with them since his childhood, the Jesuits would perpetuate their independence from this Roman congregation in Canada. There could be no question of appointing a titular bishop for Canada. Consequently difficulties of all sorts were raised, until finally it was proposed to the court of France to create a vicariate in New France rather than a bishopric. The court obtained the Jesuits' assent and that of M. de Laval himself on this question. (It has been claimed, incorrectly, that the Jesuits had suggested this expedient themselves.) The appointment of a simple vicar apostolic would make the church and the mission in Canada, including the Jesuits, directly subordinate to the Congregation for the Propagation of the Faith and thus to the Holy See; for Bishop Laval and the Jesuits it would have the advantage of withdrawing them, at least in theory, from the jurisdiction of the archbishop of Rouen, which would yield to the more universal jurisdiction of the pope.

The bulls appointing François de Laval vicar apostolic were signed in Rome on 3 June 1658. Bishop Laval chose 4 October, the feast-day of St Francis of Assisi, for his consecration.

The archbishop of Rouen, who considered that he was the rightful bishop of Canada, where he had had a vicar general for ten years, seems to have known nothing of the steps taken to endow this part of his diocese with a see. Being, moreover, an ardent Gallican, he took the news of the dispatch of his bulls to François de Laval very badly. All the more since this dignity of vicar apostolic, newly created in the church and most often obtained by stealth and under false pretences, had been the subject of earnest deliberations in the assembly of the clergy of France, which finally recommended to the bishops that they refuse to

consecrate these prelates if they applied to them. On 25 Sept. 1658 at Paris, before a special assembly of the clergy, Harlay brought up the question of the bulls delivered to François de Laval and succeeded in having a circular letter sent to the bishops urging them to refuse to consecrate him, in conformity with the recommendations of the plenary assembly and because of the prejudice which this intervention on the part of Rome caused the Gallican church. The three bishops who had already promised François de Laval their co-operation immediately desisted.

In addition to the support of the church of France, Harlay sought that of the *parlements*, the jealous and punctilious defenders of the "liberties," rights, privileges, and immunities of the Gallican church. He himself had a seat in the *parlement* of Rouen. On 3 Oct. 1658, on the eve of the day set for Bishop Laval's consecration, he obtained a decree forbidding the latter to "take upon himself the functions of vicar apostolic in Canada," and declaring that in this matter the pope's good faith had obviously been abused.

François de Laval, who had maintained silence up till then, continued to do so even now; his allies the Jesuits and the papal nuncio to Paris, Monsignor Piccolomini, however, got around the difficulty. Rome had the right of appointing vicars apostolic in mission countries; the claims of the archbishop of Rouen were not based on legal grounds or recognized by Rome; and finally, the queen mother and the young king were favourable to their candidate. They decided therefore to go ahead in secret with Bishop Laval's consecration in a church that was exempt from the ecclesiastical jurisdiction of the kingdom. On 8 Dec. 1658, in the Lady-chapel (which no longer exists) of the abbey of Saint-Germain-des-Prés, the nuncio laid hands upon François de Laval, who was 35 at that time.

As soon as this consecration was known, the Gallican reaction was not long in coming. The archbishop of Paris, who was offended because François de Laval had been consecrated in his diocese without his permission, and the archbishop of Rouen, for whom Mazarin refused to convene the assembly of the clergy of France for reasons having nothing to do with this affair, fell back upon the *parlement* of Paris. The *parlement* agreed with their views and considered that the rights of the episcopate and the liberties of the Gallican church had been infringed. On 16 December it issued a decree calling upon François de Laval to transmit his bulls to the court and forbidding him to claim authority through them before receiving the letters patent necessary in such a case. Bishop Laval was served this decree on 19 December. On 23 December the *parlement* of

Rouen in its turn renewed its decree of 3 October, forbade any of the king's subjects to recognize M. de Laval as vicar apostolic, and ordered all the officers of the kingdom to resist him in his attempt and prevent him from fulfilling any function. Once more Bishop Laval remained silent: he clearly saw that in all this affair he was only the pretext or the occasion for a battle that had long been shaping up and which others were involving him in.

After vainly threatening the archbishop of Rouen with penalties, Rome advised Monsignor Piccolomini in December 1658 and January 1659 to rely henceforth upon "Their Majesties," Anne d'Autriche and young Louis XIV. It was the only way out, as the queen mother had approved the Jesuits' plan from the beginning. This time Archbishop Harlay did feel that he was being threatened. On 3 March 1659 he suggested to Mazarin a compromise which resulted in the letters patent of 27 March requested by Anne d'Autriche to annul the decree of the *parlement*. These letters directed that Bishop Laval be recognized "to fulfil the functions of the bishop, *without prejudice to the rights of the regular jurisdiction*, and that he do so while awaiting the establishment of a bishopric *whose titular incumbent will be suffragan of the archbishop of Rouen*." This ran entirely counter to the plan of the Jesuits and the Congregation for the Propagation of the Faith. Could the queen mother, who was present at the king's council, be unaware of this? On 30 March, perhaps at the nuncio's suggestion, she recognized her error. She wrote to Voyer d'Argenson, the governor of New France, giving him strict injunctions to have Bishop Laval recognized as vicar apostolic and "to see that he is obeyed in all the functions of the bishop," and even "to prevent any ecclesiastic or other person from exercising or holding any ecclesiastical jurisdiction except by the orders or consent" of Bishop Laval. Thus, at least in theory, the authority of the archbishop of Rouen was eliminated from Canada.

Bishop Laval took the oath of loyalty to the king and sailed from La Rochelle on 13 April 1659. He had neither sought nor rejected the dignity of bishop; the worst storms had raged about him without his intervening in any way whatsoever to calm them, leaving the direction of his life entirely to God's care. One thing was henceforth certain: God wanted him in New France. He was on his way, his sole income an allowance of 1,000 *livres* with which the queen-regent had favoured him.

Thus, in detachment from worldly goods and in poverty, began a great and laborious adventure, the building of a Canadian church.

Canada in 1659 was, in truth, of little account.

Its French population did not amount to 2,000 people, divided among three centres of settlement over a distance of more than 60 leagues. The region of Quebec, formed of the town proper and the seigneuries of Beauport, Beaupré, Notre-Dame-des-Anges, and Lauson, offered the largest concentration of population with nearly 1,200 inhabitants; a few hundred settlers were established at Trois-Rivières or in the neighbouring seigneuries of Cap-de-la-Madeleine, Sainte-Anne, and Champlain, which were barely beginning to develop; the island of Montreal, an outpost, was the last inhabited centre.

The numerical weakness of its population illustrates how little the colony had progressed since its foundation by Champlain* in 1608. The companies holding monopolies, on to which the state shifted the entire responsibility for the destinies of New France, completely neglected to meet their obligations, with the exception of the Compagnie des Cent Associés (1627), which, however, got off to a disastrous start from which it never recovered. The Communauté des Habitants took over entire responsibility for the country from 1645 on but did scarcely any better, as a result of the war with the Iroquois which almost completely paralysed the fur trade. An insufficient population, administrative institutions which had remained at the embryonic stage, the repeated attacks by the Iroquois, an economic crisis that had no solution, all these factors made even the most optimistic fear for the future of the colony.

As well as being a French colony, New France was a mission country. The Recollets had arrived first, in 1615; the Jesuits had joined them 10 years later. After the treaty of Saint-Germain-en-Laye in 1632 the Jesuits came back to New France alone. Henceforth they represented the church there, as their superior was the highest ecclesiastical authority in the country. The missions made remarkable progress: in a few years they extended to Acadia, Lac Saint-Jean, the Great Lakes, the Iroquois country. The Jesuits similarly ministered to the French. The mission was in better shape than the colony.

The Jesuits attempted, moreover, to make up for the weaknesses of the Compagnie des Cent Associés and the Communauté des Habitants. In their annual *Relations* they became propagandists for the mission, but also for the colony, preventing Canada from falling into oblivion. They attracted settlers and established them on their seigneuries. They aroused in rich and powerful people an interest in New France and were thus able to endow the colony with a college in 1635, a seminary for girls and a hospital in 1639. Missionaries, parish priests, teachers, propagandists, colonizers, explorers, interpreters, on occasion ambassadors, the Jesuits—whose superior was in addition an *ex officio* member of the council—were everywhere, being involved in civil affairs just as much as in purely religious matters. The mission kept the colony going; the contrary would have been more normal.

The vicar apostolic, who reached Quebec on 16 June 1659, landed the next day and went to work without delay. He could count upon a limited number of ecclesiastics: 17 Jesuits, 4 Sulpicians, and 6 secular priests and lay brothers, one of whom had received only the tonsure. To the Jesuits he left the Indian missions, to the Sulpicians the care of the parish of Montreal, where they had been installed since 1657. The lay brothers were for their part to take charge of the ministry to the parishes in the region of Quebec, with Trois-Rivières temporarily under the spiritual guidance of the Jesuits. The bishop's see would be at Quebec.

Bishop Laval's first preoccupation was to have his authority recognized. He was obsessed by the idea that he might encounter in the colony the opposition that he had known in France. He was quite well aware of the activities of Abbé Queylus, who was for a time the archbishop of Rouen's vicar general in Canada, and he particularly feared some attempt against his authority by the Sulpicians of Montreal. He was not mistaken. The biography of Abbé Queylus [Thubières*] relates the many episodes of the long jurisdictional dispute from which the vicar apostolic, supported by the Congregation for the Propagation of the Faith, was to emerge victorious. Now, the arrival of a letter from Louis XIV to M. d'Argenson and dated 14 May 1659 provided Bishop Laval with an unhoped-for opportunity. In this letter the king directed the governor to have the authority of the vicar apostolic recognized everywhere and not to allow any vicar general appointed by the archbishop of Rouen to "take it upon himself to exercise any jurisdictional function." Bishop Laval had this letter published and posted up from one end of the country to the other.

Around this time also the prelate set up an officiality, an ecclesiastical court which would deal with all disputes involving a member of the secular or regular clergy and judge all matters falling under the jurisdiction of the bishop. The haste with which the vicar apostolic created this tribunal—three months after his arrival—seems rather surprising when one considers, for example, that not a single parish was set up canonically. Bishop Laval was arming himself against possible opponents. In the context of Gallicanism, however, this measure looked like a challenge to the civil authority.

"Great disagreements among the authorities" soon arose as a result of the presence of the officiality, but also of numerous quarrels over precedence. Today these disputes may seem trifling. But French society in the 17th century was sensitive about the concept of honour. It was imbued with respect for everything that appertained to the monarch or concerned him directly or indirectly. In this society which was, furthermore, built on a strongly hierarchical system, all the king's representatives, from the governor down to the humblest legal officer, had precise roles to play to which were attached certain allotted honours that had been minutely evaluated and rigidly fixed. Supplementary honours, whether conferred by the state or by the church, were an enviable reward and sometimes took the place of a salary. Consequently, anyone who felt that he was being wronged in a question of position defended himself bitterly.

For 25 years many ways of doing things had been adopted in New France which were not always in conformity with the customs observed in the kingdom or which could be attributed to the absence of a bishop. Thus the governor had his *prie-dieu* in the place of greatest honour in the choir of the church and regularly attended, as honorary churchwarden, discussions of the parish council of Quebec. Bishop Laval, who was anxious to suppress abuses and defend his young church against inopportune interference by the state, decided to put things in order before it was too late. His intention was laudable. But perhaps, in the ardour of his 36 years and his somewhat impetuous zeal, he did not use enough tact and diplomacy and was needlessly abrupt with a governor who was jealous of his own privileges and who was, moreover, ill disposed towards this young prelate whose first act had been to set up an ecclesiastical court in the face of civil justice. The governor became stubborn and absolutely refused to give way, as did the bishop. Constantly refueled with new incidents, which were most often provoked by Bishop Laval, the conflict grew worse month by month. "We thought it would end in violence," observed the superior of the Jesuits, who discreetly blamed the bishop.

At the root of these quarrels there was doubtless a burning desire in Bishop Laval to see his authority recognized and his church out of the reach of the state's enterprises; for this, as Louis XIV was to write in 1665, it was absolutely necessary "that the right balance be maintained between the temporal authority, which resides in the person of the king and those who represent him, and the spiritual, which resides in the person of His Excellency the Bishop and the Jesuits, in such a way, however, that the latter authority be subordinate to the other." But there was also, on the part of the governor and several settlers, a refusal to accord the vicar apostolic the same authority as a bishop sitting at the head of his diocese. For them the Bishop of Petraea could not be the bishop of Quebec. At first the religious communities had hesitated themselves: must they obey this "apostolic commissioner" who had come to Canada "under the foreign title of Bishop of Petraea," or the vicar general of the archbishop of Rouen? When they finally accepted Bishop Laval's authority, the nuns did not bring with them the adherence of the whole population—far from it. Montreal in particular remained more or less hostile to the vicar apostolic.

All were in agreement, however, about Bishop Laval's personal qualities. His deep piety, his charity, his humility were praised. "He lives like a saint and apostle," wrote Marie de l'Incarnation. Despite his illustrious origins and his new dignity, he performed the most humble services, as he had done formerly in Paris and Caen, caring for the ill, making their beds, administering the last sacrament to the Indians. In the autumn of 1659, for example, an epidemic, brought by a ship, broke out. Bishop Laval was constantly at the hospital, despite the efforts made to dissuade him and the obvious danger of being stricken himself. He did not spare his energies, and he was prodigal of his own possessions when it came to aiding the poor. He who had only 1,000 *livres* of guaranteed income distributed enormous sums secretly (10,000 *écus* in three years, according to Louis Bertrand* de Latour). He lived shabbily, moreover, first in seclusion with the Nuns Hospitallers, then with the Ursulines, and finally with the Jesuits, before acquiring in 1662 an old house where he brought together his little group of ecclesiastics.

Despite the numerous difficulties he encountered, Bishop Laval was extremely active. In 1660 he had completed his first pastoral visit, which had begun at Gaspé, where he had stopped off at the time of his crossing to Canada. He had conferred the sacrament of confirmation upon hundreds of whites and Indians. He had, in addition, attacked from its very beginnings the trade in spirits: being an enemy of half measures and having the support of his clergy, whom he had consulted about this question on three occasions, he had fulminated an excommunication against refractory traffickers. This energetic intervention on his part incurred the opposition of the businessmen, which was open, and that of the governor, more or less

admitted. It added more fuel to the already existing "disagreements." Seeing that he would never stamp out this trade without the powerful aid of the king, Bishop Laval decided in 1662 to go to explain to Louis XIV both his viewpoint on the liquor trade and also the most urgent needs of his church.

He received a sympathetic welcome at court. Louis XIV gratified all his wishes: he promised to forbid explicitly the trade in spirits and to recall Dubois* Davaugour, who had favoured it; he even invited the prelate to choose the new governor; and finally, he appointed Bishop Laval as of then (1662) to the bishopric of Quebec.

It is reasonable to believe that Louis XIV and Bishop Laval discussed at length the reorganization of New France, which would be put under the direct authority of the king. Probably the prelate was likewise consulted about the idea of creating a Conseil Souverain (1663), in which he was to be the second personage, right after the governor. Abbé Bertrand de Latour, Bishop Laval's earliest biographer, even goes so far as to affirm that "the Conseil Souverain of Canada was the work of its first bishop." However that may be, Bishop Laval received from the king political powers which put him in certain respects on an equal footing with the governor: "conjointly and in agreement" with him, he was charged with appointing councillors and granting seigneuries. More than that, when he returned to New France in 1663 in company with the new governor, Saffray* de Mézy, and a royal commissioner, Gaudais-Dupont*, it was he whom the king had entrusted with the responsibility of bringing to Canada the edict creating the Conseil Souverain.

Was this Louis XIV, who in 1662 and 1663 interested himself in building up the political power of the Canadian church, the same person who from 1665 on was to take umbrage at any interference in civil affairs, real or supposed, by the church of the colony, and who was to concern himself so much with keeping the clergy in a state of subordination to the state for fear that the bishop and the Jesuits "might establish their authority too firmly through the fear of excommunication and through an excessively severe way of life that they wish to maintain"? Did not Louis XIV go so far as to make grave accusations, as if he had forgotten events that were, however, recent: "To maintain their position [in the colony] they [the Jesuits] were very pleased to designate the Bishop of Petraea to carry out the duties of bishop there since he was entirely under their domination, and up till now they have even designated governors for the King in that country, where they have employed all means

Laval

possible to obtain the recall of those who had been chosen for that post without their participation . . ."? Is the king's attitude in 1662 and 1663 to be explained by his ignorance of the abnormal politico-religious situation which still prevailed in Canada at that time? Or must this radical change be attributed to Colbert, who had become minister of the Marine just previously and who was a convinced Gallican? The fact remains that Louis XIV contributed greatly to setting the church and the state in the colony at odds. The quarrels and acts of violence over the composition of the council which characterized M. de Mézy's government were prepared by the king himself. One day Louis XIV was to regret the extreme liberality towards the church in Canada that marked the beginning of his reign. In 1677 Colbert echoed this feeling when he wrote: "I see that the bishop of Quebec pretends to an authority a little too independent of the royal authority, and for this reason it would perhaps be good that he not have a seat on the council. . . ."

Strong in his appointment to the future see of Quebec and the knowledge that he had acquired of the religious situation in New France, Bishop Laval had not wanted to leave Paris without laying the foundations of his church. To assure the colony of the priests that it needed, he conceived the idea of a seminary, which for years was to be the centre and soul of religious life in Canada. By an ordinance published in Paris on 26 March 1663 and confirmed by the king the following month, the vicar apostolic founded the seminary of Quebec.

In Bishop Laval's mind the seminary of Quebec was, to be sure, a theological seminary, "in which will be educated and formed the young clerics who appear fitted to God's service and to whom, for this purpose, will be taught the way to administer the sacraments properly, the method of catechizing and of doing missionary preaching; they will be taught moral theology, the ceremonies, the Gregorian plain-song, and other things pertaining to the duties of a good ecclesiastic." But Bishop Laval's seminary was much more than that: "We are setting up," declared the prelate, "a seminary which will act as the clergy for this new church, . . . a reserve from which we can draw pious and capable persons, to send them on all occasions and when need arises to the parishes and other places in this country in order to fulfil the functions of a parish priest and any others for which they have been intended and whom we can withdraw from the same parishes and functions when the moment is judged opportune. . . ." Bishop Laval conceived his seminary then as a true community of secular priests "which will be directed and governed by the superiors whom we or the bishops of New France who succeed us appoint to it, and according to the regulations which we establish to this purpose." Clergy and seminary were all one in Bishop Laval's mind: the seminary of Quebec would be the clergy of New France.

The prelate specified that the future chapter of the bishopric of Quebec would be constituted "within the said seminary and clergy"; all pastoral charges would be united with the seminary, to which the tithes would be paid; the seminary would provide for the needs of the parish priests and would promise to support them "in sickness as in health, either in the exercise of their functions or in the community when they are recalled to it." In return for this promise the seminary would demand the renunciation of property, that is to say, the pooling of all its members' wealth and revenues. Membership in the seminary was nevertheless free for secular priests; Abbés Le Sueur* and Le Bey, who had already been in the colony in 1659, did not join it. But in practice it was difficult for anyone who dreamed of receiving a charge not to join the seminary first.

At Bishop Laval's request the seminary of Quebec was affiliated on 29 Jan. 1665 with the Séminaire des Missions Étrangères in Paris, with which it was to maintain close links of friendly collaboration.

Bishop Laval's seminary corresponded perfectly to the needs of the church in Canada in 1663 and in addition ensured admirable unity in it. It rendered great services as long as Bishop Laval directed it himself; but of necessity it was, in certain respects, provisional in nature. With the development of the colony and once the parishes were able to support the parish priests, this diocesan community of the clergy no longer had any reason to exist. Under Bishop Laval, whose prestige was great, and because of the strong friendship which united him with his priests, the prelate and the seminary collaborated closely and in the most complete harmony. But under a new bishop everything would perhaps not go so well; it would first be necessary that this bishop agree to exercise his authority over the clergy and the parishes only through the intermediary of the directors of the seminary. Bishop Laval's successor, Bishop Saint-Vallier [La Croix], refused categorically to do so.

The ordinance which founded the seminary of Quebec and which was registered at Quebec on 10 Oct. 1663 instituted the tithe in Canada at the same time. Bishop Laval set it at a 13th, an amount to which the king gave his approval. Unfortunately the prelate deemed it fitting a month later to make an exception for the members of the parish of Quebec: they were dispensed from paying the tithe for the year 1663, and it was set for them alone at a 20th for the following six years. Immediately, in every part of the colony, people began to hope for a similar reduction; in the meantime they refused to provide for the needs of the clergy. This was the cause of great difficulties and serious disputes. M. de Mézy supported the settlers. Bishop Laval first extended to the whole country the privilege that had been granted to the parish of Quebec, then he set the tithe at a 20th for his lifetime, and finally he postponed until 1665 the application of this regulation. Nevertheless the tithe remained unpaid until 1667, when, on 23 August, Prouville* de Tracy set it at a 26th for 20 years and a 20th after that. Willy-nilly, the settlers submitted to these arrangements rather than be dragged before the courts. In 1707, after many changes, the tithe was finally set at a 26th. In this whole affair Bishop Laval, who was so firm and intractable when questions of principle or morality were threatened, proved to be easy to deal with and understanding, even a little weak in the face of the settlers' resistance. That alone would be sufficient to warrant a revision of certain opinions of his character.

When M. de Mézy died, after a reconciliation with the bishop and the clergy, there began for Bishop Laval a short period of peace, if not of perfect harmony, with the representatives of the state. M. de Tracy's presence contributed greatly to it. The prelate, who had established the parish of Quebec canonically in 1664, consecrated its church in 1666. During these few years he gave his attention to introducing into Canada a certain number of devotions, such as that to the Holy Family, to which he was particularly attached, and that to Saint Anne. On 9 Oct. 1668, at Quebec, he founded his Petit Séminaire, called the Seminary of the Infant Jesus. Eight young Canadians who were destined for the ecclesiastical calling and six Hurons whom it was proposed to acculturate were its first pupils. They were accommodated and brought up at the Petit Séminaire and took their courses at the Jesuit college. Around the same period Bishop Laval set up at Saint-Joachim a trades school, as well as a primary school where children would learn reading and arithmetic.

Suddenly, on 10 Oct. 1668, a new crisis began to build up. But here it is advisable to go back a little.

In 1657, by a decree of his council the king had confirmed the prohibition of the trade in spirits which had been in effect in the colony since Champlain's time. On 5 May 1660 Bishop Laval had in turn forbidden, under pain of excommunication *ipso facto*, the giving of intoxicating beverages to the Indians. Some time later he had excommunicated by name the trafficker Pierre Aigron*, *dit* Lamothe. Since the trade had ceased, under the double threat of civil and ecclesiastical sanctions, Bishop Laval lifted his general excommunication in October 1661, to reimpose it on 24 Feb. 1662, shortly after the governor-general, Davaugour, had in an unreflecting moment announced that he was in favour of this commerce. Just previously in Paris the theologians of the Sorbonne, who had been called upon by the vicar apostolic to consider the question, had expressed the opinion that "in view of the disorders which arise from the sale of such beverages to the Americans [i.e. the Indians], the ordinary or prelate may, under pain of excommunication *ipso facto*, forbid the Europeans to sell such beverages and may treat those who are disobedient and refractory as being under excommunication." As a result of Davaugour's conciliatory attitude, however, the trade had reached such proportions and the disorders had become so serious that Bishop Laval had decided to go to France to seek Louis XIV's support.

When he returned to Quebec in 1663 the vicar apostolic noted with satisfaction that the traffickers had given in under the effect of the terror produced by the great earthquake of 1663. M. de Mézy, the new governor, and Bishop Laval agreed to forbid conjointly the trade in alcoholic beverages. The union of church and state on this matter lasted until 10 Oct. 1668. Then, at Intendant Talon*'s instigation, the Conseil Souverain permitted trade in spirits, although forbidding the Indians to get drunk, which was an absurdity, considering their particular dispositions. In answer to this, on 21 April 1669 Bishop Laval made a reserved sin of getting Indians drunk and giving them alcoholic beverages to take to their villages.

At that moment the great quarrel of the trade in spirits broke out. Until then, in fact, and except for the incident caused by Davaugour, the church and the state had had a common policy, at least officially. But from then on Bishop Laval, the missionaries, and the clergy were under constant attack from all those—and they were numerous—who were in favour of the trade. They were accused of interfering in a matter of commercial policy which rested exclusively with the civil police. The bishop in particular was reproached for his reserved sin. In 1674 Bishop Laval again submitted the question to the theologians of the Sorbonne. The reply, dated 8 March 1675, decided in his favour on the two points that had been

Laval

proposed: the trade in spirits constituted a mortal sin, and the ordinary had the right to take appropriate measures to curtail this commerce, such as making a reserved sin of it.

In his fights against the civil authority, particularly in those which he waged against the trade in spirits, Bishop Laval found his episcopal authority questioned everywhere, owing to the fact that he was only the vicar apostolic. Until 1664 he himself had not doubted that he had all the powers of an ordinary; consequently he created in all good faith an officiality, a seminary, and the parish of Quebec. When he finally discovered the limitations on his office, he besought Rome to establish a see at Quebec, so that he could organize his church and confront with greater powers the "perpetual and scornful rivals of the ecclesiastical authority" in Canada.

At first this request did not seem to be of a nature to stir up any objections. In 1662 Louis XIV had assured Bishop Laval of his appointment to the future see of Quebec, which shortly afterwards he asked the pope to establish. The vicar apostolic had lost no time in backing up this initiative. Thereupon the Congregation for the Propagation of the Faith had expressed the opinion that the time had come, indeed, to endow New France with a diocese. But Louis XIV had finally given such proportions to the incident of the Corsican guard (20 Aug. 1662), that relations between Rome and Paris had deteriorated completely; after that the Congregation for the Propagation of the Faith had proven to be more reticent about the plan for a see, no longer promising to do other than examine it attentively.

The king soon demanded that the future see of Quebec should be attached to that of Rouen. Not being willing to give way on this point, Rome paid no attention to the matter for two years, from 1664 to 1666. But from Quebec Bishop Laval was sending urgent letters to the Holy See, setting forth the activities of the Compagnie des Indes Occidentales which, on the pretext that there was no ordinary in Canada, was preparing to send priests there, set up parishes, and appoint priests to them. Besides, the settlers were contesting the vicar apostolic's right to institute and collect tithes. In 1666 Rome resumed its examination of the matter, but a new demand from Louis XIV again slowed it up: this time the king wanted the establishment of the see of Quebec to be carried out in a manner which would respect the privileges of the Gallican church. While Bishop Laval was fretting vainly in Quebec, Rome finally sent Paris, on 18 June 1668, a model of a bull, "to receive thereon the King's orders." The document was studied, then sent back to the Holy See. The chief obstacle continued to be the question of subordination to the archbishopric of Rouen.

In 1669, tired of waiting and seeing his church threatened with ruin, Bishop Laval made the supreme concession: he wrote to Rome and accepted that the future see be subordinated to Rouen if the cardinals considered that it should be. That same year Louis XIV and Colbert, realizing that the discussions with the Holy See would never end, gave up the condition that they had maintained till then for the establishment of the see of Quebec, that is to say the subordination to Rouen!

The matter was proceeding extremely well in 1670, but Bishop Laval found it impossible to pay the high costs of the creation of his diocese. Not having a personal fortune, he wrote one plea after another, requesting that his bulls be sent him free of charge. Having become anxious, he went to France in 1671 with the determination never to return to Canada unless the diocese was established. Rome finally agreed to reduce the costs. The bulls were not sent until 4 Oct. 1674. Bishop Laval took the oath of loyalty to the king and sailed for Canada at the end of May 1675.

From that time on the diocese of Quebec escaped completely from the claims of the archbishop of Rouen, but not yet from those of the archibishop of Paris, the same Harlay de Champvallon, who had been promoted from Rouen to Paris. This time Harlay tried to make Quebec subordinate to the "principal" diocese of France. But in 1679 he had to give up this project, to which Rome would never have given its approval.

Bishop Laval landed at Quebec at the beginning of September 1675, after an absence of four years. As titular bishop he took possession of his cathedral, renewed several of his ordinances, confirmed the creation of the officiality and the parish of Quebec, and formed a temporary chapter, since he could not establish it canonically. He drew his canons from the seminary; shortly before leaving Paris he had renewed the act of union of the seminary with the Séminaire des Missions Étrangères. Then in the spring of 1676 he set out to visit his parish.

At the moment when Bishop Laval was ensuring greater stability for his church, Louis XIV was reorganizing the Conseil Souverain of Quebec. On 5 June 1675 he raised the number of councillors to seven—in addition to the governor, the bishop, and the intendant—who would henceforth be appointed by the king for life. Bishop Laval got back the second place, which had been his before the arrival of Jean Talon. The state therefore maintained an important role for the church in civil affairs in Canada.

Bishop Laval was perfectly aware of the numerous quarrels which, during his absence from 1672 to 1675, had sorely tried the union of church and state and which were one of the reasons for the reorganization of the council. Now in 1676 two important questions still set the "authorities" against each other: the trade in spirits and the creation of parishes. The bishop considered it was necessary to assign to Paris a trusty and devoted representative who would defend the position of the church in Canada and reply to the attacks of Louis de Buade* de Frontenac and his allies. He chose Abbé Jean Dudouyt*.

The mission that was entrusted to M. Dudouyt was all the more necessary since the clergy in New France was no longer as united as it had been earlier. Indeed, in 1670 the Recollets had returned to Canada on Jean Talon's instigation and had been commissioned by the state to counterbalance the authority and severity of the Jesuits and the secular clergy in Canada, who were accused of "tormenting people's consciences." These worthy religious, who from 1672 on were patronized by Frontenac, took their role seriously and became docile tools of the governor. On the trade in spirits, the creation of parishes, the tithe, they adopted and preached up Frontenac's opinions, being moreover entirely at his orders rather than the bishop's. Bishop Laval, who knew the reasons for their coming, had nevertheless received them charitably, had assigned them missionary fields, and continued to lavish marks of esteem upon them. It was to no avail. The Recollets surpassed Frontenac's clan in the calumnies spread at court against the bishop and the Jesuits—who, it was said, had forbidden the trade in spirits simply to engage in it themselves on a greater scale and who were more interested in converting beaver skins than in converting souls.

Bishop Laval had taken advantage of his stay in Paris to consult the theologians of the Sorbonne again on the question of trafficking in spirits. He received from them an opinion favourable in every respect to his own thesis. In the hope of obtaining a contrary opinion, his adversaries applied to the theologians of the University of Toulouse. The reply differed entirely from that given by the Sorbonne: "The Bishop of Quebec cannot legally make a mortal sin, and even less a reserved sin, of the sale of spirits." This conclusion was likely to harm Bishop Laval's cause. Therefore, upon his arrival in Paris M. Dudouyt requested an interview with Colbert. On 27 April 1677 he explained to him the reasons for Bishop Laval's attitude but did not convince him. A second audience on 11 May left some hope, as the minister had listened to him more patiently. He

therefore recommended that the bishop prepare a complete report on the question; the court had sent a similar request to the intendant, Duchesneau*.

Obviously Louis XIV was determined to settle the dispute. He ordered Frontenac to convoke 20 of the leading inhabitants of Canada and collect their opinions on the trade in spirits. The Conseil Souverain chose these representatives, who met on 28 Oct. 1678. Since almost all of them were engaged in commerce, the majority declared themselves in favour of complete freedom for the trade in spirits. The council charged Messrs NICOLAS DUPONT and Jean-Baptiste de PEIRAS with taking the result of the consultation to the court. The situation was critical for the church in Canada. Despite infirmities which were becoming more and more overwhelming, Bishop Laval sailed immediately for France, in an ultimate effort to convince the king of the rightness of his cause.

Louis XIV entrusted to his confessor, Father La Chaise, and the archbishop of Paris the task of studying the reports received from Canada on the trafficking in alcoholic beverages. Then, on 24 May 1679 he published an ordinance forbidding trade in spirits outside the French settlements. Bishop Laval promised to bring the case of reserved sin into accord with the dispositions of the ordinance. This outcome of a struggle that had lasted 20 years was enough to disappoint the old bishop profoundly; he could, nonetheless, gather some solace from the fact that the traffickers in alcohol would no longer be able legally to seek out the Indians even in their most remote villages.

The question of the creation of parishes was likewise debated in France during the winter of 1678–79, in Bishop Laval's presence. In confirming the founding of the seminary of Quebec in 1663 Louis XIV had approved the double principle of the removability of parish priests and the payment of tithes to the seminary, which assumed responsibility for redistributing them equitably to the officiating priests of the various parishes. Now, with time and, it seems, under the influence of Jean Talon, this system—the only one which could be applied to New France at that period—was criticized and then violently opposed. Bishop Laval was accused of not wanting to set up parishes. To that there were two replies: on the one hand, as long as he was vicar apostolic Bishop Laval did not have the necessary powers for setting up parishes—which he found out only after he had "erected" that of Quebec in 1664; on the other hand he could set up parishes only if the subsistence of the parish priests was assured. Around the period 1675–80 no "parish" was yet

Laval

capable of keeping a parish priest, not to speak of building a church or a presbytery. To assure the neccessary income it would have been necessary to increase considerably the number of parishioners by extending indefinitely the boundaries of the parishes, which would consequently have become mission territories again.

On the question of parishes, just as on that of the trade in spirits, Bishop Laval had to give in to the king's will. In May 1679 Louis XIV signed an edict concerning "tithes and fixed parishes": the tithes would in the future belong to the priest of the parish, "in which he would be established permanently, in place of the removable priest who ministered to it previously." Bishop Laval carried this edict out without any bad grace. As early as 1678 he had consulted with Frontenac and Duchesneau on the manner of assuring the subsistence of the parish priests. Shortly afterwards he had created seven parishes. "In most of these parishes," he wrote, "the settlers have not been willing to conform to the decision of the conference concerning the feeding and upkeep of their priests. No matter; I have sent my missionaries to spend the winter among them, binding myself to furnish them what they would need." Working in conjunction with the intendant, Bishop Laval created six new parishes in 1684; again, not one of them was capable of providing for the upkeep of its priest. Help from the seminary and the state was necessary. This was abundant proof of Bishop Laval's wisdom when he conceived his seminary in 1663; despite the new regime, which was instituted in principle by the edict of 1679, the seminary continued nevertheless to support the parishes.

Bishop Laval returned to Canada in the autumn of 1680, after being busy for more than a year with other questions concerning his church, in particular with the canonical union of the abbeys of Maubec and Lestrées with his bishopric—which, however, he was not able to bring about. In 1681 he visited his diocese.

The year 1681 saw the beginning of new difficulties between the bishop and the Recollets. The latter had just obtained from the king the site of the former seneschal's court, with a view to building on it a hospice, which would serve as a retreat for them when they were staying in Quebec. Bishop Laval received this project favourably but specified, in conformity with the royal document, that this place of retreat was not to be transformed into a convent or used for public religious services. The religious nonetheless made a convent of it, topped it with a belfry [see HENRI LE ROY], held services for the public, and openly disregarded the bishop's instructions. The latter rescinded the

authorization he had given them to build a hospice; in retaliation the Recollets gave up their missions. Bishop Laval was finally compelled to forbid them to exercise any ecclesiastical functions. Once more the king had to settle the dispute: he ordered the belfry to be destroyed, but the convent continued to exist. Conciliatory as usual, Bishop Laval had, at the beginning of this dispute, invited a Recollet, Father Adrian LADAN, to preach the Advent sermons at the cathedral. The religious took advantage of this to reprimand the intendant and Frontenac's adversaries; Bishop Laval's warnings had no effect on him. The Recollets were conscientiously playing the role that the state had entrusted them with. . . .

With the exception of the Recollets and, for a time, the Sulpicians, Bishop Laval's relations with the various religious communities in his diocese were always excellent and were characterized by mutual esteem and respect. The prelate, it is true, was not always in agreement with the superiors of the different communities, but their harmony was never disturbed by that. For example, Bishop Laval was not very much in favour of the multiplication of religious orders in his diocese: he would have liked to join together the two communities of nuns hospitallers, just as he wanted to unite the nuns of the Congrégation de Notre-Dame with the Ursulines. In the meantime he helped each group as best he could and finally acknowledged the separate existence of each. From 1668 on he was on good terms with the Sulpicians, even making M. de Queylus, whom he had allowed to return to Montreal, his vicar general. His charity and humility left no room in Bishop Laval for rancour or shabby actions.

On his return from his pastoral visit in 1681 the prelate, who was exhausted, fell seriously ill: "Within two weeks all hope had been given up." He would soon be 60, and his health was declining. He became convinced that a younger and more robust bishop would do more good than he from then on and that he had to present his resignation to the king. Before doing so he wanted to complete some aspects of his work. He saw to the founding of six new parishes, set his chapter up canonically in 1684, and entrusted to the seminary the executing of some projects, leaving 8,000 *livres* for the construction of the seminary chapel, foreseen in the plans for the building which had been started in 1678, 4,000 *livres* for the construction of a church at Saint-Joachim, and 8,000 *livres* for the upkeep of the priest who would minister to this parish and would direct the arts and crafts school that he had created there. In the autumn he sailed for France.

When his resignation had been accepted, Bishop

Laval agreed to remain bishop of Quebec until the consecration of his successor, Abbé Saint-Vallier, whom he had chosen with the utmost care. However, as the strained relations existing at the time between Paris and Rome did not permit the bulls to be sent immediately, Abbé Saint-Vallier went to Canada in 1685 with the title of vicar general. On his return to Paris in January 1687 he had some disputes with Bishop Laval about the seminary of Quebec. At that point the old bishop realized that his successor intended to alter profoundly the organization of the church in Canada, of which his beloved seminary was the keystone. Only one solution was open to him to save his work: induce Abbé Saint-Vallier, who had not yet received his bulls, to renounce his see. Bishop Laval had the most influential personages intervene, but in vain; Abbé Saint-Vallier would not give in, but contented himself with explaining his attitude and promising to be moderate.

In the spring of 1687 Bishop Laval was preparing to leave for Canada, where he wanted to finish his days. The Marquis de Seignelay prevented him from doing so, fearing that his presence there would be a source of quarrels and division. Bishop Laval wrote to Father La Chaise, to Seignelay himself, but had no success in moving them. From then on he gave himself over to God's will and wrote his priests an admirable letter full of resignation before this immense trial which he accepted "with a heart filled with joy and consolation."

Abbé Saint-Vallier was consecrated bishop on 25 Jan. 1688. Bishop Laval became *Monseigneur l'Ancien*. With the support of the new bishop and after promising not to cause him any difficulty, Bishop Laval received permission to return to Quebec. He arrived there on 3 June, and Bishop Saint-Vallier on 31 July.

Monseigneur l'Ancien's return to the colony delighted not only his priests but the whole population, over which, according to the governor-general, BRISAY de Denonville, he had "great influence because of his character and his reputation for saintliness." Though certain representatives of the civil authority and most of the businessmen, who were interested in the trade in spirits, were opposed to him, the settlers, despite the difficulties caused by the establishment of tithes, sincerely loved and venerated this courageous bishop who was completely devoted to his church and whose piety, humility, and above all immense charity they were well acquainted with. People everywhere were conscious of the progress accomplished under Bishop Laval: from 5 in 1659 the number of parishes had become 35 in 1688; the number of priests had increased from 24 to 102

(36 Jesuits, 19 Sulpicians, 14 Recollets, and 33 secular priests), and from 32 the number of nuns had risen to about 97. Nor were people indifferent to the fact that 13 Canadian priests were already at work in Canada and that 50 Canadian nuns had pronounced their perpetual vows in the various communities at Quebec and Montreal. In addition to laying the bases of a national church, Bishop Laval had made a very successful start on its erection.

He went back to the seminary to live. A *donné*, Brother Hubert Houssart, was assigned to serve him. The prelate no longer gave thought to anything but prayer and mortification, limiting his outside activities entirely to acts of charity, a charity that was, moreover, very unobtrusive. He gave away everything he owned, asking for nothing that was not for his poor, for whom he even kept the greater part of his meals. When he had nothing left, he knew that his end was near. He attended all the parish services, being the first in the church every morning, well before sunrise and even in the coldest weather. He was completely withdrawn from church affairs and was no longer interested in anything but his beloved seminary, upon which he continued to lavish his counsels, and the seminarists, whose progress he followed closely, and with whom he was fond of chatting during their periods of relaxation. BOCHART de Champigny, the intendant, described aptly the old bishop's new existence in one short sentence: "He lived in his retirement in a saintly manner, concerning himself only with the direction of his seminary."

His seminary! How much grief it was to cause him in his last years! At first, Bishop Saint-Vallier was violently opposed to the parishes being united with it, and finally, in 1692, he obtained from the king a complete separation, the seminary being reduced to nothing more than an institution for training future priests. This meant the destruction of Bishop Laval's great work. It had to happen sooner or later, it is true; but who would think of reproaching the old bishop for his attachment to his life's work—this seminary to which he had made over all his landed property—especially after Bishop Saint-Vallier's severity towards him and his collaborators? At the height of the bishop's quarrel with the seminary, Bishop Laval had prudently withdrawn to Saint-Joachim to avoid having to intervene and oppose his successor openly. In the attitude of Bishop Saint-Vallier, whose personal sincerity he recognized, he saw almost the action of some evil power bent upon destroying this new church. The prospect wrung cries of pain from him. But on learning the news of the re-formation of his seminary, he submitted

La Vallière

as usual to the ways of providence, forgetting himself to console his priests and incite them to submission. Even though he was wounded to the depths of his soul, he preached reconciliation and peace: never had his virtue been more heroic.

The wounds caused by the re-formation of the seminary were not yet healed when a new disaster fell upon this institution. On 15 Nov. 1701 a fire destroyed in a few hours the seminary, the chapel, and the presbytery. This was a painful trial for Bishop Laval. As he was very old, would he see his seminary standing again? The rebuilding was done with great fervour; everything but the chapel was soon restored. But scarcely was the end of the work in sight when on 1 Oct. 1705 almost all the seminary was again destroyed by fire. His Excellency, wrote Brother Houssart, "did not lose for a single moment his peace, his joy, or his tranquillity, because these accidents were not matters capable of affecting his patience and his virtue, which were far above all that." And the humble brother added that "only the interests of God, virtue, and religion were capable of moving him," which illustrates perfectly this bishop's whole life.

In the middle of these harsh trials Bishop Laval had to come out of his retreat somewhat to fulfil on occasion the episcopal functions of Bishop Saint-Vallier, who had left in 1700, not to return to the colony until 1713. *Monseigneur l'Ancien* had, besides, always helped his bishop, without ever revealing in public his feelings on questions which were likely to set him against Saint-Vallier. In his successor's absence he particularly insisted always upon attending services in the cathedral, to enhance them by a bishop's presence. It was in so doing that during Holy Week of 1708 he contracted a chilblain on his heel which became worse and soon brought him to death's door. He died on 6 May, at half past seven in the morning. His body lay in state in the cathedral.

"Immediately after his death the people canonized him, as it were," wrote Intendant Raudot, "having had the same veneration for his body as for those of the saints, when they had come in crowds from all parts while he was exposed on his bed of state and in the church, to touch him with their chaplets and prayer-books. They even cut off pieces of his robe, which several have had enshrined in silver, and they treat them as relics."

The funeral took place on 9 May. M. Glandelet pronounced the funeral oration. Then the first bishop of Quebec was buried under the cathedral.

André Vachon

It is impossible to list here in detail the thousands of documents concerning Bishop Laval's long career;

that would require an almost complete inventory of the archives of the 17th century preserved at the AAQ, the ASQ, and to a lesser degree at the AQ. Fortunately the principal documents of interest have been published in the following work: *Quebecen. Beatificationis et Canonizationis Ven. Servi Dei. Francisci de Montmorency-Laval Episcopi Quebecencis (†1708). Altera Nova Positio Super Virtutibus Ex Officis Critice Disposita*, Typis Polyglottis Vaticanis, MCMLVI. In this are to be found, in addition to the documents drawn from the archives mentioned above, long extracts from the *JJ* and *JR*, the correspondence of the governors, intendants, and Marie de l'Incarnation, the *Jug. et délib.*, the *Mandements des évêques de Québec* (Têtu et Gagnon), I, the *Annales de l'Hôtel-Dieu de Québec* by Mother Juchereau, etc., as well as the earliest biography of this bishop, *Mémoires sur la vie de M. de Laval, premier évêque de Québec*, by Bertrand de Latour, published in 1761, and the useful letter from Brother Houssart on the last years and death of Laval.

Studies on Bishop Laval are also numerous. All the general histories devote much space to him; we shall not list them here, contenting ourselves with mentioning the following studies. Émile Bégin, *François de Laval* (Québec, 1959). [Faillon], *Histoire de la colonie française*. Auguste Gosselin, *L'Église du Canada*, I; *Henri de Bernières, premier curé de Québec* (Les Normands au Canada, Québec, 1902); *Vie de Mgr de Laval*. Rochemonteix, *Les Jésuites et la N.-F. au XVIIᵉ siècle*, I, II, III. H. H. Walsh, *The church in the French era (A history of the Christian church in Canada*, ed. J. W. Grant, I, Toronto, 1966).

LA VALLIÈRE. *See* Leneuf

LA VÉRENDRYE, JEAN-BAPTISTE GAULTIER DE. *See* Gaultier

LEAKE, SIR JOHN, admiral of the fleet; commodore of the Newfoundland convoy and temporary governor, 1702; b. 1656 at Rotherhithe, Kent; 2d son of Captain Richard Leake; married Christian, daughter of Captain Richard Hill; d. 21 Aug. 1720, at Greenwich; buried at Stepney.

As a young man Leake saw much active service, and by 1689 was in command of the *Dartmouth* at the relief of the besieged city of Londonderry. Soon after the War of the Spanish Succession was declared, Leake was appointed captain of the *Exeter* and commodore of the Newfoundland convoy for 1702. He received instructions to ascertain the strength of the French and the state of their forts in Newfoundland, to attack their fishing harbours and their ships at sea, and to assist the fishing admirals. Commissioned as temporary governor and commander-in-chief of the land forces in Newfoundland, Leake sailed from Plymouth, 22 July 1702, with five ships of the line of 50 guns, two galleys of 32 guns, a fireship and a sloop. On 26 August the fleet reached Bay Bulls to learn that two French ships were loading at Trepassey Bay and that two enemy warships were lying at Placentia (Plaisance). Leake ordered the *Montague* and *Lichfield* to chase four strange sails just then sighted; three of these French ships were captured. Meanwhile Leake and the rest of his fleet proceeded to Trepassey. On 29 August landing parties were sent ashore. They drove out the French and burned their houses, stores, and fish-drying stages. Leake proceeded to St John's and was joined there on 19 September by the *Assistance*, whose crew had wrecked the fort and settlement on Saint-Pierre [*see* LE GOUÈS]. Other ships of the squadron were also active, and by October 51 French ships had been sunk or captured, and several settlements destroyed.

Leake had been supplied by the Board of Trade and Plantations with a number of Heads of Enquiry. The board was much concerned about the inhabitants' disregard of the Newfoundland act of 1699, as reported by Leake's predecessors, Commodores Fairborne and GRAYDON. It therefore required Leake to apply "the best remedies . . . for the prevention of [such] mischiefs" as the illegal trade with New England and the enticement of English seamen from the fisheries.

Leake in his long report noted the usual problems: fishing admirals acted unjustly in settling disputes; there were no provisions in the act of 1699 for enforcing any regulations; the inhabitants passed the long winters in idleness and "debauchery," and the amount of drink sold by public and "suttling" houses had evil effects. (He observed, however, that the beer made from spruce and molasses was cheaper and more wholesome than beer made with malt.) The soldiers of the garrison of Fort William, while not complaining of ill treatment by their officers, were dissatisfied with their poor pay—the engineer Michael RICHARDS obliged them to work on the fortifications for sixpence a day—and were understandably depressed at having been kept so long in Newfoundland with little prospect of returning to England. They were short of clothing and provisions; desertions, probably to Placentia, were not infrequent. Leake also mentioned that he had improvised a temporary boom for the protection of the harbour of St John's but he was not confident that the inhabitants would stay to defend the harbour if an assault were made on it. As far as the French fisheries were concerned, Leake could not supply the board with much information, except to observe that the salt used by the French fishermen was cheaper and more efficient than that used by the English.

Leake returned to England and, in December 1702, was promoted to rear-admiral, and to vice-admiral the following March. In February 1704 he was knighted and that year took part in the assault and capture of Gibraltar under Admiral Rooke. He particularly distinguished himself in the relief of the British garrison of the rock in the subsequent siege by the Spaniards and French. Leake was promoted admiral in January 1708, and admiral of the fleet in December of that year. His son, Captain Richard Leake, was appointed commodore of the Newfoundland convoy in 1713.

Not long after the death of Queen Anne, Leake fell out of favour with the government, who treated him shabbily in the matter of pension, and he retired to a villa he had built at Greenwich. He has been described as a "virtuous, humane and gallant man, and one of the greatest admirals of his time."

A portrait by Kneller of Sir John Leake hangs in the Painted Hall at the Royal Naval College, Greenwich, and another in the guildhall, Rochester.

MICHAEL GODFREY

[Sir John is not to be confused with Capt. Andrew Leake of the *Hampshire* who was sent to Newfoundland in 1699 as commander-in-chief at land. M.G.]

[Stephen Martin Leake], *The life of Sir John Leake rear-admiral of Great Britain*, ed. Geoffrey Callender (2v., Navy Records Soc., LII, LIII, London, 1920), I, 99–104 for Nfld. service; II, 462–66 for a chronology of his career. PRO, Adm. 51/325 (captain's log of H.M.S. *Exeter*); C.O. 194/2; *CSP, Col., 1702*; *B.T.Journal, 1708/9–1714/15*, 602 (Richard Leake's answers, 1713). Charnock, *Biographia navalis*, II. DNB. Lounsbury, *British fishery at Nfld.*, 215–16. Prowse, *History of Nfld.*

LEBEAU, CLAUDE, adventurer and traveller; dates and places of birth and death unknown.

Little is known about Lebeau's life, apart from the somewhat fanciful details that he recounted himself. He claimed that he came from Morlon, in the canton of Fribourg (Switzerland). His father, who was serving in the Swiss Guards of the household of the king of France, brought Lebeau to France. He studied law and was called to the bar of the *parlement* of Paris on 8 Aug. 1724. Having lost his mother, who, he declared, had been "as gentle as his father was unbending," and having no cases to plead, he seems to have worked for an attorney. He apparently quarrelled with his father, and the latter, a friend of Intendant Hocquart*, possibly decided to entrust Lebeau to the intendant to act as his secretary during his service in Canada.

Lebeau claimed that he left Paris 10 April 1729,

Le Ber

to be presented to his protector at La Rochelle. The facts, however, are rather different. Indeed, on 28 May 1728 an order from the king dispatched Lebeau to Bicêtre; in this prison, reserved for wrong-doers of inferior social condition, he was to be detained, "no doubt for libertinism", until further notice, "in consideration of a sum of 100 *livres* for his keep, which will be paid by his father." He was transferred on an unknown date to the Hôpital Général, since on 29 April 1729 the king wrote to the administrators of that institution instructing them to hand over François Legrand, Jean and Antoine Tancré, Claude Lebeau, and others to the corporals of the watch. On the same day, an order from the king prescribed that these individuals should be transferred to Canada, "to remain there for the rest of their lives."

On 2 May 1729 Maurepas wrote to Beauharnois* de La Boische, the intendant of the Marine at Rochefort, to send him the list of the 15 prisoners who were to be embarked on the flute *Eléphant*. "You will see," added the minister, "that some of them are attached to persons of rank and that the others are for the most part sons of good families who have been imprisoned for libertinism." It was therefore in a convoy of prisoners that Lebeau left Paris for La Rochelle. He could not have reached Quebec on 18 June 1729, as he claimed, for the *Eléphant*, under the command of Lieutenant-Commander Vaudreuil [Rigaud*], did not sail until 28 June, at 3 o'clock in the morning, having embarked the prisoners at Île d'Aix. After a long crossing, the vessel was shipwrecked at about 8 in the evening on 1 September at Cape Brûle, some 30 miles from Quebec. The crew and passengers were saved.

Lebeau claimed that he was appointed a clerk in the Beaver Office (Bureau du Castor) and then chief clerk in the king's warehouses on the recommendation of Father Dubois*, the Recollets' provincial, in whose residence he was living. He became bored, his job not being important enough to induce him to remain in Canada, and as he was sunk in "an indescribable depression," he attempted to run away. Unable to obtain a passport, he says that he stole gunpowder from the warehouses and set off in the direction of New England. On 14 Nov. 1730 Intendant Hocquart issued a warrant for his arrest, promising a reward of 300 *livres* for his capture. Hocquart described Lebeau as follows: "of small stature, wearing a brown wig, with a pock-marked face, small, black, rather deep-set eyes, and a slight stammer." Nevertheless Lebeau managed to escape, tried to abduct a young Abenaki girl who refused to follow him, and reached Boston, whence he sailed for Holland. On 12 Jan. 1731, Hocquart sentenced the

Sieur Lebeau in his absence "for the crime of fraudulent circulation of counterfeit card money"; he was to be hanged and garotted until he was dead. This judgement was executed the following day; since Lebeau had fled he was hanged in effigy.

In 1738 there appeared at Amsterdam, in two volumes, a work entitled *Aventures du s. C. Le Beau, avocat en Parlement, ou Voyage curieux et nouveau parmi les Sauvages de l'Amerique septentrionale dans lequel on trouvera une description du Canada avec une relation très particulière des anciennes coutumes, mœurs et façons de vivre des barbares qui l'habitent et de la manière dont ils se comportent aujourd'huy*. This work, which belonged to a type of exotic literature popular from the second half of the 17th century on, must have enjoyed a certain success, since a German translation of it was published at Frankfurt in 1752.

Lebeau does not lack talent as a writer, and his book is pleasant reading; but its originality is slight, for he borrows generously from his predecessors. The *Journal de Trévoux* published a severe review, calling the work a novel; it does however concede that the author deserves credit for painting an exact picture of the customs and character of the Canadians, although his geographical knowledge is poor. The best chapters are those that discuss the habits of beaver and the religious ideas of the Indians. Taken all round, the work is more indicative of the author's imagination than of a scientific spirit, which is in any event seldom found in travel accounts of this period.

ÉTIENNE TAILLEMITE

AN, O¹, 72, f.201; X¹ᵃ, 9327; Col., B, 53, ff.152, 172, 548v, 572, 573; C¹¹ᴬ, 51, ff.103–6, 237–39, 387–88, 398, 476; E, 265 (dossier Lebeau). *Dictionnaire géographique de la Suisse* (6v., Neuchâtel, 1902–10), III, article Morlon. *Dictionnaire historique et biographique de la Suisse* (8v., Neuchâtel, 1921–34), IV. J.-E. Roy, "Des fils de famille envoyés au Canada — Claude Le Beau," *RSCT*, 2d ser., VII (1901), sect.I, 6–33.

LE BER, JACQUES, merchant, seigneur, ennobled in 1696; b. *c.* 1633 in the parish of Pistre, diocese of Rouen, son of Robert Le Ber and Colette Cavelier, who may have been related to Cavelier* de La Salle; d. 25 Nov. 1706 in Montreal.

Le Ber came to Canada in 1657 and took up residence in Montreal. A brother, François, also settled there around the same time, and a sister, Marie, became an Ursuline nun in Quebec. The Iroquois were then intensifying their war against the colony and Jacques, living in the area most exposed to their incursions, risked his life on many expeditions against these Indians. In 1663, he and François were members of the militia of the Holy

374

Family which Chomedey* de Maisonneuve had organized for the defence of the island.

Le Ber, however, was not primarily a soldier but a businessman. On 7 Jan. 1658, he had wed Jeanne Le Moyne, sister of Charles Le Moyne* de Longueuil et de Châteauguay, and shortly afterwards he went into business with his brother-in-law. By 1664, the two partners owned stores in Montreal and Quebec and their affairs were in a flourishing state. Le Ber's activities, however, were not limited to the fur trade and the sale of merchandise. He was keenly interested in Canada's other economic resources and was one of the principal pioneers of their development. He engaged in the cod fisheries, in trade with the West Indies, was one of the first men to send staves and sheathing to France, and experimented with the transplanting of European fruit trees.

By the 1670s Le Ber was one of the key figures in the closely knit group of wealthy and ambitious businessmen which had emerged in Canada. Among his associates was Charles Bazire*, the partner of CHARLES AUBERT de La Chesnaye, with whom he engaged in various commercial ventures. In 1674, Governor Louis de Buade* de Frontenac leased to the two men the post he had founded at Cataracoui, which was strategically located for trade with the Iroquois and some of the western tribes. The following year, however, the governor arranged for the transfer of the lease to Cavelier de La Salle. Le Ber, who had previously acted as a staunch ally of Frontenac, now became one of his chief adversaries. With Le Moyne, La Chesnaye, and Philippe Gaultier* de Comporté, who also felt slighted by Frontenac's policy, he appears to have organized a rival fur-trading network. In 1682, this group of powerful merchants gained the favour of Le Febvre* de La Barre. The new governor promptly placed Le Ber and La Chesnaye in possession of Fort Frontenac (Cataracoui, now Kingston, Ont.) and also encouraged the formation of the Compagnie du Nord, in which Le Ber and Le Moyne invested 21,357 *livres*.

By the 1680s, Le Ber was one of the wealthiest and most respected men in New France. He owned a store in Montreal and each year sent large quantities of fur and bills of exchange to France. In 1693 alone, those drawn on the state and private parties amounted to 79,380 *livres*. He was also the seigneur of two-thirds of Île Saint-Paul near Montreal, whose value was given as 18,400 *livres* in an inventory of 1694, and of Senneville, an estate of 200 *arpents* on Lac des Deux Montagnes. Le Ber himself lived on Rue Saint-Paul in Montreal, in a two-storey house whose grounds were enclosed by a wooden fence. When he entertained at dinner his guests were probably served on silver plates worth 2,140 *livres* and waited upon by Jacques, a Negro slave. In 1696, Louis XIV placed a number of letters of nobility on sale in order to replenish his depleted finances. Le Ber promptly purchased his for 6,000 *livres* and proudly added the title esquire to his name. In August 1715 a decree of the council of state revoked all letters of nobility sold since 1689, but Le Ber's descendants obtained letters patent exempting them from this law.

Le Ber's wealth gave him considerable influence in the affairs of the colony. He was one of the 20 notables summoned by Frontenac in 1678 to give their opinion on the brandy trade with the Indians. The majority view was that no restrictions should be placed on this trade, but Le Ber and four others maintained that it should be forbidden outside the confines of the main settlements. The question was temporarily settled the following year when Louis XIV issued an edict that reflected this minority opinion. In 1684, Le Ber sat on another assembly of notables; along with the others present on this occasion, he opposed replacing the tax of 25 per cent on beaver pelts and of 10 per cent on moosehides by a head tax (*capitation*) and impositions on foodstuffs and property.

When the Iroquois renewed their war on New France in the early 1680s, Le Ber and his family once more came to the defence of the colony. In 1686, he built a stone mill on the island of Montreal near the Ottawa River to provide the inhabitants of that area with a shelter in case of attack by the Five Nations. In 1693, he joined a war party of 300 Canadians, 100 soldiers, and 230 Indians that attacked the Mohawks in their own territory.

Le Ber died in Montreal on 25 Nov. 1706. According to the report of JACQUES RAUDOT on the financial status of the principal shareholders of the Compagnie de la Colonie, he was then a wealthy man. Le Ber's wife had died on 8 Nov. 1682, and two sons had also predeceased him: Louis, Sieur de Saint-Paul, who died in the early 1690s in La Rochelle where he had acted as his father's business agent, and Jean-Vincent, Sieur Du Chesne, fatally wounded during an encounter with an English and Iroquois war party near Fort Chambly in 1691. Three children survived their father: JEANNE, the famous recluse, PIERRE, and Jacques, Sieur de Senneville. While serving in France as aide-de-camp in the 1690s, Senneville dissipated his share of 40,000 *livres* from his father's estate. Following his return to Canada, he was made a captain in the colonial regular troops and soon became a successful fur-trader and merchant. When he died in 1735, he and

Le Ber

Toussaint Pothier, with whom he had formed a partnership in 1731, had 64,000 *livres* in cash in their Montreal store.

YVES F. ZOLTVANY

AJM, Greffe d'Antoine Adhémar; Greffe de Bénigne Basset; Greffe de Claude Maugue [the most significant documents from these *greffes* are: Le Ber's marriage contract, dated 29 Dec. 1657; a 60-page document, the inventory of his assets and liabilities as of 1 Dec. 1694; his will, dated 25 June 1701 — the first two documents were drawn up by Basset, the third by Adhémar]; Registre d'état civil de Notre-Dame de Montréal, 1693–1696, 200. AJQ, Greffe de J.-B. Peuvret Demesnu, 30 juillet 1658. [In this document Le Ber is called Jacques Le Ber, sr. de la Roze, but he seems to have stopped using this title after his arrival in Canada.] AN, Col., B, 19, 22, 39; C^{11A}, 4–20, 125; F³, 5, f.75; 6, f.148.

Dollier de Casson, *History of Montreal* (Flenley). *Jug. et délib.*, I, II, III, IV, V. *NYCD* (O'Callaghan and Fernow), IX. P.-G. Roy, *Inv. concessions*, II, 99–101, 103, 128f. Eccles, *Frontenac*. [É.-M. Faillon], *L'héroïne chrétienne du Canada; ou, Vie de Mlle Le Ber* (Ville-Marie [Montréal], 1860); *Histoire de la colonie française*, III.

LE BER, JEANNE, famed recluse; b. 4 Jan. 1662 at Montreal, daughter of Jacques Le Ber and Jeanne Le Moyne; d. 3 Oct. 1714 at Montreal.

Jeanne Le Ber was baptized the day she was born by Abbé Gabriel Souart*, Maisonneuve [Chomedey*] being her godfather and Jeanne Mance* her godmother. At an early age she was interested in a religious vocation and frequently visited Jeanne Mance and the Hospitallers. To complete her formal education she spent three years, 1674 to 1677, as a boarder with the Ursulines in Quebec where her aunt, Marie Le Ber de l'Annonciation, taught. The Ursulines were impressed by her many acts of self-denial and were disappointed when, at the age of 15, she returned to her family in Montreal. She was a pensive, withdrawn, and introverted young lady, who daily spent much time in prayer and in adoration of the Sacrament. A friendship with Marguerite Bourgeoys* was greatly to influence her future.

Jeanne Le Ber seemed to savour the social status of her family, however, and always enjoyed prominence and praise for her virtues and talents. As the only daughter (she had three younger brothers) of Jacques Le Ber, with a dowry of approximately 50,000 *écus*, she was rightly considered the most eligible girl in New France.

The death of one of the sisters of the Congrégation de Notre-Dame in 1679 profoundly affected her; she sought the guidance of Abbé Seguenot, Sulpician parish priest at Point-aux-Trembles (Montreal) who was to remain her confessor, and decided to live a secluded life for a five-year period. With her parents' permission she retired to a cell at the rear of the church of the Hôtel-Dieu, which served as parish church at that time. Her practices of self-mortification increased: she wore an undergarment of haircloth and corn-husk shoes, she refused to communicate with her family or friends, and she reportedly practised self-flagellation. She left her seclusion only to attend daily mass.

Jeanne Le Ber remained undecided about entering a regular order and taking permanent vows; nevertheless, her determination to shun the attractive life her family offered became evident. In November 1682 she refused to leave her cell to attend her dying mother and later refused to assume the management of the household for her widowed father.

Instead, on 24 June 1685 she took a simple vow of perpetual seclusion, chastity, and poverty. Her spiritual directors, the Abbés DOLLIER de Casson and Seguenot, encouraged her to continue her pious observances. Her poverty and seclusion, however, were somewhat tempered by the fact that, befitting her social rank, she retained throughout her years of withdrawal from the world an attendant, her cousin Anna Barroy, who saw to her physical requirements and accompanied her to mass. Pleading frailty, she did not abstain from meat as did strict observers in the 17th century. When her brother Jean was killed by the Iroquois in August 1691, her vows did not prevent her viewing his body and assisting with funeral arrangements. At the same time she attended to a number of business matters, for she had not felt obliged by her vows to divest herself of her property. She ceded the farm at Pointe Saint-Charles to the Hôpital Général of the Charon brothers. Her self-imposed rule of silence was subject to amendment by her spiritual director, and she does not seem to have been refused permission to receive visitors whenever she desired. In 1693, for example, she had a long conversation with M. de LA COLOMBIÈRE who wished to re-enter Saint-Sulpice.

When she heard that the sisters of the Congrégation planned to build a church on their property she gave them generous financial assistance on condition that they reserve for her a three-room apartment directly behind the altar, so that she could view the blessed sacrament without leaving her quarters. The apartment was built to her specifications, one room at each of three levels: the lower storey, a vestry for confessions and communion, with a door to the sisters' garden; the second storey, a simple bedchamber; the upper level, a workroom. Dollier de Casson witnessed the agreement drawn up by the notary Basset, whereby the sisters of the Congrégation promised to supply food, clothing, and fuel, to offer daily intercessions, and to wait on her whenever her lady-in-waiting was absent. In return Jeanne Le Ber provided the capital funds for building and decorating the church and an annual income of 75 *livres*.

On 5 Aug. 1695 she took the solemn vows of a recluse at a ceremony attended by scores of curious colonists. She spent much time in making church vestments and altar cloths and in fine embroidery. Six or seven hours a day were devoted to prayer and meditation, communion was received four times a week; and when the sisters of the Congrégation retired for the night Jeanne Le Ber would spend hours prostrate before the altar of the deserted and silent church. According to her confessor she did not find complete consolation in her self-abnegation and her religious exercises were always burdensome to her.

She introduced the practice of the perpetual adoration of the Blessed Sacrament and made a gift of 300 *livres* to the sisters of the Congrégation for its observance. Another 8,000 *livres* provided for perpetual masses. She also presented them with the tabernacle, ciborium, chalice, ostensorium, and a silver lamp for the chapel.

Throughout the colony she enjoyed a great fame and continued to receive distinguished visitors from time to time. In 1698, Bishop Saint-Vallier [LA CROIX], returning from France, accompanied two English gentlemen, one of them a Protestant minister, on a visit to her. Her father visited her twice a year. His request to be buried in the church of the sisters of the Congrégation to be near his daughter was granted, but Jeanne, to the disappointment of the curious, did not attend his funeral.

When a final illness overtook her in September 1714 she divested herself of her remaining possessions. The sisters of the Congrégation received 18,000 *livres*, the revenue of which maintained seven boarders, and all her furniture. She died on 3 October and was buried next to her father.

C. J. JAENEN

ACND, M¹, Écrits autographes de sœur Marguerite Bourgeois. AHDM, Annales. AHDQ, Annales, 1636–1716. *Jug. et délib.*, VI, 671. "Éloges de quelques personnes mortes en odeur de sainteté à Montréal, en Canada, divisés en trois parties," APQ *Rapport, 1929–30*, 143f. Norah Story, *The Oxford companion to Canadian history and literature* (Toronto, 1967), 446. Marie Beaupré, *Jeanne LeBer, première recluse du Canada français (1662–1714)* (Montréal, 1939). [É.-M. Faillon], *The christian heroine of Canada; or, life of Miss Le Ber* (Montréal, 1861), a translation of *L'héroïne chrétienne du Canada; ou, Vie de Mlle Le Ber* (Ville-Marie [Montréal], 1860). C.-H. Barbeau, "Jeanne Le Ber, sainte artisane," *CF*, 2e sér., XXVI (février 1939), 514–28.

LE BER, PIERRE, painter, son of JACQUES LE BER and Jeanne Le Moyne; baptized 11 Aug. 1669 at Montreal; d. 1 Oct. 1707 at Pointe-Saint-Charles, near Montreal.

Through his parents he belonged to the two richest families in Montreal. He was as generous as he was pious, and made substantial gifts to all the communities of the town, in particular to the Congrégation de Notre-Dame, where his sister JEANNE was a recluse, and to the Brothers Hospitallers of which he was a founder, along with CHARON and Fredin, and to which he belonged, without pronouncing any vows.

The Le Bers were interested in the arts. His sister practised embroidery, and his brother Jacques, Sieur de Senneville, a professional soldier and merchant, devoted his leisure moments to painting, as is attested by his "Éducation de la Vierge" (1723), which is today in the church of Sainte-Anne-de-Bellevue.

Pierre Le Ber was for a long time considered as a well-meaning but untalented amateur; he suddenly became famous, however, as the result of the discovery in 1965 of the original of the portrait of Marguerite Bourgeoys*, hailed as one of the masterpieces of Canadian art. There is, of course, no comparison between this canvas—completely repainted on two occasions—and the formal portrait as the great century conceived it, but its accent of truth and the economy of the means employed could not fail to appeal to modern taste. According to eye-witnesses, Le Ber was apparently seized by a sudden inspiration and executed his work with extraordinary facility. Be that as it may, he rendered with unusual force the human qualities that the early Montrealers saw in Sister Bourgeoys. It is in truth a great work, worthy of the subject that inspired it, and certainly a good likeness.

Was it merely a stroke of luck? There is in any case no doubt that Le Ber, who was probably trained at Quebec, devoted the major part of his time to artistic work. Proof of this is to be seen in the substantial amount of painter's equipment and the abundance of artist's supplies enumerated in the inventory of his possessions made after his death. Moreover, his will informs us that he concerned himself with ornamentalist architecture. It refers to the chapel of St Anne—a stone building which he had had constructed at Pointe-Saint-Charles to match the one at Bonsecours—and mentions a tabernacle for which he had furnished

Le Blanc

the design to a carver from Ange-Gardien, no doubt Charles Vézina.

In "Ma Saberdache," Jacques Viger transcribes a text by Abbé Sattin which relates that during the building of the Hôpital Général Le Ber "himself worked at the interior decoration by contributing a large number of pictures painted by his own hand," and adds "that only one of them remains [in 1843], that it is a daub, and that the others have wisely been burned." Despite this statement, it is doubtful that the Sisters of Charity resorted to such an *auto-da-fé*. The question is obscure. When in 1719 Brother Chrétien [Turc*] succeeded Charon at the head of the Hospitallers, he had an inventory of the establishment drawn up; no painting is listed in it, except a "picture representing a crucifix," which was apparently a framed print. On the other hand, when Mother Youville [Dufrost*] took possession of the hospice in 1747, the inventory mentioned the presence of 27 pictures in the sacristy and the church. If one can go by the titles, only two of these would seem still to exist in the mother house of the Sisters of Charity: a "St Catherine" and a "Jésus au jardin des oliviers." According to accounts of the time, it seems that the others were lost in the fire of 1765, and that they were not deliberately destroyed. Finally, to Le Ber are attributed various works which are to be found at the Congrégation de Notre-Dame, particularly an "Enfant Jésus" painted for Sister BARBIER.

JULES BAZIN

AJM, Greffe d'Antoine Adhémar, 23 oct. 1692, 11 mars 1707; Greffe de Bénigne Basset, 17 oct. 1692, 9 sept. 1697; Greffe de Louis-Claude Danré de Blanzy, 4–18 sept. 1747; Greffe de Pierre Raimbault, 3 oct. 1707. ANDM, Registres des baptêmes, mariages et sépultures. ASQ, Fonds Verreau, "Ma Saberdache." É.-Z. Massicotte, "Inventaire des documents et des imprimés concernant la communauté des frères Charon et l'Hôpital Général de Montréal sous le régime français," APQ *Rapport, 1923–24*, 168, 169, 195. Tanguay, *Dictionnaire*, I, 356. [É.-M. Faillon], *L'héroïne chrétienne du Canada; ou, Vie de Mlle Le Ber* (Ville-Marie [Montréal], 1860), 160, 164, 218f., 329f. Harper, *Painting in Canada*. Gérard Morisset, *Coup d'œil sur les arts en Nouvelle-France* (Québec, 1941), 32, 51; *La peinture traditionnelle au C.f.*, 30f., 45. Jules Bazin, "Le vrai visage de Marguerite Bourgeoys," *Vie des Arts* (Montréal), XXXVI (1964), 12–17.

LE BLANC (Le Bland), JEAN. *See* OUTOUTAGAN

LEBLOND, JEAN JACQUIÉS, *dit. See* JACQUIÉS

LEBLOND DE LATOUR, JACQUES, painter and wood-carver who taught at the school of arts and crafts at Saint-Joachim, parish priest of Baie-Saint-Paul; b. 14 Jan. 1671 at Bordeaux; d. 29 July 1715 at Baie-Saint-Paul.

His father, Antoine Leblond de Latour (b. *c.* 1630; d. 9 Dec. 1706) played a very important role in the artistic life of Bordeaux; in 1665 he was painter to the city hall of Bordeaux, in 1682 a member of the royal academy of painting in Paris, and in 1691 a founding member of the academy of painting and sculpture of Bordeaux (the only one outside Paris) and its first teacher; he was also a writer, having published in 1699 a *Lettre du sieur Leblond de Latour à un de ses amis, contenant quelques instructions touchant la peinture*. Jacques' older brother, Marc-Antoine (1668–1744), succeeded his father in his functions as painter to the city hall of Bordeaux, holding this position from 1690 to 1742. His younger brother, Pierre, born in 1673, went to America at the beginning of the 18th century as engineer in ordinary to the king; in 1720 we meet him again, in Louisiana.

Jacques Leblond de Latour is believed to have arrived in New France on 24 May 1690 when he was 19. There are no documents giving any information about his artistic training at that time, but it may readily be supposed that he did his apprenticeship as a painter with his father. He must have been well acquainted also with wood-carving, since there were numerous cabinet-makers skilled in wood-carving at Bordeaux. Possibly his departure had been motivated by his brother Marc-Antoine's appointment to his father's office; the number of masterships in a craft was limited at that period, and it was traditionally the eldest son who succeeded his father.

It is difficult to determine the exact date of the founding of the school of arts and crafts at Saint-Joachim. The institution, which had been created by Jean Talon* and Bishop LAVAL, was linked with the founding of the Petit Séminaire of Quebec in 1668. This school was situated near the site of the first church at Saint-Joachim, more than 25 miles from Quebec: "Instruction is given there in woodworking, wood-carving, painting, gilding, church decoration, masonry, and carpentry. There are also stone-cutters, shoemakers, edge-tool makers, locksmiths, and roofers who teach their trades to the Canadian youth. . . ." This document, cited by Amédée Gosselin, dates from 1685, but by 1675 various artisans were arriving in Canada, including "Michel Fauchois, apprentice wood-carver, hired for four years," and "Samuel Genner, a wood-carver, engaged for three years." They obviously came to lend their help to the

378

school which was being set up, since they were engaged by the seminary of Quebec. Bishop Saint-Vallier [LA CROIX], who visited the premises in 1685, wrote: "My main concern at Cap-Tourmente was to examine, each one in turn, 31 children whom two ecclesiastics from the Seminary were bringing up, 19 of them being directed to studying, and the remainder to learning a trade."

It was after Leblond de Latour's arrival in 1690 that the school experienced its years of greatest success, years during which the chapel of the seminary of Quebec was built. Nothing remains of this chapel, which was destroyed by fire in 1701. However, LE ROY de La Potherie's description gives us an idea of what it was like: "The wood carving in it, which is evaluated at 10,000 *écus*, is very beautiful; it was done by the members of the Seminary, who spared no expense to ensure that the work was perfect. The high altar is an architectural work in Corinthian style; the walls are covered with wainscoting and wood carving in which are set several large pictures. The decorations which go with them end up under the cornice of the severy vaulting, under which are diamond-shaped compartments adorned by painted and gilded wood carvings."

It is impossible to evaluate exactly Leblond de Latour's share in the work on the chapel of the seminary and the retables at Château-Richer, Sainte-Anne de Beaupré, and Ange-Gardien. No piece of wood carving can be attributed to him with certainty. When considering what remains today of the work at Ange-Gardien and Sainte-Anne de Beaupré, it must be kept in mind that these were undertakings in which the pupils from the school and wood-carvers such as Denis MALLET, Charles Vézina, and Pierre-Gabriel Le Prévost* participated.

The retable at Sainte-Anne de Beaupré was done around 1700 by the wood-carvers from the school at Saint-Joachim. The present-day commemorative chapel preserves what remains of it, including four pillars, a tabernacle, and two wooden statues representing St Magdalen and St John. A photo taken by Livernois in 1877 shows us the original lay-out of the retable before the church was demolished in 1878: one must refer to it to get an idea of the whole work, the architectural aspect of which was carefully worked out. The pillars, which are decorated at their base with garlands of flowers, enable us to link this work with that at Ange-Gardien, where similar pillars are to be found. The statues of St Magdalen and St John are by the same hand that did the two small angels of the Annunciation which decorate the tabernacle. The latter constitutes the principal feature of the whole work: even if it includes few outstanding decorative motifs, it strives for great architectural effect. In it are to be found various types of pillars, cornices, pediments, domes, balustrades, etc. Everything seems to be contrived to furnish an example of all the architectural elements which can enter into the composition of a tabernacle.

The retable at Ange-Gardien was much more richly decorated than that at Sainte-Anne de Beaupré; nevertheless, the same motifs are to be found in it. This retable, which was also done towards 1700, was altered several times prior to the burning of the church in 1931: at that time the parishioners saved most of it, and it was put back in the new church, where it remained until 1963. The high altar remains one of the most important pieces of wood carving in French Canada; much more elaborate than that at Sainte-Anne, it is also more subtle in its conception. Two large statues decorated the retable, those of St Michael and the Guardian Angel. They are of different workmanship from that of the statues at Sainte-Anne and seem to have been executed by a professional wood-carver who had been trained in Europe. On the other hand, the statuette which occupied the central niche of the high altar, a Virgin and Child, is certainly the work of a wood-carver who had received his training at Saint-Joachim: its stiffness and naïveté make it one of the most interesting pieces of wood-carving of this period.

Jacques Leblond de Latour took the ecclesiastical habit in 1696. He was not ordained a priest until 1706, and was appointed parish priest at Baie-Saint-Paul. There is little probability that he then continued to practise his craft as a wood-carver. But he was not only a wood-carver: his family background destined him to be a painter. Gérard Morisset attributes several works to him, among them a portrait of Bishop Laval which is preserved in the archbishop's palace in Quebec, and a portrait of Bishop Saint-Vallier in the Hôpital Général of Quebec.

JEAN TRUDEL

Archives municipales de Bordeaux, Registre des baptêmes de la cathédrale Saint-André. ASQ, MSS, 6. IOA, Dossier Jacques Leblond. Marius Barbeau, *Au cœur de Québec* (Montréal, 1934). Amédée Gosselin, *L'instruction au Canada sous le régime français (1635–1760)* (Québec, 1911), 361–63. Jean Palardy, *Les meubles anciens du Canada français* (Paris, 1963), 369–71. Harper, *Painting in Canada*. Morisset, *La peinture traditionnelle au C.f.*, 28–29. Charles Braquehaye, "Les peintres de l'hôtel de ville de Bordeaux," *Réunion des Sociétés des Beaux-Arts des Départements*, XXII (1898), 902–54; XXIII (1899), 595–639. Gérard Morisset, "L'école des Arts et Métiers de Saint-Joachim," SGCF *Mémoires*, XVI (1965), 67–73;

Le Bourguignon

"Généalogie et petite histoire, un maître-maçon d'autrefois, Claude Baillif," SGCF *Mémoires*, XVI, 131–37.

LE BOURGUIGNON, PIERRE COUTURIER, *dit*. See COUTURIER

LE BROCHET. *See* KINONGÉ

LE CASTOR. *See* LARGILLIER

LECHASSEUR, JEAN, secretary of Louis Buade* de Frontenac and of Intendant de MEULLES, lieutenant general of Trois-Rivières, seigneur of Rivière-du-Loup (Louiseville); b. *c.* 1633; d. 1 Sept. 1713, a bachelor.

Jean Lechasseur arrived in Canada in September 1672 with Frontenac, whom he served as a secretary for ten years. On 17 July 1683 Intendant de Meulles described him as the "former secretary to His Excellency the Comte de Frontenac, then governor of this country, and afterwards secretary to His Excellency the intendant," and specified that he had served his first master "honourably and faithfully."

The intendant retained his services until 1686. In the summer of that year, after Gilles de Boyvinet, the lieutenant general of Trois-Rivières, was drowned in the port of Quebec on his way back from France, Lechasseur was sent to Trois-Rivières to assume his office, according to Denonville [BRISAY] (10 Nov. 1686). On 19 August he took the oath before the Conseil Souverain.

Talon* had granted to the Sieur de Mannereuil, who was an officer in the Carignan regiment, the seigneury of Rivière-du-Loup. But as the beneficiary had not fulfilled his obligations, the land had reverted to the king's domain. On 20 April 1683 Le Febvre* de La Barre and de Meulles made it over to Lechasseur, adding two leagues to its depth, "considering that a large part of the said land grant is covered every spring by flood waters."

Lechasseur took possession of his domain on 17 July 1683. On 15 May 1688 he sold his seigneury to the explorer Nicolas PERROT. The latter did not pay the purchase price, however, and Lechasseur went to court to obtain either the payment of what was owed him or the reconveyance of his property. On 11 Oct. 1700 the Conseil Souverain, to which Perrot appealed after losing his case in the court of first instance, sentenced the explorer to return the seigneury or to pay 1,400 *livres* in beaver furs, representing the interest for seven years on the purchase price of 4,000 *livres*, plus 385 *livres*, 10 *sols*, 3 *deniers* to cover costs of ploughing and sowing. Lechasseur took back the property, which he sold again in 1701, to Michel Trottier, *dit* Beaubien.

Perrot was not the only person whom Lechasseur summoned before the courts. When he left for France in 1682, the governor owed his secretary wages amounting to 4,157 *livres*. To discharge his debt, the proud but impecunious governor had handed over to Lechasseur a bill for 2,000 *livres*, which Frontenac held against Cavelier* de La Salle. The latter although he recognized the debt could not honour it. On 14 May 1699 Lechasseur again importuned the Conseil Souverain, desperately trying to have this old debt repaid.

The burial certificate entered in the registry of the parish of Trois-Rivières on 2 Sept. 1713 gives Lechasseur's age as 80.

HERVÉ BIRON

AJTR, Registres d'état civil de Trois-Rivières, 2 sept. 1713. AQ, NF, Foi et hommage, I, 128. *Jug. et délib.* P.-G. Roy, *Inv. concessions*, III, 61–64; IV, 248. Jouve, *Les Franciscains et le Canada: aux Trois-Rivières*. P.-G. Roy, *La ville de Québec*, I, 379–80, 393; II, 418. Sulte, *Mélanges historiques* (Malchelosse), X, 7–65. P.-G. Roy, "Biographies canadiennes," *BRH*, XXI (1915), 284–85.

LECLERC, JEAN-BAPTISTE, king's carpenter at Trois-Rivières; baptized 23 Aug. 1681 at Quebec; eldest son of Robert Leclerc (1653–1731), the king's carpenter at Quebec, and Marie Jallais; d. 17 June 1739 at Trois-Rivières.

Leclerc moved to Trois-Rivières as a young man and there married Marguerite Pepin of Champlain on 10 Nov. 1704. Leclerc lived in the lower town and worked as a joiner, barn-builder, and house-framer. He took care of his aged father and acted as the latter's attorney. Like many craftsmen, both father and son were illiterate.

Jean-Baptiste Leclerc had been employed on crown projects before his appointment on 21 March 1739 by Intendant Hocquart* as king's carpenter in the town of Trois-Rivières. His official duties were to include the construction and maintenance of canoes and the heavy supply transports called *bateaux du cent*. He was to oversee the boatyard and personally to tour the forests to select and cut timber for the king's works. It was also understood that he would do general carpentry and, should the need arise, erect the carcan and gallows for the punishment of criminals. Leclerc died soon after his appointment and his son, Jean-Baptiste Le Clair (b. 1711, fl. 1743), who was a land surveyor and carpenter, was named as his father's successor.

PETER N. MOOGK

AJQ, Registres d'état civil de Notre-Dame de Québec, 1680–1685, f.100. AJTR, Greffe de Pierre Petit,

15 mars 1723, 7 juillet 1728; Greffe de J.-B. Pottier, 24 déc. 1703; Greffe d'Étienne Véron de Grandmesnil, 6 avril 1712; Registres d'état civil de Trois-Rivières, 1699–1727, 85f.; 1728–1740, 217. ASQ, Seigneuries, VII, 64. P.-G. Roy, *Inv. ord. int.*, I, 235; II, 265, 297. A. J. E. Lunn, "Economic development in New France, 1713–1760," unpublished Ph.D. thesis, McGill University, 1943, 278.

LE CONTE DUPRÉ, LOUIS (the name was sometimes written **Leconte, Lecompte, Dupré,** *dit* **Le Conte**), farmer, landowner, fur-trader, merchant and bourgeois at Bécancour, Champlain, and Montreal; b. in the parish of Pouzauges, in the province of Poitou, in 1654; d. in Montreal, in 1715.

Le Conte Dupré was the son of Charles Le Conte and Anne Defosse, both of the parish of Pouzauges. The date of his arrival in New France is unknown, but by 1672 he was established at Bécancour and probably engaged in farming. In the 1681 census he is described as a resident of Champlain, aged 27, the owner of one musket and three head of cattle, and having 18 acres under cultivation. He took up permanent residence in Montreal in 1683 and purchased land near Place du Marché and Rue Saint-Louis in 1694.

His marriage contract was drawn up on 29 Oct. 1683, but was not registered until 4 Nov. 1704. His wife was Marie-Catherine de Saint-Georges, the daughter of Adrien de Saint-Georges, esquire and member of the king's body-guard, and of Jeanne Guernon. They had a total of 16 children, some of whom, however, died young.

Little direct evidence of Le Conte Dupré's commercial activities exists. He was granted a fur-trading licence for the *pays d'en haut* in 1686, but sold it. He had business connections with CHARLES AUBERT de La Chesnaye, through whom he purchased on 26 Oct. 1681 the seigneury of Terrebonne belonging to André Daulier, Sieur Des Landes, an absentee landowner. Le Conte Dupré did not develop his lands, and in 1707 the intendant, JACQUES RAUDOT, permitted his tenants to build a mill. After Le Conte Dupré's death, his widow sold the lands to François-Marie BOUAT.

Property sales and seizures after his death and the commercial-marital links forged during his lifetime indicate that he was a man of some substance. He died in Montreal on 13 July 1715 at the age of 61.

CAMERON NISH

AJM, Greffe d'Antoine Adhémar; Greffe d'Hilaire Bourgine. AJQ, Greffe de Louis Chambalon, 9 nov. 1708, 13 août 1712. Collection Lafontaine (Sir George Williams Univ., Montréal), Registre de la cure de Montréal; Registre de la paroisse Notre-Dame de Montréal. *Les origines de Montréal* (Société hist. de Montréal, *Mémoires*, XI, 1917).

LE DORZ, BÉNIN (Bénigne), priest, Recollet, missionary at Louisbourg from 18 Sept. 1724 to 6 Oct. 1727; fl. 1718–36.

We do not know the dates of Le Dorz' birth and death. The only information that we have is for the years 1718–36. On 20 Aug. 1718, at the chapter of Pontivy, he was elected lecturer in theology and novice-master of that convent; subsequently he held various offices: novice-master of the convent of Bernon in 1719, guardian of that convent the following year, and guardian of Pontivy in 1721 and 1722. The registers of the parish of Notre-Dame-des-Anges at Louisbourg record his first act as a missionary on 14 Feb. 1724, when he baptized François, son of Joseph Lartigue* and Jeanne Dihars. The same year, in similar acts, he called himself parish priest (18 September), then superior and vicar general (1 October). The last act in which he entered the title of vicar general is dated 10 May 1725.

In 1726 Le Dorz, who was then superior of the Recollets of Île Royale, was suspended by Abbé Fornel* under peculiar circumstances. The Recollets of Louisbourg had a chapel which served as a parish church for the local settlers. Because of its diminutive size, they planned to build a church and a presbytery. As the first missionaries in the locality, they did not anticipate that the construction of a new church would call in question the authorization already acquired to have a parish there. Alleging as a pretext irregularities in the solemnizing of "three indefensible marriages" by Father Le Dorz, parish priest, and crediting without serious inquiry "all that the most malignant slander and calumny had brought to his ears," Bishop Saint-Vallier [LA CROIX] sent his vicar general, Abbé Fornel, to Louisbourg, with letters of appointment dated 3 Sept. 1726, to suspend the parish priest. This manœuvre had only one object: to transfer to the secular clergy a parish which the king, with the previous agreement of the bishop, had entrusted to the Recollets of Brittany. So it came about: on a fine November Sunday when nobody expected it, Abbé Fornel, at the end of high mass and in the presence of the parishioners, suspended Le Dorz from the execution of all his parish duties and appointed in his place Father Isidore Caulet, who refused the post.

On 11 March 1727, after a thorough scrutiny of the documents relating to this affair, the council of Marine decided to recall Father Le Dorz to France. The latter had already asked to be recalled, and as his mandate as superior was finished his return appeared to be the only way to calm the

Lefebvre

storm which had risen against the Recollets of Brittany. For these reasons Father Dirop, his provincial, while wishing that Father Le Dorz might be able to justify himself in the bishop's eyes, recalled him. In November or December 1727 Father Le Dorz returned to France, leaving the parish to the care of his *confrère*, Father Michel Le Duff. The Recollets of Brittany were to exercise their ministry at Louisbourg until the end of the French régime in Île Royale.

As for Father Le Dorz, he was re-elected guardian of Pontivy at the chapter of Port-Louis on 18 July 1733, and was still holding this office on 10 Aug. 1736.

JACQUES VALOIS

AN, Col., C¹¹ᴮ, 4, f.76; 8, ff.120, 125; 10, f.12. Hugolin [Stanislas Lemay], "Table nominale des Récollets de Bretagne, missionnaires et aumôniers dans l'île Royale (1713–1759)," *RSCT*, 3d ser., XXV (1931), sect.ɪ, 81–100; "Les Récollets de la province de Saint-Denis et ceux de la province de Bretagne à l'île Royale, de 1713 à 1731," *RSCT*, 3d ser., XXIV (1930), sect.ɪ, 77–113.

LEFEBVRE, THOMAS, voyageur, "seigneur of Koessanouskek, king's interpreter for the Abenaki language"; b. *c.* 1647, son of Jacques Lefebvre, cooper, and of Anne Anjoult, from Rouen (province of Normandy); d. sometime between 1713 and 1715.

We have no information about Lefebvre prior to 8 Sept. 1669, date of his contract of marriage in Quebec with Geneviève Pelletier (Peltier), Vincent Verdon's widow. After his marriage Lefebvre lived near the reservation at Sillery, where his first two children were baptized, and he established friendly relations with the Abenakis. By 1692 he was officially serving as an interpreter. Six years later he was in charge of an important fur-trading expedition which involved him in protracted differences with a creditor, Louis CHAMBALON, who had advanced the supplies both for the trip and for trading. In 1702 he was delegated by Brouillan [MOMBETON], the governor of Acadia, to go to Boston, and he was kept a prisoner there for some time.

To protect the frontier between continental Acadia and New England, which had been left in a precarious situation by the treaty of Ryswick (1697), the governor and the intendant, on 7 May 1703, granted as a seigneury to Thomas Lefebvre the territory of Koessanouskek (or Kouesanouskek), situated between Meniekec (today Owl's Head, opposite Rockland, Maine, on Penobscot Bay) and the St George River. The following year Colonel Benjamin CHURCH, who had set out from Boston, surprised and captured the interpreter and

two of his sons, Thomas and Timothée; they were not exchanged until the autumn of 1706. The buildings put up by Lefebvre and his sons had been burned down, and the war that followed prevented them from enjoying further use of their seigneury. The seigneury was, moreover, lost through the Anglo-Abenaki peace treaty of 1727.

HONORIUS PROVOST

AJQ, Greffe de François Genaple, 17 mars 1703. Church, *King Philip's war* (Dexter), II, 146–50, 154. *Coll. de manuscrits relatifs à la N.-F.*, II, 425, 427, 453, 455, 462, 602f. *Jug. et délib., passim*, especially VI, 560–67. Maine Hist. Soc., *Coll.*, 1st ser., IV (1856), 326; IX (1887), 79. P.-G. Roy, *Inv. des concessions*, IV, 178–79; *Inv. contrats de mariage*, IV, 88. J. P. Baxter, *The pioneers of New France in New England, with contemporary letters and documents* (Albany, 1894), 341–46. Coleman, *New England captives*, I, 93.

LEFEBVRE, *dit* **Laciseraye, MICHEL,** master-mason, land-surveyor and builder; born at Trois-Rivières in 1654, son of Pierre Lefebvre and of Jeanne Aunois; married Catherine Trottier of Champlain on 3 Nov. 1683, and had eight children; buried at Trois-Rivières 21 Oct. 1708.

Presumably this typical artisan-builder followed the normal practice of his kind and day, travelling about the colony to work on various buildings as opportunity afforded; occasionally too he surveyed land in the vicinity of Trois-Rivières. His only recorded activity as an artisan, however, is on the second parish church of Trois-Rivières in 1682–83, and on the first parish church of Lachine in 1702–3. A contract for the Trois-Rivières church exists, made between the Recollets under whose aegis it was built, and René Pelletier, carpenter; and there is also a notation in the *greffe* of Severin AMEAU giving Lefebvre the task of sheathing the building with boards and shingles for which the parish council gave him 350 *livres* plus the materials. Lefebvre being also a master-mason, it is reasonable to assume that he was responsible for the exterior appearance of the Trois-Rivières church. It has vanished without trace, but presumably it was similar to the one Lefebvre built at Lachine, whose appearance (aside from the bell-tower, rebuilt in 1718) is known from a drawing made before its demolition in 1869 (reproduced as Plate XXIX in Alan Gowans' *Church architecture in New France*).

It would be an error, however, to imagine that Lefebvre was its architect in any modern sense. Lefebvre represented the traditional "form-transmitting" folk builder, as contrasted with the modern idea of a "form-giving" architect. He incorporated in his architecture proportions and

Le Gardeur de Courtemanche

structure inherited through apprenticeship from a collective folk tradition (presumably that of Normandy, since his father came from Rouen) rather than any expression of personal taste or aesthetic ideas.

ALAN GOWANS

A. Roy, *Inv. greffes not.*, XI, 120, 121, 135, 224. É.-Z. Massicotte, "Les arpenteurs de Montréal," *BRH*, XXV (1919), 223. Tanguay, *Dictionnaire*, I, 365; VI, 263. Désiré Girouard, *Lake St. Louis, old and new, and Cavelier de La Salle* (Montréal, 1893), 45ff. Alan Gowans, *Church architecture in New France* (Toronto, 1955), 90, 131. Jouve, *Les Franciscains et le Canada: aux Trois-Rivières*, 32–34.

LE FEVRE, FRANÇOIS, priest, Sulpician, superior of the seminary of Saint-Sulpice in New France, grand vicar of the bishop of Quebec, ecclesiastical superior of the Hôtel-Dieu at Montreal, 1676–78, and of the sisters of the Congrégation de Notre-Dame, 1676–77; b. at Écouis, in the diocese of Rouen; d. 1718 at the Abbaye Saint-Victor, Paris.

Le Fevre entered the seminary of Saint-Sulpice in Paris in March 1667, and remained there until he received holy orders. He left for New France in July 1672, and for the next three years performed the functions of superior of the seminary of Saint-Sulpice in Montreal. Much to the annoyance of the missionaries of Kenté (Quinte) and the Sulpician superior in Paris, Le Fevre ordered the abandonment of the Kenté mission. In 1675 he returned to France, perhaps to explain his decision, but came back to the colony the following year as the official superior of the Sulpicians in New France.

Although Le Fevre's haughty and inconsiderate manner offended many of those with whom he worked during his remaining two years in the colony, his fervour, regularity, and strictness brought much-needed order to the Montreal seminary. In September 1677, he presented the letters of establishment for the Montreal seminary to the Conseil Souverain for registration. Before returning to France in October of the following year, he wisely refused Bishop LAVAL's offer of Île Jésus, on the basis that the seminary already held enough undeveloped land.

The various positions held by Le Fevre during the next few years seem indicative of his inability to work harmoniously with others. He was first posted to the Bourges seminary as director, but left for the Orient to work as a missionary in 1683. He probably never reached this destination for he was back in France in 1685 after having served in Rome for a short period as the representative of the bishops of the Levant. Three years later he entered an annex of the Paris seminary for ailing members of the order. This *Petite Communauté* was abolished in 1690, and Le Fevre then moved to the seminary where he died in 1718.

C. J. RUSS

ASSM, Biographies: François Le Fevre; Correspondance générale, 2e partie, lettres de M. Tronson, I, 8, 19. *Jug. et délib.*, II, 163f. Allaire, *Dictionnaire*, I, 332. Henri Gauthier, *Sulpitiana* (Montréal, 1926), 227.

LE GARDEUR DE COURTEMANCHE, AUGUSTIN, soldier, ambassador to the English and the Indians, commandant on the coast of Labrador; b. at Quebec, 16 Dec. 1663, fifth child of JEAN-BAPTISTE LEGARDEUR de Repentigny and Marguerite Nicollet, daughter of Jean Nicollet* de Belleborne; d. 29 June 1717.

Courtemanche's career falls into two periods: his military service and his life in Labrador. He was commissioned ensign in 1690, half-pay lieutenant in 1691, lieutenant in 1692, midshipman in January 1694, and given command of a company 1 April 1702. In 1689–90 he served under RENÉ ROBINAU de Portneuf on his expedition into New England, distinguishing himself during the capture of the fort at Casco Bay (near Portland, Me.). In 1690 he participated in the defence of Quebec when it was attacked by the English under William Phips*. In April the following year Governor Frontenac [Buade*] sent Courtemanche to Michilimackinac to inform the Indians of the upper nations of the great French victory.

In 1693 Courtemanche served under NICOLAS D'AILLEBOUST de Manthet against the Mohawks, and later that same year was given command of the post among the Miamis on the St Joseph River. In 1698 the governor of Montreal, Louis-Hector de CALLIÈRE, sent him to France to inform the king of Frontenac's death, and to request that Callière be promoted governor of New France in his place. Because he was successful in pleading Callière's cause over his rivals, Philippe de RIGAUD de Vaudreuil and Jean BOCHART de Champigny, Courtemanche was made captain in the governor's guards on his return.

Courtemanche's marriage on 20 July 1697 changed the whole course of his life. His wife, Marie-Charlotte Charest, was the widow of Pierre-Gratien Martel de Brouague whose brother, RAYMOND MARTEL, had commercial interests in Labrador. Courtemanche soon became interested in these and helped organize an expedition to the Labrador coast to explore the fishing and trading possibilities. In the autumn of 1700 he and Jean ENJALRAN were sent to the Ottawas to persuade

383

Legardeur de Repentigny

them to come down to Montreal to participate in treaty negotiations with the Iroquois. In the following spring, while he was still away, his wife engaged Pierre Constantin to go to the Rivière des Esquimaux (St Paul River) to trade with the Indians and set up a post on his behalf. On 17 Oct. 1702 Courtemanche was granted a concession (sometimes wrongly referred to as a seigneury) situated along the present-day Quebec and Labrador coast adjacent to the Strait of Belle Isle. It extended from the Kegaska River (Kégashka) to the Kessessakiou (Hamilton River), and gave Courtemanche for ten years the exclusive right to trade with the Indians and hunt for seals as well as permission to fish for whales and cod.

Courtemanche probably went to Labrador himself in 1704 and the following year wrote a memoir to the intendant, JACQUES RAUDOT, in which he enthusiastically described his explorations. He wrote glowingly of the superabundance of geese, ducks, caribou, beaver, seals, salmon, cod, and trout. That same year he moved his first post from Old Fort Bay to Baye de Phélypeau (Brador Bay) and built a new fort, Fort Pontchartrain. His plan to set up a whale fishery was well received by the king as whale oil was always a useful commodity in France.

Courtemanche was also on good terms with the Indians in the area. About 30 Montagnais families lived on his land, and were employed as hunters and trappers. In 1708 the minister informed him that the king had heard of his success with the Indians and hoped that he would also be as successful with the Eskimos, who had been extremely troublesome to the French fishing interests along the coast.

In 1711 Pontchartrain sent a dispatch to Courtemanche asking him to warn the governor that the English were preparing to attack New France with a large fleet under the command of Sir Hovenden WALKER. Courtemanche immediately sent his lieutenant, François Margane de Lavaltrie, with two Indians to warn Vaudreuil. Fortunately, however, the English expedition was wrecked in the Gulf of St Lawrence by fogs and gales.

In 1712 the Kegaska-Kessessakiou concession expired, but in 1714 the king granted Courtemanche for the rest of his life "la baye de Phelypeau" and "four leagues of frontage on the said coast to be taken two leagues above and two leagues below the said bay by four leagues in depth, and the islands in the said bay opposite the coast thus granted, with the exclusive right to take seals in the area and to fish concurrently with the other French subjects in the area . . . and to trade with the Indians." On 12 November of that

same year Courtemanche was appointed commandant for the king on the coast of Labrador with the authority to "settle and adjust the disputes which arise between His Majesty's subjects in connection with the situations of fisheries on the said coast."

Courtemanche planned to voyage to France to tell the new minister of Marine in person of all the advantages the crown could expect to extract from the Labrador coast, and also to lodge some complaints, chiefly about the trespass on his concession committed by his former employee, Pierre Constantin. Just as he was about to set sail a party of some 800 Eskimos appeared in the vicinity of his fort, causing much damage and stealing everything that was movable. He abandoned his plans and Madame Courtemanche went to France in his place. An anonymous writer of the period said: "The vigilance and gallantry displayed by M. de Courtemanche in opposing himself to a fleet of some 800 Indians [sic] and putting them to flight are well worth some recognition, at least a few presents; a man who is willing, for the service of the state, to live, practically alone, in an uninhabited country like Labrador, is almost priceless."

In 1716 Courtemanche wanted to build another fort on the Kessessakiou River to impress the Eskimos and protect the fishermen from attack. He petitioned Vaudreuil for permission to enlist 12 men to garrison the fort and requested an officer to command it. Unfortunately, the following year, a month after capturing the Eskimo girl, ACOUTSINA, Courtemanche died. His stepson, François Martel* de Brouague was appointed commandant in his place. Courtemanche's concession passed into the hands of Brouague (one quarter), Madame Courtemanche (one quarter), and their three daughters (one sixth each). Later, in 1722 when the concession was augmented, the family was to retain the same percentage of their holdings.

NORA T. CORLEY

"L'Ambassade de M. LeGardeur de Courtemanche: chez les Outaouais en 1691," APQ *Rapport, 1921–22,* 233–36. G.B., Privy Council, Judicial Committee, *In the matter of the boundary between the Dominion of Canada and the colony of Newfoundland in the Labrador peninsula . . .* (12v., London, 1926–27), VII, 3511–27. P.-G. Roy, *Inventaire de pièces sur la côte de Labrador conservées aux Archives de la Province de Québec* (2v., Québec, 1940–42), I; "La famille Legardeur de Repentigny," *BRH,* LIII (1947), 195–216. W. G. Gosling, *Labrador: its discovery, exploration and development* (London, 1910), 131–53.

LEGARDEUR DE REPENTIGNY, JEAN-BAPTISTE (also **Legardeur d'Arpentigny**), esquire, midshipman, councillor in the Conseil Souverain, son of Pierre Legardeur* de Repentigny and Marie Favery; b. 1632 at Thury-Harcourt in the province of Normandy; d. 9 Sept. 1709 at Montreal.

Legardeur arrived in Canada in 1636 with his parents. At an early age he was associated with the fur trade, and in 1660 was accused by Jean Peronne* Dumesnil of having killed Dumesnil's son Michel by a kick full in the face, following a dispute over the bartering of furs for alcohol. There was, however, no sequel to this accusation, which, well founded or otherwise, seems to have had no influence on his career. Indeed, on 6 Oct. 1663 he was elected the first mayor of Quebec, although he occupied this office for only one month, because the Conseil Souverain considered it unnecessary. On 2 May 1670 he received from his mother the seigneury of Repentigny, which the Compagnie de la Nouvelle-France had granted to her husband in 1647.

True to the military tradition of the Legardeur family, in 1665 he commanded a company of volunteers that succeeded in delivering Trois-Rivières, which was threatened by the Iroquois. In January 1666 he took part in the unfortunate expedition led by Rémy* de Courcelle against the Iroquois; in the autumn of the same year, he was in command of the Quebec militiamen during Prouville* de Tracy's campaign in the same region. He became a lieutenant in the colonial regular troops in 1688, a half-pay captain in 1692, and a midshipman in 1694. Callière wrote in regard to him in 1701 that he was a man "of good conduct and capable." When he retired in 1702 he drew an annual pension of 600 *livres*. He was appointed a councillor in the Conseil Souverain the following year, and was installed only on 16 Nov. 1705. Buade* de Frontenac had for him "a particular esteem and friendship."

In 1656 Legardeur had married Marguerite Nicollet, daughter of Jean Nicollet* de Belleborne, by whom he had 21 children. This large family was the cause of endless financial troubles which Frontenac, in his letters to the minister, often advanced as a reason for requesting from the king a pension for his "loyal servant." Despite the large number of fiefs that Legardeur had, he found himself, like the majority of the military and legal officers, often "reduced to dire straits."

ROBERT LAHAISE

AJM, Greffe de Claude Maugue, 21 sept. 1679. "Correspondance de Frontenac (1689–1699)," APQ *Rapport, 1927–28*, 85. *Jug. et délib.* Recensement du Canada, 1666 (APQ *Rapport*). P.-G. Roy, "Ce que Callières pensait de nos officiers," 326; *Inv. concessions*, I, 62; II, III, 26. Ivanhoë Caron, "Les censitaires du côteau Sainte-Geneviève (banlieue de Québec) de 1636 à 1800," *BRH*, XXVII (1921), 98. P.-G. Roy, "La famille Legardeur de Repentigny," *BRH*, LIII (1947), 195–98.

LEGARDEUR DE REPENTIGNY, MARIE-JEANNE-MADELEINE, *dite* **de Sainte-Agathe,** Ursuline nun; baptized 31 Jan. 1698 at Montreal, daughter of PIERRE LEGARDEUR de Repentigny and Agathe de Saint-Père*; d. 25 Feb. 1739 at the Ursuline convent in Quebec.

After her studies at the boarding-school of the Ursulines of Quebec, Madeleine Legardeur returned to her family, and soon began to shine in Montreal society. She was to marry her cousin, an officer in the colonial regular troops, but he died accidentally. At first she was deeply afflicted; then she began once more to frequent balls and promenades. In July 1717, perhaps because she had not recovered her peace of mind, she asked to be admitted to the Ursuline order of Quebec.

The annals of the convent relate that during the first years she underwent "the most violent temptations to renounce her vocation." To overcome them, she placed her trust in Notre-Dame du Grand Pouvoir; the annals add that her fits of anguish vanished. Mother Sainte-Agathe decided to offer a permanent testimony of her gratitude towards the Madonna. Thus, in 1724, was lighted "the lamp which does not go out." Her brother Jean-Baptiste-René gave 300 *livres* for the maintenance of the light.

Mother Sainte-Agathe died on 25 Feb. 1739 following a long illness, the germs of which she had been carrying, according to the annals of the convent, since she entered the noviciate.

MARIE-EMMANUEL CHABOT

AMUQ, Annales manuscrites. L.-A. Paquet, *Madones du diocèse de Québec* (Québec, 1929), 69–80. P.-G. Roy, *La ville de Québec*, II, 99f. *Les Ursulines de Québec* (1863–66), II, 105, 132–37, 234–36.

LEGARDEUR DE REPENTIGNY, PIERRE, military officer and seigneur; b. 10 March 1657 at Quebec, eldest son of JEAN-BAPTISTE LEGARDEUR de Repentigny and Marguerite Nicollet; d. 18 Nov. 1736 at Montreal.

Pierre Legardeur de Repentigny began his military career as a "petty officer"; in 1685, after serving for some years in this capacity, he was made an ensign in the colonial regular troops; he is thought to have served as such for two years. In April 1687 he obtained a commission, granted by BRISAY de Denonville, as a militia captain. It was probably in this capacity that he took part in the

Legardeur de Saint-Pierre

expedition against the Iroquois in the summer of 1687. In 1688 he received a commission as half-pay lieutenant which the king ratified on 16 March 1691.

At the time when the Iroquois were taking their revenge, spreading terror throughout the colony with the Lachine massacre, Denonville decided to abandon Fort Frontenac, which was vulnerable to Iroquois attacks. Legardeur de Repentigny offered his services to the governor to go and take the withdrawal order to the commandant of the fort, CLÉMENT Du Vuault de Valrennes. In 1691 Buade* de Frontenac gave him a commission as lieutenant on the active list; the king confirmed this commission two years later. In February 1693 he was in charge of a party made up of 600 Frenchmen and Indians; during the expedition three Mohawk villages were burned down and several prisoners were taken. The following year he was made a midshipman.

Finally, on 27 May 1706, Legardeur de Repentigny obtained the rank of captain in the colonial regular troops. His good service as a soldier earned him high praise; RIGAUD de Vaudreuil made this commendation of the old officer: "He is still a very good officer, although more fitted to serve in a fort than to march on a campaign." This was in 1722, when Legardeur was 65. In April 1733 his record of service was given final consecration in the form of the highest military honour bestowed in New France: he was made a knight of the order of Saint-Louis.

He was also a seigneur. On 20 Sept. 1680 his father made over to him Île Bourdon, which was near the family domain. To this property was added, on 4 June 1706, the sixth part of the Repentigny seigneury, a gift from his uncle Ignace Legardeur de Repentigny; Pierre thus became co-seigneur of Repentigny. And on 3 May 1715, at his wife's earnest request, he acquired the Lachenaye seigneury by auction, with a bid of 38,300 *livres*. He seems to have properly discharged his seigneurial duties towards the state, the church, and his copyholders.

On 26 Nov. 1685, at Repentigny, he had married Agathe de Saint-Père*, daughter of Jean de Saint-Père* and Mathurine Godé. As he was inclined to be indolent, and was rather easy-going, he was sometimes overshadowed by his active wife. Seven daughters and one boy were born of their marriage. He died on 18 Nov. 1736 at Montreal, and was buried the next day in the church there.

PAUL-ANDRÉ DUBÉ

AQ, NF, Aveux et dénombrements, 1, ff.136–44; NF, Foi et hommage, 2, ff.94–96; NF, Registre du Cons. sup., 29, ff.155f., 166v, 167, 167v, 168, 176v, 177; 30, ff.90, 90v; 32, ff.11v, 12, 41, 41v, 42; 36, ff.28v, 29; 39, ff.11, 11v, 12, 167; 40, ff.131v, 132, 132v; 45, f.58. ASQ, Fonds Verreau, Famille Le Gardeur de Repentigny et autres alliés; MSS, 132–33, 189. Baugy, *Journal* (Serrigny), 85. Lahontan, *Nouveaux voyages*, I, 176, 195. P.-G. Roy, *Inv. concessions*, I, 257–69; *Inv. ord. int.*, I, 79, 188, 259; II, 94, 106, 123, 192.

Bonnault, "Le Canada militaire," 474f. Fauteux, *Les chevaliers de Saint-Louis*, 128. Lorin, *Le comte de Frontenac*, 349f. P.-G. Roy, *Fils de Québec*, I, 44f. É.-Z. Massicotte, "Agathe de Saint-Père, dame Le Gardeur de Repentigny," *BRH*, L (1944), 202–7. P.-G. Roy, "La famille Legardeur de Repentigny," *BRH*, LIII (1947), 165–76, 195–216, 227–47.

LEGARDEUR DE SAINT-PIERRE, JEAN-PAUL, officer, fur-trader, interpreter, seigneur, son of JEAN-BAPTISTE LEGARDEUR de Repentigny and Marguerite Nicollet; b. at Quebec, 3 Oct. 1661; d. winter of 1722–23, probably at Chagouamigon (Chequamegon Bay in Lake Superior). Often confused with his brothers and cousins, he was usually referred to as Saint-Pierre or Sieur de Saint-Pierre.

In 1688 Saint-Pierre became an ensign, and for the rest of his life was prominent in military affairs. After 1690 most of his career was spent in the western country. He was at Fort Frontenac in 1689, however, and assisted in an attack on the Iroquois near Rivière des Prairies in 1695. CALLIÈRE, Frontenac [Buade*], and Vaudreuil [RIGAUD] consistently praised Saint-Pierre and gave him difficult missions in the west.

Saint-Pierre figured prominently in the LE PESANT affair in Detroit, 1706–7. Le Pesant, after instigating the Ottawa-Miami brawl at Detroit, fled to Michilimackinac. Saint-Pierre was instructed by Vaudreuil to apprehend him. This he did, but only after many trips between Montreal, Detroit, and Michilimackinac, numerous councils with the Indians, and much friction with Cadillac [LAUMET]. Cadillac accused Saint-Pierre of plotting against Detroit—in favour of Michilimackinac—but Vaudreuil's reports show that this was unlikely. One reason for Cadillac's anger was that Saint-Pierre had exposed Cadillac's brandy monopoly at Detroit.

In March 1711, Saint-Pierre was sent to Michilimackinac and Baie des Puants (Green Bay) to escort a party of Indians to a council at Montreal. In the fall of 1714 he was sent to Michilimackinac, where he helped LE MARCHAND de Lignery prepare for a spring offensive against the Foxes. Saint-Pierre acted as interpreter for LA PORTE DE Louvigny in the Fox war of 1716, and in the fall of that year he went to western Lake Superior to invite the Chippewas to a council in Montreal.

Saint-Pierre and the Chippewas met with Vaudreuil in July 1718. Fearing that the Fox-Chippewa feuds would disrupt the fur trade, Vaudreuil ordered Saint-Pierre, now a captain, to re-establish the post at Chagouamigon. Vaudreuil wrote in 1719 that "Saint-Pierre . . . has succeeded so well in pacifying them [the Chippewas] that they are now bent on keeping the peace."

Saint-Pierre visited with Charlevoix* at Michilimackinac in 1721, and probably went to Montreal several times before his death. It is likely that he died at his post in the winter of 1722–23. For 30 years he had been a reliable, intelligent, diplomatic officer in the western country. His greatest achievement had been as commandant at Chagouamigon. Because of his military ability and excellent relations with the Indians, this vital fur-trading centre was to know years of peace.

On 15 Sept. 1692, he had married Marie-Josette, daughter of MICHEL LENEUF de La Vallière, the elder; they had five children, of whom one, Jacques*, was to become more famous than his father.

DONALD CHAPUT

AN, Col., C¹¹ᴬ, 26, ff.75, 138. AQ, Coll. P.-G. Roy, Legardeur. Charlevoix, *History* (Shea), V, 190, 237n. "Correspondance de Frontenac (1689–99)," APQ *Rapport, 1927–28,* 19, 26, 58. "Correspondance de Vaudreuil," APQ *Rapport, 1939–40,* 389. *Découvertes et établissements des Français* (Margry), English MS translation, VI. *Michigan Pioneer Coll.,* XXXIII, 342–50, 354–58, 366–67, 582–83, 588–89. *NYCD* (O'Callaghan and Fernow), IX. Wis. State Hist. Soc. *Coll.,* XVI, 304–5, 311–12, 377, 380–81; XVII, 165–66. É.-Z. Massicotte, "Congés et permis déposés ou enregistrés à Montréal sous le régime français," APQ *Rapport, 1921–22,* 193, 195, 196, 199, 201, 203. "Répertoire des engagements pour l'Ouest," 202, 225. P.-G. Roy, "La famille Legardeur de Repentigny," *BRH,* LIII (1947), 195–216. E. M. Sheldon, *Early history of Michigan,* 271–75.

LEGARDEUR DE TILLY, PIERRE-NOËL, captain in the colonial regular troops, councillor of the Conseil Souverain, son of Charles Legardeur* de Tilly, also a member of the Conseil Souverain, and of Geneviève Juchereau de Maur; baptized 24 Dec. 1652 at Sillery; buried 13 Aug. 1720 at Saint-Antoine de Tilly.

He was the eldest son of a family of soldiers and he too had an honourable military career: ensign in the colonial regular troops in 1688, half-pay lieutenant a year later, lieutenant on the active list in 1692, midshipman in 1694, lieutenant in 1700, captain in command of a company in 1710. In 1701 CALLIÈRE makes mention of him as "a good officer."

In 1689 he was appointed councillor of the

Conseil Souverain in his father's absence; in 1695, however, he gave his position over to CHARLES AUBERT de La Chesnaye in payment of a debt of 6,500 *livres* that he and his father had contracted with Aubert.

All his life Legardeur de Tilly was beset by multiple pecuniary difficulties which he tried vainly to cope with through numerous real estate dealings. He even engaged in trade; he had cause to rue it, for on 29 Nov. 1679, four days after his offence, the Conseil Souverain sentenced him to a fine of 2,000 *livres* for trading in furs "in the Indian settlements and in the depths of the woods."

In 1675 he had married Marguerite Volant, who bore him two daughters. In 1680 he married again, this time with Madeleine, the daughter of Pierre BOUCHER, the former governor of Trois-Rivières. Thirteen children were born of this marriage. At his death his wife and children were left destitute.

ROBERT LAHAISE

AJM, Greffe de Jacques Bourdon, 24 nov. 1680. Caron, "Inventaire de documents," APQ *Rapport, 1940–41,* 444. *Jug. et délib.,* II, 343; III, 398, 404. Recensement du Canada, 1666 (APQ *Rapport*). P.-G. Roy, *Inv. coll. pièces jud. et not.,* II, 14; *Inv. concessions,* II, 137; III, 88; IV, 102; *Inv. ins. Cons. souv.,* 78; *Inv. jug. et délib., 1717–1760,* VI, 165, 218f., 222; *Inv. testaments,* II, 46; "Les conseillers au Conseil souverain de la Nouvelle-France," *RSCT,* 3d ser., IX (1915), sect.I, 173–87.

LÉGER DE LA GRANGE, JEAN, surgeon, ship's captain, merchant, and privateer; b. 19 June 1663 (N.S.), at Abiac, diocese of Limoges, son of Élie Léger and Jeanne Félix; married first to Louise Fauvel (1691), and later to Marie Des Reaux; d. possibly in 1736, in France.

Beginning his life in Canada as a surgeon, La Grange must have turned to the sea early, for by 1696 he was commandant of one of PIERRE LE MOYNE d'Iberville's ships, the *Wesp,* in the expedition against Newfoundland. By 1700 he had command of ships of the Compagnie du Canada and at the same time was known as a merchant in Quebec. Late in 1703, with business falling off and little to satisfy the need for adventure felt by the youth of the colony, La Grange obtained permission from RIGAUD de Vaudreuil and François de Beauharnois* de La Boische to lead another expedition against the English in Newfoundland. He interested some merchants such as NICOLAS DUPONT de Neuville, Louis PRAT, and Antoine PASCAUD in the venture, and thus bought and equipped two ships; La Grange also found at least 26 men willing to provide their own arms and sign on as crew with no wages but with the

Le Gouès de Sourdeval

expectation of a share in the booty. MOREL de La Durantaye and DENIS-JOSEPH JUCHEREAU de La Ferté were part of this crew. One of the merchants, Claude Pauperet of Quebec, and La Grange were to captain the two ships, the *Joybert* and the *Philipeau*. La Grange had over-all command. Attacking the port of Bonavista on 29 Aug. 1704 (18 August, o.s.), they burned two smaller ships and captured the 250-ton *Pembroke Galley* of London, which was armed but burdened with about 2,500 quintals of dry cod. The attack was bravely but vainly resisted by Captain Michael GILL.

The booty was divided up at Quebec, each man of the crew receiving about 40 *écus*; some cod was sold there to lighten the ship in case of attack en route to Europe. Ironically, the ship was re-captured by the English between Bilbao and La Rochelle after the fish had been sold. La Grange's daring example inspired ALEXANDRE LENEUF de Beaubassin and others to enter privateering, though none seems to have matched La Grange's success. La Grange was rewarded with a captaincy in the king's navy, a rank he held for several years.

He is reported to have been at Fort Bourbon on Hudson Bay during the winter of 1709–10. Later he served for a long time as chief surgeon at Louisbourg until illness forced his retirement in 1736. He died in France, possibly later that year.

DAVID LEE

AN, Col., B, 19, f.20; 27, f.94v; 30, f.16; 49, f.162v; 64, f.117; C¹¹A, 21, f.50ff.; 22, ff.4, 71; C¹¹B, 18, f.115. PAC, FM 6, A 2, 3c (Minutes Rivière et Soulard), X, pp.252–68. Charlevoix, *History* (Shea), V, 169–70. "Correspondance de Vaudreuil," APQ *Rapport, 1938–39*, 128, 147. [Jérémie], *Twenty years of York Factory* (Douglas and Wallace). Gagnon, "Noms propres au Canada français," 119. Le Jeune, *Dictionnaire*. Prowse, *History of Nfld.*, 239–40. [P.-G. Roy], "Un corsaire canadien: Jean Léger de La Grange," *BRH*, XXIV (1918), 33–48, 65–76, 97–104.

LE GOUÈS DE SOURDEVAL, SÉBASTIEN, commandant on Île Saint-Pierre; b. 1657 at Bayeux in the lower part of the province of Normandy; d. 1710 at Saint-Malo.

According to the census of the French settlers on the south coast of Newfoundland in 1698, there was living at Petit Plaisance a certain Sébastien Le Gouès, Sieur de Sourdeval, aged 41. He owned six muskets, a cow, a house, and a fishing room (section of beach) capable of taking the catch of six shallops. Being a nobleman, he asked to be exempted from the corvées required of the fishermen. In a report dated April 1700 Pontchartrain, who was secretary of state for the Marine, decided to maintain him in his fishing establishment.

Two years later, on 1 March 1702, the Sieur de Sourdeval was appointed "commandant for the king on the Îles Saint-Pierre," with the pay of a company ensign, namely 480 *livres*. In a long letter dated 11 Oct. 1702, Sourdeval recounts the events which followed his taking over of the islands. Having arrived at Saint-Pierre on 25 July, he organized "an enclosure measuring 100 paces" built by a settler, and fortified it as best he could. On 7 October two English ships of 60 guns landed a detachment which burned the church and two houses. With a small cannon he forced them to re-embark, but the next day the English returned with 400 men, who laid siege to the tiny fort. Sourdeval was subjected to their fire for several hours. The English called upon him to surrender, threatening to put all the settlers to the sword. As his gun-carriages were broken and he had only 25 muskets, 2 swords, and 2 pistols, Sourdeval capitulated. The English left him 5 muskets and some bread, and set off again after burning everything. They handed over to him 52 prisoners whom they had taken at Trepassey Bay and whom they did not know what to do with (*see* LEAKE). At the end of his letter, Sourdeval implored the king to give him the means to build a strong fort to protect the settlers from their enemies. Finally he asked for an increase in his salary.

In his official correspondence PASTOUR de Costebelle, the governor of Placentia (Plaisance), often praised Sourdeval, declaring him to be punctilious and vigilant in everything concerning His Majesty's service. He considered that the salary given to Sourdeval should be raised to 600 *livres*.

On 1 Dec. 1707 Sourdeval reported that Île Saint-Pierre had again been attacked by the English, who had landed a number of men to hunt for him in the woods, where he had taken refuge with a few settlers. He added "that he inflicted losses on one of their parties that he surprised as it was moving forward unwarily." The commander of the English vessel summoned him to surrender, threatening otherwise to burn everything, but when Sourdeval refused to give in, the commander did not carry out his threat and sailed away, leaving all his prisoners on land and having burned nothing.

In 1709 Sourdeval again asked for an increase in his salary, which was still that of a company ensign. He also wished to be granted the cross of the order of Saint-Louis, pointing out that his family was related to several noble families of France, among others the La Rochefoucaulds, La Vieuvilles, Vitrys, and Matignons. (Furthermore, according to Costebelle, Sourdeval had come to Newfoundland following family setbacks.) These requests do not seem to have been listened to.

Sourdeval must have been in poor health at that period. He returned to France and died at Saint-Malo, where he was buried on 9 March 1710.

CHARLES DE LA MORANDIÈRE

[In 1694 Sébastien Le Gouès de Sourdeval had married Catherine Le Baudy, the widow of Germain de Tour. One of the daughters by the first marriage, Anne de Tour, in her turn married Pastour de Costebelle, who later on occasionally referred to Sourdeval as his father-in-law; in reality the latter was his father-in-law only indirectly. C. M.]

Archives d'Ille-et-Vilaine (Rennes), E, État civil de Saint-Malo. AN, Col., B, 22, 23, 25, 27, 29, 30; C^{11C}, 3, 5; C^{11D}, 7. BN, MS, NAF 9283 (Margry). Le Blant, *Philippe de Pastour de Costebelle.*

LE MARCHAND DE LIGNERY, CONSTANT, esquire, lieutenant and midshipman in France, lieutenant and captain in Canada, knight of the order of Saint-Louis, twice commandant at Michilimackinac, town major of Trois-Rivières; b. *c.* 1663 at Charentilly, near Tours; d. 19 Feb. 1731 at Trois-Rivières.

He was the son of Joseph Le Marchand de Lignery, esquire and Marguerite Du Sillar. He began his military career as a lieutenant in the Régiment d'Auvergne in 1675. In 1683 he transferred to the navy and served as a midshipman in the port of Rochefort. Four years later he came to Canada as a half-pay lieutenant.

Lignery did not play a prominent part in the Iroquois war, but he did make a favourable impression on his superiors for he is frequently referred to as a "good officer" in the colony's military rolls. He was promoted to the rank of lieutenant in 1688 and to that of captain in 1705. Five years later, Philippe de RIGAUD de Vaudreuil planned to send Louvigny [LA PORTE] and Lignery together to reoccupy the strategic post of Michilimackinac, abandoned by royal orders since 1696. Lignery at first was to serve in a subordinate capacity, but the governor expected him to become fully conversant with the affairs of the post and qualified to take command there in a year or two. In 1712, when war with the Fox Indians broke out and Louvigny found himself unable to leave for the west, Vaudreuil decided to send Lignery at the head of a small party to take possession of the post.

In 1715 Lignery was chosen by Claude de RAMEZAY, acting governor of New France, to command a major expedition against the Foxes. Ramezay instructed him to assemble the coureurs de bois and northern Indians and to lead them to the Chicago portage. There they would join forces with a second corps, recruited among the native tribes of the southern Great Lakes, and together move against the enemy. Unfortunately, a series of mishaps prevented the execution of this project. The southern contingent failed to assemble as planned and Lignery himself never left Michilimackinac with his army. The supply convoy he was expecting from Montreal did not arrive on time, and he was unable to control the unruly French volunteers, most of whom preferred trading with the Indians to making preparations for war. Although a disappointed Ramezay criticized Lignery for his actions at Michilimackinac, the primary cause of the campaign's failure was not faulty leadership but bad planning and lack of discipline in the army, which because of the court's refusal to subsidize the venture had to be made up entirely of Indians and coureurs de bois.

In 1722, shortly after having been awarded the cross of the order of Saint-Louis, Lignery returned to command at Michilimackinac after an absence of approximately three years. The Foxes had just resumed their war against the French and their allies and were delivering their most destructive blows against the white and native populations of the Illinois country, which formed part of Louisiana. Lignery appears to have been unmoved by the plight of the sister colony, for he adopted a policy of conciliation towards the Foxes that was primarily designed to preserve peace in Canada's part of the west. Such conduct reflected Vaudreuil's desire to spare Canada the calamity of another Indian war and perhaps also Lignery's fear that such a conflict would disrupt the fur trade, in which he was now actively engaged. In 1724, Lignery negotiated the notorious treaty by virtue of which the Foxes ended their war on the Chippewas but continued the one they were waging on the Illinois Indians. Although he claimed that he had done his best to include the latter in the settlement, the officials in Louisiana and Versailles felt, perhaps with some justification, that Vaudreuil and Lignery had sacrificed the southern colony to the Foxes to prevent it from sharing in the western fur trade. In 1726, Lignery was sent back to Baie des Puants (Green Bay) by CHARLES LE MOYNE de Longueuil, acting governor of Canada, to renegotiate the treaty. This time, the commandant of Michilimackinac reported that he had obtained from the Foxes the promise that they would remain at peace with all the French allies.

Late in 1726 a new governor, Charles de Beauharnois* de La Boische, arrived in Canada apparently determined to begin his administration with a resounding military victory that would

Le Moyne d'Iberville

establish his reputation among all the Indian tribes. In 1728 he sent against the Foxes an army of 450 French and over 1,000 Indians under the command of Lignery. This force, the largest ever to advance so far into the interior, failed to come to grips with the elusive enemy. The latter fled westward, and the French and their allies had to be satisfied with burning their villages and ruining their crops. Beauharnois blamed Lignery for the army's failure to engage the Foxes in battle and made such serious accusations against him in his report to the ministry that Maurepas decided to have him tried by a council of war. Lignery stood accused of having mismanaged the supplies and of having marched his men at such a leisurely pace that the Foxes had been given ample time to make good their escape; of having refused, in spite of a disabling illness from which he was suffering, to allow Beaujeu [Liénard*], his first lieutenant, to assume command of operations in enemy territory; of having abandoned large quantities of merchandise at Michilimackinac on the return trip to Canada to make room, it was suggested, for beaver pelts. After hearing several witnesses and reviewing all the evidence, the council of war unanimously dismissed these charges as unfounded and acquitted Lignery, but the ordeal had apparently been too much for the old officer. He died a few months later in Trois-Rivières where he had been named town major in 1728.

In Montreal, on 10 Nov. 1691, he had married Anne Robutel de La Noue, daughter of the seigneur of Île Saint-Paul. Seven sons and two daughters were born of their marriage. The best known of these was François-Marie*, captain in the colonial regular troops and knight of the order of Saint-Louis, who was fatally wounded by the English during an engagement near Fort Niagara in the summer of 1759.

YVES F. ZOLTVANY

AJM, Greffe de Bénigne Basset, 17 nov. 1691 (Lignery's marriage contract). AN, Col., B, 33, 34, 35, 36, 37, 44, 45, 47, 48, 50, 52, 53, 54; C¹¹ᴬ, 22, 31, 34, 35, 44, 46, 47, 48, 49, 51, 56; D²ᶜ, 47, 49, 222; E, 125 (dossier de Lignery); F³, 9.

Emmanuel Crespel, *Travels in North America* (London, 1797). Father Crespel*, a Recollet friar, accompanied the expedition of 1728 against the Foxes as chaplain; his book contains an account of this campaign. The most important documents relating to Lignery's career in the west are printed in Wis. State Hist. Soc. *Coll.*, XVI, XVII. Massicotte, "Répertoire des engagements pour l'Ouest." P.-G. Roy, *Les officiers d'état-major*, 162–66. Kellogg, *French régime*. P.-G. Roy, "A propos des Le Marchand de Lignery ou Ligneris," *BRH*, XLIX (1943), 300–3.

LE MOYNE D'IBERVILLE (from a fief held by his father's family, near Dieppe, in the province of Normandy) **ET D'ARDILLIÈRES** (from a property he acquired in the province of Aunis near Rochefort), **PIERRE,** soldier, ship's captain, explorer, colonizer, knight of the order of Saint-Louis, adventurer, privateer and trader, the most renowned son of New France; baptized 20 July 1661 at Ville-Marie (Montreal); d. probably at Havana, Cuba, probably on 9 July 1706 of an unspecified illness, buried the same day, at Havana, in the Church of San Cristóbal.

Pierre Le Moyne d'Iberville was the third and most famous son of Charles Le Moyne* de Longueuil et de Châteauguay and of Catherine Thierry. He had two sisters and eleven brothers; nearly all of his brothers rose to military fame in America, and several died in battle. Iberville was accompanied by one or more of his brothers in all save two of his major campaigns.

Iberville's father, Charles Le Moyne, was a notable of the colony, a director of the Compagnie du Nord. Coming from Dieppe to New France at the age of 15 in 1641, the elder Le Moyne began as an indentured servant of the Jesuit missionaries, serving in the distant Huron missions where he learned several dialects of the Huron and Iroquois language group. In 1646 he had settled at Ville-Marie where he took part with other members of the community in frequent skirmishes against the Indians. On more peaceful occasions he served as official interpreter and emissary to the Indians on behalf of the authorities of New France. His varied services were rewarded by large grants of land in the Montreal area, most of them south of the island, and in 1668 by letters patent of nobility. He was active in the fur trade, particularly after the founding of the Compagnie du Nord in 1682, in which he held an investment of 4,440 *livres* at his death in 1685. His house was the finest in Montreal, and he was reputed to be among the wealthiest citizens of Montreal of his day.

Little is known of the youth of Pierre Le Moyne d'Iberville save that he was confirmed by Bishop LAVAL in Montreal in May 1669. Judging from his later correspondence, whatever formal schooling he received must have been rudimentary. It would seem that he prepared from an early age for a career as a seaman. He apparently sailed frequently in his father's boat on the St Lawrence, and went to France on several occasions. In 1683, for example, Governor Le Febvre* de La Barre entrusted him with his dispatches to the court. In 1686, just as he had begun his career as a fighting man as part of the expedition led by the Chevalier de Troyes* to James Bay, a paternity suit was brought against Iberville by the guardians of one Jeanne-Geneviève Picoté de Belestre. She accused him of seducing her under promise of marriage, and named him as the father of her expected child. In spite of the considerable influence of Iberville's family in the colony, the personal intervention of Governor Denonville [BRISAY], and his own prestige following the James Bay campaign, the Conseil Souverain found him guilty in October 1688 and ordered him to take charge of the child, a daughter, until her 15th year. In order to have her honour fully restored, Mademoiselle de Belestre desired Iberville to marry her; he was not bound by the council to do so. It was not until 8 Oct. 1693, after a long courtship, that he finally married Marie-Thérèse, the daughter of François Pollet* de La Combe-Pocatière (d. 1672), who in 1665 had come to New France with the Carignan-Salières regiment; her mother was Marie-Anne Juchereau de Saint-Denis. At the time of her marriage to Iberville she was 21 years old, "a lovely and very sensible Canadian woman."

Iberville's career in the service of France in America began in 1686, when he, along with two of his brothers, Jacques*, Sieur de Sainte-Hélène and PAUL, Sieur de Maricourt, took part in an expedition against the English posts of the Hudson Bay region. In the 1660s the French fur-traders Médard Chouart* Des Groseilliers and Pierre-Esprit RADISSON had come to the daring conclusion that the best furs were to be found in the colder regions of the north and that access to these furs could most easily be had via Hudson Bay. They failed, however, to interest their own compatriots in increasing the already heavy costs of administration and defence. The adventurers then made a dramatic bid to generate some enthusiasm for the scheme in England. In spite of difficulties the *Nonsuch*, with Groseilliers on board, was sent to Hudson Bay in 1668, and two years later Charles II granted a charter to the "Governor and Company of Adventurers of England tradeing into Hudson's Bay." By the terms of its charter, the company was granted lordship over the soil and exclusive trade in all the lands of the Hudson Bay drainage basin. Stations were established at the mouths of the rivers and soon the Indians of the area found it more convenient to carry their furs to the English nearby than to the French at Montreal. Following this pre-empting of the fur trade of Hudson Bay, a group of merchants, led by CHARLES AUBERT de La Chesnaye, founded the rival Compagnie du Nord in 1682. At the same time, there developed among the officials and leading merchants of New France a movement, inspired in part by imperial considerations but mostly by the commercial interest of the company, to drive the English by force from Hudson Bay. Ironically, meanwhile, in London, the two crowns were attempting to settle

their respective claims in North America, and, pending a definite settlement, to prevent any acts of hostility between their subjects. When word of these negotiations reached Quebec, however, Governor Denonville had already authorized the company to organize an expedition to seize interlopers and set up rival French posts at the mouths of the rivers flowing into the northern bay. To the 70 or so Canadian voyageurs under the Le Moyne brothers, who were entrusted by the company with its interests, Denonville, by way of official support from the crown, added 30 regular troops. He placed the expedition under the overall command of Pierre de Troyes, whom he was later to describe as the colony's most able captain. Despite Troyes' ability, the success of the venture resulted from the voyageurs' expertness in the northern wilderness and their respect for the enterprise of their leaders, in particular for that of Jacques de Sainte-Hélène and Pierre d'Iberville. Indeed had it not been for the endurance of all these men, inured to the forests and waterways and having had wide experience in winter travel over long distances, the party would probably never have reached James Bay.

The journey was made by way of the turbulent Ottawa River route to Lake Temiscaming, thence by a chain of lakes and streams and exhausting portages to the Moose River. After 85 days of incredible hardship and constant peril, during which the men at times sank into a despair bordering on mutiny, the expedition arrived before Moose Fort (modern Moose Factory) on Hayes Island at the mouth of the Moose River on the south shore of James Bay. Unmindful of their orders and violating the peace which reigned officially between the two crowns, the troops stormed the fort. Though the post was quickly subdued, one perilous incident occurred which founded Iberville's reputation for bravery. Leading the way inside the palisade through the gate, with sword in one hand and pistol in the other, Iberville found himself alone inside the stockade with the defenders, who had reclosed the gate before his companions could follow. Flailing away while his men laboured to batter the gate open again, Iberville held the English at bay until his companions finally entered. The 17 Englishmen, left leaderless by John Bridgar*'s departure the day before for Charles Fort (modern Rupert House), quickly surrendered. Troyes then determined to strike as well as the three James Bay posts still in English hands: Charles Fort, 100 miles east by land, Albany Fort, 95 miles northwest, and a storage depot on Charlton Island. While he and Sainte-Hélène took Charles Fort on 3 July, Iberville and 13 men captured Bridgar's vessel, the

Le Moyne d'Iberville

Craven, anchored in the harbour, after which the party returned to Moose Fort. Despite dwindling food supplies the expedition decided to push on to Albany Fort. Its 30 defenders were promptly forced to surrender unconditionally on 25 July and to see its defences put to the torch, as were those on Charlton Island. Having thus completely disrupted English trade at the "Bottom of the Bay," Troyes departed, leaving 40 Canadians under Iberville, who was made governor of the three posts, now renamed Saint-Louis (Moose), Saint-Jacques (Rupert) and Sainte-Anne (Albany). Iberville and his brother Sainte-Hélène had unquestionably been the outstanding figures of the campaign. A new era of Anglo-French relations in North America had begun.

Iberville took up his new command in August 1686. Despite the presence of the English in the Port Nelson region, and the much more serious threat of dwindling foodstuffs, he and his men wintered at Moose Fort. When no supplies had arrived by the late summer of 1687, Iberville returned south, first to Quebec, then to France, leaving a dozen men at James Bay. His task in France during the winter of 1687–88 was twofold: to put forward the advantages of the sea approach to the fur trade of Hudson Bay, in which he personally was greatly interested, and to solicit on behalf of the Compagnie du Nord the assistance required to strengthen its newly acquired position, particularly a shipment of trade goods with which to lure the Indians away from Port Nelson. In this mission he was successful, and, most important, he obtained for the company an excellent escort vessel, the *Soleil d'Afrique*, of which he himself took command. Returning to James Bay by way of Quebec in the summer of 1688, he prepared for immediate shipment of the furs that had accumulated.

Iberville's next encounter with the enemy occurred in September 1688 when the English tried to recoup their losses of 1686. Just as he was leaving Fort Sainte-Anne in a small vessel carrying a shipment of furs for the Compagnie du Nord, two armed English vessels, attempting to re-establish Albany Fort, blockaded him before he could sail out of the Albany River. The onset of winter froze all three vessels in the river, thus prolonging the confrontation to the following summer. The winter of 1688–89 was characterized by treachery and bad faith on both sides. Iberville made himself notorious in this regard, refusing the English permission to hunt for fresh game, and thus encouraging the spread of scurvy among them. Furthermore, when the dread epidemic did break out, the French commander invited the English surgeon to leave camp and hunt for fresh

meat, and then promptly took him prisoner. Only three Englishmen were lost in actual fighting, but 25 died of scurvy and exposure. Under these circumstances, the English were finally compelled to capitulate; Iberville's 16 Canadians, as ruthless as their leader, were better suited to this particular kind of warfare than were their 85 foes, who, far from being fighting men, were merely dispirited civilian servants of the English company. Iberville left James Bay in September 1689, after capturing another English vessel in July. Though the English still remained in possession of Port Nelson, he had frustrated their attempt to re-establish themselves in the bottom of the bay. He arrived in Quebec on 28 October, toughened by the strenuous campaign which had begun in March 1686, and laden down with English prisoners and booty, and, more important, with prize furs.

Iberville had returned to Quebec from James Bay just in time to take part in the winter campaign of 1690 which Governor Frontenac [Buade*] was organizing against the English colonies to the south. In Europe, the league of Augsburg had declared war on France in May 1689 and the conflict had extended to the colonies as well. In America the war became a *guerre de course* characterized by rapid hit-and-run attacks. The Iroquois, encouraged, supplied, and armed by the English colonies, had resumed their attacks on the Canadian settlements along the south shore of the St Lawrence. In a devastating surprise attack in August 1689 (news of the declaration of war had reached the English colonies before it reached Canada) the Iroquois ravaged the countryside around Lachine. In the wake of this incident and the several that preceded and followed it into the autumn of 1689, Frontenac, who had returned as governor for a second term in October 1689, determined to restore the prestige of France among her Indian allies and carry her vengeance to the heart of the English colonies. In the absence of assistance from France, her hands tied by the conflict in Europe, Frontenac gathered three raiding-parties of Canadian irregulars and Indian allies. One detachment was to attack either Albany or Corlaer (Schenectady, N.Y.) under the joint command of Jacques Le Moyne de Sainte-Hélène and NICOLAS D'AILLEBOUST de Manthet. Iberville served as second in command, and a third brother, François Le Moyne* de Bienville also accompanied the expedition. Of the 210 men, 114 were Canadians and 96 were Indians.

The force arrived unnoticed at Corlaer about midnight on 18 February. Finding no sentinels posted and one of the gates of the stockade ajar ("ye inhabitants being so negligent & Refractory"), the men silently took up stations at strategic points throughout the village in order to prevent any escape which might carry the alarm prematurely to Albany, a few miles to the south. Then, two hours before dawn, the invaders, with savage war cries, threw themselves ruthlessly on the sleeping inhabitants, just as the Iroquois had done at Lachine the previous August. Virtually the entire settlement was pillaged and burned; some 60 inhabitants were massacred, 25 were taken prisoner and about 50 were spared. Before the day was out the attackers had turned their backs on the scene of devastation, and had set off again for Montreal, taking 50 horses loaded with plunder. The return journey was characterized by much over-confidence, straggling, and general insubordination on the part of both the Canadians and the Indians. Almost within sight of Montreal a band of Mohawks caught up with the troop and captured 18 stragglers. Troyes had deplored similar misconduct during the 1686 journey to James Bay. The guerilla exploits recorded at James Bay in 1686 and at Corlaer in 1690 shed light on the personalities of men such as the Le Moyne brothers, especially on that of Iberville himself. Inspired by the techniques, the endurance, and even the cruelty of the Indians, they and their followers had come to be as ruthless—if not more so—than the Iroquois themselves. No other circumstance seems to have been more instrumental in delaying the eventual fall of New France until 1760 than the presence on its frontiers of small bands of hardy men adapted to the peculiarities of warfare and travel in America, and of leaders capable of overcoming their insouciance. Certainly the Canadians led by men like Iberville were far better soldiers, under North American conditions, than were the regular troops sent from France.

Iberville was rewarded for his part in the raid on Corlaer with a grant of land on Baie des Chaleurs, which he promptly disposed of. He was neither interested in nor temperamentally suited to the life of a seigneur, especially while the Hudson Bay question remained unsettled. Fortunately, in 1690, with France and England at war, the task of expelling his English rivals from the northern regions was made easier for Iberville. In accordance with his 1689 commission to command throughout the northern sea, Iberville left Quebec for Hudson Bay in July 1690, but with an inadequate complement of three small vessels carrying only 30 guns and 80 men. Arriving before York Fort in late August, he found the English on the alert, and was forced to flee from an enemy ship of 36 guns. He escaped and decided to attack instead New Severn (Neue Savanne), an outpost of York Fort, some 250 miles southeast. This

station was so weak that its commander, Thomas Walsh, blew up the buildings and fled without resisting. Iberville claimed he salvaged 100,000 *livres* worth of pelts, a figure which E. E. Rich feels is exaggerated. Iberville probably wintered in James Bay before returning to Quebec in October 1691 and thence to France. Yet the goal of the French remained unattained for the English flag still flew at York Fort.

The expulsion of the English from Hudson Bay was to elude Iberville for several years to come. He spent the following winter preparing his 1692 campaign to the bay, and received general assurances of naval support. The favourable dispositions of the ministry of Marine were frustrated, however, when Iberville's two frigates were ordered, for reasons of economy, to convoy supply ships to New France. Thus hampered and delayed, his squadron did not reach Quebec until 19 August, too late to continue to York, a further journey of 50 days, before the early winter ice. Frontenac therefore ordered Iberville's vessels to patrol New England's shores for the purpose of harassing the English settlements. All along the coast, however, from New York to Pemaquid, every settlement was awaiting the French. Iberville sailed for France in November 1692 having to his credit for the campaign only three prizes, although one was a richly laden Dutch vessel.

Iberville's forays against the English in Hudson Bay had been crippled, by delays and the early northern winters, for the second consecutive season. Furthermore, his contemporaries were beginning to suggest that the struggle in the northern regions was contributing not a little to his own growing sluggishness and indifference. The 1693 season was to be a repetition of the preceding one, as contrary winds and the supply ships he was to convoy delayed his arrival at Quebec until 23 July. Once again, Frontenac, with the directors of the Compagnie du Nord, decided it was too late in the season to take York Fort and sail away before winter set in. Though he was not alone responsible for the decision to postpone the expedition, there is little doubt that Iberville had lost his zeal for Hudson Bay, so long at least as that objective involved other burdensome duties, such as convoying the annual supplies to Quebec, instead of sailing directly from France to Hudson Bay. Nevertheless, he was appointed to head the 1694 expedition to York Fort, for the fourth season. By this time the situation had worsened, for the English had recaptured Albany Fort in 1693 and had completely driven the French from the north. Iberville set sail from Rochefort in mid-May 1694 and with the usual delays arrived at Quebec only in mid-July. It was undoubtedly

Le Moyne d'Iberville

fortunate for French plans that the arrangements for the campaign of 1694 included several stipulations which Iberville himself had shrewdly proposed, presumably with a view to reviving his own enthusiasm for Hudson Bay. In return for Iberville's assuming responsibility for his crews' wages and supplies, the crown was providing the vessels and military stores. Most important, he was to share all booty and the profits of the fur trade *à la flibustière* with his men. As a further incentive, he was granted the monopoly of trade in Hudson Bay to July 1697. This latter provision, of course, greatly irritated the directors of the Compagnie du Nord, whose Canadian and French members were in constant disagreement. Though they claimed Iberville had obtained the monopoly "under false pretences . . . and had used their funds for the furthering of his own undertaking," they had in fact contributed only 15,000 *livres* to the 1694 expedition. Iberville blamed their shortsighted and avaricious financial policy for the repeated losses they had suffered since 1686.

Leaving Quebec on 10 August 1694 in command of the *Poli*, with his brother JOSEPH, Sieur de Serigny, commanding the *Salamandre*, Iberville arrived at the mouth of the Hayes River on 24 September. He immediately landed a party to reconnoitre York Fort, and began preparations for a long winter siege. The English were summoned to surrender on 13 October (3 October, O.S.), and Henry KELSEY was sent to negotiate terms. The following day, Thomas Walsh, the governor, "basely surrendered," as the HBC governors in England later asserted. Though well supplied with men, heavy cannon, food, and trade goods, the commander had neglected to lay in firewood, ignoring earlier warnings of an impending French attack. Amid much hardship on both sides, the expedition and its prisoners wintered at York Fort, renamed Fort Bourbon. Iberville has been accused of some violations of the terms of surrender; there is reason to believe, for example, that in order to relieve the food situation he turned the English garrison, with the exception of Walsh and two or three others, loose to face the harsh northern winter. By the time the Hayes River (renamed Sainte-Thérèse) was free of ice in mid-June 1695, scurvy had taken the lives not only of a great many Englishmen but of French sailors and Canadians as well. Iberville, furthermore, had lost his young brother, Louis*, Sieur de Châteauguay, the third Le Moyne to have given his life in combat in America. The expedition stayed on for the summer in the hope of seizing the annual supply ships from England. When these had not appeared by September, Iberville decided to leave Hudson Bay in the charge of Gabriel

Testard* de La Forest and 70 men; he himself sailed to La Rochelle, arriving there on 9 October. During the campaign of 1694–95, the Indians had brought 450 canoe loads of pelts to Fort Bourbon.

Iberville had finally effected the capture of the Hudson Bay Company's most lucrative station, and his own star now shone more brightly than ever. Nevertheless, the effects of the campaign had been nullified by James KNIGHT's recapture in 1693 of Albany Fort and by the subsequent driving of the French from the Bottom of the Bay. The entire situation was further aggravated when the English reversed the position at York in 1696. With five vessels and 400 men under Captain William Allen, they recaptured their station and furs worth 136,000 *livres*. Iberville's brother, Serigny, arrived at York just two hours after the English, and seeing them in possession of the Hayes River, quickly returned to France, leaving Fort Bourbon to defend itself.

In the meantime, following his return to France in the autumn of 1695, Iberville was called upon to make ready to attack the English stations along the Atlantic coast from Fort William Henry (Pemaquid), on the disputed New England-Acadia boundary, to St John's, the fortified English settlement in Newfoundland. After the tiring northern campaigns of the preceding ten years, the scheme apparently coincided with Iberville's own preferences. He had, furthermore, learned a good deal about the profits to be derived from fishing during his patrol in the North Atlantic in 1692. He accordingly set out from France with three vessels in the spring of 1696. After dispatching his brother Maricourt to Quebec to recruit Canadians for a winter campaign against Newfoundland, he sailed with two frigates to the relief of Governor Joseph Robinau* de Villebon of Acadia, whom the English were blockading at the mouth of the Saint John River. Adept manœuvres resulted in the capture of one English frigate and the flight of two others in August. Iberville then besieged Fort William Henry, some 200 miles west of the Saint John, with 25 regulars from Acadia and 240 Abenakis under the legendary Baron de Saint-Castin [JEAN-VINCENT D'ABBADIE]. The expedition was piloted by Pierre MAISONNAT, *dit* Baptiste. Though certainly strong enough to have resisted "for some time if there had been any brave men inside," the English fort, under its commander Captain Pascoe Chubb, capitulated almost as soon as the French had set up their batteries, on 15 August.

After destroying Fort William Henry and transporting the garrison of 92 men to Boston, Iberville sailed with his three vessels to Placentia (Plaisance), the French capital of Newfoundland. Both English and French fishermen exploited the Grand Banks fishery from their respective settlements on Newfoundland under the sanction of the treaty of 1687, but the purpose of the new French expedition of 1696 was nevertheless to expel the English from the island. According to the somewhat ambiguous instructions of the minister, the campaign was to be under the overall command of Jacques-François de MOMBETON de Brouillan, the governor of Placentia, while Iberville was to lead the men recruited by Maricourt in Quebec. A serious conflict of personalities and ambitions was to develop between the two commanders, caused by Brouillan's apparent jealousy of the authority of Iberville and envy of his claims to the booty accruing from the campaign. There can be little doubt of Brouillan's rapaciousness: an official report of 1692 describes the governor's activities as ranging from general monopolizing of trade to actual seizure of troops' wages, wine, and other provisions. As it turned out, these antagonisms did not seriously impede the campaign, thanks in part to the intervention of Captain Nicolas DANEAU de Muy.

After considerable preliminary wrangling, the parties of both commanders left Placentia, Governor Brouillan by sea on 29 October, Iberville overland on 1 November. Meeting some 50 miles south of St John's, at Ferryland, both detachments began the march north to the English capital, which surrendered on 30 November following a brief siege. After setting fire to St John's, Iberville's Canadians under Jacques TESTARD de Montigny almost totally destroyed the English fisheries along the eastern shore of the island. Small raiding parties terrorized the hamlets hidden away in remote bays and inlets, burning, looting, and taking prisoners. By the end of March 1697, only Bonavista and Carbonear remained in English hands. At the latter place William PYNNE, a local merchant, actually organized a successful defence against the French. In four months of raids, Brouillan and Iberville, but primarily Iberville, were responsible for the destruction of 36 settlements. Two hundred persons were killed and 700 were taken prisoner. Even before leaving France Iberville had hoped to market 200,000 quintals of cod, and there is little doubt that he must have approached that estimate. The Newfoundland campaign had been the cruelest and most destructive of Iberville's career. It also illustrated perfectly the peculiar conditions of the North American frontier and the adaptability of the hardened voyageurs. Unfortunately for Iberville and his men, however, the effects were to be short-lived, for even as he was campaigning the ministry of Marine was gloomily facing the task of reversing the events of 1696 in Hudson Bay. Once again, as so many times before, the authorities looked to the Canadian adventurer as the most likely person to restore French fortunes in the northern regions. Accordingly, before he could consolidate his victories by driving the English out of Newfoundland entirely, Iberville and his detachment joined the squadron which his brother Serigny had brought to Placentia from France. Almost immediately following his departure, an English squadron and 2,000 land troops, commanded by Sir John GIBSONE and Sir John Norris*, arrived at St John's and provided sufficient cover to induce the displaced fishermen to return to their devastated villages, rebuild their homes, and resume fishing.

After an arduous navigation north, Iberville's lead ship, the *Pélican*, became separated from the others in fog in Hudson Strait. This was to be the occasion for what was probably the most gallant single action of Iberville's career. The *Pélican*, having preceded the squadron to the mouth of the Hayes River on 4 September, was attacked the following day by three English warships, the *Hampshire*, a man-of-war carrying 56 guns, the *Dering* of 36, and the *Hudson's Bay* [I] of 32 guns. It was, of course, essential for the success of the French venture that the *Pélican*, with her 44 guns, prevent reinforcements from reaching the English at York Fort. Iberville accordingly engaged the enemy despite a most unfavourable position. After two and a half hours of inconclusive sparring, the adversaries met finally in a duel during which Iberville carried out brilliant naval manœuvres that culminated in the sinking of the *Hampshire* by the *Pélican*. Following this action the *Hudson's Bay* was captured without resistance, though she too soon sank. Only the *Dering* (Capt. Michael GRIMINGTON, senior) fled unpursued, for the *Pélican* had to be abandoned as well, its hull having been opened at the waterline by the *Hampshire*'s guns. As the *Pélican* was being abandoned and its men regrouped in a camp slightly to the south of the English fort, the three remaining ships of the French squadron arrived including the direly needed supply ship, the *Profond*. Then, after five days of lively skirmishing, the English under Henry BALEY, governor of Hudson Bay, surrendered on 13 September; Kelsey again negotiated the terms. This had been Iberville's swiftest and most brilliant campaign. He put Serigny in command of Hudson Bay, and left hastily in late September 1697; if he wished to escape the early winter ice, he could not afford to sail south to recapture Albany Fort. This was the last time he would see the northern regions which had thus far been the major theatre of his military, naval, and commercial endeavours.

Le Moyne d'Iberville

The peace of Ryswick, signed in September 1697, had stipulated that the Bottom of the Bay should revert to France, and York Fort to the Hudson's Bay Company, but Albany remained in British hands, and Bourbon remained French until 1713, when the Ryswick terms were superseded by those of Utrecht, and England was confirmed in her possession of the whole of the Hudson Bay drainage region. Thus, somewhat ironically, after all the effort expended at Hudson Bay, the naval exploits of the French in 1697 played no role in the settlements reached at the negotiating table at Utrecht 16 years later. Iberville returned to France in November 1697. Though he managed to have his monopoly at Fort Bourbon extended to the summer of 1699, the hero of Hudson Bay was about to be drawn into an entirely new theatre of adventure: Louisiana, which was henceforth to play an important role in France's revised imperial designs.

In the 1690s, the policy of the government of Louis XIV became openly expansionist and it aimed at hemming the British in to the east of the Appalachians. The French hoped that by extending French interests beyond the St Lawrence valley and the basin of the Great Lakes, so that they included the whole Mississippi basin to the Gulf of Mexico, English settlement might be contained within a narrow strip along the Atlantic seaboard. It was this prospect which greeted Iberville upon his return from Hudson Bay in November 1697. Impressed by his accomplishments in the bay and during his other Canadian campaigns, the minister felt that he was ideally suited to lead an expedition to the Mississippi, the chief purpose of which was to find "the mouth [of the Mississippi] ... select a good site which can be defended with few men, and ... block entry to the river by other nations." Past ventures to the Mississippi, particularly Cavelier* de La Salle's voyage of 1682, had involved sailing down the river from New France; Iberville was to sail up the river from the Gulf of Mexico. The ultimate purpose of the project was, of course, to lay the foundations of a French colony along the gulf coast, thus securing for France one more avenue to the interior of the continent. After months of the usual delays, during which some crew members deserted and Iberville fell ill, four vessels, including the frigates *Badine* and *Marin*, left Brest in late October 1698. Iberville, accompanied this time by another brother, Jean-Baptiste Le Moyne* de Bienville, sailed first to Saint-Domingue, arriving 4 December, thence north to Florida and west along the northern shore of the Gulf of Mexico to the Mississippi. On the way he observed the installations of the Spaniards at Pensacola and made soundings of possible French harbour sites. As he continued along the coast, his party was driven during a storm on 2 March 1699 into the Birdfoot sub-delta of the Mississippi. The misleading descriptions by Chrestien Le Clercq* in his *Établissement de la foy* ..., however, conflicted with Iberville's own observations, and for this reason he continued to sail up the river in search of some indisputable sign that this was indeed the Mississippi. It was only after meeting Indians who recalled La Salle's expedition and gave physical proof of his having passed among them, that Iberville was finally satisfied. Having thus achieved the first aim of the expedition, Iberville built a temporary fort on Biloxi Bay (Fort Maurepas, modern Ocean Springs, Miss.), strategically situated between the Mississippi and the Spanish base at Pensacola. Then on 3 May 1699, Iberville sailed for France, leaving behind a garrison of 81 men, among whom was his brother Bienville.

In France, after being presented with the cross of the order of Saint-Louis, which he was the first person of Canadian birth to receive, Iberville recommended immediate colonization and exploitation of Louisiana. He based his recommendations less on natural resources, which alone would hardly have warranted a generous effort, than on the urgent need to counter the threat of imminent English expansion from the Carolinas. Although they were attracted by the proposal, the authorities were hampered by seriously limited financial resources. Furthermore, the minister could not formally commit the crown to the project for fear of offending the Spaniards, who were France's allies in the thorny question of the Spanish succession, and whose claims in America included Louisiana. The minister did make available, however, the means to undertake a second exploratory voyage in October 1699 and issued instructions to contain by covert means any designs the English might have in the region. He hoped that further exploration might facilitate a decision on the merits and precise nature of a major colonization effort. Iberville arrived at Biloxi in January 1700 and proceeded to build a second fort (Fort Mississipi) on the Mississippi about 40 miles upstream. He also sought to secure the allegiance of the several Indian tribes of the region and to unite them in a common front against the English threat from the Carolinas. Then, leaving Biloxi at the end of May, Iberville returned to France by way of New York where he allegedly unloaded 9,000 pelts which he had bought from Canadian trappers who, rather than return to Montreal, had brought them to Iberville

Le Moyne d'Iberville

in Louisiana. The fact that both coureurs de bois and Indians from the northwestern tribes were showing interest in Louisiana was to be the principal reason for the hostility which the Mississippi adventure was beginning to arouse among the officials and merchants of Canada. They claimed Louisiana was being encouraged at the expense of the still meagre population and trade of Canada. Though they attempted to discredit Iberville in the eyes of both the officials at Versailles and the northwestern tribes, their efforts were to be of no avail for, under the new colonial policy, coureurs de bois and Indians were officially encouraged to come to Louisiana. In their trading with the Mississippi tribes, it would be in the interest of both to drive out rival English traders, and thus they would in effect become agents of the new French imperialism. This was, of course, Iberville's thinking. He spent from August 1700 to September 1701 in France, therefore, arguing the case for a strong commitment to Louisiana and for resistance to English expansion west of the Appalachians. In the meantime, Louis XIV's grandson Philippe d'Anjou had in 1700 become king of Spain and Iberville had accordingly hoped for a Franco-Spanish alliance which would allow joint use of the Spanish base at Pensacola. Despite the weakness of this base, however, Spain did not welcome an alliance which left her clearly subject to France. As an alternative Iberville urged the founding of a strong naval base at Mobile to serve as the centre of French influence in the Gulf of Mexico. The crown authorized a third expedition to proceed with the founding of Mobile, and approved an active Indian policy conceived by Iberville to protect the Mississippi basin from English expansion west of the Appalachians. Although his resources were quite disproportionate to his ambitious programme, Iberville nevertheless set sail from La Rochelle with three vessels on 29 Sept. 1701. Forced by illness to put in at Pensacola he found the Spanish fort and garrison in a deplorable state, and the Spaniards frankly hostile to French encroachments on their zone of influence. Notwithstanding this official hostility Iberville undertook construction of a modest installation at Mobile, to be called Fort Saint-Louis.

France's official foothold in Louisiana remained precarious despite her desire and some well-intentioned efforts to make a strong showing. Attempts by Iberville to establish a colony in the Mobile area had all but failed; it would be many years before settlers could be attracted in numbers sufficient to provide the required population. On the other hand, the unofficial endeavours of missionaries, traders, and explorers, particularly in the interior, had by 1702 already asserted the French presence in the Mississippi Basin. A notable contribution in this direction had been Iberville's Indian diplomacy. As befitted a son of Charles Le Moyne, indeed any Canadian schooled on the beaver frontier of North America, Iberville believed that contact with the native population and mingling with the Indians were essential to any sound diplomacy. He had no illusions that well-manned and well-equipped military strongholds could ever replace the friendship and support of the Indians. Thus, he hoped to weld all the Indians between the Appalachians and the Mississippi into an alliance with the French and thus to contain English expansion into the west. His plan called for missionaries to live and labour in key Indian villages. To be sure, they were more valuable to Iberville's scheme as political counsellors and conciliators than as spiritual advisers to the Indians. By the time he left Louisiana in April 1702, Iberville had taken the first steps towards implementing his Indian programme. In this he was assisted by HENRI TONTY who, as La Salle's lieutenant, had travelled extensively in the Mississippi basin, and knew the Indians well. Though he had been bitterly disappointed when Iberville, and not he, had been chosen to lead the expedition to the Mississippi in 1698, Tonty agreed to exert his influence towards the reconciling of the region's hostile tribes in an effort to mount a common front against British ambitions in the Mississippi basin.

When he departed in April 1702, Iberville bade farewell to Louisiana. Though he prepared to lead several expeditions to the colony, his plans were thwarted, either by his own deteriorating health, by the straits of the French treasury, or by the state of French shipping, already acutely strained before the War of the Spanish Succession. Between attacks of malaria which recurred several times from 1702 to 1705, Iberville maintained an untiring interest in Louisiana. In fact the minister called on him for counsel on several occasions, and Iberville obliged in a succession of long memoirs in which he repeated and further refined his theory for French expansion in America. These memoirs, however, contain a noticeable amount of fanciful material (for example, on Indian policy and on the reduction of English strength along the entire seaboard), as compared to the generally lucid and well-documented observations of Iberville's earlier career. There may indeed be a relationship between these lapses after 1702, and the illness which progressively undermined his resistance until his premature death.

Despite poor health, however, Iberville was well enough in 1705 to be entrusted with the

Le Moyne d'Iberville

preparation of an armament considerably more important than he himself had dared expect, given the European preoccupation with the War of the Spanish Succession. He left for America with a squadron of 12 vessels early in 1706, to continue his harassment of the English—this time in the West Indies. When Iberville arrived at Martinique on 9 March, he found that the Comte de Chavagnac, commander of one of the two divisions, had decided to attack Nevis, a small island in the Leeward chain, while awaiting the rest of the squadron. Unable to disembark at Nevis, Chavagnac turned his attention to neighbouring St Christopher, which he ravaged mercilessly. Chavagnac's impatience thus served no military purpose; indeed it compromised Iberville's campaign by prematurely alarming all the British bases in the Caribbean. The most important of these was Jamaica, whose defences were such that only a surprise attack would have been successful.

From Martinique, Iberville sailed to Guadeloupe where he disposed his force of about 2,000 regular troops, colonial militia, Canadians, and West Indian buccaneers for the campaign against Nevis. The squadron arrived on 1 April and the troops disembarked at Charlestown, the capital, that same night. The following day a single skirmish resulted in the fall of the island to French arms. Iberville's capitulation terms were harsh, in keeping with the weak resistance of the English detachment of 250 men, who had fled almost as soon as the French force came ashore. The entire population—nearly 800 men, including soldiers and sailors, more than 300 women, 600 children, and 6,000 negro slaves—was taken prisoner, 24 English vessels were captured in the harbour, and the plantations, merchandise, official papers, and the buildings of the colony were seized. Once again, as in so many of Iberville's previous campaigns, there was much bad faith and ruthless looting; by the time the French departed on 22 April, Nevis, the garden of the Caribbean, had been completely desolated. The campaign had spread terror not only throughout the British West Indies but all along the Atlantic seaboard from Carolina to Newfoundland. Indeed, Iberville had planned upon leaving Nevis to carry fire and sword to the other English possessions in America. As suddenly as he himself was accustomed to strike, however, Iberville's career was cut short by his death.

Complicating the military facts of the capture of Nevis was the suspicion of fraudulence which surrounded the entire expedition, involving Iberville and Serigny and their agents, a number of French merchants, and practically every officer of the entire squadron, including Chavagnac. Even as the squadron was sailing towards the West Indies early in 1706, the minister of Marine appointed a commission to inquire into what the expedition's suppliers alleged were malpractices surrounding the initial outfitting of the ships. As well, merchandise had been embarked in France for the purpose of illicit trade, and the administration of the profits from the booty and prizes taken at Nevis was suspect. The inquiry was frustrated by countless delays and unbelievable confusion, which caused the case to drag on for 30 years or more. To begin with, Iberville died suddenly, as did the squadron commissary before he could put his accounts of the expedition in order. Furthermore, the storekeepers of each vessel did not keep accounts of foodstuffs and merchandise consumed during the expedition. Nor did the French port officials take inventory of the vessels on their return. Also, the captains refused to declare their returning cargoes. The outcome of the whole matter was a host of convictions and orders to make restitution. Iberville, though dead, was severely dealt with, as was his widow, who had to make restitution on behalf of her deceased husband. Iberville was found guilty of carrying merchandise, chiefly iron, for illicit trade at considerable profit in Saint-Domingue and Havana. To a lesser degree, he, and especially the agents who saw to his interests after he died, were involved in contraventions respecting prizes and booty and charged with evasion of the prescribed taxes to the crown and admiral. Iberville's most serious offence, however, was the embezzlement of large amounts of foodstuffs provided by the outfitters, which he sold on his own account. The whole affair caused a great deal of resentment and distrust of the Le Moynes in Louisiana, Canada, and above all in the ministry of Marine. Indeed the minister was so displeased that promotions for the Le Moyne brothers, especially for Serigny, whose guilt was most evident, were delayed for several years.

The Nevis affair offers the most comprehensive illustration of Iberville's considerable commercial ambitions and his shrewd business sense. Though it is not easy to pinpoint the exact range of these interests and the extent of their effect upon his activities, it is evident they were considerable, dating back to his early adventures in Hudson Bay. Indeed, Governor Frontenac, who found him boastful and presumptuous, was convinced Iberville "has his interests and his trade much more in view than the king's service." The monopoly which allowed him to exploit the fur trade from 1694 to 1700 (except from September 1696 to September 1697) provided him with regular and substantial profits. Even before leaving France for the Newfoundland campaign of 1696–97, Iberville had made arrangements to dispose of what fish he would catch. To this end, he spent nearly two months in Placentia marketing the cod and other booty he had amassed, and supervising the fishery he had organized on his own account, using not only his own men but prisoners from the English fishing settlements as well. When Iberville sought the governorship of Newfoundland in 1697, his main purpose was probably to resume his interest in the fishery, which he hoped to combine with his monopoly of the fur trade at Fort Bourbon. He was turned down, not so much because he was Canadian-born, as because of the current redefinition of French colonial policy in America: Iberville could serve France better as developer of Louisiana than as administrator of the tiny, albeit important, outpost of Newfoundland. It was in Louisiana especially that Iberville and his brothers, with a view to reconciling the general development of the colony and their own individual interests, apparently sought to master all aspects of trade. Iberville's commissary in Louisiana, Nicolas de La Salle, posthumously accused him of various malpractices including the manipulation of the king's stores. It is known that Iberville invested part of his Louisiana profits in property in Saint-Domingue, where he purchased a lucrative cocoa plantation in 1701. In France he obtained in Aunis the seigneuries of Ardillières, near Rochefort, which became the residence of his wife and family, and Duplessis, valued together at 90,000 *livres*. Though, as it would seem, there is ample evidence of a general nature to suggest Iberville had become wealthy, his sudden death in July 1706—in Havana, where he had gone presumably to dispose of part of the iron he had taken from France for the purpose of his illicit trade—had prevented him from putting his affairs in order.

It is difficult to establish with certainty the details surrounding the family born to Iberville and Marie-Thérèse Pollet. In the sparse evidence available there are conflicting details relating to dates of birth on the one hand and to Iberville's whereabouts at the probable times of conception of his children on the other. Tentatively it would seem there were five children: Pierre-Joseph-Louis, b. 1694 off the Grand Banks bound for Quebec; Jean-Baptiste, b. 1698 at La Rochelle; Marie-Thérèse, b. 1700; Jean-Charles, b. 1701 at La Rochelle; François-Jean, b. 1705 at La Rochelle. Madame d'Iberville appears to have lived mostly in France after her marriage in 1693. Following her husband's death, she was reported to be living in Paris in June 1707, and was described then as having "undoubtedly great merit . . . [she] sins only by the lofty attitudes she has acquired from her family."

The following year she married Louis, Comte de Béthune, aged 49, naval captain and knight of the order of Saint-Louis, who, despite his promotion in 1720 to commodore and in 1734 to honorary lieutenant-general, soon proved to be a financial liability. By Béthune she had two children, Marie-Armande, b. 1709 in Paris; and Armand, b. 1711 at Ardillières. Far from benefitting from the wealth Iberville had accumulated, Marie-Thérèse Pollet was to be caught up in the repercussions of the Nevis affair until her death. Though she used every intrigue and took every possible precaution to evade the onerous task of restitution, she nevertheless was forced finally to submit. The amount Iberville had fraudulently acquired during the campaign of 1706 exceeded his share of the legitimate profits by 112,000 *livres*. This debt, which devolved upon his widow, was still unpaid in 1730. By the time of her death in 1737 (her second husband had predeceased her by four and a half years, "being demented"), the entire Iberville fortune had been used up either in settling the latter's affairs, or in maintaining her second husband in his high station in life.

In the past hundred years, there have been over a dozen works—both book-length and shorter monographs—devoted to Pierre Le Moyne d'Iberville. Of these only Guy Frégault's *Iberville le conquérant* (Montréal, 1944) makes an impressive scholarly contribution. Those published before 1944 are of little value; indeed they are seldom more than religio-nationalistic panegyrics or pretentious popularizations whose aim is to highlight Iberville's military prowess against the English. Nellis Crouse, *Le Moyne d'Iberville, soldier of New France* (Ithaca, 1954) is a somewhat improved popularization but, as such, contributes little that is new. Even Frégault for that matter, though his work represents a scholarly effort at painstaking scrutiny and rigorous appraisal of available sources, succumbs to the temptation of the drum-and-trumpet or powder-blackened-faces form of biography, as may be judged from his title. Writing in 1944, Frégault, of course, did not have the opportunity of utilizing such important general studies as those of W. J. Eccles on New France, of Marcel Giraud on Louisiana and of E. E. Rich on the Hudson's Bay Company. The contribution these scholars have brought to the general context would suggest the timeliness of a revised full-length treatment of the life and career of Iberville. Documentary sources, especially economic ones, continue to be discovered, and older holdings are constantly being reappraised. The results of research carried out over the past

Le Moyne d'Iberville

quarter century will permit a more specific grasp, for instance, of Iberville's commercial ambitions, and a fuller account of his trading operations. A more critical examination of lengthy and detailed dispatches to the minister of Marine between 1702 and 1705 on French expansion and English containment in America would also seem to be required. Finally, the place of Iberville in the context of North America in the late 17th and early 18th centuries needs to be reviewed and redefined. Particular attention should be given to contemporary opinions of Iberville. He and the members of his family reputedly generated a great deal of antipathy, as well as affection, in New France, Louisiana, and France.

In the present appraisal of the career of an undoubtedly remarkable man, it is significant that, in spite of Iberville's outstanding energy and ability and incredible feats of heroism, so little was to survive by way of permanent benefit to the French empire in America. Indeed, his valiant efforts in Hudson Bay during more than half of his 20 years in the service of France were doomed even as he undertook his final campaign in 1697. Though the French were to remain in *de facto* possession of Fort Bourbon for 16 years, the treaty of Utrecht irrevocably secured to Great Britain the possession of the entire Hudson Bay basin. Similarly, the capture in 1696 of Fort William Henry, situated in the disputed zone between New England and Acadia, and the destruction of the English settlements in Newfoundland in 1696 and 1697, were to be of no consequence for French imperial history. Like Hudson Bay, both Acadia and Newfoundland were ceded to Britain in 1713, and as early as 1697, as Iberville left Newfoundland, the English population returned to its former settlements. Iberville's Louisiana adventure from 1698 to 1702 was doomed to a similar fate. Indeed, French initiative there was conceived not so much as a positive undertaking but as a means of preventing the English from acquiring a foothold in the Mississippi basin. Despite Iberville's success in attracting southwards many Indian tribes from the northwest, his effort to retain the populous English within their narrow strip along the Atlantic seaboard became more and more futile, and Iberville's thinking in this respect showed itself to be increasingly unrealistic. So too the capture of Nevis, although it served to terrorize for a time the English islands in the Caribbean, was but a temporary reversal of Britain's long-term prospects in America. Of all Iberville's campaigns, only the 1690 raid on Corlaer (Schenectady) was a comparative French success. Limited human and material resources did not allow France to retain for long territory beyond the St Lawrence valley, but the 1690 raids demonstrated the ability to hold, at least for some time to come, the Canadian colony which was already established. The fate of French imperial designs depended upon French resources and support. These, in the century following 1660, were better suited in America to the compact colony of Colbert than to a policy of expansion.

However devoid of military or political consequence the career of Pierre Le Moyne d'Iberville may now appear, his achievements are nevertheless of lasting significance. Indeed Iberville's exploits, like those of no other in New France, illustrate the physical and moral strength, the resourcefulness and adaptability that were required in some measure of the whole colonial society to survive and prosper in the exacting wilderness conditions of North America. The fierce patriotism, the bravery, even the savage cruelty, which characterized Iberville's campaigns against the English, were to a lesser degree the qualities essential to all life and progress in early North America. In this context, Iberville is an important figure, and is beyond doubt the first truly Canadian hero.

BERNARD POTHIER

[AAQ, Registre des confirmations, 58. Archives de la Charente-Maritime (La Rochelle), B 5714, 5921. Archives Maritimes, Port de Rochefort, 6E2, liasse 1. AN, V[7], carton 214 (official inquiry into the Nevis affair); Col., B, C[11A], C[11C], C[11D], C[11E], C[13A], C[13C], F[3]; Marine, B[2], B[4], C[1], 3JJ. ASQ, Lettres, M, 21, 38; N, 28. BN, MS, Cabinet des titres, Coll. Chérin, 31700; Clairambault; NAF. Some of Iberville's letters can be found in the Chicago Historical Society, Gunther and O. J. Schmidt Colls., and in the Newberry Library, Ayer Coll. There are at least two copies of an alleged original portrait: an engraving by La Guillermie (1841–1934), and a canvas by Flornoy (1894–?), which hangs in the Archives of Quebec.

Charlevoix, *Histoire* (1744), I, II. *Découvertes et établissements des Français* (Margry), IV. *Documentary hist. of New York* (O'Callaghan). *Documents relating to Hudson Bay* (Tyrrell). Paul Du Ru, *Journal of Paul Du Ru (February 1 to May 8, 1700)* . . . , trans., with Intro. and notes, R. L. Butler (Chicago, 1934). Léon Guérin, *Histoire maritime de France* . . . (6v., Paris, 1851), IV, 469–79, which contains "Mémoire succinct de la naissance et des services de . . . Iberville. . . ." HBRS, XI, XX (Rich and Johnson). [Nicolas Jérémie], "Relation du Détroit et de la Baie d'Hudson par Monsieur Jérémie," with Intro. by J.-H. Prud'homme, Société hist. de Saint-Boniface *Bull.*, II (1912). *Journal de l'abbé Beaudoin* (Gosselin). *Jug. et délib.*, III [Picoté de Belestre affair]. *Kelsey papers* (Doughty and Martin). La Potherie, *Histoire* (1753), I. *MPA* (Rowland and Sanders), I, II. Chevalier de Troyes, *Journal* (Caron).

General works pertaining to New France are: E. H. Borins, "La Compagnie du Nord, 1682–1700,"

Le Moyne de Longueuil

(unpublished M.A. thesis, McGill University, 1968); Eccles, *Canada under Louis XIV*, and *Frontenac*; Parkman, *A half-century of conflict*, I. On the Louisiana frontier, *see* V. W. Crane, *The southern frontier, 1670–1732* (Durham, N.C., 1928); Jean Delanglez, *Hennepin's Description of Louisiana, a critical essay* (Institute of Jesuit History pub., Chicago, 1941); W. E. Dunn, *Spanish and French rivalry in the Gulf region of the United States, 1678–1702* . . . (Austin, [1917]); Charles Gibson, *Spain in America* (New York, [1966]); Giraud, *Histoire de la Louisiane française*, I; and O'Neill, *Church and state in Louisiana. See also* Jean Delanglez, "Tonti letters," *Mid-America*, XXI (1939; new series, X), 209–38; P. J. Hamilton, *Colonial Mobile* (Boston, 1897; rev. ed., New York, 1910); Jonathan Pearson *et al.*, *A history of the Schenectady patent in the Dutch and English times* . . . , ed. J. W. MacMurray (Albany, 1883); and Justin Winsor, *The Mississippi basin . . . the struggle in America between England and France, 1697–1763* (Boston and New York, 1895).

About 15 biographies of Iberville have been written, but most are of little value. The most important biography is Guy Frégault, *Iberville le conquérant* (Montréal, [1944]), which is, however, out of date. Worthy of some mention, nevertheless, are Alexandre Jodoin and J.-L. Vincent, *Histoire de Longueuil et de la famille de Longueuil* (Montréal, 1889); L.-M. Le Jeune, *Le chevalier Pierre Le Moyne, Sieur d'Iberville* ([Ottawa], 1937); and N. M. Crouse, *Lemoyne d'Iberville: soldier of New France* (Toronto, [1954]).

Two articles of some interest are: Emmanuel de Cathelineau, "Les beaux mariages d'une canadienne," *NF*, VI (1931), 144–86; and "Pierre Le Moyne d'Iberville et Mlle Picoté de Belestre," *BRH*, XXI (1915), 224. B.P.]

LE MOYNE DE LONGUEUIL, CHARLES, the only native Canadian made a baron in New France, officer, delegate of the French to the Indians, governor of Trois-Rivières and later of Montreal, acting administrator of New France; baptized 10 Dec. 1656 at Montreal, son of Charles Le Moyne* de Longueuil et de Châteauguay and Catherine Thierry (Primot); d. 7 June 1729 at Montreal.

The eldest of the famous Le Moyne brothers was brought up in France as a page of one of Buade* de Frontenac's relatives, the Maréchal d'Humières. He very early took up a military career, and in 1680 became a lieutenant in the Régiment de Saint-Laurent. A year later, at Paris or Versailles, he married Claude-Élisabeth Souart d'Adoucourt, a lady's maid in the service of Madame de France (the Princess Palatine, Charlotte-Élisabeth de Bavière) and a niece of the Sulpician Gabriel Souart*, the first parish priest of Montreal.

In 1683 he was back in New France, since on 4 November Le Febvre* de La Barre recommended him without success to Seignelay, to replace the drunkard Jacques Bizard* in the post of town major of Montreal. At the beginning of the following year Charles Le Moyne de Longueuil, junior, received from his parents the seigneury of Longueuil and its outbuildings, and set about developing it without delay. In parallel fashion he was soon to begin to rise through the ranks of the military hierarchy in Canada and to give proof of the bravery characteristic of his family. Having become an infantry lieutenant in the regular troops in March 1687, he commanded four companies in the army which Brisay de Denonville launched against the Senecas. Longueuil acquitted himself so well that the governor, as soon as he returned to Montreal, reported him to the minister as being one of the two most remarkable officers in that campaign. In the most flattering terms he recommended that the rank of captain be granted to Longueuil, who, however, did not obtain it for four years.

At the beginning of August 1689, just after the Lachine massacre, Longueuil had his arm shattered by a musket shot while pursuing the Iroquois. The following year he distinguished himself, with his brother Le Moyne* de Sainte-Hélène, at the siege of Quebec by Phips*. The two brothers, at the head of 200 Montreal volunteers, attacked the English advance guard which was moving towards the town along the Saint-Charles River. Under the steady fire of the Canadians hidden in the thickets, the enemy had to fall back at the end of an afternoon of bitter fighting. It was there that Longueuil received a wound in the side which might have been fatal, had it not been for the protection given by his powder horn. The fracture in his arm had not yet even healed; in the spring of 1691 he had to go to the waters of Barèges, in France, to treat it.

During the Franco-Iroquois peace negotiations of 1694, the great Onondaga chief Teganissorens solemnly declared on 24 June that the Five Nations had adopted as their children Charles Le Moyne de Longueuil and Paul Le Moyne de Maricourt, replacing their father who had died. In their letter of 15 Oct. 1698, Frontenac and Bochart de Champigny earnestly requested the king to elevate the seigneury of Longueuil to a barony in consideration of Charles Le Moyne's loyal services and the enormous expenditures he had incurred in its establishment. "His fort, his house, and all that goes with them [give] us, when we see them," the governor and the intendant said, "an idea of the fortified castles of France." On 26 Jan. 1700 Louis XIV therefore signed letters patent by which he made Charles Le Moyne and

Le Moyne de Longueuil

his descendants barons of Longueuil. This constituted striking recognition of the merits of the Le Moyne family and of the remarkable way in which the baron had developed his seigneury, "where he is endeavouring to establish three parishes," said the king, "and to protect the said settlers in time of war he has had built at his own expense a fort flanked by four strong towers, the whole in stone and masonry with a guard-house, several large main buildings, and a very fine church, the whole embellished with all the marks of nobility . . . , and with all this there is a considerable number of servants and horses and sundry attendants, and all these buildings have cost him more than 60,000 *livres*, so much so that the said seigneury is at present one of the finest in the whole country, and the only one fortified and built in this way, which has greatly contributed to the protection of all the settlers on the neighbouring seigneuries. . . ."

On 3 July 1703 the cross of the order of Saint-Louis was added to the royal favours of which Le Moyne de Longueuil was to continue to show himself worthy, particularly as ambassador to the Onondagas. For since war had broken out between France and England in May 1702 over the Spanish succession, there was reason to fear an English invasion of New France from New York, in collaboration with the Indians of the Five Nations, who were neighbours of Albany. For this reason, and to preserve the fur trade in the west for the French, it was important to keep the Iroquois neutral. In the spring of 1704 RIGAUD de Vaudreuil therefore instructed Longueuil to go among the Iroquois "to offset the influence of the English who are continually in their villages." Then in June 1709, disturbed by the speeding up of war preparations at Albany and by the manœuvres of Abraham Schuyler, who had been sent among the Onondagas "to begin the war chant" and "to present the hatchet" on behalf of his Britannic majesty, the governor put the whole colony in a state of alert. In the autumn, Longueuil, who had been town major of Montreal since May 1706, offered to return among the Onondagas, who had invited him by a wampum belt to come and "set to rights the matters that the Flemish had upset." His embassy was a success. The Oneidas, Cayugas, and Onondagas received him with enthusiasm, "each endeavouring to caress him." They assured him they would resist both the threats and the promises of the English, and abstain from taking part in hostilities. At the time of the meeting of 17 July 1710, Longueuil managed to maintain the Onondaga and Oneida sachems in the same frame of mind.

However, the fall of Port-Royal in October 1710

shook the Indians' confidence in French power: in the spring of 1711 Longueuil was once more sent among the Iroquois. He secured the loyalty of a number of them, but several remained susceptible to the enticements of the British. The Onondagas, however, made him a present of a piece of ground on which he built himself a lodge in their midst. He returned to Quebec during the summer, accompanied by representatives of this tribe. On 7 November the authorities of the colony wrote to the minister: "His majesty must be assured of the Sieur de Longueuil's zeal for all that concerns his service; since the death of his brother, the Sieur de Maricourt, he has been obliged, in order to humour the Iroquois, to travel many times to see them, and even to stay for some time among them, willingly neglecting his family and all his affairs to go and humour these nations; his negotiations with them have always succeeded, with the happiest results that one can expect with nations like that; he is very sensible, Your Excellency, of the favour you obtained for him last year, and the Sieurs Vaudreuil and RAUDOT can assure you in advance that he will deserve all those that you give him cause to hope for." This favour was the king's lieutenancy at Montreal, which had been bestowed on Longueuil on 5 May 1710. The following July he received another favour: a second enlargement of his seigneury of Longueuil, the first dating from 25 Sept. 1698. In addition, on 24 March 1713, Vaudreuil and Bégon* increased "by one league of land fronting on the Richelieu River and going back to a depth of one and a half leagues . . ." the Belœil seigneury which he had bought on 25 Feb. 1711.

On 7 Nov. 1716 RAMEZAY and Bégon, on the basis of some information supplied by Longueuil who visited the Iroquois every year, informed the council of Marine of the need to build a post north of Niagara. The following year the baron, who on 7 May 1720 had succeeded Gallifet* as governor of Trois-Rivières, was entrusted with the task of securing Iroquois approval for the construction project of the French.

On 9 Sept. 1724 the skilful negotiator became governor of Montreal, and continued subsequently to use his influence with the Five Nations. What was particularly important at that time was to prevent the establishing at the mouth of the River Chouaguen (Oswego?) of an English fort which could ruin French trade with the *pays d'en haut*.

On Vaudreuil's death in 1725, Longueuil was made responsible for the general administration of New France, until a new governor was appointed. The baron hoped to be chosen, deeming it normal to proceed, as CALLIÈRE and Vaudreuil had done, from the governorship of Montreal to that of the colony. He was disappointed. It was decided not to place a Canadian at the head of New France because of the nepotism which had been displayed by Vaudreuil and his wife; the latter had been born in the colony.

In 1727, having become a widower, Longueuil, at the age of 71, married Marguerite Legardeur de Tilly, widow of Louis-Joseph Le Gouès de Grais and of Pierre de SAINT-OURS. By his first wife Longueuil had had several children, among them Charles*, second baron and third seigneur of Longueuil, and Joseph, commonly called the Chevalier de Longueuil, from whom is descended the second branch of the Le Moyne de Longueuil family.

The first Baron de Longueuil died on 7 June 1729. He had been a brilliant soldier, a venture-some colonizer, and a remarkable instrument of Vaudreuil's Indian policy.

CÉLINE DUPRÉ

AN, Col., C¹¹ᴬ, 10–16, 21–47; E, 290 (dossier Charles Le Moyne, 1ᵉʳ baron de Longueuil). Baugy, *Journal* (Serrigny). *Coll. de manuscrits relatifs à la N.-F.*, I. "Correspondance de Frontenac (1689–99)," APQ *Rapport, 1927–28*, 3–196. "Correspondance de Vaudreuil," APQ *Rapport, 1938–39*, 12–180; *1939–40*, 355–463; *1942–43*, 399–443; *1946–47*, 371–460; *1947–48*, 135–339. *Lettres de noblesse* (P.-G. Roy), I, 261–73. *NYCD* (O'Callaghan and Fernow), V, IX. PAC *Report, 1899*. P.-G. Roy, *Inv. concessions*, II, 59–62; IV, 80. Taillemite, *Inventaire analytique, série B*, I.

Bonnault, "Le Canada militaire," 276f. P.-G. Roy, *Les officiers d'état-major*, 170–75. [François Daniel], *Histoire des grandes familles françaises du Canada* (Montréal, 1867), 177–83. Émile Falardeau, ... *Les pionniers de Longueuil et leurs origines, 1666–1681* (Montréal, 1937), 35. Fauteux, *Les chevaliers de Saint-Louis*, 95f. A. Jodoin et J. L. Vincent, *Histoire de Longueuil et de la famille de Longueuil* (Montréal, 1889), 161–230. Lanctot, *Histoire du Canada*, II, 158; III, 37f.

LE MOYNE DE MARICOURT, PAUL, officer, interpreter, negotiator with the Indians; b. at Montreal, 15 Dec. 1663; d. at Montreal, 21 March 1704.

Maricourt was principally a man of the sword, one of the several Le Moyne brothers whose collective military exploits eventually extended to the far corners of France's North American empire. He, like his more famous brothers—PIERRE, Sieur d'Iberville, JOSEPH, Sieur de Serigny, and Jacques*, Sieur de Sainte-Hélène—enjoyed a spectacular career. He was the fourth of 12 sons born to Charles Le Moyne* de Longueuil et de Châteauguay and Catherine Thierry. Although there is only fragmentary evidence to indicate

how he passed his youth or to what extent he was formally educated, there can be no doubt that he was thoroughly tutored in the special skills required for military activity in the Canadian setting. He travelled with his brothers, mastered the Indian dialects and became one of the best canoemen in New France. Perhaps this latter ability had much to do with his being selected to act as adjutant on the Chevalier de Troyes*'s 1686 expedition to Hudson Bay—an undertaking aimed at reasserting French claims in that area in the face of English inroads. During the arduous overland trek, "without a doubt one of the worst journeys in the world," Maricourt suffered a series of accidents and narrowly escaped drowning on two occasions. Yet when the party of 30 French regulars and 70 Canadians finally arrived at the bottom of James Bay and began systematically to attack the three English forts located there, he, along with Iberville and Sainte-Hélène, was consistently in the forefront of the action. His performance won praise from the Chevalier, and when Iberville was left to command in the area, Maricourt was chosen to act as one of two lieutenants. After spending the winter there, the Le Moynes returned by land to Quebec, where Maricourt, on Governor BRISAY de Denonville's recommendation, was promoted second lieutenant of the troops.

His military career had thus begun auspiciously and, between 1688 and 1696, he was provided with still greater opportunities, both in the far north and in the war with the Iroquois, to show his mettle under fire. In the autumn of 1688 he sailed to Hudson Bay aboard the *Soleil d'Afrique*, a royal vessel recently put under Iberville's command for the protection of the interests of the Compagnie du Nord. At the Sainte-Anne (Albany) river he encountered two English vessels that ultimately became trapped in the ice. A pro-tracted and bizarre struggle ensued, lasting through most of the winter and ending with Iberville's forcing the English to surrender. Much of the credit for this victory belonged to Maricourt, who effectively employed a small detachment of Canadians to continually harass and thoroughly demoralize the enemy. He received a wound during one of the more lively exchanges but had recovered sufficiently by September 1689 to be left in charge of the bay posts when Iberville, under orders, returned to Quebec with the larger of the English prizes. On 15 May 1690, Governor Frontenac [Buade*] officially confirmed Mari-court as commander in Hudson Bay in the event of Iberville's absence or death.

Within months, however, Maricourt himself returned to Quebec, arriving just as William

Le Moyne de Maricourt

Phips* was organizing a siege of the town. Forewarned of the presence of the English, he abandoned the French vessel on which he had been travelling at Tadoussac and, in company with his brother CHARLES LE MOYNE de Longueuil and some Indian auxiliaries, advanced to the Beauport shore in a small skiff, easily escaping the pursuit of the surprised English. Once within the fortress of Quebec, Maricourt, according to a contemporary account, joined another officer in directing the French artillery. Nor did he display any traces of amateurism in the use of ordnance, for very few of his volleys were wasted and one of the first carried away the flag of Phips's own command vessel, providing the defenders with a morale-boosting omen, especially when the flag was recovered from the water and was borne in triumph to the cathedral. In 1691, Maricourt was rewarded for his part in the defence of Quebec by promotion to the rank of captain; in January 1693, he became a midshipman and on 15 Jan. 1694 a sub-lieutenant in the navy. The intendant, BOCHART de Champigny, described him, along with three other captains, as "those who are incapable of greed and who are inviolably loyal. . . ." Indeed, the colonial officials relied heavily on his talents, employing him in 1695 to patrol with a small force in the Chambly area to guard against Iroquois raids; in 1696, to raise a corps of the best militia for Iberville's Newfoundland campaign; and, in that same year, to command the Abenaki and Sault-Saint-Louis Indians during Governor Frontenac's expedition against the Iroquois. So confident were they of his resourcefulness on this latter occasion, that when momentary consideration was given to leaving a garrison to winter in the captured villages, he was one of the few considered capable of withstanding such an ordeal.

For several years following the 1696 campaign, Maricourt was obliged to remain close to his home, called *Pres de Ville*, on the outskirts of Montreal. There were a number of reasons for this. For one thing, he had been married on 29 Oct. 1691 to Marie-Madeleine, daughter of NICHOLAS DUPONT de Neuville, a member of the Conseil Souverain, and while he had no offspring of his own, he was apparently responsible for the children of Sainte-Hélène, who had been killed in the fighting at Quebec in 1690. Then too, he was intimately involved in the supervision of his invalid father's large estate; it was he, for instance, who, in the absence of several of his brothers, sold the seigneury of Île Perrot in 1703. Maricourt also had business affairs of his own. During the 1690s he participated in a number of transactions concerning seigneuries and was evidently involved in the affairs of the Compagnie du Nord. But his most serious commercial interest was as the silent partner in a trading society with the Sieur Louis LE CONTE Dupré, a prominent Montreal merchant and fur-trader. Not to be overlooked either are his duties as captain of a company of troops which formed part of the Montreal garrison. But in addition to the obvious burden of these family, business, and military responsibilities, there was an even more compelling reason for Maricourt's continued presence at Montreal during the late 1690s—his great influence with the Five Nations Indians, influence put to excellent use by the French governors in their efforts to secure a lasting peace with this traditional enemy.

Maricourt's prestige among the Iroquois, particularly the Onondagas, stemmed partly from the reputation his father had enjoyed among them and partly from his own understanding of their language and mentality. His fearless bearing and gift for symbolic oratory were much to the Iroquois taste. He was an adopted son of the Onondagas, being called by them Taouestaouis, and on their many visits to Montreal, they frequently went first to his home. The French governors compensated him for his hospitality on such occasions and encouraged further liaison with them. Governors Frontenac and CALLIÈRE repeatedly made use of him as their emissary to the Onondagas during the long negotiations leading to the peace of 1701. First, he worked closely with Callière from 1698 to 1700 to discredit the English in Iroquois eyes, particularly by questioning the sincerity of the Albany authorities in reclaiming Iroquois prisoners from the French. Then, in the critical discussions of 1700 and 1701, he, Father BRUYAS, and CHABERT de Joncaire, were continually active at the Iroquois council fires; now mocking the proud chiefs for even listening to the arrogant English agents seeking to prevent the peace by treating the Iroquois as slaves; now bribing the more intransigent families to hand over their French prisoners, many of whom were reluctant to depart. The Earl of Bellomont, governor of New York, all but admitted in his dispatches to the Board of Trade and Plantations that he had no one who could match these subtle French negotiators. When the ceremonies formally ratifying the peace were held at Montreal in the summer of 1701, Maricourt served as the plenipotentiary of the Onondagas. It was he, too, who returned to the Onondaga canton in 1702 to ensure that the Jesuit missionaries asked for by the Iroquois were well established. In fact, he continued under Governor RIGAUD de Vaudreuil to represent French interests among the Five Nations and to parry Albany's intrigues.

Le Moyne de Martigny

Such a symbol had he become to the English colonial leaders that their dispatches mistakenly credited him with leading the bloody attack on Deerfield in 1704.

Maricourt died on 21 March 1704. He left behind a 17-year-old bride of less than five weeks, Françoise Aubert de La Chesnaye, his first wife having died in April 1703. As Governor Vaudreuil remarked, the public loss was no less painful, for Maricourt was one of that small but unique group of men who were responsible for the physical extension and maintenance of France's vast North American empire. Possessing all the colour and reckless courage so typical of the French officer-nobleman of the *ancien régime*, he was also endowed with the powers of endurance and extra measure of savage guile peculiar to the coureur de bois. It was this combination that served him so well in battling the enemies of France, whether on the frozen surface of Hudson Bay, from the batteries of Quebec, or in the forests of New York. These were also the qualities that earned him the trust of four successive governors, the friendship of the habitants, and the respect of the fiercely independent Iroquois—a respect that enabled him to crown his career with a significant diplomatic triumph.

DONALD J. HORTON

AN, Col., B, 16, 19; C¹¹ᴬ, 10, 13–14, 18–22, 28; D²ᶜ, 222/2; F³, 2–8. BN, MS, Clairambault 881, ff.178–81; Fr. 31700, ff.2–8. Charlevoix, *History* (Shea), IV, V. *Coll. de manuscrits relatifs à la N.-F.*, I, II. Juchereau et Duplessis, *Histoire de l'Hôtel-Dieu de Québec*; *Annales* (Jamet). *Jug. et délib.*, V. La Potherie, *Histoire* (1722). Le Blant, *Histoire de la N.-F.* "Un mémoire de Le Roy de La Potherie sur la Nouvelle-France adressé à M. de Pontchartrain, 1701–1702," *BRH*, XXII (1916), 214–16. *NYCD* (O'Callaghan and Fernow), IV, IX. PRO, *CSP, Col., 1704–5*. P.-G. Roy, *Inv. concessions*, II, 213; *Inv. contrats de mariage*, IV. P.-G. et A. Roy, *Inv. greffes not.*, I, V, VI, XVIII. *1690, Sir William Phips devant Québec* (Myrand). Chevalier de Troyes, *Journal* (Caron). Wis. State Hist. Soc. *Coll.*, XVI, 164.

Le Jeune, *Dictionnaire*, II, 236–37. É.-Z. Massicotte, "Congés et permis déposés ou enregistrés à Montréal sous le régime français," APQ *Rapport, 1921–22*, 191. Tanguay, *Dictionnaire*. Charles Bourel de La Roncière, *Une épopée canadienne* (Paris, 1930). Eccles, *Frontenac*. Frégault, *Iberville*. Alex. Jodoin et J.-L. Vincent, *Histoire de Longueuil et de la famille de Longueuil* (Montréal, 1889). Lorin, *Le comte de Frontenac*. Rochemonteix, *Les Jésuites et la N.-F. au XVIIᵉ siècle*, III, 293–305. P.-G. Roy, *La famille Dupont de Neuville* (Lévis, 1934). Antoine d'Eschambault, "La vie aventureuse de Daniel Greysolon, sieur Dulhut," *RHAF*, V (1951–52), 337. É.-Z. Massicotte, "La Compagnie du Nord," *BRH*, XXIV (1918), 275–76; "Histoire du fief de Maricourt," *BRH*, XXXVIII (1932), 631; "Madame Boisberthelot de Beaucours," *BRH*, XXI (1915), 239. P.-G. Roy, "Le sieur de Sauvolles," *BRH*, XIV (1908), 93.

LE MOYNE DE MARTIGNY ET DE LA TRINITÉ, JEAN-BAPTISTE, military officer, seigneur, commander at Fort Bourbon; baptized 2 April 1662 at Montreal; d. July 1709 at Fort Albany. Martigny was one of at least seven children of Jacques Le Moyne de Sainte-Marie and Mathurine Godé, and a nephew of Charles Le Moyne* de Longueuil et de Châteauguay. He married Marie-Élisabeth Guyon de Rouvray on 1 July 1691 at Quebec, by whom he had one son, Jacques, born 20 March 1692.

Jean-Baptiste Le Moyne de Martigny was associated for the major part of his career with the campaigns of the French in Hudson Bay, from 1686 to 1709. In 1686, he took part in the expedition of 70 Canadians and 30 regular troops which Pierre de Troyes* led against the English fur-trading installations on James Bay. Leaving Montreal on 30 March, the party journeyed by the Ottawa route and through a chain of lakes and streams and difficult portages to James Bay, arriving on 18 June. The party captured the four Hudson's Bay Company posts of Moose Fort Charles Fort, Albany Fort, and the depot on Charlton Island.

When Troyes departed in August, he left behind 40 Canadians, including Martigny, under the command of PIERRE LE MOYNE d'Iberville, Martigny's cousin. Martigny remained at James Bay throughout 1687 and most of 1688. On 10 October of that year, he was dispatched with a companion and two Indian guides to bring news of the north both to the authorities in Quebec and to the directors of the Compagnie du Nord, whose interests in the fur trade of the region had provided the principal impetus for the 1686 expedition.

The journey was one of incredible hardship. Their food ran out, their muskets misfired, they were continually forced off the trail to seek subsistence from the wilderness. Then, fearing an attack by Iroquois reported to be in the area, their guides refused to continue along the most direct route but headed instead for Sault Ste Marie, where they arrived in May 1689. It was only in mid-June that Martigny and his companion finally trudged into Montreal.

We lose sight of Martigny until February 1694, when he and other officers were accused before the Conseil Supérieur "of having roamed through the streets of the Lower Town [of Quebec] after an orgy, breaking in and smashing window-panes and sashes in the homes of various citizens." Before this incident, however, he was probably

Le Moyne de Serigny

included in Iberville's abortive preparations in 1690, 1692, and 1693 to capture the one remaining English post in the north, York Fort. Martigny finally returned to Hudson Bay in 1694 as part of the successful expedition which captured the English station in that year. When Iberville, after wintering in the north, sailed away in September 1695, he left 70 men at Fort Bourbon (York Fort) under Gabriel Testard* de La Forest, with Martigny as the latter's lieutenant. The following year, however, the English recaptured their station. Martigny, along with the garrison, was sent as a prisoner to England.

In 1697, the French, undismayed, began preparing once more to try to regain York Fort. JOSEPH LE MOYNE de Serigny, Iberville's brother, was appointed to take a squadron from France to Placentia (Plaisance), where the latter was concluding his destruction of the English fishery in Newfoundland. Martigny was released from captivity in England in time to return to France and join the campaign, for he sailed with Serigny that summer. After taking on Iberville and his Canadian soldiers at Placentia in July, the squadron of five vessels continued to Hudson Bay. After the brilliant victory of Iberville's lead ship, the *Pélican*, over three English warships, the French laid siege to York Fort in September 1697. On the 11th of that month, Iberville picked Martigny to go into the fort under a flag of truce, and an English-imposed blindfold, to demand the release of French prisoners. Governor BALEY refused, and the French resumed their fire; after two days the English commander surrendered the fort to the French.

Iberville immediately prepared to leave Hudson Bay for the last time. He appointed Martigny commander of Fort Bourbon, effective on the departure of the higher-ranking Serigny; however, the latter was detained until the autumn of 1698 while awaiting a replacement for his ship's rudder. This was Martigny's first command; he had under him 20 Canadians and a trading establishment of 10 men under Nicolas JÉRÉMIE.

It is not known when Martigny left Fort Bourbon; he was in Quebec on 22 April 1702 when he purchased from his three sisters and two of his three brothers their portions of the family seigneury of Cap-de-la-Trinité, thus becoming the sole proprietor and seigneur of La Trinité. In 1706, he was reported living in Montreal.

We lose sight of Martigny from 1706 to 1709. In the latter year he joined a party of 100 Canadians under NICOLAS D'AILLEBOUST de Manthet on a journey to James Bay in an effort to recapture Albany Fort (Fort Sainte-Anne), which had first been captured by the French during Martigny's first campaign in 1686, and had been recaptured by James KNIGHT in 1693. Unlike his earlier campaigns, the 1709 venture was a disaster: nearly all of the party died either in battle or from hunger or exposure, and both Martigny and Ailleboust de Manthet were struck down in the very first skirmish. In his observations to the minister, Governor RIGAUD de Vaudreuil pointed out the Canadians' perennial reckless disregard for danger, and their inadequate knowledge of the area. The intendant, JACQUES RAUDOT, confirmed this opinion, mentioned Manthet's "excessive bravery," and deplored the party's failure to equip themselves properly, particularly with a battering ram and fascines for setting fire to the English fort.

After his father's untimely and tragic death, Jacques Le Moyne assumed his name, and became seigneur of La Trinité.

BERNARD POTHIER

AN, Col., C¹¹ᴬ, 10, 13, 15, 30. Charlevoix, *Histoire* (1744), III. [Nicolas Jérémie], "Relation du Détroit et de la Baie d'Hudson par Monsieur Jérémie," with Intro. by J.-H. Prud'homme, Société historique de Saint-Boniface *Bull.*, II (1912). *Jug. et délib.*, III, IV, V. *Kelsey papers* (Doughty and Martin). La Potherie, *Histoire* (1753), I. P.-G. Roy, *Inv. concessions*, II. Frégault, *Iberville*. HBRS, XXI (Rich).

LE MOYNE DE SERIGNY ET DE LOIRE, JOSEPH, naval officer, knight of the order of Saint-Louis, joint commander of Louisiana, governor of Rochefort, baptized 22 July 1668 at Montreal; d. 12 Sept. 1734 at Rochefort. He was the sixth son of Charles Le Moyne* de Longueuil et de Châteauguay and Catherine Thierry, and a younger brother of PIERRE LE MOYNE d'Iberville. Serigny married Marie-Élisabeth Héron at Rochefort, and by her had at least two sons and one daughter.

Joseph Le Moyne de Serigny began his service in 1686; on 28 May he was appointed a midshipman at Rochefort. In November 1687, he acted as interpreter for the Iroquois captives taken during Governor BRISAY de Denonville's campaign that year and sent to Marseilles to serve in the galleys. Denonville's tactlessness in shipping these Indians to France was corrected the following year, and in 1689 Serigny was again dispatched to escort the Iroquois from Marseilles to La Rochelle, where they embarked for New France.

It is difficult to ascertain how long Serigny continued to serve at Rochefort; he may well have taken part in the preparations for Iberville's abortive campaigns against the English at York Fort in Hudson Bay in 1690 and 1692. He became a sub-lieutenant in the navy on 1 Jan. 1692, and in 1693 he saw service aboard his brother's vessel, the *Poli*. When the expedition to York Fort finally materialized in 1694, with Iberville again in command of the *Poli*, Serigny was appointed to command the *Salamandre*. Leaving Rochefort in May 1694, the two frigates came first to Quebec, where Serigny shared with his brother the task of recruiting the 110 Canadians who took part in the campaign and of drawing up contracts with them. The party left Quebec on 10 August, and by 13 October Iberville, after reconnoitering the English installations, was in a position to demand the surrender of the fort. The following day, the commander, Thomas Walsh, "basely surrendered." Louis*, Sieur de Châteauguay, Serigny's brother and his ensign on the *Salamandre*, was lost in the action. After wintering at Fort Bourbon (York Fort), both Iberville and Serigny sailed for France in September 1695; the latter arrived at La Rochelle on 11 October, with a prize of 80 tons in tow.

The following season, Serigny, who had been promoted lieutenant-commander on 1 Jan. 1696, was ordered to sail to Hudson Bay to bring supplies to Fort Bourbon and to attempt the capture of the one remaining English post in the north, Albany Fort (Sainte-Anne), which had been recaptured by James KNIGHT in 1693. He sailed from La Rochelle on 9 May 1696 and, after leaving Iberville at Placentia (Plaisance) on 21 June, departed for Hudson Bay on 8 July with two vessels, the *Hardi* and the *Dragon*. After being delayed by heavy ice, he finally arrived before Fort Bourbon on 2 September, only to find that an English squadron had preceded him by just two hours. After cruising for several days in sight of Bourbon and the enemy squadron, Serigny finally resigned himself to the futility of any counter action. Leaving Fort Bourbon to defend itself, he sailed away to France, arriving at Île d'Aix in October 1696.

Undismayed by their rapid ouster from Fort Bourbon, the French authorities immediately decided to restore their fortunes by seizing Hudson Bay's most lucrative fur-trading station. During the following winter, Serigny prepared to take a squadron of five vessels to Iberville, who joined the expedition at Placentia and took over the command from his brother. After an arduous voyage north, Serigny in the *Palmier* lost his rudder on a sand-bar, and barely arrived before York Fort in time for the siege. He was twice dispatched on 12 September to demand that the English surrender. After being refused the first time, Serigny returned the same afternoon, this time telling the commander, Henry BALEY, "that it would be the last time that he [would come]."

The following day, the French flag flew once more at Bourbon.

Though Serigny was to have sailed immediately with Iberville, he was detained until the following autumn awaiting a replacement from France for his damaged rudder. In the meantime, as the highest ranking officer, he assumed command of Hudson Bay. Despite his inexperience in commercial matters, he was associated closely enough with his brother's interests to trade in furs on his behalf for a year. When his rudder and 50 additional crew members arrived the following summer, Serigny sailed first to Quebec, and then to La Rochelle where he arrived in November 1698.

In the spring of 1699, Serigny was ordered to sail a frigate to Hudson Bay to evacuate Fort Bourbon which was being exchanged for the James Bay posts, in conformity with the terms of the treaty of Ryswick. Before leaving, however, he received orders to sail instead with reinforcements for Iberville, who had embarked upon his Louisiana adventure. Nevertheless Serigny apparently did not go to Louisiana until 1701, when he accompanied his brother on the latter's third voyage. He left France in September of that year commanding the *Palmier* once again. After erecting a storehouse and other buildings on Île Dauphine, and probably engaging in trade, Serigny left Louisiana for France in April 1702.

Like Iberville, he did not return again to the New World until 1706. There is no record of his being in the royal service in France during this period, but there are several suggestions that his Louisiana voyage had been a profitable one. He made a number of important investments, particularly the purchase of the seigneury of Loire in Aunis and, with Iberville, of a number of "captaincies in the coast guards" from the royal treasury. As might be expected, the Le Moynes, a close-knit family pursuing successful careers and accumulating in the process substantial wealth in new and distant colonies, were beginning to be a source of much jealousy. There is as well ample evidence to suggest that they had in fact enjoyed the benefit of illicit gains.

When Iberville led an armament to harass the British in the West Indies in 1706, Serigny was placed in command of the *Coventry*, one of 12 vessels in the powerful squadron. After part of the force ravaged St Christopher (St Kitts), Iberville attacked and mercilessly pillaged the small island of Nevis from 1 April 1706. Of more importance to Serigny's career than the sacking of Nevis was his involvement in various fraudulent enterprises during the campaign. After a thorough investigation by the crown into the alleged malpractices, Serigny's and Iberville's guilt emerged,

Leneuf de La Vallière

as did that of their agents and outfitters in France and nearly every officer of the entire squadron. In close association with Iberville, Serigny had made illicit profits from the sale of merchandise and supplies, which the crown had furnished for the expedition, and from the disposal of Nevis booty. The supplies which he was to take to Louisiana following the capture of Nevis provide a good example of his activities. Instead of sailing directly to the Mississippi colony, Serigny called at Vera Cruz, where he unloaded not only his share of the Nevis booty but a substantial portion of the supplies so direly needed in Louisiana, at a net profit later estimated at 60,000 *piastres*. Despite such unequivocal evidence of guilt, Serigny employed every stratagem to evade costly restitution. The widespread resentment and distrust to which these irregularities gave rise in Louisiana, New France, and especially in the ministry of Marine, compromised for many years the normal advancement in the service of Serigny and his brothers Jean-Baptiste*, Sieur de Bienville and Antoine, Sieur de Châteauguay. Indeed, it was Serigny himself, after the death of Iberville in July 1706, who most personified to the minister the atmosphere of fraudulence that surrounded the whole campaign.

Serigny's activities are virtually unknown for the next ten years; it was not until 1716 or 1717 that the first indication of renewed ministerial favour appeared. In July 1718 he was ordered to sail a vessel of the Compagnie des Indes Occidentales to Louisiana and to remain there for two years serving with Bienville as joint commander of the colony. He was accompanied in this campaign by his son, the Chevalier de Loire, a midshipman at Rochefort. In May 1719, soon after his arrival and with France at war with Spain, he attacked the Spanish base at Pensacola with 3 vessels and 150 men. The Spaniards surrendered easily and although Serigny's brother, Châteauguay, was compelled to return the base to a superior force the following August, a French squadron arrived in September, and promptly regained the town. Following this campaign Serigny was promoted, on 1 Feb. 1720, naval captain and was awarded the coveted cross of Saint-Louis at about the same time.

Serigny was to have returned to France in 1720, but the council of commerce of Louisiana requested in April that he delay his departure pending the return of the more competent officers of the colony from captivity in Havana. Though it is not certain when he did sail, this was the last time he was to see the New World.

In France, Serigny took up residence in the Rochefort area. He was appointed governor of that important port in 1723 and because of its role in shipping to America, he no doubt retained his interest in both Canada and Louisiana. Though the record of his remaining years is spotty, it would seem that at the time of his death at Rochefort on 12 Sept. 1734 he was still governor. He was buried at Loire.

BERNARD POTHIER

Archives de la Charente-Maritime (La Rochelle), E; Minutes Rivière et Soulard. Archives Maritimes, Port de Rochefort, 1E, 340. AN, V⁷, carton 214; Col., B, 19, 20, 33, 39, 42 bis, 59; C¹¹A, 8, 10, 13, 14, 15; C¹³A, 1–6; Marine, B², 183, 187; B³, 132. BN, MS, Fr. 31700; NAF 9294, 22811, 22814, 22815. Charlevoix, *Histoire* (1744), III. *Découvertes et établissements des Français* (Margry), IV. *HBRS*, XI, XX (Rich and Johnson); XXI (Rich). [Nicolas Jérémie], "Relation du Détroit et de la Baie d'Hudson par Monsieur Jérémie," with Intro. by J.-H. Prud'homme, Société hist. de Saint-Boniface *Bull.*, II (1912). *Jug. et délib.*, III. *Kelsey papers* (Doughty and Martin). La Potherie, *Histoire* (1753), I. *MPA* (Rowland and Sanders). Le Jeune, *Dictionnaire*.

Frégault, *Iberville*. Charles Gibson, *Spain in America* (New York, [1966]). Giraud, *Histoire de la Louisiane française*, I, II. Pierre Heinrich, *La Louisiane sous la Compagnie des Indes, 1717–1731* (Paris, [1908]). Alex. Jodoin and J.-L. Vincent, *Histoire de Longueuil et de la famille de Longueuil* (Montréal, 1889). Thérèse Prince-Falmagne, *Un marquis du grand siècle, Jacques-René de Brisay de Denonville, gouverneur de la Nouvelle-France, 1637–1710* (Montréal, 1965).

LENEUF DE LA VALLIÈRE DE BEAUBASSIN, ALEXANDRE, naval captain, knight of the order of Saint-Louis; b. 22 June 1666 and baptized 2 Feb. 1667 at Trois-Rivières, eldest son of MICHEL LENEUF de La Vallière de Beaubassin, governor of Acadia, and of Marie, daughter of Nicolas Denys*; d. 1712.

Like his father, he was a good sailor and became a daring sea-captain. In May 1685, in his father's name, he arrested Bergier Des Ormeaux on Île Royale (Cape Breton Island) and seized his pelts; the latter was the son of Clerbaud Bergier*, the director of the Compagnie des Pêches Sédentaires de l'Acadie.

Leneuf became a sub-lieutenant in 1690. In May 1691, on Buade* de Frontenac's orders, he went by boat from Quebec to Beaubassin to take gifts to the Indians. This mission seems to have been criticized by the king in a memorandum of April 1693 addressed jointly to the governor and the intendant; the king accused the person responsible for distributing the gifts to the Indians in this region of having used for his personal advantage the powder which was intended for them; according to some authors, this was one of the causes of the defection of a certain number of Acadian Indians.

Leneuf was promoted to lieutenant on 1 March 1693. In a letter to the minister on 25 Oct. 1694, concerning a petition by La Vallière, the governor supported him as follows: "Everything he says therein is true; he is a very fine lad, liked and esteemed by everybody here, and has distinguished himself in several encounters."

During the winter of 1698–99 he carried on fur-trading by boat in Baie Verte. The year 1703 gave him an opportunity to take vengeance for the destruction of Beaubassin by CHURCH in 1696. RIGAUD de Vaudreuil sent him in the direction of Boston with a detachment of Abenakis and French. On 21 August (10 August, o.s.) Leneuf and his men made a surprise attack on the little town of Wells and took possession of it. According to François de Beauharnois* de La Boische and Vaudreuil, they laid waste more than 15 leagues of enemy country and killed or captured more than 300 persons. Casco was saved thanks to the resistance put up by Captain Southack* and John MARCH.

On 12 Oct. 1705 RAMEZAY recommended La Vallière to the minister for promotion. In 1707 he became associated with Guillaume GAILLARD, and as commander of the *Nostre-Dame-de-Victoire*, he set out from Quebec in July for Newfoundland, with Thomas MOORE, HENRI-LOUIS DESCHAMPS de Boishébert, and a crew of 100 Canadians, in search of Englishmen. He arrived there on 20 August. This privateering venture had little success, since no prizes were taken during it.

Alexandre was raised to the rank of naval captain on 5 May 1710. He was captured on the *Neptune* and taken as a prisoner to England in August 1711, when he was returning from France to bring aid to Acadia. In October he found himself penniless in Paris. The king recognized his services by granting him the cross of the order of Saint-Louis in June 1712. He died at sea on the *Héros*, in September of the same year.

Alexandre's naval career continued the tradition of the La Vallière family, which up to the period of the conquest furnished an unbroken line of distinguished soldiers and sailors.

J.-ROGER COMEAU

AJTR, Registres d'état civil de Trois-Rivières, 1636–99 (copy in PAC, MG 24, B 14, Papiers Lafontaine). AN, Col., B, 16, ff.193v, 237; 32, f.33v; 34, f.45; C¹¹ᴬ, 11, ff.222, 267; 13, f.77; 21, f.13; 22, f.341; C¹¹ᶜ, 5, f.114; 7, ff.97–98; C¹¹ᴰ, 1, f.192; 3, f.226; C¹¹ᴳ, 3, ff.153–54; D²ᶜ, 222/1, p.36 (copy in PAC); E, 277 (dossier de La Vallière), pièce 21; F¹ᴬ, 17, f.17. AQ, NF, Coll. de pièces jud. et not., liasse 57, pièce 2268. *NYCD* (O'Callaghan and Fernow), IX, 745, 756, 762. Gagnon, "Noms propres au Canada français," 121. Pierre Daviault, *Le baron de Saint-Castin, chef abénaquis* (Montréal, 1939), 152, 209. Fauteux, *Les chevaliers de Saint-Louis*, 105. Sylvester, *Indian wars*, III, 41–45. Samuel Niles, "History of the Indian and French wars," *Mass. Hist. Soc. Coll.*, 3d ser., VI (1837), 248–50.

LENEUF DE LA VALLIÈRE DE BEAU-BASSIN, MICHEL (the elder), captain, commandant and governor of Acadia, major, seigneur of Beaubassin; baptized 31 Oct. 1640 at Trois-Rivières, third son of Jacques Leneuf* de La Poterie, governor of that town, and of Marguerite Legardeur; d. in 1705.

After studying in France, La Vallière returned to Canada in 1657. According to Charlevoix* he was in command on Île Royale (Cape Breton Island) in 1666, under Nicolas Denys*. His first marriage, probably in 1666, was to Marie, only daughter of Denys, and his second, around 1683, was to Françoise, daughter of Simon Denys* de La Trinité. He had eight children, all by his first wife.

In 1672 he is supposed to have set up a fur-trading post on the isthmus of Chignecto, while devoting part of his time to the fishing industry, farming, settlement, and soldiering. On 24 Oct. 1676 Buade* de Frontenac granted him a piece of land 10 square leagues in area, constituting the Beaubassin seigneury. Later this region was to become one of the strategic points in the struggles between French and English in Acadia.

On 7 May 1676, on Frontenac's orders, he set off to cruise along the Acadian coasts to spy on the enemy. While thus occupied, with his brother-in-law Sieur Richard Denys* de Fronsac as his second in command, he seized three English ketches from Boston that were taking on coal at Cape Breton: two of them were declared lawful prizes.

La Vallière was promoted commandant of Acadia in 1678, replacing Pierre de Joybert*. He enjoyed the favour of Frontenac, who in 1681 recommended him to the minister as a future governor, being "a nobleman who has all the qualities of mind and heart necessary to acquit himself well in such a post." Duchesneau* looked with disapproval on this protection, which subsequently was the cause of a disagreement between Duchesneau and Frontenac. Appointed governor in 1683, La Vallière exercised his functions for one year only at Port-Royal (Annapolis Royal, N.S.), after which he returned to his residence at Beaubassin.

The numerous differences in which he was

Leneuf de La Vallière

involved appear to have done him harm. The most serious one was with Bergier*, who since 1682 had been running the Compagnie des Pêches Sédentaires de l'Acadie. Bergier reproached him with creating difficulties for his undertaking by distributing fishing licences too readily to Bostonians, thus preparing the way for the loss of Acadia. Despite everything, Intendant de MEULLES continued to support La Vallière, but the court, yielding to the company's representations, replaced him by François-Marie Perrot* who was named governor in April 1684.

La Vallière maintained good relations with the governor of Boston, Simon Bradstreet; on 8 August 1684 he expressed to him his regret on learning from Bergier, who had made a trip to France, that trade between the two colonies would shortly be forbidden.

In the autumn of 1685 he had the honour of receiving Jacques de Meulles at Beaubassin, on an official visit to Acadian soil. The intendant had to spend the winter with La Vallière, whom he considered to be the person best qualified to give him information about the colony. It was thanks to La Vallière's little sailing-boat, the *Saint-Antoine*, which was assigned to coastal traffic between Port-Royal and Baie Française (Bay of Fundy), that de Meulles was able to go to Port-Royal in the spring of 1686. On BRISAY de Denonville's orders, La Vallière went to France in the autumn to report on the situation in Acadia. On that occasion Denonville expressed to the minister his doubts about the charges levelled against La Vallière in Acadia.

During 1687 La Vallière entrusted his seigneurial domain to his future son-in-law, CLAUDE-SÉBASTIEN DE VILLIEU, and came back to Canada. He was made a midshipman in April of the same year, and received a double promotion in 1689: in June, lieutenant in Acadia, then in October, captain of Frontenac's guards. At the time of the siege of Quebec by Phips*, in 1690, he was responsible for the exchange of prisoners at Pointe de Lévis, in particular Pierre Bécart de Granville and Abbé TROUVÉ. He performed this task so well that Frontenac recommended him for promotion to the rank of major.

In 1691 he became a captain in place of M. d'Escairac (Desquerac), and in August 1695 he was left in command of Fort Cataracoui (Frontenac) with 48 men; his orders were to try to reach an accord with the Iroquois. He returned to Quebec in the spring of 1696, and in June embarked on the *Bouffonne*, with two of his sons, ALEXANDRE and Jacques, and Charles BÉCART de Fonville as officers, and with a crew of 150, in order to go to harass the enemy along the coasts of Acadia. It was in September of the same year that CHURCH attacked Beaubassin and laid it waste.

The king appointed La Vallière town major of Montreal on 28 May 1699. In the autumn CALLIÈRE entrusted him and Father BRUYAS with a diplomatic mission to the governor of Boston, Bellomont; it was to discuss the repatriation of French prisoners and to ascertain his attitude towards the Indians. In 1700, according to a joint report by Callière and BOCHART de Champigny to the minister, dated 6 November, La Vallière was in bad financial straits, and they recommended him to the minister's protection. Two years later the king granted him a gratuity of 500 *livres* to set up in Acadia an establishment for porpoise fishing, but it is not believed that La Vallière ever carried out this plan.

In the autumn of 1704 La Vallière returned to France, bearing official letters from RIGAUD de Vaudreuil and François de Beauharnois* de La Boische. They delegated him to go because of his profound knowledge of Canada's needs, of the Indians, and of the troops; also according to them, because he could expect to be favourably received by the minister. There is every reason to believe that he took advantage of this opportunity to solicit the ratification of the original grant of his seigneurial domain of Beaubassin (1676), which was not in fact ratified until 2 June 1705. This decree confirmed La Vallière's seigneurial claims to Beaubassin and Chipoudy, at the same time recognizing the rights of occupation of the original settlers of these places. Thus ended the disputes which two groups of Acadians from Port-Royal had carried on with him; one group, led by the surgeon Jacques BOURGEOIS, had settled at Beaubassin before La Vallière, and the other led by Pierre TIBAUDEAU had arrived at Chipoudy in 1698.

La Vallière's death probably occurred in July 1705 while he was crossing from France to Canada.

Michel Leneuf de La Vallière had an eventful career, for he was at one and the same time a sailor, traveller, fur-trader, seigneur, colonizer, diplomat, and governor. This deserving native of Trois-Rivières, Frontenac's confidential agent, left his work at Beaubassin unfinished; it is regrettable that none of his four sons continued it.

J.-ROGER COMEAU

[Some authors have claimed that La Vallière took part in an expedition headed for Hudson Bay in 1661, with Fathers Dablon* and Druillettes* (see Jean Delanglez, *Life and voyages of Louis Jolliet* (Chicago, 1948), 151, and Marie de Saint-Jean d'Ars, "A la recherche de la mer du Nord, 1661," *RHAF*, VIII (1954–55), 220–35). P.-G. Roy affirmed this at first (see *BRH*, XXII (1916), 26), but later stated that

La Vallière could not have been present (*Les officiers d'état-major*, 126–28). The account of the journey in *JR* (Thwaites), XLVI, 252ff., does not mention La Vallière. Thus there seems to be little evidence that he took part in the expedition. J.-R.C.]

AN, Col., B, 8, f.30v; 15, f.83; 20, f.228v; 22, f.99; 23, f.64; 25, ff.117, 117v; C¹¹ᴬ, 5, ff.268, 274, 304; 8, ff.150–51; 11, ff.92, 97, 221; 13, f.379; 14, ff.16, 185–86; 18, f.24; 22, ff.23, 341; C¹¹ᴰ, 1, f.148; 5, ff.10, 81–83; E, 277 (dossier de La Vallière), pièces 7, 55; F³, 4, ff.493–94; Section Outre-Mer, G¹, 466 (Recensement de l'Acadie, 1686). AQ, NF, Coll. de pièces jud. et not., liasse 5, pièce 242. PAC, MG 9, B 9, 2. PRO, C.O. 1/55, 37⁴. *Acadiensia Nova* (Morse), I, 24–26, 92f.; II, 56–58. Charlevoix, *Histoire* (1744), I, 388. *Coll. de manuscrits relatifs à la N.-F.*, I, 291–96, 298–99. "Correspondance de Frontenac (1672–82)," *APQ Rapport*, 1926–27, 111, 137. *NYCD* (O'Callaghan and Fernow), IX, 304. Webster, *Acadia*, 206–8.

P.-G. Roy, *Les officiers d'état-major*, 13, 124–46. Tanguay, *Dictionnaire*, I, 381. Bernard, *Le drame acadien*, 128–48. Rameau de Saint-Père, *Une colonie féodale*, I, 145, 167–82, 243–46, 267–70. Azarie Couillard Després, "Les gouverneurs de l'Acadie sous le régime français, 1600–1710," *RSCT*, 3d ser., XXXIII (1939), sect.ι, 263–65. Philéas Gagnon, "Noms propres au Canada français," 121. Ganong, "Historic sites in New Brunswick," 278, 304–5, 315–16. B. T. McCully, "The New England–Acadia fishery dispute and the Nicholson mission of August, 1687," Essex Institute, Salem, Mass., *Hist. Coll.*, XCVI (1960), 278–80.

LENEUF DE LA VALLIÈRE DE BEAU-BASSIN, MICHEL (the younger), captain, major, knight of the order of Saint-Louis, fourth son of MICHEL LENEUF de La Vallière de Beaubassin, governor of Acadia, and of Marie Denys; baptized 28 Oct. 1677 at Trois-Rivières; married Renée Bertrand, daughter of François Bertrand and Jeanne Giraudin; d. 11 Oct. 1740 at Louisbourg.

He distinguished himself particularly in Newfoundland and on Île Royale (Cape Breton Island). In 1701 CALLIÈRE dispatched him with orders to Brouillan [MOMBETON] in Acadia; the latter retained him in his service until 1704. In June 1703 the minister informed Brouillan that he could use La Vallière to command the militia. In the autumn of 1704 La Vallière went to Quebec, then to Placentia (Plaisance), on board the *Wesp*, with several other Canadians and some Abenakis. It was at Placentia that, under AUGER de Subercase's orders, he served with JEAN-BAPTISTE HERTEL de Rouville and François Picoté de Belestre. The governor of Placentia judged him to be a good officer and an upright man; before long, therefore, he recommended him for the first vacant post of ensign.

Promoted to this rank in 1706, La Vallière was active in watching over the coasts of Newfoundland and privateering against the English. He took part in all the cruises against the enemy; the Indians who were with him had boundless confidence in him. Thanks to his courage and foresight, he kept the governor constantly informed of the movements and intentions of the English. Consequently PASTOUR de Costebelle did not hesitate to state that La Vallière had no equal as a privateer, and that he could not serve more usefully elsewhere than in that colony. The minister himself wrote to La Vallière on 30 June 1707, urging him to continue his good service and assuring him of his protection. During a reconnaissance trip which he had been instructed to carry out at St John's that same autumn he was almost drowned. He escaped "only by one of those miraculous strokes of luck reserved for adventurers." In 1708 Costebelle sent him to France to acquaint the minister with the state of the colony, but the latter, while expressing his satisfaction with La Vallière's report, advised Costebelle not to entrust any further such missions to officers, for they weakened the garrison and entailed expenditures.

In 1712, after the fall of the French colony of Newfoundland, La Vallière was entrusted with important missions to the English commandant. During the useful and numerous services that he rendered in Newfoundland, his superiors continually sought promotion for him. At the beginning of 1713, the king counted him among the best of his soldiers and among those who were to take part in the founding of a new colony on Île Royale. On 5 March he was promoted lieutenant; in that capacity he was to serve in the company at Placentia, under Captain Louis Denys* de La Ronde, which was destined to be transferred soon to Île Royale. La Vallière was sent to Île Royale on board the *Semslack*, and his name appeared among those who signed the official taking-over of the site of the future Louisbourg, on 2 Sept. 1713.

He displayed considerable activity at Port-Toulouse (St Peters, N.S.). As early as 1715 he concerned himself with the handful of Acadian families who were trying to found a new settlement there. He was in the settlement at various times and in various capacities, even that of commandant until 1732. His presence gave rise to complaints on the part of certain settlers. In a petition addressed to the minister and dated 1 Oct. 1730, they accused him of seizing control of trade, to their detriment. If we can judge by the correspondence exchanged between Governor Saint-Ovide de Brouillan [Mombeton*] and the minister, such complaints were unfounded, and attributable,

Lenoir

according to Saint-Ovide, particularly to the local missionary.

La Vallière was appointed assistant town major in July 1720, and became a captain in March 1723. In 1728, during Jacques D'ESPIET de Pensens' absence, he was in command on Île Saint-Jean (Prince Edward Island). Two years later the king conferred on him the cross of the order of Saint-Louis.

The minister took an interest in his family, for in 1732 La Vallière obtained from him the assurance that his two sons, Louis and Philippe, would receive promotion at the right moment; moreover, in the spring of 1736, the minister approved the action of Saint-Ovide de Brouillan in sending two of La Vallière's children to spend the winter with Father Maillard* at Maligouèche (Malagawatch, N.S.), to learn the Indian language.

On 1 April 1737 La Vallière obtained a commission as major. From Louisbourg, where he was located, he wrote on 30 June 1738, to the minister in the absence of Major Le Coutre* de Bourville, the acting governor, to inform him of the deplorable state of the colony and of the necessity of sending fishermen to France, because there was a shortage of provisions. Two years later Bourville notified the minister of La Vallière's death, which occurred on 11 Oct. 1740 after an illness of six weeks. He added that he was a good officer who right up to his death had amply demonstrated his ability and his zeal in the king's service. In submitting a request for a pension for his widow, the governor and the financial commissary of Louisbourg paid tribute in their turn to his excellent conduct during his 40 years of service.

J.-ROGER COMEAU

AJTR, Registres d'état civil de Trois-Rivières, 1636–99 (copy in PAC, MG 24, B 14, Papiers Lafontaine). AN, Col., B, 23, f.254; 27, ff.283, 308; 29, ff.159v–160, 438; 35, ff.16, 233; 42, f.477; 52, ff.593v–594; 54, f.503v; 57, f.756v; 61, f.612v; 64, f.479v; C¹¹ᴮ, 1, f.11; 11, f.217; 12, f.26; 20, ff.81–82; 22, f.166; C¹¹ᶜ, 4, ff.163, 167, 220–21; 5, ff.39–40, 87–88, 163; 6, f.361; 7, ff.173, 184; D²ᶜ, 222/2, p.287 (copy in PAC); E, 277 (dossier de La Vallière), pièces 23, 25 bis; Section Outre-Mer, G¹, 407/1, f.57; G³, carton 2054, no. provisoire 8/176, pièce 2.
Fauteux, Les chevaliers de Saint-Louis, 126–27. Robert Le Blant, Philippe de Pastour de Costebelle, 103f., 196. McLennan, Louisbourg, 11.

LENOIR, dit Rolland, FRANÇOIS, soldier, businessman, builder of Fort Rolland at Lachine; b. c. 1642, son of Rolland Lenoir, a bourgeois of Moras in the province of Dauphiné, and of his wife Claudine; buried 6 May 1707 at Montreal.

As a soldier in the company commanded by Henri de Chastelard de Salières, Lenoir had left La Rochelle at the end of May 1665 with part of the troops of the Carignan-Salières regiment, and had landed at Quebec on the following 18 August, after a stormy crossing.

When he received his discharge from the army, Lenoir launched into the fur trade. In 1669 he asked the Sulpicians of Montreal to grant him, for business reasons, a piece of land situated above the Sault Saint-Louis rapids, on the present site of Lachine. His request was granted, but the official transfer was not made until 6 May 1675. As early as 1669, however, he had had a factory built there, which was protected by a stockade. This post, called "Fort Rolland", subsequently became a very thriving business location. Lenoir's frequent contacts with the Indians gave him a thorough knowledge of these primitive tribes; that is perhaps one of the reasons why Buade* de Frontenac took him along on his 1673 expedition to the pays d'en haut. Later, in 1686, Lenoir was to take part in another official expedition, that led by the Chevalier de Troyes* to Hudson Bay.

Lenoir owned several properties in the region around Montreal. On 1 Jan. 1675 he received from Gabriel de Berthé, Sieur de La Joubardière, a grant of land in the Bellevue fief (island of Montreal). Shortly afterwards, Lenoir took legal proceedings against Berthé in connection with a piece of land and a road. The lawsuit was concluded only on 30 Aug. 1683; it ended with Lenoir having to pay 400 livres to Berthé. The following year, on 15 Feb. 1684, François-Marie Perrot* granted him the island called "le petit pain" (one of the Îles aux Pins, near Île Perrot); he then received a further grant of land in 1686.

Lenoir is chiefly known for his clashes with several of his fellow citizens and for his numerous lawsuits. In 1676, for example, he was excommunicated by the Sulpician Étienne GUYOTTE, the parish priest of Lachine, for having traded spirits to the Indians. On 19 December of that year, Lenoir addressed a petition to Intendant Duchesneau*, in which he asserted his right as a settler to trade with the Indians, and asked permission to take legal action against those persons who, at Guyotte's request, had expelled him from the church on 29 November. Having received the intendant's authorization, Lenoir took the matter before the courts. A judgement was finally rendered in his favour in 1677, by which the Conseil Souverain forbade the parish priest Guyotte or any other ecclesiastic to read or cause to be read outside or inside churches "any text other than those concerned with ecclesiastical matters."

Lepailleur de Laferté

In 1681 Lenoir had four servants in his employ, and owned 40 acres under cultivation, 10 muskets, and 2 oxen. But despite his business and his trips to the west, he did not become wealthy. Perhaps his many lawsuits involved a heavy loss of time and money. In any event, he found himself obliged in 1698 to assign Fort Rolland, its outbuildings and all his accounts receivable as security for a loan made to him by CHARLES DE COUAGNE. Lenoir was unable to re-establish himself financially and died penniless in 1707.

His wife, Marie-Madeleine Charbonner, had borne him three children.

IN COLLABORATION WITH ÉMILE FALARDEAU

AJM, Greffe d'Antoine Adhémar; Greffe de Bénigne Basset; Greffe de Claude Maugue; Registres d'état civil de Notre-Dame de Montréal, 2 janv. 1673. *Jug. et délib.* Recensement du Canada, 1681 (Sulte). Gagnon, "Noms propres au Canada français," 121. Tanguay, *Dictionnaire*, I, 381. Sulte, *Mélanges historiques* (Malchelosse), VIII.

LEPAILLEUR DE LAFERTÉ, MICHEL, legal practitioner, court officer, jail-keeper, acting clerk of court, royal notary, judge of seneschal's court, deputy to the king's attorney, acting lieutenant-general for civil and criminal affairs; b. *c.* 1656; he came originally from the parish of Saint-Eustache, Paris, and was the son of Jean Lepailleur and Marie de Lamotte; buried 10 April 1733 at Montreal.

Few legal officers of the French régime can have performed as many different functions, within the judicature itself, as Michel Lepailleur. Yet he did not start on his career until he was about 44 years old. On 3 Nov. 1688, at Batiscan, he had married Catherine Jérémie, Jacques Aubuchon's widow. He had then settled at Quebec, where he was in 1690. He owned a house there, on Rue de la Fontaine Champlain, adjoining Louis Jolliet*'s house, which he rented on 15 June 1693 for five years.

Lepailleur was well thought of: Champigny [BOCHART], in 1698, called him "wise and intelligent." On 25 April 1695 the churchwardens of Quebec had given him powers of attorney to proceed against the debtors of the parochial council, even to the extent of bringing them to court. When the notion of establishing an admiralty court at Quebec was mooted, in 1698, it was to Lepailleur that the intendant gave a commission as clerk of court for that jurisdiction, but the project came to nought. In 1700 Lepailleur was court officer to the Conseil Souverain; in the following year he began to sit as judge of the seneschal's court for the Lauson seigneury; finally in 1702 he was practising as a notary in the region of Quebec. Lepailleur preferred however to go and live at Montreal. He left the capital in the autumn of 1702, turning over to Louis CHAMBALON the minutes of the 70 acts which he had received that year.

At that period Montreal offered many more opportunities than Quebec, where legal officers and candidates for the judicature were numerous. Lepailleur arrived at Montreal with a commission as royal notary dated 20 Oct. 1702; furthermore he remained court officer to the Conseil Supérieur. In 1703 and again in 1705 and 1717, he served as acting clerk of court. From 1703 on, Lepailleur was in addition prison-keeper (jailer). This was an important responsibility, which the authorities did not rate lightly. Lepailleur realized this for the first time in 1709, when a prisoner "of note" managed to escape. On 22 March he was censured and dismissed, but as his successor was still more unlucky than he, Lepailleur was reinstated the following 9 July. On another occasion, in 1731, three prisoners who had been condemned to death took to flight. Lepailleur was himself put in prison for a while. Intendant Hocquart*, however, finally pardoned him on 30 Dec. 1732, but this was the end of Lepailleur's career as a jailer. He was 76 years old.

On 7 Dec. 1706 JACQUES RAUDOT had appointed Lepailleur court crier at Montreal, a post that he held until July 1722. Bégon*, on 24 April 1715, had in addition given him a commission as deputy to the king's attorney. On 13 July 1722 Raudot had, it is true, offered him the post of king's attorney, but on condition that he ceased practising as a notary. Lepailleur refused to do this, and contented himself with acting as deputy king's attorney until 1730. In 1715, 1720, and 1726 he also officiated as acting lieutenant-general. A long and fruitful career, if we bear in mind that his minute-book contains 4,776 notarial acts.

Lepailleur resigned as a notary on 12 Jan. 1733 in favour of his son François-Michel. He died three months later. In 1740 Hocquart wrote of Lepailleur's widow that she had "long striven to fathom the secrets of Indian medicine."

ANDRÉ VACHON

AJQ, Greffe de Louis Chambalon, 15 juin 1693, 25 avril 1695, 26 oct. 1700, Greffe de Gilles Rageot, 5 mai, 18 juillet 1690. AQ, NF, Coll. de pièces jud. et not., 2036; NF, Ins. Cons. sup., III, 9f.; NF, Ord. des int., III, 29v *et seq.*, 66v *et seq.*; VI, 167; VIII, 172; 12b, 1f. É.-Z. Massicotte, "Une lettre du juge Raimbault en 1731," *BRH*, XXII (1916), 242f. L.-G. Verrier, "Les registres de l'amirauté de Québec," *APQ Rapport, 1920–21*, 107f. Massicotte, "Les tribunaux et les officiers de justice," *BRH*, XXXVII

413

Le Pape Du Lescöat

(1931), 188f., 191, 302–4, 307. Tanguay, *Dictionnaire*, I, 383. J.-E. Roy, *Histoire du notariat*, I.

LE PAPE DU LESCÖAT, JEAN-GABRIEL-MARIE (also spelled **Du Lescouat, de Lescöat,** he signed **Du Lescöat)**, priest, Sulpician, nephew of M. Le Nobletz, a famous 17th-century missionary; b. 1639 at Léon (Saint-Malo, in Brittany); d. 7 Feb. 1733 at Montreal.

M. Du Lescöat arrived in Montreal in 1717. He was first the parish priest at Pointe-aux-Trembles (Montreal), in 1718–19, then he was attached to Notre-Dame church in Montreal and was officially priest of the parish from 1725 to 1730. It is believed that it was he who carried on his shoulders the wooden cross that was set up on Mount Royal at that time. Imbued with the spirituality of M. Olier (the founder of the Sulpician order), he was the embodiment of the Sulpician spirit in its first vigour: zeal, humility, charity. He personally taught the guard-house soldiers, whose ignorance was notorious; he visited the sick and the bereaved. As spiritual director of Madame d'Youville [Dufrost*] he inculcated in her a sturdy piety based on the spirit of faith which subsequently was to blossom out in an all-embracing charity.

M. Du Lescöat passed away at 44 years of age. M. Montgolfier*, the superior of the Sulpician seminary in Montreal, wrote in M. Du Lescöat's record after his death: "He was a great man and a saint. All his life he carried out his duties zealously and successfully." Popular veneration made his tomb a place of pilgrimage. Several miraculous cures were attributed to him. His maxim for living, inspired by Pascal, was inscribed as his epitaph: "Flee the world, belong to God."

ALBERTINE FERLAND-ANGERS

AHDM, Lettres circulaires, nécrologies, fondateurs, sœurs de France et de Montréal, 1690–1747, I. ANDM, Registre d'état civil de Ville-Marie, 1720–1730. ASGM, Pour les vénérables Sœurs de l'Hôpital Général de Montréal par leur respectueux serviteur I. Paquin, ptre, curé de St Eustache . . . , 10 mars 1844. ASSM, Étienne Montgolfier, Catalogue historique et chronologique de Saint-Sulpice de Montréal. ASQ, Polygraphie, II, 27. [É.-M. Faillon], *Vie de Mme d'Youville, fondatrice des Sœurs de la Charité de Villemarie dans l'Île Montréal en Canada* (Ville-Marie [Montréal], 1852); *Vie de Mademoiselle Mance et histoire de l'Hôtel-Dieu de Villemarie dans l'île de Montréal en Canada* (2v., Ville-Marie [Montréal], 1854), II, 180; *Vie de la Sœur Bourgeoys, fondatrice de la Congrégation de Notre-Dame de Villemarie en Canada suivie de l'histoire de cet institut jusqu'à ce jour* (2v., Ville-Marie [Montréal], 1853), II, 329. Albertine Ferland-Angers, *Mère d'Youville* (Montréal, 1945). Henri Gauthier, *Sulpitiana* (Montréal, 1926).

LE PESANT ("The Heavy," so-called because of his corpulence; also known as **"The Bear"),** the leading chief of the Ottawas du Sable, he provoked inter-tribal warfare at Detroit in 1706; fl. 1703–12.

In his attempt to build up Detroit at the expense of Michilimackinac, Cadillac [LAUMET] lured Le Pesant's band there shortly after 1701. The chief and other Ottawas went to Montreal in the summer of 1703 to complain to RIGAUD de Vaudreuil of their situation: Cadillac had promised that Jesuits would come to Detroit, and none had yet arrived. Le Pesant also complained that Detroit was not the great centre that Cadillac had promised, and he feared that prices at Detroit would soon rise. He repeated these charges in front of Cadillac later that year.

In June 1706 an incident occurred that became known as the Le Pesant affair. There had been bad feeling, for which MISCOUAKY and others later gave several reasons, between the Ottawa tribes and the Miamis and Hurons also living around Detroit. Then, while on their way to make war against the Sioux, the Ottawas learned that the Miamis and Hurons planned to take advantage of this absence to plunder their camps. The Ottawas returned to Detroit and were joined by Le Pesant and OUTOUTAGAN, who presumably were returning from Michilimackinac. Led by these chiefs, the Ottawas surprised eight Miami chiefs near the fort and slew seven of them. The eighth escaped to warn his people, and the Miamis and Hurons sought refuge in the fort. Father Constantin DELHALLE and a soldier, La Rivière, were accidentally killed by the Ottawas. Cadillac, not expecting a crisis, was in Quebec at this time. VÉNIARD de Bourgmond, the ensign left in charge, decided not to take any action. For the next few weeks skirmishes continued between the Miami-Huron forces and the Ottawas. Intervening in the warfare undoubtedly would have been dangerous for the small garrisons at Detroit and Michilimackinac, but the cost of French inaction was the failure of many attempts at negotiations and the death of scores of Indians. When Cadillac returned, Le Pesant and other Ottawas fled to Michilimackinac, realizing that the death of two Frenchmen would lead to punishment.

The western country remained in turmoil during the next year, as delegations of chiefs and Frenchmen moved between Michilimackinac, Montreal, and Detroit. Vaudreuil insisted that Le Pesant, who was blamed for the entire affair, be turned over to the French. The Ottawa chiefs were reluctant to comply, though they admitted that he should be punished. Outoutagan warned Vaudreuil in June 1707 that the "great bear" had alliances with all the tribes of the *pays d'en haut*. The very nature of tribal organization also stood in the way, as Vaudreuil recognized, for "the savages have no sufficient authority over each other to be able to hand anyone over." Faced with the alternative of a punitive war which would drive the Ottawas into the arms of the Iroquois, he avoided an immediate decision and asked Cadillac to deal with the situation on the spot. In a council held at Detroit in August 1707, the Ottawas finally agreed to help the French secure Le Pesant. JEAN-PAUL LEGARDEUR de Saint-Pierre and PIERRE D'AILLEBOUST d'Argenteuil, accompanied by KINONGÉ, KOUTAOILIBOE, and other chiefs, went to Michilimackinac, apprehended Le Pesant, and sent him to Detroit.

Vaudreuil had given Cadillac authority to deal with Le Pesant, assuming that the chief would be executed. Soon after Le Pesant arrived at Detroit, he escaped by climbing the palisade. Vaudreuil did not believe that the chief—70 years old and corpulent—could thus escape from a heavily guarded fort, and suspected that Cadillac had engineered the escape. But Cadillac had arrested Le Pesant, thus establishing French authority, and by allowing him to escape, had regained favour with the Ottawas, old allies of the French and important partners in the fur trade. Vaudreuil agreed that it was probably right for Cadillac to have freed Le Pesant, since the Ottawas would be needed in case of a union between the Miamis, Hurons, and Iroquois against the French. Yet in his reports to the minister, Vaudreuil pointed out that because of Cadillac's consistent dishonesty, it was difficult to understand the situation. He also suspected that Cadillac was trying to create an empire for himself in the *pays d'en haut*.

Le Pesant is the villain in most versions of the affair, although the Ottawas apparently had just cause to suspect Miami treachery. If this circumstance had been admitted, however, Cadillac's leadership at Detroit would have seemed inadequate. He appears to have found a scapegoat in Le Pesant, with whom he had already had differences. Certainly Cadillac was unjust in putting all blame for the initial attack on the chief. As CLAIRAMBAULT d'Aigremont remarked to the Ottawas in his final report on the affair, "their chiefs have no right to say to the others—'Do so and so,' but only—'It would be advisable to do such and such a thing,' without naming anyone, for otherwise they would not do it at all, as they hate all compulsion." Although respected and feared, Le Pesant could not have led the others to attack had they been unwilling. But by making the chief entirely responsible Cadillac turned the affair to his advantage: in return for pardoning

him Cadillac insisted that the Ottawas still at Michilimackinac settle at Detroit, away from the Jesuits whom he disliked.

Even Vaudreuil admitted in 1707 that Cadillac, in spite of his schemes, seemed to have settled the affair satisfactorily. Events soon proved otherwise. In 1708 Le Pesant was again living at Detroit, and the Miamis, angry that he had not been executed as promised, attacked the fort in revenge. According to Vaudreuil, Cadillac, "thinking to do something brilliant which he believed must do him honour, has spoilt everything." Le Pesant remained at Detroit for the next few years, but did not figure prominently in the affairs of the fort. In 1712 Father JOSEPH-JACQUES MAREST, writing from Michilimackinac, reported that Le Pesant had left Detroit to settle on Manitoulin Island, traditional home of the Ottawa nation.

DONALD CHAPUT

Contemporary accounts by a half-dozen leading participants, Indian and French, do not agree on the cause of the attack, the attribution of guilt, and the roles of Cadillac and Vaudreuil. Secondary studies reflect this confusion.

AN, Col., C^{11A}, 24, f.259; 26, ff.75–79, 106–16, 124, 138–41; 28, ff.3–60; 29, ff.25ff. Charlevoix, *History* (Shea), V, 185–90. "Correspondance de Vaudreuil," APQ *Rapport*, 1939–40, 389. *Découvertes et établissements des Français* (Margry), English MS translation, V, 432–33. *Michigan Pioneer Coll.*, XXXIII, 258–85, 288–94, 319–36, 342–67, 383–86, 395–99, 401–52, 553–54; the complete story can be found in documents printed in this volume, but the arrangement is poor, and some of the translations are inadequate. *NYCD* (O'Callaghan and Fernow), IX, 809. Wis. State Hist. Soc. *Coll.*, XVI, 240–43.

C. M. Burton, "Fort Pontchartrain du Detroit—1701 to 1710—under Cadillac," *Michigan Pioneer Coll.*, XXIX (1899), 240–317, contains a long summary of the affair which usually accepts uncritically Cadillac's version of events. The best secondary account is in Jean Delanglez, "Cadillac, proprietor of Detroit," *Mid-America*, XXXII (1950), 226–58, but the author, a Jesuit, is far from objective when discussing Cadillac's role, and there are errors in ethnological details. Sheldon, *Early history of Michigan*, combines narrative with primary sources; the translation is inferior, however, dates are often missing, and the interpretation is erroneous. [D.C.]

LE PICARD DU MESNIL DE NORREY, JACQUES (Dumesnil-Pâté; he signed as "dumesnj de noré" and "dumesnj noré"), garrison adjutant (*major des troupes*) of the troops in Canada (1706–13), knight of the order of Saint-Louis, co-seigneur of the Saint-Denis fief; b. *c.* 1659, son of Auguste-Philippe Le Picard de Norrey, a soldier, and of Madeleine de Gédouin

Le Picard Du Mesnil

(Gédout), both of Norrey (department of Calvados) in the bishopric of Bayeux; m. Marie-Renée Chorel de Saint-Romain, *dit* d'Orvilliers, on 17 Feb. 1692 at Champlain; they had four children; d. 27 Oct. 1713 at Montreal.

Jacques Le Picard's title was derived from the Norman hamlet of Norrey although his right to use the noble prefix "de" has been questioned. He was, according to Louis-Hector de CALLIÈRE, a native of Caen who was made a midshipman in 1677. He served at Brest and at Rochefort, where in 1684 he was a sub-lieutenant in the navy. In the same year he came to Canada and was promoted to the rank of captain in the colonial regular troops. His first command in the colony was at Trois-Rivières, and there he married a local merchant's daughter. In 1692, the year of his marriage, he advanced to the rank of lieutenant-commander.

When he participated in Governor Louis de Buade* de Frontenac's 1696 expedition against the Iroquois, Le Picard was described as one of the four "senior captains" who each commanded a battalion of regular troops. The notarial archives indicate that he became a resident of Montreal soon afterward. Another source describes him as commandant of Fort Lachine in 1690–91, 1694, and 1696–98.

In 1699, after 15 years of service in Canada without leave, Le Picard received permission to return to France because his father had died and he was anxious to look after his own interests. His wife went with him and did not come back to the colony until 1707. Le Picard was in New France in 1706 when he was appointed garrison adjutant to replace DANEAU de Muy.

The ministry of Marine depended on the garrison adjutant for detailed information on the military personnel in Canada, and Le Picard was instructed to provide this. Every year Le Picard received a dispatch from the minister reminding him to send in his annual report and directing his attention to particular matters in the colony such as the distribution of reinforcements, work on fortifications, and the state of the militia. The promotion of junior officers was strongly influenced by Le Picard's remarks and recommendations. Although, as was customary, he asked for an ensign's commission for his son, he did not abuse his power. "I am quite convinced," wrote the minister in 1708, "that what you have written about their [the officers'] good and bad qualities is free from favouritism." Upon the recommendation of the governor and intendant, Le Picard was made a knight of the order of Saint-Louis on 10 June 1708. The cross of Saint-Louis was a small comfort to Le Picard in the face of his hardships. He was denied leave to visit France again because,

in the minister's opinion, "his presence in Canada is essential." The post of garrison adjutant involved weighty responsibilities and regular travel between Quebec and Montreal. It was not, however, included in the traditional civil and military list of New France so that, because he occupied an "extraordinary" post, Le Picard had to subsist on a captain's salary with irregular bonuses. In 1710 his wife asked the minister of Marine to pay her husband a regular and substantial honorarium in Canada. In the following year Le Picard suggested that he be given the command of Fort Chambly with its perquisites because, he wrote, "I have difficulty maintaining my family on my captain's pay and my gratuity is always held back."

It would be a mistake to picture Le Picard eking out a lean existence. He had been one of the shareholders in the Compagnie de la Colonie in 1700. He was able to provide a nun's dowry for one of his daughters and he seems to have maintained homes in Quebec and Montreal. Five months before his death, he paid 500 *livres* for half of a fief in the seigneury of Contrecœur.

Le Picard's relations with his superiors were generally good. They described him as a gentleman and a loyal subject of his majesty; the minister, for example, expressed his concern when Le Picard suffered a severe injury in 1710. This amicable relationship was strained when, in 1708, Le Picard assembled the company commanders without consulting the intendant in order to name a provisional surgeon-major for Montreal after the death of Pierre BAUDEAU. The minister was shocked by his presumption and blamed the governor for allowing Le Picard to create "a cabal of officers against this intendant [JACQUES RAUDOT]."

After Le Picard's death in 1713, the governor and Intendant Bégon* wrote that "he had served his majesty in this country with distinction for 30 years, having been a model officer. He leaves a widow burdened with four children and without resources; she now has recourse to the honour of your protection, as much for the promotion of her eldest son, a company ensign, as to obtain a pension from his majesty that might give her the means of raising her family. His [Le Picard's] name is known to you, my lord, for he has three brothers who are officers in the Marine." In a letter to Le Picard's brother, the Chevalier de Norrey, the minister assured him that "when I confer with the King on the affairs of . . . [New France] I shall remember to give an account of his services to him and I shall gladly do everything within my power to obtain the favours of his majesty for his wife and children." The minister

Le Poupet de La Boularderie

was true to his word. Le Picard's widow received a pension of 400 *livres* until her death in 1717 and his eldest son, Louis Le Picard de Letéland Du Mesnil was assured of a career in the Marine.

PETER N. MOOGK

AJM, Greffe d'Antoine Adhémar, 1er oct. 1699; 21 juin 1713; 21 févr. 1714; Greffe de Pierre Raimbault, 25 juin, 9 juillet 1714. AJQ, Greffe de Jacques Barbel, 21 mai 1713; Greffe de Louis Chambalon, 22 oct. 1697; 12 oct. 1700; Greffe de Pierre Rivet, 8 mai 1717. AJTR, Greffe de Daniel Normandin, 17 févr. 1692; Greffe de J.-B. Pottier, 27 févr. 1689. AN, Col., B, 27, f.279v; 29, ff.3–6, 107, 405v; 33, f.367; 36, ff.101, 101v, 391; C¹¹A, 14, f.65; 31, f.237; 32, ff.118–19.

"Correspondance de Vaudreuil," APQ *Rapport*, *1921–22*, 372; *1938–39*, 111, 121, 122, 156, 170, 171; *1942–43*, 406, 435; *1947–48*, 170, 223, 260f., 271, 286, 288. *Jug. et délib.*, VI, 909, 920, 923, 1100, 1127. *NYCD* (O'Callaghan and Fernow), IX, 650. PAC *Report, 1899*, Supp. P.-G. Roy, "Ce que Callières pensait de nos officiers," *BRH*, XXVI (1920), 323; *Inv. concessions*, IV, 87ff. Taillemite, *Inventaire analytique, série B*, I.

Fauteux, *Les chevaliers de Saint-Louis*, 102. Gagnon, "Noms propres au Canada français," 57. "La famille Le Picard Dumesny Noré," *BRH*, XLI (1935), 65–7. Raymond Douville, "Deux officiers 'indésirables' des troupes de la Marine," *Cahiers des Dix*, XIX (1954), 71. J.-E. Roy, "Le patronage dans l'armée," *BRH*, II (1896), 114. P.-G. Roy, "La compagnie de sieur Dumesny," *BRH*, X (1904), 128, 159; "Le sieur Dumesny-Noré," *BRH*, XIV (1908), 126f.

LÉPINAY (L'Épine). *See* COUILLARD

LE POUPET DE LA BOULARDERIE, LOUIS-SIMON, knight of the order of Saint-Louis, commandant at Port d'Orléans, Île Royale (North Bay Ingonish, Cape Breton Island), 1719–1738, naval officer, soldier, and colonizer; b. *c.* 1674, probably in Paris; d. 6 June 1738 on Île Royale.

La Boularderie was the son of Antoine Le Poupet, Seigneur de Saint-Aubin, king's secretary, and Jacqueline Arnoulet. In 1702 he married Madeleine Melançon at Port-Royal, Acadia (Annapolis Royal, N.S.); they had two known children, Antoine* and Marie-Madeleine (Mme Jacques Mazière).

He entered the colonial regular troops in 1693 and served as an ensign and later lieutenant to PASTOUR de Costebelle at Plaisance (Placentia), Newfoundland, taking part in the military operations conducted in that theatre by PIERRE LE MOYNE d'Iberville in 1696–97. Four years later he was serving at Port-Royal where he was appointed captain of a company and attained the naval rank of sub-lieutenant, both on 1 Feb. 1702.

In the second of two sieges launched against Port-Royal by Massachusetts forces under John MARCH in 1707, he was wounded while leading a gallant but imprudent sortie and returned to France with his family.

Because of the decay of the French navy following its disastrous defeat at La Hougue (1692), La Boularderie now found employment as a naval officer increasingly difficult and promotion impossible. In 1712 he collected private capital to outfit the king's ship, the *Héros*, which carried the intendant, Bégon*, to Canada; this service failed, however, to gain him hoped-for preferment. Thereafter he turned to merchant shipping, but this on occasion involved him in naval operations. At Quebec to pick up cargo in 1713, he was persuaded by Bégon to carry troops and badly needed supplies to Saint-Ovide de Brouillan [Mombeton*], sent by the French court to take possession of Île Royale and to found the port of Louisbourg.

Two years later La Boularderie used another trading vessel to relieve the starving garrison of Port Toulouse (St Peters, N.S.). This earned him the favour of the admiral of France, the Comte de Toulouse, who had ordered the relief action and to whom La Boularderie subsequently proposed the establishing of an agricultural settlement on Île Royale at Île de Verderonne (Boularderie Island) and the adjacent eastern shore of La Petite Brador (St Andrew's Channel). He also asked for the right to establish a fishery at Port d'Orléans, the harbour of the bay of Niganiche, a cod-drying station some 30 miles north of Île de Verderonne. The fishery would provide return cargoes for ships provisioning Île de Verderonne, which would in time supply Louisbourg. La Boularderie would undertake the necessary transport of fishermen and colonists provided that a naval ship, the *Paon*, were put at his disposal for two years.

The Comte de Toulouse lent his support to the project, and La Boularderie received his concession along La Petite Brador as the seigneury of Boularderie by a brevet of 15 Feb. 1719. He was granted priority right to beaches sufficient for drying the catch of 100 fishermen at Port d'Orléans and was made commandant there and in his seigneury. On 27 Feb. 1720 the shore privilege was transferred to the nearby island of Niganiche (Ingonish) because of the overcrowding of the beaches at Port d'Orléans.

After twice failing, La Boularderie succeeded in 1723 in forming a company at Saint-Malo to provide the capital necessary to exploit his concessions. The enterprise began inauspiciously when he and the company's director, a M. Le Brun,

Le Rat

were captured by pirates and set adrift in a small boat 100 miles from Île Royale. In 1726 La Boularderie had the new company evicted from his concessions because he believed, rightly or wrongly, that for three years it had neglected the duty of settlement while exploiting the lucrative fishery. Le Brun defiantly continued operations from Port d'Orléans and was still there in 1729. In that year a new company was formed with eight merchants of Rouen and Le Havre. La Boularderie returned to Île Royale with 100 winterers, both colonists and fishermen.

The population of La Petite Brador was 13 in 1726, 21 in 1734 and 32 in 1737, by which year La Boularderie had built a water-driven mill. Three years previously he had marketed unmilled grain at Louisbourg. At Niganiche stone warehouses and other buildings were erected. The company claimed to have invested 500,000 *livres* in its establishments and to employ 300 men in shipping, fishing, and cultivation. Unfortunately a managerial crisis in France caused the stoppage of supplies and obliged La Boularderie to return there in 1732 and 1735. The quarrelling associates dissolved their company, and La Boularderie returned to La Petite Brador to establish a shipyard.

This last and most visionary of La Boularderie's projects, which was to begin with the construction of a 1,200-ton vessel for the king of Spain, was blighted at the outset by La Boularderie's shipwreck in the St Lawrence with necessary supplies, and by the withdrawal of his associate, the Sieur Gombert. At the time of his death the ever-resourceful La Boularderie was soliciting support for a road to be built from La Petite Brador to Louisbourg and had persuaded the local authorities to purchase from him coal and materials for fortifications.

Although denied high naval rank, La Boularderie had the unfailing support of the French government for his colonizing and development plans. Even local officials, sceptical of the utility of seigneurial land grants, defended him against detractors. Like most primary colonizing ventures, La Boularderie's required an enormous expenditure of money and effort for little result. Yet the debt-burdened seigneury left by this resilient pioneer was a not inconsiderable monument to his endeavours before it was burned, first by the English, then by the French, in the War of the Austrian Succession.

DALE MIQUELON

AN, Col., B, 40–46; C¹¹ᴬ, 64; C¹¹ᴮ, 1–22; E, 240 (dossier La Boularderie); Marine, C¹. BN, MS, Cabinet des titres, dossiers bleus, 541; dossier 14.145. Charlevoix, *History* (Shea), V, 199. "Correspondance de Vaudreuil," APQ *Rapport, 1947–48*, 228, 230. *Documents relating to Canadian currency during the French period* (Shortt), I, 161. [Samuel Holland], *Holland's description of Cape Breton Island and other documents*, ed. D. C. Harvey (Halifax, 1935), 65–66. Le Jeune, *Dictionnaire* [this biography contains numerous errors, but gives some interesting genealogical material]. J. G. Bourinot, *Historical and descriptive account of the island of Cape Breton and of its memorials of the French régime* (Montreal, 1892), 92n. McLennan, *Louisbourg*, 11, 52, 57–58, 58n. Murdoch, *History of Nova-Scotia*, I, 267, 293.

LE RAT. *See* KONDIARONK

LE ROUGE, JEAN, mason and surveyor; b. in France 1639; buried 30 Sept. 1712 at Charlesbourg.

It was Talon* who on 5 Nov. 1672 conferred upon Le Rouge "the office of surveyor in the [. . .] seigneurial jurisdiction of Quebec and in other parts of this country, to have, hold, and exercise the aforementioned office in conformity with the customary law of Paris." Mason by trade, he was for many years Claude Baillif*'s partner.

The minute-books of the notaries Pierre Duquet* and François GENAPLE disclose the numerous contracts that were entrusted to Jean Le Rouge, who proved himself an ingenious artisan whose talents were often utilized.

These contracts are detailed; it is stipulated, for example, that a house shall be "built upon the former traces and foundations," and that it "shall have two storeys in stonework above the ground floor." Then there are details concerning the doors and windows: "There shall be two window frames to hold glass, and the others only to hold paper"; and also concerning the oven, which is to have a capacity "of about two bushels." Finally, the requirement is sometimes laid down that he "render and deliver, in a finished and perfect state, with the key handed over," for a given date. On 12 Aug. 1685 he signed a contract before the notary Genaple for the building of a powder magazine in one of the bastions of Fort Saint-Louis.

In 1693 Frontenac [Buade*] entrusted to Jean Le Rouge and Pierre Janson*, *dit* Lapalme, the construction of the first Saint-Louis gate to Quebec, which stood until 1878. Then in 1695 Le Rouge built a water-mill in the seigneury of Saint-Ignace, "on the Berger River," at the request of the Reverend Mothers Hospitallers.

He married Jeanne Poitevin, by whom he had four daughters, two of whom died in infancy; the oldest was born at Quebec in 1669.

MAURICE CARRIER

418

AJQ, Greffe de Claude Auber, 3 janv. 1689; Greffe de Romain Becquet, 24 févr. 1679; Greffe de Pierre Duquet, 17 juillet 1672, 30 juin 1683; Greffe de François Genaple, 3 déc. 1682, 22 avril 1683, 9 sept. 1688, 3 juin 1693, 22 avril 1695; Registres d'état civil de Charlesbourg, 30 sept. 1712. IOA, Portes, A-2. *Jug. et délib.*, I, II, III, IV, V. *Ord. comm.* (P.-G. Roy), I, 128f. Recensement du Canada, 1681 (Sulte). Tanguay, *Dictionnaire*, I, 386. P.-G. Roy, *La ville de Québec*, I, 521–22, 539; II, 424–25.

LEROUX, VALENTIN, priest, Recollet, provincial commissioner; b. 1642 in Paris; d. 2 April 1708, also in Paris.

Valentin Leroux entered the Recollet order in 1660, and on 19 May 1663, in Paris, was tonsured and given the minor orders by Guillaume Leboux, bishop of Dax, the Paris see being vacant. On 22 Oct. 1669, at Châlons-sur-Marne, he received episcopal approval to preach sermons and hear confessions, and in 1673 became guardian of the convent at Vitry.

A newcomer to the mission fields, Father Leroux landed at Quebec in September 1677 with the impressive title of provincial commissioner and guardian of the convent at Quebec, thus succeeding Father Potentien OZON. Since their return to New France in 1670, the Recollets had been confined to their sole convent, Notre-Dame-des-Anges, in Quebec. During his six-year term of office, Father Leroux was busily engaged in obtaining the required religious and civil authorizations as well as the land necessary for establishing his religious at Montreal and Trois-Rivières, and in the Upper Town of Quebec.

In 1678, a few months after his arrival in the colony, he had the first chapel of the Third Order constructed at Quebec, and arranged for the solemn transportation to the vault of the convent of Notre-Dame-des-Anges of the bodies of the religious and laymen who had been buried in the first Recollet cemetery. In May of the same year, Father Leroux heard the religious profession of Father JOSEPH DENYS, the first Canadian Recollet, and on 3 February of the following year he conferred the habit on Brother Didace Pelletier*, also a Canadian.

Although he was a peace-loving and conciliatory man, Valentin Leroux, by reason of his office, was involved in 1681 in the "sermon affair," in which Father Adrien LADAN was implicated, and in 1683 in the "bell-turret affair" [*see* HENRI LE ROY]. The latter marked the end of his career in Canada. His successor, Father Henri Le Roy, tried in vain from August 1683 to November of the same year to break the deadlock brought about by Bishop LAVAL in the matter of the bell-tower of the hospice. On 11 November Leroux and Le Roy sailed for France; the former provincial commissioner took with him, among other things, the specifications of the buildings of the famous hospice.

In France Leroux devoted himself to preaching, while at the same time holding other offices: guardian of the convent at Bethléem-les-Meizières in 1684, guardian of the convent in Paris in 1688, custodian and novice-master in 1689, and provincial definitor in 1695. He remained in contact with his friends in Canada, particularly with Buade* de Frontenac, who gave him news of the colony in a letter dated 1 May 1691.

Valentin Leroux was wrongly accused by Louis HENNEPIN, the author of the *Description de la Louisiane*, of publishing under a borrowed name, that of Chrestien Le Clercq*, an account of the taking of Quebec in 1629, a description of the missionary activity of the Recollets before the arrival of the Jesuits in New France, and a work denouncing the intrigues hatched in Canada. Hennepin claimed that he had entrusted to Leroux in 1681 his journal recounting the discovery of the Mississippi in 1680. Hennepin, who considered the name Le Clercq to be a pseudonym, accused Leroux of having attributed to Zénobe Membré excerpts of this journal. This accusation, however, like the first, was false.

Valentin Leroux died on 2 Aug. 1708 in Paris at the age of 66, after 48 years of religious life.

JACQUES VALOIS

Louis Hennepin, *A description of Louisiana*, ed. J. G. Shea (New York, 1880), 62, 269f. Le Clercq, *Premier établissement de la foy*, I, 408; II, 125; *Nouvelle relation de la Gaspésie*, 289f. Hugolin [Stanislas Lemay], *Bibliographie du père Louis Hennepin, récollet* (Montréal, 1937), 14f., 42, 44. Joseph Trudelle, *Les jubilés et les églises et chapelles de la ville et de la banlieue de Québec, 1608–1901* (2v., Québec, 1901–3), II, 1.

LE ROY, HENRI, priest, Recollet, provincial commissioner; b. 1639; d. 28 April 1708 at Paris.

In 1670 Father Henri Le Roy and 19 other Recollets were put in charge of the chaplain services at the military camp of Saint-Sébastien. Two years later he took part in the campaign in Holland as chaplain to the troops. We meet him again in 1677 at Nantes, where he was confessor to the nuns of the order of St Clare.

In 1681 Le Roy was elected provincial commissioner of the Recollet mission in New France. Father Pacôme Perrault, who had been appointed to this office, had declined it. Le Roy was going to succeed Father Valentin LEROUX; but for reasons that are unknown to us his departure was delayed until 1683. He arrived in Quebec on 25 August and was to remain only two and a half months in Canada. Bishop LAVAL's intransigence in the famous "affair of the bell-turret" made him so disgusted that he went back to France, never to return.

It is not easy to elicit the facts of this "affair of the bell-turret," and even less easy to decide between the good and bad faith of the parties concerned. It must be noted that the difficulties that the Recollets encountered never bore upon the authorizations to build the famous hospice; these had been received from the king and the bishop. They bore essentially on the following three points: the real reasons which caused the Recollets to ask for the construction of a hospice; the bishop's restrictive *placet*; the use that the Recollets were alleged to make of the hospice.

An unsigned report, which the historian Jouve attributes to Father Exupère Dethunes*, lists nine reasons proving the necessity for this hospice. The basic argument can be summed up thus: the convent at Notre-Dame-des-Anges was too remote from the centre of Quebec; the ministry was becoming very difficult, for it was necessary to return to the convent every evening; religious who were ill were too far from doctors; the population was complaining of the constraint being exercised on people's consciences, and because of the bishop's niggling demands penitents were reduced to meeting the Recollets secretly; alms-giving was insufficient; and finally, the chaplains to the fort in Upper Town were too far from their source of income.

In the act granting the site of the seneschal's court to the Recollets, dated 28 May 1681, Louis XIV specified that "their house being half a league distant from the town of Quebec, they would need to have in the town a hospice to which to retire when darkness and bad weather overtake them in the exercise of the functions of their institution, whereas they could continue with them more easily if it pleased us to grant them a site that is not necessary to our service. . . ." The king did not speak of an infirmary intended solely for the sick, but rather of a sort of relay station which would facilitate for the religious their ministry in the Upper Town.

It was difficult for Bishop Laval to refuse what the king had granted, but he was going to limit as much as he could the consequences of the royal grant. In his written authorization, given at Quebec on 27 Oct. 1681, he declared that "for your comfort and consolation we give you permission, when you have a house built on the aforesaid site and when one of your religious is detained there by malady, to have holy mass celebrated there by one of your religious in private, and when

the infirm are convalescent, to celebrate mass themselves until they are able to return to the aforementioned convent." The Recollets were not taken in by the bishop's craftiness. Employing expressions such as "ill-will" and "jealousy" with regard to the prelate, the author of the report mentioned previously foresaw by two years the multiple vexations to which the Recollets were to be subjected. "He [the bishop] was biding his time with this to trouble us and find fault with us according to his restriction in this sort of hospice which we would have at Quebec, to raise incidents and subjects of reproach every day when our religious would stop over there, since it is not a regular house. . . ."

With the aid of Buade* de Frontenac, the Recollets' syndic, the construction of the hospice went on for two years, under the displeased eye of the bishop, who was only waiting for a pretext to intervene. This pretext came as a godsend when, at the end of March 1683, the Recollets wanted to add a bell-turret, "which was then and still is today nothing more than four sticks enclosed with boards, without a cross or a weather-cock, without a bell, large or small, and without any construction prepared for hanging it, being in a word only a simple lantern-turret intended to support a small bell such as religious have in every infirmary."

In vain the Recollets protested that they had never had the intention, and never would have it, of saying mass other than in private, *januis clausis*, nor of exercising their functions publicly without the bishop's permission; in vain they claimed that, if ever it was hung in the bell-turret, the little bell would not be used to call the people to services; in vain they said that they were ready to tear down the tiny bell-turret; nothing was of any effect. The bishop suspended all the religious except the superior and laid the hospice under interdict.

The construction of the hospice was carried out under the provincialate of Father Valentin Leroux. When his successor, Father Le Roy, arrived at Quebec on 25 Aug. 1683, things were completely deadlocked and he was being counted on to find a solution. From August till October the new provincial commissioner had at least four interviews, either with the bishop or with the vicars general, and the ordinances that resulted from these interviews attribute to Le Roy obvious absurdities, even to the extent of claiming that he did not know that Recollets were living in the hospice, when he was the superior of these religious.

The ordinance of 24 Oct. 1683 makes a more precise accusation, which some historians, in particular Bertrand* de Latour, were to believe without question. The Recollets were accused "of having administered the sacraments of penitence and communion to lay persons." Names were even given. In a report to the court Bishop Laval wrote: "It was considered an established fact that Mademoiselle D'Aillebout had received communion to fulfil a vow that she had made to St Anthony of Padua." Being aware of the false accusations that were being brought against the Recollets, this lady of high rank, wife of Charles-Joseph d'Ailleboust* Des Muceaux, insisted upon declaring before the notary Maugue*, in the presence of witnesses, that on 20 October, when she had gone to the Recollets' hospice, "Fathers Luc and Joseph" told her "that they did not confess or give communion to anyone." Marie Pournin, wife of the Sieur de La Marque, who accompanied her when this vow was taken, confirmed Madame d'Ailleboust's declarations before the same notary.

The bishop decided to have recourse to the king; the Recollets did the same. They prepared a file on the affair which was certified and confirmed by the intendant, de MEULLES. Father Le Roy sailed on 11 Nov. 1683, convinced that this whole affair arose simply "from the antipathy which His Excellency the Bishop has always had for them." Fathers Valentin Leroux, Luc Buisset, Maxime Le Clercq, and probably Adrien LADAN and Luc FILIASTRE, who were still under suspension, left New France with him.

In the spring of 1684 the king made the following points in a letter on 10 April to the governor and the intendant: he did not want the Recollets to establish a regular convent under the guise of the hospice, but he considered it right that they have a place to betake themselves to in town, since their convent was far away. As for the bell-tower, they were not to build one against the bishop's wishes, but he felt that permission to celebrate mass in private should be granted to them. Finally, he expressed his great surprise that the bishop refused the Recollets the necessary authorizations to go on missions and to carry out their functions outside their convent since, in so doing, he was depriving the settlers of help which he could not furnish through other ecclesiastics. During the year 1684 several reports were drawn up by the Recollets and sent either to the intendant or to the bishop. In particular they said that they were ready to pull down the bell-tower for the peace and welfare of the population. We do not know whether, in fact, the famous bell-turret was ever torn down, but just before he went to the court the bishop restored to the Recollets the authority to preach and confess in his diocese, while the hospice continued to be closely watched by the ecclesiastical authorities to see that no religious lived there permanently.

In France Father Henri Le Roy can be found among the chaplains of the royal armies which besieged and captured the city of Luxemburg in the spring of 1684. He was appointed superior of the convent of Clamecy, in the former province of Nivernais, in the same year. He was guardian of the convent of Versailles twice, from 1703 till the chapter of the province held at Paris on 18 April 1704, and again from 3 July 1707 till his death, which occurred at that convent on 28 April 1708.

JACQUES VALOIS

AAQ, Registres d'insinuation A, 203, 204, 206, 211, 223, 299. AN, Col., B, 11, ff.2v, 4v; 21; 71, f.34; C^{11A}, 6, ff.240, 399; F^3, 6, f.37; 142A, ff.109–10. *Découvertes et établissements des Français* (Margry), I, 3–33. Caron, "Inventaire de documents," *APQ Rapport, 1939–1940*, 249–54. Hyacinthe Lefebvre, *Histoire chronologique de la province des Récollets de Paris, sous le titre de Saint-Denys, en France, depuis 1612, qu'elle fut érigée jusqu'en l'année 1676* (Paris, 1677), 139–42, XX. Le Tac, *Histoire chronologique de la N.-F.* (Réveillaud), 199–208, 222.

LE ROY DE LA POTHERIE, *dit* **Bacqueville de La Potherie (La Poterie), CLAUDE-CHARLES,** historian; b. 15 May 1663 in Paris, son of Charles-Auguste Le Roy de La Potherie de Bacqueville and Françoise Du Sicquet d'Esmainville; d. 18 April 1736 at Guadeloupe.

We know very little about La Potherie's youth except that he must have had a very good education, for he quoted classical authors readily, particularly Virgil and Horace. The first post that he held was that of chief writer in the Marine at Brest, in 1691. He owed this perhaps to family influence, since the La Potheries were connected on the female side with the Phélypeaux, one of whom, Louis, was minister of Marine at that period. Claude-Charles held the post of writer until 1697. He was then appointed commissary of the Marine on board the squadron which, under PIERRE LE MOYNE d'Iberville's direction, was to drive the English out of Hudson Bay. After Iberville's brilliant victory, of which he has left us a detailed and enthusiastic account, La Potherie went back to France. On 1 May 1698 he was appointed comptroller of the Marine and of the fortifications in Canada, and arrived at Quebec on 28 November, just in time to attend Buade* de Frontenac's funeral. La Potherie never ceased to consider the latter as the ideal governor, the father of the country. Having a high, perhaps too high, conception of his role, he was vexed that he was not consulted on the occasion of the peace parleys which were held in 1699–1700 with the Indians. He complained about it to the minister, Jérôme

Le Roy de La Potherie

Phélypeaux. This letter appears in his *Histoire* but without the passages that were too confidential; the latter have been published by Joseph-Edmond Roy.

On 11 March 1700 La Potherie and Élisabeth de Saint-Ours signed their marriage contract before the notary Antoine ADHÉMAR. Three sons at least were born of this marriage: Charles-Auguste, Pierre-Denis, and Marc-René-Augustin; we know little about them. On 5 July he acquired a piece of land and a farm in the seigneury of Saint-Ours, with the intention of settling in Canada, but he left New France in 1701. The historian Claude de Bonnault asserts that his recall was due to differences with certain authorities in the colony, and Robert Le Blant states that his appointment on 31 May 1701 to a lieutenancy of a company in the "Islands" was "an elevation in rank that hardly constituted a promotion."

From then on La Potherie lived in Guadeloupe, while making a few trips to France. In 1705 he tried to get himself appointed military commandant of Guadeloupe and obtained only the post of adjutant; he again sought advancement, but the minister thought his requests extravagant. Furthermore, numerous reports that he addressed to the court about magistrates, military expeditions, his differences with other personalities in the Islands, and the establishment of a parish at Gros Morne did not have any better results. He died at Guadeloupe on 18 April 1736 without ever returning to New France, and 17 years after his wife, whom he had lost on 4 Oct. 1719. It is by his *Histoire de l'Amérique septentrionale* that La Potherie passed into history. The reading of this work gives the impression of a sincere, educated, cultured man, endowed with keen sensitivity and strongly attached to France and her institutions.

During a journey to Paris in 1702 La Potherie submitted his manuscript to the royal censor, who received it favourably. But Jérôme Phélypeaux, the minister of Marine, in a letter to Michel Bégon (senior), opposed La Potherie's dedicating the manuscript to Phélypeaux, and still more his having it printed. The War of the Spanish Succession (1701–13) was apparently the reason for this; France was not desirous of giving information on a country coveted by the English. The author had to wait 14 years for the *privilège*. Some people have put forward the hypothesis that La Potherie had left two works: *Nouveau Voyage du Canada, ou de la Nouvelle-France et les Guerre des Français avec les Anglais et les originaires du pays*, and the *Histoire de l'Amérique septentrionale*. According to Fevret de Fontette the first work dated from 1716, but no copy of it is known to us. The text in question is perhaps a first

incomplete edition of the *Histoire de l'Amérique septentrionale*. Be that as it may, the existence of a manuscript is vouched for by Fontenelle [Le Bovier] in 1702, and it is in a sense confirmed by the king's *privilège*, which in 1721 granted Firmin-Didot permission to "continue to print" a work entitled *Histoire de l'Amérique septentrionale*. This work, which we know, is from 1722, and there exists another edition of it dated 1753. Joseph-Edmond Roy has compared these two editions: same number of pages, same characters, same page breaks, same errors of case. The 1753 title page has a variant in the colour of the ink; an engraving announced in 1722 is lacking; another which was not announced is there in 1753. After making this comparison, Roy wonders whether the 1753 edition is not merely a bookseller's trick.

Of the four volumes of the *Histoire*, volumes I, III, and IV are in the form of letters; the first is the best written and the most trustworthy. Here La Potherie is an eye witness and an excellent observer. His letters on the governments of Quebec, Trois-Rivières, and Montreal offer a fairly complete picture of Canada. The descriptions of places and of the settlers' way of life, the notes on individuals, the statistics on population and sources of revenue show that nothing escaped La Potherie's attention and that he wanted his readers to be well informed. He notes the rivalry between Quebec and Montreal, but without stressing it. If he narrates, he does not refrain from judging. It is not to France's interest, he affirms, to keep Hudson Bay; Canadian trade would suffer. He regrets that Montreal has not been made the capital of Canada.

The portrait that he traces of the Canadian of that time is moderate and just: "The Canadian has tolerably good qualities; he likes war more than anything else, he is physically brave, he has an aptitude for the arts, and given a modicum of instruction he learns easily what he is taught; but he is inclined to be vain and presumptuous; he likes money and spends it somewhat ill-advisedly."

The purpose of volume II, which is divided into chapters and written in a less careful style, is to make known the principal Indian nations and their relations with the French colony. La Potherie had intended to go and study on the spot the problems that he tackles here. As his state of health did not permit that, he contented himself with gathering his information from reliable witnesses: Louis Jolliet*, the Jesuit missionaries, and especially Nicolas PERROT. According to Father Jules Tailhan, a Jesuit and editor of Perrot's *Mémoire*, the latter may not only have given La Potherie verbal information but even have made accessible to him accounts that today are no longer to be found. His view is worth quoting: "... La Potherie knew Perrot in Canada, and ... received from him the most exact data ... almost the whole of his second volume can have been written only with the help of information supplied by Perrot, whose voyages, adventures, and even numerous harangues to the Indians are reported there at length ... except for a very small number of pages, the style in this same volume is noticeably different from that of the other three, and by its loose, incorrect, and involved texture is at most times undistinguishable from that of Perrot; this would not be accounted for by the hypothesis of purely verbal communications made by the latter to La Potherie."

Volumes III and IV are devoted particularly to an account of the Iroquois wars and of the peace parleys which resulted in the general treaty of 1701. For events prior to 1698, the date of his arrival in Canada, La Potherie relied on his informants, whose statements were trustworthy, but not always complete. From 1698 to 1701, although he took no official part in the peace parleys, he followed them closely. During the summer of 1701 he was at Montreal and Sault-Saint-Louis. He also had access to documents which he quotes readily. He summarizes the speeches of CALLIÈRE and of the chiefs of the various nations. He recounts the illness, death, and burial of the Huron chief KONDIARONK (The Rat): "I cannot convey to you, sir, the affliction felt by his nation at the loss of a man possessed of so many good qualities. Few could have a greater acuteness of mind than he, and had he been born a Frenchman he was the type of man to manage the most ticklish affairs of a flourishing state."

To evaluate La Potherie's work properly we must first point out that he lacked one of the essential qualities of the true historian: a concern for attaching a precise date to the events he recounts. Desrosiers wrote, with justification: "The absence of dates in the *Histoire de l'Amérique septentrionale* partakes of the fabulous. With very rare exceptions the reader never knows in what year he is—with La Potherie one can pass from 1665 to 1695 without receiving any warning." Moreover, the general title of the work is inexact. A lot of good will would be required to see in it a history of North America. For the facts prior to his arrival in Canada, the author is content to give a summary according to what was known of them at the time. The title of volume II is equally deceptive. One would expect to find in it a fairly substantial history of the Abenaki nations, whereas the lion's share goes to the Indians of the west, Nicolas Perrot's particular field of activity.

La Potherie's *Histoire* precedes by 20 years that of Charlevoix*. The latter has judged it thus: "This work ... contains somewhat ill-digested reports ... on a good part of the history of Canada. One can count on what the author says as an eye witness; he appears sincere and without passion, but he has not always been well informed as to the rest." The comment of the *Bibliothèque des Voyages* is more generous: "Bacqueville is the first to have written exactly about the settling of the French at Quebec, Montreal, and Trois-Rivières; in particular he has revealed in great detail, in a narration to which he has added much interest, the customs, usages, precepts, form of government, and method of making war and contracting alliances of the Iroquois nation, so famous in this country of North America. These observations have also been extended to some other tribes, such as the Abenaki nation." For his part Robert Le Blant wrote: "The *Histoire de L'Amérique septentrionale* has been underestimated by modern authors. The sincerity of the accounts of which it is composed is confirmed by official correspondence [volume IX of the *NYCD* takes into account the documents quoted by La Potherie]. It [the *Histoire* ...] constitutes to a large extent an original source which must be utilized for the writing of a history of New France that is as exact as possible." This opinion of Le Blant is echoed here. If, instead of seeking in La Potherie's work an historical method such as we define it today, we consider it as a serious source of information on the period, it holds agreeable surprises in store for researchers. Emma Helen Blair realized this clearly when she annotated the narratives published in *Indian tribes*; her explanations are based in very large measure on the writings of Nicolas Perrot and La Potherie.

La Potherie had dreamed of one day writing the history of his own country. He did not do so. "He stands before posterity," writes Joseph-Edmond Roy, "with his four volumes of the *Histoire de l'Amérique septentrionale*."

LÉON POULIOT

AJM, Greffe d'Antoine Adhémar, 11 mars 1700. AN, Col., C¹¹ᴬ, 18, ff.98–129. *Indian tribes* (Blair). La Poterie, *Histoire* (1722). Le Blant, *Histoire de la N.-F. NYCD* (O'Callaghan and Fernow), IX, 622. Nicolas Perrot, *Mémoire sur les mœurs, coustumes et religion des sauvages de l'Amérique septentrionale*, éd. Jules Taillon (Leipzig et Paris, 1864). Taillemite, *Inventaire analytique, série B*, I. *DBF*, IV, 1131f. L.-P. Desrosiers, "La Potherie," in *Centenaire de l'Histoire du Canada de François-Xavier Garneau* (Montréal, 1945), 291–308. J.-E. Roy, "Claude-Charles de la Potherie," *RSCT*, 2d ser., III (1897), sect.ɪ, 3–44.

Le Roy Desmarest

LE ROY DESMAREST, CLAUDE-JOSEPH (usually signed **Desmarest** and rarely **Leroy Desmarest**), royal notary, clerk of the admiralty court and of the Conseil Supérieur of Île Royale (Cape Breton Island), king's attorney of the bailliff's court at Louisbourg; b. *c.* 1695 at Trévoux in the province of Burgundy, son of Catherin Le Roy, notary, and Jeanne-Marie Boyat; d. 1 July 1737 at Louisbourg, Île Royale.

There is no mention of Desmarest's presence in the colony before 8 April 1728 when he married, at Louisbourg, Marie-Suzanne de La Bazanière of La Rochelle. She was the daughter of Pierre de La Bazanière, a navigator, and of Louise Briet, and the widow of François Lorent of Louisbourg. By her Desmarest had at least six children.

That same month, April 1728, he became the colony's royal notary and continued to serve in this capacity until his death. In March 1729, he was appointed clerk of the admiralty court of Île Royale. He subsequently became as well the clerk of the Conseil Supérieur of Île Royale, and he is referred to in this way as early as September 1730. In May 1735 Desmarest was appointed king's attorney of the bailliff's court of Louisbourg and at the time of his death in 1737 he exercised all four of the above functions. In 1741 a detailed inventory was prepared of the property and goods he held in common with his wife.

BERNARD POTHIER

AN, Col., B, 52–65; C¹¹ᴮ, 10–19; E, 126; Section Outre-Mer, G¹, 406/1, pp.145–46; 406/2, pp.29, 112, 171. 248; 406/3, pp.419, 481, 568; 466/3, p.53 (copies in PAC); G³, 2037–2039 (which contain Desmarest's notarial papers).

LERRY. *See* LORIT

LESCÖAT. *See* LE PAPE

L'ESPÉRANCE, CHARLES - LÉOPOLD - ÉBÉRARD DE, Baron of the Holy Roman Empire, lieutenant in the Swiss Régiment de Karrer; b. *c.* 1700 at Montbéliard, illegitimate son of Léopold-Ébérard, Prince de Montbéliard; d. 1738 at Louisbourg.

The Régiment de Karrer, created in 1720 for colonial service, could, like other Swiss regiments, recruit troops from among the people of central and northern Europe, and especially those of the small states on the Rhine frontier. L'Espérance enlisted as a second lieutenant on 28 July 1722, and in 1724 he went with a detachment of 50 men to Île Royale (Cape Breton Island); this brought up to 100 the number of Swiss employed on fortification work in the new colony. He was promoted lieutenant on 19 Feb. 1726, and continued to serve at Louisbourg, under the orders of Captains Merveilleux and François-Joseph de Cailly*, until his death.

There, on 26 Feb. 1725, he married Marguerite, daughter of Gabriel Dangeac, captain of a company of colonial regular troops. In 1731 he solemnly renounced his Lutheran- faith; this action, as he wrote in a petition for a pension, may have caused him to be disinherited. One may well doubt this, in view of the special circumstances of his birth.

The French-speaking principality of Montbéliard, which had gone over to the Reformation in the 16th century and was under the domination of the German house of Württemberg, maintained until 1748 a purely theoretical independence. Léopold-Ébérard, Prince de Montbéliard, of the younger branch of the house of Württemberg, who reigned from 1698 to 1723, chose as concubines four sisters, the daughters of a former tailor and soldier named Richard Curie, and they bore him some 23 children. The prince elevated the Curie sisters to the rank of baronesses of the Holy Roman Empire with the name of L'Espérance, a name borne by all the children, although the mothers had been provided with husbands to gloss over the scandal. Sébastienne, the eldest, Charles-Léopold-Ébérard's mother, died around 1715. She had married a certain Sifert, and the name Sandersleben which her son attributed to him was that of the husband of Henriette-Edwige, another of the Curie daughters. The Jean Fleury of whom Charles-Léopold-Ébérard claimed to be the son does not seem to have existed. As all the certificates of baptism were forgeries to start with and were later falsified for inheritance purposes, one cannot be more precise, but the abundance of evidence leaves no doubt as to the illegitimate origin of the L'Espérance children.

On the prince's death in 1723, the children of an earlier morganatic wife, together with those born of a late marriage to Henriette-Edwige de L'Espérance, claimed the estate. The emperor dismissed their claims, and the principality passed to the principal branch of the house of Württemberg. They continued to conduct endless lawsuits, both in Vienna and in Paris, to obtain their share of the workable domain of the seigneuries. Léopold-Ébérard did not recognize the children born of Sébastienne, and the name of the Louisbourg officer does not appear among the claimants. His son, Charles-Gabriel-Sébastien*, who was to become governor of the Islands of Saint-Pierre and Miquelon and brigadier-general in 1788, does not seem to have had any share in the inheritance either.

After an obscure career and several years of illness, the Baron de L'Espérance died on 10 Nov. 1738 at Louisbourg, leaving his family in dire straits.

LOUISE DECHÊNE

AN, K^XI, carton 1785; Col., C^11B, 1–26; E, 281 (dossier de L'Espérance); Section Outre-Mer, G^1, 406–7, 466; G^3, carton 2058 (copies in PAC). SHA, corps de troupes, Sous-série X^I, cartons 31, 33. Louis de Rouvroy de Saint-Simon, *Mémoires* (7v., Paris, 1958), VI, 586–88; VII, 303–5. L.-G. Michaud, *Biographie universelle ancienne et moderne* . . . (85v., Paris, 1811–62), XXIX, 466–68; LI, 278–79. McLennan, *Louisbourg*. John Viénot, *La vie fantastique de Léopold-Ebérard, prince de Montbéliard, 17 février 1698–25 mars 1723* (Montbéliard, 1934).

LESPINAY (L'Espinay). *See* COUILLARD

LESPINAY, JEAN-MICHEL DE, officer in Canada, then governor of Louisiana; he came originally from the region of Fougères in the province of Brittany; d. 3 Jan. 1721 at Fort-Royal (Martinique).

He became a midshipman at Rochefort on 25 July 1683, went to Canada as an ensign in the troops in 1687, was promoted lieutenant on half-pay in 1690, and lieutenant on the active list in 1691. The same year, at his request, he was appointed by Buade* de Frontenac port captain of Quebec. He had volunteered "to be responsible for preventing the said port from being befouled by the great amount of filth thrown into it by various individuals." This function did not carry any emoluments with it, and on 24 Oct. 1694 Frontenac renewed a request for a commission from the king, stating that the post of port captain was "something which will be useful for the public and no liability to the king." But Lespinay was considering leaving Canada, where he had served for eight years, and asked for permission to go to France to look after his family affairs. Frontenac did try to retain him by dangling the prospect of promotion before him, but without success. On 20 April 1695 he received a year's leave, and he did not return. Indeed, on 1 May 1698 he obtained permission to remain in France to serve at Rochefort as a sub-lieutenant, a rank which he had obtained on 5 May 1695. We know nothing of his activities during the years that followed, except that he was promoted to lieutenant-commander on 1 Nov. 1705.

After Louis XIV's death he enjoyed the protection of the Comte de Toulouse, president of the council of Marine, and of the financier Crozat, who had in September 1714 a company holding the trading monopoly of Louisiana. Lespinay was appointed governor of the colony on 12 March 1716. He left France on 21 December on board the *Ludlow*, which he commanded, and reached his post in February 1717. To attach Lespinay to his interests Crozat granted him fairly extensive financial advantages, in particular two per cent interest on all products exported by the colony.

Before leaving France, the new governor had sought the cross of the order of Saint-Louis, out of a concern, as he claimed, for increasing his prestige in the eyes of the Indians, the latter "knowing that it is a mark of distinction among military men in France." His request was granted on 21 Oct. 1716. Powers appreciably more extensive than those of his predecessor, Cadillac [LAUMET] had been conferred upon him; this change gave rise to a dissatisfaction in the colony that was the more keen because, having barely set foot ashore, he did not hesitate to exceed his instructions and to assume complete control over finance and justice. Complaints were soon voiced about his arrogance and his harshness towards the various groups in the population. He pursued an ill-advised policy towards the natives which, according to Marcel Giraud, "revealed an elementary ignorance of the mentality of the original inhabitants." Behaviour of this kind would tend to prove that during his stay in Canada he had had few contacts with the Indians. In Louisiana he was arrogant and avaricious in his treatment of them; stingy with the annual gifts, he reserved the distribution of them for himself, thus wiping out Le Moyne* de Bienville's felicitous influence. Moreover, he remained too short a time in the country to be able to visit all the posts.

Lespinay restricted the activities of the newly created Conseil Supérieur, forced it to sit at his personal domicile, and in actual fact stripped it of its judicial and administrative functions. He did, however, interest himself in the prospecting being carried out in the interior, but lack of funds slowed down exploration. All that was done was to send help to Fort Rosalie in the Natchez country and to create a new post among the Alibamus.

The financial commissary, Hubert, even expressed doubts about the honesty of the governor, whom he accused of leading a scandalous life. All these criticisms, Crozat's resignation, and the passing of Louisiana into the control of John Law's Compagnie d'Occident, brought about Lespinay's recall at the end of 1717. Nevertheless he did not fall into disgrace, since on 1 Nov. 1717 he was nominated governor of Grenada. He did have some difficulties, however. On 20 Sept. 1718 Jean-Baptiste Duché, a director of the Compagnie d'Occident, sent a report to the Comte de Toulouse

Lessard

concerning Lespinay's conduct in Louisiana: "If it is true, as we are informed, that after 11 months in authority he is bringing back with him 15,000 *piastres*, I hope that Your Highness will consider it right to make an example of him." His possessions were sequestered at Rochefort, and he remained in France during the whole of 1719. Was he a victim of slander, or did he have the benefit of powerful protection? We do not know. In any case no sanction was pronounced against him.

On 18 May 1720 he left the Île d'Aix on the *Atalante* to go and take up his new command on Grenada, where he landed on 28 June but did not hold office long there, since he died six months later.

Lespinay seems to have been an active but overbearing official, vain, and more concerned with his own interests than with those of the service.

ÉTIENNE TAILLEMITE

AN, Col., B, 16, ff.26, 192v; 17, f.236v; 20, f.64; 38, f.329; 39, f.451; C⁸ᴬ, 27, f.75; 28, f.1; C¹¹ᴬ, 13, ff.42v, 66; C¹³ᴬ, 4, 5; D²ᶜ, 49, ff.31v, 36, 41v; E, 278; F³, 241, f.141; Marine, B¹, 9, ff.444, 458, 461, 554, 645; 19, ff.493, 495; C¹, 150, ff.298, 353, 451; 161; C⁷, 181. Giraud, *Histoire de la Louisiane française*, II. O'Neill, *Church and state in Louisiana*, 106–14.

LESSARD, ÉTIENNE DE, pioneer of the Beaupré shore, seigneur of Île-aux-Coudres and co-seigneur of Lanoraie, donor of the land on which the first three churches of Sainte-Anne de Beaupré were built; b. 1623 at Chambois, in the province of Normandy; d. 19 April 1703.

He arrived in New France before 16 June 1646, and on 10 Feb. 1651 obtained the title to his domain, called Saint-Étienne, which was at Petit-Cap on the Beaupré shore (now Sainte-Anne de Beaupré). On 8 April 1652 he married Marguerite Sevestre, daughter of Charles Sevestre*, procurator-syndic of the Communauté des Habitants. Twelve children were born of this marriage.

On 8 March 1658, according to a deed of gift, "because of the desire and the pious wish that the settlers of Beaupré have long had for a church or chapel in which they can share in divine service and participate in the sacraments of our Holy Mother Church, [he] gives to the parish priests who will be appointed a piece of land with a frontage of two *arpents* and a depth of one and a half leagues. The said gift is made on condition that in the present year 1658 the settlers ... will begin without delay and will continue the building of a church or chapel on the said land." This church, the site of which was blessed on 13 March 1658 by Abbé Guillaume Vignal* in the presence of the acting governor Louis d'Ailleboust*, was

serving as a parish church in 1660. But in 1661 the damage wrought by high tides forced Bishop LAVAL to build a second church, in half-timbered field-stone, on new ground farther from the shore, to the east, at the foot of the great slope; this ground was also given by Étienne de Lessard. On the same ground, in 1676, Bishop Laval was to build a third church, of stone. Étienne de Lessard's house served as a boarding-house for pilgrims.

On 4 March 1677 Buade* de Frontenac granted him Île-aux-Coudres as a fief and seigneury. As Étienne de Lessard did not intend to establish settlers there, he sold it for 100 *livres* to the seminary of Quebec on 19 Oct. 1687. He became co-seigneur of Lanoraie on 27 April 1688, but on 12 March 1698 he sold his share to Louis de Niort. He died on 19 April 1703 at Sainte-Anne de Beaupré.

LUCIEN GAGNÉ

Archives de la Basilique de Sainte-Anne de Beaupré, Cartulaires, PA-19: L-1; PA-33: LE (E), D-5; Registres, 19 avril 1703. ANDQ, Registres des baptêmes, mariages et sépultures, 8 avril 1652. ASQ, Documents Faribault, 78; Paroisses diverses, 72, 73, 75; Procure, carton Ste-Anne, 15; Seigneurie. JJ (Laverdière et Casgrain), 89, 100, 232–33. Provost, *Le Séminaire de Québec: documents et biographies*, 97–99. P.-G. Roy, *Inv. concessions*, I, 162–63; III, 54; IV, 23–25. P.-G. et A. Roy, *Inv. greffes not.*, I, 71, 149. Alphonse Lessard, "Le berceau de la famille de Lessard," *BRH*, XXXV (1929), 75–78. Gustave Ouimet, "La dévotion à sainte Anne au Canada," *BRH*, VIII (1902), 218f. M. de Ste-A., "La première chapelle de Sainte-Anne de Beaupré," *BRH*, IX (1903), 210–13. Lucien Serre, "L'ancêtre des Lessard," *BRH*, XXXIII (1927), 549–53.

LESTRINGANT DE SAINT-MARTIN (Viabon), ALEXANDRE-JOSEPH, ensign, lieutenant, captain; b. c. 1660 at Saint-Benoît-le-Fleury-sur-Loire, son of Nicolas de Lestringant and Anne Jacquier; d. 1722.

Lestringant de Saint-Martin came to New France as a soldier in 1684. He became a lieutenant on the active list on 1 March 1688, a half-pay captain in 1691, a naval sub-lieutenant on 5 May 1695, commander of the Quebec battalion during Buade* de Frontenac's campaign against the Onondagas in 1696, and a captain in the colonial regular troops on 12 May 1697. On 11 Nov. 1702 Beauharnois* de La Boische recommended him to the minister for the position of town major of Trois-Rivières, saying that he was the protégé of the Comte de Saint-Florentin et de La Vrillière; this recommendation came to nothing.

On 1 Sept. 1694, at Montreal, Lestringant de Saint-Martin married Louise-Madeleine, daughter of Nicolas Juchereau* de Saint-Denis, seigneur of

Beauport, and of Marie-Thérèse Giffard. Two boys and two girls were born of this marriage, but only the latter, Marie-Anne-Josette and Madeleine-Thérèse, survived their father, the two boys having died soon after birth.

In August 1706 Lestringant de Saint-Martin and his wife instituted proceedings against the Jesuits over a question of precedence in the church at Beauport, but after a month's debate the two parties reached an agreement. On 7 Jan. 1711, Marie-Anne-Josette, still a minor, provoked a scandal in the region of Quebec by a marriage "à la gaumine" with Louis de Montéléon, an officer in the colonial regular troops. This marriage gave rise to two lawsuits, one before the officiality of Quebec, the other before the civil authorities. On 16 February, however, the affair was settled by a religious marriage, celebrated at Beauport.

It seems that Lestringant de Saint-Martin, after his wife's death in June 1721, went to France, where on 8 June 1722 he received the cross of the order of Saint-Louis. He died during the same year, probably in France.

ROLAND-J. AUGER

AJM, Greffe d'Antoine Adhémar, 1er sept. 1694. AQ, Famille Lestringant de Saint-Martin. "Estat des employs vaquans ausquels Monsieur le comte de Frontenac . . . a pourvue en l'année 1691 en attendant les commissions de sa majesté," BRH, XIII (1907), 339. Jug. et délib., III, V, VI. "Lettre du gouverneur de Beauharnois au ministre," BRH, LI (1945), 300–9. "Les mariages à la gaumine," APQ Rapport, 1920–21, 366–407. PAC Report, 1899, 94, 281, 328. Bonnault, "Le Canada militaire," 278, 296, 300. Tanguay, Dictionnaire, I, 175; III, 330. Fauteux, Les chevaliers de Saint-Louis, 120. J.-E. Roy, "Le patronage dans l'armée," BRH, II (1896), 115. P.-G. Roy, "Les deux capitaines de Saint-Martin," BRH, XXVI (1920), 353–58.

LE SUEUR, PIERRE-CHARLES, donné of the Jesuits, explorer, trader, coureur de bois, judge; b. 1657 in Artois, France; d. at sea 1704.

While still a youth, Le Sueur came to Canada under the auspices of the Jesuits, who sent him as a donné to their mission at Sault Ste Marie. The lure of the fur trade was too great for the youth to resist, and in 1680 he was denounced as a coureur de bois. He was soon involved in trade with the Sioux on the upper Mississippi, became thoroughly schooled in frontier life, and was popular among the Indians. On 12 Sept. 1682, in Montreal, he entered into an agreement with others for a voyage to Michilimackinac. In 1689 he was at Fort Saint-Antoine, Baie des Puants (Green Bay, Wis.), when Nicolas PERROT proclaimed the French king's sovereignty over the area. Le Sueur married, in 1690, Marguerite, daughter of Michel

MESSIER, and a relative of PIERRE LE MOYNE d'Iberville; they had a son and four daughters.

Despite the opposition of BOCHART de Champigny, who regarded him as little more than Buade* de Frontenac's ally in the fur trade, Le Sueur obtained in 1693 from Frontenac a commission to reopen the routes from Lake Superior to the Mississippi, to build a post at La Pointe (Chequamegon Bay), to maintain peace between the Chippewas and the Sioux, and to protect the latter from attacks by their enemies, the Foxes and Mascoutens. Le Sueur was undoubtedly a successful trader, but his knowledge of the Sioux and Chippewa languages and his familiarity with the geography of the upper Mississippi enabled him also to play a role in Indian diplomacy. In the summer of 1695 he returned from the west, bringing with him a great Sioux chief to make an alliance with Frontenac, and a Chippewa chief who ratified peace between the two nations. The Sioux died in Montreal.

It was probably early in 1697 that Le Sueur presented a report to the king proposing a permanent post among the Sioux. He mentioned the advantages of copper and lead mines in the area, the lucrative fur trade, and the availability of wood for construction purposes; he suggested that he be appointed commandant at La Pointe with exclusive trading rights for ten years and with permission to take arms to the Sioux; he requested a guard of 20 men for the fort and an equal number for mining. Le Sueur's proposals were rejected; the Illinois Indians opposed the giving of arms to their enemies, the Sioux, and the officials in New France claimed that Le Sueur's request for mining privileges was but a pretext for trading.

Undaunted, Le Sueur went to France in 1697 and finally obtained permission to take 50 men with him into Sioux country to open mines and engage in limited trade; he was specifically forbidden to trade in beaver. He formed a company, but misfortune dogged him. Champigny railed against the grant to Le Sueur: "I think the only mines that he seeks in those regions are mines of beaver-skins." It is possible that, during his stay in Paris, Le Sueur communicated the results of his explorations of the Mississippi to the cartographer, FRANQUELIN.

It is difficult to trace Le Sueur's movements during the next two years. He returned to France at least once, and in 1698 was captured by the English, but later released. At the French court his fortunes varied according to the changes in official policy: the trading permit granted him on 21 May 1698 was revoked on 27 May 1699, when it was decided to abandon trade with the Sioux because of Fox opposition. While in France Le

Le Sueur

Sueur gave information to Guillaume Delisle which was incorporated into one of his maps.

The antagonism of the officials in New France blocked Le Sueur's way until 1699. In that year, with the support of his wife's relative, Iberville, who no doubt expected Le Sueur to be of considerable service in the organization of the Louisiana trade, he obtained royal permission to undertake an expedition from the colony to the Sioux country to exploit mines. Le Sueur now formed a *compagnie des Sioux*, of which Iberville and the farmer-general Alexandre L'Huillier were members. He recruited men and artisans at La Rochelle and accompanied Iberville on his second expedition to Louisiana. They arrived there in December 1699.

In 1700, with two boats manned by 19 men including the carpenter Pénigaut, Le Sueur started up the Mississippi. He reached the mouth of the Rivière Saint-Pierre (Minnesota) on 19 September and continued up it to the Rivière Verte (also called Rivière Bleue, now Blue Earth River). There he built Fort L'Huillier. The following spring Le Sueur left a detachment of men under Éraque at the fort, and returned to Mobile with a cargo of furs and minerals. His activities during this period, particularly his open disregard of the prohibition against the beaver trade, further irritated the authorities in New France and led to a fresh series of accusations by CALLIÈRE. In April 1702 Le Sueur returned to France with Iberville.

Le Sueur gave an account of his expedition to the minister and showed his caissons of minerals. He presented a *mémoire* summarizing his activities during a 15-year period of exploring the upper Mississippi. He now asked for a commission as judge at newly established Mobile, permission to employ men in further discovery work, a substantial salary, and the transportation of his family to Louisiana. Iberville supported these requests for he still wanted to use Le Sueur to win a share of the Mississippi Valley trade for Louisiana, at the expense of both Canada and the English colonies if necessary. Although Pontchartrain denounced Iberville's projects and also those of Le Sueur, the king appointed the latter judge at Mobile, permitted him to recruit men for exploratory purposes, and agreed to pay him for his work among the Sioux and Illinois. Le Sueur was supposed to leave France on the *Loire* in 1703 but he did not actually sail until the spring of 1704 aboard the *Pélican*. The ship, which was carrying nurses and women to Louisiana, stopped at Havana where the plague was raging. The *Pélican* reached Louisiana in July, but Le Sueur had been "mortally and fatally" striken by the plague and had died at sea.

His wife had applied for permission to go with her children to Louisiana. This was granted in a royal *mémoire* to RIGAUD de Vaudreuil dated 14 July 1704. Madame Le Sueur probably reached Mobile in 1705 and may not have heard of her husband's death until her arrival in Louisiana. Their son, Jean-Paul, may have been the Le Sueur, known as "the Canadian," who was later active with Le Moyne* de Bienville against the Natchez.

Pierre-Charles Le Sueur helped to arouse French interest in the discovery of mines and contributed in an important way to the cartography of the upper Mississippi region. His connection with Frontenac and later with Iberville in Louisiana made him a controversial figure in the political and commercial rivalries of his day.

A. P. NASATIR

Le Sueur's "Mémoires" (extracts of letters and notes on conversations with him by Guillaume Delisle) are in AN, Marine, 2JJ, 56 (formerly Archives du Service Hydrographique de la Marine, 115ˣ, no 9). Margry's extracts from these "Mémoires" are in BN, MS, NAF 9296 (Margry), 47, published in *Découvertes et établissements des Français* (Margry), VI, 69ff.; parts are translated in Wis. State Hist. Soc. *Coll.*, XVI, 177ff. The most significant document in the "Mémoires" is a letter dated 4 April 1700; this takes the form of a journal beginning at La Rochelle, 16 Oct. 1699, and describing the journey to Louisiana and up the Mississippi (*see* BN, NAF 21395 (Arnoul), 5–13). Pénigaut incorporated Le Sueur's narration into his own "Journal" which is printed in *Découvertes et établissements des Français* (Margry), V, 375–586. Several translations of parts of the Pénigaut journal have been made, but most satisfactory is the complete translation: *Fleur de Lys et calumet: being the Pénicaut narrative of French adventure in Louisiana*, ed. and tr. R. G. McWilliams (Baton Rouge, La., 1953).

Guillaume Delisle's "Carte de la Rivière de Mississipi, 1702," based on the "Mémoires" of Le Sueur, is in BN, Cartes et plans, Portefeuille 138², div.3, no. 2. An anonymous map, apparently illustrating Le Sueur's voyage of 1700–1, is to be found at the Service historique de la Marine (Paris), LXIX, no.27.

See also: AN, Col., C¹¹ᴬ, 15, f.127v. N. M. M. Surrey, *Calendar of manuscripts in Paris archives and libraries relating to the history of the Mississippi valley to 1803* (2v., Washington, 1926, 1928). Marc de Villiers Du Terrage, "Noms de lieux Sioux tirés d'un dictionnaire inédit et probablement perdu de Le Sueur," Société des Américanistes de Paris J., nouv. série, XIV (1922), 220–21. Giraud, *Histoire de la Louisiane française*, I. P. J. Hamilton, *Colonial Mobile* (Boston, 1897; rev. ed., 1910). Kellogg, *French régime*. N. M. M. Surrey, *Commerce of Louisiana during the French régime, 1699–1763* (New York, 1916). Thomas Hughes, "Site of Le Sueur's Fort L'Huillier," Minn. Hist. Soc. *Coll.*, XII (1905–8), 283–95. Doane Robinson, "The Le Sueur tradition," S.D. Hist. Soc. *Coll.*, IX (1918), 336–46.

LE TAC, XISTE (Sixte), priest, Recollet, missionary; b. *c.* 1650 at Rouen; d. 10 Aug. 1718 in his native city.

Xiste Le Tac sailed for Canada in June 1676. He served as a priest in the Quebec region until January 1678, then went to Trois-Rivières, which was created a parish by Bishop LAVAL on 30 Oct. 1678; he officiated there as priest. In his first year in the parish, Le Tac supervised the building of a residence for the Recollets, and in 1682 the construction of a new church, more modest than the preceding one, which had not been completed. During this year 1682 Gaultier de Bruslon had been appointed parish priest of Trois-Rivières; Xiste Le Tac continued, however, to serve the parish as vicar. In 1683 he returned to Quebec, and remained there until 1689; for a certain time he was director of the Third Order and novice-master. In June he went to Placentia (Plaisance), together with Father JOSEPH DENYS and Bishop Saint-Vallier [LA CROIX]; the latter, who wanted to establish the Recollets in Newfoundland, appointed Le Tac superior of the mission and Father Denys priest of the parish of Plaisance.

Soon after 7 September of the same year, Le Tac returned to France. His task was to deliver to the king letters from the bishop of Quebec, who was asking for Recollets for the Acadian missions. But Le Tac's quarrel with M. Parat*, the governor of Plaisance, about the use of the fishing rooms, was perhaps the principal reason why he left for Europe. He was not to see New France again, and he died on 10 Aug. 1718 at the convent of the Recollets in Rouen.

Xiste Le Tac owes his notoriety to Eugène Réveillaud, who, having found an anonymous manuscript in the departmental archives of Seine-et-Oise, published it in 1888, stating that this *Histoire chronologique* was Le Tac's work. Réveillaud based his argument on the manuscript's writing "compared with other documents"; Benjamin Sulte corroborated the statement, after comparing the manuscript with the parish registers of Trois-Rivières, in which Le Tac had entered several certificates of baptism, marriage, and burial. Can one on that account declare so categorically that Le Tac was the author of this manuscript? This similarity of writing misled Réveillaud on another occasion. Among the documents that he published after the *Histoire chronologique* he attributed one to Le Tac—"Estat de la mission des PP Recollets de Canada"—which he dated 1682. But O.-M. Jouve, basing his opinion on evidence derived from a collation of

documents and of statements contained in this text, concluded that the manuscript dated from the years 1685–86, and that Father Exupère Dethunes* was probably its author. Jouve's argument seems much more convincing than Réveillaud's explanation.

To return to the *Histoire chronologique*, if the author of this work is Le Tac why did he, when depicting in great detail various regions of New France, not even mention in his description of Trois-Rivières the building of a residence and a church, in which he played an active part? And why was the manuscript, which again according to Réveillaud was begun in 1689, during Le Tac's stay in Newfoundland, and finished when he was back in France, not published before 1888? Because it was swallowed up, "without hope of ever seeing the light of day again, in the archives of the convent at Saint-Germain-en-Laye"? Yet Le Tac remained in France until his death in 1718!

The author of the *Histoire chronologique de la Nouvelle-France* did not write an original work. He admitted in his preface: "I found these authors [Lescarbot*, Champlain*, Sagard*, Du Creux*] so obscure that I thought I would render some service to the public if I discussed in greater detail what has happened up to this time . . . and passed over a number of things that I did not believe needed to be recorded"; he did not want to follow the example of the Jesuits, and write "books crammed with tales . . . to deceive the public." He proposed to write his history in three parts, devoting the first to "what has taken place since the French began to frequent Canada up to . . . the year 1629, and even . . . up to 1632. . . . The second [would extend] from 1632 to 1670, when the Recollet Fathers returned, and the third from 1670 until the present year." The author finished only the first part, however, and only partially fulfilled his promise. In the first two chapters he gives us a "general idea of America and New France," and in the 14 others he contents himself with providing a "summary" of the authors "who happened to be in his study"; he had not forgotten to mention, in his preface, that the Jesuits had crossed the sea "to bend all their zeal to the destruction of a small community of religious of the order of St Francis."

Such is the work that Le Tac is supposed to have written: a manuscript of 47 pages which had lain dormant for perhaps 200 years in the archives until Réveillaud discovered it and published it. He attributed its authorship to Le Tac on the flimsiest evidence, if not on mere presumption. The identification proposed by Réveillaud seems doubtful, yet it is not easy to suggest another possible author. If, as Réveillaud claims, the

Levasseur

handwriting of the 1682 document resembles that of the *Histoire chronologique*, then might one not conclude that Father Dethunes is the author of both? However that may be, this *Histoire chronologique de la Nouvelle-France* is in Biggar's judgement—"apart from the interesting description of New France in 1689 . . . of little or no value."

MICHEL PAQUIN

Archives des Franciscains de Québec, Dossier Exupère Dethunes; Dossier Xiste Le Tac. Archives de Seine-et-Oise (Versailles), H (clergé régulier): Chronologie de la Nouvelle-France; Eugène Réveillaud published this manuscript under the title of *Histoire chronologique de la Nouvelle-France, ou Canada, depuis sa découverte (1504) jusques en l'an 1632, par le Père Sixte Le Tac, Récollet* (Paris, 1888). Archives de la Seine-Maritime (Rouen), H (clergé régulier) récollet, ff.13–14. ASQ, MSS 200. Recensement du Canada, 1681 (Sulte). Le Jeune, *Dictionnaire*.

H. P. Biggar, *The early trading companies of New France* (Toronto, 1901), 287–90. Hugolin [Stanislas Lemay], *L'établissement des Récollets de la province de Saint-Denis à Plaisance en l'île de Terre-Neuve, 1689* (Québec, 1911); *Le père Joseph Denis, premier récollet canadien (1657–1736)* (2v., Québec, 1926), I, 183. Jouve, *Les Franciscains et le Canada: aux Trois-Rivières.* Sulte, *Mélanges historiques* (Malchelosse), I, 56. H.-A. Scott, "Au berceau de notre histoire," *RSCT*, 3d ser., XVI (1922), sect.i, 51–54.

LEVASSEUR, MICHEL, silversmith, born in France, resident of New France from 1699 to *c.* 1709; married Madeleine Vilers, and had seven children; the eldest, a girl, was born in Quebec in 1700.

Levasseur was the first member of his craft working in Quebec during the French colonial period whose activities have been documented. The records of Notre-Dame de Québec show that in 1707 he cleaned the silver and the following year he repaired a chalice and a ciborium. In 1709 he made a sanctuary lamp for the Quebec seminary. Shortly after this he returned to France where he had difficulty in finding work because of the opposition of the silversmiths of Rochefort.

During his ten-year stay in New France Levasseur followed the traditional pattern of the master silversmith in teaching his craft to others. According to a deed of 2 May 1708, he signed an agreement to teach his craft to Pierre Gauvreau and "to no one else." Shortly afterwards, he was released from this contract by the Intendant JACQUES RAUDOT and allowed to take another apprentice, Jacques Pagé, *dit* Carcy. Under the terms of such indentures, the master silversmith, in return for a sum of money from the parents, undertook to take the apprentice into his household for a period

of seven years, teach him the "mystery" of his craft, and provide shelter, food, and clothing; he also assumed certain obligations for his education and attendance at church. No wages were paid to the apprentice.

To date no examples of Levasseur's work during his stay in Canada have been identified.

JOHN LANGDON

Jug. et délib., V. Taillemite, *Inventaire analytique, série B,* I, 205. Tanguay, *Dictionnaire*, I. John Langdon, *Canadian silversmiths 1700–1900* (Lunenburg, 1966); *Canadian silversmiths and their marks 1667–1867* (Lunenburg, 1960). Ramsay Traquair, *The old silver of Quebec* (Toronto, 1940). Marius Barbeau, "Deux cents ans d'orfèvrerie chez nous," *RSCT*, 3d ser., XXXIII (1939), sect.i, 183–91. Alfred Jones, "Old church silver in Canada," *RSCT*, 3d ser., XII (1918), sect.ii, 135. Gérard Morisset, "L'orfèvre Michel Levasseur," *Revue de l'université d'Ottawa,* XVII (1947), 339–49.

LEVASSEUR, NOËL, master wood-carver, b. 1680 at Quebec, son of Noël Levasseur, carpenter, and Marguerite Guay and grandson of Jean Levasseur*, *dit* Lavigne, carpenter; d. 13 Dec. 1740 at Quebec.

Little is known about Noël Levasseur's apprenticeship years, but it can be supposed that he learned the trade of carpenter with his father, and that he was introduced to wood-carving by the masters of the school at Saint-Joachim. By his marriage contract with Marie-Madeleine Turpin, dated 3 April 1701, we can place him at Montreal, where he had probably been living for some time to complete his training. Indeed he was in Montreal and in such close contact with the carver Charles CHABOULIÉ, who was at the time a bachelor, that the latter undertook in 1702 to leave all his property to the first-born of the Levasseur couple. Unfortunately none of Chaboulié's work permits an assessment of his possible influence upon Noël Levasseur.

After finally settling at Quebec in 1703, Noël Levasseur raised a family of 13 children, and acquired a clientele among the parishes and communities of Quebec and the surrounding districts. He also worked for individuals, however; for example, Levasseur "promises and undertakes to set out immediately for Cap Saint-Ignace, in which place he will do all the carving and ornamentation required for the ship which the said [Captain Louis] PRAT is having built there. . . ." Although no trace has come down to us of ship-carvings of the 18th century, we must not forget that secular carving was practised in the French colony. Moreover, to Noël Levasseur are attributed two scrolls in polychrome carved wood representing the royal coat of arms of France; one of these is in the Quebec museum, the other in the Public Archives of Canada. Scrolls are supposed to have been ordered by Gaspard-Joseph Chaussegros* de Léry in 1727 to embellish the gates and administrative buildings of the town of Quebec.

Although the name of Levasseur is to be found in the account books of many parishes around Quebec, unfortunately few examples remain to testify to his work. This is the case at Saint-Laurent (Île d'Orléans), where he made a retable in 1711, at Lauson, where he carried out the same kind of work from 1730 to 1733, at Saint-Augustin, where he worked in 1731, at Notre-Dame in Quebec for 1732, and at Beauport for 1733. He had also worked at Varennes in 1726, at Pointe-aux-Trembles (Montreal) in 1727, and at Boucherville in 1729. It is difficult to trace today the "Vierge à l'Enfant" at Notre-Dame de la Jeune-Lorette which bore an inscription beginning as follows: "I am given by Noël Levasseur, wood-carver, and his wife Marie Madeleine Turpin on 1 March 1729, to be carried in the procession of the scapular and the rosary. . . ." Similarly we cannot track down "two wooden figures representing the Holy Virgin and St Joseph and two others representing the ox and the ass," which were carved in 1733 for the church of Sainte-Croix de Lotbinière.

Besides the high altar of L'Islet, probably done by Noël Levasseur in 1728, two works of outstanding importance have survived which we can attribute to him with certainty: the high altar in the chapel of the Hôpital Général in Quebec (1722), and the retable of the Ursuline chapel (1732–36). The first of these was no doubt executed with the help of his eldest son François-Noël, and the second with the help of Jean-Baptiste-Antoine as well. These two carvers owed their entire training to their father, and worked with him until his death. This family venture continued for a long time, for after 1740 the Levasseur sons shared the same workshop and carried on their craft in the same places.

The tabernacle of the high altar in the chapel of the Hôpital Général constitutes a work unique in its kind. It is an architectural structure in gilded wood, of great simplicity of design: on a predella is a forepart, which extends forward in steps; it has a curved arch supported by ten Corinthian columns; this forepart is surmounted by a dome, a lantern-tower, and a flying angel, and has two incurvated wings at the base of which are eight niches set in between Corinthian columns, the upper portion being made up of three levels embellished with open-work decorative motifs. The base of the forepart bears the arms of Bishop Saint-Vallier [La Croix], who donated this high altar to the nuns of the Hôpital Général. The eight niches in the wings and the five in the dome contain statuettes which are still a puzzle today: they were not done by the same carver. The statuettes of the dome seem to have been entrusted to one carver and those of the wings to another; one of the two might have been Noël Levasseur. This is only an hypothesis, however, for the necessary studies of the styles have not yet been carried out and documentation is lacking.

The retable of the Ursuline chapel constitutes one of the major pieces of carving in French Canada. The Levasseurs, father and sons, were perhaps assisted by their cousin Pierre-Noël. The work in question is a retable in the Recollet manner (see Juconde Drué), the style of which was slightly modified during a renovation in 1902. It is composed in traditional fashion, being divided into three parts separated by Corinthian columns; the centre part encloses the high altar, which is surmounted by a picture of the Annunciation and by an aedicule, topped with an arched fronton, which contains a statue of St Joseph holding the infant Jesus. In the right and left panels are incorporated the sacristy doors, which are surmounted by niches containing statues of St Foy and St Augustine. Right at the top, on the entablature, two angels in adoration form the link with the centre part of the retable. The five carvings modelled in the round are perhaps by François-Noël Levasseur. The pedestals of the columns and the sacristy doors are decorated with reliefs. The latter seem more clumsily done than the carvings modelled in the round. The tabernacle of the high altar displays a much more ornate style than that of the Hôpital Général. It is an architectural composition made up of three foreparts; on the centre one is a relief representing the Good Shepherd. A pulpit with a sounding-board completes this ensemble of carved, gilded, and painted wood.

If Noël Levasseur was not the only one to work at this retable, which is in Louis XIV style, he was certainly its guiding spirit. The same style, although simplified, is to be found in his sons' works after 1740. Indeed through his two sons, François-Noël and Jean-Baptiste-Antoine, and their cousin Pierre-Noël, Noël Levasseur was to dominate Canadian wood-carving in the 18th century long after his death.

JEAN TRUDEL

IOA, Dossiers Levasseur. *Jug. et délib.*, I, III, IV, V. Tanguay, *Dictionnaire*, V, 387f. Ramsay Traquair, *The old architecture of Quebec* (Toronto, 1947). Marius Barbeau, "Les Le Vasseur, maîtres menuisiers, sculpteurs et statuaires (Québec, *circa* 1648–1818),"

Levasseur de Neré

Les Archives de Folklore (Québec), III (1948), 35–49. Gérard Morisset, "Une dynastie d'artisans: Les Levasseur," *La Patrie* (Montréal), 8 janv. 1950.

LEVASSEUR DE NERÉ, JACQUES, military engineer, knight of the order of Saint-Louis, captain and sub-lieutenant; b. 1662 or 1664 in Paris; d. after 1723.

Nothing is known of Levasseur's family background except that he had a brother who was a clerk in the ministry of Marine. In 1680, Levasseur entered the royal academy at Rennes. Four years later, he joined the corps of royal engineers and was appointed to the king's works at Bayonne. After serving at Saint-Jean-Pied-de-Port he was promoted sub-engineer and spent a year at La Rochelle followed by a year at Nancy. Between 1691 and 1693 he served in several sieges under Vauban. On 1 March 1693 he was appointed to replace Robert de Villeneuve* as royal engineer of New France. Prior to this date, he had married Marie-Françoise Chavenault, and the poverty occasioned by his large family was a factor leading to his appointment to New France. While in Canada his wife bore him ten more children (his first child born in New France was baptized 23 Oct. 1691 with Buade* de Frontenac as godfather). This additional responsibility goaded Levasseur to make constant demands for additional appointments and gratuities throughout his career. In April 1694, before leaving France, he had received commissions as sub-lieutenant in the navy and captain of a company of colonial regular troops.

Levasseur de Neré's importance lies in his activities as royal engineer of New France. Upon his arrival in 1694, he found that much of the earlier defence construction at Quebec was defective; it was decided, therefore, to surround the town with an earth wall, to construct a strong redoubt on Cape Diamond, and to erect batteries in Lower Town. Beginning the following spring, work proceeded under the engineer's supervision. By the end of 1696 Bochart de Champigny, the intendant, could report that Levasseur was a "man of merit, a good officer, and an experienced and capable king's engineer." In 1697, however, poor health forced him to return to France and remain there until September 1700. During his absence new works were recommended, but little actual construction was carried out on the fortifications. On his return he was once more busily engaged in plans for the defence of Canada. In 1701, these plans received royal approval and 20,000 *livres* were set aside each year for expenses. The following year news of the outbreak of the War of the Spanish Succession was received;

Levasseur continued to work on the colony's fortifications.

In 1704 Levasseur was made a knight of the order of Saint-Louis. The following year he applied for permission to return to France, but was refused on the grounds that his work could not be interrupted then, when an invasion from the south was feared. By 1706, however, his recurring poor health meant that permission could no longer be withheld, and he returned to France, but a year later he was again in the colony. His last stay in New France as royal engineer was full of conflict. He was accused of being Rigaud de Vaudreuil's creature and of ungentlemanly conduct during Carnival. His attacks on Boisberthelot* de Beaucours, his assistant, and the counter attacks by Jacques Raudot, the intendant, were more serious. The engineer was described as "[a] muddle-headed, bad-tempered man, unfit for command because of his vanity" and as suffering from delusions of grandeur. His critics claimed that he had designed fortifications that would require 6,000 troops to man and take nine years to complete.

At the end of 1709 he went back to France although the fortifications at Quebec were still unfinished. It was expected that Levasseur would return to New France in 1712, but he requested and was granted permission to retire. He continued, however, to take an interest in New France, and criticized the plans of the new engineer, Chaussegros* de Léry. Levasseur returned to New France in 1717 on family matters, but his former patron, Vaudreuil, asked that he be transferred elsewhere because of his fault-finding. His permission to remain in the colony was extended to 1720, and the next year he was in France. With the rank of half-pay captain he drew his pension until 1723—the last time that his name appears in the colonial estimates. He probably died in 1723 or shortly thereafter.

James S. Pritchard

AN, Col., B, 17, ff.57, 61v; 19, ff.101v, 113v; 22, ff.213v, 233v; 23, ff.81v, 97v; 25, ff.99v, 110v, 141v, 151v; 27, ff.90, 90v; C¹¹ᴬ, 13, ff.443–47; 18, ff.164, 165; 19, f.187; 20, ff.132, 141; 22, f.354; 27, f.25; 30, ff.174, 174v, 192v, 193; 37, f.101; 38, ff.140, 141v; 40, ff.88v, 216, 216v; 113, ff.133, 181, 185, 213–31; 120, ff.4, 223; Col., D²ᶜ, 47, ff.218, 334; 112; 137; 190, ff.306, 307; Col., F¹ᴬ, 20; Marine, B², 8, f.535v; Section Outre-Mer, Dépôt des fortifications des colonies, carton 7, no.367. BN, MS, Clairambault 532, ff.629, 700, 709. [Jean-Baptiste Colbert], *Lettres, instructions et mémoires de Colbert*, éd. P. Clément (8v., Paris, 1861–82), III, 1ʳᵉ part., 317; 2ᵉ part., 220. "Correspondance de Frontenac (1689–99)," APQ *Rapport, 1927–28*, 171; *1928–29*, 289, 343–44, 349. "Correspondance de Vaudreuil," APQ *Rapport*,

1938–39, 17, 430, 443; 1947–48, 146. *Jug. et délib.*, VI, 299. "Lettre de Vauban à Louis XIV," *BRH*, XXII (1916), 121–22. Fauteux, *Les chevaliers de Saint-Louis*, 96. P.-G. Roy, *La ville de Québec*, I, 523.

LE VERRIER DE ROUSSON, FRANÇOIS,

town major of Montreal, king's lieutenant at Quebec, knight of the order of Saint-Louis; b. *c.* 1656 in Paris, son of Nicolas Le Verrier, seigneur of Boisguibert, and Madeleine Houdon; buried 7 Nov. 1732 at Quebec.

Le Verrier first had a rather long military career in France. In 1672 he was serving in the first company of the King's Musketeers. He was appointed a cornet in the Régiment de Varennes in 1675, then a half-pay lieutenant and a lieutenant on the active list in the Régiment de la Valette in 1682. He was wounded in the eye in 1684, was put on half-pay two years later, and on 17 March 1687 he was appointed a captain in the colonial regular troops. It was in this capacity that he came to New France in the same year.

On 10 Sept. 1688 Le Verrier accidentally killed his friend, Jacques Boucher de Montizambert, a son of Pierre BOUCHER. The victim's parents were convinced that it was simply a hunting accident and solemnly declared: "we are perfectly aware of his innocence in this matter. . . . For our part therefore we exonerate the aforementioned Sieur Le Verrier of the said death."

Le Verrier's military career was not affected by this accident and continued to advance. He was wounded twice in the campaigns against the Iroquois in 1689 and 1693. This did not however slow down his advancement: in January 1693 he was a midshipman; he was promoted ship's captain with a commission in March 1694, and sub-lieutenant on 5 March 1695.

On 6 Sept. 1697 the governor of Montreal, CALLIÈRE, sent him "to the foot of the Long Sault on the great river to take up position on the north side in the place that in his judgement is the most suitable for defending both shores" in order to stop all passing canoes. If possible, he was to construct a log fort there, or at least an abatis for protection against the enemy. Le Verrier seems to have carried out his mission unsatisfactorily, since the king blamed him in a personal letter for his lack of zeal in performing his duty.

This did not prevent him from being made a Chevalier of Saint-Louis in 1713 "on account of his services," and from being appointed town major of the troops at Montreal on 12 May 1714. That same year an anonymous note described him thus: "He is a fairly good officer and has dignity." In 1724 he received a pension of 400 *livres* in recognition of the wounds that he had received. The following year he replaced Louvigny [LA PORTE] as king's lieutenant at Quebec. He was given the highest praise by the intendant, CLAUDE-THOMAS DUPUY, in a letter of 20 Oct. 1727: "M. Le Verrier, the king's lieutenant at Quebec, who was in command there during the absence of the governor general Beauharnois* de La Boische, has conducted himself with all the ardour, vivacity, and experience of an officer of long-standing; he has seen war waged by M. de Turenne, consequently in an expert manner. This appears in everything he does, his vigilance is unceasing, and no one is firmer or more constant than he in observing the regulations of the service." In 1730 Vaudreuil [RIGAUD] also stressed his zeal and his activity and noted that Le Verrier "loves and enforces discipline." But all these commendations were not sufficient to obtain for Le Verrier the post of governor of Trois-Rivières which he coveted.

In 1704 François Le Verrier de Rousson married Charlotte de Fleury Deschambault, daughter of Jacques-Alexis de FLEURY and Marguerite de Chavigny. They had one daughter and a son, Louis*, who, like his father, took up a military career. In 1743 Le Verrier's widow took as her second husband Pierre de Rigaud* de Vaudreuil de Cavagnial, the last governor of New France.

NIVE VOISINE

AN, Col., B, 33–37; C^{11A}, 34, 49, 53. "Correspondance de Vaudreuil," APQ *Rapport*, 1946–47, 443; 1947–48, 137–339. P.-G. Roy, "Ce que Callières pensait de nos officiers," 321–33. Fauteux, *Les chevaliers de Saint-Louis*, 106. P.-G. Roy, *Les officiers d'état-major*, 146–55. Tanguay, *Dictionnaire*, V, 395. Claude de Bonnault, "Notes sur MM. Leverrier, père et fils," *BRH*, XXXV (1929), 288–91. Montarville Boucher de La Bruère, "La mort de Jacques Boucher de Montizambert," *BRH*, XXXIV (1928), 12–19.

LEVILLIERS, CHARLES PETIT DE. *See* PETIT

LEVINGSTON. *See* LIVINGSTON

L'HERMITTE (Lhermitte, L'Hermite, Lhermite), JACQUES, engineer, staff officer and cartographer; town major and engineer of Placentia (Plaisance), 1695–1714; king's second lieutenant and engineer for Île Royale (Cape Breton Island), 1714–15; king's lieutenant for Trois-Rivières, 1715–25; b. *c.* 1652, in France; died in the wreck of the *Chameau* 27 Aug. 1725.

L'Hermitte claimed that in 1690 he had interrupted some nine years' service in the corps of engineers in France to take part in the Irish

L'Hermitte

campaign as an infantry captain. Although afterwards he rejoined the corps, he had lost his seniority, and thus he was one of 60 officers who were victims of an establishment cut in 1694. (There is no record of this in the Archives du Génie.) It happened, however, that the Duc de Gramont had selected him as cartographer and engineer aboard SAINT-CLAIR's flagship, the *Gaillard*, fitted out at Bayonne (where L'Hermitte was serving) for an expedition during the summer of 1694 against the English in Newfoundland. L'Hermitte's work on this occasion, especially his map of Placentia Bay, attracted the attention of the governor of Placentia, Jacques-François de MOMBETON de Brouillan. Chiefly at his instigation, the minister of Marine appointed L'Hermitte in 1695 to the post of town major and engineer of Placentia.

His engineering duties were the more onerous, but in addition to them he performed the usual tasks of the town major, which included detailing the guards, inspecting the garrison, distributing military stores, and dispensing military justice. Moreover, Brouillan arranged to have him designated as third in command, after the governor and the king's lieutenant. Brouillan held him in high esteem, which may have caused Joseph de MONIC to dislike him. Friction between them came to a head in 1701 when Monic had L'Hermitte thrown in jail for three weeks for having a servant copy letters from the commandant's private office. Considering Monic's behaviour to be excessive, the minister recalled him while L'Hermitte escaped with a mild reprimand.

With occasional interludes, such as mapping expeditions, or the raid on St John's under AUGER de Subercase during the winter of 1704–5, L'Hermitte spent 17 frustrating years trying to put the fortifications of Placentia into a state of readiness. It was a losing battle against the climate, the isolation of the place, an inadequate financial policy, the apathy of the fishermen, and the ignorance of local officials. Piecemeal allocations of funds for replacing old, wood-revetted earthworks with masonry were dissipated largely in repairing each summer the damage which winter gales, waves, and frost had done to the previous summer's work. Although the court at Versailles exhorted the owners of fishing vessels (especially the Basques) to supplement royal transport to Placentia by carrying building materials, beasts of burden, and seasonally employed craftsmen, their cooperation was niggardly, even under the threat of the king's displeasure. L'Hermitte's local superiors sometimes disregarded his technical advice or ignored the accounting procedures normally followed in the corps of engineers. He even wrote at one point that henceforth he would adhere strictly to his instructions; otherwise "I should only be rebuked." Yet events often proved his judgment to be right.

L'Hermitte was recognized as a good draftsman, surveyor, and cartographer. In 1698 he was sent to Acadia to survey potential harbour facilities and natural resources (especially timber for the navy) on the Atlantic coast and on both sides of the Bay of Fundy (Baie Française); and to examine the need for fortifications at the mouth of the Saint John River. Shortly after his posting to Trois-Rivières in 1715, he was asked to survey and map much of Île Royale and environs. In 1724, he carried out a survey of the timber resources of the Gaspé region.

At the cession of Placentia in 1713, L'Hermitte played an important role in the establishment of the new colony of Île Royale. He made a quick study of several natural harbours for the purpose of selecting the best site for the fortified capital of the cod-fishery; he constructed provisional fortifications and buildings at Louisbourg in readiness for the arrival of colonists from Placentia and possibly from Acadia; and he participated in the first attempts to arrange for the transfer of Acadians to Île Royale.

By this time, he was past 60; he could no longer work at a younger man's pace; and his injuries and ailments were having their cumulative effect. Over his protests, the minister created for him the post of king's lieutenant of Trois-Rivières which, apart from his special survey expeditions, was almost a sinecure. In 1718 the council of Marine awarded him the cross of the order of Saint-Louis and assured him that the chief engineer of New France, Chaussegros* de Léry, would have no authority over his work.

In the summer of 1725, the old engineer was drowned off Cape Breton while returning home on board the ill-fated *Chameau* after making an oral report in France on the results of his Gaspé survey. Since his body was not identified, it is not known whether he was one of the 180 buried by the missionary at La Baleine (Baleine Cove). He left Marie Chevalier, whom he had married at Placentia about 1706, and their children with few assets and substantial debts. This is not surprising, because during his 30 years' service in New France he had attempted to live mainly off his salary, which few officers were able to do. He had been constantly complaining that his income could not meet colonial living costs. Even a small family pension ended in 1702 at his father's death—an event which precipitated a legal battle in France with his brothers over the succession.

His chief bequest to posterity is his cartography. Contemporary examples of his work which have survived in France bear evidence of its high quality. As an engineer, however, two factors tended to lessen his general effectiveness: the "system" and his own weakness of character. Colonial improvements played second fiddle to European hegemony, and recognition in colonial careers owed too much to influence and too little to ability. On the other hand, L'Hermitte was apparently so sensitive that he interpreted every criticism of his work, every disregard for his views, as proof that his talents were not recognized.

F. J. THORPE

[Most writers who have mentioned Jacques L'Hermitte have for some unstated reason given the year of his birth as 1670. But a note, dated 1722, in AN, Col., C¹¹ᴬ, 120, tome 2, states "âgé de 70 ans ou Environ." Moreover this tallies with other evidence from primary sources bearing on age and career. It is probable that he enlisted in the army in the early 1670s and became an engineer, as he stated himself (AN, Col., C¹¹ᶜ, 4, f.71), about 1681. F.J.T.]

AJQ, Greffe d'Étienne Dubreuil, 5 oct. 1725. AN, Col., B, 17, 19, 20, 22, 23, 25, 27, 29, 30, 32, 34, 35, 36, 37, 40; 48, p.862; C¹¹ᴬ, 37, 38, 40, 45, 46, 48; 120, t.2; C¹¹ᴮ, 1; C¹¹ᶜ, 2–7; C¹¹ᴰ, 3, ff.78, 81, 99, 101, 118; E, 285; Section Outre-Mer, Dépôt des fortifications des colonies, carton 2, nos.99, 103, 106, 107, 109–15; carton 3, nos.134, 135. Comité technique du génie (Paris), Archives, art.14 (Louisbourg), no.1. PAC, FM 6, Archives maritimes, Port de Rochefort, 1E, 43, f.18. Le Blant, *Histoire de la N.-F.*, 253. P.-G. Roy, *Inv. testaments*, II, 69.

[F. Aubert de La Chesnaye-Desbois], *Dictionnaire militaire* (Lausanne et Genève, 1743; 2ᵉ éd., 2v., Dresde, 1751), II, 210. Le Blant, *Philippe de Pastour de Costebelle*. McLennan, *Louisbourg*. P.-G. Roy, "Jacques L'Hermitte," *BRH*, XI (1905), 175–80; "Les officiers d'état major," *RC*, 3ᵉ sér., XXIV (1919), 55–61.

LIETTE, PIERRE-CHARLES DE (di Lietto, Deliette, Desliettes), aide to HENRI TONTY, commandant at Fort Saint-Louis and Chicago, captain in the colonial regular troops; fl. 1687–1721.

The precise dates of de Liette's birth and death are not known; moreover, there is no record of a marriage. He was of Italian descent and a cousin of Henri and ALPHONSE TONTY, whose mother's name before her marriage was di Lietto. His parents possibly moved to France around 1650 with the Tontys, who fled there after taking part in an unsuccessful rebellion in Italy. De Liette probably immigrated to New France with his cousin, Alphonse, in 1685.

De Liette's 15 years of service under Henri Tonty began with his arrival at Fort Saint-Louis at Le Rocher (Starved Rock) in 1687. The following year he accompanied a band of Illinois on a buffalo hunt in order to familiarize himself with their language and customs. In a memoir which he wrote at a later date, de Liette explained that his "great youth" at the time of this hunt was to his advantage, as he experienced little difficulty in adjusting to the new environment. Within three years, Tonty was sufficiently satisfied with the progress of his cousin to entrust him with the command of Fort Saint-Louis and later to appoint him to supervise the resettlement of the Illinois. When in 1692 the fort was evacuated, both the garrison and the Illinois village were moved to a new location at Pimitoui (now Peoria). De Liette must have acquitted himself satisfactorily in these duties, for he served as interim commandant at Chicago, where Tonty maintained a warehouse, and at Fort Pimitoui (sometimes also called Saint-Louis) until 1702.

In that year Henri Tonty and François DAUPHIN de La Forest retired from the Illinois country with their garrison. However, because the Indians of that area were too important commercially and militarily to be abandoned to their own devices, de Liette remained among them as a lonely agent of French influence. When he returned to Montreal in 1711 he enjoyed great prestige in the councils of the Illinois.

In 1712 the entire French western alliance system was threatened with destruction by the outbreak of the Fox war. It was imperative that the Illinois and Miamis remain at peace with each other within the French sphere of influence, as their geographical location rendered them vulnerable to both the English and the Foxes. Accordingly, Governor RIGAUD de Vaudreuil complied with the recommendations of missionaries stationed among the Illinois and with the requests of an Illinois chief, CHACHAGOUESSE, and dispatched de Liette to nullify English trade overtures to the Illinois, and to discourage war with the Miamis. Relations between the two tribes, however, deteriorated in 1713 when the Miamis conducted a surprise attack on the Illinois. The following year, New France's hold on their allegiance was again threatened when both tribes encountered the English of Carolina. Such a development was of great significance to the colony, as Vaudreuil was hoping to enlist 1,500 Illinois and Miami warriors in the war against the Foxes. Fortunately, de Liette's long association with the Illinois tipped the scales in favour of New France, and in 1715 he was able to return to Montreal, having successfully completed his assignments. This visit was a short one. Early in

Lignery

1716, Governor Claude de RAMEZAY of Montreal sent de Liette back to re-establish the old fort Saint-Louis at Starved Rock, and to maintain peace in the area.

When the Illinois country was annexed to Louisiana in 1717, de Liette was still labouring in the French interest among the Indians. He was commissioned captain in the Louisiana regular troops in 1720, but almost immediately resigned from this position and returned to Montreal. A notarial deed, signed 9 June 1721, on the eve of his departure for the west, is the last positive record of Pierre-Charles de Liette; afterwards, the documentary evidence becomes fragmentary and, to a degree, contradictory. Charlevoix* claimed that de Liette died among the Natchez, some time before December 1721. He may have been mistaken, however, since a de Liette served in the Natchez and Illinois areas between 1722 and 1728. Was this Pierre-Charles? Perhaps, but he may also have been a son of Alphonse Tonty (other than Charles-Henri-Joseph Tonty*, Sieur de Liette, who was active in the west after 1728); or again, just as FRANÇOIS-MARIE BISSOT de Vinsenne and Philippe-Thomas Chabert* de Joncaire replaced their fathers among the Miamis and Senecas respectively, it is possible that a son of Pierre-Charles, perhaps from an Illinois mother, replaced him among the Illinois.

During one of his visits to Montreal de Liette wrote the "De Gannes Memoir," preserved in the Ayer Collection, Newberry Library, Chicago. Although someone named De Gannes signed the memoir, internal evidence alone proves de Liette's authorship. Almost 50 printed pages in length, this document is a valuable account of the Illinois and Miami Indians, and of the country in which they lived. Furthermore, it provides the reader with an itinerary of de Liette's early years in the west.

Except for an occasional visit to Montreal, Pierre-Charles de Liette had spent his entire adult life in the west, arbitrating intertribal disputes and helping maintain the connection between New France and the Illinois Indians. Although material on his career is relatively scarce, what there is suggests that he did his work well.

C. J. RUSS

AJM, Greffe d'Antoine Adhémar, 18 août 1692, 11 août 1700; Greffe de Jacques David, 9 juin 1721. AN, Col., B, 42, ff.337v–38, 381v–82; 43, f.47, 461; 48, f.741; C^{11A}, 33, pp.85–91, 164–66; 34, p.305, 356–57; 35, pp.37–39, 150–55; 40, pp.23–24; 42, p.21, 61–68; 48, p.332, 336; 51, p.169; C^{11G}, 1, p.95 (PAC transcripts); C^{13A}, 1, f.27; 7, ff.73v–74, 124, 173, 307v, 311; 11, ff.89v–96v.

Charlevoix wrote in his *Histoire* (1744), IV, 235, that when he reached the Natchez at the end of 1722,

de Liette was dead; this is an error, as letter 30 reproduced in VI, 165–91 shows that Charlevoix reached Natchez at the end of 1721. "Correspondance de Vaudreuil," APQ *Rapport, 1938–39*, 133, 152; *1947–48*, 225, 230, 291. *Découvertes et établissements des Français* (Margry), III, 495. "Memoir of De Gannes concerning the Illinois country," Ill. State Hist. Lib. *Coll.*, XXIII, 302–95. *NYCD* (O'Callaghan and Fernow), IX, 865. Wis. State Hist. Soc. *Coll.*, XVI, 300–7, 332–33, 378. Tanguay, *Dictionnaire*.

Sister Marie Celeste, "The Miami Indians prior to 1700," *Mid-America*, XVI (1933–34; new ser., V), 225–34. Jean Delanglez, "The voyages of Tonti in North America, 1678–1704," *Mid-America*, XXVI (1944; new ser., XV), 255–300. Sister Mary Borgias Palm, "Kaskaskia, Indian mission village, 1703–1718," *Mid-America*, XVI (1933–34; new ser., V), 14–25.

LIGNERY, CONSTANT LE MARCHAND DE. *See* LE MARCHAND

LINO. *See* MARTIN

LINTOT, MICHEL GODEFROY DE. *See* GODEFROY

LINVILLIERS (L'Invilliers). *See* PETIT

LISLOYE, PAUL DUPUY DE. *See* DUPUY

LIVILLIERS. *See* PETIT

LIVINGSTON, JOHN (Levingston), colonel in the Connecticut militia, participant in the attempts to take Canada during Queen Anne's War (War of the Spanish Succession), and intermediary for the New England colonies in prisoner exchanges with the French at Quebec; b. New York 26 April 1680 (o.s.), the eldest of nine children of Robert and Alida Schuyler Livingston (widow of Nicholas Van Rensselaer); married at New London, Conn., in April 1701 Mary Winthrop, who died 8 Jan. 1712/13; and at Boston on 1 Oct. 1713 Elizabeth Knight, who died 17 March 1735/36; there were no children by either marriage; d. London 19 Feb. 1719/20.

Livingston's marriage to Governor Fitz-John Winthrop's daughter was no doubt instrumental in his taking up residence in New London and subsequently receiving a commission in the Connecticut militia. He had served previously in the New York militia. When not occupied by military affairs, Livingston was a merchant. In 1701 he owned the sloop *Mary*, in partnership with his brother-in-law, Samuel VETCH. They became involved in the illegal but profitable trade with Canada, a trade which soon came to the attention of colonial authorities. As late as 1706

436

it was rumoured that Livingston was still involved in such nefarious activities. During 1706–7 Livingston represented New London as a deputy to the general assembly. He also speculated in Indian lands during this period.

Livingston's restless nature suited him well for the life of a soldier. Known as "the Mohauk," he acquired great influence among the New England Indians, especially the Five Nations. His ability to control the Indians marked him as a valuable asset to colonial commanders. In August 1704 after the outbreak of Queen Anne's War, he commanded a company of "Volunteers English & Indians to reinforce the Frontiers." A month later Livingston had his "first adventure" in "a publick capassety" when his father-in-law appointed him "to visit the 5 Nations" with commissioners appointed by Governor Dudley of Massachusetts. Though the commissioners gained assurances that the Five Nations would "take up the Hatchet," this support was not utilized at the time.

Livingston was serving as a Connecticut officer on the Massachusetts frontier early in 1705 when he learned that Dudley was sending a delegation to Quebec to negotiate an exchange of prisoners. Livingston volunteered and was sent overland from Albany to begin negotiations. Although "the Expense and Industry of our Commissioners in this Affair was very great," release was obtained for only a few of the 117 captives, most notably the Reverend John WILLIAMS. Livingston, termed a "very honourable man" by Governor RIGAUD de Vaudreuil, returned to New England in June 1705 with Captain AUGUSTIN LE GARDEUR de Courtemanche, the French governor's agent for the exchange of prisoners, who continued the negotiations with Dudley.

In 1709 Livingston, now a major, prepared to take part in the still-born Vetch expedition against Quebec. A year later he was again with Vetch, this time as commander of a party of Indians which flanked the main body of troops in the successful expedition led by Francis NICHOLSON against Port-Royal (Annapolis Royal, N.S.). With AUGER de Subercase's surrender in October 1710, a council of war resolved that Livingston, accompanied by the Baron de Saint-Castin [BERNARD-ANSELME D'ABBADIE], "should go to the Governour of Canada, about the exchange of Captives, and inform him how Matters were" at Annapolis Royal. Livingston was, as Vetch put it, "perhaps the only Brittish subject of any figure or character capable of such extraordinary undertakings." The "Journall" that he kept attests to the arduous nature of this mission, which would have come to an early end had not Saint-Castin intervened to save Livingston from death "in a barbarous manner" at the hands of a distraught Indian. After almost two months' hard travel, Livingston arrived in December 1710 at Quebec where he was received "with all imaginable marks of civillity." His time in Quebec was well spent. While awaiting the arrival from Montreal of HERTEL de Rouville and Simon Dupuy, agents whom Vaudreuil was sending to New England to continue the negotiations and "to obtain information through them of the movements of our enemies," Livingston prepared notes for "A View of Canada," an account of the fortifications and troops at Quebec. This was probably the chief purpose of the mission, for a successful expedition against Quebec had long been in Vetch's mind.

Livingston returned to New England late in February 1710/11 and at Vetch's urging prepared to leave for England. It was hoped that his knowledge of Canada could be used to persuade the court to renew plans for a general assault on New France. Stormy weather postponed his trip and word from England that another expedition was under way made it unnecessary.

As preparations for the WALKER expedition began, Livingston's knowledge of Quebec was utilized by both Admiral Walker and General JOHN HILL. Livingston was questioned by the general "about the situation and works of Quebec, and was thought to give a very good account of it." The failure of Walker to navigate the St Lawrence successfully meant that Livingston's knowledge of Quebec could not be put to use.

Having "a verry great sway amongst them," Livingston, now a colonel, spent the better part of the next year and a half recruiting Iroquois for scouting work around Annapolis Royal and as a result was "considerably out of pockett." The fort was deprived of the officer best able to control the Indians when Livingston left at the end of 1712. He returned to New London where he was granted the right to erect a saw-mill in 1713. He liquidated his holdings there in 1718 and sailed for England where he hoped to recoup the money he had lost in supplying the garrison at Annapolis Royal. His early death denied him the honour of succeeding his father as the second lord of the Livingston manor in New York.

Although he was tied by blood or marriage to some of the most important families in New England, Livingston remains an obscure figure who moved only at the edges of the important events of his time; a figure who appeared to be more at home with the Indians than with his fellow colonials.

JOHN DAVID KRUGLER

Mass. Hist. Soc., Gay papers, I (transcript of Livingston's journal). *Boston News-Letter*, no.17, 14 Aug.

Lloyd

1704; no.50, 2 April 1705; no.56, 14 May 1705; no.60, 11 June 1705. Charlevoix, *History* (Shea), V, 175, 233–34. *Coll. de manuscrits relatifs à la N.-F.*, II, 426, 428–32, 435, 449. Connecticut, *The public records of the colony of Connecticut, 1636–1776* (15v., Hartford, Conn., 1859–90), V (1706–16), 1, 17, 29, 37, 38, 93, 197. Hutchinson, *Hist. of Mass.-bay* (Mayo), II, 135–39. J. F. Kenney, "A British secret service report on Canada, 1711," *CHR*, I (1920), 48–54, contains a transcript of Livingston's journal. Mass. Hist. Soc. *Coll.*, 6th ser., III (1889), 66, 68, 241, 253, 263, 267–70, 294–97, 321, 511; V (1892), 142, 225, 283; *Proc.*, 1st ser., V (1860–62), 230–35. "Lettres et mémoires de F.-M.-F. Ruette d'Auteuil," 46–47. *NYCD* (O'Callaghan and Fernow), IX, 854. N.Y. State, Secretary of State, *Calendar of historical manuscripts*, ed. E. B. O'Callaghan (2v., Albany, 1865–66), II, 276. N.S. Hist. Soc. *Coll.*, IV (1884), 23, 39–41, 47, 94. *Penhallow's Indian wars* (Wheelock), 25, 29–30, 52–53, 57–58. PRO, *CSP, Col.*, *1710–11*, *1711–12*. *Walker expedition* (Graham).

F. M. Caulkins, *History of New London, Connecticut* (New London, 1895), 364, 365, 375, 404. Coleman, *New England captives*. S. A. Drake, *The border wars of New England, commonly called King William's and Queen Anne's wars* (New York, 1897), 262. L. H. Leder, *Robert Livingston 1654–1728 and the politics of colonial New York* (Chapel Hill, N.C., 1961). E. B. Livingston, *The Livingstons of Livingston Manor . . .* (New York, 1910), 132–38, 541–43. H. L. Osgood, *The American colonies in the eighteenth century* (4v., New York, 1924–25), I, 416–20. Waller, *Samuel Vetch*.

LLOYD, THOMAS, commander of the garrison at St John's, Newfoundland; d. 1710.

Of Welsh origin, Lloyd was commissioned second lieutenant in the Newfoundland Independent Company, 16 May 1701. He acted as paymaster, rose to be senior lieutenant, and, on the departure of Captain Michael RICHARDS in 1703, succeeded to the command of a garrison of 88 men. He rapidly became unpopular for many reasons: he tried to mobilize the inhabitants of St John's for war purposes, forcing them to build guard houses, to help in fortification works, to undertake guard duty, and to contribute financially towards maintaining spies at Placentia (Plaisance); he forbad the soldiers to buy from the inhabitants and made them purchase rum and other necessities from him; he sold the garrison's provisions and commodities to the colonists at high prices; he hired out the soldiers for fishing in the summer season, taking most of the hiring-fee for himself. Many of these activities were not unusual for military officers posted overseas, but in Newfoundland their effect was more oppressive because of the lack of local magistrates. Lloyd's violent temper and vindictiveness further contributed to his unpopularity. He could be efficient, courageous, and capable of a degree of military initiative, but he was willing to let his men and his command decline to pursue his financial interests. His violent quarrels with the choleric chaplain, the Reverend John JACKSON, helped to range town and garrison into two camps of which Lloyd's was much the smaller. Described by some as a cheerful man, Lloyd was defiantly unconventional; he refused to attend church, and scandalized many by playing the flute on the Lord's day.

When Captain Timothy BRIDGES came out as convoy commodore in the summer of 1704 to inspect the island and exercise a measure of judicial authority, he found inhabitants and fishing captains united against Lloyd. His soldiers were threatening to desert unless he was removed, and his second-in-command, Lieutenant John MOODY, expressed his sympathy with them. Bridges decided in October to take Lloyd home with him, though later he denied having formally suspended him. In the long dispute which followed, Lloyd behaved with great astuteness. He obtained favourable testimonials, and explained that the soldiers were mutinying not against him but against their superiors in England who had kept them too long (since 1696) in Newfoundland. He made light of the personal charges levelled against him, maintaining that they resulted only from the essential disciplinary measures he had instituted. Bridges himself reported that Lloyd had "acted like a man of honour and [a] good governor." Although suspicion remained, the board could do no other than report that "the evidence . . . does not prove the misbehaviour alleged against him." Lloyd succeeded in persuading the board that the commodores of the annual convoy, who were "not acquainted with the discipline of land forces," should no longer be given authority over the military forces in Newfoundland, but his request to be allowed to try offences by courtmartial was refused. It was decided that a new company should be raised to replace the old. Lloyd's commission was dated 1 May and he received his brevet as major on 20 July. In June 1705 news came that Moody had bravely and successfully held Fort William when the French had attacked St John's the previous January; this enabled Lloyd to demand more troops and stores for a punitive expedition against Placentia. Delays, however, held back the proposed sailing until September and the expedition was countermanded.

Lloyd arrived with his new company in mid-October, to the astonished anger of some of his old opponents. Yet from 1705 to 1708 Lloyd behaved with great circumspection. He made a close alliance with the more influential residents and visiting fishing captains, such as Arthur HOLDSWORTH. They, in turn, mobilized support for memorials in his favour—memorials often strongly reminiscent of Lloyd's own style of writing. His attempts to blacken Moody's reputation in 1706 brought a revival of the old charges, and on 29 March of that year the Board of Trade declared that Lloyd had behaved badly to his soldiers and that his charges against Moody were malicious. The secretary of state, however, was more concerned with Lloyd's military conduct, which seemed satisfactory. He had chased off raiding parties during the winter of 1705–6 and planned, but did not carry through, an overland attack on Placentia. In 1707 he cooperated in a combined operation with the naval squadron against the northern French fishery. A militia was being built up, local commanders were appointed, and defence measures taken against French raids. The new fort in St John's was constructed, and, by the end of the fishing season in 1708, the bulk of the population was induced to retire there for winter quarters. The commodore in 1706 and 1707, Captain John Underdown, spoke highly of Lloyd, though he afterwards admitted that Lloyd had evaded all attempts to get him to account for the provisions in his possession. Early in 1708, there were fresh complaints by a small group of Newfoundlanders led by William Taverner* who maintained that the colonists were "spit upon, kicked, beaten, wounded," and exploited by Lloyd. However, the commodore for 1708, John Mitchell, whose military control over the garrison had been restored, wrote enthusiastically about Lloyd to the Board of Trade and added, "I do not apprehend any danger for the winter." This letter was read by the Board of Trade on 19 Jan. 1709, four weeks after Lloyd's garrison had been overwhelmed by the French, and about three weeks before news of the disaster reached England.

The French at Placentia, primed through an exchange of prisoners, sent Saint-Ovide de Brouillan [Mombeton*] with 170 men to attack St John's late in 1708. About 4 A.M., 22 December, the French crept into the covered way in front of the main gate of Fort William with their scaling ladders and were pouring over the ramparts and pulling open the half-secured gate when the sentinels gave the alarm. Lloyd, who had bad a cheerful farewell to a friend at midnight, ran out in his nightgown to the ramparts shouting "Fight, Boys!" but there was no serious opposition to the attacking forces. Lloyd himself was overwhelmed and bundled into his quarters, where he was seen sometime later "very heavy ey'd and little notice taken of him." The militia from the new fort could not get into Fort William to help as the sally port was locked. Captain George VANE failed to force the men to come out of the guard-room and engage the French, and the fort surrendered after only a few shots were fired. The new fort made some resistance but surrendered on reasonable terms. The disaster could not have been more complete. The French took nearly four months to destroy St John's and to shift guns and equipment to Placentia. They retired before the fishing fleet came in under convoy (Commodore Joseph TAYLOUR). Lloyd and his nephew, Thomas Phillips, were shipped to Placentia. From there he wrote several letters, asking to be exchanged and to stand court-martial. Taken to Quebec in a sloop in May, he put in again at Placentia in November on his way to La Rochelle. At Placentia he managed to send a letter giving details of French dispositions in Canada and denouncing what he described as the cowardice and treachery of Vane.

At the inquests after the disaster it became clear that Lloyd had neglected his company until it was ineffective and its morale low. Although he had some staunch supporters in St John's, most of the men under his command hated him. After the surrender of St John's to the French, accusations of treachery were made against Lloyd, but it seems more likely that the fort was taken "by neglect." Lloyd had consistently exploited and maltreated his troops, and, according to Vane, some of them said that they were glad the French had taken St John's "provided Major Lloyd was hanged as they hoped he would be."

By October 1710 news of Lloyd's death in France—apparently in a duel—had reached England. In March 1711 his outstanding pay and allowances were impounded because of the corruption which had by then been proved against him. His brother, David, was unable to clear his reputation.

D. B. QUINN

PRO, *Acts of P.C., col. ser., 1680–1720*; *B.T.Journal, 1704–1708/9, 1708/9–1714/15*; *CSP, Col., 1702, 1702–3, 1704–5, 1706–8, 1708–9, 1710–11, 1711–12*; *C.T.Books, 1704–5, 1705–6, 1706–7, 1708, 1712*; *C.T.Papers, 1702–7*. Dalton, *English army lists*, V. M. A. Field, "The development of government in Newfoundland, 1638–1713," unpublished M.A. thesis, University of London, 1924. La Morandière, *Hist. de la pêche française de la morue*, I. Prowse, *History of Nfld*. Rogers, *Newfoundland*.

LOM D'ARCE DE LAHONTAN, LOUIS-ARMAND DE, third baron of Lahontan, esquire (he sometimes signed himself **Darce**, but more frequently **Lahontan**; the name also appears as **Lahontang, La Hontan** and **La Hontaa**), seigneur

439

Lom d'Arce

of Esleix, in Canada from 1683 (?) to 1693, officer in the colonial regular troops, king's lieutenant at Placentia (Plaisance) in Newfoundland in 1693; author of voyages, memoirs, and philosophical dialogues; b. 9 June 1666 at Lahontan (department of Basses-Pyrénées), eldest son of Isaac de Lom d'Arce and of his second wife, Françoise Le Fascheux de Couttes; d. in Europe before 1716.

Lahontan's father, Isaac de Lom d'Arce, born about 1594, had devoted 18 years of his life and vast sums of money to deepening and straightening the mountain torrent known as the Gave de Pau, making it navigable from Pau to the port of Bayonne. Showered with honours for his achievement, Isaac de Lom d'Arce acquired the domain of Esleix and the barony of Lahontan, where he took up residence. Childless by his first wife, Jeanne Guérin, this vigorous septuagenarian had three children by his second wife before dying, heavily in debt, on 4 Nov. 1674.

Lom d'Arce's eldest son was probably born at the château of Lahontan, and was baptized Louis-Armand de Lom d'Arce. When he was three years old, the infant Lahontan underwent on 15 July 1669 a more formal ceremony in St Martin's church in Pau, at which were present his godfather, Armand de Gramont, Comte de Guiche and acting governor of Béarn, and a representative of his godmother, Marguerite-Louise-Suzanne de Béthune, Comtesse de Guiche. The exalted rank of the godparents attests to the social status of Lahontan's family, which was also related to the Bragelonnes in Paris, one of whose members, Claude, had been one of the Cent-Associés.

Lahontan's life falls unevenly into three parts: the years before he came to Canada, his ten years in North America, and his European wanderings after 1693. Of the first of these we know nothing, except that he must have heard tales of Canada, for many fishing and whaling crews set sail for Newfoundland from Bayonne, near the birthplace of JEAN-VINCENT D'ABBADIE, Baron de Saint-Castin.

Lahontan claims to have come to Canada at the age of 17 with the three companies of colonial regular troops which left La Rochelle on the *Tempête* on 29 Aug. 1683 and arrived at Quebec on 7 November of that year. There is, however, no proof that he travelled on this ship or that he was an officer at this time. If, as he also asserts, he was on arrival billeted on the *côte* of Beaupré, he may have lived in the house of Charles Bélanger (1640–92), seigneur of Bonsecours and a prosperous settler; this hypothesis would explain Lahontan's statement that "the Boors of those Manors live with more ease and conveniency, than an infinity of the Gentlemen in France," and might also throw light on a bequest provided for Bélanger in a *donation* signed by Lahontan the following year.

In May 1684, Lahontan visited Île d'Orléans, Quebec, and its surrounding Indian villages before being sent with his company to Montreal, where Governor Le Febvre* de La Barre's expedition against the Iroquois was being assembled. Late in June Lahontan left Montreal by canoe in the advance party led by Captain Dutast, and arrived at Fort Frontenac (Cataracoui) in mid-July. He witnessed the ill-fated negotiations at Anse de La Famine (Mexico Bay, near Oswego), in September 1684, and heard the speech of Otreouti*, "La Grande Gueule."

The winter of 1684–85 was spent by Lahontan in garrison at Montreal, although during each winter season he managed lengthy periods of hunting with Indian parties. On 25 Nov. 1684 he signed before the notary Claude Maugue* in Montreal an autograph *donation* in which he appointed his widowed mother executrix of his estate and provided for numerous bequests. At the end of March 1685, he crossed the St Lawrence with a small detachment and was stationed for a month and a half at Fort Chambly, probably to exercise surveillance over fur-trading canoes. In mid-September of that year he was sent to winter quarters at Boucherville, where he appears to have remained until May 1687 except for periods spent in hunting; during the winter of 1685–86, for example, he was absent for three months while moose-hunting with a party of Indians 40 leagues north of the St Lawrence.

In June 1687 Lahontan left Montreal with Governor BRISAY de Denonville's expedition against the Senecas. Arriving at Fort Frontenac on 1 July, he was distressed to find among the Iroquois seized by BOCHART de Champigny an Indian who had befriended him during La Barre's expedition; when Lahontan protested against the treatment accorded these prisoners, he earned himself several days of confinement to his tent. He accompanied Denonville's forces along the south shore of Lake Ontario, and on 11 July was a reluctant witness of the summary execution of the captured Canadian deserter Abel Marion, *dit* La Fontaine. Having participated in the skirmish which followed the Iroquois ambush on 13 July, Lahontan has left us a colourful description of the confusion among the French forces, although exaggerating the losses on both sides.

The campaign over, Lahontan hoped to return to France to settle his family affairs, but Denonville ordered him, because of his knowledge of Algonkian, to take a detachment to Fort Saint-

Joseph, established on the west shore of the Sainte-Claire River the previous year by DANIEL GREYSOLON Dulhut. Leaving Fort Niagara at the beginning of August, Lahontan and his party reached Fort Saint-Joseph in mid-September, and he took over command of the fort.

After spending an isolated winter there, he set out on 1 April 1688 for Michilimackinac, ostensibly in search of supplies for his men but probably seeking relief from boredom. He was at Michilimackinac in early May when Abbé Jean CAVELIER, Father Anastase DOUAY, Henri Joutel, and other survivors of René-Robert Cavelier* de La Salle's tragic expedition to the Mississippi arrived on their way back to Montreal. Here too he met KONDIARONK (The Rat), whom he was later to portray in his dialogues, and was present at the execution of the Iroquois slave turned over by Kondiaronk to DENIS-JOSEPH JUCHEREAU de La Ferté.

Lahontan returned to Fort Saint-Joseph only on 1 July 1688, after a roundabout journey that had carried him northward from Michilimackinac to Sault Ste Marie to recruit 40 young Ojibwa (Sauteux) braves, and thence eastward to Manitoulin Island. Hastily unloading sacks of grain at the fort, he set out southward two days later with his Ojibwa and Ottawa allies, following the south shore of Lake Erie and engaging in skirmishes with bands of Cayugas. Returning to his fort on 24 August, he learned that the garrison at Niagara had suffered badly from scurvy and that RAYMOND BLAISE Des Bergères de Rigauville with a handful of survivors had been ordered to abandon the fort and retire to Fort Frontenac. Having sufficient supplies and ammunition for only two months, Lahontan decided that his fort could not hold out alone: on 27 August he and his men burned it and left for Michilimackinac. Reaching there on 10 September, Lahontan decided against undertaking the journey to Quebec so late in the season, but began instead to plan an exploration trip to the south.

On 24 September 1688, he set out with his detachment of soldiers and five Ottawa hunters on travels for which no documentary confirmation is available. He appears to have crossed Lake Michigan (Lac des Illinois) and to have proceeded via Baie des Puants (Green Bay) and the Rivière aux Renards (Fox River) to the Wisconsin River, which he descended to the Mississippi. He then ascended the Mississippi to a river flowing from the west which he calls the Long River (La Rivière longue) and which he claims to have explored for some hundreds of miles westward, meeting Indian tribes bearing such names as Eokoros (probably the Arikaras), Essanapes, and Gnacsitares. Re-

turning to the Mississippi on 2 March 1689, Lahontan tells us he next paddled downstream as far as the mouth of the Ouabache (Wabash River), then back up to the Illinois River and thence by way of the Chicago portage into Lake Michigan and back to Michilimackinac, which he reached on 22 May 1689.

The trip to the Long River constitutes the most controversial episode in Lahontan's career in North America, and despite the air of veracity with which much of the voyage is recounted, most historians have concluded that this narrative of a 4,000-mile journey made in winter and spring over frozen or swollen waterways is partly, if not largely, imaginary.

Early in June 1689 Lahontan left Michilimackinac and was never to return to the west. He reached Montreal on 9 July after a narrow escape at Sault-Saint-Louis (Caughnawaga) where Philippe de RIGAUD de Vaudreuil saved him from drowning. Going on to Quebec later that summer, he was present on 12 October when Louis de Buade* de Frontenac arrived to begin his second term as governor. Having learned that the barony of Lahontan had passed out of his hands, Lahontan once again sought permission to return to France. Frontenac claimed his services, however, and, perhaps recalling his own family connections with southwestern France, offered Lahontan his table and access to his purse.

The next spring (1690) Frontenac asked Lahontan to carry offers of peace to the Iroquois, but the wily baron declined; the chevalier Pierre d'Aux (Eau), Sieur de Jolliet, was sent instead, and met the hostile reception Lahontan had foreseen. In June 1690 Lahontan, increasingly in Frontenac's favour, accompanied the governor to Montreal and was still there in October when a message arrived that the English fleet commanded by Sir William Phips* was sailing up the St Lawrence. Following Frontenac back to the capital in haste, Lahontan fought with the French forces posted in the woods during the English landings below Quebec. After the withdrawal of the English, four French merchant ships which had hidden from the invaders arrived at Quebec, but the St Lawrence froze over before they could be turned about. By mid-November, however, a warm spell had melted the ice in the channel, and Frontenac decided to risk sending dispatches to France to report his victory. Champigny contracted on 25 Nov. 1690 with captain Jean Gancleau to pay him a generous bonus for the winter crossing and Frontenac sent Lahontan to France on the *Fleur de May*. The frigate sailed from Quebec at the end of November and reached La Rochelle in mid-January 1691.

Lom d'Arce

Landing in France, Lahontan learned of the death of Seignelay, to whom Frontenac had given him a letter of recommendation. At Versailles Lahontan waited on the new minister, Pontchartrain, who refused his request for compassionate leave and required him to return to Quebec by the end of the summer. Indeed, Lahontan's only satisfaction during his visit was his being promoted, on 31 May, half-pay captain of a company in Canada. In Paris he found his family affairs hopelessly entangled, and his illustrious relations, the Bragelonnes, of little help. Lahontan tells us that he was at this time received into the Order of Our Lady of Mount Carmel and St Lazarus, but no documentary confirmation of this is available. Thoroughly disillusioned by his efforts to obtain preferment, he made his way back to La Rochelle, and at the end of July set sail on the *Honoré*, landing at Quebec on 18 September.

With Lahontan there had travelled on the same ship the Chevalier Guillaume de Maupeou (1664–1725), a relative of Pontchartrain, whose presence at Quebec, together with that of the distinguished English prisoner John NELSON, made the winter of 1691–92 a memorable one at the Château Saint-Louis. It was apparently during this winter that Frontenac attempted to arrange a marriage between Lahontan and his 18-year-old goddaughter, Geneviève Damours, daughter of Mathieu Damours* de Chauffours, but despite the financial advantages of the match, Lahontan, after reflection, withdrew.

The following summer Lahontan resubmitted to Frontenac an earlier proposal for the arming of the western frontier by establishing a chain of three forts, one near the mouth of the Niagara River, a second at Saint-Joseph on the Sainte-Claire River and a third in Georgian Bay, the three centres to be linked by light troop transport vessels manned by 50 Basque sailors. Frontenac was at first attracted by the proposal, and authorized Lahontan to sail to France on the *Sainte-Anne* on 27 July 1692 to carry the idea to the court.

The *Sainte-Anne* put in at Placentia (Plaisance) on 18 August and waited there for a month for the Basque fishing boats she was to convoy to France. On 14 September news was received that five English ships were approaching Placentia. Governor Jacques-François de MOMBETON de Brouillan prepared to defend the port and stationed Lahontan with 60 Basque sailors at an advance post called La Fontaine, less than a mile from the fort. On the 17th a landing by several boatloads of English sailors was prevented by Lahontan's Basques. The following day Lahontan and Philippe PASTOUR de Costebelle were cordially received on board the English commander's ship,

the *St Alban's*, to arrange an exchange pf prisoners; a day of bombardment (19 September) followed and then the English withdrew in discouragement. Thus on 6 October, for the second time in two years, Lahontan sailed for France bearing news of a French victory and of his own part in it.

After a 17-day crossing, he landed at Saint-Nazaire on 23 October and hurried to Versailles. His proposal to fortify the Great Lakes received little attention there but his gallantry at Placentia earned him admission on 1 March 1693 to the Marine guards and appointment on 15 March as king's lieutenant at Placentia, with the perquisites of a company of 100 men. While awaiting a ship for his return to Newfoundland that spring, Lahontan tells us he had long conversations with a Portuguese doctor about the independent origin of the American Indians and their eventual salvation or damnation, questions that were to be taken up again in his *Dialogues*. Re-embarking at Saint-Nazaire on 12 May 1693, Lahontan captured off Newfoundland an English ship laden with tobacco before landing at Placentia on 20 June.

On his return, Lahontan was badly received by Brouillan, who was surprised and annoyed to learn of his new appointment. Disagreements between the two men multiplied. Brouillan sent unfavourable reports to the minister, claiming that Lahontan neglected his responsibility as king's lieutenant for the distribution of supplies, that he questioned Brouillan's authority and disciplinary decisions, and that he tried to divert soldiers from their duties to gather his firewood. In short, wrote Brouillan, "M. de Lahontan doesn't bother about anything here except what can contribute to his pleasures." Lahontan, for his part, reproached his superior with inhumane treatment of his men and with profiteering, and composed "scurrilous songs" about the governor. Seeking to rid himself of the troublesome Lahontan, Brouillan slyly proposed that he be put in command of the island of Saint-Pierre. Suddenly matters came to a head: on 20 Nov. 1693, while Lahontan was entertaining guests at supper, Brouillan and his valets entered, wearing masks, and upset tables and cupboards, breaking bottles and glasses. During the next few days there were clashes between Brouillan's valets and Lahontan's, and Brouillan charged with desertion two of Lahontan's soldiers who were working in the district. Despite these provocations, Lahontan took the advice of the Recollets and sought an accommodation with the governor. Fearing the consequences of Brouillan's reports about him, however, Lahontan made a desperate decision. He tells us he paid the captain of the only

442

ship left in port a thousand *écus*—an unbelievable sum for an officer earning only 90 *livres* a month—to carry him to Europe, and thus he fled his post at Placentia.

His North American career having abruptly ended, and a royal order having been issued for his arrest, Lahontan began at the age of 27 the European peregrinations that were to occupy the remainder of his life. Set down at Viana do Castelo in Portugal at the end of January 1694, he went from there to Oporto, Coimbra, and Lisbon, and in April sailed for Holland. After visiting Rotterdam and Amsterdam he went by boat to Hamburg, where he wrote a letter on 19 June 1694 that he never published: in it he claimed to have met there two Frenchmen who had been on La Salle's last expedition. When Pontchartrain instructed the French resident in that city, Abbé Bidal, to investigate the story, however, no confirmation could be obtained.

That same month, Lahontan left for Copenhagen, where the French minister, François Dusson de Bonrepaus, presented him at the Danish court, and gave him letters to courtiers at Versailles. Nevertheless, when Lahontan went to Versailles in December 1694, Pontchartrain refused to receive him. A voyage to Béarn in 1695 was equally disillusioning: the château of Lahontan having been sold, the former baron found himself a stranger in his native land. While engaged in legal business visits in the neighbouring towns, Lahontan received a message that an order had been issued for his arrest, and he fled in disguise over the Pyrenees into Spain. The last letter included in his published works is dated from Saragossa on 8 Oct. 1695.

We know little of Lahontan's last years. In 1697 he appealed unsuccessfully for reinstatement in his command "au pays des Outaouais." A letter from M. de Bonrepaus, found in the archives of the Ministère des Affaires Étrangères, reports his presence at The Hague on 18 Sept. 1698 and his willingness to serve as a French agent in Spain for the modest sum of 400 *écus* a year. Two other letters, written by Lahontan to the Duke of Jovenazo on 1 and 7 Sept. 1699, confirm his return to Lisbon, whence he was forwarding to the Spanish court documents about the Mississippi. One of these was a copy of the *Journal* of Abbé Jean Cavelier, written in Lahontan's own hand. By 1702 he was presumably in Holland, arranging for his *Nouveaux voyages* . . . to be published there early in 1703. But before the volumes were printed, he had crossed to England, where he may have composed some memoirs on North America that have been attributed to him. We then lose track of Lahontan until November 1710, when Gottfried

Wilhelm Leibniz mentions him as being at the court of the Elector of Hanover and in frail health. It is usually thought that Lahontan died in 1715, although no proof of this date exists beyond the fact that in 1716 Leibniz published a pamphlet written by him, apparently as a posthumous tribute.

During the decade he had spent in North America, Lahontan had not lacked opportunities to distinguish himself. He had taken part in two campaigns against the Iroquois, had twice been besieged by the English, had visited almost all parts of New France and may well have reached the Mississippi at a time when few Frenchmen had seen it. But he appears to have made little mark; except during his final months at Placentia, the official correspondence of the time scarcely mentions him.

Indeed, had Lahontan been merely an officer and traveller, his name would be forgotten today. But while serving and travelling in New France he had done something few of his fellow officers thought to do: "In the course of my Voyages and Travels, I took care to keep particular Journals of every thing . . . ," sometimes even making notes on birch-bark. From these diaries he was able later to compose the three books which were to make him, next to Louis HENNEPIN, the most widely read author on North America in the first half of the 18th century.

Lahontan's works appeared at a time when travel narratives were enjoying an extraordinary vogue in Europe and when interest in North America, aroused by the *Jesuit Relations* and whetted by the voyages of Hennepin and HENRI TONTY, was greater than ever before.

His *Nouveaux voyages dans l'Amérique septentrionale* and their sequel, *Mémoires de l'Amérique septentrionale*, were published in January 1703 at The Hague and were twice pirated within a few months. A third volume, entitled *Supplément aux voyages* . . . and containing dialogues possibly written in collaboration in England, appeared later in 1703 in both English and French, the two earlier volumes having meantime been translated into English. New French editions were published in 1704 and 1705; the 1705 version was a considerably revised and expanded one, probably the work of the defrocked Benedictine anticlerical Nicolas Gueudeville (1650–1720), who had been living at The Hague since 1699. Other editions followed almost yearly, with a German abridgement being issued in 1709 and a Dutch one in 1710. By 1758, 25 editions or condensed versions had appeared, raising bibliographical problems which continue to puzzle bibliographers today.

Lahontan's three volumes embraced a wide

variety of subject-matter. The *Nouveaux voyages . . .* recounted in the then popular epistolary form his ten years in New France; midway through the narrative a letter four or five times as long as the rest told a fanciful tale of his imaginary voyage up the Long River. The *Mémoires* provided a lively geographical account of New France, followed by an anthropological study of its Indian inhabitants and completed by a linguistic commentary and glossary of the Algonkian language. In the third volume the travel narrative was resumed, this time in little-known European states: Portugal, Aragon, Holland, the Hansa cities, and Denmark. The remainder of the book was made up of five imaginary dialogues with an Indian chief whose name, Adario, was a partial anagram of that of the recently deceased Kondiaronk. The dialogues treated Christian belief, French laws and society, medicine, and marriage.

Lahontan's writings, in his first two volumes at least, were based on personal observation of events and practices in New France, of Indian customs, and of flora and fauna. They included an impressive wealth of detail and, except for some exaggeration in the numbers of persons involved, were remarkably accurate in their information. The infrequent occasions on which Lahontan retailed hearsay—for example in his jesting page on the marriageable girls sent out to New France, or in his tale of the Long River—have drawn refutations which by their violence bear witness to his relative veracity elsewhere.

But Lahontan's gifts were not merely descriptive. His identification of the eight abuses prevalent in New France is perceptive and sound. His assessment of the best method of fortifying the Great Lakes, his awareness of the loss to the colony of the talents of the Huguenots, his appreciation of the common interest of France and England in encouraging trade, his realization of the unwisdom of attempting to destroy the Iroquois, and his vision of the future greatness of North America demonstrate his powers of judgement and imagination, and his grasp of the situation in New France.

Quite apart from the information and opinions they communicated about North America, moreover, Lahontan's works were a compendium of early 18th-century "philosophic" ideas about the folly of superstitions, the vices of European society, the illogicalities of Christian dogma and the virtues of the "noble savage." The same ideas, better expressed, would be found in the writings of major 18th-century authors: in the fourth book of Swift's *Gulliver's Travels* (1726), in Rousseau's *Discours sur les origines de l'inégalité . . .* (1755),

in Voltaire's *L'Ingénu* (1767), or in Diderot's posthumously published *Supplément au voyage de Bougainville*. More than a century after their author's death, Lahontan's books lived on: in Chateaubriand's *Les Natchez* (1826), one of the chief figures is called Adario, and the names of all Chateaubriand's Indian characters are taken from Lahontan's Algonkian glossary.

In our own century, Lahontan's works are no longer widely read, and he himself has become a shadowy figure. There is no extant portrait of him, and we know only that he was tall, lean, and pale. Proud and independent, impulsive and inconstant, he chafed under the restraints of military discipline and never accepted those of marriage. He loved the open-air life of the forests of New France, where he could please himself, spending one day with his Indian hunters and the next with Anacreon or Petronius: "a solitary Life is most grateful to me, and the manners of the Savages are perfectly agreeable to my Palate." In Europe he led of necessity a more sociable existence: "He is witty and has a Gascon vivaciousness about him that puts him on good terms with everyone he meets . . . ," wrote Bonrepaus, "the most responsible people open their homes to him and are delighted to have his company." Among his admirers were two of the greatest minds of his time, Sir Hans Sloane and Leibniz.

Indeed, the pendulum of Lahontan's life had more than once swung between solitude and society, between Europe and North America. As a youthful subject of Louis XIV he had left the Old World for the New; as an early writer of the Enlightenment he brought the New World to the Old.

DAVID M. HAYNE

AE, Hollande, 176, ff.464–65v; 180, ff.122–24v [published by Henri Froidevaux, "Un document inédit sur Lahontan," *Journal de la Société des Américanistes de Paris*, IV (1902–3), 196–203]. AJM, Greffe de Claude Maugue, 25 nov. 1684. AJQ, Greffe de Gilles Rageot, 25 nov. 1690. AN, Col., B, 16, ff.64v, 202, 206, 206v; 17, ff.25, 36v–37, 227v; C11A, 120, f.22v; C11C, 1, ff.201–4v, 210, 243v, 244v–45, 276v–77v; D2C, 222 (Alphabet Laffilard); Marine, B2, 99, f.74; C1, 161; C7, 160. PAC, FM 18, K 1.

[Jean Cavelier], *The journal of Jean Cavelier, the account of a survivor of La Salle's Texas expedition, 1684–1688*, trans. and annotated by Jean Delanglez (Chicago, 1938), 5, 7, 39–49, 129, 134, 141, 163. Charlevoix, *History* (Shea), I, 86–87; III, 286; IV, 223–24; VI, 127. *Coll. de manuscrits relatifs à la N.-F.*, II, 62, 145. *Découvertes et établissements des Français* (Margry), IV, 6–8. Le Blant, *Histoire de la N.-F.*, 21–61. [Louis-Armand de Lom d'Arce,] Baron de Lahontan, . . . *Dialogues curieux entre l'auteur et un sauvage de bon sens qui a voyagé, et Mémoires de l'Amérique septentrionale*, éd. Gilbert Chinard (Baltimore, Paris, London, 1931); *New voyages* (Thwaites); *Nouveaux voyages* [The "Angel" (or Renommée) 1703 edition is apparently the original one; the other two, the "sphere" and "ornament" editions, are probably pirated. The edition published by François de Nion under the title *Un outre-mer au XVIIe siècle; voyages au Canada du baron de La Hontan* (Paris, 1900) is incomplete and worthless. D.M.H.]. É.-Z. Massicotte, "Un document inédit du baron de Lahontan [donation du 25 nov. 1684]," *BRH*, XXVI (1920), 11–13. (This document is also reproduced, with slight differences in readings, in *The Oakes collection. New documents by Lahontan concerning Canada and Newfoundland*, ed. with Intro. by Gustave Lanctot (Ottawa, 1940).) Numerous other documents concerning Lahontan are reproduced in J.-E. Roy, *Le baron de Lahontan* (Lévis, 1903) (first published in *RSCT*, 1st ser., XII (1894), sect.I, 63–192).

DAB, X, 548. Le Jeune, *Dictionnaire*, II, 39–42. L.-G. Michaud, *Biographie universelle ancienne et moderne* . . . (85v., Paris, 1811–62), XIX, 593. Tanguay, *Dictionnaire*, I, 338, note 1. F. C. B. Crompton, *Glimpses of early Canadians: Lahontan* (Toronto, 1925). Gustave Lanctot, "Un fantaisiste du mensonge," in *Faussaires et faussetés en histoire canadienne* (Montréal, [1948]), 96–129; *Filles de joie ou filles du roi: étude sur l'émigration féminine en Nouvelle-France* (Montréal, 1952). L. I. Bredvold, "A note on La Hontan and the *Encyclopédie*," *Modern Language Notes* (Baltimore), XLVII (1932), 508–9. A. H. Greenly, "Lahontan: an essay and bibliography," *Papers of the Bibliographical Society of America*, XLVIII (1954), 334–89. Stephen Leacock, "Baron de Lahontan, explorer," *Canadian Geographical Journal*, IV (1932), 281–94; "Lahontan in Minnesota," *Minnesota History*, XIV (1933), 367–77. D. R. McKee, "Lahontan and critical deism," *Modern Language Notes* (Baltimore), LVI (1941), 522–23. Séraphin Marion, "Les ouvrages de La Hontan," in *Relations des voyageurs français en Nouvelle-France au XVIIe siècle* (Paris, 1923), 243–52. E. Meyer, "Une source de l'*Ingénu*: les *Voyages* du baron de Lahontan," *Revue des cours et conférences* (Paris), XXI (1929–30), 561–76, 746–62. J. S. Patrick, "Memoirs of a seventeenth-century spy," *Canadian Geographical Journal*, XXII (1941), 264–68. Roger Picard, "Les aventures et les idées du baron de Lahontan," *Revue de l'université d'Ottawa*, XVI (1946), 38–70. Viateur Ravary, "Lahontan et la Rivière Longue," *RHAF*, V (1951–52), 471–92. M. E. Storer, "Bibliographical information on Foigny, Lahontan and Tyssot de Patot," *Modern Language Notes* (Baltimore), LX (1945), 143–56.

LONGUEUIL, CHARLES LE MOYNE DE. *See* LE MOYNE

LOPPINOT, JEAN-CHRYSOSTOME, notary, clerk of court and king's attorney at Port-Royal (Annapolis Royal, N.S.), then clerk of court at Plaisance (Placentia); fl. 1699–1712.

Loppinot, who came originally from the parish of Saint-Nicolas, in Paris, received a commission as clerk of court at Port-Royal on 5 April 1699. In the disputes between Brouillan [MOMBETON] and Abbé Maudoux* he took the side of the parish priest, and thus incurred the governor's hostility, but afterwards he was reconciled with him. On 4 May 1704 he was appointed king's attorney, and the following year went to France as the representative of the Acadians, who were asking for Brouillan's recall. On 15 Dec. 1706 he obtained from AUGER de Subercase the grant of a seigneury at Cap Fourchu (Yarmouth, N.S.). As a salary he received only 100, then 150 *livres* a year, so that he had to engage in trading to exist. His dwelling at Port-Royal, which was destroyed by fire in 1708, was again destroyed in June 1710. A few months later NICHOLSON seized Port-Royal. Loppinot then emigrated to Plaisance, where he obtained the post of clerk of court in 1712. But soon the treaty of Utrecht ceded Newfoundland to England. Loppinot must have returned to France after that, for we lose trace of him. A small part of his notarial acts is preserved in the French national archives. By his marriage with Jeanne (or Marie) Doucet, Judge Dubreuil's widow, he had had five children; two of his sons, Jean-Chrysostome* and Louis, served later at Louisbourg, in the colonial regular troops.

RENÉ BAUDRY

AN, Col., B, 20, 25, 27, 29, 32, 36; C¹¹D, 4–6; E, 290 (dossier Loppinot); F³, 54, f.447; Section Outre-Mer, G³, 2040 (notaires d'Acadie); 2054–55 (greffe de Plaisance).

LORI. *See* LORIT

LORIMIER DE LA RIVIÈRE, GUILLAUME DE (Lorimier, Lormier), captain in the colonial regular troops, seigneur of Les Bordes (Boyne) in Gâtinais, commandant of Fort Rolland; b. *c.* 1655, son of Guillaume de Lorimier, also seigneur of Les Bordes and a captain in the troops, and of Jeanne Guilbaut, of the parish of Saint-Luc et Saint-Gilles in Paris; m. Marie-Marguerite Chorel de Saint-Romain, *dit* d'Orvilliers, at Champlain on 27 Jan. 1695; buried 29 July 1709 at Montreal.

Guillaume de Lorimier the younger continued the military tradition of a family of the minor nobility as well as establishing the Lorimier family in Canada. It has been suggested that he came to the colony with his father in 1685, and that the latter subsequently returned to France. It is more likely, however, that he came out with the reinforcements of 1685 along with Captain Pierre de Troyes*, to whom Lorimier was assigned as a

Lorit

company lieutenant. According to one contemporary memoir, in 1686 "Sieur de Lorimier, who was only a sergeant, was promoted captain to replace Sieur de Flours [chevalier de Saint-Flour], who died in the Hôtel-Dieu at Quebec." In 1701 Governor Louis-Hector de CALLIÈRE summarized his early career slightly differently: "Sieur Lorrimier, native of Paris, 46 years old, made second lieutenant of the Régiment de la Reine, 20 March 1673, lieutenant in the same regiment 15 Sept. 1676, lieutenant of the first company of grenadiers in the same regiment 2 Sept. 1679, captain in Canada 10 Sept. 1685." He was first stationed on Montreal Island.

In February 1691, while at a gathering of officers in Lower Town, Quebec, Lorimier fell into an argument with Pierre PAYEN de Noyan over the winnings in a game of chance. Violent words were followed by the use of swords and Lorimier was seriously wounded in the back. For his part in the duel, Lorimier was deprived of his command and was ordered to give 50 *livres* to charity.

This punishment was little more than a gesture for Lorimier was reinstated in 1692 and he received the honorary post of midshipman at Rochefort the following year. He is said to have participated as captain in the 1696 expedition led by Frontenac [Buade*] against the Iroquois. He was at that time stationed at Lachine and in 1705 he was the commander of nearby Fort Rolland, where he had served in 1692.

Lorimier's second major encounter with the law came in 1707, when he was convicted of having maliciously accused Henri Catin, a Montreal butcher, of maligning Governor Philippe de RIGAUD de Vaudreuil and of beating the butcher with the flat of his sword. Although Lorimier was heavily fined for this outrage, a rumour reached the minister of Marine that Vaudreuil had prevented collection of the fine. This story was cited as proof that the governor protected his officers from the normal course of the law. Vaudreuil denied both the story and the charge of favouritism.

Lorimier's superiors described him as "ill-tempered" and "wedded to wine but a good officer." In 1707 he was informed that "the King is acquainted with the services that you have rendered up to the present, both in France and in Canada, and His Majesty is satisfied with them." His widow, by whom he had had four children, was awarded a belated pension of 75 *livres*, and his son, Claude-Nicolas (1705–1770), received a commission in the colonial regular troops.

PETER N. MOOGK

AJM, Greffe de Claude Maugue, 17 sept. 1686; 9 févr. 1687. AJTR, Greffe de François Trotain, 26 janv. 1695. AN, Col., B, 11, f.82; 12, ff.5, 45; 29, f.107; F³, 5, ff.12–23. PAC, FM 30, D 65. *Coll. de manuscrits relatifs à la N.-F.*, I; 560. "Correspondance de Frontenac (1689–99)," APQ, *Rapport, 1927–28*, 86, 110. "Correspondance de Vaudreuil," APQ *Rapport, 1939–40*, 420, 436; *1942–43*, 423, 434; *1946–47*, 372, 385. *Jug. et délib.*, III, 493, 503, 508, 510f.; V, 29, 527, 584f., 586. PAC *Report, 1899*, Supp. P.-G. Roy, "Ce que Callières pensait de nos officiers," 323; *Inv. coll. pièces jud. et not.*, I, 44. Taillemite, *Inventaire analytique, série B*, I, 28, 31, 32, 158.

Raymond Douville, "Deux officiers 'indésirables' des troupes de la Marine," *Cahiers des Dix*, XIX (1954), 71. É.-Z. Massicotte, "La famille De Lorimier," *BRH*, XXI (1915), 10–12. P.-G. Roy, "Le duel sous le régime français," *BRH*, XIII (1907), 132, 133.

LORIT (Lori, Lerry, Lorris), *dit* **Gargot, FRANÇOIS,** settler, process-server, serjeant-at-law in the bailiff's court of Montreal; b. *c.* 1646 at Celle, in the bishopric of Poitiers, son of César Lory and Richarde Grimère; buried 6 Jan. 1702 at Lachine.

Lorit arrived in Canada in 1664 as a voluntary indentured worker, and was sent to the Jesuits' seigneury at Cap-de-la-Madeleine. Probably because of a speech defect which earned him the nickname of "Gargot," the religious felt sympathetic towards him, and on 23 March 1665 made him a grant of land in their Batiscan seigneury, a grant which he sold to Nicolas Rivard on 3 Dec. 1666. He endeavoured unsuccessfully to establish himself in the neighbouring seigneuries. François Lorit was not cut out for the task of clearing land and felt at ease only in the company of men of law. Being fairly well educated, he gave valuable help to the illiterate people around him. For several years he was a process-server in the jurisdiction of the Cap; in the same period he acted as a witness for numerous notarial contracts and as an arbitrator in disputes. These various occupations were far from making him wealthy, and to avoid the visit of one of his writ-serving colleagues he had to sell, in 1680, his only remaining property, a land grant at Champlain.

He went then to the island of Montreal, where the 1681 census mentions his presence and that of his wife and three children. In official documents he was styled serjeant of the bailiff's court of Montreal, process-server, and sometimes "vicegerent." In these various capacities he had become acquainted with the private lives of almost all the families in the colony. Thus in 1687 and 1688 he was entrusted with serving some of the numerous legal papers resulting from the proceedings instituted against PIERRE LE MOYNE d'Iberville for taking advantage of Geneviève Picoté de Belestre.

446

On 1 Oct. 1670, at Quebec, François Lorit had married a king's girl (*fille du roi*), Perrette Parement, who originally came from Troyes, and who bore him four children, two of them boys. He married again on 29 Jan. 1685; his second wife was Marie-Thérèse Le Gros.

RAYMOND DOUVILLE

AJM, Greffe d'Antoine Adhémar, 17 sept. 1674, 19 oct. 1701; Greffe de Claude Maugue, 2 mai, 6, 24 août 1682, 3 août 1689. AJTR, Greffe de Jean Cusson, 10 oct. 1676; Greffe de Jacques de La Touche. *Jug. et délib.*, II, III. É.-Z. Massicotte, "La maréchaussée à Montréal," *BRH*, XXII (1916), 17.

LORMIER (Lorrimier). *See* LORIMIER

LOTBINIÈRE, RENÉ-LOUIS CHARTIER DE. *See* CHARTIER

LOUET, JEAN-CLAUDE, royal notary and clerk of the admiralty court at Quebec, son of Jean Louet and Catherine Thierry, of the parish of Saint-Maclou (Rouen); b. 1681; buried at Quebec 28 July 1739.

On 15 July 1707, at Quebec, Louet married Anne Morin, widow of René Deneau*. On 15 May 1717, an ordinance issued by Bégon* allowed him "in the name and as the husband of Anne Morin, widow of the late René Deneau, to choose a location in the Port-Daniel seigneury where he could engage in inshore fishing."

On the preceding 22 March, after the death of Louis CHAMBALON, Louet had succeeded him as royal notary. Two years later he became clerk of the admiralty court at Quebec. In fact Louet was the first holder of this office, for Charles GUILLIMIN, who had been appointed in 1717 when the jurisdiction was created, had refused it; it was thus only two years after the admiralty court had been constituted officially that it really began to carry out its functions.

On 16 and 20 April 1734, Louet sat as judge of the provost court of Quebec, "in view," as the register specifies, "of the indisposition of the lieutenant-general and the king's attorney." After being stricken with paralysis, Louet had retired. On 14 April 1738 the minister informed the intendant that he was granting Louet a pension of 400 *livres*, and that he was entrusting the office of clerk of court to BRICAULT de Valmur, the secretary of Hocquart*. But the new incumbent died 28 June 1738 at Quebec, and Jean-Claude Louet junior succeeded him on 20 April 1739.

Louet senior was buried 28 July 1739. He had three children; the above-mentioned son, having become enamoured of a young English girl, had addressed three "respectful summonses" to his father, the last two of which, dated 23 and 24 Jan. 1733, begged him to grant permission for the marriage, in order that the girl's honour might be saved. The wedding took place on 16 February following.

HERVÉ BIRON

AQ, NF, Ord. des int., VI, 272; XXVII, 28; Paroisses, Notre-Dame de Québec; NF, Registres de la Prévôté de Québec, 16, 20 avril 1734. P.-G. Roy, *Inv. ord. int.*, I, 168f. "Les 'sommations respectueuses' autrefois," *APQ Rapport, 1921–22*, 60f. L.-G. Verrier, "Les registres de l'amirauté de Québec," *APQ Rapport, 1920–21*, 106–31. P.-G. Roy, "Les secrétaires des gouverneurs et des intendants de la Nouvelle-France," *BRH*, XLI (1935), 104. J.-E. Roy, *Histoire du notariat*, I, 122, 351f.

LOUISE *dite* **DE SAINT-AUGUSTIN.** *See* SOUMANDE

LOUVIGNY, LOUIS DE LA PORTE DE. *See* LA PORTE

LOYARD, JEAN-BAPTISTE, priest, Jesuit, missionary for more than 20 years to the Malecites of the Saint John River (N.B.); b. 18 Oct. 1678 at Pau; d. in the night of 24–25 June 1731 at Médoctec (Meductic, N.B.).

Jean-Baptiste Loyard entered the noviciate of Bordeaux on 31 Aug. 1695 and arrived in Canada on 14 June 1704. Around 1709 he succeeded Father Aubéry* as missionary to the Malecites of the Saint John River. For a long time he had to assemble the faithful in a chapel made of bark, since the government did not have the necessary resources to build a church. In 1715 he applied to Intendant Bégon*, insisting that the provision of a fine church for the loyal subjects of Médoctec was of vital concern to the welfare of the state. Twelve hundred *livres* would be enough, he wrote, together with the voluntary gifts made by the Abenakis, to complete the sum needed. His request was met. In 1718 he was entrusted by RIGAUD de Vaudreuil with authority to grant lands on the Saint John River to any Acadians who wished to settle there. Few moved, however.

In his "Mémoire sur l'état présent des Abnaquis," which dates from the years 1720–22, Loyard insisted on the necessity for France to retain the attachment of this Indian nation. The report begins with these words: "Of all the Indians of New France it is the Abnaquis who have rendered and are in a position to render the most services." Speaking particularly of their three villages in Acadia, he wrote: "These three villages, each using its own route via a river, are only a

447

Lynvilliers

few days' journey from Quebec. This is what makes their situation so important in relation to Canada." He observed that the English, who by virtue of the treaty of Utrecht owned the peninsula of Acadia (Nova Scotia), were not thinking of farming it, but were trying to take possession by force of the lands of the Abenakis which had not been made over to them. They probably wanted in this way to get closer to Canada. He suggested that the problem should be studied at the congress of Cambrai which was meeting in 1722. According to a dispatch sent by Vaudreuil to the court on 17 Oct. 1722, Father Loyard, on his return from France where he had been sent by the governor, was devoting his attention to deciding upon the bounds which it would be advisable to set to the activities of the English. Things nevertheless remained as they were, perhaps because, at the time when Loyard was writing, Charlevoix* was already on an official mission in Canada (1720–23); the main purpose of his voyage was precisely to study the thorny problem of the Acadian frontiers, a source of constantly recurring conflict between France and England. Paris thought it advisable not to make any decision before having Charlevoix's report.

Loyard died at Médoctec among his Indians, during the night of 24–25 June 1731. In his obituary letter Father Jean-Baptiste Duparc* had already written of Father Loyard that "even in the depths of the woods he found means to build a fine church in stone, adorn it suitably, and furnish it abundantly with sacred vessels and quite rich frontals."

In 1890 a stone was found, bearing a Latin inscription which testified that the Malecites to whom Father Loyard had preached the gospel had built the church at Médoctec in 1717. According to the documentary evidence at present available, this stone church was the first Catholic place of worship erected on the territory of New Brunswick.

LÉON POULIOT, S.J.

AN, Col., B, 59, f.439; C¹¹ᴬ, 42, f.8; 45, f.69; C¹¹ᴮ, 12, f.36. ASJCF, 559. *NYCD* (O'Callaghan and Fernow), IX, 911f. Rochemonteix, *Les Jésuites et la N.-F. au XVIIᵉ siècle*, III, 436ff. W. O. Raymond, "The old Meductic fort," N.B. Hist. Soc. *Coll.*, I (1894–98), 221–72.

LYNVILLIERS. *See* PETIT

M

MACARD (Maquard), CHARLES, business man, member of the Conseil Supérior of New France; b. 16 Dec. 1656 at Quebec; d. 1732. His father, Nicolas Macard, *dit* Champagne, son of Thomas Macard and Marguerite Hardy, of Mareuil-sur-Dié, had married Marguerite Couillard, daughter of Guillaume Couillard* and widow of Jean Nicollet*.

In a will received by the notary Becquet* on 14 Dec. 1677, Charles Bazire* "gives to his brother-in-law, Charles Macart, 2,000 *livres*, as well as the title-deed to Charlesville, with the farm and outlying buildings." This small fief, situated near Montmorency Falls, had been granted by Bishop LAVAL on 21 July 1677 to Bazire and CHARLES AUBERT de La Chesnaye.

Macard was one of the founders and administrators of the Compagnie de la Colonie du Canada, which was created in 1700 to carry on trade in beaver furs in Canada and Europe. But as the market price for these furs had completely collapsed, the company went bankrupt.

On 14 June 1704, Louis XIV, in a letter addressed to RIGAUD de Vaudreuil and Beauharnois* de La Boische, announced the appointment of Charles de MONSEIGNAT to the office of court clerk to the Conseil Supérieur, which with the death of the Sieur CHARLES DENYS de Vitré left two vacancies on the council. "[His Majesty] has granted the seats, one to the Sieur Maccart, one of the deputies of the company, at present in France, who is ordered to return to Canada, and the other to the Sieur Juchereau du Chesnay [IGNACE JUCHEREAU]." Macard was not installed until 16 Nov. 1705.

The company's affairs failed completely; on 7 Nov. 1711 Vaudreuil and JACQUES RAUDOT informed the King that Macard and Guillaume GAILLARD had been named to be present as representatives of the administration of the company at the inventory of its assets.

As the Sieur François-Madeleine-Fortuné de RUETTE d'Auteuil had been suspended in 1707 from his office of attorney general, Macard replaced him temporarily. Subsequently Jessé Leduc Des Fontaines was appointed to succeed Ruette d'Auteuil. He arrived on 8 Sept. 1710 and died on 22 September. Macard therefore continued to hold this office. Vaudreuil and Raudot, although with some reservations, proposed that his appointment be made permanent: "... it is true that he lacks the brilliant qualities that may be found in others, but often those who have them have nothing else, and do not possess that solidity which engenders in men justice, equity, and uprightness." The minister seemed to look favourably upon this suggestion, but on 14 June 1712 he named Mathieu-Benoît COLLET to occupy the post as of 14 October. He concluded by promising that his majesty "will remember the Sieur Maccart when the time comes."

Macard remained a member of the Conseil Supérieur until his death on 9 Dec. 1732. He had already been almost helpless for four years, according to Intendant DUPUY; the latter, in a report on the incidents following the death of Bishop Saint-Vallier [LA CROIX], speaks "of the second councillor, the Sieur Maquard, who for three years has suffered from paralysis of the tongue, and who can give his opinion only by nodding his head. . . ."

On 20 Dec. 1686 Macard had married Jeanne-Renée Gourdeau de Beaulieu, daughter of Jacques Gourdeau de Beaulieu and Éléonore de Grandmaison*; she died in 1717 after bearing him several children, who did not reach adult age.

HERVÉ BIRON

"Correspondance de Vaudreuil," APQ *Rapport, 1938–39*, 36; *1946–47*, 389. *Documents relating to Canadian currency during the French period* (Shortt), 1070. *Jug. et délib.*, IV, 167, 179, 239. "Mémoire de M. Dupuy, Intendant de la Nouvelle-France, sur les troubles arrivés à Québec en 1727 et 1728, après la mort de Mgr Saint-Vallier, évêque de Québec," APQ *Rapport, 1920–21*, 91. A. Roy, *Inv. greffes not.*, III, 157. Cahall, *Sovereign Council of New France*, 102–4. J. Delalande, *Le Conseil souverain de la Nouvelle-France* (Québec, 1927), 213–27. N.-E. Dionne, "Les caveaux de la basilique Notre-Dame de Québec," *BRH*, IV (1898), 102–3. É.-Z. Massicotte, "M. de Charlesville," *BRH*, XX (1914), 267. J.-E. Roy, "Les conseillers au Conseil souverain de la Nouvelle-France," *BRH*, I (1895), 178, 185–86.

MAGOS (Magesse), JEAN MARTEL DE. *See* MARTEL

MAISONNAT, *dit* Baptiste, PIERRE (usually referred to as Baptiste), shipmaster, privateer who operated along the coast of Acadia and New England; pilot for several expeditions against New England; b. 1663 in France at Bergerac, son of Hélie Maisonnat and Jeanne Ségure (Chignac?); d. after August 1714.

Baptiste was married twice: first, to Judith Soubiran, who lived at Port-Royal (Annapolis Royal, N.S.) and died in 1703; second, to a widow,

Marguerite Bourgeois (daughter of JACQUES), with whom he was still living at Beaubassin on 29 Aug. 1714 (N.S.). However, [Buade*] de Frontenac in a letter to Pontchartrain, written 2 Nov. 1695, stated that he had heard that Baptiste had several other wives in France and Holland, and that RIGAUD de Vaudreuil knew a wife of Baptiste who lived near his home in Languedoc.

The first reference to Baptiste in Robinau* de Villebon's journals relates that he had put in at Passamaquoddy Bay on 5 Jan. 1692, with a prize which he was taking to Port-Royal. There were quite a number of privateers like Baptiste based at Port-Royal and Beaubassin at this time [*see* GUION]. They gathered their crews from among the young Acadians of these settlements who were attracted by their free life and the hope of plunder. The activities of the privateers were opposed by the clergy who felt that they had a bad influence on the local youth. Baptiste had apparently been operating on these coasts for some time, for he was said to have made a long stay in Boston, including two periods of imprisonment, and to have been familiar with Manate (New York) as well.

Baptiste reported to Villebon at the Saint John River on 4 May 1692. His two small vessels were outfitted there and he set out again on 10 May. By 22 June he was back, having captured within sight of Boston a brigantine of 45 tons loaded with wheat and flour. This made at least nine English vessels he had taken in six months. In October SIMON-PIERRE DENYS de Bonaventure and PIERRE LE MOYNE d'Iberville arrived at Baie Verte with the ships *Poli* and *Envieux*. Villebon met them there, and, when they decided to join the squadron commanded by Jean Du Paty (Patés) for a raid on New England, he arranged a rendezvous with Baptiste at Pentagoet (on Penobscot Bay). Baptiste was to act as pilot and take part in the raids. He failed to keep the rendezvous, however, because English activity at Port-Royal made it impossible for him to refit there.

In October 1693 Frontenac wrote the minister of Marine that Baptiste would go to Paris to confer with him about plans for attacking New England and Boston. This visit must have been a decided success, for Baptiste returned to Acadia in 1694 in command of the corvette the *Bonne*. He soon captured five prizes off the New England coast. He continued successfully to harass English shipping until the end of May 1695, when he was attacked in Migascor (Musquash, N.B.) harbour by an English frigate and another armed vessel. After a long fight he and his crew escaped ashore; his corvette was taken but sank within 12 hours.

Maleray de Noiré

Baptiste went to France later that year to account to the king for the vessel he had lost.

In the summer of 1696 he was with Iberville and Bonaventure on 14 July when they captured the English frigate *Newport* near the mouth of the Saint John River. He also acted as pilot for the expedition which captured Fort William Henry at Pemaquid on 15 August (5 August, o.s.). Baptiste owned a homestead near Fort Nashwaak (Naxouat) in partnership with Jean MARTEL and he was there when an English force under Colonel John Hathorne attacked the fort on 18 October of that same year. On Villebon's instructions Baptiste joined the Indians and directed them during the brief siege. When the English withdrew they abandoned two pirogues which Baptiste took to Minas where he outfitted them and recruited crews for a raid on the New England coast. In March 1697 he captured six fishing smacks south of Casco Bay. He returned to Minas for supplies and set out on another raid on 17 May. This time he was captured and taken to Boston, where he was held for some time after news was received that the treaty of Ryswick had been signed. A letter from Frontenac to the Earl of Bellomont, written 8 June 1698, demanded the release of Baptiste; Villebon reported him back on the Saint John River on 21 June. Baptiste's partnership with Martel dissolved a few years later.

English fishermen were forbidden by the treaty to fish off the coast of Acadia, and Baptiste may have been commissioned to capture those who ignored this ruling. At any rate he was a prisoner in Boston again in 1702, and the Massachusetts council was threatening to hang him as a pirate because he had been taken in time of peace. He was kept in close confinement until 1706 when he was exchanged for the Reverend John WILLIAMS, who had been captured in a French and Indian raid on Deerfield, Mass., in 1704.

Baptiste returned to Acadia and settled at Beaubassin. He was thereafter employed as a port captain, and sailed the coast between Port-Royal and Placentia (Plaisance). In 1709 and 1711 he took part in the fitting out of privateers at Placentia, and in 1714 he gave advice on the choice of a military site on Cape Breton Island (Île Royale).

W. AUSTIN SQUIRES

AN, Col., C¹¹ᴰ, 5; Section Outre-Mer, G¹, 466 (Recensements de l'Acadie, 1693, 1700); G³, cartons 2053, 2054. *Coll. de manuscrits relatifs à la N.-F.*, II, 108, 147–48, 151–53, 159, 163, 173, 202, 244, 246, 298, 395, 432, 436, 453, 454. "Correspondance de Frontenac (1689–99)," APQ *Rapport, 1927–28,* 156, 191. *NYCD* (O'Callaghan and Fernow), IV, IX. Webster, *Acadia,* 35–36, 38, 39, 42–46, 53, 54, 56, 57, 70, 75, 78, 92, 94, 100–3, 111, 112, 114, 144, 148, 154, 160–62. Bernard, *Le drame acadien,* 189, 194, 220, 237. Casgrain, *Les Sulpiciens en Acadie.* Coleman, *New England captives.* Murdoch, *History of Nova-Scotia,* I, 210, 215, 230, 232, 233, 255, 279. Régis Roy, "Le flibustier Baptiste," *BRH,* V (1899), 8–17; *see also BRH,* III (1897), 112; VI (1900), 121–23.

MALERAY DE NOIRÉ DE LA MOLLERIE, JACQUES (usually referred to as the Sieur de La Mollerie), officer in the colonial regular troops in Canada; named ensign in 1685 or 1687; lieutenant, 1691 (1693); midshipman, 1694; commanded at Fort Lachine in 1690, 1701; b. 1657 in Poitou, son of Isaac Maleray de La Périne and Marie Tessier; m. Françoise Picoté de Belestre, 6 Jan. 1687; d. 26 or 27 July 1704 on board the *Seine.*

Before coming to Canada, Jacques served as second lieutenant in the Régiment de Noailles (1675) and was made a lieutenant in 1677. He came to the colony in 1685 to escape the consequences of having killed the Sieur Guillot de La Forest in a sword fight in Poitiers that year. On 15 Jan. 1689 the seneschal's court of Poitou declared him contumacious and condemned him to be decapitated. With the king's permission, Jacques returned to France in 1693 to request letters of pardon. Considering that he received support from Frontenac [Buade*], CALLIÈRE, Champigny [BOCHART], and his brother-in-law HENRI TONTY, and that good officers were in great demand at the time, it is not surprising that the king granted his request. In the letters of pardon, signed in April 1695 and registered by the Conseil Souverain in Quebec on 14 October the same year, the king praised Jacques for having "distinguished himself on all possible occasions against the English and Iroquois, as well as in the commanding of forts entrusted to him."

In the year he was married, 1687, Jacques laid a criminal charge of rape and seduction against PIERRE LE MOYNE d'Iberville, on behalf of his sister-in-law, Jeanne-Geneviève Picoté de Belestre, a minor. Jeanne-Geneviève, who had a child as a result of the affair, maintained that she had weakened in the face of Iberville's promise to marry her. Either Iberville's influence was too great, or else Jeanne-Geneviève's reputation was questionable, for Jacques failed to persuade the Conseil Souverain to force Iberville to marry his sister-in-law. He did manage to prevent Iberville's marriage to another woman for several years, and to obtain in 1688 a court order requiring the adventurer to support Jeanne-Geneviève's daughter until she was 15 years of age.

In 1701 or 1702 Jacques took his wife and two of his children to France where he obtained an extension of his leave to look after some business and recover from an illness. The ship on which he was returning to Canada, the *Seine*, was captured after an engagement with the escorts of an English convoy, and Jacques was killed during an exchange of musket fire. Governor Callière, in his memoir of 1701 on the officers in Canada, had described the Sieur de La Mollerie as a "good officer."

Jacques Maleray de La Mollerie has frequently been confused with two of his sons, Jacques (bap. 6 Feb. 1689) and Louis-Hector (bap. 3 July 1692). Like their father before them, both Jacques and Louis-Hector participated in duels in which the survivors were condemned to be beheaded and were later pardoned. Louis-Hector died on 16 Dec. 1714 in Montreal from a wound sustained the previous day in a duel with Jean d'Ailleboust d'Argenteuil. Jacques killed Charles Fustel in September 1716 in Quebec and was granted letters of pardon in October 1720.

Some researchers have erroneously referred to Jacques Maleray, the father, as the son of a Duchesse de La Mollerie. The source of this error is probably a mistranscription in the Public Archives of Canada copy of a council of Marine memoir dated 19 March 1720 (AN, Col., C¹¹ᴬ, 41, p.144 [PAC transcript]). Reference is made to a "Duchesse" de la Mollerie who requested that her son be granted letters of grace for having killed one Fustel in a duel in Quebec. The original document (AN, Col., C¹¹ᴬ, 41, f.221) refers only to Dᵉ de la Mollerie. The transcriber erroneously assumed Dᵉ to be an abbreviation of Duchesse, instead of simply "Dame." In fact, the woman was Françoise Picoté de Belestre, the wife, and not the mother, of the Jacques Maleray who died on board the *Seine* in 1704. And the man who killed Fustel in Quebec was their son Jacques.

S. DALE STANDEN

AN, Col., B, 23, ff.119, 265; C¹¹ᴬ, 12, p.706; 41, p.144 (f.221); D²ᶜ, 47, pp.69, 93 (copies in PAC); Marine, B³, 123, ff.573–76, 577, 589; B⁴, 26, ff.96, 98–101. BN, MS, Fr. 22803, ff.285, 290, 316. *Jug. et délib.*, III, 194–97, 231–34, 237–39, 241–43, 258–64, 1057, 1060–64; VI, 923, 935. "Les officiers des troupes du Canada en 1701," *BRH*, XXVII (1921), 276. Aegidius Fauteux, *La famille d'Ailleboust* (Montréal, 1917), 89–94. É.-Z. Massicotte, "Les Maleray de la Mollerie?" *BRH*, XXV (1919), 122.

MALLET, DENIS, master wood-carver and carpenter; son of Louis-Denis Mallet and Renée Padouillet, originally from the parish of Notre-Dame in Alençon, diocese of Laix (France); interred 1 Nov. 1704 in Montreal.

It is not impossible that Mallet came to Canada at the same time and in the same circumstances as LAJOÜE, with whom he shared a house in 1692. We have no clue as to his age, but we may suppose that he was in his twenties when he arrived around 1688. On 14 Oct. 1695 at Quebec he contracted to marry Marie-Madeleine Jérémie, daughter of Noël Jérémie*, by whom he had three children who died at an early age. On 10 Nov. 1699 at Sainte-Foy he remarried, his second wife being Geneviève Liénard, and went to live at *côte* Saint-François-Xavier. Two daughters and a son were born of this marriage, all of whom attained adulthood.

The earliest of Mallet's known contracts was that by which he undertook to build a tabernacle ten feet wide and seven feet high, canopy included, for the sum of 600 *livres*. This contract, dated 24 Dec. 1693, which was concluded before Frontenac [Buade*], the protector of the Recollets, for whom the work was intended, specified that the tabernacle "will be movable . . . and that in place of the roof of the tabernacle there will also be a niche consisting of three angels holding up a royal crown, and that he will also make five figures for the niches in the said tabernacle." The tabernacle for the main altar of the church at Ange-Gardien, which is preserved in the provincial museum at Quebec and which was done at the same period by Jacques LEBLOND de Latour, no doubt permits us to visualize the work by Mallet, which has disappeared. It is not until 1700 that we again find a mention of Mallet practising as a wood-carver; at that time he carved a lion to decorate a Montreal merchant's bark.

The following year he ran foul of the law. He was sentenced and imprisoned, along with the notary GENAPLE, a former carpenter, for disrespect and failure to obey the authorities. He had, in fact, given expression a little too noisily to his desire to undertake a trip to the Mississippi region without waiting for the governor's permission. Worn out, perhaps by his misfortunes or by a malady contracted during a recent escapade, he died in November 1704 in Montreal, far from his wife, who was then in France. In the inventory of his belongings are listed "twelve small tools used in wood-turning, some old mortise chisels for carpentry work . . . of little value in all." It is on this quiet note that Mallet's career, which we have difficulty in following, comes to a premature end. It must, however, have left its mark on contemporary wood-carving at Quebec; indeed, during a lawsuit with the Jesuits, the testimony rendered in his favour by Juconde DRUÉ and Leblond, two important figures in Canadian art, proves the significance of his role.

Mallet's activity corresponded to the period when the Jesuit and Recollet monasteries were

Mandeville

being built and decorated, and was limited in great part to those programmes, of which we know very little. Undoubtedly he spent the rest of his time on day-to-day carpentry work and minor wood-carving orders; his role as a teacher at Saint-Joachim is hypothetical and not very likely. Richard Short*'s views of the interiors of the Jesuit and Recollet churches and the panels in the Quebec museum attributed to Mallet show the extent to which decorating was carried on in New France and prove that this art stands comparison with that in France from which it descended.

PIERRE MAYRAND

AJQ, Greffe de Louis Chambalon, 10 mai 1694; Greffe de François Genaple; Greffe de Florent de La Cetière, 13 mai 1705; Greffe de Guillaume Roger, 14 oct. 1694, 9 nov. 1699. IOA, Dossier Mallet. *Jug. et délib.,* IV, 478; V. Morisset, *La qeinture traditionnelle au C.f.,* 28. J.-E. Roy, *Histoire du notariat,* I, 124.

MANDEVILLE. *See* PHILIPPE(S)

MANTHET, NICOLAS D'AILLEBOUST DE. *See* AILLEBOUST

MAQUARD. *See* MACARD

MARAIS. *See* MAREST

MARCH, JOHN (occasionally written **Marsh, Mark** or **Martch**), innkeeper and ferry operator at Newbury, Mass., ship-builder, colonel in the Massachusetts Bay militia, and active participant in many battles between the French and Indians and the English; b. 10 June 1658 (o.s.) in Newbury, the fourth child of Judith and Hugh March; married at Newbury 1 Oct. 1679 to Jemima True; d. July 1712 in Woodbridge, N.J.

In 1690 March was captain of a company of volunteers which participated in the unsuccessful expedition against Quebec under Sir William Phips*. He completed construction of Fort William Henry at Pemaquid from 1692 to 1693 and was "commander of their Maties Fort" until 1695. In November 1694 March was instrumental in the capture of Bomoseen, the Norridgewock chief, when the latter came to Pemaquid for a parley. He was again in the service of the bay colony in 1697. Fearing a formidable French invasion by both land and sea, Lieutenant-Governor Stoughton attempted "to put the whole province into a posture of defence." March, now a major, was sent with about 500 soldiers to prevent any descent of the enemy along the eastern frontiers of Maine. On 9 September 1697 he encountered and successfully repulsed a war party of 200 Indians and "several French" on the banks of the Damariscotta

River. This, coupled with the failure of the French expedition under the Marquis de Nesmond to invade New England by sea, temporarily brought peace to the frontiers.

Major March, moving his family and possessions with him, became in 1702 "commander and Truckmaster at the Fort at Casco Bay" (Fort Loyal, Falmouth, now Portland, Me.) on "the utmost Frontier." He was wounded and lost most of his property when, a year later, the fort came under severe attack by Abenakis led by ALEXANDRE LENEUF de Beaubassin. For his "brave defence" March was promoted lieutenant-colonel. He commanded the fort at Casco Bay until 1707.

Massachusetts' Governor Joseph Dudley appointed Colonel March to lead the proposed expedition against Port-Royal (Annapolis Royal, N.S.) in 1707, describing him as "a very good officer, & so well esteemed that I hope to impress no man into the service." In many respects it proved an unfortunate choice. A mutinous spirit among subordinate officers, raw troops, and March's indecisiveness in command doomed the expedition to failure. Colonels Francis Wainwright and Winthrop HILTON were given command of two regiments of militia. The force of over 1,100 troops cast anchor in Port-Royal basin on 26 May 1707 (6 June, N.S.). The Port-Royal forces under the command of Daniel d'AUGER de Subercase were meagre—about 200 men, strengthened somewhat by a small detachment of about 60 men who had arrived shortly before under the command of Louis Denys* de La Ronde and AMIOT de Vincelotte. A few days after the fighting began, BERNARD-ANSELME D'ABBADIE de Saint-Castin arrived with Abenaki recruits. The French and Indian forces put up a spirited defence. Finally, after many councils, the New England troops re-embarked on 5 June with "little ... done in annoying the enemy." March retired to Casco where he was virtually relieved of his command by three commissioners sent by Governor Dudley. On the second attempt to take Port-Royal in August, March's health and spirits gave way and he turned his command over to Colonel Wainwright. The French forces, again led by Subercase and Saint-Castin, were well prepared this time and resisted the English threat. Subsequently a court martial was ordered, but so many officers were guilty of infractions that it never convened. To counter the charges of cowardice levelled against March by his irate and disappointed contemporaries, the judgement of Penhallow (1726) should suffice: March "was a Man of good Courage ... But the Business that he undertook, was too weighty for his Shoulders to bear."

His death was reported in the *Boston News-*

Letter: "New York, July 28th Last week dyed Col. John March of Newbury at Woodbridge in New Jersey."

JOHN DAVID KRUGLER

AN, Col., C^{11D}, 6. *The acts and resolves, public and private, of the province of the Massachusetts bay* (21v., Boston, 1869–1922), VII, 377, 404–9, 571, 601; VIII, 668–96, 715–18, 722–51. *Boston News-Letter*, no.433, 4 Aug. 1712. Charlevoix, *History* (Shea), V, 194–96, 200. *Coll. de manuscrits relatif à la N.-F.*, II, 464–70, 477–81. Dièreville, *Relation of voyage to Port Royal* (Webster), 209–15, 318–20. *Documentary hist. of Maine*, IV, 24–25, 150, 187–88, 243; IX, 164–65, 167, 183–84; XXIII, 9. *Extracts from John Marshall's diary, January, 1689–December, 1711*, ed. S. L. Green (Cambridge, 1900), 19, 23. Mass. Hist. Soc. *Coll.*, 3d ser., V, 189–96; 5th ser., VI, 127–29; 6th ser., III, 374, 388–92. Mather, *Magnalia Christi Americana*, II, 611, 619, 628, 632, 637–38. New Hampshire provincial papers, *Documents and records relating to the province of New Hampshire* (40v. in progress, 1867–   ), II, 247–50, 269, 492, 506–7. *Penhallow's Indian wars* (Wheelock), 6, 9, 41–43. PRO, *CSP, Col., 1693–96, 1696–97, 1702, 1702–3, 1706–8*. *1690, Sir William Phips devant Québec* (Myrand), 229. *Vital records of Newbury Massachusetts to the end of the year 1849* (2v., Salem, 1911), I, 306; II, 315.

S. L. Bailey, *Historical sketches of Andover ... Massachusetts* (Boston, 1880), 58–59, 180, 183–84. J. J. Currier, *"Ould Newbury": historical and biographical sketches* (Boston, 1896), 64, 69, 157–59, 175–76, 180, 184–86. S. A. Drake, *The border wars of New England, commonly called King William's and Queen Anne's wars* (New York, 1897), 72, 85, 129–30, 159–60, 227–28. Hutchinson, *Hist. of Mass.-bay* (Mayo), II, 78, 123–27. Everett Kimball, *The public life of Joseph Dudley: a study of the colonial policy of the Stuarts in New England, 1660–1715* (New York, 1911), 121–23. Murdoch, *History of Nova-Scotia*, I. Daniel Neal, *The history of New-England, ... to the year 1700 ...* (2v., London, 1720), II, 555–56. Rameau de Saint-Père, *Une colonie féodale*, I, 330–34, 339–40. Essex Institute, Salem, Mass., *Hist. Coll.*, XXXV (1899), 136; LVIII (1922), 80–81, 85–86.

MAREST, JOSEPH-JACQUES, Jesuit missionary, brother of PIERRE-GABRIEL; b. in France, diocese of Chartres, 19 March 1653; d. in Montreal, October 1725.

Joseph-Jacques Marest entered the Jesuit noviciate 25 Sept. 1671, and taught at Vannes, La Flèche and the Collège Louis Le Grand in Paris. He came to Canada about 1686 and spent the next two years at Sillery learning Indian languages. In 1688 he was sent to Michilimackinac, and the following year was a member of Nicolas PERROT's mission to the Sioux country. On 8 May 1689, Perrot took formal possession, for France, of the vast upper Mississippi region. On the

document recording this significant event the first signature is that of Joseph-Jacques Marest, "Missionary among the Nadouesioux [Sioux]."

Michilimackinac, where Joseph Marest was to earn repute as cleric-diplomat, played a threefold role—Jesuit mission, garrison post, and rendezvous for fur-traders. The Ottawas, over whom Marest became superior, occupied their own village in the area, as did the Hurons, under the care of Father Étienne de CARHEIL. The military commandant of the post between 1694 and 1697 was Antoine LAUMET, *dit* de Lamothe Cadillac. His "brandy diplomacy" brought him into sharp verbal conflict with Marest.

Cadillac favoured Detroit rather than Michilimackinac as a focal point for the lucrative fur trade, and with the support of the minister of Marine, Jérôme Phélypeaux, Comte de Pontchartrain, he was able to set up a post there in 1700. Transfer of the Michilimackinac Indians to Detroit was included in Cadillac's plan which Father Marest was at first willing to support, "with the feeble aid of my prayers." A change of attitude on Marest's part resulted in a vendetta, marked by rivalry and intrigue, until Cadillac was appointed governor of Louisiana in 1710.

When Marest received instruction from his superior to go to Detroit in 1703 he asked his Indians for their "precise and decided" answer about removal. They wanted three days to consider, and much to his surprise announced they would never go—rather, they would die at Michilimackinac. Encouraged by these "strong reasons" Marest visited Quebec where he was to make a staunch ally of the new governor, Philippe de RIGAUD de Vaudreuil.

By the following year (1704), however, the wheel of fortune had turned in favour of Cadillac. The Hurons and many of the Ottawas had gone to Detroit. Although Father de Carheil abandoned his mission in the straits of Mackinac in 1706 Marest remained, as active in intrigue as in priestly duty. He continued to keep the governor abreast of affairs through emissaries including the chiefs KOUTAOILIBOE and MISCOUAKY and the Montreal merchant M. Boudor.

By 1719 Joseph-Jacques Marest, aged 66, was growing infirm, and a missionary was sent to assist him. A year or more later (1721) his name appeared in the work of the eminent Jesuit historian, Pierre-François-Xavier de Charlevoix*, to whom Marest spoke of the Sioux and their country.

Marest was favoured to pass the biblical allotment of threescore and ten, for he died at the age of 72 in Montreal, October 1725.

MAUD M. HUTCHESON

Marest

Charlevoix, *History* (Shea), III, 35; V, 180. *JR* (Thwaites), LXVI; LXXI, 156, 228. *Michigan Pioneer Coll.*, XXXIII. *NYCD* (O'Callaghan and Fernow), IX, 418. Wis. State Hist. Soc. *Coll.*, XVI. Rochemonteix, *Les Jésuites et la N.-F. au XVIIᵉ siècle*, III, 480.

MAREST, PIERRE-GABRIEL (Maret, Marais), Jesuit, missionary; b. 14 Oct. 1662; d. at Kaskaskia, Illinois, in 1714.

Marest became a Jesuit novice in Paris, October 1681, and spent the next six years as an instructor at Vannes. After several years of additional study in Bourges and Paris he was sent to Canada in 1694. At this time an expedition under the command of PIERRE LE MOYNE d'Iberville was outfitting to try to wrest Hudson Bay from English control. Marest was assigned to the post of chaplain; "contrary to my inclinations" wrote the young priest, who was eager to serve among the savages.

On 10 August the expedition set sail from Quebec in two frigates, the *Poli* and the *Salamandre*. Keenly alert to the new experience, Marest kept a running account of the voyage. About the end of the month they reached the strait leading into Hudson Bay; by 24 September they entered the Nelson (Bourbon) River. Also emptying into the bay at this point was the Hayes (Sainte-Thérèse) River on which the English had built York Fort. The *Poli* was berthed on the Nelson and the *Salamandre* under Iberville's command on the Hayes, "whither I followed," wrote Marest; the vessel was "near being lost" before it was finally anchored. Iberville urged Marest, who was running a fever, to go ashore, but the conscientious priest was unwilling to leave the ship as long as it was in danger.

While preparations advanced for the siege, Marest took his share in duties far from ministerial, helping to build cabins and unload the ships. On 13 October when the French were ready to bombard the fort, they summoned the English to surrender. The following morning, led by Thomas Walsh, his lieutenant Philip Parsons, and Henry KELSEY, the besieged brought their "conditions," drawn up in Latin by the minister, Thomas Anderson. Gabriel Marest interpreted the terms of this capitulation for his French compatriots who took formal possession of the fort and re-named it Fort Bourbon. Marest said mass "and we chanted the Te Deum" and "wondered at the marvelous ordering of divine Providence."

Marest continued his ministrations to those under his care through the dreary months of an arctic winter. Scurvy broke out among the crew and Marest was himself afflicted. So far, oppor-

tunities for learning the language of the savages had been few and interrupted. He had been supplied by "Monsieur de la Motte" (Nicolas, son of Pierre Aigron*, *dit* Lamothe?) with a good many words, and "an Englishman [probably Henry Kelsey] who knows the language very well has given me many more." Marest carefully made a dictionary of all these words, "according to our alphabet" and translated the sign of the cross, the Pater, the Ave, the Credo and the ten commandments.

In the summer of 1695, Iberville returned to France with his English prisoners. Marest chose to remain behind to serve the 80 men left in garrison and when, in September 1696, the Hudson's Bay Company's ships retook the fort, he was sent to England to spend some months in prison.

Marest returned to Canada (probably early in 1697) to find that his life's ambition was to be realized. In 1698 he was assigned to the Illinois country, to the mission of the Immaculate Conception, founded by Father Jacques GRAVIER, which served a confederacy of tribes including the Kaskaskias, Cahokias, Peorias, Tamaroas, and Michigameas.

From the beginning Marest displayed "the finest talent in the world for these missions," and learned the language of the local tribes in a few months. His colleague, Father Julien Bineteau, who thought that Father Marest could endure "an incredible amount of fatigue," felt that he was "somewhat too zealous"; he lived only on a little boiled corn mixed with beans and made a beverage of watermelon. The duties of a typical day included mass before sunrise, teaching the catechism to the children, visiting the sick, saying public prayers, and individual counselling. With a pen that had lost none of its descriptive power he reported on life and conditions in this distant colony. Although many were embracing "our holy religion" his heart was troubled by lack of response from the young men. The women and girls, however, were disposed to receive baptism and the children "give us great hopes for the future."

In the autumn of 1700 the Kaskaskias decided to move south to be closer to the French for protection. Marest and Gravier accompanied them. After four days' travel they halted at the mouth of the Des Pères River, almost opposite the Cahokia or Tamaroa mission, served by the priests of the Séminaire des Missions Étrangères. The spot proved somewhat close for amicable relations, for the Jesuits considered that the Seminarians had encroached upon their field of labour. The matter of jurisdiction over the Illinois missions was referred to Versailles, and when an ecclesiastical commission decided that the Cahokia mission belonged to the Séminaire des Missions Étrangères the Kaskaskias once more continued the trek. The village which they finally established in the spring of 1703 was to earn renown as Kaskaskia.

The new community had to face many problems—among them drink and its attendant vices. Marest was obliged to seek help from Jean-Baptiste Le Moyne* de Bienville, governor of Louisiana, because Canadian traders were openly debauching the Illinois women. In response to this request, a sergeant and 12 men arrived, one being the diarist André Pénigaut.

Relations with the Peorias had been strained for some time following the death of Father Jacques Gravier in 1708 and the Peoria mission had been closed. Hearing that the tribe was repentant, Marest and his confrères, Jean MERMET and Jean-Marie de VILLES, decided it was time to put the mission again "on its old footing"; this was to be discussed during a visit to the superior at Michilimackinac, Father JOSEPH MAREST.

Gabriel Marest set out for Michilimackinac on Friday of Easter week, 1711, accompanied by several Indians who cared for him with kindness on the journey. He spent a fortnight in the village of the Peorias, then continued by the St Joseph River to the mission of the Potawatomis which was under Father Jean Chardon. There he found his brother Joseph who had come part way to meet him. They had not seen each other for 15 years. Father Chardon shared their joy and kept them with him a week before they embarked by canoe for Michilimackinac, where it took about two months to finish their "business," on which Father Gabriel Marest has left no comment.

On his return journey Marest spent a fortnight with Father Chardon, and stopped again at the village of the Peorias where he received a tumultuous welcome. He arrived at Kaskaskia on 10 September. Marest then wrote a lengthy account of his travels to Father Barthélemi Germon, a brother Jesuit. He dwelt on the isolation of the new world, where "our life is passed in threading dense forests, in climbing mountains, in crossing lakes and rivers in canoes. . . ."

Conversion of the savages was very difficult, wrote Marest; he found them indolent, treacherous, inconstant, thievish. Yet in his opinion they did not lack intelligence. He thought them "naturally inquisitive" and able to "turn a joke in a fairly ingenious manner." Nearly all the inhabitants of Kaskaskia village were Christians, he reported. The settlement had grown; many Frenchmen had been attracted there and some had married Illinois women.

On 15 Sept. 1714 Marest died during an epidemic, after an illness of only eight days. He was deeply mourned, the French singing his requiem while the Indians expressed their sorrow through symbolic gifts of fur. The following year a circular announcing his death was issued by Father Jean Mermet. In 1727 his remains were reinterred in the new Kaskaskia church by Father Jean-Antoine Le Boullenger.

His many writings are his monument. His scholarship earned praise from his fellow workers who also attested to his unselfish devotion.

MAUD M. HUTCHESON

Documents relating to Hudson Bay (Tyrrell). *Early voyages up and down the Mississippi, by Cavelier, St. Cosme, Le Sueur, Gravier, and Guignas,* ed. with intro. and notes by J. G. Shea (Albany, 1861). [André Pénigaut], *Fleur de Lys and calumet: being the Pénicaut narrative of French adventure in Louisiana,* ed. and tr. R. G. McWilliams (Baton Rouge, La., 1953). HBRS, XXI (Rich). [Jérémie], *Twenty years at York Factory* (Douglas and Wallace). *JR* (Thwaites), LXV, LXVI. *Lettres édifiantes et curieuses, escrites des missions étrangeres par quelques missionaires de la Compagnie de Jésus* (30v., Paris, 1707–73; nouv. éd., 26v., Paris, 1780–83), VI.

Chapters in frontier history; research studies in the making of the west (Milwaukee, [1934]). Delanglez, *French Jesuits in Louisiana.* Sister Mary Borgias Palm, *The Jesuit Missions of the Illinois Country, 1673–1763* (n.p., 1933). Rochemonteix, *Les Jésuites et la N.-F. au XVIIIᵉ siècle.* Marc de Villiers Du Terrage, *La découverte du Missouri et l'histoire du fort d'Orléans (1673–1728)* (Paris, 1925). Joseph Wallace, *The history of Illinois and Louisiana under the French rule* (Cincinnati, 1893). G. J. Garraghan, "New light on old Cahokia," *Ill. Catholic Hist. Review* [*Mid-America*], XI (1928–29), 99–146. J. J. Thompson, "Illinois, the cradle of christianity and civilization in Mid-America," *Ill. Catholic Hist. Review,* XI (1928–29), 65–85, 215–38, 329–48.

MARGANE DE BATILLY, FRANÇOIS-MARIE, ensign; b. 13 Nov. 1672 at Montreal, son of Séraphin Margane de Lavaltrie and Louise Bissot; killed in the raid of 28 Feb. 1704 at Deerfield, Mass. On the paternal side he was the grandson of a lawyer in the *parlement* of Paris who came from an old family of Vendôme; on his mother's side he was connected with the first families in New France, such as the Bissot de Vinsenne and the Couillard-Després.

His father Séraphin Margane came to New France in 1665 with the Carignan-Salières regiment. In 1672, in recognition of his services, he obtained the Lavaltrie seigneury. But his activity did not cease with this award, since in 1684 he was in command at the Michilimackinac post.

Marguerite

Séraphin Margane died in 1699 at Montreal, leaving a complicated estate which his widow refused, and which was still not finally settled in 1735.

François-Marie Margane de Batilly—not to be confused with his younger brother François Margane de Lavaltrie, the widower of Angélique Guyon, who took holy orders—obtained a commission as ensign in the colonial regular troops maintained by the French king in Canada. Following savage attacks made by the English colonies in the autumn of 1703, RIGAUD de Vaudreuil sent 250 men against New England under the command of JEAN-BAPTISTE HERTEL de Rouville, to whom the Sieur de Batilly was responsible. The force left Montreal, proceeded to Lake Champlain, then crossed the Allegheny mountains, and in the night of 28 Feb. 1704 (10 March, N.S.) fell upon Deerfield, on the Massachusetts border. All the inhabitants were taken prisoner or killed, and their houses set ablaze. M. de Rouville had lost only three Canadians, one being the ensign Margane de Batilly, and a few Indians. In the official correspondence we read that François-Marie Margane de Batilly was "a very brave man and the second of his family to give his life for his country."

Many prisoners from Deerfield became true Canadians and did not want to return to their native village. The king of France conferred letters of naturalization on them, they took on French ways, and married Canadian women. Several French-Canadian families of the present day are directly descended from these English pioneers and do not even suspect their origin. We might mention especially the Phaneuf (Fansworth), the Stébenne (Stebbin) and the French families.

The ensign Margane de Batilly's heroic death was thus to bring a real harvest of life to Canada, his fatherland.

ROLAND-J. AUGER

AJM, Greffe d'Antoine Adhémar, 7, 8, 11 août 1699; Greffe de C.-R. Gaudron de Chevremont, 10 juin 1735. AJQ, Greffe de Romain Becquet, 11 août 1668, 3 oct. 1677. AN, Col., C¹¹ᴬ, 22, f.4. C. A. Baker, *True stories of New England captives carried to Canada during the old French and Indian wars* (Cambridge, Mass., 1897). Coleman, *New England captives*, II, 33–131. Garneau, *Histoire du Canada*, I. J. G. Palfrey, *History of New England* (4v., Boston, 1858–75), IV, 261–64. Francis Parkman, *A half-century of conflict*; *Rivals for America* (Boston, 1915), 41, 49. G. A. Sheldon, *History of Deerfield, Massachusetts* . . . (2v., Deerfield, 1895–96). Sylvester, *Indian wars*, III. "An Account of Ye Destruction at Derefeld," *Mass. Hist. Soc. Proc.*, 1st ser., IX (1867), 478. P.-G. Roy, "La famille Margane de Lavaltrie," *BRH*, XXIII (1917), 33–53, 65–80.

MARGUERITE DE SAINT-JEAN-BAPTISTE. *See* BOURDON

MARIAUCHAU D'ESGLY (d'Esglis), FRANÇOIS, garrison adjutant, commandant of Fort Chambly, king's lieutenant at Trois-Rivières, knight of the order of Saint-Louis; b. *c.* 1670 in the parish of Saint-Benoît in Paris, son of Pierre Mariauchau d'Esgly, a lawyer in the *parlement*, and of Élisabeth Groën; buried 10 Jan. 1730 in the cemetery of the Hôtel-Dieu of Quebec.

He served first in the Régiment du Dauphiné as ensign in the colonel's company, and came to New France in 1689. Buade* de Frontenac immediately appointed him first corporal of his guards, and two years later granted him a commission as half-pay lieutenant, which was confirmed by the king on 1 March 1693. On 1 May 1696 he became lieutenant of one of the companies of colonial regular troops in New France.

On 20 Oct. 1699 Governor CALLIÈRE and Intendant BOCHART de Champigny wrote to the minister, Pontchartrain: "The Sieur d'Esgly, also a lieutenant, to whom in the past some attachment for a woman of this town was imputed, does not now give cause for such suspicions; he is applying himself to his service in Montreal, where he is almost all the time, and is discharging with diligence his duty and the functions of adjutant which he exercises; this testimony we are obliged to offer to His Majesty."

In 1703 RIGAUD de Vaudreuil instructed him to go to inform the king of Governor Callière's death. During his stay in the mother country d'Esgly managed to secure for himself a company in the colonial regular troops. The flute called the *Seine*, on which he was returning at the end of June, was surrounded by English units and captured. The officer was taken prisoner with the whole crew and the other passengers, including Bishop Saint-Vallier [LA CROIX]. After being held captive in England for more than a year, he got back to France, where he stayed for some months before returning to Canada in 1705, holding the rank of captain in Vaudreuil's guards.

In 1713 he is said to have been commandant of Fort Chambly, which had recently been rebuilt in stone. On 3 July of that year Pontchartrain informed Mariauchau d'Esgly that he was recommending him for the cross of Saint-Louis, but on the 17 May following he admitted to him that the king was not granting any crosses that year. At that time the minister also urged him to put a stop to illegal trading with the English at Chambly.

On 2 Jan. 1716 d'Esgly succeeded LA CORNE de Chaptes in the post of town major of Trois-Rivières. On 7 May 1720 he was promoted garrison adjutant at Quebec. He was decorated with the cross of Saint-Louis on 23 Dec. 1721, a decoration for which the governor had been recommending him since 1712. In 1717 Vaudreuil had insisted further with the reminder that "the Sieur d'Esgly, town major at Trois-Rivières, is the only officer at headquarters who does not have a cross of Saint-Louis. It appears necessary to him in the post that he occupies because it commands more respect and submission on the part of the settlers and Indians. He was moreover on the list of those whom M. de Pontchartrain was to propose to the king at the time of His Majesty's death."

The last position which he held was that of king's lieutenant at Trois-Rivières, an appointment he obtained on 23 April 1726. He was admitted as a patient to the Hôtel-Dieu of Quebec on 6 Jan. 1730, died there on 8 January, and on 10 January was buried in the paupers' cemetery of the institution.

On 7 Jan. 1708, at Quebec, he had married Louise-Philippe Chartier de Lotbinière, daughter of René-Louis CHARTIER de Lotbinière, first councillor in the Conseil Souverain, and of Marie-Madeleine Lambert. His wife died young, and as the officer seemed to have little concern for the upkeep of his five children, his brother-in-law, Louis-Eustache Chartier* de Lotbinière, archdeacon, vicar general, and member of the Conseil Souverain, successfully demanded that 600 *livres* be withheld from his annual salary of 1,800 *livres* in order to provide for their needs.

HERVÉ BIRON

AHDQ, Registre mortuaire. "Correspondance de Vaudreuil," APQ *Rapport, 1938–39*, 99f., 122. Tanguay, *Dictionnaire*. Fauteux, *Les chevaliers de Saint-Louis*. P.-G. Roy, *La famille Mariauchau d'Esgly* (Lévis, 1908), 3–8.

MARIAUCHAU D'ESGLY (d'Esglis), FRANÇOIS-LOUIS, baptized 17 Dec. 1708 at Quebec, son of FRANÇOIS MARIAUCHAU d'Esgly and Louise-Philippe Chartier de Lotbinière; d. a bachelor 25 March 1736 in the Chickasaw country.

On 29 March 1725 Mariauchau d'Esgly was given an expectancy of a second ensign's commission; this rank was granted officially on 23 April 1726. On 10 Nov. 1731 Charles de Beauharnois* de La Boische recommended him to the minister, Maurepas, for service in Louisiana as a lieutenant. This rank was conferred on him on 17 Aug. 1732, and in the autumn of the same year Mariauchau went to the French colony in the south.

In 1736 the governor of Louisiana, Jean-Baptiste Le Moyne* de Bienville, organized a punitive expedition against the Chickasaws who had given refuge to the Natchez chiefs responsible for the slaughter that had taken place at Fort Rosalie at the end of 1729. His plan was to set out from Mobile and go up the Tombigbee River, coming on the Chickasaw villages from the south, while the adjutant, Pierre d'Artaguiette, advancing from the Illinois country with a party made up of 140 Frenchmen, including Mariauchau d'Esgly, and 266 Indians would approach from the northwest [*see* FRANÇOIS-MARIE BISSOT de Vinsenne]. Bienville was slow in appearing, and on 25 March d'Artaguiette, having been in enemy territory for three weeks and seeing his food running low, decided to attack three Chickasaw villages. After having taken two of these villages the party was surrounded; Artaguiette and his officers, among whom was Mariauchau, were seized by the Chickasaws, tortured, and burned.

HERVÉ BIRON

AN, Col., C¹¹ᴬ, 54, f.416. Charlevoix, *Histoire* (1744), II, 501f. Le Jeune, *Dictionnaire*, I, 600f. Antoine Bernard, *Histoire de la Louisiane* (Québec, 1953), 125f. Guy Frégault, *Le grand marquis, Pierre de Rigaud de Vaudreuil et la Louisiane* (Montréal, 1952), 144–48. Charles Gayarré, *Histoire de la Louisiane* (2v., New Orleans, 1846–47), I, 314. P.-G. Roy, *Fils de Québec*, I, 174–76.

MARICOURT, PAUL LE MOYNE DE. *See* LE MOYNE

MARIE DE L'ASSOMPTION. *See* BARBIER

MARIE DES ANGES. *See* SAYWARD

MARIE-CATHERINE DU SAINT-SACREMENT. *See* CHARLY

MARIE-JEANNE-MADELEINE DE SAINTE-AGATHE. *See* LEGARDEUR

MARIE-JOSEPH-ANGÉLIQUE, negro slave; b. *c.* 1710; hanged 21 June 1734 in Montreal.

This slave, the property of FRANÇOIS POULIN de Francheville, was baptized 28 June 1730 at Montreal. At that time she was the mistress of César, Ignace GAMELIN's negro, by whom she had a son in January 1731 and twin boys in May 1732. Then she fell in love with a white man, Claude Thibault, and decided to flee with him to New England, since she had reason to believe that Francheville's widow was thinking of selling her. In the night of 10–11 April 1734, perhaps to cover her flight, she set fire to the Francheville house on

Marie-Madeleine

Rue Saint-Paul. The fire spread and turned into a conflagration: 46 houses and the Hôtel-Dieu were destroyed. The slave was caught by the constabulary (Thibault was never found), thrown into prison, and on 4 June was sentenced to make honourable amends, to have her hand cut off, and to be burnt alive. When the case was appealed, the Conseil Supérieur on 12 June mitigated somewhat the horror of the punishment: she was to be taken in a rubbish cart to the church door, where she was to make a formal confession of guilt; then she was to be hanged, before her body was burned. This sentence was carried out in Montreal on 21 June, after the slave had first been tortured. Her ashes were cast to the winds.

ANDRÉ VACHON

AQ, NF, Dossier du Cons. sup., Mat. crim., IV, 237; NF, Registre criminel, IV, 24–26. P.-G. Roy, *Inv. jug. et délib., 1717–1760*, II, 147f. Marcel Trudel, *L'esclavage au Canada français; histoire et conditions de l'esclavage* (Québec, 1960), 226–29.

MARIE-MADELEINE DE SAINT-LOUIS. *See* MAUFILS

MARIGNY. *See* PHILIPPE(S)

MARIN DE LA MALGUE (La Margue, La Marque, La Marche), CHARLES-PAUL DE, b. 1633 in the parish of Notre-Dame de Saint-Sulpice, diocese of Toulon, son of Jacques de Marin and Hélène Gorel; buried 14 April 1713 at Montreal.

Marin de La Malgue set out from Fort Frontenac in 1682 to go among the Iroquois, in order to make inquiries "about the death of one of the important members of the Seneca tribe, murdered among the Kiskakons at Michilimackinac by an Illinois." In 1688 he obtained permission to go to France.

Having returned to Canada, he married Catherine Niquet on 5 July 1691, at Saint-François-du-Lac. They had six children, four of whom reached adult age. His first wife was buried on 15 March 1703, and on 6 July 1703, at Sorel, he remarried, his second wife being Louise Lamy, daughter of Joseph Lamy and Marie Decheuraineville, who bore him three sons and three daughters.

In a letter of 7 Aug. 1693, Governor Louis de Buade* de Frontenac and Intendant BOCHART de Champigny alluded to Marin as "commander of the *Indiscret*," who with PIERRE LE MOYNE d'Iberville was to attack Fort Nelson on behalf of the Compagnie du Nord. According to the signatories, the expedition was countermanded because of the inadequate tonnage and poor condition of the ships.

Marin is normally referred to as a knight of the order of Saint-Louis, but Aegidius Fauteux exposes this error and mentions among the members of the order only his son, Paul*, and his grandson. He adds that Marin had not risen above the rank of ensign by the time of his death. The historian also notes, with some likelihood of being correct, that the biography of this personage was altered by his immediate heirs.

In his second marriage contract, drawn up by the notary ADHÉMAR, Marin is called esquire and officer in the colonial regular troops.

HERVÉ BIRON

AJM, Greffe d'Antoine Adhémar, 6 juillet 1703. AN, Col., C^{11A}, 6, f.24. "Correspondance de Frontenac (1689–1699)," APQ *Rapport*, *1927–28*, 147ff. *Royal Fort Frontenac* (Preston and Lamontagne), 43, 141, 145, 337, 342. Fauteux, *Les chevaliers de Saint-Louis*, 56–67. Régis Roy, "Les capitaines de Marin, sieurs de la Malgue," *RSCT*, 2d ser., X (1904), sect.i, 25–34.

MARK (Marsh). *See* MARCH

MARSON, LOUISE-ÉLISABETH DE JOYBERT DE SOULANGES ET DE. *See* JOYBERT

MARTCH. *See* MARCH

MARTEL, RAYMOND, merchant of Quebec, partner of AUGUSTIN LE GARDEUR de Courtemanche in the development of Labrador; b. 1663, son of Pierre Martel de Berhouague and Jeanne de Hargon of Bastide-Clérance in Navarre (diocese of Bayonne); d. 1 Nov. 1708 at Saint-François, Île-Jésus.

There is no record of when Martel came to New France. He first appears in July 1697 as a witness to the marriage contract between Courtemanche and Marie-Charlotte Charest, widow of his elder brother, Pierre-Gratien Martel de Brouague. This document marks the beginning of an association which, although it resulted in complicated legal and financial difficulties, ultimately was concluded to the satisfaction of both men.

It appears that before her second marriage, Marie Charet possessed considerable financial assets, probably inherited from her first husband. On 14 Aug. 1697 she signed an agreement with Courtemanche whereby he and Raymond Martel were authorized to use her money for business purposes. On 23 October the two men entered into a commercial partnership with François PROVOST for the export of furs to France. By 1700, after a large outlay of capital, the enterprise had failed.

In 1702 the creditors of Martel and Courtemanche descended upon them in full force. Martel, who apparently had handled most of the business arrangements, was ordered by the Conseil Souverain to produce letters of exchange and notes for money owed to various merchants of La Rochelle. This he was unable to do, so both debtors and creditors sought arbitration before the Conseil Souverain.

The legal proceedings dragged on intermittently for nearly three years. In the meantime the two men were not inactive. In 1701 they had jointly purchased the Lachenaie seigneury from CHARLES AUBERT de La Chesnaye and, that same year, resolved to establish a fishing and trading post on the Labrador coast. There is no way of knowing whose idea the latter project was but, as before, it was Martel who worked out the practical details. On 31 Oct. 1701 he asked CALLIÈRE for permission to send ships and canoes to Labrador "to win over the Eskimos who are very unapproachable . . . and to see whether one could not establish trade with them." The following year he borrowed 12,178 *livres*, asked the minister of Marine for a ship to be put at his disposal, and obtained from the king cannon, powder, and balls for the Labrador fort.

As fast as Courtemanche, and particularly Martel, spent money, claims were filed against them. In 1703 both their wives, probably at their instigation, sued to the Conseil Souverain for the division of their husbands' estates, claiming that neither had had the right to risk the wife's portion if it jeopardized the livelihood of their families. The two women won their point, and Madame Courtemanche was able to get her agreement with her husband declared null and void on the grounds that when she signed it she was still a minor.

On 3 Dec. 1702 Martel ceded to Courtemanche his share in the Labrador post and all claims to the fishing and trading concession. Although for some time afterwards he continued to act as Courtemanche's agent in Quebec, this effectively ended his active participation in the development of Labrador. In return, it seems that Courtemanche surrendered his share of the Lachenaie seigneury, for Martel was in sole possession of it by 1707.

As a seigneur Martel again demonstrated his business acumen. On 17 Jan. 1708 he requested that the lieutenant-general of Montreal force his tenants to limit themselves to the land allotted to them. From that time until his death he systematically reviewed their contracts, drawing up new ones whenever he deemed it necessary.

On 1 Nov. 1708 Martel died, leaving his wife, Marie-Anne Trottier, whom he had married in 1697, and three children, Nicolas, Louise-Catherine, and Pierre. He left his family deeply in debt, for seven years after his death the Lachenaie property was seized and awarded to PIERRE LEGARDEUR de Repentigny.

Martel's place in the history of New France is small but significant. His brief career illustrates the resourceful, and sometimes unscrupulous, business dealing that frequently took place behind the scenes in the exploration and development of French North America. The achievements of men like Courtemanche owed much to the daring and enterprise of merchants like Martel.

JOHN BRYDEN

AJQ, Greffe de François Genaple, 14 août 1697. AN, Col., B, 23, ff.50–52; C11A, 19, ff.23–25; 20, f.63v. *Documents relating to Canadian currency during the French period* (Shortt), I, 117–21. G.B., Privy Council, Judicial Committee, *In the matter of the boundary between the Dominion of Canada and the colony of Newfoundland in the Labrador peninsula . . .* (12v., London, 1926–27), VII, 3680–82. *Jug. et délib.*, IV, 913–14, 922, 925, 951, 966, 990–93, 998, 1020; V, 5, 7, 10–21, 53, 90–93, 116, 145, 274–76, 283–84. A. Roy, *Inv. greffes not.*, XVII, 23, 25, 26; XVIII, 348, 350; XIX, 25, 66, 178. P.-G. Roy, *Inv. concessions*, I, 264–65, 268; V, 173. Tanguay, *Dictionnaire*, I, 414; V, 528–29.

MARTEL DE MAGOS (Magesse), JEAN, soldier, merchant, trader, seigneur, clerk in the king's stores, b. *c.* 1650 in France, d. 7 Nov. 1729 at Quebec.

Martel came to Canada in 1672 as a soldier in the personal guard of Governor Frontenac [Buade*]. After his discharge he settled in Acadia, and in 1683 was granted the seigneury of Magos (Magesse; Machias, Me.), half of which he ceded on 8 May 1683 to Pierre Chenet Dubreuil. He married Marie-Anne Robinau, believed to be the illegitimate daughter of Joseph Robinau* de Villebon, commandant of Acadia. Martel engaged in trade and, frequently, in transport on behalf of the crown, in partnership with Pierre MAISONNAT, *dit* Baptiste, who had acquired Dubreuil's half of the Magos seigneury. As was usual in Acadia, Martel engaged in illicit trade with New England, and in 1692 Villebon had him arrested and seized a cargo of merchandise he was carrying in a small vessel belonging to the Boston merchant, John NELSON, who since 1674 had represented in Acadia the interests of his uncle, Sir Thomas Temple*.

In the spring of 1694 Martel began, with Baptiste, to clear a homestead on the Saint John River, opposite Fort Nashwaak (Naxouat). Though in 1695 he reportedly undertook improvements "with great care," it would appear that both he and Baptiste continued to devote the better part of their energies to other enterprises. In 1696 he had harvested "but a small quantity of wheat," and the following year he still raised no livestock. When the Martel-Baptiste partnership was dissolved in 1701, Martel moved to Quebec.

If P.-G. Roy's information is accurate, Martel became a clerk in the king's stores in Quebec. He resided in 1716 in the Faubourg Saint-Nicolas or Du Palais. He must have enjoyed some measure of standing, for in 1717 he and his wife were godparents for Jeanne-Élisabeth Bégon, the infant daughter of the intendant, Michel Bégon*. Two years later, the same Mademoiselle Bégon was a godparent, along with the governor's son, François de Rigaud* de Vaudreuil, for Martel's own son, Pierre-Michel*.

Jean Martel died in Quebec on 7 Nov. 1729, and was buried the following day. His wife continued to reside in Quebec, where she is mentioned in 1745, and appears to have died by 1747. Several of Martel's eight sons became prominent, notably François (b. 1703), parish priest of Saint-Laurent, Île d'Orléans; Jean-Urbain (b. 1708), a director of the Saint-Maurice ironworks; Jean-Baptiste-Grégoire* (1710–67), keeper of the king's stores in Montreal; Pierre-Michel (1719–89), financial commissary in Montreal; and Joseph-Nicolas (b. 1721), first a Jesuit in France, later parish priest at Saint-Laurent and at Contrecoeur. Both Jean-Baptiste-Grégoire and Pierre-Michel were implicated in the notorious "Affaire du Canada," and served brief sentences in the Bastille in the early 1760s.

BERNARD POTHIER

AN, Col., B, 23, ff.50–52; C¹¹ᴬ, 19, f.25; C¹¹ᴰ, 3, ff.116–16v, 157; Section Outre-Mer, G³, 2040. P.-G. Roy, *Inv. concessions*, III, 241–42. Webster, *Acadia*, 34–35, 144, 148. La Morandière, *Hist. de la pêche française de la morue*, II, 706. P.-G. Roy, *La famille Martel de Brouage* (Lévis, 1934), 5–6. *BRH*, VI (1900), 21–24.

MARTIGNY ET DE LA TRINITÉ, JEAN-BAPTISTE LE MOYNE DE. *See* LE MOYNE

MARTIN, CHARLES-AMADOR, musician, the second native Canadian to be ordained a priest; b. in Quebec, 7 March 1648, son of Abraham Martin*, *dit* L'Écossais, and Marguerite Langlois, godson of Charles de Saint-Étienne* de La Tour; d. at Sainte-Foy near Quebec, 19 June 1711.

Martin obtained his elementary and theological education from the Jesuits in Quebec. As part of his training, on 15 July 1667 he and his fellow student Pierre FRANCHEVILLE engaged in a public disputation "on the whole of Philosophy, with honour, and in presence of a considerable audience." Ordained a priest by Bishop LAVAL on 14 March 1671, Martin spent his career in or near Quebec. His first position was that of parish priest at Beauport; in 1672, while he was incumbent, the wooden church there was replaced with a stone building. Later he was pastor at Sainte-Famille, again at Beauport, at Château-Richer and Ange-Gardien-de-Montmorency. In 1673 he assisted in the conduct of elections at the Quebec Hôtel-Dieu, the first native priest to do so. He spent several years as teacher at the Quebec Seminary where from 1678 to 1681 he also acted as bursar, in charge of food supplies, repairs and the account books of the farm. On 8 November 1684 Bishop Laval appointed Martin one of eight canons of the new chapter of Quebec. Allaire asserts that, "as a gifted musician, Martin was able to raise greatly the level of the performance of the religious ceremonies at the Quebec cathedral." He resigned from this office in 1697 and the following year entered his last and longest assignment, that of priest of the newly established parish of Notre-Dame-de-Sainte-Foy. He held this position until his death during a purple fever epidemic. His remains were buried in the cathedral at Quebec.

As early as 1662 Father Jérôme Lalemant* refers to one "Amador" as a singer. Sister Régnard* Duplessis de Sainte-Hélène, who had come to Quebec nine years before Martin's death, states that Monsieur Martin, an able singer, composed the chant for the mass and the Office of the Holy Family celebration, which had been established by Laval in 1665. A musical manuscript preserved at the Hôtel-Dieu of Quebec includes the prose of the Office. Though it is unsigned and undated, local tradition claims that it is in Martin's handwriting. Comparison of it with Martin's known handwriting makes this appear a possibility, but establishes no definite proof. Dated 18th-century copies survive at other Quebec institutions and the music was printed with slight modifications in the 1827 and later editions of the *Graduel romain*. It was sung on the appropriate occasion at the Quebec basilica until the middle of the 20th century. In 1902 Ernest Gagnon, former organist of the church, judged it a piece of plain-chant of undeniable beauty and remarkable correctness, from the point of view of both rhythm and modality.

Recent investigators reject the claim that Martin also wrote the music for the mass of the Holy Family celebration. Judging by what is known about the writing of the words, the musical composition of the prose "Sacræ familiæ felix spectaculum" should be dated near the turn of the century rather than about 1679, as previously assumed. Indeed, no conclusive evidence has been found that Martin is the composer of Canada's earliest preserved musical composition.

HELMUT KALLMANN

AHDQ, Messe de la Sainte-Famille, Prose: "Sacræ familiæ felix spectaculum" (the ASQ and AMUQ have copies of this manuscript dated 1748, 1783, and 1810.); Sœur Duplessis de Sainte-Hélène, Notice sur la fête de la Sainte-Famille, 11. Caron, "Inventaire de documents," APQ *Rapport, 1939–40*, 206, 209, 213, 215, 258, 303, 324, 334. *Graduel romain* (2e éd., Québec, 1827), 203ff. (This contains the plain-chant prose "Sacræ familiæ felix spectaculum" without composer's name or any reference to its origin; the first edition (1800) of the *Graduel romain* does not contain this prose.) *JR* (Thwaites), XLV, 119, 271; XLVII, 295; L, 213. Juchereau, *Annales* (Jamet), 177. Provost, *Le Séminaire de Québec: documents et biographies*, 65, 420.

Allaire, *Dictionnaire*, IV, 8. [Allaire gives the most complete description of Martin's career as a priest. H.K.] Ernest Gagnon, *Louis Jolliet, découvreur du Mississipi et du pays des Illinois, premier seigneur de l'île d'Anticosti* (Montréal, 1946). Helmut Kallmann, *A history of music in Canada, 1534–1914* (Toronto, 1960), 22, 23.

MARTIN, GEORGE, commodore of the British fleet at the capture of Port-Royal (Annapolis Royal, N.S.), 1710; d. 22 Oct. 1724 (o.s., or less likely 22 Nov. 1732).

From 1692 on, Martin obtained several commissions in the Royal Navy. On 7 March 1708/9 he received orders to carry Colonels Samuel VETCH and Francis NICHOLSON to North America with other commissioned officers of a projected joint British and colonial expedition against the French colonies. Through the summer Martin's vessel lay in Boston harbour while the colonials made preparations and awaited the arrival of the promised fleet and troops from England. Finally in October the *Enterprise* arrived with news that the proposed expedition had been set aside. Despite entreaties by colonial officials, Martin refused to take part in a less ambitious colonial operation against Port-Royal, claiming he had orders to sail back to England. At the last moment Nicholson sailed with him to plead once again for a combined operation against the French colonies.

Nicholson obtained support for an expedition against Port-Royal or other French colonies. Martin, this time commodore of the fleet, set sail 19 May 1710, carrying Nicholson and other officers to Boston. Over the summer the possibility of a larger venture against the whole of Canada arose. Viscount Shannon began preparations in

England, but by the end of August these were abandoned, forcing a reversion to the original plan.

On 18 September the *Dragon* sailed "from Nantaskett with his Majt's ships Falmouth, Lowestaffe [*Lowestoft*], Feversham, and Starrbomb, the Province Gally, two Hospital ships, and 31 saile of Transports with two thousand troops on board for Port Royall." The fleet anchored at the entrance to Port-Royal harbour 24 September and after a council of war the siege began. On the 27th the *Starrbomb* (*Star Bomb*) "at 7 began to bombard with gt success which," according to Martin, "chiefly was the occasion of the fort's capitulating," although the artillery fire and the deployment of the land force were probably the decisive factors.

On 1 October the preliminaries of the capitulation were settled, and on the 5th AUGER de Subercase marched out of the fort. The next week was spent "setting the affairs of the Fortt and territory adjacent" and "supplying the garrison of Annapolis Royal with provisions from the severall men of war and the three transports appointed to carry the Garrison of Port Royall to old France." The *Dragon*, with Martin as captain, accompanied the New England transports to Boston, and later sailed for England. It was lost on the "Gaskets" (Channel Islands, the Casquets?) 11 May 1711. Although Martin survived, he did not command other ships after this date.

The capture of Port-Royal provided a victory to raise sagging British morale. Contemporary observers noted the successful cooperation between land and sea forces under Nicholson and Martin, and the dispatch with which Martin had "executed his orders most fully and completely." Martin, however, had reason to regret his North American tour of duty. In 1712 he complained of a stop in pay at the ticket office, imposed for his ordering that the ships' provisions be given to the garrison left at Annapolis Royal. The outcome of his petition is not known.

GEORGE C. INGRAM

PRO, Adm. 1/2094, 1/2095 (captain's letters); C.O. 5/9, ff.101–4, 111, 119–20, 159 (copies in PAC, MG 11). "Journal of Colonel Nicholson at the capture of Annapolis, 1710," N.S. Hist. Soc. *Coll.*, I (1878), 59–104. Campbell, *Lives of the admirals*, IV, 130–31. Thomas Lediard, *The naval history of England . . . from the Norman conquest . . . to the conclusion of 1734* (2v., London, 1735). Charnock, *Biographia navalis*, III, 199–201, 346–47. G.B., Admiralty, *List of sea officers, 1660–1815*, II, 604. John Hardy, *A chronological list of the Captains of His Majesty's Royal Navy with the dates of the first commissions, promotions, and other occurrences (beginning) the first June 1673 in the reign of King Charles* (London, 1784), 23, 27. Waller, *Samuel Vetch.*

Martin

MARTIN, MATHIEU, weaver, seigneur of Cobequid (Truro, N.S.); b. 1636 or 1637, son of Pierre Martin and Catherine Vigneau; did not marry; d. sometime before April 1724, probably on his seigneury.

At the same time as he plied his trade as a weaver, Martin concerned himself with the affairs of the dealers in pelts, both at Port-Royal (Annapolis Royal, N.S.), where he lived with his father, and in the Minas Basin. It is possible that his trips to the far end of the Baie Française (Bay of Fundy) had something to do with the land grant at Cobequid which was made to him in March 1689 and which he named Saint-Mathieu. He had to overcome certain difficulties created by Mathieu de GOUTIN, who was laying claim to Cobequid, as he wanted to set up there an outlet for spirits as an aid to the fur trade with the Indians. Martin, a man of foresight and determination, knew how to make his land grant prosper. Having first concerned himself with preparing the ground, he allowed three families to come in from Port-Royal around 1699. Four years later, in 1703, 19 families were to be found there and in 1714 there were 23.

Although the censuses do not mention him between 1693 (when he was at Port-Royal) and 1714 when he was at Cobequid, Martin must have chosen to reside on his seigneury from the time that his first tenant-farmers arrived. It was doubtless there that he died.

Several persons claimed to be his heirs, but the Nova Scotia Council declared that the seigneury should pass to the English crown. In 1732 the lieutenant-governor, Lawrence ARMSTRONG, wishing to put an end to the claims, stipulated that Mathieu Martin's will should be disregarded, because "during his lifetime he never would acknowledge this Government." It is nevertheless true that he had taken the oath of allegiance at Port-Royal in 1695. Thus all the rights attached to this seigneury passed to England.

CLARENCE J. D'ENTREMONT

AN, Col., C¹¹ᴰ, 2, f.126; Section Outre-Mer, G¹, 466 (Recensements de l'Acadie, 1671, 1693, 1698, 1700, 1701, 1703, 1707, 1714). "Mass. Archives," II, 540. *N.S. Archives, II,* 94; *III,* 53, 196, 199. PRO, *CSP, Col., 1732.* P.-G. Roy, *Inv. concessions,* IV, 38–39. Arsenault, *Hist. et généal. des Acadiens,* I, 46, 58, 78–79, 458. W. P. Bell, *The "foreign protestants" and the settlement of Nova Scotia* (Toronto, 1961), 73, 82–83. Murdoch, *History of Nova-Scotia,* I, 182, 416, 474, 475, 479. Rameau de Saint-Père, *Une colonie féodale,* I, 189–92; II, 318, 323, 328–29. Archange Godbout, "Les trois sœurs Esmard," SGCF *Mémoires,* I (1944–45), 197–200.

MARTIN DE LINO, ANTOINE (baptized **Guillaume**), priest, Recollet; b. 7 Aug. 1690 at Quebec, son of MATHIEU-FRANÇOIS MARTIN de Lino, a merchant, and of Catherine Nolan; died at the time of the 1733 epidemic, probably at Quebec.

The future Recollet, the fourth child of the family, entered the Petit Séminaire of Quebec on 8 Nov. 1700, with his younger brothers Charles and Jean-Marie; driven out of the seminary by the fire of 1705, the boy Guillaume continued his classical training at the Jesuit college. At the end of his studies he entered the Canadian Recollet order. Bishop Saint-Vallier [LA CROIX] admitted him into the priesthood on 24 Aug. 1714.

During the 19 years of his ministry, Martin de Lino was at different times a parish priest, missionary, and officiating priest in various parishes. The first post assigned to him was the parish of Lotbinière, to which he went on 1 Nov. 1715. The following year, on 3 Aug. 1716, the Conseil Supérieur appealed to his knowledge and requested him to "draw a map of the mouth of the Duchesne River where it flows into the St Lawrence, showing the dwellings" located in the area, to be used in an action pending before the tribunal.

Father Antoine continued his ministry in the parishes of Chambly, Trois-Rivières, Beauport, Batiscan, and Saint-Jean (Île d'Orléans), and was even at Detroit from 12 Nov. 1719 to March 1722. On 2 Jan. 1728 he was present at Bishop Saint-Vallier's funeral at the Hôpital Général, where in February he became the confessor to the nuns. We find him next at Sainte-Famille (Île d'Orléans), on 26 June, then again at the Hôpital Général, on 21 May 1729. Then from 1 Nov. 1730 to 31 July 1731 he was at Trois-Rivières. In the autumn of the latter year he travelled to France, and returned in 1732, with the title of master of novices of the convent of Quebec. It was no doubt while discharging this important duty that he died, during the epidemic of 1733.

Martin de Lino was a painter in his leisure moments. Gérard Morisset sums up his talent thus: "decorative canvases, totally lacking in contrast."

JACQUES VALOIS

AAQ, Registres d'insinuations C, 1, 2, 4, 5. AQ, NF, Ins. du Cons. sup., II, 136v; V, 52v; VI, 102. Jouve, *Les Franciscains et le Canada: aux Trois-Rivières,* 116. Gérard Morisset, *Coup d'œil sur les arts en Nouvelle-France* (Québec, 1941), 52. "La famille Martin de Lino," *BRH,* XLI (1935), 257f. Henri Têtu, "Le chapitre de la cathédrale de Québec et ses délégués en France (1723–1773)," *BRH,* XVI (1910), 228.

MARTIN DE LINO, JEAN-FRANÇOIS (sometimes called Jean-François-Mathieu), Quebec merchant, king's attorney of the provost court (1716–21) and the admiralty court (1717–21); b. 13 April 1686 at Quebec, son of MATHIEU-FRANÇOIS MARTIN de Lino and Catherine Nolan; m. 3 Nov. 1712 Angélique Chartier de Lotbinière; four children; buried 5 Jan. 1721 in the crypt of the church of Notre-Dame de Québec.

Jean-François Martin de Lino was the eldest son of a member of the governing class of New France, and he was trained to be an administrator and merchant like his father. He was educated at the Petit Séminaire in Quebec and at the Jesuit college, and he undoubtedly received informal lessons in book-keeping and law. At the age of 24 he joined the mercantile partnership of Pierre de Lestage and Antoine PASCAUD. De Lino severed his connections with the other merchants three years later.

De Lino's father and another member of the Conseil Supérieur, NICOLAS DUPONT de Neuville, decided that Jean-François ought to marry Dupont's grand-daughter, Marie-Jeanne Renaud d'Avène Desmeloizes. Jean-François was willing but the young lady, who was a former Ursuline novice, was reluctant. The matchmakers appeared before a notary on 4 May 1711 to declare that "for private reasons known to themselves" the marriage would be postponed but that if it did not take place by the end of the following September, the recalcitrant party would forfeit 10,000 *livres*.

Marie-Jeanne still would not budge and, by an agreement made on 8 May 1711, her exasperated grandfather gave young de Lino a house on Rue Saint-Pierre which he valued at 10,000 *livres*. Jean-François, for his part, promised Dupont a life annuity of 500 *livres*. Legal action was taken by Louis-Eustache Chartier* de Lotbinière, the brother-in-law of Mademoiselle Desmeloizes, to invalidate the agreement. It was argued that Dupont had acted out of "feelings of vengeance against her" and had, in effect, disinherited her. The matter was settled out of court in 1716 and de Lino retained the house. Mademoiselle Desmeloizes never did marry nor did she return to the cloister but by a curious turn of fate her brother Nicolas-Marie* married Jean-François de Lino's widow in 1722.

Young de Lino's parents arranged an equally advantageous marriage for their son in 1712. The bride was Eustache Chartier's sister, Angélique, the daughter of yet another member of the Conseil Supérieur, René-Louis CHARTIER de Lotbinière. At the formal signing of the wedding contract and in the presence of the highest officials of New France, Jean-François listed as his assets the house on Rue Saint-Pierre, 20,000

livres from his partnership with de Lestage and Pascaud, and an advance of 5000 *livres* from his parents' estate.

De Lino took his first step in the *cursus honorum* at the age of 30. He was appointed king's attorney of the Quebec provost court by royal letters dated 27 April 1716. Though his commission spoke of de Lino's capability, legal experience, and devotion to the king, some credit for the appointment is probably due to his family connections. As king's attorney, he prepared briefs for the instruction of the *lieutenants* who passed judgement. In addition to presenting cases to the court, he had a general mandate to uphold the legal interests of the king and, when an admiralty court was established at Quebec in 1717, it was natural that de Lino became its king's attorney. Maritime cases were formerly heard in the provost court and at first the new court was merely the old court sitting in special sessions.

Jean-François seems to have been a conscientious and, perhaps, a compassionate man. When New France was threatened with a famine in 1717 he tried to execute his orders to oversee the grain trade and to prevent the export of flour. The intendant, Michel Bégon*, stood in his way and, according to de Lino, told him "that it was dangerous to anticipate things" as the merchants might complain to the court at Versailles. Nevertheless, although he himself was a merchant, de Lino appealed to France for an order to stop the further exportation of food-stuffs from New France.

De Lino made a notable contribution to the welfare system in Canada. Because the urban Bureaux des Pauvres (office for the needy) boards had been abolished, the unfortunate were again dependent on church institutions and private charity. The problem of illegitimate births was of special concern to the authorities for such births were often concealed and an unwed mother might kill or abandon her child.

De Lino's interest in the fate of bastards was aroused when a woman tried to reclaim an illegitimate child that she had given to the Indians at Lorette. De Lino deplored the practice of giving illegitimate children to Indians because it reversed the policy of Frenchifying the native peoples, allowed the mother to return to an immoral life, increased the number of potential enemies, and would probably produce poor Catholics. He begged the council of Marine "to consider this evil practice and order that foundlings and abandoned bastards be raised under his care or that of the other king's attorneys . . . so that, when their age permits, they might be apprenticed or indentured to honest settlers." In France royal

Martin de Lino

officers had been made responsible for the care of foundlings by the edict of November 1706 and it was a matter of applying this law to the colony.

De Lino's proposal seems to have been adopted in a modified form. In Montreal during the 1730s, for example, the king's attorney and his deputy placed illegitimate children in private homes. In return for a gratuity, the foster parents promised "to feed and maintain the child, whether in sickness or in health, to instruct and raise the child in the Catholic, Apostolic, and Roman religion . . . and to teach the child to earn a living . . . until the said child attains the age of eighteen years."

It is likely that, had de Lino not died at the age of 34, he would have risen in the administration. Governor Vaudreuil [RIGAUD] recommended him for a seat on the Conseil Supérieur in 1717 but, perhaps because his father was already on the council or because others had precedence, he did not receive the appointment. The male line of the de Lino family survived through Jean-François and his son, Ignace-François-Pierre*, the last chief road officer in New France.

PETER N. MOOGK

AJQ, Greffe de Jacques Barbel, 8 mai 1711, 18 avril 1722; Greffe de Louis Chambalon, 4 mai 1711, 14 nov. 1713, 18 août 1714, 4 mai 1716; Greffe de J.-É. Dubreuil, 24 janv. 1722; Greffe de Florent de La Cetière, 30 oct. 1712; Greffe de J.-C. Louet, 13 août 1722; Greffe de Pierre Rivet, 8 mai 1711, 16 janv. 1714, 4 sept. 1716, 10 sept. 1717, 28 oct. 1718. AN, Col., C¹¹A, 38, pp.207–12 (copy in PAC). AQ, NF, Coll. de pièces jud. et not., 551¾. *Jug. et délib.*, VI, 1198, 1202–3. P.-G. Roy, *Inv. ins. Cons. souv.*, 131, 147, 148, 164; *Inv. jug. et délib., 1717–1760*, I, 32, 33, 71, 72; *Inv. ord. int.*, I, 216. Charland, "Notre-Dame de Québec: le nécrologe de la crypte," 177. Gareau, "La prévôté de Québec," 107–9. P.-G. Roy, *La famille Martin de Lino* (Lévis, 1935); *La ville de Québec*, I, 418; II, 86, 238, 299, 435; "La famille Renaud d'Avène Des Méloizes," *BRH*, XIII (1907), 166–67. "La famille Martin de Lino," *BRH*, XLI (1935), 257–80. Juliette Lalonde-Remillard, "Angélique Lalonde-Remillard," *RHAF*, XIX (1965–66), 520.

MARTIN DE LINO, MATHIEU-FRANÇOIS (also known as **Mathurin**, and **Mathurin-François**), merchant, fur-trader, seigneur, interpreter in English, member of the Conseil Souverain, member of the Compagnie du Nord and the Compagnie de la Colonie; b. 1657 in the parish of Saint-Nizier, Lyons; d. 5 Dec. 1731 in Quebec.

By birth and education Mathieu-François Martin de Lino was eminently qualified for a career in business. Both his father Claude and his mother Antoinette Chalmette had a middle-class background. The Chalmettes, moreover, were involved in Canadian commerce; Jean-François Chalmette, an uncle of Mathieu-François, was a wholesale fur-trader in Paris and held the lease of the Tadoussac trade in the early 1690s.

While he was still in his teens de Lino was sent to England and Holland by his father to study the languages of those countries. He was fluent in both by the age of 20, and no doubt was influenced by the way of life in those two great commercial nations. He came to New France in 1679 and, after a voyage to France in 1681, settled in Quebec. In that town on 30 April 1685 he married Catherine Nolan, daughter of the merchant Pierre Nolan. Soon afterwards he began to engage in various commercial activities. In 1688 he acquired part of Jean Gitton's interest in the Compagnie du Nord. The following year, he and a group of Canadian merchants, including CHARLES AUBERT de La Chesnaye, were granted the seigneury of Blanc Sablon in Newfoundland by the governor and intendant in order to enable them to pursue the cod and whale fishery.

During the war with the English colonies which began in 1689 de Lino, with his knowledge of English, was able to assist the colonial authorities by translating correspondence and questioning prisoners. His linguistic skill, however, also got him into serious trouble. In 1691 an English shipowner named John NELSON, whose vessel had been captured in the Bay of Fundy, was sent to Quebec by the governor of Acadia, Joseph Robinau* de Villebon. Frontenac [Buade*], showing more courtesy than caution, allowed him considerable freedom of movement of which Nelson took advantage to inspect the fortifications and relay information on them to New England. De Lino had served Nelson as interpreter and was suspected of having been his accomplice. He was arrested on 8 Jan. 1693, while in France on a business trip, and was clapped in the Bastille where he remained for six weeks. Following his release the minister informed Frontenac and BOCHART de Champigny that de Lino was a man to be watched closely, but the latter was able to regain the confidence of the government. De Lino was granted a seigneury on the coast of Acadia opposite Île Saint-Jean (Prince Edward Island) in 1697, and was appointed to the Conseil Souverain on 8 May 1702.

In 1700 de Lino had become a shareholder of the newly formed Compagnie de la Colonie and also a member of its board of directors. Later that year he left for France with Aubert de La Chesnaye to revise the terms of the agreement which Antoine PASCAUD had concluded a short time before with the banking firm of Jean Pasquier, Nicolas Bourlet, and Nicolas Gayot (Goy), which acted

Martinet de Fonblanche

as the company's correspondents in Paris. On 26 Feb. 1701, a new agreement was concluded under which Pasquier, Bourlet, and Gayot made extra credit available to the Compagnie de la Colonie and reduced their interest rate by 2 per cent. In spite of these more favourable terms the company remained in a precarious position. Its financial base was inadequate, the beaver market was depressed, and there were growing doubts about the soundness of the whole undertaking. It may have been to check an incipient panic that de Lino declared publicly both in France and in Canada that company affairs were in excellent shape. By thus resorting to what can be described only as gross misrepresentation he momentarily succeeded in restoring confidence in the operation.

De Lino also engaged in some rather sharp practices on his own behalf while he was in France. He appropriated funds from the company's account and offered an overpriced old bark as reimbursement. He also sent Jean Gitton to Hamburg to purchase some defective gunpowder and second-grade merchandise. These goods were then brought to Canada aboard a German vessel and sold to the Compagnie de la Colonie by a third party, who was apparently nothing more than a straw man for de Lino.

Pontchartrain eventually became aware of these activities, and he decided to punish de Lino for his misdemeanours. Despite JACQUES RAUDOT's attempt to excuse him, de Lino was suspended from his seat on the Conseil Supérieur and ordered to return to France to account for his actions. The businessman complied and no doubt pleaded his case with considerable skill for he succeeded in partly vindicating himself. He was allowed to return to Canada in 1707 and to resume his seat on the Conseil Supérieur. The minister, however, warned Raudot that "this man whether through ignorance or malice is dangerous" and he instructed the intendant neither to seek nor to accept his counsel in the administration of the colony's affairs.

This episode left its mark on de Lino's personality. The slick businessman of years past became studious and self-effacing. He read books on law and jurisprudence, wrote reports on questions of legal reform, and came to be regarded as one of the most competent members of the Conseil Supérieur. In 1715 Pontchartrain passed from the scene, and de Lino quickly won the confidence of the new administration. In 1716 and 1717 he served as the agent in New France of Néret and Gayot, the surviving partners of the three-man syndicate which had acquired control of the Canadian beaver trade in 1706. In 1719 he was named first councillor and appointed keeper

of the king's seal in 1727. He died four years later leaving an estate that was barely adequate to cover his debts.

De Lino's wife, Catherine, gave birth to 12 sons and 5 daughters, but only 4 sons and 3 daughters lived to adulthood. JEAN-FRANÇOIS served as king's attorney of the Quebec provost and admiralty courts, and married Angélique, daughter of René-Louis CHARTIER de Lotbinière; Guillaume became a Recollet priest, taking the name ANTOINE, and served in Trois-Rivières and Chambly; Charles, Sieur de Balmont, lived in France, probably in La Rochelle; Jean-Marie, Sieur de Murier, moved to La Rochelle where he married Marie-Anne, daughter of Antoine Peyrant, councillor of the local presidial. Catherine de Lino married JEAN-FRANÇOIS HAZEUR; Marie-Anne was still alive in 1757 but little is known about her. Finally, Geneviève-Françoise married Gaspard Adhémar* de Lantagnac, a lieutenant in the colonial regular troops.

YVES F. ZOLTVANY and C. J. RUSS

AJQ, Greffe de Pierre Duquet, 2 avril 1685; Greffe de Gilles Rageot, 28 août 1688. AN, Col., B, 25, 29–40, 54; C¹¹A, 2, 12, 14, 18–41, 57; C¹¹G, 2–4. Bibliothèque de l'Arsenal (Paris), Archives de la Bastille, 10496, ff.158–68. "Correspondance de Frontenac, 1689–99,' APQ Rapport, 1927–28, 135, 151, 163. "Correspondance de Vaudreuil," APQ Rapport, 1947–48, 319. "Lettres et mémoires de F.-M.-F. Ruette d'Auteuil." P.-G. Roy, Inv. concessions, IV, 39, 136. Le Jeune, Dictionnaire, I, 482. Tanguay, Dictionnaire, I, 416. E. H. Borins, "La Compagnie du Nord, 1682–1700," unpublished M.A. thesis, McGill University, 1968. "La famille Martin de Lino," BRH, XLI (1935), 257–93. Guy Frégault, "La Compagnie de la Colonie," Revue de l'université d'Ottawa, XXX (1960), 5–29, 127–49.

MARTINET DE FONBLANCHE, JEAN (sometimes and quite wrongly called **Tourblanche**), surgeon of the Hôtel-Dieu of Ville-Marie, medico-legal expert in that town, founder of a school for surgeon apprentices; b. 1645, son of Paul Martinet, a merchant from Moustier Saint-Jean in the diocese of Langres, and of Catherine Ducas; d. 7 Nov. 1701.

Martinet became a surgeon of the Hôtel-Dieu of Ville-Marie on 20 Aug. 1681, when he signed with that institution the same contract as did Antoine FORESTIER. Not content with looking after the patients of the Hôtel-Dieu, he frequently acted as a medico-legal expert. His signature is attached to numerous reports, the most curious being no doubt the one concerning the inquest in the Talus case. A certain Julien Talus, dit Vendamont, had returned to his home at Lachine on the night of 9–10 July 1684 and had found his

Maufils

wife in bed with a person named Antoine Roy *dit* Desjardins. The husband killed the lover and gave himself up. It was Jean Martinet who took charge of the post-mortem examination. The trial was held, and on 14 October following Vendamont was condemned to death, but lodged an appeal.

At an early date Martinet had opened a school of surgery at Montreal and was accepting apprentices: Paul Prud'homme was enrolled on 15 Jan. 1674, and François Tardy on 16 December of that year; there is a record of other apprentices in 1686 and 1691.

Medicine at that time made extensive use of medicinal herbs. Thus it is interesting to note that in the contract by which he agreed to sell a piece of land containing some three acres to the Recollets on 17 April 1681, Martinet stipulated that the sale included the trees and plants growing in the field, but not the medicinal herbs.

On 14 July 1670, at Montreal, he had married Marguerite Prud'homme, then 14 years old, the daughter of Louis Prud'homme*, a brewer and captain of the militia, and of Roberte Gadoys. Two children were born of this union.

CHARLES-MARIE BOISSONNAULT

AJM, Greffe de Bénigne Basset, 13 juillet 1670, 15 janv. 1674; Greffe de Claude Maugue, 20 août 1681. *Jug. et délib.*, II, 369, 601, 965–70, 972f., 980f.; III, 440; IV, 531. É.-Z. Massicotte, "Les chirurgiens, médecins, etc., de Montréal, sous le régime français, *APQ Rapport, 1922–23*, 135, 149. A. Roy, *Inv. greffes not.*, IX. Abbott, *History of medicine*, 19, 20. Ahern, *Notes pour l'histoire de la médecine*, 403–8. M. R. Charlton, "Outline of the history of medicine in Lower Canada under the French régime, 1608–1757, and under the English régime," *Annals of Medical History* (New York), V (1923), 150, 263; VI (1924), 22, 312. Ignotus [Thomas Chapais], "La profession médicale au Canada," *BRH*, XII (1906), 143. É.-Z. Massicotte, "Les chirurgiens de Montréal au XVIIᵉ siècle, *BRH*, XX (1914), 255; XXVIII (1922), 247.

MAUFILS, MARIE-MADELEINE, *dite* **de Saint-Louis,** Religious Hospitaller at the Hôtel-Dieu of Quebec; baptized 21 Dec. 1671 at Sainte-Anne de Beaupré, daughter of Pierre Maufils and Madeleine Poulain; buried 5 Dec. 1702.

She joined the Religious Hospitallers of Quebec in 1687. In the *Annales de l'Hôtel-Dieu de Québec* it is said of her that she "had much wit, humour, skill, and was extraordinarily expert in all sorts of learning. She had been taught to paint." The annalist affirms that "there are still some landscapes in the house which are her work; her death prevented her from finishing several that she had sketched out." Gérard Morisset believes that it

was she who painted some panels in the chapel of the Hôpital Général in Quebec. In *Painting in Canada: a history*, J. R. Harper remarks: "While artistically of no great importance, Mother Maufils ... deserve[s] mention for the secular notes introduced into [her] subject-matter."

Marie-Madeleine Maufils died a victim to her devotion, at the time of a smallpox epidemic which filled the Hôtel-Dieu of Quebec with patients during the winter of 1702–3.

HÉLÈNE BÉRNIER

Juchereau, *Annales* (Jamet). Tanguay, *Dictionnaire*. Maximilien Bibaud, *Le panthéon canadien*, éd. Adèle et Victoria Bibaud (Montréal, 1891). Casgrain, *Histoire de l'Hôtel-Dieu de Québec*, 584. Harper, *Painting in Canada*. Gérard Morisset, *Coup d'œil sur les arts en Nouvelle-France* (Québec, 1941), 50.

MAUMOUSSEAU, FRANÇOISE, nun, sixth superior of the Nuns Hospitallers of Saint-Joseph at Montreal; b. 1657 at Château-Gontier (department of Mayenne), daughter of Jean Maumousseau, a merchant, and of Renée Verron; d. 16 Jan. 1704 at Ville-Marie.

In 1681, two years after she had entered the noviciate of the Hôtel-Dieu of Beaufort-en-Vallée, Anjou, Sister Maumousseau arrived in Montreal with Sister Charlotte GALLARD. An energetic missionary and an active woman, Sister Maumousseau discharged the most difficult duties at the Hôtel-Dieu. When Bishop Saint-Vallier [LA CROIX] assumed charge of his diocese in 1688, he asked the Religious Hospitallers to build a larger hospital, capable of meeting the colony's needs. Sister Maumousseau, who was then the depositary, laid the foundations of an Hôtel-Dieu that was similar in almost every respect to the plans established for communities in France.

But on 24 Feb. 1695, barely three months after the inauguration of the Hôtel-Dieu, a fire destroyed the entire building. The reconstruction of the hospital and the convent was undertaken immediately. The work had not yet been completed when, in the spring of 1696, Sister Maumousseau was appointed superior. She then had to share with Sister MORIN, the depositary, the financial worries attached to such an undertaking. And it cannot have been an easy task, according to what CALLIÈRE and BOCHART de Champigny wrote to the Comte de Pontchartrain on 18 Oct. 1700 about "the extreme poverty of the Religious Hospitallers of Montreal, which makes it almost impossible for them to support themselves, the interior of their house being only half rebuilt. ..." Consequently, on 24 Sept. 1701, Sister Maumousseau, in her capacity as superior, signed an "État des charges et besoins des religieuses hospitalières de Montréal." This report was addressed to the minister with a view to obtaining increased financial assistance from his majesty.

Despite their extreme poverty, in June 1702 the Religious Hospitallers undertook the rebuilding of their church. Sister Maumousseau had the joy of seeing it almost completed: she died on 16 Jan. 1704, only a few months before its inauguration.

HÉLÈNE BERNIER

AAQ, Copies de documents, Série A: Église du Canada, III, 35. AHDM, Mère Chauvelier, Livre ou second recueil de lettres circulaires, 187. Caron, "Inventaire de documents," APQ *Rapport, 1940–41*, 341. Mondoux, *L'Hôtel-Dieu de Montréal*, 221.

MAUR. See AUBERT DE LA CHESNAYE, FRANÇOIS

MAUR, PAUL-AUGUSTIN JUCHEREAU DE. *See* JUCHEREAU

MÉNAGE, PIERRE, master carpenter, son of François Ménage, a merchant in Poitiers, and Françoise Lunette; b. *c.* 1648 in the bishopric of Poitiers; buried 15 April 1715.

We know nothing about the circumstances under which he came to New France when he was about 21, during Talon*'s administration. His presence at Quebec is first mentioned in 1669, when he bought a house on the Saint-Charles River. In 1675 he built François Jacquet's small house (which is still standing today at the corner of Rue Saint-Louis and Rue Desjardins) in exchange for a piece of land on the Saint-Charles River.

His principal achievements date from about 1680, when he formed a partnership with Jean Caillé, who came from Soissons. During the following ten years they were busy building the Jesuits' house near the harbour of Quebec (1684), on one of the best sites in Lower Town, the Comporté [Gaultier*] house (1685), the Pachot [Viennay-Pachot*] house (1686), sited on Place Royale which was dedicated in the same year. In 1688 he took part in the rebuilding of the Ursuline convent, built the belfry of Notre-Dame-de-la-Victoire church in 1690, and also that of the cathedral according to plans by La Rivière [BERNARD]. The drawing which is attached to the Comporté contract shows the importance of half-timbering in the period and gives evidence of sure craftsmanship utilizing simple and traditional means. His contribution to the building of the Hôtel-Dieu (1691) and of the Château Saint-Louis (1692) marks the high point of his career. His

building activity came to an end with a contract on Île d'Orléans (1701).

In 1670 Pierre Ménage married Dorothée Brassard. After this marriage was annulled, he married Anne Leblanc in 1672. Several children, including two boys, Jean-Baptiste and François, and several daughters, were born of this marriage. Two of his daughters, Marie-Anne and Anne, married François de LAJOÜE (1689) and Pierre Levasseur (1696) respectively. Ménage died 15 April 1715 at Quebec.

Although he was not pre-eminent (he was illiterate and unable to sign his name), Ménage nevertheless played an important role in construction during the last quarter of the 17th century, a role that is linked to that of his privileged colleagues, Baillif*, Lajoüe, La Rivière, etc.

PIERRE MAYRAND

AJQ, Greffe de Romain Becquet, 17 nov. 1669, 30 nov. 1672, 2 déc. 1674, 28 févr. 1675; Greffe de Louis Chambalon, 28 févr. 1701; Greffe de François Genaple, 7 févr., 20 déc. 1683; 5 déc. 1685; 4, 12 déc. 1686; 5 janv., 18 nov. 1688; 2 nov. 1692; 17 mars 1696; Registres d'état civil de Notre-Dame de Québec, 15 avril 1715. P.-B. Casgrain, "Une autre maison Montcalm à Québec (1759)," *BRH*, VIII (1902), 330–33.

MENEVAL, LOUIS-ALEXANDRE DES FRICHES DE. *See* DES FRICHES

MERIEL, HENRI-ANTOINE (Meriel de Meulan), priest, Sulpician, director and confessor of the pupils of the sisters of the Congrégation de Notre-Dame, chaplain of the Montreal Hôtel-Dieu, converted many New England captives to Roman Catholicism; b. 1661, in the diocese of Chartres; d. 12 Jan. 1713, probably in Paris.

Very little is known about Meriel de Meulan. He entered the seminary of Saint-Sulpice in Paris around the year 1685. He arrived in Montreal in July of 1690, and by 1695 had been appointed confessor of the pupils of the sisters of the Congrégation de Notre-Dame. Apparently he found confessions difficult to conduct at first, for words of encouragement on this subject can be found in the letters he received from Louis Tronson, superior of the Sulpician seminary in Paris.

It is likely that Meriel had some command of English when he came to New France in 1690, for he had not been long in the colony before he began to convert New England captives to Roman Catholicism. In 1699 he sought permission from his superior to travel to New England in search of French prisoners to bring them back to the colony, but his request was refused. Soon after he was placed in charge of the sick of the Hôtel-Dieu in Montreal.

J.-B.-A. Allaire, in his *Dictionnaire biographique du clergé canadien-français*, writes that Meriel died in Paris. This would mean that Meriel left the colony to return to France between 1707 and 1713.

C. J. RUSS

ASSM, Correspondance générale, 2e partie, lettres de M. Leschassier, 272; lettres de M. Tronson, VI, 114, 156, 231, 246. Allaire, *Dictionnaire*, I, 383. Henri Gauthier, *Sulpitiana* (Montréal, 1926), 233f. Coleman, *New England captives*.

MERMANDE. *See* SAGEAN

MERMET, JEAN, Jesuit missionary in the Illinois country, 1698–1716; b. 23 Sept. 1664 in Grenoble; d. 15 Sept. 1716, at Kaskaskia (Illinois).

Mermet became a novice at Avignon in 1683, studied at Embrun, 1685–86, and then taught successively at Carpentras, Roanne, and Vesoul. He completed his theological studies at Dole, 1692–96, spent a final year at Salins, and came to Canada in 1698.

He was immediately sent to the west, where he assisted at the Guardian Angel mission (Chicago) and at nearby Miami-Illinois villages. Father François Pinet, head of the Guardian Angel mission, spent the summers there, but wintered farther down the Illinois River or with the Indians on their winter hunts. Mermet may have followed this practice, although Father Marc BERGIER wrote in 1702 of the misery to which Mermet had been reduced in his winter quarters at Chicago. By this time Mermet was in charge of the mission, for Pinet had joined the Kaskaskias in 1700. When Mermet left Chicago in the spring of 1702, the Guardian Angel mission ended.

Mermet, in 1702, became an assistant to Father Claude AVENEAU at the Miami mission on the St Joseph River (Mich.). In April of that year Mermet wrote to Cadillac [LAUMET] at Detroit that the Miamis were urging the English to establish a post near the St Joseph River, implying that French reinforcements should be sent to the St Joseph post. Cadillac felt this was merely another Jesuit scheme to strengthen their position and to minimize his efforts at Detroit. "He writes through Michilimackinac," Cadillac sarcastically noted, "and there is reason for astonishment that he is not already in Quebec, and the English with the Miamis."

During the summer of 1702, Mermet—now with the Kaskaskia mission—was assigned as chaplain to the expedition of CHARLES JUCHEREAU de Saint-Denys, who had a concession to establish a tannery near the confluence of the Ohio and Mississippi rivers. Juchereau's party picked up Mermet at Kaskaskia in August 1702, and arrived at its destination (near Cairo, Ill.) in late autumn. The Jesuits were directed to assist Juchereau as well as they could. Even with this help, a flourishing post never developed. PIERRE-GABRIEL MAREST wrote in November 1702: "The Father [Mermet] who is with him is not very pleased. He is neither a missionary, for there are no Savages, nor a chaplain, for there is no stipend."

However, a tribe of Mascoutens soon settled nearby, probably attracted by the new post. Mermet worked among them, but was unable to break the power of the medicine men. He engaged a Mascouten shaman in a celebrated theological discussion. The shaman worshipped the bison as his manitou. Mermet convinced him that he did not worship the bison, but the spirit which animated all bison, and that man, the master of all animals, must necessarily be animated by the greatest of all manitous. Mermet concluded that if this were so, why not invoke Him who is master of all others? Marest later wrote: "This reasoning disconcerted the Charlatan, and that is all the effect it produced."

An epidemic soon swept the Mascouten village and the post. Mermet did his best to care for the sick but was rewarded only with abuse; the few Indians he managed to baptize died shortly thereafter. More than half the tribe died in the epidemic, which also caused the death of Juchereau (1703). Mermet apparently left the post in 1704, although a few French survivors remained at least through 1706.

Mermet's movements after he left Juchereau's post are unclear, although he may have served briefly at a Miami mission. Cadillac referred to Mermet in November 1704, as "the missionary of the village of the Aoyatanuons [Wea] Miamis." Mermet arrived at the Kaskaskia (Ill.) mission in 1705 or 1706 and remained there until his death in 1716.

In 1706 Mermet cared for Father Jacques GRAVIER, who was ambushed, wounded, and kept captive by some Peorias. He operated on Gravier's arm, nursed him, and sent him to Mobile. Gravier wrote (1707) that Mermet "can hardly work, owing to his ruined state of health after having spent all his strength by excess of zeal." At Kaskaskia Father Marest also wrote of Mermet's dedication: "In spite of his feeble health . . . he is the soul of this Mission."

Mermet's years at Kaskaskia were busy and fruitful. His duties consisted of officiating at baptisms, marriages, and funerals, ministering to nearby Indian villages, and trying to convince the hostile Peorias to become friendly. In February 1715, Mermet wrote of the death of his beloved colleague, Pierre-Gabriel Marest, "a missionary of incomparable zeal." In the same year Mermet wrote several letters to officials in Montreal, warning them of the English scheme to move into the Mississippi-Ohio region.

Mermet died at Kaskaskia 15 Sept. 1716. His remains were reinterred in the new parish at Kaskaskia by Father Jean-Antoine Le Boullenger in December 1727. Mermet's career involved no major scandals, controversies, successes, or failures. Yet he exemplifies the dedicated missionary who, in spite of physical limitations, performed mission work on the frontier for a long period of time. His lack of success at the Juchereau post was primarily due to causes beyond his control. The great success of the Illinois missions was mainly the result of the work of Gravier and Marest, but they both acknowledged Mermet's usefulness and devotion. Mermet had the joy of being part of a missionary endeavour of which Gravier wrote: "They have hardly time to breathe, on account of the increasing number of neophytes and their great fervor."

DONALD CHAPUT

ARSI, Francia 25/II, 298v–99; Gallia 15/I, 67–68; 110/II, 261–64. ASQ, Lettres, R, 52. Wis. State Hist. Soc. (Madison), Lettres circulaires de Canada, Letter from Gabriel Marest and Jacques L'Argilier to R. P. Germain, 25 Feb. 1715. *Découvertes et établissements des Français* (Margry), V, 446–48, 581–82. *JR* (Thwaites), LXVI, 38–41, 51–56, 121–23, 127–29, 207–9, 237–41, 255, 267, 339; LXXI, 159–60, 339. "Kaskaskia church records," Ill. State Hist. Soc. *Trans.*, 1904, 396. *Michigan Pioneer Coll.*, XXXIII, 118–19, 234. *NYCD* (O'Callaghan and Fernow), IX, 931. Wis. State Hist. Soc. *Coll.*, XVI, 317–18, 333. *Liste des missionnaires-jésuites, Nouvelle-France et Louisiane, 1611–1800* (Montréal, 1929), 57.

G. J. Garraghan, *Chapters in frontier history: research studies in the making of the west* (Milwaukee, [1934]), 39–40. Gérard Malchelosse, *Le poste de la rivière Saint-Joseph (Michigan) 1691–1781* (Montréal, 1959). Sister Mary Borgias Palm, *The Jesuit missions of the Illinois country, 1673–1763* (n.p., 1933), 30, 40, 46, 119n. Rochemonteix, *Les Jésuites et la N.-F. aux XVIIe siècle*, III, 513–14, 544, 547–50. N. W. Caldwell, "Charles Juchereau de St. Denys: A French pioneer in the Mississippi valley," *Mississippi Valley Hist. Review*, XXVIII (1942), 563–80. J. B. Culmens, "Missionary adventures among the Peorias," *Ill. Catholic Hist. Review [Mid-America]*, V (1922), 27–40. J. P. Dunn, "Letter to the Editor," *Magazine of Western History*, XII (1890), 578–79. G. J. Garraghan, "Catholic beginnings in Chicago," *Mid-America*, XVI (1933; new ser., V), 33–44; "The ecclesiastical rule of old Quebec in Mid-America," *Catholic Hist. Review* (Washington), XIX (1933), 17–32. W. N. Moyers, "A story of southern Illinois, the soldiers' reservation, including the Indians, French traders and some early Americans," Ill. State Hist. Soc. J., XXIV (1931), 54–76. Floyd Mulkey, "Fort St. Louis at Peoria," Ill. State Hist. Soc. J., XXXVII (1944), 301–16. M. T. Scott, "Old Fort Massac," Ill. State Hist. Soc. *Trans.*, 1903, 38–44.

MESSIER, *dit* **Saint-Michel, MICHEL,** lieutenant of militia, seigneur, fur-trader; b. 1640 at Saint-Denis-le-Thiboult in the diocese of Rouen, son of David Messier and Marguerite Bar; buried 3 Nov. 1725 at Saint-Anne de Varennes.

Messier seems to have come to New France with Chomedey* de Maisonneuve's contingent, which arrived at Ville-Marie in the middle of November 1653. His uncle, Jacques Messier, his aunt Martine Messier*, wife of Antoine Primot, and his cousin Catherine Thierry, daughter of Guillaume and Élisabeth Messier from Saint-Denis-le-Thiboult and adoptive child of the Primot couple, were already there. Although his name does not appear on the muster-roll of indentured workers, he must have crossed the ocean with them, for on 10 December he signed as a witness to the promise of marriage between his cousin, Catherine Thierry, and Charles Le Moyne* de Longueuil et de Châteauguay.

With the arrival of this contingent of 120 settlers, the fear of having to abandon Ville-Marie, which was exposed to frequent and violent Iroquois attacks, was removed. The settlers left the fort to go and live in their little houses, and they resumed work in the fields with renewed vigour. The Iroquois, however, continued to harass the settlers, killing and capturing them on occasion. Thus, in the autumn of 1654, young Michel Messier was captured; he was set free the following summer and taken to Ville-Marie by a Mohawk captain named "La Grande Armée," at the time when some Iroquois captains, held in the fort, were exchanged for all the French prisoners.

Subsequently Messier became interested in land clearing, and on 4 Nov. 1657, when he was 17, he bought from Charles Le Moyne, for 900 *livres*, a 30-acre piece of land called "la provençale." On 18 Feb. 1658, before the notary Bénigne Basset* and in the presence of the notables of the town, he signed his marriage contract with Anne Le Moyne, Charles' sister. On 25 February the marriage was solemnized in the chapel of the Hôtel-Dieu. Eight daughters and four sons were born of this marriage.

In 1661, after a short respite due to Dollard* Des Ormeaux's exploit at the Long-Sault, the Iroquois raids on Ville-Marie started up again. On 24 March Michel Messier was again captured

Meulles

with a few settlers. On 22 June some Iroquois who had come to Montreal stated that Messier had been burned by the Onondagas and that they did not know whether he was still alive. But at the end of 1663 he was back again with his family after having made his escape.

On 26 Nov. 1665 the Sulpicians made over to him a 30-acre piece of land above the one that he already owned. In the deed of grant he is called Michel Messier, *dit* le grand Saint-Michel. The 1667 census shows him as having 7 head of cattle and 30 acres under cultivation. On 14 May 1668 Messier and his brother-in-law Jacques Le Moyne de Sainte-Marie received conjointly the fief of Cap-de-la-Trinité, which they divided between them on 1 Aug. 1676; Le Moyne's portion was called Notre-Dame or Cap-de-la-Trinité, and Messier's, Cap-Saint-Michel. On 5 Aug. 1678 Messier, a lieutenant of militia at Ville-Marie, gave evidence in an inquiry launched by Buade* de Frontenac, the object of which was to ascertain what principle determined the allocation of the sites on which temporary booths, called "mobile shops," were put up at the time of the fur-trading fair. On 4 October Messier bought the fief of La Guillaudière, which was 30 *arpents* long by a league in depth, and which adjoined his own.

In 1684 Messier took part in Le Febvre* de La Barre's expedition against the Iroquois. On 14 August, at the time of the military review held at Fort Frontenac, he was listed as being the commander of the bark the *Générale*. On his return Messier received from the governor a fur-trading licence for the Ottawa country. He went there the following year, after making his will on 25 May. In 1692 Frontenac granted him another licence, and on 2 May, prior to his departure, Messier gave a power of attorney to his wife before the notary Bénigne Basset. During this trip Messier was exposed to grave dangers. He does not seem to have obtained further licences, hence it is possible that he settled subsequently on one of his fiefs, which in 1692, with the fiefs of Cap-de-la-Trinité, Varennes, and Île Sainte-Thérèse, made up the parish of Sainte-Anne de Varennes.

On 3 Nov. 1725, at the age of 85, Messier was buried in the parish of Sainte-Anne de Varennes, a few months after his wife. On 4 Jan. 1726 an inventory of his possessions was drawn up by the notary Marien Tailhandier, *dit* La Beaume. New France thus lost one of its pioneers who had taken an active part in the defence of the colony, the clearing of the land, and the fur trade.

Claude Perrault

AJM, Greffe de Bénigne Basset, 4 nov. 1657, 18 févr. 1658, 20 mars, 20 mai 1660, 17 sept. 1676, 2 mai 1692; Greffe de Hilaire Bourgine, 25 mai 1685; Greffe de Lambert Closse, 10 déc. 1653; Greffe de Claude Maugue, 4 oct. 1678; Greffe de Marien Tailhandier, 4 janv. 1726; Registres d'état civil de Boucherville, 31 janv. 1679; Registres d'état civil de Notre-Dame de Montréal, 1658, 1661. Archives judiciaires de Richelieu, Registre d'état civil de Sainte-Anne de Varennes. Dollier de Casson, *Histoire du Montréal*, 80, 111, 155, 241. "Ordonnances de Mr Paul de Chomedey, sieur de Maisonneuve, premier gouverneur de Montréal," in *Mémoires et documents relatifs à l'histoire du Canada*, [Société hist. de Montréal, *Mémoires*], III (1860), 142. P.-G. Roy, *Inv. concessions*, II, 117f. Tanguay, *Dictionnnaire*, I, 427. R.-J. Auger, *La grande recrue de 1653* (SGCF pub., I, Montréal, 1955), 29. Sulte, *Hist. des Can. fr.*, IV. M.-A. Bernard, "Sainte-Anne de Varennes," *BRH*, IV (1898), 129.

MEULLES, JACQUES DE, seigneur of La Source, chevalier, intendant of New France (1682–1686), son of Pierre de Meulles, king's councillor, treasurer-general of war supplies; d. 1703.

In 1674 Jacques de Meulles's career in the royal service was assured by his marriage to a daughter of Michel Bégon. He thereby became related, by marriage, to Jean-Baptiste Colbert, the great minister of Louis XIV. At that time family ties were very close and men in high places were expected to advance the careers of their relatives. When it was decided to recall the intendant of New France, Jacques Duchesneau*, Colbert appointed the son of Michel Bégon—also named Michel—to the vacant post, but at the last minute decided to send him to the West Indies instead. De Meulles, Bégon's brother-in-law, was then appointed in his place, his commission being dated 1 May 1682.

Before leaving for La Rochelle to take ship for Quebec both de Meulles and Le Febvre* de La Barre, the governor general appointed to succeed Louis de Buade*, Comte de Frontenac, were carefully briefed by the Marquis de Seignelay, Colbert's son, who was now in charge of Canadian affairs, on the manner in which they must discharge their new responsibilities. The one thing that Louis XIV and Colbert were most insistent on was that they must avoid, at all costs, the bitter disputes that had paralysed the colony's civil administration under Frontenac and Duchesneau. Tranquillity and order had to be restored to ensure the well-being of the settlers, which had suffered greatly in the past. De Meulles was instructed that his conduct towards La Barre had to be very different from that which Duchesneau had displayed towards Frontenac. Although the king was sure that La Barre would not behave as Frontenac had been wont to do, de Meulles was bluntly told that if this should occur then he could only remonstrate with the governor, and if this were to be to no avail, submit, then report the matter to the minister for him to deal with.

Despite this briefing, when de Meulles and La Barre arrived at Quebec in early October, they were quite taken aback by the intensity of the factional strife in the colony. What came as an even greater shock was to discover that the Iroquois were on the verge of war with the French, had already begun attacking their allies in the west and pillaging French canoes and trading posts, and that the colony was without defences. They immediately called an assembly of the leading men in the colony who informed them that for some time the Iroquois had made plain their intention to drive the French out of the west and divert the fur trade from Montreal to Albany, with themselves playing the role of middleman. And to the north the Hudson's Bay Company, now well entrenched in its posts on the shores of the bay, was luring the northern tribes to trade there rather than with the French. The members of this assembly were all of the opinion that the only way the Iroquois could be restrained was by adopting a much firmer policy than La Barre's predecessor had employed. A show of force, they declared, and if that failed, the use of it, was the only way to prevent the Iroquois crushing the western allies, one by one, then launching their full strength against New France.

La Barre and de Meulles were convinced. They decided that a campaign to attack the Iroquois in their villages was the only sure way of halting their aggression. They immediately sent an urgent appeal to the minister, requesting that 200 or 300 regular troops be sent to defend the settlements, along with 150 indentured labourers to work on the land while the militia were under arms. To curb the threat from the Hudson Bay posts, they issued permits to Canadians to trade with the tribes likely to defect to the English and sent orders to one of the leading western traders, DANIEL GREYSOLON Dulhut, to use all his influence to deter them from taking their furs to the English company.

Once these steps had been taken to meet the external threats to the colony La Barre and de Meulles could do little more until they received the reinforcements and the minister's approval for the Iroquois campaign. Meanwhile, they turned their attention to internal matters. De Meulles certainly found enough here to keep him busy. He declared that the lower law courts were very corrupt and he took a great deal of litigation out of their hands and dealt with it himself. In the first month he adjudicated at least 200 petty cases thereby saving the litigants considerable time and expense. He did this only when both parties to a suit were in agreement that he should. He wryly commented, "It is said that the more doctors there are in a town, the more sickness there is. It is the same with judges. . . . No wiser step was ever taken than to forbid lawyers to practise here." In contrast, he was gravely perturbed by the shortage of priests in the colony. He informed the minister: "At least three-quarters [of the habitants] do not hear Mass four times a year, which means that often they die without the sacraments and are no better instructed in our religion than the Indians, who never hear of it. This has filled me with extraordinary compassion."

With Bishop LAVAL, and the clergy in general, de Meulles appears to have been on good terms from the outset; certainly they voiced no complaints on his conduct of affairs. With La Barre too his relations were at first excellent, but after some months friction developed. It is difficult to say which of them was more to blame. La Barre certainly displayed a tendency to behave in an autocratic manner and de Meulles accused him of seeking to usurp powers that belonged to the office of the intendant, but a sharp rebuke from the minister was enough to make the governor mend his ways. De Meulles, on the other hand, was by no means so discreet. He quickly revealed a marked propensity for intrigue but was not very adroit in this subtle art. As La Barre made it increasingly obvious that he lacked the ability and strength of character needed to cope with the serious problems facing the colony, de Meulles began to criticize him in dispatches to the minister in terms that bordered on contempt. When warned by the minister that if he were to continue in this fashion he would be recalled, he was foolish enough to reiterate his charges in more detail. De Meulles left no doubt that he wished to have the governor's powers reduced and his own enhanced. Despite his close family ties with the minister, upon which he may have placed too much reliance, he overreached himself when he requested the minister to instruct the members of the Conseil Souverain to recognize only the intendant's authority and not the governor's. Upon receiving this dispatch Seignelay became furious. It appeared that the one thing Louis XIV and the minister had been anxious to avoid, an open conflict between governor and intendant which would open old wounds, was in the making. De Meulles was informed in the next dispatches that anyone who could seriously suggest such a thing clearly demonstrated that he lacked the capacity for the intendant's post. This was enough to convince de Meulles that he had overstepped the bounds and he immediately ceased to make overt attacks on the governor.

A few months later, however, La Barre's ineptitude, Seignelay's carelessness, the Iroquois, and disease combined to destroy the governor's career far more effectively than the intendant could have done. The urgent pleas from La Barre and de Meulles for military reinforcements to cope with the Iroquois threat met with a meagre response. In 1683 Seignelay neglected to deal with the Canadian dispatches at all. A junior official took it on himself to have 150 hastily recruited colonial regular troops sent, but on arrival only 120 were found fit for service, and most of the weapons and supplies sent with them proved to be worthless. Yet, when in 1684 the Iroquois made a direct assault on Fort Saint-Louis in the Illinois country, La Barre came under pressure from all sides to attack the Iroquois villages to prevent their overrunning the west. In July he left Montreal with all the available troops and militia, nearly 800 men, and 378 allied Indians. The expedition got no farther than Fort Frontenac (Cataracoui) where an epidemic of Spanish influenza reduced it to helplessness. La Barre was forced to treat for peace with the Iroquois and accept their humiliating conditions.

In his dispatches to the minister, dated 15 July and 14 August, whilst the expedition was underway, de Meulles, with rare prescience, expressed the fear that La Barre would not attack the Iroquois but would come to terms. When Louis XIV and the minister learned that this was indeed what had happened orders were immediately issued recalling La Barre, and the intendant's judgement appeared to be vindicated. De Meulles, however, had little time to gloat. He had his hands full coping with a drastic situation in the colony. As intendant he was directly responsible for the welfare of its settlers and they were now in a sorry plight. The disease that had incapacitated the army spread through the colony with a heavy death toll. That summer four more companies of troops arrived but without arms, adequate supplies, or cash for their pay. De Meulles raised what money he could and when that was exhausted he released the soldiers to work on the land for wages. From this time on the curious practice of using regular troops as a civilian labour force, and the civilian militia for military operations, was to endure. Once the harvest was in, however, the habitants did not need this labour and de Meulles had to resort to another expedient to pay the troops. He deserves a good deal of credit for the imaginative and ingenious device that he now inaugurated: the issuing of the first paper money to circulate in North America. He took packs of playing cards,

of which there seems to have been a plentiful supply, and made money of them by writing an amount on the face, with his signature. He issued an ordinance declaring that the cards would be redeemed as soon as the ships arrived from France with the annual supply of funds; meanwhile they had to be accepted at face value. This paper money had greater success and a longer life than de Meulles could ever have anticipated. There was always a shortage of currency in the colony (beaver skins were much used in lieu of it), and the card money filled a real need. In the years that followed, no sooner was the card money redeemed than necessity, or convenience, caused it to be reissued. The colony thus had a unique but viable monetary system of its own; one that, on the whole, served it well.

While performing this useful service de Meulles sent detailed accounts of La Barre's Iroquois campaign to the minister, claiming that but for the governor's pusillanimity the enemy would have been crushed, blaming all the mishaps on La Barre, and claiming that the colony was all but lost. He was careful to add, however, that despite all this he was on the best of terms with the governor.

In the summer of 1685 La Barre's replacement as governor general, Jacques-René BRISAY de Denonville, arrived. He was a very different type of man from La Barre and he wasted no time making detailed plans to cope with the serious problems that beset the colony. Among other things, it was brought to his attention that de Meulles had been guilty of serious malversation. In one of his first dispatches to the minister he declared that the intendant was so greedy for personal gain that he was regarded with contempt by the people. He stood accused of selling fur-trading licences (*congés*) for 1,000 *livres* each, and Denonville found the king's stores in a state of total confusion. To stop the intendant trafficking in these goods Denonville had triple locks placed on the warehouse, requiring the attendance of himself, de Meulles, and the storekeeper before anything could be removed. When the governor had accumulated sufficient evidence against de Meulles he faced him with his charges and offered to say nothing to the minister provided the intendant would mend his ways. De Meulles, however, merely protested his complete innocence and showed no inclination to heed the governor's advice or warnings. Denonville therefore felt that he had no recourse but to give a detailed report to both the minister and the Marquis de Menars, an influential member of the Colbert clan and a close relative of de Meulles's wife.

While Denonville was writing these reports, a

task which he clearly found distasteful, de Meulles was on his way down the St Lawrence by bark to make a tour of Acadia. The minister had instructed him to report on the resources of the area and particularly on the possibility of establishing sedentary fishing stations, which would provide employment for the Canadians and a market for the colony's agricultural produce. De Meulles was away from Quebec from early October until the following September. Upon his return he received a rude shock—a curt dispatch from the king ordering him to return to France. On 23 September, he appeared at a meeting of the Conseil Souverain for the first time since his departure for Acadia, but only to preside over the meeting while the commission of his successor, Jean BOCHART de Champigny was registered. That done, he took his leave of the council, was escorted out of the chamber by two councillors in the usual manner, and shortly afterwards set sail for France.

When he subsequently sought an interview with the minister, he was refused. He was understandably bitter at this turn of events. He claimed that Denonville had grossly slandered him and would one day be brought to account for it. It is impossible to say with any certitude whether his plea was justified, but Denonville was a very scrupulous man, and no fool. He may have accepted false testimony and grossly misjudged de Meulles, but this does not seem likely. Yet the sisters of the Hôtel-Dieu wrote in their journal that de Meulles had been maligned and had discharged his responsibilities in an exemplary manner. Whether or not they were in a position to know all that had occurred is open to doubt. Certainly de Meulles in his criticism of La Barre had shown a marked lack of scruples, moderation and sagacity, although much of what he said had been justified. Had Denonville's accusations not been well substantiated, given de Meulles's close family connections with the minister, it is unlikely that they would have been entertained.

On the credit side of de Meulles's ledger stands the fact that he was intendant of New France during an extremely difficult period; and had to deal with a governor who was clearly incompetent, and a minister, Seignelay, who made no real attempt to understand, let alone deal with, Canadian problems until compelled to do so by the failure of La Barre to cope with the Iroquois threat. De Meulles did show considerable flexibility and originality in his response to some of these problems, particularly his employing the colonial regular troops as a labour force during an emergency, and his introduction of card money. In addition, it was he who was responsible for the acquisition by the crown of Jean Talon*'s derelict brewery, beginning its renovation and conversion into the Palais de Justice.

Back in France, he retired to Orléans, where he had purchased the post of chief magistrate, and there he appears to have remained until his death in May 1703.

W. J. ECCLES

AN, Col., B 8–11; C¹¹ᴬ, 6, 7; F³, 2, f.130. ASQ, Lettres, M, 62, 71. BN, MS, Clairambault 849, f.73; Fr. 22669, f.322. Caron, "Inventaire de documents," APQ *Rapport, 1939–40*, 247, 251, 261. *Coll. de manuscrits relatifs à la N.-F.*, I, 345. *Documents relating to Canadian currency during the French period* (Shortt), I. Juchereau, *Annales* (Jamet). *Jug. et délib.*, II. "Lettre de l'intendant de Meulles à M. Peuvret de Mesnu," *BRH*, XXXV (1929), 179. *Ord. comm.* (P.-G. Roy). Eccles, *Canada under Louis XIV*. Lanctot, *Histoire du Canada*, II.

MIATT. *See* MYATT

MILLET, PIERRE, priest, Jesuit, missionary; b. 19 Nov. 1635 at Bourges; d. 31 Dec. 1708 at Quebec.

Pierre Millet entered the noviciate of Paris on 3 Oct. 1655, and from 1659 to 1663 taught junior classes at La Flèche and Compiègne. He studied theology in Paris for four years and was ordained in 1668. He arrived at Quebec on 5 Aug. 1668. As Onondaga ambassadors had made a plea for missionaries, the newcomer was assigned to the Onondagas. He lived among them with Father Julien GARNIER, learned their language rapidly, and in 1671 made his profession at that mission. The following year he became a missionary to the Oneidas, an ill-tempered tribe. Millet's skill and pleasant disposition gained him the affection of his hosts, among whom he founded a Confrérie de la Sainte-Famille in 1676.

The Senecas had attacked the Illinois and killed several French traders at the end of February 1684. The Jesuit played a prominent role in the great Iroquois council, held a few months later, which considered means whereby the French might be appeased. He was sent as a representative, together with Father JACQUES DE LAMBERVILLE, to Governor Le Febvre* de La Barre, when the latter was going to Fort Frontenac (Cataracoui) on his way to punish the Senecas. He took part in the negotiations at Anse de La Famine (Mexico Bay, near Oswego), on 2 Sept. 1684.

Father Millet then resumed his ministry among the Oneidas, but he was recalled in 1685, with the majority of the missionaries to the Iroquois country, in anticipation of the expedition which had been prepared by BRISAY de Denonville against the Senecas. The governor entrusted to him the task of interpreter at the great council

Mille-Vaches

called for 1687 at Fort Frontenac. The 1687 expedition made it impossible for the missionaries to return to the Iroquois country. Millet had to remain at Fort Frontenac as chaplain until the spring of 1688, after which he went to Fort Niagara to replace Father JEAN DE LAMBERVILLE. On 15 September he had to leave again, because this post was being abandoned.

In June 1689, by a ruse, the Iroquois captured him at Fort Frontenac, along with the surgeon Pélerin de Saint-Amant. The prisoners were subjected to the usual ill treatment, and were taken as far as the island of Toniata (Grenadier Island, near Brockville), where a council of four of the Iroquois tribes was held. The Jesuit was handed over to the Oneidas, who took him into their country. Thanks to the good offices of certain Christian notables, Millet was finally adopted and was given the name of Odatsighta, to commemorate a founder of the Iroquois confederation. This favour conferred upon him a lofty rank in the councils. He was thus enabled to continue the ministry he had abandoned in 1685, but he was exposed to slander from the other tribes and from the English, who feared his influence. The Oneidas resisted these pressures and protected him. During this period Father Millet was in touch with Peter SCHUYLER of New York, and particularly with Godfrey Dellius, the pastor at Fort Orange (Albany, N.Y.).

As warfare persisted between the English and French, the Iroquois harassed the French colony. On several occasions, however, they made a show of desiring peace. In May 1694 a delegation from the Five Cantons came to see Buade* de Frontenac, requesting that negotiations be opened. The governor demanded the liberation of the prisoners. Thus, in October, the Jesuit returned to Quebec.

He first resided at the college, then in 1696 he assisted Joseph-Louis GERMAIN in his ministry at Lorette. The following year he acted as parish priest at the same place. Finally, we come across him again among the Iroquois at Sault-Saint-Louis (Caughnawaga), where from 1698 on he spent the last years of his active life. In 1704 he returned, a sick man, to the college in Quebec, where he lived for another four years.

LUCIEN CAMPEAU

ASJCF. Coll. de documents relatifs à la N.-F., I, 488, 571, 595; II, 59, 80, 87. NYCD (O'Callaghan and Fernow), III, IV, IX. Campbell, Pioneer priests, 246–61. Rochemonteix, Les Jésuites et la N.-F. au XVIIᵉ siècle, III, 185–200.

MILLE-VACHES. See AUBERT DE LA CHESNAYE, FRANÇOIS

MINGAN, JEAN-BAPTISTE JOLLIET DE. See JOLLIET

MISCOMOTE (Miscamote), a Maskegon Cree, son of Noah (captain of the Moose River Indians); d. 1721.

Miscomote is first mentioned as a Moose River Indian in the Albany account books for 1694. A few years later he must have decided to settle at Albany where he became captain of the Home Indians. He hunted for the factory and was hired by Governor BEALE as a look-out at Cockispenny Point to give warning of French raiders.

He had four children: one son of about 13 died 29 Nov. 1712 and was buried in English fashion in Albany graveyard. A little black dog was killed by Miscomote and laid on the coffin. Another son died 19 May 1713. Miscomote and his wife were pensioners on the factory from 1711 to 12 Sept. 1721 when Miscomote died, badly "afflicted with gout." He was interred near the fort "that he might be buried nigh the Englishmen." His wife was a pensioner until at least 1728–29. Miscomote's other children evidently had been killed or had died before 8 Oct. 1715 since there is a reference at that date to the fact that he had no children to support him.

Miscomote's career illustrates the mutual respect that developed between the company and some of the leading Indians, and the responsibility accepted by the company for the maintenance of faithful old servants.

G. E. THORMAN

HBC Arch. B.3/a/1–5, 9–10 (Albany journals between 1705 and 1722); B.3/d/2, 4–5, 7, 11, 13–15, 17–29, 32–33, 37 (Albany account books between 1693 and 1729).

MISCOUAKY (Miskouaky, also miscopied as **Misconky, Miscoualzy),** minor Ottawa chief at Detroit and then at Michilimackinac; sent to Montreal in 1706 to report on the Ottawa-Miami skirmishes at Detroit; fl. 1700–13.

Miscouaky and Mekaoua arrived at Montreal in June of 1700 as emissaries of the Ottawa elders. They had come to make amends for an Ottawa attack on an Iroquois hunting band. This blow and a Miami attack on the Senecas had violated a truce for negotiations arranged by Governor CALLIÈRE with the Iroquois. The Ottawa ambassadors pleaded ignorance of the negotiations and promised to surrender ten Iroquois captives from the band which, they said, had encroached on Ottawa hunting territory.

Miscouaky's second mission to Montreal in 1706 was infinitely more important. The peace established in 1701 between the Iroquois, the

French, and the western tribes was threatened by a feud that broke out among the French Indian allies. A clash between the Ottawas and Miamis brought the threat of intervention by the Iroquois, as a Miami ally, against the Ottawas. This would have destroyed the balance of forces created in 1701, and just when New France was threatened with attack by the English of New York.

The feud, according to Miscouaky and OUTOUTAGAN, and to CLAIRAMBAULT d'Aigremont, had several causes. The Miamis had never made reparation for seven Ottawas they had killed. The French authorities at Detroit had not reconciled their allies and, during Cadillac's [LAUMET] absence, the temporary commandant of Detroit, VÉNIARD de Bourgmond, had fatally injured an Ottawa who had struck the officer's dog. When the Ottawa warriors prepared to set out for war against the Sioux in June of 1706, they heard that the Miamis intended to massacre their women and children three days after their departure. Bourgmond gave the Ottawas no reassurance and merely increased their distrust of the French. Violence erupted when LE PESANT, who was paramount chief of the Ottawas, led his notorious preventive attack on the Miamis. The first victims were eight Miami chiefs encountered by chance. One of these escaped to warn his people, who took shelter in Fort Pontchartrain. There was a *mêlée* beneath the fort's walls, and a French soldier and the Recollet missionary, Constantin DELHALLE, were killed. In the series of raids, ambushes, and counter-attacks which followed, the Miamis were joined by the Hurons. The Ottawas retreated in mid-August to their other village at Michilimackinac, after losing 26 men. There, they received a pledge of support from most of the western tribes allied to the French before sending Miscouaky to Montreal.

In giving his account to Governor RIGAUD de Vaudreuil in September, Miscouaky dissociated himself and his "brother" Outoutagan from Le Pesant's initiative in attacking first. Miscouaky claimed to have aided the escape of the Miami chief who survived the original attack, and said that he alone had restrained the young men from shooting fire arrows into the French fort. Vaudreuil, since he had not yet received Cadillac's report on the affair, temporized. He refused Miscouaky's gifts, for "the blood of Frenchmen is not to be paid for by beaverskins." The Ottawas were advised to keep the peace, and the next June Outoutagan himself came to Montreal to hear Vaudreuil's decision. The death of the two Frenchmen had prevented the governor from acting as a disinterested conciliator of the warring tribes. Vaudreuil had to obtain a public submission by

the Ottawas to satisfy his honour and to appease the Miamis and Hurons. In order to retain all the French Indian allies, he rejected Cadillac's wish for a punitive war and exploited dissension among the Ottawa chiefs. What he demanded and received from the Ottawas in 1707 was the surrender of Le Pesant into French hands.

Miscouaky came on a third mission to Montreal in 1713, accompanied by two other Michilimackinac Ottawas. They requested the replacement of LE MARCHAND de Lignery and the return of LA PORTE de Louvigny as commandant at Michilimackinac. They also reported their losses in war against the Fox tribe, and presumably sought French support.

PETER N. MOOGK

AN, Col., C^{11A}, 18, pp.42–45; 24, pp.25–64, 243–50, 255–56 (copies in PAC). "Correspondance de Vaudreuil," APQ *Rapport, 1947–48,* 229. *Michigan Pioneer Coll.*, XXXIII, 273–74, 282, 288, 294–95, 299–301, 307, 313, 319–20, 323, 329. *NYCD* (O'Callaghan and Fernow), IX, 723, 780, 810. Wis. State Hist. Soc. *Coll.*, XVI, 238.

MOG (Heracouansit, Warracansit, Warracunsit, Warrawcuset), a noted warrior, subchief, and orator of the Norridgewock (Caniba) division of the Abenakis, son of Mog, an Abenaki chief killed in 1677; b. *c.* 1663, killed 12 Aug. 1724 (o.s.) at Norridgewock (Narantsouak; now Old Point in south Madison, Me.). In the La Chasse* census of 1708, Mog is listed under the name Heracouansit (in Abenaki, *welák^{w}ansit,* "one with small handsome heels").

During King William's and Queen Anne's Wars Mog took part in the numerous raids on English settlements by Abenakis and carried captives and scalps to Quebec. Following the peace of Utrecht in April 1713, Mog, Bomoseen, Moxus, Taxous, and other chiefs concluded a peace with New England at Portsmouth, N.H., on 11–13 July. The Abenakis pledged allegiance to Anne, though "it is safe to say that they did not know what the words meant" (Parkman). They also admitted the right of the English to land occupied before the war. The English, on their side, promised that the Indians could settle any individual grievances with them in English courts. Mog and the others then sailed with six New England commissioners to Casco Bay, where the treaty and terms of submission were read to 30 chiefs, in the presence of 400 other Abenakis, on 18 July. "Young Mogg" was described as "a man about 50 years, a likely Magestick lookt Man who spake all was Said." The Abenakis expressed surprise when told that the French had surrendered all the Abenaki lands to the English: "wee wonder how they would give

Mog

it away without asking us, God having at first placed us there and They having nothing to do to give it away." Father Sébastien RALE, the Jesuit missionary at Norridgewock, reported a month later that he had convinced the Indians the English were deceiving them with an ambiguous phrase, for England and France still disagreed about the limits of "Acadia." Apparently the Indians remained disturbed, however, when the English offered to show them the official text of the European treaty in the presence of their missionaries.

The New England government and settlers did not delay in advancing into coastal Maine and the lower Kennebec River, erecting forts to support their claims to Abenaki land. In a parley at Boston in January 1713/14, Mog and Bomoseen repeated their willingness to have the English resettle lands which they had formerly occupied. Another conference was held at Portsmouth on 23 July 1714, but Mog did not attend because he was sick. In August 1715 some Abenakis—including possibly Mog—vainly tried to prevent John Gyles* from constructing a new post, Fort George (now Brunswick, Me.), on the Androscoggin River. Two years later, at Georgetown on Arrowsic Island, WOWURNA repeated the Abenakis' fears for their land. At the same meeting Mog complained of dishonest trading, a leading cause of discontent, by Captain John Lane, the commander of Fort Mary (now Biddeford Pool). Governor Shute of Massachusetts promised them trading-posts, but the fur trade remained in the hands of unscrupulous official and private traders who defrauded the Indians and debauched them with rum. The elders of the tribe, Father Rale, and some English authorities made efforts to curb the liquor traffic, but in vain.

Although the governor had promised to respect the Abenakis' claims, more English settlements and forts were established on their lands. In the summer of 1716 the Abenakis sent a delegation to Quebec. Governor RIGAUD de Vaudreuil reported to Paris that the Abenaki orators—probably Mog and Wowurna—asked him whether they could count on the French, whom they had always aided in time of need, if force was needed to dislodge the English. By the terms of Utrecht he could not openly help them, but the governor promised arms, and when pressed by the delegates, the aid of French Indians. The Abenakis wanted a promise of troops, however, and retorted "with an ironical laugh" that they could expel, if they wished, all foreigners "be they who they may." The governor reassured them that he would lead them himself if necessary, and the Norridgewocks left apparently satisfied but unsure of his sincerity.

Their report agitated the entire Abenaki nation, more convinced than ever that they had been used as a cat's-paw by both alien peoples. The building of Fort Richmond (Richmond, Me.) in 1718 aggravated the situation further.

The Iroquois secretly solicited the embittered Abenakis to join them in a war against the French, and but for their Catholicism and the persuasiveness of Father Rale a pro-French party might have ceased to exist. An English party appeared for the first time at Norridgewock, including Bomoseen and Nagiscoig (Captain John), a younger brother of Wowurna. Mog formed with Wowurna and others a nativist and neutralist party. Still others, like Ouikouiroumenit, wanted peace at any price. Tension between the English and the Abenakis grew, for the situation of the Indians was deteriorating in several respects. The continuous warfare was ruining their agriculture and thinning out local game, while their access to fish and game on the coast was being hampered by the rapidly spreading English settlements. Moreover, their economy depended more and more on the fur trade with the English, and this too was faltering.

In November 1720 Mog and Wowurna led a delegation to Georgetown to protest the advance of settlement to Merry Meeting (Merrymeeting Bay, Me.), but were forced to promise payment of 200 skins and to send four hostages to Boston as security for damage done by young men of the tribe. After this, however, relations between the English and the Abenakis degenerated into small raids. Finally, in July 1722 Massachusetts declared war on the Indians, although there was opposition to this move both within the colony, and among the Connecticut English who held that "the War [was] not just on the English Side."

Weakened by war and disease, the Abenakis could muster fewer than 500 men, but they had Indian allies, including the Hurons of Lorette, Micmacs, Malecites, Ottawas, and the mission Iroquois of Canada, all encouraged by Vaudreuil. The governor of New France also sent secretly both arms and ammunition, although he could not get permission from Louis XV to send troops. The English attempted to enlist the aid of the Iroquois and Mahicans against the Abenakis, but these nations refused to be involved. In September 1722 the Norridgewocks, about 160 Hurons of Lorette, Canadian Abenakis, and other Indians formed a party of 400 which laid waste all the English settlements on the lower Kennebec. Scores of skirmishes kept the frontier aflame from eastern Maine to the Connecticut valley.

In October the Canadian Indians returned home, accompanied by some Norridgewocks who told Vaudreuil that they could not resist the

English without help. Most of them came to Canada for the winter, leaving only Rale and about 15 others to protect the village. Mog, Wowurna, and other chiefs again requested that Vaudreuil aid them with men. The Norridgewocks returned to the Kennebec in the spring and made minor raids until the summer of 1724.

One of the major engagements of the war was the English expedition against Norridgewock on 12 Aug. 1724. That afternoon the village was surprised by Captain Jeremiah Moulton, 100 English soldiers, and 3 Mohawk mercenaries, the leader of whom was named Christian. About 50 Abenaki warriors were in the village. When the alarm was given the Indians ran for their guns, fired wildly, and then followed the women and children in a rush for the river. Some drowned or were shot down in the water, but most escaped to the woods on the opposite shore. Mog and a few others remained behind with Rale. Mog was trapped in his wigwam with his family, and fired from within at one of the Mohawks. He did not kill the Iroquois, but the man's brother broke in, shooting Mog dead before he could reload his gun. At that moment some English soldiers ran in and killed his wife and two children. Their four scalps were taken with those of 22 other Abenakis and that of Father Rale to Boston, where the lot brought £505 in bounties.

FRANK T. SIEBERT, JR.

[Accounts of the Norridgewock campaign are greatly at variance. The counter-claims of Vaudreuil and Dummer are echoed by Charlevoix, Penhallow, and Thomas Hutchinson, the first historians of the incident. Although he tried to ascertain the truth by interviewing Moulton years later, Hutchinson left much unexplained and made a number of errors, including the statement that Mog killed one of the Mohawks. In the 19th century Williamson compared some of the earlier reports, and Baxter sharply criticized Charlevoix's account, but many contradictions remain unresolved. F.T.S.]
Newberry Library, Ayer Coll., La Chasse census (1708). Charlevoix, *Histoire*, II, 383. *Coll. de manuscrits relatifs à la N.-F.*, II, 562–64. *Documentary hist. of Maine*, IX, 340–42; X, 106–14, 215–16, 229–30, 244–45, 250–54, 292–96, 368; XXIII, 23–26, 30–31, 37–57, 64–80, 83–87, 89–93, 97–108, 110–46. *George Town on Arrowsick Island, a conference of His Excellency the governor with the sachems and chief men of the Eastern Indians, Aug. 9, 1717* (Boston, 1717). [John Gyles], *Memoirs of odd adventures . . .* (Boston, 1736), "Appendix." Hutchinson, *Hist. of Mass.-bay* (1768), 218–21, 241, 244–45, 261–63, 269, 294, 296, 302–3, 309–13. Maine Hist. Soc. *Coll.*, 1st ser., III (1853), 112, 361–75. *NYCD* (O'Callaghan and Fernow), IX, 878–81, 903–6, 909–12, 933–39. Penhallow, *Hist. of wars with Eastern Indians* (1726), 74–81, 83, 89–91, 94, 105. [Thomas Westbrook, *et al.*], *Letters of Colonel Thomas Westbrook and others relative to Indian affairs in Maine 1722–26*, ed. W. B. Trask (Boston, 1901), 76–77. *Lane genealogies*, comp. Jacob Chapman and J. H. Fitts (3v., Exeter, N.H., 1891–1902), I, 227–32. J. P. Baxter, *The pioneers of New France in New England, with contemporary letters and documents* (Albany, 1894), 341–46 [this work is valuable for the documents it contains, but they do not entirely support Baxter's conclusions. F.T.S.]. Frederick Kidder, *The Abenaki Indians; their treaties of 1713 and 1717 . . .* (Portland, 1859), 19–28. Parkman, *A half-century of conflict* (1893), I, 213.

MOIREAU (Moreau), CLAUDE, Recollet, missionary in Canada and in Acadia; b. *c.* 1637; d. 14 Oct. 1703 at Nemours (department of Seine-et-Marne).

Moireau made his religious profession in 1654 and arrived on 10 Sept. 1671 at Quebec, with the second group of Recollets who came to Canada after the re-establishment of that order. A few months after his arrival he was appointed to Trois-Rivières, where he discharged the duties of a parish priest for three years. There he became acquainted with the family of MICHEL LENEUF de La Vallière senior, whom he was to meet again at Beaubassin (Chignecto) some years later. He also visited a number of posts on the south shore, among them Nicolet.

He was appointed a missionary in Acadia in 1675, and stayed there until 1686. When he arrived, Acadia had only one other missionary, Abbé PETIT, who was at that time parish priest of Port-Royal (Annapolis Royal, N.S.), and very old. Father Moireau therefore had to minister to the whole of what is now New Brunswick and the northern part of Nova Scotia, from the Saint John River to the Minas Basin. His mission register, which is preserved at the archbishopric of Quebec, indicates the stages in his journeyings. He visited the French settlers and the Indians on the Saint John River, from Menagouesche to Médoctec. He stopped off at Jemseg, which at that period enjoyed a certain importance, because of its fort and a small garrison commanded by Pierre de Joybert* de Soulanges. There Father Moireau baptized several Indians and Marie-Anne Denys, daughter of Richard Denys* and his first wife Anne Parabego (Partarabego). He also visited Les Mines (Grand Pré, N.S.), and went as far as Gaspé, when in 1680 he replaced Father Chrestien Le Clercq*. In this work of evangelization among the Micmacs he utilized the symbolic characters invented by Le Clercq.

Between his journeys he lived usually at Beaubassin, of which he became the first resident parish priest. On 2 Sept. 1678 the local seigneur, Michel Leneuf de La Vallière, made over to the

Mombeton de Brouillan

Recollets a piece of land with a frontage of 6 *arpents* on the river "Brouillée," so that a chapel and a residence could be built. Father Moireau had a small church erected there, dedicated to Notre-Dame de Bonsecours. Bishop Saint-Vallier [LA CROIX] visited this modest church in 1686, and said that it was made "of cob surrounded with stone" and had a thatched roof. But by that time Father Moireau was no longer living there; he had been recalled to Quebec to become the superior of his community.

Father Moireau then served at Cap Saint-Ignace and L'Islet from 1686 to 1688. In 1690 he was also at Pointe-aux-Trembles and Cap-Santé. Subsequently he returned to France, and died in 1703 at Nemours.

RENÉ BAUDRY

AAQ, Registres d'insinuation A (Acadie), 1678–86 (copies in PAC, FM 16, B 2, 1, and Archives de l'université de Moncton). Archives des Yvelines (Versailles), H 57. BN, MS, Fr. 13875. Le Clercq, *New relation of Gaspesia* (Ganong), 132, 150, 314. Le Tac, *Histoire chronologique de la N.-F.* (Reveillaud), incorrectly locates the concession given the Recollets by La Vallière at Percé. Tanguay, *Répertoire du clergé*, 60. Jouve, *Les Franciscains et le Canada: aux Trois-Rivières*, 21–24, 28, 302. Ganong, "Historic sites in New Brunswick," 315.

MOMBETON DE BROUILLAN, JACQUES-FRANÇOIS DE, governor of Placentia (Plaisance) and of Acadia, knight of the order of Saint-Louis; b. 1651; d. 22 Sept. 1705 at Chedabouctou (Guysborough, N.S).

Brouillan belonged to a family of Protestant noblemen named Mombeton that came from Gascony. His grandfather married Isabeau de Brouillan, the last to inherit this title, and took the name, which their descendants also bore. Jacques-François was the son of Jacques de Mombeton de Brouillan and Georgette Pouy. He was sometimes given the surname Saint-André. Seven of his brothers died in battle. He himself joined the colonial regular troops, was made captain then adjutant, and received several wounds from which he suffered all his life.

Brouillan came to Canada in 1687, as captain of a company. He had previously been a Protestant, but was baptized at Quebec. He returned to France in 1689 at the same time as BRISAY de Denonville, who recommended him strongly. On 1 June of that year he was appointed governor of Placentia with a salary of 1,200 *livres*. Several untoward events delayed his departure; he did not receive his orders until 1 Feb. 1691, and he left in the spring on a king's ship, the *Joly*. The French settlements in Newfoundland were at that time in a deplorable

state, and the minister of Marine had decided to make an attempt to reorganize the colony.

Brouillan arrived at the beginning of the summer of 1691 with supplies and munitions, a contingent of 23 soldiers, and 25 fisher lads. He completed a stockade already begun by Louis Pastour, and set up batteries, using the cannon fished up from the bay. These preparations had not been finished before a small English ship attempted to surprise the settlers. Brouillan spent the winter completing his defences and began the construction of a new fort. These were wise precautions, for the following year Placentia was subjected to a more serious attack. In September a squadron of five ships, commanded by Commodore Francis Gillam (Williams), appeared before the fort. The garrison still comprised only 50 men, but the governor obtained the help of the captains of the fishing boats and of 120 members of their crews. A frigate, with Lahontan [LOM D'ARCE] aboard, had also just arrived from Quebec. The governor had a redoubt built on the top of an adjoining hill, and set up a battery at the entry to the port. After due notice and an exchange of envoys, Brouillan gave orders to open fire. The attackers fired 2,000 shots, without doing much harm. The besieged, who were short of powder and cannon-balls, could fire only 300, but their well-aimed fire seriously damaged the enemy flagship. The attackers weighed anchor and went to burn the buildings at Pointe Verte (Point Verde). Lahontan hastened to carry the news of this success to the court.

The winter of 1692–93 was long and arduous. The supply ship had been shipwrecked. In the month of February several settlers were totally without food, and the governor had to have searches made in order to unearth hidden provisions and succour those most in need. The king expressed great satisfaction with the governor's activity, and granted him a gratuity of 500 *livres*. The court also sent Lahontan back as king's lieutenant. The governor disapproved of this promotion; he accused Lahontan of having intrigued to obtain it, and thought that Lahontan wanted to replace him; consequently a sharp rivalry sprang up between the two men.

During the summer of 1693 the governor completed the town's defensive system; he added to the fort's batteries, rebuilt the mountain redoubt in stone, and constructed retrenchments along the shore. These preparations proved useful, for on 28 August an English fleet of 24 ships, serving under Sir Francis Wheler, cast anchor in the bay. Brouillan again had the entry to the fort blocked off and had cannons hauled up to the mountain redoubt; the next day he opened fire on the fleet.

As the ships were preparing to force their way in, he had a fly-boat sunk in the middle of the channel and placed a row of merchant ships there. The timely outbreak of a storm drove the enemy ships between the cannon of the fort and the reef. After being under fire for four hours, the admiral deemed it more prudent to weigh anchor. A detachment went to burn down the establishments on the island of Saint-Pierre and captured two merchant ships.

The following years brought a respite, during which the colony was able to breathe a little and regain its strength. The population remained more or less stable. The censuses of that period list some 50 resident families, including about 150 persons. The garrison, increased to 60 soldiers, received 40 more in 1694; the two companies thus formed were commanded by Saint-Ovide de Brouillan [Mombeton*] and Philippe Pastour de Coste-belle. An engineer, Jacques L'Hermitte, arrived in 1695.

Since 1692 Brouillan had been recommending to the court the organization of a naval expedition against St John's. Two attempts, those of Digoine in 1692 and Saint-Clair in 1694, had failed. The governor, who went to France in the autumn of 1695, took up his idea again. Furthermore, Pierre Le Moyne d'Iberville also put forward a plan of attack by land. The court decided to combine the two operations, but a regrettable animosity between Brouillan and Iberville prevented the plan of campaign from being carried out exactly. The orders provided that Brouillan should look after the general conduct of the operations and should direct the expedition at sea and that Iberville should command the expedition by land. Brouillan received a frigate, and a privateer from St Malo gave him the use of four merchant vessels fitted out for war, with two corvettes and two fire-ships. The governor therefore had under his command some 10 ships and 300 or 400 men.

At the beginning of September, as Iberville, who was detained at Pemaquid, had not yet appeared, Brouillan decided to try his hand alone. He left Placentia on the ninth, took first Bay Bulls (Baie des Taureaux) then Ferryland (Forillon), and occupied Firmoose (Fermeuse), whose inhabitants had taken to the woods. He set up his base at Renews (Renoose) but did not succeed in taking possession of St John's. The site of the town was defended by three forts, and warships rode at anchor in the harbour. Brouillan tried to force his way in, but bad weather intervened, and the sailors from St Malo decided not to risk their ships. Brouillan blamed them for his failure and had some of them court-martialed. This severity did

not help at all. He consoled himself by taking some 30 fishing barks and boats, a number of prisoners, and several thousand codfish. He returned to Placentia on 17 October, with the intention of making up for his defeat by a winter campaign.

The negotiations between Iberville and Brouillan gave rise to bitter arguments. The disagreement concerned at one and the same time the leadership of the undertaking, the plan of campaign, and the sharing of the booty. In this dispute Brouillan displayed a great deal of harshness and gave expression to inadmissible demands. Finally, Iberville agreed to attack St John's rather than Carbonear, and the governor gave up the leadership of the expedition to Iberville. During this campaign Brouillan fought bravely, but neither he nor his soldiers, whom the Canadians ironically called "the jokers from Placentia" ["Messieurs les Plaisantins"], played the leading part. The campaign was nevertheless completely successful. After defeating a party of enemy scouts, the troops overcame 80 men concealed behind some rocks, and took the advanced posts. They were preparing for an assault on the principal fort of St John's by burning down the surrounding houses, when the commandant decided to surrender, on condition that he be granted two vessels to make his way to England. The fort was burned to the ground, and Brouillan returned to Placentia by sea, while Iberville was continuing his campaign against the other Newfoundland posts.

Brouillan went to France the following summer, and Joseph de Monic commanded in his absence. As the treaty of Ryswick soon brought peace, he took advantage of this to prolong his stay and take care of his health. He also attended to his interests: he received a gratuity of 500 *livres*, acquired for himself the cross of Saint-Louis, and obtained the reimbursement of 16,000 *livres* advanced during the St John's campaign. During the four years that he spent in France, Brouillan kept the title of governor and drew the salary that went with it. He continued to correspond with the minister and with Placentia, but did not forget his own affairs, recruiting Basque fishermen and employing seven fishing shallops in Newfoundland.

As Robinau* de Villebon's death in July 1700 left the government of Acadia vacant, the king appointed Brouillan to this command on 28 March 1701. This appointment represented a promotion for him, for his salary increased to 4,000 *livres*. It did not, however, give him the title of governor, but only that of commandant, to mark the subordination of Acadia to the governor of Quebec. In possession of a supplementary gratuity of 500 *livres*, Brouillan set out at the beginning of

Mombeton de Brouillan

May with a contingent of 40 soldiers and munitions of war. Contrary winds forced his ship to put in at Chibouctou (Halifax, N.S.), so Brouillan took the opportunity to visit this fort, which delighted him. He then decided to go to Port-Royal (Annapolis Royal, N.S.) by land, proceeding via Les Mines (Grand Pré). He admired the prosperity of this village, but felt little sympathy for the independent spirit of its inhabitants, whom he described as "true republicans." He persuaded them to open up a route towards Port-Royal, in order to help the capital in case of an attack. A war was indeed expected soon. Neither the minister nor the governor wanted it, for they were well aware of the colony's weakness. Hence the king had enjoined Brouillan to maintain peace and to do nothing to provoke hostile acts on the part of the Indians.

As soon as he reached Port-Royal, Brouillan called a meeting of the inhabitants, but he found them as intractable as those of Les Mines. However, he managed to obtain their cooperation for the building of a fort. He then left for the Saint John River, where he judged the fort to be useless and badly sited. He therefore had it pulled down, and shipped the materials to Port Royal on the *Gironde*. During the autumn he had a temporary *enceinte* constructed, with a sunken road round it. Inside the *enceinte* he also built living quarters for the soldiers, and he organized the settlers into a militia company. That same autumn he sent to the court a long report, a sort of programme in which he set forth his ideas on the problems of the colony. Its chief resources consisted of wood and fish. The shipping of masts, which had been begun in 1701, could supply cargo for a number of vessels. Fishing might well become the country's principal industry, but it had been completely ruined by 50 years of war and privateering. The settlers no longer possessed barks or riggings; they were discouraged, and no longer even knew how to fish. Brouillan offered to build barks, asked for rope to make nets with, and suggested bringing in fishermen from Placentia to initiate the Acadians in the art of fishing. Above all, one or two frigates were needed to cruise along the shores, in order to protect the fishermen. Taking up the proposals of Razilly*, Brouillan suggested establishing a powerful fort at La Hève (Lahave), which would become the chief post in the country. It would serve as a fishing port, but also as a naval base for relations with France, and it could intercept communications between England and her colonies. The settlers were strongly opposed to trade monopolies. Moreover the court, at this time, had already decided not to renew the privileges of the Compagnie de la Pêche Sédentaire de l'Acadie,

and to make trading free. Brouillan also asked for the title of governor, and obtained it in February 1702.

The War of the Spanish Succession broke out on 15 May 1702. This war, however, despite some sudden alarms and the capture of several supply ships by English privateers, did not result in an immediate attack on Port-Royal. The delay gave the governor time to complete the fortification. The minister had approved the plans of a new fort, partly in stone and partly in earthworks, and had authorized an annual grant of 20,000 *livres*. He also sent masons and carpenters, as well as an engineer named Labat. During this intermediary period the notables of Port-Royal, following their detestable custom, devoted their spare time to hearty squabbling. The first skirmish took place between the governor and the parish priest, Abbé Abel Maudoux*, over a public market and the relocation of the church. In a second dispute Labat and Brouillan were at odds concerning the plans of the fort and the direction of the construction work. Finally Mathieu de GOUTIN, that incorrigible haggler, who was at one and the same time a writer, a judge, and a commissary of the Marine, was in daily conflict with the governor over the way justice was being administered and money was being used. Despite this wrangling the fortifications advanced, and in 1704 were almost completed. The garrison was then composed of 200 soldiers divided into four companies, and the settlers formed six militia companies. The governor had had a lime-kiln, a mill, barks, and a frigate constructed.

At the first threat of war, the practice of making annual gifts to the Indians had been revived. Despite the absence of JEAN-VINCENT D'ABBADIE de Saint-Castin, who was then in France, the Abenakis of Pentagouet (on the Penobscot River) remained loyal; but those on the Kennebec River let themselves be won over by their New England neighbours. In order to restore French prestige, the governor of Canada, RIGAUD de Vaudreuil, launched several expeditions which ravaged the villages between Casco and Wells and sacked Deerfield [*see* Rev. John WILLIAMS]. By way of reprisal the governor of Boston, Joseph Dudley, organized a naval expedition, and as always this expedition proceeded in the direction of Acadia, the nearest and most vulnerable part of New France. It was made up of 3 warships and some 15 transports, manned by 550 militiamen. The commander, Benjamin CHURCH, had already directed a similar expedition and ravaged Beaubassin, eight years before. The fleet set out from Boston at the end of May 1704, sailed along the coast, and destroyed the French settlements in the

480

Mombeton de Brouillan

neighbourhood of Passamaquody Bay and Penta-gouet. After taking some prisoners, among them a daughter of Saint-Castin, the Bostonians headed for Port-Royal. The French and English accounts (the latter by Church) present different versions of the events that followed. According to French sources, the English entered the basin on 2 July, burned down a few isolated houses, killed some cattle, and captured a number of settlers. On 8 July a party went to ravage Les Mines. The settlers put up some resistance, killing some men as the latter landed, and then taking to the woods with their cattle. The enemy burned down the houses and broke the dikes, thus flooding the land under cultivation. Another party went to Beau-bassin, where it burned some 20 houses. Meanwhile the main body of the fleet, which had stayed at Port-Royal, attempted some landing operations. But Brouillan had sent parties of soldiers, settlers, and Indians to maintain firing along the banks. Church, after 18 days of waiting, unsure of his militiamen, and having no precise orders to attack Port-Royal, called a council of war, which decided on returning to Boston. Port-Royal therefore got off lightly, but the ravaged colony suffered from famine the following winter.

Just before the siege Brouillan had obtained permission to go to France. Several reasons impelled him to do so. First his health: he was afflicted with gout, and a fragment of broken bone, the result of old wounds, protruded from his cheek. He also wanted to make known the state of the colony and to obtain reinforcements of men, equipment, and ships. But a more pressing motive required his presence at court. His authoritarianism and corrupt practices had provoked a host of complaints against him: he was taxed with having employed workmen from the fort on personal tasks, having seized a settler's land in order to set up a menagerie on it, and having melted silver coinage to make plates and dishes; with carrying on trade through intermediaries and selling at excessive prices, protecting a liaison between SIMON-PIERRE DENYS de Bonaventure and Madame de Freneuse [Louise Guyon*], and himself keeping Madame Barrat [see Claude BARRAT]. Denunciations rained down so thick and fast that the minister began to show his disapproval. Among other excesses, the governor had subjected to torture three soldiers accused of stealing, by having matches burned between their fingers. One of them, who had remained crippled and had subsequently been acknowledged innocent, had gone to show the court his mutilated hands, and the king, "horrified at this cruelty," had sentenced Brouillan to allot half pay to this soldier out of his own salary. Brouillan, whose three-year term had just expired, felt it necessary to go and avert the thunderbolt which threatened to strike him.

After using a part of the winter to look after his health, Brouillan spent three months in Paris and Versailles. He succeeded in clearing himself of several charges, but the minister, not content with giving him rules of personal conduct, had delivered to him a statement signed by the king which contained precise instructions on several contentious points. However, despite the rebukes that he probably deserved, Brouillan's prestige remained quite high at court. His oft-displayed valour, his energy, his success in repelling enemy attacks, had acquired for him the reputation of a brave soldier, on whom one could rely in this time of war. Provided with good recommendations, Brouillan therefore set out again, after obtaining a ship and reinforcements of men and munitions.

But he was not to have the chance to utilize them. Still sick, he had had to delay his sailing several times. He finally sailed on the *Profond*, but had to go ashore at Chedabouctou, where he died on 22 Sept. 1705. His body was committed to the sea, like that of a sailor, and his heart was taken to Port-Royal, where Bonaventure, the acting commandant, had it buried near the cross on the cape. A few months later de Goutin wrote, by way of a funeral oration, that the country deemed itself well rid of a tyrant. This hasty judgement reveals the surly character of Goutin more than it expresses reality. In fact, despite his defects and his undeniable corruption, Brouillan, both at Placentia and at Port-Royal, proved himself a very effective governor. He organized the defence of these two posts and supported them courageously. He displayed remarkable activity in several fields, and was original enough to seek to promote the economic growth of Acadia by developing the fisheries, exploiting the forests, and building ships. No doubt he often confused his personal interests and those of the king; no doubt he showed himself to be ambitious, authoritarian, and excessively hard towards his subordinates. But his irritability is explicable by his bad health, and there is no denying his bravery, or his devotion to the king's service.

RENÉ BAUDRY

AN, Col., B, 15–17; C¹¹ᴬ, 22; C¹¹ᶜ, 1–2; C¹¹ᴰ, 3–5; F³, 7, 54; Marine, B³, 70, f.146. BN, MS, Clairambault 1306, f.218 *bis. Acadiensia Nova* (Morse), II, 1–5. Charlevoix, *History* (Shea), IV, 223, 275; V, 34ff., 157, 170–72. *Coll. de manuscrits relatifs à la N.-F.*, II, 37–38, 332–34, 416ff. *Journal de l'abbé Beaudoin* (Gosselin). Lahontan, *New voyages* (Thwaites), letters XXIII, XXV. Bernard, *Le drame acadien*, 212–26. J.-M. Cazauran, *La baronie de Bourrouillan* (Paris, 1887). Frégault, *Iberville*, 209–35. La Morandière,

481

Monceaux

Hist. de la pêche française de la morue, I, 445–83. Le Blant, *Philippe de Pastour de Costebelle*, 70–71. Parkman, *A half-century of conflict* (1893), 116–20. Rameau de Saint-Père, *Une colonie féodale*, I, 310–13; II, 307–10. Robert Rumilly, *Histoire des Acadiens* (2v., Montréal, [1955]), I, 159–72. J.-E. Roy, "Le baron de Lahontan," *RSCT*, 1st ser., XII (1894), sect.I, 63–192.

MONCEAUX,   FRANÇOIS - MADELEINE - FORTUNÉ DE RUETTE D'AUTEUIL ET DE. *See* RUETTE

MONCOURS (Moncourt), PIERRE HERTEL DE. *See* HERTEL

MONIC, JOSEPH DE, military officer and administrator, acting governor of Placentia (Plaisance), 1697–1702; b. probably in the 1650s, the son of Jean de Monic and Marguerite de Cornet, of Oloron in Béarn; married 13 Dec. 1691 at Quebec, Jeanne Dufresnoy Carion; d. 17 Oct. 1707, at Bayonne.

Before coming to Canada in 1687 as a captain in the colonial regular troops, Monic had held a commission in the regular armies, having served in Flanders, Germany, and Lorraine as a subaltern in the Régiment de Champagne since 1675 and having been promoted captain in 1686. Three years after his arrival in the colony, he took part in the defence of Quebec against Phips*. In March 1691, because of his experience and conduct, he became garrison adjutant at Quebec; and in December of the same year married the widow of the illustrious Jacques Le Moyne* de Sainte-Hélène. Having gone to France in 1693, he was allowed to remain there to take the waters for his health and to attend to personal affairs, and eventually was posted to duty at the port of Rochefort. In 1697 he was attached to Placentia as interim commandant in the absence of the governor, Jacques-François de Brouillan [MOMBETON]. This responsibility continued until 1702 (although Monic was permitted to spend some of his winters in France) and for all concerned these were five stormy years.

Arrogant and hot-tempered, Monic insisted a great deal on the recognition of his position, perhaps because his authority in the colony was temporary. Had he worked in greater harmony with his staff, he might have been accorded the title and prestige of the position as well as its responsibilities; Pontchartrain indicated on more than one occasion that he was high on the list to succeed Brouillan. But when the time came to appoint a successor, the choice fell on AUGER de Subercase, who had replaced Monic at Quebec; and it did so largely because of the events of 1700 and 1701.

In spite of reports from other officers reflecting on his honesty, Monic had headed the list in 1699 of possible candidates for the governorship. By 1700, however, the hardships which were part of life at Placentia were aggravated by personal friction between the commandant and his senior lieutenants, and echoes of their quarrels reached Versailles. PASTOUR de Costebelle, wrote Monic, had no sense of service or any regular military background; and it was intolerable that such a low-born person as L'HERMITTE had risen to a position of authority. For his part, Costebelle accused Monic of harsh treatment; so did Joseph de Saint-Ovide de Brouillan [Mombeton*], DURAND de La Garenne, and L'Hermitte—all of whom the commandant had imprisoned for weeks at a time. Monic's attempts to alleviate food shortages by buying emergency rations from the Huguenot, Faneuil of Boston (the father or uncle of Peter), were construed by his fellow officers as illicit trade for personal gain although Monic's motives may have been a mixture of altruism, good management, and personal profit. Since few officers were innocent of seeking to augment their incomes through trade, Pontchartrain was inclined to be lenient on that score, but he had already warned Monic that unless he treated his subordinates fairly, Placentia would be his last command. Privately he blamed Monic more than the others for the quarrels, although officially he reprimanded the subordinates for their conduct. No doubt the minister felt that temperament and insubordination were interfering with effective handling of such problems as rapid construction and repair of fortifications, ensuring adequate defence of the colony during this construction, financing a hospital, increasing the number of missionaries, recruiting tradesmen for the garrison's companies, rotating personnel between Canada and Newfoundland, equitably assigning to residents shore space for drying fish, preventing the English from hunting at Trinity and trading at Placentia, controlling the cabarets, and checking the profiteering which officers carried on at their men's expense.

By March of 1702 Pontchartrain decided to recall Monic. Early in 1703 the latter returned to France where, after a visit to Bayonne, he went back to serve at Rochefort. He was made a knight of the order of Saint-Louis on 9 May 1707 and died at Bayonne on 17 October of the same year.

F. J. THORPE

[Le Blant (p.88), citing BN, MS, NAF 9277 (Margry), f.88, states that Monic's marriage took place on

13 Oct. 1691. This is impossible if the marriage contract was signed on 12 Dec. 1691 (AJM, Greffe d'Antoine Adhémar). The marriage probably took place on 13 Dec. 1691. F.J.T.]

AJM, Greffe d'Antoine Adhémar, 12 déc. 1691, 31 mai 1692; Greffe de Bénigne Basset, 1er déc. 1692, 14 juillet 1695. AN, Col., B, 16, f.26; 17, f.64; 19, ff.158v, 162v; 20, ff.115v, 156, 172v, 176v, 190v; 22, ff.65, 133v, 187v, 198, 211v, 220, 221; 23, ff.31v, 129, 161, 163, 165, 172v, 178v, 184v, 293, 295v, 302v; 27, f.334v; C11C, 2, ff.156, 160; 3, ff.3, 16, 24, 39, 69, 152, 172, 216, 227, 264, 268, 291; D2C, 47 (1692, 1693, 1694, 1699); 222; F3, 4, f.343; Marine, C7, 213, ff.1, 2. P.-G. et A. Roy, *Inv. greffes not.*, I, 301, 309; V, 150, 160, 174. La Morandière, *Hist. de la pêche française de la morue*. Le Blant, *Philippe de Pastour de Costebelle*.

MONSEIGNAT, CHARLES DE (Monseignac), manager for Robert Cavelier* de La Salle, clerk and deputy director of the king's domain (1681–82), first secretary of Governor Louis de Buade* de Frontenac, comptroller of the navy and fortifications in New France (1701–18), secretary councillor and chief clerk of the Conseil Supérieur (1705–18), resident agent and director for the tax farmers of the Domaine d'Occident (1707–18); b. c. 1652, son of Jean de Monseignat and Hélène Perchot of the parish of Saint-Jacques-la-Boucherie in Paris; m. 28 Sept. 1693 at Quebec Claude de Sainte (d. 1702) by whom he had seven children; m. 23 Feb. 1704 Marguerite Delesnerac; buried 21 Oct. 1718 in the crypt of Notre-Dame de Québec.

Charles de Monseignat's career was full of the chicanery that characterized the civil service of Louis XIV. His experience in financial and legal matters was gained in the Chambre des Comptes at Paris. He also served with several public and private financial agencies before coming to Canada with La Salle as the explorer's business manager. His primary responsibility was to hold off La Salle's creditors and he frequently had to appear in court to delay the seizure of his employer's property for debt. After two trying years in La Salle's service, he sought work elsewhere.

In 1681 Monseignat was at Quebec working as a clerk in the office of Josias Boisseau*, the turbulent agent general of the tax farmers of the king's domain. He was a deputy director in the same office the following year. Since La Salle and Boisseau were protégés of Frontenac, it is likely that he came to the governor's attention while in their employ.

Monseignat returned to France soon after Frontenac was recalled from the colony in 1682. While there he served in a variety of offices, ranging from camp commissary to deputy director of a military hospital. He was employed as an auditor in the head office of the tax farms at Paris when Frontenac, reinstated as governor, invited him to return to Canada as his secretary.

During Frontenac's second administration (1689–98), Monseignat and the junior secretary, Barthélemy-François Bourgonnière de Hauteville, handled his entire correspondence. Monseignat also acted as Frontenac's publicity agent, writing the celebrated "Account of the most remarkable occurrences in Canada" which credited the deliverance of New France from her enemies in 1689–90 to the governor. This stirring chronicle was highly successful; it was reprinted in CLAUDE-CHARLES LE ROY de La Potherie's *Histoire de l'Amérique septentrionale* and has been the source for most accounts of the defeat of Phips*. Monseignat composed it in the form of a private letter and it has been suggested that the Marquise de Maintenon was the recipient. Since the first secretary had written other chronicles for Frontenac's wife, it is more likely that this account was intended for the use of the Comtesse de Frontenac, her husband's advocate at the court of France. Later, when the king and Pontchartrain began to take a disturbing interest in Frontenac's conduct, Monseignat was selected in 1696 to carry to Versailles a glowing eye-witness description of the governor's campaign against the Oneidas and Onondagas.

Frontenac repaid Monseignat for his services by granting him certain favours. On 24 Oct. 1694, the Intendant Jean BOCHART de Champigny wrote to the minister of Marine that "M. de Frontenac's secretary obtains large profits from the permits granted for trade with the Ottawas . . . otherwise, he has always seemed an honourable enough man to me." It appears, however, that the governor was unable to influence the minister on his secretary's behalf. In 1692 Monseignat twice petitioned for a gratuity but apparently with no success. In 1696 he was recommended by Frontenac for a naval commissary's commission without salary. The minister replied with a polite refusal—"His Majesty wishing not to create new naval commissaries nor to appoint persons who have not passed through the ranks." In the light of future events, this reply was full of irony.

In their dispatch of 20 Oct. 1699, CALLIÈRE and Champigny reported that "Monsieur de Frontenac, just before his death, recommended to the Sieur de Champigny the Sieur de Monseignat, who had served as his secretary for ten years and with whom he was pleased. There is no vacant post here that would suit him." From this statement one can speculate that Monseignat was too

Monseignat

closely associated with the deceased governor to find favour in the eyes of his successors.

In the will drawn up just before his death in November 1698, Frontenac had selected Monseignat and a mutual friend, FRANÇOIS HAZEUR, as his executors. There now remained little for Monseignat to do in New France other than to wind up the governor's estate. This done, he and his son departed for France, followed in 1700 by his wife and daughter. Like a stone thrown at his heels, a case was initiated in the Montreal court by NICOLAS PERROT against Monseignat for alleged misuse of a fur-trading licence.

Monseignat's search for a new appointment took over a year but the result was gratifying. By letters of provision granted on 1 June 1701, he was named comptroller of the navy and fortifications in New France. The comptroller was the senior financial official in the colony under the intendant. His duties were "to keep a register of revenues and expenditures for the Marine and fortifications in Canada, to sign contracts and acknowledgements for work done, to verify contractors' receipts; and to perform those other functions of a comptroller in the same manner as those naval comptrollers established in our ports and arsenals in France." The new post carried a yearly salary of 1,000 *livres*. Monseignat hastened back to Canada in that same year, accompanied by François CLAIRAMBAULT d'Aigremont, the new naval commissary.

Monseignat's enjoyment of his new post was brief. Like Job in his tribulations, Monseignat learned that the king gave and the king took away. He was informed by the minister's dispatch of 10 May 1702 that "the king has created 100 posts of commissary of the navy and galleys which must be purchased at 30,000 *livres* apiece [in return] for a salary of 2,000 *livres* and 1,000 *livres* in the exercise of one's duties, with the prerogatives listed in the edict that M. de Beauharnois [François*] will show you. Since these commissaries have to perform the functions of comptroller, your office will be abolished and you will not be retained in it if you do not buy one of these posts. Therefore, take the necessary steps to find the required sum and let me know what you can do by the first ships available because I shall be obliged to make the appointment next year." As if this were not enough trouble, Monseignat's wife died a few months later.

Purchased offices were exceptional in New France but the king's need for money took precedence over custom. It was little comfort to Monseignat that his *confrère*, d'Aigremont, had received a similar letter. This ultimatum was, as one contemporary statement expressed it, "a most

distressing extremity" for Monseignat. "He has," the governor and intendant said, "few possessions, a large family, and he has just been bankrupted of his liquid assets. He hopes ... that His Majesty will kindly retain him in his post without converting it into a [venal] office or, at least, reduce for his benefit the price at which they are set."

Monseignat was retained as acting comptroller at half pay and, by way of compensation, he was appointed to the Conseil Supérieur on 1 June 1703. The minister represented this as a great favour. He informed Monseignat that his majesty "is thus consenting to let you keep by means of these two posts the same salary that you had as comptroller." In truth, the combined salaries were 200 *livres* short of his former income.

Monseignat could not leave well enough alone. His next request noted that the minister was not too accurate in his addition and, in the same breath, asked that he grant him "the post of clerk which pays 500 *livres* so that his emoluments might equal those that he had."

The minister was most obliging; he appointed Monseignat chief clerk of the Conseil Supérieur on 1 June 1704. The catch, intentional or not, was that the commission for this post was worded in such a way as to deny Monseignat the formal title of secretary councillor and chief clerk. On top of this, he could not be paid for this position until his installation on 1 Dec. 1705 and, because he had had no official orders to carry on as acting comptroller, he had received nothing for his services in that capacity since 1703. How he survived is a mystery; one suspects that he enjoyed the private charity of someone like Philippe de RIGAUD de Vaudreuil. The senior officials of the colony, in their dispatch of 19 Oct. 1705, asked on Monseignat's behalf for an amended clerk's commission "identical to those of his predecessors" and for permission to let him draw the comptroller's salary for the years 1704 and 1705 since he had not been paid for those years. JACQUES RAUDOT suggested that the orders to serve as acting comptroller be sweetened with the commission of *écrivain du Roi* with pay.

At this point the minister of Marine hesitated to let Monseignat go on accumulating functions like burs. Raudot's proposal was turned down. Monseignat received an amended commission as chief clerk in 1707 with a note from the minister which read as follows: "I am also sending you an order to perform the comptroller's duties, but I have not promised to give you a salary for that office since you have been clerk of the Conseil Supérieur, because the comptroller's office was given only to do you honour in Canada." A second letter from the minister rejected Monseignat's own appeal for a reward for his services as comptroller "because the time is not favourable." The time only became favourable nine years later when the venality of the naval commissary's office was abolished. On 7 July 1717 Monseignat was reinstated as comptroller after having performed the functions of the office for 14 years at half or no pay.

Monseignat was neither a fool nor an incompetent and yet he endured exceptionally bad treatment from the crown. As a good father he trained Louis-Denis, the elder of his two sons, to follow him in his positions; qualified sons of royal officials in New France enjoyed a preference when their father's successor was selected. Such had been the case when in March 1693 Alexandre PEUVRET de Gaudarville was appointed *en survivance* to replace his father as clerk of the Conseil Souverain. Thus Monseignat was acting on an established precedent when in 1711, and again in 1712, he sought to secure the succession of his office as chief clerk of the Conseil Supérieur for his son.

In 1714 the minister answered Monseignat's petitions with a flat refusal: "I have already let it be known that the king was absolutely determined not to grant any survivorships for posts in New France . . . it is useless for you to ask again." On one last hope, Monseignat now begged for the survivorship of his post of comptroller or, at least, an order making Louis-Denis the comptroller's understudy. The response was, as before, negative.

Charles de Monseignat's cat and mouse game with the ministry of Marine may have been diverting but it was not profitable. His appointments had increased while his official income had declined. To meet the demands of his accumulated functions he employed deputies like his son and René Hubert whom, in 1711, he authorized to serve as his assistant and to act as chief clerk in his absence. Hubert was replaced in 1713 by Monseignat's trusted friend, Pierre RIVET, who was also his chief clerk in the Quebec office of the Domaine d'Occident.

Monseignat had been the agent and director for the tax farmers of the Domaine d'Occident since July 1707. He needed the private income and he was also the best qualified man for the position. He had already worked for tax farmers in Quebec and Paris and had served as receiver-general of excise taxes in Champagne and as a collector of bridge and road taxes in France. In Canada the tax farmers leased the right to collect import duties and to exercise certain privileges in return for a promise to pay selected salaries and subsidies in the colony. Monseignat, as director of the tax farm, managed the collection of the revenues and made the required payments.

Since Monseignat represented the king and the tax farmers at the same time, any financial conflict between the two caught him in the middle. When such a situation arose, however, he generally resolved the matter in the king's favour. In 1709, for example, he seized the estate of the Marquis de CRISAFY under the right of *aubaine*. Since the late marquis was legally a foreigner his property fell to the king but, in this case, it was claimed by the tax farmers who had leased the crown's fiscal privileges. Unfortunately, the king had already given Crisafy's estate to the Comte d'Averne and Monseignat, as comptroller, had to recover the assets from himself as director of the domain. The minister in 1711 complimented him on his handling of the estate "and the exact account of that part which reverts to the Comte d'Averne."

A similar conflict arose over the right to salvage the ships of Sir Hovenden WALKER's expedition which were wrecked off Île-aux-Oeufs in 1711. The tax farmers claimed the privilege under article 382 of their lease while Georges REGNARD Duplessis, receiver of the admiralty, claimed it by virtue of the royal ordinance of August 1681. While the dispute simmered in the admiralty court, Monseignat and Duplessis came to a private understanding and dispatched a joint expedition to begin the salvage operation.

In a letter of 9 Nov. 1712, Monseignat reported to the minister that the goods obtained had barely paid the costs of the expedition but that there were several items which remained to be sold. The minister, however, ordered the Conseil Supérieur of New France to register the decree of the king's council of 10 March 1691 by which "the vessels and goods of the state's enemies which are washed up onto the shores of the kingdom are declared to belong to His Majesty alone." A substitute comptroller, named for the duration of the case, summoned the salvagers to the admiralty court on the basis of this decree. The judgement ordered Monseignat and Duplessis to surrender to the king all that had accrued from the salvage operation and to pay court costs.

The tax farmers did not fire Monseignat; he had betrayed their interests because he had more to fear from the crown than from the tax farmers. No one could really expect to win a case against the king or those representing his power.

The Domaine d'Occident was like the goose that laid the golden eggs. The crown often gave it a severe plucking but stopped short of killing it. When card money threatened to bankrupt the domain, the government intervened. As card money depreciated, people paid the tax farm in this currency at or near face value while those who were paid by the farm demanded payment at real

Montigny

value. The director of the domain, Monseignat, had to match expenditures with revenue. The tax farmers had given him orders to pay out card money at the same rate as he had received it. The clergy and the officers whose incomes came out of the domain objected and he tried to appease them with partial payment in letters of credit. As a result the domain began to fall into arrears.

When the intendant and governor demanded that the domain pay senior officers double in card money in 1717, Monseignat stood fast and received the minister's support. His position became impossible after the king's declaration of 21 March 1718 reduced the value of card money by half. The disproportion between revenues and expenditures had to be remedied. On 13 July 1718 Monseignat asked the intendant for an order to compel importers to pay the farm in hard cash or, if in cards, double. An intendant's ordinance was issued on the same day against three importers.

No man was better suited than Monseignat to supervise the destruction of card money. As comptroller, he had been authorized since 1710 to recover for burning the cards issued by Champigny in 1702. Worn out cards of later issues were replaced but it was hoped that the provisional money would be phased out. When new and larger issues of card money defeated this plan, the crown turned to official devaluation.

In a reference to the natural devaluation of card money, Monseignat wrote that "those who are on salaries from the king suffer greatly and cannot provide themselves with a quarter of the necessities of life." But his work for the tax farmers had already freed him from dependence on the crown and it is likely that he used his offices to procure additional income. Moreover, he had engaged in a small number of private trading ventures in the late 17th century and he seems to have had commercial interests when he died. Le Roy de la Potherie, the former comptroller, had told the minister in 1702 that Monseignat "will calmly let the money flow out because he has grandiose views on commerce which hardly befit a comptroller." There must have been a grain of truth in this for Monseignat's estate was appraised at over 17,000 French *livres* in 1718.

PETER N. MOOGK

AJM, Greffe de Claude Maugue, 20 mai 1682. AJQ, Greffe de Louis Chambalon, 10 janv. 1699, 23 févr. 1697; Greffe de François Genaple, 8 janv., 21 févr. 1704; Greffe de Florent de La Cetière, 5 déc. 1718. AQ, NF, Coll. de pièces jud. et not., 2026, 3345. AN, Col., B, 22, ff.135, 276v–77; 23, ff.104v, 216v–17, 235v; 27, f.288; 29, f.110; 33, ff.382v–83; 36, f.407–8; C¹¹A, 30, f.36–37; 33, ff.151–53; 11, pp.3–99; 17, pp.36, 143; 19, pp.1–38, 122–31; 31, pp.188–89; 33,

pp.273–76; 34, pp.323, 448–51; 39, pp.7, 153–56; D²C, 47/2, p.333 (copies in PAC). BN, MS, Clairambault 884, f.456. *Documents relating to Canadian currency during the French period* (Shortt). *Jug. et délib.*, II, III, IV, V, VI. *Ord. comm.* (P.-G. Roy), I, 288. Recensement de Québec, 1716 (Beaudet), 15. P.-G. Roy, *Inv. ins. Cons. souv.; Inv. jug. et délib., 1717–1760*, I, VI, VII; *Inv. ord. int.*, I. Gareau, "La prévôté de Québec," 117–19. P.-G. Roy, "Charles de Monseignat," *BRH*, XI (1905), 292–98; "Les secrétaires des gouverneurs et intendants de la Nouvelle-France," *BRH*, XLI (1935), 82–83.

MONTIGNY. *See* PAPINEAU

MONTIGNY, JACQUES TESTARD DE. *See* TESTARD

MONTPLAISIR, MICHEL-IGNACE DIZY, *dit. See* DIZY

MOODY, JOHN, lieutenant-colonel; deputy-governor of Placentia; b. *c.* 1677; d. 1736.

Moody was appointed lieutenant in Captain Michael RICHARDS' Independent Company in Newfoundland, 18 Feb. 1703. By the time Moody arrived at St John's, Richards was preparing to leave with Commodore GRAYDON, who appointed Thomas LLOYD to the command of the garrison. When the commodore for the following year, BRIDGES, arrived, he found the inhabitants and the soldiers complaining bitterly about Lloyd's conduct. In October 1704, Bridges returned to England taking Lloyd with him, and Moody was left in charge of the military forces in St John's.

Trouble had always arisen between the residents at St John's and the military commanders, because the latter regarded themselves as entitled to certain perquisites and privileges. Although prohibited by orders from so doing, every military commander speculated profitably in trade in provisions, fish, and oil on his own account. As the commander's position gave him special advantages, the residents strongly objected. It was not long therefore before accusations similar to those against Lloyd were levelled against Lieutenant Moody. But the winter of 1704–5 was to provide grounds for more precise and spectacular accusations against Moody. In December Moody ordered that Christian, a charwoman employed by John JACKSON's daughter, Margaret, should be whipped—allegedly for the theft of some rum and brandy. The exact details of the case are lost in a mass of contradictory reports, but it may well be that Christian's real crime was that she knew too much about Moody's private life. At all events, she died a few days after her ordeal, and a number of the inhabitants accused Moody of causing her

486

death. The following summer Moody demanded a trial, which was presided over by Commodore Bridges. The court found that the allegations were "malicious and unfounded"; the woman—according to the court—had died from venereal disease.

The winter of 1704–5 had afforded Moody the opportunity to prove his military courage and determination. In January 1704/5 with a very small detachment of the Independent Company, he was besieged in Fort William by some 600 French troops, under AUGER de Subercase, from Placentia (Plaisance). With only 50 or 60 men he repulsed the enemy, who retired with the loss of 200 men. Moody was admirably supported during the siege by his lieutenant (and later personal enemy), Robert LATHAM.

In October, Lloyd returned as commander of the land forces, and on 21 Nov. 1705, Moody sailed for England with Commodore Bridges in the *Looe*. In the same convoy went John Jackson with whom, despite the episode with Christian, Moody had maintained a steady friendship. The *Looe* was wrecked on the Isle of Wight, with some loss of life, but Moody and Bridges survived. On 14 March 1707, as a result of his gallant defence of Fort William, Moody was commissioned lieutenant in the Coldstream Guards, and soon afterwards was appointed second adjutant.

After the cession of Placentia to Britain by the treaty of Utrecht in 1713, Moody was promoted brevet lieutenant-colonel, and appointed deputy-governor of Placentia, under the governor of Nova Scotia, Colonel NICHOLSON. By an ordinance of Queen Anne, the French residents at Placentia were permitted to sell their estates, and Moody purchased a considerable amount of land and property from them including the lands of the former French governor, PASTOUR de Costebelle. Like William Taverner*, he incurred the wrath of the visiting English fishing captains by so doing.

In 1717 the comptrollers of the army accounts recommended that Moody be ordered to return home with Commodore William Passenger to answer the many charges against him, and to settle the accounts of the garrison. Lieutenant-colonel Martin Purcell was appointed lieutenant-governor of Placentia to supersede Moody. The latter returned to England, letting his lands to various tenants. He resided in London (a sufferer from gout), and received army half-pay until his death in 1736. At this date his widow, Mrs. Ann Moody, was placed on the widows' pension list.

MICHAEL GODFREY

Moody kept a diary or "Relation" of the siege of January 1704/5; this has been preserved in the Public Record Office, London (C.O. 194/3/H.10).

PRO, C.O. 194/3, 194/4, 194/5, Index to Nfld.

corresp. 8234; W.O. 24/662–24/682 (half pay registers, 1717–34); 24/806 (widows' pensions); *CSP, Col., 1704–5, 1706–8, 1708–9, 1712–14, 1714–15, 1716–17, 1717–18*. Dalton, *English army lists*, IV.

MOORE, THOMAS, the name of several sea captains active in the Hudson Bay area between 1674 and the early 18th century.

A Thomas Moore was employed by the HBC from 1671 to 1678. Originally a sailor, Moore was promoted to trader, and, while accompanying Charles Bayly* on his 1674 exploratory voyage from Rupert River to Cape Henrietta Maria, he probably prepared a rough draft of the west coast of James Bay—the only map which locates Albany Fort on Bayly Island. Moore returned to England and sought employment again in 1680, but he was not re-engaged.

This may well be the same man as the Thomas Moore who, six years later (1686), was hired by the Compagnie du Nord. A son of Edward Moore, master gunner at Dover Fort, England, and Cécile (Cecilia?) Richardson, Thomas (born c. 1654) abjured his Anglican faith at Quebec, 19 March 1690 (N.S.). The same year he married Jeanne Lemelin; the marriage contract is dated 7 Jan. 1690, but the ceremony was not performed until 6 April. The couple took up residence in the village of Saint-Laurent on the Île d'Orléans. They had six children, the last born in 1709.

Thomas Moore probably conducted ships to Hudson Bay either as a master or as a pilot for PIERRE LE MOYNE d'Iberville in 1688–89. In 1706 he was commander of the *Maria*, and pilot of a privateer in 1707. Later the same year (1707) he was engaged by Guillaume GAILLARD "to go privateering aboard *La-Nostre-Dame-de-Victoire* against the enemies of the state, in the vicinity of Cape Breton, Newfoundland, the Grand Banks, and elsewhere." In 1713 he was master pilot on a ship sailing to Labrador. Moore must have died some time between 1713 and 1724; the marriage certificate of his son, Pierre, dated 1724, states that the father was dead.

In 1687 a third Thomas Moore was mate of the Hudson's Bay Company ship the *Huband* (Capt. Richard Smithsend*) on the voyage to Hudson Bay. The *Huband* remained in the bay until captured by Iberville in 1689; it is not known whether Moore died, deserted, or was captured. Unless there is some error in the records this Thomas Moore cannot be identified as the one who was hired by the Compagnie du Nord.

G. E. THORMAN

AJQ, Greffe de François Genaple, 7 janv. 1690; Greffe de Louis Chambalon, 6 mai, 7 juillet 1707.

Moreau

BM, Add. MS 5027A, f.64 (Moore's map of James Bay). *Coll. de manuscrits relatifs à la N.-F.*, II, 452–56. HBRS, V, VIII (Rich); XI (Rich and Johnson). A. Roy, *Inv. greffes not.*, VII, 67; XIX, 204, 218, 244. Tanguay, *Dictionnaire*, VI, 79. P.-G. Roy, "Le sieur Thomas Moore," dans *Les petites choses de notre histoire* (Lévis, 1931), VI, 116–19. *BRH*, XXIX (1923); XXX (1924); XXXI (1925). G. E. Thorman, "An early map of James Bay," *Beaver* (Winnipeg), outfit 291 (Spring 1961), 18–22.

MOREAU. *See* MOIREAU

MOREAU DE CABANAC, FRANÇOIS DESJORDY. *See* DESJORDY

MOREL DE LA DURANTAYE, OLIVIER, esquire, captain, commandant, councillor, seigneur; b. 17 Feb. 1640 at Notre-Dame-de-Grâce, near Nantes, son of Thomas Morel, Sieur de La Durantaye, and of Alliette Du Houssaye; d. 28 Sept. 1716.

Morel de La Durantaye arrived in Canada in June 1665 as a captain in the Carignan-Salières regiment, although his commission dated only from 10 Dec. 1665. He worked with his company on the building of Fort Sainte-Anne, and in September 1666 he took part in Prouville* de Tracy's expedition against the Mohawks. He returned to France in 1668, and on 25 March 1669 he contracted to raise a company of 50 men; in August 1670 he was back in Canada. On 14 September, at Quebec, he married Françoise Duquet, the surgeon Jean Madry*'s widow, who was fairly well off and who owned the arriere-fief of Grand-pré in the seigneury of Notre-Dame-des-Anges. They were to have 10 children, who were all baptized, from 1671 to 1685, at Quebec.

From 1670 to 1683 Morel de La Durantaye was attached to the Quebec garrison, where he commanded one of the six companies of colonial regular troops. Fur-trading was also one of his occupations, since for eight years he owned a fur-trading site at Montreal.

On 29 Oct. 1672 he obtained from Talon* the seigneury of La Durantaye, which was to be enlarged in 1693 and 1696; on 15 July 1674 Buade* de Frontenac granted him the seigneury of Kamouraska, which he was to sell in 1680 to CHARLES AUBERT de La Chesnaye, after having vainly tried to fish there.

On 10 Oct. 1682 Morel de La Durantaye took part in a meeting of religious and lay notables held at Quebec by Le Febvre* de La Barre to discuss the best course of action to follow in face of the Iroquois peril. The following spring, at the governor's request and accompanied by Louis-Henri de BAUGY, he went to the Great Lakes region and the Illinois country to put a stop to the corrupt practices of the coureurs de bois, who were trading in furs without licences. He was also instructed to invite the Indians of this region to come to Montreal to trade their furs and meet the new governor; finally, he received orders to inquire into the activities of Cavelier* de La Salle, as there was a likelihood that the latter would lose the authority which he held over the forts in that area. In July 1683 Morel de La Durantaye took over the command of Michilimackinac, a position that he was to occupy until 1690, and in August of the same year Baugy replaced HENRI TONTY as commandant of Fort Saint-Louis.

On 19 July 1684 Morel de La Durantaye left the fort, at the head of a party of 500 men laboriously mustered with the help of DANIEL GREYSOLON Dulhut and Nicolas PERROT, to join La Barre's expedition against the Iroquois. They were supposed to meet at Niagara. On the way, Durantaye was informed by a messenger of the conclusion of the unfavourable peace signed at Anse de La Famine (Mexico Bay, near Oswego, N.Y.). On 6 June 1686 he was instructed to set up a post at Detroit and another at the "Toronto portage." It was not possible to establish the latter, which was to bear the name Fort Rouillé (Toronto), until 1750. On 7 June 1687, acting on BRISAY de Denonville's instructions, he went to the south of Lake Erie "to repeat the formal taking over of the said posts" which had first been done by La Salle. On 10 July, with Dulhut and Henri Tonty, he joined up with Denonville's army to the south of Lake Ontario; he was at the head of a party composed of 160 Frenchmen, 400 allies, and 60 prisoners. A few days later he helped to burn down and destroy the Seneca villages.

In 1690 he persuaded 400 or 500 Indians to go to trade in furs at Montreal, and according to BOCHART de Champigny he marshalled 100 canoes for this purpose. The same year he was relieved of his post as commandant of Michilimackinac and replaced by LA PORTE de Louvigny, because he had apparently been too well disposed towards the Jesuits. The following year he obtained permission to trade in furs in the west, and signed an agreement with Jean Fafard. In 1694 he was again at the head of a company with instructions to clear the neighbourhood of Montreal of Iroquois; at that time he was promoted captain on the active list. The king granted him a gratuity of 1,500 *livres* in 1700, and on 18 May 1701 a pension of 600 *livres* with permission to leave the service.

In 1702 François de Beauharnois* de La Boische recommended him for appointment to the Conseil

Souverain. The appointment was made on 16 June 1703; he received his commission on 29 October and was installed on 26 Nov. 1703. He had already sat on the council on 8 October, because of a shortage of judges. Late in the autumn of 1704 he went to France. As he had not returned by 1706, his wife claimed separate maintenance, because her own assets had been seized to pay her husband's debts. The separation was granted in 1713. In 1708 Morel returned to sit on the council, and except for being absent twice in the winters of 1710 and 1711 he sat until 31 Aug. 1716, when he presided over the assembly and signed the minutes.

Morel de La Durantaye died on 28 Sept. 1716, after giving his son Joseph-François half of his La Durantaye seigneury. He was buried on 30 September in the church of Saint-Philippe, now Saint-Vallier.

Governors, intendants, and Jesuits had spoken of him in very flattering terms. High praise was given to his tact in dealing with the Indians, his uprightness, and his loyalty to the king.

BERNARD WEILBRENNER

AQ, Seigneuries, Notre-Dame-des-Anges. *Jug. et délib.* "Mémoire de la dépense faite par le sieur de La Durantaye aux Outaouais . . . ," *BRH*, XXX (1924), 49. P.-G. Roy, *Inv. coll. pièces jud. et not.*, I, 112, 197; *Inv. concessions*, I, 22. Le Jeune, *Dictionnaire*, II, 22–26. É.-Z. Massicotte et Régis Roy, *Armorial du Canada français* (2ᵉ série, Montréal, 1918), 82. Antoine d'Eschambault, "La vie aventureuse de Daniel Greysolon, sieur Dulhut," *RHAF*, V (1951–52), 334–37. P.-G. Roy, "Olivier Morel de La Durantaye, capitaine au régiment de Carignan," *BRH*, XXVIII (1922), 97–107, 129–36.

MORIN, GERMAIN, first Canadian to be ordained priest, secretary of the bishopric of Quebec, parish priest, canon; baptized 15 Jan. 1642 at Quebec, son of Noël Morin, master wheelwright, and of Hélène Desportes*, widow of Guillaume Hébert; d. 20 Aug. 1702 at the Hôtel-Dieu, Quebec.

There is documentary evidence of Germain Morin's presence at the Jesuit college on 15 Nov. 1659. He was one of the four pupils whose board was paid by the parish of Quebec, to ensure that masses were served and that there were choirboys to sing at mass. Bishop LAVAL even judged it fitting to confer the tonsure and the minor orders on him, despite his youth. This was done on 2 Dec. 1659, and was the first ceremony of its kind in Canada. After receiving the subdiaconate on 6 Aug. 1662, Morin continued to live with the Jesuits and served as sacristan for the parish. When Morin was old enough, Bishop Laval

conferred the diaconate on him on 21 March 1665 and the priesthood on 19 September.

From the time of his entry into the ecclesiastical state in 1659 he was secretary to the bishopric, then from 20 Oct. 1663 clerk to the officiality of the diocese. In this capacity he was responsible for keeping the official registers and for transcribing and initialling the bishop's pastoral letters. He continued to hold these offices until at least 1665, for until 1670 he is not known to have had any other ministry but that of vicar at the cathedral. After that he served the parishes of Champlain, Neuville (Pointe-aux-Trembles), Repentigny, Saint-Joseph de la Pointe-de-Lévy, Sainte-Anne de Beaupré, and Saint-Michel. He was rewarded for this missionary life by being appointed a canon on 20 Sept. 1697. He died in 1702.

HONORIUS PROVOST

ASQ, Chapitre, 138; Documents Faribault, 1ᵃ; Lettres, M, 29; O, 23; Paroisse de Québec, 129; Polygraphie, XXII, 22; Séminaire, I, 12, 40; XCII, 19. Charland, "Notre-Dame de Québec: le nécrologe de la crypte," 150. Laurent Morin, *Le chanoine Germain Morin, premier prêtre canadien* (Québec, 1965). "Le drapeau du camp de la Canardière," *BRH*, II (1896), 61. P.-G. Roy, "St-François de Sales de la Pointe-aux-Trembles," *BRH*, III (1897), 129.

MORIN, MARIE, first Canadian nun, Hospitaller of St Joseph, superior of the Hôtel-Dieu of Montreal (1693–96, 1708–11), annalist; b. 19 March 1649 at Quebec; daughter of Noël Morin, seigneur of Saint-Luc, and of Hélène Desportes*, god-daughter of Louis d'Ailleboust* de Coulonge; d. and buried 8 April 1730 at Montreal.

Marie Morin was one of a family of 12 children, the eldest of whom, GERMAIN, whose godmother was the mother of the famous explorer Louis Jolliet*, became the first Canadian priest.

Marie Morin was educated at the convent of the Ursulines in Quebec. She was a boarder there when in 1659 the monastery welcomed, on their arrival from France, Jeanne Mance* and the first three Religious Hospitallers chosen by Jérôme Le Royer to found the Hôtel-Dieu of Ville-Marie. The meeting with these missionaries must have made a deep impression on the little girl. What is certain is that at the age of 11 she decided to enter the order of the Religious Hospitallers of Ville-Marie. Her parents were opposed to the idea, stating that she could achieve her object just as well by joining the Hospitallers of St Augustin, who were established at Quebec. The young girl pleaded her case so well that after two years' resistance she obtained the authorization of Bishop LAVAL, although he disapproved of the founding

489

of a new community of Hospitallers at Montreal. At the age of 13, Marie Morin therefore entered the noviciate of the Religious Hospitallers of Ville-Marie.

When she pronounced her solemn vows on 27 Oct. 1671, Sister Morin became the first Canadian-born cloistered nun in Montreal. Her talents as a business woman were soon recognized, since in 1672 she was appointed depositary. She was to be appointed to this office again in 1676, 1681, 1689, and 1696. Sister Morin explained this appointment modestly: she knew the country better than the Frenchwomen who were her companions, and she could obtain materials of better quality and more cheaply. In 1693 she became the first Canadian superior of the Hôtel-Dieu of Montreal. She was to be elected superior again in 1708.

By these titles and functions, Sister Morin was intimately connected with the expansion of the Hôtel-Dieu, begun in 1689. She experienced the incredible worries involved in the construction of an edifice 200 feet long by 31 wide, 3 storeys high, and with 2 pavilions each 25 feet by 31 added to it in the form of a T. The new hospital was blessed on 21 Nov. 1694, and on Thursday 24 Feb. 1695, three months after its opening, it was destroyed by fire from top to bottom. Marie Morin was the superior at that time, and the following year she was appointed depositary to look after the rebuilding.

It was at this period of her life, in 1697 to be precise, that she began to write the annals of the Hôtel-Dieu, and she continued to do so until 1725. She died on 8 Aug. 1730 as a result of a long illness.

Marie Morin wrote her memoirs at the request of the Nuns Hospitallers of St Joseph in France, who wanted to learn about the life and work of their companions who had gone to New France. ". . . I have more knowledge of these things than many others, without speaking rashly, and being the first girl that they received into their company in the third year after their arrival in Canada, I have had the good fortune to be an eye witness of almost everything that they have done and suffered, and do not think, my Sisters, that I exaggerate, but be assured, as is the case, that this is only the smallest part [of what could be told], and that it is for your recreation that I take pleasure in writing this."

In the preface she apologizes for all her faults of style, for at that time she was the depositary and had to see to the expenses and construction work connected with the house: "The carpenters, masons, stone-cutters, and joiners needed to speak to me often, and that distracted me from my subject and caused me to make untimely repe-

titions and cut too short an account I had already begun. . . ." Then she reviewed the nuns of the Hôtel-Dieu of Montreal, first the founders, who had come from France, then the Canadian nuns. She outlined the sometimes picturesque circumstances of their entry into religion, since some came in "by night" to escape their parents' opposition. The preface ends with a description of Montreal Island.

Sister Morin then divided her narrative into 46 chapters of unequal length to which she gave titles describing the contents. In these pages is a detailed account of the founding of the community of Religious Hospitallers of St Joseph in France and of the Hôtel-Dieu of Montreal; biographers of Jérôme Le Royer de La Dauversière, Paul Chomedey* de Maisonneuve, and Jeanne Mance can draw abundant material from it, although it must be borne in mind that a concern for moral edification shapes Sister Morin's judgements on people and events. To these pages, which have been published by the Société historique de Montréal, are added 108 more, in which Marie Morin recounts the fire of 1695, that of 1721, the siege of Quebec in 1690, and the wreck of Sir Hovenden WALKER's fleet at Île-aux-Oeufs in 1711.

What is most interesting in these annals is the information that Marie Morin gives concerning the daily life of her period and the intimate opinions that she expresses about her contemporaries. Herein lie the charm and the principal value of this "domestic" chronicle. Thus she tells of the arrival of Sisters Andrée de Ronceray, Renée Le Jumeau, and Renée Babonneau at Montreal in 1669: "M. Souart[*] our confessor took them to see the Indian mission at the place called La Montagne where they were received with shouts and cries of joy which were heard afar; for their part the Sisters gave them many marks of affection, and ate of the food that had been prepared, consisting of *sagamité* made of corn meal boiled in water, pumpkins baked in the ashes, and ripe Indian corn on the cob, which are delicious dishes."

Speaking of the difficulties encountered in establishing the Hôtel-Dieu at Montreal, Sister Morin wrote: "Believe me, Sisters, much courage and strength were necessary to endure them, together with all the other troubles that accompanied them; the cold that they have suffered for more than 28 years is extreme; you must know that the cold of this country can be understood only by those who are subjected to it. Their house having holes in more than 200 places, the wind and snow easily passed through them . . . so that when there had been wind and snow during the night, one of the first things to be done in the morning was to take wooden shovels and the broom to throw out the snow around the doors and windows . . . and the water that was put on the table for drinking froze within a quarter of an hour."

In the writings of the annalist occurs also the story of the pecuniary worries of the depositary, and there is interesting information on the financial resources available to the Religious Hospitallers of the Hôtel-Dieu of Montreal.

Sister Morin, appointed depositary in 1689, found herself at that time responsible for the reconstruction of the first Hôtel-Dieu, which was falling to pieces. A report by BRISAY de Denonville and BOCHART de Champigny addressed to the king on 3 Oct. 1687, in order to obtain help for the hospital in Montreal, gives an idea of the financial difficulties which the depositary had to face: "The 16,000 *livres* which remain from the foundation are in the hands of the Sieur Desbordes who pays us an annuity of 800 *livres* from it each year, which, with the 400 derived from the land where the Hôtel-Dieu stands, constitute all the revenue of this establishment. The nuns who spend it are still more to be pitied. When Madame de Bullion gave 20,000 *livres* for their maintenance, the Sieur de La Dauversière, the receiver of taxes at La Flèche, to whom this sum was handed over, undertook to use it for the purchase of an annuity of 1,000 francs. In the meantime, he took it to the royal treasurer to be credited to his receipts of royal tax funds, with the idea of replacing it when he had found reliable people with whom to invest it. But as he died soon afterwards, and owed the king more than he possessed in assets, the 20,000 *livres* which he had on deposit went into His Majesty's coffers, and the nuns' endowment was lost. From the accounts that the Abbé de Saint-Vallier has examined, it appears that the disbursements total 8,000 *livres* a year. In this way it can be seen that the expenditure exceeds the income, and that short of special assistance this house will inevitably perish."

And Bishop Saint-Vallier [LA CROIX] wrote to France in 1688: ". . . It is surprising that their community and their hospital have not perished so far, and I attribute to their virtue the extraordinary resources that they have found from time to time in divine providence, which seems to have provided unexpected help for them in proportion to their needs and their sufferings."

The hospital, which was built despite everything and thanks to "unexpected help," was destroyed by fire on 24 Feb. 1695, barely three months after its opening. The very next day collections were begun for the reconstruction, which was undertaken immediately under the direction of the architect GÉDÉON DE CATALOGNE.

Sister Morin gives the names of the benefactors and the amounts of their donations, adding that there should also be named all those who gave wood, stone, grain, or days of work, whether it be that of men or of horses. But "towards the end of July, they began to question whether they should not abandon the work that had been started, the money from the collections being already exhausted." Borrow? Impossible, said Sister Morin, for "the state in which we were did not prompt anyone to entrust large sums to us, added to which money is scarce in this country."

Most fortunately, Governor Louis de Buade* de Frontenac, who foresaw an expedition against the Iroquois and the fact that he would need the Hôtel-Dieu for wounded soldiers, intervened personally to have the work of reconstruction resumed. Sister Morin, who was then the superior, received him: "The Comte de Frontenac walked through our humble buildings, and having examined everything he appeared quite satisfied with the diligence of the workers. He then asked for the superior, to tell her that it was absolutely necessary to have the work of rebuilding her convent continue, and as she offered as her excuse the lack of means to meet the expense of it, he told her that he would make us a present of 100 *écus*, but on condition that we should not become discouraged."

The nuns occupied their new house on 21 Nov. 1695, but the construction work was far from completed. Sister Morin, who was again the depositary in 1696 and who remained so until 1702, was once more to experience great financial worries and encounter unforeseen obstacles: "The second year after our fire we lost a whole year's income that was ours in France and that had been spent on supplies for us, such as cut cloth, wine, liquor, and ironwork necessary for the country; the ship on which these things were loaded was captured by the English, which to my knowledge has happened several other times when we lost everything that was coming to us from France. . . . It is the English who have gained from our losses at sea."

Marie Morin devoted the last 25 pages of her *Annales* to an account of the second fire, which destroyed the Hôtel-Dieu in 1721. She was 72 years old at that time, and with her companions she experienced the distress of seeing the survival of their work endangered for lack of financial resources.

As the fire ravaged "all the Lower Town . . . no general collections were made throughout the town as on the first occasion when we burned down, because those who might have given us something are almost ruined by the fire. . . ."

491

Muy

The Religious Hospitallers, lodged in the hospice of the Charon Brothers, had to wait for two years before beginning the work of reconstruction. To help themselves to survive, they worked their farm: "The most vigorous of our nuns have many times been to help them to gather hay, in the middle of the day, and to thrash the grain during the harvests, in the blazing sun, because there was not the wherewithal to pay men." Bishop Saint-Vallier asked the superior to "do her utmost to see that they pushed on with the rebuilding despite the shortage of resources," but "as he gave no money, we did not hurry. . . . What can be done without money?" The king, for his part, after allowing them a gratuity of 2,000 *livres*, sent to the intendant "an order to stop the construction work." RIGAUD de Vaudreuil and Bégon* offered only 800 *livres*, and even then this was in the form of an advance payment of the pension of the sick soldiers, a pension which was "11 sous a day, with which we had to be content and manage as best we could."

Finally, on 11 Nov. 1724, thanks to a substantial gift of 5,000 *livres* made by Bishop Saint-Vallier, to the generosity of the Sulpician seminary in Paris, and to the initiative of Louis Normant, the nuns' chaplain, who undertook "a collection which lasted a week" and with which "he seemed quite pleased," the Hôtel-Dieu was again able to open its doors.

The following year the building was completed, thanks above all to a loan from the merchant Lespérance. The former depositary could not help but worry about the debts: "Let whoever can pay them do so. I greatly fear that we shall have cause to regret them." But she closed her *Annales* with a serene prayer and these simple words: "I am writing this on 16 Sept. 1725."

The *Annales*—a manuscript saved from all the fires that devastated the Hôtel-Dieu—constitute today, by their authenticity and interest, a very precious treasure for the history of Montreal and of Canada. Through these pages, we rediscover the remarkable personality of Sister Morin, a type of heroic woman produced by the early days of New France.

HÉLÈNE BERNIER

AHDM, Annales de sœur Véronique Cuillerie, 1725–1747; Lettre de sœur Morin aux sœurs de France relatant le tremblement de terre de 1663; Marie Morin, Histoire simple et véritable de l'établissement des Religieuses Hospitalières de Saint-Joseph en l'Ile de Montréal, dite à présent Ville-Marie, en Canada, de l'année 1659 . . . [this manuscript has been published under the title *Annales de l'Hôtel-Dieu de Montréal*, éd. A. Fauteux, É.-Z. Massicotte et C. Bertrand (Société historique de Montréal, Mémoires, XII, 1921)]. Biblio-

thèque municipale de Montréal, Fonds Gagnon, Lettres autographes de Sœur Morin à Monsieur de Villeray, 23 sept. 1693.

Mandements des évêques de Québec (Têtu et Gagnon), I. Esther Lefebvre, *Marie Morin, premier historien canadien de Villemarie* (Montréal, Paris, 1959). Mondoux, *L'Hôtel-Dieu de Montréal*. É.-Z. Massicotte, "Le premier écrivain né en Canada," *BRH*, XXXVII (1931), 202. Léo Pariseau, "Pages inédites du premier écrivain canadien," *Le Journal de l'Hôtel-Dieu de Montréal*, 1937.

MUY, NICOLAS DANEAU DE. *See* DANEAU

MYATT (Miatt), JOSEPH, HBC employee from 1708; d. 1730.

Myatt, who came from Cheshire, England, joined the HBC as a landsman in May 1708 signing a contract for four years at £10 per annum for the first year with annual increases of £2. He distinguished himself (perhaps as a gunner, a position he contracted for in 1714) when John FULLARTINE commanded the defence of Albany against a French attack in 1709. Myatt was a competent, trustworthy servant, and in 1714–15, having become conversant with the Indian languages, he traded for the HBC on the East Main. His wages were raised but because his terms were so high he was recalled in 1719.

He returned in 1720 to succeed Nathaniel BISHOP as deputy to Thomas McCliesh*, governor of Albany. After wintering on the East Main he succeeded McCliesh as governor in 1721. A 50 per cent drop in trade in 1721–22 because French coureurs de bois prevented any of the leading upland Indians from coming to Albany, and some false and malicious reports, led the London committee to send out Richard Staunton* as governor in 1723; Myatt was demoted to deputy governor. He filled this position for two years as well as conducting the trade on the East Main, where he completed the building of a new factory. Staunton's favourable reports dispelled the London committee's bad opinion of Myatt although the members were still annoyed at Myatt for teaching an Indian boy to read and write.

For reasons of health Myatt spent the 1725–26 season in England. He returned to Albany as governor in 1726, a position he held until his death of "gout in the stomach" on 9 June 1730. In 1727 Myatt had suggested that Moose Factory be re-established, citing the case of SCATCHAMISSE, who drowned making the perilous trip from Moose to Albany, to support his proposal. In July 1728, he sent Joseph ADAMS and William BEVAN to survey Moose River for a possible site. The company acceded to Myatt's request and in

1730 sent out a sloop with orders for the establishment of Moose Factory. As Myatt died before the orders arrived, the task of re-establishing Moose fell to Joseph Adams who succeeded him as governor.

G. E. THORMAN

HBC Arch. A.6/3 (letters outward, 10 June 1713, 25 May 1714); A.6/4 (letters outward, 30 May 1718, 1719, 1 June 1720, 26 May 1721, 24 May 1722, 17 May 1723, 20 May 1724, 24 May 1725, 25 May 1726); A.6/5 (letters outward, 25 May 1727, 24 May 1728, 21 May 1729, 15 May 1730); B.3/a/4–5, 9–18 (Albany journals between 1712 and 1730); B.3/d/24–27 (Albany account books, 1715–19). HBRS, XXV (Davies and Johnson).

N

NAPPER, JAMES, carpenter, later ship's captain in the service of the HBC; d. 7 Aug. 1737.

Napper is first mentioned as carpenter aboard the company ship *Hudson's Bay* [III] (Capt. Richard WARD), on which he made voyages from England to York Fort in 1716 and 1718 and probably, in 1717, to Churchill River. In 1719 he again sailed to Churchill on the *Hudson's Bay*, which was later wrecked off Cape Tatnum. In consequence Napper, who had evidently mastered the pilot's art, remained in the bay in command of the *Prosperous* hoy, which he took to England in 1721. Apparently desirous of regular employment in the New World, he applied for the command of a vessel stationed in the bay. The company preferred, however, to appoint him to serve in the *Hannah*, on the transatlantic run of 1722, as first mate to Capt. Gofton, who was unfamiliar with bay navigation. In 1723 Napper again sailed to Hudson Bay as first mate aboard either the *Hudson's Bay* [IV] or the *Mary* [I]. There he succeeded John SCROGGS as captain of the *Whalebone* sloop, plying between York Fort and Churchill River. In 1725 he took a cargo of whale oil to England, and the following year made the round trip from England to Albany. After sailing on the *Hannah* to Churchill in 1727, he took command of the *Martin* sloop serving the bay posts. When his contract expired in 1729 he was re-engaged for another year; then, though wishing to return to England, he was persuaded to remain until 1732, when he sailed home bearing Governor Richard Norton*'s testimonial to the excellence of his services.

In 1733 Napper was re-engaged to serve as second-in-command to Norton, who was then supervising the construction of Prince of Wales Fort on the Churchill River. Napper's salary of £40 per annum with a bonus of 50 guineas on the satisfactory completion of the five-year contract suggests that his services were highly valued by his employers. It was stipulated that, if so required, he was to work as a shipwright. In 1734 he was in addition assigned to the command of the *Churchill* sloop, should she be sent from the factory. Napper commanded the Churchill post during Norton's absence in 1735–36.

In 1736 the company, goaded by its celebrated critic, Arthur Dobbs*, undertook to search for an ocean passage leading westward from the bay, and authorized a voyage of reconnaissance northward to Roe's Welcome. The company endeavoured to make the enterprise profitable by combining commerce with discovery, and the leaders of the expedition were assured that promotion of trade was the first objective. Ten seamen were sent out that year from England expressly to assist in the projected voyage. Orders reached Churchill too late, however, to be carried out in 1736, and departure the following summer was retarded by ice at the river mouth. Finally, on 4 July 1737, James Napper, who had been given command of the expedition, sailed in the sloop *Churchill*, accompanied by Robert Crow in the *Musquash*. In five weeks the expedition got no farther than Whale Point, latitude 62°15′N, and there, on 7 August, Napper died. The sloops turned homeward on 15 August. The *Churchill* under the command of Alexander Light* reached Churchill on the 18th, and Crow in the *Musquash* four days later.

Capt. Christopher Middleton*'s assertion that the crews employed on this voyage "were not duly qualified for such an Undertaking" may without unkindness be applied to the captain as well as to his men. Napper's record of service with the company is that of a subaltern, hard working and zealous, but with little aptitude for independent command, least of all on a mission of hazard and uncertainty.

L. H. NEATBY

HBRS, XXV (Davies and Johnson). Morton, *History of the Canadian west*, 208. Williams, *The British search for the northwest passage*, 39–46.

NELSON, JOHN, Boston merchant and statesman; b. 1654 in or near London, England, son of Robert Nelson, and of Mary Temple, sister of Sir Thomas Temple*; married Elizabeth Tailer, niece of William Stoughton, governor of Massachusetts; d. 15 Nov. 1734, in Boston.

Nelson came to Boston from England about 1670, and by his own admission became involved that same year in the trade his uncle, Sir Thomas Temple, was conducting with the French in Acadia and New France. He became Temple's principal heir after the latter died in 1674. Nelson was so familiar with the French colonies that he was sent to Quebec in 1682 to negotiate a settlement of grievances between New England and New France. Nelson resolved the dispute temporarily and emerged with permission, effective to 1684, to sell fishing and trading permits for the Acadian coast.

Nelson's name next crops up in 1689, when he played a major role in the overthrow of Sir Edmund Andros and the Dominion of New England. A year later he proposed an expedition against Port-Royal (Annapolis Royal, N.S.). When William Phips* was chosen leader instead of himself, Nelson refused to have anything more to do with the venture. Nevertheless, in 1691, after Port-Royal's capture, he and six other merchants concluded an agreement with the Massachusetts government to provide a garrison there in exchange for a monopoly of the area's trade for the next five years. Nelson had been on such good terms with the French authorities that he had been able thus far to maintain a warehouse in Port-Royal. While trading in Acadia in 1691, however, Nelson and a number of other New Englanders were captured by a French cruiser, and Nelson was sent to Quebec. Among the others taken were Colonel Edward Tyng*, newly appointed governor of Acadia, and John ALDEN, the latter apparently a colleague of Nelson, as he was one of the backers of Nelson's original proposal to seize Port-Royal.

While at Quebec Nelson was treated with the utmost courtesy, but his vast knowledge of New France apparently precluded his release during King William's War (War of the League of Augsburg). His privileged position came to an end after he bribed two French soldiers to smuggle word to Boston of an impending border raid. Nelson's actions became known to the French when the soldiers were later captured after an abortive attempt on the life of JEAN-VINCENT D'ABBADIE de Saint-Castin in 1692. Shortly thereafter he was sent to France, where he languished for several years in prison, first in a dungeon of the castle of Angoulême and then in the Bastille.

In 1694 he was released on parole and sent to London to transmit a French proposal for the neutrality of America. When the French plan was peremptorily rejected, Nelson turned propagandist, and advanced several proposals of his own for the union of New York and New England, and for the capture of Canada. He also proposed that the St George River, and not the Kennebec, be recognized as the boundary between Acadia and New England. The Board of Trade showed some interest in the schemes, but no serious steps were taken to implement them. At the end of the war in 1697 Nelson returned to Boston, resuming his trade with Acadia, which he pursued until at least 1706. He continued to be active in New England and continental affairs for some time, and in 1731 finally sold the claims to Nova Scotia which he had inherited from Temple.

DONALD F. CHARD

AN, Col., F³, 2. BM, Lansdowne MS 849. "Mass. Archives," XXVI, 108. PANS, MS docs. II, 30. *Coll. de manuscrits relatifs à la N.-F.* "Journal of expedition against Port Royal, 1690." *Mémoires des commissaires*, I, 56, 61; II, 286, 328–29, 330–33; and *Memorials of the English and French commissaries*, I, 127, 138–39, 571, 615, 617–19. *NYCD* (O'Callaghan and Fernow), IV, IX. PRO, *CSP, Col., 1689–92, 1696–97.* Webster, *Acadia.*

DAB. Brebner, *New England's outpost.* A. H. Buffington, "John Nelson's voyage to Quebec in 1682: a chapter in the fisheries controversy," in Col. Soc. Mass., *Trans., 1924–26* (Pub., XXVI, Boston, 1927), 431. B. T. McCully, "The New England-Acadia fishery dispute and the Nicholson mission of August, 1687," Essex Institute, Salem, Mass., *Hist. Coll.,* XCVI (1960), 280.

NERÉ, JACQUES LEVASSEUR DE. *See* LEVASSEUR

NESCAMBIOUIT (Ascumbuit, Assacambuit, Nessegombewit), an Abenaki chief from Pequawket (or Pigwacket; Pégouakki in French; today Fryeburg, Me.), who was received at Versailles; b. *c.* 1660; d. 1727.

Nescambiouit had a great reputation among the Abenakis, according to J.-A. Maurault, for the word "Naskâmbi8it" means "he who is so important and so highly placed because of his merit that his greatness cannot be attained, even in thought." Bacqueville de La Potherie [LE ROY], who had doubtless met him, described him in the following terms: "He is a well-built man, 38 to 40 years old. His features have a martial cast. His actions and his manners reveal that he has the sentiments inspired by a noble soul. His sang-froid is so great that he has never been seen to laugh. So far he has taken by himself more than 40 scalps." Among the New Englanders, too, he was well known. They called him "a bloody devil" and "that insulting monster," and claimed that he had killed over 150 men, women, and children.

In 1693 Nescambiouit went to Pemaquid for negotiations with the English. However, hostilities reopened the following spring. Nescambiouit accompanied PIERRE LE MOYNE d'Iberville to the siege of Fort William at St John's, Newfoundland, in November 1696. He wanted to find out whether Iberville "waged war against the English better than he did himself," and he followed him in everything he did. According to Charlevoix*, he was one of the people who most distinguished themselves in this campaign, in which Captain Jacques TESTARD de Montigny also served.

The historian Samuel Penhallow reports that in 1703, at the beginning of Queen Anne's war (War of the Spanish Succession), Nescambiouit and WENEMOUET, members of a force led by ALEXANDRE LENEUF de Beaubassin, approached the fort at Casco Bay under a flag of truce, but with hatchets concealed in their clothing. They attacked the commander, John MARCH, when he advanced to meet them, but he escaped and held the fort. Two years later Nescambiouit was again in Newfoundland. The new governor of Placentia (Plaisance), AUGER de Subercase, assigned to one of his officers, Testard de Montigny, the task of ravaging the entire coast of the island. On this occasion Nescambiouit distinguished himself, "as usual," wrote Charlevoix again.

In the autumn of 1705 Montigny went to France and took along with him his faithful Nescambiouit. The latter was received at the court of Versailles, made much of and showered with presents by King Louis XIV. He was given the title of Prince of the Abenakis: "Indeed, he had the appearance and the bravery of a great man." In 1706 he was back among his people. The account that he gave them of all the wonders he had seen in France had a good effect upon them. Thus the minister, Pontchartrain, wrote to Montigny on 30 June 1707 that he had been pleased to learn of his return to Quebec with the Abenaki chief. The following year Nescambiouit took part in the expedition which, under the leadership of Jean-Baptiste de Saint-Ours* Deschaillons and JEAN-BAPTISTE HERTEL de Rouville, went to ravage Haverhill on the Merrimack River. He performed wonders with a sabre that Louis XIV had given him; he was, however, shot in the foot.

Some years later the minister wrote to RIGAUD de Vaudreuil in his letter of 23 May 1710: "I should be very glad to be informed as to what has become of the Abenaki Indian chief whom the Sieur de Montigny brought to France five years ago and whether he is still as well disposed and on our side.

He was sufficiently well treated when he was here for us to believe that he will not have changed. Please give me news of him." Vaudreuil informed the minister that he had sent Nescambiouit with Montigny, François-Antoine Pécaudy* de Contrecoeur, and a score of the best soldiers in Canada to help Subercase, who was expecting to be attacked by the English at Port-Royal in Acadia (Annapolis Royal, N.S.). Nescambiouit's part in that expedition is not known. In 1714, however, a year after Governor Dudley of Massachusetts had concluded a general peace with the Abenaki tribes [see MOG], Nescambiouit offered his own submission. He asked for a trading post at Salmon Falls (Rollinsford, N.H.), but added meaningfully that the fraudulent dealing of the English traders had often prompted the Indians to turn to the French.

In 1716 Nescambiouit went to live among the Fox Indians, west of Lake Michigan, after they were subdued by the French [see OUACHALA]. Vaudreuil learned the dangers of such visits in 1719, when a former chief of the Saint-François mission (near Trois-Rivières), Nenangoussikou, brought his tribe an invitation from the Foxes to hunt in the *pays d'en haut*. The governor had to intervene to prevent the departure of 40 Abenaki warriors, which would have weakened Quebec's defences against New England, and strengthened the unruly Foxes. In 1721 Montigny was posted to Green Bay where he doubtless renewed his acquaintance with Nescambiouit. Montigny assured Vaudreuil that the Abenaki chief remained completely loyal to the French, and that his descriptions of France had impressed upon the Foxes the power of the French king.

Vaudreuil's fears seemed justified nevertheless when Nescambiouit returned in 1723 with a message from Nenangoussikou for the Saint-François Abenakis, inviting them to join the Foxes in a war against the Ottawas. The governor received Nescambiouit coldly, and upbraided him for his part in such dealings, but the Indian pleaded that he was only a messenger, that he did not endorse the Fox request, and that he intended to settle again among his own people. Placated by this plea and by Montigny's testimony, Vaudreuil persuaded the elders of Saint-François to accept Nescambiouit, who wished to "give up his dissolute ways and to marry before the church the woman he had brought with him." The message from the Foxes went unanswered. Joseph Aubéry*, the missionary at Saint-François, wrote that the mission chief and all the Abenakis, even the young men, rejected with horror this invitation to take part in a fratricidal war. " 'We have,' they said, 'another war, a just and necessary one, to wage against the English, without wanting to launch into an unjust and pernicious one.' " Nevertheless, Nescambiouit's mission worried the minister in Paris, who instructed Vaudreuil that he must in future allow no Abenaki voyages to the *pays d'en haut,* for "that is not at all acceptable."

According to a newspaper of the time, the *New-England Weekly Journal,* Nescambiouit died in 1727. It has been claimed that he had been made a knight of the order of Saint-Louis. Thomas Hutchinson, in his history published in 1767, recounts that when Nescambiouit appeared at the court of Versailles he stretched forth his arm and boasted of having killed with it 150 of His Majesty's enemies. The king was so pleased that he knighted him and assigned him a life pension of eight *livres* per day. Aegidius Fauteux has refuted this claim. "What must be denied," he wrote, "because it is perfectly ridiculous, is that Louis XIV even thought of placing the cross of the order of Saint-Louis, whose prestige he so jealously guarded, upon the paint-daubed breast of an Indian, whatever interest he might have aroused. . . . The story of a life pension of eight *livres* per day to a man of the woods, a pension larger than that of most of the commanders of the order of Saint-Louis, is scarcely any more reasonable than that of an Indian knight." P.-G. Roy, who had first accepted this story, subsequently concurred in Fauteux' conclusion.

THOMAS CHARLAND, O.P.

AN, Col., B, 29, f.109; C^11A, 29, f.135; 45, ff.146–55, 406–7. Charlevoix, *Histoire* (1744), II, 193, 300, 326; *History* (Shea), V, 42–44, 174, 207 (*see* especially Shea's note on La Poterie, p.42). *Coll. de manuscrits relatifs à la N.-F.,* I, 614. "Correspondance de Vaudreuil," APQ *Rapport,* 1946–47, 379, 397. *Documentary hist. of Maine,* XXIII, 5, 58–60. *Documents relating to Hudson Bay* (Tyrrell), 164–67 (translation of La Poterie). Hutchinson, *Hist. of Mass.-bay* (Mayo), II, 122. *JR* (Thwaites), LXVII, 128. La Poterie, *Histoire* (1722), I, 27–32. Mather, *Magnalia Christi Americana,* II, 558. *New-England Weekly Journal* (Boston), no.13, 19 June 1727. Penhallow, *Hist. of wars with Eastern Indians* (1824), 24, 53. Fauteux, *Les chevaliers de Saint-Louis,* 57–58. *Handbook of American Indians* (Hodge), I, 102.

T.-M. Charland, *Histoire des Abénakis d'Odanak* (Montréal, 1964), 50–51, 94. Coleman, *New England captives,* I, 57, 287, 353. S. G. Drake, *Biography and history of the Indians of North America from its first discovery* (Boston, 1848), pt.III, 110, 139–41. J.-A. Maurault, *Histoire des Abénakis depuis 1605 jusqu'à nos jours* (Sorel, 1866), 330. P.-G. Roy, "Chevalier de Saint-Louis?" dans *Toutes petites choses du régime français* (2v., Québec, 1944), I, 241; "L'otage Stobo et le seigneur Duchesnay," in *Toutes petites choses de notre histoire* (Lévis, 1919), I, 216; "Un sauvage chevalier de Saint-Louis?" *BRH,* XLVII (1941), 212.

NEUVILLE, NICOLAS DUPONT DE. *See* DUPONT

NEUVILLETTE, DANIEL ROBINAU DE. *See* ROBINAU

NICANAPÉ. *See* CHACHAGOUESSE

NICHOLSON, FRANCIS, soldier, conqueror and later governor of Nova Scotia, colonial administrator; b. 12 Nov. 1655 (o.s.), at Downholme, Yorkshire; died a bachelor 5 March 1727/28 in London; buried in the parish of St George, Hanover Square.

Nicholson's parentage is uncertain; probably he was a son or close relative of Thomas Nicholson, successively governor of the Houses of Correction at Richmond and at Thirsk. He had a sister of whom nothing is known save her married name, Phipps. He was reared in the Anglican communion and in later life supported the work of the Society for the Propagation of the Gospel. Nicholson's formal education remains obscure. His correspondence indicates he received some elementary instruction in his boyhood, possibly at a free school in Richmond, near his birthplace. During his youth he became a page of Charles Paulet (Powlett), Lord St John of Basing (afterwards Marquis of Winchester), thereby gaining the patronage of that courtier and of his son-in-law, John Egerton, Earl of Bridgewater.

On 16 Jan. 1677/78 he was gazetted ensign in the King's Holland regiment, and served in Flanders till the regiment's recall and disbandment toward the end of December. He rejoined the army 13 July 1680 as lieutenant in the Earl of Plymouth's regiment, a unit created especially for reinforcing Tangier against attack by the Moorish emperor. At Tangier he was in due course selected for courier service. Upon Tangier's evacuation in February 1683/84 he was ordered back to London, later rejoining his regiment in which he continued to serve as a subaltern till early in 1686.

With James II's creation of the Dominion of New England, Nicholson, now captain of a company of foot, sailed that fall for Boston as assistant to Sir Edmund Andros, the governor-in-chief. Less than two years thereafter he won appointment as lieutenant-governor, under Andros, at New York. In August 1687 he was sent by Andros to Port-Royal (Annapolis Royal, N.S.) to seek the restoration of a New England fishing ketch captured off Acadian shores. He failed to recover the boat, but did manage to gain some knowledge of military and other affairs in Acadia. The

Dominion's collapse in April 1689, on reports of James's deposition, set off an insurrection in Manhattan, causing Nicholson to hasten away in hope of mending his fortunes at Whitehall. Embroiled in war with France, William III responded readily to the urgings of Winchester (now Duke of Bolton) by commissioning Nicholson lieutenant-governor of Virginia on 14 November. For 15 years he served there as a royal administrator and persistently championed the defence of New York's frontier against Canadian raids. He was recalled from this post in April 1705 after many charges of fiscal maladministration had been made against him by the colonists.

Because of his colonial and military experience he became associated as a volunteer in 1709 with Samuel VETCH, whose scheme for Canada's conquest by an inter-colonial land and sea invasion was ordered into effect by the Whig ministry on 1 March. Following their joint appearance in Manhattan, Nicholson accepted command of the Connecticut, New York, and Jersey contingents, while Vetch laboured at Boston to mobilize New England units destined for Canada via the St Lawrence with British naval support. By late July Nicholson had advanced up the Hudson and deployed his troops in stockaded forts from Stillwater (north of Albany, N.Y.) to the foot of Lake Champlain, whence with Iroquois assistance he could threaten Montreal, thus diverting soldiery from Quebec's defence. The governor of New France, RIGAUD de Vaudreuil, apprehending this stratagem, dispatched a reconnoitering force southward under Claude de RAMEZAY, whose report after a skirmish off Scalping Point (Pointe-à-la-Chevelure, opposite Crown Point, N.Y.) confirmed Vaudreuil's fears. However, all chance of success for the English vanished with the ministry's cancellation of its original naval orders. Before these tidings arrived, Nicholson's force had become so demoralized by fatigue, supply shortages, and disease that they abandoned their outposts and streamed homeward.

Nicholson, after a conference at Rehoboth, Mass., sailed for Britain to press for another invasion attempt or an assault from New England on Port-Royal. The latter proposal, promising tangible returns at no great cost to the crown, won ministerial approval. Commissioned 18 March 1709/10 commander-in-chief of an expedition to recover Nova Scotia for the queen, Nicholson set forth in May with 500 marines in a flotilla under Commodore GEORGE MARTIN, consisting of frigates, transports, and a bomb-ketch. At Boston Nicholson's force was augmented by provincial troops under Vetch, and by additional supplies and sail. On 18 September he embarked, and on reaching Nova Scotia's north shore entered the basin leading to Port-Royal. Under cover of Martin's guns Nicholson disembarked his infantry beyond range of the fort, beginning a siege which terminated 2 October (13 October, N.S.), with AUGER de Subercase surrendering in the face of overwhelming odds. The articles of capitulation gave the English control over the Port-Royal fort (now renamed Annapolis Royal) and over the inhabitants living within a three-mile radius of the fort. The latter were given the freedom to move to Placentia (Plaisance) or New France if they so desired. Those who remained were to take the oath of allegiance to Queen Anne. The state of the rest of Acadia was not spelled out, but in effect the English regarded the Acadians as their subjects and expected them to provide any necessary services. The military weakness of the Annapolis Royal garrison, however, rendered the English control of Acadia rather ineffectual.

About a month after the fall of Port-Royal, Nicholson published a lengthy journal of the expedition in the *Boston News-Letter*. Returning to England in triumph that winter, he was promptly ordered back to North America with the rank of lieutenant-general by Secretary Henry St John, who persuaded Anne's new Tory ministry that British military and naval power could subjugate Canada within the framework of Vetch's original design. Delayed in the Channel by contrary winds, Nicholson put in to Nantasket on 8 July 1711, barely two weeks ahead of Admiral WALKER's squadron, whose projected advance up the St Lawrence with seven crack English regiments seemed to assure Quebec's capture. Although Nicholson, with the middle colonies and Connecticut supplying the substance, again threatened to split Canada's defensive system via Lake Champlain, he was forced to withdraw when Walker and the other officers abandoned the naval attack after the fleet ran aground on the Île-aux-Oeufs in the St Lawrence.

Slightly over a year later, in October 1712, Nicholson was appointed royal commissioner to audit colonial accounts, named governor of Nova Scotia and Placentia, and authorized to dispose of equipment brought home in Walker's store-ships. These assignments, the brain-child of Lord Treasurer Oxford, were hopelessly grandiloquent in scope and resulted in Nicholson's undoing. His proceedings at Boston in auditing provincial accounts embroiled him with the ex-governor, Vetch, whom Nicholson had accused of maladministration, and with two supply agents of the Annapolis Royal garrison, John Borland and Thomas Steel. To enforce compliance Nicholson brought suit in court, but Vetch evaded this by

Nicholson

taking off for Britain. The signing of the treaty of Utrecht in the spring of 1713, by which England was given Acadia "within its antient boundaries," had added greater stability to the English presence in Acadia. The uncertainty about the location of these "boundaries," however, was to cause difficulties later on. Nicholson was instructed by Queen Anne in June 1713 to see to it that those Acadians who wished to remain in their homes were protected, and that those who wished to leave the country could freely do so. No term was set for this latter concession. In this and most other matters, Nicholson relegated the administration of the province to his lieutenant-governor, Thomas CAULFEILD. In fact, Nicholson spent only a few months in Nova Scotia while he was governor, from 11 Aug. to 18 Oct. 1714. In August, Nicholson was present when Jacques d'ESPIET de Pensens and Louis Denys* de La Ronde came to seek permission to transport to Île Royale (Cape Breton Island) all Acadians who wanted to migrate to French territory. Nicholson let the emissaries speak to the inhabitants of several settlements and most showed a desire to go to Île Royale. When the agents requested a period of one year to effect the move Nicholson referred the question to London, saying that he did not know whether he could grant this request.

Soon after George I's accession Nicholson sailed home where the Whigs, now entrenched in office, conducted lengthy investigations of his conduct in response to complaints from many of his recent subordinates at Annapolis Royal, including Caulfeild. The general tenor of these charges was that Nicholson had neglected to see to the needs of the Annapolis Royal garrison. No doubt Nicholson's Tory sympathies weighed against his cause as well. Nicholson was dismissed and Vetch was appointed to succeed him. In 1720, Nicholson received his last colonial appointment as governor of South Carolina and remained in that post until 1725 when he returned to England to stay.

Nicholson alienated many contemporaries by his vehement temper and a show of vindictiveness which critics readily exaggerated. Robert Hunter complained of his vanity, Vetch (once his admiring collaborator) termed him an illiterate madman, while Robert Beverly in Virginia ridiculed his pretensions as a town-planner. By contrast, his field-officers, fellow-governors (such as Gurdon Saltonstall of Connecticut), and most Anglican clergymen extolled his generosity, consideration, and bravery. Modern scholarship has yet to produce a satisfactory treatment of his career. His personal appearance is unknown, but there is ample evidence that he was a man of robust physique endowed with unique stamina and energy.

BRUCE T. McCULLY

BM, Add. MS 26626; Sloane MS 3603, ff.14b, 20b, 39a. Mass., Archives, Council records, V, 54–55, 59–87, 88, 111–13, 116–17, 187, 257–59, 268, 272–73, 276–77, 279, 395–96, 401–3, 423–24; VI, 101–4, 117, 139–40, 143–50, 152–55, 161–65, 169–73, 175–76, 180–88, 193–99, 207–10, 213–16, 230–32, 259, 268, 270–71, 278–79, 285. "Mass. Archives," II, 164, 446–48a, 449, 452; LI, 217–24a; LXXI, 500, 502, 543, 561, 862; CVIII, 74. Mass. Hist. Soc., Parkman papers. Museum of the City of New York, Letter Book of Samuel Vetch, ff.1–17, 44, 60–63, 67–71, 75, 77–82. N.B. Museum, Vetch papers, Webster Coll., shelf 40, pkt. 63. N.Y. State, Archives, Col. MSS, LIII, 60, 67, 69–70, 71b, 74b, 74d, 75a, 80b, 101, 103a, 142; LV, 8, 24, 37–38, 42; 49, 60–61, 63, 65, 67, 73, 83, 93, 95, 101, 103a, 107b, 111, 117, 141, 167, 174, 182–83; LVI, 13, 17, 32, 46, 54, 58, 78, 87, 89–90, 92, 94b, 108–9, 112, 113b, 155b. PAC, Nova Scotia A, 4, pp.35–36, 57–60, 71–72, 76–79, 85, 96, 116–17, 130–34, 145–57, 197–99, 200, 205–12, 231–35, 238–45, 252–53; 5, pp.10, 15, 128, 133–35, 187 (calendared in PAC Report, 1894); 8, pp.6–7, 99–100, 109–10. PANS, MS docs., V, no.10, ff.18–20; no.11, ff.21–22; VI, nos.10–11, 13, 27; VII, nos.1–10; VII½, nos.4, 23; VIII, no.69, ff.126–28; IX, no.1. PRO, Adm. 1/4317; 2/435, ff.268–69; 2/438, ff.28–30, 50, 57, 104, 156, 161, 211–12, 239, 274, 308, 310–11, 323, 346, 350, 366, 382, 438, 472, 518; 51/269, pt.1; 52/211, f.4; 52/124, f.7; C.O. 5/1357, f.302; 323/24, f.11; S.P. 44/175, f.269; 44/213; T.1/139; 1/147, nos.33, 65, 65(a); 1/151, nos.15B, 17, 31, 48; 1/152; 1/154, no.11; 1/159; 1/167; 1/177; 1/207 (report on papers relating to Port-Royal garrison submitted to council, 22 June 1717); T.48/15, f.3; 48/16, f.3 (royal bounty to Nicholson, 3 Feb. 1711, for Port-Royal expedition); W.O. 26/14, ff.44–48, 75 (instructions from Secretary Wyndham concerning Placentia and Port-Royal garrisons); 30/89, ff.275–76, 277–79, 286–87. Franklin D. Roosevelt Library (Hyde Park, N.Y.), Livingston-Redmond Coll., Robert Livingston Papers (1714–15), 1 A, box 8. Somerset House, P.C.C., Brooke, f.91 (will of Francis Nicholson, March 1728). Suffolk County Court House (Boston, Mass.), Court files, Suffolk, LXXXIII, f.8387; XCIII, f.9575; XCIV, f.9734; XCVIII, f.10310.

Boston News-letter, 30 Oct.–6 Nov. 1710. [Thomas (John) Buckingham], "A diary of the grand expedition against Crown Point in the year 1711," *Roll and Journal of Connecticut service in Queen Anne's War, 1710–11* (Acorn Club of Connecticut pub., XIII, Hartford, Conn., 1916), 31–43. Josiah Burchett, *A complete history of the most remarkable transactions at sea, from the earliest accounts of time to the conclusion of the last war with France* (London, 1720), 765–67. *Calendar of council minutes, 1668–1763* (N.Y. State Lib., *Bull.* LVIII, Hist. VI, Albany, 1902), 228, 230, 243–44. "Correspondance de Vaudreuil," *APQ Rapport, 1942–43*, 441–42; *1946–47*, 413–14; *1947–48*, 155, 167, 252–53, 262, 268, 284. *Documentary hist. of*

New York (O'Callaghan), III, 675–76, 706–7. "Documents relating to the administration of Jacob Leisler," N.Y. Hist. Soc. *Coll.*, [3d ser.], I (1868), 241–89. *Journal of the legislative council of the colony of New York 1691–1775*, Intro. E. B. O'Callaghan (2v., Albany, 1861), I, 278–80, 312, 326. "Journal of the Rev. John Sharpe," *The Pennsylvania Mag. of Hist. and Biog.* (Philadelphia), XL (1916), 276–80. *London Gazette*, 9–11, 13–16, 20–23 May 1710; 29–31 March, 14–17 April 1711. *Memorials of the English and French commissaries*, I, 33, 451, 481, 771; *see also*, *Mémoires des commissaires*, I, xxviii; II, 642; IV, 318, 322–32, 413, 415–32. *NYCD* (O'Callaghan and Fernow), V, 72–74, 81, 262–63, 265, 279–81, 462–63, 469–70, 509, 642; IX, 857–58, 859. N.Y. State, Secretary of State, *Calendar of historical manuscripts*, ed. E. B. O'Callaghan (2v., Albany, 1865–66), II. *N.S. Archives*, II, 1–16, 20–31, 38–39. N.S. Hist. Soc. *Coll.*, I (1878), 59–104. PRO, *Acts of P.C., col. ser., 1720–45*; *B.T.Journal, 1708/9–1714/15, 1714/15–1718*; *CSP, Col., 1685–88, 1689–92, 1708–9, 1710–11, 1712–14, 1714–15*; *C.T.Books, 1716*, XXX, pt.2; *C.T.Papers, 1708–1714, 1714–1719*. *Walker expedition* (Graham).

DAB. DNB. Dalton, *English army lists*, I, 169, 221, 323; II, 27, 82, 83; VI, 20, 283–92. R. P. Bond, *Queen Anne's American kings* (Oxford, 1952), I, 46–47, 52, 122, 123–24. Brebner, *New England's outpost*. Dalton, *George the First's army*, II, 55–62. Murdoch, *History of Nova-Scotia*, I. Waller, *Samuel Vetch*; *see also* his article, "Samuel Vetch and the glorious enterprize," N.Y. Hist. Soc. *Q.*, XXXIV (1950) 101–23. B. T. McCully, "Catastrophe in the wilderness: new light on the Canada expedition of 1709," *William and Mary Q.* (Williamsburg, Va.), 3d ser., XI (1954), 441–46; "From the north riding to Morocco: the early years of Governor Francis Nicholson, 1655–1685," *William and Mary Q.*, 3d ser., XIX (1962), 534–56; "The New England-Acadia fishery dispute and the Nicholson mission of August, 1687," Essex Institute, Salem, Mass., *Hist. Coll.*, XCVI (1960).

For detailed contemporary maps of the Hudson-Champlain corridor *see* especially the N.Y. Hist. Soc. collection, which contains a remarkable sketch of the region from Albany to Crown Point around 1757, measuring 61 by 16 inches; in addition, *see* A. B. Hulbert, *The Crown collection of photographs of American maps* (5v., Cleveland, 1904–8), I, 15, which reproduces a map "to show the way from Albany to Canada . . . ," drawn about 1720. Captain John Redknap's plan of Annapolis Royal, executed after the siege in October 1710, may be found in PRO, M.P.G. 274.

NIMIMITT (Nimiquid). *See* WENEMOUET

NOIRÉ DE LA MOLLERIE, JACQUES MALERAY DE. *See* MALERAY

NORMANDIN, DANIEL, soldier, court officer, clerk of court, royal notary; b. *c.* 1660 at Rochefort, France, son of Jacob Normandin and Marie Briant; buried 18 Sept. 1729 at Batiscan.

He arrived in Canada in October 1684 as a soldier in the Marquis de Rompré's company, but lost no time in replacing the musket by the pen. By 1687, equipped with a portable writing-desk, he was travelling through the countryside on both banks of the St Lawrence River, from Montreal to Batiscan. He was at one and the same time a tabellion, public recorder, reader of letters, and adviser on legal matters. He determined his fees in a somewhat erratic manner, which called down upon him the wrath of his *confrères*. In his acts he designated himself as "royal notary and tabellion of the King our Sire," and was active throughout a wide area. In 1715 he tried to establish himself at Montreal, but the local notaries opposed this move, on the grounds that there were enough of them already. Normandin then settled permanently in the region of Trois-Rivières, more particularly at Batiscan, and held simultaneously all the posts necessitating a minimum of legal knowledge.

Normandin had married Louise Hayot in 1687 at Sorel; she bore him five children. By a holograph will dated 6 May 1728, he bequeathed to his daughter Madeleine's husband, Guillaume Billy, the greater part of his possessions, including "all the minutes and originals of all kinds of contracts and acts owned by me in my capacity of royal notary from my reception of office until the day of my death."

RAYMOND DOUVILLE

AJTR, Greffe de Charles Le Sieur, 1687–1729; Greffe de Daniel Normandin, 1684–1729; Registre d'état civil de Batiscan. *Jug. et délib.*, IV, V, VI. Cloutier, *Histoire de la paroisse de Champlain*, I. J.-E. Roy, *Histoire du notariat*, I, 203.

NORO (le Porc-épic, the Porcupine), chieftain of the Fox (Outagami) Indians; delegate to the 1701 peace conference at Montreal; fl. 1700–1701.

In response to Governor CALLIÈRE's invitation, the Fox Indians of the western prairies sent a delegation to the conference of Indian tribes held in Montreal in the summer of 1701. The purpose of the conference was to discuss the terms of a peace treaty between the Indian allies of New France and the Iroquois. The Fox delegation was under the ceremonial leadership of Miskouensa, who had his face painted red and who saluted the governor by flourishing "an old rusty wig" in the courtly manner for want of a hat. For all practical purposes, Noro was the effective negotiator of his people. LE ROY de La Potherie's *Histoire* is the single source which speaks of Noro by name.

Noro presented two requests on behalf of his tribe. He first sought redress from the Chippewas, another ally of the French, for the murder of one of his people. Ouabangué, chief of the Chippewas, replied that the murder was to revenge the death of a Chippewa, said to have been killed by the Foxes. Noro hotly denied the guilt of his tribesmen and said that, at that time, he had been at war with the Sioux. He modestly noted, in passing, that he himself had killed 40 Sioux. The Chippewa chief then admitted that since the fatal arrow was not of Fox making, Noro might be right in suggesting that a Chippewa was to blame for the murder of the Fox. The two tribes ate together afterward to demonstrate their reconciliation and Noro later accepted a gift to erase the memory of his murdered tribesman. The issue was closed when he smoked the peace pipe "in order to swallow the vengeance which he might have claimed."

Noro gave Governor Callière a packet of beaver pelts with the wish of the Fox Indians that the governor would send them a Jesuit missionary, a blacksmith to mend their axes and firearms, and Nicolas PERROT. As Noro said, "Perrot is our father, he discovered our land, he made us knowledgeable and has now left us." The governor received their petition but gave only vague promises in return. The interpreter and agent, Perrot, was never sent back to live among the Foxes.

PETER N. MOOGK

AN, Col., C¹¹ᴬ, 19, pp.78–86 (copy in PAC). *Indian tribes* (Blair), II, 225. Charlevoix, *History* (Shea), V, 151. La Poterie, *Histoire* (1722), IV, 214–16, 255. L. P. Phelps, "The Fox Indians during the French regime," Wis. State Hist. Soc. *Proc., 1907*, 142–88.

NORREY, JACQUES LE PICARD DU MESNIL DE. *See* LE PICARD

NOUVEL, HENRI, priest, Jesuit, missionary; b. 1621 or 1624 at Pézenas (department of Hérault); d. sometime between 8 Oct. 1701 and 28 Oct. 1702, probably at Baie des Puants (Green Bay, Wis.).

Henri Nouvel entered the noviciate of Toulouse on 28 Aug. 1648 and arrived in New France on 4 Aug. 1662. He appears to have spent the first year at Quebec studying the Amerindian languages. The *Journal des Jésuites* mentions no sermon by Father Nouvel or any particular ministry by him among the whites at this time.

This Jesuit became famous for his voyages to the countries of the Montagnais and Papinachois, among whom he spent many years. He has left us the complete account of his first voyage. He set out from Quebec on 19 Nov. 1663, accompanied by Charles Amiot*, and went to Île Verte, where 60 Montagnais and Papinachois were waiting for him. On 8 December they reached Île Saint-Barnabé. It was not until 21 December, after they had made certain that the Iroquois were no longer in the vicinity, that they went inland, following the Rimouski River, which was already frozen, to its source. They spent the Christmas season near a large lake which is difficult to identify; it is possible that it was Trout Lake or Lake Ferré, or else Lake Macpès. On 5 Jan. 1664 they left this resting-place to go to look for a livelihood in a more comfortable spot. It was not until 27 February that they began to return to the St Lawrence, and in March they reached its shores. They spent the Easter fortnight on Île-aux-Basques. Father Nouvel wrote: "It bears the name of Île-aux-Basques because of the whale-fishing which the Basques formerly carried on there. . . . All around can still be seen the big ribs of whales that they killed."

On 21 April Father Nouvel began the second part of his voyage. He accompanied the Papinachois on a most difficult trip on the north shore of the St Lawrence. He wrote: "We made a full day's portage, sometimes climbing mountains, sometimes traversing woods through which we had difficulty making our way, since we were all as heavily loaded as we could be." They reached the Rivière Manikouaganistikou (Manicouagan), "which the French call the black river because of its depth," and it was there, facing a high mountain, that he celebrated "the first sacrifice which has been offered in this country, where no European had ever been seen." On 9 June he reached Lake Manicouagan, which he named Lake Saint-Barnabé, and on 23 June they started on the way back. "The river is so rapid that in four days we arrived back safely on the shore of the great river, where we found the French and Papinachois waiting for us. Finally, two days and two nights of a good northeast wind brought us to Quebec."

This voyage, which lasted seven months, was a real achievement, especially if one takes into account the fact that Father Nouvel, who came from the south of France, was ill prepared to face variations of temperature ranging from the extreme cold of winter to the extreme heat of summer. His companions had first excluded him from the trip to Lake Manicouagan, alleging the fatigues and dangers which it entailed. But he insisted, and pleaded his case so well that he was accepted and bore a large share of the labour. Before coming back he gathered information about the tribes farther north who would one day have to be evangelized. He had no regrets. In fact, he thanked his superior for having chosen him for this mission: "It seems to me that I have never known God except in the dense forests of Canada, where all the eternal truths that I have meditated upon elsewhere appeared to me with extraordinary clarity." Father Nouvel remained in these missions until 1669, making occasional trips to Quebec. The most important event was no doubt the visit which Bishop LAVAL made to Tadoussac in 1668. The bishop was received with great pomp; he visited the sick and the chieftains, and administered the sacrament of confirmation to some 150 neophytes who had been prepared by Father Nouvel.

In 1669–70 Father Nouvel was at the college of Quebec. The parish register of Boucherville records his passing through during the summer of 1671. He was at that time on his way to the missions to the Ottawas on the Great Lakes. He was to devote the last 30 years of his life to these missions, of which he was the superior from 1672 to 1681 and again from 1688 to 1695. During that time he had under his direction a whole team of remarkable missionaries, among whom were Fathers Jacques Marquette*, Claude Allouez*, Claude Dablon*, Claude AVENEAU, Étienne de CARHEIL. This apostolate was much more difficult than that to the Montagnais; the Ottawas were much less prepared to receive the faith, were divided among themselves, and were under the influence of the English and the Iroquois. The 1672 *Relation* gives us the account of Father Nouvel's first voyages to his new missionary territory. He left Sault-Sainte-Marie on 31 Oct. 1671 and in six months travelled through the missions north of Lake Huron as far as Lake Nipissing, a distance of more than 600 leagues. Even when he was superior he followed the Indians during the winter, as he had done formerly in the region of Tadoussac, and he was always an attentive observer of the beauties and riches of nature. In his capacity as superior he sent a letter on 29 May 1673 to Governor Buade* de Frontenac, in which he praised his Indians and drew the governor's attention to the efforts of the turn-coat Médard Chouart* Des Groseilliers to sow dissension among the Indian allies of New France and to detach them from the French. It was also Father Nouvel who in 1677 received at the Saint-Ignace mission the remains of Father Marquette, which had been buried two years earlier at the place of his death, near Ludington, Mich.

During Father Nouvel's second term of office, in 1694, Cadillac [LAUMET], Frontenac's friend and protégé, was appointed commandant at Fort Michilimackinac, the centre of the Ottawa missions. Although the commandant did not have the same ideas as the missionaries of how to behave towards the Indians, at the beginning all went as well as could be wished. Cadillac's great concern was to protect the fort against English and Iroquois marauders and to keep the sympathies of the friendly Indians. One day he asked the Ottawas to make a raid against the Iroquois. They returned victorious and presented the commandant with some 30 scalps. The chieftain asked Cadillac to regale his valiant warriors with spirits. Cadillac assented to this request. The Indians were not content with that but also obtained spirits from other Frenchmen, and the festivities went on noisily all night. According to Cadillac, everything went off in an orderly fashion. But the missionaries thought otherwise. In unequivocal terms Father Carheil reproached Cadillac with having disobeyed the king's orders and compromised the results of the missionaries' work. Father Pierre-François Pinet took up the matter in two sermons which Cadillac considered insulting to him personally and to the authority vested in him. He demanded a complete apology. For the sake of keeping peace, or because he was convinced that his subordinate had gone too far, Father Nouvel offered his apologies to Cadillac. After 1695 he became a simple missionary and applied himself with his customary zeal to the duties that were assigned him.

Father Nouvel, one of our great missionaries, gave 40 years of his life to Canada. The pages of his journal, preserved for us in the *Relations*, reveal a man of courage, with a serenity that nothing could perturb, and with a remarkable unworldly mind. In 1676 he wrote: "O missionary vocation, how precious you are to these dear missions! How many treasures you conceal amidst your pains and fatigues!" He was a missionary to the end. Indeed, the uncertainty which formerly prevailed concerning the place and date of his death seems no longer to have any basis today. Margry has published a letter sent by Father Jean MERMET to Cadillac and dated 8 Oct. 1701, at Michilimackinac. In it we read that Father Jean-Baptiste Chardon sailed for Baie des Puants in order to bring aid to Father Nouvel, "who is burdened with his more than 80 years and several infirmities." In addition, in a letter which he sent from Quebec to the general of the Society of Jesus on 28 Oct. 1702, Father François de CRESPIEUL lamented the recent death of Father Nouvel. Father Nouvel died then sometime between 8 Oct. 1701 and 28 Oct. 1702. Until evidence to the contrary is received, it is permissible and even normal to think that he died at his mission at Baie des Puants.

LÉON POULIOT, S.J.

ASJCF, D-7, Crespieul, 6. *Découvertes et établissements des Français* (Margry), V. *JR* (Thwaites),

Noyan

XLVIII, XLIX, LVI, LVII, LX. *Mission du Canada. Relations inédites de la Nouvelle-France (1672–1679) pour faire suite aux anciennes relations (1615–1672),* [éd. Félix Martin] (2v., Paris, 1861), I, 343; II, 126. *NYCD* (O'Callaghan and Fernow). George Paré, *The Catholic church in Detroit, 1701–1888* (Detroit,

1951). Rochemonteix, *Les Jésuites et la N.-F. au XVIIe siècle,* III, 480ff.

NOYAN, PIERRE-JACQUES PAYEN DE. *See* PAYEN

O

OCHAGAC (Ochagach, Ochakah). *See* AUCHAGAH

OHONSIOWANNE (La Grande Terre, "Great World," Tohonsiowanne, Ouhensiouan, Ohoengewaene), Onondaga sachem, chief of the Onondaga old men and warriors, fl. 1699–1704.

In January 1699, Ohonsiowanne and the Oneida Odatsighta went to Montreal to try to persuade Governor CALLIÈRE to end the war of the French-allied, western Indians against the Iroquois. They returned in March 1699 with belts from Callière stating that only a direct exchange of prisoners would end the hostilities. That summer the Onondagas heard of an intended attack on the Senecas, and Ohonsiowanne was part of a war party that went to assist them. A Seneca pro-French faction then persuaded him to go again to Callière, but the governor demanded that a group more representative of the Five Nations be sent. In July 1700, Ohonsiowanne and ARADGI with four Senecas, including AOUENANO and TONATAKOUT, appeared in Montreal again to ask for peace and to request that a general exchange of prisoners be made.

Ohonsiowanne was sent to Quebec in October 1703 by TEGANISSORENS to receive Governor RIGAUD de Vaudreuil's messages on the possibility of continuing the peace between New York and Canada despite the war in Europe. Ohonsiowanne was described by Vaudreuil as being "as zealous a partizan of the French as Teganissorence is of the English." In September 1704 Ohonsiowanne (having been in Albany in May) relayed a message from Peter SCHUYLER to Vaudreuil in Montreal. The governor used this opportunity to enlist Ohonsiowanne as Father François VAILLANT de Gueslis' escort to the Seneca country. After 1704 nothing more is heard of Ohonsiowanne.

D. H. CORKRAN

[Claude-Charles Le Roy de Bacqueville de La Potherie], *Voyage de l'Amérique* (4v., Amsterdam, 1723), IV, 117–30. *Livingston Indian records* (Leder), 194, 198. *NYCD* (O'Callaghan and Fernow), IV, 491, 558, 564, 572, 658, 694; IX, 742–45.

ONANGUICÉ (Onanguisset). *See* OUNANGUISSÉ

ONTANIENDO. *See* ATECOUANDO

ORVILLIERS. *See* GUILLOUET

OTOUTAGON (Ottoutagan). *See* OUTOUTAGAN

OUACHALA (Ouachalard, Ouashala, Ouashalas, Ouechala), chief of the Fox tribe and leader of the peace faction; fl. 1716–27.

In 1716 RIGAUD de Vaudreuil dispatched lieutenant LA PORTE de Louvigny to the upper lakes to impose a peace on the Foxes. This tribe resented the French arming of their enemies, the Illinois and Chippewas, and blamed the French for the Ottawa massacre of a Fox village near Fort Pontchartrain (Detroit) in 1712. With over 400 Frenchmen Louvigny attacked the Fox villages and forced Ouachala, a Fox chief, to come to terms in the name of the tribe. The Foxes agreed to make peace with all the tribes allied to the French, and "by forcible or friendly means" to induce the Kickapoos and Mascoutens to do the same. The first condition of the French was that all prisoners be returned, which was done immediately; they required also that slaves be captured in "distant regions" to replace any casualties. The final term, an agreement "to hunt to pay the expenses of the military preparations made for this war," suggests an attempt to draw the Foxes into the orbit of French trade. As a guarantee, Louvigny brought back six hostages.

PEMOUSSA and another of the hostages died of smallpox in Montreal, and word of the disease kept the other Fox chiefs from coming down to ratify the peace. In 1717 Louvigny returned to Michilimackinac to reassure them, and the hostage who accompanied him reproached Ouachala for failing to appear at Montreal. The chief admitted that he was at fault and agreed to come down the next year; and OUENEMEK promised to use his influence with the Foxes to persuade them to carry out the French terms. It was only in 1719, however, after the return of 12 more Fox prisoners in 1718, that Ouachala was persuaded to come to Montreal to cement the peace.

The peace of 1716 proved fragile, in part, it seems, because the Illinois and Chippewa allies of the French attacked the Foxes. Ouachala complained that he was unable to control his young men; apparently they despised him "because he seemed too well-affected towards the French." In 1722 he led an attack on the Illinois who had killed his nephew Minchilay, but in 1723, when he could not restrain his men from attacking Chippewa raiders at the St Joseph River, he accompanied them to ensure "that the French there would not be harmed."

Vaudreuil was reluctant to get embroiled in an Indian war and claimed that "the Foxes are less to blame than the Illinois." LE MOYNE DE LON-GUEUIL, his successor, wanted to end war between the Illinois and Foxes by alliance, and detach the latter from the Sioux. With these ends in mind, on 7 June 1726 LE MARCHAND de Lignery gathered the Fox, Sauk, and Winnebago chiefs at Baie des Puants (Green Bay) to reaffirm the peace. Ouachala suggested that a "French leader" ["chef françois"] be sent among them to act as a check on his men. Convinced of Ouachala's good faith the French began planning for a gathering of representatives from the western tribes at Montreal to seal a formal pact. Within a year, however, the new governor, Charles de Beauharnois* de La Boische wrote, "we can no longer rely on the promises the Foxes made to M. de Lignery to live in peace, especially since the death of their chiefs, which has unleashed the war parties that they have sent out and still send out daily." Because the fur trade of the Illinois was more important to the French in the west than that of the Foxes, plans were made to force the Foxes into submission. Since peace was not restored until after 1734 when the French subdued the Foxes and deported their war chief KIALA, it seems likely that Ouachala was one of the chiefs whose death was noted in 1727.

Ouachala was referred to by the French as "the great chief" or "the principal chief" of the Foxes. Apparently he was one of the civil chiefs, whose authority was superseded in time of conflict by that of the war chiefs. In such cases the civil chiefs often represented, as Ouachala did, a peace faction in the tribe, at variance with the more warlike elements. In exploiting this division of influence the French were following a policy which marked European dealings with Indians up to the end of the nineteenth century.

DAVID LEE and TERRY SMYTHE

AN, Col., C¹¹ᴬ, 36, ff.71–76; 38, f.103; 39, f.143; 42, f.164; 44, f.441; 45, f.136; 48, f.419; 49, ff.120, 564.

OÜAOURENÉ. *See* WOWURNA

OUASHALA (Ouashalas, Ouechala). *See* OUACHALA

OUENANGUENET. *See* WENEMOUET

OUENEMEK (Ouilamek, Haouilamek, Ouilameg, Wilamak), Potawatomi chief of St Joseph River; born of either Sauk or Fox parents; fl. 1695–1717.

Although described by Governor RIGAUD de Vaudreuil as "a man of intrigue," Ouenemek was a consistent ally of the French at least during the early phase of his career. In 1696, for example, he was a prominent member of a war party that drove off a large band of Iroquois, who had come to Michilimackinac to trade with the Hurons and Ottawas in hopes of luring them out of the French alliance. Later, Father JOSEPH-JACQUES MAREST, a missionary at that post, suggested that Ouenemek was so necessary for preserving the allegiance of the Potawatomis that it would be wise for the governor to pay him a small subsidy.

In 1701 Ouenemek attended the peace conference held in Montreal between the French, their Indian allies, and the Iroquois. Besides displaying his natural bargaining skill during the commercial negotiations, he again demonstrated his loyalty to the French by seconding the efforts of his fellow chief, OUNANGUISSÉ, in securing the peace pledges of all the tribes of the upper lakes.

After 1701, however, the new French policy, based on fairly extensive withdrawal from the west, heralded a change in Ouenemek's attitude. During a series of embassies to Governor Vaudreuil between 1705 and 1712 and in conversations with the missionaries at St Joseph River, he contended that, without a strong French garrison, it was impossible to restrain the young men of his tribe from engaging in the ever more widespread intertribal strife. He complained too of the harsh treatment and poor prices his people received at Detroit and insisted with increasing urgency that a canoe of Frenchmen with a permanent commandant be sent immediately to the Potawatomis.

No doubt chagrined by Vaudreuil's failure to meet these demands completely, and conscious of his own family ties, Ouenemek was reluctant to aid the French in their war of extermination against the Foxes. In July of 1712, at Montreal, he argued against KOUTAOILIBOE and prophesied to Vaudreuil that it would be easier to start a total war with the Foxes than to end one, for that tribe was fiercely brave and had many allies, notably the Sauks. He repeated this warning in 1714. Because of his detached stand, he was employed as a peace envoy by the Foxes in 1717. At the same time, he

Ouhensiouan

promised the governor that he would use his great influence with the Foxes and Sauks to persuade OUACHALA and their other chiefs to ratify the terms of the 1716 peace. His son, who was later to become a noted Potawatomi chief, was taken prisoner by the Foxes in 1721 but was returned for ransom by some Mascouten intermediaries.

DONALD J. HORTON

AN, Col., C¹¹A, 22, ff.262v–63; 28, ff.161–63v, 171v; 30, ff.90–90v; 33, ff.81–83v; 42, f.320. Charlevoix, *History* (Shea), IV, 278; V, 143. "Correspondance de Vaudreuil," APQ *Rapport, 1947–48*, 265. *Indian tribes* (Blair), I, 270. La Poterie, *Histoire* (1722), IV, 207. *Michigan Pioneer Coll.*, XXXIII, 385, 501, 554, 559–67, 570, 590. *NYCD* (O'Callaghan and Fernow), IX, 646. Wisc. State Hist. Soc. *Coll.*, XVI, 301, 397; XVII, 396. Y. F. Zoltvany, "New France and the west," 301–22.

OUHENSIOUAN. *See* OHONSIOWANNE

OUILAMEG (Ouilamek). *See* OUENEMEK

OUNANGUISSÉ (Onanguisset, Onanguicé), a pro-French Potawatomi chief of St Joseph River, probably of Sauk origin, and an important leader among the tribes of the Great Lakes; fl. 1695–1716.

Ounanguissé was one of the most influential and independent spokesmen for the Indian allies of the northwest. Described by Charlevoix* as "a talented man and a good speaker," he was regarded by the colonial officials as a vital link in maintaining their influence among the Great Lakes tribes. In 1695 he depicted himself to Governor Buade* de Frontenac as a lifelong ally of the French, and warned him privately against the treachery of the Foxes and Mascoutens, whose spokesmen were also present. A few days later Iroquois were reported near Montreal, and Ounanguissé and the other Indians from the Baie des Puants (Green Bay) area accompanied DANEAU de Muy and a force of 700–800 men to Île Perrot. After a week during which no enemy was sighted, Ounanguissé and his men tired of the campaign and returned to Montreal. Frontenac chided him for leaving the army while under orders, but gave the Indians presents and sent them off in good temper. In 1697 Ounanguissé boldly warned Frontenac that if the French persisted in prohibiting traders from coming to his people, they would never again carry their furs or come to parley at Montreal. Nor was this considered an idle threat for, as LE ROY de La Potherie suggested, Ounanguissé, by virtue of hereditary ties and his general prestige, was capable of leading several tribes out of the French alliance.

In 1701, at the peace conference in Montreal

between the French, their allies, and the Iroquois, Ounanguissé represented the Sauks and Illinois as well as the Potawatomis, and, on certain key issues, he spoke on behalf of nearly all the Great Lakes tribes. Shrewdly aware that the French were counting heavily on his influence, he joined the Fox chief NORO in requesting that Governor CALLIÈRE send Nicolas PERROT back to St Joseph River in order to assure the implementation of the peace. He further disconcerted the French officials by vividly outlining to his fellow chiefs the serious difficulties that could arise if the Iroquois, who had failed to bring their prisoners, should prove insincere. At the formal ratification of the treaty he was singularly impressive, wearing the head of a bull buffalo with the horns hanging over his ears.

In 1716, Governor RIGAUD de Vaudreuil credited Ounanguissé with leading part of an allied war party that inflicted defeats on two large bands of Mascoutens and Foxes. His son and namesake was also a Potawatomi chief and was active as late as 1747.

DONALD J. HORTON

AN, Col., C¹¹A, 19, ff.42–42v. Charlevoix, *History* (Shea), V, 69, 143–44, 151–52. *Indian tribes* (Blair), II, 255. La Poterie, *Histoire* (1722), III, 301–2; IV, 53–57, 206–11, 212–13, 224–26, 234, 245–46, 249. *Michigan Pioneer Coll.*, XXXIII, 576. *NYCD* (O'Callaghan and Fernow), IX, 620–23, 673, 723. Wis. State Hist. Soc. *Coll.*, XVI, 160–65, 168; XVII, 490–92. Eccles, *Frontenac*, 328–33.

OUTAOULIBOY. *See* KOUTAOILIBOE

OUTOUTAGAN (Outoutaga, Otoutagon, Ottoutagan; better known as **Jean Le Blanc** or **Jean Le Bland** because of the whiteness of his mother's skin), an important chief of the Ottawas du Sable, and son of the chief Le Talon; figured prominently in the Ottawa-Miami feud at Detroit in 1706; fl. 1698–1712.

Imperial expansion by the French into the west victimized the Ottawas, their oldest ally among the tribes of that area. These were a mercantile people whose trade route between the upper lakes and Montreal ran along the river which still bears their name. They had replaced the Hurons as the leading Indian middlemen in the western fur trade and, by the end of the 17th century, they were being replaced by French traders in the west. Outoutagan endeavoured to preserve the alliance that his father, the chief Le Talon, had made with the French, while still protecting the trade interests of the Ottawas.

Outoutagan's great loyalty to the French is evident in his reaction to the post and new settlement at Detroit. The development of Detroit by Cadillac [LAUMET] as the central *entrepôt* of the western fur trade undermined the older post of Michilimackinac, around which most of the Ottawas lived; it reduced their role as middlemen and it bypassed their trade route to Montreal. Yet in 1701 Outoutagan promised CALLIÈRE that, in compliance with the governor's request, he would move with his people to Detroit. The promise was fulfilled after 1702 by the majority of the Ottawas, despite some apprehension about the transfer.

In early June of 1706, mutual distrust between the Ottawas and the Miamis at Detroit exploded in the LE PESANT affair. According to his brother MISCOUAKY, Outoutagan had opposed Le Pesant's attack on the Miamis. He shared no responsibility for the death of Constantin DELHALLE, the missionary whom he had released from his captors, saying "my father, go to the fort and tell the French not to fire at us and that we wish them no harm." The friar, however, was shot dead by a vengeful Ottawa as he approached the fort. It was Outoutagan who entered the fort under a flag of truce in a vain effort to restore peace. A month or two later, he was drawn to a sham peace conference where he was shot and wounded just as he accepted the hand of Quarante Sols*, the Huron chief.

At a later conference at Montreal on 18 June 1707, Outoutagan offered his own body to Governor RIGAUD de Vaudreuil to appease his anger over the murder of the missionary and the soldier by the Ottawas. The governor refused his submission and the offer of two Ottawas as slaves. Instead, he demanded the head of Le Pesant, who was blamed for the entire affair. Vaudreuil believed that Outoutagan was the sole Ottawa capable of overthrowing the paramount chief, a fellow Ottawa du Sable. Outoutagan would consent only to a repudiation of Le Pesant's leadership. He was then told to go to Detroit via the Iroquois lands to offer Cadillac the two slaves and to let him determine the form of further reparation.

At Detroit, Cadillac demanded the unconditional surrender of Le Pesant and Outoutagan protested "he is my brother, my own brother." The Ottawas were stricken with famine and they desperately needed a reopening of trade to obtain food supplies. A resumption of the war would have been as distasteful to them as to the French. Before presenting Cadillac's demand to the Ottawa council at Michilimackinac, Outoutagan waited until their assembled allies had departed so that they might not protest. The council decided that Le Pesant would be put to death if he refused to go to Detroit, and KINONGÉ and other Ottawas helped the French to apprehend him. He was given to Cadillac as a slave with the plea of his people that his life be spared.

In spite of Le Pesant's subsequent escape from Fort Pontchartrain the Ottawas had been humiliated to preserve the French alliance system in the west and none of their grievances against the Miamis had been answered. Nevertheless they did gain two advantages from reconciliation with their allies. Trade was resumed and the Iroquois, who were anxious to destroy the Ottawas, were deprived of an opportunity to intervene between the western tribes. With peace restored, some Ottawas returned to Detroit. In 1712, Father JOSEPH-JACQUES MAREST reported that continued insecurity had led most of these, including Outoutagan's wife (probably Mme Techenet), to come back to Michilimackinac. Outoutagan remained at Detroit.

Two apocryphal tales about Outoutagan's quick tongue survive. CLAIRAMBAULT d'Aigremont reported that the chief had once told Buade* de Frontenac that he was "a good-for-nothing weakling since he needed a horse to carry him." In another encounter with the governor recorded by Charlevoix*, Frontenac asked Outoutagan, "a bad Christian and a great drunkard," what he thought liquor was made of. The Ottawa is said to have replied that "it was an extract of tongues and hearts, for when I have had a drink, I fear nothing and I speak like an angel." This last anecdote is probably a fabrication. At the 1701 peace conference at Montreal, Outoutagan opposed liquor sales to the young Indians visiting the town and he begged in vain for an end to the traffic in alcohol with Indian allies of the French. "It is a drink that ruins our minds," he said.

Outoutagan's importance in French Indian policy is suggested by the differing accounts of his character. Cadillac portrayed the chief as a treacherous hypocrite and described his wife, Mme Techenet, as a bigamous slut who was pro-English to boot. Part of this hostility may have been engendered by the testimony of Outoutagan's sister about the misdeeds of Cadillac and Étienne VOLANT de Radisson at Detroit. On the other hand, Vaudreuil spoke of "the submissive and apparently sincere manner in which Outoutagan has always spoken to me, together with the blind obedience he has shown to my orders and in doing my will." Perhaps the best assessment was made by Charlevoix, who wrote: "this Indian possessed much talent, and though strongly attached to the French nation, he saw more clearly than desirable . . . where many things had to be passed over and much left to circumstances." Outoutagan could do little, however, to arrest the decline in Ottawa trading fortunes, and his devotion to the French produced no compensation. He did not succeed to Le Pesant's authority and it is evident that by 1712 he commanded few followers.

PETER N. MOOGK

[Manuscript references are legion, but the most important are AN, Col., C¹¹ᴬ, 19, p.82; 24, pp.27–30; 28, p.144; 29, pp.26–101; 30, pp.82–88; 33, pp.71–79 (copies in PAC); also 39, ff.44, 50v, 52v. "Correspondance de Vaudreuil," APQ *Rapport, 1938–39*, 10–179; *1939–40*, 355–463; *1942–43*, 399–443; *1946–47*, 371–460; *1947–48*, 137–339. Charlevoix, *Histoire*, II, 276 and *passim*; III, 306 and *passim*; *History* (Shea), V, 144 and *passim*. La Poterie, *Histoire* (1722), IV, 258 and *passim*. *Michigan Pioneer Coll.*, XXXIII, 328–29, 333 and *passim*. Fragmentary excerpts from series C¹¹ᴬ are also to be found in *NYCD* (O'Callaghan and Fernow), IX, and Wis. State Hist. Soc. *Coll.*, XVI, but the excerpts in these volumes are much less useful and less complete than those in the *Michigan Pioneer Collections* and the APQ *Rapports*. P.N.M.]

OUWOORANA. *See* WOWURNA

OZON, POTENTIEN, priest, Recollet, provincial commissioner for Canada; b. *c.* 1627 at Montargis (France); d. 16 June 1705 in Paris.

In 1645, when he was 18, Ozon made his religious profession in the Recollet house in Paris. He was appointed guardian of the convent at Châteauvillain in 1661 and in 1663 he exercised this office at the convent of Saint-Denis, at Paris. That same year he became a lecturer in theology. He was sent to Rome in 1667–68 as a delegate with an eye to the raising of the Recollet convents of the province of Artois into an ecclesiastical province. In 1671 he appears again, as novice master, then as guardian, of the convent at Saint-Germain-en-Laye, and at the same time as superior of the convent at Versailles.

On becoming provincial visitor of the mission in Canada, he sailed from La Rochelle in June 1675 and reached Canada on 27 September. There he received two recruits who were to become famous, Father Joseph DENYS and Brother Didace Pelletier*. He returned to France in December 1675.

In June 1676 he was appointed provincial commissioner for Canada; he visited the missions from Fort Frontenac (Kingston) on Lake Ontario to Percé. He returned to France in the autumn of 1677.

In 1683 he was guardian of the convent at Rouen, and in 1691 he was elected provincial of the Recollets of the province of Saint-Antoine in Artois, then in 1695 provincial of the province of Saint-Denis at Paris. In the latter capacity he presented to Bishop Saint-Vallier [LA CROIX], who was then in Paris, a request to have the local and personal interdict removed which the bishop had cast upon the convent in Montreal the preceding year, as a result of the affair of the *prie-dieu* [*see* JOSEPH DENYS]. The bishop of Quebec assented to his request on 15 July 1695.

Ozon was re-elected provincial in 1701 and died at the convent in Paris 16 June 1705 at 78 years of age and after 60 years of life in holy orders.

GABRIEL-M.-RÉAL DUMAS

Archives des Franciscains de Québec, Dossier Potentien Ozon. ANDQ, Registres des baptêmes, mariages et sépultures. BN, MS, Fr. 13875, 15775, f.3. *Jug. et délib.*, II, 97, 105–8. Le Clercq, *First establishment of the faith* (Shea); *New relation of Gaspesia* (Ganong). Le Tac, *Histoire chronologique de la N.-F.* (Réveillaud). Gosselin, *L'Église du Canada*, I, 117ff. Rochemonteix, *Les Jésuites et la N.-F. au XVIIᵉ siècle*, III, 639. *France franciscaine* (Lille), I (1912), 111. Hugolin [Stanislas Lemay], "L'établissement des Récollets à l'isle Percée 1673–1690," *BRH*, XVII (1911), 346.

P

PACAUD. *See* PASCAUD

PAILLARD, *dit* **Le Poitevin, LÉONARD (Paillart, Paillé,** *dit* **Paillard, Paillet),** master carpenter and millwright; b. 1647, son of André Paillard and Catherine Geoffroy of Bersac parish (department of Haute-Vienne); m. in 1678 at Beauport Louise-Marie Vachon, by whom he had nine children; buried 6 Jan. 1729 at the Hôpital Général of Montreal.

Léonard Paillard possessed the very Canadian traits of ambition, versatility, and mobility. As a millwright, he met one of the most urgent needs of the colony. He probably came to Canada about 1670 as an indentured worker. In October 1672 he became the apprentice of Jean Lemire*, a carpenter living on Grande Allée near Quebec. It is likely that he learned the millwright's craft from Lemire. He completed his apprenticeship in carpentry in 1675 under Pierre Mercereau, who had purchased Paillard's indenture for 60 *livres*. Paillard subsequently became Mercereau's journeyman.

Paillard married a notary's daughter in 1678 and settled at Petite-Auvergne in Beauport seigneury "about a league" from Quebec. On his farm he tilled the soil and worked at his trade. In 1684 he took up residence on Rue du Sault-au-Matelot in Lower Town, Quebec. He still did carpentry outside the city.

In May 1686 Paillard contracted to build a windmill near Boucherville. The opportunities in the Montreal region evidently pleased him for he wound up his affairs at Quebec and moved his family to Ville-Marie the following year. He also bought a farm at *côte* Saint-Jean, which he leased out for a small rental. At Ville-Marie, Paillard and his family occupied rented lodgings until the completion of their new home near Notre-Dame de Bonsecours chapel in 1692.

The mass of notarized building contracts entered into by Paillard testifies to his prodigious activity. In the Quebec area he occasionally took on more projects than he could complete and was forced to transfer the surplus to other carpenters. Paillard constructed houses, roof frames, and barns. His specialization in mills evolved slowly and it was in the Montreal region that this skill came to the fore. This part of the colony was destined to be the lumbering and grain-growing centre of New France and the existence of sawmills and grist-mills was essential if the colony was to feed itself and to export timber and flour. The millwright's knowledge of wooden cogged mechanisms was invaluable in a country with many technological deficiencies.

Léonard branched out into other activities like the grain trade and water transport. He bought a half interest in a small merchant vessel in 1692 and acted as agent for one or two mills.

Paillard did not work alone. He was assisted by a servant on his Beauport farm and when he built mills he concentrated on the fine details while other hands performed the heavier work. He worked with other carpenters and in 1698, for example, he and Jean La Croix of Montreal went into formal partnership for one year. Help came from the odd apprentice and, at times, from his son-in-law and sons. In this way Charles and Gabriel Paillard learned their father's craft.

Even at the age of 74, this energetic millwright went off to distant Detroit by canoe to repair a windmill and to do miscellaneous bits of carpentry. Small wonder that on his deathbed he looked like an ancient of ninety.

PETER N. MOOGK

AJM, Greffe d'Antoine Adhémar, 28 août 1688, 17 janv. 1700, 15 déc. 1712; Greffe d'Hilaire Bourgine, 28 juillet 1686; Greffe de Jacques David, 7 août 1721; Greffe de Michel Lepailleur de Laferté; Greffe de Claude Maugue, 4 janv. 1688, 28 mars 1689, 3 juillet 1692; Greffe de Michel Moreau, 14 oct. 1686; Greffe de J.-B. Pottier, 10 avril 1690; Greffe de Pierre Raimbault, 13 nov. 1698; Greffe de Nicolas Senet, 11 juin 1719; Greffe de Marien Tailhandier, 12 févr. 1705. AJQ, Greffe de Claude Auber, 26 juin 1678; Greffe de Pierre Duquet, 14 sept. 1675; Greffe de Michel Fillion, 12 avril 1684; Greffe de Gilles Rageot, 26 oct. 1672, 14 oct. 1674, 24 mai 1686, 13 mars 1687. AQ, NF, Coll. de pièces jud. et not., 3308. ASQ, Polygraphie, I, 88. *Jug. et délib.*, II, 375, 988–89, 1029–30, 1040; III, 10, 127–28, 171–73, 407, 799, 878–79, 1041–42; IV, 766–67; VI, 960. Recensement du Canada, 1681 (Sulte), 83.

PAPINEAU, *dit* **Montigny, SAMUEL,** soldier, copyholder of the Sulpicians on the *côte* Saint-Michel, Montreal Island; b. at Montigny in the province of Poitou, son of Samuel Papineau, a merchant, and of Marie Delain (Delair); buried 23 April 1737 at Sault-au-Récollet.

Samuel Papineau was a soldier in the company of the Sieur d'Andresy, which arrived at Quebec in 1688; the latter, who died during the crossing, was replaced by ALOIGNY de La Groye. For ten years Papineau served faithfully under Frontenac [Buade*] and CALLIÈRE, and was then discharged. On 25 April 1699 he acquired from the Sulpicians a land grant of 60 acres on the *côte* Saint-Michel. In 1705 he sold this land to Jean Guillebert, *dit* Laframboise, and in 1711 obtained ownership of a new grant of land at Rivière-des-Prairies which he retained until his death in 1737. He left only a few possessions, as is shown by the inventory drawn up after his death.

On 6 June 1704, at Rivière-des-Prairies, Samuel Papineau had married Catherine Quevillon (1686–1781), by whom he had nine children. When she was young, Catherine had been carried off by the Iroquois, and ransomed after several years of captivity. She married four times and died at the age of 95.

Samuel Papineau was only a private soldier; he concerned himself particularly with the land grants which were made to him from 1699 on. He is the ancestor of the Papineau families in Canada.

ROLAND-J. AUGER

AJM, Documents judiciaires, 29 juillet 1738; Greffe d'Antoine Adhémar, 5 nov. 1705; Greffe de Jacques David, 11 mars 1720; Greffe de Pierre Raimbault, 25 avril 1699, 8 juin 1704, 29 janv. 1711, 29 juillet 1738. Registre des audiences, 31 juillet 1739, 12 janv. 1740. Jean Leclerc, "Les capitaines d'infanterie 1683–1689," SGCF *Mémoires*, XI (1960), 163–67. D.-B. Papineau, "Samuel Papineau," et "Généalogie de la famille Papineau au Canada," BRH, XXXIX (1933), 331–46, 483–94.

Paradis

PARADIS, JEAN, sea captain; b. 22 July 1658 at Quebec, son of Pierre Paradis, cutler, and of Barbe Guyon; d. before 1725 at La Rochelle, where he had settled.

After studying at the Jesuit college in Quebec, Jean Paradis followed the courses given by Martin Boutet*, the king's hydrographer, in the same town. In July 1678 he bought for 1,200 *livres* the two houses of Jean Talon* situated in Rue Buade at Quebec, and bounded at the back "by the Place d'Armes of the Château Saint-Louis." Louis Rouer* de Villeray acted in this instance as proxy for Talon, who had returned to France.

There is no doubt that this is the Jean Paradis who commanded the *Sainte-Anne,* which was wrecked on the reefs of the Manicouagan River in the autumn of 1704; the intendant, JACQUES RAUDOT, ordered the sale of the wreckage of this ship in October 1705. It was also Jean Paradis who, sailing from La Rochelle in 1711 at the helm of the *Neptune,* was intercepted by Admiral WALKER and forced to pilot his ship the *Edgar.* We know the disaster that resulted for the English fleet off Île-aux-Oeufs. Some historians have accused the pilot Paradis of treachery on this occasion. Was he really a traitor? He would then have deserved the disdainful remark made by Admiral Walker to Colonel Samuel VETCH: "I thanck you for your caution concerning the French Pilot, but I never intended to trust him any farther then I could throw him."

Two years later, in 1713, Jean Paradis, captain of the *Phénix* bound for the West Indies, was recruiting indentured workers for that colony. In 1720 an order issued by Michel Bégon* declared right and proper the seizure by Étienne Amiot de Lincourt, one of the guards of the Domaine d'Occident, of spirits smuggled by Jean Paradis, captain of the *Généreuse.*

Jean Paradis died before 1725. He had settled at La Rochelle, where on 8 June 1693 he had married Catherine Batailler, daughter of Pierre Batailler, a deceased sea captain, and of Angélique Roy. They had eight children, one being a son whose first name was also Jean and who was a ship's pilot like his father and his maternal grandfather.

ROLAND-J. AUGER

AJQ, Greffe de Romain Becquet, 15 juillet 1678; Greffe de Gilles Rageot, 9 févr. 1688. Juchereau, *Annales* (Jamet), 365f. P.-G. Roy, *Inv. ord. int.,* I, 3, 191. *Walker expedition* (Graham). Gabriel Debien, *Le peuplement des Antilles françaises au XVIIᵉ siècle. Les engagés partis de La Rochelle (1683–1715)* [Cairo, 1942], 165f. Ernest Myrand. *M. de la Colombière, orateur: historique d'un sermon célèbre prononcé à Notre-Dame de Québec le 5 novembre 1690, à l'occasion de la levée du siège de cette ville ...* , *suivi des relations officielles de Frontenac, Monseignat et Juchereau de Saint-Ignace ...* (Montréal, 1898). Archange Godbout, "Paradis," SGCF *Mémoires,* I (1944), 30–33. Ernest Myrand, "Le capitaine Paradis," *BRH,* IV (1898), 221f. P.-G. Roy, "Qui était le capitaine Paradis," *BRH,* XLIX (1943), 65–68. Victor Tremblay, "Au sujet du capitaine Paradis," *BRH,* L (1944), 208f.

PASCAUD (Pacaud), ANTOINE, prominent merchant of Montreal and La Rochelle; b. at La Prade in Angoumois, *c.* 1665; d. at La Rochelle in January 1717.

The son of Guillaume Pascaud and Catherine Berteau, Antoine Pascaud arrived in Canada in the early 1680s and took up residence in Montreal. In 1688 Catherine Thierry, the widow of Charles Le Moyne* de Longueuil et de Châteauguay, formed a partnership with him for a period of three years. The understanding was that Pascaud, for one-third of all the profits, would help the widow manage the business of her late husband, valued at 58,215 *livres.* Quite possibly, Pascaud used the money he realized during those years to begin a business of his own, for he was a prominent member of the Canadian mercantile community by the 1690s. He then supplied merchandise to the Compagnie du Nord and to such leading fur traders as Pierre-Charles LE SUEUR, Antoine LAUMET, *dit* de Lamothe Cadillac, and the TONTY brothers, HENRI and ALPHONSE.

Pascaud played a very important role in the foundation of the Compagnie de la Colonie in 1700, which placed control of the fur trade in Canadian hands for the first time since the demise of the Compagnie des Habitants in the 1650s. In 1699 the Canadians, rather than accept the reduced price scale for beaver suggested by the farmers of the Domaine d'Occident, who held a monopoly on the purchase of the pelts, sent Pascaud and CHARLES JUCHEREAU de Saint-Denys to France to obtain for the colony the right to dispose freely of its skins on the metropolitan market. Pascaud, however, did not limit himself to carrying out these instructions. To prevent a market glut he also purchased the Domaine d'Occident's stock of unsold pelts for 350,000 *livres,* a sum which he borrowed from the Paris bankers Pasquier, Bourlet, et Gayot (Goy). The minister of Marine then decided that the ownership of these pelts and control of the beaver trade should be placed in the hands of a Canadian company that would issue low cost shares to enable as many settlers as possible to join it. The minister's proposal and Pascaud's transactions were ratified in October 1700 by an assembly of some 90 leading Canadians summoned by the governor and the intendant. Thus the Compagnie de la Colonie came into being. According to the minister, this experiment might have enabled Canada to secure the internal autonomy of a French *pays d'état* but it was unfortunately doomed to failure by the unfavourable economic conditions of the early 18th century. In 1704 Pascaud was again sent to France, this time by Governor RIGAUD de Vaudreuil and Intendant Beauharnois* de La Boische, to explain the company's plight to the minister, but his mission was in vain. The Compagnie de la Colonie was liquidated in 1706 and the beaver monopoly was transferred to the French firm of Aubert, Néret, et Gayot.

In addition to the fur trade and his Montreal store Pascaud took an interest in lumbering and the growing of hemp, but he owned no seigneuries and does not appear to have made cash loans to the settlers. Unlike CHARLES AUBERT de La Chesnaye, he preferred to invest in France the money he earned in Canada. Towards 1710 he moved his base of operations to La Rochelle where he took up residence with his wife and family. A partner, Pierre de Lestage, remained in Canada to manage his affairs.

In La Rochelle Pascaud further expanded his role in the French North American trade. He obtained government contracts to supply wheat and peas to Plaisance and Acadia and, with an associate named Jacques Le Clerc, discounted at 10 per cent bills of exchange drawn on Néret and Gayot, the surviving members of the partnership formed in 1706. In 1715, this firm discovered that it lacked the funds to redeem 150,000 *livres* of bills of exchange held by Pascaud and Le Clerc. It therefore agreed to let the two men seize beaver shipments arriving from Canada and, in the future, to honour their bills of exchange before dealing with those held by others. News of this transaction caused a storm of protest in Canada. Merchants from Montreal and Quebec claimed that "M. Pascaud is seeking only to ruin all the businessmen of this country ... he hopes to reduce all the merchants of this country to the necessity of directing to no others but himself the bills of exchange for the goods which they need for their trade."

Pascaud died in La Rochelle in January 1717. He was survived by his wife, Marguerite Bouat, daughter of Abraham Bouat, an innkeeper, and Marguerite de Névellet, whom he had married in Montreal on 21 Jan. 1697, and by five of eight children. Under the very able management of the widow and the two sons, Antoine and Joseph-Marie, the affairs of the family firm continued to prosper. In 1741 it was estimated that Canadians owed approximately 450,000 *livres* to French merchants, of which 300,000 *livres* were owed to the Compagnie des Indes and the widow Pascaud. The two sons, for a time, held the monopoly of the Îles de la Madeleine (Magdalen Islands) seal fisheries and frequently acted as carriers of state supplies between France and Canada. They used part of their profits to purchase positions in the government and thus entered the ranks of the nobility of the robe. Antoine was successively a judge of the royal mint and a judge-treasurer; his brother was a judge-treasurer of the generality of La Rochelle, mayor of the city of La Rochelle from 1749 to 1750, and a secretary of the king in 1758.

YVES F. ZOLTVANY AND DONALD J. HORTON

AJM, Greffe d'Antoine Adhémar; Greffe de Bénigne Basset; Greffe de J.-B. Pottier. AJQ, Greffe de Louis Chambalon; Greffe de François Genaple; Greffe de Gilles Rageot. AN, Col., B, 22, ff.102v, 141–43v, 144, 145–47; 74, ff.426, 482, 483; 76, ff.389, 389v; 78, ff.303, 303v, 320, 320v; C¹¹A, 12, 18, 19, 20, 21, 22, 31, 36, 76, 77, 78, 80, 125. *Documents relating to Canadian currency during the French period* (Shortt). *Jug. et délib.*, III, IV, V.

F. M. Hammang, *The Marquis de Vaudreuil, New France at the beginning of the eighteenth century* (Bruges, 1938). Aegidius Fauteux, "La famille Pascaud," *BRH*, XXXIII (1927), 84–88. Guy Frégault, "La Compagnie de la colonie," *Revue de l'université d'Ottawa*, XXX (1960), 5–29, 127–49. É.-Z. Massicotte, "La famille Bouat," *BRH*, XXX (1924), 10–13. P.-G. Roy, "La famille Guillimin," *BRH*, XXIII (1917), 97–116. Régis Roy, "Pacaud, secrétaire du roi," *BRH*, XXXIII (1927), 17–18.

PASTOUR DE COSTEBELLE, PHILIPPE, French officer, governor of Placentia (Plaisance), then of Île Royale (Cape Breton Island); b. 1661 in Languedoc; d. 1717 at Louisbourg.

Philippe Pastour de Costebelle was born in 1661, before 8 November, and probably at Saint-Alexandre, a village in the diocese of Uzès near Pont-Saint-Esprit, where reference is made to his family as early as the year 1400. He was the second son of François-Barthélemy, lawyer in the *parlement* of Languedoc, captain and castellan of the baronies of Thorrenc and Andance in Vivarais, and of Marie Du Plessis, second wife of François-Barthélemy. He is known to have had three brothers: Louis, the eldest, Joseph and Barthélemy, the younger ones, and a sister named Françoise.

Like the majority of the minor provincial nobility, Philippe was destined for a military career. In 1683 we find him at Toulon as a midshipman. In 1692 he was made a lieutenant and

Pastour de Costebelle

posted to the company that his brother Louis commanded at Placentia. Louis Pastour de Costebelle was born in 1658, and after having also been a midshipman had first served in the fleet, fighting in the Mediterranean against the Barbary pirates. He had been appointed an infantry lieutenant in 1687, and had been instructed to bring to Placentia 25 soldiers as reinforcements; since that time he had scarcely left Newfoundland.

Philippe's voyage in 1692 was not an untroubled one, for the vessel on which he was sailing, the *Joly*, was shipwrecked 20 leagues from Placentia. Crew and passengers had to find shelter on an island, where Governor MOMBETON de Brouillan sent his nephew Saint-Ovide [Mombeton*] with a shallop to pick them up. But the poor lieutenant had lost his baggage and arrived completely destitute. The two brothers hardly caught a glimpse of each other, since Louis went back almost immediately to France, where he was to serve again in the Marine before retiring to his estates in 1696.

The French colony of Newfoundland, which had fortunately emerged from its anarchical situation since Brouillan's arrival in 1691, remained nonetheless vulnerable to the assaults of its English neighbours, so that Pastour de Costebelle did not have too long to wait before displaying his qualities and his bravery. In September the French had to repulse an attack by five British ships. Costebelle distinguished himself in the affair with the ardour of his 30 years, so much so that Brouillan was able to write about him that he had "done his duty too well." From an expedition to Trinity Bay in the spring of 1693 Costebelle brought back six prisoners. Thus he familiarized himself with the war of skirmishes and sudden attacks which the French and English were waging against each other in Newfoundland. But the affair of August 1693 was more serious, since this time some 20 English vessels, under the command of Sir Francis Wheler, were trying to force the entry to Placentia. There was an artillery battle from 28 to 31 August, and the English fleet finally withdrew, without having been able to put its landing companies ashore. Costebelle was sent to Versailles with the governor's report.

On 25 Jan. 1694 he was appointed captain of the company which he had already been commanding in fact since his brother Louis' departure. But when he returned to Placentia, another of his brothers, Joseph, commonly called Pastour de Mérieu, accompanied him. All the Costebelle brothers were to see service in Newfoundland, since the last, Barthélemy, was to die there that same year. A close understanding seems to have existed between the governor and the captain of the regular troops; indeed Brouillan wrote to the minister that Pastour de Costebelle would be perfectly capable of replacing him, and on his side Costebelle did not fail to pay tribute to his superior's qualities. As the Baron de Lahontan [LOM d'Arce], then king's lieutenant at Placentia, had left his post in 1693, Costebelle was appointed in his place on 13 March 1695. The new king's lieutenant immediately concerned himself with improving the living conditions of the settlers and making more equitable regulations for economic relations with the seasonal fishermen.

Pastour de Costebelle, having gone to France in 1696, did not take part in the successful expedition of Brouillan and PIERRE LE MOYNE d'Iberville which sacked almost all the English settlements in Newfoundland. When he returned on 18 Aug. 1697 he hoped to replace Brouillan, who was leaving to have his wounds cared for. But Joseph de MONIC was chosen instead to govern in the interim. Costebelle accepted this and made ready to serve his new chief to the best of his ability. Monic was himself absent from October 1698 to August 1699, which enabled Costebelle to take over his duties in the meantime, under difficult conditions, for he had only meagre resources with which to repair the dilapidated fortifications. He also established land communication with the settlers of St Mary's Bay. When Monic returned, fundamental differences of opinion on the defence of the colony and the regrouping of the settlers opposed the two men. Was this the reason why Costebelle went back to France in 1700? He was at Versailles on 13 Jan. 1701 and at Pont-Saint-Esprit on 23 February, and sailed again from La Rochelle on 11 May. By the time Costebelle got back to Placentia on 8 September, Monic, by his despotic and harsh authority, had created an untenable situation there, so much so that at the beginning of 1702 the court terminated his mission. Once more Costebelle's hopes were disappointed, since on 1 April 1702 Daniel d'AUGER de Subercase was appointed governor. Costebelle's character could not show up to better advantage than in these lines, taken from a letter of 14 October: "I would willingly serve under the command of an officer in whose conduct or outstanding merit I recognized some air of distinction, even if his lack of seniority were to make me feel some aversion for him." In reality the new governor did not take up his office until the spring of 1703, and Costebelle continued to act in the interim. There had been a sharp alarm at Placentia in September 1702, when it was learned that 13 English vessels, well armed with cannon, were cruising in St Mary's Bay. But this fleet headed for Saint-Pierre, which the English ravaged once again. On 8 November Costebelle gave a war commission to the Sieur Du Tilly, a privateer captain, who in December and March went to pillage the English settlements in Trinity Bay. Meanwhile he had again been obliged to rebuild the half-destroyed fortifications.

Subercase finally arrived, and right away the new governor and the king's lieutenant found themselves in complete harmony. Despite a fresh alarm, the year 1703 was calm, and Costebelle must have reflected that at 42 it was time to take a wife. On 1 Feb. 1704, at Placentia, he did in fact marry Anne de Tour, daughter of Germain de Tour, commandant of Saint-Pierre. This did not prevent the king's lieutenant from taking part the following winter in Subercase's daring expedition against St John's. But poor Costebelle, accidentally hurt and sorely tried by the cold, had to be evacuated to Petty Harbour (Petit-Havre).

Thanks to Subercase's military and administrative qualities, he was called on in 1706 to become governor of Acadia, and Costebelle finally became governor of Placentia. He benefited from his predecessor's experiments in farming, for when he took up office he found himself the owner of 7 cows, 3 bulls, 15 ewes, and 2 rams, and a large main building on the shore at Placentia. The development of the colony was moreover in full swing. The land under cultivation was yielding well. New settlers were arriving. The seasonal activity of the Basque and Saint-Malo fishermen was not too greatly obstructed by the English or Dutch cruisers. Numerous ships put into the port. However, scarcity more than once made itself felt, when the convoys did not arrive from Quebec or France. Costebelle devoted all his energies to keeping up Fort Saint-Louis and consolidating its defences. For if he had little fear of an attack by land, from the woods which were patrolled by militiamen and Micmacs, he dreaded an action from the ships which, despite his vigilance, might have forced the narrows. His relations with the English authorities of St John's were sometimes courteous, for by virtue of a special agreement prisoners were exchanged reciprocally. In June 1708 the governor was made a knight of the order of Saint-Louis.

But if Costebelle could more or less protect himself against the English, he scarcely had the resources to launch a significant operation against them. The putting in of the *Phénix*, a ship destined for Hudson Bay, the presence of two brigantines from Quebec, and especially the arrival of the frigate *Vénus*, which had just captured a boat from Boston and had on board 20 soldiers from Acadia and some privateers from Martinique, were going to give him the opportunity. Forthwith the governor assembled a column of about 170

men, an amazing mixture of soldiers, sailors, fishermen, privateers, and settlers, under the command of Saint-Ovide, the new king's lieutenant. The expedition left Placentia on 14 Dec. 1708 and made its way overland to St John's, where it arrived at dawn on 1 Jan. 1709. The forts were taken in a few hours, and the town was occupied during the day. But how was such a conquest to be held, with only 155 able-bodied men and 800 prisoners? Saint-Ovide was very much at a loss. Consequently Costebelle made up his mind to have St John's abandoned as soon as March came; the *Vénus* took on guns and ammunition and the forts were blown up. Louis XIV could not fail to approve the governor's decision. As a counter-offensive from the English was to be feared, substantial reinforcements arrived from Placentia on 10 June 1709: the vessel the *Fidèle*, the flute *Rutland*, and 200 regular soldiers. Meanwhile Costebelle received the land grant at Point Verde (Pointe-Verte) which he had asked for, and Saint-Ovide was made a knight of the order of Saint-Louis. Although the English did not react immediately, the scarcity of provisions made itself felt so severely during the winter it could well be called a famine. The first merchant ships finally arrived on 27 April 1710.

Thereupon Costebelle, who naturally had intelligence agents in Boston, learned that Queen Anne, on pretext of aiding her threatened American colonies, wanted above all to impose her sovereign authority on them, through a governor appointed by her and furnished with full powers, "these peoples having acted up to now as little Republicans governed by their own sovereign council." Consequently Costebelle suggested to Versailles that diplomatic action calculated to encourage the Americans' liking for independence be undertaken, so that they would be induced to negotiate their affairs directly with the French. As Pontchartrain shared these views, Costebelle entrusted Louis Denys* de La Ronde, former commander of the *Vénus*, with this delicate mission. Towards the end of November 1710 La Ronde therefore went to Boston, but he arrived at an inauspicious time, and had no success. Indeed, the port was full of the ships of Admiral WALKER's fleet, whose intentions were distinctly bellicose, and the instructions of the court of France fell into the hands of the admiral himself! Arrested and condemned to be hanged, La Ronde owed his salvation only to the complicity of Joseph Dudley, the governor of Massachusetts.

With the reinstatement of an English governor at St John's, and with the British establishments put to rights, the skirmishing at sea started again worse than ever. The settlers of Placentia and

511

Pastour de Costebelle

Saint-Pierre, and the Basque, Norman, and Breton fishermen suffered by it, despite the cruises made by French sailors and privateers; meantime scarcity of foodstuffs became a more or less permanent part of existence. The French colony of Newfoundland was dying, and despite his foresight Costebelle could meet only the most pressing demands. On 22 Oct. 1712 news of the cessation of hostilities reached Placentia. On 16 April 1713 the treaty of Utrecht was signed, giving Acadia, Newfoundland, and Hudson Bay to England. Costebelle received an order to evacuate the French from Newfoundland to Cape Breton Island, or Île Royale, where the aim was to re-establish the lucrative Grand Banks fishing industry. It was hoped also that the Acadians would be attracted there, so that for the first time the cod industry would enjoy the support of a solid agricultural base.

Saint-Ovide, sent by Costebelle to explore the area, decided on a point on the east shore, the Havre-à-l'Anglais, where the town of Louisbourg was later to rise. The difficulties which the new governor of Île Royale had to face can be readily imagined. In the first year, 1713–14, it was necessary to provide winter quarters and supplies for more than 160 persons. The evacuation of Placentia, of the other settlements, and of the islands of Saint-Pierre and Miquelon could not of necessity be carried out until the summer of 1714. Costebelle himself was the last to sail, on 25 September, on board the *Héros*. Provisions were lacking; so were the materials for building the most modest kind of shelter, and during this time, from 1713 to 1716, the population reached almost 3,000 persons. Despite these difficulties the Newfoundlanders, whose fishing unquestionably depended upon their links with metropolitan France, went there almost with one accord. On the other hand the Acadians, who were for the most part farmers, and who were less dependent on the mother country and were also more sceptical, in the main refused to move, preferring their farms "which are under cultivation" to "unworked, new land, where it is necessary to uproot the standing timber," as Félix Pain* wrote.

Costebelle was a widower when he arrived at Île Royale, but we do not know when he lost his wife. He remarried on 12 Feb. 1716—thus when he was 55—at Port Dauphin (Englishtown, N.S.). His wife was Anne Mius d'Entremont, a widow of 22; she was the daughter of Jacques Mius d'Entremont, second Baron de Pobomcoup, and of Anne de Saint-Étienne de La Tour, both from old Acadian families. His young wife had been the widow of her first husband, the Chevalier de Saillans, since the age of 13!

The year 1716 was spent in feverish activity to get the new colony started: they had to transport cannon, erect forts and dwellings, re-establish the fisheries, parcel out the beaches, build flakes and stages, explore the shores, and mark out the fairways. To these normal difficulties were added the indecision of the court at Versailles as to the site of the new colony's chief town: after approving the choice of Louisbourg, a sudden decision was made in 1715 in favour of Port Dauphin, to which the administration, the garrison, and the principal services of the colony had to be transferred. In 1718, however, the order was given to bring the capital back to Louisbourg.

Costebelle, who had watched over everything and given his efforts unsparingly, finally ruined his health, which was already impaired. He accordingly decided to go to France: he wanted to give the king an account of his administration, and family affairs required his presence. On 23 Nov. 1716 he left Louisbourg with his wife, and on 25 December landed at Belle-Isle, whence he travelled to Nantes, and then to Paris. On 11 April 1717, in Paris, Madame de Costebelle gave birth to a daughter, Marie-Josèphe, who was baptized the next day in the church of Saint-André-des-Arts. In June the Costebelles were at Pont-Saint-Esprit.

On 9 Aug. 1717 the governor of Île Royale sailed from La Rochelle on the frigate *Atalante* to return to his post. During the crossing his health became so bad that he felt it necessary to dictate his will from his bed to the ship's writer. This was on 6 September. Exhausted, he died soon after his arrival at Louisbourg, at the beginning of October. He left his widow in the most complete penury, for if he had served his king well, going so far as to dip into his pocket to keep open house for English officers taken prisoner, he had scarcely given any thought to his own fortune. Overwhelmed by grasping creditors, Madame de Costebelle, when the repayments that she believed she had a right to expect did not arrive, experienced hardship bordering on destitution. She went back to France at the end of 1717 to plead her case before the king. She finally retired to Béarn to await the settlement of her affairs. On 20 Aug. 1719 she married a third time; her husband was a seigneur of Béarn in comfortable circumstances, the Chevalier Laurent de Navailles, Baron of Labatut.

By his first marriage Philippe Pastour de Costebelle had had a daughter, Anne-Catherine; on 2 Sept. 1719, at Lyons, she married Jacques de Bertaut, a receiver of salt-taxes, and after becoming a widow she joined the Carmelite order at Trévoux (principality of Dombes). His other daughter, Marie-Josèphe, was to marry, in

January 1737, François de Rivière, Marquis de Giscaro.

GEORGES CERBELAUD SALAGNAC

AN, Col., B, 12–38; C¹¹ᴬ, 25, ff.116f; C¹¹ᴮ, 1–2; C¹¹ᶜ, 1–7; C¹¹ᴰ, 6, f.157; E, 93 (dossier Costebelle); F³, 54; Section Outre-Mer, Dépôt des fortifications des colonies, carton 2, nos.81–82, 116–17; carton 3, no.144; carton 5, no.263; G², 188, ff.347–54. BN, MS, Clairambault 875, f.245; NAF 9283, ff.394–96, 404. "Mass. Archives," XXXVIIIA, 12–15. *Coll. de manuscrits relatifs à la N.-F.*, II, III. "Une lettre inédite de la fille de Philippe Pastour de Costebelle du 1ᵉʳ oct. 1726," and "Pastour de Costebelle et les officiers de la garnison de l'île Royale," *NF*, II (1926–27), 33, 177–80. *NYCD* (O'Callaghan and Fernow), IX.

Robert Le Blant, *Un colonial sous Louis XIV: Philippe de Pastour de Costebelle* (Paris et Dax, 1935), represents the most complete biography of Costebelle. La Morandière, *Hist. de la pêche française de la morue*, I, 439ff. McLennan, *Louisbourg*. Robert Le Blant, "Les trois mariages d'une Acadienne, Anne d'Entremont (1694–1778)," *NF*, VII (1932), 211–29.

PAYEN DE NOYAN, PIERRE, captain in the colonial regular troops, sub-lieutenant in the navy; b. in the diocese of Avranches, province of Normandy, 7 Oct. 1663, son of Pierre Payen, chevalier, seigneur of Chavoy; d. in 1707, probably at sea.

Payen came to Canada as a lieutenant in the colonial regular troops in 1687 and was commissioned captain on half pay in 1690. In 1691 he was fined 50 *livres* for fighting a duel with Guillaume de LORIMIER de la Rivière. Governor Frontenac [Buade*] added to the penalty by relieving the two of their commands. The following year, however, Frontenac remarked that he was pleased to be able to return their commands "for they are good officers."

Payen's whole life changed in 1694 when he married Catherine-Jeanne Le Moyne de Longueuil et de Châteauguay with both Frontenac and the intendant, Jean BOCHART de Champigny, attending the ceremony. Payen was immediately accepted into the energetic and clannish Le Moyne family; indeed, he received a one-ninth share in the estate of Louis Le Moyne* de Châteauguay, who had died two months before the wedding. In 1697 Payen was an officer in the military expedition to Newfoundland led by PIERRE LE MOYNE d'Iberville, and when Iberville subsequently moved his base of operations to France, Payen followed him. When Iberville and his four brothers sailed from France to secure the French colony of Louisiana in 1701, Payen, then a sub-lieutenant in the navy, served on the ship commanded by JOSEPH LE MOYNE de Serigny. In 1706 he accompanied Iberville on his final expedition to the West Indies, this time commanding his own ship. Payen died early in 1707 after going with his ship to relieve starving colonists at Mobile Bay. This time he was serving under the command of yet another brother-in-law, Jean-Baptiste Le Moyne* de Bienville; Iberville had died only a few months previously.

DAVID LEE

AN, Col., B, 13, f.212; C¹¹ᴬ, 11, f.252; 15, f.169. BN, MS, Fr. 30713, 31715. Bernard de La Harpe, *Journal historique de l'établissement des Français à la Louisiane* (New Orleans, 1831), 97–102. "Correspondance de Frontenac, 1689–99," APQ *Rapport, 1927–28*, 110. *Découvertes et établissements des Français* (Margry), IV, 469; V, 470–72.

PAYNE, SAMUEL, Montreal silversmith; b. 1696 in the parish of St James (Clerkenwell), London; son of the Rev. Lawrence Payne and Mary Rivers; lived in Stepney, then a suburb of London; resident in Montreal 1725–32.

Payne was the son of the protestant chaplain to Lieutenant-General Sir William Cadogan, an officer in Marlborough's army. He may have been related to the 18th-century London silversmiths, Humphrey and John Payne. Payne's life before and after his sojourn in Montreal is fertile ground for hypothesis. He was, apparently, converted to Roman Catholicism before his marriage on 30 July 1725 to Marguerite, daughter of the Montreal merchant Pierre Garau. Six children born of this marriage were baptized in Montreal.

Payne purchased a house and shop in 1726 from the widow of the silversmith Jean-Baptiste Saint-Mars or Saint-Marc. He worked at his craft in this one-storey wooden house on Rue Saint-Joseph (now Saint-Sulpice) until 1730, when he sold the property. In 1731 he employed Jacques Dache, "garçon orfèvre," as his assistant for four months. To date, a cup and a spoon have been attributed to Payne. The spoon bears a very Parisian touch-mark of a crowned fleur de lis over the letters SP.

Payne evidently left Montreal and the colony after 1732. The last record of the silversmith is the baptismal record of his son François-Amable, dated 12 July 1732 and signed by Payne. When this child was buried on 8 October of the same year, Payne's sister-in-law represented the family. The absence of any later record of Payne's immediate family and the disorder in which he left his affairs hint at a hasty departure from Montreal. É.-Z. Massicotte suggested that Payne might have accompanied his Sulpician friend, Abbé Claude Chauvreulx* to Acadia in 1733. Negative evidence in church registers suggests that

Peiras

he did not go to Louisbourg or Île Saint-Jean (Prince Edward Island). It would be natural for a silversmith to seek employment in a town because silversmithing was a luxury craft.

Another possible explanation is that Samuel Payne of London and Montreal and a Samuel Payne (fl. 1711–1748) of Braintree, Mass. are one and the same person. The second Payne had a family in Braintree but is not known to have been a silversmith. He was, it seems, captured by French mission Indians in 1721 while serving with the New England militia in the defence of Georgetown, Me. This Payne was listed in "An Account of sundry English Prisoners brought in [to Boston harbour] from Louisbourg . . . in a schooner *Britannicus* where [they] were Transported there from Canada," dated 6 Oct. 1748. It is possible that he was taken to Montreal in 1721 as a captive of the Caughnawaga Indians who had participated in the Georgetown raid.

PETER N. MOOGK

AJM, Greffe de J.-B. Adhémar, 1 mars 1726; Greffe de N.-A. Guillet de Chaumont, 30 mars 1730; Greffe de J.-C. Raimbault, 21 mai 1731; Registres d'état civil de Notre-Dame de Montréal. Mass. Hist. Soc. *Proc.*, 2d ser., XIV (1900–1), 27. Coleman, *New England captives.* John Langdon, *Canadian silversmiths, 1700–1900* (Lunenburg, 1966), 113. Parkman, *A half-century of conflict* (new ed., 1v., New York, 1962), 159–68. Ramsay Traquair, *The old architecture of Quebec* (Toronto, 1947), 30. É.-Z. Massicotte, "Deux orfèvres d'autrefois," *BRH*, XLVI (1940), 353–54; "Orfèvres et bijoutiers du régime français," *BRH*, XXXVI (1930), 32.

PEIRAS, JEAN-BAPTISTE DE, councillor in the Conseil Souverain of New France; b. *c.* 1641 in Paris, son of Jean de Peiras, king's counsellor, and of Denise Marion; d. September 1701 at Quebec.

After his father's death, Jean-Baptiste de Peiras went to New France around 1670 with his mother (who was to be buried at Quebec in 1677) and his sisters Marie-Madeleine and Denise; the former was to marry PAUL DENYS de Saint-Simon and the latter Joseph Giffard, son of Robert Giffard*, first seigneur of Beauport. The young man had inherited his father's capabilities in legal matters, and lost no time in winning official recognition of them. Protected by Buade* de Frontenac, he was appointed to the Conseil Souverain in January 1673 in place of Nicolas de Mouchy*, and two years later the king appointed him a councillor for life. In 1674 two famous cases were heard by the council: those of Abbé de Fénelon [Salignac*] and of the Sieur Perrot*. These two took exception to Peiras and two of his other colleagues because they were "tools of M. de Frontenac, their only

enemy." In 1675 Peiras was involved in a quarrel over precedence between the parish priest of Pointe-Lévy, the notary François GENAPLE, the churchwardens, and the settlers.

On 6 May 1675, wishing to give recognition to his protégé's talents or to reward him for his loyal services, Frontenac granted the Sieur de Peiras a fief with a frontage of two leagues on the St Lawrence River, "beginning in the middle of the river called Mitis . . . and going down the said river . . ." and having a depth of two leagues, taking in the three Îles Saint-Barnabé. The whole was a land grant in the form of a fief, with rights of seigneury and justice. The king confirmed this grant on 12 May 1677. Once he had become a seigneur, Peiras concerned himself with fur-trading, and bought a number of properties at Quebec and Sillery. After some years he was in a position to lend money, lease out his farms, and obtain from the governor several fur-trading licences for the *pays d'en haut*. In 1696 Frontenac, as syndic of the Recollets of Quebec, arranged for him, on very advantageous terms, the exchange of a house situated in Rue Saint-Louis at Quebec. Five years later, on 6 Sept. 1701, Peiras was buried in the paupers' cemetery of the Hôtel-Dieu. On 8 May 1702 he was replaced on the Conseil Souverain by MATHIEU-FRANÇOIS MARTIN de Lino.

On 18 Aug. 1671, at Quebec, Jean-Baptiste de Peiras had married Anne Thirement, daughter of Jacques Thirement and Marie Hubert of the parish of Saint-Sulpice in Paris; by her he had a daughter, Élisabeth, who inherited the Peiras seigneury, and two sons, of whom the elder, Louis, had Frontenac as a godfather. It seems that the two sons spent their life in France after their father's death. Anne Thirement died prematurely in 1679, leaving in Paris an annuity of 10 *livres* of which Catherine de Peiras, Jean-Baptiste's aunt and attorney, received the arrears in 1689.

ROLAND-J. AUGER

AJQ, Greffe de Romain Becquet, 10 nov. 1677, 26 avril, 30 oct. 1678; Greffe de Pierre Duquet, 9 nov. 1680; Greffe de François Genaple, 6 oct. 1696; Greffe de Gilles Rageot, 6 mars 1691. AQ, Jean-Baptiste Peiras; NF, Ins. Cons. sup., I, 160; VI, 163, 187, 207–9. *Ord. comm.* (P.-G. Roy), I, 306. "Le procès de l'abbé de Fénelon devant le Conseil souverain de la Nouvelle-France en 1674," APQ *Rapport, 1921–22*, 154, 164. PAC *Report 1899*, Supp., 62, 64, 66f., 257, 362. P.-G. Roy, *Inv. concessions*, III, 149–53. J.-E. Roy, *Histoire de la seigneurie de Lauzon* (5v., Lévis, 1897–1904), I, 281.

PÉLERIN, AMBROISE, baptized **Pierre**, priest, Recollet; b. at Trois-Rivières and baptized 10 July

514

1656, eldest son of Pierre Pélerin, Sieur de Saint-Amant, a soldier in the garrison of Trois-Rivières, and of Louise de Mousseaux; d. 12 Dec. 1708 in Paris.

Ambroise Pélerin began his studies at the Jesuit college in Quebec, for his parents had moved to this town around 1661; then he was one of the first group of eight pupils of the Petit Séminaire of Quebec, which opened its doors 1 Oct. 1668.

In 1673 Pélerin entered the Recollet order and had to go to France to do his noviciate, since the Recollets did not yet have a noviciate in Quebec. The following year he made his profession, thus becoming the first Canadian Recollet. He received the diaconate 23 Sept. 1679 at the seminary in Sens (France), and the priesthood probably the following year.

He returned to Canada in 1684 and on 6 October of that year he was at the convent of Notre-Dame-des-Anges in Quebec as a missionary. In 1684 and 1685 he was in charge of the parish of Saint-Joseph de la Pointe-Lévy, in whose records his name appears. In 1686 he replaced the parish priest of Trois-Rivières, M. de Bruslon. From October 1687 to November 1688 he carried out the duties of parish priest at Champlain, near Trois-Rivières. On 11 Dec. 1688 he was again in Quebec. After that we lose sight of him until 17 Nov. 1704; at that time he was a discreet (counsellor) in the convent of Quebec, where, along with other religious, he signed an attestation of a cure attributed to Brother Didace Pelletier*.

In 1705 he returned to France, where he served as a preacher. On 12 Dec. 1708 he died in the Recollet convent in Paris at 52 years of age and after 35 years of life in holy orders.

GABRIEL-M.-RÉAL DUMAS

AAQ, Registres d'insinuation A, 237, 248. AJTR, Registres d'état civil de Trois-Rivières. Archives de Seine-et-Oise (Versailles), H (clergé régulier): récollets. ASQ, Cahier 524. BN, MS, Fr. 13875. Odoric-M. [Jouve], *Le Frère Didace Pelletier, Récollet* (Québec, 1910). *L'Abeille* (Québec), I, 22 mars 1849.

PEMOUSSA, great war chief of the Fox Indians; d. during the winter of 1716–17 in Montreal.

Pemoussa was one of the leaders of the group of Fox Indians that migrated from Baie des Puants (Green Bay) to Detroit in 1709 or 1710. Lamothe Cadillac [LAUMET] had invited them to settle there although a number of other tribes disliked them. According to RIGAUD de Vaudreuil, the Foxes had moved simply to be nearer to the Iroquois and the English. After their arrival the Foxes behaved arrogantly. Fearing trouble, Vaudreuil advised them at a meeting in August 1711 to return to their village. This advice was not heeded and war soon followed.

The battle of Detroit in May 1712 marks the start of the Fox war that plagued New France for the next 25 years. Though RENAUD Dubuisson, the commander of the fort, blamed Fox restlessness on English intrigue, the fighting had its origin in the animosities between the Mascoutens and the Ottawas who clashed on the St Joseph River early in 1712. The Mascoutens fled to Detroit where they sought the protection of the Foxes. The Ottawas and Potawatomis, accompanied by several southern tribes under the leadership of Saguina* and Makisabi pursued them, but feared to attack the Foxes. The insolent Foxes quarrelled with some of the French inhabitants and entering Fort Pontchartrain attempted to assassinate a French man and woman. Dubuisson drove them out and joined the Ottawas and others in attacking the fortified Fox village.

The battle lasted 19 days. During that time two parleys aimed at ending hostilities were held at the request of the Foxes. At the first one, Pemoussa offered a necklace and two slaves to appease the allies, and asked for a two-day truce so that the Fox old men could hold a council. Dubuisson agreed on condition that three Indian women prisoners held by the Foxes were released; on their release Dubuisson went back on his promise. Three or four days later Pemoussa led a larger group of chiefs from both the Foxes and Mascoutens to a second parley. According to Dubuisson's account, their spokesman (perhaps Pemoussa) acknowledged their defeat and signified their readiness to die. They asked only that their women and children be spared and offered the allies six necklaces to signify that they placed themselves in servitude to the victors. This gesture was refused by the allied chiefs. According to the account of Gaspard-Joseph Chaussegros* de Léry, compiled from second-hand reports, it was probably at this parley that a Fox chief (again perhaps Pemoussa) challenged 80 allies to do battle with 20 of his own. The victor would receive the vanquished as slaves. Apparently this offer was also refused.

The Foxes and Mascoutens finally escaped from their fort under cover of a dark, rainy night, only to be pursued and surrounded on a peninsula on Lake St Clair. Except for 150 men who escaped all were either destroyed or enslaved.

In the summer of 1716 Louis de LA PORTE de Louvigny led an expedition against the Foxes. Having defeated them, he took Pemoussa and others back to Montreal as hostages. Pemoussa died there in the winter of 1716–17 in the smallpox epidemic then sweeping the colony. Apparently he had been favourable to peace between the Foxes and the French: Vaudreuil wrote in 1717 that "it was he [Pemoussa] on whom I relied most to make the Fox Indians carry out all the conditions to which they are bound." His passing may have weakened the peace party among the Foxes.

D. H. CORKRAN

Kellogg, *French régime*, 280–2. *Michigan Pioneer Coll.*, XXXIII, 537–52. Wis. State Hist. Soc. *Coll.*, V, 78–80, 81–5; XVI, 293–5. Zoltvany, "New France and the west," 301–22.

PENSENS, JACQUES D'ESPIET DE. *See* ESPIET

PEPPERRELL, WILLIAM, merchant, father of Sir William Pepperrell*, who commanded the New England forces against Louisbourg in 1745; b. c. 1647, son of Andrew and Joan Pepperrell of Revelstoke, Devonshire; married Margery Bray, daughter of a prosperous shipbuilder of Kittery Point, Me., by whom he had eight children; d. 15 Feb. 1733/34 at Kittery Point.

Of William Pepperrell's early years little is known. Coming to the Isles of Shoals (off the Maine–New Hampshire coast) about 1675, probably by way of Newfoundland, he was, by one account, engaged in fishing until his marriage in 1680, when he moved to Kittery Point and embarked on a mercantile career. His first recorded venture was a trading voyage to Newfoundland, where in September 1682 he was among the New England traders who were required to furnish bonds not to carry English subjects from the island, a practice which the authorities were, however, unable to stop [*see* William ARNOLD]. Later, he traded at Canso (Canseau, N.S.) and Port-Toulouse (St Peters) as well. By 1696, when his second son, William, was born, he had extended his commercial activities to the southern colonies, the West Indies, Portugal, and the Canary Islands.

Appointed a justice of the Court of Common Pleas in 1695, Pepperrell served as magistrate for the next 25 years. He twice represented Kittery in the provincial assembly, was nine times chosen to be a selectman of the town, and for many years commanded the county militia regiment with the rank of colonel.

By the time he died, Pepperrell was numbered among the most prominent men of the province, and was one of the wealthiest merchant-ship-owners of New England.

BYRON FAIRCHILD

For the elder William Pepperrell, the most valuable documentary sources are the Pepperrell papers of the Maine Hist. Soc. (Portland, Me.), and those of the New England Historic Genealogical Society (Boston, Mass.); also the Kittery town records, Maine, Books I–II.

For published sources, *see Province and court records of Maine*, IV, and York county, Me., *Register of deeds*, ed. H. W. Richardson *et al.* (18v. in progress, Portland, 1887–   ), III, IV. See also, PRO, CSP, Col., 1681–85, and *Genealogical dictionary of Maine and New Hampshire*, ed. Sybil Noyes *et al.* (Portland, Me., 1928–39).

Secondary accounts are in Byron Fairchild, *Messrs. William Pepperrell: merchants at Piscataqua* (Ithaca, N.Y., 1954), and Usher Parsons, *The life of Sir William Pepperrell, Bart.* (2d ed., Boston, 1856).

PERRIN, ANTOINE, royal court officer; son of Jacques Perrin, notary and tabellion of the parish of Saint-Pierre de Monastier (Le Puy-en-Velay), and of Catherine Boissières; baptized 1697; d. c. 1738, probably at Montreal.

Perrin perhaps came to Canada as a soldier; at least that is what he was in 1719 when he received a commission as "process-server within the jurisdiction of Montreal." Intendant Bégon* wrote of him, in his letter of 26 Oct. 1722, that "he is well intentioned but not very capable; inclined to drink."

On 25 June 1720, he married Marie-Anne Chotard, daughter of Jean-Baptiste Chotard and Marie-Catherine Fortin of Lachine. They had seven children. As a marriage settlement Perrin gave her 400 *livres*, and Jean-Baptiste Chotard undertook to provide a small dowry for his daughter. A few years later, Perrin gave proof of his common sense when on 16 March 1729 he withdrew "the criminal suit brought by him" against the blacksmith François Jobin, who had "insulted and struck" him, and agreed to forget the insult on payment of 60 *livres*.

Perrin died probably in or around 1738, the last year during which he discharged his duties as court officer; his wife married again in 1741, her second husband being Jacques Rondort.

ROBERT LAHAISE

AJM, Greffe de Jacques David, 13 sept., 11 oct. 1720; 17 mai 1724, 15 avril 1726; Greffe de J.-C. Raimbault, 16 mars 1729. A. Roy, *Inv. greffes not.*, XII, 96, 106, 211, 238; XXI, 59. P.-G. Roy, *Inv. ord. int.*, I, 179. "Liste des officiers de justice de la Nouvelle-France (1722)," *BRH*, XXXVI (1930), 155. É.-Z. Massicotte, "Les tribunaux et les officiers de justice," *RSCT*, 3d ser., X (1916), sect.I, 273–303. Tanguay, *Dictionnaire*, VI, 309.

PERROT, NICOLAS, explorer, interpreter, fur-trader, commandant at Baie des Puants (Green

Bay) and seigneur; b. *c.* 1644 in France, son of François Perrot, lieutenant responsible for justice in the barony of Darcey in the province of Burgundy, and of Marie Sivot; d. 13 Aug. 1717 at Bécancour and buried the next day in the parish church.

Perrot seems to have come to New France in 1660 as a *donné* of the Jesuits and thus had the opportunity to visit Indian tribes and learn their languages. In 1665, according to CLAUDE-CHARLES LE ROY de La Potherie, he left the missionaries and visited the Potawatomis and the Foxes. In 1666 he was a domestic in the house of a widow, then a servant of the Sulpicians at Montreal. On 12 Aug. 1667, after forming a trading company with Toussaint Baudry, Jean Desroches, and Isaac Nafrechoux, Perrot undertook further voyages among the various nations of Baie des Puants and Wisconsin; he was well received by each of them, and took advantage of this to do some fur-trading, although he did not derive much profit from it. He was often the first Frenchman to visit them and to win their affection.

On 3 Sept. 1670, when he returned from one of these trips, he was asked by Intendant Talon* to accompany as an interpreter Daumont* de Saint-Lusson, a commissary assigned "to the country of the Ottawas, Amikwas, Illinois, and other Indian natives discovered and to be discovered in North America in the direction of Lake Superior or Freshwater Sea, in order to search out and discover mines of all kinds there, particularly copper mines ... in addition to taking formal possession in the king's name of all the inhabited and uninhabited country...." Perrot then formed a new trading company, this time with Jean Dupuis, Denis Masse, Pierre Poupart, Jean Guytard and Jacques Benoît, and set out with Saint-Lusson. The two travellers stayed at Montreal for some time, and in October went to Lake Huron via the Ottawa River, Lake Nipissing, and French River. They spent the winter on Manitoulin Island, and the following spring Perrot dispatched Indian emissaries to the northern nations with authority to invite them to Sault Ste Marie "in order to hear the king's words which the Sieur Saint-Lusson was bringing to them and to all nations"; for his part, he went among the nations in Baie des Puants to invite them to this important gathering.

On 4 June 1671, before the representatives of 14 nations, Saint-Lusson officially took possession of these territories. The report of this ceremony was signed by Saint-Lusson, Perrot, Claude Dablon*, Claude Allouez*, and Gabriel Druillettes*, as well as by the Frenchmen who were in the locality, being "engaged in fur-trading."

Before leaving Sault Ste Marie, Perrot did some more trading with the Indians. However, on 3 September his furs were seized at Quebec, on Saint-Lusson's orders.

On 11 Nov. 1671, in the presence of the notary Guillaume de LARUE, Perrot signed a marriage contract with Madeleine, daughter of Ildebon Raclot and Marie Viennot. While still continuing to take an interest in the fur trade, he settled at Champlain, and on 2 Dec. 1677 he went to live on the river Saint-Michel, on a land grant made to him by Charles-Pierre Legardeur de Villiers, seigneur of Bécancour.

The same year a certain Nicolas Perrot, *dit* Joly-Cœur, had attempted to poison Cavelier* de La Salle at Fort Frontenac (Kingston, Ont.), shortly after Governor Buade* de Frontenac had reviewed the soldiers of the fort on 7 September. This individual, whose nickname alone was on the muster-roll of the soldiers but who was subsequently identified, confessed his crime and was put in irons; in January 1679, according to Benjamin Sulte, he was still in the prison at Quebec. Historians such as Margry and Parkman, basing themselves on the narrative of a friend of Abbé René de Bréhant* de Galinée, attributed to Eusèbe Renaudot, have seen in this man Perrot the explorer and fur-trader. Now this narrative, which is the account of alleged conversations that took place in 1678 in Paris between La Salle and Renaudot in the presence of friends, is not an original document, but a copy whose author and date are unknown to us. Strong doubts can be cast on such testimony; the confusion which has existed up to now has all the less justification because the nickname Joly-Cœur was never applied to our personage in notarial acts, registries of births, marriages, and deaths, or the *Jesuit Relations*. He therefore has nothing to do with this incident.

Although Perrot had established his small family on a farm—the 1681 census showed him as having six children—his journeys to the west did not stop because of that; in fact they continued until 1698. In 1684 Le Febvre* de La Barre, convinced of Perrot's ascendancy over the nations of the west, entrusted him with the mission of inducing them to take part in the war that he was planning against the Iroquois. Not without difficulty, Perrot succeeded in bringing the warriors of several nations to Niagara, where the meeting with the governor's army was to take place. When the peace signed by La Barre was announced, the Indians expressed their dissatisfaction at having to return to their country without having fought.

In the spring of 1685 Perrot was appointed commandant in chief of Baie des Puants and the neighbouring regions. Before he left he gave his wife a power of attorney, authorizing her to act in his name. Just as he was making his way from Montreal towards Michilimackinac, whence he would proceed to the post which had just been entrusted to him, war broke out between the Foxes on the one hand and the Sioux and Chippewas on the other. The latter had even been completely beaten already in a first battle, and their allies the Ottawas were preparing to avenge their defeat. Perrot sought an effective means of re-establishing peace between these tribes. He speedily found it once he had ascertained the causes of the conflict. The daughter of a Chippewa chief had been kept prisoner for a year among the Foxes, and the latter had persistently rejected the gifts which all the nations of the bay had been offering for her ransom. The Foxes had decided to burn the young Indian girl to avenge the death of one of their principal chiefs who had been killed by the Chippewas. The new commandant, accompanied by his 20 men and the young girl's father, went to Baie des Puants. Relying on the esteem in which he was held by the Foxes, he went among them alone, asked them to hand over the captive, and got them to do so. Having received her from their hands, he restored her to her father, on condition that the latter intervene with the Indians of his nation and their allies to make them renounce all hostile acts against the Foxes; this the chief faithfully carried out.

After having thus reconciled these nations, at least temporarily, Perrot, who from that time on was nicknamed Metaminens (the man with the iron legs), left Baie des Puants with his men and went up the Fox River as far as the village of the Mascoutens and Miamis. From there he made the portage which separated the Mascouten and Wisconsin Rivers, went down the latter as far as the Mississippi, and, turning north, went up this river to the beginning of the territory occupied by the Sioux, where he stopped and built Fort Saint-Antoine.

Perrot soon lost part of the powers that La Barre had conferred on him. In the autumn of 1685 the new governor, BRISAY de Denonville, placed under the authority of Olivier MOREL de La Durantaye, the commandant at Michilimackinac, all the Frenchmen who were in the *pays d'en haut*; at the same time he ordered Perrot to go down to the bay and to gather together as he went all allied Indians and Frenchmen, for an attack on the Senecas. Again with difficulty, Perrot persuaded the nations of the bay and the Ottawas to follow him.

In the spring of 1687, after depositing at the Saint-François-Xavier mission the yield from his fur-trading, Perrot went with his party to rejoin the French in the region of Detroit, then he headed for the Seneca country, where he took part in the destruction of five villages. But while he was taking part in this expedition fire broke out at the Jesuit mission in the bay; the church, the adjoining buildings, and the 40,000 *livres* worth of furs that Nicolas Perrot had stored there were destroyed in the blaze. Perrot, completely ruined, returned to Montreal. He had barely arrived before he set about renewing his merchandise in order to resume fur-trading with the Indians of the west, among whom he once more occupied his post as commandant. Having come back to Montreal in the spring of 1688, he served as an interpreter for the treaty of 15 June between the governor and the Onondaga chief Otreouti* (La Grande Gueule), who promised the neutrality of the Onondagas, the Cayugas, and the Oneidas. Shortly before the treaty Perrot had bought from Jean LECHASSEUR, for 4,000 *livres* worth of beaver furs, the seigneury of Rivière-du-Loup (Louiseville), with rights of *haute, moyenne, et basse justice*; he was to hand this back to its former owner a few years later, having been unable to make the payments on it.

On 8 May 1689, after building Fort Saint-Nicolas at the mouth of the Wisconsin, Perrot took possession in the name of Louis XIV "of Baie des Puants, the lake and rivers of the Outagamis and Mascoutens, the Ouiskouche and Mississippi rivers, the country of the Nadouessioux, Rivière-Sainte-Croix and Saint-Pierre and other more distant places. . . ." The following year Frontenac instructed him to bring into alliance with the French the Ottawas and the other nations of the west, who since the Lachine massacre wanted to join the Iroquois. While carrying out this mission, Perrot re-established some kind of peace among these nations. In the course of this journey he discovered, 21 leagues above Mouingouena, the lead mines whose existence had twice been drawn to his attention by the Miami chiefs.

In 1692 Perrot received an order to settle among the Indians of Marameg (Maramet), "to set up between the Miamis and the other nations who might be susceptible to offers from the English a barrier which would thwart all such plans." Three years later, at the governor's request, he brought to Montreal the Miami chiefs of Marameg and those of the Sauks, the Menominees, the Potawatomis, and the Foxes. On that occasion Frontenac urged them to make war against the Iroquois, adding that Perrot and LA PORTE de Louvigny, the commandant of Michilimackinac, were both required to account to him for their conduct. Finally Frontenac asked the Miamis of Marameg to live together with the Miamis of Saint-Joseph, their brothers, and this was done. The meeting over, Perrot returned to the west, and during his last three years among the Indians his constant concern was to maintain unity and peace among them, his advice to them being to fight rather with the Iroquois. He managed to safeguard France's interests there, but not without danger to his life, since on two occasions he was almost sent to the stake, first among the Mascoutens and then among the Miamis.

After the suppression of fur-trading licences and the evacuation of the western posts in 1696, Perrot settled permanently on his land grant at Bécancour. The Indian chiefs whom he had known he saw again for the last time in 1701, at the time of the peace treaty signed at Montreal, when he was called upon by CALLIÈRE to serve as an interpreter for the nations of the west.

Ruined, saddled with debts because of the "extraordinary expenses" that he had incurred, and harried by numerous creditors, Perrot requested from the authorities of the colony sums which he claimed were due to him, and asked the minister for a pension in consideration of his long services, but he did not obtain any satisfaction. Often on later occasions he had to appear before the courts, sometimes to defend himself against his creditors, sometimes to resist those who claimed ownership rights to a land grant which he had acquired in 1704. Perrot's numerous lawsuits, and the post of militia captain that he held from 1708 to the end of his life, did not prevent him from allowing himself a little leisure, which he used to draft his reports, with the aid of notes taken during his travels.

His *Mémoire sur les mœurs, coustumes et relligion des sauvages de l'Amérique septentrionale* is the only one that was published. Perrot's sole object in writing it was to acquaint Intendant Michel Bégon* confidentially with the true character of the tribes that were allies or enemies of France, and with the kind of relationships that should be maintained with them. He recounted what he knew, what he had seen with his own eyes, without any literary pretension, without any concern for the favours of a public for which his work was not intended, and he stopped when he ran out of paper. The obvious imperfection of the form is amply redeemed by the truth and accuracy of his information.

The other reports, except the one on the Foxes addressed to Philippe de RIGAUD de Vaudreuil, were also delivered to Bégon. They have not come down to us, but most of them were inserted by Le Roy de La Potherie in volume II of his *Histoire de l'Amérique septentrionale*. They contain a narrative of the Iroquois war against the nations of the *pays d'en haut* and the Illinois, as well as an account of the frequent acts of treachery of which the Indians and more particularly the Hurons and Ottawas had been guilty.

Such are the memoirs consigned to paper by Perrot, who died on 13 Aug. 1717 at about the age of 74 and who was buried the next day in the church at Bécancour. Nine of his 11 children, 5 boys and 4 girls, outlived him, and none of them seems to have felt any urge to roam the woods after furs or to go exploring. His wife, who was subject to fits of mental depression, died in July 1724, having been totally insane for the last four years of her life.

Perrot, who was often unappreciated even during his lifetime, was France's best representative among the Indians of the west. His knowledge of the languages of the country, his natural eloquence, the happy blend of daring and coolness that were the essence of his character, had made it possible for him to win the esteem, confidence, and even affection of the Indians. The Potawatomis, the Menominees, the Foxes, the Miamis, the Mascoutens, and the Sioux granted him, with the honours of the pipe of peace, the rights and prerogatives enjoyed by their own chiefs. His credit was not less among the Ottawas and the Hurons. During the last four decades of the 17th century, at a time when alliance with the nations of the west was indispensable in order to ward off the Iroquois peril and allow access to new territories, Perrot, thanks to the influence that he had acquired, rendered valuable assistance to the colony.

IN COLLABORATION WITH CLAUDE PERRAULT

AJM, Greffe d'Antoine Adhémar, 4 avril, 17 mai 1685, 14 août, 5 sept. 1687, 15 mai 1688; AJM, Greffe de Bénigne Basset, 12 août 1667. AJQ, Greffe de Romain Becquet, 2 sept. 1670. AJTR, Greffe de Jean Cusson, 2 déc. 1677; Greffe de Guillaume de Larue, 11 nov. 1671. AN, Col. C¹¹ᴬ, 11, ff.86–100; 13, ff.376–88; 15, ff.3–21; 18, ff.92–108. Charlevoix, *Histoire* (1744), I, 436; II, 280f.; III, 398. *Découvertes et établissements des Français* (Margry), I, 296, 389f., 397. *JR* (Thwaites). *Jug. et délib.*, III, IV, V, VI. La Potherie, *Histoire* (1722). Nicolas Perrot, *Mémoire sur les mœurs, coustumes et relligion des sauvages de l'Amérique septentrionale*, éd. Jules Tailhan (Leipzig et Paris, 1864; Canadiana avant 1867, Toronto, 1968). P.-G. Roy, *Inv. coll. pièces jud. et not.*, I, 13, 36. Bonnault, "Le Canada militaire," 509f. Le Jeune, *Dictionnaire*, II, 429f. Lorin, *Le comte de Frontenac*. Francis Parkman, *La Salle and the discovery of the great west* (Boston, 1887), 104. Rochemonteix, *Les Jésuites et la N.-F. au XVIIᵉ siècle*, III. Sulte, *Hist. des Can. fr.*, IV, V; *Mélanges historiques* (Malchelosse)

Perrot de Rizy

I, 50, 59. Raymond Douville, "Quelques notes inédites sur Nicolas Perrot et sa famille," *Cahiers des Dix*, XXVIII (1963), 43–62. Gérard Malchelosse, "Nicolas Perrot au Fort Saint-Antoine," *Cahiers des Dix*, XVII (1952), 111–36. J.-A. Perrault, "Notes sur Nicolas Perrault," *BRH*, XLIX (1943), 145–49. J.-E. Roy, "Claude-Charles Le Roy de la Potherie," *RSCT*, 2nd ser., III (1897), sect.i, 3–44.

PERROT DE RIZY (d'Erizy, Derezy, Drisy), PIERRE, merchant, major of the Quebec militia; b. 1672 at Sainte-Famille (Île d'Orléans), son of Jacques Perrot, *dit* Vildaigre, and Michelle Le Flot; buried 18 Oct. 1740 at Quebec.

At an early age Perrot sailed the seas and served in the army; in 1697 we find him at Placentia (Plaisance), where he was apparently engaged in business; for example, he advanced 37 *livres* to the brothers Alexis, Nicolas, and Pierre Lefrançois. He then settled at Quebec, where he continued his commercial activities; various lawsuits took him before the Conseil Supérieur including a very lengthy one in 1715–16 with Marie-Renée Chorel de Saint-Romain, the widow of Jacques LE PICARD Du Mesnil de Norrey, about a house in Quebec. Several of these legal actions concerned questions of inheritances in which Perrot was involved. In 1726 he became major of the Quebec militia, and remained so until his death. In 1727 he requested the post of captain of the port of Quebec; Maurepas wrote on that occasion to Beauharnois* de La Boische and CLAUDE-THOMAS DUPUY to inquire "whether he is a man of good conduct and has the necessary ability"; however, Richard Testu* de La Richardière was appointed.

Maurepas again made inquiries about Perrot in 1731, in connection with a power of attorney from M. de Montmorency apparently instructing Perrot to sell "certain possessions which belonged to him in the colony," and from the sale of which Perrot was thought to have kept the 14,000 *livres* realized. It seems, however, that Perrot succeeded in explaining his conduct, for he retained his office.

He was married twice: first, in 1699, to Anne Jourdain, then, in 1704, to the widow of Charles Arnaut, Marie Willis, who was naturalized in 1722. He had three children who died in infancy.

NIVE VOISINE

Jug. et délib., IV, V, VI. P.-G. Roy, *Inv. coll. pièces jud. et not.,* I, 58, 89; *Inv. ord. int.,* II, 96. Bonnault, "Le Canada militaire," 263–527.

PERTHUIS, CHARLES, merchant, commercial fisherman, churchwarden, and a director of the Compagnie de la Colonie; b. 1664, son of Charles Perthuis and Anne Minet, of the parish of Saint-Saturnin in Tours; d. at Quebec in 1722.

The exact date of Perthuis's arrival in the colony is unknown. He first appears in 1694; a year later, while still a bachelor, he rented a house on Rue Notre-Dame (sous le Fort), from PAUL DENYS de Saint-Simon, and was thus a neighbour of a man whose partner he would be on many occasions, Nicolas PINAUD. At the age of 32, on 26 June 1697, Perthuis signed a marriage contract, witnessed by the political and social elite of the colony, in which he is referred to as a merchant, and on 8 July he married Marie-Madeleine Roberge, the daughter of Denis Roberge and Geneviève Auber. Perthuis had 11 or 12 children, the best known being Joseph*, his penultimate child, baptized on 30 Aug. 1714. In 1732, his widow resided at the same address, and a later census, that of 1744, indicates that his son Joseph was the owner of the house.

Perthuis's business career resembles that of many other merchants and bourgeois of the colony. His commercial activities ranged from selling groceries and supplies and being a partner in the Compagnie de la Colonie, to outfitting privateers during the War of the Spanish Succession. "Merchant capitalism" or "venturing" best describe his many activities. He (and not his son, as J.-N. Fauteux writes), was engaged in the leather business. In partnership with Nicolas Pinaud, in 1695, he signed a contract to supply flour and biscuits, and many years later, in 1715, they were engaged in the same trade. In 1716 they had a one-half interest in the *Sainte-Anne*. When the Compagnie de la Colonie was formed, Perthuis acquired 2,000 *livres* worth of shares. He soon became a director of the company, and, with Nicolas Pinaud and RENÉ-LOUIS CHARTIER de Lotbinière, was appointed to settle the debts of the company in 1708.

Perthuis also established commercial relations with merchants from La Rochelle such as Robert Butler and Charles-Joseph AMIOT de Vincelotte, the latter a ship's captain as well as "venturer," whose activities had brought him to Canada. In 1716, Perthuis acquired an interest in the *sous-ferme* of Tadoussac from the estate of Joseph Riverin. In the same year he entered into a partnership with Robert Drouard, a Quebec merchant, for the exploitation of this concession.

Perthuis was a churchwarden of the church of Notre-Dame in Quebec, and he acted on several occasions as the guardian of minors. This role, and the many requests he received to arbitrate disputes before the Conseil Souverain, indicate how much his judgement was respected.

Perthuis died in Quebec at the age of 58, and

was buried there on 5 March 1722. No papers from his estate appear to have been preserved.

CAMERON NISH

AJQ, Greffe de Louis Chambalon; Greffe de François Genaple. "Correspondance de Vaudreuil," APQ *Rapport, 1938–39. Documents relating to Canadian currency during the French period* (Shortt), I, 3. *Jug. et délib.* Charland, "Notre-Dame de Québec: le nécrologe de la crypte," 178. "Liste générale des intéressés en la compagnie de la colonie du Canada, et des actions qu'ils y ont prises," *BRH*, XL (1934), 498–512. É.-Z. Massicotte, "Congés et permis déposés ou enregistrés à Montréal sous le régime français," APQ *Rapport, 1921–22,* 189–225. Fauteux, *Essai sur l'industrie sous le régime français,* I.

PETIT, JEAN (not to be confused with Jean Petit Boismorel, court officer at Montreal), councillor, treasurer of the Marine, and seigneur; b. 1663, son of Pierre Petit, former comptroller of the annuities of the Hôtel de Ville in Paris, and of Catherine Du Bellineau, of the parish of Saint-Jean in Paris; d. 24 Feb. 1720 at Quebec and buried the next day in the cathedral of Notre-Dame de Québec.

Petit probably arrived at Quebec in the spring of 1701 as the agent of the treasurer-general of the Marine, to replace his uncle, Jacques Petit de Verneuil, who had died in Quebec on 28 Aug. 1699. On 23 Sept. 1701, on behalf of the treasurers-general of the Marine and of his father, he instituted proceedings against his uncle's widow, Marie Viel, to recover a sum of 30,000 *livres* that was missing from the treasury; he won his case on 3 Nov. 1702. Shortly afterwards he demanded that the prisons of the intendant's palace be made more secure to prevent escapes. In 1703 the intendant, Beauharnois* de La Boische, recommended him to the minister, saying that he was "a thoroughly worthy man."

On 4 July 1701, at Quebec, he married Suzanne Dupuy, who died two years later. On 13 Sept. 1706 he married Charlotte Dugué, daughter of Michel-Sidrac Dugué* de Boisbriand, a former captain in the Carignan regiment, seigneur of Mille-Îles, and a fur-trader; seven children were born of this marriage. On 5 March 1714 he obtained half the seigneury of Mille-Îles, as did his brother-in-law Charles-Gaspard PIOT de Langloiserie. This seigneury, which had been granted to his father-in-law Dugué de Boisbriand in 1683, had been attached to the king's domain a few days before, that is on 1 March 1714. The grant was confirmed on 5 May 1716.

In 1717 Jean Petit brought an action against the nuns of the Hôtel-Dieu of Quebec to obtain the concession of a piece of land on the Saint-Ignace

seigneury which consisted of a half-grant of fallow land and standing timber, and which adjoined a piece of land and a settler's farm that he had bought from Pierre Brosseau. Having lost his case before the Conseil Souverain, he appealed to the king. On 2 June 1720 a royal decree demanded that the nuns make him this land grant, under penalty of seeing the land attached to the king's domain by virtue of the decrees of Marly (1711).

On 1 July 1718 the king appointed Petit a member of the Conseil Souverain. It was not until 8 Jan. 1720, however, that the council ordered the inquiry into his character. On 15 January he was admitted to the council as the 11th councillor. He died shortly afterwards, and two years later his widow married Louis-Rémy Dugué. The inventory of his possessions was made in the presence of the notary Jacques BARBEL on 17 April 1725.

W. STANFORD REID AND BERNARD WEILBRENNER

AN, Col., C^{11A}, 21, f.96. *Jug. et délib.*, IV, 597–99, 789–98. P.-G. Roy, *Inv. concessions*, III, 266; *Inv. jug. et délib., 1717–60*, I, 82f.; VI, 257f. Charland, "Notre-Dame de Québec: le nécrologe de la crypte," 170–77. P.-G. Roy, *La famille Du Gué de Boisbriand* (Lévis, 1918). J.-E. Roy, "Les conseillers au Conseil souverain de la Nouvelle-France," *BRH*, I (1895), 178. P.-G. Roy, "Les trésoriers de la marine à Québec," *BRH*, XXXV (1929), 635.

PETIT, LOUIS, priest of the Missions Étrangères of the seminary of Quebec, vicar general for Port-Royal (Annapolis Royal, N.S.), Pentagouet, the Saint John River, and the coasts of Acadia from 1676 to 1690 and from 1691 to 1693; b. 1629 at Belzane, in the diocese of Rouen, son of Adrien Petit and Catherine Dufloc; d. 3 June 1709 at Quebec and buried in the cathedral.

Petit chose a military career when quite young. He was a captain in the Carignan-Salières regiment and arrived at Quebec on 19 June 1665. He worked on the construction of Fort Richelieu (near Sorel). While studying at the seminary he was secretary to Bishop LAVAL, who ordained him a priest at Quebec on 21 Dec. 1670. From 1670 to 1676 he was chaplain at Fort Richelieu, at the same time serving as priest at Saint-Ours and Contrecoeur. In 1676 he was appointed vicar general of Acadia, becoming the first priest to represent the bishop of Quebec there in this capacity. He took up residence at Port-Royal, which was the administrative capital and a general depot for pelts.

Petit was a remarkable promoter of teaching among the Acadians of this region. He maintained a teacher who, while instructing the boys of the parish, was at the same time a valuable companion for him. This man, whose name was Pierre Chenet

Petit

Dubreuil and who held the office of king's attorney and judge at Port-Royal in 1690, was, according to Petit, "the only person with whom I may converse freely about God, not having had any spiritual help in the neighbourhood for the nine years that I have been without a companion and having been without counsel in the midst of a thousand difficulties." In 1685 Bishop Saint-Vallier [LA CROIX] sent him, at his request, a nun of the Congrégation de Notre-Dame, who took over the direction of a boarding school for girls, and in 1686 he sent him Abbé GEOFFROY, who acted as pedagogical adviser and was responsible for building schools.

On 19 May 1690 William Phips*, who had sailed from Boston, arrived before Port-Royal and called upon the governor of Acadia, Louis-Alexandre DES FRICHES de Meneval, to surrender. The latter, lacking officers, asked Abbé Petit to negotiate the capitulation. Petit obtained honourable conditions from Phips, but they were quickly violated. The church was burned and the houses pillaged. The governor, Abbé Petit, and his assistant, Abbé TROUVÉ, were seized and carried off to captivity in Boston. In the autumn of the same year the two missionaries were put on one of the ships which Phips was taking to Quebec. The English admiral had to give up his desire for conquest, and before he left there was an exchange of prisoners, including Abbés Petit and Trouvé. Abbé Petit returned to Port-Royal to rebuild the church and presbytery there.

In 1693 he retired to the seminary of Quebec, to which he had belonged as a member of the community since 1687. From 1703 to 1705 he was parish priest at Ancienne-Lorette, but refused a canonry. He almost perished in the fire which destroyed the seminary of Quebec in 1705 and had to jump from the fourth floor. Along with Bishop Laval, he was sheltered at the Jesuit college.

Certain people, such as Perrot*, have maintained that Abbé Petit was an Anglophile and that he had agreed to the surrender of Port-Royal without difficulty. The exaggerated character of these accusations seems to be confirmed by the detailed account of the capture given by Abbés Petit and Trouvé, and also by Dubreuil and the governor. In addition, the fact that Abbé Petit was able to resume his pastoral charge after he was freed contradicts these affirmations. As for the capture of Port-Royal, the account explains the action of the French by the conditions which prevailed at the time: "Without a fort or any kind of fortification, and considering that there were only about 70 wretched soldiers, badly armed and more badly disposed, and that, through fear or for some other motive, only three of the settlers had

rallied round the governor, and that in addition [the governor's illness had reduced him to inaction], and seeing that the enemy was numerous and able to land more than 800 men in half an hour, [the governor] thought that it was fitting to enter into some sort of arrangement with them."

GÉRARD DESJARDINS

AN, Col., C¹¹D, 2, ff.169, 174. Placide Gaudet, Notes généalogiques (preserved in PAC and Archives de l'université de Moncton). *Coll. de manuscrits relatifs à la N.-F.,* II, 6–8, 12–13. "Journal of expedition against Port Royal, 1690," 54. Provost, *Le Séminaire de Québec: documents et biographies,* 419. Saint-Vallier, *Estat présent de l'Église* (1857), 102. Allaire, *Dictionnaire,* I, 429. Caron, "Prêtres séculiers et religieux," 225. Bernard, *Le drame acadien,* 184–86. Casgrain, *Les Sulpiciens en Acadie,* 66–67. Gosselin, *L'Église du Canada,* I, 85, 178. Omer Le Gresley, *L'enseignement du français en Acadie* (Mamers, 1926), 46–47. Robert Rumilly, *Histoire des Acadiens* (2v., Montréal, [1955]), I, 117, 128.

PETIT, PIERRE, merchant, seigneur, royal notary, king's attorney, clerk of court, court officer; b. *c.* 1670 at Lyon, son of François Petit, a businessman, and of Jeanne Gobin; buried 24 April 1737 at Trois-Rivières.

Having lost his parents, Pierre Petit was attracted to New France by his uncle Jean GOBIN, who was a merchant at Quebec and was associated with CHARLES AUBERT de La Chesnaye in several undertakings. He arrived around 1690 and settled at Trois-Rivières, probably in the service of the merchant Étienne VÉRON de Grandmesnil, whose daughter, Marguerite, he married in 1692.

From that time on, Pierre Petit's career progressed favourably. Charles Aubert de La Chesnaye, who among his seigneuries owned that of the Yamaska (or Les Savannes) River and 12 acres adjoining, asked Pierre Petit, who had been married only a month, to be the tenant-farmer of this land for three years. On 9 July 1694 La Chesnaye sold him the whole property for 3,333 *livres,* payable in the form of an annual rent of 166 *livres.* From then on, Pierre Petit styled himself "seigneur of the Yamaska River," while continuing his business at Trois-Rivières. In less than a year he lost his two protectors: La Chesnaye died in 1702; Jean Gobin and his wife Gabrielle Bécasseau were stricken by a cholera epidemic and died on 11 July 1703. Being a prudent man, Pierre Petit accepted the complicated estate which he inherited from his uncle only without liability to debts beyond the assets descended—this estate was involved in many ways in the still more complicated one of Charles Aubert de La Chesnaye. In 1717, to avoid legal difficulties, he agreed to pay off the price of his seigneury, that is 3,333 *livres*, to Abbé Philippe Boucher, the attorney of the Marquis de Gallifet, one of La Chesnaye's creditors.

Petit took an interest in his seigneury from the period when a few settlers from Sorel and Berthier began to establish themselves on his unoccupied land. But he only occasionally spent any time there, and continued to live at Trois-Rivières, where all his children were baptized. On 5 March 1721, however, he accompanied eight of his copy-holders and the parish priest, Jean-Baptiste Dugast, to the manor-house of Saint-François, where the commissioner, COLLET, was conducting his hearings for the district. There he constituted himself the settlers' spokesman in order to complain of the lack of help from the church and the bad state of the roads.

This amateur seigneur had other ambitions. In 1721 he secured, one after another, nearly all the official judicial offices of the government of Trois-Rivières: clerk of court, court officer, royal notary, then deputy king's attorney in place of Étienne Véron de Grandmesnil, who had died on 18 May of that year.

On 1 Oct. 1735 Petit, by then old and infirm, was replaced as notary and court officer by Hyacinthe-Olivier Pressé*. He died at the Ursulines' hospital and was buried in the cemetery of that institution. His three sons divided up his seigneurial interests among themselves.

RAYMOND DOUVILLE

AJQ, Greffe de Louis Chambalon, 28 août 1692, 9 juillet 1694, 26 oct. 1695. PAC, FM 8, F97 (Yamaska, 1718–1888). AJTR, Greffe de Pierre Petit, 1721–1735. AQ, NF, Coll. de pièces jud. et not., 2048. *Jug. et délib.* P.-G. Roy, *Inv. concessions*, II, 77; *Inv. ord. int.*, I, II. "Les notaires au Canada," 39. Vachon, "Inv. critique des notaires royaux," *RHAF*, X (1956–57), 257f. T.-M. Charland, *Histoire de Saint-François du Lac* (Ottawa, 1942). Jouve, *Les Franciscains et le Canada: aux Trois-Rivières.* J.-E. Roy, *Histoire du notariat*, I, 194. "Au sujet de Pierre Petit," *BRH*, XXXVII (1931), 447.

PETIT DE LEVILLIERS, CHARLES (the name is sometimes written **Lynvilliers, Linvilliers, L'Invilliers** or **Livilliers,** but he signed himself **Levilliers,** and on a few occasions **de Coulanges de Levilliers),** officer in the colonial regular troops, b. towards 1660 at Marigny-en-Arxois in the bishopric of Soissons, d. 1714 in Montreal.

He was the son of Robert Petit de Levilliers and Élisabeth Berruyer. He followed a military career, beginning as a midshipman in 1683. In 1687 he went to New France as an ensign in the colonial regular troops, and on 24 September of that year showed great bravery in saving a Basque officer called Amiconti in a combat with Indians. Levilliers received his commission as a half-pay lieutenant in 1690. The next year he fought in the action at La Prairie de La Magdeleine, when a surprise attack was made on the fort by a large raiding party from New York under Peter SCHUYLER on the night of 10 August. Finding the French on the alert, Schuyler withdrew his militia and Indians, but encountered a second French force in his rear. The French lost 40 men, including four officers.

In 1692 Petit de Levilliers was promoted half-pay captain. He was described as a "good officer, brave man, a bit hot-headed." In January of the next year, he took part in an operation against the Mohawks around Fort Orange, under NICOLAS AILLEBOUST de Manthet, AUGUSTIN LE GARDEUR de Courtemanche, and ROBUTEL de La Noue. On 24 Aug. 1694 he married in Montreal Madeleine Gaultier, daughter of René Gaultier* de Varennes, the late governor of Trois-Rivières. A few days later he was promoted captain. The new couple seem to have taken up residence at Boucherville for some time; from 1695 until 1708, seven children were born to them there. Levilliers went in 1695 with the Chevalier Thomas Crisafy* to Fort Frontenac (Cataracoui, now Kingston, Ont.). He received one more promotion in that year, to sub-lieutenant in the navy. In 1696 he served in Buade* de Frontenac's expedition against the Iroquois, taking part in the attack against the Oneidas led by RIGAUD de Vaudreuil. About 1711 he moved to Montreal. He asked for a year's leave in 1712, but the matter had not been decided when he died, on 30 June 1714.

Two of his sons served in Louisiana. Charles Petit de Levilliers was baptized at Boucherville on 19 June 1698. He followed the same career as his father and by 1720 was promoted lieutenant in the colony on the Mississippi. On 14 Jan. 1726 he married Étiennette-Louise Malbeque in New Orleans and the census of that year showed him living there. On 17 August he was promoted captain. He took part in the disastrous expedition led by Pierre d'Artaguiette against the Chickasaws in 1736 and, although wounded, survived [see FRANÇOIS-MARIE BISSOT de Vinsenne]. He died on 1 April 1738 as a result of an injury received in a duel with a M. de Macarty (probably Barthélemy, chevalier de Macarty).

Pierre-Louis Petit de Levilliers de Coulanges was baptized at Boucherville 3 Oct. 1699. He served as a cadet in Canada and later followed his brother to Louisiana. On 26 Feb. 1731 he married Françoise Golard in New Orleans. On 25 March 1736, as a member of the Artaguiette expedition,

Petitpas

he was captured by the Chickasaws and, with 16 of his fellow prisoners, was put to death.

C. C. J. Bond

AN, Col., C[11A], 9, ff.104, 121, 147, 177; 14; D[2C], 47, 222. "Correspondance de Vaudreuil," APQ *Rapport*, *1947–48*, 171, 225, 271, 287. *NYCD* (O'Callaghan and Fernow), IX, 550, 609, 655. Antoine Bernard, *Histoire de la Louisiane* (Québec, 1953), 156. M. Dumont de Montigny, *Mémoires historiques sur la Louisiane* (2v., Paris, 1753). Lanctot, *Histoire du Canada*, II, 165. Aegidius Fauteux, "La famille Petit de Levilliers," *BRH*, XXXIV (1928), 478ff., 602.

PETITPAS, CLAUDE, schooner captain, interpreter, known particularly for his collaboration with the English, third child of a family of 15, son of Claude Petitpas, Sieur de Lafleur, clerk of the court at Port-Royal (Annapolis Royal, N.S.), and of Catherine Bugaret; b. *c.* 1663 at Port-Royal, d. some time between 1731 and 1733.

During his youth Petitpas was closely associated in his voyages and activities with the Micmacs in the neighbourhood of Port-Royal, where he lived in his father's home until his marriage. Around 1686 he married an Indian girl of that tribe named Marie-Thérèse, born in 1668, by whom he had at least seven children, according to the 1708 census. On 7 Jan. 1721, after his first wife's death, he remarried, again at Port-Royal; his second wife was Françoise Lavergne from that town, daughter of Pierre Lavergne, Father Breslay's servant, and of Anne Bernon. She was only 17; he was about 57. She bore him four children.

While his first wife was alive Petitpas lived at Mouscoudabouet (Musquodoboit), where the Boston fishermen were active; as early as 1698, complaints arose about his association with them. In September 1718, a frigate sent from Boston by the governor of Massachusetts and commanded by Captain Thomas Smart anchored in Canso (Canseau) harbour. The English seized a fair number of French fishermen, among them Marc La Londe, the son-in-law of Claude Petitpas. The latter placed his own schooner at the disposal of the English so that they might better carry out their plan.

On 30 June 1720 the legislative council of Boston, at his request, granted him the sum of £100 for having shown "tender regard . . . to sundry English captives in the late Indian War"; he had gone so far as to obtain their liberty by paying their ransom out of his own pocket. The council further resolved that the government would pay the tuition fees of one of his sons for four years at Harvard College.

He probably went to live subsequently on Île Royale (Cape Breton Island), perhaps at Port-Toulouse (St Peters, N.S.) itself, where several of his children had settled. In 1728 Joseph de Saint-Ovide de Brouillan [Mombeton*], governor of Île Royale, went there to conduct an inquiry into the loyalty of the Indians towards the French. Claude Petitpas was apparently trying to influence the Indians, particularly the young ones, in favour of the English. Saint-Ovide therefore tried to send him to France towards the end of that same year, with two of his sons by his first marriage, in order to get rid of him. If this plan was in fact carried out, Claude Petitpas does not seem to have been absent more than two years.

He died probably some time between 1731 and 1733: his last known child was born in 1731; moreover, in May 1733 the king gave his widow a sum of money for services rendered by her husband in his capacity as interpreter. In 1747 Governor Shirley of Massachusetts called Petitpas a "faithfull subject of the crown of Great Britain . . . [who] had received marks of favour from this government for his services."

Clarence J. d'Entremont

AN, Col., B, 59, f.516; C[11B], 3, 4, 10, ff.67–69; Section Outre-Mer, G[1], 466 (Recensements de l'Acadie, 1671, 1686). Newberry Library, Ayer Coll., La Chasse census (1708). PANS, MS docs., XXVI (parish register of Port-Royal), f.63. *The acts and resolves, public and private, of the province of the Massachusetts bay* (21v., Boston, 1869–1922), IX. *Coll. doc. inédits Canada et Amérique* (CF), III (1890), 165–68. *Coll. de manuscrits relatifs à la N.-F.,* III, 38–39, 379. *NYCD* (O'Callaghan and Fernow), IX, 912.

Arsenault, *Hist. et généal. des Acadiens*, I, 442, 477. Coleman, *New England captives*. Harvey, *French régime in P.E.I.*, 215. McLennan, *Louisbourg*, 62–63. Murdoch, *History of Nova-Scotia*, I, 243.

PEUVRET DE GAUDARVILLE, ALEXANDRE, counsellor, king's secretary, chief clerk of the Conseil Souverain, son of Jean-Baptiste Peuvret* Demesnu, first chief clerk of the Conseil Souverain, and of Catherine Nau; baptized 6 Oct. 1664 at Quebec; buried there 30 Dec. 1702.

Following in his father's footsteps, he occupied at an early age the office of secretary. In 1682 he became deputy secretary to Intendant de Meulles. In 1686, after de Meulles' departure, he worked with his father at the registry of the Conseil Souverain. At the request of Frontenac [Buade*] and Champigny [Bochart], he received on 1 March 1693 the letters according him "reversion of the office of king's counsellor and secretary, and of chief clerk of the Conseil Souverain of Quebec." He held this appointment until his death.

In 1695 he adopted the name of Gaudarville,

when he inherited this seigneury; he also secured title from Frontenac, in 1693, to a fief which he had named Fossambault, after his maternal grandfather Jacques Nau de La Boissière et de Fossambault. In 1696 he married Geneviève Bouteville, who died in September 1699 at the age of 17. On 12 Jan. 1700, he married Marie-Anne Gaultier, daughter of Philippe Gaultier* de Comporté, who bore him two children: Marie-Anne and Alexandre-Joseph.

In December 1702 he was carried off by the epidemic of smallpox that ravaged Quebec at that time.

ROBERT LAHAISE

Jug. et délib., I, 993; III, 517f., 988. Recensement du Canada, 1666 (APQ *Rapport*). P.-G. Roy, *Inv. concessions*, I, 13; IV, 71f.; *Inv. ins. Cons. souv.*, 93. Gareau, "La prévôté de Québec," 51–146. P.-G. Roy, "Les conseillers au Conseil souverain de la Nouvelle-France," *RSCT*, 3d ser., IX (1915), sect.i, 173–87; "Les secrétaires des gouverneurs et intendants de la Nouvelle-France," *BRH*, XLI (1935), 95. Tanguay, *Dictionnaire*, VI, 337f. J.-E. Roy, *Histoire du notariat*, I, 48. P.-G. Roy, *La ville de Québec*, I, 293; II, 18. N.-E. Dionne, "Les caveaux de la basilique Notre-Dame de Québec," *BRH*, IV (1898), 112. P.-G. Roy, "M. Nau de Fossambault et la Nouvelle-France," *BRH*, XXI (1915), 288; "La seigneurie de Gaudarville," *BRH*, IX (1903), 246–49.

PHILIPPE(S) DE HAUTMESNIL DE MANDEVILLE, FRANÇOIS (sometimes known as the Sieur de **Marigny**), trader, officer in Louisiana; baptized 10 Oct. 1682 at Montreal, seventh of 13 children of Jean-Vincent Philippe de Hautmesnil (Hautmesnyl) de Marigny, originally of Bayeux, France, who had married Marie-Catherine Lambert de Baussy in 1671; d. 24 Oct. 1728 at New Orleans.

In 1702 François and his elder brother Gabriel-Philippe, Sieur de Saint-Lambert, with whom he is frequently confused, joined the expedition of CHARLES JUCHEREAU de Saint-Denys at Montreal. After the death of Saint-Denys, and perhaps of Gabriel as well, François worked to salvage the tannery and its products, but seems to have been largely unsuccessful. By 1705, or shortly thereafter, François had replaced Gabriel as ensign in the company of François Juchereau de Vaulezar. From 1708 to 1711 he was in Paris, where he prepared a memoir on Louisiana and received a *lettre de garde de la Marine*. Returning as a lieutenant, he was accused by Le Moyne* de Bienville of having deceived the court "by passing himself off as his deceased brother"; if so, François's reputation as second in command of the Saint-Denys expedition may be open to doubt. Mandeville later commanded his own company at

Île Dauphine (Dauphin Island, Ala.), at Mobile (where a concession is still known by his name), and at New Orleans. By 1724, he was senior captain in the colony. In 1720 he had married Madeleine Le Maire in Paris; his children included Antoine (1722–1779) and an illegitimate daughter of mixed blood. In 1727 Mandeville received the prestigious appointment of town major of New Orleans. When the Mandeville family left Mobile, the engineer Devin lamented that Madame Mandeville's departure was robbing the post of its "ornament," adding: "There is, so to speak, no more society." Mandeville was cashiered in 1721 for insubordination to the Compagnie des Indes, but was restored to rank the same year. His opposition to the controversial Bienville was termed an "exécration" by one of Bienville's supporters, but he was generally respected as a soldier.

In many ways, Mandeville was a prototype of the frontier officer: he explored, experimented, and sometimes speculated in the new country; he came to know and be respected by the Indians; he was instrumental in bringing about internal improvements; he was an arbiter of local justice, a respecter of social amenities where life was harsh and uncomfortable, and a source of knowledge to his superiors. That he engaged in the self-seeking and contentiousness of an isolated society is not surprising; what is more important, his services contributed to a measure of peace in the Louisiana colony at a time when it was most needed.

JOHN FORTIER

AN, Col., B, 43, ff.738–39; C^{13A}, 3, ff.685, 687; 7, ff.213v–14; D^{2C}, 222/2, p.45 (the Alphabet Laffilard confuses Gabriel and François). *Découvertes et établissements des Français* (Margry), V, 425–26, 438–39; VI, 184; *passim. Fleur de Lys and calumet: being the Pénicaut narrative of a French adventure in Louisiana*, ed. and tr. R. G. McWilliams (Baton Rouge, La., 1953), a translation of the Pénicaut narrative from *Découvertes et établissements des Français* (Margry). V. *MPA* (Rowland and Sanders), II, 46–52; III, 18–29; *passim*.

Bonnault, "Le Canada militaire." Massicotte, "Répertoire des engagements pour l'Ouest." Tanguay, *Dictionnaire* (Vol. I lists Jean-Vincent Philippe under Hautmesny and under Flip). Alvord, *Illinois country*. Giraud, *Histoire de la Louisiane française*. P. J. Hamilton, *Colonial Mobile* (Boston, 1897; rev. ed., 1910). N. W. Caldwell, "Charles Juchereau de St. Denys: a French pioneer in the Mississippi valley," *Mississippi Valley Hist. Review*, XXVIII (1942), 563–80. Aegidius Fauteux, "Jean-Vincent Philippe du Hautmesnil et sa descendance," *BRH*, XXXVIII (1932), 199–210. J.-J. Lefebvre, "La succession de Charles Juchereau de Saint-Denis (1655–1703), premier juge royal de Montréal (1693)," APQ

Piedmont

Rapport, 1959–60, 233–73. É.-Z. Massicotte, "Jean-Vincent Philippe de Hautmesnil," *BRH*, XXII (1916), 345–46; "M. Philippe de Hautmesny" *BRH*, XXII (1916), 40–43. Régis Roy, "Philippes de Hautmenil," *BRH*, XXII (1916), 111–12.

PIEDMONT, JOSEPH-CHARLES RAIMBAULT DE. *See* Raimbault

PIKE, The. *See* Kinongé

PINAUD (Pinolt, Pineau, Pinault), NICOLAS, merchant, commercial fisherman, seigneur, churchwarden, one of the directors of the Compagnie de la Colonie; b. *c.* 1665 in the parish of Saint-Michel, Carcassonne, son of Jean Pinaud and "honorable femme" Françoise Daret (Dazé); d. in August 1722.

Pinaud's career in New France paralleled that of his frequent associate, Charles Perthuis. They not only engaged in commercial endeavours together, but were married within a few years of each other, Pinaud in 1693 and Perthuis in 1697, and they died within six months of each other. Pinaud's marriage contract, like that of Perthuis, was witnessed by the political and economic elite of the colony. His bride was Louise Douaire de Bondy, the widow of Pierre Allemand*, and the contract, signed on 9 Jan. 1693, describes Pinaud as about 28 years old and living in the home of Mathieu-François Martin de Lino. There is no trace of any children from his marriage but, in 1710, he and his wife made a *donation* to Marie-Élisabeth Waber whom they had rescued from the Abenakis in 1702. His widow, who long survived him, died some time before 1 April 1746.

Pinaud's commercial activities were many and varied. During the year of his marriage, 1693, he acted for Guillaume Maret of Bordeaux; the following year he equipped traders for the commerce of Hudson Bay. In 1696, he engaged in fishing, a business which he continued into the 18th century. That same year he traded in tobacco with Pierre Dubuc of Bayonne; Charles de Couagne was his business representative there.

At the time of the formation of the Compagnie de la Colonie, Pinaud acquired 1,000 *livres* of shares. He was later a director of the company, and was named with Perthuis and René-Louis Chartier de Lotbinière, in 1708, to help recover the debts of the bankrupt enterprise. In the early part of the 18th century he acted as the representative in New France of Pierre Peire. Later, in 1712, he fulfilled the same role for Denis Riverin, the metropolitan agent of the Compagnie de la Colonie.

After the death of François Hazeur, Pinaud also acted as a syndic in the settlement of the latter's estate. Many times during his career in New France, Pinaud was called upon by the Conseil Supérieur to act as an arbitrator—to evaluate estates and merchandise in cases in dispute before the council. The council's repeated use of him in this capacity reflects its trust in his judgement. When, in 1708, Intendant Jacques Raudot requested a gratuity to assist Perthuis and Pinaud in establishing a chamber of commerce, no immediate results were forthcoming. In 1717, however, such a chamber was established.

In 1695 Pinaud rented a house on Rue Notre-Dame (sous le Fort); his widow was still living there at her death. He also acquired a property on Rue Porche, which he leased to the Compagnie de la Colonie in 1702; a common practice among shareholders and administrators of the company at that time. In 1714, he bought a house on Rue Saint-Paul in Montreal for speculative purposes; he sold it nine months later. In 1709, he acquired the seigneury of Île Percée, which had been seized from Charles Aubert de La Chesnaye.

Pinaud died at the age of 57 or 58, and was buried in Quebec on 19 Aug. 1722. Very few of his papers seem to have survived. The inventory of his widow's goods, drawn up in August 1746, lists only a few records pertaining to Pinaud, apart from those dealing with his property.

Cameron Nish

AJQ, Greffe de Louis Chambalon; Greffe de François Genaple. AN, Col., C¹¹A, 3, f.468. AQ, NF, Coll. de pièces jud. et not., 1433. "Correspondance de Vaudreuil," APQ *Rapport, 1938–39, 1947–48. Jug. et délib.* "Lettres et mémoires de F.-M.-F. Ruette d'Auteuil," 1–114. Recensement de Québec, 1744 (APQ *Rapport*). P.-G. Roy, *Inv. concessions*, II, 128; IV, 183f. Charland, "Notre-Dame de Québec: le nécrologe de la crypte," 178. Gagnon, "Noms propres au Canada français," 154.

PINN. *See* Pynne

PINOLT. *See* Pinaud

PIOT DE LANGLOISERIE, CHARLES-GASPARD, soldier, town major and lieutenant at Montreal and at Quebec, knight of the order of Saint-Louis, son of Martin Piot de Langloiserie and Anne Petit; baptized *c.* 1655 at Hanion, bishopric of Chartres; buried at Quebec 21 Feb. 1715.

Piot de Langloiserie arrived in New France in 1691 as captain of a company of colonial regular troops on detachment. The following year, after the death of Jacques Bizard*, Buade* de Frontenac appointed him town major of Montreal with "the power to command in the absence of the governor, as the late Sieur Bizard had had." A commission dated 15 April 1695 confirmed his appointment; at the same time, Louis XIV, informed "of the courage, experience and good conduct of the Sieur de Langloiserie," named him commandant at Montreal in the absence of CALLIÈRE and RIGAUD de Vaudreuil. In 1697 Langloiserie obtained a fur-trading licence for one year, and the following year he went to France.

On 28 May 1699 the king signed the letters confirming the appointment of the Sieur de Langloiserie as town major of Quebec, replacing François de Gallifet*. Shortly afterwards "certain evil-intentioned people" accused him of "insolent behaviour in the service." Piot de Langloiserie, "strongly protected by Monsieur de Callières" according to Vaudreuil, was immediately defended by the governor, who declared "that it is impossible for anyone to have served with more energy, zeal, and affection . . . and that his great scrupulousness must have drawn down upon him the ill-will of people who do not like to have their duty pointed out to them." This high praise did not prevent the king from refusing Langloiserie's subsequent requests, such as those he made for the lieutenancy of Trois-Rivières and a post as midshipman for his son; yet almost every letter from Callière contained requests on Langloiserie's behalf. In 1700, for example, he put him forward as commandant at Chambly, but the post was not created until a few years later At about the same period, he obtained for him the right to "be in command at Quebec and take precedence over the infantry captains."

Finally, on 1 June 1703, he became king's lieutenant at Quebec, in consideration "of the favourable testimony that you [Callière] have given of the good conduct of . . . M. de Langloiserie." But this appointment did not satisfy Langloiserie, and he again solicited increases in salary, and privileges for his sons. He continued to be the target for severe criticism, for example that of having "tried to turn officers against him [Vaudreuil] here," but the minister felt himself obliged to give him a favourable reference.

The crowning-point of Piot de Langloiserie's career finally came on 24 June 1705, when he received the cross of the order of Saint-Louis. His requests nonetheless continued to pour into the mother country, together with marks of esteem and respect, which helped him to obtain in 1710 another increase in salary, and an ensign's commission for his son.

In 1691 Piot de Langloiserie had married Marie-Thérèse Dugué de Boisbriand, daughter of Michel-Sidrac Dugué* de Boisbriand, seigneur of Mille-Îles. In 1706 Piot had bought from his brother-in-law Jean-Sidrac Dugué the fief of Île Sainte-Thérèse. On 5 March 1714 Vaudreuil granted to him, jointly with Jean PETIT, the seigneury of Mille-Îles.

Piot de Langloiserie died on 21 Feb. 1715 at Quebec. Among his 11 children were Marie-Charlotte, who had a son by Pierre de Ruette d'Auteuil de La Malotière, Louis, who seems to have made a career for himself in Louisiana, and Suzanne, who married Jean-Baptiste CÉLORON de Blainville.

NIVE VOISINE

AN, Col., B, 17, 19, 20, 22, 23, 25, 27; C^{11A}, 12, 13, 16, 17. "Correspondance de Frontenac (1689–99)," APQ *Rapport*, 1927–28, 165, 166, 195. "Correspondance de Vaudreuil," APQ *Rapport*, 1938–39, 16–179; *1939–40*, 355–463; *1942–43*, 399–443; *1946–47*, 3, 371–460; *1947–48*, 137–339. "Lettre du gouvernement de Callière au ministre (7 novembre 1700)," BRH, XXXIV (1928), 746–51. Taillemite, *Inventaire analytique*, série B, I. Fauteux, *Les chevaliers de Saint-Louis*, 97. P.-G. Roy, *Les officiers d'état-major*; *La famille Du Gué de Boisbriand* (Lévis, 1918). "Charles-Gaspard Piot de Langloiserie," BRH, XII (1906), 38–40.

PITANTOUIN. *See* TANTOUIN

PORC-ÉPIC. *See* NORO

PORTNEUF, RENÉ ROBINAU DE. *See* ROBINAU

POTTIER, JEAN-BAPTISTE, royal notary, deputy to the fiscal attorney, clerk of court, royal process-server, surveyor, and jailer, originally from Chartres, France; date of birth unknown, son of Jean Pottier and Marguerite de Sainctes; buried 11 July 1711 at Trois-Rivières.

Pottier, a resident of the parish of Saints-Anges at Lachine, was at first a precentor and schoolmaster, at a salary of 50 *livres* a year. He apparently gave up these poorly paid activities towards the end of 1686, at the time when he began to receive notarial acts by virtue of a commission granted him by the seigneurs of Montreal. On 23 May 1690 he was appointed deputy to the fiscal attorney in the bailiff's court of Montreal, an office that he held until the middle of 1693. Meanwhile, on 15 March 1693, he had obtained letters confirming his appointment as royal notary in the government of Montreal; but judging by his minute-book, possibly incomplete, his clientele did not increase in consequence. Since 14 June 1688 he had been a married man and he had a family to support. On 5 Oct. 1695, therefore, he had to rent a 60-acre settler's farm at Lachine.

Poulet

An opportunity presented itself in 1701: the intendant invited him to replace the old notary Séverin AMEAU, at Trois-Rivières, for a few months at least. Pottier decided to establish himself there. In this small town he was able to hold the offices of clerk of court, jailer, and notary at one and the same time; in addition, on 17 Oct. 1703 he became royal serjeant at law (process-server) with jurisdiction for the whole of New France. Pottier, who had a fairly large family on his hands, was perhaps little better off; in any case, on 1 May 1711 Intendant Bégon* added to his titles that of sworn surveyor.

Notaries are said to be peaceable people; Pottier had rather the aggressiveness of the process-server and the jailer. He got into trouble a few times: on 5 May 1693 PIERRE RÉMY, the parish priest of Lachine, brought an action against him for insults and threats to use force; worse still, in 1707, Pottier used physical violence against a woman named Carpentier from Champlain and was sentenced to pay damages and legal costs. The amusing thing was that Pottier had been attacked himself by Étienne Pézard de La Tousche in 1704, and had been so roughly handled that La Tousche had been obliged to pay him compensation and damages to the extent of 200 *livres*.

Pottier died in 1711 at Trois-Rivières. His widow Étiennette Beauvais, who is said to have been restored to health in 1704 through the intercession of Brother Didace Pelletier*, lived until 1753.

ANDRÉ VACHON

AJM, Greffe de Claude Maugue, 13 juin 1688, 5 oct. 1695. AJTR, Greffe de J.-B. Pottier, 1699–1711. AQ, NF, Coll. de pièces jud. et not., 400; NF, Ord. des int., V, 28; VI, 22v et seq. Jug. et délib., III, IV, V. Ord. comm. (P.-G. Roy), II, 319. A. Roy, *Inv. greffes not.*, XI, 167–258. "Les notaires au Canada," 28. É.-Z. Massicotte, "Les tribunaux et les officiers de justice," *BRH*, XXXVII (1931), 126, 183, 254. Tanguay, *Dictionnaire*, I, 495. Jouve, *Les Franciscains et le Canada: aux Trois-Rivières*. J.-E. Roy, *Histoire du notariat*, I, 147, 191f.

POULET, GEORGES-FRANÇOIS, *dit* **M. Dupont,** priest, Benedictine from Saint-Maur, Jansenist, hermit at Trois-Pistoles; known in Canada from 1714 to 1718.

During a journey to Holland, this Benedictine monk had struck up a friendship with the famous Father Pasquier Quesnel and had embraced the Jansenist doctrine. But on 8 Sept. 1713 the bull *Unigenitus* condemned 101 propositions by Father Quesnel and constrained Catholics to reject his theories. Believing himself persecuted and wishing to take cover "from the earnest searches that were being conducted for his person," Dom Poulet sailed for New France in 1714.

At Quebec, where he passed himself off as a layman, he took the name of M. Dupont. He was thought to be a rich man who was making inquiries of all kinds and who wanted to found a monastery. "One noticed a certain lack of ease about him, which made one suspect him of being a defrocked monk; he denied this as best he could [. . .]," wrote Mother JUCHEREAU de Saint-Ignace. But he found himself too much in the public eye, and decided to return to seclusion. Leclair, the parish priest of Cap-Saint-Ignace, offered him hospitality, and had a cabin built for him "a quarter of a league away in the wood, beside a river." Dom Poulet remained there only a few months, for it was very uncomfortable; he even had to go and finish the winter at the presbytery. He returned to the woods in the spring, but his cabin burned down and he did not succeed in rebuilding it immediately. It was then that in order to be "much quieter" he went farther away from Quebec, and took refuge with the seigneur Nicolas Rioux of Trois-Pistoles, who welcomed him eagerly and gave him a piece of land along the Trois-Pistoles River. Dupont again built himself a hut and lived there for two years, "alone and unknown, happy and undisturbed."

In 1717 Dom Poulet returned to Quebec, where he had serious difficulties with Bishop Saint-Vallier [LA CROIX], who vainly sought to make him sign the anti-jansenist formulary. In face of the monk's obstinacy, the bishop decided to expel him from New France, and asked for the collaboration of RIGAUD de Vaudreuil. The latter, who had received a letter from Dom Poulet's superior recommending Poulet to him "as one of his religious who was more weak-minded than of evil intent," refused to give assistance to Bishop Saint-Vallier, who was to lodge a complaint about this in France and to obtain a decree from the council of Marine.

Meanwhile the Benedictine was stricken by purpura and hospitalized at the Hôtel-Dieu. The bishop warned Thomas THIBOULT, parish priest of Quebec, to refuse him absolution if he persisted in his views; he also had him exhorted by Archdeacon LA COLOMBIÈRE. But Dom Poulet refused to retract anything, and only his recovery prevented a greater scandal. He could not however remain any longer in New France, for Bishop Saint-Vallier had issued a severe ordinance against him; he therefore decided in 1718 to return to France of his own accord.

In Europe he complained bitterly of the way he had been treated in New France, and the *Gazette de Hollande* publicized his difficulties. Dom Poulet himself drafted a "Récit simple de ce qu'un religieux bénédictin a souffert au Canada au sujet de la bulle Unigenitus," in which he made an indictment against the bishop and the Jesuits and showed himself to be more and more obdurate. Nothing is known of him after this adventure. But the misfortunes of this Benedictine monk clearly reveal how New France was protected against Jansenism, and indicate how little cause there is for surprise that this doctrine was not able to take root there.

NIVE VOISINE

"Le bénédictin dom Georges-François Poulet dans la Nouvelle-France," APQ *Rapport, 1922–23*, 274–89. Caron, "Inventaire de documents," APQ *Rapport, 1941–42*. Juchereau, *Annales* (Jamet), 404–8. *Mandements des évêques de Québec* (Têtu et Gagnon), I, 496–98. Mathias D'Amours, *Les Trois-Pistoles* (2v., Trois-Pistoles, 1946). H.-R. Casgrain, "L'hermite des Trois-Pistoles," *BRH*, V (1899), 260–65.

POULIN DE COURVAL, JEAN-BAPTISTE, king's attorney, merchant, and seigneur of Nicolet; b. 15 Jan. 1657 at Trois-Rivières, of the marriage of Maurice Poulin*, Sieur de La Fontaine and Jeanne Jallot (Jalleau); d. at Trois-Rivières, 15 Feb. 1727.

Poulin de Courval is known not only as an important merchant of Trois-Rivières, but also as a shipbuilder. On 24 May 1714, he took over as king's attorney from RENÉ GODEFROY de Tonnancour, who himself succeeded Jean LECHASSEUR as lieutenant general for civil and criminal affairs.

On 7 Jan. 1696, Courval married at Trois-Rivières Louise Cressé, eldest daughter of Michel Cressé, seigneur of Nicolet, who had died in mysterious circumstances ten years before, and of Marguerite Denys; he thus became seigneur of Nicolet. Louise Cressé, who gave him five children, died 21 March 1706; his second wife was Marie-Madeleine Forestier. Six children were born of the second marriage.

One of the chief conflicts that marked Courval's administration of the Nicolet seigneury was over the question of the boundaries between it and the seigneury of Baie-du-Febvre (Baie-Saint-Antoine). In 1702 a survey revealed that Jacques Lefebvre, the seigneur of Baie-du-Febvre, was encroaching to the extent of 27 *arpents* on the adjoining territory, 18 of these being occupied by himself and some members of his family. Courval recovered the nine *arpents* occupied by copyholders and left the remainder to those who had settled there in good faith; to compensate him for this, Lefebvre conceded to him his right to a third of the milling dues levied on grain ground at the Platon mill at Trois-Rivières belonging to Courval.

The same mill was the occasion of another conflict in 1724. René Godefroy de Tonnancour had granted the Charon Brothers, free of charge, a piece of land near Platon for the construction of a school; Courval opposed this, claiming that the building blocked the wind. An agreement was reached whereby the school could be built a little further away and the mill freed from obstruction.

Poulin de Courval died 15 Feb. 1727, at Trois-Rivières, and was buried the next day in the church. He was succeeded in his office of king's attorney by his son Louis, likewise seigneur of Nicolet.

HERVÉ BIRON

Archives de la paroisse de l'Immaculée-Conception, Trois-Rivières, Registres. AQ, NF, Doc. de la jur. des T.-R.; NF, Ins. Cons. sup. Tanguay, *Dictionnaire*, I, 497; VI, 424. J.-É. Bellemare, *Histoire de Nicolet, 1669–1924* (Arthabaska, Qué., 1924), 103, 106, 116. Jouve, *Les Franciscains et le Canada: aux Trois-Rivières*, 91, 127, 278. Sulte, *Mélanges historiques* (Malchelosse), VI. *Les Ursulines des Trois-Rivières depuis leur établissement jusqu'à nos jours* (4v., Trois-Rivières, 1888–1911).

POULIN DE FRANCHEVILLE, FRANÇOIS (he always signed, with the exception of his marriage contract, Francheville), merchant and bourgeois of Montreal, fur-trader, seigneur, entrepreneur in the Saint-Maurice ironworks; b. 7 Oct. 1692; d. November 1733 in Montreal.

Francheville was the son of Michel Poulin and Marie Jutra. His grandfather was Maurice Poulin* de La Fontaine, a fur-trader and judicial office for the Trois-Rivières area. The date when Francheville moved to Montreal is unknown, but it was here that his active career took place. His marriage contract was drawn up on 26 Nov. 1718, and the following day he married the 21-year-old Thérèse de Couagne, daughter of CHARLES DE COUAGNE and Marie Godé. Couagne had been one of the most important merchants of Montreal. Parish records indicate that Francheville had at least one child, Marie-Angélique, baptized on 3 Oct. 1719. The censuses of Montreal of 1731, two years before his death, and of 1741, after his death, do not list any children in his household.

His early commercial career is typical of the merchants and bourgeois of New France. From 1722 until his death we find him engaged in several facets of the fur trade. He acted for, or in conjunction with, several officers and commandants of forts in the colony, such as Louis Liénard* de Beaujeu, Constant LE MARCHAND de Lignery, and the merchant François Volant. The advancing of credit to merchants was a typical activity of Francheville. He also hired men for the exploitation of the fur resources of the hinterlands. Just

Pourroy de Laubervière

prior to his undertaking the development of the Saint-Maurice ironworks, his real assets were estimated by the intendant to be 30,000 *livres*.

His most ambitious undertaking was the development of the mineral resources of his seigneury at Saint-Maurice. This enterprise was greatly facilitated by the support of Intendant Gilles Hocquart*, who was sympathetic to commercial endeavours. In 1729, the year Hocquart arrived in the colony, Francheville wrote Maurepas, the minister of Marine, requesting a 20-year monopoly to mine the iron deposits at Saint-Maurice. His request was referred to Charles de Beauharnois* de La Boische and Hocquart by the minister. Both wholeheartedly supported the undertaking. A brevet was granted Francheville on 25 March 1730. He was given, as requested, a 20-year monopoly, which was to date from the initial smelting of the ore. He was also granted the right to exploit cultivated and uncultivated lands adjacent to his own. If the lands were cultivated, he was to reimburse their owners, and if they were not, he could simply expropriate them.

By 1732 the project was realized to be much greater than originally thought. Hocquart supported Francheville's request for a loan of 10,000 *livres*. This was granted in 1733, and was to be repaid within three years. To facilitate the development of the industry, and probably because he had been able to get a loan of 10,000 *livres*, he formed a company and thereby drew upon the benefits that could follow from the favouritism of the upper administrators of the colony. He associated himself with his brother Pierre Poulin*, Ignace Gamelin* Jr., a Montreal merchant, BRICAULT de Valmur, the intendant's secretary, and François-Étienne Cugnet*, the director of the Domaine d'Occident and a member of the Conseil Supérieur.

On 22 March 1733 he hired Christophe Janson, *dit* Lapalme, for three years. The latter was to make a trip to New England with the Sieur La Brèche, to examine the ironworks of that area. Janson's annual salary was 700 *livres* and he was to supply his own tools. In the previous year ore samples and castings had been sent to France; the quality of the iron was considered equal to that of Spain. Further development was momentarily halted, by Francheville's early death, at the age of 41 in November 1733 (not in 1734, as Hocquart once wrote). His widow attempted to carry on the enterprise, as is indicated by her assuming her late husband's obligations on 19 Dec. 1733. By 1735, the ironworks fell under the control of François-Étienne Cugnet.

Francheville left his widow a property 43 feet by 60 on Rue Saint-Paul, Montreal, with a two-storey stone house. He also left an irregularly shaped farm of approximately 10 by 16 *arpents* in the parish of Saint-Michel, on which there were several buildings, and of which 15 acres were cultivated and 15 were grazing lands. His wife also inherited his interests in the Saint-Maurice ironworks, which included his own investments, the seigneury of Saint-Maurice, and a small annual income derived from his having contributed these lands as a capital asset. Francheville was a typical entrepreneur in New France; his early death was a loss to the colony.

CAMERON NISH

AJM, Greffe de Jacques David; Greffe de Charles-René Gaudron de Chèvremont; Greffe de Nicolas-Augustin Guillet de Chaumont; Greffe de J.-C. Raimbault. AN, Col., B, 53, 54, 55, 57, 59; C¹¹ᴬ, 51, 57, 58, 110. Collection Lafontaine (Sir George Williams University), Registre de la cure de Montréal. *Documents relating to Canadian currency during the French period* (Shortt). Fauteux, *Essai sur l'industrie sous le régime français*. Sulte, *Mélanges historiques* (Malchelosse), VI. Albert Tessier, *Les forges Saint-Maurice 1729–1883* (Trois-Rivières, 1952). Cameron Nish, "François-Étienne Cugnet et les Forges de Saint-Maurice: Un type d'entrepreneur et d'entreprise en Nouvelle-France," *L'Actualité économique*, XLII (1966–67), 884–97.

POURROY DE LAUBERIVIÈRE, FRANÇOIS-LOUIS DE, priest, doctor of theology of the Sorbonne, fifth bishop of Quebec; b. 16 June 1711 at Grenoble, son of Claude-Joseph Pourroy de Laubervière, judge of the treasury court of the province of Dauphiné, and of Marie-Anne de Saint-Germain de Mérieux; d. 20 Aug. 1740 at Quebec.

François-Louis de Pourroy de Laubervière studied at the Jesuit college in Grenoble and at the Sulpician seminary in Paris; he was ordained a priest on 21 Sept. 1735 and became a doctor of theology on 1 April 1738. He was already a canon of the collegiate church at Romans when he was recommended to Cardinal Fleury by M. Couturier, the superior of Saint-Sulpice. On 22 March 1739 Louis XV appointed him to succeed Bishop Dosquet*, who had resigned. The bulls were dispatched on 20 July and the episcopal consecration took place at Saint-Sulpice on 16 August. On 20 June 1740 the prelate caused possession to be taken of his cathedral by a power of attorney dated 20 February.

On 10 June 1740 he sailed from La Rochelle on the *Rubis*, with his chaplain, two servants, and some priests and religious. Until they reached the Grand Banks of Newfoundland the crossing was pleasant; then sickness broke out on the ship,

530

particularly affecting the passengers of lowly status. "This sickness," Hocquart* wrote in a letter dated 6 Aug. 1740, "is an unremitting fever, accompanied by violent rushes of blood to the brain, and sometimes by eruptions." Father Canot, who witnessed this epidemic, described conditions on the ship thus: "Picture a place the size of our garrets, where the light hardly ever penetrates, and where one can barely walk upright, crammed full of mattresses, above which are canvas sheets the length of a man and two feet wide, attached by the two corners to nails, and serving likewise as beds for these poor wretches, so that there were nearly 400 of them in such a small space. In such a woeful plight, would we priests have remained idle? You can imagine what one does and what one must do in these circumstances. However, the sickness spread, and we were trying to get as near as we could to Quebec. The crew was growing weaker day by day, and we had scarcely anyone who could handle the ship. The officers were forced to do it themselves, and anybody who had the strength lent a hand. It was in vain that we hoisted the flag which is the signal that one is in distress and needs help, nobody whatever came." Many died, and the captain had to ask for sailors from Quebec to reach the port. In this desperate situation, the bishop used his energies unsparingly, along with the other priests.

At Intendant Hocquart's request, Pourroy de Lauberivière disembarked at the Île-aux-Coudres to go on to Quebec in a shallop. He arrived there on 8 Aug. 1740, a Monday evening, and was welcomed by the authorities of the colony and by the whole town. In him they saw Bishop LAVAL come back to life again. On Tuesday he rested at the seminary, visiting the house and receiving the respects of the religious. On Wednesday he was Hocquart's guest at dinner and on the 11th, a holiday, he went with the seminarists to their country house at Saint-Michel; on his return he visited the governor Beauharnois* de La Boische. The latter and the intendant wrote shortly afterwards: "His Excellency the bishop, who had arrived here in perfect health, fell ill on the 13th of this month. On the 14th and 15th, the fever showed no new symptoms. On the 16th it intensified; strokes followed; finally purpura set in; and on the 20th, at 8 o'clock in the morning, he passed away, regretted by all. He had made a favourable impression upon all classes of society. During the crossing, and in the short time that he lived among us, his virtue and his good intentions manifested themselves. He was buried the same day, without ceremony, because of the nature of his disease; and today [27 August] a solemn service is being held for him in the cathedral." In such a short time, the prelate had acquired an extraordinary reputation for virtue, which caused several favours to be attributed to his intercession.

LUCIEN CAMPEAU

C.-É. Brasseur de Bourbourg, *Histoire du Canada, de son église et de ses missions* (2v., Paris, 1859), I, 263–68. Gosselin, *L'Église du Canada*, V, 353–405. Cyprien Tanguay, *Monseigneur de Lauberivière, cinquième évêque de Québec, 1739–1740* (Montréal, 1885).

PRAT, LOUIS, innkeeper, baker, ship-owner, and port captain of Quebec; b. 1662 at Notre-Dame de Ninière (province of Languedoc); d. 22 Feb. 1726 at Quebec.

In 1695 Prat was in business as an innkeeper in Quebec, and from 1703 on as a baker. In 1704 he joined the group organized by the seafarer Jean LÉGER de La Grange "for fitting out ships for privateering against the enemies of the state." To this purpose Prat had the *Joybert* built. The undertaking was crowned with success; some months after it was launched the ship returned to Quebec in triumph, bringing with it the frigate *Pembroke Galley*, which had been taken from the English. This episode is recalled in a picture dated 1706 which was given as a votive offering to the sanctuary of Sainte-Anne de Beaupré.

When the *Joybert* was lost at sea in 1709, the Sieur Prat acquired the *Normand*. Later on he had other privateers built, with the result that he finally attracted the attention of Pontchartrain, who in 1711 appointed him port captain of Quebec, an office which consisted in enforcing observance of the regulations concerning ships entering and leaving the port. This did not prevent Prat from continuing his commerce.

It is worthy of notice that Louis Prat seems to have been one of the first ship-owners in the colony, after the period of Talon*'s administration, to undertake building ships in Canada on his own account. On 15 Nov. 1716 he wrote to the council of Marine, reminding it that it was "because of him that ship-building had been taken up here, as a result of the example that he set."

Louis Prat died at Quebec on 22 Feb. 1726 and was buried in the cathedral. He had married, on 30 July 1691, Jeanne-Angélique Gobeil. Three daughters were born of this marriage.

J. P. ASSELIN, C.SS.R.

AJQ, Greffe de Louis Chambalon, 11 mai 1692, 29 mai 1693, 22 janv. 1695, 3 sept. 1701; Greffe de Gilles Rageot, 21 juillet 1691. AQ, Manuscrits relatifs à l'histoire de la N.-F., 2e sér., VI. "Engagement de Charles Prieur, chirurgien, au sieur Louis Prat, pour s'embarquer sur le bateau normand (Rivet,

Prince Waxaway

21 avril 1716)," *BRH*, XXV (1919), 238. *Jug. et délib.*, I, II, III. P.-G. Roy, *Inv. coll. pièces jud. et not.*, I; *Inv. contrats de mariages*, V, 156; *Inventaire de pièces sur la côte de Labrador conservées aux Archives de la Province de Québec* (2v., Québec, 1940–42), I, 281. J.-P. Asselin, "Louis Prat, associé du corsaire Jean de la Grange, offre un ex-voto à sainte Anne," *Annales de Sainte-Anne de Beaupré* (avril, 1958), 105–8. P.-G. Roy, "Les capitaines de port à Québec," *BRH*, XXXII (1926), 3–12, 65–78; "Un corsaire canadien: Jean Léger de La Grange," *BRH*, XXIV (1918), 33–48.

PRINCE WAXAWAY. *See* Waxaway

PROVOST, FRANÇOIS, company lieutenant in the Carignan-Salières regiment, captain, town major then king's lieutenant at Quebec, governor of Trois-Rivières; b. 1638 in Paris, son of Charles Provost and Jeanne Du Gousset; d. 1 June 1702 at Quebec.

The first mention that we find of him is a royal warrant of 6 Aug. 1661, which appointed him lieutenant of Montoson's company in the Régiment du Poitou. Another of 6 Dec. 1664 designated him as lieutenant of Andigné* de Grandfontaine's company, and it is as such that he formed part of the Carignan-Salières regiment and landed at Quebec on 19 Aug. 1665. A document dated 22 July 1666 already referred to him as town major of Quebec, a post to which he seems to have been assigned as soon as he arrived, and in which he was confirmed by a royal commission dated 14 May 1668. He was to hold this post for more than 30 years, being responsible at the same time for other duties in the discharge of which he proved himself to be a very conscientious official. He served under six governors and cooperated with five intendants, and none of them was ever able to call in question his integrity, zeal, and loyalty. Being confined to his administrative duties, he took no part in the great military expeditions of the period, except when he accompanied Buade* de Frontenac to Lake Ontario in 1673.

Frontenac always held him in high esteem. In 1683 Le Febvre* de La Barre suggested his name as governor of Montreal, in place of Perrot*. Provost did not obtain the post, as he had no trump card at court in the game of intrigue and influence. But as soon as La Barre was recalled he became temporary governor of the country, an office which was officially ratified on 30 May 1686 pending the arrival of the new appointee and which he was to occupy on various occasions subsequently. In 1687 a royal decree named him the temporary commandant of Montreal, in Callière's absence.

Provost was the man chiefly responsible for preparing the town of Quebec to defend itself against Phips*'s attack in the autumn of 1690. As the governor was absent, the command rested with him. Aware of the danger, he set to work without delay. He sent an emissary to Montreal to warn Frontenac. A bark, handled by his brother-in-law Pierre Bécart de Granville, who knew the region better than anybody else, sped to Tadoussac, to spy out the enemy. Meanwhile the town major mobilized the inhabitants of the town and of the neighbouring parishes, and everyone set to work to dig trenches, set up batteries at strategic points, and form defence battalions. Frontenac, who arrived at top speed, was amazed to find the capital ready to face the enemy. In less than six days Provost had accomplished a task which would normally have taken two months. According to the annalist of the Hôtel-Dieu, it was Provost who went to the river's bank to receive Phips's envoy, Major Thomas Savage, and who ordered him to be blindfolded before having him taken by roundabout ways to the governor's palace. History gives Frontenac, because of his famous reply to this representative, the credit for the victory. But the governor would certainly not have been able to adopt such airs of jaunty assurance without the system of defence made ready by Provost. The king was informed of this sudden veering of fortune, and on 7 April 1691 he conveyed his satisfaction to Provost, and told him that he would create expressly for him the post of king's lieutenant at Quebec. The monarch kept his promise a few months later, on 29 Feb. 1692. On several occasions, throughout his years of service, Provost received letters of commendation for his conduct, chiefly for his exploit of 1690; these letters, signed sometimes by the king, sometimes by Pontchartrain or Maurepas, were carefully preserved by him, and are enumerated in the inventory of his possessions drawn up after his death.

The spirit of justice and uprightness that always underlay Provost's administration created some enemies for him, chiefly among the people interested in freedom of trade. Provost sometimes had to display supple diplomacy, enlivened with discreet suggestions, during the conflicts between the governor and the intendant. When Duchesneau*, in 1678, had Pierre Moreau, *dit* La Taupine, arrested for trading in furs illegally, Provost received immediately from Frontenac an order to set the trader free; this was done at once. Provost's most relentless depreciator was the engineer Robert de Villeneuve*, whom Governor Brisay de Denonville described as "a fool, a libertine, a debauchee, whom we must endure because we have business with him." Villeneuve even addressed complaints to the court about the town major's conduct, alleging malpractices on his part. Denonville was informed of it, and came forcefully to Provost's defence. In his report of 8 June 1687 the governor wrote to the minister, Seignelay: "The mischievous things that have been written to you about the Sieur Provost, town major of Quebec, must not do him harm in your mind, my lord, since beyond a doubt he is the most honest and upright man, and the least self-seeking that I have found in Canada. Up to the present, he is the only former officer I have seen who has not been involved in any commerce or been a party to any past contentions, being attentive only to his duty. . . ."

Provost had reached the age of 40 when on 1 Aug. 1679 he married Geneviève Macard, Charles Bazire*'s widow and the beneficiary of a sizeable inheritance. In 1682 he bought Intendant Talon*'s house where Intendant Duchesneau had also resided. The latter's successor, Jacques de Meulles, who wanted to live in it to be nearer the governor's palace, wanted to have the sale to the town major cancelled. Provost, wishing to avoid trouble, accepted the offer to purchase made by Bishop Saint-Vallier [La Croix], who had the building pulled down so that the bishop's palace could be enlarged. Provost realized an excellent profit on this sale. In 1697 he sank more than 13,000 *livres* into a venture for exporting furs that was started by Augustin Le Gardeur de Courtemanche, Raymond Martel, and Antoine Trottier Des Ruisseaux, the latter's father-in-law. The deed of partnership, made up as a private agreement, was very vague; Provost was never fully repaid, and the affair kept the Quebec courts busy for a long time.

On 28 May 1699 a royal commission granted François Provost the post of governor of Trois-Rivières, where he replaced Claude de Ramezay, who was appointed commander in chief of the colonial regular troops. A commentary made by Le Roy de La Potherie at the time of these transfers gives us an indication of the characters of the two men and of the opinion of the inhabitants regarding their governors. Claude de Ramezay administered "with wearisome authority" and annoyed his subjects. Consequently the inhabitants of Trois-Rivières approved of François Provost's appointment as governor. In 1702 the king's writer sent the following message to the minister of the Marine: "Your name was blessed a thousand times when you gave M. Provost the governorship of Trois-Rivières. He is a generous man, who is loved by the whole town. He seeks only opportunities to please one and all. He does not meddle in the trade in pelts carried on by the bourgeoisie, who would willingly have sung the

Te Deum in thanksgiving when you rid them of M. de Ramezay. The peoples in the colonies like to be handled gently."

By the time he was appointed governor of Trois-Rivières, Provost had reached the age of 60, and was a sick man. As early as 1689 Frontenac had observed that he was suffering "from gout and gravel." Perhaps foreseeing that his term of office would be short, he brought only the bare necessities of his household. The rest was left at Quebec, placed in crates and stored in his brother-in-law Bécart de Granville's house in Rue du Sault-au-Matelot. Provost endeavoured, through the intermediary of Governor Callière, but without success, to have Granville appointed town major of Trois-Rivières to assist him in his work. The court refused because they were related. As his disease was getting worse, the governor entered the Ursuline hospital, then returned to Quebec and placed himself under the care of his friend, the king's doctor Michel Sarrazin. He died on 1 June 1702 and was buried on 5 June in the cathedral vault. The inventory of his possessions, drawn up by the notary Chambalon, covers nearly 50 pages. Since the doctor had charged Provost no fee, his widow, "out of fairness," sent him a gratuity of eight golden *louis*. On 5 Nov. 1703 she married Charles-Henri d'Aloigny de La Groye; he was her third husband.

Contrary to what Le Jeune says, François Provost left no children. He was replaced in the post of governor of Trois-Rivières by the Marquis de Crisafy, who had already succeeded him as king's lieutenant at Quebec.

Raymond Douville

AJQ, Greffe de Romain Becquet, 22 juillet 1666; Greffe de Louis Chambalon, 13 juin, 20 oct., 8 nov. 1702, 20 janv. 1704; Greffe de Jean Lecomte, 20 juillet 1668. "Correspondance de Frontenac (1389–99)," APQ *Rapport, 1927–28,* 26–179. Juchereau, *Annales* (Jamet). Gagnon, "Noms propres au Canada français," 156. Le Jeune, *Dictionnaire,* II, 477. P.-G. Roy, *Les officiers d'état-major; La ville de Québec.* Régis Roy et Malchelosse, *Le régiment de Carignan.* P.-G. Roy, "François Prévost," BRH, XI (1905), 22–24.

PYNNE (Pynn, Pyne, Pinn), WILLIAM, member of one of the leading families of Harbour Grace and Carbonear, Newfoundland, during the period of the French wars, 1689–1713.

Of the 22 inhabitants of Harbour Grace in 1677, John Pynne (father of William?) claimed to be the oldest resident, and was nominated as collector there for a proposed tax to maintain a governor in Newfoundland. He and Robert Pynne, who followed him, tended to act as leaders of the little community in dealing with the commodores of the convoy. William Pynne and, later, his son William acted in a similar capacity at Carbonear, where the population in 1677 was 55.

These two settlements were strongly defended by their inhabitants throughout the period of the French wars. Carbonear successfully resisted an attack by PIERRE LE MOYNE d'Iberville late in 1696. When raids began again in 1702, Robert and William Pynne (the elder) were among those who organized the fortification of Carbonear Island, and petitioned on 1 Dec. 1702 for official assistance. Captain Michael RICHARDS, in command at Fort William, St John's, complained of the irregularity of their action, suggesting that they had panicked. Though the inhabitants dispersed to their homes, they kept their stronghold as a place of refuge. It served them in good stead when, in February 1704/5, TESTARD de Montigny led a band of Indians—part of AUGER de Subercase's force which was besieging Fort William—to raid the English settlements on Conception Bay. William Pynne was one of those who distinguished themselves in the defence of Carbonear Island, where the enemy was repelled, though much damage was done in the region. By November more normal conditions were restored, and William Pynne, with others, signed a letter to thank the bishop of London for providing a new minister, Jacob RICE, for St John's.

The fall of St John's in December 1708 had no immediate effect on the more northerly English settlements, but in 1709 a militia was at last organized under John COLLINS, acting governor at St John's. Eight local governors were named, with subordinate officers. William Pynne emerged as governor at Carbonear, with his son, William, as one of his lieutenants. At Harbour Grace Robert Pynne was one of the two captains under the governor there, Henry Edwards. This system was confirmed by Josias CROWE in 1711 and was continued until the end of the war. The Pynne family were pioneers in organizing the outlying English settlements for local defence and gave the lead to other areas.

D. B. QUINN

PRO, *CSP, Col., 1677–80, 1702–3, 1704–5, 1708–9.* La Morandière, *Hist. de la pêche française de la morue,* I, 456–58. Prowse, *History of Nfld.* (2d ed., 1896), 194, 245. Rogers, *Newfoundland.*

Q

QUESNEVILLE (he sometimes signed **Quesnevillé, Quenneville), JEAN,** master tailor, royal court officer for the jurisdiction of Montreal, jailer and keeper of the prisons of that town; b. *c.* 1651, son of Pierre Quesneville, master tailor in the parish of Saint-Nicolas, in the diocese of Rouen, and of Jeanne Saye; d. 23 Aug. 1701 at Montreal.

Quesneville was at first a master tailor at Montreal. He continued to practise this trade along with his judicial functions. He became precentor, then verger, and subsequently was appointed court officer in the bailiff's court of Montreal in 1681. On 25 July 1690 he became jailer and prison keeper for a period of three years, but continued as court officer. On three occasions, in 1686, 1687, and 1692, he was clerk in the court registry. He was likewise acting judge in 1691, 1692, and 1693. In 1694 he received the position of royal court officer, which he kept until his death in 1701.

On 12 Feb. 1674, at Montreal, he had married Denise Marié, daughter of Pierre Marié, fencing-master in the parish of Saint-Sulpice in Paris, and of Jeanne Lord. Ten children were born of this marriage.

ROBERT LAHAISE

AJM, Greffe de Bénigne Basset, 12 janv. 1674. ASSM, tiroir 77, 37 (premiers chefs de Ville-Marie de 1665 à 1676). *Jug. et délib.,* II, 132f. Gagnon, "Noms propres au Canada français," 156. Massicotte, "Les tribunaux et les officiers de justice," *RSCT,* 3d ser., X (1916) sect.I, 273–303. Tanguay, *Dictionnaire,* I, 504.

QUIALA. *See* KIALA

QUINIARD, *dit* **Duplessis, ANTOINE-OLIVIER,** process-server and seigneurial notary, originally from Saint-Michel in the diocese of Saint-Brieuc (Brittany); b. *c.* 1651, son of Antoine Quiniard and Jeanne Branquais; buried 17 Sept. 1738 at Quebec.

It seems that Quiniard came to Canada only a short time before his marriage, which was celebrated 3 Feb. 1701 at Sainte-Famille on the Île d'Orléans. He was a settler at Argentenay, and married a widow from this fief, Marie-Louise Bolper, who was 53. He was 50. From 1701 on, Quiniard had occasionally received notarial acts, by virtue of special ordinances from the intendants; in 1705 he was also acting as a process-server, on what authority is not known. But his situation was soon to be regularized. On 15 Jan.

1707 JACQUES RAUDOT officially appointed him process-server for St Lawrence island and countship (Île d'Orléans); furthermore, on 3 July 1711 he made him a notary, thereby ratifying all the acts which he had previously drawn up and depositing them in his registry.

Quiniard was not exactly scrupulous. In 1714 the Conseil Supérieur threatened him with suspension and a fine of 20 *livres*; again, on 3 Aug. 1722, he was censured by Intendant Bégon* for a seizure made illegally; finally, 14 May 1727, Intendant CLAUDE-THOMAS DUPUY dismissed him for life from his offices as notary and process-server, and

likewise debarred him from any other post in the judiciary.

Becoming a widower in 1728, Quiniard went to live at the Hôpital Général in Quebec, where he finished his days. His registry is lost, but a fairly large number of copies of his acts are in the archives.

ANDRÉ VACHON

AJQ, Registres d'état civil de Sainte-Famille (I.O.), 3 févr. 1701. AQ, NF, Ord. des int., I, 84; V, 41. *Jug. et délib.* P.-G. Roy, *Inv. ord. int.*, I, 227; II, 8. "Les notaires au Canada," 37. Tanguay, *Dictionnaire*, VI, 485. J.-E. Roy, *Histoire du notariat*, I, 169.

R

RADISSON, ÉTIENNE VOLANT DE. *See* VOLANT

RADISSON, PIERRE-ESPRIT, explorer, coureur de bois, one of the originators of the Hudson's Bay Company; b. *c.* 1640, in Avignon (?), France; d. 1710 in England.

Little is known of the explorer's parents, birth, and early childhood. In an affidavit dated 1697 and a petition of 1698, Radisson himself states that he was then 61 and 62 years of age respectively, thereby indicating that he was born in 1636. A 1681 census of New France, however, lists him as 41 years of age. There is considerable evidence that the Radisson family came from the lower Rhone area, in or near Avignon. A Pierre-Esprit Radisson, presumably the explorer's father, was baptized 21 April 1590 (N.S.) in Carpentras, and in 1607 was living in Avignon; the senior Radisson married Madeleine Hénaut, widow of Sébastien Hayet.

Marguerite Hayet, a daughter of Madeleine Hénaut's first marriage, was to play quite an important part in the young Radisson's life. Presumably the boy came to New France with his half sister, or as a result of her being in that new country. It is known that Marguerite was in Quebec in 1646 for at that time she married Jean Véron de Grandmesnil. This was a time of difficulty, danger, and tension in New France; the fur trade was being constantly interrupted by Iroquois raiding parties, and life was hazardous even within the confines of the settlements. It was during one of the Indian raids that Marguerite's husband was killed; in August 1653 she married again, this time Médard Chouart* Des Groseilliers, the man who became Radisson's partner in the exploration of North America.

Nothing is known, however, of Radisson's

arrival in New France. The first mention we have of his presence there is his capture by Iroquois Indians, possibly in 1651. Like his half-sister he was at that time living in Trois-Rivières.

According to Radisson's account, he was taken by his captors to a Mohawk village near present-day Schenectady, N.Y. Presumably because of his youth, he was treated kindly and adopted by an Indian family of prominence. He learned the local language readily and went on expeditions with the natives, adapting himself with remarkable facility to his new environment. Eventually, however, in somewhat treacherous circumstances, he effected his escape and almost succeeded in getting back to Trois-Rivières. Recaptured and brutally tortured, he was saved from death through the intervention of his Iroquois "family," and given an Indian name, Oninga. The following spring he went on a hunting trip with his Indian friends and later described the adventure, which included an encounter with an alligator-like reptile: "there layd on one of the trees a snake wth foure feete, her head very bigg, like a Turtle, the nose very small att the end." A little later (1653) Radisson went on another trip with his Indian friends, this time to Fort Orange, the Dutch outpost on the site of present-day Albany, N.Y. The governor there offered to ransom Radisson, but the latter refused and returned to his Indian village. He then repented his decision, escaped, and reached Fort Orange safely. He was serving there as an interpreter for the Dutch when the Jesuit priest, Joseph-Antoine Poncet*, arrived. Radisson was shipped back to Europe, arriving in Amsterdam in the early weeks of 1654. Later the same year he returned to Trois-Rivières; his brother-in-law had probably already left on a two-year venture into the interior of the continent.

Radisson

Des Groseilliers' trip is recorded in the *Jesuit Relations*, which state that there were two men in the party. It was assumed for many years that Radisson was the other man; in his own reminiscences he claims to have been his brother-in-law's companion. However the discovery of a Quebec deed of sale dated 7 Nov. 1655, and bearing Radisson's signature, makes it obvious that he could not have taken part in this expedition.

During Radisson's absence, in 1654, peace had been made "betweene the french and ye Iroquoits." In 1657 he accompanied a Jesuit missionary party, which included Father Paul Ragueneau*, to Sainte-Marie-de-Gannentaa (Onondaga), established in 1656 by Joseph-Marie Chaumonot* and Claude Dablon*, in Iroquois country, not far from the site of Syracuse, N.Y. Radisson has left a colourful account of this episode, which tells of growing Indian disaffection with the venture. Finally the Iroquois determined to get rid of the unwelcome intruders. Learning of this plan, the Frenchmen made ready to depart as soon as possible in the spring of 1658 but they realized that great caution must be used to prevent the Iroquois from discovering their intentions. Radisson's familiarity with Indian psychology and Indian language proved adequate for the task. We have several contemporary accounts of the episode, suggesting the curious stratagems used by the French to deceive the natives. Marie de l'Incarnation [Guyart*] writes: "A young Frenchman, who had been adopted by a renowned Iroquois and who had learned their language, told his [Indian] father that he had had a dream that he must provide a feast, where everything must be eaten or he should die." Obedient to the dream-message, all the Indians came to the feast, and religiously consumed the vast quantities of possibly drugged food and drink. The din of music and merriment ensured that the drowsy Indians did not hear any noise as the French prepared to escape. Father Paul Ragueneau, then in charge of the mission, adds: "He who presided at the ceremony played his part with such skill and success that each one was bent on contributing to the public joy." Charlevoix*'s account mentions that it was a young man playing on a guitar who lulled the natives to sleep and thus allowed the French to escape unharmed. It is possible, even probable, that the young hero was Radisson.

Radisson's next adventure was a trip with Des Groseilliers to the far end of Lake Superior and the unexplored wilderness south and west of that great inland sea. They set out in August 1659 and returned to Montreal on 20 Aug. 1660. Of this journey Radisson has left us an account that is exact and convincing, with enthusiastic descriptions of the countryside and detailed reports of their strange, varied, and often harrowing experiences.

Governor Argenson [VOYER] insisted that one of his men accompany Des Groseilliers and Radisson, but the two explorers managed to slip away from Trois-Rivières unnoticed. They reached Lake Superior and from there they pressed inland and spent the winter with Huron and Ottawa refugees on a smaller lake, probably Lac Courte-Oreille or Ottawa Lake. Close at hand were Sioux, the resident Indians of the area with whom the two Frenchmen became acquainted, possibly the first white men to do so. It was a hard winter with heavy snowfalls; many Indians died of starvation. Radisson tells how the Indians, unable to see Des Groseilliers' emaciated face beneath his beard, concluded that he was being fed by some Manitou, but, "for me that had no beard, they said I loved them, because I lived as well as they."

Radisson's narrative contains a most valuable account of Indian customs—including a vivid description of the great Feast of the Dead, which took place in the winter of 1659–60, and to which "eighteen severall nations" came. It was at this time that the explorers probably gained much of their knowledge of the geography of the country between their camp and Hudson Bay and of the "great store of beaver" there and to the west, which some years later became the basis of their argument for convincing Englishmen to establish the Hudson's Bay Company. After the feasting ended the two men journeyed into Sioux country where they remained six weeks. Returning to Lake Superior in the spring, they crossed to its north shore, and there visited the Cree. At this point in Radisson's narrative comes another apocryphal journey, this time to Hudson Bay. Such a trip could not have been accomplished in the time at their disposal, but later when he was writing his account Radisson was anxious to appear as knowledgeable as possible about the fur trade and exploration of North America.

The following summer, 1660, the two Frenchmen and a great company of Indians left Lake Superior for Montreal. There Des Groseilliers made a business arrangement with Charles Le Moyne*, the contract for which is dated 22 Aug. 1660; the Jesuit record for that year states that the company of Indians, 300 in number, reached Trois-Rivières on 24 August. Marie de l'Incarnation also tells of the arrival of the flotilla of canoes with their "heavenly manna" of beaver skins and reflects that this would save the colony of New France from economic ruin.

Disappointment was in store for the triumphant explorers. Radisson tells of the hard usage he and his brother-in-law suffered when greedy officials

536

confiscated a large part of the furs, threw the older man into jail, and fined both men—presumably for having gone to the west without the governor's permission. Thereupon Des Groseilliers betook himself to France, hoping to get justice, but being disappointed returned to New France. Preparations were made for another wilderness expedition and in the spring of 1662 Radisson and Des Groseilliers embarked, so they announced, for Hudson Bay. Either by pre-arrangement or by force of circumstances, however, they abandoned the trip to the north and sailed instead to New England. There they were received more affably than they had been by their compatriots, and during the next two or three years they made at least two unsuccessful attempts to get to Hudson Bay by ship. In July 1664 the commissioners of the king of England arrived in Boston on empire business. Radisson and Des Groseilliers were interviewed and persuaded to go to London; they left New England on 1 Aug. 1665 (o.s.) in the *Charles* (Capt. Benjamin Gillam).

The war between England and the Dutch states for the supremacy of the sea was raging fiercely at this time. It has been suggested (Marie de l'Incarnation and Ragueneau) that the conquest of New Holland by the New Englanders was inspired by Des Groseilliers who relied no doubt on Radisson's knowledge of the Iroquois country and its fur-trading possibilities. In any case, on leaving New England, the two explorers were caught up in the Anglo-Dutch hostilities. The *Charles* was captured by a Dutch vessel and looted; her papers were thrown overboard and her passengers and crew landed in Spain. Radisson and Des Groseilliers quickly made their way to London, where they were well received—the cost of their maintenance being paid by the king. The two explorers soon found that life in Stuart England could be as hazardous, violent, and colourful as in the untamed Iroquois country—they were witness to the Great Plague and the devastating fire of London, the gay court functions in Charles II's Oxford.

Until this point in Radisson's life we have had to rely almost exclusively on his own account—a fascinating but often dubious source—but from this point on his version can be supplemented by official documents in the archives of the HBC, which take up the story of the search for the northwest passage via Hudson Bay and of attempts to gain control of the beaver country of northern North America.

In 1668 after various set-backs the men who were to found the HBC sent out two vessels, the *Eaglet* with Radisson aboard and the *Nonsuch* carrying Des Groseilliers. Radisson's vessel was damaged in a storm and had to limp back to

England, where the explorer spent the ensuing winter writing his *Voyages* at the king's express command. After completing his narrative Radisson fruitlessly attempted again to reach Hudson Bay. Meanwhile the New England captain of the *Nonsuch*, Zachariah Gillam* (brother of Capt. Gillam of the *Charles* and probably already experienced in arctic seamanship) had been successful in his search for a way into Hudson Bay. In early October 1669 Des Groseilliers returned from the bay with a fine cargo of beaver skins, and a fresh incentive was given to the scheme for establishing the HBC. Its charter passed the great seal on 2 May 1670, and almost immediately, 31 May 1670, the two Frenchmen started once more for Hudson Bay.

The vessel on which Radisson was travelling, the *Wivenhoe* (Capt. Robert Newland), made for the mouth of the Nelson River, where possession for England was formally taken by that enigmatic figure, Charles Bayly*. Des Groseilliers, aboard the *Prince Rupert* (Capt. Zachariah Gillam) with Thomas Gorst* as a passenger, returned to his post of the preceding year at the mouth of Rupert River. There Radisson joined him shortly after difficulties had arisen in the new western colony, including the death of Capt. Newland and damages to the ship. However, the abortive expedition was not without consequences for the future. Radisson's knowledge of the place, gained from this first visit, and his insight into the vital importance for the fur trade of a base at Port Nelson, were to prove useful in 1682, when Radisson attempted to found a French colony in that location. On the other hand, this brief sojourn at Port Nelson and the formal act of possession by Bayly were subsequently to constitute England's main claim to much of central North America.

Journeying back and forth between England and Hudson Bay and advising their employers about provisions and trading commodities kept Radisson and his brother-in-law occupied until 1675. During these years there was growing apprehension in New France about the activities of the two explorers and of the HBC; the intendant, Talon*, urged an expansionist policy to counterbalance English encroachments. He sent expeditions west under Cavelier* de La Salle and Daumont* de Saint-Lusson. A further party under PAUL DENYS de Saint-Simon and the Jesuit Father Albanel* penetrated into HBC territory. In 1675, however, Albanel, by that time a prisoner in England, persuaded Radisson and Des Groseilliers to return to French allegiance.

So the two explorers slipped quietly across the channel once more followed by a volley of disparaging representations to the French court from

Radisson

the English government. They had been promised favourable treatment by the Jesuits, but they did not receive it from the French court and were sent back to Canada by Colbert to consult with Frontenac [Buade*]. The governor was suspicious of them and their Jesuit promoters, however, fearing that any favours to them would react unfavourably for his own protégé, La Salle. It was immediately obvious that nothing was to be looked for in that quarter: Des Groseilliers returned to his Trois-Rivières home and Radisson sailed for France.

Radisson now found himself without occupation in France in a period of great unemployment. He sought assistance from a powerful figure in the shadows of the French court, Abbé Claude Bernou, La Salle's attorney. The result was a place as a midshipman in an expedition of Vice-Admiral d'Estrées to capture the Dutch colonies along the coast of Africa and in the Caribbean (1677–78). For this chapter in Radisson's career we have the only known letter of any length wholly written and signed by him. After initial success, the campaign ended disastrously on hidden reefs in the Caribbean. Most of the vessels were wrecked and Radisson barely escaped with his life, after losing all his possessions. Returning to France, he petitioned for relief and received a sum of money but not the position in the navy that he says he had been promised.

Colbert had previously intimated to Radisson that one reason for his having received so little help in France was the fact that he had not brought his wife with him from England. Sometime between 1665 and 1675—probably in 1672—he had married the daughter of Sir John Kirke of the HBC, who had inherited from his father, Gervase Kirke, claim to a considerable part of the north-eastern region of North America. We know little about this woman, not even her first name, but we do know that she was not the notorious courtesan of the day, Mary Kirke, with whom she has often been confused. Disgruntled after the Caribbean fiasco, Radisson returned to England on the pretext of attempting once more to bring his wife to France. But Kirke would not allow his daughter to leave the country. Radisson then put out feelers to learn what he could hope for should he return to the HBC's service, but the results were not encouraging.

In Paris, however, a new avenue was opening for him. In 1681 Radisson was approached by the Canadian merchant, CHARLES AUBERT de La Chesnaye, who, in the following year, was granted a fur-trading charter by Colbert (Compagnie du Nord). (The minister could not openly support the scheme because of the temporarily harmonious relationship between the English and French

crowns.) The unofficial nature of this transaction, however, increased the confusion when the expedition arrived in Canada—Frontenac refusing to grant permits to La Chesnaye and Radisson.

Eventually the expedition got under way, its ultimate object being the founding of a French colony at the mouth of the Nelson River. May we assume that Radisson had learned on his recent visits to London of the HBC's intention of again founding a colony on that disputed spot? The Port Nelson contest was not, however, to be a simple French/English struggle. Interlopers from New England led by Benjamin GILLAM (a nephew of the captain of the *Charles*) also turned up in the bay in the late summer of 1682. Claims and counter-claims were soon made that this party or that one had reached the mouth of the river first and taken possession. Radisson and Des Groseilliers (who had joined him) were able by subterfuge and force, as well as by better knowledge of the countryside and its wild inhabitants, to get possession of the area, capturing among others John Bridgar*, the governor of the new English colony, and acquiring many furs for France.

Flushed with success they returned to Quebec, where an attempt to avoid paying tax on their furs resulted in their being sent by Le Febvre* de La Barre to France for "adjudication of the case." There they expected great reward from Colbert. To their consternation they learned on landing that the minister was dead, and that heed was being paid in France to the complaints of the outraged HBC. Whatever their prestige in New France, Radisson and Des Groseilliers were only small pawns in the politico-religious intrigues of late seventeenth-century Europe. Des Groseilliers soon found himself back in Canada, and within a year (1684) Radisson was again in the employ of the HBC.

Radisson's return to England was brought about by a French Protestant, a former lawyer at the *parlement* of Paris, named Gédéon Godet, an employee of Lord Preston, the English envoy extraordinary at the court of Louis XIV. Godet, a colourful but suspect character, was anxious to get out of France, where he was being persecuted for his religion; he plotted to do so by means of Radisson's defection to the English, hoping at the same time to engineer his own advancement and his daughter's marriage. Both men escaped across the Channel. Radisson was greeted rather warily by the company, which sent him immediately back to Hudson Bay, "where he hath undertaken without hostility to reduce the French . . . and to render us the quiet possessions of y^t place. . . ." There, with remarkable aplomb, he prevailed upon his nephew, Jean-Baptiste Des Groseilliers, in charge of the post at the mouth of the Nelson—which Radisson had helped to secure for the French—to go over to the English side, with all his men and a great cargo of furs. As they slipped out of the bay on their way back to England, Radisson's party only just escaped detection by French ships coming to relieve young Des Groseilliers.

The two Frenchmen went to London to a cold winter and the coronation of James II, erstwhile governor of the HBC. Subsequently Des Groseilliers' son tried several times to escape back to the French side, but his attempts were thwarted. In 1685, Denonville [BRISAY] offered a reward of 50 *pistoles* to anyone bringing Radisson to Quebec; and in 1687 Seignelay wrote urging Denonville and BOCHART de Champigny to ensure Radisson's return to the French cause—either by persuasion or by force. But the versatile explorer was destined to spend the rest of his working years in the service of the HBC.

From 1685 to 1687 Radisson was resident in Hudson Bay—his last trip to Canada. During this period he was given considerable authority in all trading matters by the company, yet before his return in 1687 many disputes had arisen between him and the other officials of the HBC.

On 3 March 1685 Radisson had married Margaret Charlotte Godet, daughter of Gédéon, in the church of St Martin's in the Fields, London. Presumably his first wife, the mother of one child, had died. Now, in 1687, Radisson returned to England to live the rest of his life as a family man in the quiet of London suburbs.

On his return to the company in 1684, he had been granted company stock, and later an annuity of £100 sterling a year. Some of this promised financial support having been withdrawn in the early 1690s, he went to court against the company and won his suit in chancery in 1697 after years of litigation, thus demonstrating once more his tenacity, audacity, and astuteness. Thereafter the company was faithful in its payments to him. In 1687 Radisson and his nephew were naturalized at the company's expense.

His life between 1700 and his death in the early summer of 1710 is a relative blank. The company's only references to him relate to the payment of his annuity and the dividends on his stocks. Some time between 1692 and 1710—probably at the delivery of a fifth child—Margaret Radisson died, and Pierre married for the third time. This wife's name was Elizabeth and she bore him three daughters, who are described in his will as "small." She survived him for many years, died in extreme poverty, and was buried, it would appear from extant records of interment, in London on 2 Jan. 1732.

On 17 June 1710 Radisson made his will, which is preserved in Somerset House, London. In it he tells not a little of his life. His wife Elizabeth is mentioned and also his "former Wifes Children," who were "by me according to my ability advanced and preferred to severall Trades." Sometime between 17 June and 2 July 1710 the old explorer died and his will was probated. The company paid his widow six pounds, presumably for funeral expenses. The exact date of his death and the place of interment are not known.

Radisson seems to have been one of those fortunate people endowed with an unquenchable zest for life and a capacity for adaptation not too greatly hampered by religious, moral, or patriotic scruples. He stands for all that is rich and colourful in an age of adventure and intrigue, brutality and imagination. As an explorer he had not only the ability to endure the mental and physical hardships of life in the wilderness, but also an instinctive insight into the potentialities of certain trading areas and routes. His uncanny appreciation of Indian psychology and his spontaneous enthusiasm for natural beauty enabled him to describe the lands he discovered, and to chronicle the life of the inhabitants. A simple coureur de bois, who had lived, hunted, and killed with the Indians, he was involved in matters of international importance, moved in court circles, and conversed with kings. Sometime French and Catholic, sometime English and (probably) Protestant, he witnessed the plague and the fire of London, the coronation of James II, the founding of the HBC. He wintered in the frozen north and went campaigning in the Caribbean. Though Radisson was an opportunist and a disturbing and unreliable character, we cannot but admire his versatility and his exuberance.

GRACE LEE NUTE

The original French manuscript of the account of his travels which Radisson wrote in the winter of 1668–69 has been lost. However an English translation must already have been completed in 1669, for in June of that year the unknown translator—possibly Nicholas Hayward, later the HBC's French translator—was paid £5 for his work. This translation has been preserved in the papers of Samuel Pepys in the Bodleian Library at Oxford, England. When Radisson wrote these reminiscences he was anxious to bolster the confidence of the men who were to found the HBC, and so he edited his account rather shamelessly, inserting the fictitious journey to Hudson Bay in 1659–60 and implying that he had been Des Groseilliers' companion in 1655. Radisson's writing is remarkably vivid and precise, except in the "edited" sections, where his vague, ambiguous style betrays him immediately. A transcription of the *Voyages* and of other of Radisson's writings appeared in 1885: [Pierre-Esprit Radisson], *Voyages of Peter Esprit*

Raffeix

Radisson, being an account of his travels and experiences among the North American Indians, from 1652 to 1684, transcribed from original manuscripts in the Bodleian Library and the British Museum, ed. G. D. Skull (Prince Soc., XVI, Boston, 1885; New York, 1943). For details of the many other manuscript sources used, from collections in France, England, Canada and the U.S.A., see Nute, Caesars of the wilderness, 359–63. [G.L.N.]

Charlevoix, Histoire. Marie Guyart de l'Incarnation, Lettres (Richaudeau). HBRS, V, VIII, IX (Rich); XI, XX (Rich and Johnson); XXI, XXII (Rich). JR (Thwaites). See also Phil Day, "The Nonsuch ketch," Beaver (Winnipeg), outfit 299 (Winter 1968), 4–17.

RAFFEIX, PIERRE, priest, Jesuit, missionary, founder of Laprairie; b. 15 Jan. 1635 at Clermont-Ferrand; d. 29 Aug. 1724 at Quebec.

Pierre Raffeix entered the noviciate of Toulouse on 23 March 1653, and taught at Aubenas (1655–56), Rodez (1657–59), Aurillac (1659–60), and Albi (1660–61). After studying theology at Toulouse, he arrived at Quebec on 22 Sept. 1663. He first lived at Sillery, where he learned the Algonkian and Montagnais languages, and in 1666 he was appointed as assistant to Father Chaumonot* at the Huron mission at Quebec. At the beginning of that same year he had accompanied Governor Rémy* de Courcelle's expedition against the Iroquois, and in September he also went with that led by the Marquis de Tracy [Prouville*]. The following year we find him teaching rhetoric and classics at the Jesuit college in Quebec. His teaching was interrupted at the end of 1667, since he went to spend the winter at the Îles Percées, or more exactly on Pierre Boucher's new farm, in anticipation of the creation of the fief of La Prairie de la Magdeleine. In 1668 he distributed the first land grants to the French, and he received the 10 or 12 future founders of the Iroquois village that it was desired to set up there. He took them to Quebec to be instructed in the faith, and in 1669 the first Indian lodges began to go up close to the fields marked out by the missionary. In 1671 he handed over this work to Father Frémin*, and went with Father Julien Garnier to start teaching the gospel to the Senecas. Despite the dangers and difficulties, he remained among them until 1679, when he was called to Quebec as procurator—sometimes of the college, sometimes of the missions, sometimes of both. He held this office first for 18 years, until 1697, then for 15, from 1700 to 1715. Between these two periods he was minister for a year, 1697–98, and assistant to the parish priest of Lorette in 1698–99. He was sent as a missionary, probably in 1699, to the colony of Mont-Louis, in the Bay of Gaspé. The failure of this undertaking in the following year caused him to return to Quebec.

In his capacity as procurator, Father Raffeix had to represent the Jesuits in numerous affairs of which the repercussions extended to the courts of law. The most important action was the one that Ignace Juchereau Duchesnay brought in 1704 over the common boundary between the seigneuries of Beauport and Notre-Dame-des-Anges. Juchereau wanted to have a change made in the bearing of the boundary, which had been set in the time of Huault* de Montmagny. This dispute between the two domains was to last a long time.

Raffeix, old and ill, spent his last years at Quebec hearing confessions in the church of the college, where he died on 29 Aug. 1724.

Lucien Campeau

ASJCF. Jug. et délib., IV, 481–84, 928, 941, 993, 1049, 1091. Campbell, Pioneer priests, 276–84. Rochemonteix, Les Jésuites et la N.-F. au XVIIᵉ siècle, II, 412; III, 284.

RAGEOT DE SAINT-LUC, CHARLES, clerk of the provost court of Quebec and royal notary; baptized 12 Aug. 1674 at Quebec, eldest son of Gilles Rageot*, royal notary and clerk of court, and of Marie-Madeleine Morin; d. and buried 18 Dec. 1702 at Quebec.

Even before the end of his studies, probably at the Jesuit college, Charles Rageot began to help his father in the registry of the provost court. Gilles Rageot, although still young, suffered a great deal from gout. When he died it was, therefore, natural to think of his son as his successor. On the recommendation of Frontenac [Buade*] and Champigny [Bochart], the king granted Charles a commission as clerk of court, dated 1 March 1693. After the customary investigation as to "character" he was admitted to office by the Conseil Souverain on 7 December following. As he was not yet 25—the age at which one attained one's majority—he had to get his mother to stand surety for him before he could practise his profession.

In 1695 Charles Rageot obtained a commission as royal notary, which has not been found. As clerk of court and royal notary, on occasion appearing for a litigant before the council, Charles was treading blithely in his father's footsteps. With his future assured, he married Marie-Geneviève Gauvreau, aged 17, on 23 May 1696. She bore him four children, two of whom, both boys, died shortly after birth. In the autumn of 1702 Rageot, like all his fellow-citizens, was getting ready for a peaceful winter; for example, on 28 October he signed a contract with a settler of Lauson for the purchase of 12 cords of wood at 50 sols a cord. But an epidemic of smallpox broke out suddenly, spreading consternation and mourning throughout the colony. The strongest and the most active were not spared: Charles Rageot succumbed 18 December and his wife on the 26th; on 5 January their younger daughter also died. The only survivor was Marie-Madeleine-Geneviève, born in 1697, who later became an Hospitaller.

This short existence had certainly not allowed Charles to amass a fortune. True, he had invested 300 *livres* in the Compagnie de la Colonie; but in 1708 JACQUES RAUDOT stated that he had "left no assets."

His brother, NICOLAS RAGEOT de Saint-Luc, succeeded him as royal notary and clerk of court.

ANDRÉ VACHON

AJQ, Greffe de Louis Chambalon, 28 oct. 1702; Greffe de Charles Rageot, 1695–1702; Greffe de Charles Royer, 3 mai 1696. AQ, NF, Ins. Cons. sup., II, 110v *et seq.*; NF, Ins. de la Prév. de Québec, I, 712. "Correspondance de Frontenac (1689–99)," APQ *Rapport, 1927–28*, 147. *Jug. et délib.*, III, IV, V. "Liste générale des intéressés en la compagnie de la colonie du Canada, et des actions qu'ils y ont prises," *BRH*, XL (1934), 506. Tanguay, *Dictionnaire*, I, 507. J.-E. Roy, *Histoire du notariat*, I, 106, 108, 132, 313. P.-G. Roy, *Fils de Québec*, I, 96f.

RAGEOT DE SAINT-LUC, NICOLAS, clerk of the provost court of Quebec and royal notary; baptized 20 Aug. 1676 at Quebec, son of Gilles Rageot*, royal notary and clerk of court, and of Marie-Madeleine Morin; buried 31 March 1703 at Quebec.

Nicolas Rageot was probably born in Lower Town, Quebec, on Rue Saint-Pierre, where his father owned a house that was destroyed in the terrible fire of 4 Aug. 1682. It is also fairly certain that he attended with his brothers the Jesuit college in Quebec, where he received a classical education before entering government service as they had done. In the autumn of 1695 he was one of the guardians in the office responsible for the "safe-guarding of the king's dues" in Canada. He had the task of supervising the loading and unloading of merchandise at the port, and of making certain that the levies due to the crown were paid before the ships set sail.

In 1693 his elder brother CHARLES had replaced his father as clerk of court, and in 1695 as notary, but he fell a victim to the smallpox epidemic which scourged the colony in 1702–3, and died 18 Dec. 1702. Nicolas Rageot was called upon to succeed him and to carry on a family tradition which went back to 1666. On 15 March 1703 he was appointed royal notary and clerk of the provost court of Quebec at the king's discretion, and was admitted to his office two days later. But, stricken almost immediately by the same illness, he died a bachelor on 31 March 1703, apparently without having had time to draw up a single notarial act.

Bishop LAVAL strongly recommended that François*, another son of Gilles Rageot, should succeed Nicolas, to which the king gave his consent the following year.

ANDRÉ VACHON

AQ, NF, Registres de la Prévôté de Québec, 17 mars 1703. *Jug. et délib.*, III, 1073. "Correspondance de Vaudreuil," APQ *Rapport, 1938–39*, 22. Gareau, "La prévôté de Québec," 113. "Les notaires au Canada," 32. Tanguay, *Dictionnaire*, I, 507. J.-E. Roy, *Histoire du notariat*, I, 106, 108, 133. P.-G. Roy, *Fils de Québec*, I, 99f.

RAIMBAULT, PIERRE, cabinet-maker, clerk of court, notary, surveyor, king's counsellor, king's attorney, acting lieutenant of police, sub-delegate of the intendant, judge in the court of Montreal; b. 11 Oct. 1671 at Montreal, son of Claude Raimbault, master-carpenter, and Marie-Thérèse Sallé; d. there 17 Oct. 1740.

Raimbault was in France 1681–96, and returned to Montreal with Jeanne-Françoise Simblin, whom he had married 8 July 1691 in Paris; he was at that time a cabinet-maker with his own business. On 17 Nov. 1697 he began his career as a notary, and pursued it until 24 Jan. 1727, leaving a registry of 3,520 acts. He was made royal notary in 1699, and the following year was appointed king's attorney on an interim basis; it was not until 1706 that he received his commission for this office, which he occupied until 1727. He was a subdelegate of the intendant from 1716 to 1730, and also the Sulpicians' business agent. Finally, having been acting lieutenant of police since 1720, he was appointed on 27 April 1727 lieutenant-general at the court of Montreal for civil and criminal affairs, for police, trade, and navigation, a post which he occupied until his death, but from which he was forced to absent himself during the last two years of his life because of his infirmities.

With this impressive legal career he combined that of an astute business man, carrying through during his lifetime no fewer than about 30 real estate transactions. According to Hocquart* he was "well versed in business matters"; further-more, wrote Intendant Bégon*, he "discharged his functions well and capably." On his death he left two properties at Montreal and a fief on Lake Champlain called La Moinaudière.

Raimbault was a man of some culture. The inventory of his possessions drawn up in 1706, at the time of his first wife's death, reveals the largest collection of books known to belong to any one individual at the beginning of the 18th century; it

541

Raimbault de Piedmont

comprised 35 works: 7 law books, 12 Greek and Latin classics, 15 books on religion, and 1 on horticulture.

On the other hand, his way of life often gave rise to criticism, especially from the numerous enemies he inevitably made for himself in discharging his duties. He was accused of not taking the sacrament at Easter and of having scandalous relations with the widow of an officer. But Hocquart points out that "the Sieur Raimbault's age, together with his infirmities and the ugliness of the widow in question, do not authorize such a presumption." And when in 1731 he had two Recollets put in prison, Bishop Dosquet* wrote that "he seized the opportunity to take vengeance on church people."

By his first marriage he had six children, of whom the eldest, JOSEPH-CHARLES, was royal notary and clerk of the court of Montreal, and the second, Paul-François, was ennobled under the name of Raimbault de Saint-Blin (or Simblin), which his descendants bore. By his second marriage, to Louise Nafrechoux in 1707, he had ten children, of whom the third, Marguerite, married Pierre Boucher* de Boucherville, the third seigneur of that name.

ROBERT LAHAISE

AJM, Greffe d'Antoine Adhémar, 20 déc. 1706; Greffe de Pierre Raimbault, 1692–1727. *Documents relating to Canadian currency during the French period* (Shortt), I, 548. *Jug. et délib.*, IV, V, VI. É.-Z. Massicotte, "Une lettre du juge Raimbault en 1731," *BRH*, XXII (1916), 242f. A. Roy, *Inv. greffes not.*, XII, XV, XVI. P.-G. Roy, *Inv. concessions*; *Inv. coll. pièces jud. et not.*, I, 37, 184; *Inv. ins. Cons. souv.*, I, 111, 182f., 227–29, 234; *Inv. ord. int.*, I, 89; II, 20–22. "Liste des officiers de justice employez dans les différents tribunaux de la Nouvelle-France (1722)," *BRH*, XXXV (1929), 111. "Liste des officiers de justice de la Nouvelle-France (1722)," *BRH*, XXXVI (1930), 155–56. É.-Z. Massicotte, "Les juges de Montréal sous le régime français," *Cahiers des Dix*, VIII (1943), 255–59. "Les notaires au Canada," 31. Tanguay, *Dictionnaire*, VI, 500.

J.-E. Roy, *Histoire du notariat*, I, 151. Montarville Boucher de La Bruère, "Les Boucherville à l'étranger," *Cahiers des Dix*, I (1936), 232. L.-P. Desrosiers, "Correspondance de M. Magnien," *Cahiers des Dix*, IX (1944), 223. Albertine Ferland-Angers, "La Citadelle de Montréal," *RHAF*, III (1949–50), 501. Auguste Gosselin, "Le clergé canadien et la déclaration de 1732," *RSCT*, 2d ser., VI (1900), sect.I, 23–52. É.-Z. Massicotte, "Le juge Pierre Raimbault et sa famille," *BRH*, XXI (1915), 78–81.

RAIMBAULT DE PIEDMONT, JOSEPH-CHARLES (he often signed **Raimbault** junior or sometimes **Piedmont**), royal notary, clerk of the court of Montreal, and on several occasions acting lieutenant-general, son of the judge PIERRE RAIMBAULT and Jeanne-Françoise Simblin; b. 1693 in France, and came to Canada with his parents not later than 1696; d. 17 Dec. 1737 at Montreal.

In January 1727 he received his commission as notary and clerk of the court; his registry contains 1,498 acts, covering the period 30 Jan. 1727 to 10 Dec. 1737. In 1727 Raimbault was also appointed king's attorney, succeeding his father who became a judge. Although according to Hocquart* he was "an unimpressive fellow," he "did his job tolerably well."

In 1732 he was condemned, under pain of a charge of extortion, to reduce his legal fees and to make restitution for any excess payments he had received. Although he resigned his post as chief clerk of court, he was nevertheless appointed acting lieutenant-general in 1733, for the third time.

His estate included, among other things, "ten books containing the corpus of law and jurisprudence," possessions valued at 566 *livres* 12 *sols*, plus "seven old mended sheets."

On 30 Nov. 1724 he had married Charlotte Damours. They had no children. Charlotte married again five months after her husband's death.

ROBERT LAHAISE

AJM, Greffe de C.-J. Porlier, 17 déc. 1737, 16 avril 1738; Greffe de J.-C. Raimbault, 1727–37. "Liste des officiers de justice employez dans les différents tribunaux de la Nouvelle-France (1722)," *BRH*, XXXV (1929), 111. A. Roy, *Inv. greffes not.*, 8. P.-G. Roy, *Inv. ord. int.*, I, 219; II, 123, 132. É.-Z. Massicotte, "Les greffiers de Montréal sous le régime français, 1648–1760," *BRH*, XXXI (1925), 118; "Les tribunaux et les officiers de justice," *RSTC*, 3d ser., X (1916), sect.I, 285, 287, 288. Tanguay, *Dictionnaire*, VI, 500. Vachon, "Inv. critique des notaires royaux," *RHAF*, XI (1957–58), 95.

RALE (Râle, Rasle, Rasles), SÉBASTIEN, priest, Jesuit, missionary to the Abenakis; b. 4 Jan. 1657 at Pontarlier, diocese of Besançon (France); killed 23 Aug. 1724 (N.S.) at Norridgewock (Narantsouak, today Old Point, South Madison, Me.).

Rale had joined the Society of Jesus at Dole (France) on 24 Sept. 1675. He arrived at Quebec 13 Oct. 1689, at the same time as Buade* de Frontenac. He was first sent to the mission at the falls of the Chaudière River which was directed by Father JACQUES BIGOT. There he learned the Abenaki language and began his Abenaki-French dictionary, as is indicated on the first page of his manuscript, which is preserved at Harvard

University. In 1691 he went to assist his *confrère* Father Jacques GRAVIER at the mission to the Illinois at Kaskaskia.

At the end of two years he was recalled and sent to Acadia, where in 1694 he founded the mission to the Abenakis at Norridgewock on the Kennebec River, almost opposite its junction with the Sandy River. The Abenakis traded with the English, who were situated closer to them than were the French, but they remained attached to the French through the bonds of the Roman Catholic religion. When the War of the Spanish Succession broke out in Europe and spread to the colonies in America, Governor Dudley of Boston called the Abenakis together at Casco Bay in 1703 and proposed to them that they remain neutral in this conflict. Moxus and ATECOUANDO were the chief spokesmen for the Indians. Rale said that he was present at this meeting and promised to encourage the Indians to maintain the peace: "My religion and my office of priest were a security that I would give them only exhortations to peace." Dudley, on the other hand, said that "their [the Indians'] Friars" did not dare to be seen on this occasion.

The Abenakis did not, however, remain neutral. In August, a party of these Indians were joined to a larger French and Indian force under ALEXANDRE LENEUF de Beaubassin and took part in a raid on the village of Wells. RIGAUD de Vaudreuil said later that the Abenakis were added to the expedition after Father Rale had assured him that his Indians would be "ready to take up the hatchet against the English whenever he [Vaudreuil] gave them the order."

There were reprisals by the English. During the winter of 1705, 275 soldiers under the command of Colonel HILTON were sent to Norridgewock to seize Father Rale and sack the village. Father Rale escaped them, but they burned his church. He later returned to Canada to found at Bécancour a mission for the Abenakis from Amassokanty (Amesoquanty; near Norridgewock, today Farmington Falls, Me.). Under the threat of famine these Indians had accepted Vaudreuil's invitation to come to settle on the shores of the St Lawrence. The minister, Pontchartrain, had moreover written on the king's behalf to the Jesuit superior Pierre de La Chasse* to have Father Rale recalled, as he was suspected of being lukewarm about the war. Rale was back at his mission at Norridgewock in 1710.

By the treaty of Utrecht (1713), which ended the War of the Spanish Succession, France gave up Acadia according to its "antient boundaries." The exact extent of these boundaries was not spelled out in the treaty, and they gave rise subsequently to continued disputes between France and England. For the English, they extended to the St George River and took in the Abenakis' territory. The Abenakis refused to accept English rule [*see* MOG], and the French encouraged them in this refusal.

The English offered to rebuild the church at Norridgewock if the Abenakis consented to receive a Protestant minister and send Father Rale back to Quebec. The church was rebuilt in time by the English, but the men who were hired to do it seem to have done a poor job. By 1720 Father Rale had finished the work with the financial assistance of the French king. Reverend Joseph Baxter was sent as a missionary to Arrowsic Island on the Kennebec, and soon entered into a heated correspondence with Rale over their respective missions. It is not known how long Baxter worked on the Kennebec, but he does not seem to have had great success with the Abenakis. Through trade, however, the English succeeded in infiltrating the Abenakis' territory. First they obtained permission to have stores, where they sold merchandise cheaply. Then they brought in hundreds of families and built forts to protect them. Rale feared for the faith of the Indians, for once the English controlled their territory, they would no longer allow any Catholic missionary to remain there.

The expansion of the English into the Kennebec area led to a conference in August 1717 at Arrowsic Island, between Governor Shute of Massachusetts and the leaders of the eastern tribes. There seem to have been both pro-English and pro-French factions in the Indian delegation, the spokesman for the latter being WOWURNA. Although the pro-English faction finally prevailed at this conference, and the Indians accepted the English presence on their lands, Father Rale encouraged the anti-English elements to continue to resist. In October 1719, he sent the chiefs of Norridgewock to Vaudreuil at Quebec to assure him that the Abenakis were opposing English encroachment on their land. In 1720, Vaudreuil and Bégon*, the intendant, reported to the minister of the Marine that "Father Râlle continues to incite the Indians of the mission at Naransouak not to allow the English to spread over their lands." In July, the Massachusetts council offered a reward of £100 for the arrest of Rale.

According to a letter of Vaudreuil and Bégon, dated 8 Oct. 1721, Rale had feared the previous spring that more and more Indians would come under the influence of the English, and wanted to ensure that "the well-disposed party among the Indians was more numerous" at a meeting which the English were intending to hold soon with the Abenakis. To this end he sent to Quebec

Rale

six Indians who were to invite the Canadian Abenakis and the Hurons of Lorette to come to the meeting. They succeeded in recruiting several canoes of Indians from the missions at Saint-François, Bécancour, and Jeune-Lorette (Loretteville). Father La Chasse was sent with them to Norridgewock and recruited more than 100 Indians from other Acadian missions. On 28 July 1721 (17 July, o.s.), more than 250 Indians, with Fathers La Chasse and Rale supporting them, appeared for the meeting with the English at Georgetown on Arrowsic Island. They presented a letter, addressed to Shute, which demanded that the English withdraw from their lands. The letter was sent on to the governor.

The English wanted to get rid of Rale and Shute urged Vaudreuil, in vain, to recall him, on the pretext that an act of the Parliament of Great Britain and the laws of the province forbade any Jesuit or Roman Catholic priest to preach or even to live in any part of the kingdom. Towards the end of January 1722, while the Abenakis were away hunting, 100 men led by Colonel Westbrook surrounded the village of Norridgewock. Warned in time by two young Indian hunters, Rale fled into the forest, where he narrowly escaped his pursuers. The soldiers pillaged his church and his house and carried off his dictionary of the Abenaki language and his papers. They found a letter affixed to the church door at Norridgewock, reputedly written by Rale, which threatened reprisals against the English settlements in the area should the church be destroyed. According to La Chasse, the Abenakis begged their priest to retire to Quebec for a while. But he refused, saying: "Alas! what would become of your faith if I should abandon you? Your salvation is dearer to me than my life."

In July of the same year, a party of Abenakis attacked the English settlements around Merrymeeting Bay, near the mouth of the Kennebec, in revenge for the English attack on Norridgewock. This act led Governor Shute to declare war on 25 July, marking the beginning of what was known, variously, as Dummer's, Lovewell's, Father Rale's, or the Three Years' War. On two occasions in March 1723 Westbrook's force again tried to seize Father Rale, without any more success.

In August of the following year, however, another attack was launched against Norridgewock which ended with Father Rale's death. The New England force, under Johnson Harmon and Jeremiah Moulton, set out from Fort Richmond (Richmond, Me.) on the lower Kennebec on 19 August (8 August, o.s.) and reached Norridgewock on the 23d. Father Rale was killed during the attack which ensued, and his scalp was taken to Boston to be redeemed. The French and English accounts of the raid disagree sharply on some points, however. The principal French account is contained in a letter of Father La Chasse of 29 Oct. 1724 (the basis of Charlevoix*'s account), and originated no doubt with Indians who witnessed the event and escaped to Quebec; that compiled by the New England historian Thomas Hutchinson is based on the testimony, taken many years later, of New Englanders who took part in the raid. According to La Chasse, the New England forces numbered about 1,100 men; the New England account states that there were only slightly more than 200, 40 of whom were left downstream to guard boats. The French contended that Rale went out into the middle of the village alone to meet the attacking English, in the hope that he might draw their attention to himself and save the Indians, and that he was shot down in the open. According to the English, however, Rale was killed in a cabin while defending himself against the attackers, and this against the orders of Moulton, who had wanted the priest to be taken alive.

In 1833 Bishop Fenwick of Boston had a monument to the memory of Father Rale erected on the spot where he is supposed to have died.

Sébastien Rale evoked strong and contrasting feelings in most of his contemporaries: for some, he was "a martyr . . . sacrificed through hatred to his ministry . . ." (La Chasse); for others, he was "a bloody incendiary" (Penhallow). The French considered him a valuable ally, the English a dangerous enemy. Many later writers have shared one or the other of these views. The deep political and religious allegiances felt by the English and French at this period undoubtedly influenced most contemporary writings, making it impossible now to construct a completely objective picture of Rale and his work.

For a period of about ten years after the treaty of Utrecht, Rale's mission at Norridgewock was at the centre of an area where the political and military interests of New France and New England met and clashed. His influence among the Norridgewock Abenakis could not be limited to his missionary work. The increasing English settlement in the Kennebec area was a threat to the Abenakis, and Father Rale consistently supported those elements in the tribe which maintained an active resistance to the English. The French, for their part, needed the Abenakis as allies who could provide protection for the eastern boundaries of New France. They could not, however, openly support the Abenakis at this time because they were officially at peace with the English. Instead they had to rely to a great extent on the influence of French missionaries. Rale shared the fate of many other missionaries of this era who, willingly or not, found themselves and their work caught up in the larger colonial struggles of France and England in the New World.

THOMAS CHARLAND, O.P.

The manuscript of Rale's dictionary, preserved at Harvard University, has no title page. The first entry reads as follows: "1691. It is now a year that I have been among the savages, I begin to set in order in dictionary form the words which I learn." (*See* Maine Hist. Soc. *Coll.*, 2d ser., VI (1895), 144ff.) The dictionary was edited in 1833 by John Pickering in the *Memoirs of the American Academy of Arts and Sciences* (I, 375–574) under the title, "A dictionary of the Abnaki language in North America by Father Sebastian Rasles."
AN, Col., B, 23, f.261; 48, f.853. Charlevoix, *History* (Shea), I, 88–89; V, 133, 167, 266–81. *Coll. de manuscrits relatifs à la N.-F.*, III, *passim*. "Correspondance de Vaudreuil," APQ *Rapport, 1938–39*, 16. *Documentary hist. of Maine*, IX; XXIII, 51–57, 89–93. *JR* (Thwaites), LXVII. [Pierre-Joseph de La Chasse], "Une relation inédite de la mort du P. Sébastien Racle, 1724," in *NF*, IV (1929), 342–50. *Lettres édifiantes et curieuses escrites des missions étrangères par quelques missionaires de la Compagnie de Jésus* (30v., Paris, 1707–73; nouv. éd., Paris, 1781), VI. Mass. Hist. Soc. *Coll.*, 2d ser., VIII (1826); 5th ser., III (1877), 245. *NYCD* (O'Callaghan and Fernow), IX, 936–39. Penhallow, *Hist. of wars with Eastern Indians* (1824). PRO, *CSP, Col., 1720–21, 1722–23, 1724–25*.
J. P. Baxter, *The pioneers of New France in New England, with contemporary letters and documents* (Albany, 1894). Campbell, *Pioneer priests*. Coleman, *New England captives*. F. Convers, "Life of Rev. Sebastian Rale," in *The library of American biography*, ed. J. Spark (25v., Boston, 1834–48), 2d ser., VII. N.-E. Dionne, "Le père Sébastien Rasles, jésuite, missionnaire chez les Abénaquis, 1657–1724," *RSCT*, 2d ser., IX (1903), 117–34. M. C. Leger, *The Catholic Indian missions in Maine, 1611–1820* (Catholic Univ. of America studies in American church history, VII, Washington, 1929). Parkman, *A half-century of conflict*, (1893), I. Rochemonteix, *Les Jésuites et la N.-F. au XVIIe siècle*, III, 434–36, 439–75, 530, 537. J. F. Sprague, *Sebastian Ralé, a Maine tragedy of the 18th century* (Boston, 1906).

RAMEZAY, CLAUDE DE, esquire, lieutenant and captain in the colonial regular troops, commander of the troops, seigneur, knight of the order of Saint-Louis, governor of Trois-Rivières and governor of Montreal, acting governor of New France from 1714 to 1716, builder of the Château de Ramezay, famous Montreal landmark; b. at La Gesse, in the province of Burgundy, 15 June 1659; d. in Quebec, 31 July 1724.
Ramezay appears to be derived from the Scottish name Ramsay. The family probably emigrated from Scotland to France in the late 15th or early 16th century and settled in Burgundy. There they acquired the fiefs of La Gesse, Montigny, and Boisfleurant and entered the nobility.
Claude de Ramezay was a son of Timothé de Ramezay and Catherine Tribouillard, daughter of Hilaire Tribouillard, intendant in charge of the extensive stables of the Prince de Condé. He came to Canada in 1685 as a lieutenant in the colonial regular troops and was promoted to the rank of captain two years later. On 8 Nov. 1690, in Quebec, he married Marie-Charlotte Denys, a daughter of PIERRE DENYS de La Ronde and Catherine Leneuf and thus became linked to one of New France's leading families. A few months earlier he had obtained the post of governor of Trois-Rivières by paying a sum of 3,000 *livres* to the destitute widow of the late incumbent, René Gaultier* de Varennes. Only five years after his arrival in the colony, Ramezay had become a member of its social and political elite.
With a population of only 358 in 1698, Trois-Rivières was nothing more than a large village; but being located halfway between Montreal and Quebec it was a convenient resting place for persons travelling between the two towns. This placed a heavy burden on the finances of the local governor, who was expected to entertain the notables passing through his district. Ramezay, however, was somewhat vain and like most members of his class regarded money chiefly as a means of achieving social status. Hosting the colony's dignitaries and being referred to as a "real gentleman" by Governor Frontenac [Buade*] himself must have greatly flattered his ego. Indeed, it may have been to impress his many guests that he embarked upon an ambitious building programme. He built a large two-storey house and a number of outbuildings on land he had purchased on the seigneury of Platon Sainte-Croix and another still larger house on the other side of town. In 1699, Bishop Saint-Vallier [LA CROIX] purchased these properties for 21,000 *livres* and transferred them to the Ursuline nuns.
Ramezay did some useful work in his official capacity. Soon after taking office he ordered the town to be fortified and this was promptly done under the supervision of the engineer, Boisberthelot* de Beaucours. The new governor, however, does not appear to have been popular with the townspeople. He was brusque and ill-tempered. Moreover, since neither his salary nor a series of gratuities ranging in amount from 300 to 2,000 *livres* sufficed to maintain his station in Canadian society and to support his large family, he turned

to the fur trade. According to LE ROY de La Potherie, the governor angered the local merchants by depriving them of high quality pelts and annoyed the Indians by interfering with their freedom of trade. La Potherie reports that there was rejoicing in Trois-Rivières in 1699 when Ramezay left to become commander of the Canadian troops.

Ramezay held this new position for five years and served satisfactorily. He returned from a voyage to France with 300 recruits in 1702 and received the cross of Saint-Louis the following year. In 1704 he succeeded Philippe de RIGAUD de Vaudreuil as governor of Montreal. His reputation as a builder had preceded him to that city, and predictably enough one of his first concerns was to provide himself with a residence worthy of his new position. He purchased a lot on Rue Notre Dame from his relative, NICOLAS D'AILLEBOUST de Manthet, and in April 1705 retained the services of the master mason and architect, Pierre COUTURIER. The latter undertook to build a house 66 feet long, three storeys high (including the attic), and with four chimney-stacks. The walls were to be three and one half feet thick below ground level and two and one half feet thick above. The building was completed the following year and the proud owner described it as "unquestionably the most beautiful in Canada."

Ramezay's extravagance coupled with the losses he suffered in 1704 when the flute *Seine* was captured by the English soon landed him in severe financial difficulties. To make ends meet he harassed the minister with requests for gratuities, tried without success to sell his house to the crown for 18,000 *livres*, borrowed large sums of money from a number of persons, including 3,000 *livres* from Samuel VETCH, and failed to repay his debts until compelled to do so by the minister of Marine or the colonial authorities. Naturally, he also engaged in the fur trade. "The Sieur de Ramezay," reads a complaint from Montreal, "is completely involved in trade and . . . he gives all the members of his numerous family the means of pursuing it in preference to all other habitants." His most interesting initiative, however, was his venture into lumbering. He had a sawmill operating at Baie Saint-Paul as early as 1702 and he built another in the Montreal area in 1706. The following year he advised Pontchartrain that over 20,000 feet of boards and sheathing could be produced in the district of Montreal every year and he suggested that this wood be used to launch the shipbuilding industry in Canada.

By 1704 Ramezay had become one of Canada's leading personalities but the position he occupied did not fully satisfy him. He was ambitious, had a factious disposition, and by his marriage had

become enmeshed in the intricate web of New France's family rivalries. Soon he was filling his dispatches with virulent attacks against another Canadianized Frenchman, Philippe de Rigaud de Vaudreuil. He accused the governor of sending agents into the west to engage in the fur trade, of being a pawn of the Jesuits, of having failed to adopt adequate security measures when a New England delegation visited the colony in 1705, and of having faltered when a riot broke out in Montreal over the high price of salt. Lamothe Cadillac [LAUMET] and RUETTE d'Auteuil joined in this campaign, and for a time they succeeded in seriously undermining Vaudreuil's position at Versailles. The governor, however, counterattacked vigorously. Ramezay, he charged, had formed a cabal with the other two in order to profit from the Detroit trade; his violent temper made him unfit to govern. Ramezay heatedly denied these charges. He had once held a sixth interest in Detroit, he admitted, but had given it up in order to avoid even the suspicion of placing his private fortune before the public good. He conceded that he had "a quick temper" but maintained that he had never mistreated anyone in 15 years, unlike Vaudreuil who in a moment of anger had been known to slap a man in the face and kick him in the stomach.

Meantime, as a result of the outbreak of the War of the Spanish Succession in Europe, a state of war existed between New France and the English colonies to the south. This exposed Quebec to naval attack, but Montreal was in a relatively secure position because of the treaty of 1701 with the Iroquois and the non-belligerent policy New York was satisfied to follow during the governorship of Lord Cornbury. But there were other problems to occupy Ramezay's attention during the early years of the conflict. Frenchmen were still deserting the colony for the west in spite of the edict of 1696, and the contraband trade between Montreal and Albany was reaching frightening proportions because of the saturated condition of the French market. Ramezay assured the minister that he was doing his best to check these practices but he met with no success. Indeed, it is difficult to see what measures he could have adopted since many of the merchants who were heavily involved in this trade were also his creditors for large amounts of money. In 1707, Ramezay did make a valuable suggestion. He urged the crown to send 40,000 *livres* of merchandise to Canada annually and to make it available to the Indians at cheap rates in order to offset the fall in beaver prices that was driving them to Albany. The French government, whose resources were entirely committed to the European war, was unfortunately unable to act on this suggestion and the contraband trade continued unabated.

In 1709 Ramezay was suddenly called upon to prove himself as a military leader. In the summer of that year New York broke the truce with New France and massed militiamen and Indian auxiliaries, under the command of Francis NICHOLSON, at the Wood Creek portage near Albany in preparation for an attack on Montreal. Ramezay, at the head of an army of 1,500 men, advanced along the Richelieu against this force. He had been instructed by Vaudreuil to avoid an engagement and to limit himself to wrecking the boats and canoes and to dumping the ammunition into the river. Surprise was of the essence for the success of the operation, but the carelessness of Ramezay's nephew, the scatter-brained Pierre-Thomas Tarieu* de La Pérade, who had been placed in charge of a scouting party, betrayed the presence of the expedition. Shortly after this mishap, Ramezay learned from a prisoner that the English army at Wood Creek numbered 3,000 men. A council of war was held to consider the situation, and the infuriated governor decided that there was nothing to do but retreat.

Fortunately for New France this uninspired performance had no harmful consequences. New York called off the expedition against Montreal after learning that the English naval squadron that was supposed to attack Quebec had been sent to another destination. However, the episode may have struck yet another blow at Ramezay's sinking political fortunes. By 1709, the governor of Montreal had lost the support of his two old allies, Auteuil and Cadillac. The former had been recalled as attorney general of the Conseil Supérieur and the latter was about to be transferred to Louisiana as a result of CLAIRAMBAULT d'Aigremont's devastating report. In 1709 also, Madame de Vaudreuil [JOYBERT] took up residence at the French court and no doubt did what she could to discredit her husband's most outspoken critic. The blow fell in 1711. In a scathing dispatch, Pontchartrain accused Ramezay of being the chief fomenter of discord in the colony and warned him that Louis XIV would already have made some "unpleasant decisions" had not the minister assured him that the governor of Montreal would mend his ways in the future. Now that his foe was crushed, Vaudreuil sportingly extended the olive branch to him. In 1712 Ramezay's third son, Charles-Hector, Sieur de La Gesse, was presented to the French court by Madame de Vaudreuil.

In September 1714 Vaudreuil went to France on leave of absence and Ramezay served as acting governor until his return to Canada in the summer of 1716. It was during this period that the British colonies, capitalizing on the recently concluded treaty of Utrecht, made their first attempt to infiltrate the Mississippi Valley and Great Lakes region and to overrun the eastern frontier of New France. Ramezay had to find ways of containing this expansion, a task made all the more difficult by a lack of precedents to indicate a solution and by the return of peace between France and England, which ruled out a military policy. Ramezay forwarded notes to Robert Hunter, the governor of New York, asking him to forbid the merchants of his provinces from sending trading expeditions to the Great Lakes, traditionally a French region, until the boundary was settled. He also sought permission from the Indians of the Mississippi to plunder English supply convoys venturing into the interior. These measures, however, were, at best, expedients. The security of New France, Ramezay informed the court, could only be assured by a favourable settlement of the intercolonial boundary, a question left open by the treaty of Utrecht. If this were not done, he warned, "the English will make greater inroads into this colony by way of Acadia, Boston, Manhattan, and the Carolinas in time of peace than when we were at war with them."

While Ramezay's analysis of the English threat was remarkably clear-sighted, his organization of the abortive campaign of 1715 against the Fox Indians showed once more that he had a mediocre military mind. Nevertheless, the acting governor cannot be held responsible for all the mishaps that befell the expedition and disrupted it before it was even properly underway. Louis de LA PORTE de Louvigny, who was supposed to serve as commanding officer, became ill and had to be replaced by the less qualified Constant LE MARCHAND de Lignery. Because of the court's refusal to finance the campaign, the army had to be made up entirely of unruly Indians and coureurs de bois. Ramezay, however, was responsible for the strategy which called for the army to advance in separate groups and meet at a point near the Fox stronghold. So complex were these preliminary manoeuvres that they had almost no chance of success. Fortunately, Ramezay learned from these mistakes. In 1716 Louvigny was sufficiently recovered to lead a second expedition against the Foxes. This time the strategy was greatly simplified and the operation was a complete success.

Following Vaudreuil's return to the colony, Ramezay went back to being governor of Montreal. The sawmill he had built several years before now began to yield attractive dividends. In 1719 he was awarded by the French government a

Ramezay

contract to supply 2,000 cubic feet of pine sheathing, 8,000 cubic feet of oak sheathing, and 4,000 feet of board annually for six years. This success appears to have whetted Ramezay's commercial appetite. In 1723 he asked for fur-trading rights at the post of Kaministiquia but his request was turned down by the minister of Marine.

In spite of the success of his lumber operation and of the praise he won for his conduct of the colony's affairs in Vaudreuil's absence, this final period of Ramezay's life does not appear to have been a happy one. Twice in five years tragedy had struck his family. In 1711 his eldest son, 19-year-old Claude junior, an ensign in the French navy, lost his life in an attack on Rio de Janeiro. His second son, Louis, Sieur de Monnoir, was killed by the Cherokees during the campaign of 1715 against the Fox Indians. It is therefore not surprising that Ramezay's character should not have mellowed with the passage of years. He quarrelled with the Jesuits when he tried to place a garrison on their mission at Sault-Saint-Louis (Caughnawaga). He charged the Brothers Hospitallers of Montreal with not doing their duty. Finally, he clashed once more with Vaudreuil. How the quarrel began is not clear but it burst into the open in 1723 when the two men publicly disagreed on a point of Iroquois policy. Angered by the manner in which Vaudreuil had spoken to him in the presence of a number of people, Ramezay was soon attacking him in old-time style. A sensational quarrel between these two leading colonial figures appeared in the making, but the governor of Montreal died before it could materialize. Vaudreuil immediately laid past differences aside and spoke warmly of the man who had been both a colleague and a rival for so many years: "He served . . . with honour and distinction" he informed the minister, "and . . . lived very comfortably, having always spent more than his salary, which is the reason he has left only a very small estate to his widow and children."

Madame de Ramezay had indeed been left in a precarious financial condition which the grant of an annual pension of 1,000 *livres* did little to improve. To raise the capital she required she tried without success to sell her house, which the intendant, Claude-Thomas Dupuy, had evaluated at 28,245 *livres*, to the government. With the assistance of a partner, Clément de Sabrevois de Bleury, she continued to operate her husband's sawmill, but floodings and the wreck of the *Chameau*, the vessel which was supposed to carry her lumber to France in 1725, resulted in losses of 10,000 *livres*. In spite of these setbacks, the Ramezays did not lose their interest in the lumber industry. When the mother died in 1742, her unmarried daughter, Françoise-Louise, carried on

and expanded the family business. By the mid 1750s she had several sawmills in operation on the seigneuries her father had acquired in the Richelieu region, and one merchant alone owed her 60,000 *livres*.

Besides Françoise-Louise, Ramezay was survived by two sons and at least five daughters. La Gesse, the elder of the sons, died on 27 Aug. 1725 in the wreck of the *Chameau* off Île Royale (Cape Breton Island). The younger, Jean-Baptiste-Roch pursued a military career and is perhaps best remembered as the man who surrendered Quebec to the British in September 1759. Of the five daughters, two became nuns and two others married officers of the colonial regular troops.

Claude de Ramezay did not leave a deep imprint on the history of New France but his career is nonetheless very significant. His marriage into a prominent Canadian family, his clashes with Vaudreuil, the role of *grand seigneur*, which he played with considerable success in Trois-Rivières and Montreal, provide valuable information on how Canadian society was formed at that time, on the nature of colonial government and politics, and on the mentality and way of life of a representative member of the Canadian upper class.

Yves F. Zoltvany

AJM, Greffe d'Antoine Adhémar, 27 avril 1705 (contract between Claude de Ramezay and Pierre Couturier for the construction of the Château de Ramezay). AJQ, Greffe de François Genaple, 7 nov. 1690 (Claude de Ramezay and Marie-Charlotte Denys' marriage contract). AN, Col., B, 13, 15, 16, 19–20, 22–23, 25, 27, 29, 33–36, 39–45, 47; C^{11A}, 9–48; C^{11G}, 1–3, 5; E, 344 (dossier de Ramezay); F^{5A}, 2; Marine, B^1, 8. "Correspondance de Frontenac (1689–99)," APQ *Rapport*, *1927–28*, 1–211; *1928–29*, 247–384. "Correspondance de Vaudreuil," APQ *Rapport*, *1938–39*, 12–179; *1939–40*, 355–463; *1942–43*, 399–443; *1946–47*, 371–460; *1947–48*, 137–39. "Un mémoire de Le Roy de La Potherie sur la Nouvelle-France adressé à M. de Pontchartrain, 1701–1702," *BRH*, XXII (1916), 214–26. P.-G. Roy, *Inv. concessions*, I, 138f.; II, 168f.; IV, 195–97, 216f., 220f.; *Inv. ord. int.*, I, 66, 106, 137, 192, 203, 248; *Les officiers d'état-major*, 209–13. Tanguay, *Dictionnaire*, I, 183; III, 351.

Fauteux, *Essai sur l'industrie sous le régime français*. P.-G. Roy, *La famille de Ramezay* (Lévis, 1910). Guy Frégault, "Politique et politiciens au début du XVIIIe siècle," *Écrits du Canada français* (Montréal), XI (1961), 91–208. Désiré Girouard, "Les anciens postes du lac Saint-Louis," *BRH*, I (1895), 165–69. É.-Z. Massicotte, "Une femme d'affaires du régime français," *BRH*, XXXVII (1931), 530; "Une soirée chez M. de Ramesay, gouverneur de Montréal, en 1704," *BRH*, XXII (1916), 252f. Victor Morin, "Les Ramesay et leur château," *Cahiers des Dix*, III (1938),

9–72. P.-G. Roy, "Josué Boisberthelot de Beaucours," *BRH*, X (1904), 301–9. Benjamin Sulte, "La Vérenderie avant ses voyages au Nord-Ouest," *BRH*, XXI (1915), 97–111.

RASLE (Rasles). *See* RALE

RAT. *See* KONDIARONK

RATTIER, JEAN, fourth official executioner in Canada; b. *c.* 1650 in France; d. 21 May 1703 at the Hôtel-Dieu of Quebec.

In 1666 he was a domestic at Trois-Rivières. There, on 6 Feb. 1672, he married Marie Rivière, who came from the small town of Le Cause, in the province of Saintonge. Five children were born of this marriage.

Jean Rattier settled at Saint-François-du-Lac on 28 Jan. 1676, where he took up farming. On 23 Oct. 1679 he was involved in a quarrel during which a girl was fatally injured. Held criminally responsible for this death, Jean Rattier was condemned at Trois-Rivières to be hanged. He appealed to the Conseil Souverain, which, on 31 Dec. 1680, confirmed the original sentence. But the executioner, Jacques Daigre, had just died, on 26 Mar. 1680, and no one had yet replaced him; besides, it was always difficult in Canada to find someone who was willing to act as executioner. The councillors therefore gave the criminal, Jean Rattier, the choice between waiting in prison until an executioner was found to hang him and accepting the office of hangman. Jean Rattier lost no time in accepting the position himself.

At that time Canadian society held in horror the person who exercised this ignoble office and considered all contact of any sort with the hangman and his family degrading; this explains why the new executioner had great difficulty in finding a dwelling for his family in Quebec. But he had scarcely moved into a house situated outside the town limits of Quebec, for he was not allowed to live within the town walls, when the inhabitants of Quebec began to take delight in approaching his dwelling to insult his wife and children. The Conseil Souverain was obliged to intervene. As a final blow, it was this same executioner who on 5 July 1695, in the public square of the Lower Town of Quebec, had to put his own wife, who had been found guilty of receiving and concealing, in the pillory. Subsequently he continued until his death to carry out sentences of corporal punishment on criminals without any other troublesome incidents.

His youngest son, Pierre (baptized 9 July 1680 at Trois-Rivières), settled for good in Canada after having entertained the idea in 1703 of leaving the country for New England. In 1704 he married Catherine Rousseau, who came from Les Sables d'Olonne in Poitou. They had seven children. Pierre Rattier succeeded in supporting his family by hiring out as a day-labourer to different employers in the region of Quebec. Rattier did not however content himself with the salary which his employers gave him; he stole various tools and materials from them. For this reason he was in prison in 1710, accused along with his wife of these thefts and of some others that he had committed in company with the hangman Jacques ÉLIE. The Conseil Souverain then offered to acquit him of the crimes of which he and his wife had been accused if he agreed to fulfil the office of executioner, since Jacques Élie had been murdered. Rattier accepted and became the sixth official executioner in Canada; like his father, he exercised the office of hangman until his death, 21 Aug. 1723, at the Hôtel-Dieu of Quebec.

ANDRÉ LACHANCE

AHDQ, Registres des malades, 1698–1709, 1709–22, 1723–39. AJQ, Registre d'état civil de Notre-Dame de Québec. AJTR, Registre d'état civil de Trois-Rivières. AQ, NF, Coll. de pièces jud. et not., 251; NF, Dossiers du Cons. sup., Mat. crim., III, 193ff.; NF, Registres de la Prévôté de Québec, 43, 1ff. *Jug. et délib.*, II, III, IV, VI. Recensements du Canada, 1666 (APQ *Rapport*), 1681 (Sulte). André Lachance, *Le bourreau au Canada sous le régime français* (SHQ, Cahiers d'histoire, XVIII, 1966), 63–66, 72–75. P.-G. Roy, "Les bourreaux de Québec sous le régime français," *BRH*, XXIX (1923), 3–12.

RAUDOT, ANTOINE-DENIS, commissary and inspector general of the Marine, economist, *Intendant des classes*, adviser on colonial affairs at the French court, expert on the North American Indians, chief clerk of the royal household, director of the Compagnie des Indes, administrator of Louisiana, councillor of the Marine, intimate of France's leading economists and geographers, intendant of New France, 1705–1710; b. in 1679; d. at Versailles, 28 July 1737.

Antoine-Denis Raudot was born into family circumstances that were very favourable to a career in the royal service. His immediate ancestors had only recently abandoned their leisurely existence in the province of Burgundy, to fill important positions in the military and in France's administrative departments. Jean Raudot, Antoine-Denis' grandfather, had been the architect of this sudden change in fortune; his advantageous marriage to a member of the Talon family—the influential advocates general of France—had made him a relative of the future minister of Marine, the Comte de Pontchartrain, and had ultimately opened his way to a post as king's

Raudot

secretary. JACQUES RAUDOT, Antoine-Denis' father, had also made good use of his opportunities and was a counsellor in the Court of Aids at Paris. Thus it is not surprising that at the age of 20, Antoine-Denis was already embarked on a career of his own, as a writer in ordinary in the Marine. He seems, moreover, to have been anxious for rapid advancement, for in 1702 he purchased a position as commissary and, on 2 Aug. 1704, acquired by the same means the post of inspector general of the Marine in Flanders and Picardy. He sold this latter office, however, in April 1705, after receiving a commission, dated 1 January of that year, appointing him and his father intendants of New France.

The commission made it clear that Antoine-Denis was being sent to the colony primarily to second his father, who was in his mid-sixties and who suffered from a number of physical disabilities. It stated, for instance, that while he was to have "entrée, séance, voix et opinions délibératives" in the Conseil Souverain immediately after Jacques, he could preside over the proceedings only when the latter was incapacitated or was more than ten leagues from Quebec. Then too, whenever they were in agreement on the decision to be rendered in a legal process, their voices were to count only as one. Other convincing indications of Antoine-Denis' secondary status are that he received no salary and that he acted as his father's secretary through most of their joint tenure. Yet it would appear likely that there were other motives, besides providing Jacques Raudot with an able assistant, behind Antoine-Denis' unusual appointment. It was rumoured at the time, for example, that the minister, Pontchartrain, was very anxious to further the career of his young relative. While this may have been the case, it could also be true that Antoine-Denis had already begun to display those qualities of intelligence and incisiveness and that ability to theorize in economic terms on a grand scale that eventually made him a powerful force in French colonial policy-making. Certainly the evidence indicates that both the Marine officials and Jacques Raudot expected him to handle the financial affairs of the intendancy and to propose solutions to New France's distressing economic problems.

Antoine-Denis assumed the responsibilities of his new post in September 1705. Soon after, the dispatches passing from the colony to Versailles began to make mention of his remarkable character. His contemporaries at Quebec were impressed with his proficiency and were amazed that a man of only 26 could be so completely the master of his emotions. One of them described him as "... extremely wise and naturally just, very restrained, and of a surprising evenness of mind, which had something of the character of the ancient stoic philosophers about it, for he was not upset by any event ... the most overwhelming misfortunes would not have been able to disturb his peace of mind." These attributes were manifested in the young intendant's correspondence with the ministry. His memoirs on finance, commerce, fortifications, defence policy, Indian relations, and other less weighty subjects all testified to his calm rationality and to his faculty for quickly penetrating to the heart of any matter. In fact, emotionally and in his interests, he was a startling contrast to his father. While Jacques, a bombastic and extremely temperamental man, was fascinated by the details of legal affairs and was most concerned with reforming the abuses in existing institutions, Antoine-Denis preferred to generalize about the colony's overall condition and to programme its future course. Yet despite their different natures, there is no indication that they ever differed on basic policy or in their view of Canadian society.

On the contrary, Antoine-Denis shared his father's low opinion of the colony's inhabitants. He complained to the minister that New France was populated by "vicious minds" and that "... virtue does not triumph in this country, only vice, scandal, and libel." Since each person was solely concerned with his own immediate advantage, there was no public spirit or cooperative commercial outlook. The intendant claimed too that the habitants were poorly disciplined and that the secondary officers, both military and administrative, were insubordinate. Partly because of these bleak social impressions, Raudot became discouraged about the prospects for a swift recovery of the colonial economy. In his earliest dispatches he had spoken enthusiastically of New France's rich resources and had even requested a master builder along with other skilled workers from France to establish solidly the shipbuilding and tar-pitch industries; his increasing awareness of the country's serious limitations in labour, capital, materials, and technical skills soon curtailed these ambitions. In 1706, he noted that the conditions of war had driven prices and wages beyond the point where shipbuilding was even possible, let alone profitable.

Worse still, each year fewer and fewer vessels were arriving at Quebec from the port cities of France, thereby making it impossible to transport the colony's lumber, fishery, and agricultural products to the mother country. Furthermore, as Raudot began to plumb the depths of the Compagnie de la Colonie's dismal financial situation, it became apparent that the merchants of New

France were in no position to finance new enterprises. Summing up the colony's economic plight in their joint dispatch of 1707, the Raudots declared: "A true picture of Canada was given you, my lord, when you were informed of its misery; everything there is poor and exists only as a result of His Majesty's gracious beneficence. The war contributes greatly to these misfortunes and only a good peace could enable the habitants to undertake some improvements." Antoine-Denis therefore devoted himself to preparations for peace—to uncovering the fundamental causes of New France's economic malaise with the aim of elaborating a long-range programme of recovery.

Raudot was an economic theorist who believed that the power of individual nations was directly related to the size and scope of their commerce and that ". . . the only thing that makes countries rich is selling more to foreign countries than they buy." It was his fidelity to this concept that helped make him an influential figure in the France of Cardinal Fleury and it lay too at the root of his proposals regarding New France. In 1705 he informed Pontchartrain that the colony's economy was languishing mainly because its commerce, so heavily dependent on furs, had been crippled as a result of the glutting of the European fur market. As long as that market had been able to absorb the yearly flow of Canadian pelts, it had been possible to ignore the dangerous implications of such a narrow commercial base; but now, with enough greasy beaver in French storehouses to last for 20 years, the disastrous effects were painfully apparent. Raudot estimated that by 1706 New France's total annual revenue had dwindled to 650,000 *livres* and all but 20,000 *livres* of that sum was derived either from the sale of furs or from the royal treasury. The colony's merchants, moreover, experienced only in the simple transactions of the fur trade, possessed neither the entrepreneurial skills nor the capital resources necessary to adjust to the new situation by applying themselves to non-fur enterprises. The habitants were also guilty, according to Raudot, of relying on the easy profits of the fur trade, while cultivating their lands with an eye to subsistence only. Consequently, though the colonial inhabitants still required merchandise from France, they had little to offer in exchange.

Although this analysis of New France's economic condition really just summarized what Marine officials had already been told times without number, Raudot's proposed solution represented a radical departure. He maintained that the colony's recovery could occur only as the result of a new economic orientation, in which the fur trade would become a mere component of a multi-faceted export commerce. He envisaged the emergence of agricultural products as the new mainstay of the colony's trade, with lumber and fishery resources playing an increasingly important role. As he explained: ". . . in future this country must regard the fur trade as merely an adjunct to its commerce, and make the principal component the products of the land, which are always an almost certain source of wealth." But Raudot emphasized that the success of such a transformation would hinge on the availability of a market for Canadian products—one that would be more accessible than France or the West Indies. In this connection, he stated: ". . . I am persuaded that the only way to set this country up again . . . is to establish a city near the Gulf of St Lawrence which can consume produce." He submitted a memoir in 1706 which depicted Cape Breton island as the ideal location for this new establishment.

Raudot's Cape Breton proposal was at once brilliant and original. Ostensibly designed to restore the troubled economy of New France, it was actually a project for the future commercial development of France's entire Atlantic empire. The intendant therefore took great care to outline the potential benefits to both colony and mother country. New France, he declared, would not only be provided with a market for her agricultural produce and a clearing house for her other exportable products, but she would also be able to acquire manufactured goods from France more cheaply and in greater abundance. Cape Breton would become her storehouse, because French merchants would take full advantage of the opportunity to carry on a safer trade, over a shorter distance, with a far better chance of obtaining a return cargo. In addition, New France's transport difficulties would be largely solved, since she would require only 30 to 80 ton vessels to carry on her trade with Cape Breton. These ships could be easily constructed by Canadian shipbuilders, with a resulting stimulus to the colony's industrial economy. Beneficial also would be the rapid growth of a three-cornered fishing operation between Quebec, the Labrador-St Lawrence fishing grounds, and Cape Breton. In sum, Raudot believed that the magnetic pull of this new establishment would, in time, completely rejuvenate New France's economy.

But France, he maintained, stood to gain even more: for the Cape Breton project would furnish her with an opportunity to augment her own commerce greatly at the expense of that of her

Raudot

European rivals, and especially of that of England. Besides consolidating a mutually beneficial commerce between the port cities, the West Indies, and New France to the exclusion of foreign interlopers, it would create possibilities for the sale of French merchandise to New England and, at the same time, for shouldering aside New England in the trade with Spain and the Spanish American colonies. Indeed, with Cape Breton acting as a safe refuge, a supply depot, and an operational base for privateering, France could conceivably edge England from the rich Newfoundland fishing areas and, in time of war, wreak havoc on her Atlantic shipping. Then too, with New France flourishing behind the protection of this gulf barrier, France could eventually ship large quantities of her forest products to the royal arsenals, enabling her to jettison her costly trade in these items with the Baltic countries. In all, Raudot described a network of commercial possibilities and strategic advantages so attractive as to immediately capture the interest of the most important Marine officials.

Even so, the Cape Breton proposal did not meet with instant acceptance. It is doubtful, for one thing, if it could have been put forward at a more inopportune time. Writing in 1707, Pontchartrain argued that the concept, while theoretically promising, took little note of France's present financial difficulties and therefore stood no chance of being implemented in the near future. The royal treasury was simply unable to supply the 100,000 *écus* yearly that would be required in the early stages. The minister also rejected Raudot's contention that the state, rather than a private company, should undertake the project. He asked the intendant to forward a second memoir that would reduce the proposed costs to their bare minimum and would play up the advantages to private investors. Raudot complied with this request, but he stressed that no matter how the project was financed it could not possibly begin prior to the negotiation of a firm peace. Accordingly, between 1706 and 1710 he limited his own activities to establishing France's legal claim over the Cape Breton area and to creating the conditions in New France that would enable her to take maximum advantage of the project, if and when it was implemented.

Raudot recognized in this regard that to achieve his goal of making agricultural produce instead of furs the mainstay of the colony's export commerce, he would have to induce the inhabitants to think along those lines. He was, like his father, a strong paternalist who believed that such changes could be best promoted through close governmental supervision. As he explained to Pontchartrain, ". . . the new settlements need to be developed the way a good father would develop his land." He therefore supported Jacques' recommendations for increased royal authority in the parishes and he issued a long series of ordinances that were intended not only to discipline the habitants better, but also to eradicate their lazy habits. This authoritarian interest, however, also made him a champion of the interests of the poor farmers. In 1706, for example, he opposed the clergy's proposal to increase the annual tithes, on the grounds that it would be too burdensome for the habitants. Similarly, he pleaded with the minister to permit and even to support Madame Legardeur de Repentigny's [Agathe de Saint-Père*] small manufacturing establishment on Montreal Island, because the rough clothing it produced was a boon to the poor.

Raudot also endeavoured to improve agricultural conditions. He supported all his father's proposals for standardizing seigneurial contracts and for reducing seigneurial obligations. In addition, he demanded that the military authorities give greater consideration to planting and harvesting priorities when selecting habitants for war-parties or for work on fortifications. To reduce the hardships caused by the shortages and price speculation that frequently followed a poor harvest, he encouraged the planting of winter crops and introduced price controls along with regulations governing the export of wheat. The intendant also favoured a number of agricultural incentives. He argued, for example, that in order to promote the production of exportable commodities like sheep's wool and hemp, the king should offer, at least in the initial stages, a high fixed price in the *magasins du roi*, thereby assuring the habitants of a market. But even more radical was the suggestion that a system of liberal grants be introduced to reward those farmers showing initiative in clearing virgin land. The funds for this would be obtained from the reintroduction of the fur-trading licences (*congés*). In other words, the fur trade would indirectly help to finance agriculture.

But Raudot did not limit to agriculture alone his efforts to foster improved conditions and more enterprising attitudes. He took a number of steps to create a more cooperative commercial outlook among the merchants of New France. He encouraged them to establish a *bourse* at Quebec where they could meet to discuss business ventures and he agreed with his father and Governor RIGAUD de Vaudreuil that when future assemblies were called to discuss matters relating to trade, only the merchants should be represented since their interests were most crucially involved. Raudot even invested his own funds in a joint enterprise with several merchants for the fitting-out of a vessel that was to carry on privateering activities against the English. Responsible financing as an inducement to trade was another of his key objectives. In 1706, he submitted a memoir calling for the stabilization of New France's currency through the maintenance of confidence in the existing card-money system. In the matter of import duties, he pleaded for a better deal for Canadian merchants importing goods from the West Indies. The intendant also issued dozens of ordinances aimed at introducing order into the urban economic milieu. These ranged from measures for the improvement of sanitary and travel conditions to provisions for the holding of a twice-weekly market in Montreal. His many police regulations, issued especially to curb moral and alcoholic abuses, bore further testimony to his ambition to mould a stable, business-first society.

In 1709, however, Raudot complained bitterly to the minister that all of these efforts to improve the colony's internal economic conditions were being undermined by the military authorities and particularly by Governor Vaudreuil. Although animosity caused by his father's fiery disputes with Vaudreuil undoubtedly played a key part in his own increasing hostility towards the governor, Antoine-Denis was shrewd enough to base his criticisms on administrative issues. He contended, for example, that New France's finances were perpetually bedevilled by Vaudreuil's extravagant defence policy and he singled out two features of that policy for special censure. First, he maintained that the governor had foolishly allowed the royal engineer, JACQUES LEVASSEUR de Neré, to build a series of fortifications at Quebec that were terribly expensive and so over-extended as to be untenable by the colony's available manpower. Secondly, and this was his most devastating indictment, he argued that Vaudreuil was prone to panic at the least rumour that an enemy force was about to attack the colony. The governor called up the habitants, dispatched war parties to New England and Hudson Bay, and took other emergency measures that not only interrupted the economic cycle of the country, but necessitated new issues of card money to cover the extraordinary expenses.

Raudot was equally critical of Vaudreuil's Indian policy. While he agreed with the governor on a number of points concerning the western allies (for example, the necessity for re-establishing the fur-trading licences), he believed New France's relations with the Iroquois Confederacy were being handled in disastrous fashion. Raudot had made a thorough study of the North American Indians, which was later published under the title *Relation par lettres de l'Amérique septentrionale, années 1707–1710*, and his investigations had instilled in him a deep respect for the Iroquois. He claimed that Vaudreuil, by placing too much faith in a corrupt agent named CHABERT de Joncaire, was provoking jealousies among the various Iroquois tribes that could result only in a general war against New France. But when he attempted to point out these errors, Vaudreuil treated him with contempt. Declaring that he was not accustomed to such abuse and that he was thoroughly exhausted, Raudot asked to be recalled. In 1710 Pontchartrain granted this request and promoted him to the prestige post of *Intendant des classes*.

It is difficult to ascertain whether or not this advancement resulted from Raudot's ingenious Cape Breton proposal, but the evidence does indicate that the Marine officials considered him, even prior to 1708, as a talented candidate for important economic posts. In 1711 he was charged with the duties of the *Garde-Côte des Invalides et des Colonies* and until 1726, when he abandoned the details of the colonies, he was an adviser on colonial affairs. During the Regency period especially, when former intendants exercised considerable influence in shaping policy, Raudot's opinion was requested on many matters relating to North America. In 1713 he was named chief clerk of the ministry of the king's household, a position which made him a powerful figure beyond the range of Marine affairs and which provided him with an *entrée* into the most influential circles at Versailles. In February 1717, a new stage in his career began with his appointment as one of three new directors of the Compagnie des Indes. For the next several years he devoted much of his energy to the economic problems of Louisiana and to projects for the discovery of a route to the western sea. In this latter regard, he corresponded with France's leading geographers and used his influence to assist them. Apparently, he was also on close terms with France's foremost economists. In 1728, he succeeded his recently deceased father as councillor of the Marine, after which he spent considerable effort on the development of France's Atlantic fisheries. He inspired comment even in death, for in his will he left almost all of a considerable fortune to his domestics.

Clearly then, Raudot's five-year tenure as intendant of New France was only the embryonic phase of a long and distinguished career; but it was a vitally important phase for it provided him with an opportunity to demonstrate his ability as

Raudot

an imaginative economic theorist—an ability which counted for much in his later successes. His plan to establish Cape Breton as a market for Canadian produce and as a commercial *entrepôt* for France's Atlantic empire was truly a master stroke and was put forward with what Charlevoix* termed ". . . admirable exactness, intelligence, order and precision, upheld by solid and thorough proofs." Yet Raudot recognized himself that to undertake such a project in time of war would be an exercise in futility. Thus by the time he left New France in 1710 the key proposal of his intendancy was still mired in the planning stage. By 1713, however, conditions had changed dramatically. The loss of both Acadia and Placentia by the terms of the treaty of Utrecht left France's remaining North American possessions extremely vulnerable and obliged French officials to reconsider the Cape Breton concept. The subsequent establishment of the great fortress of Louisbourg was the practical application of Raudot's original proposal. As one historian has remarked ". . . at the Marine . . . Raudot junior inspired the colonial policy of Louis XIV and Pontchartrain. It was he who showed the king the strategic importance of Île Royale."

DONALD J. HORTON

[For material on Antoine-Denis Raudot's family background *see* the bibliography for the article on JACQUES RAUDOT. The information about the first stages of Antoine-Denis' career is based mainly on Le Jeune, *Dictionnaire*, and [C.-M.] Raudot, *Deux intendants du Canada* (Auxerre, 1854).

Brief comments on Antoine-Denis' character and abilities, both when he was in New France and during his later career, come from Juchereau, *Annales* (Jamet) and from Guy Frégault, "Politique et politiciens au début du XVIIIe siècle," *Écrits du Canada français* (Montréal), XI (1961), 91–208. In addition, the following articles and book contain some useful asides: Jean Delanglez, "A mirage: the Sea of the West . . .," *RHAF*, I (1947–48), 554–56, 563–65; Robert La Roque de Roquebrune, "La direction de la Nouvelle-France par le Ministère de la Marine," *RHAF*, VI (1952–53), 470–88; Giraud, *Histoire de la Louisiane française*, III, 48, 130, 132, 142.

Raudot's Cape Breton memoir and many of his most interesting dispatches are found in AN, Col., C^{11G}, 1–6. Information on most of his internal economic reforms and municipal regulations is taken from AN, Col., B, 25–33; C^{11A}, 22–32, 34, 36, 110, 125; F^3, 8, 9, and from Raudot's ordinances [*see*: *Édits ord.*; *Ord. comm.* (P.-G. Roy).]. Charlevoix, *History* (Shea), V, 285–94; Garneau, *Histoire du Canada*, II, 270–73; and Thomas Jeffreys, *The natural and civil history of the French dominions in North and South America* (London, 1760), contain useful analyses of the Cape Breton project, but none of them

deals adequately with the minister's objections to certain aspects of the proposal.

When Raudot's analysis of the Indian tribes in North America was published in Paris in 1904 under the title *Relation par lettres de l'Amérique septentrionale, années 1709 et 1710*, the editor, Camille de Rochemonteix, attributed the letters to Father Antoine SILVY. However, subsequent works, especially W. V. Kinietz, *The Indians of the western Great Lakes, 1615–1760* (Ann Arbor, 1940), 235–36, 314–410, and Delanglez [*supra*], point out that it was really Raudot who wrote them, basing his account on the memoirs of Louis de LA PORTE de Louvigny, whom he greatly esteemed, and on the memoir of L. Delite, which dealt with the Illinois and the Miamis. There is no evidence to indicate that Raudot ever visited these tribes. Instead, he probably spoke with their chiefs and with French travellers at Montreal. D.J.H.]

AN, Col., C^{13A}, 2–4; D^{2C}, 49; Marine, C^1, 157. ASQ, Lettres, N, P. BN, MS, Cabinet des titres, 28, 921, 13, 21, 23, 25, 31; MS, Dossiers bleus, 557, 14,680; MS, FR. 6,793, f.200; 22,696, f.185; MS, NAF 9,273, ff.257–75, 282, 361. PAC, FM 8, A 6, 1–5; F 61. "Correspondance de Vaudreuil," APQ *Rapport*, *1938–39*, 12–180; *1939–40*, 355–463; *1942–43*, 399–443; *1946–47*, 371–460; *1947–48*, 135–339. *Documents relating to Canadian currency during the French period* (Shortt), I, 132, 227, 231, 331–32, 340; II, 780. *Documents relating to seigniorial tenure* (Munro). *Jug. et délib.* "Mémoire sur La Louisiane pour estre présentée, avec la carte de ce Pais, au Conseil Souverain de Marine, par F. Le Maire P.P.," *RHAF*, III (1949–50), 436. PAC *Report, 1911*.

Jean Delanglez, *Frontenac and the Jesuits* (Chicago, 1939), 65. Hamelin, *Économie et société en N.-F.* F. M. Hammang, *The Marquis de Vaudreuil, New France at the beginning of the eighteenth century* (Bruges, 1938), 81–108, 133–38, 182–87. Harris, *The seigneurial system*, 157–58. Lanctot, *History of Canada*, I, 153–60, 201–21. N.-E. Dionne, "Les Raudot; intendants de la Nouvelle-France," *RC*, XXXI (1895), 567–610. J.-C. Dubé, "Origine sociale des intendants de la Nouvelle-France," *Social history* (Ottawa), II (November 1968), 18–33. Guy Frégault, "La Compagnie de la Colonie," *Revue de l'université d'Ottawa*, XXX (1960), 5–29, 127–49. Lionel Groulx, "Note sur la Chapellerie au Canada sous le régime français," *RHAF*, III (1949–50), 399. Robert La Roque de Roquebrune, "La direction de la Nouvelle-France par le Ministère de la Marine," *RHAF*, VI (1952–53), 470–88. Régis Roy, "Les intendants de la Nouvelle-France," *RSCT*, 2nd ser., IX (1903), sect.I, 65–107; "Jacques et Antoine-Denis Raudot," *BRH*, IX (1903), 157–59; "Quelques notes sur les Intendants," *BRH*, XXXII (1926), 442–43. H. M. Thomas, "The relations of governor and intendant in the old régime," *CHR*, XVI (1935), 27–40. Y. F. Zoltvany, "Philippe de Rigaud de Vaudreuil, governor of New France (1703–1725)," unpublished Ph.D. thesis, University of Alberta, 1963.

RAUDOT, JACQUES, lawyer in the *parlement* of Paris, counsellor in the *parlement* of Metz, magistrate, chief clerk in the department of Marine, a director of France's maritime commerce, councillor of the Marine, honorary counsellor in the Court of Aids at Paris, intendant of New France from 1705 to 1711; b. in 1638; d. at Paris, 20 Feb. 1728.

The Raudot genealogy has been traced back as far as 1360 in the small French town of Arnay-le-Duc (in the province of Burgundy, not far from Dijon). By the middle of the 17th century the family apparently held a position of prominence in the local social hierarchy. Jacques' uncle was mayor of the town and his father, Jean, besides being seigneur of Bazernes (department of Yonne) and Coudray (department of Aisne), was ranked in the king's service as lieutenant in the election of Auxerre and clerk for extraordinary war expenses. What seems, however, to have suddenly propelled the Raudots from provincial obscurity to a role of importance in the Marine was Jean's marriage to Marguerite Talon, a member of the prestigious Parisian branch of that family. Marguerite was the daughter of Jean Talon, *receveur général des bœttes et monnoyes de France*, and her cousin Marie was married to the father of the elder Pontchartrain, minister of Marine. It was perhaps through the latter connection that Jean Raudot became a farmer-general and on 1 May 1640 a king's secretary. In any case, by the time of his death in 1660, he had prepared the way for his three sons, Jacques, Jean-Baptiste (b. 1657) and Louis-François (b. 1658), to pursue distinguished careers in the royal service. The two youngest became army officers of recognized merit, while Jacques entered the magistracy.

Little is known of Jacques' early life, except that at some stage he further entrenched himself in the legal nobility by marrying Françoise Gioux, daughter of a lawyer in the *parlement* (probably the *parlement* of Paris). By Françoise he had two sons, ANTOINE-DENIS (b. 1679) and Jacques-Denis, known as Raudot de Chalus (b. 1685), as well as one daughter, Marguerite-Françoise. Jacques evidently received an arduous training in the French judicial system, the type of thorough training that was increasingly required for Marine service by the early 1700s. Prior to 1673, he was an advocate in the *parlement* of Paris, but on 16 February of that year he became a counsellor in the *parlement* of Metz. On 26 May 1678, he was appointed counsellor in the Court of Aids at Paris where he was considered a good judge. Although his record of honourable service for over 26 years in the Court of Aids was probably enough in itself to qualify him for a colonial post, other factors must have entered into his selection. He was, after all, 66 when he received the commission on

1 Jan. 1705, appointing him conjointly with Antoine-Denis to the intendancy of New France.

Raudot's contemporaries offered a number of theories on his appointment. Some thought he was being rewarded for his distinguished legal career; others claimed that he was sent to assist his son for only a three-year period; still others believed that he was simply benefiting, as his predecessor François de Beauharnois* de La Boische had done, from his family ties with the minister. Pontchartrain, according to this last theory, was anxious to help him mend his fortune. While all of these explanations undoubtedly contain elements of truth, no single one of them is entirely adequate. It was true, for example, that Jacques was expected to assist Antoine-Denis and prepare him for future posts, but he alone received a salary and their respective commissions left no doubt that he was the man in charge. Then again, the minister never displayed any anxiety over the Raudots' financial status. On the contrary, he expected them both to live off the father's 12,000 *livres* salary and he insisted that they take half of it in Canadian letters of exchange which normally meant a loss of about 3,000 *livres*. Furthermore, even though they received none of their provisions in two different years, Pontchartrain insisted that they pay freight charges and import duties on those they received in other years. Thus it seems advisable to look beyond mere considerations of patronage to account for Raudot's selection, perhaps to his character and outlook at the moment when he became intendant.

On 7 Sept. 1705, 55 days after leaving France, the Raudots—Jacques, Antoine-Denis, and Jacques-Denis—arrived at Quebec in company with Jacques' nephew, the Chevalier Dussy. They were just in time to join Beauharnois for the long overdue ceremonies held to officially install Philippe de RIGAUD, Marquis de Vaudreuil, as governor general. Appearing thus for the first time, they must surely have impressed the citizenry of Quebec. Though young, Antoine-Denis was keenly intelligent and possessed that sort of stoical bearing that generally inspires instant respect. But at this early stage, his father was clearly the more arresting figure; nor would Jacques, a man with a strong sense of his own importance, have had it any other way. A contemporary at Quebec described him as "a distinguished elderly man, a scholar with a touch of the pedant," capable of discoursing knowledgeably on almost any subject. Certainly his dispatches to the minister, particularly those written when his violent temper was not blazing over some real or imagined slight, bear out this description by their excellent organization, abundance of detail, and easy style. Their contents

Raudot

also bespeak a man of legalistic efficiency, possessed of tremendous energy, and determined to exercise every particle of his authority.

But Jacques also appreciated the better things in life. He and his two sons lived together at Quebec in relative comfort, rapidly turning the intendant's palace into a hive of social activity. Despite his 67 years, Jacques enjoyed the company of young people and displayed a lively interest in Quebec's eligible widows—in spite of the fact that his wife didn't die until 1710. He entertained them all with musical concerts performed in the latest metropolitan style of mixed voices and instruments. In fact his choice of diversion soon offended the moral scruples of the colony's stern ecclesiasts, resulting in a series of sharp verbal exchanges that led in turn to complaints about his lack of respect for the clergy. This would not be by any means the last occasion when Jacques' personality stimulated heated opposition, but it was clear nevertheless that he was a man of unique abilities who had been appointed to New France to deal with her unique problems.

Raudot had been introduced to these problems while still in Paris. He learned from several memoirs and from discussions with Canadian officials like Denis RIVERIN, that New France was teetering on the edge of economic collapse. The long war of the Spanish Succession had imposed an unbearable strain on Marine finances, making it impossible to transfuse needed capital into a colonial economy suffering from interrupted commerce, rising prices, and a shaky monetary system. Worse still, a continuing glut of the European beaver market had all but ruined the Canadian-financed and directed Compagnie de la Colonie—a reversal which touched most of New France's merchants and administrators and which seemed to call for a new economic orientation. Actually, one of Raudot's earliest resolves was to strive to create conditions whereby the habitants would leave the hunt for furs to devote themselves more earnestly to agriculture. But economic distress was only part of the problem. Raudot's instructions indicated that the company's directors were guilty of gross malfeasance and that the officers of other institutions, such as the Conseil Souverain, had introduced abuses that were purely the products of their own self-interest and very onerous to the poorer inhabitants. Here was a preliminary picture that would have jaundiced the most optimistic eye, and it is small wonder that Jacques Raudot came to the colony looking for signs of corruption and oppression and found them in every corner.

From the beginning of his tenure in 1705 until his departure in 1711, Raudot kept up a steady barrage of criticism directed against the colonial institutions, the officials who administered them and the people who lived within them. At one time or another he recommended sweeping changes in education, agriculture, the legal system, the seigneurial system, municipal regulations, and even the form of government. He divided the inhabitants of the colony into two groups, the vested interests or "oppressors" (for Raudot they included merchants, administrators, seigneurs, and even ecclesiastics), and the habitants or "oppressed." But both groups were distinguished by poverty, avarice, insubordination, and ignorance. In fact *ignorant* was an indispensable word in Raudot's vocabulary, which he employed especially to describe royal officials from the lowliest clerk to the governor general himself. In 1709 he informed Pontchartrain that there were "very few persons in this country . . . who have the qualities necessary to direct any undertaking." The persons of quality were too concerned with their own selfish interests to care about New France's general welfare, while the habitants were utterly without discipline because of their poor upbringing and lack of school training. It was even necessary to protect the parish priests from their insults.

For Raudot, an experienced magistrate accustomed to telling others what was best for them, these social conditions represented a challenge. Entrusting the financial affairs of the intendancy to Antoine-Denis, he concentrated all his energy on public order and justice in an effort to bring both the vested interests and the habitants into complete subordination, fearing yet benefiting from his paternalistic interest. To discipline the habitants of the countryside, he proposed three major reforms: the introduction of schoolmasters in each seigneury, who would be trained at the establishment of François CHARON de La Barre in Montreal at a cost to the king of 2,000 *livres*; an increase in the authority of the militia captains as agents of royal authority in the parishes, to be effected by making them sergeants in the troops at 100 *livres* salary per year; and more rigorous enforcement of police ordinances, particularly those dealing with liquor and moral offences. This programme was crippled, however, by lack of funds, the untimely death of the Sieur Charon and the minister's refusal to accept the proposals regarding the militia captains. Although Raudot issued hundreds of ordinances attempting to regulate everything from the number of bakers in Montreal to the preservation of fruit orchards, they were not usually obeyed. In 1708, he wrote in disgust, "intendants are disliked in this country because they are responsible for public order."

But Raudot was even more concerned with

curbing the power of the vested interests. On his arrival in the colony, he had been witness to the investigation of a near-riot in Montreal caused by a greedy merchant's attempt to take advantage of a serious salt shortage. Referring to this and many similar abuses, Raudot declared to the minister: ". . . the Sieur Raudot regards, Monseigneur, these kinds of things as vexations which the superior attempts to inflict on his inferior." He vowed to eradicate them wherever they existed. This was the spirit, for example, that he brought to the affairs of the Compagnie de la Colonie. Though he recognized that the company had suffered since its organization in 1700 from two main drawbacks, the depressed European beaver market and inadequate financing, he could not believe that the Canadian directors were entirely free of responsibility for the nearly one and a half million *livres* of debt that had accumulated by 1705. Consequently, even prior to his departure from Paris, he submitted a memoir composed of recommendations including one for the company's administrative reorganization. Pontchartrain agreed, having long since concluded that the company's plight was primarily attributable to corrupt administration. He instructed Raudot to suppress the board of directors, replacing it by two delegates. Rigid austerity was to be introduced and Raudot was to guard against making the same mistakes as Beauharnois, who had loaned large sums of the king's money to the directors.

Raudot undertook to carry out these orders with his usual single-mindedness. At an assembly called to inform the directors of the minister's decisions and to elect the two new delegates, he scolded his audience for their many faults and proceeded to foist his own choice of representatives upon them. When RUETTE d'Auteuil, the attorney general of the Conseil Souverain, protested at these arbitrary proceedings, Raudot heatedly replied that the assembly had not been called to deliberate but to listen. Eventually, however, Pontchartrain learned of the intendant's bullying and ordered him to hold a new assembly in 1706, where the election was to be "freely" decided by a plurality of voices. Although in later years Raudot's attitude towards the company's directors softened considerably, he never forgave Auteuil for this humiliation and for daring to challenge his authority. In fact he became convinced that the attorney general was the prime source of corruption in the Conseil Souverain and in the legal system generally.

Auteuil, the intendant informed Pontchartrain, had come to New France determined to be master of the legal system and had achieved his goal by building up a family cabal that interfered with cases, that controlled the subordinate legal officials through their fear, and perpetuated its independence by sowing discord between the governor and intendant. Under this 20-year tyranny, the Conseil Souverain had become a tool of the vested interests, a privileged forum in which "the military officials and the seigneurs of this country . . . think they can dispense justice themselves." A poor habitant who wished to bring a legitimate lawsuit against one of these persons was inevitably stymied by any number of devices: long delays over procedural points; the threat of having the case appealed to the Council of State in France; or the refusal of the governor or commandant to grant the required permission in cases involving officers. Raudot contended further, using as his example Auteuil's extra-legal activities in connection with a sensational land-title case which involved his sister-in-law, Madame de La Forest [CHARLOTTE-FRANÇOISE JUCHEREAU], that none of the foregoing abuses could be remedied until the attorney general was recalled. In this context, Pontchartrain could do little else but support his intendant and, in 1707, he dismissed Auteuil from all his functions. In full control at last, Raudot proceeded to bring every facet of the legal system under his personal supervision. He lifted cases from the provost courts at will, handling over 2,000 himself in one 14-month period, and he publicly humiliated judges he believed to be incompetent. As usual, his arbitrary actions provoked a steady stream of complaints to Versailles.

Raudot continued to search for fertile fields for reform. The large number of disputes over land-titles brought before him for judgement had convinced him that the seigneurial system was in need of some basic revisions. He submitted that since practically nothing in the mutual dealings of the Canadians was done according to proper legal procedures, the habitants were frequently without a clear title to their lands. Some had simple letters describing their land grants and others only their seigneur's word. Accordingly, there was scarcely a concession that might not be disputed or a contract that might not be arbitrarily altered by the seigneur. Indeed, Raudot continued, the seigneurs had taken advantage of the confusion to introduce higher rentals and to exact additional obligations. Some, for instance, had included in their contracts the privilege of reclaiming their land from commoners, an obligation which gave them a decided advantage when a tenant of theirs wished to sell his land, but which had no basis in the custom of Paris. The seigneurs had also maintained largely unused obligations, like the right to operate a communal oven, in the hope of converting it into a money payment later on. Furthermore, they had exerted their influence in the Conseil Souverain to forestall the publication of at least one decree that was harmful to their interests. In sum, Raudot believed that only royal intervention could crush these abuses.

He called for two decrees that would tip the scales in favour of the habitants. The first would confirm the property rights of all landholders, together with the boundaries of their concessions, on the basis of five years' tenancy. Such a measure, Raudot reassured the minister, was a fundamental prerequisite for the colony's growth. The second decree would establish a universal fixed rental (a very low one, which took no account whatsoever of good or bad land), with payment on a more flexible schedule than was previously required and with the choice of payment in money or produce left to the habitant. In addition, obligations like the right to reclaim land from commoners, which Raudot considered as particularly harmful to the habitant, would be eliminated and the seigneur's rights to a portion of his tenant's fish catch, his woodlands, and even his corvée labour, were to be substantially reduced. Raudot sought further to humble the seigneurs by proposing that they should help finance rural education and should be entirely responsible for conducting the yearly census. He complained, too, that the seigneuries in New France were far too large and underdeveloped.

It is clear that if Raudot's seigneurial recommendations had been implemented, the nature of the system would have been considerably altered. But they were not implemented. Although the minister definitely encouraged Raudot and actually set the machinery in motion for preparing the decrees, nothing was forthcoming. The officials in France perhaps felt that Raudot had exaggerated or that his solutions were too extreme. But the intendant had focused their attention on the shortcomings of the seigneurial system and had at least made clear the necessity for reform. Raudot must therefore have viewed with some satisfaction the promulgation of the Edicts of Marly in 1711 which endeavoured to deal with the problems of overextension and underdevelopment of landholdings.

Intrinsic to all of Raudot's proposals for the reform of colonial institutions was the implication that the intendant's range of authority needed to be substantially increased. As a centralizing paternalist, Raudot hungered for more power and this led almost inevitably to conflict with the governor general, who naturally viewed such ambition as a threat to his own authority.

Actually, considering Raudot's belligerent nature, the wonder is that it took three years for an explosion to occur. Yet during that time the interests of the two officials ran more or less in tandem; each was anxious to consolidate his newly acquired position; both agreed on the necessity of crushing the Auteuil cabal; they were united in their opposition to Lamothe de Cadillac's [LAUMET] schemes; and they were confronted by grave socio-economic questions that demanded their concerted action. Hence, in 1705, the intendant was able to write that Vaudreuil favoured the advancement of his son Jacques-Denis and that the governor was "a wise and reasonable man." But by 1708, this harmony had so completely disintegrated that during the last half of his term in office Raudot was consumed by his desire to bring Vaudreuil down.

The exact origins of the dispute are unclear; it seems likely, however, that some personal insult first ignited Raudot's combustible temper. At any rate, a series of satirical songs directed at the intendant and reportedly written by FRANÇOIS MARIAUCHAU d'Esgly, Vaudreuil's captain of the guards, put the issue beyond the limits of mature discussion. Raudot fired off ordinances threatening heavy fines for anyone caught singing these songs, but he suspected that Vaudreuil was paying boys to popularize them and he complained that the salon of Madame de Vaudreuil [Louise-Élisabeth JOYBERT] had become a gathering place for slanderers. The social élite of the colony rapidly divided into factions, the military caste generally supporting Vaudreuil and the administrative officials sympathizing with Raudot. In the autumn of 1708, after the inhabitants of Quebec had been treated to several exchanges of insults and to the arrest by Vaudreuil of the Sieur de Marigny, a Raudot supporter, the dispute became an administrative one. The intendant protested that Vaudreuil had encroached on his prerogatives by supporting the decision of an assembly of Montreal military officers to cast out his appointee as the new surgeon of the troops and to replace him with their own choice. Raudot was so agitated and was so anxious to inform the minister of Vaudreuil's conduct, that he dispatched a canoe in a frantic race to overtake the last vessel bound for France.

Although the canoe failed in its mission, Pontchartrain learned by word of mouth of the deteriorating relations between the colonial officials. In his dispatch of 1709, he condemned Vaudreuil for his actions in the surgeon incident, but he upbraided Raudot even more severely for repeatedly treating small matters with excessive passion. Unrepentant, the intendant responded with an incredibly peevish document, listing in no fewer than 80 folio pages all of Vaudreuil's failings. He even made certain that his complaints would be retroactive to 1705, by explaining away all of the compliments he had earlier bestowed on the governor. Included in his charges were many of those usually levelled by Canadian intendants against the governors: Vaudreuil profited from illegal trade; he employed his interpreters to procure gifts from the Indians and to sell them liquor; he favoured his many relatives and subordinate officers, protecting them from legitimate legal pursuit; he conducted the colony's defence badly and encouraged the engineer JACQUES LEVASSEUR de Néré to build useless fortifications at great expense; he undermined the confidence of the habitants in colonial institutions by appointing criminals as militia captains. But Raudot's major complaint was that Vaudreuil carried on the colony's affairs arbitrarily, ignoring the intendant's rights. He contended, for example, that Vaudreuil appointed inspectors to the fortifications without any consultation; worse still, all too prominent amongst these inspectors were persons whom Raudot described as "singers of songs." Only the minister, he declared, could correct such behaviour and avoid cause for future strife by clearly defining their respective spheres of authority.

As might be expected, Raudot offered a number of ideas on what such a definition should contain. His suggestions are not only interesting as an aspect of his dispute with Vaudreuil, but they reflect rather well the ambitious and condescending attitude of France's legal nobility toward the old nobility at the beginning of the 18th century. He began by explaining that when Jean Talon* had left New France the governor remained in sole command, exercising the intendant's powers for a three-year period. Through the ensuing decades, according to Raudot, successive intendants had striven to win back these powers, but in disputes the governor's voice was decisive. It was this that Raudot most objected to. Using Vaudreuil as his example, he argued that while the governors were normally equipped to carry out military tasks, they were too poorly educated to be entrusted with the final say in the colony's internal affairs. The intendant, on the other hand, was specifically trained for just these matters and was, moreover, naturally suited to be the minister's "confidential agent." It seemed only fitting then that the intendant should be free of contradiction on questions relating to commerce, justice, and public order—everything in short that was not primarily military. For example, in future he should share with the governor the power to appoint militia captains

but should be solely responsible for supervising corvées, appointing inspectors and issuing licences for non-military purposes. In other words, Raudot believed that since the intendant was best qualified to govern, his powers should be increased and freed from the governor's veto.

Despite the urgency of this plea for a realignment of administrative power, Raudot did not intend to remain in the colony to fight for it. In 1709, he asked for both his and Antoine-Denis' recall, citing Vaudreuil's hostility and the extremes of the Canadian climate as prime motives. But this sudden loss of enthusiasm for further service in New France in no way diminished his overall ambition, as was demonstrated by his request for the prestige post of honorary counsellor in the Court of Aids at Paris. Pontchartrain, replying in 1710, rejected his petition as preposterous but contributed the welcome news that Antoine-Denis was to return that year to fill the position of *Intendant des classes*—an advancement out of all proportion to his age and previous service. Jacques was to follow in 1711, but he had been warned that further favours to himself and his family hinged on his willingness to leave the colony on good terms with Vaudreuil. With his own interests thus clearly at stake, Raudot managed to swallow his pride and, with the Sieur de Marigny acting as intermediary, effected a reconciliation, even meeting the governor at social functions. But it was a truce of expediency and when he departed on the *Héros* in July 1711, his successor Michel Bégon* not yet arrived and the affairs of the intendancy entrusted to CLAIRAMBAULT d'Aigremont, it was clear to all that he had never really forgiven Vaudreuil.

Thus the last three years of Raudot's intendancy had been unproductive of the initiative which characterized the first three and, from the standpoint of administrative harmony, they were a failure. Yet he could look back on his Canadian experience with great personal satisfaction. For one thing, it had paved the way for his advancement. On his return to France, he was named a chief clerk in the Marine with special responsibility for war prizes. He was also a director of maritime commerce and, by 1722, had even fulfilled his great ambition to become honorary counsellor in the Court of Aids. In 1719, moreover, he had been appointed a counsellor of the Marine, a position of great honour and importance. Scattered evidence also exists to indicate that he augmented his fortune in New France. Certainly his enemies, who were legion, accused him of profiting from manipulations involving card money as well as from illegal trade. But better evidence comes from Raudot's own feeble explanations when ordered by a French court in 1722 to account for 281,000

Raudot

livres in his possession. His statement that 113,000 *livres* were the product of savings from his salary and the sale of certain household goods prior to leaving for New France hardly rings true, especially when viewed against his many complaints of financial insolvency when he was in the colony. Yet Raudot's greatest cause for satisfaction derived from the advancement of his family in the royal service. By 1710 Antoine-Denis was well on the way to prominence in the highest circles of the legal nobility; de Chalus, who had come to the colony at 19 years of age as an ensign, left in his mid-twenties as a captain; likewise, the Chevalier Dussy, who had arrived without rank, left in 1708 on the brink of a lieutenancy. In this area, Raudot had succeeded admirably.

It is more difficult to assess the overall success or failure of Raudot's intendancy. He was unquestionably one of the most intelligent and dynamic administrators ever sent to New France. With the incorruptible will of a born authoritarian, he endeavoured to examine each colonial institution in terms of its ultimate utility. When these investigations uncovered some privilege or practice that in his judgement tended to detract from the colony's prospects for development, he sought vigorously to suppress it. His incisive dispatches on the judicial and seigneurial systems testify to his energy in this regard. Yet, as students of the seigneurial regime point out, he was guilty of gross exaggerations. Furthermore, he had a poor grasp of what was possible, often allowing his reformist zeal to blind him to the subtleties of Canadian conditions. This serious failing led him to make over-simplified recommendations that were too radical for the officials in France to adopt. But Raudot was also victimized by his own violent nature, which turned his relations with other officials into a series of petty squabbles. He considered any disagreement a personal affront and, as was the case in his relations with Vaudreuil, he inevitably allowed his emotions to take complete command. In the long run, perhaps his greatest contribution to New France was as an observer. For he focused attention on the workings of Canadian institutions and offered many lucid, if derogatory, descriptions of the colony's inhabitants. His dispatches are amongst the best sources available for the historian of the epoch.

DONALD J. HORTON

[The information on Raudot's family background and early career is based on the articles by Dionne, Dubé, Le Jeune, and Régis Roy [*see* below], plus material from the *BRH*. But much important additional information, e.g. the fact that Raudot was nine years

older than all the secondary sources indicate and the details concerning Raudot's financial situation on his return from Canada, is found in BN, MS, Cabinet des titres, P.O. 28,921, 13, 23, 25, 31; Dossiers bleus, 557, 14,680.

Many of the data on Raudot's seigneurial, judicial and administrative recommendations come from AN, Col., C¹¹ᴬ, 22–32, 34, 36, 110, 125, and C¹¹ᴳ, 1–6. It is supplemented, however, by AQ, NF, Registres du Cons. sup., and by Raudot's ordinances [*see*: *Édits ord.*; *Ord. comm.* (P.-G. Roy), II, 330–34]. *Documents relating to seigniorial tenure* (Munro) contains a shrewd assessment of his seigneurial proposals.

On Raudot's personal life and character, *see*: PAC, FM 8, F 61; Juchereau, *Annales* (Jamet); Guy Frégault, "Politique et politiciens au début du XVIIIᵉ siècle," *Écrits du Canada français* (Montréal), XI (1961), 91–208.

AN, Col., B, 25–33, and C¹¹ᴬ (*supra*) contain documents pertaining to Raudot's quarrel with Vaudreuil. Moreover, the following works treat this dispute in an interesting manner: Guy Frégault, *Le grand marquis, Pierre de Rigaud de Vaudreuil et la Louisiane* (Montréal, 1952), 69–72; F. M. Hammang, *The Marquis de Vaudreuil, New France at the beginning of the eighteenth century* (Bruges, 1938), 81–108, 133–38, 182–87; Y. F. Zoltvany, "Philippe de Rigaud de Vaudreuil, governor of New France (1703–1725)," unpublished Ph.D. thesis, University of Alberta, 1963. D.J.H.]

AN, Col., C¹³ᴬ, 2–4; D²ᶜ, 49, part.2; F³, 8–9; Marine, C¹, 157. ASQ, Lettres, N, P. PAC, FM 8, A 6. Charlevoix, *History* (Shea), V, 285–94. "Correspondance de Vaudreuil," APQ *Rapport, 1938–39*, 10–179; *1939–40*, 355–463; *1942–43*, 399–443; *1946–47*, 371–460; *1947–48*, 137–339. *Documents relating to Canadian currency during the French period* (Shortt), I, 227, 231. *JR* (Thwaites), LXIX, 301. *Jug. et délib.*, V, VI. PAC *Report, 1911*. Le Jeune, *Dictionnaire*.

Garneau, *Histoire du Canada*, II, 270–73. Harris, *The seigneurial system*, 34–35, 68–71, 157–58. Lanctot, *History of Canada*, II, 153–60, 201–21. [C.-M.] Raudot, *Deux intendants du Canada* (Auxerre, 1854). E. R. Adair, "The French-Canadian seigneury," *CHR*, XXXV (1954), 187–207. N.-E. Dionne, "Les Raudot; intendants de la Nouvelle-France," *RC*, XXXI (1895), 567–610. J.-C. Dubé, "Origine sociale des intendants de la Nouvelle-France," *Social history* (Ottawa), II (November 1968), 18–33. Guy Frégault, "La Compagnie de la Colonie," *Revue de l'université d'Ottawa*, XXX (1960), 5–29, 127–49; "Le Régime seigneurial et l'expansion de la colonisation dans le bassin du Saint-Laurent au dix-huitième siècle," CHA *Report, 1944*, 61–73. Lionel Groulx, "Le Gallicanisme au Canada sous Louis XIV," *RHAF*, I (1947), 54–90. Robert La Roque de Roquebrune, "La direction de la Nouvelle-France par le Ministère de la Marine," *RHAF*, VI (1952–53), 470–88. Régis Roy, "Les Intendants de la Nouvelle-France," *RSCT*, 2nd ser., IX (1903), sect.ɪ, 65–107; "Jacques et Antoine-Denis Raudot," *BRH*, IX (1903), 157–59; "Quelques notes sur les intendants," *BRH*, XXXII (1926),

442–43. H. M. Thomas, "The relations of governor and intendant in the old régime," *CHR*, XVI (1935), 27–40.

REGNARD DUPLESSIS, GEORGES, receiver of the Admiralty, treasurer of Marine, general and special agent for the Compagnie de la Colonie; b. in the province of Champagne; buried 31 Oct. 1714 at Quebec.

Duplessis came to New France in 1689 to work in the offices of the treasurer of Marine at Quebec. "An orderly man, good at calculating," he soon received various promotions. On 27 Oct. 1698 he was appointed by Champigny [BOCHART] receiver of the Admiralty—the clerk whose task it was to collect dues to be paid to the admiral—and on 22 June 1699 he received in addition the post of treasurer of Marine. Vaudreuil [RIGAUD] paid him this tribute: "I can assure you that he carried out his duties here in a manner that satisfies everyone."

In 1705 Duplessis was chosen, with Lotbinière [CHARTIER], to manage the affairs of the Compagnie de la Colonie, which was in difficulties. He took advantage of this situation to settle certain debts that he owed the company. An inquiry was held, and an ordinance from Intendant Begon* sentenced Duplessis to make restitution to the shareholders of the money he owed them. Duplessis got out of this situation by an arrangement with the company, which led the king to say: "He [Duplessis] must consider himself fortunate to settle his differences with the company so cheaply." This escape did not put a stop to his scheming, but he fell more and more into discredit.

In January 1713 all the treasury papers were destroyed when the intendant's palace in Quebec burned. Duplessis was held responsible for the loss of the card money, treasury bonds, bills in hand, and vouchers for expenditures—all the treasury papers—and he was obliged to make reimbursement. He died on 30 Oct. 1714, before he had finished payment, and his widow had to pay more than a million *livres*.

Georges Regnard Duplessis took part in the various commercial activities of the colony. He was also an enterprising seigneur. In October 1696 Frontenac [Buade*] granted him a piece of land in Acadia, but he did not farm it. It was as the seigneur of Lauson that he revealed his qualities. He bought this seigneury on 14 Oct. 1699 from Thomas Bertrand for 5,500 *livres* and soon showed himself to be a dynamic seigneur. In 1702 a decision by the Conseil Supérieur authorized Duplessis to repossess those lands in the seigneury which had not been improved. He had the boundaries of his property marked out, set up a court, had a bannal mill built, and where necessary obtained confirmation of his rights of precedence. When reverses of fortune forced him to sell this seigneury in March 1714, he obtained 40,000 *livres* for it from Étienne Charest.

Duplessis had married Marie Le Roy, who was originally from Chevreuse near Paris. They had seven children of whom only four lived. One of them, François-Xavier*, was a famous Jesuit preacher of his time.

NIVE VOISINE

AN, Col., B, 27, f.244; C^{11A}, 26, f.233; 33, f.300. "Correspondance de Vaudreuil," APQ *Rapport, 1942–43*, 407–13. *Documents relating to Canadian currency during the French period* (Shortt), I, 89. *Jug. et délib.* P.-G. Roy, *Inv. concessions*, I, 114; III, 97; IV, 124f.; *Inventaire des procès-verbaux des grands voyers conservés aux archives de la province de Québec* (6v., Beauceville, 1923–32), II, 204. Tanguay, *Dictionnaire*, I, 511f.; III, 544. J.-E. Roy, *Histoire de la seigneurie de Lauzon* (5v., Lévis, 1897–1904), II, 1–3. Guy Frégault, "La Compagnie de la colonie," *Revue de l'université d'Ottawa*, XXX (1960), 127–49. "Madame veuve Regnard Duplessis," *BRH*, XLII (1936), 611. "Regnard Duplessis, trésorier de la Marine," *BRH*, XXIX (1923), 362. P.-G. Roy, "La famille Regnard Duplessis," *BRH*, XV (1909), 282–85; "Les trésoriers de la marine à Québec," *BRH*, XXXV (1929), 635–37.

RÉMY (Rémy de Saint Rémy), PIERRE, priest, Sulpician, first priest to be ordained in Montreal, ecclesiastical superior of the sisters of the Congrégation de Notre-Dame, bursar of the Saint-Sulpician seminary in Montreal, parish priest of Notre-Dame de Montréal and of Lachine, missionary at Sainte-Anne, chaplain and ecclesiastical superior of the Montreal Hôtel-Dieu, school teacher, procurator of the Montreal seminary; b. 1636, in the parish of Saint-Sauveur, Paris, son of Michel Rémy, king's counsellor and "paymaster of the *gendarmerie* of France," and Élisabeth Le Moyne; d. 24 Feb. 1726 in Montreal.

On 14 July 1666, Rémy entered the seminary of Saint-Sulpice in Paris, and studied there until he left for New France as a sub-deacon in 1672. During his first four years in the colony he taught at the school for boys in Montreal and worked as bursar at the seminary. In October 1674 he was fined successively 10 and 50 *livres* for refusing to appear in court over the Salignac* affair. In May 1676, he was ordained a priest in the Montreal Hôtel-Dieu by Bishop François de LAVAL, and accepted the responsibilities of ecclesiastical superior of the sisters of the Congrégation de Notre-Dame. In July 1680, he became parish priest of Notre-Dame de Montréal, and in November of that year was appointed parish priest of Lachine, an office which included serving the mission of

Renaud Dubuisson

Sainte-Anne. His first major task in Lachine was to give some semblance of order to the parish records, which were in complete disarray. In 1685, after living in a mill for some time, he suggested that a presbytery be built, and covered the initial costs of construction with his own funds. Two years later he took in a boarder, Jean-Baptiste POTTIER, who served the parish as church cantor, school master, notary, and parish secretary.

In 1688 Rémy was appointed chaplain of the Montreal Hôtel-Dieu. In August 1689 the massacre of Lachine took place and Rémy had many of the orphaned children of the parish placed with the sisters of the Congrégation in Montreal. Within five years he was able to convince the sisters to re-establish their convent in Lachine. In 1691, Rémy was appointed ecclesiastical superior of the Montreal Hôtel-Dieu. By the time he returned to his parish in October 1692, he had significantly reduced the number of taverns operating in Montreal.

Rémy now gave his attention to the writing of an abridged catechism to prepare children for their first communion, and copied dictionaries of the Algonkian and Illinois languages for the use of young missionaries. In 1703 he relinquished his responsibilities at the Sainte-Anne mission, and, in June of 1705, decided to retire as parish priest of Lachine and live in the Montreal seminary. However, he enjoyed only a few weeks rest. There was a shortage of Sulpicians in the colony and François VACHON de Belmont, superior of the Montreal seminary, sent Rémy back to Lachine on 17 July. During the following year Rémy and many other priests experienced difficulty in collecting the tithe, and they finally appealed to Intendant JACQUES RAUDOT to issue an ordinance on the subject.

Rémy continued as parish priest of Lachine until 29 Sept. 1706, when he installed his successor, Michel de Villermaula. He remained in Lachine for one more year, assisting Villermaula during the services and replacing him when the new priest was in Montreal. Rémy was suffering from old age, however, and could hardly muster enough strength to raise the chalice. He finally returned to the Montreal seminary, where he served as procurator of the order until death took him at the age of 90, in his 51st year in the priesthood.

Pierre Rémy's life was truly one of devotion and fortitude. He sacrificed the comfortable life of a counsellor's son in Paris for the challenges of a frontier settlement on Lac Saint-Louis. He was held in high esteem by his superiors in both Montreal and Paris, and was undoubtedly loved and respected by his parishioners.

C. J. RUSS

ASSM, Biographies: Pierre Rémy; Correspondance générale, 2ᵉ partie, lettres à M. Tronson. *Jug. et délib.*, I, 862, 866, 867. Eccles, *Frontenac*, 68f. Henri Gauthier, *La Compagnie de Saint-Sulpice au Canada* (Montréal, 1912), 84, 100, 107, 112, 113, 116, 119, 121, 126; *Sulpitiana* (Montréal, 1926), 253f.

RENAUD DUBUISSON, JACQUES-CHARLES, commander in the west, town major of Trois-Rivières; b. in Paris, 1666; d. in Trois-Rivières, 1739.

Dubuisson came to Canada in 1685–86 and was a cadet until 1696: he became a half-pay ensign in that year and was made lieutenant in 1698. He was assistant town major at Quebec in 1704. In 1707 he was in temporary trouble there, charged with duelling. RIGAUD de Vaudreuil absolved him of this charge and in 1709 recommended him for promotion. From this time until his death Dubuisson was consistently praised for his military and administrative work.

In September 1710 Dubuisson was sent to Detroit to act as commandant until DAUPHIN de La Forest, who was ill, could take command. During the next year Detroit was in a constant state of friction, for Lamothe Cadillac [LAUMET], the former commandant, was still at the post and was reluctant to give up his authority and privileges. Vaudreuil complimented Dubuisson on his skill in handling the delicate situation.

In 1712 Dubuisson took part in an attack on the Fox Indians, his most important military operation. Early in the spring the bands of the Fox chiefs Lamyma and PEMOUSSA joined others of their tribe already settled at Detroit and soon after received some of their allies, the Mascoutens, who were fleeing from a war party of Ottawas and Potawatomis. When the latter arrived they insisted on attacking and Dubuisson, unable to avert the clash and in view of the threatening attitude of the Foxes, decided to support the traditional allies of the French.

They besieged the Fox camp for 19 days. Heavy firing and lack of food caused many Fox deaths. Several councils were held but no peace could be arranged until finally the enemy escaped, going north a few miles to where they were forced to make a final stand. When the Foxes surrendered, most of the male captives were butchered, and Dubuisson reported the total losses as 1,000 enemy, 60 allies, and 1 Frenchman. This victory established Dubuisson's reputation both at Quebec and among the Indians so that for 20 years he maintained a great deal of influence in the unsettled affairs of the west.

Dubuisson returned to Quebec in the fall of 1712 but, because La Forest was again ill, he continued to command at Detroit until the summer of 1715, when he was replaced by Jacques-Charles de SABREVOIS. By then Dubuisson had been promoted captain. In 1716 he was again at Quebec, in garrison, and that autumn he received permission to go to France to settle some private affairs.

In the spring of 1718 Dubuisson, having returned to the colony, was sent by Vaudreuil to the Miamis to convince them to return to their old villages on the St Joseph River (Michigan). The Miamis had moved to get away from the Foxes, but the new location (in what is now Indiana) displeased the French for it was uncomfortably close to British traders, who offered better prices. For the next ten years Dubuisson's moves are hard to follow. He did manage to persuade the Miamis to move back to their Michigan villages and at one time he commanded "at the post he established among the Miamis and at the one among the Ouyatanons [Weas]." In 1722 FRANÇOIS-MARIE BISSOT de Vinsenne was in charge of the Ouyatanons post, "under the orders of Sieur Dubuisson," and a memoir of 1723–25 also lists Dubuisson as commander of a Miami post; however, three and perhaps four posts were either known by that name or were in Miami territory.

By 1728 Dubuisson seems to have been at Michilimackinac, for a report of September 1728 blamed LE MARCHAND de Lignery for poor leadership in an attack on the Foxes, although Dubuisson was said not to have been at fault. In October 1729 Dubuisson became commandant at Michilimackinac and the following summer led a large attack on the Foxes. A memoir of 1730 reported that the expedition was a failure, but Dubuisson felt that though the Foxes were not crushed, they would starve to death before spring. Michilimackinac at this time was the leading western post: "It is to Michilimackinac that the voyageurs from all these places come to sell their furs and to buy corn and canoes. . . ." TESTARD de Montigny replaced Dubuisson there that autumn. Dubuisson was old, had been wounded three times, and claimed that the fish diet at Michilimackinac had affected his health.

Dubuisson had married Gabrielle Pinet (Desmarest) in 1699; they had five girls and one boy. His wife died in 1715 and on 29 Oct. 1717 he married Louise, daughter of Jacques Bizard* of Montreal. He was appointed town major of Trois-Rivières in April 1733, and in March 1734 he was made a knight of the order of Saint-Louis, an honour which he had long sought. He died at Trois-Rivières on 24 Dec. 1739 and was buried in the chapel of Sainte-Geneviève. Vaudreuil's comment of 1720 provides a good assessment of Dubuisson's reputation: "[He] always distinguished himself on every occasion as much against the savages as against the English."

DONALD CHAPUT

AN, Col., C¹¹ᴬ, 33, f.215; 38, f.164; 44, f.366; 51, f.158; 52, f.186; C¹¹ᴱ, 13, f.140; Marine, B¹, 50, f.496. CTG, manuscrits reliés in-folio, no.210d, f.14. Charlevoix, *History* (Shea), V, 256–65. "Correspondance de Vaudreuil," APQ *Rapport, 1942–43*, 436; *1947–48*, 160–62, 164, 225, 237, 260, 267, 269, 334. *Michigan Pioneer Coll.*, XXXIII, 483–85, 495–97, 506–8, 510–12, 517, 528–52, 554, 561, 572. P.-G. Roy, "Ce que Callières pensait de nos officiers," 321–33. Wis. State Hist. Soc. *Coll.*, V, 94; XVI, 293–98, 311–12, 382–83, 395–400; XVII, 108–9.

Gagnon, "Noms propres au Canada français," 177. Le Jeune, *Dictionnaire*. Massicotte, "Répertoire des engagements pour l'Ouest," 238–39. P.-G. Roy, *Les officiers d'état-major*, 74–80. Tanguay, *Dictionnaire*. Jouve, *Les Franciscains et le Canada: aux Trois-Rivières*, 144, 156–57. Aegidius Fauteux, "La famille Renaud Du Buisson," *BRH*, XXXVII (1931), 670–75. J.-E. Roy, "Le patronage dans l'armée," *BRH*, II (1896), 115. P.-G. Roy, "Jacques Bizard, major de Montréal." *BRH*, XXII (1916), 291–303.

RENDER, THOMAS, HBC sloop-master; master of Moose Fort, 1730–31; fl. 1729–34.

Thomas Render was sent from London in 1729 in response to a request for a mate to keep "decorum" aboard the *Beaver* sloop while her master, William BEVAN, was ashore trading with the Indians at his customary winter quarters on the Eastmain River. The following year, however, it was decided to establish a post on Moose River (an area unoccupied by the HBC since Pierre de Troyes*'s exploit of 1686). The London committee made Render master of the new sloop *Moose River* [I], which would be the transport link between Albany Fort and the new Moose Fort. The latter was sited by Render one mile above the original fort.

Because he himself could not take command at the new fort, Joseph ADAMS made Render "chief over the men"; John Jewer, the carpenter, was given charge of building operations. Apparently the discipline imposed by Render caused such unrest that in 1731 Adams replaced him by Jewer. How far the change was justified is questionable; afterwards Render was remembered by some as an honest man who would not allow his subordinates to be rogues.

In 1732, on instructions from London, Render sailed the *Moose River* (renamed *Churchill*) to Churchill River and, until he returned to England in 1734, was employed in transport work between Churchill and York Forts.

ALICE M. JOHNSON

Renon

HBRS, XXV (Davies and Johnson) contains the Moose journal (7 Sept. 1730 to 9 Aug. 1731) kept by Render.

RENON, MICHEL DU PONT DE. *See* Du Pont

REPENTIGNY, JEAN-BAPTISTE LEGARDEUR DE. *See* Legardeur

REPENTIGNY, PIERRE LEGARDEUR DE. *See* Legardeur

RICE, JACOB, minister in St John's, Newfoundland, between 1705 and 1727; b. 1683, younger son of Thomas Rice of Newcastle, County Cardigan, Wales; d. 1728.

Rice took his B.A. degree from Magdalen Hall, Oxford, in 1703, and the following year was appointed to a remote curacy in Cardiganshire. When it was decided to recall John Jackson from Newfoundland in 1705, Rice was appointed in his place by the Bishop of London. The Society for the Propagation of the Gospel proposed to sponsor Rice, but he failed to produce the required testimonials before his departure. In 1709 Rice returned to England, and on 30 May offered his services as a missionary to the society. His offer was refused—once more on the score of the lack of suitable testimonials—and the society declined to admit any responsibility where he was concerned. The society's objection to Rice seems to have been a purely technical one, since, as far as can be judged, his behaviour was irreproachable and his religious commitment unquestioned. Indeed there are in the society's records reports from merchants trading in Newfoundland that Rice lived soberly and peaceably, that he discharged his ministry with care and diligence, and that he set up a school for educating the children of the community.

Rice returned to Newfoundland as a free-lance minister. In 1712 he was having difficulties collecting his allowance of fish. Although he was supposed to get 3 quintals of "dry merchantable fish" from every shallop and a lesser quantity from smaller boats, he received a bare 100 quintals a year. The commodore of the convoy, Sir Nicholas Trevanion, confirmed his salary, and was evidently impressed by Rice's fitness for the post. On 20 June 1727, Rice was appointed chaplain to the garrison at Placentia.

Rice died in September 1728, and so was probably the same man as a Jacob Rice, "clerk," who died in September 1728 in North Cray, Kent, England.

Carson I. A. Ritchie

PRO, C.O. 194/3, 195/5, 324/36, p.60. USPG, Journal of SPG, I, 18 May 1705, 15 June 1705, 17 Aug. 1705, 16 Sept. 1709; App.A, 384; App.B, 63; Committee, I. *Classified digest of the records of the Society for the Propagation of the Gospel in foreign parts 1701–1892* (London, 1893). *Index to the Act Books of the Archbishops of Canterbury, 1663–1859,* compiled E. H. W. Dunkin, extended and edited Claude Jenkins and E. A. Fry (2v., British Record Soc., LV, LXIII, 1929, 1938), II. PRO, *Acts of P.C., col. ser., Unbound papers; CSP, Col., 1706–8, 1712–14, 1726–27.*

Alumni Oxonienses, ed. Joseph Foster (4v., Oxford, [1891–92?]). John Bacon, *Liber regis, vel thesaurus rerum ecclesiasticarum* (new ed., London, 1786). Lounsbury, *British fishery at Nfld.* Prowse, *History of Nfld.*

RICHARDS, MICHAEL, captain and engineer in Newfoundland between 1697 and 1703; later brigadier-general and surveyor-general of the Ordnance; b. 1673, son of Jacob Richards; d. 1722.

Richards received a lieutenant's commission in 1692 and saw service in Flanders with the artillery train. In 1697 he was commissioned to go with the expedition to Newfoundland under Gibsone and Norris*. On 7 June he landed at St John's and was ordered to survey the harbour with a view to fortifying it. Work commenced under considerable difficulties: Richards' superior, Gibsone, proved to be over exacting; Mr Leavis, Richards' assistant, contrived to be always drunk; the seamen were unwilling to be commanded by an army officer; and the only available equipment was in a deplorable condition. By July the fort began to assume massive proportions and 600 palisades a day were going into the fortifications; nevertheless Gibsone continued to accuse Richards of negligence, and repeatedly threatened to send him back to England. As it happened the entire expedition returned to England in October 1697, leaving only some 300 men in garrison under Thomas Handasyde.

Richards probably returned to Newfoundland in 1700 with Commodore Fairborne. When the latter suspended the garrison commander, Lieutenant William Lilburne, who had been found guilty of gross cowardice in avoiding a duel with Arthur Holdsworth, Richards signed a deposition supporting Fairborne's action. Richards found Newfoundland in a disturbed state: "the fishing so bad and debts so great," and the "perpetual war" between the inhabitants and the annual fishing fleets continuing as in former years.

For the next three years Richards continued his work as engineer in Newfoundland. A redoubt was built covering the entrance to St John's harbour, with the assistance of seamen from the fleet, and of the inhabitants, who were paid "reasonable wages." The work provided something for the inhabitants to do when the fishing season was over, but its progress was interrupted by shortage of material. Richards persuaded trading masters to bring out building stone from England free of charge as ballast in their ships. The local stone had proved unsatisfactory. Nevertheless the work was so delayed that in 1701 Richards had to send home several artificers for whom no work could be found as well as an officer to make complaints on his behalf.

Richards had hoped to return to England in the fall of 1701, and was chagrined at his failure to do so: "for I want to return from this dismal place." He found his fellow officers unscrupulous, uncouth, and much inclined to settle disagreements at sword point. By May 1702, Richards was captain of the Independent Company in Newfoundland. At that date many of the men had been in Newfoundland for six years; they were discontented and difficult to command. As only shirts and shoes had been sent out from England, Richards himself had to buy greatcoats for the men so that they could continue their work on the fortifications. Allowances for all ranks were very small; it was difficult to cook or to brew beer, and the inhabitants proved of little help in forwarding the works. In 1702 Richards wrote asking to be sent home. "I can't but mention that the extremity of the last winter took from me the use of my limbs which I cannot reasonably propose to recover here." He suggested that his assistant could finish the fortifications without him. The Board of Trade did not listen sympathetically to his plea but wrote telling him that he could not leave his post for so long, "especially considering that it is now a time of warr and danger, and that, as you write, the soldiers are too apt to mutiny or desert."

Richards was to have taken part in the attack on Placentia (Plaisance) led by Vice-Admiral GRAYDON, and was present at the council of war on 3 Sept. 1703 when it was decided to abandon the expedition. Two weeks later, having put Lieutenant LLOYD in charge of the post, he sailed home with Graydon.

Although he had now left Newfoundland for good, Richards continued to urge the development of the colony for war purposes; he advocated stricter discipline and more prompt relief of the garrison. Unlike Lloyd, who thought that the garrison commander at St John's should have supreme authority over the land forces, Richards believed that the annual naval commodore should be the commander-in-chief in Newfoundland. The Board of Trade heeded Richards' advice, and the policy of spasmodic naval rule in Newfoundland was prolonged. On 29 July 1717, as a member of the Board of Ordnance, Richards suggested that the garrison at Placentia should be reduced and the non-fishing element discouraged. On 10 Feb. 1719, he urged that fortification stone should be taken, as ballast, from England to Placentia. On 3 April 1721, shortly before his death, he was still pressing the needs of the post.

After leaving Newfoundland, Richards was a successful commander of the train in the War of the Spanish Succession. He was appointed chief engineer of Great Britain in 1711; in 1712 he was promoted to brigadier-general; and on 2 Dec. 1714 he was made surveyor-general of the Ordnance—a post of considerable responsibility. Richards died, unmarried, on 5 Feb. 1721/22; he was buried at Old Charlton, Kent.

CARSON I. A. RITCHIE

BM, Stowe MSS 463 (Richards' journal 1696–97), 464 (Richards' letter book 1700–3). PRO, C.O. 194/2; *CSP, Col., 1697–98, 1700, 1701, 1702, 1702–3, 1704–5, 1706–8, 1716–17, 1717–18, 1719–20, 1720–21.* Dalton, *English army lists*, III. *DNB.* O. F. G. Hogg, *The Royal Arsenal* (2v., London, 1963). Whitworth Porter, *History of the corps of royal engineers* (2v., London, 1889), I. Prowse, *History of Nfld.*

RICHETERRE, MICHEL DESSAILLIANT, *dit. See* DESSAILLIANT

RIGAUD DE VAUDREUIL, PHILIPPE DE, chevalier and marquis, musketeer, commander of the troops, naval captain, governor of Montreal, governor general of New France, governor of Revel in Languedoc; knight, commander, and grand cross of the order of Saint-Louis; born probably in the family château near Revel, *c.* 1643; d. in Quebec, 10 Oct. 1725.

The Rigauds were an old noble family of the province of Languedoc. The fief of Vaudreuille from which they derived their title was located in the seneschalsy of Lauragais near Toulouse and had come into their possession by marriage in the 12th century. By the late Middle Ages they appear to have enjoyed both wealth and prestige, but as their numerous domains were gradually alienated they receded into the ranks of the provincial nobility. Philippe's father Jean-Louis de Rigaud held the minor rank of cornet in the French army and was also the commandant of the arrière-ban of his seneschalsy. Nothing is known of his wife, Marie de Chateauverdun, except that she was of noble birth.

Five daughters and five sons were born of their marriage. Anne, the fourth girl, married Adhémar de Lantagnac and their son later served in the troops in Canada and Île Royale (Cape Breton Island). Two of the five brothers, Antoine and François-Aimé, entered the church, and the other

Rigaud de Vaudreuil

three, Arnaud the eldest, Philippe I, and the youngest Philippe, joined the army. Arnaud became captain of a company of the king's light horse in 1668. Philippe I began his career with the Musketeers and ultimately rose to the rank of captain with the French guards. Philippe also joined the Musketeers in 1672 and served with them during the next 15 years.

The Musketeers were one of the *élite* corps of the French army. They were divided into two companies of 500 men, all noblemen or soldiers of proven merit, and were attached to the royal household. Each company was commanded by a lieutenant-captain. The rank of captain was held by the king himself, a signal honour of which the Musketeers showed themselves worthy recipients by their gallantry in battle. War with Holland was just breaking out when Vaudreuil joined their ranks in 1672 and the two companies were sent to Flanders where they were involved in several major engagements in the years that followed. On these occasions Vaudreuil appears to have fought bravely and at times with distinction. According to the historian Charlevoix* it was the role he played in the attack on Valenciennes in 1677 that won him the king's favour. Noeufville, the 18th century historian of the French army, mentions the courage displayed by "Monsieur le chevalier de Vaubreuil [*sic*] mousquetaire" at Ypres in 1678. Following the Dutch war, Vaudreuil served for some time in Germany as aide-de-camp. Thus, by the time he left for Canada, he was a tested veteran of several European campaigns.

Except for these details about his military career, nothing else is known about Vaudreuil's years in France but certain inferences can be made about them from subsequent evidence. His schooling, for instance, must have been quite rudimentary. Only five books—including a book of devotions and the *Adventures of Robinson Crusoe*—were listed in the inventory of his belongings that was made following his death. In 1709 the intendant, JACQUES RAUDOT, described him as a military man who had studied little and who was ignorant of all subjects except military ones. It is true that Vaudreuil always remained primarily a soldier and that he tended to judge men and situations in military terms. He respected and feared the Iroquois and to a lesser degree the other Indian tribes; but he sometimes gives the impression of having contempt for the inhabitants of the English colonies, particularly those of New England whose attack on Quebec in 1690 had failed so completely.

The decision to emigrate to Canada came in 1687. Despite the fact that the Vaudreuil estate was sizable Philippe himself was poor, for by virtue of the law of primogeniture the family fortune had been inherited by Arnaud, the eldest son. Without money prospects of advancement in the French army were dim, for all commissions above that of lieutenant had to be bought, usually for large sums of money. Indeed, from the fragmentary evidence that is available on the history of the family in the late 17th century, it appears that Philippe I had to seduce Arnaud's wife, Antoinette de Colombet, to obtain the 78,000 *livres* that he required to purchase his captaincy in the guards. As for Philippe, rather than spend the rest of his life as a minor officer, he accepted an appointment as commander of the troops in Canada. His duties consisted of drilling and maintaining in discipline the several companies of soldiers that were being sent to the colony to fight the Iroquois. But already the government considered that he qualified for a higher position. In March 1687, Governor BRISAY de Denonville was instructed to appoint either Vaudreuil or Louis-Hector de CALLIÈRE, the governor of Montreal, to command in the colony in his own absence.

These instructions indicate a degree of confidence in Vaudreuil that was somewhat premature at this stage of his career. His years in France had been spent as a subordinate officer and it soon became evident that he was not qualified to step immediately into positions of high responsibility. He was acting governor of Montreal in 1689 when the massacre of Lachine occurred and his errors of judgement on this occasion were at least partly responsible for the disaster. There being a lull in hostilities, he had allowed the population of the outlying settlements to return to their isolated homesteads instead of obliging them to remain close to the forts for protection. In the hours that followed the raid his literal interpretation of Denonville's orders to remain on the defensive cost him two excellent opportunities to counterattack the Iroquois and to inflict heavy casualties on them.

When acting in a purely military capacity, however, the role that he knew best, Vaudreuil showed that he was a brave and capable soldier. He led several expeditions against the Iroquois in the 1690s and twice, at Repentigny and at the Long Sault, decisively defeated their war parties. His superiors without exception were greatly impressed by his zeal and his devotion to his duties. Frontenac [Buade*] praised his "incredible diligence" during the great campaign of 1696 against the Iroquois. The intendant, BOCHART de Champigny, for his part described the commander of the troops as "a gentleman of distinction and merit." In 1698 the court, too, recognized in signal fashion Vaudreuil's distinguished services during the Iroquois war by granting him the cross of Saint-Louis, one of France's most coveted military decorations.

Encouraged by these indications that he stood in high favour in both the mother country and the colony, the *chevalier* decided to apply for the position of governor general when Frontenac died on 28 Nov. 1698. In a letter to Jérôme de Pontchartrain, the minister of Marine, which was not very elegant in its handwriting and spelling, he described his record, gave the names of several officers under whom he had served in France as references, and asked for the appointment. His request was taken overseas by AMIOT de Vincelotte, who was urged to make speed, but it was already too late when he reached Versailles. AUGUSTIN LE GARDEUR de Courtemanche, the envoy of Callière on a similar mission, had preceded him and delivered his dispatches to François de Callières, a diplomat of note and one of the king's private secretaries. The latter was able to see Louis XIV and to obtain the appointment for his brother before Pontchartrain could present Vaudreuil's request. As a consolation, the commander of the troops was named governor of Montreal. He served in this capacity conscientiously for the next four years and gained the administrative experience which he lacked.

When Callière died on 26 May 1703, Vaudreuil immediately applied for the vacant position. This time, however, he did not merely state his request in a letter of application. During the previous months he had rallied several supporters to his cause, and these people now came forward to speak on his behalf. Among his most enthusiastic partisans were the Sulpician seigneurs of Montreal who had been greatly impressed by the steps he had taken to have the sale of liquor to the Indians prohibited in 1702. Abbé Lechassier, superior of the seminary of Saint-Sulpice in Paris, warmly recommended Vaudreuil to Pontchartrain and also asked the cardinal-archbishop of Paris, Louis-Antoine de Noailles, to mention the *chevalier*'s application to his brother, Anne-Jules, Duc de Noailles and a marshal of France, who wielded great influence in court circles. Ultimately, however, it was Pontchartrain who won the governorship for Vaudreuil by recommending him to Louis XIV as a man who not only would maintain order in the colony but also would eliminate the abuses which had crept into the administration under previous governors.

Basically, the appointment was a good one. By his exploits during the war with the Iroquois, Vaudreuil had won the respect and confidence of the Indians, in whose eyes courage was one of the supreme virtues. The people of New France too were happy with the nomination, for the new governor was a popular and well-liked figure in the colony. As commander of the troops and as governor of Montreal he had been both firm and gentle in his command and had also shown his concern for the sick and the poor. Moreover, unlike his predecessors, he was married to a second-generation Canadian, Louise-Élisabeth de JOYBERT, and was gradually acquiring roots in Canada. Indeed, Louis XIV had considered that these Canadian connections might make it difficult for him to rule impartially and for this reason had hesitated before naming him as Callière's successor. As a person, Vaudreuil was reserved and cautious, but he tended to become more assertive as the years went by and as he gained in confidence. Although his intelligence was no better than average and his education limited, he had a clear and orderly mind, 16 years of experience in Canadian affairs, and such able lieutenants as CHARLES LE MOYNE de Longueuil, CHABERT de Joncaire, and LA PORTE de Louvigny to turn to for advice. In brief, he was a man who could provide the colony with sound if unspectacular government.

Vaudreuil became governor at a difficult moment in the history of New France. Since 1702 a state of war had existed with the English colonies to the south as a result of the outbreak of the War of the Spanish Succession in Europe. This conflict, the greatest of Louis XIV's reign, was taxing France's financial resources to the utmost and leaving little to spare for North America, which French strategists regarded as remote and unimportant. To complicate the situation further the beaver trade had collapsed as a result of many years of reckless overtrading with the Indians, and this had struck a damaging blow to the entire system of native alliances. Now that the French connection had ceased to be economically lucrative, the Indian allies might well grow cool towards New France and refuse to extend military assistance to the colony in case of war. Faced with these uncertainties, Vaudreuil was obviously in no position to engage in a major conflict.

Fortunately, the external threat was not as great as it had been during Frontenac's second administration. The Iroquois, traditionally the most fearsome enemies of New France, had concluded peace with the French and their allies in 1701. Vaudreuil understood that this treaty protected the most vulnerable parts of the colony from attack and he therefore made its preservation the central part of his wartime policy. This meant that he had to refrain from sending military expeditions against New York, for these would have offended the Five Nations and invited

Rigaud de Vaudreuil

retaliation. The New York authorities for their part gladly entered into this arrangement which spared them the hardships of war and until 1708 they too abstained from committing any hostile act against New France. No less satisfied were the Montreal fur-traders who had been hard hit by the unfavourable market conditions prevailing in France. The truce with New York enabled them to send most of their beaver pelts to Albany via the contraband route.

Meantime the Abenakis and the mission Indians, led by Canadian officers and militiamen, were conducting a series of border raids against the settlements of New England. The purpose of this "little war" was not to inflict a defeat on Massachusetts Bay. It was rather a tactic devised by Vaudreuil to safeguard the alliance with these Indians. He feared that a climate of peace along the eastern frontier would enable the English to win over the Abenakis and perhaps eventually to turn them against the French. The existence of a state of war in that area, on the other hand, obviously made the conclusion of such an alliance impossible. As for the Iroquois domiciled in the Canadian missions, they frequently travelled to Albany to trade with the English and to visit with their kinsmen, and their loyalty to New France suffered during those journeys. Sending them on expeditions against New England was a way for Vaudreuil to reassert his authority over them and to make the Canadian connection profitable, in spite of the depressed beaver trade, by enabling the Indians to gather booty to satisfy their needs.

By means of these tactics the alliance with the Abenakis and the mission Iroquois was maintained, but the cruelties of the "little war" so exasperated the New Englanders that they decided to attempt the conquest of New France. Vaudreuil, who had regarded them as incompetent soldiers, had been oblivious of this danger; but the former intendant, Champigny, who was assisting Pontchartrain by commenting on the Canadian dispatches, had strongly advised against provoking Massachusetts Bay. He feared not only that this colony would counter-attack but also that it would oblige New York and the Iroquois to break their truce with New France and to join in the war. This is what happened in 1708. In response to the appeals of the long-suffering New Englanders, Great Britain agreed to send several warships to North America to join the colonial fleet for an attack on Quebec. At the same time a new governor was sent to New York to mobilize the militia and to rally the Iroquois for an attack on Montreal. By 1709, everything stood in readiness for an invasion of Canada by land and sea.

Vaudreuil, who dreaded nothing more than a third Iroquois war, was far more alarmed by the threatening attitude of the Five Nations than by that of the English, and his fears were greatly increased by the uncertain loyalty of the western allies. In the previous war, the Ottawas and Miamis had inflicted heavy losses on the Five Nations by their repeated attacks on their western flank and had greatly contributed to the final victory of the French. But by 1709 they no longer had compelling reasons to make war on the Iroquois. For the past eight years the latter had allowed them to travel to Albany to barter their furs. By means of this important economic concession, which they had stubbornly refused to make in the 17th century, the Iroquois were hoping to pacify their old enemies permanently and perhaps even to win them to their side in order to isolate New France militarily and commercially.

The governor understood the purpose of the strategy but he found it difficult to devise countermeasures, for unlike his predecessors he did not possess effective tools to deal with the western tribes. The alliance with them had been weakened economically by the collapse of the beaver trade and politically by the edict of 1696 which had abolished the 25 fur-trading licences (congés) and obliged the garrisons and commanding officers to withdraw from the principal western posts. The purpose of this legislation had been to cut off the fur trade at its source to accelerate the recovery of the market, but it had also had the unfortunate effect of removing from the interior the most important agents of French influence among the Indian tribes.

The situation in the west had been further complicated by the foundation of Detroit in 1701 by Lamothe Cadillac [LAUMET]. This former commandant of Michilimackinac had assured Pontchartrain that, by the establishment of a post on the southern portion of the Great Lakes, where a large white population would settle and where the principal western tribes would regroup, it would be possible to prevent westward expansion of the English and to overawe the Iroquois. Soon after its founding, however, Detroit began to produce results quite different from those predicted by Cadillac. In the first place, it drew the western Indians close to the Iroquois and facilitated the growth of trade relations between them, the very thing which had to be avoided if the alliance between New France and the tribes of the interior was to be maintained. Secondly, it proved impossible for such dissimilar nations as the Hurons, Miamis, and Ottawas, who had moved to Detroit in response to Cadillac's invitation, to live in close proximity to one another and remain at peace. Between 1706 and 1708 these Indians

Rigaud de Vaudreuil

came to blows and seriously threatened the continuation of peace in the west.

With unreliable allies and insufficient soldiers, Vaudreuil did his best to put the colony in a state of defence. In the district of Montreal he urged the mission Indians to stand firmly by the French, in spite of the governor of New York who was threatening them with dire consequences if they opposed the progress of the invading army. In Quebec, while the engineer JACQUES LEVASSEUR de Neré worked feverishly to strengthen the fortifications, the governor visited the outlying settlements, reviewed the militia, examined their weapons and spoke encouraging words to the population. In the villages of the Five Nations, meantime, his agents warned the Iroquois that they would expose themselves to the attacks of the western Indians if they violated the treaty of 1701. This threat still carried much weight, for the Iroquois' policy of conciliation had not yet completely overcome the old animosities of the French allies towards them, bred by a century of war. Ultimately, however, what saved the colony was the misfortune that dogged the English at every step. The operations planned for 1709 had to be postponed, when the ships promised by England failed to arrive. The invasion plans of 1711 also came to naught when Sir Hovenden WALKER's mighty fleet turned back after losing eight vessels in the fogs and high winds of the lower St Lawrence. This development prevented the land army and the 682 Iroquois assembled near Albany from advancing on Montreal.

Thus the great onslaught which could have resulted in the conquest of New France did not materialize and the colony emerged from a long war without having suffered a single attack by the English or by the Iroquois. This fact alone so impressed the court that it granted Vaudreuil the rank of commander of the order of Saint-Louis, an honour not undeserved, even if the English failure was ultimately caused by factors that were not of his making. He had carefully refrained from raising his hand against the Iroquois, in spite of their two desertions to the English, and, thus, had made possible in 1712 a reconfirmation of the treaty of 1701. Under extremely difficult conditions he had managed to preserve intact the colony's network of native alliances. This was demonstrated in 1711 when between 400 and 500 western Indians arrived in Montreal and pledged their support to New France against the English. None the less, all was not well with these allies. Without holders of fur-trading licences and soldiers to act as peacemakers in the west, quarrels and skirmishes were frequently breaking out among these undisciplined tribes. By his skilful

mediation of their differences Vaudreuil managed to maintain order; but disaster finally struck in 1712. The Fox and Mascouten Indians, perennial trouble-makers in the Great Lakes country, were attacked at Detroit by several other tribes assisted by the French garrison and a full-scale Indian war broke out. Faced with this emergency the governor decided that any further delay in reoccupying strategic points in the west would leave the Indians free to wage a war of mutual extermination. Without waiting for Pontchartrain's authorization to arrive he sent a group of men under LE MARCHAND de Lignery to reoccupy Michilimackinac and delegations under JEAN-BAPTISTE BISSOT de Vinsenne and de LIETTE to contain the Miamis and Illinois. These measures constituted an important departure from the policy set down in the edict of 1696 and prepared the way for a period of renewed expansion.

Other problems had added to the difficulties experienced by Vaudreuil during this troubled decade. He had become governor when Cadillac was at the height of his power and was enjoying the support of such leading Canadian notables as Claude de RAMEZAY, the governor of Montreal, and the formidable RUETTE d'Auteuil, the attorney general of the Conseil Supérieur. As soon as Vaudreuil showed that he was opposed to Detroit this powerful group turned against him and denounced his conduct in their letters to the minister. D'Auteuil imputed the governor's hostility towards the founder of Detroit to his "extreme displeasure to see placed in a post that might interfere with his trade a man who was put there by someone other than himself and on whom he could not count for support in his greedy designs." In spite of Vaudreuil's vigorous defence and counter-accusations Pontchartrain had become so ill disposed towards him by 1706 that he threatened him with demotion from his post. But just as victory appeared within the grasp of the governor's enemies the tide turned. In 1707, the naval commissary François CLAIRAMBAULT d'Aigremont was instructed by Pontchartrain to investigate and report on conditions in the northwest. In his report submitted the following year d'Aigremont exposed Cadillac as a profiteer and his western system as a menace to French control of the Great Lakes country. Following this there was little left for the minister to do except to remove Cadillac from the Canadian scene and to grant Vaudreuil full control of the west. Thus the governor emerged victorious from a crisis which had nearly cost him his political career.

No sooner had these clouds been dispelled than Vaudreuil became involved in another quarrel, this time with the intendants Jacques Raudot and

Rigaud de Vaudreuil

his son ANTOINE-DENIS. Differences in background made some friction between the three administrators inevitable. Whereas Vaudreuil belonged to the nobility of the sword, the Raudots were members of the legal nobility of the robe and these two branches of the second estate disliked one another. To make matters worse the two intendants regarded Canadian society, to which the governor and his wife were united by so many bonds, with a mixture of superiority and contempt. Even so, harmony might have been preserved had it not been for the humourless and choleric temper of the elder Raudot. He had been greatly offended in the spring of 1708 when satirical songs written about him by persons of Vaudreuil's entourage began to circulate in the streets of Quebec. In the fall his anger became a towering rage when the governor questioned his right to appoint the surgeon-major of the Hôtel-Dieu in Montreal. The following year the two intendants submitted long letters of complaint to Pontchartrain and once again Vaudreuil had to defend himself. This time, however, he did not reply in his dispatches to the charges made against him. Rather he sent his wife to France to present his case to the minister. This tactic paid rich dividends. Madame de Vaudreuil won the favour of Pontchartrain and used her influence to consolidate her husband's position in Canada. With her help, Vaudreuil overcame the second and last great challenge to his position. When the Raudots were recalled at their own demand in 1710 he was firmly in charge of the situation.

With the return of peace, Pontchartrain granted Vaudreuil permission to come to France on leave. Important changes in the government of the kingdom occurred during this voyage to his homeland. Louis XIV died on 1 Sept. 1715, and power passed to a council of regency headed by the Duc d'Orléans, which governed in the name of the young Louis XV. Shortly afterwards Pontchartrain and the other ministers were dismissed from office and replaced by a system of seven councils, the so-called *polysinodie*. That of the Marine, to whose care the colonies were entrusted, knew little about New France and was undoubtedly relieved to have a man of Vaudreuil's experience to turn to for advice. The governor took advantage of this situation to recommend an energetic programme of colonial consolidation that would enable the colony to repair the damages it had suffered at the peace of Utrecht. The terms of this treaty had made the lands along the New England border and the Great Lakes and Mississippi Valley regions vulnerable to English expansion. By article 12, Acadia had been ceded to Great Britain "with its ancient boundaries." According to the English

view these embraced not only Nova Scotia but also present-day Maine, New Brunswick, and the Gaspé peninsula. By article 15, the Iroquois had been declared British subjects, a tactic that was meant to lay the legal groundwork for a thrust by New York towards the Great Lakes. The same clause had also stipulated that henceforth the subjects of both France and Great Britain would be allowed to trade with the western tribes. In the eyes of the merchants and senior administrators of New France, the English, with their superior merchandise, now appeared in a good position to gain control of the western fur trade and to win the allegiance of the Indians.

Vaudreuil's programme consisted of two principal points. In the first place the population of the colony should be increased by means of a large-scale civilian and military immigration movement. He was certain that the British would eventually renew their attempt to conquer New France, in which case a much larger population would be needed to resist the attack. Secondly, the alliances with the Indians should be tightened by reviving the 25 fur-trading licences, increasing the gift fund, legalizing a limited liquor trade and authorizing the governor to establish whatever posts he might judge to be necessary in the west. These measures would not only permit the colony to defend its frontiers and hinterland against English pressures but also enable it to reorganize its fur-trading empire, a step made necessary by the long-awaited recovery of the beaver trade in 1716. For these economic and political reasons the council of Marine allowed Vaudreuil to carry out his expansionist programme, but it did add one important proviso. Since France and Great Britain had recently become allies, he should strive to maintain friendly relations with the English colonies to the south. Until the joint commission on boundaries called for by the treaty of Utrecht met to lay down a definitive demarcation line between the French and English North American colonies, he was instructed to maintain possession "gently but nevertheless firmly" of the territories which had always been deemed to belong to France. Little did the council suspect that Vaudreuil's policy of frontier defence would soon lead New France to the brink of war with New England and New York.

In October 1716, Vaudreuil landed at Quebec with a staff of 16 persons. His wife had stayed on in France to continue looking after his interests, but there must have been little left for her to do. All her sons now held commissions in the army and the navy in either Canada or France. As for the old governor, his position had never been so secure. Shortly before his return to Canada the

Rigaud de Vaudreuil

regent himself granted him an interview and promised to look after his needs and those of his family. The council of Marine, for its part, considered him to be practically indispensable in North America. In 1717 it granted him a gratuity of 6,000 *livres* and in 1721 the grand cross of Saint-Louis, one of France's highest honours. The days were clearly over when men like Cadillac, Ramezay, and d'Auteuil could criticize him with impunity for Vaudreuil was now a powerful figure whom it would have been extremely dangerous to offend. On those few occasions when he suffered minor irritations he showed himself hard and unforgiving. In 1720, for example, his nephew Adhémar* de Lantagnac married the daughter of a former tavern-keeper. Vaudreuil considered himself personally humiliated by this marriage and insisted that the newlyweds be deported to Île Royale (Cape Breton Island). Nor did he ever forgive Bishop Saint-Vallier [LA CROIX] for having authorized this marriage without having first referred the matter to him.

Although Vaudreuil now enjoyed considerable power and prestige he was not a wealthy man. During the War of the Spanish Succession he had suffered several major financial setbacks. In 1704 personal belongings valued at over 30,000 *livres* were lost when the store-ship *Seine*, en route to Canada, was captured by the English. After 1706, when the French financial system began to buckle under the war effort, his salary was paid irregularly —it was two years in arrears in 1716—and at times in depreciated paper money. With his finances in this uncertain state the governor had to maintain a large household, entertain frequently, pay pensions to his sons in the armed forces, and support the costs of an endless lawsuit over the family properties in Languedoc. Except for Arnaud, who was childless, all of his brothers had died by 1700; unless therefore he succeeded in establishing his title to the barony of Vaudreuille it might pass out of family hands for the first time in 500 years. This he was determined to prevent. By 1708, he had succeeded in nullifying the claims to the estate of his sister-in-law, Antoinette de Colombet, and of several creditors. Then began another legal battle with the consuls of the town of Revel who were, he claimed, taxing the barony at an excessive rate. To strengthen his position in this quarrel he purchased the governorship of Revel for 10,000 *livres* in 1710, but it was only in 1724 that the question was settled to his satisfaction. After 25 years of effort Vaudreuil had finally achieved his goal. The ancient barony would not be lost by foreclosure or ruined by taxation. Its possession had been assured for future generations.

In view of his need of money it is not surprising that the governor should have turned to the fur trade to supplement his income. His activities in this field, however, differed considerably from those of Frontenac in the preceding century. The latter had tried to develop a system that would have enabled him and a few partners to monopolize the bulk of the trade with the Indians. Vaudreuil, for his part, engaged in the fur trade on a modest scale before 1716. After that date, profiting from his influence at the court, he exploited two posts: Temiscaming, near the headwaters of the Ottawa, which he was granted in 1717, and Île aux Tourtres, which formed part of his seigneury at the juncture of the Ottawa and St Lawrence Rivers. From those two vantage points his agents carried on a considerable trade with Indians who would otherwise have taken their pelts to Montreal. The merchants of that city protested vigorously and Jean-Frédéric de Maurepas, minister of Marine after 1723, was finally obliged to order Vaudreuil to remove his men from these two posts. The governor grudgingly complied in the case of Île aux Tourtres but until the day of his death obstructed the efforts of the intendant, Michel Bégon*, who was attempting to carry out ministerial instructions relating to Temiscaming.

In the meantime the reconstruction of New France's trading empire was rapidly moving forward. The path for this was cleared in 1716 when a force of approximately 800 men commanded by Louvigny attacked the Fox Indians in their stronghold near Baie des Puants (Green Bay) and forced them to sue for peace. Immediately afterwards the governor issued orders to build a network of posts in the region of the western Great Lakes and the upper Mississippi Valley. He expected these establishments both to facilitate the preservation of peace among the Indian tribes and to increase French control over them at a time when the English were intensifying their pressures on the west. Furthermore, these posts would also play an important economic role. Those extending westward from Lake Superior would not only serve as a base for the discovery of the western sea, a project of interest to the council of Marine, but would also intercept the Indians en route to Hudson Bay, which had been ceded to the English by the treaty of Utrecht. The one at Baie des Puants would place New France in control of an important gateway to the far west and to new beaver breeding grounds. The Canadian merchants profited greatly from this reorganization and pacification of the interior and their indentured employees (*engagés*) left for the west in record-breaking numbers in the 1720s.

The pro-Canadian manner in which Vaudreuil governed the western hinterland involved him in

Rigaud de Vaudreuil

a quarrel with Louisiana. In 1717 the Illinois country had been annexed to Louisiana and its government afterwards considered that its jurisdiction extended northward along the entire Mississippi River as far as Lake Winnipeg. Vaudreuil maintained that the annexation had simply moved the northern frontier of Louisiana to the Illinois River and he warned its administration that traders who trespassed on Canadian territory would have their goods confiscated. The ill feeling caused by this situation increased considerably after 1721, when the Fox Indians renewed their war on the French. Louisiana suffered greatly from their raids and, jointly with Versailles, urged Vaudreuil to take measures to destroy the Foxes. But the governor of Canada was not prepared to follow such a course of action, for he feared nothing more than an Indian war that would plunge the west into turmoil, dislocate the fur trade, and force a withdrawal from the posts. Instead of declaring war on the Foxes he simply negotiated a treaty with them which won immunity for the Canadian traders and their native allies but which allowed the war on Louisiana to continue. To explain why the southern colony had not been included in the peace, he claimed that the Foxes had absolutely refused to suspend their attacks on the Illinois tribes, who lived on Louisiana territory. But this explanation did little to dispel the anger which the news of the treaty had provoked in New Orleans and Versailles. In both these places the impression grew that Canada was not only tolerating the Fox war but even arranging for it to continue in order to prevent Louisiana from sharing in the western fur trade.

The greatest problem facing Vaudreuil after 1716, however, was to prevent English expansion in the region of the Great Lakes and along the eastern frontier. Soon after the treaty of Utrecht, Albany trading missions began to travel as far as Lake Ontario in order to open direct trade with the western allies of New France. William Burnet, who became governor of New York in 1720, was determined to multiply and strengthen these commercial contacts with the Indians and eventually to destroy the French grip on the west. Meantime, New England land companies were introducing settlers on the territory east of Casco Bay and trying to win the Abenakis to their side by offering them the benefits of a lucrative trade. If their policy succeeded, New France's eastern defences would collapse and the settlements on the south shore of the St Lawrence would be exposed to devastation in wartime. In the face of this double threat Vaudreuil's task was clear. He had to prevent New York from establishing commercial links with the western tribes, which might eventually become a basis for a political alliance, and to contain New England west of Casco Bay, where Abenaki lands began. But to achieve these goals he had to control the Indian tribes, and the inability of the French economy to produce trade goods matching those of the English in quality and price placed him at a disadvantage in his dealings with the natives.

Vaudreuil observed the situation in the west for three years before deciding upon a course of action. Then in the spring of 1720 he acted swiftly. His strategy consisted of driving a wedge between New York and the west by establishing three trading houses along Lake Ontario. The principal one overlooked the Niagara portage, the route used by almost all the Indians from the southwest as they made their way towards Canada or New York. The other two were located at Toronto and Quinté. This was a sound strategical move for it placed the French in a position where they could intercept the Indians before they reached the New York settlements. But it was also a dangerous procedure, for the new trading posts were located on the hunting grounds of the Iroquois which the English could claim as their protectorate under article 15 of the treaty of Utrecht. Vaudreuil knew, however, that New York would be unable to enforce this clause without the support of the Iroquois. For this reason his agent, Joncaire, had been careful to secure their consent before proceeding with the construction of the three buildings.

Along the eastern frontier Vaudreuil gradually gained the upper hand in his struggle with Samuel Shute, the governor of Massachusetts Bay, for control of the Abenakis. Left to themselves these Indians, who had suffered great losses in past wars with New England, would probably have consented to the eastward extension of the English settlements. However, they soon succumbed to the pressure of Vaudreuil and the Jesuit missionaries who told them that the land east of Casco Bay was Indian territory and that they had to defend it against the English intruders. In 1718, the Abenakis began to destroy buildings recently put up by British settlers on the lower Kennebec. Two years later, New England opened peace negotiations with the Indians only to have them collapse as a result of Jesuit intervention. Shute finally had to recognize that the Indians could not be pacified by non-violent means and he declared war on them on 22 July 1722. Vaudreuil, who was certain that the English would withdraw from the disputed territory rather than engage in a war with the Abenakis assisted by the French, would have liked to appear openly on the side of his native allies, but Versailles refused to place the Anglo-French alliance in jeopardy by allowing him to follow such a course of action. The governor, therefore, limited himself to extending secret assistance in arms and ammunition to the Abenakis and to encouraging the Indians from the Canadian missions to send war parties to their rescue.

Along Lake Ontario, meantime, the situation had become critical. So great was the desire of the western Indians for English trade goods that they simply avoided the posts recently built by the French and continued to take a large percentage of their pelts to Albany and Schenectady. The expansionist policy followed by William Burnet made the threat to the commerce of New France still more acute. In 1724 the governor of New York decided to found a post at Oswego, on Lake Ontario, "where the chief trade with the Far Indians lie." At a conference held in September the Iroquois authorized him to carry out his project. This marked the end of their middleman policy, which had long been moribund, and the substitution for it of a strategy of balance: by alternating concessions to the French and to the English, they hoped to prevent either side from becoming unduly powerful in their territory. For once, Vaudreuil failed to grasp the true nature of Iroquois intentions. He interpreted their support of the Oswego project as proof that they were now entirely in the English interest and might soon join forces with the latter to drive the French from Niagara. Since the wooden stockade might prove too weak to resist an attack, he decided to have it replaced by a stone fort. Longueuil was selected by him to present to the Iroquois the crucial request to make this change.

As the aged Vaudreuil began his last year of life and his 23d as governor of New France, near certainty existed in his mind that peaceful Anglo-French coexistence in North America was impossible. "This colony will always be the cause of jealousy on the part of the English," he wrote prophetically to Maurepas in one of his last dispatches. ". . . we have no more dangerous enemy to fear." The use of force had been necessary to prevent New England from overrunning Abenaki lands and the use of force might soon prove to be necessary in the west to keep New York from winning over the Indian allies of New France. The stone fort planned for Niagara was Vaudreuil's supreme hope—short of war—for checking this development. If the Iroquois refused to allow Longueuil to erect the fortifications the governor thought that the French would have no choice but to defend their western empire by force of arms and he pleaded with Maurepas for more soldiers, guns, and ammunition to place the colony and the western posts on a war footing. The Five Nations, however, consented to Longueuil's demand but Vaudreuil probably never learned this. He died in Quebec on 10 Oct. 1725.

Like Frontenac and Callière, he was buried in the church of the Recollets. Two years later his heart was taken to France and interred in the cemetery of Vaudreuille, near the remains of his ancestors.

The people of New France mourned the death of their governor for they had regarded him with both esteem and affection. Canada had become his adopted country and in 1724 he had even referred to it as the "patrie" of his son Louis-Philippe*. During the War of the Spanish Succession he had maintained the alliance with the western tribes and preserved the peace with the dreaded Iroquois. After the treaty of Utrecht he had rebuilt New France's western trading empire and made it possible for the Canadian merchants to profit from the fur trade. With the determination of a tough-minded old soldier he had defended the frontiers of the colony against English expansionism. The annalist of the Ursulines was undoubtedly thinking of all this when she wrote: "We had every reason to mourn him, for under his vigilant administration Canada enjoyed a prosperity unknown until that time. For 22 years the farmer, the businessman, and the soldier alike could only bless his name." Here were the beginnings of a legend which would in no small way be responsible for the naming of another Vaudreuil [Pierre Rigaud*] as governor of New France in 1755.

While working to improve his own fortunes the Marquis had not neglected to look after the careers of his six sons. The persistent efforts he and his wife made to secure their advancement in the king's service were richly rewarded for all of them ultimately occupied important positions in the army, the navy and the colonies. The eldest, Louis-Philippe, chose to serve in the navy. As commander of the *Intrépide* he distinguished himself during an engagement with a British squadron in 1747. In 1753, he was promoted to the rank of lieutenant general of his majesty's naval forces and three years later received the grand cross of Saint-Louis from the hands of the king. Philippe-Antoine*, the second son, battalion commander in the king's infantry regiment, was killed at the siege of Prague in 1742. Jean, the third son, joined the Musketeers in 1710, transferred to the French guards in 1712, and went on to win many honours on the battle-fields of Europe. He was named lieutenant general of the king's armies in 1748 and

Rigauville

received the grand cross of Saint-Louis in 1755. The next two sons, Pierre and François-Pierre*, made their careers in North America. The former became governor of Louisiana in 1742 and of Canada in 1755; the latter was named governor of Trois-Rivières in 1748 and of Montreal in 1757. The youngest, Joseph-Hyacinthe*, joined the French guards in 1722, at the age of 16, but like his father before him found it difficult to win advancement in France. He therefore accepted the captaincy of a company of infantry in Saint-Domingue, which his mother obtained for him in 1725. In 1753, he was named governor general of all the French Leeward islands. The eldest of the three daughters, Marie-Louise, married Gaspard de Villeneuve, a nobleman of Languedoc, in 1719. Marie-Josephe and Louise-Élisabeth, her two sisters, died in France, apparently unmarried.

YVES F. ZOLTVANY

[A great quantity of documentation on Vaudreuil's public life, consisting mostly of the dispatches exchanged between the ministry of Marine and the colonial government, has been preserved in the Archives des Colonies and Archives de la Marine. See particularly AN, Col., B, C^{11A}, C^{11E}, C^{11G}, C^{13A}, D^{2C}, and F^3, and AN, Marine, B^1 and C^7. Scattered items are also to be found in AE, Archives du Séminaire de Saint-Sulpice (Paris), and ASQ. Vaudreuil's correspondence with the ministry of Marine from 1703 to 1716 has been published in APQ *Rapport, 1938–39*, 12–180; *1939–40*, 355–463; *1942–43*, 399–443; *1946–47*, 371–460 and *1947–48*, 135–339.

The documentation dealing with Vaudreuil's pre-Canadian career and his personal life is quite sparse. The most significant items are in Archives de la Haute-Garonne (Toulouse), Series 2E 608 and 2E 654; AN, E, 819, and AN, Y, 234; AJQ; BN, MS, Clairambault 873 (which contains the only autograph letter by Vaudreuil which it has been possible to locate) and 1103, and NAF 890. The governor's will and the inventory of his belongings have been published in APQ *Rapport, 1920–21*, opposite p.480; *1921–22*, 238–61; and *1957–59*, 341–55.

Two old works contain valuable information: Simon Lamorel Le Pippre de Nœufville, *Abrégé chronologique et historique de l'origine, du progrès et de l'état actuel de la maison du Roi et de toutes les troupes de France* (3v., Liège, 1734) on the Musketeers; L.-P. d'Hozier, *Armorial général de France* (8v., Paris, 1736–68) for a detailed history of the Vaudreuil family from earliest times.

No complete biography of Vaudreuil has been published. F. M. Hammang, *The Marquis de Vaudreuil, New France at the beginning of the eighteenth century* (Bruges, 1938) is sound but incomplete. There are two short works by Guy Frégault: "Un cadet de Gascogne: Philippe de Rigaud de Vaudreuil," *RHAF*, V (1951–52), 15–44, a lively sketch; and "Politique et politiciens au début de XVIIIᵉ siècle," *Écrits du*

Canada français (Montréal), XI (1961), 91–208, a perceptive study of Vaudreuil's quarrels with d'Auteuil, Ramezay, Cadillac, and the Raudots. Jean Ramière de Fortanier, *Les droits seigneuriaux dans la sénéchaussée et comté de Lauragais* (Toulouse, 1932) contains an enumeration of the Vaudreuil properties in Languedoc. For an examination of Vaudreuil's relations with the English colonies and the Indian tribes, *see* Y. F. Zoltvany, "The problem of western policy under Philippe de Rigaud de Vaudreuil, 1703–1725," CHA *Report, 1964*, 9–24; "New France and the west," 301–22; "The frontier policy of Philippe de Rigaud de Vaudreuil (1713–1725)," *CHR*, XLVIII (1967), 227–50. Y.F.Z.]

RIGAUVILLE. *See* BLAISE

RIVERIN, DENIS, secretary of Intendant Duchesneau*, representative of the farmers of the Compagnie de la Ferme du Roi, member of the Conseil Souverain, one of the directors of the Compagnie du Nord, and of the Compagnie de la Colonie, lieutenant general of the provost court of Quebec, fur-trader, landowner, and commercial fisherman; b. at Tours, *c.* 1650, the son of Pierre Riverin, a merchant and bourgeois, and of Madeleine Mahyet; d. February 1717.

Riverin came to New France in 1675 as secretary to the new intendant, Duchesneau. Like many of the *bourgeois-gentilhommes*, members of the élite in New France, he fulfilled numerous functions of the colony. He was a member of the civil administration, and engaged in a wide variety of commercial activities: the fur and fishing trades, exporting and importing.

During his early career, from roughly 1675 to the early 1680s he was Duchesneau's secretary, and at the same time he represented Jean Oudiette, the holder of the monopoly of the Compagnie de la Ferme du Roi in New France. In 1694 he became a titular member of the Conseil Souverain, and a full-fledged member in 1698. He retained the latter post until 1710, in spite of the fact that he had returned to France in 1702 and never came back to the colony. In 1710, moreover, he was named lieutenant general of the provost court of Quebec. Although he never personally carried out the duties of this appointment he drew the salary provided. These last two appointments show the kind of favouritism which Riverin enjoyed, thanks no doubt to the protection of the governors and intendants who thought well of him, at least until the arrival of RIGAUD de Vaudreuil and JACQUES RAUDOT. A further factor which helps to explain Riverin's position in the society of his time was the patronage of TANTOUIN de La Touche, a member of the ministry of Marine who had served in New France till 1701. Riverin also appears to

574

have been well thought of by the minister of Marine, Louis Phélypeaux de Pontchartrain.

Until the departure of Duchesneau in 1682, Riverin appears to have engaged in the fur trade as Oudiette's representative as well as on his own account, if we are to believe his critics, Le Febvre* de La Barre and RUETTE d'Auteuil. There is no doubt that he was, as W. J. Eccles had pointed out, "the Intendant's very able secretary," quite evidently under Duchesneau's protection. When the Compagnie de la Colonie was formed in 1700, Riverin became one of its first directors. He was named the representative of the company in France in 1702; his position was renewed in 1706 and he held this post until his death in 1717, although other directors of the company claimed that he was displaced in 1713.

To be appointed to the post of director of a company during this period, a person had to own a certain number of shares, and moreover had to be elected by the other shareholders of the company who had the right to a deliberative voice. As agent of the company in France Riverin was responsible for the metropolitan administration of the company's affairs. He was the agent who found and leased warehouse space, who placed orders for trade goods and supplies, and, perhaps most important, who arranged for the credit and the loans necessary to carry out the company's business.

His views on the fur trade were somewhat contradicted by those he later put forward on the fishing trade. When he was involved in the fur trade in New France, he championed the need for fur-trading licences (congés), and did not object to the flow of men from the colony to the pays d'en haut. As a commercial fisherman, however, he insisted that young men should be kept in the colony, albeit by colony he understood the eastern extremities.

About 1688 he extended his commercial interests to include the fishing trade. Between 1688 and 1702, we find Riverin, in association with François HAZEUR, AUGUSTIN LE GARDEUR de Courtemanche, and several others, acquiring land concessions. On 19 Jan. 1689, he was granted the seigneury of Belle-Isle; in 1696, he leased three seigneuries for seven years; he paid 1,500 livres for a bark in 1701 and in the same year, in partnership with François Hazeur, leased the fur and fishing trade of Tadoussac for 12,700 livres per year. The significance of this sum can be appreciated by comparing it with a high average annual wage for an artisan of 600 livres per year.

Riverin wrote several interesting memoirs on the fishing trade which reveal the complexity of commercial organization in New France, and

reflect what could be called an ideology of commercial imperialism. Riverin showed that the establishment of a successful commercial endeavour in the colony required the co-operation of metropolitan financiers—in this case the merchants of La Rochelle. Riverin justified the permanent extension of the frontiers of the colony, and thus its defence perimeter, by pointing out its military and economic implications. He claimed that the fishing trade could employ 500 men, but would require protection. He therefore requested assistance from the French state for his fishing stations. One thing led to another, for the logic of the situation required free shipping rights for his supplies. In 1696, he requested free transport for 20 casks. Riverin never explained, however, the possible contradiction between eastern and western expansion, which would draw men to the frontiers, and the maintenance of an adequate defence system in the heart of the colony.

The period after 1702 may be said to be different in content and in context for Riverin. Prior to this date he was personally engaged in the commercial activities and the political life of the colony. After this time his position was a little parasitical, and appears to have depended as much on influence as it did on accomplishment. When he was named deputy of the Compagnie de la Colonie in France, his salary was set at 6,000 livres per year. His services must have been satisfactory, for he was reappointed in 1706 but at a salary of 3,000 livres per year. The heyday of the company was at an end; it was in effect bankrupt. The various disputes over Riverin's character and contributions date mainly from this year. He insisted that he had a right to a full salary from 1702 to 1716, but his partners in New France rejected his claims. MATHIEU-FRANÇOIS MARTIN de Lino, who had once occupied the post then held by Riverin, suggested that the colony's interests would be better served if they were represented by one better informed and less concerned with personal gain. Ruette d'Auteuil, sometimes as unreliable a witness as Riverin, accused the latter of conniving with Aubert, Neret, and Gayot, the group that took over the monopoly of the Compagnie de la Ferme du Roi from the Compagnie de la Colonie. The acrimonious disputes over Riverin's salary can be only partially explained by the amount of money involved, although he is said to have received the not inconsiderable sum of 69,000 livres between 1702 and 1716. At the heart of the matter was the dislocation of favoured groups which took place when the upper administrators of the colony were changed. The vicissitudes of favouritism are apparent in the writings of the

Rivet Cavelier

governors and intendants of the colony. Buade* de Frontenac and Duchesneau favoured Riverin. Their successors, de MEULLES and La Barre, described Riverin as one possessing "an extraordinary spirit of gain . . . ," and accused him of trying to monopolize the fishing industry. On the other hand, BRISAY de Denonville and BOCHART de Champigny respectively depicted Riverin as "poor Riverin" and as a very well liked, honest man. Later administrators such as Vaudreuil and Raudot were extremely critical of Riverin's activities in France. It should be added that Riverin, somewhat tactlessly, although accurately, said that Vaudreuil was tied to his wife's apron strings. What is perhaps most important is that as long as Riverin had the support of influential men in the French administration he managed to retain his post and its remuneration. The year 1715 was a key date in the rise and fall of Denis Riverin; that year the king died, the council of Marine was established, and administrators and merchants in New France took their revenge. Perhaps fortunately, Riverin died, thus escaping a further reduction of his influence and income.

A just assessment of Riverin requires an appreciation of the milieu in which he lived. He was certainly able. At the same time, he was very self-seeking. When his personal interests and those of the colony coincided, his contributions were considerable; when they did not, his tendency towards acrimony made his views suspect.

In 1696, Riverin had married Angélique Gaultier, the daughter of Philippe Gaultier*, Sieur de Comporté, and of Marie Bazire. The bride's guardian was François Hazeur, an occasional business partner of Riverin. In the marriage contract, Riverin is described as a director of the "Compagnie des Pesches Sédentaires de Canada." Riverin and his wife had four children born between 1697 and 1700.

There are various opinions regarding the date of his death. Ignotus [Thomas Chapais] wrote that it occurred in 1718. Riverin's last extant writing is dated July 1716. P.-G. Roy claimed that he died in 1717. In a document dated 5 May 1717, the council of Marine referred to him as the late Denis Riverin. Shortt's date of February 1717 thus appears possible.

CAMERON NISH

AJQ, Greffe de Louis Chambalon; Greffe de François Genaple. AN, M, Lettre de Riverin sur les affaires du Canada, 21 mars 1704; Col., C11G, 1–6. AQ, Coll. P.-G. Roy, Dossier Denis Riverin; NF, Coll. pièces jud. et not., 305, 3267. "Correspondance de Frontenac (1672–82)," APQ *Rapport, 1926–27. Documents relating to Canadian currency during the French period* (Shortt). "Lettres et mémoires de F.-M.-F. Ruette

d'Auteuil." P.-G. Roy, *Inv. concessions*, III, IV, V. Gareau, "La prévôté de Québec," 51–146. Eccles, *Canada under Louis XIV*. Fauteux, *Essai sur l'industrie sous le régime français*. Cameron Nish, *Les bourgeois-gentilshommes de la Nouvelle-France 1729–1748* (Montréal, 1968). J.-E. Roy, "Les conseillers au Conseil souverain de la Nouvelle-France," *BRH*, I (1895), 171. P.-G. Roy, "Notes sur Denis Riverin," *BRH*, XXXIV (1928), 65–76, 128–39, 193–206.

RIVET CAVELIER, PIERRE, clerk of court, royal notary, acting king's attorney, legal practitioner, director of the tax-farm of the Domaine d'Occident; baptized 15 March 1684 at Lachine, under the name of Cavelier; son of Pierre Cavelier, a bourgeois, and of Louise-Anne Du Souchet; d. 8 Feb. 1721 at Quebec, buried the next day.

Rivet—we do not know exactly when or why he adopted this name—began his career in the jurisdiction of Montreal. He was clerk in the court registry there from 1699 to 1701, and acting king's attorney in the last year. He then settled at Quebec, where in 1704 he was clerk in the provost court registry. He was only 20. In 1707 François Rageot*, the head clerk of this court, grew sick of his duties; after an interregnum under LA CETIÈRE, who was soon dismissed, Rivet was appointed court clerk on 10 Nov. 1707. The king confirmed him in this office on 7 July 1711, but Rivet resigned on 17 Sept. 1714. Meanwhile, on 12 Oct. 1709, he had been made royal notary in the jurisdiction of Quebec, taking the place left vacant by the death of François GENAPLE.

Rivet had long worked under Charles de MONSEIGNAT, beginning in 1706 as chief clerk of the tax-farm of the Domaine d'Occident, and from 1 June 1713 on as clerk in the court registry of the Conseil Supérieur. On Monseignat's death he succeeded him in his two functions, as director of the tax-farm on 21 Oct. 1718, and as chief clerk of court of the council on 28 Nov. 1718. His appointment as clerk of court was ratified by the king on 3 May 1719. Rivet was admitted to his office and officially installed on the following 9 October.

When he died in 1721 Rivet was the head churchwarden of the parish of Quebec. On 28 Nov. 1708 he had married Marie-Madeleine Rageot, daughter of Gilles Rageot*, royal notary and clerk of the provost court, and sister of CHARLES, NICOLAS, and François, who were all royal notaries and provost court clerks, as was Rivet himself.

ANDRÉ VACHON

AJQ, Greffe de Louis Chambalon, 25 nov. 1708; Greffe de Pierre Rivet, 1707–19. AQ, NF, Ins. Cons. sup., III, 60f., 78v *et seq.*; V, 3, 43, 53; NF, Ins. de la

576

Prév. de Québec, III, 341; NF, Ord. des int., I, 142; III, 77v *et seq.*; VI, 321v–23; VII½, 184; NF, Registres du Cons. sup., 1719–20, 45. P.-G. Roy, *Inv. jug. et délib., 1717–1760*, VI, 177; *Inv. ord. int.*, I, 175. Gareau, "La prévôté de Québec," 116–19. Massicotte, "Les tribunaux et les officiers de justice," *BRH*, XXXVII (1931), 189, 191. J.-E. Roy, *Histoire du notariat*, I.

RIZY, PIERRE PERROT DE. *See* PERROT

ROBERT, CLÉMENT, priest, Sulpician, first visitor from Saint-Sulpice to Canada; b. at a date unknown, in the diocese of Angers; d. 1 Dec. 1730 or 30 Oct. 1736 at Angers.

We lack information about Abbé Robert. No author and no manuscript source reveal his date of birth, whereas two dates, far apart though they are, are admitted as possible for his death. No one has been able to enlighten us as to his comings and goings before his first visit to Canada in July 1723.

Henri Gauthier says of Abbé Robert that at that date he was "the teacher of the Robertins." It has not been possible to trace this community despite intensive research, and apart from Gauthier and Monsignor Tanguay, who do no more than mention the fact, authors and archives remain silent about this foundation.

What is certain is that M. Robert came to Canada the first time as a visitor from Saint-Sulpice, and was here from July 1723 to September 1724. He encouraged and renewed the fervour of the missionaries, discussed a plan for uniting the parishes of the Montreal region with the seminary of that town, a plan that was only partially realized, and "came to an understanding with the bishop on the matter of sending new missionaries to Acadia."

When he returned to Canada the second time, in 1726, he came in the company of Abbé Jean Lyon de Saint-Ferréol, a friend who had recently been appointed superior of the seminary in Quebec. As it was feared, wrongly, that Saint-Sulpice would seize control of the seminary of Quebec, Robert's friendship for the new superior appeared suspect. The visitor was subjected to the resentment of the chapter; consequently he shortened his voyage and returned to France fairly rapidly.

According to Pierre Rousseau, Abbé Robert is thought to have come to Canada a third time, in 1731, and he is supposed to have taken advantage of that opportunity to visit the mission at the Lac des Deux-Montagnes. But this visit, which is very problematic since it is not mentioned by any other author or document, would make 30 Oct. 1736 possible as the date of his death.

However that may be, it does seem that Abbé Robert was noteworthy more for the fears that he inspired than for the harm that he really did. But according to Intendant CLAUDE-THOMAS DUPUY, "[This man] who likes to impart an air of intrigue to whatever he does, and who in that way spoils everything he has undertaken in this country, far from dispelling such a suspicion, has much increased it by his schemings."

JEAN-MARC PARADIS

AN, Col., B, 51, f.30; 52, f.495½; C¹¹ᴬ, 49, ff.297–301. ASQ, Lettres, M, 48, 56, 60. Henri Gauthier, *La Compagnie de Saint-Sulpice au Canada* (Montréal, 1912); *Sulpitiana* (Montréal, 1926). Gosselin, *L'Église du Canada*, I, 421–23. Pierre Rousseau, *Saint-Sulpice et les missions catholiques* (Montréal, 1930).

ROBINAU DE BÉCANCOUR, PIERRE, second Baron de Portneuf, knight of the order of Saint-Louis, seigneur of Bécancour, king's attorney, chief road commissioner (*grand voyer*) of New France from 1689 to 1729; b. at Quebec, in 1654, eldest son of René Robinau* de Bécancour and Marie-Anne Leneuf de La Poterie; m. Marie-Charlotte Legardeur de Villiers, 15 Jan. 1684 at Quebec, and had two daughters, Marie-Anne-Geneviève and Marie-Marguerite-Renée; d. 1729.

The fief of Portneuf was created a barony in 1681. When Pierre Robinau, Baron of Portneuf, disposed of this fief on 3 Oct. 1709, before the notary LA CETIÈRE in Montreal, he decided to retain his baronetcy. Jacques Robinau, his brother, became the sole proprietor of the seigneury but the title of baron, together with the precedence accorded in church, was retained by Pierre. The property passed back into the hands of the latter's daughters when Jacques died in March 1715. Pierre's contemporaries were aware of his social rank, but because he resided on his fief of Bécancour they were "uncertain about his correct title." Even Charlevoix* said he was received by the "baron de Bécancourt," an error which was perpetuated as recently as Tanguay's genealogy.

Throughout René Robinau's term as chief road commissioner of New France there had been numerous complaints about the poor state of the roads in the colony and a clamour had arisen to withhold his modest remuneration. Aware of this general dissatisfaction with the manner in which he discharged his responsibilities, René had petitioned Louis XIV to grant Pierre the right to exercise the duties of his office during his absence, with the right of succession on his retirement. Pierre was named chief road commissioner of New France by letters of provision signed by both Louis XIV and Colbert on 24 May 1689. The

Robinau de Bécancour

Conseil Souverain instituted the usual investigation of the nominee's life and morals on 23 Jan. 1690, and when a favourable report was submitted he was sworn in, on 13 February, to act "in the absence of and in succession to" his father, who had been the first holder of this office in the colony. Pierre held the position until his death in 1729.

During his term of office, the main royal road was surveyed and ordinances were issued for its construction and maintenance. There are extant at least 29 orders, dated between 1710 and 1723, for 19 seigneuries, as well as the minutes of six disputes concerning roadways adjudicated by him between 1706 and 1722. There were, however, some complaints about the discharge of his duties. In 1702, apparently following the lodging of formal complaints that Robinau was neglecting road maintenance in the Quebec area, the intendant, François de Beauharnois* de La Boische, informed Versailles that the chief road commissioner was not required to reside in Quebec because his jurisdiction extended over the entire colony, not just the town of Quebec. Beauharnois explained that family matters had obliged Robinau to return to France, but his absence from the colony was only temporary. In any case, Robinau had appointed an agent in Quebec and another in Montreal to provide the surveying which the complainants insisted should be an available service at all times. When the quality of the surveying gave rise to further complaints, the intendant advised that orders be issued for JACQUES LEVASSEUR de Neré, the royal engineer, to take charge of it, as the king had wished. There had also been complaints about the lack of paving in the Lower Town of Quebec. This was attributed to war conditions, but repairs were promised for the near future. On 9 June 1706, Louis XIV refused to consider a petition from a complainant, Duplessis-Fabert, who wanted Pierre Robinau's position. It may be concluded from this that the king, in encouraging petitions and watchfulness over civil officials, did not tolerate actions which tended to insubordination or disorder. Also, it appears that the life of an official was a delicate balance between privilege and responsibility, and that in a hierarchical society criticism from below had to be taken seriously because it could initiate action from above.

In addition to his civil post as road commissioner, Pierre Robinau also held several military ranks from 1684 to 1701. On 12 Nov. 1684, Intendant de MEULLES recommended to the minister of Marine that Pierre Robinau be given a naval appointment as midshipman, in further recognition—along with the elevation of Portneuf to a barony—of his father's distinguished service to the state. The king granted him a commission, according to a letter of 10 March 1685, and the 31-year-old Pierre Robinau was sent to Rochefort. Buade* de Frontenac wrote to the minister in 1690 that, subject to royal confirmation, he had named "Sieur Robineau Becancour the older son to replace Sr. [René] Robineau de Portneuf the younger who has a lieutenancy in the company of Sr. de Menneval [DES FRICHES] in Acadia." It was not until 1691 that Pierre Robinau was named a lieutenant, a promotion officially confirmed by the king on 1 March 1693.

His role in the military engagements of the 1690s was not as brilliant as that of his brothers. It is known that he and two brothers, RENÉ ROBINAU de Portneuf and Jacques Robinau, were ordered by Frontenac in August 1697 to join Joseph Robinau* de Villebon, another brother, at Fort Nashwaak (Naxouat) on the Saint John River. It would appear, however, that his conduct was much better than that of his unmarried brothers, René and DANIEL de Neuvillette, who were cited for their misconduct. In May 1701 the captaincy of a company of colonial regular troops was offered Pierre if he would replace the Sieur de Noyes who was returning to France. But in 1702 Robinau asked to be relieved of his lieutenancy in favour of his brother, René, who had previously held it and had now received an official pardon. Pierre was reported to be in France in 1702 and it seems he was taken prisoner by the English on his return to Canada on board the *Seine*. Subsequently, by a royal command of 27 May 1705, he was given free passage on board the *Héros* which was sailing for New France.

Pierre was also involved in some business enterprises but their exact extent has not been established. What evidence there is is fragmentary. For example, it seems that he was engaged with his brother René in the fur trade of the Saint John River area. He loaned money to his third brother, François-Alexandre, who was killed in Vera Cruz in 1703. Nevertheless, he had some financial worries. The minutes of the Conseil Souverain of Quebec indicate he had considerable trouble with a copyholder on the seigneury of Bécancour, Jacques L'Heureux, who refused to pay his *cens et rentes*. Although he inherited some of his father's estate in the Upper Town of Quebec, near the Château Saint-Louis, on at least two occasions portions of it were expropriated for a powder house and for the extension of the fortifications.

Little is known concerning Pierre's activities after 1705. He drew public attention in July 1711 by refusing to give his consent to the marriage of one of his daughters to Jacques-René Gaultier* de

Varennes. Neither his military service nor his career in the administration were marked by outstanding success. There are no indications that his commercial exploits were any more remarkable.

C. J. JAENEN

AHDQ, Mélanges, XIII, 48–50. AJQ, Greffe de Louis Chambalon, 8 nov. 1707; Greffe de Florent de La Cetière, 3 oct. 1709. AN, Col., B, 11, f.18; 15, ff.47, 69, 75½; 16, ff.22, 59½; 19, ff.113½, 123, 157½, 196½; 22, f.199; 23, f.180½; 27, ff.10½, 79; 33, ff.86, 105½; C¹¹ᴬ, 5, ff.154, 280, 281; 6, f.14; 7, f.146; 10, f.17; 11, ff.171, 212; 14, ff.295, 296; 16, ff.28, 29; 17, ff.21, 22, 78, 138, 139; 18, f.12; 20, ff.45, 46; C¹¹ᴰ, 4; 5, ff.83–99; D²ᶜ, 49, ff.40, 48, 65, 88, 111, 125, 139; 222, ff.45, 177, 220; F³, f.90; 6, ff.331, 469–71, 498, 499; 11, f.286. AQ, NF, Ins. Cons. sup.; Procès-verbaux des grands voyers, I, ff.6–48, 63–75. Bibliothèque de l'Arsenal (Paris), Archives de la Bastille, 151, liasse 431.

Charlevoix, History (Shea), IV, 133–45, 214–15; V, 166–68. Jug. et délib., III, 383, 388; IV, VI. Lahontan, Nouveaux voyages, I, 203–5. La Potherie, Histoire (1722), III, 61–70, 76–81. P.-G. Roy, Inventaire des procès-verbaux des grands voyers conservés aux archives de la province de Québec (6v., Beauceville, 1923–32), I, II. É.-Z. Massicotte, "Les prétendus barons de Bécancour," BRH, LII (1946), 73f.

ROBINAU DE NEUVILLETTE, DANIEL, officer serving with the troops in Acadia; b. 1672 or 1673, son of René Robinau* de Bécancour and Marie-Anne Leneuf de La Poterie, godson of Governor Rémy* de Courcelle, brother of Joseph Robinau* de Villebon, governor of Acadia; d. 1702.

Neuvillette began his service in 1690 and the following year received a commission as ensign. During the winter of 1692 he was in command on the Saint John River. On several occasions he carried out liaison missions between Acadia and Quebec, and he maintained good relations with the Indians. He lent active support to his brother in various situations, particularly during the attack by the English under Hathorne on Fort Nashwaak (Naxouat) in 1696. Buade* de Frontenac requested a lieutenant's commission for him, and this was granted him on 3 April 1696. He then commanded small ships fitted out for fighting privateers and for protecting fishing, and in October 1698 he seized an English ship off Port-Royal (Annapolis Royal, N.S.). The ship however put out to sea while Neuvillette was carousing on land.

His violent nature and his dissolute conduct with Indian women brought on him the hostility of Father Simon [La Place*], the commissary de GOUTIN, and certain officers. On 9 Dec. 1698 Louis de GANNES de Falaise wrote that Neuvillette was "a hot-headed man whose only occupation is engaging in debauchery, and who associates with the soldiers in order to use them for making contacts." In 1699 he had to go to France at the king's order to give an account of his conduct. His brother, the governor, sought the minister's indulgence for "youthful indiscretions," and this intervention was doubtless efficacious, for Neuvillette was able to return to Acadia at the beginning of the following year. He won the appreciation of the next governor, Brouillan [MOMBETON], who described him as "very devoted to the service and very suitable for this country because of his knowledge of it." Brouillan proposed him for promotion to the next rank, but his death prevented this. He was killed in 1702 in a combat against a brigantine from Boston which had just captured several fishing boats.

ÉTIENNE TAILLEMITE

AN, Col., B, 20, f.155v; 22, f.41v; C¹¹ᴬ, 14, ff.13, 175; 20, f.158; C¹¹ᴰ, 3, ff.70v, 105, 125v, 132, 156, 208; 4, ff.61, 225v; D²ᶜ, 49, 222. Coll. de manuscrits relatifs à la N.-F., II. NYCD (O'Callaghan and Fernow), IX. Webster, Acadia. Le Jeune, Dictionnaire, II, 454. Tanguay, Dictionnaire, I, 523; VII, 9.

ROBINAU DE PORTNEUF, RENÉ, officer who served in Acadia and Canada; b. 3 Sept. 1659 at Quebec, son of René Robinau* de Bécancour, Baron de Portneuf, and of Marie-Anne Leneuf de La Poterie; d. during the night of 3–4 Oct. 1726 at Montreal.

In 1689 Portneuf was appointed a lieutenant in Acadia, where his brother, Joseph Robinau* de Villebon, was in command. He took an active part in the operations against the English and established close relations with the Abenaki Indian tribes. During the winter of 1689–90 Buade* de Frontenac sent him, with 50 Canadians and 60 Indians, to attack the English post at Casco (Falmouth). He was joined by JEAN-BAPTISTE HERTEL de Rouville and JEAN-VINCENT D'ABBADIE de Saint-Castin, and in June 1690 he obtained the enemy's capitulation in return for the assurance that their lives would be spared and that they would be well treated. The next night he went off towards Fort Loyal (Portland) to attack a small garrison under the command of SILVANUS DAVIS, whom he captured. But he could or would not prevent the Indians from proceeding to massacre the prisoners, which created strong feeling in the English settlements. In 1692 Portneuf again joined forces with Saint-Castin to attack the English posts on Penobscot Bay, but the enterprise was a failure, although everyone fought with great

579

Robinson

bravery, and the Indians withdrew, laying waste the whole countryside as they did so.

Numerous complaints about Portneuf began to arrive at the court of Versailles. He was accused of engaging in the fur trade and of having "carried on undesirable relations with an Indian woman, to the certain knowledge of the people who were with them." He was cashiered in 1693, which did not, however, prevent him from continuing to go to war. On 25 Oct. 1696 Intendant BOCHART de Champigny wrote that his conduct was improving. "He has not failed to go to war when the opportunity has arisen. He has even participated in the last campaign as aide-de-camp to M. de Frontenac, who has been very well satisfied with him." His disgrace was therefore relatively minor, and the court was asked to restore him to his rank without, however, sending him back to Acadia, where he had created too much of a disturbance.

In November 1700 the governor general put forward Portneuf's name for the first lieutenancy that became vacant; in 1702 CALLIÈRE wrote that he was a good officer and again recommended him, "His Majesty having pardoned the aforesaid Sieur de Portneuf some petty faults of which he had been accused." On 1 June 1703 he was again appointed lieutenant and continued to serve in Canada. In 1708 he was lieutenant with the company commanded by JOSEPH DESJORDY de Cabanac, but in reality he remained with the governor general, RIGAUD de Vaudreuil, to serve as interpreter of the Abenaki language, and he seems to have rendered great services in the performance of his duties.

In 1712 Madame de Vaudreuil [JOYBERT] asked that Portneuf be given command of a company. This request was confirmed the following year by the governor general himself, who intervened in favour of Portneuf "in consideration of his services and the fact that he is very useful to him, since he knows perfectly the language of the Abenaki Indians."

On 27 April 1716 Portneuf was promoted captain. Some time later mention is made of him as a "poor, brave, honest man." In 1725 he went to replace M. de SABREVOIS in command of the fort at Chambly, an important post which covered the Montreal region and where a stone fort had been built in 1710. But his health was seriously impaired; indeed, on 23 Sept. 1726, Governor general Beauharnois* de La Boische announced that he had had to bring Portneuf back to Montreal because he was no longer able to continue his service, "on account of his age and infirmities." He was suffering from a malady "from which it is feared he will not recover." He died a few days later.

On 26 July 1706, at Montreal, Portneuf had married Marguerite Daneau de Muy, daughter of Nicolas DANEAU de Muy; they had 12 children.

ÉTIENNE TAILLEMITE

AN, Col., C¹¹ᴬ, 12, ff.91v, 95; 14, f.201v; 15, ff.84v, 131; 16, f.114v; 18, f.24v; 19, f.72v; 30, f.352; 33, f.290; 34, f.62; 36, f.112; 47, f.74; 48, f.157; D²ᶜ, 47, 49, 222. "Correspondance de Frontenac (1689–99)," APQ *Rapport, 1928–29*, 37, 42, 57. *NYCD* (O'Callaghan and Fernow), IV, 748; IX, 362, 461, 472. Webster, *Acadia*, 186–87. Le Jeune, *Dictionnaire*. Lorin, *Le comte de Frontenac*. H. H. Peckham, *The colonial wars, 1689–1762* (Chicago, 1964), 31, 32, 43, 49, 50. P.-G. Roy, "René Robineau de Portneuf et ses enfants," *Cahiers des Dix*, XVI (1951), 171–93.

ROBINSON, SIR ROBERT, captain in the Royal Navy; prominent theorist on the fishery at Newfoundland; governor of Bermuda; b. *c.* 1624; d. 1705.

A ship-owner of unknown origins, Robinson obtained a naval commission in October 1652. He had a long, active, and successful career in the Royal Navy, serving with distinction in the second Dutch War. He achieved command of a Channel squadron in 1668 and was knighted for his naval services in 1675.

Robinson first came to Newfoundland in 1661 at the time of Lord Baltimore's attempt to establish proprietary government. He returned as commodore of the annual convoys in 1665, 1668, and 1680. From 1668 onwards he submitted many drafts on the trade and fishery, and played a prominent part in the long struggle for influence between the planters resident in Newfoundland and the West Country merchant interests. He was strongly in favour of the appointment of a governor to administer the fishery and to secure the settlements against military attack by the French. He petitioned Charles II for the post of governor in 1669, and carried on his campaign for civil government over many years.

Throughout the late 17th and early 18th centuries many similar requests and proposals for civil government were made, but none were successful. The power remained in the hands of the Western Adventurers, who were violently opposed to the establishment of a permanent civil governing body. The only outside authority they tolerated was that of the seasonal commodore of the convoy, who was to help the fishing admirals to keep order in the various ports, but not to interfere in fishing matters; the commodore's post was thus a naval one, and not the civil position advocated by Robinson and, in later years, by Sir John GIBSONE and Commodore KEMPTHORNE.

In 1682 a commission for Robinson's court-martial was issued after he had allegedly allowed the dispersal of the incoming convoy from Cadiz, but apparently no trial took place. In 1686 he was appointed governor of Bermuda. During an unhappy term of office there he was constantly charged with financial corruption, and was recalled at his own request in 1690. His active career was now over, though he put forward further tracts on Newfoundland in 1693 and 1696—merely restatements of his earlier views—and asked, without success, to be restored as governor of Bermuda. He died, on a rear-admiral's life-pension, at the age of eighty-one.

C. M. ROWE

PRO, *Acts of P.C., col. ser., 1613–80, 1680–1720*; *CSP, Col., 1661–68, 1669–74, 1675–76, 1677–80, 1685–88, 1689–92, 1699, 1700*. Charnock, *Biographia navalis*, I. C. B. Judah, *The North American fisheries and British policy to 1713* (University of Illinois studies in the social sciences, XVIII, nos. 3–4, 1932, distributed 1933). Lounsbury, *British fishery at Nfld*. Prowse, *History of Nfld*.

ROBUTEL DE LA NOUE, ZACHARIE, lieutenant on half-pay and on the active list, captain, seigneur of Châteauguay; b. 4 June 1665 at Montreal, son of Claude Robutel de La Noue, seigneur of Île Saint-Paul, and of Suzanne de Gabrielle; d. 1733 at Baie des Puants (Green Bay, Wis.).

Robutel de La Noue began to attract attention in 1686, at the time of the expedition of the Chevalier de Troyes* to Hudson Bay. He took part in it as an adjutant. "Although they [the Le Moynes and he] were reputed to be the best canoeists in Canada," La Noue twice very nearly drowned in the rapids, when his canoe broke up and he himself had difficulty reaching the bank, for he could not swim. At Hudson Bay he was one of the first, with PIERRE LE MOYNE d'Iberville and five or six others, to enter Fort Monsipi.

In 1691 he became an ensign, then a half-pay lieutenant in 1692, a lieutenant on the active list in 1710, and finally a captain in 1725. He regularly took part in various expeditions of the time. In 1692 for example, with 3 Canadians and 25 Indians, he escorted in the Ottawa River region 43 Frenchmen who were making their way from Montreal towards Michilimackinac. The following year La Noue led a party of 625 men which set out from Montreal to attack three Mohawk villages; he was wounded in the fighting. In 1709, with the Sieur de Manthet [AILLEBOUST], he commanded a party bound for the north; according to RIGAUD de Vaudreuil, "one can say that it is to his prudence that we owe what remains of this party"; hence Vaudreuil called him "a very worthy person and one of the bravest officers in the colony."

From 1717 on, Robutel de La Noue was in the governor's service, with the task of trying to discover the northern sea by an inland route through New France. He set out in July 1717, with three canoes and the order "to establish the first post on the Kanastigoya River in the northern part of Lake Superior, after which he is to go to Takamamis8n in the direction of Lac des Christinaux to set up a second, and through the Indians to obtain the necessary information for setting up the third at Lac des Assenipoëlle." He remained at Kaministiquia until 1721, and according to the testimony of Father Charlevoix* returned to Montreal that year.

A document preserved in the archives of the Chicago Historical Society contains particulars concerning the partnership entered into by Robutel de La Noue with Paul de Marin* de La Malgue for trading in furs in 1729, but we have no precise details on this subject. La Noue seems to have spent his last years at Baie des Puants, where he died in 1733; he was not commandant there though he may have been recommended for that post.

In August 1706 Robutel de La Noue had bought the seigneury of Châteauguay from the children and heirs of Charles Le Moyne*. In 1689 he had married Catherine Le Moyne, Jacques*' daughter, by whom he had nine children.

NIVE VOISINE

Caron, "Inventaire de documents," APQ *Rapport, 1941–42,* 179–298. "Correspondance de Vaudreuil," APQ *Rapport, 1938–39,* 12–179. *Découvertes et établissements des Français* (Margry), VI, 522. Provost, "Inventaire de documents," 594. Chevalier de Troyes, *Journal* (Caron).

RODRIGUE, JEAN-BAPTISTE (sometimes called **Jean de Fonds (Fond)**), king's pilot, fisherman, merchant, churchwarden of Louisbourg parish; b. apparently in the 1670s in Portugal, probably at Viana do Castelo, son of Jean de Fond and Anne Manet; d. between 15 Sept. and 16 Nov. 1733 at Quebec.

Rodrigue probably came to Acadia after 1700; in 1707 he married Anne, daughter of Alexandre Le Borgne* de Belle-Isle and Marie de Saint-Étienne de La Tour, both of prominent Acadian families. Rodrigue and his wife had at least eight children.

Rodrigue served as king's pilot at Port-Royal (Annapolis Royal, N.S.) as late as March 1709. By August 1710 he had moved to Placentia (Plaisance) whence he made raids on British shipping and engaged in trade. While cruising in Acadian waters in October 1710, he met the

Roger

English invasion fleet led by Francis NICHOLSON, and it was he who dispatched messengers to Port-Royal with the news. In March 1712, Rodrigue was still engaged in trade at Placentia. He then served as a pilot at Dunkirk, as later reported by Le Normant* de Mézy, presumably sometime between the latter date and November 1713, when he is referred to as a merchant of Quebec. In 1714 he settled at Louisbourg in the new French colony of Île Royale (Cape Breton Island). After assisting in the evacuation of Placentia, ceded to Great Britain in 1713, Rodrigue prospered in fishing, coasting, and local trade. The censuses and the admiralty records of Île Royale give an idea of Rodrigue's involvement in fishing and trade; he had only one employee in 1715, 20 in 1716, 15 in 1717, 20 in 1720, and 30 in 1724. At the time of his death in 1733 he was one of the principal merchants of the colony.

Following his death, which occurred while he was in Quebec on business in the fall of 1733, his widow and two eldest sons, Michel and Pierre, carried on the family enterprise. In 1738 his widow married Jean Duperié (or Duperier) of Louisbourg, who in 1731 had been first mate on a fishing vessel from Saint-Jean-de-Luz.

BERNARD POTHIER

Archives de la Charente-Maritime (La Rochelle), Amirauté de Louisbourg, B 265, B 266–67, B 268, ff.160–64; B 277. AN, Col., C¹¹ᴮ, 1–14; C¹¹ᶜ, 7, ff.54ff.; 15; Section Outre-Mer, G¹, 406, 467; G³, 2040, 15 May 1707, 17 March 1709; 2046; 2054, pièce 52, 14 Aug. 1710; pièce 55, 18 Aug. 1710; 2055, pièce 2, 22 Feb. 1712; pièce 118, 16 [Nov.] 1713. PANS, MS docs., XXVI (parish register of Port-Royal), 21.

ROGER, GUILLAUME, principal court officer and clerk of the Conseil Souverain, provost judge of the seigneury of Notre-Dame-des-Anges, royal notary; son of Roger Guillaume, court officer, and Élisabeth Oussaye; b. in France in 1632; buried in Quebec 22 May 1702.

From August 1674 he acted as a court officer for the Conseil Souverain, and on 15 June 1676 replaced Peuvret* Demesnu as court clerk and secretary; on 25 Oct. 1677 he again became clerk under the latter's orders. He was appointed principal court officer on 18 May 1681, and was confirmed in this post on the 11 August following. In 1679 the Jesuits appointed him provost judge of the Notre-Dame-des-Anges seigneury. He succeeded Claude Auber* in 1694 as royal notary. While holding these different offices concurrently, he also served the council, on occasion, as acting judge, attorney, and secretary.

In August 1674, Frontenac [Buade*] had the Sulpician François de Salignac* de La Mothe-Fénelon arrested at Montreal, following a sermon which he gave. He was put in prison at Quebec, under Roger's guard. In the following October Fénelon, by order of the council, was required to pay "37 *livres* to court officer Guillaume Roger for his services."

At the conclusion of an "extraordinary trial," in his capacity as judge of the Notre-Dame-des-Anges seigneury, he sentenced Jean Denis junior, *in absentia*, to be broken on the wheel for the murder of Pierre Gendron.

In 1673 he had married Ursule Levasseur; they had had nine children, only one of whom reached adult age.

ANTONIO DROLET

AJQ, Greffe de Gilles Rageot, 6 janv. 1672; Greffe de Guillaume Roger, 1694–1702; Registre d'état civil de Notre-Dame de Québec. AQ, NF, Ord. des. int., I, 290; QBC, Biens des Jésuites, Notre-Dame-des-Anges. "Informations et déclarations faites au sujet d'un sermon du sieur abbé de Fénelon prononcé le jour de Pâques, 25 mars 1674, dans l'église paroissiale de Montréal (2 mai 1674)," APQ *Rapport*, 1921–22, 157, 187. *Jug. et délib.* "Les notaires au Canada," 30. J.-E. Roy, *Histoire du notariat*, I, 132f. "La haute justice dans les justices seigneuriales: sentence contre Jean Denis fils rendu le 14 septembre 1695 par Guillaume Roger, juge prévost de Notre-Dame des Anges," *BRH*, XXIII (1917), 187–90. J.-E. Roy, "Les conseillers au Conseil souverain de la Nouvelle-France," *BRH*, I (1895), 183f.

ROLLAND, FRANÇOIS LENOIR, *dit. See* LENOIR

ROOPE, JOHN, engineer and Gentleman of the Ordnance in Newfoundland; d. 1719.

Roope served in the Irish transport and had been in Newfoundland before being assigned by the ordnance as an engineer (under Captain Michael RICHARDS) to lay a boom across St John's harbour to protect it from French attacks. He arrived in St John's on 5 Oct. 1703. When he saw the vulnerability of the colony, Roope wrote asking that 2,500 soldiers, artillery, and 15 or 16 ships of war be sent to seize the French forts in Newfoundland, especially at Placentia (Plaisance), and in Acadia (Nova Scotia). The War of the Spanish Succession had reduced the number of English vessels engaged in the fishery, had practically closed the Mediterranean market to the English, and had therefore increased the desire of merchants and planters to have the French eliminated from the fishery.

In October 1704 Roope promised to finish the boom shortly; he would have finished it long since if Captain Thomas LLOYD had given him the required assistance. In his report he criticized the New England traders "coming hither in shoals," bringing rum, and carrying off seamen; the Scots who were "prying into the trade," who worked for low wages and could undersell the English; and the garrison's officers who traded privately, and illegally, and whose conduct should be inspected yearly by the commodore and the fishing admirals. Such comments from a supporter, in the main, of the West Country interests did not sit well with the men concerned: Lloyd, John MOODY, Colin CAMPBELL, John JACKSON, and Archibald CUMINGS, all blamed Roope after AUGER de Subercase's attack on St John's 21 Jan. 1704/5. Roope and his fellow engineer, Lieutenant Robert LATHAM, were accused of dissuading the inhabitants from aiding the garrison, and Campbell accused Roope of having had treasonable communications with the French. Roope's later explanation for the French knowledge of the fort's weakness was Lloyd's barbarous treatment of his soldiers, 30 of whom had earlier deserted to the French at Placentia.

When Subercase's troops left St John's they took Roope with them. His enemies said that he went willingly, though he maintained that he was forced to go. After eight months at Placentia, Roope was exchanged for some French prisoners held at St John's. He sailed for England in November 1705.

Between January and March 1705/6, he attended several meetings of the Board of Trade, and gave his views on how Newfoundland might be better defended and governed. He urged the local election, rather than royal appointment, of the governor and of the militia. Although it had not accepted an earlier plea for local civil government, the board obviously had confidence in Roope's opinions. He had shown objectivity and insight in explaining to the board the failure of John GRAYDON's expedition in 1703, and the charges and counter-charges that bombarded the board after the capture of St John's in 1704/5. Roope requested repayment for his great losses, and further employment. In April 1706 their Lordships promised to do what they could for him.

Roope accompanied the train of artillery to Spain as a Gentleman of the Ordnance and was storekeeper at Alicante Castle after it was taken in February 1706/7. Some time later he was among those captured at Villaviciosa, where he "lost all." He was in Barcelona in 1712 when the war in Spain was virtually over and the artillery trains disbanded. In 1714, on half pay as a lieutenant, he attended the Board of Trade to present some amendments to the parliamentary act desired by the West Country traders, a paper on the curing of

fish, and an account of the island of Menorca (now also British). In September Dartmouth nominated Roope as surveyor of Newfoundland, but William Taverner* won the commission. Roope was appointed a fireworker in the Royal Artillery 26 May 1716. It appears that he lived in Menorca for several years, but his interest in Newfoundland continued until his death. On 12 Feb. 1718/19 the board consulted him for the last time, before ordering some West Country mayors to carry, as ballast, materials to build a stone redoubt at the entrance to St John's harbour.

C. P. MCFARLAND

PRO, *B.T.Journal*, *1704–1708/9*, *1708/9–1714/15*, *1714/15–1718*, *1718–22*; *CSP, Col.*, *1702–3*, *1704–5*, *1706–8*, *1712–14*; *C.T.Papers*, *1714–19*. G.B., Parliament, *Proceedings and debates respecting North America* (Stock). Dalton, *English army lists*, V, VI. Lounsbury, *British fishery at Nfld.* Bernardine Pietraszek, "Anglo-French trade conflicts in North America, 1702–13," *Mid-America*, XXXV (1953; new ser., XXIV), 146–48.

ROUER DE VILLERAY ET DE LA CARDONNIÈRE, AUGUSTIN,

first seigneur of Rimouski and councillor on the Conseil Souverain; baptized 13 June 1664 at Quebec, son of Louis Rouer* de Villeray, councillor of the Conseil Souverain, and of Catherine Sevestre; d. in the spring of 1711. He bore the name La Cardonnière until the death of his father on 6 Dec. 1700, and subsequently, as the eldest son of the family, he inherited the title of Villeray.

Since his father ranked among the most important members of the colony, Augustin received on 27 April 1684, jointly with his brother Louis Rouer* d'Artigny, the seigneury of Île Verte, having a frontage of two leagues on the St Lawrence River and extending to a depth of two leagues back, together with the islands and islets opposite this shore. The parish of Île Verte is situated today on the site of this seigneury.

On 6 Oct. 1685 Jacques de MEULLES wrote a long report to the minister, Seignelay. He requested that the post of special lieutenant on the bench of the provost court of Quebec, "together with a reasonable salary for the said office," be re-established for the benefit of his protégé Augustin de La Cardonnière. The minister did not see fit to give effect to the intendant's request.

On 24 April 1688 BRISAY de Denonville granted the seigneury of Rimouski to Augustin de la Cardonnière. The latter turned over the domain of Île Verte to his brother Artigny, and became seigneur of Rimouski. This seigneury had a frontage of two leagues on the river and extended to a

Rousson

depth of two leagues inland. To it were added Île Saint-Barnabé, and the adjoining islands and islets.

Augustin Rouer de La Cardonnière remained seigneur of Rimouski until 18 July 1694. On that date he transferred his domain to René Lepage, in exchange for a tract of land that the latter owned at Saint-François on Île d'Orléans. On 29 Oct. 1703 the Conseil Souverain of New France accepted M. de La Cardonnière, who had become M. de Villeray, as one of its members.

Villeray's burial certificate has not been found, but everything seems to indicate that he died in the spring of 1711. His first wife, whom he had married on 1 Sept. 1689, was Marie-Louise, daughter of Charles Legardeur* de Tilly, who bore him six children; then in 1706 he married Marie-Louise, daughter of François Pollet* de La Combe-Pocatière, by whom he had three children.

BÉATRICE CHASSÉ

AN, Col., C¹¹ᴬ, 7, ff.157ff. AQ, NF, Cahiers d'intendance, I, 22ff.; II, 688; Registres d'intendance, I, 13. ASQ, Séminaire, II, 1; IV, 1. *Jug. et délib.*, IV, 912ff. P.-G. Roy, *Diverses familles* (3v., Lévis, 1920), I, 53ff.

ROUSSON, FRANÇOISE LE VERRIER DE. *See* LE VERRIER

ROUVILLE, JEAN-BAPTISTE HERTEL DE. *See* HERTEL

ROY, *dit* **CHÂTELLERAULT, MICHEL,** soldier, settler, seigneurial notary, royal attorney, court officer; b. 1649 in the little town of Sénillé, near Châtellerault (Vienne), son of Michel Roy and Louise Chevalier; buried 14 Jan. 1709 at Sainte-Anne-de-la-Pérade.

Michel Roy arrived at Quebec in September 1665 as a soldier in the Carignan regiment (company of Naurois). When the troops were disbanded, he decided to settle down in the country, and on 8 Oct. 1668 he married a *fille du roi*, Françoise Hobbé, an educated Parisian of good family who was 10 years older than he. There were five children from this union. On 16 November of the same year he obtained a grant of land in the seigneury of Sainte-Anne. At the same time the seigneur Michel Gamelain* appointed him seigneurial notary and his *chargé d'affaires*. He enjoyed the confidence of successive seigneurs and attracted around him several former comrades in arms.

For 40 years this pioneer combined the functions of farmer, notary, attorney, court officer, and commander of the militia. In 1689, perhaps at his sons' request, he agreed to enter into partnership with a full-time fur-trader, Robert Rivard, *dit* Loranger; they contracted with the Compagnie du Nord for the trade of the Lacs Abitibi and Témiscamingue region. This was his only venture into the fur trade, in which he seems to have played no active role.

His registry, from which certain documents have disappeared, includes 345 deeds concerning almost exclusively the seigneuries of Sainte-Anne, Saint-Charles-des-Roches (Grondines), and Sainte-Marie.

Michel Roy was interred 14 Jan. 1709. His wife had been buried two days before him. They had five children, three girls and two boys, many of whose descendants have carried on the name Châtellerault till the present day.

RAYMOND DOUVILLE

AJQ, Greffe de Gilles Rageot, 22 janv. 1689. AJTR, Greffe de Guillaume de Larue; Greffe de Jacques de La Touche; Greffe de Michel Roy, 1669–99. Raymond Douville, *Premiers seigneurs et colons de Sainte-Anne de la Pérade (1667–1681)* (Trois-Rivières, 1946). C.-C. Lalanne, *Histoire du Châtelleraud [sic] du Châtelleraudais* (2v., Châtellerault, 1859). Régis Roy et Malchelosse, *Le régiment de Carignan*.

ROYBON D'ALLONNE, MADELEINE DE, seigneuress; b. *c.* 1646 at Montargis (department of Loiret), daughter of Jacques de Roybon d'Allonne, soldier in the king's company, then gentleman carver at the court; d. mid-January 1718 at the *côte* Saint-Martin, near Montreal.

Like many other young ladies of the lesser nobility at that period, Madeleine probably came to New France in search of a husband. She never married, but it is thanks to the love affair attributed to her by historians that she has passed into history. If there was a woman in René-Robert Cavelier* de La Salle's life, it is supposed that it was she, because the archives mention her name in close association with the discoverer's, and because she was the only spinster of her rank to live at Fort Frontenac.

The loan of 2,141 *livres* that she made to the explorer on 24 Aug. 1681, at Cataracoui, is the first proof of Mlle d'Allonne's presence in the colony; it is perhaps also an indication of her attachment to a man who was then being hounded by his creditors. At that date Madeleine had been living for perhaps a little more than two years at the fort that belonged to La Salle. The fanciful "Récit d'un ami de l'abbé de Gallinée" reports that around September 1678 the discoverer was falsely accused of indulging in debauchery in his home with a girl he had seduced in Quebec, whereas on the contrary, the "Récit" says, he was living an exemplary "family" life there. In addition, in 1679 news of La Salle's marriage spread as far as Paris, a rumour which the interested party categorically denied afterwards, protesting that he would never marry anyone before he had successfully completed his undertakings. As there is never smoke without fire, no doubt there did exist a marriageable girl in La Salle's *entourage* at the time, whether he aspired to her hand or not.

We come across Madeleine de Roybon d'Allonne again on 6 Nov. 1683 at Quebec, still in the company of the explorer, who was then preparing to leave for France. La Salle gave her an I.O.U., in which he ensured to her "the possession of the house and land that she has occupied up to now at Fort Frontenac." This is the only document written by La Salle that has come down to us in which he names the young woman.

They were never to see each other again. Madeleine returned to Cataracoui, where the local seigneur had granted her a fief and seigneury in the neighbourhood of the fort. She continued from afar to take an interest in the destiny of the man whose tragic end we know.

A few months after La Salle's murder, Mlle d'Allonne almost perished in her turn. Some Iroquois captured her and laid waste her establishment at the beginning of August 1687. Her life was spared through the mediation of Father JEAN DE LAMBERVILLE, but he was unable to have her set free. The prisoner was taken to Onondaga, then, at Thomas Dongan's request, to Albany. There she attempted to cooperate in Father François VAILLANT de Gueslis' negotiations with the governor of New York and the Indians.

The following year she was finally set free, and arrived in Montreal in July. She settled permanently in Rue Saint-Vincent, being prevented from returning to her dwelling at Fort Frontenac by the monopoly of the fur trade held there first by the Compagnie du Canada then by the crown. The woman who had invested and lost her fortune at Cataracoui insisted fiercely on her right to re-establish herself there, and argued in favour of giving the local settlers freedom to trade in pelts. She even went to France in 1706 to defend her cause. Eleven years later the matter was still before the council of Marine. On 12 Oct. 1717 RIGAUD de Vaudreuil stated in a reply to the council that the plaintiff had not availed herself of the permission granted to her by the governor in 1706 to go and redevelop her land, because she was interested only in the fur trade. Vaudreuil went on: "Moreover, Mademoiselle Dalonne is enfeebled by age, very

poor, and consequently unable to go and put in order again a piece of land that has been left deserted for 30 years. She is a worthy person; her station and the sad state to which she finds herself reduced might incline the council to agree to grant her some favour."

She passed away at about the age of 72.

CÉLINE DUPRÉ

ASQ, Polygraphie, XXVII, 60. *Découvertes et établissements des Français* (Margry), I, 296–98, 381f., 430; II, 88. *Jug. et délib.*, IV, V. *NYCD* (O'Callaghan and Fernow), III, 517, 520, 527, 529, 535, 556, 563; IX, 389–91. *Royal Fort Frontenac* (Preston and Lamontagne), 39f., 49, 136–39, 171f., 333–36, 368f. Claude de Bonnault, "Cavelier de La Salle," *Larousse mensuel illustré* (14v., Paris, 1907–57), X (1935–36), 231. Rochemonteix, *Les Jésuites et la N.-F. au XVIIe siècle*, II, 413; III, 168–70, 197–207. Jean Delanglez, "Mlle de Roybon D'Allonne: La Salle's fiancée?" *Mid-America*, XXI (1939; new ser., X), 298–313. [This article is the most important work on the subject. In it the author corrects certain errors, such as Mlle d'Allonne's alleged presence at Fort Frontenac from 1675 to 1677 and her second captivity among the Indians. C.D.] É.-Z. Massicotte, "Un fait divers d'autrefois," *BRH*, XXV (1919), 277–79; "Les testaments de Mlle de Roybon d'Alonne," *BRH*, XXVIII (1922), 94–96.

RUETTE D'AUTEUIL DE MONCEAUX, FRANÇOIS - MADELEINE - FORTUNÉ (he sometimes signed **Monceaux,** and his contemporaries often used this name), attorney general to the Conseil Souverain of Quebec from 1680 to 1707; son of Denis-Joseph Ruette* d'Auteuil and Claire-Françoise Clément Du Vuault; born at sea, probably at the end of 1657, baptized in Paris 17 Jan. 1658; d. at Quebec 10 July 1737.

In 1661 his father and his maternal grandmother, Mme Jean Bourdon, went to France and brought him back with them to Quebec. Around 1673 he returned to Paris to carry on his studies there. In March 1678 he obtained his degree in law, and the following month he was called to the bar of the *parlement* of Paris. Having returned to Quebec that same year, he worked with his father the attorney general. The latter, a victim of the ill-will of Frontenac [Buade*], whose hostility was unrelenting, had been ill for several years and in addition threatened with blindness. As early as 1676 Intendant Duchesneau*, worried by Denis-Joseph Ruette d'Auteuil's state of health, had obtained letters of appointment from Colbert providing for a deputy, in case the attorney general should die. The name of this deputy was left blank, and Colbert had authorized Duchesneau to insert that of a nominee chosen by him. On 10 Nov. 1679, feeling that his end was approaching, Auteuil wrote

Ruette d'Auteuil

to Colbert requesting him to appoint his son to succeed him. A few days later he passed away. The intendant recommended that the governor insert the name of Ruette d'Auteuil junior in the letters of appointment that he had held for two years. Frontenac would not hear of it. He pointed out, among other things, that the young Auteuil was a minor. Duchesneau retorted, in answer to the governor's objections, that his candidate's natural gifts, his brilliant studies in Paris, the diplomas that he had obtained there, and the experience he had acquired in working with his father, made him, despite his youth (he was not 22), the best qualified man in the colony to hold the office of attorney general. The matter was taken before the Conseil Souverain. It was decided that the intendant had the right to insert François-Madeleine-Fortuné d'Auteuil's name in the letters of appointment obtained in 1677, but that this appointment should not be registered until the latter had received a waiver of the age limit from the king. Auteuil lost no time in writing to Versailles. In June 1680 the king appointed him attorney general by reversion from his father. It is clear that this appointment had been made in response to the latter's petition and before the minister had learned of his death, for it was not accompanied by the waiver of the age limit that his son had requested. Nevertheless, the council registered the commission on 24 Oct. 1680, and the new attorney general took up his office the same day.

The subsequent year was marked by an unbroken series of disputes between the governor and the attorney general. François Ruette d'Auteuil was a proud and aggressive man, and was supported by the intendant and the council. Remembering not only Frontenac's opposition to his appointment but also the affronts inflicted by Frontenac on his father, Auteuil lost no opportunity to thwart his plans, harry his favourites, and protect his victims. In November 1681 Frontenac, beside himself with rage, ordered him to proceed to France and to bring back (if he could) the waiver of the age limit that he had never received. In doing this the governor thought he would ruin his enemy and get rid of him once and for all. Never was a calculation more mistaken. Despite the complaints that Frontenac had lodged at the court, the young attorney general made an excellent impression there. Equipped with his famous waiver, he returned to Quebec in the autumn of 1682, at the time when Frontenac, who had received his recall to France, was preparing to leave Canada.

Under La Barre [Le Febvre*] and Denonville [Brisay] there was a period of calm. In 1683 Auteuil married Marie-Anne Juchereau de Saint-Denis, the daughter of one of the most important citizens in the colony and the widow of François Pollet* de La Combe-Pocatière, a captain in the Carignan regiment. From that time on the attorney general made the interests of his wife's family his own.

In 1689 Frontenac returned to Canada. No dissension between him and his former enemy disturbed the first years of his administration. The attorney general, however, like his father, did not lose sight of the powers that had been conferred on the Conseil Souverain in 1663. He was firmly resolved to protect them from encroachments by the civil and even religious authorities.

In the autumn of 1692 he protested vigorously against a plan by Bishop Saint-Vallier [La Croix] that was already being carried out, namely the creation of the Hôpital Général, the administration of which was to be entrusted to nuns (the Religious Hospitallers of the Hôtel-Dieu of Quebec). This opposition was based on several considerations; the first of them directly concerned the Conseil Souverain's prerogatives. In this connection Auteuil pointed out that Bishop Saint-Vallier's plan conflicted with a decree of 1688, whereby the council had set up in each parish an office for the needy run by laymen. Furthermore, the attorney general did not fail to stress that by putting his hospital in the hands of nuns, the bishop was going against the royal ordinance that forbad the founding of new convents in Canada without the express permission of His Majesty. But the letters patent which Bishop Saint-Vallier had obtained at Versailles in March 1692 contained no "special declaration" to that effect. Although he was supported by Laval, Frontenac, and Champigny [Bochart], and although all the directors of the Bureau des Pauvres except Auteuil, had agreed to be on the board of administration of the Hôpital Général, Bishop Saint-Vallier thought it wiser not to make a frontal attack on his adversary, and to let time do its work.

In 1694 the *Tartuffe* affair put an end to the somewhat fragile peace which had prevailed for five years between Frontenac and Ruette d'Auteuil. The latter sided ostentatiously with Saint-Vallier. He had Mareuil*, whom Frontenac supported against the attacks of the bishop of Quebec, thrown into prison. Also in 1694, the attorney general took the governor to task over a tax which the latter wanted to levy on meat. The two adversaries did not fail to send their complaints to Versailles. Obviously struck by the arrogance with which Auteuil expressed himself, Pontchartrain enjoined him (in his letter of 8 June 1695) to apologize to Frontenac. This incident, however, in no way diminished the favour that the attorney general enjoyed at the court, or the preponderant influence that he exercised over the Conseil Souverain. In 1700 the king granted him a pension of 300 *livres*.

In October of the same year the members of the Compagnie de la Colonie named him as one of the directors of this undertaking, which had just been established. The attorney general's prestige and activity increased steadily during the next three years. In 1703, under CALLIÈRE (whom he had supported against Vaudreuil [RIGAUD] in 1698) he was considered for the post of first councillor. This appointment would no doubt have taken place if he had not had the unfortunate idea of demanding that his son replace him as attorney general. Pontchartrain refused to agree to this arrangement, and René-Louis CHARTIER de Lotbinière assumed the office of first councillor in 1703.

In fact, the year 1703 marked a decisive turning-point in François Ruette d'Auteuil's hitherto brilliant career. In May Callière died. On 1 August, Vaudreuil, who had no reason to be pleased with Auteuil's behaviour towards him, became governor. Also in 1703, the king decided to raise the number of members of the council from 7 to 12. The effect of this change was to diminish the influence that the attorney general exerted there. Finally, still in 1703, the Compagnie de la Colonie, on which the government had founded great hopes and of which Ruette d'Auteuil was one of the directors, was in an alarmingly unsound position. Following an inquiry, the minister concluded that the directors of the company were largely responsible for the situation in which it found itself.

In 1705 JACQUES RAUDOT and his son ANTOINE-DENIS landed at Quebec. In accordance with the detailed orders which he had received from Versailles, the new intendant set about abolishing the company, starting with its board of directors. Although he had been informed by the minister of the steps that Raudot had been ordered to take, the attorney general opposed them violently. He termed Raudot's conduct arbitrary, and endeavoured to persuade the other directors to refuse to resign.

Infuriated by Auteuil's arrogance, Raudot launched an inquiry into the way in which he exercised his judicial functions. He discovered that far from acting with integrity and impartiality, the attorney general was using the powers conferred upon him by his office to further his own affairs and those of his family, and that he was devoting more attention to his personal interests than to those of justice. A lawsuit which was in progress, and in which his sister-in-law, CHARLOTTE-FRANÇOISE JUCHEREAU, Dame de La Forest, was involved, was the last straw. Raudot drafted a long report, a "Réquisitoire" which he addressed to Pontchartrain. In it he declared that the attorney general, despite the obligations of his office, had personally backed up and guided Mme de La Forest in her differences with the council. In proof of this he mentioned the insertions and references in Auteuil's handwriting that had been found in a writ suing the intendant, in which Madame de La Forest accused the latter of "falsifying" an entry in the council register.

Despite the increasingly virulent criticisms to which he was subjected during the years 1705 and 1706, Ruette d'Auteuil did not cease to oppose with his accustomed vigour what he called "the innovations" of several parish priests in the matter of the tithe.

On 20 Jan. 1706 he presented to the council his "Conclusions" on the "Remarks" which BOULLARD, the former parish priest of Beauport, and Dufournel*, the parish priest of Ange-Gardien, had submitted to that assembly a few weeks previously. In them both asserted the right of parish priests to increase not only the usual rate of the tithe but also the number of items of produce on which it was levied.

The attorney general's "Conclusions" derived from juridical and humanitarian considerations. He stressed that the "innovations" of Boullard and Dufournel had been introduced without concern for the decrees of the Conseil Souverain and without taking into account the painful situation which the settlers often had to face.

In the autumn of 1706, foreseeing that his quarrels with Raudot might have serious consequences, Auteuil went to France in order to plead his cause before the minister, as he had done successfully a quarter of a century earlier. It was of no avail. On 7 June 1707 the king revoked his commission as attorney general. Overwhelmed by this disgrace, he settled in Paris with his wife. He spent his considerable leisure drafting *Mémoires* on Canada: "Mémoire sur l'état présent du Canada" (1712); others on "Les commerces de M. de Vaudreuil avec les sauvages" (1715), "La mauvaise administration de la justice au Canada" (1715), "Ce qui concerne le commerce des castors . . ." (1715), "La monnaie de cartes" (1715); an "addition au Mémoire fait en 1715 . . . sur l'état présent du Canada" (1719); and a "Mémoire secret à M. le Duc d'Orléans sur les limites de l'Acadie" (7 Jan. 1720).

As the title of the last memoir indicates, Ruette d'Auteuil's attention was then turning towards Acadia. Indeed, on 20 May 1719, he had obtained from the regent a warrant granting Îles Madame (eight leagues in area), and made out in his name and in that of his partners, Messrs. Duforillon [Aubert*] of Quebec and Jourdan, secretary to the

587

king. The recipients of the grant undertook to establish "settlements and inshore fishing" at the entry to the Gulf of St Lawrence and in the gulf itself. This undertaking was doomed to total failure. When he arrived at Îles Madame, around 20 Aug. 1722, together with 66 settlers and fishermen, Auteuil was dumbfounded to learn that the English were established at Canso (Canseau), and that the place where he counted on installing his fisheries was barren of fish. On 15 Nov. 1723 he wrote to Cardinal Dubois that it would be better for the settlers to devote their energies to farming. As this suggestion was not followed up, the former attorney general returned to Quebec after an absence of 18 years. He died there 13 years later, 10 July 1737, at the age of 80.

An intelligent and perhaps brilliant man, Ruette d'Auteuil showed himself to be arrogant right from the beginning of his career, and became more and more so as it progressed. Undisciplined, as were a number of Canadians (although to a lesser extent) when it was a question of obeying the representatives of the government at Versailles, he stirred up strife among them, and skilfully and stubbornly supported the local authority, that of the Conseil Souverain, upon which he exerted great influence until 1703. He was grasping, strongly attached to his interests and those of his family, and he played a more than dubious role in the affairs of the Compagnie de la Colonie. Furthermore, the circumstances attending his failure on the Îles Madame show fairly clearly that the former attorney general was devoid of practical common sense.

MARINE LELAND

[Except for two long articles which Ignotus [Thomas Chapais] published in *La Presse* (Montréal) on 8 and 12 Nov. 1902, and on which this study is based, no biography of F.-M.-F. Ruette d'Auteuil exists. There is, however, an abundance of original documents (manuscript and printed) referring to his career, as well as books which mention certain aspects of it. In these two cases only a brief list is given. M.L.]

AN, Col., B; C^{11A}, 3, 5, 6, 7, 13, 30, 33, 36; F^3. "Correspondance de Vaudreuil," APQ *Rapport, 1938–39*, 12–179. *Documents relating to Canadian currency during the French period* (Shortt), I, II. *Jug. et délib.*, III, IV. "Lettres et mémoires de F.-M.-F. Ruette d'Auteuil," 1–114. PAC *Report, 1885, 1887, 1899*. Taillemite, *Inventaire analytique, série B*, I.

Cahall, *Sovereign Council of New France*. J. Delalande, *Le Conseil souverain de la Nouvelle-France* (Québec, 1927). Eccles, *Canada under Louis XIV*; *Frontenac*. Lanctot, *Histoire du Canada*, II. *Monseigneur de Saint-Vallier et l'Hôpital Général de Québec*. P.-G. Roy, *La famille Juchereau Duchesnay*. H.-A. Scott, *Une paroisse historique de la Nouvelle-France, Notre-Dame de Sainte-Foy: histoire civile et religieuse d'après les sources* (Québec, 1902), 271 [this work contains important details on the Ruette d'Auteuil family and the Monceaux seigneury at Sillery]. Guy Frégault, "Politique et politiciens au début du XVIIIe siècle," *Écrits du Canada français* (Montréal), XI (1961), 172ff.

S

SABREVOIS, JACQUES-CHARLES DE, soldier, captain in the colonial regular troops, commandant at Detroit and at Fort Chambly, town major of Montreal, knight of the order of Saint-Louis; b. *c.* 1667 at Garancière-en-Beauce, son of Henri de Sabrevois, Sieur de Sermonville, and of Gabrielle Martin; d. 1727 at Montreal.

In 1682 Sabrevois received a commission as lieutenant on half-pay in the Régiment de La Fère. He seems to have come to New France in 1685, and there he received in 1687 an order from the king to occupy the post of lieutenant in an infantry company, replacing the Sieur Damours* de Chauffours.

It was in the company of his brother-in-law, Nicolas DANEAU de Muy, that he first served in New France. He took an active part in the campaigns against the Iroquois; during the winter of 1695–96, for example, although recently married, he accompanied Louis de LA PORTE de Louvigny on his expedition against the Iroquois of Grande Presqu'île, between the St Lawrence and Ottawa Rivers. He was also a member of Buade* de Frontenac's expedition during the summer of 1696 against the same enemies. He earned a citation as a "good officer." In 1702 he became captain of a company of colonial regular troops, replacing Daniel d'AUGER de Subercase, and a few years later, in 1709, he took part in the defence of the colony against Francis NICHOLSON, who was attacking via Lake Champlain. That same year Governor RIGAUD de Vaudreuil called him a "very good officer," and the following year he elaborated: "he is one of the best officers we have here, devoted to duty and well fitted for campaigns in this country."

Thanks to his service record, he obtained still more enviable posts. In 1712 the minister promised to name him commandant at Detroit, if François DAUPHIN de La Forest, who was sick at

Quebec, was unable to return there. Sabrevois occupied this post only from 1715 to 1717, for he had serious differences with Claude de RAMEZAY, whom he accused of preventing him from enjoying his fur-trading privilege. Rigaud de Vaudreuil, in rejecting the complaint—"knowing him to be a very selfish man, he does not think that [Sabrevois] made big profits at Detroit, but he certainly did not lose anything there"—stressed Sabrevois' "hardness," his "avarice," which proved that he "was not a proper person to govern Indians."

Recalled from Detroit, Sabrevois went to France to defend himself and to recruit "50 men in Paris" for the Canadian troops. It was not until 1720 that he returned from France to occupy the post of commandant at Fort Chambly. Vaudreuil, who judged him to be "very worn out and very grasping"—he added that he would not entrust to him "a post where there was trading to be done"—relieved him of his command in 1724, but was rebuked for this by the king. The following year Sabrevois was appointed town major at Montreal in succession to François LE VERRIER. He died there on 19 Jan. 1727. He had been made a knight of the order of Saint-Louis in 1718.

In 1695 Sabrevois had married Jeanne, daughter of Pierre BOUCHER, and six children were born of this marriage, three of them being sons: Charles, Sieur de Sabrevois; Christophe, Sieur de Sermonville; and Clément, Sieur de Bleury; the first two took up a military career.

NIVE VOISINE

AN, Col., B, 13, 23, 34, 35, 36, 40, 41, 42; C¹¹ᴬ, 8, 15, 120. Coll. de manuscrits relatifs à la N.-F., III. "Correspondance de Vaudreuil," APQ Rapport, 1942–43, 438; 1946–47, 418, 458. Fauteux, Les chevaliers de Saint-Louis. É.-Z. Massicotte, "Les commandants du Fort Chambly," BRH, XXXI (1925), 456. P.-G. Roy, Les officiers d'état-major. É.-Z. Massicotte, "Les Sabrevois, Sabrevois de Sermonville et Sabrevois de Bleury," BRH, XXXI (1925), 7–14; 40–42; 77–84.

SAGEAN (Sajan, sometimes known as Mermande), MATHIEU, soldier, adventurer, and inventor of a short-lived El Dorado; born, according to his own statement, at Lachine, the son of Jean Sagean and Marie Larrante (or Maria Rende); last identified in 1711 when he owned a lot at Fort Louis on the Rivière de la Mobile.

Early in 1700 Sagean reported to Desclouzeaux, the intendant of Marine at Brest, France, that he had discovered Acaaniba, a populous kingdom of white people situated in what would now be the southwestern part of the United States. After making the journey with La Salle [Cavelier*] to the mouth of the Mississippi, Sagean claimed to have set out, with the approval of HENRI TONTY, to make discoveries of his own. With 11 Frenchmen and 2 Mahicans he had travelled from a point on the upper Mississippi River and reached the River Milly, "river of gold," after a 14-league portage. The Milly, a wider and deeper river than the Mississippi, flowed south-southwest to Acaaniba. During their five-month sojourn in Acaaniba, the adventurers had found the people to be ingenuous and the country a veritable paradise. Gold was so plentiful that the Acaanibas made common utensils and heroic statues of pure gold, and each year sent a 3,000-ox caravan laden with gold on a six-moon journey to their market, which, Sagean hinted, might be Japan.

When news of Sagean's discovery reached Pontchartrain, he wrote to Desclouzeaux (10 March 1700), ordering him to prepare a report. As Sagean could not write, he dictated his story to Desclouzeaux's secretary. Soon Pontchartrain had Sagean moved to the Rochefort area where he was to be interrogated by PIERRE LE MOYNE d'Iberville and by Michel Bégon, the intendant at La Rochelle. Strict orders were given that Sagean, and his precious secret, be kept under lock and key.

The minister of Marine was not the only one intrigued by the Acaaniba tale. His enthusiasm was shared by the small circle of men, including the king's counsellor, Cabart de Villermont, and the Abbés Claude Bernou and Louis de Dangeau, who were permitted to hear of Sagean's discovery and read extracts from his Relation. Finally, after much discussion and hesitation, Pontchartrain ordered Bégon to send Sagean to Louisiana by the first ship bound for the Mississippi so that he could lead a party of Frenchmen back to Acaaniba.

When he arrived at Fort Maurepas, Biloxi, on 27 May 1701, Sagean was immediately impeached by Henri Tonty and Pierre-Charles LE SUEUR, and his claims refuted. Although the Kingdom of Acaaniba proved to be a golden hoax, Sagean's narrative gained for him a passage to America, which was his chief objective.

Sagean deserves to be remembered both for his ingenuity in deceiving men wiser and more learned than himself and for his skill as a storyteller. Although his narrative lacks depth and subtlety of characterization, it has a place among the exciting tales of adventure, real or fictional, written when many parts of the world were still unknown.

RICHEBOURG GAILLARD MCWILLIAMS

Sagean's dictated narrative was published many years subsequently as "Découverte et aventure de Mathieu Sagean, 1683–1699," in Découvertes et établissements des Français (Margry), VI, 95–162. Other material relevant to the Sagean story is reproduced on pages

Saint-Ange

162–74 of the same volume. *See also*: AN, Marine, B², 146, f.35; 147, f.8; 148, f.518; 149, ff.149, 155. BN, MS, Fr. 22810, f.257. *MPA* (Rowland and Sanders), II, 9–18. P. J. Hamilton, *Colonial Mobile* (Boston, 1897; rev. ed., 1910), 84 ([Chevillot]'s map "Fort Louis de la Mobille, 1706?"). R. G. McWilliams, "A kingdom beyond the Rockies: the El Dorado of Mathieu Sagean," in *The French in the Mississippi valley*, ed. J. F. McDermott (Urbana, 1965).

SAINT-ANGE. *See* CHARLY

SAINT-ANGE, ROBERT GROSTON (GROTTON) DE. *See* GROSTON

SAINT-AUBIN, JEAN SERREAU (Sarreau) DE. *See* SERREAU

SAINT-CASTIN. *See* ABBADIE

SAINT-CLAIR, PIERRE DE, naval officer, a native of Normandy (probably of Avranches); d. 20 Aug. 1736 at Le Havre.

Saint-Clair was appointed a midshipman at Rochefort 15 Feb. 1670, sub-lieutenant 28 Dec. 1673; beginning 13 Jan. 1677 he served as assistant town major at the port of Brest. On 9 Dec. 1686 he was promoted commander, and captain 15 Sept. 1689. In 1694 he received command of a squadron of 3 ships: the *Gaillard* of 54 guns, the *Pélican* of 50, and the *Aigle* of 36. This squadron was fitted out by a private company in which he himself had invested the sum of 1,000 *écus*. The force was commissioned to practise privateering in Canadian waters, to acquire information concerning the state of the English defences in Newfoundland, and if possible to attack the enemy's settlements in order to capture any ships found there and send them to Placentia (Plaisance). On 10 Sept. 1694, in company with a privateer from Saint-Malo, a fire-ship, and a small vessel rigged out as a bomb-ketch, Saint-Clair tried to attack the English post at Ferryland (Forillon), which was defended by Captain Holman. The *Aigle*, commanded by Du Vignau, entered the harbour channel, but because there was no wind it ran aground. Part of the crew, which was formed of Basque sailors who had been taken on at Placentia to make up the complement, mutinied and refused to fight. After a cannonade that lasted several hours, the French had to withdraw, but not without having refloated the *Aigle*, which had been seriously damaged.

After this failure Saint-Clair, who seems hardly to have taken part in the combat, conferred with his captains and, because of the narrowness of the channel, which was strongly defended, gave up his idea of attacking St John's, to the great rage of Brouillan [MOMBETON], governor of Placentia. It required PIERRE LE MOYNE d'Iberville's audacity to carry out a similar operation successfully two years later.

On 13 Oct. 1694 Saint-Clair left to go back to France, escorting a convoy of 34 merchant ships. Subsequently he was the naval commander at Dunkirk during the War of the Spanish Succession and retired from the service 4 May 1720, with a pension of 2,500 *livres*.

ÉTIENNE TAILLEMITE

AN, Col., B, 17, f.59v; C¹¹ᶜ, 2, ff.25, 26, 33v, 38; Marine, B⁴, 15, ff.374–82; C¹, 161. PAC *Report*, 1887, cccxiii, cccxiv; 1899, Supp., 305. Taillemite, *Inventaire analytique, série B*, I. La Morandière, *Hist. de la pêche française de la morue*, I, 454. Lounsbury, *British fishery at Nfld*. Prowse, *History of Nfld*.

SAINT-CLAUDE, PIERRE ET CLAUDE VOLANT DE. *See* VOLANT

SAINT-COSME. *See* BUISSON

SAINT-DENIS, CHARLOTTE-FRANÇOISE JUCHEREAU DE. *See* JUCHEREAU

SAINT-DENYS, CHARLES JUCHEREAU DE. *See* JUCHEREAU

SAINTE-MARIE, JEAN-JOSEPH D'ALLARD DE. *See* ALLARD

SAINT-ÉTIENNE DE LA TOUR, AGATHE (Marie-Agathe) DE (also known under the name of **Mrs Agathe Campbell** or **Campbel**), allegedly the sole heiress of her grandfather Charles de Saint-Étienne* de La Tour; b. 1690 at Cape Sable, daughter of Jacques de Saint-Étienne de La Tour and Anne Melanson; d. sometime after 1739, probably at Kilkenny (Ireland).

After Jacques de La Tour's death around 1699 his children were placed by an act of the lieutenant-general of Acadia under their mother's guardianship. Agathe spent her early years at Port-Royal (Annapolis Royal, N.S.), and married, in succession, two English subalterns attached to the garrison of the town; she first married, around 1714, Lieutenant Edmond (Edward) Bradstreet (Broadstreet), who died in December 1718 and by whom she had a son, Jean-Baptiste, born 21 Dec. 1714. Her second husband was Lieutenant James (Hugh?) Campbell.

In 1729 the governor, Richard Philipps*, expressed his desire to annul the former land grants in Nova Scotia in order to create new ones, and to this end he requested a survey of the properties. The English authorities wanted to acquire land for the British subjects—Protestants for the most part—whom they were inducing to come to settle in Nova Scotia. Mrs Campbell, who had become a widow for the second time, saw in this the means of becoming rich by asserting her rights to the former properties of Charles de Saint-Étienne de La Tour, so that she could sell them to the British crown. By the terms of the decree of 20 March 1703 issued by Louis XIV's council of state (*see* CHARLES DE SAINT-ÉTIENNE) her family had in fact received from their ancestor Charles' succession a fifth of the Cape Sable fief and two of the seven parts making up the seigneuries of Port-Royal and Les Mines (Grand Pré, N.S.). In 1730 Agathe owned only a quarter of what had fallen to her family as its share; nevertheless, in 1725 she had laid claim to all of her ancestor's seigneuries, alleging that her brother and sisters, as well as her uncles and aunts, had given their shares over to her when Acadia had become English territory. In 1730 she presented a second suit, similar to the first and accompanied by three alleged deeds of transfer on the part of an uncle and two aunts.

After Philipps ordered the payment of seigneurial dues to cease, Mrs Campbell went to London to plead for the restoration of her rights, or adequate compensation for them, and in May 1732 made her first petition to the Board of Trade. Philipps was suspicious about her claim to possess all the rights to the La Tour inheritance, as was Lieutenant-Governor ARMSTRONG. Nevertheless, in October 1733 the Board of Trade recognized the legitimacy of Mrs Campbell's claims, "partly by right of inheritance and partly by cession from her relations." In March of the following year, the board recommended that she be paid £2,000 for the purchase of all her seigneurial rights.

The British authorities openly admitted that the purchase of the La Tour lands was crucial if the government was to be able to grant any land in Nova Scotia, and the secretary of the Board of Trade, Popple, pointed out that Mrs Campbell was "in a very weak state of health, and should she dye, her right might then devolve on her children with whom it might not be possible for many years to compleat any bargain." With the purchase of Mrs Campbell's rights, the seigneurial system came to an end in Nova Scotia, although other members of the La Tour family later demanded recognition of their inheritance rights.

Agathe, who had returned to Nova Scotia to receive this money, went back to Great Britain shortly afterwards. In 1737 she declared that she was "from the town of Kilkenny" in Ireland. It was there that she is believed to have died sometime after 1739, a victim in the end of her frail health.

CLARENCE J. D'ENTREMONT

Archives of the Bishop's House, Yarmouth, N.S., Documents de la collection de H. Leander d'Entremont, Revendications des membres de la famille Jacques d'Entremont—Anne de Saint-Étienne de La Tour (1750). AN, Section Outre-Mer, G¹, 466 (Recensement de l'Acadie, 1698). "Acte de tutelle des enfants de Jacques de Saint-Étienne de La Tour," *NF*, I (1926), 214–15. *N.S. Archives,* I, 91–94; *III*, 197. PRO, *Acts of P.C., col. ser., 1720–45*, 360–62; *B.T.Journal, 1728/29–1734*; *CSP, Col., 1728–29, 1730, 1732, 1733, 1734–35*; *C.T.Books and Papers, 1731–34*.
W. P. Bell, *The "foreign protestants" and the settlement of Nova Scotia* (Toronto, 1961), 69–74, 81–82. Calnek, *History of Annapolis*, 85–87. Azarie Couillard Després, *Charles de Saint-Étienne de La Tour, gouverneur, lieutenant-général en Acadie, et son temps, 1593–1666* (Arthabaska, Qué., 1930), 453–64; *Histoire des seigneurs de la Rivière-du-Sud et leurs alliés canadiens et acadiens* (Saint-Hyacinthe, Qué., 1912), 210–48, 260. Murdoch, *History of Nova-Scotia* I, 263, 475, 477, 489, 501.

SAINT-ÉTIENNE DE LA TOUR, CHARLES DE, trader and soldier; b. between 1663 and 1668 at Cape Sable in Acadia; d. 1731 at Louisbourg.

He was one of five children of the famous Charles de Saint-Étienne* de La Tour and Jeanne Motin* d'Aulnay. Little is known of his early years. As a young man he was apparently a fur trader, with his headquarters at Cape Sable. He incurred severe losses when General Phips* took Acadia in 1690, and lodged a complaint with the Earl of Bellomont, governor of Massachusetts. Late in 1695 La Tour was cited in dispatches by Frontenac [Buade*] for bravery against the enemy. His trading activity continued for some years, as records show that in 1698, or shortly before, he had been fined for trading with the English.

In 1696 he was authorized by his brothers and sisters to plead their case for the re-establishment by the French crown of rights and possessions in Acadia inherited from their parents and long disputed by the Le Borgne family. He was largely successful in his efforts, as is shown by an *arrêt* of the Conseil d'État of 20 March 1703. The *arrêt* gave the La Tour family land at Cape Sable, Port La Tour (near Cape Sable), Port-Royal, and Les Mines (Grand Pré, N.S.); it was divided among the La Tour children [*see* AGATHE DE SAINT-ÉTIENNE].

In 1703 Charles was appointed an ensign with the French forces in Acadia. He was a member of the local garrison during the bombardment and capture of Port-Royal by NICHOLSON in 1710 and

Saint-Laurent

was severely wounded. He was promoted lieutenant and in 1714 was stationed at Île Royale. For a time he served as the official government interpreter to the Indians there. He was awarded the cross of the order of Saint-Louis in 1728 for his services and shortly after (on the death of GÉDÉON DE CATALOGNE) became captain of a company of colonial regular troops that formed part of the garrison at Louisbourg. It was there he died three years later.

In 1699 La Tour had married Angélique Loreau; they had one son, Charles. In 1732 the widow received a pension of 300 *livres* in recognition of La Tour's service to his country.

GEORGE MACBEATH

AN, Col., B, 19, f.66v; 29, f.215v; 33, f.401v; 34, f.361v; C¹¹ᴮ, 10, f.183; C¹¹ᴰ, 5, ff.104, 198v–200; D²ᶜ, 47, f.296v; Section Outre-Mer, G³, cartons 2039 (Greffe de J.-C. Desmarest, 1734), 2040 (Greffe de J.-C. Loppinot, 27 nov. 1705). *Coll. de manuscrits relatifs à la N.-F.*, II, 262, 292–93, 297, 316, 362–80, 477, 528. "Correspondance de Frontenac (1689–99)," APQ *Rapport*, 1928–29, 282. Fauteux, *Les chevaliers de Saint-Louis*, 124. Azarie Couillard Després, *Charles de Saint-Étienne de La Tour, gouverneur, lieutenant-général en Acadie, et son temps, 1593–1666* (Arthabaska, Qué., 1930), 460, 462–65. Murdoch, *History of Nova-Scotia*, I, 168.

SAINT-LAURENT, Comtesse de. *See* JUCHEREAU

SAINT-LUC. *See* RAGEOT

SAINT-MARTIN, ANTOINE ADHÉMAR DE. *See* ADHÉMAR

SAINT-MARTIN-VIABON, JOSEPH-ALEXANDRE LESTRINGANT DE. *See* LESTRINGANT

SAINT-MICHEL, MICHEL MESSIER, *dit.* *See* MESSIER

SAINT - OURS, PIERRE DE, seigneur of L'Échaillon in Dauphiné in France, of Saint-Ours, Assomption, and Saint-Jean Deschaillons in New France, chevalier, captain in the Carignan-Salières regiment and in the colonial regular troops; b. October 1640 and baptized at Grenoble; d. October 1724 on his manor of Saint-Ours and buried in the parish church of the Immaculate Conception at Saint-Ours, New France.

Pierre de Saint-Ours was the son of Henri de Saint-Ours and Jeanne de Calignon. The line descended from Pierre de Saint-Ours (Petrus de Sancto Orso), first of the name, who flourished about 1330.

From 1658 he was a cadet in the Carignan-Salières regiment and the next year was appointed ensign. In January 1664 he took possession of his father's lands. He received his commission as captain in the Carignan-Salières regiment on 7 Feb. 1665 and embarked for Canada at the end of May, arriving at Quebec with his company on 12 September. Intendant Talon* travelled with them. Saint-Ours spent the winter in the newly built fort at Sorel. He appears to have gone with Prouville* de Tracy's expedition against the Iroquois in 1666.

On 8 Jan. 1668 Saint-Ours married Marie Mullois, daughter of Thomas Mullois, at Champlain; eleven children were born of this union. About the time of his marriage he was invested with the seigneury of Saint-Ours, extending from the St Lawrence River south to the Yamaska River and lying between the lands of his brother officers M. de Saurel* and M. Pécaudy* de Contrecœur; title was granted Saint-Ours on 29 Oct. 1672. Shortly afterwards he received another seigneury on the Assomption River. In 1687 he inherited the seigneury of Saint-Jean Deschaillons, near the River Duchesne. Saint-Ours built a manor-house of timber on the St Lawrence and some of his soldiers settled around him. Saint-Ours-sur-Richelieu and its neighbours were devastated by the Iroquois in 1691. The development of the seigneury was very slow; a bannal mill was not erected until 1703.

Saint-Ours commanded a detachment in Louis Buade* de Frontenac's expedition to Lake Ontario in 1673, when Fort Cataracoui (Frontenac) was built. He sometimes engaged in trade: there is a record dated 1678 of his having a booth at the annual fair in Montreal which welcomed the fur flotilla of the Ottawas. That year he figured among the notables of the colony, being summoned to Montreal or Quebec to serve on advisory committees to the governor or intendant. In 1679 he was sent by Frontenac to command at Chambly in an attempt to inhibit trade in alcoholic liquors with New England. While there he was himself admonished for trading.

At the end of 1686 the governor general, Jacques-René de BRISAY de Denonville, reported that many families, even noble ones, were living in extreme poverty. He stated that the Saint-Ours, with ten children, had lacked wheat for eight months of the year. Saint-Ours planned to go to France to take up military service; after receiving a grant of 100 *écus*, however, he stayed in the colony. In 1687 he was given the rank of captain and command of a company of colonial regular troops. Since most of these were quartered in Montreal, he decided to move there. Nuns of the Hôtel-Dieu granted him a lot on Rue Notre-

Dame, where a one-storey timber house was erected for 1,000 *livres*. A stone residence appears to have been built later.

During Phips*' siege of Quebec in 1690 Frontenac entrusted Saint-Ours with the command of a battalion, and from 1693 he was senior captain of the colonial regular troops. The next year he obtained leave and went to France to rebuild his health by taking the waters. On his return in 1695 he was sent by CALLIÈRE to the head of Lac des Deux-Montagnes to ambush an Iroquois party; however, it evaded him. Saint-Ours, at the head of his company, led the funeral procession of KONDIARONK, great leader of the Michilimackinac Hurons, in August 1701. The king, on 14 June 1704, named Saint-Ours knight of the order of Saint-Louis. When he retired from military service on 9 June 1708 with a pension of 600 *livres*, his son Jean-Baptiste* took over his company.

Saint-Ours' first wife died in 1705. Having been thwarted in a wish to marry a 17-year-old girl, he married Marguerite Legardeur, daughter of Charles Legardeur* de Tilly and widow of an army captain, on 29 July 1708 at Batiscan. In 1710 he rented his house in Montreal and retired to the seigneury. At this time the War of the Spanish Succession was raging and his pension often fell into arrears. He sold his Montreal house in 1716 for 4,500 *livres*. The following year he was included in the list of recipients of trading permits, obtaining one jointly with Madame de Saurel. As was the custom, this was sold; each received 1,000 *livres*.

In May 1723, he sent Chaussegros* de Léry, the husband of one of his grand-daughters, to the Château Saint-Louis to swear fealty and homage on his behalf for the seigneury of l'Assomption, stating that he himself could not come because of illness and age. He died in October 1724 on his manor of Saint-Ours.

Pierre de Saint-Ours abandoned a military career and hereditary estates in France to seek his fortune in the New World. His reward was meagre. On at least three occasions, in 1679, 1706, and 1708, he sought preferment or public office in vain; and his colonization efforts did not prosper. Nonetheless, he established his family name in New France and created one manor in that chain of about a hundred that the Carignan-Salières officers built in the new land. There is a bust of Saint-Ours, by Elzéar Soucy, in the village of Saint-Ours, Quebec. The bust was unveiled in 1922; the likeness is probably imaginary.

Two sons of his union with Marie Mullois made a name for themselves: Jean-Baptiste, known as Saint-Ours Deschaillons, and his brother Pierre*, both entered military service. Three of the daughters made good marriages: Jeanne with François-Antoine Pécaudy* de Contrecœur; Marie-Anne with Jean de Mine; and Élisabeth with CLAUDE-CHARLES LE ROY de La Potherie.

C. C. J. BOND

AN, Col., C¹¹A, 8, f.144; 13, f.379; D²ᶜ, 222, f.128. PAC, FM 8, F 80, 1. "Correspondance de Frontenac," APQ *Rapport, 1926–27*, 108f., 126f., 136; *1927–28*, 192. "Correspondance de Vaudreuil," APQ *Rapport, 1938–39*, 15, 18, 27, 32, 96, 99; *1939–40*, 420, 434; *1942–43*, 436. *Jug. et délib.*, I, 777–79, 943, 1002; III, 1020f.; V, 114f., 138, 308. P.-G. Roy, "Ce que Callières pensait de nos officiers," 331; *Inv. concessions*, I, 171–73, 175; II, 171; III, 14f., 122, 175f. *Royal Fort Frontenac* (Preston et Lamontagne), 482. Azarie Couillard-Després, *Histoire de la seigneurie de St-Ours* (2v., Montréal, 1915), I. Claude de Bonnault, "Généalogie de la famille de Saint-Ours, Dauphiné et Canada," *BRH*, LV (1949), 27–43, 97–110, 168–72. Germain Lesage, "L'arrivée du régiment de Carignan," *Revue de l'Université d'Ottawa*, XXXV (1965), 11–34. É.-Z. Massicotte, "La foire des pelleteries à Montréal au XVIIᵉ siècle," *BRH*, XXVIII (1922), 376. J.-E. Roy, "Le patronage dans l'armée," *BRH*, II (1896), 116.

SAINT-PAUL, JEAN-AMADOR GODEFROY DE. *See* GODEFROY

SAINT-PIERRE. *See* DU PONT DE RENON, MICHEL

SAINT-PIERRE, JEAN-PAUL LEGARDEUR DE. *See* LEGARDEUR

SAINT-RÉMY. *See* RÉMY

SAINT-SEÜRIN (SURIN), FRANÇOIS TROTAIN, *dit. See* TROTAIN

SAINT-SÉVERIN, SÉVERIN AMEAU, *dit. See* AMEAU

SAINT-SIMON, PAUL DENYS DE. *See* DENYS

SAINT-VALLIER, JEAN-BAPTISTE DE LA CROIX DE CHEVRIÈRES DE. *See* LA CROIX

SAJAN. *See* SAGEAN

SANGOUESSY. *See* CHINGOUESSI

SARRAZIN (Sarrasin), MICHEL, surgeon, doctor, and naturalist, member of the Conseil Souverain, seigneur; b. 5 Sept. 1659 at Nuits-sous-Beaune in the province of Burgundy, son of Claude Sarrazin, an official at the Abbey of Cîteaux, and of Madeleine de Bonnefoy; d. 8 Sept. 1734 at

Sarrazin

Quebec of a malignant fever probably brought on by smallpox, which had been carried there by a ship. We know of no portrait of Michel Sarrazin, and the one that is sometimes said to be of him seems to be of a Dr Sarrazin who was living in France.

Michel Sarrazin came to New France in 1685, as a surgeon in the Marine. On 12 Sept. 1686 BRISAY de Denonville appointed him surgeon-major of the colonial regular troops. A royal decree from Versailles, dated 16 March 1691, ratified the 1686 appointment. He discharged his duties both at Montreal and at Quebec, where he lived, and he even went into the Iroquois country, as his *Histoire des plantes de Canada* testifies: "I saw plane-trees 12 or 13 years ago in the Iroquois country." The date is not given, but various indications allow us to place his trip between 1685 and 1692, most probably at the time of Denonville's expedition against the Iroquois in 1687. In 1692, during a stay at Montreal, he fell seriously ill and had to spend a month in hospital, after which he retired to Quebec to the house of his friend FRANQUELIN, the king's hydrographer. At this period there was no hint of the future naturalist. The mere mention of plane-trees is not enough to reveal the interest of a botanist: their height, which reached 100 feet, was enough to surprise any visitor from the east.

Sarrazin had fleeting visions of entering the church; Buade* de Frontenac wrote in 1697: "It is true that four years ago the Sieur Sarrazin was surgeon-major of the colonial regular troops, and that ... [he had] retired a year previously to a seminary here with the intention of becoming a priest...." The archives of the seminary of Quebec are silent on this subject. Other sources mention the Séminaire des Missions Étrangères in Paris, but with no supporting evidence. On the other hand the archives of the Sulpicians contain letters, dated 1694 and 1695, from Louis Tronson, the superior general in Paris, to DOLLIER de Casson; in them are the following passages: "I do not know the reasons that induce you to keep at the seminary M. Sarrazin, who is infirm and who still practises as a surgeon-major. Is it merely out of charity or because he can be of some use to you?" And: "M. Sarrazin has retired here [to France]. We were surprised at the advice given to him in Canada to leave his profession and become a priest. The more we have examined both his present and past state of mind, the more we have been convinced that there was no indication of a divine vocation to justify this change. Thus he has been advised to resume his former occupation if he could. I see no reason, not even an apparent one, which could have prompted M. GUYOTTE [parish priest of Notre-Dame] and M. de la Colombière

[Joseph de LA COLOMBIÈRE] to give him such advice. He is a worthy person, who is capable of doing at least as much good in his profession as in the ecclesiastical state." This correspondence settles what was until now the most obscure point about Michel Sarrazin's life.

In 1693, when Sarrazin seems to have withdrawn temporarily from society, Frontenac sent for a surgeon named BAUDEAU to replace him. Michel Sarrazin himself left for France in 1694, where for three years he studied medicine. He also frequented the Jardin Royal des Plantes, the future Muséum d'Histoire Naturelle, where he received his introduction to botany under the direction of Joseph Pitton de Tournefort, who in 1700 was to publish his famous work *Institutiones rei herbariae*; this work contained new elements contributed by Sarrazin.

Intendant BOCHART de Champigny had been asking for his return since 1695. Sarrazin did in fact return in 1697, after having obtained his doctorate of medicine at Reims. He took advantage of the ship's call at Newfoundland to observe American plants and go botanizing. From then on he sent specimens regularly to the Jardin Royal des Plantes. Thenceforth, Sarrazin proposed to confine himself no longer to his medical activities, but to explore systematically the flora, fauna, and minerals of the country. One may read in the decisions of the council of Quebec: "And as there is a strong indication that the Sieur Sarrazin, in returning to Canada, had other plans than merely that of treating the sick, since he gives much attention to dissecting the rare animals which are in this country or to seeking out unknown plants, there is every reason to believe and to fear that after he has fully satisfied himself in this matter, or rather some persons of importance in his profession who appear to us to have a considerable interest in this kind of research, he will return to France gratified by their protection and by the advancement he has obtained through them...."

The doctor. If Sarrazin became a naturalist, he nevertheless continued to practise medicine faithfully, and devoted the major part of his time to it until his death at the age of 75. On several occasions he was infected by his patients. On board the *Gironde*, on which he was travelling back to Canada with Bishop Saint-Vallier [LA CROIX] after his period of study, an epidemic of "purple" fever (purpura) broke out, and the doctor was obliged to devote himself unsparingly to the care of all. He contracted the disease, as did Bishop Saint-Vallier. In 1700 another scourge, influenza, was rife at Quebec, then in 1702 and 1703 smallpox brought by an Indian from Fort Orange (Albany, N.Y.), and in 1709 Siamese sickness (yellow fever).

Sarrazin

Each time the victims were numerous, and Sarrazin knew no respite.

At this period he is thought to have drafted a treatise on pleurisy, which Governor Barrin* de La Galissonnière spoke highly of to Pehr Kalm*. The latter, when visiting Canada in 1749, heard echoes of the high esteem in which Sarrazin's medical competence was held. Sarrazin's botanical notes, still in manuscript and entered in the *Histoire des plantes de Canada*, show his medical bias, which is normal since at that time medicine and botany were difficult to separate.

Sarrazin sometimes had to perform autopsies, and even to give expert advice in criminal matters, or for affidavits concerning miraculous cures at Sainte-Anne de Beaupré. The *Mémoires de Trévoux* of August 1728 contain an account of the autopsy of the partially preserved bodies of three nuns who were buried in 1703, 1705, and 1707. They also contain a note about a young Iroquois woman, "the second Catherine," one of whose arms, holding a crucifix, had remained intact.

L'Académie des Sciences. Sarrazin's hobby, his scientific activities, brought him into contact with the Académie Royale des Sciences de Paris, which had been founded in 1666 and was reorganized by Louis XIV in 1699. This institution brought together all French scientists and certain foreign ones, such as Herman Boerhaave and Sir Isaac Newton, most of whom were in the prime of life and at the height of their productivity. To get to know foreign countries better, particularly in the field of natural history, the academy enlisted the help of correspondents who supplied specimens and observations. On 4 March 1699 Michel Sarrazin was therefore appointed the correspondent of Tournefort, who had detected in the first items collected and in the notes made by this beginner a shrewd observer. Later, on 23 Jan. 1717, long after Tournefort's death (1708), he became the correspondent of René-Antoine Ferchault de Réaumur (1683–1757). Each year the ships from New France bore letters destined for French men of science, in particular the botanists Sébastien Vaillant, Antoine de Jussieu, and Danty d'Isnard, of the Jardin des Plantes, and also the Oratorian Abbé Bignon, king's librarian, president of the Académie des Sciences and of the Académie des Inscriptions et Belles-Lettres, and member of the French academy. The following extract from a letter addressed to Antoine de Jussieu (1686–1758) on 11 Oct. 1728 (lost since the sale of Jussieu's archives around 1936) has come down to us: "The war which we have to prosecute against the Indians known as Foxes disrupts the plan that I had of sending you plants and seeds native to the region from which

I was expecting to receive them." Sarrazin went on to enumerate the dangers of botanizing in New France at that time.

Sarrazin was interested in biology, as it was understood then. It was principally confined to the anatomical and systematic study of plants and animals, to the rudiments of plant and animal physiology, and to ethnobiological considerations. Curiously enough, Dr Arthur Vallée, in a biography of Sarrazin, confuses biology and zoology, for in his book the first of these terms is opposed to botany.

Sarrazin's relations with the academy do not seem to have been ideal, as is evidenced by his correspondence with Réaumur and Abbé Bignon. In a letter Bignon rebuked him for making criticisms that were unwarranted except with respect to Fontenelle's [Le Bovier] delay in publishing his text on the seal, an omission which Bignon proposed to rectify that very year.

The zoologist. In the field of zoology Sarrazin worked particularly as an anatomist. To carry out his dissections, Sarrazin used his set of surgical instruments and a borrowed magnifying-glass; as a result Réaumur presented him with one in 1727. Sarrazin sent communications on extremely minute dissections of Canadian animals to the academy, and these were published in part in the reports of that institution. It should be noted that several of these manuscripts have been preserved. These works deal with the following subjects: "Histoire naturelle et anatomique du Castor"; "L'histoire anatomique du carcajou"; "Histoire d'une espèce de rat d'Amérique septentrionale" (the musk-rat, which is today called *water-rat* in the islands of Lac Saint-Pierre); "L'histoire anatomique du veau-marin"; and "Observations sur le porc-épic." According to his communication on the porcupine which was presented to Réaumur in 1726, Sarrazin may also have prepared a "Monographie anatomique du siffleux," but no trace of it has been found. These contributions were favourably received by the critics of the time, and particularly by the *Journal des Sçavans*, which published summaries of them regularly in 1707, 1728, 1730, and 1733.

The botanist. The study of systematic botany offered countless pitfalls in a country beset by constant guerilla warfare. Sarrazin wrote: "I do not know whether it is believed that one botanizes in Canada under the same conditions as in France. I could more easily traverse the whole of Europe, and with less danger, than I could cover 100 leagues in Canada, a much riskier undertaking." This did not prevent him, for more than 20 years, from sending specimens which still form part of the herbarium of the Muséum d'Histoire

595

Sarrazin

Naturelle. The botanist Sébastien Vaillant (1669–1722) had preserved them in his personal herbarium, which became the basis of the herbarium at the Muséum. Vaillant had likewise dispatched specimens from Sarrazin to the English botanist William Sherard (1659–1728), and these still exist in the "Sherardian Herbarium" at Oxford University.

To the herbarium specimens Sarrazin also added seeds and living plants for the flower-beds of the Jardin des Plantes. The minister wrote to Champigny in March 1698: "The king's chief doctor has instructed the Sieur Sarrazin to collect in Canada the special plants, fruits, and other things which that country produces and which may be useful for the Jardin Royal. You are to load on the king's ships the cases and boxes which the said Sieur Sarrazin will send addressed to the first king's doctor." Putting cases down in the hold for shipment was undesirable, and the intendant had to issue special instructions for them to be set in a safe place. The bushes were to remain on deck, where the sailors were instructed to water them, when it did not rain, from the ship's meagre supply of water—when they were not drenched by a wave of salt water. It is understandable that some specimens arrived in a spoiled condition. The following letter testifies to this result: "I wanted to have shipped on a boat for Orléans [M. de Luzançay wrote from Nantes] the two cases full of earth and some Canadian plants sent by the Sieur Sarrazin, a Quebec doctor. But whatever care may have been taken of them, they were dry, or more exactly dead, so that the gardener to whom I had entrusted them thinks that it would be useless to send them. . . ."

Notes on pieces of paper were attached to the herbarium specimens in each shipment. Sébastien Vaillant, a professor at the Jardin Royal and the initiator of the natural classification of plants that was later perfected by Antoine-Laurent de Jussieu (1748–1836), studied the material carefully, arranged the notes, and added his commentaries, thus making of them a "Catalogue des plantes du Canada." It is not always easy to make out each author's contribution. This work includes discussions of a systematic nature, medical, ethnographic, and historical considerations, and also popular names used in Canada. The volume can be situated chronologically after the flora of Jacques-Philippe Cornuti, the *Canadensium plantarum* (1635), and before that to be published by Charlevoix* as an appendix to his *Histoire de la Nouvelle-France* (1744). A little later appeared the flora of Jean-François Gaultier* (1708–1756), which was composed before 1750 and also left in manuscript, and the flora of Quebec by Kalm, which was first intended to come out under the name of *Flora canadensis* but which is still unpublished. This list comprises the principal works on the flora of New France, prior to 1760, which contain in part the results of Sarrazin's research.

Among the very first plants sent by Sarrazin, Tournefort discovered a species which he dedicated to him, and which still bears the name "Sarracenia purpurea." Previously an illustration of it had appeared in a popular publication (John Joselyn, *New-England Rarities*, 1672), and there were vague references to it in other authors. Sarrazin had himself made a long description of it which Charlevoix reproduced. Sarrazin also contributed to the description of new species, which Tournefort and particularly Vaillant published, although acknowledging Sarrazin as the author.

The written work of Sarrazin that appears over his signature or in the works of other botanists comprises several titles. The *Observations de Mr. Sarrazin* contain descriptions of four Canadian maples and show that Sarrazin had a better understanding of our species than Linnaeus did. Also attributed to Sarrazin are descriptions of species included in the 1700 and 1719 editions of Tournefort's *Institutiones rei herbariae*. Furthermore, the *Établissement d'un nouveau genre de plante nommé Araliastrum duquel le gin-seng des Chinois est une espèce*, by Sébastien Vaillant, contains a description of ginseng by Sarrazin. This work also mentions other species of "aralia," the description of which is ascribed to Sarrazin. In a communication on ginseng made by Danty d'Isnard to the Académie des Sciences on 4 Dec. 1717, we read that Sarrazin had dispatched this plant in 1704 (long before Lafitau* did) under the name of "Aralia humilis fructu majore." In the *Suite de l'établissement de nouveaux caractères de plantes à fleurs composées*, by Vaillant, we come across three species the description of which is attributed to Sarrazin. In addition we must mention again the "Catalogue des plantes du Canada," written up by Vaillant with the aid of Sarrazin's notes, which is posterior to 1707 and still remains unpublished.

To this series of works we may add the list of the plants discussed in the "Catalogue"; this list, selected by Antoine de Jussieu, appears in facsimile under the title "Plantes envoyées du Canada par M. Sarrazin, conseiller du Conseil supérieur et médecin du Roy en Canada," in the biography by Dr Vallée published in 1927. This list was prepared after the manuscript of the "Catalogue" was completed. It deals not with the shipments of 1704 only, as Vaillant thought, but with a series spread out over the years 1697 to 1707 at least. In a letter written by Sarrazin on 22 Sept. 1728 (which was part of the Jussieu archives and of which only an excerpt is known to us), we read that he is "sending the catalogue of the plants from the region around Quebec. I hope that these plants will be of some use to you." Probably he is referring to the later list taken from his joint work with Vaillant, the "Catalogue des plantes du Canada," since a copy of the "Catalogue," in Vaillant's own handwriting and annotated by Jean-François Gaultier, is still in existence in Canada.

Agriculture and botanical economy. Pehr Kalm, on a visit to Quebec in 1749, learned of Sarrazin's successful attempt to grow the grain and winter barley which he had imported from Sweden. This experiment was short-lived, however, and from then on only the spring varieties were utilized. Sarrazin is thought to have pointed out the special nutritive qualities of Indian corn (maize), and he may have sent a report on the subject in 1732. No trace of this text has been found. In 1715 the Conseil Supérieur instructed him, together with M. de La Colombière, to supervise the operations of milling and conditioning flour, in order to increase the yield.

According to an opinion expressed by Benjamin Sulte and adopted by Pierre-Georges Roy and Arthur Vallée, Sarrazin was the initiator of the maple sugar industry. Pierre BOUCHER, in other respects well informed, made no mention of this industry in his work (1664). It existed in Acadia, however, at the time of DIÈREVILLE's voyage in 1699. According to a remark made by Madame Legardeur de Repentigny [Agathe de Saint-Père*] and reported to the ministry of Marine on 5 Oct. 1706 by RIGAUD de Vaudreuil and JACQUES RAUDOT, more than 30,000 pounds of maple sugar were already being manufactured annually in the Montreal region alone. Sarrazin's role, pending proof to the contrary, was confined to a scientific study of the sugar maple.

The mineralogist. Sarrazin dispatched specimens of rocks and minerals to France, but played only a secondary role in mineralogy. In 1728 he discovered a slate-quarry on his fief of Grand-Étang, which he had received from the Hazeur family at the time of his marriage 16 years before, and he analysed mineral waters at Cap-de-la-Madeleine; the results of this analysis appeared in the *Mémoires de Trévoux* of 1735 ("Extrait d'une lettre de monsieur Sarrazin au sujet des eaux du Cap-de-la-Madeleine").

The businessman. Michel Sarrazin, desirous of improving his financial situation, undertook to exploit the slate-quarry. Unfortunately the costs were heavy because of its long distance from Quebec. There was a lack of slate extractors and splitters who should have been brought from France. Moreover, the deposits at Grand-Étang proved to be of poor quality, besides which such an industry could hardly pay in a country where the material, unlike wooden shingles, was ill suited to the climatic conditions. The undertaking foundered, after absorbing a considerable portion of the scanty revenues that Sarrazin obtained from the Saint-Jean fief (corresponding to what is now part of the city of Quebec and including part of Battlefields Park), and from the other properties received as a settlement at the time of his marriage.

Being nevertheless anxious to try his luck, he went into partnership with Robert Drouard to exploit a fishing-ground in the Gulf of St Lawrence. The company's capital of 13,000 *livres*, of which he subscribed three quarters, disappeared in the collapse of the undertaking on Drouard's death. If we add to that the loss of a house by fire, which deprived him of a source of revenue, and the staggering devaluation of card money, we can have some conception of the financial difficulties of this king's doctor, whose meagre emoluments could not save him from disaster.

The public administrator. Sarrazin became a member of the Conseil Supérieur on 30 June 1707, and in this capacity shared in the administration of the colony. He sometimes had to take a stand in the conflicts between the governor, the bishop, and the intendant, but for a fairly long time he abstained from taking part in the deliberations. After having been Intendant CLAUDE-THOMAS DUPUY's friend, he quarrelled with him and the Jesuits once and for all. It seems indeed that he had been attached to the bishop's party, for after Bishop Saint-Vallier's death he ceased for a while to attend the meetings of the Conseil Supérieur. The fact that the persons concerned were living in a remote post, restricted to one another's company, did not help matters. In 1733, the year before his death, Sarrazin became keeper of the seals.

Sarrazin and his family relationships. Michel Sarrazin, still a bachelor, went back to France in 1709 and stayed there for more than a year, three months of which were spent at a spa, and did not return until the end of 1710. It was apparently his first and last trip back to his native country since 1697, when he took up residence in Canada for the second time. Only after that did he think of marriage. On 20 July 1712, at the age of 53, he married at Montreal Marie-Anne Hazeur, formerly of Quebec, who was herself 20 years old. For the occasion, the marriage certificate showed the husband as being only 40. In the records, however, he was to grow old faster than his wife, for if in the 1716 census, four years after the marriage, the latter was still only 25, Sarrazin was

Sarrazin

54. Whether we should see in the marriage certificate of 1712 coquettishness on Sarrazin's part or courtesy on the celebrant's we do not know. Marie-Anne's father, FRANÇOIS HAZEUR, an important businessman, seigneur of Malbaie, of Grande-Vallée, and of Anse-de-l'Étang in the Gaspé Peninsula, had sat on the Conseil Supérieur since 1703. Sarrazin thus received a part of the seigneuries of Grande-Vallée and of Anse-de-l'Étang.

Madame Sarrazin, who was born at Quebec and was a former pupil of the Ursulines, came to Montreal after her parents' death to live with a maternal uncle, M. Soumande, a merchant in comfortable circumstances. Madame Sarrazin had at least three brothers: Canon Thierry Hazeur*, of Quebec; Pierre Hazeur* de L'Orme, who represented in Paris the interests of the chapter of Quebec, but who lived mainly at the abbey of Bénévent; and JEAN-FRANÇOIS, a lawyer in Paris, who later became a member of the Conseil Supérieur of Quebec. Michel Sarrazin himself had two brothers, who had remained at Nuits-sous-Beaune; the one, a priest, and the other (Claude), an attorney, both died in 1731.

Of the seven children of Sarrazin and Marie-Anne Hazeur, three died in infancy. At his death the doctor left his wife, aged 42, two sons, and two daughters. As a result of her husband's financial failures, Madame Sarrazin was left without resources, but fortunately she received as a pension the annual stipend of 800 *livres* which at that time was attached to the office of king's doctor at Quebec. This pension was transferred to the eldest son and lapsed on his death in 1739; Madame Sarrazin then went to live with her brother, Canon Hazeur, at Quebec.

Sarrazin's eldest son, Joseph-Michel, who was born on 13 July 1715 at Quebec, went to Paris in 1731 to carry on his studies. He was making ready to follow in his father's footsteps, and consequently, after his general training, he studied surgery, medicine, and botany; but he died of smallpox on 22 Sept. 1739 in France, before completing his education. Claude-Michel, another of Sarrazin's sons, who was born at Quebec in 1722, returned to the country of his ancestors in 1741 after studying for eight years at the Seminary of Quebec. He first considered the ecclesiastical life, and even wore a cassock, which he later abandoned for a military career. He took part in the 1747 siege of Bergen-op-Zoom, in Holland, and thereby acquired a certain notoriety. Claude-Michel died in 1809 in Paris. One of the daughters, Marie-Jeanne, died in 1737 at the age of 19. The youngest child, and the only one to remain in Canada, was Charlotte-Louise-Angélique. Five years younger than Claude-Michel, she was 19 when in 1746 she married Jean-Hippolyte Gaultier de Varennes. She died on 16 July 1793.

A few letters left by the king's doctor in Canada have earned him the reputation of being an insatiable seeker after favours. This reproach would perhaps be justified if the court had sometimes granted his requests. A letter from the minister to Bochart de Champigny on 21 March 1698 perfectly describes the wretched situation: "His Majesty does not want to incur the expense of maintaining a doctor in Canada, and as the Sieur Sarrazin would use letters of appointment only to ask subsequently for the salary, it has seemed to me useless to speak of it to His Majesty, the more so because he refused it last year." The die was cast at Versailles. It was necessary to economize on the essentials and at the expense of those indispensable servants who were sufficiently devoted to their task not to abandon it. The replies sent to Sarrazin, however, showed more circumspection; he was always promised that consideration would be given to his requests, but there was never a sequel.

His profession earned him a very inadequate income, which corresponded to an insignificant fraction of the salary to which he was entitled. Finding the situation untenable, he even thought of going back to France, as is shown by the following extracts from four letters sent from Canada by the governor and the intendant. The first three were signed jointly by CALLIÈRE and Champigny: "We shall continue to assure His Majesty of the great services which the Sieur Sarrazin, to whom he has been pleased to grant doctor's papers, renders in the hospitals and to the sick outside. He has expressed to us some desire to return to France, because of the meagre profit that there is for him in a country which is poor and in which he is exhausting himself, but we could not agree to it because of his usefulness, for he is a man of unusual experience" (18 Oct. 1700). "We are very sensible, Your Excellency, of your kindness in increasing by 300 *livres* the Sieur Sarrazin's emoluments, but you will allow us to point out to you again that that is not enough to retain in this country a man of his ability and experience" (5 Oct. 1701). "As the Sieur de Sarrazin is the one and only doctor in the colony and also very often . . . carries out the duties of a surgeon, and as he receives a salary of only 600 *livres*, without any payment from those whom he treats, we feel obliged . . . to ask for an increase in salary for him" (3 Nov. 1702). On 31 Oct. 1725 CHARLES LE MOYNE de Longueuil and Michel Bégon* were to be more explicit: "The favour that the king has granted to the Sieur Duprat, a doctor and botanist in

Louisiana, who has a salary of 2,000 *livres*, constrains us to take the liberty to point out to you that the said Sieur Sarrazin has worked here for 15 years, without receiving any other payment in return except the 500 *livres* which he has had since 1717."

Being, along with the hydrographer Franquelin, one of the few intellectuals of New France apart from the members of the legal profession, Sarrazin belonged to the aristocracy of the colony. In the absence of a noble title, his reputation as official doctor and as a scientist gave him prominence. He was a member of the Conseil Supérieur, and hence of the administrative élite. He sought to put himself on a level with the senior officials and the rich merchants. Although he did not live on an exaggerated scale, he was obliged to maintain his position. He expected to have to provide for the education of his sons in France and for the settling of his daughters, whose future depended upon their parents' fortune, in accordance with the social habits of the time. A good deal older than his wife, he wanted to ensure a respectable life for his family after his death. He was also anxious to pay off the debts which had accumulated during the difficult years, in order not to leave the burden of them for his widow later on. To maintain his position in a society which measured worth in terms of *écus*, he plunged into risky undertakings which caused frustrations and anxieties, and ruined him.

Certainly he did not lack ambition. In the material sphere he sought a situation compatible with his rank. In the scientific sphere he hoped that his works would earn him a title superior to that of correspondent of a member of the academy. On 10 Oct. 1726 he wrote to Réaumur: "In short, sir, there is then no way of having some kind of place in the Academy, and I admit to you that not knowing the procedure I had always flattered myself that I would find some corner there before I died." An exaggerated hope, it may be thought, but if one examines the list of academicians of the period, one finds that except for a few great names there are many whose worth as scientists did not equal Sarrazin's. Dr Vallée describes him as a "taciturn man, misanthropic and always pessimistic." He had reason enough to be taciturn and pessimistic, but misanthropy hardly goes with the great kindness, the extreme devotedness, and the great unselfishness that he showed towards the sick. Some people think he had a persecution complex. One always accuses of paranoia those who are in fact the victims of relentless persecution. This sometimes made him aggressive, as is shown by the letter to Réaumur quoted above, but such a reaction was inevitable in the circumstances.

A man absorbed in his research work, for which his powers of observation specially suited him, a man with little inclination for social events, and moreover of frail health, and with a religious bent that was not devoid of a certain mysticism—this was more than enough to explain the accusation that he was "rather downcast and dreamy," as a document of the period put it.

From the ideas expressed in his personal correspondence and fragments of letters from correspondents, as well as from his handwriting—an independent study made of this has confirmed my opinion in every respect—we can form a fairly good notion of his character. These sources reveal to us an active, tenacious, conscientious, and upright man, very well disciplined, who finished what he had begun, who was capable of concentration, yet was distracted by the problems that beset him. Endowed with a certain intellectual acuteness, he nevertheless was more interested in precise facts than in great ideas, and attached much importance to details, at the expense of a comprehensive view. Fairly ambitious, he was not as modest as he thought or would have liked to appear. He did not lack sensitivity, he displayed a real spirit of charity, endeavoured to protect those who were entrusted to him, and supported worthy causes. Although neither excited nor ebullient, he was not relaxed. He did not possess great vitality; rather meticulous, not an out-going person, nervous, distrustful, somewhat vindictive, he gave the appearance of a frustration complex which was amply justified, but for all that he was not without a sense of self-defence. He did not seek to complicate things, however, and his great simplicity of character prevented him from hiding what he thought. Even if he loved seclusion and tranquillity, he was a well-bred man and a congenial companion. On occasion he displayed commonplace naïveté, as is shown by a letter to Abbé Bignon dated 5 Nov. 1717: "I am sending live ginseng roots to the Jardin royal. I am requesting Monsieur Vaillant to send dried roots to you, in order to rejuvenate you if you are old, and to prolong your youth if you are lucky enough to possess it still."

One cannot without exaggeration consider him a great scientist, despite the opinion that is sometimes voiced. He was a modest, even limited researcher, but a conscientious and meticulous one, and in no way inferior to many of the academicians of the time. Being the only person with a knowledge of natural history in a country where so many things remained to be discovered, he played an important role. Already, a century before, Pierre Boucher had extended our knowledge, without realizing the contribution he was making to the scientific world. In the field of his research, Sarrazin went much further than the skilful compiler Charlevoix, and can even be compared with the majority of English and French biologists in 19th-century Canada. He is surely the equal of Antoine de Jussieu, the first of that family of botanists, but he cannot be considered as a rival of Tournefort, and still less of Sébastien Vaillant, whose work truly marks the beginnings of modern botany. Nonetheless, in the difficult emergence of Canadian science, Sarrazin occupies an important place.

JACQUES ROUSSEAU

[The following are some details on most of the works mentioned in this biography. "Histoire naturelle et anatomique du Castor" was an address to the Académie Royale des Sciences on 13, 16, 20, 27 February, 12 March, and 16 April 1704. This address was published in part in *Histoire de l'Académie royale des sciences, 1704*, which appeared in 1706. The complete manuscript was transcribed in the Académie's *Registre* in 1706. "Histoire anatomique du carcajou," was a paper read to the Académie on 15 March 1713 and was transcribed in its *Registre*. "Histoire d'une espèce de rat d'Amérique septentrionale," was an address on 21 Feb. 1714 and was published in the *Histoire de l'Académie ... 1714*. "Histoire anatomique de veau-marin," was an address of 12 and 19 Jan. 1718. "Histoire du rat musqué d'Amérique," was an address of 28 and 31 Jan. 1722. "Addition à l'histoire du rat musqué," was an address of 2 June 1725; this paper seems to correspond to the text kept in the archives of the Académie, dated 15 Oct. 1722 and entitled "Notes sur le rat musqué."

"Extrait de divers mémoires de M. Sarrazin ... sur le rat musqué" was published in the *Histoire de l'Acaémdie ... 1725*, which appeared in 1727. "Observations sur le porc-épic" was an address of 15 and 18 May 1726 and was published in the *Histoire de l'Académie ... 1727*, which came out in 1729; this paper is kept at the Académie's archives. Moreover, at the 23 July 1729 session, a paper, "Histoire du porc-épic du Canada," was read; this was perhaps an addition to the preceding work or else simply a repetition, which occasionally happened at the Académie. "Nouvelles observations du travail que j'ai fait sur les parties naturelles du rat musqué" is a manuscript preserved in the Académie's archives. "Observations de Mr. Sarrazin" is an address given on 19 August 1730 on the maple trees of Canada. This long paper is preserved in the Académie's *Registre*, and is summarized in the *Histoire de l'Académie ... 1730*, which appeared in 1732. The Académie's *Registre* for 11 Dec. 1717 and the *Histoire de l'Académie ... 1718* should be consulted on the subject of Sarrazin's "Aralia humilis fructu majore"; Sébastien Vaillant mentions this discovery in his *Établissements d'un nouveau genre de plante nommé Araliastrum duquel le gin-seng des Chinois est une espèce* (Hanover, 1718). In his "Suite de l'établissement de nouveaux caractères de plantes à fleurs composées," published in the *Histoire de l'Académie* for the years

1719 and 1721, Vaillant mentions three species, giving credit to Sarrazin for their descriptions. Moreover, the *Mémoires de Trévoux* for August 1728 and for 1735 should be looked at. Several summaries of Sarrazin's works are published in the *Journal des Sçavans* for the years 1707, 1728, 1730, and 1733.

Many manuscripts were consulted in the archives of the Académie des Sciences, the BN, the AN, the archives of the Muséum d'Histoire naturelle, the London Royal Society, the AQ, the ASSM, and in some private collections, too numerous to list here. The following studies were used: Ahern, *Notes pour l'histoire de la médecine*. L.-E. Bois, *Michel Sarrazin* (Québec, 1856). Fauteux, *Essai sur l'industrie sous le régime français*. Alfred Lacroix, *Figures de savants* (4v., Paris, 1938), IV, 113–16. Arthur Vallée, *Un biologiste canadien, Michel Sarrazin, 1659–1735, sa vie, ses travaux et son temps* (Québec, 1927). J. C. K. Laflamme, "Michel Sarrazin: matériaux pour servir à l'histoire de la science en Canada," *RSCT*, 1st ser., V (1887), sect.IV, 1–23. G. Lavier, "Un nuiton en Nouvelle-France, Michel Sarrazin," *Taste-vin en main*, XXXV (1963), 32–33. Marie-Victorin, "Un manuscrit botanique prélinnéen: l'histoire des plantes de Canada," *Revue trimestrielle canadienne* (L'Ingénieur), XXII (1936). Jacques Rousseau, "Michel Sarrazin, Jean-François Gaulthier et l'étude prélinnéenne de la flore canadienne," *Colloque internationale du Centre Nationale de la recherche scientifique* (Paris), LXIII (1957), 149–57; "Sébastien Vaillant, a key figure in eighteenth century botany," *Biologia. An international bio-historical series*, IV (Hollande, 1966). Also, Louis Moreri, *Le grand dictionnaire historique, ou le mélange curieux de l'histoire sacrée et profane*, published in Paris, first in 1674 and revised in 1759; supplements were published between these two dates, and Sarrazin's biography appeared in the second of these (1749).

Other information was taken from various addresses: one by Jean F. Leroy to the 84th congress of the Sociétés Savantes at Dijon in 1959, entitled "Un collaborateur de Tournefort: Michel Sarrazin (1659–1734)" (published in the *Comptes-rendus*), another by Alfred Lacroix before the Académie des Sciences on 21 Dec. 1931. Finally, there are three soon-to-be-published works in which Sarrazin is mentioned: "Journal original du voyage au Canada en 1749 de Pehr Kalm," edited and translated by Jacques Rousseau and Guy de Béthune; "Flore du Canada, 1749, de Jean-François Gauthier," and "Histoire des plantes de Canada, de Sébastien Vaillant et de Michel Sarrazin," unpublished works with critical essays and remarks by Jacques Rousseau. J.R.]

SARREAU. See SERREAU

SAVAGE, ARTHUR, first secretary of the Province of Nova Scotia; fl. 1720–31.

A merchant from Boston, Savage moved to Annapolis Royal, N.S., early in 1720. In that year he was appointed secretary to the new council established by Governor Richard Philipps* to provide a form of civil government for the province. In addition he was given the post of naval officer, a minor function involving the registry of vessels trading in provincial waters.

Although he seems to have been a quiet, business-like man, Savage became embroiled in petty quarrels between the New England traders, the officers of the garrison at Annapolis Royal, and the council members. He successfully refuted the charges of Lieutenant John WASHINGTON, who accused him of exacting high fees from the Acadians and of monopolizing with Philipps the sale of provisions to the garrison. The atmosphere at Annapolis not being to Savage's liking, he returned to Boston, probably early in 1722. In 1724 he petitioned the authorities in England for his pay as secretary, claiming that Philipps had withheld his salary. He did not return to Nova Scotia, apparently holding the appointment *in absentia* until 1731.

MAXWELL SUTHERLAND

PAC, Nova Scotia A, 11, p.109; 13, pp.60, 205 210–11; 16, pp.53, 55. *Documents relating to currency in Nova Scotia 1675–1758* (Shortt). *N.S. Archives, II*, 170; *III*. PAC *Report, 1894*. Brebner, *New England's outpost*.

SAVAGE, THOMAS, Boston merchant and militia officer; b. *c.* 1640 at Boston; son of Thomas Savage and Faith (Hutchinson) Savage; married Elizabeth Scottow, probably in 1664; d. 2 July 1705 (o.s.) at Boston.

Like his father, Savage became an officer in both the Ancient and Honourable Artillery Company and the Boston militia. During King Philip's War (1675–76) he served with his father, who was the commander of the Massachusetts troops.

In the summer of 1690 Savage was persuaded to abandon temporarily his business activities to play an active role in the war against the French. In August, the Massachusetts General Court sent him with two others to Albany in an effort to enlist some Indian allies to counter the serious French-Indian threat to the colony's frontiers.

Major Savage was later appointed commander of one of the three regiments in William Phips*'s expedition against Quebec. Savage was sent ashore on 6 October (16 October, N.S.) to deliver an ultimatum to Buade* de Frontenac to surrender. Savage was "carried blindfold into a circle of martial men, who, finding a pumpkin fleet with the Union flag . . . told him their guns would answer for them." The English sent troops ashore under the command of Major John WALLEY two days later; among these were Savage's command. Their

attack was to no avail and the New England fleet retreated on 14 or 15 October.

On his return to Boston, Savage wrote a letter describing the expedition to his brother Perez in London. This letter was published in London in 1691 under the imposing title *An account of the late action of the New-Englanders, under the command of Sir William Phips, against the French at Canada*. Savage was particularly critical of the New England seamen in the expedition and also stressed that the French possessed all the important strategic advantages.

The popular merchant and militia officer died in Boston on 2 July 1705 and was given an impressive military funeral. The streets were "very much fill'd with People all along."

G. A. RAWLYK

Coll. de manuscrits relatifs à la N.-F., I, 520–21, 574. *NYCD* (O'Callaghan and Fernow), IX, 485–86. PRO, *CSP, Col., 1689–92*, 376–77, 384–86. Thomas Savage, *An account of the late action of the New-Englanders, under the command of Sir William Phips, against the French at Canada* (London, 1691). Additional material on the Phips expedition to Quebec can be found in *1690, Sir William Phips devant Québec* (Myrand), and in PAC *Report, 1912*, App. E. Eccles, *Canada under Louis XIV*, 180–81; *Frontenac*, 235–37. Parkman, *Count Frontenac and New France* (1891), 262–85. L. Park, "Old Boston families, number three, the Savage family," *New Eng. Hist. and Geneal. Register*, LXVII (1913), 199–205.

SAYWARD (Sayer), MARY (baptized **Marie-Geneviève**), *dite* **Marie des Anges,** nun of the Congrégation de Notre-Dame; b. 11 April 1681, daughter of William Sayward and Mary Rishworth; d. and buried 28 March 1717 at Quebec.

When William III acceded to the throne, hostilities broke out once again between France and England, and at the same time between their American colonies. On 25 Jan. 1692, around "10 o'clock in ye morny," the Abenakis, who were allies of the French, "fell upon York, killed about 48 persons (whereof ye rev. Mr. Dummier was one), and carried captives 73." Among the captives who were taken to Montreal and for whom the Indians hoped to obtain a ransom were Mrs. Sayward and her two daughters, Mary, aged 11, and Esther (baptized Marie-Joseph), aged seven. They were received by Sister Bourgeoys* into the house of the Congrégation de Notre-Dame, and a few months later, on 8 Dec. 1693, Mrs. Sayward was converted from Puritanism to Catholicism and was baptized, together with her two daughters, in the church of Notre-Dame in Montreal.

The exact date of Mary's entry into the Congrégation de Notre-Dame cannot be found in the

Scatchamisse

archives, but considering the customary age at which girls entered it, it may be presumed to be around 1698–1700. She took the name of Sister Marie des Anges. After making her profession she was sent to the Indian mission at Sault-au-Récollet, where several captives from New England were assembled. Since she spoke English, Sister Marie des Anges was doubtless better able to help her compatriots. Later on she went to Quebec, where she died on 28 March 1717. Her sister Esther married Pierre de Lestage, a Montreal merchant; having become a widow in 1743, she entered the Congrégation de Notre-Dame as a permanent boarder, and died there on 17 June 1770 at the age of 86.

HÉLÈNE BERNIER

Coleman, *New England captives*, I, II. Sister St Ignatius Doyle, *Marguerite Bourgeoys and her Congregation* (Gardenvale, 1940). *Histoire de la Congrégation de Montréal*, III, 275–78. Kenneth Roberts, *Trending into Main* (Boston, 1938), 20–22.

SCATCHAMISSE (Scratchemisse, Scatchamissey, Atchamissey, Catchamisse), Indian captain known to HBC; d. 1712.

Scatchamisse is first referred to by name in the Albany account books for 1702–3, as captain of the Sagamy (Sockemy, Southagames, Sagomy, Susagamis) Indians of Moose River; he had previously been sent presents inviting him to visit Albany. Each year from 1704 to 1712, apart from the season 1706–7 when he was too sick to come, Scatchamisse brought groups of Indians to trade at Albany. If made in the spring the trip was perilous because ice lay along the shore. Strong on-shore winds drove the fragile canoes on the ice; strong off-shore winds drove the canoes out into the bay. At any season of the year, the lack of provisions, the shallow water, and the vagaries of wind and tide made the trip arduous and dangerous.

In 1712 Scatchamisse made the trip with 18 to 20 canoes; his men were so starved for food that they broiled their beaver skins. On the return trip to Moose River, his canoe was driven out to sea and he drowned. His death prevented Governor BEALE sending him inland to encourage the upland Indians to trade at Albany as directed in the 1712 annual letter from London. In 1727 Joseph MYATT in his efforts to persuade the London committee to found a post at Moose River quoted the sad fate of Scatchamisse as a reason for the reluctance of Moose River Indians to travel to Albany.

G. E. THORMAN

HBC Arch. A.6/3 (letters outward, 23 May 1712); B.3/a/1 (Albany journals for 1705–6, entry for 22 May 1706); B.3/d/11, 13–15, 17–20 (Albany account books between 1699 and 1712). HBRS, XXV (Davies and Johnson).

SCHUYLER, PETER, soldier, government official, and the most influential Indian expert in New York province during his day; b. 17 Sept. 1657 (o.s.) in Beverswyck (Albany, N.Y.), second son of Philip Pieterse Schuyler, an emigrant from Amsterdam, and his wife Margarita Van Slichtarhorst; married twice: first to Engeltie Van Schaick in 1681 or 1682, and secondly, in 1691, to Maria Van Rensselaer, daughter of Jeremiah Van Rensselaer; d. 19 Feb. 1723/24.

Albany was the northernmost settlement of any size in New York province. Two hundred miles almost due north lay Montreal. Though separated by impenetrable wilderness, the two settlements were joined by an almost continuous waterway consisting of the Richelieu River, Lake Champlain, Lac Saint-Sacrement (Lake George), and the Hudson River. The French claimed all the territory whose waters found an outlet in the northern lakes and the St Lawrence, by right of discovery and occupancy. It included Lake Champlain. The English resisted the claim and asserted their right to the country as far north as the St Lawrence, through a title derived from the Five Nations. During a long period of almost continuous warfare, the Iroquois sided mostly with the English, partly because Albany was nearer their homeland and easier to trade with, and partly because of the great skill of Peter Schuyler in dealing with them.

Schuyler had important family connections at Albany. Both his mother and his second wife were daughters of directors of Rensselaerwyck, one of the founding Dutch settlements in the Albany area. When Albany was incorporated as a city in 1686, Peter Schuyler became its first mayor and *ex officio* chairman of the board of commissioners for Indian affairs. During the next several years there were raids and massacres at Lachine near Montreal, at Schenectady near Albany, and elsewhere within the disputed borderlands. In 1690 Peter Schuyler, hearing that a French delegation was treating with the Iroquois, led an English delegation to Onondaga (Syracuse, N.Y.), the Iroquois capital. The French were captured and some were killed, but at least one, the Chevalier d'Aux (Eau)—a half-pay captain who had been sent as an emissary to the Iroquois by Buade* de Frontenac, governor of Canada—was taken back to Albany by Schuyler. The Iroquois called Schuyler "Quider" (their pronunciation of Peter), and according to Parkman an Onondaga sachem declaimed: "Brethren . . . we must hold fast to our brother Quider, and look on Onontio [Frontenac] as our enemy. . . ." That same year an English expedition against Canada was assembled at Albany and placed under the command of Major-General Fitz-John Winthrop. Peter Schuyler collected a few Mohawk warriors and proceeded to Wood Creek, at the southern end of Lake Champlain, where he engaged in making bark canoes for the use of the army. Since there were not enough canoes or supplies, General Winthrop abandoned the expedition.

The following year (1691), a rumour reached the English that Frontenac had received reinforcements and supplies from France and was concentrating troops at Montreal, preparatory to a descent on Albany. In order to gain intelligence, Major Peter Schuyler led northward, in July, a party consisting of 120 white men, 80 Mohawks, and 66 River Indians (Schaghticokes). At the confluence of Lac Saint-Sacrement and Lake Champlain, called Ticonderoga, Schuyler was joined by an additional contingent of Mohawks, and the expedition proceeded down Lake Champlain and the Richelieu River until it was within ten miles of Fort Chambly, which was commanded by Jean-Vincent Le Ber Du Chesne. Scouts from the fort notified the Chevalier de CALLIÈRE, the governor of Montreal, who collected from 700 to 800 men and encamped at La Prairie de la Magdeleine on the south shore of the St Lawrence, opposite Montreal. He then sent out several scouting parties, and a few days later one of the sons of JOSEPH-FRANÇOIS HERTEL de La Fresnière brought in word that he had seen a canoe containing Mohawks in the Richelieu River. Thinking that Chambly was in danger, the governor of Montreal sent Philippe CLÉMENT Du Vuault de Valrennes to the spot with about 200 men. Nicolas DANEAU de Muy and CLAUDE GUILLOUET d'Orvilliers were in the company.

Meanwhile, Schuyler, leaving his canoes on the river-bank, had made his way overland to La Prairie de la Magdeleine, reaching that fort on the rainy night of 31 July (10 August, N.S.). An hour before daybreak on 1 August (11 August) the sentinel at the fort fired his piece and M. de Saint-Cyrque (Sircq), an old captain commanding in the absence of Callière who was ill and confined to his bed in the fort, led an advance. A musket volley mortally wounded him and the Sieur d'Escairac (Desquerac), and killed M. d'Hosta (Dosta) on the spot. The second wave of troops led by Jean BOUILLET de La Chassaigne came up at that moment and rushed headlong on the enemy who, after a vigorous resistance, retreated in good order. Another small French detachment, led by the Sieur Domerque, attacked Schuyler's retreat-

ing forces and was wiped out. Schuyler now headed for his canoes on the Richelieu River but was intercepted by the party sent out to protect Fort Chambly. Valrennes and Le Ber deployed their men behind trees and fought the English for an hour and a half. Schuyler finally succeeded in cutting his way through the enemy and reached his canoes. As he reported to the provincial council in New York a few weeks later, "We took our march homewards and found 5 Elks in the way which refreshed our whole company. . . . We lost in the expedition 21 Christians 16 Mohaques 6 River Indians & the wounded in all 25 . . . . Thought to have killed about 200 French and Indians." The bravery and competence shown by Schuyler's expedition made a favourable impression on the Indians of the Five Nations, who were now convinced that the English could fight and were willing to risk their lives in the war.

During the winter of 1692–93 Frontenac sent southward an expedition, commanded by Lieutenants NICOLAS D'AILLEBOUST de Manthet, AUGUSTIN LE GARDEUR de Courtemanche and ROBUTEL de La Noue, which destroyed three Mohawk villages and captured many women and children. Schuyler led a party which pursued the retreating French and forced them to relinquish most of their prisoners.

When peace was concluded between England and France, the Earl of Bellomont, governor of New York, sent Schuyler and the Reverend Godfrey Dellius to Quebec in May 1698 to deliver news of the peace to Count Frontenac, and also to return all French prisoners held in New York. This was Schuyler's last expedition to Canada.

Schuyler was made a lieutenant of Francis NICHOLSON for the proposed expeditions against Canada in 1709 and 1711. Their forces were to attack by way of Lake Champlain. In both cases, however, the forces never got beyond the Lake Champlain camping grounds. Early in 1710, Schuyler took four Mohawk sachems to London where they were received by Queen Anne. His aim was to emphasize the importance of retaining the friendship of the Five Nations.

Schuyler continued throughout his life to serve as Indian commissioner and as a member of the provincial council. He was acting governor of New York from July 1719 to September 1720. He was dismissed from the council by the new governor, William Burnet, but continued at the head of the Indian board until his death in 1724.

JOHN H. G. PELL

Calendar of council minutes, 1668–1783 (N.Y. State Lib., *Bull.* LVIII, Hist. VI, Albany, 1902). Charlevoix, *History* (Shea). *Coll. de manuscrits relatifs à la N.-F.,*

Scratchemisse

I, 586–88. "Correspondance de Frontenac (1689–99)," APQ *Rapport*, *1927–28*, 70; *1928–29*, 370–71. "Correspondance de Vaudreuil," APQ *Rapport*, *1947–48*, 161–66. *NYCD* (O'Callaghan and Fernow), III–VII, IX (*see* Index). PRO, *CSP*, *Col.*, *1685–88*, *1689–92*, *1710–11*, *1711–12*. *Walker expedition* (Graham). *DAB*. R. P. Bond, *Queen Anne's American kings* (Oxford, 1952). Eccles, *Frontenac*. Parkman, *Count Frontenac and New France* (1891), 198. G. W. Schuyler *Colonial New York; Philip Schuyler and his family* (2v., New York, 1885). Waller, *Samuel Vetch*. A. J. Weise, *The history of the city of Albany, New York* (Albany, 1884).

SCRATCHEMISSE. *See* SCATCHAMISSE

SCROGGS, JOHN, HBC sailor; fl. 1718–24.

After serving as second mate on a Hudson's Bay Company ship in 1718 and 1719, Scroggs returned to the bay in 1721 as master of the *Whalebone* sloop, and the next year sailed north from Churchill to explore the west coast of the bay. Although Scroggs was an inexpert navigator and an unenthusiastic explorer, his short voyage is of some importance through his discovery on Marble Island of wreckage from James KNIGHT's lost expedition, and more especially because of the significance his meagre explorations attained in the search for a northwest passage. At the expedition's farthest point north Richard Norton* reported a clear channel to the west (probably Chesterfield Inlet), which Scroggs allegedly refused to investigate. In the 1730s Christopher Middleton* and Arthur Dobbs* read Scroggs' journal, and argued that this opening might be the entrance of a passage to the Pacific—an illusion which lured several expeditions to the region until Chesterfield Inlet and the nearby coastline were surveyed in detail. Scroggs returned to England in 1723, and disappeared into obscurity. The last mention of him in the company records is a refusal in 1724 to appoint him captain of one of the company's ships.

GLYNDWR WILLIAMS

Extracts from Scroggs' journal (which is no longer in the HBC archives) were printed in Arthur Dobbs, *Remarks upon Capt. Middleton's defence* (London, 1744), 113–17. A longer summary of the journal was printed a few years later in [T. S. Drage], *An account of a voyage for the discovery of a north-west passage by Hudson's Streights, to the western and southern ocean of America* (2v., London, 1748–49), II, 174–80. Details of Scroggs' service with the HBC are given in HBRS, XXV (Davies and Johnson). The fullest account of the voyage of 1722 is in Williams, *The British search for the northwest passage*, 22–26.

SENET, *dit* **LALIBERTÉ, NICOLAS,** corporal, royal notary, son of Pierre and Suzanne Vanier, of Notre-Dame-de-Vitry (Champagne); baptized 1670; buried 17 Jan. 1732.

On 10 May 1689, at Boucherville, when he was a corporal in the army, Senet married Gertrude Daunet; they had 12 children.

In November 1698 he was secretary to the Seigneurs of Montreal. In 1704 he received from Intendant Beauharnois* de La Boische his first commission as a notary, which gave him jurisdiction in the area of Pointe-aux-Trembles and as far as the lower end of the island of Montreal, as well as in the seigneuries of Repentigny, Lachenaye, Île Jésus, Île Sainte-Thérèse, Rivière-des-Prairies, Saint-Sulpice, and Chambly. On 18 June 1706 Intendant JACQUES RAUDOT granted him another commission which extended his radius of action to the other parishes of the jurisdiction of Montreal where there was no notary. On 29 June 1721 he received from Intendant Bégon* a third commission which gave him authority throughout the government of Montreal, except in the town itself. The last minute in Senet's registry, preserved in the Archives judiciaires of Montreal, bears the date 28 Dec. 1731.

From 1706 to 1708 he had also acted as court officer. During 1709 he served as soldier of the watch under the orders of the Sieur François-Marie BOUAT, lieutenant of the marshalcy of New France.

He died at Pointe-aux-Trembles (Montreal), where he appears to have had his permanent residence.

ANTONIO DROLET

AJM, Greffe de Nicolas Senet, 1704–31. AQ, NF, Ord. des int., I, 86; VII½, 184. *Jug. et délib.*, V. A. Roy, *Inv. greffes not.*, XVII, 7f. "Les notaires au Canada," 33. J.-E. Roy, *Histoire du notariat*, I, 212. É.-Z. Massicotte, "La maréchaussée à Montréal," *BRH*, XXII (1916), 17.

SERIGNY, ET DE LOIRE, JOSEPH LE MOYNE DE. *See* LE MOYNE

SERREAU (Sarreau) DE SAINT-AUBIN, JEAN, soldier, sailor, and seigneur; b. 1621 in the province of Poitou; d. 1705, probably at Port-Royal (Annapolis Royal, N.S.).

Jean Serreau arrived in Canada around 1660, established himself in 1662 on Île d'Orléans on the Argentenay seigneury, and had been living there peacefully with his wife Marguerite Boileau for some time, when a certain Jean Terme, of Swiss origin, came and disturbed the happiness of the household by his over-intimate relations with Marguerite. Despite the husband's repeated warnings, this relationship continued for about a year and soon led to threats between the two rivals.

One day in July 1665, Jean Terme, surprised by the husband, put his hand to his sword, but the other dealt him a blow with a stick which proved fatal. As it was a case of justifiable self-defence, Saint-Aubin was completely exonerated from this slaying. He obtained a reprieve, signed by Louis XIV, and presented it in January 1667 to the Conseil Souverain of Quebec. A month later the council had the reprieve registered. In April, at the request of Madame d'Ailleboust [Boullongne*], the seigneuress of Argentenay, Saint-Aubin was expelled from the land which he occupied on Île d'Orléans.

He settled at Pesmocadie (Passamaquoddy) on the Sainte-Croix River in Acadia soon after 1676. In June 1684, he received a fairly extensive land grant which he made into a prosperous seigneury. He went to live on Île Archimagan, near what is now the town of St Andrews, N.B., and became the most influential citizen of the locality.

Here, however, difficulties of another kind awaited him. In August 1692 William Phips*, who had recently been appointed governor of Massachusetts and who wished to fortify the coast of Maine against the French, sent Major Benjamin Church with his troops in pursuit of the enemy, with orders to take as many prisoners as possible. Having set off in the direction of Penobscot Bay, Church seized Saint-Aubin and his son-in-law Jacques Petitpas, with their families, and took them to Boston. At that period the Bostonians coveted a prey that was much more valuable to them, namely Baron Jean-Vincent d'Abbadie de Saint-Castin, whom they could not abide. In order to obtain their freedom, the two heads of families pretended to accept the proposal that they should go with two deserters from Quebec to carry off or assassinate Saint-Castin. But when they reached Penobscot Bay, they tied up the two traitors and took them to Governor Robinau* de Villebon, who had them executed. Villebon rewarded the two Acadians with a sum of money sufficiently large "to enable them to deliver their wives and children from the English."

One must suppose that they were not able to secure the freedom of all the members of their families, for in a letter that Saint-Aubin sent to Boston in 1695 mention is made of a ransom of 30 *livres* for his daughter. This letter also suggests that Saint-Aubin, having been ruined by Church's raid, was thinking of going to settle elsewhere. Indeed he asked the governor of Massachusetts, whose territory included at that time the whole of Acadia, to grant him in exchange for his "land at Pesmoncady a small river which the Indians call Secoudec to build a saw-mill there." In addition, he endeavoured to obtain, facing Île Saint-Jean

(Prince Edward Island), a grant of land called Picquetou (Pictou), as well as a small river called Artigonyche (Antigonish, N.S.). The following year he asked the French authorities to confirm the grant of his "seigneury which he was forced to abandon because of the English invasion and which he is in a position to restore."

He distinguished himself also in Newfoundland, in the service of his country: this was probably during the winter of 1696–97, when Pierre Le Moyne d'Iberville, after destroying Pemaquid, set out to conquer the island, at the time when Jacques-François de Brouillan [Mombeton] was governor at Placentia (Plaisance). The latter, when he became governor of Acadia, presented Saint-Aubin in 1703 with a certificate testifying to his services, his loyalty, and his bravery, both on the continent and in Newfoundland.

Saint-Aubin went to France for a short period, no doubt to recover possession of his land, which a general decree of 1703 had taken from him. In the following year he won his case and returned to Acadia, probably to Port-Royal, where he died at the age of 84.

Clarence J. d'Entremont

AAQ, Registres d'insinuation A, 362–63. AN, Col., B, 25, 123; D²ᶜ, 47/2, f.366; Section Outre-Mer, G¹, 466 (Recensements de l'Acadie, 1686, 1693). ASQ, Séminaire, XXXVII, 62. "Mass. Archives," II, 536–38.

Church, *King Philip's war* (Dexter), II, 82–92. *Coll. de manuscrits relatifs à la N.-F.*, I, 386, 429; II, 92–96, 407. *Jug. et délib.*, I, 371–73, 375–76, 379–81, 388, 394–95; II, 25. A. Roy, *Inv. greffes not.*, III, 145. P.-G. Roy, *Inv. concessions*, IV, 116. Tanguay, *Dictionnaire*, I, 548.

Pierre Daviault, *Le baron de Saint-Castin, chef abénaquis* (Montréal, 1939), 106–7. Guy Murchie, *Saint Croix, the sentinel river: historical sketches of its discovery, early conflicts and final occupation by English and American settlers with some comments on Indian life* (New York, 1947), 92–97, 99. Murdoch, *History of Nova-Scotia*, I, 168, 214. "Un drame en l'île d'Orléans en 1665: Jean Terme tué par Jean Serreau, sieur de Saint-Aubin," *NF*, II (1927), 79–81. Ganong, "Historic sites in New Brunswick," 266, 304, 307. P.-G. Roy, "Le Suisse Jean Terme," dans *Les petites choses de notre histoire*, VI, 24–28.

SHEEPSCOT JO. *See* Wowurna

SILLY, JEAN-BAPTISTE DE, commissary of the Marine, financial commissary, and acting intendant; b. *c.* 1683 in France. He had already proved himself in the French navy when King Louis XV asked him to assume the office of commissary of the Marine in New France on 24 May 1728.

Silver

He arrived in Canada in the summer of that year, but his stay was to last only two years, for his health and the climate did not permit him to remain any longer. During those two years, however, by force of circumstances, Silly temporarily held three very important posts at the same time: commissary of the Marine at Quebec and at Montreal, and also acting intendant. Intendant CLAUDE-THOMAS DUPUY having been recalled to France, CLAIRAMBAULT d'Aigremont, the commissary at Montreal, came to Quebec to discharge the duties of intendant until the arrival of Dupuy's successor. When Aigremont died on 1 Dec. 1728, it was Silly who was instructed to replace him.

It was not long before Hocquart*, the new intendant, perceived Silly's great qualities, and on 28 Oct. 1729 he delegated to him power to "deal with all civil matters involving up to 500 *livres*" at Montreal. In addition he was to carry out or have carried out edicts, declarations, and ordinances concerning fraudulent trading, and to collaborate with the governor of Montreal with regard to the maintenance of good order in the colony.

Jean-Baptiste de Silly left some traces of his short stay in Canada: in particular he promoted the slate-quarry of Anse-des-Monts Notre-Dame, known as the slate-quarry of Grand Étang, and had occasion to help the unfortunate survivors of the *Éléphant*, which was wrecked near Cap Brûlé on 2 Sept. 1729.

He resigned on 10 Oct. 1730 for reasons of health and shortly afterwards went back to France, where he was put on half pay; his subsequent activities are not known to us, any more than is the date of his death.

In a letter of 18 Oct. 1730 to the minister, Hocquart paid tribute to Silly as follows: "He has handled all matters related to warehouses and trading posts with great efficiency, and has discharged in the same way the duties of subdelegate which I had entrusted to him. He leaves loved by all and missed by the whole body of officers and settlers; in his conduct he has shown much wisdom and unselfishness."

ROLAND-J. AUGER

JR (Thwaites), LXVIII, 206, 329f. "La perte du vaisseau du roi l'Éléphant en 1729," *BRH*, XIII (1907), 285. P.-G. Roy, *Inv. coll. pièces jud. et not.*, II, 364; *Inv. ord. int.*, II, 40. Sulte, *Hist. des Can. fr.*, VI, 141. "L'ardoisière du Grand Étang," *BRH*, XVI (1910), 185–88. P.-G. Roy, "Les commissaires ordinaires de la marine en la Nouvelle-France," *BRH*, XXIV (1918), 51–54; "Jean-Baptiste de Silly," *BRH*, XXII (1916), 313; "Les trois frères Lanoullier," *BRH*, XII (1906), 18.

SILVER, MARY (baptized **Adélaïde**), nun, Religious Hospitaller of St Joseph; b. 10 March 1694 at Haverhill in New England, daughter of Thomas Silver and Mary Williams; d. and buried 22 April 1740 at Montreal.

Mary Silver lived in the village of Haverhill, in New England, with her mother, Mary Williams, who after the death of her husband Thomas Silver had remarried, her second husband being Simon Wainwright. Mary was 14 when at the end of the summer of 1708 a detachment of soldiers from New France, under the command of JEAN-BAPTISTE HERTEL de Rouville, attacked Haverhill. Simon Wainwright, who was commandant of the fort, was killed, and Mrs. Wainwright managed to flee, but Mary was captured and taken off as a prisoner to Montreal. Father Charlevoix*, an eye-witness of the prisoners' arrival at Montreal around the middle of September, related that the captives praised the kindness of their conquerors, particularly that of Simon Dupuy, "who had been humane to the point of carrying for a good part of the way the daughter of the king's lieutenant of Hewreuil [Haverhill], who could scarcely walk at all."

The young girl had to be entrusted, as was usually the case, to the Sisters of the Congrégation de Notre-Dame. She was baptized on Sunday, 2 Feb. 1710, by Abbé Henri-Antoine MERIEL, and had as her illustrious godfather and godmother the Marquis RIGAUD de Vaudreuil, governor of New France, and Marie-Charlotte Denys de La Ronde, wife of Claude de RAMEZAY, governor of Montreal Island.

At the age of 17 Adélaïde Silver entered the order of the Religious Hospitallers of St Joseph, at the Hôtel-Dieu of Montreal, where she took her vows in 1712. The correspondence between Vaudreuil and Dudley, governor of Massachusetts, informs us of the urgent steps taken to secure Mary Silver's return to New England. Furthermore, in a letter of 22 Oct. 1713 addressed to the superior of the Hôtel-Dieu of La Flèche, Sister GALLARD wrote: "During the negotiations over the peace treaty [Utrecht] the governor came and offered to send her [Mary Silver] back to her mother, who had requested him to do this, having sent him the money to cover the cost of the journey. She answered him with generous courage. . . ."

Sister Silver was for a long time "catechist of the English persons" who, being sick, came to the Hôtel-Dieu of Montreal, where she died on 22 April 1740.

HÉLÈNE-BERNIER

AHDM, Déclaration de nos anciennes Mères pour

Silvy

constater la profession religieuse et le décès des Soeurs. Charlevoix, *Histoire* (1744), II, 324–27. "Correspondance de Vaudreuil," APQ *Rapport, 1947–48*, 252f. Coleman, *New England captives*, I. Abbé E.-L. Couanier de Launay, *Histoire des religieuses hospitalières de Saint-Joseph (France et Canada)* (2v., Paris, 1887), II, 114. Garneau, *Histoire du Canada*, II, 212. Mondoux, *L'Hôtel-Dieu de Montréal*, 262, 266.

SILVY, ANTOINE, priest, Jesuit, missionary; b. 16 Oct. 1638, at Aix-en-Provence (France); d. 24 Sept. 1711, at Quebec.

At the end of his classical studies at the Jesuit college in his native town, he joined the Society of Jesus in Lyons on 7 April 1658. After two years there, he taught in the community's houses at Grenoble, Embrun, and Bourg-en-Bresse. He completed his theological studies at Dole in the period 1667–71, and did the Third Year at Lyons (1671–72).

Silvy arrived at Quebec 30 Sept. 1673, and the following year he was assigned to the missions to the Ottawas. It was while thus engaged that he took his vows as a professed, on 15 Aug. 1675. Working out from Michilimackinac, he extended his apostolate to the tribes living south of Lake Michigan and between the Great Lakes and the Mississippi: these were the Ottawas and Mascoutens (with whom he worked as assistant to Father Claude Allouez*), the Crees, Temiscamings, Chippewas, Amikwas, Sauks, Winnebagos, Foxes, and Illinois.

Having gained recognition as a missionary "of consummate merit," Father Silvy was associated in 1678 with Father François de Crespieul in the difficult missions in the Saguenay region. This immense territory, which extended from James Bay to the Gulf of St Lawrence, comprised various separate groups, the Mistassinis, the Montagnais, the Papinachois, and the Eskimos. The Jesuit missionaries did not, however, carry on their apostolate among the Eskimos. (At the time, this name was sometimes extended to the Naskapis, as Allan Burgesse has shown.) Father Silvy worked in various mission posts: Chicoutimi (1678, 1679), Métabetchouan (1678, 1679, the winters of 1681 and 1682), Lake Mistassini (1679), Baie des Papinachois and Portneuf (winter of 1683), rapidly mastering the languages, which were, it must be added, closely related, of these different tribes. In the summer of 1679 he went to James Bay with Louis Jolliet*, and on the way back founded a mission (St François Xavier) at Nemiskau, half-way between James Bay and Lake Mistassini.

In 1684 Father Silvy was chaplain with the expedition which the Sieur Bermen de La Martinière led by sea to Hudson Bay. He kept the journal of the progress and the incidents of the voyage from the time they left Île aux Coudres, on 12 July, until their return to the Strait of Belle-Isle on 15 August of the following year. This journal, which is headed "from Belle Isle to Port Nelson" and is reproduced in the preface of the *Relation par lettres*, edited by Rochemonteix*, contains precise details concerning the ship's course and its daily position, distances and meteorological data, military operations, and other incidents of all kinds. Silvy was not averse to putting a little humour into his journal; for example, in this description of their first meeting with some Labrador Eskimos: "We noticed coming towards us like eels under water a dozen Eskimo canoes with only one man in each; besides, they cannot hold any more, since they have only a round hole in the middle to take him. They came uttering cries continuously and waving in the air a piece of their take to indicate that they wanted to trade; they have only sealskins, made into hoods or otherwise, for which they ask for nothing but knives; they do not use tobacco at all, which is quite extraordinary for savages. They are childlike in nature and extremely given to laughing, but in a puerile and silly way. If they offer a sealskin, for which they are given a small knife, no sooner have they received it than they burst into laughter, as if they had acquired a treasure, and if they give us a hood made of 2 or 3 skins which are just as big, or even bigger, and finer, and very daintily sewn, for which they are offered nothing but a small knife, they receive it with the same demonstrations of joy and the same peals of laughter as if they were making a great acquisition; their distrust is such, that they want to receive with one hand while they are letting go with the other." And on the way back Father Silvy wrote: "There we saw some Eskimos in canoes and Biscay boats who were as fat as the seals on which they live. Their eyes were so deep-set in their cheeks as to be barely visible." In Saint-Pierre harbour, "surrounded by high mountains of barren rock . . . , we found a little warmth, and a number of daddy-long-legs that were as black as Ethiopians."

Father Crespieul mentions that during the wintering-over at Port Nelson "with M. de La Martinière and 50 Frenchmen," Father Antoine Silvy "began the mission to the North in that region."

In March 1686 Father Silvy accompanied as chaplain the expedition led by the Chevalier de Troyes* which went overland to Hudson Bay to take the posts which had been set up there by the English; his knowledge of the country and the Indians of the region was very useful to the leaders

Silvy

of these operations. "Father Silvy followed me step by step and ran the same risks," wrote the Chevalier de Troyes. In a letter dated 30 July 1686 Father Silvy gave a brief but substantial account of the expedition, the text of which was to be inserted by Bishop Saint-Vallier [LA CROIX] in his report on the *Estat présent de l'Église*: "It has not been without many risks and fatigues that, with God's help, we have achieved our ends. The route from Mataoüan [Mattawa] on is extremely difficult; it is nothing but very violent rapids which are dangerous either to go up or to come down; several times I was in danger of being lost, with all those accompanying me; the carpenter Noël Le Blanc, one of our best men and whom we most needed, was swallowed up all at once, without coming to the surface again; M. d'Iberville [PIERRE LE MOYNE], who had him with him, escaped only through his skill and presence of mind, which he never lost. Others, who escaped by swimming, got off with losing their canoe, their belongings, and their supplies." After the account of the little band's brilliant military operations, Father Silvy concludes: "There, Your Excellency, are the first attempts of our Canadians, under the wise leadership of brave M. de Troyes and Messieurs Sainte-Hélène [Jacques Le Moyne*] and Iberville, his lieutenants. These two noble brothers have distinguished themselves wonderfully and the Indians, who saw what was done in so little time and with so little slaughter, are so struck with astonishment that they will never stop talking about it, wherever they are."

Father Silvy adds, on the subject of evangelizing the Indians: "I saw only a small number of Indians from various tribes, some of whom understood me, and the others did not: as we converse with them only fleetingly, because they are always on the move, there is hardly any likelihood that we can very soon christianize them; it must nevertheless be hoped that God, through His omnipotent goodness, will give them the means of being converted, if they are willing to cooperate with us in this important work." He applied himself to this apostolic work when he had more time, during the winter at Fort Monsipi (Moose Fort), which was captured 21 June 1686.

After his return to Quebec in 1687, he went back to Hudson Bay, where he carried on his ministry in the French posts, especially at Fort Sainte-Anne (Fort Albany), and among the Indians until 1693. He then returned to Quebec and spent the rest of his career there in the Jesuit college, first as a mathematics teacher, and then as minister, spiritual director, and mission adviser. He died 24 Sept. 1711.

In addition to the writings already mentioned,

we have from Father Antoine Silvy a letter written from his mission to the Mascoutens in 1676. During one of his winterings-over at Lac Saint-Jean (1678) he wrote some "catecheses," constituting a sort of list of expressions in Montagnais language which Father Claude-Godefroy Coquart* later translated and to which he added a commentary. The *Relation par lettres*, which was edited by Rochemonteix, has been attributed to Silvy; Rochemonteix wrote: "Among the Jesuits of New France we do not know a single one of that period who was in a position to know and who did know as thoroughly as Father Silvy, the French-Canadians, the Indians, all of this immense North-American country." This observation is justified, but it does not prove sufficiently the affirmation that Silvy was really the author of the text in question. Concerning Rochemonteix's affirmation, Father Arthur Melançon, the eminent archivist of the Jesuits in Canada, has made this note: "Nix, but rather Raudot (junior) [ANTOINE-DENIS RAUDOT]." This opinion carries weight. It is supported by an observation. These letters dwell at length on the Indians of the Great Lakes region, including the Iroquois, and also give details concerning those of Acadia, whom Father Silvy did not know personally, whereas they give no space, not even an allusion, to those of the Saguenay country, who presented many special traits and among whom he carried on his apostolate for seven years; that he should be silent in this way in his texts is an argument against the supposition that he was the author. He must, however, have supplied many elements of these letters to Antoine-Denis Raudot, with whom he could have been in contact for four years (1705–9).

In announcing Father Antoine Silvy's death in his report on the Canadian missions, Father Joseph-Louis GERMAIN wrote of him: "[He] spent 40 years in Canada . . . ; he always carried out worthily all his duties towards God by constant exactitude in all devotional exercises, towards his neighbour by great charity and great zeal for saving souls, and towards himself by constant mortification of his senses and passions."

Father Antoine Silvy embodied the all-round type of missionary in Canada, gifted for all sorts of functions, ready to accept everything and capable of carrying everything out successfully.

VICTOR TREMBLAY, P.D.

AAQ, Registres des missions des Postes du Roy, 1678–1711. Archives de la Société historique du Saguenay, Lorenzo Angers, "Curriculum vitae d'Antoine Silvy."

Documents relating to Hudson Bay (Tyrrell). HBRS, XXI (Rich). *JR* (Thwaites). La Poterie,

Histoire (1722), I, 147. *Relation par lettres de l'Amérique septentrionale, années 1709 et 1710*, éd. Camille de Rochemonteix (Paris, 1904). Saint-Vallier, *Estat présent de l'Église* (1688; 1857). Chevalier de Troyes, *Journal* (Caron).

DCB, I. Le Jeune, *Dictionnaire. Liste des missionaires-jésuites, Nouvelle-France et Louisiane, 1611–1800* (Montréal, 1929), 69. Frégault, *Iberville*. Rochemonteix, *Les Jésuites et la N.-F. au XVIIᵉ siècle*, III, 269. J. A. Burgesse, "Esquimaux in the Saguenay," *Primitive Man* (Washington), XXII (1949), 23–32. Camille de Rochemonteix, "Biographies canadiennes: Antoine Silvy," *BRH*, XX (1914), 83–85. P.-G. Roy, "Le chevalier de Troyes," *BRH*, X (1904), 284.

SKEFFINGTON, GEORGE, owner of a large salmon fishery in Newfoundland; fl. 1700–29.

Born probably in Bristol of Quaker parents, Skeffington was established as a small trader in Bonavista by about 1700. There he practised the trades of ship-chandler and cooper. During the winter months he sold rum and wine on credit, and was reimbursed with interest at the end of the fishing season. Soon he recognized that there was a potentially lucrative trade in freshwater fish. Although the rivers of Newfoundland were rich in salmon, few attempts had been made to develop inland fishing. Leaving a capable factor to manage the chandlery business during his absence, Skeffington, with the help of a few adventurous hired hands, was soon netting large catches of salmon. He was able to sell his fish to the merchant ships touching at Bonavista, and for a time thrived without opposition. In the winter of 1704–5, however, a French expedition, led by AUGER de Subercase, attacked the English settlements in Newfoundland. Skeffington, as one of the town's leading men, was in charge of the Bonavista settlement when news arrived of the approach of a French force under TESTARD de Montigny. Perhaps in order to save his property, perhaps because of his Quaker principles, Skeffington promptly surrendered the town and agreed to pay a ransom. When the French withdrew they took Skeffington with them, and he remained for some months at Placentia (Plaisance) before an exchange of prisoners procured his release.

On his return to Bonavista, he continued to explore the lakes and rivers north of the town, taking care not to overfish any particular water. In September 1718 Skeffington proposed to set up a joint fishery with William Keen*, a merchant of St John's. Skeffington was to organize the actual fishing, while Keen would provide the salt and necessary equipment. The enterprise was not particularly successful, however, partly because interlopers encroached on the area claimed by the partners; Keen lost £120 in the deal.

Fishing in the interior of Newfoundland was difficult and dangerous. The men had to construct dams, clear the rivers, and build houses for curing the salmon; provisions were scarce and the weather was harsh. The Beothuks frequently wandered across the fishing areas looking for ochre. In 1721 they killed some of Skeffington's men; they also broke his dams, took away his nets, and made off with his provisions and gear. During 1724 they were again troublesome, and Skeffington petitioned the government for two boats with six soldiers apiece, with which he proposed to keep the country free from Indians. He was granted a guard and no doubt contributed to the destruction of the Beothuks.

Despite the manifold problems, Skeffington's fishery was extensive. In 1720 he had successfully petitioned the crown for salmon fishing rights for 21 years in a large area around Bonavista. During this year it was estimated that he employed 30 men, and sent abroad 530 "tierces" of salmon, valued at 30s. a tierce, together with fur and seal oil to a value of £6,000. By 14 Oct. 1729 Skeffington had disposed of his fishery and, as he figures no more in the Newfoundland records, he presumably retired to England.

CARSON I. A. RITCHIE

PRO, C.O. 194/6, 194/7, 195/7. PRO, *CSP, Col., 1720–21, 1722–23, 1724–25, 1728–29*. Prowse, *History of Nfld.* Michael Godfrey, "Newfoundland salmon pioneer," *Fish Trades Gazette* (London), 4359 (7 Jan. 1967).

SLAVE WOMAN. *See* THANADELTHUR

SMART, THOMAS, naval officer who directed the attack on French fishing installations at Canso (Canceau), September 1718; d. 8 Nov. 1722 (o.s.).

Smart was appointed captain and commander of the *Squirrel* (a sixth-rate frigate of 20–22 guns, carrying 100–115 men) on 26 July 1715. He participated in Sir George Byng's anti-Jacobite operation in Scotland, 1715–16, and was on home service off the French coast, 1716–17. On 18 April 1717 he was dispatched to North America "to act in concert against pirates," and was stationed off New England from July 1717 till July 1720.

The Anglo-French contest over the possession of the Canso fishery—resulting from the ambiguity of Article XIII of the treaty of Utrecht (1713) and not definitely settled until the Peace of Paris (1763)—erupted in September 1718. In response to a bolstering of the French position at Canso and a new claim of sovereignty, Governor Shute of Massachusetts determined to assert British rights. On 26 August, the *Squirrel*, Captain Thomas Smart commander, set sail for the island of Canso and Île Royale (Cape Breton Island).

Smart was instructed to investigate conditions on the spot; to visit Île Royale, where he would request Governor Saint-Ovide [Mombeton*] to order the immediate withdrawal of the French fishermen; and, if met with a refusal, to return to Canso, demolish the French installations, confiscate the vessels and effects of the fishermen, and expel them from the area. Although there are discrepancies in the various accounts of Smart's interview with Saint-Ovide, it would seem that the latter agreed to a withdrawal only on condition that it would be no more than a temporary evacuation, delayed until the season's end, and accompanied by a similar evacuation on the part of the English. Smart thereupon returned to Canso, and from 14–25 September (25 September–6 October, N.S.), carried out the rest of his instructions. On 4 October, the *Squirrel* arrived back in Boston, escorting a brigantine, a sloop, and "several" shallops, which had been confiscated "for fishing and trading contrary to the 5th and 6th Arts. of Peace and Neutrality in America."

As advised by the Massachusetts council, the vessels were kept in harbour, the perishable part of their cargoes sold at public auction, and the proceeds of the sale deposited in bond, pending a decision from England. A squabble over these spoils, typical of the many that occurred between naval commanders and colonial governors at the time, then arose between Smart and Shute, and the French fishermen hastened to press their claims as well. Eventually, on 5 June 1719, while denying the validity of the French arguments and actually commending Smart, the Board of Trade resisted its first impulse to reject these claims. In order "to cultivate a good understanding between the two Nations," but only as "a pure act of grace and favour," the confiscated vessels and effects, or their value, were to be returned. There is no evidence, however, to show that the restitution duly ordered by the Lords Justices was actually made; and the case of the chief claimant, Joannis de HIRIBERRY, dragged on till 1722, when it petered out inconclusively.

The Canso fishery was described by both Shute and the Board of Trade as "the best in America and preferable to that of Newfoundland." Largely because of the Hiriberry case, the incident of September 1718 was the most far-reaching of the many crises in the contest for this fishery after 1713. It also revealed the New England interests at work in the contest—interests that grew increasingly influential in Nova Scotian affairs, to become at least a contributing factor in the expulsion of the Acadians during 1755.

As for Thomas Smart, neither the complaints of the French nor the sympathetic hearing given those complaints by some historians alter the fact that he only acted in accordance with his instructions. Indeed, as the Board of Trade acknowledged, if a "gentler method" might have been advisable, both he and the authorities behind his action displayed a "very laudable zeal for His Majesty's service." Apparently Smart never received the bounty he and his officers had been granted by order-in-council of 9 May 1719, "as an Encouragement to them for the Service they have perform'd and to other Commanders and Officers of His Majesty's Ships to use their best endeavours to do the like for the future." But he probably deserved the acquittal recommended by the Privy Council in the Hiriberry judgement of 1722.

Smart retired when the *Squirrel* was paid off and laid up in April 1721, and died the following year.

G. P. BROWNE

AN, Col., B, 44; C^{11B}, 1, 2, 3, 5, 6, 8; E, 233; Section Outre-Mer, Dépôt des fortifications des colonies, carton 5, nos.276, 277, 278. Mass. Hist. Soc., Gay papers, II, III. PAC, Nova Scotia A, 9, 10. PRO, Adm., 1/2451, 1/2452, 8/14; C.O. 5/867, 217/2, 217/3, 218/1. *The Byng papers*, ed. [W. C.] Brian Tunstall (3v., Navy Records Soc., LXVII, LXVIII, LXX, London, 1932), III. *Coll. de manuscrits relatifs à la N.-F.*, III, 30, 34–39. *Mémoires des commissaires*, IV, 429–35. *Memorials of the English and French commissaries*, I, 487–93. PRO, *CSP, Col., 1719–20, 1720–21*. John Chamberlayne, *Magnae Britanniae notitia* (25th ed., London, 1718). G.B., Admiralty, *List of sea officers, 1660–1815*, III. McLennan, *Louisbourg*.

SMITH, JAMES, appointed judge of the vice-admiralty court in Newfoundland, 1708; fl. 1708–15.

Nothing has been found about James Smith's background. It is known, however, that he was an agent for prizes in the fleet abroad before being appointed judge of the vice-admiralty court, which was created on 18 Sept. 1708 as part of an attempt to curb the power of the military commander in St John's, Major Thomas LLOYD. Bryan Rushworth was, at the same time, appointed registrar of the court and Thomas Hayne (or Havyne), marshal. Nothing was done, however, about salaries for the judge or the other officers, none of whom seems to have reached Newfoundland in 1708. As the court was apparently never constituted, Archibald CUMINGS, appointed preventive officer in the same year, was left quite powerless to check illegal trade.

On 25 April 1710 Smith took out his patent as judge, and in 1713, when he was appointed to inspect the rights and perquisites of the Admiralty in Nova Scotia, he applied for his Newfoundland salary, but without success. "I went abroad at my own charge," Smith wrote, "and executed my commission, and for the relief of the poor inhabitants and at their earnest desire, left deputations to such as I believed to be persons of the greatest probity and knowledge among them." Smith's visit to Newfoundland may have been made in 1714, or, more probably, in 1713 when he was on his way back from Nova Scotia. He gave a depressing account of the situation in Newfoundland. In the absence of a resident governor, the naval commodores exercised "a most absolute and tyrannical power." Smith advocated that the 1699 act be amended to afford protection and encouragement for the inhabitants, and regulations for the fishery. He alleged that some persons, who wished to engross the whole of the Newfoundland trade (he seems to mean the London fishing merchants) "had interest to get several lesser officers created," and had filled the posts "with such officers as were fit to be toolls and subservient to their designs." Smith may have had in mind the preventive officer, Archibald Cumings, but he specifies only William Taverner*, against whom he made several charges.

James Smith is clearly the "Mr Smith" who appeared with Cumings before the Board of Trade in November 1714 and January 1714/15, when his views on Newfoundland were considered. But he is not the James Smith who figures among the Newfoundland inhabitants in 1705–6.

Smith's career demonstrates how little real drive there was to build up an administrative machine in Newfoundland, and how, after the War of the Spanish Succession, the little incentive there was vanished. There is no evidence that this appointment of deputy vice-admiralty commissioners had any effect or continuity. The vice-admiralty court in Newfoundland had existed only on paper.

D. B. QUINN

PRO, Adm. 1/3673, ff.401–2 (1 May 1736); H.C.A. 30/824, no.467; *B.T.Journal, 1708/9–1714/15*; *CSP, Col., 1712–14, 1714–15*. Lounsbury, *British fishery at Nfld.*

SONONCHIEZ. *See* CHABERT

SOUBRAS, PIERRE-AUGUSTE DE, financial commissary, subdelegate of the intendant of New France, and first councillor of the Conseil Supérieur of Île Royale (Cape Breton Island), d. 9 April 1725, at Bordeaux. There is no record of his having married.

Soubras began his service as a clerk in the Marine at Rochefort in February 1703. He served as a clerk at Dunkirk from April 1705 until March 1714, when he was appointed financial commissary at Île Royale. He sailed to Louisbourg aboard the *Charente* during the summer of 1714.

As head of the civil administration of Île Royale, Soubras displayed considerable enterprise in trying to develop the colony. His first impressions were of the serious lack of discipline in the garrison, the laxity of the officers, and the general state of insubordination, which permeated the entire colony from its founding to its fall. Despite opposition, he directed a major effort at exercising some control over the sale of alcohol, which he felt was the principal cause of disorder. Early in 1715 he attempted to collect a tax to be used to establish a hospital. This aroused the widespread opposition of the powerful fishing interests within the colony and in France, which forced him to drop the tax, but an impressive hospital was eventually financed and built by the crown.

Soubras actively encouraged the development of the natural resources of Île Royale. He helped individuals build sawmills and boats for the coasting trade. He attempted to encourage Acadian farmers, on whom the hopes for a viable agriculture in the colony rested, to settle on the island, but had little success. To try to create markets he sent samples of native coal to France. It was chiefly due to his efforts that a brick-kiln was established at Port Toulouse (St Peters) in 1716; despite its inferior quality, local brick was used on the Louisbourg fortifications until 1725. He also encouraged the search for and use of local building materials such as lime and slate. Probably his most important contribution, however, was the foundation he laid for trade relations with Canada. These were later extended to such a degree that Louisbourg became a clearing-house for much of the trade between France, Canada, the West Indies, Nova Scotia, and even New England.

As was usual in French colonial administration, Soubras, in attempting to control expenditures, frequently quarrelled with the governors, PASTOUR de Costebelle and Saint-Ovide de Brouillan [Mombeton*], as well as with the engineer VERVILLE. Late in 1716 he had become so distressed as to request that the council of Marine authorize his return to France. Although the latter reassured him in July 1717 of its members' entire satisfaction with his administration, in April 1718 he was appointed financial commissary at Calais. This provoked a general protest within the colony, and in November 1718 a petition to the council requested that Soubras remain at Île Royale for the good of the colony, having "until now filled

Soulanges

[his position] worthily." Though he was to have left the colony in the autumn of 1718, his successor, Le Normant* de Mézy, did not arrive until the following year. Soubras finally took leave of Île Royale late in 1719, but only after he had lost all his personal effects in a fire. In France Soubras served at Calais until 1721. He then was financial commissary at Rochefort and in 1724 at Bordeaux, where he died on 9 April of the following year.

IN COLLABORATION

AN, Col., B, 37, 38; C¹¹ᴮ, 1, 2, 3; D²ᴰ, 222. *Documents relating to Canadian currency during the French period* (Shortt). La Morandière, *Hist. de la pêche française de la morue.* McLennan, *Louisbourg.*

SOULANGES ET DE MARSON, LOUISE-ÉLISABETH DE JOYBERT DE. *See* JOYBERT

SOULLARD, JEAN, gunsmith and goldsmith; b. 1642 at La Rochelle, France, son of Jean Soullard, master gunsmith, and Jeanne Couvreur, from Saint-Sauveur in the bishopric of La Rochelle; buried 9 July 1710 at Quebec.

The first official document that we possess, confirming Soullard's presence in New France, is dated 4 March 1666, the day on which he entered into a contract of marriage with Catherine Boutet, daughter of Martin Boutet* de Saint-Martin and widow of Charles Phélippeaux. After her death, he remarried twice. Nine children were born of the first marriage; one of the sons, Jean-Baptiste, wanted to follow in his father's footsteps, but fell ill when he was about 22. During this illness he made a will, in which he stated that he had abused his father's confidence by stealing from him.

Jean Soullard seems to have been an active and enterprising man. His name appears regularly in the discussions in the Conseil Souverain of New France between 1669 and 1710. Thus on 13 Jan. 1683 the aforesaid council decided that Soullard should make the dies for stamping the coinage with the "fleur de Lys" and with a Roman numeral related to its weight. Various documents also inform us that the armourer Soullard received the sum of 10 *livres* for repairs made to the silver plate of the cathedral of Quebec in 1686. A decree of the Conseil Souverain on 29 April 1701 stated that "Soulard, a worker in the goldsmith's trade, would appear before them in order to be heard on the value of the silver plate. . . ." It is certain, therefore, that Jean Soullard did work as a goldsmith, but like many of the craftsmen of his time he plied several trades. The majority of notarial acts give him the title of king's gunsmith, and our knowledge of Jean Soullard as a goldsmith is confined to a few imprecise documents.

ANDRÉ JUNEAU

AJQ, Greffe de Romain Becquet, 4 mars 1666; Greffe de Louis Chambalon, 18 sept. 1692; Greffe de Gilles Rageot, 15 sept. 1701; Greffe de Pierre Rivet, 23 juillet 1710; Registres d'état civil de Notre-Dame de Québec, 1682. ASQ, Paroisses diverses, 9. *Jug. et délib.* P.-G. Roy, *Inv. coll. pièces jud. et not.,* I, 49, 63. Marius Barbeau, "Deux cents ans d'orfèvrerie chez nous," *RSCT,* 3d ser., XXXIII (1939), sect.ɪ, 183–91. Jean Bruchési, "De la maison Soulard à l'hôtel Chevalier," *Cahiers des Dix,* XX (1955), 91–105.

SOUMANDE, LOUIS, priest, canon of the chapter of Quebec, director of the school at Saint-Joachim; b. 14 May 1652 at Quebec, son of Pierre Soumande, master maker of edge tools, and of Simone Côté; brother of LOUISE SOUMANDE de Saint-Augustin, the first superior of the Hôpital Général of Quebec; d. 19 April 1706 at Quebec.

Louis Soumande studied at the Jesuit college, and in 1663, when the seminary of Quebec was founded, he was one of the first students to be admitted to it. He received the tonsure at the age of 16; Bishop LAVAL conferred the major orders upon him in December 1677 and the priesthood on the 21st of the same month.

He spent his first years as a priest at the seminary of Quebec. In 1683 he served the missions of Sainte-Anne de Beaupré, Cap Tourmente, Petite-Rivière, and Baie-Saint-Paul. The following year, when the chapter of Quebec was established, he was appointed a canon, and took possession of his canonry on 18 Jan. 1685.

From 1685 on, he devoted himself entirely to the Saint-Joachim and Cap Tourmente missions. It seems that he stayed there until his death, with the dual responsibility of managing the two farms belonging to the seminary and of serving the parish church which Bishop Laval and the seminary had had built at Grande-Ferme. He concerned himself more particularly with the school of arts and crafts that the bishop of Quebec had founded in 1679. He was its director and benefactor. In 1693 he set up a fund of 8,000 *livres,* the income from which served to pay the board for three pupils, "in consideration of the spiritual and temporal good that results for the poor children of this country for whom the seminary of Quebec provides training on its property at Cap Tourmente." In 1695 he added 4,000 *livres* to this fund, and in 1701, 8,000 *livres.*

Abbé Soumande was also a builder. He concerned himself with the reconstruction of the Ursuline convent, which had been burned down in 1686. Furthermore, around 1695 he began to build a stone wall at Grande-Ferme, which was 600 feet long and 2 feet thick; it was never finished.

Since 1692 he had been a member of the com-

612

munity of the seminary. He died on 14 April 1706 at Quebec, and was buried in the cathedral.

LÉON POULIOT, S.J.

AAQ, Registres d'insinuation A, 63, 104; Registres d'insinuation B, 118. ASQ, Fonds Brouillard, 1705–11, 102, 106. Lettres, N, 100; R, 11; Séminaire, I, 40, 67–68. *Mandements des évêques* (Têtu et Gagnon), I, 116. Provost, *Le Séminaire de Québec: documents et biographies*, 424f. Gérard Morisset, *Coup d'oeil sur les arts en Nouvelle-France* (Québec, 1941), 15. P.-G. Roy, *La ville de Québec*, I, 287. *Les Ursulines de Québec* (1866–78), I, 411.

SOUMANDE, LOUISE, *dite* de Saint-Augustin, Religious Hospitaller, first superior of the Hôpital Général of Quebec; b. 16 May 1664 at Quebec, daughter of Pierre Soumande, master maker of edge tools, and of Simone Côté; d. 28 Nov. 1708 at Quebec.

At an early age Louise Soumande became a boarding pupil with the Ursulines, but she returned to her parents' home around the age of 13. She formed a friendship with the son of a merchant from Blois, who had come to Canada on business. Father Chastellain*, her confessor, who wished her to give herself to God and who feared that "their ties would grow stronger," persuaded her to enter the Hôtel-Dieu of Quebec as a boarder, for God, he said, "wanted her entirely, without sharing her with anyone." She made up her mind to this vocation on 19 March 1678, but did not intend to become a nun. The following November, however, she entered the noviciate. Two years later the community voted unanimously to allow her to take her vows. Louise Soumande was in turn Hospitaller, depositary for the poor, and assistant superior.

In 1693, following the founding of the Hôpital Général of Quebec, Bishop Saint-Vallier [LA CROIX] asked the Religious Hospitallers of the Hôtel-Dieu to supply four nuns to take charge of the new establishment. In addition to Louise Soumande de Saint-Augustin, the community chose MARGUERITE BOURDON de Saint-Jean-Baptiste and two other Hospitallers. On 26 June of the following year she was elected superior of the young community. She held her post until 1699, at which time she refused a second term. She agreed, however, to be mistress of novices.

In 1700, following the litigation over the advisability of establishing the Hôpital Général, Mother Saint-Augustin resumed charge of the community, for the titular superior, Marie-Gabrielle Denis de l'Annonciation, and two novices had to return to the Hôtel-Dieu until September 1701. In 1702 Mother Saint-Augustin again assumed the office of superior and remained in it until May 1708. On 28 November of the same year, when she was assistant superior and mistress of novices, she died after suffering violent headaches.

The Hôtel-Dieu of Quebec has a portrait of her, painted the day after her death by Michel DESSAILLIANT.

MICHEL PAQUIN

Juchereau, *Annales* (Jamet). A. Roy, *Inv. greffes not.*, VII, 89. Tanguay, *Dictionnaire*. Casgrain, *Histoire de l'Hôtel-Dieu de Québec*, 321–33, 559–65. *Monseigneur de Saint-Vallier et l'Hôpital Général de Québec*, 114–200. Morisset, *La peinture traditionnelle au C.f.*, 36. *Les Ursulines de Québec*, I, 521.

SOUPIRAN, SIMON, barber-surgeon to the hospital and public of Quebec, senior churchwarden of Notre-Dame de Québec parish (*c.* 1716); b. 1670 in Saint-Michel parish, Saint-Sever, province of Gascony; son of Antoine Soupiran and Catherine Laborde; d. 9 Feb. 1724 in Quebec.

This royal notary's son probably came to Canada as a ship's surgeon. The witnesses to his marriage at Quebec on 26 Aug. 1700, acting in lieu of family, were all crew members of the *Bien-Aimé*, a vessel anchored off Quebec. Soupiran's bride was Marthe Bélanger, a widow with five children who was to present him with five more. From 1700 to 1712, the couple lived in a rented house along Rue Cul-de-Sac, near the harbour of Quebec's Lower Town.

Surgeons in New France like Soupiran were subject to the surveillance of the local representative of the king's first barber-surgeon, who was replaced as supervisor in the early 18th century by the king's physician at Quebec. Although surgery was officially elevated from manual trade to liberal art in 1699, the social distance between surgeons and physicians remained great. Surgeons, as an occupational group, had two singular advantages; they could not be physically punished for a patient's death, and, after the church and apothecary surgeons, had a primary claim on the estate of a deceased debtor. Soupiran belonged to the second grade of surgeons, the barber-surgeons, who were trained by example and imitation as apprentices rather than as students at the royal college of surgery at Saint-Côme.

Soupiran is known to have transmitted his skills to at least four apprentices, including his eldest son. Their terms of apprenticeship were from two to four years, compared with two years in France. Canadian apprentices in surgery were, however, freed from the compulsory journeymanship of six years.

Soupiran's barbershop customers were charged per visit if they did not wish to participate in his annual subscription plan. In 1714 a Quebec gentleman could be clean shaven all year round for an annual payment of ten livres. Soupiran tended to leave the barbershop in the care of his apprentices. When there were no candidates for the razor, he agreed to take his apprentices with him on house calls or on visits to the hospital to watch him bleed, purge, medicate, or operate on patients. People of that period needed a hardy constitution to survive their illnesses and the ministrations of the surgeons. One mature apprentice and assistant, Pierre Courraud de La Coste, was permitted to go to the hospital and to use his master's surgical instruments four days of the week. In return for helping their master, the apprentices received training and varying degrees of maintenance: food was always provided, and sometimes clothes, laundry, and mending.

In the 18th century, Canadian surgeons gradually abandoned the auxiliary trades of barbering and wigmaking and came under closer regulation. Soupiran's eldest son, Simon Soupiran the younger (1704–1764), rose to become sworn surgeon of the admiralty of Quebec. He, in turn, trained his eldest son, Charles-Simon Soupiran (1728–1784), in surgery. Without a male heir after the third generation, this brief dynasty of Quebec surgeons died out.

PETER N. MOOGK

[The reader will find a concise and easy-to-read account of medicine in France in the 17th century in W. H. Lewis, *The splendid century: life in the France of Louis XIV* (Garden City, N.Y., 1957). François Millepierres, *La vie quotidienne des médecins au temps de Molière* (Paris, 1964) and Marcel Marion, *Dictionnaire des institutions de la France aux XVIIᵉ et XVIIIᵉ siècles* (Paris, 1923), 92–93, should also be consulted, as should the articles on surgery and surgeons in Diderot's *Encyclopédie ou dictionnaire raisonné des sciences, des arts et des métiers* (36v., Lausanne et Berne, 1778–81), VII, 769–73, 777–82. Abbott, *History of medicine*, and Arthur Vallée, *Un biologiste canadien, Michel Sarrazin, 1659–1735, sa vie, ses travaux et son temps* (Québec, 1927) are two good works on the history of medicine in New France. The APQ *Rapports* and the *BRH* contain notes by É.-Z. Massicotte, Raymond Douville, and other authors on certain aspects of the history of medicine. A complete modern study of this area is needed. P.N.M.]

AJQ, Greffe de Louis Chambalon, 25 août, 1700, 9 juin 1703, 30 nov. 1706, 20 mars 1707, 11 mai 1716; Greffe de Pierre Rivet, 21 oct. 1715, 18 mai 1717; Registre d'état civil de Notre-Dame de Québec. ASQ, Paroisse de Québec, 118. "Un engagement d'apprenti-chirurgien en 1715," *BRH*, XXXI (1925), 51. "Un engagement d'un apprenti chirurgien en 1717," *BRH*, XXXII (1926), 541. *Jug. et délib.*, IV, 1017; VI, 126, 468. Recensement de Québec, 1716 (Beaudet). "La famille Soupiran," *BRH*, XLI (1935), 129–60.

SOURDEVAL, SÉBASTIEN LE GOUÈS DE. *See* LE GOUÈS

SOURDY. *See* DESJORDY MOREAU DE CABANAC, FRANÇOIS

STUART (Stewart), WILLIAM, HBC trader and explorer; b. *c.* 1678; d. 25 Oct. 1719.

William Stuart first went to Hudson Bay as a youth in 1691, serving as an apprentice of the Hudson's Bay Company at York Fort and then at Albany. His term of apprenticeship ended in 1699, and he remained in the bay as a normal wage-earning servant of the company until his return to England in 1708. Stuart rejoined the company's service in 1714, and sailed that year to York [Fort Bourbon] with Governor James KNIGHT, who in September received the formal surrender of the post from the French under Nicolas JÉRÉMIE.

Thus far, Stuart's career had been uneventful, but at York he soon found himself involved in Knight's grandiose plans for an expansion of the fur-trade to the northwest. An essential preliminary was the making of peace between the Crees (the Home Indians, as they were called in the company journals) who lived along the shores of Hudson Bay from the Eastmain River to York Fort, and the Chipewyan or Northern Indians, just out of range of regular European contact in their country northwest of Churchill River. The Chipewyans' lack of firearms made them easy prey for the Crees, who were equipped with muskets and ammunition by the company's factors; the bloody defeats they had suffered at Cree hands made them wary of approaching the area of the English trading posts on the bay shores. Knight was determined to stop this destructive warfare, and by June 1715 he had persuaded about 150 Home Indians, accompanied by a Chipewyan captive, THANADELTHUR, the Slave Woman, and by William Stuart, to head towards Northern Indian territory on a peace mission. Stuart's knowledge of the Cree language made him an obvious choice, though later references by Knight to the inducements Stuart wanted before leaving make it unlikely that he volunteered for this hazardous venture.

Laden with trading goods, the peace party left York on 27 June 1715. Stuart took with him written instructions from Knight; he was to assist the Home Indians in their efforts to make peace, protect the Slave Woman, and if possible bring some Northern Indians back to York. Using the Slave Woman as his interpreter, he was to tell the Northern Indians that the company intended to build a post at the mouth of the Churchill River in 1716, and that they should keep watch along the coast there for a company ship. Stuart was to look for a wide variety of furs among the Northern Indians, but "above all," Knight told him, "you are to make a Strict Enquiry abt. there Mineralls . . . if you find any Mineralls amongst them You must seem Indifferent not letting them know nor the Indians as goes with You as it is of any Value but to bring back some of Every Sort you see." Knight was anxious for information about copper deposits, but his real quest was for the "yellow mettle" or gold, which he was convinced existed in large quantities in the interior. On the ship out to York, Knight took crucibles and other apparatus for testing mineral ores, and his interrogation of the Chipewyan captives had confirmed his belief, rapidly becoming an obsession, that somewhere west of Hudson Bay lay another El Dorado.

The peace party made slow progress at first. Indians coming into York reported that at the beginning of August it had not got beyond the Churchill River, and that most of the Indians were already sick. No further news reached York during the winter, and when the first Indians from the peace party straggled into the post in April 1716 they told a grim story of sickness, starvation, and separation. Their last sight of Stuart and the Slave Woman had been as they continued towards Northern Indian territory, accompanied only by an Indian captain and a few of his followers. Other Indians who came in during the month gave Knight harrowing descriptions of the crossing of the "Barren Mountains," where, in conditions of bitter cold, with drifting snow piling high above their shelters, they had neither fuel nor food. Some killed their dogs; others had lived on moss. On 22 April Indians arrived with a note from Stuart, but dated the previous October, when he was only about a hundred miles beyond the Churchill River. It made depressing reading: "Wee are in a Starving Condition at this time Wee still push on in our Journey The Captain is willing to go through but afraid that wee shall gett no provisions Wee have eat nothing this 8 days I do not think as I shall see you any more but I have a good heart."

The next Indians to arrive brought even gloomier news. Though they had reached wooded country on the far side of the barren lands, they had attacked a party of Northern Indians there, killing some and capturing others. If this was to be the only encounter between Crees and Chipewyans then the peace mission had worsened rather than improved relations; but on 7 May Stuart himself arrived, accompanied by the Slave Woman, the Cree captain with his little band of Home Indians, and ten Northern Indians. Knight's long, excited journal entry for the day tells the dramatic story of the party's fortunes. When Stuart's Indians, following

tracks in the snow, came across the corpses of the nine Northern Indians slain by the other band of Home Indians, all prospects of success seemed at an end. The alarmed Crees were ready to make for home, and only the joint endeavours of Stuart and the voluble Slave Woman persuaded them to agree to remain for ten days with Stuart while the woman tried to make contact with the Northern Indians. As they sheltered inside a rough stockade in the snow Stuart was hard pressed to keep the Indians to their bargain, and on the tenth day they were on the point of departing when the Slave Woman returned with no fewer than 160 Northern Indians. The killing of the nine Northern Indians was explained, the two groups of Indians smoked the pipe of peace together, exchanged gifts and hostages, and after two days parted on good terms. Stuart experienced one major disappointment: although the Northern Indians he brought back with him had knives and ornaments of copper, their only knowledge of the "yellow mettle" was that it came from a land farther west.

Knight was naturally eager to learn the geography of the country to the northwest, but Stuart's report was far from trustworthy. He informed Knight that they had travelled north-northwest 400 miles from York to latitude 63°N; from there they had headed northwest across the Barrens, and then west-northwest to a country abounding in wild life. This was the land of the Northern Indians, bordered on the south by mountainous country dotted with lakes. Stuart estimated that he and his party had travelled a thousand miles and were in latitude 67°N when they met the Northern Indians. Apart from a compass, Stuart probably had none of the instruments which later explorers took for granted, nor does he seem to have kept a journal; and Knight rightly suspected that he had placed his final position much too far north. From the descriptions given by Stuart, he appears to have reached the region just southeast of Great Slave Lake; certainly he did not go farther north than latitude 63°N. Like Samuel Hearne* on his travels across this region, Stuart was dependent on his Indian guides and hunters; and in the scanty reports of the journey it is the Chipewyan Slave Woman who emerges as the dominant character when the little party approached her home territory. Even so, Stuart played an essential supporting role during the anxious ten-day wait with the Home Indians while the Slave Woman searched for her countrymen; and during the crossing of the Barrens he must have shown a dogged, if unrecorded, perseverance. His leadership of the mission also gave an air of authority to the inducements held out to the Chipewyans to trade with the company; the Slave

Subercase

Woman reported to Knight that many more Northern Indians had been eager to accompany her back to the Cree camp "to see the English Man."

For Knight the Stuart expedition was a reconnaissance. It had achieved its main objective of bringing about a truce with the Northern Indians, but the hardships suffered and the length of time that Stuart was away demonstrated that although the prospects of trade to the northwest might be good the difficulties were proportionately great. While Knight's long-term plans turned increasingly to a sea rather than a land approach, he made preparations to establish the post at Churchill promised by Stuart to the Chipewyans for 1716. In this task Stuart was once more employed. He was the only company servant at York, other than Knight and his deputy, Henry KELSEY, to speak any Indian language, and in 1717 he accompanied the advance party north to the Churchill River, charged with "ye Manngement of the Indian Affairs." Unfortunately for Knight's hopes, the failure of the annual supply ship from England to arrive at York in 1715 [see JOSEPH DAVIS] had delayed the Churchill enterprise for a year, and by the time Stuart arrived at the mouth of the Churchill River the disappointed Chipewyans had gone. When Knight arrived on the scene in July he decided to try to regain contact, but sent out on this task the young Richard Norton* rather than Stuart. It may have been that Stuart's health was declining, for he was now ordered back to assist Kelsey at York. There he suffered a complete breakdown. In June 1718 Kelsey wrote to Knight from York that Stuart had "been lunatick 3 or 4 times insomuch that wee have been forct to tye him in his bed," and in October 1719 he died after further bouts of insanity.

Stuart's importance in the annals of the HBC lies in the part he played in bringing about a peace between the York Crees and their Chipewyan neighbours, which, though not unbroken, encouraged the gradual extension of the company's trade westward towards the Athabaska region. His more general claim to fame is that he was the first European to cross the Barrens and reach the vicinity of Great Slave Lake. It is a measure of his achievement that not until Hearne's journeys more than 50 years later did another company servant penetrate as far inland in a northwesterly direction as Stuart had done.

GLYNDWR WILLIAMS

The details of Stuart's journey are in the York Fort journals for 1714–15 and 1715–16 kept by James Knight (HBC Arch. B.239/a/1, 2). Mention of Stuart's part in the establishment of a post at Churchill is in HBC Arch. B.239/a/3, which has been edited and published as *The founding of Churchill* (Kenney). References to Stuart's illness and death are in HBC Arch. B.239/a/5.

The first historian to give Stuart his proper due as an explorer of the Canadian northwest was Morton, *History of the Canadian west*. A biographical sketch of Stuart will be found in HBRS, XXV (Davies and Johnson). Concise histories of the Crees and the Chipewyans are most easily available in Jenness, *The Indians of Canada*.

SUBERCASE, DANIEL D'AUGER DE. *See* AUGER

SUÈVE, EDMOND DE, lieutenant in the Régiment de Carignan and co-seigneur of Sainte-Anne de la Pérade; b. sometime between 1617 and 1620; buried 1 March 1707. Nothing certain is known about his origins or his life before he came to Canada.

When he arrived in 1665, Edmond de Suève was a lieutenant in Pierre de SAINT-OURS' company in the Régiment de Carignan. In 1668 he decided to settle in Canada and lived for about two years with Thomas Lanouguère* at Champlain, at the home of the seigneur of the region, François Chorel de Saint-Romain. In association with Lanouguère he acquired from Michel Gamelain* on 29 Sept. 1670 the seigneury of Sainte-Anne, half a league in frontage and a league in depth; the two purchasers received the title-deed to it on 29 Oct. 1672.

On 10 Feb. 1674, at 29 years of age, Lanouguère was appointed commandant at Montreal to replace François-Marie Perrot*, who had been imprisoned in the Château Saint-Louis at Quebec; Lanouguère died four years later. These circumstances and the roving inclination of the settlers, smitten with adventure and avid for peltries, explain Suève's failure in settling people on his lands. He was ruined in the attempt.

Intendant Duchesneau* asked for a gratuity for "the Sieur de Suève, a 60-year-old bachelor who was a lieutenant, who had always been thought to have some fortune, and who has fallen this year into great distress." This text, dated 13 Nov. 1680, confirms the co-seigneur's approximate year of birth, contrary to the census of 1681 which gives his age as 50. Apparently the favour requested by the intendant took the form of a fur-trading licence which Suève shared with Jean de Broyeux and some other traders.

According to his burial certificate Suève died at Sainte-Anne de la Pérade at 90 years of age. He made two wills in 1684 and a third in 1695, to which he added a codicil in 1703. The first two were probably made before he took up arms again as captain of the Sorel shore at the time of the expedition by Governor de La Barre (Le Febvre*) against the Iroquois.

HERVÉ BIRON

AJM, Greffe d'Antoine Adhémar, 22 mai 1682, 9, 13 juillet 1684. AJQ, Greffe de Pierre Duquet, 29 sept. 1670. AJTR, Greffe de Jean Cusson, 5 juin, 16 juin 1695; Greffe de Daniel Normandin, 11 oct. 1691; Greffe de Michel Roy, 23 août 1690; 8 août 1691; Registres d'état civil de Sainte-Anne-de-la-Pérade. *Jug. et délib.*, I, 796–98; II, 390; V, 981; VI, 947. P.-G. Roy, *Inv. concessions*, II, 145, 151, 152. P.-G. et A. Roy, *Inv. greffes not.*, II, 138; V, 53, 69. Bonnault, "Le Canada militaire," 479. É.-Z. Massicotte, "Congés et permis déposés ou enregistrés à Montréal sous le régime français," APQ *Rapport, 1921–22*, 190. Cloutier, *Histoire de la paroisse de Champlain*, I, 207f. Raymond Douville, *Premiers seigneurs et colons de Sainte-Anne de la Pérade (1667–1681)* (Trois-Rivières, 1946). P.-G. Roy, *La famille Tarieu de Lanaudière* (Lévis, 1922). Sulte, *Mélanges historiques* (Malchelosse), VIII. P.-G. Roy, "Edmond de Suève, seigneur en partie de Sainte-Anne-de-la-Pérade," *BRH*, XXVI (1920), 248–50.

SURIN. *See* TROTAIN

SWAN (Captain Swan), Indian leader who acted as middleman between the native hunters of the west and the fur factories of Hudson Bay; fl. 1715–19.

The Swan was one of the chiefs in a party of Cree Indians who met Governor James KNIGHT in council at York Fort in 1715. He told Knight of a sea beyond the headwaters of the Churchill River fed by a river on the banks of which was found "Gum or pitch." Knight sent the Swan with a party mustering 25 canoes to establish friendly relations with the Indians who dwelt between the source of the Churchill and the "West Seas" (Lake Athabasca). The Swan returned two years later (5 June 1717), reporting a friendly reception from the natives (probably Beaver Indians of the Athabasca Valley), and bringing a quantity of beaver skins which excited the admiration of Knight by their "Goodness & Largeness."

In 1719 the Swan again came to York Fort, where Henry KELSEY had replaced Knight as governor, and reported that he had wintered peacefully on a river beyond the Churchill basin. He gave Kelsey a sample of "that Gum or pitch that flows out of the Banks of that River." Thus to the Swan are due the first known references to the Athabasca oil sands.

L. H. NEATBY

Founding of Churchill (Kenney). HBRS, XXV (Davies and Johnson). Morton, *History of the Canadian west*, 133–34.

T

TAGANCOUT. *See* TEKANOET

TAILHANDIER, *dit* **La Beaume, MARIEN (Taillandier,** *dit* **La Baume,** or **Maxime de La Baume),** surgeon, seigneurial then royal notary, clerk of court and judge in the seigneurial court of Boucherville, son of Antoine Tailhandier, attorney of the judicial district of Masaye in Auvergne; b. 1665 at Clermont; d. 1738 or 1739 at Boucherville.

He landed in Canada about 1685, no doubt as a soldier, for when on 8 Jan. 1688, at Boucherville, he married Madeleine Baudry, aged 27, widow of one Puybarau, the marriage contract declared him to be a soldier-surgeon in M. DANEAU de Muy's company. We come across him again in 1721, as "major of the militia of the southern part of the government of Montreal." From 1688 on, he officiated as a notary, and in 1699 received in less than one month his commissions as notary, judge, and clerk of the seigneurial court at Boucherville where subsequently he was to buy three pieces of land. He nevertheless continued to practise his "surgeon's art" at the same time. On 7 Aug. 1702 he received from M. de Champigny [BOCHART] his commission as royal notary. His last act is dated 1730, and his registry contains 1,354 acts extending from 1688 to 1730. This registry was transferred to Montreal in 1739 on the orders of the judge, PIERRE RAIMBAULT, in whose favour Hocquart* decided against Pierre BOUCHER, seigneur of Boucherville; this resulted in a plea by the Sulpicians, in which it was stated that Tailhandier "died at Boucherville some months ago."

He had two daughters by his marriage with Madeleine Baudry; the elder married Jean-Baptiste TÉTRO.

ROBERT LAHAISE

AJM, Greffe de C.-J. Porlier, 4 nov. 1742; Greffe de Marien Tailhandier, 1688–1731; Index des sépultures catholiques, 1643–1967, IX. "Procès-verbaux du procureur général Collet" (Caron), 311. A. Roy, *Inv. greffes not.*, VIII, 5–99. Bonnault, "Le Canada militaire," 428. É.-Z. Massicotte, "Les chirurgiens de Montréal au XVIIᵉ siècle," *BRH*, XXVII (1921), 44 "Les notaires au Canada," 31. Vachon, "Inv. critique

Tantouin de La Touche

des notaires royaux," *RHAF*, XI (1957–58), 400. Abbott, *History of medicine*, 21. Ahern, *Notes pour l'histoire de la médecine*, 528f. J.-E. Roy, *Histoire du notariat*, I, 332–37. É.-Z. Massicotte, "Les chirurgiens de Montréal au XVIIe siècle," *BRH*, XXVII (1921), 44; "La justice seigneuriale de Boucherville," *BRH*, XXVIII (1922), 75.

TANTOUIN (Pitantouin or **Tantoin) DE LA TOUCHE, LOUIS,** commissary of the Marine in Canada; b. *c.* 1662, place of birth unknown; buried 9 Oct. 1722 at Juilley (department of Manche), aged about 60.

We have no information about the beginnings of La Touche's career, and the date of his arrival in Canada is unknown. In 1686 he was appointed keeper of stores at Montreal by the intendant, BOCHART de Champigny, and on 1 July 1690 he was promoted commissary of the Marine, replacing Mathieu Gaillard*.

The commissaries, who were directly under the orders of the intendant, carried out duties which were laid down under Section VIII of the ordinance of the Marine of 1689. They were required to inspect the troops regularly in order to draw up the muster-rolls necessary for issuing pay—for only those officers and soldiers present in their unit were paid—see to the distribution of clothing, take delivery of goods intended for the service and see that they were taken care of, superintend the administration of naval stores, ensure that the captains paid their soldiers regularly, and, should occasion arise, receive the complaints of those who were discontented. In Canada the commissary was in addition responsible for overseeing the trade in beaver furs authorized by licences granted by the governor general, and he had to satisfy himself that the regulations in this difficult area were properly applied. People who obtained such licences had to declare to the commissary before their departure the value of the goods that they were taking with them.

Supervisory duties of this sort in spheres of activity where cheating was frequent could not fail to provoke conflicts between commissaries and officers. La Touche, who seems to have been conscientious, did not escape them. On 21 Sept. 1692 Champigny made a note about him as "doing his duty well and being much attached, very careful and loyal," and requested an increase in his pay, which was 1,200 *livres* and with which he could not "meet the expenses that he must incur, particularly in his travelling." La Touche lived most of the time at Montreal, where from 1694 on he was subdelegate to the intendant, and therefore had to move about to visit the various garrisons in the country.

In 1697 his exactitude in carrying out his duties brought him into violent conflict with the garrison adjutant, AUGER de Subercase, who winked at dummy soldiers in the companies or had absent soldiers counted. La Touche established that the officers indulged in many kinds of cheating, inflicted various sorts of persecution upon the settlers who engaged in the fur trade, and appropriated to themselves their troops' pay. He complained of the officers' lack of discipline: "In this country it is greatly doubted that the king's ordinances are to be observed and taken as literally as in the kingdom." In 1698 he caused the seizure and sale at Montreal of the canoes laden with merchandise which were being smuggled through on behalf of Lamothe Cadillac [LAUMET] and had difficulties with Governor CALLIÈRE, "who, on the pretext of war, is interfering in legal and police matters, whilst I am the intendant's subdelegate at Montreal and there is the regular judge to render justice."

The opinions of everyone were unanimously in favour of La Touche. On 15 Oct. 1698 Buade* de Frontenac and Champigny extolled his scrupulousness and expressed their satisfaction with his refusal to accept the captains' servants in the inspections. The comptroller-general, LE ROY de La Potherie, wrote: "M. de La Touche, former commissary at Montreal, is a man beyond reproach. His conduct has been very judicious. He has often had arguments with M. de Callières, but when one is upright, one is sometimes exposed to his superiors' caprices."

On 8 Nov. 1700 Champigny requested for La Touche a reward for the services that he had rendered during the reception of some English envoys at Montreal. About the same time the commissary asked to return to France to serve in a port, for his long absence had upset his personal affairs. He was replaced by François CLAIRAMBAULT d'Aigremont. La Touche was then appointed commissary at Rochefort on 8 June 1701, but he did not hold this post long, for the following year the offices of commissaries of the Marine were made purchasable and La Touche, who was not able to get together the 30,000 *livres* needed to buy his, was dismissed on 12 Oct. 1702. He must have possessed a certain fortune, however, for during his stay in Canada he lent various sums and on his departure left his affairs in the care of the notary Pierre RAIMBAULT.

Nothing is known of the end of his career other than that he became financial secretary to the Duc de Berry, then retired to Normandy. He had married Madeleine Girard, by whom he had several children.

ÉTIENNE TAILLEMITE

AN, Col., B, 20, ff.102, 234; 22, ff.85v, 104; C^{11A}, 12, ff.60, 283, 350; 15, ff.50v, 128, 159–67; 16, ff.15, 88, 108; 17, ff.105, 107; 18, ff.42, 107, 191; 19, f.19; Marine, C², 55. "Correspondance de Frontenac (1689–1699)," APQ *Rapport, 1928–1929*, 333, 353, 377. "Un mémoire de Le Roy de La Potherie sur la Nouvelle-France adressé à M. de Pontchartrain, 1701–1702," *BRH*, XXII (1916), 215. "Daniel Auger, sieur de Subercase," *BRH*, XVI (1910), 177. É.-Z. Massicotte, "Louis Tantouin ou Pitantouin de la 'Touche'," *BRH*, XXV (1919), 127f. P.-G. Roy, "Biographies canadiennes," *BRH*, XXI (1915), 217–21.

TAYLOUR, JOSEPH, commodore of the Newfoundland convoy, 1709; b. *c.* 1662; d. 1734.

Taylour went to sea in the merchant service at the age of ten, and on 26 March 1690 entered the Royal Navy. He took command of the *Charles*, a frigate of 32 guns, in 1703 and soon began to show the skill and audacity in taking numerous prizes that were to earn him a place in naval annals. During 1708 Taylour did valuable service in Spain, and the following year was appointed commodore of the Newfoundland convoy.

Along with his commission as commander-in-chief went the usual instructions, or Heads of Enquiry, dated 9 June 1709. Taylour made little systematic attempt to answer these questions as his arrival in Newfoundland on 16 Aug. 1709 found him plunged in troubles of a more serious nature. The attack by Saint-Ovide de Brouillan [Mombeton*] in the winter of 1708–9 had devastated not only the fortifications, but the town as well. All that had not been ransomed had been burned or destroyed. The garrison commander, Thomas LLOYD, had been shipped as a prisoner to Placentia (Plaisance). Taylour had several meetings with the despondent inhabitants and persuaded them not to abandon the colony. He then proceeded to repair the fortifications, employing the crews of the *Litchfield* and of the *Rye*. It was already late in the season and materials were almost unobtainable. He drew naval stores to help him with the work, and remarked that Her Majesty had not been put to much expense. The new Fort William was 180 feet square, and included four streets of houses inside the perimeter. There were even "trunks" or chutes to send shells which fell on the ramparts down into the ditch where they would burst harmlessly. "In the opinion of all that had seen it before it was destroy'd by the enemie," said Taylour, "[it] is now much more defenceable." Captain John MOODY, viewing it the following year, bore witness to "the diligence of Commodore Taylour." Probably the value of the new fort was largely psychological. It gave the inhabitants somewhere to rebuild their huts with at least the illusion of

safety, and it must have discouraged the French to see St John's being rebuilt so soon after its wholesale destruction.

On the recommendation of the inhabitants, Taylour appointed John COLLINS as governor, and when he left Newfoundland he recommended that any of the inhabitants who would flout the governor's authority once the commodore was out of the way, should be kept in check. Taylour returned to the routine duties of a naval captain for the duration of the War of the Spanish Succession.

Joseph Taylour died on 23 May 1734. Despite Taylour's recommendations, his son, Thomas, did not achieve his father's success in the navy. To his contemporaries, as to naval historians, Joseph Taylour was an extremely successful exponent of the *petite guerre*—the single ship action; but for Canadians his importance lies in his re-establishment of St John's.

CARSON I. A. RITCHIE

G.B., Admiralty, *List of sea officers, 1660–1815*. PRO, C.O. 194/4, 195/5; *B.T.Journal, 1708/9–1714/15*; *CSP, Col., 1708–9, 1710–11*. Prowse, *History of Nfld*.

TEGANCOURT (Tegancout, Tegancouti, Teganeout). *See* TEKANOET

TEGANISSORENS (Decanesora), influential Onondaga chief, orator and diplomat; played a leading role in English-French-Iroquois relations during the last quarter of the seventeenth and first quarter of the eighteenth centuries.

Teganissorens flits through the pages of history in the dispatches of the governors of Canada, and in the Albany records of negotiations with the Five Nations Confederacy. Cadwallader Colden, the first part of whose book, *The history of the Five Indian Nations depending on the Province of New-York in America*, was published in 1727, had a high opinion of him and testified to his great gifts from personal knowledge. He wrote: "Decanesora had for many years the greatest reputation among the Five Nations for speaking, and was generally employed as their Speaker, in their negotiations with both French and English. ... He had a great fluency in speaking, and a graceful Elocution, that would have pleased in any Part of the world. His person was well made, and his Features, to my thinking, resembled much the Bustos of Cicero."

From these scattered and frequently oblique references a picture emerges of a man possessed of a commanding personality and great dignity, who was extremely astute, very adroit in negotiations, equally at ease at the resplendent dining table of the governor general at Quebec as at the council fire of the Five Nations at Onondaga; a

Teganissorens

man who was spoken of with respect, even deference, by French and English alike.

Long before Teganissorens' time the basic policy of the Five Nations was established, dictated largely by their geographic location. The various tribes in the Iroquois linguistic group were situated in three main areas. West of Lake Simcoe were the Hurons and Petuns, or Tobacco Nation; in the Niagara peninsula were the Neutrals; south of Lake Ontario and as far east as Lake Champlain were the Five Nations Confederacy comprising, in east to west order, the Mohawks, Oneidas, Onondagas, Cayugas, and Senecas. To the west of the Five Nations were the Eries, or Chats, who in the 1680s were conquered and absorbed by the Senecas and Cayugas, and to the south were the Andastes, or Susquehannocks, who merged with the Senecas in the 1670s. The Five Nations Confederacy warred with all these surrounding Iroquois tribes, except the Neutrals, as well as with the Algonkin nations. In the early 17th century they had formed a commercial alliance with the Dutch traders at Fort Orange on the Hudson River. After the English conquered New Amsterdam in 1664, renaming the colony New York and establishing a settlement and trading centre at Albany, they and the Iroquois made a commercial and military alliance known as the Covenant Chain. The Hurons and Algonkins had, a few years earlier, established a fur trade partnership with the French at Quebec. Ancient hostilities were envenomed by these economic and military alliances with rival European powers. After decades of warfare the Five Nations succeeded in destroying the Huron trading empire and aspired to drive the French out of the St Lawrence valley. Their long-range aim was to monopolize the middleman's role in the western fur trade. Since, however, their Indian foes greatly outnumbered them, they had to resort to guile, terror, even treachery, in their attempts to divide their enemies and destroy them one at a time. This required that one foe had to be immobilized by peace overtures while their own forces concentrated against another. Alliances formed against the Confederacy had to be disrupted by sowing suspicion, or by negotiating separate treaties. Thus diplomacy was every bit as important as military tactics, and the astute Iroquois diplomat, such as was Teganissorens, played a role every bit as vital as that of the warriors.

In 1682, after the western Iroquois had attacked the French allies, the Illinois and Miamis, Teganissorens came to Montreal and persuaded the governor general, Frontenac [Buade*], that the Iroquois had no intention of harming French interests, thereby disrupting a possible counter-move. The following year he was again at Quebec and when questioned more closely by Frontenac's successor, Le Febvre* de la Barre, he admitted that the Iroquois were determined to destroy the Illinois nation, declaring proudly, "They have shed our blood, they deserve to die." But he again gave assurances that the Five Nations would remain at peace with the French and their allies. Then, in 1684, the Senecas pillaged some French canoes and attacked the French fort at Saint-Louis-des-Illinois (Starved Rock). La Barre immediately launched an abortive campaign and was obliged to accept humiliating terms of peace dictated by Otréouati (Otreouti*), an Onondaga chief. When Louis XIV was informed of this he recalled La Barre and replaced him with Jacques-René de Brisay de Denonville, who invaded the Seneca canton at the head of an army in 1687, destroyed their villages, and the following year induced the Five Nations to agree to a cessation of all hostilities. In 1689, however, when England and France declared war, the Iroquois, confident of active English support, launched massive assaults against the Canadian settlements in an all out attempt to destroy the colony.

In the early years of this war they enjoyed considerable success, inflicting heavy casualties, but the French eventually gained the upper hand. The Five Nations, therefore, in 1693 began treating for peace separately with both the French and their allies, hoping to divide them and at the same time gain a respite for themselves. Frontenac, reinstated as governor general in 1689, was willing to entertain their proposals and agreed to a cessation of hostilities in 1694, but he insisted that Teganissorens must be one of the plenipotentiaries in further peace negotiations. Meanwhile, the Iroquois, with Teganissorens as their spokesman, informed the Albany authorities that unless they received more assistance they would have to make peace with the French. At the same time other Iroquois ambassadors approached the French allies, the Hurons and Ottawas, at Michilimackinac, telling them that they had been abandoned by the French who had made a separate peace behind their backs. The Hurons and Ottawas were easily convinced and they made their peace with the Iroquois. New York, dismayed at the prospect of carrying on the war alone, provided the Iroquois with more abundant supplies. With their western flank now secure the Five Nations were in a much stronger position. In the spring of 1694 Teganissorens led a delegation to Quebec and, resplendent in a scarlet coat trimmed with gold braid and a new beaver hat provided by the governor of New York, met Frontenac and his senior officers in audience "with great solemnity" and offered peace on Iroquois terms.

These terms required the French to include the allies of the Five Nations, the English colonies, in a general peace settlement to be arranged at Albany. Teganissorens, in the ninth article of the Iroquois proposals, informed Frontenac bluntly, "We will admit of no Settlement at Cadaraqui, You have had your Fire there Twice wch we have Quenched, and therefore will not consent to any rebuilding there, We clear the River that we may have a Clear Passage thro it and come freely to Onondaga." The French could not have been expected to agree and after three more days of futile discussions Teganissorens returned to Onondaga. Although Frontenac refused to admit it, the other senior French officials were convinced that they had been duped by the Iroquois who had sought to gain a respite for themselves and to split the French alliance with the western tribes. This estimate was confirmed when early the following year the Iroquois again launched savage attacks on the settlements at Montreal.

This offensive failed to crush the French who received over 400 additional regular troops from France, bringing their total to more than 1,500, in addition to over 1,500 Canadian militia. Thus reinforced, the French were again able to take the offensive. Fort Frontenac (Cataracoui, now Kingston, Ont.) was restored and garrisoned in 1695, and the following summer a French army numbering 2,150 regulars, Canadian militia, and mission Indians invaded the Onondaga and Oneida cantons. The western allies of the French refused to join in the campaign. They had been incensed by the earlier peace negotiations which Frontenac had held without their participation, and by the activities of Canadian fur-traders who were trading arms to the Sioux, ancient foes of the western Algonkian nations. When, however, in 1697, France and England ended their war in Europe, New York promptly withdrew its meagre support from the Five Nations and left them to fight on alone or make peace as best they could. The Iroquois had no choice now but to treat for peace in earnest. To arrange a firm peace was by no means easy. The French insisted that their western allies had to be included in any treaty. They were also eager to have Jesuit missionaries established in the Iroquois villages. The English of New York were always very suspicious of any negotiations between the French and the Five Nations, who were their first line of defence. They were particularly fearful of the Jesuits, regarding them as political agents of the French crown, as well as apostles of a detested brand of the Christian religion. Thus they did all they could to disrupt the negotiations. The Iroquois were also hindered by Teganissorens' temporary removal from affairs. In 1700 his wife, reputed to have been a Christian Iroquois from Caughnawaga (Sault-Saint-Louis), died as the result of an accident. In his bereavement he resolved to divest himself of all his responsibilities and live apart. However, upon the earnest entreaties of the Albany authorities, who were fearful of what might transpire at the Montreal talks if Teganissorens were not the Iroquois spokesman, he agreed to resume his office.

A particular stumbling block, one that nearly prevented the treaty being ratified, was the return of prisoners taken by the various nations during the war. The French were able to persuade their allies to give up their Iroquois prisoners, but this was not reciprocated. When taxed with this apparent lack of faith Teganissorens declared that their prisoners had been adopted by particular families and had no wish to leave; moreover, if these adopted prisoners had to be returned forcibly then the French must throw all the mission Iroquois into canoes and bring them back to the Five Nations villages. The Iroquois had suffered such heavy losses during the war it is little wonder that they were reluctant to give up even a few assimilated prisoners. In the spring of 1701 Teganissorens went to Montreal to discuss these problems and was warmly received by the governor general, Louis-Hector de CALLIÈRE. Upon his return to Onondaga he informed the Albany representatives, anxious to counter any leaning towards the French, that the governor had "received him kindly, saluting him with two kisses, telling him he was glad to see him alive, and while he was discoursing with the Governour, a person of quality came whom the Governour's interpreter told—This [is] the great Hero whose picture you have seen att Paris and further that he dined with the Governour att his table and din'd also with a Clergyman a Fryer who desired that he might have his picture drawn—That he gott many presents of the Governour, a gunn with two barrels, a lac'd coat a hatt a shirte Tobacco and sundry other things. . . ." After six days of being dined and wined in a manner which the English provincials could not emulate, Teganissorens declared his intention to return to Onondaga. Callière made no demur, but subtly stated that Teganissorens would doubtless be needed at Onondaga to send for the other Nations to meet with PAUL LE MOYNE, Sieur de Maricourt, who, along with Father Jacques BRUYAS, was to go to Onondaga to arrange for the exchange of prisoners. As a final touch Teganissorens was speeded on his way in a canoe manned by three French voyageurs, specifically instructed that their

Teganissorens

distinguished passenger was on no account to put a hand to a paddle.

Teganissorens did not allow such treatment to impress him unduly. When Maricourt arrived at Onondaga and acted in a high-handed manner Teganissorens sternly rebuked him, declaring: "You come and speak of peace and scarce are set down to smoke a pipe, but talk of coming and knocking us on the head, and therefore I say nobody knows your heart." In early August 1701, the prisoner question was resolved and the definitive peace treaty was ratified, finally ending the Iroquois wars that had endured, off and on, for nearly a century. In 1699 Richard Coote, Earl of Bellomont, governor of Massachusetts, New Hampshire, and New York, had stated: "Decanissore is . . . a brave fighting fellow that has done the French much mischief, and they have mightily endeavoured to debauch him from us, but in vain." Bellomont, newly come to the colony, appears to have believed that Teganissorens served the English interest. He was soon to be disabused. When the Albany authorities sought to establish a fort in Onondaga territory on Lake Ontario they were frustrated at every turn by Teganissorens who never gave an outright refusal but blandly put one obstacle after another in their path. Only when English interests coincided with those of the Five Nations did Teganissorens further them. Cadwallader Colden put it quite succinctly when he wrote that whenever Teganissorens represented the Iroquois cause at Albany he was always able "to make an account of an affair less disagreeable to English Ears, which had been undertaken against their advice, and contrary to their Interest."

By the time the treaty of 1701 was finally signed England and France were again at war, the War of the Spanish Succession; but one of the terms of the Iroquois treaty, to the dismay of New York, stipulated that in any such war the Five Nations would remain neutral. During the preceding decade their fighting strength had been cut in half, to an estimated 1,320, but the population of Canada had risen by half to an estimated 15,000 by the end of the century. The population of the English colonies on their southern flank was also increasing rapidly. The Iroquois could no longer hope to make gains in war, they now had to concentrate all their efforts on preserving their lands against the pressures of the rival European colonies. From this time on their policy was to preserve the peace and play off the English against the French.

At the turn of the century this suited both the French in Canada and the English in New York. Neither was strong enough to conquer the other.

The French had suffered heavy damage and casualties at the hands of the Iroquois and had no stomach for further hostilities; the devastation of the New York frontier settlements by the Canadians and their Indian allies had been so severe that the authorities at Albany were eager to accept any arrangement that would spare them more death and destruction. Moreover, the French regarded the Iroquois as an essential barrier to stop their Indian allies taking their furs to Albany rather than to the French posts in the west. When, therefore, in 1703 Teganissorens proposed to the French a treaty of neutrality between New York and Canada it met with ready acceptance from both sides. This allowed the French to take the offensive on the New England frontier to safeguard Acadia. The Iroquois protested the French attacks on the New England settlements, but to no avail. In 1709 New York was constrained to join the other colonies in a major assault on New France by land and sea, but the expeditions proved abortive. Two years later, with massive aid from Britain, fresh expeditions were mobilized. Teganissorens sent a messenger secretly to the governor general of New France, Philippe de RIGAUD de Vaudreuil, to warn him of the impending assaults. Although these expeditions failed in their objectives Teganissorens' action is a clear indication of the concern felt by the Five Nations. They had to preserve the balance of power to safeguard what remained of their own independence.

After the war the Iroquois had to resist the attempts of New York land speculators to deprive them, by all manner of ruses, of large sections of their land. Only by appeals to the crown were they occasionally able to frustrate these efforts. This may be the motive behind Teganissorens' declaration to the Albany commissioners for Indian affairs in 1715 that the Five Nations had resolved to send delegates from each nation, and some from the Mohicans, to England. He asked that a ship with proper accommodation be provided for the voyage. Apparently nothing came of this request.

In 1716, when the fur trade had begun to revive from a 20-year depression and French traders were more active in the west, Vaudreuil came to suspect that Teganissorens was urging the Miamis to take their furs to an English post in the Ohio country. There was likely little foundation to this rumour since the Iroquois claimed the Ohio country as theirs by right of conquest, a claim that the French were later constrained to recognize and the English to disregard. The long-term policy of the Five Nations, and the dilemma upon which it was based, was more clearly revealed in 1717 when French traders established a post at Irondequoit

Bay on the south shore of Lake Ontario. When the Albany commissioners protested, Teganissorens informed the governor of New York that the English had no one to blame but themselves since the French traders were supplied with their goods by the merchants of Albany. Were this contraband trade between Montreal and Albany to be stopped, he declared, the western tribes would have to take their furs to the English posts. He did not add that this would be by courtesy of the Iroquois middlemen, but it is clear that the Montreal-Albany contraband trade deprived the Iroquois of a profitable role in the northern economy.

Two years later Teganissorens informed the Albany commissioners that the French were building a fort at Niagara and were settling all around the Iroquois lands, confining them to very narrow limits. Governor Vaudreuil had earlier rejected proposals that the French build a post there on the grounds that it would bring the western nations into too close proximity with the Iroquois and likely tempt them to go on to trade with the English in the Iroquois villages, or at Albany. It was only when the English of New York began to talk seriously of building a post at Niagara that the French, moving swiftly, built Fort Niagara to forestall them. Had they allowed the English to build their post it would have given them direct contact with the western tribes and threatened the French position throughout the west.

The Senecas, however, had granted Louis-Thomas CHABERT de Joncaire permission to build only a trading post at Niagara; the Five Nations regarded the massive fort which they saw established as a serious threat. They lacked the strength to force the French to abandon it, and the English of New York could do nothing but bluster in the face of the *fait accompli*. The only recourse the Iroquois now had was to offset this French move by granting the English what they had long denied them: permission to build a fort at Oswego. In this way they restored the balance of power, but the price they had to pay was a diminution of their own sovereignty and ability to control events. The bitter truth was that the power of the French and the English was growing rapidly, that of the Iroquois was not. Yet it is difficult to see what better policy the Five Nations could have pursued. Certainly Teganissorens, their chief spokesman during these difficult years, displayed great adroitness in his dealings with the officials at Albany and Quebec.

When Teganissorens died is not known. An incident that occurred in 1716 gives cause to suspect that his faculties had begun to betray him. In June of that year he pleaded with the Albany authorities to ban the sale of rum to his people to prevent serious trouble in their villages. The request was granted, but the following September Teganissorens protested it, declaring that before the prohibition was imposed all the nations should have been informed. He demanded to know who had requested the ban. When told that he and the whole Five Nations had demanded it "in the most earnest manner," Teganissorens, not a whit abashed, asked that the ban be lifted. Five years later he was replaced as chief orator of the Onondagas, ostensibly at the request of the Albany authorities on the grounds that he was a French spy. If word of this reached the ears of the officials at Quebec they must have been rather startled. A more likely explanation would be that he was no longer capable of speaking for his nation with authority and the English demand afforded an excuse for his deposition. In 1727 Cadwallader Colden wrote: "He was grown old when I saw him, and heard him speak." The use of the past tense would seem to indicate that Teganissorens was no longer living.

At a conference held at Albany in 1694 the chief sachems of the Five Nations remarked rather plaintively that they wished some of them could read and write in order to keep accurate records of all that went on, for future reference. Had this wish been fulfilled the history of North America might well appear in a somewhat different light, and men such as Teganissorens would then take their proper place in it.

W. J. ECCLES

Charlevoix, *Histoire* (1744). Colden, *History of the Five Nations* (1958). "Correspondance de Frontenac (1689–99)," APQ *Rapport, 1927–28, 1928–29.* "Correspondance de Vaudreuil," APQ *Rapport, 1938–39, 1947–48.* La Poterie, *Histoire* (1744). *Livingston Indian records* (Leder). *NYCD* (O'Callaghan and Fernow), IV, V, IX, X. PRO, *CSP, Col.,* 1660–1726. Wraxall, *An abridgement of Indian records* (McIlwain). Eccles, *Frontenac.* G. T. Hunt, *The wars of the Iroquois* (Madison, Wis., 1940). Y. F. Zoltvany, "New France and the west," *CHR,* XLVI (1965); "The frontier policy of Philippe de Rigaud de Vaudreuil (1713–1725)," *CHR,* XLVIII (1967), 227–50.

TEGANNEHOUT. *See* TEKANOET

TEGARIHOGEN (Tegarioguen, Teharihogen, Teharihoguen). *See* TEKARIHOKEN

TEHASTAKOUT. *See* TONATAKOUT

TEKANOET (Tegannehout, Cannehouet, Cannehoot, Tegancouti, Tagancout, Tegancout, Téganeout), a Seneca war chief; fl. 1680–1701.

Tekanoet figures in the hostilities between the

Tekarihoken

Iroquois and the French and their Indian allies in the two decades prior to the general peace of 1701. He was one of the leaders of the Iroquois war party which attacked an Illinois village near Le Rocher (Starved Rock) in September 1680. By wearing clothing that made him appear to be a Jesuit, Tekanoet led the Illinois scouts to believe that the attackers were accompanied by some Frenchmen. When HENRI TONTY, in an attempt to negotiate a peace on behalf of the Illinois, was wounded by an Iroquois brave and held captive, Tekanoet strongly urged that he be burned; the pro-French Onondaga chief, Agonstot, interceded, however, and persuaded the other Iroquois to set Tonty free.

In July 1684 Tekanoet was taken hostage at Fort Frontenac by Le Febvre* de La Barre. However, with his forces beset by disease and unable to withstand an attack La Barre was forced to treat Tekanoet well. Le Barre sent Tekanoet to the Onondagas laden with gifts and accompanied by Charles Le Moyne* de Longueuil. When he arrived Tekanoet was full of praise for La Barre. Still a hostage, he went with Otreouti* to the negotiations with La Barre at Anse de La Famine (Mexico Bay, near Oswego), where his release was obtained.

At the general council of the Iroquois at Onondaga in January 1690, Tekanoet presented the terms of a treaty concluded with the Michilimackinac Ottawas the previous year. It was ratified by the council despite the presence of a delegation from Peter SCHUYLER with instructions to dissuade the Iroquois from thinking about peace.

In July 1701 Tekanoet was in Montreal at the peace negotiations between the French and Iroquois as the leader of the Seneca delegation, and is described by La Potherie [LE ROY] as the superior chief of the Senecas. One of the bases of the peace was the exchange of prisoners between the Iroquois and the western tribes. The latter had brought their captives, but the Iroquois had brought none. Tekanoet explained that most of their captives had lived so long among the Iroquois that they had been successfully assimilated into their way of life. This explanation was regarded with suspicion.

After this conference, Tekanoet disappears from view and probably died shortly thereafter.

D. H. CORKRAN

[Claude-Charles Le Roy de Bacqueville de La Potherie], *Voyage de l'Amérique* (4v., Amsterdam, 1723), IV, 216–19, 238. Colden, *History of the Five Nations* (1727), 62–63, 108–9. *NYCD* (O'Callaghan and Fernow), III, 451–52; IX, 236–39, 242–43, 252–59.

Relations et mémoires inédits pour servir à l'histoire de la France dans les pays d'outre-mer, éd. Pierre Margry (Paris, 1867).

TEKARIHOKEN (Tegarihogen, Tegarioguen, Teharihogen, Teharihoguen, Thearihogen), title of one of the sachems, or hereditary chiefs, of the Mohawks. This chief belonged to the Turtle clan and Horatio Hale says he was respected as "the first chief of the eldest among the Iroquois nations." Hale suggests that the name means "holding two offices"; this would be especially appropriate since Tekarihoken, unlike most of the other sachems, was both a civil and a military leader. L. H. Morgan gives the title in its Seneca form Dagäeogä, and suggests that it means "Neutral" or "the Shield."

A chief by the name of Tekarihoken is mentioned frequently by the French between 1653 and 1659, a period of almost continuous Iroquois guerila warfare against them and their Indian allies. In 1653 Tekarihoken led one of the Mohawk war parties that sought to avenge the killing of chief Aontarisati in Trois-Rivières the year before. His appears to have been the band that seized Father Joseph-Antoine Poncet* de La Rivière near Sillery on 20 Aug. 1653. While Father Poncet was taken back to Iroquoia, Tekarihoken remained behind and attacked Trois-Rivières on 23 and 24 August. When his party was overtaken by the French who had set out from Quebec to rescue Father Poncet, Tekarihoken agreed to exchange the cleric for some Mohawks who were being held at Montreal. To assure Father Poncet's safety, Pierre BOUCHER, governor of Trois-Rivières, offered Tekarihoken a number of presents. Tekarihoken set off for the Mohawk country and in October Poncet was returned to Montreal.

Since the destruction of Huronia, the Mohawks, Onondagas, and Oneidas had been trying to persuade the Huron refugees who were living in Quebec under the cover of Fort Saint-Louis to join their respective tribes. In May 1657, Tekarihoken visited Quebec to ask that the Hurons living there be permitted to resettle among the Mohawks. Tekarihoken's negotiations led to the departure of 14 Huron women and some children for the Mohawk country on 2 June.

In January 1658, a letter from Father Simon Le Moyne* arrived at Quebec saying that an Iroquois war-party of 1,200 men, under Tekarihoken's leadership, had set out for the territory of the Ottawas. This raid was to avenge the death of 30 Iroquois who had been killed the year before. In November, Tekarihoken and five other Mohawk envoys arrived at Quebec with Father Le Moyne. There they completed the exchange of seven Frenchmen they had recently taken prisoner for some Oneidas who had been imprisoned at Quebec. The Frenchmen had been left at Trois-Rivières.

In January 1659, Tekarihoken was reported to be with Father Le Moyne at Trois-Rivières and in April he was hunting on the islands in Lac Saint-Pierre. At that time he returned Mitewemeg and several other Algonkian prisoners to Trois-Rivières. This eventually resulted in the release of four Iroquois prisoners held at Quebec. In May, Father Simon Le Moyne left Trois-Rivières with Tekarihoken on one of his many peace missions to the Mohawks.

It seems highly unlikely that the Tekarihoken referred to in the *Jesuit* Relations is the same Tekarihoken who was living in Sault-Saint-Louis (Caughnawaga) in 1726. It was reported that year that a chief of the Indians of Sault-Saint-Louis who bore that title attended a meeting at Albany between William Burnet, the governor of New York, and the Iroquois chiefs. At that meeting the governor offered presents to the Iroquois in the hope of persuading them to pull down the post that the French had constructed at Niagara in 1720. Belts of wampum also were sent perhaps by the hand of Tekarihoken to the Iroquois living in Canada to induce them to acquiesce in this. However, the Senecas, on whose land the post was built, refused to demolish it.

In 1728 the same Tekarihoken accompanied Michel Maray* de La Chauvignerie on his visit to Oswego and Onondaga. While on this trip La Chauvignerie persuaded Tekarihoken to accompany the local Iroquois on a visit to the British fort at Oswego and to report their discussions. He described Tekarihoken as "a man on whom I place great reliance."

BRUCE G. TRIGGER

JR (Thwaites), XXXVIII, XLIII–XLV. *NYCD* (O'Callaghan and Fernow), IX, 963, 1008. E. J. Devine, *Historic Caughnawaga* (Montreal, 1922), 210. *The Iroquois book of rites*, ed. Horatio Hale (Toronto, 1963), 30, 77–78. L. H. Morgan, *League of the Ho-dé-no-sau-nee, or Iroquois* (Rochester, 1851).

TERRIOT, PIERRE (he signed thus; early forms were: **Terriau, Terrio, Thério, Therriot, Thériot, Thériaud, Terriault,** and in the feminine: **Terriote**), one of the founders of Les Mines (Grand Pré, N.S.), last-born of the seven children of Jehan Terriot and Perrine Ruau (or Bau), and husband of Cécile Landry, the daughter of René Landry and Marie Bernard; b. 1654 or 1655; d. 21 March 1725 at Grand-Pré, in the parish of Saint-Charles des Mines, without leaving any issue.

As the name Terriot was borne by copyholders of Charles de Menou* d'Aulnay who lived at Martaizé (department of Vienne), one may assume that it was under this same seigneur's influence that Jehan Terriot and his wife emigrated to Acadia around 1635. Their children, born in Acadia, married into the oldest families already established at Port-Royal (Annapolis Royal, N.S.) before 1671. Pierre, who was the only "unmarried" member of the family at that date, was 16, and his brothers and sisters had already settled on tracts of land at Port-Royal. Consequently, when the time came for him to look for a farm, he probably found no more suitable land in this area.

A man of adequate schooling—his signature appears in the parish registers—he seemed to possess a spirit of decision and initiative which prompted him to draw other young men into the great adventure that the founding of a new settlement represented. The majority of these young people were related to him, which caused Mathieu de GOUTIN, his nephew by marriage, to say: "Pierre Theriot['s] wife embraces two thirds of the colony."

Terriot chose the rich lands in the Minas Basin, and in a short time the new settlement was populated. We do not know the date of the founding of Terriot's settlement at Les Mines; it is possible, however, that Pierre Melanson (brother of Charles Melanson*) had settled in this place before him. Be that as it may, the 1686 census enumerates 57 persons there.

In 1693 Pierre Terriot, at the age of 39, was prosperous. Yet this prosperity did not come to him from the profits that he might have made at his fellow-settlers' expense. In a letter dated 9 Sept. 1694 de Goutin said that Terriot "is the most notable person at Les Mines, of which he is so to speak the founder, for he has assisted almost all those who have come to establish themselves there, and his house is the refuge of all widows and orphans and people in need." Having no children of his own, Terriot took an interest in the affairs of his nephews. Four or five of them lived with him "until such time as their own dwelling was habitable."

The prosperity of this agricultural settlement continued to grow until the expulsion of the Acadians in 1755.

YVETTE THÉRIAULT

AN, Col., B, 17, f.23v; C¹¹D, 2, f.233. Section Outre-Mer, G¹, 466 (Recensements de l'Acadie, 1671, 1752). PAC, MG 9, B 8, 12. Geneviève Massignon, *Les parlers français d'Acadie, enquête linguistique* (2v., Paris, 1962).

TESTARD DE MONTIGNY, JACQUES, officer

Testard de Montigny

in the colonial regular troops in Canada, famous for his campaigns in Newfoundland, son of Jacques Testard de La Forest and Marie Pournin; b. 1663 at Montreal, d. there in 1737.

The Testards were a family of Montreal merchants connected by marriage with the Le Moynes and the Le Bers. Orphaned at an early age, Jacques and his elder brother Gabriel Testard* de La Forest were brought up by their step-father Jacques de La Marque, whose name the younger brother seems to have borne at certain times. Jacques Testard de Montigny took part as a volunteer with the colonial regular troops in the expedition launched by Buade* de Frontenac in the direction of Fort Orange (Albany, N.Y.) and in the sacking of Corlaer (Schenectady, N.Y.). He travelled to France in 1692 on board one of Pierre Le Moyne d'Iberville's ships, and was still there when the governor received the order to reinforce the garrison of Fort Nashwaak (Naxouat) on the Saint John River, where Robinau* de Villebon was in command. A company was assigned to Lieutenant Claude-Sébastien de Villieu; Montigny, who had become an ensign with the colonial regular troops, served in this company as lieutenant. The two officers took up their post on 25 Nov. 1693, and they both applied themselves successfully to the task of leading detachments of Abenakis to harass the English settlers. Each of them participated in commerce and fur-trading, and this gave rise to conflicts of interest between the commandant and the Damours brothers (Mathieu Damours* de Freneuse, Louis and René Damours), who held large land grants in the region and with whom Montigny and Villieu were associated. In 1695, the latter had to come to Quebec to explain their conduct and promise to observe regulations more closely.

The following year, before launching his great offensive in Newfoundland, Iberville landed in Acadia; his mission was to destroy Fort Pemaquid (Fort William Henry), which the English had rebuilt at the mouth of the Kennebec River. Montigny was to support him in Acadia and then to join the Newfoundland expedition. He set off in the advance guard and neutralized some small forts which could have given the alarm, after which the combined forces of the ships and the Abenakis, who were led by Saint-Castin [Jean-Vincent d'Abbadie], readily secured the capitulation of Pemaquid. The Newfoundland campaign opened at the beginning of the winter. Montigny, experienced in all the tactics of forest fighting with the Indians, gave valuable help; this is stressed by Abbé Baudoin* who left an accurate account of the campaign. The main body of the troops, led by Iberville and Governor Jacques-François de

Brouillan [Mombeton], seized St John's on 30 Nov. 1696, set fire to the place, then returned to Placentia (Plaisance), where they got rid of the prisoners and divided up the booty. Iberville placed a detachment under Montigny, with the order to clear the English coastal area of all its establishments. Apart from St John's, which was only a village, there was nothing but some scattered fishermen's settlements and a few little clusters of storehouses at the innermost point of the harbours. Wearing snowshoes, the French went from house to house, taking prisoner those who could not flee in time, seizing the belongings which were not hidden in the woods, emptying the warehouses and storehouses of cod, and setting fire to the boats. At the end of March the English retained only Bonavista and Carbonear Island, and their fisheries were ruined.

Iberville left Newfoundland without being able to consolidate his gains there, and Montigny went back to Canada, where on 20 April 1700 he received his appointment as lieutenant. Four years later Rigaud de Vaudreuil sent him back to Acadia, where he conducted a few raids on the English establishments and worked actively at persuading the Abenakis to leave this overexposed region and come to settle in Canada.

Iberville's conquest had been short-lived, and the English very quickly reorganized their establishments in Newfoundland [see Gibsone]. Consequently in 1705 Auger de Subercase undertook a second campaign, in which Montigny again took part. This time it is he who has left us the account (5 March–6 June 1705) of this expedition, which was conducted with as much dash as the first. After raising the siege of St John's [see Moody] with the able help of François Picoté de Belestre and Étienne de Villedonné, he sent forces through the woods and by sea to gather up and disarm all the settlers along the coasts. In the deserted harbours, the houses, boats, and drying-platforms were set on fire, and the salt was thrown into the sea. Hearing that Montigny was conducting this campaign, Bonavista, following George Skeffington's advice, agreed to capitulate. The victory was complete, but it was to have no more consequences than the first one.

The next year Montigny went to France to present to the king and the court the Abenaki chief Nescambiouit, who had served with distinction at his side in the two Newfoundland campaigns. As a captain on the active list as of 23 June 1706, Montigny resumed his service in Canada and assisted Ramezay in the 1709 expedition to Pointe-à-la-Chevelure (Scalping Point). He remained attached until the end of the war to the army that Vaudreuil maintained to the south of Montreal to repel NICHOLSON's invasion. In 1712 he received the cross of the order of Saint-Louis, and the following year he was granted leave, to recover his health. In 1718, having been left a widower from his first marriage, contracted in 1698 with Marguerite Damours, he married the young Marie de La Porte de Louvigny, who bore him seven children. His family was established at Montreal, and probably Montigny served in a garrison on the island or in the neighbourhood. On two further occasions, however, despite his advanced age he was sent to distant posts, being "feared and respected by the Indians."

In 1721 Vaudreuil put him in command of Baie des Puants (Green Bay). On his way through Michilimackinac to take up his post, he met Charlevoix*, and they travelled down to the bay together. During this journey Montigny talked to the Jesuit about the outstanding achievements of his career, and the latter recorded them later in his *Histoire de la Nouvelle-France*. There was nothing remarkable about the officer's stay at the bay except a council held with the Foxes in September 1722. The following year Nescambiouit, who had been living among the Foxes since 1716, returned to the Saint-François mission, perhaps at Montigny's urging, for the latter assured the authorities of the unswerving loyalty of the Abenaki chief, who had for a moment been suspected of treason. In the autumn of 1723 Montigny was back at Montreal, but in 1730 he went up again to Michilimackinac to take over from the commandant, RENAUD Dubuisson. He was placed on half pay in 1733, and died on 9 July 1737 at Montreal. The governor and the intendant invoked his distinguished services in order to obtain a pension for his widow, who was left without means of support.

LOUISE DECHÊNE

AN, Col., B, 16, 19, 22, 27, 29, 34, 35, 44, 45, 47, 48, 50, 52–55, 57, 58; C¹¹ᴬ, 29, 32, 33, 42–67; C¹¹ᴰ, 2, 3, 4; D²ᶜ, sur fiches (états de service des officiers); Marine, C⁷, 217 (dossier de Montigny). Charlevoix, *Histoire*. "Correspondance de Frontenac (1689–99)," APQ *Rapport, 1927–28, 1928–29.* "L'expédition de M. de Montigny à Terreneuve en 1705," APQ *Rapport, 1922–23,* 293–98. *Journal de l'abbé Beaudoin* (Gosselin). Tanguay, *Dictionnaire.* Frégault, *Iberville.*

TÉTRO (Tétreau), JEAN-BAPTISTE, schoolmaster, seigneurial then royal notary, court clerk of the jurisdiction of Montreal; son of Louis Tétro and Marie-Noëlle Landeau; baptized 25 Oct. 1683, in the region of Montreal; d. between September 1728 and February 1730.

As he first intended to take up the priesthood, he received the tonsure from Bishop LAVAL in 1703. Some years later he turns up again as an itinerant schoolmaster. In 1712 he received a commission as notary for the seigneury of Boucherville. He was appointed in 1727 royal notary and clerk of court at Montreal at the same time as JOSEPH-CHARLES RAIMBAULT; his registry, which extends from 28 April 1712 to 11 Sept. 1728, contains only 104 acts.

On 8 July 1710, he married Jeanne Tailhandier, daughter of Marien TAILHANDIER, seigneurial judge of Boucherville; they had three sons. The exact date of his death is unknown, but we do know that it occurred between 11 Sept. 1728, the date of his last notarial act, and 11 Feb. 1730, when his widow took Jean Latour, a notary, as her second husband.

Tétro exemplifies two characteristics of the officers of justice of the period: he held more than one post at a time, and he married into a family of the judiciary.

ROBERT LAHAISE

AJM, Greffe de J.-B. Tétro, 1712–28; Index des sépultures catholiques, 1643–1967, IX. A. Roy, *Inv. greffes not.,* XIII, 5. P.-G. Roy, *Inv. ord. int.,* II, 21. "Les notaires au Canada," 37. Tanguay, *Dictionnaire,* VII, 285. Vachon, "Inv. critique des notaires royaux," *RHAF,* XI (1957–58), 95. J.-E. Roy, *Histoire du notariat,* I, 210.

THANADELTHUR, a Chipewyan (Northern Indian) known as the **Slave Woman** in the records of the HBC; the Indian name meaning "marten shake" was given her in the oral tradition of the Chipewyans; d. 5 Feb. 1717.

In the spring of 1713 a party of Chipewyans was attacked by Crees. At least three women were taken captive. The Slave Woman and another woman escaped from their Cree master in the fall of 1713 and attempted to make their way overland to rejoin their people. Cold and hunger forced them to turn back, and they searched for York Fort, which they had heard of but had never seen. A year of hardship and starvation caused the death of the companion five days before the Slave Woman encountered some York Fort servants who brought her to the fort on 24 Nov. 1714. Governor James KNIGHT found her arrival timely for he desperately needed an interpreter if he hoped to establish trade with the Chipewyans, who were reluctant to come to York Fort because their primitive weapons were no defence against the guns of the Crees.

On 27 June 1715 Knight sent William STUART, the Slave Woman, and a party of 150 Crees on a peace-making mission to the Chipewyans. Sickness and starvation forced the expedition to break

Thaumur de La Source

up into small parties in order to survive during the merciless winter. Most of the parties made their way back to York Fort and one of them murdered a group of Chipewyans, in self-defence they claimed later. Stuart's party came upon the scene of the massacre a few days later and were horrified at the failure of their peace mission. The Slave Woman, indomitable and indefatigable, was determined that peace should be made. She persuaded the frightened Crees in Stuart's party to remain on the spot for ten days while she set off in pursuit of her countrymen. She followed their tracks until she found a large Chipewyan band who had gathered for revenge. She talked until she was hoarse to persuade them to go back with her to meet their traditional enemies. On the tenth day she returned with a large group of her countrymen to the place where she had left the apprehensive Crees, and the palaver began. The Crees in Stuart's party protested their innocence of the massacre and invited the Chipewyans to smoke the pipe of peace. After the peace-making ceremonies were completed, some of the Chipewyans accompanied Stuart's party to York Fort. One's admiration is aroused by the determination of this remarkable woman who by "her perpetual [sic] talking" persuaded 400 Chipewyans to return with her to make peace. Both James Knight and William Stuart, no less impressed by her eloquence than her own countrymen, gave her the chief credit for establishing peace.

On 7 May 1716 Stuart and his party regained York Fort. Knight was overjoyed at the success of the mission and prepared plans to send the Slave Woman and some of her countrymen across the Barrens in the spring of 1717 to announce to the Chipewyans the establishment of a fort at Churchill River. The Slave Woman was most enthusiastic about the plan, but unfortunately she became ill during the winter and after lingering seven weeks died on 5 Feb. 1717. Governor Knight, never one to praise unduly said: "She was one of a very high Spirit and of the Firmest Resolution that every I see in any Body in my Days and of great Courage."

G. E. THORMAN

HBC Arch. B.239/a/1–3 (York Fort journals, 1714–17). *Founding of Churchill* (Kenney). HBRS, XXI (Rich); XXV (Davies and Johnson). E. S. Curtis, *The Chipewyan*, ed. F. W. Hodge (The North American Indian, XVIII, Norwood, Mass., 1928), 8–9. Morton, *History of the Canadian west*. A. M. Johnson, "Ambassadress of peace," *Beaver* (Winnipeg), outfit 283 (December 1952), 42–45. K. E. Pincott, "What Churchill owes to a woman," *Beaver* (Winnipeg), outfit 263 (September 1932), 100–3.

THAUMUR DE LA SOURCE, DOMINIQUE-ANTOINE-RENÉ, priest of the seminary of Quebec, missionary to the Mississippi region; b. at Montreal, where he was baptized 1 Aug. 1692, son of Dominique Thaumur de La Source, a surgeon, and Jeanne Bonhomme; d. 4 April 1731 at Quebec.

On 14 Aug. 1702 Thaumur de La Source entered the Petit Séminaire of Quebec, where he completed his classical studies and in 1713 took holy orders. Bishop Saint-Vallier [LA CROIX] bestowed the priesthood upon him on 20 Feb. 1717. A year later, on 10 May 1718, René Thaumur de La Source set out with two *confrères*, Abbés Goulven CALVARIN and Jean-Paul Mercier, for the mission to the Tamaroas (Cahokia, Ill.), of which he had been appointed the superior. Near the mission was a small village which Canadian coureurs de bois and fur-traders had established some 15 years earlier. Thaumur lived for ten years in the Sainte-Famille mission to the Tamaroas. In this isolated place, among Indians whose moods were changeable, a missionary's life was not without risks. In 1728 he decided to return to Quebec to obtain reinforcements. He intended to rejoin his mission as soon as possible, but illness prevented him from doing so.

Abbé Thaumur de La Source died 4 April 1731 at the Hôtel-Dieu of Quebec and was buried the next day in the cathedral. Bertrand* de Latour, who met the missionary at Quebec, relates that at his death he had "such a reputation for holiness that all those present at his funeral went to touch his body with rosaries and tore off pieces of his clothes as relics."

NOËL BAILLARGEON

AAQ, Registres d'insinuation C, 10. ASQ, Lettres, M, 67; MSS, 6, p.22; Missions, 43, 73c; Polygraphie, IX, 26; Séminaire, I, 40. Louis Bertrand de Latour, *Mémoires sur la vie de M. de Laval, premier évêque de Québec* (Cologne, 1761), 101. Charland, "Notre-Dame de Québec: le nécrologe de la crypte," 205.

THAVENET, MARGUERITE DE, b. 1646 at Bourges, daughter of Raymond de Thavenet, captain in the Régiment de Brimon, and of Élisabeth de Mancelin; d. 1708. On 22 Sept. 1664, at Montreal, she married the Sieur Joseph-François HERTEL de La Fresnière (1642–1722), king's lieutenant, who was ennobled in 1716. Fifteen children were born of this marriage.

Marguerite de Thavenet and her sister, Marie-Françoise, probably came to Canada in one of the contingents of young "noble girls" who were sent by Louis XIV and Colbert and intended for Canadian noblemen.

In 1672 Marie-Françoise de Thavenet was engaged to Jacques de Chambly*, who had arrived in Canada in 1665 with the Carignan regiment and who was appointed governor of Grenada in 1679. As marriage freed officers and soldiers from the "service," Jacques de Chambly's superior officers refused him permission to marry. He died as governor of Martinique in 1687.

By a deed signed before a notary in Paris on 11 July 1679, Jacques de Chambly made a gift to "*Demoiselle* Marie-Françoise de Thavenet" of the seigneury of Chambly in Canada, on condition that she went to live there.

It is probable that Marie-Françoise de Thavenet returned to Canada from France, for at her death, in or before 1694, the seigneury became the property of her sister Marguerite.

ROBERT LA ROQUE DE ROQUEBRUNE

AN, Y, 236, f.399; Col., C¹¹A, 2, 3, 43. [François Daniel], *Histoire des grandes familles françaises du Canada* (Montréal, 1867). Placide Gaudet, "Le capitaine Jacques de Chambly," *BRH*, XXIII (1917), 14–16. Robert La Roque de Roquebrune, "Les Demoiselles de Thavenet," *NF*, V (1930), 86–91. É.-Z. Massicotte, "Le fief Hertel," *BRH*, XXXV (1929), 67–71; "Les premiers seigneurs de Chambly," *BRH*, LI (1945), 133–35, 209.

THEARIHOGEN. *See* TEKARIHOKEN

THÉRIAUD (Thério, Thériot, Therriot). *See* TERRIOT

THIBAUDEAU (Thibodeau). *See* TIBAUDEAU

THIBOULT, THOMAS, priest, canon, parish priest at Quebec, fourth superior of the Quebec seminary; b. *c.* 1681 at Purier in the diocese of Rouen; d. 12 April 1724 at Quebec.

For 4 or 5 years Thiboult had been a priest in the seminary in Paris, in preparation for joining the missions in China; beyond that we know nothing of his birth or his education prior to his being sent to Quebec in the spring of 1710. On 6 May 1711 he was admitted as a member of the community of the seminary of Quebec. Upon the death of Pierre Pocquet, the parish priest of Quebec, the superior of the seminary, Louis ANGO Des Maizerets, with whom the appointment rested, chose the new arrival to be administrator of the charge, before bestowing upon him the title of parish priest on 2 Nov. 1713. By virtue of his office he had already become a canon on 18 March of that year.

While Dom POULET, a notorious Jansenist, was dangerously ill at the Hôtel-Dieu, Bishop Saint-Vallier [LA CROIX] gave instructions to Father Thiboult, as parish priest, concerning the conditions upon which Poulet might be admitted to the Sacrament; but the sick man would not yield. Although he was a member of the seminary, M. Thiboult was imprudent enough to agree to act as attorney for the chapter and went to France (1713–16) to settle a dispute between the chapter and the seminary to the detriment of his own house. This made of him "a sorry figure," to use his own expression, and compromised the success of his mission. Upon his return there was an attempt to appoint him honorary canon without consulting the bishop, who rebuked such procedure. Disillusioned, M. Thiboult spoke of going to the missions in the Mississippi country, but no attention was paid to this. Then the ill-health of M. de GLANDELET, superior of the seminary, led to Thiboult's being chosen as his successor in 1723. When Thiboult died, therefore, he was parish priest and superior of the seminary. The historian Latour [Bertrand*] accused him of being a follower of Jansenism, but nothing is more inconsistent with the facts.

HONORIUS PROVOST

ASQ, Chapitre, 40, 47, 177, 270, 273; Fonds Verreau, cahier 035, pièce 14; Lettres, M, 41, 42, 45–47; O, 50; Paroisse de Québec, 1–3, 40, 115. Louis Bertrand de Latour, *Mémoires sur la vie de M. de Laval, premier évêque de Québec* (Cologne, 1761), 50. Provost, *Le Séminaire de Québec: documents et biographies*, 438.

TIBAUDEAU (Thibaudeau, Thibodeau), PIERRE, miller, settler, founder of the Acadian family of that name; b. 1631 in the province of Poitou; d. 26 Dec. 1704 at Prée-Ronde.

Tibaudeau arrived in 1654 in Acadia and married Jeanne Terriot around 1660. Being a miller, he settled and built a mill near Port-Royal (Annapolis Royal, N.S.), in a canton called Prée-Ronde, and soon became prosperous.

Tibaudeau is noteworthy particularly as the founder of Chipoudy (Shepody, N.B.). At an advanced age, he decided to acquire a seigneurial domain, and in the spring of 1698, with four of his sons and a comrade, he chose his site at Chipoudy. Guillaume BLANCHARD and two of his sons accompanied them there, then settled on the Petitcodiac.

A legal dispute arose which threatened his plan when an officer from Port-Royal, CLAUDE-SÉBASTIEN DE VILLIEU, asserted that the domains claimed by Tibaudeau and Blanchard formed part of the fief belonging to his father-in-law, MICHEL LENEUF de La Vallière (the elder). The case was referred to Paris, but this did not stop Pierre Tibaudeau from carrying on with the task of beginning a settlement. The final verdict did not

Tibierge

reach Acadia until after the pioneer's death. A decree of the Conseil d'État dated 2 June 1705, defining more precisely that of 20 March 1703, confirmed La Vallière's claims. The dream of a seigneury at Chipoudy was dispelled. Nevertheless, the pioneers retained possession of their "lands and inheritances," and the settlement was able to develop: the 1706 census listed 55 persons at Chipoudy, and that of 1752, 359.

A daughter of the founder, Jeanne (Marie-Jeanne), had married the Sieur Mathieu de Goutin, naval commissary at Port-Royal and civil administrator; he wrote several letters or reports about the litigation between La Vallière and the Chipoudy settlers, and they constitute a valuable source of documentation concerning Pierre Tibaudeau.

CLÉMENT CORMIER

[Historians have used as one of their main sources for this period Rameau de Saint-Père's work, *Une colonie féodale*, which contains an interesting chapter on Pierre Tibaudeau. After years of genealogical research Placide Gaudet pointed out some errors in the family relationships described in the chapter in question. In a letter to Msgr Louis-A. Richard of Trois-Rivières, he stigmatized them as "pure invention concerning the old miller's children." Gaudet attributed these errors to the fact that Rameau had only the censuses to guide him. In preparing this biography and that of Jean-François Brossard errors in Rameau have been indicated, for example the two alleged marriages of Brossard's daughters, the first one with Pierre Tibaudeau, the other with Jacques Martin, neither of which took place. C.C.]

AN, Col., B, 27, f.153; C¹¹D, 2, f.126; 3, ff.225–26; 4, ff.178–83; 5, ff.81–83; Section Outre-Mer, G¹, 466 (Recensements de l'Acadie, 1671, 1686, 1693, 1698, 1700, 1703). PANS, MS docs., XXVI (parish register of Port-Royal, 26 Dec. 1704). P.-G. Roy, *Inv. concessions*, IV, 108.
Placide Gaudet, "Notes généalogiques" (preserved in PAC and Archives de l'Université de Moncton). Arsenault, *Hist. et généal. des Acadiens*, I, 518. Geneviève Massignon, *Les parlers français d'Acadie, enquête linguistique* (2v., Paris, 1962). E. C. Wright, *The Petitcodiac: a study of the New Brunswick river and of the people who settled along it* (Sackville, N.B., 1945), 6–14. Ganong, "Historic sites in New Brunswick," 308, 316. Placide Gaudet, "Les ancêtres de feu l'honorable Sénateur Joseph Rosaire Thibaudeau," *Moniteur Acadien* (Moncton), 8 juillet 1909. L. Jore, "Mes ancêtres acadiens," SGCF *Mémoires*, VI (1955), 270–71. P.-G. Roy, "La famille Thibaudeau," *BRH*, XXXVIII (1932), 65–67.

TIBIERGE, agent of the Compagnie de la Pêche Sédentaire de l'Acadie, author of several reports on Acadia around the period 1695 to 1703.

Biographical details about Tibierge are rare. The Compagnie de la Pêche Sédentaire de l'Acadie had brought into association a number of La Rochelle merchants, among them Bergier* (who was the owner of the ship *Saint-Louis*, and on 8 May 1684 obtained registration of a fishing concession on the Acadian coast); Tibierge himself, however, does not seem to have come originally from La Rochelle. He stayed in Acadia as an agent of the company at Fort Saint-Joseph (Nashwaak) on the Saint John River from July 1695 to July 1697. He made a trip to Les Mines (Grandpré, N.S.) and Beaubassin (Chignecto) in the autumn of 1698 and he was still in Acadia in 1703. At that time he was instructed to load on the *Éléphant*, commanded by the Sieur Petit, the merchandise which the company, now in decline, still owned in Acadia. This merchandise was to be handed over at La Rochelle to the company's mercantile agent.

Tibierge was the author of journals and reports about Acadia. The journals cover the period 1695–96, the reports are of later date. A good observer of things and people, he has left a description of Fort Saint-Joseph and of the works that were carried out there by Villebon [Robinau*] from 1696 to 1697, as well as day-to-day notations about relations between the principal officers and settlers, relations between English, French, and Indians, and the intrigues of France and England concerning the Indians. He spoke highly of Father Louis-Pierre Thury*, but censured the behaviour of the other missionaries, who, he said, neglected the garrison, busied themselves with discrediting the company in the eyes of the settlers by asserting that it was exploiting them, and encouraged trade with the English. He insisted on the necessity of forbidding officers to engage in trade, even if it meant compensating them with presents. Finally he wanted to reduce the company's profits so that the settlers might receive their due. He likewise advocated that a ship be dispatched annually from Acadia to the West Indies to supply the islands with various kinds of meal, peas, salt meat, cod, fish-oil, boards, planks, and joists. For this purpose, he reported, it would be necessary to build a warehouse for the company at Port-Royal (Annapolis Royal) and another at Les Mines.

On 21 May 1698 he received from the king a land grant in Canada a league and a half in depth. After 1703 we lose all trace of this person.

M. A. MÉNIER

AN, Col., B, 20, f.81v; 23, f.266v; C¹¹D, 3, f.216ff. Two journals and a memorial by Tibierge have been printed in Webster, *Acadia*, 141–55.

TILLY, PIERRE-NOËL LEGARDEUR DE. *See* LEGARDEUR

TISNET (Tissenay). *See* DUTISNÉ

TIWATACOUT. *See* TONATAKOUT

TOHONSIOWANNE. *See* OHONSIOWANNE

TONATAKOUT (Tiwatacout, Tehastakout), Seneca chief, fl. 1700–34.

On 18 July 1700 Tonatakout arrived in Montreal with AOUENANO and two other Seneca chiefs and the Onondagas ARADGI and OHONSIOWANNE. They had come to ask Governor CALLIÈRE to bring to an end the attacks that the western tribes, who were allied to the French, had been making on the Iroquois. These attacks, which were made in retaliation for an Iroquois raid on the Miami tribe, had resulted in the death of 55 or more Iroquois. The Seneca and Onondaga envoys also asked that Father Jacques BRUYAS, CHABERT de Joncaire, and PAUL LE MOYNE de Maricourt return to their villages with them as envoys of the governor. These envoys arrived in the Onondaga country in early August and began discussions with TEGANISSORENS and other chiefs of the four western Iroquois tribes which laid the foundations for the general peace treaty of 1701 at Montreal. Tonatakout was elected Joncaire's "father" and protector among the Senecas to replace an earlier "father" who had died. Tonatakout is described as the latter's "nearest blood relation."

Tonatakout may have been still alive in 1734. At that time the Senecas protested that they had learned from the Indians living at the Lac des Deux Montagnes that the French had been wrongly told by the Onondagas that Tonatakout was a trouble maker who worked against French interests and who should be killed. The French and the Onondagas denied that such a charge had ever been made. The genesis of this accusation is unclear. In the records recounting this incident there is also an obscure reference to Tonatakout, "whom you [the French] made chief."

BRUCE G. TRIGGER

AN, Col., C¹¹ᴬ, 18, f.81. Charlevoix, *History* (Shea), V, 101. *NYCD* (O'Callaghan and Fernow), IV; IX, 708, 710, 1041.

TONNANCOUR, RENÉ GODEFROY DE. *See* GODEFROY

TONTY, ALPHONSE (de), Baron de Paludy, commandant at Forts Michilimackinac, Frontenac, and Pontchartrain (Detroit), captain in the colonial regular troops, younger brother of HENRI

TONTY; b. *c.* 1659 in France, son of Laurent (Lorenzo) de Tonty, Baron de Paludy, and of Isabelle de Liette (di Lietto), d. 10 Nov. 1727 at Detroit.

Laurent de Tonty moved to Paris from Italy around 1650 after having taken part in an unsuccessful rebellion. In 1669 he was committed to the Bastille and remained there for eight years, probably as a result of the failure of an insurance scheme which he had presented in 1653 to Cardinal Mazarin. Laurent's eight years in the Bastille coincided with Alphonse's youth, and no doubt contributed in part to the latter's irascible temper. In 1684 Alphonse quarrelled violently with René-Robert Cavelier* de La Salle over the wages he was to be paid if he sailed with the explorer to the Gulf of Mexico. As a result he did not participate in La Salle's tragic last voyage. His disagreeable manner had perhaps spared him from an early death.

Alphonse was probably aboard the first ship to leave for New France in 1685. He took up lodgings in Montreal, where, on 17 Feb. 1689, he married Marie-Anne Picoté de Belestre, daughter of the deceased Pierre Picoté* de Belestre, fur-trader and merchant. Alphonse's income as a lieutenant in the colonial regular troops was a mere 720 *livres* per year, but he was not unaware of the potential profits to be made in the fur trade and gave his attention to the west, hiring men and outfitting canoes for the Illinois country. In 1693 he was commissioned half-pay captain, and moved from Rue Saint-Joseph to a larger home on Rue Notre-Dame. He represented his brother in any legal or financial disputes which arose from his activities in the west and continued to make his own investments in the fur trade.

In 1697 Antoine LAUMET, *dit* de Lamothe Cadillac, returned from Michilimackinac to account for his activities there. Although the minister of Marine had ordered the evacuation of the western posts because of the saturation of the beaver market, Governor Louis de Buade* de Frontenac appointed Alphonse to serve in Cadillac's place. He left Montreal with 25–30 indentured employees, and a cargo of trade goods worth approximately 35,000 *livres*. The understanding was that Alphonse would receive 50 per cent of the profit realized in their sale. His command at Michilimackinac lasted only one year, but it enabled him to meet with his cousin, Pierre-Charles de LIETTE, and his brother, Henri. On this occasion the latter ceded to him half of his share of Fort Saint-Louis (Pimitoui) in the Illinois country.

The financial outcome of Alphonse's first major trading venture is not known; similarly the returns on the purchase and sale of a house on

Tonty

Rue Saint-Paul and the purchase and lease of another on Rue Notre-Dame cannot be ascertained. Nevertheless, his financial career until 1701 could by no means be termed a success—in that year his balance sheet with one merchant alone showed a deficit in excess of 11,000 *livres*. During these years, however, he had been able to make some powerful allies, including Philippe de RIGAUD de Vaudreuil who frequently acted as his protector in later years.

In June 1701, when Cadillac led an expedition from Montreal to build a fort (Pontchartrain) on the straits between Lakes Erie and St Clair, Alphonse, who held by now the rank of captain, accompanied him as second in command. As Cadillac's presence was frequently required in Montreal and Quebec during the following four years, the command of Detroit was often entrusted to Alphonse. He discharged his military responsibilities well, averting an Iroquois attack on the fort and dissuading several bands of Indians from going to Albany to trade. Unfortunately, his salary proved insufficient to settle his debts and to maintain his family. As a result, his personal trade became so considerable that the court was obliged to intervene. Vaudreuil complied with ministerial instructions in 1705 and removed Tonty from Detroit, replacing him with Étienne de VÉNIARD de Bourgmond the following year.

In 1706 Alphonse's younger brother who resided in Paris submitted a memoir to Pontchartrain about a mine near Temiscaming which Alphonse was prepared to exploit. According to this memoir, two canoes and six men would be needed each year to convey munitions and trade goods to the Indians who traded with the English of Hudson Bay, and to bring the metal (which was not named) back to the colony. The intendants, JACQUES and ANTOINE-DENIS RAUDOT, thought the plan a good one but firmly rejected the trading privileges requested by Tonty. Pontchartrain, it would seem, endorsed their modification, for the Tontys soon dropped the matter. It is interesting to note, however, that the exploitation of minerals in this area 200 years later gave rise to the town of Cobalt.

Within 12 months of his dismissal from Detroit, Alphonse was appointed commandant of Fort Frontenac. His two-year command at this post proved to be similar to his previous appointment. He charged exorbitant prices for brandy, ruled despotically and selfishly, and had little regard for honesty. In 1708, as a result of François CLAIRAMBAULT d'Aigremont's unfavourable report, which was based on the testimony of soldiers, settlers, and Indians, Alphonse was removed from Fort Frontenac and replaced by JOSEPH-FRANÇOIS HERTEL de La Fresnière.

Alphonse's stock at the French court was now at its lowest ebb, but Vaudreuil had not deserted him. In 1711, he carried the governor's orders to Detroit, returning with a convoy of Indians and canoes, and the following year Vaudreuil submitted Tonty's name for consideration as commandant of Chambly. On 11 Sept. 1714, Tonty's wife died, 16 months after giving birth to her 13th child. He remarried on 3 May 1717, taking as his second wife Marie-Anne de La Marque, widow of Joseph-Antoine de Frenel. One month later, Alphonse left Montreal to assume command at Detroit, and before the end of the year Vaudreuil had recommended him for the cross of the order of Saint-Louis.

What occurred at Detroit during the next ten years must have come as no surprise to anyone. In order to make the money he needed to settle his debts, Alphonse behaved greedily and autocratically and was soon detested by everyone. Travellers had to buy supplies from him alone, at a mark-up of 100 per cent, and were charged room and board when they stayed at the post. Settlers paid an annual land tax, and were obliged to make money available for the purchase of gifts for the Indians. Persons wishing a permit to travel from Detroit to Montreal had to pay the commandant 500 *livres*. Numerous complaints about Tonty's conduct were sworn before notaries, and petitions were signed asking for his recall, but Vaudreuil adamantly refused to take action against his protégé. The governor's attitude no doubt seemed to confirm the allegation of Jacques BAUDRY de Lamarche that Tonty was paying Vaudreuil 3,000 *livres* a year for the command of the post.

In 1726 Alphonse farmed out the Detroit trade for 7,000 *livres* annually and requested the command of the post for three more years. This, he believed, would allow him sufficient time to clear his debts. Vaudreuil, however, was dead when he made this request, and in 1727 the Hurons threatened to leave Detroit if Alphonse were not replaced. After discussing the matter with some of the senior military officers, the new governor, Charles de Beauharnois* de La Boische, decided to recall him the following spring. Tonty, however, died before the decision could take effect.

Tonty was survived by at least 6 of his 13 children. Three of his sons became officers in the troops—Alphonse served at Île Royale (Cape Breton Island); Charles-Henri-Joseph, Sieur de Liette, served among the Illinois; and Pierre-Antoine died along with FRANÇOIS-MARIE BISSOT de Vinsenne at the hands of the Chickasaws in 1736. One daughter, Marie-Françoise, joined the

Congrégation de Notre-Dame; another, Marie-Josette, married Louis Damours de Louvières; and Thérèse married François Desjordy*.

Alphonse was undoubtedly a talented officer. On many occasions he dissuaded the Indian allies of New France from going to Albany to trade. There was, however, a streak of greediness in him and this tended to become the dominant characteristic of his personality as he strove to make the money that would have enabled him to clear his debts.

C. J. RUSS

The main documentary sources for Alphonse Tonty's life are: AN, Col., B, 29; C¹¹ᴬ, 28–52; C¹¹ᴳ, 3; and AJM, Greffe d'Antoine Adhémar. Tonty's disagreement with La Salle is detailed in Beaujeu's correspondence with de Villermont, published in *Découvertes et établissements des Français* (Margry), V. The recommended printed primary source for Tonty's term at Detroit is *Michigan Pioneer Coll.*, XXXIII, XXXIV. The best secondary sources for the period 1701–6 are the following articles by Jean Delanglez: "The genesis and building of Detroit," *Mid-America*, XXX (1948; new ser., XIX), 75–104; and "Cadillac at Detroit," *Mid-America*, XXX (1948; new ser., XIX), 152–76, 233–56. Vaudreuil's correspondence with the court may be consulted in APQ *Rapport, 1938–39, 1939–40.*

Other material consulted includes *NYCD* (O'Callaghan and Fernow), IX; Ill. State Hist. Lib. *Coll.*, XXIII; Wis. State Hist. Soc. *Coll.*, III; Tanguay, *Dictionnaire*, I, VII. [Most secondary sources are partial and incomplete. C.J.R.]

TONTY, HENRI (de), voyageur, trading post commander, lieutenant of René-Robert Cavelier* de La Salle; b. 1649–50, place unknown, eldest son of Lorenzo de Tonty, the inventor of the "tontine" system of life annuity and Isabelle di Lietto, Neapolitans who sought asylum in France after being involved in an unsuccessful revolt against the Spanish viceroy, the Duke of Arcos; d. September 1704, at Fort Louis-de-la-Louisiane, about 25 miles upriver from the present Mobile, Ala.

Tonty had two younger brothers, one of whom, ALPHONSE TONTY, came to Canada in about 1684–85, settled in Montreal, and became associated with the fur trade. The Tontys were cousins of DANIEL GREYSOLON Dulhut and CLAUDE GREYSOLON de La Tourette, both of whom made names for themselves in the new world.

In 1668–69, Henri served in the French army as a cadet. During the following four years he was a midshipman at Marseilles and Toulon, participating in seven campaigns at sea, four in warships and three in galleys. Sent to Sicily, he was made captain-lieutenant to the *maître de camp* at Messina. At "Libisso", during a Spanish attack, his right hand was shot away by a grenade and he was taken prisoner. Conducted to "Metasse", he was detained there six months, then exchanged for the governor's son. Back in France, Louis XIV granted him 300 *livres*. He returned to active service in Sicily as a volunteer in the galleys.

With the conclusion of the Dutch War (1678) Tonty returned to France, but was unable to obtain employment at court. There (probably with the help of the Sieur de Villermont) he became lieutenant to La Salle, who had just been granted permission to open up the Illinois country and discover the Mississippi's mouth.

On 15 Sept. 1678, Tonty and La Salle arrived at Quebec on the *Saint-Honoré*. By 26 December they were at the Niagara River where, during the remainder of the winter, Tonty supervised the construction of Fort Conti below the falls and of the bark, *Griffon*, above them. That summer he set out with five men by canoe along the north shore of Lake Erie, hoping to intercept a party of La Salle's men who ought to have been homeward-bound to Fort Frontenac (Kingston, Ont.) after a year of trading on the upper lakes. On 9 August he arrived at the strait between Lakes Huron and Erie, where he remained for two days until joined by La Salle in the *Griffon*.

On 27 August they all reached Michilimackinac, the cross-roads of the southwestern fur trade. Here they found most of the men for whom Tonty had searched; they had remained at Michilimackinac, dissipating more than 1,300 *livres* worth of trade goods. Six others had deserted with at least 4,000 *livres* of merchandise and were believed to be at Sault Ste Marie. On 29 August Tonty set out to round them up.

Having found and apprehended the deserters Tonty left Sault Ste Marie on 5 October to rendezvous with La Salle at the mouth of the St Joseph River (Mich.). After a very difficult passage of 38 days (probably via the eastern shore of Lake Michigan) he rejoined his commander and took part in the building of Fort Miami. After completing this task, the party pressed inland and on 15 Jan. 1680 began constructing Fort Crèvecœur on the south bank of the Illinois River, between the present Pekin and Kingston Mines (Ill.).

On 1 March La Salle placed Tonty in charge of the new post, and headed east overland in search of news of his ill-fated *Griffon* (which had already foundered with all hands). Pausing at Fort Miami, La Salle sent word back to Tonty that a new fort was to be built upriver from Fort Crèvecœur on a promontory known as Le Rocher (Starved Rock: near Utica, Ill.; this was the highest point on the

Tonty

Illinois at which navigation was always possible). Tonty immediately went to make a preliminary survey of the place. While he was absent the men at Fort Crèvecœur, dismayed by rumours of La Salle's financial difficulties, mutinied, destroying the buildings and burning a partially completed vessel intended for use on the Mississippi. After hurrying back to inspect the ruins and salvage what he could, Tonty took up residence at an Illinois village with the five men who remained faithful to him.

Tonty began to trade while awaiting La Salle's return. Meanwhile, alarmed by the prospect of the French supplying arms and ammunition to the Illinois, the Iroquois decided to make war. They struck on 10 September. At first Tonty tried to buy them off with necklaces, but received only a glancing blow from a knife for his pains. Bravely persevering and with the assistance of an Onondaga chief named Agonstot, "he gave them to understand that the Illinois were under the protection of the king of France" and persuaded them to call off their attack. Nevertheless, the Iroquois insisted that Tonty and his men immediately leave the Illinois country.

Hoping to reach Michilimackinac before winter set in, Tonty and his party arrived early in October at the site of the present city of Chicago, where they rediscovered the portage taken by Louis Jolliet* and Father Marquette* seven years before. From here they headed for Baie des Puants (Green Bay). While proceeding by canoe on Lac des Illinois (Lake Michigan), they were wrecked on 1 Nov. 1680 and during the next two weeks lived on "wild garlic," grubbed up from under the snow. Ultimately they arrived at a Potawatomi settlement where Tonty remained for the winter while his chaplain, Father Zénobe Membré*, went on to the Jesuit mission of St Francis Xavier (near the present De Pere, Wis.).

Early in June 1681 Tonty joined La Salle at Michilimackinac. He accompanied his leader part way to Montreal and then in August set out ahead of him for Fort Miami to make ready for the definitive thrust southward to the Mississippi's mouth. On 27 December, with most of the men assembled for the expedition, Tonty began to cross the Chicago portage. On 6 Jan. 1682, one day's journey from the Des Plaines River, he was rejoined by his commander. On 7 April the expedition reached the Gulf of Mexico and on the 9th, near the present Venice, La., they erected a cross and post bearing the arms of France to commemorate the occasion.

As they were short of supplies, Tonty and La Salle decided to return north immediately. When La Salle became ill and unable to travel, Tonty pressed on ahead of the main expedition to attend to trading operations in the Illinois valley. He reached the Chicago portage at the end of June, carried on to the St Joseph's mouth and with two companions continued northwards to Michilimackinac where he arrived on 22 July. La Salle joined him there in September and immediately sent his lieutenant back to the south end of Lake Michigan to build a fort upriver on the St Joseph.

Seemingly on his own initiative, Tonty ignored his leader's instructions and went into the Illinois valley to winter and trade. Joined by La Salle in December, Tonty began the construction at Le Rocher of Fort Saint-Louis. He travelled more than 100 leagues, visiting various Illinois tribes to persuade the Indians to settle near the new fort. This would provide both trading opportunities and a form of defence against future Iroquois attacks. In August La Salle set out for the east (and France), leaving Tonty in command.

While La Salle was away, the governor of New France, Joseph-Antoine Le Febvre* de La Barre, decided to confiscate all his properties in North America. As a result Tonty was replaced as commandant of Fort Saint-Louis by the governor's nominee, Louis-Henri de BAUGY, who arrived in September with 30 canoes containing munitions and trade goods as well as some soldiers. During the spring of 1684, he and Tonty successfully held off an Iroquois attack. Then, on 23 May, Tonty left for Montreal and Quebec, where he found that the governor's decision to seize La Salle's properties had been reversed. He and La Salle's other lieutenant, François DAUPHIN de La Forest (who had been in charge of Fort Frontenac since 1679) were to carry on with operations on their chief's behalf. Owing to an early freeze-up, Tonty was unable to reach the west until June 1685.

In November word reached Tonty that La Salle was in the Gulf of Mexico; on 16 Feb. 1686 he set out with 25 Frenchmen and 4 Indians to join him. La Salle was supposed to be setting up a colony at the Mississippi's mouth, but when Tonty reached there (sometime between the 8th and 13th of April) he "learned nothing of M. de La Salle except that some Indians had seen him set sail and proceed southward." Tonty dispatched canoes to the east and west, "to see if they could discover anything." Having found no sign of him after each had sailed "about thirty leagues" and being obliged to turn back "for want of fresh water," Tonty decided to return upriver: "I proposed to my men, that . . . we should follow the coast as far as Menade [Manhattan], and by this means . . . arrive shortly at Montreal . . . part of my men . . . were opposed . . . , so I decided to return the way I came."

During the summer of 1685, Jacques-René BRISAY de Denonville had replaced La Barre as governor of New France. Concluding that war with the Iroquois was inevitable, he had decided to promise the Illinois "every protection" and to summon Tonty to his side for consultation. When Tonty arrived back at Fort Saint-Louis, he left almost immediately for Montreal. There the governor told him of the campaign he proposed for the following summer and the key part he was to play in its execution. He was to "march [with the Illinois] 300 leagues overland, for those Indians are not accustomed to canoes," and attack the Iroquois in the rear, while Denonville mounted a frontal assault.

The following year Tonty was able to muster only 80 Illinois for the campaign. The rest refused to leave their homes unprotected because of rumours that the Senecas were about to attack. Consequently, he was "obliged to go to join Sieurs de l'hut [Dulhut] and de la Durantais [MOREL] at the fort on the strait, being unable to take the Senecas in the rear." Between there and Niagara, advancing with 160 Frenchmen and nearly 400 Indians, they captured 60 Englishmen from New York, plus some Indians, "on their way to seize Michilimaquinac and other posts, and to establish trade there with the Indians. . . ." Proceeding to their rendezvous on Lake Ontario, they met up with Denonville and took part in the van of the French attack against the Senecas.

After helping to establish a post at Niagara, Tonty returned to his post on the Illinois, having acquitted himself "very well." During the next two years he remained at Fort Saint-Louis, running La Salle's trading operations in partnership with La Forest. As far as he knew, things were going well with his employer's new colony on the Gulf of Mexico. Then in September 1689, Jean Couture (possibly a relation of Guillaume COUTURE) came in from the Arkansas River with positive news that La Salle had been murdered by his own men.

That December Tonty set out with four Frenchmen, one Shawnee, and two slaves to go to the aid of La Salle's abandoned settlement, which was now known to be located on Baie Saint-Louis (Matagorda Bay, Texas). He was the only person who lifted a finger to help these unfortunate people, but the ordeal of the journey proved too much for him. Half-starved and short of ammunition, he gave up the attempt after penetrating as far as the northwestern part of what is now Houston County, Texas.

In 1690 La Forest and Tonty were granted La Salle's fur-trading concession among the Illinois. So long as it functioned the Iroquois advance towards the west, and thus the advance of the English, would be held in check. Tonty spent the winter of 1690 and that of 1691 in the Illinois valley, making only one trip "out" to Michilimackinac during the intervening summer. During the latter winter, as supplies of firewood had been exhausted adjacent to Fort Saint-Louis, he began a new fort at Pimitoui (near Peoria, Ill.). La Forest joined him there in the spring with hired men and soldiers to finish it.

In the summer of 1693 Tonty went down to Quebec with a fleet of fur-laden canoes manned by Ottawas and coureurs de bois. While there he borrowed a substantial sum on behalf of his business partnership. By this time La Forest had sold half his interest to Michel Accault for 6,000 *livres*. Tonty spent the next two years exploiting his licence to trade in the Illinois valley and towards the southwest and tried to persuade the authorities in France that he should resurrect La Salle's old concept of siphoning off the wealth of the Mississippi basin through the Mississippi's mouth. Understandably, this ambition was vigorously opposed by the Montreal traders and merchants.

In an effort to upgrade the quality of their furs Tonty and his partners obtained Governor Frontenac's (Buade*) permission to trade among the Assiniboins, "who live 500 leagues towards the North from Michilimackinac." On 8 Aug. 1695 Tonty left Michilimackinac for the northwest. According to Cadillac (LAUMET), who wrote the following year, he went both to trade and get news of PIERRE LE MOYNE d'Iberville's attack on Fort Nelson. "Contrary winds long detained him on Lake Superior; then ice set in, so that he . . . only journeyed about 200 leagues [from Michilimackinac]. As soon as the ice melted, he pursued his journey and is bound for the great lake of the Assiniboin which discharges its waters into the sea through the river of Port Nelson." By the end of June 1696, Tonty had sent word back that Iberville had won Hudson Bay with the loss of only two men. How far he himself penetrated towards the northwest is not known.

The beaver glut had become serious by this time, and the authorities in France tried desperately to contain it. The fort at Pimitoui was to remain open only on condition that Tonty and his partners refrain from carrying on the beaver trade. When it was pointed out to the king that if there was to be no trade, there would be no French presence in the Mississippi valley and the road to the west would be entirely open to the English colonists on the Atlantic coast, Louis XIV relented slightly, giving Tonty permission to trade within strict limits. By 1698, however, the court had decided to counter English and Spanish designs on North America by resurrecting and modifying La Salle's original plan for a colony at the mouth of the Mississippi. They chose Iberville, the conqueror of Hudson Bay and Newfoundland, to establish Louisiana; Tonty and La Forest were to cooperate fully.

That autumn, Tonty guided a party of Jesuits [see Buisson de Saint-Cosme, 1667–1706] to the mouth of the Arkansas River, arriving about Christmas. He spent the following year at Pimitoui and Michilimackinac. Then, leaving the affairs of the Illinois country to the care of his cousin Pierre de Liette, Tonty set out with seven Canadians for Fort Mississippi (near Phoenix, La.), where he made contact with Iberville. From this time on he worked to help establish the French presence in the south. He developed trade deep into the interior, persuaded the Chickasaws to live in peace with the new colony "despite the instigation of the English," and when the Alabamus took to the warpath he, with Jean-Baptiste Le Moyne* de Bienville, took revenge on them. In 1704, a supply vessel from Havana brought yellow fever to Fort Biloxi. Sometime in September of that year Tonty contracted the disease and died at Fort Louis-de-la-Louisiane.

Tonty must be ranked as a major explorer of North America and, with La Forest, as a businessman with a practical approach to the problems of the inland fur trade. It has been said of him that "while La Salle conceived, Tonty achieved." The Indians, who called him *bras de fer*, were as much in awe of his endurance, tenacity, courage, and organizing ability as they were of his hook-shaped artificial arm. Governor Denonville, himself a veteran soldier of considerable repute, called him "a lad of great enterprise and boldness" and had no hesitation in giving him a crucial role in the execution of his campaign against the Iroquois. Iberville and Bienville relied upon him heavily to help stabilize their relationship with the Indians of Louisiana. Perhaps not a giant of his age, Tonty is nonetheless a significant figure in the history of French development of the west.

E. B. OSLER

Découvertes et établissements des Français (Margry), I–V. *Early narratives of the northwest, 1634–1699*, ed. L. P. Kellogg (Original narratives of early American history, [XVII], New York, 1917). *NYCD* (O'Callaghan and Fernow), IX. H. E. Legler, *Chevalier Henry de Tonty's exploits in the valley of the Mississippi* (Milwaukee, 1896). E. R. Murphy, *Henry de Tonti, fur trader of the Mississippi* (Baltimore, 1941). Jean Delanglez, "Tonti letters," *Mid-America*, XXI (1939; new ser. X), 209–38; "The voyages of Tonty in North-America, 1678–1704," *Mid-America*, XXVI (1944; new ser. XV), 255–97. Benjamin Sulte, "Les Tonty," 1st ser., XI (1893), sect.i, 3–31.

TOURBLANCHE. *See* Martinet

TREVANION, SIR NICHOLAS, captain in the Royal Navy; commodore of the Newfoundland convoy and temporary governor, 1712; b. *c.* 1670; d. 1737.

Believed to have been a son or collateral descendant of Captain Richard Trevanion of an ancient Cornish family who adhered to King James II and went into exile with him, Trevanion was commissioned captain of the *Dunwich* in 1696 and the *Lyme* in 1698. In 1702, in command of the *Dover*, he captured a valuable French prize off Saint-Malo. He then served in the Mediterranean squadron under Sir Cloudesley Shovell, and for his services was knighted in 1710.

In 1712, in command of the *York*, Trevanion was appointed a commodore of the Newfoundland convoy. He arrived in Newfoundland on 17 or 18 September—the exact date is not known as his log-books for 1712 are missing. His replies to the Heads of Enquiry required by the Board of Trade and Plantations are dated 29 Oct. 1712. He records that he held courts twice weekly, as had his predecessor, Commodore Josias Crowe, who had been the first to institute regular courts. He caused notices to be put up in ale houses and other public places prohibiting drunkenness and swearing. He confirmed the arrangements made by Crowe for the remuneration of the minister, Jacob Rice, but found the planters backward in paying him. He also settled a number of property disputes amongst inhabitants. The fact that he stayed only a short time at St John's may account for his generally favourable report. He noted that life there was peaceable, with no complaints of stealing, or wilful damage, or unjust apportioning of beach and harbour facilities.

Also included in his replies to the Heads were his comments on the life of the inhabitants of Newfoundland—the fishing methods, the various commodities imported, and statistical data. He recorded a population of 1,509 men, 185 women, and 323 children, and the number of ships in harbour as 66 fishing ships, 17 sack ships, and 20 from America. He also estimated the population of the French at Placentia at 500 men and 200 women and children. In compliance with the board's rules he ordered that the Lord's day be duly observed and he gave strict orders against the emptying of ballast in the harbour—a pernicious practice that destroyed the cod fry. With regard to the serious matter of enticement of English seamen and "green men" by New England shipmasters, Trevanion remarked: "as to the New Englandmen I have took good care to see them all out of port so that they may not carry away any of Her Majesty's subjects." His remedy was, however, only a temporary one; Commodores FOTHERBY and KEMPTHORNE were to find the situation as bad as ever. Trevanion noted that great care was taken to preserve the fish with good salt, but that it had been a poor season; the price of fish he quoted as "30 to 36 ryalls per quintell" and of oil—"£16 per tun."

Trevanion liked Newfoundland and its inhabitants. He asked if he could return "to settle affairs here in the spring if Placentia is to be delivered up." The goodwill seems to have been mutual; the inhabitants and merchants of Newfoundland petitioned the Earl of Dartmouth that Trevanion continue in office. His relations with the French, too, were good. When some of his ships seized some French vessels after the armistice, he quickly arranged with PASTOUR de Costebelle, governor of Placentia, for their return. With his reply Costebelle sent a case of wine. It is interesting to see throughout Trevanion's reports the distinctly amiable tone when he is discussing the French, and the hostile attitude towards New England.

Trevanion's request to be allowed to return to Newfoundland was not granted—LEAKE was commodore in 1713. After Trevanion's return to England he was not employed at sea again; in 1728 he was appointed resident commissioner for the navy at Plymouth, where he died 17 Nov. 1737.

MICHAEL GODFREY

PRO, Adm. 6 (commission and warrant books); C.O. 194/5; *CSP, Col., 1712–14.* Charnock, *Biographia navalis,* III.

TROTAIN, *dit* **SAINT-SEÜRIN (Surin), FRANÇOIS,** soldier, settler, court officer, seigneurial attorney, royal notary; b. *c.* 1634 in the little town of Saint-Seurin-d'Uzet (province of Saintonge), son of François Trotain and Jeanne Gribond; buried 11 Feb. 1731 at Batiscan.

He was a soldier in the Carignan regiment (Naurois' company) when he landed at Quebec in September 1665. When the troops were disbanded in 1668 he settled in Canada, and he and a regimental comrade, Pierre Roberol, *dit* Morin, rented the land of Pierre de La Garde at Batiscan for two years. Roberol withdrew in 1670, and on 14 Nov. 1673 Trotain bought the partly cleared land which had been granted to Michel Peltier, Sieur de La Prade. The Jesuits, who owned the seigneury, and who detected in Trotain a choice recruit, paid two-thirds of the cost of this land. Trotain was

soon a seigneurial attorney and court clerk. He also became a notary; indeed in his first known act, that of 19 March 1687, he designated himself "royal notary and tabellion at Cap-de-la-Madeleine, Champlain, Batiscan, and Sainte-Anne, living at Batiscan." Perhaps he never received a commission granting him the title of royal notary, but the authorities allowed conscientious seigneurial notaries to assume this imposing appellation.

Trotain had married Jeanne Hardy (Ardies), a native of La Rochelle, on 16 Aug. 1668 at Quebec. Five daughters were born of this marriage. He died at Batiscan at the age of 96. One of his sons-in-law, Joseph Rouillard*, who had married Marie-Charlotte in 1715 inherited his post of notary and his registry.

RAYMOND DOUVILLE

AJTR, Greffe de François Trotain. *Jug. et délib.,* VI. Vachon, "Inv. critique des notaires royaux," *RHAF,* X (1956–57), 381. J.-B.-M. Barthe, *Analyse des actes de François Trotain, notaire royal, gardenote au Cap de la Madeleine, Champlain, Batiscan et Sainte-Anne* (Trois-Rivières, s.d.). J.-E. Roy, *Histoire du notariat,* I, 203f. Régis Roy et Malchelosse, *Le régiment de Carignan.*

TROUVÉ, CLAUDE, priest, Sulpician, missionary; b. *c.* 1644 in the province of Touraine; d. 1704 at Chedabouctou (Guysborough, N.S.).

Abbé Trouvé studied theology and received the subdiaconate at the Sulpician seminary in Paris. In 1667 his superiors sent him to Canada, with Abbé François de Salignac* de La Mothe-Fénelon. Bishop LAVAL conferred the diaconate upon him 24 Sept. 1667 and the priesthood 10 June 1668.

In June 1668 the chief and a few members of the Cayuga tribe who had settled on the Bay of Quinte on the north shore of Lake Ontario had come to Montreal to request that missionaries be sent to them. The Sulpicians, who were awaiting the arrival of their superior, M. de Queylus [Thubières*], at the time in France, had not wanted to make a decision. In September, after another request from the Iroquois, Abbés Trouvé and Fénelon offered to accompany them to their country. Queylus consented to the project and sent the two young priests to Quebec to obtain the permission of the religious and civil authorities. Bishop Laval received them favourably and gave them some wise instructions. The governor and the intendant also gave their consent, and, as Abbé Trouvé recounts: "these indispensable steps having been taken, we left without further delay, because we were already well into autumn." The missionaries set off by water from Lachine on

Trouvé

2 October with two Iroquois from the village at Quinte, and 26 days later they reached their destination.

For 12 years Trouvé directed the Quinte mission. But this mission, which the Sulpicians supported at the price of the greatest sacrifices, gave small results. In 1680 the superior general, Abbé Louis Tronson, ordered that it be abandoned in favour of the mission at La Montagne, near Ville-Marie. A disappointed man, Abbé Trouvé returned to the seminary in Montreal, and Tronson asked him to exercise his ministry among the nuns of the Congrégation de Notre-Dame, of which he had just been entrusted with the direction. Trouvé stayed only a year in this post, and in the autumn of 1681 he returned to France, where his father, ill and in debt, was asking for him.

In order to aid his family, Abbé Trouvé accepted the charge of parish priest and the canonry of Le Grand Pressigny which the archbishop of Tours offered him. He remained in this parish until 1685. At that time Bishop Saint-Vallier [La Croix], who had been appointed by the king to the bishopric of Quebec, was preparing to visit his future diocese. On the advice of Tronson, his spiritual director, the new coadjutor asked Abbé Trouvé to accompany him, and to gain his assent Saint-Vallier promised to pay his family's debts. The missionary immediately put himself at his benefactor's disposal and joined him at the Séminaire des Missions Étrangères in Paris, where he met Bishop Laval and his procurator, Abbé Jean Dudouyt*, who were delighted at his decision. The former bishop of Quebec wrote of Trouvé that he "had experience of long standing and of every sort concerning the Indians, and was capable of excelling in a mission, in the settled regions of Canada and in the wilds," and that he was "fitted to direct the parish of Quebec." Dudouyt on the other hand was a little more pessimistic and revealed a certain fear of seeing Trouvé become associated with Bishop Saint-Vallier. He suspected that Trouvé would return to France with the bishop when he had finished visiting his diocese, and that is exactly what happened. It seems, however, that Abbé Trouvé had never thought of leaving the Sulpicians to join the seminary of Quebec.

In 1688 the bishop of Quebec appointed him to the missions in Acadia. Trouvé arrived at his new post during the summer and chose to establish himself at Beaubassin (Chignecto). In 1690, at the time of the attack on Port-Royal (Annapolis Royal), he was captured and taken to Boston along with Abbé Louis Petit and M. de Meneval [Des Friches], the governor of Acadia. Trouvé was released from captivity when Phips* under-took to attack New France. As he wanted to use the missionary after the conquest, he took him along on board his ship. The failure of the siege of Quebec and the exchange of prisoners allowed Trouvé to recover his liberty.

After this adventure the missionary spent nearly four years at Quebec. The bishop appointed him ecclesiastical superior of the Ursuline monastery and made use of him on several occasions as an intermediary in the conflict which opposed him at that time to the chapter and seminary of Quebec. Although he was utterly devoted to Bishop Saint-Vallier, Abbé Trouvé was made very unhappy by these regrettable dissensions and by the role that he was required to play. Louis Tronson wrote to him in March 1694: "Your letter of last year makes known to me your embarrassment . . . and I can understand that it is all the greater since you cannot express yourself about it nor write about it to M. Dollier." The superior even advised him to avoid all visits to his fellow religious in Montreal, for "that could only be done with the Prelate's permission, and I cannot believe that he would consent to it; for he is very much afraid that you would be kept there, and he believes that you can be useful to him. Besides, I see clearly what you have to fear at Quebec in the present state of affairs and as long as peace has not been restored there." This letter was all that was needed to persuade Abbé Trouvé to resume the missionary life that he had never stopped yearning for. At his entreaty, the bishop let him return to his mission at Beaubassin.

On two more occasions war caught Trouvé by surprise in the midst of his apostolic tasks. In September 1696 a fleet under the command of Major Benjamin Church of Boston attacked the region of Beaubassin, which was completely devastated. In the summer of 1704, to avenge the massacre of Deerfield (Mass.), Church again organized an expedition against the Acadian establishments on Baie Française (Bay of Fundy). As the enemy approached, the pastor of Beaubassin and his flock fled in the direction of Chedabouctou, and it was there, it is believed, that Abbé Trouvé died of exhaustion at the end of 1704.

Noël Baillargeon

AAQ, Chapitre de la cathédrale de Québec, Registre, 25; Registres d'insinuation A, 57, 62, 63, 64. AMUQ, Registre de l'examen canonique des novices (1689–1817). ASQ, Chapitre, 5, 10, 160; Lettres, M, 1, 2, 9, 101; O, 1, 12; MSS, 0478; Séminaire, V, 10; XCII, 25. Dollier de Casson, *Histoire du Montréal. Mandements des évêques de Québec* (Têtu et Gagnon), I, 73, 75f. *1690, Sir William Phips devant Québec* (Myrand). [Louis Tronson], *Correspondance de M. de Tronson*, troisième Supérieur de la Compagnie de Saint-Sulpice: Lettres choisies [16 juillet 1676–15 janv. 1700], éd. A.-L. Bertrand (3v., Paris, 1904). A.-L. Bertrand, Bibliothèque sulpicienne ou histoire littéraire de la compagnie de Saint-Sulpice (3v., Paris, 1900). Casgrain, Les Sulpiciens en Acadie.

U

URFÉ, FRANÇOIS-SATURNIN LASCARIS D'.
See LASCARIS

V

VACHON, PAUL, mason, seigneurial notary, seigneurial attorney, and clerk of court; b. *c.* 1630 at La Copechagnière (province of Poitou), son of Vincent Vachon and Sapience Vateau; d. 24 June 1703 at Beauport.

Paul Vachon is supposed to have come to Canada around 1650, at the age of 20. According to a family tradition, he arrived with a few gold pieces sewn into the lining of his coat. On 22 Oct. 1653, at Quebec, he married Marguerite Langlois, who was born in 1639 at Beauport; they had 12 children. Vachon was a mason by trade; in 1654, in association with Mathurin Roy, he was entrusted with the building of the chapel and the sick-ward of the Hôtel-Dieu of Quebec, the first stone of which was laid on 15 Oct. 1654 by the governor-general, Jean de Lauson*. Vachon was perhaps already living in the small town of Fargy, in the Beauport seigneury, where on 4 June 1655 Joseph Giffard made him a land grant of ten acres, of which he officially took possession on 23 Jan. 1656. These ten acres were doubled by another grant, made in an act dated 29 Dec. 1664.

It has been stated that the first notarial document received by Vachon bears the date of 24 March 1658, but in the archives of the Conseil Souverain there is reference to an act of 23 Oct. 1655, signed by Vachon in his capacity as notary of Notre-Dame-des-Anges. In 1659 Vachon also became notary of Beauport. He was already seigneurial attorney of the Lirec and Île d'Orléans seigneuries. In the same period he acted as secretary to Charles de Lauson* de Charny, taking care of his seigneurial land grants. Vachon was the first notary of the Île d'Orléans, where he practised in 1659 and 1660. About the same time he became, in addition, court clerk of the Beauport and Notre-Dame-des-Anges seigneuries. He certainly appears to have been the one indispensable man east of Quebec.

In 1667 two exceptional commissions were to be entrusted to him in quick succession: on 3 November Marie-Barbe de Boullongne*, Governor General d'Ailleboust*'s widow, appointed him seigneurial attorney and notary in her Argentenay fief on the Île d'Orléans; a week later, on 10 November, Bishop LAVAL named him to the same offices in his Beauport and Île d'Orléans seigneuries. The appointment which he had received from Bishop Laval was renewed on 25 April 1681 for the Île dOrléans by François Berthelot, so that Vachon carried on his profession at Beaupré and on the Île d'Orléans, as well as at Beauport and Notre-Dame-des-Anges, until he retired in 1693.

Paul Vachon did not forget, however, that he came from country stock, and never failed to work his land. In 1666 he had an "indentured domestic," Michel Aubin, 22 years of age, who probably did the farm work; in 1667 Vachon owned 7 head of cattle and 20 acres under cultivation; in 1681 he still had a domestic, Pierre, 61 years old, and owned 2 muskets, 1 pistol, 13 head of cattle, and 35 acres under cultivation. In addition to his land at Beauport, he had another four acres on the Île d'Orléans, which were worked by a farmer. In 1667 this had become eight acres under cultivation. Vachon, who had obtained the land from Charles de Lauson de Charny on 12 Aug. 1660, sold it to Denis Roberge on 14 Sept. 1678.

An exemplary settler, a craftsman, a farmer, and a law officer at one and the same time, Paul Vachon experienced the grief of seeing his family afflicted by the small-pox epidemic of 1702–3. He had been a widower since 24 Sept. 1697, and in six months he lost four of his children, one daughter-in-law, and six grandchildren. He himself succumbed to the scourge on 24 June 1703, only a few hours after his daughter Marguerite, who had married his successor, the notary and clerk of court Jean-Robert DUPRAC. He was buried the next day at Beauport.

ANDRÉ VACHON

AQ, NF, Coll. de pièces jud. et not., 321/2. ASQ, Documents Faribault, 108, 117a; Polygraphie, III, 131, 131a. Juchereau, *Annales* (Jamet), 89. *Jug. et*

Vachon

délib. Recensement du Canada, 1666 (APQ *Rapport*). Recensements du Canada, 1667, 1681 (Sulte). "Les notaires au Canada," 272f. Tanguay, *Dictionnaire*, I, 578. Jean Langevin, *Notes sur les archives de N.-D. de Beauport* (2v., Québec, 1860–63). J.-E. Roy, *Histoire du notariat*, I. Vachon, *Histoire du notariat*, 13, 22. "Le premier notaire de l'île d'Orléans," *BRH*, XXXIV (1928), 272f. Léon Roy, "Les terres de l'île d'Orléans," APQ *Rapport, 1953–55*, 21.

VACHON, PAUL, priest, chaplain of the chapter of Quebec, parish priest of Sainte-Madeleine-du-Cap; b. at Beauport and baptized 9 Nov. 1656 at Quebec, son of Paul VACHON, notary and clerk of court, and of Marguerite Langlois; d. 7 March 1729 at Cap-de-la-Madeleine.

Paul Vachon entered the Petit Séminaire of Quebec on 9 Nov. 1668, when he was 12 years old. He was one of the original eight Canadian pupils of this institution, which had been founded that same year by Bishop LAVAL. He intended to enter the priesthood; he received the tonsure and minor orders 12 Dec. 1677, was admitted to the sub-diaconate on 18 December and to the diaconate 17 Sept. 1678. He was ordained in the cathedral of Quebec 21 Dec. 1680. On 17 Dec. 1677 his father had signed a clerical deed assigning him an annual income of 75 *livres*.

During the period of his theological studies Abbé Vachon had carried out various small tasks, taking care of the linen-room (1678–79), the refectory, and the cupboards (1679). He was assigned to the parochial missions. He carried out his ministry on the south shore, below Quebec, and particularly at Cap Saint-Ignace (1683–85), just as he had first done on the north shore, above Quebec, at Dombourg (Pointe-aux-Trembles), Batiscan, Sainte-Anne, and Grondines. On 9 Nov. 1684 this humble priest was appointed by Bishop Laval chaplain of the chapter of Quebec. Being absent at the time, he did not take up his duties in the chapel of the Holy Family, in the cathedral church, until 26 June 1685. He resigned from this office 8 Oct. 1694, less than a month after his appointment as resident priest for the parish of Sainte-Madeleine-du-Cap, in the seigneury of Cap-de-la-Madeleine. It was there, in fact, that Abbé Vachon was to pursue to the end his fruitful career. From 1685 on he was simply a priest in charge of his chapel; on 18 Sept. 1694 he received his letters of appointment from Bishop Saint-Vallier [LA CROIX]. From 1685 to 1716 he also extended his ministry to the seigneury of Bécancour, on the south shore. (According to tradition he was drowned while returning from this mission in 1729; but he had ceased serving it long before that.)

This Canadian priest was the originator of the devotion to the rosary that has made Cap-de-la-Madeleine one of the great centres of pilgrimage in Canada. At his request he received from Rome, 11 May 1694, an official diploma establishing a confraternity of the Holy Rosary which he set up officially, with Bishop Saint-Vallier's consent, on 4 Oct. 1697.

Though destined to a brilliant future, Abbé Vachon's parish was nonetheless poverty-stricken. The priest had barely enough to live on. On 15 Oct. 1701, for example, the seminary had been obliged to give him 250 *livres*. He appears, therefore, as moreover do all the parish priests of his time, greatly preoccupied with the question of the tithe, which was the subject of much discussion at that moment. On 27 April 1706, acting in his own name and as the "deputy" of the parish priests of his region, he signed a collective memorandum by the Canadian clergy on the tithe, a memorandum that was sent to the court. The situation was aggravated for Abbé Vachon by the fact that he had to build a new stone church as the result of a decree issued on 13 May 1714 by Bishop Saint-Vallier. The construction work was undertaken by the carpenters of the parish but little was done and in 1719, with "the consent of the majority of the parishioners," Abbé Vachon entrusted the responsibility for it to François Dufaux of Trois-Rivières, who soon completed it.

This church, which is still standing, was the source of much expense. Consequently in 1716 Abbé Vachon resorted to having the intendant force certain settlers of Bécancour and the neighbouring fief of Dutort to pay him the tithe. But soon after, on 10 May 1716, Bishop Saint-Vallier separated this mission from the parish of Cap-de-la-Madeleine, promising Father Vachon 100 silver *écus* a year as compensation. The financial situation of the parish priests was so precarious that in 1719 we find Father Vachon attacking his colleague, Pierre Hazeur* de L'Orme, parish priest of Champlain, before the provost court of Trois-Rivières. Both of them laid claim to the tithes paid by the inhabitants of Arbre-à-la-Croix and the Prairies Marsolet. The court of Trois-Rivières decided on 22 Dec. 1719 (confirmed on 22 Jan. 1720 on appeal to the Conseil Souverain), that these settlers would pay the tithe to Father Hazeur. Abbé Vachon had good reason to be uneasy: in February 1721 he had in his parish only 16 heads of families, of whom only 11 paid the tithe!

In his will Paul Vachon left his few belongings to his parish. He was buried under the sanctuary of the church. In 1895 his skeleton was found in a perfect state of preservation.

ANDRÉ VACHON

Vachon de Belmont

AAQ, Copies de documents, Série A: Église du Canada, III, 117; Registres d'insinuations A, 103–5, 578; Registres d'insinuations B, 100, 136. AJTR, Greffe de Pierre Petit, 22 mars 1729. AQ, NF, Registres du Cons. sup., 1719–20, 63v. ASQ, MSS, 17, 477; Paroisses diverses, 41; Polygraphie, XII, 20, 22, p.5; Séminaire, I, 15; S.M.E., 6 déc. 1678, 5 sept. 1679, 25 août 1680. Édits ord., III, 174. "Procès-verbaux du procureur général Collet" (Caron), 281. Provost, Le Séminaire de Québec: documents et biographies, 427. Caron, "Prêtres séculiers et religieux," 257. Tanguay, Répertoire du clergé, 60.

Gosselin, L'Église du Canada, III, 158f. Jouve, Les Franciscains et le Canada: aux Trois-Rivières. Raymond Douville, "Quelques notes inédites sur Nicolas Perrot et sa famille," Cahiers des Dix, XXVIII (1963), 55f. É.-Z. Massicotte, "Notes diverses sur le Cap-de-la-Madeleine," BRH, XXXV (1929), 393f.

VACHON DE BELMONT, FRANÇOIS, priest, Sulpician, missionary, schoolmaster, priest of the parish of Ville-Marie, seigneur of Montreal Island, superior of the Sulpician seminary from 1701 to 1732, vicar general of the bishop of Quebec; b. 3 April 1645 in the parish of Saint-Hugues et Saint-Jean at Grenoble, in the province of Dauphiné; d. 22 May 1732 at Montreal.

His father, Ennemond de Vachon, seigneur of Belmont and Crapanoz, was a counsellor in the *parlement* of Grenoble. His mother, Honorade Prunier, was the daughter of the president of the *parlement*. The Sulpician had three sisters who took the veil and two brothers. The elder, Jean-François, succeeded his father in the *parlement* and in 1707 left François an annual income of 1,200 *livres*. The younger, Jean-Baptiste, entered the order of Malta, then obtained a dispensation and got married.

François Vachon de Belmont received a "refined education, quite in the spirit of the age of Louis XIV." He learned several languages and took up drawing and music, as well as obtaining the degree of bachelor of theology at the Sorbonne. Did he spend a part of his adolescence at the court? He is said to have been one of the queen's pages before occupying a position in the magistrature of Dauphiné.

He did not enter the Sulpician order until 18 Oct. 1672. Eight years later, at the time of his coming to Canada, he was still a deacon. Bishop Saint-Vallier [LA CROIX] attributed this to his wish to avoid ecclesiastical honours. Indeed Tronson, the superior of the Sulpician seminary in Paris, sent him to hush up the affair involving sorcerers and visions which had occurred at the mission of the Indians settled at La Montagne [see GUYOTTE], because he had had experience of similar cases in Paris.

Vachon de Belmont was ordained priest in 1681 at the age of 36, and devoted a great part of his life to teaching and preaching to the Christian Iroquois who were settled in the mission near Ville-Marie. Thanks to his talents as a draughtsman and architect, he was able to set up an attractive village for the Indians on a property with a frontage of 20 *arpents* and a depth of 30, which had been kept for this purpose. He built a chapel whose walls, in imitation red marble veined with white, were covered with panelling decorated "with urns, niches, pilasters, and pedestals." In addition, he arranged a well-stocked poultry yard, a pigeon-house, a pond frequented by ducks, geese, and bustards, an orchard, a vineyard, and a fountain. At the end of the fort stood the rows of Iroquois lodges.

In 1692, to ensure better protection for the Indians against alcohol, de Belmont organized a second mission at Sault-au-Récollet. The indifferent results obtained forced him to seek a new site farther from the dangers and temptations of the town. In 1721 he installed his protégés on the seigneury of Lac des Deux-Montagnes.

This mission, a veritable *reduccion*, aimed at the complete assimilation of the Indians; it thus differed from the traditional French colonial policy. In addition to Christian doctrine, the missionary taught singing, the French language, the European way of life, and a variety of the most useful trades. Some Indians became tailors, shoemakers, or masons; others, using the land given by Belmont, built houses and tilled their fields, following the Canadians' example. In Governor Le Febvre* de La Barre's opinion, the mission produced "good soldiers, and loyal subjects for the king, as well as . . . good Christians." The Sulpician attached great importance to religious observances: catechism every working day, masses every morning, and evening prayer together. He also attempted to adapt the Roman Catholic religion to the Indian mentality; and accompanied on the lute the singing of divine service in the native language.

He did not succeed, however, in solving the fundamental problem: spirits. He even took up his pen to protest against this scourge. In an *Histoire de l'eau-de-vie* he described the very special nature of the attraction and influence which alcohol exerted upon the Indian: "I am undertaking this short history to show that the drunkenness of Indians is a different kind from that of all other men; and to make clear a principle hitherto unknown, namely 'that they drink only to get drunk,' and that they 'get drunk only to do evil.'" And he added: "the drunkenness of Indians is a frenzy and a deliberate fury, which by giving them both courage and impunity serves as an instrument and a cover for their most heinous crimes."

His indictment ended with plans for bringing the vice under control, and with an exhortation to the Indians. By reasons drawn from religious faith and nature, he urged them to free themselves of this passion; he even resorted to scorn, stating that the tavern-keepers mixed urine with the drink. His superior in Paris advised him, however, not to denounce these abuses publicly, for fear of "antagonizing the powers against ecclesiastics"; he suggested a more direct method to him: to warn the offenders individually and to refuse them absolution.

Belmont also wrote an *Histoire du Canada*. His manuscript consisted of two parts: a purely factual account, made up merely of notes covering the period 1608–64, and a memoir on the war against the Iroquois from 1680 to 1700. Although the author lived through the war years he described, he nonetheless obtained the documentation for his history from secondary sources and repeated his predecessors' errors. On the model of the Jesuit *Relations*, and with the same aim of publication and edification, Belmont wrote "Éloges de quelques personnes mortes en odeur de sainteté à Montréal, en Canada." In addition he delivered some funeral orations, among them those of Bishop LAVAL and Governor CALLIÈRE. The Sulpician's writings were always based on a precise plan, but he used rather antiquated language.

In 1701 Vachon de Belmont was called upon, against his will, to succeed DOLLIER de Casson as superior of the Sulpicians in New France. The infrequent injunctions that came from his superior in Paris and the absence of sensational conflicts show that he was able to maintain good relations among the priests of the seminary and with the other civil and religious authorities.

He was nonetheless very active, placing his energies, his many talents, and his well-lined purse at the disposal of the Compagnie de Saint-Sulpice in Montreal. He kept an eye on the planning and building of the seminary in Rue Notre-Dame, the fort at La Montagne, a mill, the façade of Notre-Dame church, and the chapel of the Marian congregation for men, and restored the cellars and roof of the seminary. Furthermore, he met the major part of the expenses thus incurred. According to M. Magnien, the procurator in Paris, it was the money given by Belmont that enabled the company to continue to exist in New France.

During his 31 years as superior, Vachon de Belmont managed the Montreal seigneury, concerned himself with the education of young Frenchmen, organized missions among the Indians, and supervised the parish work and ministry of the Sulpicians in a dozen parishes in the region of Ville-Marie; in all of this he was apparently successful. Unfortunately, the scarcity of records at our disposal does not enable us to determine how this man, who was by nature unstable and fundamentally disturbed, was able to advance the cause of the Compagnie de Saint-Sulpice in Canada.

JACQUES MATHIEU

Vachon de Belmont's writings have been published in both French and English. His *Histoire du Canada* and *Histoire de l'eau-de-vie en Canada* were published by the Literary and Historical Society of Quebec in its series, Historical Documents (D.2, 1840). J. P. Donnelly published them in English in *Mid-America*, XXXIV (1952; new ser., XXIII), 42–72, 115–47, under the titles, *Belmont's history of brandy* and *Belmont's history of Canada*. APQ *Rapport, 1920–21*, 51–59, contains the "Éloge funèbre de Mgr de Laval," and APQ *Rapport, 1929–30*, 143–89, the "Éloges de quelques personnes mortes en odeur de sainteté à Montréal, en Canada, divisés en trois parties."

AQ, François Vachon de Belmont. ASQ, Cahier 1, 20; Fonds Verreau, Ma Saberdache, N, 4, p.15; Lettres, M, 2, 23, 34; Paroisses diverses, 54, 57, 59a, 59b. ASSM, Tiroir 72, pièce 5. PAC, FM 17, 7/2, 1. La Poterie, *Histoire* (1722), I. Saint-Vallier, *Estat présent de l'Église* (1856). É.-Z. Massicotte, "Maçons, entrepreneurs, architectes," *BRH*, XXXV (1929), 132–42.

Casgrain, *Les Sulpiciens en Acadie*. Henri Gauthier, *La Compagnie de Saint-Sulpice au Canada* (Montréal, 1912); *Sulpitiana* (Montréal, 1926). Gosselin, *L'Église du Canada*, I. Olivier Maurault, *Marges d'histoire* (3v., Montréal, 1929–30), III. Pierre Rousseau, *Saint-Sulpice et les missions catholiques* (Montréal, 1930). Pierre Saint-Ovide, *Les Dauphinois au Canada. Essai de catalogue des Dauphinois qui ont pris part à l'établissement du régime français au Canada suivi d'une étude sur un Dauphinois canadien: Antoine Pécody de Contrecœur* (Paris, 1936). *Le troisième centenaire de Saint-Sulpice* (Montréal, 1941).

L.-P. Desrosiers, "Correspondance de M. Magnien," *Cahiers des Dix*, IX (1944), 199–225. "Les disparus," *BRH*, XXXV (1929), 551. Lionel Groulx, "Un seigneur en soutane," *RHAF*, XI (1957–58), 201–17. Olivier Maurault, "1742," *Cahiers des Dix*, VII (1942), 161–84; "Deux précieux manuscrits," *Cahiers des Dix*, XXVIII (1963), 33–42; "Les origines de l'enseignement secondaire à Montréal," *Cahiers des Dix*, I (1936), 95–104; "Quand Saint-Sulpice allait en guerre," *Cahiers des Dix*, V (1940), 11–30. Victor Morin, "La date de la fondation de Montréal," *BRH*, XLII (1936), 396–410.

VAILLANT DE GUESLIS, FRANÇOIS, priest, Jesuit, missionary; b. 20 July 1646 at Orléans, France; d. 24 Sept. 1718 at Moulins.

François Vaillant de Gueslis entered the noviciate of Paris on 10 Nov. 1665 and studied philosophy; he began his theology at La Flèche in 1667. He sailed for Quebec in 1670 without finishing his studies and taught junior classes in the college there, preparing himself at the same time for the priesthood, which was conferred on him by Bishop LAVAL on 1 Dec. 1675. He was first a missionary at Lorette under the guidance of Father Chaumonot*, and left two relations of that mission, for the years 1675 and 1676.

In 1678 he went to the Mohawk country to be an assistant to Father JACQUES DE LAMBERVILLE. He had been alone there since 1682 when the war with the Iroquois forced him to return to Quebec in 1685. In 1686 he became church prefect at the college, and in 1687 minister and at the same time procurator of the mission. He accompanied BRISAY de Denonville on his expedition against the Senecas, and on 19 July 1687 set his hand to the act taking over their country. On 31 December 1687 he went as an ambassador to Thomas Dongan, the governor of New York, to try to persuade him to promote peace between the French and the Iroquois. The demands which Dongan put in the form of an ultimatum on this occasion only made more difficult the negotiations which were underway between the French and the Iroquois, and which failed completely through the fault of the Huron chief, KONDIARONK.

In 1693 Vaillant went to found a residence for the Jesuits at Montreal, and as soon as he arrived he established a community of men. This superiorship ended in 1697. After this he was again appointed procurator at Quebec, where he remained until 1701, when he was sent to set up the Indian mission at Detroit. The hostility of Lamothe Cadillac [LAUMET] forced him to return a few months later. In August 1702 he set off again, with Father Julien GARNIER, to found a mission among the Senecas.

He came back to Montreal in 1706 to assume once more the office of superior, but illness obliged him to give up this position in 1716. After another year spent in Montreal, he had to sail back to France, where he ended his days.

LUCIEN CAMPEAU

ASJCF. Rochemonteix, *Les Jésuites et la N.-F. au XVIIe siècle*, I, 99; II, 413; III, 204–8.

VALMUR, LOUIS-FRÉDÉRIC BRICAULT DE. *See* BRICAULT

VALRENNES, PHILIPPE CLÉMENT DU VUAULT (VAULT) ET DE. *See* CLÉMENT

VANE, GEORGE, engineer at St John's, Newfoundland, in 1708, and at Annapolis Royal, 1711–15; d. Bombay, India, 1 May 1722.

After serving the exiled King James II of England until his death in 1701, Vane worked as a military engineer for the Republic of Venice. The Elector of Bavaria (France's ally) sent for him as his chief engineer, a position which he assumed after eight months' imprisonment in the Tyrol under suspicion of espionage. Following Bavaria's defeat in 1703, he made his way home to England.

Appointed engineer to replace Robert LATHAM at St John's in 1707, he reached the port the following year. He had very little time to improve the defences before the French attack under Saint-Ovide de Brouillan [Mombeton*] on 22 Dec. 1708 (o.s.), although new palisades which he had built delayed the attackers briefly. Probably because of his Jacobite sympathies, some British officers suspected him of conspiracy with the French: Major Thomas LLOYD, the garrison commander, called him a "cowardly villian" [*sic*] and "a traytor." The French, who for their part allowed him as a prisoner of war to wander freely about Placentia (1709), worried that the British would make use of his knowledge of the French port's defences. Yet after being released in July 1710 from confinement in Dinan, France, he was allowed to make his way to England, where he was invited to recommend improved facilities for the defence of the various ports in Newfoundland. He advised that, although the easiest and cheapest place to fortify was Ferryland (the first preference of others, such as MOODY and CUMINGS), the harbour of St John's was the largest and best. A new fort there, on a height called the Admiral's Rock, should replace the old ones.

Sent once more to North America in 1711, Vane took part in the ill-fated WALKER expedition against Quebec, after which Brigadier-General JOHN HILL assigned him to the garrison at Annapolis. Vane's first two years there, under the governorship of Samuel VETCH, were stormy. Vetch took an early dislike to him and found his cost estimates for the fortifications excessive. Vane, on his side, in letters to the home government, denounced his superior as a good governor "for his own profit," one likely to drive away the Acadians whose agriculture the colony needed. While Vane asked for funds for fortifications, Vetch requested an official policy ruling; but the British government was apathetic.

Vane frequently angered other officers with his Jacobite opinions. On one occasion in 1712, Lawrence ARMSTRONG, "not being able longer to bear It broke a large Glass decanter full of wine upon his head and had verry near sent him to the other world." Forbearing to discipline Vane lest it appear to be personal revenge, Vetch merely complained to the Board of Ordnance; but in

Varennes

September 1713 he found a charge under which Vane could be—and was—court-martialed and suspended from duty: Vane had accused another officer (Captain John Adams) of conniving with the governor to appropriate military stores to private purposes.

Evidently the Board of Ordnance, to whom NICHOLSON referred the matter, reinstated Vane. Vane must have worked well with Nicholson who, in spite of the government's reluctance to spend money on fortifications, gave him substantial responsibility. When Vetch was reappointed to the governorship, Vane transferred to the East India Company's service as a lieutenant in a Bombay infantry regiment (1716); was promoted major of an artillery company in 1718; and in 1722 died of apoplexy in Bombay.

F. J. THORPE

AN, Col., B, 32, f.168;. C¹¹ᶜ, 6, ff.208, 259. BM, Sloane MS 3607, ff.11, 14 et seq., 16, 23v–25, 39–40v; Stowe MS 246, ff.4–5v, 18. PAC, Nova Scotia A, 3, p.287; 4, pp.21, 27; 5, pp.227–30; 6, pp.175–78; 7, pp.49, 127–29, 130–32, 133–34, 135–38; 8, pp.18, 24–26. PRO, C.O. 194/4, nos.76vii, 100ii, 109ix, 143iii, vi, 144; 194/6; 195/4, p.424. Documents relating to currency in Nova Scotia, 1675–1758 (Shortt), 42–43. PRO, B.T.Journal, 1704–1708/9, 1708/9–1714/15; CSP, Col., 1706–8, 1708–9, 1710–11, 1711–12, 1712–14, 1714–15. Dalton, English army lists, VI. Brebner, New England's outpost, 60. Waller, Samuel Vetch, 247–48.

VARENNES (Devarenne, De Varenne), JEAN-BAPTISTE GAULTIER (Gauthier, Gautier) DE.
See GAULTIER

VAUDREUIL, PHILIPPE DE RIGAUD DE.
See RIGAUD

VAUGHAN, DAVID, HBC captain; d. 1720?
The first firm date we have for David Vaughan is 15 May 1713 when he contracted to serve the HBC as a carpenter for four years at £36 for the first year and £40 thereafter. He obviously had other talents, for in June of that year he sailed for Fort Albany as mate of the Prosperous hoy. On 6 Sept. 1714 he sailed from Albany in the sloop Eastmain for York to assist James KNIGHT "to build and fortifye That Place." But a month later, 15 miles short of his destination, a storm coated the sloop so heavily with ice that to prevent her foundering she was run ashore, and Vaughan and five men walked to York Fort, where they arrived 17 October. They returned by dog team to unload the sloop on 25 October but she had vanished without trace. Vaughan remained at York until

5 June 1716 when Knight ordered him to take two men and an Indian guide and return to Fort Albany. There he was to take command of the Prosperous and, with three extra men, bring provisions and trade goods back to York Fort. On 17 September Knight, in a letter to the council, not only absolved Vaughan from any blame in the loss of the Eastmain but recommended him for another command: "you cannot have a soberer or a brisker man."

The following summer (1717) Vaughan commanded the Success which, with the Prosperous (Capt. Michael GRIMINGTON), sailed in the expedition under Knight to establish Fort Prince of Wales at the Churchill River. In July he cut his foot badly while getting timber but by mid-August he was sufficiently recovered to pilot the Prosperous out and the Hudson's Bay [III] in to Churchill. On 23 August Knight sent him to York Fort with an armourer, sawyer, and two men to help strengthen that place, and he returned to Churchill 13 September. In the summer of 1718, again with the Success, he sailed north along the western shore of the bay and opened a trade with the Eskimos. Later that year he returned to England on the frigate Albany (Capt. George BERLEY).

In 1719 he sailed from the Thames as captain of the new sloop Discovery, accompanied by Berley in the Albany, on Knight's ill-fated expedition which was wrecked on Marble Island. Presumably he died in 1720.

ERNEST S. DODGE

Founding of Churchill (Kenney). HBRS, XXI (Rich); XXV (Davies and Johnson).

VAUGHAN, GEORGE, merchant and politician, lieutenant-governor of New Hampshire, 1715–17; b. 13 April 1676 at Portsmouth, N.H., son of Major William and Margaret (Cutt) Vaughan; d. 20 Nov. 1724.

A graduate of Harvard College in 1696, Vaughan followed his father's example and became active in the commercial and political life of New Hampshire. On 8 Dec. 1698 he married Mary Belcher, who died a little more than a year later. He was married again on 9 Jan. 1700/1, this time to Elizabeth Eliot. They had nine children, the most notable being William*, who played a key role in the capture of Louisbourg in 1745.

In 1708, Vaughan went to England as agent of the New Hampshire assembly, to represent New Hampshire residents in London and to protect their rights and privileges. In 1710 he volunteered to serve in the expedition led by Francis NICHOLSON against Port-Royal (Annapolis Royal,

N.S.). Little is known about Vaughan's contribution to the expedition. However, Nicholson asserted that Vaughan "imbark'd, landed & march'd with me into the Field, & behav'd himself with good Courage & Diligence, & was the chief Gentleman Voluntier of New England in that Expedition."

In 1713 Vaughan with two other commissioners represented New Hampshire in drafting the treaty with the Abenakis, whose chief spokesman was Mog. Two years later Vaughan returned to London as agent and was appointed lieutenant-governor of New Hampshire. By stressing the royal prerogative, Vaughan alienated the political leaders of New Hampshire and was therefore removed from office in September 1717. When he died in 1724 he left an estate valued at £12,190.

G. A. RAWLYK

Documentary hist. of Maine, XXIII. PRO, *CSP, Col., 1708–9*, 21–24. *Genealogical dictionary of Maine and New Hampshire*, ed. Sybil Noyes *et al.* (Portland, Me., 1928–39). Shipton, *Sibley's Harvard graduates*, IV, 308–15. McLennan, *Louisbourg*, 367–68.

VÉNIARD DE BOURGMOND, ÉTIENNE DE, officer, coureur de bois, explorer of the Missouri; b. *c.* 1675 in the province of Normandy, son of Charles de Véniard Du Vergier and Jacqueline Jean; ennobled in 1725; d. in France.

If others before him had ventured into the region, Bourgmond can nevertheless be considered to be the first explorer of the Missouri, for he went farther up it than his predecessors and wrote down his observations in two detailed reports which furnished the material for mapping the region accurately.

Bourgmond came to Canada in 1695, and everything leads us to believe that he had been deported. At first he doubtless served as a soldier, for it was not until 1705 that he was given the expectancy of an ensign's commission. In 1702 he took part in CHARLES JUCHEREAU de Saint-Denys' expedition down the Ohio. He was attached to the garrison of Fort Pontchartrain at Detroit, and in 1706 he took command of it in the absence of Antoine LAUMET, *dit* de Lamothe Cadillac, and ALPHONSE TONTY. With about 15 soldiers it was difficult to maintain order among the tribes living nearby, who were allies of the French but who distrusted one another. When the Ottawas [*see* LE PESANT] fell unexpectedly upon a group of Miamis, Bourgmond, who had not been able to prevent the incident, shut the gates of the fort and opened fire upon the assailants. A few Miamis, 30 Ottawas, one soldier, and the Recollet Constantin DELHALLE lost their lives in the affray. Although Lamothe first praised the young officer's bravery, the authorities rebuked him instead for his blunder. The account left by the commissary CLAIRAMBAULT d'Aigremont is damning for Bourgmond. But this account was written two years later when Bourgmond had become a mere deserter who merited no consideration whatsoever. It was probably towards the end of 1706 that Bourgmond and the soldier Jolicoeur deserted to go to live in the woods with Pichon, *dit* Larose, and a French woman, the wife of a certain La Chenette. Desertions at Detroit were, indeed, a common matter; it was reported in 1703 that one third of the garrison had disappeared. When Larose was brought back to the fort and tried by court-martial in November 1707, he tried to cast all the blame on Bourgmond, in a vain attempt to save his own life. Bourgmond, he said, was caching beaver pelts on an island in Lake Erie and was "ready to go over to the English and to live with them for good." Cashiered and treated as a ne'er-do-well, Bourgmond spent the next five years in the depths of the woods, probably living in the Lake Erie region, with an 18-month stay among the Mascoutens of the Lower Ohio to trade in pelts.

It was not until 1712 that Bourgmond met the Missouri Indians, probably while accompanying some of them on their way back after they had come to the help of RENAUD Dubuisson, who had been menaced at Detroit by the Foxes [*see* PEMOUSSA]. But he did not stay long in their territory and went down to Mobile to spread the news of his new acquaintances and to offer his services, in return for payment, to bring about alliances with the various tribes of the Missouri region. His proposal was accepted, for the French were nourishing the dream of commanding an access route to New Mexico and perhaps to the Western Sea, as well as of appropriating mines that were said to be very rich. Bourgmond devoted the year 1713 to visiting Louisiana and stopped for a time with the Illinois Indians before undertaking the exploration of the Missouri in March 1714.

His appearances at the Jesuit missions in the period from 1712 to 1714 brought on an avalanche of denunciations. In unison Fathers PIERRE-GABRIEL MAREST and Jean-Marie de VILLES, the bishop, and M. de RAMEZAY wrote that he was leading a life that was not only scandalous but also criminal, in that he was causing disorders among the Illinois and was preparing to bring the English into the region. There can be no doubt about the very free morals of the coureur de bois, but there are no facts to bear out the accusation of treason. Bourgmond's dissolute life was enough, however, to rouse the wrath of the missionaries,

Véniard de Bourgmond

who were above all intent upon protecting the Illinois' morals. The minister of Marine satisfied those who were complaining by giving Cadillac secret orders to have Bourgmond arrested, but the governor of Louisiana does not seem to have been in a hurry to carry them out.

Bourgmond has left two reports on the 1714 exploration trip, which took him to the junction of the Missouri and Cheyenne Rivers. The first report contains topographical data covering the region from the mouth of the Missouri as far as the Platte River. The second completes the first with geographical and ethnographical observations, covering the area as far as the territory of the Arikaras. After he had sent off his reports, Bourgmond remained for four more years in the region, then went back to Louisiana at the time of the war against the Spanish, in which he took part. Le Moyne* de Bienville requested that he be awarded the cross of the order of Saint-Louis, and the council wanted to send him back to the Missouri country to pacify the various tribes there. But Bourgmond, whom the company still owed 4,279 *livres*, preferred to sail for France with his son, who was born around 1714 in the Missouri country.

It became evident, however, that it was more and more urgent to consolidate the French positions to the west of the Mississippi, believed to be menaced by the Spanish after Pedro de Villazur's ill-starred expedition. An end to the permanent warfare which raged between the Padoucas (Comanches), who controlled access to New Mexico, and the other tribes whom Bourgmond had won over to the side of France was especially desirable, for it was impossible to conclude an alliance with the former without alienating the others. After DUTISNÉ's failure, Bourgmond was considered to be the only person capable of carrying out this enterprise. Upon his arrival in France he was awarded a captain's commission, with the title of commandant of the Missouri country, and the cross of the order of Saint-Louis. On 17 Jan. 1722 he was commissioned by the Compagnie des Indes to establish a fortified post on the Missouri, from which it would be possible to enter into relations with the Spanish, end the war against the Padoucas, and, when his mission was completed, bring some Indians back to France to make them aware of the king's power and rekindle the public's interest in the undertakings in Louisiana. If all these conditions were fulfilled within a period of two years, Bourgmond would be authorized to live in France, where he had just been married, and would receive the patent of nobility that he was seeking.

Many delays and vexations were to characterize this second expedition. Bourgmond and his company did not arrive among the Missouris until November, just in time to prevent the Otos and Iowas from concluding an alliance with the Foxes. Despite illness and the insubordination of his lieutenants, Bourgmond succeeded in having the Fort d'Orléans built, some 450 kilometres from the mouth of the river, opposite the Missouris' village. Despite the hesitations of the officers of the colony, who now considered the undertaking chimerical and costly, Bourgmond, who had finally received supplies, embarked upon the pacification trip. Acclaimed everywhere as a chief, he rallied the Missouris, Otos, Osages, Pawnees, Iowas, and Kansas, who came in his wake to offer to make peace with the Padoucas, giving up at the same time a profitable trade in slaves. The engineer La Renaudière took part in this triumphal expedition and is believed to be the author of the account which has been preserved of it. He noted that the child whom Bourgmond had taken to France shared in all the honours bestowed upon his father, and that it was thanks to his return for good among his own people that the council of the nations, meeting at Fort d'Orléans on 5 Oct. 1724, having received assurances about the risks of the voyage, agreed to send ten delegates beyond the seas.

These delegates arrived at New Orleans with Bourgmond, but there, as an economy measure, the delegation was reduced to four persons. These were the Missouri, Osage, and Oto chiefs Menspéré, Boganientim, and Aguiguida, and the daughter of a Missouri chief, Ignon Ouaconisen, who was accompanied by her slave Pilate. The Illinois Chicagou, chief of the village of the Michigameas, went to France at the same time, but being the only Christian in the group, he was under the care of Father Beaubois*, who kept him away from Bourgmond's Indians as much as possible and obtained some private audiences for him.

They first sailed on the *Bellone*, which sank as it was leaving the roadstead, and despite the fright which this accident caused them the delegates sailed off again and arrived in Paris 20 Sept. 1725. There they were immediately received at the head office of the Compagnie des Indes, along with Bourgmond, who acted as their interpreter throughout their stay. A second and more formal audience took place on 8 November on the occasion of a directors' meeting. The comptroller-general, Charles-Gaspard Dodun, replied to the speeches of the representatives of the Three Nations and of the Illinois chief and had tobacco, Indian and sumptuous French costumes distributed to them. On 22 November they were received at Fontainebleau by the Duc de Bourbon, who presented them at court, and two days later ushered them into the king's chambers. "Our territories are yours," declared the spokesman for the Three Nations; "settle French people there, protect us, and give us White Collars [priests of the Séminaire des Missions Étrangères], or prayer leaders to give us instruction." Thereupon each took off his chief's insignia and placed it, feathers, bows, and quivers, at the monarch's feet. The king questioned Bourgmond and the Jesuit at length on the customs and religion of the Indians and had a presentation made to each delegate of a gold medal, a watch, arms, and a picture painted for the occasion and representing the audience. Before returning to Port-Louis the Indians also had the honour of going hunting with the king.

During this stay, which lasted two months, they also visited all the interesting sights of the capital; the fountains of Versailles and Marly played for them; at the Théâtre des Italiens two of the chiefs gave a performance of dances which were found rather disconcerting. Never had the city and the court received Indians with so much display, but all this show had meagre results. A year after the delegates had returned to their country, Fort d'Orléans was evacuated and abandoned to some Canadian fur-traders.

Having renounced the New World and a life of adventure, and having been ennobled by letters patent in December 1725, Bourgmond still had to claim 3,000 *livres* in salary and for reimbursement of his out-of-pocket expenses incurred in providing the Indians during their stay at New Orleans and the crossing with the rations of bread and meat that the Conseil de la Colonie had refused to issue them. "He is staying in Paris," he wrote, "only to wait for you to render him the justice that is due him." It is not known whether the Compagnie des Indes did reimburse him, for from then on Bourgmond left no trace, whilst Fort d'Orléans and the precarious peace which were his work were likewise soon forgotten.

LOUISE DECHÊNE

Véniard de Bourgmond, "Routte qu'il faut tenir pour monter la rivière du Missoury," AN, Marine, 3JJ, 201 [published by Marc de Villiers Du Terrage in *La découverte du Missouri et l'histoire du fort d'Orléans (1673–1728)* (Paris, 1925), 46–59]; "L'Exacte Description de la Louisianne, de ses ports, terres et rivières, et noms des nations sauvages qui l'occupent, et des commerces et avantages que l'on en peut tirer dans l'établissement d'une colonie," AN, Col., C¹³ᶜ, 1, ff.346–56 [published by Marcel Giraud in *Revue historique*, CCXVII (1957), 29–41]. Other sources used include: AN, Col., B, 36, 37; C¹¹ᴬ, 21, 29, 34, 35; C¹¹ᴱ, 14, 15; C¹³ᴬ, 5, 9; C¹³ᶜ, 1, 4; D²ᶜ, 49, 51, 222; E, 48 (dossier de Bourgmond); F³, 2. BN, MS, Cabinet des titres, P.O. 2959 (Bourgmond's letters of nobility); a copy of this document is published in *BRH*, XXIV (1918), 254–56. BN, MS, NAF, 2551, ff.81–82; 9304 (Margry). SHA, A¹, 2592.

Charlevoix, *Histoire* (1744). *Découvertes et établissements des Français* (Margry), VI. [Le Mascrier], *Mémoires historiques sur la Louisiane ... composés sur les mémoires de M. Dumont par M.L.L.M.* (2v., Paris, 1753). *Mercure de France* (Paris), décembre 1725. Le Jeune, *Dictionnaire*. Giraud, *Histoire de la Louisiane française*, I, II, III.

VERCHÈRES, PIERRE JARRET DE. *See* JARRET

VÉRON DE GRANDMESNIL, ÉTIENNE, militia captain, notary; b. 31 Oct. 1649 at Trois-Rivières, son of Jean Véron de Grandmesnil, who had come from Normandy, and of Marguerite Hayet; d. 18 May 1721 at Trois-Rivières.

Véron de Grandmesnil was only three years old when his father was killed by the Iroquois; his mother, who was Pierre-Esprit RADISSON's half-sister, married shortly afterwards the famous Médard Chouart* Des Groseilliers. However, "as he was the cause of several quarrels and differences between his mother and his step-father over the question of punishment, Étienne's guardian, Étienne Seigneuret, assumed responsibility for him in return for 20 *livres* a year." When he was old enough to study, the Jesuits were charged with taking him in as a boarder and teaching him "all the necessary subjects."

In 1667 he was still at Trois-Rivières. The census of that year indicates that he was living there with his mother, his brother Guillaume, his half-brother Jean-Baptiste, and his half-sister Marie-Antoinette Chouart. Grandmesnil was interested in the fur trade, since in 1676 Intendant Duchesneau* summoned him, with some 20 other notables of the colony, to a meeting to discuss fixing the prices of beaver furs.

In 1680 his mother shared his father's land with him and the 1681 census mentions that he had one servant in his employ, and that he owned 7 head of cattle and 45 acres under cultivation. In 1682 he was chosen as churchwarden of the parish of Trois-Rivières, and in that capacity he took part in the building of a new church. He was also appointed militia captain of the parish. In 1684 and 1685 he signed two contracts for the hiring out of domestic animals.

Subsequently he seems to have given up working the land since he became the secretary of Lamothe Cadillac [LAUMET]. It is very possible that Véron de Grandmesnil had a share in the founding of the post at Detroit. Having returned to Montreal, he espoused his master's interests, and as Cadillac's attorney signed many transactions, conventions,

Verreau

and agreements. In 1706 he obtained a commission as a notary, and he exercised this profession until 1720. The document confirming his commission has been lost, and there is little likelihood that he was a royal notary, for the majority of texts omit this term.

In 1677, at Trois-Rivières, Véron de Grandmesnil had married Marie-Thérèse Moral, daughter of Quentin Moral de Saint-Quentin, king's lieutenant, and of Marie Marguerie, Jacques Hertel* de La Fresnière's widow. Of the nine children born of this marriage, one was Étienne*, who became a merchant and was the receiver of His Highness Louis-Alexandre de Bourbon, Comte de Toulouse and admiral of France.

ROLAND-J. AUGER

AJM, Greffe d'Antoine Adhémar, 26 juillet 1709, 6 sept. 1710, 31 mai 1713; Greffe de J.-B. Pottier, 19 mai 1701. AJTR, Greffe de Séverin Ameau, 30 mai 1677, 5 juillet 1680, 13, 19 juillet, 29 oct. 1682, 3 oct. 1684, 25 janv. 1685; Greffe de J.-B. Pottier, 7 févr. 1702; Greffe d'Étienne Véron de Grandmesnil, 1705–20. *Jug. et délib.*, I, 273; IV, 38; V, 989; VI, 121, 130, 211. Recensements du Canada, 1666 (APQ *Rapport*), 1681 (Sulte). "Les notaires au Canada," 34. Vachon, "Inv. critique des notaires royaux," *RHAF*, X (1956–57), 388. J.-E. Roy, *Histoire du notariat*, I, 193, 369. Vachon, *Histoire du notariat*, 37.

VERREAU, BARTHÉLÉMY, clerk of court and notary; b. 12 July 1678 at Château-Richer; son of Barthélémy Verreau, *dit* Le Bourguignon, of Saint-Jean de Dijon (Burgundy), maker of edge tools or blacksmith at Château-Richer prior to his marriage with Marthe Quittel (Guittel, Quitter, Quintal) on 22 Sept. 1665; buried 3 June 1718 at Château-Richer.

Thanks to his education, probably received at the school founded by Bishop LAVAL at Château-Richer, Verreau was able to become an important person in the locality, although he started as a blacksmith, as his father had been. On 7 March 1709 the superiors of the seminary of Quebec, who were seigneurs of Beaupré, appointed him clerk of their seigneurial court, and on the 23d of the same month he was received and sworn in, in succession to Guillaume Maroist, who had died. He even officiated temporarily as a judge of this court in 1711, during Étienne JACOB's illness. Implied in the commission of a seigneurial court clerk was that of a notary; hence, although Barthélémy Verreau was not formally declared a notary until 9 Oct. 1714, his registry, which has been preserved in the Palais de Justice of Quebec, covers the period 1710–18.

On 13 Feb. 1708, he had married at Quebec Marguerite Prieur, who gave him six children.

On 18 Jan. 1721, at Château-Richer, his widow took as her second husband Pierre Gravelle.

HONORIUS PROVOST

AAQ, Registres d'insinuation A, 290, 328. AJQ, Greffe de Jacques Barbel, 13 janv. 1721; Greffe de Louis Chambalon, 12 févr. 1708; Greffe de Pierre Duquet, 31 août 1665. AQ, NF, Ins. de la Prév. de Québec, II, 268; III, 623. ASQ, Séminaire, XX–XXV. A. Roy, *Inv. greffes not.*, VII, 267. P.-G. Roy, *Inv. contrats de mariage*, III, 136; V, 173; VI, 98; *Inv. ins. prév. Québec*, III, 104; *Inv. testaments*, VII, 267. Tanguay, *Dictionnaire*, VI, 450; VII, 446f. J.-E. Roy, *Histoire du notariat*, I, 170f. "Les cinq premières années d'un pionnier de la Nouvelle-France," *Le mois généalogique* (Montréal), I (juillet, août 1948), 28f.; I (avril 1948), 14.

VERVILLE, JEAN-FRANÇOIS DE, engineer, director of fortifications for Île Royale (Cape Breton Island), 1717–1725, knight of the order of Saint-Louis; b. in France, probably after 1680; father of Louis, Chevalier de Verville (1704–1784) and Guillaume (1707–1751), distinguished members of the corps of engineers; d. 1729 at Valenciennes, France; his widow was still living in 1751.

Accepted into the corps of engineers in 1704, Verville served in Spain and Germany during the War of the Spanish Succession, being wounded at the siege of Landau in 1713. In 1714 he was appointed assistant chief engineer at Douai in Flanders. After taking part, the following year, in a reconnaissance of the island of Majorca, he accepted a North American assignment as an alternative to remaining in the Spanish theatre. Apparently upon the recommendation of the Marquis d'Asfeld, director-general of fortifications and a member of the council of Marine under the regency, Verville was named director of fortifications for Île Royale.

Following a reconnaissance of the island in 1716, Verville recommended Louisbourg as the capital and main fortress of the colony. In 1717 he directed the preparation of plans for its fortifications, and (on a smaller scale) those of Port Dauphin (Englishtown, N.S.) and Port Toulouse (St Peters). From 1719 (when the construction contract was awarded to Michel-Philippe ISABEAU) until 1724, Verville directed the work during the summer months, leaving the assistant-engineers JEAN-BAPTISTE DE COUAGNE and Pierre-Jérôme Boucher* in charge while he wintered in France. In 1724, Étienne Verrier* was appointed resident chief engineer. He worked under Verville's direction until the following year, when the latter was transferred to the fortress of Valenciennes in northern France. Verville died there in 1729.

Verville's responsibility from 1716 to 1725 was

648

to fortify the new headquarters of the French North American fishery, having due regard to the requirements of trade and strategy. Permanent fortifications, not necessarily on the European scale, were to be built in proportion to the relatively small garrison provided. Hindsight allows us to criticize Verville for not building, at low cost, well-revetted earthworks on the landward side, combined with masonry batteries for seaward defence. Such a system might well have proved effective. His *enceinte*, based on the first and simplest of the three systems of fortification developed by Sébastien Le Prestre de Vauban, the director-general of fortifications in the armies of Louis XIV, proved extremely costly because of the climate and the need to transport suitable materials, labour, and beasts of burden from France. Winter frosts and thaws hindered the setting of the mortar. Verville anticipated events in giving priority to the landward defences and in designing an excellent battery at the entrance to the harbour, but there is evidence to suggest that structural faults in the Château Saint-Louis and the Royal Battery were attributable in part to his design.

It was primarily economic and political factors which made it so difficult to construct a great masonry fortress at Louisbourg. Workers had to earn enough during the short construction season (90 to 100 days, according to Verville) to subsist for the rest of the year. The wages of skilled craftsmen were already high because of their scarcity. Even where local building materials were suitable, a mishap at what was usually the only source of supply (such as the destruction by fire of the brick-kiln at Port Toulouse in 1723) could cause prices to rise sharply. The special fortifications budget, which the financial commissary was expected to control separately from general funds, ranged from 80,000 to 150,000 *livres* a year (1718–23, and 1724 respectively), but there was no provision for those years (e.g., 1722) when the contractor had spent all the funds before the end of good weather. Attempts to continue working on private credit, which drew attention to the fiscal weakness of the colony, were not approved at Versailles. The situation was further aggravated by illegal borrowings from the fortifications account for the purpose of paying other public bills. Verville's proposed solution was to make the local treasurer of fortifications responsible directly to the corresponding treasurer-general in France. The council of Marine, however, insisted on retaining control through its own financial commissary, at the same time warning Verville of disciplinary action if he continued to break its rules.

The court did give to the construction of fortifications and public buildings priority over all other military activity until the work was finished. Skilled miners and industrious Swiss mercenaries were sent in 1723 to help. Verville's opinions as a specialist were almost always accepted over those of his critics, particularly of Saint-Ovide [Mombeton*], the governor, with whom his differences were frequent and varied. Verville, who reputedly was quick-tempered, condoned no interference with his direction of the construction (which he considered his private preserve), and on many issues ignored the governor's authority. For example, he failed to inform him that he was building small casemates (as powder magazines) in the right face of the King's Bastion although he had not included them in the original cost estimates (*devis*). For his part, the governor, who was no engineer, criticized Verville for what he considered to be fortifications far too grand for their intended purpose and unsuited to an inevitable attack from the sea. He also accused him of favouring the contractor (implying collusion for personal gain), and, after Verville's departure in the autumn, gave orders to the assistant-engineers contrary to the latter's (particularly to build houses with funds from the fortifications account).

Saint-Ovide and Le Normant* de Mézy (the financial commissary) held, with some justification, that a resident engineer was required whether Verville, as director, visited the site every summer or not. Verville's long absences were inconvenient to the orderly administration of the colony, but they also put him in closer and more frequent touch with the court than that enjoyed by the administrators of the colony themselves. The latter proposed Boisberthelot* de Beaucours as the resident engineer, praising his knowledge of colonial fortifications; but when Maurepas finally approved the post, a member of the corps of engineers, Verrier, was chosen over Beaucours.

Saint-Ovide and Mézy also pressed the case for a builder with colonial experience when bids were being invited in 1723 for the contract to construct the Royal Battery and the Island Battery. They asked Bégon*, intendant of New France, to encourage bidders from Quebec. Verville, for his part, insisted on the need for someone with European experience in constructing masonry fortifications. So he supported Isabeau and belittled the claims of the Canadians. After Isabeau's death, Verville exerted influence in the selection of François Ganet*, who had done similar work in France.

A significant area of neglect on Verville's part may have been his failure to provide an annual definitive account (*toisé définitif*) of all construction work done, which was supposed to be the legal basis for payments to the contractor.

Vetch

Verville—not his assistants—was responsible for these, but he regularly left the colony on one of the last ships for France before the work was ready for the necessary measurements to be made and the costs calculated. Meanwhile, the contractors were paid on the basis of vouchers submitted by the engineers—although only preliminary measurements had been taken—leaving the final settling of the definitive account between the king and the contractor. Not only was this delayed, to the possible detriment of the public interest, but also financial settlements between contractors (e.g., Isabeau's heirs and Ganet) were unduly protracted. A heavy burden was bequeathed to Verrier, who had to prepare final accounts on work done before his time.

The quiet transfer of Verville to Valenciennes in 1725 indicates Maurepas's belief that the objectives could be met by leaving the more conciliatory Verrier in charge of the work. On the other hand, the minister of Marine was not prepared to condone outright condemnation by the governor of an engineer who had earned his laurels on European battlefields, and whose prestige was apparently high in the *élite* unit to which he belonged.

In Canada, Verville's reputation has suffered because of the difficulties which ensued from building an elaborate European fortress on a bleak North American shore. Perhaps, not being able to predict the effects of the climate and local materials on orthodox masonry structures (as Verrier suggested in 1727), it was inevitable that he should make errors from which his successors could, to some degree, benefit. On the other hand, the prestige of the corps of engineers was so high in France that policy-makers could see little need for colonial experience in selecting engineers for the colonies. For Louisbourg in particular, they felt they had only to send out a veteran of the corps in order to have policy implemented. All this considered, Verville remains the original architect of a fortress and townsite which greatly impressed its contemporaries and which may claim, with Quebec and Montreal, to be foremost among historical sites of the French régime.

F. J. THORPE

BN, Cartes et plans, 23271, Portefeuille 131, div.10, no.1^D. Archives Maritimes, Port de Rochefort, E, 1E, 89, f.197; 90, ff.307, 517, 542; 93, ff.24, 119; 94, ff.571–72, 678, 748; 96, f.641; 97, f.9; 99, ff.223, 283, 671, 695–99; 101, ff.39, 759; 103, ff.105, 173; 105, ff.149, 475, 531. AN, Col., B, 38, f.279v; 39, ff.266–69, 302v; 40, f.568v; 41, ff.569, 587; 42, ff.481, 491v; 44, ff.60v, 179–80v, 560, 569–74v, 577v–78v; 45, ff.93v, 301, 1119, 1151; 46, ff.109, 114; 47, ff.1239, 1242, 1247; 48, ff.925, 929, 932; 49, f.703; 50, ff.570–72, 597v–99; 52, ff.588–93, 598v; 53, ff.602v–6; 54, f.16v;

C^{11B}, 1, ff.421, 438–40v, 460–61v; 2, ff.14–20v, 34–37v, 69–74, 75–83, 119, 131, 193, 251–52, 304–10; 3, ff.12–13v, 67, 115–16, 119–30v; 4, ff.15–18, 39–45, 66, 71–71v, 73–74v, 76–85, 107–8v, 120–23v, 133, 142–42v, 211–13v, 224, 235–36, 237–41v, 243–46; 5, ff.116–18, 136–43v, 148–55v, 177–79, 202–5, 206–16, 218–19, 220–23, 228, 231–33v, 235–37, 238–40v, 324, 328, 349–56, 386–88v, 414–16, 418–19, 420–21; 6, ff.30–51, 112–13, 114, 116–18, 145–48, 152, 164, 170, 178, 182, 199, 209, 235, 293, 295, 298, 325, 327; 7, ff.12–13, 59–65v, 132–33, 136–37v, 142–50, 154, 156, 194–97v, 261, 328; 8, ff.71–75, 115; 9, ff.31, 93, 141–47v; 10, ff.81, 131–40; C^{11C}, 16, pièce 6, no.15 (fortifications, 1724); F^3, 51, ff.31–40, 41–54, 57–61, 63–74, 75–85, 86, 87–92, 93–94, 105, 128–47v, 189–91v, 193–226, 227–50; Marine, C^7, carton 344 (dossier de Verville; 1723, et 15 oct. 1751); Section Outre-Mer, Dépôt des fortifications des colonies, carton 3, nos.135, 143, 145–47, 149; carton 4, nos.245–47; carton 5, nos.258, 260, 261–62, 268–69. CTG, art.3, sect.1, carton 1, pièces 4, 5, 6, 7; art.14, Majorque, carton 1, pièces 6, 7.

[M.-L.-E. Moreau de Saint-Méry], *Description topographique, physique, civile, politique et historique de la partie française de l'isle Saint-Domingue, par Moreau de St-Méry*, éd. Blanche Maurel et Étienne Taillemite (3v., Paris, 1958). A.-M. Augoyat, *Aperçu historique sur les fortifications, les ingénieurs et sur le Corps du Génie en France* (3v., Paris, 1860, 1862, 1864), I, 385, 427n., 447–48. McLennan, *Louisbourg*, 42, 50–52, 53, 57.

VETCH, SAMUEL, commander of the garrison at Annapolis Royal, governor of Nova Scotia, and proponent of a plan for the conquest of New France; b. 9 Dec. 1668 (o.s.), in Edinburgh, Scotland, second son of William Veitch, a leading Presbyterian minister, and Marion Fairly Veitch, of a respected Edinburgh family; d. 30 April 1732 in London.

At the age of 15, Vetch and his brother William were sent to Holland to join their father who had fled Charles II's persecution of the Covenanters. There they studied at Utrecht until they joined the forces of William of Orange bound for England in 1688. Vetch later acquired military experience in the battles of the War of the League of Augsburg, rising to the rank of captain. At war's end, he sailed in the ambitious Scottish expedition to Darien (Central America), was elected to the council of that ill-starred colony, and in August 1699 arrived in New York with the starving survivors of the project.

His commanding presence and natural gifts earned him easy acceptance amongst the merchant families of New York. In late 1700 he married Margaret, sister of John LIVINGSTON and daughter of the prominent Scottish merchant, Robert Livingston, Lord of the Manor of Livingston, member of the New York council, and holder of important posts in Albany. Vetch shortly began a lucrative, though illegal, trade with New France. Disclosure of his ventures, combined with political disruption of the colony and the outbreak of Queen Anne's War (War of the Spanish Succession), occasioned his removal to Boston, where by 1705 he could see the possibility of undertaking new trading ventures to Canada under the cover of negotiations for prisoner exchange. Governor Dudley entrusted him with returning AUGUSTIN LE GARDEUR de Courtemanche to Quebec in the fall of 1705; the latter was carrying the rejection of a peace proposal made by Governor RIGAUD de Vaudreuil. Vetch used the opportunity to assess the resources of New France and to attempt to re-establish trading connections. He eventually found opportunities for trade in Acadia. Combining trade with espionage, Vetch and other Boston ship-captains continued their activities until public outcry forced an end to this illegal trade. Many people were alarmed that weapons were among the articles going to Acadia. Tried and convicted by the Massachusetts General Court in 1706, Vetch went to England where, the following year, he obtained acquittal from the Privy Council on the grounds that the Massachusetts legislature had exceeded its authority.

At once Vetch advanced a larger project to Queen Anne's court; nothing less than the conquest of New France. With unusual breadth of view, he combined the schemes of 1690 and New England's efforts against Acadia in a sweeping paper, "Canada Survey'd," submitted in July 1708, in which he outlined the advantages and strategy of totally defeating France in the New World. Supported by friends he had made among the Whig lords and by letters from several colonial governors, Vetch won the queen's approval for the "Glorious Enterprise," a commission as colonel, and the promise of the governorship of Canada after it was taken.

With former Virginia governor Colonel Francis NICHOLSON as a volunteer, Vetch returned to Boston in April 1709 to get the support of the colonists for the expedition while impatiently awaiting the arrival of the promised British ships and sailors. Only in October did the dismal news come to the angered colonists that the enterprise had been cancelled owing to the demands of the war in Europe. Vetch, discredited, urged renewal of the plan, and Nicholson bore the colonial protests to England.

Nicholson returned in the spring of 1710, authorized to make a limited attack against Port-Royal in Acadia, with Vetch designated to be commander of the conquered area. The French commander, Daniel d'AUGER de Subercase, whose forces were vastly outnumbered, yielded after a brief struggle and early in October Vetch assumed command at Port-Royal (now renamed Annapolis Royal); the post amounted to little more than control of a small area around the fort, in the midst of hostile French inhabitants. The major part of the New England force departed in mid-October and Vetch was left with 200 marines and 250 colonial volunteers. The first winter at Annapolis Royal proved difficult. The fort was in a state of disrepair, necessary supplies were hard to come by, and the Acadians, sensing the precariousness of the British position, became more and more intractable. Vetch returned to Boston in January 1710/11 to seek help for his garrison, only to find that rumours were spreading that he was using his position for personal profit. He angrily denied the charges and finally managed to obtain some support for his post in the form of supplies. Returning to Annapolis Royal, he found the garrison reduced in number (now little more than 200 men) and discouraged about its situation. The Acadians and Indians were becoming more openly hostile. He began to send appeals to the New England colonies for reinforcements and continued to urge the complete reduction of Canada.

In June 1711, Vetch received news that a British regiment, supported by a large force of naval vessels, was ready in Boston and that preparations were being made, on the authority of the new Tory ministry, to revive the strategy he had advocated. Vetch was recalled to Boston and left Sir Charles HOBBY in temporary command at Annapolis Royal. The force sailed for Quebec on 30 July, under the command of Admiral Sir Hovenden WALKER, with Brigadier-General JOHN HILL as commander-in-chief of the landing forces, and Vetch as commander of the New England troops. Familiar with the St Lawrence, Vetch was asked to lead the fleet, but Walker had not relinquished the van when contrary winds and poor seamanship put nine ships on the rocks off the Île-aux-Oeufs in the Gulf of St Lawrence. The admiral, unenthusiastic from the start, needed no further excuse to abandon the enterprise, though Vetch used all his powers of persuasion to urge the still powerful force to resume its course.

On the return journey, Vetch received assurances that about 350 men from the force would be detached to replace the Nova Scotia garrison. He stopped at Annapolis Royal and left about 200 men, a military engineer, George VANE, and a replacement for Hobby, Thomas CAULFEILD. Vetch then went on to spend the winter in Boston, keeping in touch with Caulfeild in the interim. During his stay in Boston and after his return to Annapolis Royal in June, he made continual appeals to London for instructions on his duties,

Vieuxpont

for a regular garrison, and for payment of the colony's sizeable expenses, but to no avail. The condition of the colony worsened as desertions from the garrison increased. About this same time, Vane sent complaints to the home government that Vetch was extorting money from the inhabitants and treating them "more like slaves then anything else."

After passing another hard winter at Annapolis Royal, Vetch learned early in the summer of 1713 that the Tory government in England had appointed Nicholson to replace him. When Nicholson arrived in the fall with a commission as governor, Vetch found that his former comrade-in-arms had turned against him and, following Vane's complaints, was attempting to have him charged with maladministration at Annapolis Royal. To counter these accusations and collect what the government owed him, Vetch sailed for England 16 April 1714, leaving behind his wife and two children, Alida and William.

With the accession of George I and the appointment of a Whig ministry, Vetch was able to discredit the arbitrary Nicholson, justify his management of Nova Scotia, and win the governorship in January 1714/15, but he never returned to America. He was often called to advise the Board of Trade on general matters concerning America, or on the troublesome problems of his own government. Superseded by Governor Philipps* in August 1717, he devoted his final years to futile proposals for developing Nova Scotia, petitions for vacant colonial governorships, and efforts to collect his accounts. Margaret Vetch joined her husband in England in 1717 and remained with him until his death while a prisoner in King's Bench for debt. He was buried at St George's Church in Southwark (London).

Samuel Vetch was one of the few prescient Britons of his time to catch a vision of the imperial future and draw colonists and crown together in plans of action which could command the support of both. He clearly outlined the new resources of forests and furs that would provide commercial opportunities for Britain in Canada. After the capture of Nova Scotia he worked tirelessly for its development, both while he held its command and afterwards when he made personal proposals in London. Throughout his life Vetch saw the relationships between his own interest and the growing administrative, financial, and military problems of the empire. He helped provide the spark that replaced the French empire in Canada by British dominion.

The Historic Sites and Monuments Board of Canada under the chairmanship of Dr. J. C. Webster erected a monument to Vetch in 1928 on the ramparts of the old fort at Annapolis Royal. Large portraits of Vetch and his wife hang in the Museum of the City of New York.

G. M. WALLER

Vetch's personal letters are found among the Robert Livingston papers in the Livingston-Redmond Coll., Roosevelt Library, Hyde Park, N.Y. Copies of his official correspondence are in his Letter Book, Museum of the City of New York; *see* also BM, Sloane MS 3607, and PANS, MS docs. V, VII, VII½. Some of the Vetch papers are found in the New Brunswick Museum, Webster Coll., shelf 40, pkt.63–65. A letter from the citizens of Port-Royal complaining of harsh treatment by Vetch can be found in AN, Col., C¹¹D, 7, f.68.

Printed sources include: *Coll. doc. inédits Canada et Amérique* (*CF*), I (1888). *Coll. de manuscrits relatifs à la N.-F.*, II, 448–51. "Correspondance de Vaudreuil," APQ *Rapport*, 1938–39. *N.S. Archives, II. N.S. Hist. Soc. Coll.*, I (1878), IV (1884). *NYCD* (O'Callaghan and Fernow), III, IV, V, IX. PRO, *B.T.Journal*, 1704–1708/9, 1708/9–1714/15, 1714/15–1718, 1718–22, 1722/23–1728; *CSP, Col.*, 1706–8, 1708–9, 1710–11, 1711–12, 1712–14, 1714–15, 1716–17. *Walker expedition* (Graham).

DAB. DNB. Brebner, *New England's outpost.* Murdoch, *History of Nova-Scotia*, I. G. M. Waller, *Samuel Vetch, colonial enterpriser* (Chapel Hill, N.C., 1960) should be consulted for a detailed bibliography on Vetch; *see also* Waller, "Samuel Vetch and the glorious enterprise," N.Y. Hist. Soc. *Q.*, XXXIV (1950), 101–23. D. C. Harvey, "History in stone and bronze," *Dalhousie Review* (Halifax), XII (1932–33), 69–76.

VIEUXPONT (Vieux-Pont), JOSEPH GODEFROY DE. *See* GODEFROY

VILLECHAUVE, CLAUDE DE BEAUHARNOIS DE BEAUMONT ET DE. *See* BEAUHARNOIS

VILLEDONNÉ, ÉTIENNE DE, esquire, captain in the colonial regular troops, commandant at Fort Saint-Joseph, 1722–26; b. in Paris, *c.* 1666; d. in Quebec, 12 May 1726.

The son of Étienne de Villedonné, an attorney of the *parlement* of Paris, and Marie Vezins, he came to Canada in 1685 as either a cadet or a second lieutenant in the colonial regular troops. Four years later he was taken prisoner by the Iroquois who, in the course of his captivity, chewed off one of his fingers and burnt his arm. In 1692, Villedonné managed to escape. Undaunted by the treatment he had suffered at the hands of the Five Nations, he participated in several expeditions against them in the years that followed. During the War of the Spanish Succession he campaigned in Newfoundland with a detachment commanded by Jacques TESTARD de Montigny which attacked the English settlements of Trinity and Bonavista in 1705.

Villedonné was named assistant town major of Quebec in 1712 and promoted to the rank of captain the following year. He was highly regarded by Philippe de RIGAUD de Vaudreuil who appointed him commandant of Fort Saint-Joseph, off the southeastern tip of Lake Michigan, in 1722. By that time the Fox Indians had begun to attack the settlements of the Illinois country, and Villedonné became involved in the controversy between the post commandants of Canada and Louisiana who accused each other of not taking appropriate measures to end this war.

In Quebec in 1697 Villedonné had married Marie Damours, daughter of Mathieu Damours* de Chauffours and Marie Marsolet. She bore him three children and died in 1703. In 1715 he married his second wife, Françoise Roussel, daughter of the surgeon Timothée Roussel*; they had seven children.

YVES F. ZOLTVANY

AJQ, Greffe de Louis Chambalon, 28 sept. 1697. AN, Col., C¹¹ᴬ, 12, 22, 24, 25, 28, 30, 56; D²ᶜ, 222. "L'expédition de M. de Montigny à Terreneuve en 1705," APQ *Rapport*, 1922–23, 290–98. A. Roy, *Inv. greffes not.*, V, 321; XII, XVIII, XIX. P.-G. Roy, "Ce que Callières pensait de nos officiers," 328. Wis. State Hist. Soc. *Coll.*, XVI, 444–51 (some of Villedonné's correspondence during his command at Fort Saint-Joseph). Tanguay, *Dictionnaire*, I, 154, 194, 530; III, 412. [Tanguay gives Villedonné's dates as 1663–1726. In 1701, however, Callière stated that Villedonné was 35 years old, which would place his birth in 1666. Y.F.Z.]

VILLERAY ET DE LA CARDONNIÈRE, AUGUSTIN ROUER DE. *See* ROUER

VILLES (Ville), JEAN-MARIE DE (also Louis according to Sommervogel, relying on De Backer, but this seems to lack archival support), priest, Jesuit, missionary in the Illinois country; b. 6 Sept. 1670 at Auxerre; d. 25 May 1720, at Natchez.

The day after his twenty-third birthday he entered the Society of Jesus at the Paris novitiate. Three years later (1696) he began to teach in the college at Rennes, and, according to a pattern of the day, led his boys through five successive grades. In 1701 he began his theological studies at La Flèche, and was ordained a priest in 1704; he moved to Paris for his fourth and final year of theology. After the year of tertianship made in Rouen, 1705–6, he set out for Canada, and in 1708

with his calm confidence headed for the Illinois mission where he was to spend the rest of his life. Before leaving Quebec he wrote out the solemn four-vow profession of the Jesuit in an open, even, forthright hand (2 Feb. 1708).

In 1711 he replaced the late Jacques GRAVIER among the Peorias, and in 1714 he was at Kaskaskia. After the death of Jean MERMET he was named superior of the Illinois missions. Gravely concerned over the anarchy of the coureurs de bois and the incursions of Carolina English agents, he travelled down the Mississippi to confer with Jean-Baptiste Le Moyne* de Bienville; he remained in Mobile more than six months. On his return trip he paused at Natchez; his scientific conversations with Le Page Du Pratz are recorded admiringly in the latter's *Histoire*.

De Villes died, apparently of dysentery, at Natchez, 25 May 1720. (Some sources put his death in June or July.) His reports on the Illinois country were read with interest in Paris by the council of the Marine and such experts as Guillaume Delisle.

CHARLES E. O'NEILL

AN, Col., D²ᴰ, carton 10; Marine, B¹, 8, f.256v; 3JJ, 387, f.34. ARSI, Francia 17, 57; 24, ff.351, 356v 363v, 376v, 383v, 402, 423; 25/I, ff.4v, 14, 31v, 50, 54v, 57v, 62, 81, 97v, 119v, 173v, 223, 265; 25/II, ff.315v, 366, 399, 440v, 489v, 524v. François Élesban de Guilhermy, *Ménologe de la Compagnie de Jésus . . . , assistance de France, comprenant les missions de l'Archipel, de la Syrie, . . . du Canada, de la Louisiane . . .*, éd. [Jacques Terrien] (2 part., Paris, 1892), première partie, 742–44. Le Page Du Pratz, *Histoire de la Louisiane* (3v., Paris, 1758), I, 130–35. *Lettres édifiantes et curieuses escrites des missions étrangères* (nouv. éd., 14v., Lyon, 1819), IV, 218, 229. Delanglez, *French Jesuits in Louisiana*, 81–83. Giraud, *Histoire de la Louisiane française*, I, 314, 318–19, 329.

VILLIERS, NICOLAS-ANTOINE COULON DE. *See* COULON

VILLIEU, CLAUDE-SÉBASTIEN DE, officer serving in Acadia, garrison adjutant of the colony; date and place of birth and of death unknown; fl. 1690–1705.

Numerous historians have confused Villieu with his father, who bore the same given names. Born in 1633 in Turin, the father came to Canada as a lieutenant in the Carignan-Salières regiment, with which he participated in the 1666 campaign against the Iroquois. In 1672 he received from Talon* a grant of land on the shores of the St Lawrence. He died before 1692. In 1668, near Nantes, he had married Jeanne Lebreton, by whom he had several children.

Villieu

In letters to the minister dated 29 Sept. 1700 and 25 Nov. 1703, his son Claude-Sébastien states that he had been in the services since 1674 and that he had fought in Flanders, Germany, Catalonia, and Roussillon for 15 years prior to coming to Canada. On 16 Mar. 1687 he had been appointed a midshipman at Rochefort, and in 1690 he took part in the defence of Quebec. On 9 April 1692, at Quebec, he married Judith Leneuf, daughter of MICHEL LENEUF de La Vallière de Beaubassin (senior), and of Marie Denys. They had only one child, SÉBASTIEN.

In 1690 Claude-Sébastien was sent as a lieutenant to Acadia, where, on 1 March 1693, he received command of a company. In May 1694 he went to put an end to the negotiations between the English and the Indians in the region of Pentagouet (on the Penobscot). Then, considered "better suited than others for war of movement with the Indians," he distinguished himself with Bomoseen at the head of bands of Abenaki Indians during the attack in July on Oyster River (Durham, New Hampshire). Buade* de Frontenac requested a reward for him and entrusted him with the command of Fort Nashwaak (Naxouat) on the Saint John River. In August 1696 Villieu took part, along with JEAN-VINCENT D'ABBADIE de Saint-Castin, in the successful operations conducted by PIERRE LE MOYNE d'Iberville against Fort Pemaquid. On returning from this attack he was captured by Captain Hathorne, as the passport which he had obtained from the English had expired. He was taken as a prisoner to Boston but was set free at Frontenac's request. He went to France in May 1698, then returned to Acadia, where he exercised temporary command of the colony from July 1700 to December 1701, after Robinau* de Villebon's death.

From 1699 till 1705 Villieu aided his father-in-law, Michel Leneuf, in his lawsuit against Pierre TIBAUDEAU and Guillaume BLANCHARD concerning some land at Chipoudy. He was appointed garrison adjutant of Acadia on 1 Feb. 1702, then once more temporary commandant on 1 March, and received a gratuity of 1,000 *livres*. His differences with Brouillan [MOMBETON], de GOUTIN, and the missionaries brought about his suspension in 1703. As he was suffering from asthma, he received his final discharge on 1 May 1704, with a pension of 600 *livres*. He remained for a time in the country, and he again received temporary command of it on 30 Aug. 1705. Villieu returned to France soon after and sold his house at Port-Royal (Annapolis Royal, N.S.) for 4,000 *livres* to the Recollets, who turned it into a parish church. After that we lose sight of him.

Opinions about Villieu varied. He got along badly with his superiors, Governors Robinau de Villebon and Brouillan, who claimed that he was "fussy and disagreeable." They accused him of having only his own interest in mind and of trafficking with the Indians. In December 1706 AUGER de Subercase begged the minister not to send Villieu back to Acadia. But he was popular in the colony; on 15 July 1705 the notary LOPPINOT wrote: "His piety, his valour, his capacity have made him very well liked by the settlers, who entreat you to send him back to them."

ÉTIENNE TAILLEMITE

AN, Col., B, 16, f.187v; 17, f.136; 19, f.44; 22, f.177; 23, ff.124v, 141, 157, 158, 281v, 283v; 25, ff.77v, 78; 27, f.369v; C^{11A}, 11, f.93; 12, f.217; 13, ff.55, 81v, 124, 153, 285, 301, 322; 14, ff.100, 210, 246; 15, ff.3, 98v; 16, f.55v; C^{11D}, 2, ff.220, 225, 228, 230, 244, 258, 274, 277; 3, ff.27, 70, 78, 111, 128, 226; 4, ff.17, 52, 142v, 186, 234, 268, 270, 290, 320v; 5, ff.95, 136v, 213v, 251v, 253v; D^{2C}, 49, f.109v; 222; Marine, C^7, 350 (dossier de Villieu). *Coll. de manuscrits relatifs à la N.-F.*, II, 135–143. A. Roy, *Inv. greffes not.*, XVIII, 9. P.-G. Roy, *Inv. concessions*, II, 136; IV, 154–55; V, 297. *Lettres de noblesse* (P.-G. Roy), I, 69, 70; II, 78. Webster, *Acadia*.

Le Jeune, *Dictionnaire*, II. Lauvrière, *La tragédie d'un peuple*. Rameau de Saint-Père, *Une colonie féodale*, I, 243–46, 267–70.

VILLIEU, SÉBASTIEN DE, naval officer, son of CLAUDE-SÉBASTIEN and Judith Leneuf de Beaubassin; b. 1693 at Quebec; d. 27 July 1715 on board the *Paix* at La Rochelle.

Sébastien de Villieu began his service around 1698 as a cadet in his father's company in Acadia. In 1701 Governor Brouillan [MOMBETON] put his name forward for a commission as sub-lieutenant, but he did not obtain it, no doubt because of his youth. On 1 May 1704, at Rochefort, he was appointed a midshipman. He did most of his service in the navy, then transferred to the service of the Compagnie du Castor, which entrusted several of its ships to him.

In 1712 he was in command of the *Providence* carrying 16 guns and 50 crew members, which had been fitted out to sail to Hudson Bay. On 19 July he fought a brilliant battle with an English frigate of 32 guns, which had to withdraw after an explosion on board. On 20 Jan. 1713 Villieu was appointed deputy-brigadier of the Gardes de la Marine. That same year he vainly solicited a naval lieutenant's commission, then in June he received command of the frigate *Louise*, which had been fitted out by Pagès and Fleury, business men at La Rochelle. It was also in 1713 that he made an agreement with the Compagnie du Castor to take command again of the *Providence*, which was to proceed to Hudson Bay to evacuate the posts handed over to England under the terms of the treaty of Utrecht.

ÉTIENNE TAILLEMITE

AN, Col., B, 34, f.429v; 35, ff.50v, 116v, 124, 229; C¹¹D, 4, ff.62, 257v; Marine, B⁴, 36, f.40; C¹, 150. Le Jeune, *Dictionnaire*, II. Tanguay, *Dictionnaire*.

VINCELOTTE, CHARLES-JOSEPH AMIOT DE. *See* AMIOT

VINCENNES (Vinsenne). *See* BISSOT

VISSERI. *See* DUTISNÉ

VITRÉ, CHARLES DENYS DE. *See* DENYS

VOLANT DE RADISSON, ÉTIENNE, Montreal merchant and surveyor; baptized at Trois-Rivières, 29 Oct. 1664, son of Claude Volant de Saint-Claude, merchant, and Françoise Radisson; d. 14 June 1735, near Montreal, without issue. His older twin brothers, the Abbés CLAUDE and PIERRE VOLANT de Saint-Claude, were among the first pupils to enter Bishop LAVAL's Petit Séminaire.

In Sorel on 9 Dec. 1693 Volant married Geneviève Letendre, the widow of Jean-François-Xavier Pelletier, who had been killed by the Iroquois the previous year. In 1694 he received a grant of islands in Lac Saint-Pierre near Sorel as a fief and seigneury.

As royal surveyor he undertook, between 1697 and 1704, some cadastral surveys in and about Montreal. By 1699 he was established in commerce in that city. In 1701, at the time of Cadillac's [LAUMET] journey to Detroit to establish a fort there, Volant was hired by Jean BOCHART de Champigny to accompany him as storehouse keeper. Volant made another voyage to Detroit in 1703, and returned the following year. He then became one of the important merchants of Montreal, conducting his business from his two-storey residence on Rue Saint-Paul. When this building was gutted in the great fire of 1734, Volant moved to his farm on the nearby *côte* of La Visitation, where he died the next year. At that time he was colonel of the town militia in Montreal and general agent there for the Compagnie des Indes.

C. C. J. BOND

AJM, Dossier Radisson, Procès-verbaux d'arpentage; Greffe de François Lepailleur, 3 juillet 1735; Registre des audiences, 19 juin 1699, 29 juillet 1700, 10 mars 1702; Registres d'état civil de Notre-Dame de Montréal, 1735, 7. AN, Col., B, 17, f.368; C¹¹A, 61, ff.144, 150. P.-G. Roy, *Inv. concessions*, IV, 92–94. Massicotte, "Répertoire des engagements pour l'Ouest," 206, 208. P.-G. Roy, *Hommes et choses du fort Saint-Frédéric* (Montréal, 1946), 240f.

VOLANT DE SAINT-CLAUDE, PIERRE and **CLAUDE,** twin brothers, priests of the seminary of Quebec, missionaries and parish priests; b. 8 Nov. 1654 at Trois-Rivières, sons of Claude Volant de Saint-Claude and Françoise Radisson; Pierre died 3 Jan. 1710 at Quebec, Claude 8 Oct. 1719 at Varennes.

Pierre and Claude Volant de Saint-Claude were the first boarders to enrol when the Petit Séminaire of Quebec opened on 19 Oct. 1668, and they went through their studies together. Together they received the tonsure and minor orders on 12 Dec. 1677, were admitted to the subdiaconate and the diaconate on the 18th and 19th of the same month, and were finally ordained priests on 17 Sept. 1678. From this date on the pastoral ministry separated the two brothers.

Abbé Pierre Volant was appointed to the mission at Grondines. In 1682 he succeeded his brother at the mission at Sorel, and in 1684 he became the first priest of the parish of Notre-Dame-de-l'Assomption at Repentigny, which served Saint-Charles de Lachenaye and Île Jésus. The field of action of the parish priest and missionary extended likewise to Saint-Sulpice and as far as Lavaltrie on the south shore.

His brother Claude first exercised his ministry in the region of Sorel. In 1682 Bishop LAVAL entrusted to him the parishes strung out over a distance of 25 leagues from Bellechasse and La Durantaye to Lotbinière. At the end of October 1683 Abbé Claude Volant went to Batiscan. He was appointed titular priest of this parish when it was set up on 2 Nov. 1684 under the patronage of St François-Xavier, and he was installed in his charge by the vicar-general, ANGO Des Maizerets, 10 June 1685.

In 1687 Bishop Laval thought of the Volant de Saint-Claude brothers for the missions in Acadia. He proposed using Pierre to convert the Indians and Claude to serve as parish priest at Port-Royal (Annapolis Royal, N.S.), but this project was not carried out.

In 1688, when he had a disagreement with Pierre LEGARDEUR de Repentigny concerning the site of the church, Pierre Volant left his parish. The bishop of Quebec did not take away his title, but used him successively at Ange-Gardien near Quebec in 1689, at the cathedral in 1690, and at Saint-Ours in 1691. The following year Abbé Volant resumed his post at Repentigny, but the conflict with Legardeur did not end until 1702.

Voyer d'Argenson

A settlement signed 13 January stipulated that the church would be built in the centre of the seigneury, on a piece of land which the parish priest had already acquired.

Pierre Volant de Saint-Claude spent four more years at Repentigny, then retired and went to live at Quebec. He died there on 3 Jan. 1710 and was buried the next day in the chapel of Sainte-Anne in the cathedral.

In the meantime Claude Volant de Saint-Claude carried on his ministry as parish priest of Saint-Pierre at Sorel from 12 Dec. 1689 till 13 May 1693. In December 1693 he was appointed priest of the parish of Sainte-Anne at Varennes, where he died 8 Oct. 1719 and was buried 10 October in the parish church.

NOËL BAILLARGEON

AAQ, Registres d'insinuations A, 104, 105, 108; Registres d'insinuations B, 104. ASQ, Chapitre, 160; Fonds Verreau, XLVI, Histoire des cures de Montréal, 170, 171; Lettres, N, 11, 86; MSS, 457, 466f.; Paroisses diverses, 23, 24, 25, 29; Polygraphie, XXII. Mandements des évêques de Québec (Têtu et Gagnon), I, 115f. Charland, "Notre-Dame de Québec: le nécrologe de la crypte," BRH, XX (1914), 205. M.-A. Bernard, "Sainte-Anne de Varennes," BRH, IV (1898), 129. G. de Nantua, "Les deux frères Volant," BRH, III (1897), 174.

VOYER D'ARGENSON, PIERRE DE, chevalier, seigneur of Chastre and Vicomte de Mouzay, governor of New France from 1658 to 1661; baptized 19 Nov. 1625; d. probably in 1709 near Mouzay in the province of Touraine.

His family formed the younger branch of the Voyer de Paulmy et d'Argenson line, and claimed noble rank from time immemorial. The valour of an ancestor had been rewarded by a viscountship in 1569 and by strong support at court. René, the father of the future governor of New France, had a brilliant career: he succeeded Cinq-Mars as grand bailiff of Touraine, accomplished delicate missions in the provinces and in regard to the organization of the armies on Richelieu's behalf, and was appointed ambassador to Venice by Mazarin.

The father's good fortune opened up the way to success for the children: until his disgrace in 1655, Marc, the eldest, occupied in turn the positions relinquished by his father, and the youngest became lieutenant of police. As the second son, Pierre was destined for the church, but he quickly abandoned this cause and became bailiff of Touraine in 1643, an ensign in the king's guards in 1650, and then a councillor of state. Thanks to President Lamoignon's friendship, he obtained the post of governor of New France, at the age of 32, by a commission dated 27 Jan. 1657.

It is not known whether he wanted to get away temporarily from the court because of his brother's disgrace or wished to look after his infirmities, but he came to Canada in the hope of taking a rest. The colony, however, was living through the darkest hours of its history: the trade in beaver furs was leading the settlers deeper into debt; the Iroquois were making bloody forays against the colony and threatening its very existence; finally the question of the appointment of an ecclesiastical authority appeared likely to present difficulties.

The new governor arrived at Quebec on 11 July 1658, and was received with great acclamation, to the sound of cannon and muskets. On the very next day, however, an attack by a band of Iroquois made clear to him that these weapons were more often used for other purposes than for show. D'Argenson had to face hostile acts by the Iroquois during the whole length of his stay; he managed fairly well, by utilizing as best he could the slender resources put at his disposal, so much so that "Everyone would have thought himself as good as lost if Monsieur le Vicomte d'Argenson our governor had not heartened us by his courage and wise conduct, putting all the posts around Quebec in such good order that the coming of the Iroquois was desired rather than feared." He showed his courage and boldness by attacking and pursuing the enemy bands; he gave evidence of prudence, on the military front, by implementing methods of surveillance and by speeding up the means of intervention, and on the diplomatic front by adopting a policy based on firmness and mistrust.

At the time of Dollard* Des Ormeaux, flattery, boasting, arrogance, and trickery seemed good ways to protect the colony from the Iroquois menace. Thus d'Argenson, like the other governors, did not accuse his Iroquois interlocutors of making war, but put the blame on some unthinking and undisciplined nephew. His slender military resources did not prevent him from stating that he had come from France to make peace, by gentle means if possible, by severity and force if necessary. He exchanged captives with the Iroquois, but, despite promises and numerous entreaties, he always kept back a few prisoners as hostages. And in the summer of 1660 he even imprisoned some 15 Indians who came to parley; "considering them as spies rather than as ambassadors . . . [he] believed that God was putting them into his hands, so that he might derive two advantages from them: the first, to be able to do the harvesting with some assurance . . . the second, to get our French captives set free."

The precariousness of the situation in New

France did not, however, prompt d'Argenson to ask for intervention by the French armies to settle the Iroquois problem; rather he asked for farmers. According to him, the colony could not support a large number of soldiers, whereas the clearing of land beyond the outskirts and an increase in the area under cultivation would push back an enemy who sought the safety of the forest, would consolidate the position of the colony, and would contribute, at least in part, to settling a thorny economic problem.

Three months after his arrival in Canada, he wrote: "after speaking to you of the war I must mention another scourge as dangerous as that, namely poverty . . . that results partly from the debasement of the fur trade, which the settlers have degraded to such an extent that they barely receive from the Indians the cost of their merchandise, and this is a disorderly state of affairs that absolutely must be remedied." For their part the merchants had lost much of their interest in this trade because of the fall in the value of beaver furs in France. Rigorous intervention and a new plan were necessary to reactivate the economy.

D'Argenson was opposed to the half-measure recommended by the king's decree of 1657, and proposed the establishment of complete control over the trade in pelts in order to relaunch the colony's economy. He suggested that the right possessed by the settlers to trade freely in furs be withdrawn, and that a trading monopoly be entrusted to a single company of merchants. These measures would eliminate the great disadvantages of competition between the settlers; the community would realize profits, to be divided up according to the amounts invested by each person in the merchandise traded by the warehouse, and would be able to pay its debts; the merchants, enjoying a monopoly, would be less afraid of investing money and being paid only after the sale of the furs.

But the Compagnie des Cent-Associés preferred to audit the accounts of the Communauté des Habitants, and took advantage of this to restrict the legal power of the governor. The Communauté, unable to pay its debts, declared bankruptcy and handed over the fur trade to a private company.

Another financial question, although of minor importance, seems to have touched off a large-scale conflict between the civil and religious authorities, and especially between the governor and Bishop LAVAL. Knowing that he was prejudiced against them, the Jesuits had given d'Argenson a most flattering official welcome. But a legal dispute over certain fishing rights set the two sides at odds, and the bishop, backing up his faithful supporters, provoked a veritable conflict in which each party publicly dealt the other foul blows. The bishop attacked the administrator's status and prestige by having him censed by the thurifer instead of by the deacon, and after the whole choir; he next took advantage of the governor's absence from a meeting of the churchwardens to have him relieved of his function as honorary churchwarden. Embittered, d'Argenson forgot all the humility that he displayed while waiting on the sick in the hospital, and "several disrespectful words were uttered concerning the prelate." The governor thought he would have his revenge on Corpus Christi day: he allowed the soldiers to remain standing and wearing their head-dress before the Holy Sacrament, but the bishop did not stop at their station.

This tension upset many people, who preferred to give up certain customs for fear of antagonizing one of the two authorities who might have considered himself insulted or relegated to second rank. It was even necessary to give up processions because of quarrels over precedence.

The opposition between Laval and d'Argenson was not related to the method of setting up or developing the colony, for Voyer d'Argenson favoured agriculture much more than trade, and endeavoured to see that moral and Christian values were respected in the colony. Thus he sent a pregnant "king's daughter" (*fille du roi*) back to France and imposed a fine of 150 *livres* on the person who had sent her to Canada to prevent further acts of a similar nature. The opposition between the two men seems therefore to have been much more a matter of personality and division of powers than of ideology. Moreover, Voyer d'Argenson accused Laval of wanting to extend his authority to fields which did not concern him.

If d'Argenson had been happy to have an appointment in Canada, he quickly changed his tune: only three months after his arrival he was thinking about returning to France, and hoping that his three-year term would not be renewed. In 1661, alleging his infirmities as a pretext, he asked to go back to France. Marie de l'Incarnation [Guyart*] added that the absence of help from France, the complaints voiced in regard to him, and the quarrels instigated by the highest powers in the country had led him to give up his post. CHARLES AUBERT de La Chesnaye claimed later that the bishop had insisted that President Lamoignon recall the governor. In any case, d'Argenson must have been happy to leave, the more so because he left no friends behind him.

Back in France, he seems by the activity which he displayed on the battlefields to have followed in his father's footsteps. In 1709, still a bachelor, he made his will and asked to be buried at Mouzay.

At the time of his stay in New France he did not manage to win over the important personages of the colony, yet one cannot attribute to him the entire responsibility for or even the start of the conflicts with the bishop. Furthermore, he saw the problems and the obstacles attending the development of Canada, and endeavoured to provide a solution for them: a utopian one perhaps if immediate results were to be expected, but essential as a stage on the road to greater achievements. In short, the situation of the colony and the scant support received from France did not permit him to do more.

JACQUES MATHIEU

AQ, Manuscrits relatifs à l'histoire de la N.-F., 2ᵉ série, I. *Édits ord.*, III, 20. Marie Guyart de l'Incarnation, *Lettres* (Richaudeau). *JR* (Thwaites), XLIV, XLV, XLVI. "Lettres inédites du gouverneur d'Argenson," *BRH*, XXVII (1921), 298–309, 328–39. [Faillon], *Histoire de la colonie française*, II. Lanctot, *Histoire du Canada*, I. Francis Parkman, *The old regime in Canada* (29th ed., Toronto, 1893). "L'arrivée du gouverneur d'Argenson à Québec," *BRH*, XXXV (1929), 678–80. M. Berneval, "Les filles venues au Canada de 1658 à 1661," *BRH*, XLVII (1941), 97–115. "La chapelle des Jésuites à Tadoussac," *BRH*, XXXI (1925), 481. Louis-Raoul de Lorimier, "Réception de M. le gouverneur d'Argenson au collège des Jésuites à Québec," *RC*, 3ᵉ sér., XXI (1918), 401. Robert Roquebrune, "La noblesse de France," *BRH*, LVII (1951), 101–14. P.-G. Roy, "La famille Rouer de Villeray," *BRH*, XXVI (1920), 33–52; "Les familles de nos gouverneurs français," *BRH*, XXVI (1920), 257–74; "La réception de Mgr le vicomte d'Argenson," *BRH*, XXXVI (1930), 219–20; "Québec au printemps de 1660," *BRH*, XXXI (1925), 33–39.

W

WAGGONER, ROWLAND, HBC employee; d. 1740.

Waggoner, an illiterate labourer, came to York Fort with Governor James KNIGHT in 1714. In 1717 he was a member of the advance party with William STUART for the founding of Churchill. He returned to York Fort in 1718. In 1721 he accompanied John SCROGGS in the *Whalebone* sloop to winter at Churchill. However it is unlikely that Waggoner continued on the expedition from Churchill in the following year as the York Fort account book shows that he made heavy expenditures in 1721–22. He probably returned to England in 1722 or 1723. In 1724 Waggoner was at Albany, and except for the 1735–36 season which he spent in England he stayed there until his death in 1740. Though illiterate, Waggoner was one of those jacks of all trades so indispensable in the north. He worked as a sawyer, was handy with the broadaxe, and could do a cooper's work. He could hunt, trap, and shoot as well as an Indian; in 1729 he shot a French spy lurking around the factory. In addition to his versatility as a workman, the Albany journals show him possessed of a warm and hearty personality. Much of his wages went for brandy and tobacco; in a ten-year period at Albany he averaged 13.6 gallons of brandy yearly, and it has been suggested that his death was hastened by his hard drinking.

Because of his usefulness his wages were advanced steadily. In 1737 he was put on the council; in 1739 he succeeded Thomas BIRD as chief, a position he held until his death on 23 April 1740.

The London committee must have been satisfied with his performance for in 1740 he was appointed chief for three years, but he died before the orders reached Albany.

G. E. THORMAN

HBC Arch. A.6/4 (letters outward, 20 May 1724); A.6/5 (letters outward, 21 May 1729, 15 May 1730, 11 May 1732, 10 May 1733, 3 March 1734,. 2 May 1735, 20 May 1737); A.6/6 (letters outward, 18 May 1738, 11 May 1739, 1 May 1740, 23 April 1741); B.3/a/15–23, 25, 27–29 (Albany journals between 1726 and 1740); B.3/d/33–43, 45–46, 48 (Albany account books between 1724 and 1740); B.42/d/1 (Churchill account books, 1717–18); B.239/a/1, 3 (York journals between 1714 and 1717); B.239/d/7–12 (York account books, 1714–22). HBRS, XXV (Davies and Johnson).

WALKER, SIR HOVENDEN, naval commander of the British expedition against Quebec in 1711; b. 1656 or 1666; d. 1725 or 1728.

The second son of Col. William Walker of Tankardstown, Queen's County, Ireland, and of Elizabeth, daughter of Dr Peter Chamberlen, Hovenden Walker is said to have been born in 1656. It is conceivable, however, according to Sir John Laughton (who sketched Walker's adult career in the *DNB*) that the correct date is ten years later. Although historical chroniclers like John Charnock (*Biographia navalis*, II, 465–66) and Robert Beatson (*A political index*, II, 5) suggest 1725 as the possible year of his death, Laughton—this time unreservedly—asserts that

Walker died of apoplexy in Dublin in 1728. Unfortunately the source of this confident statement is lacking. Walker was twice married, and had one daughter who died, unmarried, about 1777.

Walker entered Trinity College, Dublin, in 1678, but failed to complete the course, and subsequently joined the navy. Little is known of his early service, but it seems likely that he visited North America in 1686, putting into Boston aboard the frigate *Dartmouth* (Capt. George St Lo). According to Pepys he amused the ship's company with a patriotic ballad of his own composition, attacking the Spaniards for treacherous conduct in the Caribbean.

Promoted captain on 17 Feb. 1691/92, he served off Barfleur in 1692, and four years later, when in command of the *Foresight* (50 guns), helped to fight off a superior French force near the Lizard, and thus to save the convoy. In 1701 he joined the fleet under Sir George Rooke at Cadiz, and shortly afterwards, as commodore, took command of a detachment charged with cooperating in an attack on Guadaloupe and Martinique. Hitherto, his career, if not brilliant, had been successful. In the Caribbean, the first signs of a character weakness that was subsequently to prove his undoing became apparent. After wasting more than two months at Barbados, Walker set out early in February 1702/3 for Antigua, where the governor of the Leeward Islands, General Christopher Codrington, was impatiently awaiting him with the required land force. Meanwhile, sickness, desertion, and "murther" by drink played havoc with the morale of the naval force. The condition of the troops was little better; they were short of siege weapons and the powder was of miserable quality, as were the provisions, which were in short supply. The delays, which gave the French time to prepare their defences, combined with the lack of cooperation between Walker and Codrington made the Guadaloupe failure almost inevitable. After an expensive and futile assault the expedition retired to Nevis and a few weeks later moved on to Jamaica, whence accompanied by Vice-Admiral GRAYDON a reinforced squadron sailed northwards to attack the centre of the French fishery in Newfoundland, Placentia (Plaisance). But it was well into September before the British force was assembled. A joint council of war—the customary instrument of escape from individual decision—agreed that since an assault was impracticable so late in the year, the expedition should make for England.

The failure of the Caribbean enterprise cannot in retrospect be placed on Walker's shoulders alone; nor did his seniors of that day censure him for his lack of audacity and intelligence. In 1706 he

assisted Sir John LEAKE in the relief of Barcelona, and two years later was appointed to command the squadron before Dunkirk. In March 1710/11 he was promoted to flag-rank with a knighthood thrown in for good measure, and, on 3 April, the new rear-admiral of the white squadron was made commander-in-chief of a secret expedition aimed at the conquest of Canada.

The decision of the British government to resurrect a project first initiated in 1709 had sound political as well as strategic justification. The steady propaganda appeals from New England and New York had not only influenced the government, especially the Board of Trade, but had roused considerable public interest. Moreover, the conquest of Port-Royal (Annapolis Royal, N.S.) in 1710—a mere walk-over—had whetted both colonial and British imperial appetites at a time when French naval power was reduced to a shadow of its former strength. Equally impressive was the argument that the capture of Quebec under Tory auspices would dilute, if not extinguish Marlborough's fading glories, and conceivably facilitate a more favourable peace treaty than the Duke himself could secure. There can be no denying the strong Tory urge to end the war, and the newly restored Tory ministry was not unaware of the political advantages to be reaped from a spectacular military success. Mrs. Masham had replaced the Duchess of Marlborough, and while the leader of the ministry (for all intents and purposes, the prime minister), Robert Harley, scarcely shared the enthusiasm of his secretary of state, Henry St John, he was too ill during the period of organization to interfere even had he wished.

With Harley *hors de combat*, St John had free rein. Five seasoned regiments, the cream of Marlborough's army in Flanders, were ordered to be withdrawn from the continent, despite the angry objections of the Duke whose opposition was only quelled by royal command. Furthermore, St John was responsible for the choice of the military as well as the naval commander. Col. JOHN HILL, raised to the rank of brigadier-general, was Mrs Masham's brother, but whether political reasons were responsible for the appointment of Rear-Admiral Walker, it is difficult to be certain. Walker was a Tory, but his relationship with St John was one of casual friendship rather than intimacy. In an age of savage political vendettas which shaped or shattered the careers of soldiers and sailors as well as those of statesmen, it is not easy to sort grains of truth from the chaff of controversy. On the other hand, what little we know about Walker's earlier career would scarcely seem to justify this important appointment; there were other seamen with far more distinguished records,

Walker

and the end might have been very different had Harley and not St John been at the helm of state during the spring of 1711.

Moreover, the secretary's fantastic efforts at secrecy indirectly placed the whole project in jeopardy. With the object of foxing the French, St John kept not only the commander, but the Admiralty in the dark regarding his real objectives. For example, by under-victualling the expedition, he may have temporarily put French agents off the scent, but in providing only three months' provisions (the usual quantity allowed for transporting land forces to the Mediterranean) he left it ultimately dependent on New England for food supply. All told, the numbers—some 5,300 troops, 6,000 seamen, including marines, along with the promised colonial levies—exceeded the population of Boston and its vicinity.

As might have been expected in the circumstances, the British army which arrived at Boston with the main fleet on 25 June found the cost of victuals immediately ascending. There was nothing unusual about the lust of local inhabitants to make money out of visiting soldiery, but successive battles with the Massachusetts Bay authorities over supply and price deeply prejudiced good relations between colonial and regular. Encouraged by the friction a parochial spirit of independence had begun to infect the local population, a species of "colonial nationalism" which was to reach new heights of disdain in Braddock's day.

Unversed in the procedures of large-scale organization, Walker underestimated the complications—not only problems of logistics, but labour shortages, ammunition shortages, and, above all, pilot shortages. On arrival at Boston he had expected to find any number of local captains with an adequate knowledge of the St Lawrence River, and with sufficient adventurous instinct to ascend it. To his surprise, he encountered not only much ignorance but a downright lack of enthusiasm, and in the end the governor's authority was necessary to ferret out recalcitrant or absconding pilots. Moreover, Walker was obliged to pay handsomely for the uncertain services of a French captain, Paradis by name, master of the captured sloop *Neptune*. Reliable charts were equally hard to find, although Walker was able to acquire a copy of the original journal of the Phips* expedition of 1690. Unfortunately, Phips had managed to reach Quebec more by good luck than by scientific navigation, and his hair-raising account of reefs, currents, fogs, and storms served merely to unnerve the already fretting admiral. Alarmed by all he heard and read, Walker preferred not to risk his two 80-gun ships in the river, and after transferring his flag to the 70-gun *Edgar*, he ordered the *Humber*, the *Devonshire*, and four small cruisers to remain in the gulf as protection for the rear.

Early on the morning of 30 July 1711, the expedition consisting of nine ships of war, two bomb vessels and 60 transports and tenders, British and colonial, with some 7,500 troops and marines aboard set sail from Boston. Including seamen, the total manpower must have been in the neighbourhood of 12,000. By 3 August the fleet was abreast Cape Sable, and a few days later rounded Cape Breton under the guidance of Colonel Samuel Vetch. Before settling in Albany in 1699, Vetch had been a soldier with a good record of service in the Low Countries. An able lobbyist and propagandist who urged the expulsion of the French from North America, he, like many Albany merchants, was not averse to trading with the Indians, adventures which may account for his knowledge of St Lawrence navigation. Although formally in charge of the colonial levies accompanying the British regulars, Vetch was probably the most competent pilot with the expedition; yet for reasons still impossible to fathom, he refused to lead the fleet around Gaspé into the river, and, equally incomprehensible, his admiral acquiesced.

By 13 August the fleet was well within the gulf. Thence followed light winds and calms, until on the morning of the 18th, just as the expedition was about to enter the river proper, it began to blow hard from the northwest, and Walker was forced to seek shelter in Gaspé Bay. On the morning of the 20th, however, the wind veered to the southeast, and he was able to advance slowly past the western extremity of Anticosti Island before the wind died down and thick fog blanketed both shore and fleet. By the 22d the wind had freshened from the southeast, and there were intermittent breaks in the fog, but not sufficient to give sight of land. The fleet was now well to the westward of Anticosti, probably 50 miles from the south shore and less than 20 from the north shore. After consulting his pilots, both French and English, at eight o'clock in the evening, Walker gave the signal to bring-to on the larboard tack, thus heading the fleet to the southward.

Unfortunately, the admiral was not, as he thought, in mid-stream when he issued the order, but about seven leagues north of his proper course, and in the grasp of strong currents which were bearing him relentlessly towards the northwest. Aided by an easterly wind the fleet was gradually closing on the "North Shore," which in the vicinity of Île-aux-Oeufs (Egg Island) runs almost north and south. Had this position been maintained until morning, disaster might still have been avoided. Unhappily, when, at about half past ten, the *Edgar*'s captain brought the disturbing news that land had been sighted, presumably dead ahead, Walker assumed that he was approaching the south shore, and ordered the fleet to wear, and bring-to on the other tack. Not many minutes later he was again summoned from his bed, and hurrying upon deck in dressing gown and slippers saw breakers "all round us." By that time the whole fleet was heading for the "North Shore," or more accurately, the coast to the westward; ships in the van were already plunging on the edge of the breakers.

Once recovered from the shock, Walker made all available sail, and stood from the shore towards mid-channel. Up to this time a gale had been blowing almost directly on shore, and had it continued it is doubtful if many of the fleet could have survived. Mercifully, by two o'clock in the morning of 23 August the wind dropped, and this lull was followed by a shift of wind which enabled most of the ships to slip their anchors and escape the shoals on either quarter. It speaks well for the seamanship of the crews that only seven transports and one storeship were lost. Out of a total of 1,390, 740 soldiers (including 35 women attached to the regiments) and probably 150 sailors were either drowned or died from exposure on shore.

Meanwhile, Colonel Francis NICHOLSON, a former colonial governor who had commanded the militia force during the luckless advance on Montreal in 1709 and the successful expedition against Port Royal in 1710, had once again led a supporting land force to the borders of Lake Champlain. News of the disaster along with orders to abandon the attack on Montreal came as a bitter blow, but a righteous anger which led him, so the story goes, to tear off his wig and stamp on it did not extinguish his prudence. As quickly as possible Nicholson withdrew to Albany where the troops were disbanded.

Walker cruised in the neighbourhood of Île-aux-Oeufs for two days in an effort to save what men and stores he could. Thence, following a council of war, he decided to abandon the assault on Quebec, and sailed for Cape Breton. On 4 September, the fleet made its rendezvous in the Spanish River Road (Sydney Harbour), Cape Breton, where further discussion took place on the prospects of taking Placentia. In view of his instructions, Walker had some qualms about returning to England with Quebec and Placentia both unscathed; but comforted by General Hill, who was equally loth to embark on fresh adventures, and bolstered by the unanimous verdict of a second council of war, which pointed out that only ten weeks' provisions were available, he finally resolved to sail for home and face the music. On 10 October he dropped anchor at Portsmouth, and took coach to London where he reported to the distressed but not unaffable St John. During his absence, the *Edgar* blew up with the loss of the maintenance crew and the greater part of Walker's public papers, books, journals, and charts.

Thanks to an indulgent Tory ministry, both Hill and Walker escaped official censure for their conduct of the expedition. Indeed, both were given fresh commands, which could be interpreted as tacit approval of their conduct. In March 1712 Walker was appointed commodore of the squadron in Jamaica. There he engaged in trade and politics, and quarrelled with the governor until he was summoned back to England a year later. He took a house in Huntingdonshire, where, as a justice of the peace, he lived the life of a country gentleman. But the disaster—one of the worst in 18th century naval annals—was not forgotten by the politicians. When Walker's patron fell, Anne's successor, George I, called the Whigs back to power, and within a few months the admiral's name was summarily struck off the flag list without pretence of a hearing, his half-pay was stopped, and in the same year (1715) he was ordered to furnish the government with a full account of the expedition. Hoping to mend his fortunes in the colonies he took refuge in South Carolina, whence he returned within two years to complete his *Journal* on the basis of memory, a pocket diary, and various letters and documents supplied him by the secretary of the Admiralty, Josiah Burchett. This detailed personal record is essentially an effort at self-vindication.

As the introduction to the *Journal* makes clear, Walker's inner torments had not dissolved with the years, and this misery, aggravated by peremptory dismissal from the service, helped to create something like a persecution complex. On the other hand, although he pleads his own cause with bitterness and often with melodrama, there is no attempt to suppress evidence. Indeed, Walker's naïve admissions serve to diminish his own stature as a commander. Even had he possessed the guile, he lacked the subtlety and balance to make out a convincing case for himself. Walker's nerves had been shaken before the fleet left Boston; thereafter his ability to make major decisions diminished progressively. Lacking provisions, and without competent pilots, his expedition had become a gigantic gamble long before it reached the St Lawrence river. Undoubtedly he lacked the qualities of a great commander, but, whatever the weaknesses of his leadership, the failure was not his alone. Walker was a victim of the pernicious political system of the day, a reluctant tool in the hands of a brilliant sharper, Henry St John, Viscount Bolingbroke.

Following the publication of the *Journal* in 1720, Walker seems to have moved about restlessly between Ireland and the continent. Thomas Lediard, who wrote *The naval history of England*, ran into him in Hamburg and in Hanover, and found him "a gentleman of Letters, good Understanding, ready wit, and agreable [*sic*] Conversation."

GERALD S. GRAHAM

Hovenden Walker, *A journal or full account of the late expedition to Canada* (London, 1720) has been republished by the Champlain Society and the Navy Records Society under the title *The Walker expedition to Quebec, 1711*, edited by G. S. Graham. The editor's Introduction contains detailed bibliographical references.

Many of the documents in the PRO (chiefly C.O. 5) relevant to the career of Walker have been printed at length, or in abbreviated form, in PRO, *CSP, Col., 1710–11, 1711–12*. Supplementary letters and papers, which were not available to Admiral Walker when he was writing his *Journal*, and which fill in the gaps in his account, are to be found in PRO, S.P. 42/68; 44/110, 44/111 (secretaries' letter books).

Printed sources include the following: Josiah Burchett, *A complete history of the most remarkable transactions at sea, from the earliest accounts of time to the conclusion of the last war with France* (London, 1720). Juchereau et Duplessis, *Histoire de l'Hôtel-Dieu de Québec*; *Annales* (Jamet). Thomas Lediard, *The naval history of England . . . from the Norman conquest . . . to the conclusion of 1734* (2v., London, 1735). *Letters and correspondence, public and private, of the Right Honourable Henry St. John, Lord visc. Bolingbroke during the time he was secretary of state*, ed. Gilbert Parke (4v., London, 1798). Robert Beatson, *A political index to the histories of Great Britain and Ireland* (3d ed., 3v., London, 1806). Charnock, *Biographia navalis*, II. J. S. Crone, *A concise dictionary of Irish biography* (London, 1928); it is here stated that Walker was born "about 1660." *DNB*. R. D. Merriman, "Captain George St. Lo, R.N., 1658–1718," *The Mariner's Mirror* (London), XXXI, no.1 (1945), 13–23. P.-G. Roy, "Qui était le capitaine Paradis?" *BRH*, XLIX (1943), 65–68.

WALLEY, JOHN, major in the New England militia; b. apparently in England in 1644, the son of a London clergyman; d. 11 Jan. 1711/12 (o.s.), in Boston, Mass.

After emigrating to Massachusetts Bay Walley appears as a member and later an officer of the Ancient and Honourable Artillery Company of Boston. In or about 1680 he moved to Bristol (R.I.). He was apparently living in Barnstable (Mass.) in 1690, when he was appointed second in command, and commander of the land forces, in the expedition against Quebec led by Sir William

Phips*. He commanded the force of 1,200 or more men that landed on the *côte* Beauport below Quebec on 18 October. It was withdrawn three and a half days later without accomplishing anything and leaving most of its cannon behind. Walley was criticized for the failure, but was probably no more responsible than any other of the inexperienced amateurs who planned and executed the expedition.

He became a judge of the Superior Court of Massachusetts Bay in 1700, and apparently held office until his death. At various times he was a councillor of Plymouth and of Massachusetts. In 1709 he was appointed to an artillery command in the abortive expedition against Canada.

C. P. STACEY

The sources for the expedition of 1690, as well as the events in which Walley took part, are fully discussed in the article on Phips in *DCB*, I. Walley's own rather detailed narrative of the affair is published as Appendix XXI of Hutchinson, *History of Massachusetts* (1795), I, and is also found, along with a biographical sketch and portrait of Walley, in W. K. Watkins, *Soldiers in the expedition to Canada in 1690 and grantees of the Canada townships* (Boston, 1898). *See also: Diary of Samuel Sewall, 1674–1729* (3v., Mass. Hist. Soc. *Coll.*, 5th ser., V–VII, 1878–82), II. *Appleton's Cyclopædia of American biography*, ed. J. G. Wilson and John Fiske (6v., New York, 1887–89), VI, 338. Waller, *Samuel Vetch*. Emory Washburn, *Sketches of the judicial history of Massachusetts from 1630 to the revolution in 1775* (Boston, 1840).

WANUNGONET. *See* WENEMOUET

WARD, RICHARD, seaman employed by the HBC intermittently between 1698 and 1720; d. sometime before November 1729.

In 1698 and in 1699–1700 Ward was employed at Albany and on the East Main. He left the company on his return to England in 1700 and served for some while in the Royal Navy in the War of the Spanish Succession. In February 1711 the company secured his release from the navy in order that he might command its supply ship, *Pery*. He sailed this ship to Albany that year, but ran her aground on a sand-bar in the river's mouth, where she broke up. Much of her cargo of trade goods was saved, and Ward wintered at Albany. In 1712 he sailed home as captain of the *Knight*.

Four years later he applied to the company again and was given command of the *Hudson's Bay* [III] supply-ship, which Joseph DAVIS had failed to navigate into York the previous year. Ward successfully sailed the *Hudson's Bay* [III] to York in 1716 with long-awaited provisions and trade goods for James KNIGHT, the commander of that post and the company's governor in the bay. In 1717 Ward commanded the same ship on the round trip to Churchill and in 1718 to York. In 1719 he once more sailed to Churchill, but from that post he continued his voyage to York, and was wrecked at Cape Tatnum on 24 August. He successfully reached York after abandoning his ship, wintered there, and returned to England in 1720 with Capt. Gofton on the *Hannah*. He was not again employed by the company.

RICHARD GLOVER

Founding of Churchill (Kenney). HBRS, XXI (Rich); XXV (Davies and Johnson). *Kelsey papers* (Doughty and Martin). Morton, *History of the Canadian west*.

WARRACANSIT (Warracunsit, Warrawcuset). *See* MOG

WASHINGTON, JOHN, lieutenant and engineer, assigned to the British garrison at Annapolis Royal, N.S.; fl. 1719–24.

Washington's behaviour was frequently a source of agitation in the British capital between 1719 and 1724. He neglected to keep his engineering accounts in order, ignored the orders of his superiors, and intrigued against the local authorities. In June 1721 a fellow officer noticed that Washington was spending a good deal of time in the "Necessary house" at the fort. While leaving the privy one day Washington dropped a piece of "foule Paper," which was found to contain a draft of a letter to the Board of Ordnance accusing Governor Richard Phillips* and the provincial councillors of graft and peculation. A search of Washington's quarters revealed that he had been sending such letters to England for months. The revelation of this "Villanous underhand dealing" prompted an investigation and the dispatch of voluminous denials by the councillors to the home authorities. Although Washington was obviously untrustworthy and possibly insane, the council was unwilling to take action against him since he was directly responsible to the politically powerful Board of Ordnance. Apparently he remained in Nova Scotia until the spring of 1724, when he was either recalled or persuaded to return to England.

MAXWELL SUTHERLAND

Mass. Hist. Soc., Gay papers, III, IV. PAC, Nova Scotia A, 11–16; *see especially* 13, pp.105–44, 164–85. *Documents relating to currency in Nova Scotia, 1675–1758* (Shortt). PAC *Report, 1894,* 40–55. Brebner, *New England's outpost.*

WATTS, RICHARD, first schoolmaster of the

Society for the Propagation of the Gospel in Nova Scotia; born in Scotland, 1688; died at Bristol, R.I., 15 March 1739/40.

Watts was educated at Glasgow, where he received his M.A. He was a Presbyterian schoolmaster before entering the ministry of the Church of England, into which he was ordained deacon by Bishop Edmund Gibson of London on 6 Feb. 1726/27. On 7 May 1727, he was ordained priest, and soon afterwards was appointed garrison chaplain at Annapolis Royal in Nova Scotia. The Society for the Propagation of the Gospel also appointed him its schoolmaster there.

Late in 1727, he left England for Boston, where he assisted the Reverend Samuel Miles at King's Chapel for some time. Early in 1727/28, he went to Annapolis Royal and opened his school there at Easter 1728. This was an ordinary day school and not a Sunday school, as some have claimed. The old French chapel in the fort being almost in ruins, Alexander Cosby*, the lieutenant-governor of Annapolis, gave him the use of a former barrack room for his church and school.

Watts applied to the SPG, in November 1729, for appointment as its missionary at Canso (Canseau), but he was unsuccessful; in October 1730, with the full support of Governor Richard Philipps*, he petitioned the home government for a commission as an army chaplain. His request was refused. In July 1732, he applied to Lieutenant-Governor ARMSTRONG and the council for the grant of the old French church lands in the lower town at Annapolis Royal, for the use of the Church of England. On 23 November a deed for these lands was granted as "Glebe Land for ever for the Chaplain, or, if a Parish be established, for the Parish Minister." This land is still owned by the parish of St Luke's, and was the first land granted for the endowment of a Protestant church in Canada.

In September 1737, Watts wrote to the SPG stating that he had been in the colony almost ten years, and wished to return home. Not receiving a reply, he left Annapolis Royal on 19 Jan. 1737/38 for Rhode Island, settling in Bristol, near Newport. For some months, he substituted for the Reverend James Honeyman, rector of Newport. He spent most of 1739 at Bristol as the schoolmaster; but late in that year he applied to the SPG for its vacant mission at Scituate, Mass. Before a reply could reach him, however, Watts had died at Bristol on 15 March 1739/40, in his fifty-second year. His wife Margaret returned to England in July.

Little is known of his career as a schoolmaster in Scotland, but in North America it was one of disappointment and frustration. Being the only

663

Waxaway

Protestant clergyman in Nova Scotia at that period, and serving a small Protestant community in and around the fort, Watts showed remarkable fortitude in enduring ten years in Annapolis Royal, without any relief or change. Governor Philipps thought very highly of his services, as did the rector of Newport. Although life in Rhode Island was decidedly happier for him, the disappointments of his earlier career left their mark on him.

C. E. THOMAS

Watts's tombstone (St. Michael's churchyard, Bristol, R.I.) reads: "Here lieth Intombd ye Reverd Mr Richard Watts Master of Arts died March ye 15 1739/40 In ye 52d year of his age."

Guildhall Library, London, Ordinations register diocese of London, MS 9535/3, pp.227, 228; *see also* MS ,10326B, box I, file I. PANS, MS docs., XXII. USPG, Journal of SPG, V, 21 July 1727, 29 Nov. 1729; VII, 22 Sept. 1737, 19 Jan. 1737/38; VIII, April 1740; Letters and reports of missionaries of SPG, A, XXI, 408–11; B, VII, pt.I, 29; .pt.II, 27 (copies in PANS, USPG microfilms, reels 13, 14). *The Fulham papers in the Lambeth palace library*, ed. W. W. Manross (Oxford, 1965). *N.S. Archives, III.*

WAXAWAY, (Wexar, Assurowlaway, Prince Waxaway, in Abenaki *wasálialəwe*, "Snow Tail"), *dogique*, and subchief of the Norridgewock division of the Abenakis; fl. 1694–1710.

Waxaway resided at Amassokanty (now Farmington Falls, Me.). Early in July 1694 Waxaway took part in a dog feast of war that was held there. He enlisted with Bomoseen and on the 18th (o.s.) participated in the furious attack on Oyster River (Durham, N.H.) by that chief and CLAUDE-SÉBASTIEN DE VILLIEU. Evidently deeply affected by the slaughter Waxaway later ransomed one of Bomoseen's captives, Mrs Ann Jenkins, helped several other prisoners, and thereafter inclined towards pacifism.

From 1694 to 1701 Waxaway served as *dogique*, or religious assistant, to Father VINCENT BIGOT at the Amassokanty mission. He spoke good English and was known to English prisoners as "the Indian minister" and "Prince Waxaway." In September 1698 and October 1701, he probably accompanied Bigot to Canada, visiting the Abenaki missions of Saint-François de Sales (probably modern Beauceville) and Saint-Joseph de Sillery (near Quebec). Waxaway seems to have been the English-speaking chief who attended a conference with the New England deputies at Falmouth (now Portland, Me.) on 3 and 4 June 1701. He told Father Bigot that he had valiantly defended the Roman Catholic religion to which he attributed his success in overcoming his previous

drunkenness. On 20 June 1703 he and other Abenaki chiefs signed a peace treaty with Massachusetts at Falmouth. Although war broke out less than two months later, Waxaway kept the peace and did much to alleviate the suffering of English captives.

Father Bigot had been recalled from the mission in 1701, and in 1704 many of the residents of Amassokanty moved to Canada to settle at Bécancour. Waxaway and others later moved to Norridgewock (Old Point, in south Madison, Me.). He probably spent the winter of 1708–9 in Canada, since he is not listed in the La Chasse* census of Indians on the Kennebec in November of 1708.

At Norridgewock the next winter an Indian, almost certainly Waxaway, purchased Lieutenant Josiah Littlefield of Wells, Me., from his Canadian Abenaki "master" to spare the ailing prisoner the hazardous winter trip to Canada. Littlefield wrote Governor Joseph Dudley of Massachusetts that the "Norridgewock Indian" had nursed him back to health, and had "been like a father." The following summer Littlefield's new owner led some 50 Abenakis of the peace party to Falmouth, where they complained of "unfair treatment" by English fishermen while under a flag of truce. They were not well received by the commander, Captain Samuel Moodey. Waxaway released Littlefield, but was justly disappointed when he received no reward. He told Lieutenant Joseph Bean, second in command, that "the ffrench were very Angry" with the peace party for bringing Littlefield to the fort, and "haveing now no Commerce with them [the French], were come for a Supply from the English." Again they were disappointed.

Waxaway's later life and the date of his death are not known.

FRANK T. SIEBERT, JR.

Newberry Library, Ayer Coll., La Chasse census (1708). [Vincent Bigot], *Relation de ce qui s'est passé de plus remarquable dans la mission des Abnaquis à l'Acadie, l'année 1701* (Manate [New York], 1858), 8–10. *Coll. de manuscrits relatifs à la N.-F.,* II, 495. *Documentary hist. of Maine,* IX, 276, 302–3; X, 94–95. Hutchinson, *Hist. of Mass.-bay* (1768), II, 171. *New Eng. Hist. and Geneal. Register,* XVIII (1864), 163–64. Penhallow, *Hist. of wars with Eastern Indians* (1726), 2. *Province and court records of Maine,* V, 23. E. E. Bourne, *The history of Wells and Kennebunk from the earliest settlements to the year 1820* (Portland, Me., 1875), 267–73. Coleman, *New England captives,* I, 435–37.

WENEMOUET (Wenemowet, Wenemuit, Winnenimmit, Awenemwet, Nimimitt, Nimquid; and after 1726, Wenongonet, Wenungenit, Wenog-

664

genet, **Wanungonet, Ouenanguenet),** a chief of the Penobscot division of the Abenakis; d. March 1730.

In Abenaki Wenemouet's name is *winí-mαwəwet,* meaning "weak war chief." With 13 other Abenaki chiefs he signed the peace treaty with the English at Mares Point (now Merepoint, Me.) on 7 Jan. 1698/99. He was probably one of the delegation of more than 40 Penobscots who went with the Jesuit Pierre de La Chasse* to visit Governor CALLIÈRE at Quebec in October 1702. The Penobscots were unenthusiastic about fighting with the French unless Quebec was threatened with actual conquest, which would deprive them of French support against New England. The delegation asked Callière whether he could sell them goods at a fair price, and the governor arranged with the Quebec merchants to supply them cheaply. At the end of Queen Anne's War Wenemouet and 18 other Abenaki chiefs signed a peace with the English at the second conference of Portsmouth, on 28 July 1714.

In 1722 the Penobscots joined the other Abenakis against the English [*see* MOG]. Sometime late in 1724 or early in 1725 Wenemouet became head chief of the Penobscots. He was aware that the Penobscot villages were vulnerable to attack and that the French were not actively supporting his tribe; the Penobscots consequently welcomed English overtures for peace in December 1724. The next summer the tribe sent wampum belts proposing peace with the English to their allies, the Canadian Abenakis and the Hurons of Lorette. These Indians rejected the proposals, bringing about a partial political separation of the Penobscots from other divisions of the Abenaki nation and from the French in Canada. A complete rupture did not occur, however.

After preliminary negotiations Governor Dummer of Massachusetts and Wenemouet agreed on a cease-fire east of the Kennebec River, and on 31 July 1725 Dummer ordered an end to all hostilities against the Penobscot division of the Abenakis. Wenemouet twice sent emissaries to Boston in the autumn of that year to draw up terms for a permanent peace, and agreed to urge the other Abenaki tribes to join. The Canadian Abenakis and some of their allies nevertheless continued to make raids on New England, and did not participate in the treaty which Wenemouet and about 40 of his tribesmen concluded with the English on 5 August 1726. During the lengthy conference Wenemouet spoke little because he was ill, and Saguaarum* (Loron) provided most of the oratory. Dummer reassured the Penobscots about their land titles and guaranteed them the same privileges as other English subjects.

At a meeting of the chiefs and elders of the Penobscot tribe in September 1726, Wenemouet's name was officially changed to Wenongonet to honour and perpetuate the name of a former leader, head chief from 1698 to 1724. In October Wenemouet sent two messengers, Alexis and François-Xavier, to Quebec to request the new governor, Charles de Beauharnois* de La Boische, "to arrest the hatchet of their brethren" settled in Canada, "the rebound of which would inevitably fall on them." The French in vain urged the Penobscots to continue the war against the English. The envoys visited Quebec, Bécancour, Saint-François, and Caughnawaga, and persuaded most of the Canadian Abenakis and mission Iroquois to end the war, despite the opposition of Beauharnois and Fathers Aubéry* and La Chasse. The two Penobscots arrived home in March 1727 and reported that the peace had been accepted by almost all the Canadian Indians. The only ones who remained hostile were 16 men and 2 chiefs, Gray Lock* and Onedahauet (Comhommon), of Saint-François and Missiassik (on the Missisquoi R., Vt.). Earlier in March Wenemouet had denied any knowledge of Gray Lock's activities, and he now made a complete report of the results of the Canadian mission to John Gyles*, to be relayed to Dummer.

Wenemouet was devoted to establishing a lasting peace. In late April he sent messengers to all the Abenaki tribes, the Malecites, and the Micmacs asking them to attend the Penobscot annual meeting and hear of the peace. In May he sent the Canadian Abenakis a wampum belt to confirm that he strongly opposed any further hostilities. Some of the Norridgewocks left Canada in May 1727 to resettle in their old village, and a large body of Canadian Abenakis and Iroquois camped at Taconock (now Winslow, Me.) on the Kennebec River to await arrangements for a final treaty. Dummer and a New England delegation finally established a satisfactory peace with all divisions of the Abenakis at Falmouth (now Portland, Me.) on 27 July. On behalf of the Penobscots Wenemouet asked that Gyles remain as commander of the fort at St George's River, and that they be supplied with a gunsmith.

In 1729 Wenemouet protested "tree cutting" and the encroachment of English settlement on Abenaki lands. He notified the Massachusetts authorities that "if any Pass St. Georges River to Plant we shall not thinke them to be our frinds."

Near the end of his life Wenemouet was described as "a well looking man, more like a frenchman than an Indian," who seemed "grave and reserved." He died in March 1730. By freeing the Penobscots from French ties and seeking an

Wexar

amicable accommodation with the English, he enabled his people to avoid defeat and to retain at least part of their ancient territory into modern times. Although the aged Moxus of the Norridgewocks was the nominal head chief of the Abenaki nation, Wenemouet assumed tacit leadership and induced all the Abenaki tribes to forsake their old alliance with Quebec and to seek peace. After his death, the continued encroachment of the New Englanders upon Abenaki lands once again forced his nation to resume ties with the French and the Indian allies who had supported the Abenakis in 1722.

FRANK T. SIEBERT, JR.

Joseph Baxter, *Journal of several visits to the Indians of the Kennebec River, 1717*, ed. Elias Nason (Boston, 1867), 16. *The conference with the Eastern Indians at the ratification of the peace held at Falmouth in Casco-bay in July and August 1726* (Boston, 1726). *The conference with the Eastern Indians at the further ratification of the peace held at Falmouth in Casco-bay in July 1727* (Boston, 1727). Documentary hist. of Maine, X, 317–18, 358, 365–66, 375–78, 385–87, 389–92, 408–9, 445–47, 458–68; XI, 150–51; XXIII, 235. "Journal of Edward Goddard, 1726" in *Trans.*, *1917–19* (Col. Soc. Mass. pub., XX, Boston, 1920) 128–47. Maine Hist. Soc. *Coll.*, 1st ser., III (1853), 355–58, 377–447. *New Eng. Hist. and Geneal. Register*, XXI (1867), 58. *NYCD* (O'Callaghan and Fernow), IX, 736–38, 955–56, 990–91. Penhallow, *History of wars with Eastern Indians* (1726), 118, 129. [Thomas Westbrook, *et al.*], *Letters of Colonel Thomas Westbrook and others relative to Indian affairs in Maine 1722–26*, ed. W. B. Trask (Boston, 1901), 157. Frederick Kidder, *The Abenaki Indians; their treaties of 1713 and 1717* ... (Portland, 1859), 19–21.

WEXAR. *See* WAXAWAY

WHETSTONE, SIR WILLIAM, rear-admiral; commodore of the Newfoundland convoy, 1696; d. 1711.

William Whetstone, believed to have been the son of John Whetstone, sailing master of Sir William Penn's flagship in 1695, was commissioned captain of the *Europa* in 1689. In 1696 Whetstone was appointed captain of the *Dreadnought* and commodore of the Newfoundland convoy. The convoy of 61 sail, bound for Newfoundland and New England, sailed from Plymouth 1 September, escorted by the *Dreadnought* and the *Oxford*. Apart from sighting French privateers who did not attack, the passage was uneventful though progress was slow. On 2 November, some 100 miles from Newfoundland, a French fly boat, *La Courette*, was captured. The owner of the vessel was said to be the governor of Placentia (Plaisance), Brouillan [MOMBETON]. The master, Pierre Aubert,

and 19 men were taken prisoner. It was learned that a week or two previously a powerful French force under PIERRE LE MOYNE d'Iberville had left Placentia and was moving up the coast towards St John's. The land force was backed by a French squadron under Brouillan, which included 5 heavily armed ships, with up to 70 guns each, easily capable of out-gunning both the *Dreadnought* with 64 guns and the *Oxford* with 54.

The instructions given to Whetstone by the Admiralty before he sailed included the words, "take care not imprudently to expose the ships under your command." In view of the news of the destruction of the English fishing harbours, the superiority of the French forces, and the approaching winter, it was decided, after consultation with the masters of the Newfoundland-bound merchant ships, not to risk entering the harbours but to sail to the nearest ports in Spain. The following spring, 1697, an expedition, under Sir John GIBSONE and Sir John Norris*, was sent out to recover the captured English settlements.

On the accession of Queen Anne, Whetstone was sent with a small squadron to reinforce Vice-Admiral Benbow in the West Indies. He arrived 8 May 1702. Later in the summer, in an engagement with Ducasse, Benbow was seriously injured, and deputed Whetstone, with the local rank of rear-admiral, to sit as president of the court-martial which tried Captains Kirkby and Wade for cowardice.

After Benbow's death in November 1702, Whetstone assumed command of the fleet and in the summer of the following year joined the squadron commanded by Vice-Admiral GRAYDON which was to attack the French at Placentia. Whetstone was present at the council of war which decided not to risk the attack, but—perhaps because of his services in the West Indies—he escaped the criticism heaped on the unfortunate Graydon.

On 22 Feb. 1704/5 Whetstone was knighted and spent the rest of the year on service in the Caribbean. In 1707, however, an unfortunate sequence of events led to Whetstone's being superseded in his command, and, as in the case of Vice-Admiral Graydon, he was not employed again. Sir William Whetstone died apparently in the spring of 1711. Letters of administration, wherein he is described as "of Bristol," were granted to his widow Maria.

MICHAEL GODFREY

PRO, Adm. 2/21 (orders and instructions); 51/4170, pt.7 (captain's log of H.M.S. *Dreadnought*); *CSP, Col.*, *1702*, *1702–3*, *1704–5*, *1706–8*. Charnock, *Biographia navalis*, II. *DNB*.

WILAMAK. *See* OUENEMEK

WILLIAMS, JOHN, Puritan minister and one-time Indian captive; b. 10 Dec. 1664 (o.s.) at Roxbury, Mass., son of Samuel and Theoda (Park) Williams and grandson of Robert Williams, who migrated from Norwich, England, in 1638 to Massachusetts Bay; d. 12 June 1729 at Deerfield, Mass.

John Williams attended Roxbury Latin School and graduated from Harvard College in 1683. He taught school for two years in Dorchester and studied divinity. In March 1686 he was selected as preacher at Deerfield, and was ordained as the town's first minister in October 1688. He married Eunice Mather, daughter of the Reverend Eleazar Mather of Northampton, on 21 July 1687; they had nine children, two dying in infancy.

Deerfield had been burned by Indians and deserted in King Philip's War (1675–76), and during King William's War (War of the League of Augsburg) the town was attacked almost annually by French and Indians. After the start of Queen Anne's War (War of the Spanish Succession), Williams persuaded Governor Dudley to post 20 soldiers there. Nevertheless, before dawn on 29 Feb. 1703/4 (11 March 1704, N.S.), a force of 200 French and 142 Abenakis and Caughnawaga-Mohawks (also reported as 50 French and 200 Indians) under Major JEAN-BAPTISTE HERTEL de Rouville silently approached the sleeping town. With snow piled high against the stockades, they entered the town easily, and began their attack. According to one estimate they killed 47 inhabitants and took 112 prisoners, about one-third of the population; 17 houses went up in flames. Breaking into Williams' house, the enemy killed two of his sons, one a six-week-old infant, and their Negro nurse, and took the family prisoners. In the harsh trek northward to Montreal 18 prisoners, including Mrs Williams, were killed. Williams, his sons, and daughters were parcelled out among Indian and French families and held for ransom. Governor RIGAUD de Vaudreuil redeemed Williams and tried to procure the release of his children. For a time Williams was kept at Quebec, where a serious effort was made to convert him to Roman Catholicism. By October 1706 all of his children except Eunice* had been freed, and he sailed to Boston with 54 other released captives. Pierre MAISONNAT, *dit* Baptiste, was one of the French prisoners released by New England at the same time.

Williams returned to Deerfield as minister and wrote a narrative of the Deerfield attack and of his experience in Canada, which was published at Boston in 1707 as *The redeemed captive, returning to Zion* .... According to Sibley, he was appointed chaplain to the abortive New England expedition against Port-Royal (Annapolis Royal, N.S.) in 1707, and to the local troops serving in Admiral WALKER's expedition to Quebec in 1711. At the end of the war in November 1713, Williams and Major John Stoddard* were sent to Canada by Massachusetts to ransom more captives, but had only partial success in their negotiations with Vaudreuil. Although the two commissioners stayed in Montreal and Quebec until the end of August 1714, they recovered only 26 captives.

Williams took as his second wife Abigail Bissell, daughter of Captain Thomas Allen of Windsor, Conn., in September 1707. She was a cousin of his first wife and had five children by him. Williams continued his ministry at Deerfield until his death 12 June 1729, after a stroke of apoplexy three days earlier. Three of his sons by his first wife became ministers.

HOWARD H. PECKHAM

The primary source for Williams' capture and captivity at Quebec is his own narrative, cited above, *The redeemed captive returning to Zion: or, a faithful history of remarkable occurrences in the captivity and deliverance of Mr. John Williams* ... (1st ed., Boston, 1707; 6th ed., Boston, 1795, repr. in Springfield, Mass., 1908); only eight copies of the first edition are known today. Some of Williams' letters are in the Massachusetts Historical Society library. A journal of the negotiations between Stoddard, Williams, and Vaudreuil can be found in the Houghton library, Harvard Univ., MS Am 1201.

DAB. J. L. Sibley, *Biographical sketches of graduates of Harvard University* ... , (3v., Cambridge, Mass., 1873–85), III, 249–62. Coleman, *New England captives.* Parkman, *A half-century of conflict* (1893), I. S. W. Williams, *A biographical memoir of the Rev. John Williams, first minister of Deerfield, Mass.* (Greenfield, Mass. 1837).

WILLIAMS, JOHN, captain in the garrison of Annapolis Royal, N.S., fl. 1711–18.

According to later petitions, John Williams was enrolled in one of the seven regiments which made up General JOHN HILL's land force for the WALKER expedition against Quebec in 1711. Following the disaster that terminated the expedition, Williams was included in a detachment of officers and soldiers sent to relieve the garrison of Annapolis Royal.

Being one of the "eldest officers," he was given command of one of the four companies formed from the garrison in 1712. His commission as captain (dated 16 Oct. 1712) was enclosed in the document ordering Lieutenant-Governor CAULFEILD to establish the companies. As a captain in the garrison, Williams also served on the governing

Winnenimmit

council, and thus he took part in the discussions with the French envoys, Louis Denys* de La Ronde and Jacques d'ESPIET de Pensens, sent from Île Royale in the summer of 1714.

Williams' stay at Annapolis Royal seems to have been marked by great privation. A steady round of petitions from the garrison pleaded for additional provisions and clothing allowances. At one point Williams was on his way to England with a fellow captain, Christopher Aldridge, to press the issue, but was turned back at Boston by Governor NICHOLSON.

When Lieutenant-Governor Caulfeild died 2 March 1716/17, Williams reported his death to England and apparently assumed the deceased officer's duties in an acting capacity. At the same time he sought the office on a permanent basis as "the oldest officer in this part of America by some years." As he feared, however, one of the "several persons who are now att home" received the post; John DOUCETT arrived at Annapolis Royal 28 Oct. 1717 to assume the duties of lieutenant-governor under Governor Richard Philipps*. Philipps organized the independent companies at Annapolis Royal and Placentia (Plaisance) into the 40th Foot (Colonel Richard Philipps' regiment of foot). John Williams received the commission of captain (dated 25 Aug. 1717) in the new regiment; but the following year Joseph Bennett was appointed captain "in room of John Williams" (commission dated 15 May 1718). John Williams was still at Annapolis Royal 24 June 1718, but his signature does not appear on documents after that date.

GEORGE C. INGRAM

PAC, Nova Scotia A, 3, 4, 5, 6, 7, 8. PRO, C.O. 5/9; 217/1, 217/2; *CSP, Col., 1716–17*. R. H. R. Smythies, *Historical records of the 40th (2d Somersetshire) regiment now 1st battalion the Prince of Wales volunteers (South Lancashire regiment) from its formation in 1717 to 1893* (Devonport, 1894). *Walker expedition* (Graham). Dalton, *English army lists*, VI, 190, 192n. Brebner, *New England's outpost*. Dalton, *George the First's army*, I, 312–13.

WINNENIMMIT. *See* WENEMOUET

WOWURNA (Captain Joseph, Oüaourené, Ouwoorana, Sheepscot Jo, Wiwurna), a leading chief of the Norridgewock division of the Abenakis, and an ally of the French; fl. 1670–1738.

In August 1717 Wowurna represented 20 leading Norridgewock, Penobscot, Pigwacket, and Androscoggin Indians in a meeting with Governor Samuel Shute of Massachusetts, at Georgetown on Arrowsic Island. The chief denied Shute's right to build forts and new settlements, rejected

King George I as the Indians' sovereign, and ignored Reverend Joseph Baxter, the minister Shute introduced to them. Frequently interrupted by the governor, Wowurna insisted that English claims to lands up the Kennebec River and east of it were unfounded: "We can't understand how our Lands have been purchased, what has been Alienated was by our gift." The Indians supported their case with a letter from Father Sébastien RALE, the Jesuit at Norridgewock (now Old Point in south Madison, Me.). Shute threatened to leave, and Wowurna was replaced by a conciliatory speaker. Rale later claimed that the Abenakis accepted only the words of Wowurna, who had spoken "with matchless pride."

Probably unknown to Rale, the chief visited Baxter at Georgetown a few days after the conference. Wowurna's aim may have been to gain information about the English. At any rate, he translated Baxter's preaching for his wife, his brother John (Nagiscoig), and two other Indians, and even promised to teach the minister Abenaki. He visited Baxter again at Georgetown in October and December, but then the visits ceased, and Shute condemned Rale soon after for his "Excommunicating and Unchristian Treatment of the Poor Indians for only Attending on Mr Baxters Instructions...."

As English settlement spread to Merrymeeting Bay, Swan Island, and east of the Kennebec, the Norridgewocks quarrelled with the English and killed their cattle. Both sides prepared to fight. Wowurna was probably one of the two "principal chiefs" of the village whom Rale sent to Quebec in October 1719. They told Governor RIGAUD de Vaudreuil that they were determined to resist the English, and he confirmed that France had not ceded their lands to England, and supplied them with "munitions." In January 1720 Massachusetts commissioners met the Norridgewocks at Falmouth (metropolitan Portland, Me.) to warn them and to listen to their complaints. Settlement continued, however, and Wowurna, Nathaniel, and younger Indians destroyed so many crops and farm animals in the summer of 1720 that the settlers were convinced that the Norridgewocks were planning war. On 12 October, carrying a French flag, Wowurna and another Norridgewock met English representatives at Georgetown and reluctantly agreed to a larger meeting. Wowurna was there six weeks later when the Indians declared that "If all those people were removed from Merry Meeting bay, all other Differences between us would be easily composed." But the New Englanders rejected the Abenaki claims and forced them to promise payment of 200 skins, and to give up four hostages, for the damage done.

Alarmed, Rale gathered Indian allies to support the Norridgewocks, and organized a major confrontation at Georgetown on 17 July 1721. Fathers Rale and La Chasse*, Joseph d'Abbadie* de Saint-Castin and Charles Legardeur* de Croisil accompanied 250 Indians, under French colours, into the town. In a letter to Shute, the Indians demanded the release of the hostages and removal of the English from Abenaki lands. Wowurna read the letter in Abenaki in the name of "all the Christian and Catholic Indians of this country and of Canada." The English refused the demands and prepared for war, but Vaudreuil wrote Rale: "I am quite delighted that [Wowurna] thus distinguished himself in this parley." Vaudreuil also sent a full report of the chief's exploits to France. Britain soon made an official protest to the French government about the incident.

In January 1721/22 the English attempted to seize Rale at Norridgewock. An uneasy peace prevailed until, late on the night of 14 June, Wowurna led over 40 Indians, "Arm'd & Painted for warr," in a raid on Merrymeeting Bay, where they burned some houses and a mill, stripped the inhabitants of their belongings and their clothes, and took five prisoners. They hoped to exchange these men for the Norridgewock hostages held at Boston, but Massachusetts declared war on 25 July. Wowurna apparently took an active part in Dummer's War, and when he visited Quebec early in 1723 Vaudreuil presented him with a "laced Capp" in recognition of his many services to the French. After the destruction of Norridgewock in 1724 Wowurna resided in Canada, probably at Saint-François (near the mouth of the Saint-François River). He helped lead a party of 20 Norridgewock and Arosaguntacook (Saint-François) Indians on a successful raid on Damaris Cove (probably near Boothbay Harbor, Me.) in the summer of 1725. The Indians apparently claimed later that they were unaware of the English-Abenaki truce east of the Kennebec, made that July.

In March 1727 John Gyles* heard from Canada that after WENEMOUET's messengers arrived, proposing that the Canadian Indians ratify the Penobscot peace with Massachusetts, Wowurna was to set up a trail marker above Taconick (now Winslow, Me.) on the Kennebec River, to tell Norridgewocks who planned to move back to their native village whether peace was definite. Wowurna and over 50 other Abenakis returned and camped at Taconick. In June, after waiting almost two months, they had run out of supplies and were anxious to know when the governor would meet them, for they would not come to Boston. The House of Representatives voted £300 to provision them, and Wowurna and the others ratified the peace at Falmouth on 21 July. Two years later in November 1729, Wowurna was probably among the Penobscot and Norridgewock chiefs who met the surveyor David Dunbar at Pemaquid, which he was rebuilding. Dunbar reassured them about their lands, but Wowurna and others, rightly suspicious, came to Richmond in January to ask what Dunbar planned and whether the government was involved. Wowurna's concern for the Abenakis' future showed again at Falmouth in 1732, when he intervened in discussions between Loron (Saguaarum*), the official spokesman, and Governor Belcher of Massachusetts, to the latter's chagrin. The old chief resisted the governor's proposal for an English settlement at Cushnok (Augusta, Me.), and warned that quarrels between English and Indian youths threatened the peace.

Although he knew Quebec well, Wowurna's visit to Boston in July 1738 was his first, and probably his last. As "principal of the Norridgewock tribe" he declared in the council chamber that he had reassured the people at Sheepscot (near Wiscasset, Me.) of the Indians' peaceful intentions, and complained of the high cost of trade goods. He then drank the king's health and thanked the governor for his kindness. At 67, he was a very old Indian, and perhaps resigned at last to the English presence on his ancestral lands. If he had hopes for future resistance, Wowurna, a man whom historians have described as "mannerly" (Parkman), "wily" (Baxter), and "shrewd and sagacious" (Thwaites), would not have revealed them to his old enemies.

DOUGLAS HAY

AE, Corr. pol., Angleterre, 341, f.186. AN, Col., B, 44, ff.121–24; C¹¹A, 39, ff.157–62; 40, ff.45–46v; 44, ff.131–42, 303–8; 46, ff.307–10; F³, 2, ff.413–16. Joseph Baxter, "Journal of several visits to the Indians of the Kennebec River, 1717," ed. Elias Nason, New Eng. Hist. and Geneal. Register, XXI (1867), 48–51, 58. A conference of his excellency Jonathan Belcher, ... at Falmouth in Casco-Bay, July 1732 (Boston, 1732). Documentary hist. of Maine, IX, 379, 443–49, 454, 457–59; X, 356, 363, 371, 375, 380, 383, 400–7, 449, 455, 460, 468–69; XI; XXIII, 83–87, 94–108, 190–91, 212–13, 217–31, 234, 241–57. JR (Thwaites), LXVII, 56–57, 62–63, 334. Maine Hist. Soc. Coll., 1st ser., III (1853), 361–75, 407–47; VI (1859), 260–62. "Penhallow papers—Indian affairs," New. Eng. Hist. and Geneal. Register, XXXII (1878), 21–22, 24. PRO, CSP, Col., 1722–23, 27–28, 89–91, 405, 407, 409–10, 415–16, 418–20. J. P. Baxter, The pioneers of New France in New England, with contemporary letters and documents (Albany, 1894), 68–84, 96–104, 111–18, 309–15. F. H. Eckstorm, Indian place names of the Penobscot valley and the Maine coast

Wroth

(University of Maine studies, 2d, ser., Orono, Me., 1940), 113, 145. Parkman, *A half-century of conflict* (1909), I, 224–28.

WROTH, ROBERT, officer in the 40th regiment at Annapolis Royal, N.S., 1720–29; d. *c.* 1735.

Appointed adjutant on 7 May 1719, Wroth crossed the Atlantic to Boston later that year, and when he reached Annapolis Royal in January 1719/20 he brought the welcome news of Governor Richard Philipps*' arrival at Boston. Wroth was commissioned ensign on 25 July 1722, and his commission was renewed in 1727.

On 27 Sept. 1727 Wroth was appointed by Lieutenant-Governor ARMSTRONG to proclaim King George II in the Acadian settlements up to the Bay of Fundy (Baie Française) and to tender the oath of allegiance. Wroth was to assure the Acadians that if they took the oath they would enjoy the free exercise of their religion and continued possession of their lands would be confirmed. He was directed to go first to the Saint John River and to proceed from there to Minas, Cobequid (Truro), Pisiguit, and afterwards to Chignecto, and to keep an exact journal of his expenses and of all his public transactions.

Having transported Chief Joseph Nepomoit and two other Indians to the Saint John River, Wroth proclaimed George II there on 4 October. The Indians signed a proclamation declaring that the French were great obstacles and that they were now resolved to keep the peace they had made with the British. At Chignecto, on 10 October, Wroth was greeted by more than 100 inhabitants, "Every one shewing their Loyalty, & Affection; in Low'd Husas, of God Preserve King George the Second, frequently Drinking to his Royall Health, and fireing severall Vollys of small arm's." Wroth found the Acadians at Chignecto obdurate concerning the oath, however, so he consented of his own authority to certain concessions: the free exercise of their religion, with priests sufficient to practise it, exemption from bearing arms, and continued enjoyment of their property.

At Minas on 23 October the inhabitants gave similar marks of their loyalty and affection for the king. But when it came to the oath they insisted on conditions similar to those granted at Chignecto and added a fourth: the freedom to withdraw when they thought fit, sell their goods, and be quit of their oath. At their insistence Wroth also agreed to modify the oath by translating it in such a way as to omit the word "obey." The inhabitants at Pisiquit subscribed to the oath in the same way. Not having received a reply to his letter to Cobequid, Wroth did not go there. Instead, he sent a proclamation to be posted on the church door, leaving the oath to be taken at the first suitable opportunity.

When Wroth reported on 13 Nov. 1727, the council condemned his concessions as "unwarrantable & dishonourable to His Majestys authority & Government & Consequently Null & Void" and advised Armstrong not to ratify or confirm them. The council declared, moreover, that the inhabitants who had acknowledged George II's authority over the province should have the liberties and privileges of English subjects, and that there should be free trade until the king's pleasure was known.

Eventually, on 24 June 1729, because of ill-health, Wroth resigned his appointment as adjutant in favour of Lieutenant Otho Hamilton*. Wroth returned to England that year, and apparently transferred later to Lucas' regiment in the West Indies. He had died by 1735, when the widow of Ensign Wroth of that regiment was drawing a pension of £16 *per annum.*

CHARLES BRUCE FERGUSSON

PANS, MS. docs., XXII. PRO, C.O. 217/3, f.26; 217/4, ff.322, 359; 217/5, ff.49–50, 58–59, 61–65, 146–51, 153–69, 199–200; 217/30, ff.34–35; 217/38, ff.110, 134–36, 186–94, 196, 200–1; 217/39, f.13. *Coll. doc. inédits Canada et Amérique (CF),* I (1888), 175–88. *The Fulham papers in the Lambeth palace library,* ed. W. W. Manross (Oxford, 1965), 341. *N.S. Archives, III,* 16, 19, 161–63, 168–69. PRO, *CSP, Col., 1726–27, 1728–29, 1730.* Brebner, *New England's outpost.* Dalton, *George the First's army,* II, 322. Murdoch, *History of Nova-Scotia,* I, 445.

Y

YONGE, JAMES, naval surgeon, diarist, and medical writer, who left an account of his practice in the Newfoundland fisheries; b. 27 Feb. 1646/47 in Plymouth, England; d. there 25 July 1721.

He was the second son of John Yonge (d. 13 Oct. 1679), surgeon and medical practitioner in Plymouth and his wife Joanna (1618–1700), daughter of Nicholas Blackaller of Sharpham, Devonshire. Although he had little help or encouragement from his father and his formal education was limited to two years spent at the grammar school in Plymouth, James Yonge achieved distinction in his profession, his career reaching its peak in 1702, when he was elected a fellow of the Royal Society and a licentiate of the Royal College of Physicians. He was the author of several papers published in the *Philosophical Transactions of the Royal Society*, including the first report of the use of vacuum extraction in obstetrics, a valuable technique only recently rediscovered. His introduction into surgery of the "flap technique" in amputating a limb is recorded in his book *Currus triumphalis e terebinthe* (1679). His surgical skill is also apparent in his account of successful operations on skull fractures, *Wounds of the brain proved curable* (1682).

Just before his eleventh birthday he was apprenticed for eight years to Silvester Richmond, surgeon to the naval frigate *Constant Warwick*, and when his master retired to Liverpool in 1662, Yonge returned to Plymouth and was bound apprentice for seven years to his father, a servitude he did not much like. In February 1663 he set out in the *Reformation* on his first voyage to Newfoundland as surgeon to one of the small parties of Devon men who regularly spent the summer fishing off the coast there. From his earliest days at sea he made notes and drawings of all the places he visited, afterwards digested into a narrative journal which was first published in 1963. It is to this journal that we are indebted for the account of his Newfoundland voyages. His experiences there also provided the basis for his pamphlet *Some considerations touching the debate, etc. concerning the Newfoundland trade* (1670).

In the account of his first voyage (pp.54–60) he gives a detailed description of all the tasks carried out by the fishermen. Their base was Renoose (Renews), with a smaller group at Firmoose (Fermeuse). "As soon as we resolve to fish here, the ship is all unrigged, and in the snow and cold all the men go into the woods to cut timber, fir, spruce, and birch being here plentiful. With this they build stages, flakes, cookroom, and houses." Yonge gives us a sketch (plate 4B) of the stage on which the cod was landed from the boats. "The boat is 3 or 4 tons and will carry 1,000 or 1,200 cod, but ... three men will row these great boats a long way." The splitters work at a table on the stage. "There are some that will split incredibly swift, 24 score in half an hour." The cod-liver oil is collected in a great chest and the opened fish salted and dried on the beach on flakes (plate 4B) before loading. "The men in these voyages have no wages but are paid after this manner: the owners have two thirds and the men one third; this one third is divided into so many shares as there are men in the ship. ... The manner of paying the chyrurgeon is this: the owners give

5, 6, 7, or 9 pounds on the hand [cash down] towards the chest, the master gives him a share, and every man half-a-crown, out of his share, besides which he has one hundred of poor Jack [dried fish] from the whole."

Among the "diseases of this country" which Yonge describes, the most dangerous was scurvy, which he treated by giving the sufferers a variety of green leaves steeped in beer. "The cause of this so common a malady is partly from the great mutation of the weather, which when we first come is very cold, and in July shall be intolerably hot, partly from the aqueous and crude nourishment, fish, and from sudden colds after the fatigues of labour, but mostly from the air, which is crude, foggy and scorbutick." At the height of the summer, when the men "rest not above two hours in a night," they are plagued by "muscetoes," and the men suffer violent nose-bleeds from eating too much cods' liver. "In the winter the planters employ themselves in getting fish, sawing deal boards, making oars, catching beaver and fowling. They have innumerable duck, several geese, wild pigeons, partridge, hares, etc." Yonge also mentions having seen seal and penguin.

In 1664 he again visited Newfoundland, this time in the *Robert Bonadventure*, which arrived at Petty Harbour in June with salt and left St John's in August with 20 tons of cod which was later sold in Genoa (pp.67–70). Early in June 1666, while sailing to Boston, his ship was captured by the Dutch, and Yonge was taken with the rest of the crew as prisoner-of-war to Rotterdam. His journal contains a graphic account of his sufferings (pp.90–106), but by the end of the year he was exchanged for a Dutch prisoner held in England and arrived in London while the devastated city was still smoking after the Great Fire. In 1669 he again spent the whole season in Newfoundland (pp.112–21). He names the boats and their owners, there being a total of 132 boats and 660 men; planters and "interlopers" added another 35 boats and 175 men. "I never was better employed," wrote Yonge, "nor lived happier. ... Nothing happened memorable in the season but that I got by private practice above four score pounds, that we made a reasonable voyage, so that I think for my summer's work I might have above £100."

The following season proved equally successful (pp.124–38) but severe storms and ice delayed their arrival at St John's until late April. Despite the fact that "our people brought the small pocks among the inhabitants"—all of whom recovered with Yonge's care—he had sufficient leisure to read and to draft his pamphlet on the Newfoundland trade. He tells us that the ships fishing in St John's numbered 12, with 630 men. He also

You de La Découverte

looked after the men at Petty Harbour, a nine-mile walk and "a very ill way, up hill and down hill, through marshes, over rocks, and in many places without paths." It was on one of these walks that he saw a "beaver house" which he describes. It appears that he also had at least one meal of beaver meat: "their flesh eats sweet if the fishy rancidness be boiled out, as of a turtle; but there is no venom in them as those authors ridiculously assert."

Yonge's savings from his Newfoundland practice were now sufficient to enable him to settle in practice in Plymouth and on 28 March 1671 he married Jane, daughter of Thomas Crampporn of Buckland Monachorum in Devonshire. He was the first surgeon to be appointed to the naval hospital in Plymouth and in 1674 he became deputy surgeon-general to the navy. As one of the city's leading citizens he was elected mayor of Plymouth in 1694 and a memorial to him may still be seen in the parish church of St Andrew, where his body was buried. His son James (1672–1745), the eldest of five children, married as his second wife, Mary, daughter and heir of John Upton of Puslinch in Devon. The Yonge family still resides at Puslinch, where is preserved a fine portrait of James Yonge, reproduced as the frontispiece of *Plymouth memoires*, published by the Plymouth Institution in 1951.

F. N. L. POYNTER

The article on Yonge in the *DNB*, with the sources cited there, contains errors, notably the wrong date of birth. The only authentic source of information about Yonge and his work, apart from his published writings, is his own *Journal*, the original manuscript of which is preserved in the Plymouth Athenaeum (formerly the Plymouth Institution), another copy being kept by the Yonge family at Puslinch. This journal was published in its entirety (except for some of his drawings and sketch-maps) as [James Yonge], *The journal of James Yonge [1647–1721] Plymouth surgeon*, ed. F. N. L. Poynter (London, 1963). The page references given in the article above are to this edition.

YOU DE LA DÉCOUVERTE, PIERRE (Hiou, Hyou; he signed himself de Ladescouverte), officer, adjutant, merchant; b. 1658 at La Rochelle, parish of Saint-Sauveur; son of Pierre You, a tanner, and of Marie-Renée Turcot; buried 28 Aug. 1718 at Montreal.

The first document which mentions Pierre You in New France is the deed of grant made to the Recollets in 1677 by Cavelier* de La Salle: the land grant in question bordered on that of the Sieur You, a sergeant in the garrison at Fort Frontenac (Cataracoui, now Kingston, Ont.). Pierre You was later to accompany La Salle on his expeditions of discovery; La Salle wrote that "much courage and skill were necessary for these expeditions," and he considered that his habitual companion was "a very worthy fellow." When going to find the Chevalier HENRI TONTY in 1680, he took with him only the Sieur Bourdon* d'Autray, You, and two Indians. In March 1682, after the fatigues and perils of this hazardous expedition, Pierre You had the honour of signing the proceedings of the taking over of the Arkansas country. The following year, by virtue of the privileges granted by the king to the discoverers, he adopted the title of Sieur de La Découverte, a title which was subsequently attributed to him in official government records. In 1695 Buade* de Frontenac, in his farewell harangue to the chiefs of the western tribes, named the officers serving at the Michilimackinac post whom the Indians were to obey as they would himself, and he included the Sieur de La Découverte. In 1697 we find him at Montreal, and eight years later he was in possession of a piece of land with a 50-foot frontage on Rue Saint-Paul. His house was so large that it looked like a storehouse. In 1711 he bought another lot on the Place du Marché, and on it he had a two-storey house erected.

In addition to his activities as explorer and merchant, La Découverte went in for fur-trading. In 1703 he obtained a land grant near Fort Senneville, at the western extremity of Montreal Island. From then on he lived on this remote property, which facilitated clandestine fur-trading and allowed his sons to escape into the woods; despite the ordinances, they trafficked in furs even as far as New England. In proof of this, one of them, brought before the court, admitted that he had gone there and had bought a negro and some silverware there.

La Découverte won the confidence of RIGAUD de Vaudreuil, who leased to him Île-aux-Tourtres, one of his two fur-trading factories at the juncture of the St Lawrence and Ottawa Rivers. The constant offer of spirits induced the Indians to stop there with their canoes loaded with furs. The Montreal merchants complained, and La Découverte, strong in the governor's protection, went so far as to display arrogance towards them. In 1709 Rocbert* de La Morandière, the keeper of the king's stores at Montreal, complained to JACQUES RAUDOT about the insults that La Découverte had directed at him; in the autumn mail, the intendant drew these complaints to the attention of Pontchartrain, but Vaudreuil, on the same occasion, praised his protégé: "He has always served," he said, "with distinction, he is even disabled in one arm, having been wounded in the last war." The governor did not wait for the minister's favours:

he appointed La Découverte adjutant at Montreal to assist the Sieur de Clérin [Denis d'ESTIENNE DU Bourgué], the regular adjutant. In 1710 La Découverte himself requested a lieutenancy; the minister replied that there was no vacancy, but that he would bear him in mind if the occasion arose, provided he received good reports about him.

Pierre You de La Découverte was buried on 28 Aug. 1718, and the burial certificate called him an officer of a company of the colonial regular troops. From a private he had become an officer. La Découverte's first wife, whom he had married in April 1693 at Chicago, was an Indian woman of the Miami tribe, named Élisabeth, by whom he had a daughter baptized Marie-Anne; the latter married the interpreter Jean-Baptiste Richard in 1718 at Montreal. On 15 April 1697 he had taken as his second wife Madeleine Just, a native of Brèves in the province of Burgundy and the widow of Jérôme Le Gay de Beaulieu. From this marriage were born five children, two of whom survived their father: François-Madeleine d'Youville, who died in 1730, and Philippe, who died a bachelor six years later.

François-Madeleine d'Youville succeeded his father as tenant-farmer at Île-aux-Tourtres, and he continued the same trade in spirits. Not content with the pelts from the Nipissings, he raided the furs brought by the canoes from the west. He had at his command a sergeant and six soldiers for intercepting the canoes and forcing them to go to trade at the island, to the detriment of Montreal.

On 12 Aug. 1722, at Montreal, François-Madeleine d'Youville married Marie-Marguerite Dufrost* de Lajemmerais. They had six children, only two of whom reached adult age; François and Charles-Madeleine both became priests. François-Madeleine d'Youville died on 5 July 1730, when he was barely 30 years old. He signed himself Youville without the "de", as the name was generally written at the time. Abbé Étienne-Michel Faillon did research in France to find out whether a place or a domain of that name existed there. He did not find any, and there was none in Canada at that time. No doubt it was Youville who adopted the "de" for euphony. Without being a noble name, You thus acquired a noble particle.

ALBERTINE FERLAND-ANGERS

AJM, Greffe d'Antoine Adhémar; Greffe de J.-C. Raimbault, 27 juin 1729, 24 avril, 16 juin 1731; Greffe de Marien Tailhandier; Registres d'état civil de Notre-Dame de Montréal, 1697, 1698, 1699, 1700, 1702, 1718, 1722, 1730. AN, Col., B, 27; C^{11A}, 22, 24, 30, 45; D^{2C}, 222, f.187. *Découvertes et établissements des Français* (Margry), II, 117–183; IV, 117. La Poterie, *Histoire* (1753), IV, 67. Le Tac, *Histoire chronologique de la N.-F.* (Réveillaud), 191. "Lettres et mémoires de F.-M.-F. Ruette d'Auteuil," 36–51. [É.-M. Faillon], *Vie de Mme d' Youville, fondatrice des sœurs de la Charité de Villemarie dans l'Île Montréal en Canada* (Ville-Marie [Montréal], 1852). J.-B.-A. Ferland, *Cours d'histoire du Canada (1534–1759)* (1re éd., 2v., Québec, 1861–65), II, 145. Désiré Girouard, *Lake St. Louis, old and new, and Cavelier de La Salle* (Montréal, 1893). Francis Parkman, *La Salle and the discovery of the great west* (Boston, 1887).

GENERAL BIBLIOGRAPHY AND
LIST OF ABBREVIATIONS

List of Abbreviations

AAQ   Archives de l'archevêché de Québec
ACND Archives de la congrégation de Notre-Dame, Montréal
AE   Archives du Ministère des Affaires étrangères, Paris
AHDM Archives des religieuses hospitalières de Saint-Joseph de l'Hôtel-Dieu de Montréal
AHDQ Archives de l'Hôtel-Dieu de Québec
AJJ   Archives judiciaires de Joliette
AJM   Archives judiciaires de Montréal
AJQ   Archives judiciaires de Québec
AJTR Archives judiciaires de Trois-Rivières
AMUQ Archives du monastère des Ursulines de Québec
AN   Archives nationales, Paris
ANDM Archives paroissiales de Notre-Dame de Montréal
ANDQ Archives paroissiales de Notre-Dame de Québec
APQ   Archives de la province de Québec. Now AQ
AQ   Archives du Québec
ARSI   Archivum Romanum Societatis Iesu, Rome
ASGM Archives des Sœurs Grises de Montréal
ASJ   Archives de la Société de Jésus
ASJCF Archives de la Société de Jésus, province du Canada français
ASQ   Archives du Séminaire de Québec
ASSM Archives du Séminaire de Saint-Sulpice de Montréal
BM   British Museum
BN   Bibliothèque nationale, Paris
BRH   *Bulletin des recherches historiques*

CCHA Canadian Catholic Historical Association
CF   *Canada français*
CHA   Canadian Historical Association
CHR   *Canadian Historical Review*
CTG   Archives du Comité technique du génie, Paris
DAB   *Dictionary of American Biography*
DBF   *Dictionnaire de biographie française*
DCB   *Dictionary of Canadian Biography*
DNB   *Dictionary of National Biography*
HBC   Hudson's Bay Company
HBRS Hudson's Bay Record Society
IOA   Inventaire des œuvres d'art du Québec
JJ   *Journal des Jésuites*
JR   *Jesuit Relations and allied documents*
MPA   *Mississippi Provincial Archives*
NF   *Nova Francia*
NYCD *Documents relative to the colonial history of the State of New York*
PAC   Public Archives of Canada
PANS   Public Archives of Nova Scotia
PRO   Public Record Office, London
RC   *Revue canadienne*
RHAF *Revue d'histoire de l'Amérique française*
RSCT *Royal Society of Canada Transactions*
RUL   *Revue de l'université Laval*
SCHEC Société canadienne de l'histoire de l'Église catholique
SGCF   Société généalogique canadienne-française
SHA   Archives du Service historique de l'armée, Paris
SHQ   Société historique de Québec
USPG United Society for the Propagation of the Gospel

General Bibliography

The General Bibliography is based on the sources most frequently cited in individual bibliographies in Volume II. It should not be regarded as providing a complete list of background materials for the period covered by this volume. Sections I and II, however, do give a reasonably full guide to the documentation for this period.

Section I provides a description of the principal archival sources used for this volume and is divided by country. Section II contains primary printed sources, including calendars and inventories of documentary material, and printed works of the 17th and 18th centuries which may be regarded as contemporary sources. Section III includes various dictionaries and nominal lists. Section IV contains secondary works of the 19th and 20th centuries, including a large number of general histories. Section V describes the principal journals which contain material on the French régime and lists a few articles which were used frequently in Vol. II.

I. ARCHIVES AND MANUSCRIPT SOURCES

CANADA

ARCHIVES DE LA CHANCELLERIE DE L'ARCHEVÊCHÉ DE MONTRÉAL. These archives contain photographs, maps, 634 registers divided into 17 series which include the correspondance of the bishops of Montreal, and some 500,000 separate items. The latter are particularly relevant to Volume II since they date from 1675. On the French régime there are documents concerning the diocese of Quebec; the parishes of Notre-Dame de Montréal, Saint-François-de-Sales and Saint-Vincent-de-Paul on Île Jésus, Saint-Joseph at Rivière-des-Prairies, at L'Assomption, and at Repentigny; the priests of Saint-Sulpice; the religious of the Congrégation de Notre-Dame; the Religious Hospitallers of Saint-Joseph; and the Hurons.

ARCHIVES DE LA CONGRÉGATION DE NOTRE-DAME, Montreal. In the process of being catalogued.

The principal documents used in Vol. II of the *DCB* were:

Charles Glandelet, "Le vray Esprit de Marguerite Bourgeoys et de l'Institut des Sœurs Séculières de la Congrégation de Notre-Dame établie à Ville-Marie en l'Isle de Montréal en Canada, 1701."

M[1], Écrits autographes de la sœur Marguerite Bourgeois. As the original manuscript was destroyed in a fire, there remain at the ACND only microfilms and photostats of a copy (M[1]) made for the cause of beatification (considered as the basic text), of a copy (V[2]) sent to the Vatican archives, and of another copy (V[1]), slightly different, which is also preserved at the Vatican.

ARCHIVES DE L'ARCHEVÊCHÉ DE QUÉBEC. Contains about 1,060 feet of documents, an analytical card file for all documents prior to 1940, and a Répertoire général des registres officiels de l'archevêché in 6 vols., from 1659 to the present. A partial inventory of documents for the period 1659–1730 can be found in APQ *Rapport, 1939–40*, 157–353; *1940–41*, 333–473; and *1941–42*, 179–298.

The principal series concerning the French régime used in Vol. II were:

Chapitre de la cathédrale de Québec. 1 Register and 10 cartons. 1684–1773

Copies de documents. Série A: Église du Canada (copies from Rome and Paris archives concerning Canada and Louisiana); Série B: Lettres des évêques de Québec, 1659–1852. 6 vols.

Diocèse de Québec. 10 cartons

Évêques de Québec. Cartons I, V, VI. 1659–1845

France. Carton I. 1724–1878

Gouvernement. Carton III (arrêts, proclamations, ordonnances). 1659–1838

Notre-Dame de Québec (parish). Carton I. 1655–1879

Registre des confirmations. 1659–1771

Registres d'insinuation A, B, C. 1659–1783

Registres A (Acadie). 1679–86

Registres des missions des Postes du Roy. 1673–1848. Miscellaneorum Liber

Séminaire de Québec. Carton I. 1680–1877

Vicaires généraux. Carton VI. 1720–1825

ARCHIVES DE LA SOCIÉTÉ DE JÉSUS, PROVINCE DU CANADA FRANÇAIS, Saint-Jérôme (Terrebonne). These archives were founded in 1844 by Father Félix Martin. They were housed at the Collège Sainte-Marie in Montreal originally, and were designated by the abbreviation ACSM. In 1968, they were transferred to the noviciate of the Jesuits of the ecclesiastical province of French Canada, at Saint-Jérôme, and are now designated by the abbreviation ASJCF. The year of their founding these archives received a rich gift from the religious of the Hôtel-Dieu in Quebec. They contain numerous documents relating to the history of the missions of the Society of Jesus in Canada [see ARCHIVES DU COLLÈGE SAINTE-MARIE, *DCB*, I, 686].

Vol. II of the *DCB* mentions several documents found in:

A section of 140 metal boxes containing about 8,000 numbered documents (personal papers or correspondence) in the form of original manuscripts or copies

Fonds Rochemonteix, 28 notebooks, numbered from 4,001 to 4,028, which were used in the preparation of the works of Camille de Rochemonteix, *Les Jésuites et la Nouvelle-France au XVIIe siècle* and *Les Jésuites et la Nouvelle-France au XVIIIe siècle* [see ROCHEMONTEIX, section IV]

A section of original manuscripts, written by Jesuit missionaries; these manuscripts are classified.

Section D-7 (various documents relating to the Fathers of the Society of Jesus)

ARCHIVES DE L'HÔTEL-DIEU DE QUÉBEC. In the process of being catalogued.

The principal documents used in Vol. II:
Lettres, I
Registres des malades. First 6 vols., 1689–1804
Jeanne-Françoise Juchereau de La Ferté de Saint-Ignace, "Histoire abrégée de l'établissement de l'Hôtel-Dieu de Québec." The published title for this work: *Annales de l'Hôtel-Dieu de Québec, 1636–1716* [see JEANNE-FRANÇOISE JUCHEREAU DE LA FERTÉ, section II].

ARCHIVES DES FRANCISCAINS DE QUÉBEC. Contains copies of documents concerning the Canadian Recollets, 1615–1849. These copies, gathered by Fathers Odoric-M. Jouve and Archange Godbout, are handwritten and not easily legible, and have not been completely classified. There are two sections where the classification work is more advanced: the Dossiers biographiques des Récollets and the dossiers of the parishes where these religious worked. The Dossiers biographiques were used in Vol. II.

ARCHIVES DES RELIGIEUSES HOSPITALIÈRES DE SAINT-JOSEPH DE L'HÔTEL-DIEU DE MONTRÉAL. In the process of being catalogued.

The principal documents used in Vol. II:
Annales de la sœur Véronique Cuillérier, 1725–47
Déclarations de nos anciennes Mères pour constater la profession religieuse et le décès des sœurs
Lettres circulaires, nécrologies, fondateurs, sœurs de France et de Montréal, 1690–1747
Lettre de la sœur Morin aux sœurs de France relatant le tremblement de terre de 1663
Livre de comptes, I, 1705–8
Mère Chauvelier, Livre ou Second Recueil de lettres circulaires
Marie Morin, "Histoire simple et véritable de l'établissement des Religieuses hospitalières de Saint-Joseph en l'Île de Montréal, dite à présent Ville-Marie, en Canada, de l'année 1659. . . ." The published version is entitled: *Annales de l'Hôtel-Dieu de Montréal* [see MARIE MORIN and SOCIÉTÉ HISTORIQUE DE MONTRÉAL, Section II].

ARCHIVES DES SŒURS GRISES, Montreal. The documents which were at the Hôpital Général de Montréal when Madame d'Youville came there as administratrix in 1747 make up the Fonds "Charon," and are the source of this archival repository. Subsequently, items necessary for the general administration of the community were added to this. The classification for this repository is alphabetical for the dossiers and chronological within each dossier. These archives contain thousands of documents, the earliest dating from 1683, and about 300 maps and plans.

The principal documents used in Vol. II were:
"Concession par M. Dollier, supérieur du Séminaire de Montréal à M. Charon et à ses associés d'un emplacement . . . près de Montréal pour l'établissement de la maison de charité, . . . 28 octobre 1688"
"Constitution des Frères Hospitaliers de la Croix et de Saint-Joseph"
"Lettres patentes pour l'établissement d'un hôpital à Villemarie dans l'Île de Montréal, 15 avril 1694"
"Lettres patentes pour plusieurs manufactures d'arts et métiers dans la maison et enclos des Frères hospitaliers de la ville et Île de Montréal dans la Nouvelle-France"
"Registre d'admission des pauvres, 1694–1796"

"Registre des vêtures, professions, sépultures, etc. des Frères Charon, 1701–48"

"Testament du Frère François Charon, supérieur des Frères Hospitaliers de Montréal, . . . 9 juillet 1719"

ARCHIVES DU MONASTÈRE DES URSULINES DE QUÉBEC. In the process of being catalogued. The principal documents used in Vol. II:

Annales du monastère des Ursulines de Québec, Vol. I, 1639–1822

Constitution manuscrite des Ursulines de Québec, 1647

Registre des entrées des pensionnaires, 1641

Registre de l'examen canonique des novices, 1689–1817

ARCHIVES DU QUÉBEC. At the conquest, articles 43, 44, and 45 of the capitulation of Montreal—contrary to the custom of international law at that time—permitted the administrators of New France to take back to France documents relating to the government of the colony. Only archives having a legal value for individuals were to remain in the country, and these were to suffer many misfortunes before the Bureau des Archives de la province de Québec—now the Archives du Québec—was created in 1920. (*See* Fernand Ouellet, "L'histoire des archives du gouvernement en Nouvelle-France," *RUL*, XII (1958), 397–415.) Some 3,300 feet of documents are preserved there today (official and private papers, originals and copies), the majority for the period 1663–1867. In 1968, the AQ published an *État général des archives publiques et privées du Québec* and established a new system of classification of documents. We have used this classification in this volume.

Cited in Vol. II:

Nouvelle-France

Cahiers d'intendance, 1723–25. 4 vols.

Collection de pièces judiciaires et notariales, 1638–1759. 125 vols.

Documents de la juridiction de Trois-Rivières, 1646–1759. 20 vols.

Documents de la Prévôté de Québec, 1668–1759. 17 vols.

Dossiers du Conseil supérieur, 1663–1759. 11 vols.

Foi et hommage, 1667–1759. 5 vols.

Insinuations du Conseil supérieur, 1663–1758. 10 vols.

Ordonnances des intendants, 1666–1760. 46 vols.

Procès-verbaux des grands voyers, 1668–1780. 9 vols.

Registres de la Prévôté de Québec, 1666–1759. 113 vols.

Registres d'intendance, 1672–1759. 4 vols.

Registres divers et pièces détachées du Conseil supérieur, 1664–1760. 5 vols.

Registres du Conseil supérieur, 1663–1760. 69 vols.

Québec et Bas-Canada

Biens des Jésuites, Notre-Dame-des-Anges, 1626–1887. 8 cartons and 11 registers. Vols. 60–78

Copies d'archives d'autres dépôts: Canada

Paroisses. Notre-Dame de Québec, 1608–1905.

Copies d'archives d'autres dépôts: France

Manuscrits relatifs à l'histoire de la Nouvelle-France. 2e série: manuscrits concernant la Nouvelle-France, 1614–1727. 7 vols.

Archives privées

Antoine Adhémar, 1662–93

Collection P.-G. Roy

Famille Lestringant de Saint-Martin, 1608–62

Jean-Baptiste Peiras, 1687–89

Seigneuries, 1630–1925. Documents généraux sur les seigneuries. Cartons 1–34

For more complete information on the AQ, *see*: *État général des archives publiques et privées du Québec.* Québec, 1968.

ARCHIVES DU SÉMINAIRE DE QUÉBEC. One of the most important collections of documents in North America. The archives date from the founding of the seminary in 1663, but Msgr Thomas-Étienne Hamel and Msgr Amédée Gosselin may be considered to have founded the ASQ at the end of the 19th and the beginning of the 20th century. ASQ contains some 1,172 feet of documents (seminary and private papers, the oldest from 1636 and the majority from 1675 to 1950), 2,000 maps, and 160 feet of engravings and photographs.

For Vol. II the following have been used principally:

Chapitre. 1 carton containing 340 items. 1666–1785

Congrégation Notre-Dame. 1 carton containing 70 items

Documents Faribault. 1 carton containing 330 items. 1626–1860

Évêques. 1 carton containing 227 items. 1657–1920

Fonds Amédée Gosselin. 67 boxes

Fonds Verreau. Includes Fonds Viger, hence frequently called Viger-Verreau. The collections of Abbé Hospice-Anthelme Verreau and of Jacques Viger, principally composed of about a hundred cartons, several large notebooks, and the series of Viger's manuscript volumes entitled "Ma Saberdache."

Lettres, M, 171 items; N, 181 items; O, 157 items; R, 190 items; S, 188 items

Livres de comptes, C 12, 1706; C 13, 1714–22; C 14, 1722–29

Missions. 2 cartons

Manuscrits, 6, "Transcripta, 1679–1721"; 17, "Documents relatifs à Mgr de Laval"; 29, "Histoire du séminaire de Québec," by J.-A. Tachereau; 198, "Recueil touchant la sœur Barbier"; 239, "Règlement du petit séminaire, 1795"; 360, "Second registre de Tadoussac"; 374, "Des missions iroquoises en l'année 1676"; 457, 466–67, "Annales du petit séminaire"; 0478, "Les Sulpiciens en Acadie," by Abbé Pierre Rousseau

Paroisse de Québec. 1 carton containing 156 items. 1652–1877

Paroisses diverses. 1 carton containing 101 items. 1672–1880

Polygraphie. 248 cartons

Seigneuries, I–XI, Sault-au-Matelot

Séminaire. 204 cartons

S.M.E., Résolutions du conseil du séminaire ou Plumitifs, 1766–1950

Archives du Séminaire de Saint-Sulpice, Montréal. An important archival repository for the history of the Montreal region during the French régime. On his departure in 1665 Paul de Chomedey de Maisonneuve left there the greater part of his papers, dating from 1642. This repository, divided into 49 sections, contains 190 feet of documents for the years 1586–1950, and about 1,200 maps and plans.

The following sections were used in Vol. II:

Cahiers Faillon. 24 notebooks containing copies of documents (1677–1834) made under the direction of É.-M. Faillon, with a view to continuing the writing of his *Histoire de la colonie française*

Concessions de terres et d'emplacements. About 5,000 items. 1648–1854

Correspondance générale, 2e partie: correspondance des supérieurs généraux. Copies of letters preserved at the seminary of Saint-Sulpice, Paris

Histoire et biographies, géographie, 2e partie: biographies. 88 items arranged in chronological order. 1657–1926

Archives judiciaires de Joliette. Cited in Vol. II:

Registre d'état civil

Archives judiciaires de Montréal. Cited in Vol. II:

Greffes: Antoine Adhémar, 1668–1714

J.-B. Adhémar, 1714–54

Bénigne Basset Des Lauriers, 1657–99

Jacques Bourdon, 1677–1720

Hilaire Bourgine, 1685–90

Pierre Cabazié, 1673–93

Réné Chorel de Saint-Romain, 1731–32

François Comparet, 1736–55

L.-C. Danré de Blanzy, 1738–60

Jacques David, 1719–26

Thomas Frérot, 1669–78

N.-A. Guillet de Chaumont, 1727–52

Michel Lepailleur, 1703–33

Claude Maugue, 1677–96

C.-J. Porlier, 1733–44

J.-B. Pottier, 1686–1701

J.-C. Raimbault, 1727–37

Pierre Raimbault, 1692–1727

Jean de Saint-Père, 1648–57

Simon Sanguinet, 1734–47

Nicolas Senet, 1704–31

Martin Tailhandier, 1688–1731

J.-B. Tétro, 1712–28

Documents judiciaires

Index des sépultures catholiques, 1643–1967

Registres des audiences. 28 vols.

Registres du bailliage. 2 vols.

Registres des congés. 1 vol.

Registres d'état civil

Archives judiciaires de Québec. The greffes of the notaries of the judicial district of Quebec during the French régime have been kept at the AQ only since the fall of 1968; hence the bibliographical references have not been changed for Vol. II, and the greffes are still cited by the abbreviation AJQ. Used in Vol. II:

Greffes: Claude Auber, 1652–93

Jacques Barbel, 1703–40

Claude Barolet, 1731–61

Romain Becquet, 1662–82

Laurent Bermen, 1647–49

Hilaire Bernard de La Rivière, 1692–1725

Louis Chambalon, 1692–1716

Étienne Dubreuil, 1708–39

J.-R. Duprac, 1693–1723

Pierre Duquet de La Chesnaye, 1663–84

Michel Fillion, 1660–88

Florent de La Cetière, 1702–28, and 1 carton of assorted items

François Genaple de Bellefonds, 1682–1709

Jean Lecomte, 1668

Michel Lepailleur, 1700–8

J.-C. Louet, 1718–37

J.-C. Panet, 1745–75
J.-B. Peuvret de Mesnu, 1653–59
Jacques Pinguet, 1726–48
Charles Rageot, 1695–1702
François Rageot, 1709–53
Gilles Rageot, 1666–91
Pierre Rivet, 1707–19
Guillaume Roger, 1694–99
Paul Vachon, 1644–93
Registre d'état civil

ARCHIVES JUDICIAIRES DE TROIS-RIVIÈRES. Cited in Vol. II:
Greffes: Séverin Ameau, 1651–90
Jean Cusson, 1669–1700
Laurent Du Portail, 1660–63
Claude Herlin, 1659–63
Guillaume de La Rue, 1664–76
Jacques de La Touche, 1664–68
Charles Le Sieur, 1689–96
Daniel Normandin, 1686–1729
Pierre Petit, 1721–35
J.-B. Pottier, 1699–1711
Michel Roy, 1669–99
François Trotain de Saint-Surain, 1687–1732
Étienne Véron de Grandmesnil, 1705–20
Registre d'état civil

ARCHIVES PAROISSIALES DE NOTRE-DAME DE MONTRÉAL.
Registres des baptêmes, mariages et sépultures

ARCHIVES PAROISSIALES DE NOTRE-DAME DE QUÉBEC.
Registres des baptêmes, mariages et sépultures, 1621–1742

PUBLIC ARCHIVES OF CANADA, Ottawa. In 1873 the government of Canada commissioned Abbé H.-A. Verreau to investigate the holdings of English and French archives with a view to copying documents concerning the early history of Canada. The work of transcribing and microfilming such manuscripts has proceeded since that time.

Many unpublished finding aids are available only in the archives, but the Manuscript Division has published the following *Preliminary Inventories* and *Inventories*:
Fonds des Manuscrits No 1, Archives des Colonies (1952)
Fonds des Manuscrits No 2, Archives de la Marine; *No 3, Archives nationales*; *No 4, Archives de la Guerre* (1953) (now reorganized as Service historique de l'armée; a manuscript inventory of this section is avail-

able for use at the PAC: Louise Dechêne, "Inventaire analytique des documents relatifs à l'histoire du Canada conservés en France au service historique de l'armée").
Fonds des Manuscrits No 5, Ministère des Affaires étrangères (1955)
Manuscript Group 8, Quebec provincial and local records; *Manuscript Group 9, Provincial, local and territorial records* (1961)
Manuscript Group 11, Public Record Office, London, Colonial Office papers (1961)
Manuscript Group 17, Religious archives (1967)
Manuscript Group 18, Pre-Conquest papers (1964)
Manuscript Group 21, Transcripts from papers in the British Museum (1955)
Unpublished "addenda" for the above inventories are available for consultation at the PAC. Also available are typescript copies of the following unpublished provisional inventories:
"Fonds des Manuscrits No 6, Archives départementales, municipales, maritimes et de bibliothèques (France)"
"Fonds des Manuscrits No 7, Bibliothèques de France (à Paris)"
"Manuscript Group 36, Finding aids to sources in other archival repositories"
See also "Guides to calendars of series and collections in the Public Archives," PAC *Report, 1949*, 451–59; H. P. Beers, *The French & British in the old Northwest: a bibliographical guide to archive and manuscript sources* (Detroit, 1964) and *The French in North America: a bibliographical guide to French archives, reproductions, and research missions* (Baton Rouge, 1957).

The following collections, some of which contain original manuscript material, were found useful in the preparation of Vol. II:
FM 6
A 2: Charente-Maritime (La Rochelle)
C 1: Port de Rochefort
FM 8
F: Documents relatifs aux seigneuries et autres lieux, 1633–1925
80: Saint-Ours, 1633–1907
97: Yamaska, 1718–1888
MG 9
B: Nova Scotia
8: Church records, 1679–1920
9: Local records, 1682–1917
FM 17
A: Église catholique
3: Séminaire des Missions Étrangères, Paris, 1640–1851
7–2: Séminaire de Saint-Sulpice, Paris, 1640–1872

FM 18
B: Explorations
  12: Pierre Gaultier de La Vérendrye, 1731–48
H: New France
  13: Denys family, 1654–1870
  25: Robinson collection, 1532–1899
Nova Scotia A: Correspondence, 1603–1815. 198 vols. A composite series from various sources in Great Britain, especially the PRO. Documents for the period covered by Vol. II are calendared in PAC *Report, 1894.*
Nova Scotia B: Minutes of the executive council, 1720–1785. 18 vols. A composite series taken principally from sources which are now part of either PRO, C.O. 217 or C.O. 220.

PUBLIC ARCHIVES OF NOVA SCOTIA, Halifax. These archives contain bound volumes of transcripts of documents from European archives relating to the earliest history of Acadia or Nova Scotia. *See: Catalogue or list of manuscript documents, arranged, bound and catalogued under the direction of the commissioner of public records . . .* (Halifax, 1877; 2d ed., 1886) and J. P. Edwards, *The public records of Nova Scotia* (Halifax, 1920).

ENGLAND

BRITISH MUSEUM, London. In 1753 the British Museum was established as the repository for the Sloane collection of manuscripts, which were numbered from 1 to 4,100. Since that time many collections have been acquired and variously designated. Used in the preparation of Volume II were the Sloane, Lansdowne, Stowe, and Additional manuscripts. For a brief guide to catalogues of these and other manuscript collections *see* T. C. Skeat, "The catalogues of the British Museum, 2: Manuscripts," *Journal of Documentation* (London), VII (1951), 18–60; revised as *British Museum: the catalogues of the manuscript collections* (London, 1962). For copies in the PAC of documents from the British Museum *see* PAC, *Preliminary Inventory, Manuscript Group 21* (Ottawa, 1955).

HUDSON'S BAY COMPANY ARCHIVES, London. The HBC archives comprise over thirty thousand volumes and files of records dating from the founding of the company in 1670. The archives as constituted at present were established in 1932, and the work of organization proceeded thereafter [*see* R. H. G. Leveson Gower, "The archives of the Hudson's Bay Company," *Beaver* (Winnipeg),

outfit 264 (December 1933), 40–42, 64]. A publishing programme was undertaken by the Hudson's Bay Record Society [*see* section II], and in 1949 the HBC and PAC arranged jointly to microfilm the records. Information on the PAC copies is found in PAC *Report, 1950,* 13–14; *1952,* 16–18; *1953–54,* 21–22; *1955–58,* 44–46.

Documents from the following categories were used in the preparation of Volume II:
Section A: London office records
  A.1/: Minute books of the governor and committee
  A.6/: London outward correspondence books—HBC official
  A.14/: Grand ledgers (London)
  A.15/: Grand journals (London)
Section B: North America trading posts records
  B.3/a: Albany journals
  B.3/d: Albany account books
  B.42/d: Churchill account books
  B.135/a: Moose journals
  B.239/a: York journals
  B.239/d: York account books

PUBLIC RECORD OFFICE, London. For an introduction to the contents and arrangement of these archives *see: Guide to the contents of the Public Record Office* (2v., London, 1963).

The documentary series cited in Volume II include:
Admiralty
  Adm. 1: Admiralty and secretariat, papers (1660–1938) (formerly known as Secretary's Department: In-letters.)
  Adm. 2: Admiralty and secretariat, out-letters (1656–1859)
  Adm. 6: Admiralty and secretariat, registers, returns, and certificates, various (1673–1859)
  Adm. 8: List books (1673–1893)
  Adm. 51: Admiralty and secretariat, log books, etc., captains' logs (1669–1852)
  Adm. 52: Admiralty and secretariat, log books, etc., masters' logs (1672–1840)
Colonial Office [*see* R. B. Pugh, *The records of the Colonial and Dominion offices* (PRO Handbooks, III, 1964)]
  C.O. 1: General series (1574–1757). Includes papers relating to America and the West Indies, preponderantly before 1688, from which date most of these papers are in C.O. 5.
  C.O. 5: America and West Indies, original correspondence ([1606?] to 1807). Comprises the original correspondence and entry books of the Board of Trade and the secretary of state and other papers.

C.O. 194: Newfoundland, original correspondence (1696–1922) (A manuscript 18th-century index to the volumes of Newfoundland correspondence exists in the PRO and is numbered IND. 8234.)

C.O. 195: Newfoundland, entry books (1623–1867)

C.O. 217: Nova Scotia and Cape Breton, original correspondence (1710/11–1867)

C.O. 218: Nova Scotia and Cape Breton, entry books (1710–1867)

C.O. 323: Colonies, general, original correspondence (1689–1940)

C.O. 324: Colonies, general, entry books, series I (1662–1872)

Records of the High Court of Admiralty

H.C.A. 30: Instance and prize courts, miscellanea (1531–1888)

State Paper Office, State papers domestic

S.P. 42: Naval (1689–1782)

S.P. 44: Entry books (1661–1828)

Treasury

T. 1: In-letters and files, treasury board papers (1557–1920)

T. 48: Miscellanea, Lowndes papers, Charles I to 1886

War Office

W.O. 24: Establishments (1661–1846)

W.O. 26: Miscellany books (1670–1817)

W.O. 30: Miscellanea (1684–1903)

W.O. 46: Ordnance office, out-letters (1660–1861)

W.O. 53: Ordnance office, bill books, series IV (1660–1822)

W.O. 71: Judge Advocate General's office, courts martial, proceedings (1668–1850)

From the collection of maps at the PRO the following was used:

M.P.G. 274: plan of Annapolis Royal, 1710 For copies in the PAC of documents in the Colonial Office of the PRO see PAC, *Preliminary Inventory, Manuscript Group 11* (Ottawa, 1951).

SOMERSET HOUSE, London. Located here are three government departments, two of which are of special interest:

General Register Office

Contains the records of births, marriages, and deaths in England and Wales.

Principal Probate Registry

Some original wills are preserved here (others being kept in the District Probate Registries). In addition, since 1858 a copy of every will proved in England and Wales and a record of the grant of representation have been deposited in this registry. Finally, all wills proved in the Prerogative Court of Canterbury (P.C.C.) are preserved here.

UNITED SOCIETY FOR THE PROPAGATION OF THE GOSPEL, London. Formed in 1965, the USPG is responsible for continuing the work formerly carried on by the Society for the Propagation of the Gospel in Foreign Parts (incorporated by Royal Charter, 1701) and the Universities' Mission to Central Africa (founded 1857). For copies in the PAC of documents from the archives of the USPG see PAC, *Preliminary Inventory, Manuscript Group 17* (Ottawa, 1967).

Documents from the following series were used in the preparation of Volume II:

Journals of proceedings of the Society for the Propagation of the Gospel; the fair copy of the Journals has 28 volumes, 1701–1804, and there are four Appendices: A, B, C, D

Committee Books of the Society for the Propagation of the Gospel, 54 volumes, 1702–95

Letters and reports of missionaries of the Society for the Propagation of the Gospel:

A: Contemporary letterbooks of correspondence received from the colonies and elsewhere and copies of some letters sent from the secretary in London, 1702–37, 26 volumes

B: Original letters from the colonies, 1702–86, 25 volumes

FRANCE

ARCHIVES DE LA GUERRE. See ARCHIVES DU SERVICE HISTORIQUE DE L'ARMÉE

ARCHIVES DÉPARTEMENTALES, COMMUNALES, etc. The departmental archives of France and other local repositories contain valuable information on many figures belonging to early Canadian history. For lists of analytical inventories see: France, Direction des Archives, *État des inventaires des Archives nationales, départementales, communales et hospitalières au 1er janvier 1937* (Paris, 1938), and *Supplément, 1937–54* [by R.-H. Bautier] (Paris, 1955). There is a uniform system of classification for all departmental and communal archives.

Archives départementales

The series of the Fonds anciens are numbered from A to J inclusively, as follows:

A: Actes du pouvoir souverain

B: Cours et juridiction

C: Administrations provinciales (Intendances)

D: Instruction publique; sciences; arts

E: Féodalité; communes, notaires, corporations

E supplément: Archives communales déposées aux Archives départementales

F: Fonds et collections divers

G: Clergé séculier

H: Clergé régulier

H supplément: Archives hospitalières déposées aux archives départementales

I: Archives ecclésiastiques

J: Documents entrés aux archives par voies extraordinaires

For Volume II, series A, B, E, G, and H have been found most useful.

Archives communales

Series previous to 1790 are numbered from AA to II, as follows:

AA: Actes constitutifs et politiques de la commune

BB: Administration communale

CC: Impôts et comptabilités

DD: Biens communaux

EE: Affaires militaires; marine

FF: Justice et police

GG: Cultes, instruction et assistance publiques

HH: Agriculture; industrie; commerce

II: Divers (Tabellionnage, cartes et plans etc.)

For Volume II, series BB was found useful.

The local repositories also include:

Les archives hospitalières (public property although kept in the establishments)

Les archives des Chambres de Commerce (private property)

Les archives des ports ou de l'Inscription Maritime (property of the Marine department)

Les archives des bibliothèques municipales et autres

Copies and microfilms of documents from the departmental and other local archives are available in the PAC and are classed as FM 6. A printed inventory is in preparation.

ARCHIVES DU COMITÉ TECHNIQUE DU GÉNIE, Paris. These archives, which are housed at the Château de Vincennes, were originally divided into 23 articles (i.e. series). A certain number of the original articles have been turned over to other archives, notably article 9 (Colonies françaises), which is now in AN, Section Outre-Mer (Dépôt des fortifications des colonies), and article 16 (Cartes), which has passed to the BN.

The following articles are of interest for Canadian history:

Article 3: Personnel

Article 14: Places et pays étrangers: Amérique septentrionale, Possessions anglaises, États-Unis, Louisbourg et l'île Royale.

Article 15: Histoire militaire, campagnes et sièges

ARCHIVES DU MINISTÈRE DES AFFAIRES ÉTRANGÈRES, Paris. On the holdings of the archives *see* France, Archives des Affaires étrangères, *Inventaire sommaire des archives du département des Affaires étrangères* (6v., Paris, 1883–1903). Three volumes are devoted to each of the two main divisions of the archives: Correspondance politique and Mémoires et documents. *See also*: France, Archives des Affaires étrangères, *État numérique des fonds de la correspondance politique de l'origine à 1871* (Paris, 1936); Archives publiques du Canada, *Inventaire provisoire, Fonds des manuscrits n⁰ 5* (Ottawa, 1955); and W. G. Leland *et al.*, *Guide to materials for American history in the libraries and archives of Paris*, Volume II: *Archives of the Ministry of Foreign Affairs* (Carnegie Institution of Washington publication 392, 1943).

Documents used in the preparation of Vol. II are found in:

Correspondance politique, Angleterre, 341

Mémoires et documents, Amérique, 3, 8

ARCHIVES DU SERVICE HISTORIQUE DE L'ARMÉE, Paris. This archival group was officially formed in 1688 as the Archives de la Guerre. The earliest volumes date from 1631. After several changes of locale, the Archives de la Guerre were finally brought to the Pavillon du Roi at the Château de Vincennes in Paris, where they are now housed. The present name, Service historique de l'armée, dates from 1919.

The SHA is organized as follows:

Group I: Opérations militaires

Série A:

A1: Correspondance générale, 3786 vols. For Canada this is the most important series in the SHA.

A2: Fonds de Suède, 84 vols.

A3: Fonds divers, 123 vols.

A4: Fonds provisoire, 88 cartons and portfolios

Series B to L pertain to post-Revolutionary France.

Group II: Mémoires historiques et Reconnaissances militaires, 2353 articles. The Mémoires comprise diaries of campaigns and accounts of battles and sieges, and the Reconnaissances are mostly documents of a topographic nature. A third part of this group relates to military administration and the military arts.

Group III: Archives des corps de troupes

Série X: Only sous-séries XA and XI relate to Canada.

Group IV: Archives administratives

Série Y: Sous-série YA contains memoirs and projects; YD contains the dossiers of military personnel, divided according to rank.

ARCHIVES NATIONALES, Paris. The Archives nationales were founded in 1790 to accommodate the original papers of the Constituent Assembly and later of the pre-Revolutionary administrations. The basic inventories are: France, Direction des Archives, *Inventaire sommaire et tableau méthodique des fonds conservés aux Archives nationales*, Ire partie, *Régime antérieur à 1789* (Paris, 1871), and *État sommaire par séries des documents conservés aux Archives nationales* (Paris, 1891). Recent guides to finding aids are: France, Direction des Archives, *État des inventaires des Archives nationales, départementales, communales et hospitalières au 1er janvier 1937* (Paris, 1938), and *Supplément, 1937–54* [by R.-H. Bautier] (Paris, 1955). J.-E. Roy, *Rapport sur les Archives de France relatives à l'histoire du Canada* (PAC pub., 6, 1911) and H. P. Beers, *The French in North America: a bibliographical guide to French archives, reproductions, and research missions* (Baton Rouge, La., 1957) give sketches of the history and organization of the archives. For copies in the PAC of documents in the Archives nationales *see: Inventaire provisoire, Fonds des manuscrits N° 3* (Ottawa, 1953), 13–23.

Series of documents used in the preparation of Volume II:

G^7: Contrôle général des finances, 1672–1707

K: Monuments historiques, 1540–1759

K^XI: Principauté de Montbéliard

L: Monuments ecclésiastiques

LL: Registres

M: Mélanges historiques, 1696–1789

V: Grande Chancellerie et Conseils

V^5: Grand Conseil

V^7: Commissions extraordinaires du Conseil privé, 1698–1776

X: Parlement de Paris

X^1A: Registres du Parlement civil

Y: Châtelet de Paris

AN, Archives de la Marine. After the formation of the Marine under Colbert, papers relating to the navy and to colonial affairs were collected in the Archives de la Marine. In 1884 the Archives des Colonies were separated from the Marine. Both collections are now housed in the Archives nationales. The material in the Archives de la Marine extends to 1870. For descriptions of the archives and documents *see*: Didier Neuville, *État sommaire des Archives de la Marine antérieurs à la Révolution* (Paris, 1898); Neuville et al., *Inventaire des Archives de la Marine, série B: service général* (8v., Paris, 1885–1963); J.-E. Roy, *Rapport sur les Archives de France*, 157–243; and Étienne Taillemite, *Les archives anciennes de la Marine* (Académie de Marine, Paris, 1962). For copies of the manuscripts in the PAC *see: Inventaire provisoire, Fonds des manuscrits N° 2* (Ottawa, 1953).

Series pertinent to Volume II:

B^1: Délibérations du Conseil de Marine, 1715–22, 1728–86

B^2: Ordres et dépêches, 1662–1750. The kings' and the ministers' orders to the department of the Marine, military commanders, and intendants of the Marine in French ports

B^3: Correspondence received by the minister from the ports of France and from various authorities, 1660–1789

B^4: Campagnes, 1640–1789. Material relating to naval campaigns

C: Personnel

C^1: Officiers de la Marine du Roi, 1400–1789. "Revues Laffilard" and "Alphabets Laffilard" are contained in volumes 105–7, 151, 153–55, 157, 160–61.

C^2: Personnel civil des ports, 1663–1760

C^7: Dossiers individuels, 1687–1821

2JJ: Personal papers of geographers and hydrographers of the 18th and 19th centuries (numbered catalogue available at the AN)

3JJ: Memoirs, journals, and reports concerning the exploration of North America (analytical inventory available at the AN)

AN, Archives des Colonies. These archives date from about 1669 and contain material up to 1815 (*see* AN, Section Outre-Mer). Colbert established the distinction between papers relating to the Marine and those concerning the colonies and also laid down the major series in the Archives des Colonies. These series and the many later subdivisions of series are described in Étienne Taillemite, "Les archives des colonies françaises aux Archives nationales," *Gazette des Archives* (Paris), XLVI (1964), 93–116. For copies of manuscripts in the PAC *see: Inventaire provisoire, Fonds des manuscrits N° 1* (Ottawa, 1952).

Series containing information on persons in Volume II:

B: Lettres envoyées. Dispatches of the king, the minister of the Marine, and the Conseil d'État to officials in New France. For the

17th and the first half of the 18th century *see* the following calendars: Étienne Taillemite, *Inventaire analytique de la correspondance générale avec les colonies, départ, Série B (déposée aux Archives nationales), I, registres 1 à 37 (1654–1715)* (Paris, 1959) and PAC *Report, 1899*, Supp., 245–548; *Report, 1904*, App. K, 1–312.

C11A: Correspondance générale. Letters of officials in New France to the king and the minister of the Marine and some drafts of documents sent to the colony. A calendar of documents to 1741 is published in PAC *Report, 1885*, xxix–lxxix; *Report, 1886*, xxxix–cl; *see also* PAC *Report, 1887*, ccxxv–ccxxxix and D. W. Parker, *A guide to the documents in the Manuscript Room at the Public Archives of Canada*, Vol. I (PAC pub., 10, 1914), 227ff. An unpublished index for this series exists at the PAC.

C11B: Correspondance générale, Île Royale. Letters of officials in Île Royale to the king and the minister of the Marine. Volumes I–38 (1706?–1762) calendared in Parker, *Guide*, 241–45 and in PAC, *Report, 1887*, cclxxxii–cccxciv.

C11C: Amérique du Nord. Papers concerning Newfoundland, Îles de la Madeleine, Île Royale, and Gaspé. Calendared in Parker, *Guide*, 246, and PAC *Report, 1887*, cccxciv–cccxcviii.

C11D: Correspondance générale, Acadie. Dispatches to the minister of the Marine from Acadia. *See* calendars in PAC *Report, 1887*, ccxxxix–cclxiii and in Parker, *Guide*, 238–40.

C11E: Canada, divers. Letters etc. dealing with boundary disputes, 1685–1764. Calendared in Parker, *Guide*, 240–41 and in PAC *Report 1887*, cclxiii–cclxxxii.

C11G: Correspondance Raudot-Pontchartrain et correspondance générale du Domaine d'Occident et de l'Île Royale. *See* calendars in Parker, *Guide*, 246–48 and PAC *Report, 1899*, Supp., 201–44.

C13: Louisiane

C13A: Correspondance générale, Louisiane, 1678–1803

C13B: Correspondance générale, Louisiane, 1699–1773 (Documents discovered after the principal series had been made up.)

C13C: Mémoires et projects, Louisiane, 1675–1736

An analytical inventory of series C13 is available for use at the AN and will be published in the near future.

C14: Guyane, 1664–1822 (analytical inventory available at the AN)

D2C: Troupes et milice des colonies. Many volumes contain information on officers who served in Canada; the following were particularly useful:

47: Rôle des compagnies détachées en garnison au Canada et à l'île Royale, 1656–1736

49: Liste générale des officiers d'état-major au Canada, 1694–1774

51: Revues des compagnies détachées en garnison en Louisiane, 1710–57

222: Alphabet Laffilard. Service records of officers who served in the colonies before 1740

D2D: Personnel militaire et civil. Listes générales, 1695–1789

E: Dossiers personnels. Correspondence regarding pensions, employment, and so on

F1A: Fonds des colonies, 1670–1789. Financial documents

F3: Collection Moreau Saint-Méry. Seventeenth-, 18th- and 19th-century originals and copies of documents in the C11A and B series and of others that have since disappeared. Papers relating to Canada, Louisiana, Île Royale, Saint-Pierre, and Miquelon have been copied and microfilmed by the PAC. Calendared in PAC *Report, 1899*, Supp., 39–191; *Report, 1905*, I, pt.VI, 447–505; and Parker, *Guide*, 249–53. (Note that volumes have since been renumbered to agree with AN classification.)

F5A: Missions religieuses, [1650?]–1808

G: *See* AN, Section Outre-Mer.

AN, Section Outre-Mer. The Section Outre-Mer came into being on 1 Jan. 1961 when the Ministère de la France d'Outre-Mer ceased to exist. This section was intended to house post-1815 documents, while the Archives des Colonies would house the pre-1815 material. Two important series dealing with the earlier period are, however, to be found in the Section Outre-Mer. For copies of manuscripts in the PAC *see*: *Inventaire provisoire, Fonds des manuscrits Nᵒ 1*, 17–19.

Série G

G1: Registres d'état civil, recensements et divers documents.

406: État civil de Louisbourg, 1722–38

407: État civil de Louisbourg, 1738–45

411: État civil de l'île Saint-Jean, 1721–58 (fragments)

462: Concessions pour le Canada et l'île Royale

466: Recensements de l'Acadie, de l'île Royale, du Cap Breton, et de l'île Saint-Jean, 1671, 1686, 1693, 1698, 1700, 1701, 1703, 1707, 1714, 1752.

467/1: Recensements de Saint-Pierre et Miquelon, de Plaisance et de Terre-Neuve, 1671–1711

467/3: Recensements de l'île Royale, 1713, 1715, 1724, 1726, 1734.

G²: Registres des greffes du Conseil supérieur de Louisbourg, 1711–58

181 : 1732–35

G³: Notariat, 1637–1789

2037–39: Greffe de C.-J. Leroy Desmarest, Louisbourg, 1728–36

2040: Greffe de J.-C. Loppinot, Port-Royal, 1687–1710

2046–47: Greffe de Jean de Laborde, Louisbourg, 1737–53

2053–55: Notariat de Plaisance, 1696–1714

2056–58: Greffe de Lambert Micoin, île Royale, 1715–28.

Dépôt des fortifications des colonies. This series contains technical reports, maps, reports on discoveries, fisheries, commerce, and military campaigns, as well as papers on the Compagnie des Indes. Series concerning North America are: La Louisiane, L'Amérique septentrionale, Saint-Pierre et Miquelon. A manuscript inventory of the various series is available at the AN. *See*: PAC *Report, 1905,* I, pt.III, 1–43; J.-E. Roy, *Rapport sur les archives de France,* 535–59.

BIBLIOTHÈQUE NATIONALE, Paris. The library collection of the kings of France, from the time of François I, forms the basis of the BN. In the 17th century the manuscripts and printed works were separated. From 1926 the libraries of the Arsenal, Opéra, and Conservatoire National de Musique have functioned in conjunction with the Bibliothèque nationale. The main divisions at the present time are Cartes et Plans, Estampes, Imprimés, Journaux et Périodiques, Manuscrits, Médailles, and Musique.

Most important for Volume II are the manuscripts, which number over 160,000. Most of the documents have been integrated with the Fonds français (Fr., nᵒˢ 1–33264) or with the Nouvelles acquisitions françaises (NAF, nᵒˢ 1–   ); documents most recently integrated have double numbering. Among the collections not integrated are Baluze, Cinq Cents de Colbert, Mélanges de Colbert, and Clairambault.

For an outline of the organization of the BN, *see* J.-E. Roy, *Rapport sur les archives de France relatives à l'histoire du Canada* (PAC pub., 6, 1911), 655–848. For the 18-volume catalogue to the Fr. and NAF (1–10,000) there is a *Table générale alphabétique* (6v., Paris, 1931–48). Another guide

is W. G. Leland, *Guide to materials for American history in the libraries and archives of Paris,* Volume I: *Libraries* (Carnegie Institution of Washington publication 392, 1932). See also BN, Département des manuscrits, *Catalogue des manuscrits de la collection Clairambault,* par Philippe Lauer (3v., Paris, 1923–32); *Catalogue des manuscrits de la collection des Cinq Cents de Colbert,* par Charles de La Roncière (Paris, 1908); *Catalogue des manuscrits de la collection des Mélanges de Colbert,* par Charles de La Roncière et P.-M. Bondois (2v., Paris, 1920–22); *Nouvelles acquisitions du département des manuscrits pendant les années 1898–1899, inventaire sommaire* (Paris, 1900), 49–85 ("Amérique, Canada, Nouvelle-France, Acadie, et Louisiane" [catalogue sommaire de la collection Pierre Margry], par Charles de La Roncière); Robert Latouche, "Inventaire sommaire de la collection Arnoul conservée à la Bibliothèque nationale," *Revue des bibliothèques,* XVIII (1908), 244–63.

UNITED STATES OF AMERICA

MASSACHUSETTS HISTORICAL SOCIETY, Boston, Mass. Founded in 1791, it is the oldest historical society in the United States. About half the holdings of the society are manuscripts and transcriptions. *See* S. T. Riley, *The Massachusetts Historical Society 1791–1959* (Boston, 1959) and "The manuscript collections of the Massachusetts Historical Society: a brief listing," M.H.S. *Miscellany,* no. 5 (December 1958).

Of special interest for 17th- and 18th-century Canadian history are the Parkman transcripts from European archives (1565–1768), 100 volumes, the F. L. Gay transcripts from English archives (1630–1776), 124 volumes, and a considerable collection of manuscripts concerning the expeditions against Louisbourg.

MASSACHUSETTS, SECRETARY OF THE COMMONWEALTH'S OFFICE, ARCHIVES, Boston, Mass. These archives contain primarily the records of the General Court of Massachusetts from the 17th century until the present day.

The following series of documents are of interest for 17th- and 18th-century Canadian history:
"Massachusetts Archives." This is the title usually given to the 326 volumes of legislative records rearranged in the 19th century by J. B. Felt and his successor according to subject. Excellent name card-indexes have been prepared for about 55 volumes on such subjects as colonial affairs (including letters received and sent to other North American

and West Indian colonies), commerce, depositions, foreign affairs, judicial and pecuniary matters, and maritime records.

Executive records of the Council (called Council Records), about 150 vols. For the 17th and 18th centuries, the records cover 1650–56, 1686–87, and 1692 on.

J. B. Poore's transcripts from French archives, from the discovery of America to 1780, 10 vols. Copies of these copies were published 40 years later by the Quebec legislature as *Coll. de manuscrits relatifs à la N.-F.* [*see* section II; *see also* H. P. Beers, *The French in North America: a bibliographical guide to French archives, reproductions, and research missions* (Baton Rouge, La., 1957), 153–56].

For copies of documents in the PAC *see*: *Preliminary inventory, Manuscript Group 18, pre-Conquest papers* (Ottawa, 1964).

NEWBERRY LIBRARY, Chicago. The Edward E. Ayer collection contains material on the archaeology and ethnology of the Indians of North and South America and their relations with whites.

Used in Vol. II was the census of Father Pierre de La Chasse (1708): "Recensement général fait au mois de Novembre mile Sept cent huit de tous les Sauvages de l'Acadie qui résident dans la Coste de l'Est, et de ceux de Pintagouet et de Canibeky, famille par famille, . . . comme aussy le recensement des françois Establis a la dite Coste de l'Es." (MS 751)

NEW ENGLAND HISTORIC GENEALOGICAL SOCIETY, Boston, Mass. The society specializes in family history and genealogy and its collections are on a national scale. It also has one of the largest collections on this continent of copies of English parish records.

NEW YORK STATE, ARCHIVES, Albany, N.Y. On the development and present organization of these various archives *see* E. F. Rowse, "The archives of New York," *American Archivist*, IV (no.4, 1941), 267–74, and Historical Records Survey, *Guide to depositories of manuscript collections in the United States* (Columbus, 1938), 76–77.

Of interest for 17th- and 18th-century Canadian history are the Colonial Manuscripts, transcribed from various European archives (England, France, Holland), and published in full as *Documents relative to the colonial history of . . . New York* (*see* sect.II); on this collection, *see* H.P. Beers, *The French in North America: a bibliographical guide to French archives, reproductions, and research missions* (Baton Rouge, 1957), 145–53.

OTHER FOREIGN ARCHIVES

ARCHIVUM ROMANUM SOCIETATIS IESU, Rome. Despite the destruction of a large part of these archives following the brief suppression of the order in 1773, a number of valuable documents on the history of the Society of Jesus in North America have survived. These include correspondence between the general of the order and missionaries, annual letters from America, catalogues, and death notices which provide biographical information. The archives are not open to researchers, but microfilm copies of material from ARSI relating to the Americas can be found at Saint Louis University, Missouri. The American Jesuits and the Congregation have also published certain of the more important manuscripts in ARSI. The Institutum Historicum Societatis Iesu in Rome has published the series "Monumenta Historica Missionum Societatis Iesu."

The following collections were used in the preparation of Vol. II:

Francia 17, 23, 24, 25/I, 25/II

Gallia 10, 15/I, 110/I, 110/II (microfilm copies of latter two in the PAC)

II. PRINTED PRIMARY SOURCES

Acadiensia Nova (1598–1779): new and unpublished documents and other data relating to Acadia. Edited by W. I. Morse. 2 vols. London, 1935.

ARCHIVES DU QUÉBEC PUBLICATIONS

APQ and AQ *Rapports*. Documents from the AQ—as well as from other archives—have been published in the *Rapport de l'Archiviste de la Province de Québec*. Volumes correspond to the fiscal years for 1920–21 to 1948–49 and 1959–60; those for the years 1949–51 to 1957–59 include two years; no volumes were published for 1961 or 1962, but publication was resumed in 1963 as the AQ *Rapport*.

Bulletin des recherches historiques [*see* sect. V].

Lettres de noblesse (P.-G. Roy).

Ord. comm. (P.-G. Roy).

Papier terrier de la Cie des I.O. (P.-G. Roy).

P.-G. Roy. *Index des jugements et délibérations du Conseil souverain de 1663 à 1716.* Québec, 1940.

———— *Inv. coll. pièces jud. et not.*

———— *Inv. concessions.*

———— *Inv. contrats de mariage.*

———— *Inventaire de pièces sur la côte de Labrador.*

———— *Inventaire des procès-verbaux des grands voyers.*

———— *Inv. ins. cons. souv.*

———— *Inv. ins. prév. Québec.*

———— *Inv. jug. et délib., 1717–1760.*

———— *Inv. ord. int.*

———— *Inv. testaments.*

P.-G. et Antoine Roy. *Inv. greffes not.*

[For complete descriptions see individual titles and P.-G. Roy, *infra.*]

ARCHIVES DU SÉMINAIRE DE QUÉBEC PUBLICATIONS II: Provost, *Le séminaire de Québec: documents et biographies.*

BACQUEVILLE DE LA POTHERIE. *See* LE ROY

BAILLARGEON, NOËL. "Les missions du séminaire de Québec dans la vallée du Mississippi 1698–1699," AQ *Rapport, 1965,* 13–56.

BAUGY, [HENRI DE]. *Journal d'une expédition contre les Iroquois en 1687: lettres et pièces relatives au fort Saint-Louis des Illinois.* Édité par Ernest Serrigny. Paris, 1883.

[BERTRAND DE LATOUR, LOUIS.] *Mémoires sur la vie de M. de Laval, premier évêque de Québec.* Cologne, 1761.

[BIGOT, JACQUES.] *Copie d'une lettre escrite par le père Jacques Bigot de la Compagnie de Jésus l'an 1684, pour accompagner un collier de pourcelaine envoié par les Abnaquis de la mission de Sainct François de Sales dans la Nouvelle-France au tombeau de leur sainct patron à Annecy.* Cramoisy series, no. 23. Manate [New York], 1858.

[————] *Relation de ce qui s'est passé de plus remarquable dans la mission Abnaquise de Sainct Joseph de Sillery, et dans l'establissement de la Nouvelle Mission de Sainct François de Sales, l'année 1684. Par le R. P. Jacques Bigot, de la Compagnie de Jésus.* Cramoisy series, no. 2. Manate [New York], 1857.

[————] *Relation de ce qui s'est passé de plus remarquable dans la mission Abnaquise de Sainct Joseph de Sillery, et de Sainct François de Sales, l'année 1685. Par le R. P. Jacques Bigot, de la Compagnie de Jésus.* Cramoisy series, no. 3. Manate [New York], 1858.

[————] *Relation de la Mission Abnaquise de St. François de Sales, l'année 1702, par le Père Jacques Bigot, de la Compagnie de Jésus.* Cramoisy series, no. 21. New York, 1865.

[BIGOT, VINCENT.] *Relation de ce qui s'est passé de plus remarquable dans la mission des Abnaquis à l'Acadie, l'année 1701.* Cramoisy series, no. 4. Manate [New York], 1858.

BOUCHER, PIERRE. *Histoire véritable et naturelle des mœurs et productions du pays de la Nouvelle France, vulgairement dite le Canada.* Paris, 1664. (Société hist. de Boucherville pub., I, 1964.)

BUADE DE FRONTENAC, LOUIS DE. *See* "Correspondance. . . ."

"Cadillac papers." *See Michigan Pioneer Collections.*

CAMPBELL, JOHN. *Lives of the admirals and other eminent British seamen. . . . Including a new and accurate naval history from the earliest accounts of time. . . .* 4 vols. London, 1742–44; later editions in 1750, 1761, 1779, and 1781; new, revised, and corrected edition in 8 vols., London, 1812–17.

CARON, IVANHOË. "Inventaire des documents concernant l'Église du Canada sous le régime français," APQ *Rapport, 1939–40,* 157–353; *1940–41,* 333–473; *1941–42,* 179–298.

CENSUSES. *See* RECENSEMENTS

CHAMPLAIN SOCIETY. "Founded in 1905, with headquarters in Toronto, for the purpose of publishing rare and inaccessible materials relating to the history of Canada. Its publications are issued only to elected members, limited in number. . . ." Volumes relative to this work include:

II: Denys, *Description and natural history* (Ganong).

III: *Documents relating to seigniorial tenure* (Munro).

V: Le Clercq, *New relation of Gaspesia* (Ganong).

XVI: *Journals and letters of La Vérendrye* (Burpee).

XVIII: *Documents relating to Hudson Bay* (Tyrrell).

XX: Dièreville, *Relation of a voyage to Port Royal* (Webster).

XXXII: *The Walker expedition* (Graham).

[For complete citations, see individual listings.]

CHARLEVOIX, [PIERRE-FRANÇOIS-XAVIER] DE. *Histoire et description generale de la Nouvelle-France, avec le journal historique d'un voyage fait par ordre du roi dans l'Amérique Septentrionale.* 3 vols.; another edition 6 vols. Paris, 1744.

———— *History and general description of New France.* Translated and edited, with notes, by J. G. Shea. 6 vols. New York, 1866–72, London, 1902; reprinted Chicago, 1962.

CHAUCHETIÈRE, CLAUDE. *La vie de la b. Catherine Thegakouita dite à présent la Sainte Sauvagesse.*

Cramoisy series, no. 26. Manate [New York], 1887.

CHURCH, BENJAMIN. *History of King Philip's war.* Introduction and notes by H. M. Dexter. 2 vols. Boston, 1865–67. The volumes are entitled:
I: *History of King Philip's war.* 1865.
II: *The history of the eastern expeditions of 1689, 1690, 1692, 1696, and 1704 against the Indians and French.* 1867.

CHURCH, THOMAS. *Entertaining passages relating to Philip's war which began in the month of June, 1675. As also of expeditions more lately made against the common enemy, and Indian rebels in the eastern parts of New-England: with some account of the divine providence towards Benj. Church Esqr.* Boston, 1716.

Classified digest of the records of the Society for the Propagation of the Gospel in foreign parts, 1701–1892. London, 1893.

Collection de documents inédits sur le Canada et l'Amérique, publiés par le Canada-Français. I–III (1888–90).

Collection de manuscrits contenant lettres, mémoires, et autres documents historiques relatifs à la Nouvelle-France. 4 vols. Québec, 1883–85. [*See* Massachusetts, Secretary of the Commonwealth's Office, Archives, section I.]

COLONIAL SOCIETY OF MASSACHUSETTS PUBLICATIONS, Boston, Mass. A numbered series of volumes comprising either *Transactions* or separately titled Collections. 43 vols. published to date. 1892– . *Index* for vols. I–XXV published in 1932. The following publications were found useful in the preparation of vol. II:
XV–XVI, XXI: *Harvard College records, 1636–1750.*
XXIX–XXX: *Suffolk County Court records, 1671–80.*

"Correspondance échangée entre la cour de France et le gouverneur de Frontenac, pendant sa première administration (1672–1682)," APQ *Rapport, 1926–27,* 1–144.

"Correspondance échangée entre la cour de France et le gouverneur de Frontenac, pendant sa seconde administration (1689–1699)," APQ *Rapport, 1927–28,* 3–211; *1928–29,* 247–384.

"Correspondance entre M. de Vaudreuil et la Cour," APQ *Rapport, 1938–39,* 10–179; *1939–40,* 355–463; *1942–43,* 399–443; *1946–47,* 371–460; *1947–48,* 137–339.

CRAMOISY SERIES. *See: Jesuit Relations....*

DABLON, CLAUDE. *Relation de ce qui s'est passé de plus remarquable aux missions des peres de la Compagnie de Jésus en Nouvelle-France, les années 1672 et 1673.* Cramoisy series, no.13. New York, 1861.
—— *Relation de ce qui s'est passé de plus remarquable aux missions des peres de la Compagnie de Jésus en la Nouvelle-France, les années 1673 à 1679.* Cramoisy series, no. 12. New York, 1861.

Découvertes et établissements des Français dans l'ouest et dans le sud de l'Amérique septentrionale, 1614–1754: mémoires et documents inédits. Édités par Pierre Margry. 6 vols. Paris, 1879–88. Documents reproduced here should be checked against the originals. Copies of an English translation of this work, completed in 1914, are in the possession of the Burton Historical Collection (Detroit Public Library), the Michigan Historical Commission (Lansing), and the University of Chicago.

DENYS, NICOLAS. *The description and natural history of the coasts of North America (Acadia).* Translated and edited, with a memoir of the author, collateral documents, and a reprint of the original, by W. F. Ganong. (Champlain Society publications, II.) Toronto, 1908.

DIÈREVILLE, SIEUR DE. *Relation du voyage du Port Royal de l'Acadie, ou de la Nouvelle France.* Rouen, 1708.
—— *Relation of the voyage to Port Royal in Acadia or New France.* Translated by Mrs. Clarence Webster. Edited, with notes, by J. C. Webster. (Champlain Society publications, XX.) Toronto, 1933. Includes original French text.

Documentary history of the State of Maine. Edited by William Willis *et al.* 24 vols. (Maine Historical Society *Collections,* 2d series.) Portland, 1869–1916. Not to be confused with Maine Historical Society, *Collections and Proceedings* [*q.v.*].

Documentary history of the State of New-York. Edited by E. B. O'Callaghan. 4 vols. Albany, 1850–51.

Documents relating to Canadian currency, exchange and finance during the French period. Selected and edited with notes and introduction by Adam Shortt. 2 vols. (Board of historical publications, Public Archives of Canada.) Ottawa, 1925.

Documents relating to currency, exchange and finance in Nova Scotia with prefatory documents, 1675–1758. Selected by Adam Shortt, completed with an introduction by V. K. Johnston, and revised and edited by Gustave Lanctot. (Board of historical publications, Public Archives of Canada.) Ottawa, 1933.

Documents relating to the early history of Hudson Bay. Edited by J. B. Tyrrell. (Champlain Society publications, XVIII.) Toronto, 1931.

Documents relating to the seigniorial tenure in Canada, 1598–1854. Edited, with introduction and notes, by W. B. Munro. (Champlain Society publications, III.) Toronto, 1908.

Documents relative to the colonial history of the State of New-York; procured in Holland, England and France, by John Romeyn Brodhead. . . . Edited by E. B. O'Callaghan and Berthold Fernow. 15 vols. Albany, N.Y., 1853–87.

[DOLLIER DE CASSON, FRANÇOIS.] *Histoire du Montréal 1640–1672.* Avec apostilles par Pierre Margry et notes et appendices par J. Viger. (Société historique de Montréal, *Mémoires*, IV.) Montréal, 1868.

[———] *Histoire du Montréal 1640–1672,* in *RC,* 1ʳᵉ série, VI (1869), 103–35, 196–227, 262–85, 353–75, 417–25.

[———] *Histoire du Montréal 1640–1672.* (Literary and Historical Society of Quebec, Historical Documents, D.6, 3d series.) Québec, 1871.

[———] *A history of Montreal 1640–1672 from the French of Dollier de Casson.* Edited and translated by Ralph Flenley. Toronto, 1928.

Édits, ordonnances royaux, déclarations et arrêts du Conseil d'état du roi concernant le Canada: revus et corrigés d'après les pièces originales déposées aux archives provinciales. II: *Arrêts et règlements du Conseil supérieur de Québec, et ordonnances et jugements des intendants du Canada.* III: *Complément des ordonnances et jugements des gouverneurs et intendants du Canada, précédé des commissions des dits gouverneurs et intendants et des différents officiers civils et de justice.* Québec, 1854–56.

The French foundations, 1680–1693. Edited by T. C. Pease and R. C. Werner. (Illinois State Historical Library *Collections*, XXIII, French series, I.) Springfield, Ill., [1934].

GAULTIER DE LA VÉRENDRYE, PIERRE. *See: Journals and letters. . . .*

[GRAVIER, JACQUES.] *Lettre du P. Jacques Gravier, le 23 février 1708 sur les affaires de la Louisiane.* Cramoisy series, no. 22. New York, 1865.

[———] *Relation ou journal du voyage du r.p. Jacques Gravier, de la Compagnie de Jésus, en 1700 depuis le pays des Illinois jusqu'à l'embouchure de Mississipi.* Cramoisy series, no. 11. New York, 1859.

GREAT BRITAIN, PARLIAMENT. *Proceedings and debates of the British parliaments respecting North America.* Edited by L. F. Stock. 5 vols. Washington, 1924–41.

GUYART DE L'INCARNATION, MARIE. *Lettres de la révérende Mère Marie de l'Incarnation (née Marie Guyart), première supérieure du Monastère des Ursulines de Québec.* Éditées par P.-F. Richaudeau. 2 vols. Paris, Leipzig, Tournai, 1876.

——— *Word from New France. The selected letters of Marie de l'Incarnation.* Edited and translated by Joyce Marshall. Toronto, 1967.

HENNEPIN, LOUIS. *Description de la Louisiane. . . .* Paris, 1683.

——— *Nouveau voyage d'un païs plus grand que l'Europe, avec les réflections des entreprises du Sieur de La Salle. . . .* Utrecht, 1698. A continuation of the author's *Nouvelle découverte, infra.*

——— *Nouvelle découverte d'un très grand pays situé dans l'Amérique entre le Nouveau-Mexique, et la mer glaciale. . . .* Utrecht, 1697.

——— *A new discovery of a vast country, by Father Louis Hennepin, reprinted from the second London issue of 1698.* Edited by R. G. Thwaites. 2 vols. Chicago, 1903.

——— *Voyage ou nouvelle découverte d'un tres grand pays. . . .* Amsterdam, 1704.

HUDSON'S BAY RECORD SOCIETY. Initiated in 1938 by the Hudson's Bay Company after classification of its London Archives, begun in 1932, had progressed to the point where publication was feasible. Membership in the Society is limited. Inquiries should be directed to: the Hon. Secretary, Beaver House, Great Trinity Lane, London, E.C.4, England.

PUBLICATIONS

General editor for vols. I–XXII, E. E. Rich; for vols. XXIII–XXV, K. G. Davies; for XXVI, A. M. Johnson. 26 vols. published to date. Vols. I–XII issued in association with the Champlain Society, Toronto.

V: *Minutes of the Hudson's Bay Company 1671–1674.* Edited by E. E. Rich. 1942.

VIII: *Minutes of the Hudson's Bay Company 1679–1684: first part, 1679–82.* Edited by E. E. Rich. 1945.

IX: *Minutes of the Hudson's Bay Company 1679–1684: second part, 1682–84.* Edited by E. E. Rich. 1946.

XI: *Copy-book of letters outward &c, begins 29th May, 1680, ends 5 July, 1687.* Edited by E. E. Rich and A. M. Johnson. 1948.

XII: *James Isham's observations on Hudsons Bay, 1743 and notes and observations on a book entitled A voyage to Hudsons Bay in the Dobbs Galley, 1749.* Edited by E. E. Rich and A. M. Johnson. 1949.

XX: *Hudson's Bay copy booke of letters commissions instructions outward 1688–1696.* Edited by E. E. Rich and A. M. Johnson. 1957.

XXI: Rich. *History of the HBC. I: 1670–1763.* (*see* section IV)

XXII: Rich. *History of the HBC. II: 1763–1870.*

XXV: *Letters from Hudson Bay 1703–40.*

Edited by K. G. Davies and A. M. Johnson. 1965.

HUTCHINSON, [THOMAS]. *The history of the colony of Massachuset's Bay, from the first settlement thereof in 1628, until its incorporation with the colony of Plimouth, Province of Main, &c. by the charter of King William and Queen Mary, in 1691*. 2d edition. London, 1765. The 1st edition was published in Boston in 1764 and a 3d edition in Boston in 1795.

—— *The history of the province of Massachusetts-bay, from the charter of King William and Queen Mary, in 1691, until the year 1750*. 2d edition. London, 1768. The 1st edition was published in Boston in 1767 and a 3d edition in Boston in 1795.

—— *The history of the colony and province of Massachusetts-Bay, edited from the author's own copies of volumes I and II and his manuscript of volume III, with a memoir and additional notes*. Edited by L. S. Mayo. 3 vols. Cambridge, Mass., 1936. Volumes I and II include Governor Hutchinson's corrections of the 2d editions.

The Indian tribes of the upper Mississippi Valley and region of the Great Lakes, as described by Nicolas Perrot . . . ; Bacqueville de la Potherie . . . ; Morrell Marston . . . ; and Thomas Forsyth. . . . Edited and translated by E. H. Blair. 2 vols. Cleveland, 1911, 1912.

"Inventaire des documents concernant l'Église du Canada. . . ." *See* CARON, IVANHOË

[JÉRÉMIE, NICOLAS.] *Twenty years of York Factory 1694–1714: Jérémie's account of Hudson Strait and Bay*. Translated from the French edition of 1720 with notes and introduction by R. Douglas and J. N. Wallace. Ottawa, 1926.

The Jesuit Relations and allied documents: travels and explorations of the Jesuit missionaries in New France 1610–1791: the original French, Latin and Italian texts, with English translations and notes. Edited by R. G. Thwaites. 73 vols., including 2 Index vols. Cleveland, 1896–1901. Facsimile reproduction, 73 vols. in 36, New York, 1959. [For a discussion of the *Relations*, see *DCB*, I, 455–57.]

CRAMOISY SERIES: In 1857, J. G. Shea brought out the first volume of a separate series of Jesuit Relations in 26 vols., the Cramoisy series, published in New York. All the works were from original manuscripts that had not been printed before. The following works were used in the preparation of Vol. II:

2, 3: [J. Bigot,] *Relations des missions de sainct Joseph de Sillery et sainct François de Sales, 1684, 1685*.

4: [V. Bigot,] *Relation de la mission des Abnaquis à l'Acadie, 1701*.

11: [Gravier,] *Relation du voyage en 1700 à l'embouchure du Mississipi*.

12, 13: Dablon, *Relations des missions dans la Nouvelle-France, 1673–79, 1672–73*.

20: *Relation des affaires du Canada en 1696*.

21: [J. Bigot,] *Relation de la mission de St. François de Sales, 1702*.

22: [Gravier,] *Lettre sur les affaires de la Louisiane, 1708*.

23: [J. Bigot,] *Copie d'une lettre, 1684*.

26: Chauchetière, *Vie de Catherine Thegakouita*. [For complete titles, see the individual entries in this section.]

Journal de l'expédition de D'Iberville en Acadie et à Terre-Neuve, par l'abbé Beaudoin; lettres de D'Iberville. Édité, avec une introduction, par Auguste Gosselin. (Les Normands au Canada.) Évreux, 1900.

"Journal of the expedition under Sir William Phipps against Port Royal, 1690," PAC *Report, 1912*, App. E, 54–66.

Le journal des Jésuites, publié d'après le manuscrit original conservé aux Archives du Séminaire de Québec. Édité par les Abbés Laverdière et Casgrain. 2e édition; Montréal, 1892.

Journals of the House of Representatives of Massachusetts. 38 vols. to date. (Mass. Hist. Soc. publications.) Boston, 1919–

Journals and letters of Pierre Gaultier de Varennes de La Vérendrye and his sons, with correspondence between the governors of Canada and the French court, touching the search for the Western Sea. Edited, with introduction and notes, by L. J. Burpee. (Champlain Society publications, XVI.) Toronto, 1927.

JUCHEREAU [DE LA FERTÉ] DE SAINT-IGNACE, JEANNE-FRANÇOISE, et MARIE-ANDRÉE DUPLESSIS DE SAINTE-HÉLÈNE. *Les annales de l'Hôtel-Dieu de Québec, 1636–1716*. Éditées par Albert Jamet. Québec et Montréal, 1939. The original manuscript of this work was drawn up by Mother Duplessis with the help of notes gathered by Mother Juchereau, and was printed in Montauban in 1751 by Bertrand de Latour, under the title: *Histoire de l'Hôtel-Dieu de Québec*.

Jugements et délibérations du Conseil souverain de la Nouvelle-France [1663–1716]. 6 vols. Québec, 1885–91. *Index* by P.-G. Roy. Québec, 1940.

[KELSEY, HENRY.] *The Kelsey papers*. Edited, with an introduction, by A. G. Doughty and Chester Martin. (Public Archives of Canada and Public Record Office of Northern Ireland.) Ottawa, 1929.

[KNIGHT, JAMES.] *The founding of Churchill: being the journal of Captain James Knight, governor-in-chief in Hudson Bay, from the 14th of July to the 13th of September, 1717.* Edited with a historical introduction and notes by J. F. Kenney. London, Toronto, Vancouver, [1932].

[LA CROIX DE CHEVRIÈRES DE SAINT-VALLIER, JEAN-BAPTISTE DE.] *Estat présent de l'Église et de la colonie françoise dans la Nouvelle-France, par M. l'Évêque de Québec.* Paris, 1688; Québec, 1856.

LAHONTAN. *See* LOM D'ARCE

LA POTHERIE, LE ROY DE BACQUEVILLE DE. *See* LE ROY

LA VÉRENDRYE, GAULTIER DE. *See: Journals and letters.* . . .

LE BLANT, ROBERT. *Histoire de la Nouvelle-France: les sources narratives du début du XVIIIe siècle et le Recueil de Gédéon de Catalogne.* 1 vol. paru. Dax, [1948].

LE CLERCQ, CHRESTIEN. *The first establishment of the faith in New France.* Translated by J. G. Shea. 2 vols. New York, 1881.

—— *New relation of Gaspesia with the customs and religion of the Gaspesian Indians.* Translated and edited by W. F. Ganong. (Champlain Society publications, V.) Toronto, 1910.

—— *Nouvelle relation de la Gaspésie, qui contient les mœurs & la religion des sauvages Gaspésiens.* . . . Paris, 1691.

—— *Premier établissement de la foy dans la Nouvelle-France.* 2 vols. Paris, 1691.

[LE ROY] DE BACQUEVILLE DE LA POTHERIE, [CLAUDE-CHARLES.] *Histoire de l'Amérique septentrionale.* 4 vols. Paris, 1722. Autres éditions, Rouen, 1722; Paris, 1753.

LE TAC, SIXTE. *Histoire chronologique de la Nouvelle-France ou Canada depuis sa découverte (mil cinq cents quatre) jusques en l'an mil six cents trente deux . . . publiée pour la première fois d'après le manuscrit original de 1689 et accompagnée de notes et d'un appendice tout composé de documents originaux et inédits.* Par Eugène Réveillaud. Paris, 1888.

Lettres de noblesse, généalogies, érections de comtés et baronnies insinuées par le Conseil souverain de la Nouvelle-France. Éditées par P.-G. Roy. 2 vols. Beauceville, 1920.

"Lettres et mémoires de François-Madeleine-Fortuné Ruette d'Auteuil, procureur général au Conseil souverain de la Nouvelle-France," *APQ Rapport, 1922–23,* 1–114.

LITERARY AND HISTORICAL SOCIETY OF QUEBEC/ SOCIÉTÉ LITTÉRAIRE ET HISTORIQUE DE QUÉBEC. The oldest historical society in Canada, founded 6 Jan. 1824 in Quebec. It has published (a) a lengthy series of *Transactions:* old series, I (1824/29)–V (1862); new series, I (1863)–XXX (1924); (b) another collection, Historical Documents, consisting of 12 vols. in 9 series (1838–

1915), numbered consecutively D.1, D.2, etc., irrespective of the fact that the first series contains 4 vols., while the remaining eight series contain only one vol. each; (c) *Bulletin,* I (1900)–IV (1907); *Index to the archival publications . . . 1824–1924.* Québec, 1923. Relative to this volume are:
[Dollier de Casson,] *Histoire du Montréal 1640–1672.* (Historical Documents, D.6, 3d series.)
[Vachon] de Belmont, *Histoire du Canada.* . . . (Historical Documents, D.2, 1st series; D.6, 3d series.)

The Livingston Indian records 1666–1723. Edited by L. H. Leder. Gettysburg, 1956.

[LOM D'ARCE, LOUIS-ARMAND DE,] BARON DE LAHONTAN. *New voyages to North America.* . . . Edited, with introduction and notes, by R. G. Thwaites. 2 vols. Chicago, 1905 (reprinted from English edition of 1703).

—— *Nouveaux voyages de mr le baron de Lahontan, dans l'Amérique septentrionale.* . . . 2 vols. La Haye, 1703.

MAINE HISTORICAL SOCIETY PUBLICATIONS, Portland, Maine.
Collections, 1st series. 10 vols. 1831–91.
Collections and Proceedings, 2d series. 10 vols. 1890–99.
Collections, 3d series. 2 vols. 1904–6.
Documentary history of the State of Maine [*q.v.*].
Province and court records of Maine [*q.v.*].

Mandements, lettres pastorales et circulaires des évêques de Québec. Édités par Henri Têtu et C.-O. Gagnon. 9 vols. Québec, 1887–98.

MARGRY, PIERRE, éd. *See: Découvertes et établissements.* . . .

MASSACHUSETTS HISTORICAL SOCIETY PUBLICATIONS, Boston, Mass.
Collections. 7 series of 10 vols. each plus 9 vols. published to date. 1792– .
Journals of House of Representatives [*q.v.*].
Proceedings. 2 series of 20 vols. each plus 36 vols. published to date. 1879– .
Shipton, *Sibley's Harvard graduates* [*see* section III].
As a guide to contents and indexes, see: *Handbook of the publications and photostats 1792–1935* (1937).

MASSICOTTE, É.-Z. *Répertoire des arrêts, édits, mandements, ordonnances conservés dans les Archives du Palais de Justice de Montréal, 1640–1760.* Montréal, 1919.

MATHER, COTTON. *Magnalia Christi Americana: or, the ecclesiastical history of New England, from its first planting (1620–1698).* London, 1702; 2 vols., Hartford, Conn., 1820.

Mémoires des commissaires du roi et de ceux de Sa Majesté britannique, sur les possessions & les droits respectifs des deux couronnes en Amérique; avec les actes publics & pièces justificatives. 1ʳᵉ édition. 4 vols. Paris, 1755, 1757. 2ᵉ édition. 6 vols. Paris, 1756–57. Vols. I–III (1ʳᵉ éd.) were published in 1755 and vol. IV in 1757. The latter volume is probably in answer to the English *Memorials . . .* (1755), *infra.* Vol. I contains *Mémoires sur l'Acadie et sur l'isle de Sainte-Lucie;* Vol. II, *Pièces justificatives . . . sur les limites de l'Acadie;* Vol. IV, *Les derniers mémoires sur l'Acadie.*

Memorials of the English and French commissaries concerning the limits of Nova Scotia or Acadia. 2 vols. London, 1755. Vol. I relates to Nova Scotia; Vol. II, to St Lucia. *See also: Mémoires, supra.*

Michigan Pioneer Collections. 40 vols. 1874–1929. To avoid confusion the Michigan Historical Commission, Department of State, Lansing, has standardized the citation for these volumes, which were originally published by various historical agencies and under various titles.

The following volumes were particularly useful for Volume II:
XXXIII, XXXIV: Containing "Cadillac papers." 1903, 1905.

Mississippi Provincial Archives, 1701–1740, French dominion. Edited by Dunbar Rowland and A. G. Sanders. 2 vols. Jackson, Miss., 1927–29. I: *1729–40: French-English-Indian relations; wars with the Natchez and Chickasaw Indians.* II: 1701–29.

MORIN, MARIE. *Annales de l'Hôtel-Dieu de Montréal.* Éditées par A. Fauteux, É.-Z. Massicotte et C. Bertrand. (Société historique de Montréal, Mémoires, XII.) Montréal, 1921. This is an incomplete and inexact published version of the manuscript in AHDM, *Histoire simple et véritable . . .* [*q.v.*].

NAVY RECORDS SOCIETY, London. Founded in 1893 "for the purpose of rendering accessible the sources of [Britain's] naval history." PUBLICATIONS
XCIV: *The Walker expedition* (Graham).

Nova Scotia Archives. I. Selections from the public documents of the province of Nova Scotia. Edited by T. B. Akins. Halifax, 1869.
——— *II. A calendar of two letter-books and one commission-book in the possession of the government of Nova Scotia, 1713–1741.* Edited by A. M. MacMechan. Halifax, 1900.
——— *III. Original minutes of His Majesty's council at Annapolis Royal, 1720–1739.* Edited by A. M. MacMechan. Halifax, 1908.

NOVA SCOTIA HISTORICAL SOCIETY PUBLICATIONS. *Collections.* 36 vols. published to date. 1878– .
Ordonnances, commissions, etc., etc., des gouver-
neurs et intendants de la Nouvelle-France, 1639–1706. Éditées par P.-G. Roy. 2 vols. Beauceville, 1924.

Papier terrier de la Compagnie des Indes occidentales, 1667–1668. Édité par P.-G. Roy. Beauceville, 1931.

PENHALLOW, SAMUEL. *The history of the wars of New-England with the eastern Indians. . . .* Boston, 1726. Reprinted in 1824 in New Hampshire Hist. Soc. *Coll.,* I, and in 1859, with a memoir and notes, in Cincinnati, Ohio.
[———] *Penhallow's Indian wars.* Edited by Edward Wheelock. Boston, 1924.

Pièces et documents relatifs à la tenure seigneuriale, demandés par une adresse de l'assemblée législative, 1851. 2 vols. Québec, 1852.

PRINCE SOCIETY PUBLICATIONS, Boston, 1865–1920.
XVI: Radisson, *Voyages* (Scull).

"Procès-verbaux du procureur général Collet sur le district des paroisses de la Nouvelle-France," annotés par M. l'abbé Ivanhoë Caron, APQ *Rapport,* 1921–22, 262–380.

Province and court records of Maine. Edited by C. T. Libby *et al.* 5 vols. in progress. (Maine Historical Society publications.) Portland, 1928– .

PROVOST, HONORIUS. "Inventaire des documents concernant l'histoire du Canada conservés aux archives de Chicago," *RHAF,* IV (1950–51), 294–302, 453–58, 591–600.
——— *Le Séminaire de Québec: documents et biographies.* (Archives du Séminaire de Québec publications, II.) Québec, 1964.

PUBLIC ARCHIVES OF CANADA PUBLICATIONS
BOARD OF HISTORICAL PUBLICATIONS
Documents relating to Canadian currency during the French period (Shortt).
Documents relating to currency in Nova Scotia, 1675–1758 (Shortt).
NUMBERED PUBLICATIONS
I: *Index to reports of Canadian archives from 1872 to 1908.* 1909.
VI: J.-E. ROY. *Rapport sur les archives de France relatives à l'histoire du Canada.* 1911.
VIII: H. R. HOLMDEN. *Catalogue des cartes, plans et cartes marines conservés au dépôt des cartes des archives canadiennes.* 1912.
X: D. W. PARKER. *A guide to the documents in the Manuscript Room at the Public Archives of Canada, Vol. I.* 1914.
XIII: MAGDALEN CASEY. *Catalogue of pamphlets in the PAC 1493–1931 with Index.* 2 vols. 1931–32.
OTHER PUBLICATIONS
Inventories of holdings from French and English archives in Manuscript Division. *See* PAC, section I.

The *Kelsey papers* (Doughty and Martin) [published in conjunction with the Public Record Office of Northern Ireland].

Annual *Reports.* 1881–1952 (irregular thereafter).

Union list of manuscripts in Canadian repositories. Edited by R. S. Gordon *et al.* 1968.

PUBLIC RECORD OFFICE PUBLICATIONS. The following calendars contain information on events in or affecting Canada up to the mid-18th century, and were used in the preparation of Vol. II:

Acts of the Privy Council of England. Colonial series [1613–1783]. Edited by W. L. Grant and James Munro. 6 vols. 1908–12.
I: *1613–1680.* 1908.
II: *1680–1720.* 1910.
III: *1720–1745.* 1910.
VI: *"The unbound papers,"* 1676–1783. 1912.

B.T. Journal. See: Journal . . . , infra

Calendar of state papers, colonial series. [1574–1737]. Edited by W. N. Sainsbury *et al.* 43 vols., in progress. 1860– .
V: *America and West Indies, 1661–1668.* 1880.
VII: *America and West Indies, 1669–1674.* 1889.
IX: *America and West Indies, 1675–1676, with addenda 1574–1674.* 1893.
X: *America and West Indies, 1677–1680* 1896.
XI: *America and West Indies, 1681–1685.* 1898.
XII: *America and West Indies, 1685–1688.* 1899.
XIII: *America and West Indies, 1689–1692.* 1901.
XIV: *America and West Indies, January 1693–14 May 1696.* 1903.
XV: *America and West Indies, 14 May 1696–31 Oct. 1697.* 1904.
XVI: *America and West Indies, 27 Oct. 1697–31 Dec. 1698.* 1905.
XVII: *America and West Indies, 1699.* Also *Addenda, 1621–1698.* 1908.
XVIII: *America and West Indies, 1700.* 1910.
XIX: *America and West Indies, 1701.* 1911.
XX: *America and West Indies, January–1 Dec. 1702.* 1912.
XXI: *America and West Indies, 1 Dec. 1702–1703.* 1914.
XXII: *America and West Indies, 1704–1705.* 1916.
XXIII: *America and West Indies, 1706–June 1708.* 1916.
XXIV: *America and West Indies, June 1708–1709.* 1922.

XXV: *America and West Indies, 1710–June 1711.* 1924.
XXVI: *America and West Indies, July 1711–June 1712.* 1925.
XXVII: *America and West Indies, July 1712–July 1714.* 1926.
XXVIII: *America and West Indies, August 1714–December 1715.* 1928.
XXIX: *America and West Indies, January 1716–July 1717.* 1930.
XXX: *America and West Indies, August 1717–December 1718.* 1930.
XXXI: *America and West Indies, January 1719–February 1720.* 1933.
XXXII: *America and West Indies, March 1720–December 1721.* 1933.
XXXIII: *America and West Indies, 1722–1723.* 1934.
XXXIV: *America and West Indies, 1724–1725.* 1936.
XXXV: *America and West Indies, 1726–1727.* 1936.
XXXVI: *America and West Indies, 1728–1729.* 1937.
XXXVII: *America and West Indies, 1730.* 1937.
XXXIX: *America and West Indies, 1732.* 1939.
XL: *America and West Indies, 1733.* 1939.
XLI: *America and West Indies, 1734–1735.* 1953.
XLII: *America and West Indies, 1735–1736.* 1953.
XLIII: *America and West Indies, 1737.* 1963.

Calendar of state papers, domestic series, of the reign of William and Mary. [1689–1702.] Edited by W. J. Hardy (vols. 1–8) and Edward Bateson (vols. 9–11). 11 vols. 1869–1937.
XI: *1 April 1700–8 March 1702.* 1937.

Calendar of state papers, domestic series, of the reign of Anne. [1702–4.] Edited by R. P. Mahaffy. 2 vols. 1916–25.
I: *1702–1703.* 1916.

Calendar of Treasury papers. [1556–1728.] Edited by Joseph Reddington. 6 vols. 1868–89.
III: *1702–1707.* 1874.
IV: *1708–1714.* 1879.
V: *1714–1719.* 1883.
VI: *1720–1728.* 1889.

Calendar of Treasury Books and Papers. [1729–45.] Edited by W. A. Shaw. 5 vols. 1898–1903.
II: *1731–1734.* 1898.
III: *1735–1738.* 1900.

Calendar of Treasury Books. [1660–1718]. Edited by W. A. Shaw. 32 vols., in progress. 1904– .

XIX: *January 1704–March 1705*. 1938.
XX: *April 1705–September 1706*. Parts I–III. 1952.
XXI: *October 1706–December 1707*. Parts I–II. 1952.
XXII: *1708*. Parts I–II. 1953, 1950.
XXIV: *1710*. Parts I–II. 1952, 1950.
XXVI: *January–December 1712*. Parts I–II. 1954.

Journal of the commissioners for Trade and Plantations. [1704–1782.] 14 vols. 1920–38.
I: *April 1704 to February 1708/9*. 1920.
II: *February 1708/9 to March 1714/15*. 1925.
III: *March 1714/15 to October 1718*. 1924.
IV: *November 1718 to December 1722*. 1925.
V: *January 1722/23 to December 1728*. 1928.
VI: *January 1728/29 to December 1734*. 1928.
VII: *January 1734/35 to December 1741*. 1930.

[RAḋISSON, PIERRE-ESPRIT.] *Voyages of Peter Esprit Radisson, being an account of his travels and experiences among the North American Indians, from 1652 to 1684, transcribed from original manuscripts in the Bodleian Library and the British Museum*. Edited by G. D. Scull. (Prince Society publications, XVI.) Boston, 1885; New York, 1943.

RECENSEMENTS

ACADIE

1686: "Un recensement de l'Acadie en 1686: recensement fait par M. de Meulles . . . de tous les peuples de Beaubassin, Rivière St-Jean, Port-Royal, Isle Percée, et autres côtes de l'Acadie, . . ." *BRH*, XXXVIII (1932), 677–96, 721–34. Sulte, *Hist. des Can. fr.*, VI, 6–9.

CANADA

1666: "Estat general des habitans du Canada en 1666," APQ *Rapport, 1935–36*, 3–154.
Sulte, *Hist. des Can. fr.*, IV, 51–63.
"Le premier recensement nominal de Québec," éd. P.-G. R[oy], *BRH*, XXXVII (1931), 321–31, 385–404.
1667: Sulte, *Hist. des Can. fr.*, IV, 64–78.
1681: Sulte, *Hist. des Can. fr.*, V, 53–92.
1716: *Recensement de la ville de Québec en 1716*. Édité par L. Beaudet. Québec, 1887.
1744: "Le recensement de Québec en 1744," APQ *Rapport, 1939–40*, 1–154.

TERRE-NEUVE ET PLAISANCE

1671, 1673, 1698: SGCF *Mémoires*, X (1959), 179–88.
1698, 1701, 1706, 1710, 1711: SGCF *Mémoires*, XI (1960), 69–85.
1687, 1691, 1693, 1694, 1704: SGCF *Mémoires*, XIII (1962), 204–8, 244–55.
See also Canada, Bureau of Statistics, Demo-graphy Branch. *Chronological list of Canadian censuses*. Ottawa, 1942.
[Since the printed versions of the censuses are not always accurate copies, it is preferable to consult the originals. *See*: Archives Nationales, Section Outre-Mer, série G, in section I.]

Relations des affaires du Canada en 1696. Avec des lettres des pères de la Compagnie de Jésus depuis 1696 jusqu'en 1702. Cramoisy series, no. 20. New York, 1865.

Relation par lettres de l'Amérique septentrionale, années 1709 et 1710. Édité par Camille de Rochemonteix. Paris, 1904.

RIGAUD DE VAUDREUIL, PHILIPPE DE. *See* "Correspondance. . . ."

ROY, ANTOINE. *Inv. greffes not. See* ROY, P.-G. ET ANTOINE.

ROY, P.-G. "Ce que le gouverneur de Callières pensait de nos officiers militaires en 1701," *BRH*, XXVI (1920), 321–33.

—— *Inventaire des concessions en fief et seigneurie, fois et hommages et aveux et dénombrements, conservés aux Archives de la Province de Québec*. 6 vols. Beauceville, 1927–29.

—— *Inventaire des contrats de mariage du Régime français conservés aux Archives judiciaires de Québec*. 6 vols. Québec, 1937–38.

—— *Inventaire des insinuations du Conseil souverain de la Nouvelle-France*. Beauceville, 1921.

—— *Inventaire des insinuations de la prévôté de Québec*. 3 vols. Beauceville, 1936–39.

—— *Inventaire des jugements et délibérations du Conseil supérieur de la Nouvelle-France de 1717 à 1760*. 7 vols. Beauceville, 1932–35.

—— *Inventaire des ordonnances des intendants de la Nouvelle-France conservées aux Archives provinciales de Québec*. 4 vols. Beauceville, 1919.

—— *Inventaire de pièces sur la côte de Labrador conservées aux Archives de la Province de Québec*. 2 vols. Québec, 1940–42.

—— *Inventaire des procès-verbaux des grands voyers conservés aux Archives de la Province de Québec*. 6 vols. Beauceville, 1923–32.

—— *Inventaire des testaments, donations et inventaires du Régime français conservés aux Archives judiciaires de Québec*. 3 vols. Québec, 1941.

—— *Inventaire d'une collection de pièces judiciaires, notariales, etc., conservées aux Archives judiciaires de Québec*. 2 vols. Beauceville, 1917.

ROY, P.-G. ET ANTOINE. *Inventaire des greffes des notaires du Régime français*. 21 vols. parus. Québec, 1943–64. The first two volumes edited by P.-G. and Antoine Roy; volumes 3 to 19 by Antoine Roy.

Royal Fort Frontenac. Translated by R. A.

Preston; edited by Léopold Lamontagne. (Champlain Society publications, Ontario series, II.) Toronto, 1958.

RUETTE D'AUTEUIL, F.-M.-F. DE. *See* "Lettres et mémoires. . . ."

SAINT-VALLIER, LA CROIX DE CHEVRIÈRES DE. *See* LA CROIX

1690, Sir William Phips devant Québec: histoire d'un siège. Édité par Ernest Myrand. Québec, 1893.

SOCIÉTÉ HISTORIQUE DE MONTRÉAL. The Society was founded in 1857 to collect, preserve, and publish documents relating to the history of Canada; 12 volumes of Mémoires were published between 1859 and 1921. The following have been used in this volume:

IV: [Dollier de Casson,] *Histoire du Montréal.*
XII: Morin, *Annales* (Fauteux *et al.*).

SURREY, N. M. M. *Calendar of manuscripts in Paris archives and libraries relating to the history of the Mississippi Valley to 1803.* 2 vols. Washington, 1926–28.
I: *1581–1739.*

TAILLEMITE, ÉTIENNE. *Inventaire analytique de la correspondance générale avec les colonies, départ, série B (déposée aux Archives nationales), I, registres I à 37 (1654–1715).* Paris, 1959.

[TROYES, PIERRE DE.] *Journal de l'expédition du Chevalier de Troyes à la Baie d'Hudson, en 1686.* Édité par Ivanhoë Caron. Beauceville, 1918.

TRUDEL, MARCEL. *Atlas historique du Canada français: des origines à 1867.* Québec, 1961.

—— *Atlas de la Nouvelle-France/An atlas of New France.* Québec, 1968. Described by the author as a "complete revision of [the] *Atlas historique du Canada français.* . . ."

[VACHON] DE BELMONT, [FRANÇOIS]. *Histoire du Canada . . .* in *Collection de mémoires et de relations sur l'histoire ancienne du Canada, d'après des manuscrits récemment obtenus des archives et bureaux publics en France, no 4.* (Literary and Historical Society of Quebec, Historical Documents, D.2, 1st series.) Québec, 1840. Reprinted with the title *Recueil de ce qui s'est passé au Canada au sujet de la guerre tant des Anglais que des Iroquois,* in 1871 (Historical Documents, D.6, 3d series) and in 1886 (*Transactions,* XVIII, 21–56).

The Walker expedition to Quebec, 1711. Edited with an introduction by G. S. Graham. (Champlain Society publications, XXXII; Navy Records Society publications, XCIV.) Toronto, London, 1953.

WEBSTER, J. C. *Acadia at the end of the seventeenth century: letters, journals and memoires of Joseph Robineau de Villebon, commandant in Acadia, 1690–1700, and other contemporary documents.* (New Brunswick Museum, Monographic series, I.) Saint John, 1934.

WISCONSIN STATE HISTORICAL SOCIETY PUBLICATIONS, Madison, Wisconsin.
Collections. 31 vols. 1855–1931.
XVI: *The French régime in Wisconsin, 1634–1727.* Edited by R. G. Thwaites. 1902.
XVII: *The French régime in Wisconsin, 1727–1748.* Edited by R. G. Thwaites. 1906.
XVIII: *The French régime in Wisconsin, 1743–1760; the British régime in Wisconsin, 1760–1800.* Edited by R. G. Thwaites. 1908.

WRAXALL, PETER. *An abridgement of the Indian affairs contained in four folio volumes, transacted in the colony of New York, from the year 1678 to the year 1751.* Edited with an introduction by C. H. McIlwain. (Harvard Historical Studies, XXI.) Cambridge, Mass., 1915.

III. REFERENCE WORKS

ALLAIRE, J.-B.-A. *Dictionnaire biographique du clergé canadien-français.* 6 vols. Montréal, 1910–34.

A bibliography of Canadiana: being items in the Public Library of Toronto, Canada, relating to the early history and development of Canada. Edited by F. M. Stanton and Marie Tremaine. Toronto, 1934.

A bibliography of Canadiana: a first supplement. . . . Edited by G. M. Boyle, assisted by Marjorie Colbeck. Toronto, 1959.

BONNAULT, CLAUDE DE. "Le Canada militaire, état provisoire des officiers de milice de 1641 à 1760," *APQ Rapport, 1949–51,* 261–527.

CARON, IVANHOË. "Liste des prêtres séculiers et religieux qui ont exercé le saint ministère en Nouvelle-France [1604–99]," *BRH,* XLVII (1941), 76–78, 160–75, 192–201, 225–35, 257–68, 289–99. [Title varies.]

CHARLAND, P.-V. "Notre-Dame de Québec: le nécrologe de la crypte ou les inhumations dans cette église depuis 1652," *BRH,* XX (1914), 137–51, 168–81, 205–17, 237–51, 269–80, 301–13, 333–47.

CHARNOCK, JOHN. *Biographia navalis: or, impartial memoirs of the lives and characters of officers of the navy of Great Britain, from the year 1660 to the present time; drawn from the most* authentic sources, and disposed in a chrono-logical arrangement. 6 vols. London, 1794–98.

"Le clergé de la Nouvelle-France," *BRH*, LIV (1948), 82–91, 216–23, 230–37.

CURTIS, E. S. *The North American Indian, being a series of volumes picturing and describing the Indians of the United States and Alaska.* Edited by F. W. Hodge. 20 vols. Seattle, Wash., 1907–30. [Vols. 6–20 printed in Norwood, Mass.]
XVIII: *The Chipewyan* (1928).

DALTON, CHARLES. *English army lists and commission registers, 1661–1714.* 6 vols. London, 1892–1904.

Dictionary of American biography [to 1928]. Edited by Allen Johnson and Dumas Malone. 20 vols., Index. New York, 1928–37. 2 Supplements [to 31 Dec. 1940], New York, 1944, 1958. New edition, comprising 22 vols. in 11, New York, 1959. *Concise DAB*, New York, 1964. In progress.

Dictionary of national biography [to 1900]. Edited by Leslie Stephen and Sidney Lee. 63 vols.; Supplement, 3 vols.; Index and epitome. London, 1885–1903. 5 Supplements for the 20th century. *Concise DNB*, 2 vols., 1952, 1961. In progress.

Dictionnaire de biographie française. Sous la direction de J. Balteau *et al.* 11 vols. and 1 fascicule to date ["A" to "Duprat"]. Paris, 1933– .

DIONNE. N.-E. *Inventaire chronologique des livres, brochures, journaux et revues.* . . . 4 vols. Québec, 1905–9.

Encyclopedia Canadiana. J. E. Robbins, Editor-in-chief. 10 vols. Ottawa, 1957–58.

FAUTEUX, AEGIDIUS. *Les chevaliers de Saint-Louis en Canada.* Montréal, 1940.

GAGNON, PHILÉAS. "Noms propres au Canada français: transformations de noms propres, établies par les signatures autographes ou par les écrits de contemporains où ils sont mentionnés," *BRH*, XV (1909), 17–30, 49–61, 80–94, 112–24, 143–57, 177–86.

GAREAU, J.-B. "La prévôté de Québec, ses officiers, ses registres," APQ *Rapport, 1943–44,* 51–146.

GAUTHIER, HENRI. *Sulpitiana.* Montréal, 1926.

GODBOUT, ARCHANGE. "Nos ancêtres au XVIIᵉ siècle," APQ *Rapport, 1951–53,* 449–544; *1953–55,* 445–536; *1955–57,* 379–489; *1957–59,* 383–440; *1959–60,* 227–354; AQ *Rapport, 1965,* 147–81. "A" to "Brassard" included.

——— *Origine des familles canadiennes-françaises, extrait de l'état civil francais: 1ʳᵉ série.* Lille, 1925.

GREAT BRITAIN, ADMIRALTY. *List of commissioned sea officers of the Royal Navy, 1660–1815.* Edited by D. B. Smith and R. N. College. 3 vols. [privately printed, 1954?].

HAMELIN, JEAN ET ANDRÉ BEAULIEU. *Guide de l'étudiant en histoire du Canada.* Sainte-Foy, 1964. Mimeographed.

Handbook of American Indians north of Mexico. Edited by F. W. Hodge. (Smithsonian Institute, Bureau of American Ethnology, Bulletin 30.) 2 vols. Washington, D.C., 1907, 1910; reprinted New York, 1965. The Canadian material in this work has been revised and republished as an Appendix to the tenth report of the Geographic Board of Canada, under the title *Handbook of Indians of Canada* (Ottawa, 1913).

JENNESS, DIAMOND. *The Indians of Canada.* (National Museum of Canada, Bulletin 65, Anthropological series, XV.) Ottawa, 1932; 5th edition, 1960.

LANCTOT, GUSTAVE. *L'œuvre de la France en Amérique du Nord: bibliographie sélective et critique.* Montréal, 1951.

LECESTRE, LÉON. *Liste alphabétique des officers généraux jusqu'en 1762 dont les notices biographiques se trouvent dans la Chronologie militaire de Pinard.* . . . Paris, 1903.

LE JEUNE, L.-M. *Dictionnaire général de biographie, histoire, littérature, agriculture, commerce, industrie et des arts, sciences, mœurs, coutumes, institutions politiques et religieuses du Canada.* 2 vols. Ottawa, 1931.

Liste des missionaires jésuites: Nouvelle-France et Louisiane, 1611–1800. Montréal, 1929.

MARION, MARCEL. *Dictionnaire des institutions de la France aux XVIIᵉ et XVIIIᵉ siècles.* Paris, 1923; réimprimé 1968.

MASSICOTTE, É.-Z. "Les chirurgiens de Montréal au XVIIᵉ siècle," *BRH*, XX (1914), 252–56; XXVII (1921), 41–47.

——— "Les chirurgiens, médecins, etc., de Montréal sous le régime français," APQ *Rapport, 1922–23,* 131–55.

——— "Les colons de Montréal de 1642 à 1667," *RSCT*, 3d ser., VII (1913), sect.I, 3–65 and *BRH*, XXXIII (1927), 170–92, 224–39, 379–84, 433–48, 467–82, 538–48, 613–25, 650–52.

——— "Répertoire des engagements pour l'Ouest conservés dans les Archives Judiciaires de Montréal," APQ *Rapport, 1929–30,* 191–466.

——— "Les tribunaux et les officers de justice à Montréal, sous le régime français, 1648–1760," *RSCT*, 3d ser., X (1916), sect.I, 272–303 and *BRH*, XXXVII (1931), 122–28, 179–92, 252–56, 302–13.

NATIONAL MUSEUM OF CANADA PUBLICATIONS
Bulletin 65 (Anthropological series XV): Jenness, *The Indians of Canada.*

NEW ENGLAND HISTORIC GENEALOGICAL SOCIETY PUBLICATIONS

New England Historical and Genealogical Register. Boston, 1847– . Indexes for vols. I–L were published in 1906–7 (persons), 1908 (subjects), and 1911 (places); Index for vols. LI–CXII compiled by M. W. Parsons and published in 1959.

"Les notaires au Canada sous le régime français," APQ *Rapport, 1921–22,* 1–58. Contains biographies of nearly 200 notaries.

PINARD. *Chronologie historique-militaire, contenant l'histoire de la création de toutes les charges, dignités et grades militaires supérieures.* . . . 7 vols. Paris, 1760–64. [*See* LECESTRE, *supra*].

ROY, P.-G. *Les officiers d'état-major des gouvernements de Québec, Montréal et Trois-Rivières sous le Régime français.* Lévis, 1919, and *RC,* XX (1917), 375–84; XXI (1918), 75–79, 210–20, 276–95, 373–79; XXII (1918), 214–21, 290–300, 375–81, 432–46; XXIII (1919), 53–61, 131–38, 210–20, 286–302, 366–78, 442–58; XXIV (1919), 51–55, 130–41, 218–24, 299–301, 360–75, 439–56.

——— "Les secrétaires des gouverneurs et intendants de la Nouvelle-France," *BRH,* XLI (1935), 74–107.

SHIPTON, C. K. *Sibley's Harvard graduates.* (Massachusetts Historical Society publications). 11 vols., in progress. Cambridge and Boston,

1933– . A continuation of Sibley, *infra.* Vols. IV–XIV include graduates of the years 1690 to 1760.

SIBLEY, J. L. *Biographical sketches of graduates of Harvard University, in Cambridge, Massachusetts.* 3 vols. Cambridge, 1873–85. Includes graduates of the years 1642–1689.

TANGHE, RAYMOND. *Bibliography of Canadian bibliographies/Bibliographie des bibliographies canadiennes.* Toronto, 1960. Supplements 1960–61, 1962–63. Published under the auspices of the Bibliographical Society of Canada. Pages 168–81 concern history.

TANGUAY, CYPRIEN. *Dictionnaire généalogique des familles canadiennes depuis la fondation de la colonie jusqu'à nos jours.* 7 vols. [Montréal], 1871–90.

——— *Répertoire général du clergé canadien par ordre chronologique depuis la fondation de la colonie jusqu'à nos jours.* Québec, 1868.

VACHON, ANDRÉ. "Inventaire critique des notaires royaux des gouvernements de Québec, Montréal et Trois-Rivières (1663–1764)," *RHAF,* IX (1955–56), 423–38, 546–61; X (1956–57), 93–103, 257–62, 381–90; XI (1957–58), 93–106, 270–76, 400–6.

WALLACE, W. S. *The Macmillan dictionary of Canadian biography.* 3d edition, revised and enlarged. London, Toronto, and New York, 1963.

IV. STUDIES (BOOKS)

ABBOTT, M. E. *History of Medicine in the province of Quebec.* Toronto, 1931; McGill University publications, series VIII, no. 63, 1932.

AHERN, GEORGES ET M.-J. *Notes pour servir à l'histoire de la médecine dans le Bas-Canada depuis la fondation de Québec jusqu'au commencement du XIXᵉ siècle.* Québec, 1923.

ALVORD, C. W. *The Illinois country, 1673–1818.* (Centennial History of Illinois, I.) Springfield, Ill., 1918; Chicago, 1922; reprinted (The American West, [I]), Chicago, 1965.

ARSENAULT, BONA. *Histoire et généalogie des Acadiens.* 2 vols. Québec, [1965].

BAILEY, A. G. *The conflict of European and eastern Algonkian cultures, 1504–1700: a study in Canadian civilization.* (New Brunswick Museum publications, Monographic series, 2.) Saint John, 1937. New edition, Toronto, 1969.

BERNARD, ANTOINE. *Le Drame acadien depuis 1604.* Montréal, [1936].

BIGGAR, H. P. *The early trading companies of New France.* (University of Toronto Studies in

History, edited by G. M. Wrong.) Toronto, 1901.

BREBNER, J. B. *New England's outpost: Acadia before the conquest of Canada.* New York, 1927.

CAHALL, RAYMOND DU BOIS. *The sovereign council of New France: a study in Canadian constitutional history.* (Studies in History, Economics and Public Law, edited by the Faculty of Political Science of Columbia University, LXV, no. 1.) New York, 1915.

CALNEK, W. A. *History of the county of Annapolis, including old Port Royal and Acadia, with memoirs of its representatives in the provincial Parliament, and biographical and genealogical sketches of its early English settlers and their families.* Edited and completed by A. W. Savary. Toronto, 1897. *Supplement.* . . . by A. W. Savary [*q.v.*].

CAMPBELL, T. J. *Pioneer priests of North America 1640–1710.* 2 vols. New York, 1908, 1910.

CASGRAIN, H.-R. *Histoire de l'Hôtel-Dieu de Québec.* Québec, 1878.

—— Les Sulpiciens et les prêtres des Missions Étrangères en Acadie (1676–1762). Québec, 1897.

[CLOUTIER, PROSPER.] Histoire de la paroisse de Champlain. 2 vols. Trois-Rivières, 1915–17.

COLEMAN, E. L. New England captives carried to Canada between 1677 and 1760 during the French and Indian wars. 2 vols. Portland, Maine, 1925.

CROUSE, N. M. Lemoyne d'Iberville: soldier of New France. Ithaca, N.Y., [1954].

DALTON, CHARLES. George the First's army 1714–1727. 2 vols. London, 1910–12.

DELANGLEZ, JEAN. The French Jesuits in Lower Louisiana. New Orleans, 1935.

DODGE, E. S. Northwest by sea. New York, 1961.

ECCLES, W. J. Canada under Louis XIV, 1663–1701. (Canadian Centenary Series, III.) Toronto, 1964.

—— Frontenac: the courtier governor. Toronto, 1959; reprinted 1962.

[FAILLON, É.-M.] Histoire de la colonie française en Canada. 3 vols. Villemarie [Montréal], 1865–66.

FAUTEUX, J.-N. Essai sur l'industrie au Canada sous le régime français. 2 vols. Québec, 1927.

FRÉGAULT, GUY. Le XVIIIe siècle canadien: études. (Collection Constantes, 16.) Montréal, 1968.

—— Iberville le conquérant. Montréal, [1944]; 1968.

GARNEAU, F.-X. Histoire du Canada, depuis sa découverte jusqu'à nos jours. 1re édition. 4 vols. Québec, 1845–52.

GIRAUD, MARCEL. Histoire de la Louisiane française. 3 vols. to date. Paris, 1953–66.
I: Le règne de Louis XIV (1698–1715). 1953.
II: Années de transition (1715–1717). 1958.
III: L'époque de John Law (1717–1720). 1966.

GOSSELIN, AUGUSTE. L'Église du Canada depuis Monseigneur de Laval jusqu'à la Conquête. 3 vols. Québec, 1911–14.

—— Vie de Mgr de Laval, premier évêque de Québec et apôtre du Canada, 1622–1708. 2 vols. Québec, 1890.

GOWANS, ALAN. Church architecture in New France. Toronto, 1955.

HAMELIN, JEAN. Économie et société en Nouvelle-France. (Cahiers de l'institut d'Histoire, III.) Québec, 1960.

HARPER, J. R. Painting in Canada: a history. Toronto, 1966.

HARRIS, R. C. The seigneurial system in early Canada: a geographical study. Madison, Milwaukee, London, Quebec, 1966.

HARVEY, D. C. The French régime in Prince Edward Island. New Haven, 1926.

Histoire de la Congrégation de Notre-Dame de Montréal. 9 vols. Montreal, 1910–41.

HUNT, G. T. The wars of the Iroquois: a study in intertribal trade relations. Madison, Wis., 1960.

INNIS, H. A. The cod fisheries: the history of an international economy. Revised edition, Toronto, 1954.

—— The fur trade in Canada: an introduction to Canadian economic history. New Haven, 1930; revised edition, Toronto, 1956.

JOUVE, O.-M. Les Franciscains et le Canada: l'établissement de la foi, 1615–1629. Québec, 1915.

—— Les Franciscains et le Canada: aux Trois-Rivières. Paris, 1934.

KELLOGG, L. P. The French régime in Wisconsin and the northwest. Madison, Wis., 1925.

LA MORANDIÈRE, CHARLES DE. Histoire de la pêche française de la morue dans l'Amérique septentrionale (des origines à 1789). 3 vols. Paris, 1962, 1966.

LANCTOT, GUSTAVE. Histoire du Canada. 3 vols. Montréal, 1959–64.
I: Des origines au régime royal. 1959.
II: Du régime royal au traité d'Utrecht, 1663–1713. 1963.
III: Du traité d'Utrecht au traité de Paris, 1713–1763. 1964.

—— A History of Canada. Translated by Josephine Hambleton and M. M. Cameron. 3 vols. Cambridge, Mass. and Toronto, 1963–65.

LANGEVIN, JEAN. Notes sur les archives de Notre-Dame de Beauport. 2 vols. Québec, 1860.

LAUVRIÈRE, ÉMILE. La tragédie d'un peuple: histoire du peuple acadien de ses origines à nos jours. 2 vols. Paris, 1922; nouvelle édition révisée, 1924.

LE BLANT, ROBERT. Un colonial sous Louis XIV: Philippe de Pastour de Costebelle, gouverneur de Terre-Neuve puis de l'île Royale 1661–1717. Paris et Dax, 1935.

LORIN, HENRI. Le comte de Frontenac: étude sur le Canada français à la fin du XVIIe siècle, Paris, 1895.

LOUNSBURY, R. G. The British fishery at Newfoundland 1634–1763. New Haven and London, 1934.

MCLENNAN, J. S. Louisbourg from its foundation to its fall, 1713–58. London, 1918.

MALCHELOSSE, GÉRARD. Le régiment de Carignan. . . . See RÉGIS ROY.

Mélanges historiques. See SULTE.

[MONDOUX, MARIA.] L'Hôtel-Dieu, premier hôpital de Montréal . . . 1642–1763. Montréal, 1942.

Monseigneur de Saint-Vallier et l'Hôpital Général de Québec: histoire du monastère de Notre-Dame des Anges. Québec, 1882.

MORISSET, GÉRARD. L'architecture en Nouvelle-France. Québec, 1949.

—— La peinture traditionnelle au Canada

français. (L'Encyclopédie du Canada français, II.) Ottawa, 1960.

MORTON, A. S. *A history of the Canadian west to 1870–71.* . . . London, [1939].

MURDOCH, BEAMISH. *A history of Nova-Scotia or Acadie.* 3 vols. Halifax, 1865–67.

NISH, CAMERON. *Les bourgeois-gentilshommes de la Nouvelle-France 1729–1748.* Montréal, 1968.

NUTE, G. L. *Caesars of the wilderness: Médard Chouart, Sieur Des Groseilliers and Pierre Esprit Radisson, 1618–1710.* New York, [1943].

O'NEILL, C. E. *Church and state in French colonial Louisiana: policy and politics to 1732.* London and New Haven, 1966.

PARKMAN, FRANCIS. *France and England in North America.* 8 vols. Boston, 1851–92. Many editions of each of the volumes have been published. The following were used in Vol. II:
V: *Count Frontenac and New France under Louis XIV.* 1st edition, Boston, 1877; 24th edition, 1891; new edition, Toronto, 1899.
VI: *A half-century of conflict.* 2 vols. Boston, 1892; 5th edition, 1893; new edition, 1 vol., New York, 1962.
For a summary of the various editions of Parkman's works *see*: *The Parkman reader from the works of Francis Parkman*, selected and edited by S. E. Morison (Boston and Toronto, 1955), Bibliography.

PROWSE, D. W. *A history of Newfoundland, from the English, colonial, and foreign records.* London, 1895; revised edition, 1896.

RAMEAU DE SAINT-PÈRE, [F.-E.] *Une colonie féodale en Amérique: l'Acadie (1604–1881).* 2 vols. Paris et Montréal, 1889.

RICH, E. E. *The history of the Hudson's Bay Company 1670–1870. Volume I: 1670–1763; Volume II: 1763–1870.* (Hudson's Bay Record Society publications, XXI, XXII.) London, 1958–59. Another edition, 3 vols. Toronto, 1960. A copy of this work available in the PAC contains notes and bibliographical material omitted from the printed version.

ROCHEMONTEIX, CAMILLE DE. *Les Jésuites et la Nouvelle-France au XVIIᵉ siècle.* 3 vols. Paris, 1895–96.
—— *Les Jésuites et la Nouvelle-France au XVIIIᵉ siècle.* 2 vols. Paris, 1906.

ROGERS, J. D. *Newfoundland.* (C. P. Lucas, *Historical geography of the British colonies (dominions),* V, Part IV.) Oxford, 1911; 2d edition, 1931.

ROY, J.-E. *Histoire de la seigneurie de Lauzon.* 5 vols. Lévis, 1897–1904.
—— *Histoire du notariat au Canada depuis la fondation de la colonie jusqu'à nos jours.* 4 vols. Lévis, 1899–1902.

ROY, P.-G. *La famille Juchereau Duchesnay.* Lévis, 1903.
—— *Fils de Québec.* 4 vols. Lévis, 1933.
—— *Les petites choses de notre histoire.* 7 vols. Lévis et Québec, 1919–44.
—— *La ville de Québec sous le régime français.* 2 vols. Québec, 1930.

ROY, RÉGIS ET GÉRARD MALCHELOSSE. *Le régiment de Carignan: son organisation et son expédition au Canada (1665–1668): officiers et soldats qui s'établirent en Canada.* Montréal, 1925.

ROYAL COMMONWEALTH SOCIETY PUBLICATIONS. Imperial Studies Series. General editor, G. S. Graham.
XXIV: Williams, *The British search for the northwest passage.*

SALONE, ÉMILE. *La colonisation de la Nouvelle-France: étude sur les origines de la nation canadienne-française.* Paris, 1906.

SAVARY, A. W. *Supplement to the history of the county of Annapolis.* Toronto, 1913 [*see* CALNEK].

SHELDON, E. M. *The early history of Michigan, from the first settlement to 1815.* New York, 1856.

SOCIÉTÉ HISTORIQUE DE QUÉBEC. Founded in 1937, the Society has, to date, published chiefly studies, in the series Cahiers d'histoire. 18 vols. to date. Québec, 1947– . Cited in this volume:
XVIII: ANDRÉ LACHANCE. *Le bourreau au Canada sous le régime français.* 1966.

SULTE, BENJAMIN. *Histoire des Canadiens français, 1608–1880.* 8 vols. Montréal, 1882–84.
—— *Mélanges historiques: études éparses et inédites.* Édités par Gérard Malchelosse. 21 vols. Montréal, 1918–34. Cited in Vol. II:
I (1918): [no title]
VI (1920): *Les forges Saint-Maurice.*
VIII (1922): *Le régiment de Carignan.*
IX (1922): *Le fort de Chambly.*
X (1922): [no title]
XI (1923): [no title]
XIV (1928): [no title]
XVIII (1931): *Trois-Rivières d'autrefois,* 1ʳᵉ série.
XIX (1932): *Trois-Rivières d'autrefois,* 2ᵉ série.
XX (1933): *Trois-Rivières d'autrefois,* 3ᵉ série.

SYLVESTER, H. M. *Indian wars of New England.* 3 vols. Boston, 1910.

Les Ursulines de Québec, depuis leur établissement jusqu'à nos jours. 4 vols. Québec, 1863–66; 2ᵉ édition, 1866–1878.

Les Ursulines des Trois-Rivières depuis leur établissement jusqu'à nos jours. 4 vols. Trois-Rivières, 1888–1911.

VACHON, ANDRÉ. *Histoire du notariat canadien, 1621–1960.* Québec, 1962.

701

WALLER, G. M. *Samuel Vetch, colonial enterpriser.* Chapel Hill, N.C., 1960.

WILLIAMS, GLYNDWR. *The British search for the northwest passage in the eighteenth century.* (Royal Commonwealth Society, Imperial Studies series, XXIV.) London, 1962.

V. JOURNALS AND STUDIES (ARTICLES)

Beaver. Quarterly. Winnipeg. Publication of the HBC. I (outfit 250, 1920)– .

Bulletin des recherches historiques. Lévis, Québec. Monthly journal of archaeology, history, biography, bibliography, numismatology, etc. I (1895)– . *Index:* I (1895)–XXXI (1925). 4 vols. Beauceville, 1925–26. For subsequent years see the manuscript index in AQ. In addition, a nominal index (1926–) is being prepared in the *Dictionary* offices. Founded by P.-G. Roy, the *BRH* became in March 1923 the journal of the AQ (formerly APQ).

Cahiers des Dix. Montréal. I (1936)– . Annual review published by "Les Dix," a group of historians who formed a legal association on 6 Aug. 1935.

Le Canada français. Québec. First series: Journal published under the direction of a committee of professors of l'Université Laval. I (1888)–IV (1891). Concerned with religion, philosophy, history, fine arts, science, and letters. Vols. I–III contain many documents on Acadia, under the title: *Collection de documents inédits sur le Canada et l'Amérique* [*see* sect.II]. Second series: Incorporated *Parler Français* and *La Nouvelle France.* Publication of l'Université Laval; journal of the Société du Parler français au Canada. I (1918–19)–XXXIII (1945–46). Renamed *Revue de l'université Laval* [*q.v.*].

CANADIAN HISTORICAL ASSOCIATION, Ottawa. The aims of the Association are "to encourage historical research and public interest in history; to promote the preservation of historic sites and buildings, documents, relics, and other significant heirlooms of the past; to publish historical studies and documents as circumstances may permit." Publications include: annual reports, 1915– and historical booklets.

The Canadian Historical Review. Quarterly. Toronto. I (1920)– . *General Index,* I (1920)–X 1929); XI (1930)–XX (1939); XXI (1940)–XXX (1949). Each issue includes a current bibliography of publications in English and French. A continuation of the annual *Review of Historical Publications relating to Canada.* Edited by G. M. Wrong, H. H. Langton, and W. S. Wallace. I (for 1896)–XXII (for 1917 and 1918). Indexes I–X, XI–XX.

CANADIAN CATHOLIC HISTORICAL ASSOCIATION/SOCIÉTÉ CANADIENNE D'HISTOIRE DE L'ÉGLISE CATHOLIQUE. *Report/Rapport.* Ottawa. The bilingual society, founded 3 June 1933, annually publishes French and English volumes with entirely different contents. I (1933–34)– . Separate index for 1933–59.

Ganong, W. F. "A monograph of historic sites in the province of New Brunswick," *RSCT,* 2d ser., V (1899), sect.II, 213–357.

Mid-America: an historical quarterly. Chicago, Ill. Originally entitled the *Illinois Catholic Historical Review,* the first volume of this journal was published in 1919. With volume XII (1929–30), the title was changed to *Mid-America* and a new series of volume numbers began. Both series numbers are still used when referring to this journal. From 1938 on, *Mid-America* has been published by the Institute of Jesuit history of Loyola University.

New England Quarterly: a historical review of New England life and letters. Baltimore; Portland, Me., 1928– .

La Nouvelle France. See Le Canada Français

Nova Francia. Paris. I (1925–26)–VII (1932). Organ of the Société d'histoire du Canada, founded in France in 1924. Reproduces many documents.

Revue canadienne. Monthly. Montréal. First series, I (1864)–XVI (1879). Second series, XVII (1881)–L–LI (1906), with numbering peculiar to the series, and intermittent. Third series, I–II (1908)–XXVII (1922). Indexes.

Revue d'histoire de l'Amérique française. Quarterly. Montréal. I (1947–48)– . Publication of the Institut d'histoire de l'Amérique française. Founded and directed by Canon Lionel Groulx (d. May 1967). Second director, Rosario Bilodeau.

Revue de l'université Laval. Quarterly. Québec. I (1946–47)– . Publication of the University and organ of the Société du Parler français au Canada. Continuation of the review *Le Canada Français.*

ROYAL SOCIETY OF CANADA/SOCIÉTÉ ROYALE DU CANADA. Under the patronage of the Marquess of Lorne, the society was formed in 1882 for the encouragement of literature and science in

Canada. Originally the society was composed of five sections—two for literature and three for sciences. The annual *Mémoires* of Section I and the *Transactions* of Section II include historical articles. First series: I (1882–83)–XII (1894). Second series: I (1895)–X (1904). Third series: I (1907)–LVI (1962). Fourth series: I (1963)– Indexes.

SOCIÉTÉ CANADIENNE DE L'HISTOIRE DE L'ÉGLISE CATHOLIQUE. *See* CANADIAN CATHOLIC HISTORICAL ASSOCIATION

LA SOCIÉTÉ GÉNÉALOGIQUE CANADIENNE-FRANÇAISE, *Mémoires.* Organ of the society, which was founded on the initiative of P. Archange Godbout, 3 Sept. 1943. I (1944–45)– .

SOCIÉTÉ HISTORIQUE DE SAINT-BONIFACE. Saint-Boniface, Man. *Bulletin*, 5 vols. 1911–15.

TÊTU, HENRI. "Le chapitre de la cathédrale de Québec et ses délégués en France. Lettres des chanoines Pierre Hazeur de l'Orme et Jean-Marie de la Corne (1723–1773)," *BRH*, XIII (1907), 225–43, 256–83, 299–308, 321–38, 353–61; XIV (1908), 3–22, 31–40, 65–79, 97–109, 129–46, 161–75, 193–208, 225–39, 257–70, 289–98, 321–37, 353–64; XV (1909), 1–16, 33–48, 65–79, 97–111, 129–42, 161–76, 193–211, 225–41, 257–74, 289–301, 321–28, 353–60; XVI (1910), 1–10, 33–44, 65–75, 97–109, 129–41, 161–75, 193–206, 225–40, 257–74, 289–302, 321–30, 353–64.

ZOLTVANY, Y. F. "New France and the west, 1701–1713," *CHR*, XLVI (1965), 301–22.

Contributors

ANGERS, LORENZO, PTRE. Ancien professeur de lettres et d'histoire, Séminaire de Chicoutimi, Québec.
François de Crespieul.

ASSELIN, JEAN-PIERRE, C.SS.R. Archiviste provincial des Rédemptoristes, Sainte-Anne de Beaupré, Québec.
Louis Prat.

AUGER, ROLAND-J. Directeur suppléant, Archives du Québec, Québec.
Jean-Baptiste Céloron de Blainville. Pierre Haimard. Alexandre-Joseph Lestringant de Saint-Martin. François-Marie Margane de Batilly. Samuel Papineau. Jean Paradis. Jean-Baptiste de Peiras. Jean-Baptiste de Silly. Étienne Véron de Grandmesnil.

BAILLARGEON, NOËL, PTRE. Professeur d'histoire, Séminaire de Québec, Québec.
Goulven Calvarin. Albert Davion. Nicolas Foucault. Dominique-Antoine-René Thaumur de La Source. Claude Trouvé. Pierre et Claude Volant de Saint-Claude.

BAUDRY, RENÉ. Représentant des Archives publiques du Canada en France, Paris, France.
Daniel d'Auger de Subercase. Claude Barrat. Robert Chevalier, dit Beauchêne. Louis-Alexandre Des Friches de Meneval. Durand de La Garenne. Jacques-Alexis Fleury Deschambault. Jean-Chrysostome Loppinot. Claude Moireau. Jacques-François de Mombeton de Brouillan.

BAZIN, JULES. Conservateur des Bibliothèques de la ville de Montréal, Québec.
Jean Berger. Urbain Brossard. Charles Chaboulié. Pierre Couturier, dit Le Bourguignon. René Fézeret. Pierre Le Ber.

BÉCHARD, HENRI, S.J. Vice-postulateur de la cause de béatification et de canonisation de la vénérable Kateri Tekakouitha, Montréal, Québec.
Pierre Cholenec.

BÉLANGER, NOËL, PTRE. Professeur d'histoire, Collège de Rimouski, Québec.
Charles-Henri d'Aloigny de La Groye. Charles-Joseph Amiot de Vincelotte. Charles de Glandelet.

BELLAVANCE, MARCEL. Chargé de cours d'histoire, Royal Military College of Canada, Kingston, Ontario.
Nicolas Blaise Des Bergères de Rigauville. Raymond Blaise Des Bergères de Rigauville.

BERNIER, HÉLÈNE. Professeur de littérature, Collège Sainte-Marie, Montréal, Québec.
Charlotte Gallard. Marie-Madeleine Maufils, dite de Saint-Louis. Françoise Maumousseau. Marie Morin. Mary Sayward. Mary Silver.

BIRON, HERVÉ. Éditeur adjoint, *Le Journal des Débats,* Assemblée législative du Québec, Québec.
*Pierre Baudeau. Antoine Chaudillon. Guillaume Gail-*lard. *René Godefroy de Tonnancour. Joseph Godefroy de Vieuxpont. Jean Lechasseur. Jean-Claude Louet. Charles Macard. François Mariauchau d'Esgly. François-Marie Mariauchau d'Esgly. Charles-Paul de Marin de La Malgue. Jean-Baptiste Poulin de Courval. Edmond de Suève.*

BLAIN, JEAN. Professeur agrégé d'histoire, Université de Montréal, Québec.
Nicolas d'Ailleboust de Manthet. Jean-Baptiste d'Ailleboust Des Muceaux. François-Marie Bouat.

BOISSONNAULT, CHARLES-MARIE. Écrivain, Montréal, Québec.
Michel Bertier. Antoine Forestier. Jean Martinet de Fonblanche.

BOND, COURTNEY C. J. Head, Canadian Section, Map Division, Public Archives of Canada, Ottawa, Ontario.
Pierre Hertel de Moncours. Charles Petit de Levilliers. Pierre de Saint-Ours. Étienne Volant de Radisson.

BORINS, EDWARD H. Graduate student in history, McGill University, Montreal, Quebec.
Claude de Bermen de La Martinière. Jean Gobin.

BROWNE, G. PETER. Associate professor of history, Carleton University, Ottawa, Ontario.
Joannis de Hiriberry. Thomas Smart.

BRYDEN, JOHN H. Manuscript editor, *Dictionary of Canadian Biography/Dictionnaire biographique du Canada,* University of Toronto Press, Toronto, Ontario.
Raymond Martel.

BURKE-GAFFNEY, M. W., S.J. Professor emeritus, formerly professor of astronomy and lecturer in history of science, St Mary's University, Halifax, Nova Scotia.
Jean-Baptiste-Louis Franquelin.

CAMPEAU, LUCIEN, S.J. Professeur d'histoire, Université de Montréal, Québec.
François Aubert de La Chesnaye. Jean-Pierre Aulneau de La Touche. Thierry Beschefer. Martin Bouvart. Nicolas Dupont de Neuville. Denis-Joseph Juchereau de La Ferté. Ignace Juchereau Duchesnay. Pierre Millet. François-Louis de Pourroy de Lauberivière. Pierre Raffeix. François Vaillant de Gueslis.

CARRIER, MAURICE. Professeur d'histoire, École Normale M.-L. Duplessis, Trois-Rivières, Québec.
Guillaume Baudry, dit Des Butes. Michel Dessailliant, dit Richeterre. Jean Jacquiés, dit Leblond. Jean Le Rouge.

CERBELAUD SALAGNAC, GEORGES. Homme de lettres, Paris, France.
Bernard-Anselme d'Abbadie de Saint-Castin. Jean-Vincent d'Abbadie de Saint-Castin. Philippe Pastour de Costebelle.

CHABOT, MARIE-EMMANUEL, O.S.U. Directrice des

études, Monastère des Ursulines, Québec, Québec.

Anne Bourdon, dite de Sainte-Agnès. Marie-Jeanne-Madeleine Legardeur de Repentigny, dite de Sainte-Agathe.

CHAMPAGNE, ANTOINE, C.R.I.C. Professeur en retraite, Hôpital Taché, Saint-Boniface, Manitoba.

Christophe Dufrost de La Jemerais. Jean-Baptiste Gaultier de La Vérendrye.

CHAPUT, DONALD. Editor, Michigan Historical Commission, Lansing, Michigan, U.S.A.

Pierre d'Ailleboust d'Argenteuil. Kinongé. Koutaoiliboe. Jean-Paul Legardeur de Saint-Pierre. Le Pesant. Jean Mermet. Jacques-Charles Renaud Dubuisson.

CHARD, DONALD F. Lecturer in history, University of Victoria, British Columbia.

Edmund Goffe. John Nelson.

CHARD, ELIZABETH A. Assistant professor of history, St Mary's University, Halifax, Nova Scotia.

René-Charles de Breslay.

CHARLAND, THOMAS-M., O.P. Bibliothécaire et archiviste, Couvent des Dominicains, Montréal, Québec.

Jacques Bigot. Vincent Bigot. Nescambiouit. Sébastien Rale.

CHASSÉ, BÉATRICE. Archiviste, Archives du Québec, Québec.

Augustin Rouer de Villeray et de La Cardonnière.

COMEAU, J.-ROGER. Chef, Section des archives antérieures à la Confédération, Division des manuscrits, Archives publiques du Canada, Ottawa, Ontario.

Alexandre Leneuf de La Vallière de Beaubassin. Michel Leneuf de La Vallière de Beaubassin (père). Michel Leneuf de La Vallière de Beaubassin (fils).

CORKRAN, DAVID H. 2349 N. Cleveland Avenue, Chicago, Illinois, U.S.A.

Ohonsiowanne. Pemoussa. Tekanoet.

CORLEY, NORA T. Librarian, Arctic Institute of North America, Montreal, Quebec.

Augustin Le Gardeur de Courtemanche.

CORMIER, CLÉMENT, C.S.C. Ancien recteur, Université de Moncton, Nouveau-Brunswick.

Jacques Bourgeois. Jean-François Brossard. Pierre Tibaudeau.

DANSEREAU, ANTONIO, P.S.S. Archiviste, Collège de Montréal, Québec.

Michel Barthélemy. Léonard Chaigneau. François Chèze.

DAVIES, K. G. Professor of history, University of Bristol, England.

Henry Kelsey.

DAY, GORDON M. Ethnohistorian, National Museum of Man, Ottawa, Ontario.

Atecouando. Glossary of Indian Tribal Names.

DECHÊNE, LOUISE. Professeur d'histoire, Université d'Ottawa, Ontario.

Pierre Carrerot. François Dauphin de La Forest. Marc-Antoine de Laforest. Charles-Léopold-Ebérhard de L'Espérance. Jacques Testard de Montigny. Étienne de Véniard de Bourgmond.

DE LA MORANDIÈRE, CHARLES. 9, rue du Midi, Granville (Manche), France.

Sébastien Le Goüès de Sourdeval.

D'ENTREMONT, CLARENCE J. Aumônier, Our Lady's Haven, Fairhaven, Massachusetts, U.S.A.

Mathieu Martin. Claude Petitpas. Agathe de Saint-Étienne de La Tour.

DESJARDINS, GÉRARD. Directeur de l'école Beauséjour, Moncton, Nouveau-Brunswick.

Louis Petit.

DODGE, ERNEST S. Director, Peabody Museum, Salem, Massachusetts, U.S.A.

George Berley. James Knight. David Vaughan.

DONNELLY, JOSEPH P., S.J. Professor of history, Marquette University, Milwaukee, Wisconsin, U.S.A.

Louis André. Louis d'Avaugour. Étienne de Carheil. Jean Enjalran.

DOUVILLE, RAYMOND. Sous-ministre, Secrétariat provincial, Québec.

Pierre Boucher. Guillaume Couture. Antoine de Crisafy. Pierre Dandonneau, dit Lajeunesse. Michel-Ignace Dizy, dit Monplaisir. Jacques Dugay. Joseph-François Hertel de La Fresnière. Jean-Baptiste Hertel de Rouville. Jacques Largillier. Guillaume de Larue. François Lorit, dit Gargot. Daniel Normandin. Pierre Petit. François Provost. Michel Roy, dit Châtellerault. François Trotain, dit Saint-Seürin.

DROLET, ANTONIO. Bibliothécaire en chef, Archives du Québec, Québec.

Jacques Gourdeau de Beaulieu et de La Grossardière. Paul-Augustin Juchereau de Maur. Charlotte-Françoise de Juchereau de Saint-Denis. Guillaume Roger. Nicolas Senet, dit Laliberté.

DUBÉ, JEAN-CLAUDE. Professeur d'histoire, Université d'Ottawa, Ontario.

Claude-Thomas Dupuy.

DUBÉ, PAUL-ANDRÉ. Professeur d'histoire, Collège d'Enseignement Général et Professionel de Limoilou, Québec.

Pierre Legardeur de Repentigny.

DUMAS, GABRIEL-M.-RÉAL, O.F.M. CAP. Archiviste provincial des Capucins, Provincialat des Capucins, Montréal, Québec.

Séraphin Géorgemé. Olivier Goyer. Julien Guesdron. Dominique de La Marche. Louis-Hyacinthe de La Place. Potentien Ozon. Ambroise Pélerin.

DUPRÉ, CÉLINE. Office de la langue française, Ministère des Affaires culturelles du Québec, Québec.

Marc Bergier. Jean-François Buisson de Saint-Cosme. François Dupré. Pierre Jarret de Verchères. Joannès de Chacornacle. Joseph de La Colombière. Jean-Louis de La Corne de Chaptes. Charles Le Moyne, baron de Longueuil. Madeleine de Roybon d'Allonne.

ECCLES, W. J. Professor of history, University of Toronto, Ontario.

Jean Bochart de Champigny. Jacques-René Brisay de Denonville. Philippe Clément Du Vuault de Valrennes. Jacques de Meulles. Teganissorens.

EINHORN, ARTHUR. Graduate student in anthropology, State University of New York at Buffalo, New York, U.S.A.

Glossary of Indian Tribal Names.

CONTRIBUTORS

FAIRCHILD, BYRON. Department of State, Washington, D.C., U.S.A.
William Pepperrell.

FALARDEAU, ÉMILE. Généalogiste, Montréal, Québec.
François Lenoir, dit Rolland.

FENTON, WILLIAM N. Research professor of anthropology, State University of New York at Albany, New York, U.S.A.
Kondiaronk.

FERGUSSON, CHARLES BRUCE. Archivist of Nova Scotia; Associate professor of history, Dalhousie University, Halifax, Nova Scotia.
John Alden. Thomas Caulfeild. John Doucett. John Harrison. Robert Wroth.

FERLAND-ANGERS, ALBERTINE. Sorel, Québec.
François Charon de La Barre. Jean-Gabriel-Marie Le Pape Du Lescöat. Pierre You de La Découverte.

FLINN, JOHN F. Professor of French, University College, University of Toronto, Ontario. Chairman, Committee for the English translation of French biographies, *Dictionary of Canadian Biography/Dictionnaire biographique du Canada.*

FORTIER, JOHN. Director of research, Louisbourg National Historic Park, Nova Scotia.
Charles Juchereau de Saint-Denis. François Philippe de Hautmesnil.

GAGNÉ, LUCIEN, C.SS.R. Directeur des études, Séminaire Saint-Augustin, Cap-Rouge, Québec.
Étienne de Lessard.

GALLANT, PATRICE, PTRE. Sayabec, Québec.
Michel Haché-Gallant.

GILLESPIE, BERYL C. Graduate student in anthropology, University of Iowa, Iowa City, U.S.A.
Glossary of Indian Tribal Names.

GLOVER, RICHARD G. Professor of history, Carleton University, Ottawa, Ontario.
Nathaniel Bishop. Joseph Davis. Richard Ward.

GODFREY, MICHAEL, R.N. (RETD). Public Record Office, London, England.
Robert Bouler. Timothy Bridges. John Graydon. Thomas Handasyde. John Jackson. Thomas Kempthorne. Robert Latham. Sir John Leake. John Moody. Sir Nicholas Trevanion. Sir William Whetstone.

GOWANS, ALAN. Professor of art and art history, University of Victoria, British Columbia.
Juconde Drué. Michel Lefebvre, dit Laciseraye.

GRAHAM, GERALD S. Rhodes Professor of Imperial History, University of London, England.
John Hill. Sir Hovenden Walker.

HAMELIN, JEAN. Professeur agrégé d'histoire, Université Laval, Québec.
Louis-Henri de Baugy.

HAY, DOUGLAS. Graduate student in history, University of Warwick, Coventry, England.
Wowurna. Glossary of Indian Tribal Names.

HAYNE, DAVID M. Second General Editor, *Dictionary of Canadian Biography/Dictionnaire biographique du Canada,* 1965–69; Professor of French, University College, University of Toronto, Ontario.
Louis-Armand de Lom d'Arce, baron de Lahontan.

HELM, JUNE. Professor of anthropology, University of Iowa, Iowa City, U.S.A.
Glossary of Indian Tribal Names.

HICKERSON, HAROLD. Associate professor of anthropology, State University of New York at Buffalo, New York, U.S.A.
Glossary of Indian Tribal Names.

HODY, MAUD H. Moncton, New Brunswick.
Guillaume Blanchard. Abraham Bourg.

HORTON, DONALD J. Assistant professor of history, University of Waterloo, Ontario.
Chachagouesse. Alexandre de Chaumont. Chichikatelo. Chingouessi. Charles Guillimin. Paul Le Moyne de Maricourt. Ouenemek. Ounanguissé. Antoine-Denis Raudot. Jacques Raudot.

HUMPHREYS, JOHN. Graduate student in history, Harvard University, Cambridge, Massachusetts, U.S.A.
Jean-Antoine d'Agrain. Jean-Joseph d'Allard de Sainte-Marie.

HUTCHESON, MAUD M. Research assistant, *Dictionary of Canadian Biography/Dictionnaire biographique du Canada,* University of Toronto Press, Toronto, Ontario.
Henry Baley. Benjamin Gillam. George Larkin. Joseph-Jacques Marest. Pierre-Gabriel Marest.

INGRAM, GEORGE C. Historian, National Historic Sites Service, Department of Indian Affairs and Northern Development, Ottawa, Ontario.
George Martin. John Williams.

JAENEN, CORNELIUS J. Associate professor of history, University of Ottawa, Ontario.
Jacques Bruyas. Claude Chauchetière. Joseph-Louis Germain. Jeanne-Françoise Juchereau de La Ferté, dite de Saint-Ignace. Jacques de Lamberville. Jean de Lamberville. Jeanne Le Ber. Pierre Robinau de Bécancour.

JOHNSON, ALICE M. Formerly archivist, Hudson's Bay Company, London, England.
Alexander Apthorp. Anthony Beale. William Bevan. Thomas Bird. John Fullartine. Michael Grimington (sr.). Michael Grimington (jr.). Thomas Render.

JUNEAU, ANDRÉ. Directeur des services éducatifs, Musée du Québec, Québec.
Jean Soullard.

KALLMANN, HELMUT. Supervisor of music library, Canadian Broadcasting Corporation, Toronto, Ontario.
Charles-Amador Martin.

KRUGLER, JOHN DAVID. Graduate student in history, University of Illinois, Urbana, Illinois, U.S.A.
John Livingston. John March.

LACHANCE, ANDRÉ. Professeur adjoint d'histoire, Université de Sherbrooke, Québec.
Jacques Élie. Jean Rattier.

LAHAISE, ROBERT. Professeur agrégé d'histoire, Collège Sainte-Marie, Montréal, Québec.
Jean-Baptiste Legardeur de Repentigny. Pierre-Noël Legardeur de Tilly. Antoine Perrin. Alexandre Peuvret de Gaudarville, Jean Quesneville. Pierre Raimbault. Joseph-Charles Raimbault de Piedmont. Marien Tailhandier, dit La Beaume. Jean-Baptiste Tétro.

LANGDON, JOHN E. Toronto, Ontario.
Michel Levasseur.

La Roque de Roquebrune, Robert. Écrivain et archiviste, Paris, France.
Marguerite de Thavenet.

Lee, David. Historian, National Historic Sites Service, Department of Indian Affairs and Northern Development, Ottawa, Ontario.
Antoine Gaulin. Jean Léger de La Grange. Ouachala. Pierre Payen de Noyen.

Lefebvre, Jean-Jacques. Archiviste en chef, Cour supérieure, Palais de justice, Montréal, Québec.
François de Chavigny Lachevrotière. Denis d'Estienne Du Bourgué de Clérin.

Leland, Marine. Professor emeritus of French literature and French-Canadian civilization, Smith College, Northampton, Massachusetts, U.S.A.
François-Madeleine-Fortuné Ruette d'Auteuil de Monceaux.

Lévesque, Ulric. Professeur d'histoire, Collège de Sainte-Anne, La Pocatière, Québec.
Isaac (Alexandre) Berthier. Jean Bouillet de La Chassaigne.

Lunn, A. Jean E. Director, Cataloguing Branch, National Library of Canada, Ottawa, Ontario.
Simon-Pierre Denys de Bonaventure. Pierre Denys de La Ronde. Paul Denys de Saint-Simon. Charles Denys de Vitré.

MacBeath, George. Historical resources administrator, Province of New Brunswick, Fredericton, New Brunswick.
Louis Damours de Chauffours. René Damours de Clignancour. Philippe Énault de Barbaucannes. Charles de Saint-Étienne de La Tour.

McCully, Bruce T. Professor of history, College of William and Mary, Williamsburg, Virginia, U.S.A.
Francis Nicholson.

McDermott, John Francis. Research professor of humanities, Southern Illinois University, Edwardsville, Illinois, U.S.A.
Robert Groston de Saint-Ange.

McFarland, Constance P. Editor, *Canada* Handbook, Dominion Bureau of Statistics, Ottawa, Ontario.
Colin Campbell. John Collins. John Roope.

Macpherson, K. R. Historian, Department of Public Records and Archives of Ontario, Toronto, Ontario.
Auchagah.

McWilliams, Richebourg Gaillard. Mary Collett Munger Professor of English, Birmingham-Southern College, Birmingham, Alabama, U.S.A.
Mathieu Sagean.

Mathieu, Jacques. Archiviste, Archives du Québec, Québec.
François Dollier de Casson. François Vachon de Belmont. Pierre de Voyer d'Argenson.

Maude, Mary McDougall. Textual Editor, *Dictionary of Canadian Biography/Dictionnaire biographique du Canada*, University of Toronto Press, Toronto, Ontario.
Jacques d'Espiet de Pensens. Robert-David Gotteville de Belile.

Mayrand, Pierre. Directeur-adjoint, Service des monuments historiques, Ministère des Affaires culturelles du Québec, Québec.
François de Lajoüe. Denis Mallet. Pierre Ménage.

Menier, Marie Antoinette. Conservateur aux Archives nationales, Section Outre-Mer, Paris, France.
Tibierge.

Miquelon, Dale B. Graduate student in history, University of Toronto, Ontario.
Louis-Simon Le Poupet de La Boularderie.

Moogk, Peter N. Graduate student in history, University of Toronto, Ontario.
Aouenano. Pierre Gadois. Henri Lamarre, dit Bélisle. Jean-Baptiste Leclerc. Jacques Le Picard Du Mesnil de Norrey. Guillaume de Lorimier de La Rivière. Jean-François Martin de Lino. Miscouaky. Noro. Outoutagan. Samuel Payne. Simon Soupiran.

Morel, André. Professeur agrégé de droit, Université de Montréal, Québec.
Mathieu-Benoit Collet.

Nasatir, A. P. Professor of history, San Diego State College, San Diego, California, U.S.A.
Pierre-Charles Le Sueur.

Neatby, Leslie Hamilton. Professor of classics, University of Saskatchewan, Saskatoon, Saskatchewan.
James Napper. Swan.

Nielsen, Ann Marie. Instructor in history, Nasson College, Springvale, Maine, U.S.A.
William Arnold.

Nish, Cameron. Associate professor of history, Sir George Williams University, Montreal, Quebec.
Charles de Couagne. Ignace Gamelin. Louis Le Conte Dupré. Charles Perthuis. Nicolas Pinaud. François Poulin de Francheville. Denis Riverin.

Nute, Grace Lee. Formerly professor of history, Hamline University, and director of project for the preparation of the James J. Hill and L. W. Hill papers, St Paul, Minnesota, U.S.A.
Pierre-Esprit Radisson.

Olson, Alison G. Associate professor of history, The American University, Washington, D.C., U.S.A.
Sir Charles Hobby.

O'Neill, Charles Edwards, s.j. Associate professor of history, Loyola University, New Orleans, Louisiana, U.S.A.
Jacques Gravier. Nicolas de La Salle. Jean-Marie de Villes.

Osler, Edmund Boyd. Member of Parliament (Winnipeg South Centre); vice-president, Reed Shaw Osler Ltd., Winnipeg, Manitoba.
Henri Tonty.

Paquin, Michel. Chargé de recherche, *Dictionnaire biographique du Canada/Dictionary of Canadian Biography*, Les Presses de l'université Laval, Québec.
Xiste Le Tac. Louise Soumande, dite de Saint-Augustin.

Paradis, Jean-Marc. Professeur d'histoire, Centre des Études Universitaires de Trois-Rivières, Québec.

Robert-Michel Gay. *Louis-François de La Faye. Clément Robert.*

PECKHAM, HOWARD H. Director, Clements Library, University of Michigan, Ann Arbor, Michigan, U.S.A.
Benjamin Church. John Williams.

PELL, JOHN H. G. President, Fort Ticonderoga Association, New York, U.S.A.
Peter Schuyler.

PELLETIER, JEAN-GUY. Professeur d'histoire, Collège de Thetford, Thetford Mines, Québec.
Jean Cavelier. Nicolas-Antoine Coulon de Villiers.

PERRAULT, CLAUDE. Professeur d'histoire, Collège Sainte-Marie, Montréal; Recherchiste, Ville de Montréal, Québec.
René Cuillerier. Michel Messier, dit Saint-Michel. Nicolas Perrot.

POTHIER, BERNARD, Historian, National Historic Sites Service, Department of Indian Affairs and Northern Development; formerly Research Director, *Dictionary of Canadian Biography/Dictionnaire biographique du Canada*, Ottawa, Ontario.
Michel Du Pont de Renon. François Du Pont Duvivier. Louis de Gannes de Falaise. Mathieu de Goutin. Pierre Le Moyne d'Iberville. Jean-Baptiste Le Moyne de Martigny. Joseph Le Moyne de Serigny. Claude-Joseph Le Roy Desmarest. Jean Martel de Magos. Jean-Baptiste Rodrigue.

POULIOT, LÉON, S.J. Saint-Jérôme, Québec.
Claude Aveneau. Michel-Germain de Couvert. Julien Garnier. Pierre de Lagrené. Claude-Charles Le Roy de La Potherie, dit Bacqueville de La Potherie. Jean-Baptiste Loyard. Henri Nouvel. Louis Soumande.

POYNTER, F. N. L. Director, The Wellcome Institute of the History of Medicine, London, England.
James Yonge.

PRITCHARD, JAMES S. Lecturer in history, Queen's University, Kingston, Ontario.
Jean Deshayes. Jacques Levasseur de Neré.

PROVOST, HONORIUS, PTRE. Archiviste, Séminaire de Québec, Québec.
Louis Ango Des Maizerets. Jean Basset. Jean-François Buisson de Saint-Cosme. Pierre Francheville. Jean-Baptiste Gaultier de Varennes. Étienne Jacob. Thomas Lefebvre. Germain Morin. Thomas Thiboult. Barthélémy Verreau.

QUINN, DAVID B. Andrew Geddes and John Rankin Professor of Modern History, University of Liverpool, England.
Josias Crowe. Archibald Cumings. Samuel Gledhill. Arthur Holdsworth. Thomas Lloyd. William Pynne. James Smith.

RAMBAUD, ALFRED. Professeur de première supérieure, Lycée du Parc, Lyon, France.
Jean-Baptiste de La Croix de Chevrières de Saint-Vallier.

RAWLYK, GEORGE A. Associate professor of history, Queen's University, Kingston, Ontario.
Thomas Savage. George Vaughan.

REID, W. STANFORD. Professor of history, Wellington College, University of Guelph, Ontario.
Pierre Dugué de Boisbriand. Jean Petit.

RIOUX, JEAN-ROCH. Professeur d'histoire, Université Laval, Québec.
Louis Hennepin.

RITCHIE, CARSON I. A. Senior lecturer, Division of Arts and General Studies, Woolwich Polytechnic, London, England.
John Jago. Jacob Rice. Michael Richards. George Skeffington. Joseph Taylour.

ROGERS, EDWARD S. Curator of ethnology, Royal Ontario Museum, Toronto, Ontario.
Glossary of Indian Tribal Names.

ROSENFIELD, M. C. Associate professor of history, Southeastern Massachusetts Technological Institute, North Dartmouth, Massachusetts, U.S.A.
David Bassett. Michael Gill. Winthrop Hilton.

ROUSSEAU, JACQUES. Professeur d'ethnobiologie, Centre d'études nordiques, Université Laval, Québec.
Acoutsina. Dièreville. Michel Sarrazin.

ROWE, CHRISTOPHER M. Lecturer in history, University of Victoria, British Columbia.
Charles Fotherby. Sir John Gibsone. Sir Robert Robinson.

RUSS, CHRISTOPHER J. Graduate student in history, McGill University, Montreal, Quebec.
Jacques Baudry de Lamarche. Claude-Charles Dutisné. Louis Geoffroy. Michel Godefroy de Lintot. Jean-Amador Godefroy de Saint-Paul. Étienne Guyotte. Jean-François Hazeur. Jean-Baptiste Jolliet de Mingan. François Le Fevre. Pierre-Charles de Liette. François-Mathieu Martin de Lino. Henri-Antoine Mériel. Pierre Rémy. Alphonse Tonty.

SCOTT, M. EILEEN, C.N.D. Professor of English, Marianopolis College, Montreal, Quebec.
Marie Barbier, dite de l'Assomption.

SIEBERT, FRANK T., JR. Old Town, Maine, U.S.A.
Mog. Waxaway. Wenemouet.

SMYTHE, TERRENCE B. Assistant head, Historical Research Section, National Historic Sites Service, Department of Indian Affairs and Northern Development, Ottawa, Ontario.
Ouachala.

SQUIRES, W. AUSTIN. Chief curator, The New Brunswick Museum, Saint John, New Brunswick.
François Guion. Pierre Maisonnat, dit Baptiste.

STACEY, C. P. Professor of history, University of Toronto, Ontario.
John Walley.

STANDEN, S. DALE. Graduate student in history, University of Toronto, Ontario.
Jean-Baptiste Charly Saint-Ange. Claude de Beauharnois de Beaumont et de Villechauve. Jacques Maleray de Noiré de La Mollerie.

STANLEY, GEORGE F. G. Professor of history, Mount Allison University, Sackville, New Brunswick.
Nicolas Daneau de Muy. Joseph Desjordy de Cabanac. François Desjordy Moreau de Cabanac.

STEWART, ALICE R. Professor of history, University of Maine, Orono, Maine, U.S.A.
Silvanus Davis.

SUTHERLAND, MAXWELL. Head, Historical Research Section, National Historic Sites Service, Department of Indian Affairs and Northern Development, Ottawa, Ontario.

Lawrence Armstrong. Arthur Savage. John Washington.

TAILLEMITE, ÉTIENNE. Conservateur, Archives nationales, chargé des Archives anciennes de la Marine et des Colonies, Paris, France.

François Clairambault d'Aigremont. Claude Guillouet d'Orvilliers. Rémy Guillouet d'Orvilliers. Claude Lebeau. Jean-Michel de Lespinay. Daniel Robinau de Neuvillette. René Robineau de Bécancour. Pierre de Saint-Clair. Louis Tantouin de La Touche. Claude-Sébastien de Villieu. Sébastien de Villieu.

THÉRIAULT, YVETTE. Hull, Québec.

Pierre Terriot.

THOMAS, C. E. Research assistant, Public Archives of Nova Scotia, Halifax, Nova Scotia.

Richard Watts.

THORMAN, GEORGE E. Vice-Principal, Parkside Collegiate Institute, St Thomas, Ontario.

Joseph Adams. Samuel Hopkins. Miscomote. Thomas Moore. Joseph Myatt. Scatchamisse. Thanadelthur. Rowland Waggoner.

THORPE, FREDERICK J. Chief historian, National Museum of Man, Ottawa, Ontario.

Gédéon (de) Catalogne. Joseph de Catalogne. Jean-Baptiste de Couagne. Michel-Philippe Isabeau. Jacques L'Hermitte. Joseph de Monic. George Vane. Jean-François de Verville.

TISDEL, GASTON. Directeur des recherches, *Dictionnaire biographique du Canada/Dictionary of Canadian Biography*, Les Presses de l'université Laval, Québec.

Esther Brandeau.

TREMBLAY, VICTOR, P. D. Archiviste, Société historique du Saguenay, Chicoutimi, Québec.

Pierre-Michel Laure. Antoine Silvy.

TRIGGER, BRUCE G. Associate professor of anthropology, McGill University, Montreal, Quebec.

Aradgi. Cagenquarichten. Gouentagrandi. Tekarihoken. Tonatakout. Glossary of Indian Tribal Names.

TRUDEL, JEAN. Conservateur de l'art traditionnel, Musée du Québec, Québec.

Jacques Leblond de Latour. Noël Levasseur.

VACHON, ANDRÉ. Directeur adjoint, *Dictionnaire biographique du Canada/Dictionary of Canadian Biography*; Directeur général, Les Presses de l'université Laval, Québec.

Antoine Adhémar de Saint-Martin. Séverin Ameau, dit Saint-Séverin. Jacques Barbel. Charles Bécart de Granville et de Fonville. Hilaire Bernard de La Rivière. François Bigot. Louis Boulduc. Jacques Bourdon. Pierre Cabazié. Louis Chambalon. René-Louis Chartier de Lotbinière. Jean Cusson. Jacques David. Marguerite Dizy. Jean-Étienne Dubreuil. Jean-Robert Duprac. Paul Dupuy de Lisloye. François Genaple de Bellefonds. Jacques de Horné, dit Laneuville. Florent de La Cetière. François de Laval. Michel Lepailleur de Laferté. Marie-Joseph-Angélique. Jean-Baptiste Pottier. Antoine-Olivier Quiniard, dit Duplessis. Charles Rageot de Saint-Luc. Nicolas Rageot de Saint-Luc. Pierre Rivet Cavelier. Paul Vachon (père). Paul Vachon (fils).

VALOIS, JACQUES, O.F.M. 733, rue de l'Alverne, Québec, Québec.

Michel Bruslé. Guillaume Bulteau. Gélase Champy. Nicolas-Bernardin Constantin. Constantin Delhalle. Joseph Denys. Anastase Douay. Siméon Dupont. Luc Filiastre. Adrien Ladan. François de La Frenaye. Simple Landon. Bénin Le Dorz. Valentin Leroux. Henri Le Roy. Antoine Martin de Lino.

VOGET, FRED W. Professor of anthropology, Southern Illinois University, Edwardsville, Illinois, U.S.A.

Glossary of Indian Tribal Names.

VOISINE, NIVE, PTRE. Professeur auxiliaire d'histoire, Université Laval, Québec.

François-Joseph Bissot. Étienne Boullard. Marguerite Bourdon, dite de Saint-Jean-Baptiste. Jean-Baptiste Couillard de Lespinay. Louis Couillard de Lespinay. Jean-Baptiste-François Deschamps de La Bouteillerie. François Le Verrier de Rousson. Pierre Perrot de Rizy. Charles-Gaspard Piot de Langloiserie. Georges-François Poulet, dit M. Dupont. Georges Régnard Duplessis. Zacharie Robutel de La Noue. Jacques-Charles de Sabrevois.

WAGNER, ROBERT L. Graduate student in history, University of Illinois, Urbana, Illinois, U.S.A.

John Bonner.

WALLER, GEORGE M. Professor of history, Butler University, Indianapolis, Indiana, U.S.A.

Samuel Hill. Samuel Vetch.

WEILBRENNER, BERNARD. Directeur des archives historiques, Archives publiques du Canada, Ottawa, Ontario.

Jean-Baptiste-Julien Hamare de La Borde. Olivier Morel de La Durantaye. Jean Petit.

WELLS, CLAIRE DAGNEAU. Directeur, Équipe des traducteurs français, *Dictionnaire biographique du Canada/Dictionary of Canadian Biography*, Les Presses de l'université Laval, Québec.

WILLIAMS, GLYNDWR. Reader in history, Queen Mary College, University of London, England; General Editor, Hudson's Bay Record Society.

John Scroggs. William Stuart.

WOOD, JOHN S. Gooderham Professor of French, Victoria College, University of Toronto, Ontario; Committee for the English translation of French biographies, *Dictionary of Canadian Biography/Dictionnaire biographique du Canada*.

YON, ARMAND, PTRE. Professeur en retraite, Sainte-Dorothée, Québec.

Louis-Armand Champion de Cicé. François-Saturnin Lascaris d'Urfé.

ZOLTVANY, YVES F. Associate professor of history, McGill University, Montreal, Quebec.

Charles Aubert de La Chesnaye. François-Marie Bissot de Vinsenne. Jean-Baptiste Bissot de Vinsenne. Louis-Hector de Callière. Henri-Louis Chabert de Joncaire. Charles Delaunay. Henri-Louis Deschamps de Boishébert. Claude Greysolon de La Tourette. Daniel Greysolon Dulhut. François Hazeur. Louise-Élisabeth de Joybert de Soulanges et de Marson. Kiala. Louis de La Porte de Louvigny. Antoine Laumet, dit de Lamothe Cadillac. Jacques Le Ber. Constant Le Marchand de Lignery. François-Mathieu Martin de Lino. Antoine Pascaud. Claude de Ramezay. Philippe de Rigaud de Vaudreuil. Étienne de Villedonné.

Index

Included in the index are the names of persons mentioned in Volume II. People are listed by their family names, with titles and first names following. Wives are entered under their maiden names with their married names in parentheses. Incomplete citations in the text are fully identified when possible, and an asterisk indicates that the person has received a biography in a previous volume, or will receive one in a subsequent volume. Numerals in bold face indicate the pages on which a biography appears. Titles, nicknames, variant spellings, married and religious names are fully cross-referenced.

714

INDEX

733

736